LIST OF OFFICERS
of the
Navy *of the* United States
and of the
Marine Corps
from
1775 to 1900

COMPRISING A COMPLETE REGISTER OF ALL PRESENT AND
FORMER COMMISSIONED, WARRANTED, AND APPOINTED
OFFICERS OF THE UNITED STATES NAVY, AND OF THE
MARINE CORPS, REGULAR AND VOLUNTEER

Compiled from the Official Records of
the Navy Department

EDITED BY
EDWARD W. CALLAHAN
Registrar, Bureau of Navigation, Navy Department

HERITAGE BOOKS
2011

HERITAGE BOOKS
AN IMPRINT OF HERITAGE BOOKS, INC.

Books, CDs, and more—Worldwide

For our listing of thousands of titles see our website
at
www.HeritageBooks.com

A Facsimile Reprint
Published 2011 by
HERITAGE BOOKS, INC.
Publishing Division
100 Railroad Ave. #104
Westminster, Maryland 21157

Originally published
New York
L. R. Hamersly & Co.
1901

— Publisher's Notice —
In reprints such as this, it is often not possible to remove blemishes from the original. We feel the contents of this book warrant its reissue despite these blemishes and hope you will agree and read it with pleasure.

International Standard Book Numbers
Paperbound: 978-1-58549-881-9
Clothbound: 978-0-7884-4945-1

PREFACE.

In the following publication the official records of officers of the United States Navy and Marine Corps have been brought down to January, 1901. The work contains, in alphabetical order, the names of all officers of the navy and marine corps, commissioned, warranted and appointed, including volunteer officers who have entered the service since the establishment of the navy department in 1798, showing the dates of their original entry, progressive rank, and the manner in which those no longer in the service severed their connection from it. The data has been compiled from the original manuscript records of the navy department and from the official navy registers, issued semi-annually by the department. The volume also contains a list of all midshipmen, cadet engineers and naval cadets who have entered the Naval Academy since its establishment, arranged alphabetically by classes.

A sketch of the navy from 1775 to 1798, with a register of the officers in service between those dates, as well as a complete and carefully revised list of vessels of the United States Navy from its inception to the present time, form a valuable feature of the work.

L. R. HAMERSLY.

TABLE OF CONTENTS.

	PAGE
Secretaries of the Navy from 1798 to 1897	1
Assistant Secretaries	2
Solicitors and Judge Advocates, Board of Navy Commissioners	2
Secretaries of Navy Board, Judge Advocates General	2
Departmental Organization	3
Chiefs of Bureaus from 1842 to 1901	4
Sketch of the Navy from 1775 to 1798	7
Changes in Titles of Officers	12
General Navy Register, containing the names of all officers of the Navy from 1798 to January, 1901, alphabetically arranged	15
History of the United States Naval Academy	611
Superintendents since its foundation	614
Midshipmen and Naval Cadets	615
Cadet Engineers	675
Marine Corps, Complete List of Officers of, from 1798 to January, 1901	679
The Navy of the United States, January, 1901	705
Recognition by Congress of Gallant Services of Officers and others of the Navy and Marine Corps	707
Awards of Medals Commemorating Battle of Manila Bay	715
Officers of Navy and Marine Corps Promoted and Brevetted for Distinguished Services,	717
Appointments, Promotions, Retirements, Resignations and Casualties since January 1, 1901	721
Errata and Addenda	723
List of Vessels of War in the United States Navy from 1797 to 1901	725

SECRETARIES OF THE NAVY.

Name.	State.	Date of Appointment.	By whom Appointed.
*GEORGE CABOT	Mass.	3 May, 1798.	} John Adams.
BENJ. STODDERT	Md.	21 May, 1798.	
ROBERT SMITH	Md.	26 January, 1802.	Thomas Jefferson.
PAUL HAMILTON	S. C.	7 January, 1809.	
WILLIAM JONES	Penn.	12 January, 1813.	} James Madison.
B. W. CROWNINSHIELD	Mass.	19 December, 1814.	
SMITH THOMPSON	N. Y.	30 November, 1818.	} James Monroe.
SAMUEL L. SOUTHARD	N. J.	9 December, 1823.	
JOHN BRANCH	N. C.	7 March, 1829.	
LEVI WOODBURY	N. H.	23 May, 1831.	} Andrew Jackson.
MAHLON DICKERSON	N. J.	30 June, 1834.	
JAMES K. PAULDING	N. Y.	1 July, 1838.	Martin Van Buren.
GEORGE E. BADGER	N. C.	5 March, 1841.	W. H. Harrison.
ABEL P. UPSHUR	Va.	13 September, 1841.	
†DAVID HENSHAW	Mass.	24 July, 1843.	
‡THOMAS W. GILMER	Va.	15 February, 1844.	} John Tyler.
LEWIS WARRINGTON	U. S. N.	*ad interim.*	
JOHN Y. MASON	Va.	14 March, 1844.	
GEORGE BANCROFT	Mass.	11 March, 1845.	} James K. Polk.
JOHN Y. MASON	Va.	10 September, 1846.	
WILLIAM B. PRESTON	Va.	8 March, 1849.	Zachary Taylor.
WILLIAM A. GRAHAM	N. C.	1 August, 1850.	} Millard Fillmore.
JOHN P. KENNEDY	Md.	26 July, 1852.	
JAMES C. DOBBIN	N. C.	8 March, 1853.	Franklin Pierce.
ISAAC TOUCEY	Conn.	7 March, 1857.	James Buchanan.
GIDEON WELLES	Conn.	7 March, 1861.	{ Abraham Lincoln. { Andrew Johnson.
ADOLPH E. BORIE	Penn.	9 March, 1869.	} Ulysses S. Grant.
GEORGE M. ROBESON	N. J.	26 June, 1869.	
RICHARD W. THOMPSON	Ind.	13 March, 1877.	
ALEXANDER RAMSEY	Minn.	{ Acting Secretary, 20 December, 1880.	} Rutherford B. Hayes
NATHAN GOFF, Jr	W. Va.	7 January, 1881.	
WILLIAM H. HUNT	La.	7 March, 1881.	Jas. A. Garfield.
WILLIAM E. CHANDLER	N. H.	12 April, 1882.	Chester A. Arthur.
WILLIAM C. WHITNEY	N. Y.	6 March, 1885.	Grover Cleveland.
BENJAMIN F. TRACY	N. Y.	5 March, 1889.	Benjamin Harrison.
HILARY A. HERBERT	Ala.	6 March, 1893.	Grover Cleveland.
JOHN D. LONG	Mass.	5 March, 1897.	William McKinley.

*Declined.   † Not confirmed by Senate.   ‡ Killed on board *Princeton*, 28 February, 1844.

(1)

GENERAL NAVY REGISTER.

ASSISTANT SECRETARIES OF THE NAVY.

Name.	State.	Date of Appointment.	By whom Appointed.
Gustavus V. Fox	Mass.	1 August, 1861.	Abraham Lincoln.
William Faxon	Conn.	1 June, 1866.	Andrew Johnson.
James R. Soley	Mass.	18 July, 1890.	Benjamin Harrison.
William McAdoo	N. J.	20 March, 1893.	Grover Cleveland.
Theodore Roosevelt	N. Y.	8 April, 1897.	⎫
Charles H. Allen	Mass.	10 May, 1898.	⎬ William McKinley.
Frank W. Hackett	N. H.	23 April, 1900.	⎭

JUDGE ADVOCATE GENERAL.
Created by the Act of June 8, 1880.

Name.	State.	Dates of Service.
Colonel William B. Remey, U.S.M.C.	Iowa.	9 June, 1880, to 4 June, 1892.
Captain Samuel C. Lemly, U.S.N.	N. C.	5 June, 1892. Present incumbent

SOLICITORS AND JUDGE ADVOCATES.

Name.	State	Date of Appointment.	By whom Appointed.
William E. Chandler	N. H.	9 March, 1865.	Abraham Lincoln.
John A. Bolles	Mass.	10 June, 1865.	Andrew Johnson.

BOARD OF NAVY COMMISSIONERS.
Created by the Act of February 7, 1815, and abolished by the Act of August 31, 1842.

Rank and Name.	Dates of Service.
Commodore John Rodgers	{ 25 April, 1815, to 15 December, 1824. { 8 October, 1827, to 1 May, 1837.
Commodore Isaac Hull	25 April, 1815, to 30 November, 1815.
Commodore David Porter	25 April, 1815, to 31 December, 1822.
Commodore Stephen Decatur	30 November, 1815, to 22 March, 1820.
Commodore Isaac Chauncey	{ 31 December, 1822, to 15 December, 1824 { 29 July, 1833, to 27 January, 1840.
Commodore Charles Morris	⎧ 3 March, 1823, to 1 September, 1825. ⎨ 15 May, 1826, to 1 June, 1827. ⎩ 14 July, 1832, to 1 June, 1841.
Commodore William Bainbridge	15 December, 1824, to 20 June, 1827.
Commodore Jacob Jones	15 December, 1824, to 7 August, 1826.
Commodore Lewis Warrington	{ 5 January, 1827, to 20 June, 1830. { 4 November, 1840, to 31 August, 1842.
Commodore Thomas Tingey	8 October, 1827, to 27 October, 1827.
Commodore D. T. Patterson	13 October, 1828, to 1 July, 1832.
Commodore Charles Stewart	3 November, 1830, to 5 June, 1833.
Commodore A. S. Wadsworth	29 May, 1837, to 9 September, 1840.
Commodore J. B. Nicolson	8 June, 1840, to 1 March, 1841.
Commodore William M. Crane	6 May, 1841, to 31 August, 1842.
Commodore David Conner	29 July, 1841, to 31 August, 1842.

SECRETARIES OF NAVY BOARD.

James K. Paulding	7 February, 1815, to 9 November, 1823.
Charles W. Goldsborough	10 November, 1823, to 31 August, 1842.

CHANGE OF ORGANIZATION.

The Act of Congress, approved 31 August, 1842, abolished the Board of Navy Commissioners and established in lieu thereof, the following Bureaus, viz:

1. *Bureau Navy Yards and Docks.*
2. *Bureau Construction, Equipment and Repair.*
3. *Bureau Provisions and Clothing.*
4. *Bureau Ordnance and Hydrography.*
5. *Bureau Medicine and Surgery.*

A subsequent Act of Congress, approved 5 July, 1862, established the following organization, viz:

1. *A Bureau of Yards and Docks.*
2. *A Bureau of Equipment and Recruiting.*
3. *A Bureau of Navigation.*
4. *A Bureau of Ordnance.*
5. *A Bureau of Construction and Repair.*
6. *A Bureau of Steam Engineering.*
7. *A Bureau of Provisions and Clothing.*
8. *A Bureau of Medicine and Surgery.*

By order of the Secretary of the Navy the name of the Bureau of Equipment and Recruiting was, on July 1, 1889, changed to Bureau of Equipment.

An Act of Congress, approved July 19, 1892, changed the designation of Bureau of Provisions and Clothing to Bureau of Supplies and Accounts.

The present Bureau organization is as follows:

1. *Bureau of Yards and Docks.*
2. *Bureau of Equipment.*
3. *Bureau of Navigation.*
4. *Bureau of Ordnance.*
5. *Bureau of Construction and Repair.*
6. *Bureau of Steam Engineering.*
7. *Bureau of Supplies and Accounts.*
8. *Bureau of Medicine and Surgery.*

CHIEFS OF BUREAUS.

Bureau.	Chief.	Dates of Service.
Yards and Docks.	Commodore Lewis Warrington.	1 Sept., '42, to 24 May, '46.
	Rear-Admiral Joseph Smith.	25 May, '46, to 30 April, '69.
	Rear-Admiral Daniel Ammen.	1 May, '69, to 30 Sept., '71.
	Rear-Admiral C. R. P. Rodgers.	1 Oct., '71, to 21 Sept., '74.
	Rear-Admiral John C. Howell.	22 Sept., '74, to 30 June, '78.
	Captain Richard L. Law.	1 July, '78, to 4 June, '81.
	Rear-Admiral Edward T. Nichols.	4 June, '81, to 1 March, '85.
	Rear-Admiral David B. Harmony.	27 Mar., '85, to 2 April, '89.
	Commodore George B. White.	2 April, '89, to 27 Feb., '90.
	Commodore Norman H. Farquhar.	6 Mar., '90, to 6 Mar., '94.
	Commodore Edmund O. Matthews	16 Mar., '94, to 16 Mar., '98.
	Rear-Admiral M. T. Endicott.	4 April, '98.
Equipment (formerly Bureau of Equipment and Recruiting).	Rear-Admiral Andrew H. Foote.	17 July, '62, to 3 June, '63.
	Commander Albert N. Smith.	4 June, '63, to 8 Sept., '66.
	Rear-Admiral Melancton Smith.	17 Sept., '66, to 17 July, '70.
	Rear-Admiral William Reynolds.	18 July, '70, to 31 Jan., '75.
	Commodore Robert W. Shufeldt.	1 Feb., '75, to 19 Nov., '78.
	Commodore Earl English.	20 Nov., '78, to 5 Sept., '84.
	Commodore Winfield S. Schley.	6 Sept., '84, to 31 July, '89.
	Commodore George Dewey.	1 Aug., '89, to 30 June, '93.
	Commodore French E. Chadwick.	1 July, '93, to 6 Sept., '97.
	Rear-Admiral Royal B. Bradford.	7 Sept., '97.
Navigation. (Office of Detail attached 28 April, 1865.)	Rear-Admiral C. H. Davis.	17 July, '62, to 27 April, '65.
	Captain Percival Drayton.	28 April, '65, to 4 Aug., '65.
	Admiral David D. Porter.	Ad interim.
	Rear-Admiral T. A. Jenkins.	24 Aug., '65, to 11 April, '69.
	Rear-Admiral James Alden.	12 April, '69, to 30 Sept., '71.
	Rear-Admiral Daniel Ammen.	1 Oct., '71, to 4 June, '78.
	Captain Wm. D. Whiting.	11 June, '78, to 13 Oct., '81.
	Commodore James G. Walker.	22 Oct., '81, to 31 Oct., '89.
	Rear-Admiral Francis M. Ramsay.	1 Nov., '89, to 5 April, '97.
	Rear-Admiral Arent Schuyler Crowninshield.	8 April, '97.
Ordnance. (Formerly Bureau of Ordnance and Hydrography. In the year 1862 the Hydrographic Office was transferred to the Bureau of Navigation, and on May 9, 1898, was placed under the control of the Bureau of Equipment.)	Commodore William M. Crane.	1 Sept., '42, to 18 Mar., '46.
	Commodore Lewis Warrington.	25 May, '46, to 12 Oct., '51.
	Commodore Charles Morris.	13 Oct., '51, to 21 Jan., '56.
	Captain Duncan N. Ingraham.	10 Mar., '56, to 23 Sept., '60.
	Captain G. A. Magruder.	24 Sept., '60, to 23 April, '61.
	Captain A. A. Harwood.	24 April, '61, to 22 July, '62.
	Rear-Admiral John A. Dahlgren.	22 July, '62, to 24 June, '63.
	Commander Henry A. Wise.	25 June, '63, to 1 June, '68.
	Rear-Admiral John A. Dahlgren.	22 July, '68, to 23 July, '69.
	Rear-Admiral A. Ludlow Case.	10 Aug., '69, to 9 April, '73.
	Commodore William N. Jeffers.	10 April, '73, to 7 June, '81.
	Commodore Montgomery Sicard.	1 July, '81, to 13 Jan., '93.
	Commodore William M. Folger.	12 Feb., '90, to 2 Jan., '93.
	Commodore William T. Sampson.	28 Jan., '93, to 27 May, '97.
	Rear-Admiral Charles O'Neil	1 June, '97.

CHIEFS OF BUREAUS--Continued.

Bureau.	Chief.	Dates of Service.
Construction and Repair. (Formerly Bureau of Construction, Equipment, and Repair.)	Commodore DAVID CONNER.	1 Sept., '42, to 1 Mar., '43.
	Captain BEVERLY KENNON.	2 Mar., '43, to 9 April, '44.
	Commodore CHARLES MORRIS.	10 April, '44, to 31 May, '47.
	Commodore CHARLES W. SKINNER.	1 June, '47, to 28 Feb., '52.
	Commodore WILLIAM B. SHUBRICK.	1 Mar., '52, to 30 June, '53.
	Chief Naval Con'r SAMUEL HARTT.	1 July, '53, to 16 Nov., '53.
	Chief Naval Con'r JOHN LENTHALL.	17 Nov., '53, to 22 Jan., '71.
	Chief Con'r ISAIAH HANSCOM.	23 Jan., '71, to 27 April, '77.
	Chief Con'r JAMES W. EASBY.	28 April, '77, to 13 Dec., '81.
	Chief Con'r THEODORE D. WILSON.	3 Mar., '82, to 7 July, '93.
	Rear-Admiral PHILIP HICHBORN.	23 July, '93.
Steam Engineering.	Eng'r in Chief BENJ. F. ISHERWOOD	26 Mar., '61, to 16 Mar., '69
	Eng'r in Chief JAMES W. KING.	23 Mar., 69, to 14 Mar., '73.
	Eng'r in Chief W. W. W. WOOD.	31 Mar., '73, to 3 Mar., '77.
	Eng'r in Chief WM. H. SHOCK.	4 Mar., '77, to 15 June, '83.
	Eng'r in Chief CHARLES H. LORING.	18 Jan., '84, to 8 Aug., '87.
	Rear-Admiral GEO. W. MELVILLE.	9 Aug., '87.
Supplies and Accounts. (Formerly Bureau of Provisions and Clothing.)	CHARLES W. GOLDSBOROUGH.	1 Sept., '42, to 30 Jan., '44.
	Commodore WILLIAM B. SHUBRICK.	31 Jan., '44, to 14 April, '46.
	GIDEON WELLES.	15 April, '46, to 8 July, '49.
	Purser WILLIAM SINCLAIR.	9 July, '49, to 30 Sept., '54.
	Pay Director HORATIO BRIDGE.	1 Oct., '54, to 11 July, '69.
	Paym'r-Gen. EDWARD T. DUNN.	12 July, '69, to 17 Feb., '73.
	Paym'r-Gen. JOHN O. BRADFORD.	18 Feb., '73, to 22 Feb., '77.
	Paym'r-Gen. JAMES H. WATMOUGH.	23 Feb., '77, to 17 Nov., '77.
	Paym'r-Gen. GEO. F. CUTTER.	18 Nov., '77, to 30 Aug., '81.
	Paym'r-Gen. JOSEPH A. SMITH.	27 June, '82, to 29 Jan., '86.
	Paym'r-Gen. JAMES FULTON.	17 Nov., '86, to 15 Mar., '90.
	Rear-Admiral EDWIN STEWART.	16 May, '90, to 5 May, '99.
	Rear-Admiral ALBERT S. KENNY.	5 May, '99.
Medicine and Surgery.	Surgeon WILLIAM P. C. BARTON.	1 Sept., '42, to 31 Mar., '44.
	Surgeon THOMAS HARRIS.	1 April, '44, to 30 Sept., '53.
	Surgeon WILLIAM WHELAN.	1 Oct., '53, to 11 June, '65.
	Surgeon PHINEAS J. HORWITZ.	12 June, '65, to 30 June, '69.
	Surgeon-Gen. WILLIAM M. WOOD.	1 July, '69, to 24 Oct., '71.
	Surgeon-Gen. JONATHAN M. FOLTZ.	25 Oct., '71, to 9 June, '72.
	Surgeon-Gen. JAMES C' PALMER.	10 June, '72, to 4 July, '73.
	Surgeon-Gen. JOSEPH BEALE.	5 July, '73, to 30 Dec., '76.
	Surgeon-Gen. WM. GRIER.	2 Feb., '77, to 5 Oct., '78.
	Surgeon-Gen. J. WINTHROP TAYLOR	21 Oct., '78, to 19 Aug., '79.
	Surgeon-Gen. PHILIP S. WALES.	26 Jan., '80, to 26 Jan., '84.
	Surgeon-Gen. FRANCIS M. GUNNELL	27 Mar., '84, to 26 Mar., '88.
	Surgeon-Gen. JOHN M. BROWNE.	2 April, '88, to 9 May, '93.
	Surgeon-Gen. JAMES R. TRYON.	7 Sept., '93, to 7 Sept , '97.
	Rear-Admiral WILLIAM K. VAN REYPEN.	22 Oct., '97.

THE NAVY FROM 1775 TO 1798.

For the facts connected with the events of our Revolutionary war we are indebted to the United States Naval Chronicle by Charles W. Goldsborough. We give simply the essential facts of the chronologist.
During the Revolutionary war the superintending direction of the Navy was committed, in the first instance, to a Committee of three members of Congress, viz: Messrs. Deane, Langdon and Gadsden, who were, in October, 1775, required to fit out two swift sailing vessels, the one of 10 and the other of 14 guns, and a proportionate number of swivels and men, to cruise "*eastward*" for the purpose of intercepting such transports as might be laden with munitions of war, and other supplies for the British, then in possession of the town of Boston, and for such other purposes as Congress might direct. Having resolved to fit out two more vessels (30 October), viz., one of 20, the other of 36 guns, four members—Messrs. Hopkins, Hewes, R. H. Lee and J. Adams—were added to the Committee; and when Congress, by resolution of 13 December, 1775, determined to build thirteen additional vessels of war, they increased the number of the Naval Committee, so as to make it consist of one member form each colony, to be appointed by ballot; and on the 14 December the following gentlemen were accordingly thus appointed, viz: Messrs. Bartlett, Hancock, Hopkins, Deane, Lewis, Crane, R. Morris, Read, Chase, R. H. Lee, Hewes, Gadsden and Houston.
To this Committee Naval subjects were generally referred, with an instruction to examine and report thereon, for the final decision of the House. Congress reserved to themselves the right to appoint all commission officers, as low as and including Third Lieutenants, and gave to the Committee the power of appointing all officers of subordinate rank. The Committee were authorized to give such instructions for the employment of the ships as might appear to them "most conducive to the defence of the United Colonies, and to the distress of the enemy's naval forces and vessels bringing supplies to their fleets and armies."
In performing the duties assigned to them, the Committee experienced great inconvenience for want of professional practical information, and upon the subject being brought before Congress they resolved (6 November, 1776) "that three persons, well skilled in maritime affairs, should be immediately appointed to execute the business of the Navy, under the direction of the Marine Committee, and allowed to each a salary of $1,500 per annum; and on 13 November, John Nixon, John Wharton and F. Hopkinson, Esqrs., were appointed. They were styled in the resolutions of Congress "The Continental Navy Board, or Board of Assistants of the 'Marine Committee,'" and sometimes "Board of the Middle District." There was also an "Eastern Board," consisting of three persons, who executed the instructions of the Committee in their district.
This system of administering the civil department of the Navy continued, it is believed, till October, 1779, when Congress, by resolution (28), decided that a Board of Admiralty should be established, "to consist of three Commissioners not members of Congress, and two members of Congress, and three to form a Board, for the despatch of business." Early in 1781 (11 January) we find that James Reed, Esqr., was, by resolution of Congress, invested with full power to conduct the business of the Navy Board in the "Middle Department," and soon after this (27 February) Major-General Alexander M'Dougall was elected Secretary of Marine. In the same year (29 August) it was resolved that an "Agent of Marine" should be appointed "with authority to direct, fit out, equip and employ, the ships and vessels of war belonging to the United States, according to such instructions as he shall from time to time receive from Congress;" and "that as soon as the said Agent shall enter into the execution of his office the functions and appointments of the Board of Admiralty, the several Navy Boards and all civil officers appointed under them" should cease.
In September (6) a resolution was passed, by which the duties prescribed to the "Agent of Marine," until he should be appointed, devolved on the Superintendent of Finance, Robert Morris, who, indeed, appears to have had the chief agency in the Civil Administration of the Navy during the greater part of the Revolutionary war. In the earliest periods we find that the orders of the commanders generally, near his signature, and continued to be most frequently signed by him, until a Board of Admiralty was established, when the correspondence was directed under the superintending direction of the Board by Mr. John Brown, their Secretary. After the Board of Admiralty was abolished, we again find the chief duties of the Department devolving upon Mr. Morris. It would seem that the nation could not conveniently have conducted either its naval or its fiscal operations, without the agency of this distinguished patriot.
The list of officers, appointed during the Revolutionary war, are obviously imperfect; they are, however, as complete as the information in our possession will enable us to make them. The frequent changes in the administration of the Civil Department of the Navy, the occasional resolutions of Congress conferring sometimes upon one of the Boards the power of appointing; at others given to individual members, in conjunction with commanders, authority to appoint subalterns, the destruction of papers by fires and other causes, have involved this branch of the subject in great uncertainty, and it is impossible at this day, to present a perfect list of the officers. Were the information attainable, it

(7)

GENERAL NAVY REGISTER.

would be particularly gratifying to show, not only the names of those who served in the Continental Navy, but of those also who served on board the ships fitted out at the expense of the respective colonies and on board privateers.

From the Journals of Congress and other sources, we find the following Commission Officers were appointed by them during the war.

CAPTAINS AND COMMANDERS.

When appointed.	Names.
1775, Dec. 22.	Ezekiel Hopkins.
" "	Dudley Saltonstall.
" "	Abraham Whipple.
" "	Nicholas Biddle.
1776, April 17.	John B. Hopkins.
" "	William Manly.
" "	Isaac Cozneau.
" June 6.	Thomas Thompson.
" "	Samuel Tompkins.
" "	Christopher Miller.
" "	John Barry.
" "	Thomas Read.
" "	Charles Alexander.
" "	James Nicholson.
" June 15.	Hector McNiel.
" "	Thomas Grennall.
" Aug. 13.	Elisha Hinman.
" Aug. 22.	John Hodge.
" "	John Manly.
" Oct. 10.	Lambert Wickes.
" "	William Hallock.
" "	Hoysted Hacker.
" "	Isaiah Robinson.
" "	John Paul Jones.
" "	James Josiah.
" "	Joseph Olney.
" "	James Robinson.
" "	John Young.
" "	Elisha Warner.
" "	Lieutenant Commandant J. Baldwin.
" "	Thomas Albertson.
1777, Feb. 5.	Henry Johnson.
" Mar. 15.	Daniel Waters.
" "	Samuel Tucker.
1778, May 1.	William Burke.
" June 18.	Peter Landais.
" Sept. 25.	Seth Harding.
1779, Sept. 17.	Silas Talbot.
	Samuel Nicholson.
	John Nicholson.
	Henry Skinner.

CAPTAINS, ETC.—Continued.

When appointed.	Names.	
	Benjamin Dunn.	
	Samuel Chew.	

LIEUTENANTS.

When appointed.	Names.	
1775, Dec. 22.	John Paul Jones,	1st.
" "	Rhodes Arnold,	
" "	—— Stansbury,	1st.
" "	Hoysted Hacker,	
" "	Jonathan Pitcher,	
" "	Benjamin Seabury,	2d.
" "	Joseph Olney,	"
" "	Elisha Warner,	"
" "	Thomas Weaver,	"
" "	—— McDougall,	"
" "	John Fanning,	3d.
" "	Ezekiel Burroughs,	"
" "	Daniel Vaughan,	"
1776, June 6.	Israel Turner,	1st.
" "	Joseph Doble,	2d.
" "	Mark Dennet,	3d.
" July 22.	Peter Shores,	"
" "	John Wheelwright,	"
" "	Josiah Shackford,	"
" "	David Love,	"
1776, Aug. 17.	William Barnes,	1st.
" "	Thomas Vaughan,	3d.
" Aug. 22.	Jonathan Maltby,	1st.
" "	David Phipps,	2d.
" "	—— Wilson,	1st.
" "	John Nicholson,	2d.
1777, Feb. 5.	Elijah Bowen,	1st.
" Aug. 6.	John Rodeg,	2d.
" Aug. 12.	William Molleston,	3d.
1781, July 20.	Richard Dale,	"
" "	Alexander Murray,	"
" "	—— Plunkett,	"
	Joshua Barney,	
	Isaac Buck.	
	John Stevens.	
	Aquilla Johns.	

With respect to the relative rank of the Officers, Congress by resolution of 17 April, 1776, decided that the nominations or appointments of Captain or Commander should not "establish rank." It was to be settled by Congress before the Commissions should be granted, and we find that by a resolution of 10 October, 1776, Congress established the rank and command of Captains, as follows:

1.	James Nicholson	Virginia	28	Guns.
2.	John Manly	Hancock	32	"
3.	Hector McNiel	Boston	24	"
4.	Dudley Saltonstall	Trumbull	28	"
5.	Nicholas Biddle	Randolph	32	"
6.	Thomas Thompson	Raleigh	32	"
7.	John Barry	Effingham	28	"
8.	Thomas Reed	Washington	32	"
9.	Thomas Grennall	Congress	28	"
10.	Charles Alexander	Delaware	24	"
11.	Lambert Wicks	Reprisal	16	"
12.	Abraham Whipple	Providence	28	"
13.	John B. Hopkins	Warren	32	"
14.	John Hodge	Montgomery	24	"
15.	William Hallock	Lexington	16	"
16.	Hoysted Hacker	Hamden		
17.	Isaiah Robinson	Andrew Doria	14	"
18.	John Paul Jones	Providence	12	"
19.	James Josiah			
20.	Elisha Hinman	Alfred	28	"
21.	Joseph Olney	Cabot	16	"
22.	James Robinson	Sachem	10	"
23.	John Young	Independence	10	"
24.	Elisha Warner	Fly		
	Lieutenant John Baldwin	Wasp	8	"
	Lieutenant Thomas Albertson	Musqueto	4	"

The Marine Committee were empowered to regulate the rank of Lieutenants.

MARINES.

MAJOR.

When appointed.
1776, June 25. Samuel Nichols.

CAPTAINS.

" " Andrew Porter.
" " Joseph Hardy.
" " Samuel Shaw.
" " Benjamin Deane.
" " Robert Mullin.
" " John Stewart.
——, July 22. George J. Osborne.
" " Richard Palmer.
1781, Sept. 6. William Nicholson.

LIEUTENANTS.

When appointed.
1776, June 25.	Daniel Henderson,	1st.
" "	Franklin Reed,	1st.
" "	Peregrine Brown,	"
" "	James McClure,	2d.
" "	William Gilmore,	2d.
" "	Abel Morgan,	"
" "	Hugh Montgomery,	"
" "	Thomas Pownal,	1st.
" "	Richard Harrison,	2d.
" July 22.	Stephen Meade,	1st.
" "	Nathaniel Thwing,	2d.
" "	Benjamin Thompson,	"
—— Aug. 24.	Alpheus Rice,	1st.
1779, July, 24.	Abraham Vandyke,	"
1787, " 17.	William Nicholson,	"
——, Sept. 6.	Louis de la Valette,	"

On referring to the list of Captains and Commanders, and comparing it with the list established by resolution of 10 October, 1776, it will be seen, that Congress, in arranging the rank did not include the names of Ezra Hopkins, William Manly, Isaac Cozneau, Samuel Tompkins or Christopher Miller.

It is presumed that the Commanders appointed after 10 October, 1776, ranked according to the dates of their respective appointments.

Having established the relative rank of Commanders in the Navy—with each other, Congress, on 15 November following, resolved, that the rank of Naval Officers as to the rank of Officers in the land service, should be

Admiral .... as a General.
Vice-Admiral .... as a Lieutenant-General.
Rear-Admiral .... as a Major-General.
Commodore • .... as a Brigadier-General.
Captain of a ship of 40 guns and upwards.............. as a Colonel.
"   "   20 to 40 guns .... as a Lieutenant-Colonel.
"   "   10 to 20 guns .... as a Major.
Lieutenant of a ship of 10 to 20 guns .... as a Captain.

And at the same date the following was fixed as the pay of the Officers of the Navy:

Ships of 20 guns and upwards.		*Ships of 10 to 20 guns.*
Captains per month..................	$60......................	$48
Lieutenants "	30......................	24
Master "	30......................	24
Surgeon "	25......................	21-2-3
Midshipman "	12......................	12
Gunner "	15......................	13
Chaplain "	20......................	None.
Seaman "	8......................	8

And that vessels under 10 guns should be commanded by Lieutenants, and that the pay in such vessels should be Lieutenants, $30; Mate, $15; Boatswain, Gunner, etc., $12; and the following allowances were, on 25 July, 1777, established, viz: Commanders of vessels of 10 guns and upwards, $5.33 per week for subsistence; under 10 guns, $4.00. Cabin expenses—Commanders of 10 guns and upwards, $2.66 per week whilst at sea.

Lieutenants, Surgeons, Captains of Marines and Chaplains $4 per week subsistence in domestic ports when the ships should not be in condition to receive them.

The pay of Commander-in-Chief was fixed (22 December, 1775) at $125 per month, and the pay of Surgeons was increased (16 July, 1777) so as to be equal to that of Lieutenant.

On 29 October it was *"Resolved,* That no private ship or vessel of war, merchant tures of the United States to appoint gentlemen in their respective States skillful in physics and surgery, to examine those who offer to serve as Surgeons or Surgeon's Mates, in the Army or Navy; and that no Surgeon shall hereafter receive a commission or warrant to act as such in the Army or Navy, who shall not produce a certificate from some one of the examiners, so to be appointed, to prove that he is qualified to execute his office."

On 29 October it was *"Resolved,* That no private ship or vessel of war, merchant ship or other vessels belonging to the subjects of these States, be permitted to wear pendants, when in company with Continental ships or vessels of war without leave from the commanding vessel thereof."

During the war Congress authorized the purchasing, or building and equipping, as cruisers, the following description of vessels:
1775, October 13, 2 vessels of 10 and 14 guns.
1775, October 30, 2 vessels of 20 and 36 guns.
1775, December 13, 13 vessels, 5 of 32 guns, 5 of 28 guns, and 3 of 24 guns.
1776, October 3, viz., 1 frigate and 2 cutters.
1776, November 9, 10, 3 of 74 guns, 5 of 36 guns, 1 of 18 guns, and 1 packet.
1777, January 23, 2, viz., 1 of 36 guns and 1 of 18 guns.

Eight prize vessels were, during the years 1776 and 1777, directed to be purchased and fitted out, and in the course of the war a number of cutters, dispatch boats, galleys, and fire-ships were, from time to time, authorized. The cutters and dispatch boats were generally under the direction of a Secret Committee, one of whose duties was to procure munitions of war, and who, for that purpose, were authorized to export certain articles of provisions to the West Indies. The galleys and fire-ships were for the defence of our waters, within land-locked navigation and the lakes.

The thirteen ships authorized on 13 December, 1775, were directed to be built—one in New Hampshire, two in Massachusetts Bay, one in Connecticut, two in Rhode Island, two in New York, four in Pennsylvania, and one in Maryland, and, by resolution of 6 June, 1776, they were named as follows: The Congress, Randolph, Hancock, Washington, Trumbull, Raleigh, Effingham, Montgomery, Warren, Boston, Virginia, Providence and Delaware.

Among those authorized, subsequent to 13 December, 1775, and not hereinbefore mentioned by name, we find the Columbus, 28; the Queen of France, 28; the Ranger, 18; the Alliance, 32, built at Salisbury, Mass.; the Hornet, brig, General Gates, frigates Confederacy, Deane (afterwards changed to Hague), and Ariel, sloop Saratoga Duc de Lauzun, and the America, 74.

General letters of reprisal were authorized on 23 March, 1776, and thenceforth the public and private cruisers of the United Colonies were at liberty to capture all vessels, armed or unarmed, belonging to the Crown, or to the inhabitants of Great Britain.

Late in the month of December, 1775, a small squadron, consisting of the Alfred, Commodore Ezekiel Hopkins, of 28 guns; the Columbus, Captain A. Whipple, of 14 guns; the Andrew Doria, Captain Nicholas Biddle, of 14 guns; the Sebastian Cabot, Captain John D. Hopkins, of 16 guns, and the Providence, ——Hazard, of 12 guns, with the Falcon, Scorpion and Cruiser, which were to join them at Cape Fear, were ordered to New Providence, for the purpose of seizing and transporting to the colonies a large quantity of ammunition, which, it was understood, was deposited in the Royal Magazine on that island. After landing there was some unaccountable delay, and the Governor heard of Commodore Hopkins' approach, in time to remove the powder, before he reached the town. Thus the expedition failed as to the principal object. The Governor and Lieutenant-Governor, with about 40 cannon, a quantity of shot and shell and a few brass mortars were captured. A bomb-brig of 8 guns and a schooner of 6 guns were taken by the squadron on its return.

Commodore Hopkins' conduct was inquired into by Congress, and it was found that he had not paid due regard to the tenor of his instructions, which "directed him to annoy the enemy's ships upon the coast of the Southern States." The reasons he assigned for not going from Providence to the Carolinas were not satisfactory, and on 16 August, 1776, Congress passed a vote of censure upon him. Three days afterward he was ordered to Newport, to take "command of the fleet formerly under his care." It is found, however, that Congress, in aranging the rank of the officers on 10 October following, omitted his name.

Although in the earlier periods of the Revolutionary war great embarrassments were experienced for want of an efficient marine force, still much was done by the vessels of war we then possessed, and by privateers, whose energy, enterprise and success were astonishingly great, considering the overwhelming force by which they were opposed. The number of captures in the course of the war has been stated at 803, of which there were either retaken, burnt, ransomed, sunk, restored or lost 153, leaving a gain to the nation of 650. If we estimate these as averaging 250 tons, and compute their value at $30 per ton, and their cargoes at $10,000 each, the amount of captures would be $11,375,000. Some English authors have estimated the value of the prizes taken in the year 1776 by the American cruisers at one million sterling.

That our vessels captured property worth millions of dollars is unquestionably true, but it appears impossible to form any precise estimate as to their value.

It is not in our power, nor is it the purpose of this paper, to afford particular information as to the movements of our national ships during the Revolutionary war, and we are obliged to omit giving a description of any of those brilliant achievements that occurred during that eventful period.

Of the ships of the line authorized during the Revolutionary war only one, the America, was built, and she was presented (3 September, 1782) to his Most Christian Majesty, the King of France, in testimony of the sense entertained by Congress of his generous exertions in behalf of the United States, and to replace in his service the Magnifique, which, by accident, was lost in the harbor of Boston. Of the other ships built and purchased during the Revolutionary war, the whole were either captured or destroyed by the enemy or sold by the United States. We find (21 April, 1783) that the ship Duc de Lauzun was loaned to the Minister of France for the transportation of troops from the United States; and that, after performing this service, she was to be sold. The Alliance was ordered (5 September, 1783) to be surveyed, with a view of her being repaired; but on 3 June, 1785, she was ordered to be sold ; and when she was sold the United States did not, it is believed, own a single vessel of war.

The "Agent of Marine," to whom was referred a resolution of the House of Delegates of the State of Virginia, of 26 June, 1783, reported (5 August, 1783) :

"That, although it is an object highly desirable, to establish a *respectable marine;* yet, the situation of the public treasury, renders it not advisable to purchase ships *for the present,* nor until the several States shall grant such funds for the construction of ships, *docks* and *naval arsenals,,* and for the support of the naval service, as shall enable the United States to establish their marine upon a *permanent* and *respectable footing."* In this report Congress concurred.

Upon the application of the Delegates of Virginia, Congress, by resolution (3 October, 1783), authorized that State to keep, at its own expense, two armed vessels "for the defence of the trade of that State," confining the force of each to fourteen six-pounders and seventy-five men.

The United States had but recently achieved their independence and assumed a rank among the nations of the earth—they were still greatly embarrassed with the expenses of a long, bloody, yet glorious war; when the Dey of Algiers, tempted by a spirit of cupidity, seized some of their merchant vessels, and conducted their crews to slavery. This perfidious conduct produced the strongest indignation; but it was not in the power of the nation to avenge the insult, as promptly as the feelings it excited, or as sound national policy dictated. Negotiations were of necessity resorted to, but such were the difficulties which the policy of the Dey imposed, and such was our feeble condition, with respect to arms, that years elapsed before any favorable result was produced.

In this state of things we find the origin of the Act of Congress of 27 March, 1794, authorizing six frigates to be provided—which, however, were to be suspended in the event of peace with Algiers.

The resolution of the House of Representatives (of 2 January, 1794 "that a naval force adequate to the protection of the commerce of the United States against the Algerine corsairs ought to be provided," was passed by a majority of two votes only, and the bill founded upon this resolution (27 March, 1794) was passed by a majority of eleven, but it is understood that it could not have been passed if the provision suspending all proceedings in the event of peace with Algiers had ben omitted. Under these circumstances the President, General Washington, determined to build the vessels contemplated in the first section of the Act, viz: Four 44-gun and two 36-gun frigates, and that they should be built in the following ports, viz:

At Boston.....................One 44
At New York ....One 44
At Philadelphia ....One 44
At Portsmouth, Va ....One 44
At Baltimore ....One 36
At Portsmouth, N. H..........One 36

No time was lost in making every preparatory arrangement for the building of these vessels. Mr. Joshua Humphreys, of Philadelphia, a distinguished shipbuilder of very extensive practical knowledge in his profession; Mr. John Hackett, of Salisbury, Mass., who had constructed and built the Alliance frigate, and others were consulted "upon the best properties to be adopted as a general plan for the vessels now to be built," and upon the most advisable means of procuring the frames and the materials of which the vessels ought to be built. The models submitted by Mr. Humphreys were, after much consultation and consideration, adopted; and that gentleman was on 28 June, 1794, appointed the constructor and master-builder of the 44-gun ship, to be built at Philadelphia, with a salary of $2,000 per annum, commencing on 1 May.

The President, with the advice and consent of the Senate, appointed the following gentlemen Captains of the Navy:

1. JOHN BARRY,
2. SAMUEL NICHOLSON,
3. SILAS TALBOT,
4. JOSHUA BARNEY,
5. RICHARD DALE.
6. THOMAS TRUXTON,

Ranking in the order in which their names are stated, and their appointments were communicated to them 5 June, 1794.

Captain Barney declined accepting, not from any disinclination to serve his country, but in consequence of the arrangement as to rank. This produced a vacancy, which was filled on 18 July, 1794, by the appointment of James Sever, to take rank after Captain Truxtun.

The following shows the distribution of the officers thus appointed, and the constructors and agents, for building the several ships.

Captain and Superintendent.

JOHN BARRY,
SAMUEL NICHOLSON,
SILAS TALBOT,
RICHARD DALE,
THOMAS TRUXTUN,
JAMES SEVER.

Naval Constructors.

JOSHUA HUMPHREYS.
GEORGE CLEGHORN,
FORMAN CHEESEMAN,
JOHN MORGAN,
DAVID STODDER,
JAMES HACKETT.

Navy Agents.

ISAIAH COXE,
HENRY JACKSON,
JOHN BLAGGS,
W. PENNOCK,
JEREMIAH YELLOTT,
JACOB SHEAFFE.

For Ships to be Built at

PHILADELPHIA,
BOSTON,
NEW YORK,
NORFOLK,
BALTIMORE,
PORTSMOUTH, N. H.

On 21 December, 1795, President Washington communicated to the Senate a letter from the Emperor of Morocco, recognizing the treaty of peace and friendship between the United States.

Peace with Algiers having been concluded, no farther progress could be made in building the frigates; for as we have before seen, the law directed that in such event all proceedings should be suspended.

The President called the attention of Congress to this subject, and stated that serious losses would result from a sudden suspension of the work and the discharge of the valuable corps of artificers and men employed in completing it.

In January, 1796, the Chairman of the Committee of the House of Representatives, to whom the subject of frigates had been referred, called upon the Secretary of War (then charged with the superintendence of the Navy) for information as to the progress made in building them, the expenses incured, etc.

12   GENERAL NAVY REGISTER.

The information was communicated to Congress, and on 20 April following "An Act supplementary to an Act, entitled an Act to provide a Naval Armament" passed, authorizing the President to continue the construction and equipment of the frigates of 44 guns and one frigate of 36 guns, appropriating for this purpose the unexpended balance of the $688,888,82 (which had been appropriated for the six frigates by Act of 9 June, 1794), and the sum of $80,000, which by the Act of 9 June, was appropriated for a provisional equipment of galleys, but no part of which had been expended on that object.

This Act continued the construction and equipment of three of the six frigates and discontinued the remaining three, notwithstanding such progress had been made that the whole six might have been built, launched and completely equipped within the year.

President Washington, in his speech to both Houses of Congress, 7 December, 1796, after referring to the many delays and isappointments arising out of the European war and the final arrangements made to the Dey and regency of Algiers, observes among other things, the following:

"To an active external commerce the protection of a naval force is indispensable." "To secure respect to a neutral flag requires a naval force, organized and ready to vindicate it from insult and aggression;" and asks, "Will it not, then, be advisable to begin without delay to provide and lay up the materials for the building and equipping of ships of war, and to proceed in the work by degrees, in proportion, as our resources shall render it practicable, without inconvenience; so that a future war of Europe, may not find our commerce in the same unprotectd state in which it was found by the present."

The depredations committed upon our commerce by the cruisers of European powers, particularly those of Great Britain and France, and the suffering which ensued therefrom to our seafaring citizens, were the causes of our maritime war with the latter nation, and the consequent extension of our naval establishment.

On 9 April, 1798, the Secretary of War, who was charged wth the dut yof superintending the concerns of the Navy, as well as those of the Army. addressed to the Chairman of the Committee of the House of Representatives, for the protection of commerce and the defence of the country, a letter recommending building or purchasing vessels, with estimates for building, rigging and equipping, three ships of war, to carry 22, 20 and 16 guns, together with the cost of manning and victualing the same for twelve months. Said letter and estimates were submitted to Congress early in April, 1798, and on the 27th of that month an Act passed, entitled "An Act to provide an additional armament for the protection of the trade of the United States and for other purposes," authorizing the President to cause to be built, purchased or hired, a number of vessels, not exceeding twelve, to carry not more than 22 guns each, to be armed, fitted out and manned, under his direction; and appropriating $950,000 to carry these provisions into effect.

On 30 April, 1798, the office of Secretary of the Navy was established by law.

On 3 May, 1798, Hon. George Cabot, of Massachusetts, was nominated and confirmed as Secretary of the Navy, but declined the appointment.

On 4 May, 1798, another Act was passed authorizing the building or purchasing of a number of small vessels, to be equipped as galleys or otherwise, and stationed in such ports of the United States as the President might direct. Eighty thousand dollars was appropriated for this object.

On 21 May, 1798, Benjamin Stoddert, Esq., of Georgetown, in the District of Columbia, was appointed to the office of Secretary of the Navy, and in June, 1798, entered upon the duties of his office as Secretary of the Navy.

From this date we commence the compilation of the General Register of the Navy.

CHANGE OF TITLES.

Admiral—Created by Act of Congress 25 July, 1866, and by Act of Congress 2 March, 1899.
Vice-Admiral—Created by Act of Congress 21 December, 1864.—(Terminated 31 March, 1890.)
Rear Admiral—Created by Act of Congress 16 July, 1862.
Commodore—Abolished on Active List by Act of Congress 3 March, 1899.
Master to Lieutenant Junior Grade, } By Act of Congress 3 March, 1883.
Midshipman to Ensign Junior Grade, }
Ensign Junior Grade to Ensign—By Act of Congress 26 June, 1884.
Medical Directors and Medical Inspectors, } Created by Act of Congress 3
Pay Directors, and Pay Inspectors, } March, 1871.
Purser to Paymaster—Act of Congress 22 June, 1860.
*1st Assistant Engineer to Passed Assistant Engineer, } Act of Congress ?
*2d Assistant Engineer to Assistant Engineer. } 24 February,
*3d Assistant Engineer. (Abolished Act of Congress 15 July, 1870.) } 1874.
Chief Boatswain, Chief Gunner, } Created by Act of Congress 3 March, 1899.
Chief Carpenter and Chief Sailmaker, }
Acting Master's Mates to Mates—Act of Congress 3 March, 1865.
Cadet Engineer—Act of Congress 4 July, 1864. } Changed to Naval Cadet, Act
Cadet Midshipman—Act of Congress 15 July, 1870, } of 5 August, 1882

OFFICERS OF THE LINE.

Admiral.
Rear Admiral
Commodore.—On Retired List Only.
Captain.
Commander.

Lieutenant-Commander.
Lieutenant.
Lieutenant, Junior Grade.
Ensign.
Naval Cadet.

* Engineer Corps abolished by an Act of Congress 3 March, 1899.

MEDICAL CORPS.

Medical Director.
Medical Inspector.
Surgeon.

Passed Assistant Surgeon.
Assistant Surgeon.

PAY CORPS.

Pay Director.
Pay Inspector.
Paymaster.

Passed Assistant Paymaster.
Assistant Paymaster.

OTHER COMMISSIONED OFFICERS.

Chaplain.
Professor of Mathematics.
Naval Constructor.
Assistant Naval Constructor.
Civil Engineer.

Chief Boatswain.
Chief Gunner.
Chief Carpenter.
Chief Sailmaker.

WARRANT OFFICERS.

Boatswain.
Gunner.
Carpenter.

Warrant Machinist.
Pharmacist.

GENERAL NAVY REGISTER.

ABBOT, CHARLES W.
Purser, 2 September, 1856. Pay Inspector, 3 March, 1871. Pay Director, 3 July, 1871. Retired List, 18 November, 1891.
ABBOT, FRANCIS O.
Acting Ensign, 11 May, 1864. Resigned 5 May, 1865.
ABBOT, JOEL.
Midshipman, 18 June, 1812. Lieutenant, 1 April, 1818. Commander, 8 December, 1838. Captain, 3 October, 1850. Died 14 December, 1855.
ABBOT, TREVETT.
Midshipman, 13 October, 1848. Passed Midshipman, 15 June, 1854. Master, 16 September, 1855. Lieutenant, 7 January, 1856. Lieutenant-Commander, 16 July, 1862. Commander, 12 December, 1867. Died 27 October, 1869.
ABBOT, WALTER.
Midshipman, 2 December, 1859. Ensign, 25 November, 1862. Lieutenant, 22 February, 1864. Lieutenant-Commander, 25 July, 1866. Died 3 February, 1873.
ABBOTT, CHARLES.
Acting Second Assistant Engineer, 14 August, 1864. Resigned 5 June, 1865.
ABBOTT, CHARLES F.
Acting Assistant Paymaster, 24 April, 1865. Discharged 10 December, 1865.
ABBOTT, DAVID M.
Acting Ensign and Pilot, 3 May, 1864. Acting Master and Pilot, 9 November, 1864. Honorably discharged 20 June, 1865.
ABBOTT, GEORGE C.
Boatswain, 31 January, 1862. Resigned 3 April, 1866.
ABBOTT, GEORGE P.
Mate, 17 December, 1863. Honorably discharged 12 August, 1865.
ABBOTT, ISAAC A.
Mate, 2 February, 1863. Acting Ensign, 19 January, 1864. Honorably discharged 25 December, 1865.
ABBOTT, ISAAC H.
Midshipman, 10 May, 1820. Dropped since 1824.
ABBOTT, JAMES W.
Midshipman, 1 May, 1822. Resigned 23 May, 1826.
ABBOTT, J. FRANCIS.
Midshipman, 27 December, 1837. Passed Midshipman, 29 June, 1843. Master, 14 October, 1850. Lieutenant, 22 April, 1851. Reserved List, 13 September, 1855. Commander Reserved List, 4 April, 1867. Died 1870.
ABBOTT, J. GURLEY.
Mate, 3 December, 1863. Honorably discharged 7 December, 1865.
ABBOTT, JOHN P.
Purser, 1 October, 1852. Resigned 1 September, 1856.
ABBOTT, JOHN S.
Midshipman, 23 September, 1864. Graduated June, 1870. Ensign, 13 July, 1871. Master, 8 November, 1874. Lieutenant, 27 July, 1881. Died 16 March, 1889.
ABBOTT, SAMUEL W.
Assistant Surgeon, 24 January, 1862. Resigned 27 May, 1874.
ABBOTT, STEPHEN A.
Mate, 18 April, 1864. Honorably discharged, 25 July, 1865.
ABBOTT, THOMAS C.
Midshipman, 6 December, 1814. Last appearance on Records of Navy Department, 30 September, 1815.
ABBOTT, WALTER.
Midshipman, 1 January 1812. Lieutenant, 5 March, 1817. Died 12 July, 1825.
ABBOTT, WILLIAM A.
Midshipman, 13 October, 1848. Resigned 27 October, 1852.
ABBOTT, WILLIAM A.
Mate. Acting Ensign, 13 October, 1862. Honorably discharged 30 October, 1865.
ABELE, CLARENCE A.
Naval Cadet, 6 September, 1894. Ensign, 4 April, 1900.
ABELL, JOHN H.
Acting Assistant Paymaster, 5 April, 1865. Honorably discharged 24 September, 1865.
ABELL, WALTER B.
Mate, 2 February, 1865. Honorably discharged 10 November, 1865.
ABERCROMBIE, ALEXANDER R.
Midshipman, 19 October, 1841. Dismissed 28 August, 1849.
ABERCROMBIE, J. B.
Midshipman, 1 January, 1817. Died 2 March, 1819.

(15)

ABERNATHY, ROBERT A.
Naval Cadet, 5 September, 1896. Graduated, 30 June, 1900.
ABERNETHY, AUGUSTUS H.
Acting Assistant Surgeon, 28 January, 1865. Honorably discharged 10 October, 1865.
ABERNETHY, JOHN J.
Assistant Surgeon, 9 February, 1837. Passed Assistant Surgeon, 11 March, 1843. Surgeon, 7 November, 1850. Retired List, 29 October, 1868. Medical Director Retired List, 3 March, 1871. Died 28 October, 1879.
ABERNITHE, JOHN.
Midshipman, 1 September, 1811. Resigned 20 May, 1814.
ABJORNSON, AUGUST.
Acting Third Assistant Engineer, 14 October, 1864. Honorably discharged 23 October, 1867.
ABLE, AUGUSTUS H.
Third Asistant Engineer, 21 February, 1861. Second Assistant Engineer, 21 April, 1863. First Assistant Engineer, 1 December, 1864. Chief Engineer, 20 November, 1874. Retired List, 17 February, 1899.
ABRAHAMS, BENJAMIN.
Acting Assistant Paymaster, 14 December, 1864. Discharged 24 September, 1865.
ABRAMES, ISAAC S.
Acting Third Assistant Engineer, 15 November, 1861. Resigned 11 February, 1862.
ABRAMS, JAMES.
Acting Second Assistant Engineer, 11 August, 1864. Resigned 6 June, 1865.
ABY, CHARLES W.
Midshipman, 8 February, 1840. Passed Midshipman, 11 July, 1846. Master, 23 September, 1854. Lieutenant, 24 May, 1855. Died 16 October, 1856.
ACKER, EDWARD O.
Cadet Engineer, 15 September, 1875. Graduated 10 June, 1879. Assistant Engineer, 10 June, 1881. Resigned 31 December, 1889.
ACKERMAN, ALBERT A.
Cadet Midshipman, 24 June, 1876. Graduated, 22 June, 1882. Ensign Junior Grade, 3 March, 1883.· Ensign, 26 June, 1884. Lieutenant Junior Grade, 21 July, 1892. Lieutenant, 4 September, 1896.
ACKERMAN, THOMAS F.
Acting First Assistant Engineer, 1 October, 1862. Resigned 3 June, 1864.
ACKLEY, CHARLES.
Mate, 22 November, 1862. Acting Ensign, 31 October, 1863. Acting Master, 16 July, 1864. Honorably discharged 27 June, 1868.
ACKLEY, HENRY.
Assistant Surgeon, 30 July, 1861. Retired List, 20 June, 1864. Died 1 December, 1865.
ACKLEY, ISAAC.
Acting Second Assistant Engineer, 12 May, 1864. Resigned 19 June, 1865.
ACKLEY, JOHN B.
Assistant Surgeon, 24 January, 1862. Passed Assistant Surgeon, 5 March, 1866. Surgeon, 8 June, 1873. Died 11 September, 1874.
ACKLEY, SETH M.
Midshipman, 4 October, 1862. Graduated, June, 1866. Ensign, 12 March, 1868. Master, 26 March, 1869. Lieutenant, 21 March, 1870. Lieutenant-Commander, 30 June, 1887. Commander, 4 May, 1896.
ACKWORTH, WILLIAM F.
Mate, 14 November, 1862. Acting Ensign, 5 February, 1863. Dismissed 27 June, 1863.
ADAIR, ROBERT.
Acting Ensign, 1 November, 1864. Honorably discharged 23 September, 1865.
ADAIR, WILLIAM D.
Acting Second Assistant Engineer, 26 December, 1861. Acting First Assistant Engineer, 19 November, 1863. Died 11 October, 1864.
ADAMS, ALEXANDER.
Carpenter, 18 March, 1800. Last appearance on Records of Navy Department.
ADAMS, ALFRED B.
Acting Assistant Paymaster, 2 July, 1863. Resigned 28 June, 1864.
ADAMS, ATKINS.
Master, 18 January, 1809. Last appearance on Records of Navy Department.
ADAMS, CASSILLY.
Mate, 24 January, 1863. Acting Ensign, 3 October, 1863. Honorably discharged 15 September, 1865.
ADAMS, CHARLES A.
Acting Midshipman, 23 July, 1863. Graduated June, 1868. Ensign, 19 April, 1869. Master, 12 July, 1870. Lieutenant, 8 November, 1873. Lieutenant-Commander, 11 November, 1894.
ADAMS, CHARLES C.
Acting Assistant Paymaster, 6 May, 1861. Honorably discharged 7 October, 1865.
ADAMS, CHARLES F.
Mate, 27 January, 1863. Acting Gunner, 25 June, 1864. Honorably discharged 5 May, 1865.
ADAMS, CHARLES M.
Acting Third Assistant Engineer, 4 June, 1864. Honorably discharged 20 March, 1866.
ADAMS, CHARLES W.
Mate. Acting Ensign, 25 September, 1862. Acting Master, 20 July, 1864. Honorably discharged 6 June, 1868.
ADAMS, CYRUS B.
Acting Second Assistant Engineer, 4 January, 1864. Acting First Assistant Engineer, 12 June, 1865. Honorably discharged 29 October, 1865.

GENERAL NAVY REGISTER. 17

ADAMS, DAVID P.
Chaplain, 10 May, 1811. Died September, 1823.
ADAMS, ENOS O.
Mate, 16 December, 1861. Acting Ensign, 21 January, 1863. Acting Master, 18 July, 1863. Dismissed 18 January, 1865.
ADAMS, FRANK G.
Mate. Acting Ensign, 30 May, 1863. Died 23 May, 1865.
ADAMS, GEORGE.
Midshipman, 1 January, 1818. Lieutenant, 3 March, 1827. Commander, 6 April, 1849. Reserved List, 13 September, 1855. Died 19 April, 1856.
ADAMS, GEORGE K.
Midshipman, 1 August, 1864. Graduated 2 June, 1868. Lost on board Oneida, 24 January, 1870.
ADAMS, GEORGE W.
Acting Ensign, 28 January, 1863. Acting Master, 14 January, 1865. Honorably discharged 24 February, 1866. Acting Master, 11 September, 1866. Mustered out 10 November, 1868.
ADAMS, HENRY A.
Midshipman, 14 March, 1814. Lieutenant, 13 January, 1825. Commander, 8 September, 1841. Captain, 14 September, 1855. Commodore, Retired List, 16 July, 1862. Died 11 May, 1869.
ADAMS, HENRY A., Jr.
Midshipman, 16 October, 1849. Passed Midshipman, 12 June, 1855. Master, 16 September, 1855. Lieutenant, 11 May, 1856. Lieutenant Commander, 16 July, 1862. Commander, 25 July, 1866. Captain, 28 March, 1877. Died 1 February, 1878.
ADAMS, JAMES.
Midshipman, 16 January, 1809. Dropped 1815.
ADAMS, JAMES D.
Midshipman, 27 September, 1864. Graduated 2 June, 1868. Ensign 19 April, 1869. Master, 12 July, 1870. Lieutenant, 15 September, 1873. Lieutenant-Commander, 7 September, 1894. Commander, 3 March, 1899.
ADAMS, JAMES H.
Master, 10 July, 1812. Last appearance on Records of Navy Department.
ADAMS, JAMES H.
Midshipman, 11 December, 1799. Discharged 20 May, 1801, under Peace Establishment Act.
ADAMS, JAMES M.
Third Asistant Engineer, 14 May, 1847. Second Assistant Engineer, 26 February, 1851. First Assistant Engineer, 15 December, 1853. Resigned 2 August, 1862. Acting First Assistant Engineer, 12 August, 1862. Acting Chief Engineer, 19 January, 1863. Honorably discharged 27 December, 1867.
ADAMS, JEFFREY T.
Acting Assistant Surgeon, 30 November, 1861. Appointment revoked 26 July, 1862.
ADAMS, JOHN.
Boatswain, 21 May, 1803. Last appearance on Records of Navy Department, 24 July, 1840.
ADAMS, JOHN.
Midshipman, 5 September, 1845. Dropped 7 October, 1851.
'ADAMS, JOHN.
Acting Ensign, 20 July, 1863. Acting Master, 9 March, 1864. Died 22 February, 1867.
ADAMS, JOHN Q.
Midshipman, 3 July, 1835. Passed Midshipman, 22 June, 1841. Master, 22 March, 1848. Lieutenant, 21 February, 1849. Lost in Albany, 28 September, 1854.
ADAMS, JOHN Q.
Gunner, 22 October, 1862. Resigned 18 February, 1869.
ADAMS, JOSEPH H.
Midshipman, 8 December, 1831. Passed Midshipman, 23 June, 1838. Lieutenant, 15 February, 1843. Died 4 October, 1853.
ADAMS, J. P. B.
Midshipman, 2 February, 1829. Died 28 December, 1835.
ADAMS, J. F. A.
Acting Assistant Surgeon, 2 February, 1863. Resigned 20 January, 1865.
ADAMS, J. WARREN.
Mate, 22 June, 1863. Acting Ensign, 25 June, 1864. Honorably discharged 12 December, 1865.
ADAMS, LaRUE P.
Acting Midshipman, 26 October, 1859. Ensign, 16 September, 1862. Lieutenant, 22 February, 1864. Lieutenant-Commander, 25 July, 1866. Died 11 January, 1868.
ADAMS, LAWRENCE S.
Naval Cadet, 26 September, 1890. Graduated 30 June, 1896. Assistant Naval Constructor, 1 July, 1896.
ADAMS, NAPOLEON B.
Acting Midshipman, 25 January, 1849. Dropped 12 July, 1849.
ADAMS, NEWTON H.
Assistant Surgeon, 24 January, 1862. Passed Assistant Surgeon, 5 March, 1866. Surgeon, 6 June, 1868. Died 17 November, 1869.
ADAMS, PETER.
Boatswain, 25 August, 1809. Killed in action 1 June, 1813.
ADAMS, RICHARD.
Acting Master, 6 September, 1861, without pay. Appointment revoked 25 February, 1863.
ADAMS, ROBERT.
Midshipman, 18 May, 1809. Last appearance on Records of Navy Department, 18 September, 1809.
ADAMS, ROBERT.
Acting Master, 24 December, 1861. Dismissed 27 June, 1862.

GENERAL NAVY REGISTER.

ADAMS, RODERICK R.
Midshipman, 2 May, 1815. Drowned August, 1819.
ADAMS, SAMUEL L.
Acting Assistant Surgeon. Resigned 31 May, 1864.
ADAMS, SAMUEL W.
Midshipman, 1 January, 1808. Lieutenant, 24 July, 1813. Commander, 11 March, 1829. Died 1 January, 1831.
ADAMS, SAMUEL W.
Master, 3 July, 1813. Last appearance on Records of Navy Department.
ADAMS, S. WARDELL.
Midshipman, 18 June, 1812. Resigned 18 July, 1815. Midshipman, 16 May, 1816. Died 1820.
ADAMS, SHERMAN W.
Acting Assistant Paymaster, 10 March, 1862. Resigned 11 October, 1864.
ADAMS, SILAS.
Acting Third Assistant Engineer, 13 June, 1863. Died 2 February, 1864.
ADAMS, W. H.
Midshipman, 27 April, 1832. Passed Midshipman, 8 July. 1839. Died 8 November, 1842.
ADAMS, WILLIAM.
Sailmaker, 13 July, 1836. Last appearance on Records of the Navy Department.
ADAMS, WILLIAM HENRY.
Acting Third Assistant Engineer, 14 April, 1865. Honorably discharged 26 July, 1865.
ADAMS, W. M. E.
Midshipman, 7 June, 1831. Passed Midshipman, 23 June. 1838. Dismissed 9 July, 1841.
ADAMSON, ALFRED.
Third Assistant Engineer, 13 May, 1861. Second Assistant Engineer, 17 December, 1862. First Assistant Engineer, 1 January, 1865. Chief Engineer, 19 May, 1879. Retired List, 19 September, 1898.
ADAMSON, SAMUEL E.
Mate, 10 July, 1863. Honorably discharged 30 November, 1865.
ADDICKS, JOSEPH T.
Assistant Paymaster, 23 October, 1869. Passed Assistant Paymaster, 4 March, **1875.** Died 23 March, 1886.
ADDICKS, WALTER R.
Cadet Engineer, 1 October, 1878. Resigned 6 September, 1883. Lieutenant (Spanish-American War), 2 July, 1898. Honorably discharged 3 September, 1898.
ADDISON, DAVID M.
Assistant Paymaster (Spanish-American War), 18 August. 1898. Honorably discharged 11 April, 1899. Assistant Paymaster (Regular Navy), 3 June, 1899.
ADDISON, JOHN.
Chaplain, 3 March, 1825. Resigned 25 February, 1828.
ADDISON, JOSEPH.
Acting Gunner, 7 April, 1863. Honorably discharged 29 November, 1895.
ADDISON, S. RIDOUT.
Assistant Surgeon, 20 June, 1838. Passed Assistant Surgeon. 25 November, 1844. Surgeon, 22 September, 1854. Died 28 August, 1860.
ADEE, AUG.
Surgeon's Mate, 15 July, 1824. Surgeon, 3 January, 1828. Died 23 February, 1844.
ADKINS, JOHN.
Acting Third Assistant Engineer, 26 November, 1862. Appointment revoked 18 September, 1863. Acting Second Assistant Engineer, 10 December, 1863. Honorably discharged 13 July, 1865.
ADKINS, JOHN J.
Lieutenant, Junior Grade (Spanish-American War), 1 July, 1898. Honorably discharged 8 September, 1898.
ADKINS, WILLIAM E.
Mate, 1 August, 1864. Resigned 17 February, 1865.
ADLER, AUGUST.
Mate, 12 December, 1861. Acting Ensign, 3 July, 1863. Honorably discharged 2 May, 1868.
ADLINGTON, FRANCIS.
Mate, 9 June, 1862. Died 12 November, 1862.
AGNEW, JOHN.
Acting Third Assistant Engineer, 10 December, 1864. Honorably discharged 26 August, 1865.
AGNEW, JOHN P.
Acting Assistant Surgeon, 19 March, 1864. Resigned, 12 May, 1864.
AGNEW, RICHARD.
Carpenter, 12 January, 1874. Died 8 April, 1881.
AHRENS, A. H.
Mate, 17 November, 1864. Resigned 17 June, 1865.
AIKEN, EDMUND C.
Mate 28 July, 1863. Resigned 22 June, 1864. Mate, 5 April, 1865. Appointment revoked 8 August, 1866.
AIKEN, GEORGE W.
Acting Third Assistant Engineer, 1 October, 1862. Honorably discharged 3 December, 1865.
AIKEN, JOSIAH B.
Acting Boatswain, 1 September, 1863. Appointment revoked 10 August, 1864. Appointed Mate, 3 September, 1864. Resigned 13 September, 1864. Boatswain, 24 March, 1866. Chief Boatswain, 3 March, 1899.
AIKEN, W. APPLETON.
Acting Assistant Paymaster, 10 August, 1861. Resigned 12 December, 1861.

GENERAL NAVY REGISTER. 19

AIMEE, JACOB.
Gunner, 5 December, 1861. Killed on Mercedita, 31 January, 1863.
AINSWORTH, CHARLES.
Acting Ensign, 3 August, 1863. Honorably discharged 14 July, 1866.
AINSWORTH, FRANK H.
Ensign (Spanish-American War), 21 May, 1898. Honorably discharged 17 January, 1899.
AITKEN, HUGH.
Surgeon's Mate, 15 July, 1800. Died 17 September, 1806.
ALBERT, CHARLES.
Mate, 11 January, 1862. Dismissed 3 December, 1862.
ALBERT, JOHN S.
Third Assistant Engineer, 8 September, 1855. Second Assistant Engineer, 21 July, 1858. First Assistant Engineer, 30 August, 1859. Chief Engineer, 29 October, 1861. Died 3 July, 1880.
ALBERT, SIDNEY.
Third Assistant Engineer, 11 April, 1859. Second Assistant Engineer, 17 December, 1861. First Assistant Engineer, 17 March, 1863. Chief Engineer, 21 March, 1870. Resigned 31 December, 1872.
ALBRO, GARDNER D.
Acting Second Assistant Engineer, 20 December, 1862. Honorably discharged 19 August, 1865.
ALBRO, GEORGE L.
Gunner, 14 June, 1862. Retired List, 3 April, 1896.
ALBURY, WILLIAM H.
Acting Master and Pilot, 21 November, 1864. Honorably discharged 14 September, 1865.
ALBY, SETH B.
Midshipman, 18 June, 1812. Resigned 4 March, 1814.
ALCORN, JAMES.
Master, 29 June, 1812. Discharged 18 April, 1814.
ALCORN, JAMES F.
Acting Master, 28 April, 1862. Honorably discharged 14 May, 1867. Acting Master, 29 July, 1867. Mustered out 1 July, 1868.
ALDEN, CHARLES H.
Chaplain, 23 April, 1841. Died 24 September, 1846.
ALDEN, HUMPHREY.
Master, 3 October, 1811. Resigned 8 June, 1812.
ALDEN, JAMES.
Midshipman, 1 April, 1828. Passed Midshipman, 14 June, 1834. Lieutenant, 25 February, 1841. Commander, 14 September, 1855. Captain, 2 January, 1863. Commodore, 25 July, 1866. Rear-Admiral, 19 June, 1871. Retired List, 31 March, 1872. Died 6 February, 1877.
ALDEN, JAMES M.
Acting Ensign, 26 August, 1863. Acting Master, 9 January, 1865. Honorably discharged 31 December, 1865. Secretary to Admiral Porter, 26 July, 1866.
ALDEN, ROBERT W.
Midshipman, 1 May, 1822. Dismissed 14 November, 1831.
ALDEROFT, JAMES A.
Warrant Machinist (Spanish-American War), 15 June, 1898. Honorably discharged 2 September, 1898.
ALDRICH, ARTHUR F.
Mate, 11 October, 1864. Acting Ensign, 28 June, 1865. Honorably discharged 25 October, 1867.
ALDRICH, R. G.
Mate, 28 August, 1862. Resigned 24 September, 1862.
ALDRICH, WILLIAM S.
Cadet Engineer, 1 October, 1879. Resigned 12 June, 1883. Passed Assistant Engineer (Spanish-American War), 12 May, 1898. Honorably discharged 18 October, 1898.
ALDRICK, SAMUEL.
Midshipman, 7 July, 1800. Discharged 30 April, 1801.
ALDRIDGE, EDMUND W.
Acting Second Assistant Engineer, 19 April, 1862. Appointment revoked 1 July, 1862.
ALDRIDGE, JOHN H.
Acting Assistant Surgeon, 4 December, 1863. Dismissed 28 December, 1863.
ALDRIDGE, RICHARD.
Acting Third Assistant Engineer, 28 July. Discharged 16 October, 1865.
ALEXANDER, A. A.
Midshipman, 1 September, 1811. Resigned 19 June, 1824.
ALEXANDER, ADAM C.
Acting Midshipman, 23 November, 1859. Ensign, 16 September, 1862. Died 24 February, 1864.
ALEXANDER, ALEXANDER.
Midshipman, 2 March, 1799. Resigned 6 February, 1800.
ALEXANDER, CHERIAH H.
Acting Carpenter, 2 June, 1864. Honorably discharged 9 November, 1865.
ALEXANDER, FRANCIS.
Midshipman, 27 May, 1835. Passed Midshipman, 22 June, 1841. Lieutenant, 7 March, 1849. Died 11 May, 1849.
ALEXANDER, GEORGE W.
Third Assistant Engineer, 31 October, 1848. Second Assistant Engineer, 16 February, 1852. First Assistant Engineer, 27 June, 1855. Resigned 5 April, 1861.
ALEXANDER, GERARD.
Assistant Surgeon, 1 May, 1850. Resigned 8 March, 1856.
ALEXANDER, HORACE E.
Acting Ensign, 9 June, 1863. Appointment revoked 24 December, 1863.

GENERAL NAVY REGISTER.

ALEXANDER, JOHN.
First Assistant Engineer, 4 March, 1842. Disrated to Second Assistant Engineer, 28 July, 1845. First Assistant Engineer, 26 February, 1851. Died 26 January, 1863.
ALEXANDER, JOSEPH D.
Third Assistant Engineer, 13 March, 1847. Resigned 25 August, 1847.
ALEXANDER, JOSEPH W.
Acting Midshipman, 21 September, 1853. Midshipman, 10 June, 1857. Passed Midshipman, 25 June, 1860. Master, 24 October, 1860. Lieutenant, 11 March, 1861. Dismissed 5 July, 1861.
ALEXANDER, NATHANIEL.
Midshipman, 30 November, 1814. Resigned 1 June, 1821.
ALEXANDER, NEIL.
Mate, 28 October, 1861. Deserted 20 August, 1862.
ALEXANDER, RICHARD H.
Acting Third Assistant Engineer, 20 August, 1863. Resigned 17 November, 1864.
ALEXANDER, SAMUEL.
Master, 26 November, 1814. Resigned 15 March, 1815.
ALEXANDER, WILLIAM H.
Midshipman, 1 March, 1825. Resigned 10 November, 1827.
ALEXIS, LOUIS.
Midshipman, 15 July, 1798. Lieutenant, 4 March, 1807. Commander, 10 December, 1814. Resigned 17 September, 1827.
ALFORD, EDWARD.
Acting Ensign, 1 October, 1862. Acting Master, 15 June, 1864. Honorably discharged 9 April, 1866.
ALFRED, ADRIAN R.
Assistant Surgeon, 24 November, 1890. Passed Assistant Surgeon, 24 November, 1893.
ALGER, PHILIP R.
Cadet Midshipman, 22 September, 1876. Graduated 22 June, 1882. Ensign, Junior Grade, 3 March, 1883. Ensign, 26 June, 1884. Resigned 10 Novemberr, 1890. Professor, 10 November, 1890.
ALGER, WILLIAM H.
Mate, 18 August, 1863. Honorably discharged 30 September, 1865.
ALLAN, JOHN W.
Acting Third Assistant Engineer, 6 September, 1864. Honorably discharged 5 July, 1865.
ALLDERDICE, WILLIAM H.
Cadet Engineer, 14 September, 1876. Graduated 10 June, 1880. Assistant Engineer, 10 June, 1882. Passed Assistant Engineer, 21 February, 1893. Rank changed to Lieutenant, 3 March, 1899.
ALLDERDICE, WINSLOW.
Cadet Midshipman, 17 June, 1870. Graduated 1 June, 1874. Ensign, 17 July, 1875. Resigned 31 August, 1880. Lieutenant, Junior Grade (Spanish-American War), 1 June, 1898. Discharged 19 January, 1899.
ALLEE, PRESLEY.
Midshipman, 18 May, 1809. Resigned 5 November, 1810.
ALLEN, ABRAHAM.
Acting Master, 29 October, 1861. Honorably discharged 20 September, 1865.
ALLEN, ALFRED W.
Mate, 4 March, 1870. Resigned 11 March, 1873.
ALLEN, ALECK.
Acting Master, 17 October, 1861. Dismissed 22 May, 1862.
ALLEN, ALEXANDER B.
Mate, 4 April, 1864. Discharged 12 September, 1865.
ALLEN, AMOS D.
Acting Assistant Paymaster, 21 October, 1864. Honorably discharged 3 September, 1865.
ALLEN, BART. G.
Acting Ensign, 6 December, 1864. Honorably discharged 17 September, 1865.
ALLEN, BOWEN.
Acting Master, 11 November, 1861. Honorably discharged 25 November, 1865.
ALLEN, BURGESS P.
Gunner, 21 November, 1851. Retired List, 2 December, 1876. Died 16 July, 1886.
ALLEN, CALEB.
Midshipman, 13 November, 1799. Discharged 20 May, 1801, under Peace Establishment Act.
ALLEN, CHARLES N.
Acting Third Assistant Engineer, 7 September, 1864. Honorably discharged 5 July, 1865.
ALLEN, DAVID VAN H.
Naval Cadet, 6 September, 1887. Honorably discharged 30 June, 1894. Assistant Engineer, 22 August, 1894. Passed Assistant Engineer, 8 November, 1898. Rank changed to Lieutenant, Junior Grade, 3 March, 1899.
ALLEN, DRURY N.
Midshipman, 11 May, 1802. Resigned 17 September, 1803.
ALLEN, EBENEZER.
Carpenter, 27 June, 1810. Resigned 1 May, 1811.
ALLEN, EDWARD.
Midshipman, 22 January, 1838. Dismissed 9 August, 1845.
ALLEN, EDWARD.
Acting Third Assistant Engineer, 5 July, 1862. Acting Second Assistant Engineer, 10 October, 1863. Appointment revoked 23 November, 1865.
ALLEN, EDWARD GRAY.
Acting Third Assistant Engineer, 21 February, 1865. Honorably discharged 8 February, 1870. Second Assistant Engineer, 1 December, 1870. Dropped 14 January, 1879.

GENERAL NAVY REGISTER.

ALLEN, EDWIN J.
Mate, 29 December, 1861. Acting Ensign, 30 July, 1862. Dismissed 30 September, 1862.
ALLEN, EDWIN J.
Boatswain, 3 May, 1876. Died 6 September, 1881.
ALLEN, FRANCIS B.
Third Assistant Engineer, 1 March, 1862. Second Assistant Engineer, 15 October, 1863. Resigned 18 February, 1868.
ALLEN, FRANCIS P.
Acting Master, 12 October, 1861. Died 24 May, 1863.
ALLEN, FREDERICK B.
Acting Ensign, 18 May, 1864. Honorably discharged 13 August, 1865.
ALLEN, GARDNER W.
Passed Assistant Surgeon (Spanish-American War), 23 April, 1898. Honorably discharged 28 September, 1898.
ALLEN, GEORGE E.
Acting Third Assistant Engineer, 24 December, 1863. Acting Second Assistant Engineer, 4 March, 1864. Honorably discharged 14 August, 1865.
ALLEN, GEORGE M.
Assistant Paymaster, 3 March, 1879. Passed Assistant Paymaster, 30 August, 1883. Resigned 1 November, 1884.
ALLEN, GEORGE O.
Acting Assistant Surgeon, 9 December, 1863. Honorably discharged 21 October, 1865. Assistant Surgeon, 3 March, 1868. Resigned 17 March, 1873.
ALLEN, GEORGE W.
Acting Gunner, 9 May, 1862. Appointment revoked 30 October, 1865.
ALLEN, GEORGE W.
Acting Assistant Paymaster, 22 January, 1864. Discharged 25 August, 1865.
ALLEN, HENRY.
Acting Master, 15 October, 1861. Dismissed 13 January, 1863.
ALLEN, HENRY F.
Acting Third Assistant Engineer, 14 November, 1864. Honorably discharged 26 February, 1868.
ALLEN, HENRY S.
Mate, 29 October, 1863. Honorably discharged 27 August, 1865.
ALLEN, HOWARD.
Master, 24 April, 1812. Discharged 27 July, 1815.
ALLEN, H. R.
Acting Third Assistant Engineer, 20 July, 1863. Honorably discharged 8 August, 1865.
ALLEN, ISAAC.
Mate. Died 24 May, 1865.
ALLEN, JAMES.
Acting Third Assistant Engineer, 22 April, 1863. Acting Second Assistant Engineer, 19 April, 1864. Honorably discharged 22 September, 1865.
ALLEN, JAMES N.
Acting Assistant Surgeon, 10 June, 1861. Resigned 21 October, 1861.
ALLEN, JOHN.
Boatswain, 12 November, 1798. Discharged 10 June, 1801, under Peace Establishment Act.
ALLEN, JOHN.
Master, 1 July, 1805. Dismissed 12 December, 1805.
ALLEN, JOHN.
Acting Third Assistant Engineer, 2 December, 1864. Honorably discharged 9 February, 1868.
ALLEN, JOHN B. A.
Acting Third Assistant Engineer, 3 December, 1861. Acting Second Assistant Engineer, 14 November, 1862. Honorably discharged 5 October, 1865.
ALLEN, JOHN H.
Acting Ensign, 12 December, 1862. Acting Master, 16 February, 1864. Honorably discharged 12 December, 1865.
ALLEN, JOHN J.
Mate, 18 May, 1863. Reisgned 22 August, 1864.
ALLEN, JOHN M.
ALLEN, JOHN S.
Midshipman, 1 February, 1823. Resigned 13 February, 1824.
ALLEN, LOUIS J.
Acting Assistant Paymaster, 17 December, 1861. Discharged 28 December, 1865.
Third Assistant Engineer, 3 May, 1859. Second Assistant Engineer, 6 January, 1862. First Assistant Engineer, 20 May, 1863. Chief Engineer, 4 March, 1871. Rank changed to Captain 3 March, 1899.
ALLEN, MERWIN.
Acting Ensign, 5 June, 1863. Honorably discharged 28 November, 1865.
ALLEN, MOSES.
Purser, 15 May, 1790. Discharged 18 November, 1801, under Peace Establishment Act.
ALLEN, NATHANIEL P.
Mate, 26 December, 1862. Appointment revoked 1 April, 1863.
ALLEN, OLIVER P.
Midshipman, 28 September, 1846. Dismissed 17 June, 1851.
ALLEN, ROBERT W.
Acting Assistant Paymaster, 20 January, 1864. Passed Assistant Paymaster, 23 July, 1866. Paymaster, 1 February, 1868. Pay Inspector, 25 December, 1892. Retired List, 29 March, 1895. Died 6 November, 1895.
ALLEN, SAMUEL.
Midshipman, 11 December, 1799. Discharged 30 April, 1801, under Peace Establishment Act.

ALLEN, SAMUEL.
Midshipman, 13 December, 1800. Discharged 30 April, 1801. under Peace Establishment Act.
ALLEN, SAMUEL.
Gunner, 9 May, 1836. Resigned 1 March, 1839. Gunner, 3 December. 1841. Died 22 January, 1854.
ALLEN, SHERMAN.
Mate, 21 March, 1862. Appointment revoked 6 October, 1862.
ALLEN, THEODORE.
Third Assistant Engineer, 29 July, 1861. Second Assistant Engineer, 18 December, 1862. Resigned 13 June, 1865.
ALLEN, THOMAS.
Acting Assistant Surgeon, 19 September, 1863. Died 10 February, 1865.
ALLEN, WALTER H.
Naval Cadet (Spanish-American War), 21 July, 1898. Honorably discharged 23 September, 1898.
ALLEN, WELD N.
Acting Midshipman, 24 May, 1852. Midshipman, 20 June, 1856. Passed Midshipman, 29 April, 1859. Master, 5 September, 1859. Lieutenant, 24 February, 1861. Lieutenant Commander, 2 January, 1863. Commander, 25 July, 1871. Died 7 February, 1875.
ALLEN, WILLIAM.
Mate, 18 September, 1862. Acting Boatswain, 11 March, 1863. Boatswain, 13 March, 1866. Dismissed 24 February, 1868.
ALLEN, WILLIAM.
Gunner, 20 December, 1858. Dismissed 3 March, 1860.
ALLEN, WILLIAM A. H.
Third Assistant Engineer, 21 April, 1863. Second Assistant Engineer, 25 July, 1864. First Assistant Engineer, 22 November, 1872. Passed Assistant Engineer, 24 February, 1874. Retired List, 14 June, 1890.
ALLEN, WILLIAM B.
Acting Third Assistant Engineer, 5 February, 1864. Appointment revoked 10 March, 1865.
ALLEN, WILLIAM C.
Midshipman, 2 February, 1819. Died 1831.
ALLEN, WILLIAM H.
Midshipman, 28 April, 1800. Lieutenant, 17 February, 1807. Commander, 24 July, 1813. Killed in action 14 August, 1813.
ALLEN, WILLIAM H.
Midshipman, 1 January, 1808. Lieutenant, 24 July, 1813. Killed in action with Pirates, November, 1822.
ALLEN, WILLIAM HENRY.
Acting Third Assistant Engineer, 3 September, 1864. Honorably discharged 10 January, 1867.
ALLEN, WILLIAM H.
Cadet Midshipman, 26 September, 1872. Graduated 20 June, 1876. Ensign, 25 November, 1877. Lieutenant, Junior Grade, 14 July, 1884. Lieutenant, 5 March, 1890. Lieutenant-Commander, 3 March, 1899.
ALLEY, FREDERICK C.
Acting Assistant Paymaster, 26 September, 1863. Discharged 25 August, 1865. Assistant Paymaster, 21 February, 1867. Passed Assistant Paymaster, 25 January, 1870. Died 26 October, 1879.
ALLYN, GORDON L.
Acting Master, 24 May, 1861. Appointment revoked 29 October, 1862.
ALLYN, NOAH L.
Acting Master, 14 August, 1861. Appointment revoked 5 September, 1862.
ALLIBONE, CHARLES O.
Midshipman, 24 July, 1863. Graduated, September, 1867. Ensign, 18 December, 1868. Master, 21 March, 1870. Lieutenant, 2 November, 1871. Lieutenant-Commander, 28 May, 1892. Commander, 3 July, 1898.
ALLINE, BENJAMIN.
Purser, 28 October, 1798. Died 22 September, 1804.
ALLING, GEORGE B.
Mate, 1862. Resigned 28 July, 1862.
ALLINGHAM, JAMES J.
Assistant Surgeon, 21 December, 1861. Passed Assistant Surgeon, 8 May, 1865. Died 14 October, 1865.
ALLIS, E. H.
Acting Assistant Surgeon, 25 January, 1862. Lost on Bainbridge, August, 1863.
ALLISON, BURGESS.
Chaplain, 3 March, 1823. Died 20 February, 1827.
ALLISON, JACOB S.
Midshipman, 10 May, 1820. Resigned 10 March, 1822.
ALLISON, OSCAR W.
Third Assistant Engineer, 1 February, 1862. Second Assistant Engineer, 15 October, 1863. Resigned 8 December, 1869.
ALLISON, RICHARD.
Midshipman, 6 June, 1836. Passed Midshipman, 1 July, 1842. Died 5 May, 1847.
ALLISON, RICHARD T.
Purser, 30 October, 1849. Dismissed 6 May, 1861.
ALLISON, THOMAS.
Midshipman, 15 November, 1810. Resigned 19 April, 1813.
ALLISON, WILLIAM R.
Midshipman, 1 January, 1812. Last appearance on Records of Navy Department.
ALLMAN, PHILIP.
Acting Second Assistant Engineer, 27 November, 1863. Discharged 23 January, 1866.

GENERAL NAVY REGISTER. 23

ALLPHIN, HENRY Z.
Mate, 21 March, 1864. Honorably discharged 1 November, 1865.
ALLSTON, MILLEGAN.
Midshipman, 27 October, 1798. Last Appearance on Records of Navy Department.
ALLSTON, THOMAS P.
Midshipman, 15 February, 1840. Resigned 6 October, 1840.
ALMAND, ALBERT.
Midshipman, 10 September, 1841. Passed Midshipman, 10 August, 1847. Master, 14 September, 1855. Lieutenant, 15 September, 1855. Died 31 May, 1857.
ALMEY, THOMAS A.
Mate, 1861. Killed in action 20 May, 1862.
ALMS, HERMAN.
Mate, 5 June, 1863. Resigned 31 December, 1864.
ALMY, AUGUSTUS C.
Cadet Midshipman, 7 June, 1872. Reappointed 20 October, 1874. Graduated 4 June, 1880. Ensign, Junior Grade, 3 March, 1883. Ensign, 26 June, 1884. Lieutenant, Junior Grade, 28 October, 1890. Lieutenant, 1 March, 1895.
ALMY, FREDERICK C.
Mate, 21 July, 1863. Honorably discharged 11 January, 1866.
ALMY, GEORGE B.
Acting Master, 9 October, 1861. Appointment revoked 7 July, 1864.
ALMY, JOHN J.
Midshipman, 2 February, 1829. Passed Midshipman, 3 July, 1835. Lieutenant, 8 March, 1841. Commander, 24 April, 1861. Captain, 3 March, 1865. Commodore, 31 December, 1869. Rear-Admiral, 24 August, 1873. Retired List, 24 April, 1877. Died 16 May, 1895.
ALMY, JOHN W.
Mate, 13 January, 1863. Acting Ensign, 24 May, 1864. Honorably discharged 15 December, 1868.
ALMY, THOMAS C.
Master, 26 June, 1812. Last appearance on Records of Navy Department.
ALSON, ROBERT W.
Acting Ensign, 22 May, 1863. Honorably discharged 30 November, 1865.
ALTAFFER, ISAAC M.
Acting Assistant Paymaster, 24 June, 1864. Honorably discharged 20 March, 1866.
ALTHAN, GEORGE.
Acting Third Assistant Engineer, 19 March, 1864. Honorably discharged 13 October, 1865.
ALTHOUSE, ADELBERT.
Naval Cadet, 21 May, 1887. Ensign, 1 July, 1893. Lieutenant, Junior Grade, 3 March, 1899. Lieutenant, 27 March, 1900.
ALWARD, THOMAS.
Assistant Engineer (Spanish-American War), 14 May, 1898. Honorably discharged 15 February, 1899.
ALWYN, JOHN C.
Master, 25 May, 1812. Lieutenant, 24 September, 1812. Killed in action 29 December, 1812.
AMBLER, EDWARD.
Midshipman, 2 April, 1804. Resigned 30 June, 1804.
AMBLER, JAMES M.
Assistant Surgeon, 1 April, 1874. Passed Assistant Surgeon, 15 June, 1877. Lost in the Arctic regions 1 July, 1882.
AMEE, JACOB.
Gunner, 5 December, 1861. Killed on board Mercedita, off Charleston, S. C., 31 January, 1863.
AMELUNG, HENRY.
Midshipman, 1 February, 1826. Resigned 21 March, 1828.
AMES, HOWARD E.
Assistant Surgeon, 10 April, 1875. Passed Assistant Surgeon, 7 June, 1878. Surgeon, 10 March, 1891.
AMES, HUDSON N.
Acting Second Assistant Engineer, 8 July, 1863. Appointment revoked 4 June, 1864.
AMES, JOHN H.
Third Assistant Engineer, 1 July, 1861. Second Assistant Engineer, 18 December, 1862. Resigned 30 September, 1865.
AMES, MARK B.
Acting Ensign, 17 May, 1864. Honorably discharged 29 July, 1865.
AMES, PELHAM W.
Acting Assistant Paymaster, 19 July, 1861. Discharged 25 April, 1866.
AMES, SAMUEL.
Midshipman, 23 July, 1864. Graduated 2 June, 1868. Ensign, 19 April, 1869. Master, 12 July, 1870. Resigned 3 January, 1873.
AMES, SULLIVAN D.
Acting Midshipman, 22 September, 1856. Midshipman, 15 June, 1860. Master, 19 September, 1861. Lieutenant, 16 July, 1862. Lieutenant-Commander, 25 July, 1866. Commander, 6 January, 1874. Died 22 November, 1880.
AMISS, STEPHEN.
Acting Ensign, 1 October, 1862. Dismissed 2 March, 1863.
AMMEN, DANIEL.
Midshipman, 7 July, 1836. Passed Midshipman, 1 July, 1842. Master, 10 May, 1849. Lieutenant, 4 November, 1849. Commander, 16 July, 1862. Captain, 25 July, 1866. Commodore, 1 April, 1872. Rear-Admiral, 11 December, 1877. Retired list, 4 June, 1878. Died 11 July, 1898.
AMMEN, ULYSSES G.
Assistant Paymaster, 1 October, 1897. Passed Assistant Paymaster, 23 October, 1898.

GENERAL NAVY REGISTER.

AMMERMAN, CHARLES H.
Acting Ensign, 2 January, 1863. Acting Master, 23 July, 1863. Dismissed 9 October, 1863.
AMORY, EDWARD L.
Acting Midshipman, 1 October, 1862. Graduated September, 1865. Ensign, 1 December, 1866. Master, 12 March, 1868. Lieutenant, 26 March, 1869. Lieutenant-Commander, 22 January, 1881. Retired List, 29 June, 1887.
AMORY, JOHN H.
Midshipman, 19 August, 1823. Resigned 10 May, 1824.
AMSDEN, CHARLES H.
Cadet Midshipman, 21 September, 1871. Graduated June, 1875. Ensign, 18 July, 1876. Master, 4 February, 1882. Lieutenant, Junior Grade, 3 March, 1883. Retired List, 20 May, 1887. Died 17 May, 1888.
AMSDEN, GEORGE W.
Acting Third Assistant Engineer, 5 June, 1863. Honorably discharged 8 November, 1865.
ANDERSON, ADD.
Assistant Engineer (Spanish-American War), 4 May, 1898. Honorably discharged 10 January, 1899.
ANDERSON, ADDISON D.
Midshipmen, 19 August, 1823. Resigned 17 January, 1825.
ANDERSON, ANDREW.
Boatswain, 1 August, 1898.
ANDERSON, ANTONI.
Acting Third Assistant Engineer, 17 October, 1864. Honorably discharged 18 October, 1865. Acting Third Assistant Engineer, 9 March, 1867. Mustered out 6 March, 1868.
ANDERSON, ASA.
Acting Third Assistant Engineer, 4 January, 1865. Resigned 6 June, 1865.
ANDERSON, BENJAMIN F.
Midshipman, 3 March, 1831. Resigned 23 June, 1838.
ANDERSON, CAMERON.
Purser, 29 February, 1848. Died 25 June, 1852.
ANDERSON, EDWARD C.
Midshipman, 25 November, 1834. Passed Midshipman, 16 July, 1840. Master, 30 November, 1846. Lieutenant, 27 February, 1847. Resigned 25 October, 1849.
ANDERSON, EDWIN A., JR.
Cadet Midshipman, 28 June, 1878. Ensign, 1 July, 1884. Lieutenant, Junior Grade, 30 September, 1894. Lieutenant, 28 March, 1898.
ANDERSON, FRANK.
Assistant Surgeon, 24 May, 1875. Passed Assistant Surgeon, 22 November, 1878. Surgeon, 14 November, 1891.
ANDERSON, FRANK B.
Lieutenant (Spanish-American War), 30 April, 1898. Honorably discharged 15 September, 1898.
ANDERSON, GEORGE.
Acting Ensign, 14 August, 1863. Resigned 17 April, 1865.
ANDERSON, GEORGE.
Acting Third Assistant Engineer, 26 September, 1864. Lost on Narcissus, 4 January, 1866.
ANDERSON, GEORGE C.
Mate, 27 January, 1862. Deserted 2 July, 1862.
ANDERSON, GEORGE E.
Carpenter, 14 June, 1861. Retired List, 30 November, 1885.
ANDERSON, HAROLD W.
Assistant Engineer (Spanish American War), 21 May, 1898. Honorably discharged 8 October, 1898.
ANDERSON, JAMES.
Midshipman, 2 February, 1829. Passed Midshipman, 3 July, 1835. Died 28 December, 1840.
ANDERSON, JAMES.
Gunner, 19 October, 1799. Discharged.
ANDERSON, JAMES F.
Acting Master, 10 February, 1862. Appointment revoked 21 November, 1863.
ANDERSON, JOHN.
Midshipman, 22 September, 1859. Killed in action 24 April, 1862.
ANDERSON, JOHN.
Assistant Engineer (Spanish-American War), 4 May, 1898. Honorably discharged 2 September, 1898.
ANDERSON, JOHN D.
Gunner, 7 August, 1837. Resigned 10 April, 1840.
ANDERSON, JOHN W.
Acting Second Assistant Engineer, 26 October, 1861. Resigned 25 November, 1862. Acting Second Assistant Engineer, 4 June, 1864. Dismissed 5 November, 1864.
ANDERSON, JOSEPH.
Acting Third Assistant Engineer, 1 October, 1862. Acting Second Assistant Engineer, 10 August, 1864. Honorably discharged 4 December, 1865.
ANDERSON, JUSTUS D.
Acting Ensign, 6 May, 1864. Honorably discharged 28 June, 1865.
ANDERSON, MARK T.
Midshipman, 1 January, 1825. Dismissed 31 December, 1828.
ANDERSON, MARTIN A.
Cadet Engineer, 13 September, 1877. Honorably discharged 30 June, 1883. Assistant Engineer, 1 July, 1883. Passed Assistant Engineer, 25 May, 1894. Rank changed to Lieutenant, 3 March, 1899.

GENERAL NAVY REGISTER. 25

ANDERSON, NICHOLAS.
　Mate, 7 April, 1865.　Mustered out 23 July, 1870.
ANDERSON, OSCAR.
　Assistant Engineer (Spanish-American War), 4 May, 1898.　Honorably discharged 2 September, 1898.
ANDERSON, PETER.
　Acting Second Assistant Engineer, 28 May, 1863.　Honorably discharged 7 December, 1868.
ANDERSON, RICHARD.
　Acting Third Assistant Engineer, 16 October, 1861.　Acting Second Assistant Engineer, 6 February, 1863.　Dismissed 9 March, 1865.
ANDERSON, ROBERT.
　Mate, 4 August, 1863.　Resigned 5 December, 1864.
ANDERSON, ROBERT.
　Boatswain, 16 June, 1862.　Retired List, 14 February, 1896.
ANDERSON, SAMUEL.
　Surgeon's Mate, 13 July, 1799.　Surgeon, 25 August, 1800.　Discharged 23 July, 1801, under Peace Establishment Act.
ANDERSON, SAMUEL.
　Acting Assistant Paymaster, 11 August, 1862.　Honorably discharged 8 July, 1865.
ANDERSON, S. J.
　Mate, 3 September, 1863.　Died 27 January, 1864.
ANDERSON, THOMAS.
　Midshipman, 14 January, 1818.　Resigned 3 March, 1819.
ANDERSON, THOMAS O.
　Midshipman, 14 April, 1800.　Lieutenant, 24 March, 1807.　Resigned 21 August, 1807.
ANDERSON, W. G.
　Midshipman, 2 March, 1803.　Lieutenant, 9 December, 1814.　Died November, 1822.
ANDERSON, WILLIAM.
　Midshipman, 18 June, 1812.　Resigned 15 May, 1813.
ANDERSON, WILLIAM.
　Boatswain, 12 December, 1881.　Chief Boatswain, 3 March, 1899.
ANDERSON, WILLIAM E.
　Mate, 29 May, 1861.　Resigned 30 June, 1863.
ANDERSON, W. HENRY.
　Acting Assistant Paymaster, 4 June, 1862.　Assistant Paymaster, 30 June, 1864.　Paymaster, 4 May, 1866.　Resigned 16 February, 1869.
ANDERSON, WILLIAM H.
　Acting Ensign, 31 October, 1863.　Honorably discharged 3 July, 1865.
ANDERSON, WILLIAM H.
　Acting Third Assistant Engineer, 27 August, 1862.　Acting Second Assistant Engineer, 10 June, 1864.　Honorably discharged 20 September, 1865.　Acting Second Assistant Engineer, 8 June, 1866.　Mustered out 20 January, 1868.
ANDRADE, CIPRIANO.
　Third Assistant Engineer, 1 July, 1861.　Second Assistant Engineer, 18 December, 1862.　First Assistant Engineer, 13 January, 1865.　Passed Assistant Engineer, 24 February, 1874.　Chief Engineer, 11 September, 1881.　Rank changed to Captain, 3 March, 1899.
ANDRESS, WILLIAM A.
　Acting Second Assistant Engineer, 3 January, 1863.　Acting Third Assistant Engineer, 24 January, 1862.　Honorably discharged 15 October, 1865.
ANDREW, JACKSON.
　Acting Third Assistant Engineer, 17 June, 1864.　Honorably discharged 12 August, 1865.
ANDREW, MOSES L.
　Acting Third Assistant Engineer, 28 February, 1863.　Acting Second Assistant Engineer, 9 July, 1864.　Honorably discharged 7 August, 1865.
ANDREWS, A. M.
　Midshipman, 13 April, 1814.　Furloughed 15 August, 1819.　Dead.
ANDREWS, CHARLES L.
　Ensign (Spanish-American War), 30 April, 1898.　Honorably discharged 8 September, 1898.
ANDREWS, COLLIN J.
　Mate, 29 October, 1864.　Honorably discharged 21 March, 1867.
ANDREWS, DANIEL W.
　Mate, 9 August, 1864.　Acting Ensign, 19 November, 1864.　Honorably discharged 13 May, 1868.
ANDREWS, ELIJAH T.
　Midshipman, 19 October, 1841.　Died 22 January, 1849.
ANDREWS, FRANCIS S.
　Acting Third Assistant Engineer, 21 May, 1864.　Honorably discharged 13 October, 1865.　Acting Second Assistant Engineer, 19 December, 1866.　Mustered out 21 July, 1869.
ANDREWS, GEORGE H.
　Acting Assistant Paymaster and Clerk, 24 May, 1862.　Resigned 3 May, 1865.
ANDREWS, JOHN.
　Midshipman, 28 June, 1799.　Discharged 8 June, 1801, under Peace Establishment Act.
ANDREWS, JOSEPH.
　Gunner, 24 November, 1823.　Died 19 October, 1832.
ANDREWS, N.
　Chaplain, 16 August, 1816.　Died 1826.
ANDREWS, PHILIP.
　Naval Cadet, 28 September, 1882.　Ensign, 1 July, 1888.　Lieutenant, Junior Grade, 1 November, 1896.　Lieutenant, 3 March, 1899.
ANDREWS, S. C.
　Acting Master, 9 October, 1861.　Resigned 27 November, 1861.

ANDREWS, THOMAS.
  Acting Master, 29 October, 1861. Appointment revoked 4 February, 1864. Acting Master, 19 December, 1864. Died 27 February, 1865.
ANDREWS, WILLIAM B.
  Mate, 2 December, 1862. Resigned 7 August, 1863.
ANGELL, NATHAN S.
  Sailmaker, 1 June, 1822. Resigned 3 May, 1826.
ANGENY, GRANVILLE L.
  Assistant Surgeon, 16 September, 1898.
ANGIER, CHARLES.
  Midshipman, 3 September, 1800. Discharged 6 July, 1801.
ANGUS, GEORGE W.
  Mate, 21 November, 1867. Resigned 21 May, 1869.
ANGUS, JAMES W.
  Boatswain, 14 September, 1896.
ANGUS, SAMUEL.
  Midshipman, 6 November, 1799. Lieutenant, 4 February, 1807. Commander, 24 July, 1813. Captain, 27 April, 1816. Dismissed 21 June, 1824.
ANKERS, JOHN H.
  Mate. Resigned 17 July, 1862. Acting Ensign, 27 October, 1862. Honorably discharged 28 October, 1865.
ANNAN, JOHN W.
  Cadet Engineer, 15 September, 1875. Graduated 10 June, 1879. Assistant Engineer, 10 June, 1881. Died 9 January, 1891.
ANSCHUETZ, AUGUST.
  Acting Warrant Machinist, 23 August, 1899.
ANSON, R. E.
  Mate, 22 October, 1862. Acting Ensign, 31 July, 1863. Acting Master, 8 May, 1865. Honorably discharged 30 November, 1865. Acting Master, 4 January, 1866. Resigned 13 June, 1868.
ANTHON, GEORGE.
  Midshipman, 20 June, 1806. Warrant returned 7 July, 1811.
ANTHONY, CHARLES M.
  Acting Ensign, 18 December, 1863. Acting Master, 27 July, 1865. Master, 12 March, 1868. Lieutenant, 18 December, 1868. Lieutenant-Commander, 26 April, 1878. Retired List, 20 November, 1883. Died 8 November, 1885.
ANTHONY, JOHN G.
  Midshipman, 1 July, 1830. Resigned 14 June, 1837.
ANTHONY, JOSEPH.
  Surgeon, 20 June, 1798. Discharged 1 May, 1801, under Peace Establishment Act.
ANZELIUS, HJALMER K.
  Ensign (Spanish-American War), 21 May, 1898. Honorably discharged 6 December, 1898.
APGAR, ALLEN S.
  Acting Assistant Paymaster, 1 September, 1863. Honorably discharged 19 October, 1865.
APPERBY, WILLIAM.
  Acting First Assistant Engineer, 17 December, 1862. Resigned 23 June, 1864.
APPLEGATE, FRANKLIN T.
  Gunner, 27 May, 1896.
APPLEGATE, REUBEN.
  Acting Gunner. Resigned 3 June, 1864.
APPLETON, GEORGE H.
  Mate, 2 April, 1864. Resigned 18 January, 1867.
APPOLD, SAMUEL A.
  Acting Third Assistant Engineer, 12 March, 1863. Acting Second Assistant Engineer, 14 October, 1864. Honorably discharged 1 July, 1868.
ARBECAM, HENRY P.
  Mate, 2 January, 1864. Acting Ensign, 3 November, 1864. Appointment revoked 29 July, 1865.
ARBONA, JOHN G.
  Mate. Resigned 6 March, 1863.
ARBUTHNOT, C. E.
  Acting First Assistant Engineer, 1 October, 1862. Honorably discharged 20 November, 1865.
ARCHBOLD, SAMUEL.
  Third Assistant Engineer, 27 May, 1843. Second Assistant Engineer, 28 July, 1845. First Assistant Engineer, 10 July, 1847. Chief Engineer, 11 March, 1851. Engineer-in-chief, 16 October, 1857. Resigned 25 March, 1861.
ARCHER, CARSON.
  Assistant Surgeon, 23 July, 1850. Declined 13 August, 1850.
ARCHER, EDWARD K.
  Third Assistant Engineer, 26 June, 1856. Resigned 3 November, 1860.
ARCHER, GEORGE W.
  Midshipman, 1 May, 1822. Last appearance on Records of Navy Department. Dead.
ARCHER, JOHN.
  Lieutenant, 8 November, 1798. Discharged 30 April, 1801, under Peace Establishment Act.
ARCHER, RICHARD C.
  Purser, 25 April, 1812. Died 24 June, 1824.
ARCHER, STERLING.
  Surgeon's Mate, 18 April, 1800. Surgeon, 11 April, 1803. Last appearance on Records of Navy Department, November, 1805.
ARCHER, THOMAS T.
  Acting Third Assistant Engineer, 12 March, 1863. Acting Second Assistant Engineer, 29 September, 1864. Honorably discharged 7 November, 1865.

GENERAL NAVY REGISTER.   27

AREY, ALBERT R.
Mate, 19 June, 1863. Appointment revoked 19 November, 1864.
AREY, ARTHUR B.
Mate, 13 September, 1864. Honorably discharged 23 January, 1867.
AREY, DAVID B.
Acting Ensign, 3 May, 1864. Resigned 29 May, 1865.
AREY, HENRY.
Acting Ensign, 7 July, 1862. Acting Master, 9 August, 1864. Acting Volunteer Lieutenant, 5 September, 1864. Honorably discharged 11 October, 1867.
AREY, THOMAS S.
Acting Ensign, 3 May, 1864. Honorably discharged 29 July, 1865.
AREY, WILLIAM R.
Acting Ensign, 7 September, 1864. Resigned 21 April, 1865.
ARKINS, WILLIAM.
Mate, 5 August, 1863. Honorably discharged 21 December, 1865.
ARMANT, TERRENCE.
Midshipman, 19 December, 1839. Resigned 18 July, 1840.
ARMANDT, PAUL.
Mate, 5 March, 1863. Acting Ensign, 27 July, 1863. Honorably discharged 27 February, 1866. Mate, 8 July, 1867. Mustered out 12 March, 1868.
ARMBERG, CHARLES.
Acting Second Assistant Engineer, 1 September, 1863. Honorably discharged 24 January, 1866.
ARMENTROUT, GEORGE W.
Acting Midshipman, 23 November, 1861. Graduated 22 November, 1864. Ensign, 1 November, 1866. Master, 1 December, 1866. Lieutenant, 12 March, 1868. Lieutenant-Commander, 26 March, 1869. Died 13 August, 1875.
ARMISTEAD, ROBERT.
Carpenter, 14 March, 1800. Discharged 18 July, 1801.
ARMISTEAD, ROBERT.
Midshipman, 13 July, 1814. Last appearance on Records of Navy Department. Dead.
ARMISTEAD, SAMUEL W.
Cadet Engineer, 1 October, 1879. Ensign, 1 July, 1885. Assistant Naval Constructor, 1 July, 1887. Naval Constructor, 14 March, 1892. Died 27 January, 1895.
ARMOUR, SAMUEL D.
Midshipman, 15 November, 1809. Dismissed 19 November, 1812.
ARMS, FRANK H.
Acting Assistant Paymaster, 14 April, 1864. Passed Assistant Paymaster, 23 July, 1866. Paymaster, 14 October, 1871. Drowned 15 March, 1889.
ARMS, FRANK T.
Assistant Paymaster, 14 March, 1892. Passed Assistant Paymaster, 7 February, 1894. Paymaster, 15 June, 1898.
ARMS, LYMAN.
Cadet Midshipman, 24 September, 1870. Graduated 1 June, 1874. Ensign, 17 July, 1875. Resigned 31 March, 1882.
ARMS, THEODORE J.
Assistant Paymaster, 11 June, 1898.
ARMSTRONG, AARON H.
Acting First Assistant Engineer, 10 December, 1863. Honorably discharged 18 November, 1865.
ARMSTRONG, AENEAS.
Midshipman, 2 October, 1850. Passed Midshipman, 20 June, 1856. Master, 22 January, 1858. Lieutenant, 20 September, 1860. Resigned 21 November, 1860.
ARMSTRONG, CALEB H.
Mate, 29 December, 1862. Acting Ensign, 9 September, 1863. Honorably discharged 15 December, 1868.
ARMSTRONG, CHARLES W.
Midshipman, 4 March, 1823. Passed Midshipman, 23 March, 1829. Lieutenant, 3 March, 1831. Died 27 February, 1850.
ARMSTRONG, C. W.
Acting Assistant Paymaster, 30 March, 1865. Discharged 7 October, 1865.
ARMSTRONG, EDWARD V.
Assistant Surgeon, 5 April, 1898.
ARMSTRONG, FRANCIS.
Midshipman, 2 May, 1815. Furloughed 17 July, 1821. Dead.
ARMSTRONG, FRANK C.
Naval Cadet (Spanish-American War), 16 July, 1898. Honorably discharged 2 November, 1898.
ARMSTRONG, GEORGE.
Acting Second Assistant Engineer, 22 June, 1863. Resigned 7 September, 1863.
ARMSTRONG, G. N.
Acting Ensign, 15 July, 1863. Appointment revoked 20 November, 1863.
ARMSTRONG, G. W.
Acting Carpenter, 6 December, 1862. Resigned 2 October, 1863.
ARMSTRONG, HENRY.
Acting Third Assistant Engineer, 21 December, 1861. Acting Second Assistant Engineer, 26 November, 1862. Dismissed 26 May, 1863.
ARMSTRONG, JAMES.
Midshipman, 15 November, 1809. Lieutenant, 27 April, 1816. Commander, 3 March, 1825. Captain, 8 September, 1841. Commodore, Retired List, 4 April, 1867. Died 25 August, 1868.
ARMSTRONG, JAMES.
Midshipman, 9 September, 1841. Passed Midshipman, 10 August, 1847. Died 18 September, 1854.

ARMSTRONG, JAMES F.
Midshipman, 7 March, 1832. Passed Midshipman, 23 June, 1838. Lieutenant, 8 December, 1842. Commander, 8 June, 1861. Captain, Retired List, 4 April, 1867. Captain, Active List, from 27 September, 1866. Retired List, 2 September, 1872. Died 19 April, 1873.
ARMSTRONG, J. D.
Assistant Surgeon, 27 May, 1812. Last appearance on Records of Navy Department, 1824. Dead.
ARMSTRONG, JOHN.
Boatswain, 14 May, 1800. Resigned 3 December, 1800.
ARMSTRONG, JOSEPH E.
Acting Ensign, 30 January, 1865. Honorably discharged 7 August, 1865.
ARMSTRONG, L. H.
Acting Assistant Surgeon, 28 March, 1873. Honorably discharged 30 June, 1879.
ARMSTRONG, THOMAS.
Carpenter, 17 June, 1822. Died 6 September, 1836.
ARMSTRONG, THOMAS.
Acting Third Assistant Engineer, 6 July, 1864. Honorably discharged 1 March, 1866.
ARMSTRONG, WILLIAM C.
Acting Second Assistant Engineer, 1 October, 1862. Honorably discharged 10 December, 1865.
ARMSTRONG, WILLIAM M.
Midshipman 30 November, 1814. Lieutenant, 3 March, 1821. Commander, 8 September, 1841. Reserved List, 13 September, 1855. Captain, Active List, from 24 March, 1855. Died 28 June, 1861.
ARMSTRONG, WILLIAM M.
Acting Ensign, 23 January, 1864. Honorably discharged 17 August, 1865.
ARMSTRONG, WILLIAM McN.
Midshipman, 20 November, 1848. Resigned 4 October, 1854.
ARNAUD, WILLIAM S.
Mate, 19 November, 1862. Honorably discharged 29 August, 1866.
ARNE, LOUIS.
Acting Warrant Machinist. 23 August, 1899.
ARNETT, JOHN F.
Mate, 30 January, 1862. Resigned 9 September, 1863. Mate, 16 October, 1863. Acting Ensign, 22 March, 1864. Honorably discharged 20 October, 1865.
ARNOLD, A. C.
Acting Third Assistant Engineer, 8 December, 1864. Honorably discharged 9 June, 1866.
ARNOLD, CHARLES F.
Midshipman, 14 October, 1862. Graduated June, 1866. Ensign, 12 March, 1868. Master, 26 March, 1869. Lieutenant, 21 March, 1870. Dismissed 19 October, 1875.
ARNOLD, CLARENCE L.
Naval Cadet, 5 September, 1896. Graduated 30 June, 1900.
ARNOLD, CONWAY H.
Acting Midshipman, 30 September, 1863. Graduated June, 1867. Ensign, 18 December, 1868. Master, 21 March, 1870. Lieutenant, 22 June, 1871. Lieutenant-Commander, 10 January, 1892. Commander 11 May, 1898.
ARNOLD, EDWARD A.
Acting Assistant Surgeon, 5 November, 1862. Resigned 22 August, 1863.
ARNOLD, EDWARD G.
Mate, 23 December, 1862. Dismissed 9 June, 1863.
ARNOLD, EDWARD R.
Third Assistant Engineer, 1 July, 1861. Resigned 13 April, 1864.
ARNOLD, HENRY N. T.
Midshipman, 13 March, 1839. Passed Midshipman, 2 July, 1845. Master, 6 February, 1854. Lieutenant, 12 September, 1854. Lieutenant-Commander, 16 July, 1862. Commander. 3 March, 1865. Retired List, 30 October, 1871. Died 2 April, 1881.
ARNOLD, JOHN.
Master, 3 July, 1813. Last appearance on Records of Navy Department.
ARNOLD, JOSEPH.
Midshipman, 4 March, 1823. Last appearance on Records of Navy Department, October, 1828. Dead.
ARNOLD, LEROY.
Third Assistant Engineer, 16 February, 1852. Resigned 18 February, 1856.
ARNOLD, SOLON.
Cadet Engineer, 14 September, 1876. Assistant Engineer, 1 July, 1883. Passed Assistant Engineer, 1 April, 1894. Rank changed to Lieutenant 3 March, 1899.
ARNOLD, THOMAS.
Midshipman, 11 November, 1850. Resigned 21 September, 1855.
ARNOLD, WILLIAM.
Gunner, 12 April, 1845. Died 21 March, 1863.
ARNOLD, WILLIAM.
Mate, 21 October, 1863. Honorably discharged 19 September, 1865.
ARNOLD, WILL F.
Assistant Surgeon, 18 August, 1888. Passed Assistant Surgeon, 18 August, 1891. Surgeon, 22 January, 1900.
ARRANTS, RICHARD B.
Mate. 17 December. 1861. Acting Master, 21 April, 1862. Resigned 16 August, 1865.
ARRANTS, WILLIAM B.
Mate. 4 March, 1861. Acting Ensign. 14 September, 1863. Ensign, 12 March, 1868. Master, 18 December, 1868. Retired List, 23 May, 1870. Title changed to Lieutenant, Junior Grade, 3 March, 1883. Died 13 November, 1890.

GENERAL NAVY REGISTER. 29

ARTHUR, CHARLES G.
Mate, 27 December, 1861. Acting Volunteer Lieutenant, 18 May, 1864. Dismissed 29 September, 1864.
ARTHUR, CHARLES W.
Acting Ensign, 3 November, 1862. Honorably discharged 23 October, 1865. Acting Ensign, 18 May, 1866. Discharged 31 December, 1867.
ARTHUR, ELLIOTT J.
Midshipman, 27 September, 1865. Graduated 4 June, 1869. Ensign 12 July, 1870. Master, 12 December, 1872. Lieutenant, 1 July, 1876. Retired List, 16 November, 1882. Died 26 January, 1886.
ARTHUR, GEORGE.
Assistant Surgeon, 13 February, 1877. Died 1 November, 1887.
ARTHUR, HENRY H.
Acting Third Assistant Engineer, 15 December, 1863. Acting Second Assistant Engineer, 18 March, 1865. Honorably discharged 24 January, 1868.
ARTHUR, WILLIAM A.
Acting Master, 25 March, 1862. Honorably discharged 1 March, 1866.
ARTHUR, WILLIAM S.
Acting Third Assistant Engineer, 18 March, 1865. Honorably discharged 8 February, 1870.
ARUNDEL, ROBERT.
Master, 20 May, 1812. Died 10 November, 1812.
ASH, HOWARD P.
Assistant Paymaster (Spanish-American War), 11 June, 1898. Assistant Paymaster (regular Navy), 6 March, 1899.
ASHBRIDGE, J. H.
Sailing Master, 14 August, 1813. Midshipman, 1 February, 1814. Resigned 6 November, 1819.
ASHBRIDGE, RICHARD.
Assistant Surgeon, 3 July, 1876. Passed Assistant Surgeon, 11 October, 1881. Dismissed 23 February, 1881.
ASHBURY, GEORGE.
Acting Master, 28 August, 1861. Honorably discharged 8 December, 1865.
ASHBY, GEORGE E.
Acting Second Assistant Engineer, 21 December, 1861. Resigned 28 October, 1861.
ASHCROFT, RICHARD.
Acting Second Assistant Engineer. Dismissed 22 May, 1862.
ASHCROFT, ROBERT C.
Acting Second Assistant Engineer, 8 December, 1864. Honorably discharged 27 September, 1865.
ASHER, ALLEN.
Midshipman, 1 April, 1828. Resigned 1 November, 1828.
ASHMEAD, JAMES J.
Acting Third Assistant Engineer, 18 November, 1863. Honorably discharged 3 July, 1865.
ASHMEAD, L. P.
Midshipman, 19 October, 1841. Resigned 5 November, 1845.
ASHMEAD, THOMAS E.
Mate, 12 May, 1863. Acting Ensign, 25 January, 1865. Honorably discharged 21 October, 1865.
ASHMORE, HENRY B.
Cadet Midshipman, 3 October, 1876. Graduated 22 June, 1882. Ensign Junior Grade, 3 March, 1883. Ensign 26 June, 1884. Resigned 12 October, 1890.
ASHMUN, LEWIS.
Purser, 1 February, 1851. Died 1 March, 1852.
ASHTON, FRANCIS M.
Third Assistant Engineer, 20 May, 1863. Retired List, 22 January, 1866. Active List, 19 July, 1867. Second Assistant, 25 July, 1866. Resigned 4 January, 1871. Second Assistant Engineer, 19 April, 1873. Passed Assistant Engineer, 14 December, 1878. Died 15 November, 1886.
ASHTON, GURDON C.
Midshipman, 9 December, 1823. Passed Midshipman, 23 May, 1829. Lieutenant, 21 June, 1832. Died 11 October, 1840.
ASHTON, HENRY.
Midshipman, 10 February, 1838. Died 31 January, 1846.
ASHWORTH, DANIEL.
Acting Third Assistant Engineer, 17 August, 1864. Honorably discharged 20 December, 1865.
ASHWORTH, JOHN.
Acting Third Assistant Engineer, 27 April, 1865. Honorably discharged 20 December, 1865.
ASKINS, WILLIAM E.
Acting Ensign, 9 November, 1866. Discharged 20 May, 1867.
ASl'OLD, EDWARD.
Acting Third Assistant Engineer, 8 December, 1862. Acting Second Assistant Engineer, 18 October, 1864. Honorably discharged 5 October, 1865.
ASPINWALL, JOHN.
Mate, 9 June, 1862. Acting Ensign, 28 July, 1864. Honorably discharged 4 January, 1866.
ASPINWALL, JOHN S. G.
Acting Second Assistant Engineer, 16 November, 1861. Appointment revoked 1 April, 1862. Acting Second Assistant Engineer, 4 February, 1863. Honorably discharged 21 November, 1865.

GENERAL NAVY REGISTER.

ASSERSON, PETER C.
Mate, 27 May, 1862. Acting Ensign, 24 November, 1862. Honorably discharged 28 February, 1869. Civil Engineer, 6 March, 1874. Retired 5 January, 1901, with rank of Rear-Admiral and continued on active duty.

ASSERSON, WILLIAM C.
Naval Cadet, 25 September, 1893. Ensign, 1 July, 1899.

ASTON, ALBERT.
Third Assistant Engineer, 21 February, 1861. Second Assistant Engineer, 8 December, 1862. First Assistant Engineer, 1 December, 1864. First Assistant Engineer, 25 July, 1866. Chief Engineer, 12 June, 1873. Died 10 September, 1881.

ASTON, RALPH.
Third Assistant Engineer, 9 December, 1861. Second Assistant Engineer, 8 September, 1863. First Assistant Engineer, 1 January, 1868. Passed Assistant Engineer, 24 February, 1874. Chief Engineer, 28 July, 1888. Rank changed to Captain, 3 March, 1899.

ATHEARN, IRA.
Mate, 24 January, 1863. Honorably discharged 5 January, 1866.

ATKINS, FRANCIS H.
Acting Assistant Surgeon, 9 March, 1864. Resigned 28 November, 1864.

ATKINS, ISAAC F.
Mate, 2 January, 1864. Acting Ensign, 5 October, 1864. Honorably discharged 24 October, 1865.

ATKINS, JAMES.
Third Assistant Engineer, 26 August, 1850. Second Assistant Engineer, 21 October, 1861. First Assistant Engineer, 1 October, 1863. Resigned 1 August, 1865.

ATKINS, JOHN R. P.
Mate, 11 January, 1864. Acting Ensign, 19 January, 1865. Honorably discharged 11 November, 1865.

ATKINS, THOMAS H.
Acting Assistant Surgeon, 10 March, 1863. Resigned 28 November, 1864.

ATKINS, WILL E.
Mate, 1 August, 1864. Resigned 17 February, 1865.

ATKINSON, ARTHUR H.
Acting Master, 24 August, 1862. Honorably discharged 11 May, 1865.

ATKINSON, GEORGE H.
Acting First Assistant Engineer, 1 October, 1862. Acting Chief Engineer, 30 June, 1864. Honorably discharged 20 November, 1865.

ATKINSON, FRITH B.
Mate, 5 April, 1863. Honorably discharged 13 May, 1868.

ATKINSON, JAMES.
First Assistant Engineer, 26 May, 1839. Disrated to Second Assistant Engineer, 28 July, 1845. Dropped 18 January, 1848.

ATKINSON, JOHN W.
Acting Master, 10 October, 1862. Acting Volunteer Lieutenant, 7 October, 1864. Honorably discharged 28 October, 1865.

ATKINSON, PAUL.
Boatswain, 5 January, 1856. Died 2 December, 1868.

ATKINSON, WILLIAM B.
Midshipman, 16 March, 1799. Last appearance on Records of Navy Department, 23 April, 1799. Dead.

ATKINSON, WILLIAM M.
Lieutenant (Spanish-American War), 20 May, 1898. Honorably discharged 8 September, 1898.

ATLEE, HENRY C.
Mate, 4 March, 1864. Honorably discharged 10 June, 1865.

ATLEE, LOUS W.
Assistant Surgeon, 29 March, 1886. Passed Assistant Surgeon, 29 March, 1889. Surgeon, 18 June, 1898. Resigned 20 October, 1899.

ATTMORE, CHARLES.
Mate, 1862. Resigned 18 March, 1865.

ATWATER, CHARLES.
Mate, 19 March, 1862. Dismissed 23 May, 1862.

ATWATER, CHARLES N.
Cadet Midshipman, 26 September, 1873. Midshipman, 4 June, 1880. Ensign, 10 June, 1882. Lieutenant, Junior Grade, 9 September, 1889. Lieutenant, 22 June, 1894.

ATWATER, NORMAN.
Acting Ensign, 12 September, 1862. Lost on Monitor, 30 December, 1862.

ATWOOD, A. P.
Mate, 12 December, 1861. Acting Ensign, 4 May, 1864. Resigned 17 May, 1865.

ATWOOD, BENJAMIN.
Mate, 21 November, 1862. Resigned 5 May, 1863. Mate, 26 May, 1863. Appointment revoked 7 April, 1864. Mate, 9 May, 1870. Appointment revoked 31 July, 1871.

ATWOOD, EDWARD.
Midshipman, 17 May, 1800. Warrant returned.

ATWOOD, JOSEPH B.
Acting Second Assistant Engineer, 19 January, 1864. Honorably discharged 4 September, 1865.

ATWOOD, LEONARD.
Acting Third Assistant Engineer, 31 December, 1862. Appointment revoked 31 May, 1864.

ATWOOD, M. C.
Midshipman, 17 December, 1810. Purser, 26 March, 1814. Died 12 May, 1823.

ATWOOD, ROBERT N.
Acting Assistant Surgeon, 13 August, 1861. Resigned 24 September, 1863.

GENERAL NAVY REGISTER.

ATWOOD, SAMUEL.
Acting Ensign, 12 April, 1865. Honorably discharged 3 December, 1865.
AUBERLIN, GUSTAV.
Acting Warrant Machinist, 6 July, 1899.
AUBLE, JAMES L.
Acting First Assistant Engineer, 1 October, 1862. Resigned 28 March, 1863.
AUCHINLECK, ALEXANDER.
Second Assistant Engineer, 22 March, 1848. Dismissed 28 July, 1848. Acting First Assistant Engineer, 13 January, 1862. Acting Chief Engineer, 15 September, 1863. Resigned 31 May, 1865.
AUCHMUTY, H. J.
Midshipman, 10 May, 1820. Lieutenant, 17 May, 1828. Died 8 October, 1835.
AUFERMAN, WALTER C. W.
Ensign (Spanish-American War), 7 July, 1898. Honorably discharged 12 October, 1898.
AUGUR, JOHN P. J.
Midshipman, 25 September, 1866. Graduated June, 1870. Ensign, 13 July, 1871. Master, 22 July, 1874. Lieutenant, Junior Grade, 3 March, 1883. Died 9 January, 1884.
AULD, JAMES.
Mate, 21 September, 1863. Acting Ensign, 16 August, 1864. Honorably discharged 20 October, 1865.
AULICK, HAMPTON.
Assistant Surgeon, 3 February, 1879. Passed Assistant Surgeon, 3 February, 1870. Surgeon, 22 June, 1884. Died 24 March, 1888.
AULICK, JOHN H.
Midshipman, 15 November, 1809. Lieutenant, 9 December, 1814. Commander. 3 March, 1831. Captain, 8 September, 1841. Commodore, Retired list, 4 April, 1867. Died 27 April, 1873.
AULICK, RICHMOND.
Midshipman, 19 October, 1840. Passed Midshipman, 11 July, 1846. Master, 28 April, 1854. Lieutenant, 24 November, 1854. Lieutenant-Commander, 16 July, 1862. Retired List, 27 January, 1865. Commander, 3 March, 1865. Died 8 June, 1868.
AUST, JOSEPH C.
Acting Second Assistant Engineer, 6 January, 1865. Resigned 27 June, 1865.
AUSTIN, ALVIN A.
Assistant Surgeon, 6 October, 1874. Passed Assistant Surgeon, 6 May, 1879. Died 21 July, 1889.
AUSTIN, BENJAMIN.
Surgeon's Mate, 24 July, 1813. Resigned 22 November, 1824.
AUSTIN, BENJAMIN R.
Mate, 4 February, 1862. Dismissed 25 June, 1862.
AUSTIN, CHARLES A.
Acting Master, 28 October, 1861. Resigned 14 March, 1862.
AUSTIN, EDWARD A.
Acting Third Assistant Engineer, 9 June, 1863. Dismissed 15 January, 1864.
AUSTIN, EDWARD S.
Mate, 14 October, 1862. Honorably discharged 22 March, 1866.
AUSTIN, JOHN.
Acting Second Assistant Engineer, 13 January, 1864. Appointment revoked 19 March, 1864.
AUSTIN, JOHN H.
Acting Assistant Surgeon, 10 March, 1864. Assistant Surgeon, 18 May, 1864. Resigned 14 January, 1865.
AUSTIN, WILLIAM D.
Midshipman, 3 November, 1840. Passed Midshipman, 11 July, 1846. Master, 21 June, 1854. Lieutenant, 5 February, 1855. Resigned 13 May, 1857.
AUZAL, ERNEST W.
Assistant Surgeon, 22 April, 1885. Passed Assistant Surgeon, 22 April, 1888. Resigned 1 May, 1895.
AUZE, CHARLES A.
Midshipman, 13 December, 1831. Resigned 3 September, 1836.
AVANT, JOSEPH.
Mate, 7 January, 1862. Acting Ensign, 22 October, 1862. Acting Master, 8 May 1865. Died 3 November, 1866.
AVERETT, SAMUEL W.
Acting Midshipman, 3 November, 1855. Midshipman, 9 June, 1859. Dismissed 5 June, 1861.
AVERILL, FREDERICK L.
Assistant Paymaster (Spanish-American War), 8 July, 1898. Honorably discharged 21 November, 1898.
AVERILL, HENRY D.
Assistant Surgeon (Spanish-American War), 1 July, 1898. Discharged 5 April, 1899.
AVERILL, JAMES D.
Acting Third Assistant Engineer, 11 November, 1863. Honorably discharged 21 August. 1865.
AVERY, EDWARD D.
Acting Assistant Surgeon, 30 May, 1864. Honorably discharged 10 October, 1865.
AVERY, FRANK B.
Lieutenant, Junior Grade (Spanish-American War), 1 July, 1898. Honorably discharged 10 September, 1898.
AVERY, GEORGE.
Midshipman, 28 June, 1812. Last appearance on Records of Navy Department, 7 December, 1812. Dead.

AVERY, GEORGE H.
Acting Ensign, 12 September, 1862. Acting Master, 27 May. 1864. Dismissed 14 November, 1865.
AVERY, GEORGE R.
Mate, 21 November, 1863. Resigned 15 December, 1864.
AVERY, GUY H.
Acting Master, 14 October. 1861. Dismissed 7 August, 1862.
AVERY, HENRY.
Acting Ensign, 26 December, 1862. Appointment revoked 6 July, 1863.
AVERY, JOSEPH L.
Acting Master, 1 October, 1862. Resigned 25 May, 1863.
AVERY, LATHAM B.
Midshipman, 19 December, 1831. Passed Midshipman, 15 June, 1837. Lieutenant, 8 September, 1841. Dropped 28 September, 1855.
AVERY, THOMAS.
Acting Third Assistant Engineer, 14 April, 1865. Honorably discharged 12 September, 1865.
AVERY, WILLIAM B.
Acting Ensign, 10 June, 1863. Honorably discharged 10 August, 1865.
AVESON, THOMAS S.
Boatswain, 6 March, 1899. Resigned 28 June, 1899. Gunner, 29 June, 1899.
AXE, DAVID.
Mate, 13 December, 1862. Dismissed 22 February, 1864.
AXFORD, WILLIAM.
Midshipman, 28 February, 1799. Last appearance on Records of Navy Department, 30 March, 1799.
AXTELL, A. B.
Mate, 20 January, 1862. Resigned 2 December, 1862.
AXTELL, ENOS A.
Acting Third Assistant Engineer, 20 September, 1864. Honorably discharged 18 October, 1866.
AYERS, JOSEPH G.
Acting Assistant Surgeon, 17 December, 1864. Honorably discharged 24 September, 1866. Assistant Surgeon, 18 October, 1866. Passed Assistant Surgeon, 12 October, 1869. Surgeon, 7 January, 1878. Medical Inspector, 25 February, 1895. Medical Director, 12 December, 1898.
AYDELOT, BENJAMIN.
Master, 8 May, 1812. Dismissed 2 April, 1814.
AYRE, SAMUEL.
Surgeon, 29 December, 1812. Resigned 17 April, 1817.
AYRES, SAMUEL L. P.
Third Assistant Engineer, 21 July, 1858. Second Assistant Engineer, 17 January, 1861. First Assistant Engineer, 21 April, 1863. Chief Engineer, 21 March, 1870. Retired List, 29 July, 1897
AYRES, STEPHEN T.
Mate, 22 September, 1864. Honorably discharged 14 July, 1865.
AYRES, WILLIAM P.
Acting Third Assistant Engineer, 3 April, 1862. Acting Second Assistant Engineer, 22 October, 1863. Honorably discharged 29 December, 1865.
BAART, JAMES L.
Acting Warrant Machinist, 23 August, 1899.
BAAS, WILLIAM.
Acting Third Assistant Engineer, 8 December, 1863. Honorably discharged 2 September, 1865.
BABB, THOMAS D.
Mate, 21 November, 1861. Acting Master, 11 July, 1862. Honorably discharged 26 October, 1865.
BABB, WILLIAM T.
Assistant Surgeon, 26 April, 1847. Resigned 15 July, 1850.
BABBETT, CHARLES W.
Midshipman, 25 March, 1814. Resigned 9 June, 1814.
BABBIDGE, J. P.
Midshipman, 30 November, 1814. Struck off June, 1819.
BABBITT, CHARLES W.
Carpenter, 2 July, 1847. Died 23 September, 1865.
BABBITT, EBENEZER.
Acting Third Assistant Engineer, 5 November, 1863. Resigned 27 May, 1865.
BABBITT, EDWARD B.
Midshipman, 15 November, 1809. Lieutenant, 1 May, 1815. Commander, 3 March, 1835. Died 9 September, 1840.
BABBITT, FITZ HENRY.
Midshipman, 2 April, 1804. Lieutenant, 5 June, 1810. Killed in action 15 January, 1815.
BABBITT, GEORGE H. T.
Cadet Engineer, 1 October, 1873. Graduated 21 June, 1875. Assistant Engineer, 1 July, 1877. Resigned 10 August, 1886.
BABBITT, SYLVESTER C.
Acting Third Assistant Engineer, 18 April, 1863. Honorably discharged 7 November, 1865.
BABBITT, THOMAS.
Surgeon, 21 April, 1804. Resigned 25 April, 1810.
BABBITT, W. D.
Surgeon's Mate, 28 March, 1820. Surgeon, 4 May, 1825. Died 24 May, 1826.
BABBITT, W. K.
Mate, 11 March, 1865. Resigned. 8 September, 1865.

BABCOCK, CHARLES A.
  Midshipman, 8 April, 1850. Passed Midshipman, 20 June, 1856. Master, 22 January, 1858. Lieutenant, 2 October, 1859. Lieutenant-Commander, 16 July, 1862. Commander, 28 October, 1869. Died 29 June, 1876.
BABCOCK, CLAUDE.
  Acting First Assistant Engineer, 9 March, 1863. Resigned 18 March, 1865.
BABCOCK, CONVERSE A.
  Acting Ensign, 18 July, 1864. Honorably discharged 23 May, 1865.
BABCOCK, FRANKLIN.
  Acting Third Assistant Engineer, 3 November, 1863. Honorably discharged 28 October, 1865.
BABCOCK, HENRY.
  Acting Master, 4 November, 1861. Resigned 28 June, 1862.
BABCOCK, HEPMAN.
  Assistant Surgeon, 24 September, 1862. Passed Assistant Surgeon, 30 October, 1865. Resigned 28 November, 1868.
BABCOCK, JAMES D.
  Acting Ensign, 16 August, 1864. Honorably discharged 29 July, 1865.
BABCOCK, JOHN F.
  Naval Cadet, 22 September, 1894. Ensign, 4 April, 1900.
BABCOCK, WILLIAM C.
  Midshipman, 24 September, 1867. Graduated 6 June, 1871. Ensign, 14 July, 1872. Master, 9 October, 1875. Lieutenant, Junior Grade, 3 March, 1883. Lieutenant, 11 March, 1883. Died 11 March, 1896.
BABCOCK, WILLIAM L.
  Mate, 22 January, 1862. Acting Master, 10 May, 1862. Honorably discharged 13 January, 1866.
BABER, GEORGE F. B.
  Midshipman, 24 April, 1850. Lost on Porpoise. Last intelligence from ship, 21 September, 1854.
BABIN, HOSEA J.
  Acting Assistant Surgeon, 10 February, 1865. Assistant Surgeon, 13 May, 1865. Passed Assistant Surgeon, 23 June, 1869. Surgeon, 17 March, 1876. Medical Inspector, 22 June, 1894. Medical Director, 7 May, 1898.
BABIN, PROVOST.
  Naval Cadet, 6 September, 1890. Ensign, 1 July, 1896. Lieutenant, Junior Grade, 1 July, 1899.
BABSON, CHARLES B.
  Gunner, 17 July, 1895.
BABSON, EDWIN.
  Mate, 11 November, 1861. Acting Master, 14 June, 1862. Honorably discharged 1 November, 1865. Acting Master, 11 December, 1866. Mustered out 26 March, 1869.
BACHE, ALBERT D.
  Acting Assistant Paymaster, 19 November, 1862. Passed Assistant Paymaster, 23 July, 1866. Paymaster, 11 June, 1868. Pay Inspector, 12 September, 1893. Retired 23 May, 1894. Died 11 October, 1895.
BACHE, BENJAMIN F.
  Midshipman, 1 January, 1817. Resigned 22 July, 1824.
BACHE, BENJAMIN F.
  Surgeon's Mate, 9 July, 1824. Surgeon, 3 January, 1828. Retired List, 7 February, 1863. Medical Director, Retired List, 3 March, 1871. Died 2 November, 1881.
BACHE, GEORGE M.
  Midshipman, 1 January, 1825. Passed Midshipman, 4 June, 1831. Lieutenant, 3 May, 1835. Drowned 8 September, 1846.
BACHE, GEORGE M.
  Acting Midshipman, 19 November, 1857. Midshipman, 1 June, 1861. Lieutenant, 16 July, 1862. Lieutenant-Commander, 25 July, 1866. Commander, 5 April, 1875. Retired List, 5 April, 1875. Died 11 February, 1896.
BACHE, J. G
  Mate, 6 December, 1862. Resigned 11 January, 1865.
BACHE, RICHARD.
  Midshipman, 3 June, 1829. Passed Midshipman, 3 July, 1835. Lieutenant, 25 February, 1841. Drowned 27 March, 1850.
BACHELDER, GEORGE G.
  Mate, 14 November, 1862. Appointment revoked 29 August, 1864.
BACK, WILLIAM.
  Acting Gunner, 2 May, 1864. Resigned 10 May, 1865.
BACKUS, SYLVANUS.
  Acting Midshipman, 28 September, 1857. Midshipman, 22 August, 1861. Lieutenant, 16 July, 1862. Wholly retired 31 July, 1866.
BACON, ALBERT W.
  Acting Assistant Paymaster, 7 November, 1863. Passed Assistant Paymaster, 1 August, 1866. Paymaster, 25 October, 1874. Pay Inspector, 12 February, 1898. Pay Director, 10 July, 1900.
BACON, FRANCIS H.
  Acting Ensign, 13 September, 1862. Honorably discharged 10 September, 1865. Acting Ensign, 29 March, 1866. Appointment revoked 2 December, 1868.
BACON, FRANK A.
  Midshipman, 25 May, 1832. Passed Midshipman, 23 June, 1838. Lost on Exploring Expedition 1 May, 1839.
BACON, FREDERICK A. G.
  Acting Ensign, 6 November, 1863. Honorably discharged 10 March, 1867.

3

GENERAL NAVY REGISTER.

BACON, GEORGE.
Midshipman, 1 October, 1850. Passed Midshipman, 20 June, 1856. Master, 22 January, 1858. Lieutenant, 26 October, 1858. Lieutenant-Commander, 16 July, 1862. Resigned 6 June, 1865.
BACON, GRANVILLE.
Acting Assistant Paymaster, 14 December, 1864. Discharged 15 November, 1865.
BACON, HENRY.
Sailmaker, 26 February, 1833. Appointment revoked 27 March, 1847.
BACON, JAMES G.
Acting Assistant Surgeon, 21 February, 1862. Resigned 25 November, 1863.
BACON, J. K.
Acting Assistant Surgeon, 12 March, 1864. Honorably discharged 11 October, 1865.
BACON, WILLIAM T.
Acting Ensign, 20 January, 1863. Acting Master, 10 August, 1864. Honorably discharged 28 October, 1865.
BADCOCK, GEORGE.
Purser. Discharged 29 October, 1801.
BADGER, CHARLES J.
Midshipman, 22 June, 1869. Graduated 31 May, 1873. Ensign, 16 July, 1874. Master, 1 November, 1879. Lieutenant, Junior Grade, 3 March, 1883. Lieutenant, 5 January, 1886. Lieutenant-Commander, 3 March, 1899.
BADGER, OSCAR C.
Midshipman, 9 September, 1841. Passed Midshipman, 10 August, 1847. Master, 14 September, 1855. Lieutenant, 15 September, 1855. Lieutenant-Commander, 16 July, 1862. Commander, 25 July, 1866. Captain, 25 November, 1872. Commodore, 15 November, 1881. Retired List, 12 August, 1885. Died 20 June, 1899.
BADGLEY, MORGAN.
Acting Third Assistant Engineer, 21 December, 1861. Resigned 19 November, 1862.
BADLAM, WILLIAM H.
Third Assistant Engineer, 3 May, 1859. Second Assistant Engineer, 8 October, 1861. Resigned 10 March, 1866. Passed Assistant Engineer (Spanish-American War), 14 May, 1898. Honorably discharged 31 October, 1898.
BAECHTOLD, CHARLES A.
Assistant Engineer (Spanish-American War), 1 July, 1898. Honorably discharged 6 February, 1899.
BAER, W. H.
Acting Assistant Paymaster, 7 September, 1864. Honorably discharged 11 October, 1865.
BAGBY, ANDREW H.
Acting First Assistant Engineer, 13 August, 1863. Honorably discharged 4 November, 1865.
BAGG, CHARLES P.
Assistant Surgeon, 17 March, 1892. Passed Assistant Surgeon, 17 March, 1895.
BAGG, JOHN S.
Assistant Surgeon, 7 January, 1875. Passed Assistant Surgeon, 29 May, 1878. Resigned 1 June, 1883.
BAGLEY, ANDREW H.
Acting First Assistant Engineer, 22 May, 1863. Honorably discharged 4 November, 1865.
BAGLEY, WORTH.
Naval Cadet, 5 September, 1889. Resigned 17 June, 1891. Naval Cadet, 7 September, 1891. Ensign, 1 July, 1897. Killed in action, 11 May, 1898.
BAGNELL, BENJAMIN.
Boatswain, 26 November, 1799. Discharged 23 May, 1801.
BAGOT, WILLIAM.
Master, 8 June, 1804. Dismissed 10 November, 1810.
BAILEY, ALFRED.
Midshipman, 28 January, 1841. Resigned 7 July, 1845.
BAILEY, CLAUDE.
Naval Cadet, 8 September, 1886. Ensign, 1 July, 1892. Lieutenant, Junior Grade, 3 March, 1899. Lieutenant, 1 July, 1899.
BAILEY, FREDERICK C.
Mate, 28 November, 1864. Honorably discharged 23 August, 1866. Mate, 29 August, 1866. Mustered out 27 November, 1868.
BAILEY, FRANK H.
Cadet Engineer, 1 October, 1873. Graduated 21 June, 1875. Assistant Engineer, 1 July, 1877. Passed Assistant Engineer, 7 October, 1884. Chief Engineer, 27 June, 1896. Rank changed to Lieutenant-Commander, 3 March, 1899.
BAILEY, G. R.
Acting Ensign, 10 September, 1862. Honorably discharged 4 November, 1865.
BAILEY, GEORGE W. A.
Carpenter, 28 September, 1897.
BAILEY, JAMES.
Gunner, 1 August, 1803. Last appearance on Records of Navy Department.
BAILEY, JAMES.
Midshipman, 16 January, 1809. Resigned 25 February, 1810.
BAILEY, JAMES H.
Acting First Assistant Engineer, 22 June, 1863. Dismissed 8 August, 1863.
BAILEY, JAMES M.
Acting Ensign 10 April, 1863. Honorably discharged 14 November, 1865.
BAILEY, JOHN E.
Naval Cadet, 20 May, 1895. At sea prior to final graduation.
BAILEY, JOHN R.
Mate, 27 July, 1863. Dismissed 26 July, 1864.

GENERAL NAVY REGISTER. 35

BAILEY, JOHN T.
Sailmaker, 22, December, 1875. Died 18 March, 1894.
BAILEY, JOSEPH H.
Third Assistant Engineer, 21 November, 1857. Second Assistant Engineer, 2 August, 1859. First Assistant Engineer, 17 March, 1863. Dropped 11 July, 1873.
BAILEY, LEWIS C.
Midshipman, 23 August, 1798. Lieutenant, 1 November, 1800. Discharged 20 October, 1801, under Peace Establishment Act.
BAILEY, LOUDON.
Master, 11 September, 1799. Discharged 10 June, 1801, under Peace Establishment Act.
BAILEY, MAHLON G.
Mate, 7 August, 1863. Acting Ensign, 18 January, 1864. Honorably discharged 28 October, 1865.
BAILEY, THEODORUS.
Midshipman, 1 January, 1818. Lieutenant, 3 March, 1827. Commander, 6 March, 1849. Captain, 15 December, 1855. Commodore, 16 July, 1862. Rear-Admiral, 25 July, 1866. Retired List, 10 October, 1866. Died 10 February, 1877.
BAILEY, THOMAS B.
Assistant Surgeon, 23 May, 1889. Passed Assistant Surgeon, 23 May, 1892. Died 24 February, 1898.
BAILEY, WILLIAM.
Acting Master, 12 August, 1861. Appointment revoked 2 July, 1863. Acting Ensign, 7 December, 1863. Acting Master, 24 May, 1864. Honorably discharged 19 September, 1865.
BAILIE, WILLIAM L.
Third Assistant Engineer, 16 January, 1863. Second Assistant Engineer, 28 May, 1864. First Assistant Engineer, 31 January, 1874. Retired List, 30 June, 1885.
BAIN, ROBERT M.
Carpenter, 3 July, 1849. Dismissed 4 June, 1861.
BAINBRIDGE, ARTHUR.
Midshipman, 22 February, 1815. Last appearance on Records of Navy Department, 30 December, 1822. Dead.
BAINBRIDGE, JOSEPH.
Midshipman, 8 April, 1799. Lieutenant, 16 January, 1807. Commander, 3 March, 1813. Captain, 23 November, 1814. Died 18 November, 1824.
BAINBRIDGE, WILLIAM.
Lieutenant, 3 August, 1798. Commander, 29 March, 1799. Captain, 20 May, 1800. Thanks of Congress for gallantry, good conduct and services in the capture of British frigate Java. Died 27 July, 1833.
BAIRD, GEORGE W.
Acting Third Assistant Engineer, 19 September, 1862. Third Assistant Engineer, 8 September, 1863. Second Assistant Engineer, 25 July, 1866. Passed Assistant Engineer, 17 June, 1874. Chief Engineer, 22 June, 1892. Rank changed to Commander, 3 March, 1899.
BAIRD, MARCUS.
Mate, 1 November, 1862. Resigned 9 July, 1863. Mate, 31 August, 1863. Acting Ensign, 5 November, 1863. Resigned 4 January, 1865.
BAIRD, ROBERT J.
Ensign (Spanish-American War), 27 June, 1898. Honorably discharged 21 October, 1898.
BAIRD, SAMUEL P.
Midshipman, 27 September, 1861. Graduated September, 1865. Ensign, 1 December, 1866. Master, 12 March, 1868. Lieutenant, 26 March, 1869. Resigned 9 September, 1873.
BAIRD, WILLIAM P.
Acting Assistant Surgeon, 1 October, 1862. Assistant Surgeon, 21 April, 1864. Resigned 19 June, 1867.
BAKEMAN, GEORGE R.
Mate, 1 December, 1863. Resigned 17 October, 1864.
BAKER, ABNER.
Midshipman, 17 June, 1833. Resigned 17 September, 1834.
BAKER, ANTHONY W.
Midshipman, 1 January, 1825. Resigned 13 September, 1825.
BAKER, ASHER C.
Midshipman, 30 September, 1867. Graduated 6 June, 1871. Ensign, 14 July, 1872. Master, 6 December, 1876. Lieutenant, Junior Grade, 3 March, 1883. Lieutenant, 10 January, 1884. Lieutenant-Commander, 3 March, 1899.
BAKER, CHARLES.
Mate. Dismissed 23 July, 1862.
BAKER, BENJAMIN R.
Mate, 2 January, 1864. Died 16 June, 1865.
BAKER, CHARLES H.
Third Assistant Engineer, 2 August, 1855. Second Assistant Engineer, 21 July, 1858. First Assistant Engineer, 3 August, 1859. Chief Engineer, 29 October, 1861. Retired list, 16 January, 1893. Died 6 May, 1896.
BAKER, CHARLES T.
Acting Ensign, 24 October, 1864. Honorably discharged 14 August, 1865.
BAKER, DANIEL F.
Midshipman, 28 June, 1868. Graduated 1 June, 1872. Died 15 August, 1874.
BAKER, EDWARD.
Acting Master, 27 May, 1861. Acting Volunteer Lieutenant, 31 May, 1864. Honorably discharged 7 November, 1865.

36   GENERAL NAVY REGISTER.

BAKER, EDWARD.
    Midshipman, 18 June, 1812. Last appearance on Records of Navy Department.
BAKER, EZRA.
    Surgeon, 8 July, 1809. Resigned 19 May, 1810.
BAKER, FRANCIS E.
    Midshipman, 17 July, 1832. Passed Midshipman, 23 June, 1838. Lieutenant, 11 April, 1844. Died 16 May, 1844.
BAKER, FRANCIS H.
    Midshipman, 12 October, 1848. Passed Midshipman, 15 June, 1854. Master, 15 September, 1855. Lieutenant, 16 September, 1855. Lieutenant-Commander, 16 July, 1862. Commander, 24 July, 1867. Captain, 13 November, 1878. Died 3 March, 1880.
BAKER, FREDERIC W.
    Passed Assistant Engineer (Spanish-American War), 14 May, 1898. Honorably discharged 25 February, 1899.
BAKER, FREDERICK W.
    Acting Third Assistant Engineer, 5 May, 1864. Resigned 19 July, 1864.
BAKER, GEORGE.
    Mate, 10 October, 1862. Resigned 26 March, 1863.
BAKER, GEORGE A.
    Third Assistant Engineer, 16 January, 1863. Died 6 June, 1864.
BAKER, GEORGE H.
    Gunner, 8 November, 1851. Dismissed 16 November, 1855.
BAKER, GEORGE H.
    Acting Gunner, 12 November, 1864. Honorably discharged 12 October, 1865.
BAKER, GEORGE M.
    Acting Second Assistant Engineer, 27 July, 1863. Honorably discharged 30 November, 1865.
BAKER, GEORGE S.
    Acting Third Assistant Engineer, 6 January, 1862. Deserted 20 January, 1863.
BAKER, GEORGE W.
    Acting Ensign, 23 September, 1862. Honorably discharged 15 February, 1868.
BAKER, GEORGE W.
    Acting Third Assistant Engineer, 1 October, 1862. Appointment revoked 3 October, 1863.
BAKER, HENRY.
    Acting Ensign, 23 December, 1863. Honorably discharged 3 November, 1865.
BAKER, HENRY.
    Mate, 1 October, 1862. Acting Ensign, 28 April, 1863. Acting Master, 17 July, 1864. Honorably discharged 5 November, 1865.
BAKER, HENRY.
    Mate, 20 November, 1862. Died from wounds received in action 23 February, 1863.
BAKER, HENRY R.
    Acting Ensign, 11 August, 1862. Acting Master, 6 July, 1864. Ensign, 12 March, 1868. Master, 18 December, 1868. Lieutenant, 21 March, 1870. Retired List, 2 December, 1876.
BAKER, HENRY T.
    Naval Cadet, 7 October, 1890. Assistant Engineer, 1 July, 1896. Rank changed to Ensign, 3 March, 1899. Lieutenant, Junior Grade, 1 July, 1899.
BAKER, JAMES.
    Mate, 20 January, 1862. Dismissed 29 November, 1862.
BAKER, JOHN.
    Acting Master, 26 August, 1861. Honorably discharged 4 November, 1865.
BAKER, JOHN.
    Gunner, 16 June, 1814. Died 31 December, 1819.
BAKER, JOHN C.
    Midshipman, 1 September, 1811. Last appearance on Records of Navy Department, 25 June, 1812. Dead.
BAKER, JOHN F.
    Mate, 24 February, 1864. Resigned 6 June, 1865.
BAKER, JOHN H.
    Cadet Engineer, 15 September, 1875. Graduated 10 June, 1879. Assistant Engineer, 10 June, 1881. Died 12 September, 1890.
BAKER, JOHN M.
    Mate, 13 May, 1863. Appointment revoked 9 July, 1863.
BAKER, JOHN O.
    Acting Carpenter, 24 November, 1863. Resigned 8 November, 1864.
BAKER, JOHN P.
    Midshipman, 11 February, 1847. Resigned 21 March, 1851.
BAKER, JOHN W.
    Assistant Surgeon, 6 July, 1882. Passed Assistant Surgeon, 6 July, 1885. Surgeon, 21 January, 1897. Retired List, 5 November, 1897.
BAKER, JONATHAN.
    Mate, 15 November, 1861. Acting Master, 18 June, 1862. Honorably discharged 24 May, 1868.
BAKER, LORENZO.
    Acting Master and Pilot, 1 April, 1865. Appointment revoked 9 June, 1865.
BAKER, LOTHROP.
    Acting Master, 1 April, 1862. Resigned 30 March, 1864.
BAKER, MATTHIAS W.
    Acting Third Assistant Engineer, 26 November, 1861. Appointment revoked 8 January, 1863.
BAKER, NATHAN.
    Purser, 20 May, 1803. Resigned 4 May, 1805.

BAKER, NEHEMIAH M.
Mate, 14 October, 1862. Resigned 30 May, 1865.
BAKER, NELSON R.
Midshipman, 26 November, 1828. Died 22 June, 1830.
BAKER, PHILEMON.
Assistant Surgeon, 7 March, 1838. Died 22 March, 1839.
BAKER, RICHARD B.
Midshipman, 15 January, 1801. Discharged 12 October, 1801.
BAKER, ROSWELL F.
Acting Third Assistant Engineer, 18 June, 1864. Honorably discharged 18 September, 1868.
BAKER, SAMUEL H.
Midshipman, 24 September, 1861. Graduated November, 1864. Ensign, 1 November, 1866. Master, 1 December, 1866. Lieutenant, 12 March, 1868. Lieutenant-Commander, 26 March, 1809. Commander, 26 December, 1884. Died 30 October, 1888.
BAKER, STEPHEN D.
Ensign (Spanish-American War), 22 June, 1898. Honorably discharged 23 September, 1898.
BAKER, THOMAS.
Lieutenant, 25 May, 1798. Captain, 13 July, 1799. Discharged 13 April, 1801.
BAKER, THOMAS H.
Mate, 8 January, 1862. Acting Ensign, 28 October, 1862. Honorably discharged 22 November, 1865.
BAKER, WILLIAM.
Surgeon's Mate, 2 April, 1804. Resigned 1 October, 1805.
BAKER, WILLIAM L.
Mate, 31 August, 1863. Acting Ensign, 15 September, 1864. Honorably discharged 27 November, 1865.
BAKER, WINFIELD S.
Midshipman, 30 July, 1866. Graduated June, 1870. Resigned 25 August, 1870.
BAKER, YORICK.
Midshipman, 18 June, 1812. Cashiered 30 December, 1819.
BALCH, EDWARD.
Acting Ensign, 18 June, 1863. Appointment revoked 17 November, 1864.
BALCH, FRANK K.
Acting Assistant Paymaster, 29 March, 1865. Discharged 17 October, 1866.
BALCH, GEORGE B.
Midshipman, 30 December, 1837. Passed Midshipman, 29 June, 1843. Lieutenant, 16 August, 1850. Commander, 16 July, 1862. Captain, 25 July, 1866. Commodore, 13 August, 1872. Rear-Admiral, 5 June, 1878. Retired List, 3 January, 1883.
BALCH, JOHN W.
Acting Master, 4 September, 1861. Acting Volunteer Lieutenant, 30 July, 1864. Honorably discharged 20 October, 1865.
BALCH, WILLIAM.
Chaplain, 30 October, 1799. Discharged 10 May, 1801.
BALDWIN, AUG. S.
Midshipman, 2 February, 1829. Passed Midshipman, 4 June, 1836. Lieutenant, 8 September, 1841. Reserved List, 13 September, 1855. Commander, 24 April, 1861. Captain, Retired List, 4 April, 1867. Died 1 February, 1876.
BALDWIN, CHARLES.
Appointed Acting Master's Mate for gallantry, 9 June, 1864. Honorably discharged 12 January, 1865.
BALDWIN, CHARLES E.
Mate, 15 September, 1862. Resigned 2 May, 1863.
BALDWIN, CHARLES H.
Midshipman, 24 April, 1839. Passed Midshipman, 2 July, 1845. Master, 17 January, 1853. Lieutenant, 2 December, 1853. Resigned 28 February, 1854. Acting Lieutenant, 27 December, 1861. Commander, 18 November, 1862. Captain, 12 June, 1869. Commodore, 8 August, 1876. Rear-Admiral, 31 January, 1883. Retired List, 3 September, 1884. Died 17 November, 1888.
BALDWIN, CHARLES H.
Acting Master, 22 November, 1861. Honorably discharged 10 December, 1865. Acting Master, 23 April, 1867. Resigned 4 September, 1868.
BALDWIN, E. M.
Mate, 1 October, 1861. Acting Master, 24 February, 1862. Honorably discharged 12 March, 1866.
BALDWIN, FRANCIS T.
Mate, 28 July, 1863. Resigned 25 March, 1865.
BALDWIN, FRANK P.
Naval Cadet, 8 September, 1891. Ensign, 1 July, 1897. Lieutenant, Junior Grade, 1 July, 1900.
BALDWIN, FREDERICK P.
Midshipman, 30 September, 1841. Dismissed 6 June, 1845.
BALDWIN, HENRY D.
Mate, 11 September, 1862. Honorably discharged 29 May, 1865.
BALDWIN, ISAAC.
Surgeon's Mate, 24 July, 1813. Last appearance on Records of Navy Department, 1815.
BALDWIN, JAMES F. P.
Acting Third Assistant Engineer, 1 October, 1862. Acting Second Assistant Engineer, 1 July, 1864. Honorably discharged 25 November, 1865.
BALDWIN, J. M.
Midshipman, 30 November, 1814. Died 22 July, 1815.
BALDWIN, JOSEPH F.
Mate. Resigned 7 July, 1862.

GENERAL NAVY REGISTER.

BALDWIN, JOHN B.
Acting Third Assistant Engineer, 2 July, 1863. Honorably discharged 16 November, 1865.
BALDWIN, LAURIS B.
Assistant Surgeon (Spanish-American War), 14 May, 1898. Honorably discharged 23 August, 1898.
BALDWIN, LLOYD B.
Assistant Surgeon, 1 May, 1875. Passed Assistant Surgeon, 6 May, 1879. Surgeon, 22 September, 1891. Retired List, 18 September, 1899.
BALDWIN, N. P.
Acting Chief Engineer, 1 October, 1862. Honorably discharged 7 December, 1865.
BALDWIN, O. P.
Midshipman, 8 January, 1834. Resigned 8 August, 1835.
BALDWIN, RUSSELL.
Midshipman, 7 May, 1813. Lieutenant, 13 January, 1825. Died 25 April, 1832.
BALDWIN, THOMAS.
Midshipman, 30 May, 1803. Resigned.
BALDWIN, THOMAS.
Acting Master, 1 October, 1862. Honorably discharged 8 December, 1865.
BALDWIN, THEODORE E.
Mate, 19 June, 1862. Acting Ensign, 9 August, 1862. Acting Master, 10 July, 1863. Acting Volunteer Lieutenant, 19 July, 1864. Honorably discharged 5 December, 1865.
BALDWIN, W. H.
Midshipman, 1 January, 1812. Resigned 14 July, 1816.
BALDWIN, W. H.
Sailmaker, 21 May, 1817. Resigned 21 April, 1826.
BALDWIN, WILLIAM.
Surgeon's Mate, 10 March, 1812. Surgeon, 24 July, 1813. Died 31 August, 1819.
BALDWIN, WILLIAM H.
Acting Master, 29 October, 1861. Appointment revoked 15 July, 1865.
BALDWIN, W. S.
Mate, 9 July, 1863. Honorably discharged 3 August, 1865. Mate, 12 June, 1866. Resigned 18 September, 1871.
BALDY, GEORGE A.
Acting Midshipman, 29 September, 1862. Graduated June, 1866. Ensign, 12 March, 1868. Master, 26 March, 1869. Lieutenant, 21 March, 1870. Resigned 7 April, 1874.
BALESTIER, R. S.
Mate, 22 October, 1863. Appointment revoked 6 May, 1865.
BALFOUR, GEORGE.
Surgeon, 9 March, 1798. Resigned 12 April, 1804.
BALFOUR, GILBERT.
Acting Assistant Surgeon, 22 March, 1865. Honorably discharged 10 October, 1865.
BALL, BERT C.
Passed Assistant Engineer (Spanish-American War), 24 June, 1898. Honorably discharged 10 January, 1899.
BALL, CHARLES H.
Second Assistant Engineer, 19 July, 1861. Resigned 31 August, 1865.
BALL, GEORGE W.
Mate, 30 August, 1864. Honorably discharged 21 October, 1865.
BALL, JOHN.
Boatswain, 14 October, 1824. Resigned 11 November, 1833. Boatswain, 16 June, 1837. Died 8 March, 1839.
BALL, JOHN L.
Midshipman, 4 December, 1822. Lieutenant, 27 May, 1830. Cashiered 17 January, 1840.
BALL, LYSANDER C.
Mate, 26 October, 1863. Acting Ensign, 16 March, 1865. Honorably discharged 1 November, 1865.
BALL, RICHARD T. M.
Assistant Paymaster, 16 June, 1880. Passed Assistant Paymaster, 19 June, 1888. Paymaster, 10 April, 1895.
BALL, WALTER.
Naval Cadet, 6 September, 1888. Second Lieutenant Marine Corps, 1 July, 1894. Transferred to Engineer Corps and Commissioned an Assistant Engineer, 25 February, 1895. Passed Assistant Engineer, 12 October, 1898. Rank changed to Lieutenant, Junior Grade, 3 March, 1899. Lieutenant, 29 November, 1900.
BALL, WILLIAM H.
Midshipman, 1 April, 1828. Passed Midshipman, 14 June, 1834. Lieutenant, 25 February, 1841. Died 13 September, 1861.
BALLANTINE, DAVID W.
Assistant Surgeon, 22 May, 1862. Died 10 September, 1863.
BALLARD, EDWARD.
Master, 28 February, 1800. Last appearance on Records of Navy Department.
BALLARD, EDWARD J.
Midshipman, 24 February, 1809. Lieutenant, 2 June, 1813. Killed in action 1 June, 1813. (Commission issued before news of the action was received.)
BALLARD, HENRY E.
Midshipman, 1 November, 1804. Lieutenant, 26 April, 1810. Commander, 27 April, 1816. Captain, 3 March, 1825. Died 23 May, 1855.
BALLARD, JOHN.
Lieutenant, 2 October, 1798. Resigned 15 August, 1801.
BALLARD, JONATHAN M.
Master's Mate, 14 June, 1842. Gunner, 23 November, 1847. Retired List, 28 November, 1885.

GENERAL NAVY REGISTER.

BALLARD, WILLIAM.
Midshipman, 2 March, 1803. Lieutenant, 28 March, 1807. Last appearance on Records of Navy Department. Dead.

BALLASEYUS, FRANZ A.
Lieutenant, Junior Grade (Spanish-American War), 2 June, 1898. Honorably discharged 22 October, 1898.

BALLEAU, THOMAS.
Midshipman, 1 January, 1825. Last appearance on Records of Navy Department, 30 August, 1825. Dead.

BALLS, JOHN G.
Acting Third Assistant Engineer, 20 March, 1865. Honorably discharged 14 February, 1868.

BALTHIS, DAVID V.
Mate, 21 October, 1864. Discharged 5 October, 1865.

BALTHIS, HARRY H.
Assistant Paymaster, 27 April, 1898. Passed Assistant Paymaster, 3 March, 1899.

BALTZER, ROBERT M.
Assistant Surgeon, 8 February, 1832. Passed Assistant Surgeon, 8 November, 1836. Died 4 January, 1838.

BAMFORD, CHARLES C.
Mate, 22 December, 1863. Resigned 29 May, 1865.

BAMPTON, BENJAMIN C.
Third Assistant Engineer, 21 May, 1857. Second Assistant Engineer, 2 August, 1859. First Assistant Engineer, 17 December, 1862. Retired List, 6 September, 1873.

BANCROFT, KIRK H.
Acting Assistant Surgeon, 27 January, 1864. Honorably discharged 9 November, 1865.

BANCROFT, JOHN.
Acting Boatswain, 11 September, 1852. Resigned 26 January, 1853.

BANDEL, DECATUR A.
Acting Third Assistant Engineer, 6 May, 1864. Honorably discharged 11 December, 1865. Acting Third Assistant Engineer, 10 May, 1866. Discharged 31 August, 1867.

BANG, NEILS C.
Master, 23 August, 1800. Last appearance on Records of Navy Department.

BANGS, ELI A.
Mate, 26 September, 1863. Resigned 19 August, 1864.

BANGS, W. O.
Mate, 9 October, 1863. Discharged 21 March, 1865.

BANKHEAD, J. M.
Midshipman, 28 February, 1834. Resigned 23 May, 1837.

BANKHEAD, JOHN P.
Midshipman, 10 August, 1838. Passed Midshipman, 20 May, 1844. Master, 8 May, 1851. Lieutenant, 7 April, 1852. Commander, 16 July, 1862. Captain, 25 July, 1866. Died 27 April, 1867.

BANKS, HARRISON.
Acting Ensign, 24 September, 1863. Resigned 30 November, 1864.

BANKS, JAMES.
Boatswain, 21 July, 1817. Died 10 November, 1841.

BANKSON, LLOYD.
Cadet Engineer, 13 September, 1877. Honorably discharged 30 June, 1883. Assistant Engineer, 1 July, 1883. Assistant Naval Constructor, 1 July, 1889. Naval Constructor, 30 June, 1896.

BANNAN, DOUGLAS R.
Assistant Surgeon, 22 October, 1861. Passed Assistant Surgeon, 24 April, 1865. Surgeon, 7 November, 1869. Died 13 November, 1871.

BANNING, FREEBORN.
Midshipman, 30 April, 1798. Lieutenant, 1 June, 1799. Resigned 9 February, 1802.

BANNISTER, JOHN.
Midshipman, 2 February, 1829. Died 3 June, 1835.

BANNISTER, R. B.
Assistant Surgeon, 28 June, 1838. Died 12 July, 1844.

BANNISTER, S. B.
Sailmaker, 17 July, 1826. Resigned 6 June, 1833.

BANNISTER, W. C.
Midshipman, 1 April, 1828. Resigned 6 June, 1833.

BANTEN, CLINTON.
Acting Ensign, 24 January, 1863. Resigned 7 July, 1863.

BARBER, FRANCIS M.
Acting Midshipman, 27 December, 1861. Graduated September, 1865. Ensign, 1 December, 1866. Master, 12 March, 1868. Lieutenant, 26 March, 1869. Lieutenant-Commander, 13 January, 1879. Commander, 31 March, 1889. Retired List, 28 December, 1895.

BARBER, GEORGE H.
Assistant Surgeon, 23 May, 1889. Passed Assistant Surgeon, 23 May, 1892. Surgeon, 7 June, 1900.

BARBER, JAMES S.
Assistant Paymaster, 6 March, 1899. Died 15 November, 1900.

BARBER, JOEL A.
Midshipman, 22 June, 1867. Graduated 6 June, 1871. Ensign, 14 July, 1872. Master, 8 August, 1876. Lieutenant, Junior Grade, 3 March, 1883. Resigned 1 August, 1883.

BARBOT, ALPHONSE.
Midshipman, 26 February, 1838. Passed Midshipman, 20 May, 1844. Master, 10 June, 1852. Lieutenant, 22 March, 1853. Dismissed 10 June, 1861.

BARBOUR, JAMES E.
Acting Assistant Surgeon, 6 May, 1863. Resigned 21 March, 1864.

40 GENERAL NAVY REGISTER.

BARCLAY, ALEXANDER J.
Midshipman, 14 May, 1846. Resigned 26 July, 1850.
BARCLAY, CHARLES JAMES.
Acting Midshipman, 21 September, 1860. Acting Ensign, 6 October, 1863. Master, 10 May, 1866. Lieutenant, 21 February, 1867. Lieutenant-Commander, 12 March, 1868. Commander, 25 November, 1881. Captain, 1 October, 1896.
BARCLAY, J. O.
Acting Master, 24 May, 1861. Resigned 23 April, 1864.
BARCLAY, J. O. C.
Assistant Surgeon, 17 October, 1839. Passed Assistant Surgeon, 25 November, 1844. Surgeon, 4 April, 1854. Died 7 December, 1865.
BARCLAY, JOHN D.
Acting Master, 9 November, 1861. Resigned 22 August, 1862. Acting Ensign, 18 October, 1862. Resigned 23 January, 1865.
BARCLAY, PETER.
Mate, 20 November, 1863. Honorably discharged 3 February, 1866.
BARCLAY, RICHARD R.
Acting Ensign, 22 September, 1864. Honorably discharged 5 October, 1865.
BARCLAY, WILLIAM H.
Acting Third Assistant Engineer, 3 June, 1863. Honorably discharged 28 October, 1865.
BARDEN, LEVI.
Master, 17 March, 1800. Relieved, 25 April, 1805.
BARGER, WILLIAM S.
Assistant Engineer (Spanish-American War), 1 June, 1898. Honorably discharged 16 February, 1899.
BARKENBILE, C.
Carpenter, 18 August, 1819. Discharged July, 1820.
BARKER, A. J. L.
Mate, 12 November, 1861. Acting Ensign, 14 April, 1864. Honorably discharged 1 November, 1865.
BARKER, ALBERT S.
Acting Midshipman, 25 October, 1859. Ensign, 25 November, 1862. Lieutenant, 27 February, 1864. Lieutenant-Commander, 25 July, 1866. Commander, 28 March, 1877. Captain, 5 May, 1892. Rear-Admiral, 10 October, 1899.
BARKER, EDWARD T.
Acting Assistant Paymaster, 26 December, 1863. Discharged 4 February, 1866.
BARKER, GEORGE F.
Acting Assistant Paymaster, 14 August, 1863. Resigned 4 November, 1864.
BARKER, HENRY S.
Third Assistant Engineer, 26 February, 1851. Died 25 July, 1855.
BARKER, JAMES T.
Boatswain, 27 April, 1872. Died 16 September, 1885.
BARKER, JOHN K.
Acting Ensign, 15 May, 1863. Acting Master, 31 December, 1864. Honorably discharged 18 September, 1865.
BARKER, JOHN R.
Midshipman, 11 February, 1841. Dropped 17 August, 1847.
BARKER, JOSEPH B.
Acting Ensign, 25 February, 1864. Resigned 22 May, 1865.
BARKER, JOSIAH.
Naval Constructor; date not known. Dismissed 9 July, 1846.
BARKER, J. W.
Midshipman, 1 July, 1828. Resigned 20 May, 1829.
BARKER, RICHARD.
Midshipman, 30 May, 1820. Resigned 14 February, 1821.
BARKER, STEPHEN N.
Mate, 23 July, 1863. Acting Ensign, 1 January, 1865. Resigned 15 February, 1866.
BARKER, THEODORE.
Acting Assistant Paymaster, 1 April, 1863. Discharged 7 March, 1866.
BARKER, WILLIAM.
Mate, 12 November, 1861. Appointment revoked 25 March, 1863. Acting Ensign, 23 April, 1864. Honorably discharged 23 November, 1865.
BARKER, WILLIAM S.
Mate, 29 January, 1863. Dismissed 23 November, 1863.
BARKER, WILLIAM W.
Midshipman, 26 March, 1800. Discharged 12 October, 1801, under Peace Establishment Act.
BARKMAN, F. W.
Mate, 3 September, 1863. Acting Ensign, 13 May, 1865. Honorably discharged 15 December, 1865.
BARLOW, CHARLES B.
Mate, 31 October, 1861. Acting Ensign, 17 July, 1862. Resigned 11 February, 1863.
BARLOW, FREDERICK S.
Third Assistant Engineer, 22 June, 1860. Second Assistant Engineer, 30 July, 1862. Lost on the Tecumseh, 5 August, 1864.
BARLOW, THOMAS.
Midshipman, 9 June, 1811. Resigned 29 December, 1813.
BARLOW, WALTER S.
Acting Third Assistant Engineer, 9 January, 1863. Honorably discharged 2 December, 1865.
BARLOW, WALTER S.
Acting Second Assistant Engineer, 7 July, 1863. Honorably discharged 2 December, 1865.
BARNARD, BENJAMIN H.
Mate, 15 July, 1864. Honorably discharged 24 October, 1865.

GENERAL NAVY REGISTER.

BARNARD, GEORGE A.
   Acting Third Assistant Engineer, 21 May, 1864. Honorably discharged 18 August, 1865.
BARNARD, JOHN H.
   Cadet Midshipman, 23 September, 1878. Resigned 11 August, 1883. Lieutenant, Junior Grade (Spanish-American War), 30 April, 1898. Honorably discharged 13 September, 1898.
BARNARD, LEMUEL.
   Third Assistant Engineer, 16 January, 1863. Resigned 21 March, 1866.
BARNARD, ROBERT C.
   Acting Boatswain, 25 April, 1863. Appointment revoked 11 August, 1864.
BARNARD, ROBERT C.
   Acting Gunner, 23 August, 1851. Dismissed 4 August, 1852.
BARNARD, WARREN.
   Carpenter, 28 June, 1867. Died 11 July, 1893.
BARNES, BREASTED.
   Carpenter; date not known. Died 2 November, 1819.
BARNES, CASSIUS B.
   Naval Cadet, 7 September, 1891. Ensign, 1 July. 1897. Lieutenant, Junior Grade, 1 July, 1900.
BARNES, GEORGE P.
   Acting Sailmaker, 9 November, 1874. Resigned 31 March, 1875. Acting Sailmaker, 20 February, 1878. Retired List, 11 February, 1893.
BARNES, GEORGE W.
   Mate, 24 June, 1863. Resigned 28 November, 1864.
BARNES, GEORGE W.
   Acting Third Assistant Engineer, 4 June, 1864. Appointment revoked (sick), 6 September, 1864.
BARNES, HENRY E.
   Boatswain, 4 March, 1863. Retired List, 19 December, 1876. Died 28 December, 1895.
BARNES, ISAAC M.
   Mate, 22 January, 1865. Deserted 30 September, 1865.
BARNES, JAMES.
   Acting Third Assistant Engineer, 9 January, 1862. Resigned 21 March, 1863.
BARNES, JAMES O.
   Mate, 11 February, 1862. Resigned 9 June, 1862.
BARNES, JOHN S.
   Acting Midshipman, 1 October. 1851. Midshipman, 10 June, 1854. Passed Midshipman, 22 November, 1856. Master, 22 January, 1858. Resigned 5 October, 1858. Lieutenant-Commander, 16 July, 1862. Resigned 4 February, 1869.
BARNES, LAKIN.
   Mate, 11 October, 1862. Acting Ensign, 23 August, 1863. Honorably discharged 27 October, 1865. Acting Ensign, 9 July, 1866. Mustered out 2 June, 1868.
BARNES, NATHAN, JR.
   Midshipman, 22 February, 1834. Resigned 28 August, 1839.
BARNES, NATHAN HALE.
   Midshipman, 27 July, 1863. Graduated 2 June, 1868. Ensign, 19 April, 1869. Master, 12 July, 1870. Lieutenant, 12 December, 1872. Retired List, 18 February, 1891. Died 1 January, 1899.
BARNES, SAMUEL E.
   Acting Second Assistant Engineer, 6 December, 1861. Resigned 15 February, 1862.
BARNES, WINSLOW B.
   Acting Ensign, 8 March, 1864. Resigned 26 April, 1865.
BARNETT, ALBERT E.
   Mate, 26 June, 1862. Acting Ensign, 6 July, 1863. Honorably discharged 30 September, 1865.
BARNET, EDWARD A.
   Midshipman, 24 June, 1837. Passed Midshipman, 29 June, 1843. Acting Master, 13 January, 1847. Lieutenant, 4 August, 1850. Commander, 16 July, 1862. Died 26 May, 1864.
BARNETT, JACOB.
   Acting Third Assitant Engineer, 15 June, 1864. Discharged 5 February, 1865.
BARNETT, JAMES.
   Gunner, 27 May, 1800. Not in service, 1 June, 1804.
BARNETT, WASHINGTON.
   Acting Third Assistant Engineer, 9 April, 1863. Honorably discharged 9 September, 1865.
BARNETTE, WILLIAM J.
   Midshipman, 27 July, 1864. Graduated 2 June, 1868. Ensign, 19 April, 1869. Master, 12 July, 1870. Lieutenant, 28 December, 1872. Lieutenant-Commander, 16 April, 1894. Commander, 3 March, 1899.
BARNEWELL, EDWARD.
   Midshipman, 4 July, 1817. Died 17 September, 1823.
BARNEWELL, EDWARD.
   Master, 29 January, 1814. Lieutenant, 22 July, 1814. Lost in Epervier, 1815.
BARNEY, CHARLES N.
   Assistant Surgeon (Spanish-American War), 22 May, 1898. Discharged 15 September, 1898.
BARNEY, CHARLES S.
   Acting Ensign, 27 January, 1863. Acting Master, 27 June, 1864. Honorably discharged 13 October, 1865.
BARNEY, JOSEPH N.
   Midshipman, 30 June, 1835. Passed Midshipman, 22 June, 1841. Master, 22 March, 1847. Lieutenant, 5 August, 1847. Dismissed 4 June, 1861.
BARNEY, JOSHUA.
   Midshipman, 1 January, 1818. Died 30 September, 1823.

BARNEY, JOSHUA.
Captain, 25 April, 1814. Flotilla Service. Died 1 December, 1818.
BARNEY, SAMUEL C.
Midshipman, 27 June, 1835. Passed Midshipman, 22 June, 1841. Master, 23 June, 1847. Lieutenant, 12 November, 1847. Reserved List, 12 November, 1847. Dismissed 6 March, 1863.
BARNHOUSE, AUGUSTUS.
Midshipman, 10 May, 1820. Resigned 12 May, 1825.
BARNHOUSE, W. L.
Sailmaker, 2 February, 1814. Resigned 6 July, 1815.
BARNICOAT, EDWARD W.
Carpenter, 17 December, 1841. Retired List, 16 November, 1872. Died 12 December, 1882.
BARNICOAT, J. A.
Carpenter, 7 June, 1836. Resigned 14 September, 1836.
BARNUM, AUGUSTUS.
Acting Third Assistant Engineer, 10 September, 1861. Acting Second Assistant Engineer, 13 September, 1862. Acting First Assistant Engineer, 21 July, 1864. Honorably discharged 25 October, 1865.
BARNUM, DANIEL.
Acting Second Assistant Engineer, 4 September, 1863. Dismissed 20 February, 1864.
BARNUM, MERRITT W.
Assistant Surgeon, 14 March, 1892. Resigned 6 May, 1895.
BARNUM, RICHARD.
Assistant Surgeon, 11 March, 1829. Resigned 23 September, 1829.
BARNWELL, WILLIAM J.
Surgeon's Mate, 28 July, 1810. Surgeon, 27 April, 1816. Resigned 15 December, 1823.
BARR, JOHN.
Gunner, 4 August, 1841. Died 20 April, 1846.
BARR, JOHN C.
Acting Third Assistant Engineer, 1 October, 1862. Acting Second Assistant Engineer, 23 December, 1863. Resigned 28 September, 1864. Acting Ensign, 28 September, 1864. Honorably discharged 28 February, 1866.
BARR, MICHAEL P.
Sailmaker, 4 May, 1888. Chief Sailmaker, 3 March, 1899.
BARR, WILLIAM M.
Acting Third Assistant Engineer, 19 December, 1861. Third Assistant Engineer, 17 March, 1863. Second Assistant Engineer, 1 September, 1864. Resigned 16 April, 1866. Passed Assistant Engineer (Spanish-American War), 13 July, 1898. Honorably discharged 10 February, 1899.
BARRABINO, N. C.
Assistant Surgeon, 28 February, 1833. Passed Assistant Surgeon, 1 August, 1837. Surgeon, 8 September, 1841. Died 13 April, 1852.
BARRAND, JOHN T.
Midshipman, 20 September, 1841. Passed Midshipman, 10 August, 1847. Master, 18 April, 1855. Lieutenant, 14 September, 1855. Died 29 August, 1860.
BARRELL, GEORGE.
Midshipman, 17 August, 1799. Resigned 17 April, 1810.
BARRETT, EDWARD.
Midshipman, 3 November, 1840. Passed Midshipman, 11 July, 1846. Master, 1 March, 1855. Lieutenant, 14 September, 1855. Lieutenant-Commander, 16 July, 1862. Commander, 6 February, 1866. Captain, 7 May, 1871. Commodore, 11 June, 1879. Died 31 March, 1880.
BARRETT, GEORGE W.
Mate, 2 October, 1861. Acting Ensign, 9 April, 1863. Acting Master, 24 August, 1864. Honorably discharged 28 October, 1865.
BARRET, JOHN.
Mate, 16 August, 1861. Acting Ensign, 30 September, 1863. Honorably discharged 18 July, 1868.
BARRETT, PETER.
Gunner, 7 May, 1862. Died 6 November, 1871.
BARRETT, THOMAS B.
Midshipman, 8 May, 1832. Passed Midshipman, 23 June, 1838. Lieutenant, 11 February, 1844. Died 11 November, 1847.
BARRETT, THOMAS H.
Acting Third Assistant Engineer, 25 July, 1864. Honorably discharged 19 June, 1865.
BARRETT, WALTER W.
Mate (Spanish-American War), 12 April, 1898. Ensign, 5 May, 1898. Honorably discharged 7 February, 1899.
BARRETT, WILLIAM C.
Acting Third Assistant Engineer, 16 September, 1861. Acting Second Assistant Engineer, 10 April, 1863. Appointment revoked (sick), 16 March, 1865.
BARRETT, WILLIAM H.
Carpenter, 3 October, 1872. Retired List, 10 March, 1896. Died 19 April, 1897.
BARRETT, WILLIAM M.
Mate, 22 January, 1865. Honorably discharged 20 December, 1865.
BARRINGER, JEREMIAH.
Acting Third Assistant Engineer, 18 November, 1864. Honorably discharged 17 September, 1865.
BARRINGTON, SAMUEL.
Surgeon's Mate, 3 January, 1828. Passed Assistant Surgeon, 3 March, 1835. Surgeon, 9 February, 1837. Died 4 September, 1862.
BARRINGTON, WILLIAM J.
Acting Third Assistant Engineer, 13 December, 1862. Honorably discharged 27 March, 1868.

BARRITT, WILLIAM G.
Passed Assistant Paymaster (Spanish-American War), 17 June, 1898. Honorably discharged 2 September, 1898.
BARROLL, HENRY H.
Midshipman, 28 September, 1867. Graduated 6 June, 1871. Ensign, 14 July, 1872. Master, 20 October, 1875. Lieutenant, Junior Grade, 3 March, 1883. Lieutenant, 22 May, 1883. Lieutenant-Commander, 3 March, 1899. Retired List with rank of Commander, 30 June, 1899.
BARRON, JACOB.
Acting Ensign, 12 March, 1863. Resigned, 9 November, 1863. Acting Ensign, 9 March, 1864. Acting Master, 20 April, 1865. Honorably discharged 26 December, 1865. Acting Master, 11 December, 1866. Mustered out 31 May, 1868.
BARRON, JAMES.
Lieutenant, 9 March, 1798. Captain, 22 May, 1799. Died 21 April, 1851.
BARRON, JOHN M.
Acting Third Assistant Engineer, 28 December, 1861. Acting Second Assistant Engineer, 22 January, 1864. Resigned (sick), 2 March, 1865.
BARRON, SAMUEL.
Captain, 13 September, 1798. Died 29 October, 1810.
BARRON, SAMUEL.
Midshipman, 1 January, 1812. Lieutenant, 3 March, 1827. Commander, 15 July, 1847. Captain, 14 September, 1855. Dismissed 22 May, 1861.
BARRON, WILLIAM J.
Acting Third Assistant Engineer, 19 September, 1864. Resigned 22 June, 1865.
BARROUGHCLOUGH, EDWARD.
Acting Third Assistant Engineer, 15 September, 1864. Honorably discharged 26 December, 1865.
BARROWS, HENRY C.
Acting Third Assistant Engineer, 23 March, 1865. Honorably discharged 4 January, 1870.
BARRY, EDWARD.
Master, 28 February, 1809. Died 2 May, 1830.
BARRY, EDWARD B.
Midshipman, 20 July, 1865. Graduated 4 June, 1869. Ensign, 12 July, 1870. Master, 29 January, 1872. Lieutenant, 6 April, 1875. Lieutenant-Commander, 21 March, 1897. Commander, 9 March, 1900.
BARRY, ERASTUS.
Acting Third Assistant Engineer, 16 October, 1861. Acting Second Assistant Engineer, 23 June, 1864. Honorably discharged 26 November, 1865.
BARRY, FRANCIS E.
Midshipman, 29 June, 1829. Passed Midshipman, 3 July, 1835. Lieutenant, 25 February, 1841. Died 19 August, 1844.
BARRY, GARRETT.
Chaplain, 30 May, 1809. Last appearance on Records of Navy Department, 3 May, 1813.
BARRY, GARRETT R.
Purser, 3 March, 1825. Pay Director on Retired List, 3 March, 1871. Died 26 February, 1876.
BARRY, GERARD H.
Acting Ensign, 14 May, 1863. Appointment revoked (sick), 3 October, 1864.
BARRY, GEORGE J.
Third Assistant Engineer, 26 June, 1856. Second Assistant Engineer, 3 August, 1859. First Assistant Engineer, 1 July, 1861. Chief Engineer, 10 November, 1863. Retired List, 24 March, 1874. Died 10 November, 1877.
BARRY, JAMES H.
Mate, 15 November, 1861. Acting Ensign, 24 January, 1864. Honorably discharged 16 September, 1865.
BARRY, JAMES J.
Third Assistant Engineer, 8 December, 1862. Second Assistant Engineer, 8 April, 1864. First Assistant Engineer, 1 January, 1868. Passed Assistant Engineer, 24 February, 1874. Retired List, 9 January, 1891.
BARRY, JAMES J.
Midshipman, 20 December, 1837. Resigned 20 September, 1842.
BARRY, JOHN.
Captain, 6 June, 1794. Died 13 September, 1803.
BARRY, JOHN.
Midshipman, 23 September, 1798. Last appearance on Records of Navy Department.
BARRY, JOHN.
Master, 3 August, 1831. Resigned 9 July, 1833.
BARRY, JONATHAN.
Gunner, 8 July, 1837. Resigned 5 August, 1837.
BARRY, PATRICK H.
Third Assistant Engineer, 3 May, 1862. Died 1 August, 1863.
BARRY, RALPH E.
Lieutenant (Spanish-American War), 24 May, 1898. Honorably discharged 18 January, 1899.
BARRY, ROBERT T.
Assistant Surgeon, 26 March, 1834. Passed Assistant Surgeon, 12 July, 1839. Surgeon, 23 February, 1844. Died 14 August, 1857.
BARRY, THOMAS.
Gunner, 2 July, 1814. Resigned 19 November, 1826. Master, 19 February, 1841. Killed by accident, 27 June, 1842.
BARRY, WILLIAM.
Boatswain, 7 May, 1804. Last appearance on Records of Navy Department, 3 July, 1807.

BARRY, WILLIAM A.
Carpenter, 1 May, 1873. Chief Carpenter, 3 March, 1899.
BARRY, WILLIAM W.
Acting Assistant Paymaster, 30 July, 1863. Discharged 13 September, 1865. Assistant Paymaster, 15 March, 1870. Passed Assistant Paymaster, 12 April, 1877. Paymaster, 18 December, 1886. Retired List, 15 September, 1899.
BARRYMORE, JOSEPH H.
Midshipman, 16 August, 1806. Resigned 5 December, 1808.
BARRYMORE, WILLIAM.
Mate, 4 November, 1861. Acting Ensign, 28 January, 1863. Acting Master, 23 July, 1863. Honorably discharged 13 December, 1865.
BARSTON, HAVILAND.
Third Assistant Engineer, 1 July, 1861. Second Assistant Engineer, 18 December, 1862. First Assistant Engineer, 11 October, 1866. Lost on Oneida, 24 January, 1870.
BARSTOW, ROBERT.
Mate, 22 May, 1861. Acting Ensign, 1 December, 1862. Acting Master, 9 June, 1863. Honorably discharged 18 February, 1867.
BARSTOW, SOLOMON.
Mate, 15 March, 1864. Honorably discharged 30 September, 1865.
BARSTOW, SIDNEY.
Mate, 16 June, 1865. Appointment revoked 4 August, 1865.
BARTH, OTTO.
Carpenter, 5 December, 1894.
BARTHALLOW, BENJAMIN G.
Naval Cadet, 5 September, 1896. Graduated 30 June, 1900.
BARTHOLOMEW, B.
Midshipman, 30 November, 1814. Last appearance on Records of Navy Department, 21 May, 1819.
BARTHOLOMEW, HENRY L.
Acting Assistant Surgeon, 6 November, 1863. Honorably discharged 28 November, 1865.
BARTHOLOMEW, L. S.
First Assistant Engineer, 1 September, 1845. Resigned 20 April, 1847.
BARTHOLOMEW, LYMAN.
Mate, 21 November, 1861. Acting Master, 11 April, 1862. Died 20 December, 1864.
BARTLEMAN, RICHARD M.
Third Assistant Engineer, 24 December, 1853. Second Assistant Engineer, 9 May, 1857. First Assistant Engineer, 2 August 1859. Chief Engineer, 28 October, 1861. Died 22 December, 1884.
BARTLET, FRANCIS.
Midshipman, 1 March, 1825. Passed Midshipman, 10 June, 1833. Resigned 5 December, 1838.
BARTLETT, AUBREY.
Ensign (Spanish-American War), 20 May, 1898. Honorably discharged 19 September, 1898.
BARTLETT, CHARLES H.
Assistant Paymaster, 4 December, 1869. Passed Assistant Paymaster, 25 September, 1875. Died 29 January, 1882.
BARTLETT, CHARLES WARD.
Midshipman, 2 June, 1867. Graduated 6 June, 1871. Ensign, 14 July, 1872. Master, 17 March, 1875. Lieutenant, 4 February, 1882. Lieutenant-Commander, 3 March, 1899.
BARTLETT, CORNELIUS.
Acting Ensign, 23 September, 1862. Honorably discharged 22 November, 1865.
BARTLETT, ELISHA P.
Acting Second Assistant Engineer, 4 September, 1863. Acting First Assistant Engineer, 14 February, 1864. Honorably discharged 19 November, 1867.
BARTLETT, EZRA.
Mate, 23 January, 1862. Acting Ensign, 23 November, 1864. Honorably discharged 21 March, 1866.
BARTLETT, FRANK W.
Cadet Engineer, 1 October, 1874. Graduated 20 June, 1878. Assistant Engineer, 20 June, 1880. Passed Assistant Engineer, 19 June, 1890. Chief Engineer, 19 September, 1898. Rank changed to Lieutenant, 3 March, 1899.
BARTLETT, HENRY E.
Acting Master, 23 June, 1863. Appointment revoked 8 February, 1868.
BARTLETT, JOHN K.
Boatswain, 4 September, 1858. Resigned 9 August, 1859. Reappointed 5 October, 1859. Resigned 21 March, 1873.
BARTLETT, JOHN R.
Acting Midshipman, 25 November, 1859. Ensign, 8 September, 1863. Lieutenant, 22 February, 1864. Lieutenant-Commander, 25 July, 1866. Commander, 25 April, 1877. Captain, 1 July, 1892. Retired List, 12 July, 1897.
BARTLETT, JOSEPH T.
Midshipman, 9 September, 1841. Drowned 30 March, 1846.
BARTLETT, LEWIS W.
Lieutenant (Spanish-American War), 20 May, 1898. Honorably discharged 19 September, 1898.
BARTLETT, STEPHEN C.
Acting Assistant Surgeon, 31 December, 1864. Honorably discharged 31 December, 1865.
BARTLETT, WASHINGTON A.
Midshipman, 23 January, 1833. Passed Midshipman, 8 July, 1839. Lieutenant, 22 November, 1844. Dropped 28 September, 1855.
BARTLEY, WILLIAM D.
Mate, 18 July, 1898.

GENERAL NAVY REGISTER. 45

BARTLING, CHARLES C.
Sailmaker, 9 October, 1844. Resigned 18 July, 1845.
BARTOLL, JOHN.
Mate, 24 January, 1862. Acting Ensign, 20 July, 1863. Honorably discharged 12 October, 1865.
BARTON, CHARLES C.
Midshipman, 1 December, 1824. Passed Midshipman, 14 June, 1834. Lieutenant, 25 February, 1841. Died 28 August, 1851.
BARTON, CHARLES F.
Acting Ensign, 15 February, 1865. Honorably discharged 28 October, 1865.
BARTON, EDWARD D.
Acting Assistant Paymaster, 22 July, 1861. Died 1 September, 1862.
BARTON, G. DE F.
Acting Assistant Paymaster, 5 December, 1862. Assistant Paymaster, 2 July, 1864. Paymaster, 4 May, 1866. Resigned 12 April, 1869.
BARTON, GEORGE F.
Third Assistant Engineer, 26 February, 1851. Second Assistant Engineer, 21 May, 1853. Died 4 September, 1853.
BARTON, JAMES A.
Third Assistant Engineer, 16 January, 1863. Resigned 5 March, 1868.
BARTON, JEREMIAH.
Lieutenant, 8 June, 1798. Resigned 14 September, 1800.
BARTON, JOHN K.
Cadet Engineer, 1 October, 1871. Graduated 31 May, 1873. Assistant Engineer, 23 January, 1874. Passed Assistant Engineer, 1 November, 1879. Chief Engineer, 15 January, 1895. Rank changed to Lieutenant-Commander, 3 March, 1899.
BARTON, JOHN T.
Assistant Surgeon, 30 May, 1844. Died 22 August, 1846.
BARTON, JONAHAN Q.
Acting Assistant Paymaster, 30 January, 1864. Assistant Paymaster, 2 March, 1867. Passed Assistant Paymaster, 10 February, 1870. Paymaster, 29 May, 1882. Retired List, 14 August, 1893.
BARTON, JOSEPH A.
Carpenter, 21 December, 1897.
BARTON, PHILIP H.
Acting Assistant Surgeon, 5 April, 1864. Honorably discharged 9 October, 1865.
BARTON, ROBERT R.
Surgeon, 24 July, 1813. Resigned 24 February, 1824.
BARTON, THOMAS C.
Mate, 25 October, 1862. Resigned 14 April, 1864.
BARTON, WILLIAM HENRY.
Acting Midshipman, 22 September, 1856. Midshipman, 15 June, 1860. Master, 19 September, 1861. Lieutenant, 16 July, 1862. Lieutenant-Commander, 25 July, 1866. Resigned 17 June, 1867.
BARTON, WILLIAM H.
Acting Gunner, 18 April, 1863. Honorably discharged 28 November, 1865.
BARTON, W. P. C.
Surgeon, 28 June, 1809. Died 29 February, 1856.
BARTOW, THEODORE B.
Chaplain, 8 September, 1841. Died 18 May, 1869.
BARTRAM, CHARLES H.
Acting Third Assistant Engineer, 10 November, 1863. Appointment revoked 2 June, 1865.
BARTRAM, WILLIAM H.
Acting Third Assistant Engineer, 12 July, 1864. Honorably discharged 1 November, 1865.
BASHFORD, ANDREW P.
Mate, 4 April, 1862. Acting Ensign, 10 September, 1863. Honorably discharged 2 June, 1868. Mate, 4 November, 1869. Died 30 June, 1889.
BASS, E. C.
Acting Ensign, 1 October, 1862. Resigned 19 February, 1864.
BASSETT, DAVID L.
Acting Assistant Surgeon, 18 December, 1861. Resigned 24 September, 1863.
BASSETT, EZRA.
Acting Ensign, 1 June, 1864. Honorably discharged 28 October, 1865.
BASSETT, FLETCHER S.
Midshipman, 21 September, 1865. Graduated 4 June, 1869. Ensign, 12 July, 1870. Master, 13 April, 1872. Lieutenant, 16 June, 1875. Retired List, 21 October, 1882. Died 19 October, 1893.
BASSETT, FREDERIC BREWSTER.
Naval Cadet, 19 May, 1884. Ensign, 25 July, 1890. Lieutenant, Junior Grade, 5 June, 1898. Lieutenant, 3 March, 1899.
BASSETT, H. W.
Assistant Surgeon, 26 May, 1824. Surgeon, 25 May, 1826. Killed in a duel, 20 August, 1830.
BASSETT, JAMES.
Master, 18 April, 1814. Last appearance on Records of Navy Department. Brig Enterprise, 22 April, 1815.
BASSETT, JAMES C.
Acting Assistant Surgeon, 13 January, 1865. Honorably discharged 10 October, 1865.
BASSETT, ORVILLE.
Acting Third Assistant Engineer, 15 December, 1862. Honorably discharged 9 August, 1865.

BASSETT, SIMEON S.
Midshipman, 10 September, 1841. Passed Midshipman, 10 August, 1847. Master, 14 September, 1855. Lieutenant, 15 September, 1855. Died 6 May, 1859.
BASSETT, WESLEY W.
Midshipman, 9 March, 1838. Passed Midshipman, 2 July, 1845. Master, 20 February, 1854. Dismissed 22 September, 1854. Acting Assistant Paymaster, 24 March, 1862. Resigned 14 January, 1865. Master on Retired List, 8 June, 1872. Lieutenant-Commander, Retired List, 22 March, 1875. Died 4 June, 1894.
BATCHELDER, ANDREW J.
Acting Third Assistant Engineer, 24 November, 1862. Appointment revoked (sick), 6 April, 1863.
BATCHELDER, GEORGE A.
Acting Master's Mate, 14 November, 1862. Appointment revoked 29 August, 1864.
BATCHELDER, JOSEPH C.
Acting Third Assistant Engineer, 20 December, 1863. Honorably discharged 15 February, 1866.
BATCHELLER, OLIVER A.
Acting Midshipman, 28 November, 1859. Ensign, 25 November, 1862. Master, 15 April, 1863. Lieutenant, 22 February, 1864. Lieutenant-Commander, 25 July, 1866. Commander, 25 June, 1877. Retired List 6 February, 1893. Died 30 October, 1893.
BATEMAN, ARTHUR E.
Mate, 9 October, 1867. Resigned 18 September, 1871.
BATES, ADNA A.
Mate, 31 July, 1863. Acting Ensign, 16 August, 1864. Honorably discharged 13 August, 1865.
BATES, ALEXANDER B.
Third Assistant Engineer, 16 January, 1863. Second Assistant Engineer, 28 May, 1864. First Assistant Engineer, 1 January, 1874. Passed Assistant Engineer, 24 February, 1874. Chief Engineer, 12 April, 1892. Rank changed to Commander, 3 March, 1899.
BATES, ANGUS G.
Acting Warrant Machinist, 23 August, 1899.
BATES, CHARLES J.
Assistant Surgeon, 7 March, 1838. Passed Assistant Surgeon, 22 November, 1843. Died 26 August, 1847.
BATES, FRANK.
Acting Master's Mate, 28 August, 1862. Acting Ensign, 16 February, 1863. Appointment revoked (sick), 28 August, 1863. Acting Ensign, 31 March, 1863. Resigned 13 April, 1864.
BATES, HARRY C.
Mate, 28 July, 1864. Honorably discharged 1 November, 1865.
BATES, JOHN.
Boatswain, 20 October, 1845. Dismissed 29 July, 1857.
BATES, JOHN.
Boatswain, 5 June, 1861. Dismissed 28 October, 1864.
BATES, JOHN A.
Purser, 2 March, 1831. Retired 21 December, 1861. Died 26 August, 1871.
BATS, JOHN A., JR.
Assistant Paymaster, 9 March, 1862. Paymaster, 3 August, 1865. Died 4 March, 1867.
BATES, MOSES M.
Midshipman, 9 August, 1799. Resigned and entered the Army in 1800.
BATES, NATHAN D.
Acting First Assistant Engineer, 3 October, 1861. Dismissed 16 September, 1863.
BATES, NEWTON L.
Assistant Surgeon, 24 June, 1861. Passed Assistant Surgeon, 22 June, 1864. Surgeon, 16 September, 1865. Medical Inspector, 15 January, 1881. Medical Director, 1 September, 1888. Died 18 October, 1897.
BATES, NICHOLAS B.
Acting Second Assistant Engineer, 18 December, 1861. Resigned 6 August, 1862.
BATES, PHINEAS R.
Acting Master, 12 April, 1862. Appointment revoked 18 April, 1862.
BATES, RICHARD.
Acting Ensign, 20 December, 1863. Acting Master, 20 June, 1865. Honorably discharged 31 October, 1865.
BATES, THOMAS.
Acting Master, 1 October, 1862. Dismissed 19 March, 1864.
BATES, WILLIAM.
Acting Master, 7 December, 1861. Honorably discharged 14 November, 1865.
BATES, WILLIAM H.
Acting Assistant Surgeon, 15 April, 1863. Honorably discharged 6 November, 1865.
BATH, JOHN.
Mate, 3 May, 1862. Acting Ensign, 24 January, 1863. Dismissed 9 October, 1863.
BATIONE, DOMINICK B.
Acting Assistant Paymaster, 15 March, 1865. Discharged 18 October, 1865. Passed Assistant Paymaster, 23 July, 1866. Paymaster, 26 August, 1868. Died 5 September, 1878.
BATTELLE, EVERETT.
Third Assistant Engineer, 27 June, 1862. Resigned 29 June, 1865.
BATTEN, JAMES M.
Acting Third Assistant Engineer, 22 August, 1862. Acting Second Assistant Engineer, 27 July, 1863. Honorably discharged 30 December, 1865.
BATTIN, JOHN M.
Acting Assistant Surgeon, 22 March, 1864. Honorably discharged 20 March, 1866.
BATTLE, SAMUEL W.
Assistant Surgeon, 1 October, 1875. Passed Assistant Surgeon, 20 May, 1879. Retired List, 23 April, 1884.

GENERAL NAVY REGISTER. 47

BAUER, HENRY C.
  Acting Second Assistant Engineer, 3 August, 1864. Honorably discharged 26 December, 1865.
BAUGH, RICHARD.
  Midshipman, 16 January, 1809. Resigned 15 September, 1810.
BAUGHMAN, GEORGE E.
  Assistant Paymaster, 14 July, 1870. Passed Assistant Paymaster, 8 March, 1879. Died 4 August, 1880.
BAUGHMAN, HENRY C.
  Assistant Engineer, 13 October, 1875. Retired List, 15 July, 1886.
BAULSIR, WILLIAM J.
  Acting Master, 27 November, 1861. Resigned 12 March, 1862.
BAUMGARTEN, G. H. E.
  Assistant Surgeon, 24 January, 1862. Passed Assistant Surgeon, 24 April, 1865. Resigned 5 May, 1865.
BAUMEISTER, HENRY.
  Acting Boatswain, 15 August, 1899.
BAURY, FREDERICK.
  Midshipman, 18 May, 1809. Lieutenant, 9 December, 1814. Lost in the Sloop Wasp, 1815.
BAURY, FREDERICK F.
  Mate, 1861. Acting Master, 14 May, 1862. Acting Volunteer Lieutenant, 25 August, 1864. Honorably discharged 8 February, 1869.
BAXTER, ALFRED.
  Mate, 21 August, 1862. Acting Gunner, 17 December, 1862. Appointment revoked 20 June, 1864. Mate, 26 May, 1866. Resigned 11 April, 1867.
BAXTER, CHARLES H.
  Acting Ensign, 22 October, 1862. Acting Master, 29 March, 1864. Honorably discharged 3 November, 1865.
BAXTER, J. B.
  Acting Volunteer Lieutenant, 26 August, 1861. Honorably discharged 27 December, 1865.
BAXTER, JAMES W.
  Mate, 19 February, 1864. Retired List, 19 January, 1895.
BAXTER, OSCAR F.
  Assistant Surgeon, 25 January, 1842. Resigned 17 April, 1848.
BAXTER, RODNEY.
  Acting Master, 13 May, 1861. Resigned 3 October, 1861.
BAXTER, WILLIAM J.
  Cadet Engineer, 1 October, 1879. Assistant Engineer, 1 July, 1885. Assistant Naval Constructor, 6 June, 1888. Naval Constructor, 10 August, 1893; rank of Lieutenant; rank of Commander, March 3, 1899.
BAXTER, WILLIAM T.
  Acting Third Assistant Engineer, 10 July, 1863. Honorably discharged 3 January, 1866.
BAY, NATHANIEL G.
  Midshipman, 2 February, 1829. Passed Midshipman, 3 July, 1835. Lieutenant, 1 May, 1841. Cashiered 14 October, 1842.
BAYARD, A. W. W.
  Midshipman, 5 August, 1805. Dismissed 30 October, 1805.
BAYARD, CHARLES C.
  Midshipman, 9 December, 1841. Passed Midshipman, 10 August, 1847. Died 19 February, 1850.
BAYLEY, WARNER B.
  Acting Third Assistant Engineer, 4 August, 1864. Mustered out 28 April, 1869. Second Assistant Engineer, 2 September, 1870. First Assistant Engineer, 21 September, 1877. Chief Engineer, 25 May, 1894. Rank changed to Lieutenant-Commander, 3 March, 1899.
BAYLOR, ADAM K.
  Mate, 31 August, 1864. Honorably discharged 30 July, 1868. Mate, 31 December, 1869. Resigned 5 September, 1873.
BAYNTON, EDWARD.
  Midshipman, 18 May, 1809. Dismissed 24 August, 1810.
BAYS, GEORGE.
  Acting Second Assistant Engineer, 11 March, 1863. Resigned 25 August, 1863.
BEACH, EDWARD L.
  Naval Cadet, 20 May, 1884. Assistant Engineer, 1 July, 1890. Passed Assistant Engineer, 27 June, 1896. Rank changed to Lieutenant, 3 March, 1899.
BEACH, ROBERT J.
  Cadet Midshipman, 13 September, 1877. Graduated. Honorably discharged 30 June, 1883. Restored to service 10 March, 1886. Resigned 21 April, 1886. Lieutenant (Spanish-American War), 24 May, 1898. Honorably discharged 27 September, 1898.
BEACHAM, ELISHA J.
  Gunner, 7 September, 1861. Retired List, 26 January, 1893.
BEADEL, EDWARD N.
  Midshipman, 19 October, 1841. Lost in the Grampus, March, 1843.
BEAL, THADDEUS R.
  Lieutenant, Junior Grade (Spanish-American War), 24 May, 1898. Honorably discharged 9 September, 1898.
BEALE, EDWARD F.
  Midshipman, 14 December, 1836. Passed Midshipman, 1 July, 1842. Master, 1 August, 1849. Lieutenant, 28 February, 1850. Resigned 5 March, 1852.
BEALE, GEORGE.
  Purser, 24 July, 1813. Died 4 April, 1835.

BEALE, JOSEPH.
Midshipman, 1 April, 1799. Lieutenant, 19 April, 1800. Last appearance on Records of Navy Department.
BEALE, JOSEPH.
Assistant Surgeon, 6 September, 1837. Passed Assistant Surgeon, 14 March, 1843. Surgeon, 19 April, 1848. Medical Director, 3 March, 1871. Surgeon-General, 8 July, 1873. Retired List, 30 December, 1876. Died 25 September, 1889.
BEALE, JOSEPH.
Cadet Midshipman, 12 October, 1874. Midshipman, 22 June, 1882. Ensign, Junior Grade, 3 March, 1883. Ensign, 26 June, 1884. Lieutenant, Junior Grade, 17 February, 1893. Resigned 28 October, 1895. Lieutenant (Spanish-American War), 23 April, 1898. Honorably discharged 3 September, 1898.
BEALE, RICHARD C.
Lieutenant, 9 March, 1798. Last appearance on Records of Navy Department.
BEALE, ROBERT.
Midshipman, 1 January, 1818. Last appearance on Records of Navy Department.
BEALE, THOMAS T.
Midshipman, 17 February, 1800. Resigned 2 June, 1803.
BEALL, CHARLES.
Acting Third Assistant Engineer, 20 October, 1863. Honorably discharged 27 September, 1865.
BEALL, CHARLES F.
Mate, 12 January, 1864. Honorably discharged 27 September, 1865.
BEALL, JOHN H.
Surgeon's Mate, 28 April, 1804. Resigned 15 October, 1807.
BEAM, PETER M.
Mate, 23 December, 1864. Honorably discharged 14 September, 1865.
BEAMAN, EZRA.
Acting Ensign, 9 April, 1863. Acting Master, for gallant conduct, 19 March, 1864. Honorably discharged 31 December, 1865.
BEAMAN, GEORGE W.
Acting Assistant Paymaster, 5 March, 1862. Assistant Paymaster, 11 June, 1862. Paymaster, 28 March, 1866. Pay Inspector, 12 September, 1891. Pay Director, 9 April, 1899. Retired with rank of Rear-Admiral, Junior Grade. 7 May, 1899.
BEAN, GEORGE F.
Mate, 12 February, 1864. Honorably discharged 31 October, 1865.
BEAN, WILLIAM S.
Third Assistant Engineer, 15 April, 1847. Resigned 23 October, 1847.
BEANE, JOHN W.
Midshipman, 23 June, 1869. Graduated 31 May, 1873. Ensign, 16 July, 1875. Resigned 30 June, 1878.
BEANS, SAMUEL S.
Acting Ensign, 5 October, 1864. Honorably discharged 17 January, 1866.
BEARD, ALEXANDER.
Master, 1 March, 1814. Discharged 15 April, 1815.
BEARD, GEORGE M.
Acting Assistant Surgeon, 5 March, 1864. Resigned 18 October, 1865.
BEARD, GEORGE W.
Third Assistant Engineer, 25 March, 1862. Retired List, 1 February, 1866. Assistant Engineer, Retired List, 24 July, 1867.
BEARD, GEORGE W.
Acting Third Assistant Engineer, 11 June, 1864. Honorably discharged 30 October, 1865.
BEARD, LEWIS.
Midshipman, 10 January, 1840. Resigned 23 July, 1844.
BEARD, WILLIAM C.
Midshipman, 4 July, 1805. Resigned 15 September, 1810.
BEARDSLEE, LESTER A.
Midshipman, 5 March, 1850. Passed Midshipman, 20 June, 1856. Master, 22 January, 1858. Lieutenant, 23 July, 1859. Lieutenant-Commander, 16 July, 1862. Commander, 12 June, 1869. Captain, 26 November, 1880. Commodore, 23 January, 1894. Rear Admiral, 21 May, 1895. Retired List, 1 February, 1898.
BEARDSLEY, EDWARD T.
Acting Third Assistant Engineer, 1 September, 1864. Honorably discharged 19 May, 1866.
BEARDSLEY, GROVE S.
Assistant Surgeon, 1 July, 1861. Passed Assistant Surgeon, 22 June, 1864. Surgeon, 25 July, 1866. Medical Inspector, 24 April, 1884. Medical Director, 22 January, 1891. Retired List, 22 January, 1900.
BEARDSLEY, RICHARD.
Acting Assistant Paymaster, 17 December, 1861. Resigned 27 June, 1864.
BEARDSLEY, ROBERT.
Mate, 31 October, 1861. Acting Ensign, 3 November, 1863. Honorably discharged 20 January, 1866.
BEASLEY, GEORGE F.
Acting Assistant Surgeon, 5 March, 1864. Honorably discharged 15 September, 1865.
BEATTIE, FREDERICK A.
Mate, 30 September, 1864. Honorably discharged 12 October, 1865. Mate, 12 May, 1866. Appointment revoked 20 October, 1866.
BEATTIE, LUCIUS H.
Acting Master, 1 August, 1861. Honorably discharged 7 December, 1865.
BEATTIE, WILLIAM A.
Mate, 5 June, 1862. Acting Ensign, 17 October, 1864. Honorably discharged 12 May, 1865.

GENERAL NAVY REGISTER. 49

BEATTY, F. S.
  Surgeon's Mate, 27 July, 1819. Resigned 13 December, 1823.
BEATTY, FRANCIS G.
  Midshipman, 1 March, 1825. Dismissed 10 December, 1830.
BEATTY, FRANK E.
  Midshipman, 21 September, 1871. Graduated 21 June, 1875. Ensign, 18 July, 1876. Master, 19 June, 1882. Lieutenant, Junior Grade, 3 March, 1883. Lieutenant, 23 March, 1889. Lieutenant-Commander, 3 March, 1899.
BEATTY, HORATIO.
  Midshipman, 1 January, 1812. Resigned 6 September, 1822.
BEATTY, JOHN T.
  Midshipman, 21 October, 1848. Resigned 16 September, 1850.
BEATTY, THOMAS A.
  Midshipman, 16 January, 1819. Lieutenant, 24 July, 1813. Resigned 29 November, 1814.
BEAUCHAMP, HIRAM.
  Acting Assistant Surgeon, 1 October, 1862. Resigned 7 December, 1864.
BEAUCHAMP, JOSEPH.
  Acting Ensign, 3 September, 1863. Resigned 17 November, 1864.
BEAUFORT, FRANCIS.
  Acting Gunner, 1 October, 1862. Resigned 5 June, 1863.
BEAUMART, HORATIO U.
  Assistant Surgeon, 29 April, 1864. Passed Assistant Surgeon, 26 October, 1868. Surgeon, 5 April, 1875. Died 30 April, 1887.
BEAUMONT, JOHN C.
  Midshipman, 1 March, 1838. Passed Midshipman, 20 May, 1844. Master, 30 August, 1851. Lieutenant, 29 August, 1852. Commander, 16 July, 1862. Retired List, 27 April, 1868. Captain, Active List, 10 June, 1872. Commodore, 14 June, 1874. Rear Admiral, 25 November, 1881. Retired List, 3 February, 1882. Died 2 August, 1882.
BECK, ALFRED M.
  Mate, 4 March, 1863. Resigned 9 October, 1863. Mate, 31 December, 1863. Honorably discharged 25 July, 1865.
BECK, C. E.
  Acting Ensign, 29 June, 1863. Honorably discharged 2 December, 1865.
BECK, DANIEL.
  Midshipman, 24 November, 1800. Resigned 3 January, 1801.
BECK, FRANCIS W.
  Mate, 29 April, 1863. Appointment revoked 16 January, 1864.
BECK, JOHN H.
  Midshipman, 18 May, 1809. Resigned 16 September, 1810.
BECK, MORRIS B.
  Assistant Surgeon, 2 December, 1841. Passed Assistant Surgeon, 15 March, 1847. Resigned 10 May, 1861.
BECK, SAMUEL.
  Midshipman, 12 April, 1813. Last appearance on Records of Navy Department, Neptune, 25 September, 1815.
BECK, SYDNEY S.
  Mate, Acting Ensign, 28 October, 1862. Resigned 3 February, 1864.
BECK, WILLIAM W.
  Mate, 27 May, 1864. Acting Ensign, 3 December, 1864. Honorably discharged 7 October, 1868. Mate, 24 January, 1870. Retired List, 8 September, 1881.
BECKER, JAMES.
  Mate, 20 January, 1862. Dismissed 29 November, 1862.
BECKETT, B. F.
  Acting Second Assistant Engineer, 1861. Appointment revoked 12 February, 1862. Acting Second Assistant Engineer, 20 June, 1862. Acting First Assistant Engineer, 25 February, 1863. Honorably discharged 17 November, 1867.
BECKETT, MATTHEW.
  Mate, 16 September, 1861. Resigned 17 May, 1864.
BECKHAM, J. B.
  Midshipman, 1 December, 1824. Died 11 September, 1825.
BECKLEY, NOAH.
  Acting Third Assistant Engineer, 2 July, 1862. Died Magnolia, 10 October, 1862.
BECKNER, JOHN T.
  Naval Cadet, 20 May, 1895. At sea prior to final graduation.
BECKWITH, EDWARD J.
  Midshipman, 18 June, 1812. Last appearance on Records of Navy Department.
BECKWITH, GEORGE E.
  Lieutenant, Junior Grade (Spanish-American War), 18 May, 1898. Honorably discharged 2 September, 1898.
BECKWITH, HENRY C.
  Third Assistant Engineer, 27 June, 1862. Second Assistant Engineer, 21 November, 1863. First Assistant Engineer, 1 January, 1868. Retired List, 2 December, 1876. Died 12 July, 1885.
BECKWITH, J. L. S.
  Midshipman, 16 January, 1840. Dismissed 23 September, 1844.
BECKWITH, S. M.
  Gunner, 14 March, 1843. Resigned 30 September, 1853.
BEDELL, CHARLES.
  Acting Master's Mate, 10 September, 1864. Appointment marked "Deserter," 17 December, 1864.
BEDFORD, JOSEPH.
  Midshipman, 1 April, 1804. Resigned 30 June, 1804.

4

GENERAL NAVY REGISTER.

BEE, B. F.
Acting Second Assistant Engineer, 12 February, 1862. Appointment revoked 21 July, 1862. Acting Second Assistant Engineer, 27 October, 1862. Acting First Assistant Engineer, 1 March, 1864. Honorably discharged 12 September, 1865.
BEE, EPHRAIM J.
Assistant Surgeon, 9 May, 1844. Died 7 March, 1850.
BEEBE, DANIEL G.
Assistant Surgeon, 7 July, 1898.
BEECHER, ALBERT M.
Cadet Midshipman, 11 June, 1880. Ensign, 1 July, 1886. Lieutenant, Junior Grade, 7 June, 1895. Lieutenant, 5 June, 1898.
BEECHER, MARK H.
Professor, 14 June, 1841. Retired List, 27 March, 1869. Died 25 May, 1882.
BEECHER, WILLIAM P.
Acting Assistant Paymaster, 4 November, 1862. Drowned 24 June, 1863.
BEEHLER, WILLIAM H.
Midshipman, 28 July, 1864. Graduated, 2 June, 1868. Ensign, 19 April, 1869. Master, 12 July, 1870. Lieutenant, 10 September, 1874. Lieutenant-Commander, 21 June, 1896. Commander, 22 September, 1899.
BEERS, AUGUST P.
Surgeon's Mate, 16 November, 1824. Surgeon, 4 December, 1828. Died 8 June, 1831.
BEERS, BENJAMIN F.
Acting Warrant Machinist, 23 August, 1899.
BEERS, FRANK H.
Mate, 21 November, 1861. Acting Ensign, 22 December, 1862. Resigned 10 May, 1865.
BEERS, JAMES R.
Mate, 14 November, 1861. Acting Master, 15 February, 1862. Acting Volunteer Lieutenant, 24 June, 1863. Honorably discharged 19 December, 1865.
BEERS, WILLIAM L.
Ensign (Spanish-American War), 11 May, 1898. Lieutenant, Junior Grade, 30 July, 1898. Honorably discharged 22 December, 1898.
BEETLE, DAVID S.
Acting Ensign, 1 June, 1864. Honorably discharged 28 August, 1865.
BEGGS, JOHN.
Sailmaker, 20 August, 1835. Died 27 September, 1840.
BEHM, C. F. W.
Acting Volunteer Lieutenant, 26 August, 1861. Acting Volunteer Lieutenant-Commander, 22 December, 1864. Honorably discharged 28 November, 1865.
BELCHER, JAMES A.
Mate, 25 April, 1864. Honorably discharged 19 November, 1867.
BELCHER, J. H
Professor Mathematics, 26 September, 1837. Name changed to J. Sidney Henshaw. (See that name for record of service.)
BELCHER, JOHN A.
Midshipman, 1 September, 1811. Lieutenant, 27 April, 1816. Last appearance on Records of Navy Department, 7 December, 1819. Dead.
BELCHER, THOMAS E.
Acting Third Assistant Engineer, 5 November, 1863. Resigned 3 June, 1865.
BELDEN, FREDERICK.
Mate, 19 November, 1862. Died 30 September, 1863.
BELDEN, SAMUEL.
Acting Ensign, 8 September, 1862. Acting Master, 19 February, 1864. Acting Volunteer Lieutenant, 18 May, 1865. Honorably discharged 21 March, 1866. Acting Master, 5 April, 1867. Ensign, 12 March, 1868. Master, 18 December, 1868. Lieutenant, 21 March, 1870. Lieutenant-Commander, 7 July, 1883. Commander, 25 February, 1893. Retired List, 27 April, 1898.
BELDING, NICHOLAS H.
Acting Assistant Paymaster, 13 April, 1865. Honorably discharged 15 October, 1866.
BELDING, WILLIAM S.
Lieutenant, Junior Grade (Spanish-American War), 25 May, 1898. Honorably discharged 17 September, 1898.
BELKNAP, ALFRED A.
Purser, 11 March, 1851. Dismissed 2 August, 1865. Dismissal annulled, and commissioned Pay Director, 3 March, 1871. Retired List, 27 January, 1873. Died 14 March, 1884.
BELKNAP, CHARLES.
Midshipman, 28 July, 1864. Ensign, 18 December, 1868. Master, 21 March, 1870. Lieutenant, 21 March, 1871. Lieutenant-Commander, 12 February, 1889. Commander, 6 December, 1896.
BELKNAP, GEORGE E.
Midshipman, 7 October, 1847. Passed Midshipman, 10 June, 1853. Master, 15 September, 1855. Lieutenant, 16 September, 1855. Lieutenant-Commander, 10 July, 1862. Commander, 25 July, 1866. Captain, 25 January, 1875. Commodore, 2 June, 1885. Rear Admiral, 12 February, 1889. Retired List, 22 January, 1894.
BELKNAP, REGINALD R.
Naval Cadet, 5 September, 1887. Ensign, 1 July, 1893. Lieutenant, Junior Grade, 3 March, 1899. Lieutenant, 2 July, 1899.
BELL, A. NELSON.
Assistant Surgeon, 5 March, 1847. Passed Assistant Surgeon, 1 May, 1855. Resigned 30 October, 1855.
BELL, CHARLES H.
Midshipman, 18 June, 1812. Lieutenant, 28 March, 1820. Commodore, 10 September, 1840. Captain, 12 August, 1854. Commodore, Retired List, 16 July, 1862. Rear Admiral, 25 July, 1866. Died 19 February, 1875.

GENERAL NAVY REGISTER. 51

BELL, CHARLES S.
  Midshipman, 9 September, 1841. Dismissed 28 August, 1849.
BELL, DAVID N.
  Midshipman, 23 September, 1861. Graduated September, 1865. Ensign, 1 December, 1866. Retired List, 10 July, 1868. Lieutenant on Retired List, 26 March, 1869. Died 25 March, 1870.
BELL, EDWARD B.
  Boatswain, 15 December, 1852. Died 12 January, 1875.
BELL, GEORGE.
  Gunner, 25 June, 1838. Died 7 September, 1845.
BELL, GEORGE R.
  Acting Third Assistant Engineer, 3 July, 1863. Honorably discharged 30 November, 1865.
BELL, HAMILTON.
  Acting Gunner, 22 November, 1851. Deserted in August, 1854.
BELL, HENRY H.
  Midshipman, 4 August, 1823. Passed Midshipman, 23 March, 1829. Lieutenant, 3 March, 1831. Commander, 12 August, 1854. Commodore, 16 July, 1862. Rear-Admiral, 25 July, 1866. Retired List, 12 April, 1867. Drowned 11 January, 1898.
BELL, JAMES.
  Master, 16 January, 1809. Resigned 19 December, 1809.
BELL, JAMES.
  Master's Mate, 22 July, 1816. Last appearance on Records of Navy Department.
BELL, JEFFERSON.
  Acting Second Assistant Engineer, 25 November, 1862. Dismissed 9 September, 1863.
BELL, JOHN.
  Acting Boatswain, 16 September, 1873. Resigned 19 August, 1874.
BELL, JOHN A.
  Cadet Midshipman, 13 June, 1874. Graduated 10 June, 1881. Ensign, Junior Grade, 3 March, 1883. Ensign, 26 June, 1884. Lieutenant, Junior Grade, 2 October, 1891. Lieutenant, 29 December, 1895.
BELL, JOHN H.
  Midshipman, 16 January, 1809. Lieutenant, 9 December, 1814. Commander, 3 March, 1831. Died 14 August, 1833.
BELL, JOHN R.
  Acting Ensign, 7 January, 1863. Honorably discharged 27 October, 1865.
BELL, JOSEPH G.
  Acting Assistant Surgeon, 5 April, 1864. Honorably discharged 19 September, 1865.
BELL, J. SNOWDEN.
  Acting Third Assistant Engineer, 10 August, 1894. Appointment revoked (sick), 3 December, 1864.
BELL, ROBERT B.
  Midshipman, 1 August, 1820. Dismissed 19 July, 1824.
BELL, ROWLAND W.
  Assistant Paymaster (Spanish-American War), 10 August, 1898. Honorably discharged 21 September, 1898.
BELL, THADDEUS.
  Acting Assistant Paymaster, 17 January, 1865. Discharged 15 October, 1866.
BELL, THOMAS.
  Acting Second Assistant Engineer, 10 December, 1862. Resigned 17 March, 1864.
BELL, THOMAS G.
  Boatswain, 18 June, 1838. Retired List, 3 July, 1872. Died 10 August, 1883.
BELL, THOMAS W.
  Acting Ensign, 15 September, 1862. Honorably discharged 24 September, 1865. Acting Ensign, 29 January, 1867. Mustered out 30 December, 1868.
BELL, WALTER D.
  Mate, 5 July, 1862. Resigned 6 July, 1863.
BELL, WILLIAM.
  Acting Third Assistant Engineer, 1 October, 1862. Acting Second Assistant Engineer, 16 January, 1865. Honorably discharged 25 November, 1865.
BELL, WILLIAM H.
  Assistant Surgeon, 16 September, 1898.
BELL, WILLIAM H.
  Assistant Paymaster (Spanish American War), 9 July, 1898. Honorably discharged 10 October, 1898.
BELL, WILLIAM L.
  Assistant Surgeon for temporary service, 18 June, 1898. Transferred to regular service, 16 November, 1898.
BELL, WILSON F.
  Acting Assistant Surgeon, 21 October, 1861. Resigned 17 June, 1862.
BELLANDI, E.
  Acting Ensign and Pilot, 1 October, 1864. Honorably discharged 19 February, 1866.
BELLOWS, CHARLES S.
  Mate, 23 January, 1862. Honorably discharged 2 August, 1868.
BELLOWS, EDWARD.
  Assistant Paymaster, 11 June, 1862. Paymaster, 20 February, 1866. Pay Inspector, 5 July, 1889. Pay Director, 10 July, 1898.
BELLOWS, GEORGE.
  Acting Master, 28 December, 1861. Resigned 21 November, 1863.
BELROSE, LOUIS.
  Midshipman, 20 September, 1861. Graduated September, 1865. Ensign, 1 December, 1866. Resigned 30 January, 1867.
BELT, WILLIAM.
  Surgeon's Mate, 23 September, 1811. Dismissed 7 April, 1829.

GENERAL NAVY REGISTER.

BELT, WILLIAM J.
Midshipman, 1 September, 1811. Lieutenant, 3 March, 1817. Commander, 9 February, 1837. Dismissed 2 November, 1842.
BELTON, SOLOMON D.
Midshipman, 1 January, 1825. Resigned 16 February, 1827.
BEMENT, OSCAR W.
Mate, 23 October, 1861. Resigned 20 July, 1864.
BEMIS, GEORGE F.
Acting Assistant Paymaster, 26 September, 1863. Honorably discharged as Acting Assistant Paymaster, 25 October, 1865. Assistant Paymaster, 27 February, 1867. Passed Assistant Paymaster, 2 July, 1869. Dismissed 12 May, 1875.
BENBRIDGE, RICHARD M.
Midshipman, 20 November, 1823. Last appearance on Records of Navy Department, Dead.
BENCKERT, JAMES M.
Third Assistant Engineer, 8 October, 1861. Died 28 June, 1862.
BENEDICT, GEORGE S.
Acting Assistant Paymaster, 20 August, 1862. Assistant Paymaster, 30 June, 1864. Resigned 11 August, 1865.
BENEDICT, WILLIAM B.
Professor, 31 May, 1841. Died 20 June, 1853.
BENET, LAURENCE V.
Ensign (Spanish-American War), 25 April, 1898. Honorably discharged 1 June, 1898.
BENHAM, ANDREW E. K.
Midshipman, 24 November, 1847. Passed Midshipman, 10 June, 1853. Master, 15 September, 1855. Lieutenant, 16 September, 1855. Lieutenant-Commander, 16 July, 1862. Commander, 25 July, 1866. Captain, 12 March, 1875. Commodore, 30 October, 1885. Rear-Admiral, 28 February, 1890. Retired List, 10 April, 1894.
BENHAM, CHARLES A.
Mate, 16 April, 1864. Appointment revoked 25 January, 1865.
BENHAM, COURTLANDT.
Midshipman, 31 March, 1837. Passed Midshipman, 29 June, 1843. Master, 21 September, 1850. Lieutenant, 9 April, 1851. Died 30 October, 1852.
BENHAM, HENRY K.
Naval Cadet, 19 May, 1884. Ensign, 1 July, 1890. Lieutenant, Junior Grade, 27 April, 1898. Lieutenant, 3 March, 1899.
BENHAM, TIMOTHY G.
Midshipman, 30 November, 1814. Lieutenant, 3 March, 1827. Commander, 5 February, 1848. Reserved List, 14 September, 1855. Died 17 June, 1860.
BENHAM, T. W.
Mate, 31 January, 1870. Resigned 12 February, 1876.
BENHAM, W. G.
Midshipman, 26 February, 1833. Resigned 14 November, 1837.
BENHAM, W. G.
Midshipman, 5 May, 1838. Resigned 23 August, 1838.
BENJAMIN, EVERARD.
Midshipman, 1 January, 1818. Last appearance on Records of Navy Department.
BENJAMIN, J. S.
Mate, 7 June, 1862. Acting Ensign, 20 August, 1863. Resigned 8 November, 1864.
BENJAMIN, MYRON F.
Mate, 1 October, 1862. Acting Ensign, 18 December, 1862. Resigned 5 June, 1863.
BENJAMIN, PARK, JR.
Midshipman, 23 September, 1863. Ensign, 18 December, 1868. Resigned 19 January, 1869.
BENKHARD, J. P.
Acting Assistant Surgeon, 21 October, 1861. Resigned 15 May, 1862.
BENNESON, ROBERT H.
Acting Second Assistant Engineer, 25 March, 1864. Honorably discharged 4 November, 1865.
BENNET, CORNELIUS.
Master, 9 December, 1812. Died 18 August, 1840.
BENNET, J. W. A.
Acting Ensign, 20 February, 1865. Honorably discharged, 12 October, 1865.
BENNETT, A. J.
Midshipman, 4 July, 1817. Dismissed 31 December, 1828.
BENNETT, CHARLES.
Acting Third Assistant Engineer, 28 December, 1861. Acting Second Assistant Engineer, 15 February, 1864. Resigned 5 August, 1865.
BENNETT, C. W.
Midshipman, 29 March, 1839. Dismissed 6 August, 1839.
BENNETT, C. W. B.
Midshipman, 5 April, 1837. Resgned 8 November, 1838.
BENNETT, CLARENCE L.
Carpenter, 24 May, 1898.
BENNETT, EDWARD.
Midshipman, 3 January, 1800. Lieutenant, 5 February, 1807. Died 20 December, 1810.
BENNETT, ERNEST L.
Naval Cadet, 24 September, 1889. Ensign, 1 July, 1896. Lieutenant, Junior Grade, 1 July, 1899.
BENNETT, FRANCIS M.
Cadet Engineer, 1 October, 1874. Graduated 10 June, 1879.
BENNETT, FRANK M.
Cadet Engineer, 1 October, 1874. Assistant Engineer, 10 June, 1881. Passed Assistant Engineer, 24 April, 1892. Rank changed to Lieutenant, 3 March, 1899.

GENERAL NAVY REGISTER. 53

BENNETT, GEORGE.
　Acting Third Assistant Engineer, 11 October, 1864. Honorably discharged 6 November, 1865.
BENNETT, GEORGE M.
　Acting Second Assistant Engineer, 28 December, 1861. Acting First Assistant Engineer, 15 December, 1862. Honorably discharged 5 December, 1865.
BENNETT, GEORGE R.
　Acting Third Assistant Engineer, 27 September, 1861. Acting Second Assistant Engineer, 8 July, 1862. Acting First Assistant Engineer, 16 July, 1863. Honorably discharged 21 November, 1865.
BENNETT, J. A.
　Acting Ensign, 10 December, 1864. Honorably discharged 21 October, 1865.
BENNETT, JEREMIAH H.
　Acting Ensign, 11 October, 1862. Honorably discharged 12 August, 1865.
BENNETT, JOHN F.
　Mate, 31 July, 1863. Appointment revoked 25 April, 1864.
BENNETT, JOHN W.
　Midshipman, 10 February, 1840. Passed Midshipman, 11 July, 1846. Master, 1 March, 1855. Lieutenant, 14 September, 1855. Dismissed 19 April, 1861.
BENNETT, JOHN W.
　Acting Ensign,, 12 January, 1863. Appointment revoked 4 March, 1864. Acting Ensign, 17 May, 1864. Honorably discharged 15 September, 1865.
BENNETT, KENNETH M.
　Naval Cadet, 8 September, 1891. Ensign, 1 July, 1897. Lieutenant, Junior Grade, 1 July, 1900.
BENNETT, LOREY.
　Acting Third Assistant Engineer, 15 August, 1862. Resigned 23 February, 1865.
BENNETT, L. T.
　Midshipman, 7 December, 1825. Passed Midshipman, 4 June, 1831. Resigned 18 October, 1833.
BENNETT, RUDOLPH T.
　Third Assistant Engineer, 25 March, 1862. Second Assistant Engineer, 2 February, 1865. First Assistant Engineer, 1 January, 1868. Retired List, 21 May, 1880.
BENNETT, THOMAS.
　Boatswain, 19 March, 1858. Retired List, 20 October, 1883. Died 20 June, 1890.
BENNETT, THOMAS W.
　Acting Assistant Surgeon, 23 September, 1863. Honorably discharged 24 February, 1869.
BENNETT, WILLIAM.
　Sailmaker, 23 August, 1833. Resigned 18 April, 1836. Sailmaker, 5 July, 1839. Resigned 15 May, 1861.
BENNETT, WILLIAM C.
　Acting Ensign, 1 October, 1862. Resigned 18 February, 1864.
BENNETT, WILLIAM C.
　Passed Assistant Engineer (Spanish-American War), 20 May, 1898. Honorably discharged 25 January, 1899.
BENNIS, SPIRO V.
　Acting Master, 26 August, 1861. Honorably discharged 10 May, 1865.
BENSON, BENT A.
　Mate (Spanish-American War), 12 April, 1898. Honorably discharged 8 September, 1898.
BENSON, CHARLES.
　Midshipman, 21 February, 1802. Cashiered 6 June, 1803.
BENSON, GEORGE H.
　Mate, 27 May, 1862. Died 9 October, 1863.
BENSON, JOHN C.
　Midshipman, 22 August, 1812. Last appearance on Records of Navy Department (furloughed), 7 June, 1815.
BENSON, WILLIAM S.
　Cadet Midshipman, 21 September, 1872. Graduated 18 June, 1879. Ensign, 27 July, 1881. Lieutenant, Junior Grade, 28 May, 1888. Lieutenant, 27 June, 1893. Lieutenant-Commander, 1 July, 1900.
BENT, SILAS.
　Midshipman, 1 July, 1836. Passed Midshipman, 1 July, 1842. Master, 7 January, 1849. Lieutenant, 1 August, 1849. Dismissed 25 April, 1861.
BENTHALL, JOHN D.
　Gunner, 18 October, 1839. Appointment revoked 27 March, 1847.
BENTLEY, JOHN H.
　Mate, 26 September, 1864. Honorably discharged, 24 July, 1865.
BENTLEY, JOHN W.
　Acting Master, 10 June, 1861. Died 27 May, 1864.
BENTLEY, PETER E.
　Midshipman, 12 April, 1800. Resigned 4 March, 1802.
BENTLEY, THOMAS.
　Acting Second Assistant Engineer, 10 August, 1861. Acting First Assistant Engineer, 6 January, 1865. Honorably discharged 5 July, 1866.
BENTLY, JAMES L.
　Acting Volunteer Lieutenant, 1 October, 1862. Resigned 5 February, 1863.
BENTON, FREDERICK L.
　Assistant Surgeon, 21 July, 1898.
BENTON, JOSIAH H.
　Acting Assistant Paymaster, 11 September, 1862. Honorably discharged 25 September, 1865.
BENTON, THEODORE M.
　Acting Gunner, 28 January, 1864. Honorably discharged 27 November, 1865.

BENTRICK, CHARLES.
Mate. Dismissed 1 May, 1862.
BENTSON, RASMUS.
Acting Ensign, 7 January, 1863 . Lost at sea, 4 April, 1863.
BENZON, ALBERT F.
Mate, 14 August, 1897. Appointed a Boatswain 13 July, 1898.
BERENTSON, OSCAR.
Acting Warrant Machinist, 23 August, 1899.
BERGNER, A. M.
Mate, 17 June, 1864. Resigned 8 October, 1870.
BERMINGHAM, CHARLES L.
Lieutenant, Junior Grade (Spanish-American War), 25 May, 1898. Honorably discharged 13 September, 1898.
BERNADOU, JOHN B.
Cadet Midshipman, 22 September, 1876. Graduated 22 June, 1882. Ensign, Junior Grade, 3 March, 1883. Ensign, 26 June, 1884. Lieutenant, Junior Grade, 1 July, 1892. Lieutenant, 21 June, 1896.
BERNARD, HENRY.
Midshipman, 12 November, 1800. Lieutenant, 28 February, 1807. Resigned 19 May, 1812. Captain, 24 December, 1814. Last appearance on Records of Navy Department.
BERNARD, HENRY, Jr.
Assistant Surgeon, 27 November, 1844. Passed Assistant Surgeon, 12 February, 1850. Resigned 11 October, 1850.
BERNARD, LEMUEL.
Third Assistant Engineer, 16 January, 1863. Resigned 21 March, 1866.
BERNARD, STEPHEN.
Master, 7 March, 1811. Resigned 3 August, 1813.
BERNBAUM, OLE K.
Acting Ensign, 30 May, 1864. Acting Master, 6 April, 1865. Appointment revoked 31 August, 1867.
BERNICE, GEORGE.
Acting Third Assistant Engineer, 3 December, 1861. Dismissed 19 July, 1862.
BERNIER, LOUIS L.
Passed Assistant Engineer (Spanish-American War), 14 May, 1898. Honorably discharged 1 December, 1898.
BERRETT, WILLIAM H.
Acting Assistant Surgeon, 17 May, 1864. Honorably discharged 10 October, 1865.
BERRIAN, WILLIAM L.
Mate, 22 August, 1864. Appointment revoked 15 June, 1865.
BERRIEN, FRANK D.
Naval Cadet, 5 September, 1896. Graduated 30 June, 1900.
BERRIEN, JOHN M.
Midshipman, 1 March, 1825. Passed Midshipman, 4 June, 1831. Lieutenant, 9 February, 1837. Commander, 14 September, 1855. Captain, 16 July, 1862. Commodore, 26 September, 1866. Retired List, 28 December, 1866. Died 21 November, 1883.
BERRY, ABRAHAM H.
Mate, 27 May, 1862. Acting Ensign, 14 May, 1863. Honorably discharged 6 July, 1867.
BERRY, ALBERT G.
Midshipman, 24 July, 1865. Graduated 4 June, 1869. Ensign, 12 July, 1870. Master, 27 September, 1872. Lieutenant, 20 October, 1875. Lieutenant-Commander, 21 July, 1897. Commander, 1 July, 1900.
BERRY, CHARLES.
Midshipman, 1 September, 1811. Furloughed 17 October, 1815. Last appearance on Records of Navy Department.
BERRY, DANIEL D.
Acting Second Assistant Engineer, 20 December, 1864. Honorably discharged 29 July, 1865.
BERRY, DAVID M.
Naval Cadet, 6 September, 1889. Graduated. Honorably discharged 30 June, 1895. Assistant Engineer (Spanish-American War), 3 June, 1898. Honorably discharged 7 November, 1898.
BERRY, G. H.
Acting Ensign, 9 January, 1865. Honorably discharged 3 May, 1866.
BERRY, JAMES H.
Mate, 23 December, 1862. Acting Ensign, 13 February, 1864. Honorably discharged 19 September, 1865.
BERRY, J. APPLETON.
Acting Assistant Paymaster, 9 September, 1861. Assistant Paymaster, 23 July, 1866. Appointment revoked 10 April, 1877.
BERRY, JOHN R.
Acting Third Assistant Engineer, 20 March, 1865. Honorably discharged 8 October, 1868.
BERRY, MARK.
Acting Third Assistant Engineer, 31 March, 1864. Appointment revoked 3 August, 1864.
BERRY, R. D.
Carpenter, 12 October, 1833. Dismissed 8 March, 1836.
BERRY, RICHARD.
Carpenter, 1 July, 1818. Resigned 16 January, 1824.
BERRY, RICHARD.
Sailmaker, 4 November, 1852. Died 10 April, 1861.
BERRY, RICHARD.
Mate, 2 October, 1861. Resigned 29 May, 1862.

GENERAL NAVY REGISTER.

BERRY, ROBERT L.
Naval Cadet, 20 May, 1896. Graduated 30 June, 1900.
BERRY, ROBERT M.
Acting Midshipman, 31 January, 1862. Graduated June, 1866. Ensign, 12 March, 1868. Master, 26 March, 1869. Lieutenant, 21 March, 1870. Lieutenant-Commander, 4 February, 1886. Commander, 2 February, 1895.
BERRY, THOMAS.
Carpenter, 18 December, 1816. Last appearance on Records of Navy Department.
BERRY, THOMAS C.
Boatswain, 29 September, 1854. Dismissed 11 January, 1859.
BERRY, WILLIAM.
Midshipman, 17 December, 1810. Lieutenant, 27 April, 1816. Died 17 July, 1824.
BERRY, WILLIAM.
Boatswain, 20 February, 1812. Died 26 March, 1819.
BERRY, WILLIAM C.
Acting Master, without pay, 22 November, 1862. Appointment revoked 20 January, 1863.
BERRYHILL, THOMAS A.
Assistant Surgeon, 17 June, 1886. Passed Assistant Surgeon, 17 June, 1889. Surgeon, 9 April, 1899.
BERRYMAN, E. C.
Actin Second Assistant Engineer, 13 September, 1861. Resigned 7 October, 1862.
BERRYMAN, OTWAY H.
Midshipman, 2 February, 1829. Passed Midshipman, 3 July, 1835. Lieutenant, 8 September, 1841. Died 2 April, 1861.
BERRYMAN, ROBERT.
Acting Third Assistant Engineer, 25 November, 1863. Honorably discharged 27 July, 1865.
BERT, GUSTAVE W.
Acting Third Assistant Engineer, 19 April, 1864. Appointment revoked 2 February, 1865.
BERTODY, CHARLES.
Midshipman, 3 March, 1838. Resigned 31 July, 1842.
BERTOLETT, JOHN R.
Assistant Engineer (Spanish-American War), 14 May, 1898. Honorably discharged 22 December, 1898.
BERTOLETTE, DANIEL N.
Assistant Surgeon, 23 June, 1873. Passed Assistant Surgeon, 20 April, 1877. Surgeon, 1 September, 1888. Medical Inspector, 22 January, 1900.
BERTOLETTE, J. C.
Assistant Surgeon, 4 July, 1858. Surgeon, 22 May, 1862. Retired List, 15 September, 1865. Died 1 May, 1868.
BERTOLETTE, LEVI C.
Naval Cadet, 4 September, 1883. Ensign, 1 July, 1889. Lieutenant, Junior Grade, 29 April, 1897. Lieutenant, 3 March, 1899.
BERTRAM, GEORGE.
Acting Third Assistant Engineer, 4 February, 1863. Honorably discharged 12 September, 1865.
BERTSCH, LEO.
Acting Third Assistant Engineer, 11 March, 1865. Honorably discharged 14 February, 1868.
BERWIND, EDWARD J.
Midshipman, 20 July, 1865. Graduated 4 June, 1869. Ensign, 12 July, 1870. Master, 24 March, 1872. Retired List, 14 May, 1875. Title changed to Lieutenant, Junior Grade, 3 March, 1883.
BESS, JOHN.
Gunner, 28 May, 1798. Last appearance on Records of Navy Department.
BESSE, ANSEL B.
Acting Third Assistant Engineer, 28 July, 1862. Acting Second Assistant Engineer, 9 January, 1864. Honorably discharged 12 December, 1865.
BESSE, CLAUDE.
Master, 16 September, 1813. Discharged 15 April, 1815.
BESSETT, RUSSELL.
Master, 24 August, 1812. Acting Lieutenant, 1 March, 1814. Last appearance on Records of Navy Department. Dead.
BEST, HENRY.
Acting Second Assistant Engineer, 14 September, 1861. Dismissed 10 November, 1862.
BEST, WILLIAM.
Acting Ensign and Pilot, 21 June, 1865. Honorably discharged 4 August, 1866.
BEST, WILLIAM H.
Acting Second Assistant Engineer, 20 August, 1861. Acting First Assistant Engineer, 17 June, 1863. Honorably discharged 6 March, 1866.
BEST, W. J.
Mate, 25 August, 1866. Appointment revoked 31 March, 1872.
BESWICK, DELWORTH W.
Naval Cadet, 26 September, 1883. Resigned 4 February, 1884. Naval Cadet, 20 May, 1884. Ensign, 1 July, 1890. Retired List, 20 June, 1896.
BETTNER, HENRY.
Midshipman, 14 April, 1800. Discharged 6 August, 1801.
BETTS, BARZELLA C.
Acting Gunner, 9 January, 1863. Resigned 1 September, 1864.
BETTS, CHARLES R.
Mate, 22 June, 1863. Deserted 4 July, 1863.

GENERAL NAVY REGISTER.

BETTS, CHARLES T.
Acting Ensign, 19 August, 1864. Dismissed 5 May, 1865.
BETTS, HENRY E.
Lieutenant, Junior Grade (Spanish-American War), 6 July, 1898. Honorably discharged 10 March, 1899.
BETTS, WILLIAM.
Mate, 17 September, 1861. Resigned 3 April, 1862. Mate, 12 August, 1862. Acting Ensign, 24 September, 1862. Resigned 11 October, 1864.
BEUGLESS, JOHN D.
Chaplain, 2 July, 1864. Died 31 July, 1887.
BEURET, JOHN D.
Naval Cadet, 7 September, 1888. Assistant Naval Constructor, 1 July, 1894.
BEVERLEY, W. B.
Midshipman, 9 June, 1832. Passed Midshipman, 23 June, 1838. Lieutenant, 28 June, 1843. Died 30 October, 1846.
BEVERLY, C. B.
Midshipman, 1 August, 1827. Dismissed 16 June, 1834.
BEVERLY, GEORGE W.
Acting Ensign, 19 January, 1865. Honorably discharged 8 November, 1868.
BEVERLY, McKENZIE.
Midshipman, 19 October, 1841. Struck off 17 March, 1843.
BEVINGTON, MARTIN.
Cadet Engineer, 15 September, 1875. Graduated 10 June, 1879. Assistant Engineer, 10 June, 1881. Passed Assistant Engineer, 22 June, 1892. Rank changed to Lieutenant, 3 March, 1899.
BEVINS, SETH.
Acting Third Assistant Engineer, 5 April, 1865. Honorably discharged 22 September, 1865.
BEVINS, S. H.
Mate, 31 December, 1861. Acting Ensign, 31 July, 1863. Honorably discharged 1 January, 1866.
BEYER, JULIUS F.
Acting Ensign, 9 October, 1862. Acting Master, 14 November, 1864. Honorably discharged 26 October, 1865.
BEYER, HENRY G.
Assistant Surgeon, 19 May, 1876. Passed Assistant Surgeon, 30 April, 1880. Surgeon, 11 May, 1893.
BEYERSDORFF, L.
Mate, 31 October, 1861. Resigned 25 March, 1865. Mate, 1 February, 1870. Died 1877.
BEYNON, JAMES W.
Warrant Machinist (Spanish-American War), 15 June, 1898. Honorably discharged 2 September, 1898.
BEYSE, ALBERT F.
Acting Third Assistant Engineer, 6 February, 1864. Resigned 12 May, 1865.
BIANCHINI, L. A.
Teacher, date not known. Resigned 27 July, 1846.
BIBB, PEYTON P.
Cadet Midshipman, 12 June, 1874. Graduated 4 June, 1880. Ensign, 9 January, 1883. Resigned 1 March, 1886.
BIBBER, CHARLES J.
Mate, 1 March, 1865. Died 8 October, 1883.
BIBLES, FRANK P.
Mate, 5 April, 1862. Acting Ensign, 27 January, 1863. Dismissed 14 November, 1865.
BICKERSTAFF, SAMUEL.
Acting Chief Engineer, 1 October, 1862. Acting Fleet Engineer Mississippi Squadron, 1 June, 1864. Honorably discharged 3 September, 1866.
BICKNELL, GEORGE A.
Acting Midshipman, 2 December, 1861. Graduated June, 1866. Ensign, 12 March, 1868. Master, 26 March, 1869. Lieutenant, 21 March, 1870. Lieutenant-Commander, 19 May, 1886. Commander, 5 January, 1896.
BICKSHAFFT, C. H.
Acting Ensign, 12 December, 1863. Honorably discharged 1 October, 1867.
BIDDLE, CLEMENT.
Midshipman, 12 February, 1799. Resigned 30 March, 1804.
BIDDLE, CLEMENT.
Assistant Surgeon, 18 June, 1878. Passed Assistant Surgeon, 18 June, 1882. Surgeon, 26 July, 1895.
BIDDLE, EDWARD.
Midshipman, 12 February, 1800. Last appearance on Records of Navy Department. Dead.
BIDDLE, JAMES.
Midshipman, 12 February, 1800. Lieutenant, 11 February, 1807. Commander, 5 March, 1813. Captain, 28 February, 1815. Died 1 October, 1848.
BIDDLE, JAMES S.
Midshipman, 18 October, 1833. Passed Midshipman, 8 July, 1839. Lieutenant, 29 August 1844. Resigned 25 September, 1856.
BIDDLE, SAMUEL.
Surgeon's Mate, 10 July, 1824. Died 14 February, 1826.
BIDDLE, SPENCER F. B.
Cadet Midshipman, 13 June, 1874. Graduated 4 June, 1880. Resigned 30 December, 1881. Lieutenant (Spanish-American War), 23 June, 1898. Honorably discharged 6 October, 1898.
BIEDLEMAN, DANIEL.
Mate, 7 June, 1862. Resigned 14 July, 1862.

BIEG, FREDERICK C.
Cadet Engineer, 1 October, 1874. Graduated 20 June, 1878. Assistant Engineer, 20 June, 1880. Passed Assistant Engineer, 21 October, 1890. Chief Engineer, 11 October, 1898. Rank changed to Lieutenant, 3 March, 1899.

BIELBY, PORTEUS P.
Assistant Surgeon, 31 March, 1868. Retired List, 8 July, 1873. Died 1 August, 1880.

BIER, GEORGE H.
Midshipman, 19 October, 1841. Passed Midshipman, 10 August, 1847. Master, 14 September, 1855. Lieutenant, 15 September, 1855. Resigned 23 April, 1861.

BIERER, BION B.
Naval Cadet, 24 September, 1887. Ensign, 1 July, 1893. Lieutenant, Junior Grade, 3 March, 1899. Lieutenant, 18 January, 1900.

BIGELOW ABRAHAM.
Midshipman, 18 June, 1812. Lieutenant, 28 March, 1820. Commander, 22 January, 1841. Captain, 12 September, 1854. Resigned 1 March, 1857.

BIGELOW, ALPHEUS.
Acting Third Assistant Engineer, 20 October, 1864. Honorably discharged 6 August, 1866.

BIGELOW, B. F.
Acting Assistant Engineer, 12 December, 1863. Resigned 5 May, 1865.

BIGELOW, GEORGE A.
Acting Midshipman, 26 May, 1852. Midshipman, 20 June, 1856. Passed Midshipman, 29 April, 1859. Master, 5 September, 1859. Lieutenant, 19 December, 1860. Lieutenant-Commander, 16 July, 1862. Resigned 19 March, 1867.

BIGELOW, HARRY M.
Lieutenant, Junior Grade (Spanish-American War), 25 May, 1898. Honorably discharged 9 September, 1898.

BIGLEY, JOSEPH J.
Mate, 9 September, 1862. Dismissed 17 April, 1863.

BIGGS, HENRY W.
Acting Warrant Machinist, 6 July, 1899.

BIGGS, JAMES.
Midshipman, 28 May, 1800. Resigned 21 June, 1803.

BIGGS, JOEL T.
Acting Warrant Machinist, 23 August, 1899.

BIGGS, JOSEPH L.
Midshipman, 16 January, 1809. Drowned 15 April, 1813.

BIKER, NICHOLAS.
Master, 3 July, 1813. Last appearance on Records of Navy Department.

BILISOLY, JOSEPH.
Third Assistant Engineer, 2 August, 1855. Died 3 September, 1855.

BILLARD, JULES F.
Acting Assistant Surgeon, 15 October, 1863. Honorably discharged 10 October, 1865.

BILLINGER, F.
Midshipman, 1 January, 1812. Last appearance on Records of Navy Department, 30 September, 1815.

BILLINGS, C. C.
Midshipman, 18 May, 1809. Resigned 9 May, 1814.

BILLINGS, CORNELIUS C.
Naval Cadet, 28 September, 1882. Graduated. Honorably discharged 30 June, 1888. Ensign, (Spanish-American War), 12 May, 1898. Honorably discharged 6 January, 1899.

BILLINGS, HENRY R.
Acting Master's Mate, 2 December, 1861. Acting Master, 26 May, 1862. Honorably discharged 21 December, 1865.

BILLINGS, LUTHER G.
Acting Assistant Paymaster, 24 October, 1862. Assistant Paymaster, 3 March, 1865. Paymaster, 20 October, 1864. Pay Inspector, 26 December, 1882. Pay Director, 9 January, 1895. Retired List, 14 March, 1898.

BILLS, GEORGE.
Boatswain, 7 August, 1801. Resigned 24 December, 1803.

BILLS, J. HOWLAND.
Acting Assistant Paymaster, 19 September, 1861. Naval Storekeeper, 1 August, 1863. Resigned 6 February, 1865.

BILLS, JOHN G.
Gunner, 20 June, 1862. Drowned 16 May, 1863.

BINDER, GEORGE.
Carpenter, 6 July, 1798. Master, 11 July, 1812. Dismissed 6 March, 1813. Master, 12 April, 1813. Last appearance on Records of Navy Department.

BINGHAM, EDWARD B.
Acting Assistant Surgeon, 15 March, 1864. Assistant Surgeon, 1 April, 1864. Passed Assistant Surgeon, 23 April, 1868. Died 24 February, 1872.

BINGHAM, HAMILTON.
Acting Ensign, 13 December, 1862. Acting Master, 27 June, 1864. Honorably discharged 15 August, 1865.

BINGHAM, JOHN F.
Third Assistant Engineer, 25 August, 1862. Second Assistant Engineer, 20 February, 1864. First Assistant Engineer, 1 January, 1868. Passed Assistant Engineer, 24 February, 1874. Chief Engineer, 16 May, 1889. Died 3 May, 1891.

BINGLEY, W. B.
Sailmaker, 16 November, 1821. Resigned 11 September, 1824.

BINNIX, GEORGE.
Acting Gunner, 25 June, 1863. Resigned 10 May, 1865.

BIONDI, EUGENE.
Mate, 20 November, 1861. Acting Ensign, 5 December, 1863. Acting Master, 23

GENERAL NAVY REGISTER.

BIRCH DEWITT.
   March, 1865. Honorably discharged 2 November, 1868. Mate, 13 July, 1869. Resigned 14 August, 1869.
BIRCH, WARREN.
   Surgeon's Mate, 14 July, 1824. Died 1 May, 1826.
BIRD, CHARLES M.
   Acting Ensign, 16 April, 1863. Appointment revoked (sick), 22 June, 1864.
BIRD, EDWARD.
   Mate, 19 October, 1861. Acting Ensign, 3 September, 1862. Honorably discharged 21 October, 1865.
BIRD, JOHN H.
   Mate. Honorably discharged 5 October, 1865.
BIRD, JOHN D.
   Midshipman, 17 December, 1810. Killed in action, 23 August, 1812.
BIRCHMORE, WILLIAM.
   Midshipman, 16 April, 1814. Resigned 15 June, 1814.
BIRDSALL, JOHN A.
   Surgeon's Mate, 10 January, 1815. Surgeon, 10 July, 1824. Lost in the Hornet, 10 September, 1829.
BIRDSALL, W. A.
   Sailmaker, 7 March, 1848. Died 8 July, 1884.
BIRKBECK, ALEXANDER, Jr.
   Mate, 7 March, 1867. Mustered out 30 April, 1868.
BIRKEY, HENRY W.
   First Assistant Engineer, 8 June, 1844. Chief Engineer, 2 March, 1847. Resigned 23 December, 1847.
BIRNEY, FRANK C.
   Assistant Surgeon, 10 January, 1863. Resigned 16 July, 1864.
BIRNIE, EDWARD A.
   Midshipman, 24 July, 1865. Graduated June, 1869. Died 18 July, 1871.
BIRTWISTLE, JAMES.
   Acting Assistant Paymaster, 16 December, 1861. Resigned 31 March, 1863.
BISCOE, HARRY E.
   Mate, 4 November, 1861. Acting Ensign, 27 April, 1863. Acting Master, 28 June, 1865. Honorably discharged 6 January, 1868.
BISEL, AMOS T.
   Assistant Paymaster, 23 August, 1895. Passed Assistant Paymaster, 5 February, 1898.
BISHOP, ALEXANDER McC.
   Mate, 14 February, 1864. Acting Ensign, 30 March, 1865. Honorably discharged 22 April, 1866.
BISHOP, CHARLES T.
   Assistant Paymaster 19 March, 1862. Paymaster, 22 November, 1865. Retired List, 9 March, 1870. Died 23 April, 1885.
BISHOP, CHARLES W.
   Assistant Paymaster (Spanish-American War), 12 July, 1898. Honorably discharged 1 December, 1898.
BISHOP, EDWARD G.
   Mate, 30 April, 1870. Died 31 July, 1870.
BISHOP, JOHN.
   Acting Assistant Paymaster, 22 August, 1863. Discharged 19 October, 1865.
BISHOP, JOHN.
   Midshipman, 18 March, 1827. Died 20 June, 1827.
BISHOP, JOSHUA.
   Mate, 23 December, 1861. Acting Ensign, 1 October, 1863. Honorably discharged 12 December, 1866. Acting Ensign, 26 February, 1867. Resigned 3 July, 1868. Mate, 28 May, 1870. Appointment revoked 19 September, 1871.
BISHOP, JOSHUA.
   Acting Midshipman, 20 September, 1854. Midshipman, 11 June, 1858. Passed Midshipman, 28 January, 1861. Master, 28 February, 1861. Lieutenant, 19 April, 1861. Lieutenant-Commander, 3 March, 1865. Dismissed 8 February, 1868.(?) Commissioned Lieutenant-Commander, 1 March, 1871. Commander, 25 August, 1887. Retired List, 31 December, 1896.
BISHOP, NATHANIEL W.
   Lieutenant, Junior Grade (Spanish-American War), 22 June, 1898. Honorably discharged 8 September, 1898.
BISHOP, SAMUEL C.
   Mate, 31 October, 1862. Resigned 26 March, 1863.
BISHOP, THEODORE H.
   Carpenter, 8 September, 1862. Dismissed 18 December, 1867.
BISHOP, WILLIAM H.
   Acting Third Assistant Engineer, 10 July, 1861. Acting Second Assistant Engineer, 1 October, 1862. Acting First Assistant Engineer, 17 April, 1863. Honorably discharged 31 August, 1865.
BISHOP, WILLIAM S.
   Assistant Surgeon, 11 April, 1843. Passed Assistant Surgeon, 11 May, 1845. Retired 8 May, 1861. Surgeon on Retired List, 27 March, 1866. Died 28 December, 1868.
BISPHAM, HARRISON A.
   Cadet Engineer, 1 October, 1881. Ensign, 1 July, 1887. Lieutenant, Junior Grade, 4 May, 1896. Lieutenant, 3 March, 1899.
BISPHAM, JOHN E.
   Midshipman, 13 December, 1819. Lieutenant, 17 May, 1828. Died 24 March, 1849.
BISSELL, EDWARD.
   Purser, 30 December, 1839. Resigned 11 January, 1847.
BISSELL, E. S.
   Mate, 18 November, 1862. Deserted 16 December, 1862.

GENERAL NAVY REGISTER. 59

BISSELL, FRANK.
Acting Assistant Paymaster, 14 April, 1864. Assistant Paymaster, 27 February, 1867. Passed Assistant Paymaster, 13 April, 1869. Dismissed 29 April, 1874.
BISSELL, FREDERICK W.
Third Assistant Engineer, 21 April, 1863. Second Assistant Engineer, 28 September, 1864. Resigned 22 October, 1867.
BISSELL, GEORGE B.
Midshipman, 13 March, 1838. Passed Midshipman, 20 May, 1844. Acting Master, 21 August, 1848. Died 10 September, 1848.
BISSELL, GEORGE E.
Acting Assistant Paymaster, 17 October, 1863. Honorably discharged 13 October, 1865.
BISSELL, O. J.
Acting Assistant Surgeon, 7 May, 1862. Appointment revoked 13 November, 1862.
BISSELL, SIMON B.
Acting Midshipman, 1 March, 1825. Midshipman, 4 June, 1831. Passed Midshipman, 9 February, 1837. Commissioned Lieutenant from 9 February, 1837. Reserved List, 13 September, 1855. Commander on Active List, 14 September, 1855. Captain, 16 July, 1865. Commodore, 10 October, 1866. Retired List, 1 March, 1870. Died 18 February, 1883.
BISSELL, S. S.
Mate, 17 October, 1862. Acting Ensign, 12 August, 1863. Resigned 27 April, 1865.
BISSET, EUGENE L.
Naval Cadet, 2 October, 1889. Ensign, 1 July, 1895. Lieutenant, Junior Grade, 3 March, 1899.
BISSET, GUY A.
Naval Cadet, 6 September, 1895. At sea prior to final graduation.
BISSET, HENRY O.
Naval Cadet, 6 September, 1892. Assistant Engineer, 6 May, 1898. Resigned 28 April, 1899. (See Marine Corps.)
BISSETT, FREDERICK W.
Third Assistant Engineer, 21 April, 1863. Second Assistant Engineer, 28 September, 1864. Resigned 22 October, 1867.
BISSETT, JOHN J.
Third Assistant Engineer, 12 August, 1862. Second Assistant Engineer, 15 February, 1864. First Assistant Engineer, 1 January, 1868. Retired List, 21 October, 1882.
BITLER, RUBEN O.
Cadet Midshipman, 24 June, 1875. Graduated 10 June, 1881. Ensign, Junior Grade, 3 March, 1883. Ensign, 26 June, 1884. Lieutenant, Junior Grade, 29 May, 1892. Lieutenant, 29 April, 1896.
BITTINGER, EDMUND C.
Chaplain, 30 September, 1850. Retired List, 19 March, 1881. Died 2 August, 1889.
BIXBY, GEORGE H.
Acting Assistant Surgeon, 7 November, 1862. Honorably discharged 26 September, 1865.
BIXLER, LEWIS E.
Midshipman, 26 September, 1865. Graduated June, 1869. Ensign, 12 July, 1870. Master, 29 September, 1871. Lieutenant, 1 December, 1874. Resigned 30 June, 1886.
BLACK, CHARLES E.
Acting Third Assistant Engineer, 12 January, 1864. Resigned 30 November, 1864.
BLACK, CHARLES H.
Midshipman, 21 September, 1861. Graduated September, 1865. Ensign, 1 December, 1866. Master, 12 March, 1868. Lieutenant, 26 March, 1869. Lieutenant-Commander, 5 February, 1879. Retired List, 5 November, 1883. Died 20 January, 1891.
BLACK, CLARENCE E.
Assistant Surgeon, 14 November, 1871. Passed Assistant Surgeon, 24 November, 1875. Lost at sea 21 August, 1884.
BLACK, HENRY.
Warrant Machinist (Spanish-American War), 22 June, 1898. Honorably discharged 2 September, 1898.
BLACK, JOHN.
Mate, 24 June, 1864. Resigned 18 February, 1870.
BLACK, NATHAN W.
Mate, 25 January, 1862. Acting Ensign, 11 December, 1862. Honorably discharged 12 November, 1865. Acting Ensign, 12 September, 1866. Mustered out 11 January, 1868.
BLACK, WILLIAM.
Boatswain, 30 March, 1835. Died 8 June, 1874.
BLACK, WILLIAM W.
Mate, 23 September, 1862. Resigned 14 June, 1864.
BLACKDEN, PERRY D.
Passed Assistant Engineer (Spanish-American War), 21 May, 1898. Honorably discharged 14 September, 1898.
BLACKFORD, G. D.
Sailmaker, 19 February, 1838. Resigned 20 September, 1838. Sailmaker, 12 April, 1842. Dismissed 5 July, 1861.
BLACKMER, JOHN.
Acting Assistant Surgeon, 7 December, 1863. Resigned 23 September, 1863. Reappointed 14 November, 1864. Honorably discharged 18 August, 1865.
BLACKNALL, GEORGE.
Surgeon's Mate, 3 January, 1828. Passed Assistant Surgeon, 3 March, 1835. Surgeon, 9 February, 1837. Resigned 7 May, 1861.
BLACKWELL, EDWARD M.
Assistant Surgeon (Spanish-American War), 25 April, 1898. Appointed Assistant Surgeon in regular service, 7 June, 1900.

BLACKWELL, ELMER A.
Warrant Machinist, 6 July, 1899.
BLACKWELL, ERNEST C.
Acting Third Assistant Engineer, 28 February, 1865. Honorably discharged 19 July, 1866
BLACKWELL, WILLIAM C.
Acting Assistant Paymaster, 22 September, 1862. Discharged 1 September, 1865.
BLACKWOOD, NORMAN J.
Naval Cadet, 17 May, 1883. Resigned 20 February, 1886. Assistant Surgeon, 7 July, 1890. Passed Assistant Surgeon, 7 July, 1893.
BLAGDEN, THOMAS.
Acting Ensign, 21 July, 1863. Resigned 5 October, 1863.
BLAGNE, EDWARD P.
Mate, 23 January, 1862. Honorably discharged 27 October, 1865.
BLAINE, EPHRAIM h.
Midshipman, 7 March, 1800. Resigned 21 August, 1801. Midshipman, 9 September, 1801. Broken by Court-martial, 10 November, 1804.
BLAINE, JAMES H.
Mate, 22 February, 1865. Resigned 3 May, 1865.
BLAIR, ANDREW ALEXANDER.
Acting Midshipman, 20 November, 1862. Graduated June, 1866. Ensign, 12 March, 1868. Resigned 31 August, 1869.
BLAIR, BENJAMIN F.
Acting Ensign, 13 September, 1864. Honorably discharged 3 July, 1865.
BLAIR, GEORGE.
Lieutenant, 13 March, 1799. Resigned 14 March, 1800.
BLAIR, JAMES.
Midshipman, 8 January, 1836. Passed Midshipman, 1 July, 1842. Master, 2 October, 1848. Lieutenant, 2 June, 1849. Resigned, 7 May, 1851.
BLAIR, SAMUEL.
Surgeon's Mate, 9 March, 1809. Last appearance on Records of Navy Department.
BLAIR, THOMAS.
Midshipman, 18 May, 1809. Resigned 8 July, 1810.
BLAIR, THOMAS W.
Acting Second Assistant Engineer, 1 October, 1862. Resigned 24 April, 1863.
BLAISDELL, N. J.
Acting Ensign, 25 June, 1863. Honorably discharged 30 September, 1865.
BLAKE, CHARLES.
Surgeon's Mate, 9 March, 1798. Resigned 1 September, 1799.
BLAKE, CHARLES A.
Acting Third Assistant Engineer, 8 September, 1863. Honorably discharged 29 March, 1866.
BLAKE, CHARLES F.
Acting Midshipman, 26 October, 1859. Ensign, 26 June, 1863. Master, 22 February, 1864. Lieutenant-Commander, 25 July, 1866. Retired List, 18 January, 1871. Died 20 February, 1879.
BLAKE, ELLIOTT C. V.
Acting Midshipman, 28 September, 1858. Acting Master, 24 April, 1862. Lieutenant, 1 August, 1862. Resigned 16 June, 1865.
BLAKE, FRANCIS B.
Acting Midshipman, 30 September, 1853. Midshipman, 10 June, 1857. Passed Midshipman, 25 June, 1860. Master, 24 October, 1860. Lieutenant, 4 March, 1861. Lieutenant-Commander, 2 January, 1863. Resigned 15 June, 1870.
BLAKE, FRANCIS O.
Mate, 14 January, 1863. Drowned 25 June, 1863.
BLAKE, GEORGE S.
Midshipman, 1 January, 1818. Lieutenant, 3 March, 1827. Commander, 27 February, 1847. Captain, 14 September, 1855. Commodore, 16 July, 1862. Died 24 June, 1871.
BLAKE, GORHAM B.
Acting Third Assistant Engineer, 5 July, 1864. February, 1865, discharged as Fireman.
BLAKE, HENRY J.
Acting Midshipman, 29 September, 1858. Ensign, 24 February, 1863. Lieutenant, 22 February, 1864. Resigned 21 April, 1866.
BLAKE, HENRY T.
Acting Ensign, 29 October, 1863. Resigned 1 April, 1865.
BLAKE, HOMER C.
Midshipman, 2 March, 1840. Passed Midshipman, 11 July, 1846. Master, 1 March, 1855. Lieutenant, 14 September, 1855. Lieutenant-Commander, 16 July, 1862. Commander, 3 March, 1866. Captain, 25 May, 1871. Commodore, 27 October, 1879. Died 21 January, 1880.
BLAKE, J. DAVIDSON.
Midshipman, 9 September, 1847. Passed Midshipman, 15 June, 1854. Master, 15 September, 1855. Lieutenant, 16 September, 1855. Resigned 5 February, 1862.
BLAKE, JEREMIAH.
Mate, 11 October, 1861. Acting Ensign, 2 December, 1862. Dismissed 24 March, 1864.
BLAKE, JOHN.
Chaplain, 27 February, 1847. Retired List, 20 June, 1873. Died 11 July, 1893.
BLAKE, JOHN S.
Midshipman, 16 January, 1809. Resigned 1 December, 1809.
BLAKE, JOHN W.
Acting Third Assistant Engineer, 10 May, 1864. Honorably discharged 8 September, 1865.

BLAKE, JOSEPH R.
    Midshipman, 1 January, 1818. Lieutenant, 3 March, 1827. Died 11 May, 1831.
BLAKE, JOSEPHUS.
    Acting Third Assistant Engineer, 23 January, 1863. Acting Second Assistant Engineer, 31 August, 1863. Acting First Assistant Engineer, 21 November 1864. Honorably discharged 5 December, 1865.
BLAKE, JOSHUA.
    Midshipman, 6 April, 1799. Lieutenant, 4 July, 1800. Resigned 7 April, 1809.
BLAKE, J. W.
    Mate. Resigned 21 December, 1863.
BLAKE, MARSHALL W.
    Acting Assistant Paymaster, 1 September, 1861. Resigned 13 August, 1863.
BLAKE, PHILEMON C.
    Midshipman, 16 May, 1800. Resigned 10 September, 1804.
BLAKE, WILLIAM.
    Midshipman, 31 October, 1799. Last appearance on Records of Navy Department, 14 February, 1802.
BLAKELY, JOHN R. Y.
    Naval Cadet. 29 September, 1888. Ensign, 1 July, 1894. Lieutenant, Junior Grade, 3 March, 1899.
BLAKELY, JOHNSTON.
    Midshipman, 5 February, 1800. Lieutenant, 10 February, 1807. Commander, 24 July, 1813. Captain, 24 November, 1814. Lost in Sloop Wasp, 1815.
BLAKEMAN, A. NOEL.
    Acting Assistant Paymaster, 3 August, 1861. Resigned 26 September, 1864.
BLAKEMAN, ROBERT S.
    Assistant Surgeon, 27 May, 1896. Passed Assistant Surgeon, 27 May, 1899.
BLAKEMORE, WILLIAM F.
    Acting Third Assistant Engineer, 14 May, 1864. Honorably discharged 16 October, 1865. Acting Third Assistant Engineer, 27 August, 1866. Mustered out 17 November, 1868.
BLAKISTON, HENRY R.
    Acting Master, 18 November, 1861. Resigned 22 April, 1863.
BLAMER, DeWITT.
    Naval Cadet, 19 May, 1887. Ensign, 1 July, 1893. Lieutenant, Junior Grade, 3 March, 1899. Lieutenant, 6 July, 1899.
BLANCH, HENRY.
    Acting Third Assistant Engineer, 22 July, 1864. Honorably discharged 7 July, 1865.
BLANCH, WILLIAM A.
    Acting Third Assistant Engineer, 21 July, 1864. Honorably discharged 30 December, 1865.
BLANCHARD, A. S.
    Mate, 13 May, 1861. Acting Master, 22 March, 1862. Honorably discharged 18 February, 1866.
BLANCHARD, CHARLES A.
    Mate, 15 September, 1862. Resigned 25 June, 1863. Mate, 8 April, 1864. Acting Ensign, 6 May, 1865. Honorably discharged 4 December, 1865. Acting Ensign, 29 August, 1866. Mustered out, 8 October, 1868.
BLANCHARD, E. G.
    Acting Ensign, 8 January, 1864. Honorably discharged 1 May, 1867.
BLANCHARD, E. O.
    Midshipman, 10 May, 1820. Lieutenant, 17 May, 1828. Resigned 31 December, 1835.
BLANCHARD, FRANCIS E.
    Acting Master, 21 January, 1862. Dismissed 27 July, 1863.
BLANCHARD, GEORGE.
    Boatswain, 19 May, 1832. Resigned 4 May, 1835.
BLANCHARD, GEORGE.
    Mate. Resigned 4 November, 1862.
BLANCHARD, HOLLIS H.
    Acting Master, 1 May, 1862. Appointment revoked 10 February, 1863.
BLANCHARD, HORACE A.
    Midshipman, 25 July, 1865. Graduated 4 June, 1869. Ensign, 12 July, 1870. Retired List. 14 July, 1874. Died 15 January, 1876.
BLANCHARD, HORATIO S.
    Acting Master, 22 November, 1861. Honorably discharged 20 October, 1865.
BLANCHARD, JEREMIAH F.
    Mate, 23 March, 1864. Acting Ensign, 11 August, 1864. Honorably discharged 18 January, 1868.
BLANCHARD, LUCIEN J.
    Acting Third Assistant Engineer, 1861. Died 25 July, 1863.
BLANCHARD, THOMAS.
    Acting First Assistant Engineer, 4 September, 1863. Honorably discharged 20 October, 1865.
BLAND, THEODORE, Jr.
    Midshipman, 16 July, 1821. Died 13 September, 1825.
BLANDIN, JOHN J.
    Cadet Midshipman. 28 June, 1878. Ensign, 1 July, 1884. Lieutenant, Junior Grade, 31 July, 1894. Lieutenant, 1 February, 1898. Died 16 July, 1898.
BLANEY, WILLIAM.
    Master, 3 February, 1814. Resigned 25 April, 1815.
BLANKENSHIP, JOHN M.
    Naval Cadet, 20 May, 1886. Graduated. Honorably discharged 30 June, 1892. En-

sign (Spanish-American War), 13 May, 1898. Honorably discharged 26 **September,** 1898.
BLANTON, WILLIAM L.
Midshipman, 2 January, 1834. Passed Midshipman, 16 July, 1840. **Master, 26** August, 1846. Lieutenant, 25 February, 1847. Dismissed 1 December, 1853.
BLATCHFORD, JOHN T.
Acting Master, 29 May, 1861. Dismissed 4 August, 1862. Acting Ensign, 2 September, 1862. Resigned 22 April, 1864.
BLAUVELT, JAMES L.
Mate, 6 February, 1862. Appointment revoked 1 December, 1868.
BLEAKIE, JOHN H.
Acting Third Assistant Engineer, 6 October, 1864. Honorably discharged 7 December, 1865. Acting Third Assistant Engineer, 1 December, 1866. Mustered out 23 October, 1869.
BLEECKER, G. V.
Midshipman, 16 January, 1809. Resigned 23 September, 1810.
BLEECKER, G. W.
Master, 10 May, 1820. Resigned, 2 August, 1823.
BLEECKER, JOHN VAN B.
Purser, 16 January, 1847. Died 8 November, 1864.
BLEECKER, JOHN VAN B.
Acting Midshipman, 10 October, 1863. Ensign, 18 December, 1868. Master, 21 March, 1870. Lieutenant, 21 March, 1871. Lieutenant-Commander, 30 June, 1891. Commander, 5 December, 1897.
BLEECKER, WILLIAM W.
Midshipman, 1 May, 1827. Passed Midshipman, 10 June, 1833. Lieutenant, 28 February, 1838. Lost on the Albany. Last intelligence from ship, 28 September, 1854.
BLEMM, VAN BUREN.
Mate. Appointment revoked 25 April, 1864.
BLENKINSOP, JAMES.
Acting Third Assistant Engineer, 27 May, 1862. Acting Second Assistant Engineer, 12 February, 1863. Acting First Assistant Engineer, 7 October, 1863. Resigned 10 February, 1865.
BLESSING, JAMES H.
Acting Third Assistant Engineer, 26 March, 1864. Resigned 16 March, 1865.
BLIGHT, JOHN.
Gunner, 3 May, 1821. Died 15 September, 1854.
BLISH, JOHN B.
Cadet Midshipman, 18 September, 1875. Graduated 10 June, 1881. Ensign, Junior Grade, 3 March, 1883. Ensign, 26 June, 1884. Lieutenant, Junior Grade, 19 May, 1891. Lieutenant, 15 June, 1895.
BLISS, EDWARD N.
Acting Third Assistant Engineer, 18 February, 1865. Honorably discharged 27 October, 1865.
BLISS, JAMES.
Midshipman, 16 January, 1809. Resigned 31 March, 1814.
BLISS, JOEL.
Carpenter, 21 October, 1837. Resigned 26 May, 1841.
BLISS, SAMUEL T.
Acting Ensign, 14 October, 1862. Honorably discharged 26 October, 1865.
BLISS, SYLVANUS J.
Midshipman, 19 October, 1841. Passed Midshipman, 10 August, 1847. Acting Master, 11 December, 1852. Lost in Brig Porpoise. Last intelligence from ship, 21 September, 1854.
BLISS, WILLIAM C.
Ensign (Spanish-American War), 29 June, 1898. Honorably discharged 30 **January,** 1899.
BLITZ, JOHN.
Acting Ensign, 22 February, 1863. Resigned 12 May, 1865.
BLIZZARD, JAMES C.
Acting Master, 17 December, 1861. Resigned 12 November, 1862.
BLOCH, CLAUDE C.
Naval Cadet, 6 September, 1895. At sea prior to final graduation.
BLOCKER, SMITH B.
Midshipman, 2 October, 1850. Dropped 24 January, 1851.
BLOCKI, FRANZ.
Acting Third Assistant Engineer, 14 September, 1864. Honorably discharged 3 July, 1865.
BLOCKLINGER, GOTTFRIED.
Acting Midshipman, 22 July, 1863. Graduated 2 June, 1868. Ensign, 19 April, 1869. Master, 12 July, 1870. Lieutenant, 2 April, 1874. Lieutenant-Commander, 21 May, 1895. Commander, 3 March, 1899.
BLODGET, Samuel G.
Midshipman, 24 June, 1799. Lieutenant, 17 March, 1807. Drowned 29 September, 1812.
BLODGETT, THOMAS S.
Midshipman, 15 November, 1809. Resigned 15 November, 1814.
BLODGETT, GEORGE M.
Acting Midshipman, 3 October, 1851. Midshipman, 30 June, 1856. Passed Midshipman, 29 April, 1859. Master, 5 September, 1859. Lieutenant, 3 February, 1861. Died 6 November, 1862.
BLODGETT, JOHN H.
Acting Assistant Surgeon, 10 September, 1864. Honorably discharged 5 September, 1865.

GENERAL NAVY REGISTER.

BLODGETT, S. S.
Mate, 18 February, 1867. Died 20 June, 1869.
BLONK, BENJAMIN L.
Acting Master, 25 January, 1862. Dismissed 7 February, 1862.
BLOOD, SAMUEL G.
Acting Ensign, 23 October, 1863. Honorably discharged 4 October, 1865.
BLOODGOOD, ABRAM B.
Master, 25 June, 1812. Died 12 June, 1851.
BLOODGOOD, DELAVAN.
Assistant Surgeon, 13 March, 1857. Surgeon, 24 January, 1862. Medical Inspector, 3 February, 1875. Medical Director, 22 August, 1884. Retired List, 20 August, 1893.
BLOODGOOD, FREEMAN, Jr.
Ensign (Spanish-American War), 22 June, 1898. Honorably discharged 9 September, 1898.
BLOODGOOD, W. A.
Purser, 2 May, 1834. Resigned 26 November, 1854.
BLOOMER, SAMUEL W.
Acting Third Assistant Engineer, 10 December, 1861. Resigned 16 April, 1862.
BLOOMSBURG, JOHN.
Acting Third Assistant Engineer, 3 November, 1863. Honorably discharged 5 August, 1865.
BLOOMSBURG, JOSEPH Q.
Acting Second Assistant Engineer, 7 September, 1864. Honorably discharged 30 June, 1865.
BLOSS, GILBERT.
Assistant Engineer (Spanish-American War), 18 June, 1898. Honorably discharged 14 February, 1899.
BLOUNT, A. C.
Midshipman, 12 April, 1834. Resigned 19 October, 1835.
BLOUNT, BENJAMIN.
Midshipman, 15 November, 1810. Resigned 7 May, 1811.
BLOUNT, CHARLES H.
Mate, 21 November, 1862. Acting Ensign, 18 June, 1864. Honorably discharged 12 August, 1865.
BLOUNT, IRVING.
Cadet Midshipman, 6 September, 1887. Graduated. Honorably discharged 30 June, 1893. Lieutenant, Junior Grade (Spanish-American War), 21 May, 1898. Honorably discharged 8 October, 1898.
BLOUNT, JOSEPH.
Midshipman, 20 December, 1804. Resigned 24 April, 1805.
BLOUNT, RICHARD B.
Midshipman, 10 January, 1807. Resigned 16 July, 1807.
BLOUNT, SAMUEL M.
Lieutenant (Spanish-American War), 30 April, 1898. Honorably discnarged 13 March, 1899.
BLOUNT, SILAS.
Acting Master and Pilot, 1 October, 1864. Appointment revoked 9 June, 1865.
BLOW, GEORGE P.
Cadet Midshipman, 22 September, 1876. Ensign, Junior Grade, 1 July, 1883. Ensign, 26 June, 1884. Lieutenant, Junior Grade, 22 February, 1894. Lieutenant, 16 September, 1897. Resigned 1 February, 1900.
BLOXSOM, WOODMAN, Jr.
Mate. Resigned 30 January, 1862.
BLUE, HENRY M.
Acting Midshipman, 28 September, 1854. Midshipman, 11 June, 1858. Passed Midshipman, 9 February, 1861. Master, 28 February, 1861. Lieutenant, 20 April, 1861. Lieutenant-Commander, 24 March, 1865. Died 22 August, 1866.
BLUE, VICTOR.
Naval Cadet, 17 May, 1883. Assistant Engineer, 1 July, 1889. Ensign, 12 December, 1892. Lieutenant, Junior Grade, 5 December, 1897. Lieutenant, 3 March, 1899.
BLUME, N. A.
Acting Ensign, 1 May, 1863. Acting Master, 13 March, 1865. Appointment revoked 24 February, 1869.
BLUNT, SIMON F.
Midshipman, 7 September, 1831. Passed Midshipman, 23 June, 1838. Lieutenant, 28 July, 1842. Died 27 April, 1854.
BLUNT, WILLIAM S.
Acting Assistant Paymaster and Clerk, 29 October, 1861. Assistant Paymaster, 1 October, 1862. Resigned 7 April, 1866.
BLYDENBURGH, BENJAMIN B.
Sailmaker, 4 November, 1858. Retired List, 5 November, 1872. Died 19 April, 1888.
BLYDENBURGH, LUCIUS B.
Acting Assistant Paymaster, 26 August, 1862. Resigned 10 October, 1863.
BLYE, HENRY C.
Third Assistant Engineer, 18 November, 1862. Second Assistant Engineer, 23 March, 1864. First Assistant Engineer, 1 January, 1868. Retired List, 28 October, 1874.
BLYTHE, ANDREW.
Third Assistant Engineer, 24 December, 1861. Second Assistant Engineer, 8 September, 1863. Died 19 April, 1870.
BOARDLEY, J. M.
Midshipman, 7 March, 1815. Last appearance on Records of Navy Department. Killed in a duel.

GENERAL NAVY REGISTER.

BOARDMAN, CHARLES.
Carpenter, 23 August, 1833. Dismissed 6 April, 1838. Carpenter, 7 January, 1842. Retired List. Died 2 December, 1884.
BOARDMAN, CHARLES H.
Acting Assistant Paymaster, 14 December, 1864. Honorably discharged 4 September, 1865.
BOARDMAN, FREDERICK A.
Midshipman, 20 October, 1849. Resigned 19 June, 1856.
BOARDMAN, GEORGE C.
Acting Assistant Paymaster, 23 July, 1862. Died 12 November, 1865.
BOARMAN, CHARLES.
Midshipman, 9 June, 1811. Lieutenant, 5 March, 1817. Commander, 9 February, 1837. Captain, 24 March, 1844. Reserved List, 14 September, 1855. Commodore, Retired List, 4 April, 1867. Rear-Admiral, Retired List, 15 August, 1876. Died 13 September, 1879.
BOCK, WILLIAM N.
Mate, 7 January, 1864. Resigned 5 June, 1865.
BOCKING, ADOLPH H.
Acting Ensign, 17 June, 1864. Honorably ischarged 25 January, 1866.
BODDEN, DAVID.
Acting Third Assistant Engineer, 14 September, 1864. Honorably discharged 19 July, 1865.
BODEN, WILLIAM.
Midshipman, 18 June, 1812. Drowned 6 March, 1821.
BODMAN, H. A.
Acting Assistant Surgeon, 30 January, 1863. Resigned 21 April, 1865.
BOERUM, GEORGE C.
Sailmaker, 4 September, 1852. Retired List, 4 January, 1890.
BOERUM, WILLIAM.
Midshipman, 1 September, 1811. Lieutenant, 5 March, 1817. Commander, 9 February, 1837. Drowned 2 November, 1842.
BOGAN, CHARLES H.
Carpenter, 16 March, 1881. Chief Carpenter, 3 March, 1899.
BOGAN, FRED M.
Assistant Surgeon (Spanish-American War), 13 July, 1898. Appointed Assistant Surgeon in regular service, 7 June, 1900.
BOGARDUS, A. R.
Midshipman, 26 December, 1815. Lieutenant, 28 April, 1816. Resigned 21 October, 1828.
BOGARDUS, PETER C.
Third Assistant Engineer, 27 January, 1848. Resigned 6 February, 1852.
BOGART, M.
Acting Ensign, 28 September, 1863. Honorably discharged 20 October, 1865.
BOGART, ROBERT D.
Acting Ensign, 27 June, 1864. Resigned 29 August, 1864.
BOGERT, EDWARD S.
Assistant Surgeon, 10 June, 1861. Passed Assistant Surgeon, 22 June, 1864. Surgeon, 6 April, 1866. Medical Inspector, 10 September, 1882. Medical Director, 28 November, 1889. Retired List, 7 May, 1898.
BOGERT, EDWARD S., Jr.
Assistant Surgeon, 16 April, 1890. Passed Assistant Surgeon, 16 April, 1893.
BOGERT, JACOB W.
Gunner, 14 May, 1870. Resigned 19 June, 1873.
BOGERT, J. W.
Acting Master, 6 July, 1861. Resigned 7 March, 1862.
BOGGINS, MARTIN.
Acting Third Assistant Engineer, 3 November, 1863. Resigned 27 April, 1864.
BOGMAN, JAMES.
Gunner, 14 Deceber, 1815. Resigned 17 October, 1826.
BOGGS, ARCHIBALD G.
Mate, 12 September, 1814. Honorably discharged 5 August, 1865.
BOGGS, CHARLES E.
Acting Assistant Paymaster, 19 December, 1862. Discharged 4 November, 1866. Assistant Paymaster, 27 February, 1867. Retired List, 7 May, 1869. Died 1 October, 1880.
BOGGS, CHARLES S.
Midshipman, 1 November, 1826. Passed Midshipman, 28 April, 1832. Lieutenant, 6 September, 1837. Commander, 14 September, 1855. Captain, 16 July, 1862. Commodore, 25 July, 1866. Rear-Admiral, 1 July, 1870. Retired List, 28 January, 1872. Died 22 April, 1888.
BOGGS, ELY M.
Mate, 7 November, 1863. Acting Ensign, 17 March, 1864. Honorably discharged 15 September, 1865.
BOGGS, GEORGE B.
Acting Third Assistant Engineer, 2 September, 1864. Honorably discharged 15 September, 1868.
BOGGS, LAWRENCE G.
Assistant Paymaster, 24 September, 1869. Passed Assistant Paymaster, 25 October, 1874. Paymaster, 28 January, 1886. Pay Inspector, 12 November, 1899.
BOGGS, WILLIAM BRENTON.
Purser, 30 November, 1852. Pay Director, 3 March, 1871. Retired List, 2 July, 1871. Died 11 March, 1875.
BOGGS, WILLIAM BRENTON.
Cadet Engineer, 1 October, 1871. Graduated 21 June, 1875. Assistant Engineer,

1 July, 1877. Passed Assistant Engineer, 2 December, 1885. Died, 21 June, 1886.
BOGUE, GEORGE W.
Mate. Acting Ensign, 7 November, 1862. Dismissed 28 April, 1863.
BOHRER, GEORGE.
Surgeon's Mate, 24 July, 1813. Resigned 20 January, 1814.
BOHRER, JULIUS S.
Midshipman, 31 December, 1839. Passed Midshipman, 2 July, 1845. Master, 1 March, 1854. Retired List, 24 February, 1858. Title changed to Lieutenant, Junior Grade, 3 March, 1883. Died 21 June, 1892.
BOIES, DAVID A.
Mate, 11 October, 1864. Honorably discharged 22 June, 1865.
BOLAND, LEE R.
Boatswain, 3 August, 1895.
BOIVIE, ADAM H. L.
Mate, 21 January, 1863. Acting Ensign, 17 March, 1864. Honorably discharged 28 November, 1865.
BOLAND, ANDREW.
Acting Third Assistant Engineer, 26 February, 1826. Honorably discharged 11 January, 1866.
BOLAND, W. F.
Acting Carpenter, 1 October, 1862. Resigned 6 November, 1863.
BOLANDER, AMOS.
Acting Ensign, 1 October, 1862. Resigned 19 February, 1863.
BOLANDER, JOHN G.
Acting Third Assistant Engineer, 19 September, 1861. Dismissed 25 February, 1862.
BOLEJACK, JOSEPH.
Acting Third Assistant Engineer, 2 November, 1862. Acting First Assistant Engineer, 7 December, 1863. Honorably discharged 7 November, 1865.
BOLLES, COURTLAND K.
Lieutenant (Spanish-American War), 23 June, 1898. Honorably discharged 24 January, 1899.
BOLLES, HENRY S.
Mate, 14 October, 1861. Resigned 18 October, 1864. Mate, 23 December, 1864. Resigned 16 March, 1865.
BOLLES, JOHN H.
Acting Master and Pilot, 28 October, 1864. Honorably discharged 17 September, 1865.
BOLLES, MATTHEW, JR.
Acting Midshipman, 30 July, 1863. Ensign, 18 December, 1868. Master, 21 March, 1870. Lieutenant, 29 December, 1871. Died 2 May, 1875.
BOLLES, STEPHEN.
Acting Ensign, 1 October, 1862. Resigned 23 January, 1864.
BOLLES, TIMOTHY DIX.
Midshipman, 1 October, 1864. Graduated June, 1869. Ensign, 12 July, 1870. Master, 24 May, 1872. Lieutenant, 27 June, 1875. Died 23 August, 1892.
BOLLMAN, T. W.
Acting Third Assistant Engineer, 19 September, 1862. Resigned 13 June, 1863.
BOLSON, SAMUEL.
Acting Second Assistant Engineer, 5 November, 1863. Resigned 30 May, 1865.
BOLTON, SAMUEL L.
Acting Assistant Surgeon, 1 October, 1862. Resigned 1 December, 1863.
BOLTON, WILLIAM COMPTON.
Captain, 21 February, 1831. Died 22 February, 1849.
BOLTON, WILLIAM H.
Mate, 23 December, 1863. Honorably discharged 21 March, 1868. Mate, 26 October, 1869. Resigned 20 December, 1870.
BOND, CHARLES O.
Naval Cadet, 13 September, 1886. Resigned 23 June, 1891. Ensign (Spanish-American War), 12 May, 1898. Honorably discharged 30 August, 1898.
BOND, DAVID D.
Mate, 1 October, 1862. Acting Ensign, 5 June, 1863. Honorably discharged 10 October, 1865.
BOND, EDWIN.
Acting Third Assistant Engineer, 5 January, 1864. Honorably discharged 1 July, 1865.
BOND, SAMUEL.
Midshipman, 20 June, 1806. Last appearance on Records of Navy Department, 17 April, 1811.
BOND, WILLIAM.
Third Assistant Engineer, 23 June, 1863. Resigned 25 May, 1867.
BOND, WILLIAM C.
Acting Third Assistant Engineer, 6 August, 1864. Honorably discharged 26 December, 1865.
BOND, WILLIAM S.
Acting Boatswain, 7 January, 1865. Boatswain, 22 August, 1866. Resigned 15 September, 1873.
BONE, GEORGE W.
Acting Ensign, 10 April, 1863. Acting Master, 25 July, 1864. Appointment revoked 21 February, 1865.
BONEFONSE, ANTOINE.
Master. 12 October, 1812. Dismissed 25 September, 1813.

GENERAL NAVY REGISTER.

BONN, JOSEPH.
Lieutenant (Spanish-American War), 25 May, 1898. Honorably discharged 3 September, 1898.
BONNAFFON, EDMUND W.
Assistant Paymaster, 7 November, 1896. Passed Assistant Paymaster, 15 March, 1898.
BONNELL, WILLIAM.
Midshipman, 1 January, 1812. Last appearance on Records of Navy Department. Drowned.
BONNER, JAMES C.
Acting Master, 1 October, 1862. Honorably discharged 10 January, 1866.
BONNEVILLE, T. N.
Midshipman, 1 January, 1812. Resigned 13 March, 1816.
BONNEY, HENRY M.
Acting Master, 9 October, 1861. Resigned 21 August, 1863.
BONSALL, A. G.
Third Assistant Engineer, 19 February, 1863. Appoinment revoked 12 January, 1866.
BONSALL, EDWARD.
Boatswain, 1 June, 1869. Died 10 December, 1894.
BONSALL, THOMAS W.
Mate, 27 April, 1865. Honorably discharged 24 December, 1868. Mate, 6 November, 1869. Retired List, 20 June, 1896.
BONSALL, WILLIAM R.
Acting Assistant Surgeon, 7 August, 1861. Resigned 5 February, 1863.
BOOBY, HENRY.
Mate, 1 October, 1862. Acting Ensign, 16 February, 1863. Honorably discharged 24 November, 1865.
BOOK, DWIGHT D.
Ensign (Spanish-American War), 21 May, 1898. Honorably discharged 14 October, 1898.
BOOK, GEORGE H.
Acting Ensign, 5 December, 1864. Honorably discharged 26 January, 1866.
BOOK, GEORGE MILTON.
Acting Midshipman, 23 November, 1861. Graduated September, 1865. Ensign, 1 December, 1866. Master, 12 March, 1868. Lieutenant, 26 March, 1869. Lieutenant-Commander, 28 May, 1881. Commander, 16 December, 1891. Captain, 29 March, 1890. Retired List with rank of Rear-Admiral 8 March, 1900.
BOOKWALTER, CHARLES S.
Naval Cadet, 3 September, 1890. Ensign, 1 July, 1896. Lieutenant, Junior Grade, 1 July, 1899.
BOOM, FRANCIS.
Sailmaker, 3 January, 1851. Retired List, 9 September, 1881. Died 15 August, 1892.
BOOMER, EPHRAIM.
Acting Master, 5 June, 1862. Honorably discharged 27 September, 1865.
BOONE, CHARLES.
Naval Cadet. 6 September, 1894. Ensign, 4 April, 1900.
BOONE, WILLIAM.
Carpenter, 21 December, 1897.
BOONE, WILLIAM C.
Acting Third Assistant Engineer, 26 May, 1863. Resigned 12 May, 1865.
BOOREAM, HENRY.
Midshipman, 1 November, 1826. Resigned 14 June, 1833.
BOOROM, JARED D.
Gunner, 24 September, 1853. Killed 15 May, 1862, in an engagement on the James River.
BOOROM, SYLVESTER D.
Chaplain, 9 July, 1875.
BOOTH, ALONZO G.
Acting Third Assistant Engineer, 25 February, 1864. Resigned 15 May, 1865.
BOOTH, BENJAMIN W.
Midshipman, 20 June, 1806. Lieutenant, 7 January, 1813. Commander, 28 March, 1820. Died 26 July, 1828.
BOOTH, EDEN.
Mate, 19 December, 1861. Resigned 2 May, 1862.
BOOTH, JONAS.
Acting Third Assistant Engineer, 24 September, 1862. Acting Second Assistant Engineer, 10 June, 1864. Honorably discharged 12 September, 1865.
BOOTH, J. SHAW.
Midshipman, 27 May, 1829. Dismissed 6 June, 1836.
BOOTH, L. M.
Midshipman, 1 June, 1815. Lost at sea October, 1824.
BOOTH, WILLIAM W.
Acting Warrant Machinist, 23 August, 1899.
BOPP, JAMES A.
Acting Third Assistant Engineer, 28 December, 1861. Honorably discharged 19 September, 1865.
BORCHERT, GEORE A.
Acting Midshipman, 20 September, 1855. Midshipman, 9 June, 1859. Dismissed 24 July, 1861.
BORCUM, WILLIAM H.
Acting Third Assistant Engineer, 28 December, 1861. Dismissed 18 November, 1862.

GENERAL NAVY REGISTER. 67

BORDEN, CHARLES N.
Ensign (Spanish-American War), 9 May, 1898. Honorably discharged 16 September, 1898.
BORDEN, HENRY S.
Acting Ensign, 17 October, 1862. Acting Master, 28 October, 1864. Resigned 16 March, 1865.
BORDEN, HIRAM C.
Mate, 2 December, 1861. Resigned 17 May, 1865.
BORDEN, ISAAC H.
Acting Third Assistant Engineer, 17 February, 1864. Resigned 9 May, 1865.
BORDEN, J. F.
Midshipman, 1 April, 1828. Passed Midshipman, 4 June, 1834. Lieutenant, 25 February, 1841. Drowned 5 April, 1842.
BORDEN, NELSON C.
Acting Ensign, 6 November, 1863. Honorably discharged 20 September, 1865.
BORDEN, PRINCE S.
Acting Master, 2 January, 1862. Honorably discharged 4 November, 1865.
BORDEN, RICHARD P.
Ensign (Spanish-American War), 20 May, 1898. Honorably discharged 29 September, 1898.
BORDEN, WILLIAM C.
Mate, 12 November, 1863. Acting Ensign, 29 August, 1864. Honorably discharged 15 July, 1865.
BORDLEY, THOMAS H.
Third Assistant Engineer, 26 August, 1859. Second Assistant Engineer, 16 October, 1861. First Assistant Engineer, 1 October, 1863. Died 10 December, 1865.
BORDMAN, CHARLES.
Carpenter, 23 August, 1833. Dismissed 6 April, 1838. Carpenter, 7 January, 1842. Retired List, 23 September, 1868. Died 2 December, 1884.
BORIE, FRANK J.
Assistant Engineer (Spanish-American War), 27 July, 1898. Honorably discharged 29 October, 1898.
BORLAND, EUCLID.
Assistant Surgeon, 4 April, 1831. Cashiered 22 October, 1834.
BORNER, PAUL.
Mate, 31 August, 1861. Acting Ensign, 14 March, 1863. Honorably discharged 3 February, 1866.
BORTHWICK, JOHN L. D.
Third Assistant Engineer, 8 October, 1861. Second Assistant Engineer, 3 August, 1863. First Assistant Engineer, 11 October, 1866. Passed Assistant Engineer, 24 February, 1874. Chief Engineer, 7 September, 1885. Retired List, 13 October, 1896.
BORTON, JAMES D.
Gunner, 30 March, 1861. Dismissed 18 April, 1866. Boatswain, 5 November, 1866. Died 27 January, 1867.
BOSQUE, AGENOR.
Midshipman, 1 November, 1826. Discontinued 15 July, 1833.
BOSS, EDWARD.
Lieutenant, 27 June, 1799. Discharged 30 April, 1801, under Peace Establishment Act.
BOSS, EDWIN.
Acting Assistant Paymaster, 25 November, 1864. Discharged 11 October, 1865.
BOSS, JOSEPH.
Midshipman, 2 March, 1799. Delivered up Warrant 29 July, 1800.
BOSS, ROBERT P.
Mate, 4 January, 1862. Resigned 14 May, 1864. Acting Ensign, 27 May, 1864. Honorably discharged 22 January, 1866.
BOSTICK, EDWARD D.
Midshipman, 24 September, 1870. Graduated 21 June, 1875. Ensign, 21 September, 1876. Master, 9 January, 1883. Lieutenant, Junior Grade, 3 March, 1883. Lieutenant, 15 May, 1889. Retired List, 8 October, 1898.
BOSTICK, JOHN W.
Lieutenant (Spanish-American War), 26 May, 1898. Honorably discharged 3 October, 1898.
BOSTICK, WILLIAM M.
Ensign (Spanish-American War), 26 May, 1898. Honorably discharged 3 October, 1898.
BOSTWICK, CHARLES.
Mate, 27 May, 1862. Dismissed 5 June, 1863.
BOSTWICK, D. L.
Acting Assistant Paymaster, 17 November, 1863. Discharged 1 October, 1865.
BOSTWICK, FRANK M.
Cadet Midshipman, 26 September, 1873. Graduated 18 June, 1879. Ensign, 30 August, 1881. Lieutenant, Junior Grade, 19 June, 1888. Lieutenant, 27 June, 1893.
BOSTWICK, LUCIUS A.
Naval Cadet, 7 September, 1886. Ensign, 1 July, 1892. Lieutenant, Junior Grade, 3 March, 1899. Lieutenant, 1 July, 1899.
BOSTWICK M. W.
Purser, 16 July, 1814. Lost in the Epervier, in 1815.
BOSTWICK, RICHARD.
Lieutenant, 21 March, 1799. Discharged 2 September, 1801, under Peace Establishment Act.
BOSTWICK, ROBERT C.
Mate, 8 January, 1862. Dismissed 5 June, 1863.
BOSWORTH, DANIEL.
Acting Assistant Paymaster, 5 April, 1864. Discharged 18 October, 1865.

GENERAL NAVY REGISTER.

BOSWORTH, DANIEL P.
Mate, 13 May, 1863. Acting Ensign, 30 November, 1863. Honorably discharged 20 October, 1865.
BOSWORTH, HARLAN P.
Mate, 9 November, 1864. Resigned 30 May, 1865.
BOSWORTH, NATHANIEL.
Midshipman, 5 December, 1798. Lieutenant, 30 November, 1799. Last appearance on Records of Navy Department.
BOTELER, JOSEPH C.
Acting Master's Mate, 30 August, 1864. Discharged 6 May, 1865. Mate, 5 October, 1866. Deserted 8 October, 1866.
BOTSFORD, JERARD H.
Third Assistant Engineer, 3 October, 1861. Second Assistant Engineer, 3 August, 1863. Died 25 July, 1864.
BOTTEN, C. M.
Mate, 26 July, 1863. Honorably discharged 27 July, 1865.
BOTTICHER, MORRIS.
Acting First Assistant Engineer, 27 September, 1864. Dismissed 12 April, 1865.
BOUCHARD, C. L.
Acting Second Assistant Engineer, 9 June, 1863. Appointment revoked (sick), 26 May, 1865.
BOUDINOT, W. E.
Midshipman, 1 February, 1836. Passed Midshipman, 1 July, 1842. Master, 7 March, 1849. Lieutenant, 5 September, 1849. Resigned 17 November, 1858.
BOUGHAN, J. G.
Midshipman, 11 January, 1815. Lieutenant, 13 January, 1825. Died 6 November, 1832.
BOUGHTER, FRANCIS.
Naval Cadet, 17 May, 1883. Ensign, 1 July, 1889. Lieutenant, Junior Grade, 26 September, 1897. Lieutenant, 3 March, 1899.
BOUGHTON NAPOLEON.
Acting Ensign, 31 October, 1862. Honorably discharged 30 November, 1865.
BOULTON, S. L.
Acting Assistant Surgeon, 1 October, 1862. Resigned 1 December, 1863.
BOUNTHEAN, PETER.
Midshipman, 1 March, 1799. Last appearance on Records of Navy Department.
BOURNE, BENJAMIN C.
Acting Third Assistant Engineer, 25 July, 1862. Resigned 13 June, 1863. Acting Second Assistant Engineer, 14 March, 1864. Acting First Assistant Engineer, 29 December, 1864. Honorably discharged 16 August, 1865.
BOURNE, BENJAMIN F.
Purser, 26 March, 1814. Died 10 November, 1823.
BOURNE, EDMUND L.
Mate, 4 November, 1862. Acting Ensign, 11 December, 1863. Honorably discharged 30 September, 1865.
BOURNE, GEORGE W.
Acting Ensign, 11 October, 1862. Acting Master, 20 March, 1865. Resigned 8 May, 1865.
BOURNE, WILLIAM.
Acting Ensign, 9 September, 1864. Appointment revoked 15 December, 1864.
BOUSH, CLIFFORD J.
Midshipman, 5 June, 1872. Graduated 20 June, 1876. Ensign, 1 December, 1877. Lieutenant, Junior Grade, 3 November, 1884. Lieutenant, 31 July, 1890. Lieutenant-Commander, 25 March, 1899.
BOUSH, GEORGE R.
Assistant Naval Constructor, 3 August, 1869. Naval Constructor, 12 March, 1875. Retired List, 22 October, 1887. Died 6 May, 1895.
BOUSH, JAMES.
Midshipman, 1 October, 1798. Died 24 June, 1800.
BOUTELLE, CHARLES A.
Acting Master, 5 April, 1862. Acting Volunteer Lieutenant, 24 May, 1864. Honorably discharged 14 January, 1866.
BOUTELLE, CHARLES B.
Acting Ensign, 28 January, 1865. Resigned 1 September, 1865.
BOUTWELL, EDWARD B.
Midshipman, 3 March, 1819. Lieutenant, 17 May, 1828. Commander, 2 June, 1850. Dismissed 31 July, 1861.
BOUTWELL, MINSON W.
Sailmaker, 9 July, 1861. Appointment revoked 21 August, 1861.
BOUTWELL, SAMUEL H.
Sailmaker, 10 October, 1855. Dismissed 17 June, 1861. Sailmaker, 17 February, 1876. Died 9 March, 1894.
BOWDEN, ISAIAH W.
Mate, 22 October, 1864. Resigned 27 May, 1865.
BOWDEN, JOSEPH.
Mate, 9 January, 1862. Resigned 6 August, 1862.
BOWDLE, WILLIAM J.
Acting Assistant Surgeon, 3 September, 1863. Resigned 16 June, 1865.
BOWDON, FRANK W.
Cadet Midshipman, 24 September, 1875. Graduated 22 June, 1882. Ensign, Junior Grade, 3 March, 1883. Died 24 June, 1884.
BOWEN, A. S.
Acting Master, 1 October, 1862. Resigned 17 June, 1864.
BOWEN, EDWARD F.
Mate, 22 October, 1861. Resigned 4 March, 1863.

GENERAL NAVY REGISTER.   69

BOWEN, GEORGE F.
  Acting Master and Pilot, 11 October, 1864. Appointment revoked 9 March, 1865.
BOWEN, GEORGE H.
  Mate, 1 January, 1865. Honorably discharged 20 May, 1867.
BOWEN, RICHARD T.
  Midshipman, 24 December, 1847. Passed Midshipman, 10 June, 1853. Master, 15 September, 1855. Lieutenant, 16 September, 1855. Lost in Sloop-of-War Levant, 18 September, 1860.
BOWEN, ROBERT JAMES.
  Midshipman, 20 November, 1850. Resigned 6 November, 1855.
BOWEN, THOMAS C.
  Acting Midshipman, 25 September, 1857. Midshipman, 1 June, 1861. Lieutenant, 16 July, 1862. Retired from service, with one year's pay, 20 April, 1866.
BOWEN, WILLIAM S.
  Acting Assistant Surgeon, 14 January, 1865. Honorably discharged 15 February, 1866. Assistant Surgeon, 22 July, 1867. Passed Assistant Surgeon, 16 June, 1870. Resigned 31 December, 1873.
BOWER, DANIEL C.
  Acting Ensign, 1 October, 1862. Acting Master 7 September, 1863. Honorably discharged 21 December, 1865
BOWER, GEORGE K.
  Midshipman, 28 September, 1864. Graduated 2 June, 1868. Lost on board the Oneida, 24 January, 1870.
BOWER, JAMES M.
  Ensign (Spanish-American War), 14 May, 1898. Honorably discharged 17 November, 1898.
BOWERS, EDWARD C.
  Midshipman, 2 February, 1829. Passed Midshipman, 3 July, 1835. Lieutenant, 26 April, 1841. Reserved List, 13 September, 1855. Commander, 21 July, 1861. Captain on Retired List, 4 April, 1867. Died 1 November, 1893.
BOWERS, EDWARD C., Jr.
  Mate, 8 June, 1863. Acting Ensign, 19 October, 1863. Resigned 16 February, 1865.
BOWERS, FREDERIC C.
  Cadet Engineer, 15 September, 1875. Graduated 10 June, 1879. Assistant Engineer, 10 June, 1881. Passed Assistant Engineer, 1 July, 1892. Rank changed to Lieutenant, 3 March, 1899.
BOWERS, GEORGE M.
  Mate, 7 October, 1863. Resigned 7 June, 1864. Mate, 30 June, 1870. Appointment revoked.
BOWERS, JOHN L.
  Acting Third Assistant Engineer, 18 November, 1861. Acting Second Assistant Engineer, 6 January, 1864. Honorably discharged 1 November, 1865.
BOWERS, JOHN T.
  Naval Cadet, 20 September, 1895. At sea prior to final graduation.
BOWERS, LAWRENCE M.
  Mate, 5 December, 1863. Resigned 17 June, 1864.
BOWERS, JERATHMEAL.
  Midshipman, 18 June, 1812. Resigned 6 July, 1814.
BOWERS, JOSEPH.
  Boatswain 16 September, 1841. Dropped.
BOWERS, WILLIAM L.
  Acting Ensign, 3 September, 1862. Acting Master, 23 December, 1863. Honorably discharged 30 September, 1865.
BOWIE, ARGYLE. C.
  Mate, 7 July, 1863. Resigned 26 April, 1865.
BOWIE, AUGUSTUS J.
  Assistant Surgeon, 9 February, 1837. Passed Assistant Surgeon, 14 March, 1843. Surgeon, 8 February, 1848. Resigned 1 May, 1852.
BOWIE, HENRY.
  Midshipman, 18 April, 1814. Last appearance on Records of Navy Department.
BOWIE, J. K.
  Midshipman, 1 November, 1826. Passed Midshipman, 14 June, 1834. Lieutenant, 17 January, 1840. Died 25 December, 1843.
BOWIE, WALLACE A.
  Acting Third Assistant Engineer, 28 March, 1864. Honorably discharged 27 August, 1868.
BOWLAND, JAMES D.
  Acting Ensign, 15 May, 1863. Appointment revoked 25 September, 1863.
BOWLAND, R. M.
  Midshipman, 5 March, 1834. Passed Midshipman, 22 June, 1841. Resigned 7 July, 1842.
BOWLER, JOHN R.
  Acting Assistant Paymaster, 2 June, 1863. Resigned 20 February, 1865.
BOWLES, FRANCIS T.
  Cadet Engineer, 15 September, 1875. Graduated 10 June, 1879. Assistant Naval Constructor, 1 November, 1881. Naval Constructor, 10 October, 1888.
BOWLING, JAMES T.
  Mate, 27 January, 1863. Acting Ensign, 5 September, 1864. Honorably discharged 12 May, 1868.
BOWMAN, CHARLES G.
  Midshipman, 29 July, 1865. Graduated June, 1869. Ensign, 12 July, 1870. Master, 12 July, 1871. Lieutenant, 9 August, 1874. Lieutenant-Commander, 4 May, 1896. Commander, 8 July, 1899.

GENERAL NAVY REGISTER.

BOWMAN, EDWARD C.
Acting Assistant Paymaster, 30 June, 1862. Died October, 1864.
BOWMAN, JOHN.
Mate, 31 August. 1863. Acting Ensign, 21 September, 1864. Honorably discharged 2 October, 1865.
BOWMAN, JOSEPH.
Midshipman, 8 July, 1815. Died 24 October, 1825.
BOWNE, LOUIS.
Mate, 17 June, 1863. Acting Ensign, 12 August, 1864. Appointment revoked 24 July, 1865.
BOWYER, JOHN M.
Midshipman, 28 September, 1870. Graduated 15 October, 1874. Ensign, 17 July, 1875. Master, 28 May, 1881. Lieutenant, Junior Grade, 3 March, 1883. Lieutenant, 26 May, 1887. Lieutenant-Commander, 3 March, 1899.
BOWYER, THOMAS H.
Midshipman, 1 January, 1802. Lieutenant, 5 March, 1817. Died in 1822.
BOYCE, EDWIN.
Mate, 20 November, 1863. Resigned 31 May, 1864.
BOYCE, FREDERICK S.
Lieutenant (Spanish-American War), 24 May, 1898. Honorably discharged 15 November, 1898.
BOYCE, JAMES R.
Surgeon's Mate, 22 April, 1816. Dismissed 7 April, 1829.
BOYCE, L. P.
Acting Assistant Surgeon, 26 September, 1862. Resigned 19 June, 1865.
BOYCE, THOMAS J.
Sailmaker, 12 October, 1833. Died 25 March, 1853.
BOYD, ARTHUR A.
Acting Midshipman, 10 October, 1862. Ensign, 18 December, 1868. Master, 21 March, 1870. Lieutenant, 21 March, 1871. Resigned, to take effect 1 January, 1881.
BOYD, DAVID F.
Naval Cadet, 19 May, 1893. Ensign, 1 July, 1899.
BOYD, EDWARD.
Midshipman, 19 August, 1823. Passed Midshipman, 20 February, 1830. Dismissed 5 December, 1831.
BOYD, GEORGE.
Midshipman, 13 January, 1799. Resigned 5 February, 1800.
BOYD, HENRY A.
Acting Second Assistant Engineer, 28 December, 1861. Resigned 16 May, 1862.
BOYD, JAMES.
Surgeon's Mate, 10 October, 1799. Surgeon, 1 July, 1803. Died at Sea about September, 1803.
BOYD, JAMES.
Acting Third Assistant Engineer, 24 February, 1864. Appointment revoked (sick) 18 June, 1864. Acting Third Assistant Engineer, 22 August, 1864. Honorably discharged 17 July, 1865.
BOYD, JAMES T.
Acting Third Assistant Engineer, 11 October, 1864. Honorably discharged 31 July, 1865.
BOYD, JOHN C.
Assistant Surgeon, 3 April, 1873. Passed Assistant Surgeon, 18 April, 1877. Surgeon, 18 September, 1887. Medical Inspector, 25 October, 1899.
BOYD, JOHN Q. A.
Midshipman, 13 December, 1819. Dismissed, 5 November, 1827.
BOYD, JOSHUA J.
Midshipman, 1 January, 1825. Left off, 25 November, 1827.
BOYD, LOUIS J. M.
Acting Third Assistant Engineer, 6 March, 1862. Resigned 3 August, 1863.
BOYD, ROBERT.
Assistant Surgeon, 24 June, 1891. Resigned 8 May, 1895.
BOYD, ROBERT, JR.
Midshipman, 14 January, 1850. Passed Midshipman, 20 June, 1856. Master, 22 January, 1858. Lieutenant, 23 January, 1858. Lieutenant-Commander, 16 July, 1862. Commander, 20 March, 1871. Captain, 19 June, 1882. Died 30 July, 1890.
BOYD, THOMAS J.
Surgeon's Mate, 28 March, 1820. Surgeon, 10 July, 1824. Died 26 March, 1839.
BOYD, WALTER.
Midshipman, 4 August, 1800. Last appearance on Records of Navy Department, 27 October, 1808.
BOYD, WILLIAM.
Acting Ensign, 28 August, 1863. Honorably discharged 1 June, 1865. Mate, 20 April, 1870. Retired List, 1 March, 1898.
BOYD, WILLIAM B.
Acting Third Assistant Engineer, 19 August, 1864. Resigned 31 May, 1865.
BOYDEN, JEREMIAH W.
Acting Assistant Surgeon, 5 March, 1864. Assistant Surgeon, 20 August, 1864. Died 17 August, 1866.
BOYDEN, JOHN.
Midshipman, 1 January, 1812. Last appearance on Records of Navy Department, 18 August, 1812.
BOYDEN, J. WESLEY.
Acting Assistant Surgeon, 3 March, 1864. Assistant Surgeon, 20 August, 1864. Died on Muscoota, 17 August, 1866.

GENERAL NAVY REGISTER. 71

BOYDEN, PAUL.
    Mate, 26 May, 1863. Acting Ensign, 31 December, 1864. Honorably discharged 16 December, 1868.
BOYER, CHARLES.
    Acting Ensign, 2 July, 1863. Honorably discharged 10 February, 1868.
BOYER, SAMUEL P.
    Acting Assistant Surgeon, 21 June, 1862. Acting Passed Assistant Surgeon, 19 May, 1865. Honorably discharged 8 April, 1870.
BOYLE, EUGENE.
    Midshipman, 10 May, 1831. Resigned 14 July, 1838.
BOYLE, JOHN.
    Mate, 15 April, 1862. Acting Ensign, 28 July, 1863. Honorably discharged 27 November, 1869.
BOYLE, JUNIUS J.
    Midshipman, 27 August, 1823. Passed Midshipman, 23 March, 1829. Lieutenant, 21 June, 1832. Reserved List, 13 September, 1855. Commodore on Reserved List, 4 April, 1832. Died 11 August, 1870.
BOYLE, STILES E.
    Mate, 3 October, 1864. Dismissed 15 June, 1866.
BOYLE, THOMAS.
    Master, 16 April, 1813. Resigned 8 September, 1813.
BOYLE, WILLIAM.
    Acting Third Assistant Engineer, 23 May, 1864. Honorably discharged 1 October, 1865.
BOYNTON, EDWARD S.
    Third Assistant Engineer, 26 August, 1859. Resigned 15 October, 1860. Reappointed 24 April, 1861. Second Assistant Engineer, 28 October, 1862. Resigned 7 November, 1863.
BOYNTON, JAMES A.
    Acting Third Assistant Engineer, 15 March, 1864. Honorably discharged 10 October, 1865.
BOYNTON, JAMES W.
    Acting Third Assistant Engineer, 22 May, 1862. Appointment revoked (sick) 16 April, 1863.
BOX, PHILIP M.
    Midshipman, 1 November, 1826. Dismissed 21 June, 1833.
BRACKETT, FRANK E.
    Mate, 19 December, 1861. Acting Ensign, 24 June, 1864. Honorably discharged 3 November, 1865.
BRACKETT, HORACE W.
    Acting Ensign, 21 January, 1864. Honorably discharged 6 September, 1865.
BRACKETT, JOSEPH W.
    Master, 14 March, 1833. Resigned 1 August, 1836.
BRADBURN, W. P.
    Midshipman, 31 December, 1831. Resigned 2 June, 1836.
BRADBURY, CHARLES A.
    Midshipman, 26 July, 1865. Graduated 4 June, 1869. Ensign, 12 July, 1870. Master, 6 February, 1872. Lieutenant, 1 May, 1875. Retired List, 4 September, 1896.
BRADBURY, EDWARD E.
    Mate, 20 August, 1864. Master on Retired List, 20 March, 1871. Title changed to Lieutenant, Junior Grade, 3 March, 1883.
BRADBURY, GEORGE H.
    Acting Master, 5 June, 1861. Resigned 28 February, 1862.
BRADBURY, ISAAC S.
    Mate, 2 February, 1863. Acting Ensign, 29 August, 1864. Lost on Narcissus, 4 January, 1866.
BRADBURY, W. F.
    Surgeon's Mate, 10 December, 1814. Last appearance on Records of Navy Department, 1816. Resigned.
BRADDOCK, CHARLES S., JR.
    Lieutenant (Spanish-American War), 20 May, 1898. Honorably discharged 1 December, 1898.
BRADFORD, DUNCAN.
    Professor, 4 March, 1835. Dropped 4 September, 1848.
BRADFORD, GEORGE.
    Master, 17 July, 1812. Discharged 7 May, 1813.
BRADFORD, HENRY F.
    Third Assistant Engineer, 1 July, 1861. Second Assistant Engineer, 18 December, 1862. First Assistant Engineer, 11 October, 1866. Died 16 September, 1873.
BRADFORD, HORACE S.
    Acting Assistant Paymaster, 24 February, 1862. Resigned 1 December, 1863.
BRADFORD, JAMES.
    Midshipman, 4 March, 1819. Resigned 25 June, 1827.
BRADFORD, JAMES H.
    Surgeon's Mate, 23 August, 1800. Resigned 9 July, 1803.
BRADFORD, JOHN O.
    Purser, 14 March, 1845. Pay Director, 3 March, 1871. Paymaster-General, 18 February, 1873. Retired List, 22 February, 1877. Died 27 June, 1879.
BRADFORD, JOSEPH C.
    Sailmaker, 21 July, 1846. Retired List, 6 June, 1878. Died 16 December, 1895.
BRADFORD, JOSEPH M.
    Midshipman, 10 January, 1840. Passed Midshipman, 11 July, 1846. Master, 1 March, 1855. Lieutenant, 14 September, 1855. Lieutenant-Commander, 16 July, 1862. Commander, 25 July, 1866. Retired List, 5 February, 1872. Captain, Retired List, 16 March, 1872. Died 14 April, 1872.

BRADFORD, LAWRENCE.
Mate, 2 May, 1862. Honorably discharged 12 July, 1865.
BRADFORD, ROBERT F.
Acting Midshipman, 21 May, 1852. Midshipman, 30 June. 1856. Passed Midshipman, 29 April, 1859. Master, 5 September, 1859. Lieutenant. 22 December. 1860. Lieutenant-Commander, 5 August, 1862. Commander, 3 July, 1870. Captain, 15 October, 1881. Died 9 January, 1892.
BRADFORD, ROYAL B.
Acting Midshipman, 28 November, 1861. Graduated September, 1865. Ensign. 1 December, 1866. Master, 12 March, 1868. Lieutenant, 26 March, 1869. Lieutenant-Commander, 30 November, 1878. Commander, 26 March, 1889. Captain. 3 March, 1899. Chief of the Bureau of Equipment, with the rank of Rear-Admiral.
BRADFORD, WILLIAM.
Midshipman, 24 July, 1807. Resigned 11 May, 1809.
BRADFORD, WILLIAM H.
Mate, 7 August, 1862. Died on Roebuck, 29 July, 1864.
BRADFORD, WILLIAM L.
Midshipman, 1 October, 1850. Passed Midshipman, 20 June, 1856. Master. 22 January, 1858. Lieutenant, 20 August, 1859. Resigned 17 April, 1861.
BRADLEE, B. F.
Midshipman, 1 September, 1822. Discharged 4 April, 1829.
BRADLEY, CHARLES.
Acting Third Assistant Engineer, 1 February, 1865. Honorably discharged 24 September, 1865.
BRADLEY, E. R.
Mate, 3 September, 1863. Resigned 6 May, 1865.
BRADLEY, FRANKLIN.
Mate, 17 October, 1864. Honorably discharged 21 September. 1865.
BRADLEY, GEORGE H.
Mate, 5 June, 1862. Resigned 26 May, 1863.
BRADLEY, GEORGE P.
Assistant Surgeon, 7 September, 1870. Passed Assistant Surgeon, 21 January, 1874. Surgeon, 23 August, 1883. Medical Inspector, 21 January, 1897. Medical Director, 31 May, 1900.
BRADLEY, JOHN B.
Acting Midshipman, 21 September, 1858. Killed on board Richmond, below New Orleans, 24 April, 1862.
BRADLEY, LEANDER D.
Acting Assistant Paymaster, 25 September, 1863. Discharged 20 September, 1865.
BRADLEY, MICHAEL.
Assistant Surgeon, 1 July, 1861. Dismissed 3 December, 1863. Restored 18 May, 1864. Passed Assistant Surgeon, 22 June, 1864. Surgeon, 12 June, 1865. Medical Inspector, 6 December, 1879. Medical Director, 19 June, 1888. Retired List, 29 March, 1895.
BRADLEY, WALTER.
Acting Third Assistant Engineer, 4 November, 1861. Acting Second Assistant Engineer, 2 January, 1863. Resigned 23 March, 1863.
BRADLEY, WILLIAM.
Assistant Surgeon, 20 May, 1859. Lost in the Levant, 1860.
BRADLEY, WILLIAM J.
Acting Third Assistant Engineer, 29 March, 1864. Resigned 8 May. 1865.
BRADLEY, W. W.
Acting Gunner, 8 October, 1864. Resigned 27 April, 1865.
BRADNER, THOMAS J.
Surgeon's Mate, 26 May, 1824. Killed (duel) 23 August 1827.
BRADSHAW, GEORGE B.
Naval Cadet, 4 September, 1885. Ensign, 1 July, 1891. Lieutenant, Junior Grade, 15 November, 1898. Lieutenant, 3 March, 1899.
BRADSHAW, JOHN.
Lieutenant, Junior Grade (Spanish-American War), 8 June, 1898. Honorably discharged 2 September, 1898.
BRADSTREET, NATHANIEL.
Surgeon, 23 September, 1798. Resigned 23 December, 1799.
BRADY, EDWARD.
Acting Boatswain, 13 August, 1853. Resigned 7 April, 1854.
BRADY, EDWARD.
Acting Boatswain, 11 February, 1863. Appointment revoked 2 November, 1863. Acting Boatswain, 2 February, 1865. Dismissed 7 February, 1866.
BRADY, GEORGE P.
Gunner, 27 June, 1898.
BRADY, JOHN.
Acting Master's Mate, 5 August, 1862. Resigned 18 December, 1865.
BRADY, JOHN.
Acting Boatswain, 12 April, 1876. Appointment revoked 5 February, 1878.
BRADY, JOHN R.
Naval Cadet, 6 September, 1889. Assistant Engineer, 1 July, 1895. Passed Assistant Engineer, 10 February, 1899. Rank changed to Lieutenant, Junior Grade, 3 March, 1899.
BRADY, THOMAS E.
Assistant Engineer (Spanish-American War), 4 May, 1898. Honorably discharged 10 January, 1899.
BRADY, THOMAS F.
Carpenter, 24 October, 1829. Last appearance on Records of Navy Department, 1831.

GENERAL NAVY REGISTER. 73

BRADY, WILLIAM N.
    Boatswain, 7 September, 1836. Master, 1 July, 1843. Reserved List, 14 September, 1855. Died 20 February, 1887.
BRAGDEN, CHARLES A.
    Boatswain, 4 June, 1858. Disgracefully discharged 10 October, 1896.
BRAGG, CALVIN M.
    Mate, 3 September, 1863. Acting Ensign, 4 December, 1863. Honorably discharged 14 October, 1865.
BRAGG, CHARLES P.
    Acting Ensign, 11 June, 1863. Honorably discharged 20 February, 1866.
BRAGG, IRA W.
    Assistant Surgeon, 24 January, 1862. Died 21 October, 1864.
BRAGONIER, OSCAR.
    Acting Warrant Machinist, 23 August, 1899.
BRAIDWOOD, WILLIAM.
    Acting Second Assistant Engineer. Acting First Assistant Engineer, 27 December, 1864. Dismissed 18 March, 1865.
BRAILSFORD, JOSEPH.
    Midshipman, 15 November, 1809. Drowned 30 June, 1814.
BRAILSFORD, W. H.
    Midshipman, 1 December, 1809. Lieutenant, 4 February, 1815. Last appearance on Records of Navy Department.
BRAINARD, FREDERICK R.
    Cadet Midshipman, 24 June, 1876. Graduated 22 June, 1882. Ensign, Junior Grade, 3 March, 1883. Ensign, 26 June, 1884. Lieutenant, Junior Grade, 27 June, 1893. Lieutenant, 14 March, 1897.
BRAINE, DANIEL L.
    Midshipman, 30 May, 1846. Passed Midshipman, 8 June, 1852. Master, 15 September, 1855. Lieutenant, 16 September, 1855. Lieutenant-Commander, 16 July, 1862. Commander, 25 July, 1866. Captain, 11 December, 1874. Commodore, 2 March, 1885. Rear-Admiral, 4 September, 1887. Retired List, 18 May, 1891. Died 30 January, 1898.
BRAISTED, J. M.
    Mate, 24 September, 1861. Dismissed 13 August, 1863.
BRAISTED, WILLIAM C.
    Assistant Surgeon, 24 September, 1890. Passed Assistant Surgeon, 24 September, 1893.
BRALEY, GEORGE F.
    Acting Ensign, 21 October, 1864. Honorably discharged 1 October, 1866.
BRALEY, ISAAC V.
    Acting Ensign, 2 February, 1865. Honorably discharged 22 July, 1865.
BRAME, CHARLES E.
    Midshipman, 25 January, 1840. Dropped.
BRANCH, CYRUS A.
    Midshipman, 30 November, 1814. Killed (duel) May, 1826.
BRANCH, FRANK O.
    Naval Cadet, 6 September, 1895. At sea prior to final graduation.
BRAND, CHARLES A.
    Naval Cadet, 8 September, 1885. Ensign, 1 July, 1891. Lieutenant, 3 March, 1899.
BRAND, FREDERICK B.
    Midshipman, 17 July, 1840. Passed Midshipman, 11 July, 1846. Acting Master, 6 November, 1847. Resigned 1 May, 1849.
BRANDT, JOHN D.
    Gunner, 7 July, 1849. Resigned 12 January, 1853.
BRANDT, WILLIAM W.
    Mate, 16 October, 1861. Resigned 7 December, 1864.
BRANN, JOHN.
    Mate, January, 1863. Acting Ensign, 22 February, 1865. Honorably discharged 21 November, 1865. Acting Ensign, 5 April, 1867. Mustered out 2 October, 1868.
BRANNAN, JAMES A.
    Acting Ensign, 17 March, 1863. Honorably discharged 22 December, 1868.
BRANNEN, JAMES.
    Acting Third Assistant Engineer, 7 September, 1864. Honorably discharged 10 June, 1865.
BRANNON, JAMES.
    Acting Third Assistant Engineer, 11 December, 1862. Resigned 13 March, 1863.
BRANSFORD, JOHN F.
    Assistant Surgeon, 26 June, 1872. Passed Assistant Surgeon, 21 December, 1875. Surgeon, 16 June, 1885. Resigned 4 May, 1890. Assistant Surgeon (Spanish-American War), 4 May, 1898. Passed Assistant Surgeon, 21 September, 1898. Honorably discharged 23 March, 1899.
BRANSON, WARE, JR.
    Acting Sailmaker, 23 November, 1857. Resigned 27 June, 1859.
BRANT, RICHARD B.
    Midshipman, 3 August, 1798. Master, 16 May, 1800. Resigned 22 March, 1804.
BRANTINGHAM, CHARLES H.
    Acting Midshipman, 22 September, 1859. Resigned 10 March, 1860. Mate, 10 March, 1862. Acting Ensign, 13 July, 1863. Acting Master, 3 July, 1865. Honorably discharged 18 April, 1867.
BRASHER, THOMAS M.
    Midshipman, 6 June, 1831. Passed Midshipman, 15 June, 1837. Lieutenant, 8 September, 1841. Commander, 24 April, 1861. Retired List, 2 August, 1864. Captain, Retired List, 4 April, 1867. Died 11 August, 1888.

GENERAL NAVY REGISTER.

BRASHERS, W. C.
Midshipman, 15 May, 1837. Resigned 20 December, 1839.
BRASHIERS, RICHARD.
Midshipman, 1 January, 1812. Died 4 September, 1817.
BRATHWAITE, FREDERICK G.
Assistant Surgeon, 22 June, 1891. Passed Assistant Surgeon, 22 June, 1894. Resigned 10 April, 1897.
BRATT, CARLOS.
Midshipman, 12 October, 1848. Resigned 5 July, 1850.
BRAUNERSREUTHER, WILLIAM.
Cadet Midshipman, 23 September, 1871. Graduated 23 September, 1876. Ensign, 22 January, 1880. Lieutenant, Junior Grade, 26 June, 1886. Lieutenant, 10 January, 1892. Lieutenant-Commander, 2 November, 1899.
BRAWLEY, RICHARD R.
Acting Assistant Paymaster, 4 June, 1862. Discharged 12 January, 1866.
BRAWLEY, WILLIAM P.
Assistant Paymaster, 23 May, 1895. Resigned 5 March, 1897.
BRAY, CHARLES D.
Acting Third Assistant Engineer, 10 October, 1866. Third Assistant Engineer, 2 June, 1868. Resigned 18 March, 1869.
BRAY, GUILFORD P.
Mate, 13 December, 1862. Dismissed 27 May, 1863.
BRAY, OLIVER.
Acting Second Assistant Engineer, 25 March, 1863. Honorably discharged 28 November, 1865.
BRAYTON, DANIEL C.
Sailmaker, 30 August, 1851. Retired List, 17 February, 1891.
BRAYTON, HARRY R.
Boatswain, 3 May, 1897.
BRAYTON, J. B.
Acting Assistant Paymaster, 27 September, 1863. Resigned 23 October, 1863.
BRAYTON, SAMUEL N.
Assistant Surgeon, 24 November, 1861. Resigned 8 June, 1865.
BRAYTON, W. H.
Sailmaker, 21 September, 1837. Dismissed 6 November, 1847.
BRAYTON, W. S. L.
Sailmaker, 4 November, 1852. Taken prisoner and died at Charleston, South Carolina, 22 April, 1864.
BREADIN, JAMES.
Midshipman, 27 July, 1846. Resigned 16 October, 1849.
BREAKER, CHARLES W.
Third Assistant Engineer, 17 December, 1862. Second Assistant Engineer, 8 April, 1864. Died 9 February, 1871.
BREARLEY, SPENCER C.
Carpenter, 27 July, 1892.
BRECHT, FREDERICK E.
Mate, 29 October, 1862. Resigned 23 September, 1863.
BRECHT, THEODORE C.
Third Assistant Engineer, 28 May, 1861. Second Assistant Engineer, 18 December, 1862. Resigned 18 January, 1865. Acting First Assistant Engineer, 19 January, 1865. Honorably discharged 1 October, 1868.
BRECK, CHARLES E.
Acting Ensign, 2 July, 1863. Honorably discharged 2 December, 1865.
BRECK, JOSEPH B.
Acting Ensign, 27 February, 1863. Acting Master, 8 August, 1863. Acting Volunteer Lieutenant, 16 November, 1863. Acting Volunteer Lieutenant-Commander, 25 November, 1864. Died 26 July, 1865.
BRECK, LOWELL M.
Acting Ensign, 19 March, 1863. Appointment revoked 2 June, 1863.
BRECK, RICHARD A.
Midshipman, 30 September, 1865. Graduated 4 June, 1869. Ensign, 12 July, 1870. Master, 6 March, 1872. Drowned 22 September, 1874.
BRECKENRIDGE, S. M.
Midshipman, 15 December, 1819. Lieutenant, 17 May, 1828. Died 4 June, 1829.
BRECKINRIDGE, JOSEPH C.
Naval Cadet, 28 September, 1887. Resigned 24 January, 1888. Naval Cadet, 5 September, 1888. Resigned 27 June, 1891. Naval Cadet, 8 September, 1891. Ensign, 1 July, 1897. Drowned 11 February, 1898.
BREDIN, JAMES.
Midshipman, 27 July, 1846. Resigned 16 October, 1849.
BREED, CYRUS W.
Acting Midshipman, 26 November, 1861. Graduated September, 1865. Ensign, 1 December, 1866. Master, 12 March, 1868. Lieutenant, 26 March, 1869. Resigned 30 April, 1875.
BREED, EDWIN D.
Acting Master's Mate in 1862. Died 20 March, 1863.
BREED, GEORGE.
Cadet Midshipman, 17 June, 1882. Graduated 10 June, 1886. Ensign, 1 July, 1888. Resigned 7 January, 1891. Lieutenant, Junior Grade (Spanish-American War), 17 June, 1898. Honorably discharged 24 February, 1899.
BREESE, E. MARSHALL.
Third Assistant Engineer, 25 March, 1862. Second Assistant Engineer, 1 November, 1863. Resigned 2 March, 1868.

GENERAL NAVY REGISTER.

BREESE, JOHN.
Assistant Paymaster, 1 September, 1869. Resigned 14 June, 1878.
BREESE, K. RANDOLPH.
Midshipman, 6 November, 1846. Passed Midshipman, 8 June, 1852. Master, 15 September, 1855. Lieutenant, 16 September, 1855. Lieutenant-Commander, 16 July, 1862. Commander, 25 July, 1866. Captain, 9 August, 1874. Died 13 September, 1881.
BREESE, SAMUEL L.
Midshipman, 17 December, 1810. Lieutenant, 27 April, 1816. Commander, 22 December, 1835. Captain, 8 September, 1841. Commodore, Retired List, 16 July, 1862. Rear-Admiral, Retired List, 3 September, 1862. Died 17 December, 1870.
BREESE, S. LIVINGSTON.
Midshipman, 14 May, 1846. Passed Midshipman, 8 June, 1852. Master, 15 September, 1855. Lieutenant, 16 September, 1855. Lieutenant-Commander, 16 July, 1862. Commander, 14 April, 1867. Captain, 26 April, 1878. Retired List, 30 March, 1888. Died 18 July, 1899.
BREESE, THOMAS.
Purser. 8 July, 1815. Died 12 October, 1846.
BREEZE, H. M.
Master, 12 October, 1813. Discharged 15 April, 1815.
BREEZE, THEODORE.
Acting Third Assistant Engineer, 23 September, 1863. Resigned 2 June, 1865.
BREMON, CHARLES.
Acting Second Assistant Engineer, 21 July, 1864. Resigned 15 May, 1865.
BREMON, FRANK A.
Acting First Assistant Engineer, 5 August, 1861. Resigned 21 February, 1862. Acting Second Assistant Engineer, 21 May, 1862. Acting First Assistant Engineer, 31 October, 1862. Resigned 19 December, 1864.
BRENNARD, E. C.
Acting Volunteer Lieutenant, 1 October, 1862. Killed accidentally 14 November, 1863.
BRENNEN, E. C.
Mate, 1 October, 1862. Acting Ensign, 7 February, 1863. Acting Master, 7 May, 1863. Dismissed 12 November, 1864.
BRENNEN, CHRISTOPHER.
Mate, 25 November, 1863. Deserted 19 August, 1864.
BRENNON, JOHN.
Mate, 21 January, 1864. Acting Ensign, 9 November, 1864. Honorably discharged 6 April, 1868.
BRENT, ALEXANDER.
Midshipman, 2 April, 1804. Last appearance on Records of Navy Department, 28 May, 1804.
BRENT, THOMAS W.
Midshipman, 1 March, 1825. Passed Midshipman, 4 June, 1831. Lieutenant, 3 March, 1836. Commander, 14 September, 1855. Resigned 19 January, 1861.
BRENTLEY, H. J.
Mate, 2 November, 1864. Deserted 4 November, 1864.
BRENTNALL, JOHN H. H.
Acting Assistant Surgeon, 18 December, 1861. Resigned 2 November, 1863.
BRENTON, FRANCIS J.
Acting Ensign, 30 August, 1862. Resigned 6 June, 1865.
BRERETON, JOHN A.
Surgeon's Mate, 1 September, 1808. Surgeon, 4 March, 1811. Resigned 11 July, 1815.
BRERETON, THOMAS.
Midshipman, 16 June, 1806. Resigned 21 August, 1811.
BRESLYN, JEREMIAH C.
Acting Gunner. 2 December, 1863. Appointment revoked 8 May, 1865.
BREWER, THOMAS.
Mate, 20 January, 1863. Resigned 19 August, 1863. Acting Ensign, 17 October, 1864. Honorably discharged 12 July, 1816.
BREWSTER, BENJAMIN.
Midshipman, 30 November, 1814. Last appearance on Records of Navy Department, 16 February, 1816.
BREWSTER, CHARLES W.
Acting Ensign, 13 August, 1864. Honorably discharged 4 December, 1865.
BREWSTER, N.
Acting Assistant Surgeon, 12 March, 1863. Honorably discharged 19 December, 1865.
BREWSTER, PATRICK.
Acting First Assistant Engineer, 20 June, 1863. Resigned 27 March, 1865.
BRIAN, C. T.
Mate, 9 October, 1867. Resigned 13 October, 1871.
BRIARD, GEORGE.
Midshipman, 4 March, 1823. Died 15 December, 1829.
BRICE, JOHN.
Mate, 23 August, 1861. Acting Third Assistant Engineer, 10 August, 1864. Honorably discharged 4 September, 1865.
BRICE, JOHN J.
Acting Ensign, 13 September, 1862. Acting Master, 23 March, 1865. Ensign. 12 March, 1868. Master, 18 December, 1868. Lieutenant, 21 March, 1870. Lieutenant-Commander, 10 March, 1882. Commander, 28 May, 1892. Retired List, 1 February, 1895.
BRICE, JOHN W.
Midshipman, 2 March, 1833. Resigned 1 September, 1838.

GENERAL NAVY REGISTER.

BRICE, WILLIAM H.
Mate, 15 September, 1861. Acting Ensign, 3 September, 1862. Acting Master. 16 July, 1864. Ensign, 12 March, 1868. Master, 21 December, 1868. Lieutenant, 21 March, 1870. Died 6 July, 1874.

BRICELAND, ISAAC N.
Midshipman, 23 December, 1837. Passed Midshipman, 29 June, 1843. Acting Master, 8 June, 1846. Resigned 21 January, 1850.

BRICKELL, D. WARREN.
Assistant Surgeon. 8 November, 1847. Declined 9 December. 1847.

BRICKELL, ZACHARY.
Acting Second Assistant Engineer, 25 July, 1864. Resigned 5 June, 1865.

BRICKER, WILLIAM F.
Naval Cadet, 19 September, 1896. Graduated 30 June, 1900.

BRICKETT, GEORGE T.
Acting Assistant Surgeon, 19 January, 1865. Honorably discharged 1 February, 1866.

BRICKLY, JOHN.
Acting Third Assistant Engineer, 21 September, 1863. Resigned 18 January, 1864.

BRICKNELL, D. WARREN.
Assistant Surgeon, 17 November, 1847. Resigned 6 January, 1848.

BRIDGE, EDWARD W.
Acting Midshipman, 21 September, 1863. Ensign. 18 December, 1868. Master, 21 March, 1870. Lieutenant, 21 March, 1871. Retired List, 29 June, 1887. Died 29 August, 1889.

BRIDGE, HORATIO.
Purser, 16 February, 1838. Retired List, 8 April, 1868. Pay Director, Retired List, 3 March, 1871. Died 18 March, 1893.

BRIDGE, WILLIAM K.
Midshipman, 14 January, 1841. Passed Midshipman, 10 August, 1847. Master. 1 March, 1855. Lost in Brig Porpoise, 21 September, 1854.

BRIDGER, J.
Carpenter, 12 June, 1827. Last appearance on Records of Navy Department, 1829.

BRIDGES, C. P.
Mate, 6 January, 1863. Resigned 13 May, 1865.

BRIDGES, ELISHA H.
Acting Assistant Surgeon. 23 June. 1864. Honorably discharged 10 October. 1865.

BRIDGES, ISAAC W.
Mate, 9 January, 1862. Resigned 21 January, 1862.

BRIDGES, JOHN R.
Acting Third Assistant Engineer, 17 August, 1864. Honorably discharged 17 July, 1865.

BRIDGES, RUFUS.
Sailmaker, 28 May, 1836. Last appearance on Records of Navy Department. 10 November, 1836.

BRIDGES, WILLIAM E.
Mate, 22 October, 1861. Deserted 7 June, 1865.

BRIDGMAN, WILLIAM R.
Acting Midshipman, 2 December, 1859. Ensign, 16 September. 1862. Master. 22 February, 1864. Lieutenant-Commander. 25 July, 1866. Commander, 21 September, 1876. Captain, 10 January, 1892. Died 15 September, 1894.

BRIGGS, CHARLES.
Midshipman, 30 July. 1866. Graduated June, 1870. Resigned 24 August. 1871.

BRIGGS, CHARLES G.
Acting Ensign, 1 August, 1863. Resigned 16 March, 1865.

BRIGGS, DAVID L.
Acting Gunner, 8 December. 1862. Appointment revoked 22 March, 1865.

BRIGGS, F. L.
Acting Ensign, 28 June, 1864. Honorably discharged 21 September, 1865.

BRIGGS, GEORGE W.
Mate, 2 September, 1864. Honorably discharged 27 January, 1866.

BRIGGS, JAMES G.
Acting Boatswain. 25 October, 1855. Appointment revoked 14 August, 1858.

BRIGGS, JAMES G.
Acting Boatswain, 1 November. 1864. Honorably discharged 21 September, 1865.

BRIGGS, JOHN.
Boatswain. Last appearance on Records of Navy Department, 1815.

BRIGGS, JOHN.
Acting First Assistant Engineer, 4 September, 1861. Appointment revoked 6 September, 1864.

BRIGGS, JOHN B.
Midshipman. 28 September, 1865. Graduated 4 June. 1869. Ensign, 12 July, 1870. Master, 12 July, 1871. Lieutenant. 24 October, 1874. Lieutenant-Commander. 1 November, 1896. Commander, 10 October, 1899.

BRIGGS, JOHN G.
Acting Third Assistant Engineer. 9 July, 1862. Acting Second Assistant Engineer, 29 January, 1863. Honorably discharged 4 November, 1865.

BRIGGS, JOHN W.
Acting Third Assistant Engineer, 17 May, 1864. Resigned 30 April. 1867.

BRIGGS, SAMUEL R.
Master, 3 July, 1813. Last appearance on Records of Navy Department.

BRIGGS, WILBUR G.
Naval Cadet, 6 September, 1894. Ensign, 4 April, 1900.

BRIGGS, ZENO E.
Naval Cadet, 22 September, 1894. Ensign, 4 April, 1900.

BRIGHAM, CHARLES H.
Lieutenant, Junior Grade (Spanish-American War), 23 April, 1898. Resigned 28 September, 1898.
BRIGHAM, FRANKLIN W.
Acting Assistant Surgeon, 7 May, 1863. Resigned 20 January, 1865.
BRIGHAM, GEORGE H.
Acting Assistant Paymaster, 9 June, 1864. Resigned 21 July, 1864.
BRIGHAM, LE GRAND B.
Mate, 4 October, 1862. Acting Ensign, 21 October, 1863. Honorably discharged 13 January, 1866.
BRIGHAM, LEVI L.
Acting Assistant Paymaster, 14 November, 1862. Discharged 13 March, 1866.
BRIGHT, GEORGE A.
Acting Assistant Surgeon, 18 May, 1861. Assistant Surgeon, 8 August, 1864. Passed Assistant Surgeon, 31 December, 1867. Surgeon, 12 September, 1874. Medical Inspector, 11 May, 1893. Medical Director, 19 October, 1897. Retired List, 9 April, 1899.
BRIGHT, GEORGE S.
Third Assistant Engineer, 21 May, 1857. Second Assistant Engineer, 2 August, 1859. First Assistant Engineer, 1 July, 1861. Chief Engineer, 10 November, 1863. Retired List, 5 June, 1873. Died 29 May, 1875.
BRIGHT, HENRY.
Acting Boatswain, 20 December, 1852. Resigned 11 September, 1855.
BRIGHT, JACOB L.
Third Assistant Engineer, 20 November, 1861. Second Assistant Engineer, 25 August, 1863. Resigned 18 October, 1870.
BRIGHT, WASHINGTON.
Gunner, 25 July, 1838. Died 17 October, 1846.
BRIGHTMAN, PEREZ O.
Acting Third Assistant Engineer, 19 December, 1861. Acting Second Asistant Engineer, 19 September, 1862. Acting First Assistant Engineer, 1 February, 1865. Honorably discharged 27 January, 1866.
BRIGHTMAN, SHEFFIELD.
Acting Second Assistant Engineer, 6 January, 1863. Resigned 9 February, 1863.
BRILL, CONRAD.
Acting Third Assistant Engineer, 18 February, 1865. Honorably discharged 16 June, 1866.
BRINCKERHOFF, CHARLES C.
Acting Assistant Paymaster, 10 December, 1864. Resigned 22 May, 1865.
BRINDLEY, JOHN T.
Acting Third Assistant Engineer, 1 June, 1864. Resigned 20 June, 1865.
BRINK, BENJAMIN H.
Acting Carpenter, 21 February, 1864. Honorably discharged 1 November, 1865.
BRINK, EDWARD H.
Acting Assistant Paymaster, 8 August, 1863. Resigned 18 November, 1864.
BRINKERHOFF, ISAAC.
Assistant Surgeon, 1 July, 1829. Passed Assistant Surgeon, 3 March, 1835. Surgeon, 20 February, 1838. Retired List, 28 May, 1864. Medical Director, Retired List, 3 March, 1871. Died 28 September, 1874.
BRINLEY, EDWARD.
Cadet Midshipman, 18 September, 1876. Graduated 22 June, 1882. Ensign, Junior Grade, 3 March, 1883. Resigned 25 October, 1883.
BRINLEY, EDWARD, JR
Midshipman, 14 September, 1840. Passed Midshipman, 11 July, 1846. Master, 30 June, 1854. Lieutenant, 6 February, 1855. Resigned 25 June, 1856.
BRINSER, HARRY L.
Naval Cadet, 6 September, 1895. At sea prior to final graduation.
BRINTNALL, JOHN H. H.
Acting Assistant Surgeon, 18 December, 1861. Resigned 5 November, 1862.
BRINTNALL, JOHN P.
Midshipman, 21 December, 1848. Resigned 21 June, 1854.
BRISCO, JOHN A.
Boatswain, 24 March, 1858. Retired List, 18 June, 1888.
BRISCOE, WARNER L.
Midshipman, 20 November, 1849. Dropped 3 September, 1850.
BRISCOE, W. H.
Chaplain, 30 May, 1809. Last appearance on Records of Navy Department, 1815. Furloughed.
BRISTER, JOHN M.
Assistant Surgeon, 14 December, 1900.
BRISTOL, MARK L.
Naval Cadet, 19 May, 1883. Ensign, 1 July, 1889. Lieutenant, Junior Grade, 14 March, 1897. Lieutenant, 3 March, 1899.
BRITTAIN, CARLO B.
Naval Cadet, 19 May, 1884. Ensign, 1 July, 1890. Lieutenant, Junior Grade, 6 February, 1898. Lieutenant, 3 March, 1899.
BRITTAIN, GEORGE.
Acting Second Assistant Engineer, 17 November, 1862. Appointment revoked 30 May, 1864.
BRITTAIN, M. COOKMAN.
Chaplain, 31 May, 1869. Resigned 1 March, 1871.
BRITTIN, SAMUEL.
Midshipman, 1 January, 1808. Dismissed 26 June, 1809.

GENERAL NAVY REGISTER.

BRITTINGHAM, JOHN P.
  Mate, 8 November, 1862. Acting Gunner, 17 February, 1863. Resigned 17 August, 1864.
BRITTON, SALTER.
  Midshipman, 16 January, 1809. Resigned 13 December, 1809.
BROADNIX, AMOS.
  Third Assistant Engineer, 13 December, 1850. Second Assistant Engineer, 26 February, 1851. Resigned 14 February, 1856.
BROCK, EDWARD.
  Master, 25 June, 1799. Lieutenant, 18 August, 1800. Dismissed 26 February, 1801.
BROCK, OLIVER S.
  Acting Master, 22 November, 1861. Appointment revoked 19 March, 1862. Mate, 30 October, 1863. Acting Ensign, 30 August, 1864. Honorably discharged 19 September, 1865.
BROCKWAY, JAMES H.
  Mate, 2 February, 1863. Acting Ensign, 27 January, 1864. Killed accidentally 7 December, 1864.
BRODHEAD, EDGAR.
  Midshipman, 9 July, 1846. Passed Midshipman, 8 June, 1852. Resigned 12 January, 1853. Acting Lieutenant, 13 May, 1861. Acting Volunteer Lieutenant-Commander, 22 October, 1864. Resigned 2 March, 1865.
BRODHEAD, THOMAS W.
  Midshipman, 3 March, 1841. Passed Midshipman, 10 August, 1847. Acting Master, 2 December, 1854. Died 20 February, 1855.
BRODIE, CHARLES D.
  Naval Constructor, 13 January, 1826. Died 14 October, 1845.
BRODRICK, RICHARD G.
  Assistant Surgeon, 2 August, 1893. Passed Assistant Surgeon, 2 August, 1896. Retired List, 11 November, 1899.
BROE, JOHN.
  Mate, 10 January, 1863. Resigned 26 July, 1864.
BROFEY, WILLIAM J. (alias Kelly, James V.).
  Acting Assistant Surgeon, 25 March, 1865. Appointment revoked 20 May, 1865.
BROGAN, SAMUEL H.
  Acting Third Assistant Engineer, 26 April, 1864. Resigned 6 June, 1865.
BRONAUGH, WILLIAM V.
  Cadet Midshipman, 5 June, 1873. Graduated 18 June, 1879. Ensign, 30 August, 1881. Lieutenant, Junior Grade, 1 June, 1888. Lieutenant, 27 June, 1893. Lieutenant-Commander, 1 July, 1900.
BRONSON, AMON, Jr.
  Naval Cadet, 30 September, 1892. Second Lieutenant, U. S. Marine Corps, 6 May, 1898. Ensign, 20 May, 1898.
BROOK, L. M.
  Midshipman, 1 January, 1817. Last appearance on Records of Navy Department.
BROOK, PHILIP H.
  Midshipman, 1 May, 1804. Last appearance on Records of Navy Department, May, 1805. Lost.
BROOKE, G. R. A.
  Midshipman, 1 November, 1828. Lost in the Hornet, 10 September, 1829.
BROOKE, JOHN F.
  Surgeon's Mate, 16 May, 1825. Surgeon, 4 November, 1834. Died 17 October, 1849.
BROOKE, JOHN M.
  Midshipman, 3 March, 1841. Passed Midshipman, 10 August, 1847. Master, 14 September, 1855. Lieutenant, 15 September, 1855. Dismissed 20 April, 1861.
BROOKE, SAMUEL.
  Master, 17 October, 1803. Last appearance on Records of Navy Department, 31 August, 1810.
BROOKS, BENJAMIN J.
  Acting Third Assistant Engineer. Died 25 August, 1865.
BROOKS, EDWARD W.
  Acting Third Assistant Engineer, 10 March, 1864. Resigned, 6 June, 1865.
BROOKS, EDWIN C.
  Acting Third Assistant Engineer, 12 January, 1865. Honorably discharged 11 December, 1868.
BROOKS, EDWIN F.
  Acting Ensign, 21 November, 1862. Acting Master, 6 July, 1864. Honorably discharged 20 November, 1865.
BROOKS, EMORY J.
  Third Assistant Engineer, 3 May, 1859. Second Assistant Engineer, 3 October, 1861. First Assistant Engineer, 20 May, 1863. Resigned 7 December, 1868.
BROOKS, ENOCH.
  Acting Master, 18 October, 1861. Resigned 7 February, 1863.
BROOKS, EVERETT W.
  Acting Assistant Paymaster, 12 June, 1863. Honorably discharged 25 October, 1865.
BROOKS, G. H.
  Gunner, 29 October, 1861. Dismissed 29 November, 1862.
BROOKS, HENRY.
  Boatswain, 20 May, 1847. Died 29 June, 1858.
BROOKS, HORACE.
  Mate, 30 March, 1863. Acting Ensign, 12 October, 1864. Honorably discharged 20 August, 1865.
BROOKS, JAMES.
  Chaplain, 28 December, 1818. Resigned 7 January, 1828.

BROOKS, JAMES.
Purser, 7 January, 1828. Dismissed 21 July, 1840.
BROOKS, JOHN.
Midshipman, 2 May, 1836. Passed Midshipman, 1 July, 1842. Died 4 June, 1843.
BROOKS, JOHN.
Acting Third Assistant Engineer, 17 October, 1861. Resigned 18 November, 1865.
BROOKS, JOHN A. J.
Acting Master, 17 February, 1862. Honorably discharged 7 October, 1865.
BROOKS, JOHN F.
Boatswain, 23 September, 1895.
BROOKS, JONATHAN.
Assistant Paymaster (Spanish-American War), 10 June, 1898. Honorably discharged 9 March, 1899. Assistant Paymaster (regular Navy), 22 May, 1899.
BROOKS, NELSON J.
Acting Third Assistant Engineer, 5 February, 1863. Honorably discharged 27 September, 1865.
BROOKS, R. F.
Acting Assistant Surgeon, 23 March, 1864. Acting Passed Assistant Surgeon, 13 October, 1866. Honorably discharged 25 August, 1869.
BROOKS, SAMUEL.
Lieutenant, 13 July, 1799. Discharged under Peace Establishment Act, 8 July, 1801.
BROOKS, SAMUEL A.
Mate, 12 January, 1863. Acting Ensign, 4 December, 1863. Honorably discharged 16 December, 1865. Acting Master, 15 August, 1866. Resigned 26 August, 1867.
BROOKS, SAMUEL R.
Third Assistant Engineer, 21 February, 1861. Second Assistant Engineer, 21 April, 1863. Resigned 13 December, 1865.
BROOKS, THOMAS.
Acting Third Assistant Engineer, 3 April, 1863. Resigned 17 August, 1863.
BROOKS, THOMAS M.
Carpenter, 27 May, 1800. Last appearance on Records of Navy Department.
BROOKS, WILLIAM.
Acting Master, 29 October, 1861. Died May 16, 1863.
BROOKS, WILLIAM.
Boatswain, 4 January, 1897.
BROOKS, WILLIAM B.
Third Assistant Engineer, 16 February, 1852. Second Assistant Engineer, 21 July, 1855. First Assistant Engineer, 21 July, 1858. Chief Engineer, 1 August, 1861. Retired List, 1 March, 1892.
BROOKS, WILLIAM M.
Midshipman, 1 January, 1808. Dismissed 7 April, 1814.
BROOM, JAMES M.
Midshipman, 24 July, 1807. (See Marine Corps.)
BROSE, FREDERICK F.
Midshipman, 9 September, 1847. Passed Midshipman, 10 June, 1853. Died 8 December, 1854.
BROSNAHAN, JOHN G.
Third Assistant Engineer, 11 June, 1862. Second Assistant Engineer, 21 November, 1863. Passed Assistant Engineer, 1 January, 1868. Died 12 January, 1883.
BROTHERTON, WILLIAM D.
Naval Cadet, 6 September, 1887. Ensign, 1 July, 1893. Lieutenant, Junior Grade, 3 March, 1899. Lieutenant, 29 March, 1900.
BROUGHTON, C. H.
Assistant Surgeon, 8 September, 1841. Died 22 December, 1843.
BROUGHTON, REUBEN.
Midshipman, 23 October, 1799. Discharged under Peace Establishment Act, 10 June, 1801.
BROW, WILLIAM.
Midshipman, 20 June, 1799. Resigned 12 September, 1800.
BROW, WILLIAM H.
Acting Third Assistant Engineer, 28 November, 1862. Acting Second Assistant Engineer, 14 January, 1863. Appointment revoked 4 December, 1863.
BROWEN, JOHN.
Gunner, 24 May, 1804. Last appearance on Records of Navy Department, 17 October, 1808. Dead.
BROWER, A. J.
Mate, 14 November, 1861. Appointment revoked 21 February, 1862.
BROWER, EDWARD T.
Acting Midshipman, 28 September, 1858. Lieutenant, 1 August, 1862. Lieutenant-Commander, 25 July, 1866. Died 14 September, 1869.
BROWER, MARCUS.
Acting Master and Pilot, 1 October, 1864. Honorably discharged 17 June, 1865.
BROWER, T. M.
Acting Assistant Paymaster, 9 December, 1861. Died 26 December, 1864.
BROWN, ABRAHAM.
Acting Third Assistant Engineer, 24 July, 1863. Acting Second Assistant Engineer, 18 October, 1864. Honorably discharged 5 January, 1866.
BROWN, ALFRED S.
Third Assistant Engineer, 16 November, 1861. Second Assistant Engineer, 25 August, 1863. Died 17 January, 1867.
BROWN, A. J. D.
Midshipman, 17 November, 1810. Lieutenant, 13 January, 1825. (See Dallas.)

GENERAL NAVY REGISTER.

BROWN, ALBERT D.
Assistant Engineer (Spanish-American War), 1 June, 1898. Honorably discharged 17 February, 1899.

BROWN, ALEXANDER.
Gunner, 27 January, 1820. Last appearance on Records of Navy Department, 9 May, 1820. Dead.

BROWN, ALEXANDER.
Assistant Paymaster (Spanish-American War), 30 April, 1898. Honorably discharged 2 December, 1898.

BROWN, ALLAN D.
Acting Midshipman, 29 September, 1860. Ensign, 28 May, 1863. Master, 10 November, 1865. Lieutenant, 10 November, 1866. Lieutenant-Commander, 12 March, 1868. Commander, 22 January, 1880. Retired List, 24 June, 1891.

BROWN, ANDREW J.
Mate, 14 November, 1861. Dismissed 21 February, 1862.

BROWN, AMOS.
Mate, 14 November, 1861. Resigned 11 March, 1862. Acting Ensign, 4 December, 1862. Resigned 11 November, 1863.

BROWN, ARTHUR K.
Mate, 18 December, 1861. Acting Ensign, 9 February, 1865. Honorably discharged 17 August, 1867.

BROWN, BENJAMIN F.
Acting Assistant Surgeon, 3 August, 1864. Resigned 28 April, 1865.

BROWN, CALVIN.
Civil Engineer, 6 April, 1852. Resigned 8 September, 1864. Reappointed 13 May, 1869. Retired List, 15 October, 1881.

BROWN, CHARLES A.
Mate, 25 January, 1864. Died 5 March, 1867.

BROWN, CHARLES EATON.
Acting Midshipman, 25 July, 1863. Ensign, 18 December, 1868. Lost on board the Oneida, 24 January, 1870.

BROWN, CHARLES F.
Mate, 25 May, 1870. Resigned 7 September, 1871.

BROWN, CHARLES H.
Acting Assistant Paymaster, 23 July, 1862. Dismissed 23 June, 1863.

BROWN, CHARLES H.
Acting Master, 4 November, 1861. Acting Volunteer Lieutenant, 13 May, 1863. Honorably discharged 3 December, 1865.

BROWN, CHARLES R.
Midshipman, 22 September, 1865. Graduated 4 June, 1869. Ensign, 12 July, 1870. Master, 26 October, 1871. Resigned 23 May, 1875.

BROWN, CHARLES WILLIAM.
Acting Third Assistant Engineer, 5 April, 1865. Honorably discharged 19 February, 1866.

BROWN, DANIEL.
Midshipman, 31 January, 1800. Discharged 30 April, 1801.

BROWN, DIXON.
Master, 6 February, 1809. Resigned 25 July, 1810.

BROWN, D. RODNEY.
Mate, 14 October, 1862. Acting Ensign, 16 May, 1863. Acting Master, 9 January, 1865. Honorably discharged 15 September, 1866.

BROWN, ELI.
Midshipman, 9 November, 1813. Last appearance on Records of Navy Department.

BROWN, ELI.
Master, 25 April, 1812. Died in 1820.

BROWN, ELI.
Mate, 31 October, 1861. Deserted.

BROWN, ELIPHOLET.
Acting Ensign, 15 September, 1862. Acting Master, 3 May, 1864. Honorably discharged 17 February, 1866.

BROWN, ENOCH.
Midshipman, 10 July, 1799. Discharged under Peace Establishment Act, 11 July, 1801.

BROWN, ERNEST J.
Mate, 26 August, 1898. Boatswain, 10 April, 1899.

BROWN, FORD H.
Naval Cadet, 17 May, 1883. Ensign, 1 July, 1889. Lieutenant, Junior Grade, 16 September, 1897. Lieutenant, 3 March, 1899.

BROWN, FRANCIS H.
Mate, 29 December, 1863. Acting Ensign, 13 January, 1864. Resigned 15 May, 1865.

BROWN, FRANCIS S.
Acting Midshipman, 24 September, 1856. Midshipman, 15 June, 1860. Master, 19 September, 1861. Lieutenant, 16 July, 1862. Lieutenant-Commander, 25 July, 1866. Resigned 12 October, 1869.

BROWN, FRANK O.
Acting Third Assistant Engineer, 3 March, 1864. Honorably discharged 22 August, 1865.

BROWN, FREDERIC C.
Chaplain, 21 April, 1898.

BROWN, FREDERICK E.
Third Assistant Engineer, 21 November, 1857. Resigned 24 October, 1859. Second Assistant Engineer, 14 June, 1861. Died 12 December, 1864.

BROWN, GEORGE.
Midshipman, 5 February, 1849. Passed Midshipman, 12 June, 1855. Master, 16 September, 1855. Lieutenant, 2 June, 1856. Lieutenant-Commander, 16 July, 1862. Commander, 25 July 1866. Captain, 25 April, 1877. Commodore, 4 September, 1887. Rear-Admiral, 27 September, 1893. Retired List, 19 June, 1897.
BROWN, GEORGE, Jr.
Naval Cadet, 6 September, 1893. Resigned 20 November, 1895. Assistant Paymaster, 15 November, 1897. Passed Assistant Paymaster, 3 March, 1899.
BROWN, GEORGE C.
Acting Third Assistant Engineer, 30 November, 1863. Honorably discharged 5 July, 1865.
BROWN, GEORGE H.
Gunner, 14 February, 1800. Discharged 8 June, 1801.
BROWN, GEORGE H.
Acting Third Assistant Engineer, 24 December, 1863. Honorably discharged 21 August, 1865.
BROWN, GEORGE M.
Acting Midshipman, 25 November, 1859. Ensign, 16 September, 1862. Lieutenant, 22 February, 1864. Lieutenant-Commander, 25 July, 1866. Dismissed, 22 September, 1866.
BROWN, GEORGE W.
Acting Master, 18 July, 1861. Acting Volunteer Lieutenant, 29 January, 1863. Honorably discharged 3 September, 1865.
BROWN, GEORGE W.
Acting Assistant Paymaster, 20 March, 1865. Passed Assistant Paymaster, 23 July, 1866. Died 30 July, 1873.
BROWN, GUSTAVUS.
Midshipman, 2 April, 1804. Resigned 25 March, 1806.
BROWN, GUSTAVUS R.
Surgeon's Mate, 1 March, 1809. Last appearance on records of Navy Department, 1818. Furloughed.
BROWN, GUY W.
Cadet Midshipman, 24 June, 1875. Graduated 22 June, 1882. Ensign, Junior Grade, 3 March, 1883. Ensign, 26 June, 1884. Lieutenant, Junior Grade, 16 April, 1894. Lieutenant, 26 September, 1897.
BROWN, HAWLEY.
Acting Third Assistant Engineer, 22 January, 1863. Honorably discharged 24 September, 1869.
BROWN, HENRY.
Third Assistant Engineer, 17 February, 1860. Second Assistant Engineer, 1 November, 1861. First Assistant Engineer, 1 March, 1864. Resigned 3 March, 1869.
BROWN, HENRY.
Acting Master, 26 August, 1861. Acting Volunteer Lieutenant, 6 January, 1864. Honorably discharged 28 February, 1866.
BROWN, HENRY A.
Acting Third Assistant Engineer, 27 February, 1864. Resigned 13 May, 1864.
BROWN, HENRY B.
Acting Assistant Paymaster, 15 May, 1863. Honorably discharged 27 October, 1865.
BROWN, HERBERT A.
Acting Third Assistant Engineer, 8 June, 1864. Honorably discharged 16 August, 1865.
BROWN, HEZEKIAH G. D.
Midshipman, 19 February, 1841. Resigned 28 December, 1847.
BROWN, HORACE F.
Acting Third Assistant Engineer, 30 September, 1862. Acting Second Assistant Engineer, 7 March, 1865. Honorably discharged 14 November, 1865.
BROWN, H. G. D.
Midshipman, 19 February, 1841. Resigned 28 December, 1847.
BROWN, HORACE S.
Acting Third Assistant Engineer, 10 September, 1863. Honorably discharged 11 October, 1865.
BROWN, ISAAC H.
Mate, 8 March, 1864. Honorably discharged 30 September, 1865.
BROWN, ISAAC N.
Midshipman, 15 March, 1834. Passed Midshipman, 6 July, 1840. Master, 15 August, 1846. Lieutenant, 31 October, 1846. Dismissed 25 April, 1861.
BROWN, ISAAC T.
Mate, 21 October, 1861. Resigned 28 September, 1864.
BROWN, JAMES.
Acting Master, 28 February, 1862. Resigned 5 August, 1863.
BROWN, JAMES.
Mate, 26 June, 1863. Acting Ensign, 1 May, 1864. Honorably discharged 21 September, 1865.
BROWN, JAMES.
Acting Ensign, 30 September, 1864. Honorably discharged 7 November, 1865.
BROWN, JAMES.
Boatswain, 4 January, 1862. Retired List, 22 October, 1872. Died 6 June, 1879.
BROWN, JAMES A.
Acting Third Assistant Engineer, 2 November, 1861. Acting Second Assistant Engineer, 25 August, 1862. Acting First Assistant Engineer, 6 January, 1865. Honorably discharged 10 December, 1865.
BROWN, JAMES E.
Midshipman, 1 December, 1827. Passed Midshipman, 14 June, 1834. Lieutenant, 25 February, 1841. Died 3 September, 1844.

BROWN, JAMES G.
Acting Third Assistant Engineer, 9 August, 1864. Resigned 13 April, 1865.
BROWN, JAMES H. H.
Chaplain, 23 January, 1874. Resigned 1 November, 1884.
BROWN, JAMES S.
Cadet Midshipman, 18 September, 1875. Midshipman, 22 June, 1882. Ensign, Junior Grade, 3 March, 1883. Ensign, 26 June, 1884. Resigned, 10 February, 1889. Lieutenant, Junior Grade (Spanish-American War), 26 May, 1898. Honorably discharged, 3 October, 1898.
BROWN, JAMES W.
Mate, 25 May, 1863. Acting Ensign, 8 March, 1864. Honorably discharged 27 October, 1865.
BROWN, JASON P.
Acting Third Assistant Engineer, 12 April, 1865. Honorably discharged 10 June, 1866.
BROWN, JEFFERSON.
Third Assistant Engineer, 17 December, 1862. Second Assistant Engineer, 8 April, 1864. Passed Assistant Engineer, 1 January, 1868. Chief Engineer, 19 November, 1890. Retired List, 2 August, 1892.
BROWN, JOHN.
Midshipman, 13 December, 1800. Discharged 30 April, 1801.
BROWN, JOHN.
Surgeon's Mate, 11 August, 1807. Surgeon, 3 March, 1809. Resigned 4 July, 1809.
BROWN, JOHN.
Master, 24 January, 1809. Last appearance on Records of Navy Department, 23 March, 1809. Lost.
BROWN, JOHN.
Acting Carpenter, 29 July, 1848. Died 30 September, 1849.
BROWN, JOHN.
Acting Gunner. Appointment revoked 23 September, 1864.
BROWN, JOHN.
Acting Ensign and Pilot, 1 January, 1865. Honorably discharged 14 September, 1865.
BROWN, JOHN G.
Mate, 14 April, 1862. Died at Rockland, Maine, 27 November, 1864.
BROWN, JOHN H.
Mate, 24 February, 1865. Boatswain, 25 May, 1877. Retired List, 14 June, 1895.
BROWN, JOHN H.
Ensign (Spanish-American War), 25 May, 1898. Honorably discharged 3 September, 1898.
BROWN, JOHN HOGAN.
Midshipman, 1 July, 1836. Passed Midshipman, 1 July, 1842. Master, 24 July, 1849. Lieutenant, 19 February, 1850. Died 10 May, 1861.
BROWN, JOHN L.
Carpenter, 28 September, 1816. Died 28 March, 1824.
BROWN, JOHN L.
Acting Ensign, 17 December, 1863. Honorably discharged 21 December, 1868.
BROWN, JOHN W.
Acting Master, 29 June, 1861. Appointment revoked 12 July, 1862.
BROWN, JOSEPH.
Midshipman, 25 September, 1798. Resigned 12 December, 1799.
BROWN, JOSEPH.
Mate, 24 January, 1863. Resigned 8 April, 1863.
BROWN, JOSEPH.
Mate, 25 April, 1864. Appointment revoked (sick) 8 October, 1864.
BROWN, JOSEPH R.
Midshipman, 10 July, 1819. Passed Midshipman, 14 June, 1834. Died 25 August, 1836.
BROWN, JOSEPH S.
Acting Ensign, 23 March, 1864. Resigned 16 June, 1865.
BROWN, LAFAYETTE J.
Purser, 26 March, 1860. Retired List, 15 September, 1863. Died 29 July, 1864.
BROWN, LATHAM A.
Acting Master, 22 January, 1862. Honorably discharged 19 September, 1865.
BROWN, LEWIS A.
Acting Master, 13 September, 1861. Honorably discharged 18 February, 1866.
BROWN, LOUIS H.
Mate, 21 January, 1864. Honorably discharged 26 September, 1865.
BROWN, MATTHEW.
Carpenter, 14 April, 1800. Last appearance on Records of Navy Department, 1 June, 1803.
BROWN, MORRIS H.
Naval Cadet, 19 May, 1894. Ensign, 4 April, 1900.
BROWN, MOSES.
Captain, 15 September, 1798. Discharged under Peace Establishment Act, 3 April, 1801.
BROWN, NATHAN.
Acting Third Assistant Engineer, 20 October, 1863. Resigned 1 March, 1865.
BROWN, NATHAN.
Mate, 10 November, 1864. Deserted 2 July, 1866.
BROWN, NATHAN T.
Mate, 10 December, 1863. Honorably discharged 5 November, 1865.

GENERAL NAVY REGISTER. 83

BROWN, NEWELL W.
Acting Third Assistant Engineer, 2 February, 1865. Honorably discharged 27 October, 1865.
BROWN, PETER.
Gunner, 30 October, 1812. Dismissed 20 February, 1813.
BROWN, ROBERT E.
Acting Second Assistant Engineer, 21 December, 1861. Resigned 5 July, 1862.
BROWN, ROBERT JAMES.
Midshipman, 20 November, 1850. Resigned 6 November, 1855.
BROWN, ROBERT M. G.
Midshipman, 22 July, 1864. Graduated 2 June, 1868. Ensign, 19 April, 1869. Master, 12 July, 1870. Lieutenant, 13 April, 1872. Lieutenant-Commander, 27 April, 1893. Retired List, 5 December, 1894.
BROWN, ROBERT R.
Master, 24 April, 1812. Resigned 27 January, 1813.
BROWN, ROBERT W.
Mate, 22 April, 1863. Acting Ensign, 1 January, 1864. Honorably discharged 22 November, 1865.
BROWN, ROWLAND B.
Acting Ensign, 18 April, 1864. Acting Master, 5 April, 1865. Honorably discharged 13 July, 1867.
BROWN, SAMUEL.
Carpenter, 18 December, 1816. Dismissed 10 November, 1824.
BROWN, SAMUEL A.
Assistant Surgeon, 21 November, 1871. Passed Assistant Surgeon, 19 June, 1875. Resigned 7 October, 1884.
BROWN, SAMUEL T.
Acting Assistant Paymaster, 30 September, 1862. Assistant Paymaster, 9 March, 1865. Passed Assistant Paymaster, 4 May, 1866. Paymaster, 22 March, 1867. Died 15 June, 1881.
BROWN, S. H.
Acting Assistant Surgeon, 18 December, 1861. Dismissed 23 July, 1863.
BROWN, STEPHEN T.
Acting Assistant Paymaster, 17 March, 1863. Resigned 20 December, 1864.
BROWN, STIMSON J.
Midshipman, 21 September, 1872. Graduated 20 June, 1876. Ensign, 25 November, 1877. Professor, 13 October, 1883.
BROWN, T. BENTON.
Acting Third Assistant Engineer, 24 December, 1863. Honorably discharged 16 August, 1866.
BROWN, THEODORE E.
Mate, 4 April, 1862. Resigned 13 June, 1863.
BROWN, THEODORE J.
Acting Third Assistant Engineer, 3 December, 1861. Deserted 13 February, 1863.
BROWN, THOMAS.
Midshipman, 27 April, 1801. Lieutenant, 27 March, 1807. Commander, 1 March, 1815. Captain, 3 March, 1825. Died 28 November, 1828.
BROWN, THOMAS.
Mate, 4 March, 1863. Acting Ensign, 17 January, 1865. Honorably discharged 15 December, 1865.
BROWN, THOMAS H.
Midshipman, 7 November, 1813. Last appearance on Records of Navy Department, 12 September, 1815.
BROWN, THOMAS H.
Mate, 4 December, 1862. Deserted 20 December, 1862.
BROWN, THOMAS R.
Assistant Surgeon, 27 April, 1866. Resigned 22 June, 1870.
BROWN, THOMAS S.
Midshipman, 27 December, 1810. Lieutenant, 13 January, 1825. Died 6 September, 1826.
BROWN, THOMAS W.
Boatswain, 21 November, 1873. Retired List, 18 February, 1885. Died 5 April, 1885.
BROWN, WILLIAM.
Midshipman, 9 July, 1811. Resigned 3 November, 1813.
BROWN, WILLIAM.
Gunner, 4 February, 1809. Last appearance on Records of Navy Department.
BROWN, WILLIAM.
Boatswain, 27 June, 1810. Resigned in January, 1811.
BROWN, WILLIAM.
Boatswain, 29 August, 1831. Dismissed 3 November, 1840.
BROWN, WILLIAM.
Acting Third Assistant Engineer, 23 September, 1861. Dismissed 4 June, 1862.
BROWN, WILLIAM.
Mate, 21 November, 1861. Appointment revoked 22 January, 1862.
BROWN, WILLIAM.
Acting Third Assistant Engineer. Died 17 October, 1863.
BROWN, WILLIAM.
Honorary Acting Ensign, without pay, 28 August, 1863. Resigned 16 June, 1865.
BROWN, WILLIAM.
Acting Third Assistant Engineer, 14 October, 1864. Honorably discharged 3 December, 1865.
BROWN, WILLIAM B.
Gunner, 9 December, 1825. Died 25 October, 1851.

BROWN, WILLIAM B.
Midshipman, 19 October, 1841. Died 11 August, 1843.
BROWN, WILLIAM G.
Acting Third Assistant Engineer, 19 January, 1864. Honorably discharged 18 **July,** 1865.
BROWN, WILLIAM H.
Midshipman, 1 January, 1828. Passed Midshipman, 14 June. 1834. Lieutenant, 25 February, 1841. Resigned 25 February, 1851.
BROWN, WILLIAM H.
Midshipman, 1 April, 1826. Resigned 4 April, 1831.
BROWN, WILLIAM H.
Acting Third Assistant Engineer, 3 January, 1863. Resigned 16 January, 1865.
BROWN, WILLIAM H.
Acting Third Assistant Engineer, 5 February, 1863. Acting Second Assistant Engineer, 17 March, 1864. Dismissed 6 September, 1865.
BROWN, WILLIAM H.
Mate, 8 December, 1863. Acting Ensign, 11 January, 1865. Honorably discharged 29 November, 1865.
BROWN, W. ROBERTS.
Acting Third Assistant Engineer, August, 1864. Appointment revoked (sick) 14 February, 1865.
BROWN, WILLIAM S.
Acting Third Assistant Engineer, 5 January, 1864. Honorably discharged 15 May, 1865.
BROWN, WYATT M.
Assistant Surgeon, 27 November, 1854. Resigned 11 November, 1858.
BROWN, ZACHARIAH TAYLOR.
Assistant Paymaster, 13 July, 1870. Passed Assistant Paymaster, 15 June, 1878. Died 29 August, 1883.
BROWNE, B. FRANK.
Acting Assistant Paymaster, 4 September, 1863. Died 6 June, 1864.
BROWNE, GEORGE W.
Acting Volunteer Lieutenant, 26 August, 1861. Disrated 14 May, 1862, to Acting Master. Appointment revoked (sick) 18 April, 1864.
BROWNE, JOHN M.
Assistant Surgeon, 26 March, 1853. Passed Assistant Surgeon. 13 May, 1858. Surgeon, 19 June, 1861. Medical Inspector. 1 December, 1871. Medical Director, 6 October, 1878. Retired List, 11 May, 1893. Died 7 December, 1894.
BROWNE, P. H.
Mate, 26 November, 1862. Resigned 10 March, 1863.
BROWNE, RICHARD P.
Assistant Engineer (Spanish-American War), 20 May, 1898. Honorably discharged 26 September, 1898.
BROWNE, SAMUEL T.
Acting Assistant Paymaster, 30 September, 1862. Assistant Paymaster, 9 March, 1865. Passed Assistant Paymaster, 4 May, 1866. Paymaster, 22 March, 1867. Died 15 June, 1881.
BROWNE, SYMMES E.
Acting Ensign, 1 October, 1862. Resigned 31 May, 1864.
BROWNE, W. B.
Acting Ensign, 2 December, 1864. Honorably discharged 27 September, 1865.
BROWNE, WILLIAM F.
Acting Assistant Surgeon, 25 November, 1861. Appointment revoked 6 **October,** 1863.
BROWNE, WILLIAM R.
Acting Master, 13 May, 1861. Resigned 20 November, 1861. Acting Volunteer Lieutenant, 5 February, 1864. Honorably discharged 16 September, 1865.
BROWNELL, CARL D.
Assistant Surgeon, 6 April, 1891. Passed Assistant Surgeon, 6 April, 1895.
BROWNELL, GIDEON V.
Mate, 20 January, 1865. Honorably discharged 6 March, 1868.
BROWNELL, HENRY H.
Mate, 29 December, 1863. Acting Ensign, 1 March, 1864. Acting Ensign, 7 May, 1867. Mustered out 18 November, 1868.
BROWNELL, THOMAS.
Master, 30 October, 1840. Lieutenant, 26 December, 1843. Reserved List. 26 December, 1843. Captain on Retired List, 4 April, 1867. Died 5 January, 1872.
BROWNELL, WILLIAM P.
Mate, 14 July, 1864. Resigned 21 February, 1865.
BROWNING. OWEN F.
Acting Assistant Paymaster, 4 November, 1862. Resigned 20 February, 1865.
BROWNING, R. L., Jr.
Midshipman, 8 February, 1834. Resigned 26 August, 1836.
BROWNING, ROBERT L.
Midshipman. 4 March, 1823. Passed Midshipman, 23 March, 1829. Lieutenant, 21 June, 1832. Drowned 27 March, 1850.
BROWNING, WILLIAM A.
Surgeon's Mate. 24 January, 1825. Dropped in 1826.
BROWNLEE, JAMES J.
Assistant Surgeon, 20 June, 1838. Passed Assistant Surgeon. 22 November, **1840.** Surgeon, 19 October, 1852. Resigned 31 August, 1855.
BROWNLEE, J. J.
Acting Assistant Surgeon, 21 October, 1861. Resigned 27 April. 1864.

GENERAL NAVY REGISTER. 85

BROWNLEE, JOHN J.
  Acting Assistant Surgeon, 30 October, 1861. Resigned 29 April, 1864.
BROWNING, J. D.
  Surgeon's Mate, 13 March, 1805. Resigned 10 September, 1807.
BROWNRIDGE, GEORGE T.
  Acting Warrant Machinist, 23 August, 1899.
BROWNSON, WILLARD H.
  Acting Midshipman, 29 November, 1861. Graduated September, 1865. Ensign, 1 December, 1866. Master, 12 March, 1868. Lieutenant, 26 March, 1869. Lieutenant-Commander, 14 December, 1880. Commander, 19 May, 1891. Captain, 3 March, 1899.
BRUCE, DAVID.
  Sailmaker, 25 October, 1844. Retired List, 9 August, 1876. Died 26 November, 1898.
BRUCE, HENRY.
  Midshipman, 9 November, 1813. Lieutenant, 13 January, 1825. Commander, 8 September, 1841. Reserved List, 13 September, 1855. Commodore, Retired List, 4 April, 1867. Died 9 February, 1895.
BRUCE, JAMES.
  Midshipman, 12 October, 1848. Passed Midshipman, 15 June, 1854. Dropped 28 September, 1855.
BRUCE, LEWIS E.
  Acting Gunner, 10 March, 1900.
BRUCE, W. G.
  Acting Assistant Surgeon, 6 April, 1863. Resigned 29 September, 1864.
BRUCKNER, RUDOLPH E.
  Assistant Engineer (Spanish-American War), 22 June, 1898. Honorably discharged 28 October, 1898.
BRUFF, THOMAS O.
  Midshipman, 30 November, 1818. Died 9 January, 1822.
BRUM, PHILIP.
  Master, 15 February, 1813. Dismissed 29 April, 1817.
BRUMBACK, BENJAMIN H.
  Mate, 21 May, 1864. Honorably discharged 24 October, 1865.
BRUMBY, FRANK H.
  Naval Cadet, 8 September, 1891. Ensign, 1 July, 1897. Lieutenant, Junior Grade, 1 July, 1900.
BRUMBY, THOMAS M.
  Cadet Midshipman, 27 September, 1873. Graduated 18 June, 1879. Ensign, 26 November, 1880. Lieutenant, Junior Grade, 21 April, 1887. Lieutenant, 24 August, 1892. Died 17 December, 1899.
BRUMMAGE, SAMUEL R.
  Acting First Assistant Engineer, 4 February, 1864. Honorably discharged, 5 November, 1865.
BRUNER, ELIAS D.
  Acting Master, 25 July, 1861. Acting Volunteer Lieutenant, 29 March, 1864. Honorably discharged 25 January, 1866. Acting Master, 15 August, 1866. Resigned 26 April, 1869.
BRUNS, CHRISTOPHER L.
  Midshipman, 1 July, 1867. Graduated 6 June, 1871. Ensign, 14 July, 1872. Master, 30 September, 1876. Lieutenant, Junior Grade, 3 March, 1883. Retired List, 15 January, 1884.
BRUSH, GEORGE R.
  Assistant Surgeon, 3 September, 1861. Passed Assistant Surgeon, 24 January, 1862. Surgeon, 10 February, 1872. Medical Inspector, 28 November, 1889. Died 29 November, 1894.
BRYAN, BENJAMIN.
  Midshipman, 1 January, 1812. Last appearance on Records of Navy Department.
BRYAN, BENJAMIN C.
  Cadet Engineer, 15 September, 1875. Graduated 10 June, 1879. Assistant Engineer, 10 June, 1881. Passed Assistant Engineer, 3 October, 1891. Chief Engineer, 20 January, 1899. Rank changed to Lieutenant, 3 March, 1899.
BRYAN, DANIEL L.
  Assistant Surgeon, 13 October, 1840. Passed Assistant Surgeon, 12 February, 1850. Died 14 September, 1853.
BRYAN, HENRY F.
  Naval Cadet, 2 May, 1883. Ensign, 1 July, 1889. Lieutenant, Junior Grade, 19 June, 1897. Lieutenant, 3 March, 1899.
BRYAN, T. E.
  Mate. Appointment revoked 29 January, 1862.
BRYAN, F. L.
  Mate, 25 January, 1870. Died on board Colorado, 6 January, 1871.
BRYAN, HENRY W.
  Mate, 22 April, 1863. Resigned 25 August, 1863.
BRYAN, JOHN R.
  Midshipman, 4 October, 1823. Passed Midshipman, 23 March, 1829. Resigned 5 September, 1831.
BRYAN, JOSEPH.
  Purser, 1 September, 1836. Resigned 31 May, 1854.
BRYAN, JOSEPH H.
  Assistant Surgeon, 6 July, 1880. Resigned 10 April, 1885.
BRYAN, LLOYD J.
  Midshipman, 1 January, 1828. Passed Midshipman, 14 June, 1834. Cashiered 4 December, 1838.

BRYAN, SAMUEL.
  Cadet Midshipman, 24 June, 1876. Honorably discharged 30 June, 1883. Assistant Paymaster, 14 March, 1898. Passed Assistant Paymaster, 3 March, 1899.
BRYANT, BENJAMIN.
  Master, 15 April, 1812. Resigned 20 July, 1813.
BRYANT, CHARLES R.
  Acting Ensign, 8 November, 1862. Resigned 18 August, 1863.
BRYANT, CHARLES W.
  Mate, 25 July, 1864. Resigned 20 August, 1866.
BRYANT, HENRY.
  Lieutenant, Junior Grade (Spanish-American War), 24 May, 1898. Honorably discharged, 20 December, 1898.
BRYANT, JOHN L.
  Acting Ensign, 17 December, 1862. Acting Master, 19 February, 1864. Honorably discharged 5 February, 1868.'
BRYANT, JOHN V.
  Acting Master, 21 December, 1861. Appointment revoked 22 January, 1862.
BRYANT, JOSHUA.
  Boatswain, 7 March, 1836. Appointment revoked 18 February, 1846.
BRYANT, LEON.
  Mate, 19 February, 1863. Honorably discharged 10 March, 1866.
BRYANT, NATHANIEL C.
  Midshipman, 23 December, 1837. Passed Midshipman, 29 June, 1843. Acting Master, 13 June, 1850. Lieutenant, 7 August, 1850. Commander, 16 July, 1862. Retired List. Died 19 September, 1874.
BRYANT, PATRICK H.
  Assistant Surgeon, 3 November, 1888. Passed Assistant Surgeon, 3 November, 1891. Died 26 December, 1896.
BRYANT, ROBERT.
  Midshipman, 11 December, 1847. Resigned 6 May, 1850.
BRYANT, SAMUEL W.
  Naval Cadet, 5 September, 1896. Graduated 30 June, 1900.
BRYANT, SETH H.
  Mate, 29 December, 1863. Resigned 13 May, 1865.
BRYANT, SOLON A.
  Acting Third Assistant Engineer, 17 August, 1863. Honorably discharged 2 December, 1865.
BRYANT, WILLIAM H.
  Mate, 11 October, 1861. Acting Ensign, 4 September, 1863. Honorably discharged 8 October, 1868.
BRYDEN, JAMES.
  Midshipman, 9 July, 1800. Lost in the Insurgent.
BRYER, S. G.
  Acting Ensign, 2 June, 1864. Resigned 12 April, 1865.
BRYSON, ANDREW.
  Midshipman, 1 December, 1837. Passed Midshipman, 29 June, 1843. Master, 30 January, 1851. Lieutenant, 30 August, 1851. Commander, 16 July, 1862. Captain, 25 July, 1866. Commodore, 14 February, 1873. Rear-Admiral, 25 March, 1880. Retired List, 30 January, 1883. Died 7 February, 1892.
BUBIER, JOHN.
  Midshipman, 9 November, 1813. Lieutenant, 13 January, 1825. Commander, 8 September, 1841. Resigned 3 June, 1850.
BUBIER, S. C. V.
  Mate, 11 April, 1865. Died 1 November, 1865.
BUCHAN, JOHN R.
  Ensign (Spanish-American War), 18 July, 1898. Honorably discharged, 8 October, 1898.
BUCHANAN, ALLEN.
  Naval Cadet, 6 September, 1895. At sea prior to final graduation.
BUCHANAN, FRANKLIN.
  Midshipman, 28 January, 1815. Lieutenant, 13 January, 1825. Commander, 8 September, 1841. Captain, 14 September, 1855. Dismissed 22 May, 1861.
BUCHANAN, J. L.
  Midshipman, 30 December, 1820. Resigned 2 November, 1821.
BUCHANAN, JOHN.
  Midshipman, 1 July, 1828. Resigned 19 October, 1832.
BUCHANAN, L. A.
  Midshipman, 1 March, 1825. Died 27 July, 1825.
BUCHANAN, McKEAN.
  Purser, 21 August, 1826. Died 18 March, 1871.
BUCHANAN, THOMAS McK.
  Acting Midshipman, 1 October, 1851. Midshipman, 9 June, 1855. Passed Midshipman, 15 April, 1858. Master, 4 November, 1858. Lieutenant, 18 July, 1860. Lieutenant-Commander, 5 August, 1862. Died 14 January, 1863.
BUCHANAN, T. M.
  Midshipman, 3 November, 1818. Lieutenant, 3 March, 1827. Dismissed 20 October, 1832.
BUCHANAN, W. W.
  Surgeon, 6 October, 1800. Discharged 4 August, 1801, under Peace Establishment Act.
BUCHANAN, W. W.
  Surgeon, 24 July, 1818. Resigned 8 December, 1827.

GENERAL NAVY REGISTER.   87

BUCHANAN, WILSON W.
   Cadet Midshipman, 25 June, 1875. Graduated 22 June, 1882. Ensign, Junior Grade, 3 March, 1883. Ensign, 26 June, 1884. Lieutenant, Junior Grade, 27 June, 1893. Lieutenant, 29 January, 1897.

BUCHER, WILLIAM H.
   Assistant Surgeon, 5 April, 1898.

BUCK, ALONZO P.
   Midshipman, 2 February, 1829. Resigned 26 September, 1831.

BUCK, CHARLES H.
   Acting Ensign, 12 October, 1864. Honorably discharged 15 September, 1865.

BUCK, CHARLES W.
   Acting Master, 5 July, 1862. Honorably discharged 13 February, 1866.

BUCK, GUY M.
   Cadet Midshipman, 22 September, 1877. Graduated. Honorably discharged 30 June, 1883. Lieutenant (Spanish-American War), 29 April, 1898. Honorably discharged 12 April, 1899.

BUCK, ISAAC.
   Acting Third Assistant Engineer, 9 June, 1862. Acting Second Assistant Engineer, 11 May, 1865. Honorably discharged 21 August, 1865.

BUCK, JAMES.
   Mate, 30 July, 1862. Died 1 November, 1865.

BUCK, JOSEPH W.
   Mate, 6 December, 1862. Deserted 29 February, 1864.

BUCK, JOSHUA W.
   Acting Third Assistant Engineer, 10 October, 1862. Dismissed 14 October, 1864.

BUCK, NICHOLAS.
   Acting Sailmaker, 6 September, 1839. Died 16 June, 1848.

BUCK, RICHARDSON.
   Midshipman, 1 January, 1812. Resigned 25 January, 1815.

BUCK, WILLIAM F.
   Acting Third Assistant Engineer, 4 June, 1864. Appointment revoked 1 September, 1864.

BUCK, WILLIAM H.
   Naval Cadet, 22 May, 1886. Ensign, 1 July, 1892. Lieutenant, Junior Grade, 3 March, 1899. Lieutenant, 25 March, 1899.

BUCK, WILLIAM T.
   Mate, 22 March, 1862. Acting Master, 26 May, 1862. Ensign, 12 March, 1868. Master, 18 December, 1868. Lieutenant, 21 March, 1870. Died 20 July, 1874.

BUCKELEW, CHARLES H.
   Acting Second Assistant Engineer, 17 August, 1864. Honorably discharged 22 September, 1865.

BUCKHOLDT, W.
   Acting Master, 26 August, 1861. Appointment revoked 31 July, 1863.

BUCKHONT, NATHAN W.
   Third Assistant Engineer, 28 October, 1862. Second Assistant Engineer, 15 March, 1864. Resigned 29 June, 1865.

BUCKINGHAM, BENJAMIN H.
   Midshipman, 21 July, 1865. Graduated 4 June, 1869. Ensign 12 July, 1870. Master, 12 July, 1871. Lieutenant, 23 July, 1874. Lieutenant-Commander, 28 February, 1896. Retired List, 5 October, 1898.

BUCKINGHAM, N. N.
   Acting Second Assistant Engineer, 17 May, 1861. Died 29 June, 1864.

BUCKLESS, HENRY.
   Acting Master and Pilot, 1 February, 1865. Appointment revoked 2 June, 1865.

BUCKLEY, JAMES.
   Acting Third Assistant Engineer, 20 September, 1862. Dismissed 30 April, 1864.

BUCKLEY, JOHN T.
   Acting Third Assistant Engineer, 23 November, 1861. Honorably discharged 31 March, 1868.

BUCKLEY, JOSEPH D.
   Acting Ensign, 10 December, 1862. Honorably discharged 25 November, 1865.

BUCKLEY, THOMAS.
   Mate, 2 November, 1862. Dismissed 9 May, 1864.

BUCKLEY, WILLIAM N.
   Acting Third Assistant Engineer, 19 October, 1864. Honorably discharged 31 July, 1865.

BUCKMAN, ALBION.
   Acting Third Assistant Engineer, 3 November, 1863. Acting Second Assistant Engineer, 6 January, 1865. Honorably discharged 8 August, 1865. Acting Second Assistant Engineer, 20 November, 1866. Mustered out 14 May, 1868.

BUCKNER, G. D.
   Acting Assistant Surgeon, 5 April, 1864. Honorably discharged 20 December, 1865.

BUCKNER, WILLIAM P.
   Midshipman, 9 September, 1841. Passed Midshipman, 10 August, 1847. Master, 1 March, 1855. Lieutenant, 14 September, 1855. Retired List, 4 September, 1862. Commander, Retired List, 4 April, 1867. Died 18 July, 1869.

BUDD, CHARLES A.
   Midshipman, 22 November, 1805. Lieutenant, 18 June, 1814. Died 15 March, 1827.

BUDD, GEORGE.
   Midshipman, 22 November, 1805. Lieutenant, 23 May, 1812. Commander, 28 March, 1820. Died 3 September, 1837.

BUDD, SAMUEL P.
   Third Assistant Engineer, 8 September, 1863. Resigned 10 August, 1867.

BUDD, THOMAS A.
Midshipman, 2 February, 1829. Passed Midshipman, 3 July, 1835. Lieutenant, 8 September, 1841. Resigned 29 April, 1853. Acting Lieutenant, 13 May, 1861. Killed in action 22 March, 1862.
BUDD, WILLIAM.
Acting Master, 17 May, 1861. Acting Volunteer Lieutenant, 9 May, 1862. Acting Volunteer Lieutenant-Commander, 5 November, 1864. Honorably discharged 6 January, 1866. Acting Master, 14 November, 1867. Mustered out 25 June, 1868.
BUDSON, JOSEPH.
Mate, 16 March, 1865. Honorably discharged 4 October, 1865.
BUEHLER, WILLIAM G.
Third Assistant Engineer, 21 November, 1857. Second Assistant Engineer, 8 October, 1861. First Assistant Engineer, 6 October, 1862. Chief Engineer, 10 November, 1863. Rank changed to Captain 3 March, 1899. Retired List, with rank of Rear-Admiral, 25 March, 1899.
BUEL, RICHARD H.
Third Assistant Engineer, 8 July, 1862. Second Assistant Engineer, 15 February, 1864. Resigned 8 July, 1867.
BUEL, W. F.
Mate. Appointment revoked 2 February, 1864.
BUELL, JAMES W.
Acting Third Assistant Engineer, 18 June, 1864. Dismissed 31 May, 1865.
BUELL, JAMES W.
Assistant Surgeon, 20 November, 1872. Resigned 1 September, 1876.
BUELL, JEREMIAH.
Gunner, 16 August, 1841. Dismissed 6 July, 1842.
BUELL, SALMON A.
Midshipman, 1 February, 1847. Resigned 5 August, 1850. . .
BUFFINGTON, WILLIAM J.
Acting First Assistant Engineer, 23 October, 1862. Acting Chief Engineer, 25 June, 1864. Honorably discharged 4 December, 1865.
BUFFINTON, GEORGE R. H.
Lieutenant (Spanish-American War), 23 April, 1898. Resigned 1 August, 1898.
BUFORD, MARCUS B.
Acting Midshipman, 9 October, 1861. Graduated September, 1865. Ensign, 1 December, 1866. Master, 12 March, 1868. Lieutenant, 26 March, 1869. Lieutenant-Commander, 14 September, 1881. Resigned 1 January, 1888. Lieutenant-Commander (Spanish-American War), 12 May, 1898. Honorably discharged 7 January, 1899.
BUHNER, ALBERT.
Mate, 20 November, 1861. Acting Ensign, 8 April, 1863. Acting Master, 4 August, 1865. Honorably discharged 13 July, 1866.
BULKLEY, CHARLES.
Midshipman, 31 October, 1799. Discharged under Peace Establishment Act, 10 July, 1801.
BULKLEY, HENRY W.
Third Assistant Engineer, 25 August, 1862. Second Assistant Engineer, 20 February, 1864. Resigned 14 October, 1865.
BULKLEY, J. HENRY.
Acting Assistant Paymaster, 4 November, 1862. Discharged 29 October, 1865. Passed Assistant Paymaster, 23 July, 1866. Paymaster, 13 April, 1869. Died 17 January, 1873.
BULKLEY, JONATHAN.
Midshipman, 2 January, 1800. Discharged 10 July, 1801, under Peace Establishment Act.
BULKLEY, WILLIAM F.
Midshipman, 25 July, 1865. Graduated 4 June, 1869. Ensign, 12 July, 1871. Master, 2 July, 1873. Resigned 30 June, 1878.
BULL, BENJAMIN S.
Acting Third Assistant Engineer, 23 February, 1863. Acting Second Assistant Engineer, 26 October, 1863. Honorably discharged 1 December, 1865.
BULL, CORNELIUS W.
Acting Assistant Paymaster, 15 April, 1864. Discharged 18 October, 1865.
BULL, FREDERICK, Jr.
Third Assistant Engineer, 29 July, 1861. Second Assistant Engineer, 20 May, 1863. Died 9 August, 1863.
BULL, GEORGE H.
Acting Assistant Surgeon, 17 April, 1865. Resigned 30 June, 1865.
BULL, GOOLD H.
Cadet Engineer, 1 October, 1874. Graduated 20 June, 1878. Assistant Engineer, 20 June, 1880. Resigned 29 June, 1889. Passed Assistant Engineer (Spanish-American War), 23 April, 1898. Chief Engineer, 24 June, 1898. Honorably discharged 24 December, 1898.
BULL, JAMES H.
Midshipman, 25 July, 1866. Graduated 7 June, 1870. Ensign, 13 July, 1871. Master, 3 October, 1874. Lieutenant, 22 April, 1881. Lieutenant-Commander, 3 March, 1899.
BULL, WILLIAM R.
Gunner, 11 May, 1799. Resigned 20 January, 1800.
BULLARD, ALBERT F.
Acting Third Assistant Engineer, 6 July, 1863. Honorably discharged 6 January, 1866.

GENERAL NAVY REGISTER. 89

BULLARD, JOEL A.
  Third Assistant Engineer, 22 July, 1862. Second Assistant Engineer, 15 February, 1864. Died 22 March, 1866.
BULLARD, JOSEPH A.
  Mate, 30 January, 1863. Acting Ensign, 31 August, 1863. Acting Master, 15 December, 1864. Honorably discharged 26 August, 1865.
BULLARD, WILLIAM H. G.
  Naval Cadet, 28 September, 1882. Ensign, 1 July, 1888. Lieutenant, Junior Grade, 5 September, 1896. Lieutenant, 3 March, 1899.
BULLAS, JOSEPH W.
  Gunner, 1 April, 1895. Died 21 August, 1899.
BULLAY, HENRY J.
  Acting Assistant Paymaster, 18 October, 1861. Resigned 14 December, 1864.
BULLEN, SAMUEL.
  Midshipman, 3 July, 1779. Discharged under Peace Establishment Act, 12 October, 1801.
BULLIS, JOHN.
  Surgeon's Mate, 9 March, 1798. Surgeon, 20 July, 1799. Last appearance on Records of Navy Department.
BULLIS, WILLIAM H.
  Acting Ensign, 15 October, 1862. Acting Master, 10 September, 1863. Appointment revoked 26 January, 1864. Acting Ensign, 18 June, 1864. Honorably discharged 27 September, 1865.
BULLOCH, JAMES D.
  Midshipman, 21 June, 1839. Passed Midshipman, 2 July, 1845. Master, 7 January, 1853. Lieutenant, 18 October, 1853. Resigned 5 October, 1854.
BULLOCK, CHARLES H.
  Acting Boatswain, 25 January, 1900.
BULLUS, OSCAR.
  Midshipman, 1 January, 1817. Lieutenant, 3 March, 1827. Commander, 16 May, 1848. Reserved List, 13 September, 1855. Captain, Reserved List, 11 July, 1861. Commodore, Reserved List, 4 April, 1867. Died 29 September, 1871.
BULLUS, ROBERT S.
  Midshipman, 1 January, 1818. Resigned 18 May, 1825.
BULLUS, SAMUEL H.
  Midshipman, 16 January, 1809. Lieutenant, 24 July, 1813. Resigned 28 April, 1815.
BULMER, BAYARD T.
  Naval Cadet, 5 September, 1896. Graduated 30 June, 1900.
BULMER, ROSCOE C.
  Naval Cadet, 26 September, 1890. Ensign, 1 July, 1896. Lieutenant, Junior Grade, 1 July, 1899.
BULSON, SAMUEL.
  Acting Second Assistant Engineer, 5 November, 1863. Honorably discharged 12 August, 1865.
BUMGARNER, JACOB.
  Mate, 22 April, 1863. Honorably discharged 3 0November, 1865.
BUMPUS, ELISHA M.
  Acting Third Assistant Engineer, 25 November, 1862. Resigned 17 October, 1864.
BUMPUS, SAMUEL S.
  Mate, 3 March, 1864. Honorably discharged 30 July, 1865.
BUNBERRY, M. S.
  Lieutenant, 4 August, 1798. Discharged under Peace Establishment Act, 10 July, 1801. Master, 15 September, 1813. Resigned 7 October, 1813.
BUNCE, BENJAMIN.
  Third Assistant Engineer, 19 July, 1861. Second Assistant Engineer, 18 December, 1862. Resigned 17 July, 1865.
BUNCE, FRANCIS M.
  Acting Midshipman, 28 May, 1852. Midshipman, 10 June, 1857. Passed Midshipman, 25 June, 1860. Master, 24 October, 1860. Lieutenant, 11 April, 1861. Lieutenant-Commander, 16 January, 1863. Commander, 2 November, 1871. Captain, 11 January, 1883. Commodore, 1 March, 1895. Rear-Admiral, 6 February, 1898. Retired List, 25 December, 1898.
BUNCE, ISRAEL S.
  Mate, 13 November, 1861. Acting Ensign, 11 September, 1862. Died 1 November, 1862.
BUNCE, JOHN L.
  Assistant Paymaster (Spanish-American War), 4 May, 1898. Honorably discharged 21 November, 1898.
BUNCE, RICHARD G.
  Acting Assistant Paymaster, 24 July, 1863. Resigned 8 February, 1864.
BUNKER, BENJAMIN.
  Gunner, 21 November, 1838. Dead.
BUNKER, CHARLES C.
  Acting Master, 26 April, 1862. Acting Volunteer Lieutenant, 28 April, 1865. Honorably discharged 8 November, 1865. Acting Master, 26 June, 1866. Mustered out 7 December, 1868.
BUNKER, HORACE G.
  Mate, 26 January, 1863. Acting Ensign, 29 October, 1864. Honorably discharged 25 November, 1865.
BUNKER, WILLIAM.
  Boatswain, 26 August, 1861. Died 20 March, 1865.
BUNNER, JOHN C.
  Midshipman, 1 May, 1822. Resigned 26 March, 1827.

BUNNER, JOHN C.
Acting Master, 1 October, 1862. Honorably discharged 10 July 1866.
BUNTING, JAMES H.
Mate, 28 December, 1861. Acting Ensign, 12 March, 1863. Honorably discharged 4 November, 1865. Acting Ensign, 5 July, 1866. Discharged 12 October, 1867.
BURBAGE, JOHN S.
Acting Second Assistant Engineer. Resigned 3 March, 1863.
BURBANK, CHARLES H.
Assistant Sugeon, 9 May, 1861. Passed Assistant Surgeon, 26 October, 1863. Surgeon, 24 August, 1864. Medical Inspector, 2 April, 1879. Died 30 January, 1885.
BURBIER, J. A.
Assistant Surgeon, 3 December, 1861. Resigned 11 June, 1865.
BURCH, DEWITT.
Surgeon's Mate, 14 July, 1824. Died 1 May, 1826.
BURCHAM, GEORGE E.
Carpenter, 10 August, 1861. Died 6 February, 1872.
BURCHARD, CHARLES M.
Third Assistant Engineer, 17 December, 1861., Second Assistant Engineer, 8 September, 1863. Resigned 26 July, 1865. Acting Second Assistant Engineer, 19 December, 1866. Mustered out 23 October, 1869.
BURCHARD, FRANCIS C.
Third Assistant Engineer, 8 September, 1863. Second Assistant Engineer, 1 August, 1866. Retired List, 24 April, 1877. Died 15 January, 1900.
BURCHARD, JABEZ.
Acting Third Assistant Engineer. 14 March, 1865. Honorably discharged 9 January, 1868. Second Assistant Engineer, 1 September, 1870. Retired List, 26 October, 1874.
BURCHARD, WILLIAM A.
Mate, 19 March, 1863. Acting Ensign, 26 June, 1864. Honorably discharged 28 November, 1865.
BUNCHMORE, JOHN H.
Acting Third Assistant Engineer, 24 December, 1863. Honorably discharged 27 October, 1865. Acting Third Assistant Engineer, 27 December, 1866. Mustered out 28 April, 1869.
BURCHSTEAD, B. B.
Sailmaker, 5 April, 1821. Died 11 December, 1833.
BURCHSTEAD, BENJAMIN B. (2d.)
Sailmaker, 28 April, 1838. Dismissed 7 May, 1855.
BURD, GEORGE E.
Cadet Engineer, 1 October, 1874. Graduated 20 June, 1878. Assistant Engineer, 20 June, 1880. Passed Assistant Engineer, 4 May, 1891. Chief Engineer, 8 November, 1898. Rank changed to Lieutenant, 3 March, 1899.
BURDETT, CHARLES.
Midshipman, 16 May, 1832. Resigned 25 February, 1835.
BURDICK, WILLIAM L.
Cadet Midshipman, 26 September, 1873. Graduated 18 June, 1879. Ensign, 28 November, 1882 . Lieutenant, Junior Grade, 3 January, 1890. Lieutenant, 21 July, 1894.
BURDINE, JOHN.
Acting Sailmaker, 4 March, 1836. Appointment revoked 6 July, 1846.
BURDITT, HENRY D.
Mate, 5 June, 1862. Acting Ensign, 22 September, 1863. Honorably discharged 13 January, 1866. Acting Ensign, 12 December, 1866. Mustered out 21 December, 1868
BURDITT, WILLIAM.
Acting Boatswain, 7 January, 1850. Gunner, 21 November, 1853. Resigned 26 July, 1864. Acting Master, 27 July, 1864. Honorably discharged 21 December, 1866. Reinstated as Gunner from 21 November, 1853. Retired List, 7 June, 1882.
BURGDORFF, THEODORE F.
Cadet Engineer, 1 October, 1873. Graduated 21 June, 1875. Assistant Engineer, 1 July, 1877. Passed Assistant Engineer, 22 June, 1886. Chief Engineer, 26 February, 1897. Rank changed to Lieutenant-Commander, 3 March, 1899.
BURGE, W. J.
Acting Assistant Surgeon, 25 January, 1862. Honorably discharged 14 January, 1866.
BURGER, ALBERT.
Mate, 5 March, 1862. Dismissed 14 November, 1862.
BURGER, JAMES D.
Midshipman, 24 April, 1812. Dismissed 16 August, 1813.
BURGER, THEODORE W.
Acting Assistant Paymaster, 31 July, 1863. Resigned 6 April, 1864.
BURGES, W. H.
Midshipman, 1 April, 1828. Resigned 11 December, 1834.
BURGESS, FRANCIS.
Acting Master, 21 April, 1862. Honorably discharged 18 November, 1865.
BURGESS, GEORGE O.
Acting Assistant Surgeon, 2 February, 1865. Honorably discharged 31 March, 1866.
BURGESS, HENRY C.
Acting Assistant Paymaster, 31 January, 1862. Honorably discharged 31 January, 1866.
BURGESS, WILLIAM D.
Mate, 28 March, 1864. Honorably discharged 9 August, 1865.
BURGOYNE, JOHN R.
Acting Third Assistant Engineer, 5 February, 1863. Dismissed 17 November, 1863.

GENERAL NAVY REGISTER. 91

BURGOYNE, LEONIDAS R.
Acting Third Assistant Engineer, 19 April, 1864. Acting Second Assistant Engineer, 15 July, 1865. Honorably discharged 25 March, 1866. Acting Second Assistant Engineer, 19 December, 1866. Mustered out 22 August, 1869.
BURHANS, ANDREW.
Acting Third Assistant Engineer, 27 May, 1861. Resigned 5 August, 1861.
BURHANS, LORENZO.
Acting Second Assistant Engineer, 17 May, 1861. Resigned 27 June, 1861.
BURK, MICHAEL.
Carpenter, 7 August, 1798. Resigned 22 January, 1799.
BURK, THOMAS.
Sailmaker, 9 November, 1798. Last appearance on Records of Navy Department.
BURK, WILLIAM.
Acting Third Assistant Engineer, 16 December, 1863. Honorably discharged 4 October, 1865.
BURKE, ALONZO.
Carpenter, 12 December, 1898.
BURKE, DAVID.
Acting Third Assistant Engineer, 20 January, 1865. Honorably discharged 14 April, 1868.
BURKE, EDMUND.
Midshipman, 1 March, 1827. Dismissed 17 June, 1830.
BURKE, EDMUND C.
Midshipman, 20 October, 1847. Resigned 5 December, 1850.
BURKE, JAMES.
Carpenter, 26 August, 1873. Chief Carpenter, 3 March, 1899.
BURKE, RICHARD.
Mate, 26 April, 1862. Acting Ensign, 20 January, 1863. Acting Master, 2 December, 1863. Resigned 17 May, 1865.
BURKE, WALTER S.
Naval Cadet, 17 May, 1883. Ensign, 1 July, 1889. Assistant Engineer, 12 December, 1892. Passed Assistant Engineer, 5 June, 1896. Retired List, 30 April, 1897.
BURKE, WILLIAM F.
Mate (Spanish-American War), 22 June, 1898. Honorably discharged 9 September, 1898.
BURKE, WILLIAM P.
Mate, 29 May, 1862. Acting Ensign, 26 October, 1862. Honorably discharged 4 October, 1866.
BURKE, WILLIAM P.
Boatswain, 7 June, 1867. Appointment revoked 20 December, 1870.
BURKETT, GEORGE W.
Acting Assistant Paymaster, 25 September, 1863. Resigned 17 December, 1864.
BURKETT, THEODORE F.
Acting Third Assistant Engineer, 6 August, 1864. Honorably discharged 17 July, 1865.
BURKHEAD, WILLIAM O.
Acting Second Assistant Engineer, 8 November, 1862. Resigned 21 November, 1862.
BURKS, MARTIN.
Carpenter, 26 April, 1813. Last appearance on Records of Navy Department.
BURLAND, JAMES A.
Midshipman, 19 March, 1799. Returned his Warrant 19 October, 1800.
BURLEIGH, D. C.
Acting Assistant Surgeon, 11 January, 1864. Acting Passed Assistant Surgeon, 25 May, 1866. Honorably discharged 23 April, 1869. Again Appointed 4 December, 1873. Passed Assistant Surgeon, Retired List, 30 June, 1879. Died 11 January, 1884.
BURLEY, WILLIAM.
Midshipman, 9 November, 1813. Dismissed 7 May, 1814.
BURLINGAME, REUBEN W.
Acting Third Assistant Engineer, 5 May, 1863. Honorably discharged 1 December, 1865.
BURLINGAME, WILSON D.
Mate, 7 June, 1864. Resigned 17 March, 1865.
BURLINGHAM, H. D.
Assistant Surgeon, 18 July, 1861. Passed Assistant Surgeon, 22 June, 1864. Resigned 31 May, 1865.
BURN, EUGENE I.
Lieutenant, Junior Grade (Spanish-American War), 20 May, 1898. Honorably discharged 8 September, 1898.
BURNAP, GEORGE J.
Third Assistant Engineer, 13 May, 1861. Second Assistant Engineer, 16 January, 1863. First Assistant Engineer, 1 January, 1865. Chief Engineer, 1 November, 1879. Retired List, 10 February, 1899.
BURNER, CHARLES W.
Mate, 7 June, 1864. Acting Ensign, 27 March, 1865. Honorably discharged 29 June, 1865.
BURNES, MARIA J.
Mate, 26 January, 1864. Appointment revoked 2 January, 1866.
BURNET, JAMES C.
Mate, 18 April, 1863. Appointment revoked 24 December, 1863.
BURNET, JOHN C.
Assistant Paymaster, 21 December, 1869. Passed Assistant Paymaster, 28 August, 1876. Resigned 31 August, 1881.
BURNETT, CLARENCE L.
Acting Assistant Paymaster, 17 December, 1861. Honorably discharged 20 April, 1866.

BURNETT, JAMES G.
Mate, 13 May, 1863. Resigned 19 September, 1864.
BURNETT, JEREMIAH C.
Midshipman, 27 September, 1867. Graduated 6 June, 1871. Ensign, 14 July, 1872. Master, 2 July, 1875. Lieutenant, 18 November, 1882. Retired List, 9 May, 1896.
BURNETT, J. OLIVER.
Assistant Surgeon, 2 December, 1858. Retired List, 21 June, 1862. Dismissed 18 February, 1865.
BURNETT, WILLIAM H.
Acting Assistant Surgeon, 17 May, 1864. Honorably discharged 9 October, 1865.
BURNHAM, ALBION.
Mate, 12 October, 1863. Honorably discharged 5 October, 1865.
BURNHAM, JOHN W.
Carpenter 24 March, 1880. Chief Carpenter, 3 March, 1899.
BURNIECE, WILLIAM.
Gunner, 20 December, 1847. Died 21 January, 1867.
BURNS, CHARLES M., Jr.
Acting Assistant Paymaster, 11 April, 1863. Resigned 17 April, 1865.
BURNS, FRANCIS D.
Acting Warrant Machinist, 23 August, 1899.
BURNS, JAMES.
Lieutenant, 29 October, 1798. Resigned 2 January, 1802.
BURNS, JAMES.
Acting Master, 7 December, 1861. Dismissed 23 December, 1861.
BURNS, JAMES A.
Acting Second Assistant Engineer, 22 April, 1863. Acting First Assistant Engineer, 3 August, 1863. Honorably discharged 20 September, 1865.
BURNS, JAMES W.
Acting Ensign and Pilot. Appointment revoked 14 June, 1865.
BURNS, JEROME.
Acting Carpenter, 11 June, 1863. Honorably discharged 28 October, 1865.
BURNS, JOHN.
Gunner, 1 November, 1826. Lost in the Hornet, September, 1829.
BURNS, JOHN.
Acting Third Assistant Engineer, 27 February, 1862. Deserted 1874.
BURNS, JOHN.
Ensign (Spanish-American War), 28 May, 1898. Honorably discharged 7 April, 1899.
BURNS, LEWIS.
Mate, 10 October, 1862. Died 9 July, 1873.
BURNS, OWEN.
Midshipman, 1 December, 1824. Passed Midshipman, 20 February, 1830. Lieutenant, 8 April, 1834. Resigned 30 June, 1840.
BURNS, PATRICK.
Acting Third Assistant Engineer, 3 October, 1863. Honorably discharged 7 August, 1865.
BURNS, PATRICK H.
Boatswain, 20 October, 1894. Retired List, 6 June, 1898.
BURNS, ROBERT.
Mate, 15 December, 1864. Died 20 November, 1866.
BURNS, THOMAS.
Acting Boatswain, 6 July, 1853. Resigned 1 October, 1853.
BURNS, THOMAS.
Acting Ensign, 1 October, 1862. Acting Master, 20 May, 1864. Honorably discharged 5 September, 1865.
BURNS, WILLIAM C.
Boatswain, 26 March, 1842. Resigned 10 March, 1844.
BURNS, WILLIAM H.
Master's Mate, 11 May, 1842. Second Mate, 3 March, 1849. Died 4 February, 1851.
BURNSIDE, CAMERON.
Assistant Paymaster, 12 May, 1875. Resigned 21 February, 1878.
BURNSTINE, ALBERT.
Lieutenant, Junior Grade (Spanish-American War), 21 June, 1898. Honorably discharged 19 September, 1898.
BURR, CHAUNCEY R.
Assistant Surgeon (Spanish-American War), 24 May, 1898. Appointed Assistant Surgeon in Regular Navy 7 June, 1900.
BURR, HEMAN M.
Assistant Paymaster (Spanish-American War), 21 May, 1898. Honorably discharged 19 October, 1898.
BURRAGE, GUY H.
Naval Cadet, 30 June, 1883. Ensign, 1 July, 1889. Lieutenant, Junior Grade, 7 November, 1897. Lieutenant, 3 March, 1899.
BURRITT HARVEY H.
Third Assistant Engineer, 12 August, 1861. Second Assistant Engineer, 21 April, 1863. Resigned 22 September, 1865.
BURROUGH, LEWIS F.
Ensign (Spanish-American War),29 June, 1898. Honorably discharged 17 September, 1898.
BURROUGHS, ALONZO C.
Carpenter, 9 March, 1878. Chief Carpenter, 3 March, 1899.
BURROUGHS, DANIEL W.
Mate, 7 December, 1864. Honorably discharged 1 December, 1865. Mate, 8 December, 1869. Resigned 8 December, 1871. Gunner, 8 December, 1871. Died 16 March, 1879.

GENERAL NAVY REGISTER. 93

BURROUGHS, ORSON.
Acting Second Assistant Engineer, 21 November, 1862. Appointment revoked 29 June, 1864.
BURROW, WALTER P.
Third Assistant Engineer, 26 June, 1856. Dismissed 17 May, 1860.
BURROWS, GEORGE W.
Acting First Assistant Engineer, 17 June, 1864. Honorably discharged 3 November, 1865.
BURROWS, GUSTAVUS H.
Acting Ensign, 10 September, 1864. Resigned 20 April, 1865.
BURROWS, J. F.
Mate, 26 June, 1862. Appointment revoked 19 November, 1863.
BURROWS, JOHN.
Boatswain, 4 December, 1849. Retired List, 31 January, 1881. Died 30 June, 1900.
BURROWS, STEPHEN H.
Mate, 9 April, 1864. Appointment revoked 13 May, 1864.
BURROWS, THOMAS.
Midshipman, 23 May, 1798. Discharged 12 August, 1801, under Peace Establishment Act.
BURROWS, THOMAS.
Purser, 29 December, 1817. Died 13 October, 1821.
BURROWS, WILLIAM.
Midshipman, 10 November, 1799. Lieutenant, 19 March, 1807. Killed in action 5 September, 1813.
BURSLEY, IRA.
Acting Ensign, 3 March, 1864. Acting Master, 5 November, 1864. Honorably discharged 21 September, 1865.
BURT, CHARLES H.
Acting Third Assistant Engineer, 25 March, 1863. Acting Second Assistant Engineer, 2 October, 1863. Honorably discharged 26 October, 1865.
BURT, CHARLES P.
Naval Cadet, 6 September, 1892. Assistant Engineer, 6 May, 1898. Rank changed to Ensign 3 March, 1899.
BURT, CRAMER.
Purser, 1 June, 1861. Retired List, 15 September, 1863. Died 1869.
BURT, E. C.
Mate. Resigned 7 July, 1862.
BURT, GEORGE A.
Mate, 9 September, 1864. Resigned 27 May, 1865.
BURT, JOHN O.
Assistant Surgeon, 1 July, 1861. Resigned 11 November, 1863.
BURT, NELSON.
First Assistant Engineer, 15 November, 1837. Resigned 20 October, 1839.
BURTIS, ARTHUR.
Assistant Paymaster, 14 July, 1862. Paymaster, 4 May, 1866. Pay Inspector, 21 September, 1891. Pay Director, 5 May, 1899.
BURTON, RUFUS.
Acting Third Assistant Engineer, 22 October, 1862. Honorably discharged 19 September, 1865.
BURTON, WILLIAM.
Gunner, 26 July, 1837. Died 31 May, 1853.
BURTON, WILLIAM H.
Mate, 10 September, 1864. Honorably discharged 27 August, 1865.
BURTS, ROBERT.
Midshipman, 31 May, 1833. Died 22 December, 1839.
BURTT, JOHN L.
Assistant Surgeon, 30 May, 1844. Dismissed 2 September, 1858.
BURWELL, GEORGE E.
Acting Second Assistant Engineer, 23 November, 1864. Honorably discharged 1 April, 1868.
BURWELL, W. T.
Midshipman, 27 September, 1841. Resigned 20 May, 1843.
BURWELL, WILLIAM T.
Acting Midshipman, 30 September, 1862. Graduated June, 1866. Ensign, 12 March, 1868. Master, 26 March, 1869. Lieutenant, 21 March, 1870. Lieutenant-Commander, 23 September, 1885. Commander, 7 September, 1894. Captain, 29 November, 1900.
BUSBEE, PERRIN.
Midshipman, 23 September, 1867. Graduated 6 June, 1871. Ensign, 14 July, 1872. Master, 13 May, 1875. Resigned 31 May, 1881.
BUSBEE, QUENTIN.
Purser, 27 April, 1846. Resigned 21 February, 1848.
BUSH, ARTHUR R.
Cadet Engineer, 13 September, 1877. Graduated 10 June, 1881. Honorably discharged 30 June, 1883. Restored to service 10 March, 1886, as an Assistant Engineer to rank from 1 July, 1883. Resigned 31 August, 1886.
BUSH, CHARLES G.
Midshipman, 11 January, 1832. Resigned 21 February, 1833.
BUSH, JOSEPH.
Midshipman, 30 April, 1798. Discharged under Peace Establishment Act, 12 October, 1801.
BUSH, PETER A.
Midshipman, 26 May, 1812. Dismissed 28 December, 1813.
BUSH, PHILIP A.
Midshipman, 16 January, 1809. Resigned 26 May, 1810.

BUSH, WILLIAM W.
 Cadet Midshipman, 25 September, 1880. Honorably discharged 30 June, 1886. Assistant Engineer, 28 June, 1889. Passed Assistant Engineer, 28 March, 1896. Rank changed to Lieutenant, 3 March, 1899.
BUSHER, MOSES.
 Master, 17 July, 1812. Dismissed 6 March, 1813.
BUSHNELL, EBEN.
 Purser, 31 August, 1799. Died 3 August, 1800.
BUSHONG, ISRAEL.
 Acting Assistant Surgeon, 21 October, 1862. Resigned 3 April, 1865.
BUSHNELL, EDWARD A.
 Acting Third Assistant Engineer, 18 October, 1861. Honorably discharged 20 December, 1865.
BUTLAND, FRANCIS.
 Boatswain, 11 February, 1871. Died 20 February, 1881.
BUTLER, CHARLES ST. J.
 Assistant Surgeon, 26 October, 1900.
BUTLER, EDWARD A.
 Mate, 5 March, 1862. Acting Ensign, 8 June, 1864. Honorably discharged 15 November, 1865.
BUTLER, GEORGE H.
 Acting Assistant Surgeon, 9 January, 1864. Acting Passed Assistant Surgeon, 17 August, 1866. Honorably discharged 12 November, 1868.
BUTLER, HENRY S.
 Midshipman, 15 May, 1799. Resigned 6 August, 1800.
BUTLER, H. VINCENT.
 Mate, 12 February, 1863. Appointment revoked 14 May, 1864.
BUTLER, HENRY V., JR.
 Naval Cadet, 8 September, 1891. Ensign, 1 July, 1897. Lieutnant, Junior Grade, 1 July, 1900.
BUTLER, JAMES.
 Sailmaker, 29 March, 1800. Died 27 July, 1801.
BUTLER, JAMES L.
 Midshipman, 11 April, 1848. Resigned 18 December, 1848.
BUTLER, JOHN.
 Surgeon's Mate, 28 April, 1804. Resigned 1 May, 1809.
BUTLER, JOHN.
 Acting Ensign, 14 February, 1863. Dismissed 22 March, 1864.
BUTLER, JOHN F.
 Acting First Assistant Engineer, 9 January, 1863. Honorably discharged 26 October, 1865.
BUTLER, JOHN H.
 Mate, 6 June, 1862. Dismissed 6 February, 1863.
BUTLER, JOHN J.
 Acting Ensign, 18 December, 1862. Acting Master, 15 December, 1864. Honorably discharged 18 September, 1865.
BUTLER, JOHN M.
 Mate, 3 January, 1862. Acting Master, 8 May, 1862. Carpenter, 22 October, 1841. 1868.
BUTLER, JOHN O.
 Carpenter, 5 May, 1837. Resigned 16 February, 1839. Carpenter, 22 October, 1841. Died 29 September, 1862.
BUTLER, JONATHAN W.
 Acting Ensign, 24 September, 1862. Resigned 22 June, 1864.
BUTLER, JOSEPH C
 Mate, 30 July, 1862. Dropped 6 September, 1862.
BUTLER, JOSEPH L.
 Third Assistant Engineer, 19 March, 1858. Second Assistant Engineer, 1 December, 1860. Died 14 September, 1862.
BUTLER, LEVI T.
 Mate, 15 July, 1864. Appointment revoked 6 August, 1864.
BUTLER, RICHARD.
 Master, 28 April, 1801. Resigned 4 June, 1803. Master, 24 June, 1803. Dismissed 15 February, 1808.
BUTLER, SAMUEL.
 Gunner, 6 December, 1824. Resigned 21 Septemebr, 1825.
BUTLER, SILAS.
 Purser, 29 December, 1817. Died 9 April, 1837.
BUTLER, S. P.
 Acting Ensign, 13 January, 1863. Deserted 21 March, 1863.
BUTLER, SPRAGUE J.
 Acting Ensign. Resigned 9 February, 1864.
BUTLER, WILLIAM.
 Midshipman, 4 January, 1800. Resigned 5 March, 1807.
BUTLER, WILLIAM.
 Surgeon's Mate, 10 December, 1814. Resigned 6 June, 1820.
BUTLER, WILLIAM S.
 Midshipman, 18 February, 1802. Lieutenant, 6 May, 1808. Last appearance on Records of Navy Department.
BUTLER, WINTHROP.
 Acting Assistant Surgeon, 25 April, 1862. Honorably discharged 22 November, 1865.
BUTMAN, JOHN H.
 Acting Ensign, 3 September, 1862. Appointment revoked 20 February, 1864.

GENERAL NAVY REGISTER.

BUTT, J. B.
Mate, 1 February, 1863. Resigned 12 October, 1871.
BUTT, THOMAS V.
Carpenter, 4 November, 1852. Died 22 May, 1857.
BUTT, WALTER R.
Acting Midshipman, 20 September, 1855. Midshipman, 9 June, 1859. Passed Midshipman, 31 August, 1861. Dismissed 5 October, 1861.
BUTTERFIELD, GEORGE.
Midshipman, 30 January, 1833. Resigned 8 July, 1833. Midshipman, 8 October, 1833. Dismissed 2 July, 1836.
BUTTERWORTH, JAMES.
Third Assistant Engineer, 23 May, 1861. Second Assistant Engineer, 29 October, 1862. First Assistant Engineer, 25 July, 1866. Chief Engineer, 10 March, 1881. Died 2 October, 1891.
BUTTMAN, JULIUS.
Mate, 22 June, 1863. Resigned 23 November, 1863.
BUTTRICK, GEORGE.
Mate, 24 August, 1861. Resigned 31 January, 1863.
BUTTS, MOSES P.
Mate, 29 August, 1864. Honorably discharged 4 October, 1868.
BUTTS, WILLIAM D.
Acting Third Assistant Engineer, 25 August, 1863. Honorably discharged 1 September, 1865.
BUTZ, PETER.
Ensign (Spanish-American War), 18 July, 1898. Honorably discharged 26 August, 1898.
BUXTON, JAMES D.
Acting Master, 7 October, 1861. Apopintment revoked 7 March, 1862. Acting Ensign, 18 October, 1862. Appointment revoked 10 June, 1863.
BUXTON, THOMAS S.
Acting Boatswain, 19 November, 1850. Dismissed 26 May, 1851.
BYERS, DAVID.
Midshipman, 30 April, 1800. Resigned 14 July, 1801.
BYERS, JOSIAH S.
Midshipman, 19 October, 1841. Resigned 13 August, 1849.
BYLAND, JAMES R.
Acting Third Assistant Engineer, 9 June, 1863. Honorably discharged 30 November, 1865.
BYLES, TEN EYCK.
Third Assitant Engineer, 2 August, 1855. Second Assistant Engineer, 21 July, 1858. Resigned 25 October, 1858.
BYRAM, SYDNEY W.
Mate, 7 June, 1864. Honorably discharged 3 December, 1865.
BYRENS, ALLEN T.
Midshipman, 26 February, 1841. Passed Midshipman, 10 August, 1847. Dropped 13 September, 1855. Lieutenant, 15 September, 1855. Died 14 February, 1860.
BYRD, JOHN D.
Midshipman, 16 February, 1814. Resigned 15 July, 1824.
BYRN, WILLIAM H.
Acting Assistant Paymaster, 31 March, 1863. Honorably discharged 4 December, 1865.
BYRNE, EDMUND.
Midshipman, 1 February, 1814. Lieutenant, 13 January, 1825. Commander, 8 September, 1841. Died 17 October, 1850.
BYRNE, GERALD.
Lieutenant, 17 June, 1799. Discharged 14 April, 1801.
BYRNE, JAMES.
Acting Second Assistant Engineer, 27 November, 1861. Resigned 13 March, 1862.
BYRNE, JAMES.
Ensign (Spanish-American War), 21 May, 1898. Honorably discharged 7 November, 1898.
BYRNE, JAMES E.
Cadet Engineer, 14 September, 1876. Graduated 10 June, 1881. Honorably discharged 30 June, 1883. Restored to service, 10 March, 1886, as an Assistant Engineer, to rank from 1 July, 1883. Resigned 8 November, 1887.
BYRNE, JOHN J.
Sailmaker, 11 January, 1875. Chief Sailmaker, 3 March, 1899.
BYRNES, JAMES C.
Assistant Surgeon, 2 November, 1876. Passed Assistant Surgeon, 2 November, 1880. Surgeon, 25 February, 1895.
BYRNES, WILLIAM A.
Mate, 4 October, 1862. Acting Ensign, 31 October, 1863. Honorably discharged 24 November, 1865.
CABELL, ARTHUR G.
Assistant Surgeon, 14 February, 1876. Passed Assistant Surgeon, 14 February, 1880. Surgeon, 15 June, 1895. Retired List, 8 October, 1898.
CABLE, CHARLES A.
Acting Assistant Paymaster, 1 September, 1863. Mustered out 21 November, 1865. Assistant Paymaster, 23 July, 1866. Resigned 5 December, 1866.
CABLE, WILLIAM A.
Gunner, 7 December, 1894.
CABLES, GEORGE.
Acting Master, 18 December, 1861. Honorably discharged 6 March, 1866.

CADIEN, CHARLES H.
Acting Ensign, 8 July, 1863. Acting Master, 5 September, 1864. Acting Volunteer Lieutenant, 10 July, 1865. Honorably discharged 18 November, 1865.
CADLE, JOHN.
Surgeon's Mate, 24 July, 1813. Surgeon, 27 March, 1818. Last appearance on Records of Navy Department, 1822. Dead.
CADWALLADER, H.
Appointed Midshipman, 13 December, 1833. Passed Midshipman, 8 July, 1839. Died 27 July, 1844.
CADWALLADER, ROWLAND.
Acting Assistant Surgeon, 1 October, 1862. Resigned 2 February, 1865.
CADWELL, JAMES D.
Acting Third Assistant Engineer, 9 January, 1862. Honorably discharged 4 January, 1866.
CADY, HENRY A.
Acting Third Assistant Engineer, 1 March, 1863. Acting Second Assistant Engineer, 27 May, 1864. Honorably discharged 20 November, 1865.
CADY, HORATIO N.
Appointed Midshipman, 4 March, 1823. Dismissed 8 June, 1831.
CAFLIN, LAWRENCE M.
Acting Third Assistant Engineer, 6 January, 1865. Honorably discharged 1 November, 1865.
CAGE, EDMUND.
Acting First Assistant Engineer, 9 June, 1863. Honorably discharged 1 December, 1865.
CAGE, HARRY K.
Naval Cadet, 20 May, 1896. Graduated 30 June, 1900.
CAHILL, EDWARD J.
Acting Third Assistant Engineer, 14 April, 1864. Honorably discharged 28 August, 1865.
CAHILL, JOHN.
Carpenter, 8 July, 1837. Died 24 July, 1858.
CAHILL, JOHN.
Acting First Assistant Engineer, 9 October, 1862. Resigned 3 May, 1864.
CAHILL, JOSEPH N.
Third Assistant Engineer, 21 July, 1858. Second Assistant Engineer, 17 January, 1861. First Assistant Engineer, 17 March, 1863. Killed 15 April, 1864.
CAHOON, BENJAMIN G.
Mate, 21 August, 1862. Acting Ensign, 20 July, 1863. Appointment revoked (sick) 26 March, 1864.
CAHOON, JAMES B.
Cadet Midshipman, 10 June, 1874. Graduated 10 June, 1881. Ensign, Junior Grade, 3 March, 1883. Ensign, 26 June, 1884. Retired List, 22 June, 1889.
CAHOONE, J. BENJAMIN.
Purser, 12 November, 1830. Retired List, 21 December, 1861. Pay Director Retired List, 3 March, 1871. Died 27 July, 1873.
CAIN, JOHN, Jr.
Acting Midshipman, 4 October, 1851. Midshipman, 10 June, 1854. Died 12 August, 1855.
CAIN, ROBERT.
Mate, 6 June, 1863. Resigned 31 July, 1863.
CALDEN, ALVIN R.
Acting First Assistant Engineer, 22 July, 1863. Honorably discharged 15 November, 1865.
CALDER, GEORGE.
Appointed Midshipman, 29 June, 1798. Resigned 22 March, 1802.
CALDER, GEORGE.
Appointed Master, 7 April, 1803. Resigned 26 November, 1804.
CALDWELL, ALBERT GALLATIN.
Midshipman, 23 September, 1861. Graduated 22 November, 1864. Ensign, 1 November, 1866. Master, 1 December, 1866. Lieutenant, 12 March, 1868. Lieutenant-Commander, 26 March, 1869. Resigned 7 November, 1884.
CALDWELL, C. H.
Appointed Midshipman, September, 1811. Lieutenant, 5 March, 1817. Died 9 August, 1831.
CALDWELL, C. H. B.
Midshipman, 27 February, 1838. Passed Midshipman, 20 May, 1844. Master, 13 October, 1851. Lieutenant, 4 September, 1852. Commander, 16 July, 1862. Captain, 12 December, 1867. Commodore, 14 June, 1874. Died 30 November, 1877.
CALDWELL, GEORGE W.
Acting Third Assistant Engineer, 7 March, 1864. Honorably discharged 28 September, 1865.
CALDWELL, HARRY H.
Naval Cadet, 7 September, 1887. Ensign, 1 July, 1893. Lieutenant, Junior Grade, 3 March, 1899. Lieutenant, 29 December, 1899.
CALDWELL, HENRY C.
Assistant Surgeon, 17 October, 1853. Passed Assistant Surgeon, 13 May, 1858. Died 1 December, 1859.
CALDWELL, JAMES R.
Appointed Midshipman, 22 May, 1798. Lieutenant, 1 November, 1800. Killed in action 7 August, 1804.
CALDWELL, LAFAYETTE.
Third Assistant Engineer, 20 February, 1847. Resigned 12 June, 1849.

GENERAL NAVY REGISTER.

CALDWELL, R. M.
   Midshipman, 9 September, 1847. Dismissed 16 June, 1855.
CALDWELL, THOMAS.
   Appointed Master, 23 April, 1814. Resigned 24 July, 1815.
CALDWELL, WILLIAM, JR.
   Acting Ensign, 28 August, 1863. Honorably discharged 1 August, 1865.
CALDWELL, WILLIAM H.
   Cadet Midshipman, 30 September, 1882. Graduated. Honorably discharged 30 June, 1888. Lieutenant, Junior Grade (Spanish-American War), 13 May, 1898. Honorably discharged 25 January, 1899.
CALDWELL, W. M.
   Appointed Master, 21 March, 1813. Lieutenant, 27 April, 1816. Died 16 December, 1825.
CALDWELL, W. M.
   Midshipman, 10 October, 1835. Passed Midshipman, 22 June, 1841. Master, 26 September, 1847. Lieutenant, 25 July, 1848. Resigned 10 October, 1850.
CALEB, JOHN.
   Acting Master, 26 August, 1861. Appointment revoked (sick) 17 February, 1862.
CALHOON, ADAM R.
   Acting First Assistant Engineer, 24 February, 1864. Honorably discharged 4 October, 1865.
CALHOUN, GEORGE A.
   Midshipman, 31 July, 1866. Graduated 7 June, 1870. Ensign, 13 July, 1871. Master, 8 November, 1873. Lieutenant, 1 November, 1879. Died 28 April, 1897.
CALHOUN, JAMES EDWARD.
   Appointed Midshipman, 30 May, 1816. Lieutenant, 28 April, 1826. Resigned 11 November, 1833.
CALHOUN, ROBERT H.
   Appointed Midshipman, 1 November, 1828. Resigned 21 January, 1830.
CALHOUN, WILLIAM L.
   Acting Second Assistant Engineer, 5 August, 1864. Honorably discharged 3 October, 1865.
CALKINS, CARLOS G.
   Midshipman, 24 June, 1867. Graduated 6 June, 1871. Ensign, 14 July, 1872. Master, 1 July, 1875. Lieutenant, 17 November, 1882. Lieutenant-Commander, 3 March, 1899.
CALKINS, JAMES B.
   Acting Assistant Surgeon, 6 December, 1861. Resigned 30 June, 1863.
CALL, WILLIAM R.
   Acting Third Assistant Engineer, 5 October, 1863. Acting Assistant Engineer, 9 January, 1865. Resigned 29 March, 1865.
CALLAHAN, JOSEPH.
   Acting Third Assistant Engineer, 18 February, 1864. Honorably discharged 24 August, 1865.
CALLAHER, EUGENE.
   Acting Third Assistant Engineer, 1 October, 1862. Acting Second Assistant Engineer, 16 July, 1863. Dismissed 29 September, 1864.
CALLAN, JEROME.
   Appointed Midshipman, 4 March, 1823. Passed Midshipman, 23 March, 1829. Lieutenant, 3 March, 1831. Died 29 June, 1834.
CALLAN, PETER A.
   Assistant Surgeon, 25 March, 1868. Resigned 1 March, 1872.
CALLANDER, A. F.
   Mate, 26 November, 1869. Retired List, 22 May, 1899.
CALLAWAY, LEOPOLD.
   Acting Third Assistant Engineer, 27 June, 1864. Honorably discharged 4 February, 1869.
CALLENDER, ELLIOT.
   Assistant Ensign, 1 October, 1862. Resigned 18 February, 1864.
CALLISS, CLEON.
   Appointed Midshipman, 28 June, 1804. Resigned 3 August, 1805.
CALVERT, CECIL A.
   Acting Ensign, 17 January, 1864. Honorably discharged 27 September, 1865.
CALVERT, MADISON R.
   Assistant Paymaster, 29 October, 1881. Resigned 30 June, 1892.
CALVERT, THOMAS.
   Appointed Lieutenant, 4 September, 1798. Discharged 15 April, 1801, under Peace Establishment Act.
CAMBRELING, J. P.
   Appointed Midshipman, 18 June, 1812. Lieutenant, 28 March, 1820. Last appearance on Records of Navy Department, 1821. Frigate Constellation.
CAMBRIDGE, W. E.
   Appointed Midshipman, 6 March, 1815. Last appearance on Records of Navy Department, 15 August, 1820.
CAMERON, CHARLES.
   Mate, 7 March, 1864. Resigned 11 May, 1865.
CAMERON, DANIEL.
   Appointed Midshipman, 17 January, 1826. Resigned 16 November, 1831.
CAMERON, ROBERT.
   Acting Chief Engineer, 13 June, 1863. Appointment revoked 9 October, 1863.
CAMERON, ROBERT.
   Mate, 22 April, 1863. Died at Naval Hospital, Memphis, Tennessee, 29 June, 1863.

CAMERON, ROBERT H.
Mate, 24 January, 1863. Acting Ensign, 5 September, 1863. Appointment revoked 24 August, 1864. Sick.
CAMFIELD, THOMAS.
Acting Third Assistant Engineer, 11 February, 1865. Honorably discharged 16 November, 1865. Acting Third Assistant Engineer, 4 March, 1867. Mustered out 27 August, 1868.
CAMMETT, WARREN S.
Mate, 6 July, 1863. Appointment revoked 9 November, 1864.
CAMP, BENJAMIN F., JR.
Assistant Paymaster, 23 September, 1861. Resigned 29 August, 1863.
CAMP, JOHN G.
Appointed Midshipman, 15 November, 1809. Resigned 25 May, 1811.
CAMP, WALTER T.
Ensign (Spanish-American War), 25 May, 1898. Honorably discharged 17 September, 1898. Assistant Paymaster (Regular Navy), 15 January, 1900.
CAMPBELL, ALBERT B.
Third Assistant Engineer, 26 August, 1859. Second Assistnat Engineer, 26 October, 1861. Resigned 5 May, 1863.
CAMPBELL, ALEXANDER.
Acting Third Assistant Engineer, 1 October, 1862. Acting Second Assistant Engineer, 3 July, 1864. Honorably discharged 6 November, 1865.
CAMPBELL, A. S.
Appointed Midshipman, 1 January, 1812. Lieutenant, 5 March, 1817. Died 3 June, 1836.
CAMPBELL, ALEXANDER D.
Acting Ensign, 19 August, 1862. Honorably discharged 10 October, 1867.
CAMPBELL, CHARLES.
Surgeon, 24 July, 1813. Resigned 14 July, 1814.
CAMPBEL, CHARLES W.
Mate, 17 September, 1861. Dismissed 22 October, 1863.
CAMPBELL, COLIN.
Assistant Engineer (Spanish-American War), 22 June, 1898. Honorably discharged 2 September, 1898.
CAMPBELL, DANIEL A.
Acting Master, 21 August, 1861. Recommendation of Commanding Officer, 17 August, 1864. Honorably discharged 1 December, 1865.
CAMPBELL, EBEN.
Appointed Midshipman, 25 June, 1814. Last appearance on Records of Navy Department, 4 March, 1815. Drowned.
CAMPBELL, EDWARD H.
Naval Cadet, 6 Septembr, 1889. Ensign, 1 July, 1895. Lieutenant, Junior Grade, 3 March, 1899.
CAMPBELL, EDWARD H.
Acting Warrant Machinist, 6 July, 1899.
CAMPBELL, FRANCIS D.
Mate, 24 December, 1862. Resigned 8 August, 1863. Acting Ensign, 14 June, 1864. Resigned 29 November, 1864.
CAMPBELL, GEORGE C.
Mate, 11 October, 1861. Acting Ensign, 6 October, 1863. Honorably discharged 9 April, 1868.
CAMPBELL, GEORGE W.
Passed Assistant Engineer (Spanish-American War), 22 April, 1898. Honorably discharged 4 October, 1898.
CAMPBELL, H. G.
Appointed Commander, 27 July, 1799. Captain, 16 October, 1800. Died 11 November, 1820.
CAMPBELL, HECTOR R.
Lieutenant, Junior Grade (Spanish-American War), 18 May, 1898. Honorably discharged 2 September, 1898.
CAMPBELL, HERBERT.
Gunner, 25 March, 1897.
CAMPBELL, JAMES.
Appointed Midshipman, 30 November, 1814. Last appearance on Records of Navy Department, 1815. Sloop Erie.
CAMPBELL, JAMES.
Appointed Lieutenant, 20 September, 1799. Discharged 8 July, 1801, under Peace Establishment Act.
CAMPBELL, JAMES.
Acting Third Assistant Engineer, 28 June, 1862. Honorably discharged 26 May, 1868.
CAMPBELL, JAMES.
Warrant Machinist (Spanish-American War), 18 May, 1898. Honorably discharged 2 September, 1898.
CAMPBELL, JAMES C.
Appointed Midshipman, 29 December, 1840. Resigned 7 July, 1842.
CAMPBELL, JAMES E.
Mate, 29 November, 1863. Appointment revoked 17 September, 1864. Sick.
CAMPBELL, JOSEPH.
Acting Third Assistant Engineer, 22 July, 1864. Dropped 13 August, 1864.
CAMPBELL, JOSEPH R.
Naval Cadet, 29 September, 1888. Ensign, 1 July, 1894. Died 30 May, 1898.
CAMPBELL, LOUDON.
Third Assistant Engineer, 21 July, 1858. Second Assistant Engineer, 17 January, 1861. Resigned 6 May, 1861.

GENERAL NAVY REGISTER. 99

CAMPBELL, MARSHAL C.
Midshipman, 5 February, 1850. Passed Midshipman, 20 June, 1856. Master, 22 January, 1858. Lieutenant, 23 January, 1858. Lieutenant-Commander, 16 July, 1862. Died 22 February, 1865.
CAMPBELL, N. L.
Acting Assistant Surgeon, 1 November, 1861. Acting Passed Assistant Surgeon, 30 March, 1865. Honorably discharged 22 March, 1869.
CAMPBELL, ROBERT.
Acting Gunner, 15 June, 1864. Honorably discharged 9 August, 1865.
CAMPBELL, THOMAS.
Acting Third Assistant Engineer, 4 September, 1863. Honorably discharged 21 May, 1866.
CAMPBELL, WILLIAM.
Appointed Midshipman, 16 January, 1809. Died October, 1810.
CAMPBELL, WILLIAM.
Acting Third Assistant Engineer, 27 May, 1861. Resigned 21 December, 1861. Acting Second Assistant Engineer, 9 May, 1863. Acting First Assistant Engineer, 14 February, 1865. Honorably discharged 13 March, 1866.
CAMPBELL, WILLIAM G.
Mate, 8 September, 1862. Acting Ensign, 13 October, 1863. Resigned 18 January, 1866.
CAMPBELL, WILLIAM H.
Acting Assistant Surgeon, 8 November, 1862. Resigned 9 June, 1864.
CAMPBELL, WILLIAM H.
Appointed Midshipman, 30 May, 1816. Lieutenant, 28 April, 1826. Died 6 September, 1839.
CAMPBELL, WILLIAM J.
Appointed Midshipman, 28 October, 1799. Resigned 7 April, 1802.
CAMPBELL, W. P. A.
Midshipman, 14 December, 1847. Passed Midshipman, 10 June, 1853. Master, 15 September, 1855. Lieutenant, 16 September, 1855. Dismissed 19 September, 1861.
CANA, FREDERICK.
Appointed Gunner, 4 October, 1805. Resigned 21 November, 1808.
CANADY, BENJAMIN.
Acting Second Asistant Engineer, 29 November, 1862. Resigned 23 July, 1863.
CANADAY, JEREMIAH.
Mate, 2 3April, 1864. Appointment revoked 18 May, 1865. Sick.
CANAGA, ALFRED B.
Cadet Engineer, 1 October, 1872. Graduated 30 May, 1874. Assistant Engineer, 26 February, 1875. Passed Assistant Engineer, 10 March, 1881. Chief Engineer, 6 August, 1895. Rank changed to Lieutenant-Commander, 3 March, 1899.
CANFIELD, FRANCIS A.
Third Assistant Engineer, 21 May, 1853. Resigned 30 April, 1856.
CANFIELD, JOHN P.
Mate, 16 June, 1864. Resigned 6 July, 1865.
CANFIELD, RICHARD.
Acting Ensign, 11 July, 1863. Acting Master, 9 June, 1865. Honorably discharged 4 September, 1866.
CANFIELD, WILLIAM C.
Cadet Midshipman, 23 September, 1873. Graduated 4 June, 1880. Ensign, Junior Grade, 3 March, 1883. Ensign, 26 October, 1883. Resigned 30 June, 1886.
CANN, JAMES E.
Assistant Paymaster, 14 July, 1870. Passed Assistant Paymaster, 22 October, 1878. Paymaster, 21 September, 1891.
CANNEDY, P. F.
Appointed Midshipman, 4 March, 1823. Passed Midshipman, 23 May, 1829. Lieutenant, 31 December, 1833. Died 2 January, 1834.
CANNELL, CHARLES A.
Appointed Midshipman, 1 June, 1828. Lost on Hornet, 10 September, 1829.
CANNING, JOSEPH C.
Acting Assistant Paymaster, 3 August, 1861. Honorably discharged 31 May, 1866.
CANNING, WILLIAM P.
Surgeon's Mate, 7 May, 1844. Died 7 April, 1845.
CANNON, CHARLES A.
Appointed Midshipman, 9 June, 1811. Resigned 30 January, 1813.
CANNON, CHARLES A.
Acting Ensign, 9 August, 1864. Honorably discharged 14 November, 1865.
CANNON, C. C.
Midshipman, 7 April, 1847. Dropped 25 July, 1853.
CANNON, CHARLES G.
Appointed Midshipman, 30 October, 1799. Discharged 12 October, 1861, under Peace Establishment Act.
CANNON, JOHN.
Mate, 21 August, 1863. Acting Ensign, 3 June, 1864. Died 16 July, 1865, on Gennessee.
CANNON, JOHN U.
Appointed Boatswain, 8 May, 1802. Last appearance on Records of Navy Deprtment, 18 July, 1807.
CANNON, JOHN S.
Appointed Midshipman, 26 February, 1814. Dismissed 31 December, 1828.
CANNON, JOSEPH S.
Appointed Master, 16 January, 1829. Dismissed 31 December, 1829.
CANNON, LORING.
Mate, 23 January, 1862. Honorably discharged 19 May, 1865.

GENERAL NAVY REGISTER.

CANNON, THOMAS S.
Acting Ensign, 21 November, 1864. Honorably discharged 1 August, 1865.
CANNON, WILLIAM E.
Mate, 20 May, 1863. Honorably discharged 10 January, 1866.
CAPEN, WILLIAM H.
Acting Third Assistant Engineer, 2 November, 1861. Honorably discharged 6 March, 1866.
CAPEHART, EDWARD E.
Cadet Midshipman, 27 June, 1877. Ensign, Junior Grade, 1 July, 1883. Ensign 26 June, 1884. Lieutenant, Junior Grade, 26 December, 1893. Lieutenant, 28 August, 1897.
CAPERS, WILLIAM H.
Appointed Midshipman, 27 March, 1822. Resigned 20 December, 1824.
CAPERTON, WILLIAM B.
Midshipman, 13 June, 1871. Graduated 20 June, 1876. Ensign, 3 August, 1877. Lieutenant, Junior Grade, 13 October, 1883. Lieutenant, 24 October, 1889. Lieutenant-Commander, 3 March, 1899.
CAPPS, WASHINGTON L.
Cadet Engineer, 1 October, 1880. Naval Cadet, August 5, 1882. Ensign, 1 July, 1886. Assistant Naval Constructor, 6 June, 1888. Naval Constructor (Lieutenant, Junior Grade), 28 January, 1895. Naval Constructor (Commander), August 5, 1899.
CARALL, FRANK.
Acting Boatswain, 1 March, 1900.
CARBERY, HENRY.
Purser, 9 April, 1804. Resigned 23 May, 1804.
CARDELLA, R. F.
Acting Ensign, 1 October, 1862. Resigned 24 November, 1862.
CARELS, JOSEPH H.
Acting Assistant Paymaster, 21 July, 1862. Appointment revoked 11 July, 1863. Sick.
CAREY, GEORGE T.
Mate, 28 August, 1863. Honorably discharged 1 November, 1868.
CAREY, JOHN.
Acting Third Assistant Engineer, 7 October, 1864. Honorably discharged 1 September, 1865.
CAREY, JOSEPH W.
Mate, 28 January, 1863. Appointment revoked 14 March, 1863.
CAREY, MILES.
Appointed Midshipman, 13 March, 1839. Dropped in 1840.
CAREY, RICHARD.
Appointed Midshipman, 2 July, 1801. Discharged 10 November, 1801, under Peace Establishment Act.
CAREY, ROBERT H.
Mate, 23 August, 1861. Acting Ensign, 24 October, 1863. Honorably discharged 18 December, 1868.
CAREY, STEPHEN M.
Mate, 20 July, 1863. Accidentally killed on Dragon, 22 April, 1864.
CARLETON, JOHN.
Appointed Master, 4 July, 1815. Died 12 August, 1847.
CARLEY, WILLIAM D.
Mate, 12 September, 1864. Honorably discharged 24 October, 1865.
CARLIN, JAMES W.
Midshipman, 23 July, 1864. Graduated 2 June, 1868. Ensign, 19 April, 1869. Master, 12 July, 1870. Lieutenant, 12 February, 1874. Lieutenant-Commander, 10 May, 1895. Commander, 3 March, 1899. Died 30 December, 1899.
CARLISLE, COLUMBUS C.
Acting Second Assistant Engineer, 30 May, 1863. Resigned 30 June, 1864.
CARLTON, JOHN.
Master, 4 July, 1815. Died 12 August, 1847.
CARLTON, THOMAS I.
Acting Ensign, 8 June, 1864. Resigned 30 May, 1865.
CARMAN, WILLIAM J.
Acting Third Assistant Engineer, 22 October, 1862. Honorably discharged 9 October, 1865.
CARMICHAEL, E. T.
Appointed Midshipman, 17 September, 1841. Died 7 August, 1847.
CARMODY, JOHN R.
Acting Assistant Paymaster, 27 August, 1864. Assistant Paymaster, 23 July, 1866. Passed Assistant Paymaster, 5 June, 1868. Paymaster, 22 October, 1878. Retired List, 9 April, 1889.
CARMODY, ROBERT EMMET.
Acting Midshipman, 28 November, 1861. Graduated 6 June, 1867. Ensign, 18 December, 1868. Master, 21 March, 1870. Lieutenant, 21 March, 1871. Lieutenant-Commmander, 28 February, 1890. Retired List, 6 June, 1895. Died 2 February, 1896.
CARNES, EDWIN O.
Midshipman, 24 June, 1846. Passed Midshipman, 8 June, 1852. Resigned 30 May, 1855.
CARNELL, THOMAS.
Appointed Midshipman, 2 April, 1804. Resigned 2 June, 1804.
CARNES, JAMES B.
Acting Third Assistant Engineer, 29 September, 1863. Honorably discharged 7 August, 1865.
CARNEY, BENJAMIN B.
Acting Second Assistant Engineer, 1 January, 1863. Dismissed 21 May, 1863.

CARNEY, ROBERT E.
Naval Cadet, 21 May, 1885. Assistant Engineer, 1 July, 1891. Retired List, 31 December, 1896.
CARNS, WILLIAM H.
Appointed Midshipman, 31 December, 1833. Resigned 3 July, 1837.
CARPENDER, EDWARD W.
Midshipman, 10 July, 1813. Lieutenant, 13 January, 1825. Commander, 8 September, 1841. Reserved List, 13 September, 1855. Commodore, Reserved List. Died 16 May, 1877.
CARPENTER, BENJAMIN.
Appointed Midshipman, 10 July, 1798. Died in January, 1800.
CARPENTER, BENJAMIN.
Appointed Midshipman, 10 July, 1813. Drowned 25 May, 1820.
CARPENTER, BENJAMIN O.
Mate, 29 December, 1863. Discharged 6 July, 1864.
CARPENTER, CHARLES CARROLL.
Midshipman, 1 October, 1850. Passed Midshipman, 20 June, 1856. Master, 22 January, 1858. Lieutenant, 23 January, 1858. Lieutenant-Commander, 16 July, 1862. Commander, 10 February, 1869. Captain, 25 March, 1880. Commodore, 15 May, 1893. Rear-Admiral, 11 November, 1894. Retired List, 27 February, 1896. Died 1 April, 1899.
CARPENTER, CHARLES O.
Assistant Surgeon, 30 July, 1861. Resigned 27 March, 1863.
CARPENTER, CHARLES S.
Appointed Midshipman, 27 November, 1798. Discharged 30 April, 1801, under Peace Establishment Act.
CARPENTER, DUDLEY N.
Assistant Surgeon, 24 October, 1896. Passed Assistant Surgeon, 24 October, 1899.
CARPENTER, JACOB.
Appointed Gunner, 28 May, 1836. Died 8 March, 1842.
CARPENTER, JAMES D.
Acting Second Assistant Engineer, 4 June, 1862. Died on Princeton, 19 January, 1864.
CARPENTER, JAMES H.
Mate, 17 February, 1862. Resigned 6 December, 1862.
CARPENTER, JAMES H.
Acting Midshipman, 29 November, 1862. Resigned 8 December, 1865.
CARPENTER, JAMES N.
Purser, 13 September, 1860. Pay Inspector, 3 March, 1871. Retired List, 7 March, 1879. Died 20 March, 1892.
CARPENTER, JOHN B.
Third Assistant Engineer, 17 February, 1860. Second Assistant Engineer, 28 October, 1862. First Assistant Engineer, 1 March, 1864. Chief Engineer, 11 June, 1874. Retired List, 20 December, 1883. Died 22 July, 1888.
CARPENTER, JOHN S.
Mate, 24 December, 1863. Discharged 27 April, 1864.
CARPENTER, JOHN S.
Assistant Paymaster, 29 October, 1881. Passed Assistant Paymaster, 19 November, 1891. Paymaster, 14 August, 1896. Assistant Chief of Bureau of Supply and Accounts from April, 1896, to November, 1896.
CARPENTER, MILLINGTON L.
Acting Master, 4 November, 1861. Resigned 26 May, 1862.
CARPENTER, SAMUEL.
Mate, 24 November, 1863. Acting Ensign, 26 November, 1864. Honorably discharged 31 July, 1865.
CARPENTER, THOMAS.
Acting Gunner, 15 December, 1863. Honorably discharged 28 August, 1865.
CARPENTER, T. O. H.
Surgeon's Mate, 13 October, 1798. Resigned 14 June, 1799.
CARPENTER, WILLIAM A.
Acting Assistant Paymaster, 14 January, 1865. Honorably discharged 4 November, 1865.
CARR, CLARENCE A.
Cadet Engineer, 15 September, 1875. Assistant Engineer, 10 June, 1881. Passed Assistant Engineer, 24 April, 1892. Chief Engineer, 24 February, 1899. Rank changed to Lieutenant, 3 March, 1899.
CARR, CORNELIUS.
Acting Second Assistant Engineer, 18 November, 1861. Acting First Assistant Engineer, 20 November, 1863. Honorably discharged 23 March, 1866.
CARR, EDWARD.
Appointed Boatswain, 2 October, 1799. Discharged 25 May, 1801.
CARR, HENRY P.
Acting Master, 8 June, 1861. Died at Beaufort, North Carolina, 26 December, 1863.
CARR, JAMES.
Acting Third Assistant Engineer, 26 November, 1861. Resigned 7 January, 1862.
CARR, JAMES E.
Appointed Master, 4 August, 1807. Lost in the Wasp, 1815.
CARR, JAMES E.
Acting Ensign, 3 June, 1864. Honorably discharged 15 August, 1865.
CARR, JOHN A.
Appointed Midshipman, 4 July, 1817. Lieutenant, 28 April, 1826. Died 3 May, 1837.
CARR, JOHN H.
Purser, 25 April, 1812. Resigned 30 September, 1830.

GENERAL NAVY REGISTER.

CARR, JOHN P.
Acting Master, 3 September, 1861. Honorably discharged 31 August, 1865.
CARR, NATHANIEL F.
Appointed Midshipman, 3 February, 1840. Dropped.
CARR, OLIVER.
Acting Third Assistant Engineer, 29 December, 1863. Died at New Orleans, 12 October, 1864.
CARR, OVERTON, Jr.
Appointed Midshipman, 2 April, 1804. Resigned 15 April, 1807.
CARR, OVERTON.
Midshipman, 1 March, 1827. Passed Midshipman, 10 June, 1833. Lieutenant, 8 December, 1838. Commander, 14 September, 1855. Retired List, 3 December, 1861. Captain, Retired List, 4 April, 1867. Died 5 March, 1886.
CARRAWAY, JOHN.
Appointed Master, 20 April, 1813. Last appearance on Records of Navy Department. Discharged by Captain Cassin.
CARRICK, GEORGE WASHINGTON.
Third Assistant Engineer, 10 June, 1862. Resigned 18 November, 1865.
CARRICK, SAMUEL D.
Appointed Midshipman, 11 April, 1800. Resigned 26 June, 1800.
CARRINGTON, W. C. G.
Appointed Midshipman, 6 February, 1823. Resigned 10 December, 1829.
CARRINGTON, WILLIAM F.
Assistant Surgeon, 17 June, 1848. Resigned 11 September, 1851.
CARROLL, DAVID W.
Acting Ensign, 9 October, 1862. Acting Master, 5 November, 1864. Honorably discharged 30 September, 1865.
CARROLL, DENNIS.
Mate, 11 July, 1864. Dismissed 6 January, 1865.
CARROLL, FERDINAND.
Midshipman, 4 October, 1850. Dismissed 3 March, 1851.
CARROLL, GEORGE R.
Appointed Midshipman, 2 February, 1829. Passed Midshipman, 4 June, 1836. Resigned 29 May, 1837.
CARROLL, HENRY P.
Acting Third Assistant Engineer, 23 July, 1862. Deserted 1 October, 1862.
CARROLL, JOHN.
Appointed Midshipman, 13 December, 1831. Passed Midshipman, 15 June, 1837. Lieutenant, 8 September, 1841. Died 31 March, 1842.
CARROLL, JOHN.
Third Assistant Engineer, 14 May, 1847. Died 21 December, 1852.
CARROLL, M. B.
Appointed Midshipman, 7 September, 1798. Lieutenant, 10 April, 1802. Commander, 2 February, 1815. Resigned 12 December, 1822.
CARROLL, MICHAEL J.
Acting Third Assistant Engineer, 2 December, 1864. Honorably discharged 24 September, 1865.
CARROLL, RICHARD.
Acting Carpenter, 31 August, 1863. Resigned 9 December, 1864.
CARROLL, ROYAL P.
Lieutenant, Junior Grade (Spanish-American War), 14 May, 1898. Honorably discharged 8 September, 1898.
CARROLL, WILLIAM.
Gunner, 19 July, 1899.
CARROLL, WILLIAM H.
Mate. Resigned 8 May, 1865.
CARRON, JOHN.
Acting Third Assistant Engineer, 29 August, 1861. Acting Second Assistant Engineer, 17 December, 1862. Acting First Assistant Engineer, 1 April, 1864. Honorably discharged 20 November, 1865.
CARROTHERS, JOHN K.
Acting Midshipman, 23 September, 1858. Died 23 December, 1861.
CARRY, WILLIAM H.
Ensign (Spanish-American War), 29 June, 1898. Honorably discharged 14 September, 1898.
CARSON, JOHN.
Appointed Master, 20 November, 1798. Lieutenant, 13 June, 1799. Last appearance on Records of Navy Department.
CARSON, JOHN.
Appointed Master, 26 August, 1808. Dismissed 12 December, 1809.
CARSON, MARTIN.
Acting Third Assistant Engineer, 19 October, 1861. Died on Alabama, 24 July, 1863.
CARSON, PETER.
Appointed Master, 1 November, 1816. Died in 1828.
CARSON, RICHARD.
Appointed Midshipman, 14 April, 1800. Discharged 2 June, 1801, under Peace Establishment Act.
CARSON, RICHARD.
Appointed Midshipman, 15 November, 1809. Resigned 3 January, 1812.
CARSON, ROBERT.
Appointed Midshipman, 1 February, 1814. Last appearance on Records of Navy Department, 15 March, 1815. Dead.

GENERAL NAVY REGISTER.

CARSON, SCOTT H.
Mate, 7 February, 1863. Resigned (sick) 22 August, 1863.
CARSTAIRS, JOHN.
Assistant Engineer (Spanish-American War), 18 May, 1898. Honorably discharged 2 September, 1898.
CARSTAIRS, THOMAS.
Acting Assistant Paymaster, 30 September, 1862. Appointment revoked 30 June, 1866.
CARSWELL, WILLIAM.
Acting Chief Engineer, 1 October, 1862. Resigned 24 November, 1862.
CARSWELL, WILLIAM B.
Cadet Engineer, 1 October, 1879. Resigned 18 June, 1883. Passed Assistant Engineer (Spanish-American War), 23 June, 1898. Honorably discharged 7 January, 1899.
CARTEE, SETH.
Appointed Master, date not known. Lieutenant, 18 May, 1804. Last appearance on Records of Navy Department, 17 April, 1805.
CARTER, ABIEL BEACH.
Midshipman, 24 September, 1861. Graduated June, 1866. Ensign, 12 March, 1868. Master, 26 March, 1869. Lieutenant, 21 March, 1870. Died 30 November, 1874.
CARTER, CAREY.
Midshipman, 12 October, 1848. Resigned 24 June, 1856.
CARTER, CHARLES.
Assistant Surgeon, 1 October, 1861. Resigned 6 February, 1863.
CARTER, DANIEL.
Appointed Midshipman, 1 August, 1826. Died 25 March, 1832.
CARTER, C. E.
Mate, 1 January, 1865. Honorably discharged 18 September, 1865.
CARTER, EDWARD.
Appointed Midshipman, 9 November, 1813. Last appearance on Records of Navy Department, 1814.
CARTER, EDWARD C.
Appointed Midshipman, 1 January, 1812. Resigned 9 July, 1814.
CARTER, ENOCH B.
Acting Third Assistant Engineer, 22 February, 1864. Acting Second Assistant Engineer, 11 March, 1865. Resigned 12 May, 1865.
CARTER, ERNEST.
Assistant Paymaster (Spanish-American War), 7 June, 1898. Honorably discharged 17 September, 1898.
CARTER, FIDELIO S.
Midshipman, 30 September, 1870. Graduated 21 June, 1875. Ensign, 18 July, 1876. Master, 10 March, 1882. Lieutenant, Junior Grade, 3 March, 1883. Lieutenant, 12 February, 1889. Lieutenant-Commander, 3 March, 1899.
CARTER, G. B.
Acting Master's Mate, 16 May, 1861. Resigned 17 September, 1861.
CARTER, HENRY B.
Mate, 1861. Acting Master, 8 February, 1862. Appointment revoked (sick), 21 May, 1862. Reappointed Acting Master, 21 May, 1862. Honorably discharged 11 May, 1865.
CARTER, HILL.
Appointed Midshipman, 9 November, 1813. Resigned 11 March, 1816.
CARTER, JACOB.
Appointed Gunner, date not known. Last appearance on Records of Navy Department.
CARTER, JAMES F.
Naval Cadet, 24 March, 1887. Ensign, 1 July, 1893. Lieutenant, Junior Grade, 3 March, 1899.
CARTER, JOHN C.
Midshipman, 1 January, 1825. Passed Midshipman, 4 June, 1831. Lieutenant, 9 February, 1837. Reserved List, 13 September, 1855. Commander, Active List, 14 September, 1855. Commodore, Retired List, 4 April, 1867. Died 24 November, 1870.
CARTER, JOHN K.
Appointed Master, 9 May, 1812. Last appearance on Records of Navy Department. 28 March, 1814.
CARTER, JOHN K.
Appointed Midshipman, 18 June, 1812. Lieutenant, 27 April, 1816. Died 1 February, 1831.
CARTER, JOHN M.
Mate, 23 May, 1864. Dismissed 19 August, 1864.
CARTER, JOHNSTON B.
Midshipman, 31 December, 1833. Passed Midshipman, 8 July, 1839. Lieutenant, 22 July, 1846. Dismissed 3 September, 1857.
CARTER, JONATHAN H.
Midshipman, 12 March, 1840. Passed Midshipman, 11 July, 1846. Master, 1 March, 1855. Lieutenant, 14 September, 1855. Resigned 25 April, 1861.
CARTER, JOSEPH H.
Mate, 14 May, 1864. Honorably discharged 11 October, 1865.
CARTER, JOSIAH P.
Carpenter, 19 July, 1861. Retired List, 3 February, 1890. Died 30 July, 1897.
CARTER, NATHANIEL, Jr.
Appointed Midshipman, 18 June, 1812. Lieutenant, 5 March, 1817. Died 7 September, 1823.

GENERAL NAVY REGISTER.

CARTER, RICHARD H.
Acting Third Assistant Engineer, 11 January, 1863. Resigned (sick) 1 July, 1864.
CARTER, ROBERT.
Assistant Surgeon, 2 June, 1849. Passed Assistant Surgeon, 24 February, 1857. Resigned 3 July, 1858.
CARTER, ROBERT R.
Midshipman, 30 March, 1842. Passed Midshipman, 5 August, 1848. Master, 15 September, 1855. Lieutenant, 16 September, 1855. Resigned 2 April, 1861.
CARTER, RODNEY F.
Acting Third Assistant Engineer, 16 December, 1863. Acting Second Assistant Engineer, 21 March, 1865. Honorably discharged 11 October, 1865.
CARTER, SAMUEL P.
Midshipman, 14 February, 1840. Passed Midshipman, 11 July, 1846. Master. 12 September, 1854. Lieutenant, 18 April, 1855. Lieutenant-Commander, 16 July, 1862. Commander, 25 June, 1865. Captain, 28 October, 1870. Commodore, 13 November, 1878. Retired List, 6 August, 1881. Rear-Admiral on Retired List, 16 May, 1882. Died 26 May, 1891.
CARTER, THOMAS F.
Cadet Engineer, 1 October, 1873. Graduated 10 June, 1879. Assistant Engineer, 10 June, 1881. Passed Assistant Engineer, 12 April, 1892. Rank changed to Lieutenant 3 March, 1899.
CARTER, THOMAS U.
Appointed Midshipman, 4 March, 1818. Resigned 25 January, 1819.
CARTER, WILLIAM.
Carpenter, 18 February, 1870. Appointment revoked 8 September, 1870. Carpenter, 17 June, 1874. Died 14 March, 1880.
CARTER, WILLIAM.
Appointed Midshipman, 13 July, 1831. Resigned 15 March, 1834.
CARTER, WILLIAM, Jr.
Appointed Midshipman, 28 June, 1804. Lieutenant, 28 April, 1810. Commander, 27 April, 1816. Cashiered 7 December, 1827.
CARTER, WILLIAM W.
Gunner, 21 May, 1859. Acting Master, 8 October, 1862. Honorably discharged as Acting Master 24 October, 1865, remaining in service as Gunner. Retired List, 18 March, 1895.
CARTER, WOODWARD.
Mate, 12 September, 1862. Acting Ensign, 25 January, 1864. Honorably discharged 9 October, 1868. Boatswain, 18 April, 1879. Retire List, 15 February, 1897.
CARTMELL, GEORGE.
Assistant Engineer (Spanish-American War), 15 June, 1898. Honorably discharged 2 September, 1898.
CARTON, THOMAS H.
Acting Third Assistant Engineer, 22 September, 1863. Honorably discharged 20 September, 1865.
CARTWRIGHT, THOMAS G.
Mate, 19 December, 1864. Appointment revoked 4 January, 1866.
CARTY, CHARLES L.
Acting First Assistant Engineer, 17 October 1862. Acting Chief Engineer, 19 May, 1864. Honorably discharged 29 November, 1865.
CARVER, D. M.
Mate. Acting Ensign, 5 September, 1863. Resigned 22 May, 1865.
CARVER, JESSE T.
Acting Ensign, 30 April, 1864. Honorably discharged 9 July, 1865.
CARWEN, CHRISTOPHER.
Acting Ensign, 16 December, 1862. Honorably discharged 11 November, 1865.
CASE, AUGUSTUS L.
Midshipman, 1 April, 1828. Passed Midshipman, 14 June, 1834. Lieutenant. 25 February, 1841. Commander, 14 September, 1855. Captain, 2 January, 1863. Commodore, 8 December, 1867. Rear-Admiral, 24 May, 1872. Retired List, 3 February, 1875. Died 17 February, 1893.
CASE, AUGUSTUS L., Jr.
Midshipman, 23 June, 1869. Graduated 31 May, 1873. Ensign, 16 July, 1874. Master, 1 April, 1880. Resigned 7 April, 1882.
CASE, CHARLES.
Mate, 26 June, 1862. Acting Ensign, 25 May, 1864. Honorably discharged 12 December, 1865.
CASE, CHESTER N.
Acting Assistant Paymaster, 14 January, 1865. Honorably discharged 10 September, 1865.
CASE, DANIEL R.
Midshipman, 5 June, 1872. Graduated 20 June, 1876. Resigned 8 January, 1879.
CASE, FRANCIS A.
Mate, 25 April, 1864. Lost on Narcissus, 4 January, 1866.
CASE, FRANK B.
Cadet Midshipman, 10 June, 1873. Graduated 18 June, 1879. Wholly retired 18 December, 1882. Lieutenant (Spanish-American War), 14 May, 1898. Honorably discharged 1 March, 1899.
CASE, GEORGE F.
Acting Second Assistant Engineer, 19 March, 1864. Honorably discharged 14 August, 1865.
CASE, HENRY A.
Mate, 27 September, 1864. Honorably discharged 27 September, 1865.

GENERAL NAVY REGISTER.

CASE, J. MADISON.
Acting Second Assistant Engineer, 1 December, 1862. Honorably discharged 27 September, 1865.
CASE, ROBERT L.
Acting Third Assistant Engineer, 10 October, 1864. Honorably discharged 19 April, 1866.
CASE, WILLIAM S.
Naval Cadet, 6 September, 1895. Graduated 30 June, 1900.
CASEY, CHARLES H.
Acting Ensign, 8 July, 1864. Resigned 30 May, 1865.
CASEY, CHARLES H.
Acting Warrant Machinist, 23 August, 1899.
CASEY, HENRY P.
Appointed Midshipman, 17 July, 1800. Dismissed 9 December, 1805.
CASEY, JOHN A.
Surgeon's Mate, 30 October, 1799. Permitted to retire, 24 April, 1801.
CASEY, MARTIN.
Acting Warrant Machinist, 23 August, 1899.
CASEY, SILAS.
Acting Midshipman, 25 September, 1856. Midshipman, 15 June, 1860 Master, 19 September, 1861. Lieutenant, 16 July, 1862. Lieutenant-Commander, 25 July, 1866. Commander, 14 June, 1874. Captain, 12 February, 1889. Commodore, 11 May, 1898. Rear-Admiral, **3 March, 1899.**
CASH, THOMAS M.
Acting Master, 17 May, 1861. Resigned 11 June, 1861. Reappointed 29 August, 1861. **Appointment revoked 23 November, 1861.**
CASS, ALEX. H.
Appointed Midshipman, 21 July, 1835. Died 27 May, 1839.
CASSAN, LEWIS P.
Acting Ensign, 3 June, 1864. Resigned 16 March, 1865.
CASSARD, WILLIAM G.
Chaplain, 3 April, 1897.
CASSEDY, GEORGE V.
Acting Master, 22 March, 1862. Resigned 26 May, 1863. Acting Ensign, 28 December, 1864. Honorably discharged 21 July, 1865.
CASSEDY, WILLIAM H.
Acting Master's Mate, 5 June, 1863. Honorably discharged, 1865.
CASSEL, DOUGLAS.
Acting Midshipman, 28 September, 1860. Acting Ensign, 13 October, 1863. Master, 10 March, 1866. Lieutenant, 25 July, 1866. Lieutenant-Commander, 12 March, 1868. Died 15 June, 1875.
CASSELL, ALEX. W.
Sailmaker, 18 February, 1847. Resigned 27 July, 1847. Sailmaker, 7 April, 1859. Retired List, 28 March, 1886. Died 8 October, 1897.
CASSELL, CHARLES.
Appointed Sailmaker, 27 September, 1813. Resigned 11 February, 1815. Appointed Sailmaker, 24 June, 1817. Died 30 August, 1827.
CASSELL, JACOB W.
Acting Third Assistant Engineer, 3 October, 1864. Honorably discharged 12 December, 1865.
CASSIDY, EDWARD.
Mate, 8 October, 1862. Dismissed 12 May, 1865.
CASSIDY, EDWARD A.
Carpenter, 7 April, 1854. Warranted, 18 June, 1857. Died at Baltimore, Maryland, 19 July, 1860.
CASSIDY, EDWARD R.
Ensign (Spanish-American War), 14 May, 1898. Honorably discharged 4 March, 1899.
CASSIDY, FELIX.
Acting Gunner, 8 November, 1862. Gunner, 22 October, 1863. Died 8 June, 1884.
CASSIDY, FRANCIS.
Enlisted 10 October, 1861. Discharged as Acting Master's Mate 20 November, 1864.
CASSIDY, THOMAS S.
Gunner, 4 November, 1861. Dismissed 18 July, 1864. Restored on probation 15 August, 1864. Appointment revoked 1 July, 1867.
CASSIN, CHARLES L.
Assistant Surgeon, 31 March, 1869. Passed Assistant Surgeon, 28 February, 1874. Died 14 January, 1878.
CASSIN, JOHN.
Appointed Lieutenant, 13 November, 1799. Commander, 2 April, 1806. Captain, 3 July, 1812. Died 24 March, 1822.
CASSIN, JOHN.
Appointed Midshipman, 10 May, 1820. Lieutenant, 7 May, 1828. Died 16 October, 1837.
CASSIN, JOSEPH, Jr.
Appointed Midshipman, 16 January, 1809. Lieutenant, 24 July, 1813. Died 30 November, 1826.
CASSIN, JOSEPH.
Purser, 29 December, 1807. Died in 1821.
CASSIN, NICHOLAS.
Acting Third Assistant Engineer, 11 June, 1864. Honorably discharged 2 November, 1865. Acting Third Assistant Engineer, 29 January, 1867. Died on the Tacony, 10 September, 1867.

GENERAL NAVY REGISTER.

CASSIN, ROBERT A.
Appointed Midshipman, 1 November, 1826. Resigned 9 June, 1834.
CASSIN, STEPHEN.
Midshipman, 21 February, 1800. Lieutenant, 12 February, 1807. Commander, 11 September, 1814. Captain, 3 March, 1825. Reserved List, 13 September, 1855. Died 29 August, 1857.
CASTANO, DOMINGO.
Acting Third Assistant Engineer, 15 May, 1863. Honorably discharged 8 July, 1869.
CASTELL, G. CLINTON.
Acting Third Assistant Engineer, 8 August, 1863. Acting Second Assistant Engineer, 1 April, 1865. Honorably discharged 30 August, 1867.
CASTILLO, JOAQUIM D.
Assistant Surgeon, 6 July, 1880. Resigned 3 October, 1883.
CASTLE, FREDERICK A.
Acting Assistant Surgeon, 22 September, 1862. Honorably discharged 26 September, 1865.
CASTLE, WILLIAM W.
Acting Assistant Paymaster, 6 March, 1865. Mustered out 2 September, 1866.
CASTLEMAN, KENNETH G.
Naval Cadet, 6 September, 1892. Assistant Engineer, 6 May, 1898. Rank changed to Ensign 3 March, 1899.
CASWELL, BENJAMIN F.
Mate, 28 October, 1861. Deserted 9 December, 1861.
CASWELL, DANIEL.
Appointed Carpenter, 23 August, 1836. Died 25 February, 1842.
CASWELL, ELBRIDGE G., Jr.
Mate, 4 January, 1864. Honorably discharged 5 September, 1865.
CASWELL, G. W.
Mate, 19 November, 1861. Master, 2 June, 1862. Last appearance on Records 22 March, 1865.
CASWELL, JOHN W.
Mate, 15 September, 1862. Resigned 15 September, 1864.
CASWELL, RICHARD.
Mate, 15 December, 1862. Dismissed 17 February, 1863.
CASWELL, THOMAS T.
Assistant Paymaster, 9 September, 1861. Passed Assistant Paymaster, 6 February, 1862. Paymaster, 17 September, 1863. Pay Inspector, 31 August, 1881. **Pay Director, 25 December, 1892.** Retired List, 5 June, 1899.
CATALANO, SALVADORE.
Appointed Master, 9 August, 1809. Died 5 January, 1846.
CATCHPOLE, ALFRED.
Acting Second Assistant Engineer, 24 August, 1864. Honorably discharged 21 July, 1865.
CATE, DAVID.
Acting Volunteer Lieutenant, 26 August, 1861. Died on Mississippi River 4 May, 1865.
CATHCART, ARTHUR H.
Assistant Paymaster (Spanish-American War), 27 July, 1898. Honorably discharged 30 January, 1899. Assistant Paymaster (Regular Navy), 15 May, 1899.
CATHCART, WILLIAM L.
Cadet Engineer, 1 October, 1873. Graduated 21 June, 1875. Assistant Engineer, 1 July, 1877. Passed Assistant Engineer, 24 December, 1884. Resigned 23 January, 1891. Chief Engineer (Spanish-American War), 10 June, 1898. Honorably discharged 22 October, 1898.
CATHERWOOD, ARTHUR D.
Acting Warrant Machinist, 23 August, 1899.
CATLETT, HANSON.
Surgeon's Mate, 3 August, 1798. Surgeon, 14 August, 1799. Discharged under Peace Establishment Act, 29 April, 1801.
CATON, RICHARD.
Appointed Midshipman, 9 June, 1811. Resigned 20 May, 1816.
CATON, WILLIAM.
Surgeon's Mate, 1810. Surgeon, 24 July, 1813. Died 19 October, 1819.
CAULK, JOHN.
Gunner, 2 September, 1841. Died 19 May, 1873.
CAULK, P. R.
Mate, 1861. Appointment revoked 11 March, 1862.
CAULLET, BENJAMIN.
Acting Ensign, 3 August, 1863. Honorably discharged 6 September, 1865.
CAUSLER, WILLIAM.
Appointed Master, 29 March, 1814. Last appearance on Records of Navy Department, 5 April, 1814.
CAUSTEN, JOSEPH H.
Purser, 20 December, 1817. Died 29 June, 1822.
CAVEN, CHARLES H.
Acting Chief Engineer, 1 October, 1862. Honorably discharged 30 November, 1865.
CAVENDY, EDWARD.
Boatswain, 8 April, 1849. Resigned 8 October, 1853. Acting Master, 5 May, 1861. Acting Volunteer Lieutenant, 23 September, 1861. Honorably discharged 2 October, 1865. Acting Master, 18 October, 1867. Mustered out 2 October, 1868. Boatswain, 22 May, 1869. Retired List, 4 September, 1871. Died 17 January, 1880.

GENERAL NAVY REGISTER.

CAYE, EDMUND.
 Acting First Assistant Engineer, 9 June, 1863. Honorably discharged, 1 December, 1865.
CECIL, FRANCIS M.
 Carpenter, 19 February, 1838. Died 18 April, 1864.
CENAS, HILARY.
 Acting Midshipman, 21 September, 1855. Midshipman, 9 June, 1859. Dismissed 24 August, 1861.
CENTER, FRANK P.
 Acting Ensign, 21 April, 1864. Honorably discharged 15 September, 1865.
CENTER, STURGIS.
 Acting Ensign, 5 March, 1864. Honorably discharged 15 September, 1866.
CHADSEY, ARTHUR E.
 Acting Midshipman, 2 October, 1861. Resigned 19 March, 1866.
CHADWELL, JOSEPH F.
 Acting Master, 16 September, 1862. Dismissed 16 May, 1863.
CHADWICK, B. H.
 Acting Ensign, 22 July, 1863. Honorably discharged 7 October, 1868.
CHADWICK, CHARLES.
 Acting First Assistant Engineer, 7 May, 1864. Honorably discharged 2 December, 1865.
CHADWICK, DARWIN J.
 Mate, 14 May, 1864. Honorably discharged 1 August, 1865.
CHADWICK, DAVID V.
 Assistant Paymaster, 25 April, 1899.
CHADWICK, EDMUND A.
 Acting Assistant Paymaster, 10 July, 1863. Honorably discharged 10 December, 1865.
CHADWICK, FRANK L.
 Naval Cadet, 18 May, 1889. Ensign, 1 July, 1895. Lieutenant, Junior Grade, 3 March, 1899.
CHADWICK, FRENCH E.
 Acting Midshipman, 28 September, 1861. Midshipman, 16 July, 1862. Graduated 22 November, 1864. Ensign, 1 November, 1866. Master, 1 December, 1866. Lieutenant, 12 March, 1868. Lieutenant-Commander, 26 March, 1869. Commander, 12 December, 1884. Captain, 7 November, 1897.
CHADWICK, JERE.
 Acting Master, 26 February, 1862. Honorably discharged 22 September, 1865.
CHADWICK, JOHN E.
 Acting Second Assistant Engineer, 21 October, 1864. Resigned 12 May, 1865.
CHADWICK, JOHN P.
 Acting Ensign, 3 March, 1864. Honorably discharged 31 August, 1865.
CHADWICK, JOSEPH A.
 Mate, 30 December, 1861. Acting Ensign, 20 July, 1863. Honorably discharged 6 April, 1866.
CHADWICK, JOSEPH M.
 Mate, 4 November, 1862. Acting Ensign, 20 July, 1863. Honorably discharged 31 October, 1865.
CHADWICK, WILLIAM W.
 Acting Third Assistant Engineer, 30 July, 1864. Honorably discharged 5 December, 1865.
CHAFFEE, CHARLES H.
 Acting Third Assistant Engineer, 6 June, 1864. Honorably discharged 28 October, 1865.
CHAFFEE, JEROME S.
 Assistant Surgeon, 21 July, 1898. Resigned 18 September, 1899.
CHAFFEE, JOSIAH C.
 Acting Third Assistant Engineer, 2 December, 1861. Second Assistant Engineer, 8 September, 1863. Dropped 25 July, 1872.
CHAILLE, WILLIAM H.
 Appointed Midshipman, 17 December, 1810. Last appearance on Records of Navy Department, 30 September, 1815.
CHALMERS, DAVID.
 Appointed Midshipman, 2 April, 1804. Struck off 8 May, 1806.
CHALMERS, MATTHEW.
 Assistant Surgeon, 3 December, 1861. Resigned 3 August, 1864.
CHAMBERLAIN, CHARLES C.
 Mate, 7 August, 1863. Honorably discharged 29 July, 1865.
CHAMBERLAIN, EZRA.
 Appointed Boatswain, 17 December, 1841. Dismissed 26 July, 1843. Boatswain, 10 February, 1851. Dismissed 22 March, 1851.
CHAMBERLAIN, GEORGE.
 Acting Ensign, 29 April, 1864. Honorably discharged 13 February, 1866.
CHAMBERLAIN, LEANDER S.
 Acting Assistant Paymaster, 3 June, 1863. Resigned 11 October, 1866.
CHAMBERLAIN, OTIS C.
 Acting Third Assistant Engineer, 6 May, 1864. Honorably discharged 28 October, 1865. Acting Third Assistant Engineer, 31 July, 1866. Mustered out 9 November, 1868.
CHAMBERLAIN, S. P.
 Appointed Master, 8 January, 1814. Died 8 February, 1822.
CHAMBERLAIN, W. D.
 Appointed Midshipman, 4 July, 1805. Resigned 16 January, 1808.

GENERAL NAVY REGISTER.

CHAMBERLAIN, W. R. F.
Appointed Midshipman, 9 November, 1813. Resigned 4 November, 1814.
CHAMBERS, FRANK T.
Civil Engineer, 19 July, 1897.
CHAMBERS, HENRY A.
Appointed Midshipman, 1 January, 1825. Resigned 23 June, 1826.
CHAMBERS, JOHN.
Acting Third Assistant Engineer, 7 July, 1864. Honorably discharged 1 August, 1865.
CHAMBERS, JOHN L.
Mate, 28 August, 1862. Resigned 6 May, 1865.
CHAMBERS, JOHN W.
Acting Ensign, 22 April, 1863. Honorably discharged 27 September, 1865.
CHAMBERS, MICHAEL A.
Passed Assistant Engineer (Spanish-American War), 23 June, 1898. Honorably discharged 23 November, 1898.
CHAMBERS, THOMAS.
Appointed Master, 24 February, 1812. Last appearance on Records of Navy Department.
CHAMBERS, WASHINGTON I.
Midshipman, 9 June, 1871. Graduated 20 June, 1876. Ensign, 30 November, 1878. Lieutenant, Junior Grade, 1 January, 1886. Lieutenant, 29 May, 1891. Lieutenant Commander, 1 July, 1899.
CHAMBERS, WILLIAM H.
Cadet Engineer, 1 October, 1878. Assistant Engineer, 1 July, 1884. Passed Assistant Engineer, 28 August, 1894. Rank changed to Lieutenant, 3 March, 1899.
CHAMPION, JOHN C.
Acting Master, 15 August, 1861. Honorably discharged 27 November, 1865.
CHAMPION, NEWTON.
Third Assistant Engineer, 22 October, 1860. Second Assistant Engineer, 17 December, 1862. Resigned 22 September, 1863.
CHAMPION, NEWTON.
Acting Second Assistant Engineer, 7 November, 1864. Honorably discharged 3 March, 1866.
CHAMPLIN, JABEZ.
Surgeon, 30 November, 1799. Discharged under Peace Establishment Act, 13 April, 1801.
CHAMPLIN, STEPHEN.
Master, 22 May, 1812. Lieutenant, 9 December, 1814. Commander, 22 June, 1838. Captain, 4 August, 1850. Reserved List, 13 September, 1855. Commodore on Reserved List, 4 April, 1867. Died 20 February, 1870.
CHAMPNEY, BENJAMIN.
Surgeon, 30 November, 1799. Discharged 13 April, 1801, under Peace Establishment Act.
CHANCE, FRANKLIN.
Mate, 26 November, 1863. Resigned 25 June, 1864.
CHAUNCEY, ISAAC.
Lieutenant, 17 September, 1798. Commander, 23 May, 1804. Captain, 24 April, 1806. Died 27 January, 1840.
CHAUNCEY, WOLCOTT.
Appointed Midshipman, 28 June, 1804. Lieutenant, 7 June, 1810. Commander, 5 March, 1817. Captain, 24 April, 1828. Died 14 October, 1835.
CHANDLER, B. F.
Civil Engineer, 7 July, 1852. Retired List, 15 October, 1881. Died 31 October, 1886.
CHANDLER, ISAAC A.
Acting Third Assistatant Engineer, 18 January, 1864. Honorably discharged 11 November, 1865.
CHANDLER, JOHN R.
Surgeon's Mate, 14 November, 1824. Surgeon, 4 December, 1828. Died 28 July, 1841.
CHANDLER, JOSEPH W.
Acting Ensign, 23 January, 1863. Honorably discharged 27 March, 1867.
CHANDLER, JOSIAH A.
Acting Third Assistant Engineer, 2 July, 1864. Honorably discharged 27 July, 1865.
CHANDLER, LLOYD H.
Naval Cadet, 4 September, 1884. Ensign, 1 July, 1890. Lieutenant, Junior Grade, 8 April, 1898. Lieutenant, 3 March, 1899.
CHANDLER, RALPH.
Midshipman, 27 September, 1845. Passed Midshipman, 6 October, 1851. Master, 15 September, 1855. Lieutenant, 16 September, 1855. Lieutenant-Commander, 16 July, 1862. Commander, 25 July, 1866. Captain, 5 June, 1874. Commodore, 1 March, 1884. Rear Admiral, 7 October, 1886. Died 11 February, 1889.
CHANDLER, SAMUEL.
Chaplain, date not known. Discharged 9 April, 1802.
CHANDLER, THOMAS K.
Acting Assistant Surgeon, 11 April, 1864. Acting Passed Assistant Surgeon, 9 June, 1866. Died 5 February, 1867.
CHANDLER, WILLIAM.
Midshipman, 1 August, 1820. Passed Midshipman, 28 April, 1832. Lieutenant, 23 September, 1837. Reserved List, 13 September, 1855. Commander, Active List, 14 September, 1855. Dismissed 17 October, 1861.
CHANDLER, WILLIAM.
Mate, 19 August, 1862. Acting Ensign, 8 June, 1864. Honorably discharged 14 August, 1865.

GENERAL NAVY REGISTER.

CHANEY, JAMES M.
Acting Third Assistant Engineer, 7 August, 1863. Honorably discharged 18 January 1866.
CHANEY, LOUIS.
Mate, 11 May, 1863. Resigned 14 September, 1863.
CHANNING, JOHN M.
Appointed Midshipman, 9 November, 1813. Dismissed by Court Martial, 30 August, 1819.
CHAPIN, EUGENE.
Acting Assistant Paymaster, 1 July, 1863. Discharged 25 January, 1866.
CHAPIN, FREDERICK L.
Cadet Midshipman, 29 September, 1879. Ensign, 1 July, 1885. Lieutenant, Junior Grade, 1 March, 1895. Lieutenant, 27 April, 1898.
CHAPIN, THOMAS E.
Acting Ensign, 21 August, 1862. Acting Master, 19 July, 1864. Honorably discharged 12 August, 1865.
CHAPLIN, JABEZ.
Purser, 6 August, 1799. Discharged 2 April, 1801, under Peace Establishment Act.
CHAPLIN, JAMES C.
Midshipman, 4 October, 1850. Passed Midshipman, 20 June, 1856. Master, 22 January, 1858. Lieutenant, 18 November, 1858. Lieutenant-Commander, 18 April, 1863. Died 23 September, 1866.
CHAPLIN, WILLIAM C.
Midshipman, 1 November, 1826. Passed Midshipman, 28 April, 1832. Lieutenant, 8 March, 1837. Died 30 April, 1855.
CHAPMAN, ALONZO B.
Acting Carpenter, 9 December, 1862. Resigned 9 November, 1863.
CHAPMAN, CHARLES L.
Mate, 18 April, 1863. Dismissed 30 May, 1865.
CHAPMAN, CLOYD M.
Assistant Engineer (Spanish-American War), 25 July, 1898. Honorably discharged 17 November, 1898.
CHAPMAN, GEORGE A.
Mate, 7 January, 1862. Dismissed 20 June, 1862.
CHAPMAN, GEORGE H.
Midshipman, 9 September, 1847. Resigned 14 May, 1851.
CHAPMAN, GEORGE T.
Midshipman, 16 October, 1849. Appointment revoked 15 March, 1850.
CHAPMAN, GEORGE T.
Acting Ensign, 20 July, 1863. Honorably discharged 19 September, 1865.
CHAPMAN, GEORGE W.
Midshipman, 20 September, 1832. Passed Midshipman, 23 June, 1838. Lieutenant, 8 September, 1841. Died at Philadelphia, 20 February, 1853.
CHAPMAN, JAMES H.
Assistant Paymaster, 22 March, 1881. Passed Assistant Paymaster, 12 September, 1891. Died 26 February, 1895.
CHAPMAN, JOHN H.
Mate, 7 June, 1862. Resigned 15 November, 1862. Acting Ensign, 30 September, 1864. Honorably discharged 17 November, 1868.
CHAPMAN, JONATHAN.
Appointed Captain, 10 September, 1798. Resigned 25 January, 1799.
CHAPMAN, JONATHAN.
Acting Assistant Paymaster, 4 November, 1862. Resigned 9 March, 1865.
CHAPMAN, MARCUS.
Mate, 11 May, 1864. Honorably discharged 7 November, 1865.
CHAPMAN, ROBERT T.
Midshipman, 7 April, 1847. Passed Midshipman, 10 June, 1853. Master, 15 September, 1855. Lieutenant, 16 September, 1855. Resigned 16 January, 1861.
CHAPPEL, S. ELISHA.
Acting Second Assistant Engineer, 1861. Appointment revoked 17 March, 1862. Acting Third Assistant Engineer, 21 March, 1862. Acting Second Assistant Engineer, 23 September, 1863. Honorably discharged 10 March, 1866.
CHAPPELL, RALPH H.
Naval Cadet, 22 May, 1890. Assistant Engineer, 1 July, 1896. Rank changed to Ensign, 3 March, 1899. Lieutenant, Junior Grade, 1 July, 1899. Resigned 12 October, 1900.
CHARILTON, JOHN M.
Appointed Midshipman, 18 June, 1812. Resigned 31 December, 1814.
CHARLES, EDWARD W.
Mate, 24 January, 1863. Resigned 25 June, 1863.
CHARLTON, THOMAS J.
Assistant Surgeon, 15 August, 1857. Resigned 18 December, 1860.
CHARLTON, WILLIAM.
Acting Third Assistant Engineer, 21 October, 1863. Honorably discharged 26 April, 1866.
CHARLTON, WILLIAM, Jr.
Mate, 19 Decemebr, 1863. Honorably discharged 26 Decemebr, 1865.
CHARRETTE, GEORGE.
Gunner, 15 June, 1898.
CHASE, ANTHONY.
Acting Master, 27 August, 1861. Supposed killed 21 November, 1862.

CHASE, CHARLES.
Surgeon's Mate, 10 December, 1814.   Surgeon, 3 May, 1825.   Retired 21 December, 1861.   Medical Director on Retired List, 3 March, 1871.   Died 2 March, 1877.
CHASE, CHARLES H.
Mate, 12 August, 1862.   Appointment revoked 28 December, 1869.
CHASE, CHARLES T.
Acting Master, 14 August, 1861.   Honorably discharged 17 September, 1865.
CHASE, CHARLES T.
Mate, 15 April, 1898.   Boatswain, 6 March, 1899.
CHASE, DANIEL.
Ensign (Spanish-American War), 20 May, 1898.   Commission expired 21 June, 1898. Reappointed Ensign, 27 June, 1898.   Honorably discharged 22 September, 1898.
CHASE, DAVID L.
Mate, 22 October, 1862.   Resigned 12 December, 1862.
CHASE, F. B.
Mate, 23 November, 1864.   Honorably discharged 11 September, 1865.
CHASE, GILBERT.
Naval Cadet, 6 September, 1893.   Ensign, 1 July, 1899.
CHASE, HENRY.
Acting Third Assistant Engineer, 6 December, 1862.   Resigned 24 July, 1863.
CHASE, HENRY A.
Acting Third Assistant Engineer, 5 May, 1864.   Honorably discharged 16 July, 1866.
CHASE, HENRY E.
Acting Ensign, 13 August, 1864.   Drowned in New York Harbor. 11 November, 1864.
CHASE, HENRY M.
Acting Assistant Surgeon, 18 December, 1863.   Honorably discharged 26 September, 1865.
CHASE, HENRY S.
Cadet Midshipman, 24 June, 1875.   Graduated, 10 June, 1881.   Ensign, Junior Grade, 3 March, 1883.   Ensign, 26 June, 1884.   Lieutenant, Junior Grade, 27 January, 1891.   Retired List, 10 March, 1896.   Died 19 May, 1897.
CHASE, JABEZ F.
Acting Ensign, 8 October, 1862.   Honorably discharged 16 November, 1865.
CHASE, JEHU V.
Naval Cadet, 28 September, 1886.   Ensign, 1 July, 1892.   Lieutenant, 3 March, 1899.
CHASE, JOHN W.
Acting Ensign, 13 March, 1865.   Honorably discharged 14 August, 1865.
CHASE, LUKE B.
Acting Master, 4 November, 1861.   Resigned 21 August, 1862.
CHASE, MARK S.
Acting Master, 30 November, 1861.   Dismissed 21 February, 1862.
CHASE, MOSES B.
Chaplain, 8 September, 1841.   Retired List, 21 December, 1861.   Died at Cambridge, Mass., 21 October, 1875.
CHASE, PHILANDER.
Chaplain, 29 December, 1818.   Resigned 8 August, 1820.
CHASE, SAMUEL.
Appointed Lieutenant, 21 September, 1798.   Resigned 24 December, 1799.
CHASE, S. WARREN.
Mate, 21 May, 1863.   Acting Ensign, 5 October, 1864.   Honorably discharged 30 July, 1865.
CHASE, THOMAS.
Third Assistant Engineer, 4 May, 1863.   Resigned 13 November, 1865.
CHASE, VOLNEY O.
Cadet Engineer, 1 October, 1881.   Ensign, 1 July, 1887.   Lieutenant, Junior Grade, 18 February, 1896.   Lieutenant, 13 January, 1899.
CHASE, WHITMAN.
Acting Ensign, 23 August, 1862.   Resigned 18 February, 1865.
CHASE, WILLIAM F.
Acting Ensign, 24 January, 1863.   Acting Master, gallant conduct in command of Mayflower in defence of Fort Powhatan, 7 June, 1864.   Honorably discharged 11 August, 1865.   Acting Master, 25 May, 1866.   Mustered out 1 August, 1867.
CHASMAR, JAMES HENRY.
Third Assistant Engineer, 7 April, 1862.   Second Assistant Engineer, 2 February, 1864.   First Assistant Engineer, 1 January, 1868.   Chief Engineer, 27 January, 1889.   Retired List, 11 October, 1898.
CHASON, PETER A.
Boatswain, 27 September, 1858.   Retired List, 26 October, 1866.   Died at Baltimore, Md., 5 October, 1876.
CHASSAING, BENJAMIN E.
Third Assistant Engineer, 21 May, 1857.   Second Assistant Engineer, 3 August, 1859.   First Assistant Engineer, 21 October, 1861.   Chief Engineer, 10 November, 1863.   Resigned 12 February, 1867.
CHATARD, FREDERICK.
Midshipman, 16 November, 1824.   Lieutenant, 29 March, 1834.   Commander, 14 September, 1855.   Resigned 24 April, 1861.
CHATFIELD, THOMAS.
Acting Master, 27 March, 1862.   Acting Volunteer Lieutenant, 29 April, 1865. Honorably discharged 3 November, 1865.

GENERAL NAVY REGISTER. 111

CHATFIELD, WILLIAM F.
Mate, 30 December, 1863. Acting Ensign, 23 December, 1864. Honorably discharged 14 November, 1865.
CHAUNCEY, CHARLES W.
Appointed Midshipman, 1 May, 1822. Lieutenant, 27 May, 1830. Died 10 August, 1847.
CHAUNCEY, JOHN S.
Midshipman, 1 January, 1812. Lieutenant, 13 January, 1825. Commander, 8 September, 1841. Dropped, 13 September, 1855. Commissioned Captain, 14 September, 1855. Commodore, Retired List, 4 April, 1869. Died 10 April, 1871.
CHAUVENET, WILLIAM.
Professor, 8 December, 1841. Commissioned, 8 December, 1848. Resigned 19 September, 1860.
CHAVALIER, JOHN C.
Sailmaker, 3 March, 1857. Resigned 5 October, 1857. Sailmaker, 10 August, 1861. Resigned 6 April, 1864. Sailmaker, 12 November, 1869. Retired List, 17 March, 1882. Died 9 August, 1887.
CHEATHAM, JOSEPH J.
Assistant Paymaster, 22 August, 1894. Passed Assistant Paymaster, 1 November, 1896. Paymaster, 23 December, 1899.
CHEESBOROUGH, W. E.
Appointed Midshipman, 2 April, 1804. Resigned 18 February, 1806.
CHEESEMAN, WILLIAM S.
Acting Master, 27 September, 1861. Acting Volunteer Lieutenant, good service, 28 November, 1863. Acting Volunteer Lieutenant-Commander, 9 March, 1865. Honorably discharged 30 September, 1865.
CHEEVER, DAVID A.
Midshipman, 19 October, 1841. Resigned 23 December, 1847.
CHEEVER, WILLIAM HARRISON.
Midshipman, 19 October, 1849. Passed Midshipman, 12 June, 1855. Master, 16 September, 1855. Lieutenant, 11 May, 1856. Died 13 July, 1857.
CHEEVERS, MARSHALL P.
Acting Second Assistant Engineer, 10 September, 1861. Acting First Assistant Engineer, 9 September, 1862. Acting Chief Engineer, 27 June, 1864. Honorably discharged 17 July, 1865.
CHENERY, CHARLES E.
Assistant Paymaster, 10 March, 1863. Paymaster, 4 May, 1866. Dismissed 15 September, 1868.
CHENERY, LEONARD.
Acting Midshipman, 12 December, 1861. Graduated September, 1865. Ensign, 1 December, 1866. Master, 12 March, 1868. Lieutenant, 26 March, 1869. Lieutenant-Commander, 1 November, 1879. Retired List, 20 December, 1881.
CHENEY, EDWARD.
Third Assistant Engineer, 12 August, 1862. Second Assistant Engineer, 15 February, 1864. Resigned 31 March, 1869.
CHENEY, JOHN M.
Acting Third Assistant Engineer, 4 January, 1865. Honorably discharged 30 November, 1867.
CHENEY, LUTHER.
Acting Third Assistant Engineer, 23 January, 1865. Honorably discharged 15 May, 1865.
CHENEY, WILLIAM.
Gunner, 11 October, 1860. Retired List, 15 February, 1882.
CHENOWETH, G. D.
Appointed Midshipman, 19 October, 1841. Died in April, 1847.
CHERRY, WILLIAM L.
Third Assistant Engineer, 16 November, 1861. Second Assistant Engineer, 25 August, 1863. Resigned 25 October, 1867.
CHESHIRE, JOHN B.
Appointed Midshipman, 23 March, 1805. Dismissed 31 December, 1806.
CHESLEY, JAMES A.
Mate, 21 October, 1861. Acting Ensign, 1 August, 1863. Ensign, 12 March, 1868. Master, 18 December, 1868. Lieutenant, 21 March, 1870. Retired List, 22 January, 1884. Died 17 October, 1895.
CHESNEY, JESSE H.
Acting Third Assistant Engineer, 10 September, 1864. Honorably discharged 22 May, 1869.
CHESTER, ARTHUR T.
Naval Cadet, 19 May, 1890. Ensign, 1 July, 1897. Lieutenant, Junior Grade, 1 July, 1900.
CHESTER, BENJAMIN.
Acting First Assistant Engineer, 4 June, 1864. Honorably discharged 21 October, 1865.
CHESTER, B. M.
Acting Ensign, 10 September, 1862. Honorably discharged 18 September, 1865.
CHESTER, COLBY M.
Acting Midshipman, 31 October, 1859. Acting Ensign, 21 October, 1863. Master, 10 May, 1866. Lieutenant, 21 February, 1867. Lieutenant-Commander, 12 March, 1868. Commander, 15 October, 1881. Captain, 12 June, 1896.
CHESTER, DANIEL C.
Acting First Assistant Engineer, 28 March, 1863. Honorably discharged 15 May, 1865.

GENERAL NAVY REGISTER.

CHESTER, JOHN N.
  Appointed Midshipman, 31 October, 1799.   Discharged 10 July, 1801, under Peace Establishment Act.
CHESTER, LOUIS R.
  Mate, 23 December, 1862.   Acting Ensign, 31 August, 1863.   Honorably discharged 9 December, 1868.   Master on Retired List (special Act of Congress), 3 March, 1873.   Title changed to Lieutenant, Junior Grade, 3 March, 1883.
CHESTER, WALTER M.
  Acting Assistant Paymaster, 2 June, 1863.   Resigned 4 June, 1864.
CHEVALIER, FRANCIS L.
  Mate, 20 June, 1863.   Discharged 7 July, 1864.
CHEW, JOHN.
  Appointed Midshipman, 1 December, 1809.   Cashiered 19 December, 1814.
CHEW, JOHN, of BENJAMIN.
  Appointed Midshipman, 1 February, 1814.   Last appearance on Records of Navy Department, 12 February, 1814.
CHEW, RICHARD S.
  Acting Midshipman, 25 November, 1859.   Ensign, 13 December, 1862.   Lieutenant, 22 February, 1864.   Lieutenant-Commander, 25 July, 1866.   Retired List, 2 February, 1875.   Died 10 April, 1875.
CHEW, THOMAS J.
  Purser, 25 April, 1812.   Resigned 12 March, 1832.
CHICK, AMOS C.
  Carpenter, 14 July, 1838.   Retired List, 11 June, 1862.   Died in 1882.
CHIDESTER, THOMAS.
  Surgeon, 24 July, 1813.   Died August, 1818.
CHIDWICK, JOHN P. S.
  Chaplain, 2 March, 1895.
CHILD, A. O.
  Mate, September, 1861.   Acting Ensign, 7 April, 1864.   Honorably discharged 2 October, 1865.   Acting Ensign, 5 July, 1866.   Discharged 15 August, 1867.
CHILDERS, THOMAS B.
  Appointed Midshipman, 6 February, 1846.   Resigned 8 December, 1847.
CHILDS, CALVIN C.
  Acting Master, 5 April, 1862.   Honorably discharged 30 October, 1865.
CHILDS, CHARLES B.
  Appointed Midshipman, 28 January, 1815.   Dismissed 1 May, 1828.
CHILDS, ENOS R.
  Appointed Midshipman, 18 June, 1812.   Lieutenant, 27 April, 1816.   Resigned 1 April, 1825.
CHILDS, JAMES R.
  Sailmaker, 8 June, 1822.   Retired List, 8 February, 1872.   Died 5 August, 1881.
CHILDS, JOHN B.
  Acting Ensign, 15 August, 1862.   Acting Master, 29 June, 1864, on recommendation of commanding officer.   Honorably discharged 23 May, 1869.
CHILDS, JOHN D.
  Acting Master, 26 December, 1861.   Dismissed 26 May, 1864.
CHILDS, WILLIAM H.
  Mate, 16 November, 1863.   Honorably discharged 28 October, 1866.
CHILES, SAMUEL.
  Gunner, 20 July, 1898.
CHILLAS, DAVID.
  Acting Second Assistant Engineer, 3 February, 1863.   Resigned 11 June, 1864.
CHILTON, CHARLES.
  Appointed Midshipman, 5 February, 1800.   Discharged 5 June, 1801, under Peace Establishment Act.
CHIOLA, THOMAS.
  Acting Assistant Surgeon, 13 December, 1873.   Honorably discharged 30 June, 1879.
CHIPLEY, CHARLES A.
  Acting Third Assistant Engineer, 21 July, 1858.   Resigned 28 April, 1860.   Second Assistant Engineer, 19 July, 1861.   Resigned 9 April, 1862.
CHIPMAN, A. S.
  Acting Second Assistant Engineer, 7 February, 1862.   Acting First Assistant Engineer, 16 October, 1863.   Deserted 20 June, 1864.
CHIPMAN, DANIEL W.
  Acting Second Assistant Engineer, 16 December, 1863.   Acting First Assistant Engineer, 6 January, 1865.   Honorably discharged 18 July, 1865.
CHIPMAN, GEORGE E.
  Mate, 11 April, 1863.   Resigned 7 March, 1865.
CHIPMAN, HENRY L.
  Appointed Midshipman, 14 January, 1832.   Passed Midshipman, 8 July, 1839.   Lieutenant, 12 April, 1845.   Resigned 19 September, 1846.
CHIPMAN, RICHARD H.
  Acting Assistant Paymaster, 9 June, 1864.   Honorably discharged 20 October, 1865.
CHIPMAN, WILLIAM.
  Acting Master, 12 August, 1861.   Resigned 9 April, 1862.
CHIPP, CHARLES WINANS.
  Acting Midshipman, 23 July, 1863.   Graduated 2 June, 1868.   Ensign, 19 April, 1869.   Master, 12 July, 1870.   Lieutenant, 2 December, 1872.   Lost in the Arctic Regions January, 1883.
CHIPPENDALE, ALFRED E.
  Acting Second Assistant Engineer, 9 November, 1864.   Honorably discharged 3 July, 1865.

CHISHOLM, THOMAS.
Acting Master, 11 June, 1861. Resigned 17 December, 1862.
CHOATE, CHARLES H.
Acting Ensign, 6 January, 1863. Honorably discharged 24 September, 1865.
CHOATE, ISAAC T.
Boatswain, 27 August, 1860. Retired List, 4 August, 1886. Died 24 September, 1895.
CHRISMAN, WILLMER O.
Assistant Engineer, 18 May, 1877. Retired List, 29 June, 1887.
CHRISTIAN, ABRAHAM.
Acting Master, 21 January, 1862. Acting Volunteer Lieutenant, 6 January, 1864, for gallant conduct at the battle of Port Hudson. Appointment revoked 21 September, 1864. Sick.
CHRISTIAN, FERRIER C.
Acting Third Assistant Engineer, 8 July, 1863. Honorably discharged 15 January, 1866.
CHRISTIAN, MARCELLUS P.
Assistant Surgeon, 3 September, 1858. Dismissed 5 July, 1861.
CHRISTIAN, W. A.
Purser, 13 September, 1841. Died 29 August, 1852.
CHRISTIANSON, CHARLES J.
Boatswain, 11 August, 1898.
CHRISTIE, PETER.
Surgeon's Mate, 8 July, 1812. Surgeon, 27 April, 1816. Died 5 March, 1853.
CHRISTOPHER, CHARLES H.
Acting Chief Engineer, 1 October, 1862. Honorably discharged 30 November, 1865.
CHRISTOPHER, CHARLES WILLIAM.
Acting Midshipman, 24 February, 1863. Graduated 6 June, 1867. Ensign, 18 December, 1868. Master, 21 March, 1870. Lieutenant, 21 March, 1871. Retired List, 19 September, 1882. Died 7 January, 1884.
CHRISTOPHER, HENRY C.
Third Assistant Engineer, 17 March, 1863. Retired 16 May, 1867. Second Assistant Engineer, Retired List, 24 July, 1867. Died 13 August, 1872.
CHRISTOPHERSON, OLAF.
Mate, 18 August, 1897.
CHRISTY, HARLEY H.
Naval Cadet, 24 May, 1887. Ensign, 1 July, 1893. Lieutenant, Junior Grade, 3 March, 1899. Lieutenant, 21 November, 1899.
CHRYSTIE, T. M. L.
Acting Ensign, Admiral Farragut's Staff, 9 September, 1864. Resigned 24 June, 1865.
CHUBB, HENRY S.
Carpenter, 16 November, 1875. Appointment revoked 1 May, 1876.
CHUNN, FREDERICK.
Assistant Paymaster, 4 September, 1900.
CHURCH, GEORGE HURLBURT.
Acting Midshipman, 25 February, 1863. Graduated 6 June, 1867. Ensign, 18 December, 1867. Master, 21 March, 1870. Resigned 9 November, 1871.
CHURCH, GEORGE J.
Acting Third Assistant Engineer, 10 January, 1863. Appointment revoked (sick) 8 May, 1865.
CHURCH, HENRY E.
Mate, 12 December, 1862. Acting Ensign, 15 June, 1864. Honorably discharged 30 November, 1865.
CHURCH, JAMES H.
Acting Ensign, 25 April, 1864. Honorably discharged 21 October, 1865.
CHURCH, JOHN G.
Naval Cadet, 20 May, 1896. Graduated 30 June, 1900.
CHURCH, WALTER S.
Acting Ensign, 17 February, 1864. Honorably discharged 21 October, 1865.
CHURCHILL, A. L.
Acting Third Assistant Engineer, 13 June, 1863. Honorably discharged 30 November, 1865.
CHURCHILL, CREIGHTON.
Naval Cadet, 4 September, 1883. Ensign, 1 July, 1889. Retired List, 20 June, 1896.
CHURCHILL, GARDNER A.
Acting Ensign, 15 December, 1862. Resigned 3 June, 1864. Acting Ensign, 7 October, 1864. Resigned 4 April, 1865.
CHURCHILL, HENRY.
Acting Master, 18 May, 1861. Acting Volunteer Lieutenant, 25 July, 1864. Honorably discharged 10 January, 1866.
CHURCHILL, HENRY.
Mate, 22 February, 1865. Honorably discharged 12 April, 1866.
CHURCHILL, HENRY L.
Acting Third Assistant Engineer, 9 September, 1862. Resigned 9 May, 1863. Acting Third Assistant Engineer, 3 September, 1864. Resigned 29 April, 1865.
CHURCHILL, JAMES M.
Acting Third Assistant Engineer, 14 September, 1863. Honorably discharged 18 September, 1865.
CHURCHILL, JOHN FRANKLIN.
Acting Midshipman, 24 September, 1857. Resigned 25 June, 1858.
CHURCHILL, JOHN F.
Acting Ensign, 22 June, 1864. Honorably discharged 15 November, 1868.

CHURCHILL, ROBERT B.
Acting Third Assistant Engineer, 18 February, 1865. Honorably discharged 26 October, 1865.
CHURCHILL, THOMAS L.
Acting Third Assistant Engineer, 20 April, 1863. Acting Second Assistant Engineer, 23 April, 1864. Acting First Assistant Engineer, 10 February, 1865. Honorably discharged 15 July, 1865.
CHURCHILL, WILLIAM.
Acting Ensign, 1 July, 1864. Resigned 11 June, 1865.
CHURCHILL, WILLIAM B.
Acting Master, 30 August, 1861. Dismissed 8 October, 1861.
CHURCHILL, WILLIAM H.
Acting Master, 27 September, 1861. Dismissed 2 July, 1863.
CHURCHILL, WILLIAM L.
Acting Master, 11 October, 1861. Acting Volunteer Lieutenant, recommendation of commanding officer, 6 June, 164. Honorbaly discharged, 1 January, 1866.
CILLEY, GREENLEAF.
Midshipman, 26 February, 1841. Passed Midshipman, 10 August. 1847. Master, 14 September, 1855. Lieutenant, 15 September, 1855. Lieutenant-Commander, 16 July, 1862. Retired List, 18 March, 1865. Commander on Retired List. Died 5 February, 1899.
CILLEY, JONATHAN L.
Mate, 3 September, 1864. Resigned 8 November, 1864.
CISSIN, ROBERT A.
Appointed Master, 7 March, 1842. Dismissed 1 January, 1846.
CITY, GEORGE W.
Third Assistant Engineer, 12 January, 1854. Second Assistant Engineer, 9 May, 1857. First Assistant Engineer, 2 August, 1859. Name stricken from rolls, 2 August, 1861.
CITY, SAMUEL G.
Gunner, 15 September, 1835. Died 5 September, 1860.
CLACK, JOHN H.
Appointed Midshipman, 15 November. 1809. Lieutenant, 9 December, 1814. Commander, 24 April, 1828. Captain, 28 February, 1838. Dismissed 16 April, 1842.
CLAGETT, JOHN M.
Appointed Midshipman, 16 March, 1798. Lieutenant, 25 June, 1800. Last appearance on Records of Navy Department, 25 June, 1800. Lost in Gibraltar Bay.
CLAIBORN, HENRY B.
Acting Midshipman, 22 September, 1855. Midshipman, 9 June, 1859. Dismissed 24 August, 1861.
CLAIBORNE, M. G. L.
Midshipman, 1 February, 1827. Passed Midshipman, 10 June, 1833. Lieutenant, 22 June, 1838. Resigned 1 June, 1849.
CLAIBORNE, OSMAN.
Appointed Midshipman, 19 May, 1829. Resigned 21 June, 1832.
CLANCY, MARTIN J.
Acting Warrant Machinist, 23 August, 1899.
CLAPHAM, JOHN.
Gunner, 15 November, 1837. Appointed Pyrotechnist, 24 July, 1848. Died 15 September, 1864, at Washington, D. C.
CLAPHAM, JOHN.
Gunner, 15 November, 1837. Died 15 September, 1864.
CLAPHAM, JOSEPH C.
Mate. Resigned 1 April, 1862.
CLAPHAM, JOSEPH C.
Acting Gunner, 13 December, 1862. Honorably discharged 2 December, 1865.
CLAPP, ALLEN C.
Mate, 7 December, 1863. Appointment revoked (sick) 4 October, 1864.
CLAPP, AUGUSTUS.
Acting Second Assistant Engineer, 1861. Appointment revoked 17 March, 1862. Acting Second Assistant Engineer, 7 April, 1862. Acting First Assistant Engineer, 7 January, 1863. Died on Tahoma, 7 April, 1867.
CLAPP, BENJAMIN.
Appointed Midshipman, 8 December. 1813. Last appearance on Records of Navy Department, 23 December, 1815. Resigned.
CLAPP, C. W.
Acting Assistant Paymaster, 3 February, 1864. Never finally discharged. Accounts not settled.
CLAPP, FAYETTE.
Acting Assistant Surgeon, 29 November, 1862. Dead.
CLAPP, HARVEY.
Acting Third Assistant Engineer, 10 November. 1863. Acting Second Assistant Engineer, 21 August, 1866. Honorably discharged 23 December, 1867.
CLAPP, H. N.
Mate, 16 August, 1864. Discharged 25 October, 1867.
CLAPP, SAMUEL L.
Acting Master, 17 May, 1861. Dismissed 10 June, 1862.
CLAR, JOHN.
Professor of Mathematics, 15 October, 1841. Dismissed 9 September, 1847.
CLARK, ALBERT B.
Acting Assistant Paymaster, 3 November, 1864. Discharged 1 February, 1866.
CLARK, ALLEN J.
Acting Assistant Paymaster, 22 July, 1862. Resigned 20 June, 1865.

GENERAL NAVY REGISTER.   115

CLARK, AMBROSE J.
Assistant Paymaster, 12 September, 1861. Paymaster, 19 April, 1863. Pay Inspector, 9 March, 1880. Pay Director, 21 September, 1891. Killed 24 December, 1892.

CLARK, BENJAMIN F.
Acting First Assistant Engineer, 31 March, 1863. Honorably discharged 1 December, 1865.

CLARK, CHARLES.
Appointed Midshipman, 20 February, 1801. Discharged under Peace Establishment Act, 10 April, 1801.

CLARK, CHARLES.
Acting Ensign, 28 January, 1865. Died 25 March, 1865.

CLARK, CHARLES E.
Acting Midshipman, 29 September, 1860. Acting Ensign, 21 October, 1863. Master, 10 May, 1866. Lieutenant, 21 February, 1867. Lieutenant-Commander, 12 March, 1868. Commander, 15 November, 1881. Captain, 21 June, 1896.

CLARK, CHARLES E.
Acting Ensign, 16 August, 1862. Appointment revoked 18 August, 1863. Acting Ensign, 19 September, 1864. Resigned (sick) 17 March, 1865.

CLARK, CHARLES P.
Acting Ensign, 3 October, 1862. Acting Master, 18 July, 1863. Acting Volunteer Lieutenant, highly meritorious services, 9 August, 1864. Honorably discharged 20 November, 1865.

CLARK, DANIEL H.
Mate, 8 January, 1862. Honorably discharged 6 March, 1866.

CLARK, EDWARD WERTS.
Third Assistant Engineer, 20 May, 1862. Died 1 July, 1866.

CLARK, EDWARD W.
Acting Ensign, 1 October, 1862. Died on Black Hawk, 1 April, 1863.

CLARK, ELIJAH M.
Mate, 4 November, 1862. Acting Ensign 24 March, 1864. Honorably discharged 21 September, 1865.

CLARK, ERNEST M.
Mate, 16 April, 1863. Promoted Acting Ensign, 3 October, 1863. Resigned (sick) 23 May, 1864.

CLARK, E. ST. CLAIR.
Acting Assistant Paymaster, 17 December, 1861. Mustered out 10 March, 1866.

CLARK, FRANCIS G., Jr.
Midshipman, 19 October, 1841. Dismissed 23 October, 1849. Reappointed Passed Midshipman, 10 August, 1847. Master, 18 April, 1855. Died 25 July, 1855.

CLARK, FRANK H.
Naval Cadet, 5 September, 1889. Ensign, 1 July, 1895. Lieutenant, Junior Grade, 3 March, 1899.

CLARK, FRANK H.
Assistant Paymaster, 14 July, 1870. Resigned 2 September, 1878. Resignation revoked 7 September, 1878. Passed Assistant Paymaster, 3 April, 1880. Resigned 15 June, 1891.

CLARK, GEORGE H.
Acting Second Assistant Engineer, 28 May, 1861. Resigned 29 November, 1861

CLARK, GEORGE R.
Cadet Midshipman, 9 June, 1874. Graduated 4 June, 1880. Ensign, Junior Grade, 3 March, 1883. Ensign, 24 August, 1883. Lieutenant, Junior Grade, 16 February, 1890. Lieutenant, 19 August, 1894.

CLARK, GEORGE W.
Purser, 2 June, 1858. Dismissed 2 April, 1861.

CLARK, HENRY A.
Acting Master, 26 August, 1861. Resigned 9 October, 1862.

CLARK, HENRY G.
Mate, 25 July, 1864. Dismissed 14 July, 1866.

CLARK, HENRY HOWARD.
Chaplain, 27 January, 1873.

CLARK, HUGH.
Acting Second Assistant Engineer, 27 April, 1863. Dismissed 23 July, 1863.

CLARK, ISAAC.
Appointed Midshipman, 18 June, 1812. Resigned 11 February, 1813.

CLARK, JACKSON.
Acting Third Assistant Engineer, 15 August, 1864. Resigned 15 May, 1865.

CLARK, JACKSON S.
Mate, 9 August, 1864. Honorably discharged 31 December, 1865.

CLARK, JAMES B.
Acting Third Assistant Engineer, 21 February, 1865. Honorably discharged 21 October, 1865.

CLARK, JAMES H.
Purser, 24 July, 1813. Died in September, 1844.

CLARK, JAMES M.
Third Assistant Engineer, 3 August, 1863. Second Assistant Engineer, 25 July, 1866. Died 24 April, 1872.

CLARK, JAMES W.
Acting Assistant Paymaster, 25 September, 1863. Honorably discharged 11 December, 1865.

CLARK, JOHN.
Appointed Midshipman, 18 June, 1812. Killed in action 10 September, 1813.

CLARK, JOHN.
Appointed Boatswain, 1 August, 1803. Left the service 20 September, 1804.

CLARK, JOHN.
  Acting Second Assistant Engineer, 26 August, 1863. Dismissed 7 October, 1863.
CLARK, JOHN D.
  Acting Midshipman, 22 September, 1860. Midshipman. Ensign, 28 May, 1863. Master, 10 November, 1865. Lieutenant, 10 November, 1866. Died 8 March, 1868.
CLARK, JOHN H.
  Assistant Surgeon, 19 October, 1861. Passed Assistant Surgeon, 24 April, 1865. Surgeon, 14 May, 1867. Medical Inspector, 8 January, 1885. Medical Director, 4 March, 1893. Retired List, 16 April, 1899.
CLARK, JOHN L.
  Appointed Master, 29 August, 1812. Discharged 19 June, 1813.
CLARK, JOHN P.
  Mate, 21 October, 1861. Appointment revoked 21 February, 1862.
CLARK, JOHN S.
  Acting Ensign, 17 September, 1862. Acting Master, 29 March, 1864. Honorably discharged 16 November, 1865.
CLARK, JOHN W.
  Mate, 29 July, 1863. Appointment revoked 4 June, 1864.
CLARK, JOHN W.
  Acting Warrant Machinist, 23 August, 1899.
CLARK, JOSEPH H.
  Mate, 7 June, 1862. Acting Ensign, 15 December, 1862. Honorably discharged 12 August, 1865.
CLARK, J. TUCKER.
  Appointed Midshipman, 15 May, 1790. Discharged under Peace Establishment Act, 12 October, 1801.
CLARK, L.
  Mate, 28 September, 1861. Appointment revoked 11 February, 1862.
CLARK, LEWIS.
  Midshipman, 24 September, 1861. Acting Ensign, 1 October, 1863. Master, 10 May, 1866. Lieutenant, 21 February, 1867. Lieutenant-Commander, 12 March, 1868. Commander, 20 March, 1881. Died 7 June, 1885.
CLARK, LEWIS J.
  Cadet Midshipman, 22 September, 1876. Graduated 22 June, 1882. Ensign, Junior Grade, 3 March, 1883. Ensign, 26 June, 1884. Lieutenant, Junior Grade, 15 September, 1893. Lieutenant, 4 June, 1897.
CLARK, N. BEACH.
  Third Assistant Engineer, 13 May, 1861. Second Assistant Engineer, 17 December, 1862. First Assistant Engineer, 1 July, 1865. Retired 16 October, 1868. Chief Engineer, Retired List, 3 March, 1885. Died 18 April, 1892.
CLARK, PETER G.
  Chaplain, 3 October, 1838. Died at Cheshire, Connecticut, 2 January, 1860.
CLARK, RICHARD.
  Appointed Lieutenant, 15 November, 1799. Last appearance on Records of Navy Department, 2 July, 1800.
CLARK, ROBERT.
  Acting Third Assistant Engineer, 14 February, 1863. Resigned 22 October, 1863.
CLARK, ROBERT H.
  Purser, 18 July, 1857. Pay Inspector, 3 March. 1871. Pay Director, 23 January, 1873. Retired List, 5 December, 1880. Died 20 December, 1887.
CLARK, ROBERT M.
  Mate, 21 November, 1861. Acting Ensign, 24 January, 1863. Honorably discharged 6 June, 1868.
CLARK, ROBERT W.
  Acting Assistant Surgeon, 20 April, 1864. Resigned 29 April, 1865.
CLARK, SAMUEL B.
  Acting Master, 4 November, 1861. Resigned 6 August, 1864.
CLARK, SETH.
  Appointed Master, date not known. Last appearance on Records of Navy Department.
CLARK, SIMEON.
  Acting Third Assistant Engineer, 11 November, 1862. Appointment revoked (sick) 25 June, 1863.
CLARK, STEPHEN G.
  Appointed Boatswain, 1 January, 1817. Resigned 4 October, 1825.
CLARK, STEPHEN J.
  Assistant Surgeon, 19 August, 1861. Resigned 20 May, 1865.
CLARK, THADDEUS E.
  Acting Assistant Surgeon, 19 February, 1864. Honorably discharged 6 November, 1865.
CLARK, THOMAS.
  Acting Third Assistant Engineer, 1 August, 1864. Honorably discharged 23 May, 1870.
CLARK, WALTER K.
  Assistant Engineer (Spanish-American War), 20 May, 1898. Honorably discharged 26 January, 1899.
CLARK, WILLIAM.
  Appointed Sailmaker, date not known. Last appearance on Records of Navy Department. Dead.
CLARK, WILLIAM.
  Acting Third Assistant Engineer, 13 August, 1864. Honorably discharged 25 November, 1865.

GENERAL NAVY REGISTER.

CLARK, WILLIAM.
Mate, 10 February, 1864. Acting Ensign and Pilot, 26 April, 1864. Honorably discharged 3 January, 1866.
CLARK, WILLIAM C.
Appointed Master, 28 December, 1839. Resigned 18 February, 1843.
CLARK, WILLIAM H.
Acting Master, 24 January, 1862. Resigned 13 July, 1865.
CLARK, WILLIAM J., JR.
Third Assistant Engineer, 16 November, 1861. Second Assistant Engineer, 25 August, 1863. Resigned 1 December, 1865.
CLARK, WINLOCK.
Appointed Midshipman, 5 February, 1800. Lieutenant, 4 May, 1807. Drowned 26 March, 1810.
CLARKE, ARTHUR H.
Cadet Engineer, 1 October, 1878. Graduated 30 June, 1884. Transferred to Marine Corps 30 June, 1884.
CLARKE, CHARLES A.
Midshipman, 21 July, 1864. Graduated 4 June, 1869. Ensign, 12 July, 1870. Master, 22 March, 1873. Lieutenant, 11 July, 1877. Retired List, 15 September, 1897.
CLARKE, CHARLES F.
Appointed Midshipman, 15 November, 1809. Lieutenant, 19 December, 1814. Died 14 April, 1819.
CLARKE, DAVID S.
Acting Third Assistant Engineer, 7 March, 1864. Honorably discharged 4 November, 1865.
CLARKE, EDWARD R.
Mate, 23 September, 1863. Honorably discharged 5 October, 1865.
CLARKE, E. MANSFIELD.
Acting Third Assistant Engineer, 31 July, 1863. Resigned 23 August, 1864.
CLARK, FRANK.
Acting Assistant Paymaster, 4 December, 1862. Passed Assistant Paymaster, 23 July, 1866. Paymaster, 5 June, 1868. Died 2 April, 1879.
CLARKE, FREDERICK M.
Mate, 23 July, 1863. Resigned 24 December, 1863.
CLARKE, GEORGE W.
Appointed Midshipman, 10 February, 1838. Passed Midshipman, 20 May, 1844. Resigned 9 July, 1846.
CLARKE, GEORGE W.
Purser, 2 June, 1858. Dismissed 2 April, 1861.
CLARKE, GEORGE W.
Appointed Boatswain, 17 January, 1842. Resigned 1 June, 1842.
CLARKE, HENRY G.
Mate, 25 July, 1864. Dismissed 14 July, 1866.
CLARKE, HERMON M.
Surgeon's Mate, 2 July, 1812. Resigned 19 May, 1815.
CLARKE, JAMES.
Acting Third Assistant Engineer, 8 January, 1863. Dismissed 5 January, 1864.
CLARKE, THOMAS W.
Assistant Engineer (Spanish-American War), 20 May, 1898. Honorably discharged 16 February, 1899.
CLARKE, WILLIAM B.
Appointed Midshipman, 17 December, 1810. Dismissed 6 August, 1811.
CLARKE, WILLIAM D.
Acting Third Assistant Engineer, 1 February, 1865. Honorably discharged 25 September, 1865.
CLARKE, WILLIAM M.
Surgeon's Mate, 25 November, 1809. Surgeon, 24 July, 1813. Lost in the Wasp, 1815.
CLARKE, WILLIAM R.
Acting Master, 8 May, 1861. Dismissed 24 March, 1862.
CLARKSON, CHARLES F.
Mate, 12 December, 1863. Appointment revoked (sick) 19 August, 1864.
CLARKSON, SAMUEL F.
Acting Midshipman, 20 September, 1862. Graduated June, 1866. Ensign, 12 March, 1868. Master, 26 March, 1869. Lieutenant, 21 March, 1870. Died 8 January, 1883.
CLARKSON, SAMUEL G.
Surgeon's Mate, 8 August, 1826. Died 17 May, 1829.
CLARY, ALBERT G.
Midshipman, 8 May, 1832. Passed Midshipman, 8 July, 1839. Lieutenant, 11 April, 1845. Commander, 16 July, 1862. Captain, 21 November, 1866. Commodore, 5 April, 1874. Retired List, 7 August, 1866.
CLASON, WILLIAM P.
Midshipman, 27 July, 1867. Graduated 6 June, 1871. Ensign, 14 July, 1872. Master, 14 August, 1875. Lieutenant, 1 February, 1883. Resigned 21 July, 1893.
CLAUSEN, CHARLES.
Acting Ensign, 29 July, 1863. Honorably discharged 24 August, 1865.
CLAUSEN, JOHN W.
Mate, 8 September, 1864. Honorably discharged 12 October, 1865.
CLAXTON, ALEX.
Appointed Midshipman, 20 June, 1806. Lieutenant, 8 January, 1813. Commander, 28 March, 1820. Captain, 21 February, 1831. Died 7 March, 1841.
CLAXTON, THOMAS.
Appointed Midshipman, 17 December, 1810. Killed in action 10 September, 1813.

GENERAL NAVY REGISTER.

CLAY, GEORGE GOOHUE.
Acting Midshipman, 23 July, 1863. Graduated 6 June, 1867. Ensign, 18 December, 1868. Master, 21 March, 1870. Lieutenant, 21 March, 1871. Resigned 30 November, 1881. Lieutenant (Spanish-American War), 28 May, 1898. Honorably discharged 12 December, 1898.

CLAYTON, WILLIAM D.
Mate, 23 September, 1862. Resigned 6 January, 1863.

CLEAR, MICHAEL.
Master, 28 December, 1839. Reserved List (furlough), 13 September, 1855. Died in Greenwich, Connecticut, in March, 1858.

CLEARY, JOHN E.
Acting Warrant Machinist, 23 August, 1899.

CLEARY, PETER A.
Mate, 16 April, 1864. Deserted 20 March, 1866.

CLEAVELAND, CHARLES H.
Mate, 26 February, 1864. Honorably discharged 27 September, 1869. Mate, 26 November, 1869.

CLEAVER, HENRY T.
Cadet Engineer, 1 October, 1871. Graduated 31 May, 1873. Assistant Engineer, 23 January, 1874. Passed Assistant Engineer, 19 May, 1879. Chief Engineer, 20 February, 1896. Rank changed to Lieutenant-Commander, 3 March, 1899.

CLEAVES, GEORGE W.
Mate, 8 May, 1862. Dismissed 4 May, 1864.

CLEAVES, HARRISON B.
Mate, 5 August, 1863. Acting Ensign, 20 August, 1864. Appointment revoked (sick) 25 January, 1865.

CLEAVES, MOSES H.
Mate, 26 June, 1862. Honorably discharged 28 April, 1869. Mate, 10 November, 1869. Appointment revoked 9 July, 1870.

CLEBORNE, CHRISTOPHER J.
Assistant Surgeon, 9 May, 1861. Passed Assistant Surgeon, 26 October, 1863. Surgeon, 24 November, 1863. Medical Inspector, 7 January, 1878. Medical Director, 18 September, 1887. Retired List, 10 November, 1899.

CLEBORNE, CUTHBERT J.
Assistant Paymaster, 18 September, 1899.

CLEGG, ARTHUR.
Mate, 29 May, 1863. Acting Ensign, 1 August, 1864. Honorably discharged 26 July, 1865.

CLEMENS, BENJAMIN D.
Third Assistant Engineer, 3 October, 1861. Second Assistant Engineer, 3 August, 1863. Appointment revoked 12 January, 1866.

CLEMENS, ENGLEHART R.
Acting First Assistant Engineer, 30 October, 1863. Resigned 17 March, 1864.

CLEMENT, JAMES W. L., Jr.
Naval Cadet, 27 September, 1895. At sea prior to final graduation.

CLEMENTS, ABNER B.
Cadet Midshipman, 21 June, 1875. Graduated 10 June, 1881. Ensign, Junior Grade, 3 March, 1883. Ensign, 26 June, 1884. Resigned 30 June, 1890.

CLEMENTS, ARTHUR M.
Acting Third Assistant Engineer, 15 May. 1862. Acting Second Assistant Engineer, 31 January, 1863. Honorably discharged 23 April, 1868.

CLEMENTS, JOHN W.
Acting Third Assistant Engineer, 26 August, 1864. Honorably discharged 16 January, 1868.

CLEMENTS, SAMUEL.
Appointed Midshipman, 23 September, 1799. Discharged 12 October, 1801, under Peace Establishment Act.

CLEMENTSON, JOHN.
Appointed Sailmaker, 18 July, 1828. Died 9 July, 1833.

CLEMSON, HENRY A.
Appointed Midshipman, 9 June, 1836. Passed Midshipman, 1 July, 1842. Drowned 8 December, 1846.

CLENDANIEL, WILLIAM.
Acting Assistant Surgeon, 28 July, 1862. Resigned 3 January, 1865.

CLEVELAND, CHARLES W.
Acting Ensign, 7 August, 1863. Honorably discharged 30 September, 1865

CLEVERLY, HENRY T.
Mate, 27 August, 1861. Acting Ensign, 28 September, 1863. Honorably discharged 20 September, 1865.

CLIFFORD, B. F.
Acting Master and Pilot, 14 February, 1865. Resigned 3 May, 1865.

CLIFFORD, CHARLES.
Acting Gunner, 15 July, 1864. Dismissed 10 January, 1865.

CLIFFORD, ROBERT T.
Mate, 7 September, 1863. Resigned (sick) March 20, 1865.

CLIFFORD, WILLIAM H., Jr.
Lieutenant, Junior Grade (Spanish-American War), 25 May, 1898. Honorably discharged 25 October, 1898.

CLIFT, CHARLES W.
Acting Second Assistant Engineer, 3 September, 1864. Honorably discharged 8 March, 1870.

CLIFT, NATHANIEL.
Appointed Lieutenant, 24 April, 1799. Resigned 1 August, 1800.

GENERAL NAVY REGISTER. 119

CLIFTON, GEORGE R.
Mate, 11 January, 1862. Dismissed 3 December, 1862.
CLIFTON, GERVAS.
Appointed Midshipman, 20 February, 1801. Resigned 10 December, 1807.
CLIFTON, HENRY.
Mate, 17 November, 1864. Dismissed 3 August, 1865.
CLINCH, JOSEPH.
Appointed Midshipman, 16 January, 1809. Resigned 12 January, 1810.
CLINE, HUGH H.
Third Assistant Engineer, 1 July, 1861. Second Assistant Engineer, 18 December, 1862. First Assistant Engineer, 1 January, 1868. Chief Engineer, 2 December, 1887. Retired List, 27 August, 1894. Died 5 October, 1898.
CLINE, JAMES.
Mate, 17 December, 1862. Dismissed 26 June, 1863.
CLINE, SIDNEY B.
Mate, 13 June, 1863. Acting Ensign, 7 March, 1865. Honorably discharged 5 July, 1865. Mate, 19 December, 1865. Appointment revoked 2 January, 1866.
CLINTON, FRANKLIN.
Appointed Midshipman, 1 April, 1828. Passed Midshipman, 14 June, 1834. Lieutenant, 11 December, 1839. Died 26 February, 1842.
CLINTON, JAMES H.
Appointed Midshipman, 24 April, 1815. Died in June, 1824.
CLITZ, JOHN.
Mate, 26 June, 1863. Resigned 14 February, 1865.
CLITZ, JOHN M. B.
Midshipman, 12 April, 1837. Passed Midshipman, 29 June, 1843. Master, 16 August, 1850. Lieutenant, 6 April, 1851. Commander, 16 July, 1862. Captain, 25 July, 1866. Commodore, 28 December, 1872. Rear-Admiral, 13 March, 1880. Retired List, 16 October, 1883. Died 9 October, 1897.
CLOKE, WILLIAM S.
Naval Cadet, 17 May, 1883. Ensign, 1 July, 1889. Resigned 17 October, 1894.
CLOPPER, PETER.
Appointed Sailmaker, 16 January, 1799. Last appearance on Records of Navy Department.
CLOSSON, NELSON A.
Mate, 17 February, 1863. Acting Ensign, 24 November, 1863. Honorably discharged 4 November, 1865.
CLOUD, CALEB W.
Assistant Surgeon, 31 May, 1830. Died 15 July, 1831.
CLOUGH, BENJAMIN P.
Acting Ensign, 5 May, 1864. Honorably discharged 30 September, 1865.
CLOUGH, EBEN, Jr.
Appointed Midshipman, 9 November, 1813. Dismissed 30 April, 1814.
CLOUGH, JOHN.
Appointed Master, 3 July, 1813. Died 19 March, 1847.
CLOUGH, STEPHEN.
Appointed Lieutenant, 17 February, 1800. Discharged 29 September, 1801.
CLOVER, RICHARDSON.
Acting Midshipman, 30 July, 1863. Graduated 6 June, 1867. Ensign, 18 December, 1868. Master, 21 March, 1870. Lieutenant, 21 March, 1871. Lieutenant-Commander, 19 May, 1891. Commander, 16 September, 1897.
CLOYD, JOHN B.
Acting Third Assistant Engineer, 29 November, 1862. Acting Second Assistant Engineer, 17 February, 1864. Honorably discharged 1 December, 1865.
CLUGSTON, W. P.
Acting Second Assistant Engineer, 5 June, 1863. Honorably discharged 30 November, 1865.
CLUMM, ALFRED.
Acting Second Assistant Engineer, 4 January, 1862. Honorably discharged 5 December, 1865.
CLUVERIUS, WAT T., Jr.
Naval Cadet, 20 May, 1892. Ensign, 6 May, 1898.
CLYMER, GEORGE.
Assistant Surgeon, 1 July, 1829. Surgeon, 20 February, 1838. Retired, 24 July, 1866. Medical Director on Retired List, 3 March, 1871. Died 14 April, 1881.
COAKLEY, B. D.
Appointed Master, 6 June, 1814. Last appearance on Records of Navy Department, 10 June, 1815. Discharged.
COALE, ALFRED.
Appointed Midshipman, 2 April, 1804. Resigned 3 May, 1808.
COALE, WILLIAM E.
Assistant Surgeon, 6 September, 1837. Resigned 25 January, 1843.
COAN, TITUS M.
Acting Assistant Surgeon, 27 October, 1863. Honorably discharged 21 December, 1865.
COATES, GEORGE M.
Assistant Surgeon (Spanish-American War), 25 April, 1898. Honorably discharged 13 October, 1898.
COATES, THOMAS.
Appointed Master, 6 February, 1809. Last appearance on Records of Navy Department, 26 February, 1809. Resigned.
COATS, ISAAC T.
Acting Assistant Surgeon, 9 October, 1861. Resigned 18 April, 1865.

COATS, JOHN H.
Appointed Midshipman, 2 April, 1804. Died 2 February, 1807.
COBB, ALLEN A.
Acting Ensign, 17 January, 1865. Honorably discharged 1 November, 1865.
COBB, ALPHONSO H.
Midshipman, 23 September, 1867. Graduated 6 June, 1871. Ensign, 14 July, 1872. Master, 9 October, 1876. Lieutenant, Junior Grade, 3 March, 1883. Retired List, 8 November, 1883. Active service (Spanish-American War), April, 1898, to February, 1899.
COBB, BENJAMIN, JR.
Acting Third Assistant Engineer, 21 August, 1862. Honorably discharged 27 October, 1865.
COBB, CHARLES.
Gunner, 18 January, 1833. Died 9 May, 1848.
COBB, CHARLES H.
Mate, 2 April, 1864. Acting Ensign, 27 April, 1865. Honorably discharged 12 October, 1865.
COBB, CHARLES S.
Acting Third Assistant Engineer, 30 December, 1864. Honorably discharged 29 July, 1865.
COBB, CHARLES T.
Mate. Resigned 16 June, 1862.
COBB, EDWARD.
Appointed Sailmaker, date not known. Last appearance on Records of Navy Department, 1817. Brig Jones.
COBB, GEORGE W.
Acting Second Assistant Engineer, 22 October, 1862. Resigned 15 September, 1863.
COBB, HENRY J.
Appointed Midshipman, 2 July, 1801. Resigned 31 March, 1803.
COBB, JOHN E.
Acting Assistant Surgeon, 10 September, 1861. Honorably discharged 11 September, 1865.
COBB, SCHUYLER, A.
Acting Ensign, 12 August, 1864. Resigned 19 May, 1865.
COBB, WILLIAM D.
Acting Ensign, 11 September, 1862. Acting Master, 23 December, 1863. Appointment revoked (sick) 28 October, 1864.
COBB, WILLIAM B.
Mate, 13 October, 1864. Honorably discharged 27 April, 1865.
COBB, W. R.
Chaplain, 27 September, 1869. Resigned 1 June, 1873.
COBURN, HENDERSON A.
Appointed Midshipman, 18 January, 1840. Dismissed 17 August, 1847.
COCHRAN, GEORGE.
Assistant Paymaster, 27 September, 1861. Paymaster, 12 June, 1863. Pay Inspector, 6 December, 1880. Pay Director, 19 November, 1891. Died 9 July, 1900.
COCHRAN, JACOB.
Mate, 6 November, 1862. Acting Ensign, 19 December, 1863. Honorably discharged 12 May, 1865.
COCHRAN, JAMES.
First Assistant Engineer, 11 June, 1840. Dismissed 7 November, 1845.
COCHRAN, JOHN.
Appointed Midshipman, 9 May, 1800. Discharged under Peace Establishment Act, 12 August, 1801.
COCHRAN, JOHN T.
Appointed Midshipman, 15 November, 1810. Resigned 15 December, 1810.
COCHRAN, JOSHUA W.
Appointed Midshipman, 1 February, 1814. Resigned 29 June, 1820.
COCHRAN, RICHARD.
Appointed Midshipman, 7 February, 1815. Struck off 1 March, 1825.
COCHRAN, WALTER.
Appointed Gunner, 8 January, 1822. Last appearance on Records of Navy Department, 1828. Frigate Brandywine.
COCHRANE, GEORGE S.
Acting Ensign, 24 January, 1863. Appointment revoked (sick) 22 October, 1863.
COCHRANE, HENRY C.
Mate, 7 September, 1861. Resigned 20 May, 1863.
COCHRANE, JAMES.
First Assistant Engineer, 11 June, 1840. Dismissed 7 November, 1845.
COCKE, BULLER.
Purser, 6 October, 1798. Storekeeper, date not known. Resigned 8 April, 1816.
COCKE, HARRISON H.
Midshipman, 18 June, 1812. Lieutenant, 1 April, 1818. Commander, 3 March, 1839. Captain, 22 April, 1851. Resigned 22 April, 1861.
COCKE, HERBERT C.
Naval Cadet. 20 May, 1896. Graduated 30 June, 1900.
COCKE, SAMUEL B.
Appointed Midshipman, 1 January, 1818. Lieutenant, 3 March, 1827. Died 31 May, 1835.
COCKE, SAMUEL B.
Carpenter, 11 August, 1853. Dismissed 7 June, 1855.
COCKE, WILLIAM T.
Appointed Midshipman, 25 April, 1831. Resigned 4 March, 1836.
COCKLE, THOMAS B.
Acting Assistant Paymaster, 17 June, 1863. Resigned 30 November, 1863.

COCKRAN, A. M.
    Acting Assistant Surgeon, 16 October, 1862. Died July, 1863.
CODDINGTON, ETHELBERT F.
    Midshipman, 12 October, 1848. Died 8 November, 1853.
CODREY, ABRAHAM.
    Purser, 4 September, 1804. Resigned 27 June, 1806.
CODWISE, GEORGE W.
    Surgeon's Mate, 14 May, 1825. Surgeon, 4 December, 1828. Retired 30 April, 1861. Medical Director on Retired List, 3 March, 1871. Died 20 May, 1884.
COE, ISAAC.
    Appointed Midshipman, 9 April, 1799. Discharged 8 July, 1801.
COE, WILLIAM H.
    Acting Assistant Surgeon, 27 December, 1864. Resigned 24 June, 1865.
COFFEE, THEODORE D.
    Acting Third Assistant Engineer, 4 September, 1861. Acting Second Assistant Engineer, 22 September, 1863. Acting First Assistant Engineer, 11 November, 1864. Honorably discharged 2 July, 1866.
COFFEY, JOHN.
    Mate. Dismissed 30 September, 1862.
COFFIN, EDWIN.
    Acting Master, 8 October, 1861. Acting Volunteer Lieutenant, 23 June, 1865. Honorably discharged 4 February, 1866.
COFFIN, FREDERICK W.
    Midshipman, 16 June, 1870. Graduated 21 June, 1875. Ensign, 24 December, 1876. Lieutenant, Junior Grade, 21 July, 1883. Lieutenant, 4 August, 1889. Lieutenant-Commander, 3 March, 1899.
COFFIN, GEORGE W.
    Appointed Midshipman, 1 April, 1799. Discharged 14 July, 1801.
COFFIN, GEORGE W.
    Acting Midshipman, 28 September, 1860. Acting Ensign, 1 October, 1863. Master, 10 May, 1866. Lieutenant, 25 July, 1866. Lieutenant-Commander, 12 March, 1868. Commander, 30 November, 1878. Captain, 27 September, 1893. Retired List, 15 September, 1897. Died 15 June, 1899.
COFFIN, GEORGE W.
    Acting Ensign, 9 October, 1863. Died on Owasco, 11 October, 1864.
COFFIN, HENRY.
    Appointed Sailmaker, 12 November, 1799. Discharged 18 April, 1802.
COFFIN, HENRY F.
    Acting Master, 26 August, 1861. Appointment revoked (sick) 13 February, 1863.
COFFIN, JOHN C.
    Professor of Mathematics, 14 August, 1848. Retired List, 15 September, 1877. Died 8 January, 1890.
COFFIN, JOHN H. C.
    Midshipman, 22 July, 1865. Graduated 4 June, 1869. Ensign, 12 July, 1870. Master, 25 March, 1873. Lieutenant, 3 August, 1877. Died 4 January, 1897.
COFFIN, PETER F.
    Acting Master, 21 March, 1862. Honorably discharged 7 December, 1865.
COFFIN, ROBERT B.
    Appointed Midshipman, 3 November, 1818. Died 20 March, 1822.
COFFIN, ROLAND S.
    Acting Master, 22 November, 1861. Dismissed 5 March, 1864.
COFFIN, RUFUS.
    Assistant Paymaster (Spanish-American War), 12 July, 1898. Honorably discharged 8 February, 1899.
COFFINBERRY, HENRY D.
    Mate, 1 October, 1862. Promoted Acting Ensign, 10 March, 1863. Acting Master, 15 July, 1864. Honorably discharged 24 November, 1865.
COFFMAN, De WITT.
    Midshipman, 6 June, 1872. Graduated 20 June, 1876. Ensign, 10 June, 1879. Lieutenant, Junior Grade, 19 April, 1886. Lieutenant, 27 September, 1891. Lieutenant-Commander, 1 July, 1899.
COGDELL, R. C.
    Appointed Midshipman, 9 May, 1829. Passed Midshipman, 3 July, 1835. Lieutenant, 8 September, 1841. Resigned 26 July, 1846.
COGGESHALL, GEORGE.
    Appointed Midshipman, January, 1812. Resigned 19 November, 1813.
COGGESHALL, LAWTON.
    Mate, 31 October, 1861. Appointment revoked (sick) 29 December, 1863.
COGGESHALL, SAMUEL B.
    Acting Master, 13 July, 1861. Resigned 12 August, 1862.
COGGIN, F. G.
    Third Assistant Engineer, 21 September, 1861. Second Assistant Engineer, 30 July, 1863. Retired 5 January, 1866. Passed Assistant Engineer, 24 February, 1874.
COGHLAN, JASPER.
    Boatswain, 26 October, 1855. Retired List, 27 October, 1875. Died 9 February, 1889.
COGHLAN, JOSEPH B.
    Acting Midshipman, 27 September, 1860. Graduated 28 May, 1863. Ensign, 4 June, 1863. Master, 10 November, 1865. Lieutenant, 10 November, 1866. Lieutenant-Commander, 12 March, 1868. Commander, 4 February, 1882. Captain, 18 November, 1896.
COGSWELL, JAMES KELSEY.
    Midshipman, 25 September, 1863. Graduated 2 June, 1868. Ensign, 19 April, 1869. Master, 12 July, 1870. Lieutenant, 8 April, 1874. Lieutenant-Commander, 15 June, 1895. Commander, 3 March, 1899.

GENERAL NAVY REGISTER.

COGSWELL, WILBER F.
Acting Third Assistant Engineer, 17 August, 1864. Honorably discharged 7 November, 1865. Acting Third Assistant Engineer, 12 July, 1866. Mustered out 28 August, 1868.

COHEN, HARRY R.
Cadet Midshipman, 27 June, 1877. Graduated. Honorably discharged 30 June, 1883. Lieutenant (Spanish-American War), 25 May, 1898. Honorably discharged 17 September, 1898.

COHEN, JOSEPH.
Appointed Midshipman, 1 February, 1826. Resigned 1 May, 1828.

COHEN, SOLIS I.
Acting Assistant Surgeon, 4 September, 1861. Resigned 12 January, 1864.

COHILL, JOHN.
Acting First Assistant Engineer, 21 August, 1861. Resigned 3 May, 1864.

COHN, WILLIAM O.
Ensign (Spanish-American War), 21 May, 1898. Honorably discharged 17 September, 1898.

COIT, LEVI.
Acting Third Assistant Engineer, 5 January, 1864. Resigned 3 May, 1865.

COIT, TRACEY.
Acting Assistant Paymaster, 19 October, 1861. Honorably discharged 15 April, 1866.

COITE, WILLIAM J.
Acting Assistant Paymaster, 12 June, 1862. Honorably discharged 7 November, 1865.

COKE, WILLIAM H.
Appointed Midshipman, 16 January, 1809. Lieutenant, 24 July, 1813. Killed by a shot in the Moro Castle, 7 March, 1823.

COLAHAN, CHARLES E.
Midshipman, 21 July, 1865. Graduated 4 June, 1869. Ensign, 12 July, 1870. Master, 13 August, 1872. Lieutenant, 20 July, 1875. Lieutenant-Commander, 19 June, 1897. Commander, 1 July, 1900.

COLBOURN, OLIVER.
Acting Master, 29 October, 1861. Honorably discharged 4 December, 1866.

COLBY, ARTHUR H.
Passed Assistant Paymaster (Spanish-American War), 12 May, 1898. Honorably discharged 12 December, 1898.

COLBY, EDWARD P.
Acting Assistant Surgeon, 7 April, 1863. Resigned 11 April, 1865.

COLBY, FREDERICK W.
Appointed Midshipman, 9 February, 1838. Passed Midshipman, 20 May, 1844. Died 2 November, 1847.

COLBY, GEORGE H.
Acting Ensign, 24 October, 1863. Honorably discharged 12 August, 1865.

COLBY, HARRISON G. O.
Acting Midshipman, 25 November, 1862. Graduated 6 June, 1867. Ensign, 18 December, 1868. Master, 21 March, 1870. Lieutenant, 21 March, 1871. Lieutenant-Commander, 20 November, 1891. Commander, 27 April, 1898.

COLBY, HENRY B.
Mate, 23 January, 1863. Acting Ensign, 15 February, 1864. Honorably discharged 16 May, 1866.

COLBY, HENRY G.
Acting Assistant Paymaster, 22 June, 1863. Discharged 4 December, 1865. Assistant Paymaster, 23 July, 1866. Passed Assistant Paymaster, 9 April, 1868. Paymaster, 6 September, 1878. Pay Inspector, 23 April, 1899.

COLDEN, JAMES H.
Acting Second Assistant Engineer, 7 August, 1863. Dismissed 31 August, 1864.

COLE, CYRUS W.
Naval Cadet, 20 September, 1895. At sea prior to final graduation.

COLE, DAVID.
Appointed Carpenter, 18 November, 1814. Resigned 5 February, 1816.

COLE, EDWARD.
Appointed Gunner, date not known. Last appearance on Records of Navy Department, 1817. Brig Jones.

COLE, GEORGE H.
Acting Master, 18 February, 1862. Dismissed 13 July, 1863.

COLE, GEORGE H.
Mate, 5 August, 1864. Honorably discharged 12 October, 1868.

COLE, JOHN P.
Mate, 31 August, 1862. Acting Ensign, 5 August, 1864. Honorably discharged 8 July, 1868.

COLE, LUCIUS A.
Mate, 26 November, 1863. Honorably discharged 18 October, 1865.

COLE, THOMAS B.
Acting Third Assistant Engineer, 4 June, 1862. Honorably discharged 12 October, 1865.

COLE, WILLIAM C.
Naval Cadet, 5 September, 1885. Ensign, 1 July, 1891. Lieutenant, Junior Grade, 13 January, 1899. Lieutenant, 3 March, 1899.

COLEMAN, A. H.
Appointed Midshipman, 14 March, 1829. Resigned 10 May, 1830.

COLEMAN, BENJAMIN.
Appointed Master, 6 April, 1799. Resigned 7 August, 1799.

COLEMAN, CHARLES.
Third Assistant Engineer, 18 January, 1845. Dismissed 15 December, 1851.

GENERAL NAVY REGISTER. 123

COLEMAN, DAVID.
Midshipman, 19 October, 1841. Passed Midshipman, 10 August, 1847. Resigned 13 December, 1850.
COLEMAN, EUGENE.
Mate, 24 October, 1864. Resigned 15 May, 1866.
COLEMAN, FERDINAND T.
Acting Ensign, 1 October, 1862. Acting Master, 29 May, 1863. Honorably discharged 1 December, 1865.
COLEMAN, GEORGE B.
Acting Warrant Machinist, 23 August, 1899.
COLEMAN, G. L.
Acting Ensign, 1 October, 1862. Resigned 21 May, 1863.
COLEMAN, JAMES A.
Chaplain, 8 October, 1862. Commissioned 25 March, 1863. Resigned 13 November, 1863.
COLEMAN, JOHN C.
Assistant Surgeon, 28 June, 1852. Resigned 1 February, 1858.
COLEMAN, JULIUS A.
Mate, 24 November, 1863. Honorably discharged 31 October, 1865.
COLEMAN, NOAH T.
Naval Cadet, 21 May, 1886. Ensign, 1 July, 1892. Died 21 September, 1899.
COLEMAN, SILAS B.
Acting Ensign, 1 October, 1862. Acting Master, 15 June, 1864. Honorably discharged 12 December, 1865.
COLEMAN, WILLIAM B.
Acting Assistant Paymaster, 17 February, 1863. Honorably discharged 20 November, 1865.
COLEMAN, WILLIAM B.
Ensign (Spanish-American War), 20 May, 1898. Honorably discharged 9 September, 1898.
COLES, JOHN W.
Assistant Surgeon, 6 May, 1863. Passed Assistant Surgeon, 14 January, 1867. Surgeon, 6 October, 1873. Retired List, 6 February, 1885. Died 6 April, 1895.
COLFAX, WIRT W.
Mate, 21 November, 1861. Resigned 29 September, 1862.
COLGATE, GEORGE.
Assistant Surgeon, 13 March, 1805. Resigned 16 June, 1809.
COLHOUN, EDMUND R.
Midshipman, 1 April, 1839. Passed Midshipman, 2 July, 1845. Master, 6 January, 1853. Resigned 27 June, 1853. Acting Lieutenant, 24 September, 1861. Commissioned Commander, 16 July, 1862. Captain, 2 March, 1869. Commodore, 26 April, 1876. Rear-Admiral, 3 December, 1882. Retired List, 6 May, 1883. Died 17 February, 1897.
COLHOUN, JOHN.
Midshipman, 25 January, 1821. Passed Midshipman, 24 May, 1828. Lieutenant, 27 May, 1830. Commander, 4 November, 1852. Commodore on Retired List, 4 April, 1867. Died 30 November, 1872.
COLHOUN, SAMUEL REED.
Assistant Paymaster, 28 September, 1869. Passed Assistant Paymaster, 15 January, 1875. Paymaster, 16 July, 1886. Pay Inspector, 23 December, 1899.
COLIN, ALFRED.
Third Assistant Engineer, 1 July, 1861. Second Assistant Engineer, 18 December, 1862. Resigned 27 November, 1865.
COLLAMORE, HENRY H.
Mate, 7 January, 1863. Acting Ensign, 4 April, 1864. Honorably discharged 19 September, 1865.
COLLETT, E. D.
Acting First Assistant Engineer, 22 March, 1864. First Assistant Engineer, 21 July, 1865. Honorably discharged 9 November, 1865.
COLLEY, WILLIAM H.
Acting Ensign, 14 November, 1863. Acting Master, 22 November, 1864. Honorably discharged 25 October, 1865.
COLLIER, BARNABAS H.
Acting Third Assistant Engineer, 7 July, 1864. Honorably discharged 28 November, 1865.
COLLIER, CHARLES M.
Appointed Midshipman, 25 November, 1834. •Resigned 7 August, 1834.
COLLIER, PRICE.
Ensign (Spanish-American War), 8 June, 1898. Honorably discharged 8 September, 1898.
COLLIER, THOMAS S.
Mate, 28 April, 1866. Boatswain, 9 July, 1866. Retired List, 29 October, 1883. Died 21 September, 1893.
COLLIER, WILLIAM.
Acting Second Assistant Engineer, 21 September, 1863. Appointment revoked 18 May, 1865.
COLLIER, WILLIAM A.
Assistant Paymaster (Spanish-American War), 26 July, 1898. Honorably discharged 8 February, 1899.
COLLIER, WILLIAM W.
Acting Third Assistant Engineer, 29 July, 1863. Acting Second Assistant Engineer, 1 November, 1864. Honorably discharged 1 December, 1865.
COLLINS, ADAM C.
Acting Third Assistant Engineer, 31 January, 1865. Honorably discharged 15 February, 1866.

COLLINS, B.
Appointed Master, date not known,. Discharged 20 May, 1801, under Peace Establishment Act.
COLLINS, BERTRAND R. T.
Ensign (Spanish-American War), 24 May, 1898. Honorably discharged 22 October, 1898.
COLLINS, C. A.
Acting Assistant Surgeon, 1 October, 1862. Appointment revoked (sick) 28 October, 1863.
COLLINS, CHARLES F.
Appointed Midshipman, 19 February, 1841. Resigned 8 September, 1845.
COLLINS, DANIEL S.
Acting Master, 29 October, 1861. Dismissed 28 June, 1862.
COLLINS, EDWARD.
Acting Third Assistant Engineer, 23 November, 1864. Honorably discharged 2 June, 1868.
COLLINS, FREDERICK.
Acting Midshipman, 22 July, 1863. Graduated 6 June, 1867. Ensign, 18 December, 1868. Master, 21 March, 1870. Lieutenant, 21 March, 1871. Died 27 October, 1881.
COLLINS, GEORGE S.
Acting Second Assistant Engineer, 1 October, 1862. Resigned 30 May, 1864.
COLLINS, HENRY L.
Naval Cadet, 6 September, 1893. Ensign, 1 July, 1899.
COLLINS, ISAAC.
Appointed Lieutenant, 15 June, 1799. Resigned 1 January, 1800.
COLLINS, JOHN.
Boatswain, 7 February, 1859. Dismissed 17 May, 1859.
COLLINS, JOHN.
Acting Master, 21 December, 1861. Honorably discharged 19 September, 1865.
COLLINS, JOHN B.
Midshipman, 30 July, 1866. Graduated 7 June, 1870. Ensign, 13 July, 1871. Master, 3 March, 1874. Lieutenant, 18 March, 1880. Lieutenant-Commander, 3 March, 1899.
COLLINS, JOHN H.
Acting Master and Pilot, 1 October, 1864. Honorably discharged 12 August, 1866.
COLLINS, JOHN W.
Acting Third Assistant Engineer, 14 September, 1864. Honorably discharged 28 June, 1865.
COLLINS, JOS. E.
Appointed Lieutenant, 15 November, 1799. Last appearance on Records of Navy Department.
COLLINS, J. T. S.
Appointed Midshipman, 17 June, 1834. Resigned 31 January, 1835.
COLLINS, NAPOLEON.
Midshipman, 2 January, 1834. Passed Midshipman, 16 July, 1840. Master, 15 August, 1846. Lieutenant, 6 November, 1846. Commander, 16 July, 1862. Captain, 25 July, 1866. Commodore, 19 January, 1871. Rear-Admiral, 9 August, 1874. Died 9 August, 1875.
COLLINS, ROBERT W.
Mate, 8 February, 1865. Honorably discharged 18 September, 1867.
COLLINS, W. A.
Acting Assistant Surgeon, 1 October, 1862. Appointment revoked 28 October, 1863.
COLLINS, WILLIAM.
Appointed Master, 3 February, 1814. Last appearance on Records of Navy Department.
COLLINS, WILLIAM.
Acting Ensign, 17 July, 1862. Acting Master, 14 August, 1863. Honorably discharged 20 September, 1865.
COLLINS, WILLIAM.
Mate, 23 December, 1861. Resigned 1 October, 1862.
COLLINS, WILLIAM A.
Acting Second Assistant Engineer, 9 June, 1863. Honorably discharged 7 October, 1865.
COLLINS, WILLIAM H.
Acting Second Assistant Engineer, 12 November, 1864. Honorably discharged 3 December, 1865.
COLLOM, CHARLES D.
Acting Assistant Paymaster, 2 July, 1864. Discharged 12 February, 1866.
COLLYER, JOHN.
Appointed Midshipman, 30 November, 1814. Resigned 8 February, 1816.
COLP, JACOB.
Acting Third Assistant Engineer, November, 1861. Resigned 20 June, 1863.
COLROW, CHARLES J.
Ensign (Spanish-American War), 4 May, 1898. Honorably discharged 8 September, 1898.
COLSON, AMOS.
Boatswain, 26 March, 1842. Resigned 23 February, 1843. Boatswain, 4 March, 1847. Died 17 March, 1858.
COLSTON, JOSIAH.
Purser, 28 May, 1825. Dismissed 24 March, 1840.
COLT, WILLIAM.
Appointed Master, 26 May, 1812. Last appearance on Records of Navy Department, 5 June, 1812.

GENERAL NAVY REGISTER.   125

COLTER, JAMES.
Appointed Midshipman, 30 November, 1814. Last appearance on Records of Navy Department, 1815. Frigate Guerriere.
COLTON, FREDERICK W.
Mate, 4 January, 1864. Honorably discharged 1 June, 1869.
COLTON, WALTER.
Chaplain, 6 November, 1830. Died at Philadelphia 22 January, 1851.
COLVIN, EZRA C.
Mate, 12 November, 1863. Appointment revoked (sick) 8 November, 1864.
COLVOCORESSES, GEORGE P.
Midshipman, 28 September, 1864. Graduated 4 June, 1869. Ensign, 12 July, 1870. Master, 18 June, 1872. Lieutenant, 1 July, 1875. Lieutenant-Commander, 4 June, 1897. Commander, 30 June, 1900. Served two years and two months as Captain's Clery during the Civil War.
COLVOCORESSIS, GEORGE M.
Midshipman, 21 February, 1832. Passed Midshipman, 23 June, 1838. Lieutenant, 7 December, 1843. Commander, 2 July, 1861. Captain on Retired List, 4 April, 1867. Died 3 June, 1872.
COLWELL, JAMES H.
Cadet Midshipman, 27 June, 1877. Graduated. Honorably discharged 30 June, 1883. Lieutenant (Spanish-American War), 23 June, 1898. Honorably discharged 28 October, 1898.
COLWELL, JOHN C.
Midshipman, 23 September, 1870. Graduated June, 1874. Ensign, 17 July, 1875. Master, 1 June, 1881. Lieutenant, Junior Grade, 3 March, 1883. Lieutenant, 30 June, 1887. Lieutenant-Commander, 3 March, 1899.
COMBS, JAMES R.
Naval Cadet, 6 September, 1895. At sea prior to final graduation.
COMEGYS, CORNELIUS.
Midshipman, 9 September, 1841. Dismissed 2 October, 1848.
COMEGYS, GEORGE M.
Appointed Midshipman, 27 February, 1836. Resigned 18 December, 1841.
COMFORT, JAMES H.
Naval Cadet, 20 May, 1896. Graduated 30 June, 1900.
COMINS, JOB.
Acting Third Assistant Engineer, 1 October, 1862. Resigned 22 September, 1863.
COMLY, SAMUEL P.
Midshipman, 26 July, 1865. Graduated 4 June, 1869. Ensign, 12 July, 1871. Master, 3 August, 1873. Lieutenant, 26 April, 1878. Lieutenant-Commander, 10 August, 1898.
COMMONS, WILLIAM.
Assistant Surgeon, 3 November, 1863. Resigned 24 July, 1867.
COMO, JAMES.
Acting Gunner, 4 April, 1864. Honorably discharged 9 July, 1865.
COMSTOCK, ALBERT H.
Mate, 19 November, 1861. Dismissed 2 March, 1863.
COMSTOCK, JOHN H.
Acting Midshipman, 11 January, 1858. Resigned 30 January, 1861.
COMSTOCK, THEO. A.
Mate, 2 February, 1863. Acting Ensign, 16 December, 1864. Honorably discharged 28 October, 1865.
CONANT, BENJAMIN.
Appointed Midshipman, 15 May, 1799. Discharged under Peace Establishment Act, 30 April, 1801.
CONANT, FRANK H.
Cadet Engineer, 1 October, 1878. Assistant Engineer, 1 July, 1884. Passed Assistant Engineer, 30 September, 1894. Died 16 November, 1898.
CONANT, SAMUEL.
Appointed Midshipman, 2 December, 1799. Discharged under Peace Establishment Act, 6 August, 1801.
CONANT, THADDEUS L.
Acting Ensign, 1 December, 1862. Resigned 24 April, 1863.
CONARD, CHARLES.
Assistant Paymaster, 27 April, 1898. Passed Assistant Paymaster, 3 March, 1899.
CONCKLIN, ROBERT.
Appointed Midshipman, 20 March, 1815. Last appearance on Records of Navy Department.
CONCKLIN, SYLVANUS.
Appointed Midshipman, 1 January, 1812. Dismissed 20 January, 1814.
CONCKLING, AUG.
Appointed Midshipman, 16 January, 1809. Lieutenant, 24 July, 1813. Resigned 8 February, 1820.
CONCKLING, ROBERT.
Appointed Midshipman, 16 January, 1809. Resigned 27 December, 1809.
CONDRY, DENNIS.
Acting Volunteer Lieutenant, 28 September, 1861. Appointment revoked, advanced age, 16 July, 1862. Reappointed. but declined, 9 May, 1864.
CONE, HUTCH I.
Naval Cadet, 5 September, 1890. Assistant Engineer, 1 July, 1896. Rank changed to Ensign, 3 March, 1899. Lieutenant, Junior Grade, 1 July, 1899.
CONE, OWEN S. M.
Acting Ensign, 1 April, 1865. Appointment revoked 9 October, 1866.
CONEY, CHARLES JABEZ.
Third Assistant Engineer, 16 October, 1861. Second Assistant Engineer, 3 August, 1863. Resigned 2 October, 1866.

GENERAL NAVY REGISTER.

CONEY, JOSEPH S.
　　Acting Ensign, 1 November, 1862. Acting Master, gallantry in destruction of a blockade runner, 7 September, 1863. Honorably discharged 7 November, 1865.
CONGDON, JOSEPH W.
　　Acting Master, 25 February, 1862. Honorably discharged 29 August, 1865.
CONGER, DAVID G.
　　Mate, 31 March, 1864. Resigned 26 April, 1865.
CONILL, JULIEN D.
　　Mate, 3 September, 1863. Honorably discharged 26 October, 1865.
CONINGHAM, DAVID.
　　Appointed Midshipman, 4 February, 1814. Resigned 4 May, 1824.
CONKLIN, CHARLES G.
　　Acting First Assistant Engineer, 5 January, 1864. Honorably discharged 29 August, 1865.
CONKLIN, GEORGE HENRY.
　　Acting Midshipman, 28 September, 1857. Resigned 1 May, 1858.
CONKLIN, H. B.
　　Mate, 1 September, 1861. Resigned 17 October, 1864.
CONKLIN, GORDON J.
　　Mate, 24 October, 1861. Acting Ensign, 14 September, 1863. Honorably discharged 28 October, 1865.
CONKLIN, NORMAN H.
　　Mate, 22 June, 1863. Acting Ensign, 8 March, 1864. Honorably discharged 5 November, 1865.
CONKLIN, STRONG.
　　Acting Second Assistant Engineer, 18 November, 1861. Resigned 18 September, 1862.
CONKLIN, F. A.
　　Acting Assistant Paymaster, 25 September, 1861. Dismissed 6 May, 1863.
CONLEY, JAMES H.
　　Carpenter, 30 April, 1846. Dismissed 7 June, 1850. Acting Carpenter, 17 May, 1861. Dismissed 17 July, 1861. Reappointed 13 November, 1861. Resignation accepted 25 September, 1862.
CONLY, JAMES H.
　　Carpenter, 30 April. 1846. Dismissed 7 June, 1850.
CONNALLY, JOHN KERR.
　　Acting Midshipman, 28 September, 1857. Resigned 28 February, 1859.
CONNELL, JAMES.
　　Appointed Boatswain, 28 May, 1798. Last appearance on Records of Navy Department.
CONNELLY, JOHN.
　　Acting First Assistant Engineer, 7 December, 1863. Dismissed 3 December, 1864.
CONNELLY, LOUIS J.
　　Gunner, 27 May, 1896.
CONNER, DAVID.
　　Midshipman, 16 January, 1809. Lieutenant, 24 July, 1813. Commander. 23 March, 1825. Captain, 3 March, 1835. Died at Philadelphia 20 March, 1856.
CONNER, GEO. W.
　　Acting Ensign, 24 September, 1864. Honorably discharged 20 September, 1865.
CONNER, HENRY P.
　　Acting Ensign, 16 August. 1862. Acting Master, good service, 17 December, 1863. Acting Volunteer Lieutenant. 6 April, 1865. Honorably discharged 17 January, 1866.
CONNER, JOHN.
　　Mate, 5 March, 1862. Acting Ensign, 2 June, 1864. Appointment revoked (sick) 13 September, 1864.
CONNER, JOHN E.
　　Acting Third Assistant Engineer, 28 May, 1863. Honorably discharged 6 March, 1866.
CONNER, NEWELL W.
　　Acting Second Assistant Engineer, 1 October, 1862. Appointment revoked (sick) 26 January, 1863. Acting Second Assistant Engineer, 6 May, 1864. Honorably discharged 1 November, 1865.
CONNER, THOMAS.
　　Acting Third Assistant Engineer, 7 August, 1863. Resigned 15 May, 1865.
CONNERY, THOMAS B., Jr.
　　Assistant Paymaster (Spanish-American War), 21 July, 1898. Honorably discharged 12 December. 1898.
CONNOR, ARTHUR B.
　　Lieutenant (Spanish-American War), 2 June, 1898. Honorably discharged 3 October, 1898.
CONNOR, JAMES.
　　Appointed Midshipman, 18 June, 1812. Last appearance on Records of Navy Department.
CONOVER, EDWARD D.
　　Mate, 6 April, 1864. Honorably discharged 23 August, 1866.
CONOVER, FRANCIS S.
　　Midshipman. 11 May, 1840. Passed Midshipman, 11 July, 1846. Master. 1 March, 1855. Lieutenant, 14 September, 1855. Acting Lieutenant, 13 September, 1862. Resigned 11 August, 1863.
CONOVER, GEORGE W.
　　Carpenter, 18 February, 1870. Retired List, 18 July, 1895.
CONOVER, ISAAC.
　　Acting Third Assistant Engineer, 23 May, 1863. Died on the Lenapee, 9 September, 1867.

GENERAL NAVY REGISTER. 127

CONOVER, THOMAS H.
Midshipman, 1 January, 1812. Lieutenant, 5 March, 1817. Commander, 28 February, 1838. Captain, 2 October, 1848. Commodore on the Retired List, 16 July, 1862. Died 25 September, 1864.

CONRAD, DANIEL B.
Assistant Surgeon, 20 September. 1854. Passed Assistant Surgeon, 4 May, 1860. Dismissed 10 May, 1861.

CONROY, EDWARD.
Acting Volunteer Lieutenant, 21 September, 1861. Acting Volunteer Lieutenant-Commander, 8 December, 1864. Honorably discharged 30 October, 1868.

CONSTABLE, A. W.
Mate, 27 May, 1864. Resigned 5 September, 1865.

CONSTANT, JOHN C.
Mate, 15 November. 1861. Appointment revoked (sick) 2 July, 1863. Mate, 24 October, 1863. Resigned (sick) 30 December, 1864.

CONSTANT, WALTER M.
Cadet Midshipman, 13 June, 1873. Graduated 18 June, 1879. Ensign, 14 September, 1881. Lieutenant, Junior Grade, 1 July, 1888. Died 27 October, 1890.

CONSTANTINE, WILLIAM L.
Acting Ensign, 10 July. 1863. Resigned (sick) 21 March, 1865.

CONSTIEN, EDWARD T.
Naval Cadet, 19 May, 1894. Ensign, 4 April, 1900.

CONTEE, JOHN.
Midshipman, 27 October, 1832. Passed Midshipman, 23 June, 1838. Lieutenant, 14 February, 1843. Resigned 9 January, 1854.

CONTTINEAU, HERCULES.
Appointed Midshipman, 9 November, 1813. Resigned 24 January, 1816. Midshipman, 12 April, 1817. Died 12 April, 1819.

CONVERSE, BLINN.
Acting Third Assistant Engineer, 12 September, 1864. Resigned 17 May, 1865.

CONVERSE, GEORGE ALBERT.
Acting Midshipman, 29 November, 1861. Graduated September, 1865. Ensign. 1 December, 1866. Master, 12 March, 1868. Lieutenant, 26 March, 1869. Lieutenant-Commander, 12 July, 1878. Commander, 23 March, 1889. Captain, 3 March, 1899.

CONWAY, EDWIN H.
Assistant Surgeon, 7 March, 1838. Lost in the Grampus in March, 1843.

CONWAY, JOHN.
Mate. Appointment revoked 22 January, 1866.

CONWAY, J. O.
Mate, 23 June, 1863. Resigned 26 October, 1864.

CONWAY, WILLIAM D.
Surgeon's Mate, 10 December. 1814. Resigned 11 April, 1825.

CONWAY, WILLIAM P.
Midshipman, 1 October. 1866. Graduated 7 June. 1870. Ensign, 13 July, 1871. Master, 9 August, 1874. Lieutenant, 12 March, 1881. Died 14 September, 1893.

COOCK, JOHN.
Acting Third Assistant Engineer. 26 September, 1863. Honorably discharged 2 August, 1865.

COOK, AARON F.
Appointed Midshipman, 2 March. 1799. Permitted to retire 17 December, 1801.

COOK, ALBERT.
Acting Master, 11 November. 1861. Honorably discharged 18 January, 1866.

COOK, ALBERT G.
Appointed Midshipman, 24 October, 1841. Dismissed 22 November, 1844.

COOK, ALLEN M.
Naval Cadet, 6 September, 1887. Resigned 1 February, 1888. Naval Cadet, 22 May, 1889. Assistant Engineer. 1 July, 1895. Passed Assistant Engineer, 24 February, 1899. Rank changed to Lieutenant, Junior Grade, 3 March, 1899.

COOK, ANDREW B.
Surgeon's Mate, 21 December. 1812. Surgeon. 27 March, 1818. Died 4 November, 1838.

COOK, BERNA.
Acting Third Assistant Engineer, 16 October. 1863. Acting Second Assistant Engineer, 22 February, 1865. Died at Naval Hospital, New York, 7 September, 1865.

COOK, BRENTON B.
Mate, 24 December. 1863. Deserted 3 July. 1864.

COOK, B. FRANK.
Mate, 18 June, 1861. Acting Master, 10 May, 1862. Honorably discharged 21 September, 1865.

COOK, CHARLES.
Acting Master and Pilot. 28 October. 1864. Honorably discharged 6 December, 1865.

COOK, DAVID P.
Acting Ensign. 6 July. 1864. Resigned 15 May. 1865.

COOK, FRANCIS A.
Acting Midshipman. 20 September, 1860. Acting Ensign. 1 October, 1863. Master, 10 May, 1866. Lieutenant, 21 February. 1867. Lieutenant-Commander. 12 March, 1868. Commander, 12 October, 1881. Captain, 28 February, 1896.

COOK, FRANCIS T.
Acting Third Assistant Engineer. 30 March. 1863. Appointment revoked (sick) 11 July, 1864.

COOK, FRANK C.
Assistant Surgeon, 22 December, 1893. Passed Assistant Surgeon, 22 December, 1896.

GENERAL NAVY REGISTER.

COOK, GILBERT C.
Third Assistant Engineer, 16 September, 1862. Second Assistant Engineer, 1 March, 1864. Resignd 22 July, 1865.
COOK, JAMES A
Mate, 22 March, 1862. Resigned 11 January, 1864.
COOK, JAMES B.
Acting Third Assistant Engineer, 11 March, 1865. Honorably discharged 23 October, 1867.
COOK, JOHN.
Chaplain, 19 May, 1812. Died 21 August, 1828.
COOK, JCHN.
Acting Second Assistant Engineer, 26 September, 1863. Honorably discharged 2 August, 1865.
COOK, JOHN, JR.
Acting Third Assistant Engineer, 12 September, 1864. Resigned 21 June, 1865.
COOK, JOHN A.
Appointed Midshipman, 1 January, 1812. Lieutenant, 1 April, 1818. Died 7 February, 1834.
COOK, JOHN V.
Acting Ensign, 23 June, 1864. Acting Master, 21 August, 1865. Honorably discharged, 10 October, 1868.
COOK, JOSEPH J.
Midshipman, 19 October, 1841 Passed Midshipman, 10 August, 1847. Resigned 9 December, 1851.
COOK, JOSIAH D.
Acting Master, October, 1861. Dismissed 24 June, 1862.
COOK, JOSHUA, JR.
Mate, 30 December, 1863. Acting Ensign, 7 January, 1865. Honorably discharged 14 August, 1867.
COOK, LEMUEL F.
Mate, 21 January, 1864. Honorably discharged 28 October, 1865.
COOK, LEWIS G.
Acting Master, 19 December, 1861. Honorably discharged 28 February, 1866. Acting Master, 24 May, 1866. Mustered out 8 October, 1868. Mate, 1 February, 1870. Died 4 August, 1876.
COOK, LIVINGSTON.
Acting Second Assistant Engineer, 20 July, 1863. Appointment revoked 26 January, 1864.
COOK, PARKER.
Passed Assistant Paymaster (Spanish-American War), 30 April, 1898. Honorably discharged 24 January, 1899.
COOK, SIMON.
Cadet Midshipman, 6 June, 1873. Graduated 18 June, 1879. Ensign, 15 November, 1881. Lieutenant, Junior Grade, 15 March, 1889. Lieutenant, 27 September, 1893.
COOK, THEOPHILUS.
Third Assistant Engineer, 22 May, 1863. Second Assistant Engineer, 6 January, 1866. First Assistant Engineer, 31 January, 1873. Retired List, 11 October, 1881. Died 20 July, 1893.
COOK, THOMAS.
Acting Chief Engineer, 1 October, 1862. Honorably discharged 7 June, 1866.
COOK, THOMAS W.
Acting Master's Mate, 5 June, 1862. Deserted December, 1862.
COOK, WILLIAM, JR.
Mate, 6 October, 1863. Resigned (sick) 6 December, 1864.
COOK, WILLIAM C.
Acting Assistant Paymaster, 30 June, 1862. Assistant Paymaster, 30 June, 1864. Resigned 28 June, 1866.
COOK, WILLIAM H.
Mate, 11 March, 1864. Died on the Brooklyn, from wounds, 5 August, 1864.
COOKE, AUGUSTUS P.
Acting Midshipman, 27 May, 1852. Midshipman, 20 June, 1856. Passed Midshipman, 29 April, 1859. Master, 5 September, 1859. Lieutenant, 28 December, 1860. Lieutenant-Commander, 11 August, 1862. Commander, 15 August, 1870. Captain, 25 November, 1881. Retired List, 27 May, 1892. Died 7 September, 1896.
COOKE, BENJAMIN S.
Acting Second Assistant Engineer, 23 November, 1863. Acting First Assistant Engineer, 22 March, 1865. Honorably discharged 10 October, 1865.
COOKE, GEORGE H.
Assistant Surgeon, 9 September, 1862. Passed Assistant Surgeon, 5 March, 1866. Surgeon, 20 February, 1870. Medical Inspector, 15 September, 1888. Medical Director, 29 September, 1895 Retired List, 12 December, 1898.
COOKE, JAMES W.
Midshipman, 1 April, 1828. Passed Midshipman, 14 June, 1834. Master. Lieutenant, 25 February, 1841 Resigned 2 May, 1861.
COOKE, JOHN.
Appointed Midshipman, 18 June, 1812. Last appearance on Records of Navy Department, 1815. Lake Ontario.
COOKE, JOSEPH K.
Acting Ensign, 22 April, 1864. Dismissed 8 October, 1864.
COOKE, MORRIS L.
Assistant Engineer (Spanish-American War), 14 May, 1898. Honorably discharged 23 September, 1898.
COOL, CHARLES E.
Mate, 30 June, 1863. Dismissed 13 July, 1865.

GENERAL NAVY REGISTER.

COOLEY, CHARLES M.
Mate, 17 September, 1861. Resigned 28 July, 1862.
COOLEY, E. F.
Acting Assistant Paymaster, 1861. Resigned 24 July, 1862.
COOLEY, HENRY P.
Mate, 17 September, 1861 Resigned 19 May, 1862.
COOLEY, MORTIMER E.
Cadet Engineer, 1 October, 1874. Graduated 20 June, 1878. Assistant Engineer, 20 June, 1880. Resigned 1 January, 1886. Chief Engineer (Spanish-American War), 10 May, 1898. Honorably discharged 6 February, 1899.
COOMBS, CHARLES.
Appointed Midshipman, 8 March, 1800. Last appearance on Records of Navy Department. Dead.
COOMBS, JOHN H.
Acting Third Assistant Engineer, 8 May, 1864. Resigned 10 June, 1865.
COOMBS, ROWLAND L, E.
Acting Ensign, 11 August, 1864. Honorably discharged 20 October, 1865.
COOMES, WILLIAM.
Mate, 11 August, 1862. Resigned 29 December, 1862.
COOMES, WILLIAM.
Mate, 4 August, 1863. Dismissed 14 May, 1864.
COON, EDGAR A.
Acting Ensign, 24 October, 1864. Resigned 30 May, 1865.
COONAN, JOHN N.
Acting Assistant Surgeon, 24 January, 1865. Honorably discharged 10 October, 1865. Reappointed 5 December, 1873. Honorably discharged 30 June, 1876.
COONEY, CHARLES D.
Acting Midshipman, 22 September, 1855. Resigned 16 November, 1859.
COONEY THOMAS C.
Carpenter, 27 June, 1898.
COONTZ, ROBERT E.
Cadet Midshipman, 28 September, 1881. Ensign, 1 July, 1887. Lieutenant, Junior Grade, 5 September, 1896. Lieutenant, 3 March, 1899.
COOP, HENRY J.
Acting Master, 29 October, 1861. Acting Volunteer Lieutenant, 29 November, 1864. Honorably discharged 20 September, 1868. Mate, 28 September, 1869. Resigned 25 November, 1871.
COOPER, BENJAMIN.
Midshipman, 16 January, 1809. Lieutenant, 9 December, 1814. Commander, 24 April, 1828. Captain, 28 February, 1838. Died at Brooklyn, N. Y., 1 June, 1850.
COOPER, CHARLES J.
Acting Third Assistant Engineer, 25 November, 1863. Honorably discharged 4 December, 1865.
COOPER, CHARLES S.
Appointed Midshipman, 28 November, 1837. Resigned 9 April, 1842.
COOPER, CHRISTOPHER J.
Mate, 27 August, 1897. Boatswain, 6 March, 1899.
COOPER, COLDEN.
Chaplain, 24 April, 1815. Last appearance on Records of Navy Department, 1815. Frigate Constellation.
COOPER, CON. A.
Acting Third Assistant Engineer, 19 July, 1864. Honorably discharged 5 October, 1865.
COOPER, CONRAD J.
Third Assistant Engineer, 9 December, 1861. Resigned 18 July, 1862.
COOPER, EDWARD B.
Midshipman, 6 November, 1850. Dismissed 24 January, 1851.
COOPER, FRANCIS.
Appointed Master, 22 July, 1799. Last appearance on Records of Navy Department. Dismissed.
COOPER, FRANCIS L.
Third Assistant Engineer, 1 July, 1861. Second Assistant Engineer, 18 December, 1862. Resigned 10 October, 1873.
COOPER, G. C.
Purser, 11 March, 1829. Died 2 March, 1844.
COOPER, GEORGE F.
Naval Cadet, 17 June, 1882. Ensign, 1 July, 1888. Lieutenant, Junior Grade, 5 January, 1897. Lieutenant, 3 March, 1899.
COOPER, GEORGE H.
Midshipman, 4 August, 1837. Passed Midshipman, 29 June, 1843. Master, 11 October, 1850. Lieutenant, 8 May, 1851. Commander, 16 July, 1862. Captain, 2 December, 1867. Commodore, 5 June, 1874. Rear-Admiral, 15 November, 1881. Retired List, 27 July, 1884. Died 17 November, 1891.
COOPER, GEORGE H.
Mate, 25 January, 1870. Resigned 20 November, 1878.
COOPER, HOWELL C.
Assistant Engineer (Spanish-American War), 25 May, 1898. Honorably discharged 1 March, 1899.
COOPER, IGNATIUS T.
Naval Cadet, 20 May, 1890. Assistant Engineer, 1 July, 1896. Rank changed to Ensign, 3 March, 1899. Retired List, 22 November, 1899.
COOPER, ISAAC.
Carpenter, 16 May, 1871. Died 24 December, 1895.

COOPER, JAMES.
Appointed Midshipman, 1 January, 1808. Resigned 6 May, 1811.
COOPER, JAMES.
Appointed Master, 9 July, 1812. Resigned 28 January, 1813.
COOPER, JAMES B.
Master, 9 July, 1812. Lieutenant, 22 April, 1822 Commander, 8 September, 1841. Died 5 February, 1854.
COOPER, JAMES GILBERT.
Third Assistant Engineer, 24 December, 1861. Second Assistant Engineer, 8 September, 1863. Resigned 19 December, 1865.
COOPER, JAMES M.
Gunner, 20 June, 1837. Died 24 June, 1868.
COOPER, JOHN.
Appointed Master, 3 October, 1798. Last appearance on Records of Navy Department, 10 July, 1801. Resigned.
COOPER, JOHN E.
Third Assistant Engineer, 12 August, 1861. Resigned 14 May, 1863.
COOPER, JOHN E.
Acting Second Assistant Engineer, 21 September, 1863. Acting First Assistant Engineer, 2 March, 1864. Resigned 26 January, 1865.
COOPER, JOHN P.
Acting Third Assistant Engineer, 1 August, 1862. Acting Second Assistant Engineer, 4 January, 1865. Honorably discharged 30 September, 1865. Acting Second Assistant Engineer, 31 March, 1866. Mustered out 19 December, 1867.
COOPER, LEMUEL T.
Acting Warrant Machinist, 23 August, 1899.
COOPER, LLEWELLYN.
Acting Master, 11 November, 1861. Resigned 14 May, 1862.
COOPER, MASON SINCLAIR.
Mate, 6 May, 1864. Acting Ensign, 7 April, 1865. Honoraby discharged 3 October, 1866.
COOPER, PHILIP H.
Acting Midshipman, 28 September, 1860. Acting Ensign, 28 May, 1863. Master, 10 November, 1865. Lieutenant, 10 November, 1866. Lieutenant-Commander, 12 March, 1868. Commander, 1 November, 1879. Captain, 11 April, 1894.
COOPER, RICHARD F.
Midshipman, 25 October, 1850. Dismissed 12 June, 1851.
COOPER, SAMUEL.
Appointed Midshipman, 12 January, 1801. Discharged under Peace Establishment Act, 12 October, 1801.
COOPER, SAMUEL T.
Appointed Midshipman, 10 May, 1820. Resigned 9 May, 1821.
COOPER, THEODORE.
Third Assistant Engineer, 24 December, 1861. Second Assistant Engineer, 8 September, 1863. First Assistant Engineer, 11 October, 1866. Resigned 26 July, 1872.
COOPER, THOMAS.
Appointed Midshipman, 6 April, 1803. Dismissed 20 April, 1804.
COOPER, T. H. P.
Appointed Midshipman, 15 October, 1817. Died in 1821.
COOPER, THOMAS J. W.
Acting Third Assistant Engineer, 22 October, 1863. Acting Second Assistant Engineer, 11 October, 1864. Second Assistant Engineer, 25 April, 1870. Passed Assistant Engineer, 6 July, 1876. Died 29 January, 1888.
COOPER, WALTER.
Acting Ensign, Admiral Dahlgren's Staff, 1 April, 1864. Honorably discharged 26 August, 1865.
COOPER, WILLIAM.
Mate, 1 April, 1864. Mustered out 1 May, 1869.
COOPER, WILLIAM A.
Boatswain, 25 April, 1866. Chief Boatswain, 3 March, 1899. Retired List, 15 December, 1899.
COOPER, WILLIAM RINGGOLD.
Acting Ensign, Admiral S. P. Lee's Staff, 1 September, 1864. Dishonorably discharged 2 August, 1866.
COOPER, W. M.
Appointed Boatswain, 26 March, 1836. Died 3 October, 1840.
COPE, CHARLES P.
Mate, 5 September, 1864. Honorably discharged 3 June, 1865.
COPE, WILLIAM.
Gunner, 6 November, 1851. Died 7 December, 1874.
COPELAND, G. M.
Third Assistant Engineer, 21 January, 1842. Resigned 30 November, 1844.
COFELAND, LAURISSON L.
Acting Third Assistant Engineer, 20 April, 1863. Honorably discharged 23 August, 1865.
COPELAND, ROBERT A.
Third Assistant Engineer, 20 September, 1858. Resigned 1 August, 1859. Second Assistant Engineer, 28 May, 1861. Dismissed 19 September, 1861. Acting Second Assistant Engineer, 4 December, 1862. Appointment revoked 12 December, 1864.
COPELAND, THOMAS.
First Assistant Engineer, 19 October, 1842. Dismissed 28 July, 1845.
COPP, CHARLES A.
Midshipman, 5 November, 1864. Graduated 2 June, 1868. Lost on the Oneida, 24 January, 1870.

CORBETT, P. J.
    Mate, 3 April, 1868. Resigned 20 September, 1872.
CORBIN, CLARENCE A.
    Midshipman, 27 September, 1870. Graduated 21 June, 1875. Ensign, 18 July, 1876. Discharged 27 November, 1882.
CORBIN, JOB.
    Assistant Surgeon, 9 May, 1861. Passed Assistant Surgeon, 26 October, 1863. Surgeon, 9 March, 1864. Resigned 9 May, 1867.
CORBIN, THOMAS G.
    Midshipman, 15 May, 1838. Passed Midshipman, 20 May, 1844. Master, 15 July, 1851. Lieutenant, 10 June, 1852. Commander, 16 July, 1862. Captain, 25 July, 1866 Retired List, 5 January, 1874.
CORDEIRO, FREDERICK J. B.
    Assistant Surgeon, 26 June, 1884. Passed Assistant Surgeon, 26 June, 1887. Surgeon, 19 October, 1897.
CORDIS, JOHN B.
    Appointed Lieutenant, 9 April, 1798. Discharged under Peace Establishment Act, 30 April, 1801.
CORDIS, JOHN B.
    Appointed Lieutenant, 26 July, 1804. Left the service 3 March, 1805.
CORDIS, JOSEPH.
    Appointed Midshipman, 15 May, 1799. Discharged under Peace Establishment Act, 6 July, 1801.
CORDWELL, THOMAS.
    Acting Ensign, 1 October, 1862. Honorably discharged 11 November, 1865.
COREY, ALLEN.
    Appointed Midshipman, 16 January, 1809. Resigned 1 September, 1809.
COREY, DAVID B.
    Mate, 23 December, 1861. Acting Ensign, 29 March, 1864. Resigned 13 March, 1865.
CORIELL, J. D.
    Mate, 3 September, 1863. Honorably discharged 26 October, 1865
CORINO, JACOBUS J.
    Acting Warrant Machinist, 23 August, 1899.
CORLACE, JAMES.
    Mate, 11 January, 1862. Killed accidentally, on the Daylight, 12 March, 1862
CORLIS, CHARLES
    Appointed Midshipman, 30 November, 1814. Last appearance on Records of Navy Department, 9 January, 1815.
CORMACK, ALEX.
    Acting Ensign, 25 October, 1864. Honorably discharged 19 September, 1865.
CORNELL, RICHARD M.
    Acting Ensign, 10 September, 1862. Acting Master, for good service, 17 December, 1863. Resigned 10 January, 1865.
CORNELL, RANDALL M.
    Mate, 26 December, 1863. Appointment revoked 31 October, 1865.
CORNELL, STEPHEN B.
    Acting Third Assistant Engineer, 9 September, 1862. Resigned 13 May, 1863.
CORNELL, STEPHEN H.
    Acting Master, 25 January, 1862. Resigned 25 March, 1865
CORNELL, wALTER J.
    Acting Third Assistant Engineer, 23 September, 1863. Acting Second Assistant Engineer, 16 June, 1865. Honorably discharged 28 October, 1865.
CORNELL, WILLIAM.
    Acting Third Assistant Engineer, 7 August, 1863. Acting Second Assistant Engineer, 14 February, 1865. Honorably discharged 29 August, 1866.
CORNELL, WILLIAM.
    Acting Third Assistant Engineer, 13 June, 1865. Acting Second Assistant Engineer, 15 July, 1865. Honorably discharged 22 July, 1865.
CORNELL, WILLIAM H.
    Acting Third Assistant Engineer, 16 March, 1864. Honorably discharged 22 January, 1866.
CORNER, GEORGE W. (See Conner.)
    Mate, 15 April, 1862. Acting Ensign, 21 May, 1863. Dismissed 2 August, 1864.
CORNICK, JAMES.
    Surgeon's Mate, 28 March, 1820. Surgeon, 5 March, 1825. Retired 18 June, 1861. Resigned 3 August, 1861.
CORNING, DOUGLAS.
    Acting Assistant Paymaster, 11 July, 1864. Honorably discharged 12 November, 1865.
CORNTHWAIT, ROBERT H.
    Acting Third Assistant Engineer, 17 October, 1863. Honorably discharged 10 November, 1867.
CORNTHWAITE, LOUIS A
    Mate, 18 April, 1863. Acting Ensign, 2 October, 1864. Honorably discharged 12 May, 1868.
CORNWELL, CHARLES C.
    Midshipman, 20 September, 1864. Graduated 2 June, 1868. Ensign, 19 April, 1869. Master, 12 July, 1870. Lieutenant, 1 April, 1872. Lieutenant-Commander 7 February, 1893. Commander, 25 December, 1898.
CORNWELL, FRANK S.
    Lieutenant, Junior Grade (Spanish-American War), 22 June, 1898. Honorably discharged 8 October, 1898.

CORNWELL, JOHN J.
  Midshipman, 1 February, 1847. Passed Midshipman, 10 June, 1853. Master, 15 September, 1855. Lieutenant, 16 September, 1855. Lieutenant-Commander, 16 July, 1862. Commander, 25 July, 1866. Died 12 February, 1867.
CORREIRA, ANTONIO.
  Appointed Gunner, 22 June, 1809. Died 31 December, 1823.
CORSER, CHARLES H.
  Acting Master, 17 December, 1861. Resigned 23 November, 1864.
CORSON, EDW. T.
  Assistant Surgeon, 20 May, 1859. Passed Assistant Surgeon, 23 May, 1862. Surgeon, 31 July, 1862. Died 22 June, 1864.
CORSON, E. E. W.
  Assistant Surgeon, 3 March, 1873. Dismissed 2 April, 1874.
CORSON, ELWOOD M.
  Acting Assistant Surgeon, 19 March, 1864. Assistant Surgeon, 1 April, 1864. Resigned 14 October, 1865.
CORSON, JOHN.
  Acting Third Assistant Engineer, 10 December, 1864. Honorably discharged 18 October, 1865.
CORTELGAN, J. W.
  Mate, 19 December, 1861. Dismissed 7 October, 1862.
CORTEZ, RENE EDWARD.
  Midshipman, 28 April, 1851. Dropped 16 June, 1852.
CORWALL, JOHN S.
  Appointed Midshipman, 1 January, 1812. Resigned 5 July, 1827.
CORWIN, WILLIAM A.
  Assistant Surgeon, 31 March, 1869. Passed Assistant Surgeon, 27 March, 1873. Surgeon, 10 June, 1880. Died 11 March, 1886.
CORWINE, JOHN.
  Assistant Paymaster, 3 March, 1879. Passed Assistant Paymaster, 2 November, 1885. Paymaster, 9 January, 1895. Dismissed 8 July, 1897.
CORY, WILLIAM W.
  Acting Master's Mate, 9 September, 1864. Resigned 9 June, 1865.
COSBY, FRANK C.
  Assistant Paymaster, 24 August, 1861. Paymaster, 14 April, 1862. Pay Inspector, 12 April, 1877. Pay Director, 5 July, 1889.
COSBY, JAMES S.
  Appointed Midshipman, 1 January, 1825. Resigned 29 August, 1826.
COSGROVE, JAMES.
  Appointed Gunner, 12 April, 1804. Dismissed 6 June, 1807. Appointed Gunner, 30 June, 1813. Died in October, 1825.
COSGROVE, PHILIP L., Jr.
  Mate (Spanish-American War), 10 April, 1898. Honorably discharged 17 October, 1898.
COSTELLO, EDWARD.
  Acting Second Assistant Engineer, 29 December, 1863. Resigned 7 July, 1865.
COSTELLO, JOHN.
  Boatswain, 7 November, 1888. Chief Boatswain, 3 March, 1899.
COSTER, GEORGE WASHINGTON, Jr.
  Midshipman, 20 November, 1862. Graduated June, 1866. Ensign, 12 March, 1868. Master 26 March, 1869. Lieutenant, 21 March, 1870. Resigned 16 March, 1875.
COSTER, JOHN J.
  Acting Third Assistant Engineer, 7 July, 1863. Died on the Bienville, 24 October, 1866.
COSTER, STEPHEN K.
  Acting Third Assistant Engineer, 21 October, 1861. Acting Second Assistant Engineer, 24 July, 1863. Honorably discharged 4 October, 1868.
COSTER, WILLIAM E.
  Acting Third Assistant Engineer, 24 May, 1864. Honorably discharged 25 October, 1865.
COSTIGAN, F. V.
  Appointed Master, 5 August, 1812. Dismissed 2 April, 1814.
COSTIGAN, GEORGE D.
  Assistant Surgeon, 11 August, 1896. Passed Assistant Surgeon, 11 August, 1899.
COSTON, BENJAMIN F.
  Appointed Master, 16 January, 1844. Resigned 5 August, 1847.
COTSELL, GEORGE.
  Warrant Machinist (Spanish-American War), 15 June, 1898. Honorably discharged 2 September, 1898.
COTTEN, LYMAN A.
  Naval Cadet, 6 September, 1894. Ensign, 4 April, 1900.
COTTER, JOHN.
  Acting Third Assistant Engineer, 31 January, 1865. Honorably discharged 12 October, 1868.
COTTER, THOMAS.
  Appointed Midshipman, 1 September, 1811. Resigned 6 April, 1813.
COTTMAN, VINCENDON L.
  Midshipman, 25 September, 1868. Graduated 1 June, 1872. Ensign, 15 July, 1873. Master, 9 May, 1878. Lieutenant, Junior Grade, 3 March, 1883. Lieutenant, 8 January, 1885. Lieutenant-Commander, 3 March, 1899.
COTTON, CHARLES.
  Surgeon's Mate, 3 April, 1811. Surgeon, 24 July 1813, Resigned 10 December, 1823.
COTTON, CHARLES H.
  Appointed Midshipman, 1 January, 1828. Passed Midshipman, 14 June, 1834. Resigned 1 August, 1836.

GENERAL NAVY REGISTER. 133

COTTON, CHARLES S.
  Acting Midshipman, 23 September, 1858. Ensign, 11 November, 1862. Lieutenant, 22 February, 1864. Lieutenant-Commander, 25 July, 1866. Commander, 25 April, 1877. Captain, 28 May, 1892. Rear-Admiral, 27 March, 1900.
COTTON, F. W.
  Mate, 4 January, 1864. Honorably discharged 1 June, 1869.
COTTRELL, GARDNER.
  Acting Ensign, 21 July, 1862. Acting Master, recommendation of Commanding Officer, 28 April, 1864. Resigned 4 February, 1867.
COTTRELL, ARTHUR.
  Acting Warrant Machinist, 6 July, 1899.
COTTRELL, JEREMIAH.
  Ensign (Spanish-American War), 21 May, 1898. Honorably discharged 8 December, 1898.
COTTRELL, JOSEPH T.
  Assistant Surgeon, 8 April, 1864. Resigned 23 June, 1865.
COTTRELL, J. T.
  Mate, 15 October, 1861. Appointment revoked 7 February, 1862.
COTTRELL, SIMON G.
  Acting Third Assistant Engineer, 17 May, 1864. Honorably discharged 7 August, 1865.
COTTS, DAVID.
  Acting Third Assistant Engineer, 6 January, 1863. Appointment revoked (sick) 28 May, 1864.
COUCH, GEORGE.
  Mate, 10 September, 1861. Acting Ensign, 2 August, 1864. Honorably discharged 14 October, 1865.
COUDEN, ALBERT R.
  Acting Midshipman, 26 September, 1863. Graduated 6 June, 1867. Ensign, 18 December, 1868. Master, 21 March, 1870. Lieutenant, 21 March, 1871. Lieutenant-Commander, 31 March, 1889. Commander, 14 March, 1897.
COUDON, JOHN.
  Mate, 26 September, 1863. Acting Ensign, 17 January, 1864. Honorably discharged 21 October, 1865.
COUES, SAMUEL F.
  Assistant Surgeon, 25 February, 1851. Passed Assistant Surgeon, 9 April, 1851. Surgeon, 26 April, 1861. Medical Inspector, 3 March, 1871. Medical Director, 13 August, 1876. Retired, 17 September, 1887.
COULSON, WASHINGTON C.
  Mate, 1 October, 1862. Acting Ensign, 19 September, 1863. Acting Master, 16 July, 1864. Honorably discharged 20 November, 1865.
COULTER, HENRY S.
  Surgeon's Mate, 26 May, 1826. Surgeon, 4 November, 1834. Dismissed 26 December, 1843.
COULTER, MIFFLIN.
  Surgeon's Mate, 15 August, 1826. Passed Assistant Surgeon, 3 March, 1835. Surgeon, 22 December, 1835. Died 12 October, 1840.
COULTER, WILLIAM H.
  Acting Second Assistant Engineer, 9 December, 1862. Acting First Assistant Engineer, 12 June, 1863. Resigned 30 May, 1864.
COUPLAND, CHARLES.
  Appointed Sailmaker, 18 October 1820. Resigned 22 August, 1832.
COURTIS, FRANK.
  Acting Midshipman, 25 September, 1862. Graduated June, 1866. Ensign, 12 March, 1868. Master, 26 March, 1869. Lieutenant, 21 March, 1870. Lieutenant-Commander, 2 March, 1885. Commander, 10 July, 1894. Captain, 23 July, 1900.
COURTNEY, ANTHONY.
  Acting Second Assistant Engineer, 26 September, 1863. Honorably discharged 4 November, 1865.
COURTNEY, CHARLES.
  Acting Master, 21 January, 1862. Honorably discharged 4 March, 1866. Actingg Master, 17 May, 1866. Mustered out 31 December, 1867.
COURTNEY, CHARLES E.
  Naval Cadet, 20 May, 1895. At sea prior to final graduation.
COURTNEY, JAMES.
  Mate Resigned 11 May, 1863. Mate, 15 August, 1863. Acting Ensign, 12 December, 1864. Appointment revoked 18 June, 1866.
COUSENS, JOHN H.
  Acting Ensign, 29 October, 1862. Acting Master, 17 February, 1865. Honorably discharged 22 November, 1865.
COUSH, JOHN.
  Appointed Carpenter, 28 September, 1798. Resigned 10 December, 1799.
COUTHONY, JOSEPH P.
  Acting Volunteer Lieutenant, 26 August, 1861. Died at Grand Ecore, Louisiana, from wounds received in action, 4 April, 1864.
COVELL, CHARLES H.
  Assistant Surgeon, 17 June, 1861. Died 7 August, 1861.
COVELL, EMERSON G.
  First Assistant Engineer, 21 May, 1847. Died 28 December, 1847.
COVERT, A. M.
  Acting First Assistant Engineer, 13 December, 1862 Resigned 16 May, 1863.
COVINGTON, JOHN R.
  Appointed Gunner, 1 May, 1824. Died 4 November, 1840.

GENERAL NAVY REGISTER.

COWAN, ANDREW.
Appointed Gunner, 20 May, 1800. Resigned 4 September, 1800.
COWAN, JAMES.
Chief Engineer (Spanish-American War), 15 June, 1898. Honorably discharged 2 September, 1898.
COWAN, JOHN.
Appointed Midshipman, 17 December, 1810. Died at sea, 1814.
COWAN, JOHN.
Pharmacist, 15 September, 1898.
COWAN, JOHN M.
Acting Ensign, 23 February, 1863. Honorably discharged 20 October, 1865.
COWAN, LEMUEL C.
Mate, 2 March, 1865. Honorably discharged 2 June, 1865. Mate, 10 April, 1866. Resigned 15 May, 1867.
COWAN, ROBERT H.
Assistant Paymaster (Spanish-American War), 19 July, 1898. Honorably discharged 12 April, 1899.
COWAN, WILLIAM C.
Appointed Gunner, 21 April, 1819. Dismissed 18 July, 1823.
COWAN, WILLIAM S.
Appointed Gunner, 2 August, 1830. Died 14 September, 1831.
COWARD, HENRY.
Mate, 27 December, 1861. Resigned 30 October, 1862. Mate, 17 January, 1863. Resigned 24 February, 1864.
COWDEN, SAMUEL D.
Appointed Midshipman, 19 February, 1840. Dismissed 5 August, 1842.
COWDERY, JONATHAN.
Surgeon's Mate, 1 January, 1800. Surgeon, 27 November, 1804. Died 21 November, 1852.
COWEL, JOHN G.
Appointed Master, 21 January, 1809. Died of wounds received in action 18 April, 1814.
COWELL, JOHN L.
Ensign (Spanish-American War), 4 May, 1898. Honorably discharged 2 September, 1898.
COWELL, WILLIAM G.
Acting Ensign, 12 August, 1864. Honorably discharged 11 November, 1865.
COWGILL, WARNER M.
Midshipman, 30 September, 1863. Graduated 2 June, 1868. Ensign, 18 April, 1869. Master, 12 July, 1870. Deserted 5 September, 1872.
COWIE, GEORGE, Jr.
Acting Third Assistant Engineer, 23 May, 1864. Acting Second Assistant Engineer, 22 April, 1865. Honorably discharged 19 December, 1867. Second Assistant Engineer, 9 July, 1870. Passed Assistant Engineer, 3 December, 1876. Chief Engineer, 12 September, 1893. Rank changed to Lieutenant-Commander, 3 March, 1899. Commander, 1 July, 1899. Retired List with rank of Captain, 18 August, 1900.
COWIE, JAMES W.
Acting Midshipman, 25 February, 1863. Graduated 6 June, 1867. Ensign, 18 December, 1868. Lost on board the Oneida, 24 January, 1870.
COWIE, ROBERT.
Acting Assistant Surgeon, 1 December, 1862 Honorably discharged 13 April, 1866. Reappointed 13 February, 1867. Discharged 1 June, 1868.
COWIE, THOMAS J.
Assistant Paymaster, 16 June, 1880. Passed Assistant Paymaster, 26 March, 1889. Paymaster, 11 September, 1895.
COWING, SETH W.
Acting Ensign, 23 March, 1863. Acting Master, 30 May, 1865. Honorably discharged 1 October 1867.
COWLE, WILLIAM E.
Acting Second Assistant Engineer, 17 June, 1864. Honorably discharged 24 August, 1865.
COWLES, WILLIAM.
Cadet Engineer, 1 October, 1873. Graduated 21 June, 1875. Assistant Engineer, 1 July, 1877. Resigned 31 March, 1880.
COWLES, WALTER C.
Midshipman, 22 September, 1869 Graduated 31 May, 1873. Ensign, 16 July, 1874. Master, 2 August, 1879. Lieutenant Junior Grade, 3 March, 1883. Lieutenant, 1 December, 1885. Lieutenant-Commander, 3 March, 1899.
COWLES, WILLIAM SHEFFIELD.
Acting Midshipman, 21 July, 1863. Graduated 6 June, 1867. Ensign, 18 December, 1868. Master, 21 March, 1870. Lieutenant, 26 October, 1871. Lieutenant-Commander, 5 May, 1892. Commander, 5 June, 1898.
COWLEY, CHARLES.
Acting Assistant Paymaster, 22 January, 1864. Honorably discharged 21 September, 1865.
COWLING, WILLIAM.
Mate, 7 December, 1861. Appointment revoked 27 June, 1862.
COWMAN, RICHARD H.
Assistant Surgeon, 17 September, 1852. Lost at sea in the Albany.
COWPER, WILLIAM.
Appointed Lieutenant, 9 March, 1798. Commander, 12 July, 1799. Discharged under Peace Establishment Act, 3 April, 1801.
COWRODI, LEWIS.
Appointed Master's Mate, 11 August, 1819. Resigned 1 October, 1820.

GENERAL NAVY REGISTER. 135

COX, ALBERT T.
Acting Third Assistant Engineer, 5 December, 1863. Dismissed 25 October, 1865.
COX, DANIEL B.
Acting Third Assistant Engineer, 10 April, 1863. Dismissed 20 May, 1865.
COX, DANIEL H.
Naval Cadet, 9 September, 1890. Assistant Naval Constructor, 1 July, 1896.
COX, EDWARD N.
Appointed Midshipman, 6 April, 1799. Lieutenant, 14 January, 1807. Purser, 2 March, 1820. Died 14 August, 1845.
COX, EDWIN B.
Acting Ensign, 20 December, 1862. Honorably discharged 3 August, 1865.
COX, ERSKINE H.
Assistant Engineer (Spanish-American War), 6 July, 1898. Honorably discharged 29 December, 1898.
COX, GEORGE.
Appointed Lieutenant, 15 June, 1799. Commander, 27 May, 1804. Resigned 8 April, 1808.
COX, GEORGE G.
Mate, 11 December, 1862. Acting Ensign, 20 June, 1864. Honorably discharged 3 November, 1865.
COX, JAMES.
Appointed Midshipman, 28 August, 1799. Last appearance on Records of Navy Department, 10 May, 1801.
COX, JAMES H.
Mate, 13 March, 1862. Acting Ensign, 4 August, 1862. Died at Key West, Florida, 31 August, 1864.
COX, J. E.
Acting First Assistant Engineer. Appointment revoked 23 November, 1865.
COX, JOHN C.
Acting Ensign, 3 October, 1862. Acting Master, on recommendation of Commanding Officer, 21 December, 1863. Honorably discharged 30 May, 1865.
COX, JOHN F.
Appointed Midshipman, 30 June, 1799. Discharged under Peace Establishment Act, 12 October, 1801.
COX, JOHN S. H.
Appointed Midshipman; 6 July, 1798. Lieutenant, 12 September, 1799. Resigned 26 April, 1804.
COX, JOHN W.
Appointed Midshipman, 1 March, 1825. Passed Midshipman, 4 June, 1831. Lieutenant, 3 March, 1835. Died 7 December, 1842.
COX, JOSEPH.
Carpenter, 29 May, 1834. Retired List, 21 December, 1861. Died 27 March, 1894.
COX, JOSEPH E.
Carpenter, 9 July, 1861. Retired 21 April, 1892. Died 27 March, 1894.
COX, LEONARD M.
Civil Engineer, 23 February, 1899
COX, MACKALL.
Appointed Midshipman, date not known. Resigned 2 January, 1799.
COX, SAMUEL J.
Purser, 11 July, 1799. Last appearance on Records of Navy Department.
COX, WILLIAM.
Lieutenant, Junior Grade (Spanish-American War), 9 July, 1898. Honorably discharged 23 February, 1899.
COX, WILLIAM R., Jr.
Mate, 8 January, 1862. Acting Ensign, 10 November, 1864. Honorably discharged 16 December, 1865.
COXE, JOHN R.
Appointed Midshipman, 4 July, 1817. Lieutenant, 28 April, 1826. Resigned 29 May, 1833.
COXE, J. S.
Appointed Midshipman, 10 January, 1815. Died 30 June, 1822.
COXE, RICHARD.
Appointed Midshipman, 1 March, 1825. Resigned 13 June, 1832.
COXE, RICHARD J.
Appointed Master, 23 June, 1812. Died 18 April, 1822.
COXE, WILLIAM G.
Passed Assistant Engineer (Spanish-American War), 4 May, 1898. Resigned 21 July, 1898.
COXE, WILLIAM S.
Appointed Midshipman, 16 January, 1809. Lieutenant, 24 July, 1813. Cashiered, 26 April, 1814.
COY, CHARLES S.
Mate, 15 October, 1861. Acting Ensign, 16 January, 1863. Acting Master, 27 January, 1864. Acting Volunteer Lieutenant, 12 June, 1865. Honorably discharged 12 October, 1866.
COYLE, JOHN A.
Appointed Midshipman, 1 April, 1828. Lost in the Sylph, 16 August, 1831.
COYLE, JOSEPH C.
Acting Ensign, 1 October, 1862. Promoted Acting Master, 8 May, 1863. Honorably discharged 28 September, 1865.
COYLE, NICHOLAS.
Acting Second Assistant Engineer, 6 August, 1862. Acting First Assistant Engineer, 20 June, 1863. Died on the Norwich, 24 September, 1863.

136 GENERAL NAVY REGISTER.

COYLE, PETER T.
Ensign (Spanish-American War), 30 April, 1898. Honorably discharged 8 December, 1898.
COYLE, THOMAS.
Acting Third Assistant Engineer, 3 November, 1863. Dismissed 5 May, 1865.
CRABB, HORACE N.
Midshipman, 19 October, 1841. Passed Midshipman, 10 August, 1847. Master, 14 September, 1855. Lieutenant, 15 September, 1855. Died 10 March, 1861.
CRABBE, THOMAS.
Midshipman, 15 November, 1809. Lieutenant, 4 February, 1815. Commander, 3 March, 1835. Captain, 8 September, 1841. Commodore on Retired List, 16 July, 1862. Rear-Admiral on Retired List, 25 July, 1866. Died 29 June, 1872.
CRAFT, RICHARD P.
Mate, 15 July, 1863. Honorably discharged 5 November, 1865.
CRAFTS, NATHANIEL W.
Appointed Master, 10 September, 1807. Resigned 4 August, 1808.
CRAFTS, SAMUEL P.
Acting Ensign, 19 December, 1862. Acting Master, 14 August, 1863. Acting Volunteer Lieutenant, 6 April, 1865. Honorably discharged 5 December, 1865.
CRAGG, S. WILKINS.
Third Assistant Engineer, 26 August, 1859. Second Assistant Engineer, 26 October, 1861. Dismissed 27 June, 1864. Reappointed First Assistant Engineer, 25 July, 1866. Resigned 11 April, 1870.
CRAGIN, WILLIAM S. W.
Acting Ensign, 20 January, 1865. Honorably discharged 6 September, 1866.
CRAIG, BENJAMIN F.
Mate, 29 December, 1864. Honorably discharged 4 November, 1865.
CRAIG, B. J.
Mate, 26 November, 1861. Dismissed 5 March, 1862.
CRAIG, ELLIS W.
Carpenter, 14 October, 1881. Chief Carpenter, 3 March, 1899.
CRAIG, JOSEPH EDGAR.
Acting Midshipman, 29 November, 1861. Graduated September, 1865. Ensign, 1 December, 1866. Master, 12 March, 1868. Lieutenant, 26 March, 1869. Lieutenant-Commander, 13 March, 1880. Commander, 3 January, 1890. Captain, 3 March, 1899.
CRAIG, J. P. D. H.
Appointed Midshipman, 1 May, 1800. Dismissed 5 July, 1805.
CRAIG, LOUIS B.
Assistant Engineer (Spanish-American War), 14 May, 1898. Honorably discharged 24 December, 1898.
CRAIG, PHILIP S.
Carpenter, 25 March, 1873. Died 1 August, 1881.
CRAIG, ROBERT.
Mate, 14 June, 1863. Acting Ensign, 28 July, 1864. Honorably discharged 28 October, 1865.
CRAIG, THOMAS C.
Assistant Surgeon, 9 July, 1881. Passed Assistant Surgeon, 9 July, 1884. Surgeon, 14 October, 1896. Retired List, 22 March, 1897.
CRAIG, WILLIAM.
Gunner, 20 January, 1838. Lost in the Aubany. Last intelligence, 28 September, 1854.
CRAIG, WILLIAM.
Acting First Assistant Engineer, 9 October, 1862. Dismissed 14 March, 1863.
CRAIN, CHARLES C.
Acting Third Assistant Engineer, 26 February, 1864. Honorably discharged 25 October, 1865.
CRAIN, WALTER O.
Midshipman, 27 October, 1814. Passed Midshipman, 10 August, 1847. Resigned 30 December, 1851.
CRALL, GEORGE A.
Acting Midshipman, 20 September, 1858. Acting Master, 20 June, 1862. Dismissed 20 January, 1863.
CRAM, EDWIN J.
Acting Third Assistant Engineer, 6 September, 1864. Honorably discharged 29 July, 1865.
CRAMBAUGH, SAMUEL R.
Midshipman, 20 February, 1863. Graduated 2 June, 1868. Resigned 29 June, 1868.
CRAMER, FREDERICK A.
Acting Third Assistant Engineer, 3 July, 1863. Acting Second Assistant Engineer, 7 March, 1864. Honorably discharged 28 November, 1865.
CRAMER, JOHN.
Appointed Midshipman, 1 May, 1816. Drowned 20 March, 1822.
CRANDALL, ALBERT A.
Midshipman, 1 July, 1867. Graduated 6 June, 1871. Ensign, 14 July, 1872. Resigned 25 June, 1875.
CRANDALL, CHARLES S.
Mate, 17 February, 1864. Acting Ensign, 17 February, 1864. Honorably discharged 22 November, 1865.
CRANDALL, F. H.
Mate, 17 October, 1861. Acting Ensign, 14 July, 1863. Appointment revoked 12 January, 1866.
CRANDALL, RAND P.
Assistant Surgeon, 17 January, 1888. Passed Assistant Surgeon, 17 January, 1891. Surgeon, 24 September, 1899.

GENERAL NAVY REGISTER.

CRANDALL, WILLIAM H.
Mate, 12 December, 1861. Resigned 4 September, 1862.
CRANE, ELIAS F.
Mate, 9 February, 1864. Acting Ensign, 6 December, 1864. Honorably discharged 31 October, 1865.
CRANE, HENRY A.
Mate, 1 April, 1863. Resigned 7 April, 1864.
CRANE, J. B.
Mate. Appointment revoked (sick) 10 July, 1863.
CRANE, LEMUEL G.
Acting Master, 22 May, 1861. Resigned 23 January, 1863
CRANE, WILLIAM N.
Appointed Midshipman, 23 May, 1799. Lieutenant, 20 July, 1803. Commander, 4 March, 1813. Captain, 22 November, 1814. Died 18 March, 1846.
CRANEY, WILLIAM
Appointed Midshipman, 11 January, 1832. Passed Midshipman, 23 June, 1838. Dismissed 31 May, 1839.
CRANEY, WILLIAM.
Appointed Midshipman, 3 September, 1841. Resigned 15 February, 1842.
CRANK, ROBERT K.
Naval Cadet, 6 September, 1888. Assistant Engineer, 1 July, 1894. Rank changed to Lieutenant, Junior Grade, 3 March, 1899. Lieutenant, 19 August, 1900.
CRANSTON, CHARLES.
Acting Second Assistant Engineer, 9 August, 1862. Acting First Assistant Engineer, 8 July, 1863. Honorably discharged 21 March, 1868.
CRANSTON, ROBERT Jr.
Appointed Midshipman, 1 January, 1812. Last appearance on Records of Navy Department, 23 March, 1815. Dismissed.
CRAPO, ROBERT B.
Mate, 26 June, 1862. Dismissed 15 May, 1863. Acting Ensign, 18 October, 1864. Honorably discharged 17 October, 1867.
CRARY, CHARLES W.
Acting Assistant Paymaster, 29 December, 1864. Honorably discharged 10 October, 1865.
CRARY, JOHN S.
Acting Third Assistant Engineer, 26 February, 1862. Resigned 30 April, 1862.
CRARY, LODOWICK W.
Appointed Midshipman, 1 January, 1812. Last appearance on Records of Navy Department, 23 May, 1815.
CRAVEN, ALFRED.
Acting Midshipman, 24 July, 1863. Graduated 6 June, 1867. Ensign, 18 December, 1868. Master, 21 March, 1870. Resigned 12 September, 1870.
CRAVEN, CHARLES H.
Acting Midshipman, 20 September, 1860. Midshipman. Ensign, 28 May, 1863. Master, 10 Noveber, 1865. Lieutenant, 10 November, 1866. Lieutenant-Commander, 12 March, 1868. Retired List, 21 April, 1881. Died 1 March 1898.
CRAVEN, JOHN E.
Cadet Midshipman, 24 Septemebr, 1874. Graduated 4 June, 1880. Ensign, Junior Grade, 3 March, 1883. Ensign, 26 June, 1884. Lieutenant, Junior Grade, 31 July, 1890. Lieutenant, 6 December, 1894.
CRAVEN H. SMITH.
Civil Engineer, 12 March, 1879. Died 7 December, 1889.
CRAVEN, ISHI.
Appointed Midshipman, 16 January, 1809. Resigned 13 October, 1809.
CRAVEN, McDONOUGH.
Cadet Midshipman, 21 June, 1876. Graduated. Honorably discharged 30 June, 1883. Lieutenant (Spanish-American War), 4 May, 1898. Honorably discharged 15 October, 1898.
CRAVEN, THOMAS T.
Midshipman, 1 May, 1822. Passed Midshipman, 24 May, 1828 Lieutenant, 27 May, 1830. Commander, 16 December, 1852. Captain, 7 June, 1861. Commodore, 16 July, 1862. Rear-Admiral, 10 October, 1866. Retired List, 30 December, 1869. Died 23 August, 1887.
CRAVEN, THOMAS T.
Naval Cadet, 27 September, 1890. Resigned 17 June, 1891. Naval Cadet, 19 September, 1892. Ensign, 6 May, 1898.
CRAVEN, TUNIS.
Purser, 15 August, 1812. Appointment revoked 6 March, 1813.
CRAVEN, TUNIS A. M.
Midshipman, 2 February, 1829. Passed Midshipman, 3 July, 1835. Lieutenant, 8 September, 1841. Commander, 24 April, 1861. Died 5 August, 1864.
CRAWFORD, CHARLES A.
Mate, 21 November, 1861. Dismissed 27 May, 1863.
CRAWFORD, CHARLES A.
Assistant Surgeon, 1 June, 1898.
CRAWFORD, CHARLES H.
Acting Third Assistant Engineer, 1 November, 1864. Resigned 27 May, 1865.
CRAWFORD, D. R.
Appointed Midshipman, 9 December, 1831. Passed Midshipman, 15 June, 1837. Drowned 26 July, 1841.
CRWFORD, EDGAR F.
Mate, 13 January, 1865. Appointment revoked 8 June, 1868.
CRAWFORD, GEORGE A.
Chaplain, 10 May, 1870. Retired List, 2 March, 1889.

CRAWFORD, GEORGE W.
Acting First Assistant Engineer, 18 April, 1863. Resigned 20 January, 1864.
CRAWFORD, JAMES.
Acting Master, 27 February, 1862. Appointment revoked (physically disqualified) 7 March, 1862.
CRAWFORD, JOHN.
Acting Third Assistant Engineer, 10 October, 1862. Dismissed 30 April, 1864.
CRAWFORD, JOHN J.
Acting Second Assistant Engineer, 10 June, 1864. Dismissed 31 August, 1864.
CRAWFORD, JOHN W.
Appointed Secretary to the Admiral of the Navy with rank of Lieutenant, 7 October, 1899.
CRAWFORD, JOHNSON.
Acting Third Assistant Engineer, 11 April, 1864. Appointment revoked (sick) 26 May, 1865.
CRAWFORD, J. Q. A.
Appointed Midshipman, 17 February, 1840. Dismissed 19 December, 1846.
CRAWFORD, MILLARD H.
Assistant Surgeon, 1 November, 1876. Passed Assistant Surgeon, 1 November, 1880. Surgeon, 21 August, 1893.
CRAWFORD, ROBERT.
Third Assistant Engineer, 1 July, 1863. Second Assistant Engineer, 25 July, 1866. Passed Assistant Engineer, 20 February, 1874. Retired List, 30 June, 1892.
CRAWFORD, THOMAS.
Mate, 18 January, 1864. Honorably discharged 20 August, 1865.
CRAWFORD, WILLIAM H.
Acting Third Assistant Engineer, 15 December, 1862. Acting Second Assistant Engineer, 9 December, 1864. Honorably discharged 15 August, 1865.
CRAWFORD, WILLIAM H.
Third Assistant Engineer, 19 February, 1863. Second Assistant Engineer, 20 June, 1864. Resigned 30 April, 1868.
CREAN, JOHN.
Appointed Midshipman, 1 February, 1814. Resigned 18 October, 1814.
CREE, JOSEPH C.
Acting Third Assistant Engineer, 1861. Acting Second Assistant Engineer, 18 May, 1863. Acting First Assistant Engineer, 9 June, 1864. Honorably discharged 15 July, 1866.
CREECY, LUTHER.
Appointed Midshipman, 10 November, 1835. Resigned 10 August, 1836.
CREECY, RICHARD B.
Naval Cadet (Spanish-American War), 8 July, 1898. Honorably discharged 10 October, 1898.
CREEVEY, WILLIAM S.
Acting Assistant Paymaster, 8 October, 1863. Lost on Patapsco 15 January, 1865.
CREEVY, JAMES.
Acting Third Assistant Engineer, 25 July, 1863. Honorably discharged 25 November, 1865.
CREGIER, JOHN H.
Mate. Dismissed 8 July, 1862.
CREIGHTON, JAMES M.
Mate, 7 March, 1870. Retired List, 2 June, 1899.
CREIGHTON, J. BLAKELEY.
Midshipman, 10 February, 1838. Passed Midshipman, 20 May, 1844. Master, 16 December, 1852. Lieutenant, 9 October, 1853. Commander, 23 September, 1862. Captain, 26 November, 1868. Commodore, 9 November, 1874. Rear-Admiral, 11 May, 1882. Retired List, 21 November, 1882. Died 13 November, 1883.
CREIGHTON, JOHN O.
Appointed Midshipman, 25 June, 1800. Lieutenant, 24 February, 1807. Commander, 24 July, 1813. Captain, 27 April, 1816. Died 13 October, 1838.
CREIGHTON, JOSEPH A
Mate, 19 July, 1862. Discharged 18 October, 1863.
CREIGHTON, WILLIAM H. P.
Cadet Engineer, 1 October, 1878. Assistant Engineer, 1 July, 1884. Retired List, 26 July, 1892.
CRENSHAW, ARTHUR.
Naval Cadet, 6 September, 1892. Assistant Engineer, 6 May, 1898. Rank changed to Ensign, 3 March, 1899. Resigned 15 September, 1900.
CRENSHAW, J. W.
Appointed Midshipman, 1 April, 1826. Resigned 6 November, 1827.
CRENSHAW, F. M.
Appointed Midshipman, 1 December, 1827. Died 2 October, 1828.
CRESAP, JAMES C.
Midshipman, 24 June, 1867. Graduated 6 June, 1871. Ensign, 14 July, 1872. Master, 30 September, 1876. Lieutenant, Junior Grade, 3 March, 1883. Lieutenant, 1 December, 1883. Lieutenant-Commander, 3 March, 1899.
CRESPER, WILLIAM.
Appointed Master, 24 June, 1799. Lieutenant, 3 September, 1800. Discharged under Peace Establishment Act, 17 July, 1801.
CRESSY, JOSIAH P.
Acting Volunteer Lieutenant, 12 August, 1861. Dismissed 18 July, 1862.
CRESSY, WILLIAM J.
Mate, 6 January, 1863. Resigned 14 May, 1863.

GENERAL NAVY REGISTER. 139

CRESSY, W. K.
Acting Master, 31 August, 1861. Acting Volunteer Lieutenant at capture of Warrior, 20 November, 1863. Died at Navy Yard, New York, 28 October, 1864.
CRILLON, CHARLES.
Appointed Midshipman, 1 December, 1824. (See Barton.)
CRIMMON, MATTHEW.
Mate, 31 October, 1862. Resigned 24 May, 1864.
CRIPPEN, THOMAS.
Appointed Sailmaker, 9 June, 1803. Resigned 19 May, 1806.
CRISEL, NEWTON.
Appointed Midshipman, 15 June, 1838. Dropped in 1840.
CRISSEY, EDWIN.
Acting Ensign, 24 January, 1863. Acting Master on recommendation of Commanding Officer, 1 June, 1864. Resigned 17 May, 1865. Boatswain, 4 January, 1873. Retired List, 29 December, 1894.
CRIST, FREDERICK G.
Assistant Paymaster (Spanish-American War), 9 July, 1898. Honorably discharged 1 October 1898.
CRITCHELL, ROBERT S.
Mate, 3 September, 1863. Honorably discharged 4 September, 1865.
CROCKER, ADOLPHUS C.
Acting Third Assistant Engineer, 3 March, 1864. Resigned 12 May, 1865.
CROCKER, CHARLES T.
Appointed Midshipman, 30 November, 1837. Dismissed 19 November, 1844.
CROCKER, EDWARD.
Boatswain, 16 June, 1828. Died 22 July, 1858.
CROCKER, EDWARD P.
Mate, 7 July, 1863. Mate, 3 November, 1865. Appointment revoked 2 December, 1865.
CROCKER, EDMUND J.
Acting Warrant Machinist, 23 August, 1899.
CROCKER, FREDERICK.
Acting Master, 27 May, 1861. Resigned 29 November, 1861. Reappointed 3 February, 1862. Acting Volunteer Lieutenant, for gallantry, 29 November, 1862. Acting Volunteer Lieutenant-Commander, for faithful and meritorious services during rebellion, 1 May, 1865. Honorably discharged 2 October, 1865.
CROCKER, FREDERICK WILLIAM.
Acting Midshipman, 26 September, 1862. Graduated June, 1866. Ensign, 12 March, 1868. Master, 26 March, 1869. Lieutenant, 21 March, 1870. Lieutenant-Commander, 17 January, 1886. Commander, 11 November, 1894.
CROCKER JAMES G.
Mate, 9 May, 1862. Died 17 October, 1864.
CROCKER, JAMES M.
Mate, 15 November, 1861. Acting Ensign, 14 August, 1862. Honorably discharged 14 September, 1865.
CROCKER, JONATHAN W.
Acting Ensign, 2 February, 1864. Honorably discharged 7 September, 1865.
CROCKER, NILES T.
Acting Ensign, 9 August, 1864. Honorably discharged 24 October, 1865.
CROCKER, THOMAS M.
Gunner, 14 May, 1844. Died 23 January, 1859.
CROCKETT, E.
Acting Master, 27 February, 1862. Appointment revoked 21 March, 1862.
CROCKETT, FRANK P.
Lieutenant, Junior Grade (Spanish-American War), 8 July, 1898. Honorably discharged 6 January, 1899.
CROCKETT, H. N.
Acting Ensign, 21 November, 1864. Honorably discharged 19 July, 1865.
CROFT, GEORGE.
Appointed Master, 17 August, 1814. Resigned 5 October, 1815.
CROFT, THOMAS F.
Acting Assistant Paymaster, 22 June, 1864. Honorably discharged 12 November, 1865.
CROGHAN, JOHN S.
Boatswain, 10 May, 1898.
CROLINS, SEBASTIAN.
Third Assistant Engineer, 1 July, 1861. Resigned 13 August, 1862. Acting Second Assistant Engineer, 14 February, 1863. Acting First Assistant Engineer, 20 September, 1863. Resigned 10 October, 1863.
CROMACK, WILLIAM.
Mate, 14 April, 1864. Resigned 12 May, 1865.
CROMWELL, BARTLETT J.
Midshipman, 21 September, 1857. Midshipman, 1 June, 1861. Acting Master, 5 September, 1861. Lieutenant, 16 July, 1862. Lieutenant-Commander, 25 July, 1866. Commander, 24 October, 1874. Captain, 26 March, 1889. Commodore, 10 August, 1898. Rear-Admiral, 3 March, 1899.
CROMWELL, CHARLES.
Appointed Master, date not known. Resigned 13 January, 1800.
CROMWELL, CHARLES.
Appointed Master, 21 April, 1814. Discharged 28 March, 1815.
CROMWELL, JOSEPH H.
Acting Ensign, 26 July, 1864. Honorably discharged 13 July, 1865.
CRONAN, JOHN.
Acting Carpenter, 18 April, 1863. Resigned 11 November, 1865.
CRONAN, WILLIAM PIGOTT.
Naval Cadet, 6 September, 1894. Ensign, 4 April, 1900.

CRONE, BERNARD.
Acting Master and Pilot, 1 October, 1864. Honorably discharged 31 May, 1866.
CRONE, CHRISTIAN.
Mate, 23 July, 1898. Boatswain, 10 April, 1899.
CRONIN, CORNELIUS.
Mate, 9 July, 1866. Gunner, 20 November, 1873. Retired List, 16 August, 1898.
CRONIN, FRANCIS.
Third Assistant Engineer, 21 July, 1858. Second Assistant Engineer, 21 October, 1861. First Assistant Engineer, 20 May, 1863. Resigned 10 November, 1865.
CRONIN, JOHN.
Mate, 22 October, 1863. Acting Ensign, 1 January, 1865. Honorably discharged 4 November, 1865.
CRONIN, MICHAEL J.
Acting Ensign, 16 April, 1863. Acting Master 24 November, 1863. Honorably discharged 21 November, 1865.
CRONIN, THOMAS H.
Third Assistant Engineer, 20 May, 1857. Second Assistant Engineer, 3 August, 1859. Died 8 December, 1861.
CRONK, CHARLES W.
Acting Second Assistant Engineer, 10 October, 1863. Appointment revoked (sick) 17 October, 1863. Acting Second Assistant Engineer, 21 November, 1863. Acting First Assistant Engineer, 29 October, 1864. Honorably discharged 22 December, 1868.
CRONK, VOLNEY.
Acting Second Assistant Engineer, 22 August, 1862. Honorably discharged 18 September, 1865.
CRONMILLER, THOMAS L. P.
Assistant Surgeon, 28 June, 1852. Dropped 13 May, 1858.
CRONTHERS, JAMES A.
Acting Second Assistant Engineer, 11 August, 1864. Honorably dischrged 25 July, 1865.
CRONYN, W. J.
Acting Assistant Surgeon, 12 December, 1873. Resigned 7 June, 1876.
CROOKER, CHARLES A.
Acting Master, 30 August, 1861. Honorably discharged 8 January, 1866.
CROOKER, THOMAS M.
Master's Mate, 3 March, 1841. Gunner, 14 May, 1844. Died 23 January, 1859.
CROOKS, JAMES.
Acting Third Assistant Engineer, 31 August, 1863. Honorably discharged 8 December, 1865.
CROOSMAN, ALEX. F.
Acting Midshipman, 2 October, 1851. Midshipman, 9 June, 1855. Passed Midshipman, 15 April, 1858. Master, 23 June, 1860. Lieutenant, 23 November, 1860. Lieutenant-Commander, 16 July, 1862. Commander, 1 July, 1870. Drowned 12 April, 1872.
CROPPER, S. PRESTON.
Acting Third Assistant Engineer, 6 April, 1865. Honorably discharged 10 May, 1866.
CROSBY, ATWOOD.
Acting Assistant Surgeon, 27 June, 1864. Resigned 31 May, 1865.
CROSBY, EDWARD D.
Purser, 13 September, 1841. Died 20 December, 1846.
CROSBY, ELI.
Third Assistant Engineer, 22 September, 1849. Second Assistant Engineer, 26 February, 1851. Died 24 January, 1854.
CROSBY, FREEMAN H.
Midshipman, 30 July, 1866. Graduated 7 June, 1870. Ensign, 13 July, 1871. Master, 8 November, 1874. Lieutenant, 30 August, 1881. Drowned 18 August, 1894.
CROSBY, HASKELL.
Acting Ensign, 26 December, 1862. Honorably discharged 21 September, 1865.
CROSBY, HENRY.
Mate, 3 June, 1863. Dismissed 18 November, 1864.
CROSBY, JAMES E.
Mate, 31 August, 1863. Died on Honduras, 9 July, 1864.
CROSBY, JOHN.
Boatswain, 8 February, 1848. Resigned 18 September, 1854.
CROSBY, JOHN K.
Acting Master, 15 April, 1862. Honorably discharged 16 September, 1865.
CROSBY, JOSHUA W.
Acting Master, 23 April, 1862. Honorably discharged 14 September, 1865.
CROSBY PEIRCE.
Midshipman, 5 June, 1838. Passed Midshipman, 20 May, 1844. Master, 4 November, 1852. Lieutenant, 3 September, 1853. Commander, 22 September, 1862. Captain, 27 May, 1868. Commodore, 3 October, 1874. Rear-Admiral, 10 March, 1882. Retired List, 29 October, 1883. Died 15 June, 1899.
CROSBY, THOMAS D.
Acting Second Assistant Engineer, 16 November, 1863. Honorably discharged 16 February, 1868.
CROSBY, WARREN J.
Mate, 5 March, 1862. Acting Ensign, 1 July, 1864. Honorably discharged 21 October, 1865.
CROSBY, WILLIAM B., JR.
Acting Assistant Paymaster, 7 August, 1863. Resigned 23 December, 1864.

CROSE, WILLIAM M.
    Naval Cadet, 19 May, 1884. Ensign, 1 July, 1890. Lieutenant, Junior Grade, 10 May, 1898. Lieutenant, 3 March, 1899.
CROSLEY, S. M.
    Mate, 14 September, 1863. Resigned 18 March, 1871.
CROSLEY, WALTER S.
    Naval Cadet, 9 September, 1889. Ensign, 1 July, 1895. Lieutenant, Junior Grade, 3 March, 1899.
CROSMON, NELSON E.
    Acting Third Assistant Engineer, 25 May, 1864. Resigned (sick) 11 March, 1865.
CROSS, ELLIOT W.
    Acting Third Assistant Engineer, 28 March, 1864. Honorably discharged 28 June, 1865.
CROSS, GEORGE.
    Appointed Captain, 10 September, 1798. Discharged under Peace Establishment Act, date not known.
CROSS, GEORGE.
    Gunner, 31 May, 1892. Dismissed 10 June, 1899.
CROSS, J. ARNOLD.
    Acting Ensign, 7 November, 1863. Honorably discharged 20 August, 1865.
CROSS, JOHN C.
    Third Assistant Engineer, 8 December, 1862. Second Assistant Engineer, 8 April, 1864. Resigned 21 June, 1865.
CROSS, JOHN W.
    Acting Second Assistant Engineer, 18 November, 1861. Resigned 6 November, 1862.
CROSS, JOSEPH.
    Appointed Midshipman, 9 June, 1811. Lieutenant, 27 April, 1816. Died 10 February, 1834.
CROSS, J. WESLEY.
    Acting Third Assistant Engineer, 25 September, 1863. Honorably discharged 7 October, 1868.
CROSS, ROBERT H.
    Gunner, 23 April, 1858. Retired List, 16 October, 1889.
CROSS, SAMUEL.
    Gunner, 4 January, 1862. Dismissed 10 September, 1862. Gunner, 27 August, 1872. Retired List, 11 June, 1898.
CROSS, THOMAS H.
    Acting Third Assistant Engineer, 21 October, 1863. Honorably discharged 26 July, 1865.
CROSSAN, THOMAS M.
    Midshipman, 1 July, 1836. Passed Midshipman, 1 July, 1842. Master. Lieutenant, 6 April, 1849. Resigned 1 September, 1857.
CROSSING, SAMUEL L.
    Ensign (Spanish-American War), 12 July, 1898. Honorably discharged 5 October, 1898.
CROSSMAN, JAMES A.
    Acting Ensign, 14 December, 1863. Honorably discharged 23 August, 1865.
CROSSMAN, HENRY S.
    Lieutenant, Junior Grade (Spanish-American War), 4 May, 1898. Honorably discharged 24 September, 1898.
CROTON, CHARLES.
    Mate, 22 October, 1862. Resigned 15 May, 1865.
CROW, BENJAMIN.
    Appointed Sailmaker, 5 May, 1826. Died 31 March, 1845.
CROW, JAMES.
    Appointed Midshipman, 15 November, 1809. Resigned 15 December, 1810.
CROWELL, DAVID H.
    Acting Master, 22 November, 1861. Resigned 16 May, 1863.
CROWELL, ERASTUS.
    Acting Master, 26 August, 1861. Resigned 19 October, 1861.
CROWELL, GEORGE W.
    Acting Master, 6 December, 1861. Dismissed 17 September, 1862.
CROWELL, ISAIAH E.
    Sailmaker, 3 January, 1862. Dismissed 10 April, 1882.
CROWELL, JOSEPH W.
    Acting Ensign, 31 August, 1863. Honorably discharged 21 August, 1865.
CROWELL, LEVI.
    Acting Master, 7 December, 1861. Honorably discharged 29 January, 1866.
CROWELL, MINER B.
    Acting Master, 18 January, 1862. Acting Volunteer Lieutenant, for good service, 16 March, 1864. Honorably discharged 18 December, 1865.
CROWLEY, CHARLES E.
    Midshipman, 16 January, 1809. Lieutenant, 9 December, 1814. Died at Charleston, South Carolina, 15 August, 1850.
CROWLEY, JOHN.
    Appointed Carpenter, 28 October, 1811. Dismissed 26 September, 1812.
CROWLEY, JOHN.
    Boatswain, 11 January, 1876. Appointment revoked 7 February, 1876.
CROWNINSHIELD, ARENT SCHUYLER.
    Appointed Acting Midshipman to the Naval Academy, 25 September, 1860, from New York. Graduated 28 May, 1863. Ensign, 4 June, 1863. Master, 10 November, 1865. Lieutenant, 10 November, 1866. Lieutenant-Commander, 12 March, 1868. Commander, 25 March, 1880. Captain, 21 July, 1894. Appointed Chief of the Bureau of Navigation, with rank of Rear-Admiral, 1897. Commanded U. S. S. Portsmouth, 1878 to 1881: Nautical School Ship St. Mary's, 1887 to 1891: U. S. S. Kearsarge, February, 1892 to November, 1893: Battleship Maine, 1895 to 1897.

CROWNINSHIELD, JACOB.
　Midshipman, 11 March, 1815. Lieutenant, 15 January, 1825. Commander, 8 September, 1841. Died 15 July, 1849.
CROWNINSHIELD, WILLIAM W.
　Acting Ensign, 21 January, 1863. Acting Master, for good service, 10 December, 1863. Acting Volunteer Lieutenant, 17 May, 1865. Honorably discharged 4 October, 1868.
CROZET, J. B.
　Mate, 8 November, 1869. Resigned 23 November, 1872.
CROZETT, CHARLES E.
　Acting Master's Mate, 12 September, 1864. Honorably discharged 11 September, 1865.
CROZIER, JOSEPH H.
　Ensign (Spanish-American War), 21 May, 1898. Honorably discharged 11 April, 1899.
CRUFT, JOHN.
　Appointed Lieutenant, 15 October, 1798. Commission returned.
CRUGER, EDWARD MARTINEAU.
　Acting Midshipman, 30 July, 1863. Resigned 19 March, 1866.
CRUMMEY, THOMAS.
　Third Assistant Engineer, 21 April, 1862. Resigned 5 September, 1866.
CRUMP, GEORGE T.
　Appointed Midshipman, 2 February, 1829. Died 12 April, 1832.
CRUMP, RICHARD.
　Appointed Midshipman, 20 June, 1806. Dismissed 18 February, 1808.
CRUSE, PETER N.
　Acting Master, 14 September, 1861. Resigned 17 June, 1863.
CRUSE, SAMUEL C.
　Acting Master, 18 October, 1861. Honorably discharged 5 February, 1866.
CUDDY, WILLIAM.
　Sailmaker, 2 March, 1872. Chief Sailmaker, 3 March, 1899.
CUDWORTH, WILLIAM.
　Appointed Midshipman, 16 January, 1809. Resigned 17 November, 1809.
CULBERT, EDWARD.
　Mate, 23 January, 1862. Honorably discharged 29 August, 1868.
CULBERTSON, C. J.
　Mate, 17 September, 1861. Discharged 7 April, 1862.
CULBERTSON, JAMES.
　Appointed Boatswain, 1 January, 1817. Last appearance on Records of Navy Department for 1820.
CULBERTSON, WILSON S.
　Mate, 4 April, 1864. Honorably discharged 18 November, 1865.
CULBRETH, GEORGE S.
　Assistant Surgeon, 18 June, 1866. Passed Assistant Surgeon, 14 December, 1869. Surgeon, 31 December, 1876. Lost on Huron, 24 November, 1877.
CULLATON, JOHN.
　Mate, 28 June, 1862. Acting Ensign, 25 February, 1863. Resigned 9 June, 1865.
CULLEN, EZEKIEL W.
　Purser, 4 June, 1857. Resigned 11 May, 1858.
CULLEN, JOHN.
　Acting Second Assistant Engineer, 13 August, 1863. Resigned 6 October, 1863. Acting First Assistant Engineer, 7 May, 1864. Honorably discharged 29 September, 1865.
CULLEY, GEORGE L.
　Acting Third Assistant Engineer, 14 July, 1863. Dismissed 5 May, 1865.
CULLEY, JOSEPH.
　Acting Third Assistant Engineer, 1 August, 1862. Acting Second Assistant Engineer, 22 May, 1863. Appointment revoked (sick) 11 November, 1863.
CULLIN, JOHN.
　Acting First Assistant Engineer, 29 September, 1865. Honorably discharged.
CULLINS, ASA B.
　Acting Third Assistant Engineer, 21 June, 1862. Acting Second Assistant Engineer, 20 June, 1863. Honorably discharged 15 December, 1865.
CULVER, ABRAHAM E.
　Midshipman, 6 June, 1872. Graduated 20 June, 1876. Ensign, 14 December, 1877. Lieutenant, Junior Grade. 26 December, 1884. Lieutenant. 15 October, 1890. Lieutenant-Commander, 4 June, 1899.
CULVER, CHARLES B.
　Acting Third Assistant Engineer, 14 January. 1863. Acting Second Assistant Engineer, 13 September, 1864. Honorably discharged 8 September, 1865.
CULVER, CHARLES E.
　Mate, 8 October, 1861. Resigned 9 April, 1864.
CULVER, E. B.
　Acting Assistant Paymaster, 22 July, 1863. Discharged 12 November, 1865.
CULVER, JOSIAH H.
　Assistant Surgeon, 24 March, 1863. Retired 15 July, 1867. Died 25 September, 1868.
CUMBERSON, WILLIAM M.
　Acting Third Assistant Engineer, 6 January, 1862. Resigned 5 January, 1863.
CUMING, ROCHESTER.
　Ensign (Spanish-American War), 15 June, 1898. Honorably discharged 2 September, 1898.
CUMMING, JOHN W.
　Mate. Resigned 5 September. 1862.

GENERAL NAVY REGISTER. 143

CUMMING, T. W.
Appointed Midshipman, 19 May, 1832. Passed Midshipman, 23 June, 1838. Resigned 23 February, 1841.

CUMMINGS, A. B.
Midshipman, 7 April, 1847. Passed Midshipman, 10 June, 1853. Master, 15 September, 1855. Lieutenant, 16 September, 1855. Lieutenant-Commander, 16 July, 1862. Died 18 March, 1863.

CUMMINGS, ED. P.
Acting Assistant Surgeon, 21 October, 1861. Resigned 20 February, 1862.

CUMMINGS, JOHN L.
Appointed Midshipman, 8 October, 1800. Lieutenant, 1 April, 1812. Died 24 July, 1824.

CUMMINS, JAMES.
Mate, 1 November, 1863. Resigned 8 November, 1864.

CUMMINS, JAMES A.
Acting Gunner, 30 September, 1862. Dismissed 3 February, 1864.

CUNNINGHAM, ALEXANDER.
Master, 15 November, 1815. Reserved List, 13 September, 1855. Died 26 April, 1856.

CUNNINGHAM, ANDREW C.
Cadet Midshipman, 9 June, 1874. Graduated 10 June, 1881. Ensign, Junior Grade, 3 March, 1883. Resigned 1 February, 1884. Ensign for temporary service, 13 May, 1898. Honorably discharged 28 September, 1898. Civil Engineer, 29 September, 1898.

CUNNINGHAM, CHARLES.
Acting Ensign, 28 February, 1863. Resigned 5 September, 1864.

CUNNINGHAM, FREDERICK A.
Gunner, 21 August, 1856. Deserted 20 August, 1858.

CUNNINGHAM, GEORGE.
Acting Third Assistant Engineer, 22 November, 1862. Appointment revoked (sick) 15 June, 1863.

CUNNINGHAM, G. F.
Appointed Midshipman, 14 February, 1840. Resigned 20 August, 1849.

CUNNINGHAM, HUGH.
Acting Third Assistant Engineer, 6 March. 1865. Honorably discharged 4 October, 1865.

CUNNINGHAM, JAMES.
Mate, 24 January, 1863. Honorably discharged 29 October, 1865.

CUNNINGHAM, JOHN G.
Acting Third Assistant Engineer, 4 September, 1864. Dismissed 30 April, 1867.

CUNNINGHAM, JOHN S.
Purser, 13 March, 1857. Pay Inspector, 3 March, 1871. Pay Director, 14 October, 1871. Retired List, 23 December, 1883. Died 10 May, 1894.

CUNNINGHAM, PATRICK THOMAS.
Midshipman, 26 September, 1863. Graduated 6 June, 1867. Ensign, 18 December, 1868. Master, 21 March, 1870. Lieutenant, 21 March, 1871. Resigned 9 November, 1872.

CUNNINGHAM, ROBERT B.
Midshipman, 30 November, 1814. Lieutenant, 13 January, 1825. Commander, 8 September, 1841. Captain, 14 September, 1855. Died 13 March, 1861.

CUNNINGHAM, THOMAS A.
Acting Third Assistant Engineer, 26 January, 1864. Died on Merrimac 2 July, 1864.

CUNNINGHAM, THOMAS.
Acting Third Assistant Engineer, 3 May, 1859. Second Assistant Engineer, 13 May, 1861. First Assistant Engineer, 20 May, 1863. Resigned 16 November, 1866.

CUNNINGHAM, T. S.
Appointed Midshipman, 15 November, 1809. Lieutenant, 9 December, 1814. Resigned 21 April, 1827.

CUNNINGHAM, W.
Appointed Gunner, 11 August, 1819. Died in 1823.

CUNTZ, HERMANN F.
Ensign (Spanish Quarantine Service), 22 June, 1898. Honorably discharged 23 September, 1898.

CUNTZ, JOHANNES H.
Ensign (Spanish-American War), 11 May, 1898. Honorably discharged 25 February, 1899.

CURL, HOLTON C.
Assistant Surgeon for temporary service, 18 June, 1898. Transferred to Regular Service, 14 October, 1898.

CURLEY, M. E.
Acting Carpenter, 6 May, 1865. Honorably discharged 6 August, 1865.

CURRAN, JAMES.
Acting Third Assistant Engineer, 7 July, 1863. Appointment revoked (sick) 10 February, 1864.

CURRAN, JAMES.
Acting Second Assistant Engineer, 26 April, 1866. Discharged 24 July, 1867.

CURRAN, JAMES.
Acting Third Assistant Engineer, 15 September, 1864. Acting Second Assistant Engineer, 22 February, 1865. Honorably discharged 13 November, 1865.

CURRAN, SANFORD.
Acting Third Assistant Engineer, 28 December, 1863. Died on Tallahatchie, 16 April, 1865.

CURRIE, ORMAND A.
Acting Warrant Machinist, 23 August, 1899.

GENERAL NAVY REGISTER.

CURRIER, OLIVER C.
Mate, 31 August, 1864. Honorably discharged 19 December. 1865.
CURRIER, W. A.
Mate, 4 April, 1862. Dismissed 20 August. 1863. Mate. 27 November. 1863. Appointment revoked (sick) 14 October, 1864.
CURRY, DAVID H.
Acting Carpenter, 1 October, 1862. Resigned 30 May, 1864.
CURTIN, ROLAND I.
Naval Cadet, 6 September, 1892. Ensign, 6 May, 1898.
CURTIS, ANDREW.
Acting Ensign, 14 May, 1864. Honorably discharged 12 August. 1865.
CURTIS, ASA.
Gunner, 1 March. 1825. Died at Rio de Janerio 11 September. 1858.
CURTIS, CALEB A.
Acting Master, 23 September, 1861. Resigned. accepted with regrets of the Department, 2 December, 1863.
CURTIS, CICERO B.
Acting Second Assistant Engineer, 17 October, 1863. Honorably discharged 15 August, 1865.
CURTIS, CLINTON K.
Midshipman, 28 September. 1865. Graduated 4 June, 1869. Ensign. 12 July, 1870. Master, 25 November, 1872. Lieutenant, 30 June. 1876. Lieutenant-Commander, 6 February, 1898. Commander, 11 December, 1900.
CURTIS, DAVID G.
Acting Assistant Surgeon, 19 September. 1864. Honorably discharged 24 August, 1865.
CURTIS, EDWARD.
Third Assistant Engineer, 21 October, 1861. Resigned 11 February. 1863.
CURTIS, FREDERICK R.
Acting Assistant Paymaster, 19 October, 1861. Assistant Paymaster. 12 July, 1862. Died on Pawnee, 17 April, 1863.
CURTIS, G. G.
Acting Ensign. 8 June, 1864. Honorably discharged 8 November, 1865.
CURTIS, HENRY F.
Acting Ensign, 23 May, 1864. Honorably discharged 15 November. 1865.
CURTIS, JAMES F.
Appointed Midshipman, 18 June. 1812. Lieutenant. 1 April. 1818. Resigned 19 April, 1824.
CURTIS, LLOYD .
Assistant Surgeon, 6 July, 1882. Passed Assistant Surgeon. 6 July. 1885. Surgeon, 16 February, 1897.
CURTIS, ROMAINE J.
Acting Assistant Surgeon, 3 May, 1864. Honorably discharged 21 October, 1865.
CURTIS, SAMUEL.
Actng Master, 22 January, 1862. Honorably discharged 2 February. 1866.
CURTIS, STACEY.
Appointed Sailmaker, 23 April, 1813. Resigned 21 June, 1815.
CURTIS,.THOMAS B.
Appointed Midshipman, 28 September, 1812. Resigned 13 November. 1823.
CURTIS, WILLIAM H. H.
Acting Ensign. 8 September, 1864. Honorably discharged 14 July. 1865.
CURTIS, W. SCOTT.
Mate, 19 March, 1862. Dismissed 4 April, 1863.
CURWEN, HENRY.
Acting Ensign. 1 July, 1864. Honorably discharged 4 June, 1865.
CUSHING, CALEB.
Appointed Master. 18 August, 1812. Last appearance on Records of Navy Department, 21 August, 1812.
CUSHING, CHARLES C.
Acting Ensign, on Admiral Lee's Staff, 7 November. 1864. Honorably discharged 3 October, 1865.
CUSHING, EDMUND H.
Acting Assistant Paymaster, 30 June, 1863. Passed Assistant Paymaster, 23 July, 1866. Paymaster, 16 September, 1868. Died on the Tuscarora, 11 March, 1869.
CUSHING, HENRY.
Acting Assistant Paymaster, 29 July, 1862. Discharged 3 October, 1865.
CUSHING, HENRY H.
Ensign (Spanish-American War), 9 July, 1898. Honorably discharged 14 November, 1898.
CUSHING, MILTON B.
Acting Assistant Paymaster, 20 August, 1864. Passed Assistant Paymaster, 23 July, 1866. Paymaster, 12 March, 1869. Retired List, 1 April, 1882. Died 1 January, 1887.
CUSHING, SAMUEL W.
Appointed Midshipman, 28 August, 1799. Last appearance on Records of Navy Department, 12 September, 1799. Killed in a duel.
CUSHING, STEPHEN.
Acting Assistant Surgeon, 11 June, 1864. Honorably discharged 10 October, 1865.
CUSHING, THOMAS B.
Acting Assistant Paymaster, 14 August, 1863. Resigned 9 March, 1865.
CUSHING, T. J. H.
Surgeon's Mate, 23 January, 1809. Dismissed 5 March, 1810. Surgeon's Mate, 10 December. 1814. Died 1 June, 1817.

GENERAL NAVY REGISTER. 145

CUSHING, WILLIAM BARKER.
Acting Midshipman, 25 September, 1857. Resigned 23 March, 1861. Acting Master's Mate, 1861. Lieutenant, 16 July, 1862. Lieutenant-Commander, 27 October, 1864. Commander, 31 January, 1872. Died 17 December, 1874.

CUSHMAN, ALEX.
Mate, 22 March, 1862. Dismissed 15 March, 1864.

CUSHMAN, ANSELL.
Appointed Master, 26 May, 1812. Dismissed 9 January, 1813.

CUSHMAN, CHARLES F.
Gunner, 7 April, 1856. Died 14 December, 1856.

CUSHMAN, CHARLES H.
Midshipman, 24 March, 1849. Passed Midshipman, 12 June, 1855. Master, 16 September, 1855. Lieutenant, 8 February, 1856. Lieutenant-Commander, 16 July, 1862. Commander, 25 July, 1866. Retired List, 24 April, 1877. Died 11 November, 1883.

CUSHMAN, GEORGE P.
Gunner, 18 December, 1861. Retired List, 22 July, 1891.

CUSHMAN, WALTER S.
Acting Assistant Paymaster, 27 September, 1862. Resigned 12 May, 1864.

CUSHMAN, WILLIAM H.
Third Assistant Engineer, 2 August, 1855. Second Assistant Engineer, 21 July, 1858. First Assistant Engineer, 3 August, 1859. Chief Engineer, 16 October, 1861. Died 2 November, 1865.

CUSHMAN, WILLIAM R.
Naval Cadet, 5 September, 1891. Ensign, 1 July, 1897. Lieutenant, Junior Grade, 1 July, 1900.

CUSHMAN, W. S.
Appointed Midshipman, 18 February, 1841. Resigned 31 July, 1847.

CUTBUSH, EDWARD.
Surgeon, 24 June, 1799. Resigned 10 June, 1829.

CUTBUSH, WILLIAM.
Appointed Midshipman, 9 December, 1800. Resigned 20 November, 1805.

CUTCHIN, ROBERT.
Appointed Master, 30 January, 1809. Dismissed 8 November, 1813.

CUTHBERT, LACHLAN.
Appointed Midshipman, 1 January, 1812. Died 2 September, 1820.

CUTHBERT, WAYLAND.
Third Assistant Engineer, 24 August, 1861. Second Assistant Engineer, 21 April, 1863. Resigned 22 August, 1864.

CUTHBERTSON, JAMES.
Acting Second Assistant Engineer, 4 June, 1864. Honorably discharged 28 October, 1865.

CUTHBUT, B. H.
Appointed Midshipman, 24 July, 1807. Struck off 4 September, 1808.

CUTHERELL, EDWIN J.
Warrant Machinist, 23 August, 1899.

CUTLER, ALFRED.
Appointed Midshipman, 1 January, 1825. Resigned 8 March, 1826.

CUTLER, AMOS.
Appointed Sailmaker, 24 June, 1817. Resigned in October, 1820.

CUTLER, JAMES.
Acting Third Assistant Engineer, 1 October, 1862. Acting Second Assistant Engineer, 24 August, 1863. Honorably discharged 4 November, 1865.

CUTLER, WILLIAM F.
Acting Third Assistant Engineer, 23 August, 1864. Resigned 19 May, 1865.

CUTLER, WILLIAM G.
Midshipman, 22 September, 1871. Graduated 21 June, 1875. Ensign, 18 July, 1876. Master, 1 December, 1881. Lieutenant, Junior Grade, 3 March, 1883. Lieutenant, 19 June, 1888. Lieutenant-Commander, 3 March, 1899.

CUTTER, GEORGE F.
Purser, 5 June, 1844. Pay Director, 3 March, 1871. Paymaster General, 18 November, 1877. Retired List, 30 August, 1881. Died 1 September, 1890.

CUTTER, RENSALEAR.
Acting First Assistant Engineer, 27 February, 1863. Honorably discharged 18 November, 1865.

CUTTER, WILLIAM.
Appointed Midshipman, 15 November, 1809. Last appearance on Records of Navy Department.

CUTTING, JOHN B.
Appointed Midshipman, 1 January, 1825. Passed Midshipman, 4 June, 1831. Lieutenant, 22 December, 1835. Died 20 May, 1843.

CUTTS, AUGUSTUS.
Appointed Midshipman, 9 November, 1813. Lieutenant, 13 January, 1825. Died 12 June, 1829.

CUTTS, CHARLES E.
Appointed Midshipman, 3 November, 1818. Died 7 September, 1824.

CUTTS, J. M.
Appointed Midshipman, 18 June, 1812. Resigned 1 July, 1820.

CUTTS, JOSEPH, Jr.
Appointed 6 December, 1814. Lieutenant, 13 January, 1825. Died 26 September, 1834.

CUTTS, RICHARD MALCOLM.
Acting Midshipman, 22 September, 1862. Graduated June, 1866. Ensign, 12 March, 1868. Master, 26 March, 1869. Lieutenant, 21 March, 1870. Lieutenant-Commander, 31 October, 1884. Died 3 February, 1886.

10

CUTTS, RICHARD M.
　Ensign (Spanish-American War), 26 May, 1898. Honorably discharged 25 February, 1899.
CUTTS, WALTER C.
　Appointed Midshipman, 4 March, 1823. Dismissed 17 May, 1833.
CUYLER, RICHARD M.
　Midshipman, 28 April, 1839. Passed Midshipman, 2 July, 1845. Master, 9 June, 1853. Lieutenant, 20 February, 1854. Resigned 20 December, 1859.
DABNEY, ALBERT J.
　Midshipman, 1 October, 1867. Graduated 6 June, 1871. Ensign, 14 July, 1872. Master, 6 April, 1875. Lieutenant, 16 February, 1882. Retired List, 30 June, 1885.
DABNEY, GEORGE.
　Midshipman, 9 November, 1799. Discharged 14 July, 1801, under Peace Establishment Act.
DABNEY, GEORGE.
　Midshipman, 30 March, 1802. Resigned 12 April, 1805.
DABNEY, T. S.
　Acting Assistant Paymaster, 22 September, 1863. Discharged 23 March, 1867.
DADE, ALEXANDER L.
　Midshipman, 1 November, 1827. Drowned 14 September, 1830.
DADE, FRANCIS C.
　Third Assistant Engineer, 20 January, 1849. Second Assistant Engineer, 26 February, 1851. First Assistant Engineer, 21 May, 1853. Chief Engineer, 24 October, 1859. Retired List, 26 January, 1889.
DADE, TOWNSHEND.
　Midshipman, 1 May, 1828. Resigned 8 June, 1836.
DADE, STEPHEN L.
　Mate. Resigned 29 September, 1862.
DADE, WILLIAM H.
　Mate, 23 December, 1861. Dismissed 27 September, 1862.
DAGGETT, JACOB.
　Mate, 9 January, 1862. Deserted 15 July, 1864.
DAGGETT, LLOYD E.
　Mate, 11 June, 1862. Honorably discharged 16 October, 1867.
DAGGETT, RICHMOND.
　Mate, 11 October, 1862. Acting Ensign, 10 November, 1873. Honorably discharged 30 April, 1866. Mate, 4 February, 1870. Resigned 30 April, 1870.
DAGGETT, SAMUEL.
　Gunner, 26 February, 1834. Died 9 April, 1836.
DAGGETT, THOMAS H.
　Acting Ensign, 27 October, 1863. Resigned 9 April, 1864.
DAHLGREEN, CHARLES B.
　Third Assistant Engineer, 24 December, 1861. Resigned 15 December, 1862. Acting Ensign, 15 December, 1862. Acting Master, 14 May, 1863. Resigned 1 February, 1865.
DAHLGREN, JOHN A.
　Midshipman, 1 February, 1862. Passed Midshipman, 28 April, 1832. Lieutenant, 8 March, 1837. Commander, 14 September, 1855. Captain, 16 July, 1862. Rear-Admiral, 7 February, 1863. Died 12 July, 1870.
DAIGH, CHARLES A.
　Passed Assistant Engineer (Spanish-American War), 25 May, 1898. Honorably discharged 24 December, 1898.
DAILY, CORNELIUS.
　Mate, 21 February, 1863. Deserted 9 April, 1865.
DAILY, THOMAS W.
　Midshipman, 9 November, 1813. Resigned 10 January, 1818.
DAISY, GEORGE W.
　Mate. Resigned 9 May, 1862.
DAIZLEY, WILLIAM.
　Acting Third Assistant Engineer, 9 October, 1863. Honorably discharged 17 October, 1865.
DALE, FRANK C.
　Assistant Surgeon, 6 November, 1876. Passed Assistant Surgeon, 7 August, 1880. Resigned 4 February, 1884.
DALE, GEORGE.
　Carpenter (Spanish-American War), 21 June, 1898. Honorably discharged 2 September, 1898.
DALE, JOHN B.
　Midshipman, 2 February, 1829. Passed Midshipman, 3 July, 1835. Lieutenant, 25 February, 1845. Died 24 July, 1848.
DALE, JOHN M.
　Midshipman, 18 June, 1812. Lieutenant, 1 April, 1818. Commander, 12 February, 1839. Died 14 December, 1852.
DALE, RICHARD S.
　Midshipman, 18 June, 1812. Killed in action, 23 June, 1812.
DALE, RICHARD.
　Captain, 4 June, 1794. Resigned 17 December, 1802.ETAOIN SHRDLU · SHDCM
DALE, SAMUEL.
　Acting Third Assistant Engineer, 5 May, 1864. Honorably discharged 29 August, 1865.
DALEY, JOHN.
　Mate, 19 March, 1863. Acting Ensign, 15 June, 1863. Honorably discharged 9 November, 1868.

GENERAL NAVY REGISTER. 147

DALEY, WILLIAM A.
  Acting Ensign, 22 June, 1864. Honorably discharged 10 June, 1865.
DALLAS, ALEXANDER J.
  Midshipman, 22 November, 1805. Lieutenant, 13 June, 1810. Commander, 5 March, 1817. Captain, 24 April, 1828. Died 3 June, 1844.
DALLAS, ALEXANDER J.
  Lieutenant, 13 January, 1825. Commander, 8 September, 1841. Died 12 July, 1843. (See A. J. D. Brown.)
DALLAS, ALEXANDER J., Jr.
  Midshipman, 25 January, 1840. Passed Midshipman, 11 July, 1846. Resigned 28 September, 1847.
DALLAS, ALEXANDER J.
  Midshipman, 24 March, 1846. Dismissed 12 June, 1851.
DALLAS, FRANCIS G.
  Midshipman, 8 November, 1841. Passed Midshipman, 10 August, 1847. Master, 14 September, 1855. Lieutenant, 15 September, 1855. Retired, 16 December, 1864. Commander on Retired List, 4 April, 1867. Lieutenant, Retired List, from 15 March, 1877. Died 30 September, 1890.
DALLAS, JACOB M.
  Carpenter, 22 July, 1861. Resigned 21 November, 1861.
DALE, FRANK C.
  Assistant Surgeon, 6 November, 1876. Passed Assistant Surgeon, 6 November, 1879. Resigned 4 February, 1884.
DALLY, JOHN R.
  Acting Third Assistant Engineer, 14 January, 1863. Appointment revoked 25 April, 1863.
DALTON, HAMILTON H.
  Acting Midshipman, 1 October, 1851. Midshipman, 9 June, 1855. Passed Midshipman, 15 April, 1858. Master, 4 November, 1858. Lieutenant, 16 December, 1860. Dismissed 1 July, 1861.
DALTON, JOHN H.
  Acting Third Assistant Engineer, 14 May, 1864. Discharged 12 May, 1866.
DALTON, SAMUEL W.
  Acting Third Assistant Engineer, 24 December, 1864. Appointment revoked 15 January, 1866.
DALTON, THOMAS.
  Mate, 8 June, 1863. Honorably discharged 22 January, 1866.
DALY, JOHN, Jr.
  Mate, 7 August, 1861. Acting Ensign, 15 June, 1863. Honorably discharged 9 November, 1868.
DALY, JOHN R.
  Mate, 24 August, 1897.
DALY, MICHAEL J.
  Acting Ensign, 24 June, 1863. Honorably discharged 15 August, 1865.
DAMON, ALEXANDER D.
  Mate, 25 June, 1864. Honorably discharged 30 July, 1868.
DAMON, DAVID.
  Acting Gunner, 12 December, 1864. Appointment revoked 18 September, 1865.
DAMON, ORISON B.
  Acting Assistant Surgeon, 7 June, 1863. Honorably discharged 24 January, 1866.
DAMON, SAMUEL H.
  Mate, 25 January, 1862. Dismissed 16 September, 1862. Acting Ensign, 16 September, 1864. Resigned 29 May, 1865.
DAMRE, AUGUSTUS.
  Acting Ensign, 13 September, 1864. Honorably discharged 12 February, 1866.
DANA, EDWARD F.
  Midshipman, 19 February, 1799. Resigned 5 March, 1800.
DANA, WILLIAM H.
  Midshipman, 1 May, 1850. Passed Midshipman, 20 June, 1856. Master, 22 January, 1858. Lieutenant, 1 July, 1858. Lieutenant-Commander, 16 July, 1862. Commander, 27 April, 1869. Died 5 March, 1872.
DANA, WILLIAM S.
  Acting Midshipman, 25 October, 1859. Acting Ensign, 1 October, 1863. Master, 10 May, 1866. Lieutenant, 21 February, 1867. Lieutenant-Commander, 12 March, 1868. Commander, 14 September, 1881. Died 1 January, 1890.
DANBY, ROBERT.
  Third Assistant Engineer, 18 January, 1845. Second Assistant Engineer, 10 July, 1847. First Assistant Engineer, 26 February, 1851. Chief Engineer, 26 June, 1856. Retired List, 18 August, 1883. Died 31 December, 1886.
DANCE, THOMAS L.
  Midshipman, 12 March, 1838. Passed Midshipman, 20 May, 1844. Died 21 March, 1850.
DANDREAU, CORNELIUS.
  Acting Second Assistant Engineer, 4 January, 1862. Honorably discharged 24 December, 1865.
DANDREAU, MITCHELL.
  Acting Second Assistant Engineer, 4 January, 1862. Appointment revoked (sick) 3 June, 1863.
DANDREAU, PAUL.
  Acting Third Assistant Engineer, 4 January, 1862. Honorably discharged 24 December, 1865.
DANDRIDGE, R. F.
  Surgeon's Mate, 20 March, 1820. Resigned 17 February, 1824.

DANDRIDGE, ROBERT.
   Midshipman, 1 January, 1818. Last appearance on Records of Navy Department.
DANDRIDGE, WILLIAM.
   Surgeon, date not known. Died 22 July, 1812.
DANELS, JOSEPH D.
   Midshipman, 19 October, 1841. Passed Midshipman, 10 August, 1847. Master, 14 September, 1855. Lieutenant, 15 September, 1855. Resigned 23 April, 1861. Acting Master, 5 September, 1862. Acting Lieutenant, 3 June, 1863. Acting Volunteer Lieutenant-Commander, 18 May, 1864. Lieutenant-Commander, 16 July, 1862. Died of wounds 23 March, 1865.
DANENHOWER, CHARLES.
   Mate, 4 September, 1862. Acting Ensign, 9 May, 1864. Honorably discharged 10 January, 1866.
DANENHOWER, JOHN W.
   Midshipman, 25 September, 1866. Graduated 7 June, 1870. Ensign, 13 July, 1871. Master, 27 September, 1873. Lieutenant, 2 August, 1879. Died 20 April, 1887.
DANFORTH, CHARLES H.
   Mate, 19 December, 1861. Acting Ensign, 23 November, 1864. Honorably discharged 11 May, 1865.
DANFORTH, GEORGE W.
   Naval Cadet, 7 September, 1885. Assistant Engineer, 1 July, 1891. Passed Assistant Engineer, 15 November, 1896. Rank changed to Lieutenant, 3 March, 1899. Retired List, 1 June, 1899.
DANFORTH, J. B. Jr.
   Purser, 20 August, 1857. Resigned 14 October, 1858.
DANGERFIELD, WILLIAM.
   Midshipman, 30 November, 1814. Dismissed 30 August, 1815.
DANIEL, R. P.
   Assistant Surgeon, 31 May, 1854. Passed Assistant Surgeon, 20 May, 1859. Resigned 30 June, 1859.
DANIEL, WILLIAM P.
   Midshipman, 1 January, 1812. Dismissed 18 August, 1812.
DANIELL, JERE R.
   Assistant Engineer (Spanish-American War), 24 June, 1898. Honorably discharged, 19 September, 1898.
DANIELL, DAVID H.
   Mate, 23 November, 1861. Acting Ensign, 4 December, 1863. Died at Pensacola, Fla., 14 April, 1864.
DANIELLS, WILLIAM A.
   Mate, 26 October, 1863. Honorably discharged 29 October, 1865.
DANIELS, C. H.
   Acting Master, 28 September, 1861. Resigned 21 July, 1862.
DANIELS, DAVID.
   Midshipman, 5 June, 1871. Graduated 21 June, 1875. Ensign, 22 August, 1876. Master, 17 November, 1882. Lieutenant, Junior Grade, 3 March, 1883. Lieutenant, 31 March 1889. Died 7 April, 1898.
DANIELS, JOSEPH F.
   Acting Gunner, 10 March, 1900.
DANIELS, T. J. M.
   Acting Second Assistant Engineer, 5 January, 1866. Resigned 11 July, 1866.
DANIELS, T. J. McK.
   Third Assistant Engineer, 19 July, 1861. Second Assistant Engineer, 18 December, 1862. Resigned 9 March, 1865.
DANIELSON, E. E.
   Midshipman, 2 April, 1804. Killed in a duel 15 August, 1808.
DANKER, HENRY A.
   Acting Assistant Surgeon, 15 March, 1864. Assistant Surgeon, 1 April, 1864. Died 5 August, 1864.
DANLEY, THOMAS W.
   Assistant Surgeon, July, 1818. Cashiered 30 December, 1819.
DANNER, FREDERIC W. .. r
   Midshipman, 23 June, 1869. Graduated 15 October, 1874. Ensign, 17 July, 1875. Lost on Huron, 24 November, 1877.
DANSBURY, G. M.
   Acting Second Assistant Engineer, 23 December, 1864. Honorably discharged 6 November, 1865.
DANTON, FLORANCE J.
   Acting Master, 12 August, 1861. Appointment revoked 20 January, 1862.
DARBY, EDWARD A.
   Ensign (Spanish-American War), 28 May, 1898. Honorably discharged 19 August, 1898.
DARBY, HENRY.
   Purser, 29 July, 1799. Discharged 23 September, 1801, under Peace Establishment Act.
DARBY, JOHN.
   Purser, 9 April, 1804. Last appearance on Records of Navy Department, 29 November, 1805.
DARCANTEL, HENRY.
   Midshipman, 1 April, 1826. Passed Midshipman, 28 April, 1832. Lieutenant, 8 March, 1837. Reserved List, 13 September, 1855. Died 9 March, 1857.
DARLING, JOHN A.
   Acting Master, 21 December, 1861. Appointment revoked 30 April, 1862.

DARLING, J. HOMER.
Acting Assistant Surgeon, 4 December, 1863. Honorably discharged 12 December, 1865.
DARLING, LEWIS, JR.
Acting Assistant Surgeon, 11 February, 1865. Honorably discharged 10 October, 1865.
DARLING, MARTIN V. B.
Acting Third Assistant Engineer, 3 April, 1862. Acting Second Assistant Engineer, 11 November, 1863. Honorably discharged 29 December, 1865.
DARLING, WILLIAM LEE.
Appointed in Volunteer Service, 18 December, 1861. Assistant Paymaster, 30 June, 1864. Paymaster, 4 May, 1866. Resigned 1 July, 1869.
DARLING, THOMAS.
Master, 18 August, 1812. Resigned 25 January, 1813.
DARLINGTON, B. S. B.
Midshipman, 1 April, 1828. Passed Midshipman, 14 June, 1834. Lieutenant, 25 February, 1841. Died 28 February, 1845.
DARRAH, JESSE M.
Mate, 4 August, 1863. Honorably discharged 20 October, 1865.
DARRAH, WILLIAM F.
Cadet Enginer, 1 October, 1879. Assistant Engineer, 1 July, 1885. Died 25 February, 1889.
DARRARGH, A. P.
Purser, 25 April, 1812. Died 9 January, 1831.
DART, THOMAS L.
Assistant Surgeon, 2 August, 1799. Discharged 30 June, 1801, under Peace Establishment Act.
DASHIEL, RICHARD.
Midshipman, 18 May, 1809. Lieutenant, 9 December, 1814. Died 22 June, 1823.
DASHIELL, JULIUS M.
Cadet Engineer, 1 October, 1881. Resigned 9 February, 1885. Ensign (Spanish-American War), 30 June, 1898. Discharged 28 January, 1899.
DASHIELL, ROBERT B.
Cadet Midshipman, 27 June, 1877. Ensign, Junior Grade, 1 July, 1883. Ensign, 26 June, 1884. Lieutenant, Junior Grade, 26 December, 1893. Assistant Naval Constructor, 7 February, 1895. Died 8 March 1899.
DASHWOOD, LUDLOW.
Purser, 25 April, 1812. Last appearance on Records of Navy Department, 1816. Furloughed.
DASKAM, WILLIAM.
Boatswain, 3 June, 1858. Resigned 21 July, 1858..
DATES, JAMES B.
Acting Ensign, 1 October, 1862. Resigned 10 April, 1863.
DAUBENAY, L. S.
Lieutenant, 19 September, 1798. Discharged 8 June, 1801, under Peace Establishment Act.
D'AUBIGNE, W. O. M.
Mate, 14 September, 1863. Resigned 21 September, 1864.
DAUM, IGNATIUS.
Mate, 29 June, 1863. Acting Ensign, 28 June, 1864. Honorably discharged 4 November, 1865.
DAVENPORT, FRANCIS O.
Acting Midshipman, 26 September, 1856. Midshipman, 1 June, 1861. Lieutenant, 16 July, 1862. Lieutenant-Commander, 25 July, 1866. Retired List, 19 October, 1870.
DAVENPORT, HENRY K.
Midshipman, 9 February, 1838. Passed Midshipman, 20 May, 1844. Master, 5 December, 1851. Lieutenant, 19 December, 1852. Commander, 16 July, 1862. Captain, 14 March, 1868. Died 18 August, 1872.
DAVENPORT, RICHARD G.
Midshipman, 29 September, 1864. Graduated 4 June, 1869. Ensign, 12 July, 1870. Master, 20 January, 1872. Lieutenant, 17 March, 1875. Lieutenant-Commander, 14 March, 1897. Commander, 18 February, 1900.
DAVEZAC, DEC. G.
Midshipman, 30 November, 1814. Resigned 14 July, 1819.
DAVEZAC, DEC. G.
Midshipman, 17 February, 1820. Resigned 10 January, 1821.
DAVID, WILLIAM G.
Cadet Midshipman, 25 September, 1873. Graduated 18 June, 1879. Ensign, 1 April,R 1880. Resigned 23 August, 1884. Ensign (Spanish-American War), 28 May, 1898. Honorably discharged 3 September, 1898.
DAVIDS, DAVID F.
Mate, 10 December, 1862. Acting Ensign, 8 December, 1863. Resigned 3 June, 1864.
DAVIDS, HENRY S.
Third Assistant Engineer, 26 August, 1859. Second Assistant Engineer, 16 October, 1861. First Assistant Engineer, 1 October, 1863. Chief Engineer, 5 March, 1871. Retired List, 7 June, 1884. Died 8 February, 1888.
DAVIDS, OSCAR.
Third Assistant Engineer, 26 February, 1851. Second Assistant Engineer, 21 May, 1853. Died 9 February, 1859.
DAVIDSON, ANDREW.
Carpenter, 18 February, 1814. Resigned 2 November, 1815.

DAVIDSON, CHARLES H.
  Mate. Resigned 29 October, 1862.
DAVIDSON, HUNTER.
  Midshipman, 29 October, 1841. Passed Midshipman, 10 August, 1847. Master, 14 September, 1855. Lieutenant, 15 September, 1855. Dismissed 23 April, 1861.
DAVIDSON, JOHN.
  Lieutenant, 31 January, 1799. Discharged 22 October, 1801, under Peace Establishment Act.
DAVIDSON, JOHN C.
  Midshipman, 22 November, 1825. Dismissed 25 June, 1833.
DAVIDSON, JOHN E.
  Midshipman, 15 November, 1809. Resigned 6 August, 1810.
DAVIDSON, JOHN R.
  Acting Third Assistant Engineer, 18 April, 1864. Discharged 8 January, 1866.
DAVIDSON, J. Q. A.
  Acting Ensign, 10 January, 1863. Honorably discharged 30 March, 1866.
DAVIDSON, ROBERT.
  Sailmaker, 14 January, 1806. Disappeared 20 May, 1806.
DAVIDSON, ROBERT.
  Sailmaker, 14 January, 1814. Last appearance on Records of Navy Department, 1815.
DAVIDSON, THOMAS, Jr.
  Assistant Naval Constructor, 4 May, 1863. Naval Constructor, 25 July, 1866. Died at Philadelphia, Pa., 18 February, 1874.
DAVIDSON, WASHINGTON F.
  Midshipman, 20 February, 1840. Passed Midshipman, 11 July, 1846. Dismissed 17 December, 1849.
DAVIE, WILLIAM C.
  Mate, 11 January, 1865. Acting Ensign, 5 July, 1865. Died at New York, 24 June, 1866.
DAVIDSON, WILLIAM C.
  Naval Cadet, 28 September, 1891. Ensign, 1 July, 1897. Lieutenant, Junior Grade, 1 July, 1900.
DAVIES, THOMAS E.
  Acting Third Assistant Engineer, 25 April, 1864. Honorably discharged 9 November, 1865.
DAVIN, ANTHONY.
  Acting Ensign, 17 April, 1863. Resigned (sick) 18 April, 1864.
DAVIS, A. F.
  Acting Master and Pilot, 1 October, 1864. Resigned 15 June, 1865.
DAVIS, ALBERT A.
  Acting Ensign, 24 December, 1864. Honorably discharged 5 September, 1865.
DAVIS, ALEXANDER.
  Sailmaker, 7 September, 1853. Resigned 5 June, 1854.
DAVIS, ALONZO B.
  Midshipman, 25 April, 1831. Passed Midshipman, 15 June, 1837. Lieutenant, 8 September, 1841. Died 19 September, 1854.
DAVIS, ANDREW, Jr.
  Mate, 23 June, 1864. Acting Ensign, 13 June, 1866. Honorably discharged 27 August, 1868.
DAVIS, ANDREW McF.
  Midshipman, 16 March, 1849. Resigned 8 September, 1852.
DAVIS, ARCHIBALD H.
  Naval Cadet, 17 May, 1883. Ensign, 1 July, 1889. Lieutenant, Junior Grade, 29 October, 1897. Lieutenant, 3 March, 1899.
DAVIS, CHARLES A.
  Chaplain, 16 May, 1857. Died at the Naval Hospital, Norfolk, Va., 20 February, 1867.
DAVIS, CHARLES C.
  Third Assistant Engineer, 24 December, 1861. Appointment revoked 30 December, 1863.
DAVIS, CHARLES C.
  Acting Third Assistant Engineer, 30 December, 1863. Acting Second Assistant Engineer, 23 August, 1864. Honorably discharged 20 July, 1865.
DAVIS, CHARLES H.
  Midshipman, 12 August, 1823. Passed Midshipman, 23 March, 1829. Lieutenant, 3 March, 1831. Commander, 12 June, 1854. Captain, 15 November, 1861. Commodore, 16 July, 1862. Rear-Admiral, 7 February, 1863. Died 20 February, 1877.
DAVIS, CHARLES H., Jr.
  Midshipman, 29 November, 1861. Graduated 22 November, 1864. Ensign, 1 November, 1866. Master, 1 December, 1866. Lieutenant, 12 March, 1868. Lieutenant-Commander, 30 June, 1869. Commander, 30 October, 1885. Captain, 10 August, 1898.
DAVIS, CHARLES H.
  Acting Second Assistant Engineer, 7 October, 1863. Resigned 29 July, 1864.
DAVIS, CHARLES M.
  Mate, 28 January, 1862. Resigned 26 March, 1863.
DAVIS, CHARLES O.
  Acting Second Assistant Engineer, 9 December, 1863. Honorably discharged 16 August, 1865.
DAVIS, CLELAND.
  Naval Cadet, 22 May, 1886. Ensign, 1 July, 1892. Lieutenant, 3 March, 1899.

GENERAL NAVY REGISTER. 151

DAVIS, DANIEL WAGNER.
  Midshipman, 22 September, 1862. Graduated 24 September, 1865. Ensign, 12 March, 1868. Master, 26 March, 1869. Lieutenant, 21 March, 1870. Dismissed 12 October, 1883.
DAVIS, DAVID, Jr.
  Acting Assistant Paymaster, 24 October, 1864. Honorably discharged 7 October, 1865.
DAVIS, DE WITT GILMORE.
  Third Assistant Engineer, 22 May, 1863. Lost on Patapsco, 15 January, 1865.
DAVIS, EDWARD M.
  Acting Second Assistant Engineer, 28 December, 1864. Honorably discharged 29 May, 1866.
DAVIS, EDWIN.
  Assistant Surgeon, 21 November, 1899.
DAVIS, EDWIN G.
  Assistant Engineer (Spanish-American War), 3 June, 1898. Honorably discharged 10 October, 1898.
DAVIS, ENOS R.
  Midshipman, 20 June, 1806. Lieutenant, 10 January, 1813. Died in March, 1818.
DAVIS, FRANCIS B.
  Acting Ensign, 1 November, 1862. Acting Master, 8 September, 1864. Honorably discharged 22 August, 1865.
DAVIS, FRANK.
  Mate, 23 December, 1861. Dismissed 30 April, 1862.
DAVIS, FRED E.
  Mate, 1 October, 1862. Died of wounds received in action, 17 March, 1863.
DAVIS, GEORGE.
  Surgeon, 22 July, 1799. Last appearance on Records of Navy Department, 1815. New York.
DAVIS, GEORGE.
  Master, 20 July, 1812. Last appearance on Records of Navy Department, 1815. Baltimore.
DAVIS, GEORGE.
  Gunner, date not known. Discharged in 1818.
DAVIS, GEORGE LEONARD.
  Paymaster, 16 April, 1861. Pay Inspector, 3 March, 1871. Retired List, 17 January, 1881. Died 3 December, 1884.
DAVIS, GEORGE S.
  Master, 28 July, 1813. Dismissed 14 September, 1813.
DAVIS, GEORGE THORNTON.
  Acting Midshipman, 20 September, 1860. Acting Ensign, 1 October, 1863. Master, 10 May, 1866. Lieutenant, 21 February, 1867. Lieutenant-Commander, 12 March, 1868. Commander, 1 February, 1883. Retired List, 23 October, 1889.
DAVIS, GEORGE W.
  Carpenter, 30 October, 1872. Retired List, 15 September, 1897.
DAVIS, HARVEY H.
  Acting Midshipman, 30 September, 1862. Resigned 28 June, 1864.
DAVIS, HENRY.
  Carpenter, 16 May, 1871. Died 1 February, 1893.
DAVIS, HENRY T.
  Mate, 1 October, 1863. Honorably discharged 7 August, 1867.
DAVIS, IRA L.
  Acting Assistant Surgeon, 21 March, 1865. Honorably discharged 11 October, 1865.
DAVIS, ISAAC P., Jr.
  Acting Third Assistant Engineer, 9 November, 1864. Honorably discharged 14 August, 1865.
DAVIS JAMES.
  Master, 29 June, 1812. Resigned 18 January, 1815.
DAVIS, JAMES.
  Sailmaker, 4 November, 1828. Died 26 January, 1839.
DAVIS, JAMES C.
  Gunner, 3 December, 1841. Resigned, 6 April, 1843. Gunner, 20 December, 1847. Died 20 November, 1855.
DAVIS, JESSE.
  Acting First Assistant Engineer, 1 July, 1861. Resigned 3 October, 1862.
DAVIS, JOHN.
  Purser, 14 April, 1869. Last appearance on Records of Navy Department, 26 March, 1811.
DAVIS, JOHN.
  Master, 1 March, 1814. Discharged 1 February, 1815.
DAVIS, JOHN.
  Midshipman, 7 November, 1801. Lieutenant, 26 March, 1807. Died 12 January, 1808.
DAVIS, JOHN.
  Midshipman, 17 December, 1810. Resigned 27 April, 1812.
DAVIS, JOHN.
  Acting Gunner, 11 March, 1862. Died at the Naval Hospital, New York, 17 November, 1863.
DAVIS, JOHN.
  Mate, 10 September, 1863. Killed in action on Columbine, 23 May, 1864.
DAVIS, JOHN.
  Mate, 25 November, 1863. Acting Ensign, 16 March, 1865. Honorably discharged 18 November, 1865.

DAVIS, JOHN.
Boatswain, 27 March, 1836. Dismissed 18 December, 1837.
DAVIS JOHN.
Acting Third Assistant Engineer, 2 December, 1861. Acting Second Assistant Engineer, 17 February, 1862. Dismissed 5 August, 1862.
DAVIS, JOHN.
Acting Master's Mate, 9 June, 1864. Acting Ensign, 13 December, 1864. Resigned 17 May, 1865.
DAVIS, JOHN A.
Midshipman, 4 March, 1823. Passed Midshipman, 23 March, 1829. Lieutenant, 27 February, 1833. Died in Washington City, 14 January, 1854.
DAVIS, JOHN A.
Acting Ensign, 17 October, 1862. Resigned 4 April, 1865.
DAVIS, JOHN C.
Acting Third Assistant Engineer, 24 October, 1864. Resigned 9 June, 1865.
DAVIS, JOHN L.
Carpenter, 20 November, 1869. Retired List, 19 May, 1891. Died 14 November, 1899.
DAVIS, JOHN LEE.
Midshipman, 9 January, 1841. Passed Midshipman, 10 August, 1847. Master, 14 September, 1855. Lieutenant, 15 September, 1855. Lieutenant-Commander, 16 July, 1862. Commander, 25 July, 1866. Captain, 14 February, 1873. Commodore, 4 February, 1882. Rear-Admiral, 30 October, 1885. Retired List, 3 September, 1887. Died 12 March, 1889.
DAVIS, JOHN W.
Mate, 8 January, 1864. Resigned 22 February, 1865.
DAVIS, NAILOR C.
Second Asistant Engineer, 17 January, 1842. First Assistant Engineer, 10 July, 1847. Resigned 29 October, 1859.
DAVIS, NATHANIEL R.
Mate, 8 May, 1862. Acting Ensign, 23 August, 1864. Honorably discharged 15 May, 1865.
DAVIS, NORRIS K.
Assistant Engineer (Spanish-American War), 3 June, 1898. Honorably discharged 7 February, 1899.
DAVIS, OSCAR.
Midshipman, 1 February, 1812. Resigned 30 January 1822
DAVIS, OWEN T.
Midshipman, 1 February, 1814. Resigned 4 October, 1822.
DAVIS, POLLARD.
Midshipman, 15 November, 1809. Last appearance on Records of Navy Department, 5 February, 1810. Dead.
DAVIS, RICHARD.
Boatswain, 15 April, 1799. Warrant returned 5 May. 1800.
DAVIS, ROSWELL.
Mate, 16 August, 1861. Appointment revoked (sick) 28 July. 1864.
DAVIS, SAMUEL.
Surgeon's Mate, 23 January, 1809. Last appearance on Records of Navy Department, 10 February, 1809. Drowned.
DAVIS, SAMUEL.
Mate, 23 March, 1864. Died on Kearsarge, 21 March, 1866.
DAVIS, SAMUEL.
Asistant Surgeon, 23 January, 1809. Last appearance on Records of Navy Department, 10 February, 1809. Drowned.
DAVIS, STEPHEN B.
Acting Ensign, 21 January, 1863. Acting Master, 7 November, 1864. Honorably discharged 16 May, 1865.
DAVIS, STILLMAN S.
Acting Assistant Paymaster, 1 July, 1864. Honorably discharged 12 December, 1865.
DAVIS, THOMAS.
Carpenter, 16 August, 1823. Last appearance on Records of Navy Department, 8 September, 1823. Struck off.
DAVIS, THOMAS B.
Lieutenant, 19 November, 1799. Discharged 14 May, 1801, under Peace Establishment Act.
DAVIS, THOMAS F.
Midshipman, 2 February, 1829. Resigned 27 March, 1837.
DAVIS, THOMAS H.
Mate, 19 November, 1863. Died on Clover, 17 December, 1863.
DAVIS, T. W.
Acting Ensign, Admiral Farragut's Staff, 1 February, 1864. Resigned 15 July, 1864.
DAVIS, WALTER H.
Mate, 25 January, 1862. Resigned 16 June, 1863.
DAVIS, WILLIAM.
Purser, 14 August, 1799. Discharged 8 July, 1801, under Peace Establishment Act.
DAVIS, WILLIAM,
Midshipman, 24 June, 1798. Lieutenant, 3 December, 1800. Discharged 29 October, 1801, under Peace Establishment Act.
DAVIS, WILLIAM B.
Assistant Surgeon, 23 January, 1871. Passed Assistant Surgeon, 13 April, 1875. Resigned 19 January, 1877.

GENERAL NAVY REGISTER.

DAVIS, WILLIAM C.
Midshipman, 1 January, 1808. Resigned 4 February, 1809.
DAVIS, WILLIAM P.
Acting Assistant Surgeon, 11 March, 1865. Honorably discharged 11 October, 1865.
DAVIS, WILLIS.
Third Assistant Engineer, 11 January, 1849. Resigned 4 November, 1850.
DAVISON, EMANUEL R.
Mate, 1 April, 1862. Acting Ensign, 6 November, 1863. Appointment revoked 18 March, 1864. Acting Ensign, 5 August, 1865. Honorably discharged 26 December, 1865.
DAVISON, GREGORY C.
Naval Cadet, 22 May, 1888. Ensign, 1 July, 1894. Lieutenant, Junior Grade, 3 March, 1899. Lieutenant, 1 July, 1900.
DAVISON, PLINY.
Acting Ensign, 2 September, 1864. Honorably discharged 15 November, 1865.
DAVISON, ROBERT A.
Acting First Assistant Engineer, 24 June, 1863. Dismissed 29 April, 1865.
DAVOL, GEORGE S.
Midshipman, 26 February, 1863. Graduated 6 June, 1867. Ensign, 18 December, 1868. Master, 21 March, 1870. Lieutenant, 21 March, 1871. Resigned 17 June, 1872.
DAWES, EDWARD.
Midshipman, 18 June, 1812. Resigned 27 October, 1813.
DAWES, RICHARD C.
Acting Ensign, 14 December, 1863. Honorably discharged 11 January, 1867.
DAWLEY, DAVID C.
Acting Third Assistant Engineer, 25 March, 1864.
DAWSON, FRANCIS.
Gunner, 20 March, 1848. Dismissed 21 October, 1851.
DAWSON, JOHN.
Boatswain, date not known. Last appearance on Records of Navy Department, 1816.
DAWSON, LEWIS.
Acting Gunner, 1 October, 1862. Resigned (sick) 22 August, 1863.
DAWSON, LUCIEN W.
Midshipman, 27 April, 1850. Resigned 14 May, 1855.
DAWSON, WILLIAM.
Midshipman, 16 January, 1809. Last appearance on Records of Navy Department, 21 March, 1809. Lost in a Prize.
DAY, ARTHUR H.
Lieutenant (Spanish-American War), 22 June, 1898. Honorably discharged 8 September, 1898.
DAY, BENJAMIN F.
Acting Midshipman, 20 September, 1858. Resigned 24 November, 1860. Lieutenant, 1 August, 1862. Lieutenant-Commander, 25 July, 1866. Commander, 8 August, 1876. Captain, 5 November, 1891. Rear-Admiral, 29 March, 1899. Retired List, 28 January, 1900.
DAY, EDWARD M.
Midshipman, 23 September, 1863. Ensign, 19 April, 1869. Master, 12 July, 1870. Retired List, 3 August, 1874. Died 13 June, 1879.
DAY, GEORGE C.
Naval Cadet, 19 May, 1888. Ensign, 1 July, 1894. Lieutenant, Junior Grade, 3 March, 1899.
DAY, HENRY R.
Purser, 28 March, 1859. Died 22 January, 1866.
DAY, JARED.
Acting Third Assistant Engineer, 17 October, 1861. Acting Second Assistant Engineer, 7 February, 1863. Acting First Assistant Engineer, 17 August, 1864. Honorably discharged 29 December, 1861.
DAY, JOHN H. A.
Naval Cadet, 19 May, 1893. Resigned 10 June, 1896. Ensign (Spanish-American War), 14 May, 1898. Honorably discharged 31 January, 1899.
DAY, JOHN W.
Acting Assistant Paymaster, 20 October, 1863. Discharged 2 February, 1866.
DAY, JOSEPH S.
Midshipman, 16 March, 1839. Passed Midshipman, 2 July, 1845. Master, 28 October, 1853. Lieutenant, 21 June, 1854. Died 4 November, 1856.
DAY, MURRAY S.
Midshipman, 24 September, 1861. Graduated 24 September, 1865. Ensign, 12 March, 1868. Master, 26 March, 1869. Lieutenant, 21 March, 1870. Died 27 Decemebr, 1878.
DAY, RALPH H.
Mate, 26 September, 1863. Acting Ensign, 25 July, 1864. Honorably discharged 23 November, 1865.
DAY, THOMAS.
Acting Ensign, Coast Survey Duty, 20 May, 1867. Mustered out 30 November, 1868.
DAY, WILLIAM P.
Midshipman, 21 July, 1865. Graduated 4 June, 1869. Ensign, 12 July, 1870. Master, 31 October, 1871. Lieutenant, 23 January, 1875. Lieutenant-Commander, 1 January, 1897. Commander, 12 Decemebr, 1899.

DAY, WILLIS B.
Cadet Engineer, 13 September, 1877. Assistant Engineer, 1 July, 1884. Passed Assistant Engineer, 29 January, 1895. Retired List, 2 May, 1898.
DAYERS, GERARD.
Assistant Surgeon, date not known. Surgeon, 24 July, 1813. Died 20 May, 1835.
DAYTON, EPHRAIM.
Acting Assistant Surgeon, 1 March, 1864. Honorably discharged 16 October, 1865.
DAYTON, E. G.
Acting Ensign, 9 March, 1863. Honorably discharged 18 August, 1865.
DAYTON, GILBERT.
Acting Master, 18 July, 1861. Honorably discharged 10 May, 1866.
DAYTON, JAMES HENRY.
Midshipman, 27 September, 1862. Graduated 24 September, 1865. Ensign, 12 March, 1868. Master, 26 March, 1869. Lieutenant, 21 March, 1870. Lieutenant-Commander, 8 November, 1884. Commander, 23 January, 1894. Captain, 29 March, 1900.
DAYTON, JOHN H.
Naval Cadet, 13 September, 1886. Ensign, 1 July, 1892. Lieutenant, Junior Grade, 3 March, 1899. Lieutenant, 1 July, 1899.
DAYTON, S. A.
Acting Ensign, 22 July, 1863. Honorably discharged 14 September, 1865.
DAYTON, THOMAS R.
Acting Ensign, 17 October, 1863. Honorably discharged 28 October, 1865.
DAYTON, T. W. H.
Midshipman, 1 September, 1811. Last appearance on Records of Navy Department, 1818.
DEACON, DAVID.
Midshipman, 10 October, 1799. Lieutenant, 2 March, 1807. Commander, 10 December, 1814. Captain, 24 January, 1826. Died 22 February, 1840.
DEACON, JOHN.
Carpenter, date not known. Discharged 12 July, 1825.
DEACON, JOHN.
Carpenter, date not known. Dismissed 2 December, 1830.
DEACON, ROBERT.
Midshipman, 1 January, 1828. Resigned 10 March, 1834.
DEACON, WILLIAM.
Acting Second Assistant Engineer, 29 August, 1864. Honorably discharged 30 September, 1865.
DEALY, RICHARD.
Master, 4 February, 1811. Resigned 18 October, 1826.
DEALY, RICHARD.
Midshipman, 16 December, 1814. Resigned 18 October, 1826.
DEAN, SUMNER.
Acting Assistant Surgeon, 25 November, 1863. Resigned 6 July, 1865.
DEAN, BENJAMIN C.
Acting Master, 26 August, 1861. Acting Volunteer Lieutenant, 10 December, 1864. Honorably discharged 8 December, 1865.
DEAN, FRANCIS A.
Acting Ensign, 3 March, 1865. Honorably discharged 14 September, 1865.
DEAN, GEORGE.
Boatswain, 15 April, 1859. Dismissed 14 May, 1859. Reappointed 1 May, 1861. Dismissed 13 June, 1861.
DEAN, GEORGE A.
Acting Third Assistant Engineer, 6 January, 1864. Resigned 29 March, 1865.
DEAN, GEORGE W.
Acting Second Assistant Engineer, 18 April, 1863. Resigned 10 May, 1865.
DEAN, JAMES H.
Acting Third Assistant Engineer, 27 February, 1865. Honorably discharged 22 September, 1865.
DEAN, JAMES R.
Acting Assistant Surgeon, 15 November, 1862. Resigned 10 February, 1865.
DEAN, NOAH.
Acting Carpenter, 6 December, 1862. Honorably discharged 18 December, 1865.
DEAN, RICHARD C.
Assistant Surgeon, 17 April, 1856. Passed Assistant Surgeon, 25 March, 1861. Surgeon, 1 August, 1861. Medical Inspector, 8 June, 1873. Medical Director, 10 June, 1880. Retired List, 27 May, 1895.
DEAN, SAMUEL A.
Acting Third Assistant Engineer, 2 September, 1863. Resigned 30 January, 1864.
DEAN, THADDEUS J.
Acting Ensign, 26 August, 1863. Honorably discharged 6 August, 1865.
DEANE, CUNNINGHAM W.
Assistant Surgeon, 29 September, 1875. Passed Assistant Surgeon, 7 August, 1880. Died 22 October, 1888.
DEANE, EDWARD L.
Mate, 26 January, 1863. Resigned 19 April, 1864.
DEARBORN, JOHN F.
Acting Master, 27 December, 1861. Resigned 17 March, 1866.
DEARBORNE, FREDERICK M.
Acting Assistant Surgeon, 18 August, 1862. Assistant Surgeon, 15 September, 1864. Passed Assistant Surgeon, 11 October, 1867. Surgeon, 4 May, 1875. Retired List, 10 December, 1883. Died 24 April, 1887.
DEARBORNE, JOHN G.
Acting Assistant Surgeon, 10 February, 1864. Honorably discharged 22 January, 1866.

GENERAL NAVY REGISTER. 155

DEARING, CHARLES F.
Mate, 24 January, 1862. Acting Ensign, 20 July, 1863. Honorably discharged 20 September, 1865.

DEARING, HENRY L.
Acting Assistant Surgeon, 9 March, 1864. Died 5 October, 1864.

DEAS, CHARLES.
Midshipman, 15 October, 1835. Passed Midshipman, 22 June, 1841. Master, 29 April, 1848. Lieutenant, 6 March, 1849. Died 16 April, 1859.

DEAS, FITZALLEN.
Midshipman, 4 July, 1821. Passed Midshipman, 24 May, 1828. Lieutenant, 27 May, 1830. Died at Charleston, S. C., 31 July, 1849.

DEAVER, JAMES A.
Third Assistant Engineer, 19 February, 1863. Second Assistant Engineer, 25 July, 1866. Retired List, 28 February, 1874. Died 10 February, 1887.

DEAVER, WILLIAM E.
Acting Third Assistant Engineer, 24 September, 1862. Acting Second Assistant Engineer, 1 February, 1865. Honorably discharged 12 October, 1865.

DE BEVOISE, CHARLES.
Acting Master, 14 November, 1862. Acting Volunteer Lieutenant, recommendation of Commanding Officer, 6 August, 1864. Honorably discharged 20 September, 1865.

DE BEVOISE, CHARLES.
Acting Gunner, 24 February, 1862. Resigned 15 November, 1862. Acting Master.

DEBLOIS, JAMES S.
Purser, 5 May, 1798. Died 10 December, 1803.

DEBLOIS, LEWIS.
Purser, 25 February, 1812. Dismissed 27 May, 1829.

DE BLOIS, THOMAS A.
Midshipman, 21 September, 1863. Graduated 2 June, 1868. Ensign, 19 April, 1869. Master, 12 July, 1870. Lieutenant, 25 September, 1873. Resigned 1 February, 1881.

DE BREE, ALEXANDER M.
Midshipman, 19 October, 1841. Passed Midshipman, 10 August, 1847. Master, 14 September, 1855. Lieutenant, 15 September, 1855. Dismissed 6 December, 1861.

DE BREE JOHN.
Purser, 29 December, 1817. Dismissed 19 April, 1861.

DE BUTTS, SAMUEL.
Midshipman, date not known. Last appearance on Records Navy Department.

DE CAMARA, JOSEPH B.
Acting Ensign, 11 September, 1862. Acting Master, gallant conduct in action, 1 June, 1863. Appointment revoked (sick) 11 July, 1863.

DE CAMP, EDGAR A.
Mate, 24 January, 1863. Appointment revoked (sick) 19 October, 1863.

DE CAMP, JAMES.
Mate, 1 October, 1862. Resigned 8 July, 1863.

DE CAMP JAMES W.
Mate, 26 October, 1863. Resigned 13 March, 1865.

DE CAMP, JOHN.
Midshipman, 1 October, 1827. Passed Midshipman, 10 June, 1833. Lieutenant, 28 February, 1838. Commander, 14 September, 1855. Captain, 16 July, 1862. Commodore, 8 December, 1867. Retired List, 13 March, 1868. Rear-Admiral, Retired List, 13 July, 1870. Died 24 June, 1875.

DECATUR, JAMES.
Midshipman, 21 November, 1798. Lieutenant, 20 April, 1802. Killed in action 3 August, 1804.

DECATUR, JOHN P.
Master, 4 August, 1807. Resigned 26 March, 1810.

DECATUR, JOHN P.
Midshipman, 31 August, 1836. Passed Midshipman, 1 July, 1842. Master, 5 September, 1849. Lieutenant, 19 April, 1850. Died 17 July, 1857.

DECATUR, STEPHEN.
Midshipman, 30 April, 1798. Lieutenant, 21 May, 1799. Captain, 16 February, 1804. Killed in a duel 22 March, 1820.

DECATUR, STEPHEN.
Captain, 11 May, 1798. Discharged 22 October, 1801, under Peace Establishment Act.

DECATUR, STEPHEN.
Midshipman, 17 March, 1829. Passed Midshipman, 3 July, 1835. Lieutenant, 25 February, 1841. Reserved List, 13 September, 1855. Commander Reserved List, 29 July, 1861. Captain on Reserved List, 4 April, 1867. Commodore on Retired List, 30 December, 1869. Died 9 January, 1876.

DECATUR, STEPHEN.
Cadet Midshipman, 8 June, 1870. Resigned 15 June, 1872. Lieutenant, Junior Grade (Spanish-American War), 10 May, 1898. Honorably discharged 17 January, 1899.

DECKER, BENTON C.
Naval Cadet, 17 May, 1883. Ensign, 1 July, 1889. Lieutenant, Junior Grade, 24 February, 1897. Lieutenant, 3 March, 1899.

DECKER, CORBIN J.
Assistant Surgeon, 17 June, 1886. Passed Assistant Surgeon, 17 June, 1899. Surgeon, 12 December, 1898.

DECKER, EDWARD W.
Acting Master and Pilot, 1 November, 1864. Honorably discharged 17 July, 1865.

DECKER, G. G.
Master's Mate, 16 February, 1842. Dismissed 6 July, 1842.

DECKER, PETER.
Mate, 21 December, 1861. Resigned 7 October, 1862.

DECKER, WILLIAM H.
Acting Ensign, 15 July, 1863. Honorably discharged 16 August, 1865.
DE CORDY, JOHN.
Mate. Resigned (sick) 9 May, 1862.
DE CORDY, ROBERT.
Acting Third Assistant Engineer, 29 April, 1863. Appointment revoked (sick) 1 February, 1864.
DEDERER, SAMUEL T.
Acting Ensign, 29 June, 1864. Appointment revoked 12 January, 1866.
DEE, JOHN H.
Acting Third Assistant Engineer, 19 April, 1864. Honorably discharged 28 October, 1865.
DEE, PATRICK.
Carpenter, 9 May, 1852. Died in Charlestown, Mass., 27 December, 1860.
DEE, THOMAS W.
Acting Third Assistant Engineer, 18 October, 1861. Resigned 4 January, 1863. Acting Third Assistant Engineer, 26 June, 1863. Honorably discharged 9 June, 1866.
DEERING, CHARLES W.
Midshipman, 21 June, 1869. Graduated 31 May, 1873. Ensign, 16 July, 1874. Master, 28 December, 1878. Resigned 21 May, 1881.
DEERING, FREDERICK H.
Acting Ensign, 22 October, 1864. Honorably discharged 7 August, 1865.
DEERING, GEORGE A.
Assistant Paymaster, 4 May, 1870. Passed Assistant Paymaster, 25 January, 1878. Paymaster, 10 April, 1889. Died 16 October, 1890.
DEERING, JAMES.
Acting Ensign, 15 Februray, 1864. Resigned 7 July, 1865.
DEERY, PATRICK.
Boatswain, 5 May, 1897.
DeESTIMAUVILLE, F. H.
Mate. Acting Ensign, 1 June, 1863. Died at Naval Hospital, New York, 23 February, 1865.
DE FORD, HENRY S.
Acting Assistant Surgeon, 23 March, 1864. Honorably discharged 11 September, 1865.
DE FORREST, JAMES S.
Acting Ensign, 12 February, 1864. Honorably discharged 31 October, 1865.
DeFREES, JOSEPH R.
Naval Cadet, 20 May, 1896. Graduated 30 June, 1900.
DEFRIES, FERDINAND W.
Acting Ensign, 19 December, 1862. Resigned 1865.
DEGELMAN, CHARLES F.
Acting Third Assistant Engineer, 18 November, 1862. Acting Second Assistant Engineer, 10 June, 1864. Honorably discharged 4 November, 1865.
DEGGES, BEVERLY.
Midshipman, 1 March, 1814. Discharged 1 February, 1815.
DEGN, LAUST E.
Acting Master, 11 November, 1861. Honorably discharged 14 July, 1866.
DeGRAFF, ISAAC.
Third Assistant Engineer, 9 December, 1861. Second Assistant Engineer, 8 September, 1863. Resigned 23 August, 1866.
DeGROSSE, WILLIAM H.
Mate, 21 May, 1863. Acting Ensign, 2 December, 1863. Resigned (sick) 28 March, 1865.
DeGROTT, WILLIAM H. H.
Mate, 24 October, 1863. Honorably discharged 3 June, 1865.
DeHART, GOZEN R.
Midshipman, 15 November, 1809. Last appearance on Records of Navy Department, 30 January, 1811.
DeHART, J. C.
Purser, 12 April, 1824. Last appearance on Records of Navy Department, 26 May, 1824. Dead.
DeHART, WILLIAM HENRY.
Third Assistant Engineer, 17 January, 1862. Second Assistant Engineer, 1 October, 1863. Resigned 5 November, 1869.
DeHAVEN, EDWARD J.
Midshipman, 2 October, 1829. Passed Midshipman, 3 July, 1835. Lieutenant, 8 September, 1841. Retired 6 February, 1862. Died 1 May, 1865.
DeHAVEN, JOSEPH E.
Midshipman, 19 October, 1841. Passed Midshipman, 10 August, 1847. Master, 14 September, 1855. Lieutenant, 15 September, 1855. Lieutenant-Commander, 16 July, 1862. Resigned 30 May, 1865.
DEIGNAN, OSBORN.
Acting Boatswain, 9 April, 1900.
DEINKE, WILLIAM H.
Mate, 15 August, 1864. Honorably discharged 9 November, 1867.
DeJONGH, WILLIAM F.
Midshipman, 11 March, 1837. Passed Midshipman, 29 June, 1843. Died 18 January, 1850.
DeKAY, JAMES.
Acting Master, 1 July, 1861. Appointment revoked 26 August, 1861. Mate, 1862. Acting Ensign, 30 March, 1863. Resigned 12 May, 1865.

GENERAL NAVY REGISTER. 157

DEKAY, WILLIAM.
Acting Third Assistant Engineer, 22 July, 1863. Honorably discharged 12 May, 1865.
DEKLYNE, THEO. W.
Acting Third Assistant Engineer, 5 March, 1864. Honorably discharged 20 July, 1865. Acting Third Assistant Engineer, 12 July, 1866. Mustered out 28 August, 1868.
DEKOVEN, WILLIAM.
Midshipman, 9 September, 1841. Passed Midshipman, 10 August, 1847. Died 13 May, 1851.
DEKRAFT, F. C.
Midshipman, 16 February, 1803. Resigned 14 May, 1808.
DEKRAFT, JOHN C. P.
Midshipman, 19 October, 1841. Passed Midshipman, 10 August, 1847. Master, 14 September, 1855. Lieutenant, 15 September, 1855. Lieutenant-Commander, 16 July, 1862. Commander, 25 July, 1866. Captain, 20 November, 1872. Commodore, 1 October, 1881. Rear-Admiral, 2 June, 1885. Died 29 October, 1885.
DEKRAFFT, JAMES W.
Third Assistant Engineer, 21 July, 1858. Second Assistant Engineer, 1 July, 1861. First Assistant Engineer, 17 March, 1863. Died 19 October, 1870.
DELACY, W. W.
Teacher of Language, 18 May, 1841.
DELAHAY, WILLIAM E. B.
Midshipman, 22 July, 1864. Graduated 4 June, 1869. Ensign, 12 July, 187- Master, 9 November, 1872. Lieutenant, 26 April, 1877. Retired List, 22 May, 1866. Died 20 February, 1892.
DELAN, JOSEPH R.
Mate, 23 August, 1864. Resigned 4 November, 1864.
DELAN, LEWIS P.
Acting Ensign, 1 November, 1864. Resigned 12 April, 1865.
DE LANCY, CHARLES H.
Assistant Surgeon (Spanish-American War), 8 July, 1898. Appointed Assistant Surgeon in Regular Service 7 June, 1900.
DELANEY, JAMES.
Acting Third Assistant Engineer, 24 June, 1863. Dismissed 9 December, 1863.
DELANEY, JOSEPH J.
Mate (Spanish-American War), 22 June, 1898. Honorably discharged 15 February, 1899.
DELANEY, M. G.
Assistant Surgeon, 28 February, 1833. Passed Assistant Surgeon, 1 August, 1837. Surgeon, 8 September, 1841. Died 5 April, 1866.
DELANO, ABRAHAM, Jr.
Acting Master, 15 August, 1861. Dismissed 30 July, 1862. Acting Ensign, 24 September, 1862. Appointment revoked 18 March, 1864.
DELANO, ANSEL A.
Mate, 1 March, 1864. Honorably discharged 22 June, 1866.
DELANO, BENJAMIN F.
Naval Constructor, 14 August, 1846. Retired List, 17 September, 1871. Died 30 April, 1882.
DELANO, FRANCIS H.
Midshipman, 23 September, 1863. Graduated 6 June, 1867. Ensign, 18 December, 1868. Master, 21 March, 1870. Lieutenant, 6 February, 1873. Lieutenant-Commander, 22 June, 1894. Commander, 3 March, 1899.
DELANO, HARRISON.
Mate, 21 May, 1864. Honorably discharged 30 November, 1865.
DELANO, JAMES H.
Mate, 23 December, 1863. Acting Ensign, 12 October, 1864. Honorably discharged 13 June, 1867.
DELANO, MARCUS T.
Acting Assistant Surgeon, 5 March, 1864. Resigned 8 May, 1865.
DELANO, PHILIP W.
Assistant Paymaster, 1 December, 1899.
DELANO, SAMUEL.
Mate, 14 November, 1861. Resigned 5 March, 1864.
DELANO, TIMOTHY.
Mate, 15 October, 1861. Acting Ensign, 23 August, 1862. Honorably discharged 26 January, 1866.
DELANY, EDWIN H.
Naval Cadet, 21 May, 1890. Assistant Engineer, 1 July, 1896. Rank changed to Ensign, 3 March, 1899. Lieutenant, Junior Grade, 1 July, 1899.
DELANY, P. B.
Assistant Surgeon, 5 March, 1847. Died 9 August, 1847.
DELAP, GEORGE.
Mate, 26 July, 1863. Acting Ensign 7 November, 1864. Honorably discharged 20 December, 1865. Mate, 1 October, 1869. Resigned 1 August, 1870.
DELAROCHE, GEORGE F.
Master, 3 August, 1813. Resigned 24 May, 1825.
DELBERGHE, F. V.
Midshipman, 1 April, 1828. Resigned 14 February, 1835.
DELEHANTY, DANIEL.
Midshipman, 25 September, 1862. Graduated 6 June, 1867. Ensign, 18 December, 1868. Master, 21 March, 1870. Lieutenant, 6 March, 1872. Lieutenant-Commander, 9 January, 1893. Commander, 22 November, 1898. Retired List with rank of Captain, 29 June, 1900.

DELIUS, HERMAN A.
Third Assistant Engineer, 26 August, 1859. Second Assistant Engineer, 20 May, 1863. Resigned 22 June, 1865.
DELONG, GEORGE W.
Midshipman, 1 October. 1861. Graduated 24 September, 1865. Ensign, 1 December, 1866. Master, 12 March, 1868. Lieutenant, 26 March, 1869. Lieutenant-Commander, 1 November, 1879. Lost in the Arctic Regions July, 1882. Jeannette.
DELOUISY, J. B.
Midshipman, 5 December, 1798. Discharged 12 October, 1801, under Peace Establishment Act.
DELPHY, RICHARD.
Midshipman, 18 May, 1809. Killed in action 14 August, 1813.
DE LUCE, EDMUND S.
Third Assistant Engineer, 22 September, 1849. Second Assistant Engineer, 26 February, 1851. First Assistant Engineer, 21 May, 1853. Chief Engineer, 12 October, 1859. Retired List, 13 December, 1878. Died 25 June, 1890.
DELUCE, GEORGE E.
Third Assistant Engineer, 26 February, 1851. Resigned 28 February, 1853.
DE LUCE, THEODORE F.
Acting Ensign, 1 August, 1862. Appointment revoked (sick) 14 March, 1865.
DE LYON, A. S.
Midshipman, 17 December, 1810. Last appearance on Records of Navy Department, 26 April, 1811.
DEMERITT, J. H.
Gunner, 4 December, 1815. Resigned 4 November, 1817.
DEMERIT, J. H.
Acting Assistant Paymaster, 17 February, 1863. Appointment revoked (sick) 21 October, 1863.
DEMMING, WILLIAM H.
Acting Third Assistant Engineer, 17 December, 1864. Honorably discharged 1 December, 1865.
DEMOREST, G. V.
Mate, 16 April, 1864. Acting Ensign, 22 February, 1865. Honorably discharged 13 May, 1865.
DEMOTT, ABRAHAM.
Carpenter, date not known. Last appearance on Records of Navy Department.
DEMOTT, LEWIS J.
Acting Second Assistant Engineer, 12 December, 1863. Honorably discharged 8 January, 1866.
DEMPSEY, LAWRENCE.
Mate, 17 November, 1862. Deserted 14 February, 1865.
DEMPSEY, THOMAS.
Acting Third Assistant Engineer, 16 May, 1862. Acting Second Assistant Engineer, 19 November, 1863. Dismissed 4 April, 1864.
DEMPSTER, ALEXANDER.
Acting Third Assistant Engineer, 1 September, 1864. Honorably discharged 25 September, 1868.
DENBY, EDWIN R.
Assistant Surgeon, 11 July, 1855. Passed Assistant Surgeon, 4 May, 1860. Surgeon, 1 August, 1861. Medical Inspector, 28 December, 1872. Died 3 May, 1875.
DENBY, JOHN C.
Third Assistant Engineer, 20 May, 1863. Appointment revoked 1 September, 1864.
DENCH, J. SULLY.
Mate, 8 January, 1864. Died at Naval Hospital, New York, 25 February, 1864.
DENFELD, GEORGE W.
Cadet Midshipman, 22 September, 1873. Graduated 18 June. 1879. Ensign, 22 April, 1881. Lieutenant, Junior Grade, 4 September, 1887. Lieutenant. 27 April, 1893. Lieutenant-Commander, 1 July, 1900.
DENHART, JOHN.
Acting Third Assistant Engineer, 13 April, 1864. Honorably discharged 6 August, 1865.
DENIG, ROBERT G.
Cadet Engineer. 1 October, 1871. Graduated 31 May, 1873. Assistant Engineer, 23 January, 1874. Passed Assistant Engineer, 25 March. 1880. Chief Engineer, 29 January, 1895. Rank changed to Lieutenant-Commander, 3 March, 1899.
DENIGHT, SAMUEL J.
Mate, 1 October, 1862. Acting Ensign, 22 April, 1863. Resigned 28 April, 1865.
DENIS, EMILE.
Acting Ensign, 17 December, 1862. Resigned 7 September, 1863.
DENISON, CHARLES H.
Acting Paymaster. Dismissed 30 July, 1862.
DENISON, WILLIAM E.
Acting Master, 7 February, 1862. Appointment revoked (sick) 13 February, 1863. Acting Master, 22 June, 1863. Acting Volunteer Lieutenant, recommendation of commanding officer, 2 June, 1864. Honorably discharged 26 September, 1865.
DENMAN, JOSEPH A.
Acting Ensign. 10 September, 1862. Died at Key West, Florida, 4 July, 1864.
DENNETT, ADOLPHUS.
Acting Ensign, 22 August, 1862. Honorably discharged 25 November, 1865.
DENNETT, JOHN.
Mate, 28 January, 1863. Acting Ensign, 2 April, 1864. Honorably discharged 20 November, 1865. Acting Ensign, 12 September, 1866. Mustered out 2 October, 1868.

GENERAL NAVY REGISTER.

DENNETT, JOSEPH G.
Acting Third Assistant Engineer, 12 November, 1862. Acting Second Assistant Engineer, 25 May, 1864. Honorably discharged 9 October, 1866.
DENNETT, ROBERT O.
Acting Third Assistant Engineer, 17 December, 1862. Acting Second Assistant Engineer, 1 February, 1864. Appointment revoked (sick) 10 October, 1864.
DENNING, ROTHENS.
Mate, 14 May, 1864. Honorably discharged 1 December, 1865.
DENNIS, DANIEL.
Mate, 23 May, 1864. Discharged 7 December, 1864.
DENNIS, GEORGE H.
Acting Second Assistant Engineer, 20 December, 1861. Appointment revoked (sick) 5 August, 1862.
DENNIS, JOHN, Jr.
Midshipman, 18 June, 1812. Died in 1813.
DENNIS, JOHN B.
Assistant Surgeon, 20 May, 1898.
DENNIS, JOHN S.
Acting Master, 31 August, 1861. Died on Huntress, Mississippi River, 27 February, 1865.
DENNISON, ERASMUS.
Midshipman, 26 September, 1863. Graduated 6 June, 1867. Ensign, 18 December, 1868. Master, 21 March, 1870. Died 18 April, 1873.
DENNISON, HENRY.
Purser, 25 April, 1812. Died 15 March, 1822.
DENNISON, ROBERT.
Chaplain, 28 May, 1804. Last appearance on Records of Navy Department. Furloughed.
DENNISTON, G. V.
Midshipman, 10 March, 1840. Passed Midshipman, 11 July, 1846. Master, 1 March, 1855. Lieutenant, 14 September, 1855. Died 17 February, 1858.
DENNISTON, HENRY M.
Assistant Paymaster, 9 September, 1861. Paymaster, 14 April, 1862. Pay Inspector, 19 August, 1876. Pay Director, 31 July, 1884.
DENNY, ARTHUR B.
Lieutenant (Spanish-American War), 21 May, 1898. Honorably discharged 17 September, 1898.
DENNY, EBEN D.
Midshipman, 17 September, 1841. Passed Midshipman, 10 August, 1847. Died 2 February, 1853.
DENNY, JOHN.
Surgeon's Mate, 17 August, 1826. Died 19 September, 1829.
DENMORE, JOHN H.
Acting Second Assistant Engineer, 19 December, 1863. Honorably discharged 12 July, 1865.
DENSMORE, CHARLES W.
Acting Warrant Machinist, 6 July, 1899.
DENSON, JOHN.
Acting Ensign and Pilot, 28 October, 1864. Honorably discharged 4 December, 1865.
DENT, BLAINE C.
Cadet Midshipman, 5 June, 1873. Graduated 4 June, 1880. Ensign, Junior Grade, 3 March, 1883. Ensign, 26 June, 1884. Retired List, 4 June, 1890.
DENT, HENRY A.
Assistant Paymaster, 15 March, 1894. Passed Assistant Paymaster, 10 April, 1895. Paymaster, 7 May, 1899.
DENT, JOHN H.
Midshipman, 16 March, 1798. Lieutenant, 11 July, 1799. Commander, 5 September, 1804. Captain, 29 December, 1811. Died 31 July, 1823.
DENTON, ANTHONY Y.
Midshipman, 4 July, 1805. Resigned 13 October, 1807.
DENTON, GEORGE L.
Acting First Assistant Engineer, 25 July, 1863. Dismissed 31 August, 1863.
DENTON, LEONARD.
Acting Ensign, 25 January, 1865. Honorably discharged 5 October, 1865.
DEPASS, JOSEPH.
Midshipman, 1 January, 1808. Resigned 28 November, 1808.
DEPUE, ABRAHAM.
Acting Assistant Paymaster, 1 June, 1863. Discharged 24 December, 1865.
DERBY, ALBIGENCE N.
Acting Second Assistant Engineer, 1 October, 1862. Resigned 16 January, 1863.
DERBY, CHARLES P.
Midshipman, 9 November, 1813. Died in March, 1821.
DERBY, RICHARD.
Captain, 22 February, 1799. Resigned 12 May, 1801.
DERBY, RICHARD, Jr.
Assistant Surgeon, 3 May, 1815. Died 20 December, 1815.
DERBY, RICHARD C.
Midshipman, 20 September, 1864. Graduated 2 June, 1868. Ensign, 19 April, 1869. Master, 12 July, 1870. Lieutenant, 27 October, 1872. Resigned 26 August, 1884.
DEREAMER, GEORGE.
Acting Second Assistant Engineer, 13 August, 1861. Honorably discharged 13 January, 1866.
DERR, EZRA Z.
Assistant Surgeon, 3 March, 1873. Passed Assistant Surgeon, 18 April, 1877. Surgeon, 15 September, 1888. Medical Inspector, 7 February, 1900.

DE SAMES, CHARLES.
  Acting Master, 6 December, 1861. Appointment revoked 3 May, 1862.
DE SANNO, WALTER.
  Acting Third Assistant Engineer, 16 September, 1863. Dishonorably discharged 25 May, 1864.
DE SANNO, WILLIAM P.
  Third Assistant Engineer, 21 May, 1857. Second Assistant Engineer, 2 August, 1859. First Assistant Engineer, 1 July, 1861. Dismissed 19 March, 1862.
DE SAUSURE, D. L.
  Midshipman, 9 November, 1813. Resigned 14 June, 1820.
DESLONDE, ADRIAN.
  Midshipman, 27 October, 1841. Resigned 14 June, 1849.
DESMOND, HARRY.
  Acting Warrant Machinist, 29 January, 1900.
DETURBE, JOHN.
  Acting Second Assistant Engineer, 2 December, 1864. Honorably discharged 28 August, 1865. Acting Second Assistant Engineer. Appointment revoked 12 February, 1867.
DEUNGER, ALBERT.
  Lieutenant (Spanish-American War), 25 May, 1898. Honorably discharged 16 September, 1898.
DE VALIN, CHARLES E.
  Third Assistant Engineer, 20 September, 1858. Second Assistant Engineer, 17 January, 1861. First Assistant Engineer, 17 March, 1863. Chief Engineer, 21 March, 1870. Retired List, 11 April, 1892. Died 16 April, 1892.
DEVALIN, CHARLES M.
  Assistant Surgeon, 27 January, 1892. Passed Assistant Surgeon, 27 January, 1895.
DEVANS, THOMAS.
  Midshipman, 2 March, 1799. Last appearance on Records of Navy Department, 1 April, 1799. Resigned.
DE VAUX, MAX A.
  Midshipman, 1 September, 1811. Resigned 12 October, 1818.
DEVENS, EDWARD F.
  Acting Master, 11 June, 1861. Acting Volunteer Lieutenant, at capture of Aries, 25 May, 1863. Acting Volunteer Lieutenant-Commander, 7 February, 1865. Honorably discharged 19 November, 1866.
DEVEREAUX, JOHN.
  Mate, 25 February, 1864. Died at Naval Hospital, New Orleans, 25 March, 1865.
DEVERS, WILLIAM.
  Gunner, date not known. Resigned October, 1820.
DEVERSNEY, BIAL.
  Acting Third Assistant Engineer, 4 January, 1865. Honorably discharged 1 November, 1865.
DEVEZIN, J. O.
  Midshipman, 16 October, 1824. Resigned 22 November, 1827.
DEVINE, GEORGE.
  Acting Second Assistant Engineer, 21 November, 1863. Acting Second Assistant Engineer, 19 October, 1864. Honorably discharged 26 July, 1865.
DEVINE, THOMAS.
  Mate, 6 January, 1862. Acting Ensign, 28 February, 1863. Honorably discharged 30 September, 1865.
DEVINE, THOMAS H.
  Mate, 18 September, 1863. Resigned 21 June, 1865.
DEVLAN, WILLIAM T.
  (Appointed in Volunteer Service 19 March, 1863.) Gunner, 30 July, 1870. Retired List, 10 December, 1883.
DEVLIN, JAMES.
  Acting Third Assistant Engineer, 2 March, 1865. Honorably discharged 6 August, 1865.
DEVLIN, WILLIAM T.
  Acting Gunner, 19 March, 1863. Honorably discharged 1 March, 1866.
DEVOE, JAMES B.
  Acting Ensign, 22 March, 1864. Acting Master, 28 September, 1864. Honorably discharged 22 December, 1865.
DEWEESE, CORNELIUS. JR.
  Mate, 26 November, 1863. Honorably discharged 23 November, 1865.
DEWEY, EPHRAIM H.
  Mate, 17 September, 1861. Acting Ensign, 1 May, 1863. Resigned 11 December, 1863.
DEWEY, GEORGE.
  Acting Midshipman, 23 September, 1854. Midshipman, 11 June, 1858. Passed Midshipman, 28 January, 1861. Master, 28 February, 1861. Lieutenant, 19 April, 1861. Lieutenant-Commander, 3 March, 1865. Commander, 13 April, 1872. Captain, 27 September, 1884. Commodore, 28 February, 1896. Rear-Admiral, 11 May, 1898. Admiral, 2 March, 1899.
DEWEY, ORVILLE.
  Chaplain, 5 February, 1851. Resigned 9 February, 1853.
DEWEY, THEODORE G.
  Cadet Midshipman, 25 June, 1875. Graduated 22 June, 1882. Ensign, Junior Grade, 3 March, 1883. Ensign, 26 June, 1884. Lieutenant. Junior Grade, 27 September, 1893. Lieutenant, 19 June, 1897.
DEWEY, THOMAS.
  Gunner, 14 January, 1840. Died 16 November, 1849.
DEWHURST, GEORGE.
  Acting Master, 22 November, 1861. Resigned 8 August, 1865.

GENERAL NAVY REGISTER. 161

DEWING, PAUL F.
　Acting Assistant Paymaster, 31 August, 1864. Discharged 8 November, 1865.
DeWITT, AUGUSTUS.
　Acting Third Assistant Engineer, 3 September, 1864. Appointment revoked (sick) 20 February, 1865.
DeWITT, J. B.
　Surgeon's Mate, 30 June, 1823. Resigned 15 September, 1823.
DeWITT, WALTER A.
　Mate, 2 December, 1863. Acting Ensign, 16 November, 1864. Honorably discharged 14 February, 1866.
DEWLING, ISAIAH.
　Acting Assistant Surgeon, 24 May, 1864. Assistant Surgeon, Retired List, 30 June, 1879. Died 28 May, 1894.
DeWOLF, F. L.
　Midshipman, 30 November, 1814. Resigned 30 March, 1816.
DeWOLF, LEON.
　Mate, 3 February, 1865. Died at Mobile Bay, Alabama, 13 April, 1865.
DeWOLF, WILLIAM H.
　Acting Master, 16 November, 1861. Honorably discharged 4 November, 1865.
DEXTER, ADOLPHUS.
　Acting Midshipman, 24 September, 1857. Midshipman, 1 June, 1861. Passed Midshipman. Acting Master, 22 September, 1861. Lieutenant, 16 July, 1862. Resigned 23 November, 1864.
DEXTER, DANIEL S.
　Midshipman, 9 April, 1800. Lieutenant, 13 February, 1807. Commander, 20 December, 1814. Died 10 October, 1818.
DEXTER, E. T.
　Mate, 10 December, 1862. Dismissed 4 April, 1863. Mate, 7 July, 1863. Died 2 October, 1868.
DEXTER, GEORGE H.
　Mate, 14 February, 1863. Acting Ensign, 17 January, 1865. Honorably discharged 28 October, 1865.
DEXTER, HORACE.
　Mate, 18 November, 1862. Acting Ensign, 11 November, 1863. Honorably discharged 25 September, 1865.
DEXTER, J. D.
　Acting Ensign, 1 November, 1862. Resigned 13 April, 1865.
DEXTER, JENNESS K.
　Midshipman, 23 June, 1869. Resigned 13 June, 1871. Lieutenant, Junior Grade (Spanish-American War), 2 July, 1898. Honorably discharged 8 October, 1898.
DEXTER, JOHN.
　Acting Warrant Machinist, 23 August, 1899.
DEXTER, JOHN M.
　Acting Third Assistant Engineer, 24 September, 1862. Acting Second Assistant Engineer, 15 October, 1862. Honorably discharged 11 September, 1865.
DEXTER, RODOLPHUS W.
　Acting Master, 11 November, 1861. Resigned 8 July, 1862.
DEXTER, SUMNER.
　Acting Ensign and Pilot, 12 December, 1864. Honorably discharged 5 August, 1865.
DIAMOND, JASPER H.
　Third Assistant Engineer, 1 July, 1863. Second Assistant Engineer, 25 July, 1866. Dismissed 26 July, 1876.
DIBBLE, GEORGE M.
　Midshipman, 1 March, 1841. Dismissed 15 August, 1849.
DIBBLE, JONAS.
　Carpenter, 16 June, 1838. Retired List, 16 December, 1866. Died 4 February, 1885.
DICHMAN, ERNST J.
　Acting Midshipman, 20 September, 1860. Ensign, 28 May, 1863. Master, 10 November, 1865. Lieutenant, 10 November, 1866. Lieutenant-Commander, 12 March, 1868. Resigned 31 December, 1871.
DICK, EDWARD L.
　Third Assistant Engineer, 20 September, 1858. Dismissed 28 May, 1861.
DICK, JAMES.
　Midshipman, 22 May, 1799. Discharged 3 June, 1801, under Peace Establishment Act.
DICK, JOHN B.
　Acting Second Assistant Engineer, 18 October, 1861. Honorably discharged 24 July, 1866.
DICK, ROBERT B.
　Acting Third Assistant Engineer, 3 April, 1863. Honorably discharged 27 September, 1867. Passed Assistant Engineer (Spanish-American War), 13 July, 1898. Honorably discharged 12 September, 1898.
DICK, THOMAS M.
　Naval Cadet, 5 September, 1891. Assistant Engineer, 1 July, 1897. Rank changed to Ensign, 3 March, 1899. Lieutenant, Junior Grade, 1 July, 1900. Retired List, 17 November, 1900.
DICK, WALTER B.
　Assistant Surgeon, 10 July, 1861. Resigned 28 April, 1864.
DICKASON, JOHN A.
　Carpenter, 13 December, 1825. Drowned 29 September, 1847.
DICKERMAN, C. L.
　Acting Assistant Paymaster, 27 March, 1865. Discharged 11 October, 1865.
DICKERSON, HIEL L.
　Acting Third Assistant Engineer, 28 November, 1863. Resigned 8 June, 1865.

DICKERSON, J. L.
  Mate, 21 July, 1864. Dismissed 6 August, 1864.
DICKEY, ROBERT.
  Sailmaker, 11 June, 1799. Last appearance on Records of Navy Department.
DICKEY, ROBERT.
  Assistant Paymaster, 14 July, 1870. Resigned 31 December, 1873.
DICKEY, WILLIAM E.
  Assistant Engineer (Spanish-American War), 24 June, 1898. Honorably discharged 16 May, 1899.
DICKINS, CURTIS H.
  Chaplain, 11 November, 1898.
DICKINS, FRANCIS W.
  Midshipman, 20 September, 1861. Graduated 22 November, 1864. Ensign, 1 November, 1866. Master, 1 December, 1866. Lieutenant, 12 March, 1868. Lieutenant-Commander, 12 June, 1869. Commander, 23 September, 1885. Captain, 3 July, 1898.
DICKINSON, DANIEL A.
  Acting Assistant Paymaster. 15 May, 1863. Resigned 28 January, 1865.
DICKINSON, DWIGHT.
  Assistant Surgeon, 21 April, 1869. Passed Assistant Surgeon, 6 November, 1872. Surgeon, 6 December, 1879. Medical Inspector, 29 September, 1895. Medical Director, 11 November, 1899.
DICKINSON, HOLLOWELL.
  Boatswain, 18 December, 1862. Retired List, 8 December, 1890. Died 20 June, 1892.
DICKINSON, H. J.
  Midshipman, 26 December, 1815. Resigned 20 October, 1820.
DICKINSON, JOHN R.
  Acting Master, 11 November, 1861. Dismissed 1 November, 1862. Acting Ensign, 27 December, 1862. Acting Master, favorable report of commanding officer, 25 June, 1863. Resigned 29 September, 1863.
DICKINSON, NORMAN P.
  Mate, 13 September, 1862. Resigned 8 May, 1863.
DICKINSON, P.
  Acting Master, 28 October, 1861. Honorably discharged 25 January, 1868.
DICKINSON, S. M.
  Acting Assistant Paymaster, 1861. Resigned 31 October, 1862.
DICKINSON, SOLOMON.
  Purser, 16 January, 1799. Resigned 23 January, 1799.
DICKMAN, CHARLES B.
  Acting Ensign, 18 January, 1864. Honorably discharged 15 August, 1865.
DICKS, JOHN W.
  Acting Master, 26 August, 1861. Resigned (sick) 19 July, 1864.
DICKSON, ERSKINE H.
  Ensign (Spanish-American War), 28 June, 1898. Honorably discharged 8 September, 1898.
DICKSON, JOHN A.
  Carpenter, 13 December, 1825. Drowned 29 September, 1847.
DICKSON, MENZIES.
  Mate, 22 June, 1863. Appointment revoked (sick) 1 September. 1864.
DICKSON, SAMUEL H.
  Assistant Surgeon, 19 March, 1875. Passed Assistant Surgeon, 7 August. 1880. Surgeon, 5 December, 1890.
DICKSON, THOMAS.
  Third Assistant Engineer, 21 May, 1843. Died 12 September, 1847.
DICKSON, THOMAS H.
  Acting Assistant Paymaster, 18 August, 1863. Honorably discharged 12 September, 1865.
DICKSON, WILLIAM.
  Mate, 1 September, 1864. Honorably discharged 9 September, 1865.
DIEFFENBACH, ALBERT C.
  Cadet Engineer, 1 October, 1881. Ensign, 1 July, 1887. Lieutenant, Junior Grade, 29 December, 1895. Lieutenant, 9 December, 1898.
DIEHL, OLIVER.
  Assistant Surgeon, 6 July, 1880. Passed Assistant Surgeon, 6 July, 1883. Surgeon, 20 March, 1896.
DIEHL, SAMUEL W. B.
  Midshipman, 20 September, 1869. Graduated 31 May, 1873. Ensign, 16 July, 1874. Master, 1 November, 1879. Lieutenant, Junior Grade, 3 March, 1883. Lieutenant, 9 January, 1886. Lieutenant-Commander, 3 March, 1899.
DIERMANSE, HENRY P.
  Mate, 3 November, 1864. Honorably discharged 25 April, 1868.
DIGARD, MAURICE.
  Acting Master, 22 January, 1862. Resigned 9 October, 1863. Acting Ensign, 3 March, 1864. Acting Master, 16 August, 1864. Honorably discharged 14 September, 1865.
DIGGINS, DAVID F.
  Gunner, 6 March, 1899.
DIGNON, JAMES H.
  Acting Third Assistant Engineer, 12 February, 1864. Appointment revoked (sick) 31 August, 1864.
DILL, ALBERT F.
  Acting Ensign, 29 December, 1863. Resigned 5 May, 1865.
DILL, ELI.
  Boatswain, 25 June, 1818. Died 19 December, 1831.

GENERAL NAVY REGISTER.

DILL, FRANCIS J.
Mate, 8 January, 1864. Acting Ensign, 2 February, 1865. Resigned 22 May, 1865.
DILL, J. H.
Master, 10 April, 1813. Resigned 23 February, 1821.
DILL, JOSHUA H.
Acting Master, 27 August, 1861. Appointment revoked (sick) 13 June, 1862.
DILLARD, THOMAS.
Surgeon's Mate, 15 November, 1824. Surgeon, 3 January, 1828. Retired 24 January, 1863. Died 1 March, 1870.
DILLAWAY, JAMES H., JR.
Lieutenant (Spanish-American War), 21 May, 1898. Honorably discharged 8 September, 1898.
DILLINGHAM, ALBERT C.
Midshipman, 31 July, 1865. Graduated 7 June, 1870. Ensign, 13 July, 1871. Master, 4 June, 1874. Lieutenant, 14 December, 1880. Lieutenant-Commander, 3 March, 1899.
DILLINGHAM, JAMES L., JR.
Acting Master, 9 July, 1861. Resigned 9 October, 1861.
DILLINGHAM, JOHN.
Acting Master, 24 May, 1861. Resigned 28 December, 1864.
DILLMAN, JARED W.
Acting Assistant Surgeon, 21 March, 1865. Honorably discharged 11 October, 1865. Reappointed 10 December, 1873. Honorably discharged 30 June, 1879.
DILLON, ARTHUR J.
Acting Assistant Paymaster, 11 April, 1863. Died at St. Louis, Missouri, 16 December, 1863.
DILLON, JOHN R. M.
Assistant Surgeon (Spanish-American War), 20 May, 1898. Honorably discharged 19 September, 1898.
DILLON, NICHOLAS.
Acting Third Assistant Engineer, 21 May, 1863. Died at New Orleans, 23 October, 1864.
DILLON, P. R.
Acting Ensign, on Admiral Stribling's Staff, 1 October, 1864. Honorably discharged 29 October, 1865.
DIMAN, HENRY W.
Acting Assistant Paymaster, 14 January, 1862. Resigned 13 August, 1862.
DIMMOCK, CHARLES W., JR.
Mate, 16 August, 1864. Honorably discharged 15 November, 1865.
DIMMOCK, THOMAS.
Midshipman, 4 March, 1823. Resigned 1 August, 1827.
DIMOCK, MARTIAL C.
Midshipman, 31 July, 1866. Graduated 7 June, 1870. Ensign, 13 July, 1872. Master, 1 January, 1875. Resigned 23 December, 1876.
DIMOCK, WILLIAM D. W.
Ensign (Spanish-American War), 30 April, 1898. Honorably discharged 9 September, 1898.
DIMON, EDWARD M.
Mate, 9 September, 1862. Acting Ensign, 5 July, 1863. Honorably discharged 5 August, 1868.
DIMON, THEODORE.
Assistant Engineer (Spanish-American War), 3 June, 1898. Honorably discharged 31 October, 1898.
DINGER, HENRY C.
Naval Cadet, 19 May, 1894. Ensign, 4 April, 1900.
DINSMORE, JAY.
Third Assistant Engineer, 16 January, 1863. Resigned 28 May, 1864.
DINSMORE, JOHN H.
(See Densmore.)
DINSMORE, M. D. L.
Acting Third Assistant Engineer, 4 December, 1863. Honorably discharged 23 August, 1865.
DINSMORE, ROBERT.
Acting Ensign, 17 December, 1863. Honorably discharged 1 November, 1868.
DINSMOOR, SILAS.
Purser, 31 May, 1800. Discharged 8 July, 1801, under Peace Establishment Act.
DIRHAM, EDWARD W.
Mate, 29 March, 1865. Honorably discharged 21 October, 1865.
DISERENS, ALBERT D.
Mate, 11 January, 1863. Acting Ensign, 12 February, 1864. Honorably discharged 20 October, 1865.
DISERENS, CHARLES M.
Mate, 24 January, 1863. Appointment revoked (sick) 19 March, 1863. Mate, 25 April, 1864. Honorably discharged 20 September, 1865.
DISMUKES, DOCTOR E.
Naval Cadet, 22 May, 1886. Assistant Engineer, 1 July, 1892. Passed Assistant Engineer, 1 May, 1897. Rank changed to Lieutenant, Junior Grade, 3 March, 1899. Lieutenant, 1 July, 1899.
DISNEY, EDWARD V.
Gunner, 26 April, 1839. Dismissed 6 March, 1840.
DISNEY, GEORGE.
Acting Third Assistant Engineer, 17 December, 1863. Died on Ascutney, 11 January, 1868.
DISSTON, SAMUEL.
Acting Third Assistant Engineer, 7 September, 1864. Resigned 18 May, 1865.

DITTRICH, OTTO C.
 Acting Warrant Machinist, 23 August, 1899.
DIVINE, THOMAS.
 Acting Second Assistant Engineer, 26 November, 1861. Acting First Assistant Engineer, 12 November, 1863. Honorably discharged 9 October, 1865.
DIX, JOHN.
 Assistant Surgeon, 24 July, 1813. Surgeon, 27 March, 1818. Died 16 April, 1823.
DIXON, ALBERT F.
 Second Assistant Engineer, 29 October, 1870. Passed Assistant Engineer, 4 November, 1877. Chief Engineer, 13 July, 1894. Rank changed to Lieutenant-Commander, 3 March, 1899.
DIXON, FRANCIS.
 Gunner, date not known. Last appearance on Records of Navy Department.
DIXON, HIRAM.
 Lieutenant, Junior Grade (Spanish-American War), 21 April, 1898. Honorably discharged 2 September, 1898.
DIXON, HIRAM L.
 Carpenter, 23 July, 1861. Warranted 11 December, 1861. Died at Quarantine, New York, on board Hospital Ship, 26 June, 1869 (yellow fever).
DIXON, JOHN A.
 Carpenter, 27 March, 1857. Retired List, 30 June, 1885. Died 27 February, 1888.
DIXON, ROBERT.
 Boatswain, 5 February, 1842. Died 5 April, 1875.
DIXON, WILLIAM S.
 Assistant Surgeon, 27 January, 1871. Passed Assistant Surgeon, 14 January, 1875. Surgeon, 19 June, 1884. Medical Inspector, 23 January, 1898.
DOAN, THOMAS C.
 Acting Assistant Paymaster, 17 February, 1863. Discharged 5 February, 1866.
DOAN, WILLIAM.
 Acting Second Assistant Engineer, 29 November, 1862. Resigned 22 September, 1863.
DOANE, C. C.
 Mate. Dismissed 31 July, 1862.
DOANE, GEORGE B.
 Assistant Surgeon, 10 December, 1814. Resigned 5 January, 1820.
DOANE, JOHN.
 Master, 15 July, 1812. Discharged 3 November, 1814.
DOANE, WILLIAM H.
 Acting Assistant Paymaster, 18 July, 1863. Discharged 18 December, 1865.
DOBBIN, JOHN V.
 Purser, 9 February, 1856. Resigned 17 August, 1857.
DOBBINS, DANIEL.
 Master, 16 September, 1812. Resigned 5 June, 1826.
DOBBINS, JAMES H.
 Midshipman, 18 June, 1812. Last appearance on Records of Navy Department, 21 June, 1815.
DOBBINS, WILLIAM E.
 Assistant Engineer (Spanish-American War), 12 May, 1898. Honorably discharged 26 September, 1898.
DOBBS, FREDERICK A.
 Third Assistant Engineer, 11 April, 1859. Died 29 April, 1862.
DOBBS, THOMAS.
 Acting Third Assistant Engineer, 22 June, 1863. Acting Second Assistant Engineer, 9 February, 1864. Acting First Assistant Engineer, 8 March, 1865. Honorably discharged 21 November, 1867.
DOBBS, WILLIAM H.
 Acting Second Assistant Engineer, 18 July, 1862. Acting First Assistant Engineer, 22 November, 1862. Honorably discharged 5 December, 1865.
DOBELL, WILLIAM H.
 Mate, 31 December, 1863. Honorably discharged 1 November, 1865.
DOBSON, WILLIAM S.
 Acting Third Assistant Engineer, 22 August, 1864. Appointment revoked (sick) 31 January, 1865.
DOCKRAY, WILLIAM P.
 Acting Master, 21 September, 1861. Resigned 10 November, 1863.
DOD, DANIEL.
 Acting Third Assistant Engineer, 20 July, 1863. Acting Second Assistant Engineer, 9 June, 1864. Honorably discharged 28 October, 1865.
DOD, STEPHEN.
 Midshipman, 2 February, 1829. Passed Midshipman, 4 June, 1836. Lieutenant, 8 September, 1841. Died 19 April, 1845.
DODD, ARTHUR W.
 Cadet Midshipman, 10 June, 1873. Graduated 18 June, 1879. Ensign, 28 March, 1881. Lieutenant, Junior Grade, 25 August, 1887. Lieutenant, 25 February, 1893. Lieutenant-Commander, 1 July, 1900.
DODD, EDWIN H.
 Naval Cadet, 5 September, 1896. Graduated 30 June, 1900.
DODD, JAMES.
 Acting Third Assistant Engineer 21 March, 1862. Appointment revoked (sick) 24 July, 1863.
DODD, M. M.
 Carpenter, 18 June. 1845. Died 9 March, 1859.
DODD, ROBERT J.
 Surgeon's Mate, 26 May, 1826. Surgeon, 4 April, 1831. Retired 30 April, 1861. Medical Director, on Retired List, 3 March, 1871. Died 3 February, 1876.

GENERAL NAVY REGISTER.

DODD, WILLARD L.
Naval Cadet, 28 September, 1882. Ensign, 1 July, 1888. Dismissed 30 March, 1895.
DODDRIDGE, JOHN S.
Naval Cadet, 7 September, 1889. Ensign, 1 July, 1895. Lieutenant, Junior Grade, 3 March, 1899.
DODDS, GEORGE D.
Midshipman, 30 November, 1814. Resigned 10 November, 1822.
DODGE, ALVAN.
Acting Assistant Surgeon, 21 March, 1865. Honorably discharged 11 October, 1865.
DODGE, BILLY.
Master, 3 July, 1813. Last appearance on Records of Navy Department, 7 August, 1813.
DODGE, EDWARD J.
Midshipman, 18 January, 1815. Resigned 23 November, 1815.
DODGE, EDW. R.
Assistant Surgeon, 24 January, 1862. Passed Assistant Surgeon, 25 September, 1865. Surgeon, 5 September, 1869. Died 29 March, 1871.
DODGE, GEORGE H., Jr.
Mate, 7 August, 1862. Acting Ensign, 10 July, 1863. Honorably discharged 19 September, 1865.
DODGE, GEORGE P.
Midshipman, 1 October, 1850. Dismissed 12 June, 1851.
DODGE, HENRY W.
Acting Ensign, 5 August, 1862. Dismissed 26 November, 1862.
DODGE, JAMES.
Assistant Surgeon, 29 August, 1799. Surgeon, 11 September, 1800. Discharged 4 August, 1801, under Peace Establishment Act.
DODGE, JAMES.
Surgeon, 27 November, 1804. Last appearance on Records of Navy Department.
DODGE, OMENZO G.
Cadet Midshipman, 6 June, 1873. Graduated 18 June, 1879. Ensign, 25 March, 1880. Lieutenant, Junior Grade, 13 December, 1886. Lieutenant, 19 June, 1892. Resigned 26 June, 1892. Professor of Mathematics, 29 June, 1892.
DODGE, RICHARD D.
Third Assistant Engineer, 22 July, 1862. Second Assistant Engineer, 15 February, 1864. Resigned 1 June, 1868.
DODGE, RICHARD F.
Acting Ensign, 11 June, 1864. Honorably discharged 3 November, 1865.
DODGE, THOMAS W.
Mate, 16 August, 1861. Acting Master, 18 June, 1862. Honorably discharged 14 September, 1865.- Acting Master, 19 December, 1866. Mustered out 22 April, 1869.
DODSON, WILLIAM.
Master, date not known. Discharged 15 April, 1815.
DODSWORTH, JOHN.
Midshipman, 15 November, 1809. Resigned 30 July, 1810.
DOGGETT, SAMUEL.
Gunner, 21 September, 1821. Last appearance on Records of Navy Department, 1 October, 1822.
DOHERTY, JOHN.
Acting Third Assistant Engineer, 6 February, 1865. Honorably discharged 13 February, 1868.
DOHERTY, PHILIP.
Gunner, 10 April, 1899.
DOHERTY, WILLIAM H.
Assistant Paymaster, 20 May, 1898. Passed Paymaster, 12 November, 1899.
DOHRMAN, HORATIO G.
Ensign (Spanish-American War), 30 June, 1898. Honorably discharged 24 October, 1898.
DOHRNEAN, JAMES C.
Acting Third Assistant Engineer, 9 June, 1863. Resigned 24 October, 1863.
DOIG, ALEXANDER.
Acting First Assistant Engineer, 25 November, 1861. Resigned 6 June, 1863.
DOIG, GEORGE.
Acting Assistant Surgeon, 5 March, 1864. Resigned 1 August, 1865.
DOLAN, ANDREW.
Acting Second Assistant Engineer, 9 May, 1864. Honorably discharged 20 November, 1867.
DOLEN, GEORGE B.
Acting Second Assistant Engineer, 8 June, 1864. Honorably discharged 20 June, 1865.
DOLLEY, REUBEN.
Mate, 7 January, 1862. Appointment revoked 5 December, 1862.
DOLLIVER, GEORGE C.
Mate. Killed in action, Diana, 28 March, 1863.
DOLLIVER, WILLIAM F.
Acting Ensign, 2 December, 1863. Honorably discharged 10 January, 1866.
DOMBAUGH, HARRY M.
Cadet Midshipman, 6 June, 1872. Graduated 18 June, 1877. Ensign, 12 October, 1881. Lieutenant, Junior Grade, 15 January, 1889. Lieutenant, 4 July, 1893.
DOMETT, GEORGE W.
Acting Master, 12 August, 1861. Resigned 21 April, 1864.
DOMINIC, RICHARD.
Midshipman, 30 April, 1814. Died 10 June, 1822.

GENERAL NAVY REGISTER.

DOMINY, CYRENNIUS.
Acting Volunteer Lieutenant, gallant conduct, 1 August, 1862. Resigned 20 April, 1865.
DONAHUE, HENRY W.
Acting Third Assistant Engineer, 12 October, 1861. Died 8 March, 1862.
DONALD, JAMES.
Gunner, 5 May, 1897.
DONALDSON, ANDREW.
Mate, 19 December, 1863. Honorably discharged 6 August, 1865.
DONALDSON, A. B.
Acting Master's Mate, 7 September, 1864.
DONALDSON, EDWARD.
Midshipman, 21 July, 1835. Passed Midshipman, 22 June, 1841. Master, 20 May, 1847. Lieutenant, 23 October, 1847. Commander, 16 July, 1862. Captain, 25 July, 1866. Commodore, 28 September, 1871. Rear-Admiral, 21 September, 1876. Retired List, 29 September, 1876. Died 15 May, 1889.
DONALDSON, JOHN.
Acting Third Assistant Engineer, 24 December, 1864. Honorably discharged 30 October, 1865.
DONALDSON, OLIVER.
Acting Ensign, 1 October, 1862. Honorably discharged 1 January, 1866.
DONELY, STEPHEN.
Acting Gunner, 10 March, 1900.
DONNEGAN, AUGUSTUS F.
Acting Third Assistant Engineer, 1 October, 1864. Honorably discharged 2 June, 1868.
DONNELL, HARRY H.
Ensign (Spanish-American War), 28 May, 1898. Honorably discharged 27 September, 1898.
DONNELL, RUFUS R.
Acting Ensign, 17 September, 1862. Honorably discharged 17 August, 1865.
DONNELLY, ALVIN.
Acting Third Assistant Engineer, 4 September, 1863. Honorably discharged 2 January, 1866.
DONNELLY, JOHN.
Mate, 3 April, 1865. Honorably discharged 10 October, 1868.
DONNELLY, PATRICK.
Acting Ensign, 9 April, 1863. Acting Master, 22 January, 1864. Honorably discharged 25 November, 1865.
DONOHUE, JOHN J.
Acting Third Assistant Engineer, 24 July, 1863. Honorably discharged 7 August, 1865.
DONOR, WILLIAM S.
Acting Assistant Surgeon, 23 February, 1864. Honorably discharged 10 October, 1865.
DONOVAN, HENRY.
Acting Master's Mate, 30 May, 1861. Discharged 15 August, 1861.
DONOVAN, MICHAEL.
Mate, 14 December, 1862. Deserted 12 October, 1863.
DOOLEY, EDWARD.
Mate, 13 February, 1863. Dismissed 25 August, 1863. Mate, 29 October, 1863. Honorably discharged 19 September, 1865. Mate, 18 December, 1865. Appointment revoked 23 November, 1866. Mate, 3 January, 1867. Mustered out 28 September, 1867.
DORAN, EDWARD C.
Purser, 15 September, 1845. Pay Director, 3 March, 1871. Retired List, 25 December, 1882. Died 30 October, 1883.
DORAN JAMES S.
Acting Third Assistant Engineer, 1 July, 1861. Acting Second Assistant Engineer, 23 October, 1862. Resigned 10 June, 1863.
DORAN, PETER B.
Mate, 6 December, 1862. Dismissed 19 June. 1863.
DORAN, RICHARD.
Acting Third Assistant Engineer, 27 November, 1863. Honorably discharged 25 July, 1865.
DORAN, THOMAS.
Acting Master's Mate, 29 January, 1865. Discharged 26 April, 1866.
DOREY, BENJAMIN R.
Acting Master and Pilot, 1 September, 1864. Appointment revoked 31 March, 1865.
DORGAN, ANDREW.
Master, 8 July, 1812. Resigned 15 April, 1813.
DORGAN, ANDREW.
Master, 11 September, 1813. Last appearance on Records of Navy Department, 5 October, 1813.
D'ORLEANS, PIERRE.
Honorary appointment of Acting Ensign, 28 May, 1863. Resigned 30 May, 1864.
DORN, EDWARD J.
Midshipman, 21 September, 1870. Graduated 1 June, 1874. Ensign, 17 July, 1875. Master, 30 August, 1881. Lieutenant, Junior Grade. 3 March, 1883. Lieutenant, 30 June, 1887. Lieutenant-Commander, 3 March, 1899.
DORNIN, THOMAS A.
Midshipman, 2 May, 1815. Lieutenant, 13 January, 1825. Commander, 8 September, 1841. Captain, 14 September, 1855. Commodore, on Retired List, 16 July, 1862. Died 22 April, 1874.

GENERAL NAVY REGISTER.

DORNIN, THOMAS LARDNER.
Acting Midshipman, 22 September, 1856. Midshipman, 15 June, 1860. Dismissed 4 June, 1861.

DORR, HERMAN.
Acting Assistant Paymaster, 11 July, 1864. Resigned (sick) 15 March, 1865.

DORR, JOSEPH.
Midshipman, 11 September, 1799. Discharged 1 May, 1801, under Peace Establishment Act.

DORRANCE, CHARLES B.
Acting Ensign, 7 November, 1862. Died on the Sebago, 9 October, 1864.

DORRANCE, GEORGE W.
Chaplain, 2 January, 1860. Retired List, 14 February, 1873. Died 11 December, 1888.

DORY, JOHN G.
Acting Master, 24 September, 1861. Appointment revoked (sick) 11 July, 1862.

DORSEY, GREENBERG.
Acting Third Assistant Engineer, 11 October, 1864. Honorably discharged 6 September, 1865.

DORSEY, HILL.
Midshipman, 15 November, 1810. Resigned 25 April, 1811.

DORSEY, HILL.
Midshipman, 9 September, 1811. Resigned 2 May, 1812.

DORSEY, JOHN.
Midshipman, 28 April, 1801. Killed in action 7 August, 1804.

DORSEY, JOHN W.
Assistant Surgeon. 16 July, 1803. Resigned 9 July, 1807.

DORSEY, LAWRENCE A.
(To Command on Galley.) Captain, 12 September, 1798. Died 23 January, 1800.

DORSEY, ROBERT.
Midshipman, 5 February, 1800. Discharged 6 August, 1801, under Peace Establishment Act.

DORTON, HENRY F.
Mate, 10 March, 1863. Acting Ensign, 19 November. 1863. Honorably discharged 20 September, 1865. Acting Ensign, 11 September, 1867. Mustered out 23 September, 1868.

DOTEN, CLARK W.
Acting Second Assistant Engineer, 5 May, 1863. Acting First Assistant Engineer, 19 May, 1864. Honorably discharged 24 September, 1865.

DOTY, ALBERT J.
Acting Third Assistant Engineer, 11 August, 1863. Acting Second Assistant Engineer, 2 June, 1865. Honorably discharged 19 February, 1866. Acting Second Assistant Engineer, 25 April, 1866. Mustered out 27 August, 1867.

DOTY, GEORGE W.
Midshipman, 4 January, 1833. Passed Midshipman, 8 July, 1839. Lieutenant, 13 May, 1845. Commander, Retired List, 16 July, 1862. Captain on Retired List, 4 April, 1867. Died 17 April, 1869.

DOTY, STEPHEN B.
Acting Assistant Surgeon, 31 October, 1864. Honorably discharged 22 January, 1866.

DOTY, WEBSTER.
Midshipman, 27 July, 1864. Graduated 2 June, 1868. Ensign. 19 April, 1869. Master, 12 July, 1870. Lieutenant, 27 March, 1873. Retired List 28 February, 1887.

DOUGHERTY, CHARLES.
Acting First Assistant Engineer, 2 August, 1864. Honorably discharged 30 December, 1865.

DOUGHERTY, GEORGE W.
Acting Assistant Paymaster, 18 September, 1863. Honorably discharged 1 January, 1866.

DOUGHERTY, JOHN A.
Cadet Midshipman, 2 June, 1874. Graduated 10 June. 1881. Ensign, Junior Grade, 3 March, 1883. Ensign, 26 June, 1884. Lieutenant, Junior Grade, 5 November, 1891. Lieutenant, 5 January, 1896.

DOUGHERTY, JOHN C.
Acting Third Assistant Engineer, 23 March, 1865. Honorably discharged 7 September, 1865.

DOUGHERTY, WILLIAM J.
Acting Third Assistant Engineer, 2 January, 1864. Honorably discharged 5 July, 1865.

DOUGHERTY, WILLIAM J.
Mate, 17 February, 1870. Appointment revoked 20 July, 1871.

DOUGHTY, EZRA T.
Midshipman, 3 May, 1824. Passed Midshipman, 4 June, 1831. Lieutenant, 3 March, 1835. Resigned 18 February, 1839.

DOUGHTY, G. MORRIS.
Carpenter, 10 June. 1861. Warranted 26 December, 1861. Resigned 22 October, 1863.

DOUGHTY, JOHN H.
Acting Third Assistant Engineer, 16 December, 1863. Honorably discharged 1 October, 1865.

DOUGHTY, THOMAS.
Acting First Assistant Engineer, 8 July, 1862. Acting Chief Engineer, 13 December, 1862. Resigned 22 May, 1865.

DOUGHTY, WILLIAM.
Naval Constructor, 8 February, 1813. Resigned, date not known.

DOUGLAS, RICHARD S.
    Naval Cadet, 19 May, 1888. Resigned 15 May, 1889. Naval Cadet, 3 June, 1889. Ensign, 1 July, 1895. Lieutenant, Junior Grade, 3 March, 1899.
DOUGLASS, ALEXANDER D.
    Acting First Assistant Engineer, 10 September, 1861. Resigned 11 November, 1862.
DOUGLASS, AUGUSTUS C.
    Midshipman, 11 January, 1817. Last appearance on Records of Navy Department, 1818.
DOUGLASS, DANIEL.
    Gunner, 26 May, 1845. Died 17 June, 1851.
DOUGLASS, GEORGE B.
    Midshipman, 4 September, 1841. Dismissed 17 August, 1847.
DOUGLASS, GEORGE T.
    Sailmaker, 19 February, 1870. Warranted 29 October, 1870. Retired List, 20 December, 1898.
DOUGLASS, GUSTAVUS.
    Midshipman, 4 July, 1805. Drowned 5 March, 1810.
DOUGLASS, JAMES C.
    Purser, 25 September, 1841. Resigned 24 February, 1853.
DOUGLASS, JOSEPH.
    Sailmaker, 18 March, 1803. Resigned 13 January, 1806.
DOUGLASS, RICHARD H.
    Assistant Paymaster, 31 August, 1861. Paymaster, 24 August, 1862. Died 4 June, 1868.
DOUGLASS, ROBERT.
    Midshipman, 16 January, 1809. Resigned 4 April, 1815.
DOUGLASS, SAMUEL M.
    Midshipman, 7 February, 1799. Discharged 8 June, 1801, under Peace Establishment Act.
DOUGLASS, STEPHEN W.
    Pharmacist, 15 September, 1898.
DOUGLASS, THOMAS.
    Purser, 8 October, 1811. Last appearance on Records of Navy Department.
DOUGLASS, WILLIAM B.
    Midshipman, 30 June, 1837. Resigned 14 February, 1838.
DOUW, JOHN DeP.
    Ensign (Spanish-American War), 14 May, 1898. Honorably discharged 15 August, 1898.
DOVE, BENJAMIN M.
    Midshipman, 1 December, 1826. Passed Midshipman, 10 June, 1833. Lieutenant, 9 December, 1839. Commander, 14 September, 1855. Retired 1 October, 1864. Captain on Retired List, 4 April, 1867. Died 19 November, 1868.
DOVE, GEORGE W. W.
    Third Assistant Engineer, 11 July, 1861. Resigned 10 August, 1863.
DOVE, MARMADUKE.
    Master, 11 November, 1802. Resigned 4 January, 1806.
DOVE, MARMADUKE, Jr.
    Midshipman, 1 January, 1818. Died 14 September, 1821.
DOVE, MARMADUKE.
    Master, 29 August, 1812. Died 3 July, 1846.
DOW, GEORGE S.
    Sailmaker, 2 August, 1844. Resigned 18 September, 1844.
DOW, JOHN.
    Mate, 9 February, 1863. Appointment revoked (sick) 20 May, 1864.
DOW, JOHN C.
    Lieutenant (Spanish-American War), 24 May, 1898. Honorably discharged 7 January, 1899.
DOW, LYMAN.
    Acting Assistant Surgeon, 6 March, 1865. Resigned 10 June, 1865.
DOWDING, GEORGE.
    Acting Third Assistant Engineer, 29 May, 1865. Honorably discharged 5 July, 1866.
DOWLING, JAMES.
    Boatswain, 26 August, 1895.
DOWNE, WILLIAM.
    Midshipman, 15 November, 1809. Resigned 9 February, 1811.
DOWNE, ROMANZO.
    Mate, 22 June, 1864. Died from wounds on New Hampshire, 12 September, 1864.
DOWNES, ALBERT E.
    Midshipman, 1 January, 1818. Lieutenant, 3 March, 1827. Lost in the Grampus, March, 1843.
DOWNES, CHARLES A.
    Acting Assistant Paymaster, 5 March, 1862. Discharged 18 April, 1867.
DOWNES, JAMES.
    Acting Ensign, 11 June, 1863. Appointment revoked 23 January, 1866.
DOWNES, JOHN.
    Midshipman, 1 June, 1802. Lieutenant, 6 March, 1807. Commander, 24 June, 1813. Captain, 5 March, 1817. Died 11 August, 1854.
DOWNES, JOHN, Jr.
    Midshipman, 4 September, 1837. Passed Midshipman, 29 June, 1843. Master, 26 February, 1851. Lieutenant, 30 August, 1851. Commander, 16 July, 1862. Died 21 September, 1865.
DOWNES, JOHN.
    Midshipman, 22 June, 1867. Graduated 6 June, 1871. Ensign, 14 July, 1872. Master, 25 April, 1875. Lieutenant, 11 May, 1882. Retired List, 26 January, 1891.

GENERAL NAVY REGISTER.

DOWNES, SUBAEL.
Master, 9 October, 1799. Discharged 27 October, 1801, under Peace Establishment Act.
DOWNES, SUBAEL.
Master, 12 September, 1813. Died 13 June, 1825.
DOWNES, WILLIAM.
Master, 26 May, 1812. Died 7 August, 1812.
DOWNEY, WILLIAM.
Acting Second Assistant Engineer, 9 June, 1863. Died on Queen City, 1 March, 1864.
DOWNING, M. M.
Midshipman, 8 March, 1814. Died 6 October, 1817.
DOWNING, SAMUEL W.
Midshipman, 1 September, 1811. Lieutenant, 5 March, 1817. Commander, 23 September, 1837. Captain, 27 February, 1847. Cashiered 11 September, 1854.
DOWNS, JOHN H.
Boatswain, 14 May, 1861. Died 29 November, 1864.
DOWSE, EDWARD W.
Midshipman, 17 December, 1810. Lost in the Epervier.
DOWST, FRANK B.
Cadet Engineer, 13 September, 1877. Graduated 10 June, 1881. Honorably discharged 30 June, 1883. Restored to service as an Assistant Engineer, to rank from 1 July, 1883. Resigned 29 July, 1887.
DOYLE, JACOB D.
Assistant Paymaster, 16 June, 1880. Retired List, 28 February, 1889.
DOYLE, JAMES A.
Midshipman, 4 January, 1832. Passed Midshipman, 23 June, 1838. Lieutenant, 29 March, 1844. Reserved List, 13 September, 1855. Restored to Active List, 7 August, 1860. Retired 4 December, 1861. Died 3 August, 1865.
DOYLE, JAMES G.
Cadet Midshipman, 27 June, 1877. Ensign 1 July, 1884. Lieutenant, Junior Grade, 21 July, 1894. Lieutenant, 25 January, 1898.
DOYLE, JAMES H.
Mate, 15 April, 1898. Boatswain, 6 March, 1899.
DOYLE, JOHN.
Midshipman, 17 June, 1823. Resigned 6 September, 1826.
DOYLE, JOHN.
Acting Third Assistant Engineer, 18 October, 1861. Acting Second Assistant Engineer, 9 May, 1864. Honorably discharged 30 September, 1867.
DOYLE, MICHAEL.
Acting Third Assistant Engineer, 26 August, 1864. Resigned (sick) 4 January, 1865.
DOYLE, P.
Acting Ensign, on Special Duty, 7 July, 1863. Dismissed 4 August, 1863.
DOYLE, PATRICK.
Mate, 25 April, 1863. Appointment revoked 22 January, 1866.
DOYLE, PATRICK W.
Boatswain, 30 November, 1894. Resigned, 13 July, 1896.
DOYLE, ROBERT M.
Midshipman, 21 September, 1870. Graduated 21 June, 1875. Ensign, 9 September, 1876. Master, 29 November, 1882. Lieutenant, Junior Grade, 3 March, 1883. Lieutenant, 12 May, 1889. Lieutenant-Commander, 3 March, 1899.
DOYLE, STAFFORD H. R.
Naval Cadet, 20 May, 1896. Graduated 30 June, 1900.
DOYLE, THOMAS.
Midshipman, 4 July, 1805. Last appearance on Records of Navy Department, 1815. Baltimore.
DOYLE, WILLIAM.
Acting First Assistant Engineer, 27 November, 1863. Honorably discharged 5 December, 1865.
DOYLE, WILLIAM A.
Acting Second Assistant Engineer, 1 October, 1862. Resigned 14 November, 1863.
D'OYLEY, N.
Acting Master, 18 July, 1861. Resigned (sick) 23 September, 1863.
DOXEY, BRISCOE.
Master, 20 June, 1812. Died 20 May, 1828.
DOZIER, WILLIAM GAILLARD.
Midshipman, 1 April, 1850. Passed Midshipman, 20 June, 1856. Master, 22 January, 1858. Lieutenant, 19 July, 1859. Resigned 21 December, 1860.
DRAIN, GEORGE.
Mate, 6 January, 1862. Resigned 29 May, 1865.
DRAKE, ANDREW J.
Midshipman, 5 December, 1837. Passed Midshipman, 29 June, 1843. Master, 6 April, 1851. Lieutenant, 16 October, 1851. Commander, 16 July, 1862. Retired List, 12 April, 1867. Died 4 August, 1875.
DRAKE, BENJAMIN.
Midshipman, 22 October, 1849. Dropped 3 September, 1850.
DRAKE, CHARLES D.
Midshipman, 1 April, 1827. Dismissed 30 October, 1829.
DRAKE, EDWIN A.
Midshipman, 26 June, 1834. Resigned 28 January, 1837.
DRAKE, EDWIN E.
Mate, 23 September, 1861. Acting Master, 7 March, 1862. Resigned 6 May, 1862. Reappointed, 21 May, 1862. Appointment revoked (sick) 6 March, 1863. Acting Ensign, 14 July, 1863. Lost in Bainbridge, 21 August, 1863.

GENERAL NAVY REGISTER.

DRAKE, FRANKLIN J.
Midshipman, 23 February, 1863. Graduated 2 June, 1868. Ensign, 19 April, 1869. Master, 12 July, 1870. Lieutenant, 15 November, 1872. Lieutenant-Commander, 1 October, 1893. Commander, 3 March, 1899.
DRAKE, FRANKLIN M.
Mate, 26 November, 1862. Dismissed 11 February, 1863.
DRAKE, JAMES C.
Cadet Midshipman, 24 June, 1875. Graduated 22 June, 1882. Ensign, Junior Grade, 3 March, 1883. Ensign, 26 June, 1884. Lieutenant, Junior Grade, 27 April, 1893. Resigned 15 October, 1895.
DRAKE, NELSON H.
Assistant Surgeon, 26 February, 1876. Passed Assistant Surgeon, 7 August, 1880. Surgeon, 4 March, 1893.
DRAKE, RIVERS.
Mate, 3 September, 1863. Honorably discharged 3 October, 1865.
DRAN, FRANCIS A.
Mate, 13 December, 1864. Honorably discharged 13 May, 1867. Boatswain, 21 December, 1874. Chief Boatswain, 3 March, 1899.
DRAPER, E. L. R.
Acting Assistant Surgeon, 14 April, 1863. Honorably discharged 30 November, 1865.
DRAPER, HORACE T.
Acting Master, 25 January, 1862. Resigned 9 August, 1862. Ensign, 1 October, 1862. Appointment revoked (sick) 14 January, 1865.
DRAPER, LEMUEL J.
Assistant Surgeon, 26 March, 1862. Died 30 August, 1879.
DRAPER, WILLIAM B.
Mate, 21 November, 1862. Resigned 18 September, 1863.
DRAYTON, E. F.
Assistant Surgeon, 28 June, 1852. Dropped 13 May, 1858.
DRAYTON, GLENN.
Midshipman, 20 June, 1806. Lieutenant, 9 January, 1813. Died in September, 1814.
DRAYTON, PERCIVAL.
Midshipman, 1 December, 1827. Passed Midshipman, 10 June, 1833. Lieutenant, 28 February, 1838. Commander, 14 September, 1855. Captain, 16 July, 1862. Died 4 August, 1865.
DRAYTON, PERCIVAL L.
Cadet Midshipman, 10 June, 1874. Graduated 10 June, 1881. Ensign, Junior Grade, 3 March, 1883. Ensign, 26 June, 1884. Resigned 30 April, 1886.
DRAYTON, WILLIAM S.
Midshipman, 16 July, 1832. Passed Midshipman, 23 June, 1838. Lieutenant, 1 April, 1842. Resigned 15 October, 1851.
DRENNAN, MICHAEL C.
Acting Assistant Surgeon, 15 April, 1863. Resigned 18 March, 1865. Reappointed 9 February, 1867. Assistant Surgeon, 30 June, 1868. Passed Assistant Surgeon, 13 June, 1870. Surgeon, 20 April, 1879. Medical Inspector, 28 May, 1895. Medical Director, 16 April, 1899. Retired List, 24 October, 1899.
DRESSLER, AUG.
Acting Master's Mate, 20 March, 1863. Deserted 25 March, 1863.
DRESEL, HERMAN G.
Cadet Midshipman, 22 September, 1876. Graduated 22 June, 1882. Ensign, Junior Grade, 3 March, 1883. Ensign, 26 June, 1884. Lieutenant, Junior Grade, 2 June, 1892. Lieutenant, 4 May, 1896. Died 14 November, 1898.
DREW, CHARLES.
Master, 15 February, 1809. Resigned 4 May, 1810.
DREW, EDWIN O.
Acting Ensign, 1 September, 1864. Honorably discharged 18 August, 1865.
DREW, GEORGE A.
Mate, 9 December, 1861. Acting Ensign, 15 October, 1863. Honorably discharged 27 November, 1865.
DREW, JACOB J.
Mate, 13 February, 1863. Honorably discharged 9 November, 1865.
DREW, JOHN.
Master, 6 December, 1814. Died 19 April, 1823.
DREW, NEHEMIAH.
Master, 20 January, 1809. Resigned 3 February, 1814.
DREW, SAMUEL.
Boatswain, 26 July, 1839. Died 2 February, 1857.
DRIGGS, WILLIAM H.
Midshipman, 21 July, 1865. Graduated 4 June, 1869. Ensign, 12 July, 1870. Master, 27 October, 1872. Lieutenant, 7 March, 1876. Lieutenant-Commander, 16 September, 1897. Retired List, with rank of Commander, 30 June, 1899.
DRIEN, GEORGE C.
Second Assistant Engineer, 1 March, 1871. Retired List, 19 October, 1875.
DRINKWATER, EDWARD.
Acting Ensign and Pilot, 17 May, 1865. Honorably discharged 19 July, 1865.
DRINKWATER, WILLIAM.
Acting Third Assistant Engineer, 12 March, 1863. Honorably discharged 15 November, 1865.
DRIPPS, WILLIAM AUGUSTUS.
Third Assistant Engineer, 25 August, 1862. Second Assistant Engineer, 20 February, 1864. Resigned 29 January, 1867.
DRIVER, REYNOLDS.
Third Assistant Engineer, 26 August, 1859. Second Assistant Engineer, 1 March, 1862. First Assistant Engineer, 1 October, 1863. Died 2 October, 1866.

GENERAL NAVY REGISTER. 171

DRODY, A. G.
  Mate. Dismissed 21 August, 1862.
DRONBERGER, WILLIAM C.
  Acting Warrant Machinist, 23 August, 1899.
DRUMMOND, CHARLES.
  Acting Third Assistant Engineer, 27 June, 1864. Honorably discharged 29 June, 1865.
DRUMMOND, THOMAS M.
  Acting Assistant Surgeon, 13 November, 1862. Honorably discharged 22 January, 1869.
DRURY, HIRAM E.
  Assistant Paymaster, 8 September, 1876. Passed Assistant Paymaster, 9 March, 1881. Paymaster, 25 February, 1892.
DRURY, JOHN T.
  Midshipman, 16 January, 1809. Lieutenant, 9 December, 1814. Lost in the Epervier, in 1815.
DRYBURGH, J. R.
  Second Assistant Engineer, 15 January, 1845. Disrated 28 July, 1845, to Third Assistant Engineer. Dropped 4 November, 1845.
DUANE, ALEXANDER.
  Lieutenant, Junior Grade (Spanish-American War), 9 May, 1898. Honorably discharged 19 August, 1898.
DUANE, MARTIN.
  Acting Assistant Paymaster, 1 August, 1861. Discharged 14 November, 1865.
DUBARRY, E. L.
  Surgeon's Mate, 30 January, 1823. Surgeon, 24 May, 1826. Died 12 July, 1853.
DuBOIS, BARRON P.
  Assistant Paymaster, 23 May, 1895. Passed Assistant Paymaster, 1 November, 1897. Paymaster, 10 July, 1900.
DuBOIS, FRANK L.
  Assistant Surgeon, 22 May, 1862. Passed Assistant Surgeon, 30 October, 1865. Surgeon, 20 February, 1870. Medical Inspector, 15 September, 1888. Died 24 February, 1895.
DUBOIS, JOSEPH S.
  Mate, 19 May, 1864. Appointment revoked (sick) 30 January, 1865.
DuBOIS, THEO. B.
  Acting Master, 28 October, 1861. Acting Volunteer Lieutenant, for gallant conduct in battle, 5 June, 1863. Acting Volunteer Lieutenant-Commander, 26 November, 1864. Honorably discharged 7 February, 1866.
DuBOIS, WILLIAM T.
  Mate, 24 January, 1863. Resigned 25 May, 1863.
DUBOSE, JOHN.
  Midshipman, 10 March, 1799. Discharged 6 August, 1801, under Peace Establishment Act.
DUBOSE, JOHN.
  Midshipman, 1 March, 1803. Resigned 29 April, 1804.
DuBOSE, WILLIAM G.
  Naval Cadet, 6 September, 1893. Graduated. Assistant Naval Constructor, 1 July, 1899.
DUBOSE, WILLIAM R.
  Assistant Surgeon, 16 October, 1875. Passed Assistant Surgeon, 7 August, 1880. Surgeon, 1 November, 1892.
DuBUYS, GASPARD.
  Midshipman, 4 January, 1842. Resigned 6 April, 1843.
DUCKER, GEORGE.
  Acting Third Assistant Engineer, 13 October, 1863. Resigned 12 May, 1865.
DUCKETT, WASHINGTON.
  Carpenter, 9 July, 1861. Resigned 28 May, 1862.
DUCKWORTH, HENRY.
  Acting Third Assistant Engineer, 9 May, 1864. Honorably discharged 11 January, 1866.
DUDLEY, CHARLES G. B.
  Acting Third Assistant Engineer, 14 April, 1865. Honorably discharged 25 September, 1868.
DUDLEY, CHARLES S.
  Acting Third Assistant Engineer, 26 March, 1863. Died at Farmington, Maine, 26 November, 1863.
DUDLEY, DANIEL B.
  Acting Ensign, 1 July, 1864. Honorably discharged 29 October, 1865.
DUDLEY, JAMES A.
  Midshipman, 8 February, 1809. Lieutenant, 24 July, 1813. Died in May, 1817.
DUDLEY, LINTON.
  Master, 25 January, 1809. Last appearance on Records of Navy Department, 6 February, 1809.
DUER, JOHN K.
  Midshipman, 28 December, 1836. Passed Midshipman, 1 July, 1842. Master, 3 November, 1849. Lieutenant, 20 April, 1850. Died 14 June, 1859.
DUER, RUFUS K.
  Acting Midshipman, 23 September, 1857. Midshipman. Passed Midshipman. Master. Lieutenant, 1 August, 1862. Lieutenant-Commander, 25 July, 1866. Died 29 June, 1869.
DUER, WILLIAM A.
  Midshipman, 6 May, 1799. Resigned 27 September, 1800.

DUER, WILLIAM A.
  Mate, 16 April, 1862. Acting Ensign, 15 July, 1863. Honorably discharged 3 January, 1868.
DUFF, JAMES B.
  Mate, 13 December, 1861. Dismissed 5 September, 1862.
DUFFELL, H. L.
  Midshipman, 18 June, 1812. Resigned 20 April, 1813.
DUFFEY, WILLIAM.
  Acting Gunner, 16 June, 1864. Honorably discharged 2 October, 1865.
DUFFIELD, JOHN J.
  Acting Assistant Paymaster, 15 August, 1863. Discharged 21 November, 1865.
DUFFY, HUGH J.
  Boatswain, 30 July, 1897.
DUFFY, JOSEPH J.
  Acting Warrant Machinist, 23 August, 1899.
DUGAN, CORNELIUS.
  Gunner, 30 October, 1860. Chief Gunner, 3 March, 1899.
DUGAN, DANIEL A.
  Ensign (Spanish-American War), 21 May, 1898. Honorably discharged 10 October, 1898.
DUGAS, JOHN LOUIS.
  Midshipman, 8 March, 1799. Discharged 13 August, 1800.
DUKE, JAMES.
  Acting Third Assistant Engineer, 18 May, 1865. Honorably discharged 12 October, 1865.
DUKE, NATHANIEL W.
  Midshipman, 1 May, 1822. Passed Midshipman, 24 May, 1828. Lieutenant, 3 March, 1831. Died 8 July, 1852.
DUKEHART, THOMAS M.
  Third Assistant Engineer, 3 May, 1859. Second Assistant Engineer, 13 May, 1861. First Assistant Engineer, 20 May, 1863. Resigned 9 March, 1871.
DULANY, BLADEN.
  Midshipman, 18 May, 1809. Lieutenant, 9 December, 1814. Commander, 3 March, 1831. Captain, 8 September, 1841. Died in Washington, D. C., 26 December, 1856.
DULANY, DANIEL F.
  Midshipman, 1 April, 1828. Passed Midshipman, 14 June, 1834. Lieutenant, 25 February, 1841. Dropped 13 September, 1855.
DULANY, HUGH.
  Midshipman, 30 November, 1814. Lieutenant, 13 January, 1825. Died 6 January, 1827.
DULANY, JAMES W.
  Midshipman, 1 September, 1811. Died in 1819.
DULEY, WILMOT W.
  Acting Ensign, 17 September, 1862. Honorably discharged 25 November, 1866.
DULIN, EDGAR A.
  Acting Assistant Surgeon, 21 June, 1865. Resigned 5 December, 1867.
DUMONT, EUGENE A.
  Mate, 7 June, 1864. Honorably discharged 25 October, 1865.
DUMONT, FREDERICK K.
  Mate, 24 January, 1863. Resigned 17 July, 1863.
DUMONT, WILLIAM H.
  Acting Ensign, 19 July, 1864. Dismissed 6 December, 1864. Acting Ensign, 21 February, 1865. Resigned 25 May, 1865.
DUMONT, WILLIAM J.
  Acting Gunner, 7 July, 1863. Appointment revoked 21 March, 1865. Ensign, 12 March, 1868. Resigned 11 September, 1868.
DUNBAR, A. D.
  Acting Master, 21 March, 1862. Dismissed 6 December, 1862.
DUNBAR, ARTHUR W.
  Assistant Surgeon, 10 October, 1894. Passed Assistant Surgeon, 10 October, 1897.
DUNBAR, ASAPH.
  Third Assistant Engineer, 19 February, 1863. Second Assistant Engineer, 20 June, 1864. First Assistant Engineer, 6 June, 1868. Retired 31 July, 1869. Died 23 October, 1875.
DUNBAR, CHARLES C.
  Acting Ensign, 23 December, 1864. Lost on the Narcissus, 4 January, 1866.
DUNBAR, FREDERICK.
  Boatswain, 18 November, 1852. Appointment revoked 20 December, 1853.
DUNBAR, GEORGE H.
  Lieutenant, Junior Grade (Spanish-American War), 2 June, 1898. Honorably discharged 2 November, 1898.
DUNBAR, HARRY L.
  Mate, 23 March, 1863. Honorably discharged 31 August, 1865.
DUNBAR, OLIVER.
  Assistant Surgeon, 14 October, 1799. Died 11 July, 1800.
DUNCAN, A. S. E.
  Midshipman, 1 December, 1809. Resigned 10 June, 1811.
DUNCAN, CHARLES D.
  Mate, 7 March, 1864. Acting Ensign, 22 October, 1864. Resigned 28 March, 1865.
DUNCAN, CHARLES L.
  Gunner, 3 June, 1862. Resigned 12 August, 1862. Gunner, 20 November, 1873. Resigned 22 May, 1874.
DUNCAN, FREDERICK C.
  Mate, 14 March, 1864. Appointment revoked 18 August, 1865.

DUNCAN, JAMES F.
Midshipman, 12 November, 1825. Passed Midshipman, 28 April, 1832. Died 3 August, 1835.
DUNCAN, JAMES M.
Midshipman, 8 December, 1837. Passed Midshipman, 29 June, 1843. Master, 9 April, 1851. Lieutenant, 2 December, 1851. Commander, 16 July, 1862. Died 21 August, 1864.
DUNCAN, JESSE E.
Midshipman, 9 July, 1833. Died 1 January, 1840.
DUNCAN, JOHN.
Gunner, 18 December, 1861. Dismissed 22 September, 1862.
DUNCAN, JOHN M.
Midshipman, 31 December, 1798. Discharged, date not known, under Peace Establishment Act.
DUNCAN, JOHN M.
Acting Third Assistant Engineer, 3 August, 1864. Honorably discharged 12 July, 1865.
DUNCAN, JOHN W.
Acting Master's Mate, 22 January, 1864. Record in Department incomplete.
DUNCAN, LEWIS G.
Mate, 14 April, 1865. Honorably discharged 21 September, 1865.
DUNCAN, LOUIS.
Cadet Midshipman, 11 September, 1876. Graduated 22 June, 1882. Ensign, Junior Grade, 3 March, 1883. Ensign, 26 June, 1884. Resigned 30 June, 1886.
DUNCAN, OSCAR D.
Naval Cadet, 6 September, 1893. Ensign, 1 July, 1899.
DUNCAN, ROBERT E.
Midshipman, 1 January, 1817. Last appearance on Records of Navy Department. 20 May, 1818. Dead.
DUNCAN, SILAS.
Midshipman, 15 November, 1809. Lieutenant, 9 December, 1814. Commander, 1 March, 1829. Died 14 September, 1834.
DUNCAN, WILLIAM B.
Cadet Midshipman. 7 November, 1878. Resigned 15 May, 1884. Lieutenant (Spanish-American War), 30 April, 1898. Honorably discharged 6 September, 1898.
DUNCANSON, WILLIAM.
Midshipman, 20 February, 1800. Resigned 12 November, 1808.
DUNDERDALE, CLEAVELAND F.
Mate, 26 June, 1862. Acting Ensign, 9 March, 1864. Honorably discharged 16 January, 1866.
DUNDERDALE, JOHN.
Boatswain, 5 May, 1838. Resigned 10 October, 1840. Boatswain, 28 October, 1841. Dropped 20 April, 1861.
DUNDON, MICHAEL.
Acting Second Assistant Engineer, 21 March, 1864. Resigned 31 March, 1865.
DUNGAN, JACOB S.
Assistant Surgeon, 25 February, 1851. Passed Assistant Surgeon, 9 April, 1856. Surgeon, 1 May, 1861. Medical Inspector, 3 March, 1871. Medical Director, 31 December, 1876. Retired List, 29 January, 1887.
DUNGAN, PAUL B.
Naval Cadet, 6 September, 1895. At sea prior to final graduation.
DUNGAN, WILLIAM W.
Third Assistant Engineer, 26 June, 1856. First Assistant Engineer, 2 August, 1859. Chief Engineer, 1 February, 1862. Retired List, 22 December, 1897.
DUNHAM, C. MOORE.
Acting Assistant Paymaster, 6 July, 1863. Resigned 9 November, 1864.
DUNHAM, JOSIAH F.
Acting Assistant Paymaster, 4 November, 1863. Discharged 2 December, 1865.
DUNHAM, P. K.
Midshipman, 1 January, 1812. Lieutenant, 1 April, 1818. Died in August, 1822.
DUNHAM, THOMAS M.
Mate, 2 May, 1863. Discharged 23 October, 1864.
DUNHAM, WILLIAM.
Third Assistant Engineer, 2 February, 1847. Dismissed 8 April, 1847.
DUNHAM, WILLIAM J.
Acting Third Assistant Engineer, 10 November, 1863. Honorably discharged 1 August, 1865.
DUNKLY, GEORGE R.
Acting Third Assistant Engineer, 18 November, 1861. Acting Second Assistant Engineer, 22 January, 1864. Honorably discharged 28 December, 1865.
DUNLAP, A. B.
Acting First Assistant Engineer, 14 July, 1863. Appointment revoked (sick) 27 February, 1864.
DUNLAP, ANDREW.
Midshipman, 23 April, 1862. Graduated 6 June, 1867. Ensign, 18 December, 1868. Master, 21 March, 1870. Lieutenant, 21 March, 1871. Lieutenant-Commander, 2 August, 1891. Commander, 1 February, 1898.
DUNLAP, CHARLES W.
Mate, 24 November, 1863. Honorably discharged 1 November, 1865.
DUNLAP, JOHN.
Acting Third Assistant Engineer, 3 July, 1863. Honorably discharged 12 April, 1866.
DUNLAP, THADDEUS C.
Assistant Engineer (Spanish-American War), 14 May, 1898. Honorably discharged 24 December, 1898.

GENERAL NAVY REGISTER.

DUNLAP, THOMAS J.
Acting Ensign, 3 September, 1863. Resigned 21 September, 1863.
DUNLOP, JOHN.
Acting Ensign, 18 April, 1863. Resigned 19 November, 1863.
DUNLOP, N. W.
Acting Third Assistant Engineer, 1861. Resigned (sick) 29 April, 1862.
DUNLOP, THOMAS.
Acting Gunner, 2 April, 1865. Final disposition not recorded.
DUNN, CHARLES.
Midshipman, 30 November, 1814. Drowned 31 July, 1819.
DUNN, DURIUS.
Midshipman, 14 January, 1800. Discharged 10 April, 1801, under Peace Establishment Act.
DUNN, EDWARD H.
Naval Cadet, 5 September, 1891. Assistant Engineer, 1 July, 1897. Rank changed to Ensign, 3 March, 1899. Lieutenant, Junior Grade, 1 July, 1900.
DUNN, EDWARD T.
Purser, 21 February, 1831. Chief Bureau Provisions and Clothing, 12 July, 1869. Pay Director, 3 March, 1871. Retired 22 January, 1873. Died 27 September, 1887.
DUNN, ELISHA W.
Purser, 30 March, 1858. Died 26 February, 1869.
DUNN, GEORGE.
Acting Gunner, 14 March, 1863. Acting Ensign, 7 July, 1863. Dismissed 3 February, 1865. Mate, 10 February, 1870. Gunner, 11 April, 1871. Wholly retired 28 December, 1883.
DUNN, HENRY A.
Assistant Surgeon (Spanish-American War), 25 April, 1898. Appointed Assistant Surgeon in Regular Service, 7 June, 1900.
DUNN, HENRY J.
Acting Ensign, 15 December, 1864. Honorably discharged 18 September, 1865.
DUNN, HERBERT O.
Ensign, 12 March, 1881. Lieutenant, Junior Grade, 1 July, 1887. Lieutenant, 17 February, 1893. Lieutenant-Commander, 1 July, 1900.
DUNN, JOHN F.
Acting Boatswain, 1 March, 1900.
DUNN, MARTIN.
Acting Volunteer Lieutenant, 1 October, 1862. Resigned 3 August, 1863.
DUNN, RICHARD F.
Gunner, 1 November, 1837. Died at Kittery, Maine, 1 February, 1863.
DUNN, THOMAS C.
Acting Master, 14 December, 1861. Acting Volunteer Lieutenant, on recommendation of Commanding Officer, 11 August, 1864. Honorably discharged 26 October, 1865.
DUNN, WILLIAM.
Midshipman, 30 June, 1799. Discharged 6 August, 1801, under Peace Establishment Act.
DUNN, WILLIAMSON.
Acting Midshipman, 24 September, 1860. Acting Ensign, 1 October. 1863. Resigned 8 June, 1866. Ensign (Spanish-American War), 25 May, 1898. Honorably discharged 23 March, 1899.
DUNNE, WILLIAM.
Mate, 20 June, 1862. Acting Ensign, 2 May, 1864. Drowned 28 December, 1864.
DUNNELS, HENRY F.
Mate, 26 March, 1863. Acting Gunner, 5 November, 1863. Honorably discharged 7 October, 1865.
DUNNING, E. C.
Assistant Surgeon, 21 April, 1868. Resigned 1 January, 1873.
DUNNING, WILLIAM B.
Cadet Engineer, 1 October, 1873. Graduated 20 June, 1876. Assistant Engineer, 1 July, 1878. Passed Assistant Engineer, 2 December, 1887. Chief Engineer, 29 July, 1897. Retired List, 29 October, 1898.
DUNNING WILLIAM H.
Acting Third Assistant Engineer, 28 May, 1863. Honorably discharged 1 December, 1865.
DUNNINGTON, JOHN W.
Midshipman, 10 April, 1849. Passed Midshipman, 12 June, 1855. Master, 16 September, 1855. Lieutenant, 16 October, 1856. Resigned 26 April, 1861.
DUNSCOMB, CHARLES F.
Acting Assistant Paymaster, 1 June, 1864. Discharged 15 October, 1865.
DUNSMORE, DANIEL.
Gunner, 28 August, 1861. Warranted 29 May, 1862. Resigned 5 June, 1868.
DUNSTON, WILLIAM.
Master, 3 April, 1815. Last appearance on Records of Navy Department.
DUPLAINE, BEVONI C.
Acting Third Assistant Engineer, 21 October, 1863. Acting Second Assistant Engineer, 20 June, 1864. Honorably discharged 29 November, 1865.
DUPLAINE, E. A. C.
Third Assistant Engineer, 21 May, 1857. Second Assistant Engineer, 2 August, 1859. First Assistant Engineer, 10 August, 1861. Resigned 14 May, 1867.
DU PONT, SAMUEL F.
Midshipman, 19 December, 1815. Lieutenant, 26 April, 1826. Commander, 28 October, 1842. Captain, 14 September, 1855. Rear-Admiral, 16 July, 1862. Died 23 June, 1865.
DURALD, MARTIN.
Midshipman, 6 September, 1838. Resigned 17 September, 1845.

GENERAL NAVY REGISTER. 175

DURAND, GEORGE R.
    Mate, 28 October, 1861. Acting Master. 14 April, 1862. Acting Volunteer Lieutenant, 27 June, 1866. Master, 12 March, 1868. Lieutenant, 18 December, 1868. Lieutenant-Commander, 25 November, 1877. Commander, 26 March, 1889. Retired List, 21 June, 1894.
DURAND, WILLIAM F.
    Cadet Engineer, 14 September, 1876. Graduated 10 June, 1880. Assistant Engineer, 10 June, 1882. Resigned 15 September, 1887.
DURANT, EDWARD.
    Gunner, 3 July, 1799. Last appearance on Records of Navy Department.
DURDINE, THOMAS.
    Boatswain, 30 October, 1840. Last appearance on Records of Navy Department.
DURELL, EDWARD H.
    Naval Cadet, 17 May, 1883. Ensign, 1 July, 1889. Lieutenant, Junior Grade, 21 July, 1897. Lieutenant, 3 March, 1899.
DURET, JOHN B.
    Midshipman, 6 December, 1848. Dropped 12 July, 1849.
DURFEE, RICHARD.
    Acting Second Assistant Engineer, 4 February, 1863. Appointment revoked (sick) 9 June, 1864.
DURGIN, W. F.
    Mate, 30 June, 1862. Appointment revoked 17 April, 1863.
DURHAM, ANDREW E.
    Acting Ensign, 18 August, 1864. Resigned 14 June. 1865.
DURHAM, TOLFORD.
    Acting Master, 22 November, 1861. Resigned 5 May, 1865.
DURKHAM, MOSES.
    Master, 29 November, 1799. Discharged 20 May, 1801, under Peace Establishment Act.
DURNEY, MICHAEL J.
    Mate, 11 June, 1863. Honorably discharged 22 December, 1865.
DURYEE, CHARLES H.
    Midshipman, 19 August, 1823. Passed Midshipman, 23 March, 1829. Lieutenant, 31 December, 1833. Dismissed 30 October. 1837.
DUSENBURY, SAMUEL.
    Midshipman, 16 January, 1809. Resigned 16 March, 1810.
DUSENBURY, SAMUEL.
    Midshipman, 16 July, 1814. Master, 2 June, 1820. Died 4 October, 1827.
DUSENBURY, WALTER S.
    Acting Master's Mate. 27 July, 1861. Discharged 27 December, 1861.
DUSTON, JOHN S.
    Acting Third Assistant Engineer, 7 October, 1864. Honorably discharged 10 May, 1866.
DUTCH, JOHN C.
    Acting Master, 7 December, 1861. Honorably discharged 6 April, 1866.
DUTCHER, CHARLES.
    Acting Assistant Paymaster, 26 September, 1863. Discharged 5 October, 1865.
DUTCHER, MATTHEW J.
    Gunner, 16 August, 1871. Died 3 October, 1879.
DUTTON, ARTHUR H.
    Cadet Midshipman, 28 September, 1881. Graduated. Honorably discharged 30 June, 1887. Lieutenant, Junior Grade (Spanish-American War), 26 May, 1898. Honorably discharged 10 January, 1899.
DUVALL, MARIUS.
    Assistant Surgeon, 25 January, 1842. Passed Assistant Surgeon, 22 January, 1848. Surgeon, 17 September, 1856. Medical Inspector. 3 March, 1871. Medical Director, 1 December, 1871. Retired List, 9 June, 1880. Died 9 February, 1891.
DUVALL, ROBERT C.
    Midshipman, 19 October, 1841. Passed Midshipman, 10 August, 1847. Master, 14 September, 1855. Lieutenant, 15 September, 1855. Dismissed 12 December, 1859.
DUYCKER, BERNARD.
    Gunner, 29 August, 1857. Drowned at sea, while in charge of the Prize Schooner Mary Clinton, 26 June, 1861.
DWYER, WILLIAM W. W.
    Carpenter, 10 October, 1861. Resigned 21 October, 1865.
DWYER, DANIEL.
    Carpenter, 16 July, 1869. Appointment revoked 13 May, 1870.
DWYER, JAMES.
    Boatswain, 13 April, 1896. Died 21 April, 1897.
DWYER, JOHN B.
    Mate, 1 October, 1862. Acting Ensign. 8 December, 1862. Resigned 30 May, 1864.
DWYER, JOHN F.
    Ensign (Spanish-American War), 19 July, 1898. Honorably discharged 7 November, 1898.
DWYER, JOSEPH.
    Purser, 20 February, 1838. Resigned 25 June, 1838.
DWYER, THOMAS J.
    Mate, 24 October, 1861. Acting Master. 9 May, 1862. Lost at sea in Brig Bainbridge, 21 August, 1863.
DWYER, RICHARD.
    Acting Third Assistant Engineer, 10 August. 1863. Deserted 1864.
DYCE, CHARLES F.
    Acting Third Assistant Engineer, 9 August. 1864. Honorably discharged 19 October, 1867.

DYE, CHARLES B.
Acting Assistant Paymaster, 6 November, 1863. Resigned 22 March, 1864.
DYER, BENJAMIN.
Acting Master, 22 January, 1862. Honorably discharged 12 September, 1865. Acting Master, 11 September, 1866. Died on the Fredonia (destroyed by tidal wave), 18 August, 1868.
DYER, CHARLES, JR.
Midshipman, 25 January, 1840. Passed Midshipman, 11 July, 1846. Drowned in Pensacola Bay, 23 August, 1850.
DYER, EVERETT B.
Acting Third Assistant Engineer, 11 December, 1862. Appointment revoked (sick) 4 October, 1864.
DYER, FREDERICK H.
Mate, 14 January, 1864. Died at Key West, Florida, 11 June, 1864.
DYER, GEORGE L.
Midshipman, 26 July, 1866. Graduated 7 June, 1870. Ensign, 13 July, 1871. Master, 25 September, 1873. Lieutenant, 5 February, 1879. Lieutenant-Commander, 22 November, 1898.
DYER, GEORGE P.
Assistant Paymaster, 20 May, 1898. Passed Assistant Paymaster, 23 April, 1899.
DYER, N. MAYO.
Mate, 4 April, 1862. Acting Master, 12 January, 1864. Acting Volunteer Lieutenant, 22 April, 1865. Lieutenant, 12 March, 1868. Lieutenant-Commander, 18 December, 1868. Commander, 23 April, 1883. Captain, 13 July, 1897.
DYER, WILLIAM.
Mate, 30 July, 1866. Appointment revoked 12 February, 1868.
DYER, WILLIAM B., JR.
Mate, 4 April, 1862. Dismissed 31 March, 1863.
DYES, JOHN W. W.
Master's Mate, 18 March, 1843. Died 11 September, 1855.
DYKES, FRANCIS M.
Acting Third Assistant Engineer, 14 January, 1863. Honorably discharged 29 September, 1868.
DYKES, GEORGE T.
Mate, 20 October, 1862. Resigned 28 October, 1863.
DYSON, CHARLES W.
Cadet Engineer, 1 October, 1879. Assistant Engineer, 1 July, 1885. Passed Assistant Engineer, 1 June, 1895. Rank changed to Lieutenant. 3 March, 1899.
DYSON, LOGAN.
Mate, 11 August, 1863. Acting Ensign, 21 September, 1864. Honorably discharged 15 August, 1865.
DYSON, HENRY.
Midshipman, 1 January, 1815. Died November, 1823.
EAGER, ROBERT.
Midshipman, 10 February, 1838. Resigned 4 September, 1838.
EAGER, TALLAS.
Mate, 13 July, 1863. Resigned 6 May, 1865.
EAGLE, HENRY.
Midshipman, 1 January, 1818. Lieutenant, 3 March, 1827. Commander, 4 June, 1844. Captain, 14 September, 1855. Commodore, 16 July, 1862. Retired List, 1 January, 1863. Died 26 November, 1882.
EAGLING, EPHRAIM.
Pharmacist, 30 September, 1899.
EAKIN, JAMES.
Midshipman, 21 February, 1800. Resigned 1 June, 1801.
EAKIN, JAMES.
Master, 4 August, 1807. Resigned 6 March, 1811.
EAKIN, SAMUEL A.
Midshipman, 18 June, 1812. Lieutenant, 1 April, 1818. Died 30 October, 1822.
EAKINS, OLIN M.
Assistant Surgeon, 21 October, 1899.
EAKINS, SAMUEL.
Acting Master, 24 March, 1863. Appointment revoked 15 April, 1863.
EAKLE, WILLIAM P.
Mate, 9 June, 1863. Honorably discharged 20 September, 1865.
EAMES, HAROLD H.
Cadet Midshipman, 28 June, 1878. Ensign, 1 July, 1884. Resigned 11 February, 1894.
EAMES, SAMUEL.
Master, 6 July, 1798. Resigned 7 January, 1799.
EARL, JOHN T.
Acting Third Assistant Engineer, 12 January, 1863. Resigned 15 June, 1865.
EARL, WILLIAM.
Mate, 30 December, 1863. Honorably discharged 16 September, 1865.
EARLE, JOHN.
Master, 6 December, 1805. Died 10 October, 1825.
EARLE, JOHN J., JR.
Mate. Resigned 15 December, 1862.
EARLE, RALPH.
Naval Cadet, 6 September, 1892. Ensign, 6 May, 1898.
EARLE, WILLIAM.
Acting Master, 17 December, 1861. Honorably discharged 15 January, 1866.
EARNSHAW, CHARLES.
Gunner, 12 June, 1862. Died 27 March, 1875.

GENERAL NAVY REGISTER.

EASBY, JOHN W.
Assistant Naval Constructor, 17 May, 1866. Naval Constructor, 17 June, 1870. Chief Bureau of Construction and Repair, 15 April, 1878. Retired List, 13 December, 1881. Died 17 June, 1894.

EASON, HENRY.
Mate, 14 November, 1861. Acting Ensign, 6 October, 1862. Honorably discharged 11 December, 1865.

EASTBURN, JOSEPH.
Midshipman, 9 June, 1811. Last appearance on Records of Navy Department, 1815. Frigate Essex.

EASTERBROOK, MASON C.
Mate, 28 November, 1864. Resigned 21 June, 1865.

EASTLAKE, ABRAHAM P.
Acting Assistant Paymaster, 20 January, 1864. Honorably discharged 10 November, 1865.

EASTMAN, CHARLES T.
Assistant Paymaster, 28 April, 1870. Died 29 March, 1876.

EASTMAN, FRANK S.
Mate, 25 August, 1863. Acting Ensign, 12 July, 1864. Honorably discharged 12 February, 1868.

EASTMAN, JOHN R.
Professor, 17 February, 1865. Retired List, 29 July, 1898.

EASTMAN, THOMAS H.
Acting Midshipman, 31 January, 1853. Midshipman, 20 June, 1856. Passed Midshipman, 29 April, 1859. Master, 5 September, 1859. Lieutenant, 16 January, 1861. Lieutenant-Commander, 30 September, 1862. Commander, 19 June, 1871. Retired List, 29 June, 1883. Died 18 March, 1888.

EASTON, DAVID.
Boatswain, 8 August, 1811. Died 22 February, 1840.

EASTON, JAMES W.
Acting Ensign, 8 February, 1865. Honorably discharged 12 January, 1866.

EASTWICK, PHILIP G.
Third Assistant Engineer, 18 November, 1862. Second Assistant Engineer, 23 March, 1864. Resigned 5 August, 1865.

EASTWOOD, CHARLES S.
Acting Assistant Surgeon, 19 December, 1862. Honorably discharged 22 January, 1866.

EATON, CHARLES P.
Cadet Engineer, 1 October, 1879. Ensign, 1 July, 1885. Lieutenant, Junior Grade, 6 December, 1894. Lieutenant, 13 April, 1898.

EATON, EDWIN.
Chaplain, 27 February, 1847. Resigned 3 August, 1855.

EATON, FREDERICK L.
Cadet Midshipman, 6 September, 1886. Resigned 20 February, 1890. Ensign (Spanish-American War), 9 May, 1898. Honorably discharged 30 August, 1898.

EATON, HENRY.
Acting Master, 27 June, 1862. Acting Volunteer Lieutenant, on recommendation of Commanding Officer, 23 March, 1864. Resigned 28 September, 1864.

EATON, HORACE B.
Mate, 1 June, 1864. Honorably discharged 19 June, 1868.

EATON, JOSEPH GILES.
Midshipman, 24 September, 1863. Ensign, 18 December, 1868. Master, 21 March, 1870. Lieutenant, 21 March, 1871. Lieutenant-Commander, 19 June, 1888. Commander, 10 November, 1896.

EATON, THOMAS C.
Midshipman, 9 September, 1841. Passed Midshipman, 10 August, 1847. Master, 14 September, 1855. Lieutenant, 15 September, 1855. Died 1 June, 1856.

EATON, WILLIAM B.
Acting Volunteer Lieutenant, 26 August, 1861. Acting Volunteer Lieutenant-Commander, 12 December, 1864. Honorably discharged 13 January, 1866.

EATON, WILLIAM C.
Cadet Engineer, 1 October, 1872. Graduated 30 May, 1874. Assistant Engineer, 26 February, 1875. Passed Assistant Engineer, 4 March, 1881. Chief Engineer, 1 June, 1895. Rank changed to Lieutenant-Commander, 3 March, 1899.

EAYRS, CHARLES G. A.
Acting Assistant Surgeon, 30 November, 1861. Resigned 21 July, 1862.

EBERLE, EDWARD W.
Cadet Midshipman, 28 September, 1881. Ensign, 8 August, 1887. Lieutenant, Junior Grade, 12 June, 1896. Lieutenant, 3 March, 1899.

ECCLES, JAMES.
Acting Third Assistant Engineer, 22 September, 1863. Acting Second Assistant Engineer, 27 May, 1865. Died on Glasgow, 11 September, 1867.

ECKART, WILLIAM R.
Third Assistant Engineer, 8 July, 1861. Resigned 2 May, 1864.

ECKEL, FREDERICK.
Third Assistant Engineer, 1 July, 1861. Resigned 6 September, 1863.

ECKERT, GEORGE W.
Mate, 31 August, 1863. Resigned 6 July, 1864.

ECKERT, THOMAS J.
Mate, 3 August, 1864. Honorably discharged 6 July, 1865.

ECKFORD, HENRY.
Naval Constructor, 13 July, 1817. Resigned 6 June, 1820.

GENERAL NAVY REGISTER.

ECKFORD, JOSEPH B.
　Midshipman, 1 May, 1827. Resigned 16 November, 1831.
ECKHARDT, ERNEST F.
　Naval Cadet, 5 September, 1891. Assistant Engineer, 1 July, 1897. Rank changed to Ensign, 3 March, 1899. Lieutenant, Junior Grade, 1 July, 1900.
ECKSTEIN, HENRY C.
　Assistant Surgeon, 22 December, 1862. Resigned 31 January, 1866. Acting Assistant Surgeon, 1 February, 1866. Discharged 1 August, 1869. Reappointed Assistant Surgeon, 28 September, 1870. Passed Assistant Surgeon, 17 November, 1873. Surgeon, 14 March, 1883. Retired List, 10 May, 1893.
ECKWORTH, PHILIP.
　Acting Second Assistant Engineer, 14 November, 1864. Appointment revoked 9 May, 1865.
ECOFF, SAMUEL.
　Acting Second Assistant Engineer, 1 October, 1862. Acting First Assistant Engineer, 2 July, 1864. Honorably discharged 17 November, 1865.
EDDOWES, ARCHIBALD K.
　Acting Second Assistant Engineer, 1 July, 1861. Acting First Assistant Engineer, 3 October, 1862. Acting Chief Engineer, 18 June, 1863. Honorably discharged 1 December, 1865.
EDDY, CHARLES C.
　Acting Ensign, 19 December, 1862. Honorably discharged 23 June, 1868.
EDDY, GEORGE S.
　Acting Assistant Surgeon, 11 February, 1863. Resigned 21 April, 1865.
EDDY, HAVEN B.
　Mate, 7 February, 1863. Resigned 19 November, 1864.
EDELIN, JOHN M.
　Midshipman, 1 September, 1811. Died 28 May, 1812.
EDES, BENJAMIN LONG.
　Midshipman, 23 September, 1861. Graduated September, 1865. Ensign, 1 December, 1866. Master, 12 March, 1868. Lieutenant, 26 March, 1869. Lieutenant-Commander, 22 April, 1881. Killed 29 August, 1881.
EDES, RICHARD E.
　Assistant Surgeon (Spanish-American War), 12 May, 1898. Honorably discharged 18 October, 1898.
EDES, ROBERT T.
　Assistant Surgeon, 30 April, 1861. Passed Assistant Surgeon, 24 April, 1865. Resigned 31 May, 1865.
EDGAR, HENRY.
　Boatswain, 29 July, 1839. Resigned 9 November, 1841.
EDGAR, JAMES W.
　Acting First Assistant Engineer, 2 December, 1863. Dismissed 23 April, 1864.
EDGAR, JOHN M.
　Assistant Surgeon, 9 July, 1881. Passed Assistant Surgeon, 9 July, 1884. Surgeon, 3 September, 1896.
EDGAR, RICHARD C.
　Assistant Surgeon, 23 January, 1809. Surgeon, 5 May, 1813. Last appearance on Records of Navy Department, 1823. Dead.
EDGAR, WEBSTER A.
　Cadet Midshipman, 28 September, 1881. Ensign, 1 July, 1888. Lieutenant, Junior Grade, 1 October, 1896. Lieutenant, 3 March, 1899.
EDGAR, WILLIAM.
　Mate, 8 July, 1862. Appointment revoked (sick) 23 March, 1863.
EDGAR, WILLIAM.
　Mate, 22 December, 1863. Resigned 6 May, 1865.
EDGAR, WILLIAM B.
　Ensign (Spanish-American War), 2 July, 1898. Honorably discharged 23 September, 1898.
EDGAR, WILLIAM H.
　Carpenter, 25 May, 1861. Died 27 September, 1875.
EDGECOMB, CHARLES A.
　Mate, 25 October, 1862. Dismissed 6 July, 1864.
EDGERLEY, SAMUEL.
　Acting Ensign, 22 December, 1863. Honorably discharged 2 August, 1865.
EDGREN, JOHN A.
　Acting Ensign, 24 October, 1862. Resigned 28 October, 1863. Acting Ensign, 1 July, 1864. Resigned 22 May, 1865.
EDIE, JOHN R.
　Naval Cadet, 19 May, 1886. Second Lieutenant. U. S. Marine Corps, 1 July, 1892. Ensign 21 July, 1892. Lieutenant, Junior Grade, 3 March, 1899. Lieutenant, 1 July, 1899.
EDMOND, GEORGE.
　Gunner, 21 January, 1862. Dead.
EDMONSON, WILLIAM E.
　Chaplain, 24 August, 1894.
EDMONSTON, HARRISON.
　Boatswain, 28 May, 1859. Lost in the Levant. Last intelligence from the ship, 18 September, 1860.
EDMUNDS, ELI D.
　Mate, 6 September, 1862. Acting Ensign, 9 September, 1863. Acting Master, 8 May, 1865. Honorably discharged 30 January, 1866. Acting Master, 4 April, 1866. Mustered out 9 September, 1868.

GENERAL NAVY REGISTER.   179

EDMUNDSON, JOHN W.
   Acting Third Assistant Engineer, 11 October, 1864. Honorably discharged 6 July, 1865.
EDSON, AMBROSE H.
   Acting Ensign, 1 October, 1862. Died on Tuscumbia, 8 July, 1863.
EDSON, JARVIS B.
   Acting Third Assistant Engineer, 1 November, 1864. Honorably discharged 27 August, 1868.
EDSON, JOHN T.
   Midshipman, 27 June, 1867. Graduated 6 June, 1871. Resigned 17 July, 1872. Ensign (Spanish-American War), 12 May, 1898. Honorably discharged 17 October, 1898.
EDTHOFER, FRANK H.
   Ensign (Spanish-American War), 9 May, 1898. Honorably discharged 11 April, 1899.
EDWARDS, ALEXANDER H.
   Midshipman, 4 March, 1823. Resigned 2 February, 1830.
EDWARDS, DAVID S.
   Surgeon's Mate, 25 December, 1818. Surgeon, 5 May, 1825. Retired 21 December, 1861. Medical Director, on Retired List, 3 March, 1871. Died 18 March, 1874.
EDWARDS, D. W.
   Mate, 11 April, 1865. Honorably discharged 12 July, 1865.
EDWARDS, GEORGE.
   Mate, 8 May, 1862. Acting Ensign, 23 December, 1862. Acting Master, 30 May, 1865. Honorably discharged 30 September, 1868.
EDWARDS, HENRY D.
   Mate, 25 January, 1862. Acting Ensign, 17 September, 1862. Acting Master, 25 October, 1864. Honorably discharged 19 August, 1865.
EDWARDS, JAMES L.
   Second Lieutenant Marine Corps, 18 June, 1811. Resigned in February, 1813.
EDWARDS, J. B.
   Acting Ensign and Pilot, 4 November, 1864. Acting Master and Pilot, 1 February, 1865. Honorably discharged 21 October, 1865.
EDWARDS, JOHN B.
   Acting Second Assistant Engineer, 1 October, 1862. Resigned 6 June, 1864.
EDWARDS, JOHN E.
   Acting Third Assistant Engineer, 11 January, 1864. Honorably discharged 19 February, 1868.
EDWARDS, JOHN J.
   Midshipman, 1 January, 1808. Lieutenant. 24 July, 1813. Died in 1814.
EDWARDS, JOHN R.
   Cadet Engineer, 1 October, 1871. Graduated 30 May, 1874. Assistant Engineer, 26 February, 1875. Passed Assistant Engineer, 11 September, 1881. Chief Engineer, 5 November, 1895. Rank changed to Lieutenant-Commander, 3 March, 1899.
EDWARDS, PHILIP.
   First Lieutenant Marine Corps. Killed in a duel 16 October, 1800.
EDWARDS, R. G.
   Midshipman, 1 January, 1809. Lieutenant, 9 December, 1814. Died 19 January, 1824.
EDWARDS, RICHARD F.
   Third Assistant Engineer, 1 July, 1863. Died 23 March, 1866.
EDWARDS, SAMUEL D.
   Acting Third Assistant Engineer, 28 May, 1863. Acting Second Assistant Engineer, 5 December, 1864. Honorably discharged 22 September, 1865.
EDWARDS, SAMUEL.
   Midshipman, 9 March, 1838. Passed Midshipman, 20 May, 1844. Master. 21 April, 1852. Lieutenant, 17 January, 1853. Died 23 March, 1861.
EDWARDS, SHUBAEL P.
   Acting Ensign, 11 July, 1863. Honorably discharged 6 September, 1865.
EDWARDS, THOMAS.
   Acting Master, 22 October. 1861. Acting Volunteer Lieutenant, 12 April, 1864. Honorably discharged 25 February, 1866. Dead.
EDWARDS, WILLIAM.
   Sailmaker, date not known. Last appearance on Records of Navy Department for 1815. Frigate Guerriere.
EDWARDS, WILLIAM D.
   Assistant Engineer (Spanish-American War), 14 May, 1898. Honorably discharged 5 January, 1899.
EDWARDS, W. W.
   Midshipman, 1 September, 1811. Killed in action 14 August, 1813.
EGBERT, DANIEL.
   Assistant Surgeon, 22 August, 1829. Passed Assistant Surgeon. 3 March. 1835. Surgeon, 20 February, 1838. Retired 21 December, 1861. Medical Director on Retired List, 3 March, 1871. Died 24 October, 1875.
EGBERT, DANIEL B.
   Third Assistant Engineer, 8 October, 1861. Resigned 21 January, 1865.
EGE, GEORGE A.
   Mate, 13 February, 1864. Resigned 15 June, 1865.
EGERTON, R. B.
   Midshipman, 15 November, 1809. Last appearance on Records of Navy Department.
EGERTON, RICHARD.
   Midshipman, 1 January, 1809. Resigned 21 May, 1810.
EGGERT, ERNEST F.
   Naval Cadet, 6 September, 1893. Graduated. Assistant Naval Constructor. 1 July, 1899.

180   GENERAL NAVY REGISTER.

EGGLESTON, JOHN R.
    Midshipman, 2 August, 1847. Passed Midshipman, 10 June, 1853. Master, 15 September, 1855. Lieutenant, 16 September, 1855. Resigned 22 January, 1861.
EGGLESTON, NEWTON.
    Acting Third Assistant Engineer, 26 November, 1861. Acting Second Assistant Engineer, 4 June, 1862. Acting First Assistant Engineer, 24 June, 1864. Honorably discharged 4 December, 1865.
EGNOR, FREDERIC.
    Acting Third Assistant Engineer, 7 March, 1865. Honorably discharged July, 1866.
EICHELBERGER, WILLIAM S.
    Professor of Mathematics, 15 January, 1900.
EILERS, HENRY A.
    Gunner, 5 November, 1892.
EISLER, WHITNEY I
    Ensign (Spanish-American War), 4 June, 1898. Honorably discharged 4 March, 1899.
EISWALD, GEORGE H.
    Lieutenant, Junior Grade (Spanish-American War), 29 June, 1898. Honorably discharged 8 September, 1898.
EKMAN, CHARLES.
    Mate, 17 December, 1862. Acting Ensign. Resigned 8 April, 1865.
ELBERSON, FRANCIS.
    Master, 28 April, 1813. Resigned 10 March, 1815.
ELBERT, JOHN L.
    Midshipman, 18 May, 1809. Resigned 1 July, 1811.
ELBERT, SAMUEL.
    Midshipman, 11 December, 1798. Lieutenant, 4 March, 1803. Died 20 December, 1812.
ELD, HENRY.
    Midshipman, 7 January, 1832. Passed Midshipman, 23 June, 1838. Lieutenant, 21 December, 1842. Died 12 March, 1850.
ELDER, ROBERT B.
    Mate, 17 September, 1863. Acting Ensign, 6 October, 1864. Honorably discharged 1 April, 1868.
ELDREDGE, ALPHEUS S.
    Mate, 5 March, 1862. Honorably discharged 21 January, 1866.
ELDREDGE, CHARLES H.
    Acting Assistant Paymaster, 10 July, 1861. Assistant Paymaster, 23 October, 1861. Paymaster, 6 February, 1862. Pay Inspector, 3 July, 1871. Pay Director, 31 August, 1881.
ELDREDGE, EDWARD.
    Acting Second Assistant Engineer, 30 January, 1862. Resigned 21 April, 1862. Acting Second Assistant Engineer, 5 May, 1862. Acting First Assistant Engineer 16 October, 1863. Appointment revoked (sick) 28 January, 1864.
ELDREDGE, HENRY C.
    Mate, 5 November, 1863. Acting Ensign, 20 February, 1865. Honorably discharged 20 October, 1865.
ELDREDGE, HOUSTON.
    Cadet Midshipman, 9 October, 1876. Ensign, Junior Grade, 1 July, 1883. Ensign, 26 June, 1884. Lieutenant, Junior Grade, 23 January, 1894. Retired List, 4 November, 1895.
ELDREDGE, JOHN.
    Acting Volunteer Lieutenant, 12 August, 1861. Appointment revoked 26 August, 1861.
ELDREDGE, JOSEPH C.
    Purser, 2 February, 1847. Pay Director, 3 March, 1871. Retired List, 8 March, 1880. Died 14 August, 1881.
ELDREDGE, JOSHUA H.
    Acting Master, 12 June, 1861. Acting Volunteer Lieutenant, 27 June, 1865. Honorably discharged 4 October, 1868. Mate, 8 July, 1869. Resigned 12 January, 1870.
ELDREDGE, ROBERT D.
    Acting Master, 2 August, 1861. Appointment revoked (sick) 24 July, 1862. Acting Ensign, 2 January, 1863. Resigned 2 March, 1864.
ELDREDGE, ROBERT H.
    Mate, 5 September, 1863. Honorably discharged 7 August, 1865.
ELDREDGE, SAMUEL.
    Mate, 20 February, 1864. Resigned 25 March, 1865.
ELDREDGE, SYLVESTR S.
    Acting Ensign, 8 September, 1864. Resigned 10 May, 1865.
ELDREDGE, WILLIAM J.
    Acting Ensign, 29 July, 1863. Honorably discharged 24 October, 1865.
ELDRIDGE, DANIEL.
    Master, 9 May, 1802. Resigned 17 October, 1803.
ELDRIDGE, DANIEL.
    Gunner, 10 April, 1805. Died 31 December, 1806.
ELDRIDGE, FRANK H.
    Cadet Engineer, 1 October, 1873. Graduated 21 June, 1875. Assistant Engineer, 1 July, 187. Passed Assistant Engineer, 30 June, 1887. Chief Engineer, 9 May, 1897. Rank changed to Lieutenant-Commander, 3 March, 1899.
ELIASON, CHARLES W.
    Assistant Paymaster (Spanish-American War), 7 June, 1898. Honorably discharged 30 January, 1899. Assistant Paymaster (Regular Navy), 18 September, 1899.
ELKINS, HERBERT G.
    Acting Carpenter, 10 January, 1900.
ELLEDGE, JOHN W.
    Midshipman, 29 May, 1850. Dismissed 24 January, 1851.

GENERAL NAVY REGISTER.   181

ELLERTON, GEORGE C.
  Acting Warrant Machinest, 23 August, 1899.
ELLERY, CHARLES.
  Midshipman, 8 March, 1814. Lieutenant, 13 January, 1825. Dismissed 24 November, 1830.
ELLERY, FRANK.
  Midshipman, 1 January, 1812. Lieutenant, 28 March, 1820. Reserved List, 13 September, 1855. Commodore on Retired List, 4 April, 1867. Died 24 March, 18.1.
ELLERY, FRANK, JR.
  Midshipman, 25 September, 1866. Graduated 7 June, 1870. Ensign, 13 July, 1872. Master, 23 January, 1875. Resigned 31 December, 1880. Lieutenant, Junior Grade (Spanish-American War), 24 May, 1898. Honorably discharged 1 Febhruary, 1899.
ELLERY, WILLIAM.
  Acting Master, 18 May, 1861. Resigned 2 July, 1862.
ELLERY, WILLIAM H.
  Mate, 28 September, 1861. Resigned 8 October, 1863.
ELLICOTT, JOHN M.
  Cadet Engineer, 1 October, 1879. Ensign, 1 July, 1885. Lieutenant, Junior Grade, 9 December, 1894. Lieutenant, 23 April, 1898.
ELLIOT, ALFRED.
  Midshipman, 23 September, 1864. Graduated 2 June, 1868. Ensign, 19 April, 1869. Master, 12 July, 1870. Died 10 April, 1872.
ELLIOTT, ALBERT H.
  Mate (Spanish-American War), 25 June, 1898. Honorably discharged 9 September, 1898.
ELLIOT, CHARLES W.
  Midshipman, 7 January, 1832. Resigned 1 February, 1834.
ELLIOT, SAMUEL B.
  Midshipman, 20 August, 1838. Passed Midshipman, 11 July, 1846. Resigned 21 February, 1852.
ELLIOT, STEPHEN D.
  Midshipman, 1 March, 1827. Resigned 12 September, 1832.
ELLIOT, WILLIAM G.
  Midshipman, 1 April, 1828. Died in 1831.
ELLIOT, WILSON.
  Midshipman, 9 April, 1800. Resigned 30 July, 1802.
ELLIOTT, FRANK C.
  Mate, 1 February, 1870. Appointment revoked 2 October, 1871.
ELLIOTT, FREDERICK.
  Acting Ensign, 23 October, 1862. Honorably discharged 24 September, 1868.
ELLIOTT, ETHAN A.
  Acting Master and Pilot, 1 October, 1864. Appointment revoked 9 March, 1865.
ELLIOTT, GEORGE W.
  Carpenter, 15 August, 1848. Warranted 17 July, 1850. Died at Hampton, Virginia, 16 December, 1867.
ELLIOTT, JARED L.
  Chaplain, 13 July, 1838. Resigned 18 October, 1842.
ELLIOTT, JARED L.
  Acting Master, 20 August, 1861. Appointment revoked, 7 November, 1861.
ELLIOTT, JESSE D.
  Midshipman, 2 April, 1804. Lieutenant, 23 April, 1810. Commander, 24 July, 1813. Captain, 27 March, 1818. Died 10 December, 1845.
ELLIOTT, JOHN B.
  Assistant Surgeon, 20 May, 1829. Passed Assistant Surgeon, 1 February, 1836. Retired 8 May, 1861. Died 5 June, 1869.
ELLIOTT, JOSEPH W.
  Acting Third Assistant Engineer, 24 May, 1864. Honorably discharged 25 September, 1863.
ELLIOTT, MIDDLETON S.
  Assistant Surgeon, 6 October, 1896. Passed Assistant Surgeon, 6 October, 1899.
ELLIOTT, ST. CLAIR.
  Midshipman, 2 April, 1804. Resigned 26 July, 1815.
ELLIOTT, WILLIAM.
  Midshipman, 18 May, 1809. Lieutenant, 4 February, 1815. Last appearance on Records of Navy Department, 1815. Schooner Torch.
ELLIOTT, WILLIAM.
  Lieutenant, Junior Grade (Spanish-American War), 20 May, 1898. Honorably discharged 8 September, 1898.
ELLIOTT, WILLIAM HENRY.
  Midshipman, 27 September, 1861. Graduated September, 1865. Ensign, 1 December, 1866. Master, 12 March, 1868. Lieutenant, 26 March, 1869. Resigned 27 April, 1870. Lieutenant (Spanish-American War), 11 May, 1898. Honorably discharged 31 October, 1898.
ELLIOTT, WILLIAM P.
  Midshipman, 26 September, 1867. Graduated 6 June. 1871. Ensign, 14 July, 1872. Master, 14 May, 1875. Lieutenant, 20 June, 1882. Died 25 May, 1900.
ELLIS, EDMUND C.
  Mate, 28 September, 1864. Honorably discharged 30 September, 1865.
ELLIS, ELISHA.
  Carpenter, 12 November, 1833. Dismissed 23 May, 1835.
ELLIS, FRANCIS E.
  Acting Master, 25 February, 1862. Resigned 6 April, 1865.

ELLIS, GEORGE.
Acting Third Assistant Engineer, 8 September, 1863. Honorably discharged 29 June, 1866.
ELLIS, GEORGE W.
Acting Third Assistant Engineer, 1 February, 1865. Resigned 18 October, 1867.
ELLIS, HAYNE.
Naval Cadet, 5 September, 1896. Graduated 30 June, 1900.
ELLIS, JOHN D.
Acting Ensign, Admiral Dahlgren's Staff, 6 July, 1863. Resigned 31 August, 1864.
ELLIS, JOSEPH D.
Mate, 19 November, 1861. Acting Ensign, 27 October, 1863. Honorably discharged 17 December, 1865.
ELLIS, LEMUEL K.
Acting Gunner, 11 September, 1862. Honorably discharged 5 February, 1866.
ELLIS, LEONARD K.
Gunner, 3 February, 1853. Resigned 31 January, 1859. Gunner, 18 February, 1861. Dismissed 11 February, 1862. Boatswain, 8 June, 1866. Retired List, 7 October, 1876. Died at Washington, D. C., 3 July, 1877.
ELLIS, MARK ST. C.
Naval Cadet, 1 July, 1892. Ensign, 6 May, 1898.
ELLIS, RICHARD.
Acting Ensign, 1 October, 1862. Died on the Great Western, 5 September, 1863.
ELLIS, ROBERT N.
Third Assistant Engineer, 8 August, 1861. Second Assistant Engineer, 8 December, 1864. Resigned 15 October, 1867.
ELLIS, SAMUEL B.
Acting Assistant Engineer, 7 June, 1862. Acting Second Assistant Engineer, 30 December, 1864. Honorably discharged 12 January, 1866.
ELLIS, SAMUEL W.
Midshipman, 1 April, 1828. Resigned 6 April, 1829.
ELLIS, THOMAS.
Midshipman, 23 February, 1799. Discharged 10 July, 1801, under Peace Establishment Act.
ELLIS, WILLIAM P.
Acting Third Assistant Engineer, 14 September, 1863. Acting Second Assistant Engineer, 9 February, 1865. Honorably discharged 27 October, 1865.
ELLISON, F. H.
Lieutenant, 10 July, 1798. Discharged 9 September, 1801, under Peace Establishment Act.
ELLISON, FRANCIS B.
Midshipman, 28 May, 1819. Lieutenant, 17 May, 1828. Commander, 29 May, 1850. Captain, 2 March, 1857. Retired 1 October, 1864. Commodore on Retired List, 4 April, 1867. Died 25 January, 1884.
ELLISON, FARNCIS H.
Master, 3 July, 1813. Died 18 May, 1843.
ELLITER, JULIUS.
Acting Third Assistant Engineer, 1 October, 1862. Acting Second Assistant Engineer, 9 October, 1863. Honorably discharged 5 December, 1865.
ELLMORE, CHARLES F.
Mate, 14 September, 1863. Honorably discharged 20 February, 1866.
ELLMS, FRANKLIN.
Acting Ensign, 4 May, 1863. Honorably discharged 4 November, 1868.
ELLSMORE, THOMAS.
Mate, 2 December, 1863. Honorably discharged 20 October, 1865.
ELLSWORTH, JOHN T.
Midshipman, 1 March, 1799. Discharged 12 October, 1801, under Peace Establishment Act.
ELMER, HORACE
Midshipman, 27 September, 1861. Graduated 22 November. 1864. Ensign, 1 November, 1866. Master, 1 December, 1866. Lieutenant, 12 March, 1868. Lieutenant-Commander, 27 April, 1869. Comander, 2 March, 1885. Died 26 April, 1898.
ELMER, MACOMB K.
Assistant Surgeon, 18 July, 1900.
ELSEFFER, HARRY S.
Cadet Engineer, 8 October, 1874. Graduated 10 June, 1879. Assistant Engineer, 10 June, 1881. Died 21 March, 1886.
ELSON, HERMAN J.
Naval Cadet, 19 May, 1894. Ensign, 4 April, 1900.
ELSTON, JOHN W.
Acting Assistant Surgeon, 7 October. 1870. Resigned 1 August, 1874
ELTON, JOHN H.
Midshipman, 4 July, 1805. Lieutenant. 8 June. 1810. Commander, 5 March. 1817. Died 28 September, 1822.
ELTRINGHAM, ALEXANDER.
Mate, 28 June, 1865. Honorably discharged 1 October, 1865.
ELWELL, ALONZO.
Mate, 23 January, 1862. Acting Ensign, 7 March, 1864. Honorably discharged 11 November, 1865.
ELWELL, CHARLES A.
Mate (Spanish-American War), 12 May, 1898. Honorably discharged 29 August. 1898.
ELWELL. ROBERT W.
Acting Ensign, 21 August, 1863. Resigned 5 May, 1865.
ELWELL. WILLIAM H.
Acting Ensign, 31 August, 1863. Honorably discharged 7 October, 1865.

GENERAL NAVY REGISTER.

ELWYN, THOMAS O. L.
Midshipman, 19 September, 1825. Died 1 August, 1831.
ELY, GRISWOLD L.
Acting Assistant Paymaster, 23 September, 1863. Honorably discharged 31 March, 1866.
ELY, GUY.
Midshipman, 16 January, 1809. Last appearance on Records of Navy Department, 1815. Portland, Massachusetts.
ELY, JOHN H.
Mate, 28 September, 1864. Honorably discharged 19 August, 1865.
ELY, ROBERT B.
Mate, 12 September, 1861. Acting Master, 31 January, 1862. Acting Volunteer Lieutenant, on recommendation of Commanding Officer, 9 September, 1864. Honorably discharged 20 May, 1865.
ELY, THEODORE R.
Third Assistant Engineer, 26 June, 1856. Second Assistant Engineer, 2 August, 1859. Died 23 September, 1861.
EMANUEL, JONATHAN MANLY.
Third Assistant Engineer, 25 August, 1862. Second Assistant Engineer, 20 February, 1864. First Assistant Engineer, 6 June, 1869. Passed Assistant Engineer, 6 June, 1889. Retired List, 7 April, 1891.
EMERSON, ANDREW L.
Acting Ensign, 15 September, 1862. Acting Master, on recommendation of Commanding Officer, 19 May, 1864. Honorably discharged 6 August, 1865.
EMERSON, ARTHUR W.
Acting Master, 26 December, 1861. Resigned 25 June, 1862.
EMERSON, A. W.
Acting Ensign, 13 February, 1865. Honorably discharged 21 October, 1865.
EMERSON, GEORGE.
Mate, 9 January, 1865. Honorably discharged 15 July, 1865.
EMERSON, GEORGE A.
Acting Assistant Paymaster, 22 June, 1863. Discharged 25 November, 1865.
EMERSON, GEORGE T.
Mate, 25 February, 1864. Appointment revoked 28 February, 1865.
EMERSON, ISAAC E.
Lieutenant (Spanish-American War), 25 May, 1898. Honorably discharged 2 November, 1898.
EMERSON, LORING G.
Acting Ensign, 11 August, 1862. Acting Master, on recommendation of Commanding Officer, 15 January, 1864. Honorably discharged 28 February, 1869.
EMERSON, THOMAS A.
Acting Assistant Paymaster, 16 October, 1863. Discharged 25 November, 1865.
EMERSON, THOMAS L.
Midshipman, 4 March, 1823. Resigned 24 November, 1825.
EMERSON, WILLIAM H.
Cadet Midshipman, 10 October, 1876. Graduated 22 June, 1882. Ensign, Junior Grade, 3 March, 1883. Ensign, 26 June, 1884. Resigned 4 October, 1884.
EMERY, ALFRED E.
Acting Assistant Surgeon, 28 March, 1863. Appointment revoked 29 June, 1863. Reappointed 21 August, 1863. Resigned 9 February, 1865.
EMERY, ALFRED J.
Mate, 18 February, 1864. Resigned 12 January, 1865.
EMERY, CALEB J.
Purser, 18 April, 1855. Pay Director, 3 March, 1871. Retired List, 26 May, 1882. Died 5 June, 1886.
EMERY, CHARLES E.
Third Assistant Engineer, 11 July, 1861. Second Assistant Engineer, 18 December, 1862. Resigned 26 December, 1867.
EMERY, GEORGE R.
Acting First Assistant Engineer, 19 September, 1861. Resigned 9 December, 1861.
EMLEY, E. C.
Mate, 22 November, 1864. Honorably discharged 9 November, 1865.
EMMERICH, CHARLES F.
Midshipman, 26 September, 1866. Graduated 7 June, 1870. Ensign, 13 July, 1872. Master, 30 Janaury, 1875. Lieutenant, 6 November, 1881. Died 3 February, 1894.
EMMET, CHRISTOPHER T.
Midshipman, 1 October, 1814. Last appearance on Records of Navy Department, 15 March, 1822. Dead.
EMMETT, WILLIAM L.
Cadet Midshipman, 5 July, 1876. Graduated. Honorably discharged 30 June, 1883. Lieutenant, Junior Grade (Spanish-American War), 12 May, 1898. Honorably discharged 24 August, 1898.
EMMONS, GEORGE D.
Third Assistant Engineer, 3 May, 1859. Second Assistant Engineer, 21 April, 1862. First Assistant Engineer, 20 May, 1863. Chief Engineer, 5 March, 1871. Retired List, 31 October, 1879. Died 28 April, 1886.
EMMONS, GEORGE F.
Midshipman, 1 April, 1828. Passed Midshipman, 14 June, 1834. Lieutenant, 25 February, 1841. Commander, 28 January, 1856. Captain, 7 February, 1863. Commodore, 20 September, 1868. Rear-Admiral, 25 November, 1872. Retired List, 23 August, 1873. Died 23 July, 1884.
EMMONS, GEORGE T.
Midshipman, 4 June, 1870. Graduated 15 October, 1847. Ensign, 17 July, 1875. Mas-

ter, 15 October, 1881. Lieutenant, Junior Grade, 3 March, 1883. Lieutenant, 1 November, 1887. Retired List, 12 January, 1899.

EMMONS, HORATIO N.
Assistant Engineer (Spanish-American War), 14 May, 1898. Honorablyd ischarged 22 April, 1899.

EMMONS, WILLIAM.
Acting Third Assistant Engineer, 26 August, 1862. Honorably discharged 16 September, 1865.

EMORY, WILLIAM HENSLEY.
Midshipman, 23 September, 1862. Graduated June, 1866. Ensign, 12 March, 1868. Master, 26 March, 1869. Lieutenant, 21 March, 1870. Lieutenant-Commander, 26 May, 1887. Commander, 29 December, 1895.

EMRICH, CHARLES R.
Naval Cadet, 19 May, 1887. Assistant Engineer, 1 July, 1893. Passed Assistant Engineer, 22 December, 1897. Rank changed to Lieutenant, Junior Grade, 3 March, 1899. Died 23 February, 1900.

ENDICOT, CHARLES.
Acting Master, 12 August, 1861. Appointment revoked 20 January, 1862.

ENDICOTT, MORDECAI F.
Civil Engineer, 13 July, 1874. Chief of the Bureau of Yards and Docks, with the rank of Rear-Admiral.

ENFER, EMILE J.
Acting Ensign, 3 May, 1864. Honorably discharged 15 June, 1867.

ENGARD, ALBERT C.
Acting Third Assistant Engineer, 1861. Resigned 11 October, 1862. Third Assistant Engineer, 17 March, 1863. Second Assistant Engineer, 25 July, 1865. First Assistant Engineer, 11 January, 1873. Chief Engineer, 3 October, 1892. Retired List, 23 February, 1899.

ENGELL, WILLIAM K.
Mate, 12 September, 1861. Acting Ensign, 1 March, 1865. Honorably discharged 10 January, 1869.

ENGGREN, CHARLES A.
Acting Third Assistant Engineer, 21 September, 1864. Honorably discharged 19 October, 1867.

ENGLAND, CLARENCE.
Naval Cadet, 5 September, 1890. Ensign, 1 July, 1896. Lieutenant, Junior Grade, 1 July, 1899.

ENGLANDER, SAMUEL.
Pharmacist, 15 September, 1898.

ENGLE, FREDERICK.
Midshipman, 6 December, 1814. Lieutenant, 13 January, 1825. Commander, 8 September, 1841. Captain, 14 September, 1855. Commodore on Retired List, 16 July, 1862. Rear-Admiral, Retired List, 25 July, 1966. Died 12 February, 1868.

ENGLES, S. ALLEN.
Assistant Surgeon, 24 July, 1849. Pased Assistant Surgeon, 24 July, 1854. Surgeon, 24 April, 1861. Retired 12 August, 1863. Died 28 February, 1865.

ENGLISH, EARL.
Midshipman, 25 February, 1840. Passed Midshipman, 11 July, 1846. Master, 1 March, 1855. Lieutenant, 14 September, 1855. Lieutenant-Commander, 16 July, 1862. Commander, 25 July, 1866. Captain, 28 September, 1871. Chief Bureau Equipments and Recruiting, 20 November, 1878. Commodore, 25 March, 1880. Rear-Admiral, 4 September, 1884. Retired List, 18 February, 1886. Died 16 July, 1893.

ENGLISH, GEORGE B.
Second Lieutenant Marine Corps, 1 March, 1815. Resigned in 1817.

ENGLISH, HENRY C.
Acting Midshipman, 29 September, 1862. Ensign, 18 December, 1868. Died 15 August, 1869.

ENGLISH, JOHN T.
Acting Third Assistant Engineer, 22 April, 1863. Honorably discharged 26 November, 1865.

ENGLISH, MORGAN H.
Third Assistant Engineer, 21 November, 1857. Second Assistant Engineer, 2 August, 1859. Died 23 December, 1862.

ENGLISH, WILLIAM H.
Mate, 29 June, 1863. Honorably discharged 1 January, 1866.

ENOS, ALBERT G.
Midshipman, 7 November, 1840. Dismissed 10 December, 1840.

ENTWISTLE, JAMES.
Third Assistant Engineer, 29 October, 1861. Second Assistant Engineer, 3 August, 1863. First Assistant Engineer, 11 October, 1866. Chief Engineer, 1 July, 1887. Rank changed to Captain, 3 March, 1899. Rear-Admiral on Retired List, 8 July, 1899.

EPPES, JAMES H.
Acting Third Assistant Engineer, 12 March, 1863. Appointment revoked 13 December, 1864.

EPPLE, LOUIS.
Assistant Paymaster (Spanish-American War), 21 May, 1898. Honorably discharged 11 October, 1898.

ERBEN, HENRY.
Midshipman, 17 June, 1848. Passed Midshipman, 12 June, 1855. Master, 16 September, 1855. Lieutenant, 27 December, 1856. Lieutenant-Commander, 16 July, 1862. Commander, 6 May, 1868. Captain, 1 November, 1879. Commodore, 3 April, 1892. Rear-Admiral, 31 July, 1894. Retired List, 6 September, 1894.

GENERAL NAVY REGISTER.

ERICKSON, CHRISTIAN.
   Master, 15 August, 1812. Last appearance on Records of Navy Department, 17 February, 1814.
ERICKSON, CONRAD.
   Acting Ensign, 2 July, 1863. Honorably discharged 6 November, 1865.
ERNEST, JAMES E.
   Mate, 1 October, 1862. Acting Ensign, 15 June, 1864. Resigned 16 June, 1865.
ERNEST, WILLIAM M.
   Mate, 22 April, 1863. Acting Ensign, 5 June, 1863. Honorably discharged 11 December, 1865.
ERSKINE, JOHN F.
   Gunner, 7 February, 1848. Died 10 September, 1849.
ERVIN, HENRY J.
   Acting Carpenter, 19 February, 1864. Honorably discharged 25 December, 1865.
ESENWEIN, AUGUSTUS.
   Acting Assistant Paymaster, 3 August, 1861. Dismissed 6 December, 1864.
ESHLEMAN, SIDNEY ST. J.
   Lieutenant, Junior Grade (Spanish-American War), 20 May, 1898. Honorably discharged 15 September, 1898.
ESKERIDGE, VERNON.
   Chaplain, 11 March, 1851. Died of Yellow Fever, at Portsmouth, Virginia, 11 September, 1855.
ESKRIDGE, ALEX.
   Midshipman, 1 January, 1812. Lieutenant, 5 March, 1817. Died 17 March, 1832.
ESLER, JAMES.
   Acting Third Assistant Engineer, 18 April, 1864. Honorably discharged 23 July, 1866.
ESPY, JAMES P.
   Professor of Mathematics, 7 May, 1842. Resigned 5 July, 1845.
ESSEX, EDWIN.
   Midshipman, 15 November, 1809. Last Appearance on Records of Navy Department, 28 April, 1817. Dead.
ESSEX, JAMES.
   Midshipman, 4 July, 1818. Died 10 February, 1819.
ESTABROOK, EDWARD L.
   Mate, 14 October, 1864. Honorably discharged 19 May, 1866.
ESTABROOKE, ETHAN.
   Professor, 30 October, 1843. Dropped 4 September, 1848.
ESTES, SEPH.
   Acting Ensign, 18 November, 1864. Honorably discharged 15 May, 1865.
ETTING, EMLEN P.
   Assistant Paymaster (Spanish-American War), 1898. Honorably discharged 24 January, 1899.
ETTING, HENRY.
   Midshipman, 1 January, 1818. (See Purser.)
ETTING, HENRY.
   Purser, 7 November, 1826. Pay Director on Retired List, 3 March, 1871. Died 15 February, 1876.
ETTING, THEODORE M.
   Midshipman, 25 November, 1862. Graduated 2 June, 1868. Ensign, 19 April, 1869. Master, 12 July, 1870. Lieutenant, 3 March, 1874. Resigned 1 July, 1877.
ETTRINGHAM, ROBERT J.
   Mate, 1 October, 1862. Acting Ensign, 29 January, 1863. Honorably discharged 1 December, 1865.
EUSTIS, ALEXANDER B.
   Midshipman, 4 January, 1833. Resigned 8 June, 1835.
EUSTIS, GEORGE F.
   Ensign (Spanish-American War), 6 May, 1898. Honorably discharged 22 November, 1898.
EVANS, AMOS A.
   Assistant Surgeon, 1 September, 1808. Surgeon, 20 April, 1810. Resigned 15 April, 1824.
EVANS, BARUCH M.
   Carpenter, date not known. Last appearance on Records of Navy Department, 21 June, 1819. Dead.
EVANS, BENJAMIN.
   Boatswain, date not known. Last appearance on Records of Navy Department.
EVANS, CHARLES.
   Lieutenant (Spanish-American War), 28 May, 1898. Honorably discharged 24 December, 1898.
EVANS, CLARENCE A.
   Third Assistant Engineer, 17 March, 1863. Resigned 4 September, 1865.
EVANS, EDWARD A.
   Midshipman, 1 January, 1808. Last appearance on Records of Navy Department, 25 March, 1808.
EVANS, FRANCK T.
   Naval Cadet, 6 September, 1894. Ensign, 4 April, 1900.
EVANS, GEORGE.
   Master, 11 June, 1812. Resigned 10 April, 1815.
EVANS, GEORGE B.
   Midshipman, 21 May, 1800. Lost in the Insurgent.
EVANS, GEORGE R.
   Cadet Engineer, 1 October, 1881. Ensign, 1 July, 1887. Lieutenant, Junior Grade, 9 June, 1896. Lieutenant, 3 March, 1899.

EVANS, GEORGE W.
Assistant Surgeon, 30 June, 1834. Lost in the steamer Pulaski. June, 1838.
EVANS, HERBERT H.
Naval Cadet, 6 September, 1895. At sea prior to final graduation.
EVANS, HOLDEN A.
Naval Cadet, 5 September, 1888. Ensign, 1 July, 1894. Assistant Naval Constructor, 1 July, 1896.
EVANS, ISAAC S.
Acting Third Assistant Engineer, 30 December, 1864. Honorably discharged 15 May, 1865.
EVANS, JOEL C.
Gunner, 7 February, 1889. Chief Gunner, 3 March, 1899.
EVANS, JOHN.
Midshipman, 17 December, 1810. Lieutenant, 27 April, 1816. Died 5 February, 1835.
EVANS, JOHN, Jr.
Midshipman, 1 January, 1811. Killed in action 1 June, 1813.
EVANS, JOHN.
Acting Second Assistant Engineer, 28 October, 1863. Resigned 16 July, 1864. Acting Second Assistant Engineer, 6 March, 1865. Honorably discharged 12 July, 1866.
EVANS, JOHN.
Mate, 1 February, 1864. Resigned August, 1865.
EVANS, RICHARD.
Acting Second Assistant Engineer, 25 February, 1864. Honorably discharged 19 November, 1865.
EVANS, RICHARD L.
Mate, 12 February, 1864. Honorably discharged 14 August, 1865.
EVANS, ROBLEY D.
Acting Midshipman, 20 September, 1860. Acting Ensign, 1 October, 1863. Master, on Retired List, 10 May, 1866. Lieutenant on Retired List, 25 July, 1866. Active List, 25 January, 1867. Lieutenant-Commander, 12 March, 1868. Active List. Commander, 12 July, 1878. Captain, 27 June, 1893.
EVANS, SAMUEL.
Midshipman, 11 May, 1798. Lieutenant, 25 November, 1799. Commander, 24 April, 1806. Captain, 4 July, 1812. Died 2 June, 1824.
EVANS, SHELDON G.
Assistant Surgeon, 18 November, 1890. Passed Assistant Surgeon, 18 November, 1893.
EVANS, S. W.
Acting Second Assistant Enginer, 26 September, 1863. Deserted 16 April, 1865.
EVANS, JAMES.
Boatswain, 1 January, 1819. Died 9 July, 183—.
EVANS, THOMAS.
Midshipman, 23 October, 1820. Resigned 4 February, 1825.
EVANS, WALDO.
Naval Cadet, 7 September, 1887. Ensign, 1 July, 1893. Lieutenant, Junior Grade, 3 March, 1899. Lieutenant, 12 December, 1899.
EVANS, WILLIAM.
Mate, 24 May, 1865. Honorably discharged 9 November, 1865.
EVANS, WILLIAM E.
Acting Midshipman, 4 June, 1852. Midshipman, 20 June, 1856. Passed Midshipman, 29 April, 1859. Master, 5 September, 1859. Resigned 2 February, 1861.
EVERDEAN, CHARLES S.
Mate, 20 August, 1863. Honorably discharged 29 May, 1868.
EVERDING, JOHN.
Third Asistant Engineer, 2 December, 1861. Second Assistant Engineer, 25 August, 1863. Resigned 19 June, 1864.
EVERED, CHARLES P.
Acting Second Assistant Engineer, 2 September, 1864. Resigned 5 May, 1865.
EVERETT, ALFRED.
Acting Master and Pilot. 1 October, 1864. Honorably discharged 15 November, 1865.
EVERETT, DELOS.
Acting Third Assistant Enginer, 26 July, 1864. Resigned (sick) 28 October, 1864.
EVERETT, JAMES.
Chaplain, 28 December, 1818. Resigned 12 April, 1837.
EVERETT, THOMAS H.
Midshipman, 1 January, 1818. Last appearance on Records of Navy Department, 1818. Resigned
EVERETT, WILLIAM B.
Midshipman, 1 February, 1823. Dismissed 8 June, 1831.
EVERETT, WILLIAM E.
Third Asistant Engineer, 1 September, 1845. Second Asistant Engineer, 10 June, 1847. First Assistant Engineer, 31 October, 1848. Chief Engineer, 30 August, 1852. Resigned 30 November, 1859.
EVERETT, WILLIAM H.
Midshipman, 23 July, 1863. Graduated 2 June, 1868. Ensign, 19 April, 1869. Master, 12 July, 1870. Lieutenant, 12 December, 1873. Lieutenant-Commander, 6 December, 1894. Commander, 3 March, 1899.
EVERHARDT, JOHN H.
Acting Second Assistant Engineer, 1 October, 1862. Acting First Assistant Engineer, 28 November, 1863. Honorably discharged 20 November, 1865.
EVERHART, JOHN J.
Mate, 19 April, 1862. Dismissed 2 July, 1864.
EVERHART, LAY H.
Naval Cadet, 29 September, 1885. Cadet, 20 May, 1886. Ensign, 1 July, 1892. Lieutenant, Junior Grade, 3 March, 1899. Lieutenant, 1 July, 1899.

GENERAL NAVY REGISTER.   187

EVERS, EDWARD.
　Assistant Surgeon, 5 October, 1872. Resigned 12 June, 1874.
EVERSFIELD, CHARLES.
　Assistant Surgeon, 29 May, 1843. Passed Assistant Surgeon, 12 February, 1850. Surgeon, 15 August, 1857. Medical Inspector, 3 March, 1871. Medical Director, 29 June, 1872. Died 5 October, 1873.
EVERSON, ALBERT.
　Acting First Assistant Engineer, 16 December, 1862. Resigned 11 August, 1863.
EVERSON, ALFRED.
　Acting Master, 3 December, 1861. Resigned 6 April, 1865.
EVERSON, BENJAMIN.
　Acting First Assistant Engineer, 1 October, 1862. Honorably discharged 1 December, 1865.
EVERSON, LINUS J.
　Acting Third Assistant Engineer, 19 December, 1862. Acting Second Assistant Engineer, 17 November, 1864. Honorably discharged 17 September, 1865.
EWART, HORATIO.
　Carpenter, date not known. Last appearance on Records of Navy Department.
EWELL, EDWARD.
　Acting Third Assistant Engineer, 5 January, 1864. Honorably discharged 6 December, 1865.
EWELL, THOMAS.
　Surgeon, 16 January,1808. Resigned. 5 May, 1813.
EWEN, WARREN.
　Acting Third Assistant Engineer, 7 January, 1862. Acting Second Assistant Engineer, 13 December, 1862. Acting First Assistant Engineer, 12 November, 1863. Honorably discharged 13 November, 1865.
EWER, G. W.
　Acting Master, 18 November, 1861. Appointment revoked (sick) 22 September, 1864.
EWER, JOHN.
　Acting Master, 7 August, 1861. Resigned 16 October, 1863.
EWING, JOHN M.
　Mate, 5 February, 1864. Resigned (sick) 15 September, 1864.
EWING, ROBERT T
　Acting Third Assistant Engineer, 17 August, 1863. Last Record in Department, 13 January, 1865.
EYCKE, EMIL H.
　Boatswain, 23 June, 1898.
EYRE, MANNING K.
　Cadet Midshipman, 22 September, 1876. Graduated 22 June, 1882. Ensign, Junior Grade, 3 March, 1883. Ensign, 26 June, 1884. Resigned 30 June, 1894.
EYSTER, CHARLES W.
　Acting Third Assistant Engineer, 1 October, 1862. Resigned (sick) 1 March, 1865.
EYTINGE, HENRY S.
　Acting Volunteer Lieutenant, 26 August, 1861. Appointment revoked 1 December, 1863.
EYTINGE, HENRY S., Jr.
　Mate, 1 December, 1862. Deserted 1 April, 1865.
FABENS, GEORGE O.
　Acting Ensign, 30 May, 1863. Honorably discharged 11 May, 1865.
FADER, DAVID.
　Mate, 8 October, 1862. Honorably discharged 13 January, 1869. Mate, 27 January, 1870. Resigned 6 June, 1871.
FAGAN, HENRY.
　Third Assistant Engineer. 5 September, 1860. Name stricken from the rolls of the Navy 8 July, 1861
FAGAN, JAMES.
　Acting Third Assistant Engineer, 6 January, 1862. Acting Second Assistant Engineer, 24 February, 1863. Honorably discharged 19 November, 1865.
FAGEN, PETER W.
　Mate, 11 December, 1861. Acting Ensign, 16 November, 1864. Honorably discharged 20 March, 1868.
FAHS, CHARLES M.
　Cadet Engineer, 1 October, 1880. Ensign, 1 July, 1886. Lieutenant, Junior Grade, 5 November, 1895. Lieutenant, 15 November, 1898.
FAHS, CHARLES T.
　Assistant Surgeon. 19 April, 1851. Passed Assistant Surgeon, 10 April, 1856. Surgeon, 1 May, 1861. Dismissed 13 November, 1861.
FAILING, W. A.
　Mate, 19 July, 1867. Resigned 15 July, 1870.
FAIN, NICHOLAS.
　Midshipman, 15 November, 1809. Resigned 1 October, 1810.
FAIR, JOHN.
　Gunner, 8 July, 1815. Resigned 14 June, 1825.
FAIRBAIRN, JOHN O.
　Acting Third Assistant Engineer, 23 April, 1863. Acting Second Assistant Engineer. 29 October, 1863. Honorably discharged 19 May, 1866.
FAIRBANK, ALLEN.
　Mate, 18 September, 1866. Mustered out 8 September, 1868.
FAIRCHILD, CHARLES.
　Acting Assistant Paymaster, 15 March, 1862. Assistant Paymaster, 30 June, 1864. Resigned 6 December, 1864.

FAIRCHILD, J. B.
Mate, 1 September, 1862. Acting Ensign, 2 April, 1863. Honorably discharged 3 November, 1865.
FAIRCHILD, LOUIS.
Midshipman, 20 June, 1806. Appointed Purser, 29 September, 1813. Lost in the Wasp, 1815.
FAIRCOIT, CHARLES O.
Acting Third Assistant Engineer, 22 October, 1863. Honorably discharged 12 October, 1865.
FAIRFAX, ARCHIBALD B.
Midshipman, 4 August, 1823. Passed Midshipman, 23 March. 1829. Lieutenant, 13 July, 1832. Commander, 22 August, 1855. Dismissed 18 April, 1861.
FAIRFAX, DONALD, McN.
Midshipman, 12 August, 1837. Passed Midshipman, 29 June, 1843. Master, 4 August, 1850. Lieutenant, 26 February, 1851. Commander, 16 July, 1862. Captain, 25 July, 1866. Commodore, 24 August, 1873. Rear-Admiral, 11 July, 1880. Retired List, 30 September, 1881. Died 10 January, 1894.
FAIRFAX, OCTAVIUS.
Midshipman, 1 January, 1828. Passed Midshipman, 3 July, 1835. Died 4 January, 1837.
FAIRFAX, REGINALD.
Midshipman, 28 May, 1839. Passed Midshipman, 2 July, 1845. Master, 3 September, 1853. Lieutenant, 28 April, 1854. Resigned 15 April, 1861.
FAIRFIELD, JASON W.
Acting Assistant Paymaster, 5 November, 1862. Passed Assistant Paymaster, 23 July, 1866. Died 5 September, 1867.
FAIRFOWL, H. W.
Acting First Assistant Engineer, 31 March, 1863. Honorably discharged 7 November, 1865.
FAIRLIE, ROBERT Y.
Midshipman, 4 May, 1816. Resigned 25 August, 1823.
FAILING, WILLIAM A.
Mate, 19 July, 1867. Resigned 15 July, 1870.
FALCONER, R. T.
Assistant Surgeon, 28 March, 1820. Resigned 12 May, 1824.
FALCONER, WALTER M.
Naval Cadet, 6 September, 1893. Ensign, 1 July, 1899.
FALES, CHARLES.
Gunner, 30 October, 1827. Dropped 23 May, 1834.
FALES, N.
Acting Master, 28 January, 1862. Died from injuries received on the Minnesota, 1 September, 1862.
FALES, PLINY H.
Acting Third Assistant Engineer, 19 September, 1862. Honorably discharged 10 June, 1868.
FALES, WILLIAM.
Acting Master, 9 October, 1861. Honorably discharged 2 November, 1865.
FALLER, GUY W.
Naval Cadet, 19 May, 1894. Ensign, 4 April, 1900.
FALLON, JAMES E.
Third Assistant Engineer, 17 December, 1862. Second Assistant Engineer, 8 April, 1864. Resigned 21 May, 1866.
FANNING, J. B.
Purser, 29 December, 1817. Died 24 October, 1822.
FANNING, NATHANIEL.
Lieutenant, 5 December, 1804. Died 30 September, 1805.
FARENHOLT, AMMEN.
Assistant Surgeon. 29 May, 1894. Passed Assistant Surgeon, 29 May, 1897.
FARENHOLT, OSCAR W.
Acting Ensign, 19 August, 1864. Ensign, 12 March, 1868. Master, 18 December, 1868. Lieutenant, 21 March, 1870. Lieutenant-Commander, 11 May, 1882. Commander, 19 June, 1892. Captain, 25 September, 1899.
FARGO, RANSOM J.
Mate, 5 June, 1863. Resigned 29 July, 1863.
FARIES, GEORGE G.
Midshipman, 17 December, 1810. Resigned 6 June, 1811.
FARLEY, WILLIAM.
Mate, 25 December, 1863. Deserted April, 1864.
FARMER, BENJAMIN A.
Acting Third Assistant Engineer, 1 October, 1862. Acting Second Assistant Engineer, 5 July, 1864. Honorably discharged 28 September, 1865.
FARMER, EDWARD.
Third Assistant Engineer, 3 May, 1859. Second Assistant Engineer, 16 October, 1861. First Assistant Engineer, 20 May, 1863. Chief Engineer, 4 March, 1871. Retired 1 March, 1898.
FARMER, HENRY.
Acting Third Assistant Engineer, 17 October, 1861. Acting Second Assistant Engineer, 26 February, 1864. Honorably discharged 24 August, 1866.
FARMER, JOHN W.
Acting Ensign, 14 December, 1863. Honorably discharged 29 August, 1865.
FARNHAM, BELA M.
Acting Assistant Paymaster, 23 September, 1864. Discharged 7 June, 1865.

GENERAL NAVY REGISTER.   189

FARNSWORTH, JOHN.
Midshipman, 25 September, 1869. Graduated 1 June, 1874. Resigned 30 June, 1877. Ensign (Spanish-American War), 4 May, 1898. Honorably discharged 12 September, 1898.

FARON, EDWARD.
Third Assistant Engineer, 1 September, 1845. Second Asistant Engineer, 10 July, 1847. First Assistant Engineer, 31 October, 1848. Resigned 1 June, 1849. Acting Chief Engineer, 13 March, 1863. Appointment revoked 21 July, 1863.

FARON, GEORGE.
Acting First Assistant Engineer, 9 May, 1861. Honorably discharged 24 May, 1868.

FARON, JOHN.
Third Assistant Engineer, 31 October, 1848. Second Assistant Engineer, 26 February, 1851. First Assistant Engineer, 21 May, 1853. Chief Engineer, 23 April, 1859. Lost on the Tecumseh, 5 August, 1864.

FARON, JOHN, Jr.
First Assistant Engineer, 15 November, 1837. Chief Engineer, 13 January, 1840. Resigned 3 April, 1848.

FARON, ROBERT D.
Acting Third Assistant Engineer, 7 October, 1862. Acting Second Assistant Engineer, 29 September, 1864. Appointment revoked (sick) 9 December, 1864.

FARQUHAR, NORMAN H.
Acting Midshipman, 27 September, 1854. Midshipman, 9 June, 1859. Lieutenant, 31 August, 1861. Lieutenant-Commander, 5 August, 1865. Commander, 12 December, 1872. Captain, 4 March, 1886. Commodore, 21 July, 1897. Rear-Admiral, 25 December, 1898.

FARQUHARSON, A. J.
Assistant Surgeon, 26 April, 1847. Passed Assistant Surgeon, 26 April, 1852. Resigned 21 September, 1855.

FARRAGUT, DAVID G.
Midshipman, 17 December, 1810. Lieutenant, 13 January, 1825. Commander, 8 September, 1841. Captain, 14 September, 1855. Rear-Admiral, 16 July, 1862. Vice-Admiral, 31 December, 1864. Admiral, 26 July, 1866. Died 14 August, 1870.

FARRAGUT, GEORGE.
Master, 2 March, 1807. Dismissed 25 March, 1814.

FARRAGUT, W. A. C.
Midshipman, 16 January, 1809. Lieutenant, 9 December, 1814. Dropped 13 September, 1855. Commissioned Lieutenant from 9 December, 1814, on Reserved List. Died 20 December, 1859.

FARRAND, EBENEZER.
Midshipman, 4 March, 1823. Passed Midshipman, 23 March, 1829. Lieutenant, 3 March, 1831. Commander, 10 July, 1854. Resigned 21 January, 1861.

FARRAND, JAMES B.
Acting Second Assistant Engineer, 12 November, 1862. Acting First Assistant Engineer, 26 May, 1865. Honorably discharged 7 October, 1868.

FARRAR, JARVIS G.
Mate, 11 July, 1863. Drowned near Bogue Inlet, North Carolina, 10 June, 1864.

FARRAR, WILLIAM C.
Midshipman, 1 April, 1826. Passed Midshipman, 28 April, 1832. Died 24 February, 1835.

FARRELL, EDWARD.
Mate, 12 October, 1863. Deserted 17 October, 1863.

FARRELL, JAMES.
Boatswain, 30 July, 1875. Died 1 August, 1891.

FARRELL, JAMES W.
Acting First Assistant Engineer, 3 September, 1863. Honorably discharged 9 July, 1865.

FARRELL, RODGER.
Mate, 5 September, 1863. Acting Ensign, 19 January, 1864. Appointment revoked 17 November, 1865.

FARRELL, THOMAS M.
Acting Ensign, 27 December, 1862. Acting Master, 29 June, 1863. Honorably discharged 7 December, 1865.

FARRER, FRANK M.
Acting First Assistant Engineer, 8 January, 1864. Honorably discharged 29 July, 1865.

FARRER, GEORGE W.
Acting First Assistant Engineer, 10 September, 1861. Acting Chief Engineer, 19 January, 1863. Honorablyd ischarged 16 October, 1865.

FARRER, SOLON.
Acting First Assistant Engineer, 4 October, 1861. Acting Chief Engineer, 19 January, 1863. Honorably discharged 16 October, 1865.

FARRIS, JOHN.
Gunner, 23 September, 1813. Last appearance on Records of Navy Department for 1815. Sloop Frolic.

FARROAT, THOMAS G.
Acting Third Assistant Enginer, 20 December, 1861. Appointment revoked (sick) 8 November, 1864.

FARRON, JAMES.
Acting Third Assistant Engineer, 24 November, 1863. Honorably discharged 22 August, 1865.

FARROW, WILLIAM.
Boatswain, 5 May, 1838. Resigned 16 July, 1839.

FARWELL, AUGUSTUS.
Mate. Dismissed 9 January, 1863.

GENERAL NAVY REGISTER.

FARWELL, JOSEPH M.
Acting Master, 24 June, 1861. Resigned 19 April, 1862.
FARWELL, WILLIAM. G.
Assistant Surgeon, 10 November, 1868. Passed Assistant Surgeon, 23 January, 1874. Surgeon, 15 January, 1881. Medical Inspector, 28 February, 1896. Medical Director, 22 January, 1900.
FASSETT, THOMAS O
Sailmaker, 5 June, 1861. Retired List, 31 December, 1894. Died 14 December, 1897.
FASSIG, B. F.
Assistant Surgeon, 14 July, 1871. Died 10 May, 1875.
FASSOUX, PETER JR.
Midshipman, 16 January, 1809. Resigned 18 February, 1812.
FATIO, L. C.
Midshipman, 8 March, 1822. Resigned 7 July, 1829.
FAUCON, EDWARD H.
Acting Master, 23 July, 1861. Acting Volunteer Lieutenant, 4 October, 1862. Honorably discharged 4 September, 1865.
FAUL, WILLIAM J.
Acting Third Assistant Engineer, 9 December, 1863. Honorably discharged 9 November, 1865. Acting Third Assistant Engineer, 1 December, 1866. Mustered out 12 December, 1868.
FAULKNER, WILLIAM D.
Acting Chief Engineer, 1 October, 1862. Resigned 10 October,1 864.
FAUNCE, GEORGE A.
Mate, 25 January, 1862. Acting Ensign, 20 July, 1863. Honorably discharged 11 November, 1865.
FAUNCE, PETER.
Mate, 12 October, 1861. Acting Ensign, 15 June, 1863. Honorably discharged 15 July, 1867.
FAUNTLEROY, C. M.
Midshipman, 3 March, 1838. Passed Midshipman, 20 May, 1844. Master, 16 October, 1851. Lieutenant, 2 November, 1852. Dismissed 13 May, 1861.
FAUNTLEROY, D.
Purser, 7 July, 1834. Died 31 August, 1853.
FAUNTLEROY, W. H.
Midshipman, 2 March, 1841. Passed Midshipman, 10 August, 1847. Resigned 16 August, 1849.
FAUST, WILLIAM H.
Naval Cadet, 28 September, 1882. Ensign, 1 July, 1888. Lieutenant, Junior Grade, 10 November, 1896. Lieutenant, 3 March, 1899. Retired List, 23 September, 1899.
FAUTH, HENRY.
Third Assistant Engineer, 16 February, 1852. Second Assistant Engineer, 27 June, 1855. Resigned 29 August, 1856.
FAWDRY, D. C.
Acting Assistant Surgeon, 7 September, 1864. Honorably discharged 10 October, 1865.
FAWKES, THOMAS.
Acting Second Assistant Engineer. Appointment revoked (sick) 22 September, 1864.
FAXON, JOSIAH.
Sailmaker, 22 October, 1841. Died 30 June, 1844.
FAXON, WILLIAM H.
Acting Assistant Surgeon, 23 July, 1865. Honorably discharged 31 November, 1870.
FAY, JONAS.
Assistant Surgeon, 30 June, 1799. Commission returned 21 September, 1800.
FAY, JOSIAH S.
Acting Third Assistant Engineer. Resigned 10 December, 1862.
FAY, W. GASTON.
Acting Assistant Paymaster, 31 December, 1862. Resigned 25 November, 1863.
FEARING, WILLIAM G.
Mate, 2 January, 1864. Resigned 14 March, 1865.
FEASTER, JOSEPH.
Assistant Naval Constructor, 29 July, 1875. Naval Constructor, 10 October, 1888. Retired List, 5 August, 1899.
FEATHERSTON, JOHN.
Boatswain, 7 December, 1841. Warranted 1 December, 1846. Died 30 October, 1852.
FEBIGER, JOHN C.
Midshipman, 4 September, 1838. Passed Midshipman, 20 May, 1844. Master, 13 July, 1852. Lieutenant, 30 April, 1853. Commander, 27 August, 1862. Captain, 6 May, 1868. Commodore, 9 August, 1874. Rear-Admiral, 4 February, 1882. Retired List, 1 July, 1882. Died 9 October, 1898.
FECHTELER, AUGUSTUS F.
Cadet Midshipman, 5 June, 1873. Graduated 18 June, 1879. Ensign, 23 November, 1880. Lieutenant, Junior Grade, 6 March, 1887. Lieutenant, 21 July, 1892. Lieutenant-Commander, 27 March, 1900.
FEEHAN, HENRY.
Acting Boatswain, 28 September, 1899.
FEGAN, JOHN R.
Mate, 21 December, 1861. Dismissed 28 June, 1862.
FEILBURG, ULRIC.
Acting Ensign, 9 June, 1863. Honorably discharged 18 September, 1865.
FELCH, CHEEVER.
Chaplain, 12 May, 1815. Resigned 29 August, 1825.
FELCH, C. L.
Mate, 4 December, 1867. Appointment revoked 14 March, 1872.

FELIX, AMBROSE.
Mate, 20 November, 1861. Acting Ensign, 14 May, 1863. Honorably discharged 21 December, 1865.
FELL, ROBERT.
Carpenter, 6 June, 1803. Resigned 14 February, 1820.
FELLOWS, CALEB.
Mate, 8 September, 1862. Resigned 24 September, 1863.
FELT, JOHN.
Carpenter, 9 June, 1803. Resigned 16 May, 1806.
FELTAS, WILLIAM H.
Midshipman, 1 September, 1811. Last appearance on Records of Navy Department, 1815. Brooklyn.
FELTER, JACOB.
Midshipman, 10 July, 1805. Broke by Court Martial, 2 March, 1808.
FENDALL, BENJAMIN.
Master, 26 September, 1800. Discharged 8 June, 1801, under Peace Establishment Act.
FENDALL, JOHN.
Midshipman, 10 July, 1805. Resigned 4 January, 1808.
FENDALL, T. H. M.
Assistant Surgeon, 28 August, 1800. Discharged 8 June, 1801, under Peace Establishment Act.
FENGAR, ALVAN A.
Acting Master 11 June, 1861. Resigned 7 August, 1861.
FENGER, RICHARD.
Acting Second Assistant Engineer, 10 October, 1863. Honorably discharged 18 December, 1865.
FENNELL, DAVID D.
Acting Third Assistant Engineer, 14 December, 1863. Acting Second Assistant Engineer, 17 March, 1865. Honorably discharged 19 December, 1867.
FENNER, EDWARD B.
Naval Cadet, 20 May, 1895. At sea prior to final graduation
FENNER, JEREMIAH.
Lieutenant, 9 March, 1799. Discharged 9 July, 1801, under Peace Establishment Act.
FENNIMORE, WESLEY.
Third Assistant Engineer, 4 May, 1863. Resigned 12 October, 1865.
FENNO, GEORGE.
Midshipman, 20 June, 1799. Resigned 30 May, 1800.
FENTON, ASHBEL.
Purser, 14 October, 1799. Discharged 18 November, 1801, under Peace Establishment Act.
FENTON, THEODORE C.
Cadet Engineer, 1 October, 1881. Ensign, 1 July, 1887. Lieutenant, Junior Grade, 5 January, 1896. Lieutenant, 25 December, 1898.
FENTRESS, WALTER E. H.
Mate, 11 December, 1861. Acting Ensign, 27 August, 1862. Acting Master, 24 January, 1863. Honorably discharged 13 September, 1867.
FEREBEE, N. McPHERSON.
Assistant Surgeon, 12 September, 1872. Passed Assistant Surgeon, 11 January, 1876. Surgeon, 12 March, 1886. Medical Inspector, 2 September, 1898.
FERGUSON, DONALD.
Ensign (Spanish-American War), 18 July, 1898. Honorably discharged 26 August, 1898.
FERGUSON, HOMER L.
Naval Cadet, 21 May, 1888. Graduated. Assistant Naval Constructor, 1 July, 1894.
FERGUSON, EDWARD R.
Acting Third Assistant Engineer, 16 September, 1861. Acting First Assistant Engineer, 29 May, 1862. Dismissed 13 January, 1863.
FERGUSON, JAMES.
Midshipman, 22 May, 1800. Discharged 4 June, 1801, under Peace Establishment Act.
FERGUSON, JAMES.
Sailmaker, 24 February, 1835. Died at Philadelphia, 22 July, 1869.
FERGUSON, JAMES.
Master, 27 May, 1814. Reserved List, 10 October, 1855. Died at Rio de Janeiro, 4 December, 1858.
FERGUSON, JAMES L.
Midshipman, 9 September, 1841. Resigned 5 March, 1847.
FERGUSON, JOHN F.
Acting Master, 11 July, 1861. Resigned 20 March, 1862.
FERGUSON, WILLIAM.
Acting Ensign, 24 January, 1863. Acting Master 18 January, 1864. Honorably discharged 20 November, 1865.
FERGUSON, WILLIAM B., Jr.
Naval Cadet, 20 May, 1896. Graduated 30 June, 1900.
FERGUSON, WILLIAM J.
Gunner, 3 August, 1861. Retired List, 16 November, 1883. Died 21 March, 1900.
FERMIER, GEORGE L.
Naval Cadet, 21 May, 1885. Ensign, 1 July, 1891. Died 19 November, 1898.
FERNALD, BENJAMIN E.
Carpenter, 20 February, 1872. Retired List, 7 November, 1894.
FERNALD, CHARLES C.
Acting Third Assistant Engineer, 6 September, 1864. Honorably discharged 21 September, 1865.

GENERAL NAVY REGISTER.

FERNALD, CHARLES H.
Mate, 28 April, 1863. Acting Ensign, 6 August, 1864. Honorably discharged 20 August, 1865.
FERNALD, FRANK L.
Assistant Naval Constructor, 4 May, 1871. Naval Constructor, 12 March, 1875. Retired List, 11 November, 1897.
FERNALD, JOSEPH.
Acting Second Assistant Engineer, 25 August, 1863. Honorably discharged 5 July, 1865.
FERNALD, MARK.
Lieutenant, 10 June, 1879. Last appearance on Records of Navy Department.
FERNALD, THEODORE.
Boatswain, 15 March, 1836. Resigned 6 October, 1836.
FERNEY, THOMAS H.
For duty at N. Rendezvous, New Bedford, Massachusetts, 11 June, 1862. Appointment revoked, Rendezvous having closed, 21 April, 1865. Acting Ensign, Coast Survey Duty, 19 May, 1866. Mustered out 30 November, 1868.
FERRALL, PETER.
Midshipman, 26 March, 1800. Discharged 14 July, 1801, under Peace Establishment Act.
FERRALL, THOMAS C.
Carpenter, 31 May, 1850. Warranted 19 May, 1853. Dismissed 6 April, 1859.
FERRELL, JOSEPH L.
Acting Assistant Paymaster, 1 November, 1864. Honorably discharged 15 October, 1865.
FERRELL, J. W.
Acting Third Assistant Engineer, 10 July, 1863. Honorably discharged 20 November, 1865.
FERRIER, WILLIAM A.
Acting Gunner, 4 December, 1862. Resigned 21 September, 1864. Acting Gunner, 10 February, 1865. Honorably discharged 9 August, 1866. Mate, 11 January, 1870. Gunner, 8 July, 1872. Retired List, 10 February, 1892. Died 21 October, 1899.
FERRIS, GEORGE.
Acting Master, 21 October, 1861. Resigned 28 February, 1865.
FERRIS, HENRY R.
Mate, 24 November, 1863. Resigned 23 May, 1865.
FERRIS, JOHN.
Boatswain, 30 July, 1833. Last appearance on Records of Navy Department.
FERRIS, JOHN D.
Mate, 3 September, 1863. Resigned 7 November, 1863.
FERRIS, JOHN D.
Acting Third Assistant Engineer, 9 July, 1864. Honorably discharged 2 October, 1865.
FERRISS, JONATHAN D.
Master, 28 February, 1809. Lieutenant, 13 July, 1832. Died 13 November, 1855.
FESLER, JAMES W.
Naval Cadet (Spanish-American War), 5 July, 1898. Honorably discharged 8 December, 1898.
FEWEL, CHRISTOPHER C.
Naval Cadet, 2 October, 1889. Ensign, 1 July, 1895. Lieutenant, Junior, Grade, 3 March, 1899.
FEWKES, THOMAS.
Acting Second Assistant Engineer, 10 August, 1863. Appointment revoked 22 September, 1864.
FICKBOHM, HERMAN F.
Midshipman, 31 July, 1866. Graduated 7 June, 1870. Ensign, 13 July, 1871. Master, 6 January, 1874. Lieutenant, 24 February, 1880. Lieutenant-Commander, 3 March, 1899. Retired List, with rank of Commander, 30 June, 1899.
FICKETT, LEVI S.
Acting Ensign, 17 September, 1862. Acting Master, on recommendation of commanding officer, 26 April, 1864. Honorably discharged 7 December, 1868.
FIEHL, JOHN.
Acting Third Assistant Engineer, 9 May, 1864. Honorably discharged 18 July, 1866.
FIELD, AMBROSE D.
Midshipman, 1 December, 1809. Last appearance on Records of Navy Department, 1815. Frigate Constitution.
FIELD, CHARLES A.
Acting Gunner, 12 September, 1863. Drowned 6 October, 1863.
FIELD, EDWARD.
Assistant Surgeon, 6 August, 1799. Last appearance on Records of Navy Department, 6 July, 1801.
FIELD, EDWARD A.
Midshipman, 22 July, 1865. Graduated 4 June, 1869. Ensign, 12 July, 1870. Master, 26 December, 1871. Lieutenant, 10 February, 1875. Died 27 December, 1884.
FIELD, HARRY A.
Cadet Engineer, 1 October, 1879. Ensign, 1 July, 1885. Lieutenant, Junior Grade, 23 April, 1895. Lieutenant, 1 May, 1898.
FIELD, JACOB T.
Acting Assistant Surgeon, 9 March, 1863. Honorably discharged 13 October, 1865.
FIELD, JAMES G.
Assistant Surgeon, 23 May, 1887. Retired List, 26 June, 1893.

GENERAL NAVY REGISTER.

FIELD, JOHN H.
   Mate, 24 October, 1861. Acting Ensign, 28 October, 1862. Resigned 29 October, 1863.
FIELD, JOSEPH.
   Midshipman, 7 December, 1799. Discharged 9 June, 1800, under Peace Establishment Act.
FIELD, MANNSELL B.
   Midshipman, 25 February, 1863. Graduated June, 1866. Ensign, 12 March, 1868. Master, 26 March, 1869. Lieutenant, 21 March, 1870. Resignation accepted 1 April, 1873.
FIELD, ROBERT.
   Midshipman, 1 September, 1811. Lieutenant, 27 April, 1816. Resigned 4 October, 1822.
FIELD, SAMUEL H.
   Acting Ensign, 17 September, 1862. Appointment revoked (sick) 25 May, 1863. Acting Ensign, 2 October, 1863. Acting Master, on recommendation of commanding officer, 2 April, 1864. Honorably discharged 5 July, 1865.
FIELD, TIMOTHY B.
   Midshipman, 1 March, 1825. Resigned 18 July, 1831.
FIELD, WELLS LAFLIN.
   Acting Midshipman, 20 November, 1862. Ensign, 18 December, 1868. Master, 21 March, 1870. Lieutenant, 21 March, 1871. Lieutenant-Commander, 5 November, 1891. Commander, 27 April, 1898.
FIELD, WILEY ROY MASON.
   Cadet Midshipman, 28 June, 1878. Ensign, 1 July, 1884. Lieutenant, Junior Grade, 16 September, 1894. Lieutenant, 14 March, 1898.
FIELD, WILLIAM.
   Mate, 29 September, 1862. Acting Ensign, 15 June, 1863. Honorably discharged 12 April, 1868.
FIELD, WILLIAM.
   Mate, 26 April, 1865. Honorably discharged 15 September, 1866.
FIELD, WILLIAM H.
   Mate. Appointment revoked 20 May, 1863.
FIELDER, FRANK S.
   Assistant Surgeon (Spanish-American War), 9 May, 1898. Honorably discharged 27 September, 1898.
FIFE, GEORGE S.
   Acting Assistant Surgeon, 20 October, 1863. Assistant Surgeon, 10 November, 1866. Dropped 31 December, 1867.
FIFE, JOSEPH A.
   Acting Assistant Surgeon, 22 May, 1863. Resigned 9 September, 1864.
FILLEBROWN, GEORGE B.
   Mate, 1 November, 1861. Appointment revoked 5 February, 1862.
FILLEBROWN, THOMAS SCOTT.
   Midshipman, 19 October, 1841. Passed Midshipman, 10 August, 1847. Master, 14 September, 1855. Lieutenant, 15 September, 1855. Lieutenant-Commander, 16 July, 1862. Commander, 25 July, 1866. Captain, 6 January, 1874. Commodore, 7 May, 1883. Died 26 September, 1884.
FILLMORE, JOHN H.
   Cadet Midshipman, 24 September, 1874. Graduated 4 June, 1880. Ensign, 25 November, 1881. Retired List, 2 January, 1891. Died 8 January, 1893.
FINCH, WILLIAM B.
   Midshipman, 20 June, 1806. Lieutenant, 4 January, 1813. Commander, 28 March, 1820. Captain, 21 February, 1831. (See Bolton.)
FINCKE, FREDERICK O. G.
   Mate, 1 June, 1864. Appointment revoked 5 May, 1865. Mate, 1 July, 1865. Appointment revoked 27 September, 1865.
FINDLEY, DAVID G.
   Warrant Machinist (Spanish-American War), 15 June, 1898. Honorably discharged 2 September, 1898.
FINDLAY, JAMES.
   Acting Second Assistant Engineer, 23 March, 1864. Honorably discharged 28 September, 1865.
FINGER, ROBERT.
   Acting Third Assistant Engineer, 26 October, 1861. Resigned 20 December, 1862.
FINK, JOSEPH H.
   Acting Carpenter, 10 July, 1863. Acting Ensign, 22 April, 1865. Honorably discharged 21 March, 1866.
FINLEYSON, JAMES.
   Mate. Dismissed 15 September, 1862.
FINN, DENNIS.
   Mate. Dismissed 22 June, 1864.
FINN, JAMES H.
   Acting Third Assistant Engineer, 17 July, 1864. Honorably discharged 24 August, 1869.
FINN, W. H.
   Mate, 11 February, 1864. Resigned (sick), 13 May, 1864.
FINN, WILLIAM.
   Acting Third Assistant Engineer, 10 September, 1864. Honorably discharged 13 October, 1868.
FINNEGAN, PATRICK.
   Acting Third Assistant Engineer, 13 January, 1862. Resigned 12 August, 1862.
FINNEGAN, WILLIAM.
   Acting Gunner, 2 May, 1864. Dismissed 29 October, 1864.

FINNEGAN, WILLIAM.
　Acting Third Assistant Engineer, 15 September, 1864. Honorably discharged 15 Decemebr, 1865.
FINNEMORE, THOMAS E.
　Midshipman, 20 February, 1813. Lost in the Epervier, 1815.
FINNEY, ELKANAH C.
　Mate, 12 May, 1864. Honorably discharged 9 August, 1867.
FINNEY, GEORGE.
　Acting Master, 27 December, 1861. Honorably discharged 28 October, 1865.
FINNEY, ROBERT.
　Mate, 25 January, 1862. Resigned 12 October, 1863.
FINNIE, THOMAS.
　Acting Second Assistant Engineer, 4 May, 1864. Honorably discharged 30 November, 1865.
FISCHER, CHARLES H.
　Naval Cadet, 6 September, 1895. At sea prior to final graduation.
FISCHER, FREDERICK H.
　Acting Ensign, 15 November, 1864. Dismissed 17 November, 1865.
FISH, H. PORTER.
　Mate, 8 April, 1864. Honorably discharged 20 October, 1865.
FISH, WILLIAM W.
　Acting Third Assistant Engineer, 16 May, 1864. Honorably discharged 20 September, 1865.
FISHER, ALBERT H.
　Mate, 4 November, 1863. Honorably discharged 20 August, 1865.
FISHER, ARTHUR H.
　Third Assistant Engineer, 17 February, 1860. Second Assistant Engineer, 27 June, 1862. First Assistant Engineer, 1 March, 1864. Resigned 26 September, 1870.
FISHER, CHARLES.
　Mate, 25 May, 1863. Boatswain, 19 June, 1863. Dismissed 6 December, 1865.
FISHER, CHARLES A.
　Acting Third Assistant Engineer, 5 June, 1863. Acting Second Assistant Engineer, 16 December, 1863. Honorably discharged 13 December, 1865.
FISHER, CHARLES F.
　Mate, 5 January, 1864. Resigned 27 April, 1865.
FISHER, CLARK.
　Third Assistant Engineer, 3 May, 1859. Second Assistant Engineer, 1 July, 1861. First Assistant Engineer, 20 May, 1863. Chief Engineer, 23 January, 1871. Resigned 27 March, 1872.
FISHER, EDWIN N.
　Gunner, 6 March, 1899.
FISHER, ELSTNER N.
　Midshipman, 21 September, 1872. Graduated 20 June, 1876. Ensign, 27 October, 1879. Resigned 15 January, 1885.
FISHER, FRANK.
　Mate, 5 June, 1862. Acting Ensign, 17 April, 1863. Honorably discharged 13 November, 1865.
FISHER, HENDRICK.
　Lieutenant, 20 March, 1799. Last appearance on Records of Navy Department, 30 May, 1799.
FISHER, HENRY.
　Acting Third Assistant Engineer, 9 December, 1863. Honorably discharged 7 August, 1866.
FISHER, JOHN.
　Master, 12 May, 1798. Last appearance on Records of Navy Department.
FISHER, JOHN.
　Carpenter, 20 March, 1823. Dismissed 18 June, 1838.
FISHER, JOHN.
　Midshipman, 1 November, 1826. Died 11 November, 1828.
FISHER, JOHN.
　Mate, 23 January, 1862. Resigned 9 September, 1862.
FISHER, JOHN.
　Mate, 6 December, 1862. Acting Ensign, 3 May, 1864. Honorably discharged 31 October, 1865.
FISHER, JOHN D.
　Midshipman, 18 June, 1812. Died October, 1817.
FISHER, JOHN E.
　Midshipman, 19 June, 1799. Discharged 11 May, 1801, under Peace Establishment Act.
FISHER, JOHN F.
　Master. 11 May, 1799. Last appearance on Records of Navy Department.
FISHER, JOHN P.
　Assistant Surgeon, 22 September, 1800. Resigned 5 June, 1801.
FISHER, JOHN P.
　Mate, 12 January, 1864. Honorably discharged 6 November, 1865.
FISHER, JOSEPH.
　Midshipman, 1 December, 1809. Resigned 18 March, 1811.
FISHER, LEE D.
　Assistant Engineer (Spanish-American War), 14 May, 1898. Honorably discharged 22 May, 1899.
FISHER, RODNEY.
　Midshipman, 15 August, 1814. Resigned 19 October, 1814.
FISHER, THOMAS L.
　Mate, 3 November, 1863. Honorably discharged 6 January, 1866.

GENERAL NAVY REGISTER.

FISHER, WILLIAM.
Acting Third Assistant Engineer, 3 July, 1863. Appointment revoked (sick) 12 October, 1864.
FISHER, WILLIAM H.
Acting Third Assistant Engineer, 10 December, 1864. Honorably discharged 12 September, 1865.
FISHER, WILLIAM W.
Gunner, 16 November, 1848. Resigned 14 November, 1853.
FISK, ADDISON.
Acting Gunner, 8 December, 1864. Honorably discharged 30 September, 1865.
FISK, JAMES W.
Acting Ensign, 12 October, 1864. Resigned 27 April, 1865.
FISK, PHOTIUS.
Chaplain, 14 March, 1842. (See Kavasales.) Retired List, 18 July, 1864. Died 7 February, 1890.
FISK, SQUIRE.
Master, 7 May, 1812. Dismissed 23 August, 1816.
FISK, S. N.
Acting Assistant Surgeon, 28 May, 1861. Resigned 25 January, 1864.
FISK, TIMOTHY W.
Midshipman, 2 March, 1839. Died 16 February, 1845.
FISK, WILLIAM.
Acting Gunner, 14 November, 1862. Died 6 August, 1863.
FISKE, BRADLEY A.
Midshipman, 22 September, 1870. Graduated 1 June, 1874. Ensign, 17 July, 1875. Master, 2 February, 1881. Lieutenant, Junior Grade, 3 March, 1883. Lieutenant, 26 January, 1887. Lieutenant-Commander, 3 March, 1899.
FISKE, CHARLES N.
Assistant Surgeon, 15 May, 1900.
FISKE, EDWARD W.
Mate, 5 October, 1861. Resigned 11 April, 1864.
FISKE, SAMUEL.
Third Assistant Engineer, 9 March, 1858. Resigned 12 June, 1858.
FISTER, THOMAS D.
Acting Midshipman, 29 September, 1855. Resigned 23 May, 1859.
FITCH, B. F. D.
Acting Assistant Paymaster, 24 May, 1862. Resigned 15 October, 1864.
FITCH, CHARLES T.
Acting Assistant Paymaster, 17 December, 1861. Died on Tioga, 22 June, 1864.
FITCH, CLAUDE E.
Lieutenant, Junior Grade (Spanish-American War), 7 June, 1898. Honorably discharged 1 October, 1898.
FITCH, ELISHA.
Professor of Mathematics, 25 September, 1831. Died 15 October, 1839.
FITCH, HENRY W.
Third Assistant Engineer, 3 May, 1859. Second Assistant Engineer, 3 October, 1861. First Assistant Engineer, 20 May, 1863. Chief Engineer, 4 March, 1871. Retired List, 29 September, 1894.
FITCH, Le ROY.
Acting Midshipman, 1 October, 1851. Passed Midshipman, 29 April, 1859. Master, 5 September, 1859. Lieutenant-Commander, 21 September, 1862. Commander, 28 August, 1870. Died 13 April, 1875.
FITCH, REUBEN.
Third Assistant Engineer, 26 August, 1859. Second Assistant Engineer, 29 October, 1861. First Assistant Engineer, 1 October, 1863. Resigned 19 April, 1869.
FITCH, THOMAS W.
Third Assistant Engineer, 23 June, 1863. Second Assistant Engineer, 25 July, 1866. First Assistant Engineer, 8 October, 1873. Resigned 31 December, 1875.
FITCHETT, SYLVANS W.
Mate, 30 December, 1861. Resigned 14 August, 1862.
FITHIAN, CHARLES B.
Lieutenant, Junior Grade (Spanish-American War), 2 June, 1898. Honorably discharged 24 January, 1899.
FITHIAN, EDWIN.
Third Assistant Engineer, 31 October, 1848. Second Assistant Engineer, 26 February, 1851. First Assistant Engineer, 15 December, 1853. Chief Engineer, 23 October, 1859. Retired List, 13 December, 1882.
FITTS, HENRY B.
Assistant Surgeon, 6 July, 1882. Passed Assistant Surgeon, 6 July, 1885. Surgeon, 23 March, 1897.
FITTS, JAMES H.
Cadet Engineer, 1 October, 1878. Assistant Engineer, 1 July, 1884. Resigned 30 June, 1885.
FITZGERALD, EDWARD.
Purser, 25 April, 1812. Died 27 February, 1857.
FITZGERALD, EDWARD T.
Naval Cadet, 13 September, 1892. Assistant Engineer, 6 May, 1898. Rank changed to Ensign, 3 March, 1899.
FITZ GERALD, PLANT.
Ensign (Spanish-American War), 28 June, 1898. Honorably discharged 19 August, 1898.

FITZGERALD, THOMAS.
Acting Second Assistant Engineer, 13 June, 1864. Honorably discharged 9 September, 1865.
FITZGERALD, WILLIAM H.
Mate, 14 June, 1864. Honorably discharged 13 November, 1865.
FITZGERALD, WILLIAM B.
Midshipman, 30 January, 1838. Passed Midshipman, 20 May, 1844. Master, 21 November, 1851. Lieutenant, 4 November, 1852. Reserved List, 13 September, 1855. Resigned 15 April, 1861.
FITZHUGH, ANDREW.
Midshipman, 9 June, 1811. Lieutenan , 27 April, 1816. Commander, 9 February, 1837. Captain, 14 February, 1843. Died 2 October, 1850.
FITZHUGH, C. C.
Midshipman, date not known. Last appearance on Records of Navy Department.
FITZHUGH, COLE.
Midshipman, 15 November, 1809. Resigned 23 April, 1810.
FITZHUGH, GEORGE.
Master, 10 July, 1812. Last appearance on Records of Navy Department, 17 July, 1812. Discharged.
FITZHUGH, JOHN, JR.
Assistant Surgeon, 28 December, 1818. Died 6 July, 1826.
FITZHUGH, ROBERT.
Midshipman, 1 January, 1825. Passed Midshipman, 4 June, 1831. Resigned 18 December, 1833.
FITZHUGH, W. E.
Midshipman, 2 February, 1847. Dismissed 7 July, 1847.
FITZHUGH, WILLIAM E.
Midshipman, 20 November, 1848. Passed Midshipman, 15 June, 1854. Master, 16 September, 1855. Lieutenant, 15 December, 1855. Lieutenant-Commander, 16 July, 1862. Commander, 25 July, 1866. Captain, 25 November, 1876. Commodore, 25 August, 1887. Died 3 August, 1889.
FITZOSBORN, HENRY W.
Gunner, 9 May, 1857. Resigned 24 December, 1864.
FITZPATRICK, JAMES.
Acting Master, 1 October, 1862. Honorably discharged 30 December, 1865.
FITZPATRICK, JAMES.
Acting Third Assistant Engineer, 26 February, 1864. Honorably discharged 9 December, 1868.
FITZPATRICK, JOHN F.
Acting Third Assistant Engineer, 22 October, 1863. Acting Second Assistant Engineer, 4 November, 1864. Honorably discharged 3 August, 1865.
FITZPATRICK, MICHAEL F.
Acting Second Assistant Engineer, 8 December, 1863. Honorably discharged 19 November, 1865.
FITZSIMONS, PAUL.
Assistant Surgeon, 19 December, 1871. Passed Assistant Surgeon, 4 January, 1876. Surgeon, 4 March, 1884. Medical Inspector, 19 October, 1897. Medical Director, 19 November, 1900.
FITZSIMMONS, WILLIAM J.
Assistant Second Engineer, 28 December, 1863. Appointment revoked (sick) 7 February, 1865.
FLAGG, GEORGE A.
Midshipman, 21 September, 1861. Graduated, 22 November, 1864. Ensign, 21 November, 1866. Master, 1 December, 1866. Lieutenant, 12 March, 1868. Died 20 June, 1869.
FLAGG, H. C., JR.
Midshipman, 1 April, 1828. Passed Midshipman, 14 June, 1834. Lieutenant, 25 February, 1841. Reserved List, 13 September, 1855. Commander, 19 July, 1861. Died 23 August, 1862.
FLAGG, SAMUEL D.
Assistant Surgeon, 30 July, 1861. Retired List, 20 June, 1864.
FLAGG, WILLIAM.
Lieutenant, 7 March, 1799. Discharged 15 April, 1801, under Peace Establishment Act.
FLAGLIE, BERNARD.
Acting Carpenter, 25 April, 1863. Appointment revoked 17 August, 1864.
FLANDERS, TIMOTHY.
Acting Third Assistant Engineer. 16 June, 1862. Honorably discharged 27 April, 1866.
FLANNER, F. W.
Acting Master, 1 October, 1862. Dismissed 2 March, 1863.
FLANNIGAN, M. E.
Acting Ensign. 9 April, 1863. Resigned 14 June, 1864.
FLANSBERG, JOHN W.
Acting Ensign, 22 August, 1863. Honorably discharged 4 October, 1865.
FLEET, HENRY.
Mate, 19 July, 1864. Discharged 26 June, 1865.
FLEETWOOD, WILLIAM.
Master, 7 May, 1812. Last appearance on Records of Navy Department, 30 June, 1812.
FLEMING, CHARLES E.
Midshipman, 15 January, 1835. Passed Midshipman, 22 June, 1841. Master, 12 January, 1848. Lieutenant, 2 October, 1848. Dismissed 6 February, 1857.

GENERAL NAVY REGISTER.

Reappointed Lieutenant, 13 December. 1859. Lieutenant-Commander, 16 July, 1862. Died 26 September, 1867.
FLEMING, CHARLES R.
   Mate, 8 November, 1861. Acting Ensign, 16 September. 1864. Honorably discharged 2 July, 1868.
FLEMING, JAMES.
   Acting Chief Engineer, 1 October, 1862. Honorably discharged 3 December, 1865.
FLEMING, JOHN J.
   Sailmaker, date not known. Died in October, 1820.
FLEMING, MATTHEW.
   Acting Second Assistant Engineer, 17 December. 1862. Resigned 7 June, 1864.
FLEMING, ROBERT.
   Acting Second Assistant Engineer, 8 March, 1864. Resigned (sick) 6 October, 1864.
FLEMING, WILLIAM.
   Sailmaker, date not known. Died in November, 1824.
FLEMING, WILLIAM.
   Midshipman, 20 February, 1799. Discharged 5 June, 1801, under Peace Establishment Act.
FLEMING, WATSON B.
   Acting Third Assistant Engineer, 1 October, 1862. Appointment revoked (sick) 19 May, 1863.
FLENNER, JOHN P.
   Chaplain, 25 February, 1828. Resigned 23 September, 1833.
FLETCHER, ARTHUR HENRY.
   Midshipman, 29 November, 1861. Graduated September, 1865. Ensign, 1 December, 1866. Master, 12 March, 1868. Lieutenant, 26 March. 1869. Retired List, 11 October, 1881.
FLETCHER, FRANK F.
   Midshipman, 22 September, 1870. Graduated 15 October, 1874. Ensign, 18 July, 1876. Master 1 April, 1882. Lieutenant, Junior Grade, 3 March. 1883. Lieutenant, 19 February, 1889. Lieutenant-Commander, 3 March, 1899.
FLETCHER, FRANK H.
   Third Assistant Engineer, 22 October, 1860. Second Assistant Engineer, 9 July, 1863. Resigned 6 Februray, 1869.
FLETCHER, GEORGE G.
   Acting Master, 21 May, 1861. Resigned 6 August, 1862.
FLETCHER, GEORGE H.
   Mate, 7 July, 1863. Acting Ensign, 23 February, 1865. Honorably discharged 6 December, 1865.
FLETCHER, JAMES R.
   Midshipman, 26 September, 1864. Graduated 2 June, 1868. Resigned 1 September, 1868.
FLETCHER, JOHN D.
   Gunner, 5 October, 1861. Warranted 24 April, 1862. Died at Phipsburg, Me., 24 November, 1867.
FLETCHER, JOSEPH B.
   Carpenter, 5 February, 1885. Chief Carpenter, 3 March, 1899.
FLETCHER, MONTGOMERY.
   Third Assistant Engineer, 24 June, 1850. Second Assistant Engineer, 26 February, 1851. First Assistant Engineer, 20 June, 1856. Chief Engineer, 25 October, 1859. Retired List, 15 February, 1892.
FLETCHER, NATHAN.
   Midshipman, 26 September, 1798. Resigned 10 January, 1800.
FLETCHER, N. C.
   Chaplain, 7 April, 1845. Resigned 9 June, 1845.
FLETCHER, PATRICK.
   Lieutenant, 9 July, 1798. Captain, 11 September, 1798. Lost in the Insurgent, in 1800.
FLETCHER, RUFUS.
   Midshipmna, 30 May, 1816. Last appearance on Records of Navy Department.
FLETCHER, WILLIAM B.
   Cadet Midshipman, 22 September, 1877. Ensign, 1 July, 1884. Lieutenant, Junior Grade, 13 May, 1894. Lieutenant, 29 October, 1897.
FLETCHER, WILLIAM M.
   Acting Third Assistant Engineer, 4 December, 1862. Acting Second Assistant Engineer, 2 July, 1864. Honorably discharged 10 February, 1866.
FLICK, GEORGE T.
   Mate, 6 June, 1862. Acting Gunner, 20 December, 1862. Appointment revoked 21 October, 1863.
FLINN, JAMES M.
   Acting Third Assistant Engineer, 27 January, 1863. Acting Second Assistant Engineer, gallant conduct in battle, 22 May. 1863. Honorably discharged 1 September, 1865. Ensign (Spanish-American War), 28 June, 1898. Honorably discharged 30 December, 1898.
FLINT, JAMES M.
   Acting Assistant Surgeon, 14 April, 1862. Assistant Surgeon, 26 October, 1863. Passed Assistant Surgeon, 31 December, 1867. Surgeon, 24 June, 1874. Medical Inspector, 4 March, 1893. Medical Director, 6 June, 1897. Retired List, 7 February, 1900.
FLOOD, CHRISTOPHER.
   Acting Ensign, 6 November, 1862. Acting Master, 9 June, 1865. Honorably discharged 23 October, 1865.

FLOOD, JAMES M.
Acting Assistant Paymaster, 24 August, 1864. Discharged 25 November, 1865.
FLOOD, SAMUEL D.
Ensign (Spanish-American War), 7 June, 1898. Honorably discharged 16 September, 1898.
FLOOD, THOMAS. S.
Mate, 10 December, 1864. Dismissed 24 July, 1865.
FLOOD, WILLIAM H.
Mate, 14 October, 1863. Acting Ensign, 29 March, 1865. Honorably discharged 16 January, 1866.
FLORENCE, CHARLES H.
Mate, 29 June, 1864. Appointment revoked (sick) 22 September, 1864.
FLOURNOY, J. J. R.
Midshipman, 1 March, 1825. Resigned 20 September, 1825.
FLOURNOY, THOMAS.
Midshipman, 10 February, 1841. Dropped.
FLOWERS, EDWARD K.
Mate, 6 February, 1862. Killed on Maratanza, 11 October, 1862.
FLOWRY, LEWIS H.
Acting First Assistant Enginer, 14 September, 1861. Honorably discharged 18 October, 1865.
FLOYD, JOHN.
Naval Constructor, 11 July, 1820. Last appearance on Records of Navy Department, 8 September, 1830.
FLOYD, JOHN A.
Acting Boatswain, 22 December, 1864. Honorably discharged 11 August, 1865.
FLOYD, WILLIAM B.
Mate, 30 June, 1864. Honorably discharged 18 September, 1865.
FLUDDER, GEORGE M.
Mate, 4 April, 1862. Appointment revoked 28 November, 1862.
FLUSSER, CHARLES W.
Midshipman, 19 July, 1847. Passed Midshipman, 10 June. 1853. Master 15 September, 1855. Lieutenant, 16 September, 1855. Lieutenant-Commander, July, 1862. Killed on board the Miami, 19 April, 1864.
FLYE, WILLIAM.
Professor, 7 December, 1841. Commissioned 14 August, 1848. Resigned 7 March, 1857.
FLYE, WILLIAM.
Acting Volunteer Lieutenant, 6 December, 1861. Acting Volunteer Lieutenant-Commander, 18 July, 1865. Honorably discharged 24 December, 1865.
FLYNN, JOHN, JR.
Acting Assistant Surgeon, 17 December, 1862. Honorably discharged 24 October, 1866.
FLYNN, ROBERT.
Midshipman, 12 November, 1799. Discharged 12 October, 1801, under Peace Establishment Act.
FLYNNE, LUCIAN.
Midshipman, 22 September, 1870. Graduated 1 June, 1874. Ensign, 17 July, 1875. Master, 22 April, 1881. Lieutenant, Junior Grade, 3 March. 1883. Lieutenant, 6 March, 1887. Retired List, 24 January 1898.
FLYNT, JAMES M.
Mate, 1 October, 1862. Acting Ensign, 24 April, 1863. Resigned 23 October, 1863. Acting Ensign, 7 June, 1864. Honorably discharged 5 November, 1865.
FOBES, EDWIN A.
Acting Assistant Surgeon, 1 April, 1865. Honorably discharged 27 July, 1865.
FOGG, GRANVILLE W.
Mate, 27 January, 1863. Died on Mercedita, 30 July, 1863.
FOGG, WILLIAM H.
Mate, 25 February, 1863. Acting Ensign, 31 December. 1864. Honorably discharged 3 November, 1865.
FOLEY, MICHAEL J.
Mate, 13 March, 1865. Resigned 5 March, 1866.
FOLEY, PAUL.
Naval Cadet, 5 September, 1896. Graduated 30 June, 1900.
FOLEY, THOMAS.
Acting Third Assistant Engineer, 14 May, 1864. Acting Second Assistant Engineer, 2 June, 1865. Honorably discharged 8 December. 1865.
FOLEY, WILLIAM J.
Gunner, 10 April, 1899.
FOLGER, JAMES.
Acting Third Assistant Engineer, 26 November, 1862. Died on Silver Cloud, 7 October, 1864.
FOLGER, JAMES.
Acting Master, 9 October, 1861. Died on Roebuck from wounds, 15 April, 1863.
FOLGER, WILLIAM MAYHEW.
Midshipman, 21 September, 1861. Graduated 22 November, 1864. Ensign, 1 November, 1866. Master, 1 December, 1866. Lieutenant. 12 March, 1868. Lieutenant-Commander, 27 April, 1869. Commander, 1 March, 1885. Captain, 6 February, 1898.
FOLLANSBIE, JOSHUA.
Third Assistant Engineer, 17 January, 1842. Second Assistant Engineer, 20 July, 1845. First Assistant Engineer, 10 July, 1847. Chief Engineer, 31 October, 1848. Resigned 1 May, 1865.

GENERAL NAVY REGISTER. 199

FOLLET, BENJAMIN.
Midshipman, 6 December, 1814. Died in 1823.
FOLLETT, FLETCHER M.
Acting Assistant Surgeon, 17 January, 1863. Honorably discharged 13 October, 1865.
FOLLINS, RICHARD.
Boatswain, 15 November, 1850. Resigned 15 November, 1853.
FOLSOM, CHARLES.
Chaplain, 12 May, 1816. Last appearance on Records of Navy Department, 1818.
FOLSOM, CHARLES.
Acting Master, 31 October, 1861. Resigned 8 February, 1864.
FOLSON, JOHN.
Midshipman, 10 July, 1799. Resigned 6 March, 1800.
FOLSON, SAMUEL.
Midshipman, 28 August, 1799. Resigned 8 April, 1800.
FOLTZ, JONATHAN M.
Assistant Surgeon, 4 April, 1831. Passed Assistant Surgeon, 8 December, 1838. Surgeon, 8 December, 1838. Medical Director, 3 March, 1871. Chief Bureau, Medicine and Surgery, 25 October, 1871. Retired List, 25 April, 1872. Died 12 April, 1877.
FONTAINE, M.
Midshipman, 10 July, 1809. Resigned 2 November, 1811.
FOOT, JOHN.
Lieutenant, 26 August, 1800. Last appearance on Records of Navy Department, 29 December, 1801. Lost.
FOOT, SAMUEL C.
Midshipman, 4 April, 1850. Resigned 20 December, 1850.
FOOTE, ANDREW H.
Midshipman, 4 December, 1822. Passed Midshipman, 24 May, 1828. Lieutenant, 27 May, 1830. Commander, 19 December, 1852. Captain, 29 June, 1861. Rear-Admiral, 16 July, 1862. Died 26 June, 1863.
FOOTE, JOHN P.
Acting Master and Pilot, 1 October, 1864. Honorably discharged 6 December, 1865.
FOOTE, SAMUEL E.
Mate, 6 June, 1862. Died 12 June, 1862.
FORBES, CHARLES W.
Acting Third Assistant Engineer, 2 December, 1864. Honorably discharged 29 Februray, 1868.
FORBES, CORNELIUS A.
Third Assistant Engineer, 18 May, 1847. Resigned 5 November, 1847.
FORBES, FRANK H.
Mate, 18 July, 1864. Honorably discharged 10 July, 1865.
FORBES, HENRY H.
Passed Assistant Surgeon (Spanish-American War), 12 May, 1898. Resigned 5 July, 1898.
FORBES, JAMES J.
Midshipman, 30 August, 1831. Passed Midshipman, 15 June, 1837. Lieutenant, 8 September, 1841. Resigned 23 November, 1844.
FORBES, WILLIAM D.
Acting Third Assistant Engineer, 4 September, 1861. Acting Second Assistant Engineer, 29 September, 1862. Acting First Assistant Engineer, 6 November, 1863. Honorably discharged 25 November, 1865.
FORCE, HORACE W.
Acting Third Assistant Engineer, 19 July, 1864. Honorably discharged 16 December, 1867.
FORD, AUGUSTUS.
Master, 28 March, 1810. Died 4 August, 1855.
FORD, CHARLES M.
Acting Assistant Surgeon, 17 May, 1861. Resigned 11 April, 1862.
FORD, EDWARD.
Midshipman, 3 March, 1799. Last appearance on Records of Navy Department, 20 June, 1799.
FORD, FRANKLIN E.
Acting Ensign, 3 August, 1863. Honorably discharged 20 January, 1866.
FORD, F. CODMAN.
Ensign (Spanish-American War), 13 July, 1898. Honorably discharged 26 August, 1898.
FORD, GEORGE.
Gunner, 6 March, 1899.
FORD, GEORGE T.
Mate, 16 September, 1862. Acting Ensign, 25 July, 1863. Acting Master, 11 May, 1865. Honorably discharged 15 December, 1868.
FORD, JEFFERSON.
Acting Master, 26 August, 1861. Died at Beaufort, N. C., 18 June, 1864.
FORD, J. MALACHI.
Midshipman, 18 January, 1841. Resigned 17 April, 1848.
FORD, JOHN.
Mate, 25 March, 1863. Resigned 11 August, 1863.
FORD, JOHN D.
Third Assistant Engineer, 12 August, 1862. Second Assistant Engineer, 15 February, 1864. First Assistant Engineer, 6 June, 1868. Chief Engineer, 27 December, 1899. Rank changed to Commander, 3 March, 1899.

FORD, JOHN Q. A.
Acting Third Assistant Engineer, 10 October, 1866. Third Assistant Engineer, 2 June, 1868. Second Assistant Engineer, 2 June, 1869. Passed Assistant Engineer, 19 February, 1875. Died 23 February, 1878.
FORD, JOHN W. D.
Midshipman, 2 February, 1829. Dismissed 2 June, 1836.
FORD, LEIGHTON M.
Midshipman, 27 September, 1861. Ensign, 1 December, 1866. Died 22 February, 1868.
FORD, OSCAR R.
Acting Second Assistant Engineer. Resigned 28 November, 1862.
FORD, WILLIAM G.
Cadet Midshipman, 11 September, 1877. Graduated. Honorably discharged 30 June, 1883. Lieutenant (Spanish-American War), 22 June, 1898. Honorably discharged 22 November, 1898.
FORD, WILLIAM H. H.
Acting Ensign, 1 October, 1862. Resigned 10 April, 1863.
FOREE, ALFRED.
Acting Midshipman, 17 April, 1862. Ensign, 18 December, 1868. Master, 21 March, 1870. Drowned 12 April, 1872.
FORGEY, ALFRED V.
Mate, 24 November, 1863. Honorably discharged 28 October, 1865.
FORGHAM, CHARLES B.
Assistant Engineer (Spanish-American War), 12 May, 1898. Honorably discharged 18 February, 1899.
FORLAW, JAMES L.
Acting Master and Pilot, 15 November, 1864. Appointment revoked 9 March, 1865.
FORMAN, CHARLES W.
Naval Cadet, 6 September, 1895. At sea prior to final graduation.
FORMAN, ISAAC B.
Midshipman, 1 August, 1800. Discharged 18 June, 1801, under Peace Establishment Act.
FORMAN, M. V.
Mate, 14 November, 1861. Appointment revoked 1 February, 1862.
FORMAN, SAMUEL R.
Assistant Surgeon, 1 September, 1861. Resigned 20 September, 1864.
FORNANCE, JOHN.
Third Assistant Engineer, 3 October, 1861. Second Assistant Engineer, 3 August, 1863. Lost on the Oneida, 24 January, 1870.
FORREST, B. G.
Midshipman, 16 January, 1809. Last appearance on Records of Navy Department, 15 December, 1809. Dead.
FORREST, D. A.
Midshipman, 3 March, 1841. Passed Midshipman, 10 August, 1847. Master, 15 September, 1855. Lieutenant, 16 September, 1855. Dismissed 6 December, 1861.
FORREST, DULANEY A.
Midshipman, 3 March, 1841. Passed Midshipman, 10 August, 1847. Master, 15 September, 1855. Lieutenant, 16 September, 1855. Dismissed 7 December, 1861.
FORREST, DULANY.
Midshipman, 18 May, 1809. Lieutenant, 9 December, 1814. Died 1 October, 1825.
FORREST, FRENCH.
Midshipman, 9 June, 1811. Lieutenant, 5 March, 1817. Commander, 9 February, 1837. Captain, 30 March, 1844. Dismissed 19 April, 1861.
FORREST, HENRY.
Mate, 24 April, 1863. Deserted 20 August, 1863.
FORREST, JAMES W.
Midshipman, 15 November, 1809. Resigned 17 April, 1810. Midshipman, 30 May, 1810. Cashiered 29 April, 1814.
FORREST, MOREAU.
Acting Midshipman, 22 September, 1858. Lieutenant, 1 August, 1862. Lieutenant-Commander, 25 July, 1866. Died 24 November, 1866.
FORREST, RICHARD.
Midshipman, 1 November, 1828. Passed Midshipman, 14 June, 1834. Lieutenant, 25 February, 1841. Reserved List, 13 September, 1855. Died 31 August, 1859.
FORREST, SAMUEL.
Purser, 8 October, 1836. Died 15 March, 1860.
FORREST, THOMAS.
Acting Third Assistant Enginer, 13 June, 1864. Dismissed 20 December, 1865.
FORRESTER, GEORGE B.
Midshipman, 1 January, 1818. Resigned 10 June, 1822.
FORSE, CHARLES THOMAS.
Midshipman, 24 September, 1863. Graduated 2 June, 1868. Ensign, 19 April, 1869. Master, 12 July, 1870. Lieutenant, 11 February, 1873. Lieutenant-Commander, 22 June, 1894. Commander, 3 March, 1899.
FORSHEW, ROBERT P.
Cadet Midshipman, 21 June, 1876. Graduated. Honorably discharged 30 June, 1883. Lieutenant (Spanish-American War), 22 June, 1898. Honorably discharged 8 October, 1898.
FORSYTH, JAMES M.
Entered Volunteer Service, 25 September, 1861. Master, 12 March, 1868. Lieu-

GENERAL NAVY REGISTER.

tenant, 18 December, 1868. Lieutenant-Commander, 9 May, 1878. Commander, 12 February, 1889. Captain, 3 March, 1899.
FORSYTH, JAMES N.
Midshipman, 1 November, 1826. Lost in the Hornet, September, 1829.
FORT, CHARLES.
Acting Master's Mate, 19 November, 1861. Resigned 31 July, 1865.
FORT, ISAAC B.
Third Assistant Engineer, 8 September, 1863. Died 1 December, 1865.
FORT, WILLIAM F.
Third Assistant Engineer, 27 June, 1861. Second Assistant Engineer, 18 December, 1862. Resigned 21 April, 1865.
FORT, WILLIAM S.
Asistant Surgeon, 24 January, 1862. Passed Assistant Surgeon, 28 June, 1865. Died 24 March, 1873.
FORTUNE, THOMAS H.
Gunner, 18 January, 1862. Died 16 December, 1882.
FOSDICK, JOHN H.
Midshipman, 17 December, 1810. Resigned 16 March, 1812.
FOSDICK, STEPHEN.
Boatswain, 6 September, 1850. Resigned 14 July, 1851.
FOSS, CYRUS D.
Acting Third Assistant Engineer, 10 October, 1866. Third Assistant Engineer, 2 June, 1868. Second Assistant Engineer, 2 June, 1869. Resigned 1 November, 1873.
FOSS, La ROY.
Mate, 20 January, 1870. Resigned 1 December, 1870.
FOSS, STEPHEN.
Acting Assistant Surgeon, 1 October, 1862. Resigned 24 November, 1862.
FOSSETT, LORING H.
Acting Ensign, 27 November, 1863. Honorably discharged 14 September, 1865.
FOSTER, AMOS P.
Acting Master, 23 September, 1861. Acting Volunteer Lieutenant, for gallant conduct, 10 September, 1862. Honorably discharged 2 September, 1865.
FOSTER, CHARLES A.
Midshipman, 1 August, 1866. Graduated 6 June, 1871. Ensign, 14 July, 1872. Master, 15 March, 1876. Lieutenant, Junior Grade, 3 March, 1883. Lieutenant, 24 August, 1883. Retired List, 22 April, 1895.
FOSTER, CHRISTOPHER H.
Mate, 8 January, 1864. Appointment revoked (sick) 1 December, 1864.
FOSTER, EDWARD.
Acting Paymaster, 5 June, 1861. Assistant Paymaster, 23 October, 1861. Paymaster, 6 February, 1862. Pay Inspector, 23 January, 1873. Died 11 April, 1877.
FOSTER, ELIEZER.
Boatswain, 4 August, 1841. Dismissed 26 January, 1849.
FOSTER, GEORGE.
Acting Third Assistant Engineer, 19 September, 1863. Appointment revoked (sick) 4 June, 1864.
FOSTER, GEORGE B.
Mate, 15 September, 1864. Honorably discharged 3 October, 1865.
FOSTER, GEORGE N.
Acting Second Assistant Engineer, 20 July, 1863. Acting First Assistant Engineer, 8 June, 1864. Honorably discharged 1 September, 1865.
FOSTER, GRAHAM P.
Acting Master, 22 November, 1861. Appointment revoked (sick) 11 February, 1863.
FOSTER, HENRY H.
Mate, 6 March, 1862. Acting Master, 8 May, 1862. Honorably discharged 4 November, 1865.
FOSTER, HENRY P.
Mate, 8 January, 1862. Acting Ensign, 9 September, 1862. Honorably discharged 9 January, 1869. Mate, 3 August, 1869. Resigned 25 March, 1870.
FOSTER, JAMES.
Gunner, 12 April, 1815. Died 5 August, 1818.
FOSTER, JAMES.
Midshipman, 3 March, 1838. Passed Midshipman. 20 May, 1844. Died 11 November, 1847.
FOSTER, JAMES P.
Midshipman, 14 May, 1846. Passed Midshipman, 10 June, 1853. Master, 15 September, 1855. Lieutenant, 16 September, 1855. Lieutenant-Commander, 16 July, 1862. Commander, 25 July, 1866. Died 2 June, 1869.
FOSTER, JESSE W.
Mate, 1 October, 1862. Acting Ensign, 1 September, 1864. Honorably discharged 28 November, 1865.
FOSTER, JOHN C.
Mate, 21 October, 1864. Resigned 26 March, 1866.
FOSTER, JOHN G.
Gunner, 25 November, 1861. Retired List. 5 November, 1896.
FOSTER, JOHN H.
Acting Second Assistant Engineer, 21 September, 1863. Acting First Assistant Engineer, 8 July, 1864. Honorably discharged 11 October, 1865.
FOSTER, JOHN K.
Acting Third Assistant Engineer, 14 November, 1864. Honorably discharged 29 July, 1865.

GENERAL NAVY REGISTER.

FOSTER, J. W.
Mate, 26 November, 1869. Discharged 2 February, 1871.
FOSTER, JOSEPH.
Acting Assistant Paymaster, 19 October, 1863. Assistant Paymaster, 23 July, 1866. Passed Assistant Paymaster, 10 May, 1867. Paymaster, 23 February, 1877. Pay Inspector, 15 June, 1898.
FOSTER, ROBERT C., Jr.
Midshipman, 1 October, 1850. Resigned 21 October, 1851.
FOSTER, THOMAS J.
Acting Third Assistant Engineer, 17 May, 1864. Honorably discharged 19 June, 1865.
FOSTER, WILLIAM.
Midshipman, 1 February, 1814. Lieutenant, 28 April, 1826. Cashiered 28 December, 1827.
FOSTER, WILLIAM C.
Acting Assistant Surgeon, 16 February, 1863. Resigned 4 October, 1864.
FOSTER, WILLIAM E.
Acting Assistant Paymaster, 30 July, 1862. Resigned 25 February, 1865.
FOSTER, WILLIAM J.
Acting Master, 26 August, 1861. Died at New York, April, 1862.
FOSTER, WINSLOW.
Master, 10 March, 1811. Last appearance on records of Navy Department, 8 January, 1814.
FOULK, GEORGE C.
Midshipman, 14 June, 1872. Graduated 20 June, 1876. Ensign, 25 November, 1877. Lieutenant, Junior Grade, 1 May, 1884. Resigned 10 February, 1889.
FOUNTAIN, JAMES.
Acting Third Assistant Engineer, 17 October, 1861. Died at New York, 20 October, 1863.
FOUNTAIN, JAMES.
Acting Master and Pilot, 14 October, 1864. Appointment revoked 27 May, 1865.
FOUSE, GEORGE.
Gunner, 13 May, 1862. Chief Gunner, 3 March, 1899. Retired List, 10 December, 1899.
FOUTLY, GEORGE W.
Acting Master, 1 October, 1862. Died at Hospital, Fort Donelson, 10 April, 1863.
FOWLE, CHARLES W.
Midshipman, 15 November, 1809. Died 15 March, 1811.
FOWLE, WILLIAM W.
Acting Master, 26 February, 1862. Resigned 12 May, 1865.
FOWLER, ALBERT C.
Acting Ensign, 13 May, 1864. Honorably discharged 15 September, 1865.
FOWLER, ARCHIBALD C.
Acting Assistant Surgeon, 18 June, 1863. Honorably discharged 27 October, 1866.
FOWLER, BENJAMIN W.
Acting Second Assistant Engineer, 27 June, 1864. Honorably discharged 25 February, 1868.
FOWLER, CHARLES S.
Acting Third Assistant Engineer, 10 November, 1863. Acting Second Assistant Engineer, 9 December, 1863. Appointment revoked (sick) 17 December, 1864.
FOWLER, GEORGE M.
Midshipman, 1 November, 1828. Drowned 2 May, 1832.
FOWLER, GILBERT.
Midshipman, 23 June, 1869. Graduated 31 May, 1873. Died 22 August, 1874.
FOWLER, RICHARD.
Acting Third Assistant Engineer, 17 May, 1864. Resigned 12 May, 1865.
FOWLER, SAMUEL.
Acting Third Assistant Engineer, 26 January, 1863. Resigned 9 May, 1863. Acting Third Assistant Engineer, 1 September, 1863. Honorably discharged 19 October, 1865.
FOWLER, THOMAS.
Lieutenant, 20 March, 1799. Last appearance on Records of Navy Department.
FOWLER, WILLIAM.
Gunner, date not known. Last appearance on Records of Navy Department, 1815. Frigate Guerriere.
FOYE, EDWARD.
Mate, 4 March, 1862. Resigned 23 August, 1862.
FOX, ALMOND F.
Acting Second Assistant Engineer, 13 April, 1863. Resigned 11 June, 1864.
FOX, CHARLES E.
Midshipman, 23 June, 1868. Graduated 1 June, 1872. Ensign, 15 July, 1873. Master, 25 November, 1877. Lieutenant, Junior Grade, 3 March, 1883. Lieutenant, 2 August, 1884. Lieutenant, Commander, 3 March, 1899.
FOX, GUSTAVUS V.
Midshipman, 12 January, 1838. Passed Midshipman, 20 May, 1844. Master, 29 August, 1851. Lieutenant, 9 July, 1852. Resigned 10 July, 1852.
FOX, IRVIN.
Acting Second Assistant Engineer, 18 March, 1863. Acting First Assistant Engineer, 9 June, 1863. Honorably discharged 3 January, 1866.
FOX, JAMES A.
Acting Second Assistant Engineer, 13 January, 1862. Discharged 31 March, 1865.
FOX, JAMES E.
Acting Third Assistant Engineer, 29 August, 1861. Acting Second Assistant Engineer, 20 November, 1862. Resigned 28 November, 1862. Acting Second Assistant Engineer, 15 December, 1862. Acting First Assistant Engineer, 16 November, 1863. Discharged 31 March, 1865.

FOX, JOHN L.
Assistant Surgeon, 9 February, 1837. Passed Assistant Surgeon, 6 June, 1842. Surgeon, 16 August, 1847. Died 17 December, 1864.
FOX, JOSEPH W.
Mate, 28 February, 1865. Honorably discharged 27 August, 1865.
FOX, JOSIAH.
Naval Constructor, 1 August, 1798. Appointment revoked 2 August, 1799.
FOX, JOSIAH.
Carpenter, 4 May, 1804. Last appearance on Records of Navy Department.
FOX, THOMAS J.
Acting Third Assistant Engineer, 24 October, 1864. Honorably discharged 2 November, 1865.
FOX, WILLIAM S.
Professor of Mathematics, 30 December, 1841. Drowned 28 October, 1844.
FOXCROFT, SAMUEL.
Midshipman, 18 June, 1812. Dismissed 24 November, 1814.
FOY, HARRY L.
Acting Warrant Machinist, 23 August, 1899.
FRAILEY, JAMES M.
Midshipman, 1 May, 1828. Passed Midshipman, 4 June, 1836. Lieutenant, 8 September, 1841. Commander, 24 April, 1861. Captain, 6 February, 1866. Commodore, 2 March, 1870. Died 26 September, 1877.
FRAILEY, LEONARD A.
Acting Assistant Paymaster, 20 August, 1864. Passed Assistant Paymaster, 23 July, 1866. Paymaster, 29 January, 1869. Pay Inspector, 24 May, 1894. Pay Director, 29 August, 1899.
FRAILEY, WILLIAM B. H.
Midshipman, 22 July, 1863. Ensign, 18 December, 1868. Resigned 15 February, 1870.
FRANCE, RICHARD.
Mate, 20 July, 1863. Deserted 17 October, 1863.
FRANCIS, GEORGE E.
Acting Assistant Surgeon, 15 May, 1863. Honorably discharged 28 October, 1865.
FRANCIS, HENRY B.
Mate, 27 May, 1862. Acting Ensign, 14 June, 1863. Honorably discharged 12 September, 1865.
FRANCIS ISAAC, Jr.
Acting Ensign, 17 October, 1862. Died at Beaufort, North Carolina, 18 May, 1863.
FRANCIS WILLIAM.
Enlisted 1 January, 1862. Promoted to Acting Master's Mate 9 March, 1864. Discharged 7 March, 1865.
FRANK, ADAM.
Assistant Surgeon, 26 September, 1867. Resigned 25 July, 1872.
FRANK, A. J.
Acting Master, 18 November, 1861. Honorably discharged 26 January, 1866.
FRANK, JOHN A.
Acting Third Assistant Engineer, 24 November, 1863. Honorably discharged 26 July, 1865. Acting Third Assistant Engineer, 24 March, 1866. Mustered out 27 August, 1868.
FRANKLAND, GEORGE W.
Sailmaker, 16 May, 1859. Died 25 April, 1882.
FRANKLAND, HENRY W.
Sailmaker, 2 November, 1848. Resigned 16 October, 1858. Reappointed 27 February, 1861. Retired List, 1 October, 1884. Died 14 October, 1899.
FRANKLIN, BENJAMIN H.
Acting Assistant Paymaster, 24 December, 1863. Discharged 22 November, 1865.
FRANKLIN, CHARLES LOVE.
Acting Midshipman, 23 October, 1854. Midshipman, 11 June, 1858. Lieutenant, 19 April, 1861. Lieutenant-Commander, 3 March, 1865. Commander, 24 May, 1872. Died 18 September, 1874.
FRANKLIN, GUSTAVUS S.
Assistant Surgeon, 22 May, 1862. Passed Assistant Surgeon, 30 October, 1865. Resigned 2 November, 1868.
FRANKLIN, JAMES.
Midshipman, 26 September, 1865. Graduated 4 June, 1869. Ensign, 12 July, 1870. Master, 29 December, 1871. Lieutenant, 8 February, 1875. Retired List, 9 March, 1880.
FRANKLIN, JOHN, Jr.
Third Assistant Engineer, 10 June, 1862. Second Assistant Engineer, 21 November, 1863. Resigned 26 June, 1865.
FRANKLIN, JOHN S.
Mate, 15 August, 1863. Honorably discharged 15 August, 1865.
FRANKLIN, JOHN S.
Sailmaker, 15 August, 1873. Died 1 July, 1897.
FRANKLIN, SAMUEL R.
Midshipman, 18 February, 1841. Passed Midshipman, 10 August, 1847. Master, 18 April, 1855. Lieutenant, 14 September, 1855. Lieutenant-Commander, 16 July, 1862. Commander, 25 July, 1866. Captain, 13 August, 1872. Commodore, 28 May, 1881. Rear-Admiral, 24 January, 1885. Retired List, 24 August, 1887.
FRANKLIN, WILLIAM B.
Naval Cadet, 20 May, 1884. Ensign, 1 July, 1890. Resigned 8 June, 1896. Lieutenant, Junior Grade (Spanish-American War), 25 May, 1898. Honorably discharged 17 September, 1898.

FRANKS, WILLIAM J.
　Mate, gallant conduct in action at Yazoo City, 14 April, 1864. Honorably discharged 27 August, 1865.
FRANZEN, ASA A.
　Mate, 17 February, 1862. Acting Ensign, 22 July, 1864. Died on Mahaska, 10 September, 1867.
FRARY, WILLIAM H.
　Boatswain, 18 April, 1879. Retired List, 10 December, 1888.
FRASER, JOHN.
　Acting Second Assistant Engineer, 19 December, 1861. Killed in action at Sabine Pass, 8 September, 1863.
FRASERS, ALEXANDER B.
　Second Assistant Engineer, 21 September, 1861. First Assistant Engineer, 15 October, 1863. Retired List, 24 March, 1874.
FRASIER, DAVID.
　Acting First Assistant Engineer, 19 December, 1861. Honorably discharged 4 October, 1868.
FRAVEL, THEOPHILUS A.
　Acting Assistant Paymaster, 28 January, 1865. Honorably discharged 20 September, 1865.
FRAZER, ALEXANDER.
　Assistant Surgeon, 14 December, 1809. Last appearance on Records of Navy Department. Resigned.
FRAZER, ARCHIBALD.
　Midshipman, 16 April, 1799. Discharged 5 June, 1801, under Peace Establishment Act.
FRAZER, DAVID H.
　Assistant Surgeon, 21 February, 1815. Died October, 1818.
FRAZER, JAMES.
　Sailmaker, 11 December, 1841. Lost in the Albany. Last intelligence, 28 September, 1854.
FRAZER, JAMES F.
　Acting Third Assistant Engineer, 23 May, 1864. Honorably discharged 12 July, 1865.
FRAZER, PERSIFOR.
　Acting Ensign, 25 October, 1864. Honorably discharged 3 October, 1865.
FRAZER, REAH.
　Assistant Paymaster, 15 July, 1875. Passed Assistant Paymaster, 27 October, 1879. Paymaster, 19 January, 1892.
FRAZER, RICHARD.
　Purser, 19 April, 1803. Died 25 March, 1804.
FRAZER, THOMAS.
　Master, 1 July, 1807. Dismissed 2 August, 1809.
FRAZIER, JAMES.
　Master, 4 March, 1809. Discharged 7 April, 1814.
FRAZIER, JOHN.
　Boatswain, 7 September, 1798. Last appearance on Records of Navy Department.
FRAZIER, JOHN B.
　Chaplain, 2 March, 1895.
FRAZIER, SOLOMON.
　Lieutenant, Flotilla service, 26 April, 1814. Last appearance on Records of Navy Department, 6 February, 1815. Discharged.
FREANEY, JOHN.
　Acting Third Assistant Engineer, 21 October, 1862. Resigned 15 July, 1864.
FREDERIC, LOUIS.
　Acting Gunner, 1 October, 1862. Honorably discharged 12 December, 1865.
FREDERICKSON, GEORGE.
　Mate, 15 November, 1861. Acting Ensign, 31 October, 1862. Lost at sea on Monitor, 30 December, 1862.
FREEBUGHER, ISAAC.
　Acting Third Assistant Engineer, 16 October, 1862. Resigned 15 May, 1863.
FREELAND, EDWARD H.
　Assistant Surgeon, 11 March, 1829. Died 3 June, 1834.
FREELON, THOMAS W.
　Midshipman, 12 June, 1812. Lieutenant, 28 March, 1820. Commander, 8 September, 1841. Died 10 May, 1847.
FREEMAN, ALBERT T.
　Midshipman, 24 September, 1868. Graduated 1 June, 1872. Ensign, 15 July, 1873. Master, 25 November, 1877. Lieutenant, Junior Grade, 3 March, 1883. Died 11 October, 1883.
FREEMAN, CHARLES C.
　Sailmaker, 15 January, 1874. Died 3 June, 1896.
FREEMAN, CHARLES S.
　Naval Cadet, 5 September, 1896. Graduated 30 June, 1900.
FREEMAN, COREY C.
　Acting Third Assistant Engineer, 30 December, 1864. Honorably discharged 19 June, 1865.
FREEMAN, EDGAR.
　Midshipman, 9 June, 1811. Lieutenant, 5 March, 1817. Resigned 14 November, 1828.
FREEMAN, EDWARD R.
　Cadet Engineer, 1 October, 1873. Assistant Engineer, 1 July, 1877. Passed Assistant Engineer, 26 January, 1886. Chief Engineer, 8 February, 1897. Rank changed to Lieutenant-Commander, 3 March, 1899.

GENERAL NAVY REGISTER.

FREEMAN, FRANK H.
Mate, 26 June, 1862. Acting Ensign, 21 July, 1864. Honorably discharged 18 February, 1866.

FREEMAN, FREDERICK N.
Naval Cadet, 9 September, 1891. Assistant Engineer, 1 July, 1897. Rank changed to Ensign, 3 March, 1899. Lieutenant, Junior Grade, 1 July, 1900.

FREEMAN, GEORGE R.
Assistant Surgeon (Spanish-American War), 13 June, 1898. Appointed Assistant Surgeon in Regular Service 7 June, 1900.

FREEMAN, ISAAC.
Sailmaker, 24 July, 1827. Last appearance on Records of Navy Department, 1831. Sloop Erie.

FREEMAN, ISAAC D.
Sailmaker, 9 July, 1838. Died 24 March, 1863.

FREEMAN, JAMES M.
Midshipman, 24 May, 1814. Died in October, 1820.

FREEMAN, JOHN.
Master, 11 May, 1839. Resigned 26 August, 1846.

FREEMAN, JOHN.
Boatswain, 10 May, 1830. Resigned 20 July, 1836.

FREEMAN, JOSEPH M.
Third Assistant Engineer, 16 February, 1852. Resigned 8 October, 1853.

FREEMAN, JULIUS C.
Midshipman, 4 October, 1866. Graduated 6 June, 1871. Ensign, 14 July, 1872. Master, 11 July, 1877. Lieutenant, Junior Grade, 3 March, 1883. Retired List, 23 April, 1884.

FREEMAN, MARTIN.
Acting Volunteer Lieutenant and Pilot, 18 October, 1864. Honorably discharged 20 January, 1867.

FREEMAN, M. B.
Carpenter, 28 April, 1840. Last appearance on Records of Navy Department.

FREEMAN, NATHANIEL CHAPMAN.
Acting Assistant Paymaster, 17 February, 1863. Resigned 24 February, 1864.

FREEMAN, NATHANIEL W.
Mate, 12 February, 1864. Resigned 17 May, 1865.

FREEMAN, PETER.
Gunner, 13 December, 1841. Dismissed 7 June, 1842.

FREEMAN, ROBERT J.
Assistant Surgeon, 6 July, 1859. Dismissed 4 June, 1861.

FREEMAN, ROMEYN.
Acting Assistant Paymaster, 3 June, 1863. Discharged 26 November, 1865.

FREEMAN, SIMEON N.
Acting Master, 14 August, 1861. Appointment revoked 28 July, 1865.

FREEMAN, THADDEUS S. K.
Chaplain, 4 June, 1897. Died 12 September, 1898.

FREEMAN, VIRGINIUS.
Third Assistant Engineer, 26 February, 1851. Second Assistant Engineer, 21 May 1853. First Assistant Engineer, 9 May, 1857. Name stricken from the Rolls of the Navy, 8 July, 1861.

FREEMAN, WATSON, JR.
Acting Master, 26 February, 1862. Resigned 19 September, 1863.

FREEMAN, WILLIAM.
Boatswain, 10 July, 1823. Resigned 6 October. 1823.

FREEMAN, WILLIAM D.
Acting Master, 6 July, 1861. Resigned 5 May, 1864.

FREMONT, J. C.
Professor of Mathematics, 4 April, 1837. Dropped.

FREMONT, JOHN C.
Midshipman, 24 June, 1868. Graduated 1 June, 1872. Ensign, 15 July, 1873. Master, 25 November, 1877. Lieutenant, Junior Grade, 3 March, 1883. Lieutenant, 2 September, 1884. Lieutenant-Commander, 3 March, 1899.

FRENCH, ABEL E. C. P.
Acting Third Assistant Engineer, 18 March, 1863. Acting Second Assistant Engineer, 7 July, 1864. Honorably discharged 1 December, 1865.

FRENCH, ANTHONY.
Acting Third Assistant Engineer. Appointment revoked (sick) 13 July, 1863.

FRENCH, CHARLES A.
Acting Master, 13 August, 1861. Acting Volunteer Lieutenant, mark of appreciation of gallantry, 18 December, 1862. Acting Volunteer Lieutenant-Commander, 30 May, 1865. Honorably discharged 21 October, 1865.

FRENCH, GUSTAVUS E.
Mate, 3 March, 1862. Acting Ensign, 1 September, 1863. Resigned 23 June, 1866.

FRENCH, GEORGE H.
Mate, 4 April, 1862. Acting Ensign, 30 May, 1864. Honorably discharged 23 February, 1866.

FRENCH, GEORGE R.
Cadet Midshipman, 24 June, 1875. Graduated 22 June, 1882. Ensign, Junior Grade, 3 March, 1883. Ensign, 26 June, 1884. Retired List, 26 June, 1893. Died 13 August, 1895.

FRENCH, HAYDEN T.
Acting Midshipman, 2 December, 1859. Ensign, 1 July, 1863. Lieutenant, 22 February, 1864. Died 1 March, 1865.

FRENCH, HENRY.
Midshipman, 1 January, 1828. Passed Midshipman, 14 June, 1834. Lieutenant, 15 April, 1840. Commander, 14 September, 1855. Retired 24 June, 1865. Captain on Retired List, 4 April, 1867. Died 22 May, 1867.
FRENCH, JAMES A.
Acting Third Assistant Engineer, 15 March, 1865. Honorably discharged 20 July, 1865.
FRENCH, JAMES S.
Acting Master, 29 August, 1861. Acting Volunteer Lieutenant, recommendation of Commanding Officer, 15 July, 1864. Honorably discharged 22 December, 1865.
FRENCH, JEFFERSON A.
Acting Volunteer Lieutenant, 1 October, 1862. Resigned 17 June. 1864.
FRENCH, JOHN A.
Mate, 27 January, 1863. Acting Ensign, 31 August, 1863. Acting Master, recommendation of Commanding Officer, 15 July, 1864. Honorably discharged 26 November, 1865.
FRENCH, MATTHEW.
Midshipman, 14 April, 1800. Discharged 18 June, 1801, under Peace Establishment Act.
FRENCH, ORATUS S.
Acting Second Assistant Engineer, 8 January. 1864. Honorably discharged 20 April, 1866.
FRENCH, R. H.
Mate, 5 June, 1863. Appointment revoked (sick) 26 June, 1863.
FRENCH, ROBERT.
Assistant Surgeon, 16 January, 1808. Resigned 28 April, 1809.
FRENCH, ROBERT F.
Midshipman, 11 June, 1814. Resigned 18 January, 1815.
FRENCH, THOMAS.
Acting Chief Engineer, 1 October, 1862. Resigned 27 December, 1862.
FRENCH, WALTER S.
Midshipman, 27 July, 1866. Graduated 6 June, 1871. Ensign, 14 July. 1872. Master, 22 August, 1876. Lost on board Huron, 24 November, 1877.
FRENCH, WILLIAM F.
Assistant Paymaster (Spanish-American War), 21 July, 1898. Honorably discharged 12 December, 1898.
FRENCH, WILLIAM H.
Gunner, 26 July, 1861. Died 30 December, 1868.
FRICK, HORACE E.
Assistant Engineer, 11 March, 1875. Passed Assistant Engineer, 3 March, 1882. Retired List, 18 June, 1890.
FRICK, WILLIAM, JR.
Third Assistant Engineer, 26 June, 1856. Second Assistant Engineer, 2 August, 1859. First Assistant Engineer, 6 January, 1862. Resigned 12 April, 1862.
FRIEL, PATRICK H.
Acting Third Assistant Engineer, 8 March, 1864. Honorably discharged 7 September, 1865.
FRIELE, DANIEL.
Acting Ensign, 5 October, 1864. Honorably discharged 30 October, 1865.
FRIELL, WILLIAM O.
Mate, 3 November, 1865. Resigned 22 December, 1865.
FRIEND, JOSEPH L.
Midshipman, 27 October, 1841. Passed Midshipman, 10 August, 1847. Died 18 October, 1851.
FRIES, BRA. T.
Mate, 6 April, 1864. Acting Ensign, 23 January. 1865. Honorably discharged 30 July, 1868.
FRIES, FREDERICK.
Acting Third Assistant Engineer, 21 November, 1863. Resigned 18 May, 1864.
FRIES, OTTO.
Gunner, 22 August, 1895.
FRISBIE, CHARLES H.
Acting Ensign, 4 August, 1863. Acting Master, 5 September, 1864. Acting Volunteer Lieutenant, 2 June, 1865. Honorably discharged 4 October, 1865.
FRISBIE, EDGAR H.
Mate, 23 June, 1863. Acting Ensign, 1 July, 1864. Honorably discharged 13 December, 1865.
FRISBIE, J. T.
Acting Assistant Surgeon, 21 November, 1861. Appointment revoked 28 December, 1863.
FRISBY, EDGAR.
Professor, 11 June, 1878. Retired List, 22 May, 1899.
FRITMAN, MARTIN.
Acting Boatswain, 25 January, 1900.
FRIZELLE, SEYMOUR C.
Acting Assistant Paymaster, 9 December, 1861. Dismissed 2 August, 1862.
FROCK, JOHN E.
Acting Assistant Paymaster, 14 December, 1864. Honorably discharged 24 October, 1865.
FROST, CHARLES.
Sailmaker, 7 January, 1842. Resigned 10 February, 1843.
FROST, CHARLES T.
Sailmaker, 10 August, 1848. Warranted 6 November, 1851. Lost in the Levant. Last intelligence from the ship 18 September, 1860.

GENERAL NAVY REGISTER.

FROST, G. W.
    Acting Master, 26 August, 1861. Honoraby discharged 14 December, 1865.
FROST, JOHN A.
    Boatswain, 1 January, 1839. Died 20 October, 1842.
FROST, JOHN N.
    Acting Ensign, 26 July, 1864. Honorably discharged 12 October, 1865.
FROST, JOSEPH.
    Acting Ensign, 10 September. 1862. Resigned 27 June, 1865.
FROST, LESLIE D.
    Assistant Surgeon, 10 April, 1866. Resigned 27 November, 1866.
FROST, NATHANIEL.
    Chaplain, 5 October, 1844. Died in New York 14 July, 1868.
FROST, HARRISON O.
    Mate. Appointment revoked 10 January, 1865.
FROST, WILLIAM.
    Assistant Surgeon, date not known. Discharged 14 July, 1801, under Peace Establishment Act.
FROST, WILLIAM.
    Mate, 6 February, 1862. Resigned 20 June, 1863.
FROST, WILLIAM C.
    Mate, 19 December, 1863. Acting Ensign. 29 November, 1864. Honorably discharged 4 November, 1865.
FROST, WOODBURY G.
    Acting Assistant Surgeon, 4 June, 1864. Honorably discharged 6 November, 1865.
FROTHINGHAM, EDWARD.
    Acting Assistant Surgeon 25 April, 1866. Assistant Surgeon, 23 May, 1866. Lost in the Oneida, 24 January, 1870.
FRY, ALFRED B.
    Passed Assistant Engineer (Spanish-American War), 30 April, 1898. Honorably discharged 13 September, 1898.
FRY, HENRY.
    Purser, 27 February, 1813. Last appearance on Records of Navy Department, 1816. Furloughed.
FRY, JOSEPH.
    Midshipman, 15 September, 1841. Passed Midshipman, 10 August, 1847. Master, 14 September, 1855. Lieutenant, 15 September, 1855. Resigned 1 February, 1861.
FRY, PEARSON L.
    Acting Third Assistant Engineer, 14 November, 1862. Acting Second Assistant Engineer, 22 November, 1863. Acting First Assistant Engineer, 9 September, 1864. Resigned 28 February, 1865.
FUGITT, WILLIAM B.
    Sailmaker, 29 January, 1848. Warranted 17 July, 1850. Died in New York 28 March, 1860.
FUHR, ISAAC H.
    Acting Third Assistant Engineer, 12 April, 1864. Honorably discharged 1 September, 1865.
FULCHER, JOHN H.
    Acting Third Assistant Engineer. 28 August, 1863. Honorably discharged 17 October, 1865.
FULL, JOHN S.
    Mate, 1 October, 1862. Acting Ensign, 12 February, 1864. Appointment revoked 3 June, 1864.
FULLAM, WILLIAM F.
    Cadet Midshipman, 24 September, 1873. Graduated 18 June, 1879. Ensign, 13 March, 1880. Lieutenant, Junior Grade, 7 October, 1886. Lieutenant, 28 May, 1892. Lieutenant-Commander, 29 December, 1899.
FULLER, AUG. H.
    Mate, 25 January, 1862. Acting Ensign, 5 September, 1864. Honorably discharged 19 September, 1865.
FULLER, CHARLES M.
    Mate, 10 January, 1863. Acting Ensign, 16 February, 1864. Honorably discharged 5 September, 1865.
FULLER, DARIUS S.
    Acting Third Assistant Engineer, 4 October, 1864. Honorably discharged 17 July, 1865.
FULLER, EDWARD C.
    Midshipman, 27 September, 1870. Graduated 1 June, 1874. Resigned 9 September, 1874.
FULLER, GEORGE K.
    Acting Third Assistant Engineer, 20 June, 1862. Dismissed 11 September, 1862.
FULLER, GEORGE W.
    Mate, 30 October, 1863. Resigned 30 May, 1865.
FULLER, HENRY C.
    Mate, 28 July, 1862. Honorably discharged 23 November, 1868. Mate, 4 February, 1870. Retired List, 3 April, 1899.
FULLER, HORACE F.
    Ensign (Spanish-American War), 21 May, 1898. Honorably discharged 19 September, 1898.
FULLER, ICHABOD C.
    Acting Ensign, 26 September, 1864. Honorably discharged 30 September, 1865.
FULLER, JAMES.
    Midshipman, 15 November, 1809. Resigned 24 August, 1810.

FULLER, JOHN.
Acting Master, 10 September, 1861. Resigned 6 February, 1863.
FULLER, JOHN.
Mate, 8 July, 1864. Resigned 9 June, 1865.
FULLER, JOHN J., JR.
Mate, 21 September, 1864. Resigned 22 May, 1865.
FULLER, JOHN JOSEPH.
Acting Warrant Machinist, 23 August, 1899.
FULLER, WALTER.
Acting Assistant Paymaster, 9 October, 1863. Discharged 29 January, 1866.
FULLER, WILLIAM A.
Acting Third Assistant Engineer, 23 March, 1864. Honorably discharged 18 December, 1865.
FULLER, WILLIAM H.
Third Assistant Engineer, 23 May, 1861. Resigned 16 November, 1861.
FULLER, ZACHEUS R.
Carpenter, 12 April, 1815. Dismissed 30 June, 1829.
FULLINWIDER, SIMON P.
Naval Cadet, 21 May, 1890. Ensign, 1 July, 1896. Lieutenant, Junior Grade, 1 July, 1899.
FULMER, DAVID M.
Third Assistant Engineer, 4 May, 1863. Second Assistant Engineer, 28 September, 1864. Passed Assistant Engineer, 8 December, 1872. Retired List, 26 April, 1884.
FULPER, WILLIAM H.
Passed Assistant Paymaster (Spanish-American War), 23 May, 1898. Honorably discharged 31 December, 1898.
FULTON, ALBERT K.
Third Assistant Engineer, 6 January, 1862. Second Assistant Engineer, 1 October, 1863. Resigned 25 April, 1864.
FULTON, GEORGE W.
Acting First Assistant Engineer, 1 October, 1862. Honorably discharged 4 November, 1865.
FULTON, JAMES.
Purser, 20 November, 1858. Pay Inspector, 3 March, 1871. Pay Director, 28 August, 1876. Died 9 April, 1895.
FULTON, JAMES B.
Acting Chief Engineer, 1 October, 1862. Honorably discharged 15 January, 1867.
FULTON, THOMAS C.
Acting First Assistant Engineer, 1861. Resigned 31 October, 1862.
FUNCK, JOHN M.
Midshipman, 5 May, 1806. Killed in action 25 October, 1812.
FURBER, EDWARD G.
Acting Midshipman, 2 October, 1854. Midshipman, 11 June, 1858. Resigned 25 August, 1860. Mate, 16 January, 1862. Acting Master, 11 April, 1862. Honorably discharged 21 January, 1866.
FURBUSH, FREDERICK.
Mate, 27 May, 1862. Acting Ensign, 25 July, 1863. Died 27 October, 1863, on board Tennessee.
FURCH, WILLIAM.
Acting Second Assistant Engineer, 1 October, 1862. Honorably discharged 30 November, 1865.
FUREY, JOHN.
Acting Assistant Paymaster, 6 October, 1863. Passed Assistant Paymaster, 23 July, 1866. Paymaster, 24 October, 1871. Retired List, 10 September, 1895.
FURLONG, FRANCIS M.
Assistant Surgeon for Temporary Service, 13 June, 1898. Transferred to Regular Service, 16 September, 1898.
FURLONG, JOSEPH.
Acting Gunner, 31 March, 1863. Honorably discharged 13 May, 1865.
FURLONG, WALTER A.
Assistant Engineer (Spanish-American War), 20 May, 1898. Honorably discharged 30 September, 1898.
FURNISS, HARTMAN K.
Acting Master, 18 July, 1861. Acting Volunteer Lieutenant, for gallant conduct, 11 November, 1861. Dismissed 12 September, 1863.
FURNISS, LEON.
Acting Assistant Paymaster, 1 July, 1863. Resigned 13 October, 1863.
FUSSELL, LINNEAS.
Acting Assistant Surgeon, 1 March, 1865. Acting Passed Assistant Surgeon, 29 July, 1868. Resigned 3 September, 1874.
FYFFE, JOSEPH.
Assistant Paymaster, 28 December, 1896. Passed Assistant Paymaster, 30 March, 1898.
FYFFE, JOSEPH P.
Midshipman, 9 September, 1847. Passed Midshipman, 15 June, 1854. Master, 15 September, 1855. Lieutenant, 16 September, 1855. Retired List, 3 June, 1865. Lieutenant-Commander from 16 July, 1862. Commander, 2 December, 1867. Captain, 13 January, 1879. Commodore, 28 February, 1890. Rear-Admiral, 10 July, 1894. Retired List, 20 July, 1894. Died 25 February, 1896.
GABRIELSON, ERIC.
Mate, 13 December, 1861. Acting Ensign, 20 May, 1863. Honorably discharged 30 September, 1865.

GENERAL NAVY REGISTER. 209

GADSDEN, CHRISTOPHER, Jr.
Midshipman, 22 February, 1799. Lieutenant, 12 January, 1807. Commander, 10 July, 1812. Died 28 August, 1812.
GADSDEN, THOMAS.
Purser, 21 July, 1840. Resigned 31 March, 1843.
GAEDICKE, H. J.
Midshipman, 19 August, 1823. Died 17 December, 1829.
GAGE, GEORGE S.
Mate, 6 March, 1865. Honorably discharged 2 October, 1865.
GAGE, HOWARD.
Cadet Engineer, 1 October, 1874. Graduated 20 June, 1878. Assistant Engineer, 20 June, 1880. Passed Assistant Engineer, 19 November, 1890. Chief Engineer, 12 October, 1898. Rank changed to Lieutenant, 3 March, 1899.
GAGE, LEMUEL.
Acting Master, 10 October, 1861. Dismissed 8 May, 1862.
GAGER, E. V.
Acting Master, 17 May, 1861. Resigned 8 July, 1862.
GAGG, WILLIAM.
Acting Third Assistant Engineer, 16 February, 1865. Resigned 15 June, 1865.
GAILLARD, AUGUSTIN.
Midshipman, 30 November, 1814. Resigned 16 June, 1815.
GAILLARD, D. S.
Midshipman, 1 February, 1815. Resigned 25 August, 1815.
GAILLARD, SAMUEL.
Midshipman, 10 May, 1820. Resigned 28 January, 1823.
GAINES, JAMES H.
Assistant Surgeon, 20 December, 1873. Passed Assistant Surgeon, 15 June, 1877. Surgeon, 10 July, 1888. Retired List, 18 March, 1891.
GAINSFORD, CHARLES.
Mate, 5 June, 1862. Died 29 May, 1880.
GAIRY, GEORGE.
Acting Ensign, 28 October, 1863. Appointment revoked (sick) 16 January, 1865.
GALBRAITH, GILBERT S.
Naval Cadet, 8 September, 1890. Ensign, 1 July, 1896. Lieutenant, Junior Grade, 1 July, 1899.
GALBRAITH, WILLIAM.
Acting Second Assistant Engineer, 12 June, 1863. Honorably discharged 8 November, 1865.
GALE, GEORGE W.
Acting Assistant Surgeon, 19 April, 1862. Acting Passed Assistant Surgeon, 6 July, 1865. Honorably discharged 29 June, 1869.
GALE, JOHN.
Midshipman, 19 October, 1841. Dismissed 9 September, 1848.
GALE, WILLIAM.
Acting Assistant Surgeon, 18 October, 1862. Acting Passed Assistant Surgeon, 13 June, 1865. Honorably discharged 2 August, 1868.
GALE, WILLIAM A.
Acting Assistant Paymaster, 25 April, 1865. Discharged 12 October, 1865.
GALINDO, EDWARD A.
Mate, 5 March, 1862. Resigned 15 March, 1865.
GALLAGHER, JAMES.
Mate, 8 February, 1862. Dismissed 22 January, 1863.
GALLAGHER, JAMES G.
Sailmaker, 27 November, 1829. Died at the Naval Hospital, Chelsea, Massachusetts, 8 March, 1865.
GALLAGHER, JOHN.
Master, 16 January, 1809. Lieutenant, 24 July, 1813. Commander, 2 March, 1825. Captain, 22 December, 1835. Died 1 November, 1842.
GALLAGHER, JOHN.
Third Assistant Engineer, 21 January, 1842. Second Assistant Engineer, 22 January, 1846. Resigned 17 February, 1847.
GALLAGHER, JOHN L.
Acting Chief Engineer, 24 February, 1864. Dismissed 6 July, 1864.
GALLAGHER, JOSEPH P.
Acting Ensign, 2 November, 1863. Honorably discharged 15 May, 1865.
GALLAGHER, LAWRENCE.
Boatswain, 15 November, 1828. Died at Naval Hospital, New York, 3 December, 1861.
GALLAGHER, LAWRENCE B.
Mate, 12 February, 1870. Died 6 February, 1898.
GALLAGHER, WILLIAM F.
Acting Third Assistant Engineer, 5 January, 1865. Resigned 7 November, 1865.
GALLAHER, BENJAMIN F.
Purser, 15 July, 1852. Dismissed 22 August, 1862.
GALLETLY, ALLAN.
Carpenter (Spanish-American War), 23 April, 1898. Honorably discharged 2 September, 1898.
GALLGHER, DARIUS F.
Acting Third Assistant Engineer, 5 November, 1862. Dismissed 15 July, 1863.
GALLISHAN, CHARLES A.
Acting Ensign, 20 January, 1865. Deserted 22 May, 1866.
GALLOUP, JOHN L.
Mate, 23 December, 1863. Resigned 2 August, 1866.

14

GALLOWAY, CHARLES D.
Midshipman, 22 September, 1866. Graduated 6 June, 1871. Ensign, 14 July, 1872. Master, 9 December, 1875. Lieutenant, Junior Grade, 3 March, 1883. Lieutenant, 25 June, 1883. Retired List, 21 February, 1894.

GALLOWAY, JOHN.
Midshipman, 28 February, 1799. Died 22 September, 1804.

GALLOWAY, THOMAS.
Acting Third Assistant Engineer, 24 September, 1862. Acting Second Assistant Engineer, 14 January, 1863. Honorably discharged 1 May, 1866.

GALT, FRANCIS L.
Assistant Surgeon, 2 October, 1855. Passed Assistant Surgeon, 4 May, 1860. Resigned 20 March, 1861.

GALT, ROBERT W.
Assistant Engineer, 12 October, 1871. Passed Assistant Engineer, 24 February, 1879. Chief Engineer, 26 December, 1894. Retired List, 19 November, 1898.

GALT, ROGERS H.
Midshipman, 20 June, 1868. Graduated 1 June, 1872. Ensign, 15 July, 1873. Master, 11 December, 1877 Lieutenant, Junior Grade, 3 March, .1883. Lieutenant, 3 November, 1884. Lieutenant-Commander, 3 March, 1899.

GALT, WILLIAM W.
Assistant Paymaster, 25 January, 1878. Passed Assistant Paymaster, 15 October, 1881. Paymaster, 26 September, 1893.

GALVEN, JOHN.
Lieutenant, 3 June, 1800. Discharged 18 June, 1801, under Peace Establishment Act.

GAMBLE, FRAS. B.
Midshipman, 18 May, 1809. Lieutenant, 19 December, 1814. Died 29 September, 1824.

GAMBLE, JOHN L.
Acting Ensign, 2 August, 1862. Acting Master, favorable report of services, 24 February, 1864. Honorably discharged 11 April, 1866.

GAMBLE, JOHN M.
Midshipman, 16 January, 1809. Appointed Second Lieutenant Marine Corps, 16 January, 1809. First Lieutenant, 5 March, 1811. Captain, 18 June, 1814. Major by Brevet, 18 April, 1816. Major, 1 July, 1834. Lieutenant-Colonel, by Brevet, 3 March, 1827. Died 11 September, 1836.

GAMBLE, JOSEPH G.
Master, 19 March, 1812. Dismissed 5 January, 1814.

GAMBLE, PETER.
Midshipman, 16 January, 1809. Lieutenant, 17 March, 1814. Killed in action 11 September, 1814.

GAMBLE, ROBERT M.
Midshipman, 9 May, 1803. Lieutenant, 21 February, 1809. Last appearance on Records of Navy Department, 28 August, 1811.

GAMBLE, THOMAS.
Midshipman, 2 April, 1804. Lieutenant, 27 April, 1810. Commander, 27 April, 1816. Died 10 October, 1818.

GAMBLE, WILLIAM H.
Third Assistant Engineer, 8 July, 1862. Died 26 August, 1862.

GAMBLE, WILLIAM M.
Midshipman, 1 March, 1841. Passed Midshipman, 1 August, 1847. Master, 14 September, 1855. Lieutenant, 15 September, 1855. Lieutenant-Commander, 16 July, 1862. Retired 26 April, 1866. Commander on Retired List, 4 April, 1867. Died 19 October, 1896.

GAMBLE, W. P.
Midshipman, 10 October, 1832. Died 3 September, 1838.

GAMBRILL, AMOS G.
Assistant Surgeon, 10 June, 1829. Passed Assistant Surgeon, 3 March, 1835. Surgeon, 20 February, 1838. Died 12 February, 1854.

GAME, MARK.
Carpenter, 20 November, 1799. Discharged 25 May, 1801.

GAMMON, THOMAS B.
Mate, 8 November, 1861. Resigned 12 September, 1863. Mate, 26 April, 1870. Resigned 23 March, 1871.

GANNON, SINCLAIR.
Naval Cadet, 3 July, 1896. Graduated 30 June, 1900.

GANSEVOORT, GUERT.
Midshipman, 4 March, 1823. Passed Midshipman, 28 April, 1832. Lieutenant, 8 March, 1837. Commander, 14 September, 1855. Captain, 16 July, 1862. Retired List, 28 January, 1867. Commodore, Retired List. Died 15 July, 1868.

GANSEVOORT, HUNN.
Midshipman, 8 May, 1823. Passed Midshipman, 23 June, 1838. Lieutenant, 27 February, 1842. Lost in the Grampus, March, 1843.

GANSEVOORT, P. L.
Midshipman, 1 June, 1828. Drowned 7 March, 1832.

GANSEVOORT, STANWIX.
Midshipman, 3 November, 1841. Resigned 9 October, 1847.

GANTT, BENJAMIN S.
Midshipman, 16 June, 1834. Passed Midshipman, 16 July, 1840. Master, 26 August, 1846. Lieutenant, 25 February, 1847. Died 12 March, 1852.

GANTT, JOSEPH.
Midshipman, 18 June, 1799. Discharged 18 June, 1801, under Peace Establishment Act.

GANTT, RICHARD.
  Midshipman, 18 June, 1799. Lost in the Insurgent.
GARABEDIAN, H. PAUL.
  Acting Third Assistant Engineer, 6 August, 1864. Honorably discharged 19 August, 1865.
GARDINER, A. F.
  Acting Third Assistant Engineer, 1 October, 1862. Dismissed 13 October, 1864.
GARDINER, CHARLES A.
  Acting Assistant Paymaster, 20 August, 1862. Honorably discharged 7 September, 1865.
GARDINER, CARLOS A.
  Naval Cadet, 20 May, 1896. Graduated 30 June, 1900.
GARDINER, EBEN G.
  Acting Third Assistant Engineer, 25 June, 1862. Apointment revoked (sick) 31 July, 1863.
GARDINER, GEORGE N.
  Lieutenant (Spanish-American War), 14 May, 1898. Honorably discharged 28 September, 1898.
GARDINER, HENRY R.
  Mate, 29 September, 1864. Honorably discharged 3 October, 1865.
GARDNER, A. S.
  Acting Master, 26 August, 1861. Dismissed 13 July, 1865.
GARDNER, CHARLES F.
  Acting Assistant Paymaster, 18 August, 1864. Honorably discharged 9 September, 1865.
GARDNER, EDWARD C.
  Master, 18 August, 1812. Dismissed as Supernumerary 6 March, 1813.
GARDNER, FRANCIS.
  Gunner, 7 September, 1832. Died 1 May, 1835.
GARDNER, FRANK P.
  Mate, 1862. Died 25 March, 1862.
GARDNER, GILBERT.
  Master, 15 December, 1817. Resigned 1 February, 1822.
GARDNER, J. W.
  Acting Assistant Paymaster, 17 February, 1863. Resigned 12 November, 1864.
GARDNER, JAMES E.
  Assistant Surgeon, 3 July, 1876. Passed Assistant Surgeon, 7 August, 1880. Surgeon, 15 August, 1893.
GARDNER, JAMES W.
  Mate, 21 September, 1863. Honorably discharged 6 July, 1865.
GARDNER, JOHN M.
  Midshipman, 1 May, 1799. Lieutenant, 19 January, 1807. Commander, 4 February, 1815. Died 1 September, 1815.
GARDNER, JOHN M.
  Midshipman, 1 June, 1826. Passed Midshipman, 18 April, 1832. Lieutenant, 8 March, 1837. Died 27 November, 1847.
GARDNER, JOHN WESLEY.
  Third Assistant Engineer, 21 April, 1863. Second Assistant Engineer, 28 September, 1864. Passed Assistant Engineer, 31 December, 1872. Retired List, 18 February, 1889. Died 16 September, 1891.
GARDNER, LAFAYETTE.
  Acting Ensign, 22 June, 1863. Honorably discharged 26 July, 1865.
GARDNER, ROBERT M.
  Acting First Assistant Engineer, 24 August, 1863. Resigned 3 November, 1863.
GARDNER, SAMUEL H.
  Mate, 16 November, 1864. Discharged 24 August, 1865.
GARDNER, SAMUEL W.
  Boatswain, 22 April, 1896.
GARDNER, THOMAS C.
  Assistant Surgeon, 10 December, 1814. Last appearance on Records of Navy Department, 1820. Died in New York.
GARDNER, THOMAS M.
  Acting Master, 13 June, 1861. Master, 12 March, 1868. Lieutenant, 18 December, 1868. Lieutenant-Commander, 2 February, 1878. Retired List, 22 January, 1884. Died 28 January, 1887.
GARDNER, WALTER.
  Midshipman, 6 December, 1814. Resigned 16 July, 1817.
GARDNER, WALTER.
  Midshipman, 1 January, 1818. Died 21 February, 1820.
GARDNER, WILLIAM H.
  Midshipman, 6 December, 1814. Lieutenant, 13 January, 1825. Commander, 8 September, 1841. Captain, 14 September, 1855. Commodore on Retired List, 16 July, 1862. Died 19 December, 1870.
GARDNER, WILLIAM ROSS.
  Midshipman, 29 December, 1831. Passed Midshipman, 15 June, 1837 Lieutenant, 8 September, 1841. Died 22 April, 1857.
GARFIELD, WALTER H.
  Acting Master, 4 October, 1861. Acting Volunteer Lieutenant, recommendation of Rear-Admiral Dahlgren, 25 May, 1864. Honorably discharged 4 August, 1867.
GARLAND, HUDSON M.
  Midshipman, 20 November, 1848. Passed Midshipman, 12 June, 1855. Master, 16 September, 1855. Lieutenant, 17 October, 1856. Died 26 February, 1861.

GARLICK, GEORGE W.
Mate, 1 October, 1862. Acting Ensign, 5 August. 1863. Resigned (sick) 28 January, 1865.
GARLICK, JOHN.
Midshipman, 26 July, 1799. Discharged 12 August, 1801, under Peace Establishment Act.
GARNER, JOHN M.
Acting Assistant Surgeon, 2 February, 1863. Acting Passed Assistant Surgeon, 18 May, 1865. Honorably discharged 10 October, 1865.
GARNETT, ALGERNON S.
Assistant Surgeon, 16 May, 1857. Dismissed 10 May, 1861.
GARNETT, A. Y. P.
Assistant Surgeon, 8 September, 1841. Resigned 21 October, 1850.
GARNETT, JAMES.
Acting Assistant Paymaster, 28 August, 1863. Resigned 19 January, 1865.
GARNER, JOHN C.
Acting Third Assistant Engineer, 19 September, 1863. Resigned 27 April, 1865.
GARRARD, WILLIAM, Jr.
Midshipman, 1 January, 1808. Last appearance on Records of Navy Department, 12 June, 1809.
GARRECHT, WILLIAM H.
Acting Third Assistant Engineer, 18 October, 1864. Honorably discharged 9 September, 1865.
GARRETT, LE ROY M.
Cadet Midshipman, 18 September, 1875. Graduated 10 June, 1881. Ensign, Junior Grade, 3 March, 1883. Ensign, 26 June, 1884. Lieutenant, Junior Grade, 19 February, 1891. Lieutenant, 21 May, 1895.
GARRETT, LEIGH O.
Cadet Midshipman, 13 September, 1875. Graduated 10 June, 1881. Ensign, Junior Grade. 3 March, 1883. Ensign, 26 June, 1884. Resigned 8 August, 1884.
GARRETT, THOMAS J.
Mate (Spanish-American War), 29 June, 1898. Honorably discharged 21 February, 1899.
GARRETSON, ISAAC.
Purser, 25 April, 1812. Died 30 January, 1830.
GARRIGAN, MICHAEL.
Acting Third Assistant Engineer, 15 February, 1865. Honorably discharged 27 October, 1865.
GARRISON, DANIEL M.
Naval Cadet, 1 June, 1891. Assistant Engineer, 1 July, 1897. Rank changed to Ensign, 3 March, 1899. Lieutenant, Junior Grade. 1 July, 1900.
GARRISON, GEORGE W.
Mate, 18 November, 1861. Resigned 3 May, 1862. Acting Ensign. 23 January, 1863. Acting Master, 1 September, 1864. Appointment revoked 12 January, 1866.
GARRISON, J. C.
Assistant Surgeon, 22 December, 1812. Died 18 November, 1820.
GARRISON, SAMUEL.
Midshipman, 11 January, 1832. Cashiered 20 October, 1834.
GARRISON, WILLIAM H.
Acting Third Assistant Engineer, 7 September, 1864. Honorably discharged 29 November, 1865.
GARST, PERRY.
Midshipman. 28 July, 1863. Graduated 2 July, 1868. Ensign, 19 April, 1869. Master, 12 July, 1870. Lieutenant, 5 April, 1874. Lieutenant-Commander, 7 June, 1895. Commander, 3 March, 1899.
GARTHWAITE, GEORGE W.
Acting Assistant Paymaster, 10 June, 1864. Drowned on Sassacus, 5 April, 1865.
GARTLEY, ALONZO.
Cadet Midshipman. 22 May, 1886. Graduated. Honorably discharged 30 June. 1892. Lieutenant (Spanish-American War), 23 June, 1898. Honorably discharged 8 September, 1898.
GARTLEY, WILLIAM H.
Cadet Engineer, 13 September, 1877. Graduated 10 June, 1881. Honorably discharged 30 June, 1883. Restored to service 10 March. 1886, as an Assistant Engineer to rank from 1 July, 1883. Resigned 1 May, 1886.
GARTON, WILL M.
Assistant Surgeon, 27 July, 1898.
GARTS, PETER.
Purser, 29 August, 1799. Last appearance on Records of Navy Department.
GARVIN, BENJAMIN F.
Third Assistant Engineer, 29 March, 1847. Second Assistant Engineer, 31 October, 1848. First Assistant Engineer, 26 February, 1851. Chief Engineer, 11 May, 1858. Retired List, 14 February, 1885. Died 22 January, 1892.
GARVIN, JOHN.
Midshipman, 22 July, 1865. Graduated 4 June, 1869. Ensign, 12 July, 1870. Master, 12 July, 1871. Lieutenant, 3 October, 1874. Retired List, 12 May, 1894. Died 24 December, 1894.
GASKILL, VINCENT H.
Acting Assistant Surgeon, 19 February, 1864. Resigned 18 May, 1865.
GASKINS, D'ARCY M.
Mate, 21 March, 1862. Acting Ensign, 2 May, 1864. Honorably discharged 30 December, 1865.
GASKINS, JOHN.
Gunner, 20 April, 1857. Retired List, 3 March, 1895.

GASSAWAY, JOHN.
Midshipman, 16 January, 1809. Appointed Second Lieutenant Marine Corps, 18 June, 1810. Resigned 29 December, 1810.
GASSOWAY, ELMORE S.
Mate, 10 September, 1864. Honorably discharged 26 October, 1865.
GATES, ARTHUR O.
Acting Warrant Machinist, 23 August, 1899.
GATES, GEORGE S.
Acting Third Assistant Engineer, 10 October, 1866. Third Assistant Engineer, 2 June, 1868. Second Assistant Engineer, 2 June, 1869. Passed Assistant Engineer, 29 October, 1874. Retired List, 7 June, 1884.
GATES, HERBERT G.
Naval Cadet, 4 September, 1884. Ensign, 22 October, 1890. Lieutenant, Junior Grade, 7 June, 1898. Lieutenant, 3 March, 1899.
GATES, JAMES A.
Gunner, 26 December, 1855. Warranted 21 March, 1857. Died 13 December, 1857.
GATES, MANLEY F.
Assistant Surgeon, 27 March, 1889. Passed Assistant Surgeon, 27 March, 1892. Surgeon, 7 June, 1900.
GATES, V. BRUCE.
Mate, 25 July, 1864. Dismissed 29 December, 1864.
GATEWOOD, JAMES D.
Assistant Surgeon, 6 July, 1880. Passed Assistant Surgeon, 6 July, 1883. Surgeon, 28 February, 1896.
GATEWOOD, RICHARD.
Purser, 10 January, 1812. Last appearance on Records of Navy Department.
GATEWOOD, RICHARD.
Cadet Engineer, 15 September, 1875. Graduated 10 June, 1879. Assistant Naval Constructor, 20 August, 1881. Naval Constructor, 10 October, 1888. Died 15 December, 1890.
GAUL, ANDREW K.
Acting First Assistant Engineer, 27 July, 1863. Honorably discharged 7 August, 1865.
GAUL, WILLIAM.
Acting Third Assistant Engineer, 30 December, 1863. Reduced to Fireman, 14 November, 1864.
GAULT, JOHN.
Midshipman, 16 January, 1799. Resigned 23 January, 1799.
GAULT, JOHN.
Midshipman, 19 March, 1799. Last appearance on Records of Navy Department.
GAUNTT, CHARLES.
Midshipman, 1 September, 1811. Lieutenant, 5 March, 1817. Commander, 9 February, 1837. Captain, 24 February, 1847. Died at New Brunswick, New Jersey, 21 August, 1855.
GAUTIER, THOMAS N.
Lieutenant, 15 February, 1800. Discharged 20 October, 1801, under Peace Establishment Act.
GAUTIER, THOMAS N.
Master, 4 August, 1807. Resigned 25 November, 1814.
GAVAGAN, THOMAS.
Acting Third Assistant Engineer, 16 May, 1863. Acting Second Assistant Engineer, 2 February, 1865. Honorably discharged 9 August, 1865.
GAVARET, EMILE.
Acting Assistant Surgeon, 1 October, 1862. Honorably discharged 21 October, 1865.
GAVIN, MICHAEL F.
Acting Assistant Surgeon, 11 September, 1863. Appointment revoked 17 October, 1863.
GAY, ALPHONSE.
Acting Warrant Machinist, 6 July, 1899.
GAY, CHARLES W.
Midshipman, 27 October, 1818. Resigned 11 April, 1828.
GAY, EDWARD.
Third Assistant Engineer, 24 August, 1861. Second Assistant Engineer, 21 April, 1863. Died 19 January, 1870.
GAY, GEORGE W.
Midshipman, 1 April, 1828. Dismissed 28 November, 1828.
GAY, JAMES W.
Acting Ensign, 14 July, 1863. Appointment revoked 19 November, 1863.
GAY, JESSE.
First Assistant Engineer, 20 February, 1847. Chief Engineer, 31 October, 1848. Resigned 22 October, 1859.
GAY, JOHN.
Carpenter, 1 September, 1803. Last appearance on Records of Navy Department.
GAY, THOMAS S.
Mate, 30 March, 1864. Acting Ensign, 27 October, 1864. Honorably discharged 4 November, 1868. Sailmaker, 6 December, 1871. Resigned 3 March, 1873.
GAY, TIMOTHY.
Midshipman, 6 June, 1815. Last appearance on Records of Navy Department, 1821. Ship Independence.
GAYLE, JOHN H.
Mate, 20 May, 1864. Resigned 4 October, 1864.
GAYLE, RICHARD H.
Midshipman, 13 October, 1848. Resigned 27 June, 1853.

GAYLOR, CHARLES H.
Mate, 10 December, 1863. Acting Ensign, 22 November. 1864. Resigned 15 May, 1865.
GAYLORD, CHARLES.
Acting Assistant Surgeon, 10 August, 1864. Honorably discharged 22 May, 1866.
GAYLORD, FRANK B.
Ensign (Spanish-American War), 9 May, 1898. Honorably discharged 26 August, 1898.
GAYRING, DAVID.
Acting Second Assistant Engineer, 12 October, 1863. Honorably discharged 15 September, 1866.
GEARING, HENRY C.
Midshipman, 12 June, 1872. Graduated 20 June, 1876. Ensign, 25 November, 1877. Lieutenant, Junior Grade, 10 January, 1884. Lieutenant, 28 February, 1890. Lieutenant-Commander, 3 March, 1899.
GEARY, ALEXANDER M.
Acting Second Assistant Engineer, 1 February, 1864. Honorably discharged 22 November, 1865.
GEARY, AMOS H.
Mate, 20 January, 1863. Dismissed.
GEBHARDT, BERNARD.
Acting Warrant Machinist, 23 August, 1899.
GEDDES, C. WRIGHT.
Third Assistant Engineer, 15 November, 1847. Second Assistant Engineer, 11 January, 1849. First Assistant Engineer, 26 February, 1851. Resigned 5 September, 1855. Reappointed Second Assistant Engineer, 27 August, 1859. Declined appointment 31 August, 1859.
GEDDES, GEORGE H.
Midshipman, 14 October, 1799. Lieutenant, 28 April, 1809. Resigned 24 January, 1811.
GEDDES, HENRY.
Captain, 24 September, 1799. Discharged 11 April, 1801, under Peace Establishment Act.
GEDDES, HENRY, JR.
Midshipman, 16 January, 1809. Last appearance on Records of Navy Department, 15 March, 1809.
GEDDIS, GEORGE WILLIAM.
Third Assistant Engineer, 8 July, 1862. Resigned 9 March, 1864.
GEDDIS, HENRY, JR.
Midshipman, 30 April, 1800. Discharged 12 October, 1801, under Peace Establishment Act.
GEDNEY, JONATHAN.
Carpenter, 1 August, 1809. Last appearance on Records of Navy Department, 18 December, 1815.
GEDNEY, THOMAS R.
Midshipman, 4 March, 1815. Lieutenant, 13 January, 1825. Commander, 8 September, 1841. Died 30 November, 1857.
GEE, SAMUEL.
Mate, 12 November, 1869. Retired List, 10 September, 1895.
GEER, ABRAM.
Acting Third Assistant Engineer, 14 April, 1864. Honorably discharged 10 July, 1866.
GEER, EDWIN.
Lieutenant (Spanish-American War), 25 May, 1898. Honorably discharged 9 September, 1898.
GEER, GEORGE S.
Acting Third Assistant Engineer, 19 January, 1863. Acting Second Assistant Engineer, 6 June, 1864. Honorably discharged 1 December, 1865.
GEER, SHUBAEL.
Acting Third Assistant Engineer, 31 January, 1865. Honorably discharged 15 February, 1866.
GEISINGER, DAVID.
Midshipman, 15 November, 1809. Lieutenant, 9 December, 1814. Commander, 11 March, 1829. Captain, 24 May, 1838. Reserved List, 13 September, 1855. Died 5 March, 1860.
GELATT, JOSEPH S.
Acting Ensign, 16 December, 1862. Acting Master, recommendation of Commanding Officer, 16 April, 1864. Honorably discharged 1 November, 1865.
GELM, GEORGE E.
Naval Cadet, 22 May, 1890. Ensign, 1 July, 1896. Lieutenant, Junior Grade, 1 July, 1899.
GENET, CHARLES EDMUND.
Midshipman, 22 February, 1841. Dismissed 13 February, 1850.
GENTHER, SAMUEL.
Acting Second Assistant Engineer, 1 August, 1862. Acting First Assistant Engineer, 12 November, 1862. Dismissed 3 February, 1865.
GEORGE, ENOCH.
Acting Second Assistant Engineer, 18 August, 1864. Honorably discharged 22 September, 1865.
GEORGE, F. A. R.
Third Assistant Engineer, 11 April, 1859. Resigned 13 August, 1862. Acting Second Assistant Engineer, 11 December, 1862. Acting First Assistant Engineer, 7 January, 1863. Dismissed 8 June, 1864.

GEORGE, HARRY.
    Cadet Midshipman, 16 June, 1879. Ensign, 1 July, 1885. Lieutenant, Junior Grade, 14 February, 1895. Lieutenant, 27 April, 1898.
GEOGHEGAN, JOHN.
    Master, 16 September, 1813. Discharged 15 April, 1815.
GEOLTZ, LEWIS.
    Mate, 7 October, 1863. Acting Ensign, 17 March, 1865. Honorably discharged 8 October, 1868.
GERMAIN, CHARLES.
    Acting Master, 17 May, 1861. Resigned 23 June, 1863.
GERMAIN, GEORGE.
    Acting Third Assistant Engineer, 21 October, 1862. Resigned (sick) 13 February, 1865.
GERMAIN, JOHN.
    Acting First Assistant Engineer, 21 October, 1862. Acting Chief Engineer, 19 January, 1863. Honorably discharged 2 December, 1866.
GERMAN, JAMES B.
    Acting Third Assistant Engineer, 31 August, 1863. Resigned 16 November, 1864.
GERMAN, LEWIS.
    Midshipman, 15 November, 1809. Lieutenant, 24 July, 1813. Died 12 April, 1819.
GEROULD, M. L.
    Acting Assistant Surgeon, 22 September, 1863. Honorably discharged 7 December, 1865.
GERRAND, HENRY.
    Acting Assistant Paymaster, 1 July, 1862. Assistant Paymaster, 27 February, 1867. Passed Assistant Paymaster, 26 August, 1868. Died 8 July, 1872.
GERRANS, CHARLES.
    Acting Third Assistant Engineer, 18 November, 1863. Acting Second Assistant Engineer, 28 May, 1864. Honorably discharged 25 November, 1865.
GERRARD, GEORGE.
    Acting Ensign, 6 January, 1863. Honorably discharged 2 December, 1865. Acting Ensign, 12 March, 1867. Resigned 29 May, 1867.
GERRISH, DAVID F.
    Acting Assistant Engineer, 25 November, 1863. Honorably discharged 26 August, 1865.
GERRISH, FRANCIS.
    Assistant Surgeon, 10 December, 1814. Died 12 April, 1819.
GERRY, CHARLES M. S.
    Acting Third Assistant Engineer, 30 January, 1864. Honorably discharged 28 September, 1865.
GERRY, JAMES T.
    Midshipman, 20 December, 1815. Lieutenant, 28 April, 1826. Commander, 17 April, 1842. Lost on the Albany, 28 September, 1854.
GERRY, MARTIN H.
    Acting Third Assistant Engineer, 19 September, 1862. Acting Second Assistant Engineer, 23 October, 1863. Resigned 12 March, 1866. Assistant Engineer (Spanish-American War), 1 June, 1898. Honorably discharged 16 November, 1898.
GERRY, OLIVER H.
    Carpenter, 29 May, 1861. Warranted 11 December, 1861. Died at sea on board the Iroquois, 10 August, 1867.
GERRY, SAMUEL R.
    Master, 17 January, 1809. Last appearance on Records of Navy Department, 1820.
GERRY, THOMAS R.
    Midshipman, 6 December, 1814. Resigned 27 August, 1833.
GETLIFFE, FRED C.
    Passed Assistant Engineer (Spanish-American War), 27 June, 1898. Honorably discharged 8 September, 1898.
GETTY, ROBERT.
    Acting Volunteer Lieutenant, 1 October, 1862. Resigned 21 August, 1863.
GETTY, ROBERT H.
    Midshipman, 16 June, 1837. Passed Midshipman, 29 June, 1843. Died 6 July, 1847.
GETZ, GEORGE.
    Midshipman, 1 January, 1812. Resigned 5 February, 1814.
GEUTSH, FERDINAND H.
    Midshipman, 22 July, 1866. Graduated 7 June, 1870. Resigned 22 May, 1873.
GHEEN, EDWARD HICKMAN.
    Acting Midshipman, 25 September, 1862. Graduated June, 1867. Ensign, 18 December, 1868. Master, 21 March, 1870. Lieutenant, 21 March, 1871. Lieutenant-Commander, 2 October, 1891. Commander, 28 March, 1898.
GHERARDI, BANCROFT.
    Midshipman, 26 June, 1846. Passed Midshipman, 8 June, 1852. Master, 15 September, 1855. Lieutenant, 16 September, 1855. Lieutenant-Commander, 16 July, 1862. Commander, 25 July, 1866. Captain, 9 November, 1874. Commodore, 3 November, 1884. Rear Admiral, 25 August, 1887. Retired List, 10 November, 1894.
GHERARDI, WALTER R.
    Naval Cadet, 4 September, 1891. Ensign, 1 July, 1897. Lieutenant, Junior Grade, 1 July, 1900.
GIBBON, ERNEST H.
    Ensign (Spanish-American War), 19 July, 1898. Honorably discharged 29 August, 1898.
GIBBON, FREDERICK S.
    Midshipman, 9 June, 1811. Lieutenant, 1 April, 1818. Died 3 December, 1825.

GIBBON, JAMES.
Midshipman, 20 June, 1799. Lieutenant, 21 January, 1807. Died in December, 1811.
GIBBON, LARDNER.
Midshipman, 22 December, 1837. Passed Midshipman, 29 June, 1843. Master, 10 April, 1851. Lieutenant, 5 December, 1851. Resigned 15 May, 1857.
GIBBONS, JOHN H.
Cadet Midshipman, 18 September, 1875. Graduated 10 June, 1881. Ensign, Junior Grade, 3 March, 1883. Ensign, 26 June, 1884. Lieutenant, Junior Grade, 16 December, 1891. Lieutenant, 28 February, 1896.
GIBERSON, CHARLES H.
Assistant Surgeon, 19 October, 1861. Passed Assistant Surgeon, 24 April, 1865. Resigned 9 November, 1868.
GIBERSON, ROBERT D.
Acting Third Assistant Engineer, 21 October, 1863. Acting Second Assistant Engineer, 16 June, 1864. Honorably discharged 27 August, 1867. Acting Second Assistant Engineer, 14 March, 1866. Mustered out 27 August, 1867.
GIBBS, ALBION P.
Acting Ensign, 22 February, 1864. Honorably discharged 28 October, 1865. Mate, 21 January, 1876. Appointment revoked 30 October, 1871.
GIBBS, BENJAMIN F.
Assistant Surgeon, 12 November, 1858. Passed Assistant Surgeon, 22 May, 1862. Surgeon, 22 May, 1862. Medical Inspector, 17 March, 1876. Died 9 September, 1882.
GIBBS, CHARLES J.
Acting Master, 8 February, 1862. Acting Volunteer Lieutenant, good service, 4 February, 1864. Honorably discharged 5 January, 1866.
GIBBS, GEORGE T.
Acting Second Assistant Engineer, 27 July, 1864. Honorably discharged 2 November, 1865.
GIBBS, HENRY L.
Acting Assistant Surgeon, 2 February, 1864. Resigned 3 June, 1865.
GIBBS, JOHN B.
Assistant Surgeon (Spanish-American War), 25 April, 1898. Died 12 June, 1898.
GIBBS, JOHN W.
Midshipman, 16 January, 1809. Lieutenant, 9 December, 1814. Resigned 26 February, 1816.
GIBBS, LUCIUS T.
Assistant Engineer (Spanish-American War), 12 May, 1898. Honorably discharged, 2 November, 1898.
GIBBS, PAUL C.
Acting Master, 15 April, 1862. Resigned 5 October, 1863.
GIBBS, SETH D.
Ensign (Spanish-American War), 15 June, 1898. Honorably discharged 12 October, 1898.
GIBBS, WILLIAM C.
Acting Master, 26 February, 1862. Resigned 21 February, 1863.
GIBBS, WILLIAM R.
Acting Master, 26 December, 1861. Appointment revoked 25 July, 1864.
GIBNEY, JAMES C.
Mate, 25 January, 1862. Acting Ensign, 21 July, 1862. Resigned 12 October, 1863.
GIBSON, ADAM.
Warrant Machinist, 23 August, 1899.
GIBSON, ALEXANDER.
Midshipman, 4 July, 1822. Passed Midshipman, 24 May, 1828. Lieutenant, 28 February, 1838. Reserved List, 13 September, 1855. Commissioned Commander on Active List, 14 September, 1855. Captain on Retired List, 4 April, 1867. Died 8 August, 1872.
GIBSON, A. J.
Acting Ensign, Admiral Farragut's Staff, 28 August, 1864. Resigned 14 April, 1865.
GIBSON, EDWARD K.
Acting Assistant Paymaster, 4 June, 1862. Discharged 24 June, 1865.
GIBSON, JAMES.
Carpenter, date not known. Last appearance on Records of Navy Department.
GIBSON, JAMES.
Acting Third Assistant Engineer, 9 March, 1865. Honorably discharged 12 May, 1865.
GIBSON, JOHN.
Cadet Midshipman, 9 June, 1874. Graduated 10 June, 1881. Ensign, Junior Grade, 3 March, 1883. Ensign, 26 June, 1884. Lieutenant, Junior Grade, 27 September, 1891. Lieutenant, 28 December, 1895. Retired List, with rank of Lieutenant-Commander, 30 June, 1900.
GIBSON, JOHN D.
Purser, 8 June, 1840. Retired List, 10 December, 1867. Died 3 September, 1869.
GIBSON, JOHN J.
Assistant Surgeon, 4 July, 1860. Surgeon, 22 September, 1863. Died 19 February, 1870.
GIBSON, OTIS W.
Acting Assistant Surgeon, 10 September, 1861. Appointment revoked 2 December, 1862.
GIBSON, THOMAS.
Acting Ensign, 24 February, 1863. Acting Master, 5 December, 1863. Honorably discharged 21 October, 1865.
GIBSON, THOMAS W.
Midshipman, 8 February, 1832. Dismissed 30 April, 1835.

GENERAL NAVY REGISTER. 217

GIBSON, WILLIAM.
Midshipman, 11 February, 1841. Passed Midshipman, 10 July, 1847. Master, 14 September, 1855. Lieutenant, 15 September, 1855. Lieutenant-Commander, 16 July, 1862. Retired 26 April, 1867. Commander on Retired List, 27 April, 1867. Lieutenant-Commander, Active List, 12 December, 1878. Commander, Active List, 13 January, 1879. Retired List, 25 May, 1887. Died 23 October, 1887.

GIBSON, WILLIAM B.
Assistant Surgeon, 2 November, 1861. Died 8 November, 1862.

GIBSON, WILLIAM C.
Entered Volunteer Service, 15 December, 1862. Ensign, 12 March, 1868. Master, 18 December, 1868. Lieutenant, 21 March, 1870. Lieutenant-Commander, 13 July, 1884. Commander, 4 July, 1893. Captain, 18 February, 1900. Retired, with rank of Rear-Admiral, 23 July, 1900.

GIBSON, WILLIAM H.
Acting Ensign, 16 November, 1863. Resigned 27 March, 1865.

GIDDEONS, WILLIAM.
Midshipman, 20 June, 1799. Last appearance on Records of Navy Department.

GIDDINGS, JOHN E.
Acting Master, 20 August, 1861. Resigned 16 May, 1863. Acting Ensign, 3 August, 1864. Acting Master, 10 July, 1865. Honorably discharged 29 July, 1865. Acting Master, 1 May, 1866. Mustered out 4 September, 1868.

GIDEON, CASPAR P.
Boatswain, 8 May, 1826. Resigned 3 June, 1826.

GIDEON, GEORGE, JR.
Third Assistant Engineer, 31 October, 1848. Second Assistant Engineer, 26 February, 1851. First Assistant Engineer, 21 May, 1853. Chief Engineer, 23 April, 1859. Died 16 June, 1863.

GIET, GEORGE W.
Sailmaker, 3 October, 1861. Died 30 August, 1877.

GIET, JOHN N.
Acting Master, 23 September, 1861. Resigned 6 December, 1862.

GIFFORD, CHARLES P.
Acting Ensign, 2 September, 1864. Appointment revoked (sick) 24 April, 1865.

GIFFORD, GEORGE P.
Mate, 25 February, 1864. Appointment revoked 8 April, 1868. Mate, 27 January, 1870. Resigned 9 September, 1870.

GIFFORD, JOHN L.
Acting Ensign, 11 October, 1862. Acting Master, faithful manner of performing duties, 31 October, 1863. Acting Volunteer Lieutenant, recommendation of Commanding Officer, 1 May, 1865. Honorably discharged 29 November, 1865.

GIFFORD, ROBINSON.
Acting Ensign, 9 August, 1864. Honorably discharged 27 October, 1865.

GIFFORD, R. W.
Acting Assistant Surgeon, 3 March, 1863. Resigned 28 April, 1865.

GIFFORD, THOMAS H.
Acting Master, 10 June, 1861. Dismissed 23 August, 1861.

GIFT, GEORGE W.
Midshipman, 30 November, 1847. Resigned 10 January, 1851.

GIGNILLIAT, THOMAS H.
Cadet Midshipman, 23 September, 1878. Graduated. Honorably discharged 30 June, 1885. Lieutenant, Junior Grade (Spanish-American War), 7 July, 1898. Honorably discharged 1 November, 1898.

GIHON, ALBERT L.
Assistant Surgeon, 2 May, 1855. Passed Assistant Surgeon, 4 May, 1860. Surgeon, 1 August, 1861. Medical Inspector, 7 November, 1872. Medical Director, 20 August, 1879. Retired List, 28 September, 1895.

GILBERT, DANIEL D.
Acting Assistant Surgeon, 8 November, 1861. Assistant Surgeon, 25 January, 1863. Resigned 8 August, 1864.

GILBERT, FOSTER B.
Acting Assistant Paymaster, 3 June, 1864. Honorably discharged 28 November, 1865.

GILBERT, JOHN.
Acting Third Assistant Engineer, 22 October, 1863. Appointment revoked (sick) 8 August, 1864.

GILBERT, JOHN P.
Acting Assistant Surgeon, 18 December, 1861. Appointment revoked 12 November, 1862.

GILBERT, JOSEPH L.
Passed Assistant Engineer (Spanish-American War), 9 May, 1898. Chief Engineer, 25 July, 1898. Honorably discharged 8 September, 1898.

GILBERT, PHILIP J.
Acting Assistant Surgeon, 20 February, 1865. Appointment revoked 7 June, 1865.

GILBERT, WILLIAM N.
Acting Third Assistant Engineer, 28 December, 1864. Honorably discharged 14 September, 1865.

GILCHRIST, EDWARD.
Assistant Surgeon, 26 January, 1832. Passed Assistant Surgeon, 8 November, 1836. Surgeon, 27 September, 1840. Died 6 November, 1869.

GILDERDALE, GEORGE D.
Mate, 22 October, 1862. Acting Ensign, 14 August, 1863. Honorably discharged 20 September, 1865.

GILDERSLEEVE, BENJAMIN.
Acting Third Assistant Engineer, 28 December, 1861. Resigned 24 June, 1862.

GILDERSLEEVE, THOMAS J.
Mate, 20 November, 1862. Deserted 31 October. 1863.
GILES, ALPHA E.
Acting First Assistant Engineer, 1 October, 1862. Resigned 17 June, 1864.
GILES, EDWARD.
Midshipman, 10 May, 1800. Resigned 25 April, 1804.
GILES, MELVIN P.
Acting Third Assistant Engineer, 10 March, 1865. Honorably discharged 24 October, 1865.
GILES, WILLIAM D.
Mate, 28 July, 1864. Resigned 3 April, 1866.
GILES, WILLIAM W.
Midshipman, 17 December, 1810. Dismissed 8 August, 1812.
GILFILLAN, WILLIAM J.
Acting Assistant Surgeon, 17 April, 1863. Dismissed 27 December, 1864.
GILL, CHRISTOPHER C.
Acting Ensign, 16 August, 1862. Acting Master, 25 July, 1863. Resigned 25 February, 1864. Acting Ensign, 4 April, 1864. Acting Master, recommendation of Commanding Officer, 11 August, 1864. Honorably discharged 26 October, 1865. Acting Master, 30 April, 1866. Discharged 13 August, 1866.
GILL, CLIFFORD B.
Midshipman, 25 September, 1862. Graduated 22 November, 1864. Ensign, 12 March, 1868. Master, 26 March, 1869. Lieutenant, 21 March, 1870. Resigned 19 June, 1882.
GILL, JOHN H.
Carpenter, 21 December, 1897.
GILL, J. W.
Acting Master, 23 September, 1861. Resigned 24 November, 1863.
GILL, THOMAS A.
Chaplain, 22 December, 1874.
GILL, WILLIAM A.
Cadet Midshipman, 24 June, 1875. Graduated 10 June, 1881. Ensign, Junior Grade, 3 March, 1883. Ensign, 26 June, 1884. Lieutenant. Junior Grade, 25 June, 1891. Lieutenant, 4 October, 1895.
GILL, WILLIAM L.
Midshipman, 8 March, 1814. Resigned 21 January, 1815.
GILLAN, DAVID.
Mate, 6 March, 1865. Resigned 15 June, 1865.
GILLAN, JAMES.
Mate, 4 November. 1861. Dismissed 24 October, 1864.
GILLANDER, ALEXANDER.
Acting Third Assistant Engineer, 21 May, 1862. Dismissed 14 March, 1863.
GILLASPY, GEORGE.
Surgeon, 13 March, 1798. Discharged 15 April. 1801, under Peace Establishment Act.
GILLESPIE, E. C.
Mate, 12 October, 1866. Resigned 13 January, 1869.
GILLESPIE, EDWARD.
Acting Third Assistant Engineer, 4 January, 1862. Resigned 22 November, 1862. Acting Third Assistant Engineer, 4 May, 1863. Resigned 18 April, 1864. Acting Third Assistant Engineer, 27 August, 1864. Honorably discharged 21 July, 1865.
GILLESPIE, GEORGE.
Acting First Assistant Engineer. 14 July, 1863. Honorably discharged 3 May, 1868.
GILLESPIE, JOHN E.
Assistant Surgeon, 29 June, 1868. Died 29 June, 1872.
GILLESPIE, WILLIAM, Jr.
Acting Assistant Paymaster, 4 December, 1862. Resigned 28 October, 1863.
GILLESPIE, WILLIAM T.
Acting Master, 26 August, 1861. Acting Volunteer Lieutenant, 13 March, 1865. Honorably discharged 29 December, 1865.
GILLESS, WALTER V.
Midshipman, 27 October, 1841. Passed Midshipman. 10 August, 1847. Died 11 June, 1853.
GILLET, SAMUEL T.
Midshipman, 1 December, 1826. Passed Midshipman, 28 April, 1832. Lieutenant, 9 February, 1837. Appointed Chaplain. 8 September, 1841. Resigned 19 January, 1843.
GILLETT, FRANCIS T.
Acting Assistant Paymaster, 20 October, 1863. Passed Assistant Paymaster, 23 July, 1866. Paymaster, 23 January, 1873. Died 15 February, 1878.
GILLETT, SIMEON P.
Acting Midshipman, 20 September, 1856. Midshipman, 15 June, 1860. Lieutenant, 16 July, 1862. Lieutenant-Commander, 27 April, 1866. Resigned 30 December. 1871.
GILLETTE, ROBERT H.
Acting Assistant Paymaster, 21 July, 1863. Killed on Gettysburg, 16 January, 1865.
GILLEY, JOHN H.
Mate, 24 December, 1861. Honorably discharged 14 October, 1865.
GILLEY, WILLIAM L.
Mate, 28 November, 1863. Acting Ensign, 14 November, 1864. Honorably discharged 8 October, 1868. Mate, 9 March, 1870. Died 24 May, 1875.
GILLIAM, HENRY.
Midshipman, 16 January, 1809. Lieutenant, 9 December, 1814. Last appearance on Records of Navy Department, 1823. New Orleans.

GENERAL NAVY REGISTER. 219

GILLIAM, JAMES S.
Assistant Surgeon, 26 April, 1847. Resigned 2 December, 1858. Reappointed 11 March, 1869. Lost in the Levant, June, 1861.

GILLILAND, CHRISTOPHER C.
Acting Carpenter, 15 October, 1863. Resigned 12 January, 1865.

GILLILAND, DAVID.
Acting Third Assistant Engineer, 12 April, 1864. Honorably discharged 29 August, 1865.

GILLILAND, SAMUEL.
Assistant Surgeon, 1 August, 1809. Resigned 13 June, 1812.

GILLINGHAM, EDWARD E.
Acting Third Assistant Engineer, 10 August, 1864. Resigned 29 October, 1864.

GILLIS, IRVIN V.
Naval Cadet, 6 September, 1890. Ensign, 1 July, 1896. Lieutenant, Junior Grade, 1 July, 1899.

GILLIS, JAMES H.
Midshipman, 12 October, 1848. Passed Midshipman, 15 June, 1854. Master, 16 September, 1855. Lieutenant, 17 September, 1855. Lieutenant-Commander, 16 July, 1862. Commander, 25 July, 1866. Captain, 30 September, 1876. Commodore, 29 January, 1887. Retired List, 14 May, 1893.

GILLISS, JAMES M.
Midshipman, 1 March, 1827. Passed Midshipman, 10 June, 1833. Lieutenant, 28 February, 1838. Reserved List, 17 September, 1855. Commander, Reserved List, 19 July, 1861. Captain, 16 July, 1862. Died 8 February, 1865.

GILLISS, JOHN.
Acting Second Assistant Engineer, 1 October, 1862. Resigned 30 May, 1864.

GILLISS, JOHN P.
Midshipman, 12 December, 1825. Passed Midshipman, 4 January, 1831. Lieutenant, 9 February, 1837. Commander, 14 September, 1855. Captain, 16 July, 1862. Retired List, 24 September, 1864. Commodore on Retired List, 28 September, 1866. Died 25 February, 1873.

GILLMARTIN, PETER P.
Acting Assistant Surgeon, 12 June, 1863. Resigned 28 September, 1864.

GILLMOR, HORATIO G.
Naval Cadet, 5 September, 1887. Assistant Naval Constructor, 1 July, 1893.

GILLMORE, JOHN.
Acting Third Assistant Engineer, 9 February, 1864. Honorably discharged 22 August, 1865.

GILLMORE, JAMES C.
Midshipman, 20 September, 1871. Graduated 20 June, 1876. Ensign, 30 January, 1879. Lieutenant, Junior Grade, 17 January, 1886. Lieutenant, 30 June, 1891. Lieutenant-Commander, 1 July, 1899.

GILPATRICK, W. WILBERFORCE.
Midshipman, 30 September, 1862. Graduated 22 November, 1864. Ensign, 12 March, 1868. Master, 26 March, 1869. Lieutenant, 21 March, 1870. Lieutenant-Commander, 1 July, 1887. Commander, 12 June, 1896. Died 10 October, 1896.

GILMAN, AUGUSTUS H.
Paymaster, 1 June, 1861. Pay Inspector, 3 March, 1871. Pay Director, 15 May, 1879. Retired List, 9 August, 1886. Died 21 May, 1895.

GILMAN, HENRY M.
Mate, 22 June, 1863. Resigned 30 September, 1863.

GILMAN, O. B.
Acting Assistant Paymaster, 31 December, 1862. Honorably discharged 27 September, 1865.

GILMAN, WILLIAM H.
Acting Assistant Paymaster, 22 September, 1862. Discharged 5 July, 1866.

GILMAN, WILLIAM M.
Passed Assistant Engineer (Spanish-American War), 4 June, 1898. Honorably discharged 6 September, 1898.

GILMARTIN, MICHAEL W.
Gunner, 28 October, 1890.

GILMER, JAMES B.
Naval Cadet, 19 May, 1894. At sea prior to final graduation.

GILMER, WILLIAM W.
Cadet Midshipman, 16 June, 1880. Ensign, 1 July, 1887. Lieutenant, Junior Grade, 4 September, 1896. Lieutenant, 3 March, 1899.

GILMEYER, JACOB E.
Midshipman, 1 January, 1813. Resigned 20 February, 1822.

GILMORE, A. N.
Acting Second Assistant Engineer, 3 November, 1863. Honorably discharged 2 October, 1868.

GILMORE, FERNANDO P.
Acting Midshipman, 28 February, 1863. Graduated. Ensign, 18 December, 1868. Master, 21 March, 1870. Lieutenant, 21 March, 1871. Lieutenant-Commander, 23 March, 1889. Commander, 1 January, 1897.

GILMORE, JOHN W.
Assistant Engineer (Spanish-American War), 14 May, 1898. Honorably discharged, 17 September, 1898.

GILMORE, OTIS H.
Gunner, 10 June, 1861. Dismissed 7 May, 1862.

GILMORE, THOMAS S.
Mate, 8 September, 1864. Honorably discharged 12 September, 1865.

GILPIN, CHARLES E.
Naval Cadet, 6 September, 1892. Ensign, 6 May, 1898.

GINGLEN, HUMPHREY.
Acting Third Assistant Engineer, 29 December, 1864. Honorably discharged 22 September, 1865.
GIPSON, JAMES C.
Acting Ensign, 1 October, 1862. Acting Master, 24 October, 1863. Acting Volunteer Lieutenant, 9 July, 1864. Honorably discharged 14 November, 1865.
GIRAUD, HENRY E.
Mate, 17 November, 1863. Resigned 12 May, 1865.
GIRAUD, JAMES S.
Appointed Volunteer Service, 12 December, 1864. Passed Assistant Paymaster, 23 July, 1866. Paymaster, 2 July, 1869. Dismissed 25 March, 1871.
GIRAUD, PIERRE.
Acting Master, 26 August, 1861. Acting Volunteer Lieutenant, gallant conduct on Montauk, 5 August, 1863. Acting Volunteer Lieutenant-Commander, 9 December, 1864. Honorably discharged 15 January, 1869.
GIRAULT, ARSENE N.
Professor, 14 August, 1848. Retired List, 25 December, 1863. Died 2 May, 1874.
GIRTY, DAVID.
Acting Third Assistant Engineer, 3 September, 1864. Appointment revoked (sick) 1 December, 1864.
GIRTY, THOMAS.
Acting Second Assistant Engineer, 1 November, 1862. Acting First Assistant Engineer, 13 May, 1863. Honorably discharged 8 November, 1865.
GISE, WILLIAM K.
Naval Cadet, 14 June, 1889. Ensign, 1 July, 1895. Lieutenant, Junior Grade, 3 March, 1899.
GIST, MORDECAI.
Midshipman, 14 April, 1800. Discharged 31 August, 1801, under Peace Establishment Act.
GIST, SPENCER C.
Midshipman, 1 May, 1826. Passed Midshipman, 28 April, 1832. Lieutenant, 8 March, 1837. Died 22 October, 1847.
GIST, W. FERGUSON.
Midshipman, 19 November, 1799. Permitted to retire, 1 August, 1801.
GIVAN, GEORGE W.
Mate, 10 September, 1863. Appointment revoked (sick) 8 March, 1864.
GIVEN, ROBERT.
Chaplain, 13 October, 1855. Retired List, 10 April, 1881. Died 4 June, 1895.
GLADDING, WILLIAM H.
Acting Third Assistant Engineer, 21 July, 1864. Dismissed 13 May, 1865.
GLADDING, WILLIAM O.
Mate, 21 December, 1863. Resigned 29 May, 1865.
GLADDING, WILLIAM H.
Third Assistant Engineer, 20 September, 1858. Dropped 4 August, 1863.
GLASS, CARSEN.
Mate, 18 May, 1865. Honorably discharged 7 October, 1865.
GLASS, GEORGE.
Acting Ensign, 14 September, 1864. Honorably discharged 30 June, 1879.
GLASS, HENRY.
Acting Midshipman, 24 September, 1860. Ensign, 28 May, 1863. Master, 10 November, 1865. Lieutenant, 10 November, 1866. Lieutenant-Commander, 12 March, 1868. Commander, 27 October, 1879. Captain, 23 January, 1894.
GLASSCOCK, THOMAS O.
Midshipman, 17 July, 1832. Resigned 11 May, 1839.
GLASSELL, WILLIAM T.
Midshipman, 15 March, 1848. Passed Midshipman, 15 June, 1854. Master, 15 September, 1855. Lieutenant, 16 September, 1855. Dismissed 6 December, 1861.
GLASSFORD, HENRY A.
Acting Volunteer Lieutenant, 3 December, 1862. Honorably discharged 29 November, 1865.
GLASSON, JOHN J.
Midshipman, 1 February, 1823. Passed Midshipman, 4 June, 1831. Lieutenant, 9 February, 1837. Reserved List, 13 September, 1855. Commissioned Commander on Active List, from 14 September, 1855. Retired 1 October, 1864. Commodore, Retired List, 4 April, 1867. Died 12 March, 1882.
GLASTER, JAMES.
Sailmaker, 6 June, 1803. Last appearance on Records of Navy Department.
GLEASON, HENRY M.
Naval Cadet, 20 May, 1895. At sea prior to final graduation.
GLEASON, JOHN H.
Mate, 18 December, 1861. Dismissed 15 July, 1864.
GLEAVES, ALBERT.
Cadet Midshipman, 10 June, 1873. Graduated 18 June, 1879. Ensign, 1 January, 1881. Lieutenant, Junior Grade, 26 May, 1887. Lieutenant, 9 January, 1893. Lieutenant-Commander, 25 May, 1900.
GLEAVES, JOHN W.
Midshipman, 16 January, 1809. Resigned 15 July, 1811.
GLENDY, WILLIAM M.
Midshipman, 1 January, 1818. Lieutenant, 3 March, 1827. Commander, 25 February, 1847. Captain, 14 September, 1855. Commodore, 16 July, 1862. Retired 16 July, 1862. Died 16 July, 1873.
GLENN, NOBLE W.
Midshipman, 2 July, 1801. Resigned 23 April, 1804.

GENERAL NAVY REGISTER. 221

GLENN, MARSHALL.
    Midshipman, 22 May, 1800. Resigned 25 March, 1802.
GLENNEY, DANIEL W.
    Acting Ensign, 8 October, 1862. Acting Master, 2 October, 1863. Deserted 4 November, 1864.
GLENNON, JAMES H.
    Cadet Midshipman, 24 September, 1874. Graduated 4 June, 1880. Ensign, 4 February, 1882. Lieutenant, Junior Grade, 26 March, 1889. Lieutenant, 26 December, 1893.
GLENNON, MARTIN.
    Acting Third Assistant Engineer, 21 October, 1862. Honorably discharged 2 December, 1866.
GLENTWORTH, H. N.
    Assistant Surgeon, 11 March, 1829. Passed Assistant Surgeon, 3 March, 1835. Surgeon, 9 February, 1837. Died 15 August, 1847.
GLENTWORTH, J. B.
    Midshipman, 19 August, 123. Resigned 21 January, 1831.
GLIDDEN, GEORGE D. B.
    Acting Midshipman, 23 September, 1860. Acting Ensign, 1 October, 1863. Master, 10 May, 1866. Lieutenant, 21 February, 1867. Lieutenant-Commander, 12 March, 1868. Died 25 January, 1885.
GLISSON, HENRY Y.
    Acting Assistant Paymaster, 11 December, 1862. Resigned 14 March, 1865.
GLISSON, OLIVER S.
    Midshipman, 1 November, 1826. Passed Midshipman, 28 April, 1832. Lieutenant, 8 March, 1837. Commander, 14 September, 1855. Captain, 16 July, 1862. Commodore, 25 July, 1866. Rear-Admiral, 10 June, 1870. Retired 18 January, 1871. Died 20 November, 1890.
GLOVER, WILLIAM.
    Master, date not known. Discharged 13 April, 1801, under Peace Establishment Act.
GLOVER, WILLIAM F.
    Ensign (Spanish-American War), 24 May, 1898. Honorably discharged 3 November, 1898.
GLYNN, DOMINICK.
    Boatswain, 30 June, 1891.
GLYNN, JAMES.
    Midshipman, 4 March, 1815. Lieutenant, 13 January, 1825. Commander, 8 September, 1841. Reserved List, 13 September, 1855. Commissioned Captain on Active List, from 14 September, 1855. Commodore on Retired List, 4 April, 1867. Died 13 May, 1871.
GLYNN, JOHN J.
    Boatswain, 13 May, 1887. Retired List, 28 January, 1895. Died 5 February, 1895.
GOBLE, EDWARD H.
    Acting Second Assistant Engineer, 7 November, 1862. Appointment revoked (sick) 17 September, 1864.
GOBLE, SAMUEL B.
    Acting Chief Engineer, 1 October, 1862. Appointment revoked (sick) 21 June, 1864.
GODBY, WILLIAM.
    Carpenter, 16 January, 1802. Died 26 November, 1808.
GODDARD, JOHN.
    Surgeon, 28 August, 1800. Died 31 December, 1802.
GODDARD, WILLIAM.
    Acting Third Assistant Engineer, 20 January, 1862. Dismissed 18 November, 1862.
GODDING, W. W.
    Acting Assistant Surgeon, 12 September, 1865. Resignation accepted 30 October, 1865.
GODFREY, GEORGE.
    Mate. Resigned 6 March, 1862.
GODFREY, JOHN W.
    Acting Master, 21 November, 1861. Resigned 12 September, 1863.
GODFREY, JONES.
    Acting Third Assistant Engineer, 10 October, 1866. Third Assistant Engineer, 2 June, 1868. Dismissed 27 September, 1873.
GODFREY, THOMAS.
    Master, 8 April, 1815. Died 13 February, 1820.
GODFREY, WASHINGTON.
    Acting Master, 16 December, 1861. Acting Volunteer Lieutenant, gallant conduct at Port Hudson, 7 March, 1864. Honorably discharged 4 December, 1865.
GODMAN, HAMILTON.
    Midshipman, 19 December, 1837. Resigned 15 May, 1839.
GODMAN, STEWART A.
    Midshipman, 4 November, 1841. Resigned 4 May, 1842.
GODON, VICTOR L.
    Assistant Surgeon, 23 February, 1835. Passed Assistant Surgeon, 8 July, 1841. Resigned 20 September, 1844.
GODON, SYLVANUS W.
    Midshipman, 4 March, 1819. Lieutenant, 17 December, 1836. Commander, 14 September, 1855. Captain, 16 July, 1862. Commodore, 2 January, 1863. Rear-Admiral, 25 February, 1866. Retired List, 18 June, 1871. Died 17 May, 1879.
GODWIN, JOHN.
    Midshipman, 2 January, 1800. Died 2 June, 1804.
GOE, WILLIAM.
    Master, 15 April, 1799. Resigned 19 May, 1801.

GOFF, ALBERT H.
  Acting Third Assistant Engineer, 25 March, 1864. Honorably discharged 25 November, 1865.
GOFF, JOSEPH W.
  Acting Third Assistant Engineer, 30 December, 1864. Honorably discharged 14 July, 1865.
GOFF, WILLIAM F.
  Acting Second Assistant Engineer, 24 February, 1863. Resigned 21 March, 1865.
GOIN, JOHN W.
  Acting Master, recruiting duty at New York, 16 April, 1863. Appointment revoked 25 August, 1864.
GOIN, THOMAS.
  Master, 23 November, 1839. Died 14 March, 1847.
GOLD, CORNELIUS B.
  Acting Assistant Paymaster, 31 October, 1864. Discharged 1 March, 1866.
GOLD, JOSEPH.
  Midshipman, 1 July, 1836. Resigned 27 February, 1839.
GOLDEN, LUCAS.
  Acting Third Assistant Engineer, 29 May, 1863. Honorably discharged 20 September, 1865.
GOLDEN, WILLIAM H.
  Acting Second Assistant Engineer, 21 October, 1862. Acting First Assistant Engineer, 6 November, 1862. Honorably discharged 2 December, 1866.
GOLDING, THOMAS.
  Acting Ensign, 22 September, 1863. Honorably discharged 27 April, 1869.
GOLDINGAY, THOMAS.
  Ensign (Spanish-American War), 21 May, 1898. Honorably discharged 8 October, 1898.
GOLDSBOROUGH, JOHN R.
  Midshipman, 16 November, 1824. Passed Midshipman. 28 April. 1832. Lieutenant, 6 September, 1837. Commander, 14 September, 1855. Captain. 16 July, 1862. Commodore, 13 April, 1867. Retired 2 July, 1870. Died 22 June. 1877.
GOLDSBOROUGH, LOUIS M.
  Midshipman, 18 June, 1812. Lieutenant, 13 January, 1825. Commander. 8 September, 1841. Captain, 14 September, 1855. Rear-Admiral, 16 July, 1862. Retired List, 6 October, 1873. Died 20 February, 1877.
GOLDSBOROUGH, McGILL, R.
  Assistant Paymaster, 25 April, 1899.
GOLDSBOROUGH, R. W.
  Purser, 30 April, 1804. Last appearance on Records of Navy Department, 21 March, 1810. Died at Norfolk.
GOLDSBOROUGH, WORTHINGTON.
  Acting Assistant Paymaster, 30 September, 1862. Assistant Paymaster, 2 July, 1864. Paymaster, 4 May, 1866. Pay Inspector, 24 November, 1891. Retired List, 9 October, 1896.
GOLDSBOROUGH, W. S.
  Midshipman, 5 May, 1806. Last appearance on Records of Navy Department, May, 1807.
GOLDSMITH, ISAAC N.
  Mate, 5 June. 1863. Acting Ensign, 5 September, 1863. Honorably discharged 8 November, 1865.
GOLDSMITH, NATHAN A.
  Mate, 6 June, 1864. Honorably discharged 22 June, 1866.
GOLL, JOHN J.
  Acting Third Assistant Engineer, 18 December, 1861. Resigned 3 April, 1862.
GOLLET, JAMES M.
  Master, 18 October, 1798. Discharged 10 April. 1801. under Peace Establishment Act.
GOLSTEN, EMILE H.
  Acting Third Assistant Engineer. 24 November, 1863. Acting Second Assistant Engineer, 5 December, 1864. Honorably discharged 28 September, 1865.
GOOD, GEORGE.
  Mate, 6 March, 1862. Resigned 27 August, 1862.
GOOD, SAMUEL.
  Mate, 14 November. 1861. Canceled 22 January, 1862.
GOODHUE, DAVID P.
  Acting Assistant Surgeon, 4 January, 1864. Honorably discharged 9 October. 1865.
GOODING, FREDERICK A.
  Mate. 29 January, 1863. Resigned 18 November, 1865.
GOODING, GEORGE H.
  Acting Ensign, 19 August, 1864. Honorably discharged 21 August, 1865.
GOODING, P. C.
  Acting Ensign, 15 February, 1865. Honorably discharged 30 September, 1865.
GOODING, WILLIAM T.
  Mate. 1862. Resigned 28 June. 1862.
GOODING, W. M.
  Acting Assistant Surgeon, 12 September, 1865. Resigned 1 November, 1866.
GOODLOE, JOHN J.
  Midshipman. 14 October, 1845. Resigned 1 June, 1846.
GOODLOE, JOSEPH A.
  Acting Third Assistant Engineer. Resigned 13 April, 1864.
GOODMAN, RICHARD F.
  Acting Assistant Paymaster, 3 February, 1864. Honorably discharged 23 August, 1865.

GENERAL NAVY REGISTER. 223

GOODMAN, WILLIAM.
 Assistant Engineer (Spanish-American War), 25 June, 1898. Honorably discharged 31 October, 1898.
GOODMANSON, GEORGE H.
 Mate, 21 December, 1863. Honorably discharged 30 September, 1865.
GOODMANSON, JOHN P.
 Acting Master, 26 August, 1861. Dismissed 20 January, 1863.
GOODRICH, CASPAR FREDERICK.
 Midshipman, 10 December, 1861. Graduated 22 November, 1864. Ensign, 1 November, 1866. Master, 1 December, 1866. Lieutenant, 12 March, 1868. Lieutenant-Commander, 26 March, 1869. Commander, 27 September, 1884. Captain, 16 September, 1897.
GOODRICH, GEORGE F.
 Mate, 25 January, 1862. Appointment revoked (sick) 24 August, 1864.
GOODRICH, ISAIAH W.
 Mate, 11 March, 1863. Resigned (sick) 12 November, 1863. Acting Ensign, 1 December, 1864. Honorably discharged 16 September, 1865.
GOODRICH, JAMES M.
 Acting Third Assistant Engineer, 3 November, 1863. Honorably discharged 8 July, 1865.
GOODRICH, WILLIAM M.
 Ensign (Spanish-American War), 30 April, 1898. Honorably discharged 21 September, 1898.
GOODRIDGE, DANIEL M.
 Lieutenant, Junior Grade (Spanish-American War), 22 June, 1898. Honorably discharged 22 September, 1898.
GOODSOE, AUGUSTUS O.
 Carpenter, 3 June, 1861. Retired List, 7 December, 1894.
GOODSUM, JAMES.
 Midshipman, 18 June, 1812. Lieutenant, 1 April, 1818. Died 9 May, 1836.
GOODWIN, BENJAMIN.
 Master, 16 January, 1809. Last appearance on Records of Navy Department, 22 October, 1810. Drowned at sea.
GOODWIN, C. G.
 Midshipman, 17 October, 1799. (See Ridgely.)
GOODWIN, CHARLES.
 Acting Third Assistant Engineer, 11 May, 1863. Acting Second Assistant Engineer, 4 May, 1864. Acting First Assistant Engineer, 22 March, 1865. Honorably discharged 4 December, 1865.
GOODWIN, CHARLES J.
 Acting Ensign, 30 December, 1862. Appointment revoked (sick) 21 March, 1864. Acting Ensign, 16 December, 1864. Honorably discharged 7 August, 1865.
GOODWIN, CHARLES M.
 Acting Third Assistant Engineer, 11 November, 1862. Honorably discharged 16 September, 1865.
GOODWIN, DANIEL.
 Midshipman, 30 November, 1814. Struck off 3 January, 1825.
GOODWIN, EDWARD M.
 Acting Assistant Surgeon, 4 January, 1864. Honorably discharged 21 October, 1865.
GOODWIN, EZRA S.
 Acting Master, 7 December, 1861. Resigned 5 April, 1867.
GOODWIN, FRANCIS C.
 Third Assistant Engineer, 12 July, 1861. Second Assistant Engineer, 18 December, 1862. Retired List, 2 March. 1868. Died 24 April, 1886.
GOODWIN, HENRY B.
 Acting Third Assistant Engineer, 10 February, 1863. Acting Second Assistant Engineer, 21 January, 1865. Honorably discharged 19 March, 1866.
GOODWIN, J. K.
 Mate, 20 August, 1863. Resigned 17 May, 1865.
GOODWIN, JOHN.
 Midshipman, 27 May, 1800. Resigned 29 December, 1802.
GOODWIN, JOHN D., JR.
 Midshipman, 16 January, 1809. Last appearance on Records of Navy Department, 1815. Philadelphia.
GOODWIN, JOSEPH B.
 Acting First Assistant Engineer, 1 October, 1862. Honorably discharged 21 October, 1865.
GOODWIN, JOSEPH W.
 Mate, 12 September, 1862. Acting Ensign, 12 November, 1863. Honorably discharged 27 August, 1865.
GOODWIN, MONTGOMERY M.
 Chaplain, 19 March, 1894. Resigned 30 November, 1897.
GOODWIN, NATHANIEL.
 Acting Master, 31 August, 1861. Resigned 30 June, 1862.
GOODWIN, WILLIAM.
 Midshipman, 2 April, 1804. Drowned 7 June, 1808.
GOODWIN, W. WALLACE.
 Acting Assistant Paymaster, 4 October, 1861. Honorably discharged 3 March, 1866.
GOODWIN, WALTON.
 Acting Midshipman, 26 February, 1863. Graduated. Ensign, 18 December, 1868. Master, 21 March, 1870. Lieutenant, 21 March, 1871. Lieutenant-Commander, 15 October, 1890. Commander, 21 July, 1897.

GOODWYN, GEORGE.
   Midshipman, 18 June. 1812. Last appearance on Records of Navy Department, 14 December, 1812. Resigned.
GOOLD, JOHN.
   Master, 16 July, 1812. Discharged 7 May, 1813.
GORDAN, ALEXANDER G.
   Midshipman, 1 January. 1818. Lieutenant. 3 March. 1827. Commander, 14 March, 1849. Died 11 October, 1849.
GORDON, BENJAMIN.
   Boatswain, 8 November, 1814. Resigned 9 March, 1815.
GORDON, CHARLES.
   Midshipman, 24 June. 1799. Lieutenant, 16 January, 1800. Commander, 25 April, 1806. Captain, 2 March, 1813. Died in 1817.
GORDON, EDWARD.
   Midshipman, 21 September, 1841. Dismissed 21 August, 1849.
GORDON, FREDERICK T.
   Pharmacist, 25 July, 1900.
GORDON, JAMES.
   Acting Second Assistant Engineer, 15 August, 1864. Appointment revoked (sick) 8 March, 1865.
GORDON, JAMES B.
   Acting Master, 10 June, 1861. Appointment revoked 24 August. 1861. Acting Master, 28 August, 1861. Dismissed 21 March, 1862.
GORDON, JAMES H.
   Mate, 11 October, 1862. Resigned 17 January, 1863. Mate, 1 August, 1863. Resigned 2 December, 1864.
GORDON, JOHN.
   Acting Assistant Surgeon, 5 June, 1864. Honorably discharged 16 December, 1865.
GORDON, JOHN H.
   Assistant Surgeon, 24 July, 1813. Surgeon, 27 March, 1818. Resigned 27 March, 1827.
GORDON, JOHN S.
   Acting Master, 26 April, 1862. Dismissed 7 June, 1863.
GORDON, JOSEPH R.
   Acting Master, 10 June, 1861. Resigned 1 February, 1862.
GORDON, OLIVER A.
   Mate. Resigned 29 March, 1865.
GORDON, ROBERT F.
   Acting Third Assistant Engineer, 28 March, 1865. Honorably discharged 12 April, 1866.
GORDON, ROBERT H.
   Acting Third Assistant Engineer, 26 May, 1863. Dismissed 2 May, 1864.
CORDON, SAMUEL.
   Mate, 28 July, 1864. Acting Ensign, 15 September, 1865. Honorably discharged 13 February, 1866.
GORDON, THOMAS.
   Midshipman, 7 April, 1799. Discharged 10 June. 1801. under Peace Establishment Act.
GORDON, TOMBIGBEE.
   Midshipman, 3 June, 1823. Resigned 12 August, 1824.
GORDON, WILLIAM.
   Mate, 5 August, 1863. Resigned 17 May, 1865.
GORDON, WILLIAM A.
   Assistant Engineer (Spanish-American War), 27 July. 1898. Honorably discharged 19 November, 1898.
GORDON, WILLIAM L.
   Midshipman, 15 November, 1809. Lieutenant. 9 December, 1814. Commander, 24 April, 1828. Died 25 May, 1834.
GORGAS, ALBERT C.
   Assistant Surgeon, 30 August, 1856. Passed Assistant Surgeon. 25 March, 1861. Surgeon, 13 October, 1861. Medical Inspector, 6 October, 1873. Medical Director, 4 March, 1884. Retired List, 7 June, 1895. Died 29 June, 1895.
GORGAS, JOHN A., JR.
   Lieutenant, Junior Grade (Spanish-American War), 20 May, 1898. Honorably discharged 28 January, 1899.
GORGAS, MILES C
   Cadet Midshipman, 18 September, 1875. Graduated 22 June, 1882. Ensign, Junior Grade, 3 March, 1883. Ensign, 26 June, 1884. Lieutenant, Junior Grade, 15 May, 1893. Lieutenant, 5 January, 1897.
GORMAN, DANIEL.
   Acting Third Assistant Engineer, 19 December, 1863. Appointment revoked (sick) 8 November, 1864.
GORMAN, JOHN.
   Mate, 23 January, 1862. Acting Ensign, 8 June, 1863. Honorably discharged 30 September, 1865.
GORMAN, MAURICE M.
   Acting Ensign, 30 November, 1864. Honorably discharged 6 May, 1868.
GORMLEY, HENRY.
   Acting Second Assistant Engineer, 14 May, 1861. Honorably discharged 15 September, 1865.
GORRINGE, HENRY H.
   Mate, 13 July, 1862. Acting Ensign, 1 October, 1862. Acting Master, 26 September, 1863. Acting Volunteer Lieutenant, 27 April, 1864. Acting Volunteer Lieutenant-Commander, 10 July, 1865. Lieutenant, 12 March, 1868. Lieutenant-Commander, 18 December, 1868. Resigned 21 February, 1883.

GRAHAM, WILLIAM R.
  Midshipman, 2 April, 1804. Resigned 18 April, 1805.
GRAHAM, W. R.
  Midshipman, 18 June, 1812. Discharged 19 June, 1813.
GRAIL, THOMAS.
  Acting Gunner, 15 December, 1863. Honorably discharged 11 March, 1868.
GRAINGER, JOHN R.
  Gunner, 23 November, 1861. Chief Gunner, 3 March, 1899.
GRANDISON, C. F.
  Master, 20 September, 1805. Dismissed 12 January, 1808.
GRANDISON, CHARLES.
  Master, 25 March, 1812. Dismissed 1 May, 1813.
GRANGER, BROWNELL.
  Civil Engineer, 14 July, 1874. Removed 22 January, 1877.
GRANGER, H. M.
  Midshipman, 23 August, 1836. Resigned 28 April, 1837.
GRANGER, LYMAN C.
  Acting Assistant Surgeon, 24 June, 1863. Died September, 1864.
GRANT, ALBERT W.
  Cadet Midshipman, 9 June, 1873. Graduated 18 June, 1879. Ensign, 17 May, 1881. Lieutenant, Junior Grade, 1 November, 1887. Lieutenant, 9 May, 1893. Lieutenant-Commander, 1 July, 1900.
GRANT, ALEXANDER M.
  Acting Master, 1 October, 1862. Resigned 23 July, 1863.
GRANT, CHARLES H.
  Lieutenant (Spanish-American War), 18 June, 1898. Honorably discharged 7 October, 1898.
GRANT, DANIEL J.
  Acting Ensign, 22 December, 1862. Honorably discharged 22 October, 1865.
GRANT, FRANKLIN.
  Mate, 7 October, 1863. Honorably discharged 13 May, 1867.
GRANT, GOUGH W.
  Midshipman, 30 May, 1833. Passed Midshipman, 8 July, 1839. Lieutenant, 1 March, 1845. Resigned, 15 July, 1850.
GRANT, JOEL.
  Professor of Mathematics, 15 October, 1839. Resigned 2 October, 1843.
GRANT, JOHN.
  Midshipman, 18 June, 1812. Resigned 23 February, 1813.
GRANT, JOHN W.
  Acting Third Assistant Engineer, 10 August, 1864. Honorably discharged 30 October, 1866.
GRANT, JOSEPH.
  Boatswain, 27 November, 1801. Not in service, 31 December, 1803.
GRANT, KELLUM D.
  Acting Warrant Machinist, 23 August, 1899.
GRANT, WILLIAM.
  Purser, 12 October, 1844. Commission expired 3 March, 1845.
GRANT, WILLIAM.
  Acting Second Assistant Engineer, 5 August, 1864. Honorably discharged 4 November, 1865.
GRANT, WILLIAM L.
  Lieutenant, Junior Grade (Spanish-American War), 8 June, 1898. Honorably discharged 2 September, 1898.
GRANTZOUR, F. W
  Acting Ensign, 8 June, 1864. Honorably discharged 22 March, 1866.
GRATTAN, J. W.
  Acting Ensign, Admiral Porter's Staff, 6 December, 1863. Discharged 20 April, 1865.
GRAVATT, CHARLES U.
  Assistant Surgeon, 27 September, 1871. Passed Assistant Surgeon, 24 March, 1874. Surgeon, 21 November, 1883. Medical Inspector, 6 June, 1897.
GRAVES, BENJAMIN F.
  Mate, 3 June, 1864. Resigned 20 August, 1864.
GRAVES, CHARLES J.
  Acting Midshipman, 17 December, 1853. Midshipman, 10 June, 1857. Passed Midshipman, 25 June, 1860. Master, 24 October, 1860. Lieutenant, 8 April, 1861. Dismissed 24 December, 1861.
GRAVES, GEORGE W.
  Acting Master, 11 July, 1861. Acting Volunteer Lieutenant, 29 January, 1863. Honorably discharged 10 February, 1866.
GRAVES, HIRAM B.
  Mate, 22 June, 1863. Acting Ensign, 26 August, 1863. Honorably discharged 6 December, 1865.
GRAVES, JAMES C.
  Mate 3 November, 1863. Acting Assistant Paymaster 2 March, 1864. Mustered out 2 May, 1867.
GRAVES, JOHN.
  Master, 6 July, 1812. Resigned 29 October, 1813.
GRAVES, SEWELL F.
  Mate, 29 December, 1863. Acting Ensign, 27 July, 1864. Resigned 10 June, 1865.
GRAY, ANDREW F. V.
  Midshipman, 15 October, 1829. Passed Midshipman, 3 July, 1835. Lieutenant, 8 September, 1841. Died 15 March, 1860.

GRAY, CHARLES.
Midshipman, 19 October, 1841. Passed Midshipman, 10 August, 1847. Dropped 13 September, 1855.
GRAY, EDWIN F.
Midshipman, 8 April, 1846. Passed Midshipman, 8 June, 1852. Master, 15 September, 1855. Lieutenant, 16 September, 1855. Resigned 29 December, 1857.
GRAY, EZRA.
Acting Third Assistant Engineer, 23 March, 1864. Resigned 24 June, 1865.
GRAY, GEORGE.
Midshipman, 14 April, 1800. Last appearance on Records of Navy Department, 5 September, 1800. Resigned.
GRAY, GEORGE R.
Midshipman, 1 November, 1826. Passed Midshipman, 10 June, 1833. Lieutenant, 8 December, 1838. Reserved List, 13 September, 1855. Died 2 October, 1866.
GRAY, GEORGE W.
Midshipman, 1 January, 1812. Resigned 10 August, 1814.
GRAY, G. HARRISON.
Acting Assistant Surgeon, 16 June, 1871. Resigned 4 October, 1872.
GRAY, HARRY P.
Passed Assistant Engineer (Spanish-American War), 27 June, 1898. Honorably discharged 8 September, 1898.
GRAY, HENRY.
Midshipman, 1 January, 1812. Lieutenant, 1 April, 1818. Last appearance on Records of Navy Department. Dead.
GRAY, HOWARD P.
Acting Third Assistant Engineer, 29 September, 1863. Honorably discharged 16 October, 1865.
GRAY, JAMES.
Cadet Midshipman, 24 September, 1874. Resigned 23 June, 1876. Cadet Midshipman, 22 September, 1876. Midshipman, 22 June, 1882. Ensign, Junior Grade, 3 March, 1883. Resigned 31 March, 1884. Lieutenant (Spanish-American War), 9 May, 1898. Honorably discharged 6 October, 1898.
GRAY, JAMES L.
Mate. Dismissed 23 January, 1862.
GRAY, ROBERT F.
Mate, 18 May, 1864. Resigned 16 November, 1864.
GRAY, S. C.
Acting Master, 22 May, 1861. Dismissed 22 August, 1864.
GRAY, SIDNEY N.
Mate, 8 May, 1862. Acting Ensign, 21 November, 1864. Honorably discharged 10 November, 1865.
GRAY, W. H. H.
Midshipman, 2 February, 1829. Resigned 4 June, 1829.
GRAY, WILLIAM F.
Carpenter, 8 July, 1869. Died 13 December, 1871.
GRAY, WILLIAM H.
Mate, 11 June, 1863. Honorably discharged 7 August, 1865.
GRAY, WILLIAM T.
Cadet Midshipman, 28 June, 1878. Honorably discharged 30 June, 1885. Assistant Paymaster, 27 April, 1898. Passed Assistant Paymaster, 9 April, 1899.
GRAYDON, JAMES W.
Midshipman, 22 July, 1865. Graduated 4 June, 1869. Ensign, 12 January, 1870. Master, 27 March, 1873. Lieutenant, 25 November, 1877. Resigned 15 September, 1884.
GRAYSON, JOHN.
Midshipman, 26 June, 1799. Resigned 18 October, 1800.
GRAYSON, JOHN R.
Master, 14 February, 1809. Resigned 29 March, 1815.
GRAYSON, WILLIAM R.
Midshipman, 20 June, 1806. Resigned 2 April, 1808.
GREATON, JOHN.
Midshipman, 6 December, 1814. Resigned 23 February, 1815.
GREATOREX, HENRY.
Acting Third Assistant Engineer, 22 February, 1864. Acting Second Assistant Engineer, 18 April, 1865. Honorably discharged 13 June, 1866.
GREATRAKE, C. L.
Second Assistant Engineer, 15 March, 1847. Resigned 25 October, 1847.
GREELEY, ALFRED J.
Acting Assistant Paymaster, 21 October, 1864. Discharged 20 November, 1865. Acting Assistant Paymaster, 2 March, 1867. Passed Assistant Paymaster, 10 February, 1870. Retired 30 June, 1875. Died 10 August, 1875.
GREEN, ALLEN J.
Midshipman, 6 January, 1800. Resigned 17 January, 1803.
GREEN, ARCHIBALD.
Midshipman, 1 March, 1825. Resigned 19 October, 1827.
GREEN, BENNETT W.
Assistant Surgeon, 21 August, 1859. Dismissed May, 1861.
GREEN, CARL M.
Passed Assistant Engineer (Spanish-American War), 10 June, 1898. Honorably discharged 7 January, 1899.
GREEN, CHARLES.
Midshipman, 1 May, 1826. Passed Midshipman, 28 April, 1832. Lieutenant, 8 March, 1837. Commander, 14 September, 1855. Captain, 16 July, 1862. Retired 15 November, 1862. Commodore, Retired List, 4 April, 1867. Died 7 April, 1881.

GREEN, CHARLES.
Acting Third Assistant Engineer, 3 October, 1864. Resigned 13 January, 1865.
GREEN, CHARLES L.
Acting Assistant Surgeon, 31 May, 1864. Assistant Surgeon, 23 June, 1864. Passed Assistant Surgeon, 11 October, 1867. Resigned 15 January, 1870.
GREEN, DAVID.
Boatswain, 24 January, 1848. Dismissed 26 June, 1850.
GREEN, EDWARD H.
Assistant Surgeon, 11 March, 1875. Surgeon, 11 November, 1890.
GREEN, ELLIOTT.
Carpenter, 17 August, 1823. Died 14 November, 1834.
GREEN, ELLIS L.
Midshipman, 3 July, 1798. Resigned 18 December, 1798.
GREEN, FARNIFOLD.
Midshipman, 1 May, 1822. Dismissed 17 December, 1827.
GREEN, FRANCIS M.
Acting Master, 18 June, 1861. Acting Volunteer Lieutenant, 2 April, 1864. Honorably discharged 24 May, 1866. Acting Volunteer Lieutenant, 3 September, 1866. Lieutenant, 12 March, 1868. Lieutenant-Commander, 18 December, 1868. Commander, 7 July, 1883. Retired List, 23 February, 1897.
GREEN, GEORGE.
Acting Third Assistant Engineer, 4 August, 1864. Resigned 12 May, 1865.
GREEN, HENRY A.
Acting Ensign, 27 July, 1863. Acting Master, 30 November, 1864. Honorably discharged 26 September, 1865.
GREEN, HENRY B.
Acting Third Assistant Engineer, 19 September, 1862. Acting Second Assistant Engineer, 3 March, 1864. Resigned (sick) 22 March, 1865.
GREEN, HENRY D.
Mate, 3 September, 1863. Acting Ensign, 10 December, 1863. Honorably discharged 11 November, 1865.
GREEN, HENRY L.
Midshipman, 21 July, 1866. Graduated 7 June, 1870. Ensign, 13 July, 1871. Master, 23 May, 1874. Died 7 July, 1883.
GREEN, HENRY W.
Acting Master, 10 June, 1861. Dismissed 6 July, 1861.
GREEN, JAMES E.
Acting Carpenter, 1 October, 1862. Appointment revoked 29 October, 1863.
GREEN, JAMES.
Acting Master's Mate, 3 October, 1864. Deserted 3 December, 1864.
GREEN, JAMES G.
Mate, 11 May, 1861. Acting Ensign, 27 November, 1862. Acting Master, 11 August, 1864. Master, 12 March, 1868. Lieutenant, 18 December, 1868. Lieutenant-Commander, 3 July, 1870. Commander, 6 March, 1887. Captain, 3 March, 1899.
GREEN, JOHN.
Purser, 5 April, 1805. Last appearance on Records of Navy Department, 11 January, 1811.
GREEN, JOHN.
Carpenter, 23 January, 1833. Died 12 January, 1864.
GREEN, JOHN F.
Acting Warrant Machinist, 6 July, 1899.
GREEN, JOHN M.
Gunner, 23 November, 1828. Resigned 8 September, 1836.
GREEN, JOHN P.
Third Assistant Engineer, 24 February, 1862. Appointment revoked 1 March, 1862.
GREEN, JOHN R.
Purser, 25 April, 1812. Died 24 August, 1812.
GREEN, JOSEPH F.
Midshipman, 1 November, 1827. Passed Midshipman, 10 June, 1833. Lieutenant, 28 February, 1838. Commander, 14 September, 1855. Captain, 16 July, 1862. Commodore, 2 December, 1867. Rear-Admiral, 13 July, 1870. Retired List, 25 November, 1872. Died 9 December, 1897.
GREEN, JOSEPH STORY.
Third Assistant Engineer, 11 February, 1862. Second Assistant Engineer, 15 October, 1863. Retired 24 May, 1867.
GREEN, LEVI R.
Third Assistant Engineer, 19 March, 1858. Second Assistant Engineer, 1 December, 1860. First Assistant Engineer, 15 October, 1863. Resigned 2 August, 1869.
GREEN, NATHANIEL.
Acting Midshipman, 28 May, 1852. Midshipman, 1 October, 1856. Passed Midshipman, 29 April, 1859. Master, 5 September, 1859. Lieutenant, 27 February, 1861. Lieutenant-Commander, 2 January, 1863. Retired List, 21 January, 1873. Died 22 March, 1873.
GREEN, RICHARD.
Boatswain, 12 December, 1799. Discharged 1 August, 1800.
GREEN, SAMUEL.
Master, 19 January, 1809. Appointment revoked 8 May, 1809.
GREEN, SAMUEL N.
Midshipman, 1 April, 1828. Resigned 9 July, 1828.
GREEN, SAMUEL S.
Sailmaker, 1802. Last appearance on Records of Navy Department, 19 December, 1803.
GREEN, STEPHEN S.
Acting Assistant Surgeon, 5 March, 1864. Honorably discharged 5 December, 1865.

GREEN, THOMAS B.
Acting Third Assistant Engineer, 28 October, 1861. Acting Second Assistant Engineer, 26 December, 1863. Acting First Assistant Engineer, 3 October, 1864. Honorably discharged 20 March, 1866.
GREEN, THOMAS H.
Acting Gunner, 14 September, 1863. Honorably discharged 16 October, 1865.
GREEN, WILLIAM.
Master, 26 June, 1812. Last appearance on Records of Navy Department, 1815. Lake Champlain.
GREEN, WILLIAM.
Boatswain, 30 September, 1861. Warranted 30 September, 1862. Appointment revoked 19 May, 1869.
GREEN, WILLIAM.
Midshipman, 1 January, 1818. Lieutenant, 3 March, 1827. Commander, 17 May, 1847. Reserved List, 13 September, 1855. Resigned 6 May, 1861.
GREEN, WILLIAM H.
Acting First Assistant Engineer, 11 June, 1862. Acting Chief Engineer, 21 July, 1863. Resigned 15 August, 1863.
GREEN, WILLIS M.
Midshipman, 30 November, 1814. Resigned 14 June, 1819.
GREEN, W. M., Jr.
Midshipman, 16 December, 1836. Dismissed 19 September, 1840.
GREENE, ALBERT S.
Third Assistant Engineer, 17 February, 1860. Second Assistant Engineer, 17 November, 1862. First Assistant Engineer, 1 March, 1864. Chief Engineer, 5 March, 1871. Retired List, 9 August, 1893. Died 8 March, 1896.
GREENE, BENJAMIN F.
Professor, 21 March, 1873. Retired List, 25 October, 1879. Died 22 November, 1895.
GREENE, CHARLES H.
Midshipman, 13 May, 1848. Passed Midshipman, 15 June, 1854. Master, 15 September, 1855. Lieutenant, 16 September, 1855. Lieutenant-Commander, 16 July, 1862. Wholly retired 17 May, 1867.
GREENE, CHRISTOPHER N.
Midshipman, 1 February, 1827. Resigned 23 October, 1827.
GREENE, DANIEL S.
Assistant Surgeon, 18 October, 1833. Passed Assistant Surgeon, 1 August, 1837. Surgeon, 8 September, 1841. Dismissed 2 May, 1861.
GREENE, DAVID M.
Third Assistant Engineer, 23 May, 1861. Second Assistant Engineer, 28 October, 1862. First Assistant Engineer, 1 January, 1865. Resigned 16 September, 1869.
GREENE, EDWARD K.
Mate, 21 November, 1864. Honorably discharged 6 May, 1867. Mate, 26 November, 1869. Deserted 16 April, 1872.
GREENE, FRANCIS E.
Midshipman, 25 September, 1867. Graduated 6 June, 1871. Ensign, 14 July, 1872. Master, 16 June, 1875. Lieutenant, 2 July, 1882. Lieutenant-Commander, 3 March, 1899. Died 10 January, 1900.
GREENE, FRANCIS V.
Acting Assistant Surgeon, 19 December, 1862. Acting Passed Assistant Surgeon, 14 August, 1865. Passed Assistant Surgeon, Retired List, 30 June, 1879.
GREENE, FRANK C.
Acting Gunner, 5 August, 1863. Honorably discharged 6 December, 1865.
GREENE, GEORGE MAXON.
Third Assistant Engineer, 25 August, 1862. Second Assistant Engineer, 20 February, 1864. First Assistant Engineer, 1 January, 1868. Died 2 June, 1878.
GREENE, GEORGE W.
Carpenter, 16 November, 1875. Resigned 8 November, 1879.
GREENE, HUGH W.
Purser, 28 February, 1839. Resigned 15 May, 1851.
GREENE, JAMES C.
Acting Ensign, 11 November, 1862. Dismissed 7 June, 1863. Acting Ensign, 8 November, 1864. Honorably discharged 29 July, 1865.
GREENE, JAMES M.
Surgeon's Mate, 20 April, 1825. Surgeon, 4 December, 1828. Retired 21 December, 1861. Medical Director on Retired List, 3 March, 1871. Died 9 June, 1871.
GREENE, PAUL.
Acting Ensign, 17 September, 1864. Honorably discharged 13 July, 1865.
GREENE, R. H.
Acting Assistant Surgeon, 5 November, 1863. Resigned 18 May, 1865.
GREENE, SAMUEL DANA.
Acting Midshipman, 21 September, 1855. Midshipman, 9 June, 1859. Lieutenant, 31 August, 1861. Lieutenant-Commander, 11 August, 1865. Commander, 12 December, 1872. Died 11 December, 1884.
GREENE, SAMUEL D.
Cadet Midshipman, 16 June, 1879. Graduated 8 June, 1883. Ensign, 1 July, 1885. Resigned 19 February, 1888. Lieutenant, Junior Grade (Spanish-American War), 30 April, 1898. Honorably discharged 6 September, 1898.
GREENE, STEWART.
Acting Second Assistant Engineer, 28 March, 1863. Resigned 10 April, 1863. Acting Second Assistant Engineer, 21 May, 1863. Honorably discharged 19 October, 1865.
GREENE, THEODORE P.
Midshipman, 1 November, 1826. Passed Midshipman, 28 April, 1832. Lieutenant, 20 December, 1837. Commander, 14 September, 1855. Captain, 16 July, 1862. Com-

GENERAL NAVY REGISTER.

modore, 24 July, 1867. Retired 1 November, 1871. Rear-Admiral, Retired List, 24 May, 1872. Died 30 August, 1887.
GREENE, WILLIAM A.
Assistant Surgeon, 7 March, 1838. Died November, 1839.
GREENE, WILLIAM R.
Acting Second Assistant Engineer, 17 December, 1861. Killed in action at Galveston, Texas, 1 January, 1863.
GREENHALGH, JOHN.
Acting Ensign, 19 December, 1863. Honorably discharged 5 May, 1868.
GREENHOUGH, J. W. B.
Assistant Surgeon, 7 March, 1838. Resigned 10 September, 1844. Reappointed 24 April, 1847. Passed Assistant Surgeon, Retired 14 May, 1861. Dismissed 5 July, 1861.
GREENLAW, JAMES.
Midshipman, 18 June, 1813. Last appearance on Records of Navy Department, 15 November, 1814.
GREENLEAF, CHARLES H.
Third Assistant Engineer, 3 October, 1861. Second Asistant Engineer, 3 August, 1863. First Assistant Engineer, 11 October, 1866. Retired List, 18 July, 1885.
GREENLEAF, FREDERICK W.
Midshipman, 29 July, 1863. Graduated 1 June, 1867. Ensign, 18 March, 1868. Master, 21 March, 1870. Lieutenant, 31 October, 1871. Retired List, 30 April, 1884.
GREENLEAF, JONATHAN.
Midshipman, 31 October, 1799. Died 30 June, 1800.
GREENOW, JOHN.
Carpenter, date not known. Last appearance on Records of Navy Department.
GREENOW, SAMUEL.
Carpenter, 15 April, 1799. Warrant returned 1 May, 1801.
GREENSLADE, JOHN W.
Naval Cadet, 20 May, 1895. At sea prior to final graduation.
GREENWAY, C. HUNTER.
Mate, 5 May, 1870. Resigned 21 November, 1871.
GREENWAY, WILLIAM W. T.
Acting Assistant Paymaster, 1 August, 1861. Dismissed 4 December, 1863.
GREENWELL, EDWARD.
Midshipman, 9 June, 1811. Dismissed 4 December, 1819.
GREENWOOD, CHARLES H.
Mate. Deserted 25 April, 1866.
GREENWOOD, E. L.
Midshipman, 1 December, 1826. Resigned 13 May, 1833.
GREENWOOD, GEORGE W.
Acting Third Assistant Engineer, 14 May, 1864. Honorably discharged 10 August, 1865.
GREENWOOD, JOHN T.
Acting Third Assistant Enginer, 8 October, 1863. Honorably discharged 23 October, 1868.
GREENWOOD, THALES.
Midshipman, 1 January, 1808. Dismissed 6 November, 1809.
GREER, ALEXANDER.
Third Assistant Engineer, 1 December, 1854. Second Assistant Engineer, 9 May, 1857. First Assistant Engineer, 2 August, 1859. Chief Engineer, 21 May, 1863. Died 10 September, 1867.
GREER, JAMES A.
Midshipman, 10 January, 1848. Passed Midshipman, 15 June, 1854. Master, 15 September, 1855. Lieutenant, 16 September, 1855. Lieutenant-Commander, 16 July, 1862. Commander, 25 July, 1866. Captain, 26 April, 1876. Commodore, 19 May, 1886. Rear-Admiral, 3 April, 1892. Retired List, 28 February, 1895.
GREETHAM, WILLIAM D.
Acting Gunner, 10 March, 1900.
GREEVES, THOMAS.
Midshipman, 9 November, 1813. Died in 1817.
GREGG, JOHN.
Mate, 24 January, 1863. Acting Ensign, 13 Feruary, 1864. Honorably discharged 12 December, 1865.
GREGG, WILLIAM.
Mate, 24 January, 1863. Appointment revoked (sick) 1 August, 1863.
GREGG, WILLIAM W.
Mate, 23 September, 1862. Dismissed 4 February, 1863. Mate, 4 February, 1864. Deserted 29 April, 1865. Mate, 22 April, 1870. Appointment revoked 24 September, 1870.
GREGORY, FRANCIS.
Midshipman, 23 May, 1840. Passed Midshipman, 11 July, 1846. Died 27 February, 1852.
GREGORY, FRANCIS H.
Midshipman, 16 January, 1809. Lieutenant, 28 June, 1814. Commander, 28 April, 1828. Captain, 18 January, 1838. Rear-Admiral on Retired List, 16 July, 1862. Died 4 October, 1866.
GREGORY, FRANK F.
Mate, 27 April, 1864. Acting Ensign, 18 May, 1865. Honorably discharged 18 July, 1865.
GREGORY, GEORGE A.
Mate, 3 June, 1864. Honorably discharged 13 May, 1866.

GREGORY, HENRY S.
  Acting Assistant Paymaster, 31 October, 1863. Honorably discharged 21 November, 1865.
GREGORY, H. M.
  Acting Assistant Surgeon, 2 August, 1861. Resigned 27 February, 1862.
GREGORY, H. P.
  Third Assistant Engineer, 21 September, 1861. Second Assistant Engineer, 30 July, 1863. Resigned 27 April, 1865.
GREGORY, HUGH M.
  Acting Master 27 May, 1861. Acting Volunteer Lieutenant, 13 October, 1862. Resigned 6 February, 1864.
GREGORY, JOHN H.
  Mate, 4 November, 1861. Acting Ensign, 1 April, 1864. Honorably discharged 30 November, 1865. Acting Ensign, 22 August, 1867. Mustered out 9 December, 1868.
GREGORY, JOSEPH, JR.
  Mate, 24 December, 1861. Honorably discharged 24 October, 1865.
GREGORY, JUSTUS E.
  Acting Assistant Surgeon, 16 February, 1864. Honorably discharged 9 October, 1865.
GREGORY, LUTHER E.
  Civil Engineer, 5 April, 1898.
GREGORY, MICHAEL B.
  Acting Master, 24 July, 1861. Dismissed 1 October, 1861.
GREGORY, RICHARD C.
  Assistant Surgeon, 24 July, 1813. Last appearance on Records of Navy Department.
GREGORY, ROBERT.
  Mate, 20 June, 1863. Deserted 18 September, 1863.
GREGORY, SAMUEL B.
  Acting Master, 3 October, 1861. Resigned 15 November, 1864.
GREGORY, THOMAS B.
  Acting Volunteer Lieutenant, 1 October, 1862. Honorably discharged 30 October, 1865.
GREGORY, WESTON.
  Mate, 5 March, 1862. Acting Ensign, 26 December, 1862. Resigned 8 May, 1863.
GREGORY, WILLIAM D.
  Acting Master, 20 August, 1861. Dismissed 6 September, 1861. Reappointed 3 October, 1861. Appointment revoked 27 June, 1862.
GREGORY, WILLIAM D.
  Mate, 7 January, 1864. Honorably discharged 21 May, 1866.
GRENLICK, JOSEPH.
  Mate, 17 May, 1864. Dismissed 3 August, 1865.
GRENNEL, SLOSS H.
  Midshipman, 30 April, 1800. Lieutenant, 19 February, 1807. Dismissed 1 August, 1807.
GRENNEL, SLOSS H.
  Master, 24 April, 1812. Died 24 March, 1813.
GREPPIN, JOSEPH.
  Acting Second Assistant Engineer, 10 December, 1862. Honorably discharged 28 March, 1867.
GREY, HENRY W.
  Mate, 10 September, 1864. Honorably discharged 4 October, 1865.
GRICE, FRANCIS.
  Naval Constructor, 7 May, 1817. Chief Naval Constructor, 1 December, 1846. Died in 1865.
GRICE, JOSEPH.
  Carpenter, 19 February, 1819. Last appearance on Records of Navy Department, 24 February, 1819.
GRIDLEY, CHARLES VERNON.
  Acting Midshipman, 26 September, 1860. Acting Ensign, 1 October, 1863. Master, 10 May, 1866. Lieutenant, 21 February, 1867. Lieutenant-Commander, 12 March, 1868. Commander, 10 March, 1882. Captain, 14 March, 1897. Died 5 June, 1898.
GRIDLEY, JOHN P. V.
  Naval Cadet (Spanish-American War), 14 July, 1898. Honorably discharged 6 December, 1898.
GRIER, EDWARD H.
  Mate, 17 December, 1864. Honorably discharged 26 October, 1865.
GRIER, GEORGE W.
  Acting Third Assistant Engineer, 11 February, 1864. Honorably discharged 9 October, 1865.
GRIER, HENRY F.
  Acting Third Assistant Engineer, 19 October, 1863. Honorably discharged 7 October, 1865.
GRIER, JOHN A.
  Third Assistant Engineer, 2 August, 1855. Second Assistant Engineer, 21 July, 1858. First Assistant Engineer, 3 August, 1859. Chief Engineer, 31 January, 1862. Resigned 15 November, 1865.
GRIER, JOHN W.
  Chaplain, 3 March, 1825. Resigned 15 October, 1859.
GRIER, WILLIAM.
  Assistant Surgeon, 7 March, 1838. Passed Assistant Surgeon. Surgeon, 14 April, 1852. Medical Director, 3 March, 1871. Surgeon-General, Retired List, 5 October, 1878.
GRIEVE, CHARLES.
  Mate, 9 January, 1864. Acting Ensign, 30 August, 1864. Acting Master, 6 April, 1865. Honorably discharged 7 July, 1866.

GENERAL NAVY REGISTER.

GRIFFEN, JOEL D.
Carpenter, 1 February, 1896.
GRIFFIN, ALLEN.
Midshipman, 1 January, 1812. Lieutenant, 1 April, 1818. Died 18 September, 1828.
GRIFFIN, CHARLES E. L.
Midshipman, 2 November, 1828. Passed Midshipman, 14 June, 1834. Dismissed 11 January, 1840.
GRIFFIN, COLUMBUS L.
Acting Third Assistant Engineer, 1 August, 1862. Appointment revoked (sick) 15 September, 1862.
GRIFFIN, GEORGE B.
Mate, 27 February, 1863. Acting Ensign, 17 April, 1864. Honorably discharged 25 October, 1865.
GRIFFIN, GEORGE W.
Acting Assistant Paymaster, 14 January, 1862. Resigned 19 September, 1864.
GRIFFIN, ISRAEL S.
Midshipman, 4 March, 1823. Dismissed 8 June, 1831.
GRIFFIN, JAMES.
Gunner, 26 February, 1840. Appointment revoked 12 December, 1840.
GRIFFIN, JOHN.
Master's Mate, 20 June, 1861. Mate, 8 May, 1862. Acting Ensign, 31 August, 1863. Honorably discharged 6 November, 1865. Mate, 15 March, 1867. Retired List, 17 May, 1896.
GRIFFIN, LARKIN.
Assistant Surgeon, 8 September, 1802. Surgeon, 27 November, 1804. Died 1 November, 1814.
GRIFFIN, LEVI.
First Assistant Engineer, 1 November, 1842. Disrated to Second Assistant Engineer, 28 July, 1845. Resigned 2 November, 1847.
GRIFFIN, ROBERT NECHOLS.
Midshipman, 21 January, 1862. Graduated 22 November, 1864. Died 7 September, 1867.
GRIFFIN, ROBERT S.
Cadet Engineer, 1 October, 1874. Graduated 20 June, 1878. Assistant Engineer, 20 June, 1880. Passed Assistant Engineer, 25 August, 1889. Chief Engineer, 1 March, 1898. Rank changed to Lieutenant, 3 March, 1899.
GRIFFIN, SAMUEL L.
Acting Ensign, 7 October, 1863. Resigned 3 December, 1866.
GRIFFIN, SAMUEL P.
Midshipman, 9 September, 1841. Passed Midshipman, 10 August, 1847. Dismissed 15 June, 1854.
GRIFFIN, THOMAS D.
Midshipman, 20 September, 1872. Graduated 20 June, 1876. Ensign, 1 November, 1879. Lieutenant, Junior Grade, 19 May, 1886. Lieutenant, 20 November, 1891. Lieutenant-Commander, 22 September, 1899.
GRIFFIN, THOMAS J.
Second Assistant Engineer, 28 May, 1861. Resigned 6 April, 1863.
GRIFFIN, TIMOTHY J.
Sailmaker, 13 May, 1846. Resigned 6 April, 1852.
GRIFFIN, WILLIAM.
Acting Third Assistant Engineer, 13 February, 1865. Honorably discharged 16 September, 1865.
GRIFFIN, WILLIAM P.
Midshipman, 1 October, 1827. Passed Midshipman, 10 June, 1833. Lieutenant, 28 February, 1838. Died 4 December, 1851.
GRIFFING, GEORGE H.
Acting Assistant Paymaster, 18 November, 1864. Passed Assistant Paymaster, 23 July, 1866. Paymaster, 3 October, 1874. Pay Inspector, 26 September, 1897. Died 11 November, 1899.
GRIFFITH, ALBERTO.
Midshipman, 1 November, 1826. Passed Midshipman, 28 April, 1832. Lieutenant, 6 September, 1837. Died 20 December, 1842.
GRIFFITH, ALFRED.
Assistant Surgeon, 16 October, 1867. Resigned 13 October, 1871.
GRIFFITH, MILTON.
Acting Ensign, 31 March, 1863. Appointment revoked 10 January, 1865.
GRIFFITH, SAMUEL H.
Assistant Surgeon, 15 December, 1877. Passed Assistant Surgeon, 15 December, 1880. Surgeon, 30 March, 1895.
GRIFFITH, STUART W.
Ensign (Spanish-American War), 12 May, 1898. Honorably discharged 8 September, 1898.
GRIFFITH, THEOPHILUS.
Mate, 23 January, 1862. Resigned 9 September, 1862.
GRIFFITH, WILLIAM.
Acting Gunner, 5 August, 1863. Deserted 19 November, 1863.
GRIFFITH, WILLIAM.
Midshipman, 17 February, 1800. Lost on the Insurgent.
GRIFFITHS, DOMINICK E.
Mate, 2 November, 1863. Discharged 22 April, 1864.
GRIFFITHS, HERBERT M.
Carpenter, 25 September, 1861. Retired List, 17 March, 1898.
GRIFFITHS, ISAAC J.
Third Assistant Engineer, 16 January, 1863. Resigned 20 February, 1863.

GRIFFITHS, JOHN J.
Acting Assistant Paymaster, 16 September, 1862. Resigned 30 May, 1864.
GRIFFITHS, JOHN W.
Acting Ensign, 27 April, 1864. Honorably discharged 29 October, 1865.
GRIFFITHS, MONTGOMERY P.
Acting Third Assistant Engineer, 15 September, 1864. Honorably discharged 4 September, 1865.
GRIFFITHS, OLIVER W.
Carpenter, 16 September, 1862. Resigned 15 October, 1868.
GRIFFITHS, WALTER B.
Acting Gunner, 13 December, 1862. Resigned 19 August, 1864.
GRIGGS, CHARLES D.
Mate, 2 September, 1864. Honorably discharged 3 October, 1865.
GRIGGS, GEORGE H.
Acting Third Assistant Engineer, 15 January, 1862. Resigned 24 March, 1862. Acting Third Assistant Engineer, 12 June, 1862. Resigned 16 December, 1862.
GRILLO, OSCAR.
Ensign Spanish-American War), 18 July, 1898. Honorably discharged 26 August, 1898.
GRIMBALL, JOHN.
Acting Midshipman, 23 September, 1854. Midshipman, 11 June, 1858. Resigned 24 December, 1860.
GRIMBALL, WILLIAM.
Midshipman, 1 September, 1811. Resigned 20 December, 1813.
GRIMES, JAMES M.
Midshipman, 28 July, 1863. Graduated June, 1867. Ensign, 18 December, 1868. Master, 21 March, 1870. Lieutenant, 26 December, 1871. Retired List, 22 May, 1886.
GRIMES, JOHN.
Acting Third Assistant Engineer, 16 April, 1863. Honorably discharged 13 October, 1865. Acting Third Assistant Engineer, 6 August, 1866. Mustered out, 5 March, 1868.
GRIMKE, BENJAMIN S.
Midshipman, 30 November, 1814. Lieutenant, 13 January, 1825. Drowned in November, 1825.
GRIMSHAW, E. S.
Midshipman, 4 August, 1823. Resigned 16 October, 1823.
GRINNELL, H. WALTON.
Mate, 23 June, 1862. Acting Ensign, 11 November, 1862. Acting Master, 6 January, 1864. Acting Volunteer Lieutenant, 3 May, 1865. Ensign, but did not accept, 12 March, 1868. Honorably discharged 25 July, 1868. Lieutenant (Spanish-American War), 4 May, 1898. Honorably discharged 10 January, 1899.
GRISCOM, JOHN S.
Mate, 12 October, 1862. Acting Ensign, 22 February, 1864. Killed on the Mackinaw, 25 December, 1864.
GRISWOLD, CHARLES DENNING.
Midshipman, 20 November, 1861. Graduated 22 November, 1864. Ensign, 1 December, 1866. Died 5 July, 1868.
GRISWOLD, DAVID H.
Mate, 20 December, 1861. Resigned (sick) 3 December, 1862.
GRISWOLD, EDWARD D.
Lieutenant, 31 October, 1799. Resigned 29 September, 1800.
GRISWOLD, GEORGE R.
Purser, 15 September, 1853. Died 5 April, 1857.
GRISWOLD, GEORGE R.
Mate, 2 May, 1862. Deserted 30 March, 1963.
GRISWOLD, WILLIAM N.
Acting Master, 9 July, 1861. Honorably discharged 18 September, 1865.
GRIVETT, JOHN W.
Acting Master and Pilot, 1 October, 1864. Honorably discharged 27 December, 1865.
GROESBECK, WILLIAM G.
Naval Cadet, 4 September, 1891. Graduated. Assistant Naval Constructor, 1 July, 1897.
GROOMS, ROBERT L.
Acting First Assistant Engineer, 11 May, 1863. Dismissed 5 August, 1863.
GROSS, CHARLES W.
Mate, 29 June, 1863. Appointment revoked 13 April, 1864.
GROSS, DANIEL H.
Mate, 8 January, 1862. Acting Ensign, 23 May, 1863. Dismissed 5 December, 1863.
GROSS, F. A.
Acting Ensign, 30 May, 1863. Acting Master, 8 May, 1865. Honorably discharged 23 December, 1865.
GROSS, FREDERICK A., Jr.
Mate, 29 December, 1863. Honorably discharged 25 October, 1865.
GROSS, THOMAS H. P.
Mate, 5 September, 1863. Resigned 30 June, 1865.
GROSVENOR, G. H.
Mate, 27 April, 1865. Honorably discharged 24 December, 1865. Mate, 26 May, 1866. Resigned 13 October, 1866.
GROTH, THEODORE A.
Acting Third Assistant Engineer, 22 March, 1865. Honorably discharged 7 October, 1865.
GROUT, JOHN K.
Midshipman, 21 November, 1848. Dropped 12 July, 1849.
GROVE, FRANCIS H.
Acting Master, 22 January, 1862. Honorably discharged 23 November, 1865.

GENERAL NAVY REGISTER.

GROVE, JAMES R.
 Mate, 29 December, 1863. Resigned 6 May, 1865.
GROVE, THOMAS G.
 Acting Master, 18 June, 1862. Acting Volunteer Lieutenant, 4 February, 1865. Ensign, 12 March, 1868. Master, 18 December, 1868. Lieutenant, 21 March, 1870. Died 26 July, 1881.
GROVE, WASHINGTON B.
 Assistant Surgeon, 3 June, 1897. Passed Assistant Surgeon, 3 June, 1900.
GROVER, ELDRIDGE H.
 Acting Third Assistant Engineer, 11 March, 1864. Appointment revoked (sick) 8 November, 1864.
GROVES, CHARLES L.
 Acting Third Assistant Engineer, 2 September, 1864. Honorably discharged 30 June, 1865.
GROVES, GEORGE J.
 Acting Master, 1 October, 1862. Honorably discharged 11 December, 1865.
GROW, ARTEMUS L.
 Acting Third Asistant Engineer, 25 July, 1863. Honorably discharged 31 October, 1868.
GROW, EUGENE J.
 Assistant Surgeon, 8 June, 1898.
GROZIER, WILLIAM W.
 Acting Master, 28 October, 1861. Honorably discharged 24 December, 1865.
GRUB, GEORGE G.
 Midshipman, 4 June, 1801. Discharged 17 March, 1804.
GRUBB, WILLIAM H.
 Acting Ensign, 15 August, 1864. Honorably discharged 18 August, 1865.
GRUMLEY, WILLIAM R.
 Mate, 24 October, 1861 Resigned 25 February, 1862.
GRUNDY, FELIX.
 Midshipman, 21 October, 1845. Dismissed 12 June, 1851.
GRUNWELL, ALFRED G.
 Assistant Surgeon, 7 July, 1898.
GRYMES, WILLIAM F.
 Midshipman, 4 March, 1823. Dismissed 8 June, 1831.
GSANTNER, OTTO C.
 Cadet Engineer, 1 October, 1878. Graduated 30 June, 1884. Honorably discharged 30 June, 1884. Restored to service 10 March, 1886, as an Assistant Engineer to rank from 1 July, 1884. Resigned 17 April, 1886.
GUDENRATH, WILLIAM.
 Acting Third Assistant Engineer, 18 February, 1865. Honorably discharged 1 September, 1865.
GUDGEON, WILLIAM H.
 Acting Ensign, 10 March, 1863. Resigned 22 April, 1963.
GUERNSEY, DAVID W.
 Acting Assistant Paymaster, 23 October, 1863. Honorably discharged 12 September, 1865.
GUERNSEY, THOMSON.
 Acting Third Assistant Engineer, 1 October, 1862. Honorably discharged 15 December, 1865.
GUERARD, RICHARD D.
 Third Assistant Engineer, 11 January, 1849. Dismissed 20 July, 1850.
GUERTIN, FRANK.
 Midshipman, 1 July, 1867. Graduated 6 June, 1871. Ensign, 14 July, 1872. Master, 3 August, 1877. Lieutenant, Junior Grade, 3 March, 1883. Resigned 1 August, 1885.
GUEST, JOHN.
 Midshipman, 16 December, 1837. Passed Midshipman, 20 June, 1843. Master, 16 July, 1850. Lieutenant, 24 December, 1850. Commander, 16 July, 1862. Captain, 25 July, 1866. Commodore, 12 December, 1872. Died 12 January, 1879.
GUEST, MIDDLETON S.
 Assistant Surgeon, 19 November, 1891. Passed Assistant Surgeon, 19 November, 1894.
GUILD, CHARLES F.
 Acting Assistant Paymaster, 8 October, 1864. Assistant Paymaster, 12 December, 1864. Paymaster, 1 September, 1865. Pay Inspector, 16 July, 1886. ' Retired List, 14 September, 1888. Died 1 January, 1897.
GUILD, CHARLES M.
 Acting Assistant Paymaster, 19 September, 1861. Mustered out 28 April, 1869.
GUILD, HENRY A.
 Acting Third Assistant Engineer, 3 September, 1864. Honorably discharged 18 December, 1865.
GUILD, SAMUEL E.
 Acting Third Assistant Engineer, 25 August, 1864. Honorably discharged 5 January, 1866.
GUILFORD, HENRY M.
 Mate, 15 December, 1864. Dismissed 13 March, 1866.
GUILLON, C. T.
 Assistant Surgeon, 9 February, 1837. Passed Assistant Surgeon, 6 June, 1842. Surgeon, 28 August, 1847. Resigned 15 September, 1854.
GUION, JOHN A.
 Assistant Surgeon, 20 June, 1838. Resigned 30 January, 1843.
GUISE, PHILANDER N.
 Pharmacist, 15 September, 1898.

GUITERAS, DANIEL M.
Assistant Surgeon, 3 June, 1879. Passed Assistant Surgeon, 3 June, 1882. Surgeon, 28 May, 1895. Retired List, 13 October, 1896.
GULICK, CHARLES H.
Mate, 1 October, 1862. Acting Ensign, 22 June, 1863. Honorably discharged 30 November, 1865.
GULICK, JOHN S.
Purser, 1 February, 1851. Pay Director, 3 March, 1871. Retired List, 14 May, 1879. Died 6 November, 1884.
GUMPERT, P. P.
Carpenter, 30 October, 1828. Resigned 26 April, 1831.
GUMPHERT, WILLIAM.
Acting Third Assistant Engineer, 4 December, 1863. Acting Second Assistant Engineer, 19 April, 1864. Honorably discharged 18 August, 1865.
GUNDENRATH, WILLIAM.
Acting Third Assistant Engineer, 18 February, 1865. Honorably discharged 1 September, 1865.
GUNDERSON, MORGAN.
Acting Master, 27 December, 1861. Dismissed 14 January, 1862.
GUNN, JOHN.
Mate, 6 June, 1862. Acting Ensign, 28 May, 1863. Honorably discharged 22 January, 1869.
GUNN, JOHN C. C.
Midshipman, 17 December, 1810. Appointed Second Lieutenant,, Marine Corps, 12 September, 1812. Last appearance on Records of Navy Department. Resigned.
GUNN, WILLIAM E.
Lieutenant (Spanish-American War), 22 June, 1898. Honorably discharged 4 November, 1898.
GUNNELL, FRANCIS M.
Assistant Surgeon, 22 March, 1849. Surgeon, 23 April, 1861. Medical Inspector, 3 March, 1871. Medical Director, 3 February, 1875. Surgeon-General, U. S. Navy, 1884. Retired List, 27 November, 1889.
GUNNELL, ROBERT H.
Third Assistant Engineer, 17 February, 1860. Second Assistant Engineer, 27 June, 1862. First Assistant Engineer, 1 March, 1864. Retired 8 July, 1873.
GUNNING, JOSIAH H.
Assistant Surgeon, 2 September, 1861. Resigned 29 April, 1865.
GUNNING, WILLIAM.
Midshipman, 16 January, 1809. Lost at sea 5 October, 1811.
GUNNING, WILLIAM H.
Ensign (Spanish-American War), 9 May, 1898. Honorably discharged 19 August, 1898.
GURLEY, ROYAL.
Midshipman, 2 December, 1799. Resigned 25 February, 1801.
GUTHRIE, JOHN J.
Midshipman, 28 February, 1834. Passed Midshipman, 16 July, 1840. Master, 22 March, 1847. Lieutenant, 7 July, 1847. Dismissed 13 July, 1861.
GUTHRIE, JOSEPH A.
Assistant Surgeon, 27 January, 1892. Passed Assistant Surgeon, 27 January, 1895.
GUTTIN, HENRY.
Assistant Engineer (Spanish-American War), 29 June, 1898. Honorably discharged 1 November, 1898.
GUYENNE, THOMAS.
Midshipman, 27 April, 1799. Resigned 9 August, 1800.
GUYER, GEORGE H.
Acting Second Assistant Engineer, 22 September, 1862. Appointment revoked 15 July, 1865.
GWATHMEY, WASHINGTON.
Midshipman, 21 July, 1832. Passed Midshipman, 23 June, 1838. Lieutenant, 28 June, 1843. Dismissed 17 April, 1861.
GWIN, WILLIAM.
Midshipman, 7 April, 1847. Passed Midshipman, 19 June, 1853. Master, 15 September, 1855. Lieutenant, 16 September, 1855. Lieutenant-Commander, 16 July, 1862. Killed in battle, 3 January, 1863.
GWINN, JOHN.
Midshipman, 18 May, 1809. Lieutenant, 27 April, 1816. Commander, 9 February, 1837. Captain, 17 April, 1842. Died 4 September, 1849.
GWINNER, HENRY W.
Midshipman, 2 October, 1861. Graduated 22 November, 1864. Ensign, 1 December, 1866. Master, 12 March, 1868. Lieutenant, 26 March, 1869. Died 26 September, 1872.
HAAS, CLEMENT J.
Mate. 18 November, 1861. Died 1863.
HAAS, HAROLD H.
Assistant Surgeon, 28 December, 1897. Passed Assistant Surgeon, 28 December, 1900.
HAAS, JEROME.
Acting Third Assistant Engineer, 24 December, 1863. Honorably discharged 4 November, 1865.
HABERSHAM, ALEXANDER W.
Midshipman, 3 March, 1841. Passed Midshipman, 10 August, 1847. Master, 14 September, 1855. Lieutenant, 15 September, 1855. Resigned 30 May, 1860.
HABIGHURST, CONRAD J.
Third Assistant Engineer, 1 July, 1863. Second Assistant Engineer, 2 September, 1865. First Assistant Engineer, 17 September, 1873. Chief Engineer, 2 March, 1892. Retired List, 7 November, 1898.

GENERAL NAVY REGISTER. 237

HABIRSHAW, WILLIAM M.
    Third Assistant Engineer, 29 July, 1861. Appointment revoked 5 February. 1862.
HACKETT, FRANK W.
    Acting Assistant Paymaster, 11 September, 1862. Resigned 6 October, 1864.
HACKETT, SAMUEL H.
    Acting Midshipman, 28 September, 1855. Midshipman, 9 June, 1859. Dismissed 18 July, 1861.
HACKLEY, GEORGE S.
    Midshipman, 3 January, 1801. Died 8 July, 1805.
HADDAWAY, EDWARD H.
    Midshipman, 20 June, 1806. Lieutenant, 9 December, 1814. Died 15 June, 1817.
HADDAWAY, W. H.
    Midshipman, 20 June, 1806. Lieutenant, 9 December, 1814. Died 30 March, 1815.
HADDEN, G. W.
    Acting Ensign and Pilot, 26 July, 1864. Honorably discharged 30 September, 1865.
HADDEN, WILLIAM A.
    Midshipman, 28 September, 1865. Graduated June, 1869. Ensign, 12 July, 1870. Master, 1 January, 1872. Lieutenant, 12 March, 1875. Died 19 January, 1886.
HADDOCK, WILLIAM J.
    Mate. Resigned 30 June, 1863.
HADDOCK, WORCESTER.
    Acting Third Assistant Engineer, 24 March, 1865. Appointment revoked 16 June, 1865.
HADFIELD, JOSEPH.
    Acting Ensign, 7 October, 1863. Honorably discharged 26 August, 1865.
HADFIELD, WILLIAM.
    Acting Third Assistant Engineer, 16 September, 1864. Honorably discharged 21 August, 1865.
HADLEY, FRANCIS J.
    Acting Third Assistant Engineer, 10 January, 1863. Acting Second Assistant Engineer, 7 October, 1864. Honorably discharged 24 December, 1865.
HADLEY, S. W.
    Acting Master and Pilot, 28 October, 1864. Honorably discharged 6 December, 1865.
HAESELER, FRANCIS J.
    Cadet Midshipman, 22 September, 1876. Graduated 22 June, 1882. Ensign. Junior Grade, 3 March, 1883. Ensign, 26 June, 1884. Lieutenant, Junior Grade, 9 January, 1893. Lieutenant, 11 October, 1896. Died 20 October, 1900.
HAFFINGTON, JESSE.
    Master, 15 September, 1813. Discharged 15 April, 1815.
HAFNER, JOSEPH.
    Acting Third Assistant Engineer, 18 February, 1865. Honorably discharged 25 October, 1865.
HAGAN, PATRICK.
    Acting Third Assistant Engineer, 23 September, 1863. Honorably discharged 27 July, 1865.
HAGENMAN, JOHN WILLIAM.
    Midshipman, 21 July, 1863. Graduated June, 1867. Ensign, 18 December. 1868. Master, 21 March, 1870. Lieutenant, 21 March, 1871. Retired List, 3 May. 1889.
HAGER, ELIJAH W.
    Chaplain, 1 March, 1873. Died 7 July, 1880.
HAGERUP, ANTHONY.
    Acting Ensign, 3 September, 1863. Honorably discharged 17 October, 1865.
HAGGERTY, FRANCIS S.
    Midshipman, 17 February, 1832. Passed Midshipman, 23 June, 1838. Lieutenant, 19 December, 1843. Commander, 11 October, 1861. Retired 5 May, 1862. Captain on Retired List, 4 April, 1867. Died 25 September, 1899.
HAGGINS, EDMUND H.
    Acting Third Assistant Engineer, 8 December, 1863. Honorably discharged 12 October, 1865.
HAHN, JACOB.
    Mate, 2 February, 1863. Dismissed 31 December, 1863.
HAIGHT, JAMES.
    Midshipman, 21 October, 1799. Resigned 27 July, 1802.
HAIGHT, SAMUEL.
    Midshipman, 1 March, 1827. Resigned 17 March, 1829.
HAIN, FRANKLIN K.
    Third Assistant Engineer, 21 November, 1857. Resigned 9 August, 1858. Third Assistant Engineer, 23 May, 1861. Second Assistant Engineer, 29 October, 1862. Resigned 24 January, 1863.
HAINES, MATTHIAS R.
    Acting Ensign, 13 December, 1862. Honorably discharged 10 December, 1865.
HAINES, EDWARD L.
    Acting Master, 7 December, 1861. Honorably discharged 11 January, 1866.
HAINES, HIRAM.
    Third Assistant Engineer, 16 February, 1852. Resigned 25 July, 1854.
HAINES, MARTIN V. B.
    Acting Ensign, 22 January, 1863. Acting Master, 4 December, 1863. Honorably discharged 16 September, 1865. Acting Master, 11 December, 1866. Mustered out 27 August, 1868.
HALCRA, EDWARD W.
    Mate, 5 March, 1862. Acting Ensign, 27 November, 1863. Honorably discharged 3 February, 1866. Acting Ensign, 5 April, 1866. Appointment revoked 6 February, 1867.

GENERAL NAVY REGISTER.

HALD, VIGO L. T.
Mate, 21 June, 1862. Dismissed 17 December, 1862.
HALDEMAN, ROBERT A.
Acting Third Assistant Engineer, 19 July, 1864. Appointment revoked (sick) 30 January, 1865.
HALE, BENJAMIN P.
Mate, 12 April, 1865. Dismissed 2 March, 1866.
HALE, CHARLES R.
Chaplain, 10 March, 1863. Resigned 26 March, 1871.
HALE, DAVID W.
Acting Assistant Paymaster, 24 May, 1862. Resigned 3 March, 1863. Acting Assistant Paymaster, 25 September, 1863. Mustered out 17 November, 1865.
HALE, E. W., Jr.
Mate, 23 September, 1861. Resigned 10 July, 1863.
HALE, HOWARD.
Mate, 24 January, 1863. Acting Ensign, 17 January, 1864. Honorably discharged 1 December, 1865.
HALE, MARK.
Midshipman, 1 March, 1825. Resigned 29 May, 1832.
HALE, THOMAS G.
Mate, 2 October, 1861. Acting Master, 31 March, 1862. Dismissed 4 November, 1862. Mate, 20 February, 1863. Acting Ensign, 22 April, 1864. Acting Master, 26 May, 1865. Honorably discharged 31 August, 1865.
HALEY, JAMES I.
Carpenter, 22 July, 1897.
HALEY, PATRICK.
Boatswain, 18 October, 1878. Chief Boatswain, 3 March, 1899.
HALFORD, WILLIAM.
Gunner, 14 April, 1871. Chief Gunner, 3 March, 1899.
HALL, ALBERT B.
Acting Ensign, 5 December, 1864. Honorably discharged 7 August, 1865.
HALL, ALFRED L.
Midshipman, 26 September, 1872. Graduated 18 June, 1879. Ensign, 28 October, 1881. Lieutenant, Junior Grade, 12 February, 1889. Lieutenant, 22 July, 1893. Died 2 April, 1896.
HALL, ANDREW F.
Boatswain (Spanish-American War), 23 June, 1898. Honorably discharged, 25 January, 1899.
HALL, ASAPH.
Professor, 2 May, 1863. Retired List, 15 October, 1891.
HALL, ASHTON S.
Midshipman, 9 November, 1813. Lost in the Wasp in 1815.
HALL, CHARLES.
Master, 11 June, 1799. Resigned 8 February, 1800.
HALL, CHARLES.
Mate, 13 June, 1863. Acting Ensign, 10 September, 1864. Honorably discharged 30 November, 1865. Acting Ensign, 18 May, 1866. Mustered out 22 September, 1868.
HALL, CHARLES H.
Ensign (Spanish-American War), 25 May, 1898. Honorably discharged 9 September, 1898.
HALL, CHARLES H. H.
Assistant Surgeon, 1 May, 1874. Passed Assistant Surgeon, 6 December, 1878. Resigned 1 November, 1890.
HALL, CHARLES N.
Mate, 7 August, 1862. Acting Ensign, 24 February, 1863. Resigned 2 July, 1864. Acting Ensign, 3 October, 1864. Honorably discharged 21 July, 1865. Acting Ensign, 1 February, 1867. Mustered out 17 July, 1868.
HALL, CRAWFORD W.
Midshipman, 1 June, 1826. Resigned 16 January, 1827.
HALL, DAVID.
Master, 17 August, 1812. Last appearance on Records of Navy Department. Discharged.
HALL, DAVID A.
Mate, 9 June, 1863. Acting Ensign, 9 July, 1864. Honorably discharged 8 August, 1868.
HALL, DAVID H.
Mate, 7 October, 1864. Resigned 17 May, 1865.
HALL, ELDRIDGE D.
Mate, 2 March, 1870. Carpenter, 3 July, 1870. Retired List, 16 November, 1883. Died in 1886.
HALL, EUGENE F.
Assistant Paymaster (Spanish-American War), 9 July, 1898. Honorably discharged 8 February, 1899. Assistant Paymaster (Regular Navy), 27 May, 1899.
HALL, FRANCIS C.
Midshipman, 2 March, 1803. Resigned 23 September, 1805.
HALL, FRANK C.
Acting Ensign, 4 October, 1864. Honorably discharged 30 July, 1868. Ensign (Spanish-American War), 21 May, 1898. Honorably discharged 15 December, 1898.
HALL, GEORGE.
Acting Third Assistant Engineer, 5 November, 1864. Resigned 10 May, 1865.
HALL, GEORGE B.
Mate, 29 December, 1863. Honorably discharged 20 December, 1865.
HALL, GEORGE F.
Assistant Paymaster, 11 June, 1862. Died 2 September, 1862.

GENERAL NAVY REGISTER.

HALL, GEORGE O.
Acting Second Assistant Engineer, 18 August. 1864. Honorably discharged 28 January, 1866.
HALL, GEORGE S.
Acting Second Assistant Engineer, 4 June, 1864. Dismissed 5 November, 1864.
HALL, GEORGE W.
Mate, 9 June, 1863. Dismissed 19 March, 1864.
HALL, GEORGE W.
Third Assistant Engineer, 3 May, 1859. Second Assistant Engineer, 3 October, 1861. First Assistant Engineer, 25 July, 1866. Resigned 16 November, 1866.
HALL, GEORGE W.
Third Assistant Engineer, 21 September, 1861. Second Assistant Engineer, 3 August, 1863. First Assistant Engineer, 11 October, 1866. Chief Engineer, 15 February, 1885. Died 16 June, 1889.
HALL, HARRY.
Cadet Engineer, 14 September, 1876. Graduated 10 June, 1880. Assistant Engineer, 10 June, 1882. Passed Assistant Engineer, 14 December, 1892. Rank changed to Lieutenant, 3 March, 1899.
HALL, H. CLAY.
Acting Master, 12 April, 1862. Dismissed 28 August, 1862.
HALL, ISAAC.
Sailmaker, 1 April, 1822. Died 18 April, 1828.
HALL, JAMES C.
Acting Ensign, 28 April, 1863. Honorably discharged 23 November, 1865.
HALL, JOHN.
Boatswain, 15 January, 1802. Last appearance on Records of Navy Department.
HALL, JOHN.
Boatswain, 16 March, 1866. Died 22 February, 1880.
HALL, JOHN.
Midshipman, 11 January, 1832. Passed Midshipman, 28 June, 1838. Lieutenant, 28 June, 1843. Reserved List, 13 September, 1855. Died 5 October, 1860.
HALL, JOHN C.
Sailmaker, 25 August, 1829. Last appearance on Records of Navy Department, 11 March, 1833.
HALL, JOHN H.
Assistant Surgeon, 31 March, 1874. Passed Assistant Surgeon, 9 November, 1877. Surgeon, 28 November, 1889. Retired List, 25 September, 1891. Died 21 October, 1895.
HALL, JOHN L.
Mate, 19 April, 1864. Lost on Narcissus, 4 January, 1866.
HALL, JOHN L.
Acting Ensign, 24 February, 1864. Acting Master, 8 April, 1865. Honorably discharged 11 November, 1865.
HALL, JOHN P.
Midshipman, 29 December, 1840. Passed Midshipman, 11 July, 1846. Master, 1 March, 1855. Dropped 13 September, 1855. Died 8 September, 1862.
HALL, JOHN R.
Gunner, 29 August, 1861. Died 10 September, 1866.
HALL, JOHN T.
Acting Master, 12 August, 1861. Resigned 23 May, 1862.
HALL, LEONARD.
Master, 7 September, 1813. Last appearance on Records of Navy Department. Dead.
HALL, MARSHALL W.
Ensign (Spanish-American War), 29 June, 1898. Honorably discharged 3 September, 1898.
HALL, MARTIN E.
Midshipman, 19 September, 1865. Graduated June, 1869. Ensign, 12 July, 1870. Master, 12 December, 1873. Lieutenant, 1 November, 1879. Lieutenant Commander, 25 December, 1898. Retired List, with rank of Commander, 30 June, 1900.
HALL, MICHAEL.
Boatswain, 18 April, 1842. Died 22 August, 1864.
HALL, MOSES.
Boatswain, 11 June, 1847. Died 13 February, 1851.
HALL, NATHANIEL, Jr.
Mate, 1 July, 1864. Resigned 9 June, 1865.
HALL, REYNOLD T.
Assistant Engineer, 22 April, 1880. Passed Assistant Engineer, 9 January, 1889. Chief Engineer, 7 February, 1898. Rank changed to Lieutenant, 3 March, 1899. Lieutenant-Commander, 11 January, 1900.
HALL, RICHARD R.
Acting Assistant Surgeon, 1 October, 1862. Resigned 16 June, 1863.
HALL, ROBERT E.
Passed Assistant Engineer (Spanish-American War), 24 May, 1898. Honorably discharged 9 September, 1898.
HALL, SAMUEL.
Acting Master, 25 January, 1862. Honorably discharged 24 November, 1865.
HALL, SAMUEL G.
Acting Second Assistant Engineer, 6 June, 1864. Honorably discharged 3 July, 1865.
HALL, SIDNEY.
Mate, 4 September, 1861. Acting Ensign, 21 May, 1863. Honorably discharged 12 December, 1866.
HALL, THOMAS G.
Mate, 21 May, 1862. Killed in action. Diana, 28 March, 1863.

HALL, THOMAS N.
Acting First Assistant Engineer, 12 August, 1863. Honorably discharged 28 September, 1865.
HALL, V. R.
Boatswain, 15 November, 1836. Died 27 September, 1857.
HALL, WARREN.
Midshipman, 17 December, 1810. Last appearance on Records of Navy Department, 1814.
HALL, WESLEY B.
Acting Third Assistant Engineer, 30 August, 1864. Honorably discharged 8 October, 1865.
HALL, WILBURN B.
Acting Midshipman, 9 June, 1855. Midshipman, 20 September, 1855. Resigned 7 March, 1861.
HALL, WILLIAM.
Midshipman, 1 January, 1812. Last appearance on Records of Navy Department, 3 November, 1812. Dead.
HALL, WILLIAM.
Midshipman, 16 January, 1809. Last appearance on Records of Navy Department, 10 July, 1812.
HALL, WILLIAM B.
Midshipman, 1 January, 1808. Dismissed 3 May, 1813.
HALL, WILLIAM D.
Acting Ensign, 11 June, 1863. Dismissed 20 October, 1864.
HALL, WILLIAM G.
Acting Warrant Machinist, 23 August, 1899.
HALL, WILLIAM H.
Mate, 4 December, 1867. Mustered out 20 April, 1869.
HALL, W. H.
Acting Master's Mate, 2 June, 1864. Deserted 28 February, 1865.
HALL, WILLIAM K.
Third Assistant Engineer, 15 November, 1847. Second Assistant Engineer, 11 January, 1849. First Assistant Engineer, 26 February, 1851. Resigned 15 February, 1853.
HALLADAY, CHARLES S.
Acting Assistant Paymaster, 7 June, 1864. Appointment revoked, 3 June, 1865.
HALLET, F. A.
Midshipman, 13 September, 1841. Resigned, 1 December, 1845.
HALLETT, CHARLES.
Acting Master, 4 November, 1861. Honorably discharged 22 August, 1865.
HALLETT, DANIEL B.
Mate, 11 September, 1862. Acting Ensign, 20 December, 1863. Resigned 12 May, 1864.
HALLETT, GEORGE H.
Acting Ensign, Coast Survey, duty 30 November, 1866. Mustered out 30 November, 1868.
HALLETT, JAMES H.
Acting Master, 12 August, 1861. Resigned 30 July, 1862.
HALLETT, OLIVER.
Mate. Resigned 27 June, 1862.
HALLETT, WARREN.
Acting Ensign, 15 December, 1862. Resigned 1 June, 1863.
HALLIGAN, JOHN, Jr.
Naval Cadet, 6 September, 1894. Ensign. 4 April, 1900.
HALLOCK, ISAAC.
Mate, 23 October, 1861. Acting Ensign, 2 April, 1864. Acting Master, 25 May, 1865. Honorably discharged 8 June, 1868.
HALLOWAY, JAMES C.
Mate, 13 February, 1864. Resigned 11 June, 1864.
HALLOWELL, FRANCIS P.
Third Assistant Engineer, 8 September, 1863. Resigned 12 November, 1867.
HALLOWELL, GEORGE A.
Master, 4 October, 1798. Disappeared till 5 December, 1812. Appointed Master, 5 December, 1812. Last appearance on Records of Navy Department, 1820. Furloughed.
HALPIN, JOHN.
Acting Third Assistant Engineer, 7 October, 1862. Appointment revoked (sick) 13 November, 1863. Acting Third Assistant Engineer, 20 April, 1864. Resigned 5 May, 1865.
HALPINE, NICHOLAS J. L. T.
Midshipman, 9 June, 1871. Graduated 18 June, 1879. Ensign, 1 October, 1881. Lieutenant, Junior Grade, 31 October, 1888. Lieutenant, 4 July, 1893. Retired List, 4 November, 1895.
HALSALL, JOSHUA.
Acting Third Assistant Engineer, 20 August, 1864. Lost on Narcissus, 4 January, 1866.
HALSALL, WILLIAM F.
Mate, 1 November, 1862. Appointment revoked (sick) 4 June, 1863.
HALSEY, GEORGE W.
Midshipman, 31 October, 1799. Resigned 2 October, 1800.
HALSEY, JOHN M.
Purser, 25 April, 1812. Died 2 January, 1838.
HALSEY, RICHARD E.
Third Assistant Engineer, 16 January, 1863. Resigned 30 October, 1863.

GENERAL NAVY REGISTER. 241

HALSEY, WILLIAM F.
Midshipman, 21 September, 1869. Graduated 31 May, 1873. Ensign. 16 July, 1874. Master, 18 March, 1880. Lieutenant, Junior Grade, 3 March, 1883. Lieutenant, 4 March, 1886. Lieutenant Commander, 3 March, 1899.

HALSEY, WILLIAM S.
Passed Assistant Engineer (Spanish-American War), 14 May, 1898. Honorably discharged 7 November, 1898.

HALSTEAD, ALEXANDER S.
Cadet Engineer, 1 October, 1879. Assistant Engineer, 1 July, 1885. Passed Assistant Engineer, 11 September, 1895. Rank changed to Lieutenant, 3 March, 1899.

HALSTEAD, ISRAEL T.
Acting Ensign, 10 September, 1862. Resigned 11 May, 1865.

HALSTEAD, W. H. R.
Midshipman, 1 November, 1828. Resigned, 10 December, 1829. Mate. Resigned 3 April, 1862. Acting Ensign, 12 October, 1863. Honorably

HALSTED, FRANK W.
discharged 4 November, 1865.

HAMBLEN, ANDREW T.
Acting Ensign, 16 October, 1862. Honorably discharged, 2 October, 1865.

HAMBLETON, JOHN N.
Chaplain, 26 October, 1819. Purser. 26 May, 1824. Retired 21 December, 1861. Died 5 December, 1870.

HAMBLETON, SAMUEL.
Purser, 25 April, 1812. Died 18 January, 1851.

HAMBRICK, JAMES W.
Mate, 15 December, 1863. Acting Ensign, 21 April, 1865. Honorably discharged 10 February, 1866.

HAMELL, BENJAMIN F.
Acting Assistant Surgeon, 27 October, 1863. Resigned 31 August, 1864. Acting Assistant Surgeon, 1 November, 1864. Honorably discharged, 16 April, 1866.

HAMER, THOMAS M.
Midshipman, 26 June, 1847. Resigned 24 August, 1849.

HAMERSLY, GEORGE W.
Midshipman, 18 May. 1809. Lieutenant, 3 May, 1815. Died 12 September, 1823.

HAMERSLY, GEORGE W.
Midshipman, 1 September, 1837. Passed Midshipman, 29 June, 1843. Resigned 11 June, 1850.

HAMERSLY, LEWIS R.
Mate, 4 February, 1862. Acting Ensign, 3 December, 1863. Honorably discharged 23 July, 1866.

HAMERSLY, ROBERT.
Midshipman, 1 January, 1812. Died in March, 1815.

HAMERSLY, THOMAS S.
Master, 14 January. 1812. Lieutenant, 27 April, 1816. Dismissed 16 July, 8831.

HAMILTON, ALANSON.
Mate, 11 June, 1863. Honorably discharged 7 August, 1865.

HAMILTON, ALEXANDER.
Acting Master, 28 October, 1861. Dismissed 23 September, 1862.

HAMILTON, ARCHIBALD.
Midshipman, 18 May, 1809. Lieutenant, 24 July, 1813. Killed in action, 15 January, 1815.

HAMILTON, BURT.
Acting Third Assistant Engineer, 24 December, 1864. Honorably discharged, 27 July, 1865.

HAMILTON, C. B.
Asistant Surgeon, 2 April, 1811. Surgeon, 15 April, 1814. Resigned 12 April, 1826.

HAMILTON, CHARLES C.
Acting Third Assistant Engineer, 1 October, 1862. Dismissed 21 September, 1863.

HAMILTON, CHARLES H.
Acting Master, 17 September, 1861. Resigned 7 February, 1865.

HAMILTON, CLEASON F.
Acting Third Assistant Engineer, 20 July, 1864. Honorably discharged 20 January, 1866.

HAMILTON, EDWARD W.
Midshipman, 18 June, 1812. Last appearance on Records of Navy Department, 1822.

HAMILTON, F. T.
Acting Third Assistant Engineer, 28 May, 1863. Discharged 26 April, 1864.

HAMILTON, HENRY.
Gunner, 20 August, 1861. Appointment revoked 23 September, 1868.

HAMILTON, JAMES.
Acting Gunner. 24 March. 1864. Appointment revoked 9 January, 1865.

HAMILTON, JAMES.
Acting First Assistant Engineer, 30 July, 1862. Deserted 5 February, 1863.

HAMILTON, JAMES.
Assistant Surgeon, 22 July, 1844. Died 6 September, 1854.

HAMILTON, JAMES A.
Acting Ensign. 20 December, 1862. Acting Master, recommendation of Commanding Officer, 16 July. 1864. Honorably discharged 1 March, 1866.

HAMILTON, JAMES F.
Acting Assistant Paymaster, 19 May. 1863. Assistant Paymaster, 3 March, 1865. Paymaster, 29 June. 1866. Resigned 14 January, 1875.

HAMILTON, JAMES T.
Acting Ensign, 22 October, 1864. Honorably discharged 29 August, 1865.

HAMILTON, JOHN.
Midshipman, 4 July, 1818. Lieutenant, 3 March, 1827. Lost in the Hornet, September, 1829.
HAMILTON, JOHN R.
Midshipman, 8 September, 1845. Passed Midshipman, 6 October, 1851. Master, 19 September, 1855. Lieutenant, 16 September, 1856. Resigned 15 December, 1860.
HAMILTON, JOHN R.
Acting Master, 18 January, 1862. Honorably discharged 15 January, 1866.
HAMILTON, JOHN W.
Acting Assistant Surgeon, 44 November, 1861. Honorably discharged 4 August, 1865.
HAMILTON, ROBERT.
Master, 1 March, 1814. Resigned 21 November, 1814.
HAMILTON, ROBERT.
Acting Third Assistant Engineer, 13 September, 1861. Resigned 11 February, 1862.
HAMILTON, ROBERT B.
Mate, 6 March, 1865. Honorably discharged 9 September, 1865.
HAMILTON, ROBERT W.
Lieutenant, 17 September, 1798. Resigned 25 January, 1802.
HAMILTON, THOMAS H.
Acting Third Assistant Engineer, 17 May, 1864. Honorably discharged 21 July, 1865.
HAMILTON, THOMAS J.
Acting Third Assistant Engineer, 15 August, 1864. Honorably discharged 30 October, 1865.
HAMILTON, WILLIAM.
Acting Master, 26 August, 1861. Acting Volunteer Lieutenant, 12 April, 1864. Acting Volunteer Lieutenant-Commander, 17 July, 1865. Honorably discharged 15 April, 1866.
HAMILTON, WILLIAM F.
Acting Master, 1 October, 1862. Acting Volunteer Lieutenant, 10 October, 1862. Resigned 6 April, 1863.
HAMILTON, WILLIAM H.
Gunner, 15 June, 1850. Died 18 September, 1865.
HAMILTON, WILLIAM J.
Acting Second Assistant Engineer, 1 October, 1862. Acting First Assistant Engineer, 29 March, 1864. Honorably discharged 3 November, 1865.
HAMLEN, EWING W.
Ensign (Spanish-American War), 2 July, 1898. Honorably discharged 15 October, 1898.
HAMLIN, BENJAMIN N.
Mate, 6 July, 1863. Lost at sea 21 August, 1863.
HAMLIN, JOHN C.
Mate, 11 October, 1861. Acting Ensign, 7 October, 1862. Acting Master, consideration of good service, 19 November, 1863. Appointment revoked 7 December, 1865.
HAMMAR, ALRIK.
Pharmacist, 15 September, 1898.
HAMMATT, CHARLES H.
Acting Assistant Paymaster, 5 September, 1863. Honorably discharged 27 January, 1866.
HAMMETT, CHARLES.
Mate. Dismissed 24 September, 1862.
HAMMETT, WILLIAM, Jr.
Mate, 5 March, 1863. Acting Ensign, 18 November, 1863. Honorably discharged 9 November, 1865.
HAMMOND, CHARLES.
Acting Warrant Machinist, 23 August, 1899.
HAMMOND, CHARLES E.
Assistant Paymaster, 14 November, 1861. Died 27 February, 1862.
HAMMOND, C. L. O.
Midshipman, 8 November, 1847. Resigned 23 March, 1854.
HAMMOND, GEORGE F.
Acting Master, 7 December, 1861. Resigned 5 May, 1864.
HAMMOND, G. W.
Acting Ensign, Admiral Dahlgren's Staff, 20 August, 1864. Resigned 11 January, 1865.
HAMMOND, JOSEPH H.
Acting Master, 27 December, 1861. Resigned 2 April, 1862.
HAMMOND, JOSIAH.
Mate, 28 October, 1861. Acting Master, 18 February, 1862. Dismissed 6 June, 1862.
HAMMOND, NATHAN W.
Acting Master, 1 April, 1862. Acting Volunteer Lieutenant, 29 November, 1862. Honorably discharged, 8 August, 1865.
HAMMOND, SAMUEL.
Ensign (Spanish-American War), 8 July, 1898. Honorably discharged 21 January, 1899.
HAMMOND, W.
Midshipman, 29 December, 1840. Resigned 27 October, 1846.
HAMRE, HENRY.
Mate, 1 September, 1862. Acting Ensign, 31 July, 1863. Honorably discharged 21 January, 1866.
HANAWAY, JAMES W.
Mate, 4 November, 1864. Honorably discharged 21 July, 1865.
HANCOCK, FRANK B.
Assistant Surgeon (Spanish-American War), 25 April, 1898. Honorably discharged 25 November, 1899.

GENERAL NAVY REGISTER. 243

HANCOCK, JOHN.
  Mate, 21 March, 1862. Acting Ensign, 8 October, 1863. Honorably discharged 8 November, 1865.
HAND, BAYARD E.
  Midshipman, 7 April, 1847. Passed Midshipman, 10 June, 1853. Master, 15 September, 1855. Lieutenant, 16 September, 1855. Died 16 July, 1859.
HAND, BENJAMIN.
  Acting First Assistant Engineer, 17 November, 1862. Appointment revoked (sick) 17 March, 1864.
HAND, CLAYTON F.
  Acting Carpenter, 10 January, 1900.
HAND, GEORGE DALLAS.
  Midshipman, 9 September, 1847. Resigned 28 April, 1853.
HAND, HENRY W.
  Acting Master, 13 November, 1861. Honorably discharged 21 February, 1866. Acting Master, 1 May, 1866. Mustered out 1 February, 1869.
HAND, JAMES A., JR.
  Naval Cadet, 6 September, 1894. Ensign, 4 April, 1900.
HAND, JASPER.
  Surgeon, 7 March, 1809. Dismissed 9 April, 1810.
HAND, SAMUEL T.
  Acting Third Assistant Engineer, 13 August, 1864. Resigned 29 May, 1865.
HAND, SETH.
  Acting Ensign, 1 July, 1863. Honorably discharged 21 October, 1868.
HAND, S. S.
  Mate, 7 June, 1862. Acting Ensign, 10 December, 1863. Honorably discharged 7 September, 1866.
HAND, WILLIAM H.
  Mate, 23 August, 1862. Acting Ensign, 4 April, 1863. Honorably discharged, 6 April, 1869.
HANDLAN, EUGENE Y.
  Acting Ensign, 1 October, 1862. Resigned 17 April, 1863.
HANDREN, JOHN W.
  Acting Third Assistant Engineer, 17 May, 1861. Resigned 23 April, 1862.
HANDS, ROBINSON W.
  Third Assistant Engineer, 1 February, 1862. Lost on the Monitor, 31 December, 1862.
HANDY, ALBERT G.
  Master, 28 September, 1838. Last appearance on Records of Navy Department. Dead.
HANDY, BETHUEL G.
  Acting Master, 4 November, 1861. Disrated to Acting Ensign, 28 August, 1862. Resigned 2 September, 1862.
HANDY, CHARLES O.
  Purser, 29 December, 1817. Resigned 4 June, 1846.
HANDY, EDWARD L.
  Midshipman, 1 June, 1826. Passed Midshipman, 28 April, 1832. Lieutenant, 8 March, 1837. Commander, 14 September, 1855. Dismissed 14 June, 1861.
HANDY, JAMES H.
  Acting Ensign, 2 June, 1864. Honorably discharged 20 October, 1865.
HANDY, HENRY O.
  Midshipman, 28 July, 1865. Graduated June, 1869. Ensign 12 July, 1870. Master, 12 July, 1871. Lieutenant, 9 November, 1874. Died 23 December, 1884.
HANDY, LEVIN.
  Midshipman, 1 June, 1828. Passed Midshipman, 14 June, 1834. Lieutenant, 25 February, 1841. Died 14 September, 1842.
HANDY, ROBERT.
  Midshipman, 1 February, 1826. Passed Midshipman, 28 April, 1832. Lieutenant, 8 March, 1837. Reserved List, 13 September, 1855. Commander on Active List, 14 September, 1855. Retired List, 6 February, 1862. Commodore, Retired List, 4 April, 1867. Died 7 June, 1884.
HANDY, SEWALL.
  Midshipman, 28 August, 1800. Resigned 12 April, 1804.
HANDY, THOMAS B.
  Midshipman, 28 January, 1814. Died 27 October, 1824.
HANES, SAMUEL.
  Acting Master, 21 September, 1861. Honorably discharged 30 October, 1866.
HANEY, HUGH.
  Acting Third Assistant Engineer, 28 September, 1863. Honorably discharged 1 September, 1865.
HANFORD, FRANKLIN.
  Midshipman, 29 November, 1862. Graduated June, 1866. Ensign, 12 March, 1868. Master, 26 March, 1869. Lieutenant, 21 March, 1870. Lieutenant-Commander, 30 October, 1885. Commander, 30 September, 1894.
HANFORD, WILLIAM C.
  Mate, 4 April, 1862. Acting Ensign, 4 December, 1862. Appointment revoked (sick) 10 August, 1863. Acting Ensign, 2 September, 1863. Resigned 10 June, 1864.
HANKS, A. P. R.
  Mate, 9 October, 1867. Resigned 27 August, 1871.
HANLEY, JAMES E.
  Assistant Engineer (Spanish-American War), 14 May, 1898. Honorably discharged 2 November, 1898.
HANLEY, PETER.
  Gunner, 21 October, 1889. Retired List, 26 October, 1898.

HANNA, BENJAMIN.
Midshipman, 7 January, 1813. Resigned 16 March, 1814.
HANNA, GEORGE H.
Midshipman, 2 April, 1804. Resigned 30 December, 1806.
HANNA, H. MELVILLE.
Assistant Paymaster, 11 June, 1862. Resigned 13 February, 1865.
HANNA, THOMAS.
Acting Third Assistant Engineer, 18 August. 1864. Resigned 17 June, 1865.
HANNAH, WILLIAM A.
Mate, 15 September, 1863. Honorably discharged 25 October, 1865.
HANNEGAN, S. L.
Midshipman, 2 January, 1834. Dismissed 8 July, 1839.
HANNIFER, THOMAS S.
Boatswain, 16 September, 1828. Died 3 January. 1880.
HANNIGAN, THOMAS.
Acting Third Assistant Engineer, 6 July, 1864. Resigned 23 March, 1865.
HANNON, HORACE A.
Mate, 19 October, 1862. Acting Ensign. 12 November, 1863. Honorably discharged 19 November, 1865.
HANNUM, JAMES.
Midshipman, 30 April, 1800. Dismissed 4 September, 1801.
HANNUM, JOHN LEWIS.
Third Assistant Engineer, 21 April, 1863. Second Assistant Engineer, 28 September, 1864. First Assistant Engineer, 23 November, 1872. Chief Engineer, 4 May, 1891. Rank changed to Commander, 3 March. 1899. Captain on Retired List. 30 June, 1899.
HANNUM, JOSIAH A.
Acting Master, 27 May, 1861. Honorably discharged 26 October, 1865. Acting Master, 5 February, 1867. Mustered out 30 December, 1868.
HANNUM, WILLIAM G.
Midshipman, 23 September, 1872. Ensign, 2 August. 1879. Lieutenant, Junior Grade, 6 May, 1886. Lieutenant, 2 October, 1891. Retired List, 23 October, 1900.
HANRAHAN, DAVID C.
Naval Cadet,. 19 May, 1894. Ensign. 4 April, 1900.
HANRAHAN, THOMAS.
Acting Master, 5 May, 1862. Honorably discharged 9 February, 1866.
HANSCOM, ISAIAH.
Naval Constructor, 14 March, 1856. Chief Bureau Construction and Repair, 28 January, 1871. Retired List, 29 June, 1877. Died 5 March, 1880.
HANSCOM, JOHN F.
Assistant Naval Constructor, 29 July, 1875. Naval Constructor, 10 October, 1888.
HANSCOM, LEONARD.
Carpenter, 14 May, 1866. Retired List, 8 May, 1893.
HANSCOM, WILLIAM L.
Naval Constructor, 15 October, 1853. Resigned 4 January, 1866. Reinstated 17 April, 1871. Retired List, 15 August, 1874. Died 3 September, 1881.
HANSEN, ALEXANDER.
Acting Ensign, 1 October, 1863. Honorably discharged 27 October, 1865.
HANSEN, HERMAN.
Sailmaker, 17 January, 1876. Retired List, 24 January, 1889.
HANSEN, PETER.
Acting Ensign, 2 September, 1864. Honorably discharged 20 August, 1865.
HANSFORD, C. H.
Midshipman, 10 May, 1820. Lieutenant, 17 May, 1828. Died 3 September, 1830.
HANSFORD, JEFFERSON.
Midshipman, 4 December, 1821. Died 10 September, 1826.
HANSON, AARON Y.
Acting Assistant Surgeon, 6 October, 1863. Honorably discharged 19 January, 1866.
HANSON, BARTHOLD C. H.
Acting Third Assistant Engineer, 27 February, 1865. Honorably discharged 5 September, 1865.
HANSON, CHARLES H.
Mate, 3 July, 1863. Acting Ensign. 26 July, 1864. Honorably discharged 2 November, 1865.
HANSON, FREDERICK W.
Acting Assistant Paymaster, 14 April, 1864. Honorably discharged 25 November, 1865.
HANSON, JAMES W.
Acting Assistant Paymaster, 17 January, 1865. Honorably discharged 1 November, 1865.
HANSON, JOHN.
Acting Master, 27 March, 1862. Honorably discharged 16 December, 1865.
HANSON, JOHN J.
Midshipman, 21 September, 1841. Passed Midshipman, 10 August, 1847. Died 25 August, 1853.
HANSON, ROBERT W.
Acting Ensign, 12 November, 1863. Honorably discharged 12 December, 1865.
HANSOM, SAMUEL. of S.
Purser, 30 March, 1804. Dismissed 16 July, 1811.
HANSON, WILLIAM.
Acting Master, 22 January, 1862. Appointment revoked 2 July, 1867.
HANSON, WILLIAM.
Acting Ensign, 1 September, 1864. Honorably discharged 20 September, 1865.

GENERAL NAVY REGISTER.   245

HANUS, GUSTAVUS C.
    Midshipman, 26 July, 1865. Graduated 6 June, 1871. Ensign, 14 July, 1872. Master, 3 May, 1875. Lieutenant, 19 June, 1882. Lieutenant-Commander, 3 March, 1899. Retired List with rank of Commander, 30 June, 1899.
HAPSGOOD, CHARLES B.
    Mate, 20 September, 1864. Honorably discharged 26 October, 1865.
HARADON, A. F.
    Mate, 23 January, 1862. Resigned 15 April, 1863.
HARALSON, C. L.
    Midshipman, 10 September, 1847. Resigned 13 December, 1854.
HARBEN, JAMES W.
    Mate, 12 September, 1864. Resigned (sick) 20 April, 1865.
HARBENSON, HENRY.
    Acting Third Assistant Engineer, 5 November, 1862. Acting Second Assistant Engineer, 6 May, 1864. Honorably discharged 27 October, 1865.
HARBER, GILES B.
    Midshipman, 24 July, 1865. Graduated June, 1869. Ensign, 12 July, 1870. Master, 12 July, 1871. Lieutenant, 19 September, 1874. Lieutenant-Commander, 4 September, 1896. Commander, 25 September, 1899.
HARBERSON, S. H.
    Mate, 24 January, 1863. Acting Ensign, 17 June, 1864. Honorably discharged 9 December, 1865.
HARBY, LEVI M.
    Midshipman, 18 June, 1812. Resigned 4 December, 1827.
HARCOURT, CHARLES.
    Mate, 17 December, 1864. Appointment revoked 22 April, 1865.
HARCOURT, WILLIAM.
    Gunner, 1 June, 1853. Dismissed 12 January, 1852. Reappointed Gunner, 1 June, 1853. Dismissed 13 August, 1855. Mate, 22 January, 1862. Acting Ensign, 25 February, 1863. Acting Master, 26 April, 1864. Honorably discharged 10 November, 1865.
HARDEN, JOHN F.
    Acting Master, 26 August, 1861. Acting Volunteer Lieutenant, recommendation of Admiral Farragut, 29 March, 1864. Honorably discharged 12 December, 1865. Acting Master, 24 April, 1867. Mustered out 15 September, 1868.
HARDEN, WALTER S.
    Acting Third Assistant Engineer, 21 July, 1862. Appointment revoked (sick) 6 March, 1863.
HARDEN, WILLIAM N.
    Acting First Assistant Engineer, 1 October, 1862. Honorably discharged 4 November, 1865.
HARDENBURGH, T. R.
    Midshipman, 29 February, 1799. Struck off in January, 1805.
HARDESTY, JAMES H.
    Acting Master, 30 October, 1861. Dismissed 27 May, 1863.
HARDIE, DAVID.
    Third Assistant Engineer, 11 May, 1860. Second Assistant Engineer, 28 October, 1862. Retired List, 15 March, 1867. Died 20 March, 1889.
HARDING, JAMES R.
    Acting Ensign, 1 December, 1864. Honorably discharged 8 August, 1865.
HARDING, JEREMIAH.
    Acting Boatswain, 5 April, 1865. Honorably discharged 11 September, 1865. Boatswain, 21 May, 1866. Died 27 June, 1885.
HARDING, SAMUEL, Jr.
    Mate, 31 October, 1861. Acting Ensign, 22 June, 1863. Dismissed 6 July, 1864.
HARDING, THOMAS W.
    Acting Second Assistant Engineer, 4 January, 1863. Honorably discharged 14 January, 1866.
HARDING, WILLIAM A.
    Mate. Resigned 20 February, 1862.
HARDING, WILLIAM P.
    Carpenter, 23 March, 1896.
HARDISON, WILLIAM.
    Gunner, 30 August, 1861. Dismissed 29 June, 1864.
HARDMAN, JAMES W.
    Acting Third Assistant Engineer, 5 March, 1864. Resigned 31 May, 1864.
HARDWICH, CHARLES.
    Acting Third Assistant Engineer, 9 September, 1862. Resigned 4 May, 1863.
HARDWICK, THOMAS.
    Master, 21 April, 1814. Discharged 22 May, 1815.
HARDY, ALBERT W.
    Acting First Assistant Engineer, 1 October, 1862. Acting Chief Engineer, 15 January, 1863. Honorably discharged 30 November, 1865.
HARDY, CHARLES S.
    Mate, 9 November, 1863. Resigned 27 April, 1865.
HARDY, E. S.
    Acting Master, 11 June, 1861. Dismissed 27 March, 1862.
HARDY, HENRY.
    Acting Third Assistant Engineer, 21 April, 1864. Honorably discharged 11 June, 1865.
HARDY, ISHAM G.
    Acting First Assistant Engineer, 2 February, 1863. Acting Chief Engineer, 10 June, 1864. Honorably discharged 10 October, 1865.
HARDY, J. L. C.
    Midshipman, 18 June, 1812. (See Marine Corps.)

HARDY, OTIS B.
Acting Third Assistant Engineer, 12 April, 1865. Honorably discharged 30 October, 1865.
HARDYMAN, TYLER.
Midshipman, 28 June, 1804. Resigned 27 July, 1805.
HARE, GEORGE H.
Midshipman, 19 October, 1841. Passed Midshipman, 10 August, 1847. Master, 14 September, 1855. Lieutenant, 15 September, 1855. Died 24 July, 1857.
HARE, JAMES.
Acting Third Assistant Engineer, 29 August, 1863. Honorably discharged 17 August, 1865.
HARGIS, THOMAS G.
Acting Ensign, 1 May, 1863. Died at Naval Hospital, Norfolk, Virginia, 19 May, 1864.
HARGOUS, PETER J.
Mate, 11 October, 1861. Acting Master, having distinguished himself on the Congress, 14 June, 1862. Resigned 17 March, 1865.
HARKER, JOHN C.
Midshipman, 1 March, 1826. Dismissed 9 July, 1833.
HARKINS, HENRY.
Acting Ensign, 1 October, 1862. Resigned 25 January, 1864.
HARKNESS, GEORGE.
Acting Master, 27 August, 1861. Resigned 29 November, 1861.
HARKNESS, WILLIAM.
Professor, 24 August, 1863. Retired List, with rank of Rear-Admiral, 17 December, 1899.
HARLAN, DAVID.
Assistant Surgeon, 23 February, 1835. Passed Assistant Surgeon, 8 July, 1841. Surgeon, 6 December, 1845. Medical Director, 3 March, 1871. Retired List, 3 November, 1871. Died 12 July, 1893.
HARLAN, J. C.
Acting Assistant Surgeon, 21 May, 1861. Resigned 15 August, 1861.
HARLIN, W. H.
Acting Assistant Surgeon, 11 April, 1863. Dismissed 5 May, 1864.
HARLOE, MATTHEW.
Acting Second Assistant Engineer, 30 August, 1864. Honorably discharged 22 July, 1865.
HARLOW, ALEXANDER H.
Acting Ensign, 26 August, 1863. Honorably discharged 10 December, 1865.
HARLOW, CHARLES H.
Cadet Midshipman, 18 September, 1875. Midshipman, 10 June, 1881. Ensign, Junior Grade, 3 March, 1883. Ensign, 26 June, 1884. Lieutenant, Junior Grade, 29 May, 1891. Lieutenant, 1 September, 1895.
HARLOW, LUCIUS.
Acting Third Assistant Engineer, 23 July, 1863. Honorably discharged 25 July, 1866.
HARMAN, DANIEL.
Acting Assistant Paymaster, 22 July, 1862. Resigned 4 September, 1862.
HARMON, ANDREW.
Acting Gunner, 17 November, 1862. Honorably discharged 6 May, 1866. Gunner, 9 February, 1870. Retired List, 20 March, 1894.
HARMON, EUGENE M.
Cadet Midshipman, 27 June, 1877. Graduated. Honorably discharged 30 June, 1883. Lieutenant (Spanish-American War), 24 May, 1898. Honorably discharged 9 September, 1898.
HARMON, GEORGE E. H.
Assistant Surgeon, 20 December, 1873. Passed Assistant Surgeon, 25 May, 1877. Surgeon, 25 March, 1888. Medical Inspector, 11 November, 1899.
HARMONY, DAVID B.
Midshipman, 7 April, 1847. Passed Midshipman, 7 April, 1847. Master, 10 June, 1853. Lieutenant, 16 September, 1855. Lieutenant-Commander, 16 July, 1862. Commander, 25 July, 1866. Captain, 4 February, 1875. Commodore, 23 September, 1885. Rear Admiral, 26 March, 1889. Retired List, 26 June, 1893.
HARMONY, JOSEPH H.
Third Assistant Engineer, 8 July, 1862. Second Assistant Engineer, 25 July, 1866. First Assistant Engineer, 1 January, 1868. Died 27 November, 1877.
HARMONY, PETER.
Mate, 17 February, 1865. Resigned 3 April, 1866. Mate. 7 January, 1867. Resigned 10 July, 1868.
HARNETT, JOHN W.
Acting Third Assistant Engineer, 26 January, 1863. Resigned 12 October, 1863. Acting Third Asistant Engineer, 19 January, 1864. Acting Second Assistant Engineer, 25 February, 1864. Resigned 25 March, 1865.
HARNISH, WILLIAM M.
Mate, 18 December, 1863. Appointment revoked 19 February, 1864.
HARPER, JOHN S.
Acting Third Assistant Engineer, 10 December, 1862. Acting Second Assistant Engineer, 23 December, 1863. Acting First Assistant Engineer, 22 March, 1865. Honorably discharged 11 November, 1865.
HARPER, JOSEPH L.
Midshipman, 4 June, 1812. Last appearance on Records of Navy Department, 1818. Dead.
HARPER, WILLIAM.
Master, 23 January, 1809. Resigned 25 June, 1814.
HARPER, W. J.
Midshipman, 1 September, 1811. Last appearance on Records of Navy Department, 1815. Philadelphia.

GENERAL NAVY REGISTER.

HARRELL, ABRAM DAVIS.
Midshipman, 4 January, 1834. Passed Midshipman, 16 July, 1840. Master, 22 March, 1847. Lieutenant, 17 May, 1847. Dropped 14 September, 1855. Commissioned Commander, 16 July, 1862. Retired 9 February, 1867. Captain on Retired List, 4 April, 1867. Died 16 December, 1871.

HARRELL, JOHN R.
Cadet Midshipman, 25 September, 1880. Resigned 7 August, 1884. Ensign (Spanish-American War), 2 June, 1898. Honorably discharged 12 September, 1898.

HARRIDEN, NATHANIEL.
Master, 30 June, 1799. Lieutenant, 31 March, 1807. Commander, 27 April, 1816. Died 9 January, 1818.

HARRIGAN, MICHAEL T.
Acting Third Assistant Engineer, 28 December, 1864. Resigned 3 May, 1865.

HARRIMAN, CHARLES W.
Acting Master, 22 January, 1862. Appointment revoked 25 November, 1862.

HARRIMAN, GEORGE A.
Mate, 21 March, 1862. Acting Ensign, 1 March, 1863. Honorably discharged 20 December, 1865.

HARRIMAN, HORACE M.
Acting Assistant Paymaster, 11 September, 1862. Honorably discharged 29 January, 1866.

HARRINGTON, CHARLES H.
Acting Second Assistant Engineer, 29 August, 1861. Acting First Assistant Engineer, 5 February, 1863. Resigned 5 December, 1864.

HARRINGTON, DANIEL C.
Mate, 17 November, 1862. Dismissed 11 November, 1864. Mate, 11 February, 1870. Resigned 19 May, 1871.

HARRINGTON, DENNIS.
Acting Third Assistant Engineer, 17 August, 1863. Honorably Discharged 17 August, 1865.

HARRINGTON, EBEN.
Carpenter, 1 April, 1822. Resigned 25 June, 1823.

HARRINGTON, ELIOT C.
Mate, 5 February, 1868. Resigned 20 November, 1870.

HARRINGTON, JAMES.
Mate, 30 November, 1863. Resigned 13 May, 1865.

HARRINGTON, JOHN C.
Acting Ensign, 6 April, 1864. Honorably discharged 12 October, 1865.

HARRINGTON, PURNELL F.
Acting Midshipman, 20 September, 1861. Acting Ensign, 1 October, 1863. Master, 10 May, 1866. Lieutenant, 21 February, 1867. Lieutenant-Commander, 12 March, 1808. Commander, 28 May, 1881. Captain, 1 March, 1895.

HARRINGTON, W. H.
Midshipman, 17 December, 1810. Resigned 12 April, 1813.

HARRIS, ABRAHAM W.
Acting First Assistant Engineer, 27 August, 1864. Honorably discharged 20 June, 1865.

HARRIS, AMOS.
Acting Third Assistant Engineer, 16 August, 1864. Honorably discharged 28 August, 1865.

HARRIS, ANDREW.
Acting Third Assistant Engineer, 8 August, 1863. Acting Second Assistant Engineer, 28 October, 1864. Honorably discharged 21 August, 1865.

HARRIS, ARNOLD.
Acting Ensign, 24 March, 1863. Resigned 21 February, 1865.

HARRIS, ARNOLD G.
Acting Master, 26 October, 1861. Dismissed 17 July, 1862.

HARRIS, BENJAMIN G.
Assistant Surgeon, 1 January, 1800. Last appearance on Records of Navy Department, 17 February, 1800.

HARRIS, CHARLES.
Mate, 23 October, 1861. Died 7 February, 1862.

HARRIS, CHARLES R.
Mate, 15 November, 1861. Acting Master, 24 April, 1862. Honorably discharged 17 December, 1865.

HARRIS, DWIGHT J.
Acting Assistant Surgeon, 13 May, 1864. Resigned 1˙May, 1865.

HARRIS, E. RAYMOND.
Mate, 1862. Appointment revoked 14 May, 1862.

HARRIS, FIELDER.
Midshipman, 20 June, 1806. Last appearance on Records of Navy Department, 3 July, 1807. Dead.

HARRIS, FRANCIS L.
Mate, 21 January, 1862. Acting Ensign, 19 December, 1862. Honorably discharged 28 October, 1865.

HARRIS, GEORGE.
Acting Master. 29 October, 1861. Dismissed 17 December, 1862.

HARRIS, GEORGE.
Acting Third Assistant Engineer, 27 June, 1864. Honorably discharged 5 December, 1865.

HARRIS, GEORGE D.
Acting Assistant Surgeon, 12 November, 1863. Resigned 1 May, 1865.

HARRIS, GEORGE J.
Mate, 9 October, 1867. Mustered out 22 September, 1871.

GENERAL NAVY REGISTER.

HARRIS, GEORGE L.
Acting Third Assistant Engineer, 28 January, 1862. Acting Second Assistant Engineer, 20 October, 1862. Acting First Assistant Engineer, 17 June, 1863. Honorably discharged 17 November, 1867.

HARRIS, GWINN.
Purser, 25 April, 1812. Resigned 29 September, 1830.

HARRIS, HATTON N. T.
Assistant Surgeon, 13 June, 1887. Passed Assistant Surgeon, 13 June, 1891. Surgeon, 21 October, 1899.

HARRIS, H. T. B.
Acting Assistant Paymaster, 1 November, 1864. Honorably discharged 13 September, 1865. Assistant Paymaster, 21 February, 1867. Passed Assistant Paymaster, 17 February, 1869. Paymaster, 18 January, 1881. Pay Inspector, 29 August, 1899.

HARRIS, IRA.
Acting Midshipman, 22 September, 1860. Ensign, 28 May, 1863. Lieutenant, 25 July, 1866. Lieutenant-Commander, 12 March, 1868. Resigned 21 March, 1871. Lieutenant-Commander (Spanish-American War), 11 May, 1898. Honorably discharged 17 January, 1899.

HARRIS, JAMES M.
Third Assistant Engineer, 16 September, 1853. Second Assistant Engineer, 9 May, 1857. Died 6 October, 1864.

HARRIS, J. GEORGE.
Purser, 19 August, 1845. Pay Director, 3 March, 1871. Retired List, 23 October, 1871. Died 8 May, 1891.

HARRIS, J. LOUIS.
Mate, 2 March, 1864. Acting Ensign, 6 April, 1864. Honorably discharged 8 October, 1868.

HARRIS, JOHN.
Midshipman, 27 May, 1800. Last appearance on Records of Navy Department. Resigned.

HARRIS, JOHN.
Acting Second Assistant Engineer, 16 September, 1861. Acting First Assistant Engineer, 18 April, 1863. Honorably discharged 7 October, 1865.

HARRIS, JOHN H.
Mate, 4 June, 1862. Acting Ensign, 1 August, 1862. Acting Master, 16 July, 1864. Honorably discharged 18 January, 1866.

HARRIS, JOSEPH W.
Acting Midshipman, 1 January, 1853. Midshipman, 20 June, 1856. Passed Midshipman, 29 April, 1859. Master, 5 September, 1859. Lieutenant, 12 January, 1861. Died 24 August, 1861.

HARRIS, MARTIN J.
Acting Master, 11 November, 1861. Dismissed 23 November, 1861.

HARRIS, REUBEN.
Midshipman, 25 January, 1840. Passed Midshipman, 11 July, 1846. Master, 24 November, 1854. Lieutenant, 8 August, 1855. Died 28 October, 1857.

HARRIS, ROBERT.
Assistant Surgeon, 17 July, 1798. Surgeon, 7 Novemebr, 1799. Resigned 5 December, 1802.

HARRIS, ROBERT, JR.
Midshipman, 1 January, 1818. Died in 1822.

HARRIS, ROBERT L.
Third Assistant Engineer, 3 May, 1859. Second Assistant Engineer, 29 July, 1861. First Assistant Engineer, 20 May, 1863. Chief Engineer, 4 March, 1871. Died 15 May, 1889.

HARRIS, T. A.
Acting Master, 27 May, 1861. Acting Volunteer Lieutenant-Commander, 27 April, 1863. Honorably discharged 24 October, 1865.

HARRIS, THOMAS.
Surgeon, 6 July, 1812. Died 5 March, 1861.

HARRIS, THOMAS.
Mate, 9 November, 1864. Resigned 1 November, 1865.

HARRIS, THOMAS C.
Midshipman, 9 September, 1841. Passed Midshipman, 10 August, 1847. Master, 14 September, 1855. Lieutenant, 15 September, 1855. Lieutenant-Commander, 16 July, 1862. Commander, 25 July, 1866. Captain, 12 December, 1872. Died 24 January, 1875.

HARRIS, THOMAS DeF.
Assistant Paymaster, 15 June, 1900.

HARRIS, THOMAS J.
Midshipman, 1 May, 1822. Resigned 27 May, 1830.

HARRIS, THOMAS J.
Third Assistant Engineer, 27 January, 1848. Dismissed 7 July, 1849.

HARRIS, THOMAS R.
Mate, 1 May, 1861. Acting Master, 12 April, 1862. Acting Volunteer Lieutenant, 11 November, 1863. Honorably discharged 22 September, 1865.

HARRIS, THOMPSON S.
Chaplain, 23 April, 1841. Died 28 December, 1842.

HARRIS, URIAH R.
Midshipman, 22 July, 1865. Graduated June, 1869. Ensign, 12 July, 1870. Master, 1 January, 1872. Lieutenant, 11 February, 1875. Lieutenant-Commander, 24 February, 1897. Commander, 31 December, 1899.

HARRIS, WILLIAM.
Acting Ensign, 31 October, 1862. Honorably discharged 28 February, 1866.

GENERAL NAVY REGISTER. 249

HARRIS, WILLIAM A.
  Assistant Surgeon, 27 November, 1844. Passed Assistant Surgeon, 4 February, 1851. Retired List, 8 May, 1861. Died 25 October, 1881.
HARRIS, WILLIAM B.
  Midshipman, 16 January, 1809. Resigned 18 August, 1809.
HARRIS, WILLIAM H.
  Third Assistant Engineer, 21 September, 1861. Second Assistant Engineer, 30 July, 1863. First Assistant Engineer, 11 October, 1866. Chief Engineer, 27 December, 1883. Rank changed to Captain, 3 March, 1883. Retired List, with rank of Rear-Admiral, 30 June, 1900.
HARRIS, WILLIAM J.
  Midshipman, 1 September, 1811. Last appearance on Records of Navy Department, 19 November, 1811. Resigned.
HARRIS, WILLIAM S.
  Midshipman, 30 November, 1814. Lieutenant, 13 January, 1825. Commander, 8 September, 1841. Died 15 May, 1848.
HARRISON, A. C.
  Midshipman, 26 June, 1799. Master, 7 June, 1803. Lieutenant, 3 February, 1807. Discharged 16 February, 1809.
HARRISON, BENJAMIN.
  Midshipman, 1 January, 1812. Last appearance on Records of Navy Department, 1816. Furloughed.
HARRISON, C. P. C.
  Midshipman, 4 June, 1823. Last appearance on Records of Navy Department. Drowned.
HARRISON, GEORGE R.
  Midshipman, 2 October, 1850. Dismissed 12 June, 1851.
HARRISON, GUSTAVUS, Jr.
  Midshipman, 27 October, 1841. Passed Midshipman, 10 August, 1847. Resigned 3 November, 1854.
HARRISON, G. W.
  Midshipman, 21 June, 1839. Died 6 June, 1844.
HARRISON, G. W.
  Midshipman, 20 January, 1832. Passed Midshipman, 23 June, 1838. Lieutenant, 2 November, 1842. Resigned 17 April, 1861.
HARRISON, HENRY F.
  Cadet Engineer, 1 October, 1874. Resigned 23 May, 1877. Lieutenant (Spanish-American War), 25 May, 1898. Honorably discharged 10 October, 1898.
HARRISON, H. H.
  Midshipman, 21 September, 1837. Resigned 25 April, 1845.
HARRISON, HORACE W.
  Cadet Midshipman, 26 September, 1872. Graduated 18 June, 1879. Ensign, 11 June, 1881. Lieutenant, Junior Grade, 22 May, 1888. Lieutenant, 10 June, 1893. Lieutenant-Commander, 1 July, 1900.
HARRISON, H. N.
  Midshipman, 1 April, 1828. Passed Midshipman, 3 July, 1835. Lieutenant, 8 September, 1841. Reserved List, 28 September, 1855. Died 29 March, 1861.
HARRISON, JAMES F.
  Assistant Surgeon, 5 March, 1847. Passed Assistant Surgeon, 26 April, 1852. Surgeon, 5 March, 1861. Resigned 15 June, 1861.
HARRISON, JOHN.
  Assistant Surgeon, 16 January, 1805. Died 4 March, 1825.
HARRISON, NAPOLEON B.
  Midshipman, 27 February, 1838. Passed Midshipman, 20 May, 1844. Master, 2 April, 1852. Lieutenant, 6 January, 1853. Commander, 16 July, 1862. Captain, 28 April, 1868. Died 27 October, 1870.
HARRISON, RANDOLPH.
  Assistant Surgeon, 4 August, 1851. Resigned 1 April, 1856.
HARRISON, RICHARD.
  Midshipman, 7 July, 1800. Lost in the Insurgent.
HARRISON, RICHARD J.
  Assistant Surgeon, 6 September, 1837. Died 28 February, 1842.
HARRISON, R. M.
  Midshipman, 9 November, 1825. Died 5 April, 1828.
HARRISON, ROBERT.
  Master, 13 July, 1799. Lieutenant, 14 October, 1799. Discharged 8 July, 1801, under Peace Establishment Act.
HARRISON, THOMAS.
  Acting Third Assistant Engineer, 7 September, 1863. Honorably discharged 5 October, 1865.
HARRISON, THOMAS LOCKE.
  Acting Midshipman, 29 September, 1856. Midshipman, 15 June, 1860. Dismissed 26 July, 1861.
HARRISON, THOMAS S.
  Acting Assistant Paymaster, 10 July, 1861. Appointment revoked April, 1863.
HARRISON, TIMOTHY J.
  Chaplain, 2 October, 1829. Died 10 March, 1865.
HARRISON, T. P.
  Midshipman, 9 June, 1811. Resigned 29 January, 1820.
HARRISON, WILLIAM D.
  Assistant Surgeon, 25 April, 1848. Surgeon, 22 April, 1861. Dismissed 3 February, 1863.
HARRISON, WILLIAM K.
  Naval Cadet, 23 May, 1885. Ensign, 1 July, 1891. Lieutenant, 3 March, 1899.

HARRISON, WILLIAM H.
　　Mate, 24 May, 1862. Appointment revoked (sick) 28 August. 1862. Acting Ensign, 1 October, 1862. Acting Master, 16 June, 1863. Appointment revoked 21 November, 1864.
HARRISON, WILLIAM H.
　　Mate, 13 December, 1861. Acting Ensign. 11 March, 1865. Appointment revoked 23 November, 1865.
HARRISON, WILLIAM HENRY.
　　Third Assistant Engineer, 29 July, 1861. Second Assistant Engineer, 18 December, 1862. First Assistant Engineer, 30 January, 1865. Resigned 8 October, 1872.
HARRISON, W. P.
　　Midshipman, 19 October, 1841. Resigned 10 June, 1843.
HARRISS, JOHN L.
　　Midshipman, 30 November, 1814. Resigned.
HARSEN, ELISHA.
　　Third Assistant Engineer, 1 July, 1861. Second Assistant Engineer, 20 April, 1863. Lost on the Tecumseh, 5 August, 1864.
HARSHMAN, WALTER S.
　　Professor, 25 August, 1900.
HART, BENJAMIN F.
　　Purser, 8 February, 1838. Died 2 November, 1842.
HART, BENJAMIN F., JR.
　　Passed Assistant Engineer (Spanish-American War), 21 May, 1898. Honorably discharged 30 December, 1898.
HART, EDWIN M.
　　Acting Assistant Paymaster, 19 August, 1862. Passed Assistant Paymaster, 23 July, 1866. Resigned 18 July, 1868.
HART, EZEKIEL B.
　　Midshipman, 30 April, 1814. Killed in action 26 August, 1814.
HART, FRANKLIN W.
　　Assistant Paymaster, 20 May, 1898. Passed Assistant Paymaster, 6 June, 1899.
HART, GEORGE W.
　　Acting Second Assistant Engineer, 11 March, 1864. Honorably discharged 28 October, 1865.
HART, HENRY C.
　　Midshipman, 1 September, 1827. Resigned 29 December, 1834.
HART, JOHN.
　　Midshipman, 1 January, 1825. Dismissed 31 December, 1828.
HART, JOHN.
　　Assistant Surgeon, 10 September, 1798. Last appearance on Records of Navy Department. Dead.
HART, JOHN E.
　　Midshipman, 23 February, 1841. Passed Midshipman, 10 August, 1847. Master, 14 September, 1855. Lieutenant, 15 September, 1855. Lieutenant-Commander, 16 July, 1862. Killed in battle 11 June, 1863.
HART, SAMUEL.
　　Naval Constructor, 1 June, 1819. Last appearance on Records of Navy Department, 6 December, 1839.
HART, SIMEON.
　　Midshipman, 8 June, 1799. Discharged 12 October, 1801, under Peace Establishment Act.
HART, THOMAS C.
　　Naval Cadet, 19 May, 1893. Ensign, 1 July, 1899.
HART, WILLIAM.
　　Boatswain, 2 December, 1831. Died 26 February, 1861.
HARTE, FRANCIS J.
　　Carpenter, 7 October, 1895.
HARTER, LA FAYETTE.
　　Acting Assistant Paymaster, 31 December, 1862. Honorably discharged 4 December, 1865.
HARTFORD, RICHARD F.
　　Mate, 21 January, 1864. Acting Ensign, 3 December, 1864. Honorably discharged 26 August, 1865.
HARTIGAN, WILLIAM.
　　Midshipman, 11 April, 1799. Discharged 30 April, 1801, under Peace Establishment Act.
HARTLEB, LOUIS.
　　Mate. Resigned 1 March, 1865.
HARTLEY, JOHN.
　　Midshipman, 20 March, 1800. Resigned 2 January, 1802.
HARTLEY, WILLIAM W.
　　Acting Third Assistant Engineer, 9 September, 1863. Appointment revoked (sick) 24 October, 1864.
HARTMAN, JOSEPH.
　　Boatswain, 6 December, 1897. Died 24 November, 1898.
HARTMAN, W. B.
　　Acting Assistant Surgeon, 4 April, 1864. Honorably discharged 21 October, 1865.
HARTNETT, JOHN M.
　　Acting Second Assistant Engineer, 3 July, 1863. Honorably discharged 6 November, 1865.
HARTRATH, ARMIN.
　　Naval Cadet, 4 September, 1884. Assistant Engineer, 1 July, 1890. Passed Assistant Engineer, 1 May, 1898. Rank changed to Lieutenant, Junior Grade, 3 March, 1899.

GENERAL NAVY REGISTER. 251

HARTSHORN, ANDRE.
Mate, 21 January, 1862: Acting Ensign, 22 June, 1863. Honorably discharged 30 June, 1866
HARTSHORN, J. H.
Acting Ensign, 27 November, 1862. Died on Katahdin, 18 August, 1863.
HARTSTENE, HENRY J.
Midshipman, 1 April, 1828. Passed Midshipman, 14 June, 1834. Lieutenant, 23 February, 1840. Commander, 14 September, 1855. Resigned 9 January, 1861.
HARTT, CLARK.
Acting Third Assistant Engineer, 27 April, 1863. Acting Second Assistant Engineer, 6 March, 1865. Honorably discharged 6 October, 1866.
HARTT, EDWARD.
Naval Constructor, 25 July, 1866. Died 12 September, 1883.
HARTT, LAWRENCE G.
Acting Third Assistant Engineer, 5 January, 1864. Honorably discharged 31 March, 1868.
HARTT, SAMUEL T.
Naval Constructor, 15 July, 1847. Died 18 December, 1860.
HARTT, SETH.
Acting Third Assistant Engineer, 9 March, 1864. Honorably discharged 7 August, 1865.
HARTUNG, RENWICK J.
Naval Cadet, 6 September, 1887. Ensign, 1 July, 1893. Retired List, 20 June, 1896.
HARTUPER, JOHN W.
Acting First Assistant Engineer, 1 October, 1862. Acting Chief Engineer, 22 April, 1863. Honorably discharged 15 December, 1865.
HARTWELL, CHARLES F.
Mate, 19 May, 1864. Honorably discharged 15 August, 1865.
HARTWELL, SAMUEL N.
Acting First Assistant Engineer, 20 December, 1861. Appointment revoked 17 March, 1862. Acting First Assistant Engineer, 24 March, 1862. Acting Chief Engineer, 24 March, 1863. Honorably discharged 22 January, 1866.
HARTWELL, SETH E.
Acting Assistant Paymaster, 8 February, 1865. Mustered out 4 October, 1865.
HARTWELL, W. B.
Purser, 11 November, 1845. Died at sea 12 July, 1849.
HARTWIG, HENRY.
Acting Chief Engineer, 1 October, 1862. Honorably discharged 2 December, 1865.
HARTWIG, PETER R.
Acting Chief Engineer, 1 October, 1862. Honorably discharged 11 November, 1865.
HARTY, JOHN D.
Acting Master, 14 May, 1863. Acting Volunteer Lieutenant, 9 April, 1864. Resigned 28 March, 1865.
HARTZELL, FRANKLIN K.
Assistant Surgeon, 10 November, 1868. Resigned 31 December, 1873.
HARVEY, ALEXANDER J.
Acting Third Assistant Engineer 10 November, 1863. Resigned 22 June, 1865.
HARVEY, ANDREW W.
Mate, 27 August, 1863. Acting Ensign, 2 November, 1864. Honorably discharged 29 October, 1865.
HARVEY, CHARLES.
Sailmaker, 27 January, 1842. Resigned 18 April, 1846.
HARVEY, CLINTON D.
Acting Assistant Paymaster, 4 December, 1862. Died at New York 15 December, 1864.
HARVEY, DAVID.
Mate, 20 January, 1862. Resigned 14 May, 1863.
HARVEY, HENRY P.
Assistant Surgeon, 28 May, 1872. Passed Assistant Surgeon, 12 June, 1876. Surgeon, 18 December, 1886. Died 25 December, 1892.
HARVEY, JOSEPH S.
Acting Assistant Paymaster, 11 September, 1862. Resigned 13 April, 1866.
HARVEY, LUTHER ROGL.
Third Assistant Engineer, 11 February, 1862. Second Assistant Engineer, 15 October, 1863. First Assistant Engineer, 1 January, 1868. Died 11 June, 1886.
HARVEY, RICHARD M.
Midshipman, 24 June, 1830. Passed Midshipman, 15 June, 1837. Dismissed 30 July, 1841.
HARVEY, THOMAS.
Gunner, 22 June, 1810. Resigned 9 January, 1811.
HARVEY, THOMAS E.
Mate, 26 June, 1862. Acting Ensign, 21 January, 1864. Honorably discharged 8 May, 1866.
HARVEY, WILLIAM.
Midshipman, 30 November, 1814. Resigned 18 October, 1817.
HARVIE, JACQUELINE B.
Midshipman, 2 January, 1804. Lieutenant, 25 February, 1809. Resigned 28 April, 1812.
HARWOOD, ANDREW A.
Midshipman, 1 January, 1818. Lieutenant, 3 March, 1827. Commander, 2 October, 1848. Captain, 14 September, 1855. Commodore, 16 July, 1862. Retired List, 9 October, 1864. Rear-Admiral, Retired List. Died 28 August, 1884.

HARWOOD, FRANKLIN B.
Ensign (Spanish-American War), 2 June, 1898. Honorably discharged 28 January, 1899.
HARWOOD, JAMES K.
Purser, 24 November, 1852. Dismissed 31 May, 1861.
HARWOOD, NICHOLAS.
Assistant Surgeon, 9 July, 1803. Surgeon, 3 March, 1809. Died 15 September, 1812.
HASBROUCK, RAYMOND D.
Naval Cadet, 25 September, 1888. Assistant Engineer, 1 July, 1894. Passed Assistant Engineer, 11 October, 1898. Rank changed to Lieutenant, Junior Grade, 3 March, 1899.
HASCALL, BAILEY.
Acting Assistant Paymaster, 30 June, 1862. Discharged 9 September, 1865.
HASELTON, JOHN B.
Acting Assistant Paymaster, 4 November, 1862. Dismissed 22 April, 1863.
HASKELL, CHARLES W.
Midshipman, 23 June, 1870. Graduated 1 June, 1874. Ensign, 17 July, 1875. Resigned 28 March, 1879.
HASKELL, CYRUS A.
Mate, 24 March, 1865. Honorably discharged 6 October, 1868.
HASKELL, ELIJAH.
Gunner, 13 September, 1845. Retired List, 10 December, 1865. Died 27 March, 1877.
HASKELL, FORBES B.
Mate, 18 June, 1863. Honorably discharged 22 August, 1865.
HASKELL, FRANK A.
Mate, 25 July, 1863. Honorably discharged 14 August, 1865. Mate, 21 March, 1866. Resigned 14 May, 1867.
HASKELL, OTIS L.
Acting Ensign, 27 January, 1865. Resigned 10 June, 1865.
HASKELL, PORTER D.
Cadet Midshipman, 22 September, 1876. Graduated 22 June, 1882. Ensign, Junior Grade, 3 March, 1883. Resigned 18 August, 1883.
HASKELL, THOMAS H.
Acting Assistant Paymaster, 14 October, 1861. Discharged 5 February, 1866.
HASKER, CHARLES H.
Boatswain, 28 March, 1857. Dismissed 4 June, 1861.
HASKIN, BENJAMIN F.
Acting Midshipman, 2 November, 1859. Ensign, 25 November, 1862. Dropped 7 July, 1864.
HASKIN, HARRY R.
Midshipman, 18 June, 1812. Resigned 30 April, 1814
HASKINS, CHARLES R.
Mate, 2 October, 1863. Acting Ensign, 9 December, 1864. Honorably discharged 27 June, 1868.
HASKINS, GEORGE S.
Sailmaker, 19 November, 1870. Died 14 May, 1895.
HASLER, ADOLPH.
Gunner, 19 July, 1899.
HASLER, CHARLES A.
Assistant Surgeon, 4 November, 1834. Passed Assistant Surgeon, 12 July, 1839. Surgeon, 22 July, 1844. Drowned 27 November, 1846.
HASLET, JOHN.
Assistant Surgeon, 26 May, 1824. Surgeon, 23 May, 1826. Resigned 5 December, 1845.
HASLETT, ANDREW.
Midshipman, 17 December, 1810. Last appearance on Records of Navy Department, 1815. Frigate Chesapeake.
HASSELTENO, D. CARLOS.
Acting First Assistant Engineer, 27 July, 1863. Acting Chief Engineer, 18 May, 1864. Honorably discharged 7 May, 1866.
HASSLER, CHARLES W.
Assistant Paymaster, 29 August, 1861. Paymaster, 14 April, 1862. Resigned 9 February, 1870.
HASSON, WILLIAM F. C.
Cadet Engineer, 14 September, 1876. Graduated 10 June, 1880. Assistant Engineer, 10 June, 1882. Resigned 1 February, 1893.
HASTINGS, CHARLES.
Civil Engineer, 1852. Commissioned 28 March, 1867. Resigned 23 April, 1874.
HASTINGS, FRANK F.
Acting Assistant Paymaster, 22 September, 1862. Discharged 26 March, 1866.
HASTINGS, JOHN.
Assistant Surgeon, 8 September, 1841. Passed Assistant Surgeon, 13 March, 1846. Passed Assistant Surgeon, 15 March, 1847. Resigned 9 May, 1850.
HASTINGS, LOVEN W.
Mate, 23 July, 1863. Acting Ensign, 6 April, 1865. Honorably discharged 1 December, 1865.
HASWELL, CHARLES H.
Chief Engineer, 12 July, 1836. Engineer-in-Chief, 3 October, 1844. Successor appointed, 1 December, 1850. Dropped from the Navy List, 14 May, 1852.
HASWELL, GOUVERNEUR K.
Acting Midshipman, 22 September, 1859. Ensign, 7 October, 1862. Lieutenant, 22 February, 1864. Lieutenant-Commander, 25 July, 1866. Retired List, 23 November, 1876.

GENERAL NAVY REGISTER. 253

HASWELL, JOHN M.
Midshipman, 15 October, 1800. Lieutenant, 26 February, 1807. Last appearance on Records of Navy Department, 24 May, 1810.
HASWELL, ROBERT.
Lieutenant, 4 March, 1799. Last appearance on Records of Navy Department, 13 April, 1801.
HATCH, CHARLES B.
Naval Cadet, 6 September, 1895. At sea prior to final graduation.
HATCH, CHARLES F.
Mate, 25 July, 1863. Resigned 5 August, 1864.
HATCH, GEORGE W.
Acting Assistant Surgeon, 9 May, 1863 Resigned 18 March, 1865.
HATCH, WILLIAM.
Carpenter, 1 November, 1831. Discharged 29 January, 1836.
HATCH, WILLIAM.
Mate, 16 December, 1861. Dismissed 6 January, 1863.
HATCH, WILLIAM L.
Acting Ensign, 16 March, 1864. Honorably discharged 20 August, 1865.
HATCH, WILLIAM S.
Gunner, 16 August, 1854. Dismissed 24 September, 1858.
HATCH, WILLIAM W.
Acting Ensign, 13 March, 1865. Honorably discharged 21 August, 1865.
HATCHER, JACKSON R.
Third Assistant Engineer, 24 September, 1847. Second Assistant Engineer, 26 February, 1851. Died 23 December, 1853.
HATFIELD, CHARLES H.
Acting Boatswain, 10 August, 1861. Dismissed 4 January, 1862.
HATFIELD, CHESTER.
Acting Midshipman, 21 May, 1852. Midshipman, 20 June, 1856. Passed Midshipman, 29 April, 1859. Master, 5 September, 1859. Lieutenant, 23 January, 1861. Lieutenant-Commander, 2 October, 1862. Commander, 28 October, 1870. Died 15 December, 1879.
HATFIELD, DANIEL.
Assistant Surgeon, 5 May, 1810. Surgeon, 15 September, 1814. Last appearance on Records of Navy Department, 23 April, 1814.
HATFIELD, JOHN.
Midshipman, 18 June, 1812. Killed in action 27 April, 1813.
HATFIELD, ROBERT F.
Third Assistant Engineer, 24 August, 1861. Resigned 18 July, 1862.
HATFIELD, W. B.
Assistant Surgeon, 24 March, 1809. Last appearance on Records of Navy Department, 8 March, 1811.
HATHAWAY, FREDERICK M.
Acting Ensign, 28 February, 1863. Honorably discharged 5 December, 1865.
HATHAWAY, F. W.
Mate, 10 June, 1865. Honorably discharged 16 June, 1866.
HATHAWAY, HENRY P.
Acting Ensign, 19 May, 1864. Honorably discharged 18 February, 1866.
HATHAWAY, JAMES H.
Acting Assistant Paymaster, 6 August, 1862. Honorably discharged 10 March, 1866.
HATHAWAY, JOSEPH T.
Acting Third Assistant Engineer, 18 June, 1862. Acting Second Assistant Engineer, 12 November, 1862. Acting First Assistant Engineer, 16 May, 1863. Honorably discharged 18 August, 1866.
HATHAWAY, WILLIAM R.
Acting Master, 30 July, 1861. Acting Volunteer Lieutenant, 27 June, 1865. Died 11 February, 1867.
HATHORNE, EBEN.
Midshipman, 16 January, 1809. Resigned 6 December, 1810.
HATHORNE, W. H.
Acting Assistant Paymaster, 31 March, 1863. Honorably discharged 3 October, 1865.
HATHORNE, WILLIAM H.
Mate, 16 November, 1863. Resigned 30 December, 1864.
HATTON, RICHARD.
Assistant Paymaster, 2 March, 1895. Passed Assistant Paymaster, 26 September, 1897. Paymaster, 20 January, 1900.
HAVEN, WILLIAM H.
Mate, 8 April, 1864. Resigned 26 May, 1865.
HAVENS, JOSEPH A.
Mate, 22 January, 1862. Resigned 25 August, 1862. Acting Ensign, 12 December, 1863. Honorably discharged 12 October, 1865.
HAVERFIELD, H. D.
Warrant Machinst (Spanish-American War), 15 June, 1898. Honorably discharged 2 September, 1898.
HAVERLY, LEWIS A.
Third Assistant Engineer, 19 July, 1861. Died 29 August, 1862.
HAVERSFIELD, JOHN.
Acting Third Assistant Engineer, 28 October, 1862. Honorably discharged 27 October, 1865.
HAVILAND, E. M.
Mate, 3 November, 1865. Appointment revoked 5 December, 1865.
HAWES, ASA T.
Mate, 11 September, 1862. Died 26 November, 1863.

HAWES, BENJAMIN F.
Acting Third Assistant Engineer, 24 September, 1862. Acting Second Assistant Engineer, 25 July, 1863. Acting First Assistant Engineer, 19 October, 1864. Honorably discharged 14 November, 1865.
HAWES, DAVID B.
Acting Ensign, 17 June, 1863. Resigned 31 May, 1866.
HAWES, FRANKLIN.
Acting Third Assistant Engineer, 11 March, 1865. Honorably discharged 19 January, 1866.
HAWES, SANFORD B.
Acting Third Assistant Engineer, 28 May, 1863. Appointment revoked (sick) 5 November, 1863.
HAWES, WILLIAM H.
Mate, 26 June, 1862. Acting Ensign, 13 June, 1866. Honorably discharged 27 June, 1868. Mate, 6 December, 1869. Resigned 14 October, 1871.
HAWES, WILLIAM H. H.
Acting Third Assistant Engineer, 8 June, 1864. Honorably discharged 14 June, 1865.
HAWK, GEORGE F.
Naval Cadet, 17 June, 1882. Ensign, 1 July, 1888. Retired List, 26 June, 1893. Died 10 February, 1894.
HAWKE, J. ALBERT.
Assistant Surgeon, 24 June, 1867. Passed Assistant Surgeon, 26 February, 1873. Surgeon, 1 May, 1879. Medical Inspector, 8 June, 1895. Medical Director, 24 September, 1899.
HAWKESWORTH, GEORGE T.
Master, 11 April, 1815. Last appearance on Records of Navy Department, 18 April, 1815.
HAWKEY, JAMES.
Acting Third Assistant Engineer, 7 October, 1863. Honorably discharged 6 August, 1866.
HAWKEY, THOMAS.
Acting Second Assistant Engineer, 31 May, 1861. Dismissed 20 September, 1862.
HAWKINS, ABSALOM W.
Assistant Surgeon, 1 July, 1861. Passed Assistant Surgeon, 22 June, 1864. Resigned 28 July, 1866.
HAWKINS, BENJAMIN.
Acting Third Assistant Engineer, 24 September, 1863. Appointment revoked (sick) 25 May, 1864.
HAWKINS, CHARLES E.
Midshipman, 4 March, 1818. Resigned 17 October, 1826.
HAWKINS, CHARLES E.
Acting Master's Mate, 26 June, 1861. Acting Master, 26 May, 1862. Honorably discharged 29 November, 1865. Boatswain, 11 February, 1871. Chief Boatswain, 3 March, 1899. Retired List, 29 August, 1899.
HAWKINS, GEORGE N.
Midshipman, 1 March, 1826. Passed Midshipman, 28 April, 1832. Died 7 July, 1837.
HAWKINS, H. C.
Mate, Resigned 12 May, 1863.
HAWKINS, JOHN.
Acting Third Assistant Engineer, 13 September, 1862. Acting Second Assistant Engineer, 25 May, 1864. Honorably discharged 5 August, 1865.
HAWKINS, JOHN S.
Third Assistant Engineer, 29 July, 1861. Second Assistant Engineer, 18 December, 1862. First Assistant Engineer, 30 January, 1865. Resigned 18 January, 1869.
HAWKINS, JOSEPH.
Sailmaker, 25 June, 1800. Warrant returned 10 July, 1800.
HAWKINS, ROBERT M.
Mate, 24 November, 1863. Resigned (sick) 8 November, 1864.
HAWKINS, SAMUEL.
Acting Third Assistant Engineer, 1 October, 1864. Resigned 12 May, 1865.
HAWKINS, S. B.
Sailmaker, 18 March, 1834. Died 27 July, 1844.
HAWKS, PHILO P.
Mate, 14 February, 1863. Acting Ensign, 14 January, 1864. Resigned 3 May, 1865.
HAWKSWORTH, DAVID.
Acting Second Assistant Engineer, 24 July, 1862. Resigned 30 May, 1864.
HAWLER, ISAAC.
Master, 7 July, 1814. Resigned 25 September, 1815.
HAWLEY, CHARLES E.
Midshipman, 3 December, 1849. Passed Midshipman, 12 June, 1855. Master, 16 September, 1855. Lieutenant, 26 June, 1856. Retired List, 10 August, 1864. Lieutenant-Commander on Retired List, 4 April, 1867. Died 19 December, 1898.
HAWLEY, FRANCIS M.
Acting Assistant Paymaster, 30 August, 1862. Resigned 4 April, 1863.
HAWLEY, JOHN MITCHELL.
Midshipman, 23 July, 1863. Graduated June, 1868. Ensign, 19 April, 1869. Master, 12 July, 1870. Lieutenant, 6 January, 1874. Lieutenant-Commander, 9 December, 1894. Commander, 3 March, 1899.
HAWTHORN, JOSEPH W.
Acting Ensign, 22 July, 1862. Resigned 4 May, 1863.
HAWTHORNE, EUGENE P.
Mate, 6 January, 1863. Acting Ensign, 17 March, 1863. Resigned 28 October, 1863.

GENERAL NAVY REGISTER.

HAWTHORNE, HARRY L.
Cadet Engineer, 1 October, 1878. Graduated 30 June, 1884. Honorably discharged 30 June, 1884. Restored to service 22 June, 1886. Resigned as of date of 30 October, 1884.

HAWTHORNE, WYMAN G.
Assistant Engineer (Spanish-American War), 25 May, 1898. Honorably discharged 24 December, 1898.

HAXTUN, MILTON.
Midshipman, 19 October, 1841. Passed Midshipman, 10 August, 1847. Master, 14 September, 1855. Lieutenant, 15 September, 1855. Lieutenant-Commander, 16 July, 1862. Commander, 12 January, 1867. Captain, 2 February, 1878. Retired List, 7 February, 1883. Died 26 May, 1898.

HAY, EDWARD H.
Acting Third Assistant Engineer, 11 March, 1865. Resigned 30 May, 1865.

HAY, EDWARD H.
Carpenter, 31 March, 1874. Resigned 19 August, 1874. Carpenter, 1 January, 1875. Chief Carpenter, 3 March, 1899.

HAY, WILLIAM G.
Assistant Surgeon, 12 September, 1854. Passed Assistant Surgeon, 20 May, 1859. Surgeon, 1 August, 1861. Resigned 18 February, 1862.

HAYAUGA, G. A.
Acting Assistant Surgeon, 8 September, 1863. Honorably discharged 9 October, 1865.

HAYDEN, DAVID H.
Acting Master, 17 December, 1861. Dismissed 29 November, 1862.

HAYDEN, D. H.
Acting Assistant Surgeon, 15 May, 1863. Honorably discharged 2 December, 1865.

HAYDEN, EDWARD D.
Acting Assistant Paymaster, 27 September, 1862. Honorably discharged 2 February, 1866.

HAYDEN, EDWARD E.
Cadet Midshipman, 21 June, 1875. Graduated 10 June, 1881. Ensign, Junior Grade, 3 March, 1883. Ensign, 26 June, 1884. Retired List, 30 June, 1885. Restored to Active List as Lieutenant by act approved 19 January, 1901.

HAYDEN, HENRY F.
Acting Third Assistant Engineer, 30 October, 1861. Appointment revoked 13 December, 1861. Acting Third Assistant Engineer, 3 January, 1862. Acting Second Assistant Engineer, 16 July, 1863. Honorably discharged 17 September, 1867.

HAYDEN, HENRY J.
Sailmaker, 4 November, 1861. Resigned 16 February, 1865.

HAYDEN, JOHN.
Carpenter, 1 November, 1837. Appointment revoked 7 July, 1840.

HAYDEN, JOHN C.
Boatswain, 20 September, 1852. Dismissed 2 November, 1857.

HAYDEN, JOHN W.
Acting Second Assistant Engineer, 9 January, 1865. Honorably discharged 14 October, 1865.

HAYDEN, N. S.
Acting Ensign. 6 May, 1863. Died on Penguin. 6 July, 1864.

HAYDEN, REYNOLDS.
Naval Cadet (Spanish-American War), 6 August, 1898. Honorably discharged 22 November, 1898.

HAYDEN, TIMOTHY.
Warrant Machinist (Spanish-American War), 15 June, 1898. Discharged 6 August, 1898.

HAYES, CHARLES H.
Cadet Midshipman, 25 September, 1880. Honorably discharged 30 June, 1886. Assistant Engineer, 28 June, 1889. Passed Assistant Engineer, 29 January, 1896. Rank changed to Lieutenant, 3 March, 1899.

HAYES, DENNIS.
Acting Third Assistant Engineer, 27 June, 1864. Honorably discharged 10 July, 1865.

HAYES, DENNY M.
Mate, 7 June, 1864. Acting Ensign, 18 November, 1864. Honorably discharged 21 October, 1865. Acting Ensign, 5 July, 1866. Appointment revoked 7 December, 1867.

HAYES, HENRY H.
Chaplain, 3 March, 1827. Resigned 18 April, 1833.

HAYES, HENRY S.
Mate, 31 October, 1861. Resigned 20 September, 1862.

HAYES, JACOB L.
Acting Ensign, 10 April, 1863. Honorably discharged 14 September, 1865.

HAYES, JAMES.
Gunner, 11 September, 1863. Retired List, 24 March, 1895.

HAYES, JOHN J.
Acting Carpenter, 1 October. 1862. Resigned 28 March, 1864.

HAYES, PETER.
Acting Volunteer Lieutenant, 23 August, 1862. Honorably discharged 26 October, 1865.

HAYES, PETER.
Mate, 21 October, 1863. Dismissed 21 September, 1864.

HAYES, THOMAS.
Midshipman, 16 June, 1814. Resigned 25 November, 1814.

HAYES, WILLIAM G.
Midshipman, 25 September, 1811. Resigned 28 March, 1812.

HAYES, WILLIAM LEE.
Acting Master, 15 August, 1861. Honorably discharged 3 October, 1865.

HAYMAN, ANTHONY W.
Master, 22 April, 1813. Discharged 7 July, 1814.
HAYMAN, GEORGE M.
Acting Third Assistant Engineer. 12 August. 1863. Honorably discharged 4 November, 1865.
HAYNES, JOHN.
Boatswain, 11 September, 1799. Discharged 1 May, 1801.
HAYNES, JOHN.
Mate, 22 November. 1862. Deserted 15 August. 1863.
HAYNE, PAUL H.
Midshipman, 10 May, 1820. Lieutenant. 17 May, 1828. Died 14 September, 1831.
HAYNSWORTH, JOHN H.
Mate (Spanish-American War), 25 April, 1898. Appointment revoked 3 February, 1899.
HAYS, ADAM.
Surgeon, 28 September, 1811. Resigned 4 December. 1811.
HAYS, CHARLES W.
Midshipman, 12 March, 1838. Passed Midshipman. 20 May, 1844. Master, 25 November, 1852. Lieutenant, 9 September. 1853. Dismissed 5 June, 1861.
HAYS, JOHN.
Gunner, 14 March, 1800. Last appearance on Records of Navy Department, 15 May, 1800. Resigned.
HAYS, JOHN S.
Acting Third Assistant Engineer, 26 April, 1864. Acting Second Assistant Engineer, 1 February, 1865. Honorably discharged 5 October, 1865.
HAYS, WALTER W.
Midshipman, 3 August, 1838. Died 9 November, 1839.
HAYS, WILLIAM R.
Midshipman, 7 November, 1845. Died 10 August, 1849.
HAYTER, SAMUEL G.
Mate, 5 March, 1862. Resigned 24 November, 1862.
HAYWARD, ADDISON S.
Acting Third Assistant Engineer, 20 July, 1864. Honorably discharged 7 November, 1865.
HAYWARD, GEORGE N.
Naval Cadet, 19 May, 1884. Ensign. 1 July, 1890. Lieutenant. Junior Grade, 13 April, 1898. Lieutenant. 3 March, 1899.
HAYWARD, GEORGE W.
Acting Midshipman, 26 September, 1857. Midshipman, 1 June. 1861. Lieutenant, 16 July, 1862. Lieutenant-Commander. 25 July, 1866. Commander. 9 November, 1874. Died 16 January, 1886.
HAYWARD, RICHARD.
Chaplain, 2 October, 1876. Resigned 2 January, 1887.
HAYWOOD, JOLEY.
Boatswain, 4 May, 1828. Dismissed 18 April, 1832.
HAYWOOD, PHILEMON.
Midshipman, 19 October, 1841. Dismissed 28 August, 1849.
HAYWOOD, SAMUEL.
Captain (to command a Galley). 2 September, 1798. Appointed Lieutenant. 29 January, 1800. Discharged 1801, under Peace Establishment Act.
HAZARD, ALFRED.
Midshipman, 23 March, 1800. Dismissed 22 April, 1809.
HAZARD, ANDREW R.
Acting Ensign, 30 November, 1864. Honorably discharged 28 October, 1865.
HAZARD, DANIEL.
Midshipman, 20 January, 1814. Resigned 6 April, 1815.
HAZARD, FREDERICK R.
Acting Boatswain, 1 March, 1900.
HAZARD, JOHN A.
Purser, 12 March, 1799. Died 21 July, 1799.
HAZARD, JOSIAH.
Master, 23 October, 1799. Dismissed 16 June. 1803.
HAZARD, SAMUEL F.
Midshipman, January, 1823. Passed Midshipman, 4 June, 1831. Lieutenant, 9 February, 1837. Commander. 14 September, 1855. Captain, 16 July, 1862. Retired 3 November, 1863. Died 15 January, 1867.
HAZARD, STANTON.
Midshipman, 16 January, 1799. Resigned 23 January, 1799.
HAZARD, WILLIAM S.
Acting Third Assistant Engineer, 30 October, 1861. Appointment revoked 13 December, 1861.
HAZAZEN, S. J.
Acting Master's Mate, 16 November, 1861. Dismissed 11 September, 1862.
HAZELL, WILLIAM.
Midshipman, 1 January, 1808. Resigned 28 June, 1810.
HAZELTINE, CHARLES W.
Cadet Midshipman, 14 June, 1880. Graduated. Honorably discharged 30 June, 1886. Lieutenant, Junior Grade (Spanish-American War), 3 April, 1898. Lieutenant, 22 November, 1898. Honorably discharged 23 November, 1898.
HAZELTINE, EDWARD C.
Acting Midshipman, 22 September, 1859. Ensign. 27 December, 1862. Lost on the Housatonic, 17 February, 1864.
HAZELTON, JOHN A.
Mate, 5 September, 1864. Resigned 20 June, 1865.

GENERAL NAVY REGISTER. 257

HAZELTON, ISAAC.
   Assistant Surgeon, 17 September, 1861. Resigned 11 September, 1865.
HAZLETT, GEORGE J.
   Acting Ensign, 13 May, 1863. Resigned 1 March, 1865.
HAZLETT, H. K.
   Acting Master, 1 October, 1862. Appointment revoked (declined) 29 January, 1863.
HAZLETT, ISAAC.
   Midshipman, 27 September, 1861. Graduated 24 September, 1865. Ensign, 1 December, 1866. Master, 12 March, 1868. Lieutenant, 26 March, 1869. Lieutenant-Commander, 21 December, 1881. Retired List, 8 November, 1886.
HAZLITT, JAMES W.
   Mate, 6 November, 1861. Dismissed 25 May, 1863.
HAZZARD, WILLIAM S.
   Acting First Assistant Engineer, 24 September, 1863. Honorably discharged 16 August, 1865.
HEACOCK, WILLIAM C.
   Midshipman, 22 September, 1868. Graduated 1 June, 1872. Ensign, 15 July, 1873. Resigned 21 November, 1877.
HEALD, EPHRAIM.
   Carpenter, 24 July, 1827. Discharged 8 November, 1828.
HEALD, EUGENE DE F.
   Midshipman, 30 September, 1863. Graduated June, 1867. Ensign, 18 December, 1868. Master, 21 March, 1870. Lieutenant, 21 March, 1871. Lieutenant-Commander, 28 February, 1890. Commander, 4 June, 1897. Died 27 March, 1898.
HEALEY, E. C.
   Acting Master, 28 February, 1862. Honorably discharged 4 March, 1866.
HEALEY, JOHN.
   Acting Third Assistant Engineer, 28 March, 1863. Killed in action 20 April, 1863.
HEALEY, WILLIAM J.
   Acting Assistant Paymaster, 23 September, 1863. Honorably discharged 2 November, 1865. Assistant Paymaster, 27 February, 1867. Passed Assistant Paymaster, 19 July, 1868. Died 11 July, 1873.
HEANY, JOHN.
   Acting Third Assistant Engineer, 7 October, 1862. Resigned 12 March, 1863.
HEAP, JAMES L.
   Midshipman, 5 June, 1830. Passed Midshipman, 14 June, 1836. Died 15 January, 1839.
HEAP, JOSEPH L. K.
   Acting First Assistant Engineer, 1 October, 1862. Acting Chief Engineer, 23 November, 1863. Honorably discharged 25 October, 1865.
HEAP, SAMUEL D.
   Assistant Surgeon, 5 April, 1804. Surgeon, 27 November, 1804. Resigned 25 December, 1825.
HEAP, SAMUEL L.
   Assistant Paymaster, 1 April, 1882. Passed Assistant Paymaster, 15 August, 1893. Paymaster, 5 February, 1898.
HEARN, FREDERICK W.
   Acting Ensign, 24 October, 1862. Honorably discharged 12 November, 1865.
HEARSON, FREDERICK L.
   Acting Third Assistant Engineer, 24 December, 1864. Honorably discharged 17 July, 1865.
HEARTIE, ISAAC.
   Master, 6 July, 1815. Last appearance on Records of Navy Department.
HEATH, ALLEN S.
   Acting Assistant Surgeon, 28 May, 1861. Resigned 14 August, 1862.
HEATH, BENJAMIN, JR.
   Mate, 8 February, 1864. Honorably discharged 1 December, 1865.
HEATH, BYRON S.
   Acting Third Assistant Engineer, 4 October, 1864. Resigned 3 June, 1865.
HEATH, DANIEL C.
   Midshipman, 28 March, 1799. Resigned 18 April, 1805.
HEATH, DAVID P.
   Acting Master, 4 November, 1861. Resigned 13 March, 1865.
HEATH, FRANK R.
   Cadet Midshipman, 23 September, 1873. Graduated 18 June, 1879. Ensign, 28 May, 1881. Lieutenant, Junior Grade, 2 January, 1888. Died 12 June, 1889.
HEATH, HENRY.
   Mate. Resigned 29 April, 1862.
HEATH, LUCIUS E.
   Mate, 27 May, 1863. Resigned 17 May, 1865.
HEATH, MARCELLUS C.
   Acting Third Assistant Engineer, 22 November, 1862. Acting Second Assistant Engineer, 19 November, 1863. Honorably discharged 21 January, 1868.
HEATH, NATHAN B.
   Acting Master, 9 September, 1861. Acting Volunteer Lieutenant, 18 August, 1865. Honorably discharged 8 May, 1866.
HEATH, RICHARD S.
   Midshipman, 17 December, 1810. Lieutenant, 27 April, 1817. Killed in a duel 2 June, 1817.
HEATH, SAMUEL C.
   Mate, 8 May, 1862. Resigned 28 March, 1864.
HEATH, WILLIAM.
   Midshipman, 20 June, 1806. Resigned 5 June, 1809.

17

HEATH, WILLIAM R.
Assistant Paymaster (Spanish-American War), 15 July, 1898. Honorably discharged 21 November, 1898.
HEATLEY, THOMAS.
Lieutenant, 20 March, 1799. Discharged 13 March, 1802, under Peace Establishment Act.
HEATON, WILLIAM WARFORD.
Third Assistant Engineer, 2 December, 1861. Second Assistant Engineer, 8 September, 1863. First Assistant Engineer, 11 October, 1866. Chief Engineer, 26 January, 1886. Died 31 May, 1895.
HEBARD, HENRY.
Chief Engineer, 6 February, 1840. Died 4 August, 1846.
HEBARD, GEORGE F.
Second Assistant Engineer, 27 January, 1848. First Assistant Engineer, 26 February, 1851. Dropped 17 September, 1856. Acting First Assistant Engineer, 21 October, 1863. Acting Chief Engineer, 1 March, 1864. Honorably discharged 10 April, 1866.
HEBARD, JOHN H.
Acting Second Assistant Engineer, 24 November, 1863. Honorably discharged 20 October, 1867.
HEBBARD, SAMUEL.
Gunner, 23 January, 1822. Died 9 July, 1832.
HEBERTON, EDWARD P.
Acting Assistant Paymaster, 25 September, 1861. Appointment revoked (sick) 23 April, 1863.
HEBRON, THOMAS.
Acting First Assistant Engineer, 1 October, 1862. Acting Chief Engineer, 20 November, 1862. Honorably discharged 11 November, 1865.
HEBURN, PATRICIUS.
Midshipman, 18 June, 1812. Dismissed 8 March, 1814.
HEBURN, PATRICIUS.
Midshipman, 1 January, 1818. Resigned 23 February, 1821.
HECKLE, JOHN.
Sailmaker, 9 November, 1831. Died 15 January, 1847.
HEDDEN, EDWARD F.
Acting Third Assistant Engineer, 4 December, 1862. Honorably discharged 5 August, 1865.
HEDGE, CORNELIUS G.
Mate, 9 May, 1863. Deserted 20 May, 1863.
HEDGER, WILLIAM.
Acting Master, 9 April, 1862. Honorably discharged 11 January, 1866.
HEDGES, FREDERICK E.
Midshipman, 9 June, 1811. Last appearance on Records of Navy Department, 1815. Georgetown, D. C.
HEDGES, JAMES D.
Acting Third Assistant Engineer, 1 October, 1864. Appointment revoked (sick) 29 April, 1865.
HEDRICKS, ALFRED.
Third Assistant Engineer, 13 May, 1861. Second Assistant Engineer, 19 February, 1863. Resigned 9 August, 1865.
HEEDE, PETER.
Acting Ensign, 17 December, 1862. Resigned 14 March, 1864. Acting Ensign, 30 June, 1864. Dismissed 31 August, 1864.
HEENAN, THOMAS.
Acting Third Assistant Engineer, 23 November, 1861. Acting Second Assistant Engineer, 17 October, 1863. Acting First Assistant Engineer, 28 April, 1865. Honorably discharged 4 February, 1866.
HEEP, JOSEPH K.
Acting First Assistant Engineer, 1 October, 1862. Acting Chief Engineer, 23 November, 1863. Honorably discharged 25 October, 1865.
HEERMAN, LEWIS.
Surgeon's Mate, 8 February, 1802. Surgeon, 27 November, 1804. Died 19 May, 1833.
HEFFENGER, ARTHUR C.
Assistant Surgeon, 19 March, 1875. Passed Assistant Surgeon, 4 June, 1878. Retired List, 20 October, 1890.
HEFFORDS, WILLIAM.
Acting Master, 14 November, 1861. Acting Volunteer Lieutenant, for duty as Pilot, 13 November, 1863. Honorably discharged 23 October, 1865.
HEGER, ANTON.
Assistant Surgeon (Spanish-American War), 25 April, 1898. Honorably discharged 15 September, 1898.
HEILEMAN, JULIUS G.
Midshipman, 10 March, 1848. Passed Midshipman, 15 June, 1854. Master, 15 September, 1855. Lieutenant, 16 September, 1855. Resigned 31 December, 1856.
HEILGE, CHARLES C.
Acting Third Assistant Engineer, 14 December, 1863. Appointment revoked (sick) 12 September, 1864.
HEILNER, LEWIS C.
Midshipman, 25 July, 1866. Graduated 7 June, 1870. Ensign, 13 July, 1871. Master, 27 September, 1873. Lieutenant, 2 June, 1879. Lieutenant-Commander, 9 December, 1898.
HEINEN, GEORGE M.
Acting Warrant Machinist, 6 July, 1899.

GENERAL NAVY REGISTER. 259

HEINS, GEORGE M.
　Ensign (Spanish-American War), 23 June, 1898. Honorably discharged 6 September, 1898.
HEISER, HENRY DILLON.
　Third Assistant Engineer, 21 December, 1861. Resigned 22 April, 1865.
HEISKELL, HORACE M.
　Purser, 13 September, 1841. Pay Director, 3 March, 1871. Retired List, 24 September, 1875. Died 26 December, 1891.
HEISKELL, SIDNEY O.
　Passed Assistant Surgeon (Spanish-American War), 30 April, 1898. Honorably discharged 9 December, 1898.
HEITMAN, BARTHOLD H.
　Mate, 12 July, 1865. Resigned 2 March, 1866.
HEIZERMAN, JOHN B.
　Acting Ensign, 1 October, 1862. Honorably discharged 11 November, 1865.
HEKEY, PETER.
　Carpenter, 19 October, 1799. Drowned at sea 12 March, 1800.
HELLEN, CLIFTON.
　Assistant Paymaster, 8 November, 1861. Paymaster, 16 November, 1862. Resigned 15 February, 1865.
HELLER, EDWARD L.
　Acting Third Assistant Engineer, 22 October, 1863. Honorably discharged 1 September, 1865.
HELLWEG, JULIUS F.
　Naval Cadet, 5 September, 1896. Graduated 30 June, 1900.
HELM, FRANCIS T.
　Midshipman, 16 January, 1809. Resigned 5 March, 1810.
HELM, FRANK F., Jr.
　Naval Cadet, 20 May, 1895. At sea prior to final graduation.
HELM, JAMES M.
　Midshipman, 29 September, 1871. Graduated 21 June, 1875. Ensign, 18 July, 1876. Master, 25 November, 1881. Lieutenant, Junior Grade, 3 March, 1883. Lieutenant, 1 June, 1888. Lieutenant-Commander, 3 March, 1899.
HELMS, GEORGE.
　Carpenter, 10 December, 1894.
HELMS, WILLIAM T.
　Chaplain, 4 February, 1898.
HEMENWAY, PETER.
　Carpenter, 11 November, 1813. Resigned 10 August, 1814.
HEMPHILL, J. A.
　Midshipman, 4 March, 1823. Resigned 24 January, 1826.
HEMPHILL, JOSEPH NEWTON.
　Midshipman, 29 September, 1862. Graduated June, 1866. Ensign, 12 March, 1868. Master, 26 March, 1869. Lieutenant, 21 March, 1870. Lieutenant-Commander, 26 January, 1887. Commander, 15 June, 1895.
HEMPSTEAD, WILLIAM D.
　Acting Assistant Paymaster, 19 October, 1861. Appointment revoked 16 May, 1862.
HENSLEY, JAMES T.
　Mate, 26 September, 1864. Honorably discharged 20 September, 1865.
HENCK, E. W.
　Mate, 8 April, 1865. Honorably discharged 5 August, 1866.
HENCKE, JACOB.
　Acting Third Assistant Engineer, 29 January, 1864. Resigned 1 May, 1865.
HENDEE, GEORGE E.
　Acting Assistant Paymaster, 25 March, 1864. Passed Assistant Paymaster, 23 July, 1866. Paymaster, 27 February, 1869. Pay Inspector, 9 January, 1895. Pay Director, 1 September, 1899.
HENDERSON, ALBERT D.
　Acting Ensign, 8 April, 1864. Honorably discharged 9 December, 1865.
HENDERSON, ALEXANDER.
　Third Assistant Engineer, 26 February, 1851. Second Assistant Engineer, 21 May, 1853. First Assistant Engineer, 9 May, 1857. Chief Engineer, 28 June, 1861. Retired List, 12 July, 1894.
HENDERSON, ALEXANDER M.
　Midshipman, 1 April, 1827. Resigned 17 July, 1833.
HENDERSON, ANDREW A.
　Assistant Surgeon, 8 September, 1841. Surgeon, 1 March, 1856. Medical Director, 3 March, 1871. Died 4 April, 1875.
HENDERSON, ANDREW H.
　Third Assistant Engineer, 8 September, 1863. Dismissed 17 April, 1866.
HENDERSON, B. L. T.
　Midshipman, 2 January, 1840. Resigned 6 April, 1846.
HENDERSON, CHARLES.
　Midshipman, 6 April, 1830. Resigned 12 March, 1832.
HENDERSON, E. F.
　Mate, 11 October, 1861. Dismissed 31 May, 1862.
HENDERSON, FRANCIS.
　Acting Second Assistant Engineer, 3 April, 1863. Acting First Assistant Engineer, 8 April, 1864. Dismissed 12 November, 1864.
HENDERSON, GEORGE.
　Midshipman, 1 May, 1828. Resigned 13 September, 1834.
HENDERSON, GEORGE D.
　Chaplain, 2 July, 1864. Died 20 May, 1875.

HENDERSON, GERARD.
Carpenter, 19 April, 1845. Resigned 1 February, 1850.
HENDERSON, JAMES B.
Mate, 17 May, 1862. Acting Ensign, 11 August, 1863. Dismissed 28 November, 1865.
HENDERSON, JAMES L.
Midshipman, 1 June, 1828. Passed Midshipman, 14 June, 1834. Lieutenant, 6 July, 1840. Commander, 14 September, 1855. Resigned 18 April, 1861.
HENDERSON, JOHN A.
Assistant Engineer, 3 July, 1876. Retired List, 20 November, 1884.
HENDERSON, JOHN E.
Acting Third Assistant Engineer, 23 March, 1864. Honorably discharged 13 October, 1865.
HENDERSON, JOSEPH W.
Acting Third Assistant Engineer, 7 March, 1864. Honorably discharged 1 November, 1865.
HENDERSON, MOSES K.
Mate, 26 March, 1863. Honorably discharged 27 October, 1870. Gunner, 27 August, 1872. Retired List, 13 October, 1896. Died 23 January, 1897.
HENDERSON, RICHARD.
Midshipman, 25 September, 1872. Graduated 20 June, 1876. Ensign, 1 July, 1878. Lieutenant, Junior Grade, 13 May, 1886. Lieutenant, 5 November, 1891. Lieutenant-Commander, 9 September, 1899.
HENDERSON, ROBERT.
Acting Ensign, 23 December, 1863. Honorably discharged 5 August, 1865.
HENDERSON, ROBERT W.
Naval Cadet, 22 September, 1893. Ensign, 1 July, 1899.
HENDERSON, THOMAS.
Acting Third Assistant Engineer. Dismissed 22 August, 1863.
HENDERSON, WILLIAM.
Midshipman, 6 March, 1800. Resigned 20 March, 1800.
HENDERSON, WILLIAM.
Mate, 21 March, 1862. Acting Ensign, 16 March, 1864. Dismissed 28 November, 1864.
HENDERSON, WILLIAM F.
Acting Third Assistant Engineer, 11 September, 1863. Honorably discharged 8 January, 1866.
HENDERSON, YANDELL.
Ensign (Spanish-American War), 13 June, 1898. Resigned 8 August, 1898.
HENDRICKS, WILLIAM.
Mate, 4 June, 1863. Acting Ensign and Pilot, 29 April, 1864. Dismissed 3 June, 1864.
HENDRICKSON, WILLIAM W.
Acting Midshipman, 26 September, 1860. Acting Ensign, 1 October, 1863. Master, 10 November, 1865. Lieutenant, 10 November, 1866. Lieutenant-Commander, 12 March, 1868. Resigned 12 June, 1873. Professor, 21 March, 1873.
HENDRIE, STRATHCARN.
Ensign (Spanish-American War), 9 May, 1898. Honorably discharged 26 August, 1898.
HENDRIX, FREMONT M.
Midshipman, 21 March, 1862. Graduated September, 1865. Ensign, 1 December, 1866. Master, 12 March, 1868. Retired List, 11 November, 1871. Died 11 June, 1880.
HENDRY, GEORGE B.
Mate, 15 April, 1898. Boatswain, 10 April, 1899.
HENDRY, THOMAS, Jr.
Midshipman, 1 January, 1808. Lieutenant, 8 March, 1813. Resigned 16 December, 1819.
HENEBERGER, LUCIEN G.
Assistant Surgeon, 17 June, 1874. Passed Assistant Surgeon, 10 November, 1877. Surgeon, 5 May, 1890.
HENERY, SAMUEL.
Acting Third Assistant Engineer, 20 May, 1864. Honorably discharged 2 November, 1865.
HENEY, JOHN C.
Mate, 19 September, 1862. Resigned 31 March, 1865.
HENKLE, FRANKLIN.
Acting Assistant Surgeon, 8 August, 1861. Resigned 20 September, 1862.
HENLEY, CHARLES.
Acting Master's Mate, 22 June, 1863. Reduced to landsman by General Court Martial, 27 October, 1864, and discharged as Coxswain 24 October, 1867.
HENLEY, JOHN D.
Midshipman, 14 October, 1799. Lieutenant, 3 January, 1807. Commander, 24 July, 1813. Captain, 5 March, 1817. Died 23 May, 1835.
HENLEY, P. T.
Midshipman, 1 January, 1818. Last appearance on Records of Navy Department, 2 April, 1824. Dead.
HENLEY, SAMUEL.
Midshipman, 16 January, 1809. Lieutenant, 24 July, 1813. Died 14 July, 1825.
HENLEY, WILLIAM.
Purser, 22 January, 1812. Last appearance on Records of Navy Department.
HENLEY, WILLIAM D.
Midshipman, 20 August, 1800. Discharged 12 August, 1801, under Peace Establishment Act.

HENLY, ROBERT.
Midshipman, 8 April, 1799. Lieutenant, 29 January, 1807. Commander, 12 August, 1814. Captain, 3 March, 1825. Died 7 October, 1828.
HENNESSEY, DAVID F.
Boatswain, 5 December, 1894. Died 19 November, 1899.
HENNESSEY, E. J.
Mate, 23 March, 1863. Honorably discharged 10 July, 1865.
HENNESSEY, JAMES M.
Acting Third Assistant Enginer, 30 July, 1864. Honorably discharged 20 July, 1865
HENNESSEY, WILLIAM.
Acting Assistant Paymaster, 24 January, 1862. Appointment revoked (sick) 11 March, 1863.
HENNESSY, DAVID.
Acting Third Assistant Engineer, 24 December, 1863. Honorably discharged 15 July, 1865.
HENNESSY, J. B.
Midshipman, 20 June, 1799. Last appearance on Records of Navy Department. Dead.
HENNIG, PAUL.
Acting Boatswain, 25 January, 1900.
HENOP, LEWIS W.
Midshipman, 17 June, 1799. Last appearance on Records of Navy Department, 27 June, 1800.
HENOP, PHILIP.
Midshipman, 26 November, 1799. Resigned 6 August, 1801.
HENRICKS, EDWARD WILLIAM.
Midshipman, 23 September, 1863. Graduated June, 1867. Ensign, 18 December, 1868. Master, 21 March, 1870. Resigned 13 October, 1871. Lieutenant (Spanish-American War), 10 May, 1898. Honorably discharged 24 December, 1898.
HENRICKSON, CHARLES A.
Acting Ensign, 25 February, 1864. Honorably discharged 24 October, 1865.
HENRIQUES, ARTHUR J.
Ensign (Spanish-American War), 21 May, 1898. Honorably discharged 28 September, 1898.
HENRIQUES, FREDERIC D.
Acting Third Assistant Engineer, 18 January, 1864. Acting Second Assistant Engineer, 14 October, 1864. Honorably discharged 8 October, 1865.
HENRY, BERNARD.
Assistant Surgeon, 27 November, 1844. Passed Assistant Surgeon, 1 April, 1850. Resigned 11 October, 1850.
HENRY, CHARLES J.
Acting Third Assistant Engineer, 30 September, 1863. Acting Second Assistant Engineer, 9 September, 1864. Honorably discharged 19 July, 1865.
HENRY, CHARLES P.
Passed Assistant Surgeon, 18 May, 1886. Retired List 20 December, 1889.
HENRY, EDMUND W.
Midshipman, 7 April, 1842. Passed Midshipman, 5 August, 1848. Master, 15 September, 1855. Lieutenant, 16 September, 1855. Lieutenant-Commander, 16 July, 1862. Retired 19 March, 1867. Commander on Retired List, 23 April, 1867. Died 8 March, 1872.
HENRY, EDWARD T.
Acting Third Assistant Engineer, 19 April, 1864. Honorably discharged 20 October, 1865.
HENRY, HENRY.
Master, 1 July, 1812. Lieutenant, 5 March, 1817. Commander, 9 February, 1837. Captain, 27 February, 1847. Died 26 July, 1857.
HENRY, ISAAC.
Assistant Surgeon, 9 March, 1798. Surgeon, 12 July, 1799. Last appearance on Records of Navy Department.
HENRY, JAMES.
Master, 16 June, 1814. Resigned 19 October, 1818.
HENRY, JAMES B., Jr.
Naval Cadet, 6 September, 1892. Assistant Engineer, 6 May, 1898. Rank changed to Ensign, 3 March, 1899. Resigned 15 September, 1900.
HENRY, J. CASSIN.
Midshipman, 6 March, 1833. Passed Midshipman, 8 July, 1839. Lieutenant, 17 May, 1844. Died 18 February, 1846.
HENRY, JOHN.
Acting Third Assistant Engineer, 29 August, 1861. Acting Second Assistant Engineer, 19 November, 1863. Resigned 19 May, 1865.
HENRY JOHN.
Acting Third Assistant Engineer, 22 June, 1863. Honorably discharged 19 January, 1866.
HENRY, JOHN B.
Midshipman, 30 October, 1804. Dismissed 13 July, 1808.
HENRY, JOHN B.
Master's Mate, 23 April, 1805. Dismissed 26 May, 1806.
HENRY, JOHN F.
Acting Assistant Surgeon, 22 March, 1864. Dismissed 9 June, 1865.
HENRY, MORRIS H.
Acting Assistant Surgeon, 17 May, 1861. Resigned 8 July, 1863.
HENRY, ROBERT.
Acting Third Assistant Engineer, 19 December, 1863. Honorably discharged 1 March, 1866.

HENRY, ROBERT.
Acting First Assistant Engineer, 22 January, 1862. Appointment revoked 29 January, 1863.
HENRY, S. R. D.
Midshipman, 26 April, 1798. Last appearance on Records of Navy Department, 11 December, 1798.
HENRY, WILKES.
Midshipman, 18 December, 1837. Killed by South Sea Islanders, 24 July, 1840.
HENRY, WILLIAM.
Mate. Appointment revoked (sick) 26 July, 1862. Mate, 9 September, 1862. Acting Ensign, 6 October, 1862. Honorably discharged 29 August, 1865.
HENRY, WILLIAM.
Boatswain, 20 February, 1815. Dismissed 2 October, 1816.
HENRY, WILLIAM A.
Midshipman, 5 December, 1817. Passed Midshipman, 29 June, 1843. Died 14 December, 1844.
HENRY, WILLIAM P.
Mate, 12 February, 1863. Resigned 10 February, 1864.
HENSE, FREDERICK.
Acting Third Assistant Engineer, 1 October, 1862. Resigned 2 March, 1863. Acting Third Assistant Engineer, 13 August, 1863. Appointment revoked (sick) 20 July, 1864.
HENSHAW, H. CLAY.
Acting Third Assistant Engineer, 19 December, 1861. Resigned 17 September, 1863.
HENSHAW, J. SIDNEY.
Professor of Mathematics, 26 September, 1837. Resigned 10 April, 1841. Reappointed 1 July, 1842. Dropped 4 September, 1848.
HENSLEY, ALEXANDER C.
Chaplain, 9 September, 1890. Whilly retired 1 November, 1892.
HENSLEY, EDWARD M.
Mate, 8 July, 1863. Resigned 30 January, 1864. Mate, 12 February, 1864. Resigned 8 June, 1865.
HENSLEY, J. T.
Acting Master's Mate, 4 October, 1864. Honorably discharged, 20 September, 1865.
HENTIG, GEORGE.
Acting Master, 1 October, 1862. Dismissed 6 June, 1863.
HENTON, WILLIAM.
Boatswain, 10 July, 1875. Retired List, 12 October, 1876. Died 4 May, 1890.
HEPBURN, ARTHUR J.
Naval Cadet, 22 September, 1893. Ensign, 1 July, 1899.
HEPBURN, RICHARD.
Acting Ensign, 2 December, 1863. Honorably discharged 13 January, 1866.
HEPPNER, ALBERT H.
Assistant Surgeon (Spanish-American War), 20 May, 1898. Honorably discharged, 7 November, 1898.
HERBER, JACOB.
Acting Second Assistant Engineer, 1 December, 1863. Dismissed 21 July, 1864.
HERBERT, HILARY A., JR.
Naval Cadet (Spanish-American War), 28 May, 1898. Honorably discharged 5 December, 1898.
HERBERT, JOHN C.
Sailmaker, 10 June, 1861. Chief Sailmaker, 3 March, 1899. Retired List, 11 August, 1900.
HERBERT, JOSHUA.
Midshipman, 13 November, 1798. Last appearance on Records of Navy Department, 29 April, 1801. Resigned.
HERBERT, JOSHUA.
Master, 4 August, 1807. Last appearance on Records of Navy Department.
HERBERT, PERCY.
Acting Boatswain, 25 January, 1900.
HERBERT, THEODORE C.
Sailmaker, 15 June, 1842. Resigned 10 August, 1849. Reappointed 21 November, 1850. Retired List, 20 March, 1876. Died 4 July, 1890.
HERBERT, THOMAS.
Master, 9 September, 1814. Discharged 4 May, 1815.
HERBERT, WILLIAM C.
Cadet Engineer, 1 October, 1879. Assistant Engineer, 1 July, 1885. Passed Assistant Engineer, 6 August, 1895. Rank changed to Lieutenant, 3 March, 1899.
HERBERT, WILLIAM H.
Mate, 7 August, 1862. Resigned 23 March, 1863.
HERIOT, JAMES.
Midshipman, 1 April, 1828. Resigned 20 March, 1830.
HERIOT, THOMAS.
Midshipman, 17 December, 1810. Resigned 1 August, 1812.
HERMANS, HALSTEAD.
Mate, 28 June, 1864. Resigned 20 May, 1865.
HERNDON, CUMBERLAND G.
Assistant Surgeon, 3 May, 1874. Passed Assistant Surgeon, 23 March, 1878. Surgeon, 8 February, 1890.
HERNDON, PRESTON.
Lieutenant, Junior Grade (Spanish-American War), 18 July, 1898. Honorably discharged 13 September, 1898.

GENERAL NAVY REGISTER.

HERNDON, W. L.
  Midshipman, 1 November, 1828. Passed Midshipman, 14 June, 1834. Lieutenant, 25 February, 1841. Commander, 14 September, 1855. Lost 12 September, 1857.
HEROLD, JAMES.
  Boatswain, 21 January, 1862. Warranted 30 September, 1862. Died at Washington, D. C., 10 July, 1869.
HERON, JAMES.
  Midshipman, 19 October, 1841. Dismissed 3 March, 1849.
HERON, JAMES.
  Mate, 4 June, 1866. Boatswain, 16 April, 1873. Retired List, 30 June, 1885. Died 27 March, 1893.
HERR, BENJAMIN W.
  Mate, 24 November, 1863. Acting Ensign, 13 March, 1865. Honorably discharged 12 October, 1865.
HERRICK, EDWARD.
  Acting Master, 19 April, 1862. Dismissed 8 March, 1865.
HERRICK, RICHARD P.
  Mate, 3 August, 1863. Resigned 13 March, 1865.
HERRING, BENJAMIN.
  Third Assistant Engineer, 11 August, 1860. Dismissed 8 July, 1861.
HERRING, WILLIAM H.
  Mate, 9 January, 1862. Gunner, 4 February, 1863. Warranted 8 March, 1864. Dismissed 18 July, 1864. Restored on probation. Dismissed 8 June, 1865.
HERRING, WILLIAM J.
  Acting Ensign, 1 July, 1864. Honorably discharged 15 November, 1868.
HERRON, JAMES O.
  Acting Third Assistant Engineer, 29 September, 1864. Honorably discharged 30 October, 1865.
HERRON, JOHN.
  Acting Second Assistant Engineer, 12 March, 1863. Honorably discharged 29 October, 1865.
HERRON, JOHN E.
  Midshipman, 1 January, 1816. Resigned 28 August, 1822.
HERRON, THOMAS G.
  Mate, 1 October, 1862. Acting Ensign, 16 February, 1864. Honorably discharged 5 September, 1865.
HERRON, WILLIAM C.
  Mate, 1 October, 1862. Promoted to Acting Ensign, 6 June, 1863. Resigned 22 August, 1863.
HERSHEY, ANDREW H.
  Acting Assistant Surgeon, 2 July, 1862. Died 6 February, 1863.
HERSHEY, BENJAMIN J.
  Acting Assistant Surgeon, 14 December, 1861. Resigned 31 August, 1864.
HERTY, JAMES W.
  Assistant Surgeon, 30 November, 1859. Dismissed 17 December, 1861.
HERWIG, HENRY.
  Assistant Engineer, 9 September, 1874. Passed Assistant Engineer, 22 May, 1880. Chief Engineer, 21 March, 1895. Retired List, 28 January, 1896. Died 21 June, 1898.
HESLER, FREDERICK A.
  Assistant Surgeon, 3 June, 1884. Passed Assistant Surgeon, 3 June, 1888. Surgeon, 7 May, 1898.
HESLEWOOD, FREDERICK.
  Mate, 22 January, 1864. Appointment revoked (sick) 17 June, 1864. Mate, 24 August, 1864. Died at New Orleans, Louisiana, 25 September, 1867.
HASLIP, JOSEPH.
  Midshipman, 16 January, 1809. Resigned 16 May, 1809.
HESSE, FREDERICK G.
  Professor, 18 May, 1861. Resigned 2 May, 1863.
HESSELBACHER, C. C.
  Mate, 1 February, 1870. Resigned 9 July, 1873.
HESTER, ISAAC W.
  Midshipman, 12 October, 1848. Passed Midshipman, 15 June, 1854. Master, 15 September, 1855. Lieutenant, 16 September, 1855. Died 18 January, 1859.
HETH, JOHN.
  Midshipman, 25 June, 1814. Resigned 1 May, 1822.
HETHERINGTON, JAMES H.
  Cadet Midshipman, 9 June, 1874. Graduated 4 June, 1880. Ensign, Junior Grade, 3 March, 1883. Ensign, 26 June, 1884. Lieutenant, Junior Grade, 20 September, 1890. Lieutenant, 9 December, 1894.
HETHERINGTON, JOHN.
  Mate, 18 December, 1863. Deserted 7 June, 1865.
HETRICK, SAMUEL S.
  Acting Second Assistant Engineer, 16 August, 1862. Resigned 5 April, 1865.
HEWES, CHARLES H.
  Cadet Engineer, 1 October, 1880. Graduated, 4 June, 1884. Ensign, 1 July, 1886. Resigned 5 June, 1888. Appointed Assistant Naval Constructor, 6 June, 1888. Died 18 March, 1890.
HEWES, JOSHUA D.
  Acting Second Assistant Engineer, 28 September, 1863. Honorably discharged 9 August, 1865.
HEWETT, HAROLD H.
  Ensign (Spanish-American War), 25 May, 1898. Resigned 1 August, 1898.

HEWITT, EDWARD L.
　Third Assistant Engineer, 24 February, 1862.   Second Assistant Engineer, 15 October, 1863.   Resigned 2 November, 1866.
HEWITT, ISAAC B.
　Acting Second Assistant Engineer, 1 November, 1862.   Acting First Assistant Engineer, 3 October, 1863.   Honorably discharged 24 September, 1865.
HEWITT, THOMAS.
　Midshipman, 29 June, 1798.   Resigned 23 November, 1798.
HEWITT, WILLIAM.
　Midshipman, 31 March, 1840.   Resigned 26 December, 1840.
HEWLETT, FELIX.
　Boatswain, 25 August, 1851.   Warranted 2 July, 1853.   Died 1 August, 1854.
HEWRIE, DANIEL.
　Midshipman, 4 January, 1833.   Resigned 5 May, 1838.
HEWSON, ALBERT.
　Mate.   Resigned 10 August, 1863.
HEWSON, ALFRED H.
　Acting Boatswain, 31 August, 1899.
HEWSON, MICHAEL J.
　Ensign (Spanish-American War), 13 July, 1898.   Honorably discharged 22 November, 1898.
HEYDON, CALEB.
　Carpenter, 5 November, 1814.   Resigned 2 March, 1815.
HEYERMAN, OSCAR FREDERICK.
　Midshipman, 30 November, 1861.   Graduated 22 November, 1864.   Ensign, 1 November, 1866.   Master, 1 December, 1866.   Lieutenant, 12 March, 1868.   Lieutenant-Commander, 13 October, 1869.   Commander, 19 May, 1886.   Retired List, 14 June, 1895.   Died 27 October, 1895.-
HEYL, THEODORE C.
　Assistant Surgeon, 21 March, 1870.   Passed Assistant Surgeon, 10 October, 1874.   Surgeon, 15 October, 1881.   Retired List, 3 December, 1891.   Died 21 March, 1896.
HEYLIN, L. C.
　Midshipman, 1 January, 1817.   Resigned 16 January, 1826.
HEYWOOD, CHARLES.
　Midshipman, 1 November, 1826.   Passed Midshipman, 28 April, 1832.   Lieutenant, 8 March, 1837.   Died 16 January, 1853.
HIBBEN, HENRY B.
　Chaplain, 2 July, 1864.   Died 13 June, 1890.
HIBBERT, STEPHEN D.
　Third Assistant Engineer, 26 February. 1851.   Second Assistant Engineer, 21 May, 1853.   First Assistant Engineer, 9 May, 1857.   Chief Engineer, 29 June, 1861.   Retired List, 24 August, 1889.   Died 12 March, 1897.
HIBBETT, CHARLES T.
　Assistant Surgeon, 15 January, 1875.   Passed Assistant Surgeon, 30 April, 1880.   Surgeon, 26 December, 1892.
HIBBS, FRANK W.
　Naval Cadet, 4 September, 1883.   Assistant Engineer, 1 July, 1889.   Assistant Naval Constructor, 1 July, 1891.   Naval Constructor, 11 November, 1897.
HICHBORN, PHILIP.
　Assistant Naval Constructor, 26 June, 1869.   Naval Constructor, 12 March, 1875.   Chief Constructor, 12 July, 1893, to 4 March, 1901.
HICKEY, CHARLES.
　Acting Third Assistant Engineer, 18 April, 1863.   Acting Second Assistant Engineer, 27 January, 1865.   Honorably discharged 9 November, 1865.
HICKEY, JAMES A.
　Acting Warrant Machinist, 23 August, 1899.
HICKEY, JOHN K.
　Acting Third Assistant Engineer, 18 May, 1863.   Acting Second Assistant Engineer, 12 November, 1863.   Honorably discharged 21 August, 1865.
HICKEY, MICHAEL.
　Mate, 12 September, 1861.   Acting Master, 19 November. 1863.   Honorably discharged 27 December, 1865.   Boatswain, 9 July, 1866.   Died 30 April, 1876.
HICKS, A. H.
　Mate, 12 November, 1861.   Acting Ensign, gallant conduct in action, 1 June, 1863.   Resigned 30 March, 1865.
HICKS, CHARLES N.
　Acting Ensign, 13 September, 1862.   Honorably discharged 20 September, 1868.
HICKS, THOMAS H.
　Assistant Paymaster, 27 May, 1892.   Passed Assistant Paymaster, 7 April, 1894.   Paymaster, 10 July, 1898.
HICKMAN, EDWARD.
　Midshipman, 18 June, 1812.   Resigned 8 November, 1812.
HIDER, ARTHUR J.
　Acting Ensign, 24 October, 1863.   Honorably discharged 25 July, 1865.   Acting Ensign, 11 September, 1866.   Resigned 4 May, 1867.
HIERDAHL, CHARLES.
　Gunner, 10 April, 1899.
HIERMAN, LEWIS.
　Assistant Surgeon, 8 February, 1802.   Surgeon, 27 November, 1804.   Died 19 May, 1833.
HIFFREN, WILLIAM.
　Acting Third Assistant Engineer, 22 April, 1863.   Resigned 18 April, 1864.
HIGBEE, JONAS S.
　Acting Master, 22 October, 1861.   Resigned 23 April, 1864.

GENERAL NAVY REGISTER.

HIGBEE, L. P.
  Midshipman, 1 November, 1826. Resigned 28 June, 1833.
HIGBEE, WILLIAM H.
  Acting Assistant Paymaster, 14 January, 1862. Resigned 16 January, 1864.
HIGBEE, WILLIAM P.
  Mate, 24 January, 1863. Acting Ensign, 4 February, 1864. Honorably discharged 8 September, 1865.
HIGDON, BENEDICT.
  Midshipman, 1 January, 1812. Discharged 5 May, 1814.
HIGGINBOTHAM, GEORGE B.
  Acting Assistant Surgeon, 24 September, 1861. Honorably discharged 13 February, 1866.
HIGGINBOTHAM, J. L.
  Midshipman, 31 October, 1799. Lieutenant, 18 March, 1801. Last appearance on Records of Navy Department, 3 January, 1801. Furloughed.
HIGGINBOTHAM, WILLIAM H.
  Acting Ensign, Admiral Farragut's Staff, 1 April, 1864. Killed in battle, 5 August, 1864.
HIGGINS, ANTHONY.
  Acting Third Assistant Engineer, 14 July, 1864. Honorably discharged 9 August, 1865.
HIGGINS, EDWARD.
  Midshipman, 23 January, 1836. Passed Midshipman, 1 July, 1842. Master, 30 May, 1849. Lieutenant, 20 August, 1849. Resigned 16 February, 1854.
HIGGINS, ELIAS B.
  Mate, 28 October, 1862. Appointment revoked (sick) 26 August, 1863.
HIGGINS, JAMES.
  Midshipman, 13 March, 1839. Passed Midshipman, 2 July, 1845. Master, 25 February, 1854. Lieutenant, 6 October, 1854. Resigned 31 December, 1856.
HIGGINS, JAMES.
  Acting Third Assistant Engineer, 13 May, 1864. Discharged 20 August, 1864.
HIGGINS, JESSE.
  Midshipman, 1 January, 1812. Last appearance on Records of Navy Department, 1815. Furloughed.
HIGGINS, ROBERT B.
  Cadet Engineer, 1 October, 1878. Honorably discharged 30 June, 1884. Assistant Engineer, 1 July, 1884. Passed Assistant Engineer, 15 January, 1895. Rank changed to Lieutenant, 3 March, 1899.
HIGGINS, THOMAS.
  Acting Assistant Paymaster, 29 August, 1864. Honorably discharged 23 August, 1865.
HIGGINS, WILLIAM P.
  Acting Third Assistant Engineer, 9 September, 1862. Resigned 28 April, 1865.
HIGGINSON, FRANCIS J.
  Acting Midshipman, 21 September, 1857. Graduated 18 July, 1862. Acting Master. Lieutenant, 1 August, 1862. Lieutenant-Commander, 25 July, 1866. Commander, 10 June, 1876. Captain, 27 September, 1891. Commodore, 10 August, 1898. Rear-Admiral, 3 March, 1899.
HIGH, WARREN, E. G.
  Assistant Surgeon (Spanish-American War), 13 July, 1898. Appointed Assistant Surgeon in Regular Service, 7 June, 1900.
HIGINBOTHAM, D.
  Midshipman, 18 June, 1812. Died 15 October, 1817.
HIGMAN, WILLIAM.
  Acting Second Assistant Engineer, 24 August, 1864. Honorably discharged 30 November, 1865.
HILAND, MARTIN.
  Acting Third Assistant Engineer, 31 December, 1864. Honorably discharged 4 October, 1865.
HILAND, THOMAS.
  Assistant Surgeon, 22 November, 1861. Passed Assistant Surgeon, 28 June, 1865. Surgeon, 7 June, 1869. Retired List, 13 March, 1883.
HILDBURG, LOUIS.
  Mate. Resigned 31 December, 1862.
HILDERBRAND, BALTHASER.
  Acting Third Assistant Engineer, 28 August, 1862. Resigned 11 March, 1863.
HILDRETH, C. F. P.
  Acting Assistant Surgeon, 28 October, 1862. Resigned 4 February, 1864.
HILL, ALONZO A. T.
  Assistant Surgeon, 14 March, 1848. Resigned 6 April, 1854.
HILL, CHARLES H.
  Acting Assistant Paymaster, 26 December, 1863. Mustered out 12 April, 1866.
HILL, CHARLES H.
  Cadet Midshipman, 24 September, 1875. Graduated 22 June, 1882. Ensign, Junior Grade, 3 March, 1883. Resigned 30 June, 1884.
HILL, CHARLES J.
  Mate, 8 May, 1862. Acting Ensign, 5 June, 1863. Resigned 20 March, 1866.
HILL, EBEN B.
  Acting Third Assistant Engineer, 18 March, 1863. Acting Second Assistant Engineer, 20 May, 1864. Honorably discharged 5 November, 1865.
HILL, FRANK K.
  Cadet Engineer, 1 October, 1880. Ensign 1 July, 1886. Lieutenant, Junior Grade, 15 June, 1895. Lieutenant, 7 June, 1898.

HILL, FREDERICK P.
Ensign (Spanish-American War), 13 July, 1898. Honorably discharged 30 September, 1898.
HILL, FREDERICK S.
Acting Master, 12 July, 1861. Acting Volunteer Lieutenant, 11 December, 1862. Honorably discharged 12 May, 1865.
HILL, GEORGE E.
Acting Master, 7 October, 1861. Honorably discharged 13 September, 1865.
HILL, HENRY.
Acting Second Assistant Engineer, 17 October, 1861. Acting First Assistant Engineer, 4 February, 1863. Dismissed 16 September, 1863.
HILL, HENRY D.
Master, 16 June, 1814. Died 10 March, 1820.
HILL, JAMES.
Mate, 19 March, 1870. Retired List, 16 September, 1897.
HILL, JAMES.
Acting Third Assistant Engineer, 31 August, 1864. Resigned 9 June, 1865.
HILL, JOHN, JR.
Midshipman, 6 February, 1809. Lieutenant, 27 April, 1816. Discharged by Court-martial, 6 October, 1819.
HILL, JOHN.
Mate, 7 January, 1862. Dismissed 16 August, 1862.
HILL, JOHN.
Acting Ensign, 1 October, 1862. Resigned 5 March, 1864.
HILL, JOHN.
Acting Ensign, 25 November, 1863. Honorably discharged 5 December, 1865.
HILL, JOHN A.
Acting Third Assistant Engineer, 15 February, 1862. Appointment revoked 4 November, 1862. Acting First Assistant Engineer, 30 June, 1863. Honorably discharged 8 December, 1865.
HILL, JOHN.
Acting Warrant Machinist, 23 August, 1899.
HILL, JOHN S.
Acting Third Assistant Engineer, 18 December, 1863. Honorably discharged 28 October, 1865.
HILL, JOHN W.
Acting Assistant Paymaster, 4 November, 1862. Died on the Sea Foam, 1 October, 1863.
HILL, JOSEPH.
Gunner, 23 March, 1895.
HILL, JUSTUS.
Boatswain, 4 April, 1827. Last appearance on Records of Navy Department, 1832. Dead.
HILL, LEONARD W.
Acting Master, 28 August, 1861. Resigned 25 February, 1865.
HILL, OREN T.
Acting Third Assistant Engineer, 9 February, 1864. Appointment revoked (sick) 8 August, 1864.
HILL, OWEN.
Acting Gunner, 10 March, 1900.
HILL, PATRICK.
Gunner, 29 October, 1898.
HILL, RICHARD J.
Gunner, 28 April, 1860. Retired List, 19 February, 1883.
HILL, ROBERT.
Midshipman, 16 January, 1809. Resigned 30 October, 1809.
HILL, STEPHEN C.
Acting Ensign, 13 May, 1863. Resigned 25 April, 1865. Acting Ensign, 19 December, 1866. Mustered out 10 June, 1868.
HILL, THOMAS K.
Acting Third Assistant Engineer, 9 June, 1863. Honorably discharged 21 August, 1865.
HILL, THOMAS QUINCEY.
Acting Assistant Paymaster, 17 December, 1861. Resigned 1 August, 1863.
HILL, WILLIAM.
Sailmaker, 8 June, 1798. Warrant returned.
HILL, WILLIAM E.
Midshipman, 28 June, 1804. Resigned 2 April, 1808.
HILL, WILLIAM L.
Boatswain, 19 September, 1881. Chief Boatswain, 3 March, 1899.
HILLAR, BENJAMIN.
Lieutenant, 31 October, 1798. Commander, 8 February, 1800. Last appearance on Records of Navy Department.
HILLARD, CHARLES C.
Acting Master, 16 May, 1861. Died on Relief, 3 February, 1862.
HILLER, EDWARD.
Acting Master's Mate, 26 July, 1861. Dismissed 29 October, 1861. Mate, 24 September, 1869. Resigned 28 February, 1870
HILLIARD, JOHN E.
Acting Third Assistant Engineer, 27 July, 1863. Acting Second Assistant Engineer, 15 September, 1864. Honorably discharged 24 August, 1867.
HILLIARD, JOSEPH L.
Acting First Assistant Engineer, 1 October, 1862. Honorably discharged 7 November, 1865.

GENERAL NAVY REGISTER.

HILLING, CHARLES J.
　Acting Third Assistant Engineer, 5 June, 1863. Acting Second Assistant Engineer, 12 June, 1863. Honorably discharged 29 November, 1865.
HILLMAN, JAMES C.
　Acting Third Assistant Engineer, 14 September, 1864. Resigned 30 May, 1865.
HILLMAN, JULIUS.
　Acting Third Assistant Engineer, 3 March, 1864. Honorably discharged 9 August, 1865.
HILLS, FREDERICK C.
　Acting Assistant Paymaster, 11 September, 1862. Resigned 12 December, 1864.
HILLS, WILLIAM D.
　Sailmaker, 4 October, 1831. Resigned 27 July, 1832.
HILTON, OSGOOD H.
　Carpenter, 5 February, 1886. Chief Carpenter, 3 March, 1899. Retired List, 6 August, 1900.
HINCKLEY, ALEXANDER.
　Acting Ensign, 13 May, 1864. Honorably discharged 19 September, 1865.
HINCKLEY, NATHANIEL B.
　Mate, 7 March, 1864. Resigned 17 May, 1865.
HINCKLEY, SAMUEL P.
　Assistant Engineer (Spanish-American War), 25 May, 1898. Honorably discharged 19 September, 1898.
HINCKLEY, THOMAS G.
　Acting Third Assistant Engineer, 10 December, 1861. Resigned 3 April, 1862.
HINDMAN, JAMES W.
　Acting First Assistant Engineer, 7 January, 1864. Honorably discharged 7 December, 1865.
HINDS, ALFRED W.
　Naval Cadet, 6 September, 1890. Assistant Engineer, 1 July, 1896. Rank changed to Ensign, 3 March, 1899. Lieutenant, Junior Grade, 1 July, 1899.
HINE, E. CURTISS.
　Gunner, 3 August, 1850. Resigned 1 November, 1852.
HINE, ROBERT B.
　Third Assistant Engineer, 24 August, 1861. Second Assistant Engineer, 21 April, 1863. First Assistant Engineer, 11 October, 1866. Chief Engineer, 14 December, 1882. Retired List, 20 February, 1893. Died 27 June, 1895.
HINES, BENJAMIN A.
　Mate, 13 February, 1864. Resigned 3 June, 1864.
HINES, GEORGE S.
　Mate, 20 December, 1861. Resigned 14 August, 1862.
HINES, JOHN C.
　Second Assistant Engineer, 21 November, 1837. Resigned 31 December, 1848.
HINES, JOHN F.
　Naval Cadet, 21 May, 1888. Ensign, 1 July, 1894. Lieutenant, Junior Grade, 3 March, 1899. Lieutenant, 1 July, 1900.
HINES, HAROLD K.
　Naval Cadet, 2 October, 1882. Ensign, 1 July, 1888. Lieutenant, Junior Grade, 18 November, 1896. Lieutenant, 3 March, 1899.
HINES, RICHARD B.
　Mate, 6 February, 1862. Acting Master, 26 May, 1862. Honorably discharged 7 February, 1866.
HINES, SAMUEL D.
　Gunner, 10 June, 1861. Retired List, 5 November, 1883. Died 23 October, 1884.
HINGERTY, ALFRED.
　Boatswain, 27 January, 1842. Retired List, 12 May, 1865. Died 27 July, 1875.
HINMAN, FRANK H.
　Acting Assistant Paymaster, 31 March, 1863. Assistant Paymaster, 2 July, 1864. Paymaster, 4 May, 1866. Retired List, 9 April, 1889. Died 19 December, 1897.
HINMAN, JOEL R.
　Mate, 27 September, 1862. Resigned 16 April, 1863.
HINSDALE, SOLOMON R.
　Acting Assistant Paymaster, 28 June, 1862. Resigned 3 April, 1863.
HINSLEY, HOWARD E.
　Passed Assistant Paymaster (Spanish-American War), 17 June, 1898. Honorably discharged, 22 September, 1898.
HINTON, ABIJAH J.
　Midshipman, 17 February, 1800. Discharged 12 January, 1802, under Peace Establishment Act.
HINTON, A. C.
　Midshipman, 1 February, 1827. Resigned 28 October, 1833.
HINTON, STEPHEN.
　Acting First Assistant Engineer, 15 December, 1863. Honorably discharged 26 July, 1865.
HINSLINE, THOMAS W.
　Acting Third Assistant Engineer, 3 April, 1863. Acting Second Assistant Engineer, for cool and gallant conduct under fire of the enemy, 22 July, 1864. Honorably discharged 10 January, 1866. Acting Second Assistant Engineer, 17 March, 1866. Mustered out 27 August, 1867.
HIPKINS, B. G.
　Master, 4 August, 1807. Dismissed 28 July, 1812.
HIPKINS, LEROY.
　Master, 4 August, 1807. Died in October, 1808.

GENERAL NAVY REGISTER.

HIRSCH, CHARLES F.
  Acting Third Assistant Engineer, 17 February, 1864. Acting Second Assistant Engineer, 10 February, 1865. Honorably discharged 31 October, 1865.
HITCH, ANSEL S.
  Mate, 5 March, 1862. Acting Ensign, 11 October, 1864. Honorably discharged 6 March, 1868.
HITCHBORN, J. B.
  Lieutenant, 3 March, 1799. Last appearance on Records of Navy Department, 17 April, 1799.
HITCHBORN, J. B.
  Midshipman, 8 August, 1799. Resigned 26 May, 1801.
HITCHCOCK, JAMES D.
  Acting Third Assistant Engineer, 4 September, 1861. Appointment revoked (sick) 28 March, 1863.
HITCHCOCK, ROBERT B.
  Midshipman, 1 January, 1825. Passed Midshipman, 4 June, 1831. Lieutenant, 3 March, 1835. Commander, 14 September, 1855. Captain, 16 July, 1862. Commodore, 16 July, 1862. Retired List, 25 September, 1866. Died 24 March, 1888.
HITCHCOCK, ROSWELL D., Jr.
  Midshipman, 18 January, 1862. Graduated September, 1865. Ensign, 1 December, 1866. Master, 12 March, 1868. Lieutenant, 26 March, 1869. Lieutenant-Commander, 26 November, 1880. Commander, 15 October, 1890. Died 3 December, 1892.
HITCHCOCK, WILLIAM.
  Mate. Dismissed 11 March, 1862.
HITCHCOCK, WILLIAM A.
  Chaplain, 8 October, 1862. Resigned 25 November, 1867.
HITE, JACOB.
  Midshipman, 2 April, 1804. Died 17 May, 1813.
HITE, JOHN M.
  Assistant Engineer (Spanish-American War), 14 May, 1898. Honorably discharged 22 December, 1898.
HITTINGER, GEORGE.
  Gunner, 28 October, 1890. Killed 13 June, 1892.
HIVLING, W. H.
  Mate, 23 June, 1862. Died on Magnolia, 12 September, 1862.
HIXON, JOHN V.
  Midshipman, 29 June, 1835. Resigned 4 February, 1841.
HIXON, SAMUEL C.
  Master, 30 April, 1814. Died 9 September, 1840.
HOAGLAND, FRANK L.
  Gunner, 13 February, 1893.
HOAKE, GEORGE F.
  Acting Third Assistant Engineer, 12 August, 1863. Appointment revoked (sick) 23 November, 1863.
HOARD, SAMUEL.
  Sailmaker, 10 July, 1823. Resigned 6 October, 1823.
HOBAN, EDWARD.
  Midshipman, 1 February, 1823. Resigned 13 April, 1830.
HOBAN, FRANCIS P.
  Midshipman, 28 April, 1831. Resigned 31 August, 1837.
HOBART, DAVID.
  Acting Master, 1 October, 1861. Appointment revoked (sick) 28 October, 1861.
HOBART, GEORGE.
  Midshipman, 6 December, 1814. Last appearance on Records of Navy Department, 15 December, 1815.
HOBBS, GEORGE E.
  Acting Third Assistant Engineer, 24 October, 1864. Honorably discharged 28 October, 1865.
HOBBS, H. H.
  Midshipman, 4 March, 1815. Lieutenant, 13 January, 1825. Died 3 April, 1836.
HOBBS, JAMES.
  Acting Ensign, 1 December, 1864. Honorably discharged 4 January, 1865.
HOBBS, I. GOODWIN.
  Acting Assistant Paymaster, 31 August, 1864. Mustered out 18 July, 1865. Assistant Paymaster, 21 February, 1867. Passed Assistant Paymaster, 16 September, 1868. Paymaster, 15 May, 1879. Pay Inspector, 7 May, 1899.
HOBBS, NATHANIEL.
  Mate, 17 May, 1861. Acting Gunner, 22 September, 1862. Died on Tennessee, 8 July, 1863.
HOBBS, SETH J.
  Acting Third Assistant Engineer, 29 June, 1864. Honorably discharged 2 June, 1868.
HOBBY, JAMES M.
  Third Assistant Engineer, 31 October, 1848. Second Assistant Engineer, 26 February, 1851. Resigned 21 June, 1855. Second Assistant Engineer, 4 June, 1861. First Assistant Engineer, 2 May, 1863. Retired List, 19 October, 1870. Died 17 November, 1882.
HOBBY, THOMAS F.
  Acting Warrant Machinist, 23 August, 1899.
HOBREEKER, THOMAS.
  Acting Third Assistant Engineer, 3 July, 1863. Resigned 5 October, 1863.
HOBSON, JOSEPH B.
  Midshipman, 25 July, 1865. Graduated June, 1869. Ensign, 12 July, 1870. Master, 2 November, 1871. Lieutenant, 25 January, 1876. Resigned 10 October, 1880.

HOBSON, RICHMOND P.
    Naval Cadet, 21 May, 1885. Assistant Naval Constructor, 1 July, 1891. Naval Constructor, 23 June, 1898.
HOCKETT, JONATHAN W.
    Acting Third Assistant Engineer, 4 February, 1863. Acting Second Assistant Engineer, 21 July, 1864. Honorably discharged 11 December, 1865.
HODDER, ERNEST.
    Mate, 31 July, 1862. Appointment revoked 23 December, 1862. Mate, 3 June, 1863. Appointment revoked (sick) 14 September, 1863.
HODEMAN, JOHN D.
    Acting Ensign, 28 November, 1863. Honorably discharged 20 October, 1865.
HODGDON, CHARLES A.
    Acting Ensign, 31 March, 1863. Dismissed 17 April, 1866.
HODGDON, CHARLES O.
    Acting Assistant Paymaster, 27 December, 1864. Mustered out 25 September, 1865.
HODGDON, J. H.
    Acting Master, 21 May, 1861. Died 23 April, 1862.
HODGE, GEORGE.
    Boatswain, 11 May, 1798. Died 19 September, 1820.
HODGE, GEORGE B.
    Midshipman, 16 December, 1845. Resigned 25 January, 1850.
HODGE, KOSKY.
    Mate, 1 February, 1863. Resigned 5 May, 1863.
HODGE, S. A.
    Acting Ensign, 25 July, 1862. Dismissed 21 February, 1863.
HODGES, BEN W.
    Cadet Midshipman, 23 September, 1873. Graduated 18 June, 1879. Midshipman, 18 June, 1879, to 24 February, 1881. Ensign, 24 February, 1881. Lieutenant, Junior Grade, 30 June, 1887. Lieutenant, 7 February, 1893. Lieutenant-Commander, 1 July, 1900.
HODGES, HARRY M.
    Midshipman, 29 September, 1870. Graduated 21 June, 1875. Ensign, 11 July, 1877. Lieutenant, Junior Grade, 24 August, 1883. Lieutenant, 9 September, 1889. Lieutenant-Commander, 3 March, 1899.
HODGES, HENRY L. M.
    Acting Second Assistant Engineer, 26 April, 1864. Honorably discharged 17 October, 1865.
HODGES, JAMES.
    Midshipman, 9 November, 1813. Died in March, 1824.
HODGES, JAMES B.
    Midshipman, 13 October, 1848. Resigned 14 January, 1852.
HODGKINS, CHARLES F.
    Acting Ensign, 8 October, 1863. Acting Master, 27 March, 1865. Honorably discharged 31 July, 1865. Acting Master, 9 October, 1867. Mustered out 23 February, 1869.
HODGKINSON, WILLIAM F.
    Acting Ensign, 27 June, 1864. Honorably discharged 19 November, 1868.
HODGSON, ALBON C.
    Midshipman, 5 June, 1871. Graduated 21 June, 1875. Ensign, 18 July, 1876. Master, 15 November, 1881. Lieutenant, Junior Grade, 3 March, 1883. Lieutenant, 28 May, 1888. Lieutenant-Commander, 3 March, 1899.
HODGSON, RICHARD M.
    Third Assistant Engineer, 9 December, 1861. Second Assistant Engineer, 8 September, 1863. Resignation accepted 6 January, 1866.
HODSON, DANIEL W.
    Mate, 4 April, 1862. Acting Ensign, 23 October, 1863. Died at New Orleans, La., 24 September, 1866.
HOEHLING, ADOLPH A.
    Assistant Surgeon, 24 January, 1862. Passed Assistant Surgeon, 5 March, 1866. Surgeon, 2 October, 1867. Medical Inspector, 31 January, 1885. Medical Director, 11 May, 1893. Retired List, 14 June, 1895.
HOEL, WILLIAM R.
    Acting Volunteer Lieutenant, 29 April, 1862. Acting Volunteer Lieutenant-Commander, 10 November, 1864. Honorably discharged 30 December, 1865.
HOES, ROSWELL R.
    Chaplain, 26 July, 1882.
HOFF, ARTHUR B.
    Naval Cadet, 28 September, 1885. Ensign, 1 July, 1891. Lieutenant, Junior Grade, 17 July, 1898. Lieutenant, 3 March, 1899.
HOFF, HENRY K.
    Midshipman, 28 October, 1823. Passed Midshipman, 23 March, 1829. Lieutenant, 3 March, 1831. Commander, 6 February, 1854. Captain, 30 June, 1861. Commodore, 16 July, 1862. Rear-Admiral, 13 April, 1867. Retired List, 19 September, 1868. Died 25 December, 1878.
HOFF, JEREMIAH B.
    Acting Assistant Paymaster, 26 August, 1864. Mustered out 7 November, 1865.
HOFF, WILLIAM.
    Boatswain, 23 October, 1841. Resigned 8 December, 1849.
HOFF, WILLIAM BAINBRIDGE.
    Acting Midshipman, 24 October, 1860. Acting Ensign, 1 October, 1863. Master, 10 May, 1866. Lieutenant, 21 February, 1867. Lieutenant-Commander, 12 March, 1868. Commander, 7 August, 1881. Captain, 10 May, 1895. Retired List, 13 March, 1897.
HOFFAN, W. B.
    Acting Assistant Surgeon, 9 December, 1862. Resigned 23 December, 1863.

HOFFMAN, BENJAMIN A.
  Acting Second Assistant Engineer, 1 October, 1862. Promoted Acting First Assistant Engineer, 7 February, 1863. Honorably discharged 20 September, 1865.
HOFFMAN, B. V.
  Midshipman, 4 July, 1805. Lieutenant, 21 May, 1812. Commander, 5 March, 1817. Captain, 7 March, 1829. Died 10 December, 1834.
HOFFMAN, FRANK J.
  Cadet Engineer, 1 October, 1872. Graduated 30 May, 1874. Assistant Engineer, 26 February, 1875. Passed Assistant Engineer, 16 September, 1881. Resigned 11 June, 1889.
HOFFMAN, J. D.
  Civil Engineer, 18 August, 1866. Commissioned, 28 March, 1867. Resigned 12 July, 1868.
HOFFMAN, JOHN C.
  Acting Carpenter, 13 September, 1862. Appointment revoked 20 February, 1864.
HOFFMAN, OGDEN.
  Midshipman, 31 December, 1814. Last appearance on Records of Navy Department, February, 1816. Resigned.
HOFFMAN, R. K.
  Surgeon, 16 July, 1814. Resigned 16 July, 1825.
HOFFMAN, WILLIAM D.
  Acting Assistant Surgeon, 3 December, 1862. Resigned 23 December, 1863. Acting Assistant Surgeon, 7 March, 1864. Honorably discharged 1 September, 1865.
HOFFMAN, W. G.
  Midshipman, 19 October, 1841. Passed Midshipman, 10 August, 1847. Resigned 14 August, 1851.
HOFFNER, GEORGE D.
  Acting Master, 18 October, 1861. Resigned 7 February, 1863.
HOFSTRAND, OSKAR.
  Warrant Machinist (Spanish-American War), 15 June, 1898. Honorably discharged, 2 September, 1898.
HOFFNER, RICHARD J.
  Acting Master, 28 September, 1861. Died 21 September, 1865.
HOGAN, THOMAS J.
  Cadet Engineer, 1 October, 1874. Graduated 10 June, 1881. Honorably discharged, 30 June, 1883. Restored to service 10 March, 1886, as an Assistant Engineer, to rank from 1 July, 1883. Resigned 12 October, 1886.
HOGE, FRANCIS L.
  Acting Midshipman, 20 September, 1856. Midshipman, 15 June, 1860. Dismissed 4 June, 1861.
HOGG, CHARLES B.
  Mate, 14 March, 1864. Deserted 2 May, 1864.
HOGG, JAMES M.
  Mate, 14 May, 1862. Gunner, 10 July, 1862. Retired List, 17 March, 1887. Died 7 February, 1888.
HOGG, WILLIAM S.
  Midshipman, 24 September, 1872. Graduated 20 June, 1876. Ensign, 10 March, 1880. Lieutenant, Junior Grade, 5 August, 1886. Lieutenant, 5 May, 1892. Lieutenant-Commander, 8 December, 1899.
HOGGATT, WILFORD B.
  Cadet Midshipman, 11 June, 1880. Ensign, 1 July, 1886. Lieutenant, Junior Grade, 21 May, 1895. Resigned 1 August, 1898.
HOHN, GEORGE T.
  Mate, 10 January, 1865. Deserted 20 July, 1866.
HOLBROOK, ELIPHALET.
  Mate, 5 March, 1862. Resigned 2 June, 1864.
HOLBROOK, HENRY E.
  Mate, 20 November, 1862. Resigned 30 June, 1863. Mate, 9 June, 1864. Appointment revoked 9 July, 1864.
HOLBROOK, JOHN A.
  Sailmaker, 3 January, 1862. Died 2 January, 1866.
HOLBROOK, SAMUEL F.
  Acting Master, 21 March, 1862. Appointment revoked 27 June, 1864.
HOLBROOK, S. F.
  Carpenter, 27 June, 1815. Last appearance on Records of Navy Department, 30 June, 1815.
HOLCOMB, JOHN.
  Midshipman, 1 September, 1811. Last appearance on Records of Navy Department, 13 July, 1812. Dead.
HOLCOMB, RICHMOND C.
  Assistant Surgeon, 2 December, 1898.
HOLCOMB, WILLIAM L.
  Acting Ensign, 10 October, 1862. Acting Master, 16 June, 1864. Honorably discharged 4 January, 1866.
HOLCOMBE, ALBERT A.
  Midshipman, 1 April, 1828. Passed Midshipman, 14 June, 1834. Lieutenant, 25 February, 1841. Reserved List, 13 September, 1855. Died 9 August, 1858.
HOLCOMBE, JOHN H. L.
  Cadet Midshipman, 27 June, 1874. Graduated 4 June, 1880. Ensign, 1 July, 1882. Lieutenant, Junior Grade, 24 October, 1889. Lieutenant, 10 July, 1894.
HOLDEN, EDGAR.
  Assistant Surgeon, 3 October, 1861. Resigned 12 October, 1864.
HOLDEN, EDWARD S.
  Professor, 21 March, 1873. Resigned 1 June, 1882.

GENERAL NAVY REGISTER.

HOLDEN, JOHN J.
    Boatswain, 27 November, 1896.
HOLDEN, JONAS H.
    Naval Cadet, 20 May, 1892. Ensign, 6 May, 1898.
HOLDEN, OLIVER B.
    Acting Gunner, 25 June, 1862. Resigned 30 May, 1863. Acting Ensign, 28 November, 1864. Honorably discharged 19 August, 1865.
HOLDEN, WILLIAM R.
    Acting Second Assistant Engineer, 10 July, 1863. Appointment revoked (sick) 23 February, 1865.
HOLDEN, W. S.
    Mate, 16 May, 1864. Resigned 17 January, 1865.
HOLDSWORTH, WILLIAM F.
    Boatswain, 1 March, 1900.
HOLLAND, DICK. V. B.
    Midshipman, 23 February, 1849. Dropped 12 July, 1849.
HOLLAND, JAMES G.
    Acting Assistant Paymaster, 8 July, 1863. Mustered out 9 January, 1866.
HOLLAND, JOHN.
    Acting Third Assistant Engineer, 20 March, 1865. Appointment revoked 8 January, 1866.
HOLLAND, JOHN C.
    Purser, 1 June, 1838. Resigned 24 November, 1844.
HOLLAND, THOMAS.
    Mate, 19 May, 1862. Acting Gunner, 18 September, 1863. Honorably discharged 15 January, 1866.
HOLLAND, WILLIAM.
    Acting Third Assistant Engineer, 2 December, 1864. Honorably discharged 2 November, 1868.
HOLLAND, WILLIAM.
    Acting Assistant Paymaster, 6 April, 1865. Honorably discharged 17 October, 1865.
HOLLAND, WILLIAM.
    Second Assistant Engineer, 23 March, 1848. First Assistant Engineer, 26 February, 1851. Died 18 August, 1856.
HOLLAND, ZACH.
    Midshipman, 1 June, 1827. Passed Midshipman, 10 June, 1833. Lieutenant, 28 February, 1838. Discharged 30 October, 1848.
HOLLER, FRANK.
    Mate, 17 April. 1866. Retired List, 27 December, 1894.
HOLLEY, ROBERT Y.
    Acting Master, 3 September, 1861. Honorably discharged 14 January, 1868.
HOLLIDAY, WALTER S.
    Midshipman, 27 June, 1866. Graduated 7 June, 1870. Ensign, 13 July, 1871. Master, 2 December, 1873. Died 29 January, 1875.
HOLLIHAN, JAMES W.
    Third Assistant Engineer, 8 December, 1862. Second Assistant Engineer, 8 April, 1864. First Assistant Engineer, 6 June, 1868. Retired List, 31 October, 1879.
HOLLINGSWORTH, CHARLES F.
    Third Assistant Engineer, 29 October, 1861. Second Assistant Engineer, 3 August, 1863. Resigned 11 September, 1865.
HOLLINGSWORTH, JAMES.
    Acting Third Assistant Engineer, 18 April, 1863. Honorably discharged 24 November, 1865.
HOLLINGSWORTH, WILLIAM.
    Purser, 21 May, 1799. Resigned 4 November, 1799.
HOLLINGSWORTH, WILLIAM.
    Purser, 22 September, 1800. Discharged 21 September, 1801, under Peace Establishment Act, at his request.
HOLLINS, GEORGE N.
    Midshipman, 1 February, 1814. Lieutenant, 13 January, 1825. Commander, 8 September, 1845. Captain, 14 September, 1855. Dismissed 6 June, 1861.
HOLLINS, JOHN.
    Third Assistant Engineer, 25 July, 1854. Second Assistant Engineer, 9 May, 1857. Died 4 June, 1858.
HOLLINS, THOMAS.
    Mate, 8 August, 1862. Dismissed 25 October, 1864.
HOLLIS, GEORGE F.
    Acting Ensign, 20 August, 1862. Acting Master, 7 June, 1864. Honorably discharged 10 September, 1865.
HOLLIS, IRA N.
    Cadet Engineer, 1 October, 1874. Graduated 20 June, 1878. Assistant Engineer, 20 June, 1880. Passed Assistant Engineer, 19 February, 1889. Resigned 30 September, 1893.
HOLLOWAY, EDWARD O.
    Ensign (Spanish-American War), 25 May, 1898. Honorably discharged 15 September, 1898.
HOLLOWAY, GEORGE W.
    Acting Second Assistant Engineer, 9 September, 1862. Acting First Assistant Engineer, 20 September, 1862. Resigned 30 April, 1864. Acting First Assistant Engineer, 14 October, 1864. Honorably discharged 6 October, 1865.
HOLLOWAY, GIDEON E.
    Acting Ensign, 20 July, 1863. Acting Master, 25 May, 1865. Honorably discharged 27 May, 1869.

HOLLYDAY, RICHARD C.
  Civil Engineer, 15 March, 1894.
HOLM, SOREN G.
  Acting Ensign, 22 June, 1864. Honorably discharged 15 June, 1865.
HOLMAN, FREDERIC R.
  Naval Cadet, 19 May, 1893. Ensign, 1 July, 1899.
HOLMAN, GEORGE F. W.
  Midshipman, 25 July, 1866. Graduated 7 June, 1870. Ensign 13 July, 1871. Master, 14 June, 1874. Lieutenant, 1 January, 1881. Lieutenant-Commander, 3 March, 1899.
HOLMAN, JASPER.
  Acting Second Assistant Engineer, 3 October, 1863. Dismissed 27 May, 1865.
HOLMAN, JEROME B.
  Acting Third Assistant Engineer, 22 June, 1863. Honorably discharged 26 September, 1865.
HOLMAN, SAMUEL.
  Acting Assistant Surgeon, 22 June, 1864. Honorably discharged 2 October, 1865.
HOLMES, ALFRED C.
  Acting Gunner, 18 June, 1863. Honorably discharged 19 December, 1865.
HOLMES, ANTHONY F.
  Acting Ensign, 19 August, 1862. Acting Master, consideration of good service, 9 May, 1864. Honorably discharged 24 April 1869.
HOLMES, A. R.
  Acting Assistant Surgeon, 12 April, 1862. Acting Passed Assistant Surgeon, 14 May, 1866. Honorably discharged 3 July, 1868.
HOLMES, CHARLES M.
  Mate, 21 January, 1863. Resigned 31 December, 1863.
HOLMES, EDWARD W.
  Boatswain, 14 July, 1884. Resigned 22 January, 1886.
HOLMES, FRANK H.
  Midshipman, 29 June, 1870. Graduated 1 June, 1874. Ensign, 17 July, 1875. Master, 24 February, 1881. Lieutenant, Junior Grade, 3 March, 1883. Lieutenant, 29 January, 1887. Lieutenant-Commander, 3 March, 1899.
HOLMES, GEORGE H.
  Acting Master, 28 December, 1861. Honorably discharged 26 October, 1865.
HOLMES, HENRY.
  Third Assistant Engineer, 29 October, 1861. Second Assistant Engineer, 3 August, 1863. Resigned 11 September, 1865.
HOLMES, HERMAN G.
  Mate, 8 January, 1864. Honorably discharged 27 October, 1865.
HOLMES, JAMES F.
  Mate, 5 March, 1862. Acting Ensign, 6 December, 1862. Dismissed 1 October, 1863.
HOLMES, JAMES M.
  Acting Ensign, 17 December, 1862. Acting Master, 21 July, 1864. Honorably discharged 16 September, 1865.
HOLMES, JAMES M.
  Acting Ensign, 17 December, 1862. Resigned 2 June, 1863.
HOLMES, JOHN W.
  Carpenter, 7 March, 1815. Resigned 19 May, 1815.
HOLMES, J. WHELDEN.
  Acting Assistant Paymaster, 16 May, 1864. Mustered out 3 October, 1865.
HOLMES, LEWIS.
  Carpenter, 14 December, 1848. Dismissed 29 May, 1861.
HOLMES, PHILANDER J.
  Acting Third Assistant Engineer, 12 November, 1862. Honorably discharged 24 August, 1866.
HOLMES, ROBERT.
  Master, 24 March, 1809. Resigned 15 May, 1809.
HOLMES, SAMUEL P.
  Ensign (Spanish-American War), 9 May, 1898. Resigned 17 June, 1898.
HOLMES, SHEPLEY R.
  Acting Ensign, 26 October, 1863. Dismissed 13 April, 1864.
HOLMES, SILAS.
  Assistant Surgeon, 28 June, 1838. Passed Assistant Surgeon, 22 November, 1843. Drowned 21 May, 1849.
HOLMES, URBAN T.
  Naval Cadet, 13 September, 1886. Assistant Engineer, 1 July, 1892. Passed Assistant Engineer, 8 February, 1897. Rank changed to Lieutenant, 3 March, 1899.
HOLMES, WILLIAM.
  Acting Second Assistant Engineer, 18 April, 1863. Appointment revoked 18 May, 1864.
HOLMES, WILLIAM.
  Midshipman, 20 February, 1802. Died September, 1802.
HOLMES, WILLIAM.
  Midshipman, 9 June, 1811. Resigned 22 January, 1812.
HOLMES, WILLIAM C.
  Midshipman, 25 August, 1823. Passed Midshipman, 23 March, 1829. Resigned 18 October, 1832.
HOLMES, WILLIAM H.
  Acting Assistant Surgeon, 10 September, 1861. Honorably discharged 18 September, 1865.
HOLMES, WILLIAM W.
  Midshipman, 21 September, 1841. Passed Midshipman, 10 August, 1847. Dismissed 13 May, 1851.

GENERAL NAVY REGISTER. 273

HOLSINGER, GERALD L.
   Naval Cadet, 3 October, 1889. Graduated. Honorably discharged 30 June, 1895. Ensign (Spanish-American War), 14 May, 1898. Honorably discharged 4 February, 1899.
HOLT, ALFRED C.
   Assistant Surgeon, 5 June, 1844. Resigned 18 November, 1844.
HOLT, FREDERICK V. R.
   Acting Second Assistant Engineer, 8 September, 1863. Honorably discharged 25 July, 1865.
HOLT, GEORGE H.
   Acting Assistant Paymaster, 20 May, 1861. Resigned 7 July, 1862. Acting Assistant Paymaster, 2 July, 1863. Honorably discharged 2 December, 1865.
HOLT, GEORGE R.
   Third Assistant Engineer, 16 October, 1861. Second Assistant Engineer, 3 August, 1863. Resigned 4 May, 1869.
HOLT, JOHN E., JR.
   Midshipman, 4 March, 1823. Dismissed 25 June, 1833.
HOLT, RICHARD J.
   Mate, 4 February, 1865. Honorably discharged 28 October, 1865.
HOLT, SAMUEL L.
   Acting Third Assistant Engineer, 3 August, 1864. Honorably discharged 6 September, 1865.
HOLT, THOMAS.
   Acting Third Assistant Engineer, 17 December, 1864. Honorably discharged 14 July, 1865.
HOLTON, GEORGE.
   Acting Third Assistant Engineer, 1 September, 1864. Honorably discharged 1 March, 1868.
HOLTON, THOMAS.
   Acting Third Assistant Engineer, 22 August, 1864. Honorably discharged 5 August, 1866.
HOLTZ, DAVID.
   Acting Third Assistant Engineer, 21 October, 1863. Appointment revoked (sick) 8 August, 1864. Acting Third Assistant Engineer, 10 December, 1864. Resigned 11 March, 1865.
HOLTZMAN, A. J.
   Mate, 9 January, 1865. Appointment revoked 14 April, 1865.
HOLWAY, WESLEY O.
   Chaplain, 2 June, 1868.
HOMAN, ANDREW J.
   Acting Third Assistant Engineer, 2 January, 1864. Acting Second Assistant Engineer, 22 March, 1865. Honorably discharged 18 January, 1866.
HOMAN, EDWARD A.
   Acting Third Assistant Engineer, 11 March, 1864. Appointment revoked (sick) 20 July, 1864.
HOMAN, WILLIAM F.
   Acting Second Assistant Engineer, 23 November, 1862. Resigned 25 July, 1863.
HOMANS, CHARLES A.
   Acting Ensign, 14 February, 1863. Resigned 12 January, 1864.
HOMANS, J. T.
   Midshipman, 3 December, 1819. Lieutenant, 17 May, 1828. Resigned 15 May, 1843.
HOMANS, JOHN.
   Assistant Surgeon, 13 December, 1861. Resigned 17 September, 1862.
HOMANS, JOHN W.
   Acting Third Assistant Engineer, 10 May, 1864. Resigned 23 June, 1865.
HOMANS, THOMAS.
   Midshipman, 28 August, 1799. Resigned 20 May, 1801.
HOMER, ARTHUR B.
   Mate, 13 February, 1863. Acting Ensign, 14 February, 1864. Honorably discharged 18 November, 1865.
HOMER, CHARLES W.
   Gunner, 6 January, 1858. Died 6 November, 1872.
HOMER, WILLIAM H.
   Midshipman, 30 November, 1814. Lieutenant, 13 January, 1825. Died September, 1829.
HONKOMP, HENRY.
   Mate, 14 May, 1864. Honorably discharged 13 November, 1865.
HOOD, GEORGE N.
   Acting Master, 16 December, 1861. Appointment revoked 7 May, 1862.
HOOD, JOHN.
   Cadet Midshipman, 12 June, 1874. Reappointed 10 September, 1875. Graduated 10 June, 1881. Ensign, Junior Grade, 3 March, 1883. Ensign, 26 June, 1884. Lieutenant, Junior Grade, 5 December, 1890. Lieutenant, 28 April, 1895.
HOODLESS, GERRETT L.
   Acting Assistant Paymaster, 3 November, 1864. Mustered out 24 February, 1867.
HOODLESS, WILLIAM J.
   Acting Assistant Paymaster, 30 September, 1862. Resigned 9 June, 1865.
HOOE, EMMET R.
   Midshipman, 1 January, 1828. Passed Midshipman, 14 June, 1834. Lieutenant, 17 December, 1840. Died 25 September, 1847.
HOOE, GEORGE M.
   Midshipman, 21 October, 1824. Passed Midshipman, 20 February, 1830. Lieutenant, 31 December, 1833. Died 10 April, 1845.

18

HOOE, SEYMOUR.
Midshipman, 14 April, 1800. Resigned 30 July, 1801.
HOOE, WILLIAM F.
Midshipman, 1 August, 1825. Passed Midshipman, 4 June, 1831. Died 14 August, 1833.
HOOGEWERFF, JOHN A.
Cadet Midshipman, 27 June, 1877. Ensign, Junior Grade, 1 July, 1883. Ensign, 26 June, 1884. Lieutenant, Junior Grade, 5 November, 1893. Lieutenant, 21 July, 1897.
HOOK, WILLIAM.
Gunner, 17 November, 1801. Broke by Court-martial 30 May, 1808.
HOOKER, EDWARD.
Acting Master, 19 July, 1861. Acting Volunteer Lieutenant, 19 September, 1862. Acting Volunteer Lieutenant-Commander, 7 February, 1865. Lieutenant, 12 March, 1868. Lieutenant-Commander, 18 December, 1868. Commander, 9 February, 1884. Retired List, 25 December, 1884.
HOOKER, RICHARD CAMPBELL.
Midshipman, 25 September, 1861. Graduated 24 September, 1865. Ensign, 1 December, 1866. Master, 12 March, 1868. Lieutenant, 26 March, 1869. Resigned 30 June, 1876. Lieutenant (Spanish-American War), 28 May, 1898. Honorably discharged 18 November, 1898.
HOOLE, JAMES LINGARD.
Acting Midshipman, 22 September, 1856. Midshipman, 15 June, 1860. Dismissed 4 June, 1861.
HOON, WILLIAM A.
Acting Third Assistant Engineer, 18 December, 1862. Resigned 25 November, 1863.
HOOPER, JOSEPH.
Purser, 24 September, 1798. Discharged 15 September, 1801, under Peace Establishment Act.
HOOPER, QUINCEY A.
Acting Master, 27 August, 1861. Acting Volunteer Lieutenant, 25 September, 1862. Resigned 4 January, 1865.
HOOPES, EDWARD T.
Naval Cadet, 6 September, 1893. Resigned 25 February, 1897. Ensign (Spanish-American War), 14 May, 1898. Honorably discharged 3 November, 1898.
HOOPES, JOSEPH.
Third Assistant Engineer, 16 September, 1862. Second Assistant Engineer, 1 March, 1864. Died 18 March, 1866.
HOOVER, HENRY.
Constructor, 4 June, 1850. Appointment revoked 10 July, 1865.
HOOVER, JOHN B.
Acting Carpenter, 22 May, 1861. Dismissed 25 September, 1861.
HOOVER, JOHN B.
Assistant Naval Constructor, 29 July, 1875. Naval Constructor, 10 October, 1888. Retired List, 23 June, 1898.
HOPE, HENRY C.
Acting Third Assistant Engineer, 3 September, 1863. Died at New Orleans, La., 20 November, 1863.
HOPE, JAMES S.
Assistant Surgeon, 10 July, 1891. Passed Assistant Surgeon, 10 July, 1894. Died 30 June, 1896.
HOPEWELL, POLLARD.
Midshipman, 4 June, 1812. Killed in action 1 June, 1813.
HOPKINS, ALFRED.
Acting Midshipman, 1 October, 1851. Midshipman, 9 June, 1855. Passed Midshipman, 15 April, 1858. Master, 4 November, 1858. Lieutenant, 31 May, 1860. Lieutenant-Commander, 16 July, 1862. Commander, 2 March, 1871. Captain, 11 May, 1882. Dismissed 21 November, 1882.
HOPKINS, ANDREW J.
Acting Third Assistant Engineer, 1861. Resigned 30 October, 1862.
HOPKINS, CHARLES.
Acting Third Assistant Engineer, 10 September, 1863. Last appearance on Records, 22 April, 1864.
HOPKINS, CHARLES F.
Midshipman, 19 October, 1841. Passed Midshipman, 10 August, 1847. Dismissed 23 October, 1849. Reappointed 27 September, 1850. Resigned 6 November, 1851.
HOPKINS, CHARLES M.
Midshipman, 9 August, 1824. Died in 1825.
HOPKINS, EDWARD.
Midshipman, 1 April, 1828. Killed by accident 31 January, 1831.
HOPKINS, EDWARD A.
Midshipman, 22 January, 1840. Resigned 1 July, 1845.
HOPKINS, EDWARD A.
Acting Third Assistant Engineer, 12 February, 1863. Lost on Narcissus, 4 January, 1866.
HOPKINS, FARLEY.
Acting Ensign, 17 July, 1863. Resigned 13 February, 1865.
HOPKINS, FORTESQUE S.
Acting Ensign, 15 February, 1864. Honorably discharged 4 August, 1866.
HOPKINS, FRANKLIN.
Acting Master, 16 April, 1862. Dismissed 25 November, 1864.
HOPKINS, GEORGE.
Acting Assistant Surgeon, 1 October, 1862. Honorably discharged 13 October, 1865.

HOPKINS, HORACE L.
　Acting Assistant Paymaster, 21 January, 1864. Honorably discharged 15 October, 1865.
HOPKINS, JAMES B.
　Mate, 22 January, 1863. Honorably discharged 26 October, 1865.
HOPKINS, JAMES N.
　Mate, 23 January, 1862. Resigned 3 November, 1862.
HOPKINS, J. L.
　Midshipman, 26 February, 1814. Last appearance on Records of Navy Department, 1815. Resigned.
HOPKINS, JOHN H.
　Acting Third Assistant Engineer, 9 September, 1863. Dismissed 21 November, 1864.
HOPKINS, JOSHUA W.
　Acting Ensign, 10 September, 1864. Honorably discharged 30 October, 1868.
HOPKINS, J. PAGE.
　Assistant Surgeon, 30 September, 1850. Resigned 9 June, 1857.
HOPKINS, RICHARD.
　Mate, 9 February, 1864. Honorably discharged 26 October, 1865.
HOPKINS, RUFUS H.
　Mate, 21 January, 1864. Honorably discharged 3 August, 1865.
HOPKINS, SAMUEL.
　Acting Master, 29 May, 1861. Dismissed 21 January, 1862.
HOPKINS, SMITH K.
　Acting Ensign, 28 August, 1863. Honorably discharged 12 October, 1865.
HOPKINS, TOWNSEND.
　Mate, 9 June, 1863. Accidentaly killed on the Choctaw, 15 January, 1864.
HOPKINS, WARREN M.
　Lieutenant (Spanish-American War), 22 April, 1898. Resigned 1 July, 1898.
HOPKINS, WILLIAM.
　Acting Third Assistant Engineer, 23 September, 1863. Resigned 20 June, 1865.
HOPKINS, WILLIAM E.
　Midshipman, 13 November, 1839. Passed Midshipman, 2 July, 1845. Master, 2 December, 1853. Lieutenant, 10 July, 1854. Lieutenant-Commander, 5 August, 1862. Commander, 4 November, 1863. Captain, 1 July, 1870. Commodore, 1 December, 1877. Retired List, 10 January, 1883. Died 24 October, 1894.
HOPKINSON, A. H.
　Midshipman, 25 September, 1817. Lieutenant, 28 April, 1826. Died 11 August, 1827.
HOPKINSON, HENRY E.
　Mate, 23 January, 1863. Acting Ensign, 15 July, 1864. Died on the J. S. Chambers, 13 August, 1864.
HOPKINSON, JOSEPH.
　Assistant Surgeon, 13 October, 1840. Passed Assistant Surgeon, 22 January, 1848. Resigned 17 September, 1852.
HOPPER, WILLIAM W.
　Third Assistant Engineer, 11 April, 1859. Second Assistant Engineer, 26 December, 1861. First Assistant Engineer, 17 March, 1863. Resigned 22 November, 1866.
HOPPIN, SAMUEL B.
　Acting Assistant Surgeon, 2 November, 1861. Appointment revoked 29 July, 1864.
HOPSON, JOHN E.
　Midshipman, 25 September, 1840. Dismissed 9 October, 1846.
HORAN, JOHN J.
　Acting Warrant Machinist, 23 August, 1899.
HORD, WILLIAM T.
　Assistant Surgeon, 1 November, 1854. Passed Assistant Surgeon, 23 May, 1859. Surgeon, 1 August, 1861. Medical Inspector, 6 July, 1872. Medical Director, 1 May, 1879. Retired List, 3 March, 1893.
HORN, WILLIAM.
　Acting Third Assistant Engineer, 13 January, 1865. Honorably discharged 27 September, 1865.
HORNBY, WILLIAM.
　Mate, 13 May, 1863. Deserted 2 April, 1864.
HORNE, DAVID B.
　Acting Master, 3 July, 1861. Dismissed 19 May, 1863.
HORNE, FREDERICK J., Jr.
　Naval Cadet, 20 May, 1895. At sea prior to final graduation.
HORNE, GUSTAVUS H.
　Acting Assistant Paymaster, 8 July, 1864. Honorably discharged 8 November, 1865.
HORNE, JOSEPH V.
　Acting Third Assistant Engineer, 19 January, 1864. Acting Second Assistant Engineer, 21 March, 1865. Honorably discharged 31 October, 1865. Acting Second Assistant Engineer, 9 July, 1866. Appointment revoked 22 November, 1866.
HORNER, ALFRED T.
　Acting Third Assistant Engineer, 4 March, 1864. Honorably discharged 20 August, 1865.
HORNER, FREDERICK.
　Assistant Surgeon, 1 May, 1851. Passed Assistant Surgeon, 10 April, 1856. Resigned 15 May, 1857. Reappointed 12 May, 1858. Retired List, 8 May, 1861.
HORNER, GUSTAVUS R. B.
　Surgeon's Mate, 26 May, 1826. Surgeon, 4 April, 1831. Retired List, 18 June, 1866. Medical Director, Retired List, 3 March, 1871. Died 8 August, 1892.
HORNER, RICHARD B.
　Midshipman, 4 March, 1823. Resigned 10 September, 1823.

GENERAL NAVY REGISTER.

HORNSBY, ALFRED.
Mate, 31 December, 1861. Acting Ensign, 24 July, 1863. Resigned 3 March, 1865.
HORSELEY, SAMUEL.
Assistant Surgeon, 9 March, 1809. Surgeon, 5 April, 1814. Died 8 September, 1821.
HORST, ELIAS VANDER.
Midshipman, 10 September, 1841. Passed Midshipman, 10 August, 1847. Died 17 March, 1850.
HORTON, FREDERICK V. D.
Acting Assistant Paymaster, 14. October, 1861. Resigned 3 June, 1865.
HORTON, SAMUEL.
Midshipman, 30 November, 1814. Died 7 August, 1815.
HORTON, SAMUEL J.
Mate, 15 February, 1862. Dismissed 15 September, 1862. Mate. 11 July, 1863. Resigned 22 March, 1864.
HORTON, WILLIAM F.
Mate, 1 May, 1862. Resigned 18 March, 1865. Mate, 3 April. 1867. Mustered out 3 November, 1868.
HORTON, W. S.
Midshipman, 19 October, 1841. Dropped.
HORTSMAN, D.
Carpenter, 4 December, 1815. Last appearance on Records of Navy Department, 11 March, 1816.
HORWITZ, PHINEAS J.
Assistant Surgeon, 8 November, 1847. Surgeon, 19 April, 1861. Chief Bureau of Medicine and Surgery, from 11 July, 1865, to 1 July, 1869. Medical Inspector 3 March, 1871. Medical Director, 30 June, 1873. Retired 3 March, 1884.
HOSACK, ALEXANDER.
Midshipman, 22 January, 1816. Resigned 8 August, 1822.
HOSEA, WILLIAM W.
Mate, 30 May, 1864. Dismissed 19 May, 1865.
HOSFORD, JAMES H.
Acting Third Assistant Engineer, 28 October, 1861. Acting Second Assistant Engineer, 2 July, 1863. Died at Hospital, Beaufort, North Carolina, 30 December, 1864.
HOSFORD, WILLIAM S.
Acting Assistant Paymaster, 12 August, 1861. Mustered out 6 August, 1867.
HOSKINS, CHARLES.
Acting Third Assistant Engineer, 20 July, 1863. Honorably discharged 15 November, 1865.
HOSLEY, HARRY H.
Midshipman, 22 September, 1871. Graduated 21 June, 1875. Ensign, 18 July, 1876. Master, 2 June, 1882. Lieutenant, Junior Grade, 3 March, 1883. Lieutenant, 17 March, 1889. Lieutenant-Commander, 3 March, 1899.
HOSMER, FRANCIS E.
Acting Third Assistant Engineer, 21 October, 1863. Honorably discharged 17 July, 1866.
HOSMER, CHARLES E.
Acting Assistant Surgeon, 3 March, 1865. Honorably discharged 13 October, 1865.
HOSSACK, ABRAHAM.
Midshipman, 1 January, 1817. Last appearance on Records of Navy Department, 6 March, 1822. Dead.
HOSUNG, CHARLES H.
Acting Warrant Machinist, 23 August, 1899.
HOTCHKIN, FRANK S.
Midshipman, 28 June, 1867. Graduated 1 June, 1872. Ensign, 15 July, 1873. Master, 5 June, 1878. Lieutenant, Junior Grade, 3 March, 1883. Wholly retired 16 June, 1885.
HOTCHKISS, FREEMAN D.
Acting Second Assistant Engineer, 16 September, 1864. Honorably discharged 19 February, 1866.
HOTCHKISS, R. G.
Mate, 27 June, 1863. Lost at sea in Bainbridge, 21 August, 1863.
HOTCHKISS, SOLOMON.
Master, 18 July, 1798. Resigned 16 March, 1799.
HOTCHKISS, WILLIAM J.
Acting Master, 31 July, 1861. Died at Piankatank River, Virginia, 17 August, 1863.
HOUGH, ANDREW J.
Carpenter, 30 August, 1861. Died 2 September, 1864.
HOUGH, EBEN E.
Gunner, 25 March, 1814. Resigned 11 February, 1815.
HOUGH, HENRY H.
Naval Cadet, 6 September, 1887. Ensign. 1 July, 1893. Lieutenant. Junior Grade, 3 March, 1899. Lieutenant, 10 October, 1899.
HOUGHTON, AUSTIN D.
Assistant Engineer (Spanish-American War), 7 June, 1898. Honorably discharged 4 November, 1898.
HOUGHTON, GEORGE A.
Acting First Assistant Engineer, 9 November, 1862. Resigned 27 December, 1862.
HOUGHTON, THOMAS F.
Acting Assistant Paymaster, 12 December, 1864. Honorably discharged 26 October, 1865.
HOURAND, JOSEPH.
Acting Assistant Surgeon, 13 July, 1863. Dismissed 26 December, 1863.

HOURIGAN, PATRICK W.
    Cadet Midshipman, 24 June, 1876. Graduated 22 June, 1882. Ensign, Junior Grade, 3 March, 1883. Ensign, 26 June, 1884, Lieutenant, Junior Grade, 30 June, 1892. Lieutenant, 12 June, 1896.
HOUSE, JEROME B.
    Midshipman, 23 July, 1864. Graduated 2 June, 1868. Ensign, 19 April, 1869. Master, 12 July, 1870. Lieutenant, 24 August, 1873. Died 9 January, 1881.
HOUSE, WILLIAM S.
    Midshipman, 18 June, 1812. Lost in the Wasp, 1815.
HOUSEL, LOUIS V.
    Midshipman, 15 February, 1862. Graduated June, 1866. Ensign, 12 March, 1868. Master, 26 March, 1869. Lieutenant, 21 March, 1870. Resigned 31 March, 1874. Lieutenant (Spanish-American War), 25 May, 1898. Discharged 13 September, 1898.
HOUSTON, ALBERT.
    Ensign (Spanish-American War), 14 May, 1898. Honorably discharged 14 January, 1899.
HOUSTON, EDWIN SAMUEL.
    Midshipman, 18 April, 1862. Graduated September, 1865. Ensign, 1 December, 1866. Master, 12 March, 1868. Lieutenant, 26 March, 1869. Lieutenant-Commander, 29 March, 1881. Commander, 27 September, 1891. Captain, 3 March, 1899.
HOUSTON, GEORGE P.
    Third Assistant Engineer, 21 May, 1857. Resigned 28 January, 1860.
HOUSTON, H. M.
    Midshipman, 12 May, 1824. Passed Midshipman, 20 February, 1830. Lieutenant, 24 June, 1834. Died 2 July, 1839.
HOUSTON, HORATIO B.
    Acting Second Assistant Engineer, 1 February, 1864. Resigned (sick) 6 July, 1864.
HOUSTON, ISAAC H.
    Mate, 4 February, 1864. Deserted 1864.
HOUSTON, J. BUCHANAN.
    Third Assistant Engineer, 21 May, 1857. Second Assistant Engineer, 3 August, 1859. First Assistant Engineer, 9 December, 1861. Resigned 28 July, 1865.
HOUSTON, JOHN C.
    Acting First Assistant Engineer, 1 January, 1864. Resigned 15 November, 1864.
HOUSTON, NELSON T.
    Midshipman, 28 July, 1865. Graduated June, 1869. Ensign, 12 July, 1870. Master, 6 September, 1872. Lieutenant, 9 October, 1875. Lieutenant-Commander, 7 June, 1898. Retired List with rank of Commander, 30 June, 1900.
HOUSTON, SAMUEL H.
    Third Assistant Engineer, 26 February, 1851. Second Assistant Engineer, 21 May, 1853. Died 16 June, 1854.
HOUSTON, THOMAS T.
    Midshipman, 26 August, 1845. Passed Midshipman, 6 October, 1851. Master, 15 September, 1855. Lieutenant, 16 September, 1855. Died 26 June, 1860.
HOUSTON, VICTOR S.
    Naval Cadet, 22 September, 1893. Ensign, 1 July, 1899.
HOUSTON, WILLIAM.
    Acting Assistant Surgeon, 23 June, 1873. Honorably discharged 30 June, 1879.
HOVEY, CHRISTOPHER P.
    Mate, 5 December, 1861. Resigned 14 February, 1865.
HOVEY, MYRON M.
    Acting Assistant Paymaster, 10 February, 1865. Resigned 21 June, 1865.
HOVEY, WALLACE W.
    Acting First Assistant Engineer, 19 August, 1862. Resigned 5 August, 1863.
HOW, ANDREW P.
    Second Assistant Engineer, 24 September, 1847. Resigned 7 August, 1849.
HOWARD, AUSTIN.
    Mate, 10 October, 1862. Resigned 24 April, 1863.
HOWARD, CHARLES M.
    Mate. Dismissed 17 June, 1862.
HOWARD, CHARLES R.
    Midshipman, 28 May, 1834. Dismissed 11 January, 1840.
HOWARD, CHARLES R.
    Acting Assistant Paymaster, 7 August, 1863. Honorably discharged 15 November, 1865.
HOWARD, CHARLES W.
    Mate, 7 October, 1862. Acting Ensign, 1 May, 1863. Acting Master, gallant conduct in face of enemy, 16 October, 1863. Died of wounds received in action, at Charleston, S. C., 10 October, 1863.
HOWARD, EDWARD.
    Acting Master's Mate, 23 October, 1861. Paid in full 16 June, 1862.
HOWARD, GEORGE B.
    Mate, 1862. Resigned 10 January, 1863.
HOWARD, H. Z.
    Acting Ensign, 17 February, 1864. Honorably discharged 2 September, 1866.
HOWARD, JOHN.
    Captain (to command a Galley), 20 March, 1799. Last appearance on Records of Navy Department.
HOWARD, JOHN C.
    Mate, 11 January, 1865. Appointment revoked 10 January, 1872.
HOWARD, PETER.
    Mate, gallantry, 24 April, 1863. Acting Ensign, 18 November, 1863. Honorably discharged 24 November, 1867.

GENERAL NAVY REGISTER.

HOWARD, SAMUEL.
Acting Master, 9 October, 1861. Acting Volunteer Lieutenant, 5 June, 1862. Honorably discharged 4 November, 1868.

HOWARD, THOMAS B.
Midshipman, 24 June, 1869. Graduated 31 May, 1873. Ensign, 16 July, 1874. Master, 13 January, 1879. Lieutenant, Junior Grade, 3 March, 1883. Lieutenant, 7 November, 1885. Lieutenant-Commander, 3 March, 1899.

HOWARD, THOMAS C. B.
Lieutenant, Junior Grade (Spanish-American War), 25 May, 1898. Honorably discharged 24 September, 1898.

HOWARD, WILLIAM A.
Midshipman, 1 January, 1825. Resigned 12 April, 1832.

HOWARD, WM. C.
Mate, 28 December, 1863. Discharged 27 May, 1865.

HOWARD, WILLIAM H.
Acting Assistant Surgeon, 1 October, 1862. Honorably discharged 9 November, 1865.

HOWARD, WILLIAM H.
Mate, 28 December, 1861. Acting Ensign, 9 April, 1864. Honorably discharged 11 December, 1865.

HOWARD, WILLIAM H.
Mate, 17 December, 1863. Discharged 21 June, 1864.

HOWARD, WILLIAM H.
Mate, 25 October, 1864. Honorably discharged 20 October, 1865.

HOWARD, WILLIAM J.
Acting Second Assistant Engineer, 13 December, 1862. Honorably discharged 19 August, 1865.

HOWARD, WILLIAM L.
Midshipman, 10 January, 1815. Lieutenant, 28 April, 1826. Commander, 29 February, 1844. Resigned 18 December, 1852.

HOWARD, WILLIAM L.
Cadet Midshipman, 22 September, 1877. Ensign, 1 July, 1884. Lieutenant, Junior Grade, 7 September, 1894. Lieutenant, 10 March, 1898.

HOWARD, WILLIAM W.
Acting Assistant Surgeon, 1 October, 1862. Honorably discharged 9 November, 1865.

HOWATT, JAMES.
Mate, 10 November, 1865. Deserted 1 August, 1866.

HOWATT, JOSEPH H.
Assistant Engineer (Spanish-American War), 23 June, 1898. Honorably discharged 4 January, 1899.

HOWDEN, ROBERT.
Mate, 11 June, 1863. Promoted Acting Ensign, 9 October, 1863. Honorably discharged 24 October, 1865.

HOWE, ALFRED L.
Midshipman, 28 September, 1870. Graduated 21 June, 1875. Resigned 8 December, 1877.

HOWE, CHARLES C.
Acting Third Assistant Engineer, 25 August, 1863. Acting Second Assistant Engineer, 2 December, 1864. Honorably discharged 26 July, 1865.

HOWE, CHARLES M.
Assistant Engineer (Spanish-American War), 14 July, 1898. Honorably discharged 29 December, 1898.

HOWE, GEORGE W.
Acting Third Assistant Engineer, 7 October, 1861. Appointment revoked 13 December, 1861. Acting Third Assistant Engineer, 20 September, 1862. Acting Second Assistant Engineer, 25 May, 1864. Honorably discharged 19 May, 1866. Acting Second Assistant Engineer, 22 September, 1866. Resigned 6 September, 1867.

HOWE, JAMES.
Carpenter, 3 July, 1799. Discharged 6 July, 1801, under Peace Establishment Act.

HOWE, JOSEPH H.
Acting Gunner, 1 August, 1864. Appointment revoked 10 May, 1865.

HOWELL, CHARLES P.
Cadet Engineer, 7 October, 1867. Graduated 8 June, 1868. Second Assistant Engineer, 15 August, 1870. Passed Assistant Engineer, 4 December, 1876. Chief Engineer, 10 November, 1893. Rank changed to Lieutenant-Commander, 3 March, 1899. Commander, 8 July, 1899. Died 7 December, 1899.

HOWELL, DAVID N.
Acting Third Assistant Engineer, 17 October, 1861. Dismissed 20 August, 1863.

HOWELL, EDWARD A.
Acting Master, 9 January, 1862. Honorably discharged 30 November, 1865.

HOWELL, EDWARD F.
Midshipman (acting as Lieutenant), 17 December, 1810. Killed in action 15 January, 1815.

HOWELL, GEORGE H.
Assistant Surgeon, 8 November, 1847. Passed Assistant Surgeon, 22 April, 1854. Died 7 October, 1859.

HOWELL, JOHN.
Third Assistant Engineer, 24 December, 1853. Resigned 3 May, 1856.

HOWELL, JOHN ADAMS.
Acting Midshipman, 27 September, 1854. Midshipman, 11 June, 1858. Passed Midshipman, 28 January, 1861. Master, 28 February, 1861. Lieutenant, 18 April, 1861. Lieutenant-Commander, 3 March, 1865. Commander, 6 March, 1872. Captain, 1 March, 1884. Commodore, 21 May, 1895. Rear-Admiral, 10 August, 1898.

HOWELL, JOHN C.
Midshipman, 9 June, 1836. Passed Midshipman, 1 July, 1842. Master, 21 February,

GENERAL NAVY REGISTER. 279

1849. Lieutenant, 2 August, 1849. Commander, 16 July, 1862. Captain, 25 July, 1866. Commodore, 29 January, 1872. Chief, Bureau Yards and Docks, 22 September, 1874. Rear-Admiral, 25 April, 1877. Retired List, 24 November, 1881. Died 12 September, 1892.

HOWELL, JOHN F.
 Midshipman, 1 February, 1814. Last appearance on Records of Navy Department, 6 February, 1821. Dead.
HOWELL, J. RUSSELL.
 Mate, 7 February, 1862. Resigned 18 March, 1863.
HOWELL, ROBERT B.
 Cadet Midshipman, 28 September, 1881. Resigned 1 June, 1887. Lieutenant, Junior Grade (Spanish-American War), 19 May, 1898. Honorably discharged 2 December, 1898.
HOWELL, R. S.
 Mate, 3 October, 1863. Acting Ensign, 19 May, 1864. Honorably discharged 4 November, 1865.
HOWELL, SAMUEL H.
 Acting Ensign, 4 October, 1864. Honorably discharged 22 January, 1868.
HOWELL.
 Surgeon, date not known. Discharged 4 June, 1801, under Peace Establishment Act.
HOWELL, WILLIAM.
 Assistant Surgeon, 30 July, 1861. Died 26 July, 1862.
HOWELLS, WILLIAM M.
 Sailmaker, 13 June, 1861. Retired List, 20 November, 1883. Died 18 February, 1899.
HOWES, D. H.
 Acting Ensign, 29 November, 1864. Honorably discharged 30 June, 1865.
HOWES, FREDERICK ALOA.
 Midshipman, 24 September, 1863. Graduated June, 1867. Ensign, 18 December, 1868. Master, 21 March, 1870. Resigned 8 December, 1873.
HOWES, GEORGE F.
 Acting Ensign, 24 February, 1863. Honorably discharged 29 January, 1869.
HOWES, WILLIS.
 Acting Ensign, 2 September, 1864. Acting Master, 5 October, 1865. Honorably discharged 1 October, 1866.
HOWISON, HENRY L.
 Acting Midshipman, 26 September, 1854. Midshipman, 11 June, 1858. Passed Midshipman, 9 February, 1861. Master, 2 March, 1861. Lieutenant, 19 April, 1861. Lieutenant-Commander, 3 March, 1865. Commander, 19 August, 1872. Captain, 2 March, 1885. Commodore, 21 March, 1897. Rear-Admiral, 30 September, 1898. Retired List, 10 October, 1899.
HOWISON, JOHN W.
 Mate, 24 October, 1861. Acting Ensign, 11 May, 1865. Resigned 7 February, 1866.
HOWISON, NIEL M.
 Midshipman, 1 February, 1823. Passed Midshipman, 23 March, 1829. Lieutenant, 13 July, 1832. Died 23 February, 1848.
HOWLAND, CALVIN.
 Acting Third Assistant Engineer, 16 October, 1861. Resigned 26 November, 1862.
HOWLAND, CHARLES H.
 Mate, 21 March, 1862. Resigned 12 October, 1863.
HOWLAND, CHARLES H.
 Cadet Engineer, 1 October, 1878. Graduated 30 June, 1884. Honorably discharged 30 June, 1884. Restored to service 10 March, 1886, as an Assistant Engineer, to rank from 1 July, 1884. Resigned 3 May, 1886.
HOWLAND, ELIJAH K.
 Mate, 28 August, 1863. Acting Ensign, 1 September, 1864. Honorably discharged 14 August, 1865.
HOWLAND, E. S. D.
 Mate, 8 May, 1862. Resigned (sick) 10 October, 1864.
HOWLAND, JOSEPH.
 Acting Master, 23 December, 1861. Resigned 21 May, 1862.
HOWLAND, SAMUEL C.
 Mate, 25 January, 1862. Resigned 26 June, 1862.
HOWLAND, WALTER S.
 Mate, 2 October, 1863. Acting Ensign, 9 April, 1865. Honorably discharged 12 August, 1865.
HOWLAND, WARREN.
 Acting Third Assistant Engineer, 9 April, 1863. Honorably discharged 31 October, 1865.
HOWLAND, WILLIAM H.
 Mate, 2 September, 1864. Honorably discharged 1 September, 1867.
HOWORTH, GEORGE.
 Mate. Resigned 11 November, 1862. Acting Ensign, 13 December, 1862. Acting Master, 12 August, 1864. Honorably discharged 30 September, 1865. Acting Master, 22 August, 1867. Died at Naval Hospital, New York, 29 March, 1868.
HOWORTH, WILLIAM L.
 Mate, 29 April, 1863. Acting Master, gallant service in assisting to destroy Ram Albemarle, 27 October, 1864. Honorably discharged 20 October, 1865. Acting Master, 17 May, 1866. Ensign, 12 March, 1868. Resigned 4 April, 1869.
HOXIE, ALLEN.
 Mate, 13 December, 1861. Acting Master, 11 February, 1862. Resigned 15 February, 1865.
HOXIE, WILLIAM H.
 Mate, 6 February, 1862. Resigned 19 July, 1862.

HOXSEY, THOMAS D.
Assistant Paymaster, 1 September, 1876. Passed Assistant Paymaster, 18 January, 1881. Died 24 October, 1888.
HOY, JAMES, JR.
Assistant Paymaster, 11 October, 1861. Paymaster, 18 October, 1864. Pay Inspector, 29 May, 1882. Retired List, 18 January, 1892.
HOYT, AHIRA B.
Acting Assistant Surgeon, 21 October, 1861. Resigned 10 September, 1862.
HOYT, ALFRED.
Acting Third Assistant Engineer, 10 December, 1863. Acting Second Assistant Engineer, 26 July, 1864. Honorably discharged 23 October, 1865.
HOYT, EBEN.
Acting Master, 20 January, 1862. Acting Volunteer Lieutenant, recommendation of Commanding Officer, 23 May, 1864. Honorably discharged 23 January, 1866
HOYT, EBEN, JR.
Third Assistant Engineer, 21 May, 1857. Second Assistant Engineer, 2 August, 1859. First Assistant Engineer, 1 July, 1861. Chief Engineer, 10 November, 1863. Killed 19 October, 1867.
HOZAGER, S. J.
Mate, 27 November, 1861. Dismissed 11 September, 1862.
HOZIER, ENOS.
Acting First Assistant Engineer, 1 October, 1862. Honorably discharged 15 December, 1866.
HUBBARD, AUSTIN T.
Acting Assistant Paymaster, 16 December, 1864. Assistant Paymaster, 21 February, 1867. Died, Exeter, N. H., 12 June, 1868.
HUBBARD, CHARLES T.
Assistant Surgeon, 23 October, 1861. Resigned 5 September, 1865.
HUBBARD, DANIEL B.
Acting Ensign, 12 July, 1864. Honorably discharged 15 March, 1866.
HUBBARD, EDWARD H.
Midshipman, 4 March, 1823. Resigned 8 May, 1832.
HUBBARD, EDWARD R.
Acting Third Assistant Engineer, 9 January, 1864. Acting Second Assistant Engineer, 21 March, 1865. Honorably discharged 12 December, 1865.
HUBBARD, ELISHA.
Mate, 30 July, 1863. Resigned 20 April, 1865.
HUBBARD, GEORGE C.
Assistant Surgeon, 5 July, 1895. Died 21 March, 1898.
HUBBARD, JOHN.
Midshipman, 27 July, 1866. Graduated 7 June, 1870. Ensign, 13 July, 1871. Master, 15 September, 1873. Lieutenant, 28 December, 1878. Lieutenant-Commander, 6 October, 1898.
HUBBARD, JOHN F.
Naval Cadet, 5 September, 1884. Ensign, 1 July, 1890. Lieutenant, Junior Grade, 14 March, 1898. Lieutenant, 3 March, 1899.
HUBBARD, JONATHAN.
Gunner, 10 July, 1823. Died 29 January, 1824.
HUBBARD, JOSEPH S.
Professor, 7 May, 1845. Died 16 August, 1863.
HUBBARD, LEWIS H.
Mate, 30 November, 1867. Mustered out 30 November, 1868.
HUBBARD, NATHANIEL M.
Cadet Midshipman, 22 September, 1877. Resigned 1 June, 1884. Ensign (Spanish-American War), 10 May, 1898. Lieutenant, Junior Grade, 20 July, 1898. Honorably discharged 19 November, 1898.
HUBBARD, RICHARD.
Midshipman, 1 January, 1812. Resigned 22 January, 1814.
HUBBARD, SOCRATES.
Midshipman, 21 December, 1861. Graduated September, 1865. Ensign, 1 December, 1866. Master, 12 March, 1868. Lieutenant, 26 March, 1869. Lieutenant-Commander, 27 October, 1879. Retired 18 June, 1888.
HUBBELL, CHARLES F.
Mate, 5 March, 1862. Deserted 28 April, 1862.
HUBBELL, E. L.
Mate, 13 December, 1861. Resigned 24 October, 1863.
HUBBELL, ROBERT K.
Acting Ensign, 1 October, 1862. Dismissed 22 April, 1864.
HUBBS, WILLIAM H.
Acting Master, 4 November, 1861. Honorably discharged 10 December, 1865.
HUBLEY, GEORGE.
Midshipman, 15 November, 1810. Last appearance on Records of Navy Department, 27 June, 1811. Entered Army.
HUBLITZ, PHILLIP.
Acting Third Assistant Engineer, 17 February, 1862. Honorably discharged 3 August, 1865.
HUCKINS, PETER.
(See Peter Huckins Smith.)
HUDGINS, JOHN M.
Naval Cadet, 8 September, 1890. Assistant Engineer, 1 July, 1896. Rank changed to Ensign, 3 March, 1899. Lieutenant, Junior Grade, 1 July, 1899.
HUDSON, ADRIAN.
Assistant Surgeon, 30 July, 1861. Passed Assistant Surgeon, 22 June, 1864. Surgeon,

GENERAL NAVY REGISTER.

17 August, 1865. Medical Inspector, 10 June, 1880. Medical Director, 10 July, 1888. Died 7 February, 1890.
HUDSON, EDWARD.
Assistant Surgeon, 14 September, 1843. Surgeon, 29 July, 1858. Died 23 January, 1859.
HUDSON, FREDERICK N.
Midshipman, 5 July, 1799. Discharged 12 October, 1801, under Peace Establishment Act.
HUDSON, GEORGE, Jr.
Acting Assistant Paymaster, 24 December, 1863. Honorably discharged 10 November, 1865.
HUDSON, HARRY A.
Mate, 26 December, 1862. Resigned 2 June, 1863. Reappointed 9 November, 1863. Honorably discharged 26 May, 1864.
HUDSON, HENRY.
Boatswain, 27 August, 1889. Chief Boatswain, 27 August, 1899.
HUDSON, JOHN G.
Acting Ensign and Pilot, 1 October, 1864. Acting Master and Pilot, 1 October, 1864. Honorably discharged 10 March, 1866.
HUDSON, JOHN MORELY.
Acting Master, 28 March, 1862. Dismissed 7 June, 1863. Acting Ensign, 10 May, 1864. Honorably discharged 15 September, 1865.
HUDSON, ROBERT.
Chaplain, 29 April, 1874. Resigned 15 January, 1891
HUDSON, STEPHEN R.
Acting Master, 15 November, 1861. Dismissed 28 June, 1862.
HUDSON, WILLIAM H.
Midshipman, 16 July, 1838. Passed Midshipman, 20 May, 1844. Resigned 22 April, 1852.
HUDSON, WILLIAM L.
Midshipman, 1 January, 1816. Lieutenant, 28 April, 1826. Commander, 2 November, 1842. Captain, 14 September, 1855. Died 15 October, 1862.
HUESTIS, JAMES F.
Assistant Surgeon, 30 September, 1850. Resigned 9 June, 1857.
HUEY, SAMUEL B.
Acting Assistant Paymaster, 25 February, 1864. Resigned 12 January, 1866.
HUFF, CHARLES P.
Naval Cadet, 5 September, 1896. Graduated 30 June, 1900.
HUFF, JAMES.
Acting Third Assistant Engineer, 9 June, 1863. Dismissed 8 July, 1863.
HUFF, JOHN.
Acting Second Assistant Engineer, 1 October, 1862. Died from wounds received in action, 7 April, 1863.
HUGENIN, ROBERT, Jr.
Midshipman, 13 February, 1851. Resigned 12 June, 1852.
HUGER, FRANCIS.
Midshipman, 1 June, 1826. Passed Midshipman, 28 April, 1832. Lieutenant, 8 March, 1837. Died 6 January, 1849.
HUGER, THOMAS B.
Midshipman, 5 March, 1835. Passed Midshipman, 22 June, 1844. Master, 16 July, 1847. Lieutenant, 24 February, 1848. Resigned 11 January, 1861.
HUGG, JOSEPH.
Assistant Surgeon, 5 September, 1861. Passed Assistant Surgeon, 8 May, 1865. Surgeon, 23 December, 1871. Retired List, 17 March, 1887. Died 24 December, 1889.
HUGG, MARION.
Acting Ensign, 7 October, 1864. Honorably discharged 29 July, 1865.
HUGGINS, CHARLES.
Acting Master, 14 August, 1861. Honorably discharged 24 April, 1866. Acting Master, 30 July, 1867. Mustered out 18 August, 1868.
HUGGINS, E. CLARENCE.
Mate, 25 March, 1863. Acting Ensign, 18 January, 1864. Honorably discharged 15 November, 1868.
HUGHES, AARON K.
Midshipman, 20 October, 1838. Passed Midshipman, 20 May, 1844. Master, 19 December, 1852. Lieutenant, 18 October, 1853. Lieutenant-Commander, 16 July, 1862. Commander, 16 November, 1862. Retired List, 24 October, 1864. Captain, Active List, 10 February, 1869. Commodore, 4 February, 1875. Rear-Admiral, 2 July, 1882. Retired List, 31 March, 1884.
HUGHES, CHARLES F.
Naval Cadet, 6 September, 1884. Ensign, 1 July, 1890. Lieutenant, Junior Grade, 27 April, 1898. Lieutenant, 3 March, 1899.
HUGHES, DANIEL.
Assistant Surgeon, 5 March, 1799. Surgeon, 20 December, 1799. Resigned 15 May, 1800.
HUGHES, EDWARD.
Acting Boatswain, 11 August, 1864. Appointment revoked 12 March, 1866.
HUGHES, EDWARD.
Boatswain, 25 February, 1874. Retired List, 14 June, 1882. Died 24 January, 1888.
HUGHES, EDWARD M.
Midshipman, 26 July, 1866. Graduated 7 June, 1870. Ensign, 13 July, 1871. Master, 12 December, 1873. Lieutenant, 16 December, 1879. Lieutenant-Commander, 3 March, 1899.

HUGHES, GEORGE.
Purser, 12 October, 1798. Last appearance on Records of Navy Department, 5 November, 1798.
HUGHES, GEORGE W.
Acting Third Assistant Engineer, 14 November, 1864. Honorably discharged 28 August, 1865.
HUGHES, JAMES.
Boatswain 18 September, 1809. Last appearance on Records of Navy Department, 1815. Schooner Nautilus.
HUGHES, JAMES.
Acting Third Assistant Engineer, 13 May, 1864. Dismissed 12 August, 1864.
HUGHES, JAMES F.
Mate, 5 November. 1863. Acting Ensign, 2 June, 1864. Appointment revoked 8 August, 1864.
HUGHES, JOHN A.
Acting Third Assistant Engineer, 17 August, 1864. Appointment revoked 4 January, 1865.
HUGHES, JOHN T.
Mate, 23 October, 1861. Acting Ensign, 9 December, 1862. Lost on Bainbridge, 31 October, 1863.
HUGHES, OTHELLO D.
Acting Third Assistant Engineer, 20 October, 1863. Acting Second Assistant Engineer, 15 December, 1864. Dismissed 10 October, 1865.
HUGHES, PATRICK J.
Acting Third Assistant Engineer, 22 October, 1863. Resigned 12 June, 1865.
HUGHES, RICHARD M.
Cadet Midshipman, 25 September, 1874. Graduated 4 June, 1880. Ensign, 19 June, 1882. Lieutenant, Junior Grade, 4 August, 1889. Lieutenant, 22 June, 1894.
HUGHES, SAMUEL.
Lieutenant, Junior Grade (Spanish-American War), 21 May, 1898. Honorably discharged 21 November, 1898.
HUGHES, THOMAS W.
Gunner, 8 June, 1798. Midshipman, 21 April, 1800. Master, 13 April, 1801. Resigned 9 May, 1801.
HUGHES, WALTER S.
Midshipman, 24 September, 1870. Graduated 21 June, 1875. Ensign, 18 July, 1876. Master, 16 February, 1882. Lieutenant, Junior Grade, 3 March, 1883. Lieutenant, 15 January, 1889. Lieutenant-Commander, 3 March, 1899.
HUGHES, WILLIAM G.
Acting Third Assistant Engineer, 24 December, 1863. Honorably discharged 10 August, 1865. Acting Third Assistant Engineer, 14 March, 1866. Mustered out 19 February, 1868.
HUGHES, WILLIAM H.
Acting Third Assistant Engineer, 4 December, 1862. Honorably discharged 19 August, 1865.
HUGHES, WILLIAM W.
Mate, 16 December, 1861. Resigned 14 August, 1862.
HUGLE, JOHN R.
Mate, 29 October, 1863. Honorably discharged 24 October, 1865.
HUGUNIN, D. C.
Midshipman, 3 March, 1841. Drowned in November, 1846.
HUIE, JAMES.
Master, 11 March, 1803. Discharged 21 April, 1803.
HULBURD, JOHN.
Master, 11 February, 1809. Last appearance on Records of Navy Department, 3 January, 1816.
HULBURT, JAMES E.
Mate, 12 June, 1863. Acting Ensign, 19 July, 1864. Honorably discharged 20 July, 1865.
HULE, P. M.
Midshipman, 1 January, 1825. Died 4 June, 1826.
HULING, EDWARD J.
Acting Assistant Paymaster, 12 May, 1864. Honorably discharged 11 November, 1865.
HULL, CHARLES F.
Mate, 2 February, 1864. Acting Ensign, 23 August, 1864. Honorably discharged 17 July, 1865.
HULL, DAVID.
Mate, 14 July, 1863. Died in prison, Texas.
HULL, FREDERICK B.
Midshipman, 30 September, 1865. Graduated 5 June, 1869. Resigned 1 February, 1872.
HULL, ISAAC.
Lieutenant, 9 March, 1798. Commander, 18 May, 1804. Captain, 23 April, 1806. Died 13 February, 1843.
HULL, JAMES COOPER.
Midshipman, 24 July, 1863. Graduated June, 1868. Lost in the Oneida, 24 January, 1870.
HULL, JAMESON COX.
Third Assistant Engineer, 16 February, 1852. Second Assistant Engineer, 27 July, 1855. Resigned 22 September, 1856. Reinstated as Second Assistant Engineer, 30 April, 1861. First Assistant Engineer, 23 June, 1863. Resigned 15 January, 1866.

GENERAL NAVY REGISTER.

HULL, JOSEPH B.
　Midshipman, 9 November, 1813. Lieutenant, 13 January, 1825. Commander, 8 September, 1841. Captain, 14 September, 1855. Retired List, 21 December, 1861. Commodore on Retired List, 16 July, 1862. Died 17 January, 1890.

HULL, ROBERT C.
　Cadet Midshipman, 25 September, 1883. Resigned 4 February, 1884. Reappointed 20 May, 1884. Dropped 6 September, 1887. Lieutenant, Junior Grade (Spanish-American War), 25 May, 1898. Honorably discharged 26 November, 1898.

HULL, WATSON H.
　Assistant Surgeon, 16 September, 1861. Resigned 13 July, 1864.

HULL, WILLIAM.
　Acting Ensign, 13 December, 1862. Acting Master, 19 October, 1864. Honorably discharged 13 September, 1865.

HULME, WALTER O.
　Cadet Engineer, 1 October, 1880. Ensign, 1 July, 1886. Lieutenant, Junior Grade, 4 October, 1895. Lieutenant, 10 August, 1898.

HULSE, JOHN I.
　Assistant Paymaster (Spanish-American War), 20 May, 1898. Honorably discharged 11 October, 1898.

HULSE, ISAAC.
　Surgeon's Mate, 26 May, 1824. Surgeon, 6 May, 1825. Died 9 August, 1856.

HULSE, NATHANIEL S.
　Mate, 16 February, 1863. Resigned 8 July, 1863.

HULSE, THEODORE D.
　Acting Third Assistant Engineer, 21 December, 1861. Acting Second Assistant Engineer, 20 October, 1863. Appointment revoked (sick) 22 April, 1864.

HUME, JAMES H.
　Acting Third Assistant Engineer, 9 October, 1863. Honorably discharged 6 November, 1865.

HUMPHREY, ALVIN H.
　Acting Assistant Paymaster, 9 January, 1865. Mustered out 10 October, 1865.

HUMPHREY, F. M.
　Midshipman, 2 March, 1839. Resigned 14 May, 1846.

HUMPHREY, JOSEPH F.
　Actig Third Assistant Engineer,. 8 May, 1863. Honrably discharged 18 November, 1865.

HUMPHREYS, A. Y.
　Chaplain, date not known. Purser, 22 July, 1815. Died 6 February, 1826.

HUMPHREYS, CHARLES F.
　Carpenter, 17 September, 1869. Died 8 January, 1883.

HUMPHREYS, HORACE.
　Midshipman, 1 September, 1811. Appointment revoked 24 September, 1812.

HUMPHREYS, JOHN.
　Acting Volunteer Lieutenant, 12 August, 1861. Resigned 18 November, 1861.

HUMPHREYS, JOSHUA.
　Naval Constructor, date not known. Last appearance on Records of Navy Department, 26 October, 1801.

HUMPHREYS, JOSHUA.
　Midshipman, 2 February, 1829. Passed Midshipman, 3 July, 1835. Lieutenant, 25 February, 1841. Died 27 June, 1853.

HUMPHREYS, JULIUS.
　Midshipman, 16 January, 1809. Last appearance on Records of Navy Department, 1815. Wilmington, North Carolina.

HUMPHREYS, P. W.
　Midshipman, 2 February, 1829. Resigned 7 June, 1836.

HUMPHREYS, SAMUEL.
　Naval Constructor, 17 April, 1813. Chief Naval Constructor, 25 November, 1826. Died 16 August, 1846.

HUMPHREYS, SAMUEL.
　Carpenter, 16 December, 1815. Resigned 9 May, 1823.

HUMPHREYS, STERNE.
　Midshipman, 1 January, 1818. Lieutenant, 3 March, 1827. Resigned 1 October, 1834.

HUMSTONE, EDWIN.
　Acting Third Assistant Engineer, 2 June, 1864. Honorably discharged 16 August, 1865. Acting Third Assistant Engineer, 12 July, 1866. Mustered out 23 July, 1867.

HUNICKE, FELIX H.
　Cadet Midshipman, 22 September, 1877. Resigned 1 June, 1883. Lieutenant, Junior Grade (Spanish-American War), 14 May, 1898. Lieutenant, 21 February, 1899. Honorably discharged 21 February, 1899.

HUNKER, JACOB J.
　Midshipman, 30 July, 1866. Graduated 7 June, 1870. Ensign, 30 July, 1872. Master, 14 January, 1875. Lieutenant, 15 October, 1881. Lieutenant-Commander, 3 March, 1899.

HUNKER, JOHN JACOB.
　Midshipman, 18 April, 1862. Graduated June, 1866. Ensign, 12 March, 1868. Master, 26 March, 1869. Lieutenant, 21 March, 1870. Lieutenant-Commander, 2 October, 1885. Commander, 16 September, 1894. Captain, 11 December, 1900.

HUNNEWELL, L. J.
　Midshipman, 6 June, 1803. Resigned 29 July, 1805.

HUNSICKER, JOSEPH L.
　Midshipman, 25 June, 1867. Graduated 6 June, 1871. Ensign, 14 July, 1872. Master, 12 March, 1875. Lieutenant, 21 December, 1881. Resigned 1 September, 1884.

GENERAL NAVY REGISTER.

HUNSTABLE, HENRY.
　Mate, 1 January, 1864.　Appointment revoked 6 October, 1864.
HUNT, ABRAM H.
　Acting Assistant Surgeon, 28 February, 1865.　Honorably discharged 18 August, 1865.
HUNT, ANDREW M.
　Cadet Engineer, 15 September, 1875.　Graduated 10 June, 1879.　Assistant Engineer, 10 June, 1881.　Passed Assistant Engineer, 5 April, 1892.　Resigned 31 July, 1894.
HUNT, CHARLES SEDGWICK.
　Third Assistant Engineer, 22 July, 1862.　Resigned 9 June, 1863.
HUNT, CLEMENT S.
　Purser, 25 April, 1812.　Died 4 April, 1837.
HUNT, CYRUS H.
　Acting Third Assistant Engineer, 29 August, 1863.　Honorably discharged 10 November, 1865.
HUNT, DANIEL.
　Midshipman, 2 February, 1829.　Last appearance on Records of Navy Department, 18 November, 1831.　Dead.
HUNT, EDMUND B.
　Acting Ensign, 16 January, 1863.　Dismissed 21 April, 1865.
HUNT, FRANCIS W.
　Lieutenant, Junior Grade (Spanish-American War), 25 May, 1898.　Resigned 1 August, 1898.
HUNT, GEORGE P.
　Third Assistant Engineer, 1 July, 1861.　Second Assistant Engineer, 18 December, 1862.　First Assistant Engineer, 30 January, 1865.　Chief Engineer, 4 July, 1880.　Died 5 April, 1887.
HUNT, HENRY.
　Assistant Surgeon, 2 April, 1811.　Resigned 31 August, 1813
HUNT, HENRY.
　First Assistant Engineer, 17 January, 1842.　Chief Engineer, 14 May, 1847.　Died 10 April, 1861.
HUNT, HENRY.
　Gunner, 5 July, 1819.　Last appearance on Records of Navy Department, 14 September, 1819.
HUNT, HENRY J.
　Midshipman, 23 June, 1870.　Graduated 21 June, 1875.　Ensign, 30 September, 1876.　Lieutenant, Junior Grade, 11 March, 1883.　Died 5 May, 1886.
HUNT, JAMES P.
　Midshipman, 20 June, 1798.　Resigned 10 December, 1800
HUNT, JOHN H.
　Third Assistant Engineer, 1 July, 1861.　Second Assistant Engineer, 18 December, 1862.　First Assistant Engineer, 30 January, 1865.　Died 21 November, 1868.
HUNT, JOHN M.
　Midshipman, 30 November, 1814.　Resigned 29 January, 1819.
HUNT, JOHN W., Jr.
　Midshipman, 1 May, 1822.　Resigned 25 January, 1828.
HUNT, JOSEPH.
　Acting Third Assistant Engineer, 12 December, 1864.　Resigned 27 June, 1865.
HUNT, JOSEPH.
　Mate, 1 June, 1864.　Resigned 20 May, 1865.
HUNT, LEWIS.
　Midshipman, 2 March, 1803.　Resigned 20 September, 1808.
HUNT, LIVINGSTON.
　Assistant Paymaster, 29 October, 1881.　Passed Assistant Paymaster, 24 November, 1891.　Paymaster, 10 October, 1896.
HUNT, MONTGOMERY.
　Midshipman, 17 January, 1832.　Passed Midshipman, 23 June, 1838.　Lieutenant, 9 December, 1842.　Lost in Albany, 28 September, 1854.
HUNT, NATHANIEL.
　Gunner, 15 January, 1800.　Last appearance on Records of Navy Department.
HUNT, RIDGELY.
　Midshipman, 21 September, 1870.　Graduated 21 June, 1875.　Ensign, 25 November, 1877.　Lieutenant, Junior Grade, 1 December, 1883.　Lieutenant, 7 January, 1890.　Retired List, 15 September, 1897.
HUNT, SYMMES H.
　Acting Midshipman, 23 November, 1859.　Ensign, 16 December, 1862.　Lieutenant, 22 February, 1864.　Resigned 11 December, 1865.
HUNT, THEODORE.
　Midshipman, 2 September, 1798.　Lieutenant, 4 April, 1802.　Resigned 11 May, 1811.
HUNT, THOMAS.
　Midshipman, 14 April, 1800.　Resigned 26 August, 1807.
HUNT, THOMAS D.
　Mate.　Appointment revoked 8 October, 1866.
HUNT, TIMOTHY A.
　Midshipman, 1 March, 1825.　Passed Midshipman, 4 June, 1831.　Lieutenant, 17 December, 1836.　Commander, 14 September, 1855.　Captain, 16 July, 1862.　Commodore, 2 January, 1863.　Retired List, 23 July, 1877　Died 21 January, 1884.
HUNT, WALTER M.
　Naval aCdet, 12 September, 1895.　At sea prior to final graduation.
HUNT, WILLIAM E.
　Midshipman, 28 October, 1823.　Passed Midshipman, 23 March, 1829.　Lieutenant, 21 June, 1832.　Reserved List, 13 September, 1855.　Commissioned a Commander on

GENERAL NAVY REGISTER.

HUNTER, ROBERT.
Sailmaker, 12 July, 1845. Died 12 January, 1866.
HUNTER, ROBERT.
Mate, 13 February, 1865. Died 5 September, 1865.
HUNTER, SAMUEL V.
Purser, 4 June, 1858. Cashiered 11 January, 1859.
HUNTER, THOMAS T.
Midshipman, 1 July, 1828. Passed Midshipman, 14 June, 1834. Lieutenant, 25 February, 1841. Commander, 23 December, 1856. Dismissed 23 April, 1861.
HUNTER, WILLIAM.
Mate, 8 February, 1862. Acting Ensign, 8 April, 1863. Discharged 1 September, 1865.
HUNTER, WILLIAM.
Gunner, 29 March, 1836. Deserted in May, 1836.
HUNTER, WILLIAM M.
Midshipman, 16 January, 1809. Lieutenant, 24 July, 1813. Commander, 21 March, 1826. Captain, 9 February, 1837. Died 5 March, 1849.
HUNTER, WILLIAM R.
Mate, 3 July, 1862. Honorably discharged 31 January, 1866.
HUNTER, WILLIAM W.
Midshipman, 1 May, 1822. Passed Midshipman, 24 May, 1828. Lieutenant, 27 May, 1830. Commander, 6 January, 1853. Resigned 29 April, 1861.
HUNTINGTON, ARTHUR F.
Assistant Paymaster, 27 April, 1898. Passed Assistant Paymaster, 3 March, 1899.
HUNTINGTON, CHARLES L.
Acting Midshipman, 29 September, 1858. Acting Master, 13 May, 1862. Lieutenant, 1 August, 1862. Lieutenant-Commander, 25 July, 1866. Commander, 14 April, 1875. Died 14 October, 1890.
HUNTINGTON, ELON O.
Assistant Surgeon, 24 May, 1898.
HUNTINGTON, ERASTUS.
Midshipman, 1 February, 1827. Appointment revoked 3 February 1832.
HUNTINGTON, GEORGE W.
Acting Assistant Paymaster, 30 October, 1863. Honorably discharged 22 November, 1865.
HUNTINGTON, JOSHUA.
Assistant Surgeon, 20 June, 1838. Resigned 19 April, 1847.
HUNTINGTON, ROBERT PALMER.
Acting Midshipman, 24 September, 1858. Acting Ensign, 9 October, 1862. Resigned 20 January, 1865.
HUNTINGTON, SEPTIMUS.
Midshipman, 15 November, 1799. Resigned 27 September, 1800.
HUNTINGTON, THOMAS B.
Acting Ensign, 30 July, 1864. Honorably discharged 10 July, 1865.
HUNTINGTON, WILLIAM H.
Pharmacist, 15 September, 1898.
HUNTLEY, JOHN C.
Third Assistant Engineer, 12 August, 1861. Died 20 October, 1863.
HUNTLEY, WILLIAM.
Acting First Assistant Engineer, 14 February, 1863. Honorably discharged 28 October, 1865.
HUNTOON, FITZ A.
Cadet Midshipman, 15 September, 1875. Graduated 22 June, 1882. Ensign, Junior Grade, 3 March, 1883. Ensign, 26 June, 1886. Resigned 14 April, 1890.
HUNTRESS, JOSIAH.
Mate, 29 April, 1862. Dismissed 18 October, 1862.
HUNTRESS, JOSIAH.
Mate, 22 April, 1863. Dismissed 24 June, 1863.
HUNTRESS, ROBERT.
Gunner, 1 September, 1803. Resigned 31 July, 1809.
HUNTT, J. G. T.
Assistant Surgeon, 19 April, 1804. Surgeon, 27 November, 1804. Resigned 10 December, 1823.
HURD, CHARLES H.
Acting Ensign, 16 July, 1863. Died at New Orleans, La., 23 January, 1865.
HURD, EDWARD L.
Acting Ensign, 4 June, 1864. Honorably discharged 28 October, 1865.
HURD, EUGENE A.
Acting Third Assistant Engineer, 4 January, 1862. Dismissed 6 October, 1862.
HURD, FREEMAN A.
Acting Third Assistant Engineer, 16 October, 1863. Discharged 1865.
HURD, ISAAC N.
Pharmacist, 15 September, 1898.
HURD, JAMES H.
Mate, 1 October, 1862. Resigned 24 February, 1864.
HURD, JAMES M.
Mate, 3 September, 1863. Resigned 24 February, 1864.
HURD, JOSEPH H.
Mate, 31 March, 1863. Resigned 30 March, 1864.
HURD, J. S.
Acting Volunteer Lieutenant, 1 October, 1862. Resigned 13 April, 1864.
HURD, LUCIUS D.
Assistant Paymaster, 21 March, 1870. Resigned 20 September, 1873.

GENERAL NAVY REGISTER. 285

HUNT, WILLIAM F.
Active List, from 22 August, 1855. Lost in Sloop of War Levant, 18 September, 1860.
HUNT, WILLIAM H.
Mate, 16 November, 1861. Acting Master, 3 July, 1862. Honorably discharged 9 February, 1866.
HUNT, WILLIAM N.
Mate, 25 October, 1862. Resigned 19 February, 1864.
HUNT, WILSON.
Third Assistant Engineer, 24 December, 1853. Second Assistant Engineer, 9 May, 1857. First Assistant Engineer, 2 August, 1859. Chief Engineer, 19 February, 1863. Retired List, 8 February, 1871. Died 25 June, 1889.
HUNTER, A. E.
Midshipman, 20 February, 1840. Resigned 5 September, 1840.
HUNTER, ANDREW.
Acting Master, 26 August, 1861. Honorably discharged 26 February, 1866.
HUNTER, BALDWIN M.
Chaplain, 5 March, 1811. Died 24 February, 1823.
HUNTER, B. F. B.
Midshipman, 17 December, 1831. Resigned 20 August, 1835.
HUNTER, BUSHROD W.
Midshipman, 20 August, 1835. Passed Midshipman, 22 June, 1841. Master, 7 July, 1847. Lieutenant, 28 November, 1847. Resigned 17 January, 1850.
HUNTER, CHARLES.
Midshipman, 1 November, 1827. Passed Midshipman, 10 June, 1833. Lieutenant, 28 February, 1838. Reserved List, 13 September, 1855. Resigned 23 April, 1861.
HUNTER, CHARLES.
Midshipman, 25 April, 1831. Passed Midshipman, 15 June, 1837. Lieutenant, 8 September, 1841. Reserved List. Commander, 9 June, 1862. Retired List, 21 June, 1866. Captain, Retired List. Died 22 November, 1873.
HUNTER, CHARLES C.
Acting Ensign, 1 October, 1862. Resigned 6 May, 1863.
HUNTER, CHARLES G.
Midshipman, 2 July, 1842. Passed Midshipman, 5 August, 1848. Dismissed 9 September, 1848. Restored as Passed Midshipman. Died in May, 1853.
HUNTER, CHARLES G.
Midshipman, 16 November, 1824. Passed Midshipman, 20 February, 1830. Lieutenant, 24 June, 1834. Dismissed 29 January, 1855.
HUNTER, DAVID.
Midshipman, 18 June, 1812. Resigned 20 July, 1818.
HUNTER, GEORGE W.
Midshipman, 1 February, 1814. Last appearance on Records of Navy Department, 1815. Frigate Guerriere.
HUNTER, GODFREY M.
Acting Midshipman, 20 September, 1861. Graduated 24 September, 1865. Ensign, 1 December, 1866. Master, 12 March, 1868. Lieutenant, 26 March, 1869. Died 26 September, 1873.
HUNTER, HENRY C.
Midshipman, 10 September, 1841. Passed Midshipman, 10 August, 1847. Resigned 27 April, 1854.
HUNTER, HENRY CHRISTIE.
Midshipman, 3 September, 1863. Graduated 6 June, 1867. Ensign, 18 December, 1868. Master, 21 March, 1870. Lieutenant, 21 March, 1871. Died 10 June, 1881.
HUNTER, HENRY D.
Midshipman, 30 November, 1814. Resigned 12 January, 1825.
HUNTER, HENRY St. G.
Midshipman, 19 November, 1841. Passed Midshipman, 10 August, 1847. Died 24 September, 1854.
HUNTER, JAMES.
Mate, 5 March, 1862. Acting Ensign, 1 December, 1863. Honorably discharged 8 November, 1865.
HUNTER, JOHN.
Boatswain, 8 February, 1842. Resigned 9 March, 1844.
HUNTER, JOHN.
Boatswain, 11 June, 1847. Appointment revoked 14 May, 1850.
HUNTER, JOHN.
Acting Boatswain. Appointment revoked 31 January, 1865.
HUNTER, JOHN.
Chief Engineer (Spanish-American War), 4 May, 1898. Honorably discharged 2 September, 1898.
HUNTER, JOHN C.
Purser, 29 May, 1851. Resigned 14 August, 1856.
HUNTER, JOHN W.
Midshipman, 10 May, 1820. Resigned 18 November, 1825.
HUNTER, LEWIS B.
Assistant Surgeon, 3 January, 1828. Passed Assistant Surgeon, 3 March, 1835. Surgeon, 9 February, 1837. Retired List, 9 October, 1866. Medical Director, Retired List, 3 March, 1871. Died 24 June, 1887.
HUNTER, M. H.
Midshipman, 18 June, 1812. Resigned 1 October, 1822.
HUNTER, RICHARD S.
Midshipman, 1 September, 1811. Lieutenant, 5 March, 1817. Died 28 March, 1825.
HUNTER, ROBERT.
Mate, 9 January, 1863. Acting Ensign, 17 January, 1865. Honorably discharged 2 July, 1868.

GENERAL NAVY REGISTER. 287

HURD, PIERSON.
Midshipman, 1 December, 1828. Resigned 29 May, 1829.
HURD, WILLIAM L.
Acting Ensign, 28 January, 1863. Drowned 31 July, 1863.
HURLBERT, JAMES S.
Mate, 22 June, 1863. Promoted Acting Ensign, 5 October, 1863. Resigned 30 May, 1865.
HURLBUT, S. DENNISON.
Acting Assistant Paymaster, 6 April, 1865. Mustered out 9 October, 1865. Assistant Paymaster, 2 March, 1867. Passed Assistant Paymaster, 12 February, 1870. Wholly retired 27 July, 1886.
HURLBUT, SAMUEL R.
Naval Cadet, 4 September, 1883. Ensign, 1 July, 1889. Resigned 28 October, 1897. Ensign (Spanish-American War), 20 May, 1898. Honorably discharged 8 October, 1898.
HURLEY, HENRY.
Acting Master, 17 December, 1861. Died 17 September, 1862.
HURLEY, ROBERT E.
Acting Third Assistant Engineer, 11 May, 1864. Acting Second Assistant Engineer, 15 March, 1865. Honorably discharged 18 August, 1865.
HURON, THOMAS G.
Acting Ensign, 1 October, 1862. Honorably discharged 20 September, 1865.
HURST, GEORGE.
Midshipman, 1 January, 1825. Passed Midshipman, 4 June. 1831. Lieutenant, 9 February, 1837. Reserved List, 13 September, 1855. Died 9 July, 1860.
HURST, WILLIAM D.
Midshipman, 2 February, 1829. Passed Midshipman, 15 June, 1837. Lieutenant, 8 September, 1841. Died 7 August, 1855.
HUSBANDS, J. D., JR.
Acting Assistant Paymaster, 21 July, 1862. Resigned 14 September, 1863.
HUSE, HARRY McL. P.
Cadet Midshipman, 30 September, 1874. Graduated 4 June, 1880. Ensign, 2 June, 1882. Lieutenant, Junior Grade, 27 June, 1889. Lieutenant, 13 May, 1894.
HUSE, SAMUEL
Acting Master, 3 September, 1861. Acting Volunteer Lieutenant, 7 May, 1863. Acting Volunteer Lieutenant-Commander, 31 May, 1865. Honorably discharged 31 March, 1866.
HUSSEY, A. S.
Acting Master, 1 April, 1862. Honorably discharged 21 October, 1866.
HUSSEY, CHARLES L.
Naval Cadet, 21 May, 1888. Ensign, 1 July, 1894. Lieutenant, Junior Grade, 3 March, 1899. Lieutenant, 1 July, 1900.
HUSSEY, EDWARD B.
Acting Master, 18 January, 1862. Honorably discharged 15 February, 1868.
HUSTACE, RICHARD.
Acting Master, 24 March, 1862. Honorably discharged 4 February, 1866.
HUSTEAD, J. W.
Assistant Surgeon, 24 July, 1813. Died 23 May, 1814.
HUSTON, JOSEPH T.
Professor, 7 September, 1836. Dropped 4 September, 1848.
HUSTON, MATTHEW.
Acting Ensign, 10 March, 1863. Honorably discharged 28 October, 1865.
HUSTON, ROBERT M.
Second Assistant Engineer, 4 October, 1873. Resigned 15 May, 1874.
HUTCHINS, ALEXANDER.
Assistant Surgeon, 30 July, 1861. Resigned 24 June, 1863.
HUTCHINS, CHARLES THOMAS.
Midshipman, 2 January. 1862. Graduated June, 1866. Ensign, 12 March, 1868. Master, 26 March, 1869. Lieutenant, 21 March, 1870. Lieutenant-Commander, 30 June, 1887. Commander, 28 February, 1896.
HUTCHINS, EDWARD R.
Acting Assistant Surgeon, 19 December, 1862. Honorably discharged 1 December, 1865.
HUTCHINS, HAMILTON.
Midshipman, 31 June, 1870. Graduated 1 June, 1874. Ensign, 17 July, 1875. Master. 22 May, 1881. Lieutenant, Junior Grade, 3 March, 1883. Lieutenant, 21 May, 1887. Lieutenant-Commander, 3 March, 1899.
HUTCHINS, JOHN F.
Mate, 6 November, 1865. Honorably discharged 16 May, 1867.
HUTCHINS, W. H.
Lieutenant, 3 July, 1798. Resigned 9 May, 1801.
HUTCHINSON, CALVIN G.
Acting Assistant Paymaster, 24 October, 1862. Mustered out 15 April, 1866.
HUTCHINSON, EDWARD S.
Third Assistant Engineer, 3 October, 1861. Appointment revoked 26 January, 1862.
HUTCHINSON, FREDERICK A.
Acting Second Assistant Engineer, 22 July, 1863. Honorably discharged 4 November, 1865.
HUTCHINSON, HENRY M.
Acting Third Assistant Engineer, 4 March, 1864. Honorably discharged 1 September, 1865.
HUTCHINSON, JAMES.
Gunner, 19 September, 1850. Retired List, 5 November, 1883. Died 31 May, 1894.

HUTCHINSON, JAMES W.
Third Assistant Engineer, 5 November, 1861. Second Assistant Engineer, 25 August, 1863. Resigned 6 April, 1865.
HUTCHINSON, J. P. O.
Mate, 29 March, 1865. Discharged 9 July, 1867.
HUTCHINSON, ROBERT E. L.
Lieutenant, Junior Grade (Spanish-American War), 22 June, 1898. Honorably discharged 12 October, 1898.
HUTCHINSON, THOMAS C.
Acting Assistant Paymaster, 29 May, 1863. Honorably discharged 29 December, 1865.
HUTCHINSON, WILLIAM F.
Acting Assistant Surgeon, 28 April, 1863. Acting Passed Assistant Surgeon, 4 August, 1865. Honorably discharged 3 July, 1868.
HUTCHINSON, W. T.
Midshipman, 24 September, 1847. Died 7 February, 1848.
HUTCHISON, BENJAMIN F.
Naval Cadet, 5 September, 1885. Ensign, 1 July, 1891. Lieutenant, Junior Grade, 10 August, 1898. Lieutenant, 3 March, 1899.
HUTSON, T. OGIER.
Assistant Surgeon (Spanish-American War), 20 May, 1898. Honorably discharged 8 September, 1898.
HUTTER, EDWARD S.
Midshipman, 24 February, 1832. Passed Midshipman, 23 June, 1838. Resigned 22 September, 1841.
HUTTER, GEORGE F.
Midshipman, 21 June, 1870. Graduated 1 June, 1874. Ensign, 17 July, 1875. Retired List, 3 February, 1882.
HUTTON, DAVID.
Acting Third Assistant Engineer, 29 August, 1861. Resigned 30 December, 1862.
HUTTON, JOHN H.
Acting Third Assistant Engineer, 29 July, 1863. Acting Second Assistant Engineer, 3 September, 1864. Honorably discharged 14 November, 1865. Acting Second Assistant Engineer, 2 April, 1866. Mustered out 5 November, 1869.
HUTTON, JOHN S.
Master, 24 February, 1809. Last appearance on Records of Navy Department, 1815. Lake Ontario.
HUXLEY, JOHN H.
Third Assistant Engineer, 19 July, 1861. Second Assistant Engineer, 28 December, 1862. Resigned 16 June, 1865.
HYDE, FREDERICK GRISWOLD.
Midshipman, 23 September, 1863. Graduated 5 June, 1867. Ensign, 18 December, 1868. Master, 21 March, 1870. Lieutenant, 21 March, 1871. Resigned 24 June, 1883.
HYDE, GEORGE W.
Acting Master, 28 October, 1861. Honorably discharged 2 January, 1867.
HYDE, HENRY M.
Acting Assistant Paymaster, 24 May, 1862. Died, Brooklyn, N. Y., 15 February, 1864.
HYDE, JAMES N.
Acting Assistant Surgeon, 14 July, 1863. Assistant Surgeon, 26 October, 1863. Passed Assistant Surgeon, 31 December, 1867. Resigned 27 February, 1869.
HYDE, JAMES S.
Mate, 18 December, 1861. Dismissed 10 September, 1862.
HYDE, MARCUS D.
Midshipman, 25 November, 1865. Graduated 7 June, 1870. Ensign, 13 July, 1871. Master, 7 July, 1874. Resigned 25 November, 1877.
HYDE, WILLIAM.
Carpenter, 27 January, 1851. Died 4 March, 1865.
HYDE, WILLIAM D.
Acting Third Assistant Engineer, 26 February, 1864. Honorably discharged 11 January, 1866.
HYLAND, JOHN J.
Naval Cadet, 19 September, 1896. Graduated 30 June, 1900.
HYLAND, MARTIN.
Acting Third Assistant Engineer, 31 December, 1864. Honorably discharged 4 October, 1865.
HYMAN, JOHN M.
Acting Second Assistant Engineer, 1 July, 1863. Honorably discharged 4 November, 1865.
HYNARD, WILLIAM A.
Mate, 30 August, 1864. Resigned 30 May, 1865.
HYNSON, JOHN R.
Midshipman, 5 March, 1829. Passed Midshipman, 2 July, 1845. Drowned 8 December, 1846.
HYSLOP, JOHN.
Acting Third Assistant Engineer, 21 October, 1862. Honorably discharged 2 December, 1866.
IASCHKE, FREDERICK R.
Mate, 21 January, 1864. Acting Ensign, 1 December, 1864. Honorably discharged 19 August, 1866.
IDE, GEORGE ELMORE.
Acting Midshipman, 27 September, 1861. Graduated September, 1865. Ensign, 1 December, 1866. Master, 12 March, 1868. Lieutenant, 26 March, 1869. Lieuten-

GENERAL NAVY REGISTER. 289

ant-Commander, 12 October, 1881. Commander, 5 November, 1891. Captain, 25 March, 1899.
IGLEHART, EDMUND B.
   Assistant Paymaster (Spanish-American War), 13 June, 1898. Honorably discharged, 18 January, 1899.
IGLEHART, OSBORN S.
   Assistant Surgeon, 29 August, 1860. Dismissed 28 January, 1862.
IGO, JAMES.
   Acting Ensign, 17 July, 1863. Acting Master, 25 May, 1865. Honorably discharged 20 December, 1865.
IGOE, JAMES J.
   Lieutenant (Spanish-American War), 26 May, 1898. Honorably discharged 8 September, 1898.
ILSLEY, EDWARD D.
   Acting Assistant Paymaster, 18 August, 1862. Resigned 27 July, 1864.
ILSLEY, FREDERICK.
   Midshipman, 2 February, 1829. Dropped.
ILSLEY, FREDERICK.
   Acting Ensign, Coast Survey duty, 21 June, 1867. Mustered out 30 November, 1868.
IMLAY, FREDERICK C.
   Acting Assistant Paymaster, 6 December, 1862. Mustered out 19 December, 1867.
IMLAY, JOHN H.
   Surgeon's Mate, 16 November, 1824. Resigned 5 September, 1831.
IMPEY, ROBERT E.
   Acting Midshipman, 21 September, 1861. Graduated September, 1865. Ensign, 1 December, 1866. Master, 12 March, 1868. Lieutenant, 26 March, 1869. Lieutenant-Commander, 1 October, 1882. Commander, 25 January, 1893. Captain, 2 November, 1899.
INCE, HORACE L.
   Acting First Assistant Engineer, 1 October, 1862. Honorably discharged 30 November, 1865.
INCH, PHILIP.
   Third Assistant Engineer, 21 November, 1857. Second Assistant Engineer, 2 August, 1859. First Assistant Engineer, 1 July, 1861. Chief Engineer, 10 November, 1863. Retired List, 6 August, 1898. Died 18 October, 1898.
INCH, RICHARD.
   Third Assistant Engineer, 8 September, 1863. Second Assistant Engineer, 15 October, 1865. Passed Assistant Engineer, 28 September, 1874. Chief Engineer, 3 August, 1892. Rank changed to Commander, 3 March, 1899.
INDERWICKE, JAMES.
   Surgeon, 24 July, 1813. Last appearance on Records of Navy Department, 1815. Brig Epervier.
INGALLS, EMERY G.
   Acting Third Assistant Engineer, 15 August, 1864. Honorably discharged 17 July, 1865.
INGALLS, GEORGE W.
   Mate. Resigned 11 March, 1862.
INGERSOLL, DANIEL S.
   Mate, 20 April, 1863. Resigned 11 April, 1865.
INGERSOLL, HARRY.
   Midshipman, 28 February, 1824. Passed Midshipman, 20 February, 1830. Lieutenant, 8 April, 1834. Resigned 18 April, 1850.
INGERSOLL, JONATHAN.
   Midshipman, 4 March, 1823. Passed Midshipman, 23 May, 1829. Lieutenant, 3 March, 1831. Resigned 25 August, 1838.
INGERSOLL, ROYAL R.
   Midshipman, 23 July, 1864. Graduated June, 1868. Ensign, 19 April, 1869. Master, 12 July, 1870. Lieutenant, 13 April, 1872. Lieutenant-Commander, 25 February, 1893. Commander, 3 March, 1899.
INGERSOLL, WILLIAM A.
   Purser, 1 May, 1856. Died 25 August, 1865.
INGHAM, WILLIAM.
   Mate, 3 March, 1862. Dismissed 23 April, 1862.
INGLEHART, PHILIP.
   Acting Ensign, 9 April, 1863. Dismissed 29 July, 1863.
INGLIS, ANDREW.
   Acting Third Assistant Engineer, 23 February, 1864. Honorably discharged 21 November, 1865.
INGLIS, ROBERT A.
   Acting Third Assistant Engineer, 23 November, 1864. Resigned 15 February, 1866.
INGRAHAM, D. G.
   Midshipman, 16 January, 1809. Resigned 5 May, 1813.
INGRAHAM, DUNCAN N.
   Midshipman, 18 June, 1812. Lieutenant, 13 January, 1825. Commander, 8 September, 1841. Captain, 14 September, 1855. Resigned 4 February, 1861.
INGRAHAM, EDWARD.
   Boatswain, 1 November, 1826. Dismissed 12 June, 1830.
INGRAHAM, JAMES A.
   Mate, 11 May, 1864. Died on Vanderbilt, 21 June, 1866.
INGRAHAM, JAMES D.
   Acting Master, 29 October, 1861. Resigned 8 July, 1862.
INGRAHAM, JOHN D.
   Acting Master, 23 September, 1861. Resigned 17 December, 1862.

19

INGRAHAM, JOSEPH.
Lieutenant, 14 June, 1799. Last appearance on Records of Navy Department.
INGRAHAM, WILLIAM.
Midshipman, 20 July, 1799. Discharged 12 October, 1801, under Peace Establishment Act.
INGRAM, NELSON.
Acting Assistant Surgeon, 27 February, 1865. Honorably discharged 13 January, 1868.
INMAN, WILLIAM.
Midshipman, 1 January, 1812. Lieutenant, 1 April, 1818. Commander, 24 May, 18⁻⁻ Captain, 2 June, 1850. Reserved List, 13 September, 1855. Commissioned Captain on Active List from 2 June, 1850. Retired List, 1 December, 1861. Commodore, Retired List, 4 April, 1867. Died 23 October, 1874.
INNES, ROBERT.
Midshipman, 28 August, 1800. Drowned in 1802.
INNES, WILLIAM J.
Mate, 9 March, 1870. Resigned 18 August, 1870.
INNIS, PETER.
Acting Third Assistant Engineer, 21 October, 1863. Dismissed 5 December, 1864.
INSKEEP, P. H.
Midshipman, 1 April, 1828. Resigned 20 March, 1835.
INSLEE, PHINEAS J.
Acting Third Assistant Engineer, 18 December, 1861. Resigned 14 August, 1862.
INSLEY, HUGH R.
Assistant Paymaster (Spanish-American War), 11 June, 1898. Assistant Paymaster (Regular Navy), 6 March, 1899.
IPSEN, HANS J.
Acting Ensign, 29 July, 1863. Acting Master, 27 March, 1865. Honorably discharged 1 August, 1865.
IRELAN, AARON B.
Acting Boatswain, 31 August, 1899.
IRELAND, GEORGE COOKMAN.
Third Assistant Engineer, 16 September, 1862. Second Assistant Engineer, 1 March, 1864. Resigned 10 November, 1865.
IRELAND, JOHN.
Chaplain 16 August, 1816. Last appearance on Records of Navy Department, 1823. New York Navy Yard.
IRISH, CHARLES H.
Acting Third Assistant Engineer, 17 September, 1862. Dismissed 22 July, 1863.
IRVIN, ROLAND C.
Acting Midshipman, 29 September, 1860. Acting Ensign, 1 October, 1863. Master, 10 May, 1866. Resigned 25 September, 1866.
IRVIN, RICHARD.
Acting First Assistant Engineer, 10 December, 1863. Resigned 13 April, 1864.
IRVINE, ARTHUR.
Acting Third Assistant Engineer, 22 October, 1863. Appointment revoked (sick) 27 June, 1864.
IRVINE, EDWARD T.
Lieutenant, Junior Grade (Spanish-American War), 8 June, 1898. Honorably discharged 2 September, 1898.
IRVINE, JOHN C.
Midshipman, 26 September, 1864. Graduated June, 1868. Ensign, 19 April, 1869. Master, 12 July, 1870. Lieutenant, 3 June, 1873. Resigned 17 November, 1892.
IRVINE, KENNETH.
Midshipman, 16 January, 1809. Dismissed 29 April, 1809.
IRVINE, THOMAS.
Midshipman, 20 September, 1841. Dropped.
IRVING, EDGAR.
Midshipman, 1 November, 1826. Resigned 31 August, 1832.
IRVING, OSCAR.
Midshipman, 1 January, 1817. Resigned 11 October, 1824.
IRVING, PHILIP H.
Mate, 20 October, 1863. Discharged 21 June, 1864, as seaman. Mate, 30 July, 1867. Mustered out 9 April, 1868.
IRVING, THOMAS.
Mate, gallant conduct at Fort Moultrie, 17 November, 1863. Discharged 6 January, 1865.
IRVING, WASHINGTON.
Paymaster, 1 June, 1861. Wholly retired 11 February, 1870.
IRVING, WASHINGTON.
Cadet Midshipman, 18 September, 1875. Dropped 11 October, 1877. Lieutenant, Junior Grade (Spanish-American War), 21 May, 1898. Honorably discharged 8 October, 1898.
IRVING, W. F.
Midshipman, 1 January, 1825. Passed Midshipman, 4 June, 1831. Died 4 November, 1832.
IRWIN, ANDREW N.
Midshipman, 1 March, 1825. Resigned 3 November, 1827.
IRWIN, DAVID.
Midshipman, 4 March, 1834. Died 8 October, 1834.
IRWIN, JEREMIAH.
Acting Ensign, 1 October, 1862. Acting Master, 25 June, 1863. Honorably discharged 27 October, 1865.

GENERAL NAVY REGISTER.

IRWIN, JOHN.
Midshipman, 9 September, 1847. Passed Midshipman, 10 June, 1853. Master, September, 1855. Lieutenant, 16 September, 1855. Lieutenant-Commander, 16 July, 1862. Commander, 25 July, 1866. Captain, 15 May, 1875. Commodore, 4 March, 1886. Rear Admiral, 19 May, 1891. Retired List 15 April, 1894.

IRWIN, JOHN, Jr.
Assistant Paymaster, 5 September, 1895. Passed Assistant Paymaster, 12 February, 1898.

IRWIN, JOHN J.
Mate, 23 July, 1863. Acting Ensign, 3 November, 1864. Honorably discharged 13 December, 1865.

IRWIN, JOHN W.
Acting Gunner, 28 August, 1863. Appointment revoked 14 June, 1865.

IRWIN, NOBLE E.
Naval Cadet, 29 September, 1887. Ensign, 1 July, 1893. Lieutenant, Junior Grade, 3 March, 1899. Lieutenant, 8 December, 1899.

IRWIN, WILLIAM.
Midshipman, 20 June, 1806. Resigned 24 February, 1810.

IRWIN, WILLIAM M.
Midshipman, 29 June, 1867. Graduated 6 June, 1871. Ensign, 14 July, 1872. Master, 1 May, 1875. Lieutenant, 2 June, 1882. Lieutenant-Commander, 3 March, 1899.

ISAAC, EUGENE M.
Boatswain, 16 July, 1898.

ISAACS, EDWARD.
Midshipman, 1 January, 1812. Dismissed 23 September, 1813.

ISAACS, GEORGE W.
Midshipman, 1 January, 1812. Lieutenant, 5 March, 1817. Last appearance on Records of Navy Department, 6 March, 1822. Dead.

ISAACS, JOHN L.
Acting Assistant Paymaster, 23 December, 1861. Resigned 9 May, 1863.

ISAACS, WALTER G.
Chaplain, 25 April, 1888.

ISBESTER, RICHARD THORNTON.
Cadet Engineer, Naval Academy, 15 September, 1875. Graduated 10 June, 1879. Assistant Engineer, 10 June, 1881. Wholly retired 7 January, 1886.

ISHERWOOD, BENJAMIN F.
First Assistant Engineer, 23 May, 1844. Appointment revoked 22 January, 1846. Second Assistant Engineer, 22 January, 1846. First Assistant Engineer, 10 July, 1847. Chief Engineer, 31 October, 1848. Engineer-in-Chief, 26 March, 1861. Successor appointed 16 March, 1869. Retired List, 6 October, 1884.

ISRAEL, ISRAEL.
Midshipman, 9 November, 1813. Resigned 26 February, 1818.

ISRAEL, JOSEPH.
Midshipman, 15 January, 1801. Died with honor in the service 4 September, 1804.

ITRICH, FRANZ A.
Carpenter. 29 September, 1898.

IVERS, HENRY KING.
Cadet Engineer, 1 October, 1874. Graduated 10 June, 1879. Assistant Engineer, 10 June, 1881. Resigned 1 July, 1885.

IVERSON, ANDREW J.
Mate, 19 March, 1863. Acting Ensign, 6 October, 1864. Honorably discharged 8 December, 1866. Ensign, 12 March, 1868. Master, 18 December, 1868. Lieutenant, 21 March, 1870. Lieutenant-Commander, 19 June, 1882. Commander, 4 December, 1892. Retired List, 4 January, 1897.

IVES, RAIFORD W.
Midshipman, 7 April, 1847. Died 25 March, 1850.

IVES, THOMAS BOYNTON.
Acting Master, 3 September, 1862. Acting Volunteer Lieutenant, efficient and gallant conduct, 26 May, 1863. Acting Volunteer Lieutenant-Commander, 7 November, 1864. Died at Havre, France, 17 November, 1865.

IVES, WILBUR.
Acting Assistant Paymaster, 16 October, 1863. Honorably discharged 3 January, 1866.

IZARD, ALLEN C.
Midshipman, 2 October, 1850. Passed Midshipman, 20 June, 1856. Resigned 29 May, 1857.

IZARD, GEORGE, Jr.
Midshipman, 1 January, 1818. Lieutenant, 3 March, 1827. Resigned 4 May, 1833.

IZARD, RALPH, Jr.
Midshipman, 2 October, 1799. Lieutenant, 27 January, 1807. Resigned 28 April, 1810.

IZARD, R. D.
Midshipman, 7 November, 1834. Passed Midshipman, 16 July, 1840. Lieutenant, 31 October, 1846. Resigned 4 August, 1847.

JACK, CHARLES E.
Acting Master, 16 December, 1861. Honorably discharged 1 January, 1866.

JACKAWAY, JOSEPH A.
Mate, 21 October, 1861. Acting Master, 15 May, 1862. Honorably discharged 20 September, 1865.

JACKSON, A. M. D.
Purser, 23 May, 1832. Died 31 October, 1840.

GENERAL NAVY REGISTER.

JACKSON, ALBERT.
Third Assistant Engineer, 13 May, 1861. Second Assistant Engineer, 15 April, 1864. Resigned 23 September, 1865.

JACKSON, ALBERT H.
Mate, 8 August, 1864. Dismissed 21 April, 1865.

JACKSON, ALBERT R.
Assistant Engineer (Spanish-American War), 9 May, 1898. Honorably discharged 8 September, 1898.

JACKSON, ALONZO C.
Midshipman, 23 February, 1841. Passed Midshipman, 10 August, 1847. Died 31 March, 1853.

JACKSON, ANDREW.
Mate, 4 October, 1861. Acting Ensign, 24 June, 1862. Honorably discharged 6 December, 1867.

JACKSON, CALVIN C.
Purser, 17 July, 1857. Pay Inspector, 3 March, 1871. Pay Director, 24 October, 1871. Retired List, 27 August, 1876. Died 27 June, 1883.

JACKSON, CHARLES H.
Midshipman, 8 March, 1818. Lieutenant, 3 March, 1827. Commander, 14 September, 1848. Reserved List, 13 September, 1855. Commodore, Retired List, 4 Apr., 1867. Died 3 August, 1878.

JACKSON, DAVID W.
Mate, 23 October, 1861. Acting Ensign, 1 October, 1862. Resigned 27 April, 1863.

JACKSON, E. B.
Acting Assistant Surgeon, 18 December, 1861. Resigned 9 February, 1863.

JACKSON, EDWARD, Jr.
Naval Cadet, 22 May, 1896. Graduated 30 June, 1900.

JACKSON, EDWIN F.
Acting Third Assistant Engineer, 6 May, 1863. Dismissed 14 July, 1863.

JACKSON, GEORGE.
Gunner, 2 February, 1810. Last appearance on Records of Navy Department, 1825.

JACKSON, GEORGE.
Gunner, 14 December, 1825. Died in November, 1831.

JACKSON, HENRY.
Acting Ensign, 15 May, 1863. Killed at Calcasieu, La., 6 May, 1864.

JACKSON, JAMES M.
Acting Ensign, 28 January, 1865. Honorably discharged 2 April, 1867.

JACKSON, JOHN.
Midshipman, 12 December, 1812. Dismissed 5 January, 1814.

JACKSON, JOHN B.
Cadet Midshipman, 26 September, 1879. Graduated 8 June, 1883. Ensign, 1 July, 1885. Resigned 30 June, 1886.

JACKSON, JOHN H.
Mate, 16 May, 1864. Honorably discharged 18 September, 1865.

JACKSON, JOSEPH H.
Mate, 8 March, 1862. Acting Ensign, 24 September, 1862. Resigned (sick) 30 September, 1864.

JACKSON, LOTHROP.
Mate, 3 March, 1865. Deserted, 1867.

JACKSON, MARCELLUS.
Mate, 9 October, 1862. Acting Ensign, 27 November, 1863. Honorably discharged 8 November, 1865.

JACKSON, MORTON.
Midshipman, 1 January, 1808. Died 1 July, 1809.

JACKSON, ORTON P.
Naval Cadet, 18 May, 1889. Ensign, 1 July, 1895. Lieutenant Junior Grade, March, 1899.

JACKSON, RICHARD H.
Naval Cadet, 4 June, 1883. Graduated 10 June, 1887. Honorably discharged 30 June, 1889. Restored to service and commissioned Ensign, 1 July, 1890. Lieutenant, Junior Grade, 3 July, 1898. Lieutenant, 3 March, 1899.

JACKSON, SAMUEL.
Surgeon's Mate, 10 July, 1812. Surgeon, 27 March, 1818. Died 16 March, 1859.

JACKSON, SAMUEL.
Assistant Surgeon, 20 June, 1838. Passed Assistant Surgeon, 22 November, 1843. Surgeon, 2 September, 1852. Medical Director, 3 March, 1871. Retired List, 1 April, 1879.

JACKSON, THOMAS.
Boatswain, 23 September, 1813. Dismissed 3 January, 1814.

JACKSON, THOMAS A.
Third Assistant Engineer, 31 October, 1848. Second Assistant Engineer, 1 October, 1852. First Assistant Engineer, 26 June, 1856. Name stricken from the rolls 6 May, 1861.

JACKSON, VICTOR S.
Assistant Paymaster, 9 June, 1899.

JACKSON, W. H.
Acting Second Assistant Engineer, 5 June, 1863. Resigned 21 September, 1863.

JACKSON, WILLIAM G.
Chaplain, 19 October, 1842. Resigned 27 July, 1850.

JACKSON, WILLIAM H.
Acting Third Assistant Engineer, 24 March, 1865. Resigned 16 June, 1865.

JACKSON, WILLIAM H. H.
Mate, 18 April, 1863. Resigned 22 August, 1863.

JACOB, EDWIN SAMUEL.
Midshipman, 15 October, 1862. Graduated June, 1867. Ensign, 18 December, 1868. Master, 21 March, 1870. Lieutenant, 21 March, 1871. Retired List, 7 January, 1885.
JACOB, LOUIS.
Acting Third Assistant Engineer, 18 February, 1865. Honorably discharged 19 February, 1868.
JACOBS, BELA.
Carpenter, 22 April, 1799. Died 23 July, 1799.
JACOBS, BENJAMIN F.
Mate, 21 March, 1862. Resigned 26 May, 1864.
JACOBS, BENJAMIN F.
Ensign (Spanish-American War), 20 May, 1898. Honorably discharged, 6 January, 1899.
JACOBS, EDWARD.
Midshipman, 30 November, 1814. Resigned 24 October, 1815.
JACOBS, J. M.
Midshipman, 18 June, 1812. Resigned 30 April, 1814.
JACOBS, NATHANIEL P.
Mate, 10 December, 1863. Dismissed 20 May, 1865.
JACOBS, SIMON.
Gunner. 15 June, 1898.
JACOBS, WILSON, JR.
Midshipman, 7 October, 1798. Resigned 10 April, 1800.
JACOBS, WILSON.
Lieutenant, 27 October, 1798. Discharged 30 April, 1801, under Peace Establishment Act.
JACOBSON, FREDERICK D.
Acting Ensign, 25 April, 1864. Honorably discharged 19 July, 1865.
JACOBSON, JACOB.
Acting Carpenter, 9 February, 1900.
JACOBY, HENRY M.
Midshipman, 27 July, 1866. Graduated 7 June, 1870. Ensign, 13 July, 1871. Master, 8 April, 1874. Lieutenant, 11 July, 1880. Retired List, 16 November, 1883.
JACOBY, JAMES H.
Mate, 18 December, 1863. Honorably discharged 11 November, 1865.
JACQUES, GERSHOM R.
Surgeon's Mate, 21 May, 1800. Discharged 4 August, 1801, under Peace Establishment Act. Reappointed Surgeon's Mate, 18 February, 1802. Surgeon, 27 November, 1804. Struck off 25 April, 1808.
JAFFE, CHARLES E.
Gunner, 11 July, 1898.
JAGGARD, WILLIAM W.
Assistant Surgeon, 9 July, 1881. Resigned 1 December, 1881.
JAMES, BENJAMIN.
Acting Third Assistant Engineer, 10 September, 1861. Acting Second Assistant Engineer, 21 January, 1864. Honorably discharged 19 January, 1868.
JAMES, DANIEL.
Gunner, 10 June, 1837. Died 14 April, 1851
JAMES, DANIEL.
Carpenter, 8 February, 1848. Died 5 June, 1852.
JAMES, FRANKLIN.
Mate. Resigned 26 March, 1864.
JAMES, HENRY.
Acting Third Assistant Engineer, 30 December, 1864. Honorably discharged 1 November, 1865.
JAMES, HIRAM H.
Acting Assistant Surgeon, 28 April, 1863. Appointment revoked 15 Dectmber, 1863. Acting Assistant Surgeon, 15 January, 1864. Resigned 1 July, 1864.
JAMES, LELAND F.
Naval Cadet, 9 September, 1889. Assistant Engineer, 1 July, 1896. Rank changed to Ensign, 3 March, 1899. Lieutenant, Junior Grade, 1 July, 1899.
JAMES, MILTON.
Acting Assistant Surgeon, 23 November, 1863. Honorably discharged 20 November, 1865.
JAMES, NATHANIEL T.
Midshipman, 27 June, 1868. Graduated 1 June, 1872. Resigned 20 May, 1874.
JAMESON, JACOB.
Assistant Surgeon, 3 January, 1828. Died 10 January, 1830.
JAMESON, JOHN A.
Assistant Paymaster (Spanish-American War), 12 July, 1898. Honorably discharged 12 December, 1898.
JAMESON, WILLIAM.
Midshipman, 1 September, 1811. Lieutenant, 5 March, 1817. Commander, 9 February, 1837. Captain, 4 June, 1844. Reserved List, 13 September, 1855. Commodore, Retired List, 4 April, 1867. Died 6 October, 1873.
JAMESON, WILLIAM.
Acting Ensign, 26 September, 1862. Honorably discharged 28 October, 1865.
JAMESON, WILLIAM H.
Midshipman, 14 March, 1838. Passed Midshipman, 20 May, 1844. Died 8 December, 1845.
JAMIESON, JOSEPH.
Acting Third Assistant Engineer. 15 April, 1863. Acting Second Assistant Engineer, 31 August, 1864. Resigned 15 June, 1865.

JAMIESON, WILLIAM C.
  Mate, 12 February, 1864. Honorably discharged 3 October, 1865.
JAMISON, JOHN C.
  Mate, 9 February, 1870. Appointment revoked 14 January, 1871.
JAMISON, JAMES.
  Acting Third Assistant Engineer, 9 October, 1861. Appointment revoked (sick), 17 November, 1863.
JAMISON, THOMAS W.
  Acting Assistant Surgeon, 19 February, 1863. Dismissed 1 August, 1864.
JANDON, CHARLES B.
  Surgeon's Mate, 12 July, 1824. Resigned 4 May, 1826.
JANVIN, EDWARD.
  Acting Ensign, 25 September, 1862. Honorably discharged 28 October, 1865.
JAQUES, SAMUEL C.
  Acting Ensign, 30 December, 1862. Resigned 8 December, 1863.
JAQUES, WILLIAM HENRY.
  Midshipman, 30 September, 1863. Graduated June, 1867. Ensign, 18 December, 1868. Master, 21 March, 1870. Lieutenant, 21 March, 1871. Resigned 31 October. 18?
JARBOE, CHARLES W.
  Midshipman, 20 September, 1864. Graduated June, 1868. Ensign, 19 April, 1869. Master, 12 July, 1870. Lieutenant, 11 September, 1873. Died 17 March, 1880.
JARBOE, WALTER S.
  Acting Third Assistant Engineer, 27 June, 1864. Honorably discharged 3 July, 1869.
JARDINE, AUGUSTUS E.
  Midshipman, 21 September, 1870. Graduated 20 June, 1876. Ensign, Junior Grade, 3 March, 1883. Wholly retired 31 December, 1883.
JARRETT, FREDERICK.
  Midshipman, 8 March, 1814. Lieutenant, 13 January, 1825. Died 17 July, 1825.
JARRETT, HENRY C.
  Acting Boatswain, 25 January, 1900.
JARVIS, GEORGE W.
  Carpenter, 13 October, 1859. Appointment revoked 28 December, 1859.
JARVIS, JAMES.
  Mate, 9 January, 1864. Deserted 20 August, 1864.
JARVIS, JAMES C.
  Midshipman, 23 March, 1799. Last appearance on Records of Navy Department, March, 1799.
JARVIS, JOHN.
  Carpenter, 21 November, 1850. Lost in the Levant. Last intelligence from the Ship, 18 September, 1860.
JARVIS, JOHN A.
  Midshipman, 3 December, 1830. Died in 1834.
JARVIS, JOSEPH R.
  Midshipman, 18 June, 1812. Lieutenant, 28 March, 1820. Commander, 8 September, 1841. Captain, 24 May, 1855. Reserved List, 13 September, 1855. Commodore on Retired List, 16 July, 1862. Died 12 August, 1869.
JARVIS, JOSEPH W.
  Midshipman, 1 January, 1825. Passed Midshipman, 4 June, 1831. Lieutenant, February, 1837. Died 18 September, 1842.
JARVIS, PHILIP.
  Lieutenant, 1 November, 17998. Left the service 10 September, 1799.
JARVIS, WILLIAM B.
  Acting Gunner, 10 August, 1864. Honorably discharged 26 October, 1865.
JASPER, ROBERT T.
  Midshipmen, 21 July, 1864. Graduated June, 1868. Ensign, 19 April, 1869. Master, 12 July, 1870. Lieutenant, 27 October, 1872. Lieutenant-Commander, 4 July, 1893. Commander, 3 March, 1899. Retired List, 21 September, 1899.
JASPER, WILLIAM.
  Midshipman, 1 January, 1808. Last appearance on Records of Navy Department, 1815. Wilmington, N. C.
JAY, MOSES.
  Carpenter, 1 October, 1800. Last appearance on Records of Navy Department.
JAYNE, JOSEPH L.
  Cadet Midshipman, 28 June, 1878. Ensign, 1 July, 1884. Lieutenant, Junior Grade, 10 July, 1894. Lieutenant, 17 December, 1897.
JAYNE, WILLIAM.
  Acting Third Assistant Engineer, 24 November, 1863. Honorably discharged August, 1865.
JEFFARES, RICHARD.
  Acting Warrant Machinist, 23 August, 1899.
JEFFERIES, JOHN T.
  Mate, 17 September, 1864. Resigned 8 May, 1865.
JEFFERS, JOHN Y.
  Mate, 26 June, 1864. Discharged.
JEFFERS, SAMUEL.
  Master, 8 May, 1812. Resigned 31 December, 1814.
JEFFERS, WILLIAM N.
  Midshipman, 25 September, 1840. Passed Midshipman, 11 July, 1846. Master, 12 June, 1854. Lieutenant, 30 January, 1855. Lieutenant-Commander, 16 July, 1862. Commander, 3 March, 1865. Captain, 13 July, 1870. Commodore, 26 February, 1878. Died 23 July, 1883.
JEFFERS, WILLIAM NICHOLSON.
  Naval Cadet, 20 September, 1895. Graduated 30 June, 1900.

GENERAL NAVY REGISTER. 295

JEFFERSON, JAMES S.
Assistant Engineer (Spanish-American War), 29 July, 1898. Honorably discharged 28 September, 1898.
JEFFERSON THOMAS R.
Acting Third Assistant Engineer, 18 November, 1863. Resigned 27 April, 1865. Acting Third Assistant Engineer, 31 July, 1866. Deserted 22 August, 1866.
JEFFREY, ARCHIBALD.
Warrant Machinist (Spanish-American War), 18 May, 1898. Honorably discharged 2 September, 1898.
JEFFREY, RICHARD W.
Assistant Surgeon, 17 October, 1839. Passed Assistant Surgeon, 25 November, 1844. Dismissed 28 September, 1861.
JEFFRIES, ALFRED.
Cadet Midshipman, 9 June, 1873. Graduated 18 June, 1879. Ensign, 7 August, 1881. Dismissed 16 July, 1885.
JELLEY, WILLIAM E.
Mate, 17 March, 1864. Honorably discharged 1 November, 1865.
JEMESSON, SKEFF.
Midshipman, 18 June, 1812. Died 11 November, 1823.
JENKINS, A. H.
Midshipman, 25 November, 1834. Passed Midshipman, 16 July, 1840. Resigned 12 March, 1844.
JENKINS, CHARLES.
Acting Second Assistant Engineer, 4 June, 1864. Resigned (sick) 14 February, 1865.
JENKINS, DAVID J.
Assistant Engineer (Spanish-American War), 14 May, 1898. Honorably discharged 29 October, 1898.
JENKINS, EDMUND.
Midshipman, 2 February, 1829. Passed Midshipman, 3 July, 1835. Lieutenant, 8 September, 1841. Died 26 September, 1850.
JENKINS, EVANS.
Boatswain, 12 May, 1810. Last appearance on Records of Navy Department, 1815. Norfolk.
JENKINS, FRIEND W.
Naval Cadet, 28 September, 1882. Ensign, 1 July, 1888. Lieutenant, Junior Grade, 5 January, 1897. Drowned 15 February, 1898.
JENKINS, GEORGE W.
Acting Master, 29 May, 1862. Honorably discharged 13 September, 1865.
JENKINS, HOWARD.
Acting Assistant Paymaster, 24 September, 1863. Mustered out 15 November, 1865.
JENKINS, JOHN D.
Master, 26 May, 1812. Last appearance on Records of Navy Department, 1815. New York.
JENKINS, JOHN T.
Midshipman, 4 March, 1823. Passed Midshipman, 23 March, 1829. Lieutenant, 2 December, 1832. Died 6 February, 1836.
JENKINS, JOSEPH H.
Acting Assistant Paymaster, 11 September, 1862. Resigned 21 April, 1865.
JENKINS, J. W. M.
Midshipman, 1 August, 1826. Resigned 22 January, 1828.
JENKINS, MICAH.
Mate (Spanish-American War), 17 June, 1898. Honorably discharged 8 February, 1899.
JENKINS, STEPHEN.
Midshipman, 20 September, 1871. Graduated 20 June, 1876. Ensign, 9 May, 1878. Resigned 1 January, 1880. Lieutenant (Spanish-American War), 14 May, 1898. Honorably discharged 29 December, 1898.
JENKINS, THOMAS L.
Cadet Midshipman, 19 May, 1886. Resigned 15 May, 1889. Reappointed 31 May, 1889. Dismissed 1 March, 1890. Ensign (Spanish-American War), 25 April, 1898. Resigned, 13 September, 1898.
JENKINS, THORNTON A.
Midshipman, 1 November, 1828. Passed Midshipman, 14 June, 1834. Lieutenant, 9 December, 1839. Commander, 14 September, 1855. Captain, 16 July, 1862. Commodore, 25 July, 1866. Rear-Admiral, 15 August, 1870. Retired List, 11 December, 1873. Died 9 August, 1893.
JENKINS WILLIAM D.
Carpenter, 24 March, 1840. Retired List, 14 November, 1870. Died 14 April, 1883.
JENKINS, W. H.
Midshipman, 18 June, 1812. Resigned 28 January, 1815.
JENKINS, W. H.
Midshipman, 18 June, 1812. Died in August, 1820.
JENKINS, WILLIAM J.
Midshipman, 1 March, 1825. Dismissed 26 October, 1831.
JENKS, ALONZO A.
Acting Third Assistant Engineer, 5 November, 1862. Acting Second Assistant Engineer, 10 December, 1863. Resigned 5 June, 1865.
JENKS, F. M.
Acting Second Assistant Engineer, 3 July, 1863. Resigned 18 June, 1864.
JENKS, HOLLIS B.
Acting Master, 11 December, 1861. Dismissed 30 April, 1862.
JENKS, JOHN H.
Mate, 21 March, 1862. Acting Ensign, 9 June, 1863. Resigned 5 May, 1865.

GENERAL NAVY REGISTER.

JENKS, NORMAN F.
Mate, 29 December, 1863. Appointment revoked 25 June, 1864.
JENKS, THOMAS H., Jr.
Mate, 15 July, 1863. Honorably discharged 17 January, 1869.
JENKS, THOMAS M.
Acting Third Assistant Engineer, 29 August, 1863. Appointment revoked (sick) 10 April, 1865.
JENKS, W. C.
Lieutenant, 2 October, 1799. Dismissed 28 May, 1804.
JENNEY, ANSEL.
Midshipman, 16 January, 1809. Last appearance on Records of Navy Department, 14 May, 1809. Dead.
JENNEY, JONATHAN.
Acting Ensign, 1 June, 1864. Honorably discharged 25 September, 1866.
JENNEY, SIMPSON.
Acting Ensign, 18 December 1863. Honorably discharged 24 October, 1865.
JENNEY, WILLIAM.
Mate, 19 November, 1861. Acting Ensign, 27 November, 1863. Honorably discharged 11 January, 1866. Mate, 6 December, 1869. Retired List, 26 September, 1899.
JENNINGS, ANTHONY T.
Mate, 13 January, 1865. Honorably discharged 15 November, 1868.
JENNINGS, DANIEL.
Purser, 20 June, 1799. Died 13 November, 1800.
JENNINGS, EDWARD M.
Assistant Engineer (Spanish-American War), 3 June, 1898. Honorably discharged 9 January, 1899.
JENNINGS, HORNER.
Mdshipman, 24 February, 1799. Resigned 5 February, 1801.
JENNINGS, JOHN.
Purser, 6 August, 1799. Resigned 20 August, 1799.
JENNINGS, LEWIS.
Acting Ensign, 7 September, 1864. Honorably discharged 28 August, 1865.
JENNINGS NATHANIEL.
Master, 30 March, 1812. Last appearance on Records of Navy Department, 1815. New York Navy Yard.
JENNINGS, THOMAS S.
Acting Second Assistant Engineer, 25 July, 1863. Resigned 3 May, 1864. Acting Second Assistant Engieer, 20 October, 1864. Honorably discharged 24 September, 1865.
JENNINGS, WILLIAM.
Acting Ensign, 22 October, 1862. Acting Master, 28 March, 1865. Honorably discharged 30 August, 1865.
JENNINGS, WILLIAM
Acting Third Assistant Engineer, 3 October, 1864. Resigned (sick) 16 January, 1865.
JENNINGS, WILLIAM H.
Mate, 24 January, 1863. Acting Ensign, 17 November, 1863. Honorably discharged 22 February, 1869. Mate, 26 November, 1869. Resigned 30 June, 1873.
JENSON, HENRY N.
Naval Cadet, 6 September, 1893. Ensign, 1 July, 1899.
JEPSON, H. E.
Mate, 3 August, 1866. Resigned 24 September, 1869.
JERNEGAN THOMAS.
Acting Assistant Paymaster, 1 May, 1863. Mustered out 16 November 1865.
JERRALD, SAMUEL G.
Midshipman, 3 July, 1799. Resigned 2 September, 1800.
JERRAULD, S. G.
Master, 14 March, 1809. Died 4 May. 1812.
JERVEY, THOMAS H.
Master, 18 January, 1809. Resigned 26 January, 1809.
JERVEY THOMAS H.
Master, 5 January, 1813. Left the service 23 August, 1813.
JESSOP, EARL P.
Naval Cadet, 6 September, 1892. Ensign, 6 May, 1898.
JESSURUN, SAMUEL.
Mate, 8 September, 1863. Dismissed 22 February, 1864.
JEVENS, CHARLES E.
Acting Third Assistant Engineer, 8 July, 1863. Honorably discharged 26 August, 1865.
JEWELL, CHARLES T.
Naval Cadet, 19 May, 1887. Ensign, 1 July, 1894. Lieutenant, Junior Grade, 3 March. 1899. Lieutenant, 1 July, 1900.
JEWELL, HENRY C.
Third Assistant Engineer, 16 February, 1852. Resigned 11 January, 1854.
JEWELL, THEODORE F
Acting Midshipman, 29 November, 1861. Graduated. November. 1864. Ensign, 1 November, 1866. Master, 1 December, 1866. Lieutenant, 12 March, 1868. Lieutenant-Commander, 26 March, 1869. Commander, 26 January, 1885. Captain, 1 February, 1898.
JEWETT, AMOS M.
Acting Ensign, Coast Survey Duty. 9 July, 1867. Discharged 1 November, 1867.
JEWETT, CHARLES.
Lieutenant, 30 October, 1799. Discharged 8 June, 1801, under Peace Establishment Act.

GENERAL NAVY REGISTER.

JEWETT, DAVID.
Commander, 6 April, 1799. Discharged 3 June, 1801, under Peace Establishment Act.

JEWETT, GEORGE.
Midshipman, 31 October, 1799. Discharged 10 July, 1801, under Peace Establishment Act.

JEWETT, HENRY C.
Acting Third Assistant Engineer, 28 January, 1864. Appointment revoked (sick) 9 November, 1865.

JEWETT, HENRY E.
Assistant Paymaster, 27 May, 1892. Passed Assistant Paymaster, 24 May, 1894. Paymaster, 9 April, 1899.

JEWETT, THOMAS S.
Assistant Paymaster, 14 March, 1892. Passed Assistant Paymaster, 2 February, 1894. Paymaster, 30 March, 1898.

JIMMESON, JACOB.
Assistant Surgeon, 3 January, 1828. Died 10 July, 1830.

JOBSON, FRANCIS G.
Mate, 19 July, 1862. Resigned 26 July, 1862. Acting Ensign, 24 January, 1863. Honorably discharged 2 December, 1865.

JOCELYN, AMMARIAH.
Captain (to command a Galley), 23 January, 1800. Last appearance on Records of Navy Department, 15 June, 1800.

JOHNS, WALTER S.
Mate, 24 July 1862. Resigned 16 September, 1864.

JOHNSEN, HANS.
Gunner, 27 June, 1900.

JOHNSON, A. M.
Acting Assistant Surgeon, 1861. Resigned 12 December, 1862.

JOHNSON, ALFRED W.
Naval Cadet, 20 May, 1895. At sea prior to final graduation.

JOHNSON, AMOS.
Acting Master, 17 October, 1861. Acting Volunteer Lieutenant, 31 January, 1863. Honorably discharged 14 September, 1865.

JOHNSON, ANDREW W.
Midshipman, 19 October, 1841. Passed Midshipman, 10 August, 1847. Master, 14 September, 1855. Lieutenant, 15 September, 1855. Lieutenant-Commander, 16 July, 1862. Commander, 25 July, 1866. Captain, 5 April, 1874. Retired List, 8 February 1884. Died 14 June 1887.

JOHNSON, ARTEMAS.
Surgeon's Mate, 10 December, 1814. Resigned 12 June, 1815.

JOHNSON, CARROLL W.
Mate 9 December, 1862. Acting Ensign, 7 March, 1864. Honorably discharged 8 December, 1865.

JOHNSON, CHARLES C.
Mate, 1 October, 1862. Resigned 21 August, 1863. Mate. 27 April, 1864. Acting Ensign, 14 February, 1865. Honorably discharged 24 November, 1865.

JOHNSON, DANIEL.
Acting Third Assistant Engineer, 28 December, 1861. Acting Second Assistant Engineer, 31 October, 1862. Honorably discharged 24 November, 1869.

JOHNSON, EDWARD C.
Third Assistant Engineer, 18 November, 1862. Resigned 3 September, 1862.

JOHNSON, EDWARD S.
Midshipman, 30 November, 1814. Lieutenant, 13 January, 1825. Commander, 8 September, 1841. Died 23 June, 1843.

JOHNSON, ELIAS H.
Acting Assistant Paymaster, 18 April, 1864. Honorably discharged 7 August, 1866.

JOHNSON, FAYETTE.
Midshipman, 18 May, 1809. Resigned 22 September, 1810.

JOHNSON, FRANK.
Carpenter, 26 August, 1896.

JOHNSON, FREDERICK H.
Mate, 21 November, 1863. Honorably discharged 6 October, 1866.

JOHNSON, GEORGE A.
Mate, 11 February, 1863. Acting Ensign, 10 December, 1864. Honorably discharged 12 November, 1865.

JOHNSON, GEORGE R.
Third Assistant Engineer, 16 February, 1852. Second Assistant Engineer, 27 July, 1855. First Assistant Engineer, 21 July, 1858. Chief Engineer, 31 July, 18. Retired List, 9 November, 1890. Died 16 September, 1898.

JOHNSON, GORHAM S.
Mate, 5 August, 1863. Acting Ensign, 16 November, 1864. Honorably discharged 28 August, 1865.

JOHNSON, HAROLD A.
Assistant Surgeon (Spanish-American War), 2 May, 1898. Honorably discharged 8 September, 1898.

JOHNSON, HENRY.
Acting Assistant Surgeon, 26 March, 1862. Resigned 28 April, 1865.

JOHNSON, HENRY J.
Acting Third Assistant Engineer, 15 April, 1862. Acting Second Assistant Engineer, 10 January, 1865. Honorably discharged 24 December, 1865.

JOHNSON, HENRY L.
Acting Midshipman, 30 September, 1859. Ensign, 28 April, 1863. Lieutenant, 22

GENERAL NAVY REGISTER.

February, 1864. Lieutenant-Commander, 25 July, 1866. Commander, 25 November, 1876. Dismissed 24 January, 1893.
JOHNSON, ISAAC.
Acting Third Assistant Engineer, 29 August, 1861. Acting Second Assistant Engineer, 15 October, 1862. Resigned 30 December, 1864.
JOHNSON, ISAIAH.
Mate, 22April, 1863. Resigned (sick) 22 August, 1863.
JOHNSON, JAMES B.
Acting Third Assistant Engineer, 21 April, 1864. Honorably discharged 31 October, 1865.
JOHNSON, JAMES S.
Acting Ensign, 17 June, 1864. Honorably discharged 14 July, 1865.
JOHNSON, JEROME B.
Mate, 20 December, 1861. Dismissed 12 February, 1863.
JOHNSON, JOHN.
Acting Third Assistant Engineer, 22 August, 1862. Acting Second Assistant Engineer, 29 May, 1863. Appointment revoked (sick) 21 March, 1864.
JOHNSON, JOHN.
Third Assistant Engineer, 21 May, 1857. Second Assistant Engineer, 2 August, 1859. First Assistant Engineer, 1 July, 1861. Chief Engineer, 10 November, 1863. Retired 10 June, 1876. Died 15 February, 1897.
JOHNSON, JOHN.
Gunner, 6 May, 1813. Died 11 August, 1818.
JOHNSON, JOHN.
Purser, 28 August, 1850. Dismissed 20 April, 1861.
JOHNSON, JOHN.
Boatswain, 13 March, 1866. Appointment canceled 11 September, 1867.
JOHNSON, JOHN H.
Midshipman, 19 October, 1841. Resigned 29 January, 1846.
JOHNSON, JOHN N.
Acting Third Assistant Engineer, 22 March, 1864. Honorably discharged 9 October, 1865.
JOHNSON, JOHN O.
Mate, 4 October, 1861. Acting Ensign, 13 September, 1862. Acting Master, gallant conduct in action, 1 June, 1863. Honorably discharged 15 September, 1865.
JOHNSON, JOSEPH E.
Assistant Engineer (Spanish-American War), 24 June, 1898. Honorably discharged 1 November, 1898.
JOHNSON, JOSEPH S.
Acting Ensign, 26 September, 1862. Lost on Patapsco.
JOHNSON, JOSHUA.
Master, 6 August, 1799. Discharged 9 June, 1801, under Peace Establishment Act.
JOHNSON, J. SMITH.
Midshipman, 1 December, 1809. Dismissed 17 September, 1813.
JOHNSON, LORENZO B. T.
Naval Cadet (Spanish-American War), 15 June, 1898. Honorably discharged 17 September, 1898.
JOHNSON, LOUIS D.
Acting Carpenter, 1 October, 1862. Resigned 29 August, 1863.
JOHNSON, MILLER H.
Acting Master, 22 October, 1861. Died 8 July, 1864.
JOHNSON, MORTIMER L.
Acting Midshipman, 2 December, 1859. Ensign, 16 September, 1862. Lieutenant, 22 February, 1864. Lieutenant-Commander, 25 July, 1866. Commander, 26 April, 1878. Captain, 9 May, 1893.
JOHNSON, MOULTON K.
Naval Cadet, 10 June, 1889. Resigned 28 June, 1893. Assistant Surgeon, 12 November, 1895. Passed Assistant Surgeon, 12 November, 1898.
JOHNSON, NATHANIEL F.
Acting Second Assistant Engineer, 28 November, 1864. Honorably discharged 3 December, 1865.
JOHNSON, OSCAR F.
Midshipman, 14 August, 1846. Passed Midshipman, 8 June, 1852. Master, 15 September, 1855. Lieutenant, 16 September, 1855. Dismissed 22 April, 1861.
JOHNSON, OTTO.
Acting Warrant Machinist, 23 August, 1899.
JOHNSON, PETER.
Boatswain, 23 November, 1871. Retired List, 30 June, 1885.
JOHNSON, PETER.
Midshipman, 2 February, 1829. Dismissed 26 July, 1830.
JOHNSON, PHILIP C., JR.
Midshipman, 31 August, 1846. Passed Midshipman, 8 June, 1852. Master, 15 September, 1855. Lieutenant, 16 September, 1855. Lieutenant-Commander, 16 July, 1862. Commander, 25 July, 1866. Captain, 14 June, 1874. Commodore, 28 July, 1884. Died 28 January, 1887.
JOHNSON, PURLEY H.
Acting Assistant Surgeon, 11 February, 1865. Honorably discharged 26 June, 1866.
JOHNSON, R. H.
Acting Assistant Surgeon, 9 November, 1861. Resigned 4 December, 1861.
JOHNSON, RICHMOND.
Surgeon's Mate, 2 April, 1811. Surgeon, 1 March, 1815. Resigned 12 February, 1817.
JOHNSON, ROBERT.
Master, 10 May, 1813. Last appearance on Records of Navy Department, 1815. Norfolk.

GENERAL NAVY REGISTER.

JOHNSON, ROBERT E.
  Midshipman, 1 October, 1827. Passed Midshipman, 10 June, 1833. Lieutenant, 12 February, 1839. Died 4 February, 1855.
JOHNSON, SAMUEL.
  Acting Third Assistant Engineer, 29 April, 1864. Resigned 10 August, 1865.
JOHNSON, SAMUEL.
  Gunner, date not known. Discharged 1 May, 1801, under Peace Establishment Act.
JOHNSON, SAMUEL.
  Gunner, 9 March, 1802. Dismissed 14 June, 1802.
JOHNSON, SAMUEL C.
  Acting Assistant Surgeon, 9 August, 1864. Honorably discharged 6 November, 1865.
JOHNSON, SAMUEL H.
  Mate, 31 October, 1861. Appointment revoked 23 December, 1865.
JOHNSON, SETH.
  Midshipman, 16 January, 1809. Dismissed 18 November, 1809.
JOHNSON, SMITH J.
  Midshipman, 1 December, 1809. Dismissed 23 September, 1813.
JOHNSON, SPENCER H.
  Mate, 1 October, 1862. Acting Ensign, 9 November, 1863. Honorably discharged 28 November, 1865.
JOHNSON, THOMAS.
  Carpenter, 10 June, 1844. Resigned 17 March, 1848.
JOHNSON, THOMAS.
  Purser, 22 March, 1800. Resigned 9 December, 1806.
JOHNSON, THOMAS L.
  Naval Cadet, 19 May, 1894. Ensign, 4 April, 1900.
JOHNSON, THOMAS W.
  Acting Master, 9 October, 1861. Appointment revoked 25 February, 1862.
JOHNSON, W. H. B.
  Midshipman, 16 February, 1832. Resigned 29 December, 1836.
JOHNSON, WILLIAM.
  Acting Third Assistant Engineer, 4 February, 1863. Honorably discharged 20 July, 1866.
JOHNSON, WILLIAM.
  Surgeon's Mate, 16 August, 1826. Surgeon, 4 April, 1831. Retired List, 4 January, 1866. Medical Director, 3 March, 1871. Died 7 April, 1876.
JOHNSON, WILLIAM, JR.
  Assistant Surgeon, 3 September, 1855. Surgeon, 10 August, 1861. Dismissed 19 February, 1870.
JOHNSON, WILLIAM.
  Master, 11 February, 1811. Resigned 17 February, 1818.
JOHNSON, WILLIAM.
  Gunner, 4 July, 1817. Last appearance on Records of Navy Department, 17 March, 1821. Dead.
JOHNSON, WILLIAM.
  Master, 6 June, 1815. Died 27 April, 1821.
JOHNSON, WILLIAM.
  Gunner, 16 January, 1802. Last appearance on Records of Navy Department. Resigned.
JOHNSON, WILLIAM.
  Mate, 14 August, 1897. Boatswain, 10 April, 1899.
JOHNSON, WILLIAM.
  Acting Boatswain, 1 March, 1900.
JOHNSON, WILLIAM H.
  Acting Second Assistant Engineer, 5 June, 1863. Honorably discharged 5 November, 1865.
JOHNSON, WILLIAM H.
  Assistant Surgeon, 22 June, 1862. Resigned 23 July, 1868.
JOHNSON, WILLIAM H.
  Acting Second Assistant Engineer, 13 September, 1864. Honorably discharged 1 December, 1865.
JOHNSON, WILLIAM H.
  Assistant Engineer (Spanish-American War), 25 June, 1898. Honorably discharged 10 March, 1899. Warrant Machinist (Regular Navy), 6 July, 1899.
JOHNSON, WILLIAM HENRY.
  Acting Boatswain, 25 January, 1900.
JOHNSON, WILLIAM W.
  Acting Third Assistant Engineer, 6 January, 1865. Honorably discharged 11 August, 1865.
JOHNSON, WILSON H.
  Acting Second Assistant Engineer, 6 January, 1865. Honorably discharged 5 November, 1865.
JOHNSTON, ALEXANDER M.
  Acting Assistant Surgeon, 1862. Resigned 12 December, 1862.
JOHNSTON, BENJAMIN L.
  Acting Master, 9 September, 1861. Resigned 22 April, 1862.
JOHNSTON, CHARLES.
  Boatswain, 21 May, 1839. Retired List, 24 March, 1869. Died 14 March, 1874.
JOHNSTON, ELLIOT.
  Midshipman, 17 September, 1841. Resigned 16 August, 1849.
JOHNSTON, FREDERICK A.
  Mate, 21 November, 1863. Honorably discharged 6 October, 1866.
JOHNSTON, HARRY H.
  Acting Ensign, 12 August, 1863. Resigned 27 April, 1864. Mate, 27 September, 1867. Resigned 20 May, 1869. Mate, 4 November, 1869. Died 28 October, 1874.

JOHNSTON, HUNTINGTON.
Naval Cadet, 19 September, 1896. Graduated 30 June, 1900.
JOHNSTON, JAMES D.
Midshipman, 30 June, 1832. Passed Midshipman, 23 June, 1838. Lieutenant, 24 June, 1843. Resigned 10 April, 1861.
JOHNSTON, JAMES L.
Midshipman, 27 September, 1841. Dismissed 12 June, 1848.
JOHNSTON, JAMES N.
Mate, 6 September, 1861. Resigned 4 August, 1863.
JOHNSTON, JOHN.
Purser, 28 August, 1850. Dismissed 20 April, 1861.
JOHNSTON, JOHN.
Acting First Assistant Engineer, 5 June, 1863. Honorably discharged 5 September, 1865.
JOHNSTON, JOHN E.
Acting Master, 3 December, 1861. Dismissed 28 February, 1862.
JOHNSTON, JOHN E.
Mate, 19 December, 1864. Honorably discharged 4 December, 1867.
JOHNSTON, JOHN E.
Midshipman, 9 August, 1848. Passed Midshipman, 15 June, 1854. Resigned 22 March, 1855.
JOHNSTON, JOHN V.
Acting Volunteer Lieutenant, 1 August, 1862. Resigned 23 June, 1864.
JOHNSTON, JOSEPH S.
Acting Sailmaker, 19 June, 1861. Died 27 June, 1861.
JOHNSTON, MARBURY.
Cadet Midshipman, 30 September, 1878. Ensign, 1 July, 1884. Lieutenant, Junior Grade, 22 June, 1894. Lieutenant, 7 November, 1897.
JOHNSTON, RUFUS Z., JR.
Naval Cadet, 10 September, 1891. Ensign, 1 July, 1897. Lieutenant, Junior Grade, 1 July, 1900.
JOHNSTON, STEPHEN.
Midshipman, 28 June, 1823. Passed Midshipman, 23 March, 1829. Lieutenant, 3 March, 1831. Died 2 April, 1848.
JOHNSTON, THOMAS M.
Boatswain, 13 May, 1887. Gunner, 25 January, 1888. Chief Gunner, 3 March, 1899.
JOHNSTON, WILLIAM.
Acting First Assistant Engineer, 26 August, 1863. Honorably discharged 28 August, 1865.
JOHNSTON, ZACHARIAH F.
Midshipman, 1 January, 1818. Lieutenant, 3 March, 1827. Commander, 27 February, 1847. Dropped 13 September, 1855. Commissioned Captain on Active List, 14 September, 1855. Died 17 March, 1859.
JOHNSTONE, GASTON DeP.
Gunner, 9 April, 1897.
JOHNSTONE, JOHN A.
Acting Master, 4 December, 1861. Acting Volunteer Lieutenant, 12 November, 1863. Acting Volunteer Lieutenant-Commander, 19 May, 1865. Honorably discharged 9 December, 1865.
JOINS, JOHN.
Sailmaker, 26 September, 1837. Retired List, 26 May, 1865. Died 26 September, 1877.
JONES, ALBERT K.
Mate, 4 November, 1861. Acting Ensign, 4 September, 1862. Acting Master. favorable report of Commanding Officer, 2 March, 1861. Honorably discharged 12 October, 1865. Acting Master, 28 April, 1866. Mustered out 17 July, 1868.
JONES, ALONZO.
Carpenter, 18 November, 1831. Died 17 January, 1843.
JONES, BENJAMIN F.
Mate, 25 January, 1862. Acting Master, 3 February, 1862. Dismissed 7 June, 1863.
JONES, BENJAMIN L.
Midshipman, 24 January, 1815. Resigned 2 May, 1815.
JONES, BENNET.
Acting Third Assistant Engineer, 8 December, 1863. Honorably discharged 10 May, 1868.
JONES, CADWALLADER.
Midshipman, 20 June, 1806. Resigned 4 August, 1807.
JONES, CATESBY AP R.
Midshipman, 18 June, 1836. Passed Midshipman, 1 July, 1842. Master, 14 September, 1848. Lieutenant, 12 May, 1849. Resigned 17 April, 1861.
JONES, CAVE.
Chaplain, 26 May, 1824. Died 29 January, 1829.
JONES, CHARLES.
Midshipman, 6 July, 1803. Last appearance on Records of Navy Department, 1815. Norfolk.
JONES, CHARLES A.
Mate, 5 June. 1862. Appointment revoked (sick) 16 February, 1863.
JONES, CHARLES B.
Mate, 27 November, 1863. Honorably discharged 20 July, 1865.
JONES, CHARLES C.
Mate, 16 December, 1862. Appointment revoked (sick) 24 July, 1863. Mate, 2 September, 1863. Resigned (sick) 2 December, 1864.

JONES, CHARLES D.
  Acting Midshipman, 23 November, 1859. Ensign, 25 November, 1862. Lieutenant, 22 February, 1864. Died 19 December, 1865.
JONES, CHARLES H.
  Sailmaker, 7 January, 1875. Chief Sailmaker, 3 March, 1899.
JONES, CHARLES R.
  Acting Third Assistant Engineer, 24 January, 1863. Acting Second Assistant Engineer, 12 May, 1864. Honorably discharged 19 October, 1865.
JONES, CHARLES W.
  Acting Ensign and Pilot, 3 May, 1864. Honorably discharged 30 September, 1865.
JONES, CHARLES W.
  Midshipman, 6 January, 1800. Discharged 12 August, 1801, under Peace Establishment Act.
JONES, C. M.
  Acting Ensign, 29 December, 1864. Honorably discharged 14 September, 1865.
JONES, COPELAND P.
  Midshipman, 21 September, 1841. Resigned 16 May, 1848.
JONES, DANIEL.
  Carpenter, 9 December, 1847. Retired List, 27 July, 1869. Died 5 June, 1877.
JONES, DANIEL.
  Master, 8 May, 1812. Died 21 May, 1826.
JONES, DANIEL.
  Acting Ensign, 22 April, 1863. Dismissed 19 March, 1864.
JONES, DANIEL W.
  Acting Assistant Surgeon, 25 September, 1863. Appointment revoked 15 February, 1865.
JONES, DAVID P.
  Third Assistant Engineer, 25 March, 1862. Second Assistant Engineer, 1 November, 1863. First Assistant Engineer, 1 January, 1868. Chief Engineer, 9 January, 1889. Retired List, 21 June, 1892.
JONES, EDWARD.
  Master, 26 January, 1809. Last appearance on Records of Navy Department, 1815. Charleston, S. C.
JONES, EDWARD.
  Acting Master, 3 October, 1861. Resigned 5 May, 1864.
JONES, EDWARD.
  Mate, 31 October, 1861. Dismissed 16 May, 1863.
JONES, EDWARD C.
  Acting Second Assistant Engineer, 25 March, 1864. Honorably discharged 7 November, 1865.
JONES, EDWARD T.
  Acting Master, 13 November, 1861. Dismissed 14 July, 1862.
JONES, ENOCH.
  Surgeon's Mate, 10 December, 1814. Resigned 2 March, 1815.
JONES, ENOCH A.
  Midshipman, 16 January, 1809. Lieutenant, 5 May, 1817. Resigned 26 April, 1827.
JONES, GARDNER I.
  Lieutenant (Spanish-American War), 2 July, 1898. Honorably discharged 10 September, 1898.
JONES, GEORGE.
  Chaplain, 20 April, 1833. Died 22 January, 1870.
JONES, GEORGE E.
  Acting Assistant Surgeon, 29 May, 1863. Resigned 4 April, 1864.
JONES, GEORGE W.
  Assistant Paymaster, 18 March, 1881. Died 21 June, 1881.
JONES, HARRY W.
  Chaplain, 6 June, 1896.
JONES, HENRY.
  Acting Third Assistant Engineer, 30 September, 1863. Acting Second Assistant Engineer, 9 September, 1864. Honorably discharged 7 September, 1865.
JONES, HENRY D.
  Mate, 6 February, 1863. Resigned 24 November, 1863.
JONES, HILARY P., JR.
  Cadet Midshipman, 25 September, 1880. Ensign, 1 July, 1886. Lieutenant, Junior Grade, 16 October, 1895. Lieutenant, 10 August, 1898.
JONES, HIRAM H.
  Acting Assistant Surgeon, 15 January, 1864. Resigned 1 July, 1864.
JONES, HORACE EUGENE.
  Midshipman, 30 September, 1863. Graduated June, 1867. Ensign, 18 December, 1868. Master, 21 March, 1870. Resigned 18 May, 1871.
JONES, HORACE W.
  Cadet Engineer, 1 October, 1880. Honorably discharged 30 June, 1886. Assistant Engineer, 28 June, 1889. Passed Assistant Engineer, 20 February, 1896. Rank changed to Lieutenant, 3 March, 1899.
JONES, H. LeROY.
  Acting Assistant Paymaster, 2 August, 1861. Honorably discharged 13 July, 1867.
JONES, HUGH.
  Mate, 21 November, 1862. Acting Ensign, 21 May, 1863. Honorably discharged 4 May, 1867.
JONES, JACOB.
  Midshipman, 10 April, 1799. Lieutenant, 22 February, 1801. Commander, 20 April, 1810. Captain, 3 March, 1813. Died 3 August, 1850.

JONES, J. ALEXANDER.
Mate, 6 November, 1863. Acting Ensign, 17 July, 1864. Honorably discharged 15 November, 1865.
JONES, JAMES.
Carpenter, 12 January, 1832. Resigned 12 October, 1832.
JONES, JESSE E.
Acting Warrant Machinist, 23 August, 1899.
JONES, JOHN.
Mate, 24 December, 1862. Deserted 2 January, 1865.
JONES, JOHN.
Acting Master's Mate, 6 October, 1864. Disrated, 11 May, 1866. Discharged as seaman 30 June, 1866.
JONES, JOHN C.
Midshipman, 12 May, 1818. Resigned 6 November, 1823.
JONES, JOHN C.
Acting Third Assistant Engineer, 12 December, 1862. Acting Second Assistant Engineer, 8 July, 1864. Honorably discharged 1 December, 1865.
JONES, JOHN H.
Acting Third Assistant Engineer, 28 May, 1863. Acting Second Assistant Engineer, 9 June, 1864. Died 2 October, 1864.
JONES, JOHN H.
Lieutenant, 12 June, 1799. Resigned 11 June, 1801.
JONES, JOHN J.
Purser, 21 November, 1849. Dismissed 30 September, 1858.
JONES, JOHN P.
Mate, 7 August, 1861. Acting Ensign, 8 March, 1861. Honorably discharged 22 July, 1867.
JONES, JOHN W.
Mate, 13 December, 1861. Resigned 12 November, 1862.
JONES, JOSEPH E.
Acting Master, 9 October, 1861. Ensign, 12 March, 1868. Master, 18 December, 1868. Lieutenant, 21 March, 1870. Retired List, 21 May, 1883. Died 16 December, 1887.
JONES, JOSEPH E.
Mate, 26 November, 1861. Acting Ensign, 25 September, 1863. Honorably discharged 20 November, 1868.
JONES, J. PEMBROKE.
Midshipman, 19 October, 1841. Passed Midshipman, 10 August, 1847. Master, 1 March, 1855. Lieutenant, 14 September, 1855. Dismissed 29 April, 1861.
JONES, KINSEY.
Midshipman, 1 January, 1823. Last appearance on Records of Navy Department, 29 July, 1825. Drowned.
JONES, LEWIS B.
Acting Third Assistant Engineer, 5 June, 1863. Honorably discharged 19 October, 1865.
JONES, LEWIS B.
Naval Cadet, 21 May, 1890. Ensign, 1 July, 1896. Lieutenant, Junior Grade, 1 July, 1899.
JONES, MEREDITH D.
Assistant Surgeon, 17 May, 1871. Passed Assistant Surgeon, 6 February, 1875. Surgeon, 11 April, 1884. Resigned, 15 June, 1885.
JONES, MERIWETHER P.
Midshipman, 9 September, 1841. Passed Midshipman, 10 August, 1847. Master, 14 September, 1855. Lieutenant, 15 September, 1855. Lieutenant-Commander, 16 July, 1862. Died 11 April, 1866.
JONES, NEEDHAM L.
Naval Cadet, 6 September, 1893. Ensign, 1 July, 1899.
JONES, MICHAEL G.
Mate, 7 May, 1864. Honorably discharged 26 July, 1865.
JONES, OLIVER C.
Carpenter, 6 June, 1899.
JONES, OWEN.
Third Assistant Engineer, 19 February, 1863. Second Assistant Engineer, 20 June, 1864. Resigned 22 December, 1866.
JONES, P. A. J. P.
Midshipman, 16 January, 1809. Lieutenant, 24 July, 1813. Cashiered 18 August, 1820.
JONES, R. B.
Midshipman, 29 March, 1802. Resigned 6 February, 1808.
JONES, RICHARD A.
Midshipman, 18 June, 1812. Lieutenant, 26 April, 1820. Commander, 29 March, 1844. Died 17 April, 1846.
JONES, RICHARD K.
Midshipman, 16 January, 1809. Resigned 30 January, 1810.
JONES, ROBERT.
Midshipman, 4 March, 1823. Dismissed 8 June, 1831.
JONES, ROBERT CLARENDON.
Master, 4 March, 1823. Master, not in line of promotion, 7 June, 1844. Reserved List, 14 September, 1855. Died 18 October, 1893.
JONES, ROBERT J.
Acting Third Assistant Engineer, 14 September, 1864. Honorably discharged 23 November, 1865.
JONES, ROBERT L. M.
Mate, 3 April, 1863. Acting Ensign, 27 March, 1865. Honorably discharged 24 October, 1867.

GENERAL NAVY REGISTER. 303

JONES, ROBERT W.
Midshipman, 1 January, 1818. Lieutenant, 3 March, 1827. Died 19 May, 1837.
JONES, SAMUEL J.
Assistant Surgeon, 19 December, 1860. Surgeon, 22 September, 1863. Resigned 1 March, 1868.
JONES, SANFORD N.
Mate, 1 October, 1862. Resigned 14 April, 1863.
JONES, STEPHEN.
Gunner, 3 April, 1826. Died 8 February, 1834.
JONES, STEPHEN.
Gunner, 6 May, 1813. Last appearance on Records of Navy Department till 1826.
JONES, STEPHEN.
Mate, 5 November, 1862. Acting Ensign, 14 February, 1865. Honorably discharged 10 January, 1869.
JONES, THEODORE W.
Mate, 23 January, 1862. Mustered out 6 February, 1869.
JONES, T. G.
Acting Third Assistant Engineer, 20 June, 1863. Resigned 22 May, 1865.
JONES, THOMAS.
Midshipman, 10 July, 1799. Lost in the Insurgent.
JONES, THOMAS.
Sailmaker, 20 November, 1799. Discharged 25 May, 1801.
JONES, THOMAS A. C.
Midshipman, 22 November, 1805. Lieutenant, 24 May, 1812. Commander, 28 March, 1820. Captain, 11 March, 1829. Reserved List, 13 September, 1855. Died 30 May, 1858.
JONES, THOMAS C.
Mate. Resigned 12 February, 1863.
JONES, THOMAS J.
Third Assistant Engineer, 26 June, 1856. Second Assistant Engineer, 21 July, 1858. First Assistant Engineer, 3 August, 1859. Chief Engineer, 19 January, 1863. Dismissed 19 October, 1875.
JONES, THOMAS P.
Mate, 20 November, 1861. Honorably discharged 22 January, 1866.
JONES, TRUMAN M.
Third Assistant Engineer, 8 October, 1861. Second Assistant Engineer, 3 August, 1863. First Assistant Engineer, 11 October, 1866. Died 22 November, 1872.
JONES, VICTOR W.
Mate, 23 January, 1862. Acting Ensign, 5 September, 1863. Honorably discharged 10 November, 1868.
JONES, WALTER F.
Midshipman, 11 June, 1814. Resigned 2 November, 1821.
JONES, WALTER F.
Midshipman, 20 September, 1841. Passed Midshipman, 10 August, 1847. Died 20 August, 1855.
JONES, WILLIAM.
Acting Master and Pilot, 24 October, 1863. Resigned 29 December, 1864.
JONES, WILLIAM.
Boatswain, 31 July, 1866. Retired List, 10 December, 1883.
JONES, WILLIAM.
Boatswain, 26 July, 1852. Lost in Sloop of War Albany, September, 1854.
JONES, WILLIAM A.
Acting Master, 2 November, 1861. Mustered out 24 December, 1861.
JONES, WILLIAM A.
Midshipman, 13 July, 1831. Passed Midshipman, 15 June, 1837. Lieutenant, 8 September, 1841. Resigned 13 May, 1845.
JONES, WILLIAM C.
Assistant Paymaster (Spanish-American War), 20 May, 1898. Honorably discharged 11 October, 1898.
JONES, WILLIAM E.
Acting Ensign, 24 June, 1864. Honorably discharged 3 July, 1865.
JONES, WILLIAM G.
Acting Ensign, 14 January, 1864. Dismissed 13 February, 1865.
JONES, WILLIAM H.
Acting Assistant Surgeon, 6 April, 1863. Assistant Surgeon, 12 August, 1863. Passed Assistant Surgeon, 26 December, 1866. Surgeon, 5 July, 1873. Medical Inspector, 14 November, 1891. Retired List, 21 January, 1894. Died 13 December, 1900.
JONES, WILLIAM P.
Midshipman, 1 January, 1827. Passed Midshipman, 10 June, 1833. Died 15 July, 1834.
JONES, WILLIAM P.
Surgeon's Mate, 10 December, 1814. Last appearance on Records of Navy Department, 1818. Furloughed.
JORDAN, CHARLES E.
Mate, 23 August, 1864. Appointment revoked 23 December, 1864.
JORDAN, CHARLES W.
Third Assistant Engineer, 4 April, 1861. Name stricken from the Rolls of the Navy, 6 May, 1861.
JORDAN, CHRISTOPHER.
Carpenter, 24 April, 1838. Retired List, 25 September, 1866. Died 28 March, 1881.
JORDAN, CRIS. P.
Boatswain, 29 September, 1813. Resigned 7 March, 1815.
JORDAN, FRANK.
Mate, 27 October, 1862. Acting Ensign, 10 August, 1864. Honorably discharged 23 May, 1866.

GENERAL NAVY REGISTER.

JORDAN, FRANK A.
Acting Assistant Surgeon, 7 March, 1864. Honorably discharged 26 October, 1865.
JORDAN, GEORGE L.
Mate, 3 February, 1864. Acting Ensign, 30 March, 1864. Honorably discharged 24 October, 1865.
JORDAN, JAMES.
Acting Ensign, 22 September, 1864. Resigned 24 March, 1866.
JORDAN, JOHN.
Acting Third Assistant Engineer, 28 December, 1861. Acting Second Assistant Engineer, 2 January, 1864. Honorably discharged 1 September, 1865.
JORDAN, JOHN N.
Cadet Midshipman, 5 June, 1873. Graduated 18 June, 1879. Ensign, 11 October, 1880. Lieutenant, Junior Grade, 1 March, 1887. Lieutenant, 1 July, 1892. Lieutenant-Commander, 9 March, 1900.
JORDAN, JOHN P.
Mate, 23 August, 1864. Dismissed 7 January, 1865.
JORDAN, JOHN W.
Assistant Paymaster, 21 March, 1870. Passed Assistant Paymaster, 27 September, 1877. Paymaster, 19 June, 1888. Retired List, 19 August, 1889. Died 24 December, 1889.
JORDAN, JOSEPH.
Acting Third Assistant Engineer, 17 May, 1864. Honorably discharged 18 August, 1865.
JORDAN, MARSHALL P.
Third Assistant Engineer, 24 December, 1853. Second Assistant Engineer, 9 May, 1857. Dismissed 20 May, 1861.
JORDAN, MELETIAH.
Acting Master, 26 February, 1862. Honorably discharged 20 August, 1865.
JORDAN, SAMUEL.
Acting Assistant Paymaster, 14 February, 1862. Mustered out 1865.
JORDAN, SCOTT D.
Acting Ensign, 22 April, 1863. Honorably discharged 22 November, 1865.
JORDAN, SIMON.
Boatswain, 9 October, 1819. Died 10 June, 1830.
JORDAN, WILLIAM.
Carpenter, 21 March, 1837. Died 5 June, 1845.
JORGENSON, LOUIS.
Acting Assistant Paymaster, 21 February, 1863. Honorably discharged 26 June, 1865.
JOSEPH, PETER.
Gunner, 18 September, 1809. Dismissed 24 April, 1813.
JOSEPH, WILLIAM H.
Mate, 26 May, 1864. Honorably discharged 17 July, 1865.
JOSEPHTHAL, LOUIS M.
Assistant Paymaster (Spanish-American War), 12 May, 1898. Honorably discharged 5 October, 1898.
JOSLIN, GEORGE T.
Mate, 26 March, 1863. Acting Ensign, 18 April, 1864. Resigned 28 April, 1865.
JOSSELYN, FRANCIS.
Acting Master, 29 April, 1862. Acting Volunteer Lieutenant, 15 March, 1865. Honorably discharged 12 June, 1868.
JOUETT, JAMES E.
Midshipman, 10 September, 1841. Passed Midshipman, 10 August, 1847. Master, 14 September, 1855. Lieutenant, 15 September, 1855. Lieutenant-Commander, 16 July, 1862. Commander, 25 July, 1866. Captain, 6 January, 1874. Commodore, 11 January, 1883. Rear-Admiral, 19 February, 1886. Retired List, 27 February, 1890.
JOUETT, LANDON P.
Midshipman, 31 July, 1866. Graduated 7 June, 1870. Ensign, 13 July, 1871. Master, 1 December, 1874. Lieutenant, Junior Grade, 3 March, 1883. Discharged 18 February, 1889.
JOY, STEPHEN D.
Acting Master, 27 December, 1861. Appointment revoked 5 December, 1863.
JOYCE, CHARLES R.
Acting Third Assistant Engineer, 1861. Appointment revoked (sick) 3 June 1862.
JOYCE, LEMUEL B.
Acting Third Assistant Engineer, 15 September, 1864. Honorably discharged 21 September, 1865.
JOYCE, MYLES.
Gunner, 8 May, 1897.
JOYCE, NOAH D.
Acting Ensign, 27 January, 1865. Honorably discharged 14 August, 1867.
JOYCE, WILLIAM.
Passed Assistant Engineer (Spanish-American War), 18 May, 1898. Honorably discharged 2 September, 1898.
JOYNER, FRANCIS E.
Midshipman, 1 April, 1828. Resigned 27 May, 1833.
JUBE, WILLIAM O.
Acting Assistant Paymaster, 10 October, 1863. Honorably discharged 1 January, 1866.
JUDD, CHARLES H.
Midshipman, 23 September, 1862. Graduated 12 June, 1866. Ensign, 12 March, 1868. Master, 26 March, 1869. Lieutenant, 21 March, 1870. Retired List, 18 December, 1885.
JUDD, JOHN C.
Acting Third Assistant Engineer, 4 September, 1863. Dismissed 9 October, 1863.

GENERAL NAVY REGISTER. 305

JUDKINS, E. D.
　Acting Assistant Surgeon, 21 October, 1861.　Appointment revoked 5 March, 1862.
JUDSON, ADONIRAM B.
　Assistant Surgeon, 30 July, 1861.　Surgeon, 26 December, 1866.　Resigned 11 May, 1868.
JUDSON, E. J. C.
　Midshipman, 10 February, 1838.　Resigned 8 June, 1842.
JUDSON, ELNATHAN.
　Surgeon, 27 March, 1818.　Died 8 May, 1829.
JUDSON, HERBERT H.
　Mate, 7 June, 1862.　Died on Hartford, 22 January, 1863.
JUMP, LEVI L.
　Acting Master, 29 May, 1862.　Dismissed 10 September, 1862.　Acting Master and Pilot, 1 January, 1865.　Appointment revoked 10 August, 1865.
JUNGEN, CARL W.
　Cadet Midshipman, 24 September, 1874.　Graduated 10 June, 1879.　Midshipman, 10 June, 1881.　Ensign, Junior Grade, 3 March, 1883.　Ensign, 26 June, 1884.　Lieutenant, Junior Grade, 20 May, 1891.　Lieutenant, 1 August, 1895.
JUNKIN, DAVID X.
　Chaplain, 2 November, 1859.　Resigned 31 October, 1864.
JUNKIN, WILLIAM M.
　Acting Assistant Paymaster, 27 April, 1863.　Died 28 September, 1863.
JUNKINS, NATHAN H.
　Carpenter, 20 February, 1872.　Retired List, 13 November, 1896.
JUSTICE, JOHN.
　Carpenter, 17 January, 1826.　Resigned 6 July, 1826.
JUSTIN, JOSHUA H.
　Midshipman, 30 November, 1814.　Died 8 April, 1829.
KAEMMERLING, GUSTAV.
　Cadet Engineer, 13 September, 1877.　Assistant Engineer, 1 July, 1883.　Passed Assistant Engineer, 10 August, 1893.　Rank changed to Lieutenant, 3 March, 1899.
KAFER, JOHN C.
　Third Assistant Engineer, 16 January, 1863.　Second Assistant Engineer, 28 May, 1864.　First Assistant Engineer, 26 October, 1872.　(The title First Assistant Engineer was changed to Passed Assistant Engineer about 1874.)　Retired List, 18 June, 1888.
KAFER, PETER M.
　Acting Third Assistant Engineer, 21 May, 1864.　Honorably discharged 21 October, 1865.
KAIL, ARTHUR C.
　Acting Gunner, 1 August, 1900.
KAISER, JULIUS A.
　Third Assistant Engineer, 8 September, 1863.　Second Assistant Engineer, 25 July, 1866.　Retired List, 8 July, 1873.
KAISER, LOUIS A.
　Naval Cadet, 20 May, 1885.　Ensign, 1 July, 1891.　Lieutenant, Junior Grade, 25 December, 1898.　Lieutenant, 3 March, 1899.
KALBACH, ANDREW E.
　Naval Cadet, 1 July, 1892.　Ensign, 6 May, 1898.
KALBFUS, EDWARD C.
　Naval Cadet, 20 May, 1895.　At sea prior to final graduation.
KALINSKI, ACHILLES.
　Mate, 16 August, 1864.　Acting Ensign, 8 May, 1865.　Honorably discharged 26 October, 1866.
KANE, ALOYSIUS J.
　Mate, 22 December, 1863.　Acting Ensign, 20 September, 1864.　Resigned 1 March, 1871.
KAMMERER, GEORGE E.
　Mate (Spanish-American War), 22 June, 1898.　Honorably discharged, 8 September, 1898.
KANE, ELISHA K.
　Assistant Surgeon, 21 July, 1843.　Died 16 February, 1857.
KANE, FRANK.
　Acting Master and Pilot, 1 October, 1864.　Honorably discharged 8 January, 1866.
KANE, HENRY.
　Mate, 25 March, 1864.　Acting Ensign, 16 March, 1865.　Honorably discharged 28 May, 1868.
KANE, JAMES J.
　Mate, 8 August, 1861.　Acting Ensign, 28 October, 1862.　Honorably discharged August 31, 1865.　Chaplain, 6 June, 1868.　Retired List, 30 October, 1896.
KANE, JOHN L.
　Midshipman, 9 June, 1811.　Last appearance on Records of Navy Department, 1814.
KANE, LEWIS J.
　Mate 14 March, 1861.　Resigned 8 April, 1862.
KANE, PATRICK J.
　Boatswain, 21 May, 1897.
KANE, SAMUEL N.
　Midshipman, 20 September, 1862.　Graduated June, 1866.　Ensign, 12 March, 1868.　Resigned 30 November, 1868.　Ensign (Spanish-American War), 3 May, 1898.　Lieutenant, 10 May, 1898.　Honorably discharged 15 November, 1898.
KANE, THEODORE F.
　Acting Midshipman, 27 September, 1855.　Midshipman, 9 June, 1859.　Lieutenant, 31 August, 1861.　Lieutenant-Commander, 22 September, 1865.　Commander, 28 December, 1872.　Captain, 19 May, 1886.　Retired List, 20 June, 1896.

20

KANEY, OWEN.
Acting Third Assistant Engineer, 3 October, 1863. Honorably discharged 27 July, 1865.
KARLOWSKI, M. H.
Acting Ensign, 18 May, 1863. Dismissed 17 September, 1864.
KARMANY, LINCOLN.
Cadet Midshipman, 12 September, 1877. Graduated 10 June, 1881. Second Lieutenant, Marine Corps, 1 July, 1883. (See Marine Corps.)
KARNS, FRANKLIN D.
Naval Cadet, 30 September, 1891. Assistant Engineer, 1 July, 1897. Rank changed to Ensign, 3 March, 1899. Lieutenant, Junior Grade, 1 July, 1900.
KASE, SPENCER M.
Cadet Midshipman, 22 September, 1877. Graduated. Honorably discharged 30 June, 1883. Ensign (Spanish-American War), 24 May, 1898. Honorably discharged 1 December, 1898.
KASSON, MAHLON O.
Passed Assistant Engineer (Spanish-American War), 24 June, 1898. Honorably discharged 19 October, 1898.
KATZ, EDWARD M.
Midshipman, 8 June, 1872. Graduated 20 June, 1876. Ensign, 2 February, 1878. Resigned 1 August, 1884.
KAUFMAN, WINFIELD S.
Acting Third Assistant Engineer, 3 February, 1865. Honorably discharged 27 August, 1869.
KAUTZ, ALBERT.
Acting Midshipman, 28 September, 1854. Midshipman, 11 June, 1858. Passed Midshipman, 28 January, 1861. Master, 28 February, 1861. Lieutenant, 21 April, 1861. Lieutenant-Commander, 31 May, 1865. Commander, 3 September, 1872. Captain, 2 June, 1885. Commodore, 6 April, 1897. Rear-Admiral, 24 October, 1898.
KAUTZ, AUSTIN.
Naval Cadet, 19 May, 1893. Ensign, 1 July, 1899.
KAVANAGH, ARTHUR G.
Naval Cadet, 20 May, 1890. Ensign, 1 July, 1896. Lieutenant, Junior Grade, 1 July, 1899.
KAVANAUGH, BENJAMIN.
Third Assistant Engineer, 3 May, 1859. Resigned 21 December, 1861. Acceptance of resignation canceled, 15 April, 1862. Retired List, 3 April, 1862.
KAVANAUGH, JOHN F.
Mate, 14 November, 1862. Acting Ensign, 1 July, 1864. Honorably discharged 28 December, 1865.
KAY, SAMUEL W.
Acting Assistant Paymaster, 11 July, 1864. Honorably discharged 29 September, 1865.
KAY, WILLIAM S.
Acting Third Assistant Engineer, 22 July, 1863. Honorably discharged 12 May, 1865.
KEAN, WILLIAM.
Midshipman, 4 January, 1800. Discharged 12 October, 1801, under Peace Establishment Act.
KEAR, CARLETON R.
Naval Cadet, 20 May, 1896. Graduated 30 June, 1900.
KEARNEY, ARCHIBALD K.
Midshipman, 2 May, 1800. Lieutenant, 21 February, 1807. Resigned 5 July, 1808.
KEARNEY, JAMES A.
Mate, 1 October, 1862. Acting Ensign, 30 January, 1863. Resigned 24 August, 1863.
KEARNEY, JOHN A.
Surgeon's Mate, 3 March, 1809. Surgeon, 24 July, 1813. Died 27 August, 1847.
KEARNEY, LAWRENCE.
Midshipman, 24 July, 1807. Lieutenant, 6 March, 1813. Commander, 3 March, 1825. Captain, 20 December, 1832. Retired List, 14 November, 1861. Commodore, Retired List, 4 April, 1867. Died 29 November, 1868.
KEARNEY, ROBERT S.
Surgeon's Mate, 16 January, 1808. Surgeon, 28 July, 1810. Died 27 June, 1826.
KEARNEY, THOMAS A.
Naval Cadet, 6 September, 1892. Ensign, 6 May, 1898.
KEARNS, EDWARD.
Mate, 22 November, 1864. Honorably discharged 28 January, 1867.
KEARNS, JAMES H.
Mate, 15 October, 1861. Acting Ensign, 6 August, 1862. Honorably discharged 28 October, 1865.
KEARNY, EDMUND.
Acting Midshipman, 4 October, 1851. Dismissed 21 April, 1855.
KEARNY, GEORGE H.
Acting Third Assistant Engineer, 10 October, 1866. Third Assistant Engineer, 2 June, 1868. Second Assistant Engineer, 2 June, 1869. Passed Assistant Engineer, 1 January, 1876. Chief Engineer, 27 June, 1893. Rank changed to Commander, 3 March, 1899.
KEARNY, ROBERT S.
Assistant Surgeon, 16 January, 1808. Surgeon, 28 July, 1810. Died 7 June, 1826.
KEARON, JOHN W.
Acting Third Assistant Engineer, 27 March, 1865. Honorably discharged 27 August, 1868.
KEASBY, JOHN R.
Midshipman, 4 November, 1814. Died 3 March, 1818.
KEATE, EDWARD J.
Mate, 22 April, 1863. Resigned 30 November, 1863.

GENERAL NAVY REGISTER.

KEATING, ARTHUR B.
    Naval Cadet, 19 September, 1896. Graduated 30 June, 1900.
KEATING, JOHN.
    Boatswain, 20 June, 1872. Died 23 July, 1881.
KEELE, HENRY.
    Master, 13 February, 1812. Discharged 12 May, 1815.
KEELER, JOHN D.
    Midshipman, 23 July, 1866. Graduated 7 June, 1870. Ensign, 13 July, 1871. Master, 6 January, 1874. Lieutenant, 22 January, 1880. Resigned 15 June, 1885.
KEELER, WILLIAM F.
    Acting Assistant Paymaster, 17 December, 1861. Honorably discharged 25 April, 1866.
KEELER, WILLIAM J.
    Civil Engineer, 17 March, 1863. Services no longer required from 5 September, 1864.
KEELING, HENRY.
    Gunner, 25 August, 1829. Appointment revoked 22 March, 1845.
KEELING, WILLOUGHBY H.
    Mate (Spanish-American War), 2 May, 1898. Honorably discharged 13 September, 1898.
KEEN, ANSEL.
    Boatswain, 7 June, 1867. Dismissed 12 December, 1876.
KEEN, GEORGE D.
    Mate, 11 April, 1865. Honorably discharged 3 January, 1866.
KEEN, JOSIAH E.
    Carpenter, 9 March, 1878. Chief Carpenter, 3 March, 1899. Retired List, 17 November, 1900.
KEEN, LAWRENCE.
    Midshipman, 9 December, 1800. Last appearance on Records of Navy Department. Dead.
KEEN, WILLARD S.
    Mate, 12 December, 1861. Acting Ensign, 20 July, 1863. Honorably discharged 12 May, 1865.
KEENAN, ERNEST C.
    Naval Cadet, 6 September, 1893. Ensign, 1 July, 1899.
KEENAN, FRANCIS.
    Mate, 28 July, 1863. Resigned 21 June, 1864.
KEENAN, WILLIAM.
    Midshipman, 18 May, 1809. Appointment revoked 6 December, 1809.
KEENAN, WILLIAM.
    Acting Third Assistant Engineer, 31 March, 1864. Honorably discharged 4 September, 1865.
KEENE, HENRY C.
    Acting Master, 21 September, 1861. Acting Volunteer Lieutenant, 17 December, 1862. Resigned 8 September, 1863. Acting Volunteer Lieutenant, 27 April, 1864. Honorably discharged 25 April, 1865. Reappointed 10 June, 1865. Lieutenant, 20 March, 1871. Retired List, by special Act of Congress.
KEENE, HENRY T.
    Mate, 6 February, 1862. Acting Ensign, 3 April, 1863. Acting Master, 6 March, 1864. Honorably discharged 5 January, 1866.
KEENE, JESSE.
    Midshipman, 19 March, 1805. Resigned 7 April, 1807.
KEENE, LAWRENCE.
    Midshipman, 2 March, 1803. Resigned 27 February, 1809.
KEENE, LEANDER M.
    Acting Ensign, 6 October, 1864. Resigned 12 May, 1865.
KEENE, LEWIS.
    Midshipman, 1 January, 1812. Last appearance on Records of Navy Department, 1815. Brig Enterprise.
KEENER, CHARLES H.
    Acting Third Assistant Engineer, 2 March, 1864. Honorably discharged 1 August, 1865.
KEENEY, JAMES F.
    Assistant Surgeon, 1 March, 1888. Died 10 February, 1894.
KEER, JOHN.
    Midshipman, 28 June, 1804. Drowned 18 May, 1811.
KEESHAN, M. F.
    Mate, 9 March, 1864. Resigned 7 May, 1865.
KEFUSS, JACOB.
    Acting Third Assistant Engineer, 3 July, 1863. Resigned 3 June, 1864.
KEGEL, GEORGE.
    Acting Third Assistant Engineer, 9 January, 1865. Honorably discharged 21 September, 1865.
KEITH, ALBERT M.
    Acting Master, 27 March, 1862. Honorably discharged 26 December, 1865.
KEITH, ALBION S.
    Cadet Midshipman, 26 September, 1879. Graduated 8 June, 1883. Honorably discharged 30 June, 1885. Ensign, Retired List, 10 February, 1887. Died 18 April, 1891.
KEITH, CHARLES F.
    Acting Ensign, 15 September, 1862. Acting Master, 1 April, 1864. Honorably discharged 26 October, 1865.
KEITH, EDWIN H.
    Acting Third Assistant Engineer, 9 September, 1862. Acting Second Assistant Engineer, 6 June, 1864. Honorably discharged 20 January, 1866.
KEITH, LEWIS G.
    Midshipman, 1 July, 1825. Passed Midshipman, 4 June, 1831. Lieutenant, 17 March, 1836. Died 1 May, 1846.

KEITH, MELVILLE C.
Acting Ensign, 3 December, 1863. Resigned 3 May, 1865.
KEITH, RUEL.
Professor, 8 July, 1845. Resigned 11 July, 1856.
KEITH, THEODORE S.
Acting Assistant Surgeon, 13 January, 1863. Acting Passed Assistant Surgeon, 6 April, 1866. Honorably discharged 2 July, 1868.
KEITH, WILLIAM.
Master, 25 May, 1798. Last appearance on Records of Navy Department, 27 June, 1798. Dead.
KEITH, WILLIAM.
Boatswain, 21 February, 1814. Last appearance on Records of Navy Department, 9 February, 1816.
KEITH, WILLIAM.
Boatswain, 5 October, 1812. Dismissed 20 February, 1813.
KELBORN, JOHN.
Midshipman, 16 December, 1812. Resigned 21 June, 1815.
KELEHER, JAMES T.
Third Assistant Engineer, 17 February, 1860. Second Assistant Engineer, 17 December, 1862. Appointment revoked 10 December, 1865. Resignation accepted 17 March, 1868.
KELL, JOHN.
Midshipman, 9 September, 1841. Passed Midshipman, 10 August, 1847. Master, 14 September, 1855. Lieutenant, 15 September, 1855. Resigned 23 January, 1861.
KELLEHER, JEREMIAH J.
Mate, 29 January, 1863. Acting Ensign, 4 January, 1865. Honorably discharged 22 October, 1868.
KELLER, GEORGE W.
Acting Third Assistant Engineer, 16 January, 1864. Died on U. S. Steamer Don, 30 October, 1867.
KELLER, JERRY.
Mate, 5 February, 1864. Appointment revoked (sick) 26 October, 1864.
KELLEY, EDWARD.
Acting Third Assistant Engineer, 4 January, 1865. Honorably discharged 5 April, 1866.
KELLEY, JAMES D. J.
Midshipman, 5 October, 1864. Graduated 2 June. 1868. Ensign, 19 April. 1869. Master, 12 July, 1870. Lieutenant, 13 August, 1872. Lieutenant-Commander, 27 June, 1893. Commander, 3 March, 1899.
KELLEY, JAMES P.
Acting Assistant Paymaster, 4 December, 1862. Mustered out 20 December, 1865.
KELLEY, JAMES W.
Acting Assistant Paymaster, 20 July, 1863. Honorably discharged 16 December, 1865.
KELLEY, JOHN A.
Acting Ensign, 6 December, 1864. Resigned 8 May, 1865.
KELLEY, LEVI B.
Acting Ensign, 23 February, 1865. Honorably discharged 16 September, 1865.
KELLEY, ROBERT L.
Acting Master, 22 January, 1862. Killed in action at Port Hudson. 14 March, 1863.
KELLEY, THOMAS C.
Acting Ensign, 23 January, 1865. Honorably discharged 12 November, 1865.
KELLEY, THOMAS J.
Mate, 31 January, 1863. Acting Ensign, 2 June, 1866. Died on Wachusett, 13 August, 1866.
KELLOG, FREDERICK.
Midshipman, 23 February, 1841. Resigned 13 October, 1847.
KELLOGG, AUGUSTUS G.
Acting Midshipman, 21 September, 1860. Ensign, 28 May, 1863. Master, 10 November, 1865. Lieutenant, 10 November, 1866. Lieutenant-Commander, 12 March, 1868. Commander, 11 July, 1880. Retired List, 15 December, 1891.
KELLOGG, EDWARD N.
Acting Midshipman, 24 September, 1858. Ensign, 8 September. 1863. Lieutenant, 22 February, 1864. Lieutenant-Commander, 25 July, 1866. Died 6 October, 1874.
KELLOGG, EDWARD S.
Naval Cadet, 18 May, 1888. Honorably discharged 30 June, 1894. Assistant Engineer, 22 August, 1894. Passed Assistant Engineer, 30 October, 1898. Rank changed to Lieutenant, Junior Grade, 3 March, 1899.
KELLOGG, FRANK W.
Cadet Midshipman, 24 June, 1875. Graduated 10 June, 1881. Ensign, Junior Grade, 3 March, 1883. Ensign, 26 June, 1884. Lieutenant, Junior Grade, 5 May, 1892. Lieutenant, 3 April, 1896.
KELLOGG, GEORGE C.
Mate, 5 August, 1862. Appointment revoked 23 February, 1864.
KELLOGG, JOHN.
Acting Master, 3 October, 1861. Honorably discharged 30 October, 1865.
KELLOGG, MORTIMER.
Third Assistant Engineer, 16 February, 1852. Second Assistant Engineer, 27 July, 1855. First Assistant Engineer, 3 August, 1859. Chief Engineer, 8 November, 1861. Died 16 November, 1870.
KELLOGG, S. WILSON.
Assistant Surgeon, 6 September, 1837. Passed Assistant Surgeon, 14 March, 1843. Surgeon, 26 August, 1848. Died 7 January, 1867.
KELLOGG, WAINWRIGHT.
Midshipman, 27 September, 1865. Graduated 4 June, 1869. Ensign, 12 July, 1870.

GENERAL NAVY REGISTER. 309

Master, 3 September, 1872. Lieutenant, 29 September, 1875. Lieutenant-Commander, 13 July, 1897. Died 3 June, 1899.
KELLS, DE WITT C.
Mate, 24 December, 1861. Acting Ensign, 16 October, 1862. Acting Master, recommendation of Commanding Officer, 18 March, 1864. Acting Volunteer Lieutenant, 9 June, 1865. Master, 12 March, 1868. Lieutenant, 18 December, 1868. Lieutenant-Commander, 2 March, 1870. Dismissed 4 February, 1879.
KELLY, CHARLES V., JR.
Mate, 19 October, 1861. Acting Ensign, 20 May, 1863. Honorably discharged 2 July, 1867.
KELLY, DANIEL.
Gunner, 29 March, 1836. Died 9 June, 1841.
KELLY, DANIEL.
Gunner, 17 May, 1826. Discharged 3 November, 1828.
KELLY, DANIEL F.
Acting Third Assistant Engineer, 23 May, 1864. Honorably discharged 7 August, 1865.
KELLY, JAMES V. (alias BROFEY, WILLIAM J.)
Acting Assistant Surgeon, 25 March, 1865. Appointment revoked 20 May, 1865.
KELLY, JOHN.
Midshipman, 1 February, 1814. Lieutenant, 13 January, 1825. Commander, 8 September, 1841. Captain 14 Septemebr, 1855. Commodore on Retired List, 16 July, 1862. Died 6 February, 1863.
KELLY, JOHN A.
Acting First Assistant Engineer, 28 November, 1863. Resigned (sick) 14 March, 1865.
KELLY, JOHN M.
Acting Ensign, 13 March, 1863. Honorably discharged 4 March, 1866.
KELLY, JOHN P.
Third Assistant Engineer, 24 August, 1861. Second Assistant Engineer, 21 April, 1863. First Assistant Engineer, 11 October, 1866. Chief Engineer, 12 March, 1883. Died 27 January, 1890.
KELLY, JOHN W.
Acting Midshipman, 31 January, 1853. Midshipman, 10 June, 1857. Passed Midshipman, 25 June, 1860. Master, 24 October, 1860. Lieutenant, 18 April, 1861. Lost on Tecumseh, 5 August, 1864.
KELLY, JOSEPH.
Boatswain, 15 November, 1810. Dismissed 9 March, 1811.
KELLY, MARTIN.
Mate, 11 June, 1863. Resigned 30 May, 1864.
KELLY, MICHAEL.
Acting First Assistant Engineer, 1 October, 1862. Resigned 8 December, 1863.
KELLY, M. J.
Acting Ensign, 2 May, 1864. Honorably discharged, 21 June, 1865.
KELLY, ROBERT S.
Mate. Resigned 11 December, 1861.
KELLY, THADDEUS W.
Sailmaker, 2 August, 1844. Appointment revoked 29 May, 1846.
KELLY, WILLIAM, JR.
Acting Ensign, 13 June, 1864. Honorably discharged 22 August, 1865.
KELLY, WILLIAM H.
Third Assistant Engineer, 16 January, 1863. Second Assistant Engineer, 28 May, 1864. Cashiered from the service, 20 November, 1866.
KELLY, WILLIAM W. J.
Purser, 1 April, 1852. Resigned 21 January, 1861.
KELSEY, A. WARREN.
Acting Assistant Paymaster, 19 October, 1861. Appointment revoked (sick) 28 October, 1863.
KELSEY, JOHN W.
Acting Second Assistant Engineer, 12 December, 1861. Acting First Assistant Engineer, 15 February, 1864. Honorably discharged 10 October, 1865.
KELSO, JOSEPH K.
Mate, 8 September, 1864. Resigned 14 April, 1865.
KELVEN, JAMES.
Acting Second Assistant Engineer, 18 January, 1864. Dismissed 12 August, 1865.
KEMBLE, ARTHUR.
Acting Assistant Surgeon, 12 August, 1861. Resigned 16 May, 1862.
KEMBLE, ARTHUR N.
Ensign (Spanish-American War), 25 May, 1898. Honorably discharged 8 October, 1898.
KEMBLE, EDMUND.
Mate, 24 January, 1862. Acting Master, 26 May, 1862. Honorably discharged 26 August, 1865.
KEMBLE, FRANK.
Mate, 16 August, 1861. Dismissed 13 August, 1863. Mate, 20 October, 1863. Acting Ensign, 1 June, 1864. Honorably discharged 20 October, 1865.
KEMBLE, PETER.
Midshipman, 19 December, 1840. Resigned 24 June, 1845.
KEMP, JACOB.
Mate, 27 June, 1860. Appointment revoked 27 July, 1866.
KEMP, WILLIAM T.
Acting Assistant Surgeon, 8 May, 1863. Assistant Surgeon, 5 September, 1863. Died 31 March, 1864.
KEMPER, S. M.
Master, 30 October, 1812. Cashiered 30 December, 1819.

GENERAL NAVY REGISTER.

KEMPFF, CLARENCE S.
Naval Cadet, 19 May, 1893. Ensign, 1 July, 1899.
KEMPFF, LOUIS.
Acting Midshipman, 25 September, 1857. Graduated 1862. Lieutenant, 1 August, 1862. Lieutenant-Commander, 25 July, 1866. Commander, 9 March, 1876. Captain, 19 May, 1891. Rear-Admiral, 3 March, 1899.
KEMPTON, ABNER W.
Acting Master, 29 October, 1861. Honorably discharged 23 March, 1866.
KEMPTON, FRANCIS.
Acting Ensign, 17 December, 1862. Honorably discharged 14 December, 1865.
KEMPTON, SILAS W.
Mate, 9 May, 1864. Drowned 23 March, 1865.
KEMPTON, W. L.
Acting Master, 31 March, 1862. Honorably discharged 28 October, 1865.
KEMPTON, ZACCHEUS.
Acting Master, 28 May, 1861. Honorably discharged 25 October, 1865.
KENDALL, ANDREW J.
Mate, 11 September, 1863. Acting Ensign, 17 December, 1864. Honorably discharged 20 October, 1865.
KENDALL, GEORGE.
Acting Ensign, 6 October. 1862. Resigned 22 September, 1863. Acting Ensign, 14 October, 1863. Resigned 20 December, 1864.
KENDALL, LUCIAN H.
Acting Assistant Surgeon, 21 June, 1862. Acting Passed Assistant Surgeon, 26 May, 1865. Honorably discharged 24 September, 1866.
KENDRICK, CHARLES S.
Acting Master, 1 October, 1862. Died 13 August, 1863.
KENDRICKEN, PAUL.
Acting Third Assistant Engineer, 20 June, 1862. Acting Second Assistant Engineer, 6 November, 1863. Honorably discharged 3 September, 1866.
KENEALY, JOHN F.
Acting Third Assistant Engineer, 10 May, 1862. Acting Second Assistant Engineer, 16 March, 1865. Honorably discharged 5 September, 1865.
KENNARD, JOEL S.
Midshipman, 10 March, 1837. Passed Midshipman, 29 June, 1843. Master, 4 January, 1850. Lieutenant, 18 October, 1850. Resigned 23 April, 1861.
KENNARD, PERRY G.
Assistant Paymaster, 13 January, 1900.
KENNEDY, A. E.
Assistant Surgeon, 3 January, 1828. Died 13 June, 1833.
KENNEDY, CHARLES H. A. H.
Midshipman, 10 February, 1819. Passed Midshipman, 4 June, 1831. Lieutenant, 3 March, 1835. Commander, 14 September, 1855. Dismissed 14 June, 1861.
KENNEDY, CHARLES W.
Midshipman, 25 September, 1861. Graduated 22 November, 1864. Ensign, 1 November, 1866. Master, 1 December, 1866. Lieutenant, 12 March, 1868. Lieutenant-Commander, 26 March, 1869. Died 30 November, 1883.
KENNEDY, DUNCAN.
Midshipman, 20 July, 1864. Graduated 2 June, 1868. Ensign, 19 April, 1869. Master, 12 July, 1870. Lieutenant, 18 June, 1872. Lieutenant-Commander, 15 May, 1893. Commander, 3 March, 1899.
KENNEDY, EDMUND C.
Midshipman, 17 September, 1830. Resigned 15 June, 1839.
KENNEDY, EDMUND P.
Midshipman, 22 November, 1805. Lieutenant, 9 June, 1810. Commander, 5 March, 1817. Captain, 24 April, 1828. Died 28 March, 1844.
KENNEDY, FRANCIS M.
Acting Third Assistant Engineer, 30 December, 1864. Honorably discharged 24 October, 1869.
KENNEDY, H. H.
Master, 26 June, 1812. Resigned 24 May, 1813.
KENNEDY, JAMES C.
Acting Third Assistant Engineer, 27 December, 1861. Resigned 28 November, 1862. Acting Second Assistant Engineer, 30 July, 1864. Resigned 13 April, 1865.
KENNEDY, JOHN T.
Assistant Surgeon, 15 January, 1900.
KENNEDY, JOSEPH.
Acting Second Assistant Engineer, 4 April, 1864. Honorably discharged 3 October, 1865.
KENNEDY, JOSIAH W.
Acting Carpenter, 3 October, 1863. Honorably discharged 30 October, 1865.
KENNEDY, MICHAEL.
Acting Third Assistant Engineer, 13 February, 1865. Dismissed 1 August, 1865.
KENNEDY, ROBERT M.
Naval Cadet, 21 May, 1885. Resigned 26 May, 1887. Assistant Surgeon, 18 June, 1890. Passed Assistant Surgeon, 18 June, 1893.
KENNEDY, STEPHEN D.
Assistant Surgeon, 9 May, 1861. Surgeon, 5 January, 1866. Medical Inspector, 15 October, 1881. Dismissed 20 November, 1883.
KENNEDY, STEWART.
Assistant Surgeon, 1 October, 1855. Surgeon, 1 August, 1861. Died 8 March, 1864.
KENNEDY, THOMAS.
Mate, 26 November, 1862. Honorably discharged 27 December, 1865.

GENERAL NAVY REGISTER. 311

KENNEDY, THOMAS.
Acting Third Assistant Engineer, 5 December, 1864. Honorably discharged 23 March, 1866.
KENNETT, JOHN C.
Midshipman, 2 October, 1861. Graduated 22 November, 1864. Ensign, 1 November, 1866. Master, 1 December, 1866. Lieutenant, 12 March, 1868. Lieutenant-Commander, 26 March, 1869. Resigned 31 December, 1880.
KENNEY, A. J.
Mate, 8 May, 1866. Appointment revoked 19 September, 1866. Mate, 13 October, 1869. Resigned 10 April, 1873.
KENNEY, EDWARD.
Boatswain, 20 July, 1853. Died 18 August, 1888. Retired List 11 March, 1881.
KENNEY, EDWARD J.
Acting Third Assistant Engineer, 2 August, 1864. Resigned 9 July, 1865.
KENNEY, GEORGE W.
Acting Carpenter, 8 June, 1863. Honorably discharged 6 June, 1866.
KENNEY, LEWIS.
Mate, 1863. Acting Ensign, 3 October, 1863. Honorably discharged 19 December, 1868.
KENNEY, STEPHEN B.
Acting Assistant Surgeon, 4 November, 1863. Honorably discharged 15 March, 1866.
KENNISON, D. K.
Acting Master and Pilot, 29 October, 1864. Honorably discharged 8 August, 1865.
KENNISON, WILLIAM W.
Mate, 28 August, 1861. Acting Master, 1 February, 1862. Acting Volunteer Lieutenant, gallant conduct in action between Merrimac and Cumberland, 26 March, 1862. Honorably discharged 4 May, 1866. Acting Master, 20 August, 1866. Mustered out 16 November, 1868.
KENNON, BEVERLY.
Midshipman, 18 May, 1809. Lieutenant, 24 July, 1813. Commander, 24 April, 1828. Captain, 9 February, 1837. Killed by accident 28 February, 1844.
KENNON, BEVERLY.
Midshipman, 22 August, 1846. Passed Midshipman, 8 June, 1852. Master, 15 September, 1855. Lieutenant, 16 September, 1855. Resigned 23 April, 1861.
KENNON, GEORGE T.
Surgeon, 24 July, 1813. Resigned 20 December, 1823.
KENNON, JOHN T.
Surgeon, 24 July, 1813. Resigned 20 December, 1823.
KENNON, RICHARD.
Midshipman, 10 May, 1820. Resigned 4 June, 1822.
KENNON, RICHARD.
Surgeon's Mate, 17 November, 1824. Resigned 12 November, 1833.
KENNON, WILLIAM H.
Purser, 5 June, 1844. Dismissed 16 November, 1849.
KENNON, WILLIAM H.
Midshipman, 1 January, 1817. Lieutenant, 28 April, 1826. Resigned 16 December, 1840.
KENNY, ALBERT S.
Assistant Paymaster, 19 March, 1862. Paymaster, 9 March, 1865. Pay Inspector, 31 July, 1884. Pay Director, 26 September, 1897.
KENNY, JOHN.
Midshipman, 1 January, 1808. Resigned 10 August, 1809.
KENOWER, SANFORD K.
Assistant Engineer (Spanish-American War), 22 June, 1898. Honorably discharged 10 November, 1898.
KENSIL, LEWIS M.
Acting Second Assistant Engineer, 1861. Dismissed 25 September, 1862.
KENT, GEORGE E.
Cadet Midshipman, 27 June, 1877. Graduated. Honorably discharged 30 June, 1884. Lieutenant (Spanish-American War), 24 May, 1898. Honorably discharged 5 October, 1898.
KENT, JAMES W.
Acting Third Assistant Engineer, 22 September, 1864. Resigned 15 May, 1865.
KENT, JOSEPH.
Mate, 4 October, 1861. Died on Pensacola, 5 December, 1863.
KENT, LEWIS A.
Mate, 19 April, 1864. Honorably discharged 13 November, 1865.
KENWORTHY, WILLIAM S.
Acting Third Assistant Engineer, 7 September, 1864. Resigned 4 April, 1865.
KENYON, ALBERT J.
Third Assistant Engineer, 21 September, 1861. Second Assistant Engineer, 30 July, 1863. First Assistant Engineer, 11 October, 1866. Chief Engineer, 7 October, 1884. Died 27 July, 1888.
KENYON, CHARLES W.
Acting Third Assistant Engineer, gallantry, 25 October, 1862. Honorably discharged 26 September, 1865.
KENYON, HENRY.
Lieutenant, 3 August, 1798. Discharged 8 July, 1801, under Peace Establishment Act.
KENYON, JOHN.
Mate, 24 August, 1897. Gunner, 10 April, 1899.
KENZ, JOSEPH.
Surgeon's Mate, 28 March, 1820. Last appearance on Records of Navy Department, 1824. West India Station.
KEOGH, MATTHEW.
Midshipman, 6 December, 1814. Lost at sea in 1821.

KEOGH, PATRICK.
Sailmaker, 27 November, 1807. Last appearance on Records of Navy Department. Dead.
KEFLER, GEORGE W.
Mate, 10 September, 1864. Honorably discharged 24 March, 1866.
KERLEY, BERNARD.
Acting Third Assistant Engineer, 7 March, 1862. Honorably discharged 12 November, 1865.
KERNS, LUCIEN B.
Acting First Assistant Engineer, 9 February, 1864. Appointment revoked (sick) 12 April, 1864.
KERR, EDWARD A.
Midshipman, 1 June, 1821. Died in November, 1824.
KERR, DAVID B.
Assistant Surgeon, 1 June, 1898.
KERR, LEEDS C.
Assistant Paymaster, 16 June, 1880. Passed Assistant Paymaster, 25 February, 1887. Paymaster, 30 March, 1895.
KERR, THOMAS.
Assistant Gunner, 13 February, 1864. Appointment revoked 9 May, 1865.
KERR, WILLIAM A.
Acting Midshipman, 20 September, 1854. Midshipman, 11 June, 1858. Passed Midshipman, 28 January, 1861. Master, 28 February, 1861. Resigned 24 April, 1861.
KERSHAW, HERBERT E
Acting Warrant Machinist, 6 July, 1899.
KERSHNER, EDWARD.
Assistant Surgeon, 24 January, 1862. Surgeon, 7 November, 1872. Medical Inspector, 22 January, 1891. Dismissed 19 March, 1896.
KERVAN, LAWRENCE.
Carpenter, 14 October, 1834. Resigned 30 November, 1835.
KESSLER, WALTER.
Assistant Engineer (Spanish-American War), 3 June, 1898. Honorably discharged 5 October, 1898.
KETLER, PHILIP.
Acting Third Assistant Engineer, 17 June, 1863. Acting Second Assistant Engineer, 8 April, 1865. Honorably discharged 7 November, 1865.
KEY, ALBERT L.
Cadet Midshipman, 27 June, 1877. Ensign, 1 July, 1884. Lieutenant, Junior Grade, 19 August, 1894. Lieutenant, 6 February, 1898.
KEY, DANIEL M.
Midshipman, 28 November, 1833. Died 22 June, 1836.
KEY, HENRY H.
Midshipman, 10 September, 1841. Resigned 2 May, 1848.
KEY, FRANCIS S.
Midshipman, 15 May, 1823. Resigned 21 February, 1827.
KEY, JAMES.
Purser, 16 September, 1799. Discharged 18 November, 1801, under Peace Establishment Act.
KEYES, WILLIAM E.
Acting Gunner, 19 February, 1863. Honorably discharged 16 September, 1865.
KEYES, WILLIAM S. P.
Lieutenant, Junior Grade (Spanish-American War), 8 June, 1898. Honorably discharged 2 September, 1898.
KEYSER, EDWARD S.
Acting Ensign, 20 September, 1862. Acting Master, favorable report of Commanding Officer, 19 February, 1864. Acting Volunteer Lieutenant, 6 April, 1865. Master, 12 March, 1868. Lieutenant, 18 December, 1868. Lieutenant-Commander, 25 January, 1870. Died 11 March, 1881.
KEYSER, HENRY.
Acting Master, 7 August, 1863. Honorably discharged 25 November 1865.
KEYSER, HENRY C.
Acting Third Assistant Engineer, 16 February, 1865. Honorably discharged 26 July, 1865.
KID, CHARLTON B.
Third Assistant Engineer, 21 May, 1857. Second Assistant Engineer, 2 August, 1859. First Assistant Engineer, 1 February, 1862. Resigned 30 December, 1867.
KIDD, ELIJAH M.
Acting Second Assistant Engineer, 22 September, 1863. Honorably discharged 28 October, 1865.
KIDD, JAMES P.
Midshipman, 21 September, 1821. Resigned 21 October, 1824.
KIDD, JOHN M.
Master, 17 June, 1817. Last appearance on Records of Navy Department, 1822. Norfolk.
KIDD, THOMAS.
Acting Third Assistant Engineer, 20 October, 1863. Honorably discharged 1 October, 1865.
KIDDALL, JOHN.
Master, 6 October, 1813. Discharged 15 April, 1815.
KIDDALL, JOHN.
Midshipman, 29 November, 1800. Discharged 9 June, 1801, under Peace Establishment Act.
KIDDER, BENJAMIN H.
Assistant Surgeon, 24 January, 1862. Surgeon, 2 March, 1868. Medical Inspector, 30 January, 1887. Medical Director, 21 August, 1893. Retired List, 23 January, 1898.

GENERAL NAVY REGISTER. 313

KIDDER, GEORGE E.
Mate, 22 October, 1863. Acting Ensign, 19 August, 1864. Honorably discharged 3 December, 1865.
KIDDER, GEORGE W.
Acting Third Assistant Engineer, 6 December, 1862. Acting Second Assistant Engineer, 26 July, 1864. Honorably discharged 4 January, 1868.
KIDDER, JEROME H.
Acting Assistant Surgeon, 27 April, 1866. Assistant Surgeon, 18 June, 1866. Surgeon, 19 May, 1876. Resigned 18 June, 1884.
KIEHL, CHARLES I.
Ensign (Spanish-American War), 20 May, 1898. Honorably discharged 19 September, 1898.
KIELY, THOMAS J. C.
Acting Assistant Surgeon, 21 October, 1861. Resigned 2 July, 1862.
KIERSTED, ANDREW J.
Third Assistant Engineer, 26 June, 1856. First Assistant Engineer, 3 August, 1859. Chief Engineer, 12 November, 1861. Retired List, 25 December, 1894.
KIERSTED, CHARLES D.
Acting Third Assistant Engineer, 29 August, 1861. Acting Second Assistant Engineer, 15 February, 1862. Dismissed 4 August, 1864.
KIERSTED, DAVID C.
Mate, 30 September, 1862. Acting Ensign, 20 October, 1864. Honorably discharged 5 November, 1865.
KIERSTED, GEORGE W.
Acting Third Assistant Engineer, 21 May, 1863. Acting Second Assistant Engineer, 13 February, 1865. Honorably discharged 8 September, 1866.
KIHLBORN, JOHN N.
Mate, 20 January, 1863. Acting Ensign, 28 July, 1864. Resigned 10 May, 1865.
KILBURN, WILLIAM.
Midshipman, 5 December, 1865. Graduated 4 June, 1869. Ensign, 13 July, 1871. Master, 18 December, 1874. Lieutenant, 12 October, 1881. Lieutenant-Commander, 3 March, 1899. Retired List with rank of Commander, 30 June, 1900.
KILBY, JAMES A.
Mate, 11 June, 1863. Resigned (sick) 7 November, 1863. Mate, 7 December, 1863. Acting Ensign, 16 January, 1864. Appointment revoked (sick) 18 July, 1864.
KILEY, TIMOTHY EDWARD.
Carpenter, 17 November, 1896.
KILGORE, WILLIAM F.
Acting Ensign, 3 December, 1864. Honorably discharged 2 April, 1868.
KILLGORE, EDWIN R.
Warrant Machinist (Spanish-American War), 15 June, 1898. Honorably discharged 2 September, 1898.
KILLIN, JOHN J.
Boatswain, 23 October, 1877. Chief Boatswain, 3 March, 1899.
KILPATRICK, THOMAS.
Third Assistant Engineer, 23 March, 1848. Second Assistant Engineer, 13 September, 1849. First Assistant Engineer, 26 February, 1851. Resigned 22 August, 1853.
KILPATRICK, WILLIAM H.
Third Assistant Engineer, 11 February, 1862. Second Assistant Engineer, 15 October, 1863. Resigned 9 February, 1866.
KILTY, AUGUSTUS H.
Midshipman, 4 July, 1821. Passed Midshipman, 28 April, 1832. Lieutenant, 6 September, 1837. Reserved List, 13 September, 1855. Commander, Active List, 6 January, 1859. Captain, Active List, 16 July, 1862. Commander, 25 July, 1866. Retired List, 25 November, 1868. Rear-Admiral, 13 July, 1870. Died 10 November, 1879.
KIMBALL, AMBROSE.
Acting Third Assistant Engineer, 1 December, 1863. Resigned 12 April, 1865.
KIMBALL, F. W.
Mate, 30 May, 1863. Honorably discharged 2 May, 1868.
KIMBALL, GEORGE.
Acting Master, 25 May, 1861. Died 30 November, 1863.
KIMBALL, GRANVILLE.
Passed Assistant Engineer (Spanish-American War), 14 May, 1898. Honorably discharged 1 December, 1898.
KIMBALL, HENRY H.
Third Assistant Engineer, 20 May, 1863. Resigned 29 June, 1869.
KIMBALL, HILL J.
Acting Assistant Surgeon, 27 October, 1863. Died 6 February, 1864.
KIMBALL, H. S.
Acting Master. 5 July, 1862. Resigned 2 March, 1863.
KIMBALL, JACOB.
Acting Master, 22 January, 1862. Acting Volunteer Lieutenant, 8 April. 1865. Honorably discharged 4 January, 1866. Acting Master, 16 October, 1866. Mustered out 10 September, 1868.
KIMBALL, JAMES B.
Third Assistant Engineer, 8 September, 1853. Second Assistant Engineer, 26 June, 1856. First Assistant Engineer, 2 August, 1859. Chief Engineer, 5 August, 1861. Died 18 May, 1879.
KIMBALL, S.
Mate. Resigned 14 September, 1861.
KIMBALL, THOMAS W.
Mate, 31 October, 1861. Acting Ensign, 1 April, 1864. Honorably discharged 20 December, 1867.

KIMBALL, WILLIAM W.
Midshipman, 31 July, 1865. Graduated 4 June, 1869. Ensign, 19 October, 1870. Master, 14 October, 1871. Lieutenant, 18 December, 1874. Lieutenant-Commander, 6 December, 1896. Commander, 8 December, 1899.
KIMBER, GEORGE W.
Acting Second Assistant Engineer, 1 October, 1862. Acting First Assistant Engineer, 6 December, 1862. Resigned (sick) 5 November, 1863.
KIMBERLY, HENRY D.
Acting Assistant Paymaster, 3 August, 1861. Mustered out 9 January, 1866.
KIMBERLY, LEWIS A.
Midshipman, 8 December, 1846. Passed Midshipman, 8 June, 1852. Master, 15 September, 1855. Lieutenant, 16 September, 1855. Lieutenant-Commander, 16 July, 1862. Commander, 25 July, 1866. Captain, 3 October, 1874. Commodore, 27 September, 1884. Rear-Admiral, 26 January, 1887. Retired List, 2 April, 1892.
KIMBERLY, VICTOR A.
Naval Cadet, 6 September, 1895. At sea prior to final graduation.
KIMMELL, HARRY.
Cadet Midshipman, 28 September, 1874. Graduated 4 June, 1880. Ensign, 19 December, 1882. Lieutenant, Junior Grade, 7 January, 1890. Lieutenant, 31 July, 1894.
KINDLEBERGER, CHARLES P.
Assistant Surgeon, 9 July, 1894. Passed Assistant Surgeon, 9 July, 1897.
KINDLEBERGER, DAVID.
Assistant Surgeon, 20 May, 1859. Surgeon, 14 August, 1862. Medical Inspector, 13 August, 1876. Medical Director, 30 January, 1887. Retired List, 2 September, 1896.
KING, ALLEN A.
Mate, 6 October, 1864. Honorably discharged 30 September, 1865.
KING, AMOS.
Surgeon's Mate, 10 December, 1814. Last appearance on Records of Navy Department for 1815. New York.
KING, CHARLES.
Mate, 1 October, 1862. Acting Ensign, 19 February, 1863. Resigned 20 April, 1865.
KING, CHARLES A. E.
Cadet Engineer, 14 September, 1876. Graduated 10 June, 1880. Assistant Engineer, 10 June, 1882. Passed Assistant Engineer, 27 June, 1893. Rank changed to Lieutenant, 3 March, 1899. Died 25 December, 1900.
KING, DAVID J.
Mate, 11 May, 1863. Honorably discharged 10 July, 1865.
KING, DANIEL L.
Acting First Assistant Engineer, 22 February, 1864. Honorably discharged 14 October, 1867.
KING, EDWARD M.
Acting Volunteer Lieutenant, 31 October, 1863. Honorably discharged 18 July, 1867.
KING, EZEKIEL.
Midshipman, 16 January, 1809. Struck off 26 August, 1809.
KING, FREDERICK T.
Acting Master, 14 August, 1861. Honorably discharged 29 December, 1865.
KING, GEORGE LEWIS.
Acting Third Assistant Engineer, 6 September, 1864. Resigned 27 April, 1865.
KING, GEORGE S.
Midshipman, 25 March, 1842. Passed Midshipman, 5 August, 1848. Dropped 13 September, 1855.
KING, GLENDY.
Third Assisant Engineer, 2 August, 1855. Second Assistant Engineer, 21 July, 1858. Resigned 7 September, 1858. Second Assistant Engineer, 9 May, 1861. Declined. Appointment revoked 13 June, 1861.
KING, HUGH E.
Ensign (Spanish-American War), 30 July, 1898. Honorably discharged 23 January, 1899.
KING, JAMES S.
Passed Assistant Surgeon (Spanish-American War), 8 June, 1898. Honorably discharged 14 September, 1898.
KING, JAMES W.
Third Assistant Engineer, 2 September, 1844. Second Assistant Engineer, 10 July, 1847. First Assistant Engineer, 13 September, 1849. Chief Engineer, 12 November, 1852. Engineer in Chief, 15 March, 1869. Retired List, 26 August, 1881.
KING, JOHN.
Master, 16 April, 1800. Last appearance on Records of Navy Department.
KING, JOHN.
Sailmaker, 27 August, 1853. Dismissed 22 October, 1864.
KING, JOHN A. B.
Acting Third Assistant Engineer, 18 February, 1863. Acting Second Assistant Engineer, 7 April, 1864. Honorably discharged 22 March, 1868.
KING, JOHN F.
Acting Third Assistant Engineer, 26 September, 1862. Resigned 7 May, 1863.
KING, JOHN H.
Mate, 20 August, 1863. Acting Ensign, 5 October, 1864. Honorably discharged 31 July, 1867.
KING, JOHN L.
Acting Warrant Machinist, 23 August, 1899.
KING, JOHN M.
Acting Third Assistant Engineer, 6 May, 1863. Appointment revoked (sick) 26 February, 1864.
KING, JOHN W.
Acting Ensign, 2 August, 1864. Honorably discharged 30 November, 1865.

GENERAL NAVY REGISTER. 315

KING, L. B.
    Acting Ensign, 17 September, 1862. Acting Master, 7 November, 1863. Honorably discharged 2 January, 1869.
KING, MILES.
    Lieutenant, 13 July, 1799. Discharged 11 May, 1801, under Peace Establishment Act.
KING, ROBERT S.
    Gunner, 5 April, 1842. Resigned 3 July, 1846. Gunner, 6 April, 1859. Lost in the Levant, 18 September, 1860.
KING, STEPHEN G.
    Sailmaker, 27 March, 1857. Died 18 January, 1860.
KING, SYLVESTER W.
    Acting Third Assistant Engineer, 27 July, 1863. Honorably discharged 7 October, 1865.
KING, THOMAS.
    Boatswain, 11 June, 1799. Last appearance on Records of Navy Department.
KING, THOMAS.
    Acting Third Assistant Engineer, 5 March, 1864. Dismissed 23 April, 1864.
KING, THOMAS.
    Master's Mate, date not known. Died in 1821.
KING, THOMAS.
    Acting Master, 25 February, 1862. Resigned 8 February, 1864.
KING, THOMAS.
    Midshipman, 4 March, 1815. Last appearance on Records of Navy Department, 1821. Dead.
KING, THOMAS W.
    Acting Second Assistant Engineer, 18 October, 1864. Appointment revoked 18 January, 1866.
KING, WILLIAM.
    Acting Third Assistant Engineer, 2 June, 1862. Resigned 20 June, 1863.
KING, WILLIAM C.
    Mate, 10 September, 1863. Resigned 3 February, 1866.
KING, WILLIAM C.
    Mate, 27 May, 1863. Acting Ensign, 30 December, 1864. Honorably discharged 15 May, 1865.
KING, WILLIAM HENRY.
    Third Assistant Engineer, 6 February, 1851. Second Assistant Engineer, 26 February, 1851. First Assistant Engineer, 21 May, 1853. Died 25 April, 1859.
KING, WILLIAM HERVEY.
    Third Assistant Engineer, 20 May, 1857. Second Assistant Engineer, 2 August, 1859. First Assistant Engineer, 2 December, 1861. Chief Engineer, 10 November, 1863. Died 11 March, 1883.
KING, WILLIAM M.
    Assistant Surgeon, 3 December, 1858. Surgeon, 22 May, 1862. Medical Inspector, 4 May, 1875. Retired List, 5 December, 1879. Died 14 March, 1880.
KING, WILLIAM NEPHEW.
    Cadet Midshipman, 21 June, 1875. Resigned 10 May, 1884. Lieutenant, Junior Grade (Spanish-American War), 12 May, 1898. Honorably discharged 9 November, 1898.
KING, WILLIAM R.
    Cadet Engineer, Naval Academy, 1 October, 1872. Graduated 21 June, 1875. Assistant Engineer, 1 July, 1877. Passed Assistant Engineer, 17 March, 1887. Retired List, 18 March, 1891.
KINGSBURY, CHARLES C.
    Acting Master, 15 April, 1862. Acting Volunteer Lieutenant, 24 April, 1865. Honorably discharged 2 January, 1866.
KINGSBURY, GEORGE L.
    Acting Second Assistant Engineer, 14 August, 1862. Resigned 8 July, 1863.
KINGSLEY, JACKSON.
    Mate, 9 October, 1862. Discharged 2 October, 1864.
KINGSLEY, JOHN FLAVIL.
    Acting Third Assistant Engineer, 24 May, 1864. Honorably discharged 28 April, 1869.
KINGSLEY, LOUIS A.
    Midshipman, 28 September, 1861. Graduated September, 1865. Ensign, 1 December, 1866. Master, 12 March, 1868. Lieutenant, 26 March, 1869. Lieutenant-Commander, 25 November, 1881. Commander, 5 May, 1892. Died 4 January, 1896.
KINGSTON, S. B.
    Midshipman, 1 January, 1817. Resigned 16 December, 1826.
KINGSTON, SIMON.
    Master, 29 June, 1812. Died in July, 1825.
KINKAID, THOMAS WRIGHT.
    Cadet Engineer, 14 September, 1876. Graduated 10 June, 1880. Assistant Engineer, 10 June, 1882. Passed Assistant Engineer, 11 November, 1892. Rank changed to Lieutenant, 3 March, 1899.
KINKEAD, JOSEPH B.
    Midshipman, 19 October, 1841. Resigned 26 August, 1843.
KINLOCH, THOMAS L.
    Midshipman, 1 July, 1836. Passed Midshipman, 1 July, 1842. Master, 25 August, 1849. Died 25 December, 1849.
KINNAN, HENRY R.
    Mate. Dismissed 16 September, 1862. Mate, 22 November, 1862. Died 10 January, 1863.
KINNEAR, JAMES.
    Acting Carpenter, 5 June, 1861. Resigned 3 October, 1861.
KINNIER, JAMES.
    Acting Assistant Surgeon, 25 July, 1862. Honorably discharged 2 April, 1866.

KINNEY, ALBERT B.
Acting Third Assistant Engineer, 6 March, 1862. Acting Second Assistant Engineer, 16 September, 1864.
KINNEY, WILLIAM H.
Acting Assistant Surgeon, 5 March, 1864. Resigned 7 September, 1865.
KINNICUTTE, J. C.
Midshipman, 8 October, 1798. Last appearance on Records of Navy Department, 25 March, 1800.
KINNY, HARLOW.
Acting Carpenter, 1 October, 1862. Honorably discharged 27 September, 1865.
KINSEY, THOMAS.
Passed Assistant Paymaster (Spanish-American War), 18 May, 1898. Honorably discharged 2 September, 1898.
KIP, ISAAC.
Surgeon's Mate, 13 March, 1805. Dismissed 16 August, 1805.
KIRBY, ABSALOM.
Third Assistant Engineer, 3 October, 1861. Second Assistant Engineer, 3 August, 1863. Retired 22 January, 1866. Restored to Active List by Act of Congress, 3 March, 1873. First Assistant Engineer, 11 October, 1866. Chief Engineer, 2 December, 1886. Retired List, 15 February, 1898.
KIRBY, BENJAMIN.
Master's Mate, 1 February, 1816. Last appearance on Records of Navy Department.
KIRBY, NICHOLAS.
Acting Master, 29 October, 1861. Acting Volunteer Lieutenant, 20 April, 1864. Honorably discharged 14 November, 1865.
KIRK, EDWIN P.
Carpenter, 2 November, 1892.
KIRK, JAMES A.
. Midshipman, 1 May, 1822. Died 9 May, 1823.
KIRK, MORDECAI L.
Mate, 4 March, 1864. Honorably discharged 25 October, 1865.
KIRKBY, GEORGE.
Acting Ensign, 4 November, 1862. Died 22 June, 1863.
KIRKBY, WILLIAM J.
Acting Ensign, 22 December, 1863. Honorably discharged 21 November, 1865.
KIRKENDALL, CHARLES H.
Acting Assistant Paymaster, 25 September, 1861. Mustered out 15 November, 1865.
KIRKHAM, AUSTIN P.
Mate. Resigned 13 April, 1863.
KIRKLAND, JAMES.
Acting Carpenter, 1 October, 1862. Dismissed 10 June, 1863.
KIRKLAND, WILLIAM A.
Midshipman, 2 July, 1850. Passed Midshipman, 20 June, 1856. Master, 22 January, 1858. Lieutenant, 18 March, 1858. Lieutenant-Commander, 16 July, 1862. Commander, 2 March, 1869. Captain, 1 April, 1880. Commodore, 27 July, 1893. Rear Admiral, 1 March, 1895. Retired List, 3 July, 1898. Died 12 August, 1898.
KISKADDEN, HARVEY J.
Mate, 24 January, 1863. Resigned 30 May, 1864.
KISNER, WILLIAM.
Mate, 23 June, 1863. Acting Ensign, 11 March, 1865. Honorably discharged 19 November, 1865.
KISSAM, B. P.
Surgeon, 24 July, 1813. Died 6 October, 1828.
KISSAM, FRANKLIN.
Acting Third Assistant Engineer, 16 June, 1864. Appointment revoked 12 May, 1865.
KISSAM, J. J. ASTOR.
Acting Assistant Paymaster, 18 September, 1862. Resigned 23 July, 1863.
KISSAM, SAMUEL M.
Surgeon, 24 July, 1813. Died August, 1822.
KITCHEN, JOHN S.
Assistant Surgeon, 1 May, 1855. Surgeon, 1 May, 1861. Died 8 May, 1872.
KITCHEN, THEODORE S.
Acting Assistant Paymaster, 12 September, 1863. Resigned 2 December, 1864.
KITCHING, WILLIAM H., Jr.
Mate, 28 July, 1863. Resigned 22 April, 1865.
KITE, ISAAC W.
Assistant Surgeon, 1 April, 1886. Passed Assistant Surgeon, 1 April, 1889. Surgeon, 2 September, 1898.
KITTELLE, SUMNER E W.
Naval Cadet, 19 May, 1885. Ensign, 1 July, 1891. Lieutenant, Junior Grade, 10 August, 1898. Lieutenant, 3 March, 1899.
KITTREDGE, JOHN W.
Acting Volunteer Lieutenant, 26 August, 1861. Dismissed 27 October, 1863.
KITTS, JOHN.
Master, 15 May, 1813. Died 6 August, 1819.
KLECKNER, CHARLES C.
Cadet Engineer, Naval Academy, 1 October, 1871. Graduated 21 June, 1875. Assistant Engineer, 1 July, 1877 Passed Assistant Engineer, 30 June, 1887. Resigned 5 July, 1889.
KLEMANN, JOHN V.
Naval Cadet, 10 September, 1891. Ensign, 1 July, 1897. Lieutenant, Junior Grade, 1 July, 1900.

GENERAL NAVY REGISTER.   317

KLINE, GEORGE W.
Cadet Engineer, 1 October, 1881. Ensign, 1 July, 1887. Lieutenant, Junior Grade, 12 March, 1896. Lieutenant, 3 March, 1899.
KLINEHAUSE, GEORGE H.
Mate, 22 February, 1864. Appointment revoked (sick) 11 August, 1864.
KLOCK, GEORGE H.
Pharmacist, 15 September, 1898.
KLOEPPEL, HENRY.
Acting Ensign, 9 September, 1862. Honorably discharged 23 August, 1866.
KNAPP, BENJAMIN.
Midshipman, 10 October, 1799. Died 8 July, 1800.
KNAPP, B. F.
Lieutenant, 10 October, 1799. Discharged 6 July, 1801, under Peace Establishment Act.
KNAPP, HARRY S.
Cadet Midshipman, 26 June, 1874. Graduated 4 June, 1880. Ensign, 16 February, 1882. Lieutenant, Junior Grade, 31 March, 1889. Lieutenant, 23 January, 1894.
KNAPP, JOHN.
Carpenter, 30 June, 1829. Last appearance on Records of Navy Department. Deserted.
KNAPP, JOHN J.
Cadet Midshipman, 9 June, 1874. Graduated 4 June, 1880. Ensign, Junior Grade, 3 March, 1883. Ensign, 26 June, 1884. Lieutenant, Junior Grade, 15 October, 1890. Lieutenant, 2 February, 1895.
KNAPP, LYMAN M.
Mate, 24 January, 1863. Resigned 3 June, 1864.
KNAPP, MYRON H.
Third Assistant Engineer, 5 November, 1861. Second Assistant Engineer, 25 August, 1863. Resigned 8 July, 1867.
KNAPP, ROBERT A.
Midshipman, 7 December, 1837. Passed Midshipman, 29 June, 1843. Cashiered 17 May, 1845.
KNAPP, ROBERT A.
Acting Lieutenant, 27 July, 1861. Resigned 18 November, 1861.
KNAPP, SAMUEL.
Boatswain, date not known. Last appearance on Records of Navy Department.
KNAPP, WILLIAM.
Acting Ensign, 27 August, 1862. Acting Master, 7 December, 1863. Honorably discharged 6 May, 1868.
KNAPP, WILLIAM, JR.
Mate, 8 May, 1862. Appointment revoked (sick) 30 March, 1863.
KNEASS, CHRISTIAN.
Assistant Surgeon, 16 May, 1804. Resigned 24 April, 1805.
KNEELAND, WILLIAM.
Acting Gunner, 28 July, 1864. Honorably discharged 28 October, 1865.
KNEELAND, WILLIAM.
Mate, 18 December, 1866. Resigned 7 May, 1868.
KNEPPER, CHESTER M.
Cadet Engineer, 1 October, 1880. Ensign, 1 July, 1886. Lieutenant, Junior Grade, 28 April, 1895. Lieutenant, 11 May, 1898.
KNEPPER, ORLO S.
Naval Cadet, 4 September, 1891. Ensign, 1 July, 1897. Lieutenant, Junior Grade, 1 July, 1900.
KNIGHT, AUSTIN M.
Midshipman, 30 June, 1869. Graduated 31 May, 1873. Ensign, 16 July, 1874. Master, 27 October, 1879. Lieutenant, Junior Grade, 3 March, 1883. Lieutenant, 19 December, 1885. Lieutenant-Commander, 3 March, 1899.
KNIGHT, CARLOS W.
Acting Assistant Surgeon, 18 March, 1864. Honorably discharged 18 May, 1868.
KNIGHT, HENRY.
Acting Third Assistant Engineer, 6 July, 1863. Honorably discharged 11 August, 1865.
KNIGHT, JAMES D.
Midshipman, 16 January, 1809. Resigned 20 April, 1810.
KNIGHT, JAMES D.
Midshipman, 30 November, 1814. Lieutenant, 13 January, 1825. Commander, 8 September, 1841. Died 19 July, 1851.
KNIGHT, JAMES S.
Assistant Surgeon, 30 July, 1861. Surgeon, 29 July, 1866. Retired List, 21 June, 1884. Died 21 March, 1886.
KNIGHT, JOHN.
Boatswain, 24 February, 1835. Dismissed 13 May, 1836.
KNIGHT, JOSEPH.
Third Assistant Engineer, 21 September, 1863. Disrated 13 January, 1865.
KNIGHT, THOMAS.
Acting Third Assistant Engineer, 11 December, 1863. Deserted 29 February, 1864.
KNIGHT, WILLIAM.
Acting Ensign, 12 December, 1863. Honorably discharged 3 November, 1865.
KNIGHT, WILLIAM.
Carpenter, 17 July, 1839. Resigned 22 April, 1861.
KNIGHT, WILLIAM.
Master, 2 October, 1799. Died 22 July, 1834.
KNIPE, THOMAS J.
Acting Master, 8 January, 1862. Resigned 28 August, 1862.
KNOWLES, CHARLES.
Acting Ensign, 17 December, 1862. Died in Hospital, New York, 9 April, 1866.

KNOWLES, CHARLES R.
    Acting Master, Admiral Lee's Staff, 28 October, 1864. Resigned 15 June, 1865.
KNOWLES, JAMES P.
    Mate, 24 February, 1863. Resigned 28 March, 1864.
KNOWLES, OLIVER P.
    Mate, 23 January, 1863. Acting Ensign, 24 October, 1864. Honorably discharged 14 September, 1865.
KNOWLES, WILLIAM H.
    Mate, 2 December, 1863. Appointment revoked 4 April, 1864.
KNOWLTON, B. B.
    Mate, 28 September, 1861. Acting Ensign, 23 July, 1862. Acting Master, 4 March, 1864. Resigned 1 October, 1864.
KNOWLTON, DAVID M.
    Acting Ensign, 16 May, 1864. Honorably discharged 2 July, 1865.
KNOWLTON, GEORGE K.
    Mate, 16 October, 1862. Honorably discharged 26 January, 1864.
KNOWLTON, INGERSOLL F.
    Third Assistant Engineer, 18 November, 1862. Resigned 17 March, 1865.
KNOWLTON, MINOR N.
    Third Assistant Engineer, 18 November, 1862. Second Assistant Engineer, 23 March, 1864. Resigned 22 November, 1872.
KNOWLTON, WILLIAM H.
    Mate, 18 November, 1862. Resigned 17 August, 1864.
KNOX, DANIEL E.
    Mate, 22 September, 1864. Appointment revoked 8 September, 1866.
KNOX, DUDLEY W.
    Naval Cadet, 6 September, 1892. Ensign, 6 May, 1898.
KNOX, HARRY.
    Midshipman, 2 March, 1863. Graduated 6 June, 1867. Ensign, 18 December, 1868. Master, 21 March, 1870. Lieutenant, 21 March, 1871. Lieutenant-Commander, 2 January, 1888. Commander, 1 October, 1896.
KNOX, HENRY J.
    Midshipman, 30 April, 1798. Lieutenant, 20 June, 1799. Last appearance on Records of Navy Department, 24 August, 1820.
KNOX, M. D.
    Acting Assistant Surgeon, 11 September, 1861. Appointment revoked 2 November, 1861.
KNOX, MORRISON A.
    Acting Ensign, 11 June, 1863. Appointment revoked (sick) 26 July, 1864.
KNOX, ROBERT.
    Sailing Master, 20 July, 1812. Reserved List, 13 September, 1855. Died 24 February, 1857.
KNOX, ROBERT.
    Acting Gunner, 22 November, 1864. Honorably discharged 14 July, 1866.
KNOX, SAMUEL R.
    Midshipman, 1 April, 1828. Passed Midshipman, 15 June, 1837. Lieutenant, 8 September, 1841. Reserved List, 13 September, 1855. Captain on Reserved List, 4 April, 1867. Died 21 November, 1883.
KNOX, SIMON B.
    Third Assistant Engineer, 20 February, 1847. Second Assistant Engineer, 26 February, 1851. Died 19 September, 1855.
KNOX, WILLIAM E.
    Mate, 18 February, 1862. Dismissed 5 August, 1862.
KOEHL, CHARLES C.
    Acting Third Assistant Engineer, 25 March, 1863. Acting Second Assistant Engineer, 27 October, 1864. Honorably discharged 27 March, 1868.
KOEHL, EDWARD W.
    Third Assistant Engineer, 30 July, 1861. Second Assistant Engineer, 18 December, 1862. Dropped 9 January, 1867. Acting Second Assistant Engineer, 29 January, 1867. Died 27 August, 1867.
KOEHLER, JOHN G.
    Mate, 15 October, 1861. Acting Ensign, 4 August, 1863. Honorably discharged 13 May, 1867. Mate, 20 April, 1870. Appointment revoked 16 July, 1870.
KOESTER, OSCAR W.
    Naval Cadet, 26 September, 1883. Resigned 4 February, 1884. Naval Cadet, 5 April, 1884. Assistant Engineer, 1 July, 1890. Passed Assistant Engineer, 21 June, 1896. Rank changed to Lieutenant, 3 March, 1899.
KOLB, GEORGE A.
    Assistant Engineer (Spanish-American War), 22 April, 1898. Honorably discharged 24 October, 1898.
KOLLOCK, MATTHEW H.
    Acting Assistant Surgeon, 19 December, 1862. Deserted 7 February, 1864.
KOONES, ALBERT L.
    Acting Third Assistant Engineer, 29 September, 1862. Acting Second Assistant Engineer, 29 October, 1863. Honorably discharged 27 December, 1865.
KORTE, FRED J.
    Acting Warrant Machinist, 23 August, 1899.
KRECKER, FREDERICK.
    Acting Assistant Surgeon, 15 March, 1864. Assistant Surgeon, 1 April, 1864. Resigned 23 January, 1867.
KREIDER, MARION E.
    Ensign (Spanish-American War), 30 July, 1898. Honorably discharged 13 September, 1898.
KREPS, JOHN.
    Midshipman, 16 January, 1809. Resigned 15 May, 1809.

GENERAL NAVY REGISTER. 319

KRESS, JAMES C.
Naval Cadet, 20 May, 1897. Graduated 30 June, 1900.
KRETZ, CHARLES H.
Assistant Engineer (Spanish-American War), 15 June, 1898. Honorably discharged 7 November, 1898.
KRIM, JAMES.
Carpenter, 17 June, 1861. Died 1 September, 1862.
KROEHL, JULIUS H.
Acting Volunteer Lieutenant, 4 December, 1862. Appointment revoked 8 August, 1863.
KRUGE, A. O.
Acting Ensign, 30 November, 1863. Honorably discharged 28 December, 1865.
KRUSE, CHRISTIAN.
Mate, 19 July, 1864. Acting Ensign, 3 May, 1865. Honorably discharged 23 July, 1865.
KRUSE, HENRY G. C.
Acting Ensign, 27 November, 1863. Honorably discharged 10 August, 1865.
KUENZLI, HENRY C.
Naval Cadet, 6 September, 1887. Ensign, 1 July, 1893. Lieutenant, Junior Grade, 3 March, 1899. Lieutenant, 24 September, 1899.
KUHL, HUGH.
Mate, 10 December, 1862. Acting Ensign, 21 August, 1863. Resigned 30 May, 1864.
Mate, 29 November, 1869. Retired List, 10 June, 1897.
KUHLWEIN, LEONARD J. G.
Gunner, 7 June, 1894.
KUHN, ADAM S.
Midshipman, 1 February, 1814. Died 24 August, 1820.
KUNHARDT, CHARLES P.
Midshipman, 31 July, 1866. Graduated 7 June, 1870. Resigned 22 March, 1873.
KUTZ, GEORGE F.
Third Assistant Engineer, 26 June, 1856. First Assistant Engineer, 3 August, 1859. Chief Engineer, 10 November, 1861. Retired List, 26 June, 1896.
KYLE, JOHN M.
Midshipman, 17 December, 1810. Resigned 16 October, 1811.
KYLE, ROBERT A.
Acting Third Assistant Engineer, 1 December, 1863. Honorably discharged 26 July, 1865.
LaBACH, PAUL M.
Naval Cadet, 26 September, 1890. Resigned 15 February, 1893. Ensign (Spanish-American War), 11 June, 1898. Honorably discharged 6 October, 1898.
LABDON, CHARLES.
Mate, 8 May, 1862. Appointment revoked (sick) 27 February, 1863.
La BLANC, THOMAS.
Third Assistant Engineer, 1 February, 1862. Second Assistant Engineer, 15 October, 1863. Resigned 28 September, 1867.
LABREE, BENJAMIN.
Acting Second Assistant Engineer, 31 August, 1863. Honorably discharged 4 December, 1865.
LACY, CHARLES.
Midshipman, 16 January, 1809. Lieutenant, 5 March, 1817. Died 18 June, 1824.
LACKEY, HENRY E.
Naval Cadet, 20 May, 1895. At sea prior to final graduation.
LACKEY, OSCAR H.
Third Assistant Engineer, 21 July, 1858. Second Assistant Engineer, 17 January, 1861. First Assistant Engineer, 17 March, 1863. Chief Engineer, 21 March, 1870. Retired List, 16 November, 1882. Died 21 May, 1883.
LADD, JAMES M.
Midshipman, 2 March, 1839. Passed Midshipman, 2 July, 1845. Died 26 November, 1847.
La DIEU, SETH L.
Acting Ensign, 7 November, 1863. Honorably discharged 24 August, 1865.
LAESCH, LEWIS C. F.
Third Assistant Engineer, 17 March, 1863. Resigned 24 May, 1864.
La FEBRA, JAMES H.
Acting Third Assistant Engineer, 14 March, 1863. Resigned 11 September, 1863.
LAFFINER, THOMAS.
Gunner, 29 December, 1853. Dismissed 26 June, 1855.
LAFORGE, W. T.
Acting Gunner, 14 June, 1864. Appointment revoked 18 April, 1865.
LAGOW, JOHN H.
Midshipman, 31 March, 1848. Resigned 19 October, 1852.
LAHA, THOMAS, Jr.
Mate, 24 January, 1862. Acting Ensign, 18 February, 1863. Dismissed 19 June, 1863.
LAIGHTON, ALFRED S.
Acting Ensign, 19 December, 1863. Killed on Gettysburg, 16 January, 1865.
LAIGHTON, WILLIAM F.
Carpenter, 7 April, 1849. Retired List, 13 November, 1877. Died 25 June, 1879.
LAIGHTON, WILLIAM M.
Carpenter, 29 September, 1836. Retired List, 15 April, 1872. Died 23 May, 1873.
LAINE, R. W.
Mate, 13 September, 1865. Acting Ensign, 4 April, 1866. Resigned 15 June, 1868.
LAING, THOMAS.
Midshipman, 2 March, 1800. Discharged 7 July, 1801, under Peace Establishment Act.
LAIRD, CHARLES.
Midshipman, 29 September, 1869. Graduated 21 June, 1875. Ensign, 18 July, 1876.

GENERAL NAVY REGISTER.

Master, 1 February, 1882. Lieutenant, Junior Grade, 3 March, 1883. Lieutenant, September, 1888. Lieutenant-Commander, 3 March, 1899.
LAIRD, J. CLARENCE.
Mate, 22 June, 1863. Resigned 23 December, 1863.
LAIRD, ROBERT W.
Acting Ensign, 28 April, 1864. Honorably discharged 30 August, 1865.
LAKE, PETER.
Mate, 18 December, 1863. Acting Ensign, 17 March, 1865. Honorably discharged 26 November, 1865.
LAKERMAN, JOHN.
Mate, 21 February, 1863. Died at Pensacola, Florida, 15 September, 1863.
LAKIN, DANIEL W.
Mate, 25 October, 1862. Acting Ensign, 18 August, 1864. Honorably discharged 25 September, 1865.
LALOR, JOHN W.
Mate, 7 February, 1863. Acting Ensign, 11 November, 1863. Honorably discharged 20 October, 1865.
LAMB, GEORGE.
Acting Ensign, 14 May, 1863. Honorably discharged 14 September, 1865.
LAMBERT, DANIEL.
Boatswain, 10 June, 1837. Last appearance on Records of Navy Department.
LAMBERT, D. R.
Midshipman, 16 February, 1838. Passed Midshipman, 20 May, 1844. Master, 29 August, 1852. Lieutenant, 9 June, 1853. Died 27 May, 1859.
LAMBERT, GEORGE W.
Acting Third Assistant Engineer, 14 April, 1863. Resigned 8 October, 1863.
LAMBERT, HENRY S.
Mate, 12 June, 1861. Acting Ensign, 25 September, 1862. Acting Master, 9 November, 1864. Honorably discharged 26 October, 1865.
LAMBERT, THOMAS R.
Chaplain, 29 December, 1833. Resigned 11 September, 1856.
LAMBERT, WILLIAM.
Midshipman, 1 December, 1826. Passed Midshipman, 28 April, 1832. Lieutenant, 8 March, 1837. Died 15 March, 1840.
LAMBERTON, BENJAMIN P.
Acting Midshipman, 21 September, 1860. Graduated 22 November, 1864. Ensign, 1 November, 1866. Master, 1 December, 1866. Lieutenant, 12 March, 1868. Lieutenant-Commander, 27 April, 1869. Commander, 2 June, 1885. Captain, 11 May, 1898.
LAMBERTON, BENJAMIN P., Jr.
Naval Cadet (Spanish-American War), 20 July, 1898. Honorably discharged 6 December, 1898.
LAMBERTSON, GARRET J.
Acting Third Assistant Engineer, 4 February, 1863. Dismissed 15 March, 1864.
LAMDIN, JAMES F.
Third Assistant Engineer, 24 December, 1853. Second Assistant Engineer; 9 May, 1857. First Assistant Engineer, 2 August, 1859. Chief Engineer, 8 December, 1862. Dismissed 5 March, 1867.
LAMDIN, NICHOLAS H.
Third Assistant Engineer, 21 April, 1863. Retired 22 June, 1869. Restored to Active List by Act of Congress, 17 July, 1872. Second Assistant Engineer, same date. Passed Assistant Engineer, 3 June, 1879. Died 15 November, 1885.
LAMDIN, WILLIAM J.
Third Assistant Engineer, 6 February, 1851. Second Assistant Engineer, 1 October, 1852. First Assistant Engineer, 9 May, 1857. Chief Engineer, 1 October, 1861. Retired List, 29 June, 1887. Died 12 October, 1888.
LAMIE, W.
Acting Ensign and Pilot, 28 October, 1864. Honorably discharged 21 September, 1865.
LAMON, JAMES.
Acting Gunner, 27 June, 1864. Honorably discharged 28 October, 1865.
La MOTTE, HENRY.
Assistant Surgeon, 27 January, 1892. Retired List, 15 September, 1897.
LAMPHIER, RICHMOND H.
Acting Ensign, 14 July, 1864. Honorably discharged 9 December, 1868.
LAMPORT, GEORGE H.
Mate, 1 October, 1862. Resigned 8 January, 1863.
LAMPORT, RICHARD T.
Mate, 16 February, 1863. Acting Ensign, 14 June, 1864. Honorably discharged 10 December, 1865.
LAMSON, CHARLES W.
Acting Master, 8 July, 1861. Appointment revoked 25 February, 1865.
LAMSON, ROSWELL H.
Acting Midshipman, 20 September, 1858. Graduated, 1862. Lieutenant, 1 August, 1862. Resigned 6 July, 1866. Reappointed 9 January, 1895. Retired List, 15 April, 1895.
LANAHAN, DAVID J.
Acting Third Assistant Engineer, 8 September, 1863. Honorably discharged 9 October, 1865.
LANCASHIRE, BENJAMIN.
Acting Master and Pilot, 1 October, 1864. Honorably discharged 26 January, 1866.
LANCASTER, SILAS H.
Acting Third Assistant Engineer, 3 November, 1864. Resigned 6 June, 1865.
LANDENBERGER, GEORGE B.
Naval Cadet, 20 May, 1896. Graduated 30 June, 1900.

LANDERGREEN, ADOLPHUS.
  Mate, 24 July, 1863. Acting Ensign, 3 December, 1864. Honorably discharged 14 September, 1865.
LANDIS, IRWIN F.
  Naval Cadet, 6 September, 1893. Ensign, 1 July, 1899.
LANDON, GEORGE W.
  Acting Third Assistant Engineer, 28 March, 1864. Resigned 12 May, 1865.
LANDON, WILLIAM.
  Sailmaker, 4 December, 1815. Last appearance on Records of Navy Department.
LANDRAM, CLARENCE E.
  Naval Cadet, 5 September, 1896. Graduated 30 June, 1900.
LANE, ANTHONY J.
  Acting Third Assistant Engineer, 4 September, 1863. Acting Second Assistant Engineer, 16 February, 1864. Honorably discharged 5 November, 1865.
LANE, CHARLES M.
  Acting Master and Pilot, 31 October, 1864. Appointment revoked 9 February, 1865.
LANE, DAVID M.
  Acting Third Assistant Engineer, 24 April, 1862. Acting Second Assistant Engineer, 29 January, 1863. Resigned 13 February, 1864.
LANE, GEORGE W.
  Mate, 22 November, 1861. Honorably discharged 2 October, 1865.
LANE, L. COOPER.
  Assistant Surgeon, 17 April, 1856. Resigned 20 October, 1859.
LANE, MOSES A.
  Gunner, 28 January, 1852. Retired List, 11 January, 1885. Died 31 October, 1888.
LANE, NINIAN E.
  Midshipman, 1 April, 1828. Dismissed 11 July, 1835.
LANE, N. B.
  Midshipman, 18 June, 1832. Resigned 27 February, 1833.
LANE, SANDS N.
  Acting Ensign, 3 August, 1864. Honorably discharged 21 July, 1865.
LANE, SIMEON.
  Mate, 5 February, 1862. Dismissed 29 June, 1863.
LANE, S. CUSHING.
  Acting Third Assistant Engineer, 19 April, 1862. Third Assistant Engineer, 8 December, 1862. Dropped 8 April, 1865.
LANE, WILLIAM N.
  Acting Assistant Surgeon, 21 October, 1861. Appointment revoked 21 February, 1862.
LANE, WEBSTER.
  Third Assistant Engineer, 23 May, 1861. Second Assistant Engineer, 3 August, 1863. Resigned 22 March, 1867.
LANFARE, ROBERT O.
  Mate, 8 May, 1862. Acting Ensign, 24 August, 1864. Honorably discharged 12 December, 1865.
LANG, CHARLES J.
  Naval Cadet, 6 September, 1889. Ensign, 1 July, 1895. Lieutenant, Junior Grade, 3 March, 1899.
LANG, HUGH.
  Acting Third Assistant Engineer, 20 November, 1862. Resigned 27 December, 1862.
LANG, JAMES.
  Warrant Machinist (Spanish-American War), 18 May, 1898. Honorably discharged 2 September, 1896.
LANG, RICHARD.
  Boatswain, date not known. Last appearance on Records of Navy Department.
LANGDON, H. S.
  Midshipman, 18 June, 1812. Killed in action, 28 June, 1814.
LANGDON, JOSHUA B.
  Purser, 5 December, 1809. Died 3 July, 1810.
LANGER, PHILIP JOSEPH.
  Third Assistant Engineer, 18 November, 1862. Second Assistant Engineer, 23 March, 1864. Resigned 28 April, 1870.
LANGHORNE, CARY D.
  Assistant Surgeon, 7 July, 1898.
LANGHORNE, JOHN D.
  Midshipman, 6 July, 1842. Passed Midshipman, 5 August, 1848. Resigned 21 November, 1853.
LANGLANDS, ROBERT H.
  Acting Ensign, 22 October, 1863. Honorably discharged 30 September, 1865.
LANGLEY, CHARLES F.
  Acting Ensign, 14 April, 1863. Acting Master, recommendation of Captain J. L. Worden, 19 November, 1863. Honorably discharged 14 September, 1865.
LANGLEY, FREEMAN.
  Mate, 8 May, 1863. Resigned 19 April, 1864.
LANGLEY, JOHN W.
  Acting Assistant Surgeon, 3 September, 1862. Resigned 1 September, 1864.
LANGLIN, EDWARD.
  Acting Third Assistant Engineer, 20 January, 1865. Honorably discharged 28 October, 1865.
LANGLOIS, AUGUST.
  Acting Assistant Surgeon, 30 January, 1863. Honorably discharged 6 August, 1866.
LANGSTAFF, JAMES.
  Mate, 4 February, 1862. Dismissed 14 April, 1862.

LANGTHORNE, AMOS R.
Acting Master, 16 December, 1861. Acting Volunteer Lieutenant, 29 January, 1863. Honorably discharged 6 March, 1866.
LANGTON, JOHN B. F.
Boatswain, 25 November, 1861. Chief Boatswain, 3 March, 1899. Retired List, 8 October, 1900.
LANGTON, THOMAS.
Mate, 16 June, 1862. Dismissed 5 May, 1863.
LANGWORTHY, ANDREW B.
Mate, 7 August, 1861. Resigned 13 June, 1863. Mate, 22 December, 1864. Honorably discharged 17 June, 1867.
LANIER, EDMUND.
Midshipman, 9 July, 1831. Passed Midshipman, 15 June, 1837. Lieutenant, 8 September, 1841. Commander, 29 April, 1861. Retired List, 23 July, 1864. Captain on Retired List, 4 April, 1867. Died 24 February, 1872.
LANIHAN, JAMES.
Acting Third Assistant Engineer, 14 April, 1864. Appointment revoked (sick) 26 May, 1864.
LANING, HARRIS.
Naval Cadet, 19 May, 1891. Ensign, 1 July, 1897. Lieutenant, Junior Grade, 1 July, 1900.
LANMAN, JOSEPH.
Midshipman, 1 January, 1825. Passed Midshipman, 4 June, 1831. Lieutenant, 3 March, 1835. Commander, 14 September, 1855. Captain, 16 July, 1862. Commodore, 29 August, 1862. Rear-Admiral, 8 December, 1867. Retired List, 18 July, 1872. Died 13 March, 1874.
LANMAN, R. Y.
Mate, 22 September, 1864. Appointment revoked 19 April, 1866.
LANMAN, WILLIAM.
Acting Third Assistant Engineer, 1 September, 1862. Acting Second Assistant Engineer, 31 March, 1864. Honorably discharged 8 September, 1865.
LANNING, JAMES.
Acting Volunteer Lieutenant, 1 October, 1862. Resigned 13 February, 1865.
LANSDALE, PHILIP.
Assistant Surgeon, 5 March, 1847. Surgeon, 20 January, 1861. Medical Inspector, 3 March, 1871. Medical Director, 8 June, 1873. Retired List, 30 April, 1879. Died 21 August, 1894.
LANDSDALE, PHILIP V.
Cadet Midshipman, 6 June, 1873. Graduated 18 June, 1879. Ensign, 1 June, 1881. Lieutenant, Junior Grade, 31 March, 1888. Lieutenant, 15 May, 1893. Killed in action 1 April, 1899.
LANSING, EDWARD A.
Midshipman, 18 June, 1812. Died 15 August, 1821.
LANSING, GEORGE.
Midshipman, 1 November, 1828. Resigned 1 February, 1833.
LANTZ, DANIEL.
Acting Second Assistant Engineer, 29 April, 1863. Appointment revoked 20 October, 1863.
LAPHAM, HENRY K.
Acting Master, 3 October, 1861. Honorably discharged 17 November, 1867.
LAPOINT, ALFRED.
Acting First Assistant Engineer, 20 June, 1862. Honorably discharged 8 April, 1866. Acting First Assistant Engineer, 13 April, 1866. Resigned 24 April, 1867.
LARDNER, JAMES B.
Midshipman, 4 December, 1822. Died 8 April, 1829.
LARDNER, JAMES L.
Midshipman, 10 May, 1820. Lieutenant, 17 May, 1828. Commander, 21 November, 1851. Captain, 19 May, 1861. Commodore, 16 July, 1862. Retired List, 20 November, 1864. Rear-Admiral on Retired List, 25 July, 1866. Died 12 April, 1881.
LARDNER, JOHN.
Acting Third Assistant Engineer, 27 May, 1861. Acting Second Assistant Engineer, 20 September, 1862. Honorably discharged 24 September, 1865.
LARDNER, LYNFORD.
Acting Assistant Paymaster, 5 December, 1862. Resigned 23 December, 1864.
LARIMER, EDGAR B.
Naval Cadet, 6 September, 1895. At sea prior to final graduation.
LARKIN, FRANCIS E.
Boatswain, 30 January, 1895.
LARKIN, JOHN.
Midshipman, 18 June, 1812. Resigned 6 January, 1814.
LARKIN, JOSHUA W.
Midshipman, 1 December, 1824. Died 20 May, 1829.
LARKIN, SAMUEL.
Midshipman, 1 April, 1828. Passed Midshipman, 14 June, 1834. Lieutenant, 1 July, 1840. Commander, 14 September, 1855. Died 22 December, 1856.
LARKINS, JOHN S.
Acting Third Assistant Engineer, 26 September, 1864. Honorably discharged 7 July, 1866.
LARMAND, WILLIAM.
Gunner, 20 November, 1799. Last appearance on Records of Navy Department.
LARSEN, NILES.
Acting Ensign, 28 April, 1863. Honorably discharged 5 October, 1865.
LARSON, CHARLES.
Mate, 15 April, 1898. Appointment revoked 23 August, 1899.

GENERAL NAVY REGISTER.

LASHER, OLIVER.
Mate, 23 December, 1862. Acting Ensign and Pilot, 30 April, 1864. Appointment revoked 4 April, 1865.

LASHER, OREN E.
Midshipman 29 September, 1868. Graduated 1 June, 1872. Ensign, 15 July, 1873. Master, 1 July. 1878. Lieutenant, Junior Grade, 3 March, 1883. Lieutenant, 2 March, 1885. Retired List, 9 March, 1898. Died 28 April, 1899.

LASSALLE, S. B.
Midshipman, 4 November, 1814. Resigned 6 October, 1823.

LATCH, EDWARD B.
Third Assistant Engineer, 20 September, 1858. Second Assistant Engineer, 8 October, 1861. First Assistant Engineer, 17 March, 1863. Chief Engineer, 21 March, 1870. Retired List, 22 November, 1878.

LATHAM, FRANKLIN J.
Acting Ensign, 13 November, 1863. Honorably discharged 19 January, 1866.

LATHAM, GEORGE W.
Chaplain, 14 April, 1815. Died 22 January, 1847.

LATHAM, GEORGE W.
Acting Third Assistant Engineer, 24 December, 1863. Honorably discharged 28 October, 1865.

LATHAM, WILLIAM H.
Acting Master, 25 May, 1861. Acting Volunteer Lieutenant, 19 July, 1864. Resigned 22 March, 1865.

LATHROP, ALFRED G.
Acting Assistant Paymaster, 4 February, 1864. Mustered out 23 November, 1865.

LATHROP, JOHN.
Acting Third Assistant Engineer, 11 February, 1865. Resigned 6 July, 1865.

LATHROP, SUMNER P.
Acting Master, 29 October, 1861. Died 15 June, 1863.

LATHROPE, JOHN P.
Chaplain, 2 October, 1843. Died 29 December, 1843.

LATIMER, ARTHUR.
Midshipman, 1 January, 1812. Died 8 September, 1815.

LATIMER, CHARLES.
Midshipman, 9 September, 1841. Passed Midshipman, 10 August, 1847. Resigned 2 December, 1854.

LATIMER, JOHN.
Lieutenant, 14 July, 1799. Last appearance on Records of Navy Department, 18 August, 1800.

LATIMER, JULIAN L.
Naval Cadet, 30 September. 1886. Ensign, 1 July, 1892. Lieutenant, Junior Grade, 3 March, 1899. Lieutenant, 1 July, 1899.

LATIMER, ROE.
Midshipman, 5 October, 1798. Resigned 1 August, 1799.

LATIMER, SAMUEL C.
Third Assistant Engineer, 1 December, 1854. Died 24 August, 1855.

LATIMER, WILLIAM A. R.
Third Assistant Engineer, 11 January, 1849. Second Assistant Engineer, 26 February, 1851. Resigned 31 May, 1858. Second Assistant Engineer, 21 October, 1861. Resigned 26 August, 1862. Acting First Assistant Engineer, 26 August, 1862. Acting Chief Engineer, 7 July, 1863. Honorably discharged 28 September, 1867.

LATIMER, WILLIAM K.
Midshipman, 15 November, 1809. Lieutenant, 4 February, 1815. Commander, 2 March, 1833. Captain, 17 July, 1843. Reserved List, 13 September, 1855. Commodore on Retired List, 16 July, 1862. Died 15 March, 1873.

LATON, JAMES R.
Acting Assistant Surgeon, 11 November, 1861. Resigned 24 October, 1863.

LATSON, JOHN R.
Acting Assistant Surgeon, 3 November, 1864. Honorably discharged 9 October, 1865.

LATTA, SAMUEL W.
Assistant Surgeon, 24 March, 1868. Resigned 4 November, 1873. Acting Assistant Surgeon, 6 December, 1876. Honorably discharged 30 June, 1879.

LAUB, EDWIN.
Midshipman, 1 December, 1828. Lost in the Hornet, 10 September, 1829.

LAUB, HENRY.
Midshipman, 16 January, 1809. Killed in action 10 September, 1813.

LAUBACK, ALFRED.
Acting Assistant Surgeon, 27 October, 1863. Died 21 April, 1865.

LAUBER, LEWIS.
Acting Assistant Surgeon, 12 August, 1861. Dismissed 19 April, 1862.

LAUGHLIN, JOHN J.
Midshipman, 1 May, 1847. Resigned 22 September, 1852.

LAUGHTON, WILLIAM.
Midshipman, 25 August, 1809. Lieutenant, 9 December, 1814. Died 22 July, 1825.

LAURENS, JOHN.
Midshipman, 13 November, 1841. Resigned 27 July, 1846.

LAURIAT, GEORGE R.
Ensign (Spanish-American War), 17 June, 1898. Honorably discharged 26 November, 1898.

LAUTERBACH, ROBERT.
Acting Assistant Surgeon, 6 May, 1865. Honorably discharged 27 August, 1866.

LA VALLETTE, ELIE A. F.
Sailing Master, 25 June, 1812. Lieutenant, 9 December, 1814. Commander, 3 March,

1831. Captain, 23 February, 1840. Rear-Admiral, Retired List. 16 July, 1862. Died 18 November, 1862.
LAVALLETTE, S. D.
Midshipman, 8 December, 1835. Died 14 February, 1845.
LAVEN, JAMES.
Acting Boatswain, 16 May, 1900.
LAVENDER, ALBERT W.
Assistant Paymaster (Spanish-American War), 12 July, 1898. Honorably discharged 2 March, 1899.
LAVERTY, ROBERT.
Acting Third Assistant Engineer, 14 February, 1863. Appointment revoked 30 June, 1864.
LAVERY, RICHARD.
Acting First Assistant Engineer, 1861. Resigned 24 May, 1862.
LAVERY, THOMAS J.
Third Assistant Engineer, 20 September, 1862. Acting Second Assistant Engineer, 17 March, 1864. Resigned 23 February, 1865.
LAVERY, WILLIAM.
Boatswain, 2 December, 1857. Died 31 December, 1861.
LAW, BENJAMIN.
Master, 23 June, 1812. Died 17 August, 1812.
LAW, GEORGE E.
Acting Midshipman, 4 October, 1851. Midshipman, 9 June, 1855. Passed Midshipman, 15 April, 1858. Master, 5 November, 1858. Lieutenant, 19 July, 1860. Resigned 18 December, 1860. Lieutenant, 21 April, 1861. Dismissed 27 November, 1861.
LAW, HOMER L.
Assistant Surgeon, 9 July, 1870. Surgeon, 22 August, 1884. Retired List 17 December, 1886.
LAW, LYMAN R.
Midshipman, 5 February, 1838. Retired List. Died 11 January, 1869.
LAW, RICHARD.
Commander, 16 December, 1799. Discharged 2 April, 1801, under Peace Establishment Act.
LAW, RICHARD.
Acting Third Assistant Engineer, 3 December, 1864. Honorably discharged 9 December, 1865.
LAW, RICHARD L.
Midshipman, 17 February, 1841. Passed Midshipman, 10 August, 1847. Master, 1 March, 1855. Lieutenant, 14 September, 1855. Lieutenant-Commander, 16 July, 1862. Commander, 26 September, 1866. Captain, 11 December, 1877. Retired List 12 December, 1886. Died 8 June, 1891.
LAW, WILLIAM FRANCIS.
Third Assistant Engineer, 16 November, 1861. Died 24 September, 1863.
LAWARSON, JAMES.
Master, 3 July, 1812. Discharged 23 March, 1813.
LAWLER, JAMES.
Mate, 4 March, 1864. Resigned 25 January, 1865.
LAWLESS, R. T.
Mate, 2 February, 1870. Resigned 21 July, 1873.
LAWRANCE, JAMES P. S.
Assistant Engineer, 22 March, 1875. Passed Assistant Engineer, 16 June, 1883. Chief Engineer, 5 June, 1896. Rank changed to Lieutenant-Commander, 3 March, 1899.
LAWRASON, SAMUEL C.
Assistant Surgeon, 8 February, 1832. Surgeon, 9 December, 1839. Died 14 July, 1849.
LAWRENCE, ALEXANDER W.
Professor, 29 July, 1853. Dismissed 22 April, 1861.
LAWRENCE, ALBERT.
Passed Assistant Engineer (Spanish-American War), 13 June, 1898. Honorably discharged 7 October, 1898.
LAWRENCE, ALVIN.
Acting Third Assistant Engineer, 16 January, 1864. Honorably discharged 17 September, 1865.
LAWRENCE, CHARLES.
Sailmaker, 21 August, 1861. Resigned 18 February, 1864. Acting Master, 18 February, 1864. Resigned 13 June, 1864.
LAWRENCE, CHARLES H.
Acting Third Assistant Engineer, 24 December, 1863. Honorably discharged 12 June, 1865.
LAWRENCE, CHRISTIAN S.
Mate, 4 April, 1862. Acting Ensign, 20 December, 1863. Honorably discharged 2 November, 1865. Acting Ensign, 6 December, 1866. Mustered out 24 August, 1868.
LAWRENCE. C. K.
Master, 6 October, 1814. Resigned 27 February, 1815.
LAWRENCE, DAVID B.
Mate, 1 October, 1862. Dismissed 24 December, 1863.
LAWRENCE, GEORGE.
Assistant Paymaster, 31 August, 1861. Paymaster, 6 February, 1862. Resigned 7 October, 1864.
LAWRENCE, GEORGE M.
Acting Ensign and Pilot, 18 June, 1864. Resigned 2 August, 1864.
LAWRENCE, GEORGE W.
Acting Third Assistant Engineer, 5 January, 1864. Resigned 29 April, 1864.

LAWRENCE, HENRY R.
 Third Assistant Engineer, 21 September, 1861. Resigned 9 November, 1861. Third Assistant Engineer, 28 October, 1862. Resigned March, 1863.
LAWRENCE, JAMES.
 Midshipman, 4 September, 1798. Lieutenant, 6 April, 1802. Commander, 3 November, 1810. Captain, 4 March, 1813. Died 5 June, 1813, of wounds received in action.
LAWRENCE, JOHN.
 Ensign (Spanish-American War), 10 June, 1898. Honorably discharged 31 August, 1898.
LAWRENCE, JOHN B.
 Mate, 21 December, 1863. Acting Boatswain, 7 June, 1864. Acting Ensign, 12 December, 1864. Honorably discharged 5 November, 1865.
LAWRENCE, JOHN C. E.
 Third Assistant Engineer, 28 October, 1850. Second Assistant Engineer, 26 February, 1851. Resigned 2 June, 1856.
LAWRENCE, JOHN D.
 Mate, 11 July, 1863. Appointment revoked 1 April, 1864.
LAWRENCE, N. C.
 Midshipman, 1 May, 1822. Passed Midshipman, 24 May, 1828. Lieutenant, 3 March, 1831. Died 12 July, 1837.
LAWRENCE, THOMAS H.
 Mate, 5 December, 1861. Resigned 23 May, 1862. Mate, 21 July, 1864. Dismissed 28 January, 1865.
LAWRENCE, WALTER.
 Midshipman, 7 July, 1800. Discharged 30 April, 1801, under Peace Establishment Act.
LAWRENCE, WALTER.
 Mate, 17 September, 1864. Honorably discharged 5 July, 1865.
LAWRENCE, WILLIAM J. B.
 Mate, 23 January, 1862. Resigned 5 May, 1863.
LAWBACH, ALFRED S.
 Acting Assistant Surgeon, 27 October, 1863. Died 21 April, 1865.
LAWRIE, CRANSTOUN.
 Midshipman, 1 November, 1826. Resigned 4 April, 1833.
LAWS, ALEXANDER.
 Midshipman, 25 August, 1802. Lieutenant, 8 January, 1807. Resigned 13 April, 1807.
LAWS, ALEXANDER.
 Midshipman, 15 May, 1800. Discharged 12 August, 1801, under Peace Establishment Act.
LAWS, CHARLES A.
 Acting Third Assistant Engineer, 23 November, 1863. Acting Second Assistant Engineer, 1 February, 1865. Honorably discharged 27 October, 1865.
LAWS, ELIJAH.
 Third Assistant Engineer, 19 March, 1858. Second Assistant Engineer, 1 December, 1860. Dismissed 27 May, 1863. Appointed Second Assistant Engineer, 31 March, 1864, from 1 December, 1860. First Assistant Engineer, 25 July, 1866. Chief Engineer, 23 June, 1870. Retired List, 20 March, 1895.
LAWS, GEORGE W.
 Naval Cadet, 21 May, 1887. Assistant Engineer, 1 July, 1893. Passed Assistant Engineer, 16 February, 1898. Rankanchanged to Lieutenant, Junior Grade, 3 March, 1899.
LAWS, JAMES.
 Assistant Surgeon, 29 June, 1855. Surgeon, 1 August, 1861. Resigned 24 March, 1866.
LAWSON, ELIAS.
 Acting Ensign, 10 November, 1864. Honorably discharged 17 July, 1865.
LAWSON, FREDERICK B.
 Acting Assistant Surgeon, 16 September, 1862. Resigned 25 October, 1865.
LAWSON, R. H. L.
 Midshipman, 4 October, 1798. Lieutenant, 16 January, 1800. Resigned 8 March, 1804.
LAWSON, THOMAS.
 Assistant Surgeon, 1 March, 1809. Resigned 12 January, 1811.
LAWTON, ANDREW.
 Third Assistant Engineer, 24 June, 1850. Second Assistant Engineer, 26 February, 1851. First Assistant Engineer, 21 May, 1853. Chief Engineer, 23 April, 1859. Died 17 March, 1871.
LAWTON, BENJAMIN.
 Mate. Resigned 23 March, 1864.
LAWTON, CHARLES E.
 Ensign (Spanish-American War), 29 June, 1898. Honorably discharged 24 September, 1898.
LAWTON, ELBRIDGE.
 Third Assistant Engineer, 23 March, 1848. Second Assistant Engineer, 13 September, 1849. First Assistant Engineer, 26 February, 1851. Chief Engineer, 26 June, 1856. Retired List, 3 March, 1881. Died 21 July, 1889.
LAWTON, E. L.
 Surgeon, 24 July, 1813. Last appearance on Records of Navy Department, 1819. Furloughed.
LAWTON, NELSON H.
 Third Assistant Engineer, 17 March, 1863. Resigned 25 April, 1865.
LAWTON, THEODORE E.
 Acting Ensign, 17 May, 1864. Honorably discharged 21 October, 1865.
LAWTON, WILLIAM.
 Master, 10 September, 1812. Discharged in 1815.

LAWYER, AUG. F.
Assistant Surgeon, 20 June, 1838. Resigned 31 August, 1847.
LAY, JOHN L.
Second Assistant Engineer, 8 July, 1861. First Assistant Engineer, 15 October, 1863. Resigned 22 May, 1865.
LAYCOCK, THOMAS F.
Mate, 26 January, 1863. Acting Ensign, 7 April, 1864. Acting Master, 20 March, 1865. Honorably discharged 2 December, 1865.
LAYTON, JOSEPH R.
Acting Assistant Surgeon, 28 January, 1864. Honorably discharged 11 September, 1865.
LEA, EDWARD.
Acting Midshipman, 2 October, 1851. Midshipman, 9 June, 1855. Passed Midshipman, 15 April, 1858. Master, 4 November, 1858. Lieutenant, 22 November, 1860. Lieutenant-Commander, 16 July, 1862. Killed in battle 1 January, 1863.
LEA, PETER L.
Mate (Spanish-American War), 19 June, 1898. Honorably discharged 15 February, 1899.
LEACH, ABRAHAM.
Mate, 22 October, 1863. Acting Ensign, 9 March, 1865. Honorably discharged 26 August, 1865.
LEACH, BOYNTON.
Midshipman, 30 July, 1866. Graduated 7 June, 1870. Ensign, 13 July, 1871. Master, 8 November, 1874. Lieutenant, 7 August, 1881. Wholly retired 1 April, 1884.
LEACH, FRANK.
Acting Third Assistant Engineer, 3 August, 1864. Honorably discharged 12 October, 1865.
LEACH, FRANKLIN S.
Mate, 12 December, 1861. Acting Ensign, 13 October, 1864. Dismissed 14 April, 1865.
LEACH, GEORGE H.
Boatswain, 17 July, 1854. Deserted 15 January, 1857.
LEACH, PHILIP.
Assistant Surgeon, 9 July, 1881. Passed Assistant Surgeon, 9 July, 1884. Surgeon, 15 November, 1896.
LEACH, PHINEAS.
Acting Master, 16 November, 1861. Honorably discharged 4 March, 1866.
LEACH, ROWLAND.
Carpenter, 22 October, 1855. Lost in the Albany. Last intelligence, 28 September, 1854.
LEACH, THOMAS W.
Assistant Surgeon, 29 July, 1858. Surgeon, 22 May, 1862. Medical Inspector, 5 April, 1875. Retired List, 7 January, 1885. Died 29 December, 1894.
LEACOCK, RICHARD W.
Assistant Surgeon, 9 February, 1837. Passed Assistant Surgeon, 6 June, 1842. Died 31 March, 1853.
LEACRAFT, J. R.
Master, 5 May, 1812. Discharged 1 June, 1815.
LEAHY, WILLIAM D.
Naval Cadet, 19 May, 1893. Ensign, 1 July, 1899.
LEAMAN, CHARLES H.
Mate, 29 November, 1863. Honorably discharged 5 November, 1865.
LEAMAN, JOHN A.
Mate, 11 June, 1863. Appointment revoked 22 December, 1864.
LEAMAN, EDWARD.
Acting Assistant Surgeon, 1 October, 1862. Appointment revoked 25 November, 1863.
LEAR, JOHN.
Mate, 26 February, 1861. Acting Master, 26 February, 1862. Honorably discharged, 24 February, 1864.
LEARY, BASIL W.
Acting Master, 7 December, 1861. Honorably discharged 31 January, 1866.
LEARY, JOHN J.
Ensign (Spanish-American War), 24 May, 1898. Honorably discharged 24 September, 1898.
LEARY, RICHARD P.
Acting Midshipman, 20 September, 1860. Ensign, 1 October, 1863. Master, 10 May, 1866. Lieutenant. 21 February, 1867. Lieutenant-Commander, 12 March, 1868. Wholly retired 2 March, 1874. Findings of Board set aside and restored to Active List. Promoted to Commander, 2 June, 1882. Captain, 6 April, 1897.
LEAVITT, ALEXANDER.
Mate, 16 July, 1863. Resigned 21 August, 1863.
LEAVITT, ALMOND O.
Assistant Surgeon, 19 July, 1861. Retired List, 24 June, 1862.
LEAVITT, EDWARD D.
Third Assistant Engineer, 24 August, 1861. Second Assistant Engineer, 21 April, 1863. Resigned 25 May, 1867.
LEAVITT, WILLIAM A.
Acting Third Assistant Engineer, 23 April, 1862. Acting Second Assistant Engineer, 23 September, 1863. Acting First Assistant Engineer, 10 January, 1865. Honorably discharged 21 November, 1865.
LEAVITT, W. W.
Assistant Surgeon, 10 June, 1861. Resigned 23 July, 1863.
LEAVITT, WILLIAM H.
Mate, 6 July, 1863. Appointment revoked 23 November, 1865.
LEAYCRAFT, J. R.
Midshipman, 11 May, 1802. Dismissed 14 March, 1810.

GENERAL NAVY REGISTER. 327

LE BARON, FRED. L.
    Mate, 14 February, 1863. Appointment revoked (sick) 28 July, 1863.
LE BARRON, FRANCIS.
    Assistant Surgeon, 31 January, 1800. Last appearance on Records of Navy Department.
LE CHEVALER, O.
    Surgeon's Mate, 10 December, 1814. Died 16 October, 1822.
LECKIE, JAMES.
    Carpenter, 24 November, 1841. Died 12 November, 1842.
LECOMPT, CHARLES.
    Midshipman, 16 June, 1813. Last appearance on Records of Navy Department, 10 November, 1815.
LECOMPT, CHARLES.
    Midshipman, 18 May, 1809. Dismissed 30 April, 1813.
LE COMPT, GRENVILLE B.
    Acting Assistant Surgeon, 20 January, 1865. Assistant Surgeon, 3 November, 1865. Died 6 September, 1870.
LE COMPT, SAMUEL W.
    Midshipman, 4 June, 1812. Lieutenant, 28 March, 1820. Commander, 8 September, 1841. Reserved List, 13 September, 1855. Died 28 January, 1862.
LECONTE, ROBERT G.
    Assistant Surgeon (Spanish-American War), 25 May, 1898. Honorably discharged 12 September, 1898.
LEDBETTER, ROBERT E.
    Assistant Surgeon, 19 October, 1900.
LEDYARD, NATHANIEL L.
    Mate, 11 October, 1861. Appointment revoked (sick) 30 June, 1863.
LEE, ALEXANDER P.
    Mate, 31 March, 1863. Dismissed 14 December, 1863.
LEE, CALEB E.
    Third Assistant Engineer, 4 April, 1861. Second Assistant Engineer, 16 January, 1863. First Assistant Engineer, 1 January, 1865. Retired List, 2 December, 1876.
LEE, CHARLES W.
    Acting Master, 14 August, 1861. Honorably discharged 28 October, 1865.
LEE, COLUMBUS W.
    Third Assistant Engineer, 26 February, 1851. Resigned 2 June, 1855.
LEE, DAVID.
    Mate, 31 August, 1863. Acting Ensign, 22 July, 1864. Honorably discharged 8 November, 1865. Acting Ensign, 11 December, 1866. Mustered out 27 March, 1869.
LEE, GEORGE G.
    Lieutenant, 2 December, 1799. Left the service 6 March, 1895.
LEE, GEORGE P.
    Mate, 14 September, 1861. Acting Master, 15 May, 1862. Honorably discharged 28 October, 1865.
LEE, JAMES D.
    Third Assistant Engineer, 8 September, 1863. Resigned 10 November, 1866.
LEE, JOHN.
    Midshipman, 28 August, 1799. Resigned 15 October, 1799.
LEE, JOHN F.
    Acting Assistant Paymaster, 23 July, 1863. Mustered out 26 December, 1865.
LEE, JOHN H.
    Midshipman, 18 June, 1812. Lieutenant, 5 March, 1817. Died 30 June, 1832.
LEE, JOHN L.
    Acting Master, 15 April, 1862. Honorably discharged 5 October, 1865.
LEE, JOHN R.
    Mate, 14 April, 1864. Resigned 15 May, 1865.
LEE, J. R.
    Mate, 15 November, 1861. Acting Master, 9 May, 1862. Resigned 7 October, 1862.
LEE, JOSEPH.
    Surgeon, 10 October, 1798. Discharged 4 May, 1801, under Peace Establishment Act.
LEE, LARKIN F.
    Mate, 12 April, 1864. Appointment revoked 16 February, 1882.
LEE, ROBERT G.
    Acting Master, 3 July, 1861. Honorably discharged 19 September, 1865.
LEE, SAMUEL B.
    Midshipman, 28 January, 1835. Resigned 20 November, 1837.
LEE, SAMUEL PERRY.
    Acting Master, 8 June, 1861. Dismissed 6 July, 1861.
LEE, S. PHILLIPS.
    Midshipman, 22 November, 1825. Passed Midshipman, 4 June, 1831. Lieutenant, 9 February, 1837. Commander, 14 September, 1855. Captain, 16 July, 1862. Commodore, 25 July, 1866. Rear-Admiral, 22 April, 1870. Retired List, 13 February, 1873. Died 5 June, 1897.
LEE, SIDNEY SMITH.
    Midshipman, 30 December, 1820. Lieutenant, 17 May, 1828. Commander, 4 June, 1850. Dismissed 22 April, 1861.
LEE, THEODORIC.
    Midshipman, 29 September, 1841. Passed Midshipman, 10 August, 1847. Master, 14 September, 1855. Lieutenant, 15 September, 1855. Resigned, 25 April, 1857.
LEE, THOMAS.
    Acting Third Assistant Engineer, 6 June, 1864. Honorably discharged 18 June, 1865.
LEE, THOMAS.
    Acting Third Assistant Engineer, 29 January, 1867. Mustered out 1 July, 1868.

LEE, THOMAS N.
Midshipman, 13 October, 1863. Graduated, 2 June, 1868. Ensign, 18 April, 1869. Master, 12 July, 1870. Lieutenant, 23 January, 1874. Died 21 July, 1878.
LEE, WILLIAM.
Carpenter, 31 May, 1841. Died 31 July, 1853.
LEE, WILLIAM.
Master, 30 April, 1815. Resigned 20 December, 1824.
LEE, WILLIAM A.
Midshipman, 9 June, 1811. Lieutenant, 3 April, 1817. Died 9 July, 1817.
LEE, WILLIAM F.
Mate, 8 May, 1865. Mate, 16 September, 1869. Resigned 7 October, 1870.
LEE, WILLIAM P.
Mate, 1 August, 1863. Dismissed 21 October, 1864.
LEECH, DANIEL, Jr.
Acting Assistant Paymaster, 13 October, 1862. Resigned 1 February, 1864.
LEECH, JOHN.
Lieutenant, Junior Grade (Spanish-American War), 28 May, 1898. Honorably discharged 15 December, 1898.
LEECH, THOMAS F.
Acting Assistant Surgeon, 22 March, 1864. Honorably discharged 9 October, 1865.
LEEDS, BENJAMIN.
Mate, 25 January, 1863. Honorably discharged 18 December, 1865.
LEEDS, JOHN.
Mate, 21 October, 1861. Appointment revoked (sick) 29 July, 1864.
LEEDS, WILLIAM E.
Boatswain, 17 October, 1862. Died 2 November, 1869.
LEEKINS, CHARLES W.
Mate, 1861. Appointment revoked 11 February, 1862.
LEEMAN, WILLIAM.
Acting First Assistant Engineer, 1861. Resigned 26 April, 1862.
LEES, JOHN S.
Acting Assistant Surgeon, 17 April, 1863. Resigned 25 November, 1863.
LEES, THOMAS.
Acting Third Assistant Engineer, 7 September, 1864. Honorably discharged 8 July, 1865.
LEES, WILLIAM J.
Acting Ensign, 1 October, 1862. Acting Master, 14 June, 1864. Honorably discharged 15 November, 1865.
LEEVER, JOSEPH H.
Acting Ensign, 24 November, 1863. Honorably discharged 3 October, 1865.
LEFAVOR, FREDERICK H.
Midshipman, 27 July, 1866. Graduated 7 June, 1870. Ensign, 14 July, 1872. Master, 9 March, 1876. Lieutenant, Junior Grade, 3 March, 1883. Lieutenant, 8 July, 1883. Retired List, 12 April, 1898.
LEFFLER, DANIEL S., Jr.
Acting Third Assistant Engineer, 12 September, 1863. Acting Second Assistant Engineer, 3 October, 1864. Honorably discharged 7 August, 1865.
LEGARE, JAMES D.
Midshipman, 26 December, 1848. Resigned 13 December, 1852.
LEGARE, JAMES E.
Midshipman, 18 June, 1812. Lieutenant, 1 April, 1818. Dismissed 22 June, 1827.
LEGG, JOHN.
Midshipman, 2 January, 1800. Discharged 12 May, 1801, under Peace Establishment Act.
LEGGE, THOMAS W.
Second Lieutenant, 16 August, 1812. First Lieutenant, 18 June, 1814. Last appearance on Records of Navy Department, 1816. Ship Independence.
LEGGETT, WILLIAM.
Midshipman, 4 December, 1822. Resigned 17 April, 1826.
LEGROS, HENRY.
Midshipman, 2 April, 1894. Resigned 22 June, 1804.
LEIB, THOMAS J.
Midshipman, 1 September, 1811. Lieutenant, 28 April, 1826. Commander, 30 March, 1844. Died 14 July, 1851.
LEIGH, RICHARD H.
Naval Cadet, 6 September, 1887. Ensign, 1 July, 1893. Lieutenant, Junior Grade, 3 March, 1899. Lieutenant, 9 March, 1900.
LEIGH, WILLIAM.
Midshipman, 1 November, 1828. Passed Midshipman, 14 June, 1834. Lieutenant, 30 May, 1840. Resigned 3 September, 1852.
LEIGHTON, JOHN.
Boatswain, 31 January, 1800. Last appearance on Records of Navy Department.
LEIGHTON, N. G.
Master, date not known. Last appearance on Records of Navy Department, 8 May, 1815. Discharged.
LEINAS, GEORGE H.
Acting Master, 21 March, 1862. Appointment revoked 28 April, 1866.
LEIPER, CHARLES L.
Naval Cadet, 6 September, 1892. Assistant Engineer, 6 May, 1898. Rank changed to Ensign, 1899.
LEIPER, EDWARDS F.
Cadet Midshipman, 25 June, 1875. Graduated 22 June, 1882. Ensign, Junior Grade, 3 March, 1883. Ensign, 26 June, 1884. Lieutenant, Junior Grade, 25 February, 1893. Lieutenant, 18 November, 1896.

LEITCH, ROBERT R.
Cadet Engineer, Naval Academy, 10 October, 1871. Graduated, 30 May, 1873. Assistant Engineer, 23 January, 1874. Chief Engineer, 30 September, 1894. Retired List, 19 February, 1896. Died 13 March, 1899.

LELAND, GEORGE W.
Mate, 17 November, 1863. Appointment revoked 13 August, 1864.

LELAND, L. B.
Acting Second Assistant Engineer, 9 February, 1863. Appointment revoked 6 January, 1866.

LELAR, HENRY.
Acting Master, 29 August, 1861. Honorably discharged 9 February, 1866.

LELAR, ROBERT G.
Acting Master, 17 September, 1861. Honorably discharged 20 October, 1865.

LEMAN, JAMES.
Acting Third Assistant Engineer, 1861. Resigned 6 August, 1862.

LEMAN, WALTER J.
Mate, 13 April, 1865. Honorably discharged 26 June, 1865.

LEMASSENA, WILLIAM H.
Mate, 6 December, 1862. Resigned 11 March, 1863.

LEMLY, SAMUEL C.
Midshipman, 26 June, 1869. Graduated 31 May, 1873. Ensign, 16 July, 1874. Master, 24 February, 1880. Lieutenant, Junior Grade, 3 March, 1883. Lieutenant, 20 January, 1886. Lieutenant-Commander, 3 March, 1899. Judge-Advocate-General, with rank of Captain, from 5 June, 1892.

LEMMON, RICHARD.
Midshipman, 17 August, 1814. Resigned 17 April, 1815.

LEMOINE, G. D.
Midshipman, 21 September, 1838. Resigned 3 January, 1840.

LEMOINE, G. D.
Midshipman, 16 June, 1840. Dismissed 14 March, 1841.

LEMON, SAMUEL.
Acting Second Assistant Engineer, 15 December, 1862. Honorably discharged 8 October, 1865.

LENHART, JOHN S.
Chaplain, 27 February, 1847. Lost in Cumberland, 8 March, 1862.

LENNAN, FRANKLIN G. R.
Acting Ensign, 16 February, 1864. Honorably discharged 23 January, 1867.

LENOX, JOHN.
Gunner, date not known. Last appearance on Records of Navy Department.

LENT, ADOLPH C.
Assistant Surgeon, 31 December, 1798. Resigned 10 August, 1799.

LENTHALL, JOHN.
Naval Constructor, 8 February, 1838. Chief Bureau Construction and Repair, 28 April, 1863. Reappointed Chief, 28 July, 1866. Retired List, 16 September, 1869. Died 11 April, 1882.

LEON, JOSEPH S.
Mate, 31 July, 1863. Honorably discharged 5 March, 1868. Mate, 20 December, 1869. Appointment revoked 2 March, 1870.

LEONARD, EZRA.
Acting Master, 27 December, 1861. Acting Volunteer Lieutenant, 19 May, 1864. Ensign, 12 March, 1868. Master, 18 December, 1868. Lieutenant, 21 March, 1870. Died 29 July, 1870.

LEONARD, FRANK.
Acting Second Assistant Engineer, 9 August, 1864. Honorably discharged 4 September, 1865.

LEONARD, FREDERICK A.
Master, 17 June, 1809. Last appearance on Records of Navy Department, 9 March, 1813. Dead.

LEONARD, GEORGE.
Assistant Surgeon, 28 May, 1804. Resigned 5 April, 1808.

LEONARD, GEORGE.
Mate, 12 December, 1861. Acting Ensign, 27 November, 1863. Honorably discharged 18 December, 1865.

LEONARD, HENRY S.
Third Assistant Engineer, 19 July, 1861. Second Assistant Engineer, 16 January, 1863. Lost on the Tecumseh, 5 August, 1864.

LEONARD, JAMES T.
Midshipman, 26 February, 1799. Lieutenant, 13 January, 1807. Commander, 4 July, 1812. Captain, 4 February, 1815. Died 9 November, 1832.

LEONARD, JOHN C.
Cadet Engineer, 1 October, 1878. Assistant Engineer, 1 July, 1884. Passed Assistant Engineer, 14 February, 1895. Rank changed to Lieutenant, 3 March, 1899.

LEONARD, LORRANUS.
Midshipman, 27 June, 1799. Resigned 18 March, 1800.

LEONARD, SAMUEL H.
Assistant Engineer, 25 October, 1881. Passed Assistant, 3 August, 1892. Rank changed to Lieutenant, 3 March, 1899.

LEONARD, WILLIAM.
Acting Third Assistant Engineer, 26 October, 1863. Honorably discharged 23 August, 1865.

LEONARD, WILLIAM E.
Mate, 18 April, 1865. Dismissed 19 April, 1866.

LEONARD, WILLIAM H.
Acting Third Assistant Engineer, 22 February, 1864. Honorably discharged 12 February, 1869.
LEONARD, WILLIAM W.
Mate, 29 November, 1861. Acting Ensign, 3 October, 1863. Honorably discharged 13 August, 1865.
LEOPOLD, HARRY G.
Cadet Engineer, 1 October, 1878. Assistant Engineer, 1 July, 1884. Passed Assistant Engineer, 26 December, 1894. Rank changed to Lieutenant, 3 March, 1899.
LE PINE, FREDERICK C.
Acting Carpenter, 10 January, 1900.
LEPS, HENRY M.
Assistant Engineer (Spanish-American War), 1 June, 1898. Honorably discharged 7 February, 1899.
LE ROY, WILLIAM E.
Midshipman, 11 January, 1832. Passed Midshipman, 23 June, 1838. Lieutenant, 13 July, 1843. Commander, 1 July, 1861. Captain, 25 July, 1866. Commodore, 3 July, 1870. Rear-Admiral, 5 April, 1874. Retired List, 24 March, 1880. Died 10 December, 1888.
LESHER, HENRY.
Midshipman, 1 January, 1812. Resigned 20 July, 1812.
LESLIE, ADAM J.
Midshipman, 2 February, 1829. Resigned 31 October, 1831.
LESLIE, HENRY C.
Mate, 7 October, 1861. Acting Ensign, 9 March, 1864. Honorably discharged 13 April, 1866. Acting Ensign, 7 June, 1861. Appointment revoked 6 December, 1866.
LESLIE, HENRY P.
Carpenter, 15 October, 1833. Retired List, 12 February, 1876. Died 20 May, 1887.
LESTER, C. H.
Mate, 30 December, 1861. Acting Ensign, 27 August, 1863. Honorably discharged 30 September, 1865.
LESTER, DANIEL.
Mate, 6 June, 1862. Acting Ensign, 8 June, 1864. Died 2 January, 1865.
LESTER, GEORGE D.
Acting Master, 26 August, 1861. Dismissed 4 November, 1861.
LESTER, JOHN W.
Acting Carpenter, 11 June, 1863. Honorably discharged 19 December, 1865.
LESTER, JOSEPH L.
Acting Second Assistant Engineer, 17 May, 1861. Resigned 11 June, 1861.
LETHERBURY, CHARLES W.
Acting Ensign, 6 June, 1863. Honorably discharged 31 August, 1865.
LEUCKART, SIGISMUND.
Pharmacist, 15 September, 1898. Died 21 November, 1900.
LEUTZE, EUGENE H. C.
Midshipman, 4 March, 1863. Graduated 6 June, 1867. Ensign, 18 December, 1868. Master, 21 March, 1870. Lieutenant, 21 March, 1871. Lieutenant-Commander, 26 March, 1889. Commander, 5 January, 1897.
LEUTZE, TREVOR W.
Assistant Paymaster, 15 April, 1899.
LEVAY, WILLIAM H.
Chief Engineer (Spanish-American War), 3 May, 1898. Honorably discharged 4 January, 1899.
LEVELY, GEORGE.
Midshipman, 6 May, 1800. Lost in the Insurgent.
LEVERETT, GEORGE H.
Midshipman, 18 June, 1812. Last appearance on Records of Navy Department, 1823.
LEVIN, CHARLES.
Mate, 25 January, 1870. Died Philadelphia, 3 September, 1874.
LEVINDSELLER, THOMAS H.
Mate, 21 December, 1861. Dismissed 29 November, 1862.
LEVINS, C. W.
Mate, 12 April, 1870. Appointment revoked 3 January, 1874.
LEVY, CHARLES H.
Third Assistant Engineer, 21 November, 1857. Second Assistant Engineer, 2 August, 1859. Name stricken from the Rolls of the Navy, 8 July, 1861.
LEVY, MEARS.
Master, 8 May, 1812. Last appearance on Records of Navy Department, 5 June, 1813. Dead.
LEVY, URIAH P.
Sailing Master, 21 October, 1812. Lieutenant, 5 March, 1817. Commander, 9 February, 1837. Captain, 29 March, 1844. Died 22 March, 1862.
LEWERENZ, ALFRED C.
Civil Engineer, 23 February, 1899.
LEWERS, J. HENRY.
Third Assistant Engineer, 28 October, 1862. Resigned 29 June, 1868.
LEWIS, A. A.
Acting Master, 14 June, 1862. Honorably discharged 22 August, 1865.
LEWIS, ALBERT H.
Mate, 6 September, 1864. Honorably discharged 13 August, 1867.
LEWIS, ALEXANDER.
Acting Ensign, 30 January, 1865. Honorably discharged 20 September, 1865.
LEWIS, AMOS.
Sailmaker, 3 January, 1825. Dismissed 7 September, 1832.
LEWIS, ANDREW J.
Midshipman, 29 September, 1841. Lost in Grampus, March, 1843.

GENERAL NAVY REGISTER. 331

LEWIS, ARCHIBALD S.
  Gunner, 27 September, 1834. Dismissed 15 January, 1859.
LEWIS, ARTHUR.
  Midshipman, 18 June, 1812. Lieutenant, 28 April, 1826. Furloughed 19 July, 1843. Died 29 November, 1854.
LEWIS, BENJAMIN F.
  Acting Third Assistant Engineer, 11 July, 1864. Honorably discharged 17 October, 1867.
LEWIS, CALLENDER I.
  Assistant Paymaster, 23 June, 1877. Passed Assistant Paymaster, 31 August, 1881. Died 8 August, 1883.
LEWIS, DAVID O.
  Assistant Surgeon, 8 April, 1874. Passed Assistant Surgeon, 22 November, 1878. Surgeon, 22 January, 1891.
LEWIS, D. T.
  Acting Assistant Surgeon, 1 September, 1861. Died 3 September, 1862.
LEWIS, EDWARD S.
  Midshipman, 10 May, 1820. Died 25 July, 1826.
LEWIS, EDWIN F.
  Acting Third Assistant Engineer, 12 August, 1862. Acting Second Assistant Engineer, 20 August, 1864. Honorably discharged 24 September, 1865.
LEWIS, ELNATHAN.
  Acting Master, 3 October, 1861. Appointment revoked 1 March, 1864.
LEWIS, ENOS E.
  Assistant Paymaster, 21 December, 1869. Wholly retired 23 July, 1874.
LEWIS, ENOS M.
  Third Assistant Engineer, 17 February, 1860. Second Assistant Engineer, 3 August, 1863. First Assistant Engineer, 25 July, 1866. Died 12 January, 1872.
LEWIS, FREDERICK B. A.
  Assistant Surgeon, 6 September, 1861. Resigned 15 June, 1865.
LEWIS, GRENVILLE.
  Acting Third Assistant Engineer, 24 March, 1862. Acting Second Assistant Engineer, 19 April, 1864. Honorably discharged 21 January, 1866. Acting Second Assistant Engineer, 31 July, 1866. Mustered out 17 November, 1868.
LEWIS, HENRY H.
  Midshipman, 1 May, 1828. Passed Midshipman, 23 June, 1838. Lieutenant, 28 October, 1842. Dismissed 20 April, 1861.
LEWIS, HOLMES.
  Carpenter, 14 December, 1848. Dismissed 29 May, 1861.
LEWIS, JACOB M.
  (Flotilla Service.) Commander, 27 November, 1812. Captain, 26 April, 1814. Last appearance on Records of Navy Department, 7 January, 1815. Discharged.
LEWIS, JAMES.
  Mate, 22 October, 1861. Resigned 20 January, 1862.
LEWIS, JAMES B.
  Midshipman, 31 March, 1831. Passed Midshipman, 15 June, 1837. Lieutenant, 8 September, 1841. Reserved List, 13 September, 1855. Dismissed 23 May, 1861.
LEWIS, JESSE N.
  Midshipman, 12 April, 1800. Out of Servce 31 December, 1800.
LEWIS, JOHN E.
  Naval Cadet, 6 September, 1895. At sea prior to final graduation.
LEWIS, J. J. H.
  Midshipman, 10 January, 1809. Last appearance on Records of Navy Department, 1815. Navy Yard, Washington.
LEWIS, JOHN K.
  Chaplain, 29 November, 1869. Retired List, 18 March, 1897.
LEWIS, JOHN M.
  Midshipman, 15 November, 1809. Resigned 12 October, 1812.
LEWIS, JOHN W.
  Master, 7 March, 1814. Dismissed 11 July, 1814.
LEWIS, JOHN W.
  Acting Ensign, 13 May, 1863. Appointment revoked (sick) 10 February, 1864. Acting Ensign, 16 May, 1864. Dismissed 8 June, 1865.
LEWIS, JOSEPH.
  Boatswain, 6 September, 1839. Died 23 January, 1865.
LEWIS, JOSEPH C.
  Acting Third Assistant Engineer, 15 January, 1862. Acting Second Assistant Engineer, 14 April, 1864. Honorably discharged 24 October, 1865. Acting Second Assistant Engineer, 31 July, 1866. Resigned 6 November, 1867.
LEWIS, JOSEPH G.
  Acting Master, 18 December, 1861. Resigned 22 March, 1862.
LEWIS, MONTGOMERY.
  Midshipman, 1 November, 1828. Passed Midshipman, 14 June, 1834. Lieutenant, 25 February, 1841. Reserved List, 13 September, 1855. Died 21 January, 1857.
LEWIS, OSCAR C.
  Third Assistant Engineer, 1 July, 1861. Second Assistant Engineer, 18 December, 1862. First Assistant Engineer, 11 October, 1866. Resigned 28 September, 1868.
LEWIS, ROBERT.
  Purser, 10 December, 1798. Last appearance on Records of Navy Department.
LEWIS, ROBERT F. R.
  Midshipman, 19 October, 1841. Passed Midshipman, 10 August, 1847. Master, 14 September, 1855. Lieutenant, 15 September, 1855. Lieutenant-Commander, 16 July, 1862. Commander, 29 January, 1867. Captain, 26 February, 1878. Died 23 February, 1881.

LEWIS, ROBERT G.
Acting Third Assistant Engineer, 7 April, 1864. Honorably discharged 9 July, 1865.
LEWIS, RODMAN.
Chaplain, 13 March, 1839. Died 30 May, 1869.
LEWIS, SAMUEL A.
Acting Third Assistant Engineer, 28 October, 1862. Lost on the Monitor, 31 December, 1862.
LEWIS, SAMUEL W.
Mate, 10 December, 1863. Resigned 3 May, 1865.
LEWIS, STITH.
Assistant Surgeon, 23 January, 1809. Last appearance on Records of Navy Department, 1815. Frigate President.
LEWIS, THEODORE F.
Acting Second Assistant Engineer, 19 November, 1862. Acting First Assistant Engineer, 19 February, 1864. Honorably discharged 30 October, 1865.
LEWIS, THOMAS.
Gunner, 14 August, 1838. Resigned 14 January, 1845.
LEWIS, THOMAS.
Midshipman, 15 November, 1809. Resigned 26 January, 1810.
LEWIS, THOMAS M.
Mate, 13 August, 1863. Acting Ensign, 20 July, 1864. Honorably discharged 9 November, 1865.
LEWIS, WILLIAM.
Midshipman, 3 September, 1798. Resigned 21 May, 1800.
LEWIS, WILLIAM.
Midshipman, 31 August, 1802. Lieutenant, 14 March, 1807. Commander, 3 March, 1815. Lost in the Epervier, 1815.
LEWIS, WILLIAM.
Master, 22 February, 1809. Last appearance on Records of Navy Department, 12 September, 1812.
LEWIS, WILLIAM B.
Acting Assistant Surgeon, 9 March, 1864. Honorably discharged 16 September, 1865.
LEWIS, WILLIAM G.
Midshipman, 18 June, 1812. Died 30 December, 1817.
LEWIS, WILLIAM J.
Acting Ensign, 1 December, 1864. Honorably discharged 4 October, 1865.
LEWIS, WILLIAM J.
Mate, 7 December, 1863. Appointment revoked 9 June, 1865.
LEWIS, WILLIAM T.
Mate, 28 February, 1863. Dismissed 3 June, 1863.
LEWIS, WILLIAM W.
Acting Third Assistant Engineer, 16 May, 1864. Honorably discharged 12 May, 1865.
LEYS, JAMES F.
Assistant Surgeon, 22 June, 1893. Passed Assistant Surgeon, 22 June, 1896.
L'HOMMEDIEU, N. C.
Sailmaker, 16 February, 1835. Resigned 25 July, 1839.
LIBAIRE, CHARLES.
Mate, 23 September, 1862. Honorably discharged 19 August, 1865.
LIBBY, ARTHUR.
Acting Third Assistant Engineer, 9 January, 1863. Resigned 14 May, 1864.
LIBER, SAMUEL A.
Midshipman, 9 June, 1811. Lost at sea 5 October, 1811.
LIDDELL, JAMES F.
Acting Third Assistant Engineer, 4 September, 1863. Resigned 5 April, 1865.
LIEBER, ALFRED H.
Midshipman, 2 October, 1850. Dropped 24 January, 1851.
LIGGET, JOHN J.
Assistant Surgeon, 2 December, 1869. Resigned 2 April, 1870.
LIGGETT, GEORGE W.
Midshipman, 2 April, 1804. Resigned 6 July, 1804.
LILLESTON, JAMES A.
Gunner, 30 July, 1852. Dismissed 17 November, 1855. Reappointed 23 December, 1856. Died 26 May, 1872.
LILLIE, ABRAHAM B. H.
Midshipman, 25 September, 1862. Graduated June, 1866. Ensign, 12 March, 1868. Master, 26 March, 1869. Lieutenant, 21 March, 1870. Lieutenant-Commander, 29 January, 1887. Commander, 1 September, 1895.
LIMA, CHARLES DE C.
Acting Master, 6 January, 1862. Resigned 29 April, 1862.
LINCOLN, ABEL, Jr.
Midshipman, 15 May, 1799. Discharged 12 October, 1801, under Peace Establishment Act.
LINCOLN, AMASA.
Lieutenant, 12 October, 1804. Discharged 10 April, 1805.
LINCOLN, DAVID F.
Acting Assistant Surgeon, 5 September, 1862. Resigned 10 February, 1864.
LINCOLN, EDWARD T.
Mate, 3 September, 1863. Appointment revoked 28 November, 1864.
LINCOLN, EDMUND.
Third Assistant Engineer, 6 January, 1862. Second Assistant Engineer, 1 October, 1863. Resigned 4 February, 1868.
LINCOLN, GATEWOOD S.
Naval Cadet, 20 May, 1892. Assistant Engineer, 6 May, 1898. Rank changed to Ensign, 3 March, 1899.

LINCOLN, LEVI, Jr.
Midshipman, 1 November, 1827. Resigned 3 June, 1836.
LINCOLN, ROBERT B., Jr.
Acting Third Assistant Engineer, 27 December, 1864. Honorably discharged 19 October, 1865.
LIND, ERIK G.
Ensign (Spanish-American War), 28 May, 1898. Honorably discharged 2 December, 1898.
LINDEE, JACOB.
Acting Master and Pilot, 15 December, 1864. Honorably discharged 30 December, 1865.
LINDEMANN, CHRISTIAN.
Acting Ensign, 10 December, 1863. Honorably discharged 14 September, 1868.
LINDLEY, WILLIAM L.
Mate, 22 December, 1862. Resigned (sick) 6 September, 1864.
LINDSAY, CLEMENT.
Midshipman, 2 January, 1800. Discharged 6 August, 1801, under Peace Establishment Act.
LINDSAY, HUGH.
Carpenter, 4 November, 1840. Dismissed 9 December, 1853.
LINDSAY, JAMES E.
Assistant Surgeon, 2 May, 1860. Dismissed 10 October, 1861.
LINDSAY, WILLIAM.
Midshipman, 1 January, 1825. Died in 1825.
LINDSEY, JOSEPH.
Master, 17 March, 1814. Died 19 May, 1826.
LINDSLEY, A. B.
Midshipman, 28 June, 1804. Dismissed 21 April, 1807.
LINDSLEY, HENRY.
Acting Ensign, 16 May, 1865. Mustered out 28 August, 1868.
LINDSLEY, JAMES P.
Acting Master, 2 October, 1861. Resigned 23 March, 1864.
LINDSLY, CLELAND.
Third Assistant Engineer, 1 October, 1852. Resigned 30 August, 1856. Second Assistant Engineer, 3 October, 1861. First Assistant Engineer, 25 July, 1866. Resigned 12 December, 1874.
LINING, GEORGE D.
Third Assistant Engineer, 20 September, 1858. Second Assistant Engineer, 17 January, 1861. Resigned 18 April, 1861.
LINING, CHARLES E.
Assistant Surgeon, 1 July, 1858. Resigned 11 January, 1861.
LING, SAMUEL.
Midshipman, 28 February, 1799. Discharged 14 July, 1801, under Peace Establishment Act.
LINGLE, WILLIAM.
Acting Third Assistant Engineer, 19 January, 1864. Resigned 6 June, 1865.
LINK, JOHN.
Acting Third Assistant Engineer, 26 May, 1864. Honorably discharged 20 October, 1865.
LINN, JAMES.
Carpenter, 31 October, 1848. Died 27 April, 1855.
LINN, JAMES H.
Acting First Assistant Engineer, 12 June, 1863. Honorably discharged 22 December, 1865.
LINN, SAMUEL H.
Acting Third Assistant Engineer, 9 February, 1864. Acting Second Assistant Engineer, 13 April, 1865. Honorably discharged 1 June, 1866.
LINNARD, JOSEPH H.
Cadet Midshipman, 27 June, 1877. Assistant Naval Constructor, 1 July, 1883. Naval Constructor, 3 March, 1891.
LINNEKIN, THOMAS J.
Acting Master, 16 August, 1861. Honorably discharged 9 December, 1865.
LINSCOTT, EDWARD.
Boatswain, 29 March, 1809. Last appearance on Records of Navy Department, 14 April, 1827. Dead.
LINSCOTT, JOHN H.
Mate, 27 May, 1862. Acting Ensign, 7 December, 1863. Honorably discharged 21 December, 1865. Acting Ensign, 19 December, 1866. Mustered out 20 November, 1867.
LINSLEY, PETER.
Acting Third Assistant Engineer, 8 February, 1865. Honorably discharged 26 October, 1867.
LINSLEY, JARED, Jr.
Acting Assistant Paymaster, 11 July, 1864. Passed Assistant Paymaster, 23 July, 1866. Paymaster, 24 February, 1872. Died 24 January, 1878.
LIPPINCOTT, GEORGE C.
Assistant Surgeon, 28 September, 1875. Retired List, 17 December, 1886.
LIPPINCOTT, J. S.
Midshipman, 16 January, 1809. Drowned 5 October, 1811.
LIPPIT, AUGUST.
Mate, 18 January, 1862. Resigned 24 September, 1863.
LIPPITT, THOMAS McC.
Assistant Surgeon, 27 June, 1898.
LISCOMB, JOHN F.
Acting Assistant Surgeon, 19 September, 1864. Resigned 2 October, 1864.

LISLE, JOSEPH T.
Acting Assistant Paymaster, 25 September, 1861. Assistant Paymaster, 11 July, 1862. Died 25 September, 1863.
LISLE, RICHARD M.
Midshipman, 26 September, 1862. Graduated June, 1866. Ensign, 12 March, 1868. Master, 26 March, 1869. Lieutenant, 21 March, 1870. Retired List, 24 January, 1883.
LISLE, ROBERT P.
Acting Assistant Paymaster, 2 November, 1863. Assistant Paymaster, 2 July, 1864. Passed Assistant Paymaster, 4 May, 1866. Paymaster, 11 December, 1867. Pay Inspector, 19 January, 1892. Pay Director, 6 June, 1899.
LITCHFIELD, HARRY.
Acting Third Assistant Engineer, 16 August, 1864. Honorably discharged 11 December, 1868.
LITCHFIELD, HENRY.
Mate, 18 April, 1863. Resigned 21 October, 1863.
LITHERBURY, CHARLES W.
Acting Ensign, 6 June, 1863. Honorably discharged 31 August, 1865.
LITHERBURY, JOHN W.
Mate, 24 January, 1863. Acting Ensign, 23 June, 1864. Resigned 17 November, 1864.
LITTELL, EUGENE.
Acting Assistant Paymaster, 3 July, 1863. Resigned 21 March, 1864. Acting Assistant Paymaster, 16 March, 1865. Mustered out 17 October, 1865.
LITTELL, WILLIAM J.
Assistant Paymaster, 15 March, 1894. Passed Assistant Paymaster, 11 September, 1895. Paymaster, 1 September, 1899.
LITTIG, JAMES G.
Acting Third Assistant Engineer, 4 February, 1863. Resigned 16 July, 1863. Third Assistant Engineer, 3 August, 1863. Second Assistant Engineer, 25 July, 1866. Retired List, 14 July, 1874.
LITTIG, NICHOLAS B.
Third Asistant Engineer, 21 May, 1857. Second Assistant Engineer, 2 August, 1859. First Assistant Engineer, 1 July, 1861. Lost on the Oneida, 24 January, 1870.
LITTIG, PHILIP.
Acting Third Assistant Engineer, 3 February, 1865. Honorably discharged 21 August, 1865. Acting Third Assistant Engineer, 14 December, 1866. Appointment revoked 8 January, 1867. Acting Third Assistant Engineer, 5 July, 1867. Mustered out 22 August, 1869.
LITTLE, CHARLES.
Acting Assistant Surgeon, 24 December, 1863. Honorably discharged 9 October, 1865.
LITTLE, GEORGE.
Captain, 4 March, 1799. Discharged 22 October, 1801, under Peace Establishment Act.
LITTLE, GEORGE D.
Acting Ensign, 7 November, 1862. Acting Master, 11 June, 1864. Resigned 3 March, 1865.
LITTLE, HORATIO M.
Acting Third Assistant Engineer, 15 December, 1862. Acting Second Assistant Engineer, 17 October, 1863. Honorably discharged 16 February, 1868.
LITTLE, JAMES C.
Acting Master, 30 January, 1863. Resigned 16 June, 1863.
LITTLE, JEREMIAH R.
Assistant Surgeon, 10 July, 1861. Resigned 30 July, 1864.
LITTLE, JOHN H.
Midshipman, 1 January, 1818. Lieutenant, 3 March, 1827. Died 28 August, 1852.
LITTLE, JOHN W.
Acting Third Assistant Engineer, 30 August, 1864. Honorably discharged 5 July, 1865.
LITTLE, LEMUEL.
Master, 9 August, 1799. Discharged 9 June, 1801, under Peace Establishment Act.
LITTLE, WILLIAM.
Midshipman, 30 September, 1863. Graduated 6 June, 1867. Ensign, 18 December, 1868. Lieutenant, 21 March, 1871. Retired List, 26 June, 1889.
LITTLE, WILLIAM A.
Midshipman, 8 April, 1850. Died 24 August, 1852.
LITTLE, WILLIAM McC.
Midshipman, 4 March, 1863. Graduated June, 1866. Ensign, 12 March, 1868. Master, 26 March, 1869. Lieutenant, 21 March, 1870. Retired List 16 May, 1884.
LITTLE, WILLIAM N.
Cadet Engineer, Naval Academy, 1 October, 1873. Graduated 21 June, 1875. Assistant Engineer, 1 July, 1877. Passed Assistant Engineer, 17 October, 1885. Chief Engineer, 14 December, 1896. Rank changed to Lieutenant-Commander, 3 March, 1899.
LITTLEFIELD, A. D.
Acting Master, 24 March, 1862. Honorably discharged 30 September, 1865.
LITTLEFIELD, CHARLES H.
Mate, 8 May, 1862. Acting Ensign, 6 February, 1864. Honorably discharged 6 February, 1866.
LITTLEFIELD, CHARLES E.
Lieutenant (Spanish-American War, 23 June, 1898. Honorably discharged 9 March, 1899.
LITTLEFIELD, CHARLES W.
Assistant Paymaster, 8 September, 1876. Passed Assistant Paymaster, 16 June, 1881. Paymaster, 25 December, 1892

LITTLEFIELD, GEORGE O.
  Warrant Machinest, 6 July, 1899.
LITTLEFIELD, WILLIAM C.
  Mate, 8 May, 1862. Appointment revoked (sick) 17 April, 1863.
LITTLEFIELD, WILLIAM L.
  Naval Cadet, 30 September, 1892. Assistant Engineer, 6 May, 1898. Rank changed to Ensign, 3 March, 1899.
LITTLEJOHN, ELLIOTT.
  Acting Assistant Paymaster, 3 August, 1863. Resigned 7 June, 1865.
LIVERMORE, CHARLES W.
  Assistant Engineer, 26 February, 1875. Retired List, 16 November, 1882.
LIVERMORE, HENRY S.
  Acting Ensign, 14 October, 1862. Appointment revoked 24 March, 1864. Acting Ensign, 2 September, 1864. Honorably discharged 14 August, 1865.
LIVERMORE, SAMUEL.
  Purser, 26 March, 1814. Last appearance on Records of Navy Department, 1816. Furloughed.
LIVINGSTON, CORDT.
  Midshipman, 15 November, 1809. Killed in action 1 June, 1813.
LIVINGSTON, DE GRASSE.
  Midshipman, 7 March, 1848. Passed Midshipman, 15 June, 1854. Master, 16 September, 1855. Lieutenant, 18 November, 1855. Resigned 28 October, 1858. Acting Lieutenant, 30 September, 1861. Appointment revoked 18 October, 1861. Reappointed, but declined, 6 November, 1861.
LIVINGSTON, GEORGE B.
  Acting Master, 8 June, 1861. Acting Volunteer Lieutenant, 30 August, 1864. Ensign, 12 March, 1868. Master, 18 December, 1868. Lieutenant, 2 March, 1870. Lieutenant-Commander, 4 February, 1882. Died 19 September, 1890.
LIVINGSTON, JOHN.
  Midshipman, 30 July, 1799. Last appearance on Records of Navy Department.
LIVINGSTON, JOHN W. (See Turk.)
  Midshipman, 4 March, 1823. Passed Midshipman, 23 March, 1829. Lieutenant, 21 June, 1832. Commander, 24 May, 1855. Commodore, 16 July, 1862. Retired List, 12 May, 1866. Rear-Admiral, Retired List, 26 May, 1868. Died 10 September, 1885.
LIVINGSTON, LINDLEY H.
  Mate, 23 October, 1861. Resigned 2 July, 1863.
LIVINGSTON, P. F.
  Midshipman, 1 September, 1811. Resigned 18 May, 1815.
LIVINGSTON, R. J.
  Midshipman, 15 April, 1824. Resigned 30 April, 1828.
LIVINGSTON, R. P.
  Midshipman, 29 March, 1815. Last appearance on Records of Navy Department.
LIVINGSTON, SAMUEL A.
  Acting Third Assistant Engineer, 18 December, 1863. Acting Second Assistant Engineer, 18 January, 1865. Honorably discharged 27 October, 1865.
LIVINGSTON, W. M.
  Midshipman, 31 December, 1798. Lieutenant, 6 March, 1803. Resigned 15 April, 1804.
LIVINGSTON, W. P.
  Midshipman, 1 March, 1825. Dismissed 8 July, 1829.
LJUNGQUIST, CONRAD W.
  Acting Gunner, 10 March, 1900.
LLOYD, EDWARD. Jr.
  Cadet Midshipman, 17 June, 1874. Graduated 4 June, 1878. Ensign, 11 May, 1882. Lieutenant, Junior Grade, 13 June, 1889. Lieutenant, 16 April 1894.
LLOYD, JOHN G.
  Acting Master, 18 December, 1861. Resigned 7 July, 1863. Acting Ensign, 15 November, 1864. Honorably discharged 1 December, 1865.
LLOYD, JOHN W.
  Mate, 9 June, 1864. Appointment revoked 9 September, 1864.
LLOYD, THOMAS.
  Acting Third Assistant Engineer, 4 May, 1863. Resigned 20 March, 1865.
LLOYD, THOMAS.
  Mate, 1 December, 1862. Dismissed 18 August, 1864.
LOAN, WILLIAM F.
  Mate, 1 October, 1862. Acting Ensign, 26 August, 1863. Honorably discharged 13 January, 1869.
LOCKE, FREDERICK J.
  Mate, 18 May, 1863. Acting Ensign, 27 August, 1864. Honorably discharged 9 May, 1866. Acting Ensign, 6 February, 1867. Mustered out 28 August, 1868.
LOCKE, JOHN.
  Assistant Surgeon, 18 August, 1818. Resigned 4 November, 1818.
LOCKE, JOHN H.
  Mate, 9 January, 1864. Resigned 23 June, 1864.
LOCKE, LEWIS S.
  Mate, 13 December, 1861. Appointment revoked 19 January, 1863.
LOCKERT, JAMES M.
  Midshipman, 1 April, 1828. Passed Midshipman, 4 June, 1834. Lieutenant, 21 December, 1840. Died 10 April, 1845.
LOCKWOOD, CHARLES H.
  Acting Assistant Paymaster, 28 February, 1862. Assistant Paymaster, 21 February, 1867. Passed Assistant Paymaster, 27 February, 1869. Dismissed 25 March, 1871.

LOCKWOOD, DENNISON A.
Acting First Assistant Engineer, 11 December, 1862. Dismissed 16 November, 1864.
LOCKWOOD, HENRY H.
Professor, 4 November, 1841. Retired List, 18 August, 1876. Died 7 December, 1899.
LOCKWOOD, JAMES.
Acting Third Assistant Engineer, 3 September, 1863. Honorably discharged 29 September, 1865.
LOCKWOOD, JOHN A.
Assistant Surgeon, 8 February, 1832. Surgeon, 13 October, 1840. Resigned 13 March, 1865.
LOCKWOOD, JOSHUA.
Midshipman, 20 June, 1806. Died 3 April, 1808.
LOCKWOOD, SAMUEL.
Midshipman, 12 July, 1820. Lieutenant, 17 May, 1828. Commander, 18 October, 1850. Retired List, 1 October, 1864. Commodore on Retired List, 4 April, 1867. Died 5 July, 1893.
LOCKWOOD, W. K.
Midshipman, 18 May, 1809. Resigned 18 December, 1810.
LODEN, M. J.
Acting Third Assistant Engineer, 18 April, 1863. Honorably discharged 1 December, 1865.
LODGE, AUGUSTUS.
Midshipman, 22 August, 1846. Resigned 30 December, 1850.
LODGE, EDWARD.
Acting Third Assistant Engineer, 1 October, 1862. Resigned 19 March, 1864.
LODGE, GEORGE C.
Naval Cadet (Spanish-American War), 25 April, 1898. Ensign, 15 September, 1898. Honorably discharged 16 September, 1898.
LOEFFLER, JOHN L.
Acting Third Assistant Engineer, 26 September, 1864. Honorably discharged 2 July, 1865.
LOGAN, GEORGE.
Surgeon, 21 April, 1810. Resigned 16 June, 1829.
LOGAN, GEORGE T. W.
Third Assistant Engineer, 31 October, 1848. Second Assistant Engineer, 26 February, 1851. Dropped 29 August, 1856.
LOGAN, GEORGE W.
Naval Cadet, 3 September, 1883. Ensign, 1 July, 1889. Lieutenant, Junior Grade, 16 May, 1897. Lieutenant, 3 March, 1899.
LOGAN, LEAVITT C.
Midshipman, 28 February, 1863. Graduated 6 June, 1867. Ensign, 18 December, 1868. Master, 21 March, 1870. Lieutenant, 12 June, 1871. Lieutenant-Commander, 16 December, 1891. Commander, 1 May, 1898.
LOGAN, ROBERT.
Warrant Machinest (Spanish-American War), 22 June, 1898. Dropped 9 August, 1898.
LOGUE, DANIEL C.
Acting Assistant Surgeon, 25 January, 1862. Resigned 7 October, 1862.
LOGUE, WILLIAM O.
Acting Second Assistant Engineer, 10 December, 1862. Acting First Assistant Engineer, 2 December, 1863. Honorably discharged 28 November, 1865.
LOHMAN, JOHN H.
Gunner, 13 June, 1898.
LOISONS, AUGUSTUS F.
Mate, 23 November, 1863. Resigned 30 June, 1866.
LOMAX, FRANCIS C.
Acting Third Assistant Engineer, 11 July, 1863. Honorably discharged 1 September, 1865.
LOMAX, SAMUEL F.
Acting Ensign and Pilot, 14 November, 1864. Honorably discharged 9 November, 1868. Mate, 5 January, 1879. Died 18 May, 1892.
LOMBARD, BENJAMIN M.
Cadet Midshipman, 21 September, 1881. Graduated. Honorably discharged 30 June, 1887. Ensign (Spanish-American War), 24 May, 1898. Lieutenant, Junior Grade, 11 February, 1899. Honorably discharged 11 February, 1899.
LOMBARD, JOHN E.
Acting Master, 29 October, 1861. Resigned 19 June, 1862. Lieutenant (Spanish-American War), 25 July, 1898. Honorably discharged 24 January, 1899.
LONG, ANDREW K.
Midshipman, 1 January, 1818. Lieutenant, 3 March, 1827. Commander, 12 October, 1844. Reserved List, 13 September, 1855. Captain, Active List, 14 September, 1855. Retired List, 1 October, 1864. Died 6 October, 1866.
LONG, ANDREW T.
Naval Cadet, 17 May, 1883. Ensign, 1 July, 1889. Lieutenant, Junior Grade, 13 July 1897. Lieutenant, 3 March, 1899.
LONG, CHARLES F.
Ensign (Spanish-American War), 25 May, 1898. Honorably discharged 8 October, 1898.
LONG, CHRISTOPHER.
Gunner, 17 September, 1861. Resigned 10 June, 1864.
LONG, GEORGE W.
Assistant Paymaster, 22 October, 1868. Passed Assistant Paymaster, 19 March, 1870. Retired List, 30 June, 1875. Died 8 April, 1892.

GENERAL NAVY REGISTER.   337

LONG, JAMES.
 Third Assistant Engineer, 16 November, 1861. Second Assistant Engineer, 25 August, 1863. Resigned 17 April, 1865.
LONG, JOHN A.
 Sailmaker, 2 April, 1881. Chief Sailmaker, 3 March, 1899.
LONG, JOHN C.
 Midshipman, 18 June, 1812. Lieutenant, 5 March, 1817. Commander, 25 February, 1838. Captain, 2 March, 1849. Commodore on Retired List, 16 July, 1862. Died 2 September, 1865.
LONG, JOHN H.
 Third Assistant Engineer, 6 November, 1849. Resigned 5 November, 1850. First Assistant Engineer, 15 June, 1861. Chief Engineer, 10 November, 1863. Died 2 March, 1882.
LONG, ROBERT.
 Master's Mate, 16 November, 1816. Resigned 9 January, 1819.
LONG, ROBERT H.
 Third Assistant Engineer, 11 January, 1849. Second Assistant Engineer, 26 February 1851. First Assistant Engineer, 21 May, 1853. Chief Engineer, 26 June, 1856. Resigned 31 October, 1863.
LONG, R. M.
 Acting Gunner, 3 December, 1862. Dismissed 7 March, 1863.
LONG, SAMUEL.
 Carpenter, 24 May, 1804. Resigned July, 1807.
LONG, WILLIAM.
 Boatswain, 8 May, 1861. Retired List, 29 October, 1883.
LONG, WILLIAM A.
 Acting Third Assistant Engineer, 8 September, 1864. Appointment revoked (sick) 9 November, 1864.
LONGACRE, ORLEANS.
 Third Assistant Engineer, 1 July, 1861. Second Assistant Engineer, 18 December, 1862. First Assistant Engineer, 1 January, 1865. Resigned 6 June, 1866.
LONGLY, JOHN.
 Midshipman, 30 June, 1799. Discharged 6 August, 1801, under Peace Establishment Act.
LONGMAYER, EMANUEL.
 Acting Third Assistant Engineer, 4 September, 1863. Appointment revoked 22 October, 1863.
LONGNECKER, EDWIN.
 Midshipman, 24 September, 1861. Graduated September, 1865. Ensign, 1 December, 1866. Master, 12 March, 1868. Lieutenant, 26 March, 1869. Lieutenant-Commander, 30 August, 1881. Commander, 2 October, 1891. Captain, 3 March, 1899.
LONGNECKER, HENRY C.
 Midshipman, 30 July, 1864. Graduated 4 June, 1869. Retired List, 5 November, 1872. Promoted to Ensign on Retired List, 26 June, 1884.
LONGSHAW, WILLIAM, Jr.
 Acting Assistant Surgeon, 25 June, 1862. Assistant Surgeon, 9 November, 1862. Killed in battle 15 January, 1865.
LONGSTREET, CORNELIUS H.
 Acting Assistant Paymaster, 11 September, 1862. Mustered out 3 October, 1865.
LONGWELL, GEORGE.
 Acting Second Assistant Engineer, 26 July, 1864. Honorably discharged 18 Sept., 1865.
LOOBY, THOMAS A.
 Acting Third Assistant Engineer, 3 May, 1863. Acting Second Assistant Engineer, 27 February, 1865. Dismissed 5 September, 1865.
LOOK, GEORGE.
 Acting Master and Pilot, 28 October, 1864. Appointment revoked 9 March, 1865.
LOOKENS, EZRA B.
 Mate, 22 October, 1861. Dismissed 5 June, 1862.
LOOKER, THOMAS H.
 Midshipman, 6 November, 1846. Resigned 24 November, 1852. Purser, 31 August, 1853. Pay Director, 3 March, 1871. Assistant to Secretary of the Navy, 1877-8. Paymaster General and Chief of Bureau P. and C., with rank of Commodore, 1890. General Inspector of Pay Corps, 1889-90. Retired List, 23 November, 1891.
LOOMIS, EDMUND U.
 Cadet Engineer Naval Academy, 1 October, 1872. Graduated 21 June, 1875. Lost on the Huron, 24 November, 1877.
LOPEZ, ROBERT F.
 Cadet Midshipman, 29 September, 1874. Graduated 10 June, 1881. Ensign, Junior Grade, 3 March, 1883. Ensign, 26 June, 1884. Lieutenant, Junior Grade, 16 April, 1892. Lieutenant, 1 April, 1896.
LORD, ARCHIBALD B.
 Midshipman, 9 July, 1799. Dismissed 28 December, 1803.
LOOMIS, FREDERIC J.
 Cadet Engineer, 1 October, 1880. Ensign, 1 July, 1886. Resigned 30 June, 1890.
LOOMIS, J. PORTER.
 Acting Assistant Paymaster, 27 October, 1863. Assistant Paymaster, 21 February, 1867. Passed Assistant Paymaster, 29 January, 1869. Paymaster, 6 December, 1880. Pay Inspector, 6 June, 1899.
LORD, ARCHIBALD B.
 Master, 1 February, 1809. Resigned 19 December, 1810.
LORD, ARCHIBALD B.
 Master, 18 July, 1812. Discharged 5 August, 1815.
LORD, GEORGE W.
 Acting Ensign, 3 March, 1865. Resigned 29 May, 1865.

LORD, GEORGE P.
　Acting Volunteer Lieutenant, 1 October, 1862. Honorably discharged 20 February, 1866.
LORD, JOHN.
　Gunner, 17 June, 1817. Last appearance on Records of Navy Department till 7 July, 1828. Died 9 July, 1829.
LORD, JOHN.
　Boatswain, date not known. Last appearance on Records of Navy Department.
LORD, JOHN C.
　Acting Ensign, 22 June, 1864. Honorably discharged 23 August, 1867.
LORD, JOHN M.
　Acting Third Assistant Engineer, 28 January, 1865. Appointment revoked 5 September, 1865.
LORD, LEVI.
　Acting Third Assistant Engineer 20 January, 1864. Honorably discharged 14 August, 1865.
LORD, WILLIAM R.
　Midshipman, 1 February, 1814. Resigned 5 September, 1817.
LORDAN, WILLIAM.
　Acting Gunner, 16 December, 1863. Appointment revoked 30 December, 1863. Acting Gunner, 6 January, 1864. Dismissed 12 November, 1864.
LORIGAN, JOHN L.
　Mate, 12 June, 1866. Resigned 13 August, 1866.
LORING, BENJAMIN W.
　Acting Master, 6 February, 1862. Acting Volunteer Lieutenant, 29 June, 1863. Honorably discharged 17 February, 1866.
LORING, CHARLES F.
　Mate. Dismissed 18 January, 1862. Mate, 2 January, 1863. Appointment revoked (sick) 21 October, 1863.
LORING, CHARLES G.
　Acting Master, 3 October, 1861. Honorably discharged 30 September, 1865.
LORING, CHARLES H.
　Third Assistant Engineer, 26 February, 1851. Second Assistant Engineer, 21 May, 1853. First Assistant Engineer, 9 May, 1857. Chief Engineer, 25 March, 1861. Engineer-in-Chief July, 1884. Retired List, 26 December, 1890.
LORING, DAVID.
　Gunner, 8 May, 1802. Last appearance on Records of Navy Department.
LORING, ELIPHALET.
　Acting Ensign, 1 October, 1862. Resigned 5 February, 1863.
LORING, HENRY W.
　Mate, 11 May, 1861. Resigned 24 June, 1862. Mate, 17 September, 1862. Acting Ensign, 1 October, 1863. Honorably discharged 29 August, 1865.
LORING, LEWIS W.
　Acting Assistant Surgeon, 11 April, 1865. Honorably discharged 9 October, 1865.
LORING, STANTON D.
　Acting Third Assistant Engineer, 1 November, 1862. Resigned 11 March, 1863.
LORING, WADSWORTH.
　Midshipman, 18 June, 1812. Resigned 6 January, 1814.
LOSSING, EDWIN J.
　Gunner, 5 November, 1892. Appointment revoked 25 July, 1895.
LOTHROP, ANSEL D., JR.
　Lieutenant, Junior Grade (Spanish-American War), 28 May, 1898. Honorably discharged 26 November, 1898.
LOTHROP, CYRUS E.
　Lieutenant, Junior Grade (Spanish American War), 9 May, 1898. Honorably discharged 24 August, 1898.
LOUCH, ABRAHAM J.
　Mate, 13 June, 1862. Acting Ensign, 6 August, 1862. Acting Master, 19 October, 1864. Honorably discharged 20 October, 1865.
LOUCKS, CHARLES.
　Acting Assistant Paymaster, 6 February, 1864. Honorably discharged 17 October, 1865.
LOUGEE, WILLIAM T.
　Acting Third Assistant Engineer, 3 August, 1864. Honorably discharged 27 October, 1865. Acting Third Assistant Engineer, 22 August, 1866. Mustered out 5 March, 1868.
LOUIS, LEOPOLD G.
　Pharmacist, 15 September, 1898. Retired List 30 September, 1899. Died 25 May, 1900.
LOUNSBERRY, GEORGE H.
　Mate, 1861. Killed in action at Vicksburg, Mississippi, August, 1862.
LOURIE, JOHN.
　Acting Ensign, 12 November, 1863. Honorably discharged 17 December, 1868.
LOURIS, JAIRUS.
　Master, 11 November, 1812. Resigned 6 February, 1821.
LOVE, AUGUSTUS.
　Assistant Surgeon, 13 March, 1805. Resigned 23 January, 1806.
LOVE, AUGUSTUS.
　Assistant Surgeon, 27 September, 1807. Last appearance on Records of Navy Department.
LOVE, CHARLES J.
　Midshipman, 13 November, 1838. Resigned 11 March, 1839.

GENERAL NAVY REGISTER.   339

LOVE, JOHN.
Lieutenant, 29 November, 1799. Discharged 4 August, 1801, under Peace Establishment Act.
LOVE, LAWSON C.
Midshipman, 1 April, 1828. Resigned 17 February, 1830.
LOVE, RICHARD L.
Midshipman, 17 September, 1830. Passed Midshipman, 15 June, 1837. Lieutenant, 8 September, 1841. Reserved List 14 September, 1855. Died 7 April, 1856.
LOVEAIRE, HENRY F.
Acting Third Assistant Engineer, 3 December, 1861. Third Assistant Engineer, 8 September, 1863. Resigned 26 October, 1868.
LOVEDAY, JOHN.
Midshipman, 1 January, 1812. Last appearance on Records of Navy Department, 1818. Dead.
LOVEJOY, JOSEPH H.
Mate, 13 September, 1864. Resigned 1 February, 1865.
LOVELL, EDWARD D.
Mate, 22 June, 1863. Honorably discharged 1 December, 1865.
LOVELL, HALE S.
Midshipman, 9 November, 1813. Lost in the Wasp, 1815.
LOVELL, JOHN P.
Master, 17 August, 1802. Died 15 March, 1808.
LOVELL, JOHN Q.
Assistant Paymaster, 26 July, 1882. Passed Assistant Paymaster, 12 September, 1893. Paymaster, 12 February, 1898.
LOVELL, ROBERT P.
Midshipman, 11 May, 1833. Passed Midshipman, 16 July, 1840. Died 7 May, 1845.
LOVELL, S. O.
Mate, 19 March, 1863. Acting Ensign, 20 March, 1865. Resigned 15 June, 1865.
LOVELL, WILLIAM S.
Midshipman, 8 November, 1847. Passed Midshipman, 10 June, 1853. Master, 15 September, 1855. Lieutenant, 16 September, 1855. Resigned 3 May, 1859.
LOVERING, FRANCIS J.
Third Assistant Engineer, 20 May, 1857. Second Assistant Engineer, 2 August, 1859. First Assistant Engineer, 1 July, 1861. Resigned 26 June, 1865.
LOVERING, PHILLIPS A.
Assistant Surgeon, 18 June, 1875. Passed Assistant Surgeon, 10 December, 1878. Surgeon, 4 December, 1891.
LOVETT, ISRAEL E.
Mate, 12 January, 1864. Honorably discharged 5 September, 1865.
LOVETT, JOHN A.
Gunner, 1 September, 1857. Dismissed 8 June, 1861.
LOW, BENJAMIN O.
Mate, 23 January, 1862. Acting Ensign, 25 December, 1863. Honorably discharged 21 October, 1865. Acting Ensign, 19 April, 1866. Mustered out 11 October, 1867.
LOW, PHILIP B.
Acting Ensign, 16 August, 1862. Resigned 7 August, 1863.
LOW, ROBESON L.
Ensign (Spanish-American War), 4 June, 1898. Honorably discharged 12 October, 1898.
LOW, RUFUS.
Master, 6 December, 1799. Last appearance on Records of Navy Department.
LOW, WILLIAM F.
Midshipman, 21 July, 1865. Graduated, 4 June, 1869. Ensign, 20 December, 1870. Master, 2 April, 1873. Lieutenant, 25 November, 1877. Lieutenant-Commander, 5 June, 1898. Retired List with rank of Commander, 30 June, 1900.
LOW, WILLIAM R.
Midshipman, 3 November, 1838. Died in August, 1845.
LOW, WILLIAM W.
Midshipman, 3 March, 1841. Passed Midshipman, 10 August, 1847. Master, 1 March, 1855. Lieutenant, 14 September, 1855. Lieutenant-Commander, 16 July, 1862. Commander, 25 July, 1866. Captain, 29 January, 1872. Died 24 June, 1877.
LOWBER, WILLIAM.
Assistant Surgeon, 8 November, 1847. Surgeon, 18 April, 1861. Medical Inspector, 3 March, 1871. Retired List, 5 July, 1872. Died 24 February, 1888.
LOWE, EDWARD S.
Mate. Appointment revoked (sick), 18 May, 1863. Mate, 19 November, 1863. Acting Ensign, 15 December, 1863. Acting Master, 8 April, 1865. Appointment revoked 7 July, 1865.
LOWE, ENOCH.
Midshipman, 1 September, 1811. Died 15 August, 1817.
LOWE, FRANK.
Mate, 1 October, 1862. Dismissed 8 July, 1863.
LOWE, JOHN.
Third Assistant Engineer, 12 August, 1861. Second Assistant Engineer, 21 April, 1863. First Assistant Engineer, 11 October, 1866. Chief Engineer, 16 June, 1883. Rank changed to Captain, 3 March, 1899. Retired List with rank of Rear-Admiral, 11 December, 1900.
LOWE, JOHN L.
Acting Second Assistant Engineer, 21 March, 1864. Honorably discharged 22 December, 1865.
LOWE, VINCENT.
Master, 20 March, 1813. Last appearance on Records of Navy Department, 1815. Philadelphia.

LOWE, WILLIAM.
Master, 19 November, 1812. Lieutenant, 9 December, 1814. Died 2 May, 1826.
LOWELL, ABNER J.
Acting Ensign, 7 August, 1863. Honorably discharged 29 August, 1865.
LOWELL, GEORGE B.
Acting Ensign, 17 November, 1864. Honorably discharged 27 September, 1865.
LOWELL, JOHN B.
Acting Second Assistant Engineer, 3 December, 1861. Acting First Assistant Engineer, 12 November, 1863. Honorably discharged 24 August, 1865.
LOWELL, RICHARD.
Carpenter, date not known. Died in November, 1824.
LOWNDES, CHRISTOPHER.
Midshipman, 1 January, 1817. Died in 1822.
LOWNDES, C. G.
Acting Assistant Paymaster, 6 August, 1862. Mustered out 21 November, 1865.
LOWNDES, CHARLES.
Midshipman, 18 March, 1815. Lieutenant, 13 January, 1825. Commander, 8 September, 1841. Captain, 14 September, 1855. Retired List, 21 December, 1861. Commodore on Retired List, 16 July, 1862. Died 14 December, 1885.
LOWNDES, CHARLES.
Assistant Surgeon, 5 December, 1857. Dismissed 7 May, 1861.
LOWNDES, CHARLES H. T.
Assistant Surgeon, 30 March, 1889. Passed Assistant Surgeon, 30 March, 1892. Surgeon, 13 August, 1900.
LOWNDES, RICHARD H.
Midshipman, 25 June, 1831. Passed Midshipman, 15 June, 1837. Resigned 18 June, 1841.
LOWRY, FRANCIS.
Midshipman, 3 August, 1831. Passed Midshipman, 23 June, 1838. Lieutenant, 4 July, 1843. Reserved List, 13 September, 1855. Captain on Retired List, 4 April, 1867.
LOWRY, HENRY M.
Carpenter, 26 March, 1847. Died 17 May, 1868.
LOWRY, MORROW M.
Mate, 10 April, 1863. Resigned 11 June, 1863.
LOWRY, MORROW P.
Acting Assistant Paymaster, 25 June, 1864. Mustered out 8 October, 1865.
LOWRY, OSWIN W.
Midshipman, 25 June, 1868. Graduated, 1 June, 1872. Ensign, 15 July, 1873. Master, 26 April, 1878. Lieutenant Junior Grade, 3 March, 1883. Lieutenant, 26 December, 1884. Died 13 March, 1898.
LOWRY, PHILIP W.
Acting Midshipman, 22 September, 1859. Ensign, 16 September, 1862. Died 12 February, 1866.
LOWRY, REIGART B.
Midshipman, 31 January, 1840. Passed Midshipman, 11 July, 1846. Master, 1 March, 1855. Lieutenant, 14 September, 1855. Lieutenant-Commander, 16 July, 1862. Commander, 25 July, 1866. Captain, 2 November, 1871. Commodore, 1 April, 1880. Died 25 November, 1880.
LOYALL, BENJAMIN P.
Midshipman, 5 March, 1849. Passed Midshipman, 12 June, 1855. Master, 16 September, 1855. Lieutenant, 28 January, 1856. Dismissed 5 October, 1861.
LOYD, JOHN.
Acting Third Assistant Engineer, 24 September, 1861. Acting Second Assistant Engineer, 30 March, 1863. Acting First Assistant Engineer, 20 October, 1863. Appointment revoked 7 December, 1863. Acting First Assistant Engineer, 8 March, 1864. Honorably discharged 27 September, 1867.
LOZIER, EDWARD.
Acting Second Assistant Engineer, 1 October, 1862. Honorably discharged 5 November, 1865.
LOZIER, GEORGE T.
Sailmaker, 30 October, 1840. Retired List, 11 May, 1874. Died 17 August, 1878.
LUBBE, CHARLES BETHEL.
Cadet Engineer, Naval Academy, 15 September, 1875. Graduated 10 June, 1879. Drowned 4 August, 1879.
LUBY, JOHN F.
Cadet Midshipman, 25 June, 1875. Graduated, 22 June, 1822. Ensign, Junior Grade, 3 March, 1883. Ensign, 26 June, 1884. Lieutenant, Junior Grade, 22 July, 1893. Lieutenant, 16 May, 1897.
LUBY, JOHN McC.
Naval Cadet, 8 September, 1890. Ensign, 1 July, 1896. Lieutenant, Junior Grade, 1 July, 1899.
LUCAS, JAMES B.
Acting Third Assistant Engineer, 19 August, 1863. Appointment revoked (sick) 6 October, 1864. Acting Third Assistant Engineer, 8 October, 1864. Honorably discharged 19 June, 1865.
LUCAS, JOHN B.
Acting Third Assistant Engineer, 15 September, 1864. Apointment revoked 6 October, 1864.
LUCE, GEORGE I.
Lieutenant, Junior Grade (Spanish-American War), 18 May, 1898. Honorably discharged 2 September, 1898.
LUCE, HIRAM C.
Mate, 12 December, 1862. Appointment revoked 19 January, 1863.

GENERAL NAVY REGISTER. 341

LUCE, PRESBURY N.
 Acting Ensign, 21 September, 1864. Honorably discharged 30 September, 1865.
LUCE, SHUBAEL K.
 Mate, 8 January, 1862. Acting Ensign, 17 September, 1862. Acting Master, 5 November, 1864. Honorably discharged 22 August, 1865. Acting Master, 9 April, 1866. Discharged 14 May, 1867.
LUCE, STEPHEN B.
 Midshipman, 19 October, 1841. Passed Midshipman, 10 August, 1847. Master, 15 September, 1855. Lieutenant, 16 September, 1855. Lieutenant-Commander, 16 July, 1862. Commander, 25 July, 1866. Captain, 28 December, 1872. Commodore, 25 November, 1881. Rear-Admiral, 5 October, 1885. Retired List, 25 March, 1889.
LUCE, WILLIAM.
 Second Assistant Engineer, 24 May, 1843. Disrated to Third Assistant Engineer, 28 July, 1845. Resigned 29 May, 1847.
LUCK, JOHN T.
 Assistant Surgeon, 24 January, 1862. Resigned 23 June, 1868.
LUCKETT, ALEXIS.
 Master, 15 December, 1812. Died 27 August, 1821.
LUCKETT, JAMES M.
 Midshipman, 17 December, 1810. Resigned 15 June, 1819.
LUDLOW, ABRAHAM.
 Lieutenant, 1 October, 1799. Discharged 8 July, 1801, under Peace Establishment Act.
LUDLOW, ALBERT S.
 Mate, 18 February, 1864. Acting Ensign, 31 July, 1865. Honorably discharged 20 July, 1868.
LUDLOW, AUGUSTUS C.
 Midshipman, 2 April, 1804. Lieutenant, 3 June, 1810. Died of wounds received in action, 1 June, 1813.
LUDLOW, CHARLES.
 Midshipman, 29 November, 1798. Lieutenant, 22 April, 1802. Resigned 24 August, 1811. Reappointed Lieutenant, 10 September, 1811. Commander, 24 December, 1811. Resigned 1 May, 1813.
LUDLOW, FRANCIS L.
 Midshipman, 24 July, 1866. Graduated 7 June, 1870. Ensign, 13 July, 1872. Retired List, 20 November, 1877. Disappeared in 1889.
LUDLOW, JAMES H.
 Midshipman, 15 November, 1809. Resigned 9 November, 1818.
LUDLOW, JAMES H.
 Midshipman, 19 May, 1819. Resigned 23 May, 1819.
LUDLOW, NICOLL.
 Acting Midshipman, 28 October, 1859. Ensign, 1 October, 1863. Master, 10 May, 1866. Lieutenant, 21 February, 1867. Lieutenant-Commander, 12 March, 1868. Commander, 1 October, 1881. Captain, 21 May, 1895. Retired List, with rank of Rear-Admiral, 1 November, 1899.
LUDLOW, ROBERT C.
 Purser, 25 April, 1812. Died 15 May, 1826.
LUDLOW, W. B.
 Midshipman, 1 May, 1827. Passed Midshipman, 10 June, 1833. Lieutenant, 8 December, 1838. Died 29 November, 1839.
LUFBOROUGH, A. W.
 Midshipman, 18 June, 1812. Last appearance on Records of Navy Department, 15 March, 1816.
LUKE, JOHN L.
 Midshipman, 4 March, 1819. Cashiered 12 March, 1821.
LUKESH, GEORGE M.
 Assistant Paymaster, 17 March, 1898. Passed Assistant Paymaster, 3 March, 1899.
LULL, EDWARD P.
 Acting Midshipman, 7 October, 1851. Midshipman, 9 June, 1855. Passed Midshipman, 15 April, 1858. Master, 4 November, 1858. Lieutenant, 30 October, 1860. Lieutenant-Commander, 16 July, 1862. Commander, 10 June, 1870. Captain, 1 October, 1881. Died 5 March, 1887.
LULL, J. K.
 Mate, 10 March, 1863. Resigned 25 November, 1864.
LUM, JOSEPH.
 Gunner, date not known. Discharged 20 May, 1824.
LUMPKINS, GEORGE W.
 Acting First Assistant Engineer, 9 May, 1864. Appointment revoked (sick) 14 March, 1865.
LUMSDEN, GEORGE P.
 Assistant Surgeon, 2 November, 1876. Passed Assistant Surgeon, 2 November, 1879. Surgeon, 12 May, 1894.
LUNDT, W. C.
 Acting Master, 26 August, 1861. Resigned 17 December, 1864.
LUNG, GEORGE A.
 Assistant Surgeon, 18 August, 1888. Passed Assistant Surgeon, 18 August, 1892.
LUNT, GEORGE.
 Acting Master, 12 August, 1861. Resigned 11 February, 1862.
LUNT, HENRY.
 Acting Assistant Paymaster, 31 August, 1864. Mustered out 2 September, 1865.
LUSCOMB, CHARLES P.
 Mate, 8 January, 1863. Resigned 3 March, 1865.

LUSCOMB, JOHN W.
　Acting Ensign, 19 August, 1863. Honorably discharged 14 January, 1866.
LUSK, ANDREW.
　Acting Third Assistant Engineer, 7 January, 1863. Honorably discharged 31 October, 1865.
LUTHER, CHARLES.
　Acting Third Assistant Engineer, 9 March, 1865. Honorably discharged 22 September, 1865.
LUTHER, GEORGE H.
　Acting Third Assistant Engineer, 12 March, 1863. Acting Second Assistant Engineer, 25 July, 1864. Honorably discharged 18 January, 1866.
LUTKEN, HAROLD I.
　Acting Warrant Machinist, 23 August, 1899.
LUTTON, MORGAN.
　Acting Third Assistant Engineer, 26 July, 1864. Honorably discharged 10 July, 1866.
LUTZ, FREDERICK C.
　Acting Warrant Machinist, 23 August, 1899.
LYDDON, WILLIAM.
　Mate, 21 October, 1861. Acting Ensign, 6 September, 1862. Appointment revoked 5 June, 1865.
LYDE, NATHANIEL.
　Purser, 25 April, 1812. Died 7 July, 1828.
LYETH, CLINTON H.
　Midshipman, 26 June, 1868. Graduated 1 June, 1872. Ensign, 15 July, 1873. Master, 2 February, 1878. Lieutenant, Junior Grade, 3 March. 1883. Retired List, 20 May, 1887. Died 8 March, 1895.
LYLE, VICTOR R.
　Ensign (Spanish-American War), 10 May, 1898. Resigned 13 December, 1898.
LYMAN, CHARLES H.
　Midshipman, 28 July, 1866. Graduated 7 June, 1870. Ensign, 13 July, 1871. Master, 24 October, 1874. Died 28 January, 1897.
LYMAN, GAD.
　Acting First Assistant Engineer, 25 August, 1864. Honorably discharged 30 June, 1865.
LYMAN, JAMES R.
　Midshipman, 16 July, 1814. Last appearance on Records of Navy Department, 1819.
LYMAN, JOHN.
　Acting Third Assistant Engineer, 4 September, 1861. Resigned 18 January, 1862.
LYMAN, WILLIAM C.
　Assistant Surgeon, 24 June, 1861. Resigned 8 December, 1865.
LYNAM, ELBRIDGE V.
　Lieutenant, Junior Grade (Spanish-American War), 21 June, 1898. Honorably discharged 13 March, 1899.
LYNCH, A. M.
　Assistant Surgeon, 12 October, 1850. Resigned 14 January, 1861.
LYNCH, BERNARD S.
　Mate. Dismissed 13 February, 1862.
LYNCH, DOMINICK.
　Midshipman, 2 February, 1829. Passed Midshipman, 3 July, 1835. Lieutenant, 8 September, 1841. Reserved List, 13 September, 1855. Commander on Retired List, 21 July, 1861. Captain on Retired List, 4 April, 1867. Captain on Active List, 20 January, 1871. Retired List, 30 January, 1872. Died 10 October. 1884.
LYNCH, DOMINICK H.
　Midshipman, 6 November, 1846. Dismissed 12 June, 1851.
LYNCH, GREEN.
　Midshipmn, 16 January, 1809. Died in September, 1817.
LYNCH, JOHN P.
　Purser, 8 January, 1801. Discharged 8 July, 1801, under Peace Establishment Act.
LYNCH, JOHN.
　Mate, 7 January, 1862. Killed 13 October, 1862.
LYNCH, NICHOLAS.
　Sailmaker, 3 June, 1861. Retired List, 12 May, 1884.
LYNCH, PATRICK.
　Gunner, 15 August, 1877. Chief Gunner, 3 March, 1899.
LYNCH, ROBERT.
　Mate, 17 April, 1866. Appointment revoked 12 June, 1866.
LYNCH, THOMAS.
　Third Assistant Engineer, 12 August, 1861. Second Assistant Engineer, 21 April, 1863. Resigned 21 June, 1869.
LYNCH, THOMAS E.
　Acting Third Assistant Engineer, 13 October, 1862. Acting Second Assistant Engineer, 1 April, 1865. Honorably discharged 28 September, 1869.
LYNCH, WILLIAM F.
　Midshipman, 26 January, 1819. Lieutenant, 17 May, 1828. Commander, 5 September, 1849. Captain, 2 April, 1856. Resigned 21 April, 1861.
LYNCH, WILLIAM F., Jr.
　Third Assistant Engineer, 20 February, 1847. Dismissed 5 February, 1852.
LYNE, LEONARD H.
　Midshipman, 10 September, 1841. Passed Midshipman, 10 August, 1847. Master, 14 September, 1855. Lieutenant, 15 September, 1855. Dismissed 7 October, 1857.
LYNE, W. B.
　Midshipman, 4 March, 1823. Passed Midshipman, 23 May, 1829. Lieutenant, 13 July, 1832. Drowned 30 April, 1841.

GENERAL NAVY REGISTER.   343

LYNE, WILLIAM H.
    Midshipman, 5 June, 1848. Resigned 16 October, 1849.
LYNG, DENNIS.
    Acting Third Assistant Engineer, 30 May, 1863. Resigned 5 April, 1865.
LYNN, JOHN M.
    Assistant Surgeon, 24 July, 1813. Resigned 5 September, 1814.
LYON, AMOS M.
    Mate, 22 October, 1861. Resigned 27 April, 1865.
LYON, AUGUSTUS J.
    Mate, 28 December, 1861. Resigned 16 April, 1864.
LYON, FRANK.
    Naval Cadet, 20 May, 1890. Assistant Engineer, 1 July, 1896. Rank changed to Ensign, 3 March, 1899. Lieutenant, Junior Grade, 1 July, 1899.
LYON, GEORGE A.
    Assistant Paymaster, 11 June, 1862. Paymaster, 23 January, 1866. Pay Inspector, 15 September, 1888. Pay Director, 15 March, 1898. Retired List (Rear-Admiral), 23 December, 1899.
LYON, HENRY.
    Acting Third Assistant Engineer, 18 April, 1864. Honorably discharged 9 November, 1865.
LYON, HENRY W.
    Midshipman, 7 October, 1862. Graduated June, 1866. Ensign, 12 March, 1868. Master, 26 March, 1869. Lieutenant, 21 March, 1870. Lieutenant-Commander, 3 November, 1884. Commander, 1 October, 1893. Captain, 27 March, 1900.
LYON, JAMES.
    Acting Second Assistant Engineer, 24 August, 1862. Dismissed 7 January, 1863.
LYON, JOHN.
    Purser, 17 February, 1807. Last appearance on Records of Navy Department.
LYON, JOHN W.
    Acting Third Assistant Engineer, 25 August, 1864. Honorably discharged 11 December, 1865. Acting Third Assistant Engineer, 25 June, 1866. Mustered out 2 October, 1868.
LYON, LUTHER M.
    Assistant Surgeon, 19 October, 1861. Surgeon, 6 August, 1870. Retired List, 22 December, 1871. Died 7 May, 1874.
LYON, SOUTHWELL.
    Acting Third Assistant Engineer, 22 April, 1863. Honorably discharged 1 November, 1865.
LYONS, CHARLES S.
    Mate, 26 September, 1863. Resigned 30 June, 1865.
LYONS, DANIEL.
    Acting Third Assistant Engineer, 6 July, 1863. Appointment revoked (sick) 12 August, 1863.
LYONS, DAVID.
    Gunner, 30 July, 1897.
LYONS, DAVID E.
    Acting Third Assistant Engineer, 3 November, 1869. Appointment revoked 3 July, 1865.
LYONS, EDWARD.
    Boatswain, 12 February, 1842. Resigned 30 August, 1843.
LYONS, LAWRENCE, J.
    Acting Third Assistant Engineer, 25 March, 1864. Honorably discharged 16 November, 1869.
LYONS, RICHARD.
    Mate, 11 May, 1864. Appointment revoked 13 December, 1865.
LYONS, TIMOTHY A.
    Acting Midshipman, 2 January, 1862. Graduated September, 1865. Ensign, 1 December, 1866. Master, 12 March, 1868. Lieutenant, 26 March, 1869. Lieutenant-Commander, 16 December, 1879. Commander, 4 August, 1889. Retired List, 15 May, 1897.
LYONS, WILLIAM R.
    Mate, 30 June, 1863. Resigned 30 May, 1865.
LYTTLE, ROBERT E.
    Acting Master, 26 August, 1861. Dismissed 16 October, 1861.
LYTTLE, ROBERT S.
    Acting Third Assistant Engineer, 19 April, 1864. Honorably discharged 22 March, 1866.
MABEE, GEORGE J. W., JR.
    Mate, 3 May, 1864. Acting Ensign, 25 August, 1864. Honorably discharged 16 September, 1865.
MACABUM, JOHN.
    Acting Third Assistant Engineer, 19 October, 1863. Honorably discharged 21 September, 1865.
MACARTHUR, ARTHUR, JR.
    Naval Cadet, 6 September, 1892. Ensign, 6 May, 1898.
MACAY, JAMES.
    Midshipman, 25 August, 1800. Resigned 18 November, 1803.
MACCARTY, GILBERT M. L.
    Third Assistant Engineer, 8 July, 1861. Second Assistant Engineer, 18 December, 1862. First Assistant Engineer, 30 January, 1865. Chief Engineer, 16 September, 1881. Retired List, 20 June, 1896.
MACCONNELL, CHARLES J.
    Third Assistant Engineer, 29 October, 1861. Second Assistant Engineer, 30 July,

1863. First Assistant Engineer, 11 October, 1866. Chief Engineer, 2 December, 1885. Retired List, 19 January, 1899.

MACCOUN, ROBERT T.
Assistant Surgeon, 7 November, 1844. Passed Assistant Surgeon, 4 February, 1851. Surgeon, 21 September, 1858. Medical Inspector, 3 March, 1871. Medical Director, 7 November, 1872. Retired List, 19 April, 1879. Died 20 March, 1890.

MACDANIEL, ALBERT.
Midshipman, 27 August, 1823. Resigned 9 May, 1831.

MACDEARMID, JOHN.
Acting Master, 24 May, 1861. Acting Volunteer Lieutenant, gallant conduct, 1 August, 1862. Acting Volunteer Lieutenant-Commander, 3 March, 1865. Honorably discharged 28 October, 1866.

MACDONALD, JAMES P.
Acting Third Assistant Engineer, 6 January, 1865. Honorably discharged 15 May, 1869.

MACDONALD, WILLIAM.
Carpenter, 4 November, 1892.

MACDONOUGH, THOMAS.
Midshipman, 5 February, 1800. Lieutenant, 6 February, 1807. Commander, 24 July, 1813. Captain, 11 September, 1814. Died 10 November, 1825.

MACDOUGALL, WILLIAM D.
Naval Cadet, 19 May, 1885. Ensign, 1 July, 1891. Lieutenant, Junior Grade, 15 November, 1898. Lieutenant, 3 March, 1899.

MacEVITT, JOHN C.
Passed Assistant Surgeon (Spanish-American War), 24 May, 1898. Honorably discharged 9 September, 1898.

MACFARLAND, HORACE G.
Naval Cadet, 6 September, 1887. Ensign, 1 July, 1893. Lieutenant, Junior Grade, 3 March, 1899. Lieutenant, 18 February, 1900.

MACFARLANE, EDWARD O.
Midshipman, 3 October, 1864. Graduated June, 1869. Resigned 31 October, 1871.

MACFARLANE, JAMES.
Lieutenant Junior Grade (Spanish-American War), 12 May, 1898. Honorably discharged 9 September, 1898.

MACFARLANE, JOHN.
Carpenter, 3 October, 1861. Died 1 April, 1889.

MACHESNEY, WILLIAM.
Midshipman, 1 September, 1811. Dismissed 13 April, 1813.

MACHETTE, HENRY C.
Acting Assistant Paymaster, 16 April, 1864. Mustered out 4 March, 1866. Assistant Paymaster, 27 February, 1867. Passed Assistant Paymaster, 26 February, 1869. Paymaster, 16 June, 1881. Retired List, 13 August, 1896.

MACINTIRE, BENJAMIN F.
Mate, 6 January, 1863. Acting Ensign, 31 August, 1863. Appointment revoked (sick) 19 January, 1865.

MACINTYRE, L. C.
Acting Master, 5 April, 1862. Honorably discharged 18 December, 1865.

MACK, ALEXANDER.
Boatswain, 5 June, 1872. Retired List, 20 December, 1889.

MACK, DAVID.
Assistant Surgeon, 26 October, 1863. Resigned 12 May, 1870.

MACK, EUGENE.
Acting Third Assistant Engineer, 24 November, 1863. Acting Second Assistant Engineer, 28 October, 1864. Appointment revoked 22 January, 1866.

MACK, EUGENE.
Gunner, 10 September, 1849. Died 25 July, 1883.

MACK, HENRY S.
Acting Third Assistant Engineer, 19 October, 1864. Honorably discharged 7 July, 1865.

MACK, JEREMIAH.
Gunner, 30 December, 1841. Died 17 December, 1842.

MACK, JOHN.
Mate, 30 November, 1864. Appointment revoked 9 June, 1868.

MACK, WILLIAM J.
Acting Third Assistant Engineer, 22 March, 1864. Honorably discharged 11 January, 1866.

MACKALL, RICHARD.
Midshipman, 1 January, 1812. Resigned 12 May, 1823.

MACKAY, D. H.
Midshipman, 16 April, 1813. Lieutenant, 13 January, 1825. Lost in the Hornet, 10 September, 1829.

MACKAY, DONALD S.
Mate, 21 October, 1861. Appointment revoked 1 September, 1862.

MACKAY, GEORGE.
Acting Master's Mate and Mate (volunteer), 2 February, 1864, to 9 June, 1865. Civil Engineer (regular), 11 April, 1890.

MACKAY, WILLIAM H.
Assistant Engineer (Spanish-American War), 13 May, 1898. Honorably discharged 4 January, 1899.

MACKENZIE, ALEXANDER.
Acting Assistant Surgeon, 21 November, 1863. Honorably discharged 18 December, 1866.

MACKENZIE, ALEXANDER S.
Midshipman, 1 January, 1815. Lieutenant, 13 January, 1825. Commander, 8 September, 1841. Died 13 September, 1848.

GENERAL NAVY REGISTER. 345

MACKENZIE, ALEXANDER S.
   Acting Midshipman, 29 September, 1855. Midshipman, 9 June, 1859. Lieutenant, 31 August, 1861. Lieutenant-Commander, 29 July, 1865. Killed in battle, 13 June, 1867.
MACKENZIE, ALLAN S.
   Gunner, 5 January, 1897.
MACKENZIE, MORRIS R. S.
   Midshipman, 29 September, 1862. Graduated June, 1866. Ensign, 12 March, 1868. Master, 26 March, 1869. Lieutenant, 21 March, 1870. Lieutenant-Commander, 26 December, 1884. Commander, 16 April, 1894. Captain, 1 July, 1900.
MACKIE, ADAM.
   Assistant Surgeon, 18 October, 1870. Died 1 July, 1873.
MACKIE, ALFRED R.
   Carpenter, 21 December, 1897.
MACKIE, BENJAMIN S.
   Assistant Surgeon, 21 April, 1869. Surgeon, 20 August, 1879. Died 25 July, 1895.
MACKIE, J. H.
   Acting Assistant Surgeon, 17 May, 1861. Resigned 28 February, 1862.
MACKIE, JOHN P.
   Midshipman, 5 December, 1798. Resigned 13 May, 1799. Midshipman, 31 May, 1799. Warrant returned 24 August, 1799.
MACKIE, J. WALTER.
   Mate, 21 December, 1861. Appointment revoked (sick) 11 March, 1864.
MacKNIGHT, THOMAS M.
   Lieutenant, Junior Grade (Spanish-American War), 19 July, 1898. Honorably discharged 13 March, 1899.
MacLACHLAN, JOHN.
   Passed Assistant Engineer (Spanish-American War), 14 May, 1898. Honorably discharged 14 September, 1898.
MACLAY, WILLIAM W.
   Acting Midshipman, 4 October, 1860. Ensign, 28 May, 1863. Master, 10 November, 1865. Lieutenant, 10 November, 1866. Lieutenant-Commander, 12 March, 1868. Resigned 13 October, 1871.
MACLEAN, ARCHIBALD.
   Midshipman, 1 November, 1828. Resigned 19 January, 1830.
MacLAURIN, B. R.
   Acting Ensign, 10 September, 1863. Dismissed 1 October, 1864.
MacMAHON, JOHN.
   Acting Assistant Paymaster, 11 November, 1864. Assistant Paymaster, 23 July, 1866. Passed Assistant Paymaster, 11 December, 1867. Paymaster, 17 September, 1877. Died 11 September, 1893.
MACOMB, A. W.
   Master, 25 July, 1818. Resigned 19 May, 1826.
MACOMB, DAVID B.
   Third Assistant Engineer, 11 January, 1849. Second Assistant Engineer, 26 February, 1851. First Assistant Engineer, 26 June, 1856. Chief Engineer, 21 September, 1860. Retired List, 27 February, 1889.
MACOMB, EDWARD.
   Acting Assistant Surgeon, 25 February, 1865. Honorably discharged 8 November, 1865.
MACOMB, F. A. N.
   Midshipman, 14 March, 1833. Resigned 9 April, 1833.
MACOMB, S. G.
   Carpenter, 25 January, 1838. Resigned 18 January, 1839.
MACOMB, WILLIAM H.
   Midshipman, 10 April, 1834. Passed Midshipman, 16 July, 1840. Lieutenant, 27 February, 1847. Commander, 16 July, 1862. Captain, 25 July, 1866. Commodore, 1 July, 1870. Died 12 August, 1872.
MACOMBE, NEHEMIAH.
   Master, 15 May, 1799. Resigned 4 August, 1800.
MACOMBER, GEORGE.
   Midshipman, 1 May, 1828. Died 8 October, 1834.
MACOMBER, JAMES H.
   Assistant Surgeon, 30 July, 1861. Passed Assistant Surgeon, 30 July, 1864. Died 18 February, 1865.
MACOMBER, R. P.
   Assistant Surgeon, 13 July, 1824. Surgeon, 4 December, 1828. Died 16 June, 1831.
MACOMBER, S. P.
   Midshipman, 20 June, 1806. Lieutenant, 4 March, 1813. Drowned 6 March, 1820.
MACPHERSON, HUGH.
   Ensign (Spanish-American War), 28 May, 1898. Honorably discharged 13 March, 1899.
MACRAE, JOHN.
   Midshipman, 17 December, 1810. Resigned 25 January, 1812.
MACREADY, C. S., Jr.
   Mate, 18 November, 1861. Resigned 3 April, 1862.
MacVICAR, JOHN L.
   Passed Assistant Engineer (Spanish-American War), 25 May, 1898. Honorably discharged 17 January, 1899.
MACY, GILBERT D.
   Sailmaker, 20 June, 1867. Retired List, 10 September, 1896.
MACY, HENRY G.
   Acting Ensign, 17 December, 1862. Acting Master, 16 December, 1864. Ensign, 12

MACY, NELSON.
   March, 1868. Master, 18 December, 1868. Lieutenant, 21 March, 1870. Died 1 December, 1872.
MACY, NELSON.
   Assistant Engineer (Spanish-American War), 14 May, 1898. Honorably discharged 18 October, 1898.
MACY, ULYSSES S.
   Naval Cadet, 6 September, 1894. Ensign, 4 April, 1900.
MADDEN, WILLIAM.
   Acting Third Assistant Engineer, 3 November, 1863. Honorably discharged 30 May, 1867.
MADDOCK, JOHN.
   Mate, 5 November, 1862. Discharged 4 November, 1864.
MADDOCKS, W. D.
   Acting Ensign, 18 July, 1863. Acting Master, 2 October, 1865. Honorably discharged 6 June, 1868.
MADDOX, JOSHUA.
   Master, 4 August, 1807. Appointment revoked 2 May, 1809.
MADGE, THOMAS I.
   Lieutenant (Spanish-American War), 11 May, 1898. Honorably discharged 22 September, 1898.
MADIGAN, JOHN.
   Midshipman, 19 February, 1840. Passed Midshipman, 11 July, 1846. Master, 1 March, 1855. Dropped 13 September, 1855. Lieutenant, Active List, 14 September, 1855. Lieutenant-Commander, 16 July, 1862. Commander, 22 September, 1865. Died 22 October, 1870.
MADISON, J. H. M.
   Midshipman, 23 December, 1837. Resigned 4 November, 1842.
MADISON, JOHN R.
   Midshipman, 28 June, 1804. Lieutenant, 24 July, 1813. Lost in the Lynx.
MADISON, WILLIAM F.
   Midshipman, 16 January, 1809. Died 16 July, 1812.
MADISON, ZACHARIAH H.
   Naval Cadet, 6 September, 1894. At sea prior to final graduation.
MAFFIT, JOHN N.
   Midshipman, 25 February, 1832. Passed Midshipman, 23 June, 1838. Lieutenant, 25 June, 1848. Reserved List, 14 September, 1855. Lieutenant on Active List, 25 June, 1843. Resigned 2 May, 1861.
MAFFIT, SAMUEL.
   Purser, 25 April, 1812. Last appearance on Records of Navy Department. Dead.
MAFFIT, WILLIAM H.
   Midshipman, 30 May, 1846. Dismissed 12 June, 1851.
MAGAR, BENJAMIN S.
   Acting Master, 20 August, 1861. Disrated to Acting Ensign, 9 April, 1863. Acting Master, 23 August, 1863. Honorably discharged 1 October, 1865.
MAGAW, SAMUEL.
   Midshipman, 23 November, 1841. Passed Midshipman, 10 August, 1847. Master, 14 September, 1855. Lieutenant, 15 September, 1855. Lieutenant-Commander, 16 July, 1862. Commandr, 10 October, 1866. Retired List, 29 October, 1868. Died 19 May, 1884.
MAGAW, WILLIAM P.
   Acting Third Assistant Engineer, 2 December, 1861. Acting Second Assistant Engineer, 24 October, 1862. Dismissed 22 July, 1865.
MAGEE, ALEXANDER.
   Acting First Assistant Engineer, 1 October, 1862. Honorably discharged 16 February, 1867.
MAGEE, EDWARD A.
   Third Assistant Engineer, 27 June, 1862. Second Assistant Engineer, 21 November, 1863. First Assistant Engineer, 1 January, 1868. Chief Engineer, 28 February, 1889. Retired List, 4 November, 1895.
MAGEE, GEORGE W.
   Third Assistant Engineer, 4 April, 1861. Resigned 30 March, 1863. Restored 1 June, 1863, as Third Assistant Engineer from 4 April, 1861. Second Assistant Engineer, 16 January, 1863. First Assistant Engineer, 1 December, 1864. Chief Engineer, 11 June, 1876. Retired List, 26 June, 1893.
MAGEE, JAMES.
   Acting Third Assistant Engineer, 18 December, 1863. Appointment revoked (sick), 6 October, 1864.
MAGEE, S. H.
   Acting Second Assistant Engineer, 28 August, 1863. Mustered out 24 August, 1869.
MAGER, NICHOLAS.
   Carpenter, 9 July, 1847. Retired List, 9 November, 1871.
MAGER, PHILIP T.
   Carpenter, 15 November, 1873. Chief Carpenter, 3 March, 1899.
MAGHU, JOHN.
   Mate. Dismissed 28 November, 1862.
MAGIE, THEODORE B.
   Mate, 30 December, 1861. Resigned 29 May, 1862.
MAGILL, BERNARD.
   Mate, 13 October, 1863. Acting Ensign, good conduct, 7 April, 1864. Honorably discharged 5 December, 1865.
MAGILL, B. T.
   Assistant Surgeon, 7 March, 1838. Died at sea in 1841.
MAGILL, JAMES.
   Carpenter, 2 April, 1842. Died 14 April, 1848.

GENERAL NAVY REGISTER. 347

MAGILL, SAMUEL G. JR.
   Naval Cadet, 19 May, 1893. Ensign, 1 July, 1899. Died 30 June, 1900.
MAGONE, E. A.
   Acting Ensign, 15 August, 1862. Acting Master, 12 August, 1864. Honorably discharged 19 September, 1865.
MAGRATH, HUMPHREY.
   Midshipman, 1 January, 1800. Master, 9 May, 1803. Lieutenant, 3 February, 1809. Purser, 25 April, 1812. Resigned 4 June, 1814.
MAGRUDER, ALEXANDER F.
   Assistant Surgeon, 21 April, 1871. Surgeon, 8 January, 1885. Retired List, 14 November, 1896.
MAGRUDER, CHARLES B.
   Mate, 3 August, 1866. Gunner, 26 August, 1870. Chief Gunner, 3 March, 1899.
MAGRUDER, GEORGE A.
   Midshipman, 1 January, 1817. Lieutenant, 28 April, 1826. Commander, 14 February, 1843. Captain, 14 September, 1855. Dismissed 22 April, 1861.
MAGRUDER, T. C.
   Midshipman, 2 April, 1804. Resigned 22 January, 1812.
MAGRUDER, THOMAS P.
   Naval Cadet, 3 September, 1885. Ensign, 1 July, 1891. Lieutenant, Junior Grade, 9 October, 1898. Lieutenant, 3 March, 1899.
MAGRUDER, THOMAS W.
   Midshipman, 2 February, 1829. Died 4 July, 1835.
MAGRUDER, T. W.
   Midshipman, 18 May, 1809. Lieutenant, 9 December, 1814. Last appearance on Records of Navy Department, 1816. Franklin, 74.
MAGUNE, JAMES H.
   Acting Master, 14 August, 1861. Acting Volunteer Lieutenant, 17 August, 1864. Honorably discharged 29 November, 1865.
MAHAN, ALFRED T.
   Acting Midshipman, 30 September, 1856. Midshipman, 9 June, 1859. Lieutenant, 31 August, 1861. Lieutenant-Commander, 7 June, 1865. Commander, 20 November, 1872. Captain, 23 September, 1885. Retired List, 17 November, 1896.
MAHAN, DENNIS H.
   Midshipman, 20 July, 1865. Graduated June, 1869. Ensign, 12 July, 1870. Master, 14 February, 1873. Lieutenant, 21 September, 1877. Lieutenant-Commander, 11 May, 1898.
MAHAN, WILLIAM.
   Acting Third Assistant Engineer, 7 February, 1862. Acting Second Assistant Engineer, 3 October, 1863. Honorably discharged 20 February, 1866.
MAHATHA, ROBERT.
   Acting First Assistant Engineer, 1 October, 1862. Honorably discharged 28 November, 1865.
MAHON, DAVID.
   Assistant Surgeon, 28 March, 1820. Resigned 27 November, 1823.
MAHON, THOMAS D.
   Midshipman, 10 September, 1841. Dismissed 28 December, 1842.
MAHONEY, CHARLES.
   Gunner, 6 September, 1839. Discharged 7 November, 1840.
MAHONEY, JAMES E.
   Cadet Midshipman, 22 September, 1876. Graduated 10 June, 1881. Second Lieutenant, Marine Corps, 1 July, 1883. (See Marine Corps.)
MAHONEY, JOHN.
   Mate, 15 April, 1898. Boatswain, 10 April, 1899.
MAHONEY, KAEN M. A.
   Carpenter, 8 January, 1881. Retired List, 2 March, 1898.
MAHONEY, MICHAEL.
   Midshipman, 30 November, 1814. Last appearance on Records of Navy Department, 1821. Navy aYrd, Portsmouth, New Hampshire.
MAHONEY, SAMUEL.
   Boatswain, 2 March, 1848. Resigned 30 September, 1848.
MAHONY, DANIEL S.
   Naval Cadet, 6 September, 1893. Ensign, 1 July, 1840.
MAHONY, WILLIAM M.
   Sailmaker, 15 November, 1850. Dismissed 8 June, 1861.
MAIES, WILLIAM H.
   Mate, 6 August, 1861. Acting Master, 26 May, 1862. Acting Volunteer Lieutenant, 6 April, 1865. Honorably discharged 15 May, 1866. Acting Master, 23 April, 1867. Resigned 16 July, 1868.
MAIN, HERSCHEL.
   Acting Third Assistant Engineer, under instruction Naval Academy, 10 October, 1866. Third Assistant Engineer, 2 June, 1868. Second Assistant Engineer, 2 June, 1869. Passed Assistant Engineer, 20 November, 1874. Chief Engineer, 11 November, 1892. Retired List, 10 September, 1895.
MAINE, WILLIAM A.
   Acting Master, 27 February, 1862. Honorably discharged 21 January, 1866.
MAIRS, JOHN.
   Assistant Surgeon, 10 December, 1814. Last appearance on Records of Navy Department, 1815. New York.
MAITLAND, EDWARD J.
   Acting Ensign, 30 December, 1864. Honorably discharged 22 October, 1868.
MAJOR, DANIEL G.
   Acting Master, 27 July, 1861. Resigned 17 April, 1863.

MAJOR, JAMES.
Professor, 12 November, 1844. Resigned 3 September, 1859.
MAJOR, SAMUEL I. M.
Naval Cadet, 20 September, 1895. At sea prior to final graduation.
MAKINS, GEORGE B.
Acting Third Assistant Engineer, 20 May, 1864. Honorably discharged 16 August, 1865.
MALBON, THOMAS J.
Acting Second Assistant Engineer, 22 June, 1863. Acting First Assistant Engineer, 3 May, 1864. Honorably discharged 1 December, 1865.
MALBONE, W. F.
Master, 4 April, 1814. Died 6 October, 1826.
MALCOMB, JAMES R.
Acting Master, 9 October, 1861. Appointment revoked 7 March, 1862.
MALEY, PATRICK F.
Acting Assistant Surgeon, 1 October, 1862. Resigned 24 November, 1862.
MALEY, WILLIAM.
Lieutenant, 1 August, 1799. Resigned 12 November, 1800.
MALLABY, FRANCIS.
Master, not in line of promotion, 3 July, 1813. Reserved List, 13 September, 1855.
MALLAM, JOHN.
Acting Assistant Surgeon, 8 March, 1865. Honorably discharged 25 September, 1865.
MALLARD, WILLIAM H.
Acting Master, 21 January, 1862. Honorably discharged 27 May, 1867.
MALLARY, FRANCIS.
Midshipman, 1 May, 1822. Resigned 17 January, 1826.
MALLERY, GEORGE L.
Gunner, 31 March, 1896.
MALLETT, E. B.
Acting Master, 29 October, 1861. Honorably discharged 14 September, 1865.
MALLETT, GEORGE F.
Assistant Naval Constructor, 22 January, 1872. Naval Constructor, 13 January, 1885. Died 1 January, 1886.
MALLISON, GEORGE.
Naval Cadet, 21 May, 1888. Ensign, 1 July, 1894. Lieutenant, Junior Grade, 3 March, 1899.
MALLON, JOHN H.
Mate, 2 January, 1863. Appointment revoked 26 December, 1865.
MALLORY, CHARLES K.
Naval Cadet, 25 September, 1891. Assistant Engineer, 1 July, 1897. Rank changed to Ensign, 3 March, 1899. Lieutenant, Junior Grade, 1 July, 1900.
MALLORY, DWIGHT F.
Ensign (Spanish-American War), 25 May, 1898. Honorably discharged 3 September, 1898.
MALLORY, JOHN S.
Acting Assistant Paymaster, 9 March, 1863. Resigned 1 April, 1864.
MALLORY, STEVENSON B.
Midshipman, 12 June, 1872. Graduated 20 June, 1876. Died 14 November, 1878.
MALLOY, CHARLES F.
Acting Third Assistant Engineer, 26 April, 1864. Appointment revoked 17 June, 1865.
MALONE, JOHN D.
Acting Assistant Surgeon, 20 October, 1864. Honorably discharged 2 May, 1868.
MALONE, S. B.
Assistant Surgeon, 11 August, 1826. Surgeon, 14 April, 1831. Resigned 20 September, 1831. Surgeon, 17 May, 1832. Resigned 16 April, 1834.
HALONEY, FRANCIS R.
Assistant Paymaster (Spanish-American War), 2 September, 1898. Honorably discharged 7 March, 1899.
MALONEY, PATRICK.
Acting Third Assistant Engineer, 9 February, 1864. Honorably discharged 27 October, 1865.
MALOON, SOLON H.
Carpenter, 16 November, 1875. Retired List, 27 August, 1894.
MANCHESTER, ALBERT A.
Acting Third Assistant Engineer, 6 March, 1865. Honorably discharged 5 April, 1866.
MANCK, EDWARD A.
Acting Warrant Machinist, 6 July, 1899.
MANDELL, AUGUST H.
Mate, 1862. Acting Ensign, 4 March, 1864. Resigned (sick) 18 March, 1865.
MANIER, JOHN T.
Ensign (Spanish-American War), 6 July, 1898. Honorably discharged 19 August, 1898.
MANION, WALTER J.
Naval Cadet, 6 September, 1890. Ensign, 1 July, 1896. Lieutenant, Junior Grade, 1 July, 1899.
MANKINS, JOHN.
Sailmaker, 17 February, 1809. Last appearance on Records of Navy Department, 1815. Furloughed.
MANLEY, HENRY DeH.
Acting Midshipman, 25 September, 1856. Midshipman, 15 June, 1860. Master, 19 September, 1861. Lieutenant, 16 July, 1862. Lieutenant-Commander, 25 July, 1866. Commander, 5 April, 1874. Retired List, 31 January, 1883. Died 29 November, 1893.
MANLOVE, DAVID.
Master, 24 May, 1814. Last appearance on Records of Navy Department, 1815. Philadelphia.

GENERAL NAVY REGISTER. 349

MANN, ALLEN A.
Mate, 3 September, 1863. Honorably discharged 23 August, 1865.
MANN, ALBERT L.
Acting Third Assistant Engineer, 1 October, 1862. Acting First Assistant Engineer, 13 May, 1863. Resigned 5 June, 1865.
MANN, GEORGE.
Midshipman, 15 June, 1801. Lieutenant, 26 March, 1809. Resigned 1 October, 1811.
MANN, GEORGE R.
Acting Assistant Surgeon, 21 September, 1861. Died 20 August, 1864.
MANN, LEVI S.
Mate, 27 August, 1862. Resigned 21 August, 1863.
MANN, W. H.
Midshipman, 15 November, 1809. Resigned 19 August, 1811.
MANN, WILLIAM A.
Acting Assistant Paymaster, 20 August, 1862. Mustered out 1 January, 1866.
MANN, WILLIAM M.
Mate, 25 July, 1863. Resigned 12 April, 1864. Acting Ensign, 9 August, 1864. Appointment revoked 30 August, 1864.
MANNEY, HENRY N.
Midshipman, 24 September, 1861. Graduated June, 1866. Ensign, 12 March, 1868. Master, 26 March, 1869. Lieutenant, 21 March, 1870. Lieutenant-Commander, 7 October, 1886. Commander, 10 May, 1895.
MANNING, CHARLES E.
Cadet Engineer, 14 September, 1876. Graduated 10 June, 1880. Assistant Engineer, 10 June, 1882. Resigned 30 January, 1891.
MANNING, CHARLES H.
Third Assistant Engineer, 19 February, 1863. Second Assistant Engineer, 25 July, 1866. First Assistant Engineer, 26 October, 1872. Retired List, 4 June, 1884.
MANNING, EDWARD.
Mate, 16 February, 1864. Acting Ensign, 18 August, 1864. Honorably discharged 14 October, 1865. Acting Ensign, 4 August, 1866. Mustered out 15 August, 1867.
MANNING, EDWARD S.
Midshipman, 9 November, 1813. Resigned 24 November, 1814.
MANNING, EDWARD W.
Third Assistant Engineer, 21 May, 1853. Second Assistant Engineer, 25 June, 1855. First Assistant Engineer, 21 July, 1858. Dismissed 6 May, 1861.
MANNING, JAMES D.
Acting Ensign, 23 May, 1863. Died on the Courier, 25 September, 1863.
MANNING, JOHN.
Acting Chief Engineer, 1 December, 1862. Resigned 9 February, 1863.
MANNING, JOHN.
Midshipman, 10 May, 1820. Lieutenant, 17 May, 1828. Commander, 3 October, 1851. Reserved List, 13 September, 1855. Resigned 23 May, 1861.
MANNING, JOHN H.
Mate, 17 June, 1863. Resigned 21 April, 1864.
MANNING, THOMAS.
Acting Carpenter, 1 October, 1862. Resigned 20 April, 1865.
MANNING, THOMAS J.
Midshipman, 1 January, 1817. Lieutenant, 28 April, 1826. Commander, 24 July, 1843. Died 7 January, 1857.
MANNING, WILLIAM.
Mate, 6 February, 1862. Dismissed 4 November, 1862.
MANNING, WILLIAM.
Boatswain, 3 January, 1873. Chief Boatswain, 3 March, 1899. Retired List, 17 March, 1899.
MANNIX, D. PRATT.
Mate, 18 April, 1863. Acting Ensign, 30 November, 1863. Resigned 22 February, 1865.
MANNIX, DANIEL P.
Naval Cadet, 20 May, 1897. Graduated 30 June, 1900.
MANSER, EDWARD.
Acting Ensign, 22 April, 1863. Resigned 31 May, 1864.
MANSFIELD, CHARLES D.
Acting Assistant Paymaster, 19 August, 1864. Assistant Paymaster, 22 July, 1866. Passed Assistant Paymaster, 23 December, 1866. Paymaster, 25 September, 1875. Retired List, 18 June, 1888. Died 2 October, 1892.
MANSFIELD, HENRY B.
Midshipman, 27 February, 1863. Graduated June, 1867. Ensign, 18 December, 1868. Master, 21 March, 1870. Lieutenant, 21 March, 1871. Lieutenant-Commander, 3 January, 1890. Commander, 16 May, 1897.
MANSFIELD, HENRY T.
Acting Assistant Paymaster, 14 August, 1863. Resigned 30 January, 1865.
MANSFIELD, NEWTON.
Naval Cadet, 7 September, 1891. Assistant Engineer, 1 July, 1897. Rank changed to Ensign, 3 March, 1899. Lieutenant, Junior Grade, 1 July, 1900.
MANSFIELD, ROBERT H.
Acting Third Assistant Engineer, 20 January, 1865. Honorably discharged 11 September, 1865.
MANSFIELD, WILLIAM F.
Acting Third Assistant Engineer, 29 August, 1864. Honorably discharged 21 May, 1866.
MANSON, CHARLES A.
Acting Assistant Surgeon, 13 August, 1864. Resigned 23 November, 1864. Acting Assistant Surgeon, 18 January, 1865. Appointment revoked 28 June, 1865.

MANSON, CHARLES H.
Third Assistant Engineer, 26 February, 1851. Resigned 25 November, 1853.
MANSON, JOHN C.
Master, 15 July, 1812. Discharged 10 June, 1815.
MANSON, LUTHER.
Carpenter, 9 May, 1842. Died 20 September, 1867.
MANTER, EVERETT T.
Mate, 23 December, 1861. Acting Ensign, 4 December, 1862. Honorably discharged 20 September, 1865.
MANTON, BENJAMIN D.
Acting Lieutenant, 21 October, 1861. Resigned 10 September, 1863.
MANTZ, EZRA.
Midshipman, 29 July, 1800. Discharged 26 November, 1801, under Peace Establishment Act.
MAPES, CHARLES A.
Third Assistant Engineer, 17 August, 1847. Died 12 November, 1847.
MAFES, DANIEL T.
Third Assistant Engineer, 16 August, 1847. Second Assistant Engineer, 26 February, 1851. Resigned 21 June, 1855.
MAPLES, CHARLES R.
Acting Third Assistant Engineer, 8 June, 1863. Acting Second Assistant Engineer, 17 June, 1863. Dismissed 3 May, 1864.
MAPLES, EDWARD W.
Acting Third Assistant Engineer, 28 May, 1864. Resigned 11 January, 1865.
MAPLES, ISAAC B.
Acting Third Assistant Engineer, 18 December, 1861. Resigned 14 August, 1862. Acting Third Assistant Engineer, 13 November, 1862. Acting First Assistant Engineer, 14 July, 1863. Honorably discharged 21 February, 1866.
MAPLES, WILLIAM L.
Carpenter, 8 December, 1880. Retired List, 6 December, 1895.
MARA, WILLIAM.
Acting Third Assistant Engineer, 18 November, 1861. Acting Second Assistant Engineer, 7 October, 1862. Acting First Assistant Engineer, 29 September, 1864. Honorably discharged 3 September, 1865.
MARATTA, JAMES M.
Acting Second Assistant Engineer, 31 December, 1863. Honorably discharged 7 September, 1865.
MARBLE, CHARLES H.
Mate, 18 December, 1862. Dismissed 27 May, 1863. Mate, 24 March, 1864. Dismissed 29 June, 1864.
MARBLE, FRANK.
Naval Cadet, 4 September, 1884. Ensign, 1 July, 1890. Lieutenant, Junior Grade, 25 January, 1898. Lieutenant, 3 March, 1899.
MARBLE, RALPH N., Jr.
Naval Cadet, 19 May, 1894. Ensign, 4 April, 1900.
MARBLE, THOMAS D.
Mate, 24 July, 1863. Honorably discharged 5 June, 1865.
MARBURY, A. H.
Midshipman, 14 July, 1824. Passed Midshipman, 20 February, 1830. Lieutenant, 23 June, 1834. Died 6 December, 1843.
MARCELLIN, GEORGE A.
Midshipman, 4 June, 1801. Lieutenant, 3 March, 1807. Died 10 September, 1810.
MARCELLIN, H. F.
Midshipman, 20 June, 1806. Resigned 9 June, 1810.
MARCELLIN, H. F.
Midshipman, 4 June, 1812. Dismissed by Court-martial, 5 March, 1814.
MARCH, EDWARD D.
Acting Master, 26 February, 1862. Resigned 11 April, 1866.
MARCH, J. HOWARD.
Midshipman, 19 October, 1841. Passed Midshipman, 10 August, 1847. Dropped 13 September, 1855. Lieutenant on Active List, 15 September, 1855. Died 21 December, 1858.
MARCHAND, JOHN B.
Midshipman, 1 May, 1828. Passed Midshipman, 14 June, 1834. Lieutenant, 29 January, 1840. Commander, 14 September, 1855. Captain, 16 July, 1862. Commodore, 25 July, 1866. Retired List, 27 August, 1870. Died 13 April, 1875.
MARCHAND, NICHOLAS.
Midshipman, 30 November, 1814. Resigned 12 February, 1824.
MARCHANT, ELIJAH.
Gunner, date not known. Last appearance on Records of Navy Department.
MARCHANT, GEORGE W.
Mate, 6 April, 1864. Honorably discharged 2 September, 1866.
MARCHANT, WILLIAM B.
Acting Ensign, 8 April, 1864. Appointment revoked (sick) 17 December, 1864. Acting Ensign, 8 February, 1865. Honorably discharged 1 December, 1865.
MARCOUR, RAPHAEL O.
Assistant Surgeon (Spanish-American War), 29 June, 1898. Appointed Assistant Surgeon in Regular Service 7 June, 1900.
MARCY, SAMUEL.
Midshipman, 16 March, 1838. Passed Midshipman, 20 May, 1844. Master, 26 April, 1851. Lieutenant, 2 April, 1852. Died 28 January, 1862.
MARCY, WILLIAM G.
Purser, 1 April, 1853. Dismissed 25 March, 1871.

GENERAL NAVY REGISTER. 351

MARDEN, FREDERICK A.
Mate, 7 June, 1862. Dismissed 20 November, 1862.
MARFIELD, GEORGE W.
Acting Third Assistant Engineer, 16 July, 1863. Honorably discharged 29 October, 1865.
MARGORUM, D. B.
Midshipman, 30 April, 1800. Resigned 26 October, 1800.
MARIE, LOUIS E.
Ensign (Spanish-American War), 23 June, 1898. Honorably discharged 24 September, 1898.
MARIN, MATTHIAS C.
Midshipman, 3 January, 1832. Lieutenant, 29 March, 1844. Commander, 18 October, 1861. Retired List, 15 August, 1864. Captain, Retired List, 4 April, 1867. Died 22 January, 1895.
MARIX, ADOLPH.
Midshipman, 26 September, 1864. Graduated June, 1868. Master, 12 July, 1870. Lieutenant, 24 May, 1872. Lieutenant-Commander, 9 May, 1893. Commander, 3 March, 1899.
MARKHAM, BENJAMIN.
Carpenter, 8 January, 1881. Chief Carpenter, 3 March, 1899. Died 8 February, 1900.
MARKHAM, F. P.
Assistant Surgeon, 10 December, 1814. Last appearance on Records of Navy Department, 1822. Dead.
MARKLEY, ARTHUR D.
Acting Assistant Surgeon, 14 September, 1861. Resigned 12 April, 1862.
MARKOE, P. J.
Mate, 8 May, 1862. Acting Ensign, 14 January, 1864. Resigned 21 April, 1865.
MARKS, A. J.
Mate, 28 March, 1865. Honorably discharged 28 October, 1865.
MARKS, GEORGE H.
Mate, 30 December, 1862. Acting Ensign, 14 April, 1864. Honorably discharged 21 August, 1865. Mate, 26 January, 1870. Drowned 7 March, 1872.
MARKS, JAMES.
Acting Master, 1 August, 1861. Appointment revoked 10 December, 1861.
MARKS, THOMAS H.
Acting Ensign, 23 August, 1864. Resigned (sick) 2 February, 1865.
MARLEY, JOHN.
Boatswain, 7 January, 1862. Warranted 29 August, 1862. Dismissed 31 December, 1865.
MARMION, ROBERT A.
Assistant Surgeon, 14 April, 1868. Surgeon, 3 June, 1879. Medical Inspector, 15 June, 1895. Medical Director, 25 October, 1899.
MARMION, WILLIAM V.
Acting Assistant Surgeon, 27 April, 1866. Assistant Surgeon, 18 June, 1866. Resigned 10 January, 1871.
MARNER, RICHARD.
Lieutenant, 1 March, 1799. Last appearance on Records of Navy Department.
MARPLE, CHARLES R.
Mate, 23 November, 1863. Honorably discharged 2 September, 1865. Mate, 14 August, 1867. Mustered out 27 August, 1868. Mate, 12 November, 1869. Appointment revoked 9 July, 1870.
MARPLE, DAVID.
Carpenter, 13 October, 1840. Resigned 3 October, 1848.
MARR, ROBERT A.
Midshipman, 29 April, 1840. Passed Midshipman, 11 July, 1846. Master, 5 May, 1854. Lost in the Albany, 28 September, 1854.
MARRAST, A. B.
Midshipman, 21 March, 1829. Dismissed 10 December, 1830.
MARRAST, AUGUSTUS.
Midshipman, 1 January, 1825. Resigned 4 December, 1830.
MARRAST, J. F.
Midshipman, 29 March, 1834. Lieutenant, 16 July, 1840. Dismissed by Court-martial, 15 October, 1841.
MARROW, HENRY C.
Acting Third Assistant Engineer, 4 December, 1863. Honorably discharged 15 May, 1865.
MARS, EDWARD.
First Assistant Engineer, 21 September, 1861. Resigned 11 February, 1862.
MARS, PHILIP L.
First Assistant Engineer, 1 July, 1861. Dismissed 2 November, 1861.
MARS, ROBERT W.
Acting Third Assistant Engineer, 10 September, 1862. Acting Second Assistant Engineer, 24 October, 1864. Honorably discharged 18 February, 1866.
MARSDEN, CHARLES.
Acting Ensign, 15 July, 1863. Honorably discharged 5 November, 1865.
MARSDEN, CHARLES.
Acting Ensign, 5 August, 1863. Honorably discharged 5 November, 1865.
MARSH, C. F.
Acting Master's Mate, 14 September, 1864. Discharged 1 August, 1865.
MARSH, CHARLES C.
Cadet Midshipman, 18 September, 1875. Graduated 10 June, 1881. Ensign, Junior Grade, 3 March, 1883. Ensign, 26 June, 1884. Lieutenant, Junior Grade, 14 May, 1891. Lieutenant, 7 June, 1895.

GENERAL NAVY REGISTER.

MARSH, EDWARD T. T.
  Acting Assistant Surgeon, 9 February, 1864. Honorably discharged 29 March, 1868.
MARSH, FRANCIS.
  Acting First Assistant Engineer, 1 November, 1862. Honorably discharged 15 September, 1865.
MARSH, FRANK.
  Acting Third Assistant Engineer, 16 July, 1863. Acting Second Assistant Engineer, 30 November, 1864. Honorably discharged 25 January, 1866.
MARSH, HAZARD.
  Mate, 13 December, 1861. Acting Ensign, 18 December, 1862. Honorably discharged 19 December, 1865.
MARSH, HENRY C.
  Mate, 25 February, 1864. Honorably discharged 5 November, 1865.
MARSH, ISRAEL.
  Acting First Assistant Engineer, 12 December, 1863. Honorably discharged 17 December, 1865.
MARSHALL, ALBERT W.
  Naval Cadet, 6 September, 1892. Assistant Engineer, 6 May, 1898. Rank changed to Ensign, 3 March, 1899.
MARSHALL, BENJAMIN.
  Acting Assistant Surgeon, 12 August, 1861. Honorably discharged 28 July, 1866.
MARSHALL, ELBERT P.
  Mate, 21 November, 1863. Honorably discharged 26 October, 1865.
MARSHALL, E. Y.
  Midshipman, 1 January, 1818. Last appearance on Records of Navy Department, 1822.
MARSHALL, FRANK.
  Mate, 12 January, 1863. Acting Ensign, 24 November, 1863. Honorably discharged 19 September, 1865.
MARSHALL, GEORGE.
  Gunner, 15 July, 1809. Master, 19 February, 1841. Resigned 26 August, 1846. Gunner from 15 July, 1809, to 7 December, 1846. Died 2 August, 1855.
MARSHALL, G. J.
  Gunner, 19 March, 1841. Died 11 November, 1847.
MARSHALL, JAMES.
  Midshipman, 9 May, 1803. Resigned 18 May, 1810.
MARSHALL, JAMES.
  Acting Master, 29 June, 1863. Resigned 14 September, 1864.
MARSHALL, JAMES L.
  Acting Third Assistant Engineer, 12 November, 1862. Acting Second Assistant Engineer, 19 November, 1863. Dismissed 5 April, 1864.
MARSHALL, JAMES W.
  Midshipman, 1 March, 1825. Resigned 19 May, 1826.
MARSHALL, JOHN.
  Gunner, 6 July, 1798. Last appearance on Records of Navy Department.
MARSHALL, JOHN.
  Midshipman, 1 January, 1818. Lieutenant, 3 March, 1827. Resigned 18 September, 1838.
MARSHALL, JOHN.
  Midshipman, 4 July, 1805. Died 22 October, 1809.
MARSHALL, JOHN F.
  Naval Cadet, 8 September, 1891. Assistant Engineer, 1 July, 1897. Rank changed to Ensign, 3 March, 1899. Lieutenant, Junior Grade, 6 July, 1900.
MARSHALL, JOHN H.
  Acting Ensign, 18 March, 1865. Honorably discharged 13 May, 1865.
MARSHALL, JOHN H.
  Midshipman, 10 May, 1820. Lieutenant, 17 May, 1828. Died 1 June, 1850.
MARSHALL, JOSHUA H.
  Acting Assistant Paymaster, 26 February, 1863. Honorably discharged 23 October, 1865.
MARSHALL, LOUIS J.
  Mate, 8 August, 1864. Honorably discharged 28 August, 1865.
MARSHALL, ROBERT.
  Midshipman, 21 November, 1815. Drowned 20 March, 1822.
MARSHALL, SAMUEL.
  Midshipman, 1 May, 1822. Died 24 August, 1823.
MARSHALL, S. R.
  Assistant Surgeon, 14 May, 1799. Surgeon, 16 January, 1800. Died 20 May, 1828.
MARSHALL, THOMAS.
  Assistant Surgeon, 13 December, 1800. Died 17 November, 1808.
MARSHALL, THOMAS.
  Gunner, date not known. Died in August, 1822.
MARSHALL, THOMAS R.
  Mate, 20 June, 1863. Resigned 8 May, 1865.
MARSHALL, WILLIAM A.
  Midshipman, 27 June, 1867. Graduated 6 June, 1871. Ensign, 14 July, 1872. Master, 22 April, 1875. Lieutenant, 15 April, 1882. Lieutenant-Commander, 3 March, 1899.
MARSHMAN, C. P.
  Acting Master, 1 June, 1861. Resigned 18 August, 1862.
MARSILLOT, MALCOLM G.
  Acting Third Assistant Engineer, 7 June, 1864. Resigned (sick) 21 March, 1865.
MARSLAND, CHARLES F.
  Third Assistant Engineer, 8 December, 1862. Resigned 6 September, 1865.

GENERAL NAVY REGISTER. 353

MARSLAND, EDWARD.
First Assistant Engineer, 14 August, 1861. Resigned 4 June, 1864.
MARSTELLER, EMLYN H.
Assistant Surgeon, 12 January, 1876. Passed Assistant Surgeon, 12 January, 1880. Surgeon, 22 June, 1894.
MARSTERS, GEORGE W.
Acting Assistant Surgeon, 14 March, 1865. Honorably discharged 10 October, 1865.
MARSTON, J. J.
Assistant Surgeon, 15 August, 1821. Last appearance on Records of Navy Department.
MARSTON, JOHN.
Midshipman, 15 April, 1813. Lieutenant, 13 January, 1825. Commander, 8 September, 1841. Captain, 14 September, 1855. Retired List, 21 December, 1861. Commodore, Retired List, 16 July, 1862. Rear-Admiral on Retired List, 28 March, 1881. Died 8 April, 1885.
MARTENS, K. F.
Ensign (Spanish-American War), 2 June, 1898. Honorably discharged 6 January, 1899.
MARTHON, JOSEPH.
Mate, 20 May, 1863. Acting Ensign, 26 October, 1863. Acting Master, recommendation of Commanding Officer, 5 August, 1864. Honorably discharged 31 December, 1865. Acting Master, 19 April, 1866. Ensign, 12 March, 1868. Master, 18 December, 1868. Lieutenant, 21 March, 1870. Lieutenant-Commander, 1 July, 1882. Died 19 November, 1891.
MARTIN, BERNARD.
Acting Second Assistant Engineer, 19 February, 1864. Honorably discharged 4 December, 1865.
MARTIN, BYARD
Acting Carpenter, 15 December, 1862. Honorably discharged 1 November, 1865.
MARTIN, CHARLES.
Assistant Surgeon, 5 September, 1848. Surgeon, 22 April, 1861. Medical Inspector, 3 March, 1871. Medical Director, 6 October, 1873. Retired List, 21 August, 1884. Died 14 January, 1892.
MARTIN, DANIEL B.
First Assistant Engineer, 17 January, 1842. Chief Engineer, 14 May, 1847. Engineer-in-Chief, 18 October, 1853. Relieved as Engineer-in-Chief, 17 October, 1857. Resigned November, 1859.
MARTIN, EDWARD D.
Mate, 6 February, 1862. Acting Ensign, 17 July, 1863. Honorably discharged 29 November, 1865.
MARTIN, EDWIN M.
Assistant Surgeon, 12 April, 1875. Died 20 August, 1878.
MARTIN, ELIAS G.
Acting Master, 26 February, 1862. Honorably discharged 3 December, 1865.
MARTIN, ERASTUS F.
Acting Third Assistant Engineer, 25 November, 1861. Resigned 25 May, 1863.
MARTIN, ERNEST D.
Acting Assistant Surgeon, 9 March, 1865. Honorably discharged 9 October, 1865. Acting Assistant Surgeon, 27 April, 1866. Assistant Surgeon, 18 June, 1866. Died 17 July, 1868.
MARTIN, E. S.
Mate, 29 March, 1870. Appointment revoked 7 November, 1870.
MARTIN, FRANCIS.
Gunner, 19 November, 1892.
MARTIN, GEORGE E.
Acting Assistant Paymaster, 7 February, 1865. Mustered out 21 November, 1865.
MARTIN, GEORGE M.
Acting Master, 28 January, 1862. Dismissed 27 June, 1864.
MARTIN, GEORGE R.
Acting Assistant Paymaster, 30 June, 1862. Assistant Paymaster, 30 June, 1864. Paymaster, 4 May, 1866. Dismissed 26 September, 1877.
MARTIN, HENRY F.
Acting Ensign, 20 October, 1864. Honorably discharged 23 August, 1865.
MARTIN, HENRY M.
Assistant Surgeon, 21 March, 1870. Surgeon, 24 April, 1884. Retired List, 4 December, 1890. Died 16 January, 1891.
MARTIN, H. L.
Midshipman, 11 December, 1802. Resigned 6 December, 1805.
MARTIN, JAMES.
Master, date not known. Discharged 15 April, 1815.
MARTIN, JAMES.
Acting Ensign, 1 October, 1862. Resigned 9 February, 1863. Acting Ensign, 29 June, 1863. Honorably discharged 9 April, 1866.
MARTIN, JAMES.
Mate, 5 July, 1863. Resigned 28 September, 1864.
MARTIN, JAMES C.
Acting Carpenter, 1 October, 1862. Resigned 30 January, 1863.
MARTIN, JOHN.
Cadet Midshipman, 28 September, 1882. Resigned 14 June, 1883. Reappointed 4 September, 1883. Resigned 7 January, 1887. Ensign (Spanish-American War), 24 May, 1898. Honorably discharged 20 September, 1898.
MARTIN, JOHN.
Gunner, 3 March, 1832. Resigned 24 December, 1832. Gunner, 6 April, 1838. Died 5 November, 1856.

23

MARTIN, JOHN.
Sailmaker, 26 October, 1872. Retired List, 21 June, 1894. Died 15 August, 1894.
MARTIN, JOHN.
Purser, 5 October, 1798. Resigned 7 October, 1801.
MARTIN, JOHN C.
Pharmacist, 15 September, 1898.
MARTIN, JOHN R.
Assistant Surgeon, 9 May, 1815. Resigned 18 December, 1815.
MARTIN, JOHN R.
Assistant Paymaster, 14 June, 1878. Passed Assistant Paymaster, 30 January, 1882. Paymaster, 2 February, 1894.
MARTIN, JOSEPH.
Boatswain, 2 December, 1799. Last appearance on Records of Navy Department.
MARTIN, LUTHER.
Midshipman, 9 March, 1838. Resigned 23 April, 1840.
MARTIN, LUTHER D.
Carpenter, 1 February, 1896. Resigned 10 June, 1899.
MARTIN, LUTHER L.
Carpenter, 3 October, 1872. Chief Carpenter, 3 March, 1899.
MARTIN, NEILL.
Acting Gunner, 27 August, 1863. Honorably discharged 9 July, 1865.
MARTIN, ROBERT F.
Midshipman, 1 May, 1814. Died 3 July, 1825.
MARTIN, SAMUEL G.
Acting Master, 5 September, 1861. Resigned 11 February, 1862.
MARTIN, SIMEON, JR.
Midshipman, 1 March, 1799. Resigned 19 August, 1800.
MARTIN, THOMAS S.
Ensign (Spanish-American War), 4 June, 1898. Honorably discharged 28 September, 1898.
MARTIN, WILLIAM.
Master, 12 January, 1814. Discharged 15 April, 1815.
MARTIN, WILLIAM.
Acting Assistant Surgeon, 10 January, 1874. Honorably discharged 30 June, 1879.
MARTIN, WILLIAM.
Acting Master, 12 May, 1862. Honorably discharged 15 December, 1865.
MARTIN, WILLIAM.
Mate, 10 March, 1863. Resigned 16 November, 1863.
MARTIN, WILLIAM.
Assistant Surgeon, 14 April, 1882. Surgeon, 1 October, 1890. Retired List, 25 December, 1893.
MARTIN, WILLIAM J.
Acting First Assistant Engineer, 15 November, 1862. Appointment revoked (sick) 11 December, 1863.
MARTINDALE, FRANK E.
Acting Assistant Surgeon, 27 May, 1861. Resigned 5 April, 1864.
MARTINE, ALFRED H.
Acting Ensign, 3 January, 1865. Honorably discharged 30 July, 1868.
MARTINE, CHARLES A.
Acting Third Assistant Engineer, 27 May, 1862. Acting Second Assistant Engineer, 30 July, 1863. Honorably discharged 21 November, 1865.
MARTINE, WILLIAM L.
Acting Master, 9 October, 1861. Acting Volunteer Lieutenant, 2 December, 1864. Honorably discharged 14 December, 1865.
MARVEL, JOHN H.
Mate, 5 March, 1862. Resigned 19 August, 1862.
MARVELL, GEORGE R.
Naval Cadet, 7 September, 1885. Ensign, 1 July, 1891. Lieutenant, Junior Grade, 6 October, 1898. Lieutenant, 3 March, 1899.
MARVIN, GEORGE H.
Acting Assistant Surgeon, 20 September, 1862. Resigned 11 March, 1865.
MARVIN, JOSEPH D.
Acting Midshipman, 25 September, 1856. Midshipman, 15 June, 1860. Master, 19 September, 1861. Lieutenant, 16 July, 1862. Lieutenant-Commander, 12 April, 1866. Commander, 12 December, 1873. Died 10 April, 1877.
MASON, CHARLES H.
Acting Assistant Surgeon, 30 November, 1861. Died October, 1864.
MASON, CHARLES S.
Acting Third Assistant Engineer, 15 February, 1863. Died 13 November, 1863.
MASON, DAVID.
Mate, 18 February, 1862. Acting Ensign, 17 November, 1862. Deserted 13 September, 1864.
MASON, FREDERICK.
Acting Ensign, Admiral Farragut's Staff, 1 July, 1864. Honorably discharged 20 January, 1866.
MASON, GEORGE.
Acting Third Assistant Engineer, 27 September, 1861. Acting Second Assistant Engineer, 26 January, 1863. Appointment revoked (sick) 6 August, 1864.
MASON, GEORGE W.
Lieutenant (Spanish-American War), 30 April, 1898. Honorably discharged 14 November, 1898.
MASON, HENRY.
Third Assistant Engineer, 23 March, 1848. Second Assistant Engineer, 13 Septem-

GENERAL NAVY REGISTER. 355

MASON, JAMES—Continued.
ber, 1849. First Assistant Engineer, 26 February, 1851. Resigned 14 November, 1853. First Assistant Engineer, 31 May, 1861. Chief Engineer, 21 May, 1863. Retired List, 16 October, 1868.

MASON, JAMES.
Midshipman, 18 June, 1812. Resigned 28 December, 1816.

MASON, JOHN.
Sailmaker, 1 June, 1804. Dismissed by Court-martial 12 July, 1805.

MASON, JAMES L.
Mate. Appointment revoked 20 August, 1862.

MASON, JOHN M.
Midshipman, 31 March, 1831. Passed Midshipman, 15 June, 1837. Drowned 7 July, 1837.

MASON, JOHN T.
Assistant Surgeon, 6 September, 1837. Surgeon, 15 July, 1849. Resigned 6 May, 1861.

MASON, JOHN W.
Mate, 27 February, 1865. Resigned 12 May, 1865.

MASON, JOHN W.
Mate, 17 February, 1864. Resigned 12 May, 1865.

MASON, JOHN Y., Jr.
Purser, 18 April, 1845. Resigned 2 January, 1858.

MASON, LUCIUS M.
Midshipman, 19 October, 1841. Died 7 January, 1845.

MASON, MURRAY.
Midshipman, 14 November, 1823. Passed Midshipman, 23 March, 1829. Lieutenant, 3 March, 1831. Commander, 25 February, 1854. Reserved List, 14 September, 1855. Commander on Active List, 25 February, 1854. Resigned 16 April, 1861.

MASON, NEWTON E.
Midshipman, 22 July, 1865. Graduated June, 1869. Ensign, 12 July, 1870. Master, 12 July, 1871. Lieutenant, 8 November, 1874. Lieutenant-Commander, 10 November, 1896. Commander, 2 November, 1899.

MASON, RANDOLPH T.
Surgeon, 17 March, 1859. Dismissed 10 May, 1861.

MASON, RICHARD P.
Midshipman, 15 June, 1839. Died 10 May, 1847.

MASON, RUFUS O.
Acting Assistant Surgeon, 21 October, 1861. Resigned 2 February, 1864.

MASON, THEODORUS B. M.
Midshipman, 20 September, 1864. Graduated June, 1868. Ensign, 19 April, 1869. Master, 12 July, 1870. Lieutenant, 20 November, 1872. Lieutenant-Commander, 23 January, 1894. Retired List, 8 December, 1894. Died 15 October, 1899.

MASON, THOMAS.
Mate, 20 July, 1863. Acting Ensign, 18 August, 1864. Discharged 8 February, 1868.

MASON, THOMAS.
Mate, 13 December, 1861. Resigned 19 September, 1862.

MASON, WESTWOOD T.
Midshipman, 4 January, 1800. Resigned 21 August, 1802.

MASON, WILLIAM.
Acting Third Assistant Engineer, 20 April, 1863. Acting Second Assistant Engineer, 26 May, 1864. Honorably discharged 19 August, 1865.

MASON, WILLIAM H.
Assistant Engineer (Spanish-American War), 17 June, 1898. Honorably discharged 2 November, 1898.

MASON, WILLIAM W.
Acting Master, 22 October, 1861. Resigned 8 February, 1862.

MASSER, WILLIAM H. E.
Midshipman, 1 October, 1866. Graduated 6 June, 1871. Ensign, 14 July, 1872. Retired List, 8 May, 1876.

MASSEY, ARTHUR W.
Carpenter, 19 August, 1874. Retired List, 20 June, 1896.

MASSEY, ELEAZER.
Midshipman, 17 December, 1810. Resigned 30 April, 1814.

MASSEY, GEORGE B.
Assistant Engineer (Spanish-American War), 25 May, 1898. Honorably discharged 16 May, 1899.

MASTEN, THOMAS C.
Assistant Paymaster, 11 October, 1861. Paymaster, 14 April, 1862. Dismissed 9 February, 1870.

MASTERS, PHINEAS.
Midshipman, 16 February, 1809. Resigned 14 October, 1809.

MASURY, JOHN M.
Lieutenant, Junior Grade (Spanish-American War), 3 August, 1898. Honorably discharged 12 October, 1898.

MASURY, SAMUEL.
Gunner, 2 December, 1799. Dismissed 21 January, 1803.

MATHER, GEORGE H.
Naval Cadet, 22 May, 1888. Graduated. Honorably discharged 30 June, 1894. Ensign (Spanish-American War), 21 May, 1898. Honorably discharged 2 December, 1898.

MATHER, HENRY W.
Mate, 19 August, 1862. Acting Ensign, 27 May, 1863. Acting Master, 18 April, 1865. Honorably discharged 1 April, 1866.

MATHER, MASON W.
Third Assistant Engineer, 17 December, 1862. Second Assistant Engineer, 8 April, 1864. Resigned 3 March, 1869.
MATHER, S. W.
Acting Master, 17 May, 1861. Killed in action 22 March, 1862.
MATHES, GEORGE.
Acting Ensign, 20 September, 1862. Deserted 28 January, 1863.
MATHEWS, CLARENCE H.
Cadet Engineer, 14 September, 1876. Assistant Engineer, 1 July, 1883. Passed Assistant Engineer, 27 September, 1893. Rank changed to Lieutenant, 3 March, 1899.
MATHEWS, JAMES E.
Naval Cadet, 20 May, 1895. At sea prior to final graduation.
MATLACK, JOHN N.
Acting Third Assistant Engineer, 6 October, 1864. Honorably discharged 30 October, 1865.
MATTAIR, JAMES O.
Acting Master, 4 January, 1862. Appointment revoked (sick) 22 April, 1863.
MATTHEWS, A. P.
Mate, 23 January, 1862. Accidentally killed on Wyandank, 24 September, 1863.
MATTHEWS, CHARLES.
Boatswain, 27 December, 1834. Drowned 9 August, 1842.
MATTHEWS, BENJAMIN.
Midshipman, 2 April, 1804. Resigned 31 December, 1805.
MATTHEWS, EDWARD S.
Assistant Surgeon, 30 July, 1861. Surgeon, 8 January, 1867. Died 16 August, 1881.
MATTHEWS, EDMUND O.
Acting Midshipman, 2 October, 1851. Midshipman, 9 June, 1855. Passed Midshipman, 15 April, 1858. Master, 4 November, 1858. Lieutenant, 27 June, 1860. Lieutenant-Commander, 16 July, 1862. Commander, 22 April, 1870. Captain, 14 September, 1881. Commodore, 21 July, 1894. Rear-Admiral, 19 June, 1897. Retired List, 24 October, 1898.
MATTHEWS, JAMES.
Acting Boatswain, 31 August, 1899.
MATTHEWS, JOHN.
Midshipman, 22 February, 1838. Passed Midshipman, 20 May, 1844. Master, 30 August, 1851. Lieutenant, 13 July, 1852. Drowned 25 October, 1853.
MATTHEWS, JOHN.
Acting Assistant Surgeon, 12 August, 1861. Resigned 1 April, 1863.
MATTHEWS, JOHN.
Acting Third Assistant Engineer, 13 August, 1863. Acting Second Assistant Engineer, 16 February, 1865. Honorably discharged 24 November, 1867.
MATTHEWS, JOSEPH H.
Acting Third Assistant Engineer, 13 December, 1862. Acting Second Assistant Engineer, 2 November, 1864. Honorably discharged 20 August, 1865.
MATTHEWS, JOHN P.
Acting Third Assistant Engineer, 25 March, 1865. Honorably discharged 16 June, 1866. Acting Third Assistant Engineer, 23 February, 1867. Mustered out 8 May, 1869.
MATTHEWS, JOHN R.
Second Assistant Engineer, 17 January, 1842. First Assistant Engineer, 10 July, 1847. Resigned 17 May, 1849.
MATTHEWS, J. RUTHERFORD.
Chaplain, 24 September, 1869. Retired List, 14 August, 1893. Died 27 September, 1899.
MATTHEWS, SAMUEL.
Third Assistant Engineer, 20 February, 1847. Second Assistant Engineer, 24 January, 1848. First Assistant Engineer, 11 January, 1849. Resigned 18 July, 1849.
MATTHEWS, WILLIAM.
Acting Third Assistant Engineer, 1 February, 1864. Honorably discharged 4 December, 1865.
MATTHEWSON, ARTHUR.
Assistant Surgeon, 30 July, 1861. Passed Assistant Surgeon, 5 July, 1864. Surgeon, 14 March, 1865.
MATTICE, ASA M.
Cadet Engineer, 1 October, 1872. Assistant Engineer, 26 February, 1875. Passed Assistant Engineer, 31 May, 1880. Resigned 30 June, 1890.
MATTINGLEY, THOMAS.
Acting Third Assistant Engineer, 8 June, 1864. Honorably discharged 6 November, 1865.
MATTISON, JOSEPH.
Midshipman, 30 November, 1814. Lieutenant, 13 January, 1825. Commander, 8 September, 1841. Resigned 20 November, 1851.
MATTISON, SYLVESTER.
Acting Master, 13 November, 1861. Resigned 9 July, 1862.
MAUGHLIN, JAMES.
Third Assistant Engineer, 29 October, 1861. Second Assistant Engineer, 3 August, 1863. Resigned 11 August, 1865.
MAULL, WILLIAM N.
Sailmaker, 18 January, 1849. Retired List, 16 November, 1872. Died 24 January, 1881.
MAULSBY, GEORGE.
Assistant Surgeon, 7 March, 1838. Surgeon, 14 April, 1852. Medical Director, 3 March, 1871. Retired List, 27 December, 1872. Died 27 October, 1886.

GENERAL NAVY REGISTER. 357

MAULSBY, JOHN H.
Midshipman, 21 April, 1824. Resigned 6 April, 1829.
MAULSBY, J. H.
Midshipman, 6 April, 1827. Drowned 13 July, 1833.
MAUNDER, SAMUEL H.
Mate, 30 November, 1863. Acting Ensign, 22 July, 1864. Resigned 27 April, 1865.
MAURICE, C. STUART.
Third Assistant Engineer, 18 November, 1862. Second Assistant Engineer, 23 March, 1864. Resigned 21 December, 1865.
MAURY, ALEXANDER C.
Midshipman, 1 February, 1826. Passed Midshipman, 28 April, 1832. Lieutenant, 8 March, 1837. Died 23 June, 1840.
MAURY, JEFFERSON.
Midshipman, 9 September, 1841. Passed Midshipman, 10 August, 1847. Dismissed 10 May, 1855.
MAURY, JOHN M.
Third Assistant Engineer, 23 March, 1848. Second Assistant Engineer, 26 February, 1851. First Assistant Engineer, 26 February, 1851. Resigned 17 September, 1856.
MAURY, JOHN M.
Midshipman, 16 January, 1809. Lieutenant, 28 June, 1811. Died 25 June, 1823.
MAURY, JOHN S.
Midshipman, 10 February, 1838. Passed Midshipman, 20 May, 1844. Master, 2 November, 1852. Lieutenant, 1 August, 1853. Dismissed 18 April, 1861.
MAURY, MATTHEW F.
Midshipman, 1 February, 1825. Passed Midshipman, 4 June, 1831. Lieutenant, 10 June, 1836. Reserved List, 14 September, 1855. Commander on Active List, 14 September, 1855. Dismissed 26 April, 1861.
MAURY, WILLIAM L.
Midshipman, 2 February, 1829. Passed Midshipman, 3 July, 1835. Lieutenant, 26 February, 1841. Resigned 20 April, 1861.
MAXFIELD, EDWARD F.
Acting Third Assistant Engineer, 22 October, 1862. Resigned 15 January, 1864.
MAXSON, FRANK O.
Civil Engineer, 26 October, 1881.
MAXWELL, CHARLES D.
Assistant Surgeon, 6 September, 1837. Surgeon, 18 October, 1849. Retired List, 21 October, 1868. Medical Director, 3 March, 1871. Died 18 April, 1890.
MAXWELL, D.
Acting Master, 26 August, 1861. Resigned 6 December, 1861.
MAXWELL, GEORGE.
Master, 18 June, 1812. Dismissed as Supernumerary, 6 March, 1813.
MAXWELL, H. D.
Midshipman, 29 February, 1829. Resigned 13 May, 1830.
MAXWELL, JAMES.
Mate, 1 May, 1862. Resigned 19 August, 1862.
MAXWELL, JAMES G.
Midshipman, 15 December, 1847. Passed Midshipman, 12 June, 1855. Master, 16 September, 1855. Lieutenant, 23 December, 1856. Lieutenant-Commander, 16 July, 1862. Died 19 July, 1867.
MAXWELL, JOSEPH.
Midshipman, 1 March, 1799. Lieutenant, 18 May, 1804. Died 11 February, 1806.
MAXWELL, RICHARD T.
Assistant Surgeon, 8 September, 1841. Resigned 16 April, 1851.
MAXWELL, W. B.
Midshipman, 16 January, 1809. Resigned 23 May, 1809.
MAXWELL, WILLIAM.
Midshipman, 20 June, 1806. Resigned 20 May, 1809.
MAXWELL, WILLIAM J.
Cadet Midshipman, 9 June, 1874. Graduated 22 June, 1882. Ensign, Junior Grade, 3 March, 1883. Ensign, 26 June, 1884. Lieutenant, Junior Grade, 4 July, 1893. Lieutenant, 6 April, 1897.
MAY, EDWARD.
Assistant Paymaster, 6 September, 1861. Paymaster, 14 April, 1862. Pay Inspector, 25 September, 1875. Pay Director, 24 December, 1883. Retired List, 20 January, 1900.
MAY, JAMES R.
Acting Assistant Surgeon, 25 February, 1864. Honorably discharged 7 August, 1865.
MAY, JOHN.
Lieutenant, 23 April, 1799. Discharged 1 May, 1801, under Peace Establishment Act.
MAY, JOHN.
Gunner, 14 May, 1800. Last appearance on Records of Navy Department.
MAY, JOHN B.
Mate, 27 January, 1862. Dismissed 4 April, 1862.
MAY, LUTHER C.
Acting Midshipman, 20 September, 1854. Midshipman, 11 June, 1858. Resigned 21 August, 1858.
MAY, ROBERT L.
Midshipman, 7 November, 1849. Passed Midshipman, 12 June, 1855. Master, 16 September, 1855. Lieutenant, 26 September, 1856. Lieutenant-Commander, 16 July, 1862. Retired from the service, 21 April, 1866.
MAY, SIDNEY H.
Midshipman, 28 July, 1864. Graduated 4 June, 1869. Ensign, 12 July, 1871. Master, 24 August, 1873. Lieutenant, 9 May, 1878. Died 20 July, 1892.

MAY, WILLIAM.
Midshipman, 2 May, 1831. Passed Midshipman, 23 June, 1838. Lieutenant, 8 September, 1841. Commander, 6 June, 1861. Died 10 October, 1861.
MAYCOCK, JAMES.
Acting Master and Pilot, 1 October, 1864. Honorably discharged 25 October, 1865.
MAYER, ALBERT.
Acting Third Assistant Engineer, 19 April, 1864. Honorably discharged 29 January, 1866.
MAYER, ALVARADO.
Acting Third Assistant Engineer, 3 March, 1865. Resigned 5 May, 1865.
MAYER, AUGUSTUS. N.
Cadet Midshipman, 24 June, 1876. Graduated 22 June, 1882. Ensign, Junior Grade, 3 March, 1883. Ensign, 26 June, 1884. Lieutenant, Junior Grade, 27 June, 1893. Lieutenant, 24 February, 1897.
MAYER, C. F., Jr.
Third Assistant Engineer, 26 August, 1859. Second Assistant Engineer, 21 April, 1863. Wholly retired 5 May, 1868.
MAYER, WILLIAM G.
Midshipman, 23 July, 1866. Graduated 7 June, 1870. Ensign, 13 July, 1871. Resigned 5 March, 1874. Lieutenant, Junior Grade (Spanish-American War), 23 June, 1898. Honorably discharged 28 September, 1898.
MAYER, WILLIAM H., Jr.
Acting Ensign, 24 July, 1862. Acting Master, 11 April, 1865. Ensign, 12 March, 1868. Master, 18 December, 1868. Lieutenant, 21 March, 1870. Died 1 June, 1879.
MAYER, WILLIAM H.
Midshipman, 16 January, 1809. Last appearance on Records of Navy Department, 10 February, 1809. Dead.
MAYERS, FRANKLIN M.
Acting Second Assistant Engineer, 1 October, 1862. Honorably discharged 5 November, 1865.
MAYHUGH, JOHN.
Acting Second Assistant Engineer, 1 June, 1864. Honorably discharged 21 October, 1865.
MAYLOY, E. C.
Acting Third Assistant Engineer, 28 January, 1862. Acting Second Assistant Engineer, 29 July, 1863. Honorably discharged 13 May, 1865.
MAYNARD, C. W.
Mate, 26 April, 1865. Honorably discharged 23 November, 1865.
MAYNARD, LAFAYETTE.
Midshipman, 4 February, 1832. Passed Midshipman, 23 June, 1838. Lieutenant, 19 October, 1843. Resigned 1 April, 1852.
MAYNARD, WASHBURN.
Midshipman, 6 October, 1862. Graduated June, 1866. Ensign, 12 March, 1868. Master, 26 March, 1869. Lieutenant, 21 March, 1870. Lieutenant-Commander, 27 September, 1884. Commander, 27 September, 1893. Captain, 9 March, 1900.
MAYO, HENRY A.
Mate, 21 January, 1864. Honorably discharged 15 June, 1866.
MAYO, HENRY O.
Assistant Surgeon, 24 February, 1846. Passed Assistant Surgeon, 4 February, 1851. Surgeon, 24 January, 1859. Medical Inspector, 3 March, 1871. Medical Director, 28 December, 1872. Retired List, 2 February, 1875. Died 1 January, 1892.
MAYO, HENRY T.
Midshipman, 13 June, 1872. Graduated 20 June, 1876. Ensign, 26 February, 1878. Lieutenant, Junior Grade, 25 February, 1885. Lieutenant, 5 December, 1890. Lieutenant-Commander, 11 June, 1899.
MAYO, ISAAC.
Midshipman, 15 November, 1809. Lieutenant, 4 February, 1815. Commander, 20 December, 1832. Captain, 8 September, 1841. Dismissed 18 May, 1861.
MAYO, WILLIAM.
Midshipman, 9 June, 1811. Resigned 23 May, 1815.
MAYO, WILLIAM K.
Midshipman, 18 October, 1841. Passed Midshipman, 10 August, 1847. Master, 14 September, 1855. Lieutenant, 15 September, 1855. Lieutenant-Commander, 16 July, 1862. Commander, 25 July, 1866. Captain, 12 December, 1873. Commodore, 2 July, 1882. Retired List, 18 May, 1886. Died 9 April, 1900.
MAYRANT, RUFUS.
Midshipman, 1 January, 1808. Resigned 11 June, 1813.
MAYRANT, R. P.
Midshipman, 1 April, 1828. Resigned 11 July, 1831.
MAYSON, F. G.
Midshipman, 28 April, 1838. Resigned 12 September, 1840.
MAZYCK, P. R.
Midshipman, 9 June, 1811. Last appearance on Records of Navy Department, 1815. Charleston.
McADAM, JOHN.
Assistant Surgeon, 10 December, 1814. Last appearance on Records of Navy Department, 1818. Furloughed.
McALISTER, ADAM A.
Chaplain, 10 November, 1873.
McALLISTER, ANDREW.
Cadet Engineer, 13 September, 1877. Assistant Engineer, 1 July, 1884. Passed Assistant Engineer, 9 May, 1895. Retired List, 14 November, 1896.

GENERAL NAVY REGISTER. 359

McALLISTER, CHARLES A.
  Passed Assistant Engineer (Spanish-American War), 10 June, 1898. Honorably discharged 8 February, 1899.
McALLISTER, GATES.
  Third Assistant Engineer, 23 June, 1863. Dropped 18 March, 1867.
McALLISTER, GUY.
  Acting Third Assistant Engineer, 22 August, 1864. Honorably discharged 5 August, 1866.
McALLISTER, ISAAC.
  Acting Third Assistant Engineer, 25 August, 1863. Acting Second Assistant Engineer, 12 January, 1865. Honorably discharged 21 January, 1868.
McALLISTER, JOHN.
  Midshipman, 1 September, 1811. Last appearance on Records of Navy Department, 1815. Brig Nautilus.
McALLISTER, JOHN G.
  Acting Assistant Surgeon, 1 May, 1865. Honorably discharged 12 February, 1866.
McALLISTER, JOHN.
  Mate, 4 November, 1862. Honorably discharged 2 November, 1865.
McALLISTER, RICHARD, Jr.
  Acting Ensign, 24 November, 1863. Honorably discharged 3 September, 1865.
McALLISTER, THOMAS.
  Acting Third Assistant Engineer, 5 January, 1865. Honorably discharged 24 October, 1865.
McALLISTER, T. G.
  Assistant Surgeon, 13 March, 1805. Surgeon, 16 January, 1808. Last appearance on Records of Navy Department. Dead.
McALLISTER, W. S.
  Acting Ensign, 1 October, 1862. Resigned 5 October, 1863.
McALPINE, A. W.
  Acting Gunner, 27 September, 1861. Appointment revoked 18 November, 1861.
McALPINE, KENNETH.
  Cadet Engineer, 13 September, 1877. Assistant Engineer, 1 July, 1883. Passed Assistant Engineer, 12 September, 1893. Rank changed to Lieutenant, 3 March, 1899.
McALPINE, JAMES.
  Assistant Surgeon, 7 August, 1799. Discharged 17 June, 1800.
McARANN, ROBERT M.
  Midshipman, 11 May, 1840. Passed Midshipman, 11 July, 1846. Master, 20 September, 1854. Lieutenant, 1 May, 1855. Dismissed 22 January, 1862.
McARTHUR, DAVID.
  Acting Third Assistant Engineer, 30 April, 1862. Acting Second Assistant Engineer, 8 July, 1863. Acting First Assistant Engineer, 16 July, 1864. Dismissed 27 June, 1865.
McARTHUR, WILLIAM P.
  Midshipman, 11 February, 1832. Passed Midshipman, 23 June, 1838. Lieutenant, 8 September, 1841. Died 23 December, 1850.
McAULIFFE, JOHN.
  Acting Third Assistant Engineer, 11 July, 1864. Honorably discharged 20 January, 1866.
McAUSLAND, ALEXANDER.
  First Assistant Engineer, 20 February, 1847. Resigned 24 November, 1850. Acting First Assistant Engineer, 2 November, 1861. Acting Chief Engineer, 19 January, 1863. Honorably discharged 1 December, 1866.
McAVOY, SAMUEL.
  Acting Third Assistant Engineer, 29 November, 1862. Resigned 7 July, 1863.
McAVOY, THOMAS F.
  Sailmaker, 15 August, 1873. Dismissed 17 February, 1874.
McBLAIR, CHARLES H.
  Midshipman, 4 March, 1823. Passed Midshipman, 23 March, 1829. Lieutenant, 12 July, 1831. Commander, 18 April, 1855. Resigned 22 April, 1861.
McBLAIR, THOMAS P.
  Purser, 11 November, 1839. Died 17 February, 1857.
McBLAIR, WILLIAM.
  Midshipman, 16 November, 1824. Passed Midshipman, 20 February, 1830. Lieutenant, 31 December, 1833. Commander, 14 September, 1855. Dismissed 20 April, 1861.
McBRIDE, De WITT C.
  Acting Third Assistant Engineer, 8 October, 1863. Honorably discharged 24 October, 1865.
McCAFFERY, JOHN.
  Boatswain, 18 July, 1866. Retired List, 20 December, 1889. Died 30 September, 1897.
McCAFFREY, JOHN.
  Acting Gunner, 22 January, 1864. Honorably discharged 2 October, 1865.
McCALL, ARCHIBALD.
  Midshipman, 8 March, 1800. Resigned 13 February, 1802.
McCALL, EDWARD R.
  Midshipman, 1 January, 1808. Lieutenant, 11 March, 1813. Commander, 3 March, 1825. Captain, 3 March, 1835. Died 31 July, 1853.
McCALL, JAMES P.
  Midshipman, 1 January, 1817. Died 10 October, 1823.
McCALL, THOMAS.
  Midshipman, 4 June, 1812. Dismissed 19 March, 1814.
McCALL, WILLIAM C.
  Assistant Surgeon, 14 August, 1826. Surgeon, 4 April, 1831. Died 15 September, 1831.

GENERAL NAVY REGISTER.

McCALLA, BOWMAN H.
Midshipman, 30 November, 1861. Graduated November, 1864. Ensign, 1 November, 1866. Master, 1 December, 1866. Lieutenant, 12 March, 1868. Lieutenant-Commander, 26 March, 1869. Commander, 3 November, 1884. Captain, 3 March, 1899.

McCANN, FELIX.
Acting Ensign, 9 April, 1863. Dismissed 31 December, 1863.

McCANN, WILLIAM P.
Midshipman, 1 November, 1848. Passed Midshipman, 15 June, 1854. Master, 15 September, 1855. Lieutenant, 16 September, 1855. Lieutenant-Commander, 16 July, 1862. Commander, 25 July, 1866. Captain, 21 September, 1876. Commodore, 26 January, 1887. Retired List, 4 May, 1892.

McCARRICK, EDWARD C.
Acting Third Assistant Engineer, 4 January, 1862. Acting Second Assistant Engineer, 4 August, 1863. Dismissed 31 December, 1863.

McCART, JOSEPH.
Acting Ensign, 20 May, 1863. Acting Master, 21 November, 1864. Honorably discharged 30 September, 1865.

McCARTENEY, CHARLES M.
Midshipman, 25 September, 1869. Graduated 1 June, 1875. Ensign, 18 July, 1876. Master, 20 June, 1882. Lieutenant, Junior Grade, 3 March, 1883. Lieutenant, 26 March, 1889. Retired List, 10 December, 1891.

McCARTHY, ALBERT H.
Naval Cadet, 6 September, 1893. Ensign, 1 July, 1899.

McCARTHY, ANTHONY.
Mate, 3 December, 1862. Honorably discharged 7 December, 1865.

McCARTHY, FRANK.
Acting Third Assistant Engineer, 15 September, 1864. Resigned 4 January, 1865.

McCARTHY, J. B.
Midshipman, 9 January, 1841. Died 11 August, 1842.

McCARTHY, JOHN.
Acting Boatswain, 25 January, 1900.

McCARTHY, STEPHEN.
Boatswain, 13 May, 1887. Chief Boatswain, 3 March, 1899.

McCARTHY, TIMOTHY.
Acting Second Assistant Engineer, 18 April, 1863. Honorably discharged 15 December, 1865.

McCARTNEY, ANDREW J.
Mdshipman, 3 October, 1850. Passed Midshipman, 20 June, 1856. Master, 22 January, 1858. Lieutenant, 18 February, 1858. Dismissed 14 August, 1861.

McCARTNEY, DANIEL P.
Third Assistant Engineer, 19 July, 1861. Second Assistant Engineer, 18 December, 1862. First Assistant Engineer, 30 January, 1865. Chief Engineer, 22 August, 1881. Retired List, 10 November, 1892.

McCARTY, CHARLES H.
Acting Second Assistant Engineer, 1 October, 1862. Acting First Assistant Engineer, 18 April, 1865. Honorably discharged 9 January, 1866.

McCARTY, CHARLES S.
Mate, 6 February, 1862. Resigned 30 December, 1864.

McCARTY, EUGENE.
Mate, 31 October, 1864. Honorably discharged 12 May, 1865.

McCARTY, JOHN.
Chaplain, 3 March, 1825. Resigned 21 April, 1826.

McCARTY, JOSEPH.
Mate, 29 May, 1863. Deserted 1 February, 1864.

McCARTY, MAURICE.
Acting Third Assistant Engineer, 16 May, 1862. Honorably discharged 5 October, 1865.

McCARTY, MORRIS.
Acting Third Assistant Engineer, 14 August, 1863. Honorably discharged 16 August, 1865.

McCARTY, RUFUS H.
Assistant Surgeon, 18 June, 1875. Passed Assistant Surgeon, 13 December, 1878. Died 12 April, 1890.

McCARTY, STEPHEN A.
Acting Midshipman, 25 September, 1856. Resigned 17 October, 1859. Midshipman, 9 September, 1861. Lieutenant, 1 August, 1862. Lieutenant-Commander, 25 July, 1866. Resigned 7 November, 1874.

McCARTY, W. D.
Midshipman, 18 July, 1812. Resigned 9 November, 1813.

McCARTY, WILLIAM W.
Acting Third Assistant Engineer, 5 June, 1863. Died 15 September, 1863.

McCAULEY, CHARLES S.
Midshipman, 16 January, 1809. Lieutenant, 9 December, 1814. Commander, 3 March, 1831. Captain, 9 December, 1839. Retired List, 21 December, 1861. Commodore on Retired List, 4 April, 1867. Died 21 May, 1869.

McCAULEY, D. S.
Midshipman, 1 February, 1814. Resigned 13 February, 1825.

McCAULEY, EDWARD Y.
Midshipman, 9 September, 1841. Passed Midshipman, 10 August, 1847. Master, 1 July, 1855. Lieutenant, 14 September, 1855. Resigned 19 August, 1859. Acting Lieutenant, 11 May, 1861. Lieutenant-Commander, 16 July, 1862. Commander, 27 September, 1866. Captain, 3 September, 1872. Commodore, 7 August, 1881. Rear-Admiral, 2 March, 1885. Retired List, 25 January, 1887. Died 14 September, 1894.

GENERAL NAVY REGISTER.

McCAULEY, EDWARD, Jr.
   Naval Cadet, 8 October, 1892. Ensign, 6 May, 1898.
McCAULEY, FRANCIS G.
   Purser, 27 May, 1829. Resigned 30 September, 1852.
McCAULEY, JAMES.
   Acting Second Assistant Engineer, 29 November, 1862. Resigned 9 January, 1865.
McCAULEY, JAMES B.
   Midshipman, 8 February, 1840. Passed Midshipman, 11 July, 1846. Master, 5 February, 1855. Lieutenant, 22 August, 1855. Died 30 May, 1860.
McCAUSLAND, THOMAS.
   Acting First Assistant Engineer, 10 November, 1863. Mustered out 24 October, 1868.
McCAW, JOHN J.
   Midshipman, 1 September, 1811. Resigned 23 February, 1818.
McCAWLEY, G. M.
   Midshipman, 1 September, 1811. Lieutenant, 1 April, 1818. Died 20 February, 1827.
McCHESNEY, WILLIAM.
   Midshipman, 1 September, 1811. Dismissed by Court-martial, 5 August, 1817.
McCLAIN, CHARLES S.
   Cadet Midshipman, 3 November, 1874. Graduated 4 June, 1880. Ensign, 4 February, 1882. Died 11 January, 1887.
McCLANAHAN, REUBEN.
   Acting Second Assistant Engineer, 5 May, 1862. Honorably discharged 16 April, 1866.
McCLANAHAN, RICE K.
   Assistant Surgeon (Spanish-American War), 13 July, 1898. Appointed Surgeon in Regular Service, 7 June, 1900.
McCLANAHAN, T.
   Midshipman, 9 June, 1811. Resigned 23 August, 1811.
McCLEANE, JOHN.
   Mate, 22 April, 1863. Acting Ensign, 19 September, 1863. Dropped 3 January, 1861.
McCLEARY, ANDREW.
   Mate, 5 March, 1862. Acting Ensign, 28 April, 1863. Honorably discharged 17 January, 1869.
McCLEERY, ROBERT.
   Third Assistant Engineer, 2 August, 1855. Second Assistant Engineer, 21 July, 1858. First Assistant Engineer, 2 August, 1859. Chief Engineer, 11 August, 1862. Died 15 September, 1863.
McCLELLAN, CHARLES H.
   Mate, 16 April, 1863. Acting Ensign, 25 May, 1864. Honorably discharged 30 July, 1868.
McCLELLAN, EDWARD P.
   Midshipman, 25 September, 1863. Graduated June, 1867. Ensign, 18 December, 1868. Master, 21 March, 1870. Lieutenant, 21 March, 1871. Died 4 August, 1886.
McCLELLAN, JOSEPH W.
   Acting Assistant Paymaster, 5 November, 1862. Mustered out 25 September, 1865.
McCLELLAN, REUBEN.
   Mate, 1 October, 1862. Dismissed 28 November, 1862.
McCLELLAND, JAMES.
   Assistant Surgeon, 20 June, 1838. Surgeon, 6 March, 1853. Medical Director, 3 March, 1871. Retired List, 16 March, 1876. Died 4 August, 1877.
McCLENAHAN, WILLIAM F.
   Assistant Surgeon, 28 February, 1833. Surgeon, 8 September, 1841. Dismissed 9 May, 1861.
McCLENNAN, REDMAN.
   Lieutenant, 23 August, 1800. Last appearance on Records of Navy Department.
McCLINTOCK, H. M.
   Midshipman, 18 June, 1812. Died 28 July, 1817.
McCLINTOCK, J. J.
   Midshipman, 9 November, 1813. Lost 18 October, 1814.
McCLINTOCK, WILLIAM.
   Mate, 21 March, 1862. Acting Master, 10 October, 1862. Honorably discharged 5 November, 1865.
McCLOSKEY, JAMES D.
   Gunner, 9 April, 1855. Dismissed 28 January, 1858.
McCLOUD, JAMES.
   Boatswain, 1 August, 1809. Died 16 November, 1822.
McCLOUD, COLIN.
   Boatswain, 17 March, 1812. Last appearance on Records of Navy Department, 1816. Furloughed.
McCLUE, JAMES H.
   Mate, 23 May, 1863. Dismissed 9 June, 1865.
McCLUNEY, WILLIAM J.
   Midshipman, 1 January, 1812. Lieutenant, 1 April, 1818. Commander, 9 December, 1839. Captain, 13 October, 1851. Retired List, 21 December, 1861. Commodore on Retired List, 16 July, 1862. Died 11 February, 1864.
McCLUNG, ALEX.
   Midshipman, 1 April, 1828. Resigned 20 August, 1829.
McCLUNG, CHARLES L.
   Mate, 29 December, 1863. Acting Ensign, 31 October, 1864. Honorably discharged 6 July, 1865.
McCLURE, DAVID.
   Prifessor of Mathematics, 17 June, 1839. Died 13 April, 1842.

McCLURE, GEORGE M.
Midshipman, 23 September, 1859. Ensign, 1 October, 1863. Master, 10 May, 1866. Lieutenant, 21 February, 1867. Retired List, 9 November, 1868.
McCLURG, W. A.
Assistant Surgeon, 8 February, 1874. Surgeon, 25 January, 1889. Medical Inspector, 19 November, 1900.
McCLUSKEY, JOHN.
Acting Third Assistant Engineer, 12 October, 1861. Dismissed 27 May, 1862.
McCLYMONT, ALEXANDER.
Acting Third Assistant Engineer, 25 August, 1864. Resigned 27 May, 1865.
McCOLL, GAVIN.
Passed Assistant Engineer (Spanish-American War), 15 June, 1898. Honorably discharged 2 September, 1898.
McCOLLEY, HIRAM W.
Acting Assistant Paymaster, 22 June, 1863. Resigned 4 October, 1864.
McCOLLOM, THOMAS C.
Civil Engineer, 26 October, 1881. Retired List, 1 June, 1897.
McCOLLUM, JOHN V.
Midshipman, 26 February, 1841. Passed Midshipman, 10 August, 1847. Master, 14 September, 1855. Lieutenant, 15 September, 1855. Resigned 22 July, 1859.
McCOMB, ANDREW.
Lieutenant, 23 April, 1799. Discharged 21 November, 1800.
McCOMB, WILLIAM.
Acting Third Assistant Engineer, 14 September, 1863. Honorably discharged 14 August, 1865.
McCOMMICK, JAMES.
24 December, 1831. Midshipman, 15 June, 1837. Lieutenant, 8 September, 1841. Resigned 16 September, 1850.
McCONE, ALEXANDER.
Boatswain, 18 December, 1870. Chief Boatswain, 3 March, 1899.
McCONNELL, ARCHIBALD E.
Acting Third Assistant Engineer, 28 September, 1861. Resigned 10 December, 1861. Acting Third Assistant Engineer, 19 September, 1862. Acting Second Assistant Engineer, 5 August, 1863. Acting First Assistant Engineer, 6 March, 1865. Honorably discharged 23 September, 1865.
McCONNELL, ELLICOTT.
Assistant Engineer (Spanish-American War), 3 June, 1898. Honorably discharged 20 January, 1899.
McCONNELL, GEORGE E.
Mate, 27 August, 1861. Acting Ensign, 30 August, 1862. Acting Master, 18 March, 1865. Honorably discharged 5 June, 1868.
McCONNELL, HENRY.
Third Assistant Engineer, 5 November, 1861. Resigned 6 February, 1868.
McCONNELL, JAMES.
Mate, 3 February, 1863. Deserted 5 May, 1863.
McCONNELL, JAMES H.
Acting Third Assistant Engineer, 24 September, 1862. Honorably discharged 19 August, 1865.
McCONNELL, RICHARD G.
Naval Cadet, 20 May, 1892. Resigned 14 February, 1895. Ensign (Spanish-American War), 14 May, 1898. Honorably discharged 4 January, 1899.
McCONNELL, ROBERT.
Midshipman, 29 March, 1800. Last appearance on Records of Navy Department, 22 May, 1800.
McCONNELL, RUFUS S.
Acting Assistant Paymaster, 27 December, 1864. Assistant Paymaster, 23 July, 1866. Passed Assistant Paymaster, 27 November, 1866. Paymaster, 1 January, 1875. Retired List, 27 January, 1886. Died 7 March, 1886.
McCONNELL, WILLIAM.
Master, 2 November, 1812. Last appearance on Records of Navy Department, 1815. St. Mary's, Georgia.
McCOOL, DANIEL M.
Mate, 18 June, 1863. Resigned 22 December, 1864.
McCOOK, J. J.
Midshipman, 27 January, 1841. Died 30 March, 1842.
McCOOK, RODERICK S.
Acting Midshipman, 21 September, 1854. Midshipman, 9 June, 1859. Lieutenant, 31 August, 1861. Lieutenant-Commander, 25 December, 1865. Commander, 25 September, 1873. Died 13 February, 1886.
McCORD, CLINTON F. A.
Mate, 11 June, 1863. Acting Ensign, 25 May, 1865. Honorably discharged 30 November, 1865.
McCORD, FRANK M.
Mate, 24 November, 1863. Honorably discharged 16 December, 1865.
McCORKLE, DAVID P.
Midshipman, 21 September, 1841. Passed Midshipman, 10 August, 1847. Master, 14 September, 1855. Lieutenant, 15 September, 1855. Dismissed 17 May, 1861.
McCORMACK, EMMETT.
Midshipman, 17 April, 1862. Graduated, June, 1866. Ensign, 12 March, 1868. Master, 26 March, 1869. Lieutenant, 21 March, 1870. Died 12 September, 1873.
McCORMICK, ALBERT M. D.
Assistant Surgeon, 23 July, 1888. Passed Assistant Surgeon, 23 July, 1891. Surgeon, 11 November, 1899.

GENERAL NAVY REGISTER.

McCORMICK, ALEXANDER H.
Acting Midshipman, 21 September, 1859. Acting Master, April, 1861. Ensign, 22 December, 1862. Lieutenant, 22 February, 1864. Lieutenant-Commander, 25 July, 1866. Commander, 30 September, 1876. Captain, 3 April, 1892. Rear-Admiral, 9 September, 1899. Retired List, 26 March, 1900.

McCORMICK, BENJAMIN B.
Naval Cadet, 19 May, 1888. Ensign, 1 July, 1894. Lieutenant, Junior Grade, 3 March, 1899.

McCORMICK, CHARLES M.
Cadet Egineer, 1 October, 1881. Ensign, 1 July, 1887. Lieutenant, Junior Grade, 21 June, 1896. Lieutenant, 3 March, 1899.

McCORMICK, CHRISTOPHER.
Acting Third Assistant Engineer, 11 April, 1863. Honorably discharged 29 March, 1866.

McCORMICK, DANIEL, Jr.
Assistant Surgeon, 1 August, 1800. Resigned 10 January, 1802. Surgeon, 16 January, 1809. Last appearance on Records of Navy Department, 26 March, 1811. Dead.

McCORMICK, FREDERICK.
Midshipman, 25 September, 1860. Graduated June, 1866. Ensign, 12 March, 1868. Died 25 July, 1868.

McCORMICK, JAMES A.
Acting Second Assistant Engineer, 9 June, 1863. Honorably discharged 5 September, 1865.

McCORMICK, JOHN.
Mate, 13 February, 1863. Died at New Orleans 31 August, 1867.

McCORMICK, JOHN R.
Acting Second Assistant Engineer, 17 November, 1862. Appointment revoked (sick) 16 February, 1863.

McCORMICK, MICHAEL J.
Naval Cadet, 22 May, 1890. Resigned 17 June, 1891. Naval Cadet, 8 September, 1891. Ensign, 1 July, 1897. Lieutenant, Junior Grade, 1 July, 1900.

McCORMICK, SAMUEL.
Acting Ensign, 30 August, 1862. Dismissed 27 May, 1863.

McCORMICK, WILLIAM H.
Acting Ensign, 28 October, 1863. Honorably discharged 16 November, 1865.

McCOURT, JOHN.
Acting Third Assistant Engineer, 18 October, 1861. Acting Second Assistant Engineer, 13 October, 1863. Acting First Assistant Engineer, 30 September, 1864. Honorably discharged 8 October, 1865.

McCOY, CORNELIUS.
Acting Second Assistant Engineer, 13 August, 1860. Appointment revoked (sick) 5 December, 1863.

McCOY, JAMES S.
Mate, 25 August, 1864. Resigned 20 April, 1865.

McCOY, WILLIAM H.
Acting Third Assistant Engineer, 13 August, 1864. Honorably discharged 1 November, 1865.

McCRACKIN, ALEXANDER.
Midshipman, 27 July, 1866. Graduated 7 June, 1870. Ensign, 13 July, 1871. Master, 25 September, 1873. Lieutenant, 13 January, 1879. Lieutenant-Commander, 15 November, 1898.

McCRACKEN, V.
Midshipman, 1 May, 1827. Resigned 16 June, 1833.

McCRACKEN, WILLIAM W.
Mate, 5 September, 1864. Honorably discharged 2 August, 1865.

McCRAY, STUART B.
Acting Second Assistant Engineer, 1 October, 1862. Resigned 29 January, 1863.

McCREA, EDWARD P.
Midshipman. Passed Midshipman, 12 June, 1855. Master, 16 September, 1855. Lieutenant, 24 January, 1857. Lieutenant-Commander, 16 July, 1862. Commander, 27 May, 1868. Captain, 22 January, 1880. Died 14 October, 1881.

McCREA, HENRY.
Midshipman, 24 July, 1866. Graduated 6 June, 1871. Ensign, 14 July, 1872. Master, 10 June, 1876. Lieutenant, Junior Grade, 3 March, 1883. Lieutenant, 16 November, 1883. Lieutenant-Commander, 3 March, 1899.

McCREARY, JAMES A.
Mate, 21 December, 1863. Acting Ensign, 7 August, 1865. Honorably discharged 4 November, 1865.

McCREARY, THOMAS.
Acting Third Assistant Engineer, 22 August, 1864. Resigned 8 May, 1865.

McCREARY, WILLIAM.
Mate, 29 May, 1862. Resigned 13 May, 1865.

McCREARY, WIRT.
Cadet Midshipman, 16 June, 1879. Graduated. Honorably discharged 30 June, 1886. Ensign (Spanish-American War), 24 May, 1898. Honorably discharged 11 April, 1899.

McCREERY, GEORGE M.
Midshipman, 1 November, 1827. Passed Midshipman, 10 June, 1833. Lieutenant, 3 March, 1839. Lost in the Grampus, March, 1843.

McCREERY, STEPHEN A.
Assistant Surgeon, 20 June, 1838. Surgeon, 22 November, 1852. Lost in the Albany, 28 September, 1854.

McCREERY, JAMES M.
Mate, 6 February, 1870. Appointment revoked (sick) 13 May, 1870.

GENERAL NAVY REGISTER.

McCROHAN, W. A.
  Midshipman, 2 March, 1838. Dismissed 5 December, 1840.
McCULLOCH, G. B.
  Master, 27 July, 1813. Lieutenant, 9 December, 1814. Died 31 December, 1827
McCULLOUGH, ALEXANDER.
  Master, date not known. Killed in action 24 August, 1814.
McCULLOUGH, FRANK E.
  Assistant Surgeon, 10 August, 1898.
McCULLY, NEWTON A.
  Naval Cadet, 19 May, 1883. Ensign, 1 July, 1889. Lieutenant, Junior Grade, 6 April, 1897. Lieutenant, 3 March, 1899.
McCURDY, JOHN N.
  Acting First Assistant Engineer, 1 November, 1862. Honorably discharged 8 October, 1865.
McCURLEY, FELIX.
  Acting Master, 13 November, 1861. Acting Volunteer Lieutenant, 9 November, 1864. Master, 12 March, 1868. Lieutenant, 18 December, 1868. Lieutenant-Commander, 2 March, 1870. Commander, 26 January, 1887. Died 3 May, 1896.
McCUTCHEN, SAMUEL.
  Lieutenant, 14 November, 1799. Discharged 15 April, 1801, under Peace Establishment Act.
McCUTCHEN, S. D.
  Midshipman, 10 October, 1831. Resigned 25 June, 1832.
McCUTCHEON, JOHN F.
  Third Assistant Engineer, 13 May, 1861. Acting Second Assistant Engineer, 30 October, 1861. Appointment revokde 13 December, 1861. Acting First Assistant Engineer, 22 May, 1862. Acting Chief Engineer, 19 January, 1863. Honorably discharged 15 April, 1866. First Assistant Engineer, 20 August, 1866. Appointment revoked 22 September, 1866.
McDANIEL, CHARLES A.
  Acting Assistant Paymaster, 19 January, 1865. Mustered out 10 August, 1865. Passed Assistant Paymaster, 23 July, 1866. Paymaster, 3 September, 1871. Died 6 February, 1894.
McDEARMID, DONALD.
  Mate, 11 March, 1862. Dismissed 5 June, 1862.
McDERMOT, DAVID A.
  Midshipman, 8 November, 1841. Passed Midshipman, 10 August, 1847. Master, 1 March, 1855. Lieutenant, 14 September, 1855. Lieutenant-Commander, 16 July, 1862. Killed in action 18 April, 1863.
McDERMOTT, DENNIS A.
  Acting Third Assistant Engineer, 5 October, 1864. Honorably discharged 4 April, 1868.
McDERMOTT, GEORGE B.
  Acting Third Assistant Engineer, 31 December, 1862. Honorably discharged 28 October, 1867.
McDERMOTT, JAMES C.
  Gunner, 10 April, 1899.
McDERMOTT, SAMUEL.
  Acting Third Assistant Engineer, 17 October, 1861. Resigned 13 February, 1862.
McDERMOTT, WILLIAM.
  Acting Ensign, 14 November, 1862. Dismissed 5 March, 1863.
McDERMOTT, WILLIAM C.
  Mate, 25 April, 1863. Acting Ensign, 27 June, 1863. Dismissed 20 February, 1864.
McDEVITT, JOHN.
  Carpenter, 5 June, 1848. Died 15 April, 1849.
McDONALD, ALEXANDER.
  Acting Second Assistant Engineer, 28 December, 1863. Honorably discharged 8 August, 1865.
McDONALD, COLIN.
  Midshipman, 24 July, 1866. Graduated 7 June, 1870. Ensign, 13 July, 1872. Dropped 31 January, 1877.
McDONALD, DAVID.
  Acting Third Assistant Engineer, 22 February, 1864. Honorably discharged 1 September, 1865.
McDONALD, EDWARD H.
  Acting Ensign, 4 October, 1864. Honorably discharged 13 July, 1865.
McDONALD, EDWARD S.
  Mate, 20 April, 1864. Honorably discharged 12 December, 1865.
McDONALD, EDWIN A.
  Gunner, 29 July, 1861. Drowned 15 June, 1885.
McDONALD, JAMES.
  Acting Second Assistant Engineer, 19 December, 1862. Resigned 8 December, 1863.
McDONALD, JAMES.
  Mate, 8 January, 1862. Acting Master, 23 May, 1862. Honorably discharged 20 April, 1867.
McDONALD, JAMES.
  Mate, 14 April, 1862. Resigned 30 May, 1863.
McDONALD, JAMES P.
  Acting Chief Engineer, 1 October, 1862. Died 9 January, 1863.
McDONALD, J. E.
  Master, 21 July, 1814. Midshipman, 17 November, 1814. Lieutenant, 5 March, 1817. Last appearance on Records of Navy Department, 14 July, 1818. Dead.
McDONALD, JOHN A.
  Gunner, 13 November, 1861. Died 29 October, 1892.

GENERAL NAVY REGISTER.

McDONALD, JOHN D.
  Cadet Midshipman, 9 October, 1880. Ensign, 1 July, 1886. Lieutenant, Junior Grade, 1 September, 1895. Lieutenant, 17 July, 1898.
McDONALD, JOHN H.
  Acting Third Assistant Engineer, 12 December, 1864. Resigned 14 June, 1865.
McDONALD, JOSEPH W.
  Acting Ensign, 14 July, 1863. Honorably discharged 13 June, 1867. Mate, 2 March, 1870. Boatswain, 11 February, 1871. Retired List, 23 April, 1884. Died 11 September, 1897.
McDONALD, JOSEPH E.
  Naval Cadet, 7 September, 1888. Assistant Naval Constructor, 1 July, 1894.
McDONALD, LEVI.
  Acting Third Assistant Engineer, 15 September, 1861. Resigned 15 February, 1862.
McDONALD, MITCHELL C.
  Assistant Paymaster, 3 March, 1879. Passed Assistant Paymaster, 20 May, 1882. Paymaster, 7 April, 1894.
McDONALD, ROBERT.
  Boatswain, 25 July, 1857. Warrant canceled, 24 March, 1865. Boatswain, 23 May, 1868. Died 15 April, 1872.
McDONALD, R. D.
  Midshipman, 17 December, 1831. Resigned 26 December, 1834.
McDONALD, THOMAS H.
  Mate, 23 December, 1862. Acting Ensign, 2 February, 1865. Honorably discharged 9 December, 1865.
McDONALD, WILLIAM H.
  Assistant Surgeon, 22 April, 1871. Resigned 22 March, 1873.
McDONALL, JAMES H.
  Ensign (Spanish-American War), 15 June, 1898. Honorably discharged, 2 September, 1898.
McDONNELL, JAMES.
  Carpenter, 21 October, 1840. Retired List, 16 June, 1878. Died 23 July, 1888.
McDONNELL, JOHN E.
  Cadet Midshipman, 30 September, 1874. Graduated 4 June, 1880. Ensign, 25 June, 1883. Resigned 1 March, 1884.
McDONOUGH, CHARLES S.
  Midshipman, 8 April, 1835. Passed Midshipman, 22 June, 1841. Master, 12 August, 1847. Lieutenant, 16 May, 1848. Retired 14 April, 1862. Captain on Retired List, 4 April, 1867. Died 30 November, 1871.
McDONOUGH, JAMES T.
  Midshipman, 1 April, 1826. Passed Midshipman, 28 April, 1832. Lieutenant, 8 March, 1837. Dropped 13 September, 1855.
McDONOUGH, J. M.
  Midshipman, 16 March, 1798. Last appearance on Records of Navy Department.
McDONOUGH, JOHN.
  Mate, 6 January, 1862. Honorably discharged 2 December, 1865.
McDONOUGH, THOMAS.
  Third Assistant Engineer, 27 March, 1843. Resigned 4 November, 1844.
McDOUGAL, CHARLES J.
  Acting Midshipman, 26 May, 1852. Midshipman, 1 October, 1856. Passed Midshipman, 29 April, 1859. Master, 5 September, 1859. Lieutenant, 23 January, 1861. Lieutenant-Commander, 16 November, 1862. Commander, 19 January, 1871. Died 28 March, 1881.
McDOUGAL, DAVID.
  Midshipman, 1 April, 1828. Passed Midshipman, 14 June, 1834. Lieutenant, 25 February, 1841. Commander, 24 January, 1857. Captain, 2 March, 1864. Commodore, 12 June, 1869. Retired List, 27 December, 1871. Rear-Admiral, Retired List, 24 August, 1873. Died 7 August, 1882.
McDOUGAL, DOUGLAS C.
  Naval Cadet, 19 May, 1893. Resigned 16 June, 1894. Ensign (Spanish-American War), 14 May, 1898. Honorably discharged 4 October, 1898.
McDOUGAL, LEON.
  Midshipman, 13 March, 1839. Resigned 27 July, 1846.
McDOUGAL, P. D.
  Mate, 1 October, 1861. Acting Master, 24 March, 1862. Resigned 18 August, 1862. Acting Ensign, 9 October, 1862. Resigned 5 August, 1863.
McDOUGALL, ANGUS.
  Acting Third Assistant Engineer, 17 April, 1863. Acting Second Assistant Engineer, 17 August, 1864. Honorably discharged 11 September, 1865.
McDOWELL, CHARLES A.
  Acting Third Assistant Engineer, 8 July, 1863. Died 11 May, 1864.
McDOWELL, WILLIS.
  Naval Cadet, 19 May, 1893. Ensign, 1 July, 1899.
McDUFFIE, JARVIS.
  Professor, 6 December, 1838. Dropped 4 September, 1848.
McDUNN, EZRA.
  Mate, 27 November, 1863. Acting Ensign, 13 April, 1865. Honorably discharged 20 January, 1866.
McELHANY, J.
  Acting Assistant Surgeon, 4 December, 1862. Resigned 31 May, 1865.
McELLMELL, THOMAS A.
  Acting Third Assistant Engineer, 19 April, 1864. Acting Second Assistant Engineer, 28 March, 1865. Honorably discharged 11 September, 1868.

McELMELL, EDWARD F.
Acting Third Assistant Engineer, 29 September, 1863. Honorably discharged 5 April, 1869. Second Assistant Engineer, 7 November, 1871. Retired List, 1 November, 1878.

McELMELL, JACKSON.
Third Assistant Engineer, 2 August, 1855. Second Assistant Engineer, 6 May, 1859. First Assistant Engineer, 25 March, 1861. Chief Engineer, 2 February, 1862. Retired List, 4 June, 1896.

McELMELL, THOMAS.
Mate, 6 December, 1861. Acting Ensign, 9 October, 1862. Resigned 1 June, 1863.

McELROY, ARCHIBALD.
Lieutenant, 11 May, 1798. Out of service 10 May, 1801.

McELROY, DANIEL R.
Acting Third Assistant Engineer, 11 February, 1864. Acting Second Assistant Engineer, 13 December, 1864. Honorably discharged 18 January, 1866.

McELROY, GEORGE WIGHTMAN.
Cadet Engineer, Naval Academy, 1 October, 1874. Graduated 20 June, 1878. Assistant Engineer, 20 June, 1880. Passed Assistant Engineer, 28 January, 1890. Chief Engineer, 6 August, 1898. Rank changed to Lieutenant, 3 March, 1899.

McELROY, HORACE.
Midshipman, 25 September, 1863. Graduated June, 1868. Ensign, 19 April, 1869. Resigned 28 February, 1870.

McELROY, SAMUEL.
Third Assistant Engineer, 26 February, 1851. Resigned 20 July, 1852.

McELROY, THOMAS.
Gunner, 13 November, 1861. Warranted, 1 November, 1862. Resigned 18 January, 1864. Acting Master, 19 January, 1864. Mustered out 5 March, 1868.

McENTEE, MAURICE W.
Mate, 21 October, 1861. Acting Ensign, 18 November, 1863. Acting Master, 19 October, 1864. Honorably discharged 14 May, 1867.

McENTEE, WILLIAM.
Naval Cadet, 20 May, 1896. Graduated 30 June, 1900.

McEWAN, CAMPBELL.
Acting Third Assistant Engineer, 21 September, 1863. Acting First Assistant Engineer, 14 March, 1865. Honorably discharged 28 November, 1865.

McEWAN, JOHN.
Acting Third Assistant Engineer, 22 September, 1862. Acting Second Assistant Engineer, 8 February, 1864. Honorably discharged 23 September, 1865.

McEWEN, HENRY D.
Third Assistant Engineer, 1 July, 1861. Second Assistant Engineer, 21 April, 1863. First Assistant Engineer, 11 October, 1866. Chief Engineer, 3 March, 1882. Retired List, 13 December, 1892. Died 18 October, 1894.

McEWEN, WILLIAM G.
Acting Third Assistant Engineer, 24 December, 1863. Third Assistant Engineer, 8 March, 1865. Second Assistant Engineer, 1 January, 1868. Retired List, 24 May, 1875.

McFADDEN, W. J.
Mate, 23 November, 1864. Honorably discharged 2 June, 1865.

McFARLAN, ALEXANDER.
Chaplain, 2 March, 1802. Died 2 August, 1805.

McFARLAND, ABIAL.
Acting Master, 6 December, 1861. Honorably discharged 14 September, 1865.

McFARLAND, JOHN.
Acting Midshipman, 21 September, 1857. Midshipman, 1 June, 1861. Lieutenant, 1 August, 1862. Lieutenant-Commander, 25 July, 1866. Died 22 May, 1874.

McFARLAND, J. P.
Midshipman, 8 December, 1837. Resigned 2 July, 1845.

McFARLAND, WALTER.
Mate. Appointment revoked (sick) 21 February, 1862.

McFARLAND, WALTER MARTIN.
Cadet Engineer, Naval Academy, 15 September, 1875. Graduated 10 June, 1879. Assistant Engineer, 10 June, 1881. Passed Assistant Engineer, 15 September, 1891. Chief Engineer, 20 November, 1898. Rank changed to Lieutenant, 3 March, 1899. Resigned 5 July, 1899.

McFARLAND, WILLIAM D.
Acting Chief Engineer, 1 October, 1862. Honorably discharged 18 November, 1865.

McFATE, JOHN.
Boatswain, 15 July, 1813. Died in October, 1820.

McFAUL, WILLIAM.
Acting Third Assistant Engineer, 13 February, 1864. Honorably discharged 10 July, 1865. Acting Third Assistant Engineer, 29 January, 1867. Mustered out 5 April, 1869.

McFAWN, JOHN.
Acting Third Assistant Engineer, 6 June, 1864. Honorably discharged 29 September, 1865.

McGARRITY, THOMAS.
Acting Third Assistant Engineer, 10 March, 1864. Honorably discharged 16 December, 1865.

McGARY, CHARLES P.
Midshipman, 19 October, 1841. Passed Midshipman, 10 August, 1847. Master, 14 September, 1855. Leutenant, 15 September, 1855. Resigned 25 April, 1861.

McGEAN, J. R.
Acting First Assistant Engineer. Resigned 5 December, 1862.

GENERAL NAVY REGISTER.

McGILL, PETER.
Passed Assistant Surgeon (Spanish-American War), 20 May, 1898. Honorably discharged 1 December, 1898.
McGINN, MICHAEL.
Assistant Engineer (Spanish-American War), 18 May, 1898. Honorably discharged 2 September, 1898.
McGINNIS, EDWARD F.
Acting Third Assistant Engineer, 1 February, 1862. Appointment revoked 21 July, 1862. Acting Third Assistant Engineer, 9 September, 1862. Appointment revoked 8 December, 1864.
McGLANHON, JAMES.
Midshipman, 28 June, 1804. Died 19 July, 1813.
McGLANHON, TURNER.
Midshipman, 28 June, 1804. Resigned 16 January, 1808.
McGLATHERY, JAMES.
Mate, 8 January, 1862. Appointment revoked 17 November, 1862. Mate, 17 February, 1863. Acting Ensign, 19 September, 1863. Honorably discharged 28 November, 1865.
McGLENSEY, JOHN F.
Acting Midshipman, 28 September, 1857. Midshipman, 1 June, 1861. Lieutenant, 16 July, 1862. Lieutenant-Commander, 25 July, 1866. Commander, 8 February, 1875. Captain, 28 February, 1890. Retired List, 8 May, 1893. Died 3 May, 1896.
McGLINCEY, FRANCIS.
Mate, 16 May, 1864. Honorably discharged 8 February, 1868.
McGLOIN, WILLIAM.
Acting Master, 6 December, 1861. Acting Volunteer Lieutenant, 23 December, 1864. Honorably discharged 21 December, 1865.
McGLONE, THOMAS.
Carpenter, 12 May, 1866. Resigned 17 April, 1867. Carpenter, 18 May, 1870. Retired List, 6 April, 1894.
McGOUGH, THOMAS.
Acting Third Assistant Engineer, 21 March, 1862. Died 29 September, 1864.
McGOVERN, JOHN.
Mate, 27 May, 1863. Dismissed 10 December, 1864.
McGOVERN, JOHN B.
Acting Second Assistant Engineer, 18 March, 1864. Honorably discharged 14 September, 1865.
McGOVERN, PETER.
Acting Gunner, 28 August, 1863. Dismissed 16 July, 1864.
McGOWAN, BARTH.
Professor of Mathematics, 20 June, 1836. Dismissed 12 April, 1845.
McGOWAN, GEORGE W.
Acting Third Assistant Engineer, 1 September, 1863. Drowned 6 December, 1863.
McGOWAN, JAMES.
Midshipman, 1 September, 1811. Lieutenant, 9 December, 1814. Died 19 February, 1826.
McGOWAN, JOHN.
Mate, 8 March, 1862. Acting Master, 8 May, 1862. Master, 12 March, 1868. Lieutenant, 18 December, 1868. Lieutenant-Commander, 22 April, 1870. Commander, 29 January, 1887. Captain, 3 March, 1899.
McGOWAN, JOHN P.
Passed Assistant Surgeon (Spanish-American War), 30 April, 1898. Honorably discharged, 8 September, 1898.
McGOWAN, SAMUEL.
Assistant Paymaster, 15 March, 1894. Passed Assistant Paymaster, 30 March, 1895. Paymaster, 5 May, 1899.
McGOWAN, W. C.
Assistant Paymaster, 12 July, 1870. Passed Assistant Paymaster, 16 February, 1878. Died 25 December, 1887.
McGOWN, GILBERT LEWIS.
Mate, 18 June, 1864. Honorably discharged 30 March, 1866. Mate, 2 May, 1867. Mustered out 27 August, 1869.
McGRANN, WILLIAM H.
Naval Cadet, 20 May, 1887. Assistant Engineer, 1 July, 1893. Passed Assistant Engineer, 7 February, 1898. Rank changed to Lieutenant, Junior Grade, 3 March, 1899. Lieutenant, 2 February, 1900.
McGRATH, FENNEL J.
Mate. Resigned 20 May, 1863.
McGRATH, JOHN.
Mate, 12 April, 1898. Boatswain, 10 April, 1899.
McGRATH, WILLIAM W.
Acting Third Assistant Engineer, 15 April, 1863. Acting Second Assistant Engineer, 27 July, 1864. Resigned 12 May, 1865.
McGREGOR, CHARLES.
Acting Midshipman, 21 September, 1860. Ensign, 28 May, 1863. Master, 10 November, 1865. Lieutenant, 25 July, 1866. Lieutenant-Commander, 12 March, 1868. Commander, 5 June, 1878. Died 1 August, 1891.
McGREGOR, DAVID.
Midshipman, 11 June, 1799. Resigned 27 January, 1800.
McGREGOR, FRANK A.
Mate, 23 July, 1898. Gunner, 10 April, 1899.
McGREGOR, JAMES.
Third Assistant Engineer, 23 June, 1863. Died 22 September, 1863.

McGUIGAN, JAMES H.
 Pharmacist, 15 September, 1898.
McGUINNESS, JOHN P.
 Cadet Midshipman, 28 September, 1881. Ensign, 1 July, 1887. Lieutenant, Junior Grade, 1 April, 1896. Lieutenant, 3 March, 1899.
McGUIRE, NICHOLAS H.
 Acting Assistant Surgeon, 10 March, 1865. Honorably discharged 1 April, 1866.
McGUNNEGLE, WILSON.
 Midshipman, 10 December, 1845. Passed Midshipman, 10 June, 1853. Master, 15 September, 1855. Lieutenant, 16 September, 1855. Lieutenant-Commander, 16 July, 1862. Died 2 April, 1863.
McGUNNEGLE, WILLIAM S.
 Midshipman, 26 September, 1863. Graduated, June, 1867. Ensign, 18 December, 1868. Master, 21 March, 1870. Lieutenant, 21 March, 1871. Resigned 8 October, 1876.
McGURREN, B. J.
 Third Assistant Engineer, 21 April, 1863. Dismissed 26 October, 1863.
McHATTON, WILLIAM.
 Midshipman, 10 July, 1799. Discharged 14 July, 1801, under Peace Establishment Act.
McHENRY, THOMAS.
 Assistant Surgeon, 1 July, 1862. Died 18 August, 1863.
McILHANNEY, J.
 Acting Assistant Surgeon, 4 December, 1862. Resigned 31 May, 1865.
McILHENNY, HARRY H.
 Lieutenant (Spanish-American War), 20 May, 1898. Honorably discharged 21 September, 1898.
McILVAINE, BLOOMFIELD.
 Midshipman, 9 October, 1862. Graduated June, 1866. Ensign, 12 March, 1868. Master, 26 March, 1869. Lieutenant, 21 March, 1870. Retired List, 28 November, 1883. Died 16 April, 1884.
McILVAINE, HENRY C.
 Third Assistant Engineer, 17 February, 1860. Second Assistant Engineer, 6 January, 1862. First Assistant Engineer, 1 March, 1864. Resigned 21 June, 1869.
McILVAINE, WILLIAM D.
 Third Assistant Engineer, 16 November, 1861. Second Assistant Engineer, 25 August, 1863. Resigned 13 October, 1865.
McINTIRE, CHARLES.
 Master, 11 January, 1815. Resigned 3 April, 1815.
McINTOSH, ALEXANDER.
 Mate, 21 October, 1861. Acting Ensign, 29 August, 1862. Acting Master, good conduct on Ironclad Keokuk, 4 January, 1864. Honorably discharged 22 June, 1868. Mate, 25 January, 1870. Died 9 November, 1887.
McINTOSH, CHARLES.
 Boatswain, 14 July, 1851. Dismissed 30 July, 1851.
McINTOSH, CHARLES F.
 Midshipman, 1 November, 1828. Passed Midshipman, 14 June, 1834. Lieutenant, 25 February, 1841. Commander, 2 March, 1857. Dismissed 20 April, 1861.
McINTOSH, HAMPDEN.
 Midshipman, 26 April, 1798. Last appearance on Records of Navy Department.
McINTOSH, HORACE P.
 Midshipman, 28 June, 1867. Graduated 6 June, 1871. Ensign, 14 July, 1872. Master, 27 June, 1875. Lieutenant, 22 October, 1882. Retired List, 30 June, 1892.
McINTOSH, JAMES Mc.
 Midshipman, 1 September, 1811. Lieutenant, 1 April, 1818. Commander, 28 February, 1838. Captain, 5 September, 1849. Died 1 September, 1860.
McINTOSH, JOHN B.
 Midshipman, 27 April, 1848. Resigned 24 May, 1850.
McINTOSH, JOHN L.
 Acting Third Assistant Engineer, 19 October, 1864. Honorably discharged 19 October, 1865.
McINTOSH, THOMAS V.
 Acting Third Assistant Engineer, 4 January, 1862. Acting Second Assistant Engineer, 3 June, 1863. Honorably discharged 7 October, 1868.
McINTOSH W. A.
 Midshipman, 30 November, 1814. Resigned 29 November, 1817.
McINTOSH, WILLIAM.
 Midshipman, 30 April, 1800. Lieutenant, 2 May, 1808. Resigned 9 December, 1808.
McINTYRE, ALFRED F.
 Acting Ensign, 27 December, 1864. Appointment revoked 23 November, 1865.
McINTYRE, EDWARD W.
 Naval Cadet, 6 September, 1894. Ensign, 4 April, 1900.
McINTYRE, FRANK T.
 Acting Assistant Paymaster, 4 December, 1862. Died on De Soto, 13 October,1863.
McINTYRE, JOHN.
 Third Assistant Engineer, 22 July, 1862. Second Assistant Engineer, 15 February, 1864. Died 21 May, 1865.
McINTYRE, JOHN.
 Lieutenant, Junior Grade (Spanish-American War), 23 June, 1898. Honorably discharged 7 March, 1899.
McINTYRE, JOSEPH P.
 Chaplain, 26 July, 1889. Dismissed 24 October, 1898.
McINTYRE, SYLVANUS.
 Third Assistant Engineer, 24 August, 1861. Resigned 19 June, 1865.

GENERAL NAVY REGISTER.

McKAY, CHARLES E.
Acting Midshipman, 29 September, 1857. Midshipman, 1 June, 1861. Acting Master, 4 September, 1861. Lieutenant, 16 July, 1862. Lieutenant-Commander, 25 July, 1866. Retired List, 25 June, 1869.

McKAY, DANIEL.
Acting Ensign, 20 March, 1865. Honorably discharged 14 May, 1867.

McKAY, DONALD S.
Mate, 21 October, 1861. Appointment revoked 1 September, 1862.

McKAY, JOHN.
Acting Master, 18 May, 1861. Dismissed 6 February, 1863.

McKAY, JOHN E.
Third Assistant Engineer, 3 May, 1859. Resigned 7 July, 1860. Acting Third Assistant Engineer, 14 August, 1862. Acting Second Assistant Engineer, 13 December, 1862. Acting First Assistant Engineer, 17 May, 1864. Honorably discharged 13 October, 1868.

McKAY, LAUCHLAN.
Carpenter, 16 June, 1836. Resigned 29 August, 1840.

McKAY, WILLIAM.
Cadet Engineer, 1 October, 1881. Graduated. Honorably discharged, 30 June, 1887. Lieutenant (Spanish-American War), 8 June, 1898. Honorably discharged 25 August, 1898.

McKAY, WILLIAM. H.
Mate. Resigned 24 November, 1862.

McKAY, WILLIAM L.
Acting Third Assistant Engineer, 11 October, 1862. Resigned 23 November, 1864.

McKEAN, F. B.
Midshipman, 30 September, 1845. Resigned 10 May, 1847.

McKEAN, FREDERICK G.
Third Assistant Engineer, 19 February, 1861. Second Assistant Engineer, 21 April, 1863. First Assistant Engineer, 1 December, 1864. Chief Engineer, 25 November, 1877. Retired List, 9 November, 1893.

McKEAN, JOSIAH S.
Cadet Midshipman, 29 September, 1879. Honorably discharged 30 June, 1886. Assistant Engineer, 28 June, 1889. Passed Assistant Engineer, 5 November, 1895. Rank changed to Lieutenant, 3 March, 1899.

McKEAN, WILLIAM D., JR.
Mate, 22 April, 1863. Resigned 29 June, 1863. Mate, 28 September, 1864. Honorably discharged 16 September, 1865.

McKEAN, WILLIAM W.
Midshipman, 30 November, 1814. Lieutenant, 13 January, 1825. Commander, 8 September, 1841. Captain, 14 September, 1855. Retired List, 27 December, 1861. Commodore, on Retired List, 16 July, 1862. Died 22 April, 1865.

McKEE, HUGH W.
Midshipman, 25 September, 1861. Graduated June, 1866. Ensign, 12 March, 1868. Master, 26 March, 1869. Lieutenant, 21 March, 1870. Killed in attack upon Corea, Japan, 11 June, 1871.

McKEE, SAMUEL.
Mate, 17 December, 1863. Honorably discharged 1 November, 1865.

McKEEL, JOHN.
Midshipman, 3 August, 1805. Dismissed 17 September, 1805.

McKEEN, JAMES.
Acting Carpenter, 27 November, 1863. Honorably discharged 5 August, 1865.

McKEEVER, B. W.
Mate, 3 September, 1861. Resigned 30 September, 1863.

McKEEVER, EDWIN.
Mate. Acting Ensign, 25 May, 1863. Resigned 18 March, 1865. Acting Ensign, 14 August, 1866. Resigned 27 June, 1868.

McKEEVER, ISAAC.
Midshipman, 1 December, 1809. Lieutenant, 9 December, 1814. Commander, 27 May, 1830. Captain, 8 December, 1838. Died 1 April, 1856.

McKEIGE, E.
Acting Master, 26 August, 1861. Resigned 6 September, 1862.

McKEITHEN, W. J.
Midshipman, 3 March, 1841. Dropped.

McKELL, JAMES.
Acting First Assistant Engineer, 17 March, 1862. Resigned 8 December, 1863.

McKENDRY, WILLIAM.
Acting Ensign, 11 September, 1862. Acting Master, recommendation of Commanding Officer, 13 June, 1864. Honorably discharged 19 August, 1865.

McKENNEE, HENRY G.
Acting Ensign, 8 October, 1862. Acting Master, recommendation of Commanding Officer, 29 April, 1864. Honorably discharged 17 November, 1865.

McKENNEY, JOHN.
Acting Third Assistant Engineer, 5 January, 1864. Resigned 15 June, 1865.

McKENNEY, WILLIAM.
Chaplain, 8 September, 1841. Died 4 May, 1857.

McKENNY, W. E.
Midshipman, 9 June, 1811. Lieutenant, 5 March, 1817. Commander, 9 February, 1837. Died 24 August, 1839.

McKENSIE, LEWIS.
Acting Second Assistant Engineer. Resigned 7 June, 1864.

McKENZIE, ALLEN.
Lieutenant, 2 April, 1799. Last appearance on Records of Navy Department, 12 April, 1799.

GENERAL NAVY REGISTER.

McKENZIE, DANIEL.
Midshipman, 17 December, 1810. Resigned 19 October, 1813.
McKENZIE, DAVID B.
Mate, 4 November, 1863. Acting Ensign, 11 June, 1864. Honorably discharged 1 June, 1865.
McKENZIE, JAMES B.
Acting Third Assistant Engineer, 18 April, 1863. Honorably discharged 14 October, 1865.
McKENZIE, KENNETH.
Midshipman, 3 March, 1799. Discharged 12 August, 1801, under Peace Establishment Act.
McKENZIE, ROBERT C.
Mate, 4 October, 1862. Acting Ensign, 11 March, 1863. Acting Master, 21 November, 1864. Resigned 20 May, 1865.
McKENZIE, WILLIAM.
Midshipman, 30 November, 1814. Lost at sea in 1816.
McKENZIE, WILLIAM.
Acting Third Assistant Engineer, 20 May, 1864. Appointment revoked 3 March, 1865.
McKERNAN, JOHN.
Passed Assistant Engineer (Spanish-American War), 14 May, 1898. Honorably discharged 26 September, 1898.
McKERVALL, WILLIAM.
Captain (to command a Galley), 11 September, 1798. Discharged 4 September, 1801, under Peace Establishment Act.
McKETHAN, ALFRED A.
Naval Cadet, 5 September, 1889. Ensign, 1 July, 1895. Lieutenant, Junior Grade, 3 March, 1899.
McKEWAN, DAVID P.
Mate, 8 September, 1862. Acting Ensign, 29 April, 1863. Dismissed 13 June, 1863. Acting Ensign, 7 June, 1864. Honorably discharged 16 July, 1865.
McKIM, SMITH H.
Assistant Surgeon (Spanish-American War), 12 May, 1898. Honorably discharged 3 October, 1898.
McKINLEY, CHARLES S.
Ensign (Spanish-American War), 9 May, 1898. Honorably discharged 30 August, 1898.
McKINLEY, EDWARD.
Assistant Surgeon, 8 September, 1841. Died 2 November, 1841.
McKINLEY, FRANCIS.
Acting Third Assistant Engineer, 11 July, 1863. Resigned 28 March, 1865.
McKINLEY, ISAAC J.
Acting Ensign, 5 September, 1862. Honorably discharged 13 August, 1865.
McKINLEY, JOHN.
Boatswain, 5 April 1855. Died 20 May, 1866.
McKINNEY, WILSON R.
Midshipman, 20 March, 1834. Passed Midshipman, 16 July, 1840. Lieutenant, 3 March, 1847. Died 18 August, 1851.
McKINSTRY, JAMES P.
Midshipman, 1 February, 1826. Passed Midshipman, 28 April, 1832. Lieutenant, 9 February, 1837. Commander, 14 September, 1855. Captain, 16 July, 1862. Commodore, 25 July, 1866. Retired List, 9 February, 1869. Died 11 February, 1873.
McKIVER, JOHN H.
Acting Third Assistant Engineer, 4 August, 1864. Resigned 20 April, 1865.
McKNIGHT, GEORGE B.
Assistant Surgeon, 16 May, 1829. Surgeon, 20 February, 1838. Died 13 May, 1857.
McKNIGHT, JOHN.
Midshipman, 20 June, 1806. Dismissed 3 June, 1808.
McKNIGHT, JOSEPH.
Acting Third Assistant Engineer, 27 May, 1861. Acting Second Assistant Engineer, 28 October, 1861. Acting First Assistant Engineer, 27 January, 1863. Honorably discharged 25 October, 1865.
McKNIGHT, ROBERT.
Midshipman, 13 July, 1799. Resigned 15 July, 1800.
McKNIGHT, S. D.
Midshipman, 21 February, 1809. Lieutenant, 24 July, 1813. Last appearance on Records of Navy Department, 1815. Lost at sea.
McKNIGHT, WILLIAM.
Acting Master's Mate, 1 May, 1864. Discharged 27 February, 1865.
McKOY, ROBERT H.
Lieutenant, Junior Grade (Spanish-American War), 20 May, 1898. Honorably discharged 9 September, 1898.
McLACHLAN, JAMES.
Midshipman, 9 June, 1811. Last appearance on Records of Navy Department, 1814. Resigned.
McLACHLIN, P.
Master, 28 July, 1814. Last appearance on Records of Navy Department, 1817. Furloughed.
McLANAHAN, S. CALVIN. c
Third Assistant Engineer, 17 March, 1863. Second Assistant Engineer, 25 July, 1866. Resigned 21 June, 1869.
McLANAHAN, TENANT.
Midshipman, 12 December, 1839. Passed Midshipman, 2 July 1845. Killed 11 February, 1848.

GENERAL NAVY REGISTER. 371

McLANE, ALLEN.
  Midshipman, 25 April, 1831. Resigned 26 November, 1838. Midshipman, 24 May, 1842. Passed Midshipman, 5 August, 1848. Resigned 6 November, 1852.
McLANE, CHARLES S.
  Gunner, 26 December, 1845. Killed by bursting of a cannon at Washington Navy Yard, 13 November, 1849.
McLANE, LOUIS.
  Midshipman, 5 March, 1835. Passed Midshipman, 22 June, 1841. Lieutenant, 26 September, 1847. Resigned 21 January, 1850.
McLANE, LOUIS.
  Midshipman, 3 May, 1799. Resigned 10 February, 1802.
McLANE, WILLIAM G.
  Acting Third Assistant Engineer, 2 December, 1861. Acting Second Assistant Engineer, 19 December, 1862. Honorably discharged 9 April, 1868.
McLAREN, DONALD.
  Chaplain, 10 March, 1863. Retired List, 7 March, 1896.
McLARTY, WILLIAM A.
  Acting Third Assistant Engineer, 1 September, 1864. Honorably discharged 9 March, 1868.
McLAUGHLIN, AUGUSTUS.
  Midshipman, 11 January, 1840. Passed Midshipman, 11 July, 1846. Master, 1 March, 1855. Lieutenant, 14 September, 1855. Resigned 26 April, 1861.
McLAUGHLIN, DANIEL.
  Mate, 28 May, 1863. Dismissed 1 December, 1863.
McLAUGHLIN, EDWARD.
  Chaplain, 19 April, 1826. Dismissed 2 October, 1829.
McLAUGHLIN, JOHN.
  Boatswain, 18 November, 1881. Chief Boatswain, 3 March, 1899.
McLAUGHLIN, J. T.
  Midshipman, 1 December, 1827. Passed Midshipman, 10 June, 1833. Lieutenant, 28 February, 1838. Died 6 July, 1847.
McLAUGHLIN, MICHAEL.
  Acting Third Assistant Engineer, 16 June, 1862. Acting Second Assistant Engineer, 31 May, 1864. Honorably discharged 12 December, 1865.
McLAUGHLIN, RICHARD.
  Acting Third Assistant Engineer, 4 February, 1863. Honorably discharged 16 December, 1865.
McLAUGHLIN, R. K.
  Acting Third Assistant Engineer, 18 March, 1865. Honorably discharged 16 December, 1865.
McLAUGHLIN, THOMAS J.
  Acting Ensign, 1 October, 1862. Resigned 30 May, 1864.
McLEAN, ARTHUR E.
  Mate, 20 November, 1863. Resigned 28 February, 1865.
McLEAN, DANIEL.
  Acting Assistant Surgeon, 3 October, 1863. Honorably discharged 28 December, 1865.
McLEAN, DAVID.
  Acting Assistant Surgeon, 31 March, 1864. Resigned 12 August, 1864.
McLEAN, GEORGE W.
  Acting Assistant Paymaster, 14 December, 1864. Resigned 25 March, 1865.
McLEAN, JOHN.
  Master's Mate, 27 April, 1805. Last appearance on Records of Navy Department.
McLEAN, JOHN R.
  Acting First Assistant Engineer, 1 October, 1862. Resigned 5 December, 1862.
McLEAN, L. ROBERT.
  Acting First Assistant Engineer, 19 November, 1862. Honorably discharged 14 October, 1865.
McLEAN, RIDLEY.
  Naval Cadet, 20 May, 1890. Ensign, 1 July, 1896. Lieutenant, Junior Grade, 1 July, 1899.
McLEAN, ROBERT H.
  Midshipman, 22 June, 1868. Graduated 1 June, 1872. Ensign, 15 July, 1873. Master, 25 November, 1877. Lieutenant, Junior Grade, 3 March, 1883. Lieutenant, 13 July, 1884. Resigned 27 September, 1888.
McLEAN, THOMAS C.
  Midshipman, 21 September, 1864. Graduated June, 1868. Master, 12 July, 1870. Lieutenant, 12 December, 1872. Lieutenant-Commander, 11 April, 1894. Commander, 3 March, 1899.
McLEAN, WALTER.
  Midshipman, 6 June, 1872. Graduated 20 June, 1876. Ensign, 23 October, 1878. Lieutenant, Junior Grade, 1 December, 1885. Lieutenant, 20 May, 1891. Lieutenant-Commander, 1 July, 1899.
McLEAN, WILLIAM.
  Acting First Assistant Engineer, 14 July, 1863. Honorably discharged 15 April, 1866.
McLEAN, WILLIAM.
  Acting First Assistant Engineer, 1 October, 1862. Honorably discharged 5 December, 1865.
McLEAN, W. B.
  Midshipman, 1 January, 1812. Resigned 13 October, 1824.
McLEAN, WILLIAM H.
  Mate, 23 January, 1862. Acting Master, 6 June, 1862. Dismissed 17 July, 1863. Acting Ensign, 5 December, 1863. Appointment revoked (sick) 14 May, 1864. Acting Ensign, 28 September, 1864. Resigned 3 February, 1865.

GENERAL NAVY REGISTER.

McLEARY, THOMAS.
Acting Ensign, 23 December, 1863. Resigned 16 March, 1865.
McLELLAN, CHARLES H.
(See McClellan.)
McLEOD, DANIEL C.
Assistant Surgeon, 8 February, 1832. Surgeon, 23 July, 1841. Died 1 September, 1852.
McLEOD, NORMAN.
Mate, 8 September, 1862. Acting Ensign, 17 December, 1862. Honorably discharged 21 December, 1868.
McLOUD, FRANCIS.
Boatswain, 15 September, 1857. Died 6 May, 1866.
McMAHAN, JESSE.
Acting Third Assistant Engineer, 1 October, 1862. Resigned 24 November, 1862.
McMAHON, FRANK P.
Assistant Paymaster (Spanish-American War), 7 June, 1898. Honorably discharged 21 November, 1898.
McMAHON, JOSEPH.
Pharmacist, 15 Sepember, 1898.
McMAHON, PATRICK.
Acting Third Assistant Engineer, 23 September, 1863. Acting Second Assistant Engineer, 3 December, 1864. Acting First Assistant Engineer, 29 June, 1865. Honorably discharged 27 March, 1868. Passed Assistant Engineer (Spanish-American War), 20 May, 1898. Honorably discharged 18 February, 1899.
McMANUS, AUGUSTINE B.
Ensign (Spanish-American War), 8 June, 1898. Honorably discharged 4 March, 1899.
McMANUS, JOHN.
Mate, 7 July, 1863. Honorably discharged 12 May, 1868. Mate, 20 January, 1870. Died 13 March, 1890.
McMASTER, JAMES.
Assistant Surgeon, 8 October, 1859. Surgeon, 11 October, 1862. Died 4 July, 1873.
McMECHAN, ANDREW C.
Midshipman, 24 February, 1863. Graduated June, 1868. Master, 12 July, 1870. Lieutenant, 6 January, 1874. Retired List, 29 October, 1883.
McMICHAEL, WILLIAM D.
Mate, 11 November, 1864. Died at New Orleans, La., 15 December, 1864.
McMILLAN, CHARLES.
Acting Second Assistant Engineer, 12 August, 1863. Resigned 5 June, 1865.
McMILLAN, JAMES.
Acting Assistant Surgeon, 23 July, 1864. Resigned 24 June, 1865.
McMILLAN, JOHN T.
Cadet Midshipman, 17 June, 1882. Graduated. Honorably discharged 30 June, 1888. Lieutenant, Junior Grade (Spanish-American War), 28 May, 1898. Honorably discharged 10 February, 1899.
McMORRIS, BOLING K.
Naval Cadet, 15 September, 1890. Assistant Engineer, 1 July, 1896. Rank changed to Ensign, 3 March, 1899. Lieutenant, Junior Grade, 1 July, 1899.
McMILLAN, RODERICK.
Gunner, 1 March, 1860. Dismissed 25 May, 1860. Acting Ensign, 11 February, 1865. Honorably discharged 19 September, 1865.
McMULLIN, R. R.
Midshipman, 10 May, 1820. Lieutenant, 17 May, 1828. Killed by accident, 27 January, 1833.
McMURRAY, WILLIAM B.
Mate, 24 January, 1863. Deserted 19 May, 1863.
McMURTRIE, DANIEL.
Assistant Surgeon, 22 August, 1862. Surgeon, 29 June, 1872. Medical Inspector, 8 February, 1890. Medical Director, 3 September, 1896. Retired List, 18 June, 1898. Died 21 November, 1899.
McMURTRIE, HORACE.
Third Assistant Engineer, 3 May, 1859. Second Assistant Engineer, 29 October, 1861. First Assistant Engineer, 20 May, 1863. Resigned 28 November, 1865.
McMURTRIE, WILLIAM.
Purser, 26 May, 1824. Died 23 March, 1836.
McNABB, JAMES.
Acting Third Assistant Engineer, 23 January, 1864. Honorably discharged 27 September, 1867.
McNABOE, C. M.
Mate, 27 May, 1865. Appointment revoked 21 February, 1866.
McNAIR, ANTOINE R.
Acting Midshipman, 22 September, 1856. Midshipman, 15 June, 1860. Master, 19 September, 1861. Lieutenant, 16 July, 1862. Lieutenant-Commander, 25 July, 1866. Retired List, 26 October, 1872.
McNAIR, FREDERICK V.
Acting Midshipman, 21 September, 1853. Midshipman, 10 June, 1857. Passed Midshipman, 25 June, 1860. Master, 24 October, 1860. Lieutenant, 18 April, 1861. Lieutenant-Commander, 20 April, 1864. Commander, 29 January, 1872. Captain, 30 October, 1883. Commodore, 10 May, 1895. Rear-Admiral, 3 July, 1898. Died 28 November, 1900.
McNAIR, WILLIAM G.
Mate, 7 August, 1862. Appointment revoked (sick) 14 May, 1863.
McNALLY, JOHN.
Acting Ensign, Staff of Admiral Dahlgren, 1 May, 1865. Honorably discharged 29 July, 1865.

GENERAL NAVY REGISTER.

McNALLY, WILLIAM.
   Gunner, 23 December, 1835. Dismissed 3 January, 1837.
McNAMARA, JAMES B.
   Third Assistant Engineer, 8 December, 1862. Second Assistant Engineer, 8 April, 1864. Died 23 June, 1864.
McNAMEE, LUKE.
   Naval Cadet, 6 September, 1888. Ensign, 1 July, 1894. Lieutenant, Junior Grade, 3 March, 1899.
McNARRY, ISAAC R.
   Third Assistant Engineer, 13 May, 1861. Second Assistant Engineer, 19 February, 1863. First Assistant Engineer, 1 January, 1865. Chief Engineer, 14 December, 1878. Retired List, 11 September, 1894.
McNAUGHT, ROBERT.
   Acting Third Assistant Engineer, 14 March, 1865. Honorably discharged 3 December, 1865.
McNEELEY, J. S.
   Acting Assistant Surgeon. Resigned 1 September, 1863.
McNEELY, ROBERT W.
   Naval Cadet, 8 September, 1890. Ensign, 1 July, 1896. Lieutenant, Junior Grade, 1 July, 1899.
McNEIL, ARCHIBALD.
   Midshipman, 1 January, 1812. Lieutenant, 1 April, 1818. Died March, 1821.
McNEIL, B. P.
   Midshipman, 3 March, 1838. Resigned 5 November, 1838.
McNEIL, DANIEL.
   Captain, 17 July, 1798. Discharged 27 October, 1802, under Peace Establishment Act.
McNEIL, D., Jr.
   Midshipman, 12 January, 1799. Dismissed 9 May, 1807.
McNEIL, LEWIS W.
   Acting Third Assistant Engineer, 31 May, 1864. Honorably discharged 14 August, 1865.
McNEILLY, W. T.
   Acting Ensign, 31 October, 1862. Honorably discharged 4 October, 1865.
McNELLIS, THOMAS.
   Acting Third Assistant Engineer, 10 June, 1863. Acting Second Assistant Engineer, 18 October, 1864. Honorably discharged 7 August, 1865.
McNELLY, JOHN.
   Boatswain, 9 April, 1833. Drowned 14 July, 1839.
McNIER, JOHN.
   Boatswain, 15 January, 1800. Warrant returned.
McNIER, THOMAS.
   Midshipman, 9 June, 1811. Last appearance on Records of Navy Department, 1815. Furloughed.
McNITT, JAMES.
   Mate, 22 April, 1863. Died 11 August, 1863.
McNUTT, FINLEY A.
   Cadet Midshipman, 22 September, 1877. Graduated 10 June, 1882. Ensign, 1 July, 1884. Resigned 30 June, 1886.
McNUTT, WILLIAM F.
   Acting Assistant Surgeon, 24 December, 1862. Resigned 23 July, 1864.
McPHERSON, GEORGE E.
   Acting Assistant Surgeon. Resigned 26 May, 1865.
McPHERSON, H.
   Master, 1 April, 1814. Last appearance on Records of Navy Department, 1815. Philadelphia.
McPHERSON, JOHN F.
   Acting Assistant Paymaster, 28 January, 1862. Resigned 5 March, 1862.
McPHERSON, J. S.
   Midshipman, 20 June, 1806. Lieutenant, 26 May, 1812. Commander, 28 March, 1820. Died 28 April, 1824.
McQUADE, JAMES.
   Acting Third Assistant Engineer, 27 June, 1864. Appointment revoked 15 September, 1865.
McQUINN, CHARLES B.
   Acting Ensign, 6 November, 1863. Resigned 22 October, 1864.
McRAE, ARCHIBALD.
   Midshipman, 26 January, 1837. Passed Midshipman, 29 June, 1843. Lieutenant, 25 June, 1850. Died 17 November, 1855.
McREA, JOHN.
   Lieutenant, 10 September, 1798. Resigned 20 December, 1803.
McREADING, C. S., Jr
   Mate, 16 November, 1861. Resigned 3 April, 1862.
McREYNOLDS, J. D.
   Assistant Surgeon, 3 May, 1810. Surgeon, 2 October, 1811. Last appearance on Records of Navy Department, 1822. Philadelphia.
McRITCHIE, DAVID G.
   Acting Master, 29 October, 1861. Ensign, 12 March, 1868. Master, 18 December, 1868. Lieutenant, 21 March, 1870. Retired List, 14 June, 1884. Died 11 August, 1888.
McROBERTS, JEFFERSON.
   Midshipman, 3 March, 1841. Dismissed 27 June, 1850.
McRORIE, D. W.
   Midshipman, 1 February, 1814. Died 20 August, 1822.

GENERAL NAVY REGISTER.

McSEMPLE, ALEXANDER.
Mate, 24 January, 1863. Resigned 6 October, 1864.
McSHERRY, HENRY F.
Assistant Surgeon, 23 June, 1860. Surgeon, 22 September, 1863. Died 1 October, 1867.
McSHERRY, RICHARD F.
Assistant Surgeon, 22 November, 1843. Resigned 17 April, 1856.
McSWEENEY, EDWARD B.
Mate, 14 May, 1864. Honorably discharged 5 August, 1865.
McTHONE, HENRY.
Midshipman, 18 April, 1848. Dismissed 15 November, 1853.
McTURK, ANDREW.
Acting Third Assistant Engineer, 5 April, 1862. Acting Second Assistant Engineer, 19 January, 1864. Honorably discharged 21 August, 1865.
McVAY, CHARLES B.
Naval Cadet, 19 May, 1886. Ensign, 1 July, 1892. Lieutenant, Junior Grade, 3 March, 1899. Lieutenant, 1 July, 1899.
McVAY, JAMES.
Mate, 16 October, 1862. Acting Ensign, 25 November, 1863. Honorably discharged 14 June, 1867.
McVEY, ARCHIBALD.
Acting Assistant Paymaster, 6 January, 1864. Mustered out 26 January, 1866.
McWILLIAMS, ALEXANDER.
Assistant Surgeon, 8 February, 1802. Resigned 1 April, 1805.
McWILLIAMS, ALEXANDER S.
Acting Assistant Paymaster, 24 August, 1863. Honorably discharged 15 October, 1865.
McWILLIAMS, JOHN.
Acting Third Assistant Engineer, 3 August, 1863. Honorably discharged 30 September, 1865.
MEACHAM, JUSTIN W.
Mate, 1 October, 1862. Resigned 22 September, 1863. Acting Assistant Paymaster, 30 March, 1865. Mustered out 15 September, 1865.
MEACHAM, PETER.
Acting Gunner, 23 April, 1864. Dismissed 4 October, 1864.
MEAD, GEORGE L.
Acting Assistant Paymaster, 11 September, 1862. Passed Assistant Paymaster, 23 July, 1866. Paymaster, 25 January, 1870. Died 26 November, 1872.
MEAD, GEORGE V.
Mate, 17 January, 1863. Acting Ensign, 26 October, 1863. Honorably discharged 13 September, 1867.
MEAD, JAMES W.
Acting Third Assistant Engineer, 21 July, 1864. Resigned 18 April, 1865.
MEAD(SAMUEL H., JR.
Acting Ensign, 2 September, 1862. Acting Master, 19 November, 1864. Honorably discharged 23 January, 1866.
MEAD, WILLIAM H.
Mate, 31 October, 1861. Resigned 30 March, 1864.
MEAD, WILLIAM W.
Midshipman, 30 December, 1861. Graduated September, 1865. Ensign, 1 December, 1866. Master, 12 March, 1868. Lieutenant, 26 March, 1869. Lieutenant-Commander, 12 March, 1881. Commander, 2 August, 1891. Captain, 3 March, 1899.
MEADE, CYRUS G.
Acting Third Assistant Engineer, 15 September, 1864. Honorably discharged 7 August, 1865.
MEADE, EDWARD.
Master, 10 July, 1812. Dismissed as Supernumerary, 6 March, 1813.
MEADE, EDWARD.
Master, 3 July, 1798. Lieutenant, 29 May, 1799. Discharged 22 October, 1801, under Peace Establishment Act.
MEADE, HENRY C.
Acting Assistant Paymaster, 31 January, 1862. Passed Assistant Paymaster, 23 July, 1866. Paymaster, 9 April, 1868. Resigned 23 February, 1872.
MEADE, RICHARD M.
Midshipman, 2 April, 1804. Resigned 11 March, 1815.
MEADE, RICHARD W.
Midshipman, 1 April, 1826. Passed Midshipman, 14 June, 1834. Lieutenant on Reserved List, 20 December, 1837. Commander on Active List, 14 September, 1855. Captain on Active List, 16 July, 1862. Retired List, 11 December, 1867. Died 16 April, 1870.
MEADE, RICHARD W., JR.
Midshipman, 2 October, 1850. Passed Midshipman, 20 June, 1856. Master, 22 January, 1858. Lieutenant, 23 January, 1858. Lieutenant-Commander, 16 July, 1862. Commander, 20 September, 1868. Captain, 13 March, 1880. Commodore, 5 May, 1892. Rear-Admiral, 7 September, 1894. Retired List, 20 May, 1895. Died 4 May, 1897.
MEADER, SAMUEL B.
Acting Master, 13 November, 1861. Honorably discharged 4 February, 1866.
MEADS, JAMES.
Carpenter, 27 January, 1840. Dismissed 20 April, 1861.
MEALIUS, STEPHEN.
Acting Second Assistant Engineer, 26 November, 1861. Died 20 February, 1862.
MEANEY, CHARLES L.
Acting Ensign, 26 January, 1863. Honorably discharged 18 November, 1865.

GENERAL NAVY REGISTER.

MEANS, EDWARD J.
Midshipman, 12 October, 1848. Resigned 19 June, 1854.
MEANS, JOHN B.
Mate, 15 December, 1862. Appointment revoked (sick) 29 May, 1863.
MEANS, MARK B.
Acting Gunner, 22 July, 1863. Appointment revoked (sick) 24 April, 1865.
MEANS, VICTOR C. B.
Assistant Surgeon, 3 June, 1884. Passed Assistant Surgeon, 3 June, 1887. Surgeon, 6 June, 1897.
MEARS, HENRY B.
Acting Assistant Paymaster, 14 April, 1863. Mustered out 11 December, 1865.
MEARS, WILLIAM H.
Passed Assistant Engineer (Spanish-American War), 24 June, 1898. Honorably discharged 14 January, 1899.
MECHAM, JOHN T.
Acting Third Assistant Engineer, 1 June, 1864. Appointment revoked (sick) 29 September, 1864.
MECKLEY, THOMAS W.
Acting Assistant Surgeon, 22 October, 1862. Resigned 13 May, 1865.
MECRAY, JAMES, Jr.
Acting Assistant Surgeon, 5 November, 1862. Resigned 1 April, 1864.
MEDARY, JACOB.
Midshipman, 25 June, 1868. Graduated 1 June, 1872. Resigned 8 November, 1876.
MEDILL, R. H.
Acting Master, 1 October, 1862. Dismissed 17 April, 1863.
MEE, JOHN.
Acting Third Assistant Engineer, 28 November, 1862. Discharged 27 December, 1864.
MEEKER, CORNELIUS R.
Midshipman, 30 September, 1863. Graduated June, 1867. Ensign, 18 December, 1868. Master, 21 March, 1870. Lieutenant, 21 March, 1871. Dismissed 19 October, 1875.
MEEKER, JOSEPH R.
Acting Assistant Paymaster, 4 November, 1862. Mustered out 9 December, 1865.
MEETER, W. W.
Acting Ensign, 24 March, 1864. Honorably discharged 21 October, 1865.
MEGATHLIN, ANTHONY S.
Acting Master, 4 November, 1861. Honorably discharged 4 November, 1865.
MEGLER, JOSEPH G.
Mate, 1 October, 1862. Acting Ensign, 7 July, 1863. Honorably discharged 24 October, 1865.
MEHLMAN, AUGUST.
Assistant Engineer (Spanish-American War), 1 June, 1898. Honorably discharged 12 April, 1899.
MEHRTENS, RUDOLPH C.
Acting Boatswain, 25 January, 1900.
MEIGS, JOHN B.
Midshipman, 2 February, 1829. Dismissed 24 September, 1833.
MEIGS, JOHN F.
Midshipman, 4 October, 1862. Graduated June, 1867. Ensign, 18 December, 1868. Master, 21 March, 1870. Lieutenant, 21 March, 1871. Retired List, 3 August, 1891. Resigned 22 December, 1896.
MEIRE, JULIUS.
Professor, 9 November, 1840. Dropped 4 September, 1848.
MEISSNER, J. G.
Acting Ensign, 1 March, 1864. Honorably discharged, 6 June, 1865.
MELCHER, LEWIS M.
Mate, 9 October, 1867.
MELCHERT, ALBERT J.
Acting Ensign, 2 August, 1864. Honorably discharged 26 June, 1865.
MELDRUM, ALEXANDER.
Mate, 5 March, 1862. Dismissed 22 November, 1862.
MELISH, JOHN G.
Midshipman, 1 January, 1818. Dismissed 30 August, 1819.
MELLACH, SMANUEL.
Acting Assistant Paymaster, 18 December, 1861. Resigned 4 November, 1865. Passed Assistant Paymaster, 23 July, 1866. Paymaster, 4 March, 1875. Died 21 October, 1878.
MELLEN, THOMAS.
Sailmaker, 16 February, 1861. Resigned 28 January, 1863.
MELLEN, WILLIAM.
Acting Ensign, 25 November, 1863. Honorably discharged 30 September, 1865.
MELLOR, JAMES W.
Acting Second Assistant Engineer, 28 October, 1864. Honorably discharged 27 February, 1866. Acting Second Assistant Engineer, 10 August, 1866. Mustered out 20 January, 1868.
MELSON, WILLIAM H.
Mate, 1 April, 1862. Resigned 22 January, 1863.
MELVILLE, BENJAMIN S.
Acting Master, 18 July, 1861. Honorably discharged 1 August, 1868.
MELVILLE, GEORGE W.
Third Assistant Engineer, 29 July, 1861. Second Assistant Engineer, 18 December, 1862. First Assistant Engineer, 30 January, 1865. Chief Engineer, 4 March, 1881. Rank changed to Captain, 3 March, 1899. Chief of Bureau of Steam Engineering, with rank of Rear-Admiral.

MELVILLE, THOMAS W.
Midshipman, 1 February, 1826. Resigned 3 June, 1834.
MELVIN, JOSIAH.
Master, 17 October, 1812. Resigned 11 April, 1814.
MENCH, ISAAC S.
Acting Second Assistant Engineer, 3 May, 1864. Resigned (sick) 10 October, 1864.
MENDALL, JOHN T.
Acting Ensign, 10 September, 1862. Appointment revoked (sick) 7 October, 1863.
MENDELL, WILLIAM C.
Acting Ensign and Pilot, 28 October, 1864. Honorably discharged 13 May, 1865.
MENDENHALL, SAMUEL.
Acting Assistant Surgeon, 20 February, 1864. Honorably discharged 25 October, 1865.
MENEFEE, DANIEL P.
Cadet Midshipman, 25 September, 1874. Graduated 10 June, 1881. Ensign, Junior Grade, 3 March, 1883. Ensign, 26 June, 1884. Lieutenant, Junior Grade, 11 December, 1891. Lieutenant, 18 February, 1896.
MENNER, ROBERT T.
Naval Cadet, 5 September, 1896. Graduated 30 June, 1900.
MENOCAL, ADOLFO J.
Civil Engineer, 15 March, 1894.
MENOCAL, ANECITO G.
Civil Engineer, 15 July, 1874. Retired List, 1 September, 1898.
MENTZ, GEORGE W.
Midshipman, 26 September, 1866. Graduated 7 June, 1870. Ensign, 13 July, 1872. Master, 25 January, 1875. Lieutenant, 28 October, 1881. Lieutenant-Commander, 3 March, 1899.
MENZIES, GUSTAVUS V.
Midshipman, 21 September, 1861. Graduated November, 1864. Ensign, 1 November, 1866. Master, 1 December, 1866. Lieutenant, 12 March, 1868. Lieutenant-Commander, 25 January, 1870. Resigned 28 December, 1871.
MERCER, JOHN F.
Midshipman, 1 October, 1828. Passed Midshipman, 14 June, 1834. Lieutenant, 25 February, 1841. Died 10 February, 1844.
MERCER, JOHN F.
Midshipman, 4 June, 1799. Resigned 18 September, 1800.
MERCER, JOHN C.
Assistant Surgeon, 8 February, 1832. Passed Assistant Surgeon, 8 November, 1836. Surgeon, 9 December, 1839. Resigned 26 September, 1840.
MERCER, JOHN D.
Third Assistant Engineer, 16 February, 1852. Resigned 8 July, 1856.
MERCER, JOSEPH.
Third Assistant Engineer, 12 August, 1861. Resigned 1 May, 1862.
MERCER, LANDON.
Midshipman, 1 January, 1808. Killed in a duel 22 December, 1811.
MERCER, ROBERT.
Midshipman, 14 November, 1799. Resigned 30 December, 1800.
MERCER, SAMUEL.
Midshipman, 4 March, 1815. Lieutenant, 13 January, 1825. Commander, 8 September, 1841. Captain, 14 September, 1855. Died 6 March, 1862.
MERCER, WILLIAM R.
Midshipman, 8 December, 1841. Passed Midshipman, 22 August, 1849. Dropped 13 September, 1855. Lieutenant, Active List, 15 September, 1855. Resigned 24 January, 1859.
MERCHANT, CLARKE.
Acting Midshipman, 29 May, 1852. Midshipman, 10 June, 1857. Passed Midshipman, 25 June, 1860. Master, 24 October, 1860. Lieutenant, 18 April, 1861. Commander, 20 December, 1864. Resigned 10 August, 1865.
MERCHANT, CORNELIUS M.
Acting Master, 25 January, 1862. Honorably discharged 19 August, 1865.
MERCHANT, ROBERT.
Acting Ensign, 25 June, 1863. Resigned 3 May, 1865.
MERCHANT, SAMUEL.
Acting Ensign, 3 May, 1864. Honorably discharged 13 August, 1865.
MERCIER, WILLIAM T.
Third Assistant Engineer, 17 January, 1842. Second Assistant Engineer, 10 July, 1847. Dismissed 14 August, 1849.
MEREDITH, G. M.
Midshipman, 1 October, 1827. Died in 1828.
MEREDITH, HENRY C.
Acting Assistant Surgeon, 27 February, 1865. Honorably discharged 9 October, 1865.
MEREDITH, JOHN R.
Acting Third Assistant Engineer, 11 August, 1864. Honorably discharged 3 October, 1865.
MEREDITH, WILLIAM H.
Acting Chief Engineer, 1 October, 1862. Honorably discharged 27 May, 1866.
MEREDITH, WILLIAM T.
Assistant Paymaster, 24 August, 1861. Paymaster, 20 May, 1862. Resigned 13 June, 1866.
MERIAM, FRANK B.
Mate, 18 May, 1861. Acting Master, 31 October, 1861. Resigned 11 October, 1864.

MERIAN, HENRY WALTON.
Third Assistant Engineer, 25 August, 1862. Lost on the Weehawken, 6 December, 1863.
MERICK, F. T.
Midshipman, 9 June, 1811. Resigned 25 February, 1813.
MERO, WILLIAM.
Acting Ensign, 13 May, 1863. Honorably discharged 30 September, 1865.
MERRELL, JOHN P.
Midshipman, 20 July, 1863. Graduated June, 1867. Ensign, 18 December, 1868. Master, 21 March, 1870. Lieutenant, 21 March, 1871. Lieutenant-Commander, 28 May, 1888. Commander, 1 November, 1896.
MERRIAM, GREENLIEF A.
Midshipman, 24 July, 1866. Graduated 7 June, 1870. Ensign, 13 July, 1871. Master, 22 October, 1874. Lieutenant, 28 May, 1881. Lieutenant-Commander, 3 March, 1899.
MERRIAM, JOHN HANCOCK.
Assistant Paymaster, 18 May, 1897. Passed Paymaster, 15 June, 1898.
MERRIFIELD, CHARLES E.
Acting Assistant Paymaster, 24 February, 1864. Mustered out 1 March, 1866.
MERRIGHEW, JAMES.
Mate. Died at Pensacola, Fla., 15 September, 1863.
MERRIHEW, STEPHEN E.
Acting Ensign, 19 March, 1864. Dismissed 9 March, 1866.
MERRILL, ALEXANDER R.
Lieutenant (Spanish-American War), 9 May, 1898. Honorably discharged 15 September, 1898.
MERRILL, CHESTER R.
Acting Third Assistant Engineer, 11 May, 1864. Appointment revoked May, 1865.
MERRILL, DANIEL.
Acting Ensign, 24 June, 1864. Honorably discharged 10 July, 1865.
MERRILL, GEORGE.
Midshipman, 5 February, 1800. Lieutenant, 30 April, 1808. Died 18 August, 1822.
MERRILL, H. M.
Acting Master, 26 February, 1862. Honorably discharged 4 October, 1865.
MERRILL, J. AMOS.
Acting Ensign, 29 November, 1862. Dismissed 11 June, 1864. Mate, 17 August, 1864. Deserted 30 January, 1865.
MERRILL, JOHN M.
Acting Master, 12 August, 1861. Dismissed 26 February, 1862.
MERRILL, LAWSON C.
Assistant Paymaster, 29 August, 1861. Paymaster, 5 September, 1862. Died 10 August, 1864.
MERRILL, LOUVILLE H.
Acting Assistant Paymaster, 4 June, 1864. Honorably discharged 16 August, 1865.
MERRILL, RICHARD.
Gunner, date not known. Last appearance on Records of Navy Department.
MERRILL, SAMUEL.
Mate, 23 September, 1862. Acting Ensign, 22 September, 1862. Dismissed 12 August, 1863. Acting Ensign, 24 October, 1863. Resigned 9 March, 1864.
MERRILL, STEPHEN.
Purser, 4 December, 1799. Discharged 23 June, 1801,under Peace Establishment Act.
MERRILL, W. F.
Master, 19 July, 1812. Discharged 7 May, 1813.
MERRILL, WILLIAM.
Mate, 2 October, 1863. Resigned 3 May, 1865.
MERRIMAN, EDGAR C.
Acting Midshipman, 21 September, 1857. Resigned 7 November, 1860. Acting Master, 3 December, 1861. Acting Lieutenant, 25 September, 1863. Lieutenant from 6 July, 1862. Lieutenant-Commander, 25 July, 1866. Commander, 12 March, 1875. Captain, 31 July, 1890. Retired List, 26 September, 1891. Died 11 December, 1894.
MERRIMAN, EDWARD.
Acting Second Assistant Engineer, 1 October, 1862. Acting First Assistant Engineer, 1 December, 1862. Acting Chief Engineer, 1 February, 1863. Resigned 1 December, 1864.
MERRIMAN, JAMES E.
Mate, 31 March, 1864. Drowned from Shamrock, 1 July, 1865.
MERRIMAN, J. WALTER.
Mate, 12 December, 1861. Acting Ensign, 28 January, 1864. Honorably discharged 4 March, 1866.
MERRITHEW, WILLIAM H.
Acting Master, 4 November, 1861. Resigned 24 June, 1862.
MERRITT, DARWIN R.
Naval Cadet, 10 September, 1891. Assistant Engineer, 1 July, 1897. Drowned 15 February, 1898.
MERRITT, EDWARD D.
Acting Third Assistant Engineer, 18 October, 1861. Acting Second Assistant Engineer, 10 February, 1864. Resigned 14 June, 1865.
MERRITT, LAWSON C.
Assistant Paymaster, 29 August, 1861. Paymaster, 5 September, 1862. Retired 3 August, 1863. Died 10 August, 1864.
MERRITT, SILAS V.
Assistant Surgeon (Spanish-American War), 21 May, 1898. Honorably discharged 13 September, 1898.

MERRITT, WILLIAM A.
Assistant Paymaster, 20 May, 1898. Passed Assistant Paymaster, 7 May, 1899.
MERRITT, THEORON.
Acting Assistant Paymaster, 11 September, 1862. Assistant Paymaster, 30 June, 1864. Resigned 17 March, 1865.
MERRY, JOHN F.
Acting Ensign, 15 October, 1862. Acting Master, 23 September, 1865. Ensign, 12 March, 1868. Master, 18 December, 1868. Lieutenant, 21 March, 1870. Lieutenant-Commander, 1 December, 1883. Commander, 9 May, 1893. Captain, 29 December, 1899.
MERRY, THOMAS H.
Lieutenant, 21 June, 1799. Resigned 18 October, 1799.
MERSHON, JOHN S.
Assistant Surgeon, 10 December, 1814. Last appearance on Records of Navy Department, 1818. Furloughed.
MERTZ, ALBERT.
Midshipman, 27 June, 1867. Graduated 1 June, 1872. Ensign, 15 July, 1873. Master, 26 November, 1877. Lieutenant, Junior Grade, 3 March, 1883. Lieutenant, 27 September, 1884. Lieutenant-Commander, 3 March, 1899.
MERVINE, WILLIAM.
Midshipman, 16 January, 1809. Lieutenant, 4 February, 1815. Commander, 12 June, 1834. Captain, 8 September, 1841. Retired List, 21 December, 1861. Commodore, Retired List, 16 July, 1862. Rear-Admiral, Retired List, 25 July, 1866. Died 15 September, 1868.
MESSENGER, FRANK C.
Gunner, 26 June, 1888. Chief Gunner, 3 March, 1899.
MESSENGER, WILLIAM H.
Assistant Engineer (Spanish-American War), 14 May, 1898. Honorably discharged 10 January, 1899.
MESSICK, EDWARD R.
Acting Second Assistant Engineer, 1 September, 1864. Honorably discharged 17 June, 1865.
MESSINGER, WILLIAM H.
Second Assistant Engineer, 29 October, 1861. First Assistant Engineer, 28 September, 1864. Resigned 16 June, 1865.
MESSER, J. P.
Acting Third Assistant Engineer, 6 September, 1864. Honorably discharged 30 September, 1865.
MESSER, WILLIAM W., JR.
Mate, 15 October, 1861. Acting Master, 29 April, 1862. Dismissed 28 July, 1862.
MESSERSMITH, JOHN S.
Assistant Surgeon, 9 February, 1837. Surgeon, 13 July, 1853. Medical Director, 3 March, 1871. Retired List, 28 June, 1872. Died 16 February, 1891.
MESSETT, JAMES.
Mate, 6 June, 1863. Dismissed 14 April, 1864.
METCALF, PAUL.
Assistant Surgeon, 23 April, 1799. Resigned 4 August, 1799.
METZ, WILLIAM H.
Mate, 1 November, 1861. Acting Ensign, 11 February, 1864. Resigned 4 April, 1865.
METZGER, CHARLES.
Acting Second Assistant Engineer, 30 November, 1863. Honorably discharged 17 July, 1865.
MEYER, JOHN.
Acting Third Assistant Engineer, 20 April, 1864. Resigned 6 August, 1864.
MEYER, STEUBEN P.
Master, 18 November, 1814. Resigned 10 September, 1825.
MEYER, THEODORE.
Acting Warrant Machinest, 6 July, 1899.
MEYER, THIES N.
Mate, 15 November, 1861. Acting Master, 26 March, 1862. Honorably discharged 8 October, 1868.
MEYERS, JOHN K.
Acting Third Assistant Engineer, 22 June, 1863. Appointment revoked (sick) 20 October, 1863.
MICHAEL, WILLIAM H. C.
Mate, 11 June, 1863. Acting Ensign, 16 July, 1864. Honorably discharged 13 June, 1866.
MICHEL, LOUIS.
Acting Assistant Surgeon, 17 May, 1861. Resigned 24 August, 1861. Reappointed 4 October, 1861. Resigned 15 February, 1865.
MICHELSON, ALBERT A.
Midshipman, 28 June, 1869. Graduated 31 May, 1873. Ensign, 16 July, 1874. Master, 5 February, 1879. Resigned 30 September, 1881.
MICHENER, ABRAM.
Third Assistant Engineer, 28 October, 1862. Second Assistant Engineer, 15 March, 1864. Resigned 25 September, 1865.
MICHLER, AMBROSE K.
Assistant Paymaster, 31 October, 1877. Passed Assistant Paymaster, 1 September, 1881. Paymaster, 12 September, 1893. Resigned 3 May, 1899.
MICKLE, JOHN L.
Mate, 10 February, 1863. Acting Ensign, 15 October, 1863. Honorably discharged 13 September, 1867.

GENERAL NAVY REGISTER. 379

MICKLEY, ALBERT J.
Passed Assistant Engineer (Spanish-American War), 10 June, 1898. Honorably discharged 4 January, 1899.
MICKLEY, JOSEPH P.
Acting Third Assistant Engineer, 28 March, 1864. Honorably discharged 11 January, 1869. Second Assistant Engineer, 20 March, 1871. Passed Assistant Engineer, 24 February, 1878. Chief Engineer, 28 August, 1894. Rank changed to Lieutenant-Commander, 3 March, 1899. Retired List, with rank of Commander, 17 January, 1900.
MICKS, WILLIAM G.
Assistant Surgeon, 16 May, 1829. Resigned 18 October, 1833.
MIDDLEBROOK, LOUIS F.
Ensign (Spanish-American War), 22 June, 1898. Honorably discharged 9 September, 1898.
MIDDLETON, BENJAMIN P.
Acting Gunner, 1 August, 1900.
MIDDLETON, EDWARD.
Midshipman, 1 July, 1828. Passed Midshipman, 14 June, 1834. Lieutenant, 25 February, 1841. Commander, 14 September, 1855. Captain, 24 April, 1863. Commodore, 26 November, 1868. Retired List, 11 December, 1872. Rear-Admiral, Retired List, 15 August, 1876. Died 27 April, 1883.
MIDDLETON, ELECTUS.
Sailmaker, 15 July, 1841. Died 3 February, 1857.
MIDDLETON, FRANK.
Mate, 16 March, 1863. Acting Ensign, 18 June, 1864. Resigned 5 June, 1865.
MIDDLETON, GEORGE I.
Naval Cadet, 9 September, 1892. Resigned 14 June, 1895. Ensign (Spanish-American War), 13 June, 1898. Honorably discharged 24 December, 1898.
MIDDLETON GEORGE W.
Acting Carpenter, 23 May, 1863. Honorably discharged 10 November, 1865
MIDDLETON, HARRY E.
Assistant Engineer (Spanish-American War), 25 May, 1898. Honorably discharged 14 March, 1899.
MIDDLETON, JOHN.
Midshipman, 1 November, 1827. Died 12 April, 1833.
MIDDLETON, JOHN M.
Second Assistant Engineer, 2 May, 1843. Disrated to Third Assistant Engineer, 28 July, 1845. Second Assistant Engineer, 10 July, 1847. Dismissed 5 October, 1849.
MIDDLETON, JOHN M.
Acting Second Assistant Engineer, 9 January, 1864. Honorably discharged 1 December, 1868.
MIDDLETON JOSEPH.
Master, 31 July, 1812. Discharged under Act, 27 February, 1815.
MIDDLETON, MOSES.
Master, 18 June, 1812. Discharged 3 May, 1813.
MIDDLETON, O. H.
Midshipman, 1 January, 1817. Resigned 30 June, 1823.
MIDDLETON, ROBERT J.
Acting Second Assistant Engineer, 3 November, 1864. Honorably discharged 25 September, 1865.
MIDDLETON THOMAS K.
Mate. Appointment revoked (sick) 29 January, 1862.
MIDGET, B. F.
Acting Ensign and Pilot, 13 April, 1865. Resigned 29 March, 1866.
MIDLAM, SAMUEL C.
Acting First Assistant Engineer, 13 December, 1862. Honorably discharged 25 September, 1865.
MIDLAM, SYLVESTER W.
Acting Third Assistant Engineer, 26 January, 1863. Acting Second Assistant Engineer, 9 September, 1864. Honorably discharged 15 October, 1865.
MIESBANG, NICHOLAS.
Acting Second Assistant Engineer, 1 October, 1862. Died from wounds on Red Rover, 31 January, 1863.
MIFFLEN, HENRY.
Midshipman, 1 December, 1824. Resigned 22 April, 1831.
MILBY, ROBERT.
Acting Second Assistant Engineer, 5 August, 1864. Honorably discharged 21 October, 1865.
MILES, ASHTON.
Assistant Surgeon, 8 March, 1847. Passed Assistant Surgeon, 22 April, 1854. Dismissed 1 December, 1858.
MILES, CHARLES, Jr.
Midshipman, 24 June, 1799. Resigned 21 May, 1804.
MILES, CHARLES R.
Midshipman, 27 June, 1868. Graduated 1 June, 1872. Ensign, 15 July, 1873. Master, 26 February, 1878. Lieutenant, Junior Grade, 3 March, 1883. Lieutenant, 12 December, 1884. Died 14 January, 1889.
MILES, JOHN L.
Acting Second Assistant Engineer, 22 April, 1863. Discharged 29 May, 1864.
MILES, JOHN W.
Warrant Machinist (Spanish-American War), 18 May, 1898. Honorably discharged 2 September, 1898.
MILES, ORLANDO W.
Mate, 18 May, 1864. Resigned 26 May, 1865.

MILES, WILLIAM B.
  Mate, 9 January, 1862. Resigned 11 April, 1865.
MILK, LEWIS.
  Mate, 13 May, 1863. Resigned 8 May, 1865.
MILLARD, SAMUEL G.
  Mate, 10 February, 1870. Appointment revoked 2 October, 1871.
MILLEGEN, JOHN.
  Midshipman, 21 July, 1863. Graduated June, 1869. Deserted 16 October, 1869.
MILLEN, WILLIAM T.
  Assistant Engineer (Spanish-American War), 15 June, 1898. Honorably discharged 2 September, 1898.
MILLER, ARCHIBALD.
  Acting Second Assistant Engineer, 5 June, 1863. Resigned 9 October, 1863.
MILLER, B. W.
  Midshipman, 8 March, 1814. Resigned 29 September, 1814.
MILLER, CHARLES.
  Acting Ensign, 15 October, 1864. Honorably discharged 25 July, 1865.
MILLER, CHARLES.
  Boatswain, 13 June, 1861. Resigned 23 May, 1868. Reappointed from 13 June, 1861. Chief Boatswain, 3 March, 1899. Retired List, 2 May, 1899.
MILLER, CHARLES.
  Boatswain, 21 September, 1860. Retired List, 17 March, 1887. Died 2 July, 1887.
MILLER, CHARLES W.
  Mate, 1 October, 1862. Acting Ensign, 1 August, 1863. Acting Master, 18 May, 1864. Honorably discharged 27 September, 1865.
MILLER, CYRUS R.
  Naval Cadet, 6 September, 1893. Ensign, 1 July, 1899.
MILLER, DANIEL G.
  Acting Second Assistant Engineer, 6 August, 1864. Honorably discharged 7 October, 1865.
MILLER, EDWIN H.
  Mate, 10 March, 1862. Acting Ensign, 12 February, 1864. Master, 12 March, 1868. Lieutenant, 18 December, 1868. Lieutenant-Commander, 16 June, 1870. Died 7 November, 1874.
MILLER, FREDERICK A.
  Mate, 11 September, 1861. Acting Ensign, 24 April, 1863. Acting Master, 17 January, 1865. Ensign, 12 March, 1868. Master, 18 December, 1868. Lieutenant, 21 March, 1870. Lieutenant-Commander, 15 April, 1882. Retired List, 30 November, 1885.
MILLER, FRANKLIN.
  Acting Assistant Paymaster, 19 October, 1861. Mustered out 27 February, 1866.
MILLER, FREDERICK.
  Mate, 22 May, 1865. Died 20 August, 1876.
MILLER, FREDERICK C.
  Acting Master, 18 December, 1861. Honorably discharged 12 November, 1865.
MILLER, FREDERICK L.
  Third Assistant Engineer, 21 October, 1861. Second Assistant Engineer, 25 August, 1865. Resigned 28 May, 1868.
MILLER, GEORGE.
  Acting Ensign, 4 October, 1864. Honorably discharged 3 August, 1865.
MILLER, GEORGE G.
  Acting Ensign, 5 September, 1864. Resigned 13 March, 1865.
MILLER, GRIFFEN F.
  Mate, 22 April, 1863. Honorably discharged 4 February, 1866.
MILLER, HARRISON.
  Mate, 23 May, 1863. Resigned 16 September, 1864.
MILLER, HENRY.
  Acting Second Assistant Engineer, 5 August, 1864. Honorably discharged 25 September, 1865.
MILLER, HENRY W.
  Acting Midshipman, 29 May, 1852. Midshipman, 10 June, 1857. Passed Midshipman, 25 June, 1860. Master, 24 October, 1860. Lieutenant, 18 April, 1861. Lieutenant-Commander, 3 March, 1865. Resigned 10 April, 1866.
MILLER, HENRY W.
  Acting Second Assistant Engineer, 24 July, 1863. Resigned 23 June, 1865.
MILLER, HORACE B.
  Mate, 7 February, 1863. Resigned 13 August, 1863.
MILLER, HUGH L.
  Ensign (Spanish-American War), 20 May, 1898. Honorably discharged 8 September, 1898.
MILLER, ISAAC.
  Mate, 5 March, 1863. Acting Ensign and Pilot, 10 November, 1863. Honorably discharged 1 January, 1866.
MILLER, JACOB.
  Sailmaker, 28 May, 1798. Last appearance on Records of Navy Department. Suspended.
MILLER, JACOB W.
  Midshipman, 30 September, 1863. Graduated June, 1867. Ensign, 18 December, 1868. Master, 21 March, 1870. Lieutenant, 21 March, 1871. Resigned 2 January, 1884. Lieutenant-Commander (Spanish-American War), 5 July, 1898. Honorably discharged 17 September, 1898.
MILLER, JAMES.
  Acting Master's Mate, 25 December, 1863. Honorably discharged 31 August, 1864.

GENERAL NAVY REGISTER. 381

MILLER, JAMES.
Acting Second Assistant Engineer, 1 October, 1862. Acting First Assistant Engineer, 5 March, 1863. Acting Chief Engineer, 25 September, 1863. Honorably discharged 15 September, 1865.

MILLER, JAMES A.
Midshipman, 2 April, 1804. Dismissed 10 February, 1808.

MILLER, JAMES A.
Acting Second Assistant Engineer, 10 December, 1863. Honorably discharged 30 October, 1865.

MILLER, JAMES F.
Midshipman, 1 November, 1826. Passed Midshipman, 28 April, 1832. Lieutenant, 9 February, 1837. Reserved List, 13 September, 1855. Commander, Retired List, 1 July, 1861. Commodore on Reserved List, 4 April, 1867. Died 11 July, 1868.

MILLER, J. DICKINSON.
Assistant Surgeon, 6 December, 1836. Surgeon, 20 April, 1847. Medical Director, 3 March, 1871. Retired List, 6 November, 1872. Died 29 January, 1891.

MILLER, JOHN F.
Mate, 5 May, 1862. Resigned 3 December, 1862.

MILLER, JAMES M.
Midshipman, 24 September, 1863. Graduated June, 1867. Ensign, 18 December, 1868. Master, 21 March, 1870. Lieutenant, 21 March, 1871. Lieutenant Commander, 29 May, 1891. Commander, 26 September, 1897.

MILLER, JAMES M.
Boatswain, 21 September, 1857. Dismissed 12 June, 1861.

MILLER, J. E.
Acting Assistant Surgeon, 6 December, 1873. Resigned 5 November, 1875.

MILLER, JOHN.
Acting Third Assistant Engineer, 21 November, 1863. Acting Second Assistant Engineer, 14 October, 1864. Honorably discharged 16 September, 1865. Acting Second Assistant Engineer, 1 December, 1866. Mustered out 9 November, 1869.

MILLER, JOHN
Acting Second Assistant Engineer, 1 October, 1862. Honorably discharged 16 September, 1865.

MILLER, JOHN.
Acting Second Assistant Engineer, 21 October, 1863. Acting First Assistant Engineer, 29 April, 1864. Resigned (sick) 8 February, 1865.

MILLER, JOHN.
Boatswain, 16 August, 1838. Died 26 March, 1851.

MILLER, JOHN.
Boatswain, 20 July, 1840. Resigned 22 March, 1842.

MILLER, JOHN D.
Acting Second Assistant Engineer, 10 June, 1864. Honorably discharged 12 May, 1865.

MILLER, JOHN M.
Acting Second Assistant Engineer, 5 August, 1864. Honorably discharged 24 September, 1865.

MILLER, JOHN T.
Acting Third Assistant Engineer, 21 June, 1862. Resigned 1 March, 1865.

MILLER, JOHN T. S.
Carpenter, 1 February, 1896.

MILLER, JOHN V.
Assistant Engineer (Spanish-American War), 20 June, 1898. Honorably discharged 1 September, 1898.

MILLER, JOSEPH B.
Midshipman, 7 April, 1847. Died 19 March, 1850.

MILLER, JOSEPH E.
Carpenter, 10 December, 1853. Resigned 26 April, 1872.

MILLER, JOSEPH F.
Acting Third Assistant Engineer, 10 May, 1864. Honorably discharged 24 June, 1865.

MILLER, JOSEPH N.
Midshipman, 10 June, 1854. Passed Midshipman, 22 November, 1856. Master, 22 January, 1858. Lieutenant, 19 February, 1860. Lieutenant-Commander, 16 July, 1862. Commander, 25 January, 1870. Captain, 28 May, 1881. Commodore, 16 April, 1894. Rear Admiral, 21 March, 1897. Retired List, 22 November, 1898.

MILLER, LOUIS G.
Naval Cadet (Spanish-American War), 21 June, 1898. Honorably discharged 1 November, 1898.

MILLER, LUCAS.
Midshipman, 1 November, 1828. Died 3 January, 1830.

MILLER, M. A.
Acting Assistant Surgeon, 11 April, 1863. Honorably discharged 8 December, 1865.

MILLER, MARCUS L.
Naval Cadet, 4 September, 1884. Ensign, 1 July, 1890. Lieutenant, Junior Grade, 28 March, 1898. Lieutenant, 3 March, 1899.

MILLER, MERRILL.
Midshipman, 28 November, 1859. Ensign, 13 October, 1862. Lieutenant, 22 February, 1864. Lieutenant-Commander, 25 July, 1866. Commander, 25 November, 1877. Captain, 25 February, 1893. Rear-Admiral, 1 July, 1900.

MILLER, N. W.
Assistant Surgeon, 6 January, 1815. Resigned 18 May, 1819.

MILLER, PETER.
Mate, 8 September, 1863. Appointment revoked (sick) 19 October, 1863.

MILLER, PHILIP.
Boatswain, 16 September, 1859. Resigned 19 April, 1860.

382 GENERAL NAVY REGISTER.

MILLER, PHILIP.
　　Third Assistant Engineer, 20 May, 1862. Second Assistant Engineer, 15 February, 1864. Dropped 11 January, 1873.
MILLER, PHILIP J.
　　Boatswain, 4 June, 1856. Died 14 June, 1875.
MILLER, RICHARD D.
　　Midshipman, 10 May, 1820. Dismissed 6 April, 1829.
MILLER, ROBERT.
　　Surgeon, 24 May, 1812. Last appearance on Records of Navy Department. Dead.
MILLER, ROBERT.
　　Acting Third Assistant Engineer, 3 November, 1862. Honorably discharged 28 September, 1865. Acting Third Assistant Engineer, 29 January, 1867. Resigned 17 August, 1867.
MILLER, ROBERT.
　　Midshipman, 20 April, 1800. Discharged 5 June, 1801, under Peace Establishment Act.
MILLER, RUFUS N.
　　Mate, 28 December, 1863. Acting Ensign, 17 October, 1864. Resigned 9 June, 1865.
MILLER, SAMUEL A.
　　Midshipman, 3 January, 1840. Dismissed 9 February, 1842.
MILLER, THOMAS McL.
　　Acting Ensign 5 February, 1863. Deserted 31 July, 1865.
MILLER, THOMAS J.
　　Midshipman, 9 September, 1841. Resigned 2 February, 1847.
MILLER, WARREN H.
　　Assistant Engineer (Spanish-American War), 3 June, 1898. Honorably discharged 14 March, 1899.
MILLER, WILLIAM.
　　Master, 23 January, 1815. Died 19 May, 1847.
MILLER, WILLIAM.
　　Midshipman, 2 August, 1800. Dismissed 26 November, 1807.
MILLER, WILLIAM G.
　　Cadet Engineer, 1 October, 1881. Ensign, 1 July, 1887. Lieutenant, Junior Grade, 11 March, 1896. Lieutenant, 3 March, 1899.
MILLER, WILLIAM H.
　　Acting Third Assistant Engineer, 14 November, 1861. Resigned 10 February, 1863. Acting First Assistant Engineer, 10 July, 1863. Honorably discharged 6 September, 1865.
MILLER, WILLIAM O.
　　Acting Third Assistant Engineer, 26 June, 1863. Dismissed 24 September, 1863.
MILLER, WILLIAM S.
　　Naval Cadet, 20 September, 1895. At sea prior to final graduation.
MILLER, WILLIAM W.
　　Midshipman, 15 March, 1799. Last appearance on Records of Navy Department, 1 December, 1800.
MILLER, WILLIAM W.
　　Third Assistant Engineer, 26 August, 1859. Resigned 5 August, 1861.
MILLETT, CHARLES.
　　Acting Ensign, 17 June, 1863. Resigned (sick) 29 April, 1865.
MILLETT, FRANK.
　　Mate, 31 July, 1863. Acting Ensign, 25 December, 1863. Honorably discharged 20 October, 1865.
MILLETT, WILLIAM H.
　　Acting Ensign, 24 March, 1864. Honorably discharged 12 August, 1865.
MILLHOLLAND, THOMAS.
　　Acting Third Assistant Engineer, 21 March, 1862. Acting Second Assistant Engineer, 10 July, 1863. Resigned 17 December, 1863.
MILLIGAN, CHARLES W.
　　Acting Third Assistant Engineer, 22 December, 1863. Honorably discharged 24 October, 1865.
MILLIGAN, FRANK J.
　　Midshipman, 30 June, 1869. Graduated 1 June, 1874. Ensign, 17 July, 1876. Master, 6 November, 1881. Lieutenant, Junior Grade, 3 March, 1883. Lieutenant, 31 March, 1888. Retired List, 28 May, 1892. Died 13 January, 1897.
MILLIGAN, JAMES F.
　　Midshipman, 28 July, 1846. Resigned 4 April, 1850.
MILLIGAN, JOHN D.
　　Pharmacist, 15 September, 1898.
MILLIGAN, J. L.
　　Midshipman, 30 May, 1816. Resigned 24 April, 1818.
MILLIGAN, ROBERT.
　　Midshipman, 13 March, 1839. Resigned 8 July, 1846.
MILLIGAN, ROBERT W.
　　Third Assistant Engineer, 3 August, 1863. Second Assistant Engineer, 25 July, 1866. Passed Assistant Engineer, 25 March, 1874. Chief Engineer, 16 May, 1892. Rank changed to Commander, 3 March, 1899.
MILLIGAN, WILLIAM J.
　　Acting Third Assistant Engineer, 27 February, 1863. Acting Second Assistant Engineer, 17 December, 1863. Honorably discharged 4 December, 1865.
MILLIKEN, BENJAMIN F.
　　Acting Master, 30 August, 1861. Honorably discharged 11 February, 1866.
MILLIMAN, ANSON B.
　　Midshipman, 31 July, 1866. Graduated 7 June, 1870. Retired List, 14 July, 1874. Died 26 December, 1874.

GENERAL NAVY REGISTER. 383

MILLS, GEORGE E.
 Acting Ensign, 7 Septemer, 1864. Honorably discharged 15 September, 1865.
MILLS, HIRAM R.
 Mate, 6 July, 1864. Honorably discharged 27 June, 1865.
MILLS, JAMES H.
 Acting Assistant Surgeon, 28 March, 1863. Honorably discharged 26 September, 1865.
MILLS, JOHN.
 Carpenter, 20 July, 1861. Wholly retired 6 July, 1880.
MILLS, JOHN.
 Boatswain, 16 January, 1838. Died 26 March, 1851.
MILLS, JOHN K.
 Midshipman, 15 January, 1841. Resigned 7 July, 1841.
MILLS, OSCAR B.
 Acting Third Assistant Engineer, 31 October, 1862. Third Assistant Engineer, 16 January, 1863. Second Assistant Engineer, 28 May, 1864. Retired 26 October, 1872. Died 10 August, 1873.
MILLS, THOMAS B.
 Acting Midshipman, 31 May, 1852. Midshipman, 10 June, 1857. Passed Midshipman, 25 June, 1860. Master, 24 October, 1860. Resigned 16 January, 1861.
MILLS, WILLIAM.
 Acting Second Assistant Engineer, 1 October, 1862. Acting First Assistant Engineer, 5 February, 1863. Acting Chief Engineer, 12 December, 1863. Honorably discharged 2 December, 1865.
MILLS, WILLIAM A.
 Acting Master, 26 August, 1861. Honorably discharged 18 May, 1866.
MILNE, ANDREW.
 Boatswain, 8 May, 1861. Retired List, 12 December, 1885. Died 18 July, 1886.
MILNE, JAMES.
 Midshipman, 30 June, 1799. Discharged 12 October, 1801, under Peace Establishment Act.
MILNOR, WILLIAM.
 Assistant Surgeon, 3 January, 1828. Died 19 April, 1833.
MILSTEAD, JAMES W.
 Acting Third Assistant Engineer, 26 February, 1862. Resigned 13 August, 1862. Acting Third Assistant Engineer, 19 September, 1862. Acting Second Assistant Engineer, 1 February, 1864. Honorably discharged 1 June, 1867.
MILTON, JAMES.
 Acting Assistant Surgeon, 18 December, 1863. Honorably discharged 20 November, 1865.
MILTON, JOHN B.
 Midshipman, 30 July, 1866. Graduated 7 June, 1870. Ensign, 13 July, 1871. Master, 19 November, 1874. Lieutenant, 14 September, 1887. Lieutenant-Commander, 3 March, 1899.
MILTON, L. Q. C.
 Midshipman, 20 June, 1806. Resigned 10 February, 1808.
MILTON, THOMAS S.
 Midshipman, 14 May, 1800. Resigned 12 October, 1800.
MIMS, LEWIS.
 Lieutenant, Junior Grade (Spanish-American War), 17 July, 1898. Honorably discharged 26 August, 1898.
MINARD, CHARLES.
 Acting Third Assistant Engineer, 14 January, 1863. Resigned 4 April, 1863.
MINCHALL, GEORGE.
 Midshipman, 30 July, 1842. Lost in the Grampus, March, 1843.
MINCHIN, C.
 Midshipman, 1 January, 1812. Resigned 18 June, 1822.
MINER, DAVID C.
 Mate, 3 December, 1861. Honorably discharged 30 November, 1865.
MINER, LEO DWIGHT.
 Cadet Engineer, Naval Academy, 14 September, 1876. Graduated 10 June, 1880. Assistant Engineer, 10 June, 1882. Passed Assistant Engineer, 7 October, 1892. Rank changed to Lieutenant, 3 March, 1899.
MINER, RANDOLPH H.
 Cadet Midshipman, 24 une, 1875. Graduated 10 June, 1881. Ensign, Junior Grade, 3 March, 1883. Ensign, 26 June, 1884. Lieutenant, Junior Grade, 5 December, 1890. Lieutenant, 23 April, 1895. Resigned 11 October, 1895. Lieutenant (Spanish-American War), 24 May, 1898. Honorably discharged 1 November, 1898.
MINER, SANFORD S.
 Acting Ensign, 7 December, 1863. Acting Master, 15 March, 1865. Honorably discharged 19 November, 1865.
MINER, WILLIAM H.
 Acting Master, 1 October, 1862. Resigned 26 June, 1863.
MINETT, HENRY.
 Midshipman, 8 June, 1872. Graduated 20 June, 1876. Ensign, 1 November, 1879. Lieutenant, Junior Grade, 23 May, 1886. Lieutenant, 11 December, 1891. Lieutenant-Commander, 25 September, 1899.
MINGIS, JOHN.
 Acting Third Assistant Engineer, 12 April, 1864. Resigned 25 April, 1865.
MINNERLY, CHARLES.
 Acting Third Assistant Engineer, 20 January, 1862. Acting Second Assistant Engineer, 19 November, 1863. Honorably discharged 8 December, 1865.
MINOR, ALFRED W.
 Acting Assistant Surgeon, 16 December, 1864. Honorably discharged 26 October, 1865.

MINOR, GEORGE.
　Midshipman, 1 April, 1827. Passed Midshipman, 10 June, 1833. Lieutenant, 28 February, 1838. Commander, 14 September, 1855. Resigned 22 April, 1861.
MINOR, JAMES M.
　Assistant Surgeon, 7 March, 1838. Passed Assistant Surgeon, 22 November, 1843. Resigned 20 September, 1847.
MINOR, ROBERT D.
　Midshipman, 25 February, 1841. Passed Midshipman, 10 August, 1847. Master, 14 September, 1855. Lieutenant, 15 September, 1855. Dismissed 22 April, 1861.
MINOR, LEWIS W.
　Assistant Surgeon, 8 February, 1832. Surgeon, 8 September, 1841. Dismissed 7 May, 1861.
MINTER, CHARLES E.
　Sailmaker, 2 April, 1881. Chief Sailmaker, 3 March, 1899.
MINTON, JOHN.
　Acting Third Assistant Engineer, 20 August, 1863. Honorably discharged 31 August, 1865.
MINTOYNE, WILLIAM L.
　Assistant Naval Constructor, 5 August, 1869. Naval Constructor, 12 March, 1875. Retired List, 4 December, 1891.
MINTZER, FREDERICK W.
　Acting Ensign, 24 May, 1864. Honorably discharged 19 October, 1868.
MINTZER, WILLIAM AUGUSTUS.
　Third Assistant Engineer, 16 January, 1863. Second Assistant Engineer, 25 July, 1866. Passed Assistant Engineer, 26 September, 1874. Discharged 13 November, 1893.
MINUE, EUSEBIUS.
　Acting Third Assistant Engineer, 20 September, 1862. Acting Second Assistant Engineer, 31 August, 1864. Honorably discharged 14 November, 1865.
MINZIES, JAMES.
　Boatswain, 1 October, 1814. Resigned 1 December, 1814.
MINZIES, JAMES.
　Boatswain, 5 December, 1819. Resigned 24 October, 1825.
MINZIES, JAMES.
　Boatswain, 23 June, 1829. Resigned 29 August, 1829.
MIROW, HENRY.
　Mate, 11 July, 1862. Resigned 20 July, 1864.
MISH, SIMON C.
　Midshipman, 8 January, 1849. Resigned 25 March, 1856. Acting Lieutenant, 23 September, 1861. Dismissed 24 December, 1861.
MISSENER, HILLERY.
　Third Assistant Engineer, 19 February, 1861. Second Assistant Engineer, 16 January, 1863. Resigned 7 August, 1868.
MISSET, EDWARD.
　Acting Third Assistant Engineer, 19 March, 1864. Dismissed 14 December, 1864.
MISSIMER, WILLIAM H.
　Acting Third Assistant Engineer, 10 December, 1864. Honorably discharged 16 December, 1867.
MISSROON, JOHN S.
　Midshipman, 27 June, 1824. Passed Midshipman, 20 February, 1830. Lieutenant, 31 December, 1833. Commander, 14 September, 1855. Commodore, 16 July, 1862. Died 23 October, 1865.
MITCHELL, ALEXANDER J.
　Purser, 20 January, 1853. Died 23 December, 1857.
MITCHELL, ALEXANDER J.
　Midshipman, 9 September, 1841. Resigned 8 December, 1845.
MITCHELL, ALEXANDER N.
　Naval Cadet, 6 September, 1894. Ensign, 4 April, 1900.
MITCHELL, ARCHIBALD N.
　Acting Midshipman, 20 September, 1858. Lieutenant, 1 August, 1862. Lieutenant-Commander, 25 July, 1866. Died 14 September, 1873.
MITCHELL, A. H.
　Midshipman, 4 March, 1823. Last appearance on Records of Navy Department, 1826. Dead.
MITCHELL, AUGUSTUS.
　Third Assistant Engineer, 1 July, 1861. Resigned 1 May, 1862. Third Assistant Engineer, 6 October, 1862. Lost on the Weehawken, 6 December, 1863.
MITCHELL, BENJAMIN.
　Acting Ensign, 9 September, 1862. Honorably discharged 31 October, 1865.
MITCHELL, B. RUSH.
　Assistant Surgeon, 26 April, 1847. Passed Assistant Surgeon, 18 April, 1854. Retired List, 14 May, 1861. Dead.
MITCHELL, CHARLES E.
　Acting Master, 25 May, 1861. Honorably discharged 12 February, 1866.
MITCHELL, CHARLES E.
　Acting Assistant Paymaster, 14 May, 1863. Mustered out 14 January, 1866.
MITCHELL, CHARLES F.
　Acting Master, 18 December, 1861. Honorably discharged 18 April, 1866.
MITCHELL, CHARLES M.
　Midshipman, 19 October, 1841. Resigned 28 January, 1848.
MITCHELL, DAVID.
　Midshipman, 18 June, 1812. Last appearance on Records of Navy Department, 1818.

GENERAL NAVY REGISTER.

MITCHELL, F. J.
Midshipman, 2 March, 1803. Lieutenant, 18 February, 1809. Resigned 27 November, 1826.
MITCHELL, GEORGE.
Midshipman, 20 April, 1800. Left the service 10 April, 1805.
MITCHELL, GEORGE B.
Acting Ensign, 10 March, 1864. Appointment revoked 19 December, 1864.
MITCHELL, GEORGE G.
Naval Cadet, 7 September, 1885. Ensign, 1 July, 1891. Lieutenant, 3 March, 1899.
MITCHELL, GEORGE J.
Midshipman, 29 September, 1863. Graduated June, 1867. Ensign, 18 December, 1868. Master, 24 March, 1870. Lieutenant, 21 March, 1871. Resigned 8 August, 1874.
MITCHELL, HENRY A.
Acting Assistant Paymaster, 6 November, 1863. Honorably discharged 28 October, 1865.
MITCHELL, HENRY W.
Acting Assistant Surgeon, 27 October, 1862. Honorably discharged 26 January, 1866.
MITCHELL, JAMES.
Acting Master, 3 September, 1861. Appointment revoked 31 January, 1862.
MITCHELL, JAMES.
Acting Second Assistant Engineer, 8 December, 1863. Honorably discharged 16 December, 1865.
MITCHELL, JAMES.
Mate, 24 June, 1865. Resigned 13 July, 1867.
MITCHELL, JEREMIAH.
Mate, 23 May, 1863. Acting Ensign, 27 January, 1864. Honorably discharged 28 August, 1865.
MITCHELL, JOHN.
Acting Third Assistant Engineer, 1861. Resigned 9 April, 1862.
MITCHELL, JOHN C.
Third Assistant Engineer, 16 February, 1852. Resigned 28 April, 1853. Acceptance of resignation revoked 7 May, 1853. Resigned 16 November, 1854.
MITCHELL, JOHN G.
Midshipman, 2 October, 1850. Passed Midshipman, 20 June, 1856. Master, 22 January, 1858. Lieutenant, 23 January, 1858. Lieutenant-Commander, 16 July, 1862. Killed 22 October, 1868.
MITCHELL, JOHN K.
Midshipman, 1 February, 1825. Passed Midshipman, 4 June, 1831. Lieutenant, 22 December, 1835. Commander, 14 September, 1855. Dismissed, 27 May, 1861.
MITCHELL, JOHN R.
Mate, 23 December, 1862. Acting Ensign, 10 July, 1865. Honorably discharged 27 October, 1865.
MITCHELL, LESLIE.
Midshipman, 4 July, 1805. Resigned 26 March, 1806.
MITCHELL, LUEO.
Assistant Surgeon, 24 July, 1813. Resigned 17 July, 1822.
MITCHELL, NATHANIEL.
Midshipman, 1 September, 1811. Resigned in 1812.
MITCHELL, RICHARD.
Mate, 21 February, 1863. Resigned 30 May, 1864.
MITCHELL, RICHARD.
Midshipman, 22 July, 1864. Graduated June, 1869. Ensign, 12 July, 1870. Master, 19 April, 1873. Lieutenant, 1 December, 1877. Retired List, 4 September, 1896. Died 30 October, 1897.
MITCHELL, R. B.
Midshipman, 18 May, 1809. Resigned 27 February, 1811.
MITCHELL, ROBERT.
Midshipman, 1 September, 1811. Last appearance on Records of Navy Department, 1815. Frigate Guerriere.
MITCHELL, THOMAS B.
Sailmaker, 3 April, 1807. Resigned 26 December, 1807.
MITCHELL, T. MASON.
Third Assistant Engineer, 16 October, 1861. Resigned 6 December, 1862. Acting First Assistant Engineer, 18 July, 1864. Appointment revoked (sick) 17 January, 1865.
MITCHELL, WILLIAM.
Sailmaker, 8 April, 1828. Resigned 17 February, 1830.
MITCHELL, WILLIAM.
Sailmaker, 16 June, 1836. Dropped.
MITCHELL, WILLIAM.
Midshipman, 19 October, 1841. Passed Midshipman, 10 August, 1847. Master, 4 August, 1855. Lieutenant, 14 September, 1855. Lieutenant-Commander, 16 July, 1862. Retired List, 11 January, 1867. Commander on Retired List, 4 April, 1867. Died 16 July, 1871.
MITCHELL, WILLIAM.
Acting Master, 16 September, 1861. Resigned 22 January, 1862.
MITCHELL, WILLIAM.
Acting Third Assistant Engineer, 29 September, 1863. Died on Arizona, 19 November, 1863.
MITCHELL, WILLIAM G.
Acting Master, 2 November, 1861. Honorably discharged 4 December, 1865. Acting Master, 11 December, 1866. Mustered out 10 December, 1867.

MITCHELL, WILLIAM H.
Acting Third Assistant Engineer, 1 October, 1862. Acting Second Assistant Engineer, 26 February, 1863. Honorably discharged 12 December, 1865.
MITCHELL, WILLIAM T.
Acting Ensign, 17 November, 1863. Honorably discharged 27 March, 1866.
MITCHELL, WILLIS G.
Naval Cadet, 5 September, 1896. Graduated 30 June, 1900.
MITCHESON, JOSEPH M.
Lieutenant (Spanish-American War), 23 June, 1898. Honorably discharged 15 October, 1898.
MITTENDORFF, JOHN H.
Passed Assistant Engineer (Spanish-American War), 25 May, 1898. Honorably discharged 17 November, 1898.
MIX, ELIJAH.
Master, 12 June, 1813. Last appearance on Records of Navy Department. Furloughed.
MIX, GEORGE W.
Assistant Surgeon, 16 May, 1829. Resigned 18 October, 1833.
MIX, MERVINE P.
Master, 22 September, 1812. Lieutenant, 9 December, 1814. Commander, 3 March, 1831. Died 8 February, 1839.
MIX, THOMAS M.
Midshipman, 6 January, 1832. Passed Midshipman, 23 June, 1838. Lieutenant, 30 March, 1844. Died 24 August, 1849.
MIX, WILLIAM B.
Mate, 16 September, 1861. Acting Ensign, 2 September, 1863. Honorably discharged 16 January, 1866. Acting Ensign, 11 December, 1866. Resigned 31 December, 1866.
MIX, WILLIAM M.
Acting Third Assistant Engineer, 3 August, 1863. Acting Second Assistant Engineer, 4 March, 1865. Honorably discharged 12 February, 1866.
MIXER, HENRY M.
Acting Assistant Surgeon, 1 October, 1862. Resigned 28 February, 1865.
MOAKLER, PETER.
Mate, 15 November, 1862. Discharged 3 August, 1865.
MOALE, EDWARD, JR.
Naval Cadet, 17 June, 1882. Ensign, 1 July, 1889. Lieutenant, Junior Grade, 4 June, 1897. Lieutenant, 3 March, 1899.
MOCKABEE, JOSEPH C.
Acting Third Assistant Engineer, 1 February, 1862. Acting Second Assistant Engineer, 12 March, 1863. Honorably discharged 19 September, 1865.
MOELLER, BERNARD J.
Midshipman, 1 April, 1827. Passed Midshipman, 10 June, 1833. Lieutenant, 9 December, 1839. Reserved List, 13 September, 1855. Commander, Retired List, 19 June, 1861. Captain, Retired List, 4 April, 1867. Died 13 February, 1872.
MOFFAT, HOWARD F.
Mate, 31 July, 1861. Acting Ensign, 21 July, 1862. Acting Master, 12 November, 1864. Honorably discharged 1 January, 1869. Mate, 9 November, 1869. Master on Retired List, 24 March, 1873. Title changed to Lieutenant, Junior Grade, 3 March, 1883. Died 28 April, 1892.
MOFFATT, EDGAR R.
Acting Assistant Paymaster, 4 November, 1862. Honorably discharged 17 November, 1865.
MOFFETT, NOAH W.
Third Assistant Engineer, 17 December, 1862. Appointment revoked 16 September, 1863.
MOFFETT, WILLIAM A.
Naval Cadet, 6 September, 1886. Ensign, 1 July, 1892. Lieutenant, Junior Grade, 3 March, 1899. Lieutenant, 1 July, 1899.
MOFFETT, WILLIAM R.
Mate, 22 June, 1863. Honorably discharged 26 July, 1865.
MOFFITT, WILLIAM J.
Acting Third Assistant Engineer, 23 October, 1863. Reduced to Fireman, 16 July, 1864.
MOGNON, JOHN.
Acting Third Assistant Engineer, 20 August, 1863. Honorably discharged 20 October, 1865.
MOHUN, PHILIP V.
Assistant Paymaster, 15 March, 1894. Passed Assistant Paymaster, 14 August, 1896. Paymaster, 15 September, 1899.
MOIR, JOHN.
Acting Second Assistant Engineer, 29 August, 1864. Honorably discharged 9 July, 1867.
MOLIERE, HENRY.
Master, 1 August, 1812. Cashiered 14 February, 1818.
MOLIERE, LUCAS.
Master, 1 August, 1812. Dismissed 6 March, 1813. Master, 10 April, 1813. Last appearance on Records of Navy Department, 1815. Philadelphia.
MOLLINEAUX, JAMES.
Acting Third Assistant Engineer, 9 September, 1862. Resigned 26 May, 1865.
MOLONEY, DANIEL.
Mate, 11 January, 1864. Honorably discharged 4 November, 1865.
MOLONY, HENRY H.
Third Assistant Engineer, 19 February, 1861. Second Assistant Engineer, 16 January,

GENERAL NAVY REGISTER. 387

1863. First Assistant Engineer, 1 December, 1864. Lost at sea, on the merchant steamer Atlanta, October, 1865.
MOLONY, JOHN.
Mate, 13 August, 1863. Acting Ensign, 15 February, 1864. Honorably discharged 21 September, 1865.
MOLLOY, WILLIAM C.
Mate. Resigned 22 May, 1863.
MONAGHAN, JOHN R.
Naval Cadet, 7 September, 1891. Ensign, 1 July, 1897. Killed in action 1 April, 1899.
MONAGHAN, P. D.
Acting Third Assistant Engineer, 1861. Appointment revoked 2 December, 1861.
MONAHON, HENRY T.
Midshipman, 25 July, 1865. Graduated June, 1869. Ensign, 12 July, 1870. Master, 18 April, 1873. Lieutenant, 25 November, 1877. Died 6 January, 1890.
MONCREIF, GEORGE B.
Boatswain, 12 July, 1897.
MONKHOUSE, HOWARD.
Acting Third Assistant Engineer, 16 August, 1864. Honorably discharged 2 October, 1865.
MONROE, ANDREW F.
Midshipman, 3 March, 1841. Passed Midshipman, 10 August, 1847. Resigned 14 July, 1854.
MONROE, JAMES.
Acting First Assistant Engineer, 16 March, 1864. Honorably discharged 26 February, 1868.
MONROE, MOSES D.
Cadet Midshipman, 19 May, 1884. Resigned 1 September, 1888. Ensign (Spanish-American War), 14 May, 1898. Honorably discharged 5 January, 1899.
MONROE, WILLIAM C.
Third Assistant Engineer, 23 May, 1861. Second Assistant Engineer, 29 October, 1862. Dismissed 26 April, 1869. Dismissal revoked and resignation accepted 1 March, 1871.
MONTAGUE, DANIEL.
Boatswain, 15 June, 1898.
MONTAGUE, JAMES A.
Mate, 12 January, 1863. Acting Ensign, 21 December, 1863. Honorably discharged 27 October, 1865.
MONTAGUE, WILLIAM.
Acting Ensign and Pilot, 8 December, 1864. Resigned 12 May, 1865.
MONTEITH, W. L.
Midshipman, 1 September, 1811. Lieutenant, 9 December, 1814. Died 16 October, 1819.
MONTELL, F. M.
Acting Ensign, 11 December, 1862. Acting Master, recommendation of Commanding Officer, 3 May, 1864. Honorably discharged 14 November, 1865.
MONTGOMERY, A. M.
Assistant Surgeon, 16 July, 1814. Surgeon, 7 May, 1825. Died 3 January, 1828.
MONTGOMERY, GRENVILLE D.
Naval Cadet (Spanish-American War), 22 July, 1898. Honorably discharged 31 October, 1898.
MONTGOMERY, JOHN B.
Midshipman, 4 June, 1812. Lieutenant, 1 April, 1818. Commander, 9 December, 1839. Captain, 6 January, 1853. Retired List, 21 December, 1861. Commodore on Retired List, 16 July, 1862. Rear-Admiral, Retired List, 25 July, 1866. Died 25 March, 1873.
MONTGOMERY, N. L.
Midshipman, 17 December, 1810. Lieutenant, 9 December, 1814. Died at sea, 30 July, 1824.
MONTGOMERY, SAMUEL.
Acting Second Assistant Engineer, 22 October, 1862. Dismissed 20 December, 1862.
MONTGOMERY, W. H.
Midshipman, 21 December, 1837. Passed Midshipman, 29 June, 1843. Drowned in November, 1846.
MONTGOMERY, WILLIAM J.
Third Assistant Engineer, 23 May, 1861. Second Assistant Engineer, 29 October, 1862. First Assistant Engineer, 25 July, 1866. Resigned 25 October, 1869.
MONTGOMERY, WILLIAM S.
Acting Second Assistant Engineer, 28 February, 1862. Resigned 5 June, 1863.
MONTGOMERY, WILLIAM SLACK.
Naval Cadet, 6 September, 1889. Ensign, 1 July, 1895. Lieutenant, Junior Grade, 3 March, 1899.
MOODY, ROSCOE C.
Naval Cadet, 8 September, 1890. Assistant Engineer, 1 July, 1896. Rank changed to Ensign, 3 March, 1899. Lieutenant, Junior Grade, 1 July, 1899.
MOODY, WILLIAM.
Mate, 4 February, 1862. Acting Ensign, for cool and gallant conduct under fire of the enemy, 22 July, 1864. Honorably discharged 28 October, 1865. Acting Ensign, 23 June, 1866. Mustered out 12 March, 1868.
MOONEY, JOHN.
Midshipman, 13 December, 1831. Passed Midshipman, 15 June, 1837. Lieutenant, 8 September, 1841. Drowned 3 June, 1855.
MOONEY, JOHN.
Master, 23 January, 1809. Last appearance on Records of Navy Department, 1815. Wilmington, N. C.

MOONEY, THOMAS.
Mate, 29 March, 1870. Appointment revoked 27 January, 1873.
MOOR, HENRY.
Midshipman, 1 March, 1825. Passed Midshipman, 4 June, 1831. Lieutenant, 22 December, 1835. Killed by explosion of boiler 21 March, 1853.
MOORE, ALFRED F.
Acting Second Assistant Engineer, 5 March, 1864. Appointment revoked (sick) 16 July, 1864.
MOORE, ANDREW L.
Chaplain, 1 July, 1809. Purser, 17 September, 1811. Last appearance on Records of Navy Department.
MOORE, ANDREW M.
Assistant Surgeon, 19 April, 1869. Surgeon, 1 April, 1881. Retired List, 14 August, 1893. On duty from 25 May to 15 September, 1898. Duty at Naval Recruiting Rendezvous, Chicago, Ill., 1 March, 1901.
MOORE, AUSTIN.
Acting Third Assistant Engineer, 31 May, 1864. Honorably discharged 29 June, 1865.
MOORE, BENJAMIN D.
Midshipman, 2 February, 1829. Resigned 2 January, 1843.
MOORE, CHARLES.
Acting Ensign, 8 April, 1863. Honorably discharged 9 December, 1865.
MOORE, CHARLES.
Midshipman, 5 February, 1800. Last appearance on Records of Navy Department, 25 August, 1802. Dead.
MOORE, CHARLES B. T.
Midshipman, 28 September, 1869. Graduated 31 May, 1873. Ensign, 14 July, 1874. Master, 14 December, 1880. Lieutenant, Junior Grade, 3 March, 1883. Lieutenant, 5 August, 1886. Lieutenant-Commander, 3 March, 1899.
MOORE, CHARLES D.
Mate, 13 April, 1864. Deserted 30 June, 1865.
MOORE, CHARLES F.
Mate, 18 June, 1863. Acting Ensign, 1 July, 1864. Honorably discharged 5 November, 1865.
MOORE, CHARLES P.
Mate, 2 May, 1862. Appointment revoked 24 November, 1862. Mate, 4 August, 1863. Lost at sea, Bainbridge, 21 August, 1863.
MOORE, CORNELIUS.
Assistant Surgeon, 26 May, 1824. Dismissed 21 November, 1834.
MOORE, DELANEY S.
Midshipman, 18 July, 1814. Killed at Mahone in 1816.
MOORE, EDWARD K.
Midshipman, 1 October, 1864. Graduated June, 1868. Master, 12 July, 1870. Lieutenant, 1 March, 1873. Lieutenant-Commander, 10 July, 1894. Commander, 3 March, 1899.
MOORE, EDWIN W.
Midshipman, 1 January, 1825. Passed Midshipman, 4 June, 1831. Lieutenant, 3 March, 1835. Resigned 16 July, 1836.
MOORE, FRANK K.
Acting Assistant Paymaster, 24 May, 1862. Honorably discharged 15 January, 1867.
MOORE, GEORGE H.
Acting Third Assistant Engineer, 11 March, 1864. Acting Second Assistant Engineer, 12 June, 1865. Honorably discharged 20 November, 1867.
MOORE, GILBERT H.
Mate, 7 January, 1864. Killed in action, Stockadale, 16 May, 1864.
MOORE, G. WASHINGTON.
Acting Assistant Paymaster, 8 October, 1861. Dismissed 11 September, 1862.
MOORE, HENRY T.
Acting Volunteer Lieutenant, 26 August, 1861. Resigned 14 June, 1862.
MOORE, HENRY W.
Mate, 19 January, 1863. Dismissed 31 March, 1863.
MOORE, HENRY W.
Acting Third Assistant Engineer, 26 October, 1863. Acting Second Assistant Engineer, 2 August, 1864. Honorably discharged 28 October, 1865.
MOORE, HOMER J.
Midshipman, 4 July, 1805. Resigned 6 December, 1810.
MOORE, JAMES.
Gunner, 30 June, 1799. Last appearance on Records of Navy Department, 1 March, 1808. Gunner, 1 March, 1808. Last appearance on Records of Navy Department, 9 November, 1812.
MOORE, JAMES D.
Mate, 25 July, 1863. Acting Ensign, 14 August, 1865. Honorably discharged 8 November, 1868.
MOORE, JAMES G.
Acting Second Assistant Engineer, 5 August, 1864. Honorably discharged 25 September, 1865.
MOORE, JAMES H.
Midshipman, 10 February, 1838. Passed Midshipman, 20 May, 1844. Master, 5 April, 1852. Lieutenant, 7 January, 1853. Died 18 October, 1860.
MOORE, JOHN D.
Mate, 25 February, 1864. Honorably discharged 1 November, 1865.
MOORE, JOHN H.
Midshipman, 29 July, 1865. Graduated June, 1869. Ensign, 12 July, 1870. Master, 15 February, 1873. Lieutenant, 21 September, 1876. Lieutenant-Commander, 27 April, 1898. Retired List, with rank of Commander, 30 June, 1899.

MOORE, JOHN M.
Mate, 9 September, 1862. Acting Ensign, 3 November, 1864. Honorably discharged 11 May, 1865.
MOORE, JOHN M.
Assistant Surgeon, 11 November, 1892. Passed Assistant Surgeon, 11 November, 1895.
MOORE, JOHN S.
Acting First Assistant Engineer, 3 September, 1863. Honorably discharged 3 October, 1865.
MOORE, JOHN WHITE.
Third Assistant Engineer, 21 May, 1853. Second Assistant Engineer, 25 June, 1855. First Assistant Engineer, 21 July, 1858. Chief Engineer, 5 August, 1861. Retired List, 24 May, 1894.
MOORE, J. W.
Acting Assistant Surgeon, 29 May, 1861. Resigned 28 November, 1862.
MOORE, LEMUEL H.
Acting Third Assistant Engineer, 24 April, 1865. Honorably discharged 15 February, 1866.
MOORE, LEWIS H.
Acting Ensign March, 1865. Resigned 8 November, 1865.
MOORE, NICHOLAS E.
Mate, 11 August, 1864. Resigned 25 April, 1865.
MOORE, N. T. H.
Assistant Surgeon, 13 October, 1840. Died 25 April, 1843.
MOORE, OLIVER G.
Mate, 14 October, 1862. Dismissed 19 March, 1864.
MOORE, ROBERT.
Acting First Assistant Engineer, 27 October, 1863. Dismissed 1 November, 1863.
MOORE, ROBERT B.
Mate, 11 October, 1864. Resigned 25 May, 1865.
MOORE, ROBERT S.
Purser, 13 September, 1841. Died 3 April, 1845.
MOORE, RYDON G.
Midshipman, 2 February, 1829. Dismissed 28 February, 1834.
MOORE, SAMUEL.
Acting Third Assistant Engineer, 24 January, 1865. Honorably discharged 23 September, 1865.
MOORE, THOMAS.
Carpenter, 4 March, 1806. Died 27 August, 1807.
MOORE, THOMAS.
Acting Ensign, 31 December, 1862. Acting Master, 14 January, 1864. Honorably discharged 16 November, 1865.
MOORE, THOMAS M.
Master, 29 June, 1812. Resigned 1 November, 1814.
MOORE, WASHINGTON.
Mate, 27 August, 1863. Deserted 13 August, 1865.
MOORE, WILLIAM E.
Acting Second Assistant Engineer, 18 October, 1861. Acting First Assistant Engineer, 6 November, 1863. Resigned 29 March, 1865.
MOORE, WILLIAM G.
Gunner, 17 April, 1894.
MOORE, WILLIAM I.
Midshipman, 14 April, 1862. Graduated June, 1866. Ensign, 12 March, 1868. Master, 26 March, 1869. Lieutenant, 21 March, 1870. Lieutenant-Commander, 31 October, 1888. Commander, 18 November, 1896. Retired List, with rank of Captain, 30 June, 1900.
MOORE, W. M. A.
Midshipman, 19 August, 1823. Resigned 8 March, 1832.
MOORE, WILLIAM STURTEVANT.
Acting Third Assistant Engineer, under instruction Naval Academy, 10 October, 1866. Third Assistant Engineer, 2 June, 1868. Second Assistant Engineer, 2 June, 1869. Passed Assistant Engineer, 11 June, 1876. Chief Engineer, 10 August, 1893. Rank changed to Commander, 3 March, 1899.
MOORE, WILLIAM T.
Acting First Assistant Engineer, 5 August, 1864. Dismissed 25 May, 1865.
MOORE, WINCHESTER E.
Acting Third Assistant Engineer, 15 August, 1864. Honorably discharged 10 July, 1865.
MOORE, WINSHESTER
Acting Third Assistant Engineer, 15 August, 1864. Honorably discharged 15 July, 1865.
MOOREHEAD, JOSEPH.
Midshipman, 9 November, 1813. Lieutenant, 13 January, 1825. Commander, 8 September, 1841. Died 11 June, 1854.
MOOREHEAD, JOSEPH.
Midshipman, 1 April, 1828. Passed Midshipman, 14 June, 1834. Dismissed 15 February, 1840.
MOORES, FREDERICK W.
Master, not in line of promotion, 19 May, 1827. Reserved List, 14 September, 1855. Died 22 July, 1869.
MOORES, F. W., Jr.
Acting Third Assistant Engineer, 14 July, 1863. Honorably discharged 26 March, 1867.
MOORES, JOHN W.
Midshipman, 10 May, 1820. Lieutenant, 17 May, 1828. Resigned 22 September, 1841.

GENERAL NAVY REGISTER.

MOORES, ROBERT B.
Acting Ensign, 18 June, 1863. Honorably discharged 16 August, 1865.
MOORES, WILLIAM J.
Acting Third Assistant Engineer, 15 July, 1864. Honorably discharged 19 February, 1867.
MORALES, JOSEPH.
Midshipman, 1 January, 1812. Resigned in 1818.
MORALES, MANUEL.
Midshipman, 1 December, 1809. Dismissed 11 July, 1814.
MORAN, CHARLES.
Mate, 7 October, 1864. Honorably discharged 2 October, 1865.
MORAN, CHARLES.
Acting Gunner, 9 December, 1864. Honorably discharged 26 March, 1866.
MORAN, CHARLES.
Gunner, 7 February, 1870. Died 7 February, 1873.
MORAN, CHARLES.
Gunner, 17 June, 1858. Dismissed 22 May, 1861.
MORAN, DAVID P.
Passed Assistant Engineer (Spanish-American War), 1 June, 1898. Honorably discharged 4 March, 1899.
MORAN, EDWARD.
Acting Third Assistant Engineer, 22 August, 1863. Resigned 23 September, 1863. Acting Third Assistant Engineer, 28 July, 1864. Resignation accepted 25 April, 1865.
MORAN, JAMES.
Mate, 23 January, 1865. Honorably discharged 1 March, 1868.
MORAN, JOHN M.
Acting Third Assistant Engineer, 3 March, 1864. Honorably discharged 17 January, 1866.
MORAN, WILLIAM.
Acting Third Assistant Engineer, 20 November, 1862. Honorably discharged 11 November, 1865.
MOREHEAD, JOSEPH W.
Acting Ensign, 24 January, 1863. Acting Master, 2 December, 1863. Honorably discharged 12 September, 1865.
MOREHEAD, ROY A.
Ensign (Spanish-American War), 7 June, 1898. Honorably discharged 22 December, 1898.
MOREHOUSE, ALANSON J.
Mate, 30 January, 1862. Appointment revoked 19 February, 1862. Mate, 20 May, 1862. Died 9 April, 1874.
MORELAND, HENRY G.
Acting Second Assistant Engineer, 11 September, 1864. Honorably discharged 14 October, 1865.
MOREY, BENJAMIN F.
Acting First Assistant Engineer, 2 August, 1864. Dismissed 12 November, 1864.
MOREY, FRANK C.
Acting Third Assistant Engineer, 11 July, 1863. Acting Second Assistant Engineer, 8 March, 1865. Honorably discharged 11 November, 1865.
MORGAN, ADDISON E.
Ensign (Spanish-American War), 27 June, 1898. Honorably discharged 28 November, 1898.
MORGAN, ALBERT H.
Mate, 25 February, 1864. Appointment revoked 17 October, 1864.
MORGAN, BENJAMIN.
Midshipman, 2 November, 1835. Resigned 1 September, 1837.
MORGAN, CASEY B.
Naval Cadet, 4 September, 1884. Ensign, 1 July, 1890. Lieutenant, Junior Grade, 16 February, 1898. Lieutenant, 3 March, 1899.
MORGAN, CHARLES E.
Naval Cadet, 6 September, 1895. At sea prior to final graduation.
MORGAN, CHARLES.
Gunner, 28 October, 1890.
MORGAN, CHARLES J.
Acting Third Assistant Engineer, 17 August, 1863. Appointment revoked (sick) 25 November, 1864. Acting Third Assistant Engineer, 29 January, 1867. Mustered out 2 February, 1869.
MORGAN, CHARLES O.
Acting Third Assistant Engineer, 19 March, 1862. Acting Second Assistant Engineer, 17 June, 1863. Acting First Assistant Engineer, 14 September, 1864. Dismissed 26 January, 1865.
MORGAN, CHARLES W.
Mate, 23 June, 1864. Resigned 27 August, 1864. Mate, 21 March, 1866. Discharged 1 February, 1868.
MORGAN, CHARLES W.
Midshipman, 1 January, 1808. Lieutenant, 3 March, 1813. Commander, 15 April, 1820. Captain, 21 February, 1831. Died 5 January, 1853.
MORGAN, CYRUS R.
Third Assistant Engineer, 17 December, 1861. Resigned 2 April, 1864.
MORGAN, DAVID B.
Midshipman, 1 February, 1827. Resigned 25 March, 1833.
MORGAN, DANIEL H.
Assistant Surgeon, 27 November, 1896. Passed Assistant Surgeon, 27 November, 1899.

GENERAL NAVY REGISTER. 391

MORGAN, EDMUND.
Acting Ensign, 1 October, 1862. Acting Master, 3 March, 1864. Honorably discharged 21 September, 1865.

MORGAN, EDWARD.
Acting Master, 1 October, 1862. Acting Volunteer Lieutenant, 5 August, 1863. Honorably discharged 4 November, 1865.

MORGAN, GEORGE E.
Midshipman, 18 February, 1841. Passed Midshipman, 10 August, 1847. Master, 1 March, 1855. Lieutenant, 14 September, 1855. Died 6 January, 1856.

MORGAN, JAMES.
Gunner, 2 November, 1798. Last appearance on Records of Navy Department, 11 December, 1798.

MORGAN, JOHN B.
Acting Second Assistant Engineer, 28 December, 1861. Dismissed 16 April, 1863.

MORGAN, JOSEPH.
Third Assistant Engineer, 16 November, 1861. Second Assistant Engineer, 25 August, 1863. Resigned 5 January, 1866.

MORGAN, MORDECAI.
Assistant Surgeon, 28 December, 1818. Surgeon, 10 July, 1824. Died 22 July, 1841.

MORGAN, NATHANIEL S.
Mate, 16 November, 1861. Acting Master, 11 June, 1862. Acting Volunteer Lieutenant, 5 April, 1865. Deserted 4 September, 1866.

MORGAN, PAUL.
Mate, 1 October, 1862. Acting Ensign, 10 March, 1864. Honorably discharged 5 August, 1866.

MORGAN, PELEG W.
Mate, 4 April, 1862. Acting Ensign, 1 September, 1863. Died 14 July, 1865.

MORGAN, RICHARD.
Acting Third Assistant Engineer, 10 May, 1864. Resigned 1 July, 1865.

MORGAN, STOKELY.
Cadet Midshipman, 24 June, 1876. Graduated 22 June, 1882. Ensign, Junior Grade, 3 March, 1883. Ensign, 26 June, 1884. Lieutenant, Junior Grade, 4 December, 1892. Lieutenant, 1 October, 1896. Retired List, with rank of Lieutenant-Commander, 30 June, 1900. Died 9 November, 1900.

MORGAN, THOMAS.
Acting Ensign, 2 May, 1864. Honorably discharged 15 July, 1865.

MORGAN, VAN R.
Midshipman, 8 December, 1836. Passed Midshipman, 1 July, 1842. Master, 25 March, 1849. Lieutenant, 26 October, 1849. Reserved List, 13 September, 1855. Lieutenant on Active List, 26 October, 1849. Dismissed 28 June, 1861.

MORGAN, WILLIAM A.
Mate, 8 May, 1862. Acting Ensign, 2 June, 1863. Acting Master, 27 October, 1864. Honorably discharged 4 January, 1866. Acting Master, 13 April, 1866. Ensign, 12 March, 1868. Master, 18 December, 1868. Lieutenant, 21 March, 1870. Lieutenant-Commander, 28 July, 1884. Commander, 4 July, 1893. Retired List, 29 September, 1894. Died 28 October, 1895.

MORIARTY, DANIEL.
Acting Boatswain, 1 March, 1900.

MORITZ, ALBERT.
Cadet Engineer, 13 September, 1877. Assistant Engineer, 1 July, 1883. Passed Assistant Engineer, 13 July, 1894. Rank changed to Lieutenant, 3 March, 1899.

MORK, JAMES.
Master, 14 July, 1812. Lieutenant, 27 April, 1816. Resigned 31 July, 1818.

MORLEY, ALBERT W.
Third Assistant Engineer, 1 July, 1861. Second Assistant Engineer, 18 December, 1862. Passed Assistant Engineer, 24 February, 1874. Chief Engineer, 17 November, 1882. Retired List, 27 March, 1896.

MORLEY B.
Acting Master, 17 May, 1861. Resigned 17 October, 1861.

MORLEY, GIDEON M.
Acting Second Assistant Engineer, 6 June, 1864. Appointment revoked (sick) 24 August, 1864.

MORONG, JOHN C.
Acting Ensign, 1 April, 1863. Acting Master, 1 June, 1864. Ensign, 12 March, 1868. Master, 18 December, 1868. Lieutenant, 21 March, 1870. Lieutenant-Commander, 5 June, 1884. Commander, 27 June, 1893. Retired List, 28 August, 1897.

MORRALL, NORMAN G.
Lieutenant (Spanish-American War), 20 May, 1898. Honorably discharged 8 September, 1898.

MORRELL, HENRY.
Midshipman, 30 June, 1869. Graduated 31 May, 1873. Ensign, 16 July, 1874. Master, 11 October, 1880. Lieutenant, Junior Grade, 3 March, 1883. Lieutenant, 23 May, 1886. Lieutenant-Commander, 3 March, 1899.

MORRELL, JAMES.
Sailmaker, 12 July, 1800. Discharged 8 May, 1801.

MORRELL, JOSEPH.
Gunner, 28 March, 1814. Resigned 31 May, 1815.

MORRELL, MOSES.
Midshipman, 16 January, 1809. Last appearance on Records of Navy Department, 1815. Frigate, President.

MORRELL, ROBERT.
Surgeon, 31 May, 1810. Last appearance on Records of Navy Department, 1815. New Orleans.

MORRELL, WILLIAM.
  Midshipman, 11 May, 1798. Discharged 12 October, 1801, under Peace Establishment Act.
MORRILL, FERDINAND G.
  Acting Ensign, 1 October, 1864. Honorably discharged 16 September, 1866.
MORRILL, RICHARD.
  Gunner, 1 September, 1802. Killed by accident in the Mediterranean.
MORRILL, S. J.
  Master, 7 July, 1812. Discharged 7 May, 1813.
MORRIS, BENJAMIN F.
  Mate, 27 May, 1862. Resigned 15 December, 1863. Acting Ensign, 28 January, 1864. Honorably discharged 27 May, 1866.
MORRIS, CHARLES.
  Purser, 4 February, 1799. Discharged 18 November, 1801, under Peace Establishment Act.
MORRIS, CHARLES.
  Mate, 18 September, 1863. Died 25 September, 1863.
MORRIS, CHARLES.
  Midshipman, 1 July, 1799. Lieutenant, 28 January, 1807. Captain, 5 March, 1813. Died 27 January, 1856.
MORRIS, CHARLES, Jr.
  Assistant Paymaster, 20 May, 1898. Passed Assistant Paymaster, 20 January, 1900.
MORRIS, CHARLES MANINGAULT.
  Midshipman, 12 December, 1837. Passed Midshipman, 29 June, 1843. Master, 26 March, 1851. Lieutenant, 13 October, 1851. Resigned 29 January, 1861.
MORRIS, CHARLES V.
  Midshipman, 1 January, 1818. Resigned 20 October, 1827. Master, not in line of promotion, 19 July, 1842. Reserved List, 14 September, 1855. Died, 10 April, 1887.
MORRIS, CHARLES W.
  Midshipman, 12 September, 1829. Passed Midshipman, 3 July, 1835. Lieutenant, 25 February, 1841. Died of wounds received in action 1 November, 1846.
MORRIS, DAVID.
  Acting Third Assistant Engineer, 8 September, 1863. Acting Second Assistant Engineer, 28 September, 1864. Honorably discharged 14 December, 1865.
MORRIS, FRANCIS.
  Acting Midshipman, 27 September, 1860. Ensign, 1 October, 1863. Master, 10 May, 1866. Lieutenant, 21 February, 1867. Lieutenant-Commander, 12 March, 1868. Commander, 15 April, 1882. Died 12 February, 1883.
MORRIS, FRANK B.
  Mate, 18 October, 1864. Resigned 30 May, 1865.
MORRIS, GEORGE U.
  Midshipman, 14 August, 1846. Passed Midshipman, 8 June, 1852. Master, 15 September, 1855. Lieutenant, 16 September, 1855. Lieutenant-Commander, 16 July, 1862. Commander, 25 July, 1866. Died 15 August, 1875.
MORRIS, H. A. H.
  Midshipman, 1 January, 1817. Cashiered 22 December, 1827.
MORRIS, HENRY W.
  Midshipman, 21 August, 1819. Lieutenant, 17 May, 1828. Commander, 12 October, 1849. Captain, 27 December, 1856. Commodore, 16 July, 1862. Died 14 August, 1863.
MORRIS, ISAAC N.
  Midshipman, 7 July, 1836. Passed Midshipman, 1 July, 1842. Died 4 January, 1848.
MORRIS, ISAAC T.
  Acting Midshipman, 20 September, 1860. Graduated June, 1866. Died 25 December, 1866.
MORRIS, JACOB.
  Master, date not known. Resigned 10 December, 1824.
MORRIS, JAMES.
  Acting Third Assistant Engineer, 13 July, 1864. Appointment revoked 5 June, 1865.
MORRIS, JAMES.
  Carpenter, 28 May, 1798. Last appearance on Records of Navy Department.
MORRIS, JAMES L.
  Midshipman, 9 June, 1811. Lieutenant, 27 April, 1816. Resigned 10 September, 1827.
MORRIS, JOHN.
  Boatswain, 28 October, 1828. Retired List, 21 December, 1861. Died 13 January, 1875.
MORRIS, JOHN.
  Acting Second Assistant Engineer, 6 August, 1864. Deserted September, 1864.
MORRIS, JOHN F.
  Assistant Engineer (Spanish-American War), 3 June, 1898. Honorably discharged 31 October, 1898.
MORRIS, JOHN R.
  Naval Cadet, 1 September, 1889. Honorably discharged 30 June, 1895. Assistant Engineer, 17 April, 1896. Rank changed to Ensign, 3 March, 1899. Lieutenant, Junior Grade, 17 April, 1899.
MORRIS, JULIUS R.
  Acting Assistant Paymaster, 31 December, 1862. Resigned (sick) 20 March, 1865.
MORRIS, LEWIS.
  Assistant Surgeon, 27 June, 1891. Passed Assistant Surgeon, 27 June, 1895.
MORRIS, MILES R.
  Purser, 3 January, 1858. Dismissed 1 June, 1861.
MORRIS, NOADIAH.
  Chaplain, 5 July, 1803. Purser, 10 December, 1803. Last appearance on Records of Navy Department, 4 October, 1806. Dead.

GENERAL NAVY REGISTER. 393

MORRIS, RICHARD H.
  Midshipman, 10 May, 1820. Lieutenant, 17 May, 1828. Died 5 November, 1837.
MORRIS, RICHARD V.
  Captain, 8 June, 1798. Dismissed 14 May, 1804.
MORRIS, ROBERT.
  Acting Ensign, 3 March, 1864. Honorably discharged 19 November, 1865.
MORRIS, ROBERT.
  Naval Cadet, 5 September, 1896. Graduated 30 June, 1900.
MORRIS, ROBERT S.
  Midshipman, 28 December, 1837. Died 18 November, 1839.
MORRIS, WATSON.
  Boatswain, date not known. Discharged in 1818.
MORRIS, WILLIAM.
  Mate, 3 November, 1862. Honorably discharged 21 June, 1864.
MORRIS, WILLIAM G.
  Mate, 20 January, 1862. Acting Ensign, 2 April, 1863. Acting Master, 13 May, 1863. Honorably discharged 14 April, 1868.
MORRIS, WILLIAM H.
  Acting Third Assistant Engineer, 27 May, 1861. Acting Second Assistant Engineer, 17 February, 1863. Acting First Assistant Engineer, 18 April, 1864. Honorably discharged 7 March, 1866.
MORRISEY, JOHN, Jr.
  Acting Ensign, 28 March, 1864. Honorably discharged 16 September, 1865.
MORRISON, E. D.
  Assistant Surgeon, 24 July, 1813. Dismissed 16 February, 1818.
MORRISON, FARMER.
  Naval Cadet, 6 September, 1895. At sea prior to final graduation.
MORRISON, GEORGE F.
  Midshipman, 5 November, 1849. Passed Midshipman, 12 June, 1855. Master, 16 September, 1855. Retired List, 1 February, 1860. Promoted to Lieutenant-Commander on Retired List, 12 March, 1867.
MORRISON, GEORGE H.
  Acting Third Assistant Engineer, 28 May, 1864. Honorably discharged 27 September, 1865.
MORRISON, GUY.
  Mate, 1 June, 1863. Resigned 27 January, 1864.
MORRISON, HENRY.
  Midshipman, 1 March, 1799. Last appearance on Records of Navy Department.
MORRISON, HERBERT H.
  Assistant Engineer (Spanish-American War), 14 May, 1898. Honorably discharged 5 October, 1898.
MORRISON, JAMES.
  Midshipman, 20 June, 1806. Resigned 11 November, 1809.
MORRISON, JAMES H.
  Third Assistant Engineer, 3 May, 1859. Second Assistant Engineer, 3 October, 1861. First Assistant Engineer, 20 May, 1863. Dropped 7 December, 1872.
MORRISON, JAMES H.
  Warrant Machinist, 6 July, 1899.
MORRISON, JESSE C.
  Carpenter, 25 April, 1842. Died 16 April, 1846.
MORRISON, J. D.
  Midshipman, 8 March, 1832. Resigned 31 December, 1839.
MORRISON, ROBERT.
  Acting Third Assistant Engineer, 2 June, 1862. Acting Second Assistant Engineer, 17 October, 1863. Honorably discharged 28 October, 1865. Acting Second Assistant Engineer, 21 August, 1866. Mustered out 14 May, 1868.
MORRISON, SAMUEL.
  Gunner, 4 March, 1823. Died 31 August, 1823.
MORRISON, WILLIAM G.
  Mate (Spanish-American War), 22 June, 1898. Honorably discharged 8 September, 1898.
MORRISON, WILLIAM F.
  Chaplain, 5 May, 1881.
MORROW, JAMES.
  Acting Third Assistant Engineer, 27 May, 1861. Resigned 10 December, 1861.
MORROW, L. G.
  Acting Assistant Paymaster, 19 January, 1865. Honorably discharged 7 October, 1865.
MORROW, RICHARD P.
  Acting First Assistant Engineer, 18 March, 1864. Honorably discharged 6 November, 1865.
MORSE, EDMUND L.
  Acting Second Assistant Engineer, 16 March, 1864. Appointment revoked (sick) 3 December, 1864.
MORSE, EDWARD A.
  Mate, 4 January, 1864. Honorably discharged 14 October, 1865.
MORSE, EDWIN T.
  Pharmacist, 15 September, 1898.
MORSE, ESROM.
  Mate, 24 October, 1862. Resigned 2 March, 1863.
MORSE, De WITT C.
  Mate, 25 January, 1864. Died at Mound City, Ill., 11 December, 1864.
MORSE, FRANKLIN A.
  Acting Third Assistant Engineer, 10 November, 1863. Honorably discharged 7 November, 1865.

MORSE, GEORGE F.
Acting Ensign, 11 October, 1862. Honorably discharged 16 September, 1865.
MORSE, JEROME E.
Midshipman, 13 October, 1862. Graduated June, 1866. Ensign, 12 March, 1868. Master, 21 March, 1870. Lieutenant, 21 March, 1871. Retired 22 July, 1874.
MORSE, JOHN.
Acting Third Assistant Engineer, 19 July, 1862. Resigned 8 May, 1863.
MORSE, JOHN O.
Acting Ensign, 7 October, 1862. Acting Master, 18 June, 1864. Dismissed 17 October, 1864.
MORSE, JOHN W.
Assistant Paymaster, 12 April, 1898. Passed Assistant Paymaster, 3 March, 1899.
MORSE, JOSEPH T.
Mate, 30 November, 1863. Appointment revoked (sick) 11 February, 1864.
MORSE, La ROY F.
Acting Assistant Surgeon, 14 November, 1863. Honorably discharged 7 December, 1865.
MORSE, L. R. M.
Midshipman, 10 May, 1820. Resigned 17 October, 1820.
MORSE, THEODORE S.
Mate, 3 May, 1864. Honorably discharged 13 November, 1865.
MORSE, THOMAS M.
Lieutenant (Spanish-American War), 20 May, 1898. Honorably discharged 12 September, 1898.
MORSE, WILLIAM H.
Master's Mate, 1 July, 1839. Second Master, 3 March, 1849. Resigned 25 May, 1859.
MORSE, WILLIAM H.
Mate, 6 June, 1862. Honorably discharged 8 December, 1865.
MORSON, HUGH.
Assistant Surgeon, 4 April, 1831. Passed Assistant Surgeon, 1 August, 1837. Resigned 6 September, 1837. Assistant Surgeon, 8 September, 1841. Resigned 8 December, 1843.
MORTIMER, GEORGE.
Acting Third Assistant Engineer, 18 July, 1864. Honorably discharged 9 August, 1865.
MORTIMER, GEORGE L.
Acting Second Assistant Engineer, 13 November, 1863. Dismissed 13 June, 1864.
MORTIMER, WILLIAM.
Acting Gunner, 18 April, 1863. Appointment revoked 30 November, 1864.
MORTON, FRANCIS P.
Acting Assistant Paymaster, 11 April, 1863. Mustered out 14 December, 1865.
MORTON, FRANCIS T.
Acting Assistant Paymaster, 4 June, 1862. Resigned 29 September, 1862.
MORTON, GEORGE L.
Lieutenant (Spanish-American War), 12 May, 1898. Honorably discharged 2 November, 1898.
MORTON, GEORGE W.
Acting Assistant Paymaster, 25 September, 1861. Mustered out 7 July, 1867.
MORTON, GILBERT.
Acting Gunner, 1 October, 1862. Promoted Acting Master, 6 October, 1863. Honorably discharged 12 October, 1865. Acting Master, 30 May, 1867. Ensign, 12 March, 1868. Retired List, 14 February, 1874. Died 26 June, 1890.
MORTON, HENRY B.
Acting Ensign, 3 March, 1865. Honorably discharged 13 June, 1865.
MORTON, JAMES P.
Naval Cadet, 9 September, 1891. Assistant Engineer, 1 July, 1897. Rank changed to Ensign, 3 March, 1899. Lieutenant, Junior Grade, 1 July, 1900.
MORTON, JOHN W.
Acting Third Assistant Engineer, 21 March, 1864. Honorably discharged 9 January, 1866.
MORTON, JOSEPH B.
Mate, 22 April, 1863. Resigned 23 November, 1864.
MORTON, JOSEPH G.
Acting Assistant Paymaster, 19 November, 1864. Honorably discharged 18 October, 1865.
MORTON, PLINY.
Assistant Surgeon, 10 December, 1814. Last appearance on Records of Navy Department, 1815. Frigate United States.
MORTON, THOMAS H.
Acting Master, 26 December, 1861. Resigned 29 May, 1862.
MORTON, WILLIAM R.
Mate, 15 October, 1861. Dismissed 11 April, 1862. Mate, 24 April, 1862. Resigned 15 July, 1862.
MORY, JOSEPH.
Carpenter, 1 August, 1800. Last appearance on Records of Navy Department.
MOSELEY, JAMES C.
Acting Midshipman, 20 May, 1852. Midshipman, 1 October, 1856. Passed Midshipman, 29 April, 1859. Master, 5 September, 1859. Lost in the Levant, 18 September, 1860.
MOSELEY, JOSEPH.
Acting Master, 29 October, 1861. Resigned (sick) 21 May, 1862.
MOSELEY, JOSEPH.
Acting Ensign, 8 November, 1862. Appointment revoked (sick) 6 December, 1862.

GENERAL NAVY REGISTER.

MOSELEY, NATHANIEL S.
  Cadet Midshipman, 4 June, 1880. Graduated 4 June, 1884. Ensign, 1 July, 1886. Died 18 September, 1887.
MOSELEY, SAMUEL.
  Assistant Surgeon, 17 August, 1826. Surgeon, 4 April, 1831. Resigned 13 April, 1852.
MOSER, HENRY.
  Mate, 24 March, 1863. Appointment revoked 15 April, 1863.
MOSER, JEFFERSON F.
  Midshipman, 29 September, 1864. Graduated June, 1868. Master, 12 July, 1870. Lieutenant, 19 August, 1872. Lieutenant-Commander, 27 June, 1893. Commander, 3 March, 1899.
MOSES, ALEXANDER.
  Mate, 20 July, 1863. Resigned 7 August, 1865.
MOSES, C. LEE.
  Acting Master, 22 January, 1862. Resigned 18 August, 1863.
MOSES, EDWARD.
  Acting Master, 17 May, 1862. Died 18 May, 1864.
MOSES, JABEZ H.
  Acting Assistant Surgeon, 19 February, 1864. Honorably discharged 10 October, 1865.
MOSES, LEONARD.
  Carpenter, 6 July, 1850. Died 20 August, 1857.
MOSES, PHILIP.
  Midshipman, 17 May, 1800. Discharged 29 April, 1801, under Peace Establishment Act.
MOSES, STANFORD E.
  Naval Cadet, 6 September, 1888. Assistant Engineer, 1 July, 1894. Passed Assistant Engineer, 19 September, 1898. Rank changed to Lieutenant, Junior Grade, 3 March, 1899.
MOSHER, CHARLES R.
  Third Assistant Engineer, 20 May, 1863. Resigned 3 March, 1866.
MOSHER, WILLIAM.
  Mate, 15 July, 1864. Resigned 31 October, 1868.
MOSHER, WILLIAM.
  Midshipman, 7 March, 1814. Resigned 27 April, 1815.
MOSHIER, WILLIAM.
  Boatswain, 2 April, 1803. Discharged 8 August, 1803.
MOSIER, EDWARD T.
  Mate, 9 January, 1864. Honorably discharged 13 September, 1867.
MOSLANDER, WILLIAM.
  Acting Master, 27 December, 1861. Honorably discharged 31 October, 1865.
MOSMAN, B. FRANK.
  Acting Master, 3 July, 1861. Resigned 7 November, 1862.
MOSS, CHARLES B.
  Chief Engineer, 29 May, 1844. Dropped 30 January, 1846.
MOSS, JASPER H.
  Mate, 15 September, 1864. Honorably discharged 15 July, 1865.
MOSS, JOSEPH.
  Mate, 20 December, 1861. Acting Ensign, 15 September, 1863. Dead.
MOSS, MICHAEL.
  Acting Third Assistant Engineer, 9 October, 1861. Resigned 21 November, 1861.
MOSSINGTON, WALTER.
  Acting Third Assistant Engineer, 16 July, 1863. Honorably discharged 19 November, 1865.
MOTLEY, A.
  Midshipman, 16 January, 1809. Last appearance on Records of Navy Department, 1815. Portland, Massachusetts.
MOTT, GEORGE B.
  Acting Ensign, 1 April, 1863. Honorably discharged 17 August, 1865.
MOTT, JOHN.
  Lieutenant, 9 February, 1805. Resigned 6 February, 1806.
MOTT, WILLIAM H.
  Acting Third Assistant Engineer, 17 May, 1864. Acting Second Assistant Engineer, 2 June, 1865. Honorably discharged 11 December, 1865.
MOTT, WILLIAM H.
  Mate, 12 February, 1864. Honorably discharged 21 November, 1866.
MOTT, WILLIAM H.
  Midshipman, 7 August, 1812. Lieutenant, 1 April, 1818. Died 4 July, 1824.
MOTT, WILLIAM H.
  Midshipman, 1 January, 1812. Dismissed 7 July, 1812.
MOTT, WILLIAM H.
  Midshipman, 1 August, 1861. Resigned June, 1862. Mate, 9 July, 1862. Honorably discharged 21 November, 1866.
MOTTE, WILLIAM S.
  Midshipman, 2 March, 1799. Resigned 22 September, 1799.
MOULE, JOHN J.
  Acting Ensign, 28 January, 1864. Honorably discharged 22 October, 1865.
MOUNT, EDWARD.
  Master, 28 June, 1815. Last appearance on Records of Navy Department.
MOUNTAIN, J. M.
  Midshipman, 16 January, 1809. Resigned 19 December, 1809.
MOWATT, JAMES.
  Acting First Assistant Engineer, 15 November, 1861. Resigned 1 August, 1862.
MOWBRAY, WILLIAM.
  Gunner, 17 September, 1861. Resigned 19 July, 1865.

MOWER, HENRY K.
Midshipman, 1 March, 1825. Died in April, 1828.
MOWSON, ROBERT.
Mate, 25 January, 1865. Deserted 23 March, 1867.
MOXLEY, CALEB H.
Acting Third Assistant Engineer, 28 March, 1864. Honorably discharged 28 October, 1865.
MOXLEY, HENRY.
Acting Third Assistant Engineer, 29 December, 1863. Honorably discharged 9 December, 1865.
MOXON, HENRY C.
Acting Chief Engineer, 4 February, 1863. Died 3 August, 1863.
MOYER, JOSEPH.
Acting Ensign, 1 October, 1862. Honorably discharged 12 October, 1865.
MOYLE, SAMUEL.
Acting Third Assistant Engineer, 28 March, 1865. Honorably discharged 17 March, 1866.
MOYLES, HENRY.
Acting Second Assistant Engineer, 21 October, 1862. Acting First Assistant Engineer, 22 March, 1865. Honorably discharged 26 November, 1865.
MUCH, GEORGE W.
Assistant Naval Constructor, 17 May, 1866. Naval Constructor, 15 April, 1871. Retired List, 22 June, 1887. Died 17 August, 1894.
MUCKLE, JOHN S.
Lieutenant (Spanish-American War), 23 June, 1898. Honorably discharged 22 October, 1898.
MUDD, JOHN A.
Cadet Midshipman, 11 September, 1875. Completed course at Naval Academy, June, 1879. Midshipman, 10 June, 1881. Resigned 28 October, 1881. Assistant Paymaster, 29 October, 1881. Passed Assistant Paymaster, 19 January, 1892. Paymaster, 1 November, 1896.
MUDGE, WILLIAM C.
Mate, 26 May, 1864. Honorably discharged 25 October, 1865.
MUGAN, FRANCIS P.
Acting Warrant Machinist, 23 August, 1899.
MUHLENBURG, P., Jr.
Midshipman, 20 June, 1806. Resigned 2 May, 1808.
MUIR, ROBERT.
Acting Third Assistant Engineer, 24 January, 1865. Honorably discharged 15 September, 1868.
MUIR, WALTER.
Acting Ensign, 1 October, 1862. Resigned 10 April, 1865.
MUIR, WILLIAM C. P.
Cadet Midshipman, 24 June, 1876. Graduated 22 June, 1882. Ensign, Junior Grade, 3 March, 1883. Ensign, 26 June, 1884. Lieutenant, Junior Grade, 7 February, 1893. Lieutenant, 10 November, 1896.
MULCARE, MICHAEL.
Acting Third Assistant Engineer, 28 January, 1863. Honorably discharged 12 July, 1865.
MULDAUR, ALONZO W.
Acting Master, 18 October, 1861. Acting Volunteer Lieutenant, 24 May, 1864. Honorably discharged 19 November, 1866. Acting Master, 23 April, 1867. Lieutenant, 12 March, 1868. Lieutenant-Commander, 18 December, 1868. Lost on Oneida, Yokohama, Japan, 24 January, 1870.
MULFORD, A. B.
Acting Master, 26 August, 1861. Honorably discharged 10 November, 1868.
MULFORD, EZEKIEL.
Midshipman, 1 February, 1826. Resigned 7 June, 1830.
MULFORD, JAMES H., Jr.
Passed Assistant Paymaster, 23 July, 1866. Resigned 26 November, 1866.
MULFORD, JOSEPH W.
Acting Ensign, 12 July, 1864. Honorably discharged 6 December, 1865.
MULFORD, RICHARD.
Master's Mate, date not known. Master, 3 July, 1813. Last appearance on Records of Navy Department, 1815. New York.
MULHOLLAND, JOHN.
Acting Third Assistant Engineer, 13 September, 1862. Dismissed 21 April, 1863.
MULL, ALEXANDER M.
Midshipman, 1 January, 1818. Lieutenant, 3 March, 1827. Died 19 July, 1830.
MULL, JACOB.
Master, 13 February, 1809. Struck off 4 May, 1825. Master, 5 August, 1825. Died 29 January, 1851.
MULL, THOMAS A.
Midshipman, 1 December, 1824. Passed Midshipman, 28 April, 1832. Dismissed 12 March, 1838.
MULLAHAN, THOMAS.
Acting Second Assistant Engineer, 27 February, 1863. Dead.
MULLAN, DANIEL.
Acting Warrant Machinist, 23 August, 1899.
MULLAN, DENNIS W.
Acting Midshipman, 21 September, 1860. Ensign, 1 October, 1863. Master, 10 May, 1866. Lieutenant, 21 February, 1867. Lieutenant-Commander, 12 March, 1868. Commander, 3 July, 1882.
MULLAN, HORACE E.
Acting Midshipman, 25 September, 1857. Midshipman, 1 June, 1861. Acting Master,

GENERAL NAVY REGISTER. 397

23 September, 1861. Lieutenant, 16 July, 1862. Lieutenant-Commander, 25 July, 1866. Dropped 18 August, 1876. Restored to original position as Lieutenant-Commander, 16 July, 1878. Commander, 8 February, 1879. Dismissed 6 July, 1883.

MULLANY, J. R. MADISON.
Midshipman, 7 January, 1832. Passed Midshipman, 23 June, 1838. Lieutenant, 28 February, 1844. Commander, 18 October, 1861. Captain, 25 July, 1866. Commodore, 15 August, 1870. Rear-Admiral, 5 June, 1874. Retired List, 26 October, 1879. Died 17 September, 1887.

MULLEN, ANTHONY T. E.
Third Assistant Engineer, 12 August, 1861. Second Assistant Engineer, 21 April, 1863. First Assistant Engineer, 25 January, 1865. Died 20 September, 1877.

MULLEN, J. W.
Mate, 10 September, 1864. Resigned 15 May, 1865.

MULLEN, PHILLIP.
Boatswain, 28 November, 1896.

MULLEN, WILLIAM.
Acting Ensign, 16 March, 1865. Honorably discharged 27 August, 1865.

MULLEN, WILLIAM M.
Mate, 30 August, 1864. Honorably discharged 6 November, 1865.

MULLER, FREDERICK.
Mate, 11 April, 1898. Boatswain, 26 May, 1899.

MULLIGAN, BARRY D.
Acting Third Assistant Engineer, 18 April, 1862. Acting Second Assistant Engineer, 18 October, 1862. Resigned 17 September, 1863. Acting Third Assistant Engineer, 8 August, 1864. Honorably discharged 1 December, 1865.

MULLIGAN, RICHARD T.
Midshipman, 5 June, 1871. Graduated 20 June, 1876. Ensign, 2 January, 1880. Lieutenant, Junior Grade, 23 May, 1886. Lieutenant, 16 December, 1891. Lieutenant-Commander, 10 October, 1899.

MULLINIX, WILLIAM F.
Acting Warrant Machinist, 23 August, 1899.

MULLINS, JOHN.
Acting Master and Pilot, 9 January, 1865. Honorably discharged 11 October, 1865.

MULLOWNY, EDWARD.
Midshipman, 21 June, 1839. Last appearance on Records of Navy Department, 19 September, 1840.

MULLOWNY, JOHN.
Lieutenant, 9 March, 1798. Discharged 26 September, 1801, under Peace Establishment Act.

MULREADY, JOHN.
Acting Third Assistant Engineer, 24 July, 1863. Acting Second Assistant Engineer, 10 May, 1865. Honorably discharged 26 February, 1868.

MULREADY, ROBERT.
Acting Third Assistant Engineer, 12 November, 1862. Acting Second Assistant Engineer, 22 February, 1864. Acting First Assistant Engineer, 30 November, 1864. Honorably discharged 1 December, 1865.

MUMFORD, WILLIAM.
Purser, 13 November, 1799. Discharged 10 September, 1801, under Peace Establishment Act.

MUN, HUGH J.
Midshipman, 10 May, 1820. Died 28 May, 1821.

MUNCE, THOMAS Q.
Acting Midshipman, 22 September, 1857. Resigned 10 March, 1860.

MUNCY, MILTON B.
Mate, 8 December, 1862. Acting Ensign, 11 June, 1863. Acting Master, 25 March, 1865. Honorably discharged 12 December, 1865.

MUNDY, GEORGE.
Acting Ensign, 1 October, 1862. Resigned 24 April, 1863.

MUNDY, GEORGE.
Acting Master, 14 August, 1861. Acting Volunteer Lieutenant, 18 March, 1864. Honorably discharged 16 December, 1865.

MUNGER, JOHN A.
Acting Third Assistant Engineer, 25 November, 1861. Acting Second Assistant Engineer, 19 December, 1862. Resigned 23 May, 1863.

MUNGER, JNO. M.
Acting Master's Mate, 6 October, 1864. Discharged 13 October, 1865.

MUNN, JAMES P.
Acting Ensign, Admiral Stribling's Staff, 23 September, 1864. Honorably discharged 13 January, 1866.

MUNN, SAMUEL E.
Midshipman, 27 August, 1823. Passed Midshipman, 23 March, 1829. Lieutenant, 31 December, 1833. Died 23 November, 1854.

MUNRO, RICHARD A.
Boatswain, 25 July, 1826. Died 27 March, 1832.

MUNROE, BENJAMIN F.
Acting Assistant Paymaster, 7 September, 1863. Mustered out 27 August, 1865.

MUNROE, FRANK H.
Mate, 27 July, 1863. Honorably discharged 16 August, 1865.

MUNROE, JOHN.
Boatswain, 14 January, 1840. Resigned 9 August, 1852.

MUNROE, JOHN.
Acting Third Assistant Engineer, 1 February, 1863. Died 9 September, 1863.

MUNROE, JOSEPH W.
Acting Ensign, 1 July, 1864. Honorably discharged 16 November, 1865.

MUNROE, WILLIAM H.
    Mate, 14 April, 1862. Resigned 6 October, 1863.
MUNROE, WILLIS F.
    Acting Master, 17 September, 1861. Died from wounds received in Battle of Galveston, 1 February, 1863.
MUNSON, CHARLES A., JR.
    Mate, 16 April, 1863. Resigned 23 June, 1863.
MUNSON, JAMES.
    Acting Second Assistant Engineer, 9 June, 1863. Dismissed 7 October, 1863.
MURDAUGH, JAMES.
    Assistant Surgeon, 13 July, 1799. Permitted to retire 27 May, 1801.
MURDAUGH, WILLIAM H.
    Midshipman, 9 September, 1841. Passed Midshipman, 10 August, 1847. Master, 14 September, 1855. Lieutenant, 15 September, 1855. Dismissed 21 April, 1861.
MURDOCH, DAVIES.
    Lieutenant, Junior Grade (Spanish-American War), 30 April, 1898. Honorably discharged 21 September, 1898.
MURDOCH, JAMES.
    Lieutenant, 15 November, 1799. Discharged 14 April, 1801, under Peace Establishment Act.
MURDOCH, JAMES W.
    Lieutenant, 9 August, 1804. Out of service 25 June, 1806.
MURDOCH, JOSEPH
    Midshipman, 14 November, 1798. Last appearance on Records of Navy Department, 16 July, 1801.
MURDOCK, JOSEPH B.
    Midshipman, 26 July, 1866. Graduated 7 June, 1870. Ensign, 13 July, 1871. Master, 2 February, 1874. Lieutenant, 10 March, 1880. Lieutenant-Commander, 3 March, 1899.
MURFIN, ORIN G.
    Naval Cadet, 6 September, 1893. Ensign, 1 July, 1899.
MURPHY, BENJAMIN R.
    Acting Carpenter, 12 May, 1869. Appointment revoked 7 June, 1872.
MURPHY, CHARLES J.
    Mate, 2 November, 1864. In service.
MURPHY, DANIEL.
    Second Assistant Engineer, 12 November, 1842. Resigned 25 November, 1848.
MURPHY, DANIEL S.
    Acting Master, 18 December, 1861. Honorably discharged 31 October, 1865.
MURPHY, HENRY.
    Sailmaker, 1 August, 1809. Last appearance on Records of Navy Department, 1815. Brig Argus.
MURPHY, JEREMIAH.
    Mate, 8 January, 1862. Appointment revoked (sick) 26 February, 1864.
MURPHY, J. C.
    Mate, 17 July, 1861. Acting Ensign, 20 April, 1863. Honorably discharged 4 October, 1865.
MURPHY, JOHN D.
    Assistant Surgeon, 24 January, 1862. Died 26 October, 1867.
MURPHY, JOHN E.
    Boatswain, 15 June, 1898.
MURPHY, JOHN M.
    Midshipman, 18 February, 1841. Resigned 17 December, 1846.
MURPHY, JOHN M.
    Midshipman, 18 February, 1841. Passed Midshipman, 10 August, 1847. Resigned 10 May, 1852. Acting Lieutenant, 4 December, 1862. Resigned 30 July, 1864.
MURPHY, JOSEPH A.
    Assistant Surgeon, 3 January, 1900.
MURPHY, MICHAEL.
    Acting Ensign, 20 April, 1864. Honorably discharged 20 August, 1865.
MURPHY, MONROE.
    Third Assistant Engineer, 18 November, 1862. Second Assistant Engineer, 23 March, 1864. Resigned 6 December, 1865.
MURPHY, PATRICK.
    Acting Ensign, 12 December, 1862. Resigned 22 April, 1863.
MURPHY, PATRICK.
    Boatswain, 23 January, 1882. Retired List, 15 January, 1885. Died 1 December, 1896.
MURPHY, PATRICK J.
    Acting Third Assistant Engineer, 11 January, 1864. Honorably discharged 10 July, 1866.
MURPHY, PETER U.
    Midshipman, 12 May, 1834. Passed Midshipman, 8 July, 1839. Lieutenant, 29 May, 1846. Dismissed 21 April, 1861.
MURPHY, R. B. K.
    Acting Master and Pilot, 15 June, 1865. Honorably discharged 30 September, 1865.
MURPHY, SAMUEL W.
    Acting Third Assistant Engineer, 8 February, 1865. Honorably discharged 12 September, 1865.
MURPHY, WILLIAM K.
    Midshipman, 8 February, 1847. Appointment revoked 2 May, 1848.
MURRAY, ALBERT S.
    Third Assistant Engineer, 19 February, 1861. Second Assistant Engineer, 16 January, 1863. Killed on the Chenango, 15 April, 1864.

GENERAL NAVY REGISTER.   399

MURRAY, ALEXANDER.
Midshipman, 22 August, 1835. Passed Midshipman, 22 June, 1841. Master, 23 March, 1847. Lieutenant, 12 August, 1847. Reserved List, 13 September, 1855. Lieutenant on Active List, 12 August, 1847. Commander, 16 July, 1862. Captain, 25 July, 1866. Commodore, 19 June, 1871. Rear-Admiral, 26 April, 1876. Retired List, 30 April, 1878. Died 10 November, 1884.

MURRAY, ALEXANDER.
Captain, 1 July, 1798. Died 6 October, 1821.

MURRAY, ALEXANDER M.
Midshipman, 1 January, 1817. Last appearance on Records of Navy Department, 6 March, 1822. Dead.

MURRAY, CHARLES.
Purser, 31 March, 1843. Retired List, 6 January, 1864. Pay Director. Retired 3 March, 1871. Died 7 June, 1872.

MURRAY, CHARLES.
Mate, 11 June, 1863. Honorably discharged 12 December, 1865.

MURRAY, DANIEL.
Midshipman, 13 July, 1799. Lieutenant, 26 January, 1807. Resigned 29 October, 1811.

MURRAY, F. KEY.
Midshipman, 29 April, 1836. Passed Midshipman, 1 July, 1842. Master, 4 November, 1848. Lieutenant, 24 July, 1849. Commander, 16 July, 1862. Retired List, 8 June, 1867. Captain on Retired List, 22 June, 1867. Died 11 July, 1868.

MURRAY, GEORGE.
Midshipman, 15 November, 1809. Resigned 26 March, 1811.

MURRAY, GEORGE.
Midshipman, 6 January, 1809. Resigned 18 December, 1809.

MURRAY, GEORGE J.
Acting Master, 24 March, 1862. Appointment revoked 3 June, 1863.

MURRAY, JACOB M.
Third Assistant Engineer, 23 June, 1863. Resigned 13 May, 1865.

MURRAY, JAMES D.
Purser, 3 June, 1858. Pay Inspector, 3 March, 1871. Pay Director, 25 September, 1875. Retired List, 20 September, 1891.

MURRAY, JAMES M.
Assistant Surgeon, 29 December, 1877. Passed Assistant Surgeon, 29 December, 1877. Resigned 1 January, 1886.

MURRAY, JAMES W.
Acting Warrant Machinist, 23 August, 1899.

MURRAY, JOHN.
Acting Gunner, 19 March, 1864. Honorably discharged 21 January, 1866.

MURRAY, JOHN M.
Mate (Spanish-American War), 19 June, 1898. Honorably discharged 1 November, 1898.

MURRAY, ROBERT E.
Acting Third Assistant Engineer, 27 May, 1864. Honorably discharged 29 July, 1866. Acting Third Assistant Engineer, 3 December, 1866. Mustered out 9 December, 1867.

MURRAY, THOMAS N.
Acting Assistant Paymaster, 18 September, 1862. Mustered out 18 August, 1865.

MURRAY, WILLIAM D.
Acting Ensign, 13 September, 1864. Honorably discharged 31 July, 1865.

MUSE, JOHN.
Purser, 16 April, 1799. Discharged 18 November, 1801, under Peace Establishment Act.

MUSE, JOHN B.
Midshipman, 1 April, 1828. Resigned 3 June, 1828.

MUSE, LEWIS S.
Midshipman, 11 December, 1809. Resigned 10 December, 1810.

MUSE, THOMAS E.
Midshipman, 30 September, 1869. Graduated 31 May, 1873. Ensign, 16 July, 1874. Died 9 December, 1877.

MUSE, WILLIAM B.
Midshipman, 1 July, 1836. Passed Midshipman, 1 July, 1842. Lieutenant, 2 June, 1850. Resigned 9 June, 1852.

MUSE, WILLIAM T.
Midshipman, 1 June, 1828. Passed Midshipman, 14 June, 1834. Lieutenant, 29 December, 1840. Commander, 14 September, 1855. Dismissed 2 April, 1861.

MUSGRAVE, EDWARD G.
Acting Assistant Paymaster, 5 August, 1863. Resigned (sick) 6 September, 1864.

MUSGRAVE, WILLIAM.
Third Assistant Engineer, 3 May, 1859. Second Assistant Engineer, 1 July, 1861. First Assistant Engineer, 20 May, 1863. Resigned 12 September, 1865.

MUSHAWAY, JOHN.
Boatswain, 30 October, 1799. Resigned 1 April, 1800.

MUSSON, LEWIS F.
Midshipman, 11 March, 1835. Resigned 12 April, 1837.

MUSTIN, HENRY C.
Naval Cadet, 6 September, 1892. Ensign, 6 May, 1898.

MYDDLETON, HARRY S.
Ensign (Spanish-American War), 24 May, 1898. Honorably discharged 25 January, 1899.

MYERS, A. G.
Acting Assistant Paymaster, 5 March, 1862. Resigned 14 January, 1863.

MYERS, A. J
   Acting Assistant Paymaster, 13 June, 1864. Resigned 13 March, 1865.
MYERS, CHARLES
   Mate, 8 April, 1862. Resigned (sick) 14 June, 1864.
MYERS, E. F.
   Mate, 19 July, 1867. Resigned 23 March, 1870.
MYERS, HENRY.
   Purser, 21 June, 1854. Resigned 1 February, 1861.
MYERS, H. G.
   Midshipman, 25 November, 1825. Passed Midshipman, 4 June, 1831. Died 16 September, 1834.
MYERS, H. H.
   Midshipman, 1 April, 1819. Died 9 August, 1820.
MYERS, JOHN.
   Acting Ensign, 4 November, 1863. Acting Master, 8 July, 1864. Honorably discharged 13 August, 1865.
MYERS, JOHN C.
   Mate, 13 November, 1862. Dismissed 6 December, 1862.
MYERS, J. C.
   Acting Boatswain, 9 December, 1861. Dismissed 13 December, 1861.
MYERS, JOHN P.
   Boatswain, 24 July, 1827. Appointment revoked 8 May, 1828.
MYERS, JOHN T.
   Naval Cadet, 22 September, 1887. Assistant Engineer, 22 August, 1894. Transferred to the Marine Corps.
MYERS, JOSEPH.
   Midshipman, 6 December, 1814. Lieutenant, 13 January, 1825. Commander, 8 September, 1841. Reserved List, 13 September, 1855. Resigned 22 April, 1861.
MYERS, JOSEPH G.
   Carpenter, 4 November, 1852. Died 28 August, 1878.
MYERS, JULIAN.
   Midshipman, 2 March, 1839. Passed Midshipman, 2 July, 1845. Master, 21 February, 1854. Lieutenant, 20 September, 1854. Dismissed 6 December, 1861.
MYERS, MEREDITH.
   Midshipman, 2 February, 1829. Resigned 7 July, 1829.
MYERS, ROBERT.
   Carpenter, 9 March, 1802. Last appearance on Records of Navy Department, 19 March, 1802.
MYERS, ROSS M.
   Mate, 13 August, 1863. Resigned 25 September, 1863. Acting Third Assistant Engineer, 18 August, 1864. Resigned (sick) 30 January, 1865.
MYERS, TALLEYRAND D.
   Assistant Surgeon, 27 September, 1870. Retired List, 7 December, 1882.
MYERS, THOMAS J.
   Acting Third Assistant Engineer, 12 July, 1864. Honorably discharged 4 November, 1865.
MYERS, WILLIAM.
   Midshipman, 16 January, 1802. Last appearance on Records of Navy Department, 19 March, 1809.
MYERS, WILLIAM H.
   Gunner, 16 July, 1841. Resigned 15 December, 1847.
MYERS, WILLIAM W.
   Acting Assistant Surgeon, 27 September, 1862. Appointment revoked 7 August, 1865. Acting Assistant Surgeon, 12 December, 1873. Appointment revoked 31 December, 1874.
MYGATT, JARED P. K.
   Midshipman, 24 September, 1847. Passed Midshipman, 10 June, 1853. Master, 15 September, 1855. Lieutenant, 16 September, 1855. Resigned 16 September, 1855. Acting Lieutenant, 13 May, 1861. Resigned (sick) 12 December, 1861.
MYRICK, JOHN.
   Gunner, 8 August, 1811. Last appearance on Records of Navy Department, 1815.
MYRICK, JOHN.
   Gunner, 13 June, 1836. Died 17 September, 1862.
MYTINGER, JOHN K.
   Mate, 28 October, 1863. Died 23 September, 1864.
NABOR, FRANK W.
   Midshipman, 21 September, 1867. Graduated 6 June, 1871. Ensign, 14 July, 1872. Master, 11 February, 1875. Died 23 August, 1883.
NAGLE, AUGUSTUS F.
   Third Assistant Engineer, 3 August, 1863. Resigned 3 May, 1865.
NAGLE, CHARLES F.
   Third Assistant Engineer, 3 August, 1863. Appointment revoked 8 January, 1866. Restored to the service 12 January, 1866, with original date. Second Assistant Engineer, 25 July, 1866. Passed Assistant Engineer, 15 April, 1874. Retired List, 26 July, 1892.
NAILE, FREDERICK I.
   Acting Midshipman, 27 October, 1859. Ensign, 24 February, 1863. Lieutenant, 22 February, 1864. Lieutenant-Commander, 25 July, 1866. Retired List, 18 January, 1871.
NAILE, FREDERICK R.
   Naval Cadet, 5 September, 1896. Graduated 30 June, 1900.
NAILER, JEFFERSON.
   Midshipman, 1 January, 1825. Resigned 8 July, 1830.

NALLE, THOMAS B.
　Purser, 17 October, 1839.　Resigned 31 July, 1861.
NAPHEYS, BENJAMIN F.
　Acting Third Assistant Engineer, 3 March, 1864.　Resigned 10 May, 1865.
NAPHEYS, GEORGE H.
　Acting Assistant Surgeon, 22 July, 1864.　Resigned 8 September, 1865.
NAPIER, EDWARD.
　Mate, 1 October, 1862.　Resigned 21 August, 1863.
NASH, DAVID M. W.
　Carpenter, 30 October, 1860.　Resigned 15 February, 1862.　Carpenter, 8 January, 1880.　Retired List, 28 January, 1896.　Died 17 December, 1896.
NASH, EDWIN W.
　Cadet Midshipman, 11 September, 1876.　Graduated 22 June, 1882.　Ensign, Junior Grade, 3 March, 1883.　Resigned 24 December, 1883.
NASH, FRANCIS S.
　Assistant Surgeon, 22 December, 1877.　Passed Assistant Surgeon, 5 May, 1882.　Resigned 23 November, 1891.
NASH, JAMES.
　Mate, 3 July, 1862.　Acting Gunner, 4 February, 1863.　Resigned 25 January, 1864.　Gunner, 22 April, 1864.　Dismissed 15 October, 1864.　Acting Gunner, 6 March, 1865.　Honorably discharged 16 April, 1866.　Boatswain, 7 May, 1867.　Retired List, 3 June, 1895.
NASH, JAMES H.
　Acting Ensign, 20 January, 1863.　Honorably discharged 6 February, 1866.　Acting Ensign, 10 October, 1866.　Mustered out 31 October, 1866.
NASH, JAMES H.
　Acting Third Assistant Engineer, 29 January, 1867.　Died on Yantic, 23 November, 1867.
NASH, JAMES H.
　Acting Third Assistant Engineer, 1 September, 1863.　Honorably discharged 18 October, 1865.
NASH, OVERTON M.
　Acting Ensign, 18 June, 1864.　Honorably discharged 2 April, 1866.
NASH, RICHARD.
　Acting Third Assistant Engineer, 22 October, 1863.　Acting Second Assistant Engineer, 11 October, 1864.　Honorably discharged 15 July, 1865.
NASON, JOHN.
　Mate, 17 April, 1864.　Acting Ensign and Pilot, 4 July, 1864.　Appointment revoked 9 June, 1865.
NASSAU, E. A.
　Mate.　Dismissed 22 April, 1862.
NAUMAN, WILLIAM H.
　Second Assistant Engineer, 24 April, 1872.　Passed Assistant Engineer, 24 February, 1878.　Chief Engineer, 12 September, 1894.　Rank changed to Lieutenant-Commander, 3 March, 1899.
NAWNAH, BENJAMIN.
　Acting Second Assistant Engineer, 27 October, 1862.　Dismissed 31 October, 1863.
NAYLOR, B. B.
　Acting Master, 12 September, 1861.　Resigned 24 April, 1862.
NAYLOR, SAMUEL.
　Lieutenant, 22 May, 1798.　Resigned 3 December, 1798.
NAZRO, ARTHUR P.
　Midshipman, 30 July, 1865.　Graduated 4 June, 1869.　Ensign, 12 July, 1870.　Master, 26 July, 1871.　Lieutenant, 19 November, 1874.　Lieutenant-Commander, 18 November, 1896.　Commander, 22 November, 1899.
NAZRO, JAMES.
　Midshipman, 30 June, 1799.　Resigned 30 September, 1800.
NEAL, BENEDICT.
　Midshipman, 2 April, 1804.　Lieutenant, 4 June, 1810.　Died 1 September, 1815.
NEAL, ELIAS C.
　Acting Assistant Surgeon, 27 February, 1864.　Honorably discharged 25 December, 1865.
NEAL, WILLIAM SILVER.
　Third Assistant Engineer, 25 August, 1862.　Second Assistant Engineer, 20 February, 1864.　First Assistant Engineer, 1 January, 1868.　Resigned 3 September, 1872.
NEALE, FRANCIS D.
　Acting Third Assistant Engineer, 23 February, 1865.　Honorably discharged 17 July, 1865.
NEALE, HAMLET.
　Midshipman, 2 April, 1804.　Last appearance on Records of Navy Department, May, 1808.　Dead.
NEALIS, JAMES.
　Mate, 20 July, 1862.　Honorably discharged 24 October, 1865.
NEALL, WILLIAM B.
　Acting Second Assistant Engineer, 15 December, 1862.　Dismissed 13 August, 1863.
NEARNS, HAMILTON C.
　Acting First Assistant Engineer, 12 December, 1862.　Resigned 22 April, 1863.
NEEL, PERCY L.
　Assistant Engineer (Spanish-American War), 14 May, 1898.　Honorably discharged 28 April, 1899.
NEELD, JOHN R.
　Acting Master, 1 October, 1862.　Acting Volunteer Lieutenant, 27 May, 1865.　Honorably discharged 26 November, 1865.

NEELY, JAMES H.
  Mate, 11 November, 1863. Acting Ensign, 14 February, 1864. Honorably discharged 6 October. 1865.
NEELY, THOMAS.
  Acting Third Assistant Engineer, 13 May, 1863. Acting Second Assistant Engineer, 14 January, 1864. Honorably discharged 8 December, 1865.
NEGLEY, WILLIAM C.
  Midshipman, 26 July, 1865. Graduated 4 June, 1869. Resigned 10 August, 1872.
NEIL, CECIL C.
  Mate, 5 March, 1862. Acting Ensign, 29 March, 1864. Honorably discharged 10 July, 1865. Gunner, 3 January, 1870. Died 12 May, 1889.
NEIL, CHARLES H.
  Mate, 15 May, 1863. Resigned 14 March, 1865.
NEIL, WILLIAM.
  Acting Ensign, 9 April, 1863. Acting Master, 31 May, 1864. Honorably discharged 4 December, 1865.
NEIL, WILLIAM T.
  Acting Third Assistant Engineer 3 August, 1863. Resigned 6 March, 1865.
NEILL, ROBERT C.
  Midshipman, 7 June, 1799. Died in August, 1799.
NEILL, WILLIAM C.
  Midshipman, 16 January, 1800. Dismissed 11 January, 1811.
NEILL, JOHN E.
  Third Assistant Engineer, 26 August, 1859. Second Assistant Engineer, 21 October, 1861. Resigned 23 November, 1865.
NEILSON, EDWARD R.
  Midshipman, 27 October, 1841. Resigned 11 October, 1843.
NEILSON, FREDERICK C.
  Assistant Engineer (Spanish-American War), 14 May, 1898. Honorably discharged 19 January, 1899.
NEILSON, GEORGE CRAWFORD.
  Third Assistant Engineer, 13 October, 1863. Second Assistant Engineer, 1 January, 1868. Resigned 5 July, 1876.
NEILSON, GEORGE W.
  Mate, 24 October, 1861. Acting Ensign, 30 August, 1862. Dismissed 19 June, 1863.
NEILSON, HAROLD.
  Mate, 29 March, 1870. Retired List, 31 March, 1899.
NEILSON, JOHN L.
  Assistant Surgeon, 28 April, 1870. Passed Assistant Surgeon, 20 February, 1875. Surgeon, 22 October, 1882. Medical Inspector, 3 September, 1896. Died 1 September, 1898.
NEILSON, THOMAS P.
  Passed Assistant Engineer (Spanish-American War), 14 May, 1898. Honorably discharged 2 March, 1899.
NEILSON, WILLIAM.
  Midshipman, 20 June, 1799. Last appearance on Records of Navy Department, 6 June, 1800. Furloughed.
NEILSON, WILLIAM.
  Acting Assistant Surgeon, 10 February, 1863. Resigned 11 June, 1864.
NELLIS, CHARLES F.
  Acting Ensign, 22 September, 1863. Resigned 3 June, 1864.
NELLMAN, CHARLES.
  Acting Ensign, 8 July, 1864. Honorably discharged 10 August, 1865.
NELSON, AARON H.
  Acting Assistant Paymaster, 7 July, 1863. Resigned 28 March, 1865. Assistant Paymaster, 21 February, 1867. Passed Assistant Paymaster, 30 June, 1869. Resigned 14 December, 1871.
NELSON, ANDREW.
  Acting Ensign, 2 July, 1863. Honorably discharged 28 October, 1865.
NELSON, ARMISTEAD.
  Midshipman, 30 November, 1814. Resigned 30 June, 1817.
NELSON, BENJAMIN.
  Mate, 13 September, 1864. Honorably discharged 9 February, 1866.
NELSON, CHARLES.
  Acting Ensign, 24 February, 1863. Honorably discharged 27 September, 1865.
NELSON, CHARLES G.
  Acting Warrant Machinist, 23 August, 1899.
NELSON, CHARLES P.
  Naval Cadet, 19 May, 1894. Ensign, 4 April, 1900.
NELSON, CHRISTIAN.
  Sailmaker, 21 December, 1826. Resigned 7 August, 1835.
NELSON, GEORGE.
  Acting Second Assistant Engineer, 29 September, 1864. Honorably discharged 30 October, 1865.
NELSON, GEORGE E.
  Acting Master, 9 April, 1862. Acting Volunteer Lieutenant, 22 December, 1864. Honorably discharged 6 December, 1865.
NELSON, HENRY C.
  Assistant Surgeon, 9 May, 1861. Passed Assistant Surgeon, 26 October, 1863. Surgeon, 25 October, 1864. Medical Inspector, 20 April, 1879. Retired List, 23 April, 1884. Died 10 March, 1893.
NELSON, JOHN D.
  Midshipman, 21 September, 1799. Dismissed 30 December, 1799.

GENERAL NAVY REGISTER. 403

NELSON, JOHN L.
  Midshipman, 10 March, 1838. Dismissed 19 August, 1845.
NELSON, JOSEPH S.
  Midshipman, 16 January, 1809. Resigned 1 June, 1809.
NELSON, ROBERT S.
  Midshipman, 1 January, 1812. Discharged 16 June, 1812.
NELSON, P. T.
  Midshipman, 20 June, 1806. Last appearance on Records of Navy Department, 4 November, 1806. Furloughed.
NELSON, ROBERT T.
  Mate, 22 August, 1863. Acting Ensign, 16 July, 1864. Honorably discharged 27 October, 1865.
NELSON, THOMAS.
  Mate, 8 January, 1862. Acting Ensign, 7 November, 1862. Acting Master, 27 March, 1865. Master, 12 March, 1868. Lieutenant, 12 December, 1868. Lieutenant-Commander, 25 January, 1870. Commander, 13 December, 1886. Retired List, 5 December, 1896.
NELSON, THOMAS H.
  Acting Second Assistant Engineer, 25 March, 1864. Honorably discharged 12 May, 1865.
NELSON, THOMAS J.
  Assistant Surgeon, 7 August, 1819. Resigned 15 May, 1820.
NELSON, THOMAS N.
  Mate, 6 January, 1863. Died in New York 23 April, 1875.
NELSON, VALENTINE S.
  Cadet Midshipman, 6 June, 1873. Graduated 18 June, 1879. Ensign, 14 December, 1880. Lieutenant, Junior Grade, 21 May, 1887. Leiutenant, 18 November, 1892. Lieutenant-Commander, 1 July, 1900.
NELSON, WILLIAM.
  Mate, 19 November, 1861. Acting Ensign, 18 June, 1863. Honorably discharged 5 November, 1865.
NELSON, WILLIAM.
  Acting Master and Pilot, 1 October, 1864. Honorably discharged 23 January, 1866.
NELSON, WILLIAM.
  Midshipman, 28 January, 1840. Passed Midshipman, 11 July, 1846. Master, 19 September, 1854. Lieutenant, 18 April, 1855. Lieutenant-Commander, 16 July, 1862. Detailed for duty in United States Volunteer Army, and died as Major-General, 29 September, 1862.
NELSON, WILLIAM.
  Boatswain, 5 June, 1872. Died 8 January, 1874.
NELSON, WILLIAM A.
  Assistant Surgeon, 9 December, 1839. Surgeon, 21 November, 1854. Resigned 28 July, 1858.
NELSON, WILLIAM H.
  (See Melson.)
NES, DAVID S.
  Cadet Midshipman, 22 June, 1881. Graduated 5 June, 1885. Ensign, 1 July, 1887. Resigned 30 June, 1889.
NESBIT, THOMAS.
  Acting Third Assistant Engineer, 14 November, 1861. Resigned 13 January, 1863.
NESBITT, ANDREW.
  Acting Third Assistant Engineer, 13 February, 1862. Died 9 March, 1862.
NESEN, JOSEPH H.
  Acting Third Assistant Engineer, 17 June. 1863. Acting Second Assistant Engineer, 8 March, 1865. Died 24 October, 1866.
NESTELL, D. D. T.
  Acting Assistant Surgeon, 25 January, 1862. Appointment revoked 6 June, 1865.
NEUMANN, GEORGE G.
  Acting Gunner, 10 March, 1900.
NEVILLE, FREDERICK A.
  Midshipman, 10 May 1820. Lieutenant, 17 May, 1828. Commander, 15 July, 1851. Reserved List, 13 September, 1855. Dismissed 9 December, 1861.
NEVILLE, JOHN S.
  Midshipman, 2 May, 1823. Passed Midshipman, 18 July, 1839. Master, 31 October, 1846. Resigned 23 January, 1847. Acting Lieutenant, 13 May, 1861. Appointment revoked 12 November, 1861.
NEVILLE, ROBERT P.
  Pharmacist, 15 September, 1896.
NEVITT, JOHN.
  Midshipman, 30 May, 1803. Lieutenant, 23 February, 1809. Resigned 5 January, 1811.
NEW, JOSEPH W.
  Assistant Surgeon, 8 February, 1802. Surgeon, 28 June, 1809. Died 23 September, 1815.
NEW, PHILIP.
  Gunner, 26 March, 1800. Last appearance on Records of Navy Department.
NEW, WALTER W.
  Assistant Surgeon, 5 March, 1811. Surgeon, 6 October, 1813. Resigned 23 December, 1824.
NEWBEGIN, JOHN S.
  Mate, 5 September, 1863. Honorably discharged 16 August, 1865.
NEWBERRY, TRUMAN H.
  Lieutenant, Junior Grade (Spanish-American War), 9 May, 1898. Honorably discharged 24 August, 1898.

NEWCOMB, FRANK H.
Mate, 4 November, 1863. Resigned 6 May, 1865.
NEWCOMB, HENRY S.
Midshipman, 21 July, 1838. Passed Midshipman, 20 May, 1844. Master, 4 September, 1852. Lieutenant, 28 June, 1853. Lieutenant-Commander, 16 July, 1862. Commander, 21 September, 1862. Died 24 October, 1863.
NEWCOMB, H. S.
Midshipman, 16 January, 1809. Lieutenant, 24 July, 1813. Drowned 1 November, 1825.
NEWCOMB, JOHN B.
Mate, 31 August, 1863. Resigned 6 May, 1865.
NEWCOMB, SIMON.
Professor, 21 September, 1861. Retired 12 March, 1897.
NEWCOMB, WALTER.
Midshipman, 11 January, 1812. Lieutenant, 28 March, 1820. Last appearance on Records of Navy Department, 9 August, 1822. Dead.
NEWCOMBE, GEORGE D.
Mate, 17 November, 1862. Acting Ensign, 9 February, 1863. Appointment revoked 4 March, 1863. Reappointed 19 March, 1863. Acting Master, 29 October, 1864. Honorably discharged 30 October, 1865. Acting Master, 29 September, 1866. Resigned 5 February, 1867.
NEWCOMER, JOSEPH W.
Acting Assistant Surgeon, 15 March, 1864. Assistant Surgeon, 1 April, 1864. Resigned 24 August, 1865.
NEWELL, CHESTER.
Chaplain, 8 September, 1841. Retired List, 3 July, 1865. Died 24 June, 1892.
NEWELL, DAVID.
Acting Third Assistant Engineer, 29 July, 1863. Acting Second Assistant Engineer, 3 October, 1864. Honorably discharged 23 August, 1865.
NEWELL, FREDERICK.
Acting Ensign, 8 May, 1863. Honorably discharged 11 November, 1865.
NEWELL, HARMAN.
Third Assistant Engineer, 22 September, 1849. Second Assistant Engineer, 26 February, 1851. First Assistant Engineer, 21 May, 1853. Chief Engineer, 23 April, 1859. Died 24 March, 1880.
NEWELL, JOHN S.
Midshipman, 28 September, 1861. Graduated 24 September, 1865. Ensign, 1 December, 1866. Master, 12 March, 1868. Lieutenant, 26 March, 1869. Lieutenant-Commander, 22 January, 1880. Commander, 24 October, 1889. Died 3 September, 1896.
NEWELL, LLOYD B.
Midshipman, 10 May, 1820. Lieutenant, 17 May, 1828. Commander, 6 April, 1851. Reserved List, 13 September, 1855. Died 26 April, 1861.
NEWELL, THOMAS M.
Master, 11 September, 1813. Lieutenant, 9 December, 1814. Commander, 3 March, 1831. Captain, 28 January, 1840. Reserved List, 13 September, 1855. Resigned 18 March, 1861.
NEWHALL, RICHARD H.
Acting Third Assistant Engineer, 7 June, 1864. Honorably discharged 13 November, 1865.
NEWLIN, GEORGE.
Mate, 23 January, 1862. Appointment revoked 10 September, 1866.
NEWLIN, JOHN L.
Mate, 4 April, 1862. Dismissed 28 June, 1862.
NEWMAN, ALLEN M.
Acting Master, 9 October, 1861. Honorably discharged 26 October, 1865.
NEWMAN, CHARLES M.
Ensign (Spanish-American War), 25 May, 1898. Honorably discharged 3 September, 1898.
NEWMAN, GUSTAVUS.
Gunner, 6 September, 1836. Died 2 May, 1852.
NEWMAN, JOHN.
Midshipman, 31 October, 1799. Died 2 August, 1800.
NEWMAN, JOHN M.
Acting Third Assistant Engineer, 3 September, 1864. Honorably discharged 4 December, 1865.
NEWMAN, L. HOWARD.
Midshipman, 24 September, 1847. Passed Midshipman, 10 June, 1853. Master, 15 September, 1855. Lieutenant, 16 September, 1855. Lieutenant-Commander, 16 July, 1862. Died 31 May, 1866.
NEWMAN, MONTGOMERY.
Midshipman, 21 November, 1800. Discharged 12 May, 1801, under Peace Establishment Act.
NEWMAN, MORRIS.
Master, 1 August, 1801. Discharged 8 April, 1803.
NEWMAN, SEWELL H.
Acting Ensign, 1 October, 1863. Acting Master, 13 June, 1865. Honorably discharged 20 March, 1866.
NEWMAN, THOMAS H.
Midshipman, 1 January, 1819. Died in May, 1821.
NEWMAN, TIMOTHY.
Commander, 1 July, 1799. Died 15 August, 1800.

GENERAL NAVY REGISTER. 405

NEWMAN, WILLIAM.
Midshipman, 2 July, 1801. Resigned 14 June, 1803.
NEWMAN, WILLIAM B.
Mate, 12 October, 1861. Acting Master, 3 February, 1862. Ensign, 12 March, 1868. Master, 18 December, 1868. Lieutenant, 21 March, 1870. Lieutenant-Commander, 2 June, 1882. Commander, 1 July, 1892. Retired List, 9 November, 1896.
NEWMAN, W. D.
Midshipman, 1 February, 1814. Lieutenant, 13 January, 1825. Commander, 8 September, 1841. Died 9 October, 1844.
NEWSHAM, PETER.
Boatswain, 10 August, 1805. Last appearance on Records of Navy Department.
NEWTON, EDWIN B.
Midshipman, 1 January, 1819. Last appearance on Records of Navy Department, 20 March, 1822. Dead.
NEWTON, G. BOLTON.
Acting Assistant Paymaster, 4 June, 1863. Resigned 18 June, 1863.
NEWTON, H. C.
Midshipman, 18 June, 1812. Lieutenant, 28 March, 1820. Resigned 29 April, 1828.
NEWTON, ISAAC.
First Assistant Engineer, 15 June, 1861. Resigned 8 February, 1865.
NEWTON, JAMES J.
Acting Third Assistant Engineer, 19 September, 1862. Dismissed 15 May, 1863.
NEWTON, JOEL W.
Chaplain, 30 May, 1844. Died 29 October, 1865.
NEWTON, JOHN T.
Midshipman, 16 January, 1809. Lieutenant, 24 July, 1813. Commander, 3 March, 1827. Captain, 9 February, 1837. Died 28 July, 1837.
NEWTON, JOHN T.
Midshipman, 14 October, 1872. Graduated 20 June, 1876. Ensign, 9 May, 1878. Lieutenant, Junior Grade, 15 June, 1885. Lieutenant, 19 February, 1891. Lieutenant-Commander, 1 July, 1899.
NEWTON, JOSEPH D.
Acting Second Assistant Engineer, 10 August, 1864. Honorably discharged 3 July, 1865.
NEWTON, JOSEPH T.
Acting Second Assistant Engineer, 24 October, 1861. Resigned 17 December, 1863.
NEWTON, THOMAS.
Mate, 5 December, 1861. Deserted 27 November, 1866.
NEWTON, WILLIAM E.
Midshipman, 24 September, 1832. Struck off 15 June, 1839.
NEWTON, WILLIS H.
Acting Third Assistant Engineer, 7 March, 1863. Deserted 30 August, 1863.
NEYLAN, THOMAS F.
Mate, 26 June, 1862. Resigned 11 August, 1863.
NEYLE, CHARLES.
Midshipman, 9 May, 1800. Discharged 12 August, 1801, under Peace Establishment Act.
NIBLACK, ALBERT P.
Cadet Midshipman, 22 September, 1876. Graduated 22 June, 1882. Ensign, Junior Grade, 3 March, 1883. Ensign, 26 June, 1884. Lieutenant, Junior Grade, 24 August, 1892. Lieutenant, 5 September, 1896.
NICHOL, WILLIAM L.
Assistant Surgeon, 28 June, 1852. Resigned 21 November, 1855.
NICHOLAS, GEORGE W.
Midshipman, 20 June, 1807. Died 15 September, 1809.
NICHOLAS, J. N.
Midshipman, 1 January, 1808. Resigned 1 September, 1809.
NICHOLAS, JOHN S.
Midshipman, 6 June, 1815. Lieutenant, 28 April, 1826. Commander, 29 July, 1842. Reserved List, 14 September, 1855. Captain on Active List, 14 September, 1855. Died 18 July, 1865.
NICHOLLS, BENJAMIN R.
Midshipman, 8 July, 1833. Passed Midshipman, 8 July, 1839. Resigned 5 May, 1841.
NICHOLLS, JOSEPH B.
Acting Master, 4 November, 1861. Resigned 4 March, 1862.
NICHOLLS, ROBERT H.
Master, 12 January, 1839. Appointment revoked 10 January, 1846.
NICHOLLS, THOMAS.
Master, 6 May, 1812. Died 12 December, 1822.
NICHOLLS, W. F.
Midshipman, 17 January, 1800. Resigned 18 September, 1804.
NICHOLS, ALPHEUS.
Acting Third Assistant Engineer, 13 January, 1864. Honorably discharged 4 November, 1865.
NICHOLS, CHARLES B.
Acting Third Assistant Engineer, 1 October, 1864. Honorably discharged 28 April, 1869.
NICHOLS, CHARLES H.
Mate, 11 February, 1863. Resigned 6 June, 1864.
NICHOLS, CLEMENT.
Acting Ensign, 30 June, 1864. Honorably discharged 19 September, 1865.
NICHOLS, CYRUS B.
Acting Ensign, 2 September, 1864. Honorably discharged 17 July, 1865.

NICHOLS, DAVID C.
  Midshipman, 1 December, 1811. Resigned 16 January, 1814.
NICHOLS, EDWARD T.
  Midshipman, 14 December, 1836. Passed Midshipman, 1 July, 1842. Master, 2 August, 1849. Lieutenant, 13 March, 1850. Commander, 16 July, 1862. Captain, 25 July, 1866. Commodore, 24 May, 1872. Rear-Admiral, 26 February, 1878. Retired List, 1 March, 1885. Died 12 October, 1886.
NICHOLS, FRANCIS.
  Midshipman, 18 June, 1812. Resigned 29 November, 1813.
NICHOLS, FRANK W.
  Midshipman, 24 September, 1862. Graduated 6 June, 1867. Ensign, 18 December, 1868. Master, 21 March, 1870. Lieutenant, 21 March, 1872. Lieutenant-Commander, 25 January, 1893. Retired List, 21 June, 1894. Died 7 February, 1895.
NICHOLS, GEORGE.
  Captain (to command a Galey), 30 November, 1798. Last appearance on Records of Navy Department.
NICHOLS, HENRY E.
  Midshipman, 28 September, 1861. Graduated 24 September, 1865. Ensign, 1 December, 1866. Master, 12 March, 1868. Lieutenant, 26 March, 1869. Lieutenant-Commander, 1 January, 1881. Commander, 25 June, 1891. Captain, 3 March, 1899. Died 10 June 1899.
NICHOLS, LLOYD.
  Midshipman, 3 January, 1801. Discharged 31 August, 1801, under Peace Establishment Act.
NICHOLS, R. H.
  Purser, 19 October, 1812. Last appearance on Records of Navy Department.
NICHOLS, ROBERT H.
  Midshipman, 1 September, 1811. Resigned 1 April, 1828.
NICHOLS, ROBERT H.
  Master, 12 January, 1839. Appointment revoked 10 January, 1846.
NICHOLS, RODNEY.
  Acting Second Assistant Engineer, 31 March, 1863. Acting First Assistant Engineer, 9 February, 1864. Appointment revoked (sick) 29 June, 1864.
NICHOLS, SMITH W.
  Acting Midshipman, 27 September, 1858. Lieutenant, 1 August, 1862. Lieutenant-Commander, 25 July, 1866. Commander, 26 April, 1876. Retired List, 14 April, 1882.
NICHOLS, THOMAS L.
  Acting Second Assistant Engineer, 23 December, 1864. Honorably discharged 4 November, 1865.
NICHOLSON, A. A.
  Midshipman, 1 January, 1817. (See Marine Corps.)
NICHOLSON, D. CARROLL.
  Mate, 31 December, 1869. Resigned 26 May, 1871.
NICHOLSON, EDWARD D.
  Midshipman, 29 May, 1805. Died 15 July, 1807.
NICHOLSON, GEORGE.
  Boatswain, 8 August, 1803. Died 29 July, 1809.
NICHOLSON, HENRY C.
  Acting Assistant Surgeon, 11 May, 1863. Resigned 21 March, 1864.
NICHOLSON, JAMES.
  Midshipman, 1 January, 1812. Last appearance on Records of Navy Department, 1816. Frigate United States.
NICHOLSON, JAMES.
  Midshipman, 1 December, 1809. Lieutenant, 5 March, 1817. Last appearance on Records of Navy Department, 25 June, 1819. Dead.
NICHOLSON, JAMES.
  Midshipman, 29 July, 1800. Resigned 21 April, 1804.
NICHOLSON, JAMES.
  Acting Third Assistant Engineer, 12 July, 1864. Resigned 10 May, 1865.
NICHOLSON, JAMES.
  Master, 31 August, 1813. Discharged 15 April, 1815.
NICHOLSON, JAMES W. A.
  Midshipman, 10 February, 1538. Passed Midshipman, 20 May, 1844. Master, 11 June, 1851. Lieutenant, 24 April, 1852. Commander, 16 July, 1862. Captain, 25 July, 1866. Commodore, 8 November, 1873. Rear-Admiral, 1 October, 1881. Retired List, 10 March, 1883. Died 28 October, 1887.
NICHOLSON, JOHN.
  Acting Master and Pilot, 1 October, 1864. Appointment revoked 5 June, 1865.
NICHOLSON, JOHN.
  Midshipman, 1 May, 1800. Last appearance on Records of Navy Department, 25 August, 1802. Furloughed.
NICHOLSON, JOHN.
  Carpenter, 28 April, 1809. Died 9 September, 1814.
NICHOLSON, JOHN B.
  Midshipman, 1 May, 1800. Lieutenant, 20 February, 1807. Cashiered 8 December, 1809.
NICHOLSON, JOHN R.
  Surgeon, 22 October, 1799. Died 28 April, 1800.
NICHOLSON, JOS.
  Midshipman, 15 July, 1803. Lieutenant, 15 June, 1809. Died 29 August, 1821.
NICHOLSON, JOS. J.
  Midshipman, 2 April, 1804. Lieutenant, 4 June, 1810. Commander, 5 March, 1817. Captain, 3 March, 1827. Died 12 December, 1838.

GENERAL NAVY REGISTER. 407

NICHOLSON, JOS. M.
Midshipman, 30 August, 1816. Lieutenant, 28 April, 1826. Died 5 April, 1833.
NICHOLSON, MICHAEL J.
Mate, 23 June, 1862. Acting Ensign, 22 March, 1865. Honorably discharged 31 October, 1865.
NICHOLSON, N. D.
Midshipman, 1 January, 1808. Lieutenant, 24 July, 1813. Died 24 June, 1822.
NICHOLSON, REGINALD F.
Midshipman, 30 September, 1869. Graduated 31 May, 1873. Ensign, 16 July, 1874. Master, 22 January, 1880. Lieutenant, Junior Grade, 3 March, 1883. Lieutenant, 17 January, 1886. Lieutenant-Commander, 3 March, 1899.
NICHOLSON, SAMUEL.
Captain, 10 June, 1794. Died 29 December, 1811.
NICHOLSON, SAMUEL, Jr.
Midshipman, 30 April, 1798. Died 25 September, 1798.
NICHOLSON, SETH.
Midshipman, 20 June, 1806. Resigned 24 July, 1809.
NICHOLSON, SOMERVILLE.
Midshipman, 21 June, 1839. Passed Midshipman, 2 July, 1845. Master, 9 September, 1853. Lieutenant, 5 May, 1854. Lieutenant-Commander, 16 July, 1862. Commander, 2 January, 1863. Captain, 10 June, 1870. Commodore, 22 January, 1880. Retired List, 7 April, 1881.
NICHOLSON, WILLIAM.
Master, 14 August, 1813. Last appearance on Records of Navy Department, 1815.
NICHOLSON, WILLIAM B.
Midshipman, 17 March, 1817. Lieutenant, 13 January, 1825. (Died 15 October, 1827.
NICHOLSON WILLIAM C.
Midshipman, 18 June, 1812. Lieutenant, 3 March, 1821. Commander, 8 September, 1841. Captain, 22 August, 1855. Retired List, 21 December, 1861. Commodore on Retired List, 16 July, 1862.. Died 25 July, 1872.
NICHOLSON, WILLIAM D.
Midshipman, 4 October, 1862. Graduated June, 1867. Ensign, 18 December, 1868. Master, 21 March, 1870. Resigned 12 June, 1871.
NICHOLSON, W. R,
Midshipman, 2 March, 1803. Last appearance on Records of Navy Department, 4 June, 1803. Killed in a duel.
NICKELL, HUGH.
Master, 4 February, 1809. Resigned 15 May, 1809.
NICKELS, JOHN A. H.
Midshipman, 8 October, 1864. Graduated 4 June, 1869. Ensign, 12 July, 1870. Master, 20 November, 1872. Lieutenant, 10 June, 1876. Lieutenant-Commander, 1 February, 1898. Commander, 29 November, 1900.
NICKELS, J. FREDERICK.
Acting Volunteer Lieutenant, 26 August, 1861. Acting Volunteer Lieutenant-Commander, 6 May, 1865. Honorably discharged 26 August, 1865.
NICKERSON, ARTHUR R.
Mate, 11 April, 1898. Boatswain, 10 April, 1899.
NICKERSON, FRANKLIN.
Acting Assistant Surgeon, 16 November, 1863. Resigned 5 November, 1864.
NICKERSON, HIRAM B.
Mate, 16 October, 1862. Appointment revoked (sick) 10 February, 1863
NICKERSON, LUTHER.
Acting Master, 30 August, 1861. Died on the J. S. Chambers, 15 August, 1864.
NICKERSON, MARCUS A.
Acting Ensign, 31 March, 1864. Honorably discharged 21 October, 1865.
NICKERSON, SYLVANUS.
Acting Master, 31 March, 1862. Acting Volunteer Lieutenant, 20 February, 1865. Honorably discharged 4 April, 1868.
NICKERSON, THEODORE.
Acting Ensign, 25 April, 1864. Honorably discharged 23 November, 1865.
NICKERSON, THOMAS.
Mate, 7 March, 1864. Honorably discharged 2 October, 1865. Mate, 25 May, 1866. Resigned 8 October, 1868.
NICKERSON, WILLIAM M.
Assistant Surgeon, 2 March, 1867. Retired List, 15 March, 1874.
NICOLL, WILLIAM L.
Third Assistant Engineer, 21 October, 1861. Second Assistant Engineer 3 August 1863. First Assistant Engineer, 11 October, 1866. Chief Engineer, 17 October, 1885. Died 2 July, 1887.
NICOLSON, JOHN B.
Midshipman, 4 July, 1805. Lieutenant, 20 May, 1812. Commander, 5 March, 1817. Captain, 24 April, 1828. Died 9 November, 1846.
NICOLSON, JOHN O.
Midshipman, 24 June, 1869. Graduated 15 October, 1874. Ensign, 17 July, 1875. Master, 12 October, 1881. Lieutenant, Junior Grade, 3 March, 1883. Lieutenant, 4 September, 1887. Retired List, 31 March, 1896. Died 27 February, 1898.
NICOLSON, WILLIAM.
Master, 28 January, 1809. Resigned 3 June, 1809.
NIELDS, HENRY C.
Mate, 11 February, 1863. Acting Ensign, 11 July, 1864. Acting Master, 4 November, 1864. Master, 12 March, 1868. Lieutenant, 18 December, 1868. Lieutenant-Commander, 1 July, 1870. Died 13 December, 1880.

GENERAL NAVY REGISTER.

NILES, HEZEKIAH.
Midshipman, 10 February, 1838. Died 23 December, 1841.
NILES, KOSSUTH.
Midshipman, 22 September, 1865. Graduated 4 June, 1869. Ensign, 12 July, 1870. Master, 1 March, 1873. Lieutenant, 30 September, 1876. Lieutenant-Commander, 1 May, 1898.
NILES, MARSTON.
Acting Midshipman, 25 September, 1860. Ensign, 28 May, 1863. Master, 10 November, 1865. Lieutenant, 10 November, 1866. Lieutenant-Commander, 12 March, 1868. Resigned 25 December, 1871. Lieutenant (Spanish-American War), 18 July, 1898. Honorably discharged 14 January, 1899.
NILES, NATHAN F.
Midshipman, 28 July, 1864. Graduated 2 June, 1868. Ensign, 19 April, 1869. Master, 12 July, 1870. Lieutenant, 7 July, 1874. Lieutenant-Commander, 5 January, 1896. Commander, 25 March, 1899.
NILSON, JULIUS.
Acting Ensign, 30 November, 1863. Acting Master, 22 November, 1864. Honorably discharged 16 July, 1866.
NISBET, RICHARD.
Acting Carpenter, 13 October, 1863. Resigned 17 February, 1865.
NIXON, JOHN W.
Purser, 24 December, 1857. Resigned 15 April, 1861.
NIXON, LEWIS.
Cadet Midshipman, 21 June, 1878. Assistant Naval Constructor, 1 July, 1884. Resigned 1 May, 1891.
NIXON, Z. W.
Midshipman, 18 June, 1812. Lieutenant, 28 March, 1820. Resigned 31 March, 1826.
NOA, LOVEMAN.
Naval Cadet, 5 September, 1896. Graduated 30 June, 1900.
NOBLE, ABIJAH W.
Purser, 10 January, 1799. Resigned 26 February, 1800.
NOBLE, JAMES.
Midshipman, 27 May, 1824. Passed Midshipman, 20 February, 1830. Lieutenant, 31 December, 1833. Dropped 13 September, 1855.
NOBLE, JAMES D.
Acting Assistant Surgeon, 20 February, 1865. Honorably discharged 13 January, 1866.
NOBLE, JAMES J.
Third Assistant Engineer, 19 February, 1861. Second Assistant Engineer, 20 May, 1863. Retired 5 January, 1866. Resigned 3 March, 1866.
NOBLE, MASON.
Chaplain, 30 March, 1853. Retired List, 18 March, 1871. Died 24 October, 1881.
NOE, HENRY.
Mate. Resigned 19 June, 1863.
NOE, JAMES W.
Acting Second Assistant Engineer, 1862. Resigned 3 November, 1862.
NOEL YORK.
Midshipman, 24 September, 1870. Graduated 1 June, 1874. Ensign, 17 July, 1876. Master, 28 October, 1881 Lieutenant, Junior Grade, 3 March, 1883. Lieutenant, 2 January, 1888. Lieutenant-Commander, 3 March, 1899.
NOELL, JACOB E.
Midshipman, 3 December, 1861. Graduated 24 September, 1865. Ensign, 1 December, 1866. Master, 12 March, 1868. Lieutenant, 26 March, 1869. Lieutenant-Commander, 2 August, 1879. Resigned 30 June, 1887.
NOLAN, JOSEPH.
Acting Second Assistant Engineer. Dismissed 19 July, 1864.
NOLAN, WILLIAM.
Mate, 6 November, 1865. Dismissed 30 October, 1865.
NOLAN, WILLIAM P.
Acting Third Assistant Engineer, 29 July, 1863. Acting Second Assistant Engineer, 31 July, 1863. Acting First Assistant Engineer, 23 November, 1864. Honorably discharged 5 October, 1865.
NOLAND, C. ST. G.
Midshipman, 16 June, 1834. Passed Midshipman, 16 July, 1840. Master, 6 November, 1846. Lieutenant, 25 February, 1847. Resigned 29 June, 1854.
NOLAND, MARTIN C.
Acting Third Assistant Engineer, 8 May, 1863. Honorably discharged 15 December, 1865.
NOLAND, WILLIAM H.
Midshipman, 13 December, 1823. Passed Midshipman, 23 March, 1829. Lieutenant, 31 December, 1833. Dropped 13 September, 1855.
NOLTON, C. G.
Mate, 4 February, 1870. Resigned 25 November, 1871.
NONES, HENRY B.
Third Assistant Engineer, 23 September, 1853. Resigned 19 August, 1856. Second Assistant Engineer, 28 May, 1861. First Assistant Engineer, 1 July, 1861. Chief Engineer, 14 December, 1864. Retired List, 15 May, 1892.
NONES, J. B.
Midshipman, 1 February, 1814. Resigned 2 July, 1821.
NONES, JEFFERSON H.
Midshipman, 19 December, 1840. Appointment revoked 3 February, 1846.
NONES, WASHINGTON H.
Third Assistant Engineer, 8 March, 1850. Second Assistant Engineer, 26 February, 1851. Died 9 September, 1853.

NOONAN, DAVID A.
    Acting Third Assistant Engineer, 25 August, 1864. Honorably discharged 23 February, 1869.
NOONEY, JAMES, JR.
    Professor of Mathematics, 24 May, 1838. Resigned 13 May, 1840.
NORCOTT, EDWARD J.
    Boatswain, 11 March, 1898.
NORFLEET, ERNEST.
    Assistant Surgeon, 21 May, 1874. Surgeon, 26 September, 1891. Retired List, 31 October, 1892.
NORIE, WILLIAM.
    Acting Third Assistant Engineer, 3 September, 1863. Honorably discharged 18 October, 1865.
NORMAN, BENJAMIN F.
    Acting Second Assistant Engineer, 4 May, 1863. Resigned 5 September, 1863.
NORMAN, GEORGE H., JR.
    Lieutenant, Junior Grade (Spanish-American War), 14 May, 1898. Honorably discharged 1 October, 1898.
NORMAN, GUY.
    Ensign (Spanish-American War), 21 May, 1898. Honorably discharged 15 September, 1898.
NORMAN, HUGH K.
    Lieutenant, Junior Grade (Spanish-American War), 6 July, 1898. Honorably discharged 13 March, 1899.
NORMAN, JAMES M.
    Acting Ensign and Pilot, 3 May, 1864. Appointment revoked 8 June, 1865.
NORMAN, REGINALD.
    Ensign (Spanish-American War), 28 June, 1898. Honorably discharged 6 September, 1898.
NORRIS, CHARLES A.
    Acting Second Assistant Engineer, 21 April, 1861. Resigned 14 April, 1864.
NORRIS, CHARLES F.
    Mate, 30 March, 1870. Resigned 2 September, 1870.
NORRIS, GEORGE A.
    Midshipman, 27 September, 1862. Graduated 12 June, 1866. Ensign, 12 March, 1868. Master, 26 March, 1869. Lieutenant, 21 March, 1870. Lieutenant-Commander, 13 December, 1886. Died 29 June, 1891.
NORRIS, GEORGE E.
    Acting Third Assistant Engineer, 10 May, 1864. Honorably discharged 28 October, 1865. Passed Assistant Paymaster (Spanish-American War), 23 April, 1898. Honorably discharged 4 January, 1899.
NORRIS, JAMES.
    Assistant Surgeon, 10 December, 1814. Resigned 20 June, 1826.
NORRIS, JOHN A.
    Midshipman, 27 September, 1865. Graduated 4 June 1869. Ensign, 12 July, 1870. Master, 10 October, 1872. Lieutenant, 20 October, 1875. Lieutenant-Commander, 28 August, 1897. Commander, 1 July, 1900.
NORRIS, OTHO.
    Midshipman, 16 January, 1809. Lieutenant, 24 July, 1813. Commander, 3 March, 1827. Lost in the Hornet, 10 September, 1829.
NORRIS, THOMAS E.
    Purser, 30 June, 1840. Resigned 29 August, 1845.
NORRIS, WILLIAM H.
    Mate, 3 November, 1862. Dismissed 21 January, 1863.
NORTH, GEORGE.
    Midshipman, 10 September, 1798. Resigned 4 December, 1800.
NORTH, HENRY H.
    Acting Master and Pilot, 1 October, 1864. Honorably discharged 8 October, 1868.
NORTH, JAMES H.
    Midshipman, 29 May, 1829. Passed Midshipman, 5 July, 1835. Lieutenant, 8 September, 1841. Resigned 15 January, 1861.
NORTH, JAMES H., JR.
    Assistant Surgeon, 7 July, 1890. Resigned 8 October, 1891.
NORTH, JOHN W.
    Sailmaker, 3 July, 1849. Retired List, 15 October, 1879.
NORTH, JOSEPH.
    Purser, 24 July, 1813. Last appearance on Records of Navy Department, 1810. Frigate Macedonian.
NORTH, JOSEPH W.
    Mate, 11 August, 1861. Acting Ensign, 28 September, 1863. Honorably discharged 22 September, 1865.
NORTH, WILLIAM F.
    Acting Master, 9 September, 1861. Dismissed 19 June, 1865.
NORTHROP, JOB.
    Midshipman, 22 January, 1815. Resigned 7 October, 1816.
NORTHRUP, F. U.
    Mate, 30 March, 1863. Resigned 22 May, 1865.
NORTHUP, GOULD.
    Carpenter, 16 May, 1871. Retired List, 10 October, 1898.
NORTON, ALBERT L.
    Naval Cadet, 23 May, 1884. Ensign, 1 July, 1890. Lieutenant, Junior Grade, 1 May, 1898. Lieutenant, 3 March, 1899.

NORTON, CHARLES.
Mate, 4 April, 1862. Acting Ensign, 10 September, 1862. Acting Master, 11 August, 1863. Acting Volunteer Lieutenant, 15 February, 1865. Honorably discharged 3 February, 1867.
NORTON, CHARLES.
Acting Third Assistant Engineer, 24 August, 1864. Honorably discharged 9 July, 1865.
NORTON, CHARLES F.
Midshipman, 22 July, 1863. Graduated 2 June, 1868. Ensign, 19 April, 1869. Master, 12 July, 1870. Lieutenant, 6 January, 1875. Retired List, 3 October, 1895. Died 21 September, 1896.
NORTON, CH. M.
Midshipman, 5 May, 1806. Resigned 15 April, 1809.
NORTON, CHARLES S.
Acting Midshipman, 3 October, 1851. Midshipman, 9 June, 1855. Passed Midshipman, 15 April, 1858. Master, 4 November, 1858. Lieutenant, 24 November, 1860. Lieutenant-Commander, 16 July, 1862. Commander, 1 July, 1870. Captain, 1: October, 1881. Commodore, 31 July, 1894. Rear-Admiral, 1 February, 1898. Retired List, 10 August, 1898.
NORTON, FREDERIC H.
Acting Third Assistant Engineer, 15 February, 1865. Resigned 31 October, 1867.
NORTON, HAROLD PERCIVAL.
Cadet Engineer, Naval Academy, 1 October, 1874. Graduated 10 June, 1879. Assistant Engineer, 10 June, 1881. Passed Assistant Engineer, 12 October, 1891. Chief Engineer, 10 February, 1899. Rank changed to Lieutenant, 3 March, 1899.
NORTON, HIRAM W.
Acting Ensign, 17 May, 1864. Honorably discharged 6 February, 1866.
NORTON, ICHABOD.
Acting Assistant Paymaster, 2 October, 1863. Resigned 29 June, 1865.
NORTON, JOHN C.
Lieutenant, Junior Grade (Spanish-American War), 24 May, 1898. Honorably discharged 25 January, 1899.
NORTON, JOHN F.
Acting Assistant Surgeon, 24 December, 1862. Appointment revoked 4 September, 1863.
NORTON, LOT.
Mate, 5 June, 1864. Honorably discharged 14 June, 1867. Mate, 20 December, 1869. Supposed to have been drowned 1872.
NORTON, MICHAEL.
Acting Second Assistant Engineer, 1 October, 1862. Resigned 23 November, 1864.
NORTON, OLIVER D.
Assistant Surgeon, 22 April, 1885. Passed Assistant Surgeon, 22 April, 1888. Surgeon. 23 January, 1898.
NORTON, RICHARD C.
Chaplain, 7 August, 1815. Last appearance on Records of Navy Department.
NORTON, SHUBAL C., JR.
Acting Ensign, 20 January 1864. Honorably discharged 7 August, 1865.
NORVELL, HENDRICK.
Midshipman, 1 April, 1828. Passed Midshipman, 14 June, 1834. Died 18 May, 1837.
NORVELL, JOSEPH.
Midshipman, 13 January, 1834. Resigned 1 May, 1838.
NORWOOD, JOHN G.
Midshipman, 3 July, 1799. Discharged 12 October, 1801, under Peace Establishment Act.
NOSTRAND, WARNER H.
Midshipman, 24 September, 1870. Graduated 1 June, 1874. Ensign, 17 July, 1875. Master, 7 August, 1881. Lieutenant, Junior Grade, 3 March, 1883. Resigned 30 June, 1886. Lieutenant (Spanish-American War), 17 June, 1898. Discharged 8 February, 1899.
NOTT, HUGH.
Acting Assistant Paymaster, 17 February, 1863. Honorably discharged 12 December, 1865.
NOTTINGHAM, J. H.
Midshipman, 4 November, 1841. (See Upshur.)
NOURSE, CHARLES J.
Assistant Surgeon 1 June, 1876. Died 23 July, 1880.
NOURSE, JOSEPH E.
Professor, 21 May, 1864. Retired List, 17 April, 1881. Died 8 October, 1889.
NOURSE, RALPH F.
Acting Warrant Machinist, 23 August, 1899.
NOWLAND, J. L.
Midshipman, 1 January, 1818. Last appearance on Records of Navy Department, 1821. Ship John Adams.
NOYES, ALLEN K.
Mate, 5 October, 1861. Acting Ensign, 1 September, 1864. Honorably discharged 5 November, 1865. Acting Ensign, 14 December, 1866. Mustered out 21 December. 1868.
NOYES, BOUTELLE.
Midshipman, 26 September, 1864. Graduated 2 June, 1868. Ensign, 19 April, 1869. Master, 12 July, 1870. Lieutenant, 14 February, 1873. Killed 29 August, 1883.
NOYES, CHARLES E. P.
Acting Ensign, 16 September, 1864. Honorably discharged 24 July, 1865.
NOYES, CHARLES H.
Acting Assistant Paymaster, 28 August, 1861. Resigned 17 January, 1865.

NOYES, HENRY M.
Acting Third Assistant Engineer, 21 November, 1863. Acting Second Assistant Engineer, 13 December, 1864. Honorably discharged 21 August, 1865.
NOYES, JOSEPH.
Midshipman, 18 June, 1812. Resigned 21 June, 1813.
NOYES, WILLIAM H. D.
Acting Assistant Surgeon, 4 September, 1861. Resigned 28 November, 1862.
NUGENT, DAVID E.
Acting Third Assistant Engineer, 26 September, 1863. Resigned (sick), 21 March, 1865.
NUGENT, RICHARD.
Acting Third Assistant Engineer, 13 September 1864. Dismissed 2 December, 1864.
NULTON, CHRISTOPHER H
Acting Second Assistant Engineer, 6 December, 1866. Honorably discharged 24 September, 1869.
NULTON, CHRISTOPHER.
Acting Third Assistant Engineer, 16 June, 1862. Acting Second Assistant Engineer, 26 July, 1864. Honorably discharged 24 September, 1869.
NULTON, LOUIS McC.
Naval Cadet, 8 September, 1885. Assistant Engineer, 1 July, 1891. Passed Assistant Engineer, 4 July, 1896. Rank changed to Lieutenant, 3 March, 1899.
NULTY, THOMAS.
Mate, 13 May, 1863. Resigned 20 August, 1863.
NUNTZ, JOHN.
Master, 7 July, 1812. Died 27 December, 1824.
NUTTER, JACOB.
Gunner, 11 January, 1799. Resigned 5 February, 1800.
NUTTING, DANIEL C.
Naval Cadet, 21 May, 1889. Assistant Naval Constructor, 1 July, 1895.
NUTTING, WILLIAM G.
Acting Master, 26 August, 1861. Appointment revoked 24 March, 1865.
NUTZ, WILLIAM R.
Acting Third Assistant Engineer, 24 December, 1862. Acting Second Assistant Engineer, 14 January, 1864. Honorably discharged 15 October, 1865.
NYBORG, WILLIAM.
Acting Ensign, 30 November, 1863. Acting Master, 22 November, 1864. Honorably discharged 13 September, 1867.
NYE, EDWARD C. T.
Mate, 26 December, 1863. Acting Ensign, 12 November, 1864. Honorably discharged 4 November, 1865.
NYE, FRANKLIN K. S.
Mate, 27 July, 1863. Resigned 10 June, 1864.
NYE, HAILE C.
Midshpman, 28 July, 1866. Graduated 7 June, 1870. Ensign, 13 July, 1872. Master, 1 January, 1875. Lieutenant, 12 October, 1881. Died 30 July, 1885.
NYE, PRINCE M.
Mate, 10 December, 1863. Discharged 2 June, 1864.
NYE, WILLIAM C.
Mate, 5 March, 1862. Honorably discharged 21 January, 1866.
NYMAN, FRANK W.
Third Assistant Engineer, 19 February, 1863. Resigned 21 April, 1864.
NYMAN, JAY.
Mate, 9 April, 1864. Honorably discharged 13 November, 1865.
NYSTROM, JOHN W.
Acting First Assistant Engineer, 29 July, 1864. Acting Chief Engineer, 28 February, 1865. Resigned 8 July, 1865.
OAKES, FREDERICK.
Midshipman, 8 May, 1832. Resigned 1 May, 1837.
OAKFORD, ISAAC R.
Third Assistant Engineer, 1 July, 1861. Second Assistant Engineer, 18 December, 1862. Resigned 13 October, 1865.
OAKLEY, CHARLES H.
Midshipman, 30 March, 1842. Dismissed 2 October, 1845.
OAKLEY, CHARLES H.
Assistant Surgeon, 2 October, 1844. Died 24 July, 1851.
OAKLEY, EUGENE H.
Midshipman, 2 August, 1847. Passed Midshipman, 15 June, 1844. Master, 16 September, 1855. Lieutenant, 17 September, 1855. Resigned 9 May, 1856.
OAKLEY, FARNAM L.
Acting Assistant Paymaster, 24 February, 1864. Mustered out 10 September, 1865.
OAKLEY, HENRY.
Mate, 9 July, 1862. Acting Ensign, 3 March, 1863. Acting Master, 14 May, 1864. Resigned 21 November, 1864.
OAKS, CALVIN.
Carpenter, 12 June, 1826. Resigned 26 August, 1833.
OATES, JOHN H.
Mate, 7 January, 1862. Dismissed 13 June, 1862.
OATLEY, JOHN C.
Mate, 13 September, 1864. Acting Ensign, 27 November, 1864. Honorably discharged 15 January, 1868.
OBERLY, AARON S.
Assistant Surgeon, 30 July, 1861. Passed Assistant Surgeon, 22 June, 1864. Surgeon, 19 June, 1866. Medical Inspector, 4 March, 1884. Retired List, 24 January, 1889

OBERLY, HUBERT.
　Mate, 25 April, 1863. Acting Ensign, 7 July, 1863. Appointment revoked 22 January, 1866.
O'BRIEN, DOUGLAS F.
　Mate, 19 December, 1861. Acting Ensign, 31 July, 1863. Honorably discharged 20 July, 1865.
O'BRIEN, EDWARD.
　Midshipman, 30 October, 1799. Dismissed 11 May, 1804.
O'BRIEN, GAB. A.
　Midshipman, 1 January, 1825. Resigned 8 March, 1831.
O'BRIEN, HUGH.
　Acting Second Assistant Engineer, 28 December, 1861. Dismissed 5 May, 1862.
O'BRIEN, JAMES.
　Mate, 4 October, 1862. Dismissed 10 March, 1862.
O'BRIEN, JOHN.
　Mate (Spanish-American War), 25 June, 1898. Honorably discharged 28 October 1898.
O'BRIEN, JOHN S.
　Mate, 27 July, 1863. Honorably discharged 30 December, 1867.
O'BRIEN, OLIVER.
　Mate, meritorious conduct, 1 December, 1864. Deserted, 25 April, 1865. Charge of Desertion by Act of Congress approved 3 August, 1894.
O'BRIEN, SAMUEL A.
　Mate, 19 December, 1861. Resigned 5 August, 1863.
O'BRIEN, WILLIAM P.
　Acting Ensign, 15 August, 1862. Resigned 6 June, 1863.
O'BRYAN, ARTHUR.
　Acting Third Assistant Engineer, 21 May, 1864. Honorably discharged 16 October, 1865.
O'BRYON, EDWARD D.
　Mate, 11 June, 1863. Appointment revoked 1 December, 1864.
O'CALLAGHAN, EDWARD J.
　Acting Assistant Surgeon, 23 December, 1863. Dismissed 6 September, 1865.
O'CALLAHAN, NICHOLAS.
　Purser, 24 February, 1801. Last appearance on Records of Navy Department.
OCHILTREE, DAVID.
　Midshipman, 21 June, 1839. Passed Midshipman, 11 July, 1846. Master, 1 March, 1855. Dropped 13 September, 1855.
O'CONNELL, DENNIS J.
　Acting Boatswain, 30 January, 1900.
O'CONNER, J. C.
　Appointed Sailmaker, 21 May, 1836. Resigned 25 July, 1839.
O'CONNOR, JOHN.
　Mate, 10 February, 1863. Apointment revoked 3 January, 1866.
O'CONNOR, JOSEPH A.
　Carpenter, 27 May, 1897.
O'CONNOR, CHRIS.
　Midshipman, 18 June, 1812. Discharged 25 May, 1813.
O'CONNOR, FREDERICK A.
　Mate, 12 January, 1863. Acting Ensign, 21 January, 1864. Acting Master, 28 June, 1865. Honorably discharged 27 December, 1867.
O'CONNOR, NICHOLAS.
　Master, 25 September, 1813. Last appearance on Records of Navy Department.
O'CONNOR, NICHOLAS.
　Master, 17 October, 1812. Dismissed 25 August, 1813.
O'CONNOR, PETER.
　Mate, 19 November, 1861. Acting Ensign, 15 March, 1864. Honorably discharged 4 March, 1866. Mate, 5 October, 1866. Mustered out 27 August, 1868.
O'CONNOR, THOMAS W.
　Acting Second Assistant Engineer, 21 July, 1862. Acting First Assistant Engineer, gallantry, 25 September, 1862. Honorably discharged 12 August, 1865. Acting First Assistant Engineer, 21 May, 1866. Mustered out 23 July, 1867.
O'CONWAY, J. M. S.
　Surgeon, 27 June, 1814. Resigned 5 November, 1821.
ODBERT, HENRY S.
　Mate, 26 August, 1864. Honorably discharged 26 October, 1865.
ODELL, ALVIN A.
　Acting Third Assistant Engineer, 21 April, 1862. Honorably discharged 16 October, 1865.
ODELL, GEORGE S.
　Acting Third Assistant Engineer, 8 July, 1863. Acting Second Assistant Engineer, 29 July 1865. Honorably discharged 1 October, 1867.
ODELL, HENRY E.
　Assistant Surgeon, 8 November, 1899.
ODELL, THOMAS G.
　Assistant Surgeon (Spanish-American War), 29 June, 1898. Honorably discharged 1 December, 1898.
ODEND'HAL, JOHN.
　Mate, 20 January, 1870. Appointment revoked 4 January, 1883.
ODENHEIMER, W.
　Midshipman, 17 December, 1810. Lieutenant, 16 July, 1814. Died 13 November, 1815.
ODEON, WILLIAM J.
　Acting Second Assistant Engineer, 1862. Resigned 28 February, 1863.

GENERAL NAVY REGISTER. 413

ODIORNE, LEVI L.
    Mate, 5 October, 1863. Acting Ensign, 29 November, 1864. Resigned 29 June, 1865.
ODIORNE, WALTER C.
    Mate, 26 August, 1861. Acting Ensign, 24 April, 1863. Resigned 16 March, 1866.
O'DONNELL, JAMES.
    Mate, 22 October, 1863. Resigned 22 May, 1866.
O'DONNELL, THOMAS.
    Warrant Machinist, 6 July, 1899.
O'DRISCOLL, CORNELIUS.
    Lieutenant, 26 April, 1799. Discharged 15 April, 1801.
OELLERS, JAMES P.
    Lieutenant, 24 July, 1813. Died 20 February, 1849.
OFFLEY, CLELAND N.
    Naval Cadet, 5 September, 1885. Assistant Engineer, 1 July, 1891. Passed Assistant Engineer, 14 December, 1896. Rank changed to Lieutenant, 3 March, 1899.
OGDEN, FREDERICK N.
    Assistant Surgeon, 9 January, 1885. Resigned 11 October, 1892.
OGDEN, HENRY W.
    Midshipman, 1 September, 1811. Lieutenant, 5 March, 1817. Commander, 31 January, 1838. Captain, 5 February, 1848. Reserved List, 13 September, 1855. Died 25 August, 1860.
OGDEN, JAMES.
    Acting Third Assistant Engineer, 15 December, 1862. Acting Second Assistant Engineer, 7 June, 1864. Honorably discharged 3 October, 1865.
OGDEN, JULIEN S.
    Acting Third Assistant Engineer, under instruction Naval Academy, 10 October, 1866. Third Assistant Engineer, 2 June, 1868. Second Assistant Engineer, 2 June, 1869. Passed Assistant Engineer, 20 October, 1875. Chief Engineer, 17 January, 1893. Rank changed to Lieutenant-Commander, 3 March, 1899. Commander, 11 June, 1899.
OGDEN, LEWIS.
    Midshipman, 1 March, 1825. Dismissed 1 June, 1832.
OGDEN, WILLIAM A.
    Midshipman, 1 September, 1811. Resigned 7 May, 1812.
OGDEN, WILLIAM B.
    Acting First Assistant Engineer, 5 May, 1863. Appointment revoked (sick) 20 November, 1863.
ODDIE, JOHN.
    Acting Master's Mate, 17 September, 1861. Discharged 25 April, 1862.
OGDEN, WILLIAM H.
    Acting Second Assistant Engineer, 9 October, 1861. Appointment revoked sick) 21 April, 1863.
OGDEN, WILLIAM S.
    Midshipman, 26 July, 1820. Lieutenant, 17 May, 1828. Commander, 22 April, 1851. Retired 15 January, 1862. Died 14 August, 1866.
OGLEVIE, PETER.
    Midshipman, 6 January, 1800. Lieutenant, 18 May, 1804. Lost at sea in 1805.
OGILVIE, JAMES.
    Acting Master, 26 August, 1861. Honorably discharged 6 June, 1868.
OGILVIE, JAMES G.
    Chaplain, 15 September, 1825. Last appearance on Records of Navy Department.
O'GRADY, HENRY S.
    Mate, 13 March, 1863. Acting Ensign, 2 November, 1863. Dismissed 16 November, 1864.
O'HARA, HENRY W.
    Mate, 20 February, 1863. Acting Ensign, 6 July, 1864. Honorably discharged 2 May, 1868.
O'HARA, MICHAEL.
    Assistant Surgeon, 31 May, 1854. Resigned 30 June, 1858.
OHMSEN, AUGUST.
    Boatswain, 24 June, 1897.
OHNESORG, KARL.
    Assistant Surgeon, 27 January, 1900.
O'KANE, JAMES.
    Acting Midshipman, 30 September, 1856. Midshipman, 15 June, 1860. Master, 19 September, 1861. Lieutenant, 16 July, 1862. Lieutenant-Commander, 22 April, 1866. Commander, 6 January, 1874. Captain, 29 January, 1887. Retired List, 30 September, 1896. Died 5 January, 1897.
O'KEEFE, DANIEL J.
    Acting Third Assistant Engineer, 18 April, 1864. Honorably discharged 15 May, 1865.
O'KEEFE, JOHN F.
    Acting Third Assistant Engineer, 10 June, 1864. Honorably discharged 19 August, 1865.
O'KELL, PETER.
    Acting Ensign, 5 October, 1862. Acting Master, 5 June, 1863. Acting Volunteer Lieutenant, 8 November, 1864. Honorably discharged 24 November, 1865.
OLCOTT, E. R.
    Acting Ensign, special duty, 6 December, 1863. Appointment revoked 1 September, 1864.
OLCOTT, EUGENE S.
    Assistant Surgeon, 24 January, 1862. Resigned 6 January, 1864.
OLCOTT, FREDERIC W.
    Assistant Surgeon, 21 January, 1887. Passed Assistant Surgeon, 21 January, 1890. Surgeon, 15 January, 1900. Discharged 14 December, 1900.

OLCOTT, HENRY.
Midshipman, 5 November, 1809. Resigned 29 April, 1812.
O'LEARY, ARTHUR.
Acting Ensign, 5 June, 1863. Honorably discharged 9 December, 1868.
O'LEARY, CHARLES R.
Assistant Paymaster (Spanish-American War), 9 July, 1898. Honorably discharged 4 March, 1899. Assistant Paymaster (Regular Navy), 18 September, 1899.
O'LEARY, CORNELIUS.
Pharmacist, 15 September, 1898.
O'LEARY, TIMOTHY S.
Cadet Midshipman, 29 September, 1879. Honorably discharged 30 June, 1885. Assistant Paymaster, 26 July, 1897. Passed Assistant Paymaster, 10 July, 1898.
OLER, HENRY D.
Mate, 12 May, 1866. Resigned 15 May, 1867.
OLIPHANT, JOSEPH B.
Purser, 1 June, 1861. Died 1 September, 1862.
OLIVER, CHARLES B.
Master's Mate, 3 May, 1843. Gunner, 2 June, 1846. Dismissed 21 April, 1861.
OLIVER, EDWIN W.
Midshipman, 9 November, 1841. Resigned 1 June, 1842.
OLIVER, FRANCIS A.
Acting Ensign, 15 July, 1863. Acting Master, 3 February, 1864. Appointment revoked 31 May, 1864.
OLIVER, FRANCIS A.
Boatswain, 28 May, 1850. Dismissed 3 November, 1856.
OLIVER, HENRY H.
Acting Third Assistant Engineer, 20 January, 1864. Honorably discharged 29 August, 1866.
OLIVER, JAMES.
Acting Ensign, 9 September, 1864. Honorably discharged 25 August, 1865. Mate, 5 September, 1866. Mustered out 1 May, 1869.
OLIVER, JAMES H.
Cadet Midshipman, 12 June, 1879. Graduated 18 June, 1879. Ensign, 1 October, 1881. Lieutenant, Junior Grade, 28 September, 1888. Lieutenant, 4 July, 1893.
OLIVER, MARSHAL.
Professor, 20 May, 1881.
OLIVER, PAUL A.
Master, 25 April, 1814. Resigned 9 March, 1815.
OLMSTEAD, EDMUND F.
Master's Mate, 3 May, 1843. Second Master, 2 March, 1849. Master, 1 September, 1851. Reserved List, 10 October, 1855. Died 7 February, 1857.
OLMSTEAD, EDWARD.
Midshipman, 17 December, 1810. Last appearance on Records of Navy Department, 1815. New York.
OLMSTEAD, GEORGE A.
Mate, 20 November, 1862. Honorably discharged 24 August, 1867.
OLMSTEAD, L. L.
Third Assistant Engineer, 4 April, 1861. Resigned 22 September, 1862.
OLMSTED, PERCY N.
Naval Cadet, 21 May, 1888. Resigned 14 May, 1889. Naval Cadet, 21 May, 1889. Ensign, 1 July, 1895. Lieutenant, Junior Grade, 3 March, 1899.
OLSEN, CHRISTIAN.
Carpenter, 7 March, 1853. Died 12 June, 1855.
OLSEN, HJALMER E.
Mate, 20 August, 1897. Boatswain, 6 March, 1889.
OLSON, EDMUND.
Second Assistant Engineer, 12 July, 1861. First Assistant Engineer, 15 October, 1863. Chief Engineer, 27 October, 1874. Lost on the Huron, 24 November, 1877.
OLSSON, ANDREW.
Gunner, 16 September, 1898.
O'MALLEY, WILLIAM A.
Cadet Midshipman, 25 September, 1880. Graduated. Honorably discharged 30 June, 1886. Ensign (Spanish-American War), 14 May,1898. Honorably discharged 31 January, 1899.
OMAN, JOSEPH W.
Naval Cadet, 17 June, 1882. Ensign, 1 July, 1888. Lieutenant, Junior Grade, 11 October, 1896. Lieutenant, 3 March, 1899.
OMENSETTER, GEORGE W.
Gunner, 27 November, 1861. Resigned 27 March, 1883.
OMENSETTER, ROBERT L.
Mate, 12 July, 1862. Acting Ensign, 15 June, 1864. Honorably discharged 30 November, 1865.
OMEY, WILLIAM H.
Mate, 18 January,1864. Honorably discharged 18 January, 1868.
O'NEAL, ROBERT H.
Boatswain, 13 June, 1831. Died 4 August, 1847.
O'NEALE, JOHN.
Midshipman, 29 July, 1806. Resigned 16 July, 1807.
O'NEALE, RICHARD.
Midshipman, 1 January, 1812. Resigned 9 August, 1817.
O'NEALE, ROBERT H.
Boatswain, 13 June, 1831. Died 4 August, 1847.

GENERAL NAVY REGISTER. 415

O'NEIL, A. F.
Acting Ensign, 1 October, 1862. Acting Master, 16 February, 1863. Acting Volunteer Lieutenant, 24 October, 1863. Dismissed 30 June, 1864.

O'NEIL, CHARLES.
Mate. Acting Master, 1 May, 1862. Acting Volunteer Lieutenant, 30 May, 1865. Lieutenant, 12 March, 1868. Lieutenant-Commander, 18 December, 1868. Commander, 28 July, 1884. Captain, 21 July, 1897. Chief of Bureau of Ordnance, with rank of Rear Admiral, 1 June, 1897.

O'NEIL, JAMES.
Acting Third Assistant Engineer, 22 April, 1863. Acting Second Assistant Engineer, 30 April, 1864. Honorably discharged 26 February, 1868.

O'NEIL, JOHN. H
Acting Third Assistant Engineer, 21 October, 1862. Honorably discharged 2 December, 1866.

O'NEIL, RICHARD F.
Passed Assistant Surgeon (Spanish-American War), 21 May, 1898. Honorably discharged 24 September, 1898.

O'NEILL, CHARLES F.
Mate, 26 May, 1863. Honorably discharged 13 June, 1867.

O'NEILL, CHARLES W.
Acting Third Assistant Engineer, 16 April, 1863. Acting Second Assistant Engineer, 15 December, 1864. Honorably discharged 14 October, 1868.

O'NEILL, H. B.
Acting Ensign, 7 August, 1863. Resigned 2 March, 1865.

O'NEILL, JOHN.
Warrant Machinest, 6 July, 1899.

O'NEILL, WILLIAM J.
Acting Third Assistant Engineer, 11 October, 1864. Honorably discharged 18 September, 1865.

OPIE, LEROY.
Midshipman, 21 May, 1800. Discharged 5 May, 1801, under Peace Establishment Act.

OPP, HENRY K.
Acting Assistant Paymaster, 5 February, 1864. Honorably discharged 9 October, 1865.

ORCHARD, JOHN M.
Cadet Midshipman, 11 June, 1873. Graduated 18 June, 1879. Ensign, 11 July, 1880. Lieutenant, Junior Grade, 26 January, 1887. Lieutenant, 1 July, 1892. Lieutenant-Commander, 18 February, 1900.

ORCUTT, AUGUSTUS C.
Mate, 19 May, 1864. Resigned 24 May, 1865.

ORCUTT, JOHN A.
Mate, 7 December, 1863. Honorably discharged 2 May, 1866.

ORCUTT, WILLIAM K.
Mate, 5 August, 1863. Resigned (sick) 18 March, 1864.

ORD, JAMES.
Midshipman, 9 June, 1811. Resigned 13 April, 1813.

ORDWAY, WILLIAM A.
Mate, 9 October, 1862. Acting Ensign, 23 December, 1863. Honorably discharged 20 June, 1866.

ORGAN, DAVID.
Acting Ensign, 9 November, 1862. Acting Master, 22 December, 1864. Honorably discharged 1 November, 1865. Acting Master, 12 September, 1866. Died 18 August, 1868.

ORLOPP, MAX A.
Cadet Midshipman, 24 June, 1876. Dropped 13 June, 1881. Lieutenant, Junior Grade, (Spanish-American War), 22 June, 1898. Honorably discharged 3 September, 1898.

ORME, J. GEORGE.
Acting Assistant Paymaster, 11 May, 1864. Mustered out 21 November, 1865.

ORMOND, JOHN O.
Mate. Resigned 19 February, 1862. Acting Master, 30 April, 1862. Dismissed 1 April, 1863.

ORMSBY, GEORGE F.
Cadet Midshipman, 24 September, 1873. Graduated 4 June, 1880. Ensign, 2 July, 1882. Dismissed 15 June, 1889.

ORMSBY, ROBERT.
Purser, 25 April, 1812. Last appearance on Records of Navy Department, 1816. Furloughed.

ORNE, JOSHUA.
Midshipman, 16 January, 1809. Resigned 29 October, 1810.

O'ROURKE, WILLIAM P.
Ensign (Spanish-American War), 21 May, 1898. Honorably discharged 10 October, 1898.

ORR, HECTOR.
Surgeon, 2 March, 1799. Discharged 10 June, 1801, under Peace Establishment Act.

ORR, ROBERT H.
Cadet Engineer, 1 October, 1880. Honorably discharged 30 June, 1886. Assistant Paymaster, 20 May, 1898. Passed Assistant Paymaster, 5 May, 1899.

ORR, WILLIAM L.
Acting Second Assistant Engineer, 21 March, 1865. Resigned 18 December, 1865.

ORSWELL, GEORGE B.
Acting First Assistant Engineer, 21 February, 1862. Honorably discharged 26 December, 1865. Acting First Assistant Engineer, 7 April, 1866. Mustered out 27 August, 1867.

ORTEGA, JOHN.
Mate, 30 August, 1864. Deserted June, 1865.
ORVIS, RALPH T.
Assistant Surgeon, 27 May, 1898.
OSBORN, ARTHUR P.
Midshipman, 25 July, 1865. Graduated June, 1869. Ensign, 12 July, 1870. Master, 12 July, 1871. Lieutenant, 22 October, 1874. Lieutenant-Commander, 11 October, 1896. Retired List, 8 December, 1898.
OSBORN, FRANCIS G.
Acting Ensign, 20 August, 1863. Acting Master, 6 December, 1864. Honorably discharged 16 July, 1866.
OSBORN, JAMES.
Acting Second Assistant Engineer, 10 September, 1861. Resigned 14 February, 1863.
OSBORN, MARCUS B.
Acting Assistant Paymaster, 11 October, 1861. Resigned 16 September, 1863.
OSBORN, RALPH.
Lieutenant, Junior Grade (Spanish-American War), 4 May, 1898. Honorably discharged 2 September, 1898.
OSBORN, ROBERT H.
Naval Cadet, 23 May, 1890. Ensign, 1 July, 1896. Lieutenant, Junior Grade, 1 July, 1899.
OSBORN, VICTOR M.
Acting Third Assistant Engineer, 27 March, 1865. Resigned 20 November, 1867.
OSBORN, WILLIAM A.
Mate, 14 May, 1863. Resigned 17 May, 1865
OSBORNE, CHARLES A.
Mate, 12 June, 1863. Honorably discharged 26 August, 1865.
OSBORNE, LEONARD.
Asistant Surgeon, 24 July, 1813. Surgeon, 27 March, 1818. Died 5 October, 1837.
OSGOOD, GEORGE C.
Acting Assistant Surgeon, 26 February, 1863. Honorably discharged 19 January, 1866.
OSGOOD, JOSEPH.
Master, 3 July, 1813. Died 8 August, 1813.
O'SHANNESSY, JAMES.
Midshipman, 9 July, 1833. Resigned 27 February, 1839.
OSTERHAUS, HUGO.
Midshipman, 25 September, 1865. Graduated 7 June, 1870. Ensign, 13 July, 1871. Master, 12 February, 1874. Lieutenant, 13 March, 1880. Lieutenant-Commander, 3 March, 1899.
OSTERHAUS, HUGO W.
Naval Cadet, 20 May, 1896. Graduated 30 June, 1900.
OSTERHOULT, DAVIS D.
Acting Third Assistant Engineer, 24 August, 1864. Honorably discharged 5 October, 1865.
OSTERLOH, JOHN C.
Acting Assistant Paymaster, 22 January, 1864. Honorably discharged 6 October, 1865.
OSTERMEYER, WILLIAM.
Acting Carpenter, 28 June, 1864. Honorably discharged 21 September, 1865.
OSTRANDER, ARTHUR D.
Passed Assistant Engineer (Spanish-American War), 23 July, 1898. Honorably discharged 22 December, 1898.
OSTRANGER, A. H.
Acting Ensign, 4 January, 1864. Honorably discharged 1 August, 1865.
O'SULLIVAN, W. R.
Midshipman, 1 November, 1828. Dismissed 10 December, 1830.
OTIS, ARTHUR H.
Midshipman, 9 September, 1841. Resigned 10 August, 1849.
OTIS, JAMES F.
Acting Ensign, 29 October, 1862. Acting Master, 30 January, 1865. Honorably discharged 19 August, 1865.
OTIS, JENKS H.
Assistant Surgeon, 19 April, 1851. Passed Assistant Surgeon, 10 April, 1856. Surgeon, 2 June, 1861. Died 27 August, 1864.
OTIS, WILLIAM H.
Mate, 11 September, 1862. Acting Ensign, 30 September, 1863. Honorably discharged 11 August, 1865.
OTLEY, WILLIAM.
Acting Second Assistant Engineer, 9 February, 1864. Honorably discharged 22 August, 1865.
OTTER, WILLIAM.
Acting Carpenter, 6 July, 1864. Honorably discharged 19 February, 1866.
OTTIGNON, CHARLES F.
Acting Master, special duty as Drill Officer, 31 October, 1863. Appointment revoked 27 October, 1864.
OTTIWELL, WILLIAM.
Acting Master, 10 June, 1861. Appointment revoked (sick) 14 April, 1863. Acting Ensign, 1 October, 1863. Honorably discharged 3 December, 1865.
OURSLER, JOHN T.
Pharmacist, 15 September, 1898.

GENERAL NAVY REGISTER. 417

OVATT, JAMES.
    Mate, 1 October, 1862. Promoted Acting Ensign, 9 October, 1863. Honorably discharged 24 June, 1866.
OVERMAN, JOHN.
    Carpenter, 22 October, 1841. Died 19 March, 1845.
OVERN, JOHN.
    Acting Third Assistant Engineer, 1 August, 1862. Resigned 24 March, 1863.
OVERN, JOHN J.
    Carpenter, 2 May, 1866. Died 10 June, 1867.
OVERSTREET, LUTHER M.
    Naval Cadet, 6 September, 1893. Ensign, 1 July, 1899.
OVERTON, DANIEL B.
    Acting First Assistant Engineer, 31 August, 1864. Honorably discharged 22 September, 1865.
OVERTON, P. H.
    Midshipman, 30 November, 1814. Resigned 18 November, 1821.
OWEN, ALFRED C.
    Naval Cadet, 6 September, 1893. Ensign, 1 July, 1899.
OWEN, ALFRED M.
    Assistant Surgeon, 20 May, 1869. Passed Assistant Surgeon, 18 March, 1874. Surgeon, 2 January, 1881. Died 22 August, 1883.
OWEN, CHARLES W.
    Acting Ensign, 3 August, 1864. Honorably discharged 11 August, 1865.
OWEN, ELIAS K.
    Midshipman, 7 December, 1848. Passed Midshipman, 15 June, 1854. Master, 15 September, 1855. Lieutenant, 16 September, 1855. Lieutenant-Commander, 16 July, 1862. Commander, 25 July, 1866. Retired List, 9 June, 1876. Died 8 April, 1877.
OWEN, LEANDER C.
    Acting Ensign, 13 September, 1864. Honorably discharged 25 July, 1865.
OWEN, O. DARWIN.
    Acting Ensign, 16 February, 1865. Honorably discharged 17 September, 1867.
OWEN, SILAS.
    Mate, 9 September, 1862. Dismissed 21 May, 1863. Acting Ensign, 25 November, 1863. Acting Master, 25 July, 1865. Honorably discharged 4 November, 1865.
OWEN, WILLIAM H.
    Acting Assistant Paymaster, 30 September, 1862. Resigned 8 October, 1863.
OWEN, WILLIAM R.
    Mate, 18 April, 1863. Acting Ensign, 11 June, 1863. Resigned 13 March, 1865.
OWENS, A. A.
    Acting Master, 13 May, 1862. Honorably discharged 13 August, 1865.
OWENS, CHARLES T.
    Naval Cadet, 6 September, 1893. Ensign, 1 July, 1899.
OWENS, FORREST B.
    Acting Ensign and Pilot, 12 December, 1863. Acting Master and Pilot, 1 October, 1864. Honorably discharged 29 November, 1865.
OWENS, JAMES H.
    Carpenter, 4 November, 1852. Died 10 October, 1873.
OWENS, JOHN.
    Acting Ensign, 3 August, 1864. Honorably discharged 13 July, 1865.
OWENS, THOMAS.
    Acting Assistant Surgeon, 16 August, 1864. Honorably discharged 28 December, 1869. Acting Assistant Surgeon, 8 February, 1870. Honorably discharged 30 June, 1879. Assistant Surgeon, not in line of promotion, 3 April, 1882. Surgeon, not in line of promotion, 1 October, 1890. Retired List, 10 March, 1896. Died 8 March, 1897.
OWINGS, JOHN C.
    Master, 15 September, 1806. Resigned 22 February, 1810.
OWINGS, SAMUEL J.
    Acting Ensign, 3 September, 1863. Died at St. Louis, Mo., October, 1863.
OWINS, JOHN.
    Gunner, 7 March, 1842. Dropped 20 April, 1861.
PACE, DAVID.
    Acting Third Assistant Engineer, 13 August, 1863. Acting Second Assistant Engineer, 20 March, 1865. Appointment revoked 29 December, 1866.
PACKARD, HARRISON D.
    Mate, 21 January, 1864. Acting Ensign, 1 December, 1864. Honorably discharged 16 May, 1865.
PACKARD, HENRY.
    Acting Assistant Paymaster, 25 September, 1861. Died 29 January, 1862.
PACKARD, R. G.
    Civil Enginer, 28 November, 1866. Commissioned 28 March, 1867. Resigned 28 April, 1869.
PACKER, CHARLES H.
    Mate, 1 November, 1861. Acting Ensign, 1 February, 1864. Dismissed 10 August, 1864.
PACKETT, JOHN.
    Midshipman, 16 January, 1809. Lieutenant, 24 July, 1813. Died 29 March, 1820.
PADDOCK, SAMUEL B.
    Acting Midshipman, 26 September, 1856. Midshipman, 15 June, 1860. Acting Master, 26 June, 1861. Appointment revoked 24 July, 1861.
PAGE, BENJAMIN.
    Midshipman, 26 March, 1800. Resigned 7 July, 1803.

27

PAGE, BENJAMIN.
　Midshipman, 17 December, 1810. Lieutenant, 27 April, 1816. Commander, 22 December, 1835. Captain, 8 September, 1841. Reserved List, 13 September, 1855. Died 16 April, 1858.
PAGE, BENJAMIN.
　Acting Assistant Paymaster, 12 June, 1862. Resigned 30 December, 1865.
PAGE, BENJAMIN.
　Mate. Appointment revoked (sick) 19 May, 1862.
PAGE, CHARLES H.
　Acting Assistant Surgeon, 2 February, 1863. Surgeon, 22 September, 1863. Died 24 December, 1867.
PAGE, DAVID P.
　Acting Ensign, 2 December, 1863. Acting Master, 22 November, 1864. Honorably discharged 28 October, 1865.
PAGE, HENRY.
　Midshipman, 5 February, 1800. Resigned 7 June, 1803.
PAGE, HENRY M.
　Mate, 11 January, 1865. Resigned 30 June, 1865.
PAGE, HENRY T.
　Mate, 23 November, 1863. Acting Ensign, 4 September, 1864. Honorably discharged 3 June, 1865.
PAGE, HUGH N.
　Midshipman, 1 September, 1811. Lieutenant, 1 April, 1818. Commander, 28 February, 1838. Captain, 29 May, 1850. Reserved List, 13 September, 1855. Resigned 19 April, 1861.
PAGE, JAMES.
　Surgeon, 23 April, 1827. Died 15 March, 1832.
PAGE, JAMES.
　Assistant Surgeon, 7 September, 1807. Surgeon, 5 March, 1811. Resigned 14 June, 1824.
PAGE, JEREMIAH J.
　Acting Assistant Surgeon, 14 February, 1874. Assistant Surgeon, Retired List, 30 June, 1879.
PAGE, JOHN E.
　Assistant Surgeon, 18 June, 1890. Passed Assistant Surgeon, 18 June, 1894.
PAGE, JOHN W.
　Mate, 19 November, 1861. Resigned 29 October, 1862.
PAGE, LEWIS B.
　Midshipman, 9 March, 1809. Dismissed 8 March, 1813. Master, 6 April, 1813. Died 16 September, 1826.
PAGE, OCTAVIUS A.
　Midshipman, 6 June, 1800. Lieutenant, 9 February, 1807. Died in June, 1813.
PAGE, RICHARD L.
　Midshipman, 1 March, 1824. Passed Midshipman, 20 February, 1830. Lieutenant, 26 March, 1834. Commander, 14 September, 1855. Dismissed 18 April, 1861.
PAGE, ROBERT N.
　Midshipman, 2 May, 1800. Discharged 24 September, 1801, under Peace Establishment Act.
PAGE, THOMAS J.
　Midshipman, 1 October, 1827. Passed Midshipman, 10 June, 1833. Lieutenant, 20 December, 1839. Commander, 14 September, 1855. Dismissed 22 April, 1861.
PAGE, WILLIAM.
　Midshipman, 1 January, 1817. Resigned 3 January, 1820.
PAGE, WILLIAM M.
　Assistant Surgeon, 31 October, 1855. Passed Assistant Surgeon, 4 May, 1860. Surgeon, 1 August, 1861. Dismissed 10 October, 1861.
PAGET, JOHN H.
　Acting Third Assistant Engineer, 9 May, 1861. Acting Second Assistant Engineer, 28 May, 1863. Acting First Assistant Engineer, 8 March, 1864. Honorably discharged 28 March, 1867.
PAIGE, JOHN.
　Acting Master's Mate, 28 January, 1863. Taken prisoner, 18 August, 1863.
PAINE, AMASA.
　Midshipman, 1 May, 1822. Passed Midshipman, 24 May, 1828. Lieutenant, 3 March, 1831. Commander, 12 April, 1853. Reserved List, 13 September, 1855. Captain on Reserved List, 9 June, 1862. Died 27 July, 1863.
PAINE, A O.
　Acting Ensign, 5 January, 1863. Dismissed 27 May, 1863.
PAINE, FRANCIS M.
　Acting Ensign, 25 August, 1862. Acting Master, 9 November, 1864. Honorably discharged 13 September, 1867.
PAINE, FREDERICK H.
　Midshipman, 27 July, 1863. Graduated June, 1867. Ensign, 18 December, 1868. Master, 21 March, 1870. Lieutenant, 20 June, 1871. Resigned 1 August, 1884.
PAINE, JAMES G.
　Mate, 5 October, 1861. Appointment revoked 22 March, 1864. Mate, 22 September, 1864. Honorably discharged 20 February, 1866.
PAINE, JOHN S.
　Midshipman, 29 November, 1813. Lieutenant, 13 January, 1825. Commander, 8 September, 1841. Reserved List, 13 September, 1855. Died 2 May, 1859.
PAINE, ORRIS S.
　Midshipman, 2 July, 1814. Resigned 27 February, 1815.
PAINE, SAMUEL T.
　Mate, 16 July, 1864. Died on Kearsarge, 28 March, 1866.

GENERAL NAVY REGISTER.   419

PAINE, SUMNER C.
　Midshipman, 21 September, 1865. Graduated June, 1869. Ensign, 12 July, 1870. Master, 12 July, 1871. Lieutenant, 7 October, 1874. Lieutenant-Commander, 1 October, 1896. Retired List, 14 November, 1898. Died 21 December, 1898.
PAINE, THEODORE H.
　Acting Ensign, 17 April, 1863. Acting Master, 22 April, 1865. Honorably discharged 10 November, 1865.
PAINE, THOMAS.
　Master, 10 October, 1812. Lieutenant, 1 December, 1815. Commander, 3 March, 1835. Captain, 8 September, 1841. Reserved List, 13 September, 1855. Died 9 November, 1859.
PAINTER, FRANCIS J.
　Acting Assistant Paymaster, 17 February, 1863. Passed Assistant Paymaster, 23 July, 1866. Retired List, 13 May, 1869.
PAINTER, GEORGE.
　Carpenter, 9 April, 1804. Last appearance on Records of Navy Department, 1 September, 1809.
PAINTER, JOSEPH E.
　Acting Assistant Surgeon, 5 August, 1870. Died 15 March, 1878.
PALFREY, ROBERT B.
　Mate, 5 April, 1864. Appointment revoked 13 May, 1864.
PALLETT, ROBERT.
　Acting Third Assistant Engineer, 26 April, 1862. Acting Second Assistant Engineer, 3 March, 1863. Honorably discharged 4 September, 1865.
PALMER, ALBERT S.
　Second Assistant Engineer, 14 January, 1839. Previous appointment revoked, and appointed Second Assistant Engineer, 28 July, 1845. Resigned 15 July, 1848.
PALMER, ARCHY S.
　Acting Ensign, 15 July, 1863. Honorably discharged 8 December, 1865.
PALMER, CHARLES F.
　Mate, 25 January, 1862. Acting Ensign, 30 August, 1864. Honorably discharged 18 January, 1866.
PALMER, EUGENE P.
　Mate, 9 June, 1862. Resigned 21 October, 1862. Mate, 7 July, 1863. Acting Gunner, 9 April, 1864. Honorably discharged 31 December, 1866.
PALMER, GEORGE L.
　Acting Third Assistant Engineer, 21 January, 1862. Appointment revoked 17 March, 1862. Acting Second Assistant Engineer, 8 December, 1862. Drowned 15 January, 1865.
PALMER, GEORGE W.
　Assistant Surgeon, 18 August, 1826. Passed Assistant Surgeon, 3 March, 1835. Died 6 November, 1836.
PALMER, GEORGE W.
　Acting Master, 23 August, 1861. Dismissed 14 December, 1861.
PALMER, JAMES C.
　Assistant Surgeon, 26 March, 1834. Surgeon, 27 October, 1841. Medical Director, 3 March, 1871. Retired List, 29 June, 1873. Died 24 April, 1883.
PALMER, JAMES E.
　Cadet Engineer, 1 October, 1879. Honorably discharged 30 June, 1885. Passed Assistant Engineer, 4 April, 1898. Rank changed to Lieutenant, 3 March, 1899.
PALMER, JAMES S.
　Midshipman, 1 January, 1825. Passed Midshipman, 4 June, 1831. Lieutenant, 17 December, 1836. Reserved List, 13 September, 1855. Commander, Active List, 14 September, 1855. Captain, on Active List, 16 July, 1862. Commodore, 7 February, 1863. Rear-Admiral, 25 July, 1866. Died 7 December, 1867.
PALMER, JOHN H.
　Mate, 15 November, 1861. Resigned 21 March, 1862.
PALMER, JOHN W.
　Midshipman, 30 November, 1814. Resigned 15 April, 1828.
PALMER, JOHN W.
　Master's Mate, 1 July, 1840. Died 23 July, 1851.
PALMER, LAMBERT G.
　Midshipman, 20 July, 1863. Graduated June, 1868. Ensign, 19 April, 1869. Master, 12 July, 1870. Lieutenant, 10 November, 1872. Lost on the Huron, 24 November, 1877.
PALMER, LEIGH C.
　Naval Cadet, 6 September, 1892. Ensign, 6 May, 1898.
PALMER, MARSHALL E.
　Midshipman, 23 March, 1848. Resigned 13 May, 1853.
PALMER, ROBERT.
　Lieutenant, 6 March, 1799. Discharged 8 December, 1801, under Peace Establishment Act.
PALMER, ROBERT.
　Master, 7 May, 1812. Dismissed 2 April, 1814.
PALMER, SAMUEL B.
　Assistant Surgeon, 6 June, 1896. Resigned 15 May, 1899.
PALMER, WILLIAM H.
　Acting Assistant Paymaster, 25 October, 1864. Honorably discharged 15 October, 1865.
PANCAKE, WILLIAM D.
　Acting Third Assistant Engineer, 20 October, 1863. Honorably discharged 2 October, 1865.
PANCOAST, ALLEN A.
　Acting Assistant Paymaster, 5 August, 1861. Resigned 30 January, 1864.

PANCOAST, JOHN A.
   Acting Third Assistant Engineer, 17 February, 1864. Honorably discharged 30 August, 1865.
PANGBORN, HENRY H.
   Paymaster, 1 June, 1861. Died 31 July, 1866.
PAPANTI, FRANK L.
   Mate, 14 October, 1863. Honorably discharged 10 July, 1865.
PARDEE, JOSEPH W.
   Mate, 4 April, 1864. Appointment revoked 10 October, 1864. Mate, 4 February, 1865. Honorably discharged 15 August, 1865.
PARDEE, S. S.
   Mate, 20 December, 1861. Dismissed 1 May, 1862.
PARDINGTON, ARTHUR H.
   Assistant Paymaster (Spanish-American War), 15 May, 1898. Honorably discharged 17 September, 1898.
PARIS, RUSSEL C.
   Cadet Midshipman, 23 September, 1873. Graduated 18 June, 1879. Resigned 1 December, 1880.
PARK, CHARLES S.
   Acting Assistant Paymaster, 21 October, 1864. Honorably discharged 2 August, 1865.
PARK, DAVID B.
   Sailmaker, 2 August, 1844. Died 5 August, 1848.
PARK, EDWARD G.
   Acting Third Assistant Engineer, 27 December, 1864. Honorably discharged 30 April, 1868.
PARK, JOHN.
   Surgeon, 14 October, 1799. Discharged 6 July, 1801, under Peace Establishment Act.
PARK, STEPHEN A.
   Mate, 23 January, 1864. Honorably discharged 6 August, 1865.
PARK, THEODORE W.
   Mate, 26 February, 1863. Appointment revoked (sick) 21 October, 1863.
PARK, WILLIAM D.
   Acting Third Assistant Engineer, 22 May, 1862. Died 11 July, 1863.
PARK, WILLIAM DUNLAP.
   Third Assistant Engineer, 4 February, 1862. Dismissed 17 February, 1862. Third Assistant Engineer, 17 December, 1862. Died 11 July, 1863.
PARK, W. W.
   Acting Assistant Surgeon, 1 May, 1863. Died 3 August, 1863.
PARKE, CORNELIUS T.
   Third Assistant Engineer, 26 February, 1851. Resigned 31 May, 1854.
PARKE, JOHN G.
   Acting Assistant Surgeon, 19 February, 1862. Honorably discharged 6 November, 1865.
PARKE, THOMAS A.
   Cadet Midshipman, 21 June, 1876. Graduated 22 June, 1882. Ensign, Junior Grade, 3 March, 1883. Ensign, 26 June, 1884. Retired 30 June, 1885. Died 13 October, 1885.
PARKER, ADAMS.
   Acting Ensign, 4 March, 1863. Dismissed 17 November, 1863.
PARKER, CHARLES.
   Acting Third Assistant Engineer, 29 December, 1864. Honorably discharged 4 March, 1866.
PARKER, CHARLES H.
   Ensign (Spanish-American War), 14 May, 1898. Lieutenant, Junior Grade, 17 June, 1898. Honorably discharged 17 September, 1898.
PARKER, DELOS L.
   Passed Assistant Surgeon (Spanish-American War), 9 May, 1898. Honorably discharged 26 August, 1898.
PARKER, EDWARD G.
   Assistant Surgeon, 10 January, 1899.
PARKER, FELTON.
   Cadet Midshipman, 6 November, 1876. Graduated. Honorably discharged 30 June, 1884. Lieutenant (Spanish-American War), 22 June, 1898. Honorably discharged 17 October, 1898.
PARKER, EDWIN N.
   Mate, 6 May, 1865. Deserted 17 March, 1867.
PARKER, FORBES.
   Acting Assistant Paymaster, 19 October, 1861. Assistant Paymaster, 19 March, 1862. Paymaster, 26 August, 1865. Dropped 2 August, 1871.
PARKER, FOXHALL A.
   Midshipman, 1 January, 1808. Lieutenant, 9 March, 1813. Commander, 3 March, 1825. Captain, 3 March, 1835. Reserved List, 13 September, 1855. Died 23 November, 1857.
PARKER, FOXHALL A.
   Midshipman, 11 March, 1837. Passed Midshipman, 29 June, 1843. Acting Master, 17 November, 1847. Lieutenant, 21 September, 1850. Reserved List, 14 September, 1855. Commander, 16 July, 1862. Captain, 25 July, 1866. Commodore, 25 November, 1872. Died 10 June, 1879.
PARKER, FRANCIS H.
   Acting Midshipman, 20 September, 1861. Graduated September, 1865. Ensign, 1 December, 1866. Retired List, 17 November, 1868. Died 15 May, 1895.
PARKER, FREDERIC.
   Ensign (Spanish-American War), 28 May, 1898. Honorably discharged 31 August, 1898.

PARKER, GEORGE.
Midshipman, 3 February, 1800. Lieutenant, 30 March, 1807. Commander, 24 July, 1813. Died 11 March, 1814.
PARKER, GEORGE.
Midshipman, 6 June, 1815. Last appearance on Records of Navy Department, 1815. New Orleans.
PARKER, GEORGE.
Sailmaker, 3 July, 1841. Died 5 October, 1857.
PARKER, GEORGE A.
Acting Assistant Surgeon, 19 April, 1864. Died 18 June, 1864.
PARKER, GEORGE C.
Master, 15 July, 1812. Last appearance on Records of Navy Department.
PARKER, GEORGE O.
Acting Third Assistant Engineer, 25 March, 1864. Resigned 23 June, 1865.
PARKER, GEORGE S.
Acting Assistant Surgeon, 22 September, 1864. Resigned 9 September, 1865.
PARKER, GEORGE W.
Acting Master, 12 August, 1861. Honorably discharged 24 September, 1865.
PARKER, HIRAM, Jr.
Third Assistant Engineer, 16 November, 1861. Second Assistant Engineer, 25 August, 1863. First Assistant Engineer, 11 October, 1866. Resigned 18 February, 1875.
PARKER, JAMES, Jr.
Midshipman, 14 November, 1846. Passed Midshipman, 8 June, 1852. Master, 15 September, 1855. Lieutenant, 16 September, 1855. Resigned 2 October, 1856. Acting Lieutenant, 8 May, 1861. Lieutenant-Commander, 16 July, 1862. Resigned 31 May, 1866.
PARKER, JAMES L.
Midshipman, 6 June, 1831. Passed Midshipman, 15 June, 1837. Lieutenant, 8 September, 1841. Died 12 July, 1847.
PARKER, JAMES P.
Cadet Midshipman, 5 June, 1873. Graduated 18 June, 1879. Ensign, 10 January, 1881. Lieutenant, Junior Grade, 30 June, 1887. Lieutenant, 25 January, 1893. Lieutenant-Commander, 30 June, 1900.
PARKER, JAMES P.
Lieutenant, Junior Grade (Spanish-American War), 9 May, 1898. Honorably discharged 16 September, 1898.
PARKER, J. B.
Acting Assistant Surgeon, 16 March, 1863. Honorably discharged 12 October, 1865.
PARKER, JOHN.
Assistant Surgeon, 11 May, 1798. Last appearance on Records of Navy Department.
PARKER, JOHN.
Purser, 15 June, 1799. Died 25 June, 1799.
PARKER, JOHN C.
Mate, 4 November, 1864. Deserted 12 June, 1865.
PARKER, JOHN C.
Acting Master, 1 October, 1862. Acting Volunteer Lieutenant, 29 March, 1864. Resigned 31 May, 1865.
PARKER, JOHN F.
Midshipman, 29 September, 1870. Graduated 1 June, 1874. Ensign, 17 July, 1875. Master, 17 May, 1881. Lieutenant, Junior Grade, 3 March, 1883. Lieutenant, 21 April, 1887. Lieutenant-Commander, 3 March, 1899.
PARKER, JOHN H.
Midshipman, 30 December, 1836. Passed Midshipman, 1 July, 1842. Lieutenant, 2 June, 1850. Dismissed 18 January, 1862.
PARKER, JOHN P
Midshipman, 1 April, 1828. Passed Midshipman, 14 June, 1834. Lieutenant, 25 February, 1841. Reserved List, 13 September, 1855. Died 7 June, 1860.
PARKER, JOSEPH B.
Acting Assistant Surgeon, 16 March, 1863. Honorably discharged 12 October, 1865. Assistant Surgeon, 24 November, 1866. Passed Assistant Surgeon, 31 December, 1867. Surgeon, 13 August, 1876. Medical Inspector, 30 November, 1894. Medical Director, 18 June, 1898.
PARKER, LEWIS.
Gunner, 13 February, 1832. Died 31 August, 1845.
PARKER, NATHANIEL C.
Acting Assistant Surgeon, 23 October, 1862. Appointment revoked 3 March, 1863.
PARKER, NEHEMIAH.
Carpenter, 27 January, 1820. Died 20 August, 1839.
PARKER, ROBERT L.
Passed Assistant Surgeon (Spanish-American War), 18 May, 1898. Honorably discharged 2 September, 1898.
PARKER, R. Le ROY.
Mate, 24 February, 1862. Dead.
PARKER, ROBERT W.
Acting Ensign, 26 December, 1862. Honorably discharged 11 December, 1865.
PARKER, SAMUEL.
Lieutenant, 18 April, 1799. Discharged 13 April, 1801, under Peace Establishment Act.
PARKER, SAMUEL F.
Boatswain, date not known. Last appearance on Records of Navy Department.
PARKER, SCOLLAY.
Acting Assistant Surgeon, 9 September, 1863. Acting Passed Assistant Surgeon, 15 May, 1866. Honorably discharged 19 January, 1868.

PARKER, THOMAS D.
Naval Cadet, 3 October, 1889. Honorably discharged 30 June, 1893. Assistant Engineer, 19 April, 1898. Rank changed to Ensign, 3 March, 1899.
PARKER, THOMAS V.
Mate, 28 August, 1863. Acting Ensign, 26 November, 1864. Honorably discharged 4 October, 1865.
PARKER, WALTER R.
Ensign (Spanish-American War), 9 May, 1898. Honorably discharged 26 August, 1898.
PARKER, WILLIAM.
Gunner, 21 January, 1862. Died November, 1864.
PARKER, WILLIAM A.
Midshipman, 3 July, 1832. Passed Midshipman, 23 June, 1838. Lieutenant, 16 May, 1843. Commander, 28 June, 1861. Retired List, 23 December, 1865. Captain on Retired List, 4 April, 1867. Died 24 October, 1882.
PARKER, WILLIAM C.
Mate, 2 June, 1864. Honorably discharged 27 September, 1868.
PARKER, WILLIAM D.
Acting Third Assistant Engineer, 1 February, 1865. Honorably discharged 25 September, 1865.
PARKER, WILLIAM H.
Midshipman, 19 October, 1841. Passed Midshipman, 10 August, 1847. Master, 1 March, 1855. Lieutenant, 14 September, 1855. Dismissed 20 April, 1861.
PARKER, WILLIAM H.
Midshipman, 17 April, 1862. Graduated June, 1866. Ensign, 12 March, 1868. Master, 26 March, 1869. Lieutenant, 21 March, 1870. Lieutenant-Commander, 14 December, 1881. Died 28 May, 1891.
PARKER, WILLIAM S.
Acting Assistant Surgeon, 18 March, 1864. Resigned 8 March, 1865.
PARKES, JOHN W.
Third Assistant Engineer, 10 July, 1847. Second Assistant Engineer, 13 September, 1849. Resigned 21 May, 1853.
PARKHURST, GEORGE A.
Gunner, 3 January, 1862. Dismissed 2 March, 1863.
PARKINSON, WILLIAM L.
Midshipman, 29 September, 1832. Dismissed 15 June, 1838.
PARKS, CHARLES H.
Chaplain, 25 April, 1888. Resigned 25 January, 1900.
PARKS, CHARLES P.
Acting Second Assistant Engineer, 26 January, 1863. Died from wounds 26 April, 1864.
PARKS, CHARLES W.
Civil Engineer, 19 July, 1897.
PARKS, EDWARD W.
Acting Third Assistant Engineer, 11 January, 1864. Resigned 20 October, 1864.
PARKS, F. P.
Acting Master's Mate, 8 June, 1859. Discharged 7 November, 1860. Reappointed, 13 June, 1861. Discharged 30 May, 1863.
PARKS, GEORGE H.
Acting Third Assistant Engineer, 6 July, 1863. Killed by explosion on Tulip, 11 November, 1864.
PARKS, RUFUS.
Captain's Clerk, U. S. S. Vandalia, November, 1860, to 1 June, 1861. Acting Paymaster, 1 June, 1861. Assistant Paymaster, 12 September, 1861. Paymaster, 14 April, 1862. Pay Inspector, 23 February, 1877. Pay Director, 10 August, 1886. Retired List, 9 April, 1899, with rank of Rear Admiral.
PARKS, WILLIAM.
Mate, 9 March, 1866. Resigned 5 April, 1867.
PARKS, WILLIAM.
Mate, 7 February, 1865. Resigned 5 April, 1867.
PARKS, WYTHE M.
Assistant Engineer, 8 May, 1877. Passed Assistant Engineer, 22 June, 1884. Chief Engineer, 27 June, 1896. Rank changed to Lieutenant-Commander, 3 March, 1899.
PARMELEE, ARTHUR W.
Mate, 22 January, 1863. Appointment revoked, having been appointed Captain's Clerk, 14 February, 1863.
PARMENTER, HENRY E.
Cadet Engineer, 1 October, 1880. Ensign, 1 July, 1886. Lieutenant, Junior Grade, 12 October, 1895. Lieutenant, 10 August, 1898.
PARNELL, EDWARD.
Midshipman, 20 June, 1806. Resigned 29 December, 1806.
PARRIS, ELIAS.
Acting Third Assistant Engineer, 11 December, 1862. Resigned 26 June, 1863.
PARRISH, HORATIO N.
Acting Master, 23 September, 1861. Resigned 6 December, 1861.
PARRISH, HUGH F.
Assistant Surgeon, 23 June, 1896. Resggned 1 January, 1897.
PARRISH, JOSEPH.
Midshipman, 19 October, 1841. Dismissed 27 June, 1850.
PARROTT, ENOCH G.
Midshipman, 10 December, 1831. Pased Midshipman, 15 June, 1837. Lieutenant, 8 September, 1841. Commander, 24 April, 1861. Captain, 25 July, 1866. Commodore, 22 April, 1870. Rear-Admiral, 8 November, 1873. Retired List, 4 April, 1874. Died 10 May, 1879.
PARRY, CYRUS.
Midshipman, 18 May, 1809. Dismissed 7 May, 1813.

PARRY, JOHN.
Acting Ensign, 2 July, 1863. Honorably discharged 19 October, 1865.
PARRY, JOSEPH L.
Acting First Assistant Enginer, 3 October, 1862. Resigned 15 July, 1864.
PARSEM, JOHN.
Carpenter, 12 July, 1800. Last appearance on Records of Navy Department.
PARSONS, ALONO D.
Acting Third Assistant Engineer, 27 December, 1864. Honorably discharged 12 February, 1869.
PARSONS, ARTHUR C.
Cadet Midshipman, 24 June, 1876. Graduated. Honorably discharged 30 June, 1883. Lieutenant (Spanish-American War), 17 June, 1898. Honorably discharged 30 January, 1899.
PARSONS, ARTHUR F.
Mate, 2 January, 1862. Acting Ensign, 30 July, 1863. Honorably discharged 24 October, 1865.
PARSONS, ARTHUR H.
Midshipman, 27 July, 1864. Graduated June, 1868. Ensign, 19 April, 1869. Master, 12 July, 1870. Resigned 7 December, 1871.
PARSONS, E. D. W.
Mate, 19 November, 1862. Resigned 20 January, 1865.
PARSONS, HENRY.
Mate, 13 December, 1861. Died 18 June, 1863.
PARSONS, ISAAC B.
Cadet Engineer, 13 September, 1877. Graduated 10 June, 1883. Honorably discharged 30 June, 1883. Restored to service, 10 March, 1886, as an Assistant Engineer, to rank from 1 July, 1883. Resigned 24 November, 1887.
PARSONS, JAMES L.
Acting Third Assistant Engineer, 27 July, 1863. Acting Second Assistant Engineer, 20 February, 1864. Honorably discharged 8 November, 1865.
PARSONS, JOHN E.
Acting Assistant Surgeon, 10 October, 1863. Acting Passed Assistant Surgeon, 24 March, 1866. Resigned 8 December, 1866.
PARSONS, RICHARD.
Gunner, 10 June, 1799. Resigned 20 August, 1801.
PARSONS, SCOTT B.
Mate, 5 June, 1862. Resigned 17 December, 1862.
PARSONS, THOMAS A.
Assistant Surgeon, 4 November, 1834. Resigned 20 September, 1837.
PARSONS, USHER.
Assistant Surgeon, 6 July, 1812. Surgeon, 15 April, 1814. Resigned 23 April, 1823.
PARSONS, WILLIAM.
Assistant Surgeon, 15 May, 1799. Resigned 24 July, 1800.
PARTRIDGE, EDWIN W.
Mate, 12 October, 1861. Acting Ensign, 19 July, 1862. Appointment revoked 17 November, 1862.
PARTRIDGE, FREDERICK W.
Acting Master, 28 February, 1862. Resigned 19 March, 1862. Acting Master, 27 March, 1862. Honorably discharged 30 October, 1865.
PARTRIDGE, JOHN A.
Acting Ensign, 30 November, 1864. Honorably discharged 12 October, 1865.
PARTRIDGE, LEANDER H.
Acting Master, 18 December, 1861. Acting Volunteer Lieutenant, 8 April, 1865. Honorably discharged 20 November, 1865.
PARY, C. B.
Acting Ensign and Pilot, 18 July, 1864. Appointment revoked 12 December, 1864.
PARYS, EDMUND.
Mate, 8 May, 1862. Resigned 2 July, 1863. Mate, 3 October, 1863. Acting Ensign, 22 November, 1864. Appointment revoked 18 November, 1867. Mate, 5 November, 1869. Resigned 23 February, 1870.
PASQUELL, RICHARD.
Acting Master, 30 December, 1861. Dismissed 29 May, 1863.
PASSOW, FREDERICK M.
Commander (Spanish-American War), 15 June, 1898. Honorably discharged 2 September, 1898.
PASTUER, EDWARD W.
Midshipman, 22 January, 1841. Resigned 2 May, 1848.
PATCH, NATHANIEL J. K.
Midshipman, 20 September, 1865. Graduated June, 1869. Ensign, 12 July, 1870. Master, 27 October, 1872. Lieutenant, 9 March, 1876. Lieutenant-Commander, 26 September, 1897.
PATCHKE, GUSTAVUS A.
Mate, 27 August, 1863. Acting Ensign, 5 October, 1864. Honorably discharged 17 January, 1868. Mate, 21 January, 1870. Appointment revoked 22 September, 1871.
PATE, McCALL.
Carpenter, 27 July, 1896. Resigned 13 September, 1897. Assistant Engineer (Spanish-American War), 3 June, 1898. Honorably discharged 31 October, 1898. Carpenter, 12 December, 1898.
PATERSON, R. H. L.
Midshipman, 1 October, 1827. Resigned 12 April, 1831.
PATERSON, WILLIAM.
Passed Assistant Engineer (Spanish-American War), 15 June, 1898. Honorably discharged 2 September, 1898.

PATJENS, JOHN A.
Lieutenant, Junior Grade (Spanish-American War), 26 May, 1898. Honorably discharged 3 October, 1898.
PATTEN, EDWARD C.
Third Assistant Engineer, 3 May, 1859. Dismissed 8 January, 1861.
PATTEN, JOHN.
Midshipman, 28 May, 1800. Discharged 6 August, 1801, under Peace Establishment Act.
PATTEN, S. P.
Acting Master, 29 October, 1861. Dismissed 24 June, 1862.
PATTEN, THOMAS.
Midshipman, 9 November, 1813. Resigned 20 October, 1820.
PATTEN, WILLIAM W.
Mate, 13 December, 1861. Resigned 16 May, 1863.
PATTERSON, CARLILE P.
Midshipman, 2 September, 1830. Passed Midshipman, 4 June, 1836. Lieutenant, 8 September, 1841. Resigned 2 September, 1853.
PATTERSON, DANIEL T.
Midshipman, 20 August, 1800. Lieutenant, 24 January, 1807. Commander, 24 July, 1813. Captain, 28 February, 1815. Died 25 August, 1839.
PATTERSON, GEORGE A.
Acting Ensign, 13 January, 1863. Appointment revoked (sick) 20 July, 1863.
PATTERSON, GRIFFITH W. D.
Acting Master, 5 October, 1861. Acting Volunteer Lieutenant, 1 June, 1864. Honorably discharged 14 December, 1865. Acting Master, 13 August, 1867. Mustered out 1 July, 1868.
PATTERSON, JAMES.
Acting Third Assistant Engineer, 30 August, 1861. Acting Second Assistant Engineer, 23 May, 1862. Honorably discharged 3 April, 1868.
PATTERSON, JAMES W.
Third Assistant Engineer, 21 April, 1863. Second Assistant Engineer, 28 September, 1864. Retired 21 October, 1869.
PATTERSON, JOHN.
Boatswain, 2 April, 1832. Died 13 December, 1836.
PATTERSON, JOHN A.
Acting Third Assistant Engineer, 3 November, 1863. Acting Second Assistant Engineer, 6 October, 1864. Honorably discharged 11 February, 1866.
PATTERSON, JOHN M.
Midshipman, 1 January, 1818. Resigned 17 September, 1821.
PATTERSON, JOHN S.
Midshipman, 18 April, 1833. Passed Midshipman, 8 July, 1839. Killed 28 October, 1842.
PATTERSON, NATHANIEL P.
Third Assistant Engineer, 15 March, 1847. Second Assistant Engineer, 13 September, 1849. First Assistant Engineer, 26 February, 1851. Chief Engineer, 15 October, 1859. Name stricken from the Rolls of the Navy, 10 June, 1861.
PATTERSON, ROBERT E.
Acting Assistant Paymaster, 8 March, 1863. Honorably discharged 12 December, 1865.
PATTERSON, ROBERT O.
Acting Master, 29 May, 1861. Resigned 10 April, 1865.
PATTERSON, SAMUEL G.
Acting Second Assistant Engineer, 9 December, 1863. Honorably discharged 25 August, 1865.
PATTERSON, SILAS W.
Mate, 30 December, 1861. Dismissed 30 April, 1862.
PATTERSON, THOMAS H.
Midshipman, 5 April, 1836. Passed Midshipman, 1 July, 1842. Master, 31 October, 1848. Lieutenant, 23 June, 1849. Commander, 16 July, 1862. Captain, 25 July, 1866. Commodore, 2 November, 1871. Rear-Admiral, 28 March, 1877. Retired List, 10 May, 1882. Died 9 April, 1889.
PATTERSON, WILLIAM.
Acting Third Assistant Engineer, 3 June, 1861. Appointment revoked (sick) 24 December, 1861.
PATTERSON, WILLIAM A.
Midshipman, 1 October, 1827. Resigned 19 October, 1831.
PATTERSON, WILLIAM J.
Acting Third Assistant Engineer, 17 August, 1864. Honorably discharged 19 April, 1866.
PATTISON, THOMAS.
Midshipman, 2 March, 1839. Passed Midshipman, 2 July, 1845. Master, 17 February, 1854. Lieutenant, 19 September, 1854. Lieutenant-Commander, 16 July, 1862. Commander, 3 March, 1865. Captain, 3 July, 1870. Commodore, 11 December, 1877. Rear-Admiral, 1 November, 1883. Retired List, 8 February, 1884. Died 17 December, 1891.
PATTON, FRANCIS.
Midshipman, 27 November, 1799. Resigned 5 May, 1806.
PATTON, GEORGE.
Midshipman, 15 November, 1809. Last appearance on Records of Navy Department, 1815. Charleston, South Carolina.
PATTON, JOHN B.
Naval Cadet, 21 May, 1885. Assistant Engineer, 1 July, 1891. Passed Assistant Engineer, 14 October, 1896. Rank changed to Lieutenant, 3 March, 1899.
PATTON, ROBERT.
Midshipman, 9 September, 1841. Resigned 1 October, 1846.

PATTON, ROBERT.
  Midshipman, 2 February, 1829. Dismissed 19 June, 1837.
PATTON, WILLIAM F.
  Surgeon, 4 April, 1831. Resigned 6 May, 1861.
PATTSON, JULIUS A.
  Lieutenant (Spanish-American War), 21 April, 1898. Honorably discharged 2 September, 1898.
PAUL, ALLEN G.
  Midshipman, 23 September, 1862. Graduated June, 1866. Ensign, 18 December, 1868. Master, 21 March, 1870. Lieutenant, 2 November, 1871. Died 13 May, 1891.
PAUL, GEORGE.
  Third Assistant Engineer, 16 January, 1863. Resigned 9 September, 1865.
PAUL, HENRY J.
  Midshipman, 1 April, 1828. Passed Midshipman, 14 June, 1834. Lost at sea 10 March, 1839.
PAUL, HENRY M.
  Professor, 3 April, 1897.
PAUL, MARK W.
  Carpenter, 26 July, 1861. Resigned 13 November, 1865.
PAUL, ROBERT S.
  Chief Engineer (Spanish-American War), 21 May, 1898. Honorably discharged 25 January, 1899.
PAUL, WILLIAM, Jr.
  Acting First Assistant Engineer, 28 November, 1863. Honorably discharged 20 September, 1865.
PAUL, WILLIAM M.
  Midshipman, 24 September, 1863. Graduated June, 1867. Ensign, 18 December, 1868. Master, 21 March, 1870. Lieutenant, 21 March, 1871. Resigned 23 March, 1872. Lieutenant (Spanish-American War), 27 July, 1898. Honorably discharged 14 September, 1898.
PAULDING, GEORGE W.
  Acting Ensign, 1 October, 1862. Declined to accept. Revoked 16 February, 1863.
PAULDING, HIRAM.
  Midshipman, 1 September, 1811. Lieutenant, 27 April, 1816. Commander, 9 February, 1837. Captain, 29 February, 1844. Retired List, 21 December, 1861. Rear-Admiral, Retired List, 16 July, 1862. Died 20 October, 1878.
PAULDING, LEONARD.
  Midshipman, 19 December, 1840. Passed Midshipman, 11 July, 1846. Master, 1 March, 1855. Lieutenant, 14 September, 1855. Lieutenant-Commander, 16 July, 1862. Commander, 24 December, 1865. Died 29 April, 1867.
PAULDING, ROBERT P.
  Assistant Paymaster, 31 July, 1869. Passed Assistant Paymaster, 31 July, 1873. Resigned 3 December, 1879.
PAULL, JOHN W.
  Acting Third Assistant Engineer, 18 March, 1863. Acting Second Assistant Engineer, 13 August, 1863. Honorably discharged 19 January, 1866.
PAVY, ELI R.
  Acting First Assistant Engineer, 4 December, 1863. Honorably discharged 19 February, 1866.
PAVY, WILLIAM L.
  Mate, 23 January, 1862. Acting Ensign, 20 November, 1862. Resigned 7 October, 1863. Acting Ensign, 23 April, 1864. Resigned 30 June, 1866.
PAXSON, ISAIAH.
  Third Assistant Engineer, 17 March, 1863. Second Assistant Engineer, 1 September, 1864. Resigned 18 November, 1865.
PAYNE, CHARLES W.
  Mate, 16 June, 1864. Appointment revoked (sick) 7 November, 1864.
PAYNE, EDWARD D.
  Assistant Surgeon, 20 September, 1861. Passed Assistant Surgeon, 28 June, 1865. Surgeon, 14 November, 1871. Retired List, 13 April, 1876.
PAYNE, FRANK B.
  Assistant Paymaster (Spanish-American War), 10 June, 1898. Honorably discharged 21 November, 1898.
PAYNE, FREDERICK R.
  Naval Cadet, 21 May, 1888. Ensign, 1 July, 1894. Lieutenant, Junior Grade, 3 March, 1899.
PAYNE, JAMES.
  Captain (to command a Galley), 16 September, 1798. Last appearance on Records of Navy Department, 9 October, 1798.
PAYNE, JAMES H., Jr.
  Assistant Surgeon (Spanish-American War), 29 June, 1898. Appointed Assistant Surgeon in Regular Service, 7 June, 1900.
PAYSON, THOMAS K.
  Acting Third Assistant Engineer, 15 October, 1863. Honorably discharged 18 August, 1865.
PAYTON, GEORGE V.
  Acting Third Assistant Engineer, 9 March, 1864. Honorably discharged 3 July, 1865.
PEABODY, JOHN M.
  Acting Carpenter, 5 October, 1863. Honorably discharged 4 January, 1866.
PEABODY, JOSEPH N.
  Mate, 2 January, 1864. Acting Ensign, 1 March, 1865. Honorably discharged 19 October, 1865.
PEABODY, WILLIAM.
  Midshipman, 16 January, 1809. Resigned 7 April, 1814.

GENERAL NAVY REGISTER.

PEABODY, WILLIAM H.
    Acting Third Assistant Engineer, 27 October, 1863. Appointment revoked 16 June, 1865.
PEACHY, THOMAS G.
    Assistant Surgeon, 10 December, 1814. Resigned 6 September, 1817.
PEACO, JOHN W.
    Assistant Surgeon, 23 June, 1814. Surgeon, 10 July, 1824. Died 23 May, 1827.
PEACOCK, CHARLES A.
    Mate, 1 June, 1863. Appointment revoked 13 May, 1868.
PEACOCK, DAVID.
    Midshipman, 28 September, 1869. Graduated 15 October, 1874. Ensign, 17 July, 1875. Master, 1 October, 1881. Lieutenant, Junior Grade, 3 March, 1883. Lieutenant, 25 August, 1887. Retired List, 28 October, 1897.
PAULDING, WILLIAM.
    Mate, 16 August, 1864. Resignation accepted 19 May, 1865.
PEACOCK, JOHN R.
    Acting Ensign, 3 March, 1863. Appointment revoked 21 August, 1866.
PEAKE, EDWARD T.
    Acting Third Assistant Engineer, 24 February, 1864. Honorably discharged 17 November, 1868.
PEAKE, FRANCIS M.
    Acting Second Assistant Engineer, 8 December, 1863. Honorably discharged 14 November, 1865.
PEAKE, JOHN L.
    Acting Second Assistant Engineer, 10 September, 1861. Acting First Assistant Engineer, 2 October, 1862. Acting Chief Engineer, 1 March, 1864. Honorably discharged 22 December, 1865.
PEAKE, RICHARD N.
    Gunner, 25 August, 1852. Died 31 January, 1860.
PEAKES, THOMAS M.
    Acting Ensign, 16 July, 1862. Appointment revoked (sick) 24 August, 1864.
PEALE, GEORGE.
    Carpenter, 9 May, 1828. Dismissed 16 June, 1830.
PEARCE, ALFRED D.
    Ensign (Spanish-American War), 30 June, 1898. Honorably discharged 19 September, 1898.
PEARCE, CHARLES H.
    Mate, 4 April, 1862. Resigned 5 August, 1863.
PEARCE, GEORGE.
    Midshipman, 6 March, 1809. Lieutenant, 24 July, 1813. Died 7 August, 1827.
PEARCE, GEORGE.
    Midshipman, 20 June, 1806. Dismissed 10 May, 1808.
PEARCE, JOHN.
    Acting Master, 1 October, 1862. Acting Volunteer Lieutenant, 16 April, 1863. Honorably discharged 19 December, 1865.
PEARCE, JOHN S.
    Acting Third Assistant Engineer, 13 February, 1863. Acting Second Assistant Engineer, 26 July, 1864. Honorably discharged 18 August, 1866.
PEARCE, SAMUEL.
    Midshipman, 30 March, 1833. Passed Midshipman, 8 July, 1839. Reserved List, 13 September, 1855. Ensign on Retired List, 10 March, 1863. Captain on Retired List, 4 April, 1867. Died 29 March, 1874.
PEARCE, SAMUEL.
    Midshipman, 30 March, 1833. Passed Midshipman, 8 July, 1839. Resigned 9 June, 1841.
PEARCE, SAMUEL.
    Master, 16 January, 1809. Appointment revoked 8 May, 1809.
PEARCE, WALTER.
    Mate, 21 October, 1861. Acting Ensign, 6 March, 1863. Acting Master, 24 March, 1865. Resigned 27 April, 1865.
PEARCE, WILLIAM.
    Midshipman, 1 October, 1850. Dismissed 12 June, 1851. Acting Master, 23 November, 1861. Appointment revoked 14 June, 1862. Mate, 14 June, 1862. Acting Ensign, 24 September, 1863. Honorably discharged 29 July, 1865.
PEARCE, WILLIAM H.
    Acting Gunner, 9 February, 1864. Honorably discharged 9 May, 1865.
PEARSON, ALBERT.
    Assistant Surgeon, 26 April, 1848. Died 27 July, 1849.
PEARSON, ALEXANDER W.
    Acting Assistant Paymaster, 22 July, 1862. Mustered out 24 February, 1866.
PEARSON, FREDERICK.
    Acting Midshipman, 21 September, 1859. Ensign, 16 September, 1862. Lieutenant, 22 February, 1864. Lieutenant-Commander, 25 July, 1866. Commander, 1 December, 1877. Resigned 1 October, 1885.
PEARSON, GEORGE F.
    Midshipman, 11 March, 1815. Lieutenant, 13 January, 1825. Commander, 8 September, 1841. Captain, 14 September, 1855. Retired List, 21 December, 1861. Commodore on Retired List, 16 July, 1862. Rear-Admiral on Retired List, 25 July, 1866. Died 30 June, 1867.
PEARSON, GEORGE T.
    Acting Ensign, 12 August, 1864. Resigned 26 January, 1866.
PEARSON, HENRY A.
    Naval Cadet, 6 September, 1889. Ensign, 1 July, 1895. Lieutenant, Junior Grade, 3 March, 1899.

GENERAL NAVY REGISTER.

PEARSON, J. F.
  Acting Ensign, 30 September, 1863. Honorably discharged 12 November, 1865.
PEARSON, JEREMIAH.
  Midshipman, 31 October, 1799. Died 25 July, 1800.
PEARSON, JOHN.
  Master, not in line of promotion, 7 June, 1844. Reserved List, 14 September, 1855. Resigned 22 January, 1861.
PEARSON, JOSEPH F.
  Pharmacist, 26 March, 1900.
PEARSON, WILLIAM.
  Midshipman, 1 January, 1818. Lieutenant, 28 April, 1826. Commander, 10 December, 1843. Died 1 November, 1852.
PEARY, ROBERT E.
  Civil Engineer, 26 October, 1881.
PEASE, CHARLES.
  Acting Ensign, 1 October, 1862. Resigned 16 February, 1863.
PEASE, GEORGE W.
  Acting Ensign, 3 July, 1863. Honorably discharged 14 August, 1865.
PEASE, GILES M.
  Acting Assistant Surgeon, 18 December, 1861. Appointment revoked 19 November, 1862.
PEASE, HENRY, Jr.
  Acting Ensign, 4 December, 1863. Acting Master, 9 January, 1865. Honorably discharged 21 September, 1865. Acting Master, 18 May, 1866. Mustered out 1 February, 1868.
PEASE, ISAAC D.
  Acting Ensign, 14 July, 1864. Honorably discharged 20 May, 1865.
PEASE, JOHN P.
  Mate, 5 March, 1862. Appointment revoked 30 September, 1865.
PEASE, LEVI.
  Carpenter, 1 October, 1841. Died 12 May, 1842.
PEASE, PETER.
  Acting Ensign, 8 April, 1864. Honorably discharged 12 October, 1865.
PEASE, WILLIAM B.
  Acting Ensign, 22 October, 1864. Honorably discharged 16 September, 1865.
PEASE, WILLIAM R.
  Mate, 23 December, 1862. Dismissed 31 May, 1864.
PEASE, WILLIAM S.
  Acting Ensign, 1 October, 1862. Acting Master, 3 February, 1864. Resigned 11 January, 1865.
PECK, CHARLES F.
  Midshipman, 3 October, 1850. Passed Midshipman, 20 June, 1856. Resigned 21 July, 1856.
PECK, CHARLES W.
  Acting Assistant Surgeon, 22 May, 1863. Died 4 September, 1863.
PECK, EDWARD C.
  Acting First Assistant Engineer, 12 June, 1863. Honorably discharged 4 December, 1865.
PECK, ELISHA.
  Midshipman, 4 March, 1817. Lieutenant, 28 April, 1826. Commander, 8 September, 1843. Reserved List, 13 September, 1855. Captain on Reserved List, 14 September, 1855. Died 11 June, 1866.
PECK, GEORGE.
  Assistant Surgeon, 25 February, 1851. Passed Assistant Surgeon, 10 April, 1856. Surgeon, 30 May, 1861. Medical Inspector, 1 June, 1871. Medical Director, 7 January, 1878. Retired List, 9 July, 1888.
PECK, GEORGE P.
  Acting Assistant Paymaster, 11 June, 1863. Honorably discharged 19 December, 1865.
PECK, JOHN B.
  Acting Third Assistant Engineer, under instruction Naval Academy, 10 October, 1866. Third Assistant Engineer, 2 June, 1868. Resigned 7 June, 1869.
PECK, JOHN F.
  Acting Second Assistant Engineer, 15 December, 1862. Acting First Assistant Engineer, 12 March, 1863. Resignation accepted 22 July, 1863.
PECK, OSCAR E.
  Mate, 30 July, 1862. Dismissed 7 December, 1863.
PECK, PASCAL PAOLI.
  Midshipman, 9 May, 1803. Resigned 1 May, 1809.
PECK, RALPH E.
  Acting Ensign, 9 November, 1864. Resigned 29 April, 1865.
PECK, RANSOME B.
  Midshipman, 21 November, 1861. Graduated June, 1866. Ensign, 12 March, 1868. Master, 26 March, 1869. Lieutenant, 21 March, 1870. Died 6 November, 1885.
PECK, ROBERT G.
  Midshipman, 24 September, 1866. Graduated 7 June, 1870. Ensign, 13 July, 1871. Master, 11 September, 1873. Lieutenant, 13 November, 1878. Lieutenant-Commander, 10 August, 1898. Retired List, with rank of Commander, 30 June, 1899.
PECKHAM, CHARLES F.
  Passed Assistant Surgeon (Spanish-American War), 29 June, 1898. Honorably discharged 20 September, 1898.
PECKWORTH, J. R.
  Assistant Surgeon, 4 November, 1834. Resigned 13 November, 1838.
PECOR, WILLIAM R.
  Sailmaker, 12 April, 1852. Died 30 January, 1853.

FEDDLE, JOSEPH.
  Acting Third Assistant Engineer, 22 October, 1862. Resigned 29 September, 1863.
PEED, JOHN.
  Sailmaker, 8 April, 1840. Died 23 February, 1851.
PEED, NATHANIEL B.
  Sailmaker, 22 October, 1823. Died 9 May, 1846.
PEED, WILLIAM C.
  Mate, 18 September, 1863. Deserted 7 December, 1863.
PEEL, JOSEPH H.
  Mate, 1 March, 1863. Appointment revoked (sick) 27 July, 1863.
PEETE, GEORGE W.
  Assistant Surgeon, 2 May, 1834. Passed Assistant Surgeon, 12 July, 1839. Resigned 29 May, 1843.
PEGRAM, JOHN C.
  Acting Midshipman, 21 September, 1860. Ensign, 28 May, 1863. Resigned 18 May, 1866.
PEGRAM, ROBERT B.
  Midshipman, 2 February, 1829. Passed Midshipman, 3 July, 1835. Lieutenant, 8 September, 1841. Dismissed 17 April, 1861.
PEIRCE, BENJAMIN F.
  Assistant Surgeon, 24 January, 1862. Drowned 9 March, 1864.
PEIRCE, CHARLES H.
  Acting Ensign, 14 November, 1863. Resigned 9 February, 1865.
PEIRCE, GRANVILLE T.
  Third Assistant Engineer, 26 June, 1856. Resigned 8 August, 1857.
FEIRCE, ISAAC A.
  Mate, 8 January, 1864. Died at Newbern, N. C., 25 October, 1864.
PEIRCE, ROBERT C.
  Acting Assistant Paymaster, 12 August, 1862. Resigned 15 June, 1865.
PEIRCE, WILLIAM B.
  Acting Ensign, 13 September, 1864. Honorably discharged 25 July, 1865.
PEIRSON, ROBERT A.
  Acting Third Assistant Engineer, 20 December, 1862. Honorably discharged 18 September, 1865.
PELOT, JOHN F.
  Midshipman, 10 June, 1814. Resigned 21 July, 1821.
PELOT, THOMAS P.
  Midshipman, 2 June, 1849. Passed Midshipman, 12 June, 1855. Master, 16 September, 1855. Lieutenant, 1 January, 1857. Resigned 11 January, 1861.
PELTON, CHARLES E.
  Mate, 25 November, 1864. Honorably discharged 30 September, 1865.
PELTON, ELLSWORTH W.
  Mate, 31 December, 1861. Acting Ensign, 11 December, 1862. Honorably discharged 3 November, 1865.
PELTON, JAMES H.
  Acting Third Assistant Engineer, 15 December, 1862. Acting Second Assistant Engineer, 21 May, 1864. Honorably discharged 26 November, 1865.
PELTZ, PHILIP G.
  Third Assistant Engineer, 26 June, 1856. Second Assistant Engineer, 21 July, 1858. First Assistant Engineer, 3 August, 1859. Chief Engineer, 5 November, 1861. Died 21 August, 1868.
PELTZ, SAMUEL H.
  Assistant Surgeon, 22 August, 1862. Drowned 15 January, 1865.
PEMBERTON, JOHN, Jr.
  Third Assistant Engineer, 8 December, 1862. Second Assistant Engineer, 8 April, 1864. First Assistant Engineer, 7 May, 1873. Retired List, 14 September, 1891.
PEMBERTON, JOHN.
  Midshipman, 13 May, 1800. Discharged 14 July, 1801, under Peace Establishment Act.
PEMBLE, ALBERT G.
  Acting First Assistant Engineer, 21 March, 1862. Appointment revoked 8 May, 1862.
PENDER, BENJAMIN D.
  Carpenter, 12 December, 1898.
PENDERGRAST, AUSTIN.
  Midshipman, 14 October, 1848. Passed Midshipman, 15 June, 1854. Master, 15 September, 1855. Lieutenant, 16 September, 1855. Lieutenant-Commander, 16 July, 1862. Commander, 25 July, 1866. Died 23 October, 1874.
PENDERGRAST, GARRETT J.
  Midshipman, 1 January, 1812. Lieutenant, 3 March, 1821. Commander, 8 September, 1841. Captain, 24 May, 1855. Commodore, Retired List, 16 July, 1862. Died 7 November, 1862.
PENDEXTER, EDWARD.
  Acting Ensign, 4 December, 1862. Honorably discharged 31 October, 1865.
PENDLEBERRY, ROBERT.
  Mate, 26 November, 1862. Acting Ensign, 23 December, 1863. Appointment revoked (sick) 10 October, 1864.
PENDLETON, A. G.
  Professor, 14 August, 1848. Died 16 February, 1865.
PENDLETON, ALBERT L.
  Mate, 26 June, 1862. Resigned 13 May, 1863.
PENDLETON, CHARLES H.
  Acting Midshipman, 27 September, 1860. Ensign, 1 October, 1863. Master, 10 May, 1866. Lieutenant, 21 February, 1867. Lieutenant-Commander, 12 March, 1868. Dropped 12 July, 1884.

PENDLETON, EDWIN C.
Midshipman, 13 October, 1863. Graduated June, 1867. Ensign, 18 December, 1868. Master, 21 March, 1870. Lieutenant, 21 March, 1871. Lieutenant-Commander, 4 August, 1889. Commander, 21 March, 1897.
PENDLETON, EPHRAIM E.
Acting Master, 22 November, 1861. Honorably discharged 18 December, 1865.
PENDLETON, GEORGE H.
Acting Master, 8 July, 1861. Died 13 January, 1866.
PENDLETON, OLIVER.
Captain (to command a Galley), 4 May, 1799. Last appearance on Records of Navy Department.
PENDLETON, RALPH C. J.
Mate, 11 September, 1862. Acting Ensign, 23 April, 1863. Honorably discharged 17 May, 1867.
PENDLETON, WILLIAM D.
First Assistant Engineer, 29 October, 1861. Resigned 4 January, 1866.
PENDLETON, W. H.
Midshipman, 1 September, 1827. Resigned 7 July, 1835.
PENFIELD, CHARLES.
Acting Ensign, 26 February, 1863. Honorably discharged 16 November, 1865.
PENFIELD, GEORGE O.
Mate, 19 December, 1861. Appointment revoked 27 June, 1862.
PENFIELD, JOSEPH L.
Acting Ensign, 15 June, 1864. Dismissed 12 December, 1864.
PENFIELD, NORMAN H.
Acting Master, 17 December, 1861. Resigned 3 February, 1865.
PENFIELD, WILLIAM H.
Mate, 19 December, 1861. Acting Ensign, 17 November, 1862. Appointment revoked 28 February, 1866.
PENHALLOW, SAMUEL.
Midshipman, 1 November, 1826. Resigned 6 September, 1828.
PENN, JOHN H.
Acting Third Assistant Engineer, 4 June, 1864. Resigned (sick) 14 November, 1864.
PENNELL, ISAAC A.
Acting Master, 26 August, 1861. Acting Volunteer Lieutenant, 13 March, 1865. Dismissed 9 June, 1865.
PENNELL, WILLIAM L.
Acting First Assistant Engineer, 22 July, 1863. Honorably discharged 22 September, 1865.
PENNEY, EDGAR.
Acting Third Assistant Engineer, 13 February, 1865. Honorably discharged 6 March, 1868.
PENNICK, SOLOMON.
Master, 21 January, 1809. Appointment revoked 2 May, 1809.
PENNIMAN, LUTHER L.
Acting Assistant Paymaster, 17 December, 1861. Resigned 28 May, 1864.
PENNINGTON, CHARLES C.
Acting Second Assistant Engineer, 5 August, 1861. Dismissed 28 December, 1861.
PENNINGTON, CHARLES H.
Acting Third Assistant Engineer, 6 January, 1865. Honorably discharged 21 September, 1869.
PENNINGTON, CHARLES W.
Acting First Assistant Engineer, 19 November, 1862. Honorably discharged 19 March, 1868.
PENNINGTON, HENRY R.
Midshipman, 1 October, 1866. Graduated 7 June, 1870. Resigned 15 June, 1873.
PENNINGTON, JOHN H.
Acting Gunner, 8 November, 1862. Honorably discharged 11 April, 1866.
PENNINGTON, JOSEPH W.
Gunner, 11 March, 1837. Deserted 14 April, 1849.
PENNINGTON, LAWRENCE.
Midshipman, 22 November, 1822. Passed Midshipman, 24 May, 1828. Lieutenant, 27 May, 1830. Dropped 13 September, 1855.
PENNINGTON, LEWIS W.
Acting Master, 22 November, 1861. Acting Volunteer Lieutenant, 25 September, 1862. Acting Volunteer Lieutenant-Commander, 3 March, 1865. Honorably discharged 12 November, 1865.
PENNINGTON, ROBERT.
Midshipman, 28 March, 1800. Discharged 28 May, 1801, under Peace Establishment Act.
PENNOCK, ALEXANDER M.
Midshipman, 1 April, 1828. Passed Midshipman, 14 June, 1834. Lieutenant, 25 February, 1841. Commander, 15 December, 1855. Captain, 2 January, 1863. Commodore, 6 May, 1868. Rear-Admiral, 19 July, 1872. Died 20 September, 1876.
PENNOCK, W. H.
Midshipman, 20 April, 1815. Died 24 December, 1824.
PENNOYER, JAMES.
Acting Assistant Surgeon, 13 September, 1862. Resigned 8 May, 1865.
PENNY, THOMAS.
Boatswain, date not known. Resigned in 1820.
PENNYCOOK, JOHN T.
Acting Warrant Machinist, 23 August, 1899.
PENROSE, CHARLES W.
Assistant Paymaster, 20 May, 1898. Passed Assistant Paymaster, 23 December, 1899.

PENROSE, THOMAS N.
Assistant Surgeon, 24 January, 1862. Passed Assistant Surgeon, 28 June, 1865. Surgeon, 28 May, 1871. Medical Inspector, 25 January, 1889. Medical Director, 28 February, 1896. Retired List, 6 June, 1897.
PENTLAND, ANDREW.
Midshipman, 15 November, 1809. Dismissed 21 June, 1813.
PENTON, ABNER C.
Acting Ensign, 12 May, 1864. Honorably discharged 13 October, 1865.
PENTONY, THOMAS.
Acting Third Assistant Engineer, 22 July, 1864. Honorably discharged 11 December, 1865.
PEOPLES, CHRISTIAN J.
Assistant Paymaster, 27 March, 1900.
PEPE, NICHOLAS.
Midshipman, 16 January, 1809. Resigned 20 May, 1814.
PEPIN, FERDINAND.
Midshipman, 13 April, 1832. Died 28 October, 1838.
PERCHARD, CLEMENT H.
Acting Ensign, 5 December, 1864. Honorably discharged 1 August, 1865.
PERCIVAL, ARTHUR T.
Acting Warrant Machinist, 23 August, 1899.
PERCIVAL, GUSTAVUS.
Acting Master, 30 August, 1861. Appointment revoked (sick) 23 August, 1864. Acting Master, 17 November, 1864. Honorably discharged 8 December, 1865.
PERCIVAL, JOHN.
Master, 6 March, 1809. Lieutenant, 9 December, 1814. Commander, 3 March, 1831. Captain, 8 September, 1841. Reserved List, 13 September, 1855. Died 17 September, 1862.
PERCY, EZEKIEL D.
Acting Master, 18 December, 1861. Honorably discharged 1 December, 1865.
PERCY, HENRY T.
Acting Assistant Surgeon, 31 May, 1873. Assistant Surgeon, 30 June, 1879. Passed Assistant Surgeon, 30 June, 1882. Surgeon, 29 September, 1895.
PERKINS, AMOS G.
Acting First Assistant Engineer, 22 April, 1863. Honorably discharged 1 December, 1865.
PERKINS, CHARLES G.
Acting Volunteer Lieutenant, 1 October, 1862. Resigned 25 March, 1865.
PERKINS, CHARLES F.
Midshipman, 20 July, 1865. Graduated June, 1869. Ensign, 12 July, 1870. Master, 12 July, 1871. Lieutenant, 22 July, 1874. Lieutenant-Commander, 18 February, 1896. Commander, 8 July, 1899.
PERKINS, CON M.
Assistant Engineer, 1 July, 1883. (See Marine Corps.)
PERKINS, CYRUS.
Acting Third Assistant Engineer, 5 June, 1863. Resigned.
PERKINS, DAVID K.
Mate, 27 January, 1863. Acting Ensign, 1 April, 1864. Honorably discharged 15 November, 1865.
PERKINS, EDWARD.
Mate, 3 September, 1863. Resigned 23 May, 1864.
PERKINS, EDWARD H.
Midshipman, 1 September, 1828. Resigned 2 January, 1833.
PERKINS, E. S.
Acting Assistant Surgeon, 1 September, 1864. Honorably discharged 10 November, 1868.
PERKINS, FOSTER.
Midshipman, 18 February, 1800. Discharged 12 October, 1801, under Peace Establishment Act.
PERKINS, FREDERICK K.
Assistant Paymaster, 17 June, 1898.
PERKINS, GEORGE H.
Acting Midshipman, 1 October, 1851. Midshipman, 1 October, 1856. Passed Midshipman, 29 April, 1859. Master, 5 September, 1859. Lieutenant, 2 February, 1861. Lieutenant-Commander, 30 December, 1862. Commander, 19 January, 1871. Captain, 10 March, 1882. Retired List, 1 October, 1891. Commodore on Retired List, 9 May, 1896. Died 28 October, 1899.
PERKINS, GEORGE W.
Passed Assistant Engineer (Spanish-American War), 6 July, 1898. Honorably discharged 14 January, 1899.
PERKINS, GUSTAVUS S.
Acting Second Assistant Engineer, 20 September, 1862. Acting First Assistant Engineer, 16 March, 1864. Honorably discharged 27 September, 1865.
PERKINS, HAMILTON.
Midshipman, 24 September, 1863. Graduated June, 1867. Ensign, 18 December, 1868. Master, 21 March, 1870. Lieutenant, 14 October, 1871. Resigned 31 May, 1888.
PERKINS, ISAAC E.
Midshipman, 1 January, 1817. Drowned August, 1819.
PERKINS, JAMES F.
Mate, 20 December, 1861. Acting Ensign, 28 October, 1862. Honorably discharged 20 September, 1865.
PERKINS, JOHN H.
Assistant Surgeon, 13 December, 1800. Discharged 30 April, 1801, under Peace Establishment Act.

GENERAL NAVY REGISTER.

PERKINS, JOHN J.
    Mate, 1 October, 1862. Acting Ensign, 12 November, 1863. Appointment revoked 20 July, 1864.
PERKINS, JOHN P.
    Acting Ensign, 2 December, 1863. Honorably discharged 10 August, 1865.
PERKINS, LYMAN B.
    Cadet Engineer, 13 September, 1877. Graduated. Honorably discharged 26 June, 1883. Restored to service 10 March, 1886. Resigned 12 April, 1886. Passed Assistant Engineer (Spanish-American War), 12 May, 1898. Honorably discharged 21 February, 1899.
PERKINS, PELTIAH.
    Acting Ensign, 9 March, 1865. Honorably discharged 1 August, 1865.
PERKINS, WILLIAM H.
    Passed Assistant Engineer (Spanish-American War), 24 June, 1898. Honorably discharged 16 January, 1899.
PERKS, EDWARD.
    Lieutenant, Junior Grade (Spanish-American War), 22 June, 1898. Honorably discharged 17 January, 1899.
PERLEE, THADDEUS KOS.
    Midshipman, 12 February, 1834. Dismissed 8 July, 1839.
PERLEY, CHARLES S.
    Acting Assistant Paymaster, 18 February, 1862. Assistant Paymaster, 1 October, 1862. Paymaster, 4 May, 1866. Resigned 14 January, 1868.
PERA, JOHN S.
    Acting Third Assistant Engineer, 14 February, 1863. Acting Second Assistant Engineer, 6 October, 1863. Died 1 October, 1864.
PERRAULT, MICHAEL.
    Midshipman, 16 January, 1809. Resigned 21 March, 1814.
PERRIGO, GEORGE W.
    Mate, 22 August, 1864. Honorably discharged 26 October, 1865.
PERRILL, HARLAN P.
    Naval Cadet, 6 September, 1893. Ensign, 1 July, 1899.
PERRIMOND, XAVIER.
    Boatswain, 18 April, 1879. Retired List, 1 November, 1895.
PERRINE, H. LANSING.
    Acting Third Assistant Engineer, 17 October, 1864. Resigned 10 May, 1865.
PERROT, AUGUSTUS.
    Acting Assistant Paymaster, 18 July, 1863. Mustered out 26 August, 1865.
PERRY, ALEXANDER J.
    Midshipman, 9 June, 1811. Lieutenant, 1 April, 1818. Lost overboard 20 March, 1822.
PERRY, ALFRED H.
    Acting Third Assistant Engineer, 5 January, 1864. Resigned 2 May, 1865.
PERRY, BENJAMIN F.
    Acting Midshipman, 5 October, 1857. Died 3 July, 1860.
PERRY, BENJAMIN G.
    Mate, 3 November, 1865. Retired List, 8 September, 1894. Died 26 June, 1896.
PERRY, CHARLES B.
    Acting Assistant Paymaster, 20 May, 1863. Honorably discharged 14 January, 1866.
PERRY, CHARLES H.
    Assistant Surgeon, 24 January, 1862. Resigned 9 May, 1865.
PERRY, CHRISTOPHER R.
    Captain, 7 January, 1798. Discharged 3 April, 1801, under Peace Establishment Act.
PERRY, DAVID W.
    Carpenter, 23 June, 1869. Retired List, 14 February, 1899.
PERRY, EDWARD A.
    Acting Assistant Paymaster, 24 February, 1862. Dismissed 5 September, 1862.
PERRY, EDWARD W.
    Mate, 29 February, 1864. Honorably discharged 11 December, 1865.
PERRY, JAMES H.
    Third Assistant Engineer, 17 January, 1862. Second Assistant Engineer, 1 October, 1863. Resigned 12 April, 1866. Acting Second Assistant Engineer, 29 January, 1867. Mustered out 10 March, 1869. Second Assistant Engineer, 1 September, 1870. Passed Assistant Engineer, 25 April, 1877. Chief Engineer, 1 April, 1894. Rank changed to Lieutenant-Commander, 3 March, 1899.
PERRY, JOHN F.
    Mate, 25 August, 1863. Acting Ensign, 18 May, 1865. Mustered out 29 September, 1868.
PERRY, JOSEPH L.
    Acting First Assistant Engineer. Resigned 15 July, 1864.
PERRY, MARCUS H.
    Acting Third Assistant Engineer, 16 February, 1865. Deserted 28 February, 1866.
PERRY, MATTHEW C.
    Midshipman, 16 January, 1809. Lieutenant, 24 July, 1813. Commander, 21 March, 1826. Captain, 9 February, 1837. Died 4 March, 1858.
PERRY, MATTHEW C.
    Midshipman, 1 July, 1835. Passed Midshipman, 22 June, 1841. Master, 5 August, 1847. Lieutenant, 3 April, 1848. Reserved List, 13 September, 1855. Lieutenant on Active List, 3 April, 1848. Retired List, 14 April, 1862. Captain on Retired List, 4 April, 1867. Died 16 November, 1873.
PERRY, NATHANIEL H.
    Purser, 28 March, 1820. Died 8 May, 1832.
PERRY, OLIVER H.
    Midshipman, 28 February, 1829. Passed Midshipman, 3 July, 1835. Lieutenant, 25 February, 1841. Resigned 23 July, 1849.

PERRY, OLIVER H.
Midshipman, 7 April, 1799. Lieutenant, 15 January, 1807. Commander, 28 August, 1812. Captain, 10 September, 1813. Died 23 August, 1819.
PERRY, RAYMOND H.
Midshipman, 24 July, 1807. Lieutenant, 5 March, 1813. Died 12 March, 1826.
PERRY, R. J.
Acting Assistant Surgeon, 28 September, 1870. Honorably discharged 30 June, 1879.
PERRY, ROGER.
Midshipman, 1 July, 1828. Passed Midshipman, 14 June, 1834. Lieutenant, 25 February, 1841. Commander, 14 September, 1855. Retired List, 24 June, 1865. Captain on Retired List, 4 April, 1867. Died 5 November, 1880.
PERRY, THOMAS.
Acting Ensign, 14 July, 1864. Honorably discharged 27 October, 1865.
PERRY, THOMAS.
Midshipman, 25 September, 1861. Graduated September, 1865. Ensign, 1 December, 1866. Master, 12 March, 1868. Lieutenant, 26 March, 1869. Lieutenant-Commander, 6 November, 1881. Commander, 10 January, 1892. Captain, 11 June, 1899.
PERRY, THOMAS H.
Professor, 10 October, 1836. Dropped 4 September, 1848.
PERRY, WILLIAM C.
Acting Third Assistant Engineer, 30 November, 1862. Died 31 July, 1865.
PERRY, WILLIS G.
Mate, 8 May, 1862. Acting Ensign, 19 April, 1864. Honorably discharged 20 December, 1865.
PERSONS, REMUS C.
Assistant Surgeon, 5 March, 1872. Passed Assistant Surgeon, 13 January, 1876. Surgeon, 7 February, 1885. Medical Inspector, 18 June, 1898.
PETER, WILLIAM H.
Midshipman, 12 April, 1825. Died 8 August, 1830.
PETERKIN, WILLIAM.
Lieutenant, 11 June, 1799. Discharged 30 April, 1801, under Peace Establishment Act.
PETERKIN, WILLIAM.
Master, 1 March, 1814. Resigned 2 July, 1814.
PETERKIN, WILLIAM.
Acting Gunner, 18 April, 1863. Dismissed 13 August, 1863. Acting Gunner, 11 May, 1864. Dismissed 4 April, 1865.
PETERS, EDWARD McC.
Lieutenant (Spanish-American War), 21 May, 1898. Honorably discharged 8 October, 1898.
PETERS, GEORGE H.
Midshipman, 24 June, 1870. Graduated 1 June, 1874. Ensign, 17 July, 1875. Master, 10 January, 1881. Lieutenant, Junior Grade, 3 March, 1883. Lieutenant, 14 December, 1886. Lieutenant-Commander, 3 March, 1899.
PETERS, HERMAN.
Gunner, 30 March, 1861. Resigned 6 June, 1863. Acting Gunner, 5 January, 1864. Honorably discharged 6 December, 1865. Boatswain, 26 January, 1866. Died 26 July, 1877.
PETERS, WILLIAM.
Midshipman, 4 July, 1805. Lieutenant, 22 May, 1812. Last appearance on Records of Navy Department. Dead.
PETERS, WILLIAM D.
Acting Second Assistant Engineer, 12 October, 1861. Honorably discharged 9 October, 1865.
PETERSON, ADRIAN A.
Gunner, 25 October, 1836. Retired List, 21 December, 1861. Died in 1880.
PETERSON, ARTHUR.
Assistant Paymaster, 23 February, 1877. Passed Assistant Paymaster, 14 July, 1881. Paymaster, 15 August, 1893.
PETERSON, ERIC P.
Acting Ensign, 19 May, 1864. Honorably discharged 28 October, 1865.
PETERSON, JAMES.
Acting Third Assistant Engineer, 26 August, 1864. Honorably discharged 22 July, 1865.
PETERSON, JOHN.
Mate (Spanish-American War), 15 April, 1898. Honorably discharged 11 November, 1898.
PETERSON, JOHN F.
Mate, 31 May, 1864. Honorably discharged 17 June, 1866.
PETERSON, JOSEPH R.
Acting Third Assistant Engineer, 5 November, 1863. Honorably discharged 1 August, 1865. Acting Third Assistant Engineer, 12 April, 1866. Deserted 10 July, 1867.
PETERSON, MOSES.
Acting Second Assistant Engineer, 26 November, 1861. Died 6 October, 1864.
PETERSON, THOMAS L.
Acting Master, 8 April, 1862. Killed in action 28 March, 1863.
PETERSON, WILLIAM.
Carpenter, 21 January, 1835. Resigned 21 September, 1837.
PETERSON, WILLIAM.
Midshipman, 1 February, 1814. Last appearance on Records of Navy Department, 1816. Resigned.
PETERSON, WILLIAM G.
Acting Second Assistant Engineer, 29 August, 1861. Resigned 6 December, 1861.

GENERAL NAVY REGISTER. 433

PETHERICK, THOMAS, Jr.
   Third Assistant Engineer, 21 September, 1861. Appointment revoked 26 November, 1862.
PETIGRU, THOMAS.
   Midshipman, 1 January, 1812. Lieutenant, 13 January, 1825. Commander, 8 September, 1841. Dropped 14 September, 1855.
PETLEY, LAZARUS.
   Midshipman, 1 January, 1812. Resigned 10 December, 1813.
PETRIE, JAMES A.
   Acting Assistant Surgeon, 18 August, 1864. Honorably discharged 10 August, 1865.
PETTENGILL, GEORGE T.
   Naval Cadet, 22 September, 1894. Ensign, 4 April, 1900.
PETTERSON, JAMES C.
   Mate, 1 October, 1862. Mate, 31 March, 1863. Acting Ensign, 22 April, 1863. Resigned 23 June, 1864.
PETTIGREW, JOHN.
   Midshipman, 30 May, 1803. Lieutenant, 22 April, 1810. Drowned 6 March, 1820.
PETTINGELL, EDWARD D.
   Acting Ensign, 26 February, 1863. Honorably discharged 26 November, 1865.
PETTINGELL, SAMUEL S.
   Acting Third Assistant Engineer, 9 January, 1864. Honorably discharged 12 May, 1865.
PETTINGILL, B. G.
   Acting Master, 26 December, 1861. Dismissed 15 March, 1863.
PETTIS, DAVID.
   Sailmaker, 12 October, 1798. Last appearance on Records of Navy Department, 29 November, 1798.
PETTIS, JAMES.
   Midshipman, 5 December, 1798. Resigned 10 October, 1799.
PETTIT, CHARLES A.
   Mate, 24 April, 1861. Acting Ensign, 18 July, 1862. Acting Master, 8 November, 1864. Honorably discharged 27 October, 1865.
PETTIT, JOHN A.
   Assistant Surgeon, 5 March, 1847. Died 4 January, 1851.
PETTIT, ROBERT.
   Purser, 6 April, 1837. Retired List, 19 February, 1866. Pay Director, Retired List, 3 March, 1871. Died 19 May, 1878.
PETWAY, THOMAS M.
   Midshipman, 1 April, 1828. Resigned 2 December, 1830.
PETTEY, JOSEPH B.
   Acting Ensign, 12 December, 1862. Honorably discharged 23 November, 1865.
PETTY, CHARLES G.
   Acting Ensign, 9 January, 1863. Dismissed 14 July, 1863.
PETTY, WILLIAM.
   Chaplain, 9 March, 1807. Dismissed 18 February, 1808.
PEUGNET, MAURICE B.
   Naval Cadet, 7 September, 1889. Assistant Engineer, 1 July, 1895. Resigned 18 September, 1895. Ensign (Spanish-American War), 22 April, 1898. Resigned 5 May, 1898.
PEUROSE, JAMES.
   Midshipman, 30 November, 1799. Discharged 6 August, 1801, under Peace Establishment Act.
PEUROSE, WILLIAM.
   Lieutenant, 19 October, 1799. Discharged 10 May, 1801, under Peace Establishment Act.
PEYTON, EDWARD J.
   Purser, 11 June, 1798. Last appearance on Records of Navy Department.
PFELTZ, GUSTAVUS A.
   Third Assistant Engineer, 3 August, 1863. Resigned 25 June, 1866.
PHELAN, JOHN R.
   Midshipman, 17 April, 1862. Graduated June, 1866. Ensign, 12 March, 1868. Master, 26 March, 1869. Lost on the Oneida, 24 January, 1870.
PHELON, HENRY A.
   Acting Master, 27 February, 1862. Resigned 4 April, 1865.
PHELPS, ALFRED, Jr.
   Acting Master, 18 April, 1863. Resigned 22 February, 1864.
PHELPS, ARTHUR A.
   Mate, 6 December, 1869. Discharged 29 May, 1872. Gunner, 25 February, 1875. Chief Gunner, 3 March, 1899.
PHELPS, EDWIN F.
   Acting Ensign, 1 October, 1862. Appointment revoked (sick) 31 December, 1862.
PHELPS, HARRY.
   Cadet Midshipman, 22 September, 1876. Graduated 22 June, 1882. Ensign, Junior Grade, 3 March, 1883. Ensign, 26 June, 1884. Lieutenant, Junior Grade, 19 June, 1892. Lieutenant, 10 May, 1896.
PHELPS, JOHN.
   Acting Third Assistant Engineer, 22 May, 1863. Appointment revoked (sick) 1 December, 1863.
FHELPS, JOHN J.
   Ensign (Spanish-American War), 20 May, 1898. Honorably discharged 8 September, 1898.
PHELPS, NELSON S.
   Midshipman, 9 June, 1811. Resigned 14 January, 1814.

28

GENERAL NAVY REGISTER.

PHELPS, SAMUEL B.
Midshipman, 30 May, 1813. Lieutenant, 13 January, 1825. Resigned 2 February, 1827.
PHELPS, S. LEDYARD.
Midshipman, 19 October, 1841. Passed Midshipman, 10 August, 1847. Master, 30 June, 1855. Lieutenant, 14 September, 1855. Lieutenant-Commander, 16 July, 1862. Resigned 29 October, 1864.
PHELPS, THOMAS S.
Midshipman, 7 January, 1840. Passed Midshipman, 11 July, 1846. Master, 1 March, 1855. Lieutenant, 14 September, 1855. Lieutenant-Commander, 16 July, 1862. Commander, 5 August, 1865. Captain, 19 January, 1871. Commodore, 13 January, 1879. Rear-Admiral, 1 March, 1884. Retired List, 2 November, 1884.
PHELPS, THOMAS S., Jr.
Midshipman, 25 July, 1865. Graduated June, 1869. Ensign, 12 July, 1870. Master, 29 October, 1872. Lieutenant, 15 March, 1876. Lieutenant-Commander, 7 November, 1897.
PHELPS, WILLIAM W.
Naval Cadet, 19 May, 1885. Ensign, 1 July, 1891. Lieutenant, Junior Grade, 9 December, 1898. Lieutenant, 3 March, 1899.
PHENIX, DAWSON.
Midshipman, 30 September, 1841. Passed Midshipman, 10 August, 1847. Master, 14 September, 1855. Lieutenant, 15 September, 1855. Lieutenant-Commander, 16 July, 1862. Died 20 February, 1864.
PHENIX, LLOYD.
Acting Midshipman, 24 September, 1857. Midshipman, 1 June, 1861. Acting Master, 18 September, 1861. Lieutenant, 16 July, 1862. Resigned 27 June, 1865.
PHILBRICK, GEORGE.
Mate, 25 June, 1861. Appointment revoked (sick) 3 May, 1862.
PHILBRICK, HENRY R.
Carpenter, 8 July, 1861. Resigned 14 March, 1866. Carpenter, 12 November, 1869. Retired List, 11 October, 1889.
PHILBRICK, JOHN J.
Acting Assistant Paymaster, 23 January, 1862. Assistant Paymaster, 9 March, 1865. Resigned 28 June, 1866.
PHILIP, J. V. N.
Midshipman, 25 February, 1841. Master, 18 April, 1855. Lieutenant, 14 September, 1855. Resigned 26 June, 1857. Acting Lieutenant, 14 May, 1861. Died 3 September, 1862.
PHILIP, JOHN W.
Acting Midshipman, 20 September, 1856. Midshipman, 1 June, 1861. Acting Master, 9 July, 1862. Lieutenant, 16 July, 1862. Lieutenant-Commander, 25 July, 1866. Commander, 18 December, 1874. Captain, 31 March, 1889. Commodore, 10 August, 1898. Rear-Admiral, 3 March, 1899. Died 30 June, 1900.
PHILIPS, ABRAHAM.
Midshipman, 8 June, 1812. Drowned 15 April, 1813.
PHILIPS, DAVID S.
Boatswain, 19 July, 1837. Last appearance on Records of Navy Department.
PHILIPS, ISAAC.
Captain, 3 July, 1798. Dismissed 10 January, 1799.
PHILIPS, JOSEPH P.
Acting Third Assistant Engineer, 13 September, 1864. Resigned (sick) 3 January, 1865.
PHILIPS, SAMUEL.
Carpenter, 24 May, 1821. Died 9 October, 1839.
PHILIPS, WESLEY, J.
Acting Third Assistant Engineer, 7 October, 1863. Honorably discharged 8 January, 1866.
PHILIPS, WILLIAM A.
Acting First Assistant Engineer, 20 September, 1864. Honorably discharged 11 May, 1868.
PHILLIBER, JAMES C.
Mate, 11 June, 1863. Dismissed 4 September, 1863.
PHILLIPPI, EDWIN T.
Third Assistant Engineer, 20 May, 1862. Second Assistant Engineer, 15 February, 1864. First Assistant Engineer, 1 January, 1868. Retired List, 21 June, 1884.
PHILLIPS, ADRIAN.
Acting Ensign, Admiral Farragut's Staff, 29 March, 1865. Honorably discharged 16 July, 1866.
PHILLIPS, C. H.
Mate, 30 December, 1861. Appointment revoked 4 June, 1862.
PHILLIPS, CHARLES L.
Midshipman, 21 February, 1863. Graduated June, 1866. Ensign, 12 March, 1868. Dismissed 3 September, 1868.
PHILLIPS, CHARLES L.
Acting Warrant Machinist, 6 July, 1899.
PHILLIPS, DINWIDDIE B.
Assistant Surgeon, 8 November, 1847. Resigned 6 May, 1861.
PHILLIPS, FREDERICK H. R.
Acting Assistant Surgeon, 10 March, 1865. Honorably discharged 27 August, 1866.
PHILLIPS, GEORGE W.
Gunner, 20 July, 1898.
PHILLIPS, HENRY WRIGHT.
Third Assistant Engineer, 19 February, 1862. Second Assistant Engineer, 15 October, 1863. Resigned 28 July, 1869.

GENERAL NAVY REGISTER. 435

PHILLIPS, JAMES.
Acting Assistant Surgeon, 6 December, 1863. Honorably discharged 30 June, 1879.
PHILLIPS, JAMES D.
Acting Master, without pay, 6 September, 1861. Appointment revoked 23 February, 1863.
PHILLIPS, JAMES S.
Assistant Paymaster, 21 October, 1882. Passed Assistant Paymaster, 26 September, 1893. Paymaster, 15 March, 1898.
PHILLIPS, JOHN.
Midshipman, 16 January 1809. Resigned 27 April, 1812.
PHILLIPS, JOHN A.
Acting Master, 6 April, 1863. Appointment revoked (sick) 9 June, 1864. Acting Master and Pilot, 15 June, 1864. Appointment revoked 7 November, 1864.
PHILLIPS, MANUEL.
Assistant Surgeon, 18 July, 1809. Resigned 19 February, 1824.
PHILLIPS, SAMUEL.
Lieutenant, 4 March, 1799. Discharged 1 May, 1801, under Peace Establishment Act.
PHILLIPS, SELDEN J.
Mate, 25 November, 1863. Appointment revoked (sick) 23 June, 1864.
PHILLIPS, WILLIAM E.
Acting Ensign, 6 October, 1862. Appointment revoked (sick) 18 February, 1863.
PHILLIPS, WILLIAM L.
Third Assistant Engineer, 3 May, 1859. Resigned 6 July, 1860.
PHILLIPS, WILLIAM W.
Acting Ensign, 30 May, 1864. Resigned 22 May, 1865.
PHILP, JOHN.
Chief Engineer (Spanish-American War), 15 June, 1898. Honorably discharged 2 September, 1898.
PHINNEY, ALVIN.
Acting Master, 22 October, 1861. Acting Volunteer Lieutenant, 20 July, 1864. Honorably discharged 7 February, 1866. Acting Master, 5 April, 1867. Mustered out 7 October, 1868.
PHIPPS, DAVID.
Lieutenant, 2 July, 1798. Discharged 15 April, 1801, under Peace Establishment Act.
PHIPPS, DAVID.
Master, 1 June, 1801. Died in April, 1825.
PHIPPS, FRANCIS H.
Acting Ensign, 10 January, 1863. Honorably discharged 12 May, 1866.
PHIPPS, GARDNER E.
Mate, 21 December, 1862. Resigned 24 November, 1863.
PHIPPS, JOHN A., Jr.
Acting Ensign, 6 July, 1864. Honorably discharged 18 September, 1865.
PHYFFE, WILLIAM.
Mate, 18 October, 1864. Honorably discharged 19 September, 1865.
PHYTHIAN, ROBERT L.
Acting Midshipman, 28 January, 1853. Midshipman, 20 June, 1856. Passed Midshipman, 29 April, 1859. Master, 5 September, 1859. Lieutenant, 25 December, 1860. Lieutenant-Commander, 16 July, 1862. Commander, 13 July, 1870. Captain, 15 November, 1881. Commodore, 7 September, 1894. Retired List, 21 July, 1897.
PICK, AUGUSTUS T.
Assistant Surgeon, 25 February, 1867. Died 29 August, 1867.
PICK, JOHN.
Acting Second Assistant Engineer, 27 February, 1862. Resigned (sick) 9 August, 1864.
PICKERING, CHARLES W.
Midshipman, 1 May, 1822. Passed Midshipman, 10 June, 1833. Lieutenant, 8 December, 1838. Commander, 14 September, 1855. Captain, 16 July, 1862. Retired List, 1 February, 1867. Commodore on Retired List, 8 December, 1867. Died 29 February, 1888.
PICKERING, HORACE F.
Mate, 1 February, 1865. Resigned 24 June, 1865.
PICKERING, MARCELLUS C.
Mate, 11 June, 1863. Resigned 26 December, 1863.
PICKERING, T., Jr.
Midshipman, 17 June, 1799. Resigned 2 May, 1801.
PICKERING, THOMAS.
Acting Master, 11 May, 1861. Acting Volunteer Lieutenant, 22 August, 1863. Dismissed 8 June, 1865.
PICKETT, JAMES C.
Midshipman, 4 June, 1812. Entered the Army, 1813.
PICKETT, RICHARD.
Midshipman, 30 November, 1814. Resigned 7 January, 1819.
PICKING, HENRY F.
Acting Midshipman, 28 September, 1857. Midshipman, 1 June, 1861. Acting Master, 3 June, 1861. Lieutenant, 16 July, 1862. Lieutenant-Commander, 25 July, 1866. Commander, 25 January, 1875. Captain, 4 August, 1889. Commodore, 22 November, 1898. Rear-Admiral, 3 March, 1899. Died 8 September, 1899.
PICKINS, JOSEPH.
Boatswain, 21 April, 1819. Last appearance on Records of Navy Department.
PICKLES, STANLEY H.
Mate, 10 May, 1864. Honorably discharged 17 September, 1865.

PICKRELL, GEORGE.
Assistant Surgeon, 16 January, 1888. Passed Assistant Surgeon, 16 January, 1891. Surgeon, 19 September, 1899.
PICKRELL, JAMES McCALL.
Cadet Engineer, Naval Academy, 1 October, 1874. Graduated 10 June, 1879. Assistant Engineer, 10 June, 1881. Passed Assistant Engineer, 16 May, 1892. Rank changed to Lieutenant, 3 March, 1899.
PIDGSON, JOHN.
Mate, 11 October, 1861. Appointment revoked (sick) 26 February, 1862.
PIEPMEYER, LOUIS W.
Midshipman, 22 September, 1871. Graduated 20 June, 1876. Ensign, 3 March, 1879. Lieutenant, Junior Grade, 4 February, 1886. Died 21 May, 1888.
PIERCE, ABEL B.
Assistant Paymaster, 20 May, 1898.
PIERCE, ALLEN W.
Acting Ensign, 4 October, 1864. Honorably discharged 23 April, 1867.
PIERCE, CHARLES.
Midshipman, 1 August, 1827. Resigned 30 May, 1834.
PIERCE, CHARLES F.
Boatswain, 7 May, 1889. Chief Boatswain, 7 May, 1899.
PIERCE, CHARLES J.
Mate, 7 June, 1864. Acting Ensign, 8 May, 1865. Resigned 23 June, 1866.
PIERCE, GEORGE.
Midshipman, 15 June, 1799. Last appearance on Records of Navy Department.
PIERCE, GRANVILLE T.
Purser, 3 November, 1858. Dismissed 4 September, 1862.
PIERCE, HENRY L.
Acting Ensign, 22 September, 1864. Honorably discharged 27 June, 1865.
PIERCE, HENRY M.
Acting Ensign, 19 August, 1862. Acting Master, 27 May, 1864. Honorably discharged 13 September, 1865.
PIERCE, JOHN, Jr.
Professor, 9 October, 1838. Dropped 4 September, 1848.
PIERCE, JOSEPH.
Master, 22 May, 1813. Resigned 21 February, 1814.
PIERCE, NORVAL H.
Passed Assistant Surgeon (Spanish-American War), 14 May, 1898. Honorably discharged 30 September, 1898.
PIERCE, SAMUEL.
Sailmaker, 28 April, 1809. Last appearance on Records of Navy Department, 1815. Frigate United States.
PIERCY, WILLIAM M.
Acting Third Assistant Engineer, 17 May, 1864. Honorably discharged 29 September, 1865.
PIERCY, WILLIAM P.
Midshipman, 15 March, 1815. Lieutenant, 28 April, 1826. Commander, 29 March, 1844. Died 14 July, 1847.
PIERCY, WILLIAM P.
Midshipman, 16 January, 1809. Resigned 5 May, 1813.
PIERPONT, W. C.
Midshipman, 20 June, 1806. Last appearance on Records of Navy Department, 27 May, 1811. Dead.
PIERRUCCI, CELSO.
Acting Assistant Surgeon, 10 September, 1861. Resigned 5 June, 1863.
PIERSON, ABRAHAM B.
Acting Master, 28 December, 1861. Resigned 3 May, 1864.
PIERSON, EDWARD A.
Assistant Surgeon, 24 January, 1862. Killed in action 22 May, 1863.
PIERSON, WILLIAM H.
Acting Assistant Surgeon, 18 August, 1862. Acting Passed Assistant Surgeon, 18 May, 1865. Honorably discharged 12 January, 1869.
PIGMAN, GEORGE W.
Midshipman, 28 September, 1861. Graduated November, 1864. Ensign, 1 November, 1866. Master, 1 December, 1866. Lieutenant, 12 March, 1868. Lieutenant-Commander, 28 October, 1869. Commander, 7 October, 1886. Captain, 3 March, 1899.
PIGOTT, MICHAEL R.
Naval Cadet, 6 September, 1883. Honorably discharged 30 June, 1889. Assistant Surgeon, 22 May, 1891. Passed Assistant Surgeon, 22 May, 1894.
PIGMAN, GEORGE W., Jr.
Assistant Paymaster, 13 January, 1900.
PIKE, BOAZ E.
Third Assistant Engineer, 8 December, 1862. Resigned 6 April, 1864.
PIKE, CHARLES A.
Acting Ensign, 24 June, 1863. Honorably discharged 12 November, 1865.
PIKE, E. B.
Acting Master, 28 April, 1864. Resigned 6 May, 1865.
PITCHER, LEWIS S.
Assistant Surgeon, 14 May, 1867. Passed Assistant Surgeon, 24 June, 1870. Resigned 5 January, 1872.
PILE, CHARLES H.
Assistant Surgeon, 9 May, 1861. Died 23 December, 1862.
PILKINGTON, HUGH LOWELL.
Third Assistant Engineer, 27 June, 1862. Second Assistant Engineer, 21 November, 1863. Resigned 27 June, 1872.

GENERAL NAVY REGISTER. 437

PILLSBURY, JOHN E.
　Midshipman, 22 September, 1862. Graduated June, 1867. Ensign, 18 December, 1868. Master, 21 March, 1870. Lieutenant, 1 January, 1872. Lieutenant-Commander, 1 July, 1892. Commander, 10 August, 1898.
PILSBURY, WINGATE.
　Midshipman, 9 September, 1841. Drowned July, 1846.
PIMBLETT, THOMAS.
　Acting Second Assistant Engineer, 4 November, 1861. Deserted February, 1863.
PINCKNEY, EDWARD C.
　Midshipman, 21 November, 1815. Resigned 9 October, 1824.
PINCKNEY, RICHARD S.
　Midshipman, 3 August, 1814. Lieutenant, 13 January, 1825. Commander, 8 September, 1841. Died 9 July, 1854.
PINCKNEY, ROBERT H.
　Lieutenant (Spanish-American War), 7 June, 1898. Honorably discharged 15 September, 1898.
PINDAR, THOMAS.
　Mate, 26 February, 1864. Honorably discharged 22 April, 1867.
PINDELL, WILLIAM N.
　Acting Assistant Surgeon, 19 February, 1862. Honorably discharged 16 December, 1865.
PINDER, BENJAMIN.
　Master, 24 April, 1812. Dismissed 2 April, 1814.
PINDER, THOMAS.
　Midshipman, 1 January, 1818. Last appearance on Records of Navy Department, 20 February, 1818.
PINGREE, JOHN A.
　Acting Third Assistant Engineer, 17 June, 1862. Resigned 18 July, 1863.
PINKHAM, A. B.
　Midshipman, 17 June, 1814. Lieutenant, 13 June, 1825. Commander, 8 September, 1841. Died 23 July, 1843.
PINKHAM, R. R.
　Midshipman, 1 January, 1818. Lieutenant, 3 March, 1827. Died 27 October, 1839.
PINKERTON, JAMES.
　Gunner, 6 June, 1803. Dismissed 17 April, 1807.
PINKNEY, HENRY.
　Midshipman, 30 November, 1818. Lieutenant, 3 March, 1827. Commander, 25 February, 1847. Drowned 15 May, 1848.
PINKNEY, NINIAN.
　Assistant Surgeon, 26 March, 1834. Surgeon, 27 October, 1841. Medical Director, 3 March, 1871. Died 15 December, 1877.
PINKNEY, ROBERT F.
　Midshipman, 1 December, 1827. Passed Mdshipman, 10 June, 1833. Lieutenant, 28 February, 1838. Commander, 14 September, 1855. Resigned 23 April, 1861.
PINNER, JOSIAH D.
　Carpenter, 11 December, 1860. Lost on the Oneida, 24 January, 1870.
PINNEY, FRANK L.
　Naval Cadet, 6 September, 1894. Ensign, 4 April, 1900.
PINNEY, MARTIN.
　Mate, 14 May, 1864. Honorably discharged 2 December, 1865.
PINNEY, PETER.
　Midshipman, 4 July, 1805. Resigned 14 September, 1807.
PIPER, CHARLES H.
　Midshipman, 7 November, 1833. Resigned 8 January, 1839.
PIPER, FERDINAND.
　Midshipman, 1 November, 1827. Passed Midshipman, 10 June, 1833. Lieutenant, 7 December, 1839. Drowned 28 October, 1844.
PISHON, HENRY M.
　Mate, 13 October, 1863. Acting Ensign, 26 November, 1864. Honorably discharged 10 November, 1865.
PITCHER, M. S.
　Midshipman, 13 March, 1829. Passed Midshipman, 3 July, 1835. Resigned 24 January, 1839.
PITKIN, HENRY S.
　Assistant Surgeon, 18 July, 1862. Passed Assistant Surgeon, 30 October, 1865. Surgeon, 28 December, 1872. Died 23 June, 1874.
PITMAN, HENRY.
　Acting Master, 12 August, 1861. Resigned 26 April, 1862.
PITMAN, JOHN H.
　Mate, 4 October, 1861. Resigned 23 August, 1864.
PITT, JOHN.
　Midshipman, 18 May, 1809. Resigned 17 June, 1810.
PITTALUGA, LOUIS.
　Acting Third Assistant Engineer, 28 February, 1865. Resigned 7 June, 1865.
PITTS, SAMUEL.
　Midshipman, 16 January, 1809. Resigned 18 November, 1811.
PITTS, WILLIAM G.
　Acting Ensign, 12 July, 1864. Honorably discharged 28 October, 1865.
PIXLEY, ANDREW J.
　Acting Third Assistant Engineer, 23 May, 1864. Resigned 23 June, 1865.
PLACE, CHARLES W.
　Midshipman, 10 February, 1838. Passed Midshipman, 20 May, 1844. **Master,** 7 April, 1852. Lieutenant, 21 February, 1853. Died 9 January, 1859.

GENERAL NAVY REGISTER.

PLACE, EDWARD N. K.
Mate, 8 September, 1863. Honorably discharged 16 September, 1865.
PLACE, JOSHUA B.
Acting Third Assistant Engineer, 13 November, 1862. Acting Second Assistant Engineer, 8 September, 1864. Honorably discharged 31 August, 1865.
PLAISTED, CHARLES W.
Acting Third Assistant Engineer, 28 August, 1863. Honorably discharged 7 August, 1865.
PLANDER, G. E.
Mate, 22 June, 1866. Resigned 1 March, 1867.
PLANDER, JOHN E.
Mate, 4 January, 1864. Honorably discharged 8 January, 1866.
PLANT, JOSEPH F.
Acting Third Assistant Engineer, 19 October, 1863. Resigned 6 January, 1864.
PLANT, WILLIAM T.
Assistant Surgeon, 24 January, 1862. Resigned 4 October, 1865.
PLATT, CHARLES T.
Midshipman, 18 June, 1812. Lieutenant, 28 March, 1820. Commander, 8 September, 1841. Reserved List, 13 September, 1855. Died 12 December, 1860.
PLATT, GEORGE W.
Mate, 22 June, 1863. Acting Ensign, 21 November, 1863. Dismissed 15 November, 1864.
PLATT, JOHN H.
Acting Master, 1 April, 1862. Honorably discharged 1 November, 1865.
PLATT, RICHARD S.
Midshipman, 22 March, 1819. Died 9 July, 1822.
PLATT, ROBERT.
Acting Master, 1 March, 1863. Master, not in line of promotion, 15 June, 1878. Lieutenant, Junior Grade, 3 March, 1883. (Not in line of promotion.)
PLATT, THOMAS.
Boatswain, 9 November, 1798. Last appearance on Records of Navy Department.
PLATT, WILLIAM H.
Acting Third Assistant Engineer, 24 March, 1865. Honorably discharged 3 June, 1869. Second Assistant Engineer, 7 June, 1870. Retired List, 3 November, 1877.
PLATTENBURY, CYRUS B.
Mate, 3 October, 1863. Acting Ensign, 2 November, 1864. Honorably discharged 5 August, 1865.
PLEADWELL, FRANK L.
Assistant Surgeon, 24 October, 1896. Passed Assistant Surgeon, 24 October, 1899.
PLEASANTON, JOHN H.
Midshipman, 4 July, 1817. Died 7 September, 1825.
PLOTTS, REZEAU B.
Third Assistant Engineer, 1 July, 1861. Second Assistant Engineer, 18 December, 1862. Retired 16 January, 1866. First Assistant Engineer on Retired List, 25 July, 1866.
PLUMER, THOMAS H.
Mate, 9 December, 1863. Resigned 29 March, 1865.
PLUMLEY, JOHN L.
Third Assistant Engineer, 3 May, 1859. Resigned 29 August, 1860.
PLUMMER, EDWARD C.
Assistant Paymaster (Spanish-American War), 28 June, 1898. Honorably discharged 21 November, 1898.
PLUMMER, JONES W.
Assistant Surgeon, 20 June, 1829. Surgeon, 20 February, 1838. Died 20 August, 1859.
PLUMMER, RALPH W.
Assistant Surgeon, 17 June, 1899.
PLUMMER, SAMUEL.
Midshipman, 20 June, 1799. Master, 18 August, 1800. Discharged 18 June, 1801, under Peace Establishment Act.
PLUMSTEAD, WILLIAM.
Assistant Surgeon, 13 May, 1825. Surgeon, 4 December, 1828. Died 17 April, 1839.
PLUNKETT, CHARLES P.
Cadet Midshipman, 3 October, 1879. Ensign, 1 July, 1886. Lieutenant, Junior Grade, 5 November, 1895. Lieutenant, 15 November, 1898.
PLUNKETT, FRANK.
Assistant Paymaster, 25 September, 1875. Passed Assistant Paymaster, 4 December, 1879. Dismissed 14 October, 1881.
PLUNKETT, GEORGE.
Assistant Paymaster, 10 October, 1861. Paymaster, 6 February, 1862. Resigned 25 August, 1868. Reinstated 2 April, 1872. Died 24 October, 1874.
PLUNKETT, JAMES.
Third Assistant Engineer, 3 May, 1859. Resigned 6 February, 1861.
PLUNKETT, JAMES T.
Acting Third Assistant Engineer, 21 July, 1863. Acting Second Assistant Engineer, 4 April, 1864. Resigned 19 August, 1865.
PLUNKETT, J. L.
Mate, 12 May, 1860. Acting Master, 19 June, 1862. Honorably discharged 17 November, 1865. Mate, 26 January, 1867. Mustered out 8 September, 1868. Mate, 30 September, 1869. Appointment revoked 7 November, 1870.
PLUNKETT, M. H.
Third Assistant Engineer, 21 July, 1858. Second Assistant Engineer, 21 September, 1861. Resigned 9 May, 1865.

GENERAL NAVY REGISTER. 439

PLUNKETT, THOMAS S.
    Midshipman, 21 June, 1867. Graduated 7 June, 1871. Ensign, 14 July, 1872. Master, 9 September, 1876. Drowned 31 January, 1882.
PLURIGHT, WILLIAM.
    Master, 23 July, 1812. Resigned 10 April, 1815.
PLYMPTON, G. M.
    Third Assistant Engineer, 14 September, 1853. Resigned 19 December, 1854.
PLYMPTON, HENRY L.
    Acting Assistant Surgeon, 25 March, 1863. Assistant Surgeon, 28 April, 1863. Died 25 September, 1863.
POESSEL, LEWIS.
    Assistant Paymaster (Spanish-American War), 24 September, 1898. Honorably discharged 20 June, 1899.
POINDEXTER, CARTER B.
    Midshipman, 16 November, 1831. Passed Midshipman, 15 June, 1837. Lieutenant, 8 September, 1841. Dismissed 18 April, 1861.
POINSETT, ASA.
    Carpenter, 11 December, 1847. Died 14 September, 1859.
POLEN, GEORGE B.
    Acting Second Assistant Engineer, 6 June, 1864. Honorably discharged 20 June, 1865.
POLK, DANIEL.
    Midshipman, 16 March, 1799. Resigned 24 January, 1804.
POLK, G. W. M. R.
    Assistant Surgeon, 30 October, 1800. Resigned 8 December, 1800.
POLK, JOHN.
    Midshipman, 5 December, 1799. Lost in the Insurgent.
POLK, WILLIAM W.
    Master, 18 July, 1814. Resigned 27 July, 1825.
POLLARD, JAMES.
    Acting Third Assistant Engineer, 27 May, 1861. Acting Second Assistant Engineer, 20 July, 1863. Honorably discharged 30 October, 1865.
POLLARD, ROBERT.
    Midshipman, 15 November, 1809. Resigned 20 November, 1811.
POLLARD, WILLIAM.
    Midshipman, 8 March, 1814. Resigned 8 January, 1824.
POLLARD, WILLIAM.
    Third Assistant Engineer, 17 February, 1860. Appointment revoked 24 January, 1862. Reappointed in original position, 5 July, 1862. Second Assistant Engineer, 25 August, 1862. Dismissed 18 October, 1867.
POLLARD, WILLIAM H.
    Acting Third Assistant Engineer, 8 September, 1864. Resigned 5 June, 1865.
POLLEY, JAMES H.
    Master's Mate, 3 May, 1843. Boatswain, 27 February, 1846. Deserted September, 1850.
POLLEY, JAMES H.
    Boatswain, 20 June, 1861. Died 13 April, 1866.
POLLEYS, WOODBURY H.
    Acting Master, 29 October, 1861. Resigned 21 April, 1864.
POLLOCK, ALEXANDER.
    Acting Third Assistant Engineer, 27 May, 1861. Resigned 9 August, 1862.
POLLOCK, DAVID J.
    Acting Third Assistant Engineer, 10 September, 1861. Resigned 9 September, 1862.
POLLOCK, EDWIN T.
    Naval Cadet, 20 May, 1887. Ensign, 1 July, 1893. Lieutenant, Junior Grade, 3 March, 1899. Lieutenant, 9 September, 1899.
POLLOCK, EMMET R.
    Naval Cadet, 18 May, 1888. Assistant Engineer, 1 July, 1895. Passed Assistant Engineer, 28 February, 1899. Rank changed to Lieutenant, Junior Grade, 3 March, 1899.
POLLOCK, JOHN.
    Acting Third Assistant Engineer, 13 February, 1865. Honorably discharged 1 August, 1865.
POLLOCK, MATTHEW V.
    Acting Carpenter, 10 January, 1900.
POLLOCK, SAMUEL H.
    Mate, 19 June, 1862. Acting Ensign, 22 August, 1863. Honorably discharged 18 September, 1865.
POLLOCK, THOMAS.
    Master, 1 November, 1816. Resigned 5 January, 1819.
POLLOCK, WILLIAM W.
    Midshipman, 30 June, 1837. Passed Midshipman, 29 June, 1843. Dropped 15 December, 1847.
POLLOCK, W. WINDOR.
    Midshipman, 30 June, 1837. Passed Midshipman, 29 June, 1843. Master, 5 November, 1850. Lieutenant, 15 July, 1851. Dismissed 19 January, 1863.
POMEROY, G. P.
    Acting Ensign, 26 September, 1862. Acting Master, 14 July, 1863. Honorably discharged 10 November, 1865.
POMEROY, ARMISTEAD.
    Boatswain, 13 September, 1852. Dismissed 17 January, 1857. Boatswain, 27 February, 1858. Retired List, 22 January, 1885. Died 28 February, 1890.
POMROY, JOSEPH R.
    Third Assistant Engineer, 14 August, 1851. Dropped 20 December, 1852.

POND, CHARLES F.
Midshipman, 12 June, 1872. Graduated 20 June, 1876. Ensign, 11 July, 1878. Lieutenant, Junior Grade, 2 October, 1885. Lieutenant, 19 May, 1891. Lieutenant-Commander, 1 July, 1899.
POND, COLLIS T.
Mate. Resigned 11 March, 1862.
PONTE, JOHN.
Mate, 16 April, 1865. Honorably discharged 2 April, 1869.
POOK, SAMUEL H.
Assistant Naval Constructor, 17 May, 1866. Naval Constructor, 15 April, 1871. Retired List, 17 January, 1889.
POOK, SAMUEL M.
Naval Constructor, 1 January, 1841. Retired List, 15 August, 1866. Died 2 December, 1878.
POOK, WILLIAM.
Carpenter, date not known   Discharged in 1820.
POOL, ADDISON.
Acting Assistant Paymaster, 17 December, 1861. Appointment revoked (sick) 8 January, 1862. Acting Assistant Paymaster, 27 January, 1862. Honorably discharged 1 May, 1865.
POOL, SYLVESTER.
Acting Ensign, 1 October, 1862. Died 26 April, 1864.
POOLE, FRANCIS H.
Mate, 21 September, 1863. Died 4 December, 1886.
POOLE, ISAAC.
Acting Assistant Surgeon, 23 November, 1863. Resigned 13 May, 1865.
POOLE, LEMUEL G.
Acting Third Assistant Engineer, 13 December, 1864. Resigned 5 July, 1865.
POOLE, L. W.
Mate, 30 November, 1867. Mustered out 2 October, 1868.
POOLE, SAMUEL.
Midshipman, 30 June, 1799. Resigned 3 September, 1800.
POOR, ALBERT B.
Acting Assistant Paymaster, 26 August, 1861. Mustered out 4 September, 1865.
POOR, CHARLES H.
Midshipman, 1 March, 1825. Passed Midshipman, 4 June, 1831. Lieutenant, 22 December, 1835. Commander, 14 September, 1855. Captain, 16 July, 1862. Commodore, 2 January, 1863. Rear-Admiral, 20 September, 1868. Retired List, 9 June, 1870. Died 5 November 1882.
POOR, CHARLES H.
Mate, 10 August, 1863. Resigned 29 June, 1865.
POOR, CHARLES L.
Naval Cadet, 6 September, 1892. Ensign, 6 May, 1898.
POPE, EZRA P.
Mate, 28 September, 1864. Resigned 14 July, 1865.
POPE, JOHN.
Midshipman, 30 May, 1816. Lieutenant, 28 April, 1826. Commander, 15 February, 1843. Captain, 14 September, 1855. Retired List, 21 December, 1861. Commodore on Retired List, 16 July, 1862. Died 14 January, 1876.
POPE, LEMUEL.
Mate, 26 June, 1862. Acting Ensign, 11 February, 1864. Acting Master, 18 July, 1865. Honorably discharged 28 February, 1866.
POPE, RALPH E.
Naval Cadet, 20 May, 1895. At sea prior to final graduation.
POPE, ROBERT G.
Acting Second Assistant Engineer, 26 February, 1862. Acting First Assistant Engineer, 9 June, 1864. Honorably discharged 20 November, 1865.
POPE, WILLIAM.
Midshipman, 2 February, 1829. Passed Midshipman, 4 June, 1836. Resigned 19 June, 1839.
POPEJOY, JAMES P.
Mate, 4 September, 1864. Honorably discharged 26 October, 1865.
POPLAR, CHARLES.
Acting Carpenter, 4 January, 1863. Appointment revoked (sick), 21 June, 1864.
POPPLESTON, J. H.
Midshipman, 25 April, 1831. Resigned 19 September, 1832.
PORCHER, PHILIP.
Midshipman, 9 June, 1855. Passed Midshipman, 15 April, 1858. Master, 4 November, 1858. Lieutenant, 27 April, 1860. Resigned 2 February, 1861.
PORTEOUS, JAMES.
Mate, 27 March, 1863. Died on Niphon, 11 September, 1863.
PORTER, ABEL K.
Acting Third Assistant Engineer, 15 June, 1864. Honorably discharged 4 November, 1865.
PORTER, ALEXANDER F.
Midshipman, 19 March, 1819. Died 11 February, 1827.
PORTER, BENJAMIN H.
Acting Midshipman, 1 December, 1859. Ensign, 8 November, 1862. Lieutenant, 22 February, 1864. Killed in attack upon Fort Fisher, 15 January, 1865.
PORTER, CARLISLE P.
Acting Midshipman, 27 September, 1861. Resigned 18 January, 1864.
PORTER, CHARLES.
Mate, 28 November, 1863. Discharged 29 August, 1864.

GENERAL NAVY REGISTER. 441

PORTER, CYRUS K.
Acting Ensign, 22 February, 1864. Honorably discharged 20 October, 1865.
PORTER, DANIEL G.
Mate, 21 May, 1864. Honorably discharged 12 October, 1865.
PORTER, DAVID.
Midshipman, 16 April, 1798. Lieutenant, 8 October, 1799. Commander, 22 April, 1806. Captain, 2 July, 1812. Resigned 18 August, 1826.
PORTER, DAVID, Jr.
Master, 3 September, 1807. Last appearance on Records of Navy Department, 1 March, 1808.
PORTER, DAVID D.
Midshipman, 2 February, 1829. Passed Midshipman, 3 July, 1835. Lieutenant, 27 February, 1841. Commander, 22 April, 1861. Rear-Admiral, 4 July, 1863. Vice-Admiral, 25 July, 1866. Admiral, 15 August, 1870. Died 13 February, 1891.
PORTER, DAVID H.
Midshipman, 4 August, 1814. Lieutenant, 13 January, 1825. Resigned 26 July, 1826.
PORTER, DAVID V.
Mate, 19 November, 1863. Died 29 December, 1863.
PORTER, EDWARD E.
Acting Third Assistant Engineer, 21 November, 1863. Honorably discharged 20 July, 1865.
PORTER, FREDERICK E.
Acting Second Assistant Engineer, 25 September, 1863. Acting First Assistant Engineer, 28 October, 1864. Honorably discharged 30 July, 1865.
PORTER, HAMILTON F.
Midshipman, 12 April, 1836. Passed Midshipman, 1 July, 1842. Died 10 August, 1844.
PORTER, HENRY O.
Acting Master, 24 April, 1862. Resigned 30 September, 1863. Acting Master, 5 August, 1864. Honorably discharged 15 August, 1865.
PORTER, HENRY O.
Midshipman, 3 November, 1840. Resigned 16 August, 1847.
PORTER, HERBERT G.
Mate (Spanish-American War), 27 July, 1898. Honorably discharged 10 October, 1898.
PORTER, JAMES.
Gunner, date not known. Last appearance on Records of Navy Department.
PORTER, JAMES H.
Mate, 23 January, 1862. Acting Ensign, 23 August, 1862. Acting Master, 9 November, 1864. Honorably discharged 28 February, 1869.
PORTER, J. HAMPDEN.
Acting Assistant Surgeon, 17 October, 1861. Resigned 25 June, 1862.
PORTER, JAMES O.
Lieutenant (Spanish-American War), 14 May, 1898. Honorably discharged 1 December, 1898.
PORTER, JOHN.
Midshipman, 20 June, 1806. Lieutenant, 27 May, 1812. Commander, 28 March, 1820. Died 2 September, 1831.
PORTER, JOHN F.
Mate, 7 March, 1864. Honorably discharged 21 December, 1865.
PORTER, JOHN H.
Lieutenant (Spanish-American War), 25 May, 1898. Resigned 1 August, 1898.
PORTER, MAITLAND.
Mate, 7 June, 1862. Dismissed 26 November, 1862.
PORTER, MORTIMER S.
Acting Ensign, 1 March, 1864. Honorably discharged 21 October, 1865.
PORTER, PINKNEY J.
Midshipman, 6 March, 1848. Resigned 4 June, 1849.
PORTER, SIDNEY.
Carpenter, 29 August, 1837. Resigned 29 December, 1837.
PORTER, THEODORIC.
Midshipman, 20 September, 1865. Graduated 7 June, 1870. Ensign, 12 July, 1870. Master, 11 February, 1873. Lieutenant, 22 August, 1876. Lieutenant-Commander, 28 March, 1898.
PORTER, THOMAS K.
Acting Midshipman, 20 May, 1852. Midshipman, 20 June, 1856. Passed Midshipman, 29 April, 1859. Master, 5 September, 1859. Lieutenant, 24 January, 1861. Dismissed 18 July, 1861.
PORTER, WARREN.
Acting Ensign, 22 October, 1863. Acting Master, 8 November, 1864. Honorably discharged 23 August, 1865.
PORTER, WILLIAM B.
Lieutenant, Junior Grade (Spanish-American War), 8 June, 1898. Honorably discharged 2 September, 1898.
PORTER, WILLIAM C. B. S.
Midshipman, 29 July, 1835. Passed Midshipman, 22 June, 1841. Master, 17 June, 1848. Lieutenant, 25 March, 1849. Lost on the Levant, 18 September, 1860.
PORTER, WILLIAM D.
Midshipman, 1 January, 1823. Passed Midshipman, 29 March, 1829. Lieutenant, 31 December, 1833. Reserved List, 13 September, 1855. Commander on Active List, 14 September, 1855. Commodore, 16 July, 1862. Died 1 May, 1864.
POST, A. S.
Mate, 1 October, 1862. Resigned 24 February, 1864.
POST, CHARLES H.
Mate, 13 December, 1861. Resigned 27 February, 1863.

POST, GEORGE W.
  Mate, 29 June, 1864. Honorably discharged 20 February, 1866.
POST, JOEL A.
  Midshipman, 23 July, 1866. Graduated 7 June, 1870. Resigned 22 November, 1872.
POST, JUDSON S.
  Assistant Paymaster, 9 September, 1861. Assistant Paymaster, 6 February, 1862. Paymaster, 16 October, 1864. Dismissed 15 September, 1868.
POST, WILLIAM M.
  Acting Master, 22 November, 1861. Resigned 20 June, 1864.
POSTELL, WILLIAM R.
  Midshipman, 31 December, 1831. Passed Midshipman, 15 June, 1837. Resigned 14 June, 1839.
POSTELL, EDWARD.
  Midshipman, 30 November, 1814. Resigned 30 June, 1817.
POSTLETHWAIT, GEORGE W.
  Acting Third Assistant Engineer, 22 November, 1864. Resigned 15 June, 1865.
POTTER, CHARLES.
  Acting Master, 14 August, 1861. Resigned (sick) 30 March, 1865.
POTTER, CHARLES H.
  Mate, 23 December, 1862. Dismissed 19 March, 1863.
POTTER, DAVID.
  Assistant Paymaster, 18 February, 1898. Passed Assistant Paymaster, 3 March, 1899.
POTTER, DAVID T.
  Mate, 17 February, 1862. Dismissed 16 July, 1862.
POTTER, EDWARD E.
  Midshipman, 5 February, 1850. Passed Midshipman, 20 June, 1856. Master, 22 January, 1858. Lieutenant, 9 July, 1858. Lieutenant-Commander, 16 July, 1862. Commander, 3 June, 1869. Captain, 11 July, 1880. Commodore, 27 September, 1893. Retired List, 9 May, 1895.
POTTER, FREDERICK E.
  Assistant Surgeon, 30 July, 1861. Surgeon, 25 March, 1866. Resigned 1 April, 1875.
POTTER, GEORGE.
  Acting Third Assistant Engineer, 30 May, 1865. Honorably discharged 29 September, 1865.
POTTER, HENRY.
  Midshipman, 10 May, 1820. Resigned 27 May, 1824.
POTTER, JAMES B.
  Naval Cadet, 5 September, 1889. Graduated. Honorably discharged 30 June, 1895. Lieutenant (Spanish-American War), 25 May, 1898. Honorably discharged 17 September, 1898.
POTTER, JOHN H.
  Ensign (Spanish-American War), 12 July, 1898. Honorably discharged 30 December, 1898.
POTTER, JOSEPH.
  Mate, 8 November, 1869. Resigned 1 June, 1872.
POTTER, JOSEPH.
  Acting Gunner, 21 October, 1862. Dismissed 29 June, 1863.
POTTER, RICHARD M.
  Midshipman, 1 January, 1812. Lieutenant, 1 April, 1818. Died 11 August, 1823.
POTTER, ROBERT.
  Midshipman, 2 March, 1815. Resigned 26 March, 1821.
POTTER, SEYMOUR.
  Lieutenant, 15 August, 1800. Discharged 10 July, 1801, under Peace Establishment Act.
POTTER, THOMAS M.
  Assistant Surgeon, 17 October, 1839. Surgeon, 17 September, 1854. Medical Director, 3 March, 1871. Retired List, 12 August, 1876. Died 13 April, 1890.
POTTER, WILLIAM H.
  Acting Ensign, 30 December, 1863. Honorably discharged 2 August, 1865.
POTTER, WILLIAM H.
  Midshipman, 6 December, 1814. Resigned 8 June, 1819.
POTTER, WILLIAM P.
  Midshipman, 26 September, 1865. Graduated June, 1869. Ensign, 12 July, 1870. Master, 12 July, 1871. Lieutenant, 9 August, 1874. Lieutenant-Commander, 12 June, 1896. Commander, 9 September, 1899.
POTTENGER, CHARLES B.
  Mate, 21 October, 1861. Resigned 12 August, 1862.
POTTINGER, THOMAS.
  Midshipman, 1 January, 1812. Last appearance on Records of Navy Department.
POTTINGER, ROBERT.
  Purser, 16 July, 1825. Lost in the Hornet, 10 September, 1829.
POTTINGER, WILLIAM.
  Midshipman, 1 September, 1811. Lieutenant, 5 March, 1817. Died 5 February, 1833.
POTTS, HOWARD D.
  Third Assistant Engineer, 16 November, 1861. Second Assistant Engineer, 25 August, 1863. Retired 26 October, 1874
POTTS, JAMES.
  Boatswain, 3 July, 1799. Last appearance on Records of Navy Department.
POTTS, JAMES B.
  Master, 24 July, 1812. Died 8 May, 1839.
POTTS, JEREMIAH.
  Mate, 4 April, 1862. Acting Ensign, 28 May, 1863. Honorably discharged 17 November, 1867.

GENERAL NAVY REGISTER. 443

POTTS, JOSEPH H.
Acting Second Assistant Engineer, 6 April, 1864. Appointment revoked (sick) 20 March, 1865.
POTTS, RICHARD C.
Third Assistant Engineer, 15 November, 1847. Second Assistant Engineer, 26 February, 1851. First Assistant Engineer, 9 May, 1857. Name stricken from the Rolls 15 June, 1861.
POTTS, ROBERT.
Third Assistant Engineer, 17 February, 1860. Second Assistant Engineer, 27 June, 1862. First Assistant Engineer, 1 March, 1865. Chief Engineer, 22 January, 1873. Retired List, 8 May, 1897.
POTTS, STACY.
Cadet Engineer, Naval Academy, 1 October, 1872. Graduated 30 May, 1874. Assistant Engineer, 26 February, 1875. Passed Assistant Engineer, 12 October, 1881. Chief Engineer, 29 January, 1896. Rank changed to Lieutenant-Commander, 3 March, 1899.
POTTS, TEMPLIN M.
Midshipman, 6 June, 1872. Graduated 20 June, 1876. Ensign, 25 November, 1877. Lieutenant, Junior Grade, 9 February, 1884. Lieutenant, 28 February, 1890. Lieutenant-Commander, 3 March, 1899.
POTTS, WILLIAM P.
Midshipman, 9 June, 1811. Resigned 2 March, 1814.
POUGUET, ANDREW.
Master's Mate, date not known. Resigned in 1820.
POULSON, WILLIAM H.
Acting Third Assistant Engineer, 23 July, 1864. Honorably discharged 6 August, 1865.
POUNDSTONE, HOMER C.
Cadet Midshipman, 24 September, 1874. Graduated 10 June, 1880. Ensign, Junior Grade, 3 March, 1883. Ensign, 26 June, 1884. Lieutenant, Junior Grade, 1 July, 1892. Lieutenant, 4 July, 1896.
POWELL, ELI.
Acting Third Assistant Engineer, 22 June, 1863. Honorably discharged 4 November, 1865.
POWELL, HENRY T.
Assistant Engineer (Spanish-American War), 30 April, 1898. Honorably discharged 4 January, 1899.
POWELL, JOHN.
Mate, 1 October, 1862. Acting Ensign, 22 April, 1863. Acting Master, 18 January, 1864. Honorably discharged 15 November, 1865.
POWELL, JOHN B.
Acting Gunner, 1 September, 1864. Honorably discharged 31 December, 1865.
POWELL, JOSEPH W.
Naval Cadet, 19 May, 1893. Ensign, 28 June, 1898. Assistant Naval Constructor, 1 July, 1899.
POWELL, LEVIN M.
Midshipman, 1 March, 1817. Lieutenant, 28 April, 1826. Commander, 24 June, 1843. Captain, 14 September, 1855. Retired List, 21 December, 1861. Commodore on Retired List, 16 July, 1862. Rear-Admiral, Retired List, 13 May, 1869. Died 15 January, 1885.
POWELL, WILLIAM G.
Naval Cadet, 18 May, 1888. Resigned 6 May, 1889. Naval Cadet, 18 May, 1889. Graduated. Honorably discharged 30 June, 1895. Ensign (Spanish-American War), 14 May, 1898. Honorably discharged 21 November, 1898.
POWELL, WILLIAM E.
Carpenter, 12 December, 1898.
POWELL, WILLIAM J.
Assistant Surgeon, 8 February, 1832. Surgeon, 8 November, 1836. Died 7 February, 1848.
POWELL, WILLIAM J.
Acting Warrant Machinist, 23 August, 1899.
POWELL, WILLIAM L.
Midshipman, 20 September, 1841. Passed Midshipman, 10 August, 1847. Master, 10 July, 1855. Lieutenant, 14 September, 1855. Dismissed 20 April, 1861.
POWELSON, WILFRID V. N.
Naval Cadet, 5 September, 1889. Ensign, 1 July, 1895. Lieutenant, Junior Grade, 3 March, 1899.
POWER, ALEXANDER W.
Acting Third Assistant Engineer, 29 December, 1864. Honorably discharged 15 May, 1866.
POWER, DAVID T.
Acting Assistant Paymaster, 5 November, 1863. Mustered out 8 December, 1865.
POWER, EDWARD R.
Acting Ensign, 22 June, 1864. Honorably discharged 20 July, 1865.
POWER, JAMES T.
Master's Mate, 19 July, 1842. Died 20 August, 1853.
POWER, THOMAS.
Mate, 28 September, 1863. Appointment revoked (sick), 7 October, 1864.
POWER, WILLIAM T.
Acting Ensign, 1 October, 1862. Acting Master, 12 November, 1863. Honorably discharged 8 December, 1865.
POWERS, FRANK A.
Mate, 18 October, 1864. Resigned 22 May, 1865.

444 GENERAL NAVY REGISTER.

POWERS, HENRY P.
　Acting Second Assistant Engineer, 17 October, 1861. Honorably discharged 15 November, 1865.
POWERS, JAMES F.
　Acting Third Assistant Engineer, 5 August, 1861. Acting Second Assistant Engineer, 5 September, 1862. Honorably discharged 10 December, 1865.
POWERS, JOHN.
　Acting Second Assistant Engineer, 8 January, 1864. Honorably discharged 24 July, 1866.
POWERS, MANDEVILLE P.
　Acting Ensign, 14 December, 1864. Honorably discharged 2 December, 1867.
POWERS, ROBERT.
　Boatswain, 7 June, 1852. Resigned 16 December, 1852.
POWERS, WILLIAM AUGUSTUS.
　Third Assistant Engineer, 3 May, 1862. Resigned 3 March, 1866.
POWERS, WILLIAM J.
　Acting Master, 5 September, 1861. Appointment revoked (sick) 23 May, 1862.
POWLING, H. DEW.
　Assistant Surgeon, 4 April, 1831. Resigned 1 December, 1834.
POYER, JOHN M.
　Cadet Midshipman, 27 June, 1877. Ensign, 1 July, 1884. Lieutenant, Junior Grade, 11 November, 1894. Lieutenant, 8 April, 1898.
PRATT, ALFRED A.
　Naval Cadet, 7 September, 1889. Ensign, 1 July, 1895. Lieutenant, Junior Grade, 3 March, 1899.
PRATT, ANDREW.
　Mate, 18 January, 1870. Deserted 28 January, 1871.
PRATT, CHARLES W.
　Acting Master, 31 March, 1862. Honorably discharged 5 November, 1865.
PRATT, EDWIN B.
　Mate, 2 August, 1862. Acting Ensign, 27 May, 1863. Honorably discharged 29 January, 1866.
PRATT, GEORGE W.
　Mate, 22 October, 1862. Mustered out 1 May, 1869.
PRATT, HENRY C.
　Assistant Surgeon, 9 August, 1826. Died 10 March, 1828.
PRATT, JOHN B.
　Mate, 13 February, 1864. Acting Ensign, 31 October, 1864. Honorably discharged 31 October, 1865.
PRATT, JOHN J.
　Acting Assistant Paymaster, 6 August, 1861. Honorably discharged 30 October, 1865.
PRATT, LEONARD.
　Acting Third Assistant Engineer, 4 January, 1864. Honorably discharged 28 October, 1865.
PRATT, MAXWELL.
　Acting Third Assistant Engineer, 3 March, 1863. Appointment revoked 5 August, 1864.
PRATT, NICHOLS.
　Mate, 23 August, 1862. Acting Ensign, 2 November, 1863. Acting Master, 25 April, 1865. Honorably discharged 8 April, 1867.
PRATT, OSCAR H.
　Acting Master, 1 October, 1862. Died 13 December, 1863.
PRATT, PETER L.
　Naval Cadet, 19 May, 1893. Ensign, 1 July, 1899.
PRATT, SHUBAEL.
　Midshipman, 18 June, 1812. Last appearance on Records of Navy Department, 1815. Frigate Constitution.
PRATT, SPENCER.
　Acting Master, 1 November, 1861. Resigned 12 March, 1862.
PRATT, WILLIAM FENNELL.
　Third Assistant Engineer, 25 August, 1862. Second Assistant Engineer, 20 February, 1864. Resigned 29 July, 1865.
PRATT, WILLIAM F.
　Acting Master, 26 May, 1862. Honorably discharged 31 March, 1869.
PRATT, WILLIAM S.
　Acting Second Assistant Engineer, 20 July, 1864. Resigned 26 June, 1865.
PRATT, WILLIAM V.
　Naval Cadet, 9 September, 1855. Ensign, 1 July, 1891. Leutenant, Junior Grade, 10 August, 1898. Lieutenant, 3 March, 1899.
PRAY, CHARLES B.
　Acting Ensign, 31 December, 1862. Honorably discharged 16 December, 1865.
PRAY, EZRA.
　Acting Assistant Surgeon, 21 October, 1861. Acting Passed Assistant Surgeon, 4 August, 1865. Honorably discharged 1 March, 1866.
PRAY, JOHN H.
　Mate, 26 February, 1864. Resigned 24 June, 1865.
PRAY, RUEL B.
　Mate, 3 March, 1864. Acting Ensign, 21 March, 1864. Resigned 7 June, 1865.
PRAY, THOMAS J.
　Mate, 16 May, 1862. Resigned 29 June, 1864.
PREBLE, EDWARD.
　Lieutenant, 9 February, 1798. Captain, 15 May, 1799. Died 25 August, 1807.
PREBLE, EDWARD.
　Midshipman, 1 January, 1817. Drowned 20 March, 1822.

GENERAL NAVY REGISTER. 445

PREBLE, EDWARD E.
Active Midshipman, 29 November, 1859. Ensign, 9 August, 1864. Lieutenant, 22 February, 1864. Lieutenant-Commander, 25 July, 1866. Resigned 21 January, 1871.

PREBLE, FRANK H.
Carpenter, 21 December, 1897.

PREBLE, GEORGE H.
Midshipman, 10 October, 1835. Passed Midshipman, 22 June, 1841. Master, 15 July, 1847. Lieutenant, 5 February, 1848. Commander, 16 July, 1862. Captain, 29 January, 1867. Commodore, 2 November, 1871. Rear-Admiral, 30 September, 1876. Retired List, 25 February, 1878. Died 1 March, 1885.

PREDMORE, F.
Mate, 21 December, 1861. Last appearance on Records of Navy Department, 1 January, 1865.

PRENTISS, GEORGE A.
Midshipman, 1 March, 1825. Passed Midshipman, 4 June, 1831. Lieutenant, 9 February, 1837. Commander, 14 September, 1855. Retired List, 24 October, 1864. Commodore, Retired List. Died 8 April, 1868.

PRENTISS, JABEZ.
Master, 4 January, 1809. Last appearance on Records of Navy Department, 1815. Norfolk.

PRENTISS, JOHN, Jr.
Midshipman, 11 June, 1799. Resigned 27 January, 1800.

PRENTISS, JOHN E.
Midshipman, 9 November, 1813. Lieutenant, 13 January, 1825. Died 5 July, 1840.

PRENTISS, JOHN E.
Midshipman, 19 October, 1841. Died 31 December, 1843.

PRENTISS, NATHANIEL.
Master, 22 January, 1823. Died 20 April, 1852.

PRENTISS, NATHANIEL A.
Midshipman, 18 June, 1812. Last appearance on Records of Navy Department, 1812. Brig Prometheus.

PRENTISS, RODERICK.
Acting Midshipman, 21 September, 1854. Midshipman, 9 June, 1859. Lieutenant, 31 August, 1861. Died from wounds, 6 August, 1864.

PRENTISS, WILLIAM M.
Acting Third Assistant Engineer, 24 February, 1863. Honorably discharged 16 October, 1865.

PRESCOTT, CHARLES M.
Acting Third Assistant Engineer. Resigned (sick) 6 August, 1864.

PRESCOTT, GEORGE.
Acting Chief Engineer, 16 March, 1864. Resigned 20 October, 1864.

PRESCOTT, GEORGE H.
Mate, 9 August, 1864. Honorably discharged 11 August, 1866.

PRESCOTT, SAMUEL.
Midshipman, 30 June, 1799. Resigned 3 September, 1800.

PRESCOTT, WILLIAM A.
Mate, 26 September, 1862. Honorably discharged 7 November, 1865.

PRESSEY, ALFRED W.
Naval Cadet, 19 May, 1893. Ensign, 1 July, 1899.

PREST, EBENEZER.
Acting Third Assistant Engineer, 5 November, 1863. Honorably discharged 9 October, 1865.

PRESTON, CHARLES F.
Naval Cadet, 4 September, 1885. Resigned 17 June, 1887. Naval Cadet, 6 September, 1887. Ensign, 1 July, 1893. Lieutenant, Junior Grade, 3 March, 1899. Lieutenant, 18 February, 1900.

PRESTON, SAMUEL W.
Acting Midshipman, 4 October, 1858. Acting Master, 4 October, 1861. Lieutenant, 1 August, 1862. Killed in attack on Fort Fisher, 15 January, 1865.

PRESTON, VERNON F.
Warrant Machinist (Spanish-American War), 18 May, 1898. Honorably discharged 2 September, 1898.

PRESTON, WILLIAM M.
Assistant Paymaster, 4 November, 1869. Passed Assistant Paymaster, 1 July, 1875. Died 8 March, 1881.

PREVOST, AUGUSTUS W.
Midshipman, 1 November, 1828. Passed Midshipman, 14 June, 1834. Died 22 February, 1837.

PREVOST, B. B.
Midshipman, 30 July, 1799. Discharged 6 August, 1801, under Peace Establishment Act.

PREVOST, JAMES F.
Midshipman, 12 November, 1819. Died in 1829.

PRICE, ABEL F.
Assistant Surgeon, 10 November, 1868. Passed Assistant Surgeon, 27 March, 1873. Surgeon, 14 August, 1878. Medical Inspector, 30 March, 1895. Medical Director, 9 April, 1899.

PRICE, ALEXANDER H.
Third Assistant Engineer, 8 October, 1861. Second Assistant Engineer, 3 August, 1863. Retired List, 26 October, 1872.

PRICE, ARTHUR.
Third Assistant Engineer, 10 June, 1862. Second Assistant Engineer, 21 November, 1863. First Assistant Engineer, 1 January, 1868. Resigned 1 January, 1890.

GENERAL NAVY REGISTER.

PRICE, BENJAMIN L.
  Midshipman, 4 July, 1805. Dismissed 16 September, 1805.
PRICE, BENJAMIN S.
  Acting Assistant Paymaster, 9 December, 1861. Resigned 10 December, 1862.
PRICE, CHARLES J.
  Acting Third Assistant Engineer, 2 November, 1864. Honorably discharged 16 July, 1866.
PRICE, CICERO.
  Midshipman, 1 February, 1826. Passed Midshipman, 28 April, 1832. Lieutenant, 6 September, 1837. Commander, 14 September, 1855. Captain, 16 July, 1862. Commodore, 29 December, 1866. Retired List, 2 December, 1867. Died 24 November, 1888.
PRICE, CLAUDE B.
  Naval Cadet, 2 June, 1886. Assistant Engineer, 1 July, 1892. Passed Assistant Engineer, 26 February, 1897. Rank changed to Lieutenant, Junior Grade, 3 March, 1899. Lieutenant, 2 April, 1899.
PRICE, EDWARD.
  Midshipman, 5 April, 1813. Resigned 31 July, 1823.
PRICE, GEORGE.
  Lieutenant, 19 July, 1799. Last appearance on Records of Navy Department, 26 September, 1799. Dead.
PRICE, GEORGE.
  Acting Gunner, 4 November, 1862. Honorably discharged 16 November, 1865.
PRICE, HENRY B.
  Naval Cadet, 20 May, 1889. Assistant Engineer, 1 July, 1895. Passed Assistant Engineer, 17 November, 1898. Rank changed to Lieutenant, Junior Grade, 3 March, 1899.
PRICE, JOHN.
  Acting Master and Pilot, 1 October, 1864. Honorably discharged 8 October, 1868.
PRICE, JOS. P.
  Midshipman, 13 June, 1799. Discharged 21 April, 1801, under Peace Establishment Act.
PRICE, JOS. P.
  Master, 20 January, 1809. Resigned 2 July, 1812.
PRICE, RICHARD J. D.
  Midshipman, 9 September, 1841. Passed Midshipman, 10 August, 1847. Died 20 June, 1853.
PRICE, ROBERT.
  Mate, 31 December, 1863. Acting Ensign, 8 June, 1864. Appointment revoked 26 September, 1866.
PRICE, RODMAN M.
  Purser, 5 November, 1840. Resigned 16 December, 1850.
PRICE, THOMAS D.
  Assistant Surgeon, 1 April, 1800. Discharged 4 August, 1801.
PRICE, WILLIAM C.
  Master, 21 April, 1809. Dismissed 1 March, 1810.
PRICE, WILLIAM D.
  Acting Ensign, 21 March, 1864. Resigned 28 April, 1865.
PRICE, WILLIAM H.
  Acting Second Assistant Engineer, 1 October, 1862. Acting First Assistant Engineer, 4 February, 1863. Dismissed 23 April, 1863.
PRICE, WILLIAM N.
  Acting Ensign, 27 January, 1863. Acting Master, recommendation of Commanding Officer, 2 May, 1864. Died 7 April, 1866.
PRICKETT, NATHANIEL P.
  Midshipman, 10 June, 1848. Died 23 March, 1850.
PRIEST, JOSHUA.
  Acting Third Assistant Engineer, 6 September, 1864. Honorably discharged 4 September, 1865.
PRIME, EBENEZER S.
  Midshipman, 22 September, 1863. Graduated June, 1868. Master, 12 July, 1870. Lieutenant, 5 June, 1874. Lieutenant-Commander, 29 December, 1895. Commander, 3 March, 1899.
PRIME, WILLIAM.
  Gunner, 18 April, 1804. Dismissed 31 January, 1806.
PRINCE, A. B.
  Acting Ensign, 27 July, 1863. Honorably discharged 26 October, 1867.
PRINCE, BENJAMIN C.
  Master, 1 July, 1805. Resigned 15 September, 1807.
PRINDLE, FRANKLIN C.
  Third Assistant Engineer, 3 August, 1861. Second Assistant Engineer, 21 April, 1863. Resigned 11 September, 1865.
PRINDLE, F. C.
  Civil Engineer, 17 April, 1869. Resigned 1 January, 1876.
PRINDLE, FRANKLIN C.
  Civil Engineer, 22 July, 1879.
PRINDLE, GEORGE M.
  Acting Ensign, 20 January, 1863. Honorably discharged 18 January, 1867.
PRINDLE, GILBERT H.
  Mate, 27 January, 1865. Honorably discharged 22 June, 1867.
PRINGLE, JOEL R. P.
  Naval Cadet, 6 September, 1888. Ensign, 1 July, 1894. Lieutenant, Junior Grade, 3 March, 1899. Lieutenant, 11 December, 1900.

GENERAL NAVY REGISTER.   447

PRINGLE, JOHN J.
Midshipman, 23 September, 1840. Passed Midshipman, 11 July, 1846. Resigned 8 June, 1849.
PRIOR, FRANCIS G.
Mate, 23 January, 1862. Acting Master, 21 August, 1862. Appointment revoked (sick) 29 December, 1863.
PRIOR, GILBERT S.
Acting Third Assistant Engineer, 12 October, 1863. Resigned 26 January, 1865.
PRITCHARD, ARTHUR J.
Assistant Paymaster, 7 October, 1861. Paymaster, 9 November, 1864. Pay Inspector, 24 December, 1883. Pay Director, 10 April, 1895. Retired List 12 February, 1898.
PRITCHETT, JAMES M.
Acting Midshipman, 27 May, 1852. Midshipman, 10 June, 1857. Passed Midshipman, 5 September, 1859. Master, 25 June, 1860. Lieutenant, 3 April, 1861. Lieutenant-Commander, 2 January, 1863. Died 24 October, 1871.
PROCTER, ANDRE M.
Naval Cadet, 6 September, 1889. Assistant Engineer, 1 July, 1895. Rank changed to Lieutenant, Junior Grade, 3 March, 1899.
PROCTER, ALEXANDER.
Mate, 5 June, 1863. Honorably discharged 1 December, 1865.
PROCTOR, HENRY O.
Mate, 15 September, 1862. Acting Ensign, 19 July, 1864. Honorably discharged 4 January, 1866.
PROCTOR, STEPHEN.
Midshipman, 9 May, 1800. Resigned 27 April, 1803.
PROSPERI, AUGUSTUS.
Pharmacist, 15 September, 1898. Retired List, 23 July, 1900. Died 8 December, 1900.
PROTHERS, JOHN.
Acting Third Assistant Engineer, 26 September, 1862. Appointment revoked (sick) 21 May, 1863.
PROUDFIT, JOHN McL.
Midshipman, 24 September, 1872. Graduated 20 June, 1876. Ensign, 24 September, 1872. Died 15 December, 1879.
PROUDFIT, RANSOM S.
Mate, 6 May, 1863. Acting Ensign, 3 March, 1865. Honorably discharged 23 August, 1866.
PROVAUX, JOHN.
Midshipman, 15 January, 1801. Discharged 12 October, 1801, under Peace Establishment Act.
PROVOST, NELSON.
Acting Master, 26 August, 1861. Honorably discharged 25 February, 1866.
PRUD'HOMME, LUCIEN F.
Professor, 20 May, 1881. Retired List, 1 September, 1896.
PRYOR, CINCINNATUS.
Midshipman, 1 January, 1828. Dismissed 16 May, 1832.
PRYOR, EDWARD.
Mate, 18 March, 1865. Appointment revoked 12 December, 1865.
PRYOR, JAMES C.
Assistant Surgeon, 27 February, 1897. Passed Assistant Surgeon, 27 February, 1900.
PRYOR, WILLIAM.
Midshipman, 11 February, 1832. Murdered in April, 1833.
PUCKETT, JOHN H.
Acting Ensign and Pilot, 9 September, 1864. Resigned 8 March, 1865.
PUGH, ROBERT C.
Midshipman, 24 May, 1798. Left the service, 24 December, 1798.
PUGSLEY, HENRY S.
Passed Assistant Engineer (Spanish-American War), 20 May, 1898. Honorably discharged 30 December, 1898.
PUGSLEY, ISAAC P.
Acting Assistant Paymaster, 24 August, 1864. Honorably discharged 15 September, 1865.
PULLEN, FRED H.
Lieutenant, Junior Grade (Spanish-American War), 20 May, 1898. Died 12 October, 1898.
PULMAN, DAVID.
Mate, 24 January, 1863. Acting Ensign, 22 June, 1864. Honorably discharged 14 November, 1865.
PULSIPHER, G. M.
Acting Ensign, 18 December, 1862. Honorably discharged 23 November, 1865.
PULTZ, NORMAN S.
Mate, 16 November, 1863. Resigned 12 May, 1865.
PUNCH, JOHN S.
Purser, 23 May, 1832. Dismissed by Court-martial 2 July, 1834.
PUNCH, RICHARD D.
Mate, 23 November, 1863. Honorably discharged 2 October, 1865.
PURCELL, GREGORY.
Midshipman, 4 March, 1823. Died in June, 1824.
PURCELL, JOHN L.
Cadet Midshipman, 30 September, 1873. Graduated 10 June, 1881. Ensign, Junior Grade, 3 March, 1883. Ensign, 26 June, 1884. Lieutenant, Junior Grade, 28 May, 1892. Lieutenant, 29 April, 1896.
PURDIE, CHARLES F.
Acting Third Assistant Engineer, under instruction Naval Academy, 10 October, 1866.

Third Assistant Engineer, 2 June, 1868. Second Assistant Engineer, 2 June, 1869. Resigned 23 January, 1875.
PURDIE, WILLIAM A.
Mate, 26 December, 1862. Acting Ensign, 20 August, 1863. Honorably discharged 21 June, 1865.
PURDON, DAVID.
Acting Warrant Machinist, 23 August, 1899.
PURDY, HENRY B.
Mate, 19 December, 1863. Resigned 3 June, 1864.
PURDY, JOHN, Jr.
Third Assistant Engineer, 21 November, 1857. Second Assistant Engineer, 2 August, 1859. First Assistant Engineer, 19 February, 1863. Resigned 30 January, 1873.
PURDY, WARREN F.
Ensign (Spanish-American War), 18 June, 1898. Honorably discharged 17 September, 1898.
PURDY, WILLIAM B.
Acting Assistant Paymaster, 5 November, 1862. Mustered out 15 November, 1865.
PURKET, JOHN.
Master, 23 January, 1799. Resigned 25 July, 1799.
PURNELL, HENRY.
Midshipman, 1 January, 1808. Resigned 18 August, 1809.
PURPLE, JOHN L.
Carpenter (Spanish-American War), 3 May, 1898. Honorably discharged 8 September, 1898.
PURRINGTON, CHARLES F.
Mate, 29 January, 1864. Mustered out 1867.
PURSE, WILLIAM A.
Acting Assistant Paymaster, 28 August, 1863. Resigned 9 November, 1864.
PURSE, WILSON K.
Third Assistant Engineer, 12 August, 1858. Second Assistant Engineer, 21 September, 1861. First Assistant Engineer, 11 March, 1863. Retired List, 16 June, 1874. Died 30 December, 1882.
PURSELL, FRANCIS.
Boatswain, 27 May, 1857. Resigned 31 August, 1857.
PURSELL, P. H.
Acting Assistant Surgeon, 2 February, 1864. Resigned 28 April, 1865.
PURVIANCE, HUGH Y.
Midshipman, 3 November, 1818. Lieutenant, 3 March, 1827. Commander, 7 March, 1849. Captain, 28 January, 1856. Retired List, 21 December, 1861. Commodore on Retired List, 16 July, 1862. Rear-Admiral on the Retired List, 25 February, 1881. Died 21 October, 1882.
PURVIANCE, W. C.
Midshipman, 6 November, 1817. Died 26 July, 1822.
PURVIS, ANDREW.
Gunner, 25 November, 1799. Last appearance on Records of Navy Department.
PURVIS, WILLIAM.
Sailmaker, 15 January, 1800. Warrant returned 26 January, 1800.
PUSEY, ALFRED B.
Assistant Surgeon, 20 March, 1893. Resigned 25 June, 1896.
PUTNAM, CHARLES.
Mate, 8 September, 1862. Acting Ensign, 3 December, 1863. Honorably discharged 21 October, 1865.
PUTNAM, CHARLES F.
Midshipman, 24 June, 1860. Graduated 31 May, 1873. Ensign, 16 July, 1874. Master, 12 March, 1880. Lost in the Arctic Regions, June, 1882.
PUTNAM, CHARLES O.
Acting Third Assistant Engineer, 18 June, 1864. Honorably discharged 28 November, 1865.
PUTNAM, EDWIN.
Assistant Paymaster, 20 September, 1862. Paymaster, 4 May, 1866. Pay Inspector, 19 November, 1891. Pay Director, 7 May, 1899.
PUTNAM, W. O.
Acting Ensign, 12 August, 1862. Acting Master, recommendation of Commanding Officer, 22 April, 1864. Honorably discharged 20 September, 1865.
PUTNAM, WILLIAM S.
Mate, 19 November, 1862. Resigned 31 October, 1862.
PUTTS, WILLIAM E.
Ensign (Spanish-American War), 25 May, 1898. Honorably discharged 3 September, 1898.
PYBUS, JOHN.
Mate, 11 June, 1863. Resigned (sick) 7 March, 1865.
PYE, JAMES.
Midshipman, 18 June, 1812. Discharged 6 July, 1813.
PYKE, DAVID.
Acting Second Assistant Engineer, 14 November, 1861. Resigned 13 January, 1863.
PYLE, GEORGE W.
Acting Third Assistant Engineer, 25 April, 1864. Honorably discharged 16 April, 1868.
PYNCHON, JOSEPH H.
Acting Assistant Paymaster, 14 November, 1862. Honorably discharged 20 December, 1865.
PYNCHON, W. L.
Acting Assistant Paymaster, 28 January, 1862. Mustered out 20 December, 1865.
PYNE, CHARLES B.
Acting Ensign, 7 January, 1865. Honorably discharged 14 July, 1865.

GENERAL NAVY REGISTER.

PYNNE, GEORGE A.
　Mate, 2 April, 1864.　Appointment revoked 27 December, 1865.
QUACKENBOS, PETER.
　Midshipman, 20 June, 1806.　Resigned 27 July, 1807.
QUACKENBOSS, G. C.
　Assistant Surgeon, 10 September, 1805.　Last appearance on Records of Navy Department, 6 August, 1806.　Resigned.
QUACKENBUSH, JOHN N.
　Midshipman, 24 September, 1847.　Dismissed 3 January, 1854.　Acting Lieutenant, 16 July, 1862.　Lieutenant-Commander, 16 July, 1862.　Retired List, 17 July, 1868.　Lieutenant-Commander on Active List, from 29 September, 1862.　Commander, 25 May, 1871.　Retired List, 1 June, 1895.
QUACKENBUSH, STEPHEN P.
　Midshipman, 15 February, 1840.　Passed Midshipman, 11 July, 1846.　Master, 1 March, 1855.　Lieutenant, 14 September, 1855.　Lieutenant-Commander, 16 July, 1862.　Commander, 25 July, 1866.　Captain, 25 July, 1871.　Commodore, 13 March, 1880.　Rear-Admiral, 28 July, 1884.　Retired List, 23 January, 1885.　Died 4 February, 1890.
QUADLING, EDWARD H.
　Acting Ensign, 6 June, 1863.　Honorably discharged 17 September, 1865.
QUALTROUGH, EDWARD F.
　Midshipman, 21 September, 1867.　Graduated 6 June, 1871.　Ensign, 14 July, 1872.　Master, 1 July, 1876.　Lieutenant, Junior Grade, 3 March, 1883.　Lieutenant, 24 November, 1883.　Lieutenant-Commander, 3 March, 1899.
QUAYLE, THOMAS E.
　Mate, 20 November, 1861.　Resigned 27 April, 1865.
QUEEN, WALTER W.
　Midshipman, 7 October, 1841.　Passed Midshipman, 10 August, 1847.　Master, 15 September, 1855.　Lieutenant, 16 September, 1855.　Lieutenant-Commander, 16 July, 1862.　Commander, 25 July, 1866.　Captain, 4 June, 1874.　Commodore, 9 February, 1884.　Rear-Admiral, 28 August, 1886.　Retired List, 6 October, 1886.　Died 24 October, 1893.
QUEON, WILLIAM C.
　Mate, 13 September, 1865.　Deserted 24 May, 1867.
QUEVEDO, JOHN.
　Mate, 4 December, 1861.　Resigned 19 November, 1863.　Acting Gunner, 16 February, 1865.　Honorably discharged 24 January, 1866.　Mate, 13 February, 1866.　Mustered out 30 September, 1868.
QUICK, ROBERT B.
　Lieutenant (Spanish-American War), 20 May, 1898.　Honorably discharged 15 September, 1898.
QUIG, HENRY M.
　Third Assistant Engineer, 8 October, 1861.　Second Assistant Engineer, 3 August, 1863.　Resigned 26 November, 1869.
QUIGLEY, JAMES L.
　Acting Ensign, 27 May, 1863.　Honorably discharged 9 November, 1868.
QUIGLEY, MASSA T.
　Carpenter, 14 October, 1881.　Died 2 September, 1888.
QUILL, JAMES.
　Acting Warrant Machinist, 23 August, 1899.
QUILLIN, JOHN.
　Boatswain, 30 July, 1807.　Last appearance on Records of Navy Department, 31 July, 1807.
QUILTY, JAMES.
　Assistant Engineer (Spanish-American War), 24 May, 1898.　Honorably discharged 10 November, 1898.
QUIMBY, SAMUEL F.
　Acting Assistant Surgeon, 19 February, 1862.　Dismissed 15 August, 1863.
QUIN, JAMES N.
　Acting Third Assistant Engineer, 16 March, 1864.　Honorably discharged 12 October, 1865.
QUIN, JOHN.
　Master, 1 November, 1816.　Reserved List, 14 September, 1855.　Died 21 September, 1858.
QUIN, RICHARD B.
　Third Assistant Engineer, 21 May, 1853.　Second Assistant Engineer, 27 July, 1855.　Resigned 1 September, 1856.
QUIN, THOMAS A.
　Mate, 25 March, 1863.　Acting Ensign, 23 July, 1863.　Honorably discharged 27 September, 1865.
QUINBY, JOHN G.
　Cadet Midshipman, 12 June, 1874.　Graduated 4 June, 1880.　Ensign, 1 February, 1882.　Lieutenant, Junior Grade, 26 March, 1889.　Lieutenant, 5 November, 1893.　Lieutenant-Commander, 11 December, 1900.
QUINLAN, WILLIAM H.
　Ensign (Spanish-American War), 5 August, 1898.　Honorably discharged 27 February, 1899.
QUINN, JAMES.
　Acting Third Assistant Engineer, 24 October, 1864.　Honorably discharged 23 May, 1869.
QUINN, JOHN.
　Acting Third Assistant Engineer, 14 July, 1863.　Honorably discharged 14 August, 1865.
QUINN, JOHN.
　Boatswain, 15 September, 1873.　Dismissed 8 January, 1875.

29

QUINN, JOHN.
Midshipman, 30 May, 1803. Resigned 28 November, 1803.
QUINN, JOHN PAUL.
Assistant Surgeon, 9 May, 1861. Passed Assistant Surgeon, 26 October, 1863. Surgeon, 30 December, 1864. Died 6 June, 1869.
QUINN, MICHAEL.
Second Assistant Engineer, 15 November, 1847. First Assistant Engineer, 6 November, 1849. Chief Engineer, 15 December, 1853. Name stricken from the Rolls 18 May, 1861.
QUINN, WILLIAM E.
Acting Third Assistant Engineer, 28 April, 1863. Resigned 22 August, 1863. Acting Third Assistant Engineer, 2 October, 1863. Appointment revoked (sick) 25 January, 1864. Acting Third Assistant Engineer, 7 March, 1865. Honorably discharged 7 January, 1866.
QUINN, WILLIAM R.
Acting Warrant Machinist, 23 August, 1899.
QUINTARD, FERRIS J.
Acting Assistant Paymaster, 4 November, 1862. Resigned 22 June, 1863.
RABADAN, RAYMOND.
Mate, 21 October, 1861. Acting Ensign, 8 December, 1862. Honorably discharged 5 September, 1865.
RABY, JAMES J.
Naval Cadet, 9 September, 1891. Ensign, 1 July, 1897. Lieutenant, Junior Grade, 1 July, 1900.
RACE, CARLTON W.
Mate, 4 February, 1864. Honorably discharged 28 June, 1866.
RACK, GEORGE.
Acting Assistant Paymaster, 14 November, 1864. Honorably discharged 13 September, 1865.
RACK, THOMAS W.
Mate, 30 January, 1863. Resigned (sick) 20 April, 1865.
RACOE, FREDERICK W.
Acting Third Assistant Engineer, 10 February, 1864. Acting Second Assistant Engineer, 29 July, 1865. Honorably discharged 23 August, 1865.
RADABAUGH, GEORGE.
Acting First Assistant Engineer, 12 December, 1862. Honorably discharged 29 October, 1865.
RADCLIFFE, ALEXANDER D.
Acting Third Assistant Engineer, 27 March, 1865. Honorably discharged 22 September, 1869.
RADCLIFFE, JOHN H.
Acting Third Assistant Engineer, 24 August, 1864. Honorably discharged 5 July, 1865.
RADCLIFFE, PETER E.
Boatswain, 1 September, 1898.
RADFORD, STEPHEN K.
Assistant Paymaster, 6 July, 1878. Resigned 28 January, 1879.
RADFORD, WILLIAM.
Midshipman, 1 March, 1825. Passed Midshipman, 4 June, 1831. Lieutenant, 9 February, 1837. Commander, 14 September, 1855. Captain, 16 July, 1862. Commodore, 24 April, 1863. Rear-Admiral, 25 July, 1866. Retired List, 1 March, 1870. Died 8 January, 1890.
RAE, CHARLES W.
Acting Third Assistant Engineer, under instruction Naval Academy, 10 October, 1866. Third Assistant Engineer, 2 June, 1868. Second Assistant Engineer, 2 June, 1869. Passed Assistant Engineer, 28 December, 1875. Chief Engineer, 21 February, 1893. Rank changed to Commander, 3 March, 1899.
RAE, THOMAS WHITESIDE.
Third Assistant Engineer, 30 July, 1861. Second Assistant Engineer, 21 April, 1863. First Assistant Engineer, 11 October, 1866. Resigned 1 October, 1877.
RAEBEL, HERMAN C.
Midshipman, 23 September, 1861. Graduated November, 1864. Ensign, 1 November, 1866. Master, 1 December, 1866. Lieutenant, 12 March, 1868. Died 25 June, 1869.
RAEFLE, MAX G.
Acting Assistant Surgeon, 20 February, 1862. Resigned 18 May, 1865.
RAFFERTY, HUGH.
Acting Second Assistant Engineer, 27 August, 1861. Honorably discharged 9 August, 1865.
RAGSDALE, JAMES K. P.
Acting Midshipman, 21 September, 1860. Graduated September, 1865. Ensign, 1 December, 1866. Master, 12 March, 1868. Lieutenant, 26 March, 1869. Died 20 May, 1874.
RAINBOW, JOHN.
Carpenter, 10 June, 1837. Died 18 September, 1868.
RAINER, AMOS.
Acting Master and Pilot, 1 October, 1864. Honorably discharged 1 August, 1865.
RAINER, WILLIAM S.
Acting Third Assistant Engineer, 25 March, 1864. Honorably discharged 22 August, 1865.
RAINEY, JOHN D.
Midshipman, 19 March, 1846. Passed Midshipman, 10 June, 1853. Master, 15 September, 1855. Lieutenant, 16 September, 1855. Resigned 29 July, 1857.
RAINIER, CHARLES E.
Acting Third Assistant Engineer, 11 December, 1861. Acting Second Assistant Engineer, 19 September, 1864. Honorably discharged 30 November, 1865.

RALPH, JOSEPH P.
Mate, 28 September, 1863. Deserted January, 1864.
RAMAGE, JAMES.
Master, 1 June, 1813. Lieutenant, 9 December, 1814. Commander, 11 March, 1829. Cashiered 24 September, 1831.
RAMSAY, FRANCIS M.
Acting Midshipman and Midshipman, 5 October, 1850. Passed Midshipman, 20 June, 1856. Master, 22 January, 1858. Lieutenant, 23 January, 1858. Lieutenant-Commander, 16 July, 1862. Commander, 25 July, 1866. Captain, 1 December, 1877. Commodore, 26 March, 1889. Rear-Admiral, 11 April, 1894. Retired List, 5 April, 1897.
RAMSAY, HENRY A.
Third Assistant Engineer, 21 May, 1853. Second Assistant Engineer, 26 June, 1856. First Assistant Engineer, 2 August, 1859. Name stricken from the Rolls, 6 May, 1861.
RAMSAY, JOHN S.
Acting Assistant Surgeon, 15 March, 1864. Assistant Surgeon, 1 April, 1864. Resigned 31 December, 1867.
RAMSAY, MARTIN M.
Assistant Paymaster, 22 August, 1894. Passed Assistant Paymaster, 10 October, 1896. Paymaster, 12 November, 1899.
RAMSAY, STERRETT.
Purser, 18 November, 1830. Pay Director, Retired List. Died 23 July, 1872.
RAMSAY, WILLIAM.
Midshipman, 1 September, 1811. Lieutenant, 5 March, 1817. Commander, 9 February, 1837. Captain, 27 February, 1847. Died 10 August, 1866.
RAMSDELL, JOHN.
Mate, 22 December, 1863. Died 22 October, 1866.
RAMSDEN, FREDERICK THOMAS HULLY.
Third Assistant Engineer, 25 August, 1862. Second Assistant Engineer, 20 February, 1864. Resigned 14 April, 1869.
RAMSEY, DANIEL B.
Midshipman, 6 July, 1803. Resigined 12 December, 1808.
RAMSEY, JAMES.
Acting Second Assistant Engineer, 12 December, 1863. Resigned 27 February, 1864.
RAMSEY, J. R.
Acting First Assistant Engineer, 1 October, 1862. Honorably discharged 5 September, 1865.
RAND, GEORGE D.
Acting Assistant Paymaster, 4 December, 1862. Assistant Paymaster, 30 June, 1864. Resigned 22 December, 1865.
RAND, HOMER E.
Acting Assistant Paymaster, 22 April, 1864. Mustered out 24 September, 1865.
RAND, ISAAC H.
Midshipman, 23 January, 1815. Last appearance on Records of Navy Department, 1822. Dead.
RAND, JAMES.
Purser, 12 March, 1800. Discharged 8 July, 1801, under Peace Establishment Act.
RAND, LEONARD L.
Ensign (Spanish-American War), 24 May, 1898. Honorably discharged 6 December, 1898.
RAND, STEPHEN.
Acting Third Assistant Engineer, 17 December, 1864. Honorably discharged 8 August, 1869. Assistant Paymaster, 12 August, 1869. Passed Assistant Paymaster, 30 April, 1874. Paymaster, 31 July, 1884. Pay Inspector, 1 September, 1899.
RANDALL, ANDREW A.
Gunner, 29 August, 1843. Resigned 27 November, 1854. Mate. Died 18 January, 1865.
RANDALL, BENJAMIN W.
Acting Third Assistant Engineer, 10 March, 1864. Honorably discharged 15 July, 1865.
RANDALL, GEORGE G.
Acting Ensign, 7 December, 1864. Honorably discharged 7 November, 1865.
RANDALL, HENRY K.
Midshipman, 18 June, 1812. Resigned 1815.
RANDALL, JOSEPH P.
Acting Ensign, 6 May, 1863. Acting Master, 16 December, 1863. Resigned 15 December, 1864.
RANDALL, MILTON P.
Acting Third Assistant Engineer, 3 June, 1861. Acting Second Assistant Engineer, 16 July, 1863. Honorably discharged 24 December, 1865.
RANDALL PHILIP.
Mate, 3 July, 1866. Resigned 7 November, 1868.
RANDALL, SAMUEL A.
Acting First Assistant Engineer, 16 July, 1864. Honorably discharged 11 November, 1865.
RANDALL, SANFORD.
Mate, 19 December, 1861. Resigned 25 October, 1862.
RANDALL, THOMAS.
Midshipman, 23 September, 1799. Discharged 22 June, 1801, under Peace Establishment Act.
RANDALL, WESLEY.
Acting Second Assistant Engineer, 18 June, 1864. Honorably discharged 27 September, 1865.
RANDALL, WILLIAM P.
Acting Master, 24 July, 1861. Acting Volunteer Lieutenant, 28 May, 1862. Acting

452   GENERAL NAVY REGISTER.

Volunteer Lieutenant-Commander, 9 March, 1865. Honorably discharged 19 December, 1865. Acting Master, 7 December, 1866. Ensign, 12 March, 1868. Master, 18 December, 1868. Lieutenant, 21 March, 1870. Retired List, 15 February, 1882. Lieutenant-Commander on Retired List, 6 August, 1886.
RANDLE, WILLIAM G.
Commander (Spanish-American War), 18 May, 1898. Honorably discharged 2 September, 1898.
RANDOLPH, BEVERLY.
Midshipman, 23 July, 1839. Passed Midshipman, 2 July, 1845. Acting Master, 17 December, 1847. Resigned 18 May, 1850.
RANDOLPH, B. S.
Midshipman, 2 February, 1815. Resigned 5 September, 1817.
RANDOLPH, D. L.
Midshipman, 1 May, 1822. Resigned 6 February, 1830.
RANDOLPH, EDWARD.
Midshipman, 20 August, 1800. Discharged 14 April, 1801.
RANDOLPH, GEORGE W.
Midshipman, 31 March, 1831. Passed Midshipman, 15 June, 1837. Resigned 22 July, 1839.
RANDOLPH, JOHN B.
Midshipman, 11 June, 1833. Passed Midshipman, 8 July, 1839. Lieutenant, 29 May, 1846. Died 20 July, 1854.
RANDOLPH, J. F.
Captain (to command Galley), 13 September, 1798. Last appearance on Records of Navy Department, 23 March, 1799.
RANDOLPH, P. B.
Midshipman, 1 January, 1817. Last appearance on Records of Navy Department, 1819. Died at sea.
RANDOLPH, PEYTON H.
Acting Ensign, 11 November, 1863. Honorably discharged 21 October, 1865.
RANDOLPH, R. C.
Assistant Surgeon, 1 May, 1810. Surgeon, 15 April, 1814. Resigned 24 May, 1824.
RANDOLPH, RICHARD B.
Midshipman, 18 June, 1799. Lost in the Insurgent.
RANDOLPH, ROBERT B.
Midshipman, 15 August, 1810. Lieutenant, 27 April, 1816. Dismissed 19 April, 1833.
RANDOLPH, T. M.
Midshipman, 30 May, 1816. Resigned 28 May, 1822.
RANDOLPH, VICTOR M.
Midshipman, 11 June, 1814. Lieutenant, 13 January, 1825. Commander, 8 September, 1841. Captain, 14 September, 1855. Resigned 14 January, 1861.
RANDOLPH, W. B.
Midshipman, 1 January, 1812. Lost in the Wasp in 1815.
RANDRUP, C. E.
Acting Ensign, 17 February, 1865. Honorably discharged 15 September, 1865.
RANK, ERASTUS P.
Third Assistant Engineer, 8 December, 1862. Resigned 9 March, 1866.
RANKIN, ALEXANDER M.
Acting Third Assistant Engineer, 2 October, 1862. Resigned 29 August, 1863.
RANKIN, DAVID.
Gunner, 19 March, 1844. Dismissed 30 May, 1851.
RANKIN, WILLIAM B.
Acting Ensign, 31 July, 1863. Honorably discharged 3 November, 1865.
RANSOM, GEORGE B.
Cadet Engineer, Naval Academy, 1 October, 1871. Graduated 30 May, 1874. Assistant Engineer, 26 February, 1875. In service. Passed Assistant Engineer, 4 July, 1880. Chief Engineer, 9 May, 1895. Rank changed to Lieutenant-Commander, 3 March, 1899.
RANSOM, GEORGE M.
Midshipman, 25 July, 1839. Passed Midshipman, 2 July, 1845. Master, 28 June, 1853. Lieutenant, 21 February, 1854. Lieutenant-Commander, 16 July, 1862. Commander, 2 January, 1863. Captain, 2 March, 1870. Commodore, 28 March, 1877. Retired List, 18 June, 1882. Died 10 September, 1889.
RANSOM, HARVEY L.
Mate, 17 September, 1862. Acting Ensign, 14 September, 1863. Died 14 January, 1864.
RANSOM, T. B.
Professor of Mathematics, 2 October, 1835. Last appearance on Records of Navy Department, 1837. Frigate Constellation.
RANSOM, THEODORE S.
Mate, 14 February, 1863. Resigned 4 October, 1864.
RANTEN, HENRY H.
Midshipman, 2 April, 1804. Resigned 26 August, 1811.
RAPALJE, STEPHEN
Surgeon, 4 December, 1828. Died 11 September, 1856.
RAPP, HENRY B.
Midshipman, 15 November, 1809. Lieutenant, 24 July, 1813. Resigned 10 February, 1817.
RAPPELL, GEORGE W.
Mate. Resigned 15 October, 1863.
RATCHFORD, RICHARD.
Acting Carpenter, 18 April, 1863. Honorably discharged 17 September, 1865.
RATCLIFFE, QUINTON.
Midshipman, 1 February, 1823. Died 1 October, 1828.

GENERAL NAVY REGISTER. 453

RATHBONE, CLARENCE.
Midshipman, 28 September, 1861. Acting Ensign, 10 June, 1844. Resigned 23 December, 1865.

RATHBONE, J. B.
Midshipman, 3 March, 1841. Resigned 20 September, 1845.

RATHBORNE, SAMUEL T.
Acting Master, 26 April, 1862. Resigned 22 January, 1863.

RATHBURNE, N. W.
Acting Ensign, 8 October, 1862. Resigned 23 August, 1864.

RATTIGAN, WILLIAM E.
Mate, 21 November, 1867. Resigned 3 December, 1872.

RAWLINGS, JOHN.
Midshipman, 25 March, 1800. Discharged 14 July, 1801, under Peace Establishment Act.

RAWLINSON, FRANCIS.
Acting Second Assistant Engineer, 6 June, 1864. Honorably discharged 8 August, 1865.

RAWSON, EDWARD K.
Chaplain, 21 January, 1871. Resigned, 28 October, 1890. Professor, 28 October, 1890.

RAY, CHARLES M.
Assistant Paymaster, 3 March, 1879. Passed Assistant Paymaster, 2 April, 1882. Paymaster 7 February, 1894.

RAY, HYDE.
Assistant Surgeon, 20 July, 1809. Surgeon, 24 July, 1813. Died 7 September, 1835.

RAY, J. W. H.
Midshipman, 1 September, 1811. Lieutenant, 5 March, 1817. Died 10 November, 1824.

RAY, ROBERT C.
Midshipman, 1 October, 1872. Graduated 20 June, 1876. Ensign, 4 June, 1878. Retired List, 25 October, 1883. Died 4 December, 1889.

RAY, WHITMUL P.
Midshipman, 27 September, 1866. Graduated 7 June, 1870. Ensign, 13 July, 1871. Master, 4 August, 1874. Lieutenant, 24 February, 1881. Died 9 June, 1893.

RAY, WILLIAM.
Boatswain, 15 January, 1855. Resigned 26 October, 1855.

RAY, WILLIAM.
Acting Boatswain, 16 May, 1863. Appointment revoked 25 March, 1864.

RAY, WILLIAM.
Acting Second Assistant Engineer, 10 November, 1864. Honorably discharged 28 October, 1865.

RAYMOND, H. C.
Acting Ensign, 11 June, 1863. Resigned 31 May, 1865.

RAYMOND, JAMES H.
Mate, 15 October, 1861. Resigned 19 July, 1862.

RAYNAL, LEWIS F.
Purser, 30 May, 1800. Last appearance on Records of Navy Department.

RAYNOLDS, EDWARD V.
Lieutenant (Spanish-American War), 22 June, 1898. Honorably discharged 8 September, 1898.

RAYNOLDS, W. F., JR.
Mate, 28 March, 1862. Acting Ensign, 13 July, 1863. Resigned 12 November, 1864.

RAYNOR, JAMES B.
Mate, 22 November, 1864. Honorably discharged 4 October, 1868.

RAYNOR, RUSSELL.
Ensign (Spanish-American War), 28 June, 1898. Honorably discharged 8 September, 1898.

RAYNOR, WILLIAM.
Acting Third Assistant Engineer, 5 January, 1864. Honorably discharged 7 September, 1865.

READ, ABNER.
Midshipman, 2 March, 1839. Passed Midshipman, 2 July, 1845. Master, 12 April, 1853. Lieutenant, 6 February, 1854. Lieutenant-Commander, 16 July, 1862. Commander, 13 September, 1862. Died from wounds received in action, 12 July, 1863.

READ, CHARLES.
Midshipman, 12 December, 1799. Resigned 5 May, 1806.

READ, CHARLES W.
Acting Midshipman, 20 September, 1856. Midshipman, 15 June, 1860. Resigned 4 February, 1861.

READ, EDMUND G.
Acting Midshipman, 25 September, 1855. Midshipman, 15 June, 1860. Dismissed 1 May, 1861.

READ, FRANK DeW.
Naval Cadet, 6 September, 1889. Assistant Engineer, 1 July, 1895. Passed Assistant Engineer, 20 January, 1899. Rank changed to Lieutenant, Junior Grade, 3 March, 1899. Retired List, 11 November, 1899. Died 3 October, 1900.

READ, FREDERICK.
Acting Ensign, 24 December, 1862. Acting Master, 5 March, 1864. Honorably discharged 16 September, 1865.

READ, GEORGE C.
Midshipman, 2 April, 1804. Lieutenant, 25 April, 1810. Commander, 27 April, 1816. Captain, 3 March, 1825. Reserved List, 13 September, 1855. Rear-Admiral on Retired List, 16 July, 1862. Died 22 August, 1862.

READ, GEORGE H.
Acting Assistant Paymaster, 14 January, 1865. Mustered out 15 August, 1865. Assist-

GENERAL NAVY REGISTER.

ant Paymaster, 21 February, 1867. Passed Assistant Paymaster, 12 March, 1869. Paymaster, 31 August, 1881. Retired List, 29 March, 1898.
READ, JAMES.
Midshipman, 30 May, 1833. Passed Midshipman, 8 July, 1839. Lieutenant, 29 October, 1844. Resigned 22 June, 1847.
READ, JAMES.
Acting Gunner, 26 December, 1863. Appointment revoked 29 April, 1865.
READ, JOHN.
Acting Assistant Paymaster, 6 November, 1862. Resigned 20 March, 1865.
READ, JOHN D.
Midshipman, 16 October, 1837. Passed Midshipman, 29 June, 1843. Master, 17 September, 1850. Lieutenant, 8 April, 1851. Died 8 July, 1858.
READ, JOHN J.
Acting Midshipman, 21 September, 1858. Ensign, 25 November, 1862. Lieutenant, 22 February, 1864. Lieutenant-Commander, 25 July, 1866. Commander, 11 December, 1877. Captain, 27 April, 1893. Rear-Admiral, 29 November, 1900.
READ, JOHN W.
Acting Second Assistant Engineer, 4 June, 1864. Appointment revoked (sick) 19 January, 1865.
READ, MAURICE L.
Cadet Midshipman, 28 September, 1874. Graduated 10 June, 1881. Ensign, Junior Grade, 3 March, 1883. Ensign, 26 June, 1884. Retired List, 14 June, 1890.
READ, ROBERT R.
Mate, 11 March, 1864. Resigned 31 March, 1864.
READ, WILLIAM.
Acting Ensign and Pilot, 22 November, 1864. Appointment revoked 16 June, 1865.
READ, WILLIAM, JR.
Mate, 26 August, 1864. Honorably discharged 27 July, 1865.
READ, WILLIAM H.
Acting Ensign, 13 August, 1863. Appointment revoked (sick) 6 June, 1864.
REAGAN, JOHN J.
Acting Ensign, 23 February, 1863. Honorably discharged 6 November, 1865.
REAMEY, LAZARUS LOWREY.
Midshipman, 25 July, 1866. Graduated 7 June, 1870. Ensign, 13 July, 1871. Master, 23 July, 1874. Lieutenant, 2 February, 1881. Lieutenant-Commander, 3 March, 1899. Retired List, with rank of Commander, 30 June, 1900.
REANEY, HENRY.
Mate, 18 June, 1861. Acting Ensign, 8 October, 1862. Acting Master, 17 November, 1863. Honorably discharged 6 June, 1868.
REANEY, THOMAS J.
Acting Third Assistant Engineer, 22 August, 1864. Honorably discharged 26 July, 1865.
REANEY, WILLIAM H. I.
Chaplain, 14 March, 1892.
REARDON, WILLIAM J.
Mate, 24 February, 1870. Appointment revoked 31 August, 1871.
REARICK, PETER A.
Third Assistant Engineer, 17 February, 1860. Second Assistant Engineer, 22 July, 1862. First Assistant Engineer, 1 March, 1864. Chief Engineer, 25 March, 1874. Rank changed to Captain, 3 March, 1899. Rear-Admiral on Retired List, 17 February, 1900.
REBER, WILLIAM M.
Acting Assistant Surgeon, 6 April, 1863. Assistant Surgeon, 22 September, 1863. Resigned 19 December, 1868.
REDDING, JAMES.
Acting Master and Pilot, 1 October, 1864. Honorably discharged 20 October, 1865.
REDDING, WILLIAM F.
Acting Ensign, 31 August, 1862. Acting Master, 8 February, 1864. Honorably discharged 10 November, 1865.
REDDISH, JOSEPH S.
Mate, 25 January, 1864. Appointment revoked (sick) 1 September, 1864.
REDICK, DAVID.
Midshipman, 20 June, 1806. Dismissed 4 April, 1808.
REDFIELD, GEORGE S.
Acting Assistant Paymaster, 3 August, 1861. Resigned 3 March, 1864.
REDFIELD, J. BAYARD.
Acting Assistant Paymaster, 16 January, 1865. Honorably discharged 23 November, 1865. Assistant Paymaster, 21 February, 1867. Passed Assistant Paymaster, 11 June, 1868. Paymaster, 8 March, 1879. Pay Inspector, 5 May, 1899.
REDFIELD, JUDD F.
Mate, 2 May, 1868. Mustered out 6 February, 1869.
REDGRAVE, DEWITT C.
Cadet Engineer, 13 September, 1877. Assistant Engineer, 1 July, 1883. Passed Assistant Engineer, 1 October, 1893. Rank changed to Lieutenant, 3 March, 1899.
REDINGTON, ROBERT.
Assistant Surgeon, 29 May, 1866. Resigned 26 October, 1868.
REDMAN, CURTIS.
Acting Master, 4 November, 1861. Honorably discharged 17 September, 1865.
REDMAN, WALLACE ST. C.
Acting Third Assistant Engineer, 18 June, 1863. Acting Second Assistant Engineer, 23 November, 1863. Acting First Assistant Engineer, 17 May, 1864. Honorably discharged 31 December, 1868.

REDMOND, ANDREW J.
Acting Third Assistant Engineer, 21 May, 1863. Honorably discharged 12 November, 1868.
REDSTONE, WILLIAM.
Sailmaker, 17 January, 1876. Retired List, 13 October, 1896.
REED, ALLEN V.
Acting Midshipman, 26 September, 1854. Midshipman, 11 June, 1858. Passed Midshipman, 28 January, 1861. Master, 28 February, 1861. Lieutenant, 18 April, 1861. Lieutenant-Commander, 3 March, 1865. Commander, 1 April, 1872. Captain, 28 July, 1884. Retired List, 11 June, 1896.
REED, BENJAMIN S.
Mate, 9 November, 1864. Honorably discharged 30 June, 1865.
REED, BRADFORD D.
Mate, 31 October, 1861. Acting Ensign, 6 May, 1863. Honorably discharged 6 March, 1866.
REED, CHARLES H.
Acting Ensign, 18 April, 1863. Honorably discharged 5 December, 1865.
REED, DAVID.
Acting Third Assistant Engineer, 28 May, 1863. Honorably discharged 10 October, 1865.
REED, EDWARD W.
Mate, 26 June, 1862. Dropped 13 October, 1862.
REED, EZRA, Jr.
Midshipman, 1 April, 1828. Resigned 28 June, 1830.
REED, FREDERICK.
Acting Master's Mate, 16 April, 1864. Last appearance on records of Navy Department, 4 May, 1865.
REED, GEORGE S.
Acting Third Assistant Engineer, 9 June, 1863. Resigned 3 November, 1863.
REED, GEORGE W.
Midshipman, 13 January, 1799. Lieutenant, 10 March, 1803. Died 4 January, 1813.
REED, HETHCOTE J.
Midshipman, 31 December, 1798. Lieutenant, 16 March, 1807. Died 27 August, 1812.
REED, ISAAC.
Acting Third Assistant Engineer, 9 August, 1864. Appointment revoked (sick) 19 September, 1864.
REED, JOHN.
Acting Second Assistant Engineer, 1 October, 1862. Honorably discharged 4 November, 1865.
REED, JOHN D.
Mate, 20 December, 1862. Resigned 22 May, 1865.
REED, JOHN, Jr.
Midshipman, 30 November, 1814. Died 29 August, 1823.
REED, J. FRANK.
Acting Ensign, 5 September, 1862. Acting Master, 11 June, 1863. Honorably discharged 30 November, 1865.
REED, JOHN H.
Acting Midshipman, 28 September, 1859. Ensign, 25 November, 1862. Lieutenant, 22 February, 1864. Lieutenant-Commander, 25 July, 1866. Drowned 11 January, 1868.
REED, JOHN K., Jr.
Surgeon, 5 February, 1799. Died 28 February, 1805.
REED, JOHN W.
Acting Third Assistant Engineer, 22 November, 1862. Resigned 7 August, 1863.
REED, MILTON E.
Naval Cadet, 5 September, 1887. Assistant Engineer, 1 July, 1893. Passed Assistant Engineer, 29 July, 1897. Rank changed to Lieutenant, Junior Grade, 3 March, 1899. Lieutenant, 2 November, 1899.
REED, ROBERT R.
Mate, 14 August, 1862. Resigned 11 March, 1864.
REED, SHERWOOD B.
Mate, 26 April, 1864. Honorably discharged 12 October, 1865.
REED, THOMAS.
Acting Third Assistant Engineer, 23 November, 1863. Honorably discharged 25 November, 1865.
REED, THOMAS B.
Acting Assistant Paymaster, 19 April, 1864. Honorably discharged 4 November, 1865.
REED, THOMAS J.
Acting Second Assistant Engineer, 12 June, 1863. Resigned 31 May, 1864.
REED, THOMAS J.
Acting Assistant Surgeon, 15 March, 1864. Resigned 21 November, 1864.
REED, WALLACE W.
Mate, 10 September, 1861. Resigned (sick) 9 November, 1864.
REED, WILLIAM.
Surgeon, 9 March, 1798. Died 26 September, 1798.
REED, WILLIAM.
Acting Master and Pilot, 14 November, 1864. Resigned 17 January, 1865.
REED, WILLIAM H.
Acting Ensign, 11 February, 1865. Honorably discharged 18 September, 1865.
REEDE, WILLIAM, Jr.
Midshipman, 28 June, 1804. Last appearance on Records of Navy Department, 10 April, 1805. Broke by Court-martial.
REEDER, NATHANIEL.
Midshipman, 1 November, 1828. Dismissed 6 June, 1836.

REEDER, ROBERT D.
Midshipman, 2 April, 1804. Resigned 1 April, 1805.
REEDER, S. ANDREWS.
Acting Assistant Surgeon, 17 December, 1862. Resigned 7 October, 1864.
REEDER, WILLIAM H.
Midshipman, 20 September, 1862. Graduated June, 1867. Ensign, 18 December, 1868. Master, 21 March, 1871. Lieutenant, 31 January, 1872. Lieutenant-Commander, 4 December, 1892. Commander, 10 August, 1898.
REENSTJERNA, LARS M.
Acting Third Assistant Engineer, 11 March, 1864. Honorably discharged 10 October, 1868.
REES, CLAYTON T.
Mate, 19 September, 1864. Resigned 6 June, 1865.
REES, CORWIN P.
Midshipman, 31 July, 1866. Graduated 7 June, 1870. Ensign, 13 July, 1871. Master, 21 May, 1874. Lieutenant, 11 October, 1880. Lieutenant-Commander, 3 March, 1899.
REESE, C. M.
Surgeon, 27 April, 1816. Resigned 29 March, 1824.
REESE, ELIAS.
Acting Master, 1 October, 1862. Resigned 17 October, 1864.
REESE, L. M.
Acting Assistant Surgeon, 1 October, 1862. Died 1 September, 1864.
REESE, THOMAS.
Acting Gunner, 27 July, 1863. Honorably discharged 15 November, 1865.
REESIDE, JOHN E.
Ensign (Spanish-American War), 25 May, 1898. Honorably discharged 10 October, 1898.
REEVES, CHARLES P.
Acting Assistant Paymaster, 17 September, 1864. Mustered out 1 October, 1865.
REEVES, GEORGE W., JR.
Assistant Paymaster, 15 January, 1900.
REEVES, ISAAC S. K.
Assistant Engineer, 30 June, 1875. Passed Assistant Engineer, 16 September, 1883. Chief Engineer, 21 June, 1896. Rank changed to Lieutenant-Commander, 3 March, 1899.
REEVES, JAMES F.
Acting Assistant Paymaster, 3 January, 1865. Mustered out 9 October, 1865.
REEVES, JOSEPH M.
Naval Cadet, 8 September, 1890. Assistant Engineer, 1 July, 1896. Rank changed to Ensign, 3 March, 1899. Lieutenant, Junior Grade, 1 July, 1899.
REEVES, SAMUEL T.
Acting Second Assistant Engineer, 31 August, 1863. Honorably discharged 9 October, 1865.
REGAN, JEREMIAH.
Mate, 25 October, 1862. Deserted 8 November, 1862.
REH, OTTO E.
Acting Gunner, 1 August, 1900.
REHDER, HENRY.
Acting Master and Pilot, 1 October, 1864. Honorably discharged 25 October, 1865.
REICH, HENRY F.
Midshipman, 28 September, 1870. Graduated 1 June, 1874. Ensign, 17 July, 1875. Master, 29 March, 1881. Lieutenant, Junior Grade, 3 March, 1883. Retired List, 5 June, 1885.
REICHENBACH, W. C. F.
Third Assistant Engineer, 8 September, 1863. Resigned 27 November, 1866.
REID, BENJAMIN F.
Midshipman, 13 July, 1799. Lieutenant, 23 January, 1807. Died 6 January, 1812.
REID, CHARLES C. B.
Lieutenant (Spanish-American War), 24 May, 1898. Honorably discharged 13 September, 1898.
REID, JAMES.
Mate, 31 May, 1864. Honorably discharged 25 October, 1865.
REID, JAMES H.
Naval Cadet, 4 September, 1884. Ensign, 1 July, 1890. Lieutenant, Junior Grade, 11 May, 1898. Lieutenant, 3 March, 1899.
REID, JAMES L.
Acting Ensign, 22 June, 1863. Honorably discharged 1 December, 1865.
REID, JOHN M.
Acting Ensign, 16 April, 1863. Honorably discharged 12 September, 1865.
REID, JOSEPH.
Mate, 27 February, 1863. Acting Ensign, 10 July, 1865. Dismissed 22 September, 1866. Mate, 24 January, 1870. Died 8 December, 1882.
REID, J. W. E.
Midshipman, 26 September, 1831. Passed Midshipman, 15 June, 1837. Lost on the Exploring Expedition in May, 1839.
REID, PETER.
Mate, 29 September, 1862. Dismissed 28 November, 1862.
REID, ROBERT I.
Cadet Engineer, Naval Academy, 1 October, 1873. Graduated 21 June, 1875. Assistant Engineer, 1 July, 1878. Passed Assistant Engineer, 19 June, 1888. Chief Engineer, 22 December, 1897. Rank changed to Lieutenant, 3 March, 1899. Lieutenant-Commander, 12 December, 1899.
REID, SAMUEL C.
Master, not in line of promotion, 3 July, 1843. Reserved List, 14 September, 1855. Died 28 January, 1861.

GENERAL NAVY REGISTER.

REID, WASHINGTON.
Midshipman, 22 December, 1831. Passed Midshipman, 23 June, 1838. Lieutenant, 10 December, 1843. Died 19 February, 1850.

REID, WILLIAM.
Acting Carpenter, 22 September, 1863. Honorably discharged 1 March, 1866.

REID, WILLIAM IRVING.
Third Assistant Engineer, 2 December, 1861. Second Assistant Engineer, 8 September, 1863. Resigned 29 January, 1867.

REILEY, PETER C.
Third Assistant Engineer, 17 March, 1863. Resigned 20 October, 1863.

REILL, ROBERT B.
Midshipman, 2 September, 1835. Passed Midshipman, 22 June, 1841. Master, 17 July, 1847. Reserved List, 13 September, 1855. Lieutenant on Active List from 14 March, 1848. Retired List, 29 Sepetmber, 1864. Captain on Retired List, 4 April, 1867. Died 5 February, 1869.

REILLY, EDWARD A.
Acting Third Assistant Engineer, 8 August, 1863. Honorably discharged 9 November, 1868.

REILLY, JAMES.
Midshipman, 1 January, 1808. Lieutenant, 24 July, 1813. Lost in the Wasp, 1815.

REILLY, JOHN.
Acting Third Assistant Engineer, 9 October, 1866. Mustered out 27 August, 1868.

REILLY, JOHN.
Acting Third Assistant Engineer, 19 February, 1864. Honorably discharged 20 October, 1865.

REILLY, JOHN F.
Acting First Assistant Engineer, 19 September, 1862. Resigned 17 September, 1863. Acting First Assistant Engineer, 24 December, 1863. Acting Chief Engineer, 16 June, 1864. Honorably discharged 16 October, 1865.

REILLY, ROBERT.
Acting Third Assistant Engineer, 5 January, 1864. Honorably discharged 13 January, 1866.

REILY, JAMES.
Acting Third Assistant Engineer, 13 August, 1864. Appointment revoked 4 January, 1865.

REILY, WILLIAM.
Midshipman, 9 February, 1841. Passed Midshipman, 10 August, 1847. Acting Master, 11 December, 1852. Lost in Porpoise, 21 September, 1854.

REINBURG, LOUIS.
Mate, 28 November, 1863. Honorably discharged 8 February, 1866.

REINHARDT, AUGUSTUS.
Acting Third Assistant Engineer, 20 August, 1864. Honorably discharged 2 June, 1865.

REISINGER, WILLIAM W.
Midshipman, 21 April, 1862. Graduated 12 June, 1866. Ensign, 12 March, 1868. Master, 26 March, 1869. Lieutenant, 21 March, 1870. Lieutenant-Commander, 2 June, 1885. Commander, 21 July, 1894. Captain, 22 November, 1900.

REITER, GEORGE C.
Midshipman, 20 September, 1861. Graduated September, 1865. Ensign, 1 December, 1866. Master, 12 March, 1868. Lieutenant, 26 March, 1869. Lieutenant-Commander, 23 November, 1880. Commander, 31 July, 1890. Captain, 3 March, 1899.

RELYEA, ISAAC E.
Ensign (Spanish-American War), 1 July, 1898. Honorably discharged 8 September, 1898.

REMEY, EDWARD W.
Midshipman, 27 September, 1862. Graduated June, 1867. Ensign, 18 December, 1868. Master, 21 March, 1870. Lieutenant, 9 December, 1871. Disappeared 17 February, 1885.

REMEY, GEORGE C.
Acting Midshipman, 20 September, 1855. Midshipman, 9 June, 1859. Lieutenant, 31 August, 1861. Lieutenant-Commander, 25 June, 1865. Commander, 25 November, 1872. Captain, 30 October, 1885. Commodore, 19 June, 1897. Rear-Admiral, 22 November, 1898.

REMICK, WILLIAM C.
Acting Third Assistant Engineer, 14 April, 1864. Honorably discharged 11 November, 1865.

REMINGTON, EDWARD C.
Acting Ensign, 1 February, 1865. Honorably discharged 4 September, 1865.

REMMONDS, CHARLES T.
Mate, 29 October, 1863. Honorably discharged 13 July, 1867.

REMSEN, WILLIAM.
Midshipman, 26 July, 1866. Graduated 7 June, 1870. Resigned 5 September, 1873.

RENNELL, NUGENT T.
Acting Ensign, 1 October, 1862. Honorably discharged 28 November, 1865.

RENNELLS, FARNUM J.
Acting Ensign, 27 May, 1864. Honorably discharged 8 August, 1865.

RENNER, WILLIAM F.
Mate, 24 January, 1863. Honorably discharged 26 November, 1865.

RENNEY, WILLIAM E.
Acting Third Assistant Engineer, 19 August, 1864. Honorably discharged 5 September, 1865.

RENNOLDS, HENRY S.
Surgeon, 8 September, 1841. Retired List, 29 May, 1861. Died 27 September, 1869.

RENNOLDS, LOUIS P.
Chaplain, 31 January, 1900.

RENO, GEORGE E.
Acting Third Assistant Engineer, 13 September, 1864. Honorably discharged 9 August, 1865.
RENSFORD, CHARLES C.
Acting Third Assistant Engineer, 1 October, 1862. Resigned 28 February, 1863. Acting Third Assistant Engineer, 6 June, 1864. Honorably discharged 31 October, 1865.
RENSHAW, ALEXANDER D.
Acting Third Assistant Engineer, 14 January, 1863. Honorably discharged 8 November, 1866.
RENSHAW, C. S.
Midshipman, 1 January, 1825. Passed Midshipman, 4 June, 1831. Resigned 11 February, 1832.
RENSHAW, EDWARD.
Midshipman, 4 November, 1841. Passed Midshipman, 10 August, 1847. Master, 14 September, 1855. Lieutenant, 15 September, 1855. Died 23 November, 1857.
RENSHAW, FRANCIS B.
Midshipman, 1 November, 1828. Passed Midshipman, 3 July, 1835. Lieutenant, 8 September, 1841. Resigned 22 January, 1861.
RENSHAW, JAMES.
Third Assistant Engineer, 17 February, 1860. Second Assistant Engineer, 8 December, 1862. First Assistant Engineer, 1 March, 1864. Resigned 14 May, 1867.
RENSHAW, JAMES.
Midshipman, 7 July, 1800. Lieutenant, 25 February, 1807. Commander, 10 December, 1814. Captain, 3 March, 1825. Died 29 May, 1846.
RENSHAW, RICHARD T.
Midshipman, 26 January, 1838. Passed Midshipman, 20 May, 1844. Acting Master, 10 September, 1851. Resigned 29 June, 1852. Acting Lieutenant, 13 May, 1861. Commander, 22 September, 1862. Captain, 20 September, 1868. Retired List, 10 December, 1874. Died 22 March, 1879.
RENSHAW, SAMUEL.
Midshipman, 4 July, 1805. Died 11 October, 1826.
RENSHAW, WILLIAM B.
Midshipman, 17 November, 1831. Passed Midshipman, 15 June, 1837. Lieutenant, 8 September, 1841. Commander, 26 April, 1861. Killed in Battle 1 January, 1863.
RETTIG, AUGUST.
Boatswain, 1 September, 1898.
REUSCH, JOHN.
Acting Third Assistant Engineer, 18 February, 1865. Died 13 September, 1867.
REVELL, JOHN.
Mate, 1 October, 1862. Promoted Acting Ensign, 8 May, 1863. Resigned 17 February, 1865.
REVERE, JOSEPH W.
Midshipman, 1 April, 1828. Passed Midshipman, 4 June, 1834. Lieutenant, 25 February, 1841. Resigned 20 September, 1850.
REVILLE, JOHN M. C.
Mate, 28 March, 1862. Acting Ensign, 5 March, 1863. Resigned 29 May, 1865.
REX, GEORGE A.
Acting Third Assistant Engineer, 16 February, 1865. Honorably discharged 17 July, 1865.
REXFORD, GEORGE H.
Mate, 7 November, 1863. Acting Ensign, 11 November, 1864. Honorably discharged 27 August, 1865.
REYNER, EBENEZER.
Midshipman, 1 May, 1822. Died 28 June, 1824.
REYNOLDS, A. H.
Mate, 2 December, 1861. Acting Ensign, 30 July, 1862. Died 27 February, 1865.
REYNOLDS, ALBERT W.
Acting First Assistant Engineer, 17 May, 1861. Resigned 1 July, 1861. Acting First Assistant Engineer, 8 September, 1864. / Honorably discharged 16 August, 1865.
REYNOLDS, ALFRED.
Midshipman, 22 September, 1869. Graduated 31 May, 1873. Ensign, 16 July, 1874. Master, 1 January, 1881. Lieutenant, Junior Grade, 3 March, 1883. Lieutenant, 9 November, 1886. Lieutenant-Commander, 3 March, 1899.
REYNOLDS, CHARLES E.
Pharmacist, 15 September, 1898.
REYNOLDS, CHARLES W.
Acting Second Assistant Engineer, 21 June, 1862. Acting First Assistant Engineer, 1 July, 1864. Honorably discharged 2 November, 1865.
REYNOLDS, EDWARD.
Carpenter, 15 January, 1800. Warrant returned 11 September, 1800.
REYNOLDS, EDWARD D.
Purser, 17 October, 1846. Resigned 7 July, 1857.
REYNOLDS, EDWIN L.
Midshipman, 22 June, 1870. Graduated 1 June, 1874. Ensign, 17 July, 1875. Master, 12 October, 1881. Lieutenant, Junior Grade, 3 March, 1883. Resigned 18 April, 1886.
REYNOLDS, EZEKIEL F.
Acting Second Assistant Engineer, 1 October, 1862. Acting Second Assistant Engineer, 24 December, 1862. Acting First Assistant Engineer, 15 October, 1863. Honorably discharged 19 November, 1865.
REYNOLDS, GEORGE C.
Acting Assistant Surgeon, 19 April, 1864. Honorably discharged 7 December, 1865.

GENERAL NAVY REGISTER.

REYNOLDS, HENRY C.
Acting Third Assistant Engineer, 28 September, 1864. Honorably discharged 21 August, 1865.
REYNOLDS, JOHN.
Assistant Surgeon, 2 May, 1809. Resigned 15 November, 1811.
REYNOLDS, JULIEN S.
Mate, 4 September, 1862. Resigned 20 June, 1866.
REYNOLDS, LOVELL K.
Midshipman, 5 June, 1871. Graduated 20 June, 1876. Ensign, 28 December, 1878. Lieutenant, Junior Grade, 9 January, 1886. Lieutenant, 25 June, 1891. Died 16 February, 1893.
REYNOLDS, MATTHEW G.
Midshipman, 22 September, 1870. Graduated 1 June, 1874. Ensign, 17 July, 1875. Resigned 30 November, 1877.
REYNOLDS, RICHARD.
Sailmaker, 22 November, 1826. Resigned 8 June, 1827.
REYNOLDS, SILAS.
Acting Master, 22 May, 1861. Honorably discharged 31 October, 1865. Acting Master, 9 October, 1866. Mustered out 8 October, 1868.
REYNOLDS, THEODORE O.
Acting Third Assistant Engineer, 24 September, 1862. Acting Second Assistant Engineer, 6 October, 1863. Appointment revoked (sick) 2 December, 1864.
REYNOLDS, THOMAS.
Surgeon, 10 September, 1798. Died 11 July, 1800.
REYNOLDS, WILLIAM.
Midshipman, 17 November, 1831. Passed Midshipman, 15 June, 1837. Lieutenant, 8 September, 1841. Reserved List (sick), 24 September, 1855. Naval Storekeeper at Honolulu, 23 February, 1857. Active List, 25 April, 1861. Commander, 9 June, 1862. Captain, 25 July, 1866. Commodore, 10 June, 1870. Rear-Admiral, 12 December, 1873. Retired List, 10 December, 1877. Died 5 November, 1879.
REYNOLDS, WILLIAM H.
Naval Cadet, 6 September, 1893. Ensign, 1 July, 1899.
REYNOLDS, ZIBA W.
Naval Cadet, 21 May, 1886. Resigned 23 February, 1887. Assistant Paymaster, 27 May, 1892. Passed Assistant Paymaster, 9 January, 1895. Paymaster, 23 April, 1899.
REYNOLDS, W. L.
Boatswain, 14 June, 1822. Died 21 May, 1823.
RHIND, ALEXANDER C.
Midshipman, 3 September, 1838. Passed Midshipman, 2 July, 1845. Master, 30 April, 1853. Lieutenant, 17 February, 1854. Lieutenant-Commander, 16 July, 1862. Commander, 2 January, 1863. Captain, 2 March, 1870. Commodore, 30 September, 1876. Rear-Admiral, 30 October, 1883. Retired List, 31 October, 1883. Died 8 November, 1897.
RHOADES, ARCHIBALD C.
Assistant Surgeon, 30 July, 1861. Passed Assistant Surgeon, 22 June, 1864. Surgeon, 19 March, 1865. Retired List, 14 September, 1888.
RHOADES, HENRY E.
Acting First Assistant Engineer, 10 June, 1862. Dismissed 25 July, 1863.
RHOADES, HENRY E.
Acting Third Assistant Engineer, 11 February, 1865. Honorably discharged 3 October, 1865. Acting Third Assistant Engineer, 19 December, 1866. Mustered out 23 April, 1869. Second Assistant Engineer, 8 March, 1871. Assistant Engineer, 24 February, 1874. Lieutenant (by virtue of Personal Act), 3 March, 1899. Retired List, 30 December, 1874.
RHOADES, JOSEPH L.
Acting Third Assistant Engineer, 16 February, 1864. Honorably discharged 31 August, 1865.
RHOADES, SAMUEL.
Sailmaker, 2 August, 1845. Resigned 19 February, 1847.
RHOADES, STEPHEN W.
Acting Ensign, 21 August, 1862. Acting Master, 19 June, 1863. Honorably discharged 18 March, 1868.
RHOADES, WILLIAM W.
Acting Ensign, 19 August, 1864. Acting Master, 2 April, 1866. Ensign, 12 March, 1868. Master, 13 December, 1868. Lieutenant, 21 March, 1870. Lieutenant-Commander, 9 February, 1884. Died 30 September, 1893.
RHOADS, EDWIN C.
Lieutenant, Junior Grade (Spanish-American War), 23 June, 1898. Honorably discharged 8 October, 1898.
RHOADS, THOMAS L.
Assistant Surgeon, 27 May, 1898. Resigned 16 November, 1898.
RHODES, HENRY E.
Acting Third Assistant Engineer, 19 December, 1866. Mustered out 23 April, 1869.
RHODES, HILLARY H.
Midshipman, 10 May, 1820. Lieutenant, 17 May, 1828. Dropped 13 September, 1855.
RHODES, ROBERT.
Mate, 11 October, 1861. Acting Master, 27 January, 1862. Killed in action on Clifton, 8 September, 1863.
RHODES, STEWART.
Assistant Paymaster, 13 January, 1900.
RHODES, WILLIAM, Jr.
Midshipman, 28 February, 1799. Discharged 10 July, 1801, under Peace Establishment Act.

460　　　　　GENERAL NAVY REGISTER.

RHODES, ZACHARIAH.
　Lieutenant, 3 October, 1798. Discharged 13 May, 1801, under Peace Establishment Act.
RIBER, CHARLES L.
　Acting Third Assistant Engineer, 26 March, 1863. Resigned 7 November, 1863.
RIBLETT, JOHN.
　Acting Gunner, 22 September, 1862. Resigned 18 February, 1865.
RIBLETT, JOHN F.
　Acting Gunner, 1 October, 1862. Resigned 18 February, 1868.
RICAND, RICHARD.
　Master, date not known. Chesapeake Flotilla. Discharged 15 April, 1815.
RICARD, JAMES.
　Sailmaker, 11 September, 1799. Last appearance on Records of Navy Department.
RICE, ALBERT R.
　Acting Assistant Surgeon, 27 January, 1864. Honorably discharged 20 September, 1865.
RICE, ALEXANDER J.
　Assistant Surgeon, 5 March, 1847. Died 20 April 1851.
RICE, BERNARD.
　Acting Third Assistant Engineer, 11 October, 1864. Honorably discharged 8 August, 1865.
RICE, C. C.
　Purser, 17 October, 1839. Died 5 March, 1846.
RICE, CHARLES H.
　Acting Ensign, 23 December, 1862. Resigned 4 April, 1863. Acting Ensign, 26 September, 1863. Appointment revoked (sick) 29 February, 1864.
RICE, GEORGE B.
　Naval Cadet, 6 September, 1892. Assistant Engineer, 6 May, 1898. Rank changed to Ensign, 3 March, 1899.
RICE, GEORGE H.
　Mate, 11 June, 1861. Acting Ensign, 30 May, 1865. Honorably discharged 12 February, 1868.
RICE, GEORGE M.
　Acting Master's Mate. Dismissed 3 January, 1862.
RICE, GEORGE R.
　Midshipman, 4 July, 1805. Dismissed 21 April, 1807.
RICE, JAMES.
　Mate, 12 August, 1864. Deserted 17 October, 1865.
RICE, JAMES B.
　Acting Third Assistant Engineer, 22 June, 1863. Honorably discharged 29 July, 1865.
RICE, J. D
　Acting First Assistant Engineer. Resigned 27 December, 1862.
RICE, JOHN H.
　Acting Ensign, 30 December, 1862. Acting Master, 20 July, 1864. Honorably discharged 26 October, 1865.
RICE, JOHN M.
　Assistant Surgeon, 28 April, 1863. Died 13 July, 1868.
RICE, JOHN M.
　Professor, 26 March, 1873. Retired List, 20 October, 1890.
RICE, LAWSON E.
　Acting Assistant Paymaster, 9 October, 1863. Resigned 1 August, 1866.
RICE, M.
　Assistant Surgeon, 13 May, 1800. Last appearance on Records of Navy Department.
RICE, OLIVER B.
　Acting Master's Mate, 13 December, 1861. Dismissed 30 December, 1861.
RICE, THOMAS.
　Acting Assistant Surgeon, 1 October, 1862. Drowned 7 November, 1864.
RICE, WARREN E.
　Acting Assistant Paymaster, 2 December, 1864. Mustered out 29 September, 1867.
RICE, WILLIAM.
　Midshipman, 9 November, 1813. Lost at sea, 1 February, 1824.
RICH, ABRAHAM.
　Acting Ensign, 28 September, 1863. Acting Master, 16 January, 1865. Honorably discharged 26 September, 1865.
RICH, ALBERT F.
　Mate, 19 January, 1863. Resigned 30 March, 1865.
RICH, ANDREW J.
　Acting Ensign, 6 March, 1863. Died at Chelsea, Mass., 29 September, 1863.
RICH, CHARLES E.
　Mate, 7 January, 1862. Acting Ensign, 23 April, 1863. Honorably discharged 23 October, 1866. Boatswain, 11 August, 1873. Died 3 May, 1880.
RICH, ELIAS B.
　Mate, 19 January, 1865. Honorably discharged 16 November, 1865
RICH, ALKANAH, Jr.
　Acting Ensign, 2 July, 1863. Resigned 30 April, 1864.
RICH, GEORGE W.
　Mate, 7 May, 1863. Resigned 18 October, 1864.
RICH, JOHN A.
　Mate, 1 April, 1865. Resigned 17 May, 1865.
RICH, JOHN C.
　Midshipman, 23 September, 1862. Graduated June, 1866. Ensign, 12 March, 1868. Master, 26 March, 1869. Lieutenant, 21 March, 1870. Lieutenant-Commander, 8 June, 1885. Commander, 31 July, 1894. Died 27 December, 1895.

GENERAL NAVY REGISTER. 461

RICH, REUBEN.
Mate, 24 April, 1862. Acting Ensign, 19 March, 1866. Honorably discharged 1 May, 1868.
RICH, WILLIAM A.
Acting Ensign, 1 June, 1864. Honorably discharged 25 September, 1866.
RICHARDS, BENJAMIN S.
Midshipman, 22 October, 1861. Graduated June, 1866. Ensign, 12 March, 1868. Master, 26 March, 1869. Retired as Ensign, 17 June, 1869. Master on Active List, 26 March, 1869. Lieutenant, 21 March, 1871. Lieutenant-Commander, 25 August, 1887. Commander, 21 June, 1896. Retired List, 30 April, 1898.
RICHARDS, HENRY M. M.
Midshipman, 20 July, 1865. Graduated June, 1869. Ensign, 12 July, 1870. Master, 12 July, 1871. Resigned 31 December, 1874.
RICHARDS, HENRY, M. M.
Lieutenant (Spanish-American War), 28 June, 1898. Honorably discharged 21 October, 1898.
RICHARDS, JAMES W.
Mate, 29 June, 1863. Acting Ensign, 1 January, 1864. Honorably discharged 15 November, 1865.
RICHARDS, JOHN H.
Acting Assistant Surgeon, 19 April, 1864. Honorably discharged 9 October, 1865.
RICHARDS, JOHN M.
Mate, 20 December, 1861. Acting Ensign, 14 November, 1862. Resigned 31 December, 1864.
RICHARDS, LOUIS.
Mate, 30 July, 1862. Resigned 15 June, 1863.
RICHARDS, ROBERT G.
Mate, 11 April, 1862. Resigned 30 September, 1863.
RICHARDS, ROBERT J.
Acting Assistant Surgeon, 8 February, 1865. Honorably discharged 9 January, 1866.
RICHARDS, THEODORE W.
Assistant Surgeon, 12 November, 1894. Passed Assistant Surgeon, 12 November, 1897.
RICHARDS, THOMAS W.
Carpenter, 12 December, 1898.
RICHARDS, WALTER.
Midshipman, 15 November, 1809. Resigned 23 May, 1811.
RICHARDSON, CHARLES.
Midshipman, 19 May, 1832. Resigned 16 February, 1838.
RICHARDSON, CHARLES W.
Acting Ensign, 12 January, 1865. Honorably discharged 27 February, 1866.
RICHARDSON, EDWIN H.
Mate, 25 November, 1864. Honorably discharged 28 November, 1866.
RICHARDSON, EDWIN P.
Acting Third Assistant Engineer, 12 January, 1863. Resigned (sick) 12 April, 1863.
RICHARDSON, H. A.
Acting Assistant Surgeon, 6 August, 1861. Resigned 5 June, 1862.
RICHARDSON, HENRY.
Acting Assistant Surgeon, 3 March, 1865. Honorably discharged 10 October, 1865.
RICHARDSON, JAMES F.
Acting Master, 1 October, 1862. Acting Volunteer Lieutenant, 10 October, 1862. Resigned 31 May, 1864.
RICHARDSON, J. C.
Assistant Surgeon, 17 May, 1814. Resigned 16 July, 1819.
RICHARDSON, J. C.
Midshipman, 25 June, 1838. Died 29 September, 1841.
RICHARDSON, JOS.
Midshidman, 16 May, 1799. Dissmissed 17 May, 1803.
RICHARDSON, JOS.
Boatswain, 8 June, 1822. Last appearance on Records of Navy Department. Discharged.
RICHARDSON, JOS.
Purser, 3 August, 1796. (See Midshipmen.)
RICHARDSON, JOSEPH.
Mate, 23 December, 1862. Acting Ensign, 19 July, 1864. Honorably discharged 9 March, 1868.
RICHARDSON, JOHN H.
Acting Master, 24 May, 1862. Honorably discharged 2 June, 1866.
RICHARDSON, JOHN R.
Acting Assistant Surgeon, 22 July, 1864. Resigned 30 March, 1865.
RICHARDSON, LOUIS C.
Naval Cadet, 6 September, 1893. Ensign, 1 July, 1899.
RICHARDSON, R. JULIUS.
Assistant Paymaster, 6 September, 1861. Paymaster, 3 September, 1862. Resigned 17 October, 1864.
RICHARDSON, N. B.
Midshipman, 14 May, 1819. Died 26 July, 1822.
RICHARDSON, P. W.
Gunner, 14 May, 1842. Resigned 26 August, 1843.
RICHARDSON, WALTER G.
Cadet Midshipman, 12 June, 1876. Graduated 22 June, 1882. Ensign, Junior Grade, 3 March, 1883. Ensign, 26 June, 1884. Retired List, 22 June, 1889.
RICHARDSON, WENTWORTH R.
Assistant Surgeon, 30 July, 1861. Died 20 July, 1864.

RICHARDSON, WILLIAM.
Acting Third Assistant Engineer, 15 November, 1861. Resigned 24 January, 1863.
RICHARDSON, WILLIAM.
Acting Master, 23 May, 1862. Acting Master and Pilot, 1 October, 1864. Died 17 April, 1865.
RICHARDSON, WILLIAM W.
Carpenter, 31 March, 1873. Retired List, 1 November, 1892. Died 14 November, 1892.
RICHARDSON, W. N.
Assistant Surgeon, 10 December, 1814. Resigned 2 May, 1815.
RICHARDT, S., JR.
Master, 27 February, 1809. Last appearance on Records of Navy Department, 26 July, 1814. Dead.
RICHDALE, HENRY W.
Mate, 27 May, 1861. Acting Ensign, 17 December, 1864. Honorably discharged 19 November, 1865.
RICHEY, OLIVER G.
Acting Third Assistant Engineer, 1 October, 1862. Acting Second Assistant Engineer, 1 December, 1862. Acting First Assistant Engineer, 22 June, 1863. Honorably discharged 19 November, 1865.
RICHEY, WILLIAM B.
Acting Third Assistant Engineer, 22 April, 1863. Honorably discharged 20 February, 1866.
RICHMAN, CLAYTON S.
Midshipman, 21 July, 1865. Graduated 7 June, 1870. Ensign, 12 July, 1871. Master, 2 August, 1873. Lieutenant, 26 February, 1878. Lieutenant-Commander, 3 July, 1898. Retired List, with rank of Commander, 30 June, 1900.
RICHMOND, GILBERT.
Acting Master, 29 October, 1861. Appointment revoked 1 April, 1865
RICHMOND, JONATHAN.
Mate. Dismissed 30 December, 1862.
RICHMOND, WILLIAM H.
Mate, 15 September, 1863. Resigned 22 January, 1866.
RICHWIEN, FREDERICK H.
Acting Warrant Machinest, 23 August, 1899.
RICKARDS, WILLIAM H.
Carpenter, 7 May, 1869. Died 14 December, 1874.
RICKER, CHARLES C.
Acting Ensign, 9 September, 1862. Acting Master, 25 November, 1863. Acting Volunteer Lieutenant, 25 May, 1865. Honorably discharged 30 August, 1868.
RICKER, GEORGE P.
Midshipman, 1 September, 1828. Resigned 17 February, 1829.
RICKETSON, A.
Acting Assistant Surgeon, 13 July, 1861. Resigned 9 December, 1863.
RICKETTS, DAVID F.
Assistant Surgeon, 24 January, 1862. Died 8 January, 1866.
RIDDELL, JOHN W.
Midshipman, 12 October, 1848. Resigned 10 September, 1849.
RIDDLE, DANIEL W.
Acting Assistant Paymaster, 2 July, 1863. Mustered out 8 December, 1865.
RIDDLE, GIRARD E.
Acting Third Assistant Engineer, 29 September, 1862. Acting Second Assistant Engineer, 15 June, 1863. Honorably discharged 7 September, 1865.
RIDDLE, JAMES, JR.
Midshipman, 31 May, 1833. Dismissed 25 July, 1840.
RIDDLE, ROBERT B.
Second Lieutenant, 24 April, 1810. Died in September, 1811.
RIDDLE, THOMAS.
Midshipman, 18 June, 1812. Dismissed 1 March, 1813.
RIDDLE, WILLIAM K.
Naval Cadet, 5 September, 1896. Graduated 30 June, 1900.
RIDER, FREDERICK C.
Cadet Midshipman, 12 September, 1877. Graduated 10 June, 1881. Assistant Engineer, 1 July, 1883. Died 10 September, 1885.
RIDGATE, THOMAS.
Mate, 3 August, 1866. Resigned 7 February, 1867.
RIDGELEY, C. G.
Midshipman, 19 October, 1799. Lieutenant, 2 February, 1807. Commander, 24 July, 1813. Captain, 28 February, 1815. Died 8 February, 1848.
RIDGELEY, FRANK E.
Naval Cadet, 6 September, 1892. Ensign, 6 May, 1898.
RIDGELEY, G. W.
Midshipman, 5 December, 1799. Lost in the Insurgent.
RIDGELY, DANIEL B.
Midshipman, 1 April, 1828. Passed Midshipman, 14 June, 1834. Lieutenant, 10 September, 1840. Commander, 14 September, 1855. Captain, 16 November, 1862. Commodore, 25 July, 1866. Died 5 May, 1868.
RIDGELY, G. W.
Chaplain, 24 April, 1828. Resigned 2 September, 1830.
RIDGELY, JAMES S.
Midshipman, 11 September, 1835. Passed Midshipman, 22 June, 1841. Lieutenant, 31 October, 1848. Died 8 April, 1851.
RIDGELY, JOHN.
Surgeon, 2 July, 1803. Resigned 26 August, 1808.

GENERAL NAVY REGISTER. 463

RIDGELY, THOMAS G.
   Acting Second Assistant Engineer, 20 July, 1864. Honorably discharged 17 September, 1865.
RIDGEWAY, CHARLES M.
   Acting Third Assistant Engineer, 26 March, 1863. Resigned 5 August, 1863.
RIDGLEY, CHARLES W.
   Acting Third Assistant Engineer, 1 October, 1862. Discharged 24 January, 1863.
RIDGLY, CHARLES S.
   Midshipman, 1 November, 1826. Passed Midshipman, 10 June, 1833. Lieutenant, 22 December, 1838. Died 14 October, 1839.
RIDGWAY, EBEN.
   Midshipman, 1 January, 1812. Lieutenant, 5 March, 1817. Commander, 28 February, 1838. Died 31 October, 1841.
RIDGWAY, JOSEPH T.
   Mate, 25 June, 1862. Acting Ensign, 23 August, 1864. Resigned 21 March, 1865.
RIDOUX, LEON.
   Acting Carpenter, 11 February, 1876. Resigned 1 July, 1877. Acting Carpenter, 22 October, 1878. Appointment revoked 2 September, 1879.
RIEG, PHILIP S.
   Assistant Surgeon (Spanish-American War), 30 July, 1898. Honorably discharged 27 September, 1898.
RIGBY, HENRY.
   Carpenter, 7 December, 1878. Chief Carpenter, 3 March, 1899.
RIGG, JOHN.
   Mate, 3 February, 1863. Appointment revoked (sick) 7 November, 1864.
RIGGS, CHARLES E.
   Assistant Surgeon, 13 April, 1893. Passed Assistant Surgeon, 13 April, 1896.
RIGGS, J. MORTON.
   Assistant Paymaster (Spanish-American War), 9 June, 1898. Discharged 2 September, 1898.
RIGGS, RICHARD.
   Acting Master and Pilot, 1 October, 1864. Honorably discharged 12 August, 1866.
RIGGS, WILLIAM J.
   Assistant Surgeon, 19 December, 1873. Resigned 24 July, 1876.
RILEY, BENNET J.
   Acting Midshipman, 27 December, 1850. Midshipman, 14 July, 1852. Lost in the Albany, 28 September, 1854.
RILEY, GEORGE.
   Mate, 27 January, 1863. Acting Ensign, 25 November, 1863. Dismissed 5 August, 1864.
RILEY, GEORGE H.
   Third Assistant Engineer, 21 July, 1858. Second Assistant Engineer, 1 July, 1861. Resigned 17 October, 1865.
RILEY, JOHN.
   Acting Gunner, 20 November, 1873. Resigned 29 June, 1874.
RILEY, JOHN T.
   Acting Warrant Machinest, 23 August, 1899.
RILEY, REUBEN.
   Acting Third Assistant Engineer, 29 August, 1863. Acting Second Assistant Engineer, 18 November, 1864. Honorably discharged 20 August, 1865.
RILEY, ROBERT K.
   Acting Volunteer Lieutenant, 1 October, 1862. Resigned 16 February, 1863.
RIND, S. Z. K.
   Third Assistant Engineer, 7 September, 1855. Resigned 10 November, 1858.
RINEHART, BENJAMIN F.
   Midshipman, 26 September, 1868. Graduated 1 June, 1872. Ensign, 15 July, 1873. Master, 1 December, 1877. Lieutenant, Junior Grade, 3 March, 1883. Retired List, 26 November, 1884. Died 29 December, 1884.
RING, JAMES A.
   Assistant Paymaster, 24 January, 1870. Passed Assistant Paymaster, 23 February, 1877. Paymaster, 20 August, 1889. Pay Inspector, 10 July, 1900.
RING, JOHN L.
   Midshipman, 1 April, 1828. Passed Midshipman, 14 June, 1834. Lieutenant, 10 September, 1840. Dropped 13 September, 1855.
RING, THOMAS.
   Boatswain, 1 July, 1825. Died 25 September, 1835.
RINGGOLD, CADWALADER.
   Midshipman, 4 March, 1819. Lieutenant, 17 May, 1828. Commander, 16 July, 1849. Reserved List, 13 September, 1855. Captain on Active List, 2 April, 1856. Commodore, 16 July, 1862. Rear-Admiral, Retired List, 25 July, 1866. Died 29 April, 1867.
RINGOLD, W. S.
   Passed Midshipman, 9 December, 1841. Resigned 25 April, 1843.
RINGOLD, W. S.
   Midshipman, 1 November, 1828. Passed Midshipman, 14 June, 1834. Cashiered 4 August, 1840.
RINGOT, CHARLES.
   Acting Ensign, 14 October, 1862. Killed in action on Shawsheen, 7 May, 1864.
RINKER, JOHN M.
   Midshipman, 1 January, 1818. Lieutenant, 3 March, 1827. Died 30 May, 1833.
RINKER, SAMUEL.
   Master, 3 September, 1813. Died 10 July, 1823.

RION, PIERRE C.
Midshipman, 1 January, 1817. Last appearance on Records of Navy Department, 1821. New Orleans.
RIPLEY, CHARLES S.
Cadet Midshipman, 24 June, 1875. Graduated 10 June, 1881. Ensign, Junior Grade, 3 March, 1883. Ensign, 26 June, 1884. Lieutenant, Junior Grade, 2 August, 1891. Lieutenant, 5 November, 1895. Retired List, 22 April, 1898.
RIPLEY, HENRY E.
Mate, 13 April, 1862. Discharged 15 February, 1865.
RIPLEY, JAMES W.
Midshipman, 5 October, 1836. Passed Midshipman, 1 July, 1842. Dismissed 19 November, 1844.
RISBELL, THOMAS T.
Acting Third Assistant Engineer, 12 April, 1864. Honorably discharged 28 August, 1865.
RITCHIE, CHARLES O.
Midshipman, 18 January, 1837. Dismissed 9 May, 1839.
RITCHIE, DAVID.
Passed Assistant Engineer (Spanish-American War), 24 May, 1898. Honorably discharged 10 October, 1898.
RITCHIE, GEORGE H.
Purser, 1 April, 1853. Dismissed 29 April, 1861.
RITCHIE, JOHN T.
Midshipman, 17 December, 1810. Lieutenant, 27 April, 1816. Died 26 June, 1831.
RITCHIE, ROBERT.
Midshipman, 1 February, 1814. Lieutenant, 13 January, 1825. Commander, 8 September, 1841. Reserved List, 13 September, 1855. Captain on Active List, 14 September, 1855. Retired List, 21 December, 1861. Commodore on Retired List, 4 April, 1867. Died 6 July, 1870.
RITER, D. CLINTON.
Acting First Assistant Engineer, 27 July, 1863. Acting Chief Engineer, 9 May, 1864. Honorably discharged 5 April, 1866.
RITTENHOUSE, B. F.
Midshipman, 2 January, 1804. Died 2 September, 1804.
RITTENHOUSE, HAWLEY O.
Midshipman, 27 July, 1866. Graduated 7 June, 1870. Ensign, 13 July, 1871. Master, 10 September, 1873. Lieutenant, 5 June, 1878. Lieutenant-Commander, 10 August, 1898. Retired List, with rank of Commander, 30 June, 1899.
RITTENHOUSE, JOHN B.
Purser, 21 July, 1840. Pay Director, 3 March, 1871. Retired List, 13 October, 1871. Died 22 January, 1874.
RITTENHOUSE, WILLIAM M.
Midshipman, 30 November, 1814. Died in 1823.
RITTER, BENJAMIN F.
Mate, 13 May, 1862. Acting Gunner, 20 December, 1862. Dismissed 28 November, 1863. Mate, 20 May, 1864. Dismissed 24 May, 1866.
RITTER, HENRY.
Acting Third Assistant Engineer, 22 January, 1864. Lost on Tecumseh, 1 August, 1864.
RITTER, HENRY S.
Naval Cadet, 25 May, 1886. Ensign, 1 July, 1892. Lieutenant, Junior Grade, 3 March, 1899. Lieutenant, 4 June, 1899. Retired List, 22 August, 1900.
RITTER, JOHN C.
Gunner, 18 September, 1845. Retired List, 9 March, 1877.
RIVERS, ALONZO M.
Mate, 18 January, 1864. Discharged 13 September, 1867.
RIVERS, CHARLES W.
Midshipman, 2 April, 1804. Left the service April, 1805.
RIVERS, FRANK.
Acting Third Assistant Engineer, 1 November, 1864. Honorably discharged 8 July, 1865.
RIVERS, JAMES H.
Mate, 1 October, 1862. Acting Ensign, 25 June, 1863. Honorably discharged 28 October, 1865.
RIVES, ORAN A.
Acting Assistant Surgeon, 12 July, 1864. Honorably discharged 18 May, 1867.
RIXEY, PRESLEY M.
Assistant Surgeon, 28 January, 1874. Passed Assistant Surgeon, 18 April, 1877. Surgeon, 27 November, 1888. Commissioned Medical Inspector U. S. N., 24 August, 1900.
RIXEY, PRESLEY M., JR.
Naval Cadet (Spanish-American War), 15 June, 1898. Honorably discharged 6 December, 1898.
ROACH, JAMES.
Midshipman, 26 April, 1802. Last appearance on Records of Navy Department, November, 1805. Dead.
ROACH, JAMES T.
Gunner, 6 March, 1899.
ROACH, JOHN.
Acting Third Assistant Engineer, 13 June, 1864. Honorably discharged 24 June, 1866.
ROACH, JOHN B.
Acting Second Assistant Engineer, 4 March, 1864. Honorably discharged 10 December, 1865.
ROACH, THOMAS.
Mate, 26 September, 1863. Honorably discharged 18 November, 1865.

ROACHE, JAMES.
Midshipman, 5 December, 1798. Discharged 12 October, 1801, under Peace Establishment Act.
ROAKE, JOHN L.
Acting Third Assistant Engineer, 29 August, 1863. Appointment revoked (sick) 31 July, 1864.
ROANE, ALEXANDER H.
Third Assistant Engineer, 27 January, 1848. Resigned 11 February, 1850.
ROANE, SAMUEL B.
Acting Third Assistant Engineer, 30 May, 1864. Honorably discharged 4 February, 1868.
ROANE, WILLIAM.
Midshipman, 30 November, 1814. Resigned 25 June, 1818.
ROATH, WARRINGTON P.
Acting Master, 20 September, 1861. Acting Volunteer Lieutenant, 7 July, 1863. Resigned 7 March, 1865.
ROBB, ROBERT G.
Midshipman, 6 September, 1821. Passed Midshipman, 24 May, 1828. Lieutenant, 27 May, 1830. Commander, 2 November, 1852. Dismissed 18 April, 1861.
ROBBINS, C. A.
Acting Assistant Paymaster, 25 June, 1864. Honorably discharged 31 October, 1865.
ROBBINS, EUGENE P.
Acting Assistant Surgeon, 6 February, 1863. Resigned 23 July, 1863.
ROBBINS, EZRA L.
Mate, 24 October, 1861. Resigned 4 March, 1862. Mate, 13 January, 1863. Acting Ensign, 29 October, 1863. Acting Master, 21 November, 1864. Honorably discharged 19 February, 1866.
ROBBINS, LEVI.
Acting Third Assistant Engineer, 5 August, 1864. Honorably discharged 1 November, 1865.
ROBBINS, OCTAVIUS H.
Mate, 22 December, 1863. Resigned 9 August, 1864.
ROBBINS, WILLIAM M.
Master, 18 June, 1812. Lieutenant, 27 April, 1816. Died 18 May, 1828.
ROBEN, DOUGLAS.
Midshipman, 23 September, 1862. Graduated June, 1866. Ensign, 12 March, 1868. Master, 26 March, 1869. Lieutenant, 21 March, 1870. Retired List, 26 October, 1872.
ROBERT, WILLIAM P.
Naval Cadet, 20 May, 1890. Graduated 30 June, 1896. Assistant Naval Constructor, 1 July, 1896.
ROBERTS, ARTHUR O.
Mate, 14 October, 1861. Resigned 5 May, 1862.
ROBERTS, BENJAMIN.
Gunner, 25 July, 1861. Resigned 18 June, 1863.
ROBERTS, DAVID.
Boatswain, date not known. Last appearance on Records of Navy Department. Ship General Greene.
ROBERTS, DAVID S.
Acting First Assistant Engineer, 3 October, 1863. Honorably discharged 11 August, 1866.
ROBERTS, EDWARD.
Acting First Assistant Engineer, 13 August, 1863. Died on Rattler, 22 September, 1864.
ROBERTS, EDWARD E.
Third Assistant Engineer, 21 September, 1861. Second Assistant Engineer, 30 July, 1863. Resigned 19 June, 1865.
ROBERTS, EDWARD H.
Acting Assistant Paymaster, 1 August, 1861. Mustered out 22 March, 1866.
ROBERTS, EDWARD V.
Lieutenant (Spanish-American War), 4 May, 1898. Honorably discharged 23 January, 1899.
ROBERTS, JAMES.
Midshipman, 1 September, 1811. Last appearance on Records of Navy Department, 1818. Furloughed.
ROBERTS, JAMES S.
Acting Ensign, 16 April, 1863. Honorably discharged 15 November, 1868.
ROBERTS, J. G.
Assistant Surgeon, 4 March, 1811. Surgeon, 15 April, 1814. Resigned 30 May, 1815.
ROBERTS, JOHN.
Mate, 11 December, 1862. Acting Gunner, 27 November, 1863. Honorably discharged 12 October, 1866.
ROBERTS, JOHN.
Acting Gunner, 27 November, 1863. Honorably discharged 12 October, 1866.
ROBERTS, JOHN H.
Midshipman, 1 March, 1827. Resigned 21 June, 1834.
ROBERTS, JOS.
Purser, date not known. Discharged 10 September, 1801, under Peace Establishment Act.
ROBERTS, LOUIS C.
Ensign (Spanish-American War), 18 June, 1898. Honorably discharged 30 September, 1898.

GENERAL NAVY REGISTER.

ROBERTS, L. Q. C.
Midshipman, 16 January, 1809. Last appearance on Records of Navy Department, 1815. Charleston, S. C.
ROBERTS, MICHAEL.
Boatswain, 15 November, 1810. Dismissed 24 April, 1813.
ROBERTS, MILTON F.
Carpenter, 12 December, 1879. Chief Carpenter, 3 March, 1899.
ROBERTS, M. M.
Boatswain, 18 November, 1814. Dismissed 16 August, 1819.
ROBERTS, ORLANDO S.
Mate, 15 October, 1861. Acting Ensign, 23 August, 1862. Acting Ensign, 27 April, 1866. Resigned 23 September, 1867.
ROBERTS, THOMAS F.
Mate, 19 April, 1864. Honorably discharged 2 August, 1865.
ROBERTS, THOMAS G.
Naval Cadet, 27 May, 1890. Graduated 30 June, 1896. Assistant Naval Constructor, 1 July, 1896.
ROBERTS, THOMAS W.
Acting Ensign, 25 June, 1864. Died on Ozark, 17 August, 1864.
ROBERTS, W. H.
Mate, 24 November, 1864. Honorably discharged 12 August, 1865.
ROBERTS, WILLIAM.
Third Assistant Engineer, 2 August, 1855. Second Assistant Engineer, 21 July, 1858. First Assistant Engineer, 3 August, 1859. Resigned 24 August, 1859. First Assistant Engineer, 24 April, 1861. Chief Engineer, 21 April, 1863. Resigned 18 March, 1869.
ROBERTS, WILLIAM.
Mate, 28 July, 1863. Died 15 April, 1864.
ROBERTS, WILLIAM H.
Mate, 8 May, 1862. Acting Ensign, 20 April, 1863. Appointment revoked 23 February, 1864.
ROBERTS, WILLIAM J.
Mate, 20 January, 1863. Resigned 22 June, 1863.
ROBERTS, WILLIAM J.
Lieutenant, Temporary Service, 15 June, 1898. Honorably discharged 2 September, 1898.
ROBERTS, WILLIAM W.
Midshipman, 2 March, 1839. Passed Midshipman, 2 July, 1845. Master, 1 August, 1853. Lieutenant, 1 March, 1854. Resigned 19 May, 1860.
ROBERTSON, ASHLEY H.
Naval Cadet, 4 September, 1884. Ensign, 1 July, 1890. Lieutenant, Junior Grade, 1 February, 1898. Lieutenant, 3 March, 1899.
ROBERTSON, GEORGE W.
Acting Assistant Paymaster, 9 May, 1864. Honorably discharged 7 February, 1866.
ROBERTSON, GILBERT A.
Acting Assistant Paymaster, 14 October, 1861. Passed Assistant Paymaster, 23 July, 1866. Resigned 6 November, 1866.
ROBERTSON, HENRY P.
Midshipman, 28 June, 1832. Passed Midshipman, 8 July, 1839. Lieutenant, 14 August, 1846. Died 4 November, 1850.
ROBERTSON, JAMES P.
Acting Midshipman, 28 September, 1857. Graduated 1861. Lieutenant, 1 August, 1862. Lieutenant-Commander, 25 July, 1866. Died 19 July, 1875.
ROBERTSON, JOHN.
Master, 24 February, 1809. Dismissed 2 April, 1814.
ROBERTSON, JOHN D.
Acting Master, 27 August, 1861. Resigned 1 June, 1864.
ROBERTSON, SAMUEL.
Purser, 25 April, 1812. Died 11 August, 1820.
ROBERTSON, THOMAS.
Midshipman, 11 September, 1799. Last appearance on Records of Navy Department, 24 October, 1799. Resigned.
ROBERTSON, W. J. H.
Midshipman, 1 November, 1827. Passed Midshipman, 10 June, 1833. Lieutenant, 24 May, 1838. Died 18 December, 1843.
ROBESON, HENRY B.
Acting Midshipman, 25 September, 1856. Midshipman, 15 June, 1860. Master, 19 September, 1861. Lieutenant, 16 July, 1862. Lieutenant-Commander, 25 July, 1866. Commander, 12 February, 1874. Captain, 25 August, 1887. Commodore, 1 February, 1898. Retired List, with rank of Rear-Admiral, 28 March, 1899.
ROBESON, JOHN.
Boatswain, 1 January, 1817. Died in October, 1820.
ROBIE, EDWARD D.
Third Assistant Engineer, 16 February, 1852. Second Assistant Engineer, 27 July, 1855. First Assistant Engineer, 21 July, 1858. Chief Engineer, 30 July, 1861. Retired List, 11 September, 1893.
ROBIE, HENRY W.
Third Assistant Engineer, 3 May, 1859. Second Assistant Engineer, 9 April, 1862. First Assistant Engineer, 20 May, 1863. Resigned 25 May, 1868.
ROBINETT, DAVID.
Carpenter, 28 October, 1858. Died 15 November, 1880.
ROBINETT, RICHARD.
Midshipman, 20 August, 1814. Resigned 7 June, 1815.

GENERAL NAVY REGISTER. 467

ROBINS, D. W.
  Mate, 12 November, 1864. Appointment revoked 16 January, 1866.
ROBINS, HARRISON L.
  Assistant Paymaster, 20 May, 1898. Passed Assistant Paymaster, 1 September, 1899.
ROBINS, JOHN L.
  Mate, 9 May, 1862. Resigned 27 April, 1865.
ROBINS, ROBERT W.
  Mate, 24 September, 1863. Resigned 13 April, 1864. Mate, 12 November, 1864. Appointment revoked 16 January, 1866.
ROBINS, THOMAS.
  Midshipman, 9 August, 1798. Died 8 September, 1798.
ROBINS, WILLIAM C.
  Acting Assistant Paymaster, 3 February, 1864. Mustered out 5 March, 1866.
ROBINSON, ALEXANDER.
  Assistant Surgeon, 26 April, 1847. Died 11 March, 1849.
ROBINSON, ALEXANDER A.
  Acting Ensign, 18 October, 1864. Dismissed 23 December, 1864.
ROBINSON, ALEXANDER B.
  Acting Assistant Paymaster, 11 April, 1863. Honorably discharged 21 November, 1865.
ROBINSON, ANDREW J.
  Boatswain, 27 November, 1860. Deserted 22 July, 1861.
ROBINSON, ARTHUR L.
  Assistant Engineer (Spanish-American War), 14 May, 1898. Honorably discharged 22 December, 1898.
ROBINSON, BENJAMIN F.
  Mate, 21 January, 1864. Honorably discharged 10 August, 1865.
ROBINSON, CHARLES.
  Midshipman, 1 May, 1832. Passed Midshipman, 23 June, 1838. Dismissed 11 February, 1840.
ROBINSON, CHARLES.
  Acting Third Assistant Engineer, 4 May, 1864. Honorably discharged 11 October, 1865.
ROBINSON, CHARLES.
  Midshipman, 31 July, 1800. Resigned 23 April, 1807.
ROBINSON, CHARLES.
  Passed Assistant Engineer (Spanish-American War), 4 May, 1898. Honorably discharged 2 September, 1898.
ROBINSON, CHARLES.
  Acting Third Assistant Engineer, 12 August, 1862. Dismissed 6 March, 1863.
ROBINSON, EDWARD A.
  Acting Third Assistant Engineer, 18 June, 1864. Honorably discharged 30 April, 1868.
ROBINSON, EDWARD W.
  Mate, 23 July, 1863. Honorably discharged 27 November, 1865.
ROBINSON, EUGENE N.
  Ensign (Spanish-American War), 12 May, 1898. Honorably discharged 15 September, 1898.
ROBINSON, FREDERICK W.
  Midshipman, 14 August, 1846. Apointment revoked 12 June, 1849.
ROBINSON, G. H.
  Mate, 4 December, 1867. Appointment revoked 29 February, 1872.
ROBINSON, GEORGE M.
  Acting Third Assistant Engineer, 4 March, 1864. Honorably discharged 8 August, 1865.
ROBINSON, H. B.
  Midshipman, 1 January, 1828. Resigned 4 June, 1828.
ROBINSON, HENRY C.
  Mate, 15 September, 1863. Acting Ensign, 5 August, 1864. Honorably discharged 29 July, 1865.
ROBINSON, H. E. V.
  Mdshipman, 4 March, 1823. Passed Midshipman, 23 March, 1829. Lieutenant, 3 March, 1831. Lost in the Sylph, August, 1831.
ROBINSON, HERBERT J.
  Cadet Midshipman, 15 September, 1875. Graduated 10 June, 1881. Ensign, Junior Grade, 3 March, 1883. Died 19 June, 1883.
ROBINSON, HORATIO G.
  Mate, 12 November, 1863. Honorably discharged 21 June, 1868.
ROBINSON, HORACE.
  Gunner, 11 November, 1850. Resigned 18 July, 1851.
ROBINSON, H. S.
  Acting Third Assistant Engineer, 17 September, 1861. Appointment revoked 22 May, 1862.
ROBINSON, JAMES B.
  Acting Ensign, 1 September, 1864. Honorably discharged 10 August, 1865.
ROBINSON, JAMES W.
  Mate, 11 June, 1863. Appointment revoked (sick) 29 July, 1864.
ROBINSON, JOHN.
  Master, 27 November, 1815. Reserved List, 13 September, 1855. Died 17 March, 1868.
ROBINSON, JOHN.
  Acting Master and Pilot, 1 October, 1864. Honorably discharged 19 December, 1865.
ROBINSON, JOHN.
  Mate, 13 December, 1862. Dismissed 23 April, 1863.
ROBINSON, JOHN B.
  Midshipman, 30 July, 1864. Graduated June, 1868. Ensign, 12 July, 1870. Resigned 31 December, 1874.

ROBINSON, JOHN C.
Mate, 15 November, 1861. Resigned 24 April, 1862.
ROBINSON, JOHN F. D.
Acting Master, 12 March, 1862. Dismissed 21 November, 1863.
ROBINSON, JOHN MARSHALL.
Midshipman, 25 June, 1869. Ensign, 16 July, 1874. Master, 2 January, 1881. Lieutenant, Junior Grade, 3 March, 1883. Lieutenant, 13 December, 1886. Lieutenant-Commander, 3 March, 1899.
ROBINSON, JOSEPH E.
Acting Third Assistant Engineer, 5 November, 1862. Resigned 24 November, 1863.
ROBINSON, L. B.
Midshipman, 4 March, 1840. Resigned 12 March, 1845.
ROBINSON, LEWIS W.
Third Assistant Engineer, 21 September, 1861. Second Assistant Engineer, 30 July, 1863. First Assistant Engineer, 11 October, 1866. Chief Engineer, 19 August, 1883. Rank changed to Captain, 3 March, 1899.
ROBINSON, PETER B.
Acting Third Assistant Engineer, 10 September, 1861. Acting Second Assistant Engineer, 12 November, 1863. Resigned 2 June, 1865.
ROBINSON, RICHARD H.
Naval Cadet, 6 September, 1892. Graduated. Assistant Naval Instructor, 21 April, 1898.
ROBINSON, RICHARD P.
Master's Mate, 19 July, 1842. Deserted 6 December, 1850.
ROBINSON, ROBERT.
Mate, 23 December, 1862. Retired List, 16 April, 1897.
ROBINSON, SAMUEL.
Acting Third Assistant Engineer, 28 January, 1862. Deserted 30 June, 1863.
ROBINSON, SAMUEL.
Assistant Surgeon, 8 February, 1802. Resigned 12 December, 1803.
ROBINSON, SOMERSET.
Assistant Surgeon, 9 May, 1861. Passed Assistant Surgeon, 26 October, 1863. Surgeon, 18 December, 1864. Medical Inspector, 1 May, 1870. Retired List, 15 August, 1887. Died 19 January, 1896.
ROBINSON, THOMAS.
Gunner, 8 November, 1835. Retired List, 22 May, 1863. Died 13 December, 1882.
ROBINSON, THOMAS.
Captain, 24 September, 1799. Discharged 26 September, 1801, under Peace Establishment Act.
ROBINSON, THOMAS, JR.
Midshipman, 30 November, 1798. Lieutenant, 12 July, 1799. Commander, 10 September, 1804. Resigned 20 December, 1809.
ROBINSON, THOMAS J.
Professor, 27 January, 1860. Dismissed 15 August, 1861.
ROBINSON, WILLIAM.
Chaplain, 17 April, 1809. Dismissed 29 May, 1809.
ROBINSON, WILLIAM.
Acting Ensign, 28 October, 1862. Honorably discharged 7 July, 1865. Acting Ensign, 19 November, 1866. Mustered out 2 July, 1868.
ROBINSON, WILLIAM H.
Mate, 3 August, 1866. Mustered out 29 July, 1869.
ROBISON, JOHN K.
Naval Cadet, 20 May, 1887. Assistant Engineer, 1 July, 1893. Passed Assistant Engineer, 9 May, 1897. Rank changed to Lieutenant, Junior Grade, 3 March, 1899. Lieutenant. 8 July, 1899.
ROBISON, SAMUEL S.
Naval Cadet, 4 September, 1884. Ensign, 1 July, 1890. Lieutenant, Junior Grade, 23 April, 1898. Lieutenant, 3 March, 1899.
ROBNETT, JOHN D.
Assistant Paymaster, 13 January, 1900.
ROBSON, CLINTON.
Mate, 29 June, 1863. Resigned 9 December, 1863.
ROBY, JOHN.
Mate, 16 December, 1861. Appointment revoked 23 September, 1862.
ROCHE, GEORGE WALTER.
Third Assistant Engineer, 28 October, 1862. Second Assistant Engineer, 15 March, 1864. First Assistant Engineer, 1 January, 1868. Chief Engineer, 25 August, 1889. Retired List, 3 July, 1896.
ROCHE, JAMES R.
Midshipman, 30 May, 1850. Resigned 12 October, 1855.
ROCHE, MARTIN.
Professor, 19 December, 1835. Dropped 4 September, 1848.
ROCHELLE, JAMES H.
Midshipman, 9 September, 1841. Passed Midshipman, 10 August, 1847. Master, 14 September, 1855. Lieutenant, 15 September, 1855. Dismissed 17 April, 1861.
ROCHFORT, JOHN J.
Boatswain, 15 May, 1897.
ROCK, GEORGE H.
Naval Cadet, 20 May, 1885. Assistant Naval Constructor, 1 July, 1891. Naval Constructor, 23 June, 1898.
ROCKEFELLER, ABRAM T.
Acting Third Assistant Engineer, 4 January, 1862. Acting Second Assistant Engineer, 8 April, 1865. Honorably discharged 30 November, 1865.

ROCKEFELLER, ALFRED.
Acting First Assistant Engineer, 11 August, 1864. Resigned 19 June, 1865.
ROCKEFELLOW, SIMON.
Acting Third Assistant Engineer, 25 November, 1861. Acting Second Assistant Engineer, 12 November, 1863. Honorably discharged 25 October, 1865.
ROCKWELL, CHARLES H.
Acting Master, 5 July, 1862. Acting Volunteer Lieutenant, 16 December, 1863. Acting Volunteer Lieutenant-Commander, 29 April, 1865. Honorably discharged 8 December, 1865. Acting Master, 19 November, 1866. Master, 12 March, 1868. Lieutenant, 18 December, 1868. Lieutenant-Commander, 26 February, 1878. Commander, 31 October, 1888. Captain, 3 March, 1899.
ROCKWELL, GEORGE L.
Acting Third Assistant Engineer, 29 July, 1864. Honorably discharged 12 June, 1865.
ROCKWELL, JAMES V.
Assistant Engineer (Spanish-American War), 22 June, 1898. Honorably discharged 8 February, 1899.
ROCKWELL, JOHN E.
Acting Master, 10 June, 1861. Honorably discharged 2 October, 1865.
ROCKWOOD, HENRY.
Acting Assistant Surgeon, 6 October, 1863. Appointment revoked 16 August, 1865.
RODDY, JOHN.
Sailmaker, 27 April, 1872. Chief Sailmaker, 3 March, 1899.
RODERICK, EDMUND A.
Acting Ensign, 2 March, 1863. Acting Master, 15 December, 1864. Honorably discharged 31 March, 1869.
RODES, HENRY, E.
Acting Third Assistant Engineer, 11 February, 1865. Honorably discharged 3 October, 1865.
RODES, WILLIAM M.
Acting Third Assistant Engineer, 15 September, 1862. Acting First Assistant Engineer, 23 October, 1862. Honorably discharged 6 May, 1870.
RODGER, THOMAS.
Assistant Engineer(Spanish-American War), 3 June, 1898. Honorably discharged 6 February, 1899.
RODGERS, C. R. PERRY.
Midshipman, 5 October, 1833. Passed Midshipman, 8 July, 1839. Lieutenant, 4 September, 1844. Commander, 15 November, 1861. Captain, 25 July, 1866. Commodore, 28 August, 1870. Rear-Admiral, 14 June, 1874. Retired List, 14 November, 1881. Died 8 January, 1892.
RODGERS, FREDERICK.
Midshipman, 4 March, 1823. Died 5 April, 1828.
RODGERS, FREDERICK.
Acting Midshipman, 25 September, 1857. Midshipman, 1 June, 1861. Acting Master, 10 June, 1861. Lieutenant, 16 July, 1862. Lieutenant-Commander, 25 July, 1866. Commander, 4 February, 1875. Captain, 28 February, 1890. Commodore, 25 December, 1898. Rear-Admiral, 3 March, 1899.
RODGERS, GEORGE W.
Midshipman, 14 October, 1839. Passed Midshipman, 2 July, 1845. Acting Master, 4 November, 1846. Lieutenant, 4 June, 1850. Commander, 16 July, 1862. Killed in attack on Fort Sumter, 17 August, 1873.
RODGERS, GEORGE W.
Midshipman, 2 April, 1804. Lieutenant, 24 April, 1810. Commander, 27 April, 1816. Captain, 3 March, 1825. Died 21 May, 1832.
RODGERS, GUY G.
Cadet Midshipman, 26 September, 1876. Honorably discharged, 30 June, 1883. Assistant Paymaster, 22 August, 1864. Died 17 October, 1897.
RODGERS, HENRY.
Midshipman, 11 March, 1837. Passed Midshipman, 29 June, 1843. Master, 7 August, 1850. Lieutenant, 26 March, 1851. Lost in the Albany, 28 September, 1854.
RODGERS, JACOB D.
Acting Third Assistant Engineer, 14 November, 1861. Honorably discharged 26 June, 1866.
RODGERS, JOHN.
Midshipman, 18 April, 1828. Passed Midshipman, 14 June, 1834. Lieutenant, 28 January, 1840. Commander, 14 September, 1855. Captain, 16 July, 1862. Commodore, 17 June, 1863. Rear Admiral, 31 December, 1869. Died 5 May, 1882.
RODGERS, JOHN.
Lieutenant, 9 March, 1798. Captain, 5 March, 1799. Discharged, 23 October, 1801, under Peace Establishment Act.
RODGERS, JOHN.
Captain, 28 August, 1802. Died 1 August, 1838.
RODGERS, JOHN A.
Midshipman, 30 July, 1863. Graduated June, 1868. Master, 12 July, 1870. Lieutenant, 2 February, 1874. Lieutenant-Commander, 1 March, 1895. Commander, 3 March, 1899.
RODGERS, JOHN G.
Midshipman, 4 July, 1817. Lieutenant, 17 May, 1828. Resigned 10 February, 1834.
RODGERS, MATTHEW.
Gunner, 17 August, 1812. Cashiered 20 October, 1818.
RODGERS, RAYMOND P.
Midshipman, 25 July, 1864. Graduated June, 1868. Ensign, 19 April, 1869. Master, 12 July, 1870. Lieutenant, 10 October, 1872. Lieutenant-Commander, 4 July, 1893. Commander, 3 March, 1899.

RODGERS, SAMUEL.
Midshipman, 9 November, 1813. Last appearance on Records of Navy Department, 1824.
RODGERS, SAMUEL R.
Carpenter, 17 February, 1809. Last appearance on Records of Navy Department, 1815. Frigate President.
RODGERS, THOMAS S.
Cadet Midshipman, 24 September, 1874. Graduated 4 June, 1880. Ensign, 1 December, 1881. Lieutenant, Junior Grade, 23 March, 1889. Lieutenant, 1 October, 1893. Lieutenant-Commander, 22 November, 1900.
RODGERS, WALTER.
Midshipman, 16 May, 1811. Resigned 5 October, 1812.
RODGERS, WILLIAM L.
Cadet Midshipman, 11 June, 1874. Graduated 4 June, 1880. Ensign, 1 April, 1882. Lieutenant, Junior Grade, 4 May, 1889. Lieutenant, 4 February, 1894.
RODGERS, WILLIAM J.
Ensign (Spanish-American War), 23 June, 1898. Honorably discharged 8 September, 1898.
RODGERS, WILLIAM T.
Midshipman, 9 November, 1813. Lieutenant, 13 January, 1825. Resigned 21 April, 1827.
RODGERS, W. L.
Midshipman, 9 June, 1811. Dismissed 9 March, 1813.
RODIE, ROBERT.
Acting Third Assistant Engineer, 26 October, 1861. Resigned 28 November, 1862.
RODMAN, HUGH.
Cadet Midshipman, 18 September, 1875. Graduated 22 June, 1882. Ensign, Junior Grade, 3 March, 1883. Ensign, 26 June, 1884. Lieutenant, Junior Grade, 1 October, 1893. Lieutenant 13 July, 1897.
RODMAN, ROBERT C.
Sailmaker, 28 April, 1840. Died 19 September, 1855.
RODMAN, SAMUEL.
Master, date not known. Discharged 15 April, 1815.
RODMAN, SAMUEL S.
Assistant Surgeon, 14 December, 1900.
RODNEY, ROBERT B.
Acting Assistant Paymaster, 24 October, 1862. Passed Assistant Paymaster, 23 July, 1866. Paymaster, 30 June, 1869. Retired List, 2 September, 1871.
RODOCANICHI, LEONIDAS D.
Mate, 22 August, 1863. Honorably discharged 22 May, 1867.
RODRIQUES, P. J.
Master, 4 August, 1827. Professor Mathematics, date not known. Died 14 October, 1838.
ROE, DAVID A.
Gunner, 9 July, 1861. Retired List, 15 March, 1882.
ROE, FRANCIS A.
Midshipman, 19 October, 1841. Passed Midshipman, 10 August, 1847. Master, 8 August, 1855. Lieutenant, 14 September, 1855. Lieutenant-Commander, 16 July, 1862. Commander, 25 July, 1866. Captain, 1 April, 1872. Commodore, 26 November, 1880. Rear Admiral, 3 November, 1884. Retired List, 4 October, 1885.
ROEBUCK, CHARLES P.
Acting First Assistant Engineer, 5 October, 1863. Honorably discharged 27 November, 1865.
ROELKER, CHARLES R.
Third Assistant Engineer, 8 December, 1862. Second Assistant Engineer, 8 April, 1864. First Assistant Engineer, 1 January, 1868. Chief Engineer, 10 November, 1890. Rank changed to Commander, 3 March, 1899.
ROFFENBERG, LEWIS M.
Acting First Assistant Engineer, 3 October, 1864. Honorably discharged 29 June, 1865.
ROGERS, ALLEN G.
Cadet Midshipman, 12 June, 1874. Graduated 4 June, 1880. Ensign, Junior Grade. 3 March, 1883. Ensign, 1 December, 1883. Lieutenant, Junior Grade, 28 February, 1890. Lieutenant, 16 September, 1894.
ROGERS, BENJAMIN F.
Assistant Surgeon, 21 March, 1872. Passed Assistant Surgeon, 20 June, 1876. Surgeon, 30 January, 1887.
ROGERS, CHARLES A.
Acting Third Assistant Engineer, 19 July, 1864. Resigned 7 July, 1865.
ROGERS, CHARLES C.
Midshipman, 7 June, 1872. Graduated 20 June, 1876. Ensign, 26 April, 1878. Lieutenant, Junior Grade, 2 June, 1885. Lieutenant, 27 January, 1891. Lieutenant-Commander, 1 July, 1899.
ROGERS, CHARLES J.
Mate, 6 June, 1861. Acting Ensign, 6 May, 1863. Honorably discharged 22 December, 1865. Lieutenant (Spanish-American War), 15 June, 1898. Honorably discharged 2 September, 1898.
ROGERS, CHARLES W.
Acting Ensign, 23 September, 1863. Acting Master, recommendation of Admiral Lee, 18 August, 1864. Honorably discharged 11 November, 1865.
ROGERS, CLEMENT.
Midshipman, 16 April, 1814. Last appearance on Records of Navy Department, 1816. Resigned.

GENERAL NAVY REGISTER.

ROGERS, EDWARD.
  Mate, 15 November, 1861. Acting Ensign, 30 May, 1863. Deserted 3 May, 1865.
ROGERS, EUGENE.
  Midshipman, 25 November, 1834. Resigned 12 September, 1839.
ROGERS, EUSTACE B.
  Assistant Paymaster, 3 March, 1879. Passed Assistant Paymaster, 2 November, 1884. Paymaster, 24 May, 1894.
ROGERS, FRANK.
  Acting Third Assistant Engineer, 2 March, 1864. Honorably discharged 20 November, 1865.
ROGERS, FRANKLIN.
  Assistant Surgeon, 21 March, 1872. Passed Assistant Surgeon, 20 June, 1876. Surgeon, 30 January, 1887. Medical Inspector, 12 December, 1898.
ROGERS, FRANKLIN G.
  Acting Master's Mate, 24 August, 1864. Resigned 29 May, 1865.
ROGERS, GEORGE.
  Mate, 15 September, 1864. Deserted 24 March, 1867.
ROGERS, GEORGE B.
  Acting Third Assistant Engineer, 1 September, 1863. Honorably discharged 18 October, 1865.
ROGERS, GEORGE C.
  Acting Third Assistant Engineer, 7 July, 1863. Honorably discharged 17 October, 1865.
ROGERS, GEORGE W.
  Third Assistant Engineer, 21 July, 1858. Second Assistant Engineer, 29 October, 1861. Resigned 23 June, 1865.
ROGERS, GEORGE W.
  Acting Ensign, 1 October, 1862. Acting Master, 16 April, 1863. Acting Volunteer Lieutenant, 9 July, 1864. Honorably discharged 15 December, 1868.
ROGERS, HENRY.
  Mate, 15 September, 1863. Resigned 26 June, 1866.
ROGERS, HENRY A.
  Mate, 14 March, 1864. Honorably discharged 29 December, 1866.
ROGERS, HENRY J.
  Acting Master, 1 August, 1862. Honorably discharged 13 December, 1865.
ROGERS, HENRY M.
  Acting Assistant Paymaster, 6 November, 1862. Mustered out 25 November, 1865.
ROGERS, H. V.
  Acting Ensign, 18 April, 1863. Resigned (sick) 28 August, 1863.
ROGERS, JAMES.
  Midshipman, 12 January, 1800. Discharged 13 June, 1801, under Peace Establishment Act.
ROGERS, JAMES.
  Midshipman, 15 November, 1809. Last appearance on Records of Navy Department, 1815.
ROGERS, JAMES.
  Master, 6 April, 1810. Last appearance on Records of Navy Department, 1818. Furloughed.
ROGERS, JAMES H.
  Acting Master, 26 August, 1861. Resigned 26 April, 1864.
ROGERS, JAMES H.
  Mate, 29 December, 1862. Acting Ensign, 12 December, 1863. Honorably discharged 10 May, 1865.
ROGERS, JEROME B.
  Acting Master, 22 October, 1861. Honorably discharged 29 November, 1865.
ROGERS, JOHN.
  Midshipman, 9 June, 1811. Resigned 15 June, 1812.
ROGERS, JOHN.
  Acting Second Assistant Engineer, 10 March, 1864. Acting First Assistant Engineer, 15 July, 1865. Honorably discharged 4 December, 1865.
ROGERS, JOHN.
  Acting Ensign, 30 October, 1862. Acting Master, 21 August, 1863. Acting Volunteer Lieutenant, 16 July, 1864. Honorably discharged 21 September, 1865.
ROGERS, JOHN.
  Gunner, 27 September, 1861. Died 1 May, 1874.
ROGERS, JOHN A.
  Acting Master, 27 August, 1861. Dismissed 3 December, 1862.
ROGERS, JOHN J.
  Acting Master, 11 November, 1861. Resigned 25 February, 1865.
ROGERS, JOSEPH.
  Mate, 28 July, 1866. Died 20 December, 1888.
ROGERS, JOSEPH T.
  Lieutenant, Junior Grade (Spanish-American War), 8 June, 1898. Honorably discharged 2 September, 1898.
ROGERS, LEWIS.
  Sailmaker, 12 June, 1848. Died 17 September, 1862.
ROGERS, LLOYD.
  Mate, 21 August, 1862. Dismissed 13 January, 1863.
ROGERS, MICHAEL F.
  Acting Second Assistant Engineer, 16 December, 1864. Resigned 20 April, 1865.
ROGERS, MILFORD.
  Acting Master, 22 October, 1861. Honorably discharged 3 December, 1865.
ROGERS, RICHARD.
  Midshipman, 15 November, 1809. Killed in duel 16 October, 1810.

ROGERS, ROBERT C.
  Midshipman, 14 October, 1839. Passed Midshipman, 2 July, 1845. Acting Master, 31 August, 1852. Resigned 31 January, 1854.
ROGERS, ROBERT W.
  Mate, 30 October, 1864. Honorably discharged 20 October, 1865.
ROGERS, THOMAS M.
  Midshipman, 31 October, 1799. Discharged 10 July, 1801, under Peace Establishment Act.
ROGERS, THOMAS.
  Master, 31 October, 1899. Discharged 8 June, 1801.
ROGERS, THOMAS.
  Master, 31 October, 1799. Discharged 8 June, 1801.
ROGERS, WILLIAM.
  Gunner, 11 May, 1798. Last appearance on Records of Navy Department, 19 April, 1803.
ROGERS, WILLIAM.
  Assistant Surgeon, 8 February, 1802. Resigned 24 May, 1803.
ROGERS, WILLIAM.
  Surgeon, 27 November, 1804. Dismissed 11 August, 1807.
ROGERS, WILLIAM.
  Mate, 11 October, 1862. Acting Ensign, 13 July, 1863. Honorably discharged 16 September, 1865.
ROGERS, WILLIAM.
  Acting Chief Engineer, 25 March, 1864. Honorably discharged 20 December, 1865.
ROGERS, WILLIAM.
  Sailmaker, 17 October, 1857. Retired List, 2 December, 1876. Died 20 February, 1883.
ROGERS, WILLIAM.
  Acting Master, 26 August, 1861. Honorably discharged 23 December, 1865.
ROGERS, WILLIAM B.
  Assistant Paymaster (Spanish-American War), 9 June, 1896. Honorably discharged 8 February, 1899. Assistant Paymaster (Regular Navy), 12 June, 1900.
ROGERS, WILLIAM C.
  Acting Volunteer Lieutenant, 12 August, 1861. Acting Volunteer Lieutenant-Commander, 24 October, 1864. Honorably discharged 18 July, 1866.
ROGERS, WILLIAM P.
  Acting Master, 16 December, 1861. Acting Volunteer Lieutenant, 8 June, 1864. Honorably discharged 26 October, 1865.
ROGERS, WILLIAM S.
  Purser, 26 February, 1813. Resigned 17 February, 1834.
ROGERS, WILMOT F.
  Assistant Surgeon, 24 July, 1813. Died August, 1824.
ROGERSON, ROBERT.
  Midshipman, 1 January, 1812. Drowned 30 June, 1814.
ROGERSON, THOMAS.
  Assistant Surgeon, 25 October, 1813. Lost in the Wasp in 1815.
ROGET, EDWARD A.
  Professor, 21 May, 1864. Retired List, 1864. Died 9 November, 1887.
ROHANGE, ROBERT.
  Mate, 16 August, 1897. Appointment revoked 2 November, 1897.
ROHER, JOHN W.
  Acting First Assistant Engineer, 31 March, 1863. Dismissed 31 October, 1863.
ROHRBACHER, JOSEPH H.
  Cadet Midshipman, 24 June, 1876. Graduated 22 June, 1882. Ensign, Junior Grade, 3 March, 1883. Ensign, 26 June, 1884. Lieutenant, Junior Grade, 7 March, 1893. Lieutenant, 6 December, 1896.
ROHRER, KARL.
  Midshipman, 20 July, 1865. Graduated June, 1869. Ensign, 12 July, 1870. Master, 10 November, 1872. Lieutenant, 26 April, 1876. Lieutenant-Commander, 5 December, 1897. Commander, 22 November, 1900.
ROLAND, BENJAMIN C.
  Mate, 5 June, 1862. Dismissed 25 August, 1862.
ROLANDO, HENRY.
  Midshipman, 28 December, 1836. Passed Midshipman, 1 July, 1842. Master, 12 May, 1849. Lieutenant, 18 January, 1850. Reserved List, 28 September, 1855. Commander on Active List, 16 July, 1862. Retired List, 8 June, 1867. Died 20 March, 1869.
ROLLER, FRANK W.
  Assistant Engineer (Spanish-American War), 12 May, 1898. Honorably discharged 31 October, 1898.
ROLLER, JOHN E.
  Midshipman, 26 June, 1867. Graduated 6 June, 1871. Ensign, 14 July, 1872. Master, 24 May, 1875. Lieutenant, 1 July, 1882. Lieutenant-Commander, 3 March, 1899.
ROLLINGS, JOHN H.
  Acting Third Assistant Engineer, 26 May, 1863. Resigned (sick) 13 April, 1865.
ROLLINGS, GEORGE F. D.
  Assistant Engineer (Spanish-American War), 22 June, 1898. Honorably discharged 10 November, 1898.
ROLLINS, ANTHONY N.
  Midshipman, 10 June, 1872. Graduated 20 June, 1876. Died 10 November, 1878.
ROLLINS, HENRY S. P.
  Mate, 4 December, 1862. Acting Ensign, 28 April, 1865. Honorably discharged 28 October, 1865.
ROLLINS, LOUIS N.
  Acting Ensign, 13 December, 1864. Honorably discharged 14 October, 1865.

GENERAL NAVY REGISTER. 473

ROLLINS, THOMAS J.
Acting Ensign, 31 December, 1863. Honorably discharged 6 October, 1865.
ROMAINE, HENRY.
Acting Third Assistant Engineer, 4 August, 1864. Honorably discharged 19 July, 1865.
ROMAINE, WILLIAM H.
Acting Assistant Paymaster, 28 August, 1863. Dead.
ROMME, WILLIAM S.
Acting Ensign, 9 November, 1863. Honorably discharged 18 November, 1865.
ROMMEL, CHARLES E.
Naval Cadet, 1 October, 1878. Assistant Engineer, 1 July, 1884. Passed Assistant Engineer, 12 September, 1894. Rank changed to Lieutenant, 3 March, 1899.
RONCKENDORFF, WILLIAM.
Midshipman, 17 February, 1832. Passed Midshipman, 23 June, 1838. Lieutenant, 28 June, 1843. Commander, 29 June, 1861. Captain, 27 September, 1866. Commodore, 12 February, 1874. Retired List, 9 November, 1874. Died 27 November, 1891.
RONEY, JAMES.
Midshipman, 24 July, 1807. Last appearance on Records of Navy Department, 1815. New Orleans.
RONEY, THOMAS.
Midshipman, 3 March, 1841. Passed Midshipman, 10 August, 1847. Master, 2 March, 1855. Lieutenant, 14 September, 1855. Died 20 April, 1860.
ROONEY, WILLIAM R. A.
Midshipman, 29 September, 1870. Graduated 1 June, 1874. Ensign, 17 July, 1875. Master, 11 June, 1881. Lieutenant, Junior Grade, 3 March, 1883. Lieutenant, 30 June, 1887. Lieutenant-Commander, 3 March, 1899.
ROOP, JOHN.
Third Assistant Engineer, 3 May, 1859. Second Assistant Engineer, 17 December, 1861. First Assistant Engineer, 20 May, 1863. Resigned 15 October, 1872.
ROOSE, WILLIAM C.
Acting Third Assistant Engineer, 3 July, 1863. Appointment revoked (sick) 28 October, 1863.
ROOSEVELT, C. M.
Midshipman, 15 November, 1809. Resigned 5 March, 1810.
ROOSEVELT, NICHOLAS L.
Midshipman, 27 September, 1864. Graduated June, 1868. Master, 12 July, 1870. Lieutenant, 3 August, 1873. Resigned 1 February, 1874.
ROOT, FRANK P.
Acting Second Assistant Engineer, 10 December, 1861. Acting First Assistant Engineer, 3 October, 1863. Died 16 April, 1864.
ROOT, LYMAN.
Ensign (Spanish-American War), 22 June, 1898. Honorably discharged 17 September, 1898.
ROOT, OLIVER D.
Acting Assistant Surgeon, 30 November, 1861. Died 30 October, 1863.
ROOTE, CHARLES.
Midshipman, 1 April, 1828. Died 8 December, 1828.
ROOTES, THOMAS R.
Midshipman, 1 March, 1827. Passed Midshipman, 10 June, 1833. Lieutenant, 28 February, 1838. Commander, 14 September, 1855. Dismissed 19 April, 1861.
ROPER, JESSE M.
Midshipman, 23 June, 1868. Graduated 1 June, 1872. Ensign, 15 July, 1873. Master, 25 November, 1877. Lieutenant, Junior Grade, 3 March, 1883. Lieutenant, 5 June, 1884. Lieutenant-Commander, 3 March, 1899.
ROPER, WALTER G.
Naval Cadet, 22 September, 1894. Ensign, 4 April, 1900.
RORSCHACK, FRANK.
Gunner, 27 November, 1896.
ROSE, ALEXANDER R.
Midshipman, 25 September, 1834. Cashiered 20 May, 1836.
ROSE, EDWARD S.
Mate, 1 March, 1862. Died 6 November, 1863.
ROSE, FRANK B.
Chaplain, 3 February, 1870. Retired List, 5 April, 1898.
ROSE, JACOB H.
Acting First Assistant Engineer, 17 May, 1861. Died 12 September, 1862.
ROSE, JOHN G.
Mate, 11 October, 1862. Disrated to Landsman and discharged 23 October, 1864.
ROSE, ROBERT M.
Midshipman, 18 May, 1809. Lieutenant, 24 July, 1813. Commander, 24 April, 1828. Died 27 August, 1830.
ROSE, WALDEMAR D.
Midshipman, 5 June, 1872. Graduated 20 June, 1876. Ensign, 12 July, 1878. Lieutenant, Junior Grade, 2 August, 1885. Lieutenant, 14 May, 1891. Lieutenant-Commander, 1 July, 1899.
ROSE, WEBB V. H.
Assistant Paymaster, 20 May, 1898. Passed Assistant Paymaster, 15 September, 1899.
ROSEBUSH, OLIVER.
Acting Third Assistant Engineer, 1 October, 1862. Honorably discharged 20 February, 1866.
ROSENBLEUTH, JACOB C.
Assistant Surgeon, 14 October, 1895. Passed Assistant Surgeon, 14 October, 1898.
ROSENMILLER, D. P., Jr.
Acting Ensign, 1 October, 1862. Acting Master, 25 August, 1863. Honorably discharged 5 November, 1865.

GENERAL NAVY REGISTER.

ROSIER, JOHN.
Sailmaker, 12 November, 1833. Dismissed 16 May, 1835.
ROSLING, JOHN.
Mate, 12 September, 1862. Honorably discharged 11 June, 1867.
ROSMOND, JOHN.
Acting Second Assistant Engineer, 27 September, 1861. Honorably discharged 26 October, 1865.
ROSS, ALBERT.
Midshipman, 24 July, 1863. Graduated June, 1867. Ensign, 18 December, 1868. Master, 21 March, 1870. Retired 21 December, 1871. Lieutenant on Active List, 21 March, 1871. Lieutenant-Commander, 5 December, 1890. Commander, 28 August, 1897.
ROSS, DAVID.
Lieutenant, 9 March, 1798. Last appearance on Records of Navy Department, 30 November, 1799.
ROSS, DAVID.
Acting Second Assistant Engineer, 24 May, 1864. Honorably discharged 7 August, 1865.
ROSS, EDWIN.
Gunner, 26 July, 1847. Died September, 1849.
ROSS, ELIJAH.
Acting Master, 28 December, 1861. Resigned 11 August 1864.
ROSS, H. SCHUYLER.
Third Assistant Engineer, 18 November, 1862. Second Assistant Engineer, 23 March, 1864. First Assistant Engineer, 1 January, 1868. Chief Engineer, 28 January, 1890. Rank changed to Commander, 3 March, 1899. Retired List with rank of Captain, 30 June, 1899.
ROSS, JAMES.
Midshipman, 2 March, 1799. Resigned 8 October, 1800.
ROSS, JAMES.
Mate, 18 April, 1863. Dismissed 17 July, 1863.
ROSS, JAMES H.
Acting Third Assistant Engineer, 27 July, 1863. Resigned 15 October, 1863.
ROSS, JOHN.
Mate, 21 December, 1861. Acting Ensign, 30 July, 1862. Honorably discharged 14 September, 1865. Acting Ensign, 1 February, 1867. Mustered out 21 December, 1868.
ROSS, JOHN.
Acting Third Assistant Engineer, 4 March, 1863. Resigned 25 June, 1864. Acting Master, 8 March, 1864. Resigned 26 August, 1867.
ROSS, JOHN.
Boatswain, 21 October, 1861. Resigned 7 March, 1864.
ROSS, JOHN.
Lieutenant, Junior Grade (Spanish-American War), 21 May, 1898. Honorably discharged 24 October, 1898.
ROSS, JOHN W.
Acting Third Assistant Engineer, 24 May, 1864. Appointment revoked 23 June, 1865.
ROSS, JOHN W.
Assistant Surgeon, 21 March, 1870. Passed Assistant Surgeon, 13 May, 1875. Surgeon, 17 August, 1881. Retired List, 11 May, 1894.
ROSS, NELSON.
Third Assistant Engineer, 8 July, 1862. Second Assistant Engineer, 15 February, 1864. Retired List, 26 October, 1872. Died 6 August, 1883.
ROSS, ROBERT.
Acting Third Assistant Engineer, 12 December, 1861. Honorably discharged 25 October, 1865.
ROSS, ROBERT J.
Midshipman, 1 August, 1826. Passed Midshipman, 28 April, 1832. Resigned 13 December, 1833.
ROSS, THOMAS.
Midshipman, 17 March, 1814. Last appearance on Records of Navy Department, 1815. Furloughed.
ROSS, WILLIAM.
Acting Third Assistant Engineer, 10 December, 1861. Appointment revoked (sick) 10 February, 1863. Acting Second Assistant Engineer, 12 August, 1864. Honorably discharged 29 July, 1865.
ROSS, WILLIAM.
Mate, 20 April, 1863. Acting Ensign, 19 July, 1864. Honorably discharged 1 November, 1865.
ROSS, WILLIAM C.
Acting Master, 9 April, 1862. Dismissed 26 July, 1862.
ROSS, WILLIAM T.
Mate, 27 August, 1864. Resigned 18 May, 1865.
ROSSETER, ROBERT C.
Midshipman, 11 March, 1800. Discharged 28 April, 1801, under Peace Establishment Act.
ROSWALD, RAYMOND F.
Acting Third Assistant Engineer, 18 December, 1863. Acting Second Assistant Engineer, 19 September, 1864. Honorably discharged 18 July, 1865.
ROTHGANGER, GEORGE.
Assistant Surgeon, 24 May, 1889. Passed Assistant Surgeon, 24 May, 1892. Surgeon, 7 June, 1900.

GENERAL NAVY REGISTER. 475

ROTHWELL, N. B.
   Purser, 2 March, 1813. Last appearance on Records of Navy Department, 1816. Furloughed.
ROUMFORT, L. H.
   Midshipman, 23 December, 1831. Died at sea 21 October, 1833.
ROUND, SAMUEL.
   Warrant Machinist (Spanish-American War), 18 May, 1898. Honorably discharged 2 September, 1898.
ROUNDS, ANDRE S., JR.
   Mate, 19 February, 1863. Acting Ensign, 15 May, 1864. Honorably discharged 15 May, 1865.
ROUNDS, JAMES.
   Mate, 12 October, 1866. Appointment revoked 21 October, 1867.
ROUNSAVELLE, JOHN.
   Acting Ensign, 5 May, 1864. Honorably discharged 9 January, 1866. Mate, 12 April, 1870. Resigned 28 July, 1875.
ROUNSEVILLE, J. F.
   Acting Master, 11 November, 1861. Honorably discharged 18 February, 1866.
ROUNTREE, ROBERT W.
   Mate, 13 December, 1861. Acting Ensign, 29 September, 1862. Honorably discharged 18 August, 1865.
ROUSE, FREDERICK.
   Lieutenant, Junior Grade (Spanish-American War), 2 June, 1898. Honorably discharged 7 November, 1898.
ROUSE, JAMES W.
   Acting Carpenter, 15 July, 1863. Resigned 4 October, 1864.
ROUSSEAU, HARRY H.
   Civil Engineer, 29 September, 1898.
ROUSSEAU, J. B.
   Midshipman, 30 November, 1814. Last appearance on Records of Navy Department, 1815. Drowned.
ROUSSEAU, LAWRENCE.
   Midshipman, 16 January, 1809. Lieutenant, 24 July, 1813. Commander, 24 April, 1828. Captain, 9 February, 1837. Resigned 11 February, 1861.
ROWAN, JAMES H.
   Midshipman, 19 August, 1823. Passed Midshipman, 23 March, 1829. Lieutenant, 31 December, 1833. Commander, 14 September, 1855. Dismissed 23 January, 1857.
ROWAN, JAMES H., JR.
   Midshipman, 8 November, 1847. Resigned 28 July, 1854.
ROWAN, STEPHEN C.
   Midshipman, 1 February, 1826. Passed Midshipman, 28 April, 1832. Lieutenant, 8 March, 1837. Commander, 14 September, 1855. Commodore, 16 July, 1862. Rear-Admiral, 25 July, 1866. Vice-Admiral, 15 August, 1870. Retired List, 26 February, 1889. Died 31 March, 1890.
ROWAN, WILLIAM.
   Midshipman, 4 March, 1823. Resigned 10 November, 1829.
ROWAND, JOHN.
   Midshipman, 30 April, 1800. Discharged 16 June, 1801, under Peace Establishment Act.
ROWBOTHAM, WILLIAM.
   Second Assistant Engineer, 27 January, 1871. Passed Assistant Engineer, 25 November, 1877. Retired List, 26 September, 1893. Died 30 May, 1894.
ROWE, ALBERT M.
   Acting First Assistant Engineer, 1 October, 1862. Resigned 23 July, 1863.
ROWE, CHARLES M.
   Acting Ensign, 5 October, 1864. Honorably discharged 25 August, 1865.
ROWE, EDWARD F.
   Acting Ensign, 1 October, 1862. Honorably discharged 13 December, 1865.
ROWE, EDWARD V.
   Midshipman, 28 September, 1861. Graduated September, 1865. Ensign, 1 December, 1866. Resigned 25 February, 1867.
ROWE, HENRY B.
   Mate, 1 December, 1862. Resigned 30 December, 1863.
ROWE, JASON L.
   Mate, 17 June, 1863. Appointment revoked 2 May, 1864.
ROWE, JOHN.
   Midshipman, 2 December, 1799. Lieutenant, 21 March, 1807. Resigned 27 August, 1808.
ROWE, JOHN H.
   Acting Second Assistant Engineer, 14 May, 1861. Resigned 22 May, 1865.
ROWE, JOSHUA N.
   Acting Master, 18 December, 1861. Honorably discharged 24 October, 1865.
ROWEN, JOHN H.
   Naval Cadet, 20 May, 1887. Assistant Engineer, 1 July, 1893. Passed Assistant Engineer, 28 May, 1897. Rank changed to Lieutenant, Junior Grade, 3 March, 1899. Lieutenant, 25 September, 1899.
ROWLAND, ALEXANDER H.
   Acting Ensign, 1 October, 1862. Resigned 17 June, 1864.
ROWLAND, JOHN.
   Mate, 4 February, 1865. Deserted 3 July, 1865.
ROWLAND, JOHN H.
   Midshipman, 21 September, 1857. Graduated 1861. Lieutenant, 1 August, 1862. Lieutenant-Commander, 25 July, 1866. Dismissed 10 September, 1873.

ROWLAND, SYLVESTER.
Mate, 19 December, 1861. Resigned 11 August, 1863.
ROWLAND, THOMAS.
Surgeon, 25 July, 1798. Resigned 23 January, 1799.
ROY, CHARLES H.
Midshipman, 2 February, 1829. Resigned 25 September, 1830.
ROYALL, HILARY H.
Naval Cadet, 20 May, 1895. At sea prior to final graduation.
ROYCE, ALFRED L.
Chaplain, 18 February, 1881.
ROYCE, CHARLES C.
Mate, 16 September, 1864. Honorably discharged 26 August, 1865.
ROYCE, FRANK.
Acting Third Assistant Engineer, 10 December, 1863. Honorably discharged 20 May, 1866.
ROYCE, WESLEY.
Acting Third Assistant Engineer, 23 December, 1863. Resigned 13 June, 1864.
ROYS, JOHN H.
Naval Cadet, 6 September, 1892. Ensign, 6 May, 1898.
RUCKLEY, HENRY R.
Acting Assistant Surgeon, 15 February, 1864. Honorably discharged 19 January, 1866.
RUDD, JOHN.
Midshipman, 30 November, 1814. Lieutenant, 13 January, 1825. Commander, 8 September, 1841. Captain, 14 September, 1855. Retired List, 21 December, 1861. Commodore, Retired List, 16 July, 1862. Died 12 October, 1867.
RUDD, WILLIAM J.
Mate, 15 July, 1864. Honorably discharged 6 July, 1865.
RUDDER, WILLIAM.
Master, 4 March, 1814. Resigned 20 March, 1815.
RUDE, WILLIAM R.
Acting Master, 14 August, 1861. Dismissed 12 January, 1863. Acting Ensign, 27 February, 1863. Dismissed 8 August, 1863.
RUDENSTEIN, JOHN.
Assistant Surgeon, 24 February, 1846. Surgeon, 21 August, 1859. Died 9 December, 1869.
RUDROW, JOHN
Mate, 24 May, 1862. Honorably discharged 28 June, 1867.
RUFF, SAMUEL W.
Assistant Surgeon, 12 August, 1826. Surgeon, 4 April, 1831. Died in 1841.
RUFFIN, C. K.
Midshipman, 24 October, 1825. Died 27 July, 1831.
RUGG, CHARLES W.
Acting Third Assistant Engineer, 10 May, 1864. Appointment revoked (sick) 20 February, 1865.
RUHM, THOMAS F.
Naval Cadet, 20 May, 1886. Assistant Naval Constructor, 1 July, 1892. Naval Constructor, 1 November, 1898.
RUIZ, ALBERTO DE.
Cadet Engineer, Naval Academy, 1 October, 1873. Graduated 21 June, 1875. Assistant Engineer, 1 July, 1878. Wholly retired 31 December, 1885.
RULON, JOSEPH F.
Mate, 21 December, 1863. Honorably discharged 4 October, 1865.
RUMMELL, CHARLES V.
Mate, 23 January, 1862. Acting Ensign, 27 October, 1863. Honorably discharged 8 January, 1866.
RUMNEY, EDWARD.
Master, 18 November, 1812. Lost at sea 31 March, 1823.
RUMSEY, BENJAMIN.
Boatswain, 17 March, 1800. Discharged 8 June, 1801.
RUMSEY, HENRY B.
Acting Midshipman, 25 October, 1859. Ensign, 24 February, 1863. Lieutenant, 22 February, 1864. Lieutenant-Commander, 25 July, 1866. Resigned 31 December, 1871.
RUMSEY, HARRY E.
Naval Cadet, 28 September, 1882. Graduated 10 June, 1886. Ensign, 1 July, 1888. Drowned 26 September, 1890.
RUMSEY, OLIVER.
Carpenter, date not known. Last appearance on Records of Navy Department.
RUMSEY, WILLIAM W.
Mate, 28 December, 1863. Honorably discharged 14 October, 1865.
RUNCHEY, JOHN.
Midshipman, 1 January, 1808. Dismissed 22 June, 1809.
RUNDLETT, HOWARD M.
Acting Assistant Surgeon, 9 March, 1864. Assistant Surgeon, 14 February, 1865. Passed Assistant Surgeon, 24 April, 1868. Resigned 6 February, 1869. Assistant Surgeon from 4 November, 1865. Passed Assistant Surgeon, 13 July, 1870. Died 25 May, 1873.
RUNDLETT, THOMAS M.
Boatswain, 4 December, 1837. Resigned 29 March, 1839.
RUNDLETT, WILLIAM A.
Mate, 7 June, 1862. Deserted 9 May, 1863.
RUNNELLS, SAMUEL B.
Acting Third Assistant Engineer, 21 June, 1862. Acting Second Engineer, 25 July, 1863. Appointment revoked (sick) 6 April, 1864.

GENERAL NAVY REGISTER. 477

RUNNELS, P. R.
  Acting Ensign, 9 February, 1865. Discharged 20 October, 1867.
RUSCHENBERGER, CHARLES W.
  Midshipman, 23 July, 1864. Graduated June, 1869. Ensign, 12 July, 1870. Master, 31 January, 1872. Lieutenant, 14 April, 1875. Resigned 31 July, 1895.
RUSCHENBERGER, W. S. W.
  Surgeon, 4 April, 1831. Retired List, 4 September, 1869. Medical Director, 3 March, 1871. Died 24 March, 1895.
RUSH, CHARLES W.
  Assistant Surgeon, 30 June, 1879. Passed Assistant Surgeon, 6 July, 1883. Retired List, 14 August, 1893. Died 9 November, 1893.
RUSH, JOHN.
  Surgeon, 11 May, 1798. (See Lieutenant.)
RUSH, JOHN.
  Lieutenant, 5 March, 1799. Resigned 29 January, 1802.
RUSH, JOHN.
  Master, 10 September, 1805. Died 7 March, 1809.
RUSH, JOHN W.
  Carpenter, 25 November, 1799. Dismissed 8 May, 1802.
RUSH, LEWIS.
  Acting Third Assistant Engineer, 8 January, 1864. Resigned 28 January, 1865.
RUSH, MADISON.
  Midshipman, 15 October, 1836. Passed Midshipman, 1 July, 1842. Master, 6 April, 1849. Lieutenant, 3 November, 1849. Resigned 7 February, 1856.
RUSH, RICHARD.
  Midshipman, 30 September, 1863. Graduated June, 1867. Ensign, 18 December, 1868. Master, 21 March, 1870. Lieutenant, 21 March, 1871. Lieutenant-Commander, 27 September, 1891. Commander, 6 February, 1898. Retired List with rank of Captain, 7 July, 1899.
RUSH, WILLIAM H.
  Assistant Surgeon, 13 February, 1877. Passed Assistant Surgeon, 13 February, 1880. Surgeon, 30 November, 1894. Retired 31 October, 1900.
RUSH, WILLIAM R.
  Midshipman, 6 June, 1872. Graduated 18 June, 1879. Ensign, 15 October, 1881. Lieutenant, Junior Grade, 11 February, 1889. Lieutenant, 26 December, 1893. Lieutenant-Commander, 19 February, 1901.
RUSHMORE, WILLIAM.
  Mate, 1 December, 1862. Resigned 13 May, 1865.
RUSS, FRANCIS A.
  Mate, 12 September, 1861. Resigned 13 November, 1861. Acting Master, 23 November, 1861. Appointment revoked (sick) 26 July, 1862.
RUSS, JOHN A.
  Midshipman, 1 March, 1825. Passed Midshipman, 28 April, 1832. Lieutenant, 23 September, 1837. Cashiered 15 August, 1846.
RUSS, JOHN S.
  Mate. Acting Ensign, 19 August, 1863. Resigned 23 May, 1864.
RUSS, ROBERT F.
  Mate, 20 December, 1861. Resigned 1 May, 1863.
RUSSELL, ALEXANDER.
  Gunner, 9 December, 1834. Resigned 6 April, 1838.
RUSSELL, ALEXANDER W.
  Purser, 28 February, 1861. Pay Inspector, 3 March, 1871. Pay Director, 23 February, 1877. Retired List, 4 February, 1886.
RUSSELL, ALEXANDER W., JR.
  Ensign (Spanish-American War), 23 June, 1898. Honorably discharged 12 September, 1898.
RUSSELL, AVERLEY C. H.
  Assistant Surgeon, 3 June, 1879. Passed Assistant Surgeon, 3 June, 1882. Surgeon, 8 June, 1895.
RUSSELL, BENJAMIN.
  Mate, 20 February, 1863. Died 28 March, 1866.
RUSSELL, BENJAMIN F.
  Acting Ensign, 22 November, 1862. Appointment revoked (sick) 22 February, 1864.
RUSSELL, CHARLES C.
  Lieutenant, 8 April, 1798. Discharged 23 October, 1801, under Peace Establishment Act.
RUSSELL, CHARLES O.
  Midshipman, 18 June, 1812. Resigned 14 February, 1825.
RUSSELL, CHARLES F.
  Acting Ensign, 27 September, 1862. Honorably discharged 14 September, 1865.
RUSSELL, EDMUND M.
  Midshipman, 18 June, 1812. Lieutenant, 17 May, 1828. Died 21 July, 1838.
RUSSELL, FRANK L.
  Naval Cadet, 19 May, 1883. Ensign, 1 July, 1889. Lieutenant, Junior Grade, 17 December, 1897. Lieutenant, 3 March, 1899.
RUSSELL, FREDERICK C.
  Acting Third Assistant Engineer, 6 November, 1862. Acting Second Assistant Engineer, 13 June, 1864. Honorably discharged 30 October, 1865.
RUSSELL, GEORGE H.
  Mate, 5 December, 1864. Appointment revoked 24 December, 1866.
RUSSELL, GEORGE L.
  Acting Warrant Machinist, 6 July, 1899.
RUSSELL, GEORGE W.
  Acting Third Assistant Engineer, 24 December, 1863. Acting Second Assistant Engineer, 8 March, 1865. Honorably discharged 17 January, 1868.

RUSSELL, HENRY.
Acting Assistant Paymaster, 9 December, 1861. Mustered out 27 November, 1865.
RUSSELL, HENRY C.
Mate, 24 January, 1862. Acting Ensign, 8 October, 1862. Died 21 September, 1863.
RUSSELL, HORATIO N.
Midshipman, 1 January, 1825. Resigned 14 January, 1826.
RUSSELL, JAMES B.
Mate, 21 March, 1863. Acting Ensign, 29 March, 1864. Honorably discharged 3 November, 1867. Mate, 8 November, 1869. Appointment revoked 9 July, 1870.
RUSSELL, JAMES J.
Mate, 12 November, 1861. Acting Ensign, 5 November, 1862. Acting Master, 23 February, 1864. Honorably discharged 21 October, 1865.
RUSSELL, JOHN.
Acting Second Assistant Engineer, 17 October, 1863. Dismissed 17 November, 1863.
RUSSELL, JOHN.
Acting Gunner, 13 September, 1862. Honorably discharged 11 May, 1868. Gunner, 14 August, 1875. Retired List, 9 August, 1895. Died 26 November, 1899.
RUSSELL, JOHN H.
Midshipman, 10 September, 1841. Passed Midshipman, 10 August, 1847. Master, 14 September, 1855. Lieutenant, 15 September, 1855. Lieutenant-Commander, 16 July, 1862. Commander, 25 July, 1866. Captain, 12 February, 1874. Commodore, 30 October, 1883. Rear-Admiral, 4 March, 1886. Retired List, 27 August, 1886. Died 1 April, 1897.
RUSSELL, JOHN M.
Mate, 26 November, 1863. Resigned 27 January, 1865.
RUSSELL, ROBERT L.
Cadet Midshipman, 14 June, 1881. Ensign, 1 July, 1887. Lieutenant, Junior Grade, 29 April, 1896. Lieutenant, 3 March, 1899.
RUSSELL, STEPHEN G.
Acting Master, 19 July, 1861. Resigned 2 July, 1862.
RUSSELL, THOMAS.
Midshipman, 1 April, 1828. Died 28 August, 1830.
RUSSELL, THOMAS S.
Mate, 13 January, 1863. Acting Ensign, 29 February, 1864. Resigned 17 January, 1865.
RUSSELL, WILLIAM.
Midshipman, 1 November, 1826. Resigned 13 December, 1832.
RUSSELL, WILLIAM A.
Second Assistant Engineer, 5 March, 1872. Died 17 February, 1873.
RUSSELL, WILLIAM A.
Acting Third Assistant Engineer, 6 January, 1864. Honorably discharged 8 May, 1869.
RUST, ARMISTEAD.
Cadet Engineer, 1 October, 1881. Ensign, 1 July, 1887. Lieutenant, Junior Grade, 10 May, 1896. Lieutenant, 3 March, 1899.
RUST, EDWIN G.
Passed Assistant Engineer (Spanish-American War), 24 June, 1898. Honorably discharged 8 September, 1898.
RUST, JAMES F. P.
Acting First Assistant Engineer, 29 June, 1864. Honorably discharged 10 January, 1868.
RUSTIC, JOHN T.
Carpenter, 8 December, 1849. Dropped 20 April, 1861.
RUTH, DUDLEY L.
Acting Assistant Paymaster, 11 August, 1862. Mustered out 20 October, 1865.
RUTH, FREDERICK.
Acting Warrant Machinist, 23 August, 1899.
RUTH, MARTIN L.
Acting Third Assistant Engineer, 29 July, 1864. Resigned 20 June, 1865.
RUTH, MELANCTHON L.
Assistant Surgeon, 21 April, 1868. Passed Assistant Surgeon, 10 October, 1871. Surgeon, 2 April, 1879. Died 14 December, 1891.
RUTHERFORD, JACOB.
Mate, 1 December, 1862. Acting Ensign, 29 June, 1863. Honorably discharged 28 October, 1865.
RUTHERFORD, JESSE M.
Mate, 1 October, 1862. Resigned 13 February, 1863.
RUTHERFORD, JESSE S.
Appointed Second Assistant Engineer, 17 January, 1842. Warranted Second Assistant Engineer, 28 July, 1845. First Assistant Engineer, 26 February, 1851. Died 3 January, 1862.
RUTHERFORD, WILLIAM H.
Third Assistant Engineer, 22 September, 1849. Second Assistant Engineer, 16 February, 1852. First Assistant Engineer, 26 June, 1856. Chief Engineer, 12 August, 1861. Retired List, 26 October, 1874. Died 1 March, 1898.
RUTGERS, HERMAN.
Midshipman, 31 November, 1814. Last appearance on Records of Navy Department, 1822. Dead.
RUTLEDGE, EDWARD C.
Midshipman, 30 November, 1814. Lieutenant, 13 January, 1825. Commander, 8 September, 1841. Resigned 6 August, 1850.
RUTLEDGE, JOHN.
Midshipman, 9 April, 1835. Passed Midshipman, 22 June, 1841. Master, 22 March, 1848. Lieutenant, 7 January, 1849. Resigned 23 February, 1861.

RUTLEDGE, STATES.
   Midshipman, 1 October, 1798. Resigned 7 January, 1802.
RUTTER, EDWARD J.
   Assistant Surgeon, 6 September, 1837. Surgeon, 20 September, 1850. Drowned 30 April, 1852.
RUTTER, GEORGE H.
   Acting Third Assistant Engineer, 15 January, 1862. Acting Second Assistant Engineer, 13 October, 1863. Appointment revoked 19 August, 1864.
RUTTER, JOSIAS.
   Master, 1 March, 1814. Discharged 15 April, 1815.
RUTTER, THOMAS.
   Midshipman, 9 November, 1813. Resigned 25 March, 1814.
RUTTER, SOLOMON.
   Lieutenant (Flotilla Service), 25 April, 1814. Last appearance on Records of Navy Department, 6 February, 1815.
RUTTER, SOLOMON.
   Midshipman, 26 February, 1814. Resigned 1 February, 1822.
RUTTER, THOMAS.
   Master, 9 May, 1813. Dropped 11 December, 1826.
RYAN, DAVID.
   Midshipman, 25 January, 1828. Dropped in 1840.
RYAN, EDWARD.
   Mate, 2 January, 1862. Acting Ensign, 20 October, 1863. Resigned 24 February, 1865.
RYAN, EUGENE D.
   Naval Cadet, 4 September, 1886. Resigned 18 February, 1890. Assistant Paymaster, 29 July, 1892. Passed Assistant Paymaster, 27 February, 1895. Paymaster, 3 May, 1899.
RYAN, GEORGE P.
   Acting Midshipman, 30 September, 1857. Midshipman, 1 June, 1861. Lieutenant, 16 July, 1862. Lieutenant-Commander, 16 July, 1866. Commander, 3 October, 1874. Lost in the Huron, 24 November, 1877.
RYAN, GEORGE W.
   Naval Cadet, 6 September, 1889. Resigned 9 June, 1890. Reappointed 12 June, 1890. Resigned 14 June, 1893. Ensign (Spanish-American War), 10 May, 1898. Honorably discharged 10 February, 1899.
RYAN, JASON.
   Mate, 5 March, 1862. Acting Ensign, 26 September, 1864. Resigned 27 April, 1865.
RYAN, JOHN.
   Acting Third Assistant Engineer, 20 October, 1863. Discharged 6 August, 1865.
RYAN, JOHN J.
   Third Assistant Engineer, 22 May, 1863. Second Assistant Engineer, 25 January, 1866. Retired List, 28 October, 1874.
RYAN, JOHN P. J.
   Naval Cadet, 6 September, 1886. Resigned 25 February, 1889. Naval Cadet, 22 May, 1889. Honorably discharged 30 June, 1895. Assistant Engineer, 17 April, 1896. Rank changed to Ensign, 3 March, 1899. Lieutenant, Junior Grade, 17 April, 1899.
RYAN, M. TALMADGE.
   Mate, 26 December, 1862. Dismissed 9 May, 1863.
RYAN, ROBERT H.
   Acting Third Assistant Engineer, 22 December, 1862. Honorably discharged 11 November, 1865.
RYAN, THOMAS E.
   Acting Assistant Paymaster, 7 October, 1863. Mustered out 21 March, 1866.
RYAN, THOMAS W.
   Cadet Midshipman, 13 June, 1873. Graduated 4 June, 1880. Cadet Midshipman, 16 June, 1873. Graduated 4 June, 1880. Ensign, Junior Grade, 3 March, 1883. Ensign, 2 May, 1884. Lieutenant, Junior Grade, 31 July, 1891. Lieutenant, 12 October, 1895.
RYAN, TIMOTHY.
   Mate, 9 October, 1862. Deserted 5 July, 1864.
RYAN, WILLIAM.
   Sailmaker, 18 September, 1827. Retired List, 23 February, 1863. Died 12 November, 1872.
RYCKMAN, EDWARD.
   Mate, 26 January, 1867. Resigned 16 May, 1867.
RYCKMAN, GEORGE C.
   Acting Ensign, 29 October, 1863. Honorably discharged 9 May, 1866. Acting Master, 17 July, 1867. Mustered out 8 October, 1868.
RYDER, EDWARD M.
   Acting Ensign, 26 November, 1862. Honorably discharged 31 August, 1865.
RYDER, GEORGE N.
   Mate, 16 October, 1862. Resigned 26 March, 1863.
RYDER, JOHN H.
   Gunner, 26 September, 1837. Appointment revoked 7 July, 1840.
RYDER, JOSHUA H.
   Mate, 28 March, 1864. Honorably discharged 25 July, 1865.
RYDER, MARTIN H.
   Acting Third Assistant Engineer, 7 March, 1865. Honorably discharged 26 September, 1865.
RYDER, PRESERVED M.
   Mate, 28 November, 1861. Resigned 10 May, 1865.
RYDER, REUBEN T.
   Mate, 6 April, 1864. Resigned 3 May, 1865.

RYDER, ROYAL S.
Acting Ensign, 12 January, 1863. Appointment revoked 14 April, 1863.
RYDER, STEPHEN A.
Acting Master, 31 October, 1861. Resigned 12 March, 1862. Acting Ensign, 22 December, 1862. Honorably discharged 30 September, 1865.
RYFENBURGH, LEWIS M.
Acting Second Assistant Engineer, 3 October, 1864. Honorably discharged 29 June, 1865.
RYLAND, WILLIAM.
Chaplain, 23 May, 1829. Died 19 January, 1846.
RYLEY, THOMAS W.
Gunner, 29 January, 1827. Died 14 March, 1845.
RYLEY, GEORGE.
Mate, 24 October, 1861. Dismissed 5 January, 1863.
RYMES, GEORGE W.
Acting Third Assistant Engineer, 6 April, 1864. Honorably discharged 29 July, 1865.
SACKETT, AUGUSTINE.
Third Assistant Engineer, 3 October, 1861. Second Assistant Engineer, 3 August, 1863. Resigned 24 August, 1865.
SACKETT, FRANKLIN P.
Assistant Paymaster, 3 June, 1899.
SADLER, EVIRET J.
Naval Cadet, 20 September, 1895. At sea prior to final graduation.
SAFFORD, JOHN B.
Acting Third Assistant Engineer, 21 May, 1862. Acting Second Assistant Engineer, 12 November, 1863. Honorably discharged 23 August, 1869.
SAFFORD, LEVI T.
Third Assistant Engineer, 8 December, 1862. Second Assistant Engineer, 8 April, 1864. First Assistant Engineer, 6 June, 1868. Retired List, 11 October, 1881.
SAFFORD, S. J.
Assistant Surgeon, 24 July, 1813. Resigned 1 September, 1814.
SAFFORD, WILLIAM E.
Cadet Midshipman, 22 September, 1876. Graduated 22 June. 1882. Ensign, Junior Grade, 3 March, 1883. Ensign, 26 June, 1884. Lieutenant, Junior Grade, 4 July, 1893. Lieutenant, 21 March, 1897.
SAGEE, FRANCIS.
Carpenter, 13 April, 1831. Died 23 May, 1853.
SAILER, JOSEPH.
Passed Assistant Surgeon (Spanish-American War), 15 July, 1898. Honorably discharged 12 September, 1898.
SALADE, LEWIS A.
Acting Third Assistant Engineer, 21 July, 1864. Honorably discharged 19 August, 1865.
SALISBURY, CHARLES H.
Acting Master, Recruiting Service, 16 June, 1864. Appointment revoked 16 November, 1864.
SALISBURY, GEORGE R.
Cadet Engineer, Naval Academy, 1 October, 1874. Graduated 10 June, 1879. Assistant Engineer, 10 June, 1881. Passed Assistant Engineer, 27 July, 1892. Rank changed to Lieutenant, 3 March, 1899.
SALSTONSTALL, WILLIAM G.
Acting Master, without pay, 8 June, 1861. Acting Volunteer Lieutenant, 5 May, 1863. Acting Volunteer Lieutenant-Commander, 20 May, 1865. Honorably discharged 5 October, 1865.
SALTAR, FRANCIS.
Gunner, 27 September, 1798. Resigned 10 December, 1799.
SALTER, THOMAS B.
Surgeon's Mate, 24 July, 1813. Surgeon, 22 May, 1815. Died 6 November, 1850.
SALTER, THOMAS G.
Chaplain, 20 March, 1861. Died 25 February, 1872.
SALTER, TIMOTHY G. C.
Midshipman, 20 September, 1866. Graduated 7 June, 1870. Ensign, 13 July, 1871. Master, 9 November, 1874. Lieutenant, 30 August, 1881. Retired List, 26 June, 1893.
SALTER, WILLIAM D.
Midshipman, 15 November, 1809. Lieutenant, 9 December, 1814. Commander, 3 March, 1831. Captain, 3 March, 1839. Reserved List, 4 January, 1856. Commodore on Reserved List, 4 April, 1867. Died 1869.
SALVATOR, EMMANUEL A.
Acting Warrant Machinist, 23 August, 1899.
SAMPLE, WINFIELD SCOTT.
Cadet Engineer, Naval Academy, 14 September, 1876. Graduated 10 June, 1880. Assistant Engineer, 10 June, 1882. Resigned 27 June, 1887.
SAMPSON, ALBERT P.
Mate, 31 July, 1862. Acting Ensign, 24 October, 1863. Honorably discharged 7 September, 1865.
SAMPSON, BIAS C. B.
Cadet Engineer, 13 September, 1877. Assistant Engineer, 1 July, 1883. Passed Assistant Engineer, 14 November, 1893. Rank changed to Lieutenant, 3 March, 1899.
SAMPSON, CHARLES A.
Mate, 18 August, 1862. Appointment revoked 21 May, 1863. Acting Gunner, 21 May, 1863. Honorably discharged 8 July, 1865.
SAMPSON, DANIEL W.
Mate, 4 March, 1870. Resigned 21 April, 1873.

GENERAL NAVY REGISTER.   481

SAMPSON, FREDERICK A.
　Acting Master, 13 May, 1861.　Resigned 17 May, 1862.
SAMPSON, FREDERICK G.
　Acting Ensign, 1 October, 1862.　Acting Master, 18 July, 1864.　Honorably discharged 20 November, 1865.
SAMPSON, ISAAC F.
　Mate, 5 September, 1863.　Acting Ensign, 9 July, 1864.　Resigned 26 May, 1865.
SAMPSON, L. GRANVILLE.
　Acting Ensign, 17 January, 1865.　Honorably discharged 15 February, 1866.
SAMPSON, WILLIAM T.
　Acting Midshipman, 24 September, 1857.　Midshipman, 1 June, 1861.　Lieutenant, 16 July, 1862.　Lieutenant-Commander, 25 July, 1866.　Commander, 9 August, 1874. Captain, 26 March, 1889.　Commodore, 3 July, 1898.　Rear-Admiral, 3 March, 1899.
SAMSON, GUY.
　Third Assistant Engineer, 24 December, 1861.　Second Assistant Engineer, 8 September, 1863.　Resigned 2 April, 1869.
SANBORN, ALBION J.
　Acting Third Assistant Engineer, 9 February, 1864.　Honorably discharged 22 August, 1865.
SANBORN, BENJAMIN F.
　Acting Third Assistant Engineer, 19 January, 1864.　Discharged 19 May, 1865.
SANBORN, FRANCIS W.
　Mate, 29 July, 1861.　Acting Ensign, 10 September, 1863.　Honorably discharged 27 December, 1865.
SANBORN, GEORGE C.
　Mate, 16 November, 1861.　Honorably discharged 10 June, 1865.　Mate, 11 July, 1865. Resigned 8 September, 1871.
SANBORN, THOMAS F.
　Acting Third Assistant Engineer, 19 December, 1863.　Honorably discharged 11 October, 1865.
SANDER, JAMES.
　Midshipman, 27 August, 1800.　Discharged 12 August, 1801, under Peace Establishment Act.
SANDERS, CAMILLUS.
　Midshipman, 8 January, 1836.　Resigned 25 February, 1839.
SANDERS, CARY N.
　Assistant Paymaster, 27 October, 1869.　Passed Assistant Paymaster, 1 July, 1875. Lost on board the Huron, 24 November, 1877.
SANDERS, JAMES.
　Midshipman, 1 January, 1808.　Lieutenant, 24 July, 1813.　Died 7 December, 1816.
SANDERS, JOS.
　Lieutenant, 10 June, 1799.　Discharged, at his own request, 6 July, 1801.
SANDERS, MORTON W.
　Acting Midshipman, 20 September, 1859.　Ensign, 25 November, 1862.　Lieutenant, 22 February, 1864.　Lieutenant-Commander, 25 July, 1866.　Commander, 11 April, 1877.　Died 11 July, 1878.
SANDERSON, FRANCIS.
　Midshipman, 3 February, 1815.　Lieutenant, 13 January, 1825.　Died 23 August, 1831.
SANDERSON, GEORGE A.
　Midshipman, 26 September, 1866.　Graduated 6 June, 1871.　Resigned 31 December, 1872.
SANDERSON, JOHN W.
　Mate, 13 May, 1863.　Acting Ensign, 29 April, 1865.　Honorably discharged 21 November, 1868.
SANDERSON, JOS.
　Boatswain, 21 March, 1837.　Died 24 November, 1837.
SANDFORD, JOHN W.
　Assistant Surgeon, 28 May, 1857.　Dismissed 29 May, 1861.
SANDOZ, FRITZ L.
　Naval Cadet, 19 May, 1890.　Ensign, 1 July, 1896.　Lieutenant, Junior Grade, 1 July, 1899.
SANDS, BENJAMIN F.
　Midshipman, 1 April, 1828.　Passed Midshipman, 14 June, 1834.　Lieutenant, 16 March, 1840.　Commander, 14 September, 1855.　Captain, 16 July, 1862.　Commodore, 25 July, 1866.　Rear-Admiral, 27 April, 1871.　Retired List, 11 February, 1874. Died 30 June, 1883.
SANDS, FRANCIS.
　Master's Mate, 28 February, 1807.　Last appearance on Records of Navy Department till 2 August, 1809.
SANDS, FRANCIS P. B.
　Acting Ensign, 9 December, 1862.　Acting Master, 31 January, 1865.　Honorably discharged 18 February, 1867.
SANDS, GEORGE.
　Mate, 17 May, 1870.　Died 10 July, 1873.
SANDS, GEORGE L.
　Mate, 20 August, 1863.　Acting Ensign, 17 January, 1865.　Honorably discharged 10 August, 1865.
SANDS, JAMES H.
　Acting Midshipman, 26 November, 1859.　Ensign, 28 May, 1863.　Master, 10 November, 1865.　Lieutenant, 10 November, 1866.　Lieutenant-Commander, 12 March, 1868.　Commander, 23 November, 1880.　Captain, 7 September, 1894.
SANDS, J. H. H.
　Midshipman, 19 April, 1834.　Resigned 4 November, 1837.

31

SANDS, JOSHUA R.
Midshipman, 18 June, 1812. Lieutenant, 1 April, 1818. Commander, 23 February, 1840. Captain, 25 February, 1854. Retired List, 21 December, 1861. Commodore on Retired List, 16 July, 1862. Rear-Admiral, Retired List, 25 July, 1866. Died 2 October, 1883.

SANDS, J. WOODVILLE.
Acting Assistant Paymaster, 4 November, 1863. Honorably discharged 5 October, 1865.

SANDS, LOUIS.
Acting Assistant Paymaster, 10 July, 1861. Mustered out 25 February, 1866.

SANDS, THOMAS.
Midshipman, 10 May, 1820. Resigned 17 June, 1830.

SANDS, WILLIAM M.
Purser, 20 May, 1815. Resigned 24 March, 1832.

SANDSTROM, ERNEST V.
Mate, 11 April, 1898. Boatswain, 10 April, 1899.

SANFORD, HIRAM.
Second Assistant Engineer, 21 November, 1837. First Assistant Engineer, 6 February, 1840. Resigned 5 November, 1849. Acting Second Assistant Engineer, 16 October, 1861. Appointment revoked 28 August, 1862.

SANFORD, JOHN R.
Assistant Paymaster (Spanish-American War), 10 June, 1898. Honorably discharged 2 March, 1899. Assistant Paymaster (Regular Service), 9 June, 1899.

SANFORD, JOS.
Master, 25 June, 1812. Resigned 20 July, 1812.

SANFORD, JOSEPH P.
Midshipman, 11 February, 1832. Passed Midshipman, 23 June, 1838. Lieutenant, 2 November, 1842. Resigned 8 October, 1853. Acting Lieutenant, 13 May, 1861. Commander, 6 June, 1861. Captain, 27 September, 1866. Resigned 1 March, 1869.

SANFORD, WILLIAM.
Sailmaker, 2 August, 1809. Last appearance on Records of Navy Department, 10 August, 1812.

SANFORD, WILLIAM.
Sailmaker, 15 October, 1805. Last appearance on Records of Navy Department, 18 October, 1805.

SANFORD, WILLIAM C.
Acting First Assistant Engineer, 28 May, 1863. Honorably discharged 26 November, 1865.

SANFORD, WILLIAM C. N.
Mate, 30 July, 1864. Resigned 30 June, 1865.

SANGER, W. P. S.
Civil Engineer, 8 July, 1836. Ordered to Bureau Yards and Docks, 7 September, 1842. Retired List, 15 October, 1881. Died 16 February, 1890.

SANKEY, JOHN G.
Mate, 6 June, 1862. Appointment revoked 14 June, 1862. Acting Assistant Paymaster, 24 September, 1863. Honorably discharged 11 November, 1865.

SAPHAM, ASA.
Lieutenant, 4 October, 1799. Resigned 13 December, 1799.

SARD, WILLIAM F.
Mate, 23 December, 1863. Honorably discharged 25 October, 1866.

SARGENT, ASA.
Surgeon, 9 May, 1799. Last appearance on Records of Navy Department.

SARGENT, ELI D.
Acting Assistant Surgeon, 2 June, 1865. Honorably discharged 11 May, 1866.

SARGENT, FERNANDO C.
Acting Assistant Surgeon, 8 September, 1863. Honorably discharged 24 August, 1865.

SARGENT, HOWARD.
Mate, 22 December, 1862. Honorably discharged 15 May, 1865.

SARGENT, LEONARD R.
Naval Cadet, 6 September, 1893. Ensign, 1 July, 1899.

SRGENT, NATHAN.
Midshipman, 23 July, 1866. Graduated 7 June, 1870. Ensign, 13 July, 1871. Master, 10 July, 1874. Lieutenant, 10 January, 1881. Lieutenant-Commander, 3 March, 1899.

SARGENT, WALTER.
Mate, 21 March, 1862. Acting Ensign, 28 January, 1863. Acting Master, 25 May, 1865. Honorably discharged 28 October, 1865. Acting Master, 15 August, 1866. Ensign, 12 March, 1868. Master, 18 December, 1868. Lost on the Oneida, 24 January, 1870.

SARTORI, CHARLES W.
Acting Assistant Surgeon, 18 May, 1861. Resigned 19 July, 1864.

SARTORI, LOUIS C.
Midshipman, 2 February, 1869. Passed Midshipman, 15 June, 1837. Lieutenant, 8 September, 1841. Reserved List, 28 September, 1855. Lieutenant on Active List, 8 September, 1841. Commander, 27 April, 1861. Captain, 26 September, 1861. Commodore, 12 December, 1873. Retired List, 3 June, 1874. Died 11 January, 1899.

SASSE, PETER A.
Third Assistant Engineer, 16 November, 1861. Died 23 July, 1862.

SATTERLEE, CHARLES A.
Acting Third Assistant Engineer, 14 September, 1864. Honorably discharged 12 May, 1865.

SATTERLEE, HERBERT L.
Lieutenant (Spanish-American War), 6 July, 1898. Honorably discharged 7 November, 1898.

GENERAL NAVY REGISTER.   483

SATTERWHITE, E. F.
  Midshipman, 16 January, 1809. Purser, 25 April, 1812. Last appearance on Records of Navy Department, 1815.
SATTERWHITE, W. F.
  Midshipman, 9 November, 1813. Dismissed 24 November, 1813.
SAUER, NICHOLAS.
  Acting Third Assistant Engineer, 1 June, 1863. Honorably discharged 9 November, 1865.
SAUL, THOMAS H.
  Midshipman, 23 October, 1820. Resigned 2 November, 1821.
SAUNDERS, B. R.
  Midshipman, 2 April, 1804. Resigned 27 May, 1806.
SAUNDERS, CHARLES H. N.
  Acting Third Assistant Engineer, 6 March, 1865. Dismissed 22 April, 1865.
SAUNDERS, JOHN L.
  Midshipman, 15 November, 1809. Lieutenant, 13 January, 1825. Commander, 8 September, 1841. Reserved List, 13 September, 1855. Died 26 October, 1860.
SAUNDERS, J. W.
  Acting Master, 28 February, 1862. Honorably discharged 29 October, 1865.
SAVAGE, AUGUSTUS C.
  Acting Ensign, 11 January, 1864. Honorably discharged 2 August, 1865.
SAVAGE, HIBIJAH.
  Midshipman, 12 January, 1799. Resigned 12 August, 1801.
SAVAGE, HIBIJAH.
  Master, 31 July, 1801. Resigned 11 August, 1801.
SAVAGE, HUGH H.
  Acting Master, 16 December, 1861. Honorably discharged 27 September, 1865.
SAVAGE, L. W.
  Acting Ensign, 31 January, 1865. Honorably discharged 14 September, 1865.
SAVAGE, ROBERT.
  Midshipman, 27 March, 1840. Passed Midshipman, 11 July, 1846. Died 8 February, 1848.
SAVAGE, SAMUEL F.
  Third Assistant Engineer, 21 May, 1857. Second Assistant Engineer, 3 August, 1859. First Assistant Engineer, 8 October, 1861. Resigned 13 January, 1865.
SAVAGE, SILAS T.
  Acting Assistant Paymaster. 6 November, 1862. Appointment revoked (sick) 21 November, 1863. Acting Assistant Paymaster, 26 August, 1864. Resigned 13 January, 1865.
SAVAGE, THOMAS.
  Mate, 20 April, 1865. Mustered out 12 March, 1868. Mate, 10 December, 1869. Boatswain, 12 October, 1871. Retired List, 8 November, 1886.
SAVILLE, JOHN W., JR.
  Third Assistant Engineer, 28 October, 1862. Second Assistant Engineer, 15 March, 1864. Retired List, 1 February, 1871. Passed Assistant Engineer, Retired List, 19 June, 1884.
SAVILLE, WILLIAM O.
  Acting Third Assistant Engineer, 19 August, 1863. Honorably discharged 10 July, 1865.
SAVORY, GEORGE E.
  Acting Third Assistant Engineer, 13 November, 1863. Honorably discharged 8 July, 1869.
SAWTELL, ISAIAH L.
  Acting Third Assistant Engineer, 2 September, 1863. Died 6 May, 1864.
SAWTELLE, ARTHUR M.
  Acting Second Assistant Engineer, 3 February, 1864. Honorably discharged 11 October, 1865.
SAWYER, A. B. C.
  Acting Assistant Surgeon, 21 May, 1862. Acting Passed Assistant Surgeon, 27 April, 1865. Honorably discharged 28 October, 1865.
SAWYER, BENJAMIN A.
  Acting Assistant Surgeon, 9 February, 1865. Honorably discharged 10 October, 1865.
SAWYER, CHARLES.
  Acting Ensign, 29 August, 1864. Honorably discharged 25 December, 1865.
SAWYER, CHARLES H.
  Acting Ensign, 29 August, 1864. Honorably discharged 25 December, 1865.
SAWYER, CHARLES H.
  Mate, 9 October, 1863. Acting Ensign, 5 November, 1864. Honorably discharged 17 September, 1867.
SAWYER, DANIEL A.
  Third Assistant Engineer, 6 October, 1862. Second Assistant Engineer, 15 March, 1864. Retired List, 22 January, 1866.
SAWYER, E. A.
  Acting Ensign, 28 July, 1863. Honorably discharged 1 April, 1866.
SAWYER, FRANK E.
  Midshipman, 25 September, 1868. Graduated 1 June, 1872. Ensign, 15 July, 1873. Master, 22 July, 1878. Lieutenant, Junior Grade, 3 March, 1883. Lieutenant, 16 June, 1885. Lieutenant-Commander, 3 March, 1899.
SAWYER, FREDERICK L.
  Naval Cadet, 6 September, 1888. Ensign, 1 July, 1894. Lieutenant, Junior Grade, 3 March, 1899.
SAWYER, GEORGE A.
  Assistant Paymaster, 24 August, 1861. Paymaster, 17 September, 1863. Retired List, 29 June, 1869.

SAWYER, GEORGE F.
    Purser, 20 March, 1838. Died 24 June, 1852.
SAWYER, GEORGE F.
    Third Assistant Engineer, 8 September, 1863. Second Assistant Engineer, 15 October, 1865. Resigned 12 October, 1868.
SAWYER, HORACE B.
    Midshipman, 4 June, 1812. Lieutenant, 1 April, 1818. Commander, December, 1839. Captain, 12 April, 1853. Reserved List, 13 September, 1855. Died 14 February, 1860.
SAWYER, ISAAC.
    Mate, 22 August, 1863. Appointment revoked (sick) 19 May, 1864.
SAWYER, JAMES.
    Acting Ensign, 12 December, 1863. Acting Master, 31 July, 1865. Honorably discharged 23 November, 1865.
SAWYER JOHN C.
    Acting Assistant Paymaster, 8 February, 1864. Honorably discharged 9 November, 1865.
SAWYER, JOSEPH.
    Acting Ensign, 7 December, 1863. Honorably discharged 23 November, 1865.
SAWYER, JOS. P.
    Master, 18 July, 1812. Discharged 7 May, 1813.
SAWYER, LEWIS C.
    Midshipman, 14 August, 1846. Resigned 16 December, 1847.
SAWYER, MOSES H.
    Acting Master, 16 May, 1861. Resigned 2 May, 1862.
SAWYER, R. P.
    Acting Assistant Surgeon, 29 December, 1863. Resigned 18 May, 1865.
SAWYER, WARREN L.
    Assistant Paymaster (Spanish-American War), 20 July, 1898. Honorably discharged 21 February, 1899.
SAWYERS, JAMES H.
    Acting Midshipman, 24 September, 1866. Graduated June, 1870. Died 24 October, 1870.
SAYER, BENJAMIN.
    Master, 14 August, 1799. Discharged 8 July, 1801, under Peace Establishment Act.
SAYERS, JOHN.
    Acting Master and Pilot, 1 October, 1864. Appointment revoked 9 March, 1865.
SAYRE, JOHN S.
    Assistant Surgeon, 24 June, 1884. Passed Assistant Surgeon, 24 June, 1887. Retired List, 16 November, 1896. Died 29 November, 1899.
SAYLES, WILLIAM R., JR.
    Naval Cadet, 20 May, 1895. At sea prior to final graduation.
SCALES, ARCHIBALD H.
    Naval Cadet, 19 May, 1883. Ensign, 1 July, 1889. Lieutenant, Junior Grade, 28 August, 1897. Lieutenant, 3 March, 1899.
SCALES, DABNEY M.
    Lieutenant (Spanish-American War), 4 June, 1898. Honorably discharged 8 September, 1898.
SCALLON, WILLIAM.
    Midshipman, 2 December, 1799. Resigned 27 March, 1805.
SCANLAN, CHARLES S.
    Mate, 23 October, 1863. Honorably discharged 9 February, 1866.
SCANLAN, PATRICK.
    Acting Third Assistant Engineer, 1 October, 1862. Acting Second Assistant Engineer, 6 July, 1864. Honorably discharged 27 November, 1865.
SCANNELL, JAMES.
    Acting Master, 12 April, 1862. Dismissed 10 September, 1862. Acting Ensign, 9 December, 1862. Resigned 24 July, 1863.
SCANTLAND, ROBERT A.
    Acting Midshipman, 30 December, 1848. Dropped 12 July, 1849.
SCARLETT, JOSEPH H.
    Acting Ensign, 6 September, 1864. Honorably discharged 13 December, 1865.
SCATTERGOOD, EDWARD.
    Third Assistant Engineer, 26 August, 1859. Second Assistant Engineer, 1 March, 1862. First Assistant Engineer, 1 October, 1863. Died 20 September, 1864.
SCHAEFER, HENRY W.
    Midshipman, 21 July, 1866. Graduated 7 June, 1870. Ensign, 13 July, 1871. Master, 9 October, 1873. Lieutenant, 27 October, 1879. Died 11 May, 1889.
SCHAFER, GEORGE C.
    Assistant Paymaster, 10 July, 1898.
SCHAMBACK, HERMAN G.
    Mate, 21 July, 1864. Resigned 26 October, 1864.
SCHAUDER, ADOLPH.
    Mate. Appointment revoked 9 November, 1866.
SCHELL, FRANKLIN J.
    Cadet Engineer, Naval Academy, 1 October, 1874. Graduated 20 June, 1878. Assistant Engineer, 20 June, 1880. Passed Assistant Engineer, 16 May, 1889. Chief Engineer, 16 February, 1898. Rank changed to Lieutenant, 3 March, 1899. Lieutenant-Commander, 29 November, 1900.
SCHELLENBERGER, GEORGE W.
    Acting Third Assistant Engineer, 1 October, 1862. Acting Second Assistant Engineer, 5 December, 1863. Honorably discharged 27 November, 1865.

GENERAL NAVY REGISTER. 485

SCHELLER, JOHN F.
Lieutenant, Junior Grade (Spanish-American War), 24 May, 1898. Honorably discharged 11 January, 1899.
SCHENCK, CASPAR.
Acting Assistant Paymaster, 6 July, 1861. Assistant Paymaster, 14 September, 1861. Paymaster, 5 February, 1862. Pay Inspector, 3 March, 1871. Pay Director, 6 December, 1880. Retired List, 26 September, 1897.
SCHENCK, GEORGE R.
Acting Master, 30 October, 1861. Resigned 8 May, 1862.
SCHENCK, JAMES F.
Midshipman, 1 July, 1825. Passed Midshipman, 4 June, 1831. Lieutenant, 22 December, 1835. Commander, 14 September, 1855. Commodore, 2 January, 1863. Rear-Admiral, 21 September, 1868. Retired List, 11 June, 1869. Died 21 December, 1882.
SCHENCK, JOHN N.
Acting Third Assistant Engineer, 14 September, 1864. Honorably discharged 27 October, 1865.
SCHENCK, JOHN P.
Acting Assistant Surgeon, 7 May, 1864. Resigned 19 May, 1864.
SCHENCK, ROBERT C.
Assistant Paymaster, 20 October, 1897. Resigned 30 October, 1900.
SCHENCK, WOODHULL S.
Midshipman, 30 December, 1831. Passed Midshipman, 15 June, 1837. Lieutenant, 8 September, 1841. Died 9 May, 1849.
SCHEPEL, J. AUGUSTUS.
Mate, 6 December, 1861. Appointment revoked 11 August, 1862.
SCHERMERHORN, EDWARD.
Midshipman, 1 May, 1822. Passed Midshipman, 24 May, 1828. Lost in the Hornet, 10 September, 1829.
SCHETKY, CHARLES A.
Acting Ensign, 27 June, 1863. Honorably discharged 22 February, 1866. Master, 12 March, 1868. Lieutenant, 18 December, 1868. Lieutenant-Commander, 1 December, 1877. Commander, 4 September, 1887. Retired List, 18 March, 1889.
SCHLEY, ARTHUR.
Mate, 28 October, 1869. Resigned 5 April, 1871.
SCHLEY, WILLIAM R.
Third Assistant Engineer, 2 May, 1857. Died 25 February, 1858.
SCHLEY, WINFIELD S.
Acting Midshipman, 20 September, 1856. Midshipman, 15 June, 1860. Master, 19 September, 1861. Lieutenant 16 July, 1862. Lieutenant-Commander, 25 July, 1866. Commander, 10 June, 1874. Captain, 31 March, 1888. Commodore, 6 February, 1898. Rear-Admiral, 3 March, 1899.
SCHLUTER, WILHELM H. F.
Acting Gunner, 1 August, 1900.
SCHMIDT, EDWARD H.
Mate 24 January, 1863. Appointment revoked (sick) 20 October, 1864.
SCHMITZ, CHARLES F.
Midshipman, 19 October, 1861. Graduated November, 1864. Ensign, 1 November, 1866. Master. 1 December, 1866. Lieutenant, 12 March, 1868. Lieutenant-Commander, 26 March, 1869. Died 20 May, 1883.
SCHNEIDER, WILLIAM T.
Acting Third Assistant Engineer, 2 September, 1863. Acting Second Assistant Engineer, 6 March, 1865. Honorably discharged 15 August, 1865.
SCHOBER, FREDERICK.
Third Assistant Engineer, 23 June, 1863. Second Assistant Engineer, 25 July, 1866. Resigned 9 June, 1873.
SCHOCK, JOHN L.
Cadet Midshipman, 19 June, 1877. Graduated 10 June, 1881. Assistant Naval Constructor, 1 July, 1883. Died 23 May, 1885.
SCHOENFELD, JOHN W.
Naval Cadet, 6 July, 1896. Graduated 30 June, 1900.
SCHOFIELD, CHARLES E.
Mate, 19 September, 1864. Honorably discharged 23 June, 1866.
SCHOFIELD, FRANK H.
Naval Cadet, 21 May, 1886. Ensign, 1 July, 1892. Lieutenant, 3 March, 1899.
SCHOFIELD, JOHN A.
Naval Cadet. 6 September, 1894. Ensign, 4 April, 1900.
SCHOLES, THOMAS.
Acting Third Assistant Engineer, 19 August, 1862. Acting Second Assistant Engineer, 1 November, 1862. Resigned 11 December, 1863.
SCHOOLEY, FRANK N.
Mate, 10 September, 1864. Appointment revoked (sick) 30 January, 1865.
SCHOOLFIELD, J. J.
Assistant Surgeon, 13 March, 1805. Surgeon, 28 June, 1809. Resigned 27 October, 1817.
SCHOONMAKER. C. M.
Acting Midshipman, 28 September, 1854. Midshipman, 9 June, 1859. Lieutenant, 31 August, 1861. Lieutenant-Commander, 24 December, 1865. Commander, 14 February, 1873. Captain, 7 October, 1886. Drowned 15 March, 1889.
SCHOULER, JOHN.
Midshipman, 25 September, 1861. Graduated November, 1864. Ensign, 1 November, 1866. Master. 1 December, 1866. Lieutenant, 12 March, 1868. Lieutenant-Commander, 3 June, 1869. Commander, 8 June, 1885. Captain, 5 June, 1898. Retired with rank of Rear-Admiral, 21 November, 1899.

SCHOW, MAGNUS.
Acting Master, 12 May, 1862. Dismissed 13 October, 1862.
SCHRADER, CORNELIUS.
Acting Third Assistant Engineer, 23 January, 1865. Honorably discharged 17 June, 1866.
SCHREIBER, MARTIN M.
Acting Warrant Machinist, 23 August, 1899.
SCHROEDER, CHARLES.
Third Assistant Engineer, 24 December, 1853. Second Assistant Engineer, 9 May, 1857. First Assistant Engineer, 3 August, 1859. Name stricken from the Rolls, 18 May, 1861.
SCHROEDER, SEATON.
Acting Midshipman, 27 September, 1864. Graduated June, 1868. Master, 12 July, 1870. Lieutenant, 29 October, 1872. Lieutenant-Commander, 27 September, 1893. Commander, 3 March, 1899.
SCHRYVER, DAVID M.
Acting Third Assistant Engineer, 26 May, 1863. Honorably discharged 15 May, 1865.
SCHUETZE, WILLIAM H.
Midshipman, 23 June, 1869. Graduated 31 May, 1873. Ensign, 16 July, 1874. Master, 30 November, 1878. Lieutenant, Junior Grade, 3 March, 1883. Lieutenant, 2 October, 1885. Lieutenant-Commander, 3 March, 1899.
SCHULTICE, SIMON.
Acting First Assistant Engineer, 1 October, 1862. Acting Chief Engineer, 15 April, 1864. Honorably discharged 29 September, 1865.
SCHULTZ, WILLIAM.
Acting Ensign, 15 October, 1863. Resigned 18 April, 1865.
SCHULZE, GERHARD C.
Acting Master, 25 September, 1861. Master, 12 March, 1868. Lieutenant, 18 December, 1868. Lieutenant-Commander, 10 June, 1870. Died 28 September, 1870.
SCHUSTER, FRANCIS E.
Acting Boatswain, 20 July, 1898. Died 21 June, 1899.
SCHUYLER, P. P.
Midshipman, 20 June, 1806. Dismissed 26 June, 1809.
SCHWARTZ, EDWARD G.
Acting Third Assistant Engineer, 23 November, 1864. Honorably discharged 18 June, 1868.
SCHWENK, MILTON K.
Midshipman, 22 September, 1866. Graduated 1 June, 1872. Ensign, 15 July, 1874. Master, 23 October, 1878. Lieutenant, Junior Grade, 3 March, 1883. Lieutenant, 31 July, 1885. Retired List, 14 May, 1889. Died 28 June, 1899.
SCHWERIN, RENNIE P.
Cadet Midshipman, 25 September, 1874. Graduated 10 June, 1881. Ensign, Junior Grade, 3 March, 1883. Ensign, 26 June, 1884. Lieutenant, Junior Grade, 30 June, 1891. Resigned 6 March, 1893.
SCOBEY, GILBERT W.
Acting Third Assistant Engineer, 30 May, 1864. Honorably discharged 24 June, 1868.
SCOFFIN, CHARLES R.
Mate, 4 April, 1862. Acting Ensign, 2 May, 1864. Honorably discharged 14 December, 1865.
SCOFIELD, WALTER K.
Assistant Surgeon, 12 July, 1861. Surgeon, 19 June, 1876. Medical Inspector, 21 November, 1883. Medical Director, 8 February, 1890.
SCOFIELD, WILLIAM R.
Warrant Machinist, 6 July, 1899.
SCOT, JOHN A.
Third Assistant Engineer, 3 October, 1861. Second Assistant Engineer, 3 August, 1863. First Assistant Engineer, 11 October, 1866. Chief Engineer, 6 July, 1885. Retired List, 28 May, 1897.
SCOTT, BERNARD O.
Midshipman, 30 June, 1870. Graduated 1 June, 1874. Ensign, 17 July, 1875. Master, 14 September, 1881. Lieutenant, Junior Grade, 3 March, 1883. Lieutenant, 1 July, 1887. Lieutenant-Commander, 3 March, 1899.
SCOTT, BEVERLY R.
Midshipman, 18 June, 1812. Resigned 11 December, 1815.
SCOTT, **CHARLES P.**
Third Assistant Engineer, 18 November, 1862. Died 20 June, 1864.
SCOTT, FREDERICK.
Acting Third Assistant Engineer, 22 July, 1863. Honorably discharged 22 December, 1865.
SCOTT, GUSTAVUS H.
Midshipman, 1 August, 1828. Passed Midshipman, 14 June, 1834. Lieutenant, 25 February, 1841. Commander, 27 December, 1856. Captain, 4 November, 1863. Commodore, 10 February 1869. Rear-Admiral, 14 February, 1873. Retired List, 13 June, 1874. Died 23 March, 1882.
SCOTT, HENRY B.
Mate, 20 February, 1865. Honorably discharged 3 December, 1867.
SCOTT, H. D.
Midshipman, 30 May, 1816. Lieutenant, 28 April, 1826. Died 16 February, 1830.
SCOTT, HENRY M.
Mate, 22 April, 1863. Dismissed 19 March, 1864.

GENERAL NAVY REGISTER. 487

SCOTT, HENRY W.
　　Third Assistant Engineer, 1 July, 1861. Second Assistant Engineer, 29 April, 1863. First Assistant Engineer, 30 January, 1865. Died 10 May, 1869.
SCOTT, HORACE B.
　　Assistant Surgeon, 11 July, 1883. Passed Assistant Surgeon, 25 March, 1887. Retired List, 31 October, 1890. Died 29 May, 1900.
SCOTT, JAMES M.
　　Assistant Surgeon, 6 June, 1868. Resigned 14 August, 1874.
SCOTT, JOHN.
　　Acting Volunteer Lieutenant, 1 October, 1862. Resigned 5 October, 1864.
SCOTT, JOHN.
　　Mate, 7 May, 1863. Honorably discharged 30 June, 1866.
SCOTT, JOHN B.
　　Chaplain (Spanish-American War), 30 April, 1898. Died 15 July, 1898.
SCOTT, JOHN G.
　　Acting First Assistant Engineer, 1 October, 1862. Acting Chief Engineer, 19 May, 1864. Honorably discharged 14 October, 1865.
SCOTT, JOHN H.
　　Mate, 3 April, 1865. Honorably discharged 10 July, 1865.
SCOTT, MERRITT.
　　Midshipman, 30 November, 1814. Died in January, 1825.
SCOTT, ROBERT T.
　　Warrant Machinist, 23 August, 1899.
SCOTT, ROBERT W.
　　Midshipman, 9 September, 1841. Passed Midshipman, 10 August, 1847. Master, 15 September, 1855. Lieutenant, 16 September, 1855. Lieutenant-Commander, 16 July, 1852. Died 5 January, 1866.
SCOTT, SAMUEL P.
　　Gunner, 26 November, 1841. Appointment revoked 15 January, 1842.
SCOTT, WARBURTON S.
　　Mate, 1 October, 1862. Resigned 22 April, 1864.
SCOTT, WILLIAM.
　　First Assistant Engineer, 20 March, 1840. Disrated to Second Assistant Engineer, 22 January, 1846. Dismissed 5 June, 1850.
SCOTT, WILLIAM.
　　Boatswain, 17 June, 1850. Resigned 6 November, 1850.
SCOTT, WILLIAM.
　　Acting Gunner, 8 August, 1863. Honorably discharged 24 July, 1865.
SCOTT, WILLIAM P.
　　Naval Cadet, 20 May, 1890. Ensign, 1 July, 1896. Lieutenant, Junior Grade, 1 July, 1899.
SCOVEL, LEWIS L.
　　Acting Assistant Paymaster, 3 August, 1861. Mustered out 9 February, 1866.
SCOVELL, EDWARD H.
　　Midshipman, 19 October, 1841. Dismissed 21 January, 1850.
SCRANTON, EDISON F.
　　Naval Cadet, 20 May, 1896. Graduated 30 June, 1900.
SCRANTON, SAMUEL O.
　　Acting Master and Pilot, 1 December, 1864. Honorably discharged 8 June, 1865.
SCRIBNER, EDWARD H.
　　Cadet Engineer, Naval Academy, 1 October, 1874. Graduated 10 June, 1879. Assistant Engineer, 10 June, 1881. Passed Assistant Engineer, 2 March, 1892. Chief Engineer, 28 February, 1899. Rank changed to Lieutenant, 3 March, 1899.
SCRIBNER, JAMES E.
　　Acting Third Assistant Engineer, 18 June, 1864. Honorably discharged 8 October, 1865.
SCRIGGINS, JOHN.
　　Carpenter, 11 June, 1799. Resigned 5 February, 1800.
SCUDDER, ALEXANDER.
　　Acting Master, 4 November, 1861. Appointment revoked (sick) 27 December, 1861.
SCUDDER, THEODORE.
　　Acting Third Assistant Engineer, 30 December, 1863. Honorably discharged 12 July, 1865.
SCULLEY, JAMES.
　　Mate, 4 February, 1865. Appointment revoked 5 February, 1866.
SEABURY, PHILIP A.
　　Acting Ensign, 13 May, 1863. Resigned 23 March, 1865.
SEABURY, SAMUEL.
　　Midshipman, 20 June, 1867. Graduated 6 June, 1871. Ensign, 14 July, 1872. Master, 20 July, 1875. Lieutenant, 9 January, 1883. Retired List, 28 April, 1896.
SEAGER, EDWARD.
　　Professor, 21 May, 1864. Retired List, 8 April, 1871. Died 23 January, 1886.
SEAGRAVE, O. B.
　　Acting Assistant Paymaster, 19 October, 1863. Honorably discharged 21 October, 1865.
SEAGROVE, JAMES.
　　Gunner, 7 May, 1804. Last appearance on Records of Navy Department.
SEAL, WILLIAM.
　　Assistant Surgeon, 24 June, 1826. Died 18 December, 1829.
SEAMAN, HENRY G.
　　Mate, 24 October, 1862. Acting Ensign, 1 July, 1864. Honorably discharged 12 August, 1865.

GENERAL NAVY REGISTER.

SEAMAN, JOHN.
Acting Second Assistant Engineer, 12 January, 1863. Acting First Assistant Engineer, 9 June, 1864. Honorably discharged 26 October, 1865.
SEAMAN, JOHN.
Acting Third Assistant Engineer, 24 January, 1862. Honorably discharged 26 October, 1865.
SEAMAN, STEPHEN.
Sailmaker, 22 April, 1846. Retired List, 22 April, 1884. Died in 1886.
SEAMAN, W. R.
Acting Assistant Surgeon, 22 November, 1864. Honorably discharged 2 November, 1865.
SEARCY, ROBERT E.
Midshipman, 1 January, 1812. Lieutenant, 5 March, 1817. Died 2 November, 1822.
SEARLE, ADDISON.
Chaplain, 27 April, 1820. Died 2 August, 1850.
SEARS, AMASA C.
Acting Ensign, 5 January, 1863. Acting Master, 7 March, 1864. Honorably discharged 10 August, 1865.
SEARS, CYRUS.
Acting Ensign, 12 August, 1863. Acting Master, 16 August, 1864. Acting Volunteer Lieutenant, 15 July, 1865. Honorably discharged 27 September, 1865.
SEARS, EDWARD H.
Acting Assistant Paymaster, 27 August, 1863. Mustered out 2 June, 1868.
SEARS, E. T.
Acting Ensign, 28 August, 1863. Honorably discharged 19 August, 1865.
SEARS, JAMES H.
Midshipman, 20 September, 1871. Graduated 20 June, 1876. Ensign, 11 December, 1877. Lieutenant, Junior Grade, 2 December, 1884. Lieutenant, 20 September, 1890. Lieutenant-Commander, 29 March, 1899.
SEARS, JOHN.
Mate, 7 August, 1862. Acting Ensign, 9 April, 1863. Honorably discharged 22 February, 1869.
SEARS, JOHN D.
Midshipman, 2 April, 1804. Lost overboard 29 June, 1804.
SEARS, MYLES.
Acting Boatswain, 1 March, 1900.
SEARS, THOMAS B.
Acting Master, 22 January, 1862. Honorably discharged 18 February, 1866.
SEARS, WALTER J.
Cadet Midshipman, 24 June, 1875. Graduated 10 June, 1881. Ensign, Junior Grade, 3 March, 1883. Ensign, 26 June, 1884. Lieutenant, Junior Grade, 4 August, 1891. Lieutenant, 5 November, 1895.
SEAVER, EBEN M.
Mate, 13 June, 1863. Acting Ensign, 22 October, 1863. Dismissed 27 April, 1864.
SEAVER, JAMES T.
Acting Master, 9 January, 1862. Dishonorably discharged 21 October, 1864.
SEAVEY, EDWIN A.
Acting Ensign, 13 May, 1864. Died 25 September, 1864.
SEAVEY, FAYETTE.
Acting Third Assistant Engineer, 4 September, 1863. Acting Second Assistant Engineer, 1 December, 1863. Honorably discharged 11 March, 1866.
SEAVEY, THEODORE B.
Mate, 24 March, 1864. Resigned 29 April, 1865.
SEAWELL, JOSEPH A.
Midshipman, 3 July, 1842. Passed Midshipman, 5 August, 1848. Dropped 13 September, 1855.
SEBASTIAN, BENJAMIN.
Acting Ensign, 1 October, 1862. Acting Master, 7 March, 1863. Resigned 22 March, 1865.
SEBELIN, AUGUSTUS.
Mate, 3 September, 1864. Discharged 5 October, 1864. Acting Ensign, 8 December, 1864. Honorably discharged 14 September, 1865.
SEBREE, URIEL.
Midshipman, 25 July, 1863. Graduated June, 1867. Ensign, 18 December, 1868. Master, 24 March, 1870. Lieutenant, 21 March, 1871. Lieutenant-Commander, 26 March, 1889. Commander, 24 February, 1897.
SECCOMBE, WILLIAM S.
Lieutenant (Spanish-American War), 26 May, 1898. Honorably discharged 13 March, 1899.
SEDAM, LEWIS W.
Mate, 24 November, 1863. Honorably discharged 11 October, 1865.
SEDAM, WALKER Y.
Acting Third Assistant Engineer, 1 October, 1862. Acting First Assistant Engineer, 10 June, 1863. Resigned 10 May, 1864.
SEE, THOMAS J. J.
Professor, 10 February, 1899.
SEEGERS, LEWIS.
Mdshipman, 10 May, 1820. Resigned 28 April, 1824.
SEEKINS, CHARLES W.
Acting Ensign, 13 July, 1863. Acting Master, 9 June, 1865. Honorably discharged 8 January, 1866.
SEELEY, CHARLES W.
Acting Assistant Paymaster, 15 November, 1864. Mustered out 16 November, 1865.

GENERAL NAVY REGISTER.

SEELY, HENRY B.
Acting Midshipman, 26 May, 1852. Midshipman, 10 June, 1857. Passed Midshipman, 25 June, 1860. Master, 24 October, 1860. Lieutenant, 17 April, 1861. Lieutenant-Commander, 21 February, 1864. Commander, 24 August, 1873. Captain, 13 December, 1886. Retired List, 30 June, 1892.

SEELY, SAMUEL J.
Carpenter, 24 March, 1842. Resigned 3 April, 1848.

SEGANNY, J. B.
Midshipman, 16 January, 1809. Killed in action 14 Juy, 1813.

SEGERSTEEN, B.
Mate, 20 June, 1864. Honorably discharged 13 June, 1868.

SEGRAVE, THOMAS G.
Lieutenant (Spanish-American War), 18 May, 1898. Honorably discharged 30 August, 1898.

SEIBELS, GEORGE G.
Assistant Paymaster, 31 August, 1896. Passed Assistant Paymaster, 6 March, 1898.

SELDEN, EDWARD A.
Midshipman, 19 October, 1841. Passed Midshipman, 10 August, 1847. Dropped 13 September, 1855. Lieutenant, 24 March, 1861. Dismissed 27 November, 1861.

SELDEN, GEORGE L.
Midshipman, 1 April, 1828. Passed Midshipman, 14 June, 1834. Lieutenant, 25 April, 1841. Reserved List, 13 September, 1855. Commander, Retired List, 19 July, 1861. Died 14 February, 1864.

SELDEN, GEORGE L.
Midshipman, 27 July, 1866. Graduated 6 June, 1871. Resigned 24 July, 1872.

SELDEN, ROBERT.
Midshipman, 9 September, 1841. Passed Midshipman, 10 August, 1847. Master, 14 September, 1855. Lieutenant, 15 September, 1855. Resigned 27 December, 1860.

SELDEN, W. C.
Midshipman, 16 November, 1824. Passed Midshipman, 20 February, 1830. Lost in Sylph, August, 1831.

SELDEN, WILLIAM CAREY.
Third Assistant Engineer, 26 August, 1859. Second Assistant Engineer, 3 October, 1861. First Assistant Engineer, 1 October, 1863. Resigned 19 October, 1868.

SELFRIDGE, C. G.
Naval Constructor, 15 July, 1847. Died 30 May, 1848.

SELFRIDGE, E. A.
Mate. Resigned 29 October, 1862.

SELFRIDGE, GEORGE S.
Lieutenant (Spanish-American War), 14 May, 1898. Honorably discharged 10 October, 1898.

SELFRIDGE, JAMES R.
Midshipman, 21 July, 1864. Graduated June, 1868. Ensign, 19 April, 1869. Master, 12 July, 1870. Lieutenant, 27 September, 1873. Lieutenant-Commander, 30 September, 1894. Commander, 3 March, 1899.

SELFRIDGE, JAMES R.
Assistant Engineer (Spanish-American War), 3 June, 1898. Honorably discharged 17 January, 1899.

SELFRIDGE, THOMAS O.
Midshipman, 1 January, 1818. Lieutenant, 3 March, 1827. Commander, 11 April, 1844. Captain, 14 September, 1855. Commodore, 16 July, 1862. Retired 10 October, 1866. Rear-Admiral on Retired List, 25 July, 1866.

SELFRIDGE, THOMAS O.
Acting Midshipman, 3 October, 1851. Midshipman, 10 June, 1854. Passed Midshipman, 22 November, 1856. Master, 22 January, 1858. Lieutenant, 15 February, 1860. Lieutenant-Commander, 16 July, 1862. Commander, 31 December, 1869. Captain, 24 February, 1881. Commodore, 11 April, 1894. Rear-Admiral, 28 February, 1896. Retired List, 6 February, 1898.

SELLERS, DAVID F.
Naval Cadet, 21 May, 1890. Ensign, 1 July, 1896. Lieutenant, Junior Grade, 1 July, 1899.

SELLERS, JAMES.
Master, 27 January, 1814. Discharged 15 April, 1815.

SELLEW, EDGAR K.
Acting Assistant Paymaster, 22 September, 1864. Honorably discharged 3 October, 1865.

SELLEW, WILLIAM.
Acting Assistant Paymaster, 22 July, 1862. Mustered out 23 October, 1866.

SELLMAN, HENRY D.
Third Assistant Engineer, 19 July, 1861. Second Assistant Engineer, 18 December, 1862. Retired List, 7 November, 1871.

SELLMAN, J. HENRY.
Acting Assistant Paymaster, 5 March, 1862. Resigned 14 November, 1864.

SELLS, ELIJAH.
Acting Master, 23 June, 1863. Acting Volunteer Lieutenant, 14 May, 1864. Resigned 22 July, 1864.

SELLS, WILLIAM H.
Acting Assistant Paymaster, 9 December, 1861. Assistant Paymaster, 18 September, 1862. Resigned 16 November, 1864.

SELMER, JOHN A.
Boatswain. 2 September, 1861. Died 14 December, 1880.

SEMANS. WILLIAM R.
Acting Assistant Surgeon, 22 March, 1864. Honorably discharged 2 November, 1865.

SEMIG, B.
Acting Assistant Surgeon, 11 April, 1865. Resigned 9 June, 1866.
SEMMES, ALEXANDER A.
Midshipman, 27 October, 1841. Passed Midshipman, 10 August, 1847. Master, 14 September, 1855. Lieutenant, 15 September, 1855. Lieutenant-Commander, 16 July, 1862. Commander, 25 July, 1866. Captain, 24 August, 1873. Commodore, 10 March, 1882. Died 22 September, 1885.
SEMMES, FRANCIS J.
Assistant Paymaster, 2 March, 1895. Resigned 22 October, 1898.
SEMMES, RAPHAEL.
Midshipman, 1 April, 1826. Passed Midshipman, 28 April, 1832. Lieutenant, 9 February, 1837. Commander, 14 September, 1855. Resigned 15 February, 1861.
SEMON, E. N.
Acting Ensign, 26 December, 1862. Honorably discharged 2 September, 1865.
SEMPLE, JAMES A.
Purser, 12 October, 1844. Dismissed 15 July, 1861.
SEMPLE, J. E.
Assistant Surgeon, 22 September, 1854. Resigned 1 May, 1860.
SEMPLE, JOHN R.
Master's Mate, 25 January, 1862. Discharged 8 March, 1862.
SEMPLE, LORENZO.
Cadet Midshipman, 22 September, 1877. Graduated 10 June 1882. Ensign, 1 July, 1884. Resigned 30 June, 1890.
SENAC, FELIX.
Purser, 15 August, 1856. Dismissed 22 June, 1861.
SENATE, GEORGE.
Midshipman, 21 July, 1807. Lieutenant, 9 December, 1814. Last appearance on Records of Navy Department. Dead.
SENIOR, EDWIN.
Acting Second Assistant Engineer, 17 February, 1863. Honorably discharged 1 December, 1865.
SENN, THOMAS J.
Naval Cadet, 19 May, 1887. Ensign, 1 July, 1893. Lieutenant, Junior Grade, 3 March, 1899. Lieutenant, 31 December, 1899.
SENSNER, GEORGE W.
Third Assistant Engineer, 22 October, 1860. Second Assistant Engineer, 19 February, 1862. First Assistant Engineer, 24 August, 1864. Chief Engineer, 17 June, 1874. Retired List, 25 January, 1886.
SENTER, CHARLES W. C.
Third Assistant Engineer, 4 May, 1863. Second Assistant Engineer, 28 September, 1864. Lost on the Oneida, 24 January, 1870.
SENTER, GEORGE E.
Mate, 26 June, 1862. Resigned 8 May, 1863.
SERRA, JOHN.
Third Assistant Engineer, 29 May, 1843. Resigned 23 October, 1845. Third Assistant Engineer, 14 May, 1847. Dropped 27 February, 1851.
SERRY, AUGUSTINE.
Boatswain, 1 August, 1800. Broke by Court-martial 16 May, 1804.
SERVANT, JAMES.
Gunner, 15 April, 1799. Warrant returned 1 May, 1800.
SERVICE, DAVID.
Midshipman, 15 June, 1799. Discharged 6 July, 1801, under Peace Establishment Act.
SERVOSS, COURTNEY S.
Acting Third Assistant Engineer, 7 October, 1862. Acting Second Assistant Engineer, 29 September, 1864. Honorably discharged 17 October, 1865.
SERVOSS, SILAS M. B.
Mate, 1 October, 1862. Acting Ensign, 18 November, 1862. Honorably discharged 24 March, 1863.
SETLY, HARRY.
Mate, 10 January, 1865. Died 30 July, 1887.
SETON, HENRY.
Lieutenant, 5 February, 1799. Discharged 15 April, 1801, under Peace Establishment Act.
SETON, WILLIAM.
Midshipman, 4 July, 1817. Lieutenant, 28 April, 1826. Resigned 5 July, 1834.
SEVER, JAMES.
Captain, 11 May, 1798. Discharged 18 June, 1801, under Peace Establishment Act.
SEVERNS, ISAAC.
Mate, 5 June, 1863. Acting Ensign, 14 June, 1864. Honorably discharged 24 August, 1865.
SEVIER, ALEXANDER.
Midshipman, 18 June, 1836. Dropped.
SEWARD, WILLIAM A.
Acting Second Assistant Engineer, 28 December, 1861. Resigned 29 April, 1862.
SEWELL, GEORGE.
Acting Second Assistant Engineer, 13 March, 1847. First Assistant Engineer, 10 July, 1847. Chief Engineer, 15 July, 1852. (By Act of Congress, 15 July. 1870. Chief Engineer from 11 March, 1851.) Retired List, 17 December, 1885. Died 13 March, 1895.
SEWELL, WILLIAM.
Chief Engineer. 15 March, 1845. Resigned 10 November, 1853.
SEWELL, WILLIAM E.
Midshipman, 27 September, 1867. Graduated 6 June, 1871. Ensign, 14 July, 1872.

GENERAL NAVY REGISTER. 491

Master, 26 April, 1876. Lieutenant, Junior Grade, 3 March, 1883. Lieutenant, 13 October, 1883. Lieutenant-Commander, 3 March, 1889.
SEXTON, WALTON R.
Naval Cadet, 19 May, 1893. Ensign, 1 July, 1899.
SEYBURN, ISAAC D.
Acting Master, 30 August, 1861. Resigned 24 March, 1864.
SEYMOUR, CHARLES.
Gunner, 19 February, 1862. Dismissed 25 April, 1862.
SEYMOUR, CHARLES.
Midshipman, 28 July, 1864, Graduated June, 1869. Ensign, 19 April, 1869. Master, 12 July, 1870. Lieutenant, 4 June, 1874. Died 10 March, 1883.
SEYMOUR, CHARLES.
Mate, 3 August, 1863. Resigned 25 January, 1865.
SEYMOUR, E. H.
Third Assistant Engineer, 3 August, 1861. Died 11 April, 1864.
SEYMOUR, EDWARD.
Acting Assistant Surgeon, 5 December, 1864. Honorably discharged 10 October, 1865.
SEYMOUR, FRANK.
Mate, 27 November, 1863. Resigned 21 October, 1864.
SEYMOUR, G. CHARLES.
Acting First Assistant Engineer, 3 February, 1863. Resigned 7 November, 1863.
SEYMOUR, ISAAC K.
Cadet Midshipman, 25 September, 1880. Ensign, 1 July, 1886. Lieutenant, Junior Grade, 5 November, 1895. Lieutenant, 9 October, 1898.
SEYMOUR, WILLIAM C.
Mate, 9 November, 1863. Acting Ensign, 15 January, 1865. Honorably discharged 26 October, 1865. Gunner, 13 January, 1870. Retired List, 23 November, 1883. Died 23 October, 1896.
SHACKFORD, CHAUNCEY R.
Naval Cadet, 6 September, 1895. At sea prior to final graduation.
SHACKFORD, W. G.
Acting Ensign, 1 September, 1864. Honorably discharged 18 June, 1865.
SHACKFORD, WILLIAM.
Acting Ensign, 13 July, 1863. Acting Master, 27 October, 1864. Honorably discharged 11 November, 1865.
SHAFER, ADAM A.
Warrant Machinist, 23 August, 1899.
SHAFER, JOSEPH.
Assistant Surgeon, 12 June, 1885. Died 29 July, 1887.
SHAFFER, JAMES E.
Acting Second Assistant Engineer, 27 September, 1861. Dismissed 21 April, 1862.
SHAFFER, JOSEPH A.
Mate, 12 January, 1863. Resigned 18 May, 1865.
SHALER, EGBERT.
Midshipman, 30 November, 1814. Resigned 14 September, 1819.
SHALLENBERGER, OLIVER B.
Cadet Engineer, 13 September, 1877. Graduated 10 June, 1881. Honorably discharged 30 June, 1883. Restored to service 10 March, 1886, as an Assistant Engineer, to rank from 1 July, 1883. Resigned 23 September, 1886.
SHALLER, W. D.
Midshipman, 30 May, 1816. Resigned 10 August, 1819.
SHANE, LOUIS.
Naval Cadet, 6 September, 1894. Ensign, 4 April, 1900.
SHANK, GEORGE W.
Acting Third Assistant Engineer, 3 December, 1861. Acting Second Assistant Engineer, 18 April, 1863. Acting First Assistant Engineer, 8 January, 1864. Honorably discharged 24 October, 1864.
SHANKLAND, JOSEPH.
Boatswain, 20 June, 1861. Dismissed 10 September, 1862.
SHANKLAND, WILLIAM.
Acting Master, 16 August, 1861. Resigned 12 March, 1863.
SHANKLAND, WILLIAM F.
Acting Master, 16 June, 1861. Acting Volunteer Lieutenant, 20 April, 1864. Honorably discharged 9 September, 1867.
SHANLEY, HENRY C.
Sailmaker, 12 November, 1872. Resigned 15 March, 1873.
SHANLEY, J. D.
Surgeon, 10 September, 1798. Discharged 11 April, 1801, under Peace Establishment Act.
SHANNON, FRANCIS G.
Acting Third Assistant Engineer, 2 October, 1863. Honorably discharged 8 August, 1865.
SHANNON, FRANK P.
Mate, 4 April, 1862. Dismissed 9 September, 1862.
SHANNON, JAMES.
Gunner, 13 April, 1894.
SHANNON, JOHN.
Carpenter, 4 November, 1861. Resigned 27 July, 1863.
SHANNON, JOHN.
Boatswain, 8 March, 1838. Resigned 10 July, 1849.
SHANNON, L.
Carpenter, 14 January, 1806. Resigned 22 September, 1806. Carpenter, 25 April, 1808. Last appearance on Records of Navy Department.

SHANNON, R. C.
Assistant Surgeon, 5 July, 1799. Surgeon, 8 October, 1799. **Resigned 14 October, 1800.**
SHAPLEY, LLOYD S.
Naval Cadet, 30 May, 1895. At sea prior to final graduation.
SHAREY, SAMUEL O.
Third Assistant Engineer, 11 February, 1852. Resigned 3 June, 1854.
SHARP, ALEXANDER.
Midshipman, 21 June, 1870. Graduated 21 June, 1875. Ensign, 18 July, 1876. Master, 8 April, 1882. Lieutenant, Junior Grade, 3 March, 1883. Lieutenant, 15 March, 1889. Lieutenant-Commander, 3 March, 1899.
SHARP, ISAAC.
Midshipman, 10 July, 1799. Resigned 6 December, 1800.
SHARP, SOLOMON.
Assistant Surgeon, 15 September, 1829. Surgeon, 20 February, 1838. Retired List, 16 August, 1865. Died 7 January, 1870.
SHARP, WILLIAM, JR.
Midshipman, 9 September, 1841. Passed Midshipman, 10 August, 1847. Master, 15 September, 1855. Lieutenant, 15 September, 1855. Dismissed 17 April, 1861.
SHARPE, JOHN C.
Midshipman, 1 January, 1825. Passed Midshipman, 4 June, 1831. Lieutenant, 9 February, 1837. Cashiered 28 December, 1840.
SHARRER, WASHINGTON O.
Acting Midshipman, 27 September, 1864. Graduated June, 1868. Master, 12 July, 1870. Lieutenant, 22 March, 1873. Died 8 September, 1889.
SHATTUCK, BENJAMIN.
Midshipman, 30 June, 1799. Discharged 6 July, 1801.
SHATTUCK, BENJAMIN F.
Midshipman, 25 June, 1831. Passed Midshipman, 15 June, 1837. Lieutenant, 8 September, 1841. Died 6 July, 1859.
SHATTUCK, JOHN.
Midshipman, 2 December, 1799. Lieutenant, 20 March, 1807. Last appearance on Records of Navy Department, 27 May, 1809. Furloughed.
SHAW, A. MERRIT.
Acting Third Assistant Engineer, 20 April, 1865. Honorably discharged 26 April, 1869.
SHAW, ANDREW.
Gunner, 31 January, 1800. Last appearance on Records of Navy Department.
SHAW, BENJAMIN.
Acting First Assistant Engineer, 1861. Resigned 20 December, 1861.
SHAW, CHARLES P.
Midshipman, 26 September, 1863. Graduated June, 1867. Ensign, 18 December, 1868. Master, 21 March, 1870. Lieutenant, 21 March, 1871. Retired List, 4 June, 1883.
SHAW, DANIEL.
Acting Third Assistant Engineer, 6 June, 1864. Resigned 24 February, 1865.
SHAW, EDWARD.
Acting Volunteer Lieutenant, 1 October, 1862. Resigned 4 August, 1863.
SHAW, GEORGE J.
Carpenter, 7 October, 1895.
SHAW, HENRY.
Acting Assistant Surgeon, 25 July, 1862. Resigned 26 May, 1864. Acting Assistant Surgeon, 17 February, 1865. Acting Passed Assistant Surgeon, 17 July, 1865. Honorably discharged 2 May, 1868.
SHAW, HENRY G. C.
Midshipman, 30 July, 1842. Resigned 18 May, 1843.
SHAW, HENRY G.
Ensign (Spanish-American War), 20 May, 1898. Honorably discharged 26 August, 1898.
SHAW, JOHN.
Lieutenant, 3 August, 1798. Commander, 22 May, 1804. Captain, 27 August, 1807. Died 17 September, 1823.
SHAW, JOHN M. A.
Acting Boatswain, 24 March, 1900.
SHAW, JOHN O.
Midshipman, 31 December, 1800. Discharged 6 August, 1801, under Peace Establishment Act.
SHAW, JOHN O.
Acting Ensign, 31 July, 1863. Resigned 13 September, 1864.
SHAW, JOHN R.
Purser, 28 February, 1813. Died 17 October, 1820.
SHAW, JOSIAH.
Midshipman, 16 January, 1809. Resigned 16 April, 1809.
SHAW, ROBERT P.
Mate, 11 December, 1862. Acting Ensign, 5 November, 1863. Honorably discharged 30 November, 1865.
SHAW, ROGER C.
Midshipman, 30 November, 1814. Last appearance on Records of Navy Department, 1824. Norfolk.
SHAW, SAMUEL F.
Acting Assistant Surgeon, 9 September, 1862. Assistant Surgeon, 11 October, 1862. Surgeon, 27 January, 1873. Resigned 21 March, 1881.
SHAW, T. DARRAH.
Midshipman, 10 May, 1820. Lieutenant, 17 May, 1828. Commander, 7 August, 1850. Reserved List, 13 September, 1855. Commander on Active List, 7 August, 1850. Retired List, 26 February, 1862. Commodore on Retired List, 4 April, 1867. Died 26 July, 1874.

GENERAL NAVY REGISTER. 493

SHAW, THOMAS M.
Ensign (Spanish-American War), 22 June, 1898. Honorably discharged 19 September, 1898.
SHAW, WILLIAM.
Midshipman, 23 April, 1815. Last appearance on Records of Navy Department, 1824. West Indies.
SHAY, JOHN.
Mate, 11 April, 1866. Appointment revoked 29 December, 1866.
SHEA, DANIEL W.
Lieutenant (Spanish-American War), 9 May, 1898. Honorably discharged 15 September, 1898.
SHEAN, SAMUEL A.
Acting First Assistant Engineer, 3 January, 1865. Honorably discharged 23 July, 1865.
SHEARMAN, JOHN A.
Midshipman, 7 June, 1871. Graduated 21 June, 1875. Ensign, 8 September, 1876. Master, 28 November, 1882. Lieutenant, Junior Grade, 3 March, 1883. Lieutenant, 4 May, 1889. Lieutenant-Commander, 3 March, 1899.
SHEEAN, TIMOTHY.
Boatswain, 22 October, 1878. Chief Boatswain, 3 March, 1899.
SHEED, WILLIAM W.
Master, 5 May, 1813. Resigned 27 November, 1824.
SHEEHAN, WILLIAM.
Acting Third Assistant Engineer, 10 August, 1864. Honorably discharged 31 July, 1865.
SHEER, EDWIN H.
Mate, 5 June, 1862. Acting Ensign, 2 February, 1865. Honorably discharged 3 August, 1865.
SHEER, THOMAS W.
Mate, 7 March, 1862. Acting Ensign, 12 August, 1862. Acting Master, 15 April, 1863. Honorably discharged 12 November, 1865.
SHEETS, T. J.
Mate, 1 October, 1862. Appointment revoked (sick) 26 September, 1863.
SHEFFER, LEWIS.
Acting Third Assistant Engineer, 4 April, 1862. Dismissed 14 November, 1862.
SHEFFER, THOMAS.
Acting First Assistant Engineer, 22 June, 1863. Acting Chief Engineer, 20 May, 1864. Honorably discharged 30 October, 1865.
SHEFFIELD, E. H.
Mate, 11 October, 1861. Acting Master, 3 May, 1862. Resigned 8 May, 1865.
SHEFFIELD, FLETCHER L.
Naval Cadet, 6 September, 1893. Ensign, 4 April, 1900.
SHEFFIELD, ROBERT L.
Carpenter, 27 November, 1841. Died 17 March, 1849.
SHEFFIELD, WILLIAM E.
Carpenter, 11 November, 1829. Died 18 February, 1851.
SHELDON, CLIFFORD H.
Gunner, 3 December, 1897.
SHELDON, E. P.
Acting Assistant Paymaster, 21 January, 1865. Mustered out 30 September, 1865.
SHELDON, H. LAWRENCE.
Assistant Surgeon, 17 April, 1856. Resigned 5 July, 1861.
SHELDON, WILLIAM B.
Acting Master, 4 November, 1861. Acting Volunteer Lieutenant, 15 October, 1864. Honorably discharged 29 October, 1865.
SHEPARD, BURRITT.
Midshipman, 1 February, 1826. Passed Midshipman, 28 April, 1832. Lieutenant, 8 March, 1837. Resigned 22 June, 1849.
SHEPARD, EDWIN M.
Acting Midshipman, 25 November, 1859. Ensign, 25 November, 1862. Lieutenant, 22 February, 1864. Lieutenant-Commander, 25 July, 1866. Commander, 9 May, 1878. Captain, 15 May, 1893.
SHEPARD, GEORGE H.
Naval Cadet, 27 September, 1887. Assistant Engineer, 1 July, 1893. Retired List, 8 January, 1898.
SHEPARD, RICHARD S.
Mate, 30 March, 1863. Resigned 20 March, 1865.
SHEPHERD, EDMUND.
Midshipman, 19 October, 1841. Passed Midshipman, 10 August, 1847. Dropped 13 September, 1855.
SHEPHERD, FRANKLIN.
Acting Third Assistant Engineer, 21 November, 1862. Dismissed 17 April, 1863.
SHEPHERD, JAMES.
Acting Ensign, 1 December, 1863. Honorably discharged 10 February, 1866.
SHEPHERD, WILLIAM.
Acting Ensign, 21 January, 1863. Honorably discharged 20 October, 1865.
SHEPPARD, B. H.
Midshipman, 13 May, 1834. Dropped 12 December, 1836.
SHEPPARD, FRANCIS H.
Midshipman, 16 October, 1861. Graduated November, 1864. Ensign, 1 November, 1866. Master, 1 December, 1866. Retired List, 27 April, 1868. Lieutenant, Retired List, 12 March, 1868. Lieutenant-Commander, Retired List, 26 March, 1869.
SHEPPARD, FRANK S.
Carpenter, 14 October, 1881. Dismissed 2 October, 1895.

SHEPPARD, FREDERICK P.
Acting Assistant Surgeon, 11 March, 1865. Honorably discharged 10 October, 1865.
SHEPPARD, JAMES.
Boatswain, 8 March, 1877. Died 29 June, 1883.
SHEPPARD, JOS.
Gunner, 30 May, 1811. Resigned 27 February, 1815.
SHEPPARD, JOSEPH.
Mate, 21 March, 1865. Dismissed 26 May, 1865.
SHEPPARD, ROBERT.
Mate, 7 June, 1862. Acting Ensign, 17 December, 1863. Deserted 14 February, 1868.
SHEPPERD, FRANCIS E.
Midshipman, 16 October, 1849. Passed Midshipman, 12 June, 1855. Master, 16 September, 1855. Lieutenant, 1 January, 1857. Dismissed 8 July, 1861.
SHEPPERD, THOMPSON.
Midshipman, 2 April, 1804. Resigned 3 October, 1805.
SHERBURNE, C. F.
Midshipman, 1 September, 1811. Last appearance on Records of Navy Department, 17 July, 1812. Resigned.
SHERBURNE, J. B.
Master, 10 April, 1812. Discharged 8 May, 1813.
SHERBURNE, JOHN H.
Midshipman, 5 October, 1829. Passed Midshipman, 15 June, 1837. Lieutenant, 8 September, 1841. Died 2 November, 1849.
SHERBURNE, J. W.
Midshipman, 30 November, 1814. Lieutenant, 13 January, 1825. Died 20 November, 1830.
SHERFY, JOHN W.
Acting Assistant Surgeon, 26 August, 1861. Acting Passed Assistant Surgeon, 18 October, 1865. Honorably discharged 30 April, 1869.
SHERIDAN, JAMES.
Third Assistant Engineer, 3 May, 1859. Second Assistant Engineer, 29 October, 1861. First Assistant Engineer, 20 May, 1863. Died 24 November, 1871.
SHERIDAN, PHILIP.
Acting Second Assistant Engineer, 30 November, 1863. Honorably discharged 15 November, 1865.
SHERIDAN, PHILIP.
Acting Ensign, 27 August, 1862. Honorably discharged 30 September, 1865.
SHERMAN, FRANCIS H.
Midshipman, 20 September, 1871. Graduated 20 June, 1876. Ensign, 24 February, 1880. Lieutenant, Junior Grade, 1 July, 1886. Lieutenant, 3 April, 1892. Lieutenant-Commander, 22 November, 1899.
SHERMAN, FRANK.
Acting Ensign, 29 August, 1864. Honorably discharged 24 January, 1866.
SHERMAN, FREDERICK F.
Chaplain, 14 March, 1892. Resigned 15 May, 1896.
SHERMAN, FREEMAN A.
Mate, 18 February, 1864. Died 12 June, 1865.
SHERMAN, GEORGE W.
Mate, 15 October, 1861. Dismissed 2 May, 1862. Mate, 26 June, 1862. Acting Ensign, 23 February, 1864. Mustered out 26 August, 1868.
SHERMAN, HORACE D.
Mate, 27 August, 1863. Resigned (sick) 26 May, 1864.
SHERMAN, ROBERT.
Acting Gunner, 1 October, 1862. Honorably discharged 28 October, 1865.
SHERRAND, G. W.
Acting Third Assistant Engineer. Appointment revoked 31 March, 1863.
SHERRELL, JOHN.
Acting Master, 27 May, 1861. Acting Volunteer Lieutenant, 19 May, 1864. Honorably discharged 4 November, 1865.
SHERWIN, EDWARD.
Acting Assistant Paymaster, 31 March, 1863. Passed Assistant Paymaster, 23 July, 1866. Resigned 22 December, 1866.
SHERWOOD, CHARLES W.
Mate, 7 June, 1864. Appointment revoked (sick) 29 August, 1864.
SHERWOOD, GILBERT.
Second Assistant Engineer, 21 January, 1842. Resigned 29 October, 1845.
SHERWOOD, HENRY.
Acting Master, 30 November, 1861. Dismissed 21 February, 1862.
SHERWOOD, JOHN R.
Acting Third Assistant Engineer, 5 January, 1864. Honorably discharged 23 July, 1869.
SHERWOOD, J. R.
Midshipman, 30 May, 1803. Resigned 17 August, 1813.
SHERWOOD, WILLIAM R.
Acting Assistant Paymaster, 8 November, 1862. Resigned 12 November, 1864.
SHEWELL, WALTER.
Assistant Engineer, 27 January, 1876. Died 30 November, 1881.
SHEWERMAN, AARON H.
Acting Second Assistant Engineer, 27 December, 1864. Honorably discharged 24 September, 1865.
SHIBLEY, HOWARD C.
Acting First Assistant Engineer, 7 December, 1863. Honorably discharged 15 October, 1865.

GENERAL NAVY REGISTER. 495

SHIELDS, GEORGE W.
Acting Assistant Surgeon, 24 November, 1863. Honorably discharged 19 January, 1866.
SHIELDS, GEORGE W.
Acting Second Assistant Engineer, 30 September, 1863. Honorably discharged 11 August, 1865.
SHIELDS, JOHN.
Mate, 27 November, 1863. Disrated 6 February, 1864.
SHIELDS, JOHN.
Acting Third Assistant Engineer, 21 July, 1863. Resigned 16 June, 1864.
SHIELDS, LeROY H.
Assistant Paymaster (Spanish-American War), 21 July, 1898. Honorably discharged 11 February, 1899.
SHIELDS, THOMAS.
Midshipman, 2 January, 1804. Purser, 25 April, 1812. Died 22 May, 1827.
SHIELDS, W. C.
Midshipman, 18 May, 1809. Resigned 12 October, 1813.
SHIELDS, WILLIAM.
Acting Gunner, 16 February, 1863. Discharged 21 March, 1865.
SHIELDS, WILLIAM B.
Acting Midshipman, 2 October, 1850. Dropped 12 June, 1851.
SHIELDS, WILLIAM F.
Midshipman, 2 February, 1814. Lieutenant, 3 March, 1821. Commander, 8 September, 1841. Reserved List, 13 September, 1855. Died 30 May, 1856.
SHIELDS, WILMER.
Midshipman, 19 October, 1835. Passed Midshipman, 22 June, 1841. Master, 23 October, 1847. Lieutenant, 14 September, 1848. Resigned 6 April, 1852.
SHIFFERT, HERBERT O.
Assistant Surgeon, 26 December, 1900.
SHILLITO, WILLIAM B.
Acting Ensign, 22 August, 1863. Honorably discharged 5 September, 1865.
SHINDEL, JAMES E.
Cadet Midshipman, 22 June, 1881. Ensign, 1 July, 1887. Retired List, 31 October, 1892. Died 23 February, 1894.
SHINN, JACOB.
Mate, 28 November, 1862. Acting Ensign, 23 July, 1863. Honorably discharged 27 October, 1865.
SHINN, SAMUEL S.
Mate, 5 August, 1864. Disrated 28 October, 1864.
SHIPLEY, GEORGE T.
Assistant Surgeon, 16 September, 1861. Resigned 6 September, 1865.
SHIPLEY, GEORGE W.
Acting Third Assistant Engineer, 7 December, 1862. Resigned 16 June, 1863.
SHIPLEY, JOHN H.
Cadet Midshipman, 30 September, 1874. Graduated 4 June, 1880. Ensign, Junior Grade, 3 March, 1883. Ensign, 16 April, 1884. Lieutenant, Junior Grade, 5 March, 1890. Lieutenant, 11 November, 1894.
SHIPLEY, SAMUEL J.
Midshipman, 14 January, 1834. Passed Midshipman, 16 July, 1840. Master, 22 March, 1847. Lieutenant, 23 June, 1847. Resigned 12 July, 1852. Acting Lieutenant, 25 September, 1861. Appointment revoked (sick) 6 February, 1863.
SHIPMAN, WILLIAM W.
Acting Third Assistant Engineer, 9 August, 1862. Acting Second Assistant Engineer, 24 September, 1862. Acting First Assistant Engineer, 9 June, 1864. Honorably discharged 13 September, 1865.
SHIPMAN, WILLIAM W.
Third Assistant Engineer, 3 August, 1861. Resigned 27 February, 1862.
SHIPP, EDWARD M.
Assistant Surgeon, 20 March, 1893. Passed Assistant Surgeon, 20 March, 1896.
SHIPPEN, EDWARD.
Assistant Surgeon, 7 August, 1849. Surgeon, 26 April, 1861. Medical Inspector, 3 March, 1871. Medical Director, 17 March, 1876. Retired List, 18 June, 1888.
SHIRK, A.
Acting Assistant Surgeon, 1 July, 1862. Honorably discharged 2 July, 1866.
SHIRK, CHARLES C.
Mate, 1861. Resigned 30 September, 1862.
SHIRK, JAMES W.
Midshipman, 26 March, 1849. Passed Midshipman, 12 June, 1855. Master, 16 September, 1855. Lieutenant, 5 November, 1856. Lieutenant-Commander, 16 July, 1862. Commander, 25 July, 1866. Died 10 February, 1873.
SHIRLEY, AMBROSE.
Lieutenant, 1 August, 1798. Discharged 8 July, 1801, under Peace Establishment Act.
SHIRLEY, PAUL.
Midshipman, 25 July, 1839. Passed Midshipman, 2 July, 1845. Master, 3 December, 1853. Lieutenant, 21 July, 1854. Lieutenant-Commander, 16 July, 1862. Commander, 5 November, 1863. Captain, 1 July, 1870. Died 24 November, 1876.
SHIVELY, JOSEPH W.
Assistant Surgeon, 25 February, 1861. Surgeon, 22 September, 1863. Resigned 15 March, 1865.
SHOCK, GEORGE E.
Third Assistant Engineer, 16 February, 1852. Died 11 September, 1853.
SHOCK, JOHN L.
Cadet Midshipman, 27 June, 1877. Graduated 10 June, 1881. Assistant Naval Constructor, 1 July, 1883. Died 23 May, 1885.

SHOCK, THOMAS A.
Third Assistant Engineer, 6 February, 1851. Second Assistant Engineer, 21 May, 1853. First Assistant Engineer, 26 June, 1856. Chief Engineer, 6 December, 1860. Died 21 January, 1873.
SHOCK, WILLIAM H.
Third Assistant Engineer, 18 January, 1845. Second Assistant Engineer, 10 July, 1847. First Assistant Engineer, 31 October, 1848. Chief Engineer, 16 September, 1852. (By Act of Congress, 15 July, 1870, Chief Engineer from 11 March, 1851.) Engineer-in-Chief, 3 March, 1877. Retired List, 15 June, 1883.
SHOEMAKER, C. F.
Midshipman, 10 May, 1820. Killed in a duel 23 September, 1825.
SHOEMAKER, DAVID.
Master, 19 October, 1814. Last appearance on Records of Navy Department, 1818. Furloughed.
SHOEMAKER, FRANCIS R.
Acting Third Assistant Engineer, 3 November, 1863. Acting Second Assistant Engineer, 22 November, 1864.
SHOEMAKER, GEORGE L.
Acting Third Assistant Engineer, 7 October, 1863. Honorably discharged 9 November, 1865.
SHOEMAKER, HOWELL.
Mate, 3 September, 1863. Acting Ensign, 24 July, 1864. Appointment revoked 26 June, 1865.
SHOEMAKER, WILLIAM R.
Cadet Midshipman, 14 June, 1880. Ensign, 1 July, 1886. Lieutenant, Junior Grade, 29 October, 1895. Lieutenant, 6 October, 1898.
SHONE, JOHN H.
Mate. Resigned 14 January, 1864.
SHORE, JOHN.
Midshipman, 30 June, 1799. Resigned 3 September, 1800. Midshipman, 21 February, 1801. Resigned 8 September, 1803.
SHORT, CHARLES R.
Mate, 23 October, 1862. Deserted 30 May, 1863.
SHORT, GEORGE C.
Mate, 17 October, 1862. Resigned 26 March, 1863. Mate, 2 September, 1864. Deserted 20 February, 1865.
SHORT, HUGH S.
Acting Third Assistant Engineer, 13 December, 1862. Acting Second Assistant Engineer, 19 November, 1863. Honorably discharged 18 September, 1865.
SHORT, PERRY.
Acting Second Assistant Engineer, 4 September, 1861. Acting First Engineer, 22 October, 1862. Appointment revoked 23 February, 1864.
SHORT, TERENCE.
Mate, 20 November, 1861. Dismissed 4 November, 1862.
SHRIVER, ALBERT.
Assistant Surgeon, 28 June, 1852. Surgeon, 3 June, 1861. Retired List, 25 April, 1868. Died 21 January, 1873.
SHRYOCK, GEORGE S.
Acting Midshipman, 22 May, 1852. Midshipman, 20 June, 1856. Passed Midshipman, 29 April, 1859. Master, 3 September, 1859. Lieutenant, 9 January, 1861. Dismissed 1 July, 1861.
SHUBRICK, EDWARD R.
Midshipman, 16 January, 1807. Lieutenant, 9 October, 1813. Commander, 24 April, 1828. Captain, 9 February, 1837. Died at sea 12 March, 1844.
SHUBRICK, EDWARD R.
Midshipman, 9 February, 1849. Resigned 26 April, 1853.
SHUBRICK, EDWARD T.
Midshipman, 22 June, 1829. Passed Midshipman, 4 June, 1836. Lieutenant, 8 September, 1841. Resigned 23 April, 1852.
SHUBRICK, IRVINE.
Midshipman, 12 May, 1814. Lieutenant, 13 January, 1825. Commander, 8 September, 1841. Died 5 April, 1849.
SHUBRICK, JOHN T.
Midshipman, 20 June, 1806. Lieutenant, 20 May, 1812. Lost in the Epervier in 1815.
SHUBRICK, THOMAS B.
Midshipman, 3 March, 1841. Killed in action 25 March, 1847.
SHUBRICK, WILLIAM B.
Midshipman, 20 June, 1806. Lieutenant, 5 January, 1813. Commander, 20 March, 1820. Captain, 21 February, 1831. Retired List, 21 December, 1861. Rear-Admiral on Retired List, 16 July, 1862. Died 27 May, 1874.
SHUCK, F. A.
Acting Second Assistant Engineer, 11 June, 1847. Second Assistant Engineer, 10 July, 1847. Declined appointment 7 August, 1847.
SHUFELDT, MASON A.
Midshipman, 24 June, 1869. Graduated 31 May, 1873. Ensign, 16 July, 1874. Master, 26 November, 1880. Lieutenant, Junior Grade, 3 March, 1883. Resigned, 30 June, 1890.
SHUFELDT, ROBERT W.
Midshipman, 11 May, 1839. Passed Midshipman, 2 July, 1845. Master, 21 February, 1853. Lieutenant, 26 October, 1853. Resigned 20 June, 1854. Acting Lieutenant, 25 September, 1861. Commander, 16 July, 1862. Captain, 31 December, 1869. Commodore, 21 September, 1876. Rear-Admiral, 7 May, 1883. Retired List, 21 February, 1884. Died 6 November, 1895.

GENERAL NAVY REGISTER. 497

SHULER, DARIUS P.
    Acting Assistant Paymaster, 30 September, 1862. Mustered out 24 October, 1865.
SHULL, GEORGE C.
    Acting Third Assistant Engineer, 1 September, 1864. Honorably discharged 29 September, 1865.
SHULTIES, ROBERT H.
    Acting Third Assistant Engineer, 15 July, 1862. Resigned 8 February, 1864.
SHULTZ, GEORGE.
    Acting Third Assistant Engineer, 30 June, 1864. Honorably discharged 14 July, 1865.
SHULTZ, JAMES.
    Acting Second Assistant Engineer, 28 January, 1862. Acting First Assistant Engineer, 20 October, 1862. Died 5 October, 1863.
SHUMAN, GEORGE W.
    Mate 15 October, 1861. Dismissed 2 May, 1862.
SHUMAN, LUKE.
    Acting Third Assistant Engineer, 22 October, 1863. Honorably discharged 27 October, 1865.
SHUMAN, PARMENIO.
    Midshipman, 12 May, 1824. Resigned in 1825.
SHUMAN, WASHINGTON.
    Assistant Surgeon, 25 April, 1845. Surgeon, 13 January, 1859. Died 4 May, 1864.
SHUMATE, J. R.
    Assistant Surgeon, 4 January, 1810. Resigned 21 July, 1812.
SHUMWAY, A. DWIGHT.
    Acting Third Assistant Engineer, 31 May, 1861. Resigned 7 August, 1861.
SHUNK, WILLIAM F.
    Midshipman, 1 June, 1846. Resigned 13 March, 1850.
SHURTLIFF, BENJAMIN.
    Assistant Surgeon, 5 February, 1799. Surgeon, 23 December, 1799. Discharged 30 April, 1801, under Peace Establishment Act.
SHURTLIFF, E. S.
    Acting Ensign, 31 July, 1863. Acting Master, 7 March, 1865. Honorably discharged 22 July, 1865.
SHUTE, GEORGE.
    Midshipman, 1 January, 1817. Resigned 20 June, 1823.
SHUTE, JOHN B.
    Midshipman, 16 April, 1813. Died 26 March, 1819.
SHUTE, PEARSON.
    Midshipman, 1 January, 1812. Dismissed 13 May, 1813.
SHUTTLEWORTH, THOMAS J.
    Gunner, 1 September, 1897.
SHUWEMAN, AARON H.
    Acting Second Assistant Engineer 27 December, 1864. Honorably discharged 24 September, 1865.
SIAS, JOHN F.
    Mate, 20 February, 1863. Honorably discharged 20 September, 1867.
SIBELL, E. A.
    Acting Master's Mate, 9 February, 1864. Resigned 20 May, 1865.
SIBLEY, ARTHUR.
    Acting Assistant Paymaster, 4 December, 1862. Honorably discharged 21 September, 1865.
SIBLEY, WILLIAM E.
    Third Assistant Engineer, 20 May, 1863. Second Assistant Engineer, 7 September, 1865. Dismissed 10 December, 1874.
SICARD, MONTGOMERY.
    Acting Midshipman, 1 October, 1851. Midshipman, 9 June, 1855. Passed Midshipman, 15 April, 1858. Master, 4 November, 1858. Lieutenant, 31 May, 1860. Lieutenant-Commander, 16 July, 1862. Commander, 2 March, 1870. Captain, 7 August, 1881. Commodore, 10 July, 1894. Rear-Admiral, 6 April, 1897. Retired List, 30 September, 1898. Died 14 September, 1900.
SICKLES, HENRY.
    Mate, 5 March, 1862. Dismissed 30 July, 1863.
SICKLES, J. FREDERICK.
    Assistant Surgeon, 28 February, 1833. Surgeon, 8 September, 1841. Died 18 April, 1848.
SIDELL, GEORGE B.
    Mate, 2 December, 1861. Acting Ensign, 18 July, 1864. Honorably discharged 6 October, 1868.
SIDNEY, CHARLES.
    Mate, 22 February, 1864. Honorably discharged 17 September, 1865.
SIEGFRIED, C. A.
    Assistant Surgeon, 8 June, 1872. Passed Assistant Surgeon, 10 January, 1876. Surgeon, 31 January, 1885. Medical Inspector, 7 May, 1898. Died 14 January, 1900.
SIGNOR, MATT H.
    Naval Cadet, 21 May, 1886. Ensign, 1 July, 1892. Lieutenant, 3 March, 1899.
SIGSBEE, CHARLES D.
    Acting Midshipman, 27 September, 1859. Ensign, 1 October, 1863. Master, 10 May, 1866. Lieutenant, 21 February, 1867. Lieutenant-Commander, 12 March, 1868. Commander 11 May, 1882. Captain, 21 March, 1897.
SILL, WILLIAM.
    Acting Ensign, 7 June, 1863. Honorably discharged 8 November, 1865.
SILLIMAN, WYLLYS.
    Midshipman, 1 April, 1828. Dropped.

32

SILLMAN, THOMAS W.
Acting Third Assistant Engineer, 3 March, 1864. Honorably discharged 20 September, 1865.
SILLMAN, WILLIAM S.
Acting Second Assistant Engineer, 19 September, 1863. Resigned (sick) 15 June, 1864.
SILSBEY, SAMUEL T.
Acting Third Assistant Engineer, 29 November, 1862. Died 17 October, 1863.
SILVA, FRANCISCO.
Mate, 15 September, 1863. Discharged 21 June, 1864.
SILVA, JOSEPH F.
Mate, 27 December, 1863. Resigned 21 April, 1865.
SILVER, ROBERT.
Mate, 3 December, 1861. Died 14 January, 1888.
SILVERCAHN, CHARLES R.
Acting Second Assistant Engineer, 4 September, 1863. Honorably discharged 19 October, 1865.
SILVERS, FRANK H.
Ensign (Spanish-American War), 20 May, 1898. Honorably discharged 28 October, 1898.
SIM, DANIEL C.
Midshipman, 18 November, 1799. Resigned 8 May, 1804.
SIM, PATRICK.
Assistant Surgeon, 1 July, 1803. Died 11 October, 1806.
SIM, WILLIAM.
Midshipman, 12 June, 1802. Dismissed 4 December, 1809. Midshipman, 1 September, 1811. Resigned 16 December, 1813.
SIMES, GEORGE T.
Midshipman, 19 October, 1841. Passed Midshipman, 10 August, 1847. Resigned 7 May, 1851.
SIMMES, JOHN.
Boatswain, date not known. Last appearance on Records of Navy Department.
SIMMONDS, FREDERICK J.
Assistant Engineer (Spanish-American War), 20 June, 1898. Honorably discharged 22 December, 1898. Acting Carpenter, 10 January, 1900.
SIMMONS, ALEXANDER R.
Midshipman, 19 October, 1841. Dismissed 28 August, 1849.
SIMMONS, DAVID A.
Mate, 19 January, 1863. Resigned (sick) 9 September, 1864.
SIMMONS, GEORGE E.
Mate, 7 July, 1864. Honorably discharged 4 May, 1867.
SIMMONS, GEORGE W.
Acting First Assistant Engineer, 26 October, 1861. Resigned 13 December, 1862.
SIMMONS, GEORGE W., Jr.
Acting Assistant Paymaster, 1 June, 1863. Resigned 14 June, 1865.
SIMMONS, J. M. R.
Assistant Surgeon, 29 June, 1872. Died 16 December, 1872.
SIMMONS, JOHN W.
Acting Master, 24 August, 1861. Acting Volunteer Lieutenant, gallant conduct in battle, 3 September, 1863. Appointment revoked 24 November, 1865. Mate, 7 July, 1869. Resigned 24 July, 1869. Mate, 24 December, 1869. Boatswain, 15 November, 1870. Resigned 21 February, 1872.
SIMMONS, JOSHUA.
Mate, 15 November, 1862. Acting Ensign, 24 November, 1863. Dismissed 21 April, 1864. Acting Ensign, 26 April, 1864. Resigned 28 November, 1864.
SIMMONS, MAURICE.
Midshipman, 1 March, 1799. Resigned 20 April, 1802.
SIMMONS, MELVIN.
Naval Constructor, 25 July, 1866. Retired List, 15 June, 1868. Died 13 May, 1871.
SIMMS, CHARLES C.
Midshipman, 9 October, 1839. Passed Midshipman, 2 July, 1845. Master, 15 January, 1854. Lieutenant, 12 August, 1854. Dismissed 22 April, 1861.
SIMMS, GEORGE W.
Midshipman, 1 January, 1818. Died in October, 1823.
SIMMS, JOSEPH M.
Carpenter, 6 June, 1899.
SIMMS, JOSEPH M., Jr.
Mate, 27 August, 1863. Acting Ensign, 13 June, 1866. Honorably discharged 31 July, 1868.
SIMON, WILLIAM J.
Assistant Surgeon, 30 May, 1864. Surgeon, 3 February, 1875. Died 26 November, 1888.
SIMONDS, GUSTAVUS B.
Acting Master, 1 October, 1862. Resigned 22 April, 1863.
SIMONDS, LEWIS D.
Mate, 12 September, 1864. Resigned 31 May, 1865.
SIMONDS, LEWIS E.
Midshipman, 1 January, 1812. Lieutenant, 1 April, 1818. Commander, 22 December, 1838. Captain, 6 April, 1851. Reserved List, 13 September, 1855. Died 17 February, 1865.
SIMONDS, L. W.
Acting Second Assistant Engineer, 26 February, 1862. Resigned 19 April, 1863. Acting Third Assistant Engineer, 26 June, 1863. Dismissed 11 July, 1863.
SIMONS, ISAAC.
Mate, 1 October, 1862. Resigned 18 March, 1863.

SIMONS, JOSEPH.
Acting Gunner, 1 October, 1862. Resigned 24 April, 1863.
SIMONS, MANLY H.
Assistant Surgeon, 28 May, 1872. Passed Assistant Surgeon, 15 December, 1875. Surgeon, 16 August, 1887. Medical Inspector, 24 September, 1899.
SIMONS, MAURICE.
Midshipman, 10 December, 1839. Passed Midshipman, 2 July, 1845. Master, 29 November, 1853. Lieutenant, 30 June, 1854. Reserved List, 13 September, 1855. Resigned 7 March, 1861.
SIMONS, SIDNEY A.
Midshipman, 23 September, 1863. Graduated June, 1867. Ensign, 18 December, 1868. Master, 21 March, 1870. Lieutenant, 21 March, 1871. Lost on Huron, 24 November, 1877.
SIMONSON, JACOB.
Acting Third Assistant Engineer. Appointment revoked (sick) 7 October, 1864.
SIMONSON, ROBERT E.
Mate, 23 July, 1898. Acting Gunner, 10 March, 1900.
SIMONTON, HIRAM.
Mate, 28 November, 1863. Acting Ensign, 10 March, 1865. Resigned 7 July, 1865.
SIMPSON, CHARLES A.
Acting Gunner, 21 May, 1863. Honorably discharged 8 July, 1865.
SIMPSON, EDWARD.
Midshipman, 11 February, 1840. Passed Midshipman, 11 July, 1846. Master, 10 July, 1854. Lieutenant, 18 April, 1855. Lieutenant-Commander, 16 July, 1862. Commander, 3 March, 1865. Captain, 15 August, 1870. Commodore, 26 April, 1878. Rear-Admiral, 9 February, 1884. Retired List, 3 March, 1886. Died 1 December, 1888.
SIMPSON, EDWARD.
Cadet Midshipman, 24 June, 1876. Graduated 22 June, 1882. Ensign, Junior Grade, 3 March, 1883. Ensign, 26 June, 1884. Lieutenant, Junior Grade, 25 January, 1893. Lieutenant, 1 November, 1896.
SIMPSON, GEORGE L.
Acting Assistant Surgeon, 30 April, 1864. Acting Passed Assistant Surgeon, 19 July, 1866. Honorably discharged 19 November, 1868.
SIMPSON, GEORGE N.
Acting Assistant Paymaster, 11 April, 1863. Mustered out 9 December, 1865.
SIMPSON, GEORGE W.
Assistant Paymaster, 1 April, 1882. Passed Assistant Paymaster, 25 December, 1892. Paymaster, 26 September, 1897.
SIMPSON, GUSTAVUS.
Midshipman, 1 January, 1812. Permitted to resign 7 October, 1812.
SIMPSON, JAMES.
Boatswain, 6 June, 1838. Resigned 13 January, 1840.
SIMPSON, MAXWELL S.
Passed Assistant Surgeon (Spanish-American War), 21 May, 1898. Honorably discharged 22 October, 1898.
SIMPSON, R. G.
Acting Assistant Paymaster, 22 April, 1865. Mustered out 17 August, 1865.
SIMPSON, ROBERT.
Boatswain, 8 December, 1840. Dismissed 12 September, 1853.
SIMS, ALBERT L.
Acting Third Assistant Engineer, 21 May, 1864. Honorably discharged 2 November, 1865.
SIMS, CLIFFORD S.
Acting Assistant Paymaster, 10 March, 1863. Resigned (sick) 21 March, 1865.
SIMS, DAVID R.
Acting First Assistant Engineer, 7 May, 1864. Honorably discharged 4 November, 1865.
SIMS, GARDINER C.
Passed Assistant Engineer (Spanish-American War), 12 May, 1898. Chief Engineer, 28 May, 1898. Honorably discharged 24 January, 1899.
SIMS, R. K. H.
Assistant Surgeon, 2 December, 1828. Died 5 July, 1833.
SIMS, WILLIAM S.
Cadet Midshipman, 24 June, 1876. Graduated 22 June, 1882. Ensign, Junior Grade, 3 March, 1883. Ensign, 26 June, 1884. Lieutenant, Junior Grade, 9 May, 1893. Lieutenant, 1 January, 1897.
SINCLAIR, ARTHUR.
Lieutenant, 10 June, 1807. Commander, 2 July, 1812. Captain, 24 July, 1813. Died 7 February, 1831.
SINCLAIR, ARTHUR.
Midshipman, 4 March, 1823. Passed Midshipman, 4 June, 1831. Lieutenant, 3 March, 1835. Commander, 14 September, 1855. Dismissed 18 April, 1861.
SINCLAIR, CHARLES.
Acting Third Assistant Engineer, 20 December, 1861. Acting Second Assistant Engineer, 21 July, 1863. Deserted 1864.
SINCLAIR, CHARLES H.
Acting Ensign, 7 March, 1864. Resigned 14 June, 1865.
SINCLAIR, DANIEL.
Mate, 26 January, 1870. Resigned 27 February, 1872.
SINCLAIR, GEORGE T.
Midshipman, 23 April, 1831. Passed Midshipman, 15 June, 1837. Lieutenant, 8 September, 1841. Dismissed 16 April, 1861.

SINCLAIR, HENRY.
Mate, 5 May, 1863. Honorably discharged 3 October, 1865.
SINCLAIR, HUGH.
Gunner, 5 August, 1892.
SINCLAIR, JAMES D.
Acting Master, 1 October, 1862. Dismissed 14 November, 1863.
SINCLAIR, JOHN S.
Mate, 18 November, 1864. Boatswain, 9 July, 1866. Chief Boatswain, 3 March, 1899.
SINCLAIR, MALCOLM.
Acting Third Assistant Engineer, 31 August, 1863. Resigned (sick) 13 October, 1864.
SINCLAIR, WILLIAM.
Purser, 26 March, 1814. Died 22 May, 1858.
SINCLAIR, WILLIAM B.
Assistant Surgeon, 20 June, 1838. Surgeon, 21 June, 1852. Dismissed 10 June, 1861.
SINGER, FREDERICK.
Midshipman, 27 July, 1863. Graduated June, 1868. Ensign, 19 April, 1869. Master, 12 July, 1870. Lieutenant, 21 May, 1874. Lieutenant-Commander, 1 September, 1895. Commander, 3 March, 1899.
SINGLETON, E. B. J.
Mate, 8 May, 1862. Acting Ensign, 2 May, 1864. Honorably discharged 10 December, 1865.
SINGLETON, JACOB H.
Acting Ensign, 13 August, 1863. Honorably discharged 28 November, 1865.
SINKLER, CHARLES.
Midshipman, 24 March, 1836. Passed Midshipman, 1 July, 1842. Resigned 20 February, 1847.
SINNOTT, JOHN.
Mate, 17 April, 1866. Appointment revoked 15 November, 1866.
SIRIAN, GEORGE.
Gunner, 20 April, 1837. Retired List, 15 December, 1880. Died 21 December, 1891.
SISSON, ALEX.
Master, 13 July, 1812. Died of wounds received in action, 27 November, 1812.
SISSON, CHARLES.
Gunner, 28 June, 1837. Appointment revoked 2 September, 1837.
SISSON, CHARLES C.
Acting Master, 26 August, 1861. Resigned 29 August, 1862.
SKARDON, JAMES M.
Mate, 20 March, 1863. Resigned 11 May, 1864.
SKEEL, THERON.
Acting Third Assistant Engineer, under instruction, Naval Academy, 10 October, 1866. Third Assistant Engineer, 2 June, 1868. Retired 22 June, 1869. Resigned 12 November, 1870.
SKELDING, HENRY T.
Acting Assistant Paymaster, 31 December, 1862. Assistant Paymaster, 23 July, 1866. Passed Assistant Paymaster, 5 March, 1867. Paymaster, 19 August, 1876. Retired List, 31 October, 1896.
SKELTON, WILLIAM.
Acting Third Assistant Engineer, 22 May, 1862. Appointment revoked (sick) 27 October, 1863.
SKERITT, JOHN J.
Mate, 6 September, 1864. Resigned 6 June, 1865.
SKERRETT, JOSEPH S.
Midshipman, 12 October, 1848. Passed Midshipman, 15 June, 1854. Master, 15 September, 1855. Lieutenant, 16 September, 1855. Lieutenant-Commander, 16 July, 1862. Commander, 9 June, 1867. Captain, 5 June, 1878. Commodore, 4 August, 1889. Rear-Admiral, 16 April, 1894. Retired List, 9 July, 1894. Died 1 January, 1897.
SKIDDY, CHARLES S.
Gunner, 10 June, 1842. Dismissed 27 October, 1842.
SKIDDY, WILLIAM.
Midshipman, 9 May, 1812. Struck off 3 January, 1840.
SKILLINGS, JOHN M.
Acting Master, 11 November, 1861. Resigned 16 March, 1865.
SKINNER, AARON N.
Professor, 30 July, 1898.
SKINNER, ALFONZO.
Acting Warrant Machinist, 23 August, 1899.
SKINNER, CHARLES W.
Midshipman, 16 June, 1809. Lieutenant, 24 July, 1813. Commander, 3 March, 1827. Captain, 9 February, 1837. Reserved List, 1 October, 1855. Died 14 October, 1860.
SKINNER, DANIEL M.
Assistant Surgeon, 16 September, 1861. Resigned 15 May, 1865.
SKINNER, FRANCIS J.
Sailmaker, 27 April, 1809. Resigned 3 July, 1811.
SKINNER, HENRY.
Midshipman, 4 March, 1823. Died 31 March, 1826.
SKINNER, JOHN.
Mate, 18 November, 1861. Dismissed 11 January, 1862.
SKINNER, JOHN S.
Purser, 26 March, 1814. Last appearance on Records of Navy Department, 1815. Resigned.
SKIPWITH, GREY.
Midshipman, 4 March, 1823. Passed Midshipman, 23 March, 1829. Lieutenant, 3 March, 1831. Resigned 19 December, 1838.

SKIPWITH, GREY.
Assistant Paymaster, 13 April, 1899.
SKIPWITH, HENRY.
Midshipman, 25 June, 1831. Resigned 6 April, 1838.
SLACK, CHARLES H.
Acting Third Assistant Engineer, 19 September, 1862. Acting Second Assistant Engineer, 18 April, 1864. Acting First Assistant Engineer, 29 October, 1864. Honorably discharged 9 October, 1867.
SLACK, CLARENCE M.
Acting Assistant Surgeon, 20 April, 1865. Honorably discharged 10 October, 1865.
SLACK, JAMES T.
Acting Third Assistant Engineer, 18 January, 1864. Honorably discharged 8 November, 1865.
SLACK, JOHN.
Acting Third Assistant Engineer, 21 November, 1864. Honorably discharged 1 July, 1868.
SLACK, WILLIAM H.
Midshipman, 1 October, 1867. Graduated 6 June, 1871. Ensign, 14 July, 1872. Master, 21 November, 1877. Lieutenant, Junior Grade, 3 March, 1883. Resigned 20 July, 1883.
SLACUM, W. A.
Purser, 8 June, 1829. Died 1 November, 1839.
SLADE, CHARLES R.
Midshipman, 1 July, 1836. Resigned 17 April, 1840.
SLADE, WILLIAM O.
Midshipman, 1 April, 1828. Resigned 3 June, 1835.
SLAMM, CHARLES W.
Acting Assistant Paymaster, 4 November, 1862. Assistant Paymaster, 23 July, 1866. Passed Assistant Paymaster, 22 March, 1867. Paymaster, 28 August, 1876. Pay Inspector, 15 March, 1898. Retired List, 22 April, 1899.
SLAMM, JEFFERSON A.
Mate, 8 November, 1861. Acting Ensign, 1 April, 1863. Honorably discharged 6 November, 1865.
SLAMM, LEVI D.
Purser, 30 November, 1846. Died 6 October, 1862.
SLATER, ATWOOD.
Acting Third Assistant Engineer, 9 December, 1863. Honorably discharged 9 November, 1865.
SLATER, SANFORD A.
Acting Third Assistant Engineer, 14 January, 1863. Resigned 8 May, 1865.
SLATER, THOMAS.
Acting Third Assistant Engineer, 19 October, 1861.
SLATER, WILLIAM.
Gunner, 24 May, 1800. Deserted.
SLATTERLY, DANIEL P.
Acting Ensign, 19 March, 1863. Acting Master, 19 July, 1864. Honorably discharged 9 February, 1866.
SLAUGHTER, ALBERT G.
Midshipman, 3 November, 1819. Lieutenant, 3 March, 1827. Commander, 16 May, 1848. Died 8 September, 1853.
SLAUGHTER, N. G. C.
Midshipman, 1 March, 1825. Died 8 April, 1829.
SLEAMAN, JOHN H.
Acting Third Assistant Engineer, 21 April, 1864. Honorably discharged 18 October, 1865.
SLEEPER, HENRY J.
Acting Master, 18 December, 1861. Acting Volunteer Lieutenant, 18 June, 1864. Honorably discharged 6 January, 1866.
SLEEPER, JAMES H.
Acting Third Assistant Engineer, 9 March, 1865. Appointment revoked 14 December, 1866.
SLIDELL, ALEX.
Midshipman, 1 January, 1815. Lieutenant, 13 January, 1825. (See MacKenzie.)
SLIDELL, WILLIAM J.
Midshipman, 1 January, 1823. Died 5 April, 1828.
SLIGHT, GEORGE A.
Acting Third Assistant Engineer, 22 February, 1863. Resigned 28 December, 1864.
SLOAN, CHARLES E.
Mate. Dismissed 24 July, 1862.
SLOAN, JOHN F.
Acting Third Assistant Engineer, 28 May, 1864. Honorably discharged 28 September, 1865.
SLOAN, ROBERT S.
Cadet Midshipman 21 June, 1875. Midshipman, 10 June, 1881. Resigned 7 September, 1882. Lieutenant (Spanish-American War), 17 June, 1898. Honorably discharged 4 October, 1898.
SLOAN, THOMAS M.
Acting Second Assistant Engineer, 5 August, 1864. Honorably discharged 27 September, 1865.
SLOANE, JOHN D.
Assistant Engineer, 7 June, 1877. Retired List, 30 June, 1885.
SLOAT, GEORGE V.
Acting First Assistant Engineer, 10 September, 1861. Resigned 9 September, 1862.

SLOAT, JOHN D.
Midshipman, 12 February, 1800. Master, 10 January, 1812. Lieutenant, 24 July, 1813. Commander 21 March, 1826. Captain, 9 February, 1837. Reserved List, 27 September, 1855. Retired List, 21 December, 1861. Commodore on Retired List, 16 July, 1862. Rear-Admiral, Retired List, 25 July, 1866. Died 28 November, 1867.
SLOAT, WILLIAM.
Acting Second Assistant Engineer, 22 December, 1864. Honorably discharged 14 February, 1868.
SLOCUM, CHARLES H.
Mate, 24 January, 1863. Acting Ensign, 15 July, 1864. Honorably discharged 26 November, 1865.
SLOCUM, CHARLES M.
Acting Third Assistant Engineer, 16 January, 1864. Resigned (sick) 7 October, 1864.
SLOCUM, EBENEZER.
Gunner, 22 April, 1799. Resigned 7 July, 1801.
SLOCUM, GEORGE D.
Assistant Surgeon, 29 November, 1861. Resigned 17 January, 1864.
SLOCUM, GEORGE R.
Cadet Midshipman, 28 September, 1881. Ensign, 1 July, 1887. Lieutenant, Junior Grade, 28 February, 1896. Lieutenant, 3 March, 1899.
SLOCUM, JONAH.
Acting First Assistant Engineer, 18 April, 1863. Resigned 22 April, 1865.
SLOCUM, WILLIAM B.
Acting Ensign, 9 April, 1863. Resigned 29 December, 1863.
SLOSSON, HENRY L.
Acting Third Assistant Engineer, 29 September, 1863. Third Assistant Engineer, 13 October, 1863. Second Assistant Engineer, 1 August, 1866. Passed Assistant Engineer, 27 October, 1874. Resigned 15 September, 1883.
SLOUGH, GRANVILLE B.
Assistant Surgeon, 20 December, 1861. Resigned 26 October, 1864.
SLOUGH, JONAS S.
Acting First Assistant Engineer, 1 October, 1862. Dismissed 15 May, 1863.
SLUYTER, STEPHEN E.
Acting Ensign, 14 May, 1863. Dismissed 25 August, 1864.
SLYE, BENJAMIN S.
Midshipman, 1 March, 1825. Dismissed 9 July, 1833.
SMALL, ALONZO.
Acting Ensign, 27 June, 1863. Resigned 3 October, 1864.
SMALL, BRUCE.
Mate. Resigned 17 November, 1862.
SMALL, EDWARD A.
Acting Ensign, 11 September, 1862. Acting Master, 22 February, 1865. Honorably discharged 14 October, 1866.
SMALL, ELDRIDGE F.
Mate, 17 February, 1864. Acting Ensign, 13 May, 1865. Honorably discharged 3 September, 1865.
SMALL, GILBERT H.
Acting Master, 22 January, 1862. Resigned 5 July, 1862.
SMALL, JOHN, Jr.
Acting Ensign, 21 January, 1864. Resigned 9 June, 1865.
SMALLEY, ANTHONY.
Acting Master, 27 March, 1862. Appointment revoked (sick) 1 September, 1863. Acting Ensign, 1 December, 1863. Honorably discharged 3 August, 1865.
SMALLEY, JACOB M.
Mate. Acting Ensign, 1 December, 1862. Acting Master, 28 June, 1864. Resigned 10 February, 1865.
SMALLEY, LEONARD D.
Acting Master, 27 December, 1861. Dismissed 11 March, 1863.
SMART, HIRAM.
Acting Boatswain, 25 April, 1866. Resigned 12 June, 1866.
SMEDLEY, JOHN KINSEY.
Third Assistant Engineer, 18 November, 1862. Second Assistant Engineer, 23 March, 1864. Resigned 13 March, 1866.
SMITH, AARON W.
Acting Third Assistant Engineer, 28 November, 1863. Honorably discharged 26 July, 1865.
SMITH, ABRAM G.
Acting Third Assistant Engineer, 6 March, 1865. Honorably discharged 18 November, 1865.
SMITH, A. C.
Mate, 11 September, 1869. Deserted 15 September, 1869.
SMITH, ALBERT C.
Acting Second Assistant Engineer, 18 February, 1863. Acting First Assistant Engineer, 29 August, 1863. Died 1 September, 1863.
SMITH, ALBERT EDWARD.
Cadet Engineer, Naval Academy, 14 September, 1876. Graduated 10 June, 1880. Assistant Engineer, 10 June, 1882. Resigned 7 December, 1886.
SMITH, ALBERT M.
Acting Second Assistant Engineer, 1 October, 1862. Resigned 22 September, 1863.
SMITH, ALBERT N.
Midshipman, 26 October, 1838. Passed Midshipman, 20 May, 1844. Master, 9 July, 1852. Lieutenant, 12 April, 1853. Lieutenant-Commander, 16 July, 1862. Commander, 11 August, 1862. Died 8 September, 1866.

GENERAL NAVY REGISTER. 503

SMITH, ALBERT P.
  Acting Third Assistant Engineer, 9 June, 1864. Honorably discharged 30 October, 1865.
SMITH, ALEXANDER M.
  Acting Master, 9 October, 1861. Dismissed 21 March, 1862.
SMITH, ALFRED C.
  Mate, 16 April, 1864. Appointment revoked (sick) 21 July, 1864.
SMITH, ARCHIMEDES.
  Assistant Surgeon, 5 July, 1814. Resigned 18 April, 1818.
SMITH, ARTHUR.
  Acting Boatswain, 1 March, 1900.
SMITH, ARTHUR ST. C.
  Naval Cadet, 6 September, 1893. Ensign, 1 July, 1899.
SMITH, AUGUSTUS R.
  Acting Second Assistant Engineer, 26 April, 1864. Honorably discharged 1 November, 1865.
SMITH, AUGUSTUS W.
  Professor, 22 September, 1860. Died 21 March, 1866.
SMITH, BAXTER.
  Acting Second Assistant Engineer, 16 July, 1864. Honorably discharged 23 November, 1865.
SMITH, BEATTY P.
  Acting Midshipman, 29 September, 1854. Midshipman, 9 June, 1859. Lieutenant, 31 August, 1861. Lieutenant-Commander, 26 October, 1865. Dropped from service 9 July, 1874.
SMITH, BENJAMIN.
  Midshipman, 9 October, 1798. Lieutenant, 14 April, 1802. Died 14 October, 1807.
SMITH, BENJAMIN B.
  Mate, 16 April, 1863. Resigned (sick) 8 July, 1863.
SMITH, CHARLES.
  Acting Assistant Paymaster, 12 February, 1864. Mustered out 13 December, 1865.
SMITH, CHARLES.
  Boatswain, 24 July, 1850. Dismissed 6 August, 1853.
SMITH, CHARLES.
  Acting Master, 26 August, 1861. Resigned 19 May, 1864.
SMITH, CHARLES.
  Midshipman, 17 December, 1810. Last appearance on Records of Navy Department, 1818. Furloughed.
SMITH, CHARLES.
  Acting Master's Mate, 12 November, 1863, to 22 May, 1864.
SMITH, CHARLES, JR.
  Mate, 1 October, 1862. Acting Ensign, 6 July, 1864. Honorably discharged 5 December, 1865.
SMITH, CHARLES B.
  Midshipman, 30 November, 1846. Passed Midshipman, 8 June, 1852. Dropped 13 September, 1855.
SMITH, CHARLES G., JR.
  Mate, 3 June, 1862. Resigned 8 May, 1865.
SMITH, CHARLES H.
  Mate, good conduct at loss of Monitor, 21 April, 1864. Honorably discharged 12 May, 1865.
SMITH, CHARLES L.
  Midshipman, 27 July, 1846. Died 16 November, 1848.
SMITH, CHARLES L.
  Ensign (Spanish-American War), 10 June, 1898. Honorably discharged 12 December, 1898.
SMITH, CHARLES P.
  Carpenter, 27 May, 1827. Resigned 4 December, 1827.
SMITH, CHARLES R.
  Assistant Surgeon, 28 March, 1820. Died 8 November, 1822.
SMITH, CHARLES R.
  Midshipman, 2 September, 1835. Passed Midshipman, 22 June, 1841. Dismissed 4 December, 1843.
SMITH, CHARLES W.
  Boatswain, 8 December, 1857. Dismissed 29 June, 1859.
SMITH, CHARLES W.
  Acting Third Assistant Engineer, 6 January, 1862. Deserted 20 January, 1864.
SMITH, CRAWFORD E.
  Midshipman, 2 January, 1840. Dropped.
SMITH, DANIEL A.
  Acting Assistant Paymaster, 31 August, 1863. Passed Assistant Paymaster, 23 July, 1866. Paymaster, 23 July, 1870. Pay Inspector, 10 October, 1896. Pay Director, 20 January, 1900.
SMITH, DAVID.
  Third Assistant Engineer, 26 August, 1859. Second Assistant Engineer, 8 July, 1861. First Assistant Engineer, 1 October, 1863. Chief Engineer, 5 March, 1871. Retired List, 13 December, 1896.
SMITH, DAVID.
  Acting Second Assistant Engineer, 14 July, 1864. Honorably discharged 17 July, 1865.
SMITH, E. D.
  Acting Assistant Surgeon, 12 August, 1861. Honorably discharged 23 November, 1865.
SMITH, EDGAR S.
  Acting Assistant Surgeon, 1 September, 1861. Resigned 4 August, 1862. Acting Assistant Surgeon, 3 July, 1863. Acting Passed Assistant Surgeon, 17 June, 1865. Honorably discharged 28 April, 1866.

GENERAL NAVY REGISTER.

SMITH, EDWARD H., JR.
Acting Ensign, 24 December, 1863. Honorably discharged 19 September, 1865.
SMITH, EDWARD K.
Acting Ensign, 27 November, 1863. Honorably discharged 4 September, 1865.
SMITH, EDWARD S.
Midshipman, 16 January, 1809. Last appearance on Records of Navy Department, 10 March, 1809.
SMITH, EDWARD W.
Carpenter, 7 May, 1889. Chief Carpenter, 7 May, 1899.
SMITH, ELIAS, JR.
Mate, 23 June, 1863. Lost on Bainbridge, 21 August, 1863.
SMITH, ELIAS.
Acting Ensign, 22 December, 1862. Resigned 3 August, 1863.
SMITH, E. V. B.
Mate, 25 October, 1862. Appointment revoked (sick) 21 March, 1865. Mate, 31 May, 1866. Dishonorably discharged 30 April, 1867.
SMITH, FERDINAND.
Midshipman, 1 July, 1826. Died 21 March, 1831.
SMITH, FRANCIS G., JR.
Third Assistant Engineer, 29 July, 1861. Second Assistant Engineer, 18 December, 1862. First Assistant Engineer, 30 January, 1865. Resigned 28 July, 1869.
SMITH, FRANK.
Acting Master, 9 October, 1861. Acting Volunteer Lieutenant, 28 November, 1863. Resigned 14 December, 1864.
SMITH, FREDERICK N.
Acting Ensign, 13 October, 1862. Deserted, 4 August, 1863.
SMITH, F. W.
Midshipman, 1 January, 1808. Lieutenant, 24 July, 1813. Died 4 June, 1828.
SMITH, FREDERICK R.
Acting Midshipman, 24 September, 1858. Graduated 1862. Lieutenant, 1 August, 1862. Lieutenant-Commander, 25 July, 1866. Commander, 6 April, 1875. Retired List, 18 June, 1892.
SMITH, GEORGE.
Acting Third Assistant Engineer, 25 September, 1863. Honorably discharged 7 August, 1865.
SMITH, GEORGE.
Boatswain,, 20 October, 1845. Retired List, 19 December, 1869. Died 27 November, 1873.
SMITH, GEORGE.
Acting Ensign, 13 September, 1862. Appointment revoked 26 January, 1866.
SMITH, GEORGE A.
Mate, 22 October, 1861. Acting Master, 24 April, 1862. Acting Volunteer Lieutenant, 27 June, 1865. Honorably discharged 2 July, 1868.
SMITH, GEORGE A.
Acting Ensign, 1 December, 1862. Honorably discharged 14 December, 1865.
SMITH, GEORGE F.
Acting Third Assistant Engineer, 27 September, 1861. Acting Second Assistant Engineer, 28 October, 1864. Resigned 25 January, 1865.
SMITH, GEORGE F.
Acting Third Assistant Engineer, 16 September, 1864. Resigned 25 January, 1865.
SMITH, GEORGE L.
Acting Ensign, 5 December, 1862. Resigned 29 January, 1863. Mate, 31 March, 1863. Acting Ensign, 10 April, 1863. Resigned 15 July, 1864.
SMITH, GEORGE L.
Naval Cadet, 6 September, 1894. Ensign, 4 April, 1900.
SMITH, GEORGE M.
Acting Third Assistant Engineer, 20 July, 1863. Honorably discharged 14 November, 1865.
SMITH, GEORGE M.
Mate, 30 July, 1862. Acting Ensign, 27 July, 1863. Honorably discharged 25 May, 1867.
SMITH, GEORGE S.
Midshipman, 1 January, 1817. Last appearance on Records of Navy Department, 1819.
SMITH, GEORGE T.
Assistant Surgeon, 3 June, 1889. Passed Assistant Surgeon, 3 June, 1892. Surgeon, 24 August, 1900.
SMITH, GEORGE W.
Chaplain, 2 July, 1864. Resigned 30 September, 1876.
SMITH, GEORGE W.
Acting First Assistant Engineer, 1 October, 1862. Dismissed 8 May, 1863.
SMITH, G. GEDDES.
Mate, 27 January, 1865. Acting Ensign, 3 May, 1865. Honorably discharged 14 August, 1865.
SMITH, GIDEON H.
Mate, 25 January, 1862. Appointment revoked (sick) 22 October, 1863.
SMITH, GILBERT H.
Midshipman, 6 July, 1803. Resigned 12 September, 1805.
SMITH, HARRY E.
Naval Cadet, 20 May, 1887. Ensign, 1 July, 1893. Lieutenant, Junior Grade, 3 March, 1899. Lieutenant, 2 June, 1900.
SMITH, HARRY H.
Ensign (Spanish-American War), 23 June, 1898. Honorably discharged 12 September, 1898.

SMITH, HEBER.
Acting Assistant Surgeon, 24 June, 1861. Assistant Surgeon, 16 August, 1861. Resigned 1 March, 1865.
SMITH, HENRY.
Mate, 7 January, 1862. Dismissed 5 June, 1862.
SMITH, HENRY.
Acting Warrant Machinist, 23 August, 1899.
SMITH, HENRY, AUGUSTUS.
Third Assistant Engineer, 16 September, 1862. Second Assistant Engineer, 1 March, 1864. Resigned 28 July, 1866.
SMITH, HENRY G.
Naval Cadet, 5 September, 1887. Graduated. Assistant Naval Constructor, 1 July, 1893.
SMITH, HENRY H.
Acting Assistant Surgeon, 20 November, 1863. Resigned 21 April, 1865.
SMITH, HENRY N.
Acting Second Assistant Engineer, 12 October, 1861. Appointment revoked 27 November, 1861.
SMITH, HENRY R.
Assistant Paymaster, 1 June, 1876. Passed Assistant Paymaster, 6 December, 1880. Paymaster, 19 February, 1892. Dismissed 12 June, 1895.
SMITH, HENRY W.
Acting Third Assistant Engineer, 19 April, 1864. Honorably discharged 28 October, 1865.
SMITH, HERBERT L.
Ensign (Spanish-American War), 23 April, 1898. Honorably discharged 30 September, 1898.
SMITH, HORACE.
Master, 17 July, 1812. Last appearance on Records of Navy Department, 1816. Baltimore.
SMITH, HORACE.
Midshipman, 16 December, 1798. Resigned 23 January, 1799.
SMITH, HORATIO D.
Mate, 26 October, 1864. Honorably discharged 8 June, 1865.
SMITH, HOWARD.
Assistant Surgeon, 13 July, 1871. Passed Assistant Surgeon, 13 December, 1875. Surgeon, 11 December, 1883. Retired List, 10 November, 1890.
SMITH, HOWARD J.
Assistant Surgeon, 20 June, 1838. Passed Assistant Surgeon, 22 November, 1843. Died 5 September, 1847.
SMITH, HUNTINGTON.
Midshipman, 26 February, 1863. Graduated June, 1868. Master, 12 July, 1870. Resigned 15 May, 1873.
SMITH, INCREASE C.
Acting Third Assistant Engineer, 8 May, 1863. Acting Second Assistant Engineer, 17 August, 1864. Honorably discharged 16 September, 1865. Acting Second Assistant Engineer, 20 August, 1866. Mustered out 21 August, 1867.
SMITH, ISAAC B.
Assistant Paymaster (Spanish-American War), 16 July, 1898. Honorably discharged 21 November, 1898.
SMITH, ISAAC J.
Acting Third Assistant Engineer, 18 December, 1863. Deserted 29 April, 1864.
SMITH, ISRAEL D.
Midshipman, 1 May, 1826. Resigned 23 April, 1827.
SMITH, JACOB J.
Acting Assistant Surgeon, 14 March, 1864. Honorably discharged 9 October, 1865.
SMITH, JAMES.
Lieutenant, 28 May, 1800. Last appearance on Records of Navy Department, 9 September, 1800.
SMITH, JAMES E.
Acting Third Assistant Engineer, 21 May, 1863. Honorably discharged 21 July, 1865.
SMITH, JAMES L.
Acting First Assistant Enginer, 1 October, 1862. Resigned 31 May, 1864.
SMITH, JAMES L.
Assistant Engineer (Spanish-American War), 14 May, 1898. Honorably discharged 3 February, 1899.
SMITH, JAMES R.
Acting Ensign, 6 August, 1864. Dismissed 7 January, 1865.
SMITH, JAMES T.
Midshipman, 12 June, 1871. Graduated 21 June, 1875. Ensign, 21 November, 1877. Lieutenant, Junior Grade, 16 November, 1883. Lieutenant, 3 January, 1890. Lieutenant-Commander, 3 March, 1899.
SMITH, JAMES W.
Acting Second Assistant Engineer, 31 December, 1863. Court-Martial. Sent North, under arrest, 21 April, 1865.
SMITH, JAY WOLBERT.
Acting Third Assistant Engineer, 5 March, 1864. Honorably discharged 15 September, 1869.
SMITH, JESSE, 3d.
Midshipman, 11 March, 1815. Lieutenant, 13 January, 1825. Lost in the Hornet, 10 September, 1829.
SMITH, JESSE B.
Midshipman, 28 July, 1864. Graduated June, 1868. Ensign, 19 April, 1869. Master, 12 July, 1870. Lieutenant, 25 November, 1872. Died 18 November, 1874.

SMITH, JESSE M.
　Midshipman, 9 February, 1841.　Died 3 December, 1844.
SMITH, J. MALCOLM.
　Assistant Surgeon, 6 September, 1837.　Passed Assistant Surgeon, 14 March, 1843.
　Died 29 April, 1848.
SMITH, JOHN.
　Master, 1 December, 1812.　Resigned 12 June, 1813.
SMITH, JOHN.
　Carpenter, 11 May, 1798.　Last appearance on Records of Navy Department.
SMITH, JOHN.
　Mate.　Appointment revoked (sick) 28 August, 1862.
SMITH, JOHN.
　Lieutenant, 8 March, 1799.　Commander, 25 May, 1804.　Captain, 24 December, 1811.
　Died 31 May, 1815.
SMITH, JOHN.
　Acting Boatswain, 6 June, 1871.　Appointment revoked 9 December, 1872.
SMITH, JOHN.
　Boatswain, 7 December, 1819.　Died 7 October, 1843.
SMITH, JOHN.
　Midshipman, 30 April, 1800.　Discharged 6 August, 1801, under Peace Establishment
　Act.
SMITH, JOHN.
　Acting Boatswain, 6 September, 1862.　Honorably discharged 12 December, 1865.
　Boatswain, 24 October, 1866.　Died 11 January, 1890.
SMITH, JOHN.
　Acting Third Assistant Engineer, 22 September, 1862.　Resigned 5 April, 1865.
SMITH, JOHN.
　Boatswain, 11 August, 1819.　Resigned 19 July, 1828.
SMITH, JOHN.
　Mate, 11 February, 1864.　Deserted 2 March, 1864.
SMITH, JOHN A. B.
　Third Assistant Engineer, 21 April, 1863.　Second Assistant Engineer, 28 September,
　1864.　First Assistant Engineer, 22 January, 1873.　Chief Engineer, 16 February,
　1892.　Rank changed to Commander, 3 March, 1899.
SMITH, JOHN B. F.
　Mate, 8 May, 1862.　Acting Ensign, 9 January, 1864.　Resigned (sick) 6 September,
　1864.
SMITH, JOHN D.
　Acting Assistant Surgeon, 27 July, 1867.　Died 26 April, 1884.
SMITH, JOHN E.
　Acting Ensign, 30 December, 1864.　Honorably discharged 21 July, 1865.
SMITH, JOHN F.
　Acting Third Assistant Engineer, 18 January, 1864.　Honorably discharged 4 November, 1865.
SMITH, JOHN H.
　Midshipman, 1 January, 1815.　Lieutenant, 13 January, 1825.　Died 30 November,
　1836.
SMITH, JOHN ROTHWELL.
　Acting Second Assistant Engineer, 21 October, 1864.　Honorably discharged 7 September, 1865.
SMITH, JOHN S.
　Acting First Assistant Engineer, 27 September, 1861.　Dismissed 25 February, 1862.
SMITH, JOHN T.
　Acting Third Assistant Engineer, 12 March, 1863.　Acting Second Assistant Engineer,
　24 March, 1865.　Honorably discharged 23 June, 1870.　Second Assistant Engineer,
　17 June, 1870.　Retired as Passed Assistant Engineer, 24 February, 1875, by Act
　of Congress, approved 30 January, 1875.
SMITH, JOSEPH.
　Midshipman, 16 January, 1809.　Lieutenant, 24 July, 1813.　Commander, 3 March,
　1827.　Captain, 9 February, 1837.　Retired List, 21 December, 1861.　Rear-Admiral,
　Retired List, 16 July, 1862.　Died 17 January, 1877.
SMITH, JOSEPH.
　Gunner, 9 October, 1861.　Retired List, 10 December, 1890.
SMITH, JOSEPH.
　Midshipman, 18 June, 1812.　Resigned 17 February, 1813.
SMITH, JOSEPH, Jr.
　Purser, 1 March,, 1799.　Last appearance on Records of Navy Department, 20 March,
　1799.
SMITH, JOSEPH ADAMS.
　Assistant Paymaster, 8 October, 1861.　Paymaster, 23 August, 1862.　Pay Inspector,
　15 May, 1879.　Pay Director, 24 November, 1891.　Retired List, 1 September, 1899.
SMITH, JOSEPH B.
　Midshipman, 19 October, 1841.　Passed Midshipman, 10 August, 1847.　Master, 22
　August, 1855.　Lieutenant, 14 September, 1855.　Killed in action between Congress
　and Merrimac, 8 March, 1862.
SMITH, JOSEPH E.
　Midshipman, 1 January, 1808.　Lieutenant, 10 March, 1813.　Died 1 December, 1813.
SMITH, JOSEPH G.
　Midshipman, 15 November, 1809.　Last appearance on Records of Navy Department,
　1814.
SMITH, JOSEPH G.
　Midshipman, 1 January, 1817.　Died in June, 1823.
SMITH, JOSEPH R.
　Carpenter, 4 November, 1852.　Resigned 21 February, 1860.

SMITH, J. W.
Acting Master, 8 June, 1861. Appointment revoked 2 July, 1861. Reappointed 24 July, 1861. Acting Volunteer Lieutenant, 27 October, 1863. Acting Volunteer Lieutenant-Commander, 7 February, 1865. Honorably discharged 21 February, 1866.
SMITH, J. VAUGHAN.
Assistant Surgeon, 27 June, 1829. Surgeon, 20 February, 1838. Died 25 August, 1848.
SMITH, LAYTON F.
Lieutenant, Junior Grade (Spanish-American War), 30 April, 1898. Honorably discharged 7 December, 1898.
SMITH, LEVI W.
Mate, 28 August, 1863. Acting Ensign. Deserted 30 April, 1866.
SMITH, LOMAN.
Carpenter, 27 November, 1840. Died 20 August, 1843.
SMITH, LUTHER W.
Acting Ensign, 21 April, 1864. Honorably discharged 23 August, 1865.
SMITH, MANASSEH.
Acting Third Assistant Engineer, 16 October, 1861. Acting Second Assistant Engineer, 23 December, 1863. Resigned 3 May, 1865.
SMITH, MARSHALL J.
Midshipman, 19 October, 1841. Passed Midshipman, 10 August, 1847. Resigned 4 February, 1851.
SMITH, MELANCTHON.
Midshipman, 1 March, 1826. Passed Midshipman, 28 April, 1832. Lieutenant, 8 March, 1837. Commander, 14 September, 1855. Captain, 16 July, 1862. Commodore, 25 July, 1866. Rear-Admiral, 1 July, 1870. Retired List, 24 May, 1871. Died 19 July, 1893.
SMITH, MICHAEL J.
Acting Ensign, 17 December, 1863. Honorably discharged 23 November, 1865.
SMITH, MILO H.
Midshipman, 1 April, 1828. Resigned 3 June, 1831.
SMITH, MOSES R.
Master, 4 May, 1812. Discharged 16 June, 1815.
SMITH, NATHAN D.
Acting First Assistant Engineer, 18 March, 1864. Appointment revoked (sick) 30 January, 1865.
SMITH, NEWTON C.
Mate. Resigned 15 July, 1862.
SMITH, OSCAR G.
Acting Assistant Surgeon, 3 June, 1861. Resigned 11 September, 1861.
SMITH, OSCAR L.
Acting Third Assistant Engineer, 7 September, 1863. Honorably discharged 15 August, 1865.
SMITH, OMAR.
Mate, 18 February, 1862. Resigned 16 April, 1863.
SMITH, OWEN P.
Assistant Surgeon (Spanish-American War), 25 May, 1898. Honorably discharged 22 September, 1898.
SMITH, PETER.
Acting Third Assistant Engineer, 26 November, 1864. Honorably discharged 24 September, 1869.
SMITH, PETER HUCKINS.
Boatswain, 7 August, 1872. Chief Boatswain, 3 March, 1899.
SMITH, REGINALD K.
Assistant Surgeon, 3 April, 1895. Passed Assistant Surgeon, 3 April, 1898.
SMITH, REUBEN.
Acting Assistant Surgeon, 15 September, 1863. Honorably discharged 13 December, 1868.
SMITH, RICHARD.
Midshipman, 28 June, 1804. Last appearance on Records of Navy Department, 19 March, 1805.
SMITH, RICHARD B.
Acting Warrant Machinest, 23 August, 1899.
SMITH, RICHARD H.
Acting Ensign, 1 October, 1862. Appointment revoked 7 February, 1866.
SMITH, RICHARD L.
Midshipman, 1 January, 1812. Resigned 23 June, 1812.
SMITH, ROBERT.
Acting Third Assistant Engineer, 16 November, 1861. Dismissed 13 August, 1862.
SMITH, ROBERT B.
Mate. Acting Master, 24 March, 1862. Acting Volunteer Lieutenant, good service, 3 December, 1863. Acting Volunteer Lieutenant-Commander, 29 April, 1865. Honorably discharged 1 January, 1866.
SMITH, ROBERT B.
Mate, 19 December, 1861. Honorably discharged 7 August, 1866.
SMITH, ROBERT B.
Acting Ensign, 1 October, 1862. Acting Master, 16 February, 1863. Resigned 29 April, 1863.
SMITH, ROBERT H.
Acting Second Assistant Engineer, 10 August, 1864. Honorably discharged 7 October, 1865.
SMITH, RODNEY.
Acting Chief Engineer, 19 January, 1863. Honoraby discharged 8 January, 1866.

SMITH, ROY C.
  Cadet Midshipman, 2 October, 1874. Graduated 4 June, 1880. Ensign, 8 April, 1882. Lieutenant, Junior Grade, 12 May, 1889. Lieutenant, 22 February, 1894.
SMITH, RUSSELL.
  Carpenter, 21 December, 1841. Dismissed 28 July, 1842.
SMITH, SAMUEL.
  Acting Ensign, 14 July, 1863. Resigned 1 April, 1865.
SMITH, SAMUEL.
  Midshipman, 16 June, 1834. Resigned 21 October, 1839.
SMITH, SAMUEL C.
  Assistant Surgeon, 28 March, 1820. Resigned 28 November, 1822.
SMITH, SAMUEL D.
  Acting Assistant Surgeon, 1 April, 1863. Resigned 30 June, 1863.
SMITH, SAMUEL O.
  Midshipman, 8 May, 1799. Discharged 19 October, 1799.
SMITH, S. CHESTER.
  Acting Assistant Surgeon, 30 November, 1861. Resigned 11 November, 1864.
SMITH, SIDNEY.
  Acting Second Assistant Engineer, 2 November, 1861. Honorably discharged 5 October, 1865.
SMITH, SIDNEY.
  Midshipman, 26 July, 1800. Lieutenant, 7 March, 1807. Commander, 28 February, 1815. Died 17 May, 1827.
SMITH, SIDNEY LEE.
  Third Assistant Enginer, 21 October, 1861. Second Assistant Engineer, 25 August, 1863. First Assistant Engineer, 1 January, 1868. Resigned 29 August, 1884.
SMITH, SIMEON.
  Acting Third Assistant Engineer, 20 July, 1863. Acting Second Assistant Engineer, 3 September, 1864. Honorably discharged 12 May, 1865.
SMITH, SIMON.
  Midshipman, 28 April, 1801. Died 4 June, 1806.
SMITH, SOLON C.
  Acting Third Assistant Engineer, 9 November, 1864. Died 10 July, 1865.
SMITH, STUART FARRAR.
  Naval Cadet, 4 September, 1891. Assistant Naval Constructor, 1 July, 1897.
SMITH, SUMNER T.
  Mate, 25 April, 1864. Appointment revoked (sick) 20 July, 1864.
SMITH, S. T. C.
  Mate, 28 December, 1869. Retired List, 28 December, 1894.
SMITH, THADDEUS S.
  Third Assistant Engineer, 12 August, 1861. Resigned 8 July, 1862.
SMITH, THEODORE E.
  Acting Assistant Paymaster, 10 October, 1861. Resigned 5 January, 1865.
SMITH, THOMAS.
  Acting Master, 21 October, 1861. Appointment revoked 31 March, 1864.
SMITH, THOMAS.
  Boatswain, 24 September, 1855. Retired List, 18 February, 1874. Died 11 April, 1885.
SMITH, THOMAS.
  Acting Master and Pilot, 1 October, 1864. Honorably discharged 1 July, 1865.
SMITH, THOMAS.
  Acting Third Assistant Engineer, 12 July, 1864. Honorably discharged 4 November, 1865.
SMITH, THOMAS.
  Mate, 25 January, 1862. Resigned 14 November, 1862.
SMITH, THOMAS.
  Boatswain, 23 May, 1804. Dismissed 14 August, 1810.
SMITH, THOMAS.
  Acting Gunner, 1 August, 1900.
SMITH, THOMAS E.
  Acting Master, 22 October, 1861. Acting Volunteer Lieutenant, 29 January, 1863. Honorably discharged 28 February, 1869.
SMITH, THOMAS L.
  Assistant Surgeon, 3 January, 1828. Surgeon, 9 February, 1837. Retired List, 13 August, 1862. Medical Director, 3 March, 1871. Died 14 August, 1891.
SMITH, THOMAS M.
  Acting Ensign, 30 June, 1864. Honorably discharged 6 January, 1866.
SMITH, THOMAS P.
  Carpenter, 28 April, 1873. Retired List, 26 December, 1891. Died 29 August, 1896.
SMITH, THOMAS R.
  Boatswain, 5 November, 1814. Died 28 November, 1827.
SMITH, WALTER D.
  Third Assistant Engineer, 1 July, 1861. Second Asssistant Engineer, 18 December, 1862. First Assistant Engineer, 25 July, 1866. Chief Engineer, 25 March, 1880. Retired List, 16 March, 1887. Died 11 September, 1887.
SMITH, WALTER N.
  Mate, 5 April, 1862. Acting Ensign, 14 August, 1864. Honorably discharged 12 October, 1867. Mate, 20 January, 1870. Died 14 April, 1888.
SMITH, WATERS.
  Surgeon's Mate, 26 May, 1824. Surgeon, 3 January, 1828. Died 19 September, 1850.
SMITH, WATSON.
  Midshipman, 19 October, 1841. Passed Midshipman, 10 August, 1847. Master, 14 September, 1855. Lieutenant, 15 September, 1855. Lieutenant-Commander, 16 July, 1862. Died 19 December, 1864.

GENERAL NAVY REGISTER.

SMITH, WILBERT.
Naval Cadet, 6 July, 1896. Graduated 30 June, 1900.

SMITH, WILLIAM.
Boatswain, 2 August, 1838. Dropped 20 April, 1861.

SMITH, WILLIAM.
Midshipman, 4 March, 1823. Passed Midshipman, 23 March, 1829. Lieutenant, 3 March, 1831. Commander, 12 September, 1854. Commodore, 16 July, 1862. Retired List, 9 January, 1865. Died 29 April, 1873.

SMITH, WILLIAM.
Lieutenant, 5 March, 1799. Discharged 8 July, 1801, under Peace Establishment Act.

SMITH, WILLIAM.
Midshipman, 15 January, 1801. Discharged 6 August, 1801, under Peace Establishment Act.

SMITH, WILLIAM.
Acting Third Assistant Engineer, 5 July, 1864. Honorably discharged 28 October, 1865.

SMITH, WILLIAM.
Boatswain, 1 January, 1819. Died 7 July, 1825.

SMITH, WILLIAM A.
Acting Third Assistant Engineer, 21 June, 1862. Acting Second Assistant Engineer, 30 June, 1864. Honorably discharged 2 September, 1865.

SMITH, WILLIAM A.
Mate, 27 December, 1861. Acting Ensign, 21 November, 1863. Honorably discharged 8 October, 1865.

SMITH, WILLIAM A. F.
Ensign (Spanish-American War), 18 May, 1898. Honorably discharged 2 September, 1898.

SMITH, WILLIAM C.
Assistant Surgeon, 1 June, 1802. Resigned 13 July, 1802.

SMITH, WILLIAM G.
Mate, 5 October, 1866. Retired List, 25 May, 1897.

SMITH, WILLIAM G.
Mate, 5 May, 1863. Honorably discharged 21 December, 1865.

SMITH, WILLIAM H.
Acting Master, 21 June, 1861. Killed 11 November, 1864.

SMITH, WILLIAM H.
Midshipman, 31 July, 1840. Passed Midshipman, 11 July, 1846. Last appearance on Records of Navy Department, 1852.

SMITH, WILLIAM H.
Acting Third Assistant Engineer, 12 October, 1861. Acting Second Assistant Engineer, 23 September, 1863. Acting First Assistant Engineer, 2 February, 1865. Honorably discharged 14 February, 1866.

SMITH, WILLIAM H.
Midshipman, 31 March, 1800. Discharged 30 April, 1801, under Peace Establishment Act.

SMITH, WILLIAM H.
Midshipman, 16 October, 1845. Resigned 20 April, 1853.

SMITH, WILLIAM H.
Mate, 26 December, 1863. Honorably discharged 7 September, 1865.

SMITH, WILLIAM H.
Acting Third Assistant Engineer, 31 October, 1863. Honorably discharged 19 February, 1866.

SMITH, WILLIAM MOSHER.
Acting Third Assistant Engineer, 15 September, 1864. Resigned 5 May, 1865.

SMITH, WILLIAM M.
Midshipman, 16 January, 1809. Resigned 26 February, 1810.

SMITH, WILLIAM P.
Midshipman, 17 March, 1814. Last appearance on Records of Navy Department, 1815. Lake Ontario.

SMITH, WILLIAM P.
Master, 26 December, 1812. Resigned 1 December, 1815.

SMITH, WILLIAM P.
Midshipman, 2 January, 1800. Lieutenant, 23 March, 1807. Resigned 2 March, 1809.

SMITH, WILLIAM STROTHER.
Cadet Engineer, Naval Academy, 15 September, 1875. Graduated 10 June, 1880. Assistant Engineer, 10 June, 1882. Passed Assistant Engineer, 27 June, 1893. Rank changed to Lieutenant, 3 March, 1899.

SMITH, WILLIAM S.
Midshipman, 25 April, 1831. Passed Midshipman, 15 June, 1837. Died 13 November, 1839.

SMITH, WILLIAM S.
Third Assistant Engineer, 19 February, 1861. Second Assistant Engineer 16 January, 1863. First Assistant Engineer, 1 December, 1864. Chief Engineer, 20 October, 1875. Died 7 February, 1897.

SMITH, WILLIAM STUART.
Cadet Engineer, 13 September, 1877. Graduated 10 June, 1881. Honorably discharged 30 June, 1883. Restored to service 10 March, 1886, and commissioned Assistant Engineer to rank from 1 July, 1883. Retired List, 30 October, 1890.

SMITH, WILLIAM TAYLOR.
'shipman, 7 July, 1832. Passed Midshipman, 23 June, 1838. Lieutenant, 19 September, 1842. Resigned 17 October, 1853.

SMITH, WILLIAM V.
Mate. Resigned 2 April, 1863.

SMITH, WILLIAM WESLEY.
Acting Third Assistant Engineer, 13 June, 1864. Honorably discharged 11 October, 1865.
SMITH, WILLIAM W.
Midshipman, 1 November, 1828. Resigned 1 February, 1834.
SMITH, WILLIAM W.
Acting Ensign, 2 September, 1864. Honorably discharged 22 July, 1865.
SMITH, WILLIAM W.
Acting Second Assistant Engineer, 1 May, 1864. Resigned 5 June, 1865.
SMITTEN, CHARLES H.
Mate, 26 July, 1864. Acting Ensign, 31 January, 1865. Discharged 21 July, 1866.
SMOOT, GEORGE W.
Mate, 1 July, 1863. Resigned 7 February, 1865.
SMOOT, JOHN H.
Acting Assistant Paymaster, 20 August, 1864. Honorably discharged 19 September, 1865.
SMOOT, JOSEPH.
Midshipman, 1 December, 1809. Lieutenant, 27 April, 1816. Commander, 3 March, 1835. Captain, 8 September, 1841. Reserved List, 1 October, 1855. Died 13 March, 1857.
SMOOT, SAMUEL C.
Acting Assistant Surgeon, 5 October, 1861. Resigned 27 January, 1862.
SMOOT, WILLIAM G.
Acting Third Assistant Engineer, 4 June, 1862. Acting Second Assistant Engineer, 12 March, 1863. Appointment revoked (sick), 6 February, 1864. Acting Second Assistant Engineer, 12 October, 1864. Honorably discharged 15 February,, 1866.
SMYLIE, WILLIAM.
Sailmaker, 7 July, 1804. Died 28 September, 1805.
SMYTH, JAMES W.
Acting Third Assistant Engineer, 31 May, 1861. Acting Second Assistant Engineer, 20 July, 1863. Honorably discharged 30 December, 1865.
SMYTH, THOMAS S.
Acting Ensign, 15 August, 1862. Resigned 26 May, 1863.
SNAITH, GEORGE S.
Acting Third Assistant Engineer, 17 May, 1864. Honorably discharged 12 March, 1866.
SNARE, ELISHA W.
Acting Ensign, 22 December, 1863. Honorably discharged 21 October, 1865.
SNEDEKER, WILLIAM A.
Acting Third Assistant Engineer, 15 September, 1864. Resigned (sick) 18 March, 1865.
SNELL, ALFRED T.
Midshipman, 26 September, 1857. Midshipman, 1 June, 1861. Lieutenant, 16 July, 1862. Lieutenant-Commander, 25 July, 1866. Commander, 19 September, 1874. Died 8 September, 1876.
SNELSON, ROBERT L.
Midshipman, 1 January, 1812. Last appearance on Records of Navy Department, 1816. Frigate Java.
SNIDER, JOHN.
Carpenter, 1 January, 1818. Died 7 November, 1836.
SNOR, JOHN J.
Acting Third Assistant Engineer, 21 December, 1863. Honorably discharged 18 October, 1865.
SNOW, ALBERT S.
Midshipman, 30 November, 1861. Graduated September, 1865. Ensign, 1 December, 1866. Master, 12 March, 1868. Lieutenant, 26 March, 1869. Lieutenant-Commander, 11 July, 1880. Commander, 28 February, 1890. Captain, 3 March, 1899.
SNOW, ALLEN W.
Mate, 4 February, 1864. Appointment revoked 21 April, 1864. Mate, 23 December, 1864. Acting Ensign, 20 January, 1865. Honorably discharged 5 December, 1867.
SNOW, CARLTON F.
Naval Cadet, 19 May, 1890. Ensign, 1 July, 1896. Lieutenant, Junior Grade, 1 July, 1899.
SNOW, CHARLES W.
Acting Ensign, 21 December, 1863. Died 11 September, 1864.
SNOW, ELISHA N.
Mate, 12 September, 1862. Acting Ensign, 28 April, 1864. Honorably discharged 22 December, 1865.
SNOW, ELLIOTT.
Naval Cadet, 4 September, 1883. Ensign, 1 July, 1889. Assistant Naval Constructor, 1 July, 1891. Naval Constructor, 11 November, 1897.
SNOW, HENRY C.
Acting Ensign, 4 October, 1864. Honorably discharged 25 August, 1865.
SNOW, JAMES F.
Assistant Engineer (Spanish-American War), 1 June, 1898. Honorably discharged 19 January, 1899.
SNOW, JOHN S.
Acting Ensign, 6 August, 1864. Honorably discharged 29 July, 1865.
SNOW, JOSEPH W.
Acting Ensign, 20 May, 1864. Dismissed 26 July, 1864.
SNOW, JOSIAH, Jr.
Acting Master, 11 May, 1861. Appointment revoked 26 August, 1861.
SNOW, OLIVER C.
Acting Ensign, 25 April, 1864. Honorably discharged 10 December, 1865.

GENERAL NAVY REGISTER. 511

SNOW, RUSSELL.
Acting Master, 27 February, 1862. Resigned 19 March, 1862.
SNOW, WILLIAM A., JR.
Naval Cadet, 4 September, 1886. Ensign, 1 July, 1892. Died 12 April, 1894.
SNOW, WILLIAM B.
Acting Third Assistant Engineer, 1 September, 1864. Honorably discharged 7 July, 1865.
SNOWDEN, THOMAS.
Cadet Midshipman, 25 June, 1875. Graduated 10 June, 1881. Ensign, Junior Grade, 3 March, 1883. Ensign, 26 June, 1884. Lieutenant, Junior Grade, 10 January, 1892. Lieutenant, 11 March, 1896.
SNYDER, ASA P.
Acting Gunner, 30 March, 1863. Resigned 16 January, 1865.
SNYDER, CHARLES P.
Naval Cadet, 20 May, 1896. Graduated 30 June, 1900.
SNYDER, FREDERICK.
Acting Second Assistant Engineer, 8 August, 1863. Resigned 6 April, 1864.
SNYDER, GEORGE W.
Assistant Engineer, 9 October, 1876. Died 27 December, 1884.
SNYDER, HENRY.
Third Assistant Engineer, 25 August, 1862. Second Assistant Engineer, 21 February, 1864. First Assistant Engineer, 1 January, 1868. Resigned 21 December, 1873.
SNYDER, HENRY LEE.
Third Assistant Engineer, 19 March, 1858. Second Assistant Engineer, 16 October, 1861. First Assistant Engineer, 21 April, 1863. Chief Engineer, 14 December, 1864. Died 30 June, 1887.
SNYDER, JOHN J.
Assistant Surgeon (Spanish-American War), 25 April, 1898. Appointed Assistant Surgeon in Regular Service 7 June, 1900.
SNYDER, M. B.
Acting Master, 1 October, 1862. Dismissed 28 May, 1863.
SOCOLA, ANGELO W.
Lieutenant (Spanish-American War), 20 May, 1898. Honorably discharged 16 September, 1898.
SODENBERG, B. B.
Acting Ensign, 24 June, 1864. Honorably discharged 20 June, 1865.
SOFIELD, ISAAC.
Acting Ensign and Pilot, 19 September, 1864. Acting Master and Pilot, 1 October, 1864. Resigned 18 April, 1865.
SOFTLY, JAMES.
Mate, 3 April, 1863. Acting Ensign, 18 June, 1864. Honorably discharged 21 May, 1867.
SOLEY, JOHN C.
Midshipman, 24 September, 1862. Graduated June, 1866. Ensign, 12 March, 1868. Master, 26 March, 1869. Lieutenant, 21 March, 1870. Retired List, 24 February, 1885.
SOLEY, JAMES R.
Professor, 18 August, 1876. Resigned 16 July, 1890.
SOLOMON, BENJAMIN.
Midshipman, 16 January, 1809. Resigned 11 October, 1810.
SOLOMON, EZEKIEL.
Purser, 26 March, 1814. Last appearance on Records of Navy Department, 1816. Furloughed.
SOMERBY, JOSEPH P.
Acting Third Assistant Engineer, 10 May, 1864. Died 21 November, 1865.
SOMERS, HENRY.
Midshipman, 15 June, 1799. Last appearance on Records of Navy Department.
SOMERS, JOHN.
Mate. Appointment revoked (sick) 10 July, 1863.
SOMERS, JOSEPH N.
Mate. Resigned 31 May, 1864.
SOMERS, RICHARD.
Midshipman, 30 April, 1798. Lieutenant, 21 May, 1799. Died 4 September, 1804.
SOMERVILLE, JAMES H.
Midshipman, 10 September, 1841. Passed Midshipman, 10 August, 1847. Acting Master, 17 January, 1848. Died 4 February, 1850.
SOMES, CHARLES T.
Mate. 24 October, 1862. Acting Ensign, 21 July, 1864. Resigned 13 March, 1865.
SOMES, JOHN B.
Mate, 16 October, 1862. Honorably discharged 31 December, 1865.
SOMMERS, ROBERT.
Acting Gunner, 11 November, 1873. Chief Gunner, 3 March, 1899. Retired List, 17 December, 1899.
SOMMERS, RUDOLPH.
Mate, 16 December, 1861. Acting Ensign, 4 February, 1863. Acting Master, 8 December, 1864. Honorably discharged 27 August, 1868.
SOMMERVILLE, G. W.
Midshipman, 30 November, 1814. Died 28 August, 1832.
SONNTAG, GEORGE S.
Master, 4 August, 1807. Last appearance on Records of Navy Department, 1815. Philadelphia.
SOPER, ALFRED S.
Acting Gunner, 25 January, 1864. Dismissed 28 July, 1865.
SOPER, ANTHONY.
Mate, 21 December, 1861. Dismissed 10 September, 1862.

SOPP, LOUIS W.
Acting Boatswain, 15 August, 1899.
SOULE, H. A.
Acting Gunner, 24 March, 1864. Dismissed 29 August, 1864.
SOULE, HENRY B.
Gunner, 2 June, 1893.
SOULE, HENRY W.
Mate, 11 August, 1862. Resigned 3 December, 1862.
SOULE, THOMAS H., JR.
Mate, 25 April, 1864. Resigned 13 May, 1865.
SOUTH, PERRY.
Acting First Assistant Engineer, 27 February, 1863. Honorably discharged 22 November, 1865.
SOUTHALL, CHARLES D.
Acting Third Assistant Engineer, 11 March, 1864. Honorably discharged 1 September, 1869.
SOUTHALL, P. A.
Purser, 23 March, 1832. Dismissed 21 March, 1840.
SOUTHARD, ALLEN P.
Acting Third Assistant Engineer. Dismissed 17 April, 1863.
SOUTHARD, JAMES W.
Midshipman, 16 November, 1824. Resigned 29 April, 1831.
SOUTHERLAND, WILLIAM H. H.
Midshipman, 29 June, 1868. Graduated 1 June, 1872. Ensign, 15 July, 1873. Master, 21 November, 1877. Lieutenant, Junior Grade, 3 March, 1883. Lieutenant, 9 February, 1884. Lieutenant-Commander, 3 March, 1899.
SOUTHWICK, JOHN.
Carpenter, 21 December, 1826. Retired List, 5 November, 1866. Died 15 February, 1874.
SOUTHWORTH, ASA C.
Acting Ensign, 28 November, 1863. Honorably discharged 26 October, 1865.
SOUTHWORTH, EDWARD B.
Acting Assistant Paymaster, 19 October, 1861. Honorably discharged 27 October, 1865.
SOWERBY, J. J.
Acting Assistant Surgeon, 5 November, 1862. Acting Passed Assistant Surgeon, 12 April, 1865. Honorably discharged 18 July, 1868. Acting Passed Assistant Surgeon, 5 December, 1873. Honorably discharged 30 June, 1879.
SPAIN, RICHARD A.
Acting Third Assistant Engineer, 22 October, 1863. Appointment revoked (sick), 6 May, 1864.
SPALDING, JAMES.
Carpenter, 21 October, 1812. Resigned 21 May, 1813.
SPALDING, JAMES.
Midshipman, 9 November, 1813. Resigned 10 June, 1817.
SPALDING, JOSEPH A.
Acting Third Assistant Engineer, 27 February, 1863. Acting Second Assistant Engineer, 9 October, 1864. Honorably discharged 3 April, 1868.
SPALDING, LYMAN G.
Midshipman, 26 September, 1862. Graduated June, 1866. Resigned 16 June, 1866. Master, 28 June, 1871. Lieutenant, 10 July, 1875. Killed 29 August, 1881.
SPALDING, RUFUS C.
Paymaster, 1 June, 1861. Pay Inspector, 3 March, 1871. Dismissed 18 August, 1876.
SPALDING, RUFUS C.
Midshipman, 12 October, 1848. Resigned 1 October, 1852.
SPANBURGH, LEONARD.
Acting Third Assistant Engineer, 13 January, 1862. Resigned 25 June, 1862.
SPANGENBERG, ROBERT F., JR.
Lieutenant, Junior Grade (Spanish-American War), 18 July, 1898. Honorably discharged 26 August, 1898.
SPANGLER, DANIEL M.
Acting Third Assistant Engineer, 2 January, 1864. Honorably discharged 12 September, 1865.
SPANGLER, HENRY W.
Cadet Engineer, Naval Academy, 1 October, 1874. Graduated 20 June, 1878. Assistant Engineer, 20 June, 1880. Passed Assistant Engineer, 17 June, 1889. Resigned 11 October, 1891. Chief Engineer (Spanish-American War), 14 May, 1898. Honorably discharged 8 September, 1898.
SPANGLER, SAMUEL S.
Mate, 11 August, 1864. Honorably discharged 6 September, 1865.
SPARE, JOHN.
Acting Assistant Surgeon, 10 April, 1862. Honorably discharged 2 July, 1866.
SPARKS, CHARLES D.
Midshipman, 18 April, 1850. Died 12 April, 1853.
SPARKS, WILLIAM.
Acting First Assistant Engineer, 27 April, 1863. Dismissed 25 July, 1863.
SPARKS, WILLIAM L.
Lieutenant, Junior Grade (Spanish-American War), 7 June, 1898. Honorably discharged 19 September, 1898.
SPARROW, HERBERT G.
Naval Cadet, 6 September, 1895. At sea prior to final graduation.
SPARROW, ROSCOE D.
Acting Ensign, 30 September, 1864. Honorably discharged 18 September, 1865.
SPATES, RICHARD N.
Mate, December, 1861. Appointment revoked 27 June, 1862.

GENERAL NAVY REGISTER. 513

SPAULDING, JOSIAH C.
Acting Assistant Paymaster, 2 July, 1863. Honorably discharged 13 December, 1865.
SPAVIN, ROBERT.
Acting Master, 23 September, 1861. Resigned 5 November, 1864.
SPAVIN, ROBERT, Jr.
Mate, 20 January, 1864. Resigned (sick), 21 September, 1864.
SPEAKE, JOSEPH M.
Lieutenant, 30 July, 1798. Discharged 11 April, 1801, under Peace Establishment Act.
SPEAKE, JOSEPH M.
Master, 6 June, 1801. Resigned 14 March, 1803.
SPEAKMAN, THOMAS B.
Acting Third Assistant Engineer, 4 December, 1863. Dismissed 23 January, 1865.
SPEAR, ALDEN T.
Acting Master, 4 November, 1861. Acting Volunteer Lieutenant, 31 January, 1863. Died 18 September, 1863.
SPEAR, B. H.
Mate, 20 January, 1863. Honorably discharged 14 September, 1865.
SPEAR, GEORGE W.
Mate. Appointment revoked (sick) 10 February, 1863.
SPEAR, HARRISON.
Third Assistant Engineer, 21 April, 1863. Second Assistant Engineer, 25 July, 1866. Retired 8 July, 1873. Died 18 September, 1874.
SPEAR, JOHN C.
Assistant Surgeon, 9 May, 1861. Surgeon, 23 June, 1864. Medical Inspector, 6 October, 1878. Retired List, 14 September, 1888.
SPEAR, LAWRENCE.
Naval Cadet, 19 May, 1886. Assistant Naval Constructor, 1 July, 1892. Naval Constructor, 1 November, 1898.
SPEAR, NATHAN.
Acting Third Assistant Engineer, 26 September, 1863. Honorably discharged 28 October, 1865.
SPEAR, OLIVER A.
Acting Ensign, 1 February, 1865. Honorably discharged 23 July, 1865.
SPEAR, OTIS G.
Mate, 1 November, 1864. Appointment revoked 23 December, 1865.
SPEAR, RAY.
Assistant Paymaster, 19 February, 1900.
SPEAR, RAYMOND.
Assistant Surgeon, 22 June, 1897. Passed Assistant Surgeon, 22 June, 1900.
SPEAR, ROSCOE.
Naval Cadet, 23 May, 1890. Ensign, 1 July, 1896. Lieutenant, Junior Grade, 1 July, 1899.
SPEAR, TRUMAN W.
Mate, 4 August, 1862. Dismissed 6 October, 1862.
SPEAR, W. M.
Civil Engineer, 28 September, 1865. Died 26 July, 1873.
SPEDDEN, EDWARD T.
Midshipman, 20 November, 1848. Passed Midshipman, 15 June, 1854. Master, 15 September, 1855. Lieutenant, 16 September, 1855. Died 3 March, 1861.
SPEDDEN, ROBERT.
Midshipman, 2 April, 1804. Lieutenant, 9 December, 1814. Resigned 4 December, 1823.
SPEEL, JOHN N.
Assistant Paymaster, 1 July, 1875. Passed Assistant Paymaster, 15 May, 1879. Paymaster, 24 November, 1891.
SPEIDEN, WILLIAM.
Purser, 30 August, 1837. Died 18 December, 1861.
SPEIGHTS, HENRY W.
Acting Third Assistant Engineer, 7 February, 1865. Honorably discharged 24 August, 1869.
SPEIGHTS, JAMES EDWARD.
Third Assistant Engineer, 12 August, 1862. Dropped 21 March, 1868.
SPEIGHTS, THOMAS G.
Mate, 8 May, 1862. Appointment revoked (sick) 17 September, 1863.
SPEIRS, JAMES.
Acting Third Assistant Engineer, 18 December, 1863. Resigned 10 June, 1865.
SPENCE, G. K.
Purser, 8 April, 1814. Last appearance on Records of Navy Department, 1816. Sloop Ontario.
SPENCE, HENRY J.
Acting Third Assistant Engineer, 18 August, 1864. Resigned 6 June, 1865.
SPENCE, KEITH.
Purser, 10 May, 1800. Last appearance on Records of Navy Department, September, 1805.
SPENCE, ROBERT T.
Midshipman, 15 May, 1800. Lieutenant, 17 February, 1807. Commander, 24 July, 1813. Captain, 28 February, 1815. Died 26 September, 1826.
SPENCE, STEPHEN D.
Midshipman, 9 September, 1841. Resigned 16 March, 1849.
SPENCER, CHARLES B.
Acting Second Assistant Engineer, 27 May, 1861. Resigned 5 August, 1861.
SPENCER, FREDERICK C.
Assistant Engineer (Spanish-American War), 22 June, 1898. Honorably discharged 26 August, 1898.

33

SPENCER, GEORGE.
Mate, 18 November, 1861. Resigned 14 June, 1864.
SPENCER, J. C.
Assistant Surgeon, 16 December, 1828. Surgeon, 20 December, 1837. Resigned 19 April, 1847.
SPENCER, J. C.
Purser, 21 August, 1843. Died 29 December, 1845.
SPENCER, JOHN L.
Midshipman, 1 June, 1826. Resigned 20 April, 1833.
SPENCER, LEMUEL.
Midshipman, 30 November, 1814. Resigned 5 July, 1815.
SPENCER, LEVI T.
Second Assistant Engineer, 3 June, 1844. Resigned 18 November, 1845.
SPENCER, P. D.
Midshipman, 1 December, 1810. Resigned 9 June, 1812.
SPENCER, PHILIP.
Midshipman, 20 November, 1841. Died 1 December, 1842.
SPENCER, THOMAS C.
Midshipman, 24 July, 1866. Graduated 7 June, 1870. Ensign, 13 July, 1871. Master, 4 June, 1874. Died 13 January, 1875.
SPENCER, THOMAS S.
Acting Midshipman, 29 September, 1854. Midshipman, 9 June, 1859. Lieutenant, 31 August, 1861. Lieutenant-Commander, 3 March, 1866. Resigned 25 April, 1867.
SPENCER, T. W.
Acting Ensign, 2 March, 1863. Honorably discharged 17 August, 1865.
SPENCER, W. C.
Midshipman, 1 December, 1827. Passed Midshipman, 10 June, 1833. Cashiered 10 April, 1837.
SPENCER, WILLIAM A.
Midshipman, 15 November, 1809. Lieutenant, 9 December, 1814. Commander, 3 March, 1831. Captain, 22 January, 1841. Resigned 9 December, 1843.
SPENCER, WILLIAM B.
Mate, 13 July, 1864. Acting Ensign, 11 March, 1865. Resigned 24 September, 1866.
SPERRY, CHARLES.
Midshipman, 16 March, 1833. Resigned 1 April, 1836.
SPERRY, CHARLES.
Midshipman, 1 April, 1828. Dismissed 21 April, 1831.
SPERRY, CHARLES S.
Midshipman, 26 September, 1862. Graduated June, 1866. Ensign, 12 March, 1868. Master, 26 March, 1869. Lieutenant, 21 March, 1870. Lieutenant-Commander, 1 March, 1885. Commander, 22 June, 1894. Captain, 1 July, 1900.
SPERRY, JACOB F.
Midshipman, 27 March, 1839. Resigned 28 January, 1842.
SPERRY, ROBERT J.
Mate, 13 May, 1864. Honorably discharged 27 December, 1865. Mate, 18 April, 1866. Mustered out 12 September, 1868.
SPEYERS, ARTHUR B.
Acting Midshipman, 24 July, 1863. Graduated June, 1868. Master, 12 July, 1870. Lieutenant, 23 May, 1874. Lieutenant-Commander, 28 December, 1895. Commander, 3 March, 1899.
SPICER, WILLIAM F.
Midshipman, 21 June, 1839. Passed Midshipman, 2 July, 1845. Master, 28 June, 1853. Lieutenant, 25 February, 1854. Lieutenant-Commander, 16 July, 1862. Commander, 2 January, 1863. Captain, 22 April, 1870. Commodore, 25 April, 1877. Died 29 November, 1878.
SPICKNALL, JOSEPH.
Midshipman, 1 January, 1812. Last appearance on Records of Navy Department, 1815. Wilmington, N. C.
SPIER, JOHN.
Sailmaker, 6 June, 1816. Resigned 10 February, 1819.
SPIES, GEORGE W.
Acting Third Assistant Engineer, 19 September, 1862. Appointment revoked (sick) 3 February, 1863.
SPILLMAN, JAMES.
Master, 3 February, 1815. Last appearance on Records of Navy Department, 1820. Furloughed.
SPILLMAN, L. L.
Midshipman, 19 August, 1823. Resigned 3 September, 1829.
SPILMAN, JOHN A.
Naval Cadet, 20 May, 1896. Graduated 30 June, 1900.
SPINNEY, A. L.
Mate, 21 October, 1864. Honorably discharged 6 July, 1865.
SPINNEY, JOSEPH.
Acting Master, 2 August, 1861. Resigned 22 January, 1862.
SPONGBERG, CHARLES.
Acting Third Assistant Engineer, 28 April, 1863. Drowned 6 December, 1863.
SPOONER, CHARLES W.
Mate, 13 August, 1863. Acting Ensign, 12 February, 1864. Resigned 22 March, 1865.
SPOONER, GEORGE W.
Midshipman, 15 November, 1809. Lieutenant, 4 February, 1815. Died 31 May, 1817.
SPOONER, HENRY W.
Third Assistant Engineer, 16 February, 1852. Second Assistant Engineer, 27 July, 1855. First Assistant Engineer, 21 July, 1858. Resigned 23 May, 1859.

GENERAL NAVY REGISTER. 515

SPOTSWOOD, CHARLES F. M.
　Midshipman, 1 November, 1828. Passed Midshipman, 14 June, 1834. Lieutenant, 25 February, 1841. Dismissed 18 April, 1861.
SPOTSWOOD, GEORGE W.
　Midshipman, 15 July, 1799. Dismissed 14 May, 1803.
SPOTSWOOD, J. A.
　Commander, 15 February, 1800. Discharged 4 June, 1801, under Peace Establishment Act.
SPOTSWOOD, W. A. W.
　Assistant Surgeon, 2 December, 1828. Surgeon, 20 February, 1838. Resigned 12 January, 1861.
SPOTTS, JAMES H.
　Midshipman, 2 August, 1837. Passed Midshipman, 29 June, 1843. Master, 8 April, 1851. Lieutenant, 21 November, 1851. Commander, 16 July, 1862. Captain, 25 July, 1866. Commodore, 25 September, 1873. Rear-Admiral, 28 May, 1881. Died 9 March, 1882.
SPRAGUE, ALBERT L.
　Midshipman, 11 April, 1862. Graduated June, 1866. Ensign, 12 March, 1868. Master, Retired List, 26 March, 1869. Died 18 November, 1873.
SPRAGUE, EDWARD P.
　Acting Second Assistant Engineer, 12 January, 1863. Acting First Assistant Engineer, 2 August, 1865. Appointment revoked 30 July, 1866.
SPRAGUE, FRANK J.
　Cadet Midshipman, 29 September, 1874. Graduated 4 June, 1880. Ensign, 10 March, 1882. Resigned 15 April, 1884.
SPRAGUE, HORACE B.
　Mate, 10 April, 1863. Resigned 8 May, 1863. Mate, 13 January, 1864. Honorably discharged 5 August, 1865.
SPRAGUE, JAMES P.
　Third Assistant Engineer, 17 February, 1860. Second Assistant Engineer, 1 November, 1861. First Assistant Engineer, 1 March, 1864. Chief Engineer, 5 March, 1871. Died 15 September, 1881.
SPRAGUE, THOMAS.
　Assistant Surgeon, 24 July, 1813. Last appearance on Records of Navy Department, 1815. Frigate President.
SPRAGUE, WILLIAM.
　Acting First Assistant Engineer, 24 May, 1864. Honorably discharged 9 February, 1866.
SPRAGUE, WILLIAM H.
　Mate, 27 July, 1863. Resigned 26 May, 1864. Mate, 11 July, 1864. Resigned 25 May, 1865.
SPRATLING, LECKINSKI W.
　Assistant Surgeon, 16 April, 1890. Passed Assistant Surgeon, 16 April, 1893.
SPRIGG, HORACE S.
　Midshipman, 2 April, 1804. Resigned 17 May, 1810.
SPRIGG, JAMES.
　Midshipman, 16 January, 1809. Last appearance on Records of Navy Department, 20 March, 1809.
SPRIGGS, JOHN.
　Lieutenant, 28 December, 1804. Dismissed 28 April, 1805.
SPRIGMAN, JAMES H.
　Mate, 4 June, 1862. Resigned 13 January, 1863.
SPRINGER, CHARLES H.
　Midshipman, 1 September, 1811. Lieutenant, 27 April, 1816. Died 25 May, 1820.
SPRINGER, E. D.
　Acting Ensign, 11 August, 1864. Honorably discharged 11 December, 1865.
SPRINGER, JAMES.
　Boatswain, 13 August, 1833. Died 6 September, 1837.
SPROGELL, SYLVANUS.
　Midshipman, 16 January, 1809. Drowned 21 October, 1810.
SPROSTON, GEORGE S.
　Mate, 12 November, 1869. Appointment revoked 26 April, 1871.
SPROSTON, GEORGE S.
　Assistant Surgeon, 8 November, 1813. Surgeon, 27 March, 1818. Died 27 January, 1842.
SPROSTON, GEORGE S.
　Acting Assistant Paymaster, 27 September, 1862. Mustered out 15 January, 1867.
SPROSTON, JOHN G.
　Midshipman, 15 July, 1846. Passed Midshipman, 8 June, 1852. Master, 15 September, 1855. Lieutenant, 16 September, 1855. Killed 8 June, 1862.
SQUIBB, EDWARD R.
　Assistant Surgeon, 26 April, 1847. Resigned 4 December, 1857.
SQUIRE, WILLIAM H.
　Acting Carpenter, 20 February, 1900.
SQUIER, JESSE M.
　Mate (Spanish-American War), 22 June, 1898. Honorably discharged 13 September, 1898.
SQUIRES, THEORON W.
　Mate, 9 February, 1862. Dismissed 13 August, 1862.
STAATES, E. M.
　Acting First Assistant Engineer, 28 May, 1861. Resigned 29 November, 1861.
STAATS, PETER P.
　Acting Third Assistant Engineer, 20 January, 1862. Resigned 14 November, 1862.
STACKHOUSE, GEORGE M.
　Assistant Paymaster, 13 April, 1899.

GENERAL NAVY REGISTER.

STAFFORD, GEORGE H.
Cadet Midshipman, 10 June, 1874. Graduated 4 June, 1880. Ensign, Junior Grade, 3 March, 1883. Ensign, 13 October, 1883. Lieutenant, Junior Grade, 28 February, 1890. Lieutenant, 7 September, 1894.

STAFFORD, JAMES C.
Acting Master, 22 November, 1861. Resigned 21 February, 1863.

STAHL, ALBERT WILLIAM.
Cadet Engineer, Naval Academy, 14 September, 1876. Graduated 10 June, 1880. Assistant Engineer, 10 June, 1882. Assistant Naval Constructor, 11 August, 1887. Naval Constructor, 9 July, 1892.

STAHL, HENRY.
Acting Ensign, 5 September, 1862. Honorably discharged 15 May, 1865.

STAIGG, ALFRED.
Mate, 18 November, 1861. Acting Ensign, 23 February, 1865. Honorably discharged 30 September, 1865.

STALL, ROMEO E.
Acting Second Assistant Engineer, 14 June, 1862. Acting First Assistant Engineer, 2 March, 1864. Honorably discharged 19 December, 1867.

STALLINGS, C. T.
Midshipman, 16 January, 1809. Lieutenant, 9 December, 1814. Last appearance on Records of Navy Department, 1822. Baltimore.

STALLINGS, JOSEPH.
Midshipman, 10 May, 1820. Lieutenant, 17 May, 1829. Died 25 April, 1841.

STALLINGS, OTHO.
Midshipman, 18 June, 1812. Lieutenant, 28 March, 1820. Died 12 January, 1825.

STAMM, WILLIAM S.
Third Assistant Engineer, 26 February, 1851. Second Assistant Engineer, 21 May, 1863. First Assistant Engineer, 9 May, 1857. Chief Engineer, 29 July, 1861. Retired List, 1 December, 1887. Died 27 June, 1897.

STANCLIFFE, H. TRUMBULL.
Acting Assistant Paymaster, 20 January, 1865. Assistant Paymaster, 21 February, 1867. Passed Assistant Paymaster, 19 May, 1869. Paymaster, 2 April, 1882. Retired List, 6 April, 1894.

STANDISH, FREDERICK D.
Ensign (Spanish-American War), 9 May, 1898. Honorably discharged 30 August, 1898.

STANDLEY, WILLIAM H.
Naval Cadet, 7 September, 1891. Ensign, 1 July, 1897. Lieutenant, Junior Grade, 1 July, 1900.

STANDWOOD, NATHANIEL.
Master, 2 January, 1800. Discharged 30 April, 1801, under Peace Establishment Act.

STANFIELD, THOMAS.
Mate, 13 June, 1863. Honorably discharged 22 July, 1865.

STANFORD, HOMER R.
Civil Engineer, 20 May, 1898.

STANFORD, JOHN J.
Sailmaker, 4 November, 1848. Retired List, 7 November, 1874. Died 11 April, 1879.

STANFORD, THOMAS.
Purser, 8 January, 1800. Discharged 20 July, 1801, under Peace Establishment Act.

STANLEY, CHARLES.
Mate, 13 November, 1863. Acting Ensign, 29 January, 1864. Dismissed 14 April, 1864.

STANLEY, CHARLES.
Acting Third Assistant Engineer, 20 March, 1865. Honorably discharged 4 September, 1865.

STANLEY, CHARLES J.
Acting Ensign, 13 August, 1863. Resigned 19 November, 1863.

STANLEY, JAMES G.
Midshipman, 30 April, 1831. Resigned 11 February, 1836.

STANLEY, THOMAS.
Gunner, 16 August,1823. Resigned 16 November, 1831.

STANLEY, THOMAS.
Boatswain, 19 June, 1798. Discharged 15 June, 1799.

STANLEY, THOMAS C.
Chaplain, 27 February, 1847. Resigned 26 September, 1853.

STANLY, FABIUS.
Midshipman, 20 December, 1831. Passed Midshipman, 15 June, 1837. Lieutenant, 8 September, 1841. Reserved List, 13 September, 1855. Lieutenant on Active List, 8 September, 1841. Commander, 19 May, 1861. Captain, 25 July, 1866. Commodore, 1 July, 1870. Rear-Admiral, 12 February, 1874. Retired List, 4 June, 1874. Died 5 December, 1882.

STANNARD, JOSEPH E.
Acting Master, 22 November, 1861. Acting Volunteer Lieutenant, 8 April, 1865. Honorably discharged 15 January, 1866.

STANNARD, WILLIAM A.
Mate, 11 June, 1863. Acting Ensign, 23 February, 1865. Honorably discharged 18 June, 1867.

STANNARD, WILLIAM M.
Acting Master, 25 January, 1862. Honorably discharged 10 September, 1866.

STANSBURY, JOHN.
Midshipman, 16 January, 1809. Killed in action 11 September, 1814.

STANTON, CHARLES F.
Acting Ensign, 1 October, 1862. Resigned 24 July, 1863. Acting Ensign, 12 February, 1864. Appointment revoked 7 August, 1864.

STANTON, CURTIS.
Acting Third Assistant Engineer, 18 September, 1863. Acting Second Assistant Engineer, 10 December, 1864. Honorably discharged 26 March, 1869.

GENERAL NAVY REGISTER. 517

STANTON, OSCAR F.
Midshipman, 29 December, 1849. Passed Midshipman, 12 June, 1855. Master, 16 September, 1855. Lieutenant, 2 April, 1856. Lieutenant-Commander, 16 July, 1862. Commander, 12 December, 1867. Captain, 11 June, 1879. Commodore, 19 May, 1891. Rear-Admiral, 21 July, 1894. Retired List, 30 July, 1894.
STANTON, JOSIAH R.
Assistant Paymaster, 25 March, 1870. Passed Assistant Paymaster, 25 November, 1877. Paymaster, 26 March, 1889. Pay Inspector, 20 January, 1900.
STANWORTH, CHARLES S.
Cadet Engineer, 1 October, 1881. Ensign, 1 July, 1887. Lieutenant, Junior Grade, 29 April, 1896. Lieutenant, 3 March, 1899.
STAPLEFORD, JAMES W.
Acting Master, 24 March, 1862. Honorably discharged 21 February, 1865.
STAPLES, CHARLES B.
Mate, 4 April, 1862. Acting Ensign, 18 August, 1863. Honorably discharged 19 September, 1865.
STAPLES, JAMES C.
Mate, 24 October, 1861. Acting Ensign, 5 January, 1863. Honorably discharged 15 September, 1865.
STAPLES, JOHN L.
Mate, 14 May, 1862. Gunner, 16 July, 1862. Died 27 June, 1871.
STAPLES, J. H.
Acting Master's Mate, 24 October, 1861. Resigned 12 June, 1862.
STAPLES, WILLIAM C.
Acting Master, 22 November, 1861. Honorably discharged 15 November, 1865.
STAPLETON, JESSE J.
Acting Ensign, 19 March, 1863. Promoted Acting Master, 9 April, 1863. Appointment revoked 3 February, 1864.
STARBUCK, ALLEN W.
Acting Ensign, 31 March, 1864. Appointment revoked (sick) 8 November, 1864.
STARBUCK, DANIEL JOY.
Acting Ensign, 9 May, 1864. Honorably discharged 22 November, 1865.
STARK, DANIEL.
Acting Ensign, 25 October, 1864. Honorably discharged 19 August, 1865.
STARKE, ROBERT B.
Assistant Surgeon, 18 April, 1800. Surgeon, 28 June, 1809. Last appearance on Records of Navy Department, 16 March, 1810.
STARKE, THOMAS.
Assistant Surgeon, 9 July, 1800. Last appearance on Records of Navy Department.
STARKEY, JOHN L.
Acting Third Assistant Engineer, 6 October, 1864. Honorably discharged 21 July, 1865.
STARR, CHARLES H.
Midshipman, 3 November, 1818. Resigned 11 November, 1823.
STARR, COLIN C.
Mate, 4 November, 1861. Acting Ensign, 13 January, 1863. Resigned 23 November, 1864.
STARR, JOHN B.
Acting Ensign, 17 August, 1864. Honorably discharged 27 November, 1865.
STARR, JOHN P.
Acting Second Assistant Engieer, 14 July, 1864. Dismissed 21 October, 1864.
STARR, JOB V.
Acting First Assistant Engineer, 1 October, 1862. Acting Chief Engineer, 31 March, 1863. Honorably discharged 24 January, 1867.
STARR, PHINEAS R.
Acting Ensign, 1 October, 1862. Dismissed 3 June, 1864.
STARR, WILLIAM C.
Third Assistant Engineer, 17 February, 1860. Resigned 28 May, 1862.
STARRETT, ADRIAN C.
Gunner, 31 August, 1859. Acting Master, 13 December, 1862. Honorably discharged 13 September, 1865.
STATTON, THOMAS.
Midshipman, 4 July, 1805. Dismissed 16 September, 1805.
STAUFFER, DAVID M.
Mate, 5 January, 1864. Acting Ensign, 25 May, 1865. Honorably discharged 1 November, 1865.
STAUNTON, SIDNEY A.
Midshipman, 23 September, 1867. Graduated 6 June, 1871. Ensign, 14 July, 1872. Master, 4 February, 1875. Lieutenant-Commander, 3 March, 1899.
STAVEY, NICHOLAS H.
Assistant Paymaster, 4 December, 1869. Retired List, 1 September, 1876.
STAYTON, WILLIAM H.
Lieutenant (Spanish-American War), 18 June, 1898. Honorably discharged 28 October, 1898.
St. CLAIR, ARTHUR.
Midshipman, 15 November, 1798. Discharged as Lieutenant, 12 October, 1801.
STEADMAN, GEORGE C.
Acting Third Assistant Engineer, 30 December, 1862. Honorably discharged 21 August, 1865.
STEADMAN, HORACE B.
Acting Third Assistant Engineer, 17 May, 1864. Honorably discharged 21 July, 1865.
STEARNS, BEN W.
Naval Cadet, 17 May, 1883. Graduated 10 June, 1887. Honorably discharged 30 June, 1889.

STEARNS, CLARK D.
Naval Cadet, 5 September, 1887. Ensign, 1 July, 1893. Lieutenant, Junior Grade, 3 March, 1899. Lieutenant, 22 September, 1899.
STEARNS, DAVID.
Acting Master, 14 August, 1861. Died from wounds received in action 30 June, 1862.
STEARNS, J. B.
Midshipman, 28 September, 1814. Resigned 25 October, 1817.
STEARNS, WILLIAM, Jr.
Midshipman, 1 May, 1828. Resigned 11 February, 1832.
STEBBINS, A. W.
Midshipman, 25 April, 1838. Resigned 15 April, 1842. Midshipman, 27 April, 1842. Resigned 20 September, 1842.
STEBBINS, AUGUSTUS G.
Acting Ensign, 25 August, 1862. Lost in Bainbridge, 21 August, 1863.
STEBBINS, De WAYNE.
Mate, 15 September, 1862. Acting Ensign, 1 October, 1862. Acting Master, 22 July, 1864. Honorably discharged 29 November, 1865.
STEBBINS, JAMES H.
Acting Third Assistant Engineer, 4 May, 1863. Resigned 6 October, 1863.
STEBBINS, L. C.
Acting Assistant Paymaster, 16 May, 1864. Honorably discharged 4 November, 1865.
STEDMAN, CHARLES E.
Assistant Surgeon, 16 September, 1861. Resigned 27 April, 1865.
STEDMAN, EDWARD M.
Midshipman, 27 September, 1861. Graduated November, 1864. Ensign, 1 November, 1866. Master, 1 December, 1866. Lieutenant, 12 March, 1868. Lieutenant-Commander, 26 March, 1869. Retired List, 10 February, 1875.
STEDMAN, FRANCIS D.
Third Assistant Engineer, 19 January, 1863. Second Assistant Engineer, 20 June, 1864. Resigned 6 October, 1866.
STEDMEN, ROBERT S.
Third Assistant Engineer, 17 March, 1863. Resigned 5 April, 1865.
STEECE, TECUMSEH.
Midshipman, 26 September, 1857. Midshipman, 1 June, 1861. Lieutenant, 16 July, 1862. Died 15 July, 1864.
STEED, ROBERT.
Midshipman, 10 February, 1819. Died 4 September, 1823.
STEEDMAN, CHARLES.
Midshipman, 1 April, 1828. Passed Midshipman, 14 June, 1834. Lieutenant, 25 February, 1841. Commander, 14 September, 1855. Captain, 13 December, 1862. Commodore, 25 July, 1866. Rear-Admiral, 25 May, 1871. Retired List, 24 September, 1873. Died 13 November, 1890.
STEEL, HUGH.
Midshipman, 15 November, 1809. Dismissed 25 February, 1811.
STEEL, ISAAC.
Sailmaker, 6 July, 1798. Resigned 2 August, 1806.
STEEL, JOHN H.
Assistant Surgeon, 10 December, 1814. Resigned 8 July, 1818.
STEEL, THOMAS S.
Acting Master, 24 September, 1861. Dismissed 15 May, 1863.
STEELE, ARTHUR G.
Acting Third Assistant Engineer, 14 April, 1865. Died 9 October, 1867.
STEELE, GEORGE W., Jr.
Naval Cadet, 3 June, 1896. Graduated 30 June, 1900.
STEELE, HENRY A.
Midshipman, 1 November, 1826. Passed Midshipman, 28 April, 1832. Lieutenant, 27 February, 1837. Reserved List, 13 September, 1855. Died 29 June, 1858.
STEELE, JOHN F.
Purser, 29 August, 1845. Died 20 July, 1860.
STEELE, JOHN M.
Passed Assistant Surgeon, 30 April, 1880. Surgeon, 11 May, 1893.
STEELE, J. MURRAY.
Assistant Surgeon, 18 June, 1875.
STEELE, ROBERT.
Mate, 18 April, 1864. Resigned 12 June, 1866. Mate, 28 September, 1866. Honorably discharged 12 April, 1868.
STEELE, ROBERT E.
Chaplain, 27 June, 1898.
STEELE, ROBERT S.
Midshipman, 28 June, 1804. Resigned 1 October, 1810.
STEELE, ROBERT W.
Assistant Naval Constructor, 24 May, 1871. Naval Constructor, 13 March, 1875. Retired List, 13 April, 1893.
STEELE, RUSH C.
Acting Warrant Machinist, 23 August, 1899.
STEELE, THOMAS B.
Assistant Surgeon, 5 March, 1847. Surgeon, 29 August, 1860. Resigned 21 April, 1861.
STEELE, WILLIAM.
Midshipman, 1 January, 1812. Last appearance on Records of Navy Department, 1818. Furloughed.
STEELE, WILLIAM.
Assistant Surgeon, 13 March, 1807. Resigned 29 August, 1810.

GENERAL NAVY REGISTER. 519

STEEN, GEOGRE A.
Mate, 21 January, 1864. Ensign, 6 September, 1864. Honorably discharged 6 November, 1866.
STEERS, THOMAS.
Acting Third Assistant Engineer, 14 April, 1865. Honorably discharged 10 August, 1865.
STEEVER, CHARLES L.
Acting Third Assistant Engineer, 21 May, 1864. Acting Second Assistant Engineer, 25 February, 1865. Resigned 18 December, 1865.
STEEVER, HENRY K.
Acting Third Assistant Engineer, 1 February, 1862. Appointment revoked 21 July, 1862. Acting Third Assistant Engineer, 9 October, 1862. Acting Second Assistant Engineer, 1 February, 1865. Honorably discharged 23 January, 1866. Acting Second Assistant Engineer, 26 March, 1866. Mustered out 27 August, 1867.
STEIGER, WALTER H.
Assistant Engineer (Spanish-American War), 14 May, 1898. Honorably discharged 22 April, 1899.
STEIGHER, JOHN J.
Acting Third Assistant Engineer, 5 August, 1861. Resigned 7 June, 1862.
DE STEIGUER, LOUIS R.
Naval Cadet, 17 March, 1885. Ensign, 1 July, 1891. Lieutenant, Junior Grade, 22 November, 1898. Lieutenant, 3 March, 1899.
STEIN, EDWARD M.
Assistant Engineer, 30 July, 1861. Surgeon, 12 May, 1866. Died 13 July, 1877.
STEINBOGH, NICHOLAS.
Boatswain, 16 August, 1838. Died 20 November, 1840.
STEINBRENNER, AUGUST C.
Acting Gunner, 1 August, 1900.
STEINHAUER, G. W.
Midshipman, 18 February, 1800. Discharged 12 October, 1801, under Peace Establishment Act.
STEINS, GEORGE A.
Mate, 20 October, 1861. Acting Ensign, 23 May, 1864. Honorably discharged 8 August, 1865.
STELL, JOHN.
Third Assistant Engineer, 18 November, 1862. Resigned 18 September, 1863.
STELLWAGEN, D. C.
Master, 14 May, 1814. Died 16 November, 1828.
STELLWAGEN, HENRY S.
Midshipman, 1 April, 1828. Passed Midshipman, 14 June, 1834. Lieutenant, 2 July, 1840. Commander, 14 September, 1855. Captain, 29 August, 1862. Retired List, 24 December, 1865. Died 15 July, 1866.
STELLWAGEN, THOMAS C.
Acting Assistant Paymaster, 25 September, 1861. Resigned 4 June, 1863.
STEMBEL, ROGER N.
Midshipman, 27 March, 1832. Passed Midshipman, 23 June, 1838. Lieutenant, 26 October, 1843. Commander, 1 July, 1861. Captain, 25 July, 1866. Commodore, 13 July, 1870. Retired List, 27 December, 1872. Rear-Admiral, Retired List, 5 June, 1874. Died 20 November, 1900.
STENSON, J. FENWICK.
Midshipman, 15 December, 1837. Passed Midshipman, 29 June, 1843. Master, 24 December, 1850. Lieutenant, 29 August, 1851. Resigned 20 February, 1854.
STEPHEN, DAVID.
Mate, 20 November, 1862. Acting Ensign, 20 May, 1863. Resigned 29 March, 1865.
STEPHENS, ALEXANDER W.
Sailmaker, 15 August, 1873. Retired List, 10 December, 1883.
STEPHENS, AMMIE.
Acting Third Assistant Engineer, 5 May, 1863. Honorably discharged 28 August, 1865.
STEPHENS, DOUGLASS H.
Acting Midshipman, 1 October, 1850. Dropped 12 June, 1851.
STEPHENS, ELIHU.
Acting Third Assistant Engineer, 1 October, 1862. Acting Second Assistant Engineer, 28 January, 1863. Dismissed 17 June, 1863.
STEPHENS, JACOB.
Sailmaker, 30 September, 1844. Retired List, 20 June, 1868. Died 14 October, 1881.
STEPHENS, THOMAS A.
Third Assistant Engineer, 11 January, 1849. Second Assistant Engineer, 26 February, 1851. Resigned 6 September, 1853. Second Assistant Engineer, 13 May, 1861. Died 9 August, 1864.
STEPHENSON, ALEXANDER.
Gunner, 6 January, 1832. Died 9 May, 1847.
STEPHENSON, CHARLES A.
Acting Gunner, 7 January, 1862. Appointment revoked 12 June, 1863.
STEPHENSON, FRANKLIN BACHE.
Assistant Surgeon, 14 March, 1873. Passed Assistant Surgeon, 21 April, 1877. Surgeon, 15 September, 1888. Medical Inspector, 31 May, 1900.
STEPHENSON, GEORGE B.
Acting Master, 12 August, 1861. Resigned 16 May, 1862. Mate, 7 April, 1863. Acting Ensign, 23 July, 1863. Acting Master, 3 March, 1864. Dismissed 21 May, 1864.
STEPHENSON, JOHN F.
Mate, 14 June, 1862. Resigned 8 February, 1866.
STEPHENSON, J. W.
Midshipman, 1 May, 1822. Resigned 5 July, 1822.

STEPHENSON, RICHARD.
　Gunner, 1 December, 1802.　Last appearance on Records of Navy Department, 31 October, 1803.
STEPLETON, JESSE J.
　Acting Master, 9 April, 1863.　Appointment revoked (sick) 3 February, 1864.
STEPP, JACOB.
　Assistant Surgeon (Spanish-American War), 8 July, 1898.　Appointed Assistant Surgeon, in Regular Service 7 June, 1900.
STERRETT, ANDREW.
　Lieutenant, 25 March, 1798.　Resigned 29 June, 1805.
STERRETT, ISAAC S.
　Midshipman, 24 March, 1819.　Lieutenant, 17 May, 1828.　Commander, 5 February 1850.　Reserved List, 28 September, 1855.　Captain, 2 March, 1857.　Resigned 23 April, 1861.
STERRETT, WILLIAM M.
　Mate, 12 September, 1864.　Resigned 20 May, 1865.
STETSON, JOSEPH F.
　Acting Ensign, 19 September, 1864.　Resigned 10 May, 1865.
STEUART, A. M.
　Midshipman, 9 November, 1813.　Last appearance on Records of Navy Department 1818 Furloughed.
STEUART, EDWARD H.
　Master, 11 July, 1812.　Resigned 23 September, 1813.
STEUART, E. H.
　Midshipman, 4 July, 1805.　Resigned 28 June, 1809.
STEVENS, ABRAHAM L.
　Mate, 14 March, 1864.　Honorably discharged 20 October, 1865.
STEVENS, BENJAMIN R.
　Third Assistant Engineer, 23 June, 1863.　Lost on the Patapsco, 15 June, 1865.
STEVENS, CALVIN.
　Midshipman, 9 April, 1800.　Discharged 15 April, 1801, under Peace Establishment Act.
STEVENS, CHARLES G.
　Acting Second Assistant Engineer, 6 January, 1862.　Resigned 16 March, 1865.
STEVENS, CLEMENT W.
　Midshipman, 9 June, 1811.　Lieutenant, 5 March, 1817.　Resigned 13 September, 1823.
STEVENS, FRANCIS P.
　Mate, 15 November, 1861.　Acting Ensign, 24 May, 1864.　Honorably discharged 1 December, 1865.
STEVENS, FREDERICK.
　Purser, 13 September, 1841.　Died 14 July, 1843.
STEVENS, GEORGE A.
　Midshipman, 13 May, 1840.　Passed Midshipman, 11 July, 1846.　Master, 1 March, 1855.　Lieutenant, 14 September, 1855.　Lieutenant-Commander, 16 July, 1862.　Retired List, 20 October, 1865.　Commander, Retired List, 4 April, 1867.　Commander, Active List, 23 May, 1871.　Captain, 2 July, 1882.　Retired List, 24 November, 1883.　Died 16 February, 1892.
STEVENS, GEORGE H.
　Acting Carpenter, 1 October, 1862.　Honorably discharged 4 October, 1865.
STEVENS, HENRY.
　Acting Master and Pilot, 1 October, 1864.　Honorably discharged 5 July, 1865.
STEVENS, HENRY K.
　Midshipman, 2 March, 1839.　Passed Midshipman, 2 July, 1845.　Master, 22 March, 1853.　Lieutenant, 16 January, 1854.　Dismissed 30 September, 1861.
STEVENS, HERBERT E.
　Assistant Paymaster (Spanish-American War), 30 April, 1898.　Honorably discharged 30 January, 1899.　Assistant Paymaster (Regular Navy), 5 July, 1899.
STEVENS, ISAAC.
　Gunner, date not known.　Last appearance on Records of Navy Department, 14 May, 1803.
STEVENS, JAMES.
　Carpenter, 8 April, 1815.　Last appearance on Records of Navy Department, 1820.
STEVENS, JOHN.
　Midshipman, 8 March, 1800.　Discharged 28 April, 1801, under Peace Establishment Act.
STEVENS, JOHN C.
　Third Assistant Engineer, 24 February, 1862.　Second Assistant Engineer, 15 October, 1863.　Resigned 25 October, 1866.
STEVENS, JOSEPH.
　Master, 3 May, 1812.　Died in 1820.
STEVENS, JOSEPH.
　Acting Assistant Surgeon, 11 March, 1862.　Resigned 5 December, 1864.
STEVENS, RICHARD.
　Assistant Surgeon, 28 December, 1818.　Resigned 11 May, 1826.
STEVENS, ROBERT D.
　Midshipman, 25 June, 1867.　Graduated 6 June, 1871.　Died 5 January, 1874.
STEVENS, ROBERT E.
　Mate, 27 November, 1861.　Resigned 23 December, 1862.
STEVENS, RUEL J.
　Acting Assistant Engineer, 9 October, 1861.　Discharged 12 March, 1863.
STEVENS, THOMAS.
　Mate, 4 November, 1861.　Acting Ensign, 29 February, 1864.　Died of wounds 19 January, 1865.
STEVENS, THOMAS H.
　Midshipman, 1 October, 1863.　Graduated June, 1868.　Master, 12 July, 1870.　Lieutenant, 6 January, 1874.　Lieutenant-Commander, 2 February, 1896.　Commander, 3 March, 1899.

GENERAL NAVY REGISTER. 521

STEVENS, THOMAS H.
  Lieutenant, 24 July, 1813. Commander, 3 March, 1825. Captain, 27 January, 1836. Died 22 January, 1841.
STEVENS, THOMAS H.
  Midshipman, 14 December, 1836. Passed Midshipman, 1 July, 1842. Master, 25 July, 1848. Lieutenant, 10 May, 1849. Lieutenant on Active List, 10 May, 1849. Commander on Active List, 16 July, 1862. Captain, 25 July, 1866. Commodore, 20 November, 1872. Rear-Admiral, 27 October, 1879. Retired List, 27 May, 1881. Died 15 May, 1896.
STEVENS, WILLIAM H. H.
  Mate, 16 October, 1862. Resigned 17 February, 1864.
STEVENSON, BYRD W.
  Midshipman, 9 September, 1841. Dropped 18 December, 1854.
STEVENSON, HOLLAND N.
  Acting Third Assistant Engineer, under instruction, Naval Academy, 10 October, 1866. Third Assistant Engineer, 2 June, 1868. Second Assistant Engineer, 2 June, 1869. Passed Assistant Engineer, 13 December, 1874. Chief Engineer, 14 December, 1892. Rank changed to Commander, 3 March, 1899.
STEVENSON, JOHN.
  Midshipman, 1 February, 1814. Resigned 10 September, 1818.
STEVENSON, JOHN H.
  Acting Assistant Paymaster, 19 September, 1862. Paymaster, 13 June, 1863. Honorably discharged 8 November, 1865. Pay Inspector, 18 January, 1881. Retired List, 25 September, 1893. Died 14 June, 1899.
STEVENSON, JOHN K.
  Third Assistant Engineer, 20 May, 1863. Dismissed 2 August, 1869.
STEVENSON, LEWIS.
  Acting Third Assistant Engineer, 1 October, 1862. Resigned 24 October, 1862.
STEVENSON, WILBUR F.
  Carpenter, 27 July, 1892.
STEVENSON, WILLIAM.
  Master, 10 April, 1812. Died 28 August, 1813.
STEVENSON, WILLIAM T.
  Assistant Paymaster, 25 November, 1869. Resigned 8 August, 1872.
STEWART, ALBERT.
  Acting Third Assistant Engineer, 5 March, 1864. Honorably discharged 25 July, 1865.
STEWART, A. MURRAY.
  Acting Assistant Paymaster, 13 September, 1862. Mustered out 5 October, 1865.
STEWART, ANDREW.
  Midshipman, 8 November, 1803. Resigned 27 June, 1808.
STEWART, CHARLES.
  Lieutenant, 9 March, 1798. Commander, 19 May, 1804. Captain, 22 April, 1806. Reserved List, 14 September, 1855. Senior Flag Officer on Active List, 20 April, 1859. Retired List, 21 December, 1861. Rear-Admiral on Retired List, 16 July, 1862. Died 6 November, 1869.
STEWART, CHARLES.
  Acting Assistant Paymaster, 11 September, 1862. Mustered out 20 January, 1867.
STEWART, CHARLES A.
  Mate, 5 June, 1862. Acting Ensign, 31 August, 1863. Resigned 14 February, 1865. Acting Ensign, 16 March, 1865. Honorably discharged 21 January, 1868.
STEWART, CHARLES S.
  Chaplain, 1 November, 1828. Died 14 December, 1870.
STEWART, DAVID A.
  Midshipman, 23 October, 1862. Graduated June, 1866. Ensign, 12 March, 1868. Resigned 12 September, 1869.
STEWART, D. R.
  Midshipman, 1 February, 1814. Lieutenant, 13 January, 1825. Killed in a duel 6 August, 1835.
STEWART, EDWIN.
  Assistant Paymaster, 9 September, 1861. Paymaster, 14 April, 1862. Pay Inspector, 8 March, 1879. Pay Director, 12 September, 1891. Retired List, 5 May, 1899.
STEWART, HENRY.
  Assistant Surgeon, 22 October, 1868. Surgeon, 6 October, 1878. Retired List, 10 April, 1884.
STEWART, HENRY H.
  Third Assistant Engineer, 23 March, 1848. Second Assistant Engineer, 13 September, 1849. Irst Assistant Engineer, 26 February, 1851. Chief Engineer, 21 July, 1858. Retired List, 6 September, 1885. Died 2 May, 1893.
STEWART, JAMES M.
  Mate, 5 September, 1864. Honorably discharged 6 July, 1865.
STEWART, JOHN.
  Carpenter, date not known. Resigned in 1820.
STEWART, JOHN B.
  Midshipman, 9 September, 1841. Passed Midshipman, 10 August, 1847. Master, 14 September, 1855. Lieutenant, 15 September, 1855. Died 10 November, 1861.
STEWART, JOHN W.
  Midshipman, 29 September, 1870. Graduated 1 June, 1874. Ensign, 17 July, 1875. Master, 12 March, 1881. Lieutenant, Junior Grade, 3 March, 1883. Lieutenant, 1 March, 1887. Retired List, 26 May, 1898.
STEWART, RICHARD.
  Midshipman, 15 November, 1809. Resigned 1 March, 1824.
STEWART, ROBERT.
  Midshipman, 20 June, 1799. Lieutenant, 23 February, 1807. Last appearance on Records of Navy Department. Drowned.

STEWART, ROBERT, Jr.
  Cadet Engineer, 13 September, 1877. Assistant Engineer, 1 July, 1883. Retired List, 17 June, 1890.
STEWART, THOMAS.
  Gunner, 1 July, 1861. Retired List, 2 December, 1876. Died 14 October, 1892.
STEWART, THOMAS W.
  Mate, 5 August, 1864. Resigned 8 May, 1865.
STEWART, WALTER.
  Midshipman, 2 April, 1804. Lieutenant, 4 June, 1810. Died 12 April, 1817.
STEWART, WILLIAM.
  Acting Master and Pilot, 1 October, 1864. Honorably discharged 11 December, 1865.
STEWART, WILLIAM F.
  Acting Midshipman, 23 September, 1857. Midshipman, 1 June, 1861. Lieutenant, 16 July, 1862. Lieutenant-Commander, 25 July, 1866. Lost in the Oneida, 21 January, 1870.
STEWART, WILLIAM G.
  Midshipman, 25 November, 1802. Last appearance on Records of Navy Department. Dead.
STEWART, WILLIAM H.
  Chaplain, 10 March, 1863. Retired List, 11 July, 1893.
STEWART, WILLIAM M.
  Acting Second Assistant Engineer, 23 April, 1864. Honorably discharged 4 December, 1865.
STICHT, JOHN L.
  Naval Cadet, 7 September, 1889. Ensign, 1 July, 1895. Lieutenant, Junior Grade, 3 March, 1899.
STICKNEY, HERMAN O.
  Naval Cadet, 4 September, 1884. Assistant Engineer, 1 July, 1890. Passed Assistant Engineer, 27 June, 1896. Rank changed to Lieutenant, 3 March, 1899.
STICKNEY, JOHN E.
  Mate, 31 August, 1861. Acting Ensign, 9 June, 1863. Acting Master, 27 October, 1864. Honorably discharged 6 November, 1865.
STICKNEY, JOSEPH.
  Midshipman, 30 April, 1800. Discharged 6 July, 1801.
STICKNEY, JOSEPH L.
  Midshipman, 26 September, 1862. Graduated June, 1867. Ensign, 18 December, 1868. Master, 21 March, 1870. Resigned 6 September, 1871.
STILES, EDWARD A.
  Third Assistant Engineer, 8 September, 1863. Retired 24 October, 1866. Promoted to Second Assistant Engineer on Retired List, 15 July, 1867. Died 10 September, 1891.
STILES, EDWARD C.
  Midshipman, 13 December, 1839. Passed Midshipman, 2 July, 1845. Resigned 17 August, 1847.
STILES, TOWNSEND.
  Acting Master and Pilot, 14 May, 1861. Acting Volunteer Lieutenant, 25 June, 1863. Died 28 November, 1863.
STILES, WILLIAM H.
  Acting Third Assistant Engineer, 13 February, 1864. Resigned 21 April, 1865.
STILLINGS, SAMUEL V.
  Acting Third Assistant Engineer, 20 May, 1862. Acting Second Assistant Engineer, 16 January, 1864. Honorably discharged 8 November, 1866.
STILLMAN, J. B.
  Assistant Surgeon, 28 March, 1820. Died 24 March, 1825.
STILLSON, DANIEL C.
  Acting Third Assistant Engineer, 20 January, 1862. Resigned 22 July, 1862. Acting Second Assistant Engineer, 17 August, 1863. Acting First Assistant Engineer, 16 November, 1864. Honorably discharged 17 July, 1865.
STILLWELL, JAMES.
  Midshipman, 9 September, 1847. Passed Midshipman, 15 June, 1854. Master, 15 September, 1855. Lieutenant, 16 September, 1855. Lieutenant-Commander, 16 July, 1862. Resigned 21 December, 1867.
STILLWELL, RICHARD.
  Mate, 15 July, 1863. Resigned 18 December, 1863.
STIMERS, ALLEN C.
  Third Assistant Engineer, 11 January, 1849. Second Assistant Engineer, 26 February, 1851. First Assistant Engineer, 21 May, 1853. Chief Engineer, 21 July, 1858. Resigned 3 August, 1865.
STIMPSON, JAMES H.
  Acting Master, 8 April, 1862. Honorably discharged 20 December, 1867.
STIMPSON, MELVIN O.
  Acting Third Assistant Engineer, 20 November, 1862. Dismissed 2 August, 1864.
STIMSON, J. S.
  Acting Assistant Paymaster, 5 December, 1862. Mustered out 15 November, 1865.
STIMSON, JOHN W.
  Carpenter, 15 April, 1852. Retired 26 January, 1866.
STIMSON, OLIVER T.
  Carpenter, 26 July, 1861. Died 15 August, 1864.
STINERUCK, WILLIAM A.
  Acting Third Assistant Engineer, 14 September, 1863. Resigned (sick) 17 October, 1864.
STINESS, SAMUEL.
  Master, 27 October, 1812. Dismissed 5 January, 1814.

STINSON, HERBERT C.
  Midshipman, 30 September, 1864. Graduated June, 1868. Ensign, 19 April, 1869. Master, 12 July, 1870. Died 21 December, 1871.
STINSON, THOMAS.
  Acting Third Assistant Engineer, 16 September, 1863. Honorably discharged 15 August, 1865.
STINSON, WILLIAM P.
  Lieutenant, Junior Grade (Spanish-American War), 21 May, 1898. Honorably discharged 1 October, 1898.
STIRLING, YATES.
  Acting Midshipman, 27 September, 1860. Ensign, 28 May, 1863. Master, 10 November, 1865. Lieutenant, 10 November, 1866. Lieutenant-Commander, 12 March, 1868. Commander, 26 November, 1880. Captain, 16 September, 1894.
STIRLING, YATES, Jr.
  Naval Cadet, 6 September, 1888. Ensign, 1 July, 1894. Lieutenant, Junior Grade, 3 March, 1899.
STILES, MATTHEW.
  Acting First Assistant Engineer, 17 June, 1864. Resigned 5 October, 1864.
STITH, LAWRENCE W.
  Master, 31 January, 1809. Dismissed 26 August, 1812.
STITH, St. JOHN.
  Master, 18 June, 1812. Resigned 27 November, 1812.
STITT, EDWARD R.
  Assistant Surgeon, 23 March, 1889. Passed Assistant Surgeon, 23 March, 1892. Surgeon, 7 June, 1900.
STIVER, WILLIAM C.
  Mate, 27 January, 1864. Acting Carpenter, 1 February, 1864. Honorably discharged 19 July, 1865.
STIVERS, GEORGE W.
  Third Assistant Engineer, 2 December, 1861. Second Assistant Engineer, 8 September, 1863. First Assistant Engineer, 11 October, 1866. Chief Engineer, 18 December, 1885. Retired List, 12 October, 1898.
STIVERS, HENRY H.
  Cadet Engineer, Naval Academy, 1 October, 1873. Graduated 20 June, 1876. Assistant Engineer, 1 July, 1878. Died 24 April, 1881.
STIVERS, JAMES.
  Acting Third Assistant Engineer, 7 August, 1863. Acting Second Assistant Engineer, 30 June, 1864. Dismissed 6 December, 1865.
STIVERS, WILLIAM.
  Acting Third Assistant Engineer, 30 January, 1867. Mustered out 14 May, 1868.
St. JOHN, JOHN.
  Carpenter, 17 July, 1801. Warrant returned.
St. JOHN, G. P.
  Mate, 19 April, 1862. Acting Ensign, 6 June, 1863. Honorably discharged 24 February, 1866.
St. JOHN, OSCAR.
  Mate, 1861. Appointment revoked 23 January, 1862.
St. JOHN, HENRY.
  Acting Assistant Paymaster, 20 August, 1863. Mustered out 29 November, 1865.
St. JOHN, STEPHEN.
  Pharmacist, 15 September, 1898.
St. MEDARD, PETER.
  Surgeon, 14 July, 1799. Died in March, 1822.
STOAKLEY, JOHN W.
  Mate, 23 July, 1898. Acting Boatswain, 15 August, 1899.
STOCKBRIDGE, JOSEPH.
  Chaplain, 8 September, 1841. Retired List, 14 July, 1873. Died 16 November, 1894.
STOCKER, HENRY T.
  Sailmaker, 1 July, 1850. Retired List, 24 December, 1884. Died 20 August, 1897.
STOCKER, ROBERT.
  Naval Cadet, 4 September, 1883. Ensign, 1 July, 1889. Assistant Naval Constructor, 1 July, 1891. Naval Constructor, 11 November, 1897.
STOCKER, WILLIAM.
  Boatswain, 16 December, 1831. Resigned 14 June, 1832.
STOCKHOLM, ANDREW.
  Acting Ensign, 3 August, 1864. Dismissed 7 November, 1864.
STOCKING, R. M.
  Gunner, 22 December, 1849. Dismissed 29 September, 1856.
STOCKTON, C. C.
  Midshipman, 1 January, 1812. Resigned 20 October, 1813.
STOCKTON, CHARLES H.
  Midshipman, 14 November, 1861. Graduated September, 1865. Ensign, 1 December, 1866. Master, 12 March, 1868. Lieutenant, 26 March, 1869. Lieutenant-Commander, 15 November, 1881. Commander, 3 April, 1892. Captain, 8 July, 1899.
STOCKTON, EDWARD C.
  Midshipman, 16 October, 1849. Passed Midshipman, 12 June, 1855. Master, 16 September, 1855. Lieutenant, 7 February, 1857. Dismissed 30 June, 1858.
STOCKTON, FRANCIS B.
  Purser, 11 March, 1829. Died 15 January, 1858.
STOCKTON, H. H.
  Midshipman, 1 July, 1827. Resigned 5 September, 1833.
STOCKTON, HENRY T.
  Midshipman, 20 July, 1865. Graduated 4 June, 1869. Ensign, 12 July, 1871. Master, 3 June, 1873. Lieutenant, 2 February, 1878. Retired List, 4 January, 1886. Died 6 May, 1886.

524   GENERAL NAVY REGISTER.

STOCKTON, HORATIO.
　Midshipman, 24 January, 1815. Last appearance on Records of Navy Department, 1815. Frigate Guerriere.
STOCKTON, JOHN, JR.
　Midshipman, 2 April, 1804. Resigned 17 October, 1808.
STOCKTON, P. A.
　Midshipman, 1 February, 1823. Passed Midshipman, 23 March, 1829. Lieutenant, 3 March, 1831. Resigned 14 February, 1834.
STOCKTON, ROBERT F.
　Midshipman, 1 September, 1811. Lieutenant, 9 December, 1814. Commander, 27 May, 1830. Captain, 8 December, 1838. Resigned 28 May, 1850.
STOCKTON, S. W.
　Midshipman, 1 December, 1821. Passed Midshipman, 24 May, 1828. Lieutenant, 27 May, 1830. Died 29 November, 1836.
STOCKWELL, LEVI S.
　Assistant Paymaster, 25 November, 1861. Paymaster, 4 August, 1863. Resigned 21 November, 1865.
STOCKWELL, MARK.
　Purser, 30 August, 1800. Discharged 3 September, 1801, under Peace Establishment Act.
STODDARD, A. D.
　Midshipman, 16 January, 1809. Resigned 12 July, 1809.
STODDARD, CHARLES.
　Acting Master, 27 May, 1861. Dismissed 10 December, 1861.
STODDARD, EBEN M.
　Acting Master, 29 October, 1861. Acting Volunteer Lieutenant, 17 March, 1865. Honorably discharged 11 April, 1866.
STODDARD, JAMES.
　Mate, gallant conduct in action at Yazoo City, 14 April, 1864. Resigned 20 May, 1865.
STODDARD, J. S.
　Midshipman, 2 February, 1829. Resigned 24 November, 1832.
STODDARD, LUTHER.
　Midshipman, 1 April, 1827. Passed Midshipman, 10 June, 1833. Lieutenant, 8 December, 1838. Commander, 14 September, 1855. Died 29 August, 1859.
STODDARD, WILLIAM B.
　Acting Master, 13 November, 1861. Appointment revoked (sick) 30 November, 1864.
STODDER, LOUIS N.
　Acting Master, 26 December, 1861. Acting Volunteer Lieutenant, 10 January, 1863. Honorably discharged 20 November, 1865.
STODDER, SETH.
　Midshipman, 4 July, 1805. Resigned 3 March, 1806.
STODDERT, B. F.
　Midshipman, 8 November, 1800. Last appearance on Records of Navy Department. Resigned.
STOEVER, J. C.
　Acting Assistant Paymaster, 7 February, 1865. Mustered out 1 October, 1865.
STOKES, CHARLES F.
　Assistant Surgeon, 1 February, 1889. Passed Assistant Surgeon, 1 February, 1892. Surgeon, 31 May, 1900.
STOKES, DAVID M.
　Midshipman, 1 May, 1822. Resigned 15 April, 1833.
STOKES, M. S.
　Midshipman, 12 May, 1829. Passed Midshipman, 3 July, 1835. Resigned 6 February, 1839.
STOKES, THOMAS B.
　Acting Ensign, 8 October, 1862. Honorably discharged 31 August, 1865.
STOLLERY, WILLIAM.
　Acting Third Assistant Engineer, 3 September, 1864. Honorably discharged 10 October, 1865.
STONE, BRINTON.
　Acting Assistant Surgeon, 5 December, 1873. Died 21 January, 1875.
STONE, CHARLES A.
　Midshipman, 27 July, 1864. Graduated June, 1868. Ensign, 19 April, 1869. Master, 12 July, 1870. Lieutenant, 3 September, 1872. Retired List, 25 December, 1893. Resigned 31 January, 1897.
STONE, CHARLES F.
　Acting Master, 15 August, 1861. Dismissed 3 September, 1861.
STONE, CHARLES H.
　Second Assistant Engineer, 24 August, 1861. Resigned 10 June, 1865.
STONE, CLARENCE M.
　Naval Cadet, 25 September, 1883. Ensign, 1 July, 1889. Lieutenant, Junior Grade, 16 September, 1897. Lieutenant, 3 March, 1899.
STONE, DANIEL.
　Mate, 9 March, 1864. Died 30 August, 1864.
STONE, EDWARD E.
　Midshipman, 19 October, 1841. Passed Midshipman, 10 August, 1847. Master, 14 September, 1855. Lieutenant, 15 September, 1855. Lieutenant-Commander, 16 July, 1862. Commander, 25 July, 1866. Retired List, 5 January, 1874. Died 18 June, 1892.
STONE, EUGENE P.
　Assistant Surgeon, 5 August, 1886. Passed Assistant Surgeon, 5 August, 1889. Surgeon, 16 April, 1899.
STONE, FRANCIS.
　Midshipman, 1 May, 1822. Resigned 17 November, 1828.

GENERAL NAVY REGISTER.   525

STONE, GEORGE L. P.
    Naval Cadet, 26 September, 1890. Ensign, 1 July, 1896. Lieutenant, Junior Grade, 1 July, 1899.
STONE, GEORGE W.
    Acting Assistant Paymaster, 5 August, 1861. Mustered out 8 November, 1865.
STONE, HENRY O.
    Acting Master, 3 January, 1862. Died 17 February, 1865.
STONE, JOHN T.
    Midshipman, 17 December, 1810. Resigned 10 March, 1812.
STONE, JOHN T.
    Acting Second Assistant Engineer, 22 January, 1863. Honorably discharged 27 October, 1865.
STONE, JOSIAH.
    Acting Master, 7 September, 1861. Dismissed 10 May, 1862.
STONE, LEWIS H.
    Assistant Surgeon, 19 June, 1890. Passed Assistant Surgeon, 19 June, 1894. Retired List, 10 February, 1898.
STONE, MACK V.
    Assistant Surgeon (Spanish-American War), 24 May, 1898. Appointed Assistant Surgeon in Regular Service 7 June, 1900.
STONE, MOSES W.
    Mate. Resigned 6 February, 1863.
STONE, PHINEAS.
    Midshipman, 31 January, 1800. Discharged 30 April, 1801, under Peace Establishment Act.
STONE, PHINEAS J., JR.
    Acting Assistant Paymaster, 31 March, 1863. Mustered out 9 April, 1866.
STONE, RAYMOND.
    Naval Cadet, 5 September, 1890. Ensign, 1 July, 1896. Lieutenant, Junior Grade, 1 July, 1899.
STONE, RICHARD J.
    Acting First Assistant Engineer, 13 November, 1863. Honorably discharged 1 October, 1865.
STONE, ROBERT.
    Acting Assistant Surgeon, 1 September, 1864. Resigned 11 May, 1865.
STONE, THEODORE.
    Mate, 3 May, 1864. Appointment revoked 7 November, 1865.
STONE, WILLIAM L.
    Acting Volunteer Lieutenant, 21 September, 1861. Dismissed 29 March, 1862.
STONEALL, WASHINGTON.
    Acting Ensign, 1 October, 1862. Dismissed 21 September, 1863.
STONEY, GEORGE M.
    Midshipman, 21 September, 1870. Graduated 17 September, 1875. Ensign, 9 October, 1876. Lieutenant, Junior Grade, 25 June, 1883. Lieutenant, 27 June, 1889. Lieutenant-Commander, 3 March, 1899.
STOODLEY, NATHANIEL.
    Master, 14 August, 1813. Resigned 6 April, 1822.
STORER, EDWARD.
    Purser, 6 October, 1840. Dismissed 10 April, 1850.
STORER, FREDERICK.
    Midshipman, 20 November, 1814. Lost at sea in 1815.
STORER, GEORGE W.
    Midshipman, 16 January, 1809. Lieutenant, 24 July, 1813. Commander, 24 April, 1828. Captain, 9 February, 1837. Rear-Admiral on Retired List, 16 July, 1862. Died 8 January, 1864.
STORER, NATHANIEL.
    Master, 15 February, 1809. Appointment revoked 2 May, 1809.
STORER, ROBERT B.
    Midshipman, 4 November, 1841. Died at sea 4 July, 1847.
STORIN, JOHN F.
    Acting Warrant Machinist, 23 August, 1899.
STORM, GEORGE A.
    Mate, 4 December, 1861. Dismissed 16 May, 1863.
STORMES, JOSEPH W.
    Acting First Assistant Engineer, 13 December, 1862. Acting Chief Engineer, 19 January, 1863. Honorably discharged 7 January, 1866.
STORRS, A. H.
    Mate, 13 December, 1861. Appointment revoked (sick) 18 February, 1862.
STORRS, GEORGE S.
    Acting Midshipman, 23 September, 1854. Midshipman, 11 June, 1858. Resigned 6 March, 1860.
STORY, F. W. C.
    Midshipman, 11 March, 1815. Resigned 22 October, 1817.
STORY, REUBEN.
    Acting Second Assistant Engineer, 1 October, 1862. Honorably discharged 21 November, 1865.
STORY, THOMAS W.
    Master, 27 April, 1813. Last appearance on Records of Navy Department, 1820. Furloughed.
STOTESBURY, WILLIAM.
    Acting Third Assistant Engineer, 2 September, 1864. Acting Second Assistant Engineer, 27 October, 1864. Honorably discharged 9 December, 1865.
STOTESBURY, WILLIAM C.
    Acting Master, 25 September, 1861. Dismissed 4 November, 1861.

STOTHARD, THOMAS.
Mate. Acting Ensign, 7 November, 1862. Acting Master, 4 January, 1865. Honorably discharged 2 October, 1865. Acting Master, 5 April, 1867. Mustered out 15 December, 1868.
STOTSENBERG, JOHN H.
Mate, 15 March, 1862. Died on Honduras, 19 July, 1864.
STOTT, JOHN W.
Acting Third Assistant Engineer, 10 December, 1863. Resigned 27 April, 1865.
STOUGHTON, JAMES.
Assistant Surgeon, 20 May, 1891. Passed Assistant Surgeon, 20 May, 1894. Drowned 6 August, 1900.
STOUGHTON, SETH.
Mate, 1 October, 1862. Resigned 8 January, 1863.
STOUT, A. C.
Midshipman, 16 January, 1809. Lieutenant, 9 December, 1814. Last appearance on Records of Navy Department, 1815. Lake Erie.
STOUT, CHARLES H.
Mate, 13 August, 1863. Resigned 31 May, 1864.
STOUT, EDWARD C.
Midshipman, 18 February, 1840. Passed Midshipman, 11 July, 1846. Master, 6 October, 1854. Lieutenant 4 June, 1855. Lost in Levant, 18 September, 1860.
STOUT, GEORGE C.
Cadet Midshipman, 22 September, 1879. Graduated. Honorably discharged 30 June, 1885. Lieutenant (Spanish-American War), 23 June, 1898. Honorably discharged 8 September, 1898.
STOUT, JACOB D.
Master's Mate, date not known. Last appearance on Records of Navy Department.
STOUT, JOHN.
Boatswain, 24 July, 1850. Resigned 26 March, 1853.
STOUT, JOSEPH.
Lieutenant, 3 July, 1798. Discharged 6 July, 1801, under Peace Establishment Act.
STOUT, M. W.
Midshipman, 12 November, 1813. Died 8 August, 1820.
STOVER, ABNER D.
Acting Ensign, 18 December, 1862. Honorably discharged 9 November, 1865.
STOVER, EPHRAIM S.
Mate, 1 March, 1864. Honorably discharged 29 October, 1867.
STOVER, GEORGE H.
Acting Third Assistant Engineer, 25 October, 1862. Appointment revoked 21 March, 1864.
STOW, FREDERICK R.
Acting Assistant Paymaster, 10 July, 1863. Died 5 January, 1865.
STOWELL, ELIAS.
Mate, 8 May, 1862. Appointment revoked 25 November, 1862.
STRAIN, ISAAC G.
Midshipman, 11 December, 1837. Passed Midshipman, 29 June, 1843. Lieutenant, 27 February, 1850. Died 14 May, 1857.
STRANDBERG, F. A.
Acting Ensign, 2 May, 1863. Acting Master, 13 July, 1865. Resigned 4 September, 1868.
STRANGE, CLARENCE A.
Assistant Engineer, 30 October, 1875. Died 30 December, 1877.
STRATTON, FRANKLIN A.
Civil Engineer, 1 January, 1867. Died 18 July, 1879.
STRATTON, NORMAN.
Civil Engineer, 2 March, 1876. Retired List, 15 October, 1881. Died 11 March, 1882.
STRATTON, SAMUEL W.
Lieutenant (Spanish-American War), 24 May, 1898. Honorably discharged 22 November, 1898.
STRAUB, AMBROSE W.
Acting Third Assistant Engineer, 6 June, 1864. Honorably discharged 30 October, 1865.
STRAUCH, D. B.
Acting Third Assistant Engineer, 1 September, 1861. Resigned 8 February, 1862.
STRAUSS, JOSEPH.
Cadet Engineer, 1 October, 1881. Ensign, 1 July, 1887. Lieutenant, Junior Grade, 3 April, 1896. Lieutenant, 3 March, 1899.
STREEPEY, CHARLES C.
Acting Second Assistant Engineer, 3 July, 1863. Honorably discharged 17 November, 1865.
STREET, GEORGE.
Acting Third Assistant Engineer, 22 September, 1864. Dismissed 15 November, 1864.
STREET, GEORGE W.
Cadet Midshipman, 29 September, 1879. Graduated 8 June, 1883. Ensign, 1 July, 1885. Assistant Naval Constructor, 1 July, 1889. Died 11 January, 1895.
STREET, JOHN W.
Acting Third Assistant Engineer, 4 December, 1862. Acting Second Assistant Engineer, 17 November, 1864. Honorably discharged 4 December, 1865.
STREET, MILES.
Midshipman, 18 June, 1812. Last appearance on Records of Navy Department, 1816. Dismissed.
STREET, S. A.
Midshipman, 4 March, 1822. Resigned 7 July, 1830.

GENERAL NAVY REGISTER. 527

STREET, THOMAS.
Gunner, 12 November, 1799. Discharged 18 April, 1802.
STREET, WILLIAM T.
Acting Master, 16 December, 1861. Honorably discharged 8 December, 1865.
STREETS, T. HALE.
Assistant Surgeon, 12 April, 1872. Passed Assistant Surgeon, 27 December, 1875. Surgeon, 1 May, 1887. Medical Inspector, 16 April, 1899.
STREMMELL, HENRY.
Sailmaker, 24 June, 1857. Died 21 April, 1858.
STRIBLING, CORNELIUS K.
Midshipman, 18 June, 1812. Lieutenant, 1 April, 1818. Commander, 28 January, 1840. Captain, 1 August, 1853. Retired List, 21 December, 1861. Commodore on Retired List, 16 July, 1862. Rear-Admiral, Retired List, 25 July, 1866. Died 17 January, 1880.
STRIBLING, JOHN M.
Acting Midshipman, 7 October, 1851. Midshipman, 10 June, 1854. Passed Midshipman, 22 November, 1856. Master, 22 January, 1858. Lieutenant, 16 March, 1860. Resigned 8 January 1861.
STRICKLAND, GEORGE D.
Assistant Engineer, 12 January, 1876. Passed Assistant Engineer, 27 April, 1884. Retired List, 13 February, 1895. Died 17 June, 1896.
STRICKLAND, PAUL M.
Acting First Assistant Engineer, 1 November, 1862. Resigned 29 August, 1863.
STRICKLAND, WILLIAM R.
Assistant Engineer (Spanish-American War), 14 May, 1898. Honorably discharged 26 January, 1899.
STRIEBY, JOHN A.
Acting Third Assistant Engineer, 9 July, 1863. Honorably discharged 25 July, 1865.
STRIKER, THEODORE.
Mate, 11 October, 1861. Resigned 14 July, 1862.
STRINGER, GEORGE.
Acting Third Assistant Engineer, 23 March, 1865. Honorably discharged 16 June, 1866.
STRINGER, JOSEPH.
Acting Third Assistant Engineer, 1 January, 1865. Honorably discharged 1 October, 1865.
STRINGHAM, SILAS H.
Midshipman, 15 November, 1809. Lieutenant, 9 December, 1814. Commander, 3 March, 1831. Captain, 8 September, 1841. Retired List, 21 December, 1861. Rear-Admiral on Retired List, 16 July, 1862. Died 7 February, 1876.
STRITE, SAMUEL M.
Naval Cadet, 28 September, 1882. Ensign, 1 July, 1888. Lieutenant, Junior Grade, 1 January, 1897. Lieutenant, 3 March, 1899.
STROM, AUGUST E.
Mate, 1 January, 1899.
STRONG, AUGUSTUS R.
Midshipman, 20 June, 1823. Passed Midshipman, 23 March, 1829. Lieutenant, 21 June, 1832. Died 18 October, 1834.
STRONG, EDWARD T.
Mate, 24 November, 1862. Acting Ensign, 15 October, 1863. Acting Ensign, 5 July, 1866. Ensign, 12 March, 1868. Master, 18 December, 1868. Lieutenant 21 March, 1870. Lieutenant-Commander, 2 July, 1882. Commander, 9 January, 1893. Captain, 10 October, 1899. Retired List, with rank of Rear-Admiral, 21 November, 1900.
STRONG, FRANK L.
Acting Third Assistant Engineer, 1 September, 1864. Honorably discharged 14 August, 1865. Passed Assistant Engineer (Spanish-American War), 24 June, 1898. Honorably discharged 14 February, 1899.
STRONG, FREDERICK W.
Acting Master, 2 August, 1861. Honorably discharged 14 November, 1865.
STRONG, HENRY A.
Acting Assistant Paymaster, 25 September, 1861. Assistant Paymaster, 12 March, 1863. Resigned 15 February, 1865.
STRONG, JAMES H.
Midshipman, 2 February, 1829. Passed Midshipman, 4 June, 1836. Lieutenant, 8 September, 1841. Commander, 24 April, 1861. Captain, 5 August, 1865. Commodore, 2 March, 1870. Rear-Admiral, 25 September, 1873. Retired List, 25 April, 1876. Died 28 November, 1882.
STRONG, JOHN L. G.
Acting Assistant Paymaster, 18 September, 1862. Discharged 21 March, 1866.
STRONG, JOS. C.
Assistant Surgeon 11 October, 1799. Permitted to retire 26 May, 1801.
STRONG, PETER Y.
Midshipman, 30 November, 1814. Last appearance on Records of Navy Department, 1815. Frigate Constellation.
STRONG, WILLIAM C.
Midshipman, 22 September, 1864. Graduated June, 1868. Ensign, 19 April, 1869. Master, 12 July, 1870. Lieutenant, 14 June, 1874. Retired List, 3 July, 1896.
STROPE, WILLIAM H.
Mate, 2 December, 1862. Acting Ensign, 22 April, 1863. Honorably discharged 23 November, 1865.
STROUD, CHARLES F.
Acting Third Assistant Engineer, 19 April, 1864. Honorably discharged 8 December, 1865.

STROUD, LINCOLN B.
    Mate, 31 October, 1861. Dismissed 27 May, 1862.
STROUT, JESSE B.
    Mate, 4 October, 1864. Honorably discharged 7 June, 1865.
STROUT, LEWIS F.
    Mate, 19 July, 1864. Died 19 November, 1876.
STRUDE, SAMUEL T.
    Acting Third Assistant Engineer, 9 January, 1862. Drowned 15 October, 1863.
STRUNK, SIMON H.
    Mate, 1 October, 1862. Acting Ensign, 11 June, 1863. Honorably discharged 29 November, 1865.
STUART, ALEXANDER C.
    Acting Third Assistant Engineer, 1 July, 1863. Acting Second Assistant Engineer, 27 June, 1864. Honorably discharged 19 April, 1866.
STUART, ALLAN.
    Assistant Surgeon (Spanish-American War), 25 April, 1898. Appointed Assistant Surgeon in Regular Service 7 June, 1900.
STUART, CHARLES.
    Gunner, 22 October, 1859. Died 21 July, 1886.
STUART, CHARLES A.
    Acting Second Assistant Engineer, 19 May, 1863. Resigned (sick) 13 February, 1865.
STUART, CHARLES B.
    Engineer-in-Chief, 1 December, 1850. Resigned 30 June, 1853.
STUART, DANIEL D. V.
    Midshipman, 24 September, 1863. Graduated June, 1869. Ensign, 12 July, 1870. Master, 11 February, 1873. Lieutenant, 9 September, 1876. Lieutenant-Commander, 27 April, 1898.
STUART, E. W. B.
    Mate, 4 April, 1862. Honorably discharged 20 June, 1866.
STUART, FREDERICK D.
    Acting Master, 7 July, 1862. Acting Volunteer Lieutenant, 21 November, 1864. Honorably discharged 3 February, 1866.
STUART, FREDERICK D., JR.
    Acting Second Assistant Engineer, 13 August, 1862. Dismissed 7 January, 1863. Acting Third Assistant Engineer, 3 February, 1863. Acting Second Assistant Engineer, 17 March, 1864. Honorably discharged 1 December, 1865.
STUART, JAMES H.
    Assistant Surgeon, 29 March, 1853. Lost in Porpoise, 1853.
STUART, JOHN.
    Midshipman, 21 June, 1839. Passed Midshipman, 2 July, 1845. Master, 15 October, 1853. Died 27 October, 1853.
STUART, JOHN A.
    Acting Carpenter, 21 December, 1863. Honorably discharged 3 November, 1865.
STUART, ROBERT.
    Midshipman, 19 October, 1841. Passed Midshipman, 10 August, 1847. Master, 14 September, 1855. Lieutenant, 15 September, 1855. Resigned 16 April, 1857.
STUBBINS, VICTOR B.
    Acting Third Assistant Engineer, 15 February, 1864. Honorably discharged 9 July, 1866.
STUBBS, SAMUEL.
    Midshipman, 2 December, 1799. Resigned 9 February, 1801.
STUDEBAKER, HENRY.
    Mate, 14 January, 1864. Appointment revoked (sick) 18 July, 1864.
STUDLEY, BRADDOCK G.
    Mate, 28 January, 1864. Honorably discharged 3 April, 1868.
STUDLEY, E.
    Acting Ensign, Coast Survey duty, 21 June, 1867. Mustered out 30 November, 1868.
STUDLEY, IRA B.
    Acting Master, 12 August, 1861. Honorably discharged 3 October, 1865.
STULL, ELIE W.
    Midshipman, 1 June, 1828. Passed Midshipman, 11 June, 1834. Resigned 19 November, 1838.
STUMP, T. B. C.
    Third Assistant Engineer, 26 February, 1851. Second Assistant Engineer, 21 May, 1853. First Assistant Engineer, 9 May, 1857. Name stricken from the Roll 22 May, 1861.
STURDY, EDWARD W.
    Midshipman, 25 February, 1863. Graduated June, 1867. Ensign, 18 December, 1868. Master, 21 March, 1870. Lieutenant, 26 July, 1871. Lieutenant-Commander, 3 April, 1892. Died 7 June, 1898.
STURGEON, JOHN.
    Mate, 14 January, 1863. Resigned 27 February, 1865.
STURGES, HENRY L.
    Acting Master, 28 October, 1861. Honorably discharged 29 September, 1865.
STURGIS, JAMES B.
    Mate, 5 June, 1862. Appointment revoked 14 March, 1863. Mate, 2 September, 1863. Died 8 January, 1864.
STURMAN, F. H.
    Midshipman, 2 April, 1804. Resigned 3 October, 1808.
STURTEVANT, CHARLES.
    Acting Assistant Surgeon, 5 September, 1863. Honorably discharged 18 January, 1866.
STUTTS, HENRY P.
    Acting Third Assistant Engineer, 27 January, 1864. Honorably discharged 8 August, 1865.

GENERAL NAVY REGISTER. 529

STUYVESANT, HENRY.
Acting Assistant Paymaster, 7 October, 1863. Appointment revoked (sick) 11 November, 1864.
STUYVESANT, MOSES S.
Acting Midshipman, 29 September, 1856. Midshipman, 15 June, 1860. Master, 19 September, 1861. Lieutenant, 16 July, 1862. Lieutenant-Commander, 11 April, 1866. Resigned 18 December, 1868.
SUCH, JAMES.
Mate. Dismissed 6 June, 1862. Reappointed Mate, 6 November, 1862. Died 26 December, 1863.
SUDDARDS, JAMES.
Assistant Surgeon, 17 May, 1849. Surgeon, 24 April, 1861. Medical Inspector, 3 March, 1871. Medical Director, 5 April, 1875. Died 31 August, 1888.
SUGGETTE, T. S.
Midshipman, 1 December, 1809. Last appearance on Records of Navy Department, 1815.
SUGGS, WILLIAM B.
Midshipman, 27 February, 1799. Discharged 27 September, 1801, under Peace Establishment Act.
SUGHRUE, DANIEL H.
Ensign (Spanish-American War), 23 April, 1898. Honorably discharged 29 September, 1898.
SUGHRUE, DENNIS F.
Assistant Surgeon (Spanish-American War), 2 June, 1898. Honorably discharged 14 February, 1899.
SULLIVAN, DANIEL.
Mate, 19 February, 1864. Honorably discharged 16 September, 1865.
SULLIVAN, FRANKLIN B.
Naval Cadet, 22 May, 1886. Ensign, 1 July, 1892. Lieutenant, Junior Grade, 3 March, 1899. Wholly retired 20 November, 1899.
SULLIVAN, HARRY R.
Assistant Paymaster, 16 June, 1880. Passed Assistant Paymaster, 19 June, 1888. Paymaster, 1 November, 1897.
SULLIVAN, JAMES.
Acting Third Assistant Engineer, 14 January, 1863. Dismissed 28 August, 1863.
SULLIVAN, JAMES.
Acting Second Assistant Engineer, 30 June, 1864. Honorably discharged 10 December, 1865.
SULLIVAN, JAMES F.
Acting Third Assistant Engineer, 16 November, 1863. Resigned 26 April, 1864.
SULLIVAN, JAMES J.
Acting Third Assistant Engineer, 20 April, 1863. Acting Second Assistant Engineer, 5 December, 1864. Honorably discharged 31 November, 1865.
SULLIVAN, JEREMIAH.
Midshipman, 7 February, 1799. Resigned 28 July, 1799.
SULLIVAN, JEREMIAH C.
Midshipman, 12 October, 1848. Resigned 14 April, 1854.
SULLIVAN, JOHN.
Mate, 1 September, 1862. Acting Ensign, 11 June, 1863. Honorably discharged 31 October, 1865.
SULLIVAN, JOHN.
Acting Boatswain, 1 March, 1864. Appointment revoked 21 March, 1865.
SULLIVAN, J. B.
Midshipman, 1 December, 1814. Resigned 10 May, 1828.
SULLIVAN, JOHN CLYDE.
Assistant Paymaster, 13 July, 1870. Passed Assistant Paymaster, 6 September, 1878. Paymaster, 12 September, 1891. Dismissed 1 February, 1894. Reappointed Paymaster, 16 June, 1899.
SULLIVAN, JOHN C.
Mate, 25 January, 1862. Deserted 31 March, 1862.
SULLIVAN, JOHN M.
Midshipman, 1 March, 1813. Lieutenant, 13 January, 1825. Died 21 February, 1833.
SULLIVAN, JOHN T.
Midshipman, 10 October, 1862. Graduated June, 1867. Ensign, 18 December, 1868. Master, 21 March, 1870. Lieutenant, 21 March, 1871. Retired List, 12 May, 1886. Died 19 March, 1900.
SULLIVAN, LUCIEN.
Third Assistant Engineer, 12 July, 1861. Second Assistant Engineer, 18 December, 1862. Resigned 5 April, 1866.
SULLIVAN, ROBERT J.
Carpenter, 23 October, 1896. Died 8 August, 1897.
SULLIVAN, TIMOTHY.
Boatswain, 2 June, 1898.
SULLIVAN, TIMOTHY S.
Mate, 24 October, 1863. Died 13 March, 1872.
SULLY, JAMES R.
Midshipman, 1 February, 1827. Passed Midshipman, 10 June, 1833. Lieutenant, 9 December, 1839. Died 28 January, 1840.
SUMMERS, JAMES C.
Ensign (Spanish-American War), 21 May, 1898. Lieutenant, Junior Grade, 17 January, 1899. Honorably discharged 11 April, 1899.
SUMMERS, JOHN W.
Mate, 30 August, 1864. Resigned (sick) 21 March, 1865.

SUMMERS, L. W. P.
  Midshipman, 9 June, 1831. Lost in the Sylph, in August, 1831.
SUMMERS, R. M.
  Midshipman, 1 February, 1814. Cashiered 25 March, 1821.
SUMMERS, WILLIAM.
  Gunner, 10 June, 1861. Dismissed 17 October, 1861. Dismissal revoked 14 November, 1861. Warranted 6 March, 1862. Dismissed 30 September, 1862.
SUMMERS, WILLIAM.
  Gunner, 10 June, 1861. Dismissed 30 September, 1862.
SUMMERS, WILLIAM H.
  Acting Ensign, 15 June, 1864. Acting Master, 11 May, 1865. Honorably discharged 22 October, 1865.
SUMNER, DAVID H.
  Acting Master, 22 November, 1861. Resigned 6 January, 1865.
SUMNER, GEORGE W.
  Acting Midshipman, 20 September, 1858. Graduated 1862. Lieutenant, 1 August, 1862. Lieutenant-Commander, 25 July, 1866. Commander, 13 June, 1876. Captain, 2 October, 1891. Rear-Admiral, 3 March, 1899.
SUMWALT, FREDERICK G.
  Third Assistant Engineer, 30 August, 1853. Dismissed 29 September, 1854.
SUNDQVIST, AXEL L.
  Carpenter, 12 December, 1898.
SUNDSTRUM, OLOF.
  Mate, 5 June, 1862. Acting Ensign, 27 October, 1863. Resigned 26 April, 1864.
SUNSTROM, MARK TRUEMAN.
  Third Assistant Engineer, 1 February, 1862. Second Assistant Engineer, 15 October, 1863. Resigned 10 November, 1865.
SURRETTE, THOMAS.
  Mate, 27 November, 1863. Appointment revoked (sick) 17 March, 1864.
SUTHERLAND, ALAN P.
  Acting Third Assistant Engineer, 1 October, 1862. Dismissed 17 April, 1863.
SUTHERLAND, JOHN C.
  Lieutenant (Spanish-American War), 9 May, 1898. Honorably discharged 3 November, 1898.
SUTHERLAND, MOSHER A.
  Third Assistant Engineer, 17 March, 1863. Second Assistant Engineer, 1 September, 1864. Resigned 15 October, 1867.
SUTPHEN, EDSON W.
  Cadet Midshipman, 28 June, 1878. Graduated 10 June, 1882. Ensign, 1 July, 1884. Resigned 30 June, 1890.
SUTTON, JOHN.
  Boatswain, 23 June, 1882. Chief Boatswain, 3 March, 1899.
SVARZ, EMIL P.
  Naval Cadet, 20 May, 1896. Graduated 30 June, 1900.
SWAIN, CHARLES.
  Master, 5 December, 1798. Warrant returned by Captain Nicholson.
SWAIN, OLIVER.
  Acting Ensign, 17 May, 1864. Died 10 June, 1867.
SWAIN, SAMUEL G.
  Mate, 16 October, 1862. Acting Ensign, 16 August, 1864. Honorably discharged 26 January, 1866.
SWAIN, WILLIAM H.
  Acting Master, 8 July, 1861. Appointment revoked (sick) 22 April, 1863.
SWAN, FRANCIS H.
  Acting Assistant Paymaster, 9 December, 1861. Assistant Paymaster, 9 March, 1865. Passed Assistant Paymaster, 4 May, 1866. Paymaster, 31 August, 1865. Pay Inspector, 5 February, 1886. Retired List, 15 July, 1886.
SWAN, GEORGE H.
  Lieutenant, Junior Grade (Spanish-American War), 1 July, 1898. Honorably discharged 8 September, 1898.
SWANEY, JOHN.
  Acting Ensign, 1 October, 1862. Acting Master, 7 January, 1863. Acting Volunteer Lieutenant, 19 March, 1864. Honorably discharged 1 December, 1865.
SWANN, BENJAMIN.
  Acting Master, 14 August, 1861. Appointment revoked 20 November, 1861.
SWANN, GEORGE W.
  Chaplain, 15 June, 1844. Died 22 September, 1844.
SWANN, ROBERT.
  Assistant Surgeon, 2 May, 1874. Wholly retired 28 February, 1889.
SWANN, ROBERT P.
  Acting Ensign, 19 July, 1862. Acting Master, 25 May, 1863. Acting Volunteer Lieutenant, 13 April, 1864. Died 13 January, 1866.
SWANN, SAMUEL R.
  Assistant Surgeon, 31 May, 1854. Discharged 16 May, 1859.
SWANN, THOMAS L.
  Acting Midshipman, 8 December, 1856. Midshipman, 15 June, 1860. Master, 19 September, 1861. Lieutenant, 16 July, 1862. Lieutenant-Commander, 2 May, 1866. Commander, 6 January, 1874. Retired List, 10 July, 1877.
SWANN, WILLIAM S.
  Midshipman, 1 July, 1828. Passed Midshipman, 14 June, 1834. Lieutenant, 25 February, 1841. Lost in the Grampus, 20 March, 1843.
SWANSON, JOHN.
  Mate, 8 June, 1864. Died 23 January, 1873.

SWANSTROM, FREDERICK E.
Naval Cadet, 6 September, 1883. Graduated. Honorably discharged 30 June, 1889. Lieutenant, Junior Grade (Spanish-American War), 8 June, 1898. Honorably discharged 9 February, 1899.
SWARTWOUT, AUGUSTUS.
Midshipman, 1 January, 1812. Resigned 18 April, 1820.
SWARTWOUT, JOHN.
Midshipman, 9 November, 1813. Lieutenant, 28 April, 1826. Resigned 15 June, 1831.
SWARTWOUT, SAMUEL.
Midshipman, 1 January, 1812. Resigned 18 April, 1820. ruary, 1837. Commander, 14 September, 1855. Died 5 February, 1867.
SWARTWOUT, SAMUEL.
Acting Second Assistant Engineer, 4 January, 1862. Honorably discharged 19 December, 1865.
SWARTWOUT, THOMAS, Jr.
Midshipman, 28 May, 1800. Last appearance on Records of Navy Department, 29 April, 1801. Killed in a duel.
SWARTWOUT, WILLIAM.
Mate, 23 March, 1864. Acting Ensign, 24 October, 1864. Honorably discharged 21 November, 1865.
SWASEY, CHARLES H.
Acting Midshipman, 28 September, 1854. Midshipman, 9 June, 1859. Lieutenant, 31 August, 1861. Killed in action 4 October, 1862.
SWASEY, TRUE.
Acting Third Assistant Engineer, 24 September, 1861. Dismissed 27 January, 1862.
SWASEY, WILLIAM M.
Acting Ensign, 22 July, 1863. Honorably discharged 12 October, 1865.
SWEARENGEN, THOMAS.
Midshipman, 2 April, 1804. Dismissed by Court-martial 4 May, 1808.
SWEENEY, JOHN E.
Mate, 21 October, 1861. Resigned 30 August, 1864. Mate, 18 May, 1866. Resigned 15 April, 1867.
SWEENEY, HUGH.
Boatswain, 27 August, 1889. Chief Boatswain, 27 August, 1899.
SWEENY, HUGH C.
Midshipman, 18 June, 1812. Cashiered in 1821.
SWEENY, WILLIAM.
Gunner, 31 July, 1802. Last appearance on Records of Navy Department.
SWEET, FRANK.
Acting Ensign, 22 September, 1864. Honorably discharged 8 July, 1865.
SWEET, GEORGE C.
Naval Cadet, 22 September, 1894. Ensign, 4 April, 1900.
SWEET, GEORGE F.
Third Assistant Engineer, 20 May, 1863. Dismissed 30 January, 1869.
SWEET, GEORGE J.
Acting Assistant Surgeon, 8 October, 1861. Honorably discharged 14 December, 1865.
SWEET, JAMES P.
Acting First Assistant Engineer, 24 August, 1864. Honorably discharged 22 July, 1865.
SWEETING, CHARLES E.
Cadet Midshipman, 22 September, 1879. Graduated 8 June, 1883. Ensign, 1 July, 1885. Died 25 January, 1890.
SWEETZER, LEVI.
Acting Second Assistant Engineer, 18 September, 1861. Honorably discharged 16 October, 1865.
SWENDSON, CHARLES.
Acting Ensign, 12 March, 1863. Acting Master, 1 September, 1864. Honorably discharged 1 November, 1865.
SWETT, J. B.
Acting Master's Mate, 24 October, 1861. Acting Ensign, 1 October, 1862. Honorably discharged 23 September, 1866.
SWIFT, FRANKLIN.
Cadet Midshipman, 9 June, 1874. Graduated 22 June, 1882. Ensign, Junior Grade, 3 March, 1883. Ensign, 26 June, 1884. Lieutenant, Junior Grade, 4 July, 1893. Lieutenant, 29 April, 1897. Retired List, 1 July, 1899.
SWIFT, JONATHAN W.
Midshipman, 25 August, 1823. Passed Midshipman, 23 March, 1829. Lieutenant, 3 March, 1831. Reserved List, 13 September, 1855. Commodore on Retired List, 4 April, 1867. Died 30 July, 1877.
SWIFT, JOSEPH.
Gunner, 17 May, 1858. Retired List, 6 December, 1894. Died 22 October, 1895.
SWIFT, LE ROY E.
Acting Ensign, 26 October, 1864. Honorably discharged, 12 October, 1868.
SWIFT, ROBERT B.
Acting Second Assistant Engineer, 21 January, 1865. Honorably discharged 21 February, 1868.
SWIFT, R. R.
Midshipman, 1 November, 1827. Lost in the Hornet, 10 September, 1829.
SWIFT, THOMAS W., Jr.
Acting Ensign, 2 September, 1864. Honorably discharged 25 November, 1865.
SWIFT, WILLIAM.
Surgeon's Mate, 24 July, 1813. Surgeon, 15 April, 1814. Retired List, 25 April, 1861. Died 27 December, 1864.
SWIFT, WILLIAM C.
Acting Third Assistant Engineer, 5 June, 1863. Appointment revoked 19 December, 1863.

GENERAL NAVY REGISTER.

SWIFT, WILLIAM.
Midshipman, 25 September, 1863. Graduated June, 1867. Ensign, 18 December, 1868. Master, 21 March, 1870. Lieutenant, 21 March, 1871. Lieutenant-Commander, 24 October, 1889. Commander, 6 April, 1897.
SWIMMS, J. H.
Carpenter, 12 July, 1799. Dismissed 15 September, 1800.
SWINBURNE, WILLIAM T.
Midshipman, 29 September, 1862. Graduated June, 1866. Ensign 12 March, 1868. Master, 26 March, 1869. Lieutenant, 21 March, 1870. Lieutenant-Commander, 6 March, 1887. Commander, 28 December, 1895.
SWINNERTON, SAMUEL A.
Acting Master, 22 January, 1862. Resigned 2 September, 1863. Acting Master, 1 April, 1864. Honorably discharged 31 October, 1865.
SWINT, LEWIS F.
Acting Third Assistant Engineer, 16 August, 1862. Appointment revoked (sick) 9 April, 1863.
SWORD, EDWARD J.
Acting Third Assistant Engineer, 14 September, 1864. Honorably discharged 15 February, 1866. Acting Third Assistant Engineer, 12 April, 1866. Mustered out 27 March, 1869.
SWORDS, THOMAS A.
Acting Assistant Paymaster, 5 December, 1864. Mustered out 29 September, 1865.
SYDNEY, JOSEPH W.
Third Assistant Engineer, 3 December, 1861. Second Assistant Engineer, 8 September, 1863. Died 31 October, 1864.
SYKES, ARTHUR O.
Chaplain, 30 December, 1897.
SYKES, SAMUEL M.
Acting Second Assistant Engineer, 9 May, 1864. Honorably discharged 29 November, 1865.
SYKES, STEPHEN.
Purser, 12 September, 1800. Last appearance on Records of Navy Department. Resigned.
SYMINGTON, POWERS.
Naval Cadet, 7 September, 1888. Ensign, 1 July, 1894. Lieutenant, Junior Grade, 3 March, 1899. Lieutenant, 30 August, 1900.
SYMMES, FRANK J.
Acting Third Assistant Engineer, under instruction, Naval Academy, 10 October, 1866. Third Assistant Engineer, 2 June, 1868. Second Assistant Engineer, 2 June, 1869. Resigned 18 July, 1871.
SYMMES, J. G.
Surgeon, 9 January, 1799. Last appearance on Records of Navy Department.
SYMMES, THOMAS.
Acting Master, 30 August, 1861. Resigned 21 February, 1865.
SYMMS, G. G.
Mate, 3 June, 1864. Honorably discharged 20 November, 1867.
SYMONDS, FREDERICK M.
Midshipman, 26 September, 1862. Graduated June, 1867. Ensign, 18 December, 1868. Master, 21 March, 1870. Lieutenant, 21 March, 1871. Lieutenant-Commander, 31 July, 1890. Commander, 19 June, 1897.
SYMONDS, WILLIAM.
Acting Ensign, 11 February, 1864. Resigned 20 January, 1865.
SYPHER, ABRAM J.
Acting First Assistant Engineer, 12 January, 1864. Resigned 20 May, 1865.
SYPHER, JAY H.
Naval Cadet, 5 September, 1887. Ensign, 1 July, 1893. Lieutenant, Junior Grade, 3 March, 1899. Lieutenant, 11 January, 1900.
TAAFE, CHRISTOPHER G.
Acting Master, 8 May, 1862. Honorably discharged 25 August, 1865.
TABB, BLUCHER H.
Midshipman, 17 January, 1849. Killed 5 March, 1850.
TABER, CHARLES E.
Acting Third Assistant Engineer, 29 August, 1863. Honorably discharged 24 August, 1865.
TABER, SILAS A.
Mate, 1 May, 1863. Resigned (sick) 18 October, 1864.
TABER, WILLIAM.
Mate, 15 November, 1861. Appointment revoked (sick) 28 August, 1862.
TABER, WILLIAM D.
Acting Ensign, 14 February, 1864. Honorably discharged 6 December, 1865.
TAFFE, ARTHUR F.
Mate, 29 November, 1862. Drowned from Juniata, 6 March, 1865.
TAFT, JOHN M.
Midshipman, 25 February, 1863. Graduated June, 1866. Ensign, 12 March, 1868. Master, 26 March, 1869. Lieutenant, 21 March, 1870. Died 28 October, 1872.
TAGGART, DAVID.
Gunner, 18 June, 1834. Died at sea 13 December, 1836.
TAGGART, F. B.
Midshipman, 1 February, 1814. Resigned 4 May, 1815.
TAGGART, WILLIAM H.
Acting Assistant Surgeon, 1 October, 1864. Resigned 18 January, 1865.
TAGGART, WILLIAM.
Third Assistant Engineer, 5 January, 1843. Second Assistant Engineer, 10 July, 1837. Resigned 12 May, 1849.

GENERAL NAVY REGISTER. 533

TAINTER, DEAN W.
  Acting Ensign, 1 October, 1862. Resigned 26 April, 1865.
TAINTER, GEORGE W.
  Mate, 22 October, 1863. Acting Ensign, 22 July, 1864. Honorably discharged 3 November, 1865.
TAIT, CHARLES W.
  Assistant Surgeon, 24 July, 1837. Passed Assistant Surgeon, 14 March, 1843. Resigned 17 November, 1843.
TALBOT, CYRUS.
  Lieutenant, 21 May, 1799. Commander, 15 January, 1800. Discharged 23 October, 1801, under Peace Establishment Act.
TALBOT, JOHN G.
  Midshipman, 15 April, 1862. Graduated June, 1866. Ensign, 12 March, 1868. Master, 26 March, 1869. Lieutenant, 21 March, 1870. Drowned 19 December, 1870.
TALBOT, LAURIE H.
  Ensign (Spanish-American War), 29 June, 1898. Honorably discharged 18 January, 1899.
TALBOT, LEVI.
  Gunner, 13 July, 1831. Died 14 June, 1841.
TALBOT, MORTIMER R.
  Chaplain, 8 September, 1841. Died 21 April, 1863.
TALBOT, ROBERT S.
  Third Assistant Engineer, 22 October, 1860. Second Assistant Engineer, 26 August, 1862. First Assistant Engineer, 24 August, 1864. Resigned 24 October, 1868. Passed Assistant Engineer (Spanish-American War), 14 May, 1898. Honorably discharged 10 January, 1899.
TALBOT, SILAS.
  Captain, 11 May, 1798. Resigned 21 September, 1801.
TALBOT, ZEPHANIAL.
  Third Assistant Engineer, 3 May, 1859. Second Assistant Engineer, 13 May, 1861. First Assistant Engineer, 20 May, 1863. Resigned 16 December, 1865.
TALCOTT, CHARLES GRATIOT.
  Cadet Engineer, Naval Academy, 15 September, 1875. Graduated 10 June, 1879. Assistant Engineer 10 June, 1881. Died 25 July, 1889.
TALCOTT, GEORGE, Jr.
  Midshipman, 23 November, 1861. Graduated September, 1865. Ensign, 1 December, 1866. Master, 12 March, 1868. Lieutenant, 26 March, 1869. Lieutenant-Commander, 25 March, 1880. Resigned 15 November, 1883.
TALCOTT, HORACE.
  Acting Assistant Paymaster, 27 September, 1862. Died 8 May, 1864.
TALCOTT, MATTHEW.
  Midshipman, 26 April, 1798. Dismissed 16 August, 1798.
TALCOTT, MATTHEW.
  Midshipman, 11 September, 1799. Discharged 15 April, 1801, under Peace Establishment Act.
TALIAFERRO, HORACE D.
  Assistant Surgeon, 20 June, 1838. Passed Assistant Surgeon, 22 November, 1843. Resigned 15 November, 1844.
TALIAFERRO, A. R.
  Midshipman, 2 February, 1829. Passed Midshipman, 3 July, 1835. Lieutenant, 8 September, 1841. Cashiered 20 October, 1843.
TALLMADGE, B.
  Midshipman, 24 January, 1815. Lieutenant, 13 January, 1825. Died 20 June, 1831.
TALLMAN, BENJAMIN.
  Carpenter, 25 March, 1802. Last appearance on Records of Navy Department, 1 December, 1803. Furloughed.
TALLMAN, CHARLES E.
  Sailmaker, 9 January, 1877. Retired List, 29 October, 1898.
TALLMAN, HAMILTON M.
  Midshipman, 27 February, 1863. Graduated June, 1868. Ensign, 19 April, 1869. Master, 12 July, 1870. Retired List, 26 June, 1875. Title changed to Lieutenant, Junior Grade, 3 March, 1883. Died 19 January, 1890.
TALLMAN, HENRY C.
  Acting Midshipman, 24 September, 1857. Lieutenant, 1 August, 1862. Lieutenant-Commander, 25 July, 1866. Retired List, 9 October, 1872. Died 19 December, 1896.
TALLMAN, PELEG.
  Lieutenant, 16 April, 1799. Resigned 20 September, 1799.
TALLMAN, WILLIAM, Jr.
  Acting Master, 30 August, 1861. Honorably discharged 18 December, 1865.
TALLON, JOHN.
  Acting First Assistant Engineer, 1 May, 1863. Appointment revoked (sick) 21 April, 1865.
TANEY, J. B.
  Acting Ensign, 27 July, 1863. Honorably discharged 6 June, 1868.
TANEY, JOSEPH.
  Midshipman, 20 February, 1800. Resigned 2 January, 1801.
TANNER, HENRY N.
  Acting Assistant Paymaster, 10 July, 1862. Died 2 July, 1863.
TANNER, JOHN A.
  Assistant Surgeon, 20 October, 1875. Resigned 11 August, 1882.
TANNER, SAMUEL W.
  Acting Assistant Paymaster, 18 January, 1864. Mustered out 22 September, 1865.

GENERAL NAVY REGISTER.

TANNER, ZERA L.
Acting Ensign, 18 August, 1862. Acting Master, 29 September, 1864. Ensign, 12 March, 1868. Master, 18 December, 1868. Lieutenant, 21 March, 1870. Lieutenant-Commander, 22 February, 1883. Commander, 7 February, 1893. Retired List, 5 December, 1897.

TAPLEY, JOHN.
Midshipman, 31 January, 1800. Discharged 30 April, 1801, under Peace Establishment Act.

TAPMAN, HENRY T.
Third Assistant Engineer, 3 August, 1863. Dismissed 13 September, 1864.

TAPPAN, AMOS K.
Acting Third Assistant Engineer, 11 March, 1865. Honorably discharged 27 October, 1865.

TAPPAN, BENJAMIN.
Midshipman, 21 September, 1871. Graduated 20 June, 1876. Ensign, 5 February, 1879. Lieutenant, Junior Grade, 20 January, 1886. Lieutenant, 2 August, 1891. Lieutenant-Commander, 1 July, 1899.

TARBELL, JOHN F.
Acting Assistant Paymaster, 28 January, 1862. Mustered out 11 December, 1865. Assistant Paymaster, 21 February, 1867. Passed Assistant Paymaster, 16 September, 1868. Paymaster, 3 April, 1879. Retired List, 18 February, 1892.

TARBELL, JOSEPH.
Midshipman, 5 December, 1798. Lieutenant, 25 August, 1800. Commander, 25 April, 1808. Captain, 24 July, 1813. Died 24 November, 1815.

TARBOX, GLENNIE.
Cadet Midshipman, 1 October, 1881. Ensign, 8 August, 1887. Lieutenant, Junior Grade, 4 July, 1896. Lieutenant, 3 March, 1899.

TARDY, HENRY.
Midshipman, 9 November, 1813. Dismissed by Court-martial 5 August, 1817.

TARDY, WALTER B.
Naval Cadet, 19 May, 1894. Ensign, 4 April, 1900.

TARR, HERBERT J.
Acting Third Assistant Engineer, 19 September, 1862. Honorably discharged 8 February, 1866.

TARR, ROBERT.
Acting Master, 25 January, 1862. Acting Volunteer Lieutenant, 13 April, 1864. Honorably discharged 12 October, 1865.

TARRANT, WILLIAM T.
Naval Cadet, 6 September, 1894. Ensign, 4 April, 1900.

TATE, JAMES.
Acting Second Assistant Engineer. Resigned 17 June, 1864.

TATE, ROBERT.
Acting Chief Engineer, 1 October, 1862. Honorably discharged 19 November, 1865.

TATE, WILLIAM H.
Acting Third Assistant Engineer, 12 December, 1861. Acting Second Assistant Engineer, 9 February, 1864. Honorably discharged 7 October, 1865.

TATEM, JOSEPH F.
Ensign (Spanish-American War), 20 May, 1898. Honorably discharged 31 October, 1898.

TATEM, ROBERT L.
Sailmaker, 22 June, 1861. Dismissed 24 November, 1880.

TATEM, ROBERT S.
Master, 21 July, 1814. Died 3 January, 1844.

TATEM, SAMUEL.
Sailmaker, 30 March, 1848. Died 23 August, 1877.

TATEM, THOMAS.
Sailmaker, 10 September, 1849. Died 3 May, 1853.

TATEN, JOHN F.
Sailmaker, 21 December, 1841. Resigned 8 June, 1842.

TATEN, THOMAS.
Sailmaker, 24 November, 1841. Resigned 7 September, 1842.

TATNALL, EDWARD F.
Midshipman, 17 March, 1838. Passed Midshipman, 20 May, 1844. Died 21 July, 1850.

TATNALL, JOSIAH.
Midshipman, 1 January, 1812. Lieutenant, 1 April, 1818. Commander, 25 February, 1838. Captain, 5 February, 1850. Resigned 21 February, 1861.

TATTNALL, JOSIAH, Jr.
Purser, 28 June, 1850. Resigned 22 April, 1856.

TAUNT, EMORY H.
Midshipman, 22 July, 1865. Graduated June, 1869. Ensign, 12 July, 1870. Master, 28 December, 1872. Lieutenant, 8 August, 1876. Resigned 30 June, 1888.

TAUSSIG, EDWARD D.
Midshipman, 24 July, 1863. Graduated June, 1867. Ensign, 18 December, 1868. Master, 21 March, 1870. Lieutenant, 1 January, 1872. Lieutenant-Commander, 19 June, 1892. Commander, 10 ugust, 1898.

TAUSSIG, JOSEPH K.
Naval Cadet, 5 June, 1895. At sea prior to final graduation.

TAWRESEY, JOHN G.
Cadet Engineer, 1 October, 1881. Ensign, 1 July, 1887. Assistant Naval Constructor, 1 July, 1889. Naval Constructor, 30 June, 1896.

TAYLOE, JAMES L.
Acting Midshipman, 24 September, 1855. Midshipman, 15 June, 1860. Dismissed 5 July, 1861.

TAYLOE, JOHN.
Midshipman, 15 November, 1809. Lieutenant, 9 December, 1814. Resigned 31 July, 1823.
TAYLOR, ALBERT.
Mate, 8 May, 1862. Acting Ensign, 24 November, 1862. Acting Master, 11 March, 1865. Honorably discharged 20 January, 1866. Acting Master, 11 December, 1866. Mustered out 27 March, 1869.
TAYLOR, ALFRED.
Midshipman, 1 January, 1825. Passed Midshipman, 4 June, 1831. Lieutenant, 9 February, 1837. Commander, 14 September, 1855. Captain, 16 July, 1862. Commodore, 27 September, 1861. Rear-Admiral, 29 January, 1872. Retired List, 23 May, 1872. Died 19 April, 1891.
TAYLOR, BENJAMIN F.
Acting Third Assistant Engineer, 13 September, 1861. Acting Second Assistant Engineer, 23 October, 1862. Died 4 August, 1863.
TAYLOR, BUSHROD B.
Midshipman, 3 April, 1849. Passed Midshipman, 12 June, 1855. Master, 16 September, 1855. Lieutenant, 31 July, 1856. Lieutenant-Commander, 16 July, 1862. Commander, 14 March, 1868. Captain, 27 October, 1879. Died 22 April, 1883.
TAYLOR, CHARLES E.
Acting Assistant Paymaster, 6 February, 1862. Resigned 7 April, 1865.
TAYLOR, CHARLES F.
Mate, 5 March, 1862. Acting Ensign, 5 November, 1862. Acting Master, 6 December, 1864. Honorably discharged 27 August, 1865.
TAYLOR, CHARLES F.
Assistant Engineer (Spanish-American War), 12 May, 1898. Honorably discharged 2 November, 1898.
TAYLOR, CHARLES S.
Carpenter, 12 July, 1897.
TAYLOR, CLINTON F.
Mate, 20 July, 1864. Honorably discharged 10 April, 1866.
TAYLOR, DANIEL G.
Acting Master, 27 February, 1862. Dismissed 22 July, 1863.
TAYLOR, DAVID.
Acting Second Assistant Engineer, 2 August, 1864. Honorably discharged 19 June, 1865.
TAYLOR, DAVID P.
Acting Assistant Surgeon, 28 March, 1864. Honorably discharged 28 October, 1865.
TAYLOR, DAVID W.
Cadet Engineer, 1 October, 1881. Assistant Naval Constructor, 14 August, 1886. Naval Constructor, 5 December, 1891.
TAYLOR, DUDLEY E.
Acting Master, 18 January, 1862. Died, New Haven, Connecticut, 19 July, 1866.
TAYLOR, DUGOMIER.
Midshipman, 16 January, 1809. Lieutenant, 24 July, 1813. Died at sea 5 October, 1819.
TAYLOR, EDWARD E.
Acting Ensign, 26 February, 1863. Acting Master, 29 September, 1864. Honorably discharged 27 September, 1865.
TAYLOR, ELIAS C.
Master's Mate, 16 November, 1816. Midshipman, 1 January, 1819. Lieutenant, 17 May, 1828. Died 20 April, 1832.
TAYLOR, FITCH W.
Chaplain, 23 April, 1841. Died 23 July, 1865.
TAYLOR, FRANCIS.
Midshipman, 9 June, 1811. Drowned 5 October, 1811.
TAYLOR, FRANCIS C.
Acting Third Assistant Engineer, 4 May, 1864. Appointment revoked 23 May, 1864.
TAYLOR, FRANCIS E.
Mate, 21 April, 1865. Honorably discharged 8 January, 1866.
TAYLOR, GEORGE.
Acting Master, 21 January, 1862. Acting Volunteer Lieutenant, 16 August, 1864. Resigned 18 February, 1865.
TAYLOR, GEORGE.
Mate, 31 October, 1861. Acting Ensign, 6 January, 1863. Dismissed 5 January, 1865.
TAYLOR, GEORGE.
Acting Third Assistant Engineer, 12 July, 1862. Honorably discharged 14 April, 1868.
TAYLOR, GEORGE B.
Midshipman, 10 May, 1820. Resigned 6 January, 1821.
TAYLOR, GEORGE C.
Acting Assistant Paymaster, 10 October, 1861. Resigned 19 December, 1863.
TAYLOR, GEORGE W.
Acting Second Assistant Engineer, 1 October, 1862. Acting First Assistant Engineer, 28 November, 1863. Resigned 28 February, 1865.
TAYLOR, GEORGE W.
Midshipman, 1 November, 1827. Resigned 19 December, 1831.
TAYLOR, GORHAM C.
Mate, 24 October, 1861. Appointment revoked (sick) 31 January, 1863.
TAYLOR, HENRY.
Acting Ensign, 10 June, 1863. Acting Master, 27 December, 1864. Honorably discharged 31 January, 1866. Acting Master, 4 August, 1866. Mustered out.
TAYLOR, HENRY.
Acting Ensign, 11 December, 1863. Honorably discharged 12 May, 1867.

TAYLOR, HENRY C.
Acting Midshipman, 20 September, 1860. Ensign, 28 May, 1863. Master, 10 November, 1865. Lieutenant, 10 November, 1866. Lieutenant-Commander, 12 March, 1868. Commander, 16 December, 1879. Captain, 16 April, 1894.
TAYLOR, HENRY W.
Acting First Assistant Engineer, 28 May, 1864. Resigned 17 June, 1865.
TAYLOR, HENRY W.
Acting Third Assistant Engineer, 7 February, 1865. Honorably discharged 27 October, 1865.
TAYLOR, HIERO.
Cadet Midshipman, 30 September 1873. Graduated 18 June, 1879. Ensign 1 September, 1880. Lieutenant, Junior Grade, 29 January, 1887. Retired List, 1 June, 1892. Died 14 July, 1893.
TAYLOR, HIRAM A.
Mate, 12 August, 1864. Honorably discharged 9 August, 1865.
TAYLOR, JAMES.
Master, 19 April, 1813. Discharged 3 February, 1814.
TAYLOR, JAMES.
Acting Master, 29 May, 1861. Honorably discharged 12 February, 1866.
TAYLOR, JAMES.
Master, 13 December, 1814. Last appearance on Records of Navy Department, 1815. Dead.
TAYLOR, JAMES B.
Midshipman, 1 January, 1812. Lieutenant, 5 March, 1817. Drowned 19 March, 1819.
TAYLOR, JAMES M.
Surgeon, 9 August, 1805. Resigned 27 September, 1807.
TAYLOR, JAMES S.
Assistant Surgeon, 8 November, 1899.
TAYLOR, JAMES W.
Acting Master and Pilot, 15 November, 1864. Appointment revoked 9 March, 1865.
TAYLOR, JESSE.
Midshipman, 6 December, 1849. Passed Midshipman, 12 June, 1855. Master, 16 September, 1855. Lieutenant, 26 November, 1856. Resigned 12 September, 1859.
TAYLOR, J. H. R.
Midshipman, 8 March, 1839. Resigned 30 July, 1839.
TAYLOR, JOHN.
Midshipman, 16 January, 1809. Killed in action 23 August, 1812.
TAYLOR, JOHN.
Mate, 9 March, 1866. Resigned 5 August, 1868.
TAYLOR, JOHN H.
Mate, 10 November, 1863. Honorably discharged 5 September, 1865.
TAYLOR, JOHN L.
Midshipman, 2 February, 1829. Resigned 3 August, 1831.
TAYLOR, JOHN S.
Midshipman, 14 December, 1836. Passed Midshipman, 1 July, 1842. Master, 23 June, 1849. Lieutenant, 5 February, 1850. Reserved List, 13 September, 1855. Resigned 18 April, 1861.
TAYLOR, JOHN W.
Midshipman, 1 April, 1828. Dismissed 6 June, 1836.
TAYLOR, JOHN Y.
Assistant Surgeon, 26 September, 1853. Passed Asistant Surgeon, 1 August, 1861. Medical Inspector, 29 June, 1872. Medical Director, 20 April, 1879. Retired List, 21 January, 1891.
TAYLOR, JOSEPH.
Master, 14 July, 1812. Died 2 January, 1820.
TAYLOR, JOSEPH.
Acting Assistant Surgeon, 28 September, 1870. Honorably discharged 30 June, 1879.
TAYLOR, J. WINTHROP.
Assistant Surgeon, 7 March, 1838. Surgeon, 1 May, 1852. Medical Director, 3 March, 1871. Chief, Bureau Medicine and Surgery, 21 October, 1878. Retired List, 19 August, 1879. Died 19 January, 1880.
TAYLOR, MARTIN L.
Acting Third Assistant Engineer, 6 September, 1864. Honorably discharged 23 September, 1865.
TAYLOR, MONTGOMERY M.
Naval Cadet, 21 May, 1886. Ensign, 1 July, 1892. Lieutenant, Junior Grade, 3 March, 1899. Lieutenant, 2 June, 1899.
TAYLOR, N.
Mate, 19 June, 1865. Resigned 14 September, 1867.
TAYLOR, PERSIFER.
Carpenter, 17 April, 1800. Resigned 20 April, 1807.
TAYLOR, PETER.
Acting Third Assistant Engineer, 22 October, 1863. Acting Second Assistant Engineer, 8 March, 1865. Honorably discharged 27 September, 1865.
TAYLOR, P. HENRY.
Third Assistant Engineer, 16 February, 1852. Second Assistant Engineer, 21 May, 1853. Resigned 10 September, 1856.
TAYLOR, RICHARD, Jr.
Midshipman, 1 January, 1818. Resigned 17 January, 1825.
TAYLOR, RICHARD H.
Mate, 30 June, 1864. Honorably discharged 17 July, 1865.
TAYLOR, RICHARD L.
Mate, 30 June, 1864. Resigned 17 June, 1865.

GENERAL NAVY REGISTER. 537

TAYLOR, RICHARD N.
Acting Third Assistant Engineer, 11 March, 1863. Acting Second Assistant Engineer, 7 January, 1865. Honorably discharged 16 August, 1866.
TAYLOR, RICHARDSON.
Midshipman, 14 April, 1800. Discharged 5 June, 1801, under Peace Establishment Act.
TAYLOR, ROBERT.
Midshipman, 1 May, 1822. Died in 1823.
TAYLOR, ROBERT C.
Acting Second Assistant Engineer, 7 December, 1863. Dismissed 13 October, 1864.
TAYLOR, ROBERT D.
Third Assistant Engineer, 21 April, 1863. Second Assistant Engineer, 25 July, 1866. First Assistant Engineer, 31 January, 1873. Retired List, 23 April, 1892.
TAYLOR, ROBERT L.
Acting Third Assistant Engineer, 20 August, 1864. Honorably discharged 5 July, 1865.
TAYLOR, THOMAS E.
Acting Third Assistant Engineer, 19 February, 1864. Honorably discharged 28 October, 1865.
TAYLOR, THRUSTON M.
Midshipman, 1 April, 1828. Resigned 28 May, 1836.
TAYLOR, T. MARSTON.
Purser, 3 November, 1834. Died 6 July, 1870.
TAYLOR, WALTER.
Acting Third Assistant Engineer, 14 September, 1864. Honorably discharged 22 July, 1865.
TAYLOR, W. B. G.
Midshipman, 13 February, 1815. Resigned 9 June, 1836.
TAYLOR, W. D. S.
Midshipman, 20 June, 1806. Resigned 10 February, 1807.
TAYLOR, WILLIAM.
Gunner, 6 July, 1804. Last appearance on Records of Navy Department, 5 June, 1806.
TAYLOR, WILLIAM.
Midshipman, 1 January, 1812. Lieutenant, 5 March, 1817. Died 13 January, 1835.
TAYLOR, WILLIAM.
Midshipman, 17 December, 1810. Resigned 5 July, 1811.
TAYLOR, WILLIAM A.
Acting Ensign, 7 September, 1864. Honorably discharged 24 July, 1865.
TAYLOR, WILLIAM E.
Acting Second Assistant Engineer, 15 October, 1863. Resigned 28 June, 1865.
TAYLOR, WILLIAM E.
Assistant Surgeon, 3 July, 1859. Passed Assistant Surgeon, 22 August, 1862. Surgeon, 5 September, 1862. Medical Inspector, 31 December, 1876. Retired List, 14 January, 1881.
TAYLOR, WILLIAM P.
Midshipman, 13 June, 1831. Died 14 December, 1846.
TAYLOR, WILLIAM ROGERS.
Midshipman, 1 April, 1828. Passed Midshipman, 14 June, 1834. Lieutenant, 10 February, 1840. Commander, 14 September, 1855. Captain, 16 July, 1862. Commodore, 25 July, 1866. Rear-Admiral, 19 January, 1871. Retired List, 7 November, 1873. Died 14 April, 1889.
TAYLOR, WILLIAM V.
Lieutenant, 9 December, 1814. Commander, 3 March, 1831. Captain, 8 September, 1841. Reserved List, 13 September, 1855. Died 11 February, 1858.
TAYON, AUGUSTUS S.
Acting Master, 1 October, 1862. Resigned 16 June, 1863.
TEAL, BENJAMIN F.
Acting Third Assistant Engineer, 17 August, 1864. Honorably discharged 24 September, 1868.
TEAL, JACOB, Jr.
Mate, 17 October, 1863. Resigned 17 May, 1865.
TEAL, WILLIAM.
Acting Third Assistant Engineer, 7 July, 1863. Honorably discharged 3 January, 1866.
TELT, WILLIAM.
Sailmaker, 5 December, 1798. Last appearance on Records of Navy Department.
TEMPENNY, ELI.
Acting Third Assistant Engineer, 10 December, 1862. Honorably discharged 31 October, 1865.
TEMPLE, WILLIAM G.
Midshipman, 18 April, 1840. Passed Midshipman, 11 July, 1846. Master, 21 July, 1854. Lieutenant, 18 April, 1855. Lieutenant-Commander, 16 July, 1862. Commander, 3 March, 1865. Captain, 28 August, 1870. Commodore, 5 June, 1878. Rear-Admiral, 22 February, 1884. Retired List, 29 February, 1884. Died 28 June, 1894.
TEMPLE, WILLIAM T.
Midshipman, 1 September, 1811. Lieutenant, 1 April, 1818. Died 23 June, 1830.
TENANT, MOSES.
Midshipman, 3 July, 1798. Resigned 15 December, 1798.
TEN EICK, A. S.
Midshipman, 1 September, 1811. Lieutenant, 27 April, 1816. Commander, 9 February, 1837. Captain, 10 December, 1843. Died 28 March, 1844.
TENGWALL, CHARLES.
Mate, 27 August, 1863. Acting Ensign, 4 January, 1865. Honorably discharged 8 August, 1865.

TENLEY, WASHINGTON.
 Acting First Assistant Engineer, 31 December, 1863. Appointment revoked (sick) 16 June, 1864.
TENNANT, JOHN.
 Acting Third Assistant Engineer, 19 October, 1861. Dismissed 15 October, 1862.
TENNANT, THOMAS.
 Acting Third Assistant Engineer, 23 March, 1865. Died 4 September, 1867.
TENNENT, GEORGE W.
 Third Assistant Engineer, 17 February, 1860. Resigned 6 February, 1861.
TENNENT, JOHN C.
 Third Assistant Engineer, 10 July, 1847. Second Assistant Engineer, 31 October, 1848. Dismissed 5 July, 1849.
TENNEY, JOHN.
 Mate, 6 September, 1864. Honorably discharged 17 March, 1866.
TERHUNE, WARREN J.
 Naval Cadet, 19 May, 1885. Ensign, 1 July, 1891. Lieutenant, 3 March, 1899.
TERRELL, CHARLES.
 Acting Midshipman, 26 September, 1867. Graduated 6 June, 1871. Resigned 30 June, 1874.
TERRELL, DOUGLASS F.
 Cadet Midshipman, 25 September, 1880. Graduated 4 June, 1884. Ensign, 1 July, 1886. Died 15 April, 1891.
TERRELL, GEORGE B.
 Ensign (Spanish-American War), 22 April, 1898. Honorably discharged 16 November, 1898.
TERRELL, THOMAS C.
 Midshipman, 20 September, 1862. Graduated June, 1866. Ensign, 12 March, 1868. Master, 26 March, 1869. Lieutenant, 21 March, 1870. Died 16 May, 1881.
TERRETT, COLVILLE.
 Midshipman, 3 January, 1840. Passed Midshipman, 11 July, 1846. Master, 1 March, 1855. Lieutenant, 14 September, 1855. Lost in Levant, 18 September, 1860.
TERRILL EDWARD A.
 Acting Master, 19 April, 1862. Honorably discharged 16 December, 1865.
TERRILL FRANCIS H.
 Assistant Surgeon, 22 June, 1875. Resigned 24 April, 1884.
TERRILL, GEORGE.
 Surgeon, 22 May, 1826. Resigned 21 September, 1854.
TERRY, EDWARD.
 Acting Midshipman, 21 September, 1853. Midshipman, 10 June, 1857. Passed Midshipman, 25 June, 1860. Master, 24 October, 1860. Lieutenant, 3 April, 1861. Lieutenant-Commander, 4 January, 1863. Commander, 31 October, 1871. Died 1 June, 1882.
TERRY, FRANK D.
 Passed Assistant Engineer (Spanish-American War), 14 May, 1898. Honorably discharged 21 January, 1899.
TERRY, JAMES.
 Midshipman, 16 July, 1814. Resigned 20 April, 1815.
TERRY, JAMES.
 Master, 20 April, 1815. Cashiered 25 October, 1820.
TERRY, JOSEPH H.
 Purser, 6 June, 1815. Died 22 August, 1853.
TERRY, SILAS W.
 Acting Midshipman, 28 September, 1858. Ensign, 16 September, 1862. Lieutenant, 22 February, 1864. Lieutenant-Commander, 25 July, 1866. Commander, 11 July, 1877. Captain, 9 January, 1893. Rear-Admiral, 29 March, 1900.
TERRY, VAN RENSALEAR.
 Acting Second Assistant Engineer, 28 May, 1861. Dismissed 4 August, 1862.
TERRY, WILLIAM F.
 Assistant Surgeon, 24 January, 1862. Resigned 19 October, 1863. Assistant Surgeon, 12 July, 1866. Resigned 15 May, 1868.
TESSIMOND, C. M.
 Mate 10 September, 1864. Honorably discharged 16 August, 1865.
TEST, HENRY M.
 Acting Third Assistant Engineer, 7 December, 1863. Honorably discharged 15 August, 1865.
TESTER, ABRAHAM.
 Acting Third Assistant Engineer, 18 February, 1864. Honorably discharged 21 August, 1865.
TEW, GEORGE W.
 Midshipman, 21 February, 1799. Lieutenant, 1 April, 1800. Last appearance on Records on Navy Department, 30 April, 1801. Dead.
TEW, HENRY.
 Mate, 18 April, 1864. Died 18 August, 1877.
TEW, HENRY, Sr.
 Master, 28 March, 1814. Resigned 27 December, 1814.
TEW, HENRY.
 Master, 28 June, 1812. Resigned 27 December, 1814.
TEW, JAMES B.
 Mate, 12 January, 1863. Acting Ensign, 31 January, 1865. Honorably discharged 19 October, 1865.
TEWKSBURY, JAMES.
 Master, 14 December, 1815. Died 1 September, 1843.
THACHER, OLIVER.
 Acting Master, 4 March, 1862. Honorably discharged 21 November, 1865.

THACKARA, ALEXANDER M.
  Midshipman, 20 July, 1865. Graduated June, 1869. Ensign, 12 July, 1870. Master, 12 July, 1871. Lieutenant, 8 November, 1874. Resigned 24 October, 1882.
THAIN, WILLIAM W.
  Acting Third Assistant Engineer, 29 December, 1862. Honorably discharged 30 October, 1865.
THALL, RICHARD.
  Acting Third Assistant Engineer, 4 March, 1863. Acting Second Assistant Engineer, 1 February, 1865. Honorably discharged 20 June, 1868.
THATCHER, CALEB B.
  Mate, 18 February, 1864. Honorably discharged 6 November, 1865.
THATCHER, CHARLES.
  Acting Ensign, 4 March, 1863. Acting Master, 1 December, 1863. Murdered at Raceousi Island, La., 25 November, 1864.
THATCHER, EDWARD C.
  Assistant Surgeon, 8 July, 1867. Resigned 1 March, 1873.
THATCHER, HENRY C.
  Acting Assistant Surgeon, 3 March, 1865. Honorably discharged 19 January, 1866.
THATCHER, HENRY K.
  Midshipman, 4 March, 1823. Lieutenant, 23 March, 1829. Lieutenant-Commander, 28 February, 1833. Commander, 14 September, 1855. Commodore, 16 July, 1862. Rear-Admiral, 25 July, 1866. Retired List, 26 May, 1868. Died 5 April, 1880.
THATCHER, J. C.
  Purser, 13 September, 1841. Lost in the Grampus, March, 1843.
THATCHER, JOSEPH L.
  Carpenter, 20 February, 1872. Died 23 September, 18??.
THATCHER, JOSEPH L.
  Carpenter, 20 February, 1872. Died 23 December, 1886.
THATCHER, LEWIS C.
  Acting Third Assistant Engineer, 9 June, 1864. Acting Second Assistant Engineer, 20 March, 1865. Honorably discharged 9 December, 1865.
THAXTER, MARTIN W.
  Acting Third Assistant Engineer, 31 May, 1864. Honorably discharged 8 February, 1866.
THAYER, EWDARD N.
  Midshipman, 18 June, 1812. Resigned 8 March, 1814.
THAYER, FOSTER.
  Acting Assistant Surgeon, 17 June, 1864. Resigned 9 June, 1865.
THAYER, G. J. W.
  Midshipman, 23 October, 1832. Resigned 27 October, 1834.
THAYER, HENRY G.
  Acting Assistant Paymaster, 24 March, 1864. Honorably discharged 12 December, 1865.
THAYER, ISAAC.
  Acting Ensign, 28 March, 1864. Honorably discharged 1 August, 1865.
THAYER, JAMES.
  Boatswain, 1 April, 1822. Died 9 January, 1828.
THAYER, JAMES.
  Gunner, 27 September, 1860. Dismissed 9 November, 1864. Acting Gunner, 3 December, 1864. Dismissed 14 March, 1865. Reinstated from 3 December, 1864. Resigned 31 October, 1876.
THAYER, WILLIAM L. G.
  Acting Assistant Paymaster 17 November, 1864. Honorably discharged 15 October, 1865.
THEISS, EMIL.
  Naval Cadet, 1 October, 1878. Assistant Engineer, 1 July, 1884. Passed Assistant Engineer, 1 August, 1894. Rank changed to Lieutenant, 3 March, 1899.
THELEEN, DAVID E.
  Naval Cadet, 6 September, 1893. Ensign, 1 July, 1899.
THODE, JOHN W.
  Mate, 8 January, 1862. Resigned 23 September, 1862. Mate, 2 February, 1864. Re signed 27 June, 1865.
THOM, J. PEMBROKE.
  Assistant Surgeon, 16 March, 1853. Resigned 27 May, 1857.
THOM, WILLIAM A.
  Cadet Midshipman, 21 June, 1875. Graduated 10 June, 1881. Ensign, Junior Grade, 3 March, 1883. Ensign, 26 June, 1884. Died 11 December, 1886.
THOM, WILLIAM S.
  Purser, 15 October, 1799. Dscharged 21 May, 1802, under Peace Establishment Act.
THOMAE, GEORGE F.
  Ensign (Spanish-American War), 21 May, 1898. Honorably discharged 20 December. 1898.
THOMAS, ALBERT E.
  Lieutenant, Junior Grade (Spanish-American War), 2 July, 1898. Honorably discharged 10 October, 1898.
THOMAS, CALVIN F.
  Midshipman, 16 October, 1849. Passed Midshipman, 20 June, 1856. Master, 22 January, 1858. Lieutenant, 23 January, 1858. Died 18 February, 1860.
THOMAS, CHARLES.
  Acting Ensign, 1 September, 1864. Dismissed 21 November, 1864.
THOMAS, CHARLES.
  Midshipman, 2 February, 1829. Passed Midshipman, 3 July, 1835. Lieutenant, 8 September, 1841. Reserved List, 13 September, 1855. Captain on Retired List, 4 April, 1867. Died 24 February, 1891.

THOMAS, CHARLES M.
Midshipman, 28 November, 1861. Graduated September, 1865. Ensign, 1 December, 1866. Master, 12 March, 1868. Lieutenant, 26 March, 1869. Lieutenant-Commander, 1 April, 1880. Commander, 28 February, 1890. Captain, 3 March, 1899.

THOMAS, CHARLES W.
Chaplain, 29 October, 1853. Resigned 26 January, 1861.

THOMAS, CHAUNCEY, Jr.
Midshipman, 26 September, 1867. Graduated 6 June, 1871. Ensign, 14 July, 1872. Master, 14 April, 1875. Lieutenant, 10 March, 1882. Lieutenant-Commander, 3 March, 1899.

THOMAS, EDWARD.
Acting Assistant Surgeon, 25 January, 1862. Dismissed 7 April, 1862.

THOMAS, E. H.
Acting Ensign, 24 April, 1863. Dismissed 31 October, 1864.

THOMAS, EUGENE B.
Midshipman, 20 September, 1861. Graduated September, 1865. Ensign, 1 December, 1866. Master, 12 March, 1868. Lieutenant, 26 March, 1869. Lieutenant-Commander, 7 August, 1881. Retired List, 29 June, 1887. Died 28 June, 1896.

THOMAS, F. J.
Acting Master, 19 November, 1861. Resigned 2 September, 1862.

THOMAS, GARDNER, Jr.
Purser, 22 July, 1815. Died 25 September, 1829.

THOMAS, GEORGE.
Master, 7 July, 1812. Last appearance on Records of Navy Department. Dead.

THOMAS, GEORGE.
Sailmaker, 19 December, 1834. Retired List, 16 May, 1873. Died in 1881.

THOMAS, GEORGE.
Mate, 29 September, 1863. Acting Ensign, 22 December, 1864. Honorably discharged 2 August, 1865.

THOMAS, GEORGE E.
Mate, 14 November, 1861. Acting Ensign, 5 April, 1867. Died 24 December, 1867.

THOMAS, GEORGE E.
Ensign, 26 November, 1863. Resigned 12 May, 1865.

THOMAS, HENRY.
Midshipman, 2 January, 1804. Resigned 26 September, 1808.

THOMAS, HENRY.
Master, 25 January, 1814. Discharged 1 February, 1815.

THOMAS, HENRY G.
Carpenter, 10 February, 1844. Dismissed 27 July, 1861.

THOMAS, JAMES R.
Mate, 21 May, 1864. Resigned 19 May, 1865.

THOMAS, JOHN.
Mate, gallantry in saving life of two companions, 27 December, 1862. Died 2 October, 1863.

THOMAS, JOHN A.
Mate, 10 March, 1864. Honorably discharged 13 August, 1865.

THOMAS, JOHN D.
Acting Ensign, 23 December, 1864. Honorably discharged 21 December, 1867.

THOMAS, JOHN J.
Carpenter, 20 April, 1874. Retired List, 1 May, 1884. Died 23 June, 1884.

THOMAS, JOHN L.
Midshipman, 1 January, 1818. Lieutenant, 3 March, 1827. Lost in the Hornet, 10 September, 1829.

THOMAS, JONATHAN.
Acting Third Assistant Engineer, 17 May, 1861. Resigned 8 February, 1862.

THOMAS, JOSEPH G.
Carpenter, 16 March, 1847. Retired List, 2 December, 1878. Died 31 January, 1893.

THOMAS, JOSEPH H.
Third Assistant Engineer, 20 May, 1863. Second Assistant Engineer, 15 September, 1865. Resigned 29 November, 1873.

THOMAS, JOSIAH.
Acting Ensign, 4 October, 1864. Honorably discharged 23 September, 1865.

THOMAS, LLOYD.
Mate, 1 October, 1862. Acting Ensign, 16 April, 1863. Appointment revoked (sick) 27 July, 1864.

THOMAS, MARTIN V.
Mate, 4 October, 1862. Resigned 17 July, 1863. Mate, 7 September, 1864. Honorably discharged 18 August, 1865.

THOMAS, NATHANIEL W.
Acting Midshipman, 24 September, 1857. Lieutenant, 1 August, 1862. Lieutenant-Commander, 25 July, 1866. Died 18 September, 1866.

THOMAS, RICHARD.
Midshipman, 3 August, 1798. Resigned 11 December, 1802.

THOMAS, RICHARD.
Carpenter, 22 January, 1814. Died 10 December, 1842.

THOMAS, ROBERT G.
Carpenter, 20 June, 1853. Died 9 May, 1871.

THOMAS, SAMUEL, Jr.
Acting Assistant Paymaster, 27 July, 1863. Honorably discharged 28 October, 1865.

THOMAS, SAMUEL B.
Naval Cadet, 31 May, 1895. At sea prior to final graduation.

GENERAL NAVY REGISTER.   541

THOMAS, THOMAS.
　Midshipman, 15 November, 1809.　Last appearance on Records of Navy Department, 21 May, 1810.　Drowned.
THOMAS, WALTER S.
　Mate, 12 November, 1863.　Appointment revoked (sick) 17 February, 1865.
THOMAS, WILLIAM E.
　Acting Ensign, 25 June, 1863.　Acting Master recommendation of Commanding Officer, 6 July, 1864.　Honorably discharged 27 October, 1865.
THOMAS, WILLIAM F.
　Mate 11 August, 1864.　Honorably discharged 23 September, 1865.
THOMAS, WILLIAM H.
　Mate, 18 February, 1862.　Acting Ensign, 26 December, 1862.　Dismissed 30 December, 1864.
THOMAS, WILLIAM H.
　Acting Second Assistant Engineer, 9 June, 1864.　Appointment revoked (sick) 8 August, 1864.
THOMAS, W. R.
　Midshipman, 15 January, 1841.　Died 10 November, 1847.
THOMAS, WILLIAM S.
　Assistant Surgeon, 20 May, 1898.　Resigned 1 December, 1898.
THOMBS, JOSEPH S.
　Acting Ensign, 3 May, 1864.　Honorably discharged 9 July, 1865.
THOMPSON, ALEXANDER.
　Midshipman, 26 October, 1815.　Resigned 8 August, 1826.
TMOHPSON, ANDREW S.
　Mate, 25 November, 1863.　Honorably discharged 19 July, 1865.
THOMPSON, AUGUSTUS F.
　Gunner, 3 March, 1849.　Retired List, 3 December, 1881.　Died 3 December, 1890.
THOMPSON, AUGUSTUS F.
　Acting Master, 9 April, 1863.　Honorably discharged 20 October, 1865.
THOMPSON, BENJAMIN.
　Midshipman, 1 December, 1809.　Killed in action 27 April, 1813.
THOMPSON, CHARLES.
　Carpenter, 21 December, 1897.
THOMPSON, C. A.
　Midshipman, 1 January, 1812.　Resigned 18 April, 1813.
THOMPSON, C. A.
　Midshipman, 27 August, 1823.　Passed Midshipman, 20 February, 1830.　Resigned 27 September, 1833.
THOMPSON, CHARLES A.
　Midshipman, 30 September, 1868.　Resigned 7 March, 1873.　Ensign (Spanish-American War), 2 July, 1898.　Honorably discharged 8 February, 1899.
THOMPSON, C. C. B.
　Midshipman, 22 December, 1802.　Lieutenant, 15 February, 1809.　Commander, 27 April, 1816.　Captain, 3 March, 1825.　Died 2 September, 1832.
THOMPSON, CHARLES A.
　Midshipman, 30 September, 1868.　Graduated 1 June, 1872.　Resigned 7 March, 1873.
THOMPSON, CHARLES D.
　Mate, 28 December, 1861.　Acting Ensign, 23 April, 1863.　Deserted 4 March, 1865.
THOMPSON, CHARLES P.
　Acting Ensign, 28 October, 1862.　Died at Cape Haytien, 13 July, 1864.
THOMPSON, CHARLES P.
　Acting Assistant Paymaster, 19 January, 1865.　Assistant Paymaster, 3 March, 1865.　Passed Assistant Paymaster, 4 May, 1866.　Paymaster, 1 August, 1866.　Retired List, 24 February, 1892.
THOMPSON, D. L.
　Acting Ensign, 9 October, 1862.　Resigned (sick) 10 June, 1864.
THOMPSON, EBENEZER.
　Carpenter, 16 November, 1849.　Retired List, 6 August, 1879.
THOMPSON, EDGAR.
　Assistant Surgeon, 19 April, 1898.
THOMPSON, EDWARD.
　Master, 24 March, 1820.　Last appearance on Records of Navy Department, Columbus, 1874.
THOMPSON, EDWARD.
　Mate, 14 May, 1864.　Resigned 31 January, 1865.
THOMPSON, EGBERT.
　Midshipman, 13 March, 1837.　Passed Midshipman, 29 June, 1843.　Acting Master, 12 June, 1846.　Lieutenant, 3 October, 1850.　Commander, 16 July, 1862.　Captain, 25 July, 1866.　Retired List, 5 January, 1874.　Died 5 January, 1881.
THOMPSON, E. H.
　Mate, 15 July, 1864.　Resigned 7 April, 1865.
THOMPSON, FRANK.
　Chaplain, 16 May, 1881.
THOMPSON, F. A.
　Midshipman, 1 April, 1826.　Resigned 31 December, 1828.
THOMPSON, FRED.
　Civil Engineer, 29 September, 1898.
THOMPSON, FRED. H.
　Acting Assistant Paymaster, 18 August, 1862.　Died 5 September, 1863.
THOMPSON, G. B.
　Acting Master, 19 June, 1862.　Honorably discharged 7 February, 1866.
THOMPSON, GEORGE.
　Acting Master, 2 October, 1861　Resigned 31 May, 1862.

THOMPSON, GILBERT L.
Engineer-in-Chief, 1 September, 1842. Appointment revoked 3 October, 1844.
THOMPSON, G. M.
Midshipman, 1 February, 1826. Resigned 12 September, 1831.
THOMPSON, HARRISON.
Mate, 6 December, 1862. Appointment revoked 27 December, 1865.
THOMPSON, H. A., Jr.
Acting Assistant Paymaster, 10 February, 1865. Assistant Paymaster, 23 July, 1866. Resigned 10 December, 1866.
THOMPSON, HENRY.
Acting Master, 29 March, 1862. Dismissed 27 June, 1862.
THOMPSON, HARRY J.
Ensign (Spanish-American War), 30 July, 1898. Honorably discharged 10 October, 1898.
THOMPSON, HENRY L.
Lieutenant, Junior Grade (Spanish-American War), 23 June, 1898. Honorably discharged, 29 Decbmber, 1898.
THOMPSON, JAMES.
Chief Engineer, 14 April, 1842. Resigned 3 July, 1845.
THOMPSON, JAMES F.
Mate, 9 May, 1862. Deserted 13 March, 1863.
THOMPSON, JOHN.
Mate, 25 July, 1861. Discharged 24 November, 1861.
THOMPSON, JOHN.
Boatswain, 17 March, 1800. Last appearance on Records of Navy Department.
THOMPSON, JOHN.
Acting First Assistant Engineer, 4 December, 1863. Honorably discharged 10 October, 1865.
THOMPSON, JOHN.
Mate, 16 April, 1863. Dismissed 29 December, 1864.
THOMPSON, JOHN, Jr.
Acting Third Assistant Engineer, 24 December, 1863. Resigned 23 November, 1864.
THOMPSON, JOHN C.
Boatswain, 28 August, 1874. Retired List, 10 October, 1892.
THOMPSON, JOHN P.
Acting Ensign, 10 December, 1864. Honorably discharged 30 September, 1865.
THOMPSON, JOHN W.
Mate 5 May, 1862. Acting Ensign, 9 April, 1863. Appointment revoked 11 June, 1867.
THOMPSON, JOS.
Midshipman, 1 January, 1812. Died at Norfolk in 1813 or 1814.
THOMPSON, J. D.
Acting Third Assistant Engineer, 11 March, 1864. Resigned 5 February, 1865.
THOMPSON, JOSEPH C.
Assistant Surgeon, 19 July, 1897.
THOMPSON, J. W. B.
Midshipman, 17 February, 1810. Dismissed by Court-martial, 4 March, 1811.
THOMPSON, LEON S.
Naval Cadet, 21 May, 1888 Ensign, 1 July, 1894. Lieutenant, Junior Grade, 3 March, 1899. Lieutenant, 1 July, 1900.
THOMPSON, M. M.
Third Assistant Engineer, 24 May, 1844. Resigned 25 August, 1845.
THOMPSON, M. M.
Third Assistant Engineer, 24 May, 1844. Resigned in July, 1847.
THOMPSON, NATHANIEL.
Master, 1 July, 1812. Resigned 25 November, 1812.
THOMPSON, OTIS A.
Mate, 3 May, 1862. Acting Ensign, 24 January, 1864. Honorably discharged 22 May, 1867.
THOMPSON, OTIS P.
Acting Third Assistant Engineer, 18 November, 1862. Honorably discharged 5 November, 1865.
THOMPSON, ROBERT.
Boatswain, 9 July, 1798. Last appearance on Records of Navy Department.
THOMPSON, ROBERT M.
Midshipman, 30 July, 1864. Graduated June, 1868. Ensign, 19 April, 1869. Master, 12 July, 1870. Resigned 18 November, 1871.
THOMPSON, SAMUEL.
Passed Assistant Engineer (Spanish-American War), 14 May, 1898. Honorably discharged 4 January, 1899.
THOMPSON, SMITH, Jr.
Third Assistant Engineer, 1 June, 1842. Resigned 13 January, 1846.
THOMPSON, STRONG B.
Midshipman, 13 April, 1832. Passed Midshipman, 23 June, 1838. Lieutenant, 24 July, 1843. Resigned 24 June, 1850.
THOMPSON THEODORE S.
Acting Assistant Paymaster, 9 October, 1863. Mustered out 23 August, 1865. Assistant Paymaster, 23 July, 1863. Passed Assistant Paymaster, 1 February, 1868. Paymaster, 25 January, 1878. Pay Inspector, 10 July, 1898.
THOMPSON, THOMAS C.
Acting Ensign, 23 November, 1866. Mustered out 30 November, 1868.
THOMPSON, THOMAS H.
Acting Third Assistant Engineer, 20 August, 1864. Honorably discharged 7 July, 1865.

GENERAL NAVY REGISTER. 543

THOMPSON, THOMAS R.
  Acting Third Assistant Engineer, 6 January, 1865. Honorably discharged 30 June, 1865.
THOMPSON, VISTA R.
  Acting Gunner, 1 August, 1900.
THOMPSON, WILLIAM.
  Sailmaker, 8 June, 1812. Resigned 11 May, 1813.
THOMPSON, WILLIAM.
  Acting Master, 21 March, 1862. Honorably discharged 18 November, 1865.
THOMPSON, WILLIAM.
  Mate, 4 October, 1862. Resigned 15 September, 1864.
THOMPSON, WILLIAM C.
  Gunner, 28 July, 1846. Resigned 13 November, 1849.
THOMPSON, WILLIAM H.
  Midshipman, 27 December, 1837. Passed Midshipman, 29 June, 1843. Master, 27 September, 1850. Died 15 March, 1851.
THOMPSON, WILLIAM H.
  Assistant Paymaster, 9 September, 1861. Paymaster, 12 July, 1862. Resigned 27 March, 1866.
THOMPSON, WILLIAM H.
  Acting Second Assistant Engineer, 21 February, 1863. Acting First Assistant Engineer, 21 March, 1865. Honorably discharged 16 November, 1865.
THOMPSON, WILLIAM H.
  Mate, 23 January, 1862. Resigned 24 February, 1863.
THOMPSON, WILLIAM K.
  Mate, 5 April, 1862. Dismissed 9 June, 1862.
THOMPSON, WILLIAM S.
  Acting First Assistant Engineer, 14 October, 1863. Killed 6 April, 1865.
THOMPSON, WINFIELD SCOTT.
  Third Assistant Engineer, 16 September, 1858. Tendered resignation 7 December, 1861. No record of its acceptance. In Confederate Navy, First Assistant Engineer, 15 May, 1862.
THOMSON, CURTIS H.
  Assistant Paymaster, 21 December, 1869. Passed Assistant Paymaster, 19 August, 1876. Died 13 July, 1881.
THOMSON, ALEXANDER F.
  Warrant Machinist (Spanish-American War), 15 June 1898. Honorably discharged 2 September, 1898.
THOMSON, CHARLES F.
  Assistant Engineer (Spanish-American War), 4 May, 1898. Honorably discharged 2 September, 1898.
THOMSON, EDWARD R.
  Midshipman, 1 December, 1826. Passed Midshipman, 28 April, 1832. Lieutenant, 8 March, 1837. Commander, 14 September, 1855. Retired List, 3 December, 1861. Commodore on Retired List, 4 April, 1867. Died 12 February, 1879.
THOMSON, GEORGE A.
  Mate, 30 November, 1863. Acting Ensign, 16 December, 1864. Honorably discharged 16 September, 1865.
THOMSON, JAMES F.
  Acting Master's Mate, 26 September, 1863. Acting Ensign, 16 May, 1864. Resigned 30 May, 1865.
THOMSON, JAMES W., JR.
  Third Assistant Engineer, 26 June, 1856. First Assistant Engineer, 1 August, 1859. Chief Engineer, 2 February, 1862. Retired List, 26 June, 1896.
THOMSON ROBERT.
  Chaplain, 12 July, 1800. Last appearance on Records of Navy Department. Dead.
THOMSON, WILLIAM H., JR.
  Assistant Engineer (Spanish-American War), 22 June, 1898. Honorably discharged 17 February, 1899.
THOMSON, WILLIAM J.
  Acting Assistant Paymaster, 29 March, 1865. Assistant Paymaster, 23 July, 1866. Passed Assistant Paymaster, 20 March, 1868. Paymaster, 16 February, 1878. Pay Inspector, 9 April, 1899.
THORBURN, CHARLES E.
  Midshipman, 9 September, 1847. Passed Midshipman, 10 June, 1853. Master, 15 September, 1855. Lieutenant, 16 September, 1855. Resigned 21 July, 1860.
THORBURN, HENRY A.
  Maste, 26 August, 1863. Honorably discharged 31 August, 1865.
THORBURN, HENRY G.
  Mate, 17 May, 1864. Appointment revoked 24 July, 1866.
THORBURN, ROBERT D.
  Midshipman, 30 March, 1820. Lieutenant, 17 May, 1828. Commander, 3 October, 1850. Reserved List, 13 September, 1855. Commander on Active List, 3 October, 1850. Resigned 22 April, 1861.
THORING, FERDINAND E.
  Acting Third Assistant Engineer, 9 February, 1864. Resigned 27 September, 1864.
THORN, HERMAN.
  Purser, 24 July, 1813. Last appearance on Records of Navy Department, 1816. Furloughed.
THORN, JONATHAN.
  Midshipman, 28 April, 1800. Lieutenant, 16 February, 1807. Furloughed 18 May, 1810. Since dead.
THORN, ROBERT L.
  Assistant Surgeon, 17 June, 1806. Surgeon, 3 March, 1809. Died 18 August 1827.

GENERAL NAVY REGISTER.

THORN, SAMUEL G.
Acting Assistant Paymaster 24 February, 1862. Resigned 12 November, 1863.
THORN, WILLIAM H.
Midshipman, 2 August, 1800. Dismissed 3 May, 1805.
THORNBOROUGH, N.
Gunner, 29 November, 1798. Last appearance on Records of Navy Department.
THORNDYKE, LARKIN.
Surgeon, 3 July, 1798. Died 24 May, 1800.
THORNE, C. A.
Mate, 14 June, 1862. Dismissed 11 April, 1865.
THORNE, CHARLES H.
Mate, 6 July, 1863. Died 2 February, 1899.
THORNE, EDGAR C.
Mate, 21 January, 1863. Deserted 10 March, 1863.
THORNE, GEORGE W.
Third Assistant Engineer, 3 August, 1861. Second Assistant Engineer, 3 August, 1863. Resigned 5 November, 1863.
THORNILEY, W.
Midshipman, 30 November, 1814. Died 2 March, 1818.
THORNLEY, JOHN.
Assistant Surgeon, 13 October, 1840. Passed Assistant Surgeon, 7 March, 1846. Surgeon, 1 September, 1855. Retired List, 1 June, 1861. Medical Director, Retired List, 3 March, 1871. Died 8 November, 1887.
THORNTON, ALEXANDER B.
Acting Assistant Paymaster, 27 August, 1863. Dismissed 17 January, 1865.
THORNTON, CHARLES F.
Assistant Surgeon, 22 September, 1800. Last appearance on Records of Navy Department.
THORNTON, D. McC. F.
Purser, 3 March, 1825. Dismissed 13 June, 1850.
THORNTON, FRANCIS A.
Purser, 25 April, 1812. Died 25 February, 1862.
THORNTON, GILBERT E.
Assistant Paymaster, 6 September, 1861. Paymaster, 6 February, 1862. Pay Inspector, 14 October, 1871. Pay Director, 29 May, 1882. Died 11 September, 1891.
THORNTON, JAMES S.
Midshipman, 15 January, 1841. Passed Midshipman, 20 August, 1847. Acting Master, 7 May, 1855. Dropped 28 September, 1855. Lieutenant on Active List, 15 September, 1855. Lieutenant-Commander, 16 July, 1862. Commander, 25 July, 1866. Captain, 24 May, 1872. Died 14 May, 1875.
THORNTON, J. B.
Midshipman, 18 June, 1812. Resigned 23 May, 1815.
THORNTON, THOMAS.
Sailmaker, 5 October, 1812. Resigned 11 April, 1814.
THORNTON, WILLIAM.
Midshipman, 30 April, 1800. Discharged 12 August, 1801, under Peace Establishment Act.
THORP, ABNER.
Acting Assistant Surgeon, 15 May, 1863. Honorably discharged 1 November, 1865.
THORP, EDWIN L.
Acting Second Assistant Engineer, 9 January, 1863. Acting First Assistant Engineer, 23 July, 1863. Honorably discharged 19 December, 1867.
THRIFT, NATHANIEL.
Acting Master and Pilot, 1 October, 1864. Resigned 8 May, 1865.
THROCKMORTON, C. S.
Midshipman, 18 December, 1837. Passed Midshipman, 29 June, 1843. Resigned 4 August, 1845.
THROCKMORTON, REID R.
Acting Third Assistant Engineer, 19 November, 1864. Resigned 17 May, 1865.
THRUSTEN, EDMUND T.
Midshipman, 20 June, 1806. Resigned 25 March, 1810.
THRUSTON, GEORGE E.
Acting Master, 15 August, 1861. Dismissed 16 September, 1863.
THRUSTON, JOHN.
Midshipman, 27 October, 1841. Resigned 13 December, 1841.
THRUSTON, J. J.
Midshipman, 2 February, 1829. Resigned 6 June, 1836.
THUMBERT, JAMES E.
Acting Third Assistant Engineer, 24 October, 1864. Resigned (sick) 20 April, 1865.
THURBER, FRANK H.
Acting Third Assistant Engineer, 29 November, 1862. Acting Second Assistant, 20 February, 1864. Honorably discharged 9 August, 1865.
THURSTON, BENJAMIN E.
Cadet Midshipman, 29 September, 1879. Ensign, 1 July, 1885. Lieutenant, Junior Grade, 2 February, 1895. Died 8 June, 1896.
THURSTON, CHARLES S.
Acting Ensign, 6 December, 1864. Honorably discharged 7 August, 1865. Lieutenant, Junior Grade (Spanish-American War), 20 July, 1898. Honorably discharged 24 January, 1900.
THURSTON, CLARKE.
Acting Third Assistant Engineer, 21 July, 1864. Honorably discharged 29 September, 1865.
THURSTON, GEORGE S.
Acting Third Assistant Engineer, 12 October, 1863. Resigned 7 July, 1864.

GENERAL NAVY REGISTER. 545

THURSTON, ROBERT H.
Third Assistant Engineer, 29 July, 1861. Second Assistant Engineer, 18 December, 1862. First Assistant Engineer, 30 January, 1865. Resigned 1 April, 1872.
THURSTON, SPENCER D.
Acting Third Assistant Engineer, 22 February, 1864. Resigned 10 September, 1864.
THWING, CHESTER M.
Acting Ensign, 4 November, 1863. Honorably discharged 8 January, 1866.
THWING, SAMUEL.
Master, 14 May, 1814. Died at Washington, 1815.
TIBBATTS, ZACHARY T.
Mate, 26 November, 1863. Acting Ensign, 31 October, 1864. Honorably discharged 12 September, 1865.
TIBBETTS, HOWARD.
Acting Master, 29 October, 1861. Resigned 9 June, 1865.
TIBBITTS, HENRY.
Surgeon, 1 March, 1799. Died 22 July, 1799.
TIBBITTS, RICHARD S.
Lieutenant, 7 January, 1799. Resigned 5 February, 1800.
TICE, THEOPHILUS.
Mate, 28 March, 1862. Dismissed 15 July, 1862.
TICE, WILLIAM B.
Mate, 17 January, 1864. Resigned 30 May, 1865.
TICKNER, THOMAS.
Boatswain, 19 October, 1799. Last appearance on Records of Navy Department, 24 October, 1799.
TICKNOR BENAJAH.
Surgeon, 10 July, 1824. Died 20 September, 1858.
TIER, JAMES C.
Acting Carpenter, 23 December, 1863. Honorably discharged 1 March, 1866.
TIERNEY, JAMES W.
Assistant Paymaster (Spanish-American War), 13 June, 1898. Discharged 8 February, 1899.
TIERNEY, THOMAS.
Mate, 23 December, 1862. Acting Ensign, 24 June, 1864. Appointment revoked (sick) 22 December, 1864.
TIFFANY, DEXTER, JR.
Assistant Paymaster, 31 May, 1899.
TIFFANY, OTIS C.
Assistant Paymaster, 12 May, 1875. Passed Assistant Paymaster, 3 April, 1879. Paymaster, 19 November, 1891. Died 31 October, 1897.
TILBY, WILLIAM.
Acting Master and Pilot, 1 October, 1864. Honorably discharged 5 June, 1865.
TILDEN, ALFRED O.
Acting Second Assistant Engineer, 17 April, 1865. Honorably discharged 25 May, 1868.
TILDEN, JOHN.
Midshipman, 14 January, 1800. Resigned 24 December, 1800.
TILDEN, JOHN G.
Carpenter 4 May, 1876. Chief Carpenter, 3 March, 1899.
TILDEN, THOMAS B.
Midshipman, 11 November, 1821. Last appearance on Records of Navy Department, 1824. Boston.
TILDEN, THOMAS B.
Midshipman, 1 January, 1815. Resigned 6 February, 1820.
TILGHMAN E.
Mate. Dismissed 26 July, 1862.
TILGHMAN, EDWARD.
Acting Ensign, 14 July, 1863. Honorably discharged 29 September, 1865.
TILGHMAN, H. C.
Midshipman, 1 February, 1828. Resigned 24 July, 1835.
TILGHMAN, RICHARD L.
Midshipman, 27 October, 1830. Passed Midshipman, 4 June, 1836. Lieutenant, 8 September, 1841. Resigned 23 April, 1861.
TILGHMAN, R. L.
Midshipman 24 June, 1799. Resigned 7 December, 1802.
TILGHMAN, R. L.
Midshipman 1 May, 1828. Lost in the Hornet, 10 September, 1829.
TILLEY, BENJAMIN F.
Midshipman, 23 September, 1863. Graduated June, 1867. Ensign, 18 December, 1868. Master, 21 March, 1870. Lieutenant, 21 March, 1871. Lieutenant-Commander, 4 September, 1887. Commander, 4 September, 1896.
TILLEY, EDWARD.
Assistant Surgeon, 28 March, 1820. Died in 1822.
TILLINGHAST, ALEXANDER.
Acting Master, 5 April, 1862. Honorably discharged 22 August, 1865.
TILLINGHAST, CHARLES H.
Mate, 15 October, 1861. Resigned 7 April, 1863.
TILLINGHAST, T. G.
Midshipman, 1 January, 1808. Lieutenant, 24 July, 1813. Lost in the Wasp in 1815.
TILLMAN, EDWIN H.
Cadet Midshipman, 18 September, 1875. Graduated 10 June, 1881. Ensign, Junior Grade, 3 March, 1883. Ensign, 26 June, 1884. Lieutenant, Junior Grade, 3 April, 1892. Lieutenant, 12 March, 1896.

TILLOTSON, E. H.
 Midshipman, 1 September, 1811. Last appearance on Records of Navy Department, 16 December, 1812. Dead.
TILLOTSON, HOWARD.
 Midshipman, 3 September, 1835. Resigned 12 March, 1840.
TILLOTSON, J. L.
 Midshipman, 19 October 1841. Resigned 14 May, 1846.
TILLOTSON, JOHN H.
 Midshipman, 30 July, 1842. Resigned 15 February, 1849.
TILLOTSON, R. M.
 Midshipman, 29 May, 1833. Passed Midshipman, 6 July, 1839. Resigned 17 October, 1840.
TILLSON, ALONZO W.
 Acting Ensign, 7 January, 1863. Honorably discharged 10 December, 1865.
TILTON, EDWARD G.
 Midshipman, 1 May, 1822. Passed Midshipman, 24 May, 1828. Lieutenant, 3 March, 1831. Commander, 1 August, 1853. Died 8 February, 1861.
TILTON, NEHEMIAH.
 Midshipman, 9 November, 1813. Resigned 10 July, 1822.
TILTON, THOMAS.
 Acting Third Assistant Engineer, 11 November, 1864. Honorably discharged 19 June, 1865.
TILTON, WALTER H.
 Mate 9 December, 1862. Resigned 3 May, 1866.
TIMBERLAKE, J. B.
 Purser, 25 April, 1812. Died 2 April, 1828.
TIMBERLAKE, R. B.
 Midshipman, 16 January, 1809. Resigned 24 June, 1811.
TIMBERLAKE, R. T.
 Purser, 26 March, 1814. Last appearance on Records of Navy Department, 1815. Lake Erie.
TIMMERMAN, LOUIS F.
 Acting Master, 11 April, 1862. Honorably discharged 11 January, 1866.
TIMMONDS, R. H.
 Acting Ensign, 1 October, 1862. Acting Master, 29 January, 1863. Resigned 28 October, 1863.
TIMMONS, JOHN W.
 Naval Cadet, 3 June, 1896. Graduated 30 June, 1900.
TINELLI, JOSEPH J.
 Mate, 25 November, 1863. Resigned 22 December, 1864.
TINGEY, THOMAS.
 Captain, 3 September, 1798. Discharged under Peace Establishment Act, date not known.
TINGEY, THOMAS.
 Captain. 23 November, 1804. Died 23 February, 1829.
TINKER, CORNELIUS M.
 Acting Master, 26 February, 1862. Died on Estrella, 27 May, 1863.
TINKER, THOMAS C.
 Mate, 4 February, 1864. Acting Ensign, 9 March, 1865. Honorably discharged 31 August, 1865.
TINKHAM, HOSEA E.
 Mate, 12 December, 1861. Acting Ensign, 26 October, 1863. Honorably discharged 13 May, 1867.
TINKHAM, JAMES H.
 Assistant Surgeon, 30 July, 1861. Passed Assistant Surgeon, 22 June, 1864. Surgeon, 5 December 1865. Died 2 June, 1879.
TINSLAR, BENJAMIN R.
 Surgeon, 4 December, 1828. Died 23 November, 1864.
TIPPETT, THOMAS A.
 Midshipman, 9 June, 1811. Lieutenant, 5 March, 1817. Last appearance on Records of Navy Department, 1822. Dead.
TIPTON, WILLIAM.
 Acting Second Assistant Engineer, 18 July, 1862. Acting First Assistant Engineer, 20 October, 1863. Honorably discharged 25 December, 1865.
TISDALE, NATHANIEL.
 Assistant Surgeon, 10 March, 1799. Struck off 16 April, 1804.
TISDALE, RYLAND D.
 Naval Cadet, 28 September, 1882. Ensign, 1 July, 1888. Lieutenant, Junior Grade, 6 December, 1896. Lieutenant, 3 March, 1899. Died 1 June, 1900.
TISTADT, CHARLES.
 Acting Third Assistant Engineer, 1 October, 1862. Acting Second Assistant Engineer, 22 April, 1863. Acting First Assistant Engineer, 10 August, 1864. Honorably discharged 26 April, 1867.
TITCOMB, JONATHAN, Jr.
 Master, 15 October, 1798. Lieutenant, 20 June, 1799. Discharged 30 April, 1801, under Peace Establishment Act.
TITCOMB MICHAEL, Jr.
 Lieutenant, 15 October, 1798. Discharged 30 April, 1801, under Peace Establishment Act.
TITCOMB, OLIVER.
 Acting Chief Engineer, 1 October, 1862. Resigned 8 July, 1863.
TITCOMB, WALTER L.
 Acting Ensign, 7 October, 1863. Lost on Tecumseh, 5 August, 1864.

GENERAL NAVY REGISTER. 547

TITTCOMB, JOSEPH A.
 Acting Master, 14 August, 1861. Resigned 5 July, 1862.
TITUS, IRA.
 Midshipman, 1 September, 1811. Last appearance on Records of Navy Department, 1816. Furloughed.
TOBEY, EUGENE C.
 Assistant Paymaster (Spanish-American War), 25 May, 1898. Honorably discharged 13 March, 1899. Assistant Paymaster (Regular Navy), 28 April, 1899.
TOBEY, FRANK A.
 Mate, 26 May, 1864. Resigned (sick) 23 March, 1865.
TOBEY, JOHN G.
 Acting Assistant Paymaster, 22 June, 1864. Mustered out 19 April, 1866.
TOBIN, JOHN A.
 Second Assistant Engineer, 4 October, 1870. Passed Assistant Engineer, 2 October, 1877. Retired 20 October, 1890.
TODD, CHAPMAN C.
 Midshipman, 9 October, 1861. Graduated June, 1866. Ensign, 12 March, 1868. Master, 26 March 1869. Lieutenant, 21 March, 1870. Lieutenant-Commander, 9 November, 1886. Commander, 21 May, 1895.
TODD, CHARLES J.
 Acting Assistant Paymaster, 11 April, 1863. Mustered out 5 December, 1865.
TODD, DAVID W.
 Naval Cadet, 8 September, 1891. Ensign, 1 July, 1897. Lieutenant, Junior Grade, 1 July, 1900.
TODD, GEORGE B.
 Acting Assistant Surgeon, 17 October, 1862. Acting Passed Assistant Surgeon. 12 April, 1865. Honorably discharged 2 July, 1868. Acting Passed Assistant Surgeon, 12 December, 1873. Died 20 September, 1874.
TODD, GEORGE W., JR.
 Acting Third Assistant Engineer, 1 October, 1862. Appointment revoked (sick) 10 October, 1863.
TODD, HENRY D.
 Acting Midshipman, 28 May, 1853. Midshipman, 10 June, 1857. Passed Midshipman, 15 June, 1860. Master, 24 October, 1860. Lieutenant, 3 April, 1861. Lieutenant-Commander, 2 January, 1863. Resigned 19 October, 1866. Professor, 16 September, 1877. Retired List, 25 August, 1900.
TODD, JAMES M.
 Acting Midshipman, 2 October, 1851. Midshipman, 10 June, 1854. Died 30 December, 1855.
TODD, JOHN G.
 Midshipman, 9 June, 1811. Drowned 5 October, 1811.
TODD, JOHN G.
 Midshipman, 1 April, 1828. Resigned 25 June, 1833.
TODD, JOHN N.
 Purser, 1 March, 1815. Dismissed 11 November, 1845.
TODD, JOSHUA D.
 Midshipman, 26 June, 1835. Passed Midshipman, 22 June, 1841. Master, 13 August, 1847. Lieutenant, 16 May, 1848. Died 25 December, 1861.
TODD, WILSON L.
 Cadet Midshipman, 5 June, 1873. Graduated 4 June, 1880. Ensign, Junior Grade, 3 March. 1883. Ensign, 26 June, 1884. Resigned 1 July, 1885.
TODD, OLIVER.
 Midshipman, 1 May, 1827. Passed Midshipman, 10 June, 1833. Lieutenant, 28 February, 1838. Died at sea 1 December, 1845.
TODD SAMUEL P.
 Purser, 1 March, 1813. Died 10 May, 1858.
TODD, WILLIAM E.
 Acting Third Assistant Engineer, 8 February, 1865. Honorably discharged 8 January, 1866.
TOLE, JAMES C.
 Acting Master, 12 July, 1862. Honorably discharged 14 October, 1865.
TOLER, HUGH K.
 Midshipman, 3 March, 1779. Discharged 12 August, 1801, under Peace Establishment Act.
TOLER, WILLIAM P.
 Midshipman, 19 October, 1841. Resigned 12 December, 1848.
TOLFREE, JAMES E.
 Acting Assistant Paymaster, 13 September, 1862. Assistant Paymaster, 3 March. 1865. Paymaster, 22 January, 1866. Pay Inspector, 10 August, 1886. Pay Director, 12 February, 1898. Retired List, 29 August, 1899.
TOLLE, WILLIAM L.
 Acting Second Assistant Engineer, 1 December, 1863. Appointment revoked (sick) 9 November, 1864.
TOMB, JAMES H.
 Naval Cadet, 6 September, 1895. At sea prior to final graduation.
TOMB, WILLIAM V.
 Naval Cadet, 5 September, 1896. Graduated 30 June, 1900.
TOMPKINS, FRANCIS.
 Purser, 19 November, 1799. Discharged 6 June, 1801, under Peace Establishment Act.
TOMPKINS, GRIFFIN.
 Midshipman, 11 July, 1818. Resigned 22 May, 1826.

TOMPKINS, JOHN.
Midshipman, 30 November, 1814. Last appearance on Records of Navy Department, 1821. Furloughed.
TOMPKINS, JOHN T.
Naval Cadet, 6 September, 1890. Ensign, 1 July, 1896. Lieutenant, Junior Grade, 1 July, 1899.
TOMPKINS, WILLIAM G.
Mate, 1 September, 1862. Honorably discharged 15 February, 1866. Boatswain, 23 February, 1866. Died 3 July, 1885.
TOMLIN, GEORGE.
Midshipman, 15 November, 1809. Died 18 December, 1813.
TOMLINSON, SAMUEL.
Acting Third Assistant Engineer, 17 May, 1861. Acting Second Assistant Engineer, 15 October, 1863. Honorably discharged 26 October, 1865.
TOMLINSON, WILLIAM M.
Mate, 21 September, 1861. Appointment revoked (sick) 23 April, 1863.
TOOKER, CHARLES.
Acting Master and Pilot, 1 October, 1864. Honorably discharged 16 September, 1865.
TOOLE, JOHN.
Midshipman, 30 November, 1814. Lost in the Epervier, 1815.
TOOLEY, HENRY.
Midshipman, 1 January, 1825. Passed Midshipman, 4 June, 1831. Resigned 24 September, 1832.
TOOMBS, JAMES H.
Third Assistant Engineer, 19 February, 1861. Declined appointment 24 April, 1861.
TOOMBS, THOMAS M.
Mate, 15 March, 1862. Resigned 23 March, 1865.
TOOMER, J. L.
Midshipman, 3 February, 1837. Resigned 23 September, 1840.
TOON, WILLIAM H.
Midshipman, 21 April, 1848. Resigned 8 December, 1853.
TOOTELL, JAMES.
Purser, 5 May, 1803. Died September, 1809.
TOOTHAKER, SAMUEL G.
Acting Ensign, 20 January, 1863. Honorably discharged 10 December, 1865. Acting Ensign, 5 July, 1866. Mustered out 4 October, 1867.
TOPHAM, P. M.
Master, 27 July, 1813. Last appearance on Records of Navy Department, 1815. Newport, Rhode Island.
TOPHAM, PHILIP M.
Mate, 28 August, 1863. Appointment revoked 23 November, 1864.
TOPLIFF, JAMES C.
Acting Assistant Paymaster, 5 August, 1861. Resigned 17 July, 1862.
TOPLIFF, THOMAS.
Mate, 20 April, 1864. Resigned 4 January, 1865.
TOPPAN, FRANCIS W.
Cadet Midshipman, 22 September, 1873. Graduated 18 June, 1879. Ensign, 22 May, 1881. Retired List, 29 June, 1887.
TOPPIN, JOHN D.
Third Assistant Engineer, 1 July, 1861. Second Assistant Engineer, 18 December, 1862. Retired 11 May, 1867. First Assistant Engineer on Retired List, 24 July, 1867.
TOPPING, ROBERT R.
Mate, 20 January, 1863. Appointment revoked 9 March, 1864.
TORALLES, EDWARD.
Acting Third Assistant Engineer, 18 April, 1864. Honorably discharged 1 October, 1865.
TORBERT, WILLIAM F. A.
Acting Assistant Paymaster, 11 May, 1864. Passed Assistant Paymaster, 23 July, 1866. Paymaster, 16 September, 1868. Died 2 October, 1874.
TORNBOHM, M. S.
Acting First Assistant Engineer, 14 December, 1864. Honorably discharged 10 May, 1868.
TORNEY, GEORGE H.
Assistant Surgeon, 1 November, 1871. Passed Assistant Surgeon, 18 December, 1874. Resigned 9 July, 1875.
TORREY, JOSEPH.
Gunner, date not known. Acting Lieutenant, 27 December, 1798. Discharged 14 January, 1800.
TOSCAN, FRANK.
Midshipman, 18 June, 1812. Killed in action 28 June, 1814.
TOSCAN, NESSIDOR.
Midshipman, 1 April, 1814. Died in August, 1818.
TOTTEN, BENJAMIN J.
Midshipman, 2 March, 1823. Passed Midshipman, 20 February, 1830. Lieutenant, 29 March, 1834. Commander, 14 September, 1855. Retired List, 1 October, 1864. Commodore on Retired List, 4 April, 1867. Died 9 May, 1877.
TOTTEN, GEORGE M.
Midshipman, 5 May, 1831. Passed Midshipman, 15 June, 1837. Lieutenant, 8 September, 1841. Died 18 July, 1857.
TOTTEN, GEORGE M.
Midshipman, 29 September, 1862. Graduated June, 1866. Ensign, 12 March, 1868. Master, 26 March, 1869. Lieutenant, 21 March, 1870. Lieutenant-Commander, 26 January, 1885. Died 27 May, 1888.

GENERAL NAVY REGISTER. 549

TOTTEN, WASHINGTON.
Midshipman, 8 November, 1847. Passed Midshipman, 10 June, 1853. Died 27 December, 1854.
TOUCHSTONE, WILLIAM H.
Assistant Engineer (Spanish-American War), 26 May, 1898. Honorably discharged 24 September, 1898.
TOUCHTON, WILLIAM H.
Acting Third Assistant Engineer, 31 March, 1864. Honorably discharged 9 January, 1866.
TOUCHTON, WILLIAM H.
Acting Third Assistant Engineer, 9 October, 1866. Mustered out 28 April, 1869.
TOULMAN, H. F.
Midshipman, 1 February, 1827. Resigned 15 August, 1831.
TOURTELOTTE, J. F.
Acting Assistant Surgeon, 5 March, 1863. Honorably discharged 15 December, 1868.
TOWER, ANDREW.
Acting Assistant Paymaster, 2 July, 1863. Honorably discharged 10 December, 1865.
TOWER, GEORGE EDWARD.
Third Assistant Engineer, 17 January, 1862. Second Assistant Engineer, 1 October, 1863. First Assistant Engineer, 1 January, 1868. Chief Engineer, 30 June, 1887. Retired List, 25 February, 1897.
TOWER, GEORGE B. N.
Third Assistant Engineer, 21 November, 1857. Second Assistant Engineer, 2 August, 1859. First Assistant Engineer, 16 October, 1861. Chief Engineer, 10 November, 1863. Resigned 29 September, 1865.
TOWERS, JOHN.
Master, 29 December, 1812. Discharged 27 April, 1813.
TOWLE, HENRY R.
Acting Ensign, 12 January, 1863. Honorably discharged 10 July, 1865.
TOWLE, PHINEAS S.
Acting Assistant Paymaster, 8 February, 1864. Honorably discharged 20 November, 1865.
TOWN, JOHN.
Sailmaker, 22 May, 1804. Resigned 30 January, 1807.
TOWNE, F. WARREN.
Mate, 20 January, 1862. Acting Ensign, 20 November, 1863. Honorably discharged 30 December, 1865.
TOWNE, NATHAN P.
Third Assistant Engineer, 6 January, 1862. Second Assistant Engineer, 1 October, 1863. First Assistant Engineer, 1 January, 1868. Chief Engineer, 3 July, 1887. Resigned 31 March, 1894.
TOWNE, SAMUEL H.
Acting Third Assistant Engineer, 8 December, 1863. Acting Second Assistant Engineer, 7 March, 1865. Honorably discharged 1 March, 1866.
TOWNER, BENJAMIN.
Gunner, 7 February, 1828. Died in 1834.
TOWNLEY, CHARLES E.
Mate, 14 September, 1864. Honorably discharged 7 July, 1865.
TOWNLEY, RICHARD H.
Midshipman, 21 June, 1870. Graduated 21 June, 1875. Ensign, 8 August, 1876. Master, 2 July, 1882. Lieutenant, Junior Grade, 3 March, 1883. Retired List, 29 June, 1887.
TOWNROW, FREDERICK W.
Third Assistant Engineer, 20 May, 1863. Second Assistant Engineer, 25 July, 1866. Dropped 11 June, 1878.
TOWNSEND, ALONZO.
Mate, 18 November, 1862. Resigned 29 September, 1863.
TOWNSEND, BENJAMIN C.
Acting Ensign, 8 December, 1864. Honorably discharged 25 October, 1865.
TOWNSEND, FRANK H.
Third Assistant Engineer, 8 September, 1863. Resigned 12 April, 1866.
TOWNSEND, GERARD B.
Lieutenant, Junior Grade (Spanish-American War), 12 May, 1898. Honorably discharged 10 September, 1898.
TOWNSEND, HOWARD S.
Ensign (Spanish-American War), 20 May, 1898. Honorably discharged 8 September, 1898.
TOWNSEND, JOHN S.
Midshipman, 18 November, 1814. Died 16 April, 1820.
TOWNSEND, LEMUEL.
Carpenter, 31 December, 1836. Discharged 28 November, 1837.
TOWNSEND, ROBERT.
Midshipman, 1 August, 1837. Passed Midshipman, 29 June, 1843. Lieutenant, 11 October, 1850. Resigned 7 April, 1851. Acting Lieutenant, 17 September, 1861. Commander, 16 July, 1862. Captain, 25 July, 1866. Died 15 August, 1866.
TOWNSEND, S. D.
Assistant Surgeon, 3 May, 1815. Last appearance on Records of Navy Department, 1815. Washington, 1874.
TOY, WILLIAM D.
Carpenter, 28 October, 1858. Retired List, 8 May, 1892.
TOZER, CHARLES M.
Naval Cadet, 19 September, 1892. Ensign, 6 May, 1898.
TRACY, CHARLES W.
Acting Midshipman, 27 October, 1859. Ensign, 10 December, 1862. Lieutenant, 22 February, 1864. Lieutenant-Commander, 25 July, 1866. Retired List, 22 October, 1878.

TRACY, ELMER C.
Assistant Surgeon, 28 March, 1886. Resigned 11 February, 1888.
TRACY, N. W.
Mate, 4 September, 1863. Honorably discharged 5 October, 1865.
TRACY, THOMAS F.
Mate, 1 April, 1863. Acting Ensign, 1 September, 1863. Honorably discharged 20 December, 1865.
TRAIN, CHARLES J.
Midshipman, 28 November, 1861. Graduated November, 1864. Ensign, 1 November, 1866. Master, 1 December, 1866. Lieutenant, 12 March, 1868. Lieutenant-Commander, 30 June, 1869. Commander, 17 January, 1886. Captain, 22 November, 1898.
TRAIN, CHARLES R.
Naval Cadet, 5 September, 1896. Graduated 30 June, 1900.
TRAIN, SAMUEL F.
Acting Assistant Paymaster, 14 January, 1862. Resigned 18 June, 1862. Acting Assistant Paymaster, 28 June, 1862. Died 1 November, 1863.
TRAINOR, EDWARD.
Acting Third Assistant Engineer, 20 March, 1863. Appointment revoked 23 June, 1865.
TRANT, JAMES.
Master, 10 April, 1799. Resigned 31 March, 1802.
TRANT, JAMES.
Master, 16 May, 1804. Lieutenant, 5 May, 1817. Died 11 September, 1820.
TRAPIER, PAUL H.
Midshipman, 1 January, 1825. Resigned 28 September, 1830.
TRAPIER, RICHARD S.
Midshipman, 21 December, 1831. Passed Midshipman, 15 June, 1837. Lieutenant, 8 September, 1841. Resigned 30 December, 1846.
TRARY, WILLIAM H.
Retired List, 10 December, 1888.
TRASK, B. P.
Mate, 31 August, 1861. Acting Ensign, 8 November, 1862. Appointment revoked 6 June, 1865.
TRATHEN, CHARLES.
Mate, 5 December, 1861. Acting Ensign, 8 September, 1863. Discharged 22 November, 1867.
TRATHEN, JAMES.
Mate, 27 December, 1861. Acting Volunteer Lieutenant, 26 August, 1861. Acting Volunteer Lieutenant-Commander, 16 May, 1865. Honorably discharged 26 May, 1866.
TRAU, ADAM.
Acting Assistant Surgeon, 27 April, 1866. Assistant Surgeon, 18 June, 1866. Resigned 1 March, 1871.
TRAUT, FREDERICK A.
Naval Cadet, 19 May, 1888. Ensign, 1 July, 1894. Lieutenant, Junior Grade, 3 March, 1899. Lieutenant, 1 July, 1900.
TRAVER, LORENZO.
Acting Assistant Surgeon, 22 November, 1861. Honorably discharged 18 October, 1868.
TRAVIS, WILLIAM L.
Midshipman, 4 July, 1805. Resigned 30 March, 1808.
TREADWAY, WILLIAM.
Acting Third Assistant Engineer, 25 January, 1864. Honorably discharged 6 September, 1867.
TREADWELL, JAMES.
Acting Master's Mate, 27 November, 1861. Marked "Run" 9 December, 1862.
TREADWELL, PASSMORE.
Acting Assistant Surgeon, 30 June, 1862. Honorably discharged 28 March, 1867.
TREAT, BRADFORD E.
Mate, 2 January, 1864. Appointment revoked (sick) 14 March, 1865.
TREAT, CHARLES H.
Assistant Engineer (Spanish-American War), 3 June, 1898. Honorably discharged 31 October, 1898.
TREAT, JOHN F.
Acting Master. Died 20 October, 1863.
TREAT, RICHARD A.
Mate, 26 September, 1863. Appointment revoked 31 October, 1864.
TREBBY, SAMUEL.
Sailmaker, date not known. Last appearance on Records of Navy Department, 1824. Norfolk.
TREMAINE, HOBART L.
Midshipman, 26 September, 1864. Graduated June, 1868. Master, 12 July, 1870. Lieutenant, 26 January, 1872. Retired List, 19 May, 1891.
TRENCH, MARTIN E.
Naval Cadet, 3 October, 1889. Assistant Engineer, 1 July, 1895. Passed Assistant Engineer, 20 November, 1898. Rank changed to Lieutenant, Junior Grade, 3 March, 1899.
TRENCHARD, EDWARD.
Midshipman, 30 April, 1800. Lieutenant, 18 February, 1807. Commander, 24 July, 1813. Captain, 5 March, 1817. Died 3 November, 1824.
TRENCHARD, STEPHEN D.
Midshipman, 23 October, 1834. Passed Midshipman, 16 July, 1840. Lieutenant, 27 February, 1847. Commander, 16 July, 1862. Captain, 25 July, 1866. Commodore, 7 May, 1871. Rear-Admiral, 10 August, 1875. Retired List, 10 July, 1880. Died 15 November 1883.
TRESCOTT, PETER.
Mate, 13 April, 1863. Resigned 15 September, 1864.

GENERAL NAVY REGISTER. 551

TRESSELT, HENRY J.
　Gunner, 31 January, 1889. Retired List, 14 June, 1895.
TREVETT, JOSEPH.
　Assistant Surgeon, 2 May, 1809. Dismissed 9 April, 1810.
TREVETT, SAMUEL R., Jr.
　Surgeon, 3 March, 1809. Last appearance on Records of Navy Department, 1822. Dead.
TREVITT, BENJAMIN.
　Master, 9 September, 1812. Resigned 19 January, 1815.
TREVOR, FRANCIS N.
　Acting Third Assistant Engineer, 10 October, 1866. Third Assistant Engineer, 2 June, 1868. Resigned 26 June, 1869.
TREVORROW, WILLIAM J.
　Acting Warrant Machinist, 29 January, 1900.
TREZEVANT, PETER.
　Purser, 10 March, 1799. Discharged 18 November, 1801, under Peace Establishment Act.
TRIBOU, DAVID H.
　Chaplain, 5 February, 1872.
TRICK, JAMES.
　Mate, 6 April, 1863. Dismissed 18 May, 1863.
TRILLEY, JOSEPH.
　Third Assistant Engineer, 11 August, 1860. Second Assistant Engineer, 30 July, 1862. First Assistant Engineer, 20 July, 1864. Chief Engineer, 31 January, 1873. Rank changed to Captain, 3 March, 1899. Retired List, with rank of Rear-Admiral, 25 September, 1899.
TRIMBLE, JOHN.
　Sailmaker, 30 September, 1818. Died September, 1824.
TRIMBLE, R. M.
　Acting Assistant Paymaster, 14 October, 1861. Resigned 27 October, 1863.
TRIMBLE, RICHARD.
　Ensign (Spanish-American War), 15 June, 1898. Honorably discharged 28 September, 1898.
TRIPLER, BYRON.
　Mate, 5 October, 1863. Honorably discharged 2 August, 1868.
TRIPLETT, JAMES M.
　Mate, 12 November, 1862. Dismissed 19 December, 1862.
TRIPLETT, THOMAS.
　Surgeon, 14 October, 1799. Resigned 10 July, 1804.
TRIPLETT, THOMAS.
　Surgeon, 6 May, 1806. Resigned 5 July, 1810.
TRIPP, ALDEN W.
　Mate, 9 September, 1862. Dismissed 23 April, 1864.
TRIPP, GEORGE B.
　Acting Assistant Paymaster, 20 June, 1862. Mustered out 5 August, 1865.
TRIPP, GREENLEAF G.
　Acting Ensign, 9 June, 1864. Honorably discharged 4 September, 1865.
TRIPP, LYSANDER C.
　Acting Assistant Paymaster, 28 August, 1863. Mustered out 24 October, 1865.
TRIPPE, JOHN.
　Midshipman, 5 April, 1799. Master, 6 May, 1803. Lieutenant, 9 January, 1807. Died 9 July, 1810.
TRIST, H. B.
　Assistant Surgeon, 10 June, 1857. Resigned 2 July, 1860.
TRIVETT, HENRY J.
　Acting Ensign, 18 March, 1865. Honorably discharged 16 November, 1865.
TROTT, HENRY D.
　Acting Ensign, 26 August, 1864. Resigned 3 May, 1865.
TROTT, JOHN B.
　Acting Ensign, 20 July, 1863. Honorably discharged 27 August, 1865.
TROTT, WILLIAM S.
　Mate, 8 October, 1863. Died 2 August, 1864.
TROTTER, CHARLES.
　Acting Third Assistant Engineer, 1 October, 1862. Acting First Assistant Engineer, 9 October, 1863. Honorably discharged 20 October, 1865.
TROTTER, GEORGE A.
　Midshipman, 20 November, 1848. Died 27 December, 1849.
TROTTER, W. D. B.
　Midshipman, 1 January, 1825. Resigned 12 July, 1826.
TROUT, JACOB G.
　Mate, 21 August, 1862. Appointment revoked 9 September, 1862.
TROWBRIDGE, AMASA.
　Passed Assistant Engineer (Spanish-American War), 22 June, 1898. Honorably discharged 27 September, 1898.
TRUFANT, WILLIAM B.
　Acting Ensign, 2 April, 1863. Honorably discharged 19 August, 1865.
TRUITT, SAMUEL.
　Midshipman, 18 May, 1809. Resigned 28 June, 1810.
TRUMPBOUR, MATTHEW T.
　Acting Assistant Paymaster, 21 January, 1865. Honorably discharged 7 September, 1865.
TRUNDY, CARLTON A.
　Mate, 2 January, 1863. Honorably discharged 9 May, 1865.

TRUNDY, GEORGE A.
　Acting Volunteer Lieutenant, 26 August, 1861. Resigned 24 July, 1862.
TRUSSELL, JOHN M.
　Acting Third Assistant Engineer, 27 March, 1865. Honorably discharged 16 September, 1865.
TRUXTUN, THOMAS.
　Captain, 4 June, 1794. Resigned, date not known.
TRUXTUN, THOMAS, JR.
　Midshipman, 1 December, 1798. Resigned 11 May, 1801.
TRUXTUN, WILLIAM.
　Cadet Midshipman, 24 June, 1876. Graduated 22 June, 1882. Ensign, Junior Grade, 3 March, 1883. Ensign, 26 June, 1884. Lieutenant, Junior Grade, 18 November, 1892. Lieutenant, 5 September, 1896.
TRUXTUN WILLIAM T.
　Midshipman, 9 February, 1841. Passed Midshipman, 10 August, 1847. Master, 14 September, 1855. Lieutenant, 15 September, 1855. Lieutenant-Commander, 16 July, 1862. Commander, 25 July, 1866. Captain, 25 September, 1873. Commodore, 11 May, 1882. Retired List, 11 March, 1886. Died 25 February, 1887.
TRYON, GEORGE.
　Midshipman, 11 September, 1799. Last appearance on Records of Navy Department, 3 October, 1799.
TRYON, JAMES RUFUS.
　Acting Assistant Surgeon, 19 March, 1863. Assistant Surgeon, 22 September, 1863. Passed Assistant Surgeon, 22 December, 1866. Surgeon, 30 June, 1873. Medical Inspector, 22 September, 1891. Medical Director, 21 January, 1897. Retired List, 24 September, 1899.
TRYON, MOSES.
　Captain, 16 September, 1798. Discharged under Peace Establishment Act, date not known.
TUBBS, A. DEAN.
　Acting Assistant Surgeon, 23 January, 1864. Died 6 November, 1865.
TUBBS, SAMUEL.
　Acting First Assistant Engineer, 18 May, 1864. Honorably discharged 14 October, 1865.
TUCK, DAVIS R.
　Assistant Surgeon, 10 December, 1814. Last appearance on Records of Navy Department, 1815. Fairfax C. H., Va.
TUCK, JOHN.
　Midshipman, 16 January, 1809. Resigned 27 September, 1810.
TUCK, JOSEPH W.
　Acting Master, 14 August, 1861. Honorably discharged 16 December, 1865.
TUCKER, B. W., JR.
　Mate, 23 January, 1862. Honorably discharged 1 July, 1868.
TUCKER, ALBERT F.
　Acting Master's Mate, 23 August, 1864. Resigned 20 June, 1865.
TUCKER, CHARLES E.
　Mate, 20 November, 1861. Resigned 21 April, 1862. Mate, 17 December, 1862. Resigned 10 September, 1863.
TUCKER, GEORGE C.
　Master, 15 July, 1812. Resigned 17 March, 1813.
TUCKER, JACOB.
　Acting First Assistant Engineer, 16 October, 1861. Appointment revoked (sick) 1 September, 1864.
TUCKER, JOHN.
　Acting Third Assistant Engineer, 6 August, 1864. Discharged 21 March, 1865.
TUCKER, JOHN R.
　Midshipman, 1 June, 1826. Passed Midshipman, 10 June, 1833. Lieutenant, 20 December, 1837. Commander, 14 September, 1855. Dismissed 18 April, 1861.
TUCKER, JOHN T.
　Third Assistant Engineer, 19 February, 1861. Name stricken from the Rolls 6 May, 1861.
TUCKER, JOHNSON M.
　Mate, 13 August, 1863. Resigned 31 May, 1864.
TUCKER, THOMAS B., JR.
　Acting Ensign, 22 June, 1864. Honorably discharged 3 January, 1868.
TUCKERMAN, J. FRANCIS.
　Assistant Surgeon, 25 January, 1842. Passed Assistant Surgeon, 15 March, 1847. Resigned 3 January, 1852.
TUDOR, JACOB L.
　Acting Third Assistant Engineer, 18 April, 1865. Honorably discharged 30 September, 1865.
TUDOR, OWEN.
　Midshipman, 11 September, 1799. Discharged 10 July, 1801, under Peace Establishment Act.
TUELLS, HENRY M.
　Acting Third Assistant Engineer, 9 August, 1862. Appointment revoked (sick) 27 June, 1863.
TUFFS, JOSEPH.
　Midshipman, 4 April, 1800. Discharged 6 July, 1801.
TUKEY, WILLIAM H.
　Assistant Surgeon (Spanish-American War), 27 July, 1898. Honorably discharged 26 September, 1898.
TULLOCK, THOMAS L.
　Acting Assistant Paymaster, 11 May, 1863. Passed Assistant Paymaster, 23 July, 1866. Paymaster, 26 February, 1869. Lost in the Oneida, 24 January, 1870.

GENERAL NAVY REGISTER.   553

TUNIS, WILLIAM W.
 Acting Second Assistant Engineer, 29 May, 1862. Resigned 6 December, 1864.
TUNSTALL, J. M.
 Assistant Surgeon, 10 December, 1814. Last appearance on Records of Navy Department, 1818. Dead.
TUNSTALL, RICHARD B.
 Assistant Surgeon, 28 August, 1850. Resigned 31 October, 1854.
TUOHY, JAMES.
 Acting Ensign, 11 June, 1863. Honorably discharged 4 January, 1866.
TURBITT, FITCH.
 Midshipman, 2 December, 1799. Resigned 23 November, 1800.
TURERALL, WILLIAM.
 Gunner, 12 July, 1799. Resigned 11 August, 1800.
TURK, JOHN W.
 Midshipman, 4 March, 1823. Passed Midshipman, 23 March, 1829. Lieutenant, 21 June, 1832. (See Livingston.)
TURK, WILLIAM.
 Surgeon, 24 July, 1813. Died 20 November, 1854.
TURLEY, JOHN A.
 Midshipman, 1 May, 1826. Dismissed 29 November, 1831.
TURNBULL, FRANK.
 Midshipman, 20 September, 1861. Graduated June, 1866. Ensign, 12 March, 1868. Master, 26 March, 1869. Lieutenant, 21 March, 1870. Retired List, 10 July, 1877.
TURNBULL, JAMES S.
 Assistant Paymaster, 1 November, 1861. Died 6 February, 1862.
TURNER, BENJAMIN.
 Midshipman, 27 September, 1800. Lieutenant, 9 March, 1807. Killed in a duel 1 October, 1807.
TURNER, B. W.
 Midshipman, 21 October, 1824. Died 30 September, 1828.
TURNER, CHARLES A.
 Mate, 5 June, 1863. Appointment revoked (sick) 21 November, 1863.
TURNER, CHARLES C.
 Midshipman, 10 May, 1820. Lieutenant, 17 May, 1828. Commander, 20 July, 1851. Died 4 March, 1861.
TURNER, CHARLES P.
 Mate, 12 September, 1862. Resigned 14 March, 1864.
TURNER, DANIEL.
 Midshipman, 1 January, 1808. Lieutenant, 12 March, 1813. Commander, 3 March, 1825. Captain, 3 March, 1835. Died 4 February, 1850.
TURNER, EDWARD W.
 Purser, 25 April, 1812. Died 6 March, 1819.
TURNER, ELEAZER S.
 Acting Master, 28 May, 1861. Dead.
TURNER, ELISHA L.
 Acting Assistant Paymaster, 3 July, 1862. Resigned 21 October, 1864.
TURNER, FRANK W.
 Mate, 15 November, 1861. Resigned 18 October, 1864. Mate, 3 January, 1865. Honorably discharged 16 May, 1868.
TURNER, FREDERICK G.
 Mate, 19 November, 1862. Resigned 1 December, 1863.
TURNER, GEORGE R.
 Lieutenant, 8 January, 1799. Discharged 18 June, 1801, under Peace Establishment Act.
TURNER, HENRY E.
 Midshipman, 30 November, 1814. Died October, 1820.
TURNER, JAMES S.
 Acting Second Assistant Engineer, 16 October, 1861. Killed in action 30 January, 1863.
TURNER, JAMES W.
 Mate, 21 September, 1861. Acting Ensign, 13 September, 1862. Appointment revoked 26 September, 1864.
TURNER, JOHN.
 Acting Ensign, 13 June, 1864. Honorably discharged 25 November, 1865.
TURNER, J. M.
 Midshipman, 18 February, 1841. Dismissed by Court-martial 5 August, 1842.
TURNER, LOUIS H.
 Lieutenant (Spanish-American War), 22 June, 1898. Honorably discharged 8 September, 1898.
TURNER, L. W.
 Mate, 22 August, 1862. Resigned 28 July, 1862.
TURNER, OBED C.
 Acting Assistant Surgeon, 12 August, 1864. Resigned 6 July, 1865.
TURNER, PETER.
 Midshipman, 4 March, 1823. Passed Midshipman, 23 March, 1829. Lieutenant, 20 December, 1832. Reserved List, 13 September, 1855. Commander on Reserved List, 1 July, 1861. Commodore on Retired List, 4 April, 1867. Died 19 February, 1871.
TURNER, REUBEN A.
 Acting Ensign, 24 January, 1863. Acting Master, 21 August, 1863. Accidentally killed, 23 August, 1863.
TURNER, ROBERT M.
 Mate, 28 April, 1864. Honorably discharged 12 October, 1865.
TURNER, SAMUEL A.
 Midshipman, 2 February, 1829. Resigned 6 June, 1836.

TURNER, SAMUEL S.
Midshipman, 4 March, 1800. Died October, 1822.
TURNER, SAMUEL V.
Sailmaker, 29 December, 1857. Resigned 18 April, 1861.
TURNER, THOMAS.
Midshipman, 21 April, 1825. Passed Midshipman, 4 June, 1831. Lieutenant, 22 December, 1835. Commander, 14 September, 1855. Captain, 16 July, 1862. Commodore, 13 December, 1862. Rear-Admiral, 27 May, 1868. Retired List, 21 April, 1870. Died 24 March, 1883.
TURNER, THOMAS J.
Assistant Surgeon, 16 December, 1853. Passed Assistant Surgeon, 23 May, 1859. Surgeon, 20 June, 1861. Medical Inspector, 26 April, 1872. Medical Director, 2 April, 1879. Retired List, 21 September, 1891.
TURNER, THOMAS J.
Ensign (Spanish-American War), 15 June, 1898. Honorably discharged 2 September, 1898.
TURNER, WILLIAM.
Assistant Surgeon, 3 July, 1798. Surgeon, 31 August, 1799. Died 27 October, 1802.
TURNER, WILLIAM C.
Mate, 1 October, 1862. Acting Ensign, 8 December, 1862. Dismissed 10 June, 1864.
TURNER, WILLIAM H.
Midshipman, 22 July, 1865. Graduated June, 1869. Ensign, 12 July, 1870. Master, 13 April, 1872. Lieutenant, 13 May, 1875. Lieutenant-Commander, 16 May, 1897. Commander, 29 March, 1900.
TURPIN, EBEN A.
Mate, 7 June, 1864. Appointment revoked 24 December, 1864.
TURPIN, WALTER S.
Naval Cadet, 22 May, 1890. Ensign, 1 July, 1896. Lieutenant, Junior Grade, 1 July, 1899.
TUTHILL, SAMUEL B.
Assistant Surgeon, 30 July, 1861. Resigned 28 June, 1864.
TUTTLE, A.
Acting Ensign, 2 November, 1863. Honorably discharged 15 November, 1865.
TUTTLE, CHARLES W.
Ensign (Spanish-American War), 20 May, 1898. Honorably discharged 6 October, 1898.
TUTTLE, FRANCIS.
Mate, 22 December, 1863. Acting Ensign, 18 November, 1864. Honorably discharged 24 January, 1869. Mate, 27 January, 1870. Resigned 9 September, 1870.
TUTTLE, HORACE P.
Acting Assistant Paymaster, 17 February, 1863. Assistant Paymaster, 2 July, 1865. Paymaster, 4 May, 1866. Dismissed 3 March, 1875.
TUTTLE, JOHN P.
Midshipman, 30 November, 1814. Lieutenant, 13 July, 1825. Died 10 June, 1827.
TUTTLE, LUCIUS B.
Acting Assistant Paymaster, 31 August, 1864. Honorably discharged 21 November, 1865.
TUTTLE, REUBEN.
Acting Second Assistant Engineer, 14 July, 1863. Dismissed 31 August, 1863.
TUTTLE, ROBERT C.
Acting Assistant Surgeon, 25 September, 1863. Honorably discharged 19 January, 1866.
TUTTLE, THOMAS.
Acting Third Assistant Engineer, 8 July, 1863. Acting Second Assistant Engineer, 18 October, 1864. Appointment revoked (sick) 9 November, 1865.
TUTTLE, WILLIAM L.
Acting Master, 14 September, 1861. Resigned 28 May, 1863.
TUXBURY, JAMES.
Master, 24 January, 1809. Appointment revoked 8 May, 1809.
TUZO, LOUIS E.
Ensign (Spanish-American War), 22 June, 1898. Honorably discharged 13 October, 1898.
TWAMBLEY, HENRY B.
Acting Ensign, 1 June, 1864. Honorably discharged 3 August, 1865.
TWICHELL, THOMAS J.
Mate, 24 January, 1863. Resigned 8 August, 1863.
TWIGGS, DENNIS.
Acting Boatswain, 7 March, 1877. Appointment revoked 18 August, 1877. Acting Boatswain, 15 March, 1878. Appointment revoked, 2 September, 1879.
TWINING, NATHAN C.
Naval Cadet, 4 September, 1885. Ensign, 1 July, 1891. Lieutenant, Junior Grade, 2 August, 1898. Lieutenant, 3 March, 1899.
TWINING, THEODORE W.
Acting Assistant Paymaster, 31 July, 1863. Died 17 August, 1864.
TYLER, ASAHEL H.
Acting Second Assistant Engineer, 23 January, 1864. Honorably discharged 19 October, 1865.
TYLER, BENJAMIN S.
Assistant Surgeon, 10 December, 1814. Last appearance on Records of Navy Department, 1815. New York.
TYLER, FREDERICK H.
Midshipman, 20 June, 1868. Graduated 31 May, 1873. Ensign, 16 July, 1874. Master, 11 July, 1880. Lieutenant, Junior Grade, 3 March, 1883. Lieutenant, 19 May, 1886. Died 27 April, 1895.

GENERAL NAVY REGISTER. 555

TYLER, GEORGE S.
Acting Third Assistant Engineer, 15 December, 1862. Acting Second Assistant Engineer, 9 April, 1863. Honorably discharged 22 November, 1865.
TYLER, GEORGE W.
Midshipman, 3 October, 1864. Graduated June, 1868. Master, 12 July, 1870. Lieutenant April, 1873. Lieutenant-Commander, 31 July, 1894. Died 17 February, 1896.
TYLER, GORHAM P.
Acting Ensign and Pilot 26 November, 1864. Honorably discharged 28 July, 1865.
TYLER, HANSON R.
Midshipman, 27 July, 1866. Graduated 7 June, 1870. Ensign, 13 July, 1871. Master, 19 September, 1874. Lieutenant, 29 March, 1881. Retired List, 28 April, 1896. Died 11 May, 1900.
TYLER, RUFUS C.
Mate, 8 October, 1864. Resigned 15 June, 1865.
TYLER, TOBIAS.
Midshipman, 1 January, 1812. Last appearance on Records of Navy Department, 1815. Boston.
TYLER, THOMAS.
Boatswain, 11 June, 1839. Resigned 4 July, 1842.
TYLER, WILLIAM.
Assistant Surgeon, 23 May, 1829. Died 14 January, 1832.
TYNAN, JOHN W.
Third Assistant Engineer, 21 November, 1857. Second Assistant Engineer, 2 August, 1860. Name stricken from the Rolls, 6 May, 1861.
TYRRELL, STEPHEN R.
Acting Ensign, 15 December, 1862. Died whilst Prisoner of War, 6 May, 1864.
TYSON, ELIJAH R.
Third Assistant Engineer, 3 August, 1863. Died 23 March, 1866.
TYSON, EUGENE V.
Mate, 16 June, 1861. Honorably discharged 2 September, 1866.
TYSON, HERBERT B.
Acting Midshipman, 22 October, 1857. Lieutenant, 1 August, 1862. Resigned 14 March, 1866.
UBER, CARLTON A.
Third Assistant Engineer, 17 March, 1863. Retired 27 March, 1867. Second Assistant Engineer, Retired List, 24 July, 1867. First Assistant Engineer, Retired List, 28 May, 1872.
UBSDELL, JOHN A.
Cadet Midshipman, 6 September, 1883. Resigned 6 March, 1886. Lieutenant, Junior Grade (Spanish-American War), 24 May, 1898. Honorably discharged 9 September, 1898.
UFFORD, HENRY.
Mate, 28 September, 1864. Honorably discharged 30 September, 1865.
UHLER, WILLIAM E.
Midshipman, 27 July, 1864. Graduated 2 June, 1868. Ensign, 19 April, 1869. Lost in Oneida, 24 January, 1870.
UHLRICH, GEORGE.
Master, 4 December, 1809. Died 6 June, 1822.
ULMER, ALBERT F.
Mate, 17 January, 1863. Acting Ensign, 7 August, 1866. Honorably discharged 17 December, 1868.
ULMER, PHILIP.
Master, 6 February, 1809. Warrant revoked 8 May, 1809.
ULSH, WILLIAM H.
Assistant Surgeon (Spanish-American War), 12 May, 1898. Appointed Assistant Surgeon in Regular Service 7 June, 1900.
UNDERDOWN, THOMAS G.
Mate, 3 November, 1864. Honorably discharged 9 April, 1868.
UNDERHILL, JOSEPH G.
Mate, 16 October, 1863. Resigned 30 May, 1865.
UNDERHILL, WILLIAM C.
Mate, 23 December, 1861. Acting Ensign, 26 September, 1862. Appointment revoked 21 January, 1863. Reappointed 7 February, 1863. Honorably discharged 27 October, 1865.
UNDERWOOD, CLARK M.
Acting Carpenter, 1 October, 1862. Resigned 20 July, 1863.
UNDERWOOD, EDMUND B.
Midshipman, 26 June, 1869. Graduated 31 May, 1873. Ensign, 16 July, 1874. Master, 10 March, 1880. Lieutenant, Junior Grade, 3 March, 1883. Lieutenant, 4 February, 1886. Lieutenant-Commander, 3 March, 1889.
UNDERWOOD, JAMES P.
Midshipman, 29 June, 1869. Graduated 31 May, 1873. Ensign, 16 July, 1874. Died 9 July, 1879.
UNDERWOOD, JOHN A.
Midshipman, 7 January, 1832. Resigned 2 July, 1832.
UNDERWOOD, JOS. A.
Midshipman, 2 February, 1829. Passed Midshipman, 3 July, 1835. Killed by Fejee Islanders 24 July, 1840.
UNGER, EDWARD.
Mate, 15 September, 1863. Dismissed 24 May, 1866.
UNSWORTH, JOHN.
Boatswain, 2 July, 1803. Warrant revoked 28 February, 1805.
UPDEGRAFF, MILTON.
Professor, 5 June, 1899.

UPHAM, CHARLES C.
Purser, 30 July, 1852. Died 10 June, 1868.
UPHAM, FRANK B.
Naval Cadet, 6 September, 1889. Ensign, 1 July, 1895. Lieutenant, Junior Grade, 3 March, 1899.
UPHAM, GEORGE B.
Acting Master, 3 September, 1861. Acting Volunteer Lieutenant, 13 April, 1864. Resigned 13 May, 1865.
UPHAM, HENRY M.
Mate, 31 October, 1864. Honorably discharged 4 August, 1866.
UPHAM, JOSEPH BADGER.
Third Assistant Engineer, 18 November, 1862. Second Assistant Engineer, 23 March, 1864. First Assistant Engineer, 1 January, 1868. Retired List, 27 December, 1875. Died 13 August, 1889.
UPSHUR, A. W.
Purser, 26 March, 1843. Died in September, 1844.
UPSHUR, CUSTIS P.
Midshipman, 24 September, 1869. Resigned 13 June, 1881. Ensign (Spanish-American War), 28 May, 1898. Honorably discharged 6 February, 1899.
UPSHUR, GEORGE P.
Midshipman, 23 April, 1818. Lieutenant, 3 March, 1827. Commander, 27 February, 1847. Died 3 November, 1852.
UPSHUR, JOHN H.
Midshipman, 4 November, 1841. Passed Midshipman, 10 August, 1847. Master, 18 April, 1855. Lieutenant, 14 September, 1855. Lieutenant-Commander, 16 July, 1862. Commander, 25 July, 1866. Captain, 31 January, 1872. Commodore, 11 July, 1880. Rear-Admiral, 1 October, 1884. Retired List, 1 June, 1885.
UPSTONE, GEORGE L.
Mate, 10 September, 1864. Honorably discharged 27 August, 1865.
UPTON, DANIEL P.
Acting Volunteer Lieutenant, 21 October, 1861. Dismissed 15 August, 1863.
UPTON, FRANCIS C.
Assistant Paymaster, 14 September, 1861. Resigned 14 February, 1862.
UPTON, FREDERICK E.
Midshipman, 1 November, 1864. Graduated 2 June, 1868. Master, 3 December, 1872. Retired List, 21 November, 1877. Title changed to Lieutenant, Junior Grade, 3 March, 1883.
UFTON, GEORGE.
Mate, 24 September, 1863. Dismissed 19 June, 1865.
UPTON, WILLIAM G.
Acting Ensign, 22 December, 1863. Honorably discharged 31 July, 1865.
URANN, WILLIAM D.
Acting Master, 29 October, 1861. Acting Volunteer Lieutenant, 18 June, 1864. Honorably discharged 30 October, 1868.
URIE, JOHN F.
Assistant Surgeon, 3 July, 1888. Passed Assistant Surgeon, 3 July, 1891. Surgeon, 25 October, 1899.
URNER, EDWARD C.
Mate, 5 June, 1863. Acting Ensign, 14 December, 1864. Honorably discharged 21 November, 1865.
URQUHART, RICHARD A.
Assistant Surgeon, 7 January, 1875. Passed Assistant Surgeon, 29 May, 1878. Resigned 27 April, 1884.
USHER, JAMES D.
Midshipman, 24 March, 1837. Resigned 15 June, 1839.
USHER, NATHANIEL R.
Cadet Midshipman, 22 September, 1871. Graduated 1 June, 1875. Ensign 18 July, 1876. Master, 4 February, 1882. Lieutenant, Junior Grade, 3 March, 1883. Lieutenant, 31 October, 1888. Lieutenant-Commander, 3 March, 1899.
USHER, RICHARD R.
Midshipman, 4 March, 1823. Dismissed 22 August, 1826.
USINA, MICHAEL N.
Passed Assistant Engineer (Spanish-American War), 24 June, 1898. Honorably discharged 27 February, 1899.
USTICK, THOMAS.
Acting Third Assistant Engineer, 14 January, 1863. Second Assistant Engineer, 12 June, 1863. Drowned 5 August, 1864.
UTLEY, JOSEFH H.
Midshipman, 22 September, 1865. Graduated 7 June, 1870. Resigned 30 September, 1874.
UTTER, JOHN.
Mate, 6 December, 1861. Acting Ensign, 12 February, 1864. Acting Master, 1 November, 1864. Honorably discharged 14 February, 1866.
VAIL, ABRAHAM HOLMAN.
Midshipman, 28 September, 1861. Graduated September, 1865. Ensign, 1 December, 1866. Master, 12 March, 1868. Lieutenant, 26 March, 1869. Lieutenant-Commander, 15 October, 1881. Retired List, 4 December, 1890.
VAIL, ABRAM L.
Acting Assistant Surgeon, 17 January, 1863. Resigned 15 September, 1864.
VAIL, EDWARD H.
Mate, 23 January, 1862. Resigned 24 June, 1863.
VAIL, EDWARD M.
Midshipman, 1 December, 1821. Lieutenant, 27 May, 1830. Dismissed 3 July, 1843.

GENERAL NAVY REGISTER.

VAIL, GEORGE A.
   Midshipman, 27 September, 1867. Graduated 6 June, 1871. Retired List, 14 July, 1874. Died 7 August, 1881.
VAIL, SAMUEL.
   Midshipman, 1 January, 1809. Died 14 April, 1812.
VAILE, JOHN H.
   Acting Third Assistant Engineer, 9 September, 1862. Acting Second Assistant Engineer, 12 August, 1864. Honorably discharged 21 September, 1865.
VALDES, PEDRO C.
   Midshipman, 17 June, 1823. Passed Midshipman, 23 March, 1829. Lieutenant, 3 March, 1831. Resigned 6 February, 1834.
VALENTINE, EDWARD K.
   Mate, 5 November, 1862. Acting Ensign, 3 October, 1863. Acting Master, 27 September, 1864. Dismissed 25 August, 1868.
VALK, JACOB R.
   Midshipman, 24 July, 1798. Resigned 12 August, 1802.
VALK, WILLIAM W.
   Assistant Surgeon, 23 February, 1835. Resigned 10 October, 1838.
VALLE, BARTHOLOMEW.
   Midshipman, 28 January, 1841. Resigned 30 November, 1841.
VALLETT, J. K.
   Midshipman, 1 January, 1815. Died in 1825.
VALLETTE, E. A. F.
   Master, 25 June, 1812. Lieutenant, 9 December, 1814. Commander, 3 March, 1831. (See Lavalette.)
VALLETTE, ELI.
   Chaplain, 26 February, 1800. Discharged 8 June, 1801, under Peace Establishment Act.
VALLETTE, S. D.
   Midshipman, 8 December, 1835. (See Lavalette.)
VALLOSHER, MARTIN.
   Acting Ensign, 7 December, 1864. Honorably discharged 27 September, 1865.
VANALSTINE, CORNELIUS J.
   Midshipman, 27 February, 1833. Passed Midshipman, 8 July, 1839. Lieutenant, 11 April, 1845. Resigned 18 May, 1859. Acting Master, 31 October, 1861. Acting Volunteer Lieutenant, 12 October, 1863. Acting Volunteer Lieutenant-Commander, 14 August, 1865. Honorably discharged 30 April, 1866. Died 12 August, 1866.
VANANDA, G. J.
   Mate, 21 May, 1864. Honorably discharged 8 November, 1865.
VANARTSDALT, J.
   Midshipman, 24 September, 1799. Last appearance on Records of Navy Department.
VAN BEUREN, EGBERT.
   Master, 22 January, 1815. Resigned, 22 February, 1815.
VAN BIBBER, FREDERICK.
   Assistant Surgeon, 23 May, 1857. Dismissed 6 May, 1861.
VAN BOSKIRK, JAMES.
   Mate, 18 December, 1861. Acting Master, 14 April, 1862. Honorably discharged 14 January, 1868.
VAN BRUNT, C. H.
   Assistant Surgeon, 26 May, 1820. Died 28 July, 1825.
VAN BRUNT FRANK.
   Acting Third Assistant Engineer, 18 February, 1865. Honorably discharged 17 April, 1866. Acting Third Assistant Engineer, 9 August, 1866. Mustered out 24 September, 1868.
VAN BRUNT, GERSHOM J.
   Midshipman, 1 January, 1818. Lieutenant, 3 March, 1827. Commander, 29 May, 1846. Captain, 14 September, 1855. Commodore, 16 July, 1862. Retired List, 28 April, 1863. Died 17 December, 1863.
VAN BUREN, JOHN D.
   Third Assistant Engineer, 13 May, 1861. Second Assistant Engineer, 21 April, 1863. First Assistant Engineer, 1 January, 1865. Resigned 22 September, 1868.
VAN BUREN MARTIN.
   Acting Third Assistant Engineer, 5 July, 1862. Dismissed 11 December, 1862.
VAN BUSKIRK, J. N.
   Acting Ensign, 13 December, 1862. Honorably discharged 19 August, 1865.
VAN BUSKIRK, PHILIP C.
   Mate, 28 February, 1870. Retired List, 4 March, 1896.
VANCE, GEORGE.
   Mate, 30 July, 1863. Acting Ensign, 27 May, 1864. Died on Peosta, 4 July, 1864.
VANCE, LEWIS R.
   Acting Ensign, 2 March, 1864. Honorably discharged 21 December, 1865.
VANCLAIN, JAMES L.
   Third Assistant Engineer, 11 August, 1860. Second Assistant Engineer, 30 July, 1862. First Assistant Engineer, 20 July, 1864. Died 27 September, 1874.
VANCLEAVE, G. W.
   Midshipman, 16 January, 1809. Lieutenant, 9 December, 1814. Cashiered, 9 February, 1820.
VAN CLEEF, CHARLES H.
   Acting Midshipman, 2 October, 1850. Dropped 24 January, 1851.
VAN CLEEF, SAMUEL M.
   Acting Third Assistant Engineer, 27 February, 1863. Resigned 13 June, 1865.
VAN CLEFT, GEORGE H.
   Civil Engineer, 27 January, 1870. Dropped 2 March, 1871.

VAN CLEVE, AARON.
Acting Third Assistant Engineer, 19 April, 1864. Honorably discharged 4 October, 1865.
VAN CLEVE, JOHN W., Jr.
Acting Assistant Paymaster, 28 October, 1863. Mustered out 7 November, 1865.
VAN de CARR, WILLIAM H.
Midshipman, 26 July, 1865. Graduated 7 June, 1870. Resigned 21 November, 1873.
VANDEGRIFT, NICHOLAS G.
Acting Third Assistant Engineer, 3 August, 1864. Honorably discharged 7 August, 1866.
VANDENBERGH, WILLIAM.
Acting Third Assistant Engineer, 17 October, 1861. Resigned 17 February, 1862.
VANDENBOS, JACOB.
Sailmaker, 3 April, 1807. Last appearance on Records of Navy Department, 1815. Frigate Chesapeake.
VANDERBECK CLARENCE S.
Gunner, 2 November, 1897.
VANDERBILT, AARON.
Mate, 20 July, 1863. Acting Ensign, 1 February, 1865. Honorably discharged 12 October, 1865.
VANDERBILT, WILLIAM W.
Third Assistant Engineer, 18 November, 1862. Second Assistant Engineer, 23 March, 1864. Resigned 30 October, 1865.
VANDERFORD, H.
Boatswain, 15 October, 1830. Dismissed 10 February, 1831.
VANDER HORST, ELIAS.
Midshipman, 10 September, 1841. Passed Midshipman, 10 August, 1847. Died 17 March, 1850.
VANDERSLICE, THADDEUS L.
Third Assistant Engineer, 8 September, 1863. Second Assistant Engineer, 15 October 1865. Resigned 31 December, 1871.
VAN DEUSEN, GEORGE H.
Acting Assistant Surgeon, 14 February, 1862. Resigned 19 March, 1864.
VAN de VANTER, J. C.
Mate, 24 October, 1861. Acting Ensign, 28 Janury, 1864. Appointment revoked 12 May, 1865.
VANDEVEER, HANKERSON.
Acting Master and Pilot, 1 October, 1864. Honorably discharged 15 August, 1865.
VAN DUZER, GEORGE.
Mate, 21 June, 1862. Dismissed 6 September, 1862. Mate, 28 May, 1863. Resigned 9 February, 1865.
VAN DUZER, LOUIS S.
Cadet Midshipman, 22 September, 1876. Graduated 22 June, 1882. Ensign, Junior Grade, 3 March, 1883. Ensign, 26 June, 1884. Lieutenant, Junior Grade, 10 June, 1893. Lieutenant, 5 January, 1897.
VAN DYKE, ALEXANDER.
Midshipman, 10 May, 1820. Resigned 17 August, 1820.
VANDYKE, ALEXANDER.
Midshipman, 6 May, 1822. Resigned 10 March, 1826.
VAN DYKE, BENJAMIN G.
Mate, 11 June, 1863. Acting Ensign, 27 June, 1864. Honorably discharged 31 October, 1865.
VANDYKE, HENRY.
Midshipman, 16 March, 1798. Lieutenant, 1 May, 1800. Last appearance on Records of Navy Department, 8 September, 1802. Killed in a duel.
VANDYKE, J. C.
Midshipman, 4 March, 1823. Resigned 5 June, 1823.
VAN FORSEN, MORRIS.
Acting Third Assistant Engineer, 30 November, 1862. Resigned 31 May, 1864.
VAN GIESON, RANSFORD E.
Assistant Surgeon, 24 January, 1862. Resigned 26 May, 1863.
VAN GIESON, HENRY C.
Acting Assistant Surgeon, 10 February, 1864. Resigned 17 May, 1865.
VAN HARTEN, WILLIAM H. E.
Mate, 25 June, 1898. Honorably discharged 15 September, 1898.
VAN HOOK, B. F.
Midshipman, 2 January, 1840. Resigned 15 June, 1843.
VAN HORN, WILLIAM L.
Assistant Surgeon 4 April, 1831. Surgeon, 8 September, 1841. Died 3 April, 1854.
VAN HOUTEN, D. W.
Acting Assistant Paymaster, 7 September, 1864. Mustered out 13 December, 1865.
VAN HOVENBERG, JOHN.
Third Assistant Engineer, 12 August, 1861. Second Assistant Engineer, 21 April, 1863. First Assistant Engineer, 11 October, 1866. Chief Engineer, 23 December, 1884. Died 16 October, 1885.
VAN IDERSTINE, JARED.
Acting Third Assistant Engineer, 15 November, 1861. Resigned 21 August, 1862.
VAN MATER, GARRETT.
Sailmaker, 25 January, 1873. Chief Sailmaker, 3 March, 1899.
VAN METER, JOHN B.
Chaplain, 19 December, 1871. Resigned 1 July, 1882.
VAN NESS, RALPH G.
Mate, 15 December, 1863. Honorably discharged 9 March, 1866.

GENERAL NAVY REGISTER. 559

VAN NEST, JOHN F.
   Mate, 4 January, 1864. Drowned 18 August, 1864.
VAN PELT, ELBERT C.
   Acting Ensign, 28 November, 1862. Resigned 3 March, 1865.
VAN RENSELAER, H. H.
   Midshipman, 10 May, 1820. Dismissed 6 April, 1829.
VAN RENSALEAR, K. H.
   Lieutenant, 7 January, 1799. Last appearance on Records of Navy Department, 16 April, 1800.
VAN RENSELAER, W.
   Midshipman, 1 November, 1830. Resigned 14 September, 1839.
VAN REYPEN, WILLIAM K.
   Assistant Surgeon, 24 January, 1862. Passed Assistant Surgeon, 26 May, 1865. Surgeon, 12 May, 1868. Medical Inspector, 16 August, 1887. Medical Director, 30 March, 1895.
VANSANT, IRA.
   Midshipman, 16 January, 1809. Last appearance on Records of Navy Department, 1815. Philadelphia.
VANSANT, JOHN.
   Assistant Surgeon, 1 May, 1855. Passed Assistant Surgeon, 4 May, 1860. Resigned 22 June, 1860.
VANSANT, WILLIAM N.
   Naval Cadet, 4 September, 1884. Assistant Naval Constructor, 1 July, 1890. Died 1 January, 1893.
VAN SCHAICK, S.
   Midshipman, 30 December, 1798. Lieutenant, 18 May, 1804. Resigned 9 July, 1807.
VAN SICE, EDWARD.
   Acting Master, 26 August, 1861. Resigned 7 October, 1864.
VAN SLYCK, EDGAR.
   Acting Master, 19 July, 1861. Honorably discharged 28 October, 1865.
VANTIN, CLAUDE.
   Acting Third Assistant Engineer, 17 December, 1863. Honorably discharged 1 October, 1865.
VAN TINE, CHARLES M.
   Third Assistant Engineer, 16 January, 1863. Second Assistant Engineer, 28 May, 1864. Resigned 4 January, 1866.
VAN VELSON, HENRY.
   Mate, 26 October, 1863. Honorably discharged 4 November, 1865.
VAN VLECK, WILLIAM A.
   Acting Midshipman, 25 November, 1849. Acting Ensign, 1 October, 1863. Master, 10 May, 1866. Lieutenant, 21 February, 1867. Lieutenant-Commander, 12 March, 1868. Died 29 June, 1869.
VAN VOORHIS, BARKER.
   Acting Ensign, 9 September, 1862. Acting Master, 22 September, 1863. Honorably discharged 30 August, 1865.
VAN VOORHIS, HENRY.
   Sailmaker, 11 August, 1819. Died 30 August, 1826.
VAN VOORHIS, RICHARD.
   Sailmaker, 8 February, 1834. Retired List, 21 September, 1861. Died 12 April, 1880.
VAN VOORHIS, R. B.
   Master, 28 February, 1809. Last appearance on Records of Navy Department, 1815. New York Navy Yard.
VAN WART, EDWARD S.
   Assistant Engineer (Spanish-American War), 4 May, 1898. Honorably discharged 8 September, 1898.
VAN WERT, WILLIAM H.
   Acting Third Assistant Engineer, 25 March, 1864. Honorably discharged 14 November, 1865.
VAN WORMER, JOHN.
   Acting Third Assistant Engineer, 4 November, 1861. Resigned 17 November, 1862.
VAN WYCK, EDWARD H.
   Assistant Surgeon, 20 June, 1838. Retired List, 8 May, 1861. Died 11 September, 1887.
VAN WYCK, P. C.
   Midshipman, 4 December, 1834. Died 31 December, 1841.
VAN WYCK, P. C.
   Assistant Surgeon, 3 March, 1809. Last appearance on Records of Navy Department, 1815. Frigate Constitution.
VAN WYCK, WASHINGTON.
   Mate, 24 May, 1862. Honorably discharged 22 June, 1866.
VAN WYCK, WILLIAM.
   Midshipman, 19 October, 1841. Passed Midshipman, 10 August, 1847. Lost on the Porpoise, 21 September, 1855.
VAN ZANDT, JAMES.
   Acting Third Assistant Engineer, 1 October, 1862. Acting Second Assistant Engineer, 26 December, 1863. Honorably discharged 4 November, 1865.
VAN ZANDT, JAMES D.
   Acting Third Assistant Engineer, 8 January, 1864. Appointment revoked (sick) 19 July, 1864.
VAN ZANDT, JOSEPH A.
   Third Assistant Engineer, 20 February, 1847. Died 7 April, 1849.
VAN ZANDT, NICHOLAS H.
   Midshipman, 19 October, 1841. Passed Midshipman, 10 August, 1847. Master, 14 September, 1855. Lieutenant, 15 September, 1855. Dismissed 24 December, 1861.

VAN ZANDT, WILLIAM V. R.
  Mate, 6 September, 1862. Resigned 18 June, 1863.
VARNEY, WILLIAM H.
  Assistant Naval Constructor, 29 July, 1869. Retired List, 19 April, 1900.
VARNUM, FREDERICK.
  Midshipman, 18 June, 1812. Lieutenant, 28 March, 1820. Commander, 8 March, 1841. Dropped 13 September 1855.
VARNUM, WILLIAM L.
  Midshipman, 5 June, 1871. Graduated 20 June, 1876. Ensign, 20 November, 1878. Retired List, 20 November, 1884.
VASSALLO, L. GUSTAV.
  Acting Master, 11 January, 1862. Acting Volunteer Lieutenant, 7 November, 1864. Resigned 1 November, 1868.
VASSE, JAMES.
  Midshipman, 18 June, 1812. Resigned 13 July, 1813.
VAUGHAN, CHARLES E.
  Acting Assistant Surgeon, 15 May, 1863. Honorably discharged 21 October, 1865.
VAUGHAN, EDWIN.
  Acting Third Assistant Engineer, 11 October, 1862. Acting Second Assistant Engineer, 14 May, 1864. Honorably discharged 19 September, 1865.
VAUGHAN, HIRAM C.
  Acting Assistant Surgeon, 10 March, 1864. Honorably discharged 21 October, 1865.
VAUGHAN, WILLIAM.
  Master, 12 August, 1822. Reserved List, 14 September, 1855. Died 10 December, 1856.
VAUGHN, HENRY.
  Acting Master, 23 September, 1861. Honorably discharged 10 February, 1869.
VAUGHN, HENRY A.
  Mate, 22 June, 1863. Resigned 21 July, 1864. Acting Ensign, 24 April, 1865. Honorably discharged 26 January, 1866.
VAUGHN, JOHN A.
  Midshipman, 24 September, 1861. Graduated September, 1865. Ensign, 1 December, 1866. Master, 12 March, 1868. Resigned 6 December, 1870.
VAUGHN, NATHAN F.
  Mate, 13 August, 1863. Acting Ensign, 17 February, 1864. Honorably discharged 1 December, 1865.
VEACOCK, GILBERT W.
  Mate. Dismissed 16 March, 1863.
VEATCH, JAMES C.
  Acting Third Assistant Engineer, 10 May, 1864. Honorably discharged 12 October, 1867.
VEDDER, ALEXANDER M.
  Assistant Surgeon, 12 September, 1856. Passed Assistant Surgeon, 25 March, 1861. Surgeon, 14 November, 1861. Resigned 29 December, 1864.
VEEDER, TEN EYCK DE W.
  Midshipman, 25 September, 1868. Graduated 31 May, 1873. Ensign, 16 July, 1874. Master, 1 January, 1881. Lieutenant, Junior Grade, 3 March, 1883. Lieutenant, 7 October, 1886. Lieutenant-Commander, 3 March, 1899.
VEITCH, WILLIAM.
  Acting Third Assistant Engineer, 18 November, 1861. Acting Second Assistant Engineer, 6 November, 1863. Honorably discharged 16 October, 1865.
VEITINGER, JACOB.
  Acting Third Assistant Engineer. 30 March, 1863. Honorably discharged 16 May, 1868.
VELTMAN, WILLIAM F.
  Mate, 7 August, 1862. Resigned 6 June, 1864.
VENABLE, CHARLES H.
  Mate, 2 April, 1866. Resigned 17 August, 1867. Mate, 4 September, 1869. Gunner, 5 September, 1871. Chief Gunner, 3 March, 1899.
VENABLE, GEORGE R.
  Assistant Paymaster (Spanish-American War), 11 June, 1898. Assistant Paymaster (Regular Navy), 6 March, 1899.
VENABLE, JOHN A.
  Acting Warrant Machinist, 23 August, 1899.
VENABLE, JOSEPH G.
  Acting Gunner, 6 May, 1864. Honorably discharged 9 January, 1866.
VENABLE, THOMAS P.
  Gunner, 19 March, 1847. Resigned 15 May, 1854. Gunner, 22 October, 1855. Retired List, 25 August, 1887.
VENNARD, JOHN L.
  Mate, 9 May, 1862. Acting Ensign, 9 May, 1864. Honorably discharged 5 January, 1868. Mate, 26 April, 1870. Retired List, 9 June, 1899.
VER MEULEN, EDMUND C.
  Assistant Surgeon, 24 January, 1862. Passed Assistant Surgeon, 26 May, 1865. Surgeon, 26 April, 1872. Retired List, 21 October, 1882. Died 21 January, 1898.
VERMILLION, D.
  Carpenter, 8 June, 1822. Last appearance on Records of Navy Department. Ordered to Sloop Peacock.
VERNER, HENRY.
  Master, 5 December, 1812. Last appearance on Records of Navy Department, 1815. Charlestown, Mass.
VERNON, SAMUEL.
  Assistant Surgeon. 11 January, 1812. Discharged 5 February, 1814.

VERNON, WILLIAM G.
Acting Third Assistant Engineer, 6 September, 1864. Honorably discharged 16 July, 1865.
VERNON, WILLIAM R.
Acting Second Assistant Engineer, 28 October, 1864. Honorably discharged 23 September, 1865.
VERY, ABRAHAM A.
Acting Ensign, 5 January, 1864. Honorably discharged 22 June, 1867.
VERY, EDWARD W.
Midshipman, 20 February, 1863. Graduated June, 1867. Ensign, 18 December, 1868. Master, 21 March, 1870. Lieutenant, 29 September, 1871. Resigned 30 April, 1885.
VERY, SAMUEL, JR.
Acting Master, 2 August, 1861. Honorably discharged 6 October, 1867.
VERY, SAMUEL W.
Midshipman, 23 February, 1863. Graduated June, 1866. Ensign, 12 March, 1868. Master, 26 March, 1869. Lieutenant, 21 March, 1870. Lieutenant-Commander, 4 March, 1886. Commander, 1 March, 1895.
VESTLERY, DAVID.
Boatswain, 8 June, 1822. Died 6 November, 1828.
VEVERS, RICHARD.
Acting Master, 26 August, 1861. Resigned 25 March, 1863.
VIALL, THOMAS B.
Mate, 8 February, 1865. Appointment revoked 18 November, 1865.
VICKEREY, JACOB.
Midshipman, 25 June 1800. Resigned 6 February, 1803.
VICKERY, ROBERT J.
Acting Warrant Machinist, 23 August, 1899.
VICTOR, HENRY C.
Third Assistant Engineer, 2 August, 1855. Resigned 28 August, 1858. Reinstated in original position, 11 April, 1859. Second Assistant Engineer, 20 December, 1860. First Assistant Engineer, 1 July, 1861. Resigned 16 December, 1863.
VIENE, LOUIS.
Midshipman, 1 December, 1809. Last appearance on Records of Navy Department, 17 August, 1810.
VINALL, JOSEPH T.
Acting Third Assistant Engineer, 1 December, 1864. Mustered out 2 June, 1868.
VILAS, R. A.
Acting Assistant Paymaster, 10 January, 1865. Mustered out 7 October, 1865.
VILLAZON, MARCELINO.
Acting Third Assistant Engineer, 1 March, 1864. Acting Second Assistant Engineer, 15 December, 1864. Honorably discharged 10 May, 1866.
VINCENT, DAVID.
Mate, 23 July, 1862. Killed on the Winona, 14 December, 1862.
VINCENT, FREEMAN
Mate, 1 October, 1862. Acting Ensign, 1 September, 1863. Acting Master, 20 May, 1865. Honorably discharged 22 November, 1865.
VINCENT, ROE W.
Naval Cadet, 6 September, 1895. At sea prior to final graduation.
VINCENT, WILLIAM J.
Mate, 5 March, 1862. Appointment revoked 11 November, 1865.
VINING, SETON.
Midshipman, 16 January, 1809. Resigned 27 July, 1810.
VINTON, BENJAMIN.
Surgeon, 2 May, 1799. Resigned 31 July, 1800.
VINTON, FREDERICK B.
Cadet Midshipman, 21 September, 1871. Graduated 17 September, 1875. Ensign, 9 October, 1876. Resigned 20 September, 1883.
VINTON GEORGE A.
Acting Gunner, 23 January, 1865. Honorably discharged 1 August, 1865.
VOELKERS, FREDERICK T.
Mate, 28 September, 1866. Resigned 11 April, 1867.
VOGELGESANG, CHARLES T.
Naval Cadet, 6 September, 1886. Ensign, 1 July, 1892. Lieutenant, Junior Grade, 3 March, 1899. Lieutenant, 11 June, 1899.
VOICE, GEORGE W.
Acting Third Assistant Engineer, 29 December, 1862. Dismissed 24 December, 1863.
VOLLUM, SAMUEL.
Acting Third Assistant Engineer, 13 January, 1862. Dropped 2 May, 1863.
Von HARTEN, WILLIAM H. E.
Mate (Spanish-American War), 25 June, 1898. Honorably discharged 15 September, 1898.
Von LOESECKE, MAGNUS F. S.
Ensign (Spanish-American War), 18 July, 1898. Honorably discharged 8 September, 1898.
Von WEDEKIND, LUTHER E.
Assistant Surgeon, 3 November, 1888. Passed Assistant Surgeon, 3 November, 1892.
VOORHEES, A. H.
Midshipman, 12 July, 1800. Lost on the Insurgent.
VOORHEES, JAMES.
Midshipman 18 May, 1809. Killed in a duel 19 December, 1809.
VOORHEES, L. D. D.
Acting Master, 8 June, 1861. Acting Volunteer Lieutenant, 20 August, 1861. Appointment revoked, and appointed Acting Master, 23 September, 1861. Acting Volunteer Lieutenant, 5 November, 1864. Honorably discharged 11 November, 1865.

VOORHEES, PHILIP F.
Midshipman, 15 November, 1809. Lieutenant, 9 December, 1814. Commander, 24 April, 1828. Captain, 28 February, 1838. Reserved List, 13 September, 1855. Died 26 February, 1862.

VOORHEES, PHILIP R.
Third Assistant Engineer, 19 February, 1861. Second Assistant Engineer, 16 January, 1863. First Assistant Engineer, 1 December, 1864. Resigned 18 February, 1868.

VOORHEES, RALPH.
Midshipman, 1 September, 1811. Lieutenant, 5 March, 1817. Commander, 9 February, 1837. Died 27 July, 1842.

VOSE, EDWIN H.
Acting Assistant Surgeon, 2 December, 1863. Resigned 22 March, 1864.

VOSHEL, JAMES.
Midshipman, 1 January, 1812. Last appearance on Records of Navy Department, 1815. Furloughed.

VREELAND, BENJAMIN.
Assistant Surgeon, 9 May, 1850. Passed Assistant Surgeon, 30 March, 1857. Surgeon, 26 April, 1861. Died 20 March, 1866.

VREELAND, CHARLES E.
Midshipman, 31 July, 1866. Graduated 7 June, 1870. Ensign, 13 July, 1871. Master, 2 April, 1874. Lieutenant, 25 March, 1880. Lieutenant-Commander, 3 March, 1899.

VREELAND, CHARLES M.
Ensign (Spanish-American War), 21 May, 1898. Honorably discharged 8 October, 1898.

VULTEE, FRANCIS P.
Mate, 23 November, 1864. Discharged May, 1866.

WADDELL, CHARLES.
Midshipman, 14 March, 1840. Passed Midshipman, 11 July, 1846. Died 30 August, 1847.

WADDELL, HENRY.
Midshipman, 29 September, 1832. Passed Midshipman, 23 June, 1838. Died 27 September, 1839.

WADDELL, HENRY C.
Mate, 1861. Resigned 28 February, 1862. Mate, 15 October, 1863. Dismissed 11 May, 1864.

WADDELL, JAMES J.
Midshipman, 10 September, 1841. Passed Midshipman, 10 August, 1847. Master, 14 September, 1855. Lieutenant, 15 September, 1855. Dismissed 18 January, 1862.

WADDELL, JOHN.
Lieutenant, 15 October, 1798. Resigned 16 January, 1799.

WADE, CHARLES.
Gunner, 27 September, 1834. Died 27 February, 1841.

WADE, CHARLES T.
Naval Cadet, 5 September, 1896. Graduated 30 June, 1900.

WADE, EDWIN L.
Sailmaker, 16 May, 1871. Resigned 14 June, 1875.

WADE, EUGENE J.
Acting Third Assistant Engineer, 27 May, 1861. Resigned 22 August, 1862.

WADE, GEORGE H.
Acting First Assistant Engineer, 28 May, 1861. Honorably discharged 24 November, 1865.

WADE, GEORGE S.
Master, 29 January, 1809. Dismissed 21 July, 1810.

WADE, HENRY C.
Acting Master, 29 October, 1861. Died 12 September, 1867.

WADE, JOHN T.
Master, 6 February, 1809. Lieutenant, 9 December, 1814. Died 25 November, 1816.

WADE, JOSEPH M.
Acting Assistant Paymaster, 3 June, 1861. Never finally discharged. Accounts not settled.

WADE, RUSSELL A.
Acting Third Assistant Engineer, 24 August, 1864. Honorably discharged 10 June, 1867.

WADE, THOMAS F.
Acting Lieutenant, 8 May, 1861. Acting Volunteer Lieutenant, 28 October, 1861. Master, 12 March, 1868. Lieutenant, 18 December, 1868. Lieutenant-Commander, 1 July, 1870. Retired List 3 November, 1877. Died 20 March, 1885.

WADE, WILLIAM.
Mate, 20 August, 1864. Resigned 7 June, 1865.

WADE, WILLIAM.
Acting Gunner, 10 August, 1861. Dismissed 4 January, 1862.

WADE, WILLIAM R.
Ensign (Spanish-American War), 5 July, 1898. Honorably discharged 20 September, 1898.

WADELL, GEORGE.
Acting Third Assistant Engineer, 19 January, 1863. Acting Second Assistant Engineer, 13 August 1863. Honorably discharged 5 September, 1865.

WADHAMS, ALBION J.
Naval Cadet, 14 September, 1891. Ensign, 1 July, 1897. Lieutenant, Junior Grade, 1 July, 1900.

GENERAL NAVY REGISTER. 563

WADHAMS, ALBION V.
Midshipman, 26 September, 1864. Graduated June, 1868. Ensign, 19 April, 1869. Master 12 July, 1870. Lieutenant, 25 March, 1873. Lieutenant-Commander, 21 July, 1894. Commander, 3 March, 1899.
WADLEIGH, GEORGE H.
Acting Midshipman, 27 September, 1860. Ensign, 28 May, 1863. Master, 10 November, 1865. Lieutenant, 10 November, 1866. Lieutenant-Commander, 12 March, 1868. Commander, 13 March, 1880. Captain, 10 July, 1894.
WADSWORTH, ALEXANDER S.
Midshipman, 2 April, 1804. Lieutenant, 21 April, 1810. Commander, 27 April, 1816. Captain 3 March, 1825. Died 5 April, 1851.
WADSWORTH, CHARLES.
Purser, 28 May, 1798. Died July, 1809.
WADSWORTH, C. E.
Midshipman, 1 December, 1824. Died 8 May, 1827.
WADSWORTH, HENRY.
Midshipman, 28 August, 1799. Died 1805.
WADSWORTH, HENRY M.
Mate, 8 December, 1864. Deserted 5 July, 1865.
WADSWORTH, P
Acting Assistant Surgeon, 10 March, 1865. Resigned 3 July, 1865.
WAGER, CHARLES.
Midshipman, 2 April, 1835. Resigned 19 February, 1842.
WAGER, PETER, JR.
Midshipman, 12 February, 1840. Passed Midshipman, 11 July, 1846. Master, 1 March, 1855. Dropped 13 September, 1855.
WAGG, MAURICE.
Mate, 21 April, 1864. Honorably discharged 6 January, 1866.
WAGGENER, JAMES R.
Assistant Surgeon, 29 July, 1872. Passed Assistant Surgeon, 21 December, 1875. Surgeon, 18 March, 1887. Medical Inspector, 9 April, 1899.
WAGGENER, RICHARD.
Pharmacist, 15 September, 1898.
WAGNER, DAVID.
Mate, 13 August, 1863. Acting Ensign, 21 July, 1864. Appointment revoked 5 August, 1864.
WAGNER, FRANK E.
Assistant Surgeon (Spanish-American War), 25 May, 1898. Honorably discharged 20 October, 1898.
WAGNER, FREDERIC.
Acting Third Assistant Engineer, 3 October, 1863. Honorably discharged 21 November, 1865.
WAGNER, FREDERIC M.
Acting Third Assistant Engineer, 4 June, 1864. Honorably discharged 13 June.
WAGNER, JAMES.
Acting First Assistant Engineer, 15 October, 1863. Appointment revoked 1 June, 1864
WAGNER, JAMES J.
Acting First Assistant Engineer, 1 October, 1862. Appointment revoked (sick) 1 January, 1864.
WAGNER, PETER.
Acting First Assistant Engineer, 23 April, 1863. Honorably discharged 20 February, 1866.
WAGNER, WILLIAM.
Acting Ensign, 1 October, 1862. Honorably discharged 6 December, 1865
WAGSTAFF, ROBERT M.
Mate, 11 December, 1861. Acting Ensign, 19 January, 1863. Honorably discharged 25 September, 1867.
WAHL, JACOB.
Acting Third Assistant Engineer, 23 July, 1864. Honorably discharged 30 December, 1865.
WAILES, JOHN P.
Midshipman, 1 January, 1812. Resigned 3 May, 1813.
WAINE, THOMAS.
Purser, 24 July, 1813. Last appearance on Records of Navy Department, 1820. Frigate Java.
WAINWRIGHT, GARDNER S.
Acting Midshipman, 1 November, 1849. Dropped 3 September, 1850.
WAINWRIGHT, JOHN D.
Naval Cadet, 19 September, 1896. Graduated 30 June, 1900.
WAINWRIGHT, JONATHAN M.
Midshipman, 13 June, 1837. Passed Midshipman, 29 June, 1843. Acting Master, 10 November, 1849. Lieutenant, 17 September, 1850. Commander, 16 July, 1862. Killed in action 1 January, 1863.
WAINWRIGHT, JONATHAN M.
Midshipman, 30 July, 1863. Graduated June, 1867. Ensign, 18 December, 1868. Died 19 June. 1870.
WAINWRIGHT, JOSEPH H.
Mate, 4 April, 1862. Acting Ensign, 20 May, 1864. Honorably discharged 9 April, 1866.
WAINWRIGHT, RICHARD.
Midshipman, 11 May, 1831. Passed Midshipman, 15 June. 1837. Lieutenant, 8 September, 1841. Commander, 24 April, 1861. Killed in battle 10 August, 1862.

WAINWRIGHT, RICHARD.
Midshipman, 28 September, 1864. Graduated June, 1868. Master, 12 July, 1870. Lieutenant, 25 September, 1873. Lieutenant-Commander, 16 September, 1894. Commander, 3 March, 1899.

WAINWRIGHT, THOMAS B
Midshipman, 21 September, 1841. Passed Midshipman, 10 August, 1847. Died 4 August, 1850.

WAIT, GEORGE M.
Second Assistant Engineer, 17 May, 1861. Acting First Assistant Engineer, 3 October, 1861. Resigned 7 February, 1862.

WAIT, HORATIO L.
Assistant Paymaster, 14 July, 1862. Paymaster, 1 April, 1866. Resigned 22 July, 1870.

WAIT, ISRAEL C.
Midshipman, 28 December, 1836. Passed Midshipman, 1 July, 1842. Acting Master, 21 January, 1848. Lieutenant, 29 May, 1850. Dropped 13 September, 1855.

WAIT, NATHAN W.
Mate, 4 April, 1862. Acting Ensign, 11 September, 1863. Honorably discharged 19 November, 1865.

WAITE, CEPHAS K.
Acting Ensign, 13 January, 1864. Honorably discharged 15 May, 1867.

WAITE, FREDERICK H.
Acting Ensign, 10 July, 1863. Honorably discharged 23 November, 1868.

WAITE, HENRY.
Acting First Assistant Engineer, 7 December, 1861. Acting Chief Engineer, 19 January, 1863. Honorably discharged 29 February, 1866.

WAITE, WILLIAM H.
Acting Third Assistant Engineer, 14 January, 1865. Honorably discharged 11 November, 1864.

WAKEFIELD, CHARLES H.
Acting Third Assistant Engineer, 10 March, 1863. Honorably discharged 29 July, 1865.

WAKEFIELD, GEORGE W.
Acting Third Assistant Engineer, 22 August, 1864. Honorably discharged 11 September, 1865.

WAKEFIELD, HENRY.
Acting Ensign, 7 November, 1863. Honorably discharged 22 November, 1865.

WAKEMAN, LEWIS B.
Sailmaker, 31 October, 1855. Resigned 12 June, 1865.

WAKENSHAW, H. C.
Cadet Midshipman, 10 June, 1873. Graduated 18 June, 1879. Ensign, 2 February, 1881. Lieutenant, Junior Grade, 30 June, 1887. Died 15 February, 1890.

WALBACH, JOHN J. B.
Midshpman, 1 December, 1827. Passed Midshipman, 14 June, 1834. Lieutenant, 25 February, 1841. Dropped 28 September, 1855. Lieutenant, Active List, 25 February, 1841. Resigned 18 February, 1861.

WALBRIDGE, EDWARD N.
Ensign (Spanish-American War), 18 July, 1898. Honorably discharged 12 October, 1898.

WALCOTT, HENRY O.
Acting Second Assistant Engineer, 9 February, 1864. Appointment revoked 19 December, 1864.

WALCOTT, MORGAN.
Ensign (Spanish-American War), 15 June, 1898. Honorably discharged 2 September, 1898.

WALCOTT, W. F.
Mate, 18 January, 1865. Honorably discharged 30 October, 1865.

WALCUTT, JOHN.
Midshipman, 2 March, 1840. Passed Midshipman, 11 July, 1846. Master, 30 January, 1855. Dropped 28 September, 1855.

WALDEMAR, CHARLES F
Acting Ensign, 7 June, 1864. Died October, 1864

WALDO, CHARLES.
Master, 10 March, 1813. Killed 30 August, 1838.

WALDRON, R. R.
Midshipman, 15 June, 1837. Died 30 October 1846.

WALES, PHILIP S.
Assistant Surgeon, 7 August, 1856. Passed Assistant Surgeon, 25 March, 1861. Surgeon, 12 October, 1861. Medical Inspector, 30 June, 1873. Medical Director, 15 October, 1881. Retired List, 27 February, 1896.

WALKE, FRANK A.
Assistant Surgeon, 31 May, 1854. Resigned 6 August, 1856.

WALKE, HENRY.
Midshipman, 1 February, 1827. Passed Midshipman, 10 June, 1833. Lieutenant, 9 December, 1839. Reserved List, 13 September, 1855. Commander on Active List, 14 September, 1855. Captain on Active List, 16 July 1862. Commodore, 25 July, 1866. Rear-Admiral, 13 July, 1870. Retired List, 26 April, 1871. Died 8 March, 1896.

WALKENSHAW, SAMUEL L.
Acting First Assistant Engineer, 22 October, 1863. Honorably discharged 10 October, 1865.

WALKER, ASA.
Midshipman, 21 November, 1862. Graduated June, 1866. Ensign, 12 March, 1868. Master, 26 March, 1869. Lieutenant, 21 March, 1870. Lieutenant-Commander, 12 December, 1884. Commander, 11 April, 1894. Captain, 9 September, 1899.

GENERAL NAVY REGISTER. 565

WALKER, BENJAMIN.
Mate, 12 September, 1861. Acting Ensign, 3 March, 1863. Honorably discharged 12 October, 1865.

WALKER, CHARLES.
Boatswain, 6 June, 1803. Last appearance on Records of Navy Department.

WALKER, CHARLES H.
Mate, 26 August, 1862. Resigned 26 May, 1863. Acting Ensign, 4 June, 1863. Dismissed 7 October, 1864.

WALKER, DANIEL R.
Midshipman, 9 June, 1811. Resigned 21 November, 1820.

WALKER, DUDLEY.
Purser, 21 August, 1826. Dismissed 24 February, 1853.

WALKER EDWARD A.
Acting Midshipman, 26 September, 1855. Midshipman, 15 June, 1860. Master, 19 September, 1861. Lieutenant, 16 July, 1862. Lieutenant-Commander, 25 July, 1866. Commander, 5 June, 1874. Died 8 March, 1876.

WALKER, EDWARD H.
Mate, 1 October, 1862. Dismissed 13 December, 1862.

WALKER, GEORGE W.
Acting Chief Engineer, 1 October, 1862. Honorably discharged 12 February, 1866.

WALKER, HENRY.
Acting Third Assistant Engineer, 1 August, 1864. Honorably discharged 8 July, 1865.

WALKER, H. H.
Acting Ensign, 1 October, 1862. Resigned 24 November, 1862.

WALKER, JAMES.
Boatswain, 11 February, 1851. Retired List, 13 November, 1871. Died 21 May, 1884.

WALKER, JAMES C.
Midshipman, 12 February, 1849. Resigned 8 October, 1855.

WALKER, JAMES E.
Naval Cadet, 7 September, 1891. Ensign, 1 July, 1897. Lieutenant, Junior Grade, 1 July, 1900.

WALKER, JAMES G.
Acting Third Assistant Engineer, 7 October, 1864. Honorably discharged 20 July, 1865.

WALKER, JAMES M.
Acting Ensign, 1 October, 1862. Resigned 17 June, 1863.

WALKER, JAMES W. G.
Civil Engineer, 29 July, 1898.

WALKER, JOHN.
Mate, 11 December, 1863. Acting Ensign, 27 February, 1865. Honorably discharged 26 August, 1867.

WALKER, JOHN.
Boatswain, 6 February, 1862. Retired List, 15 August, 1877. Died 5 December, 1887.

WALKER, JOHN.
Acting Second Assistant Engineer, 16 September, 1861. Resigned 30 July, 1862.

WALKER, JOHN G.
Acting Midshipman, 5 October, 1850. Midshipman, 11 December, 1852. Passed Midshipman, 20 June, 1856. Master, 22 January, 1858. Lieutenant 23 January, 1858. Lieutenant-Commander, 16 July, 1862. Commander, 25 July, 1866. Captain, 25 June, 1877. Commodore 12 February, 1889. Rear-Admiral, 23 January, 1894. Retired List, 20 March, 1897.

WALKER, JOHN T.
Midshipman, 18 February, 1841. Passed Midshipman, 10 August, 1847. Master, 14 September, 1855. Lieutenant, 15 September, 1855. Died 25 November, 1856.

WALKER, NATHANIEL B.
Mate, 15 October, 1861. Dismissed 27 August, 1862. Mate, 22 June, 1864. Acting Ensign, 13 March, 1865. Honorably discharged 29 October, 1865. Mate, 22 June, 1866. Resigned 13 August, 1867.

WALKER, RALPH E.
Naval Cadet, 20 May, 1892. Ensign, 6 May, 1898. Second Lieutenant, Marine Corps, 20 May, 1898.

WALKER, THEODORIC L.
Midshipman, 10 September, 1841. Passed Midshipman. 10 August, 1847. Master, 26 July, 1855. Lieutenant, 14 September, 1855. Died 17 March, 1858.

WALKER, THOMAS.
Acting Third Assistant Engineer, 20 February, 1864. Honorably discharged 10 July, 1865.

WALKER, THOMAS J.
Mate, 15 June, 1863. Resigned 11 May, 1865.

WALKER, THOMAS W.
Acting Ensign, 31 March, 1863. Dismissed 23 July, 1863.

WALKER, W. D.
Acting Assistant Paymaster, 16 November, 1864. Mustered out 5 November, 1865.

WALKER, WILLIAM.
Acting Ensign, 31 October, 1862. Dismissed 19 June, 1863. Acting Ensign, 4 October, 1864. Deserted 13 January, 1865.

WALKER, WILLIAM.
Midshipman, 2 April, 1804. Appointment revoked 4 August, 1809.

WALKER, WILLIAM L.
Assistant Engineer (Spanish-American War), 1 June, 1898. Honorably discharged 20 February, 1899.

WALKER, WILLIAM M.
Midshipman, 1 November, 1827. Passed Midshipman, 10 June, 1833. Lieutenant, 8 December, 1838. Commander, 14 September, 1855. Captain, 16 July, 1862. Died 19 November, 1866.

GENERAL NAVY REGISTER.

WALKER, WILLIAM S.
Midshipman, 30 November, 1814. Lieutenant, 13 January, 1825. Captain, 8 September, 1841. Captain, 14 September, 1855. Commodore on Retired List, 16 July, 1862. Died 24 November, 1863.

WALL, A. G.
Midshipman, 1 January, 1812. Lieutenant, 1 April, 1818. Died 31 August, 1825.

WALL, AUGUSTUS.
Midshipman, 1 September, 1811. Last appearance on Records of Navy Department.

WALL, ELLICOTT C.
Midshipman, 12 February, 1842. Dismissed 2 October, 1845.

WALL, FRANCIS R.
Cadet Midshipman, 23 June, 1876. Graduated 22 June, 1882. Ensign, Junior Grade, 3 March, 1883. Ensign, 26 June, 1884. Resigned 30 June, 1888. Ensign (Spanish-American War), 24 May, 1898. Lieutenant, Junior Grade, 3 June, 1898. Honorably discharged 25 November, 1898.

WALL, JOHN.
Acting Third Assistant Engineer, 21 December, 1861. Resigned 12 February, 1864.

WALL, JOHN W.
Acting Third Assistant Engineer, 26 October, 1861. Resigned 20 December, 1862. Acting Second Assistant Engineer, 2 November, 1864. Honorably discharged 7 October, 1865.

WALL, RICHARD.
Acting Ensign, 18 May, 1863. Dismissed 8 August, 1863.

WALL, ROBERT E.
Assistant Surgeon, 27 November, 1844. Died 15 December, 1853.

WALLACE, ALEXANDER.
Acting Master, 5 July, 1862. Acting Volunteer Lieutenant, 1 May, 1865. Honorably discharged 28 November, 1865.

WALLACE, FRANCIS.
Mate, 16 July, 1862. Acting Ensign, 11 December, 1862. Honorably discharged 25 August, 1865.

WALLACE, GEORGE C.
Midshipman, 20 July, 1864. Graduated June, 1868. Resigned 26 May, 1870.

WALLACE, JAMES.
Third Assistant Engineer, 11 November, 1858. Resigned 8 August, 1859.

WALLACE, JAMES.
Acting Midshipman, 1 November, 1859. Ensign, 16 September, 1862. Died 25 February, 1864.

WALLACE, JOHN.
Acting Master, 21 January, 1862. Honorably discharged 11 August, 1865.

WALLACE, JOHN S.
Chaplain, 10 March, 1863. Retired List, 29 January, 1893.

WALLACE, JOHN T.
Midshipman, 1 March, 1825. Resigned 27 July, 1827.

WALLACE, JOSEPH W.
Mate, 9 December, 1862. Resigned 13 November, 1863. Mate, 23 August, 1864. Acting Ensign, 21 April, 1865. Honorably discharged 30 June, 1865.

WALLACE, LEVIN J.
Gunner, 30 July, 1897.

WALLACE, MATTHEW J.
Acting Third Assistant Engineer, 29 November, 1864. Honorably discharged 21 August, 1865.

WALLACE, RICHARD W.
Mate, 22 September, 1864. Resigned 20 December, 1866. Mate, 15 March, 1867. Mustered out 29 July, 1867.

WALLACE, ROBERT.
Acting Third Assistant Engineer, 20 September, 1862. Acting Second Assistant Engineer, 12 March, 1864. Honorably discharged 15 May, 1865.

WALLACE, RUSH R.
Acting Midshipman, 25 May, 1852. Midshipman, 20 June, 1856. Passed Midshipman, 29 April, 1859. Master, 5 September, 1859. Lieutenant, 17 January, 1861. Lieutenant-Commander, 1 October, 1862. Commander, 23 October, 1870. Captain, 4 February, 1882. Commodore, 11 November, 1894. Retired List, 7 November, 1897.

WALLACE, RUSH R., JR.
Naval Cadet (Spanish-American War), 11 July, 1898. Honorably discharged 2 November, 1898.

WALLACE, SAMUEL.
Acting Third Assistant Engineer, 28 September, 1864. Honorably discharged 14 August, 1865.

WALLACE, W. H.
Midshipman, 7 July, 1832. Dropped 6 December, 1836.

WALLACE, WILLIAM M.
Midshipman, 3 June, 1833. Resigned 1 November, 1833.

WALLACE, WILLIAM T.
Assistant Paymaster, 3 June, 1899.

WALLACH, CUTHBERT P.
Paymaster, 1 June, 1861. Pay Inspector, 3 March, 1871. Pay Director, 9 March, 1880. Retired List, 4 July, 1889. Died 19 May, 1895.

WALLER, LITTLETON T.
Purser, 13 September, 1841. Resigned 12 January, 1853.

WALLING, BURNS T.
Midshipman, 5 June, 1872. Graduated 20 June, 1876. Ensign, 26 November, 1877. Lieutenant, Junior Grade, 2 September, 1884. Lieutenant, 5 March, 1890. Lieutenant-Commander, 3 March, 1899.

GENERAL NAVY REGISTER. 567

WALLIS, JOHN E.
Acting Ensign, 20 July, 1863. Honorably discharged 10 September, 1865.
WALLIS, JOHN F.
Midshipman, 26 July, 1864. Graduated 20 June, 1869. Ensign, 12 July, 1870. Master, 19 August, 1872. Lieutenant, 14 August, 1875. Died 23 February, 1880.
WALLS, JAMES C.
Assistant Engineer (Spanish-American War), 15 June, 1898. Honorably discharged 2 September, 1898.
WALLS, JOHN.
Chief Engineer (Spanish-American War), 18 May, 1898. Honorably discharged 2 September, 1898.
WALPOLE, HORACE.
Midshipman, 4 July, 1805. Lieutenant, 12 June, 1810. Resigned 8 December, 1814.
WALSH, CHARLES.
Midshipman, 2 April, 1804. Resigned 6 June, 1809.
WALSH, DANIEL.
Acting Third Assistant Engineer, 29 April, 1864. Honorably discharged 28 August, 1865.
WALSH, JOHN.
Professor of Mathematics, 5 December, 1837. Last appearance on Records of Navy Department, 1839.
WALSH, JOHN D.
Acting Boatswain, 29 August, 1899.
WALSH, JOHN J.
Gunner, 18 April, 1871. Chief Gunner, 3 March, 1899.
WALSH, JOHN K.
Acting Assistant Surgeon, 5 September, 1863. Honorably discharged 6 September, 1865.
WALSH, JOSEPH C.
Midshipman, 1 November, 1828. Passed Midshipman, 14 June, 1834. Lieutenant, 9 December, 1839. Resigned 18 September, 1854. Acting Lieutenant, 11 February, 1862. Resigned 1 May, 1862.
WALSH, KEGRAN.
Midshipman, 25 November, 1799. Discharged 12 May, 1801, under Peace Establishment Act.
WALSH, S. W.
Midshipman, 13 February, 1821. Resigned 2 December, 1825.
WALSH, WILLIAM.
Gunner, 12 October, 1882. Chief Gunner, 3 March, 1899.
WALSTROM, CHARLES G.
Acting Ensign, 16 December, 1862. Resigned 27 March, 1865.
WALTER, HORACE.
Acting Ensign, 14 May, 1863. Resigned (sick) 18 August, 1864.
WALTER, JOSEPH.
Acting Third Assistant Engineer, 4 June, 1864. Resigned 6 June, 1865.
WALTER, ROBERT.
Acting Master, 20 August, 1861. Dismissed 22 October, 1864.
WALTER, R. PRICE.
Acting Master, 4 November, 1861. Honorably discharged 14 December, 1865.
WALTERS, C. P.
Mate, 2 October, 1861. Acting Ensign, 4 October, 1862. Resigned 30 March, 1864.
WALTERS, HENRY.
Acting Ensign, 19 January, 1863. Dismissed 21 November, 1863.
WALTERS, HENRY.
Mate, 20 January, 1864. Honorably discharged 1 November, 1865.
WALTERS, WILLIAM L.
Third Assistant Engineer, 21 May, 1857. Died 27 May, 1858.
WALTEMEYER, JOHN S.
Carpenter, 30 December, 1874. Chief Carpenter, 3 March, 1899.
WALTON, EDMUND W.
Mate, 7 April, 1864. Appointment revoked 14 December, 1864.
WALTON, JAMES C.
Boatswain, 9 May, 1859. Retired List, 16 October, 1883. Died 30 June, 1887.
WALTON, BENJAMIN G.
Acting Assistant Surgeon, 15 November, 1862. Appointment revoked 10 April, 1865.
WALTON, JESSE FLETCHER.
Third Assistant Engineer, 25 August, 1862. Resigned 31 March, 1865.
WALTON, THOMAS C.
Assistant Surgeon, 24 January, 1862. Passed Assistant Surgeon, 5 March, 1866. Surgeon, 22 October, 1868. Medical Inspector, 18 September, 1887. Medical Director, 28 May, 1895. Retired List, 31 May, 1900.
WALTON, THOMAS O.
Acting Assistant Surgeon, 22 April, 1873. Honorably discharged 30 June, 1879.
WALTON, WALTER.
Mate, 28 January, 1862. Acting Ensign, 23 July, 1864. Honorably discharged 20 October, 1865.
WALTON, WILLIAM.
Boatswain, 17 September, 1813. Died March, 1822.
WAMALING, C. THOMAS.
Acting Third Assistant Engineer, 30 December, 1863. Honorably discharged 30 August, 1865.
WAMALING, ROBERT LEWIS.
Third Assistant Engineer, 8 July, 1862. Resigned 17 November, 1865.

WANDELL, AUGUSTUS.
Acting Third Assistant Engineer, 14 September, 1861. Acting Second Assistant Engineer, 26 July, 1864. Honorably discharged 12 December, 1865.
WANDELL, MARTIN E.
Mate, 19 August, 1862. Acting Ensign, 21 August, 1863. Honorably discharged 2 August, 1865. Mate, 20 January, 1870. Resigned 9 August, 1871.
WANKLIN, HENRY.
Acting Second Assistant Engineer, 8 April, 1863. Honorably discharged 21 September, 1865.
WAPPENHAUS, C. F. R.
Mate, 22 December, 1862. Acting Ensign, 8 January, 1863. Acting Master, 3 May, 1865. Honorably discharged 29 September, 1868.
WARBURTON, EDGAR T.
Cadet Engineer, Naval Academy, 1 October, 1872. Graduated 21 June, 1875. Assistant Engineer, 1 July, 1878. Passed Assistant Engineer, 1 July, 1887. Chief Engineer, 28 May, 1897. Rank changed to Lieutenant-Commander, 3 March, 1899.
WARBURTON, WILLIAM F.
Acting Third Assistant Engineer, 5 July, 1861. Acting Second Assistant Engineer, 17 June, 1863. Honorably discharged 21 January, 1868.
WARD, AARON.
Midshipman, 28 September, 1867. Graduated 6 June, 1871. Ensign, 14 July, 1872. Master, 8 February, 1875. Lieutenant, 25 November, 1881. Lieutenant-Commander, 3 March, 1899.
WARD, ANDREW A.
Acting Master, 2 November, 1861. Resigned 12 October, 1863. Ensign, 27 January, 1864. Master, 27 May, 1865. Honorably discharged 1 December, 1865.
WARD, BROWNLEE R.
Assistant Surgeon, 14 January, 1893. Passed Assistant Surgeon, 13 January, 1896.
WARD, CHARLES.
Acting Third Assistant Engineer, 11 June, 1864. Deserted March, 1865.
WARD, CHARLES C.
Acting Assistant Paymaster, 1 December, 1864. Mustered out 12 August, 1865.
WARD, DANIEL.
Acting Third Assistant Engineer, 18 February, 1864. Honorably discharged 8 October, 1865.
WARD, DANIEL.
Mate, 17 January, 1862. Boatswain, 11 December, 1872. Retired List, 15 February, 1897. Died 15 October, 1898.
WARD, E. C.
Professor, 4 March, 1835. Resigned 28 April, 1848.
WARD, EDWARD C.
Midshipman, 2 February, 1829. Passed Midshipman, 3 July, 1835. Lieutenant, 8 September, 1841. Dismissed 25 March, 1851.
WARD, ELIJAH.
Acting Assistant Paymaster, 12 May, 1863. Mustered out 12 December, 1865.
WARD, GEORGE W.
Acting Master, 21 October, 1861. Dismissed 11 October, 1863.
WARD, HENRY.
Midshipman, 9 November, 1813. Lieutenant, 5 March, 1817. Died 9 July, 1825.
WARD, HENRY H.
Naval Cadet, 7 September, 1889. Ensign, 1 July, 1895. Lieutenant, Junior Grade, 3 March, 1899.
WARD, JAMES.
Acting Third Assistant Engineer, 4 January, 1862. Honorably discharged 8 December, 1865.
WARD, JAMES H.
Midshipman, 4 March, 1823. Passed Midshipman, 23 March, 1829. Lieutenant, 3 March, 1831. Commander, 9 September, 1853. Killed in action 27 June, 1861.
WARD, JOHN.
Assistant Surgeon, 28 April, 1848. Passed Assistant Surgeon, 22 April, 1854. Resigned 3 April, 1861.
WARD, JOHN H.
Acting Third Assistant Engineer, 9 January, 1865. Honorably discharged 21 October, 1865.
WARD, JOS.
Gunner, 27 December, 1834. Dismissed 8 March, 1836.
WARD, JOSEPH R.
Gunner, 11 March, 1892.
WARD, JOSIAH M.
Assistant Surgeon (Spanish-American War), 20 May, 1898. Honorably discharged 20 September, 1898.
WARD, PETER T.
Carpenter, 8 June, 1870. Chief Carpenter, 3 March, 1899.
WARD, ROBERT.
Midshipman, 18 May, 1809. Dismissed 10 October, 1811.
WARD, STILLMAN W.
Mate, 21 November, 1862. Acting Ensign, 8 August, 1864. Resigned 20 May, 1865.
WARD, THOMAS.
Sailmaker, 25 September, 1879. Resigned 7 January, 1882.
WARD, WILLIAM.
Sailmaker, 14 August, 1834. Died 24 May, 1844.
WARD, WILLIAM.
Midshipman, 1 February, 1826. Passed Midshipman, 28 April, 1832. Lieutenant, 8 March, 1837. Died 10 June, 1838.

GENERAL NAVY REGISTER. 569

WARD, WILLIAM G.
Mate, 13 March, 1865. Honorably discharged 4 September, 1865.
WARD, WILLIAM H.
Midshipman, 7 April, 1847. Resigned 10 December, 1852.
WARD, WILLIAM H.
Midshipman, 17 February, 1849. Passed Midshipman, 12 June, 1855. Master, 16 September, 1855. Lieutenant, 9 September, 1856. Dismissed 16 July, 1861.
WARD, WILLIAM S.
Mate, 1 October, 1862. Resigned 18 January, 1864.
WARDELL, Z. P.
Midshipman, 1 March, 1826. Cashiered 10 December, 1830.
WARDEN, HALSTEN.
Acting Third Assistant Engineer, 20 December, 1861. Appointment revoked (sick) 21 May, 1862.
WARDLE, R. C.
Assistant Surgeon, 10 December, 1814. Drowned in August, 1819.
WARDROP, WILLIAM.
Acting Ensign, 29 October, 1862. Appointment revoked (sick) 26 January, 1864.
WARE, CHARLES F.
Acting Ensign, 16 September, 1864. Resigned 3 May, 1865.
WARE, EDWARD H.
Acting Assistant Surgeon, 27 April, 1866. Assistant Surgeon, 18 June, 1866. Passed Assistant Surgeon, 10 June, 1870. Surgeon, 25 November, 1877. Died 13 August, 1878.
WARE, JOSEPH.
Acting Ensign, 19 May, 1864. Honorably discharged 30 September, 1865.
WARE, PAUL, JR.
Acting Ensign, 18 December, 1863. Honorably discharged 30 September, 1865.
WARE, THOMAS R.
Purser, 28 June, 1843. Dismissed 13 June, 1861.
WARFIELD, ANDERSON.
Surgeon, 1 July, 1799. Discharged 31 August, 1801, under Peace Establishment Act.
WARFIELD, LOT.
Midshipman, 16 July, 1799. Discharged 3 July, 1801.
WAREHAM, RICHARD.
Acting Third Assistant Engineer, 25 September, 1863. Acting Second Assistant Engineer, 2 June, 1865. Honorably discharged 15 November, 1865.
WARFORD, GEORGE H.
Carpenter, 18 August, 1894.
WARFORD, LEWIS S.
Acting Carpenter, 20 February, 1900.
WARING, ARCHIBALD H.
Midshipman, 19 October, 1841. Resigned 11 July, 1848.
WARING, HENRY.
Acting Ensign, 8 August, 1863. Honorably discharged 8 November, 1865.
WARING, HORATIO S.
Assistant Surgeon, 12 March, 1813. Resigned 28 June, 1813.
WARING, HOWARD S.
Midshipman, 26 June, 1867. Graduated 1 June, 1872. Ensign, 15 July, 1873. Master, 12 July, 1878. Lieutenant, Junior Grade, 3 March, 1883. Lieutenant, 2 June, 1885. Died 4 November, 1893.
WARK, DAVID.
Midshipman, 20 June, 1806. Last appearance on Records of Navy Department, 5 December, 1806.
WARLEY, ALEXANDER F.
Midshipman, 17 February, 1840. Passed Midshipman, 11 July, 1846. Master, 1 March, 1855. Lieutenant, 14 September, 1855. Resigned 24 December, 1860.
WARNER, CHARLES K.
Acting Third Assistant Engineer, 11 December, 1863. Third Assistant Engineer, 1 February, 1865. Resigned 11 October, 1866.
WARNER, FRANCIS W.
Acting Second Assistant Engineer, 3 June, 1861. Acting First Assistant Engineer, 30 July, 1863. Honorably discharged 24 December, 1865.
WARNER, FRANKLIN C.
Acting Ensign, 7 July, 1864. Resigned 26 February, 1867.
WARNER, GEORGE H.
Acting First Assistant Engineer, 16 July, 1863. Appointment revoked (sick) 22 December, 1863.
WARNER, HENRY R.
Midshipman, 28 June, 1812. Lieutenant, 5 March, 1817. Cashiered 11 December, 1824.
WARNER, HIRAM.
Acting Third Assistant Engineer, 27 September, 1862. Acting Second Assistant Engineer, 6 October, 1863. Acting First Assistant Engineer, 31 August, 1864. Resigned 7 January, 1865.
WARNER, JAMES H.
Third Assistant Engineer, 6 February, 1851. Second Assistant Engineer, 26 February, 1851. First Assistant Engineer, 26 June, 1856. Chief Engineer, 6 December, 1859. Name stricken from the Rolls, 8 July, 1861.
WARNER, JOHN.
Lieutenant, 2 October, 1798. Last appearance on Records of Navy Department, 29 November, 1798.
WARNER, JOHN.
Master, 15 September, 1813. Died 24 August, 1814.
WARNER, JOHN E.
Acting Assistant Surgeon, 28 July, 1863. Resigned 12 November, 1864.

WARNER, MURRAY.
Assistant Engineer (Spanish-American War), 21 June, 1898. Honorably discharged 20 January, 1899.
WARNER, OSWALD.
Acting Assistant Surgeon, 18 December, 1861. Resigned 9 June, 1864.
WARNER, RUSSELL.
Acting Third Assistant Engineer, 11 November, 1864. Resigned 17 May, 1865.
WARNER, SAMUEL P. N.
Acting Assistant Paymaster, 30 June, 1862. Dismissed 19 February, 1863.
WARNICK, WILLIAM F.
Mate, 9 June, 1864. Honorably discharged 6 December, 1866.
WARRELL, THOMAS W.
Midshipman, 4 July, 1805. Dismissed 7 January, 1807.
WARREN, AUGUSTUS A.
Sailmaker, 12 September, 1853. Died 24 March, 1885.
WARREN, BENJAMIN H.
Cadet Engineer, Naval Academy, 1 October, 1871. Graduated 30 May, 1874. Assistant Engineer, 26 February, 1875. Retired List, 11 June, 1878.
WARREN, CHADBURN H.
Acting Third Assistant Engineer, 20 April, 1864. Resigned (sick) 15 October, 1864.
WARREN, CHARLES S.
Acting Assistant Paymaster, 17 December, 1861. Resigned 14 November, 1862.
WARREN, EPHRAIM R.
Acting Ensign, 5 January, 1863. Honorably discharged 18 September, 1865. Acting Ensign, 1 May, 1866. Mustered out 15 October, 1867.
WARREN, GEORGE A.
Acting Assistant Surgeon, 8 July, 1864. Honorably discharged 14 September, 1865.
WARREN, H. G.
Mate, 14 December, 1862. Resigned 25 July, 1863.
WARREN, ISAAC.
Acting Master, 1861. Resigned 23 July, 1862.
WARREN, JOSEPH H.
Acting Master, February, 1862. Discharged 13 July, 1863.
WARREN, JOSHUA D.
Mate, 19 September, 1861. Acting Master, 2 October, 1861. Acting Volunteer Lieutenant, 13 May, 1863. Resigned 21 October, 1864.
WARREN, NAHUM.
Master's Mate, 6 February, 1815. Died 10 June, 1843.
WARREN, O. B.
Acting Master, 22 March, 1862. Appointment revoked (sick) 22 November, 1864.
WARREN, OGLE T.
Lieutenant, Junior Grade (Spanish-American War), 27 July, 1898. Honorably discharged 16 September, 1898.
WARREN, ROBERT.
Lieutenant, 13 July, 1799. Discharged 10 May, 1801.
WARREN, SYLVANUS.
Acting Second Assistant Engineer, 21 May, 1862. Honorably discharged 29 December, 1865.
WARRINGTON, FRANKLIN C.
Acting Third Assistant Engineer, 10 December, 1863. Honorably discharged 14 November, 1865.
WARRINGTON, JOSEPH H.
Third Assistant Engineer, 21 May, 1857. Resigned 1 February, 1860.
WARRINGTON, LEWIS, Jr.
Purser, 13 September, 1841. Dismissed 11 June, 1863.
WARRINGTON, LEWIS.
Midshipman, 6 January, 1800. Lieutenant, 7 February, 1807. Commander, 24 July, 1813. Captain, 22 November, 1814. Died 12 October, 1851.
WARRINGTON, MILES K.
Midshipman, 30 January, 1838. Passed Midshipman, 20 May, 1844. Master, 2 December, 1851. Lieutenant, 16 December, 1852. Dismissed 18 July, 1859. Lieutenant, 21 December, 1859. Died 20 Septembr, 1860.
WARTMAN, SAMUEL.
Acting Warrant Machinist, 23 August, 1899.
WASHBURN, ALFRED.
Mate, 19 September, 1861. Acting Master, 28 December, 1861. Died 14 May, 1865.
WASHBURN, HENRY W.
Acting Master, 26 February, 1862. Honorably discharged 3 April, 1866.
WASHBURN, SAMUEL B.
Acting Master, 11 November, 1861. Dismissed 30 December, 1861. Reappointed 11 January, 1862. Acting Volunteer Lieutenant, 21 January, 1864. Honorably discharged 24 October, 1865.
WASHBURNE, CHARLES P.
Acting Master, 21 January, 1862. Appointment revoked (sick) 20 July, 1864.
WASHBURNE, CORNELIUS.
Mate, 7 January, 1862. Acting Ensign, 11 December, 1862. Honorably discharged 16 December, 1865.
WASHINGTON, BAILEY.
Surgeon, 24 July, 1813. Died 4 August, 1854.
WASHINGTON, H. W. M.
Assistant Surgeon, 17 April, 1856. Passed Assistant Surgeon, 25 March, 1861. Dismissed 10 May, 1861.
WASHINGTON, POPE.
Naval Cadet, 7 September, 1892. Assistant Engineer, 6 May, 1898. Rank changed to Ensign, 3 March, 1899.

WASHINGTON, RICHARD.
Acting Assistant Paymaster, 18 July, 1861. Assistant Paymaster, 24 August, 1861. Paymaster, 14 April, 1862. Pay Inspector, 28 August, 1876. Pay Director, 5 February, 1886. Died 8 January, 1895.
WASHINGTON, S. A.
Midshipman, 1 November, 1826. Resigned 17 April, 1834.
WASHINGTON, S. S.
Midshipman, 1 December, 1828. Lost on the Hornet, 10 September, 1829.
WASHINGTON, S. W.
Midshipman, 15 November, 1809. Last appearance on Records of Navy Department, 1815. Alexandria.
WASHINGTON, T. M.
Midshipman, 21 October, 1824. Passed Midshipman, 4 June, 1831. Lieutenant, 12 January, 1836. Resigned 17 August, 1838.
WASHINGTON, THOMAS.
Naval Cadet, 17 May, 1883. Ensign, 1 July, 1889. Lieutenant, Junior Grade, 16 September, 1897. Lieutenant, 3 March, 1899.
WASHINGTON, W. S. J.
Midshipman, 5 February, 1812. Dismissed 1 May, 1828.
WASSON, ALONZO M. L.
Acting Third Assistant Engineer, 18 April, 1863. Honorably discharged 7 November, 1865.
WASSON, WILLIAM.
Acting First Assistant Engineer, 17 November, 1862. Died 7 July, 1863.
WATERBURY, SAMUEL A.
Acting Master, 8 May, 1862. Resigned 25 April, 1865.
WATERMAN, LUCIUS A.
Acting Ensign, 29 June, 1863. Honorably discharged 13 August, 1865. Acting Ensign, 11 December, 1866. Mustered out 26 March, 1869.
WATERMAN, RUFUS, Jr.
Midshipman, 25 September, 1861. Graduated June, 1866. Ensign, 12 March, 1868. Master, 21 March, 1869. Lieutenant, 21 March, 1870. Resigned 8 December, 1871. Lieutenant (Spanish-American War), 12 May, 1898. Honorably discharged 28 September, 1898.
WATERMAN, WILLIAM L.
Acting Third Assistant Engineer, 19 September, 1862. Appointment revoked 15 February, 1865.
WATERS, JOHN G.
Mate, 16 September, 1862. Acting Ensign, 28 November, 1862. Resigned 13 April, 1864.
WATERS, KIRVEN.
Midshipman, 1 September, 1811. Lieutenant, 30 June, 1814. Died, of wounds received in action, 26 September, 1815.
WATERS, NICHOLAS B.
Midshipman, 1 November, 1827. Resigned 6 October, 1832.
WATERS, WILLIAM.
Boatswain, 8 December, 1835. Died 7 September, 1851.
WATKEYS, EDWARD H.
Acting Ensign, 13 January, 1863. Died 30 July, 1864.
WATKINS, CLARENCE.
Midshipman, 1 December, 1828. Died 19 July, 1834.
WATKINS, ERASMUS.
Midshipman, 1 January, 1812. Resigned 1 December, 1817.
WATKINS, FREDERICK.
Commander (Spanish-American War), 15 June, 1898. Honorably discharged 2 September, 1898.
WATKINS, GEORGE R.
Acting Assistant Paymaster, 31 December, 1863. Honorably discharged 5 December, 1865. Passed Assistant Paymaster, 23 July, 1866. Paymaster, 10 February, 1870. Dismissed 13 June, 1888.
WATKINS, HENRY J.
Acting Third Assistant Engineer, 24 September, 1862. Acting Second Assistant Engineer, 17 August, 1864. Honorably discharged 25 September, 1865.
WATKINS, MAYO CARRINGTON.
Midshipman, 8 May, 1834. Passed Midshipman, 16 July, 1840. Master, 22 March, 1847. Lieutenant, 15 July, 1847. Died 19 September, 1860.
WATKINS, MILTON W.
Sailmaker, 18 April, 1879. Chief Sailmaker, 3 March, 1899.
WATKINS, TOBIAS.
Assistant Surgeon, 20 July, 1799. Resigned 1 January, 1801.
WATKINS, T. BASCOM.
Gunner, 5 October, 1861. Retired List, 20 May, 1889.
WATMOUGH, JAMES H.
Acting Midshipman, 24 November, 1843. Purser, 12 December, 1844. Pay Director, 3 March, 1871. Acting Paymaster-General, 1 March, 1873, to 23 February, 1877. Paymaster-General, 23 February, 1877, to 17 November, 1877. Retired List, 30 July, 1884.
WATMOUGH, PENDLETON G.
Midshipman, 20 September, 1841. Passed Midshipman, 10 August, 1847. Master, 14 September, 1855. Lieutenant, 15 September, 1855. Resigned 26 April, 1859. Acting Lieutenant, 13 May, 1861. Lieutenant-Commander, 16 July, 1862. Resigned 28 July, 1865.
WATMOUGH, WILLIAM N.
Acting Assistant Paymaster, 7 November, 1862. Assistant Paymaster, 30 June, 1864. Paymaster, 4 May, 1866. Retired List, 17 December, 1886. Died 20 January, 1887.

WATSON, ADOLPHUS E.
  Naval Cadet, 30 May, 1895. At sea prior to final graduation.
WATSON, ANDREW J.
  Purser, 1 May, 1831. Lost in Levant, 18 September, 1860.
WATSON, A. EUGENE.
  Purser, 31 August, 1836. Retired List, 15 November, 1862. Pay Director on Retired List, 3 March, 1871. Died 10 July, 1876.
WATSON, CHARLES F.
  Mate, 25 August, 1862. Acting Ensign, 19 January, 1863. Honorably discharged 9 November, 1868.
WATSON, DAVID.
  Acting Assistant Surgeon, 14 September, 1863. Resigned 3 July, 1865.
WATSON, EDWARD H.
  Naval Cadet, 26 September, 1890. Resigned 17 June, 1891. Naval Cadet, 7 September, 1891. Ensign, 1 July, 1897. Lieutenant, Junior Grade, 1 July, 1900.
WATSON, EUGENE W.
  Acting Ensign, 18 September, 1863. Ensign, 12 March, 1868. Master, 18 December, 1868. Lieutenant, 21 March, 1870. Lieutenant-Commander, 16 November, 1883. Commander, 27 April, 1893. Captain, 22 November, 1899.
WATSON, E. W.
  Acting Master, 25 June, 1862. Resigned 30 August, 1862.
WATSON, FRANK.
  Mate, 12 May, 1863. Acting Ensign, 29 March, 1864. Appointment revoked (sick) 25 January, 1865.
WATSON, FRANK.
  Sailmaker, 3 March, 1877. Chief Sailmaker, 3 March, 1899.
WATSON, GEORGE W.
  Acting Master, 27 May, 1861. Resigned 4 November, 1861.
WATSON, HENRY.
  Mate, 9 December, 1863. Honorably discharged 1 November, 1868.
WATSON, JAMES.
  Boatswain, 9 March, 1802. Resigned 9 April, 1807.
WATSON, JAMES.
  Midshipman, 18 June, 1812. Discharged from the service 6 July, 1813.
WATSON, JAMES.
  Boatswain, date not known. Died 31 December, 1819.
WATSON, JAMES M.
  Midshipman, 1 February, 1823. Passed Midshipman, 23 March, 1829. Lieutenant, 30 December, 1831. Reserved List, 13 September, 1855. Commander on Reserved List, 1 February, 1861. Commodore, Retired List, 4 April, 1867. Died 17 April, 1873.
WATSON, JAMES P.
  Lieutenant, 13 February, 1799. Last appearance on Records of Navy Department, 27 November, 1800.
WATSON, J. CRITTENDEN.
  Acting Midshipman, 29 September, 1856. Midshipman, 15 June, 1860. Master, 19 September, 1861. Lieutenant, 16 July, 1862. Lieutenant-Commander, 25 July, 1866. Commander, 23 January, 1874. Captain, 6 March, 1887. Commodore, 7 November, 1897. Rear-Admiral, 3 March, 1899.
WATSON, JOHN.
  Carpenter, 29 July, 1799. Warrant given up.
WATSON, JOHN L.
  Chaplain, 8 August, 1855. Retired List, 21 December, 1861. Died 12 August, 1884.
WATSON, JOHN S., 1st.
  Acting Master, 9 September, 1861. Acting Volunteer Lieutenant, 7 August, 1865. Honorably discharged 21 October, 1866.
WATSON, JOHN S., 2d.
  Acting Master, 17 November, 1863. Acting Volunteer Lieutenant, 3 June, 1864. Honorably discharged 30 October, 1865.
WATSON, JOSEPH.
  Purser, 26 May, 1824. Died 16 February, 1831.
WATSON, JOSEPH.
  Acting Assistant Paymaster, 18 August, 1862. Honorably discharged 7 November, 1865.
WATSON, JOSEPH.
  Acting Ensign, 1 October, 1862. Acting Master, 16 September, 1863. Discharged 14 September, 1865.
WATSON, JOSHUA.
  Midshipman, 4 July, 1805. Died 1 June, 1811.
WATSON, M. D. E. W.
  Midshipman, 21 October, 1831. Dismissed 20 May, 1836.
WATSON, REUBEN G.
  Acting Third Assistant Engineer, 4 October, 1864. Honorably discharged 29 August, 1865.
WATSON, THEODORE B.
  Gunner, 30 August, 1897.
WATSON, THOMAS G.
  Acting Ensign, 10 June, 1864. Honorably discharged 23 February, 1867.
WATSON, W. ARGYLE.
  Acting Assistant Surgeon, 21 May, 1861. Resigned 3 February, 1864.
WATSON, WILLIAM.
  Acting Master, 26 August, 1861. Resigned 29 July, 1862. Reappointed 4 August, 1862. Honorably discharged 29 October, 1865.
WATSON, WILLIAM H.
  Midshipman, 1 January, 1808. Lieutenant, 7 March, 1813. Died 13 September, 1823.

GENERAL NAVY REGISTER.

WATT, RICHARD M.
Naval Cadet, 22 September, 1887. Assistant Naval Constructor, 1 July, 1893.
WATTERS, H. H.
Midshipman, 1 June, 1826. Resigned 16 March, 1830.
WATTERS, JOHN.
Midshipman, 12 February, 1846. Passed Midshipman, 8 June, 1852. Master, 15 September, 1855. Lieutenant, 16 September, 1855. Lieutenant-Commander, 16 July, 1862. Commander, 25 July, 1866. Died 22 January, 1874.
WATTERS, JOHN S.
Cadet Midshipman, 21 June, 1876. Graduated 22 June, 1882. Ensign, Junior Grade, 3 March, 1883. Ensign, 26 June, 1884. Resigned 1 December, 1890. Lieutenant (Spanish-American War), 12 May, 1898. Honorably discharged 15 Septebmer, 1898.
WATTERS, JOSEPH.
Third Assistant Engineer, 22 October, 1860. Second Assistant Engineer, 8 December, 1862. First Assistant Engineer, 1 December, 1864. Died 13 September, 1866.
WATTERS, WILLIAM H.
Acting Third Assistant Engineer, 17 November, 1864. Honorably discharged 27 October, 1865.
WATTLES, CHARLES T.
Midshipman, 1 May, 1822. Died 10 November, 1822.
WATTS, ANDREW C.
Mate, 29 November, 1864. Resigned 9 May, 1865.
WATTS, EDWARD.
Midshipman, 18 June, 1812. Last appearance on Records of Navy Department, 25 September, 1815. Killed by a fall from masthead.
WATTS, GEORGE.
Master, 20 April, 1812. Killed in action 28 November, 1812.
WATTS, H. R.
Acting Assistant Surgeon, 29 April, 1864. Honorably discharged 2 April, 1866.
WATTS, JAMES E.
Third Assistant Engineer, 17 March, 1863. Second Assistant Engineer, 28 September, 1864. Drowned 9 July, 1871.
WATTS, JOSEPH.
Acting Third Assistant Engineer, 9 July, 1863. Acting Second Assistant Engineer, 21 October, 1864. Resigned 12 May, 1865.
WATTS, THOMAS.
Master, 9 February, 1809. Last appearance on Records of Navy Department, 1815. Charleston, S. C.
WATTS, WILLIAM.
Midshipman, 10 April, 1862. Graduated June, 1866. Ensign, 12 March, 1868. Master, 26 March, 1869. Lieutenant, 21 March, 1870. Retired List, 31 January, 1883.
WATTS, WILLIAM C.
Naval Cadet, 22 September, 1894. Ensign, 4 April, 1900.
WAUGH, ALEXANDER.
Acting Master, 6 December, 1861. Appointment revoked 13 January, 1864.
WAUGH, EDWARD J.
Gunner, 1 July, 1861. Dismissed 19 February, 1881.
WAUGH, JOS.
Midshipman, 30 November, 1814. Resigned 21 February, 1815.
WAUGH, WILLIAM F.
Assistant Surgeon, 3 April, 1873. Resigned 1 April, 1876.
WAUKLIN, HENRY.
Acting Third Assistant Engineer, 26 September, 1862. Honorably discharged 21 September, 1865.
WAUKLIN, JOHN D.
Acting Third Assistant Engineer, 6 May, 1864. Honorably discharged 9 December, 1865.
WAY, FRANCIS S.
Mate, 11 September, 1862. Dismissed 18 January, 1864.
WAYNE, CHARLES.
Assistant Surgeon, 29 August, 1825. Died 19 August, 1828.
WAYNE, T. S.
Midshipman, 1 January, 1825. Resigned 18 December, 1827.
WAYNE, WILLIAM A.
Midshipman, 27 October, 1833. Passed Midshipman, 8 July, 1839. Lieutenant, 4 June, 1844. Resigned 1 May, 1861.
WAYNE, WILLIAM C.
Midshipman, 17 December, 1810. Last appearance on Records of Navy Department, 1815. Sloop Wasp.
WEAVER, AARON W.
Midshipman, 10 May, 1848. Passed Midshipman, 15 June, 1854. Master, 15 September, 1855. Lieutenant, 11 September, 1855. Lieutenant-Commander, 16 July, 1862. Commander, 25 July, 1866. Captain, 8 August, 1876. Commodore, 7 October, 1886. Rear-Admiral, 27 June, 1893. Retired List, 26 September, 1893.
WEAVER, CHARLES H.
Mate, 7 January, 1862. Resigned 22 June, 1863.
WEAVER, CALVIN R.
Acting Second Assistant Engineer, 10 October, 1862. Honorably discharged 19 September, 1865.
WEAVER, D. EDWARD.
Acting First Assistant Engineer, 1 October, 1862. Acting Chief Engineer, 9 June, 1863. Resigned 26 July, 1864.
WEAVER, GEORGE F.
Midshipman, 3 August, 1816. Died 5 October, 1825.

574   GENERAL NAVY REGISTER.

WEAVER, JAMES B.
Midshipman, 30 November, 1861. Graduated November, 1864. Ensign, 1 November, 1866. Master, 1 December, 1866. Resigned 4 December, 1867.

WEAVER, SAMUEL.
Acting Second Assistant Engineer, 9 December, 1863. Honorably discharged 20 October, 1865.

WEAVER, WILLIAM A.
Midshipman, 4 February, 1811. Lieutenant, 27 April, 1816. Cashiered 27 November, 1824.

WEAVER, WILLIAM DIXON.
Cadet Engineer, Naval Academy, 14 September, 1876. Graduated 10 June, 1880. Assistant Engineer, 10 June, 1882. Resigned 24 January, 1892. Passed Assistant Engineer (Spanish-American War), 20 May, 1898. Honorably discharged 1 December, 1898.

WEAVER, WILLIAM H.
Midshipman, 19 October, 1841. Passed Midshipman, 10 August, 1847. Died 24 September, 1851.

WEAVER, WILLIAM L.
Mate, 7 January, 1862. Resigned 22 June, 1863.

WEBB, CHARLES.
Assistant Surgeon, 30 March, 1800. Surgeon, 19 November, 1800. Cashiered 10 July, 1801.

WEBB, CHARLES L.
Acting Assistant Paymaster, 17 December, 1861. Appointment revoked (sick) 12 December, 1862.

WEBB, FRANCIS R.
Acting Ensign, 14 October, 1862. Acting Master, 22 January, 1864. Honorably discharged 4 October, 1865.

WEBB, GILBERT.
Acting Third Assistant Engineer, 8 August, 1863. Resigned 15 August, 1865.

WEBB, HENRY.
Mate, 7 March, 1864. Dismissed 11 April, 1865.

WEBB, JAMES.
Sailmaker, 11 November, 1798. Last appearance on Records of Navy Department, 5 December, 1798. Discharged.

WEBB, JAMES P.
Midshipman, 2 April, 1804. Resigned 15 May, 1806.

WEBB, JAMES R.
Acting Second Assistant Engineer, 27 January, 1863. Honorably discharged 28 October, 1865.

WEBB, JOHN.
Boatswain, 12 November, 1799. Discharged 14 September, 1801, under Peace Establishment Act.

WEBB, JOHN B.
Acting Assistant Paymaster, 9 March, 1863. Dismissed 10 November, 1863.

WEBB, JOHN M.
Carpenter, 21 January, 1840. Died 16 June, 1847.

WEBB, JOHN S.
Midshipman, 4 June, 1799. Discharged 5 June, 1801, under Peace Establishment Act.

WEBB, ROBERT LESLIE.
Third Assistant Engineer, 11 February, 1862. Second Assistant Engineer, 15 October, 1863. Dropped 9 March, 1868. Restored to original place 6 April, 1868. Died 13 June, 1870.

WEBB, THOMAS E.
Assistant Naval Constructor, 27 February, 1865. Naval Constructor, 17 July, 1868. Retired List, 18 June, 1888.

WEBB, THOMAS F.
Lieutenant, Junior Grade (Spanish-American War), 26 May, 1898. Honorably discharged 3 October, 1898.

WEBB, THOMAS T.
Midshipman, 1 January, 1808. Lieutenant, 19 December, 1814. Commander, 8 March, 1831. Captain, 8 March, 1841. Died 11 April, 1853.

WEBB, THOMAS M.
Mate, 5 September, 1863. Appointment revoked (sick) 24 October, 1864.

WEBB, WADE F.
Ensign (Spanish-American War), 26 May, 1898. Honorably discharged 5 October, 1898.

WEBB, WILLIAM A.
Midshipman, 26 January, 1838. Passed Midshipman, 2 July, 1845. Master, 9 October, 1853. Lieutenant, 12 June, 1854. Resigned 17 May, 1861.

WEBB, WILLIAM H.
Mate, 19 June, 1862. Acting Ensign, 27 January, 1864. Ensign, 12 March, 1868. Master, 18 December, 1868. Lieutenant, 21 March, 1870. Lieutenant-Commander, 3 July, 1882. Retired List, 26 June, 1893.

WEBBER, GEORGE C.
Acting Assistant Surgeon, 14 November, 1863. Honorably discharged 12 July, 1865.

WEBBER, JOHN.
Gunner, 26 May, 1852. Died 28 November, 1869.

WEBBER, JOHN J. N.
Acting Master, 28 December, 1861. Dismissed 24 June, 1863.

WEBBER, SAMUEL G.
Assistant Surgeon, 22 May, 1862. Resigned 10 April, 1865.

WEBBER, WILLIAM E.
Acting Gunner, 9 September, 1862. Honorably discharged 28 February, 1866. Gunner, 27 August, 1872. Retired List, 29 June, 1887.

GENERAL NAVY REGISTER. 575

WEBER, LAWRENCE.
Acting Ensign, 13 January, 1864. Resigned 22 October, 1864.
WEBER, ROBERT L.
Assistant Surgeon, 20 May, 1859. Passed Assistant Surgeon, 17 December, 1862. Surgeon, 25 January, 1863. Retired List, 23 November, 1863. Died 13 December, 1884.
WEBSTER, CHARLES.
Naval Cadet, 6 September, 1890. Ensign, 1 July, 1896. Lieutenant, Junior Grade, 1 July, 1899.
WEBSTER, CHARLES F.
Assistant Surgeon, 18 January, 1888. Died 5 September, 1888.
WEBSTER, EDWIN.
Acting Assistant Paymaster, 19 April, 1864. Honorably discharged 26 September, 1865.
WEBSTER, EDWIN B.
Cadet, Midshipman, 28 September, 1874. Resigned 15 August, 1879. Assistant Paymaster, 29 October, 1881. Passed Assistant Paymaster, 25 February, 1892. Discharged 5 March, 1898.
WEBSTER, HARRIE.
Acting Third Assistant Engineer, 8 February, 1862. Third Assistant Engineer, 20 May, 1864. Retired List, 29 December, 1865. Restored to Active List as Third Assistant Engineer, with original date and position, 26 January, 1866. Second Assistant Engineer, 1 January, 1868. Passed Assistant Engineer, 29 October, 1874. Chief Engineer, 7 October, 1892. Rank changed to Commander, 3 March, 1899.
WEBSTER, H. C.
Mate, 19 September, 1861. Died 19 September, 1862.
WEBSTER, JOHN.
Acting Third Assistant Engineer, 2 July, 1862. Honorably discharged 24 December, 1865.
WEBSTER, JOHN A.
Master, 1 March, 1814. Discharged 15 April, 1815.
WEBSTER, JOHN L.
Acting Assistant Paymaster, 9 October, 1862. Resigned.
WEBSTER, LEWIS D.
Midshipman, 26 September, 1863. Graduated June, 1867. Ensign, 18 December, 1868. Master, 21 March, 1870. Lieutenant, 21 March, 1871. Resigned 28 February, 1873.
WEBSTER, MILTON.
Acting Ensign, 24 June, 1863. Honorably discharged 19 September, 1867.
WEBSTER, NELSON.
Midshipman, 16 January, 1809. Lieutenant, 9 December, 1814. Died 24 August, 1825.
WEBSTER, THADDEUS D.
Acting Third Assistant Engineer, 4 January, 1862. Resigned 19 October, 1864.
WEBSTER, WALTER A.
Acting Third Assistant Engineer, 27 December, 1864. Honorably discharged 14 September, 1865.
WEBSTER, WILLIAM E.
Acting Third Assistant Engineer, 23 March, 1863. Honorably discharged 12 November, 1868.
WEBSTER, WILLIAM T.
Cadet Engineer, 13 September, 1877. Graduated 10 June, 1881. Honorably discharged 5 October, 1883. Restored to service 10 March, 1886, as an Assistant Engineer, to rank from 1 July, 1883. Resigned 22 May, 1886.
WEDDERBURM, A. J.
Assistant Surgeon, 22 December, 1835. Passed Assistant Surgeon, 1 January, 1842. Resigned 14 June, 1844.
WEDERSTRANDT, P. C.
Midshipman, 16 March, 1798. Lieutenant, 25 June, 1800. Commander, 27 August, 1807. Resigned 2 May, 1810.
WEED, JOHN B.
Midshipman, 13 December, 1837. Dismissed 13 July, 1838.
WEED, JOSEPH D.
Mate, 23 January, 1862. Resigned (sick) 26 March, 1863.
WEEDEN, GEORGE W.
Acting Master, 4 December, 1861. Resigned 5 August, 1862.
WEEDEN, CHARLES L.
Mate, 26 March, 1863. Acting Ensign, 18 June, 1864. Resigned 2 December, 1864.
WEEKS, BENJAMIN S.
Acting Master, 20 December, 1861. Resigned 18 April, 1865.
WEEKS, EDMUND C.
Acting Master, 4 September, 1861. Resigned 6 July, 1864.
WEEKS, EDWIN C.
Lieutenant (Spanish-American War), 9 May, 1898. Honorably discharged 25 October, 1898.
WEEKS, GEORGE M.
Acting Assistant Surgeon, 1 July, 1862. Resigned 18 November, 1863.
WEEKS, JAMES C.
Acting Ensign, 22 June, 1863. Honorably discharged 5 November, 1865.
WEEKS, JOHN W.
Cadet Midshipman, 27 June, 1877. Graduated. Honorably discharged 30 June, 1883. Lieutenant (Spanish-American War), 23 April, 1898. Honorably discharged 28 October, 1898.
WEEMS, EDWARD D.
Third Assistant Engineer, 25 March, 1862. Second Assistant Engineer, 1 November, 1863. Resigned 6 September, 1867.

WEEMS, JOHN.
Midshipman, 1 March, 1825. Resigned 20 June, 1827. Midshipman, 4 August, 1827. Passed Midshipman, 10 June, 1833. Lieutenant, 22 December, 1838. Died 29 May, 1840.
WEEMS, N. T.
Assistant Surgeon, 21 September, 1802. Surgeon, 1 July, 1803. Resigned 20 February, 1806.
WEEMS, ROLLA.
Midshipman, 1 January, 1818. Died October, 1823.
WEGMANN, ALBERT.
Midshipman, 22 September, 1870. Graduated 1 June, 1874. Resigned 16 March, 1875.
WEICHERT, ERNEST A.
Naval Cadet, 6 September, 1895. At sea prior to final graduation.
WEIDENBERN, CHARLES.
Mate, 8 April, 1862. Acting Ensign, 2 September, 1863. Honorably discharged 16 September, 1865.
WEIDMAN, JOHN.
Acting Midshipman, 22 September, 1857. Midshipman, 1 June, 1861. Lieutenant, 16 July, 1862. Lieutenant-Commander, 25 July, 1866. Retired List, 30 June, 1875. Died 14 February, 1891.
WEIL, SAMUEL H.
Acting Assistant Surgeon, 13 January, 1863. Resigned 22 February, 1865.
WEIR, ANDREW.
Midshipman, 6 July, 1836. Passed Midshipman, 1 July, 1842. Master, 2 June, 1849. Lieutenant, 22 January, 1850. Resigned 8 June, 1853.
WEIR, ROBERT.
Third Assistant Engineer, 25 August, 1862. Second Assistant Engineer, 20 February, 1864. Resigned 19 June, 1865.
WEIR, ROBERT McQ.
Acting Second Assistant Engineer, 2 September, 1864. Honorably discharged 20 May, 1868.
WEISENTHALL, T. V.
Assistant Surgeon, 10 December, 1814. Dismissed 7 April, 1829.
WEISS, CHARLES L.
Mate, 11 April, 1898. Boatswain, 10 April, 1899.
WELCH, ARISTIDES.
Purser, 27 June, 1846. Resigned 9 February, 1856.
WELCH, CHARLES P.
Midshipman, 29 September, 1864. Graduated June, 1868. Ensign, 19 April, 1869. Retired List, 8 November, 1872.
WELCH, DANIEL.
Mate, 1 October, 1862. Died 18 March, 1862. Died 18 March, 1863.
WELCH, GEORGE E.
Acting Volunteer Lieutenant, 31 October, 1861. Resigned 12 April, 1862. Acting Volunteer Lieutenant, 1 July, 1862. Honorably discharged 13 September, 1865.
WELCH, JOHN H.
Acting Ensign, 16 April, 1863. Acting Master, 1 August, 1864. Honorably discharged 10 December, 1865.
WELCH, WILLIAM.
Mate, 13 June, 1864. Honorably discharged 15 May, 1866. Mate, 30 August, 1866. Ensign, 12 March, 1868. Master, 18 December, 1868. Lieutenant, 21 March, 1870. Lieutenant-Commander, 23 April, 1883. Retired List, 13 December, 1886. Died 12 January, 1887.
WELCH, WILLIAM E.
Acting Master, 4 November, 1861. Dismissed 6 August, 1862.
WELCKER, WILLIAM.
Acting Third Assistant Engineer, 4 November, 1863. Acting Second Assistant Engineer, 9 December, 1864. Honorably discharged 25 August, 1867.
WELD, A. D.
Acting Assistant Paymaster, 6 February, 1862. Dead.
WELD, FRANCIS M.
Assistant Surgeon, 22 May, 1862. Resigned 31 December, 1863.
WELD, WILLIAM W.
Mate, 19 September, 1861. Acting Ensign, 26 September, 1862. Honorably discharged 26 December, 1865.
WELDEN, JAMES.
Master's Mate, 23 April, 1805. Appointment revoked 22 May, 1805.
WELDON, WILLIAM H.
Assistant Paymaster, 25 September, 1861. Resigned 31 December, 1863.
WELLES, CHARLES.
Mate, 28 July, 1862. Acting Ensign, 19 January, 1864. Honorably discharged 24 August, 1865.
WELLES, JOSEPH D.
Mate, 12 September, 1862. Acting Ensign, 9 May, 1863. Acting Master, 7 November, 1864. Honorably discharged 22 April, 1866.
WELLES, ROGER, JR.
Cadet Midshipman, 25 September, 1880. Ensign, 1 July, 1886. Lieutenant, Junior Grade, 1 August, 1895. Lieutenant, 3 July, 1898.
WELLING, RICHARD W. G.
Ensign (Spanish-American War), 14 July, 1898. Honorably discharged 8 September, 1898.
WELLS, ALEXANDER H.
Midshipman, 14 December, 1831. Drowned 30 November, 1836.
WELLS, BENJAMIN A.
Assistant Surgeon, 10 December, 1814. Died 26 November, 1825.

GENERAL NAVY REGISTER. 577

WELLS, BENJAMIN F.
Midshipman, 22 September, 1841. Dismissed 28 August, 1849.
WELLS, BENJAMIN W., Jr.
Naval Cadet, 17 May, 1883. Ensign, 1 July, 1889. Lieutenant, Junior Grade, 21 March, 1897. Lieutenant, 3 March, 1899.
WELLS, BEZALEEL.
Midshipman, 1 July, 1825. Last appearance on Records of Navy Department, 1826. Dead.
WELLS, CHARLES.
Midshipman, 22 December, 1847. Dropped 28 February, 1849.
WELLS, CHARLES C.
Acting Master, 5 October, 1861. Honorably discharged 21 December, 1865. Acting Master, 11 December, 1866. Mustered out 16 May, 1867.
WELLS, CHARLES J. S.
Assistant Surgeon, 24 January, 1862. Passed Assistant Surgeon, 30 October, 1865. Surgeon, 6 July, 1872. Died 1 January, 1881.
WELLS, CHARLES S.
Mate, 18 December, 1863. Died 28 April, 1864.
WELLS, CHESTER.
Naval Cadet, 15 November, 1889. Honorably discharged 30 June, 1895. Assistant Engineer, 17 April, 1896. Rank changed to Ensign 3 March, 1899. Lieutenant, Junior Grade, 17 April, 1899.
WELLS, CLARK H.
Midshipman, 25 September, 1840. Passed Midshipman, 11 July, 1846. Master, 1 March, 1855. Lieutenant, 14 September, 1855. Lieutenant-Commander, 16 July, 1862. Commander, 25 July, 1866. Captain, 19 June, 1871. Commodore, 22 January, 1880. Rear-Admiral, 1 April, 1884. Retired List, 26 September, 1884. Died 28 January, 1888.
WELLS, EDWIN.
Third Assistant Engineer, 1 July, 1861. Second Assistant Engineer, 18 December, 1862. First Assistant Engineer, 30 January, 1865. Chief Engineer, 31 May, 1880. Died 8 January, 1889.
WELLS, E. G.
Mate. Dismissed 16 March, 1863.
WELLS, FRANCIS S.
Acting Master, 8 June, 1861. Acting Volunteer Lieutenant, 7 May, 1863. Acting Volunteer Lieutenant-Commander, 27 May, 1865. Honorably discharged 31 March, 1866.
WELLS, FREDERICK.
Acting Assistant Paymaster, 5 April, 1865. Honorably discharged 30 October, 1865.
WELLS, GEORGE.
Midshipman, 18 December, 1833. Passed Midshipman, 8 July, 1839. Lieutenant, 20 September, 1845. Retired 4 February, 1862. Died 27 October, 1864.
WELLS, HENRY.
Assistant Surgeon, 25 July, 1798. Surgeon, 2 August, 1799. Last appearance on Records of Navy Department.
WELLS, HENRY.
Midshipman, 20 June, 1806. Lieutenant, 6 January, 1813. Resigned 8 February, 1820.
WELLS, HENRY M.
Assistant Surgeon, 30 July, 1861. Passed Assistant Surgeon, 22 June, 1864. Surgeon, 9 October, 1866. Medical Inspector, 22 August, 1884. Medical Director, 22 September, 1891. Retired List, 20 January, 1897.
WELLS, HENRY N.
Mate, 22 April, 1863. Acting Ensign, 17 February, 1864. Honorably discharged 6 June, 1866.
WELLS, HOWARD.
Assistant Surgeon, 10 December, 1873. Passed Assistant Surgeon, 22 December, 1876. Surgeon, 19 June, 1888. Medical Inspector, 15 January, 1900.
WELLS, JAMES.
Surgeon, 24 April, 1799. Last appearance on Records of Navy Department, 11 January, 1806. Dead.
WELLS, JOHN C.
Acting Master, 26 February, 1862. Acting Volunteer Lieutenant, 10 July, 1865. Honorably discharged 21 November, 1865.
WELLS, JOHN C.
Acting Third Assistant Engineer, 17 October, 1863. Honorably discharged 2 November, 1865.
WELLS, JOHN T.
Acting Assistant Surgeon, 1 June, 1871. Resigned 1 September, 1874.
WELLS, JOSEPH E.
Acting Second Assistant Engineer, 20 June, 1864. Honorably discharged 21 August, 1865.
WELLS, LYMAN.
Acting Master, 22 November, 1861. Honorably discharged 10 February, 1869.
WELLS, ROBERT.
Master, 8 September, 1798. Last appearance on Records of Navy Department.
WELLS, WILLIAM.
Lieutenant, 17 February, 1800. Discharged 13 May, 1801, under Peace Establishment Act.
WELLS, WILLIAM.
Acting Second Assistant Engineer, 21 October, 1862. Honorably discharged 7 February, 1865.
WELLS, WILLIAM B.
Naval Cadet, 19 May, 1894. Ensign, 4 April, 1900.

WELLS, WILLIAM H.
Acting First Assistant Engineer, 24 August, 1863. Resigned 1 August, 1864.
WELLS, WILLIAM N.
Acting Master, 19 September, 1861. Honorably discharged 26 October, 1865.
WELLS, WILLIAM R.
Acting Master, 23 October, 1862. Acting Volunteer Lieutenant, 7 December, 1863. Honorably discharged 5 September, 1865.
WELLS, WILLIAM S.
Third Assistant Engineer, 18 November, 1862. Second Assistant Engineer, 23 March, 1864. Resigned 12 October, 1870.
WELSH, EDWIN.
Midshipman, 1 May, 1822. Resigned 11 August, 1825.
WELSH, GEORGE P.
Midshipman, 4 September, 1840. Passed Midshipman, 11 July, 1846. Master, 12 August, 1854. Lieutenant, 18 April, 1855. Died 26 April, 1860.
WELSH, JOHN.
Boatswain, 4 January, 1823. Died in 1825.
WELSH, JOSEPH.
Acting Assistant Surgeon, 10 September, 1864. Dismissed 18 February, 1865.
WELSH, ROBERT P.
Midshipman, 1 April, 1828. Resigned 6 July, 1835.
WELSH, THOMAS.
Mate, 6 July, 1863. Acting Ensign, 26 November, 1864. Honorably discharged 12 March, 1866.
WELSH, THOMAS.
Acting Assistant Surgeon, 1 September, 1861. Resigned 30 April, 1864.
WELTON, HENRY.
Gunner, 17 October, 1840. Resigned 23 February, 1843. Gunner, 27 March, 1847. Appointment revoked 6 March, 1848.
WELTON, HENRY.
Acting Ensign, 9 January, 1861. Acting Master, 4 January, 1865. Honorably discharged 3 October, 1865.
WELTON, HENRY.
Boatswain, 8 August, 1837. Appointment revoked 12 May, 1838.
WEMPLE, DAVID D.
Acting Midshipman, 24 September, 1858. Ensign, 25 November, 1862. Lieutenant, 22 February, 1864. Killed 24 December, 1864.
WENDELL, J. W.
Midshipman, 18 June, 1812. Resigned 16 December, 1814.
WENDELL, TUNIS D.
Mate. Resigned 13 December, 1862. Mate, 23 July, 1864. Died 22 June, 1871.
WENTWORTH, ANDREW R.
Assistant Surgeon, 22 April, 1885. Passed Assistant Surgeon, 22 April, 1889. Surgeon, 9 October, 1898.
WENTWORTH, JERE. C.
Mate, 2 March, 1863. Acting Ensign, 1 December, 1863. Acting Master, 29 June, 1864. Honorably discharged 20 May, 1865.
WENTWORTH, LEONARD.
Carpenter, 5 June, 1861. Dismissed 30 September, 1864.
WENTWORTH, WALTER W.
Acting Assistant Surgeon, 28 April, 1863. Honorably discharged 28 November, 1865.
WERDEN, REED.
Midshipman, 9 January, 1834. Passed Midshipman, 16 July, 1840. Lieutenant, 27 February, 1847. Commander, 16 July, 1862. Captain, 25 July, 1866. Commodore, 27 April, 1871. Rear-Admiral, 4 February, 1875. Retired List, 27 March, 1877. Died 11 July, 1886.
WERLHOFF, THEODORE.
Acting Master, 15 May, 1862. Honorably discharged 10 August, 1865.
WERLICK, PERCIVAL J.
Cadet Midshipman, 6 June, 1873. Graduated 18 June, 1879. Ensign, 6 November, 1881. Lieutenant, Junior Grade, 19 February, 1889. Lieutenant, 15 September, 1893.
WERNER, THEODORE J.
Mate, 1 February, 1863. Acting Ensign, 8 May, 1865. Honorably discharged 30 November, 1868.
WERNER, JOSEPH.
Acting Third Assistant Engineer, 3 January, 1863. Honorably discharged 4 October, 1865.
WERNTZ, ROBERT L.
Cadet Engineer, 1 October, 1880. Honorably discharged 30 June, 1886. Assistant Engineer, 28 June, 1889. Resigned 30 June, 1890.
WESCOTT, WILLIAM.
Master, 4 December, 1800. Last appearance on Records of Navy Department.
WESCOTT, WILIAM H.
Acting Assistant Surgeon, 4 August, 1862. Assistant Surgeon, 21 June, 1864. Resigned 27 April, 1865.
WESKETT, SAMUEL.
Acting Ensign and Pilot, 1 January, 1865. Honorably discharged 14 August, 1865.
WESSELS, FREDERICK.
Assistant Surgeon, 11 March, 1829. Died 15 November, 1834.
WESSON, GEORGE M.
Acting Assistant Paymaster, 21 July, 1862. Resigned 4 December, 1862.
WEST, ABNER.
Acting Master, 18 December, 1861. Resigned 20 June, 1863.

GENERAL NAVY REGISTER.   579

WEST, ALEXANDER F. H.
　Acting Ensign, 29 April, 1863. Resigned 25 March, 1864. Acting Ensign, 21 April, 1864. Honorably discharged 14 October, 1865. Acting Ensign, 21 November, 1866. Mustered out 14 May, 1868.
WEST, CHARLES H.
　Acting Assistant Paymaster, 9 December, 1861. Resigned 28 December, 1864.
WEST, CLIFFORD H.
　Midshipman, 22 September, 1863. Graduated June, 1867. Ensign, 18 December, 1868. Master, 21 March, 1870. Lieutenant, 21 March, 1871. Lieutenant-Commander, 31 March, 1888. Commander, 11 October, 1896.
WEST, ERNEST E.
　Cadet Midshipman, 20 May, 1884. Resigned 6 May, 1889. Ensign (Spanish-American War), 14 May, 1898. Honorably discharged 4 January, 1899.
WEST, GEORGE.
　Acting Third Assistant Engineer, 16 June, 1862. Resigned 6 June, 1863. Acting Third Assistant Engineer, 8 November, 1864. Honorably discharged 24 September, 1865.
WEST, GEORGE E.
　Midshipman, 27 March, 1839. Resigned 24 June, 1844.
WEST, GEORGE E.
　Cadet Midshipman, 12 September, 1876. Graduated 22 June, 1882. Ensign, Junior Grade, 3 March, 1883. Resigned 4 October, 1883.
WEST, GEORGE S.
　Acting Ensign, 6 December, 1862. Died 9 August, 1863.
WEST, H.
　Mate, 29 July, 1862. Appointment revoked (sick) 13 July, 1863.
WEST, JAMES.
　Mate, 4 November, 1862. Acting Ensign, 29 March, 1865. Honorably discharged 13 May, 1865.
WEST, JAMES E.
　Midshipman, 12 June, 1799. Discharged 12 October, 1801, under Peace Establishment Act.
WEST, JOB.
　Master, 12 May, 1813. Resigned 4 October, 1813.
WEST, JOHN.
　Acting Master, 24 July, 1862. Honorably discharged 26 October, 1865.
WEST, JOHN.
　Lieutenant, 4 July, 1798. Resigned 23 January, 1799.
WEST, JOHN T.
　Warrant Machinist, 23 August, 1899.
WEST, JOHN W.
　Midshipman, 3 November, 1818. Lieutenant, 3 March, 1827. Dismissed 22 November, 1844. Master, 19 March, 1847. Died 24 November, 1852.
WEST, JOHN W.
　Midshipman, 3 November, 1818. Lieutenant, 3 March, 1827. Dismissed 22 November, 1844.
WEST, LEWIS.
　Acting Master, 23 August, 1861. Resigned 25 March, 1865.
WEST, MONTGOMERY.
　Acting Third Assistant Engineer, 9 September, 1863. Honorably discharged 27 October, 1865.
WEST, NATHANIEL T.
　Midshipman, 18 February, 1844. Passed Midshipman, 10 August, 1847. Reserved List, 13 September, 1855. Ensign (retired), 10 March, 1863. Commander, Reserved List, 4 April, 1867. Died 31 October, 1881.
WEST, THOMAS.
　Acting Ensign, 2 January, 1864. Honorably discharged 28 October, 1865.
WEST, WILLIAM C.
　Midshipman, 30 January, 1841. Passed Midshipman, 10 August, 1847. Master, 14 September, 1855. Lieutenant, 15 September, 1855. Lieutenant-Commander, 16 July, 1862. Retired List, 26 April, 1866. Commander on Retired List, 4 April, 1867. Died 22 June, 1879.
WEST, WILLIAM H.
　Acting Master, 16 May, 1861. Acting Volunteer Lieutenant, 24 February, 1862. Acting Volunteer Lieutenant-Commander, 30 November, 1864. Honorably discharged 24 October, 1865.
WEST, WILLIAM H. G.
　Third Assistant Engineer, 13 May, 1861. Second Assistant Engineer, 19 February, 1863. First Assistant Engineer, 1 January, 1865. Drowned at Cape May, 19 July, 1872.
WESTCOTT, BAYSE N.
　Midshipman, 5 December, 1837. Passed Midshipman, 29 June, 1843. Master, 18 October, 1850. Lieutenant, 11 June, 1851. Retired List, 14 May, 1863. Commander, Retired List, 4 April, 1867. Died 6 December, 1891.
WESTCOTT, EDWARD R.
　Acting Ensign, 26 October, 1864. Died 9 March, 1865.
WESTCOTT, HAMPTON.
　Midshipman, 10 May, 1820. Lieutenant, 17 May, 1826. Dismissed 31 March, 1830.
WESTCOTT, JOHN J.
　Acting Ensign, 24 February, 1865. Appointment revoked 28 January, 1865.
WESTCOTT, R. T.
　Acting Ensign, 16 October, 1862. Resigned 23 October, 1863.
WESTERVELT, JACOB.
　Acting Master, 8 February, 1862. Killed in action 25 February, 1864.
WESTFALL, JOHN.
　Gunner, 8 June, 1886. Retired List, 26 July, 1892.

WESTFALL, LEWIS.
Acting Assistant Surgeon, 19 March, 1863. Honorably discharged 6 November, 1865.
WESTINGHOUSE, GEORGE, JR.
Acting Third Assistant Engineer, 1 December, 1864. Honorably discharged 1 August, 1865.
WESTINGHOUSE, JOHN.
Acting Third Assistant Engineer, 24 August, 1863. Acting Second Assistant Engineer, 11 July, 1864. Honorably discharged 31 October, 1865.
WESTON, ABIJAH.
Midshipman, 2 July, 1801. Resigned 4 November, 1805.
WESTON, ALFRED.
Mate, 28 September, 1861. Acting Master, 4 November, 1861. Acting Volunteer Lieutenant, 17 December, 1864. Honorably discharged 27 February, 1867. Acting Master, 5 April, 1867. Mustered out 2 October, 1868.
WESTON, CHARLES.
Midshipman, 11 March, 1837. Cashiered 27 October, 1842. Acting Lieutenant, 13 May, 1861. Resigned 16 August, 1861.
WESTON, CHARLES P.
Mate, 17 February, 1863. Resigned 30 June, 1865.
WESTON, DANIEL.
Acting Third Assistant Engineer, 7 July, 1864. Honorably discharged 28 October, 1865.
WESTON, GEORGE.
Gunner, 1 August, 1800. Dismissed 7 May, 1804.
WESTON, GERALD.
Mate, 27 January, 1864. Honorably discharged 1 August, 1866.
WESTON, HENRY, JR.
Mate, 12 September, 1862. Acting Ensign, 14 January, 1863. Honorably discharged 3 December, 1865.
WETHERELL, HIRAM B., JR.
Acting Assistant Paymaster, 13 July, 1863. Mustered out 25 March, 1866.
WETHERELL, MILFORD H.
Acting Assistant Surgeon, 27 April, 1865. Honorably discharged 15 March, 1866.
WETMORE, HENRY S.
Mate, 11 September, 1858. Discharged 27 December, 1858. Mate, 16 October, 1861. Resigned 2 May, 1862. Mate, 1 October, 1862. Acting Ensign, 5 December, 1862. Acting Master, 14 December, 1863. Acting Volunteer Lieutenant, 9 July, 1864. Honorably discharged 29 December, 1865.
WETMORE, WILLIAM C.
Midshipman, 18 June, 1812. Lieutenant, 13 January, 1825. Commander, 8 September, 1841. Died 7 August, 1846.
WETTENGEL, IVAN C.
Naval Cadet, 6 September, 1892. Ensign, 6 May, 1898.
WEY, RUFUS S.
Midshipman, 5 April, 1834. Resigned 15 July, 1837.
WEYMAN, E. A.
Midshipman, 30 March, 1838. Resigned 21 September, 1839.
WHALEN, DANIEL.
Acting Assistant Paymaster, 5 March, 1862. Resigned 12 February, 1866.
WHALL, CHARLES F.
Mate. Killed 5 November, 1862.
WHANN, DAVID.
Purser, 9 April, 1804. Resigned 17 April, 1809.
WHARTON, ARTHUR D.
Acting Midshipman, 23 September, 1856. Midshipman, 15 June, 1860. Dismissed 26 August, 1861.
WHARTON, BENJAMIN B. H.
Third Assistant Engineer, 21 November, 1857. Second Assistant Engineer, 3 August, 1859. First Assistant Engineer, 16 October, 1861. Chief Engineer, 10 November, 1863. Retired, 14 January, 1895.
WHARTON, J. P.
Midshipman, 19 October, 1799. Discharged 20 May, 1801, under Peace Establishment Act.
WHEATON, SETH.
Midshipman, 4 March, 1814. Last appearance on Records of Navy Department, 1816.
WHEDON, ROBERT H.
Acting Assistant Surgeon, 10 October, 1863. Honorably discharged 1 November, 1865. Acting Assistant Surgeon, 27 April, 1866. Assistant Surgeon, 18 June, 1866. Resigned 19 October, 1869.
WHEEDEN, MADISON.
Sailmaker, 19 August, 1834. Retired 27 February, 1862. Died 28 March, 1875.
WHEELEN, E. S.
Acting Assistant Paymaster, 1861. Appointment revoked 20 December, 1861.
WHEELER, BYRON C.
Mate, 15 October, 1863. Acting Ensign, 23 July, 1864. Honorably discharged 4 November, 1865.
WHEELER, EDMUND S.
Acting Assistant Paymaster, 24 September, 1863. Mustered out 31 October, 1865.
WHEELER FREDERICK L.
Acting Assistant Paymaster, 24 August, 1864. Mustered out 29 August, 1865.
WHEELER, FREDERICK A.
Mate, 5 March, 1864. Resigned 20 March, 1865.
WHEELER, HENRY.
Mate, 8 November, 1862. Acting Ensign and Pilot, 26 July, 1864. Honorably discharged 3 November, 1865.

WHEELER, HORACE K.
  Acting Assistant Surgeon, 24 May, 1862. Honorably discharged 13 August, 1866.
WHEELER, JAMES R.
  Acting Master, 29 October, 1861. Acting Volunteer Lieutenant, 7 February, 1865. Honorably discharged 11 February, 1867.
WHEELER, JOEL M.
  Acting Third Assistant Engineer, 23 July, 1863. Acting Second Assistant Engineer, 2 September, 1864. Honorably discharged 3 May, 1868.
WHEELER, MORTIMER M.
  Acting Ensign, 23 January, 1864. Honorably discharged 2 February, 1867.
WHEELER, RUSSELL M.
  Acting Third Assistant Engineer, 26 October, 1863. Acting Second Assistant Engineer, 13 February, 1865. Honorably discharged 9 December, 1865.
WHEELER, THOMAS H.
  Mate, 28 January, 1864. Acting Ensign, 2 December, 1864. Honorably discharged 28 October, 1865.
WHEELER, WILLIAM C.
  Third Assistant Engineer, 14 April, 1847. Second Assistant Engineer, 26 February, 1851. First Assistant Engineer, 26 June, 1856. Chief Engineer, 10 April, 1861. Dismissed 17 January, 1863.
WHEELER, WILLIAM K.
  Acting Midshipman, 7 December, 1859. Acting Ensign, 1 October, 1863. Master, 10 May, 1866. Lieutenant, 21 February, 1867. Lieutenant-Commander, 12 March, 1868. Died 14 March, 1876.
WHEELER, WILLIAM L.
  Assistant Surgeon, 30 July, 1861. Resigned 9 May, 1864. Acting Assistant Surgeon, 11 July, 1864. Acting Passed Assistant Surgeon, 20 September, 1866. Honorably discharged 15 November, 1868.
WHEELER, WILLIAM M.
  Assistant Surgeon, 27 May, 1896. Passed Assistant Surgeon, 27 May, 1899.
WHEELOCK, E. M.
  Acting Ensign, 1 October, 1862. Appointment revoked 27 April, 1863.
WHEELOCK, FREDERICK P.
  Midshipman, 10 March, 1840. Passed Midshipman, 11 July, 1846. Died 11 April, 1848.
WHEELWRIGHT, CHARLES W.
  Assistant Surgeon, 17 October, 1839. Surgeon, 5 April, 1854. Died 30 July, 1862.
WHELEN, HENRY.
  Midshipman, 23 September, 1862. Graduated June, 1866. Ensign, 12 March, 1868. Master, 26 March, 1869. Lieutenant, 21 March, 1870. Resigned 2 June, 1873.
WHELEN, WILLIAM.
  Assistant Surgeon, 3 January, 1828. Surgeon, 9 February, 1837. Died 11 June, 1865.
WHETCROFT, W. W.
  Midshipman, 1823. Resigned 26 November, 1827.
WHERRY, WILLIAM.
  Mate, 1 October, 1862. Resigned 20 July, 1863.
WHIDBEE, J. W.
  Midshipman, 16 January, 1800. Last appearance on Records of Navy Department, 17 March, 1800.
WHIFFLIN, JULIUS W.
  Acting Assistant Paymaster, 17 December, 1861. Resigned 23 September, 1864.
WHIPKEY, ALLEN.
  Boatswain, 18 March, 1897.
WHIPPLE, ARNOLD.
  Midshipman, 6 October, 1798. Discharged 30 April, 1801, under Peace Establishment Act.
WHIPPLE, EDWARD A.
  Third Assistant Engineer, 10 July, 1847. Second Assistant Engineer, 31 October, 1848. First Assistant Engineer, 26 February, 1851. Resigned 20 February, 1854.
WHIPPLE, EDWARD A.
  Acting First Assistant Engineer, 12 November, 1862. Acting Chief Engineer, 27 January, 1863. Honorably discharged 3 September, 1866.
WHIPPLE, GEORGE.
  Acting First Assistant Engineer, 28 July, 1862. Resigned 25 February, 1863.
WHIPPLE, GEORGE W.
  Acting First Assistant Engineer, 15 February, 1862. Resigned 25 February, 1863.
WHIPPLE, JOHN P.
  Third Assistant Engineer, 13 March, 1847. Second Assistant Engineer, 13 September, 1849. First Assistant Engineer, 26 February, 1851. Chief Engineer, 27 June, 1855. Died 26 September, 1864.
WHIPPLE, P. M.
  Midshipman, 18 June, 1812. Lieutenant, 28 March, 1820. Died 11 May, 1827.
WHISTLER, W.
  Midshipman, 30 April, 1800. Last appearance on Records of Navy Department, 9 June, 1800.
WHITAKER, CARROLL.
  Mate, 22 February, 1865. Honorably discharged 15 August, 1865.
WHITAKER, HERVEY W.
  Assistant Surgeon, 9 July, 1881. Passed Assistant Surgeon, 9 July, 1884. Resigned 5 November, 1896.
WHITAKER, JOHN G.
  Midshipman, 10 September, 1841. Resigned 22 May, 1849.
WHITE, CALEB B.
  Acting Assistant Surgeon, 3 May, 1865. Discharged 11 October, 1865.
WHITE, C. D.
  Acting Assistant Surgeon, 5 December, 1873. Honorably discharged 30 June, 1879.

WHITE, CHARLES.
Mate, 18 January, 1864. Honorably discharged 26 October, 1865.
WHITE, CHARLES H.
Assistant Surgeon, 24 January, 1862. Passed Assistant Surgeon, 30 October, 1865. Surgeon, 18 November, 1869. Medical Inspector, 10 July, 1883. Medical Director, 8 June, 1895. Retired List, 19 November, 1900.
WHITE, CHARLES W.
Acting Third Assistant Engineer, 9 December, 1863. Resigned 8 September, 1864.
WHITE, COLLINS D.
Acting Assistant Surgeon, 19 December, 1862. Honorably discharged 30 September, 1865.
WHITE, EDWARD F.
Passed Assistant Engineer (Spanish-American War), 24 June, 1898. Honorably discharged 17 January, 1899.
WHITE, EDGAR T.
Ensign (Spanish-American War), 20 July, 1898. Honorably discharged 8 September, 1898.
WHITE, EDWARD W.
Mate, 9 August, 1861. Acting Master, 21 January, 1862. Honorably discharged 15 July, 1867. Acting Master, 27 July, 1867. Mustered out 9 July, 1868.
WHITE, EDWIN.
Midshipman, 25 November, 1861. Graduated November, 1864. Ensign, 1 November, 1866. Master, 1 December, 1866. Lieutenant, 12 March, 1868. Lieutenant-Commander, 15 September, 1869. Commander, 4 March, 1886. Captain, 25 December, 1898. Retired List, with rank of Rear-Admiral, 28 December, 1899.
WHITE, GEORGE.
Acting Third Assistant Engineer, 1 February, 1863. Dismissed 13 July, 1863.
WHITE, GEORGE B.
Acting Midshipman, 28 September, 1854. Midshipman, 11 June, 1858. Passed Midshipman, 28 January, 1861. Master, 28 February, 1861. Lieutenant, 19 April, 1861. Lieutenant-Commander, 3 March, 1865. Commander, 13 August, 1872. Captain, 3 November, 1884. Died 27 February, 1890.
WHITE, GEORGE H.
Midshipman, 1 June, 1828. Resigned 17 July, 1829.
WHITE, GEORGE H.
Third Assistant Engineer, 21 July, 1858. Resigned 14 October, 1859. Third Assistant Engineer, 23 May, 1861. Second Assistant Engineer, 28 October, 1862. First Assistant Engineer, 1 January, 1865. Chief Engineer, 23 November, 1878. Retired List, 18 November, 1890. Died 23 February, 1891.
WHITE, GEORGE H.
Purser, 13 September, 1841. Retired 18 April, 1863. Died 18 November, 1867.
WHITE, GEORGE H.
Mate, 24 September, 1861. Resigned 21 June, 1864.
WHITE, GEORGE M.
Midshipman, 1 November, 1828. Passed Midshipman, 14 June, 1834. Lieutenant, 25 February, 1841. Reserved List, 13 September, 1855. Captain, Reserved List, 4 April, 1867. Died 24 May, 1882.
WHITE, GEORGE W.
Acting Assistant Paymaster, 10 February, 1865. Mustered out 27 October, 1865.
WHITE, GIDEON, Jr.
Surgeon's Mate, 10 December, 1814. Assistant Surgeon, 2 May, 1825. Dismissed 12 January, 1832.
WHITE, HENRY.
Mate, 1 November, 1864. Honorably discharged 13 June, 1867.
WHITE, HENRY C.
Midshipman, 16 October, 1861. Graduated November, 1864. Ensign, 1 November, 1866. Master, 1 December, 1866. Lieutenant, 12 March, 1868. Lieutenant-Commander, 26 March, 1869. Resigned 1 June, 1884.
WHITE, HENRY C.
Acting Second Assistant Engineer, 27 February, 1865. Honorably discharged 6 September, 1865.
WHITE, ISAAC.
Carpenter, 29 November, 1825. Discharged 15 December, 1828.
WHITE, JAMES.
Midshipman, 20 August, 1814. Resigned 22 August, 1815.
WHITE, JAMES H.
Acting Third Assistant Engineer, 3 January, 1865. Honorably discharged 10 August, 1865.
WHITE, J. HENRY.
Mate, 27 October, 1862. Resigned 11 October, 1864.
WHITE, JOHN.
Mate, 8 October, 1862. Acting Ensign, 26 August, 1863. Acting Master, 15 December, 1864. Lost on Patapsco, 15 January, 1865.
WHITE, JOHN.
Master, 24 April, 1814. Lieutenant, 27 April, 1816. Commander, 9 February, 1837. Died 14 April, 1840.
WHITE, JOHN.
Acting Master, 7 October, 1861. Died 30 October, 1861.
WHITE, JOHN.
Master, 2 December, 1813. Resigned 20 April, 1814.
WHITE, JOHN.
Mate, 8 April, 1864. Resigned (sick) 6 October, 1864.
WHITE, JOHN.
Acting Third Assistant Engineer, 16 November, 1863. Died 15 April, 1864.

GENERAL NAVY REGISTER. 583

WHITE, JOHN B.
Acting Assistant Surgeon, 12 May, 1865. Honorably discharged 27 August, 1866.
WHITE, JOHN J.
Midshipman, 1 July, 1826. Passed Midshipman, 10 June, 1833. Resigned 26 February, 1839.
WHITE, JOSEPH.
Carpenter, 29 August, 1825. Last appearance on Records of Navy Department, 1827. Frigate Constellation.
WHITE, JOSHUA.
Midshipman, 1 June, 1812. Resigned 30 January, 1817.
WHITE, LEVERETT H.
Mate, 30 August, 1861. Acting Ensign, 26 November, 1864. Appointment revoked 12 January, 1867.
WHITE, LUTHER.
Gunner, 23 August, 1800. Last appearance on Records of Navy Department.
WHITE, MICHAEL.
Boatswain, date not known. Last appearance on Records of Navy Department.
WHITE, OSCAR.
Midshipman, 21 September, 1861. Graduated October, 1865. Ensign, 1 December, 1866. Master, 12 March, 1868. Resigned 28 November, 1868. Lieutenant, Junior Grade (Spanish-American War), 24 May, 1898. Honorably discharged 12 September, 1898.
WHITE, PHILIP H.
Third Assistant Engineer, 16 October, 1861. Second Assistant Engineer, 3 August, 1863. Resigned 27 April, 1865.
WHITE, PHILIP, Jr.
Acting Third Assistant Engineer, 20 April, 1865. Honorably discharged 24 January, 1868.
WHITE, PHILO.
Purser, 11 May, 1830. Resigned 31 October, 1834. Purser, 13 April, 1837. Resigned 15 September, 1845.
WHITE, RICHARD D.
Naval Cadet, 20 May, 1895. At sea prior to final graduation.
WHITE, ROBERT H.
Acting Third Assistant Engineer, 29 September, 1862. Resigned 11 October, 1862.
WHITE, SAMUEL.
Carpenter, 4 May, 1841: Died 20 August, 1843.
WHITE, SAMUEL G.
Assistant Surgeon, 26 April, 1847. Resigned 16 May, 1849.
WHITE, SAMUEL J.
Acting Master and Pilot, 1 October, 1864. Resigned 27 March, 1865.
WHITE, STEPHEN S.
Assistant Surgeon, 19 May, 1887. Passed Assistant Surgeon, 19 May, 1890. Died 30 May, 1899.
WHITE, TRUMAN B.
Sailmaker, 25 July, 1870. Retired List, 3 November, 1898.
WHITE, U. S. G.
Civil Engineer, 22 January, 1877.
WHITE, WILLIAM.
Mate, 22 May, 1863. Honorably discharged 2 November, 1867.
WHITE, WILLIAM.
Mate, 10 February, 1864. Acting Ensign, 25 November, 1864. Honorably discharged 1 August, 1865.
WHITE, WILLIAM A.
Master, 15 July, 1812. Killed in action 1 June, 1813.
WHITE, WILLIAM C.
Ensign (Spanish-American War), 28 May, 1898. Honorably discharged 13 March, 1899.
WHITE, WILLIAM E.
Mate, 25 January, 1862. Dismissed 30 September, 1862.
WHITE, WILLIAM H.
Acting Third Assistant Engineer, 12 January, 1865. Honorably discharged 14 November, 1865. Acting Third Assistant Engineer, 4 December, 1866. Died 9 February, 1868.
WHITE, WILLIAM H.
Acting Third Assistant Engineer, 5 July, 1862. Resigned (sick) 3 November, 1864.
WHITE, WILLIAM P.
Cadet Midshipman, 30 June, 1874. Graduated 4 June, 1880. Ensign, Junior Grade, 3 March, 1883. Ensign, 9 February, 1884. Lieutenant, Junior Grade, 5 March, 1890. Lieutenant, 30 September, 1894.
WHITE, WILLIAM R.
Naval Cadet, 6 September, 1893. Ensign, 1 July, 1899.
WHITE, WILLIAM W.
Cadet Engineer, 13 September, 1877. Assistant Engineer, 1 July, 1883. Passed Assistant Engineer, 10 November, 1893. Rank changed to Lieutenant, 3 March, 1899.
WHITEHEAD, FREDERICK.
Mate, 24 August, 1864. Resigned 29 March, 1865.
WHITEHEAD, IRA C.
Acting Assistant Surgeon, 12 August, 1861. Resigned 16 March, 1865. Acting Assistant Surgeon, 25 February, 1871. Honorably discharged 30 June, 1879.
WHITEHEAD, SAVILL.
Acting Third Assistant Engineer, 11 May, 1864. Honorably discharged 2 November, 1865.
WHITEHEAD, THOMAS.
Boatswain, 27 May, 1800. Last appearance on Records of Navy Department, 8 October, 1808.

WHITEHEAD, WALTER E.
Gunner, 10 April, 1899.
WHITEHEAD, WILLIAM.
Boatswain, 5 May, 1838. Died 9 April, 1854.
WHITEHEAD, WILLIAM.
Acting Midshipman, 23 September, 1856. Midshipman, 15 June, 1860. Master, 19 September, 1861. Lieutenant, 16 July, 1862. Lieutenant-Commander, 25 July, 1866. Commander, 4 June, 1874. Captain, 4 September, 1887. Died 8 January, 1893.
WHITEHILL, J. F.
Assistant Surgeon, 16 May, 1829. Lost in the Hornet, 10 September, 1829.
WHITEHILL, ROBERT, JR.
Acting Third Assistant Engineer, 2 December, 1863. Acting Second Assistant Engineer, 16 February, 1865. Acting First Assistant Engineer, 7 March, 1865. Honorably discharged 8 August, 1865.
WHITEHOUSE, EDWARD M.
Acting Assistant Paymaster, 24 December, 1862. Assistant Paymaster, 23 July, 1866. Passed Assistant Paymaster, 6 September, 1867. Paymaster, 12 April, 1877. Retired List 4 February, 1898.
WHITEHOUSE, SAMUEL N.
Carpenter, 17 July, 1861. Retired List, 8 March, 1890. Died 2 January, 1891.
WHITESIDE, FRANKLIN W.
Mate, 17 March, 1864. Honorably discharged 1 September, 1865.
WHITESIDE, JAMES E.
Mate. Appointment revoked 30 July, 1862.
WHITESIDES, JOHN A.
Mate, 26 December, 1863. Honorably discharged 3 November, 1865.
WHITESIDES, WILLIAM.
Midshipman, 24 June, 1799. Lost in the Insurgent.
WHITFIELD, FREDERICK A.
Acting Third Assistant Engineer, 17 February, 1862. Died 14 October, 1865.
WHITFIELD, GEORGE.
Mate, 19 January, 1862. Dismissed 18 January, 1862.
WHITFIELD, JAMES M.
Assistant Surgeon, 19 June, 1890. Resigned 17 December, 1892.
WHITFIELD, W. A.
Midshipman, 16 December, 1836. Resigned 6 December, 1838.
WHITFIELD, WILLIAM E.
Midshipman, 2 June, 1870. Graduated 1 June, 1874. Ensign, 17 July, 1875. Master, 30 August, 1881. Lieutenant, Junior Grade, 3 March, 1883. Retired List, 10 December, 1883. Died 10 January, 1890.
WHITHAM, JAY M.
Cadet Engineer, 13 September, 1877. Graduated 10 June, 1881. Assistant Engineer, 1 July, 1883. Resigned 1 February, 1886.
WHITIN, LOUIS F.
Acting Assistant Paymaster, 20 January, 1865. Mustered out 10 November, 1865.
WHITING, ADONIRAM.
Mate, 8 January, 1862. Honorably discharged 4 October, 1866.
WHITING, CHARLES G.
Acting Ensign, 5 August, 1864. Honorably discharged 22 January, 1866.
WHITING, F. B.
Midshipman, 6 July, 1803. Resigned 6 December, 1805.
WHITING, GEORGE B.
Acting Chief Engineer, 28 February, 1865. Honorably discharged 31 October, 1868.
WHITING, HENRY W.
Acting Third Assistant Engineer, 19 April, 1864. Honorably discharged 3 November, 1865.
WHITING, JAMES B.
Assistant Surgeon, 1 May, 1851. Died 1 June, 1855.
WHITING, JAMES R.
Assistant Surgeon, 14 June, 1898.
WHITING, JAMES W.
Acting Gunner, 4 October, 1864. Honorably discharged 30 September, 1865.
WHITING, ROBERT.
Assistant Surgeon, 21 June, 1875. Passed Assistant Surgeon, 17 December, 1878. Surgeon, 15 December, 1891. Retired List, 15 February, 1897. Died 5 March, 1897.
WHITING, SAMUEL.
Boatswain, for duty in the Arctic Expedition, 9 May, 1855. Appointment ended with return of Expedition, 1857.
WHITING, WILLIAM.
Boatswain, 19 February, 1848. Accidentally killed 1 April, 1855.
WHITING, WILLIAM B.
Midshipman, 10 February, 1829. Passed Midshipman, 4 June, 1836. Lieutenant, 8 September, 1841. Reserved List, 28 September, 1855. Commander on Retired List, 21 July, 1861. Captain on Retired List, 4 April, 1867. Commodore, Retired List, 15 February, 1872. Died 16 December, 1883.
WHITING, WILLIAM D.
Midshipman, 1 March, 1841. Passed Midshipman, 10 August, 1847. Master, 1 May, 1855. Lieutenant, 14 September, 1855. Lieutenant-Commander, 16 July, 1862. Commander, 25 July, 1866. Captain, 19 August, 1872. Chief, Bureau Navigation, 11 June, 1878. Commodore, 12 October, 1881. Retired List, 13 October, 1881. Died 19 March, 1894.
WHITING, WILLIAM H.
Acting Midshipman, 21 September, 1860. Acting Ensign, 1 October, 1863. Master, 10 May, 1866. Lieutenant, 21 February, 1867. Lieutenant-Commander, 12 March, 1868. Commander, 2 July, 1882. Captain, 19 June, 1897.

GENERAL NAVY REGISTER. 585

WHITING, WILLIAM W.
Acting Second Assistant Engineer, 28 October, 1861. Acting First Assistant Engineer, 17 March, 1864. Honorably discharged 11 January, 1866.
WHITLOCK, E. D.
Midshipman, 1 January, 1812. Lieutenant, 1 April, 1818. Dismissed 23 May, 1832.
WHITLOCK, ISAAC.
Midshipman, 4 April, 1800. Lost in the Insurgent.
WHITMAN, C. S.
Mate, 13 December, 1861. Resigned 24 July, 1862.
WHITMAN, JOHN F.
Acting Ensign, 1 July, 1864. Honorably discharged 4 October, 1866. Acting Ensign, 11 December, 1866. Mustered out 27 March, 1869.
WHITMAN, JOSEPH A.
Mate, 17 April, 1866. Appointment revoked 27 July, 1866.
WHITMARSH, ZACHARIAH, Jr.
Boatswain, 3 February, 1849. Died 20 November, 1869.
WHITMORE, A. H.
Acting Second Assistant Engineer, 24 October, 1862. Appointment revoked (sick) 19 December, 1862.
WHITMORE, BENJAMIN.
Midshipman, 31 January, 1800. Resigned 16 February, 1801.
WHITMORE, BENJAMIN.
Acting Master, 24 March, 1862. Honorably discharged 10 November, 1865.
WHITMORE, HENRY C.
Mate, 23 December, 1861. Acting Ensign, 18 March, 1864. Honorably discharged 18 August, 1868.
WHITMORE, JOSEPH.
Master, 21 August, 1799. Discharged 30 April, 1801, under Peace Establishment Act.
WHITMORE, WALTER P.
Acting Third Assistant Engineer, 17 August, 1864. Honorably discharged 23 November, 1865.
WHITMORE, WILLIAM B.
Acting Third Assistant Engineer, 11 December, 1861. Honorably discharged 1 December, 1865.
WHITMORE, WILLIAM T.
Acting Assistant Paymaster, 18 August, 1862. Honorably discharged 3 October, 1865.
WHITNEY, ALFRED C.
Acting Second Assistant Engineer, 3 November, 1863. Acting First Assistant Engineer, 13 September, 1864. Resigned 14 June, 1865.
WHITNEY, DAVID V.
Acting Assistant Surgeon, 26 May, 1863. Assistant Surgeon, 22 September, 1863. Dismissed 8 May, 1866.
WHITNEY, FRANK H.
Gunner, 7 January, 1890. Chief Gunner, 7 January, 1900.
WHITNEY, GEORGE E.
Acting Third Assistant Engineer, 2 June, 1862. Acting Second Assistant Engineer, 7 March, 1865. Honorably discharged 6 May, 1866.
WHITNEY, ISAAC.
Sailmaker, 10 January, 1837. Appointment revoked 2 November, 1847.
WHITNEY, JOHN M.
Acting Assistant Surgeon, 27 June, 1864. Drowned 16 August, 1864.
WHITNEY, THOMAS H.
Assistant Surgeon, 30 July, 1861. Resigned 9 May, 1864.
WHITNEY, W. H.
Mate, 6 January, 1863. Dismissed 4 June, 1863.
WHITNEY, WILLIAM.
Sailmaker, 16 May, 1871. Died 3 January, 1874.
WHITAKER, EZRA J.
Third Assistant Engineer, 19 February, 1861. Second Assistant Engineer, 17 December, 1862. First Assistant Engineer, 1 December, 1864. Chief Engineer, 6 June, 1873. Retired List, 8 May, 1895. Died 20 August, 1895.
WHITTAKER, FREDERICK W. H.
Acting Third Assistant Engineer, 26 February, 1862. Resigned 16 August, 1862. Acting Third Assistant Engineer, 13 September, 1862. Acting Second Assistant Engineer, 20 July, 1863. Resigned 15 February, 1865.
WHITTAKER, JAMES.
Acting First Assistant Engineer, 21 November, 1862. Appointment revoked (sick) 12 May, 1863.
WHITTAKER, JAMES WASHINGTON.
Third Assistant Engineer, 21 November, 1857. Second Assistant Engineer, 2 August, 1859. First Assistant Engineer, 16 October, 1861. Chief Engineer, 10 November, 1863. Died 9 March, 1881.
WHITTAKER, JOHN.
Acting Third Assistant Engineer, 21 August, 1861. Acting Second Assistant Engineer, 12 November, 1863. Resigned 5 June, 1865.
WHITTAKER, JOHN A.
Acting Third Assistant Engineer, 17 February, 1862. Honorably discharged 15 August, 1865.
WHITTAKER, ROBERT.
Boatswain, 16 February, 1842. Died 27 September, 1858.
WHITTED, WILLIAM S.
Naval Cadet, 20 May, 1890. Ensign, 1 July, 1896. Lieutenant, Junior Grade, 1 July, 1899.

GENERAL NAVY REGISTER.

WHITTELSEY, WILLIAM B.
Cadet Midshipman, 28 June, 1878. Ensign, 1 July, 1884. Lieutenant, Junior Grade, 22 June, 1894. Lieutenant, 5 December, 1897.
WHITTEMORE, GEORGE H.
Acting Third Assistant Engineer, 30 December, 1863. Acting Second Assistant Engineer, 18 April, 1865. Honorably discharged 22 December, 1868.
WHITTEMORE, HARRY D.
Acting Ensign, 1 June, 1864. Appointment revoked 6 November, 1866.
WHITTEMORE, HENRY M.
Acting Assistant Paymaster, 11 July, 1863. Mustered out 12 December, 1865.
WHITTEMORE, JOHN M.
Third Assistant Engineer, 24 August, 1861. Killed in action 7 November, 1861.
WHITTEMORE, MENAUGH.
Acting Assistant Paymaster, 19 October, 1861. Died 26 April, 1862.
WHITTEMORE, THEO. W.
Acting Assistant Paymaster, 12 March, 1863. Honorably discharged 2 February, 1866.
WHITTEMORE, W. M.
Acting Assistant Paymaster, 18 August, 1862. Resigned 17 February, 1864.
WHITTEN, ELIJAH.
Gunner, 1 January, 1818. Resigned in 1825.
WHITTHORNE, DE WITT C.
Midshipman, 10 September, 1847. Resigned 12 July, 1849.
WHITTIER, A. S.
Midshipman, 8 July, 1833. Passed Midshipman, 8 July, 1839. Died 24 January, 1841.
WHITTIER, RUFUS A.
Acting Midshipman, 4 March, 1850. Dropped 24 January, 1851.
WHITTINGTON, C. S.
Midshipman, 18 June, 1812. Resigned 17 February, 1826.
WHITTINGTON, GEORGE H.
Acting Third Assistant Engineer, 26 August, 1863. Honorably discharged 26 August, 1865.
WHITTINGTON, HENRY.
Carpenter, 11 December, 1827. Died 28 January, 1828.
WHITTINGTON, S. B.
Assistant Surgeon, 7 July, 1812. Last appearance on Records of Navy Department, 1815. Sloop Ontario.
WHITTLE, JOHN S.
Assistant Surgeon, 20 June, 1838. Died 5 April, 1850.
WHITTLE, WILLIAM C.
Midshipman, 10 May, 1820. Lieutenant, 17 May, 1828. Commander, 4 August, 1850. Resigned 20 April, 1861.
WHITTLE, WILLIAM C., JR.
Acting Midshipman, 28 September, 1854. Midshipman, 11 June, 1858. Passed Midshipman, 28 January, 1861. Master, 28 February, 1861. Resigned 15 May, 1861.
WHITTLESEY, HUMES H.
Cadet Engineer, 1 October, 1880. Ensign, 1 July, 1886. Lieutenant, Junior Grade, 28 December, 1895. Lieutenant, 22 November, 1898.
WHITTLESEY, JOHN C.
Acting Master, 26 August, 1861. Resigned 21 November, 1861.
WHITTLESEY, W. C.
Surgeon, 27 April, 1816. Last appearance on Records of Navy Department, 1819. Furloughed.
WHITTON, ELISHA.
Gunner, 13 April, 1838. Died 17 June, 1849.
WHITTON, WILLIAM H.
Mate, 2 June, 1864. Appointment revoked 16 August, 1864.
WHITWORTH, HORACE.
Acting Third Assistant Engineer, 8 December, 1863. Honorably discharged 16 November, 1865. Acting Third Assistant Engineer, 26 April, 1866. Mustered out 7 December, 1868.
WHYBORN, DAVID T.
Acting Assistant Surgeon, 10 March, 1864. Resigned 9 September, 1865.
WHYTE, HARRY M.
Acting Third Assistant Engineer, 23 August, 1864. Honorably discharged 4 December, 1865.
WICHART, JOHN.
Ensign (Spanish-American War), 1 July, 1898. Honorably discharged 8 September, 1898.
WICKES, ROSCOE V.
Mate, 13 October, 1868. Resigned 19 August, 1871.
WICKES, SILAS C.
Assistant Surgeon, 24 July, 1813. Surgeon, 27 March, 1818. Died 21 August, 1819.
WICKHAM, GEORGE.
Midshipman, 5 January, 1832. Passed Midshipman, 23 June, 1838. Resigned 26 July, 1839.
WICKWISE, JONATHAN W.
Mate, 31 December, 1863. Appointment revoked 8 November, 1864.
WIDDEN, PHILON C.
Acting Assistant Surgeon, 16 December, 1863. Honorably discharged 19 October, 1865.
WIDGEON, WILLIAM.
Sailmaker, 20 June, 1812. Resigned 12 June, 1815.
WIDUP, ALLEN W.
Mate, 21 November, 1863. Resigned 24 April, 1865.
WIEBER, FRANCIS W. F.
Assistant Surgeon, 3 November, 1884. Passed Assistant Surgeon, 3 November, 1887. Surgeon, 6 November, 1897.

GENERAL NAVY REGISTER.

WIGAND, RAYMOND.
Mate, 24 January, 1863. Dismissed 30 June, 1863.
WIGGIN, ALEXANDER S.
Acting Master, 27 February, 1862. Died from wounds received in action at Bayou Teche, La., 9 February, 1863.
WIGGIN, GEORGE.
Acting Master, 3 July, 1861. Acting Volunteer Lieutenant, 3 November, 1862. Honorably discharged 25 February, 1865.
WIGGINS, ALEXANDER.
Acting Third Assistant Engineer, 14 July, 1864. Honorably discharged 11 January, 1866.
WIGHT, CHARLES L.
Cadet Engineer, Naval Academy, 1 October, 1874. Graduated 20 June, 1878. Assistant Engineer, 20 June, 1880. Resigned 1 July, 1882.
WIGHT, DANFORTH P.
Acting Assistant Paymaster, 20 January, 1864. Passed Assistant Paymaster, 23 July, 1866. Paymaster, 12 February, 1870. Retired List, 12 December, 1885. Died 12 July, 1890.
WIGHT, JAMES M.
Midshipman, 1 July, 1867. Graduated 6 June, 1871. Ensign, 14 July, 1872. Master, 30 June, 1873. Lost on Huron, 24 November, 1877.
WIGHT, LOTHROP.
Mate, 19 August, 1862. Acting Ensign, 21 May, 1863. Acting Master, 2 July, 1864. Honorably discharged 19 August, 1865.
WIGHTMAN, GEORGE A.
Acting Sailmaker, 5 June, 1861. Resigned 3 October, 1861.
WICKOFF, HOLMES.
Acting Assistant Surgeon, 29 June, 1871. Assistant Surgeon, 26 February, 1875. Died 17 July, 1878.
WILBUR, CHARLES C.
Mate, 4 January, 1864. Acting Ensign, 27 September, 1864. Honorably discharged 28 October, 1866.
WILBUR, JAMES B.
Acting Third Assistant Engineer, 24 June, 1863. Resigned 23 June, 1865.
WILCOX, ABRAHAM H.
Acting First Assistant Engineer, 21 March, 1865. Honorably discharged 6 September, 1866.
WILCOX, AMOS C.
Acting Third Assistant Engineer, 19 April, 1864. Honorably discharged 26 October, 1865.
WILCOX, B. C.
Midshipman, 1 April, 1827. Resigned 15 December, 1838.
WILCOX, CALVIN S.
Mate, 15 December, 1863. Acting Ensign, 13 December, 1864. Honorably discharged 10 August, 1865.
WILCOX, DAVID L.
Acting Master's Mate, 4 September, 1861. Appointment revoked 20 January, 1862.
WILCOX, DAVID L.
Acting Master, 14 August, 1861. Resigned 17 January, 1862.
WILCOX, HENRY F.
Acting Second Assistant Engineer, 25 January, 1864. Honorably discharged 15 August, 1865.
WILCOX, JOHN.
Mate. Dismissed 26 May, 1863.
WILCOX, RICHARD.
Mate, 15 April, 1863. Resigned 3 December, 1864.
WILCOX, SAMUEL.
Midshipman, 11 June, 1840. Resigned 17 August, 1847.
WILCOX, WILLIS B.
Assistant Paymaster, 29 October, 1881. Passed Assistant Paymaster, 19 February, 1892. Paymaster, 9 July, 1897.
WILCOXSON, JAMES.
Midshipman, 18 November, 1839. Passed Midshipman, 2 July, 1845. Drowned 21 December, 1850.
WILD, EDWARD N.
Mate, 4 April, 1864. Honorably discharged 3 November, 1865.
WILDE, GEORGE F. F.
Midshipman, 30 November, 1861. Graduated November, 1864. Ensign, 1 November, 1866. Master, 1 December, 1866. Lieutenant, 12 March, 1868. Lieutenant-Commander, 26 June, 1869. Commander, 2 October, 1885. Captain, 10 August, 1898.
WILDE, RICHARD.
Midshipman, 1 December, 1809. Resigned 1 November, 1810.
WILDER, CHARLES B.
Acting Master, 17 October, 1861. Acting Volunteer Lieutenant, 12 April, 1864. Killed in action at Smithfield, Virginia, 14 April, 1864.
WILDER, HENRY M.
Acting Gunner, 25 May, 1865. Honorably discharged 12 October, 1865.
WILDES, FRANK.
Acting Midshipman, 21 September, 1860. Ensign, 28 May, 1863. Master, 10 November, 1865. Lieutenant, 10 November, 1866. Lieutenant-Commander, 12 March, 1868. Commander, 1 April, 1880. Captain, 31 July, 1894.
WILDES, WILLIAM.
Lieutenant, 23 April, 1799. Resigned 4 August, 1800.
WILDMAN, JAMES T.
Acting Assistant Paymaster, 11 January, 1864. Honorably discharged 5 June, 1865.

WILE, JULIUS I.
Assistant Engineer (Spanish-American War), 20 May, 1898. Honorably discharged 27 February, 1899.
WILEY, CHARLES.
Acting Ensign, 4 May, 1863. Resigned 30 March, 1865.
WILEY, EDWIN H.
Midshipman, 27 July, 1865. Graduated June, 1869. Ensign, 12 July, 1870. Master, 12 July, 1871. Resigned 1 July, 1875.
WILEY, GEORGE.
Purser, 4 August, 1800. Dismissed 8 October, 1800.
WILEY, GEORGE F.
Mate, 24 June, 1867. Resigned 6 May, 1868.
WILEY, HENRY A.
Naval Cadet, 17 May, 1883. Ensign, 1 July, 1890. Lieutenant, Junior Grade, 27 May, 1898. Lieutenant, 3 March, 1899.
WILEY, JAMES.
Midshipman, 9 March, 1840. Resigned 8 June, 1847.
WILEY, J. H.
Mate, 19 September, 1861. Acting Ensign, 13 September, 1862. Dismissed 7 June, 1863.
WILEY, JOHN S.
Assistant Surgeon, 9 May, 1825. Died 20 June, 1852.
WILEY, ROBERT.
Acting Ensign, 14 August, 1862. Killed on the Montgomery, 15 January, 1865.
WILHELM, WILLIAM.
Mate, 14 April, 1862. Resigned 30 April, 1864.
WILKES, CHARLES.
Midshipman, 1 January, 1818. Lieutenant, 28 April, 1826. Commander, 13 July, 1843. Captain, 14 September, 1855. Retired List, 21 December, 1861. Commodore on Retired List from 16 July, 1862. Rear-Admiral, Retired List, 6 August, 1866. Died 8 February, 1877.
WILKES, GILBERT.
Cadet Midshipman, 22 September, 1877. Graduated 10 June, 1881. Ensign, Junior Grade, 1 July, 1883. Ensign, 26 June, 1884. Resigned 20 February, 1891. Lieutenant (Spanish-American War), 9 May, 1898. Honorably discharged 26 August, 1898.
WILKES, JOHN, Jr.
Midshipman, 9 September, 1841. Passed Midshipman, 10 August, 1847. Resigned 3 November, 1854.
WILKINS, CHARLES R.
Acting Master, 27 March, 1862 Honorably discharged 12 December, 1865.
WILKINS, GEORGE F.
Acting Ensign, 22 May, 1863. Acting Master, 5 September, 1864. Master, 12 March, 1868. Lieutenant, 18 December, 1868. Retired List, 31 October, 1879. Died 25 June, 1882.
WILKINS, HEBER C.
Acting Third Assistant Engineer, 22 June, 1864. Honorably discharged 17 July, 1865.
WILKINS, HENRY.
Mate, 5 April, 1862. Resigned 18 March, 1863.
WILKINS, HENRY H.
Acting Assistant Surgeon, 3 October, 1864. Resigned 12 May, 1865.
WILKINS, JAMES.
Acting Second Assistant Engineer, 1 October, 1862. Honorably discharged 6 December, 1865.
WILKINS, JOHN.
Gunner, 12 January, 1853. Dismissed 23 February, 1853.
WILKINS, L. M.
Midshipman, 13 June, 1831. Resigned 5 December, 1837.
WILKINS, ROBERT M.
Assistant Engineer (Spanish-American War), 15 June, 1898. Honorably discharged 31 January, 1899.
WILKINS, WILLIAM W.
Acting Assistant Surgeon, 21 October, 1861. Resigned 22 December, 1862.
WILKINSON, ALFRED.
Acting Third Assistant Engineer, 11 January, 1864. Honorably discharged 9 December, 1865.
WILKINSON, ERNEST.
Cadet Midshipman, 19 June, 1875. Graduated 22 June, 1882. Ensign, Junior Grade, 3 March, 1883. Ensign 26 June, 1884. Resigned 30 June, 1890.
WILKINSON, G. B.
Midshipman, 1 February, 1823. Died in 1825.
WILKINSON, GEORGE W.
Third Assistant Engineer, 21 September, 1861. Resigned 22 September, 1863.
WILKINSON, H.
Master, 1 January, 1812. Last appearance on Records of Navy Department, 1815. Lake Ontario.
WILKINSON, JAMES.
Acting First Assistant Engineer, 14 November, 1861. Resigned 7 January, 1863.
WILKINSON, J. B.
Purser, 26 March, 1814. Resigned 2 June, 1829.
WILKINSON, J. B.
Midshipman, 15 November, 1799. Last appearance on Records of Navy Department.
WILKINSON, JESSE.
Midshipman, 4 July, 1805. Lieutenant, 10 April, 1810. Commander, 18 April, 1818. Captain, 11 March, 1829. Reserved List, 13 September, 1855. Died 23 March, 1861.

GENERAL NAVY REGISTER. 589

WILKINSON, JOHN.
Midshipman, 18 December, 1837. Passed Midshipman, 29 June, 1843. Master, 25 June, 1850. Lieutenant, 5 November, 1850. Dismissed 20 April, 1861.
WILKINSON, JOHN H.
Mate, 30 October, 1862. Dismissed 11 July, 1863.
WILKINSON, J. M.
Midshipman, 30 November, 1814. Resigned 6 March, 1815.
WILKINSON, RICHARD.
Acting Ensign, 28 October, 1863. Honorably discharged 22 June, 1865.
WILKINSON, ROBERT.
Acting Ensign, 1 October, 1862. Honorably discharged 9 April, 1866.
WILKINSON, S. W.
Midshipman, 1 April, 1828. Passed Midshipman, 14 June, 1834. Died 14 November, 1839.
WILKINSON, T. H.
Midshipman, 1 January, 1812. Dismissed 6 May, 1812.
WILKINSON, WILLIAM W.
Midshipman, 4 November, 1841. Passed Midshipman, 10 August, 1847. Resigned March, 1851.
WILKS, FRANK H.
Mate, 22 October, 1861. Acting Ensign, 13 January, 1863. Acting Master, recommendation of Admiral Lee, 6 September, 1864. Resigned 15 March, 1865.
WILKY, THOMAS.
Lieutenant, 25 May, 1798. Last appearance on Records of Navy Department, 15 April, 1801. Declined.
WILLARD, ANDREW.
Acting Ensign, 20 July, 1864. Honorably discharged 6 August, 1865.
WILLARD, ARTHUR L.
Naval Cadet, 7 September, 1887. Ensign, 1 July, 1893. Lieutenant, Junior Grade, 3 March, 1899. Lieutenant, 8 July, 1899.
WILLARD, CHARLES F.
Mate, 13 July, 1861. Ensign, 19 July, 1862. Resigned 25 March, 1863.
WILLARD, GEORGE J.
Midshipman, 1 May, 1822. Struck off 23 August, 1828.
WILLARD, J. M.
Acting Ensign, 8 October, 1862. Honorably discharged 22 November, 1865.
WILLARD, LEWIS H.
Acting Assistant Surgeon, 29 September, 1862. Appointment revoked 9 March, 1864.
WILLARD, ROBERT.
Acting Assistant Surgeon, 6 May, 1863. Assistant Surgeon, 1 June, 1863. Resigned 31 May, 1865.
WILLARD, WILLIAM H.
Lieutenant (Spanish-American War), 4 May, 1898. Honorably discharged 7 December, 1898.
WILLCOMB, CHARLES L.
Acting Master, 14 August, 1861. Appointment revoked 17 March, 1864. Acting Ensign, 2 June, 1864. Acting Master, 7 March, 1865. Honorably discharged 20 October, 1865.
WILLCOX, WILLIAM H.
Midshipman, 30 January, 1841. Passed Midshipman, 10 August, 1847. Master, 2 March, 1855. Lieutenant, 14 September, 1855. Resigned 20 June, 1857.
WILLCOX, WILLIAM H.
Professor, 3 June, 1858. Died 20 August, 1870.
WILLCOXEN, JOHN S.
Acting Third Assistant Engineer, 1 October, 1862. Acting Second Assistant Engineer, 6 October, 1863. Honorably discharged 12 November, 1865.
WILLES, WILLIAM S.
Assistant Surgeon, 28 March, 1868. Died 29 January, 1870.
WILLETT, SAMUEL E.
Assistant Surgeon, 24 September, 1800. Last appearance on Records of Navy Department, 31 December, 1803.
WILLETT, SILAS S.
Mate, 26 December, 1862. Acting Ensign, 11 May, 1865. Honorably discharged 27 February, 1866. Acting Ensign, 27 April, 1866. Mustered out 8 February, 1868. Mate, 6 August, 1869. Resigned 15 March, 1873.
WILLETT, STEPHEN E.
Mate, 31 December, 1861. Acting Ensign, 22 November, 1864. Appointment revoked 24 July, 1866.
WILLETT, WILLIAM M., JR.
Third Assistant Engineer, 24 December, 1853. Resigned 6 March, 1857.
WILLETT, WILLIAM M.
Mate (Spanish-American War), 12 April, 1898. Ensign, 5 May, 1898. Honorably discharged 4 February, 1899.
WILLETTS, ALBERT B.
Cadet Engineer, Naval Academy, 1 October, 1872. Graduated 30 May, 1874. Assistant Engineer, 26 February, 1875. Resigned 31 December, 1879.
WILLETTS, NICHOLAS B.
Gunner, 26 July, 1858. Acting Master, 10 July, 1863. Honorably discharged 24 October, 1865. Ensign, 12 March, 1868. Died 23 March, 1868.
WILLEY, GRANVILLE C.
Acting Third Assistant Engineer, 12 January, 1864. Resigned 16 July, 1864.
WILLEY, LEVI C.
Mate, 25 May, 1863. Died 13 September, 1863.
WILLEY, O. S.
Mate, 11 July, 1861. Dismissed 27 March, 1863.

WILLEY, WILLIAM A.
Acting First Assistant Engineer, 1 October, 1862. Honorably discharged 11 November, 1865.
WILLIAMS, ALEXANDER.
Assistant Surgeon, 28 March, 1820. Resigned 14 June, 1820.
WILLIAMS, ALFRED E.
Assistant Engineer (Spanish-American War), 27 June, 1898. Honorably discharged 26 November, 1898.
WILLIAMS, ANTHONY.
Acting Third Assistant Engineer, 21 October, 1862. Acting Second Assistant Engineer, 10 September, 1864. Honorably discharged 2 October, 1866.
WILLIAMS, ARTHUR S.
Gunner, 25 January, 1896.
WILLIAMS, AUGUSTUS P.
Acting Assistant Surgeon, 30 May, 1861. Resigned 7 June, 1861.
WILLIAMS, B. T.
Midshipman, 9 November, 1813. Resigned 19 April, 1815.
WILLIAMS, B. T.
Assistant Surgeon, 27 April, 1818. Last appearance on Records of Navy Department, 1821. Schooner Lynx.
WILLIAMS, CHARLES L.
Acting Third Assistant Engineer, 22 December, 1864. Honorably discharged 7 July, 1865.
WILLIAMS, CHARLES S.
Assistant Paymaster, 16 June, 1880. Passed Assistant Paymaster, 20 August, 1889. Paymaster, 13 June, 1895
WILLIAMS, CHARLES W.
Acting Third Assistant Engineer, 19 October, 1863. Honorably discharged 22 August, 1865.
WILLIAMS, C. HENRY.
Mate. Deserted 1 May, 1862.
WILLIAMS, CLARENCE S.
Cadet Midshipman, 25 September, 1880. Ensign, 1 July, 1886. Lieutenant, Junior Grade, 10 May, 1895. Lieutenant, 27 May, 1898.
WILLIAMS, COURTLAND P.
Acting Ensign, 30 January, 1863. Acting Master, 11 November, 1863. Honorably discharged 12 August, 1866.
WILLIAMS, EDWARD, Jr.
Carpenter, 4 November, 1852. Dismissed 12 July, 1861.
WILLIAMS, E. COURT.
Mate, 1 October, 1862. Acting Ensign, 15 February, 1864. Honorably discharged 15 September, 1865.
WILLIAMS, EDWARD P.
Midshipman 9 September, 1847. Passed Midshipman, 10 June, 1853. Master, 15 September, 1855. Lieutenant, 16 September, 1855. Lieutenant-Commander, 16 July, 1862. Commander, 25 July, 1866. Lost on the Oneida, 24 January, 1870.
WILLIAMS, FLAVIUS J.
Acting Assistant Surgeon, 18 March, 1864. Appointment revoked 24 February, 1865.
WILLIAMS, FRANK C.
Assistant Engineer (Spanish-American War), 9 May, 1898. Honorably discharged 25 January, 1899.
WILLIAMS, GEORGE.
Boatswain, 12 July, 1799. Dismissed 15 September, 1800.
WILLIAMS, GEORGE.
Acting Master, 12 August, 1861. Resigned 17 December, 1864.
WILLIAMS GEORGE.
Boatswain, 11 July, 1842. Dismissed 11 November, 1851.
WILLIAMS, GEORGE C.
Mate, 10 June, 1862. Acting Ensign, 2 December, 1863. Honorably discharged 10 November, 1865.
WILLIAMS, GEORGE M.
Midshipman, 26 September, 1863. Graduated June, 1867. Ensign, 18 December, 1868. Resigned 26 October, 1869.
WILLIAMS, GEORGE R.
Mate, 5 April, 1864. Appointment revoked (sick) 16 June, 1864.
WILLIAMS, GEORGE W.
Acting Ensign, 30 January, 1863. Honorably discharged 30 September, 1865.
WILLIAMS, GEORGE W.
Naval Cadet, 6 September, 1884. Resigned 24 June, 1886. Naval Cadet. 28 September, 1886. Ensign, 1 July, 1892. Lieutenant, Junior Grade, 3 March 1899. Lieutenant, 29 March, 1899.
WILLIAMS, HENRY.
Carpenter, 1 June, 1880. Retired List, 6 February, 1896.
WILLIAMS, HENRY.
Naval Cadet, 6 September, 1894. Graduated. Assistant Naval Constructor, 4 April, 1900.
WILLIAMS, HENRY E.
Acting Master, 22 November, 1861. Dismissed 7 October, 1862.
WILLIAMS, HENRY E.
Ensign (Spanish-American War), 2 June, 1898. Dropped 24 June, 1898.
WILLIAMS, HILARY.
Naval Cadet. 6 September, 1893. Ensign, 1 July, 1899.
WILLIAMS, JAMES.
Midshipman, 1 September, 1811. Lieutenant, 28 March, 1820. Died 14 May, 1837.

WILLIAMS, JAMES.
  Mate, 6 December, 1862. Honorably discharged 28 October, 1865.
WILLIAMS, JAMES.
  Boatswain, 14 October, 1854. Dismissed 2 April, 1855.
WILLIAMS, JAMES.
  Mate, 2 March, 1866. Resigned 24 June, 1867.
WILLIAMS, JAMES.
  Acting Second Assistant Engineer, 12 April, 1864. Honorably discharged 28 August, 1865.
WILLIAMS, JAMES.
  Mate, 3 November, 1864. Appointment revoked 25 November, 1865.
WILLIAMS, JAMES B.
  Acting Ensign, 11 March, 1863. Acting Master, 1 September, 1864. Honorably discharged 20 December, 1865.
WILLIAMS, JAMES M.
  Acting Master, 30 May, 1861. Acting Volunteer Lieutenant, 12 April, 1864. Honorably discharged 2 March, 1866. Acting Master, 6 December, 1866. Mustered out 21 March, 1867. Acting Master, 6 April, 1867. Mustered out 8 September, 1868.
WILLIAMS, JAMES S.
  Mate, 4 December, 1861. Acting Ensign, 24 November, 1862. Acting Master, 26 December, 1863. Honorably discharged 7 December, 1865.
WILLIAMS, JOHN.
  Master, 7 August, 1812. Dismissed 9 March, 1813.
WILLIAMS, JOHN.
  Mate, 26 June, 1863. Discharged 4 February, 1868.
WILLIAMS, JOHN.
  Mate, 14 April, 1862. Deserted 29 September, 1862.
WILLIAMS, JOHN.
  Mate, 26 June, 1863. Resigned (sick) 19 December, 1864.
WILLIAMS, JOHN.
  Acting Ensign, 20 August, 1863. Honorably discharged 12 October, 1865.
WILLIAMS, JOHN.
  Acting Master, 4 March, 1862. Dismissed 7 May, 1862.
WILLIAMS, JOHN A.
  Acting Ensign, 24 June, 1864. Honorably discharged 14 September, 1865.
WILLIAMS, JOHN D.
  Acting Third Assistant Engineer, 26 May, 1864. Resigned 16 March, 1865.
WILLIAMS, JOHN H.
  Mate, 15 January, 1864. Deserted 13 May, 1864.
WILLIAMS, JOHN R.
  Acting Third Assistant Engineer, 1 October, 1862. Resigned 15 May, 1863.
WILLIAMS, JULES L.
  Mate, 14 December, 1863. Honorably discharged 30 October, 1864.
WILLIAMS, J. T.
  Midshipman, 1 April, 1828. Passed Midshipman, 14 June, 1834. Resigned 13 September, 1838.
WILLIAMS, LEWIS E.
  Acting Third Assistant Engineer, 17 August, 1864. Resigned 10 January, 1865.
WILLIAMS, LEWIS J.
  Assistant Surgeon, 25 January, 1842. Surgeon, 30 August, 1856. Medical Inspector, 3 March, 1871. Medical Director, 28 May, 1871. Retired List, 14 October, 1881. Died 8 April, 1888.
WILLIAMS, LLOYD A.
  Third Assistant Engineer, 16 February, 1852. Second Assistant Engineer, 9 May, 1857. First Assistant Engineer, 2 August, 1859. Retired 20 December, 1866. Chief Engineer, Retired List, 24 July, 1867. Died 28 December, 1873.
WILLIAMS, PETER.
  Mate, 25 March, 1862. Acting Ensign, 10 January, 1863. Honorably discharged 9 November, 1867.
WILLIAMS, PHILIP.
  Naval Cadet, 4 September, 1885. Ensign, 1 July, 1891. Lieutenant, 3 March, 1899.
WILLIAMS, RICHARD.
  Acting Third Assistant Engineer, 22 June, 1863. Resigned 27 August, 1863.
WILLIAMS, R M.
  Acting Ensign, 4 June, 1863. Resigned 23 December, 1863.
WILLIAMS, RICHARD B.
  Assistant Surgeon, 17 November, 1900.
WILLIAMS, ROBERT A.
  Carpenter, 26 July, 1859. Retired List, 9 August, 1890.
WILLIAMS, STEPHEN.
  22 April, 1813. Dismissed 2 April, 1814.
WILLIAMS, THEODORE S.
  Midshipman, 27 September, 1862. Graduated June, 1866. Ensign, 12 March, 1868. Master, 26 March, 1869. Died 13 June, 1871.
WILLIAMS, THOMAS.
  Captain, 17 July, 1798. Resigned 28 May, 1799.
WILLIAMS, THOMAS.
  Acting Ensign, 16 May, 1864. Resigned 20 June, 1865.
WILLIAMS, THOMAS W.
  Acting Master, 3 April, 1862. Dismissed 17 April, 1863.
WILLIAMS, WESLEY.
  Acting Midshipman, 4 October, 1850. Dismissed 12 June, 1851.

WILLIAMS, WILLIAM.
Mate, 30 September, 1861. Acting Master, 28 March, 1862. Honorably discharged 4 December, 1868.

WILLIAMS, WILLIAM C.
Mate, 24 January, 1863. Acting Ensign, 20 March, 1865. Appointment revoked 20 April, 1865.

WILLIAMS, WILLIAM C.
Acting Ensign and Pilot, 30 October, 1864. Dismissed 18 November, 1864.

WILLIAMS, WILLIAM H.
Midshipman, 8 August, 1799. Resigned 20 August, 1799.

WILLIAMS, WILLIAM H.
Acting Ensign, 15 July, 1864. Honorably discharged 11 May, 1865.

WILLIAMS, WILLIAM H. H.
Assistant Paymaster, 6 September, 1861. Paymaster, 14 April, 1862. Resigned 31 March, 1866.

WILLIAMS, WILLIAM W.
Acting Assistant Paymaster 11 July, 1861. Assistant Paymaster, 29 August, 1861. Paymaster, 6 February, 1862. Pay Inspector, 24 October, 1871. Pay Director, 26 December, 1882. Retired List, 9 July, 1898.

WILLIAMS, YANCEY S.
Naval Cadet, 6 September 1894. Ensign, 4 April, 1900.

WILLIAMS, ZALMON T.
Acting Third Assistant Engineer, 26 August, 1863. Resigned 12 November, 1864.

WILLIAMSON, ANDREW F.
Mate, 23 May, 1862. Resigned 7 February, 1865.

WILLIAMSON, CHARLES H.
Assistant Surgeon, 24 September, 1850. Passed Assistant Surgeon, 24 September, 1855. Dismissed 10 May, 1861.

WILLIAMSON, C. L.
Midshipman, 1 September, 1811. Lieutenant, 5 March, 1817. Commander, 9 February, 1837. Cashiered 27 October, 1842.

WILLIAMSON, DAVID.
Midshipman, 11 April, 1837. Resigned 10 May, 1843.

WILLIAMSON, GABRIEL G.
Midshipman, 2 June, 1824. Passed Midshipman, 20 February, 1830. Lieutenant, 29 March, 1834. Reserved List, 13 September, 1855. Commander on Active List, 14 September, 1855. Died 17 October, 1859.

WILLIAMSON, GEORGE.
Midshipman, 8 May, 1799. Discharged 5 June, 1801, under Peace Establishment Act.

WILLIAMSON, GEORGE H.
Mate, 12 November, 1863. Resigned 31 May, 1864.

WILLIAMSON, JAMES C.
Midshipman, 7 January, 1832. Passed Midshipman, 8 July, 1839. Lieutenant, 25 November, 1844. Commander, 16 July, 1862. Captain, 10 October, 1866. Died 24 July, 1871.

WILLIAMSON, J. B.
Mate, 8 July, 1862. Dismissed 25 February, 1863.

WILLIAMSON, J. D.
Midshipman, 1 September, 1811. Lieutenant, 27 April, 1816. Commander, 9 February, 1837. Died 10 April, 1844.

WILLIAMSON, J. G.
Gunner, 20 June, 1839. Appointment revoked 26 November, 1847.

WILLIAMSON, JOHN D.
Acting Second Assistant Engineer, 2 December, 1861. Acting First Assistant Engineer, 27 July, 1863. Acting Chief Engineer, 30 July, 1864. Honorably discharged 2 October, 1865.

WILLIAMSON, J. S.
Master, 4 August, 1807. Last appearance on Records of Navy Department, 1815. New Orleans.

WILLIAMSON, THOM.
Third Assistant Engineer, 21 May, 1853. Second Assistant Engineer, 25 June, 1855. First Assistant Engineer, 23 April, 1859. Chief Engineer, 5 August, 1861. Retired List, 5 August, 1895.

WILLIAMSON, THOMAS.
Assistant Surgeon, 27 May, 1818. Died 12 January, 1859.

WILLIAMSON, V. L.
Midshipman, 12 March, 1832. Died 6 September, 1834.

WILLIAMSON, WILLIAM.
Assistant Surgeon, 28 March, 1820. Resigned 2 November, 1827.

WILLIAMSON, WILLIAM C.
Third Assistant Engineer, 19 February, 1861. Second Assistant Engineer, 16 January, 1863. First Assistant Engineer, 1 December, 1864. Resigned 10 January, 1866.

WILLIAMSON, WILLIAM P.
Chief Engineer, 20 October, 1842. Name stricken from the Rolls 6 May, 1861.

WILLIAMSON, W. S.
Midshipman, 2 February, 1829. Resigned 29 June, 1836.

WILLIS, CLARENCE C.
Cadet Engineer, 1 October, 1878. Assistant Engineer, 1 July, 1884. Retired List, 28 June, 1890. Died 11 June, 1895.

WILLIS, ELIAS.
Midshipman, 4 June, 1799. Last appearance on Records of Navy Department, 24 June, 1799. Lost at sea.

WILLIS, FOSTER.
Acting Master, 22 January, 1862. Resigned 24 April, 1865.
WILLIS, GEORGE R.
Boatswain, 22 October, 1878. Retired List, 21 September, 1882. Died 7 December, 1884.
WILLIS, HENRY.
Midshipman, 10 September, 1841. Dismissed 28 August, 1849.
WILLIS, ROBERT.
Lieutenant, 14 February, 1799. Last appearance on Records of Navy Department, 3 May, 1800.
WILLIS, THOMAS N.
Midshipman, 13 August, 1799. Last appearance on Records of Navy Department, 3 December, 1800. Furloughed.
WILLISON, CHARLES.
Midshipman, 2 January, 1800. Resigned 5 July, 1803.
WILLISS, JOHN W.
Midshipman, 1 May, 1825. Resigned 7 October, 1831.
WILLISTON, JOHN.
Carpenter, 17 November, 1831. Resigned 14 October, 1836.
WILLISTON, JOSEPH.
Master, 26 November, 1814. Died 14 April, 1833.
WILLITS, ALBERT B.
Cadet Engineer, 1 October, 1872. Assistant Engineer, 26 February, 1875. Passed Assistant Engineer, 12 October, 1881. Chief Engineer, 28 March, 1896. Rank changed to Lieutenant-Commander, 3 March, 1899.
WILLITS, GEORGE S.
Cadet Engineer, Naval Academy, 1 October, 1873. Graduated 21 June, 1875. Assistant Engineer, 1 July, 1877. Passed Assistant Engineer, 1 July, 1885. Chief Engineer, 4 July, 1896. Rank changed to Lieutenant-Commander, 3 March, 1899.
WILLITSON, JOSEPH.
Midshipman, 5 June, 1799. Resigned 15 August, 1801.
WILLITSON, JOSEPH.
Midshipman, 11 June, 1799. Last appearance on Records of Navy Department, 28 November, 1800. Furloughed.
WILLMUTH, GEORGE.
Boatswain, 16 September, 1841. Retired List, 21 December, 1861. Died 5 August, 1873.
WILLMUTH, JOHN A. H.
Mate, 25 August, 1862. Acting Ensign, 19 September, 1865. Honorably discharged 9 January, 1869. Mate, 20 April, 1870. Died 28 February, 1891.
WILLSON, JOHN.
Assistant Surgeon, 30 July, 1861. Resigned 14 July, 1862.
WILLSON, WILLIAM G. G.
Assistant Surgeon, 9 December, 1839. Resigned 8 September, 1843.
WILLSON, WILLIAM G. G.
Assistant Surgeon, 1 December, 1876. Passed Assistant Surgeon, 7 August, 1880. Died 23 January, 1889.
WILLSON, WILLIAM H.
Acting Assistant Surgeon, 1 October, 1862. Resigned 9 September, 1864.
WILMAR, JAMES.
Boatswain, 9 June, 1803. Dismissed 18 June, 1807.
WILMER, ABRAHAM.
Midshipman, 4 April, 1799. Resigned 10 February, 1800.
WILMER, EMMANUEL.
Midshipman, 1 June, 1808. Resigned 18 September, 1812.
WILMER, JAMES P.
Midshipman, 27 December, 1802. Lieutenant, 16 February, 1809. Killed in action 28 March, 1814.
WILMER, J. B. B.
Chaplain, 7 March, 1839. Resigned 23 July, 1844.
WILMER, JOSEPH R.
Cadet Engineer, Naval Academy, 1 October, 1874. Graduated 20 June, 1878. Assistant Engineer, 20 June, 1880. Passed Assistant Engineer, 10 January, 1891. Retired List, 4 April, 1892.
WILMOTT, JAMES W.
Lieutenant, Junior Grade (Spanish-American War), 1 June, 1898. Honorably discharged 4 January, 1899.
WILNER, FRANK A.
Midshipman, 30 June, 1869. Graduated 31 May, 1873. Ensign, 16 July, 1874. Master, 25 March, 1880. Lieutenant, Junior Grade, 3 March, 1883. Lieutenant, 13 May, 1886. Lieutenant-Commander, 3 March, 1899.
WILSON, ALBERT.
Acting Master, 29 October, 1861. Appointment revoked (sick) 18 February, 1862.
WILSON, ALEXANDER W.
Midshipman, 27 November, 1825. Resigned 13 June, 1829.
WILSON, ANDREW.
Gunner, 24 September, 1859. Dismissed 8 January, 1866.
WILSON, ANDREW.
Acting Second Assistant Engineer, 4 September, 1863. Resigned 15 June, 1865.
WILSON, BENJAMIN F.
Acting Assistant Surgeon, 15 August, 1861. Resigned 18 February, 1864.
WILSON, BENJAMIN T.
Midshipman, 15 October, 1834. Dismissed 10 January, 1838.
WILSON, BRYCE.
Acting Third Assistant Engineer, 22 November, 1862. Acting Second Assistant Engineer, 28 December, 1863. Honorably discharged 30 December, 1868.

WILSON, BYRON.
Acting Midshipman, 31 January, 1853. Midshipman, 10 June, 1857. Passed Midshipman 25 June, 1860. Master, 24 October, 1860. Lieutenant, 16 April, 1861. Lieutenant-Commander, 5 November, 1863. Commander, 20 January, 1872. Captain, 23 April, 1883. Retired List, 24 February, 1893. Died 6 September, 1893.

WILSON, CÆSAR R.
Midshipman, 30 November, 1814. Resigned 31 December, 1816. Master, 1 January, 1817. Died November, 1820.

WILSON, CHARLES.
Acting Ensign, 21 June, 1864. Honorably discharged 19 October, 1868. Mate, 25 January, 1870. Retired List, 10 February, 1899.

WILSON, CHARLES HOWARD.
Acting Third Assistant Engineer, 14 July, 1864. Died 24 April, 1865.

WILSON, CHARLES H.
Acting Third Assistant Engineer, 3 January, 1865. Honorably discharged 2 October, 1865.

WILSON, CHARLES W.
Acting Master, 23 April, 1862. Acting Volunteer Lieutenant, 3 February, 1864. Honorably discharged 12 November, 1866.

WILSON, DAVID.
Mate, 29 April, 1864. Appointment revoked 9 August, 1865.

WILSON, DOWNS L.
Midshipman, 22 June, 1867. Graduated 6 June, 1871. Ensign, 14 July, 1872. Master, 21 September, 1876. Lieutenant, Junior Grade, 3 March, 1883. Lieutenant, 1 December, 1884. Retired List, 4 November, 1895.

WILSON, FLETCHER A.
Third Assistant Engineer, 26 August, 1859. Second Assistant Engineer, 21 October, 1861. First Assistant Engineer, 1 October, 1863. Chief Engineer, 5 March, 1871. Retired List, 7 February, 1898.

WILSON, GEORGE.
Acting Assistant Paymaster, 3 August, 1861. Resigned 19 October, 1861.

WILSON, GEORGE B.
Assistant Surgeon, 1 February, 1889. Passed Assistant Surgeon, 1 February, 1892. Surgeon, 8 February, 1900.

WILSON, GEORGE M.
Master, 24 July, 1812. Resigned 20 May, 1818.

WILSON, GEORGE T.
Acting First Assistant Engineer, 28 November, 1863. Honorably discharged 4 November, 1865.

WILSON, GEORGE W.
Mate, 9 July, 1863. Honorably discharged 13 May, 1865. Mate, 25 July, 1866. Discharged 23 April, 1867.

WILSON, GEORGE W.
Acting Assistant Surgeon, 25 September, 1862. Died 24 September, 1864.

WILSON, G. P.
Gunner, 24 July, 1827. Dropped.

WILSON, HENRY.
Acting Master, 18 November, 1862. Resigned 3 March, 1863.

WILSON, HENRY.
Midshipman, 2 October, 1847. Passed Midshipman, 10 June, 1853. Master, 15 September, 1855. Lieutenant, 16 September, 1855. Lieutenant-Commander, 16 July, 1862. Commander, 30 April, 1867. Captain, 9 May, 1878. Retired List, 30 March, 1889. Died 27 December, 1894.

WILSON, HENRY.
Acting Third Assistant Engineer, 13 February, 1865. Honorably discharged 9 August, 1866.

WILSON, HENRY.
Purser, 17 June, 1846. Resigned 11 February, 1851.

WILSON, HENRY B.
Cadet Midshipman, 22 September, 1876. Ensign, Junior Grade, 1 July, 1883. Ensign, 26 June, 1884. Lieutenant, Junior Grade, 2 February, 1894. Lieutenant, 16 September, 1897.

WILSON, HENRY D.
Assistant Surgeon, 22 April, 1892. Passed Assistant Surgeon, 22 April, 1895.

WILSON, HORATIO R.
Midshipman, 17 April, 1862. Graduated June, 1866. Ensign, 12 March, 1868. Master, 26 March, 1869. Lieutenant, 21 March, 1870. Died 23 January, 1875.

WILSON, JACOB.
Acting Second Assistant Engineer, 5 June, 1863. Appointment revoked (sick) 26 June, 1863. Acting First Assistant Engineer, 19 February, 1864. Appointment revoked (sick) 18 July, 1864.

WILSON, JAMES.
Midshipman, 2 April, 1804. Lieutenant, 19 May, 1812. Last appearance on Records of Navy Department, 1814.

WILSON, JAMES.
Midshipman, 18 May, 1809. Appointment revoked 24 July, 1809.

WILSON, JAMES.
Acting Third Assistant Engineer, 19 September, 1864. Honorably discharged 25 July, 1865.

WILSON, JAMES.
Acting Assistant Surgeon, 1 September, 1863. Assistant Surgeon, 21 June, 1864. Wholly retired 24 April, 1866.

WILSON, JAMES.
Acting Ensign, 12 November, 1863. Dismissed 18 July, 1864.

GENERAL NAVY REGISTER. 595

WILSON, JAMES.
Boatswain, 8 August, 1866. Dismissed 8 April, 1871.
WILSON, JAMES.
Mate, 21 May. 1863. Acting Ensign, 30 August, 1865. Honorably discharged 9 November, 1868.
WILSON, JAMES.
Mate, 1 October, 1864. Appointment revoked 28 September, 1866.
WILSON, JAMES.
Mate, 3 November, 1865. Appointment revoked 2 August, 1866.
WILSON, JAMES.
Acting Warrant Machinist, 23 August, 1899.
WILSON, JAMES H.
Acting Third Assistant Engineer, 28 February, 1865. Honorably discharged 12 February, 1869.
WILSON, JAMES L.
Acting Ensign, 10 December, 1864. Honorably discharged 15 September, 1865.
WILSON, JAMES P.
Midshipman, 1 January, 1817. Lieutenant, 28 April, 1826. Commander, 3 November, 1842. Died 13 March, 1848.
WILSON, JAMES R.
Purser, 25 April, 1812. Last appearance on Records of Navy Department, 1815. Furloughed.
WILSON, JAMES. W.
Acting Assistant Surgeon, 3 February, 1865. Honorably discharged 9 October, 1865.
WILSON, JARVIS.
Acting Ensign and Pilot, 26 November, 1864. Honorably discharged 4 October, 1865.
WILSON, JOHN.
Acting First Assistant Engineer, 3 May, 1864. Honorably discharged 13 October, 1865.
WILSON, JOHN.
Third Assistant Engineer, 19 February, 1861. Second Assistant Engineer, 17 December, 1862. Resigned 19 May, 1866.
WILSON, JOHN A.
Acting Second Assistant Engineer, 19 July, 1864. Honorably discharged 19 September, 1865.
WILSON, JOHN A.
Acting Master and Pilot, 1 January, 1865. Honorably discharged 1 August, 1865.
WILSON, JOHN C.
Midshipman, 20 July, 1865. Graduated June, 1869. Ensign, 12 July, 1870. Master, 9 December, 1871. Lieutenant, 3 February, 1875. Lieutenant-Commander, 5 January, 1897. Commander, 29 December, 1899.
WILSON, JOHN H.
Mate, 7 November, 1863. Resigned 17 October, 1864.
WILSON, JOHN H.
Acting Third Assistant Engineer, 22 November, 1864. Honorably discharged 27 October, 1865.
WILSON, JOHN H.
Mate, 13 June, 1865. Honorably discharged 7 September, 1865.
WILSON, JOHN J.
Acting Second Assistant Engineer, 27 December, 1864. Honorably discharged 1 December, 1865.
WILSON, JOHN K.
Midshipman, 3 March, 1841. Passed Midshipman, 10 August, 1847. Master, 14 September, 1855. Lieutenant, 15 September, 1855. Resigned 9 May, 1856.
WILSON, JOHN L.
Acting Second Assistant Engineer, 4 March, 1863. Dismissed 17 October, 1863.
WILSON, JOHN O.
Midshipman, 2 February, 1829. Resigned 1 July, 1836.
WILSON, JOHN S.
Gunner, date not known. Last appearance on Records of Navy Department, 1815. Brig Firefly.
WILSON, JOSEPH.
Purser, 24 July, 1813. Retired List, 21 December, 1861. Pay Director on Retired List, 3 March, 1871. Died 19 June, 1875.
WILSON, JOSEPH.
Sailmaker, 12 April, 1870. Died 7 August, 1889.
WILSON, JOSEPH.
Assistant Surgeon, 13 May, 1843. Surgeon, 23 May, 1857. Medical Inspector, 3 March, 1871. Medical Director, 26 April, 1872. Retired List, 6 January, 1878. Died 1 March, 1887.
WILSON, JOSIAH M.
Midshipman, 21 September, 1861. Graduated October, 1865. Ensign, 1 December, 1866. Master, 12 March, 1868. Retired List, 7 March, 1870. Died 29 October, 1871.
WILSON, MASON.
Midshipman, 1 January, 1818. Died 31 October, 1822.
WILSON, MATT. H.
Mate, 7 December, 1861. Resigned 8 March, 1865.
WILSON, MILES.
Carpenter, 21 March, 1838. Resigned 6 September, 1838.
WILSON, NATHANIEL.
Purser, 6 October, 1829. Died 26 October, 1849.
WILSON, RICHARD A.
Midshipman, 2 January, 1804. Resigned 6 December, 1805.
WILSON, RICHARD C.
Assistant Engineer (Spanish-American War), 20 May, 1898. Honorably discharged 15 September, 1898.

WILSON, ROBERT H.
Acting Midshipman, 18 June, 1850. Resigned 14 December, 1850.
WILSON, SAMUEL L.
Midshipman, 20 September, 1861. Graduated November, 1864. Ensign, 1 November, 1866. Master, 1 December, 1866. Lieutenant, 12 March, 1868. Lieutenant-Commander, 31 December, 1869. Died 1 August, 1879.
WILSON, STEPHEN.
Midshipman, 15 November, 1809. Dismissed 3 May, 1813.
WILSON, STEPHEN B.
Midshipman, 1 January, 1812. Lieutenant, 13 January, 1825. Commander, 8 September, 1841. Captain, 14 September, 1855. Died 15 March, 1863.
WILSON, THEODORE D.
Carpenter, 3 August, 1861. Resigned 24 May, 1866. Assistant Naval Constructor, 17 May, 1866. Naval Constructor, 1 July, 1873. Died 29 June, 1896.
WILSON, THOMAS.
Boatswain, 27 July, 1799. Last appearance on Records of Navy Department, 29 July, 1799.
WILSON, THOMAS.
Mate, 15 October, 1863. Appointment revoked 5 January, 1867.
WILSON, THOMAS E.
Acting Third Assistant Engineer, 4 November, 1863. Honorably discharged 12 August, 1865.
WILSON, THOMAS P.
Midshipman, 20 September, 1861. Graduated October, 1865. Ensign, 1 December, 1866. Master, 12 March, 1868. Lieutenant, 26 March, 1869. Retired List, 2 August, 1873. Died 10 March, 1877.
WILSON, THOMAS R.
Midshipman, 22 January, 1816. Killed in 1821.
WILSON, THOMAS R.
Gunner, 31 January, 1853. Retired List, 13 July, 1889. Died 25 July, 1897.
WILSON, THOMAS S.
Midshipman, 7 April, 1862. Graduated November, 1864. Resigned 28 August, 1865.
WILSON, THOMAS S.
Naval Cadet, 20 May, 1889. Ensign, 1 July, 1895. Lieutenant, Junior Grade, 3 March, 1899.
WILSON, WALTER L.
Assistant Paymaster, 15 March, 1894. Passed Assistant Paymaster, 13 June, 1895. Paymaster, 6 June, 1899.
WILSON, W. G. G.
Assistant Surgeon, 9 December, 1839. Resigned 8 September, 1843.
WILSON, WILLIAM.
Gunner, 10 June, 1861. Retired List, 22 April, 1889. Died 20 January, 1896.
WILSON, WILLIAM.
Midshipman, 1 January, 1808. (See Marine Corps.)
WILSON, WILLIAM A.
Acting Assistant Surgeon, 1 October, 1862. Resigned 9 September, 1864.
WILSON, WILLIAM E.
Mate, 2 September, 1864. Resigned 3 May, 1865.
WILSON, WILLIAM J.
Cadet Midshipman, 22 September, 1879. Graduated. Honorably discharged 30 June, 1885. Lieutenant (Spanish-American War), 14 May, 1898. Honorably discharged 14 January, 1899.
WILTBANK, JAMES.
Chaplain, 30 September, 1833. Resigned 12 October, 1833. Chaplain, 25 February, 1837. Died 19 March, 1842.
WILTON, RICHARD W.
Acting Third Assistant Engineer, 2 September, 1864. Honorably discharged 19 July, 1865.
WILTSE, GILBERT C.
Acting Midshipman, 20 September, 1855. Midshipman, 9 June, 1859. Lieutenant, 31 August, 1861. Lieutenant-Commander, 6 January, 1866. Commander, 8 November, 1873. Captain, 26 January, 1887. Died 26 April, 1893.
WILTSEE, ISAAC P.
Mate, 6 June, 1863. Acting Ensign, 4 November, 1864. Honorably discharged 30 November, 1865.
WILTZ, ALEXANDER.
Mate, 30 August, 1864. Drowned 27 August, 1864.
WILTZE, ROBERT.
Mate, 18 January, 1868. Mustered out 12 March, 1869.
WINANS, GEORGE W.
Acting Assistant Paymaster, 30 October, 1863. Drowned 1864.
WINANS, HERMAN W.
Acting Third Assistant Engineer, 8 May, 1863. Appointment revoked (sick) 18 June, 1864.
WINANS, JOHN.
Midshipman, 1 July, 1825. Died 31 January, 1831.
WINANS, NELSON.
Acting Chief Engineer, 9 March, 1863. Honorably discharged 28 September, 1865.
WINANT, WILLIAM E.
Acting Carpenter, 10 January, 1900.
WINCH, THOMAS G.
Midshipman, 20 September, 1872. Graduated 20 June, 1876. Died 8 January, 1879.
WINCHELL, WARD P.
Cadet Engineer, 1 October, 1878. Assistant Engineer, 1 July, 1884. Passed Assistant Engineer, 21 March, 1895. Rank changed to Lieutenant, 3 March, 1899.

GENERAL NAVY REGISTER. 597

WINCHESTER, FELIX.
Acting Midshipman, 25 October, 1849. Dropped 3 September, 1850.
WINCHESTER, JOHN F.
Acting Master, 9 August, 1861. Honorably discharged 30 September, 1865.
WINCHESTER, J. O.
Acting Ensign, 27 July, 1863. Honorably discharged 9 August, 1865. Acting Ensign, 11 December, 1866. Mustered out 27 March, 1869.
WINCHESTER, WILLIAM.
Boatswain, 28 October, 1858. Dismissed 17 October, 1863. Acting Boatswain, 31 July, 1869. Appointment revoked 20 December, 1869. Acting Boatswain, 21 November, 1873. Appointment revoked 11 July, 1874.
WINDER, EDWARD L.
Midshipman, 29 April, 1836. Passed Midshipman, 1 July, 1842. Master, 25 October, 1849. Lieutenant, 20 April, 1850. Dismissed 22 April, 1861.
WINDER, LEVIN W.
Midshipman, 3 June, 1799. Resigned 25 March, 1801.
WINDER, THOMAS JONES.
Surgeon, 24 September, 1799. Resigned, date not known.
WINDER, WILLIAM.
Midshipman, 21 September, 1869. Graduated 31 May, 1873. Ensign, 16 July, 1874. Master, 23 November, 1880. Lieutenant, Junior Grade, 3 March, 1883. Lieutenant, 23 May, 1886. Lieutenant-Commander, 3 March, 1899.
WINDSOR, WILLIAM AUGUSTUS.
Third Assistant Engineer, 16 September, 1862. Second Assistant Engineer, 1 March, 1864. First Assistant Engineer, 1 January, 1868. Chief Engineer, 17 June, 1889. Rank changed to Commander, 3 March, 1899.
WINES, CHARLES.
Acting Third Assistant Engineer, 24 February, 1863. Acting Second Assistant Engineer, 1 March, 1864. Appointment revoked (sick) 22 September, 1864.
WING, FRANK H.
Mate, 21 February, 1865. Honorably discharged 10 September, 1868. Mate, 18 January, 1870. Appointment revoked 8 April, 1873.
WING, GEORGE E.
Acting Ensign, 21 August, 1863. Appointment revoked 9 March, 1866.
WING, JAMES.
Acting Assistant Paymaster, 8 February, 1862. Resigned 13 August, 1862.
WING, WILLIAM.
Acting Ensign, 28 April, 1864. Honorably discharged 27 October, 1865.
WINGATE, GEORGE E.
Acting Ensign, 31 October, 1863. Master, 12 March, 1868. Lieutenant, 18 December, 1868. Lieutenant-Commander, 13 July, 1870. Commander, 26 May, 1887. Retired List, 13 June, 1897. Died 7 June, 1897.
WINGATE, HENRY T.
Midshipman, 13 December, 1831. Passed Midshipman, 15 June, 1837. Lieutenant, 8 September, 1841. Died 4 May, 1854.
WINGATE, JAMES W.
Sailmaker, 17 January, 1876. Died 10 March, 1894.
WINGATE, JOHN D.
Mate, 9 December, 1862. Honorably discharged 25 November, 1865.
WINGATE, WILLIAM H.
Acting Third Assistant Engineer, 14 October, 1864. Honorably discharged 20 October, 1867.
WINGERD, GEORGE B.
Midshipman, 1 March, 1825. Dismissed by Court-martial 6 November, 1828.
WINGET, DANIEL.
Mate, 31 March, 1863. Resigned 22 March, 1864.
WINGOOD, WILLIAM, Jr.
Mate, 28 August, 1862. Acting Ensign, 21 September, 1864. Honorably discharged 1 November, 1865.
WINLOCK, JAMES H.
Midshipman, 25 September, 1868. Graduated 1 June, 1872. Died 2 March, 1873.
WINLOCK, JOSEPH.
Professor, 26 June, 1856. Resigned 1 May, 1866.
WINN, CHARLES F.
Midshipman, 1 January, 1818. Died 3 May, 1820.
WINN, EDWARD A.
Mate, 17 August, 1866. Mustered out 4 September, 1868.
WINN, JOHN K.
Mate, 8 September, 1862. Acting Ensign, 2 June, 1863. Acting Master, 6 August, 1864. Acting Volunteer Lieutenant, 27 July, 1865. Master, 12 March, 1868. Lieutenant, 18 December, 1868. Lieutenant-Commander, 11 December, 1877. Commander, 31 March, 1888. Retired List, 31 August, 1895.
WINN, MINOR.
Midshipman, 16 January, 1806. Resigned 8 May, 1809.
WINN, TIMOTHY.
Purser, 17 May, 1815. Died 18 February, 1836.
WINN, JOSEPH.
Acting Volunteer Lieutenant, 28 September, 1861. Resigned 24 July, 1862.
WINNEMORE, EDWARD.
Acting Ensign, 6 June, 1864. Died of wounds at Fort Fisher, 24 December, 1864.
WINRAM, JOHN.
Mate, 9 June, 1863. Honorably discharged 3 October, 1865.
WINRAM, SAMUEL R.
Mate, 24 January, 1863. Resigned 31 May, 1864.

GENERAL NAVY REGISTER.

WINSHIP, ALVIN A.
Acting Second Assistant Engineer, 25 August, 1864. Honorably discharged 21 July, 1865.

WINSHIP, AMOS
Surgeon, 12 September, 1799. Last appearance on Records of Navy Department, 11 August, 1800.

WINSHIP, EMORY.
Naval Cadet, 3 June, 1890. Assistant Engineer, 1 July, 1896. Rank changed to Ensign, 3 March, 1899. Lieutenant, Junior Grade, 1 July, 1899.

WINSHIP, E. K.
Acting Assistant Paymaster, 18 December, 1862. Resigned 11 November, 1864.

WINSHIP, THOMAS.
Acting Third Assistant Engineer, 28 May, 1862. Acting Second Assistant Engineer, 27 November, 1863. Resigned 16 March, 1865.

WINSLOW, CAMERON McR.
Midshipman, 29 September, 1870. Graduated 21 June, 1875. Ensign, 18 July, 1876. Master, 21 December, 1881. Lieutenant, Junior Grade, 3 March, 1883. Lieutenant, 1 July, 1888. Lieutenant-Commander, 3 March, 1899.

WINSLOW, EDWARD D.
Acting Assistant Surgeon, 1 October, 1862. Appointment revoked 18 November, 1863.

WINSLOW, EZRA D.
Chaplain, 10 March, 1863. Wholly retired from service 11 January, 1869.

WINSLOW, FRANCIS.
Midshipman, 8 July, 1833. Passed Midshipman, 8 June, 1839. Lieutenant, 24 November, 1844. Commander, 6 May, 1862. Died 26 August, 1862.

WINSLOW, FRANCIS.
Midshipman, 26 July, 1865. Graduated 7 June, 1870. Ensign, 13 July, 1871. Master, 7 October, 1874. Lieutenant, 17 May, 1881. Retired List, 14 March, 1889.

WINSLOW, GEORGE F.
Mate, 25 January, 1862. Acting Ensign, 23 May, 1863. Acting Master, 14 January, 1864. Honorably discharged 5 January, 1868. Lieutenant (Spanish-American War), 12 July, 1898. Honorably discharged 26 November, 1898.

WINSLOW, GEORGE F.
Acting Assistant Surgeon, 26 July, 1862. Assistant Surgeon, 28 May, 1864. Passed Assistant Surgeon, 14 June, 1867. Surgeon, 2 April, 1875. Medical Inspector, 21 August, 1893. Medical Director, 23 January, 1898.

WINSLOW, HENRY A.
Mate, 26 August, 1863. Acting Ensign, 31 October, 1864. Honorably discharged 28 August, 1865.

WINSLOW, HERBERT.
Midshipman, 20 July, 1865. Graduated June, 1869. Ensign, 12 July, 1870. Master, 1 April, 1872. Lieutenant, 3 May, 1875. Lieutenant-Commander, 6 April, 1897. Commander, 27 March, 1900.

WINSLOW, JOHN A.
Midshipman, 1 February, 1827. Passed Midshipman, 10 June, 1833. Lieutenant, 9 December, 1839. Commander, 14 September, 1855. Captain, 16 July, 1862. Commodore, 19 June, 1864. Rear Admiral, 2 March, 1870. Died 29 September, 1873.

WINSLOW, J. C.
Acting Master's Mate, 2 October, 1863. Resignation accepted 26 May, 1865.

WINSLOW, WILLIAM H.
Mate, 28 June, 1862. Acting Ensign, 3 October, 1862. Acting Master, 12 September, 1863. Honorably discharged 26 October, 1865.

WINSLOW, WILLIAM R.
Acting Assistant Paymaster, 24 December, 1862. Assistant Paymaster, 2 July, 1864. Paymaster 4 May, 1866. Died 25 February, 1869.

WINSOR, GUSTAVUS A.
Acting Ensign, 14 August, 1863. Appointment revoked (sick) 8 June, 1864.

WINSOR, HORACE E.
Third Assistant Engineer, 21 May, 1853. Second Assistant Engineer, 27 July, 1855. Resigned 20 August, 1856.

WINSTON, JOHN L.
Acting First Assistant Engineer, 13 August, 1863. Honorably discharged 20 November, 1865.

WINSTON, HOLLIS T.
Naval Cadet, 5 September, 1896. Graduated 30 June, 1900.

WINTER, ASA C.
Acting Assistant Paymaster, 1 August, 1861. Died 28 June, 1864.

WINTER, JAMES.
Acting Assistant Paymaster, 10 October, 1863. Mustered out 12 October, 1865.

WINTER, RICHARD.
Midshipman, 15 November, 1809. Lieutenant, 9 December, 1814. Died January, 1819.

WINTER, WALTER.
Midshipman, 22 March, 1799. Lieutenant, 26 April, 1809. Last appearance on Records of Navy Department, 1 June, 1813. Drowned.

WINTERHALTER, ALBERT G.
Cadet Midshipman, 24 September, 1873. Midshipman, 18 June, 1879. Ensign, 11 July, 1880. Lieutenant, Junior Grade, 14 December, 1886. Lieutenant, 30 June, 1892. Lieutenant-Commander, 18 January, 1900.

WINTERS, JAMES F.
Acting Third Assistant Engineer, 22 October, 1863. Honorably discharged 23 October, 1865.

WINTON, DAVID L.
Acting Third Assistant Engineer, 21 July, 1863. Resigned 30 January, 1864.

GENERAL NAVY REGISTER. 599

WINTON, J. L.
    Mate, 24 September, 1861. Dismissed 21 April, 1862. Acting Ensign, 29 June, 1863. Dismissed 17 October, 1873.
WIRT, WILLIAM E.
    Cadet Midshipman, 25 September, 1880. Graduated. Honorably discharged 30 June, 1886. Lieutenant, Junior Grade (Spanish-American War), 15 June, 1898. Lieutenant, 28 December, 1898. Honorably discharged 29 December, 1898.
WISE, EDWARD E.
    Midshipman, 5 June, 1871. Graduated 20 June, 1876. Resigned 1 September, 1880.
WISE, FRANCIS.
    Midshipman, 25 August, 1802. Dismissed 22 December, 1803.
WISE, FREDERICK M.
    Midshipman, 23 September, 1862. Graduated June, 1867. Ensign, 18 December, 1868. Master, 21 March, 1870. Lieutenant, 21 March, 1871. Lieutenant-Commander, 25 June, 1891. Commander, 7 November, 1897.
WISE, GEORGE E.
    Acting Ensign, 28 November, 1864. Resigned 22 May, 1865.
WISE, GEORGE S.
    Purser, 25 April, 1812. Died 20 November, 1824.
WISE, HENRY A.
    Midshipman, 8 February, 1834. Passed Midshipman, 16 July, 1840. Master, 31 October, 1846. Lieutenant, 25 February, 1847. Commander, 16 July, 1862. Captain, 29 December, 1866. Died 2 April, 1869.
WISE, JOHN.
    Assistant Surgeon, 10 December, 1814. Resigned 24 August, 1818.
WISE, JOHN.
    Acting Assistant Surgeon, 1 October, 1862. Resigned 4 June, 1864.
WISE, JOHN C.
    Assistant Surgeon, 28 April, 1870. Passed Assistant Surgeon, 10 June, 1874. Surgeon, 10 September, 1882. Medical Inspector, 20 March, 1896. Medical Director, 7 February, 1900.
WISE, WILLIAM C.
    Acting Midshipman, 29 September, 1860. Ensign, 1 October, 1863. Master, 10 May, 1866. Lieutenant, 21 February, 1867. Lieutenant-Commander, 12 March, 1868. Commander, 24 February, 1881. Captain, 11 November, 1894.
WISE, WILLIAM C., JR.
    Naval Cadet (Spanish-American War), 9 July, 1898. Honorably discharged 7 October, 1898.
WISH, JOHN A.
    Midshipman, 7 December, 1810. Lieutenant, 27 April, 1816. Died 25 October, 1833.
WISHART, ALEXANDER.
    Acting Midshipman, 2 October, 1850. Resigned 22 March, 1851.
WISNER, GEORGE.
    Carpenter, 30 December, 1841. Died 24 March, 1866.
WISNER, HENRY C.
    Midshipman, 17 April, 1862. Graduated June, 1866. Ensign, 12 March, 1868. Master, 26 March, 1869. Lieutenant, 21 March, 1870. Resigned 17 April, 1873.
WISNER, ROBERT.
    Mate, 22 May, 1862. Died 28 June, 1864.
WISSING, HERMAN.
    Mate, 20 February, 1864. Resigned 8 May, 1865.
WISTER, OWEN J.
    Assistant Surgeon, 6 March, 1848. Resigned 24 July, 1852.
WISWALL, WILLIAM J.
    Midshipman, 1 January, 1825. Resigned 7 February, 1827.
WITHAM, THOMAS A.
    Acting Ensign, 29 December, 1863. Honorably discharged 2 October, 1865.
WITHERBEE, JOHN J.
    Acting Assistant Surgeon, 7 January, 1863. Died 30 August, 1863.
WITHERELL, A. D.
    Acting Third Assistant Engineer, 27 July, 1863. Acting Second Assistant Engineer, 2 May, 1864. Appointment revoked (sick), 20 April, 1865.
WITHERELL, J. B.
    Midshipman, 10 March, 1820. Died 20 October, 1822.
WITHERS, J. FRANCIS.
    Acting Third Assistant Engineer, 2 November, 1864. Honorably discharged 4 December, 1865.
WITHERSPOON, DAVID.
    Midshipman, 11 December, 1799. Resigned 1 January, 1801.
WITHERSPOON, EDWARD T.
    Naval Cadet, 28 September, 1882. Ensign, 1 July, 1888. Lieutenant, Junior Grade, 29 January, 1897. Lieutenant, 3 March, 1899.
WITHERSPOON, JOHN.
    Midshipman, 5 February, 1800. Discharged 12 October, 1801, under Peace Establishment Act.
WITHINGTON, SAMUEL L.
    Mate, 19 November, 1861. Resigned 13 February, 1865.
WITHINGTON, SUMNER.
    Acting Master, 29 October, 1861. Resigned 31 December, 1863.
WITZEL, HORACE M.
    Cadet Midshipman, 5 June, 1873. Graduated 18 June, 1879. Ensign, 18 March, 1880. Lieutenant, Junior Grade, 9 November, 1886. Lieutenant, 29 May, 1892. Lieutenant-Commander, 31 December, 1899.

WIXON, OSCAR F.
Mate, 17 December, 1862. Acting Ensign, 31 December, 1863. Resigned 10 May, 1865.
WOART, WILLIAM.
Midshipman, 29 September, 1863. Graduated June, 1868. Drowned 18 June, 1869.
WOGAN, MICHAEL.
Boatswain, 21 October, 1889. Chief Boatswain, 21 October, 1899.
WOLBERT, FREDERICK G.
Midshipman, 18 June, 1812. Lieutenant, 28 March, 1820. Cashiered 17 September, 1825.
WOLCOTT, CHRISTOPHER C.
Civil Engineer, 26 October, 1881.
WOLCOTT, OLIVER S.
Midshipman, 1 January, 1818. Resigned 13 March, 1819.
WOLD, LAURITZ.
Acting Ensign, 3 August, 1863. Honorably discharged 16 September, 1865.
WOLFE, HENRY.
Mate, 16 February, 1864. Honorably discharged 12 August, 1865.
WOLFENDEN, JOHN.
Master, 27 June, 1812. Discharged 10 June, 1815.
WOLFF, CHARLES.
Acting Third Assistant Engineer, 20 October, 1863. Honorably discharged 29 August, 1865.
WOLFLEY, LEWIS.
Assistant Surgeon, 21 June, 1832. Passed Assistant Surgeon, 8 November, 1836. Surgeon, 29 July, 1841. Died 31 July, 1844.
WOLSTENHOLME, JOHN.
Mate, 21 January, 1864. Resigned 10 May, 1865.
WOOD, ALBERT N.
Cadet Midshipman, 24 September, 1873. Graduated 4 June, 1880. Ensign, 15 April, 1882. Lieutenant, Junior Grade, 15 May, 1889. Lieutenant, 11 April, 1894.
WOOD, ALONZO D.
Acting Third Assistant Engineer, 10 November, 1863. Acting Second Assistant Engineer, 24 January, 1865. Honorably discharged 16 August, 1866.
WOOD, BENJAMIN F.
Third Assistant Engineer, 1 July, 1861. Second Assistant Engineer, 21 April, 1863. First Assistant Engineer, 11 October, 1866. Chief Engineer, 14 December, 1883. Retired List, 6 October, 1892.
WOOD, CHARLES R.
Assistant Paymaster (Spanish-American War), 7 June, 1898. Honorably discharged 12 December, 1898.
WOOD, CHESTER O.
Acting Third Assistant Engineer, 9 August, 1864. Honorably discharged 15 September, 1865.
WOOD, CLARENCE E.
Acting Warrant Machinist, 23 August, 1899.
WOOD, D. R.
Midshipman, 3 March, 1841. Resigned 26 October, 1841.
WOOD, DUNCAN M.
Naval Cadet, 30 September, 1892. Ensign, 6 May, 1898.
WOOD, EDWARD P.
Midshipman, 1 October, 1863. Graduated June, 1867. Ensign, 18 December, 1868. Master, 21 March, 1870. Lieutenant, 21 March, 1871. Lieutenant-Commander, 20 September, 1890. Commander, 13 July, 1897. Died 11 December, 1899.
WOOD, EDWIN M.
Mate, 1 October, 1862. Acting Ensign, 28 November, 1863. Honorably discharged 18 September, 1865.
WOOD, FRANCIS.
Pharmbacist, 15 September, 1898. Retired List, 20 March, 1900.
WOOD, FREDERICK.
Acting Ensign, 22 October, 1864. Honorably discharged 1 July, 1865.
WOOD, GEORGE H.
Mate, 24 April, 1862. Acting Ensign, 6 May, 1863. Honorably discharged 28 October, 1865.
WOOD, GEORGE W.
Acting Midshipman, 23 September, 1859. Ensign, 24 February, 1863. Lieutenant, 22 February, 1864. Lieutenant-Commander, 25 July, 1866. Commander, 26 February, 1878. Discharged 3 July, 1893.
WOOD, GEORGE W.
Mate 26 February, 1868. Mustered out 30 November, 1868.
WOOD, GODFREY.
Lieutenant, 16 February, 1800. Resigned 11 August, 1802.
WOOD, HENRY.
Chaplain, 11 September, 1856. Retired List, 21 December, 1861. Died 8 October, 1873.
WOOD, HENRY.
Acting Third Assistant Engineer. Dismissed 11 August, 1864.
WOOD, H. P. T.
Midshipman, 1 March, 1825. Passed Midshipman, 28 April, 1832. Died 9 October, 1836.
WOOD, ISAAC.
Paymaster, 30 May, 1861. Resigned 30 July, 1862.
WOOD, JAMES B.
Acting Master, 25 January, 1862. Honorably discharged 9 January, 1866. Acting Master, 26 June, 1866. Mustered out 9 November, 1868.

GENERAL NAVY REGISTER. 601

WOOD, JAMES D.
Acting Master, 28 September, 1861. Resigned 25 March, 1863.
WOOD, JAMES P.
Sailmaker, 24 November, 1841. Resigned 28 April, 1843.
WOOD, JOHN.
Midshipman, 18 July, 1800. Resigned 4 March, 1804.
WOOD, JOHN.
Midshipman, 7 December, 1799. Last appearance on Records of Navy Department. Dead.
WOOD, JOHN F.
Acting Assistant Paymaster, 27 September, 1862. Mustered out 17 October, 1865.
WOOD, JOHN TAYLOR.
Midshipman, 7 April, 1847. Passed Midshipman, 10 June, 1853. Master, 15 September, 1855. Lieutenant, 16 September, 1855. Dismissed 2 April, 1861.
WOOD, JOHN W.
Pharmacist, 15 September, 1898.
WOOD, JOSEPH H.
Acting Assistant Paymaster, 28 September, 1863. Mustered out 12 June, 1866.
WOOD, JOSEPH LEARNED.
Cadet Engineer, Naval Academy, 14 September, 1876. Graduated 10 June, 1880. Assistant Engineer, 10 June, 1882. Retired List, 11 November, 1893.
WOOD, LEMUEL C.
Acting Master, 22 May, 1861. Resigned 22 June, 1862.
WOOD, L. C., Jr.
Acting Assistant Paymaster, 6 April, 1865. Mustered out 3 September, 1865.
WOOD, MINARD.
Mate, 26 June, 1862. Appointment revoked 28 November, 1862.
WOOD, MOSES L.
Cadet Midshipman, 21 September, 1871. Graduated 21 June, 1875. Ensign, 18 July, 1876. Master, 1 July, 1882. Lieutenant, Junior Grade, 3 March, 1883. Lieutenant, 26 March, 1889. Lieutenant-Commander, 3 March, 1899.
WOOD, OLIVER W.
Midshipman, 30 November, 1814. Died in 1822.
WOOD, SAMUEL S.
Acting Assistant Paymaster, 27 September, 1862. Passed Assistant Paymaster, 23 July, 1866. Resigned 19 March, 1868.
WOOD, SPENCER S.
Cadet Midshipman, 28 June, 1878. Ensign, 1 July, 1884. Lieutenant, Junior Grade, 11 April, 1894. Lieutenant, 16 September, 1897.
WOOD, THEODORE T.
Midshipman, 29 September, 1864. Graduated June, 1868. Master, 12 July, 1870. Lieutenant, 2 April, 1873. Died 8 January, 1886.
WOOD, THOMAS C.
Midshipman, 30 July, 1866. Graduated 6 June, 1871. Ensign, 14 July, 1872. Resigned 31 May, 1876. Lieutenant (Spanish-American War), 20 May, 1898. Honorably discharged 28 September, 1898.
WOOD, WILLIAM H.
Acting Master, 25 July, 1861. Acting Volunteer Lieutenant, 24 December, 1864. Honorably discharged 23 February, 1866. Acting Master, 25 July, 1866. Mustered out 13 April, 1868.
WOOD, WILLIAM H.
Mate, 23 September, 1863. Honorably discharged 5 December, 1865.
WOOD, WILLIAM M.
Assistant Surgeon, 16 May, 1829. Surgeon, 20 February, 1838. Medical Director, 3 March, 1871. Retired List, 27 May, 1871. Died 1 March, 1880.
WOOD, WILLIAM MAXWELL.
Midshipman, 20 July, 1865. Graduated 7 June, 1870. Ensign, 13 July, 1871. Master, 3 August, 1873. Lieutenant, 11 December, 1877. Died 16 December, 1897.
WOOD, WILLIAM W. W.
Chief Engineer, 15 March, 1845. Chief of Bureau Steam Engineering, 20 March, 1873. Successor appointed 3 March, 1877. Retired List, 31 May, 1880. Drowned 31 August, 1882.
WOODBRIDGE, DUDLEY G.
Midshipman, 1 January, 1825. Died 21 January, 1832.
WOODBRIDGE, HENRY R.
Purser, 27 March, 1861. Died 25 October, 1861.
WOODBURY, GEORGE A.
Mate, 9 November, 1864. Honorably discharged 30 June, 1865.
WOODBURY, JESSE P.
Acting Assistant Paymaster, 14 August, 1861. Assistant Paymaster, 24 September, 1862. Resigned 18 April, 1866.
WOODBURY, JOSIAH G.
Acting Assistant Paymaster, 10 November, 1862. Killed in action 17 August, 1863.
WOODBURY, LEANDER S.
Acting Assistant Engineer, 20 January, 1865. Honorably discharged 25 September, 1865.
WOODEND, GEORGE R.
Third Assistant Engineer, 21 May, 1853. Resigend 20 April, 1857.
WOODHOUSE, SAMUEL.
Midshipman, 2 May, 1801. Lieutenant, 4 May, 1808. Commander, 27 April, 1816. Captain, 3 March, 1827. Died 16 July, 1843.
WOODHULL, MAXWELL.
Midshipman, 4 June, 1832. Passed Midshipman, 26 June, 1838. Lieutenant, 17 July, 1843. Commander, 1 July, 1861. Died 19 February, 1863.

WOODHULL, WILLIAM W.
Acting Assistant Paymaster, 13 May, 1863. Passed Assistant Paymaster, 23 July, 1866. Paymaster, 10 February, 1870. Pay Inspector, 30 March, 1895. Retired List, 15 June, 1898.
WOODLAND, CHARLES.
Boatswain, 27 June, 1848. Retired List, 12 August, 1864. Died 11 May, 1873.
WOODLAND, WESLEY..
Acting Third Assistant Engineer, 14 January, 1862. Dismissed 2 September, 1862.
WOODMAN, EDWARD.
Midshipman, 30 September, 1862. Graduated June, 1866. Ensign, 12 March, 1868. Master, 26 March, 1869. Lieutenant, 21 March, 1870. Died 2 August, 1877.
WOODMAN, JOHN.
Mate, 28 October, 1862. Drowned 27 October, 1864.
WOODROW, DAVID C.
Midshipman, 21 September, 1861. Graduated November, 1864. Ensign, 1 November, 1866. Master, 1 December, 1866. Lieutenant, 12 March, 1868. Lieutenant-Commander, 26 March, 1869. Retired List, 4 June, 1884.
WOODRUFF, ABNER.
Midshipman, 1 September, 1798. Lieutenant, 4 March, 1803. Resigned 26 November, 1803.
WOODRUFF, CHARLES E.
Assistant Surgeon, 17 May, 1886. Resigned 19 April, 1887.
WOODRUFF, HARRY.
Mate, 24 ovember, 1863. Acting Ensign, 19 May, 1864. Resigned 5 May, 1865.
WOODRUFF, JOSEPH, JR.
Midshipman, 1 February, 1827. Dropped.
WOODRUFF, TIMOTHY.
Acting Third Assistant Engineer, 9 May, 1864. Honorably discharged 4 April, 1868.
WOODRUFFE, JOSEPH.
Midshipman, 1 January, 1808. Resigned 16 January, 1809.
WOODS, ARTHUR TANNATT.
Cadet Engineer, Naval Academy, 14 September, 1876. Graduated 10 June, 1880. Assistant Engineer, 10 June, 1882. Resigned 11 July, 1887.
WOODS, BENJAMIN.
Mate, 21 March, 1862. Acting Ensign, 1 October, 1863. Resigned 15 May, 1865.
WOODS, CHARLES W.
Acting Third Assistant Engineer, 28 February, 1865. Honorably discharged 24 May, 1866.
WOODS, DAVID C.
Acting Master, 13 May, 1861. Acting Volunteer Lieutenant, 6 January, 1864. Honorably discharged 10 September, 1865.
WOODS, EDWARD.
Naval Cadet, 19 May, 1894. Ensign, 4 April, 1900.
WOODS, GEORGE W.
Mate, 12 December, 1861. Acting Ensign, 16 September, 1862. Acting Master, 6 January, 1865. Honorably discharged 10 September, 1865.
WOODS, GEORGE W.
Assistant Surgeon, 24 January, 1862. Passed Assistant Surgeon, 8 May, 1865. Surgeon, 10 December, 1869. Medical Inspector, 1 September, 1888. Medical Director, 15 June, 1895. Retired List, 24 August, 1900.
WOODS, HENRY L. R.
Mate, 3 April, 1863. Acting Ensign, 7 April, 1864. Honorably discharged 12 May, 1865.
WOODS, JOHN C.
Boatswain, 8 July, 1815. Died 31 January, 1836.
WOODS, ROBERT H.
Cadet Midshipman, 30 September, 1878. Honorably discharged 30 June, 1885. Assistant Paymaster, 20 May, 1898. Passed Assistant Paymaster, 3 May, 1899.
WOODS, STANLEY.
Naval Cadet, 20 May, 1896. Graduated 30 June, 1900.
WOODS, WILLIAM C.
Acting Third Assistant Engineer, 24 September, 1864. Honorably discharged 30 September, 1867.
WOODWARD, CLARK H.
Naval Cadet, 6 September, 1895. At sea prior to final graduation.
WOODWARD, EDWIN T.
Acting Midshipman, 23 November, 1859. Lieutenant, 23 February, 1864. Lieutenant-Commander, 25 July, 1866. Commander, 2 February, 1878. Retired List, 3 July, 1893. Died 22 February, 1894.
WOODWARD, EDWARD.
Assistant Surgeon, 10 December, 1814. Died 26 January, 1818.
WOODWARD, JAMES M.
Gunner, 8 March, 1851. Died 21 December, 1857.
WOODWARD, JOSEPH J.
Cadet Midshipman, 27 June, 1877. Assistant Naval Constructor, 1 July, 1883. Naval Constructor, 3 March, 1891.
WOODWARD, J. W.
Midshipman, 28 August, 1789. Resigned 21 April, 1800.
WOODWARD, ROLAND E.
Acting Assistant Surgeon, 15 July, 1864. Appointment revoked 6 March, 1865.
WOODWARD, THOMAS J.
Acting Master, 23 September, 1861. Acting Volunteer Lieutenant, 1 August, 1862. Honorably discharged 12 September, 1865.

WOODWARD, WILLIAM H.
Acting Third Assistant Engineer, 29 March, 1864. Honorably discharged 19 March, 1868.
WOODWARD, WILLIAM R.
Acting Assistant Paymaster, 11 May, 1863. Mustered out 4 September, 1865.
WOODWELL, BENJAMIN.
Carpenter, 31 January, 1800. Last appearance on Records of Navy Department.
WOODWORTH, HENRY W.
Acting Second Assistant Engineer, 17 May, 1861. Resigned 23 August, 1861.
WOODWORTH, ROBERT.
Assistant Surgeon, 23 February, 1835. Surgeon, 1 December, 1846. Retired List, 13 May, 1867. Died 17 March, 1870.
WOODWORTH, SELIM E.
Midshipman, 16 June, 1838. Passed Midshipman, 20 May, 1844. Resigned 11 February, 1850. Acting Lieutenant, 10 September, 1861. Commander, 16 July, 1862. Resigned 2 March, 1866.
WOODWORTH, SELIM E.
Cadet Midshipman, 30 September, 1872. Graduated 18 June, 1879. Ensign, 2 January, 1881. Lieutenant, Junior Grade, 30 June, 1887. Resigned 15 April, 1892. Lieutenant, Junior Grade (Spanish-American War), 24 May, 1898. Honorably discharged 8 February, 1899.
WOODYEAR, W. R.
Midshipman, 2 April, 1804. Resigned 10 April, 1810.
WOOLAND, CHARLES.
Boatswain, 12 November, 1833. Dismissed 8 March, 1836.
WOOLEY, CHARLES W.
Midshipman, 30 November, 1841. Passed Midshipman, 10 August, 1847. Resigned 31 December, 1854.
WOOLSEY, MELANTHON B.
Midshipman, 24 September, 1832. Passed Midshipman, 16 July, 1840. Master, 22 March, 1847. Lieutenant, 16 July, 1847. Reserved List, 13 September, 1855. Commander on Active List, 16 July, 1862. Captain, 25 July, 1866. Commodore, 25 May, 1871. Died 2 October, 1874.
WOOLSEY, M. T.
Midshipman, 9 April, 1800. Lieutenant, 14 February, 1807. Commander, 24 July, 1813. Captain, 27 April, 1816. Died 18 May, 1838.
WOOLSEY, W. G.
Midshipman, 1 January, 1817. Lieutenant, 28 April, 1826. Died 25 October, 1840.
WOOLSON, CLIFFORD G.
Assistant Engineer (Spanish-American War), 3 June, 1898. Honorably discharged 27 October, 1898.
WOOLSON, JOHN S.
Assistant Paymaster, 19 March, 1862. Resigned 13 December, 1865.
WOOLVERTON, THEORON.
Assistant Surgeon, 17 July, 1862. Passed Assistant Surgeon, 25 September, 1865. Surgeon, 23 November, 1868. Medical Inspector, 19 June, 1888. Retired List, 13 November, 1891.
WOOSTER, LUCIUS W.
Cadet Engineer, Naval Academy, 1 October, 1871. Graduated 31 May, 1873. Second Assistant Engineer, 23 January, 1874. Passed Assistant Engineer, 1 November, 1879. Retired List, 29 June, 1887.
WORCESTER, GEORGE H.
Midshipman, 27 September, 1871. Graduated 21 June, 1865. Ensign, 18 July, 1876. Master, 15 April, 1882. Lieutenant, Junior Grade, 3 March, 1883. Resigned 1 December, 1884.
WORDEN, ISAAC G.
Acting Assistant Paymaster, 1 April, 1863. Resigned 9 November, 1864.
WORDEN, JOHN L.
Midshipman, 10 January, 1834. Passed Midshipman, 16 July, 1840. Master, 15 August, 1846. Lieutenant, 30 November, 1846. Commander, 16 July, 1862. Captain, 3 February, 1863. Commodore, 27 May, 1868. Rear-Admiral, 20 November, 1872. Retired List, 23 December, 1886. Died 18 October, 1897.
WORDING, W. H.
Mate, 8 September, 1864. Dismissed 22 March, 1865.
WORK, GEORGE.
Acting Assistant Paymaster, 2 February, 1864. Lost on Tecumseh, 5 August, 1864.
WORMLEY, WALLACE.
Midshipman, 24 November, 1800. Discharged 31 August, 1801, under Peace Establishment Act.
WORMLEY, W. W.
Midshipman, 25 March, 1802. (See Marine Corps.)
WORSTELL, FRANK W.
Mate, 8 December, 1863. Acting Ensign, 11 January, 1865. Resigned 11 April, 1866.
WORTH, ALGERNON S.
Midshipman, 1 February, 1827. Passed Midshipman, 10 June, 1833. Lieutenant, 28 February, 1838. Died 3 February, 1841.
WORTH, GEORGE B.
Mate. Dismissed 31 July, 1862.
WORTH, GEORGE H.
Mate. Resigned 24 November, 1863. Mate, 13 June, 1866. Appointment revoked 27 July, 1866.
WORTH, JETHRO.
Acting Ensign, 28 October, 1863. Honorably discharged 14 August, 1865.
WORTHERSPOON, WILLIAM W.
Mate, 9 March, 1870. Resigned 9 October, 1873.

WORTHINGTON, C. T. G.
  Midshipman, 1 September, 1811. Resigned 2 July, 1812.
WORTHINGTON, EDWARD.
  Midshipman, 1 March, 1825. Died 18 July, 1827.
WORTHINGTON, HENRY.
  Master, 15 September, 1813. Discharged 15 April, 1815. Master, 2 May, 1815. Died 18 November, 1848.
WORTHINGTON, JOHN LEEDS.
  Cadet Engineer, 14 September, 1876. Graduated 10 June, 1880. Died 14 July, 1881.
WORTHINGTON, T. B.
  Midshipman, 1 January, 1817. Killed in a duel 4 February, 1822.
WORTHINGTON, THOMAS.
  Cadet Midshipman, 19 June, 1876. Graduated 22 June, 1882. Ensign, Junior Grade, 3 March, 1883. Ensign, 26 June, 1884. Resigned 30 June, 1886.
WORTHINGTON, WALTER F.
  Cadet Engineer, 1 October, 1873. Graduated 21 June, 1875. Assistant Engineer, 1 July, 1877. Passed Assistant Engineer, 19 July, 1885. Chief Engineer, 14 October, 1896. Rank changed to Lieutenant-Commander, 3 March, 1899.
WORTMAN, WARD K.
  Naval Cadet, 5 September, 1896. Graduated 30 June, 1900.
WOUTERS, CHARLES.
  Boatswain, 23 June, 1898.
WRAGG, JOS.
  Midshipman, 16 January, 1809. Lieutenant, 24 July, 1813. Died 18 April, 1825.
WRAN, JOHN.
  Acting Gunner, 17 June, 1863. Honorably discharged 23 March, 1866.
WREN, WILLIAM J.
  Carpenter, 27 July, 1896.
WRIGHT, ALBERT J., JR.
  Acting Assistant Paymaster, 23 May, 1863. Mustered out 3 December, 1865.
WRIGHT, ARTHUR H.
  Acting Midshipman, 28 September, 1860. Ensign, 1 October, 1863. Master, 10 May, 1866. Lieutenant, 21 February, 1867. Lieutenant-Commander, 12 March, 1868. Died 5 November, 1881.
WRIGHT, B. B.
  Midshipman, 10 September, 1841. Resigned 24 October, 1842.
WRIGHT, BARTON L.
  Assistant Surgeon for temporary service, 13 June, 1898. Transferred to Regular Service, 13 May, 1899.
WRIGHT, BENJAMIN.
  Cadet Midshipman, 28 September, 1881. Ensign, 1 July, 1887. Resigned 20 November, 1895. Lieutenant, Junior Grade (Spanish-American War), 24 May, 1898. Discharged 19 January, 1899.
WRIGHT, CARROLL Q.
  Chaplain, 3 March, 1885.
WRIGHT, CHARLES A.
  Acting Ensign, 1 October, 1862. Acting Master, 7 February, 1863. Acting Volunteer Lieutenant, 22 August, 1863. Honorably discharged 9 September, 1865.
WRIGHT, CHARLES B.
  Acting Third Assistant Engineer, 18 May, 1863. Acting Second Assistant Engineer, 12 November, 1864. Resigned 7 April, 1865.
WRIGHT, CLINTON.
  Midshipman, 18 May, 1809. Resigned 5 August, 1809.
WRIGHT, D. V. N.
  Acting Master and Pilot, 1 September, 1864. Appointment revoked 14 April, 1865.
WRIGHT, EDWARD.
  Midshipman, 30 November, 1814. Resigned 10 April, 1817.
WRIGHT, EDWARD E.
  Cadet Midshipman, 20 September, 1873. Graduated 18 June, 1879. Ensign, 1 January, 1881. Lieutenant, Junior Grade, 21 May, 1887. Lieutenant, 4 December, 1892. Lieutenant-Commander, 29 March, 1900.
WRIGHT, EMORY.
  Acting Assistant Paymaster, 30 June, 1862. Mustered out 4 November, 1865.
WRIGHT, F. B.
  Midshipman, 1 April, 1828. Resigned 24 August, 1833.
WRIGHT, GEORGE.
  Surgeon, 27 June, 1798. Discharged 16 June, 1801, under Peace Establishment Act.
WRIGHT, GEORGE.
  Master, 19 January, 1809. Last appearance on Records of Navy Department.
WRIGHT, GEORGE F.
  Midshipman, 20 July, 1865. Graduated June, 1869. Resigned 25 April, 1871.
WRIGHT, GEORGE P.
  Acting Assistant Surgeon, 30 September, 1863. Honorably discharged 9 October, 1865.
WRIGHT, HENRY C.
  Acting Second Assistant Engineer, 18 November, 1863. Appointment revoked 3 August, 1865.
WRIGHT, HENRY T.
  Acting Assistant Paymaster, 19 February, 1864. Passed Assistant Paymaster, 23 July, 1866. Paymaster, 10 March, 1870. Pay Inspector, 10 April, 1895. Pay Director, 23 December, 1899.
WRIGHT, HENRY T.
  Naval Cadet, 6 September, 1894. Graduated. Assistant Naval Constructor, 4 April, 1900.
WRIGHT, HENRY X.
  Third Assistant Engineer, 3 May, 1859. Name stricken from the Rolls, 6 May, 1861.

GENERAL NAVY REGISTER.

WRIGHT, JAMES.
Master, 16 February, 1814. Discharged 1 February, 1815.
WRIGHT, JAMES B.
Master, 19 November, 1813. Cashiered 15 November, 1820.
WRIGHT, JAMES B.
Midshipman, 4 March, 1819. Last appearance on Records of Navy Department, 1822. Dead.
WRIGHT, JAMES D.
Third Assistant Engineer, 21 July, 1858. Second Assistant Engineer, 17 January, 1861. Resigned 16 October, 1861.
WRIGHT, JAMES H.
Acting Third Assistant Engineer, 22 July, 1864. Honorably discharged 9 March, 1866.
WRIGHT, JAMES K.
Acting Third Assistant Engineer, 11 November, 1863. Honorably discharged 12 August, 1865.
WRIGHT, JESSE.
Acting Third Assistant Engineer, 27 October, 1863. Honorably discharged 28 October, 1865.
WRIGHT, J. H.
Acting Assistant Surgeon, 19 December, 1864. Honorably discharged 11 February, 1866.
WRIGHT, JOHN.
Midshipman, 20 December, 1804. Resigned 14 February, 1807.
WRIGHT, JOHN.
Mate, 6 December, 1862. Dead.
WRIGHT, JOHN E.
Mate, 13 August, 1863. Acting Ensign, 18 July, 1864. Honorably discharged 6 October, 1865.
WRIGHT, JOHN H.
Assistant Surgeon, 9 December, 1839. Surgeon, 18 April, 1855. Retired List, 25 April, 1861. Medical Director on Retired List, 3 March, 1871. Died 26 December, 1879.
WRIGHT, JOSEPH L.
Acting Third Assistant Engineer, 16 August, 1864. Honorably discharged 26 June, 1865.
WRIGHT, LUKE E., Jr.
Naval Cadet, 5 September, 1896. Graduated 30 June, 1900.
WRIGHT, MIERS F.
Midshipman, 1 October, 1866. Graduated 7 June, 1870. Ensign, 13 July, 1871. Master, 5 April, 1874. Lieutenant, 1 April, 1880. Died 4 March, 1890.
WRIGHT, PERRY C.
Acting Ensign, 5 June, 1863. Honorably discharged 12 November, 1865.
WRIGHT, ROBERT ARMSTRONG.
Third Assistant Engineer, 10 June, 1862. Second Assistant Engineer, 21 November, 1863. Resigned 16 October, 1865.
WRIGHT, ROBERT C.
Mate. Acting Ensign, 1 October, 1862. Resigned 10 December, 1862. Acting Ensign, 7 January, 1863. Appointment revoked (sick) 10 July, 1863. Acting Ensign, 9 October, 1863. Resigned 17 February, 1864.
WRIGHT, ROBERT D.
Acting Third Assistant Engineer, 16 March, 1864. Honorably discharged 20 January, 1866.
WRIGHT, ROBERT K.
Cadet Midshipman, 11 June, 1873. Graduated 4 June, 1880. Ensign, 18 December, 1882. Resigned 1 May, 1884. Lieutenant (Spanish-American War), 12 May, 1898. Honorably discharged 14 February, 1899.
WRIGHT, THOMAS.
Acting Ensign, 1 October, 1862. Resigned 20 May, 1863. Acting Master, 17 November, 1863. Dismissed 8 June, 1864.
WRIGHT, THOMAS.
Acting Master, 7 December, 1861. Resigned 7 April, 1863.
WRIGHT, WILLIAM.
Acting Master, 28 October, 1861. Honorably discharged 17 September, 1865.
WRIGHT, WILLIAM.
Midshipman, 4 July, 1805. Resigned 20 February, 1806.
WRIGHT, WILLIAM.
Acting Third Assistant Engineer, 9 March, 1864. Honorably discharged 22 September, 1865.
WRIGHT, WILLIAM.
Acting Third Assistant Engineer. Appointment revoked (sick) 12 December, 1863.
WRIGHT, WILLIAM F.
Acting First Assistant Engineer, 17 October, 1861. Acting Chief Engineer, 19 January, 1863. Resigned 15 May, 1865.
WRIGHT, WILLIAM G.
Acting Master, 1 October, 1861. Honorably discharged 5 May, 1866.
WRIGHT, WILLIAM G.
Acting Third Assistant Engineer, 15 June, 1864. Honorably discharged 30 October, 1865.
WRIGHTINGTON, CHARLES D.
Acting Third Assistant Engineer, 30 December, 1864. Honorably discharged 27 October, 1865.
WROTEN, W. H.
Acting Master and Pilot, 1 October, 1864. Honorably discharged 17 January, 1866.

WUNDERLICH, FREDERICK W.
Acting Assistant Surgeon, 18 May, 1864. Assistant Surgeon, 10 May, 1865. Passed Assistant Surgeon, 22 January, 1869. Resigned 21 March, 1870.
WURTS, DANIEL.
Midshipman, 31 December, 1798. Resigned 28 January, 1802.
WURTS, WILLIAM A.
Midshipman, 1 April, 1826. Passed Midshipman, 28 April, 1832. Lieutenant, 9 February, 1837. Died 6 February, 1847.
WURTSBAUGH, DANIEL W.
Naval Cadet, 20 May, 1892. Ensign, 6 May, 1898.
WYATT, LEMUEL C.
Acting Third Assistant Engineer, 11 December, 1861. Dismissed 28 May, 1862.
WYATT, ROBERT T.
Acting Master, 14 August, 1861. Honorably discharged 28 August, 1865.
WYATT, S. C.
Acting First Assistant Engineer, 1861. Resigned 19 October, 1861.
WYATT, THOMAS A.
Acting Master and Pilot, 1 October, 1864. Appointment revoked 9 March, 1865.
WYATT, THOMAS H.
Acting Master and Pilot, 15 September, 1863. Appointment revoked 9 February, 1865.
WYBRANT, JOHN.
Acting First Assistant Engineer, 22 June, 1863. Resigned 3 June, 1864.
WYCKOFF, AMBROSE B.
Midshipman, 29 September, 1864. Graduated June, 1868. Ensign, 19 April, 1869. Master, 12 July, 1870. Lieutenant, 25 October, 1872. Retired 3 July, 1893.
WYCKOFF, JOHN.
Mate, 25 January, 1870. Resigned 15 March, 1873.
WYER, EDWARD.
Midshipman, 20 April, 1798. Lieutenant, 18 March, 1800. Left the service 15 January, 1805.
WYLIE, DAVID R.
Acting Third Assistant Engineer, 25 October, 1862. Acting Second Assistant Engineer, 6 July, 1863. Honorably discharged 23 September, 1865.
WYLIE, JAMES.
Third Assistant Engineer, 19 February, 1863. Second Assistant Engineer, 20 June, 1864. Died 26 April, 1869.
WYMAN, FRANCIS S.
Acting Second Assistant Engineer, 8 August, 1864. Honorably discharged 11 December, 1865.
WYMAN, HENRY.
Mate, 24 September, 1861. Resigned 5 April, 1865.
WYMAN, HENRY L.
Naval Cadet, 6 September, 1895. Graduated 30 June, 1900.
WYMAN, JOHN.
Midshipman, 1 April, 1828. Resigned 17 March, 1829.
WYMAN, ROBERT H.
Midshipman, 11 March, 1837. Passed Midshipman, 29 June, 1843. Acting Master, 13 June, 1848. Lieutenant, 16 July, 1850. Commander, 16 July, 1862. Captain, 25 July, 1866. Commodore, 19 July, 1872. Rear-Admiral, 26 April, 1878. Died 2 December, 1882.
WYMAN, THOMAS W.
Midshipman, 17 December, 1810. Lieutenant, 27 April, 1816. Commander, 9 February, 1837. Captain, 2 November, 1842. Died 24 February, 1854.
WYNCH, GEORGE J.
Midshipman, 2 February, 1829. Passed Midshipman, 3 July, 1835. Lieutenant, 8 September, 1841. Died 24 October, 1843.
WYNDE, HENRY J.
Mate, 21 January, 1864. Honorably discharged 13 August, 1867.
WYNN, WILLIAM P.
Acting Third Assistant Engineer, 3 July, 1863. Resigned 1864.
WYSHAM, WILLIAM E.
Assistant Surgeon, 24 September, 1824. Passed Assistant Surgeon, 16 May, 1860. Dismissed 10 May, 1861.
YANCEY, A. K.
Midshipman, 1 April, 1825. Resigned 25 June, 1833.
YANCEY, BENJAMIN.
Midshipman, 14 March, 1799. Discharged 10 May, 1801.
YANCEY, C. C.
Midshipman, 1 January, 1808. Resigned 24 October, 1808.
YANCEY, C. C.
Midshipman, 18 June, 1812. Resigned 25 September, 1813.
YANCEY, CHARLES K.
Assistant Surgeon, 1 March, 1871. Passed Assistant Surgeon, 12 June, 1876. Retired List, 21 May, 1880.
YARD, EDWARD M.
Midshipman, 1 November, 1827. Passed Midshipman, 10 June, 1833. Lieutenant, 28 February, 1838. Commander, 14 September, 1855. Retired List, 18 January, 1862. Resigned 3 May, 1866.
YARD, THOMAS S.
Acting Assistant Surgeon, 25 January, 1862. Honorably discharged 24 October, 1865.
YARNALL, JOHN.
Midshipman, 16 January, 1809. Lieutenant, 24 July, 1813. Lost in the Epervier.
YARNALL, MORDECAI.
Professor 1 February, 1839. Retired List, 16 April, 1878. Died 27 February, 1879.

GENERAL NAVY REGISTER. 607

YARNELL, HARRY E.
　Naval Cadet, 6 September, 1893. Ensign, 1 July, 1899.
YATES, ALEXANDER F. H.
　Naval Cadet, 20 May, 1895. At sea prior to final graduation.
YATES, ARTHUR R.
　Acting Midshipman, 24 September, 1856. Midshipman, 10 June, 1857. Passed Midshipman, 25 June, 1860. Master, 24 October, 1860. Lieutenant, 18 April, 1861. Lieutenant-Commander, 16 November, 1864. Commander, 6 February, 1872. Captain, 9 February, 1884. Died 4 November, 1891.
YATES, CHARLES.
　Midshipman, 1 January, 1812. Last appearance on Records of Navy Department, 1815. Norfolk.
YATES, ISAAC I.
　Midshipman, 21 September, 1861. Graduated June, 1866. Ensign, 12 March, 1868. Master, 26 March, 1869. Lieutenant, 21 March, 1870. Resigned 23 November, 1883.
YATES, JAMES B.
　Midshipman, 29 December, 1841. Resigned 11 May, 1848.
YATES, JOHN.
　Acting First Assistant Engineer, 20 September, 1862. Acting Chief Engineer, 19 January, 1863. Honorably discharged 23 November, 1865.
YATES, JOHN A.
　Acting Ensign, 1 October, 1862. Promoted to Acting Master, 19 February, 1863. Resigned 3 June, 1863.
YATES, JOHN P.
　Carpenter, 21 December, 1897.
YATES, WILLIAM.
　Acting Gunner, 5 December, 1861. Dismissed 30 September, 1862.
YEAGER, CHARLES F.
　Acting Second Assistant Engineer, 5 December, 1862. Acting First Assistant Engineer, 1 November, 1864. Honorably discharged 28 November, 1865.
YEATEMAN, T. H.
　Midshipman, 1 May, 1822. Resigned 12 June, 1827.
YEATES, DONALDSON.
　Assistant Surgeon, 14 May, 1812. Died 28 October, 1815.
YEATON, JOHN H.
　Acting Ensign, 14 March, 1864. Dismissed 29 December, 1864.
YEATON, JOSEPH N.
　Mate, 18 February, 1863. Dismissed 4 December, 1863.
YEATON, SAMUEL.
　Acting Master, 26 August, 1861. Resigned 11 February, 1862.
YEATON, SAMUEL R.
　Acting Third Assistant Engineer, 22 February, 1864. Appointment revoked 21 June, 1864.
YEATON, WILLIAM HARPER.
　Mate, 30 January, 1862. Resigned 28 February, 1867.
YEISER, JOHN H.
　Midshipman, 1 May, 1822. Died in September, 1823.
YEO, WILLIAM F.
　Mate, 18 April, 1863. Resigned 25 July, 1863.
YEOMANS, JAMES.
　Carpenter, 3 November, 1798. Resigned 27 July, 1799.
YEWELL, HORACE R.
　Gunner, 23 August, 1886. Retired List, 21 February, 1894.
YOCUM, REUBEN.
　Acting Third Assistant Engineer, 3 July, 1863. Honorably discharged 2 November, 1865.
YOE, GEORGE W.
　Acting Third Assistant Engineer, 8 August, 1863. Honorably discharged 26 July, 1865.
YORK, LEWIS S.
　Acting Assistant Paymaster, 24 February, 1862. Mustered out 28 September, 1865.
YORKE, LOUIS A.
　Assistant Paymaster, 26 October, 1869. Passed Assistant Paymaster, 12 May, 1875. Discharged 24 February, 1887. Assistant Paymaster (Spanish-American War), 16 July, 1898. Honorably discharged 11 October, 1898.
YORSTON, MATTHEW M.
　Mate, 29 September, 1864. Honorably discharged 4 October, 1865.
YOU, ISAAC S. K.
　Midshipman, 3 July, 1835. Passed Midshipman, 22 June, 1841. Lost in the Grampus, March, 1843.
YOUNG, ADAM.
　Master's Mate, 29 September, 1840. Resigned 22 March, 1858.
YOUNG, ALBERT OSBORN.
　Cadet Engineer, Naval Academy, 14 September, 1876. Graduated 10 June, 1880. Assistant Engineer, 10 June, 1882. Resigned 30 June, 1888.
YOUNG, CARRINGTON A.
　Mate, 14 September, 1866. Gunner, 9 April, 1875. Retired List, 10 December, 1883.
YOUNG, DAVID C.
　Assistant Engineer (Spanish-American War), 29 June, 1898. Honorably discharged 20 December, 1898.
YOUNG, EDWARD L.
　Master, 9 May, 1812. Last appearance on Records of Navy Department, 1816. Furloughed.
YOUNG, FRANKLIN.
　Acting Ensign, 20 January, 1865. Honorably discharged 30 August, 1865.

YOUNG, GEORGE.
Lieutenant (Spanish-American War), 21 April, 1898. Honorably discharged 2 September, 1898.
YOUNG, GEORGE M.
Mate, 13 December, 1861. Deserted 26 December, 1861.
YOUNG, GEORGE W.
Acting Third Assistant Engineer, 14 April, 1864. Resigned 27 June, 1865.
YOUNG, GEORGE W.
Midshipman, 19 October, 1841. Passed Midshipman, 10 August, 1847. Master, 14 September, 1855. Lieutenant, 15 September, 1855. Lieutenant-Commander, 16 July, 1862. Commander, 25 July, 1866. Died 30 August, 1867.
YOUNG, H. A. F.
Master, 16 May, 1829. Reserved List, 14 September, 1855. Resigned 15 May, 1861.
YOUNG, HENRY C.
Acting Assistant Surgeon, 8 March, 1865. Honorably discharged 9 January, 1866.
YOUNG, HORACE S.
Acting Master, 18 July, 1861. Honorably discharged 19 September, 1865.
YOUNG, JAMES G.
Acting First Assistant Engineer, 28 July, 1862. Acting Chief Engineer, 5 July, 1863. Honorably discharged 6 May, 1866.
YOUNG, JAMES G.
Third Assistant Engineer, 27 January, 1848. Second Assistant Engineer, 6 November, 1849. First Assistant Engineer, 26 February, 1851. Resigned 14 November, 1855.
YOUNG, JAMES N.
Acting Assistant Surgeon, 8 March, 1865. Honorably discharged 23 January, 1866.
YOUNG, JEFFERSON.
First Assistant Engineer, 21 September, 1861. Retired List, 7 March, 1871. Died 3 July, 1894.
YOUNG, JOHN.
Midshipman, 4 March, 1823. Resigned 19 October, 1827.
YOUNG, JOHN.
Acting Second Assistant Engineer, 2 November, 1861. Discharged 19 July, 1862.
YOUNG, JOHN.
Boatswain, 6 April, 1838. Resigned 2 July, 1841.
YOUNG, JOHN, Jr.
Assistant Surgeon, 9 July, 1812. Last appearance on Records of Navy Department, 1815.
YOUNG, JOHN J.
Boatswain, 5 April, 1847. Resigned 12 July, 1858.
YOUNG, JOHN J.
Midshipman, 1 January, 1812. Resigned 25 May, 1814. Midshipman, 17 June, 1814. Lieutenant, 28 March, 1820. Commander, 15 April, 1840. Reserved List, 13 September, 1855. Commodore, Retired List. Died 4 November, 1875.
YOUNG, JOHN L.
Acting Third Assistant Engineer, 26 October, 1863. Honorably discharged 12 June, 1866. Acting Third Assistant Engineer, 30 January, 1867. Mustered out 6 August, 1869.
YOUNG, JOHN M.
Acting Third Assistant Engineer, 27 December, 1864. Resigned 24 January, 1867.
YOUNG, JONATHAN.
Midshipman, 19 October, 1841. Passed Midshipman, 10 August, 1847. Master, 14 September, 1855. Lieutenant, 15 September, 1855. Lieutenant-Commander, 16 July, 1862. Commander, 25 July, 1866. Captain, 8 November, 1873. Commodore, 19 June, 1882. Died 17 May, 1885.
YOUNG, JOSEPH S.
Mate, 21 November, 1862. Acting Ensign, 23 September, 1864. Honorably discharged 14 May, 1867.
YOUNG, LOUIS L.
Naval Cadet, 6 September, 1883. Resigned 20 September, 1888. Assistant Surgeon, 20 May, 1891. Passed Assistant Surgeon, 20 May, 1894. Retired List, 10 November, 1899. Died 6 October, 1900.
YOUNG, LUCIEN.
Midshipman, 21 June, 1869. Graduated 31 May, 1873. Ensign, 16 July, 1874. Master, 24 November, 1877. Lieutenant, Junior Grade, 3 March, 1883. Lieutenant, 1 May, 1884. Lieutenant-Commander, 3 March, 1899.
YOUNG, NATHAN L.
Mate, 22 June, 1863. Resigned 7 August, 1863.
YOUNG, N. C.
Mate, 9 March, 1866. Deserted 17 August, 1866.
YOUNG, PERRIT D.
Acting Second Assistant Engineer, 23 February, 1864. Died on General Lyon, 15 August, 1864.
YOUNG, PHILANDER S.
Acting First Assistant Engineer, 2 December, 1864. Resigned 20 June, 1865.
YOUNG, SAMUEL.
Purser, 24 July, 1800. Last appearance on Records of Navy Department.
YOUNG, STEPHEN.
Gunner, 1 October, 1861. Retired List, 8 November, 1883. Died 20 January, 1895.
YOUNG, THOMAS.
Midshipman, 19 October, 1841. Passed Midshipman, 10 August, 1847. Master, 14 September, 1855. Lieutenant, 15 September, 1855. Resigned 8 September, 1856.
YOUNG, V. J.
Acting Ensign, 21 May, 1864. Appointment revoked (sick) 13 December, 1864.
YOUNG, WILLIAM.
Acting Second Assistant Engineer, 28 May, 1861. Resigned 28 October, 1861.

GENERAL NAVY REGISTER. 609

YOUNG, WILLIAM.
　Mate, 17 June, 1863. Dismissed 1 August, 1863.
YOUNG, WILLIAM.
　Acting Ensign, 28 February, 1863. Honorably discharged 10 September, 1865.
YOUNG, WILLIAM S.
　Midshipman, 1 March, 1827. Passed Midshipman, 10 June, 1833. Lieutenant, 28 February, 1838. Commander, 14 September, 1855. Died 17 October, 1861.
ZAHM, FRANK B.
　Naval Cadet, 5 September, 1887. Assistant Naval Constructor, 1 July, 1893. Naval Constructor, 1 November, 1898.
ZANE, ABRAHAM V.
　Cadet Engineer, Naval Academy, 1 October, 1871. Graduated 3 May, 1874. Assistant Engineer, 26 February, 1875. Passed Assistant Engineer, 27 August, 1881. Chief Engineer, 11 September, 1895. Rank changed to Lieutenant-Commander, 3 March, 1899.
ZANTZINGER, H. D.
　Midshipman, 1 January, 1817. Died in 1822.
ZANTZINGER, JOHN P.
　Midshipman, 15 November, 1809. Lieutenant, 9 December, 1814. Commander, 3 March, 1831. Captain, 22 December, 1838. Dropped 13 September, 1855.
ZANTZINGER, W. P.
　Purser, 25 June, 1832. Dismissed 17 January, 1844.
ZANTZINGER, W. P.
　Purser, 24 July, 1813. Cashiered 31 May, 1830.
ZEIGLER, ASA H.
　Acting Assistant Surgeon, 8 March, 1865. Honorably discharged 9 October, 1865.
ZEITLER, WILLIAM.
　Gunner, 1 July, 1898.
ZELLER, THEODORE.
　Third Assistant Engineer, 15 June, 1843. Second Assistant Engineer, 10 July, 1847. First Assistant Engineer, 26 February, 1851. Chief Engineer, 27 June, 1855. Retired List, 1 December, 1885.
ZENZEN, LOUIS.
　Assistant Surgeon, 24 January, 1862. Passed Assistant Surgeon, 25 September, 1865. Surgeon, 10 May, 1867. Died 22 November, 1868.
ZEREGA, ALFRED L. B.
　Acting Master, 24 July, 1861. Resigned 1 September, 1864.
ZEREGA, RICHARD A.
　Assistant Paymaster (Spanish-American War), 20 May, 1898. Honorably discharged 11 October, 1898.
ZEREGA, THEODORE C.
　Lieutenant (Spanish-American War), 28 June, 1898. Honorably discharged 28 September, 1898.
ZETTICK, JOHN J. P.
　Acting Ensign, 24 February, 1864. Honorably discharged 25 September, 1866.
ZIEGEMEIER, HENRY J.
　Naval Cadet, 21 May, 1886. Ensign, 1 July, 1892. Lieutenant, 3 March, 1899.
ZIEGLER, DAVID H.
　Mate, 26 November, 1863. Resigned 6 June, 1864.
ZIEGLER, JOHN QUINCY ADAMS.
　Acting First Assistant Engineer, 24 February, 1862. Acting Chief Engineer, 4 February, 1863. Chief Engineer, 18 June, 1868. Died 5 July, 1885.
ZIMMERMAN, CHARLES.
　Acting Ensign, 2 June, 1864. Honorably discharged 21 February, 1866.
ZIMMERMAN, CHARLES W.
　Acting Midshipman, 20 September, 1858. Acting Master, 12 February, 1862. Lieutenant, 1 August, 1862. Killed in Battle, 1 January, 1863.
ZIMMERMAN, EUGENE.
　Acting Ensign, 13 May, 1863. Acting Master, 12 June, 1864. Honorably discharged 25 October, 1865.
ZIMMERMAN, WILLIAM.
　Mate, 18 April, 1863. Acting Ensign, 2 November, 1863. Honorably discharged 24 October, 1865.

THE
UNITED STATES NAVAL ACADEMY.

The United States Naval Academy was founded in 1845, by Hon. George Bancroft, Secretary of the Navy, in the administration of President James K. Polk. It was formally opened October 10, of that year, under the name of the Naval School, with Commander Franklin Buchanan as Superintendent. It was placed at Annapolis, Md., on the land occupied by Fort Severn, which was given up by the War Department for the purpose. The course was fixed at five years, of which the first and last only were spent at school, the intervening three being passed at sea. This arrangement was not strictly adhered to, the exigencies of the service making it necessary, in many cases, to shorten the period of study. In January, 1846, four months after the opening of the school, the students consisted of 36 Midshipmen, of the date of 1840, who were preparing for the examination for promotion; 13 of the date of 1841, who were to remain until drafted for service at sea; and 7 Acting Midshipmen, appointed since September of the previous year. The Midshipmen of the date of 1840 were the first to be graduated, finishing their limited course in July, 1846, and they were followed in order by the subsequent dates until the reorganization of the School, in 1851.

In September, 1849, a Board was appointed to revise the plan and regulations of the Naval School. The Board was composed of the following officers:

        Commodore WILLIAM B. SHUBRICK,
        Commander FRANKLIN BUCHANAN,
        Commander SAMUEL F. DUPONT,
        Commander GEORGE P. UPSHUR,
        Surgeon W. S. W. RUSCHENBERGER,
        Professor WILLIAM CHAUVENET,
        Captain HENRY BREWERTON, U. S. A.

The plan reported by the Board was approved, and went into operation July 1, 1850. The new organization provided for a course of seven years, the first two and last two at the School and the three intermediate years at sea. The School was placed under the supervision of the Bureau of Ordnance and Hydrography, and its name was changed to the United States Naval Academy. The corps of professors was enlarged, the course was extended, and the system of separate departments, with executive heads, was fully adopted. It was provided that a Board of Visitors should make an annual inspection of the Academy, and report upon its condition to the Secretary of the Navy. A suitable vessel was attached to the Academy as a practice-ship, and the annual practice-cruises were begun.

After the system had been in operation a year new changes were proposed, and the recommendations of the Academic Board on the subject were referred to the Board of Examiners of the year 1851, composed of the following officers:

        Commodore DAVID CONNER,
        Captain SAMUEL L. BREESE,
        Commander C. K. STRIBLING,
        Commander A. BIGELOW,
        Commander FRANKLIN BUCHANAN,
        Lieutenant THOMAS T. CRAVEN.

The change recommended by the Board of Examiners, and adopted by the Department, consisted mainly in leaving out the requirement of three years of sea-service in the middle of the course, thus making the four years of study consecutive. The practice-cruise supplied the place of the omitted sea-service, and gave better opportunities of training. The change went into operation in November, 1851, together with other improvements recommended by the Board. The system has continued, with slight modifications, to the present time. The first class to receive the benefit of it was that which entered in 1851. Six members of this class completed the course in three years, and were graduated in June, 1854; the rest of the class followed in 1855.

In May, 1861, on the outbreak of the war, the Academy was removed to Newport, R. I. The three upper classes were detached and ordered to sea, and the remaining Acting Midshipmen were quartered in the Atlantic House and on board the frigates Constitution and Santee. In September, 1865, the Academy was moved back to Annapolis, where it has since remained.

When the Bureau of Navigation was established, July 5, 1862, the Academy was placed under its supervision; March 1, 1867, it was placed under the direct care and supervision of the Navy Department, the administrative routine and financial management being still conducted through the Bureau. On the 11th of March, 1869, all official connection with the Bureau came to an end.

The term of the academic course was changed by law, March 3, 1873, from four to six years. The change took effect with the class which entered in the following summer.

In 1866, a class of Acting Third Assistant Engineers was ordered to the Academy for instruction. The course embraced the subjects of steam engineering, iron manufacture, chemistry, and mechanics, and practical exercises with the steam engine and in the machine shop. This class was graduated in June, 1868, together with two Cadet Engineers who had entered the Academy in 1867. After an interval of four years, in October, 1871, a new class of Cadet Engineers was admitted. This class followed a two years' course, somewhat more extended than that of the class of 1868, and was graduated in 1873. In 1872 and 1873 new classes were admitted, the first of which left the Academy in 1874 and the second in 1875. By an act of Congress approved February 24, 1874, the course of instruction for Cadet Engineers was made four years instead of two ; and the new provision was first applied to the class entering the Academy in the year 1874. This class was graduated in June, 1878.

By an act of Congress approved August 5, 1882, it was provided that from that date "there shall be no appointments of cadet midshipmen or cadet engineers at the Naval Academy, but in lieu thereof naval cadets shall be appointed from each Congressional district and at large, as now provided by law for cadet midshipmen, and all the undergraduates at the Naval Academy shall hereafter be designated and called 'naval cadets ;' and from those who successfully complete the six years' course, appointments shall hereafter be made as it is necessary to fill vacancies in the lower grades of the Line and Engineer Corps of the Navy and of the Marine Corps: *And provided further*, That no greater number of appointments into these grades shall be made each year than shall equal the number of vacancies which has occurred in the same grades during the preceding year; such appointments to be made from the graduates of the year, at the conclusion of their six years' course, in the order of merit, as determined by the Academic Board of the Naval Academy; the assignment to the various corps to be made by the Secretary of the Navy upon the recommendation of the Academic Board. But nothing herein contained shall reduce the number of appointments from such graduates below ten in each year, nor deprive of such appointment any graduate who may complete the six years' course during the year eighteen hundred and eighty-two. And if there be a surplus of graduates, those who do not receive such appointment shall be given a certificate of graduation, an honorable discharge, and one year's sea pay, as now provided by law for cadet midshipmen; and so much of section fifteen hundred and twenty-one of the Revised Statutes as is inconsistent herewith is hereby repealed.

"That any cadet whose position in his class entitles him to be retained in the service may, upon his own application, be honorably discharged at the end of the four years' course at the Naval Academy, with a proper certificate of graduation."

In 1886 a special course of instruction in physiology and hygiene was established, in accordance with an act of Congress approved May 20 of that year.

The act of Congress approved March 2, 1889, provides that "the Academic Board of the Naval Academy shall on or before the thirtieth day of September in each year separate the first class of naval cadets then commencing their fourth year into two divisions, as they may have shown special aptitude for the duties of the respective corps, in the proportion which the aggregate number of vacancies occurring in the preceding fiscal year ending on the thirtieth day of June in the lowest grades of commissioned officers of the Line of the Navy and Marine Corps of the Navy shall bear to the number of vacancies to be supplied from the Academy occurring during the same period in the lowest grade of commissioned officers of the Engineer Corps of the Navy; and the cadets so assigned to the Line and Marine Corps division of the first class shall thereafter pursue a course of study arranged to fit them for service in the Line of the Navy, and the cadets so assigned to the Engineer Corps division of the first class shall thereafter pursue a separate course of study arranged to fit them for service in the Engineer Corps of the Navy, and the cadets shall thereafter, and until final graduation, at the end of their six years' course, take rank by merit with those in the same division, according to the merit marks: and from the final graduates of the Line and Marine Corps division, at the end of their six years' course, appointments shall be made hereafter as it shall be necessary to fill vacancies in the lowest grades of commissioned officers of the Line of the Navy and Marine Corps : and the vacancies in the lowest grades of the commissioned officers of the Engineer Corps of the Navy shall be filled in like manner by appointments from the final graduates of the Engineer division at the end of their six years' course: *Provided*, That no greater number of appointments into the said lowest grades of commissioned officers shall be made each year than shall equal the number of vacancies which shall have occurred in the same grades during the fiscal year then current; such appointments to be made from the final graduates of the year, in the order of merit as determined by the Academic Board of the Naval Academy, the assignment to be made by the Secretary of the Navy upon the recommendation of the Academic Board at the conclusion of the fiscal year then current; but nothing contained herein or in the naval appropriation act of August fifth, eighteen hundred and eighty-two, shall reduce the number of appointments of final graduates at the end of their six years' course below twelve in each year to the Line of the Navy, and not less than two shall be appointed annually to the Engineer Corps of the Navy, nor less than one annually to the Marine Corps; and if the number of vacancies in the lowest grades aforesaid, occurring in any year shall be greater than the number of final graduates of that year, the surplus vacancies shall be filled from the final graduates of following years, as they shall become available.

"That after the fourth day of March, eighteen hundred and eighty-nine, the minimum age of admission of cadets to the Academy shall be fifteen years and the maximum age twenty years."

In October, 1897, a post-graduate course in Naval Architecture, for the education of officers for the Construction Corps of the Navy, was established; and a class was formed from the naval cadets that had finished the four years' course in that year.

By an act of Congress, approved March 3, 1899, "the officers constituting the Engineer Corps of the Navy" were "transferred to the Line of the Navy," thereby repealing so much of the act of Congress, approved March 2, 1889, as relates to the separation of naval cadets of the first class into Line and Engineer divisions.

This same act having limited the number of Constructors in the Navy to forty, the post-graduate course in Naval Architecture was discontinued.

SUPERINTENDENTS

OF THE

United States Naval Academy

SINCE ITS FOUNDATION.

Assumed command.

Commander Franklin Buchanan	Sept. 3, 1845
Commander George P. Upshur	Mar. 15, 1847
Commander Cornelius K. Stribling	July 1, 1850
Commander Louis M. Goldsborough	Nov. 1, 1853
Captain George S. Blake	Sept. 15, 1857
Rear Admiral David D. Porter	Sept. 9, 1865
Commodore John L. Worden	Dec. 1, 1869
Rear Admiral C. R. P. Rodgers	Sept. 22, 1874
Commodore Foxhall A. Parker	July 1, 1878
Rear Admiral George B. Balch	Aug. 2, 1879
Rear Admiral C. R. P. Rodgers	June 13, 1881
Captain F. M. Ramsay	Nov. 14, 1881
Commander W. T. Sampson	Sept. 9, 1886
Captain R. L. Phythian	June 30, 1890
Captain P. H. Cooper	Nov. 15, 1894
Rear Admiral F. V. McNair	July 15, 1898
Commander Richard Wainwright	Mar. 15, 1900

Midshipmen, Acting Midshipmen and Naval Cadets

AT THE

NAVAL ACADEMY, 1840--1900, INCLUSIVE.

ARRANGED IN CLASSES.

1840.—MIDSHIPMEN.

Aby, Charles W., 8 February, 1840. Graduated.
Alston, Thomas P., 15 February, 1840. Resigned.
Aulick, Richmond, 19 October, 1840. Graduated.
Austin, William D., 3 November, 1840. Graduated.
Barrett, Edward, 3 November, 1840. Graduated.
Beard, Louis, 10 January, 1840. Resigned.
Beckwith, James L. S., 16 January, 1840. Dismissed.
Bennett, John W., 10 February, 1840. Graduated.
Blake, Homer C., 2 March, 1840. Graduated.
Bradford, James M., 10 January, 1840. Graduated.
Brand, Frederick B., 17 July, 1840. Graduated.
Branle, Charles E., 25 January, 1840. Dropped.
Brinley, Edward, Jr., 14 September, 1840. Graduated.
Campbell, James C., 29 December, 1840. Resigned.
Carr, Nathaniel F., 3 February, 1840. Dropped.
Carter, Jonathan H., 12 March, 1840. Graduated.
Carter, Samuel P., 14 February, 1840. Graduated.
Colborn, Henderson A., 18 January, 1840. Dropped.
Conover, Francis S., 11 May, 1840. Graduated.
Cowden, Samuel D., 19 February, 1840. Dismissed.
Crawford, J. Q. A., 17 February, 1840. Dismissed.
Cunningham, George F., 14 February, 1840. Dropped.
Davidson, Washington F., 20 February, 1840. Graduated.
Denniston, Garret V., 10 March, 1840. Graduated.
Dyer, Charles, Jr., 25 January, 1840. Drowned.
English, Earl, 25 February, 1840. Graduated.
Enos, Albert G., 7 November, 1840. Dismissed.

Gregory, Francis, 23 May, 1840. Graduated.
Hammond, Washington, 29 December, 1840. Resigned.
Hall, John P., 29 December, 1840. Graduated.
Harris, Reuben, 25 January, 1840. Graduated.
Henderson, Benjamin L., 2 January, 1840. Resigned.
Hewitt, William, 31 March, 1840. Resigned.
Hopkins, Edward A., 22 January, 1840. Resigned.
Hopson, John E., 25 September, 1840. Dismissed.
Hunt, Wilson, 20 February, 1840. Resigned.
Jeffers, William N., Jr., 25 September, 1840. Graduated.
Kemble, Peter, 19 December, 1840. Resigned.
Lowry, Reigert B., 31 January, 1840. Graduated.
Marr, Robert A., 29 April, 1840. Graduated.
Madigan, John, 19 February, 1840. Graduated.
McArann, Robert M., 12 May, 1840. Graduated.
McCauly, James B., 8 February, 1840. Graduated.
McLaughlin, Augustus, 11 January, 1840. Graduated.
Miller, Samuel A., 3 January, 1840. Dismissed.
Nelson, William, 28 January, 1840. Graduated.
Nones, Jefferson H., 19 December, 1840. Dismissed.
Paulding, Leonard, 19 December, 1840. Graduated.
Phelps, Thomas S., 17 January, 1840. Graduated.
Polk, William W. (changed to Pollock,), 30 June, 1837. Graduated.
Porter, Henry O., 3 November, 1840. Resigned.
Pringle, John J., 23 September, 1840. Graduated.
Quackenbush, Stephen P., 15 February, 1840. Graduated.
Robinson, Lawrence B., 4 March, 1840. Resigned.

(615)

GENERAL NAVY REGISTER.

Savage, Robert, 27 March, 1840. Graduated.
Simpson, Edward, 11 February, 1840. Graduated.
Smith, Crawford E., 2 January, 1840. Dropped.
Smith, William Henry, 31 July, 1840. Graduated.
Stevens, George A., 13 May, 1840. Graduated.
Stout, Edward C., 18 February, 1840. Graduated.
Temple, William G., 18 April, 1840. Graduated.
Terrett, Colville, 3 January, 1840. Graduated.
Van Hook, Benjamin L. T., 2 January, 1840. Resigned.
Waddell, Charles, 14 March, 1840. Graduated.
Wager, Peter, Jr., 12 February, 1840. Graduated.
Walcutt, John, 2 March, 1840. Graduated.
Warley, Alexander F., 19 February, 1840. Graduated.
Wells, Clark H., 25 September, 1840. Graduated.
Welsh, George P., 14 September, 1840. Graduated.
Wheelock, Frederick P., 10 March, 1840. Graduated.
Wilcox, Samuel, 11 January, 1840. Resigned.
Wiley, James, 9 March, 1840. Resigned.

1841.—MIDSHIPMEN.

Abercromble, Alexander R., 19 October, 1841. Dismissed.
Allmand, Albert, 10 September, 1841. Graduated.
Andrews, Elijah T., 10 October, 1841. Died 1848.
Armstrong, James, 9 September, 1841. Graduated.
Ashmead, Lehman P., 19 October, 1841. Resigned.
Badger, Oscar C., 9 September, 1841. Graduated.
Baily Alfred, 28 January, 1841. Resigned.
Baldwin, Frederick P., 10 September, 1841. Dismissed.
Barker, John R., 11 February, 1841. Dropped.
Barrand, John T., 20 September, 1841. Graduated.
Bartlett, Joseph T., 9 September, 1841. Drowned 30 March, 1846.
Bassett, Simeon S., 10 September, 1841. Graduated.
Bayard, Charles C., 9 December, 1841. Graduated.
Beadel, Edmund N., 19 October, 1841. Lost in Grampus, March, 1843.
Bell, Charles S., 9 September, 1841. Dismissed.
Beverly, McKenzie, 19 October, 1841. Dropped.
Bier, George H., 19 October, 1841. Graduated.
Bliss, Sylvanus J., 19 October, 1841. Graduated.
Bridge, William King, 14 January, 1841. Graduated.
Brodhead, Thomas W., 3 March, 1841. Graduated.
Brooke, John M., 3 March, 1841. Graduated.
Brown, Hezekiah G. D., 19 February, 1841. Resigned.
Browne, William B., 19 October, 1841. Died 11 August, 1843.
Buckner, Washington P., 9 September, 1841. Graduated.
Burwell, William T., 27 September, 1841. Resigned.
Byers, Josiah S., 19 October, 1841. Resigned.
Byrens, Allen T., 26 February, 1841. Graduated.
Carmichael, Edward T., 17 September, 1841. Died 7 August, 1847.
Chenoweth, Gideon D., 19 October, 1841. Died April, 1847.
Chever, David A., 19 October, 1841. Resigned.
Cilley, Greenleaf, 26 February, 1841. Graduated.
Clarke, Francis G., Jr., 19 October, 1841. Graduated.
Coleman, David, 19 October, 1841. Graduated.
Collins, Charles F., 19 February, 1841. Resigned.
Comegys, Cornelius, 9 September, 1841. Dismissed.
Cook, Albert G., 27 October, 1841. Dismissed.
Cook, Joseph J., 19 October, 1841. Graduated.
Crabb, Horace N., 19 October, 1841. Graduated.
Crain, Walter O., 27 October, 1841. Graduated.
Craney, William, September, 1841. Resigned.
Cushman, William S., 18 February, 1841. Resigned.
Dallas, Francis G., 8 November, 1841. Graduated.
Danels, Joseph D., 19 October, 1841. Graduated.
Davidson, Hunter, 29 October, 1841. Graduated.
Davis, John L., 9 January, 1841. Graduated.
DeBree, Alexander M., 19 October, 1841. Graduated.
De Haven, Joseph E., 19 October, 1841. Graduated.
Dekoven, William, 9 September, 1841. Graduated.
De Krafft, J. C. P., 19 October, 1841. Graduated.
Denny, Ebenezer D., 17 September, 1841. Graduated.
Dibble, George M., 1 March, 1841. Graduated.
Desloude, Adrian, 27 October, 1841. Resigned.
Douglas, George B., 10 September, 1841. Dropped.
Duvall, Robert C., 19 October, 1841. Graduated.
Eaton, Thomas C., 9 September, 1841. Graduated.
Fauntleroy, William H., 2 March, 1841. Graduated.
Ferguson, James L., 9 September, 1841. Resigned.
Fillebrown, Thomas S., 19 October, 1841. Graduated.
Flournoy, Thomas, 10 September, 1841. Dropped.
Ford, Joseph M., 18 January, 1841. Resigned.
Forrest, Joseph A. (changed to Dulany Abell Forrest), 3 March, 1841. Graduated.

GENERAL NAVY REGISTER.

Franklin, Samuel R., 18 February, 1841. Graduated.
Friend, Joseph L., 27 October, 1841. Graduated.
Fry, Joseph, 15 September, 1841. Graduated.
Gale, John, 19 October, 1841. Graduated.
Gamble, William M., 1 March, 1841. Graduated.
Gansevoort, Stanwix, 3 November, 1841. Resigned.
Genet, Edmund C., 22 February, 1841. Resigned. Reappointed. Dismissed.
Gibson, William, 11 February, 1841. Graduated.
Gillis, Walter V., 27 October, 1841. Graduated.
Godman, Stewart A., 4 November, 1841. Resigned.
Gordan, Edward, 21 September, 1841. Dismissed.
Grafton, Edward C., 5 October, 1841. Graduated.
Graham, Charles K., 19 October, 1841. Resigned.
Gray, Charles, 19 October, 1841. Graduated.
Griffin, Samuel P., 9 September, 1841. Graduated.
Habersham, Alexander W., 3 March, 1841. Graduated.
Hallett, Frederick A., 13 September, 1841. Resigned.
Hanson, John J., 21 September, 1841. Graduated.
Hare, George H., 19 October, 1841. Graduated.
Harris, Thomas C., 9 September, 1841. Graduated.
Harrison, Gustavus, 27 October, 1841. Graduated.
Harrison, Walter P., 19 October, 1841. Resigned.
Hart, John E., 23 February, 1841. Graduated.
Haxtun, Milton, 19 October, 1841. Graduated.
Haywood, Philemon H., 19 October, 1841. Dismissed.
Heron, James, 19 October, 1841. Dismissed.
Hoffman, William G., 19 October, 1841. Graduated.
Holmes, William W., 21 September, 1841. Graduated.
Hopkins, Charles F., 19 October, 1841. Graduated.
Horton, William S., 19 October, 1841. Dropped.
Hugunin, Daniel C., 3 March, 1841. Lost in the Warrens, 13 November, 1846.
Hunter, Henry C., 10 September, 1841. Graduated.
Hunter, Henry St. George, 19 November, 1841. Graduated.
Irvine, Thomas. 10 September, 1841. Dropped.
Jackson, Alonzo C., 23 February, 1841. Graduated.
Johnson, Andrew W., 19 October, 1841. Graduated.
Johnson, John H., 19 October, 1841. Resigned.
Johnston, Elliott, 17 September, 1841. Resigned.
Johnston, James L., 27 September, 1841. Dismissed.
Jones, Copeland P., 21 September, 1841. Resigned.
Jones, John P., 19 October, 1841. Graduated.
Jones, M. Patterson, 9 September, 1841. Graduated.
Jones, Walter F., 20 September, 1841. Graduated.

Jouett, James E., 10 September, 1841. Graduated.
Kell, John, 9 September, 1841. Graduated.
Kellog, Frederick, 23 February, 1841. Resigned.
Key, Henry H., 10 September, 1841. Resigned.
Kinkead, Joseph B., 19 October, 1841. Resigned.
Latimer, Charles, 9 September, 1841. Graduated.
Laurens, John, 13 November, 1841. Resigned.
Law, Richard L., 17 February, 1841. Graduated.
Law, William W., 3 March, 1841. Graduated.
Lee, Theodoric, 9 September, 1841. Graduated.
Lewis, Andrew J., 26 September, 1841. Graduated.
Lewis, Robert F. R., 19 October, 1841. Graduated.
Luce, Stephen B., 19 October, 1841. Graduated.
Lyne, Leonard H., 10 September, 1841. Graduated.
Magaw, Samuel, 23 November, 1841. Graduated.
Mahon, Thomas D., 10 September, 1841. Dismissed.
March, John H., 19 October, 1841. Graduated.
Mason, Lucius M., 19 October, 1841. Died 7 January, 1845.
Maury, Jefferson, 9 September, 1841. Graduated.
Mayo, William K., 18 October, 1841. Graduated.
McCarthy, James B., 9 January, 1841. Died 11 August, 1842.
McCauley, Edward Y., 9 September, 1841. Graduated.
McCollum, John Van, 26 February, 1841. Graduated.
McCook, John J., 27 January, 1841. Died 30 March, 1842.
McCorkle, David P., 21 September, 1841. Graduated.
McDermut, Daniel A., 8 November, 1841. Graduated.
McGary, Charles P., 19 October, 1841. Graduated.
McKeithen, William J., 3 March, 1841. Dropped.
McRoberts, Jefferson, 3 March, 1841. Dismissed.
Mercer, William R., 8 December, 1841. Graduated.
Miller, Thomas J., 9 September, 1841. Resigned.
Mills, John K., 15 January, 1841. Resigned.
Minor, Robert D., 26 February, 1841. Graduated.
Mitchell, Alexander J., 9 September, 1841. Resigned.
Mitchell, Charles M., 19 October, 1841. Resigned.
Mitchell, William, 24 September, 1841. Graduated.
Monroe, Andrew F., 3 March, 1841. Graduated.
Morgan, George E., 18 February, 1841. Graduated.
Murdaugh, William H., 9 September, 1841. Graduated.
Murphy, John McL., 18 February, 1841. Graduated.
Neilson, Edward R., 27 October, 1841. Resigned.
Oliver, Edwin W., 9 November, 1841. Resigned.

Otis, Arthur H., 9 September, 1841. Resigned.
Patton, Robert, 9 September, 1841. Resigned.
Parker, William H., 19 October, 1841. Graduated.
Parrish, Joseph, 19 October, 1841. Dismissed.
Pasteur, Edward C., 22 January, 1841. Resigned.
Phelps, Seth L., 19 October, 1841. Graduated.
Phenix, Dawson, 30 September, 1841. Graduated.
Philip, John V. N., 25 February, 1841. Graduated.
Pillsbury, Wingate, 9 September, 1841. Drowned 25 July, 1847.
Prentiss, John E., 19 October, 1841. Died 31 December, 1843.
Price, Richard J. D., 9 September, 1841. Graduated.
Powell, William L., 20 September, 1841. Graduated.
Queen, Walter, 7 October, 1841. Graduated.
Rathbone, Samuel B., 3 March, 1841. Resigned.
Reily, William, 9 February, 1841. Graduated.
Renshaw, Edward, 4 November, 1841. Graduated.
Rochelle, James H., 9 September, 1841. Graduated.
Roe, Francis A., 19 October, 1841. Graduated.
Roney, Thomas, 3 March, 1841. Graduated.
Russell, John H., 10 September, 1841. Graduated.
Scott, Robert W., 9 September, 1841. Graduated.
Scovell, Edward H., 19 October, 1841. Dismissed.
Selden, Edward A., 19 October, 1841. Graduated.
Selden, Robert, 9 September, 1841. Graduated.
Semmes, Alexander A., 27 October, 1841. Graduated.
Sharp, William, 9 September, 1841. Graduated.
Shepherd, Edmund, 19 October, 1841. Graduated.
Shubrick, Thomas B., 3 March, 1841. Killed 25 March, 1847.
Simes, George T., 19 October, 1841. Graduated.
Simmons, Alexander R., 19 October, 1841. Dismissed.
Smith, Jesse M., 9 February, 1841. Died.
Smith, Joseph B., 19 October, 1841. Graduated.
Smith, Marshall J., 19 October, 1841. Graduated.
Smith, Watson, 19 October, 1841. Graduated.
Somerville, James H., 10 September, 1841. Graduated.
Spence, Stephen D., 9 September, 1841. Resigned.
Spencer, Philip, 20 November, 1841. Died 1 December, 1842.
Stephenson, Byrd W., 9 September, 1841. Dropped.
Stewart, John B., 9 September, 1841. Graduated.

Stone, Edward E., 19 October, 1841. Graduated.
Storer, Robert B., 4 November, 1841. Died 4 July, 1847.
Stuart, Robert, 19 October, 1841. Graduated.
Thomas, William R., 15 January, 1841. Graduated.
Thornton, James S., 15 January, 1841. Graduated.
Thruston, John, 27 October, 1841. Resigned.
Tillotson, James L., 19 October, 1841. Resigned.
Toler, William P., 19 October, 1841. Resigned.
Truxtun, William, 9 February, 1841. Graduated.
Turner, James M., 18 February, 1841. Dismissed.
Upshur, John H., 4 November, 1841. Graduated.
Vander Horst, Elias, 10 September, 1841. Graduated.
Valle, Bartholomew, 28 January, 1841. Resigned.
Van Wyck, William, 19 October 1841. Graduated.
Van Zandt, Nicholas H., 19 October, 1841. Graduated.
Waddell, James J., 10 September, 1841. Graduated.
Wager, Charles, 2 April, 1835. Resigned. Reinstated 16 March, 1841. Resigned.
Wainwright, Thomas B., 21 September, 1841. Graduated.
Walker, John T., 18 February, 1841. Graduated.
Walker, Theodoric L., 10 September, 1841. Graduated.
Waring, Archibald H., 19 October, 1841. Resigned.
Watmough, Pendleton G., 20 September, 1841. Graduated.
Weaver, William H., 19 October, 1841. Graduated.
Wells, Benjamin F., 22 September, 1841. Dismissed.
West, Nathaniel T., 18 February, 1841. Graduated.
West, William C., 30 January, 1841. Graduated.
Whitaker, John G., 10 September, 1841. Resigned.
Whiting, William D., 1 March, 1841. Graduated.
Wilcox, William Henry, 30 January, 1841. Graduated.
Wilkes, John, Jr., 9 September, 1841. Graduated.
Wilkinson, William W., 4 November, 1841. Graduated.
Willis, Henry, 10 September, 1841. Dismissed.
Wilson, John K., 3 March, 1841. Graduated.
Wood, Dallas R., 3 March, 1841. Resigned.
Woolley, Charles, 30 November, 1841. Graduated.
Wright, Benjamin B., 10 September, 1841. Resigned.
Yates, James B., 29 December, 1841. Resigned.
Young, Jonathan, 19 October, 1841. Graduated.
Young, Thomas, 27 October, 1841. Graduated.

GENERAL NAVY REGISTER. 619

1842.—MIDSHIPMEN.

Carter, Robert R., 30 March, 1842. Graduated.
Debuys, Gaspard, 4 January, 1842. Resigned.
Henry, Edmund W., 7 April, 1842. Graduated.
Hunter, Charles C., 2 July, 1842. Graduated.
King, George S., 25 March, 1842. Graduated.
Langhorne, John D., 6 July, 1842. Graduated.
McFane, Allan, 24 May, 1842. Graduated.
Minchall, George A., 30 July, 1842. Lost in the Grampus, March, 1843.
Oakley, Cyrus H., 30 March, 1842. Dismissed.
Seawell, Joseph A., 2 July, 1842. Graduated.
Shaw, Henry G. C., 30 July, 1842. Resigned.
Tillotson, John H., 30 July, 1842. Resigned.
Wall, Elliott D., 19 July, 1842. Dismissed.

1845.—MIDSHIPMEN.

Adams, John, 5 September, 1845. Dropped.
Chandler, Ralph, 27 September, 1845. Graduated.
Goodloe, John J., 14 October, 1845. Resigned.
Grundy, Felix, 21 October, 1845. Dismissed.
Hamilton, John R., 8 September, 1845. Graduated.
Hays, William B., 7 November, 1845. Graduated.
Hodge, George B., 16 December, 1845. Graduated.
Houston, Thomas T., 26 August, 1845. Graduated.
McGunnegle, Wilson, 16 December, 1845. Graduated.
McKean, Franklin B., 30 September, 1845. Resigned.
Smith, William H., 16 October, 1845. Resigned.

1846.—MIDSHIPMEN.

Allen, Oliver P., 28 September, 1846. Dismissed.
Barclay, Alexander J., 14 May, 1846. Resigned.
Braine, Daniel L., 30 May, 1846. Graduated.
Bredin, James, 27 July, 1846. Resigned.
Breese, Kidder R., 6 November, 1846. Graduated.
Breese, Samuel L., 14 May, 1846. Graduated.
Brodhead, Edgar, 9 July, 1846. Graduated.
Carnes, Edwin O., 24 June, 1846. Graduated.
Childress, Thomas B., 6 February, 1846. Resigned.
Dallas, Alexander J., 24 March, 1846. Dismissed.
Foster, James P., 14 May, 1846. Graduated.
Gherardi, Bancroft, 29 June, 1846. Graduated.
Gray, Edwin F., 8 April, 1846. Graduated.
Johnson, Philip C., Jr., 31 August, 1846. Graduated.
Johnson, Oscar F., 14 August, 1846. Graduated.
Kennon, Beverly, Jr., 22 August, 1846. Graduated.
Kimberly, Lewis A., 8 December, 1846. Graduated.
Lodge, Augustus, 22 August, 1846. Resigned.
Looker, Thomas H., 6 November, 1846. Resigned.
Lynch, Dominick H., 6 November, 1846. Dismissed.
Maffitt, William H., 30 May, 1846. Dismissed.
Milligan, James F., 28 July, 1846. Resigned.
Morris, George U., 14 August, 1846. Graduated.
Parker, James, Jr., 14 November, 1846. Graduated.
Rainey, John D., 19 March, 1846. Graduated.
Robinson, Frederick W., 14 August, 1846. Dismissed.
Sawyer, Lewis C., 14 August, 1846. Resigned.
Shunk, William F., 1 June, 1846. Resigned.
Smith, Charles B., 30 November, 1846. Graduated.
Smith, Charles L., 27 July, 1846. Died 16 November, 1848.
Sproston, John G., 15 July, 1846. Graduated.
Watters, John, 12 February, 1846. Graduated.

1847.—MIDSHIPMEN.

Baker, John P., 11 February, 1847. Resigned.
Belknap, George E., 7 October, 1847. Graduated.
Benham, Andrew E. K., 24 November, 1847. Graduated.
Blake, Joseph D., 9 September, 1847. Graduated.
Bowen, Richard T., 24 December, 1847. Graduated.
Brose, Frederick F., 9 September, 1847. Graduated.
Bryant, Robert, 11 December, 1847. Resigned.
Buell, Salmon A., 1 February, 1847. Resigned.
Burke, Edmund C., 20 October, 1847. Resigned.
Caldwell, Robert M., 9 September, 1847. Dismissed.

620 GENERAL NAVY REGISTER.

Campbell, William P. A., 14 December, 1847. Graduated.
Cannon, Chastain C., 7 April, 1847. Dropped.
Chapman, George H., 9 September, 1847. Resigned.
Chapman, Robert T., 7 April, 1847. Graduated.
Cornwell, John J., 1 February, 1847. Graduated.
Cummings, Andrew B., 7 April, 1847. Graduated.
Eggleston, John R., 2 August, 1847. Graduated.
Fitzhugh, William E., 2 February, 1847. Out of service from 7 July, 1847.
Flusser, Charles W., 19 July, 1847. Graduated.
Fyffe, Joseph P., 9 September, 1847. Graduated.
Gift, George W., 30 November, 1847. Resigned.
Gwin, William, 7 April, 1847. Graduated.
Hamer, Thomas M., 26 June, 1847. Resigned.
Hammond, Charles L. O., 8 November, 1847. Resigned.
Hand, Bayard E., 7 April, 1847. Graduated.
Hand, George D., 9 September, 1847. Resigned.
Haralson, Charles L., 10 September, 1847. Resigned.
Harmony, David B., 7 April, 1847. Graduated.
Hutchinson, William T., 24 September, 1847. Died 7 February, 1848.

Irwin, John, 9 September, 1847. Graduated.
Ives, Raiford W., 7 April, 1847. Died 25 March, 1850.
Laughlin, John J., 1 May, 1847. Resigned.
Lovell, William S., 8 November, 1847. Graduated.
Maxwell, James G., 15 December, 1847. Graduated.
Miller, Joseph B., 7 April, 1847. Died 19 March, 1850.
Mygatt, Jared P. K., 24 September, 1847. Graduated.
Newman, L. H., 24 September, 1847. Graduated.
Oakley, Eugene H., 2 August, 1847. Graduated.
Quackenbush, John N., 24 September, 1847. Dismissed.
Rowan, James H., Jr., 8 November, 1847. Resigned.
Stillwell, James, 9 September, 1847. Graduated.
Thoburn, Charles E., 9 September, 1847. Graduated.
Totten, Washington, 8 November, 1847. Graduated.
Ward, William H., 7 April, 1847. Resigned.
Wells, Charles, 22 December, 1847. Dropped.
Whitthorne, De Witt C., 10 September, 1847. Resigned.
Williams, Edward P., 9 September, 1847. Graduated.
Wilson, Henry, 22 October, 1847. Graduated.
Wood, John S., 7 April, 1847. Graduated.

1848.—MIDSHIPMEN.

Abbot, Trevett, 13 October, 1848. Graduated.
Abbott, William A., 13 October, 1848. Resigned.
Armstrong, William McN., 20 November, 1848. Resigned.
Baker, Francis H. 12 October, 1848. Graduated.
Beatty, John T., 21 October, 1848. Resigned.
Bratt, Carlos, 12 October, 1848. Resigned.
Brintnall, John P., 21 December, 1848. Resigned.
Bruce, James, 12 October, 1848. Graduated.
Butler, James L., 11 April, 1848. Resigned.
Carter, Carey, 12 October, 1848. Resigned.
Coddington, Ethelbert F., 12 October, 1848. Died 8 November, 1853.
Duret, John B., 6 December, 1848. Dropped.
Erben, Henry, Jr., 17 June, 1848. Graduated.
Fitzhugh, William E., 20 November, 1848. Graduated.
Garland, Hudson M., 20 November, 1848. Graduated.
Gayle, Richard H., 13 October, 1848. Resigned.
Gillis, James H., 12 October, 1848. Graduated.
Glassell, William T., 15 March, 1848. Graduated.
Greene, Charles H., 13 May, 1848. Graduated.
Greer, James A., 10 January, 1848. Graduated.
Grout, John K., 21 November, 1848. Dropped.
Heileman, Julius G., 10 March, 1848. Graduated.

Hester, Isaac W., 12 October, 1848. Graduated.
Hodges, James B., 13 October, 1848. Resigned.
Johnston, John E., 9 August, 1848. Graduated.
Lagow, John K., 31 March, 1848. Resigned.
Legare, James D., 26 December, 1848. Resigned.
Livingston, De Grasse, 7 March, 1848. Graduated.
Lyne, William H., 5 June, 1848. Resigned.
McCann, William P., 1 November, 1848. Graduated.
McIntosh, John B., 27 April, 1848. Resigned.
McThorne, Henry, 18 April, 1848. Dismissed.
Means, Edward J., 12 October, 1848. Resigned.
Owen, Elias K., 7 December, 1848. Graduated.
Palmer, Marshall E., 23 March, 1848. Resigned.
Porter, Pinckney J., 6 March, 1848. Resigned.
Prickett, Nathaniel P., 10 June, 1848. Died 23 March, 1850.
Riddell, John W., 12 October, 1848. Resigned.
Pendergrast, Austin, 14 October, 1848. Graduated.
Scantland, Robert A., 30 December, 1848. Dropped.
Skerrett, Joseph S., 12 October, 1848. Graduated.
Spalding, Rufus C., 12 October, 1848. Resigned.

GENERAL NAVY REGISTER. 621

Spedden, Edward T., 20 November, 1848. Graduated.
Sullivan, Jeremiah C., 12 October, 1848. Resigned.
Toon, William H., 21 April, 1848. Resigned.
Trotter, George A., 20 November, 1848. Died 29 December, 1849.
Weaver, Aaron W., 10 May, 1848. Graduated.

1849.—MIDSHIPMEN.

Adams, Henry A., Jr., 16 October, 1849. Graduated.
Adams, Napoleon B., 25 January, 1849. Dropped.
Boardman, Frederick A., 20 October, 1849. Resigned.
Briscoe, Warner L., 20 November, 1849. Dropped.
Brown, George, 5 February, 1849. Graduated.
Chapman, George T., 16 October, 1849. Appt. revoked.
Chever, William H., 19 October, 1849. Graduated.
Cushman, Charles H., 24 March, 1849. Graduated.
Davis, Andrew McF., 16 March, 1849. Resigned.
Drake, Benjamin, 22 October, 1849. Dropped.
Dunnington, John W., 10 April, 1849. Graduated.
Hawley, Charles E., 3 December, 1849. Graduated.
Holland, Dick. V. B., 23 February, 1849. Dropped.
Loyall, Benjamin P., 5 March, 1849. Graduated.
May, Robert L., 7 November, 1849. Graduated.
McCrea, Edward P., 16 October, 1849. Graduated.
Mish, Simon C., 8 January, 1849. Resigned.
Morrison, George F., 5 November, 1849. Graduated.
Pelot, Thomas P., 2 June, 1849. Graduated.
Shepperd, Francis E., 16 October, 1849. Graduated.
Shirk, James W., 26 March, 1849. Graduated.
Shubrick, Edward R., 9 February, 1849. Resigned.
Stanton, Oscar F., 29 December, 1849. Graduated.
Stockton, Edward C., 16 October, 1849. Graduated.
Tabb, Blucher, H., 17 January, 1849. Killed 5 March, 1850.
Taylor, Bushrod B., 3 April, 1849. Graduated.
Taylor, Jesse, Jr., 6 December, 1849. Graduated.
Thomas, Calvin F., 16 October, 1849. Graduated.
Tipton, John, 24 November, 1849. Appt. revoked.
Wainwright, Gardner S., 1 November, 1849. Dropped.
Walker, James C., 12 February, 1849. Resigned.
Ward, William H., 17 February, 1849. Graduated.
Winchester, Felix, 25 October, 1849. Dropped.

1850.—MIDSHIPMEN.

Armstrong, Æneas, 2 October, 1850. Graduated.
Arnold, Thomas, 11 November, 1850. Resigned.
Babcock, Charles A., 8 April, 1850. Graduated.
Baber, George F. B., 24 April, 1850. Lost in the Porpoise, 21 September, 1854.
Bacon, George, 1 October, 1850. Graduated.
Beardslee, Lester A., 5 March, 1850. Graduated.
Blocker, Smith B., 2 October, 1850. Dropped.
Bowen, Robert J., 20 November, 1850. Resigned.
Boyd, Robert, Jr., 14 January, 1850. Graduated.
Bradford, William L., 1 October, 1850. Graduated.
Campbell, Marshall C., 5 February, 1850. Graduated.
Carpenter, Charles C., 1 October, 1850. Graduated.
Carroll, Ferdinand, 4 October, 1850. Dismissed.
Chaplin, James C., 4 October, 1850. Graduated.
Cooper, Edward B., 6 November, 1850. Dismissed.
Cooper, Richard F., 25 October, 1850. Dismissed.
Dana, William H., 1 May, 1850. Graduated.
Dawson, Lucien W., 27 April, 1850. Resigned.
Dodge, George P., 1 October, 1850. Dismissed.
Dozier, William G., 1 April, 1850. Graduated.
Ellege, John W., 29 May, 1850. Dismissed.
Foot, Samuel C., 4 April, 1850. Resigned.
Foster, Robert C., Jr., 1 October, 1850. Resigned.
Harrison, George R., 2 October, 1850. Dismissed.
Izard, Allen C., 2 October, 1850. Graduated.
Kirkland, William A., 2 July, 1850. Graduated.
Lieber, Alfred H., 2 October, 1850. Dismissed.
Little, William A., 8 April, 1850. Died 24 August, 1852.
Mathias, George M., 7 October, 1850. Dropped.
McCartney, Andrew J., 3 October, 1850. Graduated.
McEntee, Maurice W., 4 October, 1850. Resigned.
McLanahan, James W., 2 October, 1850. Resigned.
Meade, Richard W., Jr., 2 October, 1850. Graduated.

Mitchell, John G., 2 October, 1850. Graduated.
Offley, Robert H., 19 October, 1850. Dismissed.
Pearce, William, 1 October, 1850. Dismissed.
Peck, Charles F., 3 October, 1850. Graduated.
Potter, Edward E., 5 February, 1850. Graduated.
Ramsay, Francis M., 5 October, 1850. Graduated.
Roche, James R., 30 May, 1850. Resigned.
Shields, William B., 2 October, 1850. Dismissed.
Smith, William H., 3 October, 1850. Resigned.
Sparks, Charles D., 18 April, 1850. Died 12 April, 1853.
Stevens, Douglas H., 1 October, 1850. Dismissed.
Simmer, Edward E., 2 October, 1850. Resigned.
Van Cleef, Charles M., 2 October, 1850. Dropped.
Walker, John G., 5 October, 1850. Graduated.
Whittier, Rufus A., 4 March, 1850. Dropped.
Williams, Wesley, 4 October, 1850. Dismissed.
Wilson, Robert H., 18 June, 1850. Resigned.
Wishart, Alexander, 2 October, 1850. Resigned.

1851.—MIDSHIPMEN.

Allen, Edmund S., 2 October, 1851. Dropped.
Armington, Adolphus G., 2 October, 1851. Dropped.
Barnes, John S., 1 October, 1851. Graduated.
Blodgett, George M., 3 October, 1851. Graduated.
Buchanan, Thomas McK., 1 October, 1851. Graduated.
Cain, John, Jr., 4 October, 1851. Graduated.
Campbell, John B., 1 October, 1851. Resigned.
Carriere, Albert, 2 October, 1851. Dropped.
Cecil, Walpole, 2 October, 1851. Dropped.
Clarke, Frederic J., 3 October, 1851. Dismissed.
Cooke, George H., 1 October, 1851. Resigned.
Cortez, Rene E., 1 October, 1851. Dropped.
Crawford, John, 2 October, 1851. Resigned.
Crosman, Alexander F., 2 October, 1851. Graduated.
Dalton, Hamilton H., 1 October, 1851. Graduated.
Dodge, George P., 1 October, 1851. Dropped.
Dooley, Edwin H., 1 October, 1851. Resigned.
Douglas, James N., 1 October, 1851. Dropped.
Dox, Henry B., 2 October, 1851. Resigned.
Erwin, Jason C., 1 October, 1851. Resigned.
Etting, J. M., 2 October, 1851. Resigned.
Fitch, Leroy, 1 October, 1851. Graduated.
Fortier, Charles E., 1 October, 1851. Dropped.
Glasson, David G. H., 1 October, 1851. Resigned.
Graham, Richard W. M., 2 October, 1851. Graduated.
Hopkins, Alfred, 1 October, 1851. Graduated.
Hubbell, S. De Witt, 3 October, 1851. Resigned.
Hugunin, Robert, 1 October, 1851. Resigned.
Jay, Joseph McD. C., 1 October, 1851. Dropped.
Kearney, Edward, 4 October, 1851. Dismissed.
Law, George E., 4 October, 1851. Graduated.
Lawson, Hiram A., 14 October, 1851. Dropped.
Lea, Edward, 2 October, 1851. Graduated.
Lull, Edward P., 7 October, 1851. Graduated.
Matthews, Edmund O., 2 October, 1851. Graduated.
McEntee, Maurice W., 1 October, 1851. Resigned.
McKee, Samuel, 1 October, 1851. Resigned.
Meeds, Benjamin N., 1 October, 1851. Dismissed.
Miller, Joseph N., 1 October, 1851. Graduated.
Noble, James, 1 October, 1851. Dropped.
Norton, Charles S., 3 October, 1851. Graduated.
Perkins, George H., 1 October, 1851. Graduated.
Porcher, Philip, 2 October, 1851. Graduated.
Seabrook, E. M., 4 October, 1851. Resigned.
Seely, Carlton W., Jr., 1 October, 1851. Dropped.
Selfridge, Thomas O., 3 October, 1851. Graduated.
Sicard, Montgomery, 1 October, 1851. Graduated.
Sloan, George J., 1 October, 1851. Resigned.
Smith, Samuel A., 2 October, 1851. Dismissed.
Stribling, John M., 7 October, 1851. Graduated.
Sumner, Edward E., 1 October, 1851. Resigned.
Taylor, John R., 1 October, 1851. Dropped.
Todd, James M., 2 October, 1851. Graduated.
White, Hamilton C., 1 October, 1851. Resigned.

1852.—MIDSHIPMEN.

Allen, Weld N., 24 May, 1852. Graduated.
Ashe, William W., 31 May, 1852. Resigned.
Barrett, Clarence L., 25 May, 1852. Resigned.
Bigelow, George A., 26 May, 1852. Graduated.
Bishop, Henry J., 20 May, 1852. Dropped.
Bradford, Robert F., 21 May, 1852. Graduated.
Brodhead, Alfred W., 25 May, 1852. Died 23 January, 1853.

GENERAL NAVY REGISTER.

Bunce, Francis M., 28 May, 1852. Graduated.
Burton, Edward H., 31 May, 1852. Dropped.
Butler, Samuel M., 25 May, 1852. Dismissed.
Cooke, Augustus P., 27 May, 1852. Graduated.
Crenshaw, Cyrus W., 20 May, 1852. Dropped.
Cushman, Charles E., 25 May, 1852. Resigned.
Dunn, Denton, 28 May, 1852. Dropped.
Emerson, William R., 24 May, 1852. Resigned.
Evans, William E., 4 June, 1852. Graduated.
Gilchrist, Miller H., 31 May, 1852. Dropped.
Gorman, Richard L., 24 May, 1852. Resigned.
Gove, Gilman D., 22 May, 1852. Graduated.
Greene, Nathaniel, 28 May, 1852. Graduated.
Hale, Matthew, 31 May, 1852. Dropped.
Hatfield, Chester, 21 May, 1852. Graduated.
Holley, Robert Y., 24 May, 1852. Dropped.
Ingraham, Henry L., 29 May, 1852. Resigned.
Johnson, Robert McA., 28 May, 1852. Resigned.
Kendall, George T., 20 May, 1852. Dropped.
Lamar, Southworth H., 26 May, 1852. Dropped.

McDougal, Charles J., 26 May, 1852. Graduated.
McEnery, Samuel D., 25 May, 1852. Resigned.
Merchant, Clarke, 29 May, 1852. Graduated.
Miller, Henry W., 29 May, 1852. Graduated.
Mills, Thomas B., 31 May, 1852. Graduated.
Morgan, William H., 25 May, 1852. Resigned.
Mosely, James C., 20 May, 1852. Graduated.
Porter, Thomas K., 20 May, 1852. Graduated.
Potter, James L., 25 May, 1852. Resigned.
Prichett, James M., 27 May, 1852. Graduated.
Ragland, Eldred B., 25 May, 1852. Dropped.
Seely, Henry B., 26 May, 1852. Graduated.
Shyrock, George S., 22 May, 1852. Graduated.
Stebbins, De Wayne, 20 May, 1852. Resigned.
Sutherland, Robert, 29 May, 1852. Resigned.
Tickner, George P., 31 May, 1852. Dismissed.
Wallace, Rush R., 25 May, 1852. Graduated.

1853.—MIDSHIPMEN.

Adams, Leonard J., 21 January, 1853. Resigned.
Alexander, Joseph W., 21 September, 1853. Graduated.
Ashe, Alexander S., 31 January, 1853. Resigned.
Barrett, Walter, 28 September, 1853. Dropped.
Beckwith, Josiah G., 1 February, 1853. Resigned.
Blake, Francis B., 30 September, 1853. Graduated.
Bond, Francis W., 30 September, 1853. Dropped.
Brown, James F., 1 April, 1853. Dropped.
Cameron, William, 1 April, 1853. Dropped.
Colt, George DeWolf, 21 September, 1853. Resigned.
Eastman, Thomas H., 31 January, 1853. Graduated.
Graves, Charles J., 17 December, 1853. Graduated.
Harris, Joseph W., 1 January, 1853. Graduated.
Hosmer, James R., 26 September, 1853. Dropped.
Hunter, Clarence, 20 September, 1853. Dropped.
Ingraham, Darius H., 24 September, 1853. Resigned.
Kelly, John W., 31 January, 1853. Graduated.
Lallande, Charles D., 26 January, 1853. Dropped.

McCandless, William G., 24 September, 1853. Resigned.
McCrabb, Alfred P., 2 April, 1853. Dropped.
McNair, Frederick V., 21 September, 1853. Graduated.
Orton, Jason R., 29 September, 1853. Dropped.
Phythian, Robert L., 28 January, 1853. Graduated.
Sawyer, George A., 27 September, 1853. Resigned.
Terry, Edward, 21 September, 1853. Graduated.
Todd, Henry D., 28 May, 1853. Graduated.
Vultee, Francis P., 3 January, 1853. Dropped.
Wagstaff, Charles S., 21 September, 1853. Resigned.
Ward, Lewis P., 29 September, 1853. Resigned.
Warren, H. L., 20 September, 1853. Resigned.
Weisman, Harry J., 7 October, 1853. Died 17 November, 1854.
Welch, William, 23 September, 1853. Dismissed.
Wheeler, Fitz Henry, 30 September, 1853. Dropped.
Wilson, Byron, 31 January, 1853. Graduated.
Worthington, James G., 1 April, 1853. Dropped.
Yates, Arthur R., 24 September, 1853. Graduated.

1854.—MIDSHIPMEN.

Adams, Samuel, 21 September, 1854. Resigned.
Andruss, Elias V., 27 September, 1854. Resigned.

Beaumont, Myron H., 28 September, 1854. Resigned.
Belknap, Alden W., 27 September, 1854. Resigned.

624 GENERAL NAVY REGISTER.

Bishop, Joshua, 20 September, 1854. Graduated.
Blue, Henry M., 28 September, 1854. Graduated.
Bradley, John, 25 September, 1854. Resigned.
Brodrick, Henry H., 25 September, 1854. Resigned.
Brown, Hamilton A., 25 September, 1854. Resigned.
Carns, Andrew, Jr., 9 October, 1854. Resigned.
Cleveland, Charles B., 28 September, 1854. Resigned.
Collum, Richard S., 20 September, 1854. Resigned.
Condict, Henry F., 29 September, 1854. Dismissed.
Davis, T. W. W., 25 September, 1854. Resigned.
De Shields, Alfred, 23 September, 1854. Resigned.
Dewey, George, 23 September, 1854. Graduated.
Ewing, Thomas, 27 September, 1854. Resigned.
Farquhar, Norman H., 27 September, 1854. Graduated.
Franklin, Charles L., 23 October, 1854. Graduated.
Furber, Edward G., 2 October, 1854. Graduated.
Gibbs, Lucius H., 23 September, 1854. Resigned.
Grimball, John, 23 September, 1854. Graduated.
Hines, Iverson A., 21 September, 1854. Resigned.
Hinman, Curtis P., 30 September, 1854. Resigned.
Holliday, Titus T., 17 October, 1854. Resigned.
Howell, John A., 27 September, 1854. Graduated.
Howison, Henry L., 26 September, 1854. Graduated.
Hulburd, Horace R., 26 September, 1854. Resigned.
Jones, Richmond L., 23 September, 1854. Resigned.
Judson, Charles O., 30 September, 1854. Graduated.
Kautz, Albert, 28 September, 1854. Graduated.
Kerr, William A., 20 September, 1854. Graduated.
Lane, Nicholas J., 28 September, 1854. Resigned.
Livingston, Charles S., 22 September, 1854. Resigned.
Mailler, Robert C., 10 October, 1854. Resigned.
Mallett, Richardson, 20 September, 1854. Resigned.
May, Luther C., 20 September, 1854. Graduated.
McCook, Edwin S., 21 September, 1854. Resigned.

McCook, Roderick S., 21 September, 1854. Graduated.
McKinstry, Arthur, 29 September, 1854. Resigned.
Merriam, Gustavus F., 30 September, 1854. Resigned.
Milliken, Samuel, 20 September, 1854. Resigned.
Mullay, John C. K., 22 September, 1854. Resigned.
Pardee, Don A., 28 September, 1854. Resigned.
Phillips, Clavius, 3 October, 1854. Resigned.
Prentiss, Roderick, 21 September, 1854. Graduated.
Reddington, Thomas, 30 September, 1854. Resigned.
Reed, Allen V., 26 September, 1854. Graduated.
Ridgley, Franklin L., 25 September, 1854. Resigned.
Ross, James, Jr., 25 September, 1854. Resigned.
Schoonmaker, Cornelius M., 28 September, 1854. Graduated.
Smith, Beatty P., 29 September, 1854. Resigned.
Smith, Philip, 20 September, 1854. Resigned.
Spencer, Thomas S., 29 September, 1854. Graduated.
Stanburrough, James L., 26 September, 1854. Resigned.
Storrs, George S., 23 September, 1854. Graduated.
Swasey, Charles H., 28 September, 1854. Graduated.
Taylor, Edmund, 29 September, 1854. Resigned.
Terry, Felix G., 9 October, 1854. Resigned.
Triplett, Wellington, 22 September, 1854. Resigned.
Van Santvoord, Westbrook, 28 September, 1854. Resigned.
Vaughan, Vernon H., 21 September, 1854. Resigned.
Wadsworth, James M., 28 September, 1854. Resigned.
Walls, Augustus S., 27 September, 1854. Resigned.
Wheeler, Charles S., 27 September, 1854. Resigned.
Wheeler, Richard T., 27 September, 1854. Resigned.
White, George B., 28 September, 1854. Graduated.
Whittle, William C., Jr., 28 September, 1854. Graduated.
Wing, Edward D. C., 25 September, 1854. Resigned.
Wright, John F., 27 September, 1854. Resigned.
Yates, Robert H., 22 September, 1854. Resigned.
Young, Henry F., 30 September, 1854. Resigned.

1855.—MIDSHIPMEN.

Ashe, Samuel A'Court, 28 September, 1855. Resigned.
Averett, Samuel W., 3 November, 1855. Graduated.
Borchert, George, 20 September, 1855. Graduated.
Boyd, Frank, 21 September, 1855. Resigned.
Bristown, Benjamin W., 21 September, 1855. Dismissed.

Brown, James T., 27 September, 1855. Resigned.
Butt, Walter R., 20 September, 1855. Graduated.
Cenas, Hilary, 21 September, 1855. Graduated.
Claiborne, Henry B., 22 September, 1855. Graduated.
Crump, Edward H., 28 September, 1855. Resigned.

GENERAL NAVY REGISTER.

Daugherty, Oliver R., 26 September, 1854. Resigned.
Fister, Thomas D., 29 September, 1855. Resigned.
French, Samuel L., 26 September, 1855. Dismissed.
Graham, Archibald, 29 September, 1855. Resigned.
Greene, Samuel D., 21 September, 1855. Graduated.
Hackett, Samuel H., 28 September, 1855. Graduated.
Hall, Wilburn B., 20 September, 1855. Graduated.
Harry, Edwin C., 20 September, 1855. Resigned.
Hodge, Kosciusko, 28 September, 1855. Resigned.
Kane, Theodore F., 27 September, 1855. Graduated.
McKenzie, Alexander S., 29 September, 1855. Graduated.
Northrop, John B., 24 September, 1855. Resigned.

Pleasants, Charles W., 24 September, 1855. Dismissed.
Read, Edmund G., 25 September, 1855. Graduated.
Remey, George C., 20 September, 1855. Graduated.
Saulsbury, Gove H., 26 September, 1855. Resigned.
Slamm, Jefferson A., 2 October, 1855. Resigned.
Snyder, David H., 21 September, 1855. Resigned.
Stanton, Clarence L., 26 September, 1855. Dismissed.
Tayloe, James L., 24 September, 1855. Graduated.
Walker, Edward A., 26 September, 1855. Graduated.
Ward, George A., 21 September, 1855. Resigned.
Weisman, F. P., 25 September, 1855. Resigned.
Wiltse, Gilbert C., 20 September, 1855. Graduated.

1856.—MIDSHIPMEN.

Adams, Thomas E. M., 25 September, 1856. Resigned.
Allen, John W., 27 September, 1856. Resigned.
Ames, Sullivan D., 22 September, 1856. Graduated.
Barton, William H., 22 September, 1856. Graduated.
Bradford, James O., 23 September, 1856. Resigned.
Brown, Francis S., 24 September, 1856. Graduated.
Burt, Louis J., 20 September, 1856. Resigned.
Carnes, William W., 30 September, 1856. 1 October, 1857. Resigned.
Casey, Silas, 25 September, 1856. Graduated.
Comstock, John H., 27 September, 1856. Resigned.
Cordell, Ernest D., 20 September, 1856. Resigned.
Davenport, Francis O., 22 September, 1856. Graduated.
Devault, Edwin R., 20 September, 1856. Resigned.
Doolittle, Ormus A., 26 September, 1856. Dismissed.
Darnin, Thomas L., 22 September, 1856. Graduated.
Dowling, John C., 22 September, 1856. Resigned.
Foot, Henry D., 30 September, 1856. Dismissed.
Foster, Lyman B., 24 September, 1856. Resigned.
Gillet, Simeon P., 20 September, 1856. Graduated.
Gregory, Benjamin, 23 September, 1856. Resigned.
Greiner, Theodore S., 27 September, 1856. Resigned.
Griswold, George R., 20 September, 1856. Resigned.
Harris, George P., 22 September, 1856. Resigned.
Harrison, Thomas L., 29 September, 1856. Graduated.
Hayward, David S., 29 September, 1856. Resigned.
Herman, Henry M., 20 September, 1856. Resigned.
Hesse, John, 23 September, 1856. Resigned.

Hoge, Francis L., 20 September, 1856. Graduated.
Hooe, Roy Mason, 27 September, 1856. Resigned.
Hoole, James L., 22 September, 1856. Graduated.
Howard, George T., 22 September, 1856. Resigned.
Hunt, Charles S., 27 September, 1856. Resigned.
Hunt, John J., 30 September, 1856. Resigned.
Jacobs, William C., 29 September, 1856. Resigned.
Kean, Charles, 20 September, 1856. Resigned.
King, Charles K., 25 September, 1856. Resigned.
Kinney, Francis S., 22 September, 1856. Resigned.
Knipe, Samuel W., 22 September, 1856. Resigned.
Lambert, Bruce, 20 September, 1856. Resigned.
Lewis, Harold, 26 September, 1856. Dismissed.
Mahan, Alfred T., 30 September, 1856. Graduated.
Manley, Henry D., 25 September, 1856. Graduated.
Marvin, Joseph D., 25 September, 1856. Graduated.
McCarty, Stephen A., 25 September, 1856. Graduated.
McKinley, John S., 26 September, 1856. Resigned.
McNair, Antoine R., 22 September, 1856. Graduated.
Meade, Robert L., 30 September, 1856. Resigned.
O'Kane, James, 30 September, 1856. Graduated.
Paddock, Samuel B., 26 September, 1856. Graduated.
Philip, John W., 20 September, 1856. Graduated.
Porter, Robert H., 23 September, 1856. Resigned.
Raynsford, Edmund J. W., 27 September, 1856. Resigned.
Read, Charles William, 20 September, 1856. Graduated.
Reardon, Simon B., 20 September, 1856. Resigned.

Robeson, Henry B., 25 September, 1856. Graduated.
Sanderson, Philip S., 29 September, 1856. Dismissed.
Schenck, Woodhull S., 24 September, 1856. Resigned.
Schley, Winfield S., 20 September, 1856. Graduated.
Shute, Francis A., 24 September, 1856. Resigned.
Smith, William W., 25 September, 1856. Dismissed.
Spencer, Julian M., 22 September, 1856. Resigned.
Stevenson, John M., 22 September, 1856. Resigned.
Stuyvesant, Moses S., 29 September, 1856. Graduated.
Swann, Thomas L., 8 December, 1856. Graduated.

Sydnor, Richard D. B., 25 September, 1856. Resigned.
Talbott, Richard P. S., 29 September, 1856. Resigned.
Wall, William H., 27 September, 1856. Resigned.
Watson, John C., 29 September, 1856. Graduated.
Webster, Isaac P., 30 September, 1856. Resigned.
Weidman, John, 25 September, 1856. Resigned.
Wharton, Arthur D., 23 September, 1856. Graduated.
Whitehead, William, 23 September, 1856. Graduated.
Whitman, Charles S., 26 September, 1856. Resigned.

1857.—MIDSHIPMEN.

Armstrong, Richard F., 21 September, 1857. Resigned.
Bache, George M., 19 November, 1857. Graduated.
Backus, Sylvanus, 28 September, 1857. Graduated.
Boggs, Robert, 30 September, 1857. Resigned.
Bowen, Thomas C., 25 September, 1857. Graduated.
Churchill, John F., 24 September, 1857. Resigned.
Clark, Andrew J., 22 September, 1857. Resigned.
Concklin, George Henry, 28 September, 1857. Resigned.
Connally, John K., 28 September, 1857. Resigned.
Cooney, Charles D., 22 September, 1857. Resigned.
Cromwell, Bartlett J., 21 September, 1857. Graduated.
Cushing, William B., 25 September, 1857. Resigned.
Dexter, Adolphus, 24 September, 1857. Graduated.
Duer, Rufus K., 23 September, 1857. Graduated.
Farrington, Thomas P., 26 September, 1857. Appt. revoked.
Fisk, James E., 28 September, 1857. Resigned.
Foster, Charles G., 21 September, 1857. Resigned.
Frierson, Thomas H., 26 September, 1857. Resigned.
Fuller, James F., 22 September, 1857. Resigned.
Graham, James D., 25 September, 1857. Graduated.
Grimes, Howard, 22 September, 1857. Resigned.
Hayward, George W., 26 September, 1857. Graduated.
Haverstick, John W., 26 September, 1857. Resigned.
Hampstead, Lyman P., 23 September, 1857. Resigned.
Hicks, William A., 23 September, 1857. Resigned.
Higginson, Francis J., 21 September, 1857. Graduated.
Hobbs, Odillon B., 26 September, 1857. Died 1 October, 1860.
Holden, John F., 21 September, 1857. Resigned.
Hooper, Thomas W., 21 September, 1857. Resigned.

Howard, Ochran H., 21 September, 1857. Resigned.
Hudgins, Albert G., 24 September, 1857. Resigned.
Ingraham, John H., 23 October, 1857. Resigned.
Jackson, Crawford M., 29 September, 1857. Resigned.
Keeney, Charles T., 28 September, 1857. Resigned.
Kempff, Louis, 25 September, 1857. Graduated.
Lee, William P., 21 September, 1857. Resigned.
Leonard, Joseph A., 18 November, 1857. Resigned.
Lester, George, 23 September, 1857. Resigned.
Lodge, Douglas, 26 September, 1857. Resigned.
Lord, George P., 24 September, 1857. Resigned.
Malin, Emery, 24 September, 1857. Resigned.
Marsh, William, 25 September, 1857. Resigned.
Martin, William, 29 September, 1857. Resigned.
McFarland, John, 21 September, 1857. Graduated.
McGlensey, John F., 28 September, 1857. Graduated.
McKay, Charles E., 29 September, 1857. Graduated.
McKinley, Robert L., 24 September, 1857. Resigned.
McVeigh, Hiram, 25 September, 1857. Resigned.
Meade, Robert L., 29 September, 1857. Resigned.
Merriman, Edgar C., 21 September, 1857. Resigned.
Moore, Thomas L., 30 September, 1857. Resigned.
Morey, Koswell E., 26 September, 1857. Appt. revoked.
Mullen, Horace E., 25 September, 1857. Graduated.
Munce, Thomas Q., 22 September, 1857. Resigned.
Munroe, Frank, 25 September, 1857. Resigned.
Nurre, John, 23 September, 1857. Resigned.
Ogden, Morgan L., 29 September, 1857. Dismissed.
Orth, Christopher H., Jr., 26 September, 1857. Resigned.

GENERAL NAVY REGISTER. 627

Perry, Benjamin F., 5 October, 1857. Died 3 July, 1860.
Phoenix, Lloyd, 24 September, 1857. Graduated.
Picking, Henry F., 28 September, 1857. Graduated.
Platt, Frank A., 26 September, 1857. Resigned.
Polhemus, Charles, 21 September, 1857. Resigned.
Robertson, James P., 28 September, 1857. Graduated.
Rodgers, Frederic, 25 September, 1857. Graduated.
Rowland, John H., 21 September, 1857. Graduated.
Ryan, George P., 30 September, 1857. Graduated.
Sampson, William T., 24 September, 1857. Graduated.
Sleeper, George A., 26 September, 1857. Resigned.
Smith, Francis, 25 September, 1857. Resigned.
Smith, Napoleon J., 25 September, 1857. Resigned.
Smyser, Charles J., 22 September, 1857. Resigned.
Snell, Alfred T., 26 September, 1857. Graduated.
Steece, Tecumseh, 26 September, 1857. Graduated.
Stewart, William F., 23 September, 1857. Graduated.
Stone, Sardine G., Jr., 29 September, 1857. Resigned.
Sturdivant, Theodore, 21 September, 1857. Resigned.
Sturgeon, Eugene B., 23 September, 1857. Resigned.
Swift, Samuel, 26 September, 1857. Died 28 November, 1860.
Talbot, Daniel, Jr., 26 September, 1857. Resigned.
Tallman, Henry C., 24 September, 1857. Graduated.
Thomas, Nathaniel W., 24 September, 1857. Graduated.
Tyson, Herbert B., 22 October, 1857. Graduated.
Van Comstock, William, 25 September, 1857. Resigned.
Walker, Clifford B., 28 September, 1857. Dismissed.
Weldman, John, 22 September, 1857. Graduated.
Wilson, Joseph D., 22 September, 1857. Resigned.
Withers, Henry, 21 September, 1857. Dismissed.
Yorke, Patton J., 28 September, 1857. Resigned.

1858.—MIDSHIPMEN.

Ahl, James W., 24 September, 1858. Resigned.
Appleton, Giles F., 20 September, 1858. Resigned.
Barnum, David, 20 September, 1858. Resigned.
Benton, Mortimer M., 28 September, 1858. Resigned.
Blake, Elliott C. V., 28 September, 1858. Promoted 1 August, 1862.
Blake, Henry J., 29 September, 1858. Promoted 24 February, 1863.
Bradley, John B., 21 September, 1858, Killed in action 24 April, 1862.
Brower, Edwin T., 28 September, 1858. Promoted 1 August, 1862.
Carrothers, John K., 23 September, 1858. Died 23 December, 1861.
Comstock, John H., 11 January, 1858. Resigned.
Cotton, Charles S., 23 September, 1858. Promoted 11 November, 1862.
Crall, George A., 20 September, 1858. Dismissed.
Crandall, Frederick H., 24 September, 1858. Appt. revoked.
Daniels, Charles H., 23 September, 1858. Resigned.
Day, Benjamin F., 20 September, 1858. Promoted 1 August. 1862.
Dougherty, Harvey H., 20 September, 1858. Resigned.
Foreman, Ivey, 25 September, 1858. Resigned.
Forrest, Moreau, 22 September, 1858. Promoted 1 August, 1862.
Foute, Robert C., 20 September, 1858. Resigned.
Grafton, Henry T., 23 September, 1858. Resigned.
Harrison, William H., 28 September, 1858. Resigned.
Hivling, William H., 20 September, 1858. Resigned.
Holt, Henry C., 21 September, 1858. Resigned.
Howard, George A., 20 September, 1858. Resigned.
Humphrey, Charles H., 22 September, 1858. Resigned.
Huntington, Charles L., 29 September, 1858. Promoted 1 August, 1862.
Huntington, Robert P., 24 September, 1858. Promoted 9 October, 1862.
Huston, Charles St. C., 22 September, 1858. Resigned.
Kellog, Edward N., 24 September, 1858. Promoted 8 September, 1863.
Lamson, Roswell H., 20 September, 1858. Promoted 1 August, 1862.
Littlepage, H. Beverly, 23 September, 1858. Resigned.
Marmaduke, Henry H., 20 September, 1858. Resigned.
Mason, Alexander M., 11 October, 1858. Resigned.
McDermott, Edward J., 23 September, 1858. Resigned.
McWilliams, Mortimer, 23 September, 1858. Resigned.
Merriwether, James A., 29 September, 1858. Resigned.
Mitchell, Archibald N., 20 September, 1858. Promoted 1 August, 1862.
Moodey, David, 22 September, 1858. Resigned.
Moon, William S., 21 September, 1858. Resigned.
Nichols, Smith W., 27 September, 1858. Promoted 1 August, 1862.
Payne, Robert, 20 September, 1858. Resigned.
Pinkney, William, 23 September, 1858. Resigned.
Preston, Samuel W., 4 October, 1858. Promoted 1 August, 1862.
Read, John J., 21 September, 1858. Promoted 25 November, 1862.
Read, William W., 27 September, 1858. Resigned.
Robinson, William O'H., 22 September, 1858. Resigned.

GENERAL NAVY REGISTER.

Roby, Francis M., 28 September, 1858. Resigned.
Ruggles, Edward S., 21 September, 1858. Resigned.
Shoemaker, Charles F., 21 September, 1858. Resigned.
Smith, Frederick R., 24 September, 1858. Promoted 1 August, 1862.
Sturgeon, Eugene B., 20 September, 1858. Resigned.
Sumner, George W., 20 September, 1858. Promoted 1 August, 1862.
Terry, Silas W., 28 September, 1858. Promoted 16 September, 1862.
Telfair, David A., 23 September, 1858. Resigned.
Trigg, Daniel, 30 September, 1858. Resigned.
Wemple, David D., 24 September, 1858. Promoted 25 November, 1862.
Winslow, William H., 23 September, 1858. Resigned.
Worth, Algernon S., 21 September, 1858. Resigned.
Zimmerman, Charles W., 20 September, 1858. Promoted 19 September, 1862.

1859.—MIDSHIPMEN.

Abbot, Walter, 2 December, 1859. Promoted 25 November, 1862.
Adams, La Rue P., 26 October, 1859. Promoted 16 September, 1862.
Alexander, Adam C., Jr., 23 November, 1859. Promoted 16 September, 1862.
Anderson, John, 22 September, 1859. Killed in Action 24 April, 1862.
Bacot, Richard H., 20 September, 1859. Resigned.
Baird, Thomas D., 22 September, 1859. Resigned.
Bartlett, John R., 28 November, 1859. Promoted 8 September, 1863.
Batcheller, Oliver A., 28 November, 1859. Promoted 25 November, 1862.
Beirne, Andrew P., 28 September, 1859. Resigned.
Blake, Charles F., 26 October, 1859. Promoted 26 June, 1863.
Brady, Alfred T., 2 December, 1859. Resigned.
Brantingham, Charles H., 22 September, 1859. Resigned.
Brice, John J., 24 September, 1859. Resigned.
Bridgman, William R., 2 December, 1859. Promoted 16 September, 1862.
Brown, George M., 25 November, 1859. Promoted 16 September, 1862.
Brunk, Frank C., 23 September, 1859. Resigned.
Burker, Albert S., 25 October, 1859. Promoted 25 November, 1862.
Camm, Robert A., 30 November, 1859. Resigned.
Carroll, Daniel, 2 December, 1859. Resigned.
Case, James S., 28 September, 1859. Resigned.
Chester, Colby M., 31 October, 1859. Promoted 21 October, 1863.
Chew, Francis T., 21 September, 1859. Resigned.
Chew, Richard S., 25 November, 1859. Promoted 13 December, 1862.
Claybrook, Joseph P., 27 September, 1859. Resigned.
Cook, William W., 26 October, 1859. Resigned.
Cooke, Henry S., 25 November, 1859. Resigned.
Craig, William J., 7 December, 1859. Resigned.
Dalton, William R., 20 September, 1859. Resigned.
Dana, William S., 25 October, 1859. Promoted 10 June, 1864.
Dayton, Charles M., 25 October, 1859. Resigned.
Dick, James A., 29 September, 1859. Resigned.
Epes, Freeman, 2 December, 1859. Resigned.
Flournoy, Robert, 24 September, 1859. Resigned.
Floyd, Richard S., 30 November, 1859. Resigned.
Ford, George E., 30 November, 1859. Resigned.
Fortune, John C., 27 September, 1859. Resigned.
French, Hayden T., 2 December, 1859. Promoted.
Garrett, Thomas G., 15 November, 1859. Resigned.
Gedney, Alexander D., 25 November, 1859. Dismissed.
Gregory, Samuel S., 24 September, 1859. Resigned.
Hammett, William, 27 September, 1859. Resigned.
Haskin, Benjamin F., 2 November, 1859. Promoted.
Haswell, Gouverneur K., 25 November, 1859. Promoted.
Hazletine, Edward C., 22 September, 1859. Promoted.
Heath, Lucius E., 25 November, 1859. Resigned.
Hiatt, Samuel S., 12 October, 1859. Resigned.
Holcombe, Isaac C., 9 November, 1859. Resigned.
Howard, George H., 1 December, 1859. Resigned.
Hunt, Symmes H., 23 November, 1859. Promoted.
Hutter, William C., 26 October, 1859. Resigned.
Jackson, William C., 28 November, 1859. Resigned.
Johnson, Henry L., 30 September, 1859. Resigned.
Johnson, Mortimer L., 2 December, 1859. Promoted.
Jones, Charles D., 23 November, 1859. Promoted.
Jones, John C., 11 October, 1859. Resigned.
Long, James C., 23 November, 1859. Resigned.
Lowry, Philip W., 22 September, 1859. Promoted.
Ludlow, Nicoll, 28 October, 1859. Promoted.
Mallory, George T., 15 November, 1859. Resigned.
Mason, William P., 23 September, 1859. Resigned.
McClure, George M., 23 September, 1859. Promoted.
McCormick, Alexander H., 21 September, 1859. Promoted.
McDaniel, Henry C., 30 November, 1859. Resigned.

GENERAL NAVY REGISTER. 629

McKenney, Ulric F., 25 November, 1859. Resigned.
Miller, Merrill, 28 November, 1859. Promoted.
Moore, John H., 27 September, 1859. Resigned.
Nalle, Frederick I., 27 October, 1859. Promoted.
Pearson, Frederick, 21 September, 1859. Promoted.
Pipkin, William M., 7 December, 1859. Resigned.
Poor, Charles H., Jr., 26 September, 1859. Dismissed.
Porter, Benjamin H., 1 December, 1859. Promoted.
Preble, Edward E., 2 December, 1859. Promoted.
Price, John R., 15 November, 1859. Resigned.
Reed, John H., 28 September, 1859. Promoted.
Robinson, William F., 28 November, 1859. Resigned.
Rumsey, Henry B., 25 October, 1859. Promoted.
Sanders, Morton W., 20 September, 1859. Promoted.
Sands, James H., 25 November, 1859. Graduated.
Scales, Dabney M., 7 December, 1859. Resigned.
Shepard, Edward M., 25 November, 1859. Promoted.
Sigsbee, Charles D., 27 September, 1859. Promoted.
Smith, Richard M., 30 November, 1859. Resigned.
Stafford, James M., 22 September, 1859. Resigned.
Thomas, Francis M., 24 September, 1859. Resigned.
Tracy, Charles W., 27 October, 1859. Promoted.
Turner, Thomas T., 25 November, 1859. Resigned.
Vance, George P., 25 November, 1859. Dismissed.
Van Vleck, William A., 25 November, 1859. Promoted.
Walker, John T., 24 September, 1859. Resigned.
Wallace, James, 1 November, 1859. Promoted.
Wheeler, William K., 7 December, 1859. Promoted.
Wilkinson, William W., 7 December, 1859. Resigned.
Willett, Silas S., 26 November, 1859. Resigned.
Wood, George W., 23 September, 1859. Promoted.
Woodward, Edwin T., 23 November, 1859. Promoted.
Wyman, Henry D., 21 September, 1859. Dropped.
Young, William, 1 December, 1859. Resigned.

1860.—ACTING MIDSHIPMEN.

Ames, William L., 23 September, 1860. Resigned.
Baldwin, James G., 29 September, 1860. Resigned.
Barclay, Charles J., 21 September, 1860. Graduated.
Berrien, Thomas M., 26 September, 1860. Resigned.
Bidlick, James B., 22 September, 1860. Dismissed.
Boyle, William O., 26 September, 1860. Dismissed.
Brantingham, Charles H., 25 September, 1860. Resigned.
Brooks, Thomas R., 20 October, 1860. Resigned.
Brown, Allen D., 29 September, 1860. Graduated.
Brown, Orris A., 23 September, 1860. Resigned.
Bryan, George D., 25 September, 1860. Resigned.
Buckmaster, Esculapius, 20 September, 1860. Resigned.
Bush, Charles G., 25 September, 1860. Resigned.
Califf, Joseph M., 27 September, 1860. Resigned.
Carmody, Robert E., 29 September, 1860. Resigned.
Carroll, William J., 21 September, 1860. Resigned.
Carter, Barron, 28 September, 1860. Resigned.
Cassell, Douglas R., 28 September, 1860. Graduated.
Clark, Charles E., 29 September, 1860. Graduated.
Clark, David J., 27 September, 1860. Resigned.
Clark, John D., 22 September, 1860. Graduated.
Clements, Courtland C., 26 September, 1860. Resigned.
Coffin, George W., 28 September, 1860. Graduated.
Coghlan, Joseph B., 27 September, 1860. Graduated.
Cook, Francis Augustus, 20 September, 1860. Graduated.
Cooper, Philip H., 28 September, 1860. Graduated.
Craven, Charles H., 20 September, 1860. Graduated.
Crowninshield, A. S., 25 September, 1860. Graduated.
Davis, George Thornton, 20 September, 1860. Graduated.
Dick, James A., 29 September, 1860. Resigned.
Dickman, Ernest J., 20 September, 1865. Graduated.
Duer, William A., 29 September, 1860. Resigned.
Dunn, Williamson, 24 September, 1860. Graduated.
English, Gustavus, 25 September, 1860. Resigned.
Evans, Robley D., 20 September, 1860. Graduated.
Fagan, Louis E., 28 September, 1860. Resigned.
Fuller, Henry D., 24 September, 1860. Dropped.
Gardner, Joseph M., 24 September, 1860. Resigned.
Garrett, Thomas G., 12 October, 1860. Resigned.
Glass, Henry, 24 September, 1860. Graduated.
Glidden, George D. B., 23 September, 1860. Graduated.
Goode, William D., 6 November, 1860. Resigned.
Goodwyn, Matthew P., 21 September, 1860. Resigned.
Gridley, Charles V., 26 September, 1860. Resigned.

630 GENERAL NAVY REGISTER.

Guthrie, Edward P., 28 September, 1860. Resigned.
Harris, Ira, 22 September, 1860. Graduated.
Heath, Benjamin, 22 September, 1860. Resigned.
Hendrickson, William W., 26 September, 1860. Graduated.
Hoff, William B., 24 October, 1860. Graduated.
Hopkins, John Adams, 20 September, 1860. Resigned.
Hill, Hugh L., 25 September, 1860. Resigned.
Hunter, William R., 29 September, 1860. Dismissed.
Irvin, Roland C., 29 September, 1860. Graduated.
Kellog, Augustus G., 21 September, 1860. Graduated.
Laughton, George H., 22 September, 1860. Resigned.
Leary, Richard Phillips, 20 September, 1860. Graduated.
Lenox, Albert H., 25 September, 1860. Dismissed.
Livingston, John S., 25 September, 1860. Resigned.
Maclay, William W., 4 October, 1860. Graduated.
Mayo, Wyndham R., 21 September, 1860. Resigned.
McClintoc, Horatio Gates, 21 September, 1860. Resigned.
McCormick, Frederick, 25 September, 1860. Graduated.
McGregor, Charles, 21 September, 1860. Graduated.
McIlvane, John Clay, 24 September, 1860. Resigned.
Meyer, Cassius, 20 September, 1860. Resigned.
Morgan, James M., 20 September, 1860. Resigned.
Morris, Francis, 27 September, 1860. Graduated.
Morris, Isaac Tompkins, 20 September, 1860. Graduated.
Morris, Thomas L., 26 September, 1860. Resigned.
Moses, Raphael, 27 September, 1860. Resigned.
Mullen, Dennis W., 21 September, 1860. Graduated.
Newlin, Alfred S., 25 September, 1860. Resigned.

Niles, Marston, 25 September, 1860. Graduated.
Osterloh, William Cooper, 20 September, 1860. Resigned.
Pearson, James M., 21 September, 1860. Resigned.
Pegram, John Combe, 21 September, 1860. Graduated.
Pendleton, Charles A., 27 September, 1860. Graduated.
Peters, James Arthur, 20 September, 1860. Resigned.
Peyton, Joseph B., 23 September, 1860. Resigned.
Phelps, Jefferson, 28 September, 1860. Resigned.
Ragsdale, James K. P., 21 September, 1860. Graduated.
Reber, John M., 21 September, 1860. Resigned.
Schultz, Charles F., 23 September, 1860. Resigned.
Sevier, Charles F., 27 September, 1860. Resigned.
Sparks, Gale W., 24 September, 1860. Resigned.
Sterling, Yates, 27 September, 1860. Graduated.
Taylor, Henry Clay, 20 September, 1860. Graduated.
Vaughn, Henry L., 24 September, 1860. Resigned.
Wadleigh, George H., 27 September, 1860. Graduated.
Washington, Le Roy H., 26 September, 1860. Resigned.
Webb, William H., 24 September, 1860. Resigned.
Whiting, William H., 21 September, 1860. Graduated.
Wildes, Frank, 21 September, 1860. Graduated.
Williams, Henry S. H., 27 September, 1860. Resigned.
Williams, Thomas, 26 September, 1860. Dropped.
Wise, William C., 29 September, 1860. Graduated.
Wright, Arthur H., 28 September, 1860. Graduated.
Wright, Augustus O., 29 September, 1860. Resigned.
Yancey, William E., 23 September, 1860. Resigned.

1861.—ACTING MIDSHIPMEN.

Adams, Stephen D., 20 September, 1861. Dropped.
Albright, Lewis M., 15 October, 1861. Resigned.
Alexander, Robert W., 2 December, 1861. Resigned.
Anderson, Thomas C., 28 November, 1861. Dismissed.
Armentrout, George W., 25 November, 1861. Graduated.
Arnold, Charles F., 14 October, 1861. Graduated.
Baird, Samuel P., 27 September, 1861. Graduated.
Baker, Albert L., 28 September, 1861. Died 3 March, 1864.
Baker, James B., 2 December, 1861. Resigned.
Baker, Samuel H., 24 September, 1861. Graduated.
Barber, Francis M., 27 December, 1861. Graduated.

Bay, Joseph L., 27 September, 1861. Resigned.
Baylies, Alfred W., 15 October, 1861. Dropped.
Beemer, Julius N., 27 September, 1861. Dismissed.
Bell, David N., 23 September, 1861. Graduated.
Belrose, Louis, 20 September, 1861. Graduated.
Bicknell, George A., 2 December, 1861. Graduated.
Bidlack, James B., 24 September, 1861. Dismissed.
Bigelow, Horatio R., 23 September, 1861. Resigned.
Black, Charles H., 21 September, 1861. Graduated.
Blake, Charles G., 30 November, 1861. Dropped.
Blake, Francis O., 27 September, 1861. Resigned.

Bolenius, Frederic H., 27 September, 1861. Dropped.
Book, George M., 23 November, 1861. Graduated.
Bradford, Royal B., 28 November, 1861. Graduated.
Breed, Edward D., 21 September, 1861. Resigned.
Breed, Cyrus W., 26 November, 1861. Graduated.
Brownson, Willard H., 29 November, 1861. Graduated.
Buckingham, Samuel C., 21 September, 1861. Resigned.
Buford, Marcus B., 9 October, 1861. Graduated.
Bussing, Peter V., 24 September, 1861. Resigned.
Caldwell, Albert G., 23 September, 1861. Graduated.
Campbell, Francis D., 27 September, 1861. Dismissed.
Cantrell, Franklin S., 25 September, 1861. Resigned.
Carmody, Robert E., 28 November, 1861. Graduated.
Carpenter, William L., 20 September, 1861. Resigned.
Carter, Abiel B., 23 September, 1861. Graduated.
Chadsey, Arthur E., 2 October, 1861. Resigned.
Chadwick, French E., 28 September, 1861. Graduated.
Chenery, Leonard E., 12 December, 1861. Graduated.
Clark, Lewis, 24 September, 1861. Graduated.
Commager, Franklin T., 21 September, 1861. Dismissed.
Conner, John Clay, 20 September, 1861. Dismissed.
Converse, George A., 29 November, 1861. Graduated.
Crabb, Junius D., 25 November, 1861. Resigned.
Craig, Joseph E., 29 November, 1861. Graduated.
Dana, George S., 28 September, 1861. Resigned.
Davies, Daniel W., 28 September, 1861. Resigned.
Davis, Charles H., 29 November, 1861. Graduated.
Day, Murray S., 24 September, 1861. Graduated.
De Camp, Edgar A., 26 November, 1861. Resigned.
De Long, George W., 1 October, 1861. Graduated.
Dickins, Francis W., 20 September, 1861. Graduated.
Dohrman, Arnold H., 23 September, 1861. Resigned.
Dolliver, William A., 2 December, 1861. Resigned.
Doughty, John C., 28 September, 1861. Resigned.
Duncan, John McK., 21 September, 1861. Dropped.
Dunn, Henry T., 25 September, 1861. Resigned.
Dunn, William H., 5 October, 1861. Resigned.
Dyer, Charles G., 20 September, 1861. Resigned.
Edes, Benjamin L., 23 September, 1861. Graduated.
Edgar, Daniel, 20 September, 1861. Resigned.
Elliott, William H., 27 September, 1864. Graduated.
Elmer, Horace, 27 September, 1861. Graduated.
Fitzgerald, Charles H., 29 November, 1861. Resigned.
Fisher, John F., 28 September, 1861. Dropped.
Flagg, George N., 21 September, 1861. Graduated.
Fletcher, Arthur H., 29 November, 1861. Graduated.
Folger, William M., 21 September, 1861. Graduated.
Foote, Francis D., 27 September, 1861. Dropped.
Ford, Leighton M., 27 September, 1861. Graduated.
Freeman, Frederick H., 20 September 1861. Dismissed.
Garrison, Oliver F., 24 September, 1861. Resigned.
Golden, Henry W., 25 September, 1861. Resigned.
Goodhue, James K., 28 November, 1861. Dropped.
Goodrich, Caspar F., 10 December, 1861. Graduated.
Gove, Francis M., 27 September, 1861. Graduated.
Graham, Wallace, 6 December, 1861. Graduated.
Griswold, Charles D., 20 November, 1861. Graduated.
Groves, William D., 5 October, 1861. Resigned.
Gwinner, Henry W., 2 October, 1861. Graduated.
Hale, James Potter, 29 November, 1861. Dropped.
Harrington, Purnell F., 20 September, 1861. Graduated.
Haskins, Peter V., 27 September, 1861. Resigned.
Hazlett, Isaac, 27 September, 1861. Graduated.
Hess, William A., 27 September, 1861. Resigned.
Heyerman, Oscar F., 30 November, 1861. Graduated.
Hicks, Amariah H., 20 September, 1861. Resigned.
Hone, Calbraith P., 28 September, 1861. Resigned.
Hooker, Richard C., 25 September, 1861. Graduated.
Hopkins, John A., 4 December, 1861. Dismissed.
Hubbard, Socrates, 24 December, 1861. Graduated.
Hull, James C., 27 September, 1861. Dropped. 24 July, 1863. Graduated.
Hunter, Godfrey, 25 September, 1861. Graduated.
Hyam, George F., 20 September, 1861. Resigned.
Ide, George E., 27 September, 1861. Graduated.
Impey, Robert, 21 September, 1861. Graduated.
James, Richard E., 21 September, 1861. Dismissed.
Jameson, William C., 27 September, 1861. Resigned.
Jewell, Theodore F., 29 November, 1861. Graduated.
Johns, Walter S., 2 November, 1861. Resigned.
Keith, Fordyce M., 21 September, 1861. Dropped.
Kelso, Joseph K., 24 September, 1861. Dropped.
Kennedy, Charles, 25 September, 1861. Graduated.
Kennett, John C., 2 October, 1861. Graduated.
Kingsley, Louis A., 28 September, 1861. Graduated.

GENERAL NAVY REGISTER.

Lain, Henry C., 21 September, 1861. Resigned.
Lamberton, Benjamin P., 21 September, 1861. Graduated.
Lathy, William E., 21 September, 1861. Dropped.
Longnecker, Edwin, 24 September, 1861. Graduated.
Lowry, Morrow M., 26 November, 1861. Resigned.
Manney, Henry N., 24 September, 1861. Graduated.
Martin, Enos T., 4 December, 1861. Resigned.
McCalla, Bowman H., 30 November, 1861. Graduated.
McKee, Hugh W., 25 September, 1861. Graduated.
McMichael, William B., 27 September, 1861. Dropped.
Mead, William W., 30 December, 1861. Graduated.
Menzies, Gustavus V., 21 September, 1861. Dropped.
Mitchell, James L., 20 September, 1861. Resigned.
Mott, William H., 25 September, 1861. Resigned.
Murray, William B., 2 December, 1861. Dropped.
Nellis, Edward P., 28 November, 1861. Resigned.
Newell, John S., 28 September, 1861. Graduated.
Nichols, Henry E., 1 October, 1861. Graduated.
Noell, Jacob E., 3 December, 1861. Graduated.
Parker, Francis H., 20 September, 1861. Graduated.
Peck, Ransome B., 21 November, 1861. Graduated.
Penhallow, Thomas W., 28 September, 1861. Resigned.
Perry, Thomas, 25 September, 1861. Graduated.
Pigman, George W., 28 September, 1861. Graduated.
Porter, Carlile P., 27 September, 1861. Resigned.
Potter, Charles H., 31 December, 1861. Resigned.
Powell, Joseph D., 21 September, 1861. Resigned.
Preston, William H., 24 September, 1861. Resigned.
Proctor, Henry O., 28 September, 1861. Resigned.
Raebel, Herman C., 23 September, 1861. Graduated.
Rathbone, Clarence, 28 September, 1861. Graduated.
Reiter, George C., 20 September, 1861. Graduated.
Reynolds, Charles W., 20 September, 1861. Resigned.
Reynolds, Robert B., 31 December, 1861. Resigned.
Richards, Benjamin S., 22 October, 1861. Graduated.
Richardson, George J., 28 November, 1861. Resigned.
Robinson, William, 7 December, 1861. Resigned.
Rodman, Edward, 27 September, 1861. Resigned.
Roth, Edward N., 19 October, 1861. Resigned.
Rowe, Edward V., 28 September, 1861. Graduated.
Russing, Peter V., 24 September, 1861. Resigned.
Schmitz, Charles F., 19 October, 1861. Graduated.
Schouler, John, 25 September, 1861. Graduated.
Schroeder, William J., 26 November, 1861. Dropped.
Shaw, Dickson C., 20 September, 1861. Resigned.
Sheppard, Francis H., 16 October, 1861. Graduated.
Sherburne, John H., 24 September, 1861. Resigned.
Smith, William H., 21 September, 1861. Resigned.
Snow, Albert S., 30 November, 1861. Graduated.
Stedman, Edward M., 27 September, 1861. Graduated.
Stockton, Charles H., 14 November, 1861. Graduated.
Stockwell, Norris P., 21 September, 1861. Resigned.
Struse, Henry F., 27 November, 1861. Resigned.
Sturtevant, Frederick, 29 November, 1861. Graduated.
Sullivan, George S. B., 27 September, 1861. Resigned.
Talcott, George, 23 November, 1861. Graduated.
Tasker, John F., 24 September, 1861. Resigned.
Taylor, Edward M., 20 September, 1861. Resigned.
Thomas, Charles M., 28 November, 1861. Graduated.
Thomas, Eugene B., 20 September, 1861. Graduated.
Todd, Chapman C., 9 October, 1861. Graduated.
Tomkins, James S., 27 November, 1861. Resigned.
Towle, Edwin S., 24 September, 1861. Dismissed.
Train, Charles J., 28 November, 1861. Graduated.
Truax, Anthony R., 26 October, 1861. Died 18 February, 1865.
Turley, Augustus R., 29 November, 1861. Resigned.
Turnbull, Frank, 20 September, 1861. Graduated.
Vail, Abraham H., 28 September, 1861. Graduated.
Vaughn, John A., 24 September, 1861. Graduated.
Washabaugh, Perry McL., 27 September, 1861. Dropped.
Waterman, Rufus, 25 September, 1861. Graduated.
Weaver, James B., 30 November, 1861. Graduated.
Whitall, Samuel R., 24 September, 1861. Resigned.
White, Edwin, 29 November, 1861. Graduated.
White, Henry C., 16 October, 1861. Graduated.
White, Oscar, 21 September, 1861. Graduated.
Whitwell, James E., 23 September, 1861. Dismissed.
Wilde, George F. F., 30 November, 1861. Graduated.
Wilson, Josiah M., 21 September, 1861. Graduated.
Wilson, Samuel L., 20 September, 1861. Graduated.
Wilson, Thomas P., 20 September, 1861. Graduated.
Woodrow, David C., 21 September, 1861. Graduated.
Wygum, James P., 20 September, 1861. Dropped.
Yates, Isaac I., 21 September, 1861. Graduated.
Yerkes, Joseph P., 28 November, 1861. Resigned.

1862.—ACTING MIDSHIPMEN.

Ackley, Seth M., 6 October, 1862. Graduated.
Adams, Clifton T., 24 September, 1862. Resigned.
Adams, James R., 7 October, 1862. Dismissed.
Amory, Edward L., 4 December, 1862. Graduated.
Anderson, Thaddeus P., 1 October, 1862. Dropped.
Babbitt, William K., 24 November, 1862. Dropped.
Baldy, George A., 29 September, 1862. Graduated.
Barnes, James A., 30 September, 1862. Resigned.
Beale, Buchanan, 4 October, 1862. Dropped.
Beebe, James E., 29 September, 1862. Resigned.
Belknap, Frederick A., 8 October, 1862. Died 20 November, 1865.
Berrian, Hobart, 22 September, 1862. Dismissed.
Berry, Robert M., 31 January, 1862. Graduated.
Blair, Andrew A., 20 November, 1862. Graduated.
Boyd, Arthur A., 10 October, 1862. Graduated.
Bradford, John M., 9 October, 1862. Resigned.
Bramhall, George W., 23 September, 1862. Resigned.
Bridge, Henry S., 25 November, 1862. Dismissed.
Brown, George J., 2 January, 1862. Resigned.
Brown, George L., 16 April, 1862. Resigned.
Browne, Keyes D., 22 September, 1862. Resigned.
Buchan, Charles J., 18 April, 1862. Dropped.
Burwell, William T., 30 September, 1862. Graduated.
Bushnell, Robert H., 25 September, 1862. Dismissed.
Carpenter, James H., 29 November, 1862. Resigned.
Cathcart, John W., 24 September, 1862. Dropped.
Chapman, George H., 4 February, 1862. Resigned.
Clark, Edward H., 22 January, 1862. Resigned.
Clarkson, Samuel F., 20 September, 1862. Graduated.
Clason, Augustus, 1 October, 1862. Resigned.
Clifton, Richard F., 20 September, 1862. Deserted.
Colby, Harrison G. O., 25 November, 1862. Graduated.
Cook, Henry T., 26 September, 1862. Resigned.
Coster, George W., 20 November, 1862. Graduated.
Courtis, Frank, 25 September, 1862. Graduated.
Crocker, Frederick W., 26 September, 1862. Graduated.
Cushman, Herbert, 23 September, 1862. Resigned.
Cutts, Richard M., 22 September, 1862. Graduated.
Dahlgren, Paul, 7 October, 1862. Resigned.
Davis, Daniel W., 22 September, 1862. Graduated.
Davis, Harvey H., 30 September, 1862. Resigned.

Dayton, James H., 27 September, 1862. Graduated.
Delehanty, Daniel, 25 September, 1862. Graduated.
Dorrance, George M., 29 September, 1862. Resigned.
Dunlap, Andrew, 23 April, 1862. Graduated.
Dunscomb, John, 20 November, 1862. Dropped.
Eames, Charles C., 29 November, 1862. Resigned.
Egbert, Smith, 29 September, 1862. Dismissed.
Emory, William H., 23 September, 1862. Graduated.
Engle, Charles McI., 17 April, 1862. Dropped.
English, Henry C., 30 September, 1862. Graduated.
Ernhout, Perry, 17 April, 1862. Dismissed.
Etting, Theodore M., 25 November, 1862. Graduated.
Fenner, Charles, 30 September, 1862. Resigned.
Flood, Thomas S., 6 October, 1862. Dropped.
Field, Stephen D., 4 October, 1862. Dropped.
Field, Wells L., 20 November, 1862. Graduated.
Folliot, Louis E., 29 November, 1862. Resigned.
Force, Alfred, 17 April, 1862. Graduated.
Frost, Louis W., 23 September, 1862. Resigned.
Gardner, Frederic W., 29 November, 1862. Resigned.
Gheen, Edward H., 25 September, 1862. Graduated.
Gill, Clifford B., 25 September, 1862. Graduated.
Gilpatrick, William W., 30 September, 1862. Graduated.
Gilpin, Frederick M., 23 September, 1862. Resigned.
Gookin, Charles B., 25 November, 1862. Resigned.
Griffin, Robert N., 21 January, 1862. Graduated.
Hall, Edward R., 25 September, 1862. Resigned.
Hall, William F., 29 September, 1862. Resigned.
Hanford, Franklin, 29 November, 1862. Graduated.
Hays, William McC., 14 October, 1862. Dropped.
Hemphill, Joseph N., 29 September, 1862. Graduated.
Hendrix, Fremont M., 21 March, 1862. Graduated.
Higbee, Daniel H., 10 April, 1862. Died 12 February, 1865.
Hitchcock, Roswell D., 18 January, 1862. Graduated.
Hollingshead, Robert K., 10 October, 1862. Resigned.
Hopkins, Robert C., 27 September, 1862. Resigned.
Housel, Louis V., 15 February, 1862. Graduated.
Houston, Edwin S., 18 April, 1862. Graduated.
Hughes, Matthew, 26 September, 1862. Resigned.
Hunker, John J., 18 April, 1862. Graduated.
Hutchins, Charles T., 2 January, 1862. Graduated.
Hutchinson, James O., 30 September, 1862. Resigned.

GENERAL NAVY REGISTER.

Jacob, Edwin S., 15 October, 1862. Graduated.
Jamar, Mitchell F., 15 April, 1862. Dropped.
Jenks, Charles H., 27 September, 1862. Died 26 February, 1866.
Jewett, Charles T., 24 September, 1862. Dropped.
Johnston, William, 22 September, 1862. Dismissed.
Judd, Charles H., 23 September, 1862. Graduated.
Kane, Samuel N., 20 September, 1862. Graduated.
Keith, Asa S., 18 April, 1862. Resigned.
Kelton, Allen C., 25 September, 1862. Resigned.
Kenney, Albert J., 1 October, 1862. Resigned.
Kessler, Simon N., 20 September, 1862. Dropped.
Kneass, Franklin, 26 September, 1862. Dismissed.
Lawrence, Samuel, 29 November, 1862. Resigned.
Lillie, Abram B. H., 25 September, 1862. Graduated.
Lincoln, Frederick L., 26 November, 1862. Dropped.
Lisle, Richard W., 26 September, 1862. Graduated.
Lull, Lewis J., 1 October, 1862. Resigned.
Lyon, Caleb, 10 February, 1862. Resigned.
Lyon, Henry W., 7 October, 1862. Graduated.
Lyons, Timothy A., 2 January, 1862. Graduated.
Mackenzie, Morris R. S., 29 September, 1862. Graduated.
Mallory, Lawrence, 22 September, 1862. Dropped.
Mansfield, H. Livingston, 29 September, 1862. Resigned.
Marsh, William L., 17 April, 1862. Resigned.
Maus, Frederick K., 20 September, 1862. Resigned.
Maynard, Washburn, 6 October, 1862. Graduated.
Mayo, Edward B., 26 September, 1862. Resigned.
Maxwell, George, 26 September, 1862. Resigned.
McCormack, Emmet, 17 April, 1862. Graduated.
McIlvaine, Bloomfield, 9 October, 1862. Graduated.
McKown, William, 24 September, 1862. Dropped.
McMurdy, John H., 21 April, 1862. Resigned.
Meigs, John F., 4 October, 1862. Graduated.
Moore, James, 29 September, 1862. Resigned.
Moore, William J., 14 April, 1862. Graduated.
Mordecai, Marion C., 26 November, 1862. Resigned.
Morrow, James F., 15 April, 1862. Resigned.
Morse, Jerome E., 13 October, 1862. Graduated.
Nichols, Frank W., 24 September, 1862. Graduated.
Nicholson, William D., 4 October, 1862. Graduated.
Norris, George A., 27 September, 1862. Graduated.
Orner, John C., 18 April, 1862. Dropped.
Parker, Erastus W., 14 April, 1862. Dropped.
Parker, William H., 17 April, 1862. Graduated.

Paul, Allen G., 23 September, 1862. Graduated.
Peck, Harold S., 29 September, 1862. Resigned.
Peirce, George, 25 September, 1862. Resigned.
Perkins, Francis W., 23 September, 1862. Dismissed.
Phelan, John R., 19 April, 1862. Graduated.
Pillsbury, John E., 22 September, 1862. Resigned.
Pond, Colles T., 23 April, 1862. Resigned.
Preston, Charles, 22 November, 1862. Dismissed.
Price, Henry W., 23 September, 1862. Resigned.
Reeder, William H., 20 September, 1862. Graduated.
Reisinger, William W., 21 April, 1862. Graduated.
Remey, Edward W., 27 September, 1862. Graduated.
Rich, John C., 23 September, 1862. Graduated.
Ridgely, Henry M., 22 November, 1862. Dropped.
Roben, Douglas, 23 September, 1862. Graduated.
Robinson, Albert F., 20 September, 1862. Resigned.
Rogers, Charles H., 4 October, 1862. Resigned.
Ross, Richard L., 4 October, 1862. Dropped.
Ryors, Robert S., 12 April, 1862. Dismissed.
Safford, George R., 26 September, 1862. Resigned.
Schuyler, Montgomery R., 30 September, 1862. Resigned.
Seager, Edward R., 22 September, 1862. Resigned.
Sedgwick, Charles H., 29 September, 1862. Dismissed.
Selby, Arthur P., 15 April, 1862. Resigned.
Silver, Marcus B., 22 January, 1862. Dropped.
Smith, Edward C., 15 April, 1862. Resigned.
Smith, Foxhall P., 20 September, 1862. Died 19 January, 1863.
Soley, John C., 20 September, 1862. Graduated.
Spalding, Lyman G., 26 September, 1862. Graduated.
Sperry, Charles S., 26 September, 1862. Graduated.
Sperry, Robert J., 26 November, 1862. Dismissed.
Sprague, Albert L., 11 April, 1862. Graduated.
Starr, Charles E., 25 September, 1862. Resigned.
Stembel, James McB., 26 September, 1862. Resigned.
Stewart, David A., 23 October, 1862. Graduated.
Stickney, Joseph L., 26 September, 1862. Graduated.
Stockbridge, Charles H., 25 November, 1862. Dropped.
Stockton, Richard, 26 September, 1862. Resigned.
Sullivan, John T., 10 October, 1862. Graduated.
Swinburne, William T., 29 September, 1862. Graduated.
Symonds, Frederick M., 26 September, 1862. Graduated.
Talbot, John G., 15 April, 1862. Graduated.
Terrell, Thomas C., 20 September, 1862. Graduated.

GENERAL NAVY REGISTER. 635

Thatcher, James S., 1 October, 1862. Resigned.
Totten, George M., 29 September, 1862. Graduated.
Townsend, Henry C., 18 January, 1862. Resigned.
Trumbull, Walter, 18 April, 1862. Resigned.
Walker, Asa, 21 November, 1862. Graduated.
Warren, Edward F. J., 18 April, 1862. Dismissed.
Watts, William, 10 April, 1862. Graduated.
Welles, Thomas G., 20 September, 1862. Resigned.
Wessells, Henry W., 20 September, 1862. Resigned.
Whelen, Henry, 23 September, 1862. Graduated.
Whelen, William N., 10 October, 1862. Resigned.

Williams, Theodore S., 27 September, 1862. Graduated.
Wilson, Downes L., 25 September, 1862. Resigned.
Wilson, Edward H., 27 September, 1862. Resigned.
Wilson, Henry H., 24 September, 1862. Dismissed.
Wilson, Horatio R., 17 April, 1862. Graduated.
Wilson, Thomas S., 7 April, 1862. Graduated.
Wise, Frederick M., 23 September, 1862. Graduated.
Wisner, Henry C., 17 April, 1862. Graduated.
Woodman, Edward, 30 September, 1862. Graduated.
Young, Robert, 24 September, 1862. Resigned.

1863.—ACTING MIDSHIPMEN.

Adams, Charles A., 24 July, 1863. Graduated.
Agnel, Francis W., 1 October, 1863. Dropped.
Alfter, Charles, 26 February, 1863. Resigned.
Allen, Daniel D., 1 October, 1863. Resigned.
Allibone, Charles O., 24 July, 1863. Graduated.
Arnold, Conway H., 30 September, 1863. Graduated.
Ashwin, Edward J., 22 July, 1863. Resigned.
Atkins, George E., 25 February, 1863. Resigned.
Austen, George, 23 September, 1863. Resigned.
Ayres, Mortimer, 23 July, 1863. Resigned.
Ballance, Charles H., 25 February, 1863. Resigned.
Barnes, Nathan H., 27 July, 1863. Graduated.
Bayer, George C., 16 October, 1863. Resigned.
Benjamin, Edward A., 29 July, 1863. Resigned.
Benjamin, Park, 23 September, 1863. Graduated.
Bennett, Daniel F., 29 July, 1863. Resigned.
Blake, Charles H. M., 25 September, 1863. Resigned.
Bleecker, John Van B., 10 October, 1863. Graduated.
Bliss, Edwin W., 23 September, 1863. Resigned.
Blocklinger, Gottfried, 22 July, 1863. Graduated.
Bolles, Matthew, 30 July, 1863. Graduated.
Bridge, Edward W., 31 July, 1863. Graduated.
Brown, Charles E., 25 July, 1863. Graduated.
Burrall, Arthur, 31 July, 1863. Resigned.
Butler, Lisle C., 29 July, 1863. Resigned.
Butler, William K., 2 March, 1863. Died 6 April, 1863.
Carr, John T., 25 September, 1863. Dropped.
Chipp, Charles W., 24 July, 1863. Graduated.
Christopher, Charles W., 24 February, 1863. Resigned.
Church, George H., 25 February, 1863. Graduated.

Clay, George G., 23 July, 1863. Graduated.
Clover, Richardson, 30 July, 1863. Graduated.
Cogswell, James K., 25 September, 1863. Graduated.
Cole, Arthur B., 26 September, 1863. Resigned.
Cole, William H., 21 July, 1863. Resigned.
Collins, Frederick, 24 July, 1863. Graduated.
Couden, Albert R., 26 September, 1863. Graduated.
Cowen, Sidney J., 20 July, 1863. Resigned.
Cowgill, Warner M., 30 September, 1863. Graduated.
Cowie, James W., 25 February, 1863. Graduated.
Cowles, William S., 22 July, 1863. Graduated.
Craven, Alfred, 24 July, 1863. Graduated.
Creecy, Edward H., 23 September, 1863. Resigned.
Cruger, Edward M., 30 July, 1863. Resigned.
Crumbaugh, Samuel R., 20 February, 1863. Graduated.
Cunningham, Patrick T., 26 September, 1863. Graduated.
Dana, Richard H., 27 February, 1863. Died 2 April, 1863.
Davol, George S., 26 February, 1863. Graduated.
Day, Edward M., 24 September, 1863. Graduated.
DeBlois, Thomas A., 21 September, 1863. Graduated.
Delano, Francis H., 23 September, 1863. Graduated.
Dennison, Erasmus, 26 September, 1863. Graduated.
Doughty, Frank S., 25 July, 1863. Resigned.
Drake, Franklin J., 23 February, 1863. Graduated.
Eaton, Joseph G., 24 September, 1863. Graduated.
Everett, William H., 23 July, 1863. Graduated.
Farrington, Edward A., 1 October, 1863. Dropped.
Field, Maunsell B., 25 February, 1863. Graduated.
Fine, John G., 26 September, 1863. Resigned.
Foote, Augustus R. S., 1 October, 1863. Resigned.

Forse, Charles T., 24 September, 1863. Graduated.
Foster, Percy R., 24 July, 1863. Resigned.
Frailey, William B. H., 22 July, 1863. Graduated.
Garsed, Robert P., 23 September, 1863. Resigned.
Gaust, Perry, 28 July, 1863. Graduated.
Gilmore, Fernando P., 28 February, 1863. Graduated.
Glen, Justin D., 31 July, 1863. Resigned.
Goldsmith, Benjamin F., 28 July, 1863. Resigned.
Goodwin, Walton, 26 February, 1863. Graduated.
Goundie, William T., 28 July, 1863. Resigned.
Greenleaf, Frederick W., 29 July, 1863. Graduated.
Grimes, James M., 28 July, 1863. Graduated.
Griswold, Frederick B., 24 February, 1863. Died 9 April, 1863.
Hagenman, John W., 21 July, 1863. Graduated.
Haines, Frederick, 28 July, 1863. Dismissed.
Hamilton, Samuel, 30 September, 1863. Dropped.
Harrington, Charles D., 24 July, 1863. Dropped.
Harrington, Perez, 21 February, 1863. Resigned.
Hawley, John M., 23 July, 1863. Graduated.
Hayden, Aaron, 30 July, 1863. Appt. revoked.
Heald, Eugene De F., 30 September, 1863. Graduated.
Henricks, Edward W., 24 September, 1863. Graduated.
Holmes, James, 24 July, 1863. Resigned.
Howes, Frederick A., 24 September, 1863. Graduated.
Hoyt, Charles C., 29 July, 1863. Dropped.
Hull, James C., 24 July, 1863. Graduated.
Hunter, Henry C., 23 September, 1863. Graduated.
Huttleston, George K., 24 February, 1863. Resigned.
Hyde, Frederick G., 23 September, 1863. Graduated.
Jaques, William H., 30 September, 1863. Graduated.
Johnson, Bradish W., 1 October, 1863. Resigned.
Jones, Horace E., 30 September, 1863. Graduated.
Jones, James, 30 September, 1863. Dropped.
Kane, John S., 29 September, 1863. Resigned.
Kearney, William, 29 July, 1863. Resigned.
Kerr, Joseph W., 28 July, 1863. Resigned.
Kirkland, Frank S., 24 February, 1863. Resigned.
Klapp, Frederick, 23 September, 1862. Resigned.
Knox, Harry, 2 March, 1863. Graduated.
Landott, Albert, 29 July, 1863 Resigned.
Lee, Thomas N., 13 October, 1863. Graduated.
Leutze, Eugene H. C., 4 March, 1863. Graduated.
Little, William, 30 September, 1863. Graduated.
Little, William McC., 11 March, 1863. Graduated.
Logan, Leavitt C., 28 February, 1863. Graduated.
Mansfield, Henry B., 27 February, 1863. Graduated.
Marlow, John A., 25 July, 1863. Dropped.
McBride, George, 26 September, 1863. Resigned.

McClennan, Edward P., 25 September, 1863. Graduated.
McElroy, Horace, 25 September, 1863. Graduated.
McGunnegle, William S., 26 September, 1863. Graduated.
McMechan, Andrew C., 24 February, 1863. Graduated.
Meeker, Cornelius R., 30 September, 1863. Graduated.
Merrell, John P., 20 July, 1863. Graduated.
Miles, George, 29 September, 1863. Resigned.
Miles, Solomon W., 31 July, 1863. Resigned.
Miller, Jacob W., 30 September, 1863. Graduated.
Miller, James M., 24 September, 1863. Graduated.
Milligen, John, 21 July, 1863. Graduated.
Missiner, John, 22 July, 1863. Dropped.
Mitchell, George J., 29 September, 1863. Graduated.
Morehead, Frank C., 25 September, 1863. Resigned.
Morgan, William G., 24 September, 1863. Resigned.
Morrison, William E., 30 September, 1863. Resigned.
Muhlenberg, John C., 24 September, 1863. Resigned.
Murray, Thompson A., 28 July, 1863. Resigned.
Neal, John P., 24 September, 1863. Resigned.
Norton, Charles F., 22 July, 1863. Graduated.
Odell, John, 30 July, 1863. Resigned.
Paine, Frederick H., 27 July, 1863. Graduated.
Palmer, Lambert G., 20 July, 1863. Graduated.
Parks, Samuel S., 30 July, 1863. Resigned.
Paul, William M., 24 September, 1863. Graduated.
Payne, Charles McD., 25 July, 1863. Resigned.
Pendleton, Edwin C., 13 October, 1863. Graduated.
Perkins, Hamilton, 24 September, 1863. Graduated.
Perry, William C. G., 20 February, 1863. Resigned.
Peshine, John H. H., 26 February, 1863. Resigned.
Phillips, Adoniram J., 26 September, 1863. Resigned.
Phillips, Charles L., 21 February, 1863. Graduated.
Post, Alfred S., 21 February, 1863. Resigned.
Prentis, Charles, 24 July, 1863. Resigned.
Prime, Ebenezer S., 22 September, 1863. Graduated.
Robinson, Francis T., 24 September, 1863. Resigned.
Rodgers, John A., 30 July, 1863. Graduated.
Rogers, Furman G., 23 September, 1863. Resigned.
Ross, Albert, 24 July, 1863. Graduated.
Rush, Richard, 30 September, 1863. Graduated.
Schenck, Woodhull S., 21 September, 1863. Resigned.
Sebree, Uriel, 25 July, 1863. Graduated.
Sedman, Thomas D., 11 March, 1863. Dropped.
Shaw, Charles P., 26 September, 1863. Graduated.
Sherman, William W., 31 July, 1863. Dropped.

Simons, Sidney A., 23 September, 1863. Graduated.
Singer, Frederick, 27 July, 1863. Graduated.
Southworth, Alvan S., 24 July, 1863. Dismissed.
Smith, Allen, 8 July, 1863. Resigned.
Smith, Dwight S., 25 July, 1863. Resigned.
Smith, Huntington, 26 February, 1863. Graduated.
Speyers, Arthur B., 24 July, 1863. Graduated.
Sprole, Henry W., 29 September, 1863. Resigned.
Stevens, Thomas H., 1 October, 1863. Graduated.
Stewart, Daniel D. V. S., 24 September, 1863. Graduated.
Stow, John B., 31 July, 1863. Dropped.
Sturdy, Edward W., 25 February, 1863. Graduated.
Swift, Willie, 25 September, 1863. Graduated.
Taft, John M., 25 February, 1863. Graduated.
Talbott, William C., 19 October, 1863. Dropped.
Tallman, Hamilton M., 27 February, 1863. Graduated.
Tausig, Edward D., 24 July, 1863. Graduated.
Taylor, Nelson, 31 July, 1863. Resigned.
Tilley, Benjamin F., 23 September, 1863. Graduated.
Tinker, John T., 24 February, 1863. Dismissed.
Tracy, Walter G., 1 October, 1863. Dropped.
Very, Edward W., 20 February, 1863. Graduated.
Very, Samuel W., 23 February, 1863. Graduated.
Wainwright, Jonathan M., 30 July, 1863. Graduated.
Washburne, Gratiot, 1 October, 1863. Resigned.
Webster, Ashburton, 28 July, 1863. Resigned.
Webster, Lewis D., 26 September, 1863. Graduated.
Weidman, Charles A., 23 September, 1863. Resigned.
West, Clifford H., 22 September, 1863. Graduated.
West, Theodore P., 25 September, 1863. Dropped.
Whittell, Alfred H., 22 September, 1863. Resigned.
Williams, George M., 26 September, 1863. Graduated.
Williams, John S., 28 July, 1863. Resigned.
Wilson, Charles R., 22 July, 1863. Resigned.
Woart, William, 29 September, 1863. Graduated.
Wood, Edward P., 1 October, 1863. Graduated.
Woodruff, Thomas S., 30 July, 1863. Resigned.

1864.—ACTING MIDSHIPMEN.

Abbott, John S., 23 September, 1864. Graduated.
Abercrombie, Frank P., 3 October, 1864. Resigned.
Adams, George K., 1 August, 1864. Graduated.
Adams, James D., 27 September, 1864. Graduated.
Agnel, Francis W., 28 September, 1864. Discharged.
Ames, Samuel, 23 July, 1864. Graduated.
Ashmun, Lewis, 25 July, 1864. Resigned.
Barnett, William J., 27 July, 1864. Graduated.
Bartlett, Edward C., 28 September, 1863. Discharged.
Beehler, William H., 28 July, 1864. Graduated.
Belknap, Charles, 20 July, 1864. Graduated.
Bladen, W. E. E., 29 September, 1864. Resigned.
Bolles, Timothy D., 1 October, 1864. Graduated.
Bower, George K., 26 September, 1864. Graduated.
Brady, Hugh, 22 November, 1864. Resigned.
Brown, Borrudial, 26 September, 1864. Resigned.
Brown, Robert M. G., 22 July, 1864. Graduated.
Bryson, Gilbert E., 25 July, 1864. Resigned.
Buckminster, William B., 1 October, 1864. Resigned.
Burrall, Arthur, 29 July, 1864. Resigned.
Carlin, James W., 23 July, 1864. Graduated.
Carpenter, Alvin R., 28 September, 1864. Dropped.
Clarke, Charles A., 21 July, 1864. Graduated.
Cofforth, Alexander, 30 July, 1864. Dropped.
Colby, Edward P., 23 July, 1864. Resigned.
Cole, Zachary T., 30 September, 1864. Appt. revoked.
Colvocoresses, George P., 28 September, 1864. Graduated.
Comstock, Archibald Y., 22 September, 1864. Resigned.
Cook, Francis B:, 28 July, 1864. Resigned.
Copp, Charles A., 5 November, 1864. Graduated.
Cornwell, Charles C., 20 September, 1864. Graduated.
Danforth, Henry W., 1 October, 1864. Resigned.
Davenport, Richard G., 27 September, 1864. Graduated.
Delahay, William E. B., 22 July, 1864. Graduated.
Derby, Richard C., 20 September, 1864. Graduated.
Derringer, Henry, 30 September, 1864. Resigned.
Doty, Webster, 27 July, 1864. Graduated.
Eaton, Joseph H., 21 September, 1864. Died 28 April, 1865.
Elliott, Alfred, 23 September, 1864. Graduated.
Fisher, Charles G., 22 September, 1864. Resigned.
Fletcher, James R., 26 September, 1864. Graduated.
Fox, Walter H., 30 September, 1864. Resigned.
Fuller, John F., 26 September, 1864. Appt. revoked.
Gay, John F., 23 July, 1864. Dropped.
Goddard, William B., 22 September, 1864. Resigned.
Goin, James D., 26 July, 1864. Resigned.
Goundie, William T., 22 July, 1864. Resigned.

Green, Charles T., 20 September, 1864. Dismissed.
Guild, Gustavus J., 3 October, 1864. Resigned.
Handy, Henry O., 26 July, 1864. App. revoked.
Harris, Charles McI., 28 September, 1864. Resigned.
Hildeburn, Hampton, 22 September, 1864. Dismissed.
Hipple, Edward H., 30 July, 1864. Resigned.
Hoffman, Julius T. C., 22 September, 1864. Resigned.
House, Gerome B., 23 July, 1864. Graduated.
Howe, George S., 21 September, 1864. Resigned.
Hubbell, George E., 26 September, 1864. Resigned.
Hunter, George Z., 21 September, 1864. Resigned.
Ingersoll, Royal R., 23 July, 1864. Graduated.
Irvine, John, 26 September, 1864. Graduated.
Jarboe, Charles W., 29 September, 1864. Graduated.
Jasper, Robert T., 21 July, 1864. Graduated.
Jerome, Roswell H., 21 September, 1864. Resigned.
Kelley, James D. J., 5 October, 1864. Graduated.
Kennedy, Duncan, 20 July, 1864. Graduated.
Kidder, Daniel S., 24 September, 1864. Resigned.
Krause, Francis A., 27 July, 1864. Resigned.
Legg, Aretus M., 23 July, 1864. Resigned.
Lichty, John S., 1 October, 1864. Resigned.
Longnecker, Henry C., 30 July, 1864. Graduated.
Macfarlane, Edward O., 3 October, 1864. Graduated.
Marix, Adolphus, 26 September, 1864. Graduated.
Mason, Theodorus B. M., 20 September, 1864. Graduated.
May, Sidney H., 28 July, 1864. Graduated.
McAllister, Patrick A., 16 November, 1864. Resigned.
McArthur, Francis H., 22 September, 1864. Resigned.
McFarland, Malcolm, 26 July, 1864. Resigned.
McLean, Thomas C., 21 September, 1864. Graduated.
Mitchell, Richard, 22 July, 1864. Graduated.
Moore, Edwin K., 1 October, 1864. Graduated.
Morgan, William G., 26 July, 1864. Resigned.
Moser, Jefferson F., 29 September, 1864. Graduated.
Mott, Charles M., 29 July, 1864. Resigned.
Moulton, Horatio F., 20 September, 1864. Resigned.
Myer, Richard E. C., 28 July, 1864. Resigned.
Myers, Stephen B., 1 August, 1864. Resigned.
Newell, Charles, 30 September, 1864. Dismissed.
Newlin, William B., 27 September, 1864. Resigned.
Nickels, John A. H., 8 October, 1864. Graduated.
Niles, Nathan E., 28 July, 1864. Graduated.

Noteware, Albert C., 20 September, 1864. Resigned.
Noyes, Boutelle, 26 September, 1864. Graduated.
Oakley, Frederick B., 27 July, 1864. Resigned.
Ogle, Alexander, 24 September, 1864. Resigned.
Parsons, Arthur H., 27 July, 1864. Graduated.
Rawdon, Frederick W., 29 September, 1861. Resigned.
Richburg, John C., 20 July, 1864. Resigned.
Robinson, John B., 30 July, 1864. Graduated.
Rodgers, Raymond P., 25 July, 1864. Graduated.
Roosevelt, Nicholas L., 27 September, 1864. Graduated.
Ruschenberger, Charles W., 23 July, 1864. Graduated.
Ryors, Robert S., 20 July, 1864. Resigned.
Sage, George E., 27 September, 1864. Resigned.
Sanford, Edwards S., 20 September, 1864. Resigned.
Schroeder, Seaton, 27 September, 1864. Graduated.
Scott, Charles N., 21 September, 1864. Resigned.
Selfridge, James R., 21 July, 1864. Graduated.
Seymour, Charles, 28 July, 1864. Graduated.
Sharrer, Washington O., 27 September, 1864. Graduated.
Shepard, Jesse C., 26 September, 1864. Discharged.
Shepard, Lorenzo B., 7 October, 1864. Deserted.
Shepherd, Charles M., 3 December, 1864. Resigned.
Shook, Luther S., 30 July, 1864. Dismissed.
Smith, Clark, 26 September, 1864. Resigned.
Smith, Jesse B., 28 July, 1864. Graduated.
Stinson, Herbert C., 30 September, 1864. Graduated.
Stone, Charles A., 27 July, 1864. Graduated.
Strong, William C., 22 September, 1864. Graduated.
Talbot, William C., 30 July, 1864. Resigned.
Taylor, Nelson, 27 July, 1864. Resigned.
Thompson, Robert M., 30 July, 1864. Graduated.
Tremain, Hobart L., 26 September, 1864. Graduated.
Turnbull, Nisbet, 29 September, 1864. Resigned.
Tyler, George W., 3 October, 1864. Graduated.
Uhler, William E., 27 July, 1864. Graduated.
Upton, Frederick E., 10 November, 1864. Graduated.
Venable, Charles H., 22 September, 1864. Resigned.
Wadhams, Albion V., 26 September, 1864. Graduated.
Wainwright, Richard, 28 September, 1864. Graduated.
Wallace, George C., 20 July, 1864. Graduated.
Wallis, John P., 26 July, 1864. Graduated.
Welch, Charles P., 29 September, 1864. Graduated.
Welles, Edward T., 23 September, 1864. Resigned.

GENERAL NAVY REGISTER. 639

Wheeler, James S., 23 September, 1864. Resigned.
Wood, Theodore T., 29 September, 1864. Graduated.
Wyckhoff, Ambrose B., 29 September, 1864. Graduated.
Yeamen, Caldwell, 24 September, 1864. Resigned.

1865.—ACTING MIDSHIPMEN.

Arthur, Elliott J., 26 September, 1865. Graduated.
Barry, Edward B., 20 July, 1865. Graduated.
Bassett, Fletcher S., 20 September, 1865. Graduated.
Bates, Charles J., 20 July, 1865. Resigned.
Berry, Albert G., 24 July, 1865. Graduated.
Berryman, William M., 21 November, 1865. Resigned.
Berwind, Edward J., 20 July, 1865. Graduated.
Birney, Frank C., 24 July, 1865. Graduated.
Bixler, Lewis E., 26 September, 1865. Graduated.
Blanchard, Horace, 25 July, 1865. Graduated.
Bowman, Charles G., 29 July, 1865. Graduated.
Bradbury, Charles A., 26 July, 1865. Graduated.
Breck, Richard A., 29 September, 1865. Graduated.
Briggs, John B., 28 September, 1865. Graduated.
Brown, Charles R., 22 September, 1865. Graduated.
Brownlee, John D., 21 July, 1865. Resigned.
Buckingham, B. H., 21 July, 1865. Graduated.
Bulkley, William F., 25 July, 1865. Graduated.
Buskirk, Floyd O., 22 September, 1865. Resigned.
Cist, William R., 22 July, 1865. Resigned.
Clason, William P., 30 September, 1865. Resigned.
Coffin, J. H. C., Jr., 21 July, 1865. Graduated.
Colohan, Charles E., 20 July, 1865. Graduated.
Comly, Samuel P., 26 July, 1865. Graduated.
Conry, Francis, 20 July, 1865. Resigned.
Crane, Ashley A., 28 July, 1865. Resigned.
Curtis, Clinton K., 27 September, 1865. Graduated.
Daniel, Henry M., 27 July, 1865. Resigned.
Day, William P., 25 July, 1865. Graduated.
Dillingham, Albert C., 20 July, 1865. Graduated.
Dimick, Otis S., 26 July, 1865. Discharged.
Driggs, William H., 20 July, 1865. Graduated.
Field, Edward A., 20 July, 1865. Graduated.
Fowler, Alfred B., 23 September, 1865. Resigned.
Fowler, Robert L., 20 July, 1865. Resigned.
Franklin, James, 23 September, 1865. Graduated.
Fuller, George H., 20 July, 1865. Resigned.
Garvin, John, 22 July, 1865. Graduated.
Gerrish, Winfield S., 21 September, 1865. Resigned.
Geutsch, Ferdinand H., 21 July, 1865. Graduated.
Graydon, James W., 21 July, 1865. Graduated.
Hadden, William A., 27 September, 1865. Graduated.
Hall, Joel, 25 July, 1865. Died 22 June, 1866.
Hall, Martin E., 19 September, 1865. Graduated.
Handy, Henry O., 25 July, 1865. Graduated.
Hanus, Gustavus C., 25 July, 1865. Graduated.
Harber, Giles B., 22 July, 1865. Graduated.
Harmon, William E., 22 July, 1865. Resigned.
Harris, Uriah R., 21 July, 1865. Graduated.
Hawley, Henry, 27 July, 1865. Resigned.
Henshaw, Edward T., 25 September, 1865. Resigned.
Hobson, Joseph B., 24 July, 1865. Graduated.
Houston, Nelson T., 27 July, 1865. Graduated.
Howe, Orin F., 28 July, 1865. Resigned.
Hull, Frederick B., 28 September, 1865. Graduated.
Hyde, Marcus D., 23 November, 1865. Graduated.
Kellogg, Germaine A., 28 July, 1865. Resigned.
Kellogg, Wainwright, 27 September, 1865. Graduated.
Kilburn, Willie, 5 December, 1865. Graduated.
Kimball, William W., 31 July, 1865. Graduated.
King, Allan A., 29 July, 1865. Discharged.
King, William S., 21 September, 1865. Resigned.
Leach, Herbert C., 28 July, 1865. Resigned.
Low, William F., 21 July, 1865. Graduated.
Mahan, Dennis H., 20 July, 1865. Graduated.
Mason, Newton E., 22 July, 1865. Graduated.
McCabe, George W., 29 September, 1865. Resigned.
McEwen, Charles A., 23 September, 1865. Resigned.
McLane, Alan E., 27 September, 1865. Resigned.
Miller, Byron H., 23 September, 1865. Discharged.
Monahon, Henry T., 25 July, 1865. Graduated.
Montgomery, Thomas C., 23 September, 1865. Resigned.
Moore, John H., 29 July, 1865. Graduated.
Morgan, Randal W., 27 September, 1865. Resigned.
Muhlenberg, Henry E., 21 September, 1865. Resigned.
Nazro, Arthur P., 20 July, 1865. Graduated.
Negley, William C., 26 July, 1865. Graduated.
Niles, Kossuth, 22 September, 1865. Graduated.
Norris, John A., 27 September, 1865. Graduated.
Norton, Charles H., 29 July, 1865. Resigned.

Noteware, Albert C., 20 July, 1865. Resigned.
Osborn, Arthur P., 25 July, 1865. Graduated.
Osterhaus, Hugo, 22 September, 1865. Graduated.
Paine, Sumner C., 21 September, 1865. Graduated.
Patch, Nathaniel J. K., 20 September, 1865. Graduated.
Perkins, Charles P., 20 July, 1865. Graduated.
Phelps, Samuel H., 21 July, 1865. Resigned.
Phelps, Thomas S., Jr., 25 July, 1865. Graduated.
Porter, Theodoric, 20 September, 1865. Graduated.
Potter, William P., 26 September, 1865. Graduated.
Pratt, John B., 27 September, 1865. Resigned.
Quinby, DeHunt G., 20 July, 1865. Resigned.
Richards, Henry M. M., 20 July, 1865. Graduated.
Richman, Clayton S., 21 July, 1865. Graduated.
Richmond, George H., 26 September, 1865. Resigned.
Rodd, Thomas, 20 July, 1865. Resigned.
Rohrer, Karl, 20 July, 1865. Graduated.
Root, Edward R., 25 September, 1865. Resigned.
Ross, Joseph H., 31 July, 1865. Resigned.
Rudd, Negley, 28 September, 1865. Resigned.
Russell, Horace G., 25 September, 1865. Resigned.
Schnur, William, 29 July, 1865. Resigned.
Scott, Wisner G., 21 July, 1865. Resigned.
Stephens, Alexander, 25 July, 1865. Discharged.
Stockton, Henry T., 20 July, 1865. Graduated.

Sweet, Frederick B., 29 July, 1865. Resigned.
Taunt, Emory H., 22 July, 1865. Graduated.
Taylor, Edward G., 20 September, 1865. Resigned.
Thackara, Alexander M., 20 July, 1865. Graduated.
Tonvelle, William W., 21 September, 1865. Resigned.
Turner, Edward P., 20 July, 1865. Resigned.
Turner, William H., 21 July, 1865. Graduated.
Utley, Joseph H., 22 September, 1865. Graduated.
Van de Carr, William H., 25 July, 1865. Graduated.
Warren, George, 28 July, 1865. Resigned.
Weld, Edward C., 30 September, 1865. Resigned.
Wheeler, James J., 19 September, 1865. Dismissed.
Wilcox, Montgomery, 25 July, 1865. Resigned.
Wiley, Edwin H., 27 July, 1865. Graduated.
Wilson, John C., 22 July, 1865. Graduated.
Wing, Halsey M., 26 July, 1865. Resigned.
Winslow, Francis, 20 July, 1865. Graduated.
Winslow, Herbert, 20 July, 1865. Graduated.
Wood, William F., 25 July, 1865. Discharged.
Wood, William M., 20 July, 1865. Graduated.
Wright, George F., 20 July, 1865. Graduated.
York, John W. E., 24 July, 1865. Resigned.
Zabriskie, George A., 28 September, 1865. Resigned.

1866.—MIDSHIPMEN.

Arnold, Philip, 1 August, 1866. Resigned.
Ashley, Pacificus L., 24 September, 1866. Resigned.
Augur, John P. J., 26 September, 1866. Graduated.
Bachus, Montgomery, 25 July, 1866. Resigned.
Baker, Winfield S., 30 July, 1866. Graduated.
Barnes, John W., 28 July, 1866. Resigned.
Barnette, Gaspar C., 23 July, 1866. Resigned.
Bassford, Warren L., 31 July, 1866. Resigned.
Belcher, Willie M., 31 July, 1866. Dropped.
Brahe, Charles H., 25 July, 1866. Resigned.
Brenen, Edward W., 28 July, 1866. Resigned.
Briggs, Charles, 30 July, 1866. Graduated.
Bull, James H., 25 July, 1866. Graduated.
Calhoun, George A., 31 July, 1866. Graduated.
Carter, James L., 25 July, 1866. Resigned.
Clark, George D., 24 September, 1866. Dismissed.
Clason, William P., 27 July, 1866. Graduated.
Collins, John B., 30 July, 1866. Graduated.
Conway, William P., 1 October, 1866. Graduated.

Crane, Ashley A., 26 July, 1866. Resigned.
Crosby, Freeman H., 30 July, 1866. Graduated.
Culver, Edwin K., 1 August, 1866. Resigned.
Danenhower, John W., 25 September, 1866. Graduated.
Darley, William B. W., 27 September, 1866. Resigned.
Dimmock, Martial C., 31 July, 1866. Graduated.
Donsman, Lyndsey W., 25 July, 1866. Resigned.
Dyer, George L., 26 July, 1866. Graduated.
Ellery, Frank, 25 September, 1866. Graduated.
Emmerick, Charles F., 26 September, 1866. Graduated.
Esmonds, Zadok T., 26 July, 1866. Resigned.
Eycleshimer, Charles S., 1 October, 1866. Resigned.
Fickbohm, Herman F., 31 July, 1866. Graduated.
Field, Philip V., 1 August, 1866. Resigned.
Foster, Charles A., 1 August, 1866. Graduated.
Foster, George, Jr., 31 July, 1866. Resigned.
Fraunces, Joseph H., 26 July, 1866. Resigned.

GENERAL NAVY REGISTER.   641

Frazer, Walter, 27 July, 1866. Resigned.
Freeman, Julius C., 4 October, 1866. Graduated.
French, Walter S., 27 July, 1866. Graduated.
Galloway, Charles D., 22 September, 1866. Graduated.
Gore, James M., 25 July, 1866. Graduated.
Gosling, Harrington L., 25 September, 1866. Resigned.
Graham, Samuel L., 27 July, 1866. Graduated.
Green, Henry L., 31 July, 1866. Graduated.
Hancock, Hiram, 23 July, 1866. Dropped.
Hargous, Frank G., 1 August, 1866. Resigned.
Harris, Henry, 1 August, 1866. Graduated.
Hart, John L., 22 September, 1866. Dismissed.
Hellner, Lewis C., 25 July, 1866. Graduated.
Heiskell, Henry L., 26 September, 1866. Dropped.
Holliday, Walter S., 27 July, 1866. Graduated.
Holman, George F. W., 25 July, 1866. Graduated.
Hoyt, George B., 31 July, 1866. Resigned.
Hubbard, John, 27 July, 1866. Graduated.
Hughes, Edward M., 26 July, 1866. Graduated.
Hunker, Jacob J., 30 July, 1866. Graduated.
Jacoby, Harry M., 27 July, 1866. Graduated.
Jarnagin, Julius S., 27 September, 1866. Resigned.
Jordan, Jacob W., 2 October, 1866. Resigned.
Jouett, Landon P., 31 July, 1866. Graduated.
Kauffman, Francis A., 31 July, 1866. Resigned.
Keeler, John D., 23 July, 1866. Graduated.
Keyes, Charles E., 27 September, 1866. Dismissed.
Kirkpatrick, Henry H., 22 September, 1866. Resigned.
Kronmiller, George, 3 October, 1866. Resigned.
Kunhardt, Charles P., 31 July, 1866. Graduated.
Leach, Boynton, 30 July, 1866. Graduated.
Lefavor, Frederick H., 27 July, 1866. Graduated.
Little, David S., 25 September, 1866. Resigned.
Long, William St. C., 25 July, 1866. Resigned.
Ludlow, Francis L., 24 July, 1866. Graduated.
Lyman, Charles H., 28 July, 1866. Graduated.
Lyon, George, 25 July, 1866. Resigned.
Masser, William H. E., 1 October, 1866. Graduated.
Mayer, William G., 23 July, 1866. Graduated.
McCracken, Alexander, 27 July, 1866. Graduated.
McCrea, Henry, 24 July, 1866. Graduated.
McDonald, Colin, 24 July, 1866. Graduated.
Mentz, George W., 26 September, 1866. Graduated.
Merriam, Greenlief A., 24 July, 1866. Graduated.

Miller, Marcellus G., 26 July, 1866. Resigned.
Milliman, Anson B., 31 July, 1866. Graduated.
Milton, John B., 30 July, 1866. Graduated.
Murdock, Joseph B., 26 July, 1866. Graduated.
Murphy, John A., 26 September, 1866. Dismissed.
Norton, Edward R., 30 July, 1866. Resigned.
Norton, James P., 25 July, 1866. Resigned.
Nye, Haile C. T., 28 July, 1866. Graduated.
Oxley, William H., 31 July, 1866. Resigned.
Peck, Robert G., 24 September, 1866. Graduated.
Pennington, Henry R., 1 October, 1866. Graduated.
Perkins, Joseph W., 26 September, 1866. Resigned.
Platt, Howard, 1 October, 1866. Resigned.
Post, Joel A., 23 July, 1866. Graduated.
Ray, Whitmul P., 27 September, 1866. Graduated.
Reamey, Lazarus L., 25 July, 1866. Graduated.
Rees, Corwin P., 31 July, 1866. Graduated.
Remsen, William, 26 July, 1866. Graduated.
Richardson, Charles S., 30 July, 1866. Resigned.
Rittenhouse, Hawley O., 27 July, 1866. Graduated.
Sanderson, George A., 26 September, 1866. Graduated.
Sargent, Nathan, 23 July, 1866. Graduated.
Sawyers, James H., 24 September, 1866. Graduated.
Schaefer, Henry W., 23 July, 1866. Graduated.
Schwenk, Milton K., 22 September, 1866. Graduated.
Scott, Frank, 24 September, 1866. Resigned.
Selden, George L., 27 July, 1866. Graduated.
Seymour, George N., 25 July, 1866. Resigned.
Shaffer, Edward L., 27 July, 1866. Resigned.
Shaffner, Benjamin M., 31 July, 1866. Resigned.
Soule, Charles E., 31 July, 1866. Dismissed.
Spears, John R., 31 July, 1866. Resigned.
Spencer, Thomas C., 24 July, 1866. Graduated.
Shump, George M., 27 July, 1866. Resigned.
Talbot, Emory H., 26 July, 1866. Resigned.
Tillinghast, Benjamin C., 31 July, 1866. Resigned.
Tyler, Hanson R., 27 July, 1866. Graduated.
Van Horn, Dick, 1 October, 1866. Resigned.
Veazie, Francis B., 23 July, 1866. Resigned.
Vedder, Albert F., 2 August, 1866. Resigned.
Vreeland, Charles E., 31 July, 1866. Graduated.
Warden, Charles P., 27 September, 1866. Resigned.
Weave, Kingsland, 26 September, 1866. Resigned.

Whipple, David, 25 September, 1866. Resigned.
Williams, Henry S., 30 July, 1866. Resigned.
Wilson, Downs S., 27 July, 1866. Graduated.

Wood, Thomas C., 30 July, 1866. Graduated.
Wright, Miers F., 1 October, 1866. Graduated.

1867.—MIDSHIPMEN.

Anderton, Robert J., 25 September, 1867. Resigned.
Babcock, William C., 24 September, 1867. Graduated.
Babcock, Zachary T., 27 June, 1867. Resigned.
Baker, Asher C., 30 September, 1867. Graduated.
Barber, Joel A., 22 June, 1867. Graduated.
Barroll, Henry H., 28 September, 1867. Graduated.
Bartlett, Charles W., 21 June, 1867. Graduated.
Brown, Charles W., 26 June, 1867. Resigned.
Brown, Julian H., 27 September, 1867. Resigned.
Bonns, Christopher, 1 July, 1867. Graduated.
Burnett, Jeremiah C., 27 September, 1867. Graduated.
Busbee, Perrin, 23 September, 1867. Graduated.
Calkins, Carlos G., 24 June, 1867. Graduated.
Carnahan, Thomas D., 21 June, 1867. Resigned.
Clark, Frank L., 27 June, 1867. Resigned.
Cobb, Alphonso H., 23 September, 1867. Graduated.
Cory, George W., 22 June, 1867. Dropped.
Crandall, Albert A., 1 July, 1867. Graduated.
Cresup, James C., 24 June, 1867. Graduated.
Dabney, Albert J., 1 October, 1867. Graduated.
Denny, Thomas C., 26 June, 1867. Resigned.
Downes, John, 22 June, 1867. Graduated.
Edson, John T., 27 June, 1867. Graduated.
Elliott, William P., 26 September, 1867. Graduated.
Ford, Melbourne H., 21 June, 1867. Resigned.
Fox, Levi, 28 June, 1867. Resigned.
Graham, Robert S., 23 September, 1867. Resigned.
Greene, Francis E., 25 September, 1867. Graduated.
Greene, Franklin L., 26 June, 1867. Resigned.
Guertin, Frank, 1 July, 1867. Graduated.
Gwynn, Winfield, 24 September, 1867. Resigned.
Harper, William M., 29 September, 1867. Resigned.
Helstand, George W., 1 July, 1867. Resigned.
Hotchkins, Frank S., 28 June, 1867. Graduated.
Hunsicker, Joseph L., 25 June, 1867. Graduated.

Irwin, William M., 29 June, 1867. Graduated.
Jenkins, Albert T., 21 September, 1867. Resigned.
Livingston, Walter T., 26 June, 1867. Resigned.
Lytle, Robert F., 31 June, 1867. Resigned.
Marshall, William A., 27 June, 1867. Graduated.
McIntosh, Horace P., 28 June, 1867. Graduated.
Mertz, Albert, 27 June, 1867. Graduated.
Montgomery, Joseph C., 26 June, 1867. Resigned.
Nabor, Frank W., 21 September, 1867. Graduated.
O'Reilly, William T. B., 22 June, 1867. Resigned.
Plunket, Thomas S., 21 June, 1867. Graduated.
Pinckney, Nelson, 26 June, 1867. Resigned.
Qualtrough,, Edward T., 21 September, 1867. Graduated.
Roller, John E., 26 June, 1867. Graduated.
Sawyer, Frank E., 23 September, 1867. Resigned.
Scott, Benjamin B., 1 July, 1867. Resigned.
Seabury, Smauel, 26 June, 1867. Graduated.
Sewell, William E., 27 September, 1867. Graduated.
Singer, Harry C., 30 September, 1867. Resigned.
Siter, William A., 1 July, 1867. Resigned.
Slack, William H., 1 October, 1867. Graduated.
Staunton, Sidney A., 23 September, 1867. Graduated.
Stevens, Robert D., 25 June, 1867. Graduated.
Terrell, Charles, 26 September, 1867. Graduated.
Thomas, Clarence, Jr., 26 September, 1867. Graduated.
Tittman, Eugene C., 27 September, 1867. Resigned.
Vandervoort, Germain B., 30 September, 1867. Dropped.
Van Horn, Robert C., 23 September, 1867. Resigned.
Vail, George A., 27 September, 1867. Graduated.
Ward, Aaron, 28 September, 1867. Graduated.
Waring, Howard S., 26 June, 1867. Graduated.
Wight, James M., 1 July, 1867. Graduated.
Worsley, Dwight L., 26 June, 1867. Resigned.

GENERAL NAVY REGISTER.

1868.—MIDSHIPMEN.

Baker, Daniel E., 26 June, 1868. Graduated.
Baldwin, William L., 25 September, 1868. Resigned.
Brown, Abel B., 25 September, 1868. Resigned.
Burns, Joel H., 26 September, 1868. Resigned.
Cottman, Vincendon L., 25 September, 1868. Graduated.
Crosswait, Charles H., 26 June, 1868. Dropped.
Dieterich, Jonathan G., 30 September, 1868. Resigned.
Dixon, Thomas F., 24 September, 1868. Resigned.
Dockery, Alfred V., 26 September, 1868. Resigned.
Fletcher, Robert H., 25 June, 1868. Graduated.
Fox, Charles E., 25 June, 1868. Graduated.
Freeman, Albert T., 26 September, 1868. Graduated.
Fremont, John C., Jr., 25 June, 1868. Graduated.
Galt, Rogers H., 23 June, 1868. Graduated.
Garrett, William H., 26 September, 1868. Resigned.
Heacock, William C., 24 September, 1868. Graduated.
Hey, George W., 30 September, 1868. Resigned.
James, Nathaniel S., 30 June, 1868. Graduated.
Keeler, Delmar R., 29 June, 1868. Resigned.
Kirkland, Alexander, 24 September, 1868. Resigned.
Lasher, Oren E., 29 September, 1868. Graduated.
Lloyd, Edward, 30 September, 1868. Resigned.
Lowry, Oswin W., 25 June, 1868. Graduated.
Lyeth, Clinton H., 26 June, 1868. Graduated.
Manley, James S., 30 September, 1868. Resigned.
Mann, Horace W., 6 October, 1868. Resigned.
McCarthy, George D., 1 May, 1868. Resigned.
McConnell, Murray D., 1 July, 1868. Dismissed.
McLean, Robert H., 29 June, 1868. Graduated.
Medary, Jacob, 26 June, 1868. Graduated.
Miles, Charles R., 29 June, 1868. Graduated.
Mitchell, Charles T., 26 September, 1868. Resigned.
Nagle, Jacob K., 29 June, 1868. Resigned.
Oliver, John Y., 1 October, 1868. Resigned.
Pitcher, William L., 30 June, 1868. Resigned.
Polmyer, William, 26 June, 1868. Resigned.
Powers, Frank H., 29 June, 1868. Resigned.
Rinehart, Benjamin F., 26 September, 1868. Graduated.
Roper, Jesse M., 25 June, 1868. Graduated.
Rosencrantz, William D., 26 June, 1868. Resigned.
Sawyer, Frank E., 25 September, 1868. Graduated.
Slough, William McL., 1 October, 1868. Resigned.
Smith, Arthur C., 29 June, 1868. Resigned.
Southerland, William H. H., 29 June, 1868. Graduated.
Thompson, Charles A., 30 September, 1868. Graduated.
Tyler, Frederick H., 23 June, 1868. Graduated.
Van Epps, Lemuel, 29 June, 1868. Resigned.
Veeder, Ten Eyck, D. W., 25 September, 1868. Graduated.
Winlock, James H., 25 September, 1868. Graduated.
Winston, George T., 1 October, 1868. Resigned.

1869.—MIDSHIPMEN.

Anderson, John E., 24 September, 1869. Resigned.
Arnold, George S., 30 June, 1869. Resigned.
Axon, Clinton, 25 June, 1869. Resigned.
Badger, Charles J., 24 June, 1869. Graduated.
Baker, Edward L., 22 September, 1869. Resigned.
Bean, John W., 24 June, 1869. Graduated.
Blakeley, James W., 29 June, 1869. Dropped.
Bremer, Charles J., 22 September, 1869. Resigned.
Burns, Worth, 24 June, 1869. Resigned.
Case, Augustus L., Jr., 24 June, 1869. Graduated.
Conet, William N., 30 June, 1869. Resigned.
Connell, Humberston S., 24 September, 1869. Resigned.
Cowles, Walter C., 22 September, 1869. Graduated.
Craig, William H., 30 June, 1869. Resigned.
Crocker, Eben B., 23 September, 1869. Resigned.
Culp, Isaac B., 24 September, 1869. Resigned.
Danner, Frederick W., 25 June, 1869. Graduated.
Davids, Lewis J., 24 September, 1869. Resigned.
Deering, Charles W., 23 June, 1869. Graduated.
Dexter, Jenness K., 23 June, 1869. Resigned.
Diehl, Samuel W. B., 21 September, 1869. Graduated.
Elliott, Isaac B., 22 September, 1869. Resigned.
Fales, Horatio C., 29 June, 1869. Resigned.
Farnsworth, John, 28 September, 1869. Graduated.
Fenn, Frank A., 23 June, 1869. Dropped.
Fisher, Irving R., 24 September, 1869. Resigned.
Fithian, Clarence E., 23 September, 1869. Resigned.

644   GENERAL NAVY REGISTER.

Fowler, Gilbert, 24 June, 1869. Graduated.
Grant, Charles V., 25 September, 1869. Resigned.
Greenough, Horatio W., 25 June, 1869. Resigned.
Gundlach, William, 29 September, 1869. Resigned.
Habersham, Richard, 24 September, 1869. Resigned.
Halsey, William F., 22 September, 1869. Graduated.
Hard, Edwin F., 23 September, 1869. Resigned.
Holder, Charles F., 29 June, 1869. Resigned.
Howard, Thomas B., 25 June, 1869. Graduated.
Hyde, George W., 22 September, 1869. Resigned.
Jackson, James M., 28 September, 1869. Resigned.
Jenkins, Frank T., 23 June, 1869. Dropped.
Johnson, John P., 23 June, 1869. Resigned.
Jouett, J. Stockett, 23 June, 1869. Resigned.
Knight, Austin M., 30 June, 1869. Graduated.
Laird, Charles, 25 September, 1869. Resigned.
Lemley, Samuel C., 26 June, 1869. Graduated.
Manley, James S., 25 June, 1869. Resigned.
McCartney, Charles M., 25 September, 1869. Resigned.
McKelvy, William, 25 September, 1869. Resigned.
Michelson, Albert A., 29 June, 1869. Graduated.
Milligan, Frank J., 30 June, 1869. Graduated.
Moore, Charles B. T., 28 September, 1869. Graduated.
Morrell, Henry, 30 June, 1869. Graduated.
Muse, Thomas E., 30 September, 1869. Graduated.
Negley, James S., 29 September, 1869. Resigned.
Nichols, John B., 29 September, 1869. Resigned.
Nicholson, John Q., 24 June, 1869. Graduated.
Nicholson, Reginald F., 30 September, 1869. Graduated.
North, George L., 25 June, 1869. Resigned.

Northcott, William A., 28 September, 1869. Resigned.
Peacock, David, 29 September, 1869. Resigned.
Pell, Herbert C., 29 June, 1869. Resigned.
Pierson, Frank, 23 September, 1869. Resigned.
Putnam, Charles F., 24 June, 1869. Graduated.
Raines, Eugene, 24 June, 1869. Resigned.
Ray, Edmund G., 24 September, 1869. Resigned.
Reynolds, Alfred, 22 September, 1869. Graduated.
Robb, John F., 23 September, 1869. Resigned.
Robinson, J. Marshall, 25 June, 1869. Graduated.
Rodman, Herman J., 23 June, 1869. Resigned.
Schuetze, William H., 23 June, 1869. Graduated.
Shaw, William F., 24 September, 1869. Resigned.
Shufeldt, Mason A., 24 June, 1869. Graduated.
Smith, Irving, 26 June, 1869. Resigned.
Strong, Rouldo D., 26 June, 1869. Resigned.
Talbot, William A., 29 September, 1866. Resigned.
Topping, William V. B., 25 June, 1869. Resigned.
Turnbull, John W., 6 October, 1869. Resigned.
Underwood, Edmund B., 26 June, 1869. Graduated.
Underwood, James P., 29 June, 1869. Graduated.
Upshur, Custis P., 24 September, 1869. Resigned.
Vail, Edward, Jr., 22 September, 1869. Resigned.
Van Vliet, Frederick C., 23 June, 1869. Resigned.
Wallingford, Charles A., 25 September, 1869. Resigned.
Way, George B., 29 September, 1869. Resigned.
White, Frank A., 24 September, 1869. Resigned.
Wilner, Frank A., 30 June, 1869. Graduated.
Winder, William, 21 September, 1869. Graduated.
Young, Lucien, 23 June, 1869. Graduated.

1870.—MIDSHIPMEN.

Allderdice, Winslow, 18 June, 1870. Graduated.
Arms, Lyman, 26 September, 1870. Graduated.
Axon, Clinton J., 23 September, 1870. Resigned.
Beuagh, Henry C., 30 September, 1870. Resigned.
Bostick, Edward D., 26 September, 1870. Graduated.
Boush, Clifford J., 25 June, 1870. Dropped.
Bowyer, John M., 30 September, 1870. Graduated.
Braekenridge, Joseph G., 24 June, 1870. Dropped.
Brown, Frederick S., 29 September, 1870. Resigned.
Brown, Beriah, Jr., 29 September, 1870. Graduated.

Bryden, James, 1 October, 1870. Resigned.
Carrow, Charles M., 22 September, 1870. Dropped.
Carter, Fidelio S., 30 September, 1870. Graduated.
Cheek, John F., 29 June, 1870. Dropped.
Clark, William G., 29 June, 1870. Resigned.
Coffin, Frederick W., 16 June, 1870. Graduated.
Coleman, William K., 22 September, 1870. Resigned.
Colwell, John C., 23 September, 1870. Graduated.
Corbin, Clarence A., 27 September, 1870. Graduated.
Craig, Corydon F., 8 June, 1870. Dropped.
Decatur, Stephen, 8 June, 1870. Resigned.

GENERAL NAVY REGISTER.

Dorn, Edward J., 22 September, 1870. Graduated.
Doyle, Robert W., 30 September, 1870. Graduated.
Dutton, William T., 8 June, 1870. Dropped.
Emmons, George T., 8 June, 1870. Graduated.
Fiske, Bradley A., 24 September, 1870. Graduated.
Fletcher, Frank F., 23 September, 1870. Graduated.
Flynne, Lucien, 1 October, 1870. Graduated.
Fuller, Edward C., 28 September, 1870. Graduated.
Gaither, Edward H., 1 October, 1870. Resigned.
Gibson, Lewis W., 22 September, 1870. Resigned.
Gillett, Joseph A., 29 September, 1870. Resigned.
Hall, Alfred L., 27 September, 1870. Resigned.
Hallowell, William H., 13 October, 1870. Resigned.
Hard, Edwin F., 30 September, 1870. Resigned.
Harrington, William G., 21 June, 1870. Dropped.
Hartman, Frederick L., 21 September, 1870. Resigned.
Haskell, Charles W., 25 June, 1870. Graduated.
Hodges, Henry M., 30 September, 1870. Graduated.
Holmes, Frank H., 30 June, 1870. Graduated.
Howe, Alfred L., 29 September, 1870. Graduated.
Hughes, Walter S., 26 September, 1870. Graduated.
Hull, Charles, 24 September, 1870. Resigned.
Hunt, Henry J., 23 June, 1870. Graduated.
Hunt, Ridgely, 21 September, 1870. Graduated.
Hutchins, Hamilton, 24 June, 1870. Graduated.
Hutter, George E., 23 June, 1870. Graduated.
Jardine, Augustus E., 22 September, 1870. Graduated.
Jones, George H., 27 September, 1870. Resigned.
Jones, John K., 21 September, 1870. Resigned.
Kinney, Robert P., 27 September, 1870. Resigned.
Laird, Charles, 29 September, 1870. Graduated.
Lewis, Harry R., 22 September, 1870. Resigned.
McCartney, Charles M., 22 September, 1870. Resigned.
McDaid, Gulford M., 30 September, 1870. Resigned.
McDowell, Wilken C., 30 June, 1870. Resigned.
McGinnis, William S., 25 June, 1870. Dropped.
McGunnegle, George K., 22 September, 1870. Resigned.
Moorman, Henry P., 21 September, 1870. Dropped.
Negley, James S., 30 June, 1870. Resigned.
Nichols, John C., 21 September, 1870. Dropped.
Noell, York, 21 September, 1870. Graduated.

Nostrand, Warner H., 24 September, 1870. Graduated.
Osgood, Hosea A., 22 September, 1870. Resigned.
Oliver, William C., 21 September, 1870. Resigned.
Parker, John F., 30 September, 1870. Graduated.
Peacock, David, 28 September, 1870. Graduated.
Peacock, Samuel M., 19 October, 1870. Resigned.
Peale, Louis T., 7 October, 1870. Resigned.
Peters, George H., 24 June, 1870. Graduated.
Powers, Stephen A., 29 September, 1870. Resigned.
Ragan, Otho H. W., 22 June, 1870. Resigned.
Ray, Edmund G., 22 September, 1870. Dropped.
Reich, Henry F., 28 September, 1870. Graduated.
Reiley, William V. W., 23 September, 1870. Resigned.
Reynolds, Edwin L., 22 June, 1870. Graduated.
Reynolds, Matthew G., 22 September, 1870. Graduated.
Rooney, William R. A., 29 September, 1870. Graduated.
Scott, Bernard O., 30 June, 1870. Graduated.
Sharp, Alexander, Jr., 21 June, 1870. Graduated.
Stewart, John W., 29 September, 1870. Graduated.
Stoney, George, 21 September, 1870. Graduated.
Strader, Joseph S., 23 September, 1870. Resigned.
Tennison, John K., 23 September, 1870. Resigned.
Thomas, John C., 23 September, 1870. Dropped.
Townley, Richard H., 21 June, 1870. Graduated.
Turner, James V., 21 June, 1870. Resigned.
Turner, William H., 29 September, 1870. Dropped.
Wanless, George J., 30 June, 1870. Resigned.
Ward, Arthur J., 29 September, 1870. Dropped.
Watkins, Samuel W., 1 October, 1870. Resigned.
Way, George B., 21 September, 1870. Resigned.
Wegmann, Albert, 22 September, 1870. Graduated.
Wells, Henry F., 29 September, 1870. Resigned.
Whipple, Edward A., 23 September, 1870. Resigned.
White, Hunter C., 13 June, 1870. Resigned.
Whitefield, William E., 22 June, 1870. Graduated.
Whitehead, Thomas C., 21 September, 1870. Dropped.
Wills, Allen W., 22 September, 1870. Resigned.
Winslow, Cameron M., 29 September, 1870. Graduated.

1871.—MIDSHIPMEN.

Amsden, Charles H., 21 September, 1871. Graduated.
Beatty, Frank E., 23 September, 1871. Graduated.
Blakesley, Mendle P., 10 June, 1871. Resigned.
Boult, Clare, 22 September, 1871. Resigned.
Brawnersreuther, William, 26 September, 1871. Graduated.
Brent, Samuel G., 22 September, 1871. Resigned.
Campbell, William, 10 June, 1871. Resigned.
Caperton, William B., 13 June, 1871. Graduated.
Chambers, Washington I., 9 June, 1871. Graduated.
Chase, Henry G., 23 September, 1871. Resigned.
Collamore, George W., 10 June, 1871. Dropped.
Collins, Frank S., 26 September, 1871. Graduated.
Crittenden, Albert B., 14 October, 1871. Resigned.
Cutler, William G., 22 September, 1871. Graduated.
Daniels, David, 12 June, 1871. Graduated.
Diggs, Robert D., 25 September, 1871. Resigned.
Drake, Charles C., 10 June, 1871. Resigned.
Dubois, Henry O., 22 September, 1871. Resigned.
Dyer, Shubael A., 6 October, 1871. Resigned.
Elder, Eustace C., 28 September, 1871. Resigned.
Ewing, Boyd, 15 June, 1871. Dropped.
Ford, Henry W., 9 June, 1871. Resigned.
Gillmore, James C., 22 September, 1871. Graduated.
Glassford, William A., 27 September, 1871. Resigned.
Goss, Edwin C., 21 September, 1871. Resigned.
Gove, Charles A., 9 June, 1871. Graduated.
Grabo, Herman F., 23 September, 1871. Resigned.
Halpine, Nicholas J. L. T., 13 June, 1871. Graduated.
Hamersly, Thomas H. S., 30 September, 1871. Resigned.
Hayward, Charles, 9 June, 1871. Resigned.
Helm, James M., 30 September, 1871. Graduated.
Hicks, Edward W., 22 September, 1871. Resigned.
Hodgson, Albon C., 9 June, 1871. Graduated.
Hasley, Harry H., 23 September, 1871. Graduated.

Hughes, Silven, 9 June, 1871. Resigned.
Hunt, Willie W., 30 September, 1871. Resigned.
Jenkins, Stephen, 21 September, 1871. Graduated.
Johns, Frank, 9 June, 1871. Resigned.
Lathrop, Frederick A., 10 June, 1871. Resigned.
Lauferty, Simon L., 22 September, 1871. Resigned.
Lewis, Robert E., 5 October, 1871. Resigned.
Manley, James S., 30 September, 1871. Resigned.
McCoy, Frank C., 9 June, 1871. Resigned.
McGunnegle, George K., 26 September, 1871. Resigned.
Mears, Samuel M., 9 June, 1871. Resigned.
Milligan, Richard T., 16 June, 1871. Graduated.
Osborne, Eben S., 30 September, 1871. Resigned.
Peacock, Samuel M., 21 September, 1871. Resigned.
Piepmeyer, Louis W., 23 September, 1871. Graduated.
Poland, Edward R., 22 September, 1871. Resigned.
Rogan, Otho H. W., 10 June, 1871. Resigned.
Reed, George H., 9 June, 1871. Resigned.
Reed, Horace, B., 6 October, 1871. Resigned.
Reynolds, Lovell K., 9 June, 1871. Graduated.
Sears, James H., 22 September, 1871. Graduated.
Seyburn, Stephen Y., 10 June, 1871. Resigned.
Sherman, Francis H., 21 September, 1871. Graduated.
Sherman, John A., 13 June, 1871. Graduated.
Slaughter, Harry A., 18 September, 1871. Resigned.
Smith, James T., 12 June, 1871. Graduated.
Tappan, Benjamin S., 22 September, 1871. Graduated.
Thompson, Cyrus H., 22 September, 1871. Resigned.
Usher, Nathaniel R., 22 September, 1871. Graduated.
Varnum, William L., 9 June, 1871. Graduated.
Vinton, Frederick B., 21 September, 1871. Graduated.
Wise, Edward E., 8 June, 1871. Graduated.
Wood, Thomas N., 10 June, 1871. Resigned.
Wood, Moses L., 23 September, 1871. Graduated.
Worcester, George H., 27 September, 1871. Graduated.

1872.—MIDSHIPMEN.

Albertson, Jonathan W., 6 June, 1872. Resigned.
Alderson, William B., 24 September, 1872. Resigned.
Allen, William H., 27 September, 1872. Graduated.
Almy, Augustus C., 7 June, 1872. Dropped.
Bailey, Morton S., 21 September, 1872. Resigned.

Benson, William S., 23 September, 1872. Graduated.
Boult, Clare, 8 June, 1872. Dropped.
Boush, Clifford J., 6 June, 1872. Graduated.
Brown, Stimpson J., 21 September, 1872. Graduated.
Butterfield, Harry N., 24 September, 1872. Dropped.

GENERAL NAVY REGISTER. 647

Cheek, John F., 8 June, 1872. Dropped.
Cherbonnier, Caleb V., 8 June, 1872. Resigned.
Chipman, William L., 1 October, 1872. Resigned.
Coffman, De Witt, 8 June, 1872. Graduated.
Conyers, James H., 24 September, 1872. Resigned.
Cruger, Eugene, 12 June, 1872. Resigned.
Culver, Abraham E., 6 June, 1872. Graduated.
Cuse, Daniel R., 6 June, 1872. Graduated.
Diggs, Robert D., 15 June, 1872. Dismissed.
Dombaugh, Harry M., 8 June, 1872. Graduated.
Donnelly, George D., 25 September, 1872. Resigned.
Duer, Francis H., 25 September, 1872. Dropped.
Eldridge, Foxall P., 25 September, 1872. Resigned.
Fegan, Charles P., 24 September, 1872. Resigned.
Fisher, Elstner N., 24 September, 1872. Graduated.
Flanigan, Willis S., 30 September, 1872. Resigned.
Fletcher, Lewis C., 26 September, 1872. Dropped.
Foulk, George C., 15 June, 1872. Graduated.
Frenzel, Arthur B., 8 June, 1872. Resigned.
Geuring, Harry C., 13 June, 1872. Graduated.
Gilder, Joseph B., 28 September, 1872. Resigned.
Goodfellow, George E., 13 June, 1872. Dropped.
Grabo, Herman F., 21 September, 1872. Graduated.
Gray, Charles H., 25 September, 1872. Resigned.
Gridley, Frederick D., 25 September, 1872. Resigned.
Griffin, Thomas D., 23 September, 1872. Graduated.
Hall, Alfred L., 21 September, 1872. Graduated.
Hall, William E. W., 14 June, 1872. Resigned.
Hammon, William G., 24 September, 1872. Graduated.
Harrison, Horace W., 26 September, 1872. Graduated.
Heap, Samuel L., 12 November, 1872. Resigned.
Henderson, Richard, 26 September, 1872. Graduated.
Henderson, William C., 25 September, 1872. Resigned.
Hodges, Fletcher, 6 June, 1872. Resigned.
Hogg, William S., 25 September, 1872. Graduated.
Horton, Cyrus W., 13 June, 1872. Resigned.
Howard, Grosvenor T., 28 September, 1872. Resigned.
Johnson, Henry A., 6 June, 1872. Graduated.
Jones, David W., 10 June, 1872. Resigned.

Jones, Horace T., 10 June, 1872. Resigned.
Katz, Edward M., 10 June, 1872. Graduated.
King, George E., 6 June, 1872. Resigned.
Leach, Edward D., 10 June, 1872. Resigned.
Lockett, William, 23 September, 1872. Dropped.
Macomb, Augustus C., 25 September, 1872. Resigned.
Mallory, Stevenson B., 13 June, 1872. Graduated.
Manadier, Thomas B., 11 June, 1872. Resigned.
Mayo, Henry T., 14 June, 1872. Graduated.
McLean, Walter, 7 June, 1872. Graduated.
McNasser, John H., 10 June, 1872. Resigned.
Messinger, Lyman B., 27 September, 1872. Resigned.
Minett, Henry, 10 June, 1872. Graduated.
Mitchell, Alexander R., 8 June, 1872. Resigned.
Munn, Charles W., 27 September, 1872. Resigned.
Newton, John T., 16 October, 1872. Graduated.
Norris, Calvin C. J., 27 September, 1872. Resigned.
O'Keefe, John T., 25 September, 1872. Dropped.
Osterhout, William B., 13 June, 1872. Resigned.
Paff, Albert F., 10 June, 1872. Resigned.
Parker, Benjamin W., 23 September, 1872. Resigned.
Pond, Charles F., 13 June, 1872. Graduated.
Potts, Templin M., 8 June, 1872. Graduated.
Proudfit, John M., 25 September, 1872. Graduated.
Ray, Robert C., 2 October, 1872. Graduated.
Ricker, Edward P., 13 June, 1872. Resigned.
Rogers, Charles C., 8 June, 1872. Graduated.
Rollins, Anthony W., 11 June, 1872. Graduated.
Rose, Wildemar D., 6 June, 1872. Graduated.
Rowan, Andrew S., 24 September, 1872. Dropped.
Rush, William R., 10 June, 1872. Graduated.
Sheeks, James D., 26 September, 1872. Resigned.
Ustick, William F., 24 September, 1872. Resigned.
Walling, Burns T., 6 June, 1872. Graduated.
Winch, Thomas G., 21 September, 1872. Graduated.
Winston, Charles, 21 September, 1872. Resigned.
Woodworth, Selim E., 1 October, 1872. Graduated.
Young, William T., 23 September, 1872. Dropped.

1873.—MIDSHIPMEN.

Ancona, John, 24 September, 1873. Resigned.
Atwater, Charles N., 26 September, 1873. Graduated.
Blodgett, Spencer L., 30 September, 1873. Resigned.
Bostwick, Frank M., 27 September, 1873. Graduated.

Brice, Jonathan K., 16 June, 1873. Graduated.
Bronaugh, William V., 7 June, 1873. Graduated.
Brumby, Thomas M., 29 September, 1873. Graduated.
Buckley, Frank S., 27 September, 1873. Resigned.

Bunn, Maurice O., 26 September, 1873. Resigned.
Burdick, William L., 27 September, 1873. Graduated.
Canfield, William C., 25 September, 1873. Graduated.
Carrington, Austin D., 25 September, 1873. Resigned.
Case, Frank B., 10 June, 1873. Graduated.
Castle, Mark C., 30 September, 1873. Resigned.
Chase, John D., 24 September, 1873. Dropped.
Constant, Walter M., 16 June, 1873. Graduated.
Cook, Simon, 10 June, 1873. Graduated.
Crenshaw, Charles R., 1 October, 1873. Resigned.
Crosby, William, 14 June, 1873. Resigned.
David, William G., 26 September, 1873. Graduated.
Denfield, George W., 24 September, 1873. Graduated.
Dent, Baine C., 16 June, 1873. Graduated.
Dickinson, Thomas, 25 September, 1873. Resigned.
Dodd, Arthur W., 10 June, 1873. Graduated.
Dodge, Omenzo G., 17 June, 1873. Graduated.
Donovan, Robert M., 16 June, 1873. Resigned.
Dunn, Herbert O., 9 June, 1873. Graduated.
Dykeman, John H., 7 June, 1873. Resigned.
Endress, William F., 26 September, 1873 Resigned.
Fauntleroy, Robert P., 25 September, 1873. Resigned.
Fechteler, Augustus F., 9 June, 1873. Graduated.
Fletcher, Lewis C., 17 June, 1873. Resigned.
Fullam, William F., 25 September, 1873. Graduated.
Gleanes, Albert, 12 June, 1873. Graduated.
Goulding, Francis S., 11 June, 1873. Dropped.
Grant, Albert W., 10 June, 1873. Graduated.
Green, Thomas, 16 June, 1873. Resigned.
Green, William, 24 September, 1873. Resigned.
Griffith, Horace P., 26 September, 1873. Resigned.
Hagar, Walter C., 4 October, 1873. Resigned.
Hall, William E. W., 16 June, 1873. Resigned.
Harkness, Thomas G., 7 June, 1873. Resigned.
Heath, Frank R., 25 September, 1873. Graduated.
Hess, George H., 25 September, 1873. Resigned.
Hodges, Benjamin W., 25 September, 1873. Graduated.
Holmes, Howard S., 10 June, 1873. Resigned.
Horton, Roscoe, 1 October, 1873. Resigned.
Jayne, Anselm H., 24 September, 1873. Resigned.
Jeffries, Alfred, 10 June, 1873. Graduated.
Jones, Henry C., 29 September, 1873. Resigned.
Jordan, John N., 10 June, 1873. Graduated.

Lansdale, Philip V., 10 June, 1873. Graduated.
Le Bron, John F., 14 June, 1873. Resigned.
Lee, Clarence E., 24 September, 1873. Resigned.
Lindley, Henry B., 10 June, 1873. Dropped.
Lockwood, John A., 27 September, 1873. Resigned.
Lull, Richard H., 25 September, 1873. Resigned.
Mason, John G., 7 June, 1873. Resigned.
McClennan, Alonzo C., 24 September, 1873. Resigned.
Morris, Frank C., 26 September, 1873. Resigned.
Nelson, Valentine S., 10 June, 1873. Graduated.
Oliver, James H., 16 June, 1873. Graduated.
Orchard, John M., 12 June, 1873. Graduated.
Ormsby, George F., 25 September, 1873. Graduated.
Paris, Russel C., 25 September, 1873. Graduated.
Parker, Benjamin W., 26 September, 1873. Dropped.
Parker, James P., 10 June, 1873. Graduated.
Purcell, John L., 30 September, 1873. Graduated.
Riorden, William C., 24 September, 1873. Dropped.
Rogers, Henry H., 16 June, 1873. Resigned.
Ryan, Thomas W., 16 June, 1873. Graduated.
Sanders, Ezra P., 24 September, 1873. Resigned.
Schoolcraft, Oliver J., 7 June, 1873. Resigned.
Seucerbox, William, 10 June, 1873. Resigned.
Stevens, William K., 30 September, 1873. Resigned.
Taylor, Bushrod W., 24 September, 1873. Resigned.
Taylor, Hiero, 30 September, 1873. Graduated.
Taylor, Thomas H., 1 October, 1873. Resigned.
Todd, Wilson L., 10 June, 1873. Graduated.
Topham, Frank W., 24 September, 1873. Graduated.
Tracy, Arthur B., 7 June, 1873. Dismissed.
Vinson, Webster, 1 October, 1873. Resigned.
Vinton, Maurice A., 7 June, 1873. Resigned.
Wakenshaw, Harry C., 12 June, 1873. Graduated.
Walsh, Charles H., 19 June, 1873. Resigned.
Werlich, Percival J., 9 June, 1873. Graduated.
Williams, Charles S., 16 June, 1873. Graduated.
Wilson, John C., 26 September, 1873. Dismissed.
Winterhalter, Albert G., 24 September, 1873. Graduated.
Witzell, Horace M., 7 June, 1873. Graduated.
Wood, Albert N., 25 September, 1873. Graduated.
Wright, Edward E., 24 September, 1873. Graduated.
Wright, Robert K., 11 June, 1873. Graduated.

GENERAL NAVY REGISTER. 649

1874.—MIDSHIPMEN.

Almy, Augustus C., 20 October, 1874. Graduated.
Bailey, Prentice, 28 September, 1874. Resigned.
Baker, Henry E., 24 September, 1874. Dismissed.
Barnard, Louis H., 13 June, 1874. Resigned.
Bartlett, David, 24 September, 1874. Resigned.
Beale, Joseph, 12 October, 1874. Graduated.
Bell, John A., 13 June, 1874. Graduated.
Belmont, Oliver H. P., 30 September, 1874. Resigned.
Bibb, Peyton B., 12 June, 1874. Graduated.
Biddle, Spencer F. B., 13 June, 1874. Graduated.
Boon, Howard C., 12 June, 1874. Resigned.
Boyd, John P., 26 September, 1874. Resigned.
Breck, Charles R., 21 October, 1874. Dismissed.
Cahoon, James B., 10 June, 1874. Graduated.
Clark, George R., 9 June, 1874. Graduated.
Conger, Pliny O., 13 June, 1874. Resigned.
Cox, William H., 26 September, 1874. Drowned.
Cramer, Ambrose, 28 September, 1874. Resigned.
Craven, John E., 24 September, 1874. Graduated.
Crosby, William, 25 September, 1874. Resigned.
Cummings, Leroy E., 24 September, 1874. Resigned.
Cunningham, Andrew C., 9 June, 1874. Graduated.
Dickinson, Thomas, 24 September, 1874. Dismissed.
Dougherty, John A., 12 June, 1874. Graduated.
Drayton, Percival L., 10 June, 1874. Graduated.
Duer, Francis H., 9 June, 1874. Resigned.
Fillmore, John H., 24 September, 1874. Graduated.
Fitzgerald, Edward D., 2 October, 1874. Resigned.
Garrett, Charles W., 24 September, 1874. Died 1877.
Gibson, John, 9 June, 1874. Graduated.
Glennon, James H., 24 September, 1874. Graduated.
Graham, William A., 28 September, 1874. Resigned.
Gray, Alfred G., 26 September, 1874. Resigned.
Gray, James, 24 September, 1874. Resigned.
Guinnep, Arthur B., 28 September, 1874. Resigned.
Hetherington, James H., 9 June, 1874. Graduated.
Holcombe, John H. L., 27 June, 1874. Graduated.
Hood, John, 12 June, 1874. Dismissed.
Hooke, Horatio H., 26 September, 1874. Died 2 January, 1881.
Hughes, Richard M., 25 September, 1874. Graduated.
Huse, Harry M. P. 30 September, 1874. Graduated.
Jungen, Charles W., 24 September, 1874. Resigned.
Kimmell, Harry, 28 September, 1874. Graduated.
Knapp, Harry S., 26 June, 1874. Graduated.
Knapp, John J., 9 June, 1874. Graduated.
Lloyd, Edward, 17 June, 1874. Graduated.
Lopez, Robert F., 29 September, 1874. Graduated.
Maury, Alfred I., 28 September, 1874. Resigned.
Maxwell, William J., 9 June, 1874. Graduated.
Mayer, Chester A., 16 June, 1874. Dismissed.
McClain, Charles S., 3 November, 1874. Graduated.
McDonnell, John E., 30 September, 1874. Graduated.
Meares, Frederick P., 25 September, 1874. Resigned.
Menefee, Daniel P., 25 September, 1874. Graduated.
Milton, Lawson D., 25 September, 1874. Dismissed.
Morey, Alfred G., 25 September, 1874. Resigned.
Paxton, Alfred N., 24 September, 1874. Resigned.
Perry, George E., 10 June, 1874. Dropped.
Perry, John A., 29 September, 1874. Resigned.
Picking, William W., 24 September, 1874. Resigned.
Poundstone, Homer C., 24 September, 1874. Graduated.
Preble, George H. R., 25 September, 1874. Resigned.
Quinby, John G., 12 June, 1874. Graduated.
Read, Maurice L., 28 September, 1874. Graduated.
Redfern, Joseph L., 14 July, 1874. Resigned.
Richardson, Samuel, 17 June, 1874. Resigned.
Rodgers, Thomas S., 24 September, 1874. Graduated.
Rodgers, William L., 11 June, 1874. Graduated.
Rogers, Allen G., 12 June, 1874. Graduated.
Rowan, Andrew S., 25 September, 1874. Resigned.
Schwerin, Rennie R., 25 September, 1874. Graduated.
Shipley, John H., 30 September, 1874. Graduated.
Skinner, Frank C., 26 September, 1874. Resigned.
Smith, Roy C., 3 October, 1874. Graduated.
Sparhawk, George, 24 September, 1874. Graduated.
Sprague, Frank J., 29 September, 1874. Graduated.
Stafford, George G., 10 June, 1874. Graduated.
Sturdivant, Harry L., 13 June, 1874. Dropped.
Swift, Franklin, 9 June, 1874. Graduated.
Tillman, Edwin H., 28 September, 1874. Resigned.
Van Horne, George, 9 June, 1874. Dropped.
Wallace, Carshena, 9 June, 1874. Died 23 December, 1874.
Webb, Lovell H., 28 September, 1874. Dismissed.
Webster, Edwin B., 28 September, 1874. Resigned.

650 GENERAL NAVY REGISTER.

Welch, George P., 24 September, 1874. Resigned.
White, William P., 30 June, 1874. Graduated.
Wilson, Llewellyn, V., 25 September, 1874. Resigned.
Young, Feramorz L., 24 September, 1874. Resigned.

1875.—MIDSHIPMEN.

Arnold, John P., 25 June, 1875. Died 18 July, 1876.
Aldrich, Stuart, 18 September, 1875. Resigned.
Bailey, John B., 18 September, 1875. Resigned.
Barkley, Richard W., 25 June, 1875. Dismissed.
Bartlett, David, 18 September, 1875. Resigned.
Berkeley, Francis L., 18 September, 1875. Dropped.
Bitler, Reuben O., 25 June, 1875. Graduated.
Blish, John B., 18 September, 1875. Graduated.
Bliss, Herbert, 18 September, 1875. Resigned.
Bonfils, Thomas L., 24 June, 1875. Graduated. Honorably discharged, 30 June, 1883.
Booth, Henry D., 18 September, 1875. Resigned.
Bowden, Frank W., 18 September, 1875. Graduated.
Breckenridge, Robert J., 18 September, 1875. Resigned.
Bridges, Mark, 24 June, 1875. Died 9 July, 1875.
Brown, Guy W., 24 June, 1875. Graduated.
Brown, James S., 18 September, 1875. Graduated.
Buchanan, Wilson W., 24 June, 1875. Graduated.
Buffington, Anson W., 18 September, 1875. Resigned.
Bullitt, Howard H., 18 September, 1875. Resigned.
Chase, Henry S., 24 June, 1875. Graduated.
Clements, Abner B., 24 June, 1875. Graduated.
Cockle, Rudolphus R., 24 June, 1875. Graduated. Honorably discharged, 30 June, 1883.
Condict, Edward C., 25 June, 1875. Resigned.
Cooke, Paul B., 18 September, 1875. Resigned.
Cooper, Robert J., 18 September, 1875. Resigned.
Dewey, Theodore G., 25 June, 1875. Graduated.
Drake, James C., 24 June, 1875. Graduated.
Fillebrown, Horatio L., 25 June, 1875. Resigned.
Finley, Henry M., 25 June, 1875. Resigned.
Franklin, Thomas B., 18 September, 1875. Resigned.
French, George R., 24 June, 1875. Graduated.
Garrett, Leigh O., 18 September, 1875. Graduated.
Garrett, Le Roy M., 18 September, 1875. Graduated.
Gibbons, John H., 18 September, 1875. Graduated.
Gill, William A., 24 June, 1875. Graduated.
Gilmore, Alexander C., 18 September, 1875. Resigned.
Godfrey, Frank L., 25 June, 1875. Resigned.
Gorgas, Miles C., 18 September, 1875. Graduated.
Gresham, William A., 25 June, 1875. Graduated.
Haines, Henry C., 3 July, 1875. Graduated. Transferred to Marine Corps.
Harlow, Charles H., 18 September, 1875. Graduated.
Harrison, George E., 24 June, 1875. Resigned.
Hasson, Alexander R., 24 June, 1875. Graduated. Honorably discharged 30 June, 1883.
Hayden, Edward E., 24 June, 1875. Graduated.
Haymond, Edgar B. W., 18 September, 1875. Resigned.
Hill, Charles H., 18 September, 1875. Graduated.
Hood, John, 18 September, 1875. Graduated.
Huntoon, Fitz Aubert, 18 September, 1875. Graduated.
Irving, Washington, 18 September, 1875. Dropped.
Jackson, Samuel L., 18 September, 1875. Resigned.
Johnston, Campbell M., 18 September, 1875. Resigned.
Jones, Richard, Jr., 25 June, 1875. Resigned.
Kellogg, Frank W., 24 June, 1875. Graduated.
Kimball, Edward F., 25 June, 1875. Resigned.
King, William N., 25 June, 1875. Resigned. Restored by Act of Congress. Graduated.
Leiper, Edwards F., 25 June, 1875. Graduated.
Levisee, Leonidas, 25 June, 1875. Resigned.
Luby, John F., 24 June, 1875. Graduated.
Marsh, Charles C., 18 September, 1875. Graduated.
Maury, W. O. N. P., 18 September, 1875. Resigned.
Mincer, Randolph H., 24 June, 1875. Graduated.
Moore, John McC., 24 June, 1875. Died 16 November, 1879.
Morse, William, 18 September, 1875. Resigned.
Mudd, John A., 18 September, 1875. Graduated.
Norris, Calvin C. J., 18 September, 1875. Resigned.
O'Connell, James, 13 September, 1875. Resigned.
Offley, Edward H., 25 June, 1875. Resigned.
Ord, Edward O. C., 18 September, 1875. Resigned.
Parsons, Frank B., 18 September, 1875. Dismissed.
Perkins, Con M., 18 September, 1875. Graduated. Transferred to Marine Corps.
Porter, John P., 18 September, 1875. Resigned.

GENERAL NAVY REGISTER. 651

Ripley, Charles S., 25 June, 1875. Graduated.
Robinson, Herbert J., 18 September, 1875. Graduated.
Rodman, Hugh, 18 September, 1875. Graduated.
Russell, William W., 18 September, 1875. Dropped.
Saunders, Nat., 3 July, 1875. Resigned.
Schrum, James A., 18 September, 1875. Resigned.
Scott, George A., 24 June, 1875. Resigned.
Sears, Walter J., 24 June, 1875. Graduated.
Sloan, Robert S., 24 June, 1875. Graduated.
Snowden, Thomas, 25 June, 1875. Graduated.
Starkloff, Emile A. von, 18 September, 1875. Resigned.
Thom, William A., 24 June, 1875. Graduated.
Thompson, Edward C., 18 September, 1875. Resigned.
Tillman, Edwin H., 18 September, 1875. Graduated.
Wike, Harvey, 18 September, 1875. Died 26 February, 1880.
Wilkinson, Ernest, 24 June, 1875. Graduated.
Winchester, William S., 18 September, 1875. Resigned.
Woodworth, Frederick A., 24 June, 1875. Dismissed.

1876.—MIDSHIPMEN.

Ackerman, Albert A., 24 June, 1876. Graduated.
Alger, Philip R., 22 September, 1876. Graduated.
Andrews, Horace B., 24 June 1876. Dropped.
Ashmore, Harry B., 9 October, 1876. Graduated.
Babcock, William F., 25 September, 1876. Resigned.
Bellinger, Oscar H., 24 June, 1876. Resigned.
Bernadou, John B., 22 September, 1876. Graduated.
Best, Wesley E., 22 September, 1876. Resigned.
Bishop, Lot C., 24 June, 1876. Resigned.
Blow, George P., 22 September, 1876. Graduated.
Brainard, Frederick R., 24 June, 1876. Graduated.
Brinley, Edward, 22 September, 1876. Graduated.
Bronner, Edmund D., 22 September, 1876. Resigned.
Bryan, Samuel, 24 June, 1876. Graduated. Honorably discharged 30 June, 1883.
Cabaniss, Charles, 24 June, 1876. Killed 19 January, 1882.
Clark, Lewis J., 22 September, 1876. Graduated.
Conness, David C. B., 22 September, 1876. Resigned.
Cooke, Abbot S., 22 September, 1876. Resigned.
Craig, Benjamin H., 14 June, 1876. Resigned.
Craven, Macdonough, 24 June, 1876. Graduated. Honorably discharged 30 June, 1883.
Deal, Edward T., 26 June, 1876. Resigned.
Dent, Sidney H., 22 September, 1876. Resigned.
Dickson, Joseph M., 24 June, 1876. Resigned.
Dillman, George L., 24 June, 1876. Resigned.
Doyen, Charles A., 24 June, 1876. Graduated. Transferred to Marine Corps.
Dresel, Herman G., 22 September, 1876. Graduated.
Duncan, Louis, 22 September, 1876. Graduated.
Eldredge, Houston, 9 October, 1876. Graduated.
Emerson, William H., 12 October, 1876. Graduated.
Emmet, William L., 5 July, 1876. Graduated. Honorably discharged 30 June, 1883.
Eyre, Manning K., 22 September, 1876. Graduated.
Firestone, Allison D., 24 June, 1876. Resigned.
Forshew, Robert P., 24 June, 1876. Graduated. Honorably discharged 30 June, 1883.
Foster, Edward W., 24 June, 1876. Resigned.
Garland, John S., 24 June, 1876. Resigned.
George, Charles P., 6 July, 1876. Graduated. Honorably discharged 30 June, 1883.
Gilliam, Donnell, 24 June, 1876. Resigned.
Gray, James, 22 September, 1876. Graduated.
Haessler, Francis J., 22 September, 1876. Graduated.
Hains, Robert P., 22 September, 1876. Graduated. Honorably discharged 30 June, 1883.
Haskell, Porter D., 22 September, 1876. Graduated.
Haymond, Edgar B. W., 22 September, 1876. Resigned.
Hourigan, Patrick W., 24 June, 1876. Graduated.
Honze, Arthur R., 24 June, 1876. Resigned.
Jones, Harry G., 24 June, 1876. Dropped.
Lindsey, John H., 24 June, 1876. Resigned.
Mahoney, James E., 22 September, 1876. Graduated. Transferred to Marine Corps.
Matthews, Thomas H., 22 September, 1876. Resigned.
Mayer, Augustus N., 24 June, 1876. Graduated.
McCrea, Alexander S., 9 October, 1876. Graduated. Honorably discharged 30 June, 1883.
Miner, John R., 24 June, 1876. Resigned.
Morgan, Stokely, 24 June, 1876. Graduated.
Muir, William C. P., 24 June, 1876. Graduated.
Murray, James B., 22 September, 1876. Died 11 August, 1878.
Nash, Edwin W., 22 September, 1876. Graduated.
Niblack, Albert B., 22 September, 1876. Graduated.
Norton, Luman S., 22 September, 1876. Resigned.
Orlopp, Max A., 24 June, 1876. Dropped.
Parke, Thomas A., 24 June, 1876. Graduated.

Parker, Felton, 9 November, 1876. Graduated. Honorably discharged 30 June, 1884.
Parsons, Arthur C., 24 June, 1876. Graduated. Honorably discharged 30 June, 1883.
Patterson, Samuel A. W., 26 June, 1876. Graduated. Honorably discharged 30 June, 1884.
Perry, George E., 22 September, 1876. Graduated. Honorably discharged 30 June, 1883.
Perry, John A., 22 September, 1876. Resigned.
Phelps, Harry, 22 September, 1876. Graduated.
Reamer, Mark M., 24 June, 1876. Dropped.
Richardson, Walter G., 22 September, 1876. Graduated.
Robinson, William M., 24 June, 1876. Graduated. Honorably discharged 30 June, 1883.
Rodgers, Guy G., 26 September, 1876. Graduated. Honorably discharged 30 June, 1883.
Rohrbacher,, Joseph H., 24 June, 1876. Graduated.
Russell, William W., 22 September, 1876. Dropped.
Safford, William E., 22 September, 1876. Graduated.
Scott, Richard H., 24 June, 1876. Resigned.
Simpson, Edward, 26 June, 1876. Graduated.
Sims, William S., 24 June, 1876. Graduated.
Taylor, John, 24 June, 1876. Resigned.
Thatcher, Herbert W., 22 September, 1876. Resigned.
Truxtun, William, 24 June, 1876. Graduated.
Vance, Zebulon B., 24 June, 1876. Graduated. Honorably discharged 30 June, 1883.
Van Duzer, Lewis S., 22 September, 1876. Graduated.
Wall, Francis R., 5 July, 1876. Graduated.
Wallace, John T., 24 June, 1876. Dropped.
Watters, John S., 24 June, 1876. Graduated.
West, George E., 22 September, 1876. Graduated.
Whitewell, Samuel E., 24 June, 1876. Resigned.
Whitfield, Jesse G., 22 September, 1876. Resigned.
Will, James F., 22 September, 1876. Resigned.
Williamson, Benjamin H., 22 September, 1876. Dropped.
Williamson, Samuel H., 22 September, 1876. Dropped.
Wilson, Henry B., 22 September, 1876. Graduated.
Wolfersberger, William H., 22 September, 1876. Resigned.
Wood, James E., 22 September, 1876. Resigned.
Worthington, Thomas, 24 June, 1876. Graduated.
Wright, Silas H., 22 September, 1876. Graduated. Honorably discharged 5 October, 1883.

1877.—MIDSHIPMEN.

Arnold, John T., 29 September, 1877. Resigned.
Ballentine, Henry L., 27 June, 1877. Graduated. Honorably discharged 30 June, 1883.
Barnett, George, 27 June, 1877. Graduated. Transferred to Marine Corps.
Bell, Everett N., 22 September, 1877. Dropped.
Bennett, Louis S., 22 September, 1877. Resigned.
Blake, Robert B., 22 September, 1877. Resigned.
Buck, Guy M., 22 September, 1877. Graduated. Honorably discharged 30 June, 1883.
Bunts, Frank E., 27 June, 1877. Graduated. Honorably discharged 30 June, 1883.
Capehart, Edward E., 27 June, 1877, Graduated.
Carroll, Eugene, 27 June, 1877. Graduated. Honorably discharged 30 June, 1883.
Clark, George, 27 June, 1877. Graduated. Honorably discharged 30 June, 1883.
Cohen, Harry R., 27 June, 1877. Graduated. Honorably discharged 30 June, 1883.
Colwell, James H., 27 June, 1877. Graduated. Honorably discharged 30 June, 1883.
Conway, John J., 22 September, 1877. Dropped.
Cooke, Abbots, 22 September, 1877. Resigned.
Crenshaw, James D., 22 September, 1877. Graduated. Honorably discharged 30 June, 1883.
Dashiell, Robert B., 27 June, 1877. Graduated.
Donnelly, Michael J., 27 June, 1877. Graduated. Honorably discharged 30 June, 1883.
Doyle, James G., 27 June, 1877. Graduated.
Dresser, James W., 27 June, 1877. Graduated. Honorably discharged 30 June, 1883.
Dudley, Charles J., 22 September, 1877. Died 8 November, 1880.
Fletcher, William B., 22 September, 1877. Graduated.
Flournoy, William F., 27 June, 1877. Graduated. Honorably discharged 30 June, 1883.
Ford, William G., 22 September, 1877. Graduated. Honorably discharged 30 June, 1883.
Forrest, Rutherford W., 22 September, 1877. Resigned.
Grambs, William J., 22 September, 1877. Graduated. Honorably discharged 30 June, 1884.
Gurley, Revere R., 22 September, 1877. Dropped.
Harmon, Eugene M., 27 June, 1877. Graduated. Honorably discharged 30 June, 1883.
Harrison, Edward H., 27 June, 1877. Graduated. Honorably discharged 30 June, 1883.
Hayden, Thomas W., 22 September, 1877. Dropped.
Hoke, William P., 22 September, 1877. Dropped.
Hoogewerff, John A., 27 June, 1877. Graduated.
Howard, William L., 22 September, 1877. Graduated.
Hubbard, Nathaniel M., 22 September, 1877. Resigned.

GENERAL NAVY REGISTER.

Hunicke, Felix H., 22 September, 1877. Resigned.
Jackson, Malcom, 22 September, 1877. Resigned.
Jones, Alexander J., 22 September, 1877. Resigned.
Karmany, Lincoln, 22 September, 1877. Graduated. Transferred to Marine Corps.
Kase, Spencer M., 22 September, 1877. Graduated. Honorably discharged 30 June, 1883.
Kennett, Percy, 22 September, 1877. Resigned.
Kent, George, 27 June, 1877. Graduated. Honorably discharged 30 June, 1884.
Key, Albert L., 27 June, 1877. Graduated.
Kimball, John A., 22 September, 1877. Graduated. Honorably discharged 30 June 1883.
Lamkin, John A., 27 June, 1877. Dropped.
Lauchheimer, Charles H., 22 September, 1877. Graduated. Transferred to Marine Corps.
Linnard, Joseph H., 27 June, 1877. Graduated.
McGiffin, Philo N., 22 September, 1877. Graduated. Honorably discharged 30 June, 1884.
McJunkin, Ira, 27 June, 1877. Graduated. Honorably discharged 30 June, 1883.
McKee, Llewelyn T., 27 June, 1877. Graduated. Honorably discharged 30 June, 1883.
McNutt, Finley A., 22 September, 1877. Graduated.
McWhorter, Jacob G., 22 September, 1877. Graduated. Transferred to Marine Corps.
Morgan, Daniel, 22 September, 1877. Graduated. Honorably discharged 30 June, 1883.
Morris, Walter E., 27 June, 1877. Resigned.
Moses, Franklin J., 22 September, 1877. Graduated. Transferred to Marine Corps.
Norton, Oliver D., 22 September, 1877. Resigned.
Oliphant, Alexander C., 22 September, 1877. Graduated. Honorably discharged 30 June, 1883.
Paine, Walter T., 22 September, 1877. Graduated. Honorably discharged 30 September, 1884.
Plythian, Charles T., 27 June, 1877. Resigned.
Pierce, Byron G., 7 June, 1877. Died 28 November, 1880.
Pleasants, Charles, 22 September, 1877. Resigned.
Poyer, John M., 27 June, 1877. Graduated.
Printup, David L., 27 June, 1877. Graduated. Honorably discharged 30 June, 1883.
Rees, John L., 27 June, 1877. Resigned.
Rider, Frederick C., 22 September, 1877. Graduated 30 June, 1883.
Schock, John L., 27 June, 1877. Graduated.
Semple, Lorenzo, 22 September, 1877. Graduated.
Slack, William Y., 27 June, 1877. Resigned.
Smies, Frederick W., 27 June, 1877. Graduated. Honorably discharged.
Smyth, James W., 27 June, 1877. Resigned.
Stahle, Frederick H., 22 September, 1877. Graduated. Honorably discharged 30 June, 1884.
Stayton, William H., 27 June, 1877. Graduated. Transferred to Marine Corps.
Stewart, Charles W., 27 June, 1877. Graduated. Honorably discharged 30 June, 1883.
Sutton, Francis E., 27 June, 1877. Graduated. Transferred to Marine Corps.
Weeks, John W., 27 June, 1877. Graduated. Honorably discharged 30 June, 1883.
Weller, Ovington E., 22 September, 1877. Graduated. Honorably discharged 30 June, 1883.
White, Harry K., 22 September, 1877. Graduated. Transferred to Marine Corps.
Whittlesey, William B., 22 September, 1877. Resigned.
Wickes, Joseph L., 22 September, 1877. Resigned.
Wilkes, Gilbert, 22 September, 1877. Graduated.
Woodward, Joseph J., 27 June, 1877. Graduated.

1878.—MIDSHIPMEN.

Anderson, Edwin A., 28 June, 1878. Graduated.
Ashby, Stephen, 28 June, 1878. Dismissed.
Barnard, John H., 30 September, 1878. Resigned.
Bedford, Samuel E., 30 September, 1878. Resigned.
Blandin, John J., 28 June, 1878. Graduated.
Carpenter, James F., 30 September, 1878. Dropped.
Dalrymple, Elton W., 28 June, 1878. Resigned.
Dovale, Arthur, 30 September, 1878. Resigned.
Duncan, William B., 7 November, 1878. Resigned.
Eames, Harold H., 28 June, 1878. Graduated.
Field, Wiley M., 28 June, 1878. Graduated.
Fowler, Hammond, 30 September, 1878. Resigned.
Gignilliat, Thomas H., 30 September, 1878. Graduated. Honorably discharged 30 June, 1885.
Gray, Willie T., 28 June, 1878. Graduated. Honorably discharged 30 June, 1885.
Gwyn, Lawrence S., 28 June, 1878. Graduated. Honorably discharged 30 June, 1884.
Hepp, Charles, 28 June, 1878. Died 11 April, 1882.
Horst, Henry A., 28 June, 1878. Resigned.
Jayne, Joseph L., 28 June, 1878. Graduated.
Johnston, Marbury, 30 September, 1878. Graduated.
Kenkel, Herman H., 28 June, 1878. Resigned.
Legare, Alexander B., 28 June, 1878. Graduated. Honorably discharged 30 June, 1885.
Lodeman, Frank F. E., 28 June, 1878. Dismissed.
Martin, Clarence, 28 June, 1878. Resigned.
Mitchell, Sidney Z., 30 September, 1878. Graduated. Honorably discharged 30 June, 1885.
Morris, John R., 30 September, 1878. Resigned.
Nixon, Lewis, 28 June, 1878. Graduated.
Philbin, Patrick H., 28 June, 1878. Graduated. Honorably discharged 30 June, 1885.

Prince, Thomas C., 28 June, 1878. Graduated. Transferred to Marine Corps.
Rankin, Harry, 28 June, 1878. Dropped.
Reynolds, Charles R., 28 June, 1878. Dropped.
Ricketts, William A., 30 September, 1878. Dropped.
Salisbury, Smith, 30 September, 1878. Dismissed.
Savage, Ledru R., 30 September, 1878. Dropped.
Schrader, George M. von. 3 October, 1878. Graduated. Honorably discharged 30 June, 1885.

Solomon, Edward E., 30 September, 1878. Resigned.
Smith, Thomas B., 28 June, 1878. Dropped.
Sutphen, Edson W., 28 June, 1878. Graduated.
Weeks, Edwin B., 30 September, 1878. Resigned.
Whittelsey, William B., 28 June, 1878. Graduated.
Wood, Spencer S., 28 June, 1878. Graduated.
Woods, Robert H., 30 September, 1878. Graduated. Honorably discharged 30 June, 1885.

1879.—MIDSHIPMEN.

Agee, Alfred P., 16 September, 1879. Graduated. Honorably discharged 30 June, 1885.
Alexander, Robert C., 29 September, 1879. Graduated. Honorably discharged 30 June, 1885.
Balthis, Harry H., 16 June, 1879. Graduated. Honorably discharged 30 June, 1885.
Bowman, William E., 26 September, 1879. Dismissed.
Brady, Cyrus T., 26 September, 1879. Resigned.
Cassiday, Edward R., 29 September, 1879. Dropped.
Chapin, Frederick L., 29 September, 1879. Graduated.
Colvin, Frank R., 26 September, 1879. Graduated. Honorably discharged 30 June, 1885.
Cooper, James J. G., 26 September, 1879. Died 16 September, 1881.
Frazier, Robert T., 26 September, 1879. Graduated. Honorably discharged 30 June, 1885.
George, Harry, 16 June, 1879. Graduated.
Greene, Samuel D., 16 June, 1879. Graduated.
Jackson, John A., 26 September, 1879. Resigned.
Jackson, John B., 26 September, 1879. Graduated.
Jastremski, Leon H., 29 September, 1879. Dismissed.
Keith, Albion S., 26 September, 1879. Graduated. Honorably discharged 30 June, 1885.
Kiefer, Edmund E., 16 June, 1879. Died 18 November, 1880.
Ledbetter, William H., 26 June, 1879. Graduated. Honorably discharged 30 June, 1885.
Lennon, Michael E., 29 September, 1879. Resigned.
Lerch, Robert L., 29 September, 1879. Graduated. Honorably discharged 30 June, 1885.
Lovensklold, A. Lee, 26 September, 1879. Dropped.

McCook, John A., 29 September, 1879. Resigned.
McCreary, Wirt, 16 June, 1879. Graduated. Honorably discharged 30 June, 1886.
McIntire, Alonzo E., 26 September, 1879. Resigned.
McKean, Josiah S., 29 September, 1879. Graduated. Honorably discharged 30 June, 1886.
Megrath, William A., 29 September, 1879. Dropped.
Mitchell, Charles R., 29 September, 1879. Resigned.
O'Leary, Timothy S., 29 September, 1879. Graduated. Honorably discharged 30 June, 1885.
Parker, Foxhall A., 26 September, 1879. Resigned.
Pefley, Harlen, 26 September, 1879. Resigned.
Pettit, Harry C., 29 September, 1879. Graduated. Honorably discharged 30 June, 1885.
Plunkett, Charles P., 3 October, 1879. Graduated.
Sparling, Frederick H., 29 December, 1879. Dropped.
Stevens, Raymond R. W. B., 22 November, 1879. Resigned.
Stout, George C., 29 September, 1879. Graduated. Honorably discharged 30 June, 1885.
Street, George W., 29 September, 1879. Graduated.
Sweeting, Charles E., 26 September, 1879. Graduated.
Temple, Edwin G., 29 September, 1879. Dropped.
Thurston, Benjamin E., 29 September, 1879. Graduated.
Toney, Tremlet V., 16 June, 1879. Died 29 December, 1884.
Wentworth, Louis M., 26 September, 1879. Resigned.
Wilson, William J., 29 September, 1879. Graduated. Honorably discharged 30 June, 1885.
Witherspoon, Thomas A., 16 June, 1879. Graduated. Honorably discharged 30 June, 1885.

1880.—MIDSHIPMEN.

Atwood, John C., 16 June, 1880. Resigned.
Barker, William A., 25 September, 1880. Resigned.
Barkley, Richard W., 16 June, 1880. Graduated. Honorably discharged 30 June, 1885.
Beecher, Albert M., 14 June, 1880. Graduated.
Blake, Henry D., 25 September, 1880. Dropped.

Bush, William W., 25 September, 1880. Graduated. Honorably discharged 30 June, 1886.
Carter, Vaulx, 25 September, 1880. Resigned.
Cook, William E., 2 October, 1880. Resigned.
Curtis, Frederick E., 25 September, 1880. Resigned.

GENERAL NAVY REGISTER.

Davis, James S., 16 June, 1880. Resigned.
Friedlander, Harry, 25 September, 1880. Resigned.
Gilmer, William W., 16 June, 1880. Graduated.
Gonong, William G., 14 June, 1880. Dropped.
Harrell, John R., 25 September, 1880. Resigned.
Hayes, Charles H., 25 September, 1880. Graduated. Honorably discharged 30 June, 1886.
Hazeltine, Charles W., 14 June, 1880. Graduated. Honorably discharged 30 June, 1886.
Hoggatt, Wilford B., 14 June, 1880. Graduated.
Johnston, William, 14 June, 1880. Graduated. Honorably discharged 30 June, 1886.
Jones, Hilory P., Jr., 25 September, 1880. Graduated.
Lamison, Jason G., 16 June, 1880. Dismissed.
Leary, Thomas H., 25 September, 1880. Resigned.
Lovenskiold, A. Lee, 7 October, 1880. Dropped.
Macpherson, Victor, 25 September, 1880. Graduated. Honorably discharged 30 June, 1886.
Maxey, John W., 16 June, 1880. Dismissed.
McCook, John A., 1 October, 1880. Resigned.
McCord, Henry H., 16 June, 1880. Resigned.
McDonald, John D., 9 October, 1880. Graduated.
McNulta, Hurbert, 14 June, 1880. Graduated. Honorably discharged 30 June, 1886.
Moseley, Nathaniel S., 4 June, 1880. Graduated.
O'Malley, William A., 25 September, 1880. Graduated. Honorably discharged 30 June, 1886.
Raichle, Frank G., 16 June, 1880. Resigned.
Sargent, Frederic H., 16 June, 1880. Resigned.
Seymour, Isaac R., 25 September, 1880. Graduated.
Shoemaker, William R., 14 June, 1880. Graduated.
Sloan, Albert B., 25 September, 1880. Resigned.
Smith, Sidney F., 25 September, 1880. Graduated. Honorably discharged 30 June, 1886.
Terrell, Douglass F., 25 September, 1880. Graduated.
Venable, Charles, 25 September, 1880. Dropped.
Wells, Roger, 25 September, 1880. Graduated.
Williams, Clarence S., 25 September, 1880. Graduated.
Williams, William P., 14 June, 1880. Resigned.
Wirt, William E., 25 September, 1880 Graduated. Honorably discharged 30 June, 1886.
Wood, John W., 25 September, 1880. Resigned.

1881.—MIDSHIPMEN.

Burnstine, Albert, 28 September, 1881. Graduated. Honorably discharged 30 June, 1887.
Clark, Harry D., 22 June, 1881. Resigned.
Coontz, Robert E., 28 September, 1881. Graduated.
Corpening, Charles M., 22 June, 1881. Graduated. Honorably discharged 30 June, 1887.
Crisfield, James A. P., 1 February, 1881. Resigned.
De Krafft, John C. F., 28 February, 1881. Dropped.
Dutton, Arthur H., 28 September, 1881. Graduated. Honorably discharged 30 June, 1887.
Eberle, Edward W., 28 September, 1881. Graduated.
Edgar, Webster A., 28 September, 1881. Graduated.
Ferris, Louis D., 28 September, 1881. Resigned.
Gibson, Robert E. L., 22 June, 1881. Resigned.
Howell, Robert B., 28 September, 1881. Resigned.
Jacobs, Benjamin, 22 June, 1881. Resigned.
Kittrell, James W., 28 September, 1881. Resigned.
Ledbetter, Thomas P., 28 September, 1881. Resigned.
Livingood, James J., 28 September, 1881. Resigned.
Lombard, Benjamin M., 21 September, 1881. Graduated. Honorably discharged 30 June, 1887.
Luzenberg, Charles K., 28 September, 1881. Dropped.
McGuinness, John P., 28 September, 1881. Graduated.
Nes, Davis S., 22 June, 1881. Graduated.
Pagin, James R., 28 September, 1881. Dismissed.
Pentz, George S., 21 September, 1881. Resigned.
Pitner, Samuel E., 28 September, 1881. Resigned.
Poe, Charles C., 28 September, 1881. Graduated. Honorably discharged 30 June, 1887.
Robinson, Leonidas L., 28 September, 1881. Dropped.
Russell, Robert L., 22 June, 1881. Graduated.
Scott, William S., 22 June, 1881. Resigned.
Shindel, James E., 22 June, 1881. Graduated.
Shipley, Richard T., 3 February, 1881. Resigned.
Slade, Thomas B., 22 June, 1881. Graduated. Honorably discharged 30 June, 1887.
Slocum, George R., 28 September, 1881. Graduated.
Stearns, John W., 28 September, 1881. Resigned.
Tarbox, Glennie, 1 October, 1881. Graduated.
Tennant, George B., 28 September, 1881. Dismissed.
Thompson, Alexander, 23 September, 1881. Resigned.
Tilden, Edward W., 22 June, 1881. Resigned.
Treadway, Henry B., 3 February, 1881. Resigned.
Van Keuren, Jerome, 22 June, 1881. Resigned.
Wright, Benjamin, 28 September, 1881. Graduated.

1882.—NAVAL CADETS.

Allen, Walter R., 17 June, 1882. Resigned.
Allison, Joseph N., 28 September, 1882. Dropped.
Andrews, Philip, 28 September, 1882. Graduated.
Beckham, Robert W., 22 June, 1882. Dropped.
Berry, John G., 17 June, 1882. Graduated. Graduated. Honorably discharged 30 June, 1888.
Bertholf, Ellsworth P., 28 September, 1882. Dismissed.
Biddle, John M., 20 June, 1882. Resigned.
Billings, Cornelius C., 28 September, 1882. Graduated. Honorably discharged 30 June, 1888.
Bird, Clare B., 28 October, 1882. Dismissed.
Breed, George, 17 June, 1882. Graduated.
Brockway, Hugh W., 3 October, 1882. Dropped.
Bullard, William H. G., 28 September, 1882. Graduated.
Caldwell, Chester L., 28 September, 1882. Resigned.
Caldwell, William H., 28 September, 1882. Graduated. Honorably discharged 30 June, 1888.
Campbell, Archibald, 28 September, 1882. Dismissed.
Cassil, Harvey H., 28 September, 1882. Resigned.
Cooper, George F., 17 June, 1882. Graduated.
Darby, Samuel E., 28 September, 1882. Resigned.
Dodd, William L., 28 September, 1882. Graduated.
Driscoll, Daniel J., 20 October, 1882. Resigned.
Faust, William H., 28 September, 1882. Graduated.
Francis, William C., 17 June, 1882. Dropped.
Gates, Edward S., 28 September, 1882. Failed to appear.
Griswold, John N., 30 September, 1882. Resigned.
Hall, Clinton L., 28 September, 1882. Resigned.
Hawk, George F., 17 June, 1882. Graduated.
Hawkes, Charles E., 17 June, 1882. Dismissed.
Heilig, Edwin A., 28 September, 1882. Dropped.
Hines, Harold K., 2 October, 1882. Graduated.
Howard, Henry L., 28 September, 1882. Resigned.
Irwin, Samuel W., 17 June, 1882. Dropped.
Jenkins, Friend W., 28 September, 1882. Graduated.

Johnson, Edwin V., 17 June, 1882. Graduated. Honorably discharged 30 June, 1888.
Knettles, John P., 28 September, 1882. Resigned.
Kress, Frederis N., 3 October, 1882. Graduated. Honorably discharged 15 October, 1888.
La Tourette, William S., 21 October, 1882. Resigned.
Levis, Frank A., 17 June, 1882. Graduated. Honorably discharged 30 June, 1888.
Martin, John J., 28 September, 1882. Resigned.
McMillan, John T., 17 June, 1882. Graduated. Honorably discharged 30 June, 1888.
Moale, Edward, Jr., 17 June, 1882. Graduated.
Moeller, Franklin, 28 September, 1882. Dismissed.
Murray, William J., 17 June, 1882. Resigned.
Oman, J. Wallace, 17 June, 1882. Graduated.
O'Neall, Miles G., 28 September, 1882. Dropped.
Parker, Frederic, 28 September, 1882. Dismissed.
Proctor, Wallace N., 17 June, 1882. Resigned.
Redfield, William N., 28 September, 1882. Resigned.
Reilly, George B., 28 August, 1882. Resigned.
Rumsey, Harry E., 28 September, 1882. Graduated.
Salter, Jasper C., 28 September, 1882. Dropped.
Stone, Clarence M., 17 June, 1882. Dropped.
Strite, Samuel M., 28 September, 1882. Graduated.
Tisdale, Ryland D., 28 September, 1882. Graduated.
Trapnell, Benjamin, 28 September, 1882. Dismissed.
Tuggle, James R., 28 September, 1882. Dismissed.
Webster, Frank D., 28 September, 1882. Resigned.
Winram, Samuel B. Jr., 17 June, 1882. Graduated. Honorably discharged 30 June, 1888.
Witherspoon, Edward T., 28 September, 1882. Graduated.
Wood, Harvey D., 17 June, 1882. Resigned.
Young, David M., 30 September, 1882. Graduated. Honorably discharGged 30 June, 1888.

1883.—NAVAL CADETS.

Alexander, John N., 19 May, 1883. Resigned.
Allen, Henry A., 4 September, 1883. Graduated. Honorably discharged 30 June, 1889.
Allen, Walter R., 6 September, 1883. Dropped.
Backman, Morris P., 4 September, 1883. Resigned.
Ballinger, James G., 6 September, 1883. Graduated. Honorably discharged 30 June, 1889.

Bertolette, Levi C., 4 September, 1883. Graduated.
Beswick, Delworth W., 27 September, 1883. Resigned.
Blackwood, Norman J., 17 May, 1883. Resigned.
Blue, Victor, 6 September, 1883. Graduated.
Bonham, William B., 1 June, 1883. Resigned.
Boughter, Francis, 17 May, 1883. Graduated.

GENERAL NAVY REGISTER. 657

Bower, James M., 15 September, 1883. Resigned.
Bristol, Mark L., 19 May, 1883. Graduated.
Brown, Ford H., 17 May, 1883. Graduated.
Brucks, Henry E., 3 September, 1883. Resigned.
Bruns, William F., 3 October, 1883. Resigned.
Bryan, Henry F., 2 May, 1883. Graduated.
Burke, Walter S., 17 May, 1883. Graduated.
Burrage, Guy H., 6 September, 1883. Graduated.
Callaghan, William C., 17 May, 1883. Resigned.
Campbell, Archie P., 6 September, 1883. Resigned.
Canaday, Walter, 10 September, 1883. Resigned.
Carden, Godfrey L., 17 May, 1883. Resigned.
Carnahan, John S., 27 September, 1883. Resigned.
Carpenter, Henry W., 6 September, 1883. Resigned.
Cash, Charles F., 17 May, 1883. Resigned.
Childs, Herbert L., 17 May, 1883. Resigned.
Churchill, Creighton, 4 September, 1883. Graduated.
Cloke, William S., 17 May, 1883. Graduated.
Cochran, Claude S., 4 September, 1883. Graduated. Honorably discharged 30 June, 1889.
Cohen, Ambrose R. W., 17 May, 1883. Graduated.
Cole, Eli K., 4 September, 1883. Graduated.
Coleman, Ross, 17 May, 1883. Graduated.
Craig, Charles C., 17 May, 1883. Resigned.
Craig, Colin S., 17 May, 1883. Graduated. Honorably discharged 30 June, 1889.
Davis, Archibald H., 17 May, 1883. Graduated.
Davis, Henry H., 26 September, 1883. Resigned.
Decker, Benton C., 17 May, 1883. Graduated.
Draper, Herbert L., 6 September, 1883. Graduated. Transferred to Marine Corps.
Durell, Edward H., 17 May, 1883. Graduated.
Edmonds, Samuel P., 19 May, 1883. Graduated. Honorably discharged 30 June, 1889.
Edmundson, Erle, 4 September, 1883. Resigned.
Ethell, John E., 6 September, 1883. Resigned.
Eyre, George W., 4 September, 1883. Resigned.
Eyre, William P., 17 May, 1883. Dismissed.
Fitzgerald, George W., 19 May, 1883. Resigned.
Frick, Oliver O., 6 September, 1883. Resigned.
Galloway, George W., 19 May, 1883. Resigned.
Gillespie, William T., 26 September, 1883. Resigned.
Gueydan, Henry L., 4 September, 1883. Dismissed.
Guthrie, Joseph A., 28 May, 1883. Resigned.
Hibbs, Frank W., 4 September, 1883. Graduated.
Hill, Alfred N., 4 September, 1883. Resigned.
Hill, Charles S., 6 September, 1883. Resigned.
Hollis, William S., 6 September, 1883. Resigned.

Hudson, Charles E., 4 September, 1883. Graduated. Honorably discharged 30 June, 1889.
Hull, Robert C., 25 September, 1883. Resigned.
Hurlbut, Samuel R., 4 September, 1883. Graduated.
Jackson, Richard H., 4 June, 1883. Graduated. Honorably discharged 30 June, 1889.
Jacobs, James I., 19 May, 1883. Resigned.
Jewett, Thomas S., 17 May, 1883. Resigned.
Johnston, Charles E., 17 May, 1883. Graduated. Honorably discharged 30 June, 1889.
Kalbach, Lewis A., 26 September, 1883. Resigned.
Kelly, Frank, 21 May, 1883. Resigned.
Kochersperger, William D., 19 May, 1883. Resigned.
Koester, Oscar W., 26 September, 1883. Resigned.
Logan, George W., 3 September, 1883. Graduated.
Long, Andrew T., 17 May, 1883. Graduated.
Luzenberg, Charles K., 11 July, 1883. Resigned.
Lynott, George E., 6 September, 1883. Resigned.
Marriott, John J. C., 26 September, 1883. Resigned.
Martin, John J., 4 September, 1883. Graduated.
McCully, Newton A., 19 May, 1883. Graduated.
McGee, Harry W., 19 May, 1883. Dropped.
McMillan, William G., 4 September, 1883. Graduated. Honorably discharged 30 June, 1889.
Moore, Frederick G., 17 May, 1883. Resigned.
Morgan, Edward P., 4 September, 1883. Resigned.
Moseley, William B., 6 September, 1883. Graduated. Honorably discharged 30 June, 1889.
Mowbray, Louis, 21 September, 1883. Resigned.
Muller, Valentine H., 4 September, 1883. Resigned.
O'Halloran, Thomas M., 17 May, 1883. Graduated. Honorably discharged 30 June, 1889.
O'Neall, Miles G., 28 September, 1883. Resigned.
Peacock, William T., 6 September, 1883. Resigned.
Peckham, Henry L., 17 May, 1883. Graduated. Honorably discharged 30 June, 1889.
Phillips, Clarence T., 6 September, 1883. Resigned.
Pigott, Michael R., 20 September, 1883. Graduated. Honorably discharged 30 June, 1889.
Porter, Alpheus L., 6 September, 1883. Resigned.
Potter, Franklin, 17 May, 1883. Resigned.
Ricketts, Joseph V., 6 September, 1883. Resigned.
Rodgers, Henry C., 19 May, 1883. Resigned.
Russell, Frank M., 19 May, 1883. Graduated.
Scales, Archibald H., 19 May, 1883. Graduated.
Seymour, William H., 17 September, 1883. Resigned.
Sims, James W., 4 September, 1883. Resigned.
Snow, Elliot, 4 September, 1883. Graduated.
Stearns, Ben W., 17 May, 1883. Graduated. Honorably discharged 30 June, 1889.

42

Steber, Benjamin, 17 May, 1883. Dismissed.
Stocker, Robert, 4 September, 1883. Graduated.
Stone, Clarence M., 25 September, 1883. Graduated.
Straub, August A., 6 September, 1883. Resigned.
Swamstrom, Frederick E., 6 September, 1883. Graduated. Honorably discharged 30 June, 1889.
Taliaferro, Edwin M., 6 September, 1883. Resigned.
Tolin, William E., 6 September, 1883. Dropped.
Ubsdell, John A., 6 September, 1883. Resigned.
Van Antwerp, William C., 19 May, 1883. Resigned.
Van De Wyngaard, James, 27 September, 1883. Resigned.
Washington, Thomas, 17 May, 1883. Graduated.
Waters, Glen, 17 May, 1883. Dismissed.
Wells, Benjamin W., 17 May, 1883. Graduated.
Welsh, Joseph J., 19 May, 1883. Resigned.
Wethered, John L., 3 September, 1883. Resigned.
Wiley, Henry A., 17 May, 1883. Graduated.
Williams, William H., 17 May, 1883. Resigned.
Wilmer, William R., 17 May, 1883. Resigned.
Young, Louis L., 6 September, 1883. Resigned.

1884.—NAVAL CADETS.

Aiken, Samuel J., 4 September, 1884. Resigned.
Alexander, James N., 6 September, 1884. Resigned.
Anderson, Louis J., 27 May, 1884. Resigned.
Bailey, Ralph, 5 September, 1884. Dismissed.
Bassett, Frederick B., 19 May, 1884. Graduated.
Baya, William P., 20 May, 1884. Resigned.
Beach, Edward L., 20 May, 1884. Graduated.
Beckwith, Henry, 4 September, 1884. Resigned.
Behse, Herman H., 21 May, 1884. Resigned.
Benham, Henry K., 19 May, 1884. Graduated.
Beswick, Delworth W., 20 May, 1884. Graduated.
Bischof, George C. W., 5 September, 1884. Resigned.
Brand, Charles A., 20 May, 1884. Resigned.
Brittain, Carlo B., 19 May, 1884. Graduated.
Campbell, Archie P., 20 May, 1884. Resigned.
Carden, Godfrey L., 19 May, 1884. Resigned.
Carpenter, Henry W., 24 April, 1884. Resigned.
Chandler, Lloyd H., 4 September, 1884. Graduated.
Clement, Edward E., 29 September, 1884. Resigned.
Close, Hiram B., 22 May, 1884. Resigned.
Coe, Robert, 5 September, 1884. Resigned.
Cramer, Stuart W., 4 September, 1884. Resigned.
Crose, William M., 19 May, 1884. Graduated.
Fairfax, Franklin E., 6 September, 1884. Resigned.
Fitch, Frederic, 4 September, 1884. Resigned.
Fitzgerald, George W., 4 September, 1884. Resigned.
Franklin, William B., 20 May, 1884. Graduated.
Frick, Oliver O., 20 May, 1884. Resigned.
Gates, Herbert G., 4 September, 1884. Graduated.
Gillespie, William T., 5 September, 1884. Dismissed.
Gould, William H., 4 September, 1884. Resigned.
Hagood, Robert W., 6 September, 1884. Resigned.
Harris, Jeptha V., 20 May, 1884. Resigned.
Hartrath, Armin, 4 September, 1884. Graduated.
Hayward, George N., 19 May, 1884. Graduated.
Hicks, Nathan W., 19 May, 1884. Resigned.
Hill, Alfred N., 20 May, 1884. Resigned.
Howze, James A., 6 September, 1884. Resigned.
Hubbard, John F., 5 September, 1884. Graduated.
Hughes, Charles F., 6 September, 1884. Graduated.
Hull, Robert C., 20 May, 1884. Dropped.
Ingate, Clarence L. A., 20 May, 1884. Graduated. Transferred to Marine Corps.
Jones, Roger C., 5 September, 1884. Resigned.
Kane, Theodore P., 19 May, 1884. Graduated. Transferred to Marine Corps.
Kemp, Henry G., 2 June, 1884. Resigned.
Kieruiff, Thomas C., 18 September, 1884. Resigned.
Kinnear, Claude H., 26 September, 1884. Resigned.
Knoernschild, Jacob L., 20 May, 1884. Dismissed.
Kochersperger, William D., 20 May, 1884. Resigned.
Koester, Oscar W., 5 April, 1884. Graduated.
Lafferty, John L., 6 September, 1884. Resigned.
Lange, Herman D., 5 September, 1884. Resigned.
Lejeune, John A., 19 May, 1884. Graduated. Transferred to Marine Corps.
Loyall, George, 24 September, 1884. Resigned.
Marble, Frank, 4 September, 1884. Graduated.
Melson, Edmund P., 20 May, 1884. Resigned.
Miller, Marcus L., 4 September, 1884. Graduated.
Monroe, Moses D., 19 May, 1884. Resigned.
Morgan, Casey B., 4 September, 1884. Graduated.
Morris, Joseph R., 19 May, 1884. Resigned.
Moses, Lawrence H., 8 September, 1884. Resigned.
Mowbray, Louis, 21 May, 1884. Resigned.
Murdough, Frank O., 20 May, 1884. Dismissed.
Murphy, Ignatius I., 8 September, 1884. Resigned.
Norton, Albert L., 23 May, 1884. Graduated.
Quinby, Edwin R., 22 May, 1884. Resigned.
Reid, James H., 4 September, 1884. Graduated.
Riley, James F., 24 April, 1884. Dismissed.

GENERAL NAVY REGISTER.   659

Robertson, Ashley H., 4 September, 1884. Graduated.
Robison, Samuel S., 4 September, 1884. Graduated.
Rowan, Willie McD., 19 May, 1884. Resigned.
Selfridge, George S., 5 September, 1884. Resigned.
Scott, James H., 1 October, 1884. Resigned.
Shaffer, Paul C., 20 May, 1884. Resigned.
Smith, Ernest F., 5 September, 1884. Resigned.
Smith, Richard M., 4 April, 1884. Resigned.
Smoak, Marcus F., 19 May, 1884. Died 11 February, 1885.
Stafford, Leroy A., 15 September, 1884. Graduated. Transferred to Marine Corps.
Stickney, Herman O., 4 September, 1884. Graduated.
Taylor, Henry, 27 May, 1884. Resigned.
Tutein, Constantine D., 6 September, 1884. Resigned.
Van Allen, John McE., 12 June, 1884. Resigned.
Van Antwerp, William C., 19 May, 1884. Resigned.
Vansant, William N., 4 September, 1884. Resigned.
Wedderburn, John, 5 September, 1884. Resigned.
West, Ernest E., 23 May, 1884. Resigned.
Wilbur, Curtis D., 19 May, 1884. Resigned.
Williams, Chester B., 23 May, 1884. Resigned.
Williams, George W., 6 September, 1884. Resigned.

1885.—NAVAL CADETS.

Alford, Harvey C., 20 May, 1885. Resigned.
Anderson, Ernest B., 22 May, 1885. Resigned.
Bradshaw, George B., 4 September, 1885. Graduated.
Brand, Charles A., 8 September, 1885. Graduated.
Bunker, Charles M., 5 September, 1885. Resigned.
Caffery, Donelson, 22 May, 1885. Resigned.
Carney, Robert E., 21 May, 1885. Graduated.
Chace, Morgan, 21 May, 1885. Resigned.
Clinton, James W., 21 May, 1885. Resigned.
Cohen, John S., 4 September, 1885. Resigned.
Cole, William C., 5 September, 1885. Graduated.
Danforth, George W., 7 September, 1885. Graduated.
Driggs, Louis L., 28 September, 1885. Resigned.
Dutton, Robert McM., 4 September, 1885. Graduated. Transferred to Marine Corps.
Emerson, Selden, 22 May, 1885. Resigned.
Everhart, Lay H., 29 September, 1885. Graduated.
Fermier, George L., 21 May, 1885. Graduated.
Fife, George B., 5 September, 1885. Resigned.
Frick, Oliver O. D., 8 September, 1885. Resigned.
Fuller, Benjamin H., 22 May, 1885. Graduated. Transferred to Marine Corps.
Gaines, Edward, 21 May, 1885. Resigned.
Gray, George R., 5 September, 1885. Dismissed.
Guest, Middleton S., 21 May, 1885. Resigned.
Harrison, William K., 23 May, 1885. Graduated.
Hobson, Richmond P., 21 May, 1885. Graduated.
Hoff, Arthur B., 28 September, 1885. Graduated.
Horne, Adrian L., 5 September, 1885. Resigned.
Horst, Elias Vander, 5 September, 1885. Resigned.
Howry, Lucien B., 7 September, 1885. Resigned.
Hutchison, Benjamin F., 5 September, 1885. Graduated.
Hyland, John A., 7 September, 1885. Resigned.
Johns, Vandyke, 25 September, 1885. Resigned.
Johnson, Sidney S., 7 September, 1885. Resigned.
Kaiser, Louis A., 20 May, 1885. Graduated.
Kemp, Henry G., 27 May, 1885. Resigned.
Kennedy, Robert M., 21 May, 1885. Resigned.
Kenney, Richard E., 28 September, 1885. Resigned.
King, Stephen G. O., 28 September, 1885. Resigned.
Kirk, George W., 7 September, 1885. Drowned 17 November, 1889.
Kittelle, Sumner E., 19 May, 1885. Graduated.
Krumbhaar, Alfred P., 5 September, 1885. Resigned.
Lewis, Frederick N., 22 May, 1885. Resigned.
Long, Charles G., 7 September, 1885. Graduated.
Lowndes, Edward R., 29 September, 1885. Graduated. Transferred to Marine Corps.
Lucas, Lewis C., 9 September, 1885. Graduated. Transferred to Marine Corps.
MacDougall, William D., 19 May, 1885. Graduated.
Magruder, Thomas P., 3 September, 1885. Graduated.
Marvell, George R., 7 September, 1885. Graduated.
McLemore, Albert S., 7 September, 1885. Resigned.
Mendell, George H., 5 September, 1885. Resigned.
Mitchell, George G., 7 September, 1885. Graduated.
Montgomery, Walace B., 5 September, 1885. Resigned.
Neumann, Bertram S., 22 May, 1885. Graduated. Transferred to Marine Corps.
Nulton, Louis McC., 8 September, 1885. Graduated.
Offley, Cleland N., 5 September, 1885. Graduated.
Patton, John B., 21 May, 1886. Graduated.
Paul, George H., 7 September, 1885. Resigned.
Pegram, George B., 29 September, 1885. Resigned.
Phelps, William W., 19 May, 1885. Graduated.
Potter, Charles W., 22 May, 1885. Dismissed.
Pratt, William V., 9 September, 1885. Graduated.
Preston, Charles F., 4 September, 1885. Resigned.
Prochazka, Julius, 7 September, 1885. Graduated. Transferred to Marine Corps.
Raymond, William W., 7 September, 1885. Resigned.
Rightor, Henry J., 4 September, 1885. Resigned.

GENERAL NAVY REGISTER.

Rock, George H., 20 May, 1885. Graduated.
Schaeffer, Adolph, 7 September, 1885. Resigned.
Schley, Oskaloosa S., 17 September, 1885. Killed 3 August, 1886.
Seeley, John B., 3 September, 1885. Resigned.
Sexton, Horatio C., 19 May, 1885. Resigned.
Seymour, William H., 27 May, 1885. Resigned.
Shannon, Robert H., 12 September, 1885. Resigned.
Staples, George K., 30 September, 1885. Resigned.
de Steiguer, Louis R., 17 March, 1885. Graduated.
Stockton, Richard, 19 May, 1885. Dismissed.
Stokes, Marcus B., 7 September, 1885. Resigned.
Terhune, Warren J., 19 May, 1885. Graduated.
Thompson, Alfred S., 5 September, 1885. Resigned.
Thomas, Cully F., 21 May, 1885. Resigned.
Twining, Nathan C., 4 September, 1885. Graduated.
Wall, Garrett B., 1 October, 1885. Resigned.
Webb, Thomas S., 2 October, 1885. Dropped.
Williams, Philip, 4 September, 1885. Graduated.
Woodward, Henry L., 19 May, 1885. Dismissed.
Woods, Howard T., 19 May, 1885. Resigned.
Woodworth, James A., 22 May, 1885. Dismissed.

1886.—NAVAL CADETS.

Ament, George H., 24 May, 1886. Resigned.
Bailey, Claude, 8 September, 1886. Graduated.
Ballschmider, Frederick W., 4 September, 1886. Resigned.
Beale, Robert W., 24 May, 1886. Resigned.
Beck, William W., 6 September, 1886. Resigned.
Berkeley, Edmund I., 19 May, 1886. Resigned.
Blankenship, John M., 20 May, 1886. Graduated. Honorably discharged 30 June, 1892.
Bond, Charles O., 8 September, 1886. Resigned.
Bostwick, Lucius A., 7 September, 1886. Graduated.
Buck, William H., 22 May, 1886. Graduated.
Butler, Charles V., 7 September, 1886. Dismissed.
Catlin, Albertus W., 24 May, 1886. Graduated. Transferred to Marine Corps.
Chandler, Porter, 7 September, 1886. Resigned.
Chappell, Roten N., 7 September, 1886. Resigned.
Chase, John V., 28 September, 1886. Graduated.
Clinton, James W., 20 May, 1886. Dismissed.
Coleman, Noah T., 21 May, 1886. Graduated.
Coulson, Benjamin LeF., 6 September, 1886. Resigned.
Davis, Cleland, 22 May, 1886. Graduated.
Dayton, John H., 13 September, 1886. Graduated.
Demarest, Melville, 24 May, 1886. Resigned.
Dinges, John W., 7 September, 1886. Died 19 September, 1888.
Dismukes, Dr. E., 21 May, 1886. Graduated.
Eaton, Frederick L., 6 September, 1886. Resigned.
Edie, John R., 19 May, 1886. Graduated.
Erd, Charles J. E., 24 May, 1886. Resigned.
Everhart, Lay H., 20 May, 1886. Graduated.
Fife, George B., 4 September, 1886. Dismissed.
Gartley, Alonzo, 22 May, 1886. Graduated. Honorably discharged 30 June, 1892.
Gibbs, George F., 19 May, 1886. Resigned.
Gowey, Frank McD., 19 May, 1886. Resigned.
Green, Henry T., 7 September, 1886. Resigned.
Harness, Conrad, 24 May, 1886. Resigned.
Holland, Frank, 22 May, 1886. Resigned.
Holmes, Urban T., 13 September, 1886. Graduated.
Horne, Adrian L., 22 May, 1886. Resigned.
Horne, Augustus F., 22 May, 1886. Resigned.
Jenkins, Thomas L., 19 May, 1886. Resigned.
Kochersperger, Frank H., 20 May, 1886. Graduated. Honorably discharged 30 June, 1891.
Kremer, Daniel H., 7 September, 1886. Resigned.
Lancaster, William L., 22 May, 1886. Resigned.
Lang, Edward E., 20 May, 1886. Dismissed.
Latimer, Julian L., 20 September, 1886. Graduated.
Leonard, Will W., 30 September, 1886. Resigned.
Litchfield, Walter D., 22 May, 1886. Resigned.
Mason, Thomas J., 13 September, 1886. Resigned.
McDonald, Edwin H., 7 September, 1886. Resigned.
McVay, Charles B., 19 May, 1886. Graduated.
Moffett, William A., 6 September, 1886. Graduated.
Moses, Lawrence H., 29 September, 1886. Graduated.
Mullen, John D. S., 25 May, 1886. Resigned.
Neville, Wendell C., 13 September, 1886. Graduated. Transferred to Marine Corps.
Norton, Walter S., 7 September, 1886. Resigned.
Okell, Frank T., 20 May, 1886. Resigned.
Paul, George H., 20 May, 1886. Resigned.
Perry, William Y., 22 May, 1886. Resigned.
Price, Claude B., 2 June, 1886. Graduated.
Radford, Cyrus S., 25 May, 1886. Graduated. Transferred to Marine Corps.
Rano, Henry W., 20 May, 1886. Resigned.
Regan, Charles F., 21 May, 1886. Resigned.
Reynolds, Ziba W., 21 May, 1886. Resigned.
Rising, Franklin S., 20 May, 1886. Resigned.
Ritter, Henry S., 25 May, 1886. Graduated.
Ruhm, Thomas F., 20 May, 1886. Graduated.

GENERAL NAVY REGISTER. 661

Ryan, Eugene D., 4 September, 1886. Resigned.
Ryan, John P. J., 6 September, 1886. Resigned.
Saunders, William T., 21 May, 1886. Resigned.
Schofield, Frank H., 21 May, 1886. Graduated.
Sheehan, John, Jr., 13 September, 1886. Resigned.
Shellabarger, Frederick, 22 May, 1886. Resigned.
Signor, Matt H., 21 May, 1886. Graduated.
Smith, Glenn S., 6 September, 1886. Resigned.
Snow, William A., 4 September, 1886. Graduated.
Soule, John L., 4 September, 1886. Resigned.
Spear, Lawrence, 19 May, 1886. Graduated.
Sullivan, Franklin B., 22 May, 1886. Graduated.
Taylor, Montgomery M., 21 May, 1886. Graduated.
Thompson, Alfred S., 20 May, 1886. Resigned.
Treadwell, Thomas C., 21 May, 1886. Graduated. Transferred to Marine Corps.
Vogelgesang, Charles T., 6 September, 1886. Graduated.
Ward, George C., 21 May, 1886. Resigned.
White, Chester B., 6 September, 1886. Resigned.
Williams, George W., 28 September, 1886. Graduated.
Williams, Henry W., 8 September, 1886. Resigned.
Willis, John G., 25 May, 1886. Resigned.
Ziegemeier, Henry J., 21 May, 1886. Graduated.

1887.—NAVAL CADETS.

Allen, Charles, 21 May, 1887. Resigned.
Allen, David Van H., 6 September, 1887. Graduated. Honorably discharged 30 June, 1894.
Althouse, Adelbert, 21 May, 1887. Graduated.
Anthon, Archibald, 9 June, 1887. Resigned.
Arison, Edgar E., 5 September, 1887. Resigned.
Beck, William W., 6 September, 1887. Resigned.
Belknap, Reginald R., 5 September, 1887. Graduated.
Bierer, Bion B., 24 September, 1887. Graduated.
Blamer, De Witt, 19 May, 1887. Graduated.
Blount, Irving, 6 September, 1887. Graduated. Honorably discharged 30 June, 1893.
Breckinridge, John C., 28 September, 1887. Resigned.
Brotherton, William D., 6 September, 1887. Graduated.
Caldwell, Harry H., 7 September, 1887. Graduated.
Camden, Bernard W., 27 August, 1887. Resigned.
Carter, James F., 24 March, 1887. Resigned.
Christy, Harley H., 24 May, 1887. Graduated.
Consaul, Charles F., 21 May, 1887. Resigned.
Cook, Allen M., 6 September, 1887. Resigned.
Cotton, Charles S., 7 September, 1887. Resigned.
Curlett, John, 8 September, 1887. Resigned.
Davis, Austin R., 7 September, 1887. Resigned.
Embrey, Wiley S., 6 September, 1887. Resigned.
Emrich, Charles R., 19 May, 1887. Graduated.
Evans, Waldo, 7 September, 1887. Graduated.
Flowers, Robert L., 7 September, 1887. Graduated. Honorably discharged 30 June, 1891.
Ford, William H., 7 September, 1887. Resigned.
Gilchrist, Clarence D., 12 September, 1887. Resigned.
Gillmor, Horatio G., 5 September, 1887. Graduated.
Goodwin, Leonard, 5 September, 1887. Resigned.
Gross, Louis H., 19 May, 1887. Dropped.
Hartung, Renwick J., 6 September, 1887. Graduated.
Hough, Henry H., 6 September, 1887. Graduated.
Irwin, Noble E., 29 September, 1887. Graduated.
Jenkins, Thomas L., 21 May, 1887. Resigned.
Jewell, Charles T., 19 May, 1887. Graduated.
Jones, Beriah E., 6 September, 1887. Resigned.
Kellogg, Thomas S., 21 May, 1887. Resigned.
Kilbourne, Joseph C., 6 September, 1887. Resigned.
Kuenzli, Henry C., 6 September, 1887. Graduated.
Lancaster, William L., 23 May, 1887. Resigned.
Lane, Rufus H., 2 June, 1887. Graduated. Transferred to Marine Corps.
Larkin, Rozier B., 7 September, 1887. Resigned.
Laws, George W., 21 May, 1887. Graduated.
Leeds, Joseph A., 19 May, 1887. Resigned.
Leigh, Richard H., 6 September, 1887. Dismissed.
Low, Robeson L., 21 May, 1887. Resigned.
Lyle, Charles W., 5 September, 1887. Dismissed.
Macfarland, Horace G., 6 September, 1887. Graduated.
Magill, Louis J., 17 June, 1887. Resigned.
Malone, John C., 6 September, 1887. Resigned.
Maurin, Timothy F., 21 May, 1887. Resigned.
McGrann, William H., 20 May, 1887. Graduated.
McKeage, Robert, 5 September, 1887. Resigned.
McKelvy, William N., 20 May, 1887. Graduated. Transferred to Marine Corps.
McLemore, Albert S., 23 May, 1887. Graduated. Transferred to Marine Corps.
McReavy, Herbert E., 7 September, 1887. Resigned.
Merrill, Clarence S., 7 September, 1887. Resigned.
Moale, John G. F., 6 September, 1887. Graduated. Honorably discharged 30 June, 1893.

Murphy, Charles K., 7 September, 1887. Resigned.
Myers, John T., 27 September, 1887. Graduated. Honorably discharged 30 June, 1894.
Ninde, Daniel B., 20 May, 1887. Graduated. Honorably discharged 30 June, 1891.
Nott, George W. Jr., 7 September, 1887. Resigned.
Owsley, Letcher, 7 September, 1887. Resigned.
Pillot, Peter S., 7 September, 1887. Resigned.
Pollock, Edwin T., 20 May, 1887. Graduated.
Preston, Charles F., 6 September, 1887. Graduated.
Reed, Milton E., 5 September, 1887. Graduated.
Reese, William J., 5 September, 1887. Resigned.
Richards, George, 12 September, 1887. Graduated. Transferred to Marine Corps.
Ridgely, Randolph, 7 September, 1887. Resigned.
Robinson, Roby, 21 May, 1887. Resigned.
Robison, John K., 20 May, 1887. Graduated.
Rowen, John H., 27 September, 1887. Graduated.
Russell, Edward G., 7 September, 1887. Resigned.
Sass, Maurice, 7 September, 1887. Resigned.
Senn, Thomas J., 19 May, 1887. Graduated.
Shepard, George H., 27 September, 1887. Graduated.
Smith, Henry E., 20 May, 1887. Graduated.
Smith, Henry G., 5 September, 1887. Resigned.
Smith, Lucien G., 3 June, 1887. Graduated. Honorably discharged 30 June, 1893.
Sparkman, Sullivan T., 24 September, 1887. Resigned.
Stearns, Clark D., 5 September, 1887. Graduated.
Sypher, Jay H., 5 September, 1887. Graduated.
Theall, Elisha, 28 May, 1887. Graduated. Transferred to Marine Corps.
Todd, Von Dyke, 21 May, 1887. Resigned.
Trickle, Edward, 20 May, 1887. Resigned.
Waller, William L., 21 May, 1887. Resigned.
Watt, Richard M., 22 September, 1887. Graduated.
Weaver, Van Wyck, 7 September, 1887. Resigned.
Wedekind, George, 7 September, 1887. Resigned.
Wells, Chester, 10 September, 1887. Resigned.
Willard, Arthur L., 7 September, 1887. Graduated.
Williams, Dion, 16 July, 1887. Graduated. Transferred to Marine Corps.
Williams, John C., 6 September, 1887. Resigned.
Zahm, Frank B., 5 September, 1887. Graduated.

1888.—NAVAL CADETS.

Allen, Charles, 15 March, 1888. Resigned.
Arison, Edgar E., 18 May, 1888. Resigned.
Baird, Lewis C., 6 September, 1888. Resigned.
Ball, Walter, 6 September, 1888. Graduated. Transferred to Marine Corps.
Bannon, Philip M., 21 May, 1888. Resigned.
Beurt, John D., 7 September, 1888. Graduated.
Bewley, Walter P., 10 September, 1888. Resigned.
Blakely, John R. Y., 29 September, 1888. Graduated.
Boltwood, Lucius, 4 April, 1888. Resigned.
Borden, Thomas S., 25 September, 1888. Graduated. Transferred to Marine Corps.
Breckinridge, Joseph C., 5 September, 1888. Resigned.
Campbell, Joseph R., 29 September, 1888. Graduated.
Chadbourne, Ralph C., 21 May, 1888. Resigned.
Childs, Albert P., 6 September, 1888. Resigned.
Churchill, Frederick A., 7 September, 1888. Resigned.
Coleman, James S., 6 September, 1888. Resigned.
Crank, Robert K., 6 September, 1888. Graduated.
Curlett, John, 15 March, 1888. Resigned.
Davis, Austin R., 21 May, 1888. Graduated.
Davison, Gregory C., 22 May, 1888. Graduated. Transferred to Marine Corps.
Dawson, William C., 6 September, 1888. Graduated. Transferred to Marine Corps.
Day, George C., 19 May, 1888. Graduated.
Dennett, Stanley P., 19 May, 1888. Resigned.
Douglas, Richard S., 19 May, 1888. Resigned.
Evans, Holden A., 5 September, 1888. Graduated.
Ferguson, Homer L., 21 May, 1888. Graduated.
Gamble, Aaron L., 5 September, 1888. Graduated. Honorably discharged 30 June, 1894.
Gibbs, Washington D., 18 May, 1888. Resigned.
Goodwin, Leonard, 18 May, 1888. Resigned.
Hasbrouck, Raymond D., 25 September, 1888. Graduated.
Hines, John F., 21 May, 1888. Graduated.
Hoblitzell, William E., 6 September, 1888. Resigned.
Hooker, James C., 18 June, 1888. Resigned.
Huffington, Howard W., 19 May, 1888. Resigned.
Hussey, Charles L., 21 May, 1888. Graduated.
Jennings, Joseph, 7 September, 1888. Resigned.
Jones, Beriah E., 19 May, 1888. Resigned.
Kaufman, Charles L., 18 May, 1888. Resigned.
Kellogg, Edward S., 18 May, 1888. Graduated. Honorably discharged 30 June 1894.
Kilbourne, Joseph C., 21 May, 1888. Resigned.
Lang, John Y., 1 June, 1888. Died 15 May, 1889.
Larkin, Rosier B., 21 May, 1888. Resigned.
Logan, William V., 6 September, 1888. Resigned.
Low, Theodore H., 18 May, 1888. Graduated. Transferred to Marine Corps.
Macklin, Charles F., 25 September, 1888. Graduated. Transferred to Marine Corps.

GENERAL NAVY REGISTER.

Mallison, George, 21 May, 1888. Graduated.
Manion, Walter J., 24 September, 1888. Resigned.
Mather, George H., 22 May, 1888. Graduated. Honorably discharged 30 June, 1894.
McCormick, Benjamin B., 19 May, 1888. Graduated.
McDonald, Joseph E., 7 September, 1888. Graduated.
McNamee, Luke, 6 September, 1888. Graduated.
McReavy, Herbert E., 18 May, 1888. Dismissed.
Moses, Stanford E., 6 September, 1888. Graduated.
Murray, William L., 21 May, 1888. Resigned.
Nevitt, Rolin R., 7 September, 1888. Resigned.
Olmsted, Percy N., 21 May, 1888. Resigned.
Payne, Frederick R., 21 May, 1888. Graduated.
Pollard, Charles T., Jr., 25 September, 1888. Resigned.
Pollock, Emmett R., 18 May, 1888. Graduated.
Porter, John S., 25 September, 1888. Graduated.
Powell, William G., 18 May, 1888. Resigned.
Pringle, Joel R. P., 6 September, 1888. Graduated.
Randolph, William B., 6 September, 1888. Resigned.
Rice, Arthur, 7 September, 1888. Resigned.
Ridgely, Randolph, 6 September, 1888. Resigned.
Rodney, Warren, 6 September, 1888. Resigned.
Russell, John H., 18 May, 1888. Graduated. Transferred to Marine Corps.
Sawyer, Frederick L., 6 September, 1888. Graduated.
Sawyer, Joshiah C. 19 May, 1888. Resigned.
Scott, Guy T., 5 September, 1888. Resigned.
Shaw, Graham, 6 September, 1888. Resigned.
Sheehan, James, 21 May, 1888. Died 20 April, 1893.
Sparks, William W., 22 May, 1888. Resigned.
Stirling, Yates, Jr., 6 September, 1888. Graduated.
Stitt, Thomas L., 5 September, 1888. Graduated. Honorably discharged 30 June, 1894.
Stopford, Frederick W., 19 May, 1888. Resigned.
Swigart, Raymond W., 5 September, 1888. Resigned.
Symington, Powers, 7 September, 1888. Graduated.
Thompson, John H., 27 September, 1888. Resigned.
Thompson, Leon S., 21 May, 1888. Graduated.
Traut, Frederick A., 19 May, 1888. Graduated.
Valentine, William S., 6 September, 1888. Resigned.
Vail, Thomas H. S., 25 May, 1888. Resigned.
Wager, George P., 6 September, 1888. Resigned.
Waldron, Hugh, 27 September, 1888. Resigned.
Wedekind, George, 5 September, 1888. Resigned.
Zillman, Christian, C. H., 27 September, 1888. Resigned.

1889.—NAVAL CADETS.

Andrews, Claude N., 5 September, 1889. Resigned.
Ashbury, Louis G., Jr., 7 September, 1889. Resigned.
Baehr, William A., 20 May, 1889. Resigned.
Bagley, Worth, 5 September, 1889. Resigned.
Baird, Lewis C., 6 September, 1889. Resigned.
Bennett, Ernest L., 24 September, 1889. Graduated.
Berry, David M., 6 September, 1889. Graduated. Honorably discharged 30 June, 1895.
Berryman, John R., 3 October, 1889. Resigned.
Bisset, Eugene L., 2 October, 1889. Graduated.
Brady, John R., 6 September, 1889. Graduated.
Campbell, Edward H., 6 September, 1889. Graduated.
Carver, Marvin, 27 September, 1889. Resigned.
Chadwick, Frank L., 18 May, 1889. Graduated.
Clark, Frank H., Jr., 5 September, 1889. Graduated.
Cobb, John A., Jr., 22 May, 1889. Resigned.
Coleman, James S., 5 September, 1889. Resigned.
Cook, Allen M., 22 May, 1889. Graduated.
Crocker, John A., 22 May, 1889. Resigned.
Crosley, Walter S., 9 September, 1889. Graduated.
Cruse, Andrew J., Jr., 18 May, 1889. Resigned.
Dailey, Harry L., 7 September, 1889. Dismissed.
Doddridge, John S., 7 September, 1889. Graduated.
Douglas, Richard S., 3 June, 1889. Graduated.
Eberle, Joseph D., 28 May, 1889. Resigned.
Elder, Edwin A., 21 May, 1889. Graduated. Honorably discharged 30 June, 1895.
Feild, Hubbard M., 20 May, 1889. Dismissed.
Fewel, Christopher C., 2 October, 1889. Graduated.
Fitch, Claude E., 7 September, 1889. Graduated. Honorably discharged 30 June, 1893.
French, Robert A., 23 May, 1889. Resigned.
Gise, William K., 14 June, 1889. Graduated.
Greer, George T., 4 October, 1889. Resigned.
Groesbeck, William G., 5 September, 1889. Resigned.
Groff, Joseph C., 3 October, 1889. Resigned.
Haines, Peter C., Jr., 18 May, 1889. Graduated. Honorably discharged 30 June, 1893.
Holsinger, Gerald L., 3 October, 1889. Graduated. Honorably discharged 30 June, 1895.

Hood, Gordon, 2 October, 1889. Resigned.
Hooker, James C., 7 September, 1889. Resigned.
Jackson, Orton P., 18 May, 1889. Graduated.
James, Leland F., 9 September, 1889. Graduated.
Jenkins, Thomas L., 31 May, 1889. Dismissed.
Johnson, John R., 4 October, 1889. Resigned.
Johnson, Moulton K., 10 June, 1889. Resigned.
Jones, Lewis B., 21 May, 1889. Resigned.
Kellogg, Thomas S., 19 October, 1889. Dropped.
Lane, Charles A., 21 May, 1889. Resigned.
Lang, Charles J., 6 September, 1889. Graduated.
Latta, Samuel G., 9 September, 1889. Resigned.
Logan, William V., 26 June, 1889. Resigned.
Magill, Louis J., 11 November, 1889. Graduated. Transferred to Marine Corps.
Manion, Walter J., 21 May, 1889. Resigned.
McKethan, Alfred A., 5 September, 1889. Graduated.
Montgomery, William S., 5 September, 1889. Graduated.
Morris, John R., 7 September, 1889. Graduated. Honorably discharged 30 June, 1895.
Neill, Charles F., 21 May, 1889. Resigned.
Nutting, Daniel C., 21 May, 1889. Graduated.
Olmstead, Percy N., 21 May, 1889. Graduated.
Parker, Thomas D., 3 October, 1889. Graduated. Honorably discharged 30 June, 1893.
Pearson, Henry A., 6 September, 1889. Graduated.
Perry, Joseph A., 6 September, 1889. Graduated. Honorably discharged 30 June, 1895.
Perkins, Frederick K., 23 May, 1889. Resigned.
Peugnet, Maurice B., 7 September, 1889. Graduated.
Potter, James B., 5 September, 1889. Graduated. Honorably discharged 30 June, 1895.
Powell, William G., 18 May, 1889. Graduated. Honorably discharged 30 June, 1893.
Powelson, Wilfried Van N., 5 September, 1889. Graduated.
Pratt, Alfred A., 7 September, 1889. Graduated.
Price, Henry B., 20 May, 1889. Graduated.
Proctor, André M., 6 September, 1889. Graduated.
Randolph, William B., 20 May, 1889. Resigned.
Read, Frank DeW., 6 September, 1889. Graduated.
Richmond, Edgar, 7 September, 1889. Resigned.
Ryan, George W., 6 September, 1889. Resigned.
Ryan, John P. J., 22 May, 1889. Graduated. Honorably discharged 30 June, 1895.
Scott, Guy T., 7 September, 1889. Resigned.
Shaw, Graham, 7 September, 1889. Resigned.
Smith, Edward P., 29 May, 1889. Resigned.
Stearns, Edward C., 21 May, 1889. Dropped
Sticht, John L., 7 September, 1889, Graduated.
Sturdevant, Richard, 6 September, 1889. Resigned.
Townsend, Arthur C., 22 May, 1889. Resigned.
Trench, Martin E., 3 October, 1889. Graduated.
Upham, Frank B., 6 September, 1889. Graduated.
Vail, Thomas H. S., 25 May, 1889. Resigned.
Valentine, William S., 20 May, 1889. Resigned.
Ward, Henry H., 7 September, 1889. Graduated.
Wells, Chester, 15 November, 1889. Graduated. Honorably discharged 30 June, 1895.
Whitman, Walter B., 20 May, 1889. Resigned.
Wilson, Thomas S., 20 May, 1889. Graduated.
Winship, Emory, 23 May, 1889. Resigned.
Wishart, William C., 20 May, 1889. Resigned.

1890.—NAVAL CADETS.

Adams, Lawrence S., 26 September, 1890. Graduated.
Andrews, Claude N., 8 September, 1890. Resigned.
Babin, Provoost, 6 September, 1890. Graduated.
Baker, Henry T., 7 October, 1890. Graduated.
Baldwin, Murray, 27 September, 1890. Resigned.
Batts, Edward L., 22 May, 1890. Resigned.
Berryman, John R., 22 May, 1890. Resigned.
Bivins, Robert F., 27 September, 1890. Resigned.
Blandy, Edwin C., 20 May, 1890. Resigned.
Bookwalter, Charles S., 27 September, 1890. Graduated.
Bulmer, Roscoe C., 26 September, 1890. Graduated.
Chappell, Ralph H., 22 May, 1890. Graduated.
Chester, Arthur T., 19 May, 1890. Graduated.
Churchill, Winston, 21 May, 1890. Resigned.
Cone, Hutch I., 5 September, 1890. Graduated.
Cooper, Ignatius T., 20 May, 1890. Graduated.
Cox, Daniel H., 9 September, 1890. Graduated.
Craven, Thomas T., 27 September, 1890. Resigned.
Crosby, Benjamin G., 26 September, 1890. Resigned.
De Jarnette, James D. C., 8 September, 1890. Resigned.
De Kay, Eckford C., 26 September, 1890. Resigned.
De Lany, Edwin H., 21 May, 1890. Graduated.
Emery, Arthur B., 22 May, 1890. Resigned.
England, Clarence, 5 September, 1890. Graduated.
Fullinwider, Simon P., 21 May, 1890. Graduated.

GENERAL NAVY REGISTER. 665

Galbraith, Gilbert S., 8 September, 1890. Graduated.
Gelm, George E., 22 May, 1890. Graduated.
Gillis, Irvin VanG., 6 September, 1890. Graduated.
Graham, Stephen V., 19 May, 1890. Graduated.
Greer, George T., 20 May, 1890. Resigned.
Griffith, Charles W., 8 September, 1890. Resigned.
Hinds, Alfred W., 6 September, 1890. Graduated.
Houk, Herman W., 8 September, 1890. Resigned.
Hudgins, John M., 8 September, 1890. Graduated.
Hull, Alexander T., 21 May, 1890. Dismissed.
Izard, Walter B., 10 September, 1890. Resigned.
Jones, Lewis B., 21 May, 1890. Graduated.
Kavanagh, Arthur G., 20 May, 1890. Graduated.
Kress, Frederick C., 6 September, 1890. Resigned.
La Bach, Paul M., 26 September, 1890. Resigned.
Lane, Charles A., 20 May, 1890. Resigned.
Luby, John McC., 8 September, 1890. Graduated.
Lyon, Frank, 20 May, 1890. Graduated.
Manion, Walter J., 6 September, 1890. Graduated.
Mann, George H., 6 September, 1890. Dropped.
McAvoy, Ballard B., 6 September, 1890. Resigned.
McCormack, Michael J., 22 May, 1890. Resigned.
McLean, Ridley, 20 May, 1890. Graduated.
McMorris, Boling K., 15 September, 1890. Graduated.
McNeely, Robert W., 8 September, 1890. Graduated.
Moody, Roscoe C., 8 September, 1890. Graduated.
Osborn, Robert H., 23 May, 1890. Graduated.

Perkins, Frederick K., 11 June, 1890. Dismissed.
Reeves, Joseph M., 8 September, 1890. Graduated.
Ridgely, Randolph, Jr., 21 May, 1890. Resigned.
Robert, William P., 20 May, 1890. Graduated.
Roberts, Thomas G., 27 May, 1890. Graduated.
Ryan, George W., 12 June, 1890. Resigned.
Sandoz, Fritz L., 19 May, 1890. Graduated.
Scott, William P., 20 May, 1890. Graduated.
Sellers, David F., 21 May, 1890. Graduated.
Shaw, Melville, J., 6 September, 1890. Graduated. Transferred to Marine Corps.
Snow, Carlton F., 19 May, 1890. Graduated.
Spear, Roscoe, 23 May, 1890. Graduated.
Stone, George L. P., 26 September, 1890. Graduated.
Stone, Raymond, 5 September, 1890. Graduated.
Talcott, Arthur J., 21 May, 1890. Resigned.
Tolfree, Herbert M., 21 May, 1890. Resigned.
Tompkins, John T., 6 September, 1890. Graduated.
Towne, Arthur E., 26 September, 1890. Resigned.
Turpin, Walter S., 22 May, 1890. Graduated.
Walker, Henry M., 8 September, 1890. Resigned.
Watson, Edward H., 26 September, 1890. Resigned.
Webster, Charles, 6 September, 1890. Graduated.
Whitted, William S., 20 May, 1890. Graduated.
Winn, Philip B., 12 September, 1890. Resigned.
Winship, Emory, 3 June, 1890. Graduated.

1891.—NAVAL CADETS.

Allison, Louis B., 9 September, 1891. Resigned.
Bagley, Worth, 7 September, 1891. Graduated.
Baldwin, Frank P., 8 September, 1891. Graduated.
Baldwin, George E., 21 May, 1891. Resigned.
Bannon, Philip M., 19 May, 1891. Graduated. Transferred to Marine Corps.
Barnes, Cassius B., 7 September, 1891. Graduated.
Bennett, Kennett M., 8 September, 1891. Graduated.
Bigelow, Harry M., 8 September, 1891. Resigned.
Billings, Frederick T., 22 May, 1891. Resigned.
Blandy, Edwin C., 19 May, 1891. Resigned.
Breckinridge, Joseph C., 8 September, 1891. Graduated.
Brumby, Frank H., 8 September, 1891. Grauated.
Butler, Henry V., Jr., 5 September, 1891. Graduated.
Carmody, Robert E., 11 September, 1891. Resigned.
Cruse, Andrew J., 22 May, 1891. Dismissed.

Cushman, William R., 5 September, 1891. Graduated.
Davidson, William C., 28 September, 1891. Graduated.
Deane, Russell A., 19 May, 1891. Resigned.
Dennett, Stanley P., 5 September, 1891. Resigned.
Dick, Thomas M., 5 September, 1891. Graduated.
Doane, Eugene P., 22 May, 1891. Resigned.
Dunn, Edward H., 5 September, 1891. Graduated.
Eckhardt, Ernest F., 5 September, 1891. Graduated.
Fairbrother, Arthur L., 21 May, 1891. Dismissed.
Fellows, Richard J., 29 September, 1891. Dismissed.
Freeman, Frederic N., 9 September, 1891. Grauated.
Garrison, Daniel M., 1 June, 1891. Graduated.
Gherardi, Walter R., 4 September, 1891. Graduated.
Gideon, Walter I., 24 September, 1891. Resigned.
Groesbeck, William G., 4 September, 1891. Graduated.

Hall, Newt H., 7 September, 1891. Graduated. Transferred to Marine Corps.
Harrison, Bruce W., 21 May, 1891. Resigned.
Henry, James B., Jr., 22 September, 1891. Resigned.
Houk, Herman W., 10 September, 1891. Resigned.
Izard, Walter B., 7 September, 1891. Resigned.
Johnston, Rufus Z., Jr., 10 September, 1891. Graduated.
Karns, Franklin D., 30 September, 1891. Graduated.
Kearney, Thomas A., 8 September, 1891. Resigned.
Kleman, John V., 10 September, 1891. Graduated.
Knepper, Orlo S., 4 September, 1891. Graduated.
Laning, Harris, 19 May, 1891. Graduated.
Liscom, Arthur C., 20 May, 1891. Resigned.
Love, James M., 20 May, 1891. Resigned.
Mackay, Francis L., 30 September, 1891. Resigned.
Mallory, Charles K., 25 September, 1891. Graduated.
Mallory, Hugh, 9 September, 1891. Resigned.
Mansfield, Newton, 7 September, 1891. Graduated.
Marshall, John F., 8 September, 1891. Graduated.
Martin, Nathaniel M., 19 May, 1891. Resigned.
McCormack, Michael J., 8 September, 1891. Graduated.
Merritt, Darwin, R., 10 September, 1891. Graduated.
Mitchell, Mason E., 9 September, 1891. Resigned.
Monaghan, John R., 7 September, 1891. Graduated.
Morgan, Alfred, 8 September, 1891. Resigned.
Morton, James P., 9 September, 1891. Graduated.

Noyes, Lauren A., 10 September, 1891. Resigned.
Olsen, Mack H., 10 September, 1891. Resigned.
Pratt, Peter L., 19 May, 1891. Resigned.
Raby, James J., 9 September, 1891. Graduated.
Rucker, William J., 12 September, 1891. Resigned.
Sayers, Joseph D., 5 September, 1891. Graduated. Honorably discharged 30 June, 1895.
Shea, Patrick F., 21 May, 1891. Resigned.
Sheffield, Fletcher L., 7 September, 1891. Resigned.
Shirley, Rufus, 9 September, 1891. Resigned.
Smith, Stuart F., 4 September, 1891. Graduated.
Standley, William H., 7 September, 1891. Graduated.
Terrell, Willie A., 24 September, 1891. Resigned.
Todd, David W., 8 September, 1891. Graduated.
Vestal, Samuel C., 19 May, 1891. Graduated. Honorably discharged 30 June, 1895.
Volkmar, Walter S., 4 September, 1891. Resigned.
Vollmer, Frederick, 10 September, 1891. Resigned.
Wadhams, Albion J., 4 September, 1891. Graduated.
Walker, Charles H., 8 September, 1891. Died 7 February, 1897.
Walker, James E., 7 September, 1891. Graduated.
Washington, Pope, 29 May, 1891. Resigned.
Watson, Edward H., 7 September, 1891. Graduated.
White, Henry H., 21 May, 1891. Resigned.
Williams, Henry C., 9 September, 1891. Resigned.
Winfield, John B., 8 September, 1891. Resigned.
Woods, Edward, 8 September, 1891. Resigned.

1892.—NAVAL CADETS.

Anding, Sheldon W., 6 October, 1892. Resigned.
Bisset, Henry O., 6 September, 1892. Graduated.
Briggs, James, 6 September, 1892. Resigned.
Bronson, Amon, Jr., 30 September, 1892. Graduated.
Brown, Morris H., 6 September, 1892. Resigned.
Burt, Charles P., 6 September, 1892. Graduated.
Bryant, John J., Jr., 20 May, 1892. Resigned.
Castleman, Kenneth G., 6 September, 1892. Graduated.
Cluverius, Wat T., 20 May, 1892. Graduated.
Cooke, Robert P. P., 6 September, 1892. Resigned.
Craven, Thomas T., 19 September, 1892. Graduated.
Crenshaw, Arthur, 6 September, 1892. Graduated.
Curtin, Roland I., 6 September, 1892. Graduated.
Deane, Russell A., 20 May, 1892. Resigned.
Doak, Henry M., Jr., 19 September, 1892. Resigned.

Earle, Ralph, 6 September, 1892. Graduated.
Ellis, Mark St. C., 1 July, 1892. Graduated.
Emory, Dennis McC., 30 September, 1892. Resigned.
Evans, Franck T., 19 September, 1892. Resigned.
Fitzgerald, Edward T., 13 September, 1892. Graduated.
Gilpin, Charles E., 6 September, 1892. Graduated.
Green, Grant, 6 September, 1892. Resigned.
Hamilton, James E., 6 September, 1892. Resigned.
Hauenstein, George J., 6 September, 1892. Resigned.
Henry, James B., Jr., 6 September, 1892. Graduated.
Hill, Frank W., 21 September, 1892. Resigned.
Holden, Jonas H., 20 May, 1892. Graduated.
Jessop, Earl P., 6 September, 1892. Graduated.
Jones, Carlos S., 9 September, 1892. Resigned.
Jones, Junius H., 19 September, 1892. Resigned.
Kalbach, Andrew E., 1 July, 1892. Graduated.

Kearney, Thomas A., 6 September, 1892. Graduated.
Kimball, Henry S., 6 September, 1892. Graduated.
Knox, Dudley W., 6 September, 1892. Graduated.
Leiper, Charles L., 6 September, 1892. Graduated.
Lincoln, Gatewood S., 20 May, 1892. Graduated.
Littlefield, William L., 30 September, 1892. Graduated.
MacArthur Arthur, 6 September, 1892. Graduated.
Marshall, Albert W., 6 September, 1892. Graduated.
McCauley, Edward, Jr., 8 October, 1892. Graduated.
McConnell, Richard G., 20 May, 1892. Resigned.
McMullen, Stanley H., 20 May, 1892. Resigned.
Middleton, George I., 9 September, 1892. Resigned.
Mitchell, Mason E., 6 September, 1892. Resigned.
Mustin, Henry C., 6 September, 1892. Graduated.
Norwood, Harold B., 6 September, 1892. Resigned.
Oglesby, Richard J., Jr., 6 September, 1892. Resigned.
Olin, Henry W., 6 September, 1892. Resigned.
Olsen, Mack H., 20 May, 1892. Dropped.
Palmer, Leigh C., 6 September, 1892. Graduated.
Poor, Charles L., 6 September, 1892. Graduated.
Reynolds, John, 20 May, 1892. Resigned.
Rice, George B., 6 September, 1892. Graduated.
Ridgely, Frank E., 6 September, 1892. Graduated.
Robinson, Richard H., 6 September, 1892. Graduated.
Roys, John H., 6 September, 1892. Graduated.
Sanford, John R., 19 September, 1892. Resigned.
Schwalbach, John A., 6 September, 1892. Resigned.
Shelton, Nathan J., 7 September, 1892. Resigned.
Spitzer, Max, 30 September, 1892. Dropped.
Stone, Frederick L., 6 September, 1892. Resigned.
Sykes, Eugene O., 8 September, 1892. Resigned.
Taussig, Paul E., 6 September, 1892. Died 23 July, 1894.
Terry, John T. M., 6 September, 1892. Resigned.
Terry, Joseph D., 20 May, 1892. Resigned.
Tozer, Charles M., 19 September, 1892. Graduated.
Volkmar, Walter S., 6 September, 1892. Resigned.
Walker, Ralph E., 20 May, 1892. Graduated. Transferred to Marine Corps.
Ward, Joshua T., 20 May, 1892. Resigned.
Washington, Pope, 7 September, 1892. Graduated.
Wettengel, Ivan C., 6 September, 1892. Graduated.
Wiley, Walter A., 6 September, 1892. Resigned.
Williams, Thomas N. M., 6 September, 1892. Resigned.
Wood, Duncan M., 30 September, 1892. Graduated.
Wurtsbaugh, Daniel W., 20 May, 1892. Graduated.

1893.—NAVAL CADETS.

Anding, Sheldon W., 19 May, 1893. Resigned.
Asserson, William C., 25 September, 1893. Graduated.
Bagby, Robert C., 22 September, 1893. Resigned.
Boyd, David F., Jr., 19 May, 1893. Graduated.
Brockway, Benjamin L., 6 September, 1893. Resigned.
Brown, George, Jr., 6 September, 1893. Resigned.
Bryant, Samuel W., 19 May, 1893. Resigned.
Buford, Charles S., 6 September, 1893. Resigned.
Buttrick, James T., 27 May, 1893. Resigned.
Chase, Gilbert, 6 September, 1893. Graduated.
Collins, Henry L., 6 September, 1893. Graduated.
Day, John A., 19 May, 1893. Resigned.
Du Bose, William G., 6 September, 1893. Graduated.
Duncan, Oscar D., 6 September, 1893. Graduated.
Eggert, Ernest F., 6 September, 1893. Graduated.
Enbody, Josiah W., 6 September, 1893. Resigned.
Eskridge, Oliver S., 6 September, 1893. Resigned.
Falconer, Walter M., 6 September, 1893. Graduated.
Falk, Julius, 6 September, 1893. Resigned.
Giles, William P., 20 May, 1893. Died 7 December, 1899.
Graeme, Joseph W., 6 September, 1893. Graduated.
Graham, Andrew T., 6 September, 1893. Graduated.
Green, Grant, 19 May, 1893. Resigned.
Hart, Thomas C., 19 May, 1893. Graduated.
Henderson, Robert W., 22 September, 1893. Graduated.
Hepburn, Arthur J., 22 September, 1893. Graduated.
Herndon, Henry R., 19 May, 1893. Resigned.
Hilleary, John F., 6 September, 1893. Resigned.
Holman, Frederic R., 19 May, 1893. Graduated.
Hoopes, Edward T., 6 September, 1893. Resigned.
Hord, Oliver S., 6 September, 1893. Resigned.
Houston, Victor S., 22 September, 1893. Graduated.
Hunter, Charles M., 6 September, 1893. Resigned.
Jeffers, William N., 19 May, 1893. Resigned.
Jenson, Henry N., 6 September, 1893. Graduated.
Jones, Needham L., 6 September, 1893. Graduated.
Kautz, Austin, 19 May, 1893. Graduated.
Keenan, Ernest C., 6 September, 1893. Graduated.

Kempff, Clarence S., 19 May, 1893. Graduated.
Kress, James C., 19 May, 1893. Resigned.
Landis, Irwin F., 6 September, 1893. Graduated.
Leahy, William D., 19 May, 1893. Graduated.
Leutze, Trevor W., 19 May, 1893. Resigned.
Magill, Samuel G., 19 May, 1893. Graduated.
Mahony, Daniel S., 6 September, 1893. Graduated.
Mayo, Henry W., 19 May, 1893. Resigned.
McCarthy, Albert H., 6 September, 1893. Graduated.
McDougal, Douglas C., 19 May, 1893. Resigned.
McDowell, Willis, 19 May, 1893. Graduated.
McMullen, Stanley H., 19 May, 1893. Resigned.
Miller, Cyrus R., 6 September, 1893. Graduated.
Morris, Bennie, 19 May, 1893. Resigned.
Morse, John W., 6 September, 1893. Resigned.
Murfin, Orin G., 6 September, 1893. Graduated.
Naylor, Charles J., 6 September, 1893. Resigned.
Oglesby, Richard J., Jr., 19 May, 1893. Resigned.
Overstreet, Luther M., 6 September, 1893. Graduated.
Owen, Alfred C., 6 September, 1893. Graduated.
Owens, Charles T., 6 September, 1893. Graduated.
Pattison, Dilby N., 6 September, 1893. Resigned.
Perrill, Harlan P., 6 September, 1893. Graduated.
Peters, Francis M., 19 May, 1893. Resigned.
Powell, Joseph W., 19 May, 1893. Graduated.
Pratt, Peter L., 19 May, 1893. Graduated.
Pressey, Alfred W., 19 May, 1893. Graduated.
Reynolds, William H., 6 September, 1893. Graduated.

Richardson, Louis C., 6 September, 1893. Graduated.
Robinson, William A., 6 September, 1893. Resigned.
Roehle, Clifton C., 6 September, 1893. Died 14 July, 1896.
Rutledge, Carl C., 6 September, 1893. Resigned.
Sargent, Leonard R., 6 September, 1893. Graduated.
Sexton, Walton R., 19 May, 1893. Graduated.
Sheffield, Fletcher L., 6 September, 1893. Graduated.
Shelton, Nathan J., 6 September, 1893. Resigned.
Smith, Arthur St. C., Jr., 6 September, 1893. Graduated.
Sykes, Eugene O., Jr., 19 May, 1893. Resigned.
Tarrant, William T., 6 September, 1893. Resigned.
Taylor, Hugh K., 6 September, 1893. Resigned.
Terry, Joseph D., 19 May, 1893. Resigned.
Theleen, David E., 6 September, 1893. Graduated.
Tonkin, John B., 6 September, 1893. Resigned.
Tottenham, John W., 6 September, 1893. Resigned.
Van Orden, George, 19 May, 1893. Graduated.
Ward, Joshua T., 19 May, 1893. Resigned.
Watson, Henry W., 19 May, 1893. Resigned.
Webber, George, 6 September, 1893. Resigned.
Wells, Horace T., 6 September, 1893. Resigned.
Wells, William B., 6 September, 1893. Resigned.
Wessels, Arthur L., 19 May, 1893. Dismissed.
White, William R., 6 September, 1893. Graduated.
Williams, Hilary, 6 September, 1893. Graduated.
Williams, Yancey S., 6 September, 1893. Resigned.
Yarnell, Harry E., 6 September, 1893. Graduated.

1894.—NAVAL CADETS.

Abele, Clarence A., 6 September, 1894. Graduated.
Applewhite, Scott C., 19 May, 1894. Resigned.
Arnold, William W., 19 May, 1894. Resigned.
Babcock, John F., 22 September, 1894. Graduated.
Ball, William G., 22 September, 1894. Resigned.
Bissell, Henry H., 6 September, 1894. Resigned.
Bonnaffon, Sylvester, 6 September, 1894. Resigned.
Boone, Charles, 6 September, 1894. Graduated.
Briggs, Wilbur G., 6 September, 1894. Graduated.
Briggs, Zeno E., 22 September, 1894. Graduated.
Brown, Josephus J., 6 September, 1894. Resigned.
Brown, Morris H., 19 May, 1894. Graduated.
Bynum, Dixson H., 19 May, 1894. Resigned.
Caffery, John M., 6 September, 1894. Resigned.

Constien, Edward T., 19 May, 1894. Graduated.
Cotten, Lyman A., 6 September, 1894. Graduated.
Cronan, William P., 6 September, 1894. Graduated.
Dinger, Henry C., 19 May, 1894. Graduated.
Durham, Raymond E., 22 September, 1894. Resigned.
Eisbein, Arthur, 19 May, 1894. Resigned.
Elson, Herman J., 19 May, 1894. Graduated.
England, William H., 6 September, 1894. Resigned.
Evans, Franck T., 6 September, 1894. Graduated.
Falk, Julius P., 19 June, 1894. Resigned.
Faller, Guy W., 19 May, 1894. Graduated.
Farrin, Thomas B., Jr., 22 September, 1894. Resigned.
Field, Francis L., 22 September, 1894. Resigned.
Fox, Lynn H., 6 September, 1894. Resigned.
Gilmer, James B., 19 May, 1894. Graduated.

GENERAL NAVY REGISTER. 669

Gleason, Henry M., 6 September, 1894. Resigned.
Graham, John S., 19 May, 1894. Graduated.
Halligan, John, Jr., 6 September, 1894. Graduated.
Hand, James A., Jr., 6 September, 1894. Graduated.
Hanrahan, David C., 19 May, 1894. Graduated.
Hord, Oliver S., 19 May, 1894. Resigned.
Hunter, Charles M., 19 May, 1894. Resigned.
Huntington, Arthur F., 12 September, 1894. Resigned.
Jeffries, James G., 6 September, 1894. Resigned.
Johnson, Thomas L., 19 May, 1894. Graduated.
Kress, James C., 6 September, 1894. Resigned.
Lehfeldt, Harry A., 19 May, 1894. Resigned.
Love, James M., Jr., 6 September, 1894. Resigned.
Macy, Ulysses S., 6 September, 1894., Graduated.
Madison, Zachariah H., 6 September, 1894. Graduated.
Mannix, David P., 6 September, 1894. Resigned.
Marble, Ralph N., Jr., 19 May, 1894. Graduated.
McCarty, Sterling H., 6 September, 1894. Resigned.
McIntyre, Edward W., 6 September, 1894. Graduated.
Mitchell, Alexander N., 6 September, 1894. Graduated.
Moore, William A., 22 September, 1894. Resigned.
Morris, Bennie, 3 March, 1894. Resigned.
Nelson, Charles P., 19 May, 1894. Graduated.
Peterson, Roscoe L., 1 June, 1894. Dropped.
Pettengill, George T., 22 September, 1894. Graduated.
Pinney, Frank L., 6 September, 1894. Graduated.
Purse, Henry A., 6 September, 1894. Died 9 April,, 1896.

Reifsnider, John, 6 September, 1894. Resigned.
Roper, Walter G., 22 September, 1894. Graduated.
Rutledge, Carl C., 19 May, 1894. Resigned.
Sayles, William R., Jr., 29 September, 1894. Resigned.
Schofield, John A., 6 September, 1894. Graduated.
Shane, Louis, 6 September, 1894. Graduated.
Shay, Louis B., 6 September, 1894. Resigned.
Shockley, Augustus W., 12 May, 1894. Resigned.
Small, Jesse McL., 12 September, 1894. Resigned.
Smith, George L., 6 September, 1894. Graduated.
Stogsdill, James E., 22 September, 1894. Resigned.
Sweet, George C., 22 September, 1894. Graduated.
Tardy, Walter B., 19 May, 1894. Graduated.
Tarrant, William T., 6 September, 1894. Graduated.
Taylor, Hugh K., 22 September, 1894. Resigned.
Thorpe, George C., 19 May, 1894. Resigned.
Tottenham, John W., 6 September, 1894. Resigned.
Turner, Laurin H., 6 September, 1894. Resigned.
Watts, William C., 22 September, 1894. Graduated.
Webber, Charles H., 19 May, 1894. Resigned.
Wells, William B., 19 May, 1894. Graduated.
Wilcox, Luther T., 19 May, 1894. Resigned.
Williams, Henry, 6 September, 1894. Graduated.
Williams, Yancey S., 6 September, 1894. Graduated.
Woods, Edward, 19 May, 1894. Graduated.
Wright, Henry T., 6 September, 1894. Graduated.

1895.—NAVAL CADETS.

Performing required sea service prior to final graduation, except otherwise stated.

Asserson, Frederick A., 6 September, 1895. Resigned.
Bailey, John E., 20 May, 1895. Graduated.
Beckner, John T., 20 May, 1895. Graduated.
Bird, Owen S., 20 May, 1895. Resigned.
Bisset, Guy A., 6 September, 1895. Graduated.
Bissett, Henry H., 30 May, 1895. Resigned.
Bloch, Claude C., 6 September, 1895. Graduated.
Bowers, John T., 20 September, 1895. Graduated.
Bowman, Everett N., 6 September, 1895. Resigned.
Branch, Frank O., 6 September, 1895. Graduated.
Brinser, Harry L., 6 September, 1895. Graduated.
Buchanan, Allen, 6 September, 1895. Graduated.

Buttrick, James T., 6 September, 1895. Resigned.
Case, William S., 6 September, 1895. Graduated.
Cashman, Frank P., 6 September, 1895. Resigned.
Clement, James W. G., Jr., 27 September, 1895. Graduated.
Cocke, Herbert C., 20 May, 1895. Resigned.
Cole, Cyrus W., 20 September, 1895. Graduated.
Combs, James R., Jr., 6 September, 1895. Graduated.
Conger, William H., Jr., 20 May, 1895. Resigned.
Courtney, Charles E., 20 May, 1895. Graduated.
Craighead, Walter B., 20 September, 1895. Resigned.
Cresap, Edward O., 20 May, 1895. Resigned.
Cull, Julius E., 20 May, 1895. Resigned.

Doyle, Stafford H. R., 6 September, 1895. Resigned.
Dungan, Paul B., 6 September, 1895. Graduated.
Evans, Herbert H., 6 September, 1895. Graduated.
Fenner, Edward B., 20 May, 1895. Graduated.
Ferguson, Garland S., Jr., 20 May, 1895. Resigned.
Fischer, Charles H., 6 September, 1895. Graduated.
Forman, Charles W., 6 September, 1895. Graduated.
Frawley, William J., 20 May, 1895. Resigned.
Gillett, Ransom H., 6 September, 1895. Resigned.
Gleason, Henry M., 20 May, 1895. Graduated.
Greenslade, John W., 20 May, 1895. Graduated.
Hatch, Charles B., 6 September, 1895. Graduated.
Helm, Frank P., Jr., 20 May, 1895. Graduated.
Horn, Frank J., 20 September, 1895. Resigned.
Horne, Frederick J., 20 May, 1895. Graduated.
Hunt, Walter M., 12 September, 1895. Graduated.
Irwin, Algernon Charles I., 6 September, 1895. Resigned.
Jeffers, William N., 20 September, 1895. Graduated.
Johnson, Alfred W., 20 May, 1895. Graduated.
Kalbfus, Edward C., 20 May, 1895. Graduated.
Kearny, Philip, 6 September, 1895. Resigned.
Kimberly, Victor A., 6 September, 1895. Graduated.
Lackey, Henry E., 20 May, 1895. Graduated.
Larimer, Edgar B., 6 Septeber, 1895. Graduated.
Lewis, John E., 6 September, 1895. Graduated.
Maguire, Charles L., 20 May, 1895. Resigned.
Major, Samuel I. M., 20 September, 1895. Graduated.
Mathews, James E., 20 May, 1895. Graduated.
McCarty, Stirling H., 11 September, 1895. Resigned.
Miller, William S., 20 September, 1895. Graduated.
Montgomery, Russell, 6 September, 1895. Resigned.
Morgan, Charles E., 6 September, 1895. Graduated.
Morris, Thomas J., 20 May, 1895. Resigned.
Morrison, Farmer, 6 September, 1895. Graduated.
Muir, John C., 6 September, 1895. Resigned.
Northup, Arthur W., 6 September, 1895. Resigned.
Osterhout, Frank M., 6 September, 1895. Dismissed.
Parrish, John W. C., 6 September, 1895. Resigned.
Pope, Ralph E., 20 May, 1895. Graduated.
Royall, Hilary H., 20 May, 1895. Graduated.
Sadler, Eviret Jay S., 20 September, 1895. Graduated.
Savidge, Albert C., 20 May, 1895. Resigned.
Sayles, William R., Jr., 20 May, 1895. Graduated.
Schmidt, Oscar, 27 May, 1895. Resigned.
Shackford, Chauncey, 6 September, 1895. Graduated.
Shapley, Lloyd S., 30 May, 1895. Graduated.
Smith, Clyde W., 6 September, 1895. Resigned.
Sparrow, Ernest A., 6 September, 1895. Graduated.
Taussig, Joseph K., 5 June, 1895. Graduated.
Thomas, Samuel B., 31 May, 1895. Graduated.
Tomb, James H., 6 September, 1895. Graduated.
Turner, Robert F., 6 September, 1895. Dropped.
Vernon, Walter N., 20 May, 1895. Resigned.
Vincent, Roe W., 6 September, 1895. Graduated.
Watson, Adolphus E., 30 May, 1895. Graduated.
Weichert, Ernest A., 6 September, 1895. Graduated.
Wells, Daniel H., Jr., 6 September, 1895. Resigned.
West, Arthur S., 20 May, 1895. Resigned.
White, Richard D., 20 May, 1895. Graduated.
Wood, Robert T., 30 May, 1895. Resigned.
Wood, Welborn C., 6 September, 1895. Killed in action 17 September, 1899.
Woodward, Clark H., 6 September, 1895. Graduated.
Wright, Luke E., Jr., 20 May, 1895. Resigned.
Wyman, Henry L., 6 September, 1895. Graduated.
Yates, Alexander F. H., 20 May, 1895. Graduated.

1896.—NAVAL CADETS.

Performing required sea service prior to final graduation, except otherwise stated.

Abernathy, Robert A., 5 September, 1896. Graduated.
Arnold, Clarence L., 5 September, 1896. Graduated.
Asmus, Allston, 5 September, 1896. Resigned.
Barthalow, Benjamin G., 5 September, 1896. Graduated.
Berrien, Frank D., 5 September, 1896. Graduated.
Berry, Robert L., 20 May, 1896. Graduated.
Blair, George F., 5 September, 1896. Resigned.
Boardman, William H., 5 September, 1896. Died 10 August, 1898.
Bricker, William F., 19 September, 1896. Graduated.
Brackett, William, 5 September, 1896. Resigned.

Browne, Claude, 5 September, 1896. Resigned.
Bryant, Samuel W., 5 September, 1896. Graduated.
Bulmer, Bayard T., 5 September, 1896. Graduated.
Caffery, John M., 5 September, 1896. Academy course not completed.
Cage, Harry K., 20 May, 1896. Graduated.
Catron, John W., 5 September, 1896. Resigned.
Church, John G., 20 May, 1896. Graduated.
Clark, Arthur W., 19 September, 1896. Resigned.
Cocke, Herbert C., 20 May, 1896. Graduated.
Comfort, James H., 20 May, 1896. Graduated.
Cox, Lewis S., Jr., 20 May, 1896. Resigned.
Cresap, Edward O., 20 May, 1896. Resigned.
Crittendon, Kirby B., 5 September, 1896. Resigned.
Day, Charles C., 5 September, 1896. Resigned.
Dearborn, Peyton B., 5 September, 1896. Resigned.
Defrees, Joseph R., 20 May, 1896. Graduated.
Dodd, Edwin H., 5 September, 1896. Graduated.
Downes, John, Jr., 3 June, 1896. Resigned.
Doyle, Stafford H. R., 20 May, 1896. Graduated.
Draper, Arthur E., 19 September, 1896. Resigned.
Ellis, Hayne, 5 September, 1896. Graduated.
Enbody, Josiah W., 5 September, 1896. Resigned.
Ferguson, William B., Jr., 20 May, 1896. Graduated.
Fitzpatrick, John J., 5 September, 1896. Resigned.
Foley, Paul, 5 September, 1896. Graduated.
Foote, Percy W., 5 September, 1896. Resigned.
Fowler, Orie W., 5 September, 1896. Resigned.
Freeman, Charles S., 5 September, 1896. Graduated.
Gannon, Sinclair, 3 June, 1896. Graduated.
Gardiner, Carlos A., 20 May, 1896. Graduated.
Harris, George S., 5 September, 1896. Resigned.
Hellweg, Julius F., 5 September, 1896. Graduated.
Howard, Abram C., 5 September, 1896. Dropped.
Huff, Charles P., 5 September, 1896. Graduated.
Hulick, Clive K., 5 September, 1896. Died 11 June, 1898.
Hyland, John J., 19 September, 1896. Graduated.
Jackson, Edward S., 22 May, 1896. Graduated.
James, John F., 5 September, 1896. Resigned.
Johnston, Huntington, 19 September, 1896. Graduated.
Kear, Carlton R., 20 May, 1896. Graduated.
Kearny, Philip, 20 May, 1896. Dismissed.

Keating, Arthur B., 19 September, 1896. Graduated.
Landenberger, George B., 20 May, 1896. Graduated.
Landram, Clarence E., 5 September, 1896. Graduated.
Mann, John F., 5 September, 1896. Resigned.
McEntee, William, 20 May, 1896. Graduated.
Menner, Robert T., 5 September, 1896. Graduated.
Miles, Harold B., 20 May, 1896. Resigned.
Miller, Benjamin F., 5 September, 1896. Resigned.
Mitchell, Willis G., 5 September, 1896. Graduated.
Morris, Robert, 5 September, 1896. Graduated.
Nalle, Frederick R., 5 September, 1896. Graduated.
Noa, Loveman, 5 September, 1896. Graduated.
O'Reilly, Philip M., 3 June, 1896. Resigned.
Osterhaus, Hugo W., 20 May, 1896. Graduated.
Pye, William S., 5 September, 1896. Resigned.
Rhea, Robert Y., 20 May, 1896. Resigned.
Rhue, John A., 5 September, 1896. Resigned.
Riddle, William K., 5 September, 1896. Graduated.
Roberts, Charles V., 3 June, 1896. Dismissed.
Roosevelt, Henry L., 6 July, 1896. Resigned.
Russell, Branch E., 20 May, 1896. Resigned.
Schoenfeld, John W., 6 July, 1896. Graduated.
Scranton, Edison E., 20 May, 1896. Graduated.
Shea, William H., 20 May, 1896. Resigned.
Sloan, James M., Jr., 20 May, 1896. Resigned.
Smith, Wilbert, 6 July, 1896. Graduated.
Snyder, Charles P., 20 May, 1896. Graduated.
Spilman, John A., 20 May, 1896. Graduated.
Steele, George W., Jr., 3 June, 1896. Graduated.
Svarz, Emil P., 29 May, 1896. Graduated.
Thompson, Scott McG., 5 September, 1896. Resigned.
Timmons, John W., 3 June, 1896. Graduated.
Tomb, William V., 5 September, 1896. Graduated.
Train, Charles R., 5 September, 1896. Graduated.
Vernon, Walter N., 5 September, 1896. Resigned.
Wade, Charles T., 5 September, 1896. Graduated.
Wainwright, John D., 19 September, 1896. Graduated.
Winston, Hollis T., 5 September, 1896. Graduated.
Wood, Robert T., 5 September, 1896. Resigned.
Woods, Stanley, 20 May, 1896. Graduated.
Wortman, Ward K., 5 Septmeber, 1896. Graduated.
Wright, Luke E., Jr., 5 September, 1896. Graduated.
Zogbaum, Rufus F., Jr., 20 May, 1896. Resigned.

1897.—NAVAL CADETS.

At Naval Academy, unless otherwise stated.

Ackerson, James L., 20 May, 1897.
Allen, Burrell C., 7 September, 1897.
Allen, William H., 20 May, 1897.
Alsop, Kelly D., 10 September, 1897. Resigned.
Andrews, Adolphus, 7 September, 1897.
Babcock, John V., 10 September, 1897.
Bass, Ivan E., 20 May, 1897.
Bertholf, Wallace, 22 September, 1897.
Blair, George F., 8 September, 1897.
Bowne, William R., 20 September, 1897. Resigned.
Brooks, Ernest A., 6 September, 1897.
Brooks, Leroy, Jr., 7 September, 1897. Resigned.
Brown, George P., 10 September, 1897. Resigned.
Browne, Claude, 11 September, 1897.
Bruff, Charles L., 20 May, 1897.
Burwell, John T., 20 May, 1897.
Castle, Guy W. S., 20 May, 1897.
Cleveland, Thomas J., 20 May, 1897. Resigned.
Colvocoresses, Harold, 20 May, 1897. Resigned.
Conway, Clarence A., 10 September, 1897.
Cook, Harold E., 20 May, 1897.
Cook, Merlyn G., 10 September, 1897.
Cooper, Oscar F., 8 September, 1897. Resigned.
Cox, Lewis S., Jr., 20 September, 1897.
Downes, John, Jr., 8 September, 1897.
Enochs, John M., 23 September, 1897.
Fairfield, Arthur P., 8 September, 1897.
Fisher, Charles W., Jr., 1 October, 1897.
Fitzpatrick, John J., 8 September, 1897.
Fogarty, William B., 20 September, 1897.
Foote, Percy W., 20 May, 1897.
Fowler, Orle W., 20 May, 1897.
Fremont, John C., Jr., 20 May, 1897.
Furer, Julius A., 10 September, 1897.
Furse, John H., 20 May, 1897.
Galbraith, William W., 20 May, 1897.
Gay, Jesse B., 9 September, 1897.
Gilmore, John J., 23 September, 1897. Resigned.
Goodrich, Caspar, 7 September, 1897.
Green, John F., 7 September, 1897.
Green, Marshall B., 13 September, 1897. Resigned.
Hamner, Edward C., Jr., 9 September, 1897.
Hannigan, John J., 9 September, 1897.
Harris, George S., 20 May, 1897.
Hastings, Russell, 9 September, 1897. Resigned.
Henry, Sidney M., 6 September, 1897.
Hileman, Joseph L., 10 September, 1897.
Howe, Alfred G., 20 May, 1897.
Hutchins, Charles T., 20 September, 1897.
Jackson, John P., 7 September, 1897.

Kerrick, Charles S., 11 September, 1897.
Keyes, Raymond S., 10 September, 1897.
King, Ernest J., 6 September, 1897.
Kittinger, Theodore A., 20 May, 1897.
Kress, James C., 20 May, 1897. Performing sea service prior to final graduation.
Kurtz, Thomas R., 6 September, 1897.
Lawrason, George C., 20 May, 1897. Resigned.
Lindsay, Joseph S., 8 September, 1897. Resigned.
Lloyd, Howard M., 10 September, 1897. Resigned.
Long, Byron A., 10 September, 1897.
Manley, Rufus S., 7 September, 1897.
Mannix, Daniel P., 20 May, 1897. Performing sea service prior to final graduation.
McBride, Lewis B., 6 September, 1897.
McCommon, Frank, 21 September, 1897.
McCrary, Frank R., 11 September, 1897.
Moore, Langdon, 17 September, 1897. Resigned.
Nauman, Arthur L., 11 September, 1897. Resigned.
Neal, George F., 20 May, 1897
Nitingale, Garrard P., 20 May, 1897.
Norris, William, 7 September, 1897.
Oakley, Owen H., 20 May, 1897.
Oliver, Frederick L., 8 September, 1897.
Perry, Newman K., Jr., 9 September, 1897.
Price, Samuel R., 10 September, 1897. Resigned.
Pye, William S., 20 May, 1897.
Rich, Albert T., 5 June, 1897. Resigned.
Richardson, Holden C., 8 September, 1897.
Robertson, William M., 20 May, 1897. Resigned.
Rodgers, John, 7 September, 1897. Resigned.
Simons, Manley H., 20 May, 1897.
Spafford, Edward E., 9 September, 1897.
Steinhagen, William H., 6 September, 1897.
Tone, Bernard L., 25 May, 1897. Resigned.
Vernon, Walter N., 20 September, 1897.
Walsh, John H., 10 September, 1897.
Weaver, David A., 11 September, 1897.
Westervelt, George C., 20 May, 1897.
Wheeler, Thomas H., 20 May, 1897. Died 7 September, 1898.
Whitlock, Guy, 20 May, 1897.
Whitney, Edward L., 20 May, 1897. Resigned.
Williams, Roger, 20 May, 1897.
Woodson, Pickens E., 20 May, 1897. Resigned.
Wygant, Benguard B., 20 September, 1897.
Yates, Isaac I., 20 May, 1897.
Zogbaum, Rufus F., Jr., 20 May, 1897.

1898.—NAVAL CADETS.

At Naval Academy, unless otherwise stated.

Abbott, John S., 10 September, 1898. Resigned.
Adams, Roe R., 12 September, 1898.
Alsop, Kelley D., 24 May, 1898. Resigned.
Ancrum, William, 23 May, 1898. Resigned.
Anderson, Edward C., 23 May, 1898.
Apted, Herbert M., 19 September, 1898. Resigned.

Arwine, John S., 22 September, 1898. Resigned.
Austin, James M., 10 September, 1898. Resigned.
Baker, Don D., 20 May, 1898. Resigned.
Baldridge, Harry A., 13 September, 1898.
Bean, Carlos, 12 September, 1898.
Bingham, Donald C., 9 September, 1898.

GENERAL NAVY REGISTER. 673

Blackburn, John H., 29 September, 1898.
Brooks, Leroy, Jr., 8 September, 1898.
Brown, George P., 13 September, 1898.
Browne, Wilson, Jr., 23 September, 1898.
Campbell, James A., 8 September, 1898.
Childs, Harold D., 12 September, 1898.
Claude, Abram, 13 September, 1898. Resigned.
Conn, William T., Jr., 9 September, 1898.
Cooper, Oscar F., 26 May, 1898.
Corning, Merritt S., 10 September, 1898.
Craft, Ralph P., 21 September, 1898.
Darst, Gilford, 21 September, 1898.
Davis, Roscoe C., 22 September, 1898.
Deering, George A., 10 September, 1898.
Diman, Walker G., 12 September, 1898.
Dowling, Otto C., 9 September, 1898.
Early, Charles W., 13 September, 1898.
Enfer, Emile P., 21 May, 1898. Resigned.
Eslick, Fred M., 8 September, 1898. Resigned.
Finney, Earl P., 17 September, 1898.
Fisher, Joseph O., 21 May, 1898.
Freyer, Frank B., 23 May, 1898.
Ghent, Daniel T., 23 May, 1898. Resigned.
Goldman, Mayer L., 7 September, 1898.
Griswold, Ralph M., 9 September, 1898.
Hall, Frank D., 23 May, 1898.
Hart, Asa E. L., 22 September, 1898. Resigned.
Henderson, Robert, 21 May, 1898.
Hepburn, Harry H., 22 September, 1898. Resigned.
Hickman, Christopher J., 8 September, 1898. Resigned.
Horning, George R., 21 September, 1898.
Johnston, Richard H., 2 June, 1898.
Kintner, Edward G., 12 September, 1898.
Klyce, Horace S., 7 September, 1898.
Lacy, Linsay H., 12 September, 1898.
Land, Emory S., 9 September, 1898.
Lannon, James P., 12 September, 1898.
Lawrason, George C., 9 September, 1898. Resigned.
Martin, Frank C., 21 May, 1898.
Marquart, Edward J., 7 September, 1898.
Meyers, George J., 23 May, 1898.
Morton, Harry T., 7 September, 1898. Resigned.
Moses, William J., 3 June, 1898.
Mott, Thomas A., 21 May, 1898. Resigned.
Murdock, James P., 10 September, 1898.
Murphy, Daniel J., 21 May, 1898. Resigned.
Nichols, Neil E., 20 May, 1898.
Nussbaum, Victor M., 24 May, 1898. Resigned.
O'Reilly, Philip M., 24 May, 1898.
O'Rourke, Maurice W., 21 May, 1898. Resigned.
Osburn, Franklin W., 27 September, 1898.
Ownby, George S., 12 September, 1898. Resigned.
Ozburn, Thomas L., 21 May, 1898.
Parker, Edward B., 9 September, 1898.
Peterson, Andrew A., 21 September, 1898.
Porterfield, Lewis B., 8 September, 1898.
Poteet, Fred H., 17 October, 1898.
Price, Clarener H., 12 September, 1898. Resigned.
Pryor, William L., 12 September, 1898.
Puleston, William D., 7 September, 1898.
Quinlan, William J., 14 September, 1898.
Read, Semmers, 3 October, 1898.
Reed, James, Jr., 8 September, 1898.
Richardson, James O., 21 September, 1898.
Rowcliff, Gilbert J., 25 May, 1898.
Simmers, Clayton M., 12 September, 1898.
Smith, William W., 8 September, 1898.
Staton, Adolphus, 12 September, 1898.
Sterling, Frank W., 24 September, 1898.
St. George, William T., 21 May, 1898. Resigned.
Symonds, Charles F., 9 September, 1898. Resigned.
Thompson, George N., 9 September, 1898. Resigned.
Townsend, Julius C., 8 September, 1898.
Wainwright, Richard, Jr., 8 September, 1898.
Wallace, Henry G. S., 27 September, 1898.
Wallace, Robert, Jr., 12 September, 1898.
Walthall, William H., 17 September, 1898. Resigned.
Whitten, Francis S., 23 May, 1898.
Woodruff, John W., 8 September, 1898.

1899.—NAVAL CADETS.

At Naval Academy, unless otherwise stated.

Abbott, John S., 12 September, 1899.
Ancrum, William, 22 May, 1899.
Anderson, Walter S., 9 September, 1899.
Arwine, John, 22 September, 1899.
Battles, Donald R., 6 September, 1899.
Belknap, Charles, Jr., 26 May, 1899.
Blakely, Charles, 9 September, 1899.
Brillhart, Charles E., 3 October, 1899.
Brisbin, Alfred T., 23 May, 1899.
Claude, Abram, 12 September, 1899. Resigned.
Cleary, Francis J., 12 September, 1899.
Clifford, Hugh J., 13 September, 1899. Resigned.
Cooke, Henry D., Jr., 9 September, 1899.
Craven, Henry S., 30 June, 1899.
Davis, Milton S., 7 September, 1899.
Donaldson, Hugh O., 23 May, 1899. Dismissed.
Eberlein, Michael G., 8 September, 1899. Resigned.
Eslick, Fred M., 8 September, 1899. Resigned.
Fretz, Paul H., 9 September, 1899.
Friedrick, Ernest, 7 September, 1899.
Gatewood, Richard D., 26 June, 1899.
Ghent, Daniel T., 23 May, 1899.
Giles, William J., 9 September, 1899.
Hays, William D., 21 September, 1899. Resigned.
Holland, Walter J., 28 September, 1899. Resigned.
Holmes, Ralston S., 21 September, 1899.
Kibbee, Austin, S., 13 September, 1899.
Koch, Ralph, 12 September, 1899.
Leahy, Lamar R., 12 September, 1899.
Loomis, Sam C., 22 September, 1899.
Maxwell, James F., 18 September, 1899. Dismissed.
McCracken, John J., 13 September, 1899.
McKenzie, Clovis H., 14 September, 1899.
McNair, Frederick V., Jr., 24 January, 1899.
Metcalf, Martin K., 12 September, 1899.
Milne, Macgillivray, 8 September, 1899.
Moses, Charles C., 21 July, 1899.
Mott, Thomas A., 21 May, 1898. Resigned.
Nelson, Theodore N., 13 September, 1899.
Neumann, William E. T., 16 September, 1899.
Ownby, George S., 23 May, 1899.
Poteet, Fred H., 7 October, 1899.
Radford, George S., 12 September, 1899.
Raudenbush, Webb R., 9 September, 1899.

43

GENERAL NAVY REGISTER.

Reid, William P., 22 September, 1899. Dismissed.
Rhea, Robert Y., 17 June, 1899. Resigned.
Rhodes, Butler Y., 13 September, 1899.
Robinson, Samuel M., 8 September, 1899.
Rodgers, John, 9 September, 1899.
Rowan, Stephen C., 26 June, 1899.
Ryden, Roy W., 11 September, 1899.
Sadler, Frank H., 23 May, 1899.
Sahm, Leo, 28 September, 1899.
Schlabach, Ross P., 11 September, 1899.
Schreiber, George E., 12 September, 1899. Resigned.
Simon, Harry A., 12 September, 1899. Resigned.
Smead, Walter A., 12 September, 1899. Resigned.
Smith, Charles E., 24 May, 1899.
Smith, William R., 14 September, 1899.
Smyth, William W., 9 September, 1899.
Stark, Harold R., 25 October, 1899.
Taylor, James A., 9 September, 1899. Resigned.
Taylor, Thomas H., 13 September, 1899.
Thackara, Alexander M., 17 June, 1899.
Thompson, George N., 25 May, 1899. Resigned.
Thompson, Rufus S., 21 September, 1899.
Van Auken, Wilbur R., 9 September, 1899.
Van Keuren, Alexander H., 11 September, 1899.
Walker, Hugh M., 13 September, 1899.
Ward, Thomas, Jr., 23 May, 1899.
Wickersham, Darrell P., 8 September, 1899. Resigned.
Willson, James D., 23 May, 1899.

1900.—NAVAL CADETS.

At Naval Academy, unless otherwise stated.

Arrowood, Milton Wallace, 8 September, 1900.
Atkinson, John Franklin, 11 September, 1900.
Bagley, David Worth, 8 September, 1900.
Barnette, Bradford, 9 July, 1900.
Bassett, Prentiss Peck, 7 September, 1900.
Baum, George Martin, 10 September, 1900.
Benjamin, Adrian Thomas, 7 September, 1900.
Blackburn, Paul Prichard, 2 July, 1900.
Burnett, William LeGrande, 2 July, 1900.
Cade, Cassius Marcellus, 28 May, 1900.
Caffee, Arthur Gill, 7 September, 1900.
Campbell, James Edwin, Jr., 3 October, 1900.
Carpenter, Reginald Thorne, 29 September, 1900.
Chafee, Earl Worden, 7 September, 1900.
Claude, Abram, 10 September, 1900.
Close, Charles Fisher, 10 September, 1900.
Coburn, Fred Gallup, 29 September, 1900.
Collins, Thomas Edward, 25 September, 1900.
Cook, Arthur Byron, 10 September, 1900.
Corey, Clement Bassett, 12 September, 1900.
Craig, Donald Bloyer, 7 September, 1900.
Craven, Henry Smith, 30 June, 1899.
Cressey, Calvin Joy, 7 September, 1900.
Dampman, Paul Edward, 7 September, 1900.
Dawes, Robert Alden, 7 September, 1900.
Dillen, Roscoe Franklin, 23 May, 1900.
Dodge, Omenzo Colby Ford, 7 September, 1900.
Dortch, Isaac Foote, 26 September, 1900.
Druley, Waldo Putnam, 7 September, 1900.
Fairchild, Herbert Bigelow, 21 July, 1900.
Fitch, Edwin Oberlin, Jr., 2 July, 1900.
Greene, Edward Forbes, 26 September, 1900.
Hage, Sigurd, 7 September, 1900.
Halsey, William Frederick, Jr., 9 July, 1900.
Hand, Chester Lyerly, 7 September, 1900.
Harrington, Charles Anthony, 2 July, 1900.
Hart, John Porter, 27 September, 1900.
Hayward, James Waldemar, 7 September, 1900.
Hazard, Stanton Leigh Hunt, 29 September, 1900.
Hilliard, Robert Bell, 2 July, 1900.
Holland, Walter John, 21 May, 1900.
Howard, Herbert Seymour, 8 September, 1900.
Hutchins, Hamilton Eugene, 20 July, 1900.
Johnson, Benjamin Kent, 7 September, 1900.
Johnson, Isaac Cureton, Jr., 25 September, 1900.
Jones, Chandler Kendall, 25 April, 1900.
Kimmell, Husband Edward, 21 May, 1900.
LeBreton, David McDougal, 9 July, 1900.
Langley, Ralph Simons, 24 May, 1900.
Lofland, John Henry, 24 September, 1900.
McCullough, Richard Philip, 24 May, 1900.
McDowell, Clyde Stanley, 27 September, 1900.
McMillan, Frank Dodd, 10 September, 1900.
McMillan, Fred Ewing, 22 May, 1900.
Maguire, Joseph Frederick, 27 September, 1900.
Mauldin, Cleon Wirt, 23 May, 1900.
Michael, Herbert Harlan, 9 July, 1900.
Morgan, Luman Edgar, 25 September, 1900.
Newcomer, Robert Hitt, 11 September, 1900.
Oak, Edson Collins, 7 September, 1900.
Otterson, John Edward, 7 September, 1900.
Pickens, Andrew Calhoun, 7 September, 1900.
Post, Nathan Woodworth, 10 September, 1900.
Powell, Halsey, 8 September, 1900.
Ramstad, Albert George, 10 September, 1900.
Reed, Allen Bevins, 24 September, 1900.
Rice, Arthur Hopkins, 24 September, 1900.
Richards, Clarence Alvin, 24 May, 1900.
Richter, Carl Albert, 7 September, 1900.
Robinson, Edward Small, 25 September, 1900.
Rodgers, Christopher Raymond Perry, September 8, 1900.
Sedgwick, William Parker, Jr., 7 September, 1900.
Shepardson, Charles Albert, 23 May, 1900.
Sherman, Edward Bragg, 20 July, 1900.
Shoup, Aubry K., 22 May, 1900.
Smead, Walter Albert, 9 July, 1900.
Smith, William Redding, 14 September, 1899.
Soule, Charles Carroll, Jr., 7 September, 1900.
Stafford, Donald Bernard, 23 May, 1900.
Stewart, Leigh Morrison, 7 September, 1900.
Stuart, Harry Allen, 24 September, 1900.
Taylor, James Alvan, 23 May, 1900.
Toaz, William Hamilton, 7 September, 1900.
Todd, Forde Anderson, 8 September, 1900.
Treadwell, Lawrence Penfield, 7 September, 1900.
Tupper, Frederick Geddings, 29 September, 1900.
Wadsworth, Alexander Scammell, Jr., 25 September, 1900.
Whetsel, Everard N., 25 September, 1900.
Whiting, Kenneth, 10 September, 1900.
Wickersham, Darrell Palmer, 22 May, 1900.
Wright, Nathaniel Hoadley, 25 September, 1900.

CADET ENGINEERS AT THE NAVAL ACADEMY.

1866.

McCarty. George D., 3 October, 1866. Transferred to be a midshipman.

Wilson, James P., 5 October, 1866. Resigned.

1867.

Howell, Charles P., 7 October, 1867. Graduated.

Steel, James, 23 September, 1867. Died 16 August, 1869.

1871.—OCTOBER 1.
Except otherwise stated.

1871.—OCTOBER 1.
Except otherwise stated.
Barton, John K. Graduated.
Boggs, William B. Graduated.
Cleaver, Henry T. Graduated.
Cumming, John A. Resigned.
Denig, Robert G. Graduated.
Edwards, John R. Graduated.
Kleckner, Charles. Graduated.
Leitch, Robert R. Graduated.

Potts, Stacy. Graduated.
Ransom, George B. Graduated.
Ruiz, Alberto de. Resigned.
Schneider, William E. Resigned.
Tiffany, William H. Dropped 24 October, 1872.
Warren, Benjamin H. Graduated.
Willetts, Albert B. Graduated.
Wooster, Lucius W. Graduated.
Zane, Abraham V. Graduated.

1872.—OCTOBER 1.
Except otherwise stated.

Canaga, Alfred B. Graduated.
Drouillard, George L. Resigned.
Eaton, William C. Graduated.
Eldridge, Frank H. Graduated.
Frizell, Charles H. Resigned.
Hoffman, Frank J. Graduated.
Jeffrey, William C., 18 November, 1872. Resigned.
King, William R. Graduated.
Little, William A. Graduated.

Loomis, Edmund N. Graduated.
Mattice, Asa. Graduated.
Meredith, Edward D. Resigned.
Morgan, Lee. Resigned.
Reid, Robert J. Graduated.
Roebling, Edmund. Dropped.
Ruiz, Alberto de. Resigned.
Schermerhorn, William E. Resigned.
Sornborger, Edwin C. Resigned.
Warburton, Edgar T. Graduated.

1873.—OCTOBER 1.

Babbitt, George Henry Thomas. Graduated.
Bailey, Frank Hughes. Graduated.
Burgdorff, Theodore Frederick. Graduated.
Carter, Thomas F. Graduated.
Cathcart, William Ledyard. Graduated.
Claude, Gordon H. Resigned.
Cowles, William. Graduated.
Dunning, William Batey. Graduated.
Eastman, Harry. Resigned.

Freeman, Edward Russell. Graduated.
Johnson, Charles N. Resigned.
Kelley, B. F. Resigned.
Olmstead, Loring. Resigned.
Ruiz, Alberto de. Graduated.
Stivers, Henry Hicks. Graduated.
White, John M. Resigned.
Willetts, George Sidney. Graduated.
Worthington, Walter Fitzhugh. Graduated.

1874.—OCTOBER 1.

Bartlett, Frank W. Graduated.
Bennett, Frank M. Graduated.
Bieg, Frederick Charles. Graduated.
Bull, George Hoyt. Graduated.

Burd, George Ell. Graduated.
Claude, Gordon Handy. Dismissed.
Cooley, Mortimer Elwyn. Graduated.
Crygier, John Ulysses. Graduated.

Dungan, Horace Greeley. Resigned.
Elseffer, Harry Smith. Graduated.
Gage, Howard. Graduated.
Gow, John London. Graduated.
Griffin, Robert Stanislaus. Graduated.
Harrison, Henry Fillmore. Resigned.
Hogan, Thomas Joseph. Graduated.
Hollis, Ira Nelson. Graduated.
Ivers, Henry King. Graduated.
McElroy, George Wightman. Graduated.

Norton, Harold Percival. Graduated.
O'Connor, Henry. Dropped. Resigned.
Pickrell, Joseph McCall. Graduated.
Salisbury, George Robert. Graduated.
Schell, Franklin Jacob. Graduated.
Scribner, Edward Herschell. Graduated.
Spangler, Harry Wilson. Graduated.
Wright, Charles Leslie. Graduated.
Wilmer, Joseph Ringgold. Graduated.

1875.—SEPTEMBER 15.
Except otherwise stated.

Acker, Edward O'Connor. Graduated.
Annan, John Wesley. Graduated.
Baker, John Howard. Graduated.
Bowers, Frederick C. Graduated.
Bartholow, Frank la Motte. Dropped.
Bevington, Martin. Graduated.
Bowles, Francis Tiffany. Graduated.
Bryan, Benjamin Chambers. Graduated.
Carr, Clarence Alfred. Graduated.
Gatewood, Richard. Graduated.
Hunt, Andrew Murray. Graduated.

Isbester, Richard Thornton. Graduated.
Lubbe, Charles Bethel. Graduated.
McFarland, Walter Martin. Graduated.
Miller, Clarence A. Dropped.
Mercier, David Isaiah. Resigned.
Noell, Michael Daniel. Died 1 January, 1878.
Smith, William Strother. Graduated.
Talcott, Charles Gratiot. Graduated.
Temple, Arthur Wallace. Resigned.
Yarnall, John Hepburn. Resigned.

1876.—SEPTEMBER 14.

Allderdice, William Hillary. Graduated.
Arnold, Solon. Graduated.
Bailey, Horace Justus. Resigned.
Belden, Charles Emory. Graduated.
Byrne, James Edwin. Graduated.
Durand, William Frederick. Graduated.
Eckel, Herman. Dismissed.
Hall, Harry. Graduated.
Hasson, William Frederick Converse. Graduated.
King, Charles Alfred. Graduated.
Kinkaid, Thomas Wright. Graduated.
Lang, William. Died 15 November, 1880.

Lillebridge, Frederick May. Resigned.
Manning, Charles Edward. Graduated.
Mathews, Clarence Herbert. Graduated.
Miner, Leo Dwight. Graduated.
Nichols, Arthur. Resigned.
Sample, Winfield Scott. Graduated.
Smith, Albert Edward. Graduated.
Stahl, Albert William. Graduated.
Weaver, William Dixon. Graduated.
Wood, Joseph Learned. Graduated.
Woods, Arthur Tannatt. Graduated.
Worthington, John Leeds. Graduated.
Young, Albert Osborn. Graduated.

1877.—SEPTEMBER 13.

Anderson, Martin Augustus. Graduated.
Arnold, Solon. Graduated.
Bankson, Lloyd. Graduated.
Beach, Robert James. Graduated.
Bush, Arthur Richmond. Graduated.
Day, Willis Bruner. Graduated.
Dowst, Frank Butland. Graduated.
Gartley, William Henry. Graduated.
Gladstone, Daniel Demarest. Dropped.
Kaemmerling, Gustave. Graduated.
McAllister, Andrew. Graduated.
McAlpine, Kennett. Graduated.
McCreary, Harry Raynor. Resigned.
Moritz, Albert. Graduated.
Nichols, Arthur. Resigned.

Parsons, Isaac Brown. Graduated.
Perkins, Lyman Burnham. Graduated.
Prevear, Herbert Banker. Resigned.
Redgrave, De Witt Clinton. Graduated.
Sampson, Bias Clay. Graduated.
Shallenberger, Olver Blackburn, Graduated.
Smith, William Stuart. Graduated.
Stewart, Robert, Jr. Graduated.
Webster, William Townsend. Graduated.
White, William Wilmot. Graduated.
Whitham, Jay Manuel. Graduated.
Whittle, Llewellyn Fairfax. Died 23 July, 1880, Naval Hospital, Philadelphia.

1878.—OCTOBER 1.

Addicks, Walter R. Resigned.
Chambers, William H. Graduated.
Clarke, Arthur H. Graduated. Transferred to Marine Corps.
Coley, Frederick E. Died 19 December, 1883.
Conant, Frank H. Graduated. Honorably discharged 30 June, 1884.
Creighton, William H. P. Graduated.
Fitts, James H. Graduated.
Ferguson, George R. Resigned.
Gatewood, Robert W. Graduated. Honorably discharged 30 June, 1884.
Gsantner, Otto C. Resigned.

Hawthorne, Harry L. R. Graduated. Honorably discharged 30 June, 1884.
Higgins, Robert B. Graduated. Honorably discharged 30 June, 1884.
Howland, Charles H. Graduated. Honorably discharged 30 June, 1884.
Leonard, John C. Graduated.
Leopold, Harry G. Graduated. Honorably discharged 30 June, 1884.
Miller, Peter. Died 3 April, 1883.
Pendleton, Joseph H. Graduated. Transferred to Marine Corps.
Quinby, Isaac H. Dropped.
Rommell, Charles E. Graduated.

Simpson, Henry L. Resigned.
Shock, Thomas A. W. Graduated. Honorably discharged 30 June, 1885.
Taylor, Edward K. Died 10 December, 1880.
Theiss, Emil. Graduated.

Willis, Clarence C. Graduated. Honorably discharged 30 June, 1884.
Winchell, Ward P. Graduated. Honorably discharged 30 September, 1884.
Youchi, Sadanori.

1879.—OCTOBER 1.

Aldrich, William S. Resigned.
Armistead, Samuel W. Graduated.
Barnes, Charles E. Resigned.
Baxter, William J. Graduated.
Carswell, William B. Resigned.
Darrah, William F. Graduated.
Duvall, Marius, Jr. Dropped.
Dyson, Charles W. Graduated.
Eaton, Charles P. Graduated.
Ellinger, Julius. Resigned.
Ellicott, John M. Graduated.
Field, Harry A. Graduated.
Gillis, Harry A. Resigned.
Glasscock, Eustace S. Resigned.
Gross, Charles J. Dropped.

Halstead, Alexander J. Graduated.
Herbert, William C. Graduated.
Lawrence, William H. Died 1 January, 1885.
Littlehales, George W. Graduated. Honorably discharged 30 June, 1885.
Palmer, James E. Graduated. Honorably discharged 30 June, 1885.
Pattison, Thomas P. Resigned.
Ryan, Philip J. Graduated. Honorably discharged 30 June, 1885.
Webster, Charles F. Graduated. Honorably discharged 30 June, 1885.
Woodruff, Charles E. Dropped.
Zinnell, George F. Resigned.

1880.—OCTOBER 1.

Barron, Charles C. Resigned.
Biddle, Andrew P. Resigned.
Capps, Washington L. Graduated.
Crisp, Richard O. Resigned.
Dargan, Milton. Dismissed.
Davis, Edward. Graduated. Honorably discharged 30 June, 1886.
Fahs, Charles M. Graduated.
Field, Horace A. Graduated. Honorably discharged 30 June, 1886.
Hewes, Charles H. Graduated.
Hill, Frank K. Graduated.
Hughes, Arthur L. Resigned.
Hulme, Walter O. Graduated.
Jones, Horace W. Graduated. Honorably discharged 30 June, 1886.
Keilholtz, Pierre O. Resigned.

Knepper, Chester M. Graduated.
Loomis, Frederick J. Graduated.
McCay, Henry K. Resigned.
Mathews, Albert C. Graduated. Honorably discharged 30 June, 1886.
Orr, Robert H. Graduated. Honorably discharged 30 June, 1886.
Parmenter, Henry E. Graduated.
Richardson, Thornton R. Graduated. Honorably discharged 30 June, 1886.
Starr, John B. Graduated. Honorably discharged 30 June, 1886.
Wedderburn, Lawrence A. Died 27 April, 1882.
Werntz, Robert L. Graduated. Honorably discharged 30 June, 1886.
Whittlesey, Humes H. Graduated.

1881.—OCTOBER 1.

Bootes, James T. Graduated. Honorably discharged 30 June, 1887.
Taylor, David Watson. Graduated.
Rust, Armistead. Graduated.
Boyd, Harry Lansdale. Resigned.
Uberroth, Preston Harry. Resigned.
Shields, William. Resigned.
Chase, Volney O. Graduated.
Fenton, Theodore C. Graduated.
Miller, William G. Graduated.
Tawresey, John G. Graduated.
McKay, William. Graduated. Honorably discharged 30 June, 1887.
Evans, George R. Graduated.

Mulford, Harry B. Dropped.
Dashiell, Julius M. Resigned.
Kline, George W. Graduated.
Stanworth, Charles S. Graduated.
Warfield, Louis E. Resigned.
McCormick, Charles M. Graduated.
McCusker, James F. Resigned.
Bispham, Harrison A. Graduated.
Joynes, Walker W. Graduated. Honorably discharged 30 June, 1887.
Dieffenbach, Albert C. Graduated.
Culver, William W. Resigned.
Stebbins, Charles W. Turned back.
Strauss, Joseph. Graduated.

COMPLETE LIST

OF ALL THE

OFFICERS OF THE MARINE CORPS,

From 1798 to the Present Time.

COMMANDANTS.

BURROWS, WILLIAM W.
Major Commandant, 12 July, 1798. Lieutenant-Colonel Commandant, 1 May, 1800. Resigned 6 March, 1804.
WHORTON, FRANKLIN.
Captain, 3 August, 1798. Lieutenant-Colonel Commandant, 7 March, 1804. Died 1 September, 1818.
GALE, ANTHONY.
Second Lieutenant, 2 September, 1798. First Lieutenant, 2 March, 1799. Captain, 24 April, 1804. Lieutenant-Colonel Commandant, 3 March, 1819. Brevet Major, 24 April, 1814. Cashiered 18 October, 1820.
HENDERSON, ARCHIBALD.
Second Lieutenant, 4 June, 1806. First Lieutenant, 6 March, 1807. Captain, 1 April, 1811. Lieutenant-Colonel Commandant, 17 October, 1820. Colonel Commandant, 1 July, 1834. Brevet Lieutenant-Colonel, 17 October, 1820. Brevet Brigadier General, 27 January, 1837. Brevet Major, 1814. Died 6 January, 1859.
HARRIS, JOHN.
Second Lieutenant, 23 April, 1814. First Lieutenant, 18 June, 1814. Captain, 13 June, 1830. Major, 6 October, 1841. Colonel Commandant, 7 January, 1859. Brevet Captain, 3 March, 1825. Brevet Major, 27 January, 1837. Died 12 May, 1864.
ZEILIN, JACOB.
Second Lieutenant, 1 October, 1831. First Lieutenant, 12 September, 1836. Captain, 14 September, 1847. Major, 26 July, 1861. Colonel Commandant, 10 June, 1864. Brigadier General Commandant, 2 March, 1867. Brevet Major, 9 January, 1847. Retired 1 November, 1876. Died 18 November, 1880.
McCAWLEY, C. G.
Second Lieutenant, 3 March, 1847. First Lieutenant, 2 January, 1855. Captain, 26 July, 1861. Major, 10 June, 1864. Lieutenant-Colonel, 5 December, 1867. Colonel Commandant, 1 November, 1876. Brevet First Lieutenant, 13 September, 1847. Brevet Major, 8 September, 1863, for gallant and meritorious services at the night attack upon Fort Sumter, to date from 8 September, 1863. Retired January 29, 1891. Died October 13, 1891.
HEYWOOD, CHARLES.
Second Lieutenant, 5 April, 1858. First Lieutenant, 1861. Captain, 23 November, 1861. Major, 1 November, 1876. Lieutenant-Colonel, 9 March, 1888. Colonel Commandant, 30 January, 1891. Brigadier General Commandant, 3 March, 1899. Brevet Major, 8 March, 1862, for distinguished gallantry in the presence of the enemy, 8 March, 1862. Brevet Lieutenant-Colonel, 5 August, 1864, for gallant and meritorious services at the Battle of Mobile Bay, to date from 5 August, 1864. In service.

OFFICERS.

ADAMS, GEORGE.
Second Lieutenant, 19 March, 1845. Brevet First Lieutenant, 12 August, 1847. Died 21 October, 1856.
ADAMS, SAMUEL C.
Second Lieutenant, 25 November, 1861. First Lieutenant, 4 November, 1862. Drowned 1 April, 1864, Cairo, Illinois.
ALEXANDER, PHILIP.
Second Lieutenant, 7 November, 1800. First Lieutenant, 1 August, 1802. Resigned 31 March, 1803.
ALLEN, AUSTIN W.
Second Lieutenant, 10 February, 1838. Transferred to the Army, 26 November, 1838.
ALLEN, NATHANIEL.
Second Lieutenant, 3 April, 1810. Resigned 24 July, 1810.
ALLEN, SAMUEL K.
Second Lieutenant, 12 March, 1868. Retired 11 May, 1880. Died 18 February, 1884, at Greensboro, N. C.

(679)

GENERAL NAVY REGISTER—MARINE CORPS.

AMORY, WILLIAM.
Second Lieutenant, 25 July, 1798. First Lieutenant, 10 November, 1799. Resigned, date unknown.

ANDERSON, JEREMIAH.
Second Lieutenant, 11 June, 1811. Dismissed in September, 1811.

ANDERSON, WILLIAM.
Second Lieutenant, 17 February, 1807. First Lieutenant, 23 June, 1809. Captain, 18 June, 1814. Brevet Major, 18 June, 1824. Brevet Lieutenant-Colonel, 24 May, 1828. Died 13 June, 1830.

ANDRESEN, CHARLES G.
First Lieutenant, 13 April, 1899. Captain, 23 July, 1900. In service.

ARMISTEAD, F. N.
Second Lieutenant, 13 November, 1830. First Lieutenant, 1 July, 1834. Died 14 April, 1841.

ARROWSMITH, THOMAS.
Second Lieutenant, 19 April, 1812. Resigned in October, 1812.

ASHTON, RICHARD W.
Second Lieutenant, 28 January, 1817. Resigned 22 January, 1821.

AUCHMUTY, RICHARD.
Second Lieutenant, 28 February, 1815. First Lieutenant, 18 April, 1817. Brevet Captain, 18 April, 1827. Resigned 1 April, 1830.

BABB, MACKER.
First Lieutenant, 23 July, 1900. In service.

BACKSTROM, THEODORE E.
Second Lieutenant, 17 February, 1900. In service.

BACON, SAMUEL.
Second Lieutenant, 14 April, 1812. First Lieutenant, 8 July, 1812. Captain, 18 June, 1814. Resigned in November, 1815.

BACOTE, THOMAS W.
Second Lieutenant, 24 June, 1813. First Lieutenant, 18 June, 1812. Resigned 4 June, 1815.

BAINBRIDGE, THEODORE.
Second Lieutenant, 24 May, 1828. Resigned 18 January, 1832.

BAKER, ADAM N.
Second Lieutenant, 12 September, 1853. First Lieutenant, 1 August, 1860. Dismissed 23 May, 1861.

BAKER, D. D.
Second Lieutenant, 20 October, 1832. First Lieutenant, 30 December, 1837. Captain, 28 September, 1847. Brevet Captain, 13 September, 1847. Died 31 August, 1853.

BAKER, JOSEPH F.
Second Lieutenant, 5 June, 1861. First Lieutenant, 1 September, 1861. Captain, 22 June, 1864. Died 2 October, 1876.

BALL, WALTER.
Second Lieutenant, 1 July, 1894. Resigned 7 March, 1895.

BIGLOW, HORATIO R.
Second Lieutenant, 6 February, 1865. Resigned 28 February, 1870.

BISHOP, HENRY J.
Second Lieutenant, 25 November, 1861. First Lieutenant, 1 April, 1864. Captain, 12 January, 1876. Died 22 December, 1884.

BISHOP, GILES, Jr.
Second Lieutenant, 23 July, 1900. In service.

BISSET, HENRY O.
Second Lieutenant, 15 February, 1899. Captain, 3 March, 1899. In service.

BLAKE, DANIEL W.
Second Lieutenant, 26 February, 1900. In service.

BLOODGOOD, W. A.
Second Lieutenant, 3 March, 1821. Appointed Purser 2 May, 1834.

BOND, FRANCIS A.
Second Lieutenant, 1 March, 1815. Resigned in November, 1816.

BOON, LEONARD J.
Second Lieutenant, 7 July, 1812. First Lieutenant, 18 June, 1814. Disbanded 18 April, 1817, under Peace Establishment Act.

BOOTES, JAMES T.
First Lieutenant, 1 July, 1899. In service.

BORDEN, THOMAS S.
Second Lieutenant, 1 July, 1894. First Lieutenant, 11 August, 1898. Captain, 3 March, 1899. In service.

BORROUGH, JEHU A.
Second Lieutenant, 5 June, 1861. First Lieutenant, 1 September, 1861. Captain, 1 September, 1864. Died 28 November, 1867, West Indies.

BOSQUE, JOSEPH.
Second Lieutenant, 28 February, 1815. Died at New Orleans, 1815.

BOURNE, WILLIAM T.
Second Lieutenant, 5 August, 1824. Died 4 March, 1826.

BOYD, WILLIAM S.
Second Lieutenant, 12 January, 1848. First Lieutenant, 13 December, 1857. Captain, 26 July, 1861. Resigned 31 July, 1865.

BOYLE, JAMES H.
Second Lieutenant, 25 June, 1809. First Lieutenant, 27 April, 1810. Resigned in 1812.

BALDWIN, SAMUEL.
Second Lieutenant, 2 January, 1800. First Lieutenant, 10 December, 1801. Last appearance in Register of 1806.

BANNING, EDMUND P.
Second Lieutenant, 2 July, 1864. Resigned 13 April, 1870.

GENERAL NAVY REGISTER—MARINE CORPS. 681

BANNON, PHILIP M.
Second Lieutenant, 1 July, 1897. Captain, 3 March, 1899. First Lieutenant by Brevet for distinguished service in the battle at Guantanamo, Cuba, 13 June, 1898. In service.
BARCLAY, THOMAS.
Second Lieutenant, 18 August, 1799. First Lieutenant, 21 October, 1801. Resigned 31 May, 1802.
BARTLETT, HENRY A.
Second Lieutenant, 25 November, 1861. First Lieutenant, 26 November, 1861. Captain, 29 November, 1867. Major, 30 January, 1891. Retired 1 February, 1898.
BARTON, THOMAS B.
Second Lieutenant, 10 June, 1817. First Lieutenant, 17 October, 1820. Resigned 13 March, 1829.
BATES, GEORGE T.
Second Lieutenant, 19 February, 1873. First Lieutenant, 12 May, 1880. Captain, 2 May, 1891. Retired 2 May, 1891.
BATES, JOHN S.
First Lieutenant, 1 July, 1899. In service.
BAYLY, ROBERT P.
Second Lieutenant, 1 July, 1809. Died 26 August, 1809.
BEARSS, HIRAM I.
*First Lieutenant, 26 May, 1899. Captain, 23 July, 1900. In service.
BEAUMONT, JOHN C.
Second Lieutenant, 26 January, 1900. First Lieutenant, 23 July, 1900. In service.
BELL, DANIEL.
Second Lieutenant, 8 November, 1800. Resigned 14 February, 1801.
BELLVUE, F. B. DE.
Second Lieutenant, 24 April, 1812. First Lieutenant, 18 June, 1814. Captain, 3 March, 1819. Resigned 6 March, 1824.
BENSON, G. ROBERT.
Second Lieutenant, 17 December, 1873. First Lieutenant, 5 June, 1880. Died 29 April, 1892, at Sitka, Alaska.
BERKELEY, RANDOLPH C.
First Lieutenant, 13 April, 1899. Captain, 23 July, 1900. In service.
BERRETT, JOHN J.
Second Lieutenant, 19 November, 1840. Resigned 5 April, 1843.
BERRYMAN, O. C.
Second Lieutenant, 24 January, 1870. First Lieutenant, 16 November, 1877. Captain, 11 July, 1892. Major, 3 March, 1899. Lieutenant-Colonel, 15 August, 1900. In service.
BETTS, CHARLES.
Second Lieutenant, 28 March, 1820. Died 7 January, 1822.
BIDDLE, WILLIAM P.
Second Lieutenant, 19 June, 1875. First Lieutenant, 24 February, 1884. Captain, 7 February, 1894. Major, 3 March, 1899. In service.
BOYD, WILLIAM L.
Second Lieutenant, 17 September, 1813. First Lieutenant, 18 June, 1814. Resigned 26 July, 1814.
BRACKETT, WILLIAM.
Second Lieutenant, 11 September, 1900. In service.
BRADFORD, C. H.
Second Lieutenant, 25 November, 1861. First Lieutenant, 26 November, 1861. Died 13 February, 1864, from wounds received in battle.
BRADFORD, E. T.
Second Lieutenant, 18 December, 1868. First Lieutenant, 20 August, 1874. Resigned 15 November, 1877.
BRADMAN, FREDERICK L.
First Lieutenant, 8 April, 1899. Captain, 23 July, 1900. In service.
BRADY, THOMAS A.
Second Lieutenant, 3 February, 1837. First Lieutenant, 3 March, 1847. Died 7 November, 1847.
BRECKENRIDGE, H. B.
Second Lieutenant, 15 April, 1812. First Lieutenant, 18 June, 1814. Captain, 10 December, 1814. Disbanded 18 April, 1817, under Peace Establishment Act.
BRECKINRIDGE, JAMES C.
First Lieutenant, 13 April, 1899. Captain, 23 July, 1900. In service.
BREESE, JAMES B.
Second Lieutenant, 18 March, 1864. First Lieutenant, 1 May, 1868. Resigned 5 December, 1879.
BREVOORT, A. N.
Second Lieutenant, 28 March, 1820. First Lieutenant, 26 September, 1823. Captain, 6 March, 1838. Brevet Captain, 26 September, 1833. Died 26 November, 1866.
BREWERTON, G. D.
Second Lieutenant, 3 March, 1819. First Lieutenant, 17 September, 1821. Died 31 January, 1827.
BREWSTER, W. H.
Second Lieutenant, 24 January, 1838. Resigned 1 February, 1839.
BREWSTER, SIDNEY W.
Second Lieutenant, 17 February, 1900. In service.
BRITTON, ABRAHAM.
Second Lieutenant, 9 September, 1818. Resigned in 1818.
BROADHEAD, J. T.
Second Lieutenant, 12 April, 1872. In service.
BRODHEAD, JOHN T.
Second Lieutenant, 12 April, 1872. Resigned 14 November, 1879.

BROATCH, JAMES W.
Second Lieutenant, 1 July, 1899. First Lieutenant, 23 July, 1900. In service.
BROOKE, B. E.
Second Lieutenant, 8 July, 1833. First Lieutenant, 7 February, 1839. Died 28 November, 1858.
BROOKE, EDMUND.
Second Lieutenant, 15 April, 1814. First Lieutenant, 18 June, 1814. Resigned 13 February, 1817.
BROOKS, JOHN, Jr
Second Lieutenant, 1 October, 1807. First Lieutenant, 30 January, 1809. Killed in action, 10 September, 1813.
BROOM, CHARLES R.
Second Lieutenant, 27 July, 1813. First Lieutenant, 18 June, 1814. Paymaster and Captain. Captain, 7 March, 1824. Major, 12 September, 1836. Brevet Lieutenant-Colonel, 7 March, 1834. Died 14 November, 1840.
BROOM, JAMES.
Second Lieutenant, 21 April, 1810. First Lieutenant, 14 April, 1812. Killed in action, 1 June, 1813.
BROOM, JAMES.
Second Lieutenant, 28 December, 1836. Cashiered 6 July, 1838.
BROOME, JOHN L.
Second Lieutenant, 12 January, 1848. First Lieutenant, 28 September, 1857. Captain, 26 July, 1861. Major, 8 December, 1864. Lieutenant-Colonel, 16 March, 1879. Brevet Major, 24 April, 1862, for gallant and meritorious services. Brevet Lieutenant-Colonel, 14 March, 1863, for gallant and meritorious services at the second Battle of Vicksburg, 15 July, 1863. Retired 8 March, 1888. Died 12 April, 1898, at Binghampton, N. Y.
BROWN, PEREGRINE.
First Lieutenant, 25 June, 1776. Disbanded with the Navy of the Revolution.
BROWN, WILLIAM.
Second Lieutenant, 16 January, 1817. Died 19 June, 1818.
BROWN, PHILIP S.
First Lieutenant, 13 April, 1899. Captain, 23 July, 1900. In service.
BROWN, THOMAS H.
Second Lieutenant, 19 March, 1900. In service.
BROWN, W. R.
Second Lieutenant, 25 November, 1861. First Lieutenant, 18 August, 1862. Captain, 18 May, 1871. Major, 11 July, 1892. Retired 5 September, 1892. Died 2 August, 1894, at Torresdale, Pa.
BROWNING, R. L.
Second Lieutenant, 24 November, 1852. First Lieutenant, 29 November, 1858. Lost in the Levant.
BROWNLOW, W. L.
Second Lieutenant, 6 July, 1812. First Lieutenant, 18 June, 1814. Captain, 17 October, 1820. Died 17 July, 1821.
BRUNZELL, ALBERT N.
Second Lieutenant, 17 February, 1900. In service.
BUCHANAN, J. A.
Second Lieutenant, 3 March, 1847. Last appearance in Register for 1850.
BURKE, THOMAS P.
Second Lieutenant, 20 November, 1830. Cashiered 3 October, 1831.
BURNHAM, JAMES D.
Second Lieutenant, 1 July, 1825. Transferred to the Army, 30 June, 1826.
BUSH, WILLIAM S.
Second Lieutenant, 3 July, 1809. First Lieutenant, 4 March, 1811. Killed in action, 19 August, 1812.
BUTLER, GEORGE.
Second Lieutenant, 11 February, 1859. First Lieutenant, 9 July, 1861. Captain, 4 November, 1862. Major, 16 March, 1879. Brevet Major, 14 January, 1865, for gallant and meritorious services at the attack upon Fort Fisher, 13, 14 and 15 January, 1865. Died 23 February, 1884, at Portsmouth, N. H.
BUTLER, SMEDLEY D.
First Lieutenant, 8 April, 1899. Captain, 23 July, 1900. In service.
BURTON, NORMAN G.
First Lieutenant, 1 July, 1899. In service.
BUTTERFIELD, WILLIAM.
Second Lieutenant, 3 March, 1847. Resigned 1 May, 1858.
BUTTRICK, JAMES T.
Second Lieutenant, 23 July, 1900. In service.
CAFFREY, St. JOHN S.
Second Lieutenant, 26 January, 1900. First Lieutenant, 23 July, 1900. In service.
CALDWELL, HENRY.
Second Lieutenant, 2 September, 1798. First Lieutenant, 2 March, 1799. Captain, 23 January, 1809. Died 12 March, 1812.
CALDWELL, R. C.
Second Lieutenant, 17 October, 1834. First Lieutenant, 3 March, 1845. Died 13 November, 1852.
CAMMACK, WILLIAM.
First Lieutenant, 1 September, 1798. Resigned 31 December, 1800.
CAMPBELL, G. W.
Second Lieutenant, 14 October, 1852. Died 23 March, 1855.
CAMPBELL, CHANDLER.
Second Lieutenant, 11 September, 1900. In service.
CARMICK, DANIEL.
Captain, 3 August, 1798. Major, 7 March, 1809. Died in 1816.

GENERAL NAVY REGISTER—MARINE CORPS. 683

CARMODY, ROBERT E.
 First Lieutenant, 13 April, 1899. Disappeared from U. S. A. T. Relief, at sea, 23 October, 1899.
CARPENTER, HENRY W.
 First Lieutenant, 13 April, 1899. Captain, 23 July, 1900. In service.
CARPENTER, CHARLES C.
 Second Lieutenant, 1 July, 1899. First Lieutenant, 23 July, 1900. In service.
CATLIN, ALBERTUS W.
 Second Lieutenant, 1 July, 1892. First Lieutenant, 18 April, 1893. Captain, 3 March, 1899. In service.
CARTER, LANDON N.
 Second Lieutenant, 26 May, 1824. First Lieutenant, 7 April, 1832. Captain, 3 March, 1847. Died 26 September, 1847.
CARTTER, W. H.
 Second Lieutenant, 1 March, 1861. First Lieutenant, 1 September, 1861. Captain, 10 June, 1864. Dismissed 12 August, 1865.
CASH, JOHN C.
 Second Lieutenant, 16 March, 1845. First Lieutenant, 21 September, 1852. Paymaster, with the rank of Major, 1861. Major, 20 November, 1862. Died 8 March, 1877.
CHAMBERLIN, PAUL E.
 Second Lieutenant, 17 February, 1900. In service.
CHURCH, F. L.
 Second Lieutenant, 12 July, 1862. First Lieutenant, 13 August, 1865. Resigned 8 August, 1868.
CHURCH, JONATHAN.
 First Lieutenant, 5 September, 1798. Resigned 26 October, 1801.
CLARK, LEMUEL.
 Captain, 3 August, 1798. Resigned 30 November, 1801.
CLARK, N. S.
 Second Lieutenant, 20 April, 1812. Resigned 1812.
CLAYPOLE, JOHN.
 Second Lieutenant, 30 March, 1799. Resigned 23 December, 1800.
CLEMENTS, JAMES M.
 Second Lieutenant, 28 January, 1817. First Lieutenant, 28 March, 1820. Died 27 May, 1822.
CLIFFORD, WILLIAM H., Jr.
 First Lieutenant, 1 July, 1899. In service.
CLINCH, B.
 First Lieutenant, 5 September, 1798. Resigned 30 June, 1803.
CLINTON, THOMAS N.
 Second Lieutenant, 23 July, 1900. In service.
COCHRANE, HENRY C.
 Second Lieutenant, 7 September, 1861. First Lieutenant, 20 August, 1865. Captain, 16 March, 1879. Major, 1 February, 1898. Colonel, 3 March, 1899. In service.
COEJMAN, S. S.
 Second Lieutenant, 28 March, 1820. First Lieutenant, 8 March, 1824. Died 26 December, 1825.
COFFIN, H. G.
 Second Lieutenant, 4 May, 1866. Dismissed 17 February, 1872.
COHEN, D. M.
 Second Lieutenant, 19 August, 1855. First Lieutenant, 1861. Captain, 26 July, 1861. Major, 5 December, 1867. In service. Retired 12 October, 1869. Died 28 May, 1891, at New York.
COLE, ELI K.
 Second Lieutenant, 1 July, 1890. First Lieutenant, 5 June, 1892. Captain.
COLLIER, GEORGE W.
 Second Lieutenant, 5 September, 1860. First Lieutenant, 1 September, 1861. Captain, 20 November, 1862. Major, 18 April, 1880. Lieutenant-Colonel, 18 August, 1889. Retired 23 October, 1889. Died 23 December, 1892, at Hagerstown, Md.
COLLUM, RICHARD S.
 Second Lieutenant, 25 November, 1861. First Lieutenant, 30 December, 1862. Captain, 13 March, 1872. Assistant Quartermaster, 4 May, 1885. Quartermaster, with the rank of Major, 20 June, 1897. Retired 26 June, 1897.
COLTON, DIAMOND.
 First Lieutenant, 5 September, 1798. Resigned 24 June, 1799.
COLVOCORESSES, HAROLD.
 Second Lieutenant, 5 September, 1900. In service.
CONTEE, JOHN.
 Second Lieutenant, 17 April, 1812. First Lieutenant, 24 July, 1812. Resigned 15 September, 1813.
COOPER, GEORGE.
 Second Lieutenant, 28 March, 1820. Died 25 September, 1823.
CORRIE, F. H.
 Second Lieutenant, 25 November, 1861. First Lieutenant, 26 November, 1861. Captain, 12 February, 1870. Brevet Captain, 14 January, 1865, for gallant and meritorious services at the attack upon Fort Fisher, 13, 14, 15 January, 1865. Retired 18 December, 1885.
COSTON, H. H.
 Second Lieutenant, 9 March, 1865. First Lieutenant, 18 May, 1871. Captain, 9 March, 1888. Retired 14 June, 1892. Died 6 November, 1896, at Pensacola, Fla.
COWAN, WILLIAM.
 Second Lieutenant, 16 April, 1812. First Lieutenant, 20 August, 1812. Resigned 22 November, 1812.
COYLE, WILLIAM R.
 Second Lieutenant, 26 January, 1900. First Lieutenant, 23 July, 1900. In service.

GENERAL NAVY REGISTER—MARINE CORPS.

COXE, CHARLES D.
  Second Lieutenant, 18 November, 1805. First Lieutenant, 4 March, 1807. Resigned 18 September, 1809.
CRABB, JOHN.
  Second Lieutenant, 31 January, 1809. First Lieutenant, 28 June, 1809. Captain, 18 June, 1814. Disbanded 18 April, 1817, under Peace Establishment Act.
CRABB, HORATIO N.
  Second Lieutenant, 7 May, 1822. First Lieutenant, 23 February, 1830. Resigned 30 December, 1837.
CRANE, ICHABOD B.
  Second Lieutenant, 26 January, 1809. First Lieutenant, 28 June, 1809. Resigned 28 April, 1812.
CRUISE, LAWRENCE.
  Second Lieutenant, 29 July, 1806. Last appearance in Register of 1806.
CUMMINS, F. D.
  Second Lieutenant, 14 April, 1810. First Lieutenant, 1 April, 1811. Resigned 21 January, 1812.
CURTIS, JOSEPH W.
  Second Lieutenant, 4 May, 1840. First Lieutenant, 16 March, 1847. Dismissed 26 August, 1852.
CUTTS, RICHARD M.
  Second Lieutenant, 1 July, 1899. First Lieutenant, 23 July, 1900. In service.
DAVIS, KENT D.
  Second Lieutenant, 2 July, 1864. Died 11 January, 1865.
DAVIS, AUSTIN R.
  Second Lieutenant, 1 July, 1894. First Lieutenant, 2 June, 1898. Captain, 3 March, 1899. Killed in action at Tientsin, China, 13 July, 1900.
DAVIS, HENRY C.
  First Lieutenant, 8 April, 1899. Captain, 23 July, 1900. In service.
DALLAS, A. H.
  Second Lieutenant, 31 October, 1854. Resigned 24 September, 1855.
DANIELS, C. L.
  Second Lieutenant, 12 July, 1862. First Lieutenant, 13 February, 1865. Resigned 20 July, 1868.
DARLEY, JOHN.
  Second Lieutenant, 8 November, 1798. First Lieutenant, 10 April, 1800. Resigned 31 October, 1800.
DAWSON, L. L.
  Second Lieutenant, 13 January, 1859. First Lieutenant, 1861. Captain, 23 November, 1861. Major, 16 May, 1878. Brevet Major, 14 January, 1865. Brevet Major, for gallant and meritorious services at the attack upon Fort Fisher, 13, 14 and 15 January, 1865. Resigned 20 December, 1880.
DAWSON, WILLIAM C.
  Second Lieutenant, 1 July, 1894. First Lieutenant, 1 February, 1898. Captain, 3 March, 1899. In service.
DAY, JOHN H. A.
  First Lieutenant, 1 July, 1899. In service.
DEANE, BENJAMIN.
  Captain, 25 June, 1776. Disbanded with the Navy of the Revolution.
DELANO, FREDERICK H.
  First Lieutenant, 26 May, 1899. Captain, 23 July, 1900. In service.
DENNY, FRANK L.
  Second Lieutenant, 16 June, 1880. First Lieutenant, 23 December, 1884. Assistant Quartermater, with the rank of Captain, 26 February, 1892. Quartermaster, with the rank of Major, 27 June, 1897. Quartermaster, with the rank of Colonel, 3 March, 1899. In service.
De GRANPRE, P. B.
  Second Lieutenant, 26 April, 1812. First Lieutenant, 18 June, 1814. Disbanded 18 April, 1817, under Peace Establishment Act.
DESHA, ROBERT M.
  Second Lieutenant, 28 February, 1816. First Lieutenant, 12 April, 1817. Died 6 November, 1862.
DEVEREUX, A.
  Second Lieutenant, 25 November, 1861. Retired 31 March, 1864.
DEVLIN, JOHN S.
  Second Lieutenant, 21 February, 1839. First Lieutenant, 3 March, 1847. Cashiered 20 September, 1852.
DEWEY, RUPERT C.
  Second Lieutenant, 23 July, 1900. In service.
DICKINS, RANDOLPH.
  Second Lieutenant, 19 May, 1876. First Lieutenant, 2 March, 1884. Captain, 2 May, 1894. Major, 3 March, 1899. In service.
DIKEMAN, RAYMOND W.
  Second Lieutenant, 23 July, 1900. In service.
DIETERICH, J. P.
  Second Lieutenant, 17 October, 1834. Cashiered 27 April, 1838.
DIX, HENRY E.
  Second Lieutenant, 13 March, 1816. First Lieutenant, 18 April, 1817. Died 21 January, 1822.
DOUGHTY, ISAAC T.
  Second Lieutenant, 26 September, 1837. First Lieutenant, 3 March, 1847. Captain, 14 March, 1856. Major, 23 November, 1861. Retired 6 June, 1864. Died 21 June, 1890, at Poughkeepsie, N. Y.

GENERAL NAVY REGISTER—MARINE CORPS. 685

DOUGLASS, RICHARD.
Second Lieutenant, 7 May, 1822. Second Lieutenant, 26 April, 1825. Captain, 7 March, 1839. Died 20 April, 1851.
DOYEN, CHARLES A.
Second Lieutenant, 1 July, 1883. First Lieutenant, 24 October, 1889. Captain, 2 June, 1898. Major, 31 January, 1900. In service.
DRAPER, HERBERT L.
Second Lieutenant, 1 July, 1889. First Lieutenant, 1 July, 1891. Captain, 3 March, 1899. In service.
DULANY, WILLIAM.
Second Lieutenant, 10 June, 1817. First Lieutenant, 19 June, 1819. Captain, 1 July, 1834. Major, 17 November, 1847. Colonel, 26 July, 1861. Brevet Captain, 19 June, 1829. Brevet Major, 3 March, 1843. Brevet Lieutenant-Colonel, 13 September, 1847. Died 4 July, 1868.
DUNCAN, JOHN H.
Second Lieutenant, 16 January, 1817. Resigned 11 August, 1817.
DUNLAP, ROBERT H.
First Lieutenant, 8 April, 1899. Captain, 23 July, 1900. In service.
DUTTON, ROBERT McM.
Second Lieutenant, 1 July, 1891. First Lieutenant, 17 March, 1893. Captain, 3 March, 1899. In service.
DUVAL, SINGLETON.
Second Lieutenant, 1 March, 1815. Resigned in October, 1816.
EDELIN, JAMES.
Second Lieutenant, 1 March, 1815. First Lieutenant, 18 April, 1817. Captain, 1 July, 1834. Major, 14 September, 1847. Lieutenant-Colonel, 7 January, 1859. Brevet Captain, 18 April, 1827. Died 13 July, 1869.
EDSON, ALVIN.
Second Lieutenant, 7 May, 1822. First Lieutenant, 14 March, 1829. Captain, 6 October, 1841. Died 15 July, 1847.
EDWARDS, JAMES L.
Second Lieutenant, 18 June, 1811. Resigned in February, 1813.
EDWARDS, PHILIP.
First Lieutenant, 3 August, 1798. Killed in a duel 26 October, 1800.
ELA, F. P.
Second Lieutenant, 24 January, 1870. Drowned in the East Indies, 19 February, 1874.
ELLIOTT, GEORGE F.
Second Lieutenant, 12 October, 1870. First Lieutenant, 30 March, 1878. Captain, 15 June, 1892. Major, 3 March, 1899. Lieutenant-Colonel, 11 September, 1899. In service.
ELLIOTT, STEPHEN.
Second Lieutenant, 1 July, 1899. First Lieutenant, 23 July, 1900. In service.
ELLSWORTH, H. G.
Second Lieutenant, 4 April, 1870. First Lieutenant, 19 November, 1877. Died 24 June, 1890, at Mare Island, Cal.
ENGLISH, GEORGE B.
Second Lieutenant, 1 March, 1815. Resigned in 1817.
ENGLISH, THOMAS S.
Second Lieutenant, 10 June, 1817. First Lieutenant, 11 August, 1819. Captain, 1 June, 1834. Major, 18 February, 1853. Brevet Captain, 11 August, 1829. Died 26 March, 1871.
ESLICK, FRED M.
Second Lieutenant, 8 December, 1899. First Lieutenant, 23 July, 1900. In service.
EVANS, FRANK E.
Second Lieutenant, 26 January, 1900. First Lieutenant, 23 July, 1900. In service.
FAGAN, LOUIS E.
Second Lieutenant, 14 June, 1862. First Lieutenant, 8 December, 1864. Captain, 16 May, 1878. Brevet First Lieutenant, 8 September, 1863, for gallant and meritorious services at the night attack upon Fort Sumter, 8 Sepember, 1863. Brevet Captain, 14 January, 1865, for gallant and meritorious services at the attack upon Fort Fisher, 13, 14, 15 January, 1865. Retired 14 June, 1892. Died 4 January, 1894, at Washington, D. C.
FAUNT LE ROY, ROBERT P.
First Lieutenant, 8 April, 1899. Assistant Quartermaster, with the rank of Captain, 27 May, 1899. In service.
FAY, WILLIAM G.
Second Lieutenant, 21 March, 1900. In service.
FELAND, LOGAN.
First Lieutenant, 1 July, 1899. In service.
FENDALL, P. R., Jr.
Second Lieutenant, 17 October, 1857. First Lieutenant, 1861. Captain, 26 July, 1861. Major, 1 November, 1876. Brevet Major, 17 June, 1870, for gallant and meritorious conduct at the Battles of Hatteras Inlet, Port Royal, Sewell's Point, Ocrakoke Inlet, Savannah and James Rivers, to date from 7 June, 1870. Retired 15 May, 1878. Died 21 March, 1879.
FENWICK, JOHN R.
Second Lieutenant, 10 November, 1799. First Lieutenant, 1 December, 1801. Captain, 13 August, 1809. Resigned 1 April, 1811.
FIELD, THOMAS Y.
Second Lieutenant, 3 March, 1847. First Lieutenant, 15 October, 1854. Captain, 30 May, 1861. Major, 10 June, 1864. Lieutenant-Colonel, 1 November, 1876. Colonel, 18 April, 1880. Brevet First Lieutenant, 13 September, 1847. Retired 17 August, 1889.

GENERAL NAVY REGISTER—MARINE CORPS.

FILETTE, T. G.
Second Lieutenant, 22 June, 1880. First Lieutenant, 16 July, 1886. Dismissed 29 June, 1894.
FISHER, H. C.
Second Lieutenant, 7 September, 1871. First Lieutenant, 27 September, 1879. Captain, 16 March, 1893. Retired 16 March, 1893.
FLINT, KINGMAN.
Second Lieutenant, 1863. Died 15 October, 1863.
FLOYD, C. C.
Second Lieutenant, 9 September, 1818. First Lieutenant, 24 March, 1821. Resigned 1 December, 1824.
FONTANE, P. H. W.
Second Lieutenant, 22 February, 1857. First Lieutenant, 1861. Captain, 26 July, 1861. Resigned 19 May, 1864.
FOOTE, YANDELL.
Second Lieutenant, 17 February, 1900. In service.
FORD, CHRISTOPHER.
Second Lieutenant, 1 March, 1815. First Lieutenant, 18 April, 1817. Resigned 13 June, 1819.
FORD, R. O'NEILL.
Second Lieutenant, 25 November, 1861. First Lieutenant, 6 February, 1864. Resigned 30 April, 1868.
FORDE, HENRY H.
Second Lieutenant, 1 February, 1809. First Lieutenant, 14 April, 1810. Captain, 18 June, 1814. Cashiered in 1816.
FORNEY, JAMES.
Second Lieutenant, 1 March, 1861. First Lieutenant, 1 September, 1861. Captain, 23 April, 1864. Major, 24 February, 1884. Lieutenant-Colonel, 30 January, 1891. Colonel, 11 July, 1892. Brevet Captain, 24 April, 1862, for gallant and meritorious services at the attack upon Forts Jackson and St. Philip, 24 April, 1862. Brevet Major, 15 April, 1869, for meritorious services in defeating a rebel raid at Gunpowder Bridge, in July, 1864. Brevet Lieutenant-Colonel, 15 March, 1870, for gallant and meritorious services in the action with the savages at Formosa, 13 July, 1867. In service.
FOSTER, JOSEPH.
Second Lieutenant, 29 June, 1809. First Lieutenant, 27 April, 1810. Last appearance in Register, 1810.
FOWLER, H. W.
Second Lieutenant, 26 May, 1824. First Lieutenant, 2 May, 1834. Resigned 8 June, 1836.
FREEMAN, W. H.
Second Lieutenant, 17 August, 1812. First Lieutenant, 18 June, 1814. Captain, 17 July, 1821. Major, 1 July, 1834. Brevet Lieutenant-Colonel, 20 February, 1832. Died 11 March, 1843.
FRENCH, L. P.
Second Lieutenant, 14 June, 1862. First Lieutenant, 23 April, 1864. Resigned 30 December, 1873.
FREYER, ELI T.
Second Lieutenant, 21 March, 1900. In service.
FULLER, BEN H.
Second Lieutenant, 1 July, 1891. First Lieutenant, 16 March, 1893. Captain, 3 March, 1899. In service.
GABAUDAN, E. C.
Second Lieutenant, 18 March, 1864. Died 25 March, 1868.
GAMBLE, JOHN M.
Second Lieutenant, 16 January, 1809. First Lieutenant, 5 March, 1811. Captain, 18 June, 1814. Major, 1 July, 1834. Brevet Major, 19 April, 1816. Brevet Lieutenant-Colonel, 3 March, 1827. Died 11 September, 1836.
GARDNER, HENRY W.
Second Lieutenant, 10 June, 1817. First Lieutenant, 8 October, 1819. Died 26 April, 1825.
GARDNER, ROBERT.
Second Lieutenant, 3 February, 1809. Died, date not known.
GARLAND, ADDISON.
Second Lieutenant, 17 October, 1834. First Lieutenant, 15 November, 1840. Captain, 15 October, 1854. Major, 26 July, 1861. Brevet Captain, 10 March, 1847. Died 20 June, 1864.
GARRARD, W. C.
Second Lieutenant, 1815. Resigned 31 May, 1815.
GASSAWAY, JOHN.
Second Lieutenant, 18 June, 1810. Resigned 29 December, 1810.
GEDDIS, S. W.
First Lieutenant, 26 July, 1798. Resigned 9 April, 1801.
GIBSON, S. H.
Second Lieutenant, 5 October, 1869. First Lieutenant, 3 October, 1876. Retired 6 January, 1888.
GILLESPIE, A. H.
Second Lieutenant, 30 October, 1832. First Lieutenant, 18 January, 1838. Captain, November, 1847. Brevet Major, 6 December, 1846. Resigned 14 October, 1854.
GILMAN, HOWARD K.
Second Lieutenant, 24 June, 1880. First Lieutenant, 19 December, 1885. Resigned 22 December, 1890.
GILMORE, WILLIAM.
Second Lieutenant, 25 June, 1776. Disbanded with the Navy of the Revolution.

GENERAL NAVY REGISTER—MARINE CORPS. 687

GILSON, ROBERT M.
First Lieutenant, 8 April, 1899. Captain, 23 July, 1900. In service.
GLISSON, H. Y.
Second Lieutenant, 27 February, 1866. Died 13 August, 1867.
GOLDSBOROUGH, L. M.
Second Lieutenant, 1 March, 1861. First Lieutenant, 1 September, 1861. Died 15 October, 1863.
GOODLOE, G. C.
Second Lieutenant, 21 April, 1869. First Lieutenant, 12 January, 1876. Paymaster, with the rank of Major, 17 March, 1877. Paymaster, with the rank of Colonel, 3 March, 1899. In service.
GOODRELL, MANCIL C.
Second Lieutenant, 9 March, 1865. First Lieutenant, 16 April, 1870. Captain, 16 July, 1886. Lieutenant-Colonel, 3 March, 1899. In service.
GRAHAM, GEORGE R.
Second Lieutenant, 27 July, 1847. First Lieutenant, 22 October, 1856. Captain, 26 July, 1861. Major, 21 June, 1864. Retired 1 January, 1876. Died 20 July, 1889, at Washington, D. C.
GRANT, OSCAR B.
Second Lieutenant, 25 November, 1861. First Lieutenant, 26 November, 1861. Resigned 23 April, 1862.
GRAYSON, ALFRED.
Second Lieutenant, 26 July, 1810. First Lieutenant, 14 April, 1812. Brevet Captain, 18 June, 1814. Died 28 June, 1823.
GRAYSON, JOHN C.
Second Lieutenant, 4 May, 1840. First Lieutenant, 16 March, 1847. Captain, 7 January, 1859. Retired 22 April, 1864. Died 3 February, 1888, at Clinton Heights, Pa.
GREEN, FARNIFOLD.
Second Lieutenant, 23 February, 1830. First Lieutenant, 19 July, 1855. Resigned 6 June, 1831.
GREEN, ISRAEL.
Second Lieutenant, 3 March, 1847. Dismissed 18 May, 1861.
GREENLEAF, ROBERT.
Second Lieutenant, 16 March, 1801. First Lieutenant, 4 April, 1805. Captain, 19 January, 1811. Died in 1815.
GREEN, RICHARD D.
Second Lieutenant, 1 March, 1815. Resigned 1 April, 1823.
GREENE, EDWARD A.
Second Lieutenant, 23 July, 1900. In service.
GRIDLEY, JOHN P. V.
Second Lieutenant, 26 March, 1900. In service.
GRIMES, JOHN H.
Second Lieutenant, 5 June, 1861. First Lieutenant, 1 September, 1861. Captain, 13 August, 1865. Dismissed 11 February, 1870.
GRYMES, CHARLES.
Second Lieutenant, 3 March, 1819. First Lieutenant, 17 July, 1821. Brevet Captain, 20 July, 1831. Died 25 July, 1834.
GULICK, LOUIS J.
Second Lieutenant, 22 June, 1874. First Lieutenant, 21 December, 1880. Captain, 18 April, 1893. Retired 18 April, 1893. Died 20 April, 1896, at New York, N. Y.
GULICK, LOUIS M.
First Lieutenant, 26 May, 1899. Captain, 23 July, 1900. In service.
GUNN, C. C.
Second Lieutenant, 12 September, 1812. Resigned in 1812.
HAINES, HENRY C.
Second Lieutenant, 1 July, 1883. First Lieutenant, 18 June, 1890. Captain, 11 August, 1898. Major, 15 August, 1900. In service.
HALE, W. H.
Second Lieutenant, 5 June, 1861. First Lieutenant, 1 September, 1861. Captain, 8 December, 1864. Died 28 August, 1867.
HALFORD, FRANK.
Second Lieutenant, 23 July, 1900. In service.
HALL, EDWARD.
Second Lieutenant, 15 April, 1799. Captain, 23 January, 1809. Resigned 13 August, 1809.
HALL, FRANCIS C.
Second Lieutenant, 5 July, 1825. First Lieutenant, 1 July, 1834. Captain, 16 March, 1847. Died 13 July, 1853.
HALL, JOSEPH C.
Second Lieutenant, 10 June, 1817. First Lieutenant, 3 March, 1819. Brevet Captain, 3 March, 1829. Died 17 May, 1833.
HALL, JOHN.
First Lieutenant, 2 August, 1798. Captain, 1 December, 1801. Major, 8 June, 1814. Disbanded 18 April, 1817, under Peace Establishment Act.
HALL, WILLIAM.
Second Lieutenant, 18 April, 1812. First Lieutenant, 24 September, 1813. Captain, 18 December, 1814. Disbanded 18 April, 1817, under Peace Establishment Act.
HALL, NEWT H.
Second Lieutenant, 1 July, 1897. Captain, 3 March, 1899. In service.
HALL, DICKINSON P.
First Lieutenant, 1 July, 1899. In service.
HAMERSLY, LEWIS RANDOLPH.
Second Lieutenant, 23 July, 1866. Resigned 21 September, 1869.
HANNA, CHARLES S.
Second Lieutenant, 23 April, 1810. First Lieutenant, 14 April, 1812. Captain, 18 June, 1814. Disbanded 18 April, 1817, under Peace Establishment Act.

GENERAL NAVY REGISTER—MARINE CORPS.

HARDING, ARTHUR E.
 First Lieutenant, 1 July, 1899. In service.
HARDING, LEOF M.
 First Lieutenant, 1 July, 1899. In service.
HARDY, J. L. C.
 Second Lieutenant, 3 March, 1823. First Lieutenant, 13 June, 1830. Captain, 3 March, 1847. Died 26 November, 1853.
HARDY, JOSEPH.
 Captain, 25 June, 1776. Disbanded with the Navy of the Revolution.
HARLLEE, WILLIAM C.
 Second Lieutenant, 17 February, 1900. First Lieutenant, 23 July, 1900. In service.
HARWOOD, RICHARD.
 First Lieutenant, 10 July, 1798. Resigned 10 November, 1799.
HARRINGTON, F. M.
 Second Lieutenant, 8 December, 1864. First Lieutenant, 13 October, 1869. Captain, 4 May, 1885. Major, 10 August, 1898. Lieutenant-Colonel, 3 March, 1899. Colonel, 15 August, 1900. In service.
HARRIS, LLOYD G.
 Second Lieutenant, 9 March, 1865. Resigned 25 April, 1868.
HARRIS, JOHN C.
 Second Lieutenant, 25 November, 1861. First Lieutenant, 16 February, 1864. Brevet First Lieutenant, 24 April, 1862, for gallant and meritorious serivecs at the attack upon Forts Jackson and St. Philip, 24 April, 1862. Resigned 31 July, 1869.
HARRISON, RICHARD.
 Second Lieutenant, 25 June, 1776. Disbanded with the Navy of the Revolution.
HASIL, ANDREW.
 Second Lieutenant, 1808. First Lieutenant, 23 January, 1809. Resigned 2 August, 1809.
HATCH, CHARLES S.
 First Lieutenant, 13 April, 1899. Captain, 23 July, 1900. In service.
HAVERSTICK, JOHN W.
 Second Lieutenant, 18 March, 1864. Resigned 27 September, 1869.
HAYCOCK, GEORGE B.
 Second Lieutenant, 10 March, 1863. First Lieutenant, 20 June, 1866. Captain, 18 April, 1880. Brevet Captain, 7 June, 1870, for gallant and meritorious services at Gunpowder Bridge, in July, 1864, to date from 7 June, 1870. Retired 19 March, 1883.
HAYES, EDGAR.
 Second Lieutenant, 23 July, 1900. In service.
HAYS, A. J.
 Second Lieutenant, 4 December, 1847. First Lieutenant, 17 July, 1857. Resigned 1 March, 1861.
HEATH, JOHN.
 Second Lieutenant, 18 April, 1811. First Lieutenant, 31 May, 1812. Captain, 18 June, 1814. Disbanded 18 April, 1817, under Peace Establishment Act.
HEBB, C. D.
 Second Lieutenant, 14 March, 1856. First Lieutenant, 1861. Captain, 26 July, 1861. Major, 12 January, 1870. Lieutenant-Colonel, 18 April, 1880. Colonel, 18 August, 1889. Retired 10 July, 1892. Died 23 June, 1897, at Washington, D. C.
HEISLER, GEORGE.
 Second Lieutenant, 25 November, 1861. Died 12 July, 1862.
HENDERSON, C. A.
 Second Lieutenant, 16 March, 1847. First Lieutenant, 10 December, 1855. Brevet First Lieutenant, 13 September, 1847. Dismissed 22 July, 1863.
HENDERSON, DANIEL.
 First Lieutenant, 25 June, 1776. Disbanded with the Navy of the Revolution.
HERBERT, HILARY A., JR.
 Second Lieutenant, 5 December, 1900. In service.
HERVILLY, D', JAMES.
 Second Lieutenant, 5 March, 1872. Resigned 1 May, 1880.
HIGBEE, JOHN H.
 Second Lieutenant, 9 March, 1861. First Lieutenant, 1 September, 1861. Captain, 10 June, 1864. Major, 18 August, 1889. Lieutenant-Colonel, 11 July, 1892. Retired 1 June, 1898. Brevet Captain, 25 May, 1863, for gallant and meritorious serivces at Port Hundson and Grand Gulf, 25 May, 1863.
HILL, CHARLES S.
 First Lieutenant, 8 April, 1899. Captain, 23 July, 1900. In service.
HIRSHINGER, HERBERT J.
 Second Lieutenant, 11 January, 1900. First Lieutenant, 23 July, 1900. In service.
HITCHCOCK, ROBERT E.
 Second Lieutenant, 5 June, 1861. Killed in action, 21 July, 1861, Bull Run.
HOFF, H. B.
 Second Lieutenant, 25 November, 1861. First Lieutenant, 26 November, 1861. Died 17 August, 1862.
HOIST, THOMAS.
 Second Lieutenant, 14 January, 1799. Last appearance in Register of 1799.
HOLCOMB, THOMAS, JR.
 Second Lieutenant, 21 March, 1900. In service.
HOLMES, GEORGE.
 Second Lieutenant, 8 March, 1849. Resigned 28 February, 1861.
HOOKER, RICHARD S.
 Second Lieutenant, 17 February, 1900. First Lieutenant, 23 July, 1900. In service.
HOOPER, THOMAS W.
 Second Lieutenant, 19 February, 1801. First Lieutenant, 1 September, 1802. Resigned 10 March, 1807.
HOPKINS, S. G.
 Second Lieutenant, 28 April, 1810. Last appearance in Register of 1810.

GENERAL NAVY REGISTER—MARINE CORPS. 689

HOPKINS, WILLIAM.
First Lieutenant, 1 July, 1899. In service.
HOUSTON, GEORGE P.
Second Lieutenant, 23 October, 1860. First Lieutenant, 1 September, 1861. Captain, 6 February, 1864. Major, 21 December, 1880. Lieutenant-Colonel, 24 October, 1889. Retired 1 February, 1891. Died 7 February, 1897, at Baltimore, Md. Brevet Major, 5 August, 1864, for gallant and meritorious services at the Battle of Mobile Bay, to date 5 August, 1864.
HOWARD, JOHN.
Second Lieutenant, 4 June, 1799. First Lieutenant, 1 July, 1801. Resigned 16 February, 1807.
HOWELL, BECKET J.
Second Lieutenant, 1 August, 1860. Resigned 1 March, 1861.
HOWLE, PARKE G.
Second Lieutenant, 1 March, 1815. First Lieutenant, 18 April, 1817. Brevet Captain, Adjutant and Inspector, with rank of Major. Captain, 1 July, 1834. Brevet Captain, 18 April, 1827. Died 16 July, 1857.
HOYT, SAMUEL.
Second Lieutenant, 5 June, 1809. Resigned 14 March, 1810.
HUEY, JAMES McE.
Second Lieutenant, 2 October, 1899. First Lieutenant, 23 July, 1900. In service.
HUGER, JACOB M.
Second Lieutenant, 1 May, 1799. Died 8 November, 1799.
HUMPHREY, C. H.
Second Lieutenant, 10 March, 1863. Resigned in 1864.
HUNTINGTON, R. W.
Second Lieutenant, 5 June, 1861. First Lieutenant, 1 September, 1861. Captain, 21 June, 1864. Major, 24 October, 1889. Lieutenant-Colonel, 2 February, 1897. Colonel, 10 August, 1898. Retired 10 January, 1899.
HYDE, BENJAMIN.
Second Lieutenant, 2 July, 1812. First Lieutenant, 1813. Died 10 February, 1815.
INGATE, CLARENCE L. A.
Second Lieutenant, 1 July, 1890. First Lieutenant, 30 April, 1892. Captain, 3 March, 1899. Died 24 December, 1899, at Agana, Guam, Lad. I.
INGRAHAM, H. L.
Second Lieutenant, 16 July, 1858. Resigned 8 March, 1861.
IRVING, EDGAR.
Second Lieutenant, 1 October, 1833. Resigned 27 February, 1835.
JACKSON, SAMUEL S.
Second Lieutenant, 22 June, 1880. First Lieutenant, 7 January, 1888. Died 26 October, 1890, at Boston, Mass.
JAMES, JAMES.
First Lieutenant, 9 August, 1798. Resigned 20 May, 1799.
JOHNSON, JOHN.
Second Lieutenant, 23 May, 1800. First Lieutenant, 1 June, 1802. Resigned in 1809.
JOHNSON, SAMUEL B.
Second Lieutenant, April, 1814. First Lieutenant, 16 July, 1814. Died 19 May, 1820.
JOLLY, WADE L.
Second Lieutenant, 2 October, 1899. First Lieutenant, 23 July, 1900. In service.
JONAS, EDWIN A.
First Lieutenant, 26 May, 1899. In service.
JONES, EDWARD.
Second Lieutenant, 7 January, 1859. Resigned 22 October, 1860.
JONES, JAMES H.
Second Lieutenant, 3 March, 1847. First Lieutenant, 1 September, 1853. Captain, 7 May, 1861. Lieutenant-Colonel, 10 June, 1864. Colonel, 16 March, 1879. Died 17 April, 1880.
JONES, ROGER.
Second Lieutenant, 26 January, 1809. First Lieutenant, 28 June, 1809. Resigned 7 July, 1812.
JUNKIN, WILLIAM D. A.
Second Lieutenant, 3 December, 1900. In service.
KANE, THEODORE P.
Second Lieutenant, 1 July, 1890. First Lieutenant, 15 June, 1892. Captain, 3 March, 1899. In service.
KARMANY, LINCOLN.
Second Lieutenant, 1 July, 1883. First Lieutenant, 18 August, 1889. Captain, 1 February, 1898. Major, 11 January, 1900. In service.
KEENE, NEWTON.
Second Lieutenant, 22 December, 1798. First Lieutenant, 1 November, 1800. Resigned 1 November, 1805.
KELLOGG, LYMAN.
Second Lieutenant, 3 July, 1812. First Lieutenant, 18 June, 1814. Captain, 3 March, 1819. Resigned 9 February, 1820.
KELTON, ALLAN C.
Second Lieutenant, 31 March, 1869. First Lieutenant, 1 April, 1875. Captain, 18 June, 1890. Major, 3 March, 1899. Lieutenant-Colonel, 11 January, 1900. In service.
KENNEDY, H. W.
Second Lieutenant, 1 March, 1815. Resigned 9 November, 1816.
KENNEDY, PHILIP C.
Second Lieutenant, 14 February, 1861. First Lieutenant, 2 September, 1861. Captain, 1864. Died 31 August, 1864.
KIDD, ROBERT.
Second Lieutenant, 25 November, 1861. First Lieutenant, 26 November, 1861. Dismissed 29 December, 1862.

44

GENERAL NAVY REGISTER—MARINE CORPS.

KINTZING, M. R.
Second Lieutenant, 8 September, 1841. First Lieutenant, 16 March, 1847. Captain, 1 August, 1860. Lieutenant-Colonel, 10 June, 1864. Colonel, 5 December, 1867. Retired 15 March, 1879. Died 9 December, 1893, at Brooklyn, N. Y.
KIPP, HOWARD H.
Second Lieutenant, 3 December, 1900. In service.
KIRKLAND, D. W.
Second Lieutenant, 26 June, 1855. Resigned 28 August, 1860.
KUHN, JOSEPH L.
Second Lieutenant, 27 July, 1813. First Lieutenant, 18 June, 1814. Captain, 25 June, 1823. Dismissed 7 April, 1832.
LANDER, FRANK C.
Second Lieutenant, 15 March, 1900. In service.
LANE, RUFUS H.
Second Lieutenant, 1 July, 1893. First Lieutenant, 28 January, 1896. Captain, 3 March, 1899. In service.
LANE, ENOCH S.
Second Lieutenant, 27 February, 1801. Died 16 July, 1804.
LANG, WILLIAM.
Second Lieutenant, 30 September, 1831. First Lieutenant, 21 June, 1836. Captain, 16 January, 1847. Died 6 May, 1850.
LAUCHHEIMER, CHARLES H.
Second Lieutenant, 1 July, 1883. First Lieutenant, 9 January, 1890. Captain, 10 August, 1898. Assistant Adjutant and Inspector with rank of Major, 3 March, 1899. In service.
LAY, HARRY R.
Second Lieutenant, 26 January, 1900. First Lieutenant, 23 July, 1900. In service.
LEE, HARRY.
First Lieutenant, 13 April, 1899. Captain, 23 July, 1900. In service.
LEE, THOMAS.
Second Lieutenant, 4 November, 1826. Resigned 30 September, 1831.
LEGGE, THOMAS W.
Second Lieutenant, 16 August, 1812. First Lieutenant, 1814. Resigned in 1816.
LEJEUNE, JOHN A.
Second Lieutenant, 1 July, 1890. First Lieutenant, 26 February, 1892. Captain, 3 March, 1899. In service.
LEMLY, WILLIAM B.
First Lieutenant, 8 April, 1899. Assistant Quartermaster with rank of Captain, 27 May, 1899. In service.
LEONARD, HENRY.
First Lieutenant, 8 April, 1899. Captain, 23 July, 1900. In service.
LEWIS, JAMES.
Second Lieutenant, 25 September, 1855. First Lieutenant, 1861. Captain, 26 July, 1861. Major, 13 October, 1869. Resigned 11 January, 1876.
LEWIS, JOHN L.
Second Lieutenant, 9 August, 1798. First Lieutenant, 24 June, 1799. Resigned 23 June, 1801.
LILLY, REUBEN.
First Lieutenant, 9 September, 1798. Died 9 April, 1800.
LINDSAY, G. F.
Second Lieutenant, 1 April, 1823. First Lieutenant, 23 September, 1831. Captain, 3 March. 1847. Died 27 September, 1857.
LINDSAY, G. F., Jr.
Second Lieutenant, 16 March, 1847. Resigned 31 December, 1852.
LINTON, THOMAS A.
Second Lieutenant, 28 February, 1815. First Lieutenant, 18 April, 1817. Captain, 7 April, 1872. Major, 12 March, 1845. Brevet Captain, 18 April, 1827. Died 17 February, 1853.
LITTLE, M. M.
Second Lieutenant, 17 May, 1822. Resigned 25 February, 1825.
LITTLE, LOUIS M.
Second Lieutenant, 1 July, 1899. First Lieutenant, 23 July, 1900. In service.
LLEWELLIN, SAMUEL.
Second Lieutenant, 12 January, 1799. First Lieutenant, 1 October, 1801. Resigned 1 August, 1805.
LOGAN, SAMUEL J.
Second Lieutenant, 26 April, 1875. First Lieutenant, 12 December, 1883. Retired 25 September, 1885.
LONG, CHARLES G.
Second Lieutenant, 1 July, 1891. First Lieutenant, 6 September, 1892. Captain, 3 March, 1899. In service.
LONG, HENRY D. F.
Second Lieutenant, 26 January, 1900. First Lieutenant, 23 July, 1900. In service.
LOOMIS, ERASTUS.
Second Lieutenant, 28 February, 1816. Resigned 15 July, 1816.
LORD, CHARLES.
Second Lieutenant, 27 September, 1813. First Lieutenant, 18 June, 1814. Died 30 October, 1821.
LOVE, MARSHALL.
Second Lieutenant, 3 April, 1830. Died 28 July, 1832.
LOVE, JOHN C.
Second Lieutenant, 20 July, 1804. First Lieutenant, 4 July, 1805. Died 13 May, 1807.
LOW, THEODORE H.
Second Lieutenant, 1 July, 1894. First Lieutenant, 3 March, 1899. Captain, 3 March, 1899. In service.

GENERAL NAVY REGISTER—MARINE CORPS. 691

LOW, WILLIAM W.
  First Lieutenant, 1 July, 1899. In service.
LOWE, DAVID.
  First Lieutenant, 25 June, 1776. Disbanded with the Navy of the Revolution.
LOWRY, H. B.
  Second Lieutenant, 25 November, 1861. First Lieutenant, 26 November, 1861. Assistant Quartermaster, with rank of Captain. Quartermaster, with the rank of Major, 4 May, 1885. Captain, 16 October, 1869. Brevet Captain, 8 September, 1863, for gallant and meritorious services at the night attack upon Fort Sumter, 8 September 1863. Retired 19 June, 1897.
LOWRY, JOHN.
  Second Lieutenant, 7 May, 1822. Resigned 30 June, 1825.
LUCAS, LEWIS C.
  Second Lieutenant, 1 July, 1891. First Lieutenant, 15 June, 1892. Captain, 3 March, 1899. In service.
LUCKET, LLOYD.
  Second Lieutenant, 5 July, 1812. Last appearance in Register of 1812.
LUCKET, NELSON.
  Second Lieutenant, 1807. First Lieutenant, 26 January, 1809. Resigned in 1812.
LYMAN, CHARLES H.
  First Lieutenant, 1 July, 1899. In service.
LYNCH, JAMES W.
  First Lieutenant, 1 July, 1899. In service.
LYONS, THOMAS F.
  First Lieutenant 16 June, 1899. In service.
MACKLIN, CHARLES F.
  Second Lieutenant, 1 July, 1894. Resigned 30 June, 1896.
MACOMBER, BENJAMIN.
  Second Lieutenant, 28 March, 1820. First Lieutenant, 2 April, 1823. Captain, 8 January, 1838. Major, 7 January, 1859. Brevet Captain, 2 April, 1833. Died in 1861.
MADDOX, W. A. T.
  Second Lieutenant, 14 October, 1837. First Lieutenant, 3 March, 1847. Assistant Quartermaster with rank of Captain. Major, 26 October, 1857. Brevet Captain, 3 January, 1847. Retired 3 January, 1880. Died 1 January, 1889, at West Washington, D. C.
MADISON, A. L. B.
  Second Lieutenant, 30 June, 1809. First Lieutenant, 16 November, 1810. Resigned 16 April, 1812.
MADISON, AMBROSE.
  Second Lieutenant, 1817. Resigned 21 July, 1818.
MAGILL, LOUIS J.
  Second Lieutenant, 1 July, 1895. First Lieutenant, 13 June, 1898. Captain, 3 March, 1899. First Lieutenant by Brevet for good judgment and gallantry in battle at Guantanamo, Cuba, 13 June, 1898. Captain by Brevet for good judgment and gallantry in battle at Guantanamo, Cuba, 13 June, 1898. In service.
MAGUIRE, JAMES.
  Second Lieutenant, 28 February, 1839. Resigned 25 January, 1842.
MAHONEY, JAMES E.
  Second Lieutenant, 1 July, 1883. First Lieutenant, 1 July, 1890. Captain, 3 March, 1899. In service.
MAINE, JOHN.
  Second Lieutenant, 12 August, 1798. Resigned 14 May, 1799.
MANNIX, D. P.
  Second Lieutenant, 30 December, 1862. First Lieutenant, 12 February, 1870. Captain, 19 December, 1885. Died 6 February, 1894, at Washington, D. C.
MANWARING, EDWARD B.
  Second Lieutenant, 23 July, 1900. In service.
MARIX, ARTHUR T.
  First Lieutenant, 13 April, 1899. Captain, 23 July, 1900. In service.
MARSTON, WARD.
  Second Lieutenant, 3 March, 1819. First Lieutenant, 30 October, 1821. Captain, 1 July, 1834. Major, 10 December, 1855. Lieutenant-Colonel, 26 July, 1861. Brevet Major, 2 January, 1847. Brevet Captain, 30 October, 1831. Retired 1 June, 1864. Died 14 April, 1882, at Roxbury, Mass.
MARTIN, NICHOLAS.
  Second Lieutenant, 26 April, 1810. Last appearance in Register of 1810.
MASSEY, LEE.
  Second Lieutenant, 1807. First Lieutenant, 28 January, 1809. Drowned 7 February, 1812.
MATHER, HERBERT.
  Second Lieutenant, 8 December, 1899. First Lieutenant, 23 July, 1900. In service.
MATHEWS, S. H.
  Second Lieutenant, 25 November, 1861. First Lieutenant, 26 November, 1861. Dismissed 1 July, 1863.
MATTHEWS, ARTHUR J.
  First Lieutenant, 13 April, 1899. Captain, 23 July, 1900. In service.
MATTHEWS, HUGH L.
  Second Lieutenant, 17 February, 1900. In service.
MAYSON, F. G.
  Second Lieutenant, 14 November, 1845. Resigned 26 January, 1850.
McARDLE, W. M.
  Second Lieutenant, 3 March, 1835. Resigned 31 January, 1837.

GENERAL NAVY REGISTER—MARINE CORPS.

McCAWLEY, EDWARD.
Second Lieutenant, 17 June, 1870. Resigned 1 April, 1873.
McCAWLEY, JAMES.
Second Lieutenant, 28 March, 1820. First Lieutenant, 6 October, 1822. Captain, 12 September, 1836. Brevet Captain, 6 October, 1832. Died 22 February, 1839.
McCAWLEY, CHARLES L.
Assistant Quartermaster, with the rank of Captain, 27 June, 1897. Assistant Quartermaster, with the rank of Major, 3 March, 1899. In service.
McCLASKEY, JOHN W.
Second Lieutenant, 5 December, 1900. In service.
McCLEAN, JAMES.
Second Lieutenant, 23 March, 1813. Resigned 20 August, 1813.
McCLEARY, W.
Second Lieutenant, 16 December, 1799. Died 31 December, 1800.
McCLINE, JOHN.
Second Lieutenant, 9 September, 1818. Last appearance in Register of 1818.
McCLURE, JAMES.
Second Lieutenant, 25 June, 1776. Disbanded with the Navy of the Revolution.
McCONNELL, RICHARD G.
Second Lieutenant, 2 October, 1899. First Lieutenant, 23 July, 1900. In service.
McCORMICK, PROVENCE, Jr.
Second Lieutenant, 11 September, 1900. In service.
McCREARY, WIRT.
Second Lieutenant, 27 July, 1899. First Lieutenant, 23 July, 1900. In service.
McDOUGAL, DOUGLAS C.
Second Lieutenant, 17 February, 1900. In service.
McDOWELL, J. E.
Second Lieutenant, 3 July, 1811. Resigned 25 March, 1812.
McGILL, JOHN F.
First Lieutenant, 26 May, 1899. Captain, 23 July, 1900. In service.
McLEMORE, ALBERT S.
Second Lieutenant, 1 July, 1893. First Lieutenant, 14 June, 1896. Captain, 3 March, 1899. In service.
McKELVY, WILLIAM N.
Second Lieutenant, 1 July, 1893. First Lieutenant, 20 June, 1897. Captain, 3 March, 1899. In service.
McKINNON, N. A.
Second Lieutenant, 21 April, 1812. Last appearance in Register of 1812.
McKNIGHT, JAMES.
First Lieutenant, 3 August, 1798. Captain, 1 September, 1798. Killed in a duel, 14 October, 1802.
McDONALD, W. J., Jr.
Second Lieutenant, 21 May, 1868. Resigned 1 September, 1879.
McELRATH, THOMAS L.
Second Lieutenant, 25 November, 1861. First Lieutenant, 26 November, 1861. Resigned 19 June, 1866.
McKEAN, W. B.
Second Lieutenant, 25 November, 1861. First Lieutenant, 26 November, 1861. Captain, 13 October, 1869. Retired 16 April, 1870. Died 30 August, 1879.
McLEAN, ALEXANDER C.
Second Lieutenant, 11 March, 1829. Resigned 8 May, 1833.
McLEAN, G. W.
Second Lieutenant, 8 May, 1833. First Lieutenant, 6 March, 1838. Resigned 7 February, 1839.
McNEILL, F. B.
Second Lieutenant, 17 October, 1834. First Lieutenant, 15 April, 1841. Died 13 March, 1856.
McSHERRY, W. K.
Second Lieutenant, 31 March, 1869. Died 13 October, 1872.
McWHORTER, JACOB G.
Second Lieutenant, 1 July, 1884. First Lieutenant, 23 December, 1890. Died 27 June, 1891, at Boston, Mass.
MEADE, ROBERT L.
Second Lieutenant, 14 June, 1862. First Lieutenant, 2 April, 1864. Captain, 22 January, 1876. Major, 6 September, 1892. Lieutenant-Colonel, 10 August, 1898. Colonel, 3 March, 1899. Brevet First Lieutenant, 8 September, 1863, for gallant and meritorious services at the night attack upon Fort Sumter, 8 September, 1863. In service.
MEADE, STEPHEN.
First Lieutenant, 22 July, 1776. Disbanded with the Navy of the Revolution.
MEEKER, E. P.
Second Lieutenant, 14 June, 1862. First Lieutenant, 17 November, 1864. Captain, 19 November, 1877. Brevet Captain, 14 January, 1865, for gallant and meritorious services at the attack upon Fort Fisher, 13, 14 and 15 January, 1865. Retired 15 March, 1893.
MEIERE, JULIUS E.
Second Lieutenant, 16 April, 1855. First Lieutenant, 1861. Dismissed 6 May, 1861.
MEMMINGER, GEORGE.
Captain, 3 August, 1798. Died 31 August, 1798.
MERCER, CARROLL.
Second Lieutenant, 22 June, 1880. First Lieutenant, 18 March, 1887. Resigned 30 June, 1890.
MERCER, SAMUEL.
Second Lieutenant, 12 March, 1866. First Lieutenant, 1 January, 1874. Captain, 24 October, 1889. Retired 27 January, 1896. Died 22 July, 1896, at Philadelphia, Pa.

GENERAL NAVY REGISTER—MARINE CORPS. 693

MILLER, E. R.
Second Lieutenant, 6 February, 1805. Retired 12 October, 1869.
MILLER, SAMUEL.
Second Lieutenant, 1 June, 1808. First Lieutenant, 7 March, 1809. Captain, 18 June, 1814. Major, 1 July, 1834. Lieutenant-Colonel, 6 October, 1841. Brevet Major, 24 August, 1814. Brevet Lieutenant-Colonel, 3 March, 1827. Died 9 December, 1855.
MILLER, LOUIS G.
Second Lieutenant, 23 February, 1900. In service.
MILLER, ELLIS B.
Second Lieutenant, 23 July, 1900. In service.
MILLS, JAMES J.
Second Lieutenant, 1 March, 1815. First Lieutenant, 18 April, 1817. Resigned 12 September, 1817.
MONELL, THEODORE.
Second Lieutenant, 23 July, 1900. In service.
MONTEGAT, T. R.
Second Lieutenant, 15 April, 1812. First Lieutenant, 18 June, 1814. Last appearance in Register of 1810.
MONTGOMERY, HUGH.
Second Lieutenant, 25 June, 1776. Disbanded with the Navy of the Revolution.
MORGAN, ABEL.
Second Lieutenant, 25 June, 1776. Disbanded with the Navy of the Revolution.
MORGAN, JOHN C.
Second Lieutenant, 10 March, 1865. First Lieutenant, 2 July, 1871. In service.
MORRIS, GOVERNEUR.
Second Lieutenant, 2 July, 1864. Died 25 December, 1865.
MOSBY, ROBERT.
Second Lieutenant, 1810. First Lieutenant, 14 April, 1812. Resigned 30 April, 1814.
MOSEBY, JOSEPH.
Second Lieutenant, 20 April, 1810. Resigned 30 April, 1814.
MOSES, FRANKLIN J.
Second Lieutenant, 1 July, 1883. First Lieutenant, 27 October, 1890. Captain, 3 March, 1899. In service.
MOSES, LAURENCE H.
Second Lieutenant, 1 July, 1892. First Lieutenant, 26 December, 1893. Captain, 3 March, 1899. In service.
MOTT, THOMAS A.
Second Lieutenant, 26 January, 1900. First Lieutenant, 23 July, 1900. In service.
MUIR, JOHN G.
Second Lieutenant, 13 January, 1900. First Lieutenant, 23 July, 1900. In service.
MULLANY, FRANK A.
Second Lieutenant 23 July, 1866. First Lieutenant, 21 June, 1872. Resigned 11 May, 1880.
MULLEN, ROBERT.
Captain, 25 June, 1876. Disbanded with the Navy of the Revolution.
MUNROE, FRANK.
Second Lieutenant, 5 June, 1861. First Lieutenant, 1 September, 1861. Captain, 10 June, 1864. Died 18 November, 1877.
MURPHY, P. ST. C.
Second Lieutenant, 19 February, 1873. First Lieutenant, 18 April, 1880. Captain, 16 March, 1893. Major, 3 March, 1899. Major by Brevet for gallant and meritorious services in the Naval Battle at Santiago, Cuba, 3 July, 1898. In service.
MURRAY, W. B.
Second Lieutenant, 2 July, 1864. First Lieutenant, 2 August, 1869. Dismissed 17 May, 1871.
MUSE, W. S.
Second Lieutenant, 18 March, 1864. First Lieutenant, 27 April, 1867. Captain, 21 December, 1880. Major, 11 July, 1898. Lieutenant-Colonel, 3 March, 1899. Colonel, 31 January, 1900. Retired 14 August, 1900.
NEALE, JOSEPH.
Second Lieutenant, 8 May, 1799. Died 22 September, 1800.
NEILL, R. R.
Second Lieutenant, 6 February, 1865. First Lieutenant, 16 October, 1869. Resigned 2 June, 1873.
NEUMANN, BERTRAM S.
Second Lieutenant, 1 July, 1891. First Lieutenant, 11 July, 1892. Captain, 3 March, 1899. In service.
NEVILLE, WENDELL C.
Second Lieutenant, 1 July, 1891. First Lieutenant, 7 February, 1894. Captain, 3 March, 1899. Captain by Brevet for conspicuous conduct at Guantanamo, Cuba, 13 June, 1898. In service.
NEVILLE, FRANCIS S.
Second lLeutenant, 22 May, 1826. Struck off 3 April, 1840.
NEVILLE, FRANCIS S.
Second Lieutenant, 30 October, 1830. Resigned 15 July, 1833.
NEWTON, EDWIN B.
Second Lieutenant, 16 January, 1817. Resigned 1 January, 1819.
NICHOLS, ROBERT H.
Second Lieutenant, 27 February, 1801. Resigned 5 April, 1801.
NICHOLS, SAMUEL.
Major, 25 June, 1776. Disbanded with the Navy of the Revolution.
NICHOLSON, A. A.
Second Lieutenant, 28 March, 1820. First Lieutenant, 27 May, 1822. Captain, 25 July, 1834. Quartermaster with the rank of Major. Brevet Captain, 27 May, 1832. Died 18 July, 1855.

GENERAL NAVY REGISTER—MARINE CORPS.

NICHOLSON, A. S.
Second Lieutenant, 16 March, 1847. First Lieutenant, 14 March, 1856. Adjutant and Inspector with the rank of Major. Major, 6 May, 1861. Brevet First Lieutenant, 13 September, 1847. Retired 1 May, 1894.

NICHOLSON, JESUP.
Second Lieutenant, 7 June, 1873. First Lieutenant, 29 November, 1874. Retired 24 February, 1887. Died 22 May, 1893, at Hamilton, Va.

NICHOLSON, JOSEPH S.
Second Lieutenant, 16 March, 1847. Brevet First Lieutenant, 13 September, 1847. Resigned 5 September, 1850.

NICHOLSON, JOSEPH.
Second Lieutenant, 13 March, 1816. Resigned 10 July, 1817.

NICHOLSON, WILLIAM.
Captain, 6 September, 1776. Disbanded with the Navy of the Revolution.

NICOLL, WILLIAM.
Second Lieutenant, 24 December, 1813. First Lieutenant, 18 June, 1814. Died 24 March, 1821.

NOKES, N. L.
Second Lieutenant, 25 November, 1861. First Lieutenant, 30 June, 1863. Captain, 20 March, 1872. Died 7 October, 1883, on board the U. S. S. Hartford, at Corinto, Nicaragua.

NORVELL, FREEMAN.
Second Lieutenant, 3 March, 1847. Brevet First Lieutenant, 13 September, 1847. Dismissed 23 June, 1855.

NOWELL, ED. S.
Second Lieutenant, 9 May, 1815. Died 7 July, 1817.

NYE, C. H.
Second Lieutenant, 25 November, 1861. First Lieutenant, 26 November, 1861. Dropped 16 November, 1864.

O'BANNON. P. N.
Second Lieutenant, 18 January, 1801. First Lieutenant, 15 October, 1802. Resigned 6 March, 1807.

O'BRIEN, A. H.
Second Lieutenant, 10 March, 1869. First Lieutenant, 29 November, 1874. Resigned 30 March, 1875.

OLCOTT, HENRY.
Second Lieutenant, 19 October, 1812. First Lieutenant, 18 June, 1814. Died 17 September, 1821.

O'LEARY, ARTHUR J.
Second Lieutenant, 23 July, 1900. In service.

OSBORN, GEORGE.
Captain, 22 July, 1776. Disbanded with the Navy of the Revolution.

OSBORN, W. S.
Second Lieutenant, 9 October, 1800. First Lieutenant, 1 July, 1802. Resigned 26 April, 1806.

PAGE, JOHN S.
Second Lieutenant, 13 March, 1816. Cashiered 12 June, 1817.

PALMER, AULICK.
Second Lieutenant, 12 March, 1866. First Lieutenant, 13 March, 1872. Resigned 26 September, 1879.

PALMER, RICHARD.
Captain, 22 July, 1776. Disbanded with the Navy of the Revolution.

PARKER, HENRY M.
Second Lieutenant, 23 January, 1809. First Lieutenant, 28 June, 1809. Resigned 28 February, 1812.

PARKER, W. H.
Second Lieutenant, 5 June, 1861. First Lieutenant, 1 September, 1861. Captain, 8 December, 1864. Brevet Major, 15 January, 1864. for gallant and meritorious services at the attack upon Fort Fisher, 13, 14 and 15 January, 1865. Retired 18 March, 1872. Died 9 May, 1872, at Washington, D. C.

PARKER, WILLIAM H.
First Lieutenant, 26 May, 1899. Captain, 23 July, 1900. In service.

PATTERSON, SAMUEL A. W.
Second Lieutenant, 11 January, 1900. First Lieutenant, 23 July, 1900. In service.

PAYNE, JOHN O.
Second Lieutenant, 2 December, 1853. Dismissed 25 October, 1858.

PEET, F. T., Jr.
Second Lieutenant, 14 June, 1862. First Lieutenant, 1 September, 1864. Resigned 28 August, 1869.

PENDLETON, JOSEPH H.
Second Lieutenant, 1 July, 1884. First Lieutenant, 28 June, 1891. Captain, 3 March, 1899. In service.

PERKINS, CON. M.
Second Lieutenant, 1 July, 1884. First Lieutenant, 30 January, 1891. Captain, 3 March, 1899. In service.

PERRY, WILLIAM F.
Second Lieutenant, 3 March, 1847. Resigned 15 November, 1848.

PICKERING, WOODELL A.
Second Lieutenant, 21 October, 1900. In service.

PILE, JONES.
Second Lieutenant, 12 July, 1862. Killed in action, 24 December, 1864.

PRIME, JOSHUA.
Second Lieutenant, 27 April, 1812. Died 7 February, 1813.

GENERAL NAVY REGISTER—MARINE CORPS. 695

PINCKNEY, THOMAS H.
Second Lieutenant 1807. First Lieutenant, 23 January, 1809. Resigned 31 August, 1811.
POPE, P. C.
Second Lieutenant, 25 November, 1861. First Lieutenant, 26 Nvember, 1861. Captain, 14 April, 1870. Major, 2 February, 1891. Lieutenant-Colonel, 2 June, 1898. Colonel, 3 March, 1899. Brevet Captain, 8 September, 1863, for gallant and meritorious services at the night attack upon Fort Sumter, 8 September, 1863. In service.
PORTER, ANDREW.
Captain, 25 June, 1776. Disbanded with the Navy of the Revolution.
PORTER, CHARLES K.
Second Lieutenant, 1817. First Lieutenant, 3 March 1819. Resigned 12 August, 1819.
PORTER, CARLISLE P.
Second Lieutenant, 20 December, 1866. First Lieutenant, 1 February, 1873. Captain, 18 August, 1889. Lieutenant-Colonel, 3 March, 1899. Retired 10 September, 1899.
PORTER, DAVID D.
First Lieutenant, 8 April, 1899. Captain, 23 July, 1900. In service.
PORTER, JAMES.
Second Lieutenant, 6 December, 1799. Resigned 30 June, 1801.
POWELL, WILLIAM G.
First Lieutenant, 1 July, 1899. In service.
POWERS, DARIUS C.
Second Lieutenant, 13 June, 1836. Dismissed 10 July, 1837.
POWNAL, THOMAS.
First Lieutenant, 25 June, 1776. Disbanded with the Navy of the Revolution.
POWELL, S. W.
Second Lieutenant, 25 November, 1861. First Lieutenant, 20 November, 1862. Resigned 12 February, 1865.
PRITCHETT, WILLIAM H.
Second Lieutenant, 2 March, 1900. In service.
PRINCE, THOMAS C.
Second Lieutenant, 1 July, 1884. First Lieutenant, 2 February, 1891. Assistant Quartermaster with the rank of Captain, 20 June, 1897. Assistant Quartermaster with the rank of Major, 3 March, 1899. In service.
PROCHAZKA, JULIUS.
Second Lieutenant, 1 July, 1891. Died 10 October, 1892, at Brooklyn, N. Y.
PURCELL, LEE B.
Second Lieutenant, 2 October, 1899. First Lieutenant, 23 July, 1900. In service.
QUACKINBUSH, S. W.
Second Lieutenant, 4 December, 1869. First Lieutenant, 8 September, 1877. Captain, 15 June, 1892. Died 13 June, 1896, at Brooklyn, N. Y.
QUEEN, HENRY W.
Second Lieutenant, 14 March, 1842. First Lieutenant, 28 September, 1847. Died at sea, 4 April, 1858.
RANDOLPH, W. A.
Second Lieutenant, 30 July, 1823. Dismissed 21 October, 1826.
RAGLAND, JAMES.
Second Lieutenant, 2 February, 1809. Resigned 17 May, 1809.
RAMSAY, ALAN.
Second Lieutenant, 1 March, 1857. First Lieutenant, 1861. Captain, 26 July, 1861. Died 15 February, 1864.
RAMSEY, FRED A.
Second Lieutenant, 5 December, 1900. In service.
RANKIN, ROBERT.
Second Lieutenant, 2 September, 1798. First Lieutenant, 2 March, 1799. Captain, 16 January, 1808. Resigned 1 January, 1809.
RASK, OLOF H.
Second Lieutenant, 2 October, 1899. First Lieutenant, 23 July, 1900. In service.
RATHBORNE, J. H.
Second Lieutenant, 25 October, 1858. Resigned 16 January, 1862.
READ, FRANKLIN.
First Lieutenant, 25 June, 1776. Dismissed with the Navy of the Revolution.
READ, JACOB.
Second Lieutenant, 3 March, 1847. First Lieutenant, 19 August, 1855. Resigned 28 February, 1861.
REBER, JOHN M.
Second Lieutenant, 14 June, 1862. Dismissed 20 June, 1863.
REDDICK, JOSIAH.
Second Lieutenant, 5 September, 1798. First Lieutenant, 25 May, 1799. Resigned 30 June, 1802.
REDLES, WILLIAM L.
Second Lieutenant, 11 September, 1900. In service.
REID, GEORGE C.
First Lieutenant, 8 April, 1899. Captain, 23 July, 1900. In service.
REID, GEORGE C.
Second Lieutenant 2 July, 1864. First Lieutenant, 29 August, 1869. Captain, 2 April, 1884. Adjutant and Inspector with the rank of Major, 2 May, 1894. Adjutant and Inspector with the rank of Colonel, 3 March, 1899. In service.
REISINGER, HAROLD C.
Second Lieutenant, 26 January, 1900. First Lieutenant, 23 July, 1900. In service.

GENERAL NAVY REGISTER—MARINE CORPS.

REMEY, W. B.
Second Lieutenant, 25 November, 1861. First Lieutenant, 17 February, 1864. Captain, 21 June, 1872. Appointed Acting Judge Advocate General of the Navy, 2 July, 1878. Appointed Judge Advocate General of the Navy with the rank of Colonel, from 9 June, 1880, to 3 June, 1892. Retired 4 June, 1892. Died 20 January, 1895, at Sommerville, Mass.

REYNOLDS, E. McD.
Second Lieutenant, 3 March, 1847. First Lieutenant, 27 November, 1853. Captain, 24 May, 1861. Brevet First Lieutenant, 13 September, 1847. Dismissed 7 December, 1864.

REYNOLDS, MICHAEL.
Second Lieutenant, 1 May, 1799. First Lieutenant, 9 April, 1801. Captain, 23 January, 1809. Resigned 30 January, 1811.

REYNOLDS, JOHN G.
Second Lieutenant, 26 May, 1824. First Lieutenant, 17 May, 1833. Captain, 3 March, 1847. Major, 1861. Lieutenant-Colonel, 26 July, 1861. Brevet Major, 13 September, 1847. Died 2 November, 1865.

RHEA, ROBERT Y.
Second Lieutenant, 31 March, 1900. In service.

RICH, JABEZ C.
Second Lieutenant, 21 June, 1834. First Lieutenant, 24 February, 1839. Captain, 27 November, 1853. Dismissed 22 May, 1861.

RICHARDS, GEORGE.
Second Lieutenant, 1 July, 1893. First Lieutenant, 2 February, 1897. Captain, 3 March, 1899. Assistant Paymaster with the rank of Major, 3 March, 1899. In service.

RICHARDSON, BENJAMIN.
Second Lieutenant, 5 June, 1813. First Lieutenant, 18 June, 1814. Resigned 1 October, 1824.

RIDDLE, ROBERT B.
Second Lieutenant, 24 April, 1810. Died in September, 1811.

RIGGS, MYRON C.
Second Lieutenant, 18 August, 1857. Resigned 9 January, 1858.

RITTENHOUSE, BENJAMIN F.
First Lieutenant, 26 May, 1899. In service.

RIXEY, PRESLEY M., Jr.
Second Lieutenant, 17 February, 1900. In service.

ROBARDS, FRANK F.
Second Lieutenant, 23 July, 1900. In service.

ROBINS, G. W.
Second Lieutenant, 26 April, 1832. First Lieutenant, 11 December, 1836. Died 1 March, 1845.

ROBINSON, E. R.
Second Lieutenant, 2 July, 1864. First Lieutenant, 28 September, 1869. Captain, 23 December, 1884. Major, 10 August, 1898. Retired 10 August, 1898.

ROGERS, AUSTIN R.
Second Lieutenant, 11 September, 1900. In service.

ROGERS, S. W.
Second Lieutenant, 3 March, 1821. Died 27 September, 1823.

ROOSEVELT, HENRY L.
Second Lieutenant, 8 December, 1899. First Lieutenant, 23 July, 1900. In service.

ROSS, ANDREW.
Second Lieutenant, 3 March, 1821. First Lieutenant, 1 October, 1824. Died 11 December, 1836, of wounds received in action.

ROUMFORT, A. L.
Second Lieutenant, July, 1817. Died in 1818.

RUSSELL, B. R.
Second Lieutenant, 16 October, 1869. First Lieutenant, 1 November, 1876. Captain, 2 February, 1891. Major, 3 March, 1899. Lieutenant-Colonel, 31 January, 1900. In service.

RUSSELL, W. W.
Second Lieutenant, 5 April, 1843. First Lieutenant, 18 November, 1847. Paymaster with the rank of Major. Brevet Captain, 10 December, 1847. Died 31 October, 1862.

RUSSELL, JOHN H.
Second Lieutenant, 1 July, 1894. First Lieutenant, 10 August, 1898. Captain, 3 March, 1899. In service.

SALLADAY, JAY M.
Second Lieutenant, 8 December, 1899. First Lieutenant, 23 July, 1900. In service.

SALTMARSH, E. G.
Second Lieutenant, 14 June, 1862. First Lieutenant, 10 June, 1864. Resigned 1 July, 1871.

SAYRE, CALVIN L.
Second Lieutenant, 3 June, 1853. Resigned 14 February, 1861.

SCOTT, FRANK.
Second Lieutenant, 9 December, 1870. First Lieutenant, 16 May, 1878. Resigned 30 June, 1883.

SCOTT, W. B.
Second Lieutenant, 4 July, 1809. Resigned 13 March, 1810.

SCOTT, HENRY H.
Second Lieutenant, 3 December, 1900. In service.

SCHAUMBURGH, J. W.
Second Lieutenant, 14 March, 1829. Cashiered 20 October, 1832.

GENERAL NAVY REGISTER—MARINE CORPS. 697

SCHERMERHORN, J.
Second Lieutenant, 10 January, 1858. First Lieutenant, 16 November, 1861. Captain, 16 November, 1861. Retired 17 May, 1871. Died 16 January, 1876.
SCHENCK, W. S.
Second Lieutenant 5 July, 1871. First Lieutenant, 2 September, 1879. Assistant Quartermaster with the rank of Captain, 4 January, 1880. Retired 12 October, 1891. Died 4 June, 1893, at Philadelphia, Pa.
SCHWABLE, FRANK J.
Second Lieutenant, 21 March, 1900. In service.
SEARS, CHARLES.
Second Lieutenant, 28 March, 1820. Died 29 May, 1821.
SEARCY, LAFAYETTE.
Second Lieutenant, 30 October, 1831. Resigned 31 December, 1841.
SELLS, DAVID M.
Second Lieutenant, 25 November, 1861. Resigned 17 July, 1863.
SEVIER, ALEXANDER.
Second Lieutenant, 27 April, 1810. First Lieutenant, 17 April, 1812. Captain, 18 June, 1814. Brevet Major, 1814. Resigned 3 April, 1816.
SHAILER, JULIUS C.
Second Lieutenant, 21 March, 1870. Resigned 15 June, 1877.
SHAW, SAMUEL.
Captain, 25 June, 1776. Disbanded with the Navy of the Revolution.
SHAW, MELVILLE J.
Second Lieutenant, 1 July, 1896. Captain, 3 March, 1899. In service.
SHERBURNE, JOHN H.
Second Lieutenant, 12 March, 1866. First lLieutenant, 20 March, 1872. In service.
SHERBURNE, W. W.
Second Lieutenant, 28 September, 1811. Resigned 1811.
SHEREDINE, M. R.
Second Lieutenant, 26 March, 1799. Resigned 31 July, 1802.
SHERMAN, C. L.
Second Lieutenant, 12 July, 1862. First Lieutenant, 9 December, 1864. Brevet First Lieutenant, 5 August, 1864, for gallant and meritorious services at the Battle of Mobile Bay, 5 August, 1864. Resigned 7 September, 1877.
SHUTTLEWORTH, W. L.
Second Lieutenant 28 February, 1839. First Lieutenant, 16 March, 1847. Captain, 28 September, 1857. Colonel, 10 June, 1864. Brevet Captain, 10 March, 1847. Died 27 September, 1871.
SIBLEY, BURTON W.
Second Lieutenant, 23 July, 1900. In service.
SIMMS, JOHN D.
Second Lieutenant, 7 October, 1841. First Lieutenant, 27 September, 1847. Captain, 1861. Brevet Captain, 13 September, 1847. Dismissed 8 July, 1861.
SINGLETARY, J. G.
Second Lieutenant 1 March, 1815. Last appearance in Register of 1815.
SLACK, W. B.
Second Lieutenant, 28 January, 1839. First Lieutenant, 3 March, 1847. Captain, 22 February, 1857. Quartermaster with the rank of Major. Major, 13 August, 1860. Brevet Captain, 10 March, 1847. Retired 3 May, 1885. Died 3 December, 1895, at Washington, D. C.
SLACK, W. B., JR.
Second Lieutenant, 12 May, 1869. Died 27 September, 1874.
SLOAN, THOMAS T.
Second Lieutenant, 17 October, 1834. First Lieutenant, 31 October, 1840. Died 10 February, 1850.
SMALLEY, E. A.
Second Lieutenant, 25 November, 1861. First Lieutenant, 26 November, 1861. Resigned 25 July, 1866.
SMITH, CONSTANTINE.
Second Lieutenant, 27 August, 1825. Transferred to the Army, 20 November, 1830.
SMITH, JACOB G.
Second Lieutenant, 1 September, 1802. Resigned 29 March, 1804.
SMITH, RICHARD.
Second Lieutenant. 20 July, 1806. First Lieutenant, 8 March, 1807. Captain, 13 March, 1812. Brevet Major, 18 June, 1814. Brevet Lieutenant-Colonel, 18 June, 1824. Cashiered 23 February, 1830.
SMITH, RICHARD L.
Second Lieutenant, 26 April, 1812. Resigned 8 July, 1812.
SMITH, WILLIAM E.
Second Lieutenant, 23 July, 1900. In service.
SMYSER, JOHN D.
Second Lieutenant, 21 March, 1870. Retired 3 May, 1878.
SNOWDEN, CHARLES.
Second Lieutenant, 1 March, 1815. Last appearance in Register of 1815.
SNYDER, HAROLD C.
Second Lieutenant, 1 July, 1899. First Lieutenant, 23 July, 1900. In service.
SOUTH, HAMILTON D.
Second Lieutenant, 23 July, 1900. In service.
SPARKS, ALEXANDER D.
Second Lieutenant, 10 December, 1855. Resigned in 1855.
SPEARING, CHARLES F.
Second Lieutenant, 7 May, 1822. First Lieutenant, 31 January, 1827. Cashiered 23 September, 1841.

GENERAL NAVY REGISTER—MARINE CORPS.

SPICER, W. F., JR.
Second Lieutenant, 13 March, 1872. First Lieutenant, 4 January, 1880. Captain, 6 September, 1892. Major, 3 March, 1899. In service.
SPRAGUE, JOHN T.
Second Lieutenant, 17 October, 1834. Resigned 3 July, 1837.
STAFFORD, LEROY A.
Second Lieutenant, 1 July, 1890. Resigned 30 June, 1892.
STARK, ALEXANDER W.
Second Lieutenant, 19 July, 1855. First Lieutenant, 28 February, 1861. Dismissed 9 January, 1862.
STARK, WILLIAM B.
Second Lieutenant, 1 July, 1831. First Lieutenant, 1 July, 1834. Captain, 16 March, 1847. Died 18 August, 1855.
STAYTON, WILLIAM H.
Second Lieutenant, 1 July, 1883. First Lieutenant, 18 June, 1890. Resigned 30 June, 1891.
STEPHEN, HENRY.
Second Lieutenant, 28 February, 1815. Resigned 20 March, 1816.
STERNE, FRANCIS W.
Second Lieutenant, 22 April, 1812. Frst Lieutenant, 24 July, 1813. Captain, 10 December, 1814. Disbanded 18 April, 1817, under Peace Establishment Act.
STEVENSON, ANDREW.
Second Lieutenant, 26 February, 1875. Resigned 25 April, 1879.
STEWART, C. G.
Second Lieutenant, 1808. First Lieutenant, 1809. Last appearance in Register of 1809.
STEWART, RICHARD.
Second Lieutenant, 23 April, 1812. Last appearance in Register of 1812.
STICKNEY, DAVID.
Second Lieutenant, 23 October, 1798. Resigned 30 September, 1801.
STILLMAN, C. H.
Second Lieutenant, 25 November, 1861. First Lieutenant, 26 November, 1861. Captain, 5 December, 1867. Retired 12 March, 1872.
STODDARD, GEORGE C.
Second Lieutenant, 14 June, 1862. First Lieutenant, 10 June, 1864, for gallant and meritorious services at the Battle of Boyd's Neck, and at the Battle of Tulifinny Cross Roads, to date from 6 December, 1864. Died 26 April, 1867.
STRONG, WILLIAM.
Second Lieutenant, 1 March, 1811. First Lieutenant, 16 April, 1812. Captain, 18 June, 1814. Resigned 23 October, 1818.
STROTHER, BENJAMIN.
First Lieutenant, 31 October, 1798. Resigned 31 October, 1800.
SQUIRES, W. I.
Second Lieutenant, 25 November, 1861. First Lieutenant, 26 November, 1861. Captain, 24 August, 1867. Resigned 12 January, 1870.
STUART, ALEXANDER.
Second Lieutenant, 1 June, 1806. Resigned 6 August, 1806.
STUART, JOHN.
Captain, 25 June, 1776. Disbanded with the Navy of the Revolution.
STURGEON, E. B.
Second Lieutenant 25 November, 1861. Dismissed 1 July, 1863.
SULLIVAN, RAYMOND B.
Second Lieutenant, 23 July, 1900. In service.
SUTHERLAND, D. J.
Second Lieutenant, 29 March, 1842. First Lieutenant, 1847. Quartermaster with rank of Major. Brevet Captain, 14 September, 1847. Dismissed 23 July, 1860.
SUTTON, FRANCIS E.
Second Lieutenant, 1 July, 1883. First Lieutenant, 9 March, 1888. Lost in wreck of U. S. S. Vandalia, 16 March, 1889, at Apia, Samoa.
SWIFT, THOMAS R.
Second Lieutenant, 1807. First Lieutenant, 27 January, 1809. Captain, 18 June, 1814. Disbanded 18 April, 1817, under Peace Establishment Act.
SWIFT, WILLIAM F.
Second Lieutenant, 1 March, 1815. Last appearance in Register of 1815.
TALLMAN, JAMES.
First Lieutenant 5 September, 1798. Dismissed 2 January, 1799.
TANSILL, ROBERT.
Second Lieutenant, 3 November, 1840. First Lieutenant, 16 March, 1847. Captain. 29 November, 1858. Brevet Captain, 17 November, 1847. Dismissed 24 August, 1861.
TATTNALL, J. R. F.
Second Lieutenant, 3 November, 1847. First Lieutenant, 22 February, 1857. Dismissed 22 November, 1861.
TAYLOR, ALGERNON S.
Second Lieutenant, 21 February, 1839. First Lieutenant, 3 March, 1847. Captain, 17 July, 1857. Brevet Captain, 27 March, 1847. Dismissed 6 May, 1861.
TAYLOR, A. S.
Second Lieutenant, 2 July, 1864. First Lieutenant, 30 July, 1868. Captain, 12 December, 1883. Retired 17 June, 1890.
TAYLOR, ROBERT D.
Second Lieutenant, 2 March, 1839. Died 13 November, 1845.
TAYLOR, CHARLES B.
Second Lieutenant, 26 January, 1900. First Lieutenant, 23 July, 1900. In service.

GENERAL NAVY REGISTER—MARINE CORPS. 699

TERRETT, GEORGE H.
Second Lieutenant, 1 April, 1830. First Lieutenant, 1 July, 1834. Captain, 16 March, 1847. Brevet Major, 13 September, 1847. Dismissed 6 May, 1861.
THAYER, COTTON.
Second Lieutenant, 25 June, 1799. Resigned 15 July, 1801.
THEALL, ELISHA.
Second Lieutenant, 1 July, 1893. First Lieutenant, 2 February, 1897. Retired 2 February, 1897.
THOMAS, FREDERICK.
Second Lieutenant, 1 July, 1825. Transferred to the Army, 14 July, 1826.
THOMPSON, BENJAMIN.
Second Lieutenant, 22 July, 1776. Disbanded with the Navy of the Revolution.
THOMPSON, GEORGE H.
Second lLieutenant, 11 March, 1865. Died at sea 2 May, 1868.
THOMPSON, GILLIES.
Second Lieutenant, 12 April, 1815. Resigned 12 December, 1815.
THOMPSON, JAMES.
Second Lieutenant, 2 May, 1799. First Lieutenant, 1 July, 1800. Captain, 23 January, 1809. Resigned 12 January, 1810.
THORNTON, FRANCIS.
Second Lieutenant, 25 April, 1810. First Lieutenant, 3 April, 1811. Resigned in 1847.
THORPE, GEORGE C.
First Lieutenant, 8 April, 1899. Captain, 23 July, 1900. In service.
THWING, NATHANIEL.
Second Lieutenant, 22 July, 1776. Disbanded with the Navy of the Revolution.
TILTON, McLANE.
Second Lieutenant, 2 March, 1861. First Lieutenant, 1 September, 1861. Captain, 10 June, 1864. Major, 9 March, 1888. Lieutenant-Colonel, 28 February, 1891. Retired 1 February, 1897.
TOWNS, THOMAS.
Second Lieutenant, 30 August, 1805. Resigned 31 March, 1806.
TUPPER, CHARLES C.
Second Lieutenant, 3 March, 1819. First Lieutenant, 21 January, 1822. Captain, 1 July, 1834. Brevet Captain, 21 January, 1832. Died 18 January, 1838.
TURNER, GEORGE P.
Second Lieutenant, 27 September, 1856. Dismissed 25 June, 1861.
TURNER, JAMES A.
Second Lieutenant, 22 June, 1880. First Lieutenant, 27 May, 1885. Retired 25 December, 1893. Died 23 January, 1895, at San Francisco, Cal.
TURNER, WILLIAM C.
Second Lieutenant, 12 March, 1875. First Lieutenant, 8 October, 1883. Suicided 31 August, 1890, on board the U. S. S. Omaha.
TRACCY, JAMES K.
Second Lieutenant, 23 July, 1900. In service.
TREADWELL, THOMAS C.
Second Lieutenant, 1 July, 1892. Frst Lieutenant, 3 May, 1894. Captain, 3 March, 1899. In service.
TURRILL, JULIUS C.
Second Lieutenant, 2 October, 1899. First Lieutenant, 23 July, 1900. In service.
TWIGGS, LEVI.
Second Lieutenant, 10 November, 1813. First Lieutenant, 18 June, 1814. Captain, 23 February, 1830. Major, 15 November, 1840. Brevet Captain, 3 March, 1825. Killed in battle 13 September, 1847.
TYLER, H. B.
Second Lieutenant, 3 March, 1823. First Lieutenant, 1 April, 1830. Captain, 12 March, 1845. Adjutant and Inspector with rank of Major. Dismissed 4 May, 1861.
TYLER, H. B., Jr.
Second Lieutenant, 2 January, 1855. Dismissed 21 June, 1861.
UDELL, FRED A.
Second Lieutenant, 11 September, 1900. In service.
URQUEHART, JOHN.
Second Lieutenant, 5 March, 1811. First Lieutenant, 30 April, 1812. Resigned in 1812.
VALETTE, LOUIS DE LA.
First Lieutenant, 24 August, 1776. Disbanded with the Navy of the Revolution.
VAN DYKE, ABRAHAM.
First Lieutenant, 22 July, 1776. Disbanded with the Navy of the Revolution.
VAN ORDEN, GEORGE.
First Lieutenant, 1 July, 1899. In service.
WADLEIGH, JOHN W.
Second Lieutenant, 26 January, 1900. First Lieutenant, 23 July, 1900. In service.
WAIT, MARMADUKE.
Second Lieutenant, 16 January, 1801. Last appearance in Register of 1801.
WALLACE, WILLIAM.
Second Lieutenant, 14 June, 1862. First Lieutenant, 10 June, 1864. Captain, 3 October, 1876. Brevet First Lieutenant, 8 September, 1863, for gallant and meritorious services at the night attack upon Fort Sumter, 8 September, 1863. Brevet Captain, 14 January, 1865, for gallant and meritorious services at the attack upon Fort Fisher, 13, 14 and 15 January, 1865. Died 11 December, 1883, at Philadelphia, Pa.
WALLACH, RICHARD.
Second Lieutenant, 24 April, 1869. First Lieutenant, 22 January, 1876. Captain, 30 January, 1891. Major, 3 March, 1899. Retired 24 July, 1899.

WALLER, LITTLETON W. T.
Second Lieutenant, 26 June, 1880. First Lieutenant, 28 September, 1885. Captain, 14 June, 1896. Major, 25 July, 1899. In service.
WALES, SAMUEL.
Second Lieutenant, 10 November, 1800. Resigned 20 February, 1801.
WALDRON, N. S.
Second Lieutenant, 13 September, 1831. First Lieutenant, 25 July, 1834. Captain, 16 March 1847. Brevet Major, 22 July, 1848. Died 21 February, 1857.
WAINWRIGHT, R. D.
Second Lieutenant 15 February, 1807. First Lieutenant, 23 January, 1809. Captain, 29 September, 1812. Lieutenant-Colonel, 1 July, 1834. Brevet Major, 3 March, 1823. Brevet Lieutenant-Colonel, 3 March, 1827. Died 5 October, 1841.
WAINWRIGHT, R. D.
Second Lieutenant, 4 December, 1869. First Lieutenant, 17 March, 1877. Captain, 5 June, 1892. Retired 17 April 1893.
WALLACE, RUSH R., JR.
Second Lieutenant, 29 December, 1899. First Lieutenant, 23 July, 1900. In service.
WALKER, GEORGE W.
Second Lieutenant, 10 June, 1817. First Lieutenant, 3 March, 1821. Brevet Captain and Quartermaster. Captain, 1 July, 1834. Brevet Captain, 3 March, 1831. Died 29 August, 1851.
WALKER, RALPH E.
Second Lieutenant, 20 May, 1898. Captain, 3 March, 1899. In service.
WARD, A. W.
Second Lieutenant, 14 June, 1862. Died 17 March, 1867.
WASHBURN, I. H.
Second Lieutenant, 18 March, 1864. First Lieutenant, 29 August, 1867. Captain, 20 March, 1883. Retired 15 July, 1886. Died 6 February, 1896, at Hot Springs, Ark.
WATKINS, T. L. C.
Second Lieutenant, 22 May, 1826. First Lieutenant, 1 July, 1834. Died 31 October, 1840.
WATSON, ARTHUR L.
Second Lieutenant, 9 March, 1865. First Lieutenant, 18 May, 1871. Retired 29 March, 1878. Died 30 June, 1882, at Portsmouth, N. H.
WATSON, HENRY B.
Second Lieutenant, 5 October, 1836. First Lieutenant, 3 March, 1847. Brevet Captain, 20 November, 1847. Resigned 1 January, 1855.
WATSON, JOSIAH.
Second Lieutenant, 21 June, 1835. First Lieutenant, 3 March, 1847. Captain, 10 December, 1855. Major, 16 November, 1861. Died 5 February, 1864.
WATSON, SAMUEL E.
Second Lieutenant, 4 July, 1812. First Lieutenant, 18 June, 1814. Captain, 28 March, 1820. Major, 1 July, 1834. Brevet Lieutenant-Colonel, 28 March, 1830. Died 17 November, 1847.
WEAVER, JAMES.
First Lieutenant, 27 September, 1798. Resigned 31 August, 1803.
WEBSTER, F. D.
Second Lieutenant, 18 March, 1864. First Lieutenant, 5 December, 1867. Captain, 8 October, 1883. Retired 1 April, 1884.
WEBSTER, LE ROY C.
Second Lieutenant, 1 July, 1874. First Lieutenant, 24 January, 1883. Captain, 18 April, 1893. Died 17 June, 1899, at San Francisco, Cal.
WEED, ELIJAH J.
Second Lieutenant, 16 January, 1817. First Lieutenant, 3 March, 1819. Captain, 1 July, 1834. Quartermaster with rank of Major. Brevet Captain, 7 November, 1828. Died 5 March, 1838.
WELCH, HENRY.
Second Lieutenant, 3 March, 1847. Died 27 August, 1847.
WELLES, GEORGE M.
Second Lieutenant, 12 July, 1862. First Lieutenant, 11 January, 1865. Retired 29 November, 1874. Died 18 October, 1883, at Fort Dodge, Iowa.
WEST, EDWARD L.
Second Lieutenant, 17 October, 1834. First Lieutenant, 6 October, 1841. Died 30 March, 1851.
WEST ERNEST E.
First Lieutenant, 1 July, 1899. In service.
WESTCOTT, CHARLES T., JR.
Second Lieutenant, 17 February, 1900. In service.
WHARTON, THOMAS.
Second Lieutenant, 28 January, 1799. First Lieutenant, 17 October, 1800. Died in 1801.
WHETCROFT, W. W.
Second Lieutenant, 19 February, 1817. Resigned 3 August, 1820.
WHIPPLE, DAVID.
Second Lieutenant, 29 May, 1871. First Lieutenant, 16 March, 1879. Died 1 March, 1884, at Norfolk, Va.
WHITE, FRANCIS B.
Second Lieutenant, 24 September, 1813. First Lieutenant, 18 June, 1814. Killed in a duel, 25 September, 1819.
WHITE, HARRY K.
Second Lieutenant, 1 July, 1883. First Lieutenant, 26 March, 1889. Captain, 2 February, 1897. Major, 11 September, 1899. In service.
WHITING, HENRY.
Second Lieutenant, 1 July, 1874. First Lieutenant, 20 March, 1883. Died 8 January, 1890, at New York, N. Y.

GENERAL NAVY REGISTER—MARINE CORPS. 701

WHITNEY, L. F.
    Second Lieutenant, 17 October, 1834. Cashiered 14 March, 1840.
WHITTIER, RUFUS A.
    Second Lieutenant, 22 October, 1856. Dismissed 30 June, 1858.
WILEY, JAMES.
    Second Lieutenant, 9 January, 1847. First Lieutenant, 27 September, 1856. Assistant Quartermaster, with the rank of Captain, 26 July, 1861. Retired 20 June, 1872. Died 7 July, 1895.
WILLIAMS, CHARLES F.
    Second Lieutenant, 14 June, 1862. First Lieutenant, 10 June, 1864. Captain, 1 November, 1876. Major, 2 February, 1897. Colonel, 3 March, 1899. Brevet Captain, 14 January, 1865, for gallant and meritorious services at the attack upon Fort Fisher, 13, 14 and 15 January, 1865. Died 30 January, 1900, at Mare Island, Cal.
WILLIAMS, H. A.
    Second Lieutenant, 28 September, 1798. Died 1 July, 1800.
WILLIAMS, JOHN.
    Second Lieutenant, 20 August, 1805. First Lieutenant, 2 March, 1807. Captain, 31 January, 1811. Died of wounds received in action, August, 1812.
WILLIAMS, JOB G.
    Second Lieutenant, 7 May, 1822. First Lieutenant, 27 December, 1825. Captain, 15 November, 1840. Died 26 September, 1856.
WILLIAMS, DION.
    Second Lieutenant, 1 July, 1893. First Lieutenant, 1 June, 1894. Captain, 3 March, 1899. In service.
WILLIAMS, RICHARD P.
    Second Lieutenant, 2 October, 1899. First Lieutenant, 23 July, 1900. In service.
WILLIAMS, ALEXANDER S.
    Second Lieutenant, 2 October, 1899. First Lieutenant, 23 July, 1900. In service.
WILMER, E. P.
    Second Lieutenant, 23 January, 1809. Resigned 19 June, 1809.
WILSON, ISAAC R.
    Second Lieutenant, 10 May, 1838. Resigned 29 Maq, 1841.
WILSON, THOMAS S.
    Second Lieutenant, 13 December, 1857. Dismissed 24 August, 1861.
WILSON, W. D.
    Second Lieutenant, 23 January, 1809. First Lieutenant, 28 June, 1809. Resigned 14 September, 1809.
WILTSE, FRANKLIN S.
    Second Lieutenant, 22 October, 1900. In service.
WINTHROP, P. W.
    Second Lieutenant, 1808. First Lieutenant, 13 February, 1809. Resigned 6 May, 1811.
WISE, FREDERIC M., JR.
    Second Lieutenant, 1 July, 1899. First Lieutenant, 23 July, 1900. In service.
WOOD, THOMAS N.
    Second Lieutenant, 1 July, 1876. First Lieutenant, 2 April, 1884. Captain, 28 January, 1896. Major, 18 June, 1899. In service.
WOODSON, JOSEPH.
    Second Lieutenant, 22 April, 1810. First Lieutenant, 2 April, 1811. Resigned 17 June, 1814.
WOOG, BENJAMIN B.
    First Lieutenant, 1 July, 1899. In service.
WORMELEY, W. W.
    Second Lieutenant, 15 August, 1805. Resigned 17 June, 1806.
WRIGHT, WILLIAM.
    Second Lieutenant, 1817. Resigned 8 May, 1818.
WRIGHT, JOHN H.
    Second Lieutenant, 2 October, 1899. First Lieutenant, 23 July, 1900. In service.
WYNKOOP, D. S.
    First Lieutenant, 16 November, 1798. Lost in the Insurgent.
WYNNE, ROBERT F.
    First Lieutenant, 26 May, 1899. Captain, 23 July, 1900. In service.
YATES, THOMAS Y.
    Second Lieutenant, 1817. Dismissed 17 August, 1817.
YOUNG, ALBERT B.
    Second Lieutenant, 18 March, 1864. First Lieutenant, 29 November, 1867. Resigned 31 January, 1873.
YOUNG, JAMES B.
    Second Lieutenant, 14 June, 1862. First Lieutenant, 22 June, 1864. Resigned 20 January, 1865.
YOUNG, JOHN F.
    Second Lieutenant, 4 April, 1838. Died 9 February, 1839.
YOUNG, J. M. T.
    Second Lieutenant, 2 July, 1864. First Lieutenant, 9 August, 1868. Captain, 24 February, 1884. Major, 10 August, 1898. Retired 10 August, 1898.
YOUNG, T. M. W
    Second Lieutenant, 20 February, 1822. Died 7 July, 1825.
YOUNG, W. L.
    Second Lieutenant, 23 February, 1835. First Lieutenant, 12 March, 1845. Brevet Captain, 13 September, 1847. Died 12 December, 1857.
YOUNGBLOOD, E. H.
    Second Lieutenant, 27 March, 1856. Resigned 28 February, 1857.
ZEILIN, W. F.
    Second Lieutenant, 19 December, 1871. First Lieutenant, 6 December, 1879. Died 4 June, 1880.

Appendix.

THE NAVY OF THE UNITED STATES.

Summarized from the Navy Register of January, 1901.

The active list of the Navy is composed of 1 admiral, 18 rear-admirals, 70 captains, 112 commanders, 170 lieutenant-commanders, 300 lieutenants, 101 lieutenants (junior grade), 111 ensigns, 18 chief boatswains, 14 chief gunners, 16 chief carpenters, 10 chief sailmakers, 111 naval cadets performing two years' service at sea, or pursuing special studies prior to final graduation, 280 naval cadets on probation at the Naval Academy.

Of the staff there are 1 surgeon-general 15 medical directors, 15 medical inspectors, 55 surgeons, 40 passed assistant surgeons, 56 assistant surgeons, 1 paymaster-general, 13 pay directors, 13 pay inspectors, 30 paymasters, 40 assistant paymasters, 24 chaplains, 12 professors of mathematics, 1 secretary for the admiral, 1 chief constructor, 19 naval constructors, 20 assistant naval constructors, and 21 civil engineers.

The warrant officers consist of 73 boatswains, 71 gunners, 46 carpenters, 100 warrant machinists, 25 pharmacists, and 8 mates.

The retired list is composed of officers of the line as follows : Forty-three rear-admirals, 8 commodores, 14 captains, 38 commanders, 22 lieutenant-commanders, 54 lieutenants, 10 lyieutenants (junior grade), 16 ensigns, 5 chief boatswains, 2 chief gunners, 2 chief carpenters, and 1 chief sailmaker. Staff officers, viz. : Thirty-two medical directors, 5 medical inspectors, 18 surgeons, 9 passed assistant surgeons, 7 assistant surgeons, 17 pay directors, 5 pay inspectors, 13 paymasters, 1 passed assistant paymaster, 2 assistant paymasters, 58 chief engineers, 37 passed assistant engineers, 30 assistant engineers, 7 chaplains, 8 professors of mathematics, 8 naval constructors, 3 civil engineers. Warrant officers, viz. : 15 boatswains, 27 gunners, 23 carpenters, 12 sailmakers, 1 pharmacist, and 20 mates.

The active list is therefore composed of 1,332 officers of the line, 414 officers of the staff, and 323 warrant officers. Total, 2,069 officers of all grades.

The retired list is composed of 215 officers of the line, 260 officers of the staff, and 98 warrant officers.

RECOGNITION BY CONGRESS

OF

Gallant Services of Officers and Others

OF THE

NAVY AND MARINE CORPS.

Resolution requesting the President to present a gold medal to Captain THOMAS TRUXTON; *and respecting the conduct of Midshipman* JAMES JARVIS.

That the President of the United States be requested to present to Captain Thomas Truxtun, a gold medal, emblematical of the late action between the United States frigate Constellation, of thirty-eight guns, and the French ship of war La Vengeance, of fifty-four; in testimony of the high sense entertained by Congress of his gallantry and good coduct in the above engagement, wherein an example was exhibited by the captain, officers, sailors, and marines, honorable to the American name, and instructive to its rising navy.

That the conduct of James Jarvis, a midshipman in said frigate, who gloriously preferred certain death to an abandonment of his post, is deserving of the highest praise, and that the loss of so promising an officer is a subject of national regret.

Approved March 29, 1800.

Resolution expressing the sense of Congress on the gallant conduct of Lieutenant STERETT, *the officers, and crew of the United States' schooner Enterprise.*

That they entertain a high sense of the gallant conduct of Lieutenant Sterett, and the other officers, seamen, and marines, on board the schooner Enterprise, in the capture of a Tripolitan corsair of fourteen guns and eighty men.

That the President of the United States be requested to present to Lieutenant Sterett a sword, commemorative of the aforesaid heroic action; and that one month's pay be allowed to all the other officers, seamen, and marines, who were on board the Enterprise when the aforesaid action took place.

Approved February 3, 1802.

Resolution expressive of the sense of Congress of the gallant conduct of Captain STEPHEN DECATUR, *the officers, and crew of the United States' ketch Intrepid, in attacking, in the harbor of Tripoli, and destroying, a Tripolitan frigate of forty-four guns.*

That the President of the United States be requested to present, in the name of Congress, to Captain Stephen Decatur, a sword, and to each of the officers and crew of the United States ketch Intrepid, two months' pay, as testimony of the high sense entertained by Congress of the gallantry, good conduct, and services of Captain Decatur, the officers and crew, of the said ketch in attacking, in the harbor of Tripoli, and destroying, a Tripolitan frigate of forty-four guns.

Approved November 27, 1804.

Resolution expressive of the sense of Congress of the gallant conduct of Commodore EDWARD PREBLE, *the officers, seamen, and marines of his squadron.*

That the thanks of Congress be, and the same are hereby, presented to Commodore Edward Preble, and through him to the officers, petty officers, seamen, and marines, attached to the squadron under his command, for their gallantry and good conduct displayed in the several attacks on the town, batteries, and naval force of Tripoli, in the year 1804.

That the President of the United States be requested to cause a gold medal to be struck, emblematical of the attacks on the town, batteries, and naval force of Tripoli by the squadron under Commodore Preble's command, and to present it to Commodore Preble in such a manner as, in his opinion, will be most honorable to him; and that the President be further requested to cause a sword to be presented to each of the commissioned officers and midshipmen who have distinguished themselves in the several attacks.
That one month's pay be allowed, exclusively of the common allowance, to all the petty officers, seamen, and marines, of the squadron, who so gloriously supported the honor of the American flag, under the orders of their gallant commander, in the several attacks.
That the President of the United States be also requested to communicate to the parents, or other near relatives, of Captain Richard Somers, Lieutenants Henry Wadsworth, James Decatur, James R. Caldwell, Joseph Israel, and Midshipman John Sword Dorsey, the deep regret which Congress feels for the loss of those gallant men, whose names ought to live in the recollection and affection of a grateful country, and whose conduct ought to be regarded as an example to future generations.
Approved March 3, 1805.

Resolutions relative to the brilliant achievements of Captains HULL, DECATUR, JONES *and Lieutenant* ELLIOTT.

1. That the President of the United States be, and he is hereby, requested to present to Captain Hull, of the frigate Constitution, Captain Decatur, of the frigate United States, and Captain Jones, of the sloop of war Wasp, each a gold medal, with suitable emblems and devices; and a silver medal, with like emblems and devices, to each commissioned officer of the aforesaid vessels, in testimony of the high sense entertained by Congress of the gallantry, good conduct, and services, of the captains, officers, and crews, of the aforesaid vessels, in their respective conflicts with the British frigates, the Guerriere and the Macedonian, and sloop of war Frolic; and the President is also requested to present a silver medal, with like emblems and devices, to the nearest male relative of Lieutenant Bush, and one to the nearest male relative of Lieutenant Funk, in testimony of the gallantry and merit of those deceased officers, in whom their country has sustained a loss much to be regretted.
2. That the President of the United States be, and he hereby is, requested to present to Lieutenant Elliot, of the Navy of the United States, an elegant sword, with suitable emblems and devices, in testimony of the just sense entertained by Congress of his gallantry and good conduct in boarding and capturing the British brigs Detroit and Caledonia, while anchored under the protection of Fort Erie.
Approved January 29, 1813.

Resolution requesting the President of the United States to present medals to Captain WILLIAM BAINBRIDGE, *and the officers of the frigate Constitution.*

That the President of the United States be, and he is hereby, requested to present to Captain William Bainbridge of the frigate Constitution, a gold medal, with suitable emblems and devices; and a silver medal, with suitable emblems and devices, to each commissioned officer of the said frigate, in testimony of the high sense entertained by Congress of the gallantry, good conduct, and services of Captain Bainbridge, his officers and crew, in the capture of the British frigate Java, after a brave and skillful combat.
Approved March 3, 1813.

An act rewarding the officers and crew of the frigate Constitution, and the officers and crew of the Wasp.

Be it enacted, etc., That the President of the United States be, and he is hereby authorized to have distributed, as prize money, to Captain Isaac Hull, of the frigate Constitution, his officers and crew, the sum of fifty thousand dollars, for the capture and destruction of the British frigate Guerriere; and the like sum, in like manner, to Captain William Bainbridge, his officers and crew, for the capture and destruction of the British frigate Java; and the sum of twenty-five thousand dollars in like manner to Captain Jacob Jones, of the sloop of war Wasp, his officers and crew, for the capture of the British sloop of war Frolic; and that the sum of one hundred and twenty-five thousand dollars, out of any money in the treasury not otherwise appropriated, be, and the same is hereby, appropriated for the purposes aforesaid.
Approved March 3, 1813.

An act to reward the officers and crew of the sloop of war Hornet, and Lieutenant ELLIOTT, *and his officers and companions.*

That the President of the United States be, and he is hereby, authorized to have distributed, as prize money, to Captain James Lawrence, late of the sloop of war Hornet, his officers and crew, or their widows and children, the sum of twenty-five thousand dollars, for the capture and destruction of the British brig Peacock; and to Lieutenant Elliott, and his officers and companions, or their widows and children, the sum of twelve thousand dollars, for the capture and destruction of the British brig Detroit: and that the sum of thirty-seven thousand dollars be, and the same is hereby, appropriated to the purpose aforesaid, to be paid out of any money in the treasury not otherwise appropriated.
Approved July 13, 1813.

Resolution relative to the brilliant achievement of Lieutenants BURROWS *and* MCCALL.

That the President of the United States be requested to present to the nearest male relative of Lieutenant William Burrows, and to Lieutenant Edward R. McCall, of the brig Enterprise, a gold medal, with suitable emblems and devices; and a silver medal, with like emblems and devices, to each of the commissioned officers of the aforesaid vessel, in testimony of the high sense entertained by Congress of the gallantry and good conduct of the officers and crew in the conflict with the British sloop Boxer, on the fourth of September, in the year eighteen hundred and thirteen. And the President is also requested to communicate to the nearest male relative of Lieutenant Burrows, the deep regret which Congress feels for the loss of that valuable officer, who died in the arms of victory, nobly contending for his country's rights and fame.
Approved January 6, 1814.

Resolution directing a sword to be presented to the nearest male relation of Midshipman JOHN CLARK.

That the President of the United States be requested to present a sword to the nearest male relation of Midshipman John Clark, who was slain gallantly combating the enemy in the glorious battle gained on Lake Erie, under the command of Captain Perry, and to communicate to him the deep regret which Congress feels for the loss of that brave officer.
Approved February 19, 1814.

Resolution expressive of the sense of Congress of the gallant conduct of Captain THOMAS MACDONOUGH, *the officers, seamen, marines, and infantry serving as marines, on board the United States' squadron on Lake Champlain.*

That the thanks of Congress be, and the same are hereby, presented to Captain Thomas Macdonough, and, through him, to the officers, petty officers, seamen, marines and infantry serving as marines, attached to the squadron under his command, for the decisive and splendid victory gained on Lake Champlain, on the eleventh of September, in the year one thousand eight hundred and fourteen, over a British squadron of superior force.
That the President of the United States be requested to cause gold medals to be struck, emblematical of the action between the two squadrons, and to present them to Captain Macdonough and Captain Robert Henley, and also to Lieutenant Stephen Cassin, in such manner as may be most honorable to them; and that the President be further requested to present a silver medal, with suitable emblems and devices, to each of the commissioned officers of the navy and army serving on board, and a sword to each of the midshipmen and sailing-masters, who so nobly distinguished themselves in that memorable conflict.
That the President of the United States be requested to present a silver medal, with like emblems and devices, to the nearest male relative of Lieutenant Peter Gamble, and of Lieutenant John Stansbury, and to communicate to them the deep regret which Congress feels for the loss of those gallant men, whose names ought to live in the recollection and affection of a grateful country.
That three months' pay be allowed, exclusively of the common allowance, to all the petty officers, seamen, marines, and infantry serving as marines, who so gloriously supported the honor of the American flag on that memorable day.

Resolutions expressive of the sense of Congress of the gallant conduct of Captain OLIVER H. PERRY, *the officers, seamen, marines, and infantry acting as such, on board his squadron.*

That the thanks of Congress be, and the same are hereby, presented to Captain Oliver Hazard Perry, and through him to the officers, petty officers, seamen, marines, and infantry serving as such, attached to the squadron under his command, for the decisive and glorious victory gained on Lake Erie, on the tenth of September, in the year eighteen hundred and thirteen, over a British squadron of superior force.
That the President of the United States be requested to cause gold medals to be struck, emblematical of the action between the two squadrons, and to present them to Captain Perry and Captain Jesse D. Elliott, in such manner as will be most honorable to them; and that the President be further requested to present a silver medal, with suitable emblems and devices, to each of the commissioned officers, either of the navy or army, serving on board, and a sword to each of the midshipmen and sailing-masters who so nobly distinguished themselves on that memorable day.
That the President of the United States be requested to present a silver medal, with like emblems and devices, to the nearest male relative of Lieutenant John Brooks, of the marines, and a sword to the nearest male relatives of Midshipman Henry Laub, and Thomas Claxton, Jr., and to communicate to them the deep regret which Congress feels for the loss of those gallant men, whose names ought to live in the recollection and affection of a grateful country, and whose conduct ought to be regarded as an example to future generations.
That three months' pay be allowed, exclusively of the common allowance, to all the petty officers, seamen, marines, and infantry serving as such, who so gloriously supported the honor of the American flag, under the orders of their gallant commander, on that signal occasion.
Approved January 6, 1814.

Resolution relative to the brilliant achievement of Captain JAMES LAWRENCE, *in the capture of the British vessel of war, the Peacock.*

That the President of the United States be requested to present to the nearest male relative of Captain James Lawrence, a gold medal, and a silver medal to each of the commissioned officers who served under him in the sloop of war Hornet, in her conflict with the British vessel of war, the Peacock, in testimony of the high sense entertained by Congress of the gallantry and good conduct of the officers and crew in the capture of that vessel; and the President is also requested to communicate to the nearest relative of Captain Lawrence the sense which Congress entertains of the loss which the naval service of the United States has since sustained in the death of that distinguished officer.
Approved January 11, 1814.

Resolutions expressive of the sense of Congress relative to the victory of the Peacock over the Epervier.

That the President of the United States be requested to present to Captain Lewis Warrington, of the sloop of war Peacock, a gold medal, with suitable emblems and devices, and a silver medal, with like emblems and devices, to each of the commissioned officers, and a sword to each of the midshipmen, and to the sailing-master of the said vessel, in testimony of the high sense entertained by Congress of the gallantry and good conduct of the officers and crew, in the action with the British Brig Epervier, on the twenty-ninth day of April, in the year one thousand eight hundred and fourteen, in which action the decisive effect and great superiority of the American gunnery were so signally displayed.
Approved October 21, 1814.

Resolution expressive of the sense of Congress relative to the capture of the British sloop Reindeer, by the American sloop Wasp.

That the President of the United States be requested to present to Captain Johnston Blakely, of the sloop Wasp, a gold medal, with suitable devices, and a silver medal, with like devices, to each of the commissioned officers, and also a sword to each of the midshipmen, and the sailing-master of the aforesaid vessel, in testimony of the high sense entertained by Congress of the gallantry and good conduct of the officers and crew, in the action with the British sloop of war Reindeer, on the twenty-eighth of June, in the year one thousand eight hundred and fourteen, in which action determined bravery and cool intrepidity, in nineteen minutes obtained a decisive victory, by boarding.
Approved November 3, 1814.

Resolutions expressive of the high sense entertained by Congress of the gallantry and good conduct of Commodore D. T. PATTERSON, *and Major D.* CARMICK, *and of the officers, seamen, and marines, under their command, in the defence of New Orleans.*

That Congress entertain a high sense of the valor and good conduct of Commodore D. T. Patterson, of the officers, petty officers, and seamen, attached to his command, for their prompt and efficient co-operation with General Jackson, in the late gallant and successful defence of the city of New Orleans, when assailed by a powerful British force.

That Congress entertain a high sense of the valor and good conduct of Major Daniel Carmick, of the officers, non-commissioned officers, and marines, under his command, in the defence of the said city on the late memorable occasion.
Approved February 22, 1815.

Resolution requesting the President to present medals to Captain JAMES BIDDLE, *and the officers of the sloop of war Hornet.*

That the President of the United States be, and he is hereby, requested to present to Captain James Biddle, of the sloop of war Hornet, a gold medal, with suitable emblems and devices, and a silver medal, with suitable emblems and devices, to each commissioned officer of the said sloop of war, in testimony of the high sense entertained by Congress of the gallantry, good conduct, and services, of Captain Biddle, his officers and crew, in capturing the British sloop of war Penguin, after a brave and skilful combat.
Approved February 22, 1816.

Resolution requesting the President to present medals to Captain STEWART *and the officers of the frigate Constitution.*

That the President of the United States be, and he is hereby, requested to present to Captain Charles Stewart, of the frigate Constitution, a gold medal, with suitable emblems and devices, and a silver medal, with suitable emblems and devices, to each commissioned officer of the said frigate, in testimony of the high sense entertained by Congress of the gallantry, good conduct, and services, of Captain Stewart, his officers and crew, in the capture of the British vessels of war, the Cyane and the Levant, after a brave and skilful combat.
Approved February 22, 1816.

GENERAL NAVY REGISTER.   711

An act rewarding the officers and crew of the sloop of war Hornet, for the capture and destruction of the British sloop of war Penguin.

That the President of the United States be, and he is hereby, authorized to have distributed, as prize-money, to Captain James Biddle, of the sloop of war Hornet, his officers and crew, the sum of twenty-five thousand dollars, for the capture and destruction of the British sloop of war Penguin; and that the sum of twenty-five thousand dollars, out of any money in the treasury not otherwise appropriated, be, and the same is hereby, appropriated for the purpose aforesaid.
Approved February 28, 1816.

An act rewarding the officers and crew of the Constitution for the capture of the British sloop of war Levant.

That the President of the United States be, and he hereby is, authorized to have distributed as prize-money, to Captain Charles Stewart, late of the frigate Constitution, his officers and crew, the sum of twenty-five thousand dollars, for the capture of the British sloop of war Levant; and that the sum of twenty-five thousand dollars, out of any money in the treasury not otherwise appropriated, be, and the same is hereby, appropriated for the purpose aforesaid.
Approved April 26, 1816.

Resolution expressive of the sense of Congress of the gallant conduct of Lieutenant DUNCAN, *of the United States Navy.*

That the provisions of the joint resolutions of Congress, passed October twenty, eighteen hundred and fourteen, entitled "Resolutions expressive of the sense of Congress of the gallant conduct of Captain Thomas Macdonough, the officers, seamen, and marines, and infantry serving as marines, on board of the United States squadron on Lake Champlain," be so construed and extended as to include the name of Silas Duncan, a lieutenant in the navy of the United States, in testimony of the sense which is entertained by both Houses of Congress, of the distinguished gallantry and good conduct of the said Lieutenant Duncan, in an action with the enemy's forces, on the sixth of September, eighteen hundred and fourteen, on the same lake.
Approved May 13, 1826.

Joint resolution of thanks to the officers, sailors and marines of the United States Navy.

That the thanks of Congress are due and are hereby tendered to the officers, sailors, and marines of the navy of the United States, for the zeal and ability with which their duty during the late war with Mexico, and especially their efficient co-operation with the army of the United States in the capture of Vera Cruz and the Castle of San Juan de Ulloa, was performed.
That the President of the United States be requested to cause the foregoing resolution to be communicated to the officers, sailors, and marines of the Navy of the United States in such terms as he may deem best calculated to give effect to the object thereof.
Approved August 7, 1848.

A joint resolution directing the presentation of a medal to Commander DUNCAN N. INGRAHAM.

That the President of the United States be, and he is hereby requested, to cause to be made a medal, with suitable devices, and presented to Commander Duncan N. Ingraham, of the Navy of the United States, as a testimonial of the high sense entertained by Congress of his gallant and judicious conduct on the second of July, eighteen hundred and fifty-three, in extending protection to Martin Koszta, by rescuing him from illegal seizure and imprisonment on board the Austrian war-brig Hussar.
Approved August 4, 1854.

A resolution conferring the rank of senior flag-officer on the active service list of the United States Navy on Captain CHARLES STEWART.

That the President of the United States, by and with the advice and consent of the Senate, be, and he is hereby, authorized and empowered to confer on Captain Charles Stewart, of the United States Navy, in recognition of his distinguished and meritorious service, the commission of senior flag officer of the United States Navy, on the active service list.
Approved March 2, 1859.

A resolution giving the thanks of Congress to the officers, soldiers, and seamen of the Army and Navy for their gallantry in the recent brilliant victories over the enemies of the United States and the Constitution.

That the thanks of Congress are due and are hereby tendered, to the officers, soldiers, seamen of the Army and Navy of the United States, for the heroic gallantry, that under the providence of Almighty God, has won the recent series of brilliant victories over the enemies of the Union and the Constitution.
Approved February 22, 1862.

UPON RECOMMENDATION OF THE PRESIDENT.

A resolution tendering the thanks of Congress to Captain SAMUEL F. DUPONT, *and officers, petty officers, seamen, and marines under his command, for the victory at Port Royal.*

That the thanks of Congress be, and they are hereby, tendered to Captain Samuel F. DuPont, and through him to the officers, petty officers, seamen, and marines attached to the squadron under his command, for the decisive and splendid victory achieved at Port Royal on the seventh day of November last.
Approved February 22, 1862.

A resolution expressive of the thanks of Congress to Captain A. H. FOOTE, *of the United States Navy, and to the officers and men under his command in the western flotilla.*

That the thanks of Congress and of the American people are due, and are hereby tendered, to Captain A. H. Foote, of the United States Navy, and to the officers and men of the western flotilla under his command, for the great gallantry exhibited by them in the attack upon Forts Henry and Donelson, for their efficiency in opening the Tennessee, Cumberland, and Mississippi Rivers to the pursuits of lawful commerce, and for their unwavering devotion to the cause of the country in the midst of the greatest difficulties and dangers.
Approved March 19, 1862.

A resolution expressive of the thanks of Congress to Lieutenant J. L. WORDEN, *of the United States Navy, and to the officers and men under his command in the Monitor.*

That the thanks of Congress and of the American people are due and are hereby tendered to Lieutenant John L. Worden, of the United States Navy, and to the officers and men of the iron-clad gunboat Monitor, under his command, for the skill and gallantry exhibited by them in the late remarkable battle between the Monitor and the rebel iron-clad steamer Merrimac.
SEC. 2. *Be it further resolved,* That the President of the United States be requested to cause this resolution to be communicated to Lieutenant Worden, and through him to the officers and men under his command.
Approved July 11, 1862.

UPON RECOMMENDATION OF THE PRESIDENT.

A resolution of thanks to Captain DAVID G. FARRAGUT, *of the United States Navy, and to the officers and men under his command.*

That the thanks of the people and of the Congress of the United States are due and are hereby tendered to Captain David G. Farragut, of the United States Navy, and to the officers and men under his command, composing his squadron in the Gulf of Mexico, for their successful operations on the lower Mississippi River, and for their gallantry displayed in the capture of Forts Jackson and St. Philip, and the city of New Orleans, and in the destruction of the enemy's gunboats and armed flotilla.
SEC. 2. *And be it further resolved,* That the Secretary of the Navy be directed to communicate this resolution to Captain Farragut, and through him to the officers and men under his command.
Approved July 11, 1862.

UPON RECOMMENDATION OF THE PRESIDENT.

A resolution tendering the thanks of Congress to Captain LOUIS M. GOLDSBOROUGH, *and officers, petty officers, seamen, and marines under his command, for the victory at Roanoke Island.*

That the thanks of Congress be, and they are hereby, tendered to Captain Louis M. Goldsborough, and through him to the officers, petty officers, seamen, and marines attached

GENERAL NAVY REGISTER.   713

to the squadron under his command, for the brilliant and decisive victory achieved at Roanoke Island on the seventh, eighth, and tenth days of February last.
Approved July 11, 1862.

UPON RECOMMENDATION OF THE PRESIDENT.

Joint resolution tendering the thanks of Congress to Captain ANDREW H. FOOTE, *of the United States Navy.*

That the thanks of Congress be, and the same are hereby, tendered to Captain Andrew H. Foote, of the United States Navy, for his eminent services and gallantry at Fort Henry, Fort Donelson, and Island Number Ten, while in command of the naval forces of the United States.

SEC. 2. That the President of the United States be, and he is hereby, requested to transmit a certified copy of the foregoing resolution to Captain Foote.
Approved July 16, 1862.

Joint resolution tendering the thanks of Congress to Commander JOHN L. WORDEN, *of the United States Navy.*

That in pursuance of the recommendation of the President of the United States, and to enable him to advance Commander John L. Worden one grade, in pursuance of the ninth section of the act of Congress of sixteenth July, eighteen hundred and sixty-two, that the thanks of Congress be, and they are hereby, tendered to Commander John L. Worden for highly distinguished conduct in conflict with the enemy in the remarkable battle between the United States iron-clad steamer Monitor, under his command, and the rebel iron-clad frigate Merrimac, in March, eighteen hundred and sixty-two.
Approved February 3, 1863.

Joint resolution tendering the thanks of Congress to Commodore CHARLES HENRY DAVIS, *and other officers of the Navy, in pursuance of the recommendation of the President of the United States.*

That the thanks of Congress be, and they are hereby, given to the following officers of the United States Navy, upon the recommendation of the President of the United States, viz: Commodore Charles Henry Davis, for distinguished services in conflict with the enemy at Fort Pillow, at Memphis, and for successful operations at other points in the waters of the Mississippi River; Captain John A. Dahlgren, for distinguished service in the line of his profession, improvements in ordnance, and zealous and efficient labors in the ordnance branch of the service; Captain Stephen C. Rowan, for distinguished services in the waters of North Carolina, and particularly in the capture of Newbern, being in chief command of the naval forces; Commander David D. Porter, for the bravery and skill displayed in the attack on the post of Arkansas, which surrendered to the combined military and naval forces on the tenth of January, eighteen hundred and sixty-three; Rear-Admiral Silas H. Stringham, now on the retired list, for distinguished services in the capture of Forts Hatteras and Clark; and that a copy of this resolution be forwarded to each of the above officers by the President of the United States.
Approved February 7, 1863.

Joint resolution tendering the thanks of Congress to Captain JOHN RODGERS, *of the United States Navy for eminent skill and zeal in the discharge of his duties.*

That in pursuance of the recommendation of the President of the United States, and to enable him to advance Captain Rodgers one grade in pursuance of the ninth section of the act of Congress of sixteenth July, eighteen hundred and sixty-two, the thanks of Congress be, and they are hereby, tendered to Captain John Rodgers for the eminent skill and gallantry exhibited by him in the engagement with the relief armed iron-clad steamer Fingal, alias Atlanta, whilst in command of the United States iron-clad steamer Weehawken, which led to her capture on June seventeenth, eighteen hundred and sixty-three; and also for the zeal, bravery, and general good conduct shown by this officer, on many occasions.
Approved December 23, 1863.

A resolution of thanks of Congress to Commodore CADWALADER RINGGOLD, *the officers and crew of the United States ship Sabine.*

That the thanks of Congress are hereby tendered to Commodore Ringgold, the officers, petty officers, and men of the United States ship Sabine, for the daring and skill displayed in rescuing the crew of the steam transport Governor, wrecked in a gale on the first day of November, eighteen hundred and sixty-one, having on board a battalion of United States marines under the command of Major John G. Reynolds, and in the search for, and rescue of, the United States line-of-battle ship Vermont, disabled in a gale upon the twenty-sixth of February last, with her crew and freight.

714   GENERAL NAVY REGISTER.

SEC. 2. That the Secretary of the Navy be directed to communicate the foregoing resolution to Commodore Ringgold, and through him to the officers and men under his command.
Approved *March 7, 1864.*

Joint resolution tendering the thanks of Congress to Admiral PORTER.

That the thanks of Congress be, and they are hereby, tendered to Admiral David D. Porter, commanding the Mississippi squadron, for the eminent skill, endurance and gallantry exhibited by him and his squadron, in co-operation with the Army, in opening the Mississippi River.
Approved *April 19, 1864.*

A resolution tendering the thanks of Congress to Captain JOHN A. WINSLOW, *United States Navy, and to the officers and men under his command, on board the United States steamer Kearsarge, in her conflict with the piratical craft the Alabama, in compliance with the President's recommendation to Congress of the fifth of December, eighteen hundred and sixty-four.*

That the thanks of Congress are due, and are hereby tendered, to Captain John A. Winslow, of the United States Navy, and to the officers, petty officers, seamen and marines of the United States steamer Kearsarge, for the skill and gallantry exhibited by him and the officers and men under his command in the brilliant action on the nineteenth of June, eighteen hundred and sixty-four, between that ship and the piratical craft Alabama, a vessel superior to his own in tonnage, in guns, and in the number of his crew.
Approved *December 20, 1864.*

A resolution tendering the thanks of Congress to Lieutenant WILLIAM B. CUSHING, *of the United States Navy, and to the officers and men who assisted him in his gallant and perilous achievement in destroying the rebel steamer Albemarle, in compliance with the President's recommendation to Congress of the fifth of December, eighteen hundred and sixty-four.*

That the thanks of Congress are due, and are hereby tendered, to Lieutenant William B. Cushing, of the United States Navy, and to the officers and men under his command, for the skill and gallantry exhibited by them in the destruction of the rebel iron-clad steamer Albemarle, at Plymouth, North Carolina, on the night of the twenty-seventh of October, eighteen hundred and sixty-four.
Approved *December 20, 1864.*

A resolution tendering the thanks of Congress to Rear-Admiral DAVID D. PORTER, *and to the officers, petty officers, seamen, and marines under his command, for their gallantry and good conduct in the recent capture of Fort Fisher.*

That the thanks of Congress are hereby presented to Rear-Admiral David D. Porter, and to the officers, petty officers, seamen, and marines under his command, for the unsurpassed gallantry and skill exhibited by them in the attacks upon Fort Fisher and the brilliant and decisive victory by which that important work has been captured from the rebel forces and placed in the possession and under the authority of the United States, and for their long and faithful services and unwavering devotion to the cause of the country in the midst of the greatest difficulties and dangers.
SEC. 2. *And be it further resolved,* That the President of the United States be requested to communicate this resolution to Admiral Porter, and through him to the officers, seamen, and marines under his command.
Approved *January 24, 1865.*

A resolution tendering the thanks of Congress to Vice-Admiral DAVID G. FARRAGUT, *and to the officers, petty officers, seamen, and marines under his command, for their gallantry and good conduct in the action in Mobile Bay on the fifth of August,* 1864.

That the thanks of Congress are eminently due, and are hereby tendered, to Vice-Admiral David G. Farragut, of the United States Navy, and to the officers, petty officers, seamen, and marines under his command, for the unsurpassed gallantry and skill exhibited by them in the engagement in Mobile Bay on the fifth day of August, eighteen hundred and sixty-four, and for their long and faithful services and unwavering devotion to the cause of the country in the midst of the greatest difficulties and dangers.
SEC. 2. That the President of the United States be requested to communicate this resolution to Vice-Admiral Farragut, and that the Secretary of the Navy be requested to communicate the same to the officers, seamen, and marines of the Navy by general order of his department.
Approved *February 10, 1866.*

GENERAL NAVY REGISTER.   715

An act in recognition of the merits and services of Chief Engineer GEORGE WALLACE MELVILLE, *United States Navy, and of the other officers and men of the Jeannette Arctic Expedition.*

Be it enacted by the Senate and House of Representatives of the United States of America in Congress assembled, That the President be, and hereby is, authorized, by and with the advice and consent of the Senate, to advance Chief Engineer George Wallace Melville, United States Navy, one grade, to take rank from the same date, but next after the junior chief engineer, having the relative rank of commander at the passage of this act, as a recognition of his meritorious services in successfully directing the party under his command after the wreck of the Arctic exploring steamer Jeannette, and of his persistent efforts through dangers and hardships to find and assist his commanding officer and other members of the expedition before he himself was out of peril, and that he be allowed the pay of a chief engineer as if he had been commissioned on the same date as the junior chief engineer, having the relative rank of commander at the passage of this act, such increased rate of pay to begin from the date of the passage of this act.

*   *   *   *   *   *   *   *   *

That suitable medals be struck at the United States Mint in commemoration of the perils encountered by the officers and men of the said Jeannette Arctic Expedition, and as an expression of the high esteem in which Congress holds their services in the said expedition; and that one of the said medals be presented to each of the survivors of said expedition, and one of the heirs of each of the deceased members.

*   *   *   *   *   *   *   *   *

Approved September 30, 1890.

Joint resolution tendering the thanks of Congress to Commodore GEORGE DEWEY, *United States Navy, and to the officers and men of the squadron under his command.*

Resolved by the Senate and House of Representatives of the United States of America in Congress assembled, That, in pursuance of the recommendation of the President, made in accordance with the provisions of section fifteen hundred and eight of the Revised Statutes, the thanks of Congress and of the American people are hereby tendered to Commodore George Dewey, United States Navy, Commander-in-Chief of the United States naval force on the Asiatic Station, for highly distinguished conduct in conflict with the enemy, as displayed by him in the destruction of the Spanish fleet and batteries in the harbor of Manila, Philippine Islands, May first, eighteen hundred and ninety-eight.

That the thanks of Congress and the American people are hereby extended through Commodore Dewey to the officers and men under his command for the gallantry and skill exhibited by them on that occasion.

Be it further resolved, That the President of the United States be requested to cause this resolution to be communicated to Commodore Dewey, and, through him, to the officers and men under his command.

Approved May 10, 1898.

Award of medals to participants in Battle of Manila Bay.

Under authority of an act of Congress approved June 3, 1898, medals commemorating the Battle of Manila Bay were conferred upon the following officers who participated in the engagement between the United States and the Spanish naval forces at Manila Bay, May 1, 1898:

COMMANDER-IN-CHIEF.

Commodore George Dewey.

PERSONAL STAFF.

Chief of Staff, Commander Benjamin P. Lamberton.
Flag Lieutenant, Lieutenant Thomas M. Brumby.
Flag Secretary, Ensign Harry H. Caldwell.
Aid, Ensign William P. Scott.

FLAGSHIP OLYMPIA.

Captain Charles V. Gridley.
Lieutenant Corwin P. Rees.
Lieutenant Carlos G. Calkins.
Lieutenant Valentine S. Nelson.
Lieutenant Stokely Morgan.
Lieutenant (junior grade) Samuel M. Strite.
Ensign Montgomery M. Taylor.
Ensign Frank B. Upham.
Ensign Arthur G. Kavanagh.
Ensign Henry V. Butler, Jr.
Medical Inspector (Surgeon of the Fleet) Abel F. Price.
Passed Assistant Surgeon John E. Page.
Assistant Surgeon Charles P. Kindleberger.

Pay Inspector (Paymaster of the Fleet) Daniel A. Smith.
Chief Engineer (Engineer of the Fleet) James Entwistle.
Passed Assistant Engineer Gustav Kaemmerling.
Assistant Engineer Edwin H. DeLany.
Assistant Engineer John F. Marshall, Jr.
Assistant Engineer Edward H. Dunn.
Chaplain John B. Frazier.
Captain of Marines (Marine Officer of the Fleet) William P. Biddle.
Gunner Leonard J. G. Kuhlwein.
Pay Clerk William M. Long.
Pay Clerk (Fleet) William J. Rightmire.

BOSTON.

Captain Frank Wildes.
Lieutenant-Commander John A. Norris.
Lieutenant Bernard O. Scott.
Lieutenant John Gibson.
Lieutenant (junior grade) William L. Howard.
Ensign Samuel S. Robison.
Ensign Lay H. Everhart.
Ensign John S. Doddridge.
Surgeon Millard H. Crawford.
Assistant Surgeon Robert S. Blakeman.
Paymaster John R. Martin.
Chief Engineer Richard Inch.
Assistant Engineer Leland F. James.
First Lieutenant of Marines Robert McM. Dutton.
Gunner Joel C. Evans.
Carpenter Osgood H. Hilton.
Pay Clerk George H. Grendle.

RALEIGH

Captain Joseph B. Coghlan.
Lieutenant-Commander Frederic Singer.
Lieutenant William Winder.
Lieutenant Benjamin Tappan.
Lieutenant Hugh Rodman.
Ensign Casey B. Morgan.
Ensign Frank L. Chadwick.
Ensign Provost Babin.
Surgeon Emlyn H. Marsteller.
Assistant Surgeon Dudley N. Carpenter.
Paymaster William W. Galt.
Chief Engineer Frank H. Bailey.
Passed Assistant Engineer Alexander S. Halstead.
Assistant Engineer John R. Brady.
First Lieutenant of Marines Thomas C. Treadwell.
Acting Boatswain Edward J. Norcott.
Acting Gunner Gaston D. Johnstone.
Acting Carpenter Timothy E. Kiley.
Pay Clerk George A. White.

BALTIMORE.

Captain Nehemiah M. Dyer.
Lieutenant-Commander John B. Briggs.
Lieutenant Frank H. Holmes.
Lieutenant Frank W. Kellogg.
Lieutenant (junior grade) John M. Ellicott.
Lieutenant (junior grade) Charles S. Stanworth.
Ensign George N. Hayward.
Ensign Noble E. Irwin.
Ensign Michael J. McCormack.
Medical Inspector John C. Wise.
Assistant Surgeon Reginald K. Smith.
Pay Inspector Edward Bellows.
Chief Engineer John D. Ford.
Passed Assistant Engineer Edward L. Beach.
Assistant Engineer Henry B. Price.
Assistant Engineer Hutch I. Cone.
Chaplain Thaddeus S. K. Freeman.
Captain of Marines Otway C. Berryman.
First Lieutenant of Marines Dion Williams.
Acting Boatswain Harry R. Brayton.
Gunner Louis J. Connelly.
Acting Gunner Levin J. Wallace.
Carpenter Otto Barth.
Pay Clerk William J. Corwin.

CONCORD.

Commander Asa Walker.
Lieutenant-Commander George P. Colvocoresses.
Lieutenant Thomas B. Howard.
Lieutenant Patrick W. Hourigan.

GENERAL NAVY REGISTER.   717

Lieutenant (junior grade) Charles M. McCormick.
Ensign Louis A. Kaiser.
Ensign William C. Davidson.
Ensign Orlo S. Knepper.
Passed Assistant Surgeon Richard G. Brodrick.
Passed Assistant Paymaster Eugene D. Ryan.
Chief Engineer George B. Ransom.
Passed Asistant Engineer Horace W. Jones.
Pay Clerk Frederick K. Hunt.

PETREL.

Commander Edward P. Wood.
Lieutenant Edward M. Hughes.
Lieutenant Bradley A. Fiske.
Lieutenant Albert N. Wood.
Lieutenant (junior grade) Charles P. Plunkett.
Ensign George L. Fermier.
Ensign William S. Montgomery.
Passed Assistant Surgeon Carl D. Brownell.
Assistant Paymaster George G. Seibels.
Chief Engineer Reynold T. Hall.

RESERVE.

McCULLOCH.

Lieutenant, U. S. Navy, William P. Elliot.
Captain, Revenue Cutter Service, Daniel B. Hodgsdon.
First Lieutenant, R. C. S., Daniel P. Foley.
Second Lieutenant, R. C. S., Walker W. Joynes
Third Lieutenant, R. C. S., Randolph Ridgely, Jr.
Third Lieutenant, R C. S., William E. Atlee.
Third Lieutenant, R C. S., John Mel.
Assistant Surgeon, Marine Hospital Service, Joseph B Greene.
First Assistant Engineer, R. C. S., William C. Meyers.
First Assistant Engineer, R. C. S., William E. Maccoun
Second Assistant Engineer, R C S., Henry F. Schoenborn.

NANSHAN (Collier.)

Lieutenant Ben W. Hodges.

ZAFIRO (Supply Vessel.)

Ensign Henry A. Pearson.

Promotions for eminent and conspicuous conduct in battle or extraordinary heroism during the war between the United States and Spain.

For eminent and conspicuous conduct at the battle of Manila Bay, May 1, 1898.

Captain FRANK WILDES, advanced five numbers.
Captain JOSEPH B. COGHLAN, advanced six numbers.
Captain CHARLES V. GRIDLEY, advanced six numbers.
Captain NEHEMIAH M. DYER, advanced seven numbers.
Captain BENJAMIN P. LAMBERTON, advanced seven numbers.
Commander ASA WALKER, advanced nine numbers.
Commander EDWARD P. WOOD, advanced ten numbers.
Commander JOHN D. FORD, advanced three numbers.
Commander RICHARD INCH, advanced three numbers.
Commander FREDERIC SINGER, advanced five numbers.
Commander JOHN B. BRIGGS, advanced five numbers.
Commander GEORGE P. COLVOCORESSES, advanced five numbers.
Commander JOHN A. NORRIS, advanced five numbers.
Lieutenant-Commander EDWARD M. HUGHES, advanced five numbers.
Lieutenant-Commander CORWIN P. REES, advanced five numbers.
Lieutenant-Commander GEORGE B. RANSOM, advanced three numbers.
Lieutenant-Commander FRANK H. BAILEY, advanced three numbers.
Lieutenant-Commander BENJAMIN TAPPAN, advanced five numbers.
Lieutenant-Commander REYNOLD T. HALL, advanced three numbers.
Lieutenant THOMAS M. BRUMBY, advanced five numbers.
Lieutenant HARRY H. CALDWELL, advanced three numbers.
Lieutenant (junior grade) WILLIAM P. SCOTT, advanced five numbers.
Ensign WILLIAM R. WHITE, advanced five numbers.
Rear-Admiral JAMES ENTWISTLE, retired, advanced two numbers.

For eminent and conspicuous conduct at the battle of Santiago, July 3, 1898.

Captain FRANCIS J. HIGGINSON, advanced three numbers.
Captain ROBLEY D. EVANS, advanced five numbers.
Captain HENRY C. TAYLOR, advanced five numbers.
Captain FRANCIS A. COOK, advanced five numbers.
Captain CHARLES E. CLARK, advanced six numbers
Captain FRENCH E. CHADWICK, advanced five numbers.
Commander ALEXANDER B. BATES, advanced three numbers.
Commander ROBERT W. MILLIGAN, advanced three numbers.
Commander CHARLES W. RAE, advanced three numbers.

Commander RAYMOND P. RODGERS, advanced five numbers.
Commander SEATON SCHROEDER, advanced three numbers.
Commander RICHARD WAINWRIGHT, advanced ten numbers.
Commander JOHN A. RODGERS, advanced five numbers.
Commander JAMES K. COGSWELL, advanced five numbers.
Commander WILLIAM P. POTTER, advanced five numbers.
Commander GILES B. HARBER, advanced five numbers.
Commander NEWTON E. MASON, advanced five numbers.
Lieutenant-Commander WARNER B. BAYLEY, advanced two numbers.
Lieutenant-Commander ALEXANDER SHARP, JR., advanced five numbers.
Lieutenant GEORGE W. MCELROY, advanced three numbers.
Lieutenant HARRY MCL. P. HUSE, advanced five numbers.
Lieutenant CLELAND N. OFFLEY, advanced four numbers.
Lieutenant (junior grade) JOSEPH M. REEVES, advanced four numbers.
Lieutenant (junior grade) FRANK LYON, advanced four numbers.
Chief Engineer CHARLES J. MCCONNELL, retired, advanced one number.
Captain JOHN L. HANNUM, retired, advanced two numbers.
Captain GEORGE COWIE, retired, advanced three numbers.

For eminent and conspicuous conduct in battle on the occasions mentioned.

Captain JOHN J. HUNKER, advanced three numbers for eminent and conspicuous conduct in proceeding on July 21, 1898, with the United States Steamship Annapolis, under his command, over a mine field supposed to exist at the entrance to the Bay of Nipe, Cuba, for the purpose of attacking Spanish vessels lying inside.
Commander CHAPMAN C. TODD, advanced three numbers for eminent and conspicuous conduct in battle in an engagement at Cardenas, May 12, 1898, and at Manzanillo, July 18, 1898.
Commander WILLIAM T. SWINBURNE, advanced two numbers for eminent and conspicuous conduct in battle in three attacks on the batteries of Tunas, July 1, 3 and 26, 1898.
Commander ADOLPH MARIX, advanced two numbers for eminent and conspicuous conduct in battle in two engagements at Manzanillo, July 1 and July 18, 1898.
Lieutenant-Commander ALBERT C. DILLINGHAM, advanced two numbers for eminent and conspicuous conduct in battle while in temporary command of the Nashville, off Cienfuegos, Cuba, May 11, 1898.
Lieutenant-Commander AARON WARD, advanced two numbers for eminent and conspicuous conduct in battle in an action with the Spanish gunboat Don Jorge Juan, July 21, 1898, at the entrance of the Bay of Nipe.
Lieutenant-Commander LUCIEN YOUNG, advanced three numbers for eminent and conspicuous conduct in battle in three engagements at Manzanillo, June 30, July 18 and August 12, 1898.
Lieutenant-Commander JAMES M. HELM, advanced five numbers for eminent and conspicuous conduct in battle on the occasion of the action between a flotilla of United States gunboats and a Spanish armed flotilla and shore batteries at Manzanillo, Cuba, on June 30, 1898.
Lieutenant CARL W. JUNGEN, advanced five numbers for eminent and conspicuous conduct in battle on the occasion of the engagement at Manzanillo, June 30, 1898.
Lieutenant CHARLES H. HARLOW, advanced two numbers for eminent and conspicuous conduct in battle and for extraordinary heroism in a successful attempt to extricate two steam launches, under his command, from a serious ambuscade by Spanish infantry near Santiago, June 17, 1898.
Lieutenant JOHN B. BERNADOU, advanced ten numbers for eminent and conspicuous conduct in battle while in command of the Winslow, at Cardenas, May 11, 1898.
Lieutenant JOHN L. PURCELL, advanced two numbers for eminent and conspicuous conduct in battle in three engagements at Manzanillo and one at Las Tunas.
Lieutenant THOMAS P. MAGRUDER, advanced five numbers for eminent and conspicuous conduct in battle on May 11, 1898, in taking in tow and bringing off two pulling launches under a heavy fire from a large force of Spanish infantry.
Lieutenant (junior grade) WALTER S. CROSLEY, advanced two numbers for eminent and conspicuous conduct in battle in an action with the Spanish gunboat Don Jorge Juan, July 21, 1898, in which the Leyden, under his command, participated.
Lieutenant (junior grade) ANDRE M. PROCTER, advanced five numbers for eminent and conspicuous conduct in battle in the engagement between the Gloucester and the Spanish torpedo boat destroyers Pluton and Furor, July 3, 1898.
Lieutenant (junior grade) JAMES P. MORTON, advanced four numbers for extraordinary heroism in entering on the night of May 28, 1898, at great personal peril, the fire room of the United States Steamship Vixen to assist in repairing one of the boilers of that vessel.
Mate FREDERICK MULLER, promoted to Boatswain for eminent and conspicuous conduct in battle in the engagement off Manzanillo, Cuba, June 30, 1898.
Lieutenant THOMAS C. WOOD (volunteer), advanced eight numbers on the list of temporary officers for eminent and conspicuous conduct in battle in the engagement between the Gloucester and the Spanish torpedo boat destroyers Pluton and Furor, July 12, 1898.
Lieutenant (junior grade) GEORGE H. NORMAN, junior (volunteer), advanced eight numbers on the list of temporary officers for eminent and conspicuous conduct in battle in the engagement between the Gloucester and the Spanish torpedo boat destroyers Pluton and Furor, July 3, 1898.
Ensign JOHN T. EDSON (volunteer), advanced eight numbers on the list of temporary officers for eminent and conspicuous conduct in battle in the engagement between the Gloucester and the Spanish torpedo boat destroyers Pluton and Furor, July 3, 1898.
Assistant Surgeon JOHN F. BRANSFORD (volunteer), advanced three numbers on the list of temporary officers for eminent and conspicuous conduct in battle in the engagement between the Gloucester and the Spanish torpedo boat destroyers Pluton and Furor, July 3, 1898.

GENERAL NAVY REGISTER.   719

Assistant Paymaster ALEXANDER BROWN (volunteer), advanced three numbers for eminent and conspicuous conduct in battle in the engagement between the Gloucester and the Spanish torpedo boat destroyers Pluton and Furor, July 3, 1898.

For extraordinary heroism on occasions mentioned.

Captain CHARLES D. SIGSBEE, advanced three numbers for extraordinary heroism on the occasion of the destruction of the Maine in the harbor of Havana, February 15, 1898, and for eminent and conspicuous conduct in battle in an engagement between the United States steamship St. Paul, under his command, and the Spanish torpedo boat destroyer Terror, off San Juan, Porto Rico, June 22, 1898.
Lieutenant-Commander CAMERON McR. WINSLOW, advanced five numbers for extraordinary heroism displayed in the cable cutting expedition off Cienfuegos Harbor, Cuba, May 11, 1898.
Lieutenant EDWIN A. ANDERSON, advanced five numbers for extraordinary heroism displayed in the cable cutting expedition off Cienfuegos Harbor, Cuba, May 11, 1898.
Lieutenant VICTOR BLUE, advanced five numbers for extraordinary heroism displayed in perilous reconnoitering duty near Santiago, Cuba.
Lieutenant WILLIAM H. BUCK, advanced eight numbers for extraordinary heroism while on service as a spy in Spain and secret service in North Atlantic, May 1 to September 8, 1898.
Lieutenant HENRY H. WARD, advanced ten numbers for extraordinary heroism while on service as a spy in Spain and Porto Rico and secret service in North Atlantic, May 1 to September 1, 1898.
Paymaster WILLIAM W. GALT, advanced one number for extraordinary heroism April 26, 1898, in proceeding from Hong Kong to Mirs Bay in a small steam launch, in the face of a northeast gale, for the purpose of conveying greaty needed machinery to the Raleigh, thus expediting her departure with the squadron for Manila.
Naval Constructor RICHMOND P. HOBSON, advanced ten numbers, and promoted to the grade of naval constructor with the rank of captain, for extraordinary heroism in sinking the collier Merrimac in the north of the harbor of Santiago de Cuba, June 3, 1898.
Naval Cadet JOSEPH W. POWELL, advanced two numbers and promoted to ensign for extraordinary heroism while in charge of a steam launch which accompanied the collier Merrimac, for the purpose of rescuing her gallant force when that vessel was sunk in the mouth of the harbor of Santiago, Cuba, June 3, 1898.

Officers of the Marine Corps advanced and brevetted for distinguished services during the war between the United States and Spain.

Lieutenant-Colonel ROBERT W. HUNTINGTON, to be advanced one number in rank, and promoted to be a colonel in the Marine Corps from the tenth day of August, 1898, for eminent and conspicuous conduct in battle.
Captain GEORGE P. ELLIOTT, to be advanced three numbers in rank from the tenth day of August, 1898, for eminent and conspicuous conduct in battle.
Captain PAUL ST. C. MURPHY, to be brevetted a major in the Marine Corps from the third day of July, 1898, for gallant service in the naval battle of Santiago.
Captain CHARLES L. MCCAWLEY, to be a major by brevet, from the eleventh day of June, 1898, for distinguished conduct and public service in the presence of the enemy at Guantanamo, Cuba.
Captain ALLAN C. KELTON, to be a major by brevet, from the eleventh day of June, 1898, for distinguished conduct and public service in the presence of the enemy at Guantanamo, Cuba.
First Lieutenant JAMES E. MAHONEY, to be a captain by brevet, from the eleventh day of June, 1898, for distinguished conduct and public service in the presence of the enemy at Guantanamo, Cuba.
First Lieutenant HERBERT L. DRAPER, to be a captain by brevet, from the eleventh day of June, 1898, for distinguished conduct and public service in the presence of the enemy at Guantanamo, Cuba.
First Lieutenant CHARLES G. LONG, to be a captain by brevet, from the eleventh day of June, 1898, for distinguished conduct and public service in the presence of the enemy at Guantanamo, Cuba.
First Lieutenant WENDELL C. NEVILLE, to be brevetted a captain in the Marine Corps from the thirteenth day of June, 1898, for conspicuous conduct in battle at Guantanamo, Cuba.
First Lieutenant LEWIS C. LUCAS, to be brevetted a captain in the Marine Corps from the thirteenth day of June, 1898, for conspicuous conduct in battle at Guantanamo, Cuba.
First Lieutenant ALBERT S. MCLEMORE, to be a captain by brevet, from the eleventh day of June, 1898, for distinguished conduct and public service in the presence of the enemy at Guantanamo, Cuba.
First Lieutenant WILLIAM N. MCKELVY, to be a captain by brevet, from the eleventh day of June, 1898, for distinguished conduct and public service in the presence of the enemy at Guantanamo, Cuba.
Second Lieutenant THOMAS S. BORDEN, to be brevetted a first lieutenant in the Marine Corps from the third day of July, 1898, for distinguished service in the naval battle of Santiago.
Second Lieutenant LOUIS J. MAGILL, to be brevetted a first lieutenant and a captain in the Marine Corps from the thirteenth day of June, 1898, for good judgment and gallantry in battle at Guantanamo, Cuba.
Second Lieutenant MELVILLE J. SHAW, to be a first lieutenant by brevet, from the eleventh day of June, 1898, for distinguished conduct and public service in the presence of the enemy at Guantanamo, Cuba.
Second Lieutenant PHILIP M. BANNON, to be brevetted a first lieutenant in the Marine Corps from the thirteenth day of June, 1898, for conspicuous service in battle at Guantanamo, Cuba.

Appointments, Promotions, Retirements, Casualties and Resignations

SINCE JANUARY, 1901.

APPOINTMENTS.

ASSISTANT PAYMASTERS.

BOWNE, WILLIAM R. 28 February, 1901.
COLBY, FREDERICK B. 28 February, 1901.
GOODHUE, EDWARD E. 28 February, 1901.
HATCH, JOHN F. 2 January, 1901.
NICHOLSON, RICHWORTH. 7 March, 1901.

CIVIL ENGINEERS.

BAKENHUS, REUBEN E., 27 February, 1901.
BELLINGER, LYLE F., 12 January, 1901.

PROMOTIONS.

LINE.

BERRY, ROBERT M. Captain 11 February, 1901.
EVANS, ROBLEY D., Rear Admiral, 11 February, 1901.
GLENNON, JAMES H. Lieutenant 22 January, 1901.
HANFORD, FRANKLIN. Captain 29 January, 1901.
JOHNSON, MORTIMER L. Rear-Admiral 29 January, 1901.
KNAPP, HARRY S. Lieutenant-Commander 11 February, 1901.
MONTGOMERY, WILLIAM S. Lieutenant 11 February, 1901.
PORTER, THEODORIC. Commander 29 January, 1901.
POWELSON, WILFIRD V. N. Lieutenant 11 February, 1901.
RODGERS, WILLIAM L. Lieutenant 19 February, 1901.
RUSH, WILLIAM R. Lieutenant-Commander 11 February, 1901.
STUART, DANIEL D. V. Commander 11 February, 1901.
TAYLOR, HENRY C., Rear Admiral, 11 February, 1901.

PAY CORPS.

BISCOE, HARRY E. Paymaster 13 January, 1901.
SEIBELS, GEORGE G. Paymaster 4 March, 1901.
SPEEL, JOHN N. Pay Inspector 4 March, 1901.

RETIREMENTS.

AIKEN, JOSIAH B., Chief Boatswain. Retired 28 January, 1901, with rank of Lieutenant (junior grade).
ASSERSON, PETER C., Civil Engineer. Retired 5 January, 1901, with rank of Rear-Admiral.
DYER, NEHEMIAH MAYO, Captain. Retired 19 February, 1901, as a Rear Admiral.
FREEMAN, EDWARD R., Lieutenant-Commander. Retired 21 January, 1901.
HICHBORN, PHILIP, Chief Constructor. Retired 4 March, 1901, with rank of Rear-Admiral.
KAUTZ, ALBERT, Rear Admiral. Retired 29 January, 1901.
PRINDLE, FRANKLIN C., Civil Engineer. Retired 27 February, 1901, with rank of Rear Admiral.
WALKER, RALPH E. Captain, United States Marine Corps. Retired 15 February, 1901.

GENERAL NAVY REGISTER.

DEATHS.

HARRIS, WILLIAM R., Commodore. Died 5 January, 1901.
HENDERSON, ALEXANDER, Chief Engineer. Died 12 January, 1901.
LOOMIS, JOEL P., Pay Inspector. Died 12 January, 1901.
PHELPS, THOMAS S., Rear-Admiral. Died 10 January, 1901.
PIGOTT, MICHAEL R., Assistant Surgeon. Died 30 January, 1901.
QUACKENBUSH, JOHN N., Commodore. Died 10 January, 1901.
REARICK, PETER A., Rear-Admiral. Died 9 February, 1901.
THOMPSON, CHARLES P., Paymaster. Died 8 January, 1901.
WHARTON, BENJAMIN B. H., Chief Engineer. Died 13 January, 1901.

RESIGNATIONS.

ANDERSON, EDWARD C., Naval Cadet. Resigned 2 January, 1901.
ATKINSON, JOHN F., Naval Cadet. Resigned 8 February, 1901.
BURNETT, WILLIAM L., Naval Cadet. Resigned 23 February, 1901.
CADE, CASSIUS M., Naval Cadet. Resigned 23 February, 1901.
CLOSE, CHARLES F., Naval Cadet. Resigned 23 February, 1901.
COOK, ARTHUR B., Naval Cadet. Resigned 23 February, 1901.
COREY, CLEMENT B., Naval Cadet. Resigned 20 February, 1901.
CRAVEN, HENRY S., Naval Cadet. Resigned 6 March, 1901.
DEERING, GEORGE A., Naval Cadet. Resigned 23 February, 1901.
DORTCH, ISAAC F., Naval Cadet. Resigned 23 February, 1901.
RAMSTAD, ALBERT G., Naval Cadet. Resigned 16 January, 1901.
ROBINSON, EDWARD S., Naval Cadet. Resigned 23 February, 1901.
SHEPARDSON, CHARLES A., Naval Cadet. Resigned 23 February, 1901.
STAFFORD, DONALD B., Naval Cadet. Resigned 23 February, 1901.
WHETSEL, EVERARD N., Naval Cadet. Resigned 23 February, 1901.
WHITING, KENNETH, Naval Cadet. Resigned 23 February, 1901.

ERRATA AND ADDENDA.

OFFICERS OF THE NAVY.

COOPER, PHILIP H.—Entry "Acting Ensign 28 May, 1863" should read "Ensign 28 May, 1863."
DOMBAUGH, HARRY M.—Add to record "Lieutenant-Commander 19 August, 1900."
DYER, N. MAYO.—Insert after first entry "Acting Ensign 20 May, 1863."
ELDREDGE, CHARLES H.—First entry should read "Acting Paymaster 10 July, 1861."
FIELD, HARRY A.—Insert after first entry "Naval Cadet 5 August, 1882."
FRANKLIN, SAMUEL R.—For "Commander 25 July, 1866" read "Commander 27 September, 1866."
FRAZER, ALEXANDER V.—Change name to read "Fraser, Alexander V." Insert "Passed Assistant Engineer 24 February, 1874."
FRAZER, REAH.—Before first entry insert "Captain's Clerk 2 November, 1872, to 29 May, 1875."
FULMER, DAVID M.—First line, change "1 May, 1863" to read "21 April, 1863."
GIHON, ALBERT L.—Change last entry to read "Retired List with rank of Commodore, 28 September, 1895."
HOOD, JOHN.—Change record to read as follows: "Cadet Midshipman 10 September, 1875; graduated 10 June, 1879; Midshipman 10 June, 1881; Ensign (junior grade) 3 March, 1883; Ensign 26 June, 1884; Lieutenant (junior grade) 5 December, 1890; Lieutenant 28 April, 1895."
HOOKER, EDWARD.—Change record to read "Promoted to Acting Volunteer Lieutenant 5 September, 1862, for gallantry in action. Acting Volunteer Lieutenant-Commander 20 January, 1865."
HUTCHINS, HAMILTON.—Date of appointment as "Midshipman" should read "24 June, 1870."
LEMLY, SAMUEL C.—Add following to record: "Reappointed Judge Advocate-General from 5 June, 1896, and 4 June, 1900."
MORRIS, ROBERT (Naval Cadet).—Entry "Graduated 30 June, 1900" should read "Graduated 3 June, 1900."
PATCH, NATHANIEL J. K.—Add following to record: "Commander 23 July, 1900."
READ, GEORGE H.—Insert following entry: "Captain's Clerk 14 October, 1861."
SMITH, ROY CAMPBELL.—Change record in accordance with following: "Cadet Midshipman 3 October, 1874; Graduated 30 June, 1878; Midshipman 4 June, 1880."
SNOW, ELLIOTT.—Name should read "Snow, Elliot."
STAUNTON, SIDNEY A.—Insert following entry in record: "Lieutenant 15 November, 1881."
STEWART, EDWIN.—Add following to record: "Appointed Paymaster-General and Chief of the Bureau of Supplies and Accounts 16 May, 1890. Reappointed 16 May, 1894, and 1 6May, 1898. Retired with rank of Senior Rear-Admiral."
STRONG, EDWARD T.—After entry "Acting Ensign 15 October, 1863" insert "Resigned 16 June, 1865."
SULLIVAN, JOHN CLYDE.—Insert in record: "Reappointed Paymaster in pursuance of an Act of Congress passed by unanimous vote of the Senate and House of Representatives, and approved by the President, March 3, 1899."
THEISS, EMIL.—For "Naval Cadet" read "Cadet Engineer."
TREMAIN, HOBART L.—Omit final "e" in surname.
VAN REYPEN, WILLIAM K.—In first line change "24 January, 1862" to read "26 December, 1861." Make following addition to record: "Surgeon-General 23 October, 1897."
VARNEY, WILLIAM H.—Insert following entry: "Naval Constructor 13 March, 1875."
WATSON, EUGENE W.—Insert following entries: "Master's Mate, 2 May, 1859; Acting Master's Mate 5 Fbruary, 1862."
WEST, CLIFFORD H.—First entry should read "Midshipman 21 September, 1863."
WHITE, EDWIN.—Change first entry to read "Midshipman 29 November, 1861."

OFFICERS OF THE MARINE CORPS.

BARTLETT, HENRY A.—Date of appointment as Second Lieutenant should read "10 September, 1861" instead of "25 November, 1861."
CAFFERY, ST. JOHN L.—Change middle initial of name to "L."
HEYWOOD, CHARLES.—Fifth and sixth lines: For "gallant and meritorious services," read "distinguished gallantry in the presence of the enemy."
HUNTINGTON, R. W.—For last entry read "Retired 10 January, 1900."
MARIX, ARTHUR T.—Insert "Second Lieutenant 26 May, 1898, to 11 February, 1899."
MURPHY, PAUL ST. C.—Change first entry in record to read "Second Lieutenant 27 January, 1873."
MUSE, WILLIAM S.—Change date of promotion to Major to read "1 June, 1898" instead of "11 July, 1898."
ROGERS, AUSTIN C.—Change middle initial of name to "C."
STILLMAN, C. A.—Change middle initial of name to "A."
WILLIAMS, DION.—Insert before first entry "Naval Cadet 17 July, 1887."

A LIST

OF THE

Vessels of War of the United States Navy.

1797–1900.

SAILING VESSELS.

Name.	Tons.	Guns.	Remarks.
Active	122	2	Purchased 1837.
Adams	530	28	Built 1799. Burned at Hampden, Me., 1814.
Adolph Hugel	269	3	Purchased 1863. Mortar Schooner.
A. Houghton	326	2	Purchased 1862. Sold.
Alabama, re-named New Hampshire	4150	15	Built 1818. Naval Militia, New York, N. Y.
Albany	1064	20	Built 1843. Foundered at Sea, 1854.
Albemarle	200		Built 1865. Sold.
Alert	300	20	Captured 1812. Broken up, 1829.
Alligator	40	4	Built 1813. Originally Gunboat 166. Sunk 1814.
Alligator, 2d		1	Purchased 1813. Captured at New Orleans, 1814.
Alligator, 3d	198	12	Built 1821. Lost at Carysfort Reef, 1823.
Amanda	368	6	Purchased 1862. Sold.
America—Yacht			Purchased 1862. Sold.
Annie	27	1	Built 1864. Wrecked on Coast of Florida, 1865.
Argus	298	16	Built 1803. Captured in British Channel, 1813.
Argus, 2d	509	18	Built 1814. Burned at Washington, 1814.
Ariel	19	1	Purchased 1863. Sold.
Ariel, 3d		1	Purchased 1812. Sold 1815.
Ariel, 3d		1	Purchased 1831. Sold 1833.
Arietta	199	3	Purchased 1862. Mortar Schooner.
Arthur	554	6	Purchased 1862. Sold.
Asp, 2d	57	2	Purchased 1813. Sold 1824.
Asp, 2d	57	3	Purchased 1813. Sold 1815.
Asp, 3d	56	3	Purchased 1813. Sold 1824.
Augusta		14	Purchased 1799. Sold 1801.
Bainbridge	259	10	Built 1842. Foundered on Atlantic Coast, 21 August, 1863.
Baltimore	422	20	Purchased 1798. Sold 1801.
Beagle	52	3	Purchased 1822. Sold 1825.
Beauregard	101	1	Captured 1862. Sold.
Ben Morgan			Purchased 1862. Sold.
Bohio	196	2	Purchased 1862. Sold.
Bonita	76	1	Purchased 1846. Sold 1849.
Boston, 3d	700	28	Built 1799. Burned at Washington, 1814.
Boston, 4th	700	18	Built 1825. Lost at Eleuthera, West Indies, 1846.
Boxer	370	14	Built 1815. Lost off Balize, 1817.
Boxer, 2d	194	10	Built 1831. Sold 1848.
Brandywine	1726	44	Built 1821. Launched 1825. Destroyed by fire at Norfolk, Va., 1864.
Brazilleras	540	6	Purchased 1862. Sold.
Buffalo		5	Purchased 1814. Sold 1820.
Bull Dog		2	Purchased 1814. Sold 1821.
Caledonia		3	Captured 1812. Sold.
Camel		5	Purchased 1814. Sold 1820.
Carmita	61		Built 1865. Condemned at Key West, 1865.
Carolina	230	14	Blew up at New Orleans, 1814.
Charles Phelps	862	1	Purchased 1862. Sold.

(725)

GENERAL NAVY REGISTER.

Name.	Tons.	Guns.	Remarks.
Charlotte	70	2	Purchased 1863. Sold.
Chippewa	390	14	Built 1815. Lost. Caycos, W. I.
Chippewa, 2d	..	44	Built 1815. Broken up or sold between 1815 and 1824.
Chesapeake	1244	36	Captured June 1, 1813.
Chesapeake	1175	14	Training Ship for Cadets. Naval Academy, Md.
Chotauk	53	1	Purchased 1862. Sold 1865.
Columbia	1508	44	Built 1814. Burned on stocks at Washington, 1814.
Columbia, 2d	1726	44	Built 1825. Launched 1836. Destroyed at Norfolk, Va., 1861.
Columbus	2480	74	Built 1816.
Concord	700	18	Built 1828. Lost on East coast of Africa, 1843.
Congress	1268	36	Built 1799. Broken up 1836.
Congress, 4th	1867	44	Built 1839. Destroyed at Hampton Roads, 1862.
Connecticut, 2d	492	24	Sold 1801.
Conquest	82	3	Purchased 1813. Sold 1815.
Consort	230	6	Built 1836. Sold 1844.
Constellation	1236	10	Rebuilt 1854. Training station, Newport, R. I.
Constitution	1335	6	Built 1797. Repaired at Philadelphia Navy-Yard, 1874. Laid up at Boston, Mass., 1901.
C. P. Williams	210	3	Purchased 1863. Mortar Schooner.
Corporation	..	2	Purchased 1814. Sold 1820.
Corypheus—Yacht	..	..	Purchased 1862. Sold.
Courier	554	3	Purchased 1862. Wrecked 4 June, 1864.
Crescent	..	36	Presented to the Dey of Algiers.
Cumberland	1726	44	Built 1825. Launched 1842. Razeed. Sunk in Hampton Roads by the Merrimac.
Cyane	..	84	Captured 1815. Broken up 1836.
Cyane, 2d	695	2	Built 1837. At Mare Island Navy Yard, 1874.
Dale	675	8	Built 1839. For use of Naval Militia, Baltimore, Md.
Dan Smith	149	3	Purchased 1862. Mortar Schooner.
Dart	94	1	Purchased 1862. Sold.
Decatur	566	16	Built 1838. Sold.
Decoy	..	6	Purchased 1822. Sold 1826.
Delaware, 2d	321	20	Purchased 1798. Sold 1801.
Delaware, 2d	2633	74	Built 1817. Destroyed at Norfolk, Va., 1861.
Detroit	400	18	Captured 1813.
Dispatch	50	2	Purchased 1814. Sold 1820.
Dolphin, 2d	198	12	Built 1821. Sold in the Pacific, 1835.
Dolphin, 3d	224	10	Built 1836. Destroyed at Norfolk, 1861.
Eagle	..	2	Purchased 1812. Captured 3 June, 1813.
Eagle, 3d	..	20	Built 1814. Sold 1824.
Eagle, 3d	..	12	Purchased 1814. Sold 1820.
Electra	248	2	Purchased 1846. Sold.
Elizabeth	..	2	Purchased 1812. Broken up 15 May, 1815.
Enterprise, 2d	135	12	Built 1799. Enlarged to 165 tons in 1811. Lost at Little Curacoa. 1823.
Enterprise, 3d	194	10	Built 1831. Sold 1845.
Epervier	477	18	Captured 1814. Lost at sea. 1815.
Erie	509	18	Built 1813. Broken up 1841.
Erie, 2d	611	4	Built 1842. Storeship. Sold.
Essex	860	32	Built 1799. Captured 1814.
Essex, Sr.	355	16	Built 1813. Sold 1815.
Ethan Allen	556	7	Purchased 1862. Sold.
Etna	139	..	Bomb Ketch. Built 1806. Lost at New Orleans, 1812.
Etna, 2d	220	11	Purchased 1813. Condemned at New Orleans, 1817.
Etna, 3d	182	..	Bomb Barge. Purchased 1846. Sold.
Eugenia—Schooner	..	..	Purchased 1862. Sold 1864.
Experiment	135	12	Built 1800. Sold 1801.
Experiment, 2nd	194	10	Built 1831. Sold 1848.
Fair America	..	2	Purchased 1812. Sold 1815.
Fairfield	700	18	Built 1826. Sold and broken up.
Falcon	80	1	Captured 1846. Sold 1849.
Falmouth	705	18	Built 1826. Sold at Aspinwall, 1863.
Farralones	882	..	Built 1863. Steamer Massachusetts altered to sailing bark. Sold.
Fear Not	1012	6	Purchased 1862. Sold 1866.
Fennimore Cooper	95	1	Purchased 1852. Sold 1856.
Fernandina	297	6	Purchased 1862. Sold.
Ferret, 2d	..	8	Purchased 1812. Lost off Stony Inlet. 1814.
Ferret, 2d	51	3	Purchased 1822. Lost in West Indies, 1825.

GENERAL NAVY REGISTER. 727

Name.	Tons.	Guns.	Remarks.
Firebrand	..	12	Purchased 1815. Condemned at New Orleans, 1819.
Firefly	333	14	Purchased 1814. Sold 1816.
Flambeau	300	14	Purchased 1814. Sold 1816.
Flying Fish	90	2	Purchased 1838. Sold 1842.
Flirt	150	2	Built 1839. Sold.
Fox	130	4	Built 1817. Condemned 1821.
Fox	80	2	Built 1864. Sold.
Fox, 2d	51	3	Purchased 1822. Condemned 1838.
Franklin	2257	74	Built 1815. Broken up 1852-53.
Fredonia	800	4	Purchased 1845. Destroyed by earthquake, 1869.
Frolic	509	18	Built 1813. Captured off Havana, 1814.
Fulton—Steamship	2000	30	Built 1814. Blew up at Brooklyn, 1829.
Ganges	504	24	Purchased 1798. Sold 1801.
Gemsbok	622	7	Built 1862. Sold.
Gem of the Sea	371	4	Purchased 1862. Sold.
General Greene	645	28	Built 1799. Burned at Washington, 1814.
General Pike	875	24	Built 1813. Sold.
George Maughan	274	3	Purchased 1862. Mortar Schooner.
George Washington	624	24	Purchased 1798. Sold 1803.
Georgiana	280	16	Captured 1813. Recaptured off coast, 1814.
Germantown	939	20	Built 1843. Destroyed at Norfolk, 1861.
Ghent	..	1	Built 1815. Sold.
G. L. Brockenborough	..	..	Built 1863. Lost 1863.
Governor Tompkins	96	6	Purchased 1812. Captured 12 August, 1814.
Grampus	184	12	Built 1821. Foundered off Charleston, S. C., 1843.
Granite	..	1	Purchased 1862. Returned to Lighthouse Board, 1865.
Greenwich	338	16	Captured 1813. Burned at Marquesas Island, 1814.
Greyhound	65	3	Purchased 1822. Sold 1824.
Growler	53	2	Purchased 1812.
Guard	925	3	Bought 1861. Originally National Guard. Laid up at New York, 1874.
Guerriere	1508	44	Captured 1814. Broken up 1841.
G. W. Blunt	121	1	Purchased 1862. Sold.
Hamilton	..	9	Purchased 1812. Capsized 10 August, 1813.
Hecla	194	..	Bomb Barge. Purchased 1846. Sold.
Helen	..	4	Purchased 1813. Lost in Delaware Bay, 1815.
Henry James	261	3	Purchased 1862. Mortar Schooner. Sold.
Herald	279	18	Purchased 1798. Sold 1801.
Hope	134	1	Purchased 1862. Sold.
Horace Beals	296	3	Purchased 1862. Sold.
Hornet, 2d	..	10	Purchased 1804. Sold 1806.
Hornet, 3d	440	18	Built 1805. Lost off Tampico, 1829.
Hudson	1728	44	Purchased 1826. Sold 1844.
Idaho	1837	7	Built 1866. Screw steamer, converted into sailing ship. Sold 1874.
Independence	1891	22	Built 1814. Razeed to a 54. Receiving Ship at Mare Island Navy Yard, Cal., 1874, 1901.
Ino	895	9	Purchased 1862. Sold 1867.
Insurgent	..	36	Captured 1799. Lost at sea, July, 1800.
Intrepid	..	4	Captured 1803. Blew up off Tripoli, 1804.
Ironsides, Jr.	200	..	Built 1864. Sold.
Jackal	47	3	Purchased 1822. Sold 1824.
James L. Davis	461	4	Purchased 1862. Sold.
James S. Chambers	401	5	Purchased 1862. Sold.
Jamestown	1150	20	Built 1845. Transferred to Marine Hospital Service.
Java	1508	44	Built 1814. Broken up 1842.
J. C Kuhn	888	5	Purchased 1862. Sold.
Jefferson	..	18	Built 1814. Sold 1821, or broken up, or unfit for repairs.
John Adams	544	28	Built 1799. Broken up 1829.
John Adams, 2d	700	18	Built 1830. Sold at Boston, 1865.
John Griffith	246	3	Purchased 1862. Mortar Schooner.
John P. Kennedy	350	3	Purchased 1853. Sold 1856.
Jones	..	18	Built 1814. Sold 1821, or broken up, or unfit for repairs.
Julia	53	2	Purchased 1812. Captured 10 August, 1813.
Julia	..	..	Built 1864. Sold.
Kingfisher	450	5	Purchased 1862. Wrecked on St. Helena Island, 28 March, 1864.
Kittatinney	421	4	Purchased 1862. Sold.

728   GENERAL NAVY REGISTER.

Name.	Tons.	Guns.	Remarks.
Lady of the Lake	89	3	Purchased 1813. Sold 1815.
Lawrence	450	20	Built 1813.
Lawrence, 2d	364	10	Built 1843. Sold 1846.
Levant, 2d	792	18	Built 1837. Lost in Pacific Ocean, 1860.
Lexington, 2d	691	18	Built 1825. Sold.
Lightning	..	..	Built 1865. Sold.
Louisiana	341	16	Purchased 1812. Broken up 1821.
Lynx	150	6	Built 1814. Lost at sea, 1820.
Macedonian	1325	38	Captured 1812. Broken up 1835.
Macedonian, 3d	1140	..	Built 1832. Launched 1836. Razeed 1852. In ordinary at Norfolk, Va., 1874. Sold Dec., 1875.
Madison	593	20	Built 1812.
Mahonese	100	1	Captured 1846. Sold 1849.
Malek Abdhel	250	10	Captured 1846. Sold 1849.
Maria A. Wood	344	2	Purchased 1863. Mortar Schooner. Sold 1866.
Marion	566	16	Built 1838. Broken up. Rebuilt as Steamer, 1874.
Maryland	380	20	Purchased 1799. Sold 1801.
Matthew Vassar	182	3	Purchased 1863. Mortar Schooner.
Matthew Vassar	182	3	Purchased 1864. Mortar Schooner.
Merrimac	530	24	Purchased 1798. Sold 1801.
Midnight	386	5	Purchased 1862. Sold.
Mohawk	..	32	Built 1814. Sold 1821, or broken up, or unfit for repairs.
Montezuma	347	20	Purchased 1798. Sold 1801.
Montgomery	..	6	Purchased 1813. Sold 1815.
Morning Light	937	8	Purchased 1862. Captured off Coast of Texas, 21 January, 1863.
Natchez	700	18	Built 1827. Broken up 1840.
National Guard	1046	4	Purchased 1862. Name changed to Guard, 1865.
Nautilus	185	12	Purchased 1803. Captured off New York, 1812.
New Hampshire	4150	2	Built 1801. Naval Militia, N. H.
New Orleans	2805	60	Built 1815. On the stocks, Sackett's Harbor, 1874.
New York	2633	74	Built 1818. Destroyed at Norfolk, 1861.
New York, 2d	1130	36	Built 1799. Burned at Washington, 1814.
Norfolk	200	18	Purchased 1798. Sold 1801.
Norfolk—Packet	349	3	Purchased 1862. Mortar Schooner.
Niagara	450	20	Built 1813.
Nightingale	1000	1	Purchased 1862. Sold 11 February, 1865.
Nonsuch	148	14	Purchased 1812. Dropped from Navy List, 1826.
North Carolina	2633	74	Built 1818. Broken up. Sold 1867.
Ohio	..	3	Built 1813. Captured 12 August, 1814.
Ohio, 2d	2700	5	Built 1820. Launched 1820. Receiving Ship. Boston, 1874. Laid up at Boston.
O. H. Lee	199	3	Purchased 1864. Sold.
Oliver H. Lee	199	3	Purchased 1863. Mortar Schooner.
Oneida	243	14	Built 1809. Sold.
On-ka-hy-e	250	2	Purchased 1843. Lost on Caycos Reef, W. I., 1848.
Ontario	509	18	Built 1813. Sold 1819.
Ontario, 2d	81	3	Purchased 1813. Sold 1815.
Onward	704	3	Purchased 1860. Storeship at Callao, Peru, 1874.
Oregon	250	2	Purchased 1841. Sold 1845.
Orvetta	171	3	Purchased 1861. Mortar Schooner.
Otsego	..	2	Built 1840. Transferred from the V Department, and returned to it, 1844-1845.
Pampero	1375	4	Purchased 1860. Sold 1867.
Para	190	3	Purchased 1860. Mortar Schooner.
Patapsco	380	20	Purchased 1799. Sold 1801.
Peacock	509	18	Built 1813. Broken up 1828.
Peacock, 2d	559	18	Built 1828. Lost at Columbia River, 1841.
Pennsylvania	3241	120	Built 1822. Launched 1837. Destroyed at Norfolk, Va., 1861.
Perry	280	10	Built 1843. Sold 1865.
Pert	..	3	Purchased 1813. Sold 1815.
Petrel	76	1	Purchased 1846. Transferred to Coast Survey, 1850.
Phenix	90	2	Purchased 1841. Sold.
Philadelphia	1240	36	Built 1799. Wrecked off Tripoli, 1803.
Pilot	120	2	Built 1836. Sold 1838.
Pinckney	195	18	Built 1798. Sold 1801.
Pioneer	230	6	Built 1836. Sold 1844.
Plattsburg	..	44	Built 1815. Broken up or sold between 1815 and 1824.

GENERAL NAVY REGISTER. 729

Name	Tons.	Guns.	Remarks.
Plymouth	989	20	Built 1843. Destroyed at Norfolk, Va., 1861.
Poinsett—Steamer	250	2	Built 1840. Transferred from the War Department and returned to it, 1844.
Porcupine		1	Built 1813.
Porpoise	198	12	Built 1820. Lost in West Indies, 1833.
Porpoise, 2d	224	10	Built 1836.
Portsmouth	593	24	Built 1798. Sold 1801.
Portsmouth, 2d	846	14	Built 1843. North Pacific Squadron, 1874. Naval Militia, New Jersey.
Potomac	1457	20	Built 1819. Launched 1821. Receiving Ship, Philadelphia, 1874. Sold May, 1877.
Preble		7	Purchased 1813. Sold 1815.
Preble, 2d	566	16	Built 1838. Burned at Pensacola, 27 April, 1863.
President	1576	44	Built 1800. Captured off New York, 1815.
President, 2d		2	Purchased 1812. Sold 1815.
rrmotheus	290	12	Purchased 1814. Sold 1819.
Pursuit	603	6	Purchased 1860. Sold.
Queen Charlotte	300	14	Captured 1813.
Racer	252	3	Purchased 1860. Mortar Schooner.
Rachel Seaman	303	2	Purchased 1860. Sold.
Ranger		14	Purchased 1814. Sold 15 May, 1821.
Ranger, 3d		1	Purchased 1814. Sold 1816.
Raritan	1726	44	Built 1842. Launched 1843. Destroyed at Norfolk, Va., 1861.
Rattlesnake	278	14	Purchased 1813. Captured at sea, 1814.
Raven—Transport	50	1	Purchased 1813. Sold 1815.
Reefer	76	1	Purchased 1846. Sold 1849.
Release	327	2	Purchased 1856. Sold.
Relief	468	2	Built 1836. Receiving Ship, Washington, 1874. Laid up.
Renshaw	80	..	Purchased 1864. Sold.
Restless	265	4	Purchased 1860. Sold.
Retaliation	107	14	Captured 1798. Recaptured in West Indies, 1798. Original name, Le Croyable.
Revenge, 3d		12	Purchased 1807. Lost off Newport, R. I., 1811.
Richmond	200	18	Purchased 1798. Sold 1801.
Roanoke	..	7	Transferred from State Department, 1814. Sold 1816.
Roebuck	455	4	Purchased 1860. Sold.
Roman	350	1	Purchased 1860. Sold.
Rosalie	28	1	Built 1864. Sold.
Sabine	1457	22	Built 1855 Receiving Ship, Portsmouth, N. H., 1874. Laid up, Portsmouth.
Saint Lawrence	1726	..	Built 1826. Launched 1847. Used as Marine Barracks at Norfolk, 1874. Sold 1875.
Saint Louis	830	18	Built 1828. Naval Militia, Philadelphia, Pa.
Saint Mary's	1025	20	Built 1843. State School Ship, New York, 1874, and 1901.
Sam Houston	66	1	Purchased 1860. Sold.
Samuel Rotan	212	2	Purchased 1860. Sold.
Santee	1475	48	Built 1855. At Annapolis Naval Academy, 1874. Gunnery Ship.
Sarah Bruen	233	3	Purchased 1860. Mortar Schooner. Sold.
Saranac	360	14	Built 1815. Sold 1818.
Saratoga	1025	4	Built 1842. Public Marine School, Philadelphia, Pa.
Saratoga, 2d		26	Built 1814. Sold 1824.
Savannah	1475	..	Built 1842. Launched 1842. Razeed. In ordinary, Norfolk, Va., 1874.
Scorpion		2	Purchased 1812. Captured 5 September, 1814.
Scourge		16	Captured 1804. Sold 1812. Originally, Transfer. a Privateer.
Scourge, 2d		10	Captured 1812 Capsized 10 August, 1813.
Sea Foam	264	3	Purchased 1860. Sold.
Sea Gull, 2d	100	2	Purchased 1838. Lost off Cape Horn, 1839
Sea Gull—Steam Galliot	150	3	Purchased 1822. Sold 1840.
Seahorse		1	Purchased 1812. Burned 1814.
Shark	177	12	Built 1821. Lost at Columbia River, 1846.
Shark	87	1	Built 1864. Name changed to George W. Rodgers.
Shepark Knapp	838	8	Purchased 1860. Wrecked at Cape Haytien, 18 May, 1863.
Somers		2	Purchased 1812. Captured 12 August, 1814.
Somers, 2d	259	10	Built 1842. Sunk off Vera Cruz, 1846.
Sophronia	217	3	Purchased 1860. Mortar Schooner.
Southampton	567	4	Built 1842. Storeship. Sold.
Spark	300	14	Purchased 1814. Sold 1826.

GENERAL NAVY REGISTER.

Name	Tons	Guns	Remarks
Spark, 2d	..	1	Purchased 1831. Sold 1833.
Spitfire, 2d	102	..	Bomb Ketch. Purchased 1805. Broken up 1820.
Spitfire, 3d	286	12	Purchased 1814. Sold 1816.
Stonewall	30	1	Captured 1864. Sold.
Stromboli	192	..	Bomb Barge. Purchased 1846. Sold.
Superior	..	44	Built 1814. Sold 1821, or broken up, or unfit for repairs.
Supply	547	4	Purchased 1846. Laid up, New York, 1874.
Surprise—Ketch	..	12	Purchased 1815. Condemned, New Orleans, 1820.
Sylph	300	16	Built 1813. Broken up 1820.
Sylph, 2d	..	1	Purchased 1831. Lost in West Indies, 1831.
Syren	250	16	Built 1803. Captured at sea, 1814.
Tampico	80	1	Captured 1846. Sold 1849.
Taney	..	1	Built 1846. Transferred from Treasury Department and returned to it.
T. A. Ward	234	3	Purchased 1860. Mortar Schooner.
Tchefonta—Block Ship	1500	22	Built 1814. Sold on stocks.
Terrier	61	3	Purchased 1822. Sold 1825.
Tickler	50	..	Bomb Ketch. Purchased 1812. Sold 1818.
Ticonderoga	..	17	Purchased 1814. Sold 1824.
Tigress	..	1	Purchased 1812. Captured 4 September, 1814.
Tom Bowline	260	12	Purchased 1814. Sold 1818.
Torch	260	12	Purchased 1814. Sold 1816.
Torpedo	..	..	Purchased 1814. Sold 1818.
Trippe	..	1	Purchased 1812. Burned.
Troup	..	16	Purchased 1812. Sold 1815.
Trumbull, 3d	400	24	Built 1798. Sold 1801.
Truxtun	331	10	Built 1842. Lost at Tuspan, 1846.
Two Sisters	54	1	Built 1864. Sold.
United States	1576	44	Built 1797. Destroyed at Norfolk, Va., 186-.
Valparaiso	402	..	Built 1864. Sold.
Velocity	..	..	Built 1863. Captured at Sabine Pass, 21 January, 1863.
Vengeance	92	..	Bomb Ketch. Purchased 1805. Broken up 1818.
Vermont	2633	16	Built 1848. Receiving Ship, New York, 1874 and 1901.
Vesuvius	92	..	Bomb Ketch. Purchased 1806. Broken up, 1829.
Vesuvius, 2d	239	..	Bomb Ketch. Purchased 1846. Sold.
Vincennes	700	18	Built 1825. Sold 1867.
Viper	..	10	Built 1804. Captured at sea, 1813.
Virginia	2633	74	Built 1818. Broken up on stocks, 1874.
Vixen	185	12	Built 1803. Captured at sea, 1812.
Vixen, 2d	..	14	Purchased 1813. Captured at sea, 1813.
Wanderer	300	4	Purchased 1860. Sold.
Warren, 2d	385	20	Built 1798. Sold 1801.
Warren, 3d	697	18	Built 1825. Sold at Panama, and used as a coal hulk by Pacific Mail Steamship Company, 1874.
Washington	2250	74	Built 1816. Broken up 1843.
Washington, 3d	2250	74	Built 1814. Broken up 1843.
Washington, 4th	..	10	Built 1843. Transferred from Treasury Department, and returned to it, 1848.
Wasp, 2d	450	18	Built 1806. Captured at sea, 1812.
Wasp, 3d	509	18	Built 1813. Lost at sea, 1817.
Wave	..	1	Purchased 1838. Sold.
Weasel	53	3	Purchased 1822. Sold 1825.
Wild Cat	48	3	Purchased 1822. Lost in the West Indies, 1824.
Wild Cat	30	1	Built 1864. Sold.
William Bacon	183	3	Purchased 1860. Mortar Schooner.
William Badger	334	1	Purchased 1860. Sold.
William G. Anderson	593	7	Purchased 1860. Sold 1866.
Yorktown	566	16	Built 1838. Lost at Cape de Verde.

REVENUE SERVICE.

Name	Tons	Guns	Remarks
Algonquin	..	..	Transferred in 1898. Returned to the Revenue Service.
Calumet	174	2	Transferred in 1898. Returned to the Revenue Service.
Corwin	424	2	Transferred in 1898. Returned to the Revenue Service.

GENERAL NAVY REGISTER. 731

Name	Tons.	Guns.	Remarks.
Diligence	187	12	Built 1798. Returned to the Revenue Service.
Eagle	187	14	Built 1798. Sold 1801.
General Greene	98	12	Built 1798.
Governor Jay	187	14	Built 1798. Returned to the Revenue Service
Grant	407	..	Transferred in 1898. Returned to the Revenue Service.
Gresham	906	..	Transferred in 1898. Returned to the Revenue Service.
Hamilton	250	1	Transferred in 1898. Returned to the Revenue Service.
Hudson	174	3	Transferred in 1898. Returned to the Revenue Service.
Manning	980	3	Transferred in 1898. Returned to the Revenue Service.
McCulloch	1280	..	Transferred in 1898. Returned to the Revenue Service.
McLean	846	..	Transferred in 1898. Returned to the Revenue Service.
Morrill	397	2	Transferred in 1898. Returned to the Revenue Service.
Perry	534	..	Transferred in 1898. Returned to the Revenue Service.
Pickering	187	14	Built 1798. Lost at sea, 1800.
Rush	695	..	Transferred in 1898. Returned to the Revenue Service.
Scammel	187	14	Built 1798. Sold 1801.
South Carolina	..	12	Built 1798. Returned to the Revenue Service.
Virginia, 2d	187	14	Built 1798. Returned to the Revenue Service.
Windom	525	1	Transferred in 1898. Returned to the Revenue Service.
Woodbury	370	7	Transferred in 1898. Returned to the Revenue Service.

STEAM VESSELS.

Abarenda	4670	4	Screw. Purchased 5 May, 1898. Pacific Station.
Abraham	700	..	Paddle. Purchased 1862-63. Sold 30 Sept., 1868.
Abeona	206	6	Paddle. Purchased 1864-65. Sold 17 Aug., 1865.
Acacia	300	4	Screw. Purchased 1863-64. Sold.
Accomac	187	2	Screw. Tug. Built 1891. Originally El Toro. Purchased 26 March, 1898. Havana, Cuba.
A. C. Powell	65	1	Screw. Purchased 1861-62. Sold 20 June, 1865.
Active	296	5	Screw. Tug. Built 1888. Purchased 18 April, 1898. Mare Island, Cal.
Adams	1400	12	Screw. Built 1874. Training Ship.
Adder	120	1	Screw. Submarine Torpedo Boat. Built 1900-1901. Building, Elizabethport, N. J.
Adela	583	6	Paddle. Purchased 1863-64. Sold 30 Nov., 1865.
Admiral	1248	5	Screw. Purchased 1863-64. Name changed to Fort Morgan, 1 September, 1864.
Advance	880	4	Paddle. Purchased 1864-65. Name changed to Frolic.
Agamenticus	3990	10	Iron-clad. Built 1861-62. Renamed Terror. Norfolk, Va.
Agawam	974	8	Paddle. Built 1861-62. Sold 1867.
Aileen	192	5	Screw. Converted Gunboat. Purchased 2 May, 1898. Naval Militia, N. Y.
Ajax	7500	4	Screw. Collier. Built 1890. Purchased 12 May, 1898. Originally Scindia. Asiatic Station.
Alabama	1261	9	Paddle. Purchased 1862-63. Sold.
Alabama	11,565	46	Two screws. Battleship. Built 1896-99. North Atlantic Station.
Alarm	800	4	Fowler Wheel. Built 1874. Torpedo Boat. Sold 23 February, 1898.
Alaska	1122	12	Screw. Built 1868. Sold 2 November, 1883.

GENERAL NAVY REGISTER.

Name.	Tons.	Guns.	Remarks.
Albany	3769	30	Two screws. Protected Cruiser. Originally Almirante Abru. Built 1898. Purchased 16 March, 1898. Asiatic Station.
Albay	151	2	Two screws. Gunboat. Transferred from War Department. Asiatic Station.
Albatros	378	4	Screw. Purchased 1861-62. Sold 8 Sept., 1865.
Albatross	..	..	Transferred from Fish Commission during Spanish-American War. Returned.
Alert	831	10	Screw. Built 1866.
Alert	1110	11	Screw. Built 1874. Mare Island, Cal.
Alert, 2d	65	2	Screw. Purchased 1863-64. Name changed to Watch, 1 October, 1865.
Alexander	6181	2	Screw. Built 1894. Collier. Originally Atala. Purchased 25 April, 1898. Asiatic Station.
Alexandria	60	2	Paddle. Purchased 1863-64. Sold 17 Aug., 1865.
Alfred Robb	75	4	Screw. Purchased 1861-62. Sold 17 Aug., 1865.
Algoma	483	2	Screw. Built 1864-65. Originally Squando. Broken up 1875.
Algonquin	974	10	Paddle. Purchased 1863-64. Sold 21 Oct., 1869.
Alice	155	2	Screw. Tug. Built 1893. Purchased 26 March, 1898. Norfolk, Va.
Alleghany	1000	..	Horizontal Hunter Paddles. Built 1845. First vessel with an iron hull in the United States' Navy. Converted into Screw, 1851. Sold 15 May, 1869.
Alliance	1375	14	Screw. Built 1873-76. Training Ship.
Alpha	..	..	Screw. Purchased 1864-65. Sold 15 Sept., 1865.
Althea	72	1	Screw. Purchased 1863-64. Sunk by torpedo, 12 March, 1865.
Alvarado	106	4	Screw. Gunboat. Captured in Spanish-American War. Portsmouth, N. H.
Amaranthus	182	3	Screw. Purchased 1864-65. Sold 5 Sept., 1865.
Ammonoosuc	3200	23	Screw. Built 1864. Name changed to Iowa. Sold 27 September, 1883.
Amphitrite	3990	20	Two screws. Monitor. Built 1874-95. Training Ship.
Anacosta	217	1	Screw. Purchased 1858. Sold 20 July, 1865.
Anemone	156	4	Screw. Purchased 1864-65. Sold 25 Oct., 1865.
Annapolis	1000	13	Screw. Gunboat. Built 1896-97. Asiatic Station.
Antelope	173	6	Paddle. Purchased 1863-64. Sold.
Antietam	2490	21	Screw. Built 1870. Store Ship, League Island. Sold 8 Sept., 1888.
Antona	565	4	Screw. Purchased 1863-64. Sold 30 Nov., 1868.
Apache	650	6	Screw. Tug. Built 1889. Originally J. D. Jones. Navy Yard, N. Y.
Arapahoe	2348	13	Screw. Built 1864-65. Not built.
Arapahoe	2200	8	Screw. Built 1863-64.
Arayat	..	..	Screw. Gunboat. Captured Philippine Islands. Asiatic Station.
Arctic	255	..	Screw. Purchased 1855. Sold.
Arctic	1358	..	Screw. Ice Boat. Built 1873. Leased 1898. Returned to City of Philadelphia, Pa. Originally Ice Boat No. 3.
Arethusa	195	2	Screw. Purchased 1864-65. Sold 3 Jan., 1866.
Arethusa	3319	..	Screw. Tank Steamer. Built 1893. Purchased in 1898. Originally Luciene. Asiatic Station.
Argosy	219	8	Paddle. Purchased 1863-64. Sold 1 Aug., 1868.
Aries	820	7	Screw. Purchased 1863-64. Sold 1 Aug., 1865.
Arizona	950	2	Paddle. Purchased 1862-63. Destroyed by fire, 27 February, 1865.
Arkansas	752	6	Screw. Purchased 1863-64. Sold 20 July, 1863.
Arkansas	3235	13	Two screws. Monitor. Built 1898-1901. Building, Newport News, Va.
Armeria	1600	2	Light-House Tender. Transferred in 1898. Returned.
Aroostook	507	4	Screw. Built 1861-62. Sold September, 1869.
Ascutney	974	8	Paddle. Built 1861-62. Sold.
Ashuelot	786	6	Paddle. Built 1865. Wrecked 17 February, 1883, in China.
Aster	..	..	Tug. Purchased 1863-64. Wrecked 8 Oct., 1864.
Atlanta	1006	4	Iron-clad. Captured 1864-65. Sold 4 May, 1862.
Atlanta	3000	21	Screw. Protected Cruiser. Built 1883-85. Navy Yard, N. Y.
Augusta	1310	8	Paddle. Purchased 1861-62. Sold.
Augusta Dinsmore	850	2	Screw. Purchased 1863-64. Sold 5 Sept., 1868.
Avenger	750	7	Ram. Built 1863-64. Sold 29 November, 1865.
Azalia	176	2	Screw. Purchased 1864-65. Sold 10 Aug., 1868.
Badger	4784	12	Screw. Auxiliary Cruiser. Built 1889. Originally Yumuri. Purchased 19 April, 1898. Transferred to War Department.

GENERAL NAVY REGISTER.

Name.	Tons.	Guns.	Remarks.
Bagley	167	3	Two screws. Torpedo Boat. Built 1898-1901. Building, Bath Iron Works.
Bailey	235	4	Two screws. Torpedo Boat. Built 1897-1900. Morris Heights, New York.
Bainbridge	420	7	Two screws. Torpedo Boat Destroyer. Built 1898-1901. Building, Neafie & Levy, Philadelphia, Pa.
Baltimore	4413	25	Two screws. Protected Cruiser. Built 1886-88. Navy Yard, N. Y.
Baltimore	500	2	Paddle. Purchased 1863-64. Sold 23 June, 1865.
Bancroft	839	20	Two screws. Gunboat. Built 1890-92. North Atlantic Station.
Banshee	533	5	Paddle. Purchased 1863-64. Sold 30 Nov., 1868.
Barcelo	66	..	Screw. Gunboat. Captured during Spanish-American War. Asiatic Station.
Basco	42	2	Screw. Gunboat. Transferred from War Department. Asiatic Station.
Barrataria	..	..	Grounded and destroyed, 7 April, 1863.
Barney	167	3	Two screws. Torpedo Boat. Built 1898-1901. Building, Bath Iron Works.
Baron de Kalb	511	13	Iron-clad. Purchased 1861-62. Sunk by torpedo, July, 1863.
Barry	420	7	Two screws. Torpedo Boat Destroyer. Built 1898-1901. Building, Neafie & Levy, Philadelphia.
Bat	530	3	Screw. Purchased 1864-65. Sold 25 Oct., 1865.
Belusan	200	..	Screw. Gunboat. Transferred from War Department. Asiatic Station.
Benefit	..	..	Paddle. Purchased 1864-65. Charter expired 1865; returned to owners.
Bennington	1710	15	Two screws. Gunboat. Built 1887-89. Asiatic Station.
Benton	1000	16	Iron-clad. Built 1861-62. Sold 29 Nov., 1865.
Berberry	163	4	Screw. Purchased 1864-65. Sold 10 July, 1868.
Bermuda	1235	3	Screw. Purchased 1863-64. Sold 21 Sept., 1868.
Biddle	167	3	Two screws. Torpedo Boat. Built 1898-1901. Building, Bath Iron Works.
Bienville	1558	10	Paddle. Purchased 1861-62. Sold 1867.
Bignonia	321	3	Screw. Purchased 1864-65. Sold 12 July, 1868.
Black Hawk	902	8	Paddle. Purchased 1862-63. Destroyed by fire, 22 April, 1865.
Blakely	165	3	Two screws. Torpedo Boat. Built 1898-1901. Building, Geo. Lawley, Boston.
Bloomer	130	2	Paddle. Purchased 1863-64. Sunk and wreck sold, 1865.
Blue Light	85	1	Screw. Purchased 1863-64. Sold 27 Sept., 1883.
Bon Homme Richard, 2d.	3713	20	Screw. Built 1864-65. Not built.
Boston	3000	21	Screw. Protected Cruiser. Built 1883-85. Mare Island, Cal.
Boxer	444	3	Paddle. Purchased 1866. Originally Tristam Shandy. Sold.
Brilliant	226	4	Stern-wheel. Purchased 1862-63. Sold 17 Aug., 1868.
Britannia	495	4	Paddle. Purchased 1863-64. Sold 10 Aug., 1868.
Brooklyn	2070	20	Screw. Built 1858. Sold 25 March, 1891.
Brooklyn	9215	42	Two screws. Armored Cruiser. Built 1893-96. Asiatic Station.
Brutus	6000	2	Screw. Collier. Originally Peter Jebson. Built 1894. Purchased June 3, 1898. Asiatic Station.
Buccaneer	160	..	Screw. Auxiliary Gunboat. Built 1888. Borrowed in 1898. Returned to William R. Hearst.
Buckthorne	128	1	Screw. Purchased 1863-64. Sold 1869.
Buffalo	6888	14	Screw. Converted Cruiser. Originally Nictheroy. Built 1892. Purchased July 11, 1898, from Brazilian government. Training vessel.
Burlington	814	..	Built 1875. Sold 27 September, 1883.
Cactus	176	1	Screw. Purchased 1863-64. Sold 20 June, 1865.
Caesar	5016	4	Screw. Collier. Originally Kingston. Built 1896. Purchased 21 April, 1898. Fortress Monroe, Va.
Cairo	512	..	Iron-clad. Purchased 1861-62. Western flotilla, sunk by torpedo, 12 December, 1862.
Calamianes	151	..	Screw. Gunboat. Transferred from War Department. Asiatic Station.
Calhoun	508	4	Paddle. Purchased 1861-62. Sold 1865.
California	14,020	62	Two screws. Armored Cruiser. Building 1901-1904, Union Iron Works, San Francisco.
Callao	208	5	Two screws. Gunboat. Captured during Spanish-American War. Asiatic Station.
Calypso	630	6	Screw. Purchased 1863-64. Sold 30 Nov., 1865.
Camanche	1875	2	Screw. Built 1862. Sold 22 March, 1889.

GENERAL NAVY REGISTER.

Name.	Tons.	Guns.	Remarks.
Cambridge	858	5	Screw. Purchased 1861-62. Sold 20 June, 1865.
Camella	198	2	Screw. Purchased 1863-64. Sold 15 Aug., 1865.
Canandaigua	955	10	Screw. Built 1861-62. Broken up in 1884.
Canonicus	1034	2	Iron-clad. Built 1864-65. Navy Yard, League Island.
Carnation	82	2	Screw. Purchased 1863-64. Sold 10 Aug., 1865.
Carondelet	512	13	Iron-clad. Built 1861-62. Western Flotilla. Sold 30 November, 1865.
Carrabasset	292	6	Paddle. Purchased 1863-64. Sold 15 Aug., 1865.
Casco	614	2	Iron-clad. Built 1863-64. Re-named Hero at Washington, 1874. Broken up 1875.
Cassius	3458	2	Screw. Collier. Built 1883. Originally Rhaetia. Purchased 24 May, 1898. Transferred to War Department. Now Transport Sumner.
Castine	1177	15	Two screws. Gunboat. Built 1890-92. Asiatic Station.
Catalpa	1900	3	Screw. Purchased 1864-65. Sold July 23, 1894.
Catawba	1034	2	Iron-clad. Built 1861-62.
Catskill	496	2	Iron-clad. Built 1861-62. League Island, Pa.
Cayuga	507	6	Screw. Built 1861-62. Sold 25 October, 1865.
Celtic	8000	2	Screw. Refrigerator Ship. Built 1891. Originally Celtic King, Asiatic Station.
Ceres	144	1	Screw. Purchased 1861-62. Sold 25 Oct., 1865.
Champion	115	4	Paddle. Purchased 1863-64. Sold 29 Nov., 1865.
Chatham		..	Paddle. Purchased 1864-65. Sold 2 Sept., 1865.
Charleston	3730	23	Two screws. Protected Cruiser. Built 1886-88. Wrecked Nov. 2, 1899, near Kamiguin Island, P. I.
Charleston	9700	68	Two screws. Protected Cruiser. Built 1901-04. Building, Newport News, Va.
Chattanooga	3000	8	Screw. Built 1863-64. Sunk by ice at League Island, and sold 27 January, 1872.
Chattanooga	3200	24	Two screws. Protected Cruiser. Built 1899-1902. Building, Lewis Nixon, Elizabeth, N. J.
Chauncey	420	7	Two screws. Torpedo Boat Destroyr. Built 1898-1901. Building, Neafie & Levy.
Chenango	974	8	Paddle. Built 1861-62. Sold.
Cherokee	606	6	Screw. Built 1863-64. Sold 1 August, 1866.
Cheyenne	145	..	Screw. Tug. Built 1885. Originally Bristol. Purchased July 8, 1898. Sold 14 Nov., 1900.
Chicago	5000	32	Two screws. Protected Cruiser. Built 1883-85. South Atlantic Station.
Chickasaw	450	4	Iron-clad. Built 1861-62. Sold.
Chickasaw	100	1	Screw. Tug. Built 1882. Originally Hercules. Purchased 25 June, 1898. Navy Yard, N. Y.
Chicopee	974	8	Paddle. Built 1861-62. Sold 1867.
Chillicothe	303	2	Iron-clad. Built 1861-62. Sold 29 Nov., 1865.
Chillicothe	203	3	Iron-clad. Built 1863-64. Sold 29 Nov., 1865.
Chimo	614	2	Iron-clad. Built 1863-64. Re-named Piscataqua. Sold 27 February, 1877.
Chippewa	507	4	Screw. Built 1861-62. Sold 30 November, 1865.
Choctaw	1000	..	Paddle. Purchased 1861-62. Sold 1866, at New Orleans.
Choctaw	350	3	Screw. Tug. Built 1892. Originally C. G. Coyle. Purchased April 19, 1898. Pensacola, Fla.
Chocura	507	4	Screw. Built 1861-62. Sold 1867.
Cimarron	860	10	Paddle. Built 1863-64. Sold.
Cimmerone	860	10	Paddle. Built 1861-62. Sold 1866.
Cincinnati	512	..	Iron-clad. Purchased 1861-62. Sold 1866.
Cincinnati	3213	24	Two screws. Protected Cruiser. Built 1890-94. Navy Yard, N. Y.
Circassian	1750	5	Screw. Purchased 1862-63. Sold 22 June, 1868.
City of Pekin	5080	2	Screw. Transport. Chartered in 1898. Returned to Pacific Mail Steamship Co.
Clara Dolson	1000	..	Paddle. Captured 1861-62. Western Flotilla. Returned to owner, 1865.
Clematis	296	3	Screw. Purchased 1864-65. Sold.
Cleveland	3200	24	Two screws. Protected Cruiser. Built 1899-1902. Building, Bath Iron Works.
Clifton	892	6	Paddle. Purchased 1861-62. Captured at Sabine Pass, 1863.
Clinton	50	..	Screw. Purchased 1864-65. Sold.
Clover	128	2	Screw. Purchased 1863-64. Sold 21 Sept., 1868.
Clyde	294	5	Paddle. Purchased 1863-64. Sold 25 Oct., 1865.
Cœur de Lion	60	2	Screw. Built 1861-62. Returned to Lighthouse Board, 1865.
Cohassett	100	2	Screw. Built 1861-62. Sold May 16, 1892.
Cohoes	614	2	Iron-clad. Built 1864-65. Broken up 1874.
Collier	177	..	Paddle. Purchased 1864-65 Sold 15 Aug., 1865.
Colossus	2127	10	Screw. Building 1866. Originally Kalamazoo. Broken up in 1884.

GENERAL NAVY REGISTER. 735

Name.	Tons.	Guns.	Remarks.
Colorado	3400	40	Screw. Built 1855. Sold 14 February, 1885.
Colorado	13,680	62	Two screws. Armored Cruiser. Built 1901-04. Building, Cramp & Sons, Philadelphia, Pa.
Columbia			Iron-clad. Wrecked off North Carolina, 1863.
Columbia, 3d			Purchased 1862-63. Sold 1867.
Columbia	7375	28	Three screws. Protected Cruiser. Built 1890-93. League Island, Pa.
Columbine	131	2	Screw. Purchased 1862-63. Captured 23 May, 1864.
Commodore	80	4	Paddle. Purchased 1863-64. Name changed to Fort Gaines, 1 September, 1864.
Commodore Barney	513	4	Paddle. Purchased 1861-62. Sold 20 July, 1868.
Commodore Hull	376	3	Paddle. Purchased 1861-62. Sold 27 Sept., 1865.
Commodore Jones	542	6	Paddle. Purchased 1862-63. Destroyed by torpedo, 6 May, 1864.
Commodore McDonough	534	6	Paddle. Purchased 1861-62. Foundered 23 August, 1865.
Commodore Morris	532	1	Paddle. Purchased 1861-62. Sold 12 July, 1865.
Commodore Perry	513	4	Paddle. Built 1861-62. Sold 12 July, 1865.
Commodore Read	650	6	Paddle. Purchased 1863-64. Sold 20 July, 1865.
Commodore Truxton			Purchased 1862-63. Sold.
Concord	1710	14	Two screws. Gunboat. Built 1887-89. Asiatic Station.
Conemaugh	955	8	Paddle. Built 1861-62. Sold 1867.
Conestoga			Iron-clad. Built 1861-62. Western Flotilla. Sold Sold 30 November, 1865.
Confiance	1380	12	Screw. Not built.
Connecticut	1800	5	Paddle. Purchased 1861-62. Sold 21 Sept., 1865.
Connecticut	1800	11	Paddle. Purchased 1864-65. Sold 21 Sept., 1865.
Contoocock	2200	8	Screw. Built 1863-64. Name changed to Albany, and sold, 1872.
Cornubia	600	3	Paddle. Purchased 1863-64. Sold 25 Oct., 1865.
Covington	224	8	Paddle. Purchased 1863-64. Captured 5 May, 1864.
Cowslip	220	3	Paddle. Purchased 1863-64. Sold 1866.
Craven, T. A. M.	146	4	Two screws. Torpedo Boat Destroyer. Built 1896-98. Newport, R. I.
Cricket	151	6	Purchased 1862-63. Sold 17 August, 1868.
Crocus			Screw. Purchased 1863-64. Wrecked on Boty's Island, August, 1863.
Crusader	549	8	Screw. Purchased 1858. Sold.
Culgoa	6500		Screw. Refrigerator Ship. Built 1889. Asiatic Station.
Curlew	196	6	Purchased 1862-63. Sold 17 August, 1868.
Cushing	105	3	Two screws. Torpedo Boat. Built 1888-89. Navy Yard, N. Y.
Currituck	193	5	Screw. Purchased 1861-62. Sold 15 Sept., 1865.
Dacotah	998	6	Screw. Built 1858. Broken up at Mare Island, 1870.
Daffodil	160	2	Paddle. Purchased 1862-63. Sold 1867.
Dahlgren	146	4	Two screws. Torpedo Boat. Built 1896-98. Newport, R. I.
Dahlia	50		Paddle. Purchased 1862-63. Sold 17 Aug., 1865.
Dai-ching	520	7	Screw. Purchased 1863-64. Grounded and destroyed, 26 January, 1865.
Daisy	50		Paddle. Purchased 1862-63. Sold 17 Aug., 1865.
Dale	420	7	Torpedo Boat Destroyer. Built 1898-1901. Building, Richmond, Va.
Dandelion	111	2	Screw. Purchased 1862-63. Sold 15 Aug., 1865.
Darlington	300		Paddle. Purchased 1861-62. Sold.
Davis	154	3	Two screws. Torpedo Boat. Built 1896-97. Navy Yard, Mare Island.
Dawn	391	3	Screw. Purchased 1861-62. Sold 1 Nov., 1865.
Daylight	682	4	Screw. Purchased 1861-62. Sold 25 Oct., 1865.
Decatur	420	7	Two screws. Torpedo Boat Destroyer. Built 1898-1901. Building Richmond, Va.
Delaware	357	3	Paddle. Purchased 1861-62. Sold 12 Sept., 1865.
De Long	166	3	Two screws. Torpedo Boat. Built 1898-1901. Building South Boston, Mass.
Delta			Screw. Purchased 1864-65. Sold 5 Sept., 1868.
Denver	3200	24	Two screws. Protected Cruiser. Built 1899-1902. Building, Neafie & Levy.
Des Moines	3200	24	Two screws. Protected Cruiser. Built 1899-1902. Building Fore River Engine Co.
De Soto	1600	9	Paddle. Purchased 1861-62. Sold.
Detroit	1380	12	Screw. Purchased 1864-65. Not built.
Detroit	2089	21	Two screws. Unprotected Cruiser. Built 1888-92. Navy Yard, Portsmouth, N. H.
Diana			Screw. Purchased 1862-63. Captured in Archipelago River, 1863.

GENERAL NAVY REGISTER.

Name.	Tons.	Guns.	Remarks.
Dictator	1750	2	Iron-clad. Built 1861-62-64. Sold 24 Sept., 1883.
Dispatch	558	..	Screw. Purchased 1855. Sold.
Dispatch	750	4	Screw. Purchased 1873. Wrecked in 1891 and sold Oct., 1891.
Dixie	6114	19	Auxiliary Cruiser. Built 1893. Originally El Rio. Training ship.
Dolphin	1486	11	Screw. Dispatch Boat. Built 1883-85. Special service.
Don	390	8	Screw. Purchased 1864-65. In service.
Donegal	1124	..	Paddle. Purchased 1864-65. Sold 27 Sept., 1868.
Don Juan de Austria	1130	12	Screw. Gunboat. Built 1887. Asiatic Station.
Dorothea	594	10	Screw. Converted Gunboat. Built 1897. League Island. Purchased 1898.
Dragon	118	1	Paddle. Purchased 1861-62. Sold 20 July, 1868.
Dunbarton	636	4	Paddle. Purchased 1864-65. Sold 1867.
Dunderberg	5090	10	Iron-clad. Built 1861-62. Sold by contractor, 1866, to French Imperial Government, and renamed the Rochambeau.
Du Pont	165	4	Two screws. Torpedo Boat. Built 1895-96, Newport, R. I.
Eagle	434	4	Screw. Converted Gunboat. Built 1890. Special service. Originally Almy. Purchased 2 April, 1898.
East Boston	631	4	Paddle. Auxiliary Gunboat. Built 1892. Purchased 2 June, 1898. Sold 19 July, 1899.
Eastport	700	8	Paddle. Built 1861-62. Grounded and destroyed, 26 April, 1864.
E. B. Hall	192	4	Screw. Purchased 1861-62. Sold 20 June, 1865.
Edith	400	2	Screw. Purchased 1847. Lost on California Coast.
Elfrida	173	..	Screw. Converted Gunboat. Built 1899. Naval Militia, New Jersey.
El Cano	560	10	Screw. Gunboat. Captured during Spanish-American War. Asiatic Station.
Elk	162	6	Paddle. Purchased 1863-64. Sold 24 Aug., 1865.
Ella	230	2	Paddle. Purchased 1861-62. Sold 15 Sept., 1865.
Ellen	341	4	Paddle. Purchased 1861-62. Sold 2 Sept., 1865.
Ellis	..	2	Paddle. Purchased 1861-62. Sold.
Emerald	30	..	Screw. Purchased 1864-65.
Emma	350	8	Screw. Purchased 1863-64. Sold 1 Nov., 1865.
Emma Henry	521	1	Paddle. Purchased 1864-65. Name changed to Wasp, 1865. Sold Jan., 1876.
Engineer	142	1	Paddle. Purchased 1836. Rebuilt 1855.
Engineer	200	..	Paddle. Purchased 1855. Sold.
Enterprise	1375	..	Screw. Built 1874. Public Marine School, Boston, Mass.
Enquirer	136	2	Screw. Auxiliary Gunboat. Built 1896. Purchased 29 June, 1898. Transferred to War Department.
Eolus	344	3	Paddle. Purchased 1864-65. Sold 1 Aug., 1865.
Epervier	831	10	Screw. Purchased 1864-65. Not built.
Epsilon	..	..	Screw. Purchased 1864-65. Sold 12 July, 1868.
Ericsson	120	4	Two screws. Torpedo Boat. Built 1891-97. Navy Yard, N. Y.
Essex	614	17	Iron-clad. Purchased 1861-62. Sold 29 Nov., 1865.
Essex	1375	..	Screw. Built 1874. Training service.
Estrella	..	..	Screw. Purchased 1864-65. Sold 1867.
Etlah	483	2	Iron-clad. Built 1863-64-65. Sold 1876.
Eureka	..	..	Screw. Purchased 1862-63. Sold 15 Sept., 1868.
Eutaw	974	8	Paddle. Purchased 1861-62. Sold 1867.
Exchange	211	7	Paddle. Purchased 1863-64. Sold 17 Aug., 1865.
Fahkee	699	3	Screw. Purchased 1863-64. Sold 10 Aug., 1865.
Fairplay	800	4	Screw. Purchased 1862-63. Sold 17 Aug., 1865.
Fairy	173	8	Paddle. Purchased 1864-65. Sold 17 Aug., 1865.
Farragut	279	4	Two screws. Torpedo Boat. Built 1896-98. Mare Island.
Fawn	174	7	Paddle. Purchased 1863-64. Sold 17 Aug., 1865.
Fern	..	2	Screw. Purchased 1862-63. Sold 17 Aug., 1865.
Fern	840	..	Screw. Built 1871. Naval Militia, Washington, D. C.
Fish Hawk	..	..	Fish Commission Vessel. Transferred during War in 1898. Returned.
Flag	963	9	Screw. Purchased 1861-62. Sold 12 July, 1865.
Flambeau	900	2	Screw. Purchased 1861-62. Sold 12 July, 1865.
Florida	1261	9	Paddle. Purchased 1861-62. Sold.
Florida	3235	16	Two screws. Built 1898-1901. Building, Elizabeth, N. J.
Foote	142	3	Two screws. Built 1895-96. Navy Yard, New York.
Forest Rose	203	6	Screw. Purchased 1862-63. Sold 17 Aug., 1865.
Fort Donelson	900	7	Paddle. Purchased 1864-65. Sold 25 Oct., 1865.
Fort Doneldson	900	5	Paddle. Purchased 1863-64. Sold 25 Oct., 1865.

GENERAL NAVY REGISTER. 737

Name.	Tons.	Guns.	Remarks.
Fort Gaines	80	4	Paddle. Purchased 1864-65. Sold 15 Aug., 1865.
Fort Henry	519	6	Paddle. Purchased 1861-62. Sold 15 Aug., 1865.
Fort Hindman	286	7	Paddle. Purchased 1863-64. Sold 17 Aug., 1865.
Fort Jackson	1770	..	Paddle. Purchased 1862-63. Sold 27 Sept., 1865.
Fort Morgan	1248	5	Screw. Purchased 1864-65. Sold 5 Sept., 1865.
Fortune	450	2	Screw. Built 1863-64. Training station, Newport, R. I.
Fox	154	3	Two screws. Torpedo Boat. Built 1896-97. Mare Island.
Franklin	3680	51	Screw. Built 1854. Receiving Ship at Norfolk, Va.
Free Lance	197	2	Screw. Auxiliary Gunboat. Built 1895. Borrowed in 1898. Returned to Augustus Schermerhorn.
Frolic	614	..	Paddle. Purchased as A. D. Vance, 1864. Sold 27 Sept., 1883.
Frolic	607	6	Screw. Converted Gunboat. Built 1892. Navy Yard, Norfolk. Originally Comanche. Purchased 28 May, 1898.
Fulton, 1st	2000	30	Paddle. Built 1814. Blew up, 1829.
Fulton, 2d		..	Paddle. Built 1835. Launched 1837.
Fuschia	180	3	Screw. Purchased 1863-64. Sold 15 Sept., 1868.
Galatia	1244	11	Screw. Purchased 1863-64. Sold 13 Oct., 1865.
Galena	910	8	Screw. Built 1872-79. Wrecked in 1891 and sold May 16, 1892.
Galveston	3200	24	Two screws. Protected Cruiser. Built 1899-1902. Building W. R. Trigg Co., Richmond, Va.
Gamage	187	6	Paddle. Purchased 1864-65. Sold 17 Aug., 1865.
Gamma		1	Screw. Purchased 1864-65. Sold 25 Oct., 1865.
Gazelle	117	6	Paddle. Purchased 1863-64. Sold 17 Aug., 1865.
General Alava	1390	6	Screw. Asiatic Station.
General Bragg	700	2	Ram. Captured 1861-62. Western Flotilla. Sold 1 Sept., 1865.
General Burnside	201	5	Paddle. Purchased 1864-65. Returned to War Department. 1 June, 1868.
General Grant	204	5	Paddle. Purchased 1864-65. Returned to War Department. 1865.
General Lyon	1200	1	Paddle. Purchased 1862-63. Sold 17 Aug., 1865.
General Pillow	500	2	Ram. Captured 1861-62. Western Flotilla. Sold 29 November, 1865.
General Price	700	..	Ram. Captured 1861-62. Western Flotilla. Sold 30 September, 1865.
General Sherman	187	5	Paddle. Purchased 1864-65. Returned to War Department, 1 June, 1868.
General Taylor	150	1	Paddle. Built 1845. Sold.
General Thomas	184	5	Paddle. Purchased 1864-65. Returned to War Department, 1 June, 1865.
Genessee	803	4	Screw. Built 1861-62. Sold 1867.
Georgia	15,320	66	Two screws. Battleship. Built 1901-1904. Building Bath, Me.
Geranium	222	3	Paddle. Purchased 1863-64. Sold 16 Oct., 1865.
Gertrude	350	8	Screw. Purchased 1863-64. Sold 30 Nov., 1865.
Gettysburg	518	2	Paddle. Purchased 1863 as Margaret and Jessie. Sold May, 1879.
Glacier	7000	..	Screw. Refrigerator Ship. Built 1891. Asiatic Station. Originally Port Chalmers. Purchased July, 1898.
Gladiolus	97	3	Screw. Purchased 1864-65. Sold 15 Sept., 1865.
Glance	80	..	Screw. Purchased 1864-65. Sold 27 Sept., 1883.
Glasgow	252	6	Paddle. Purchased 1863-64. Sold June, 1869.
Glaucus	1244	11	Screw. Purchased 1863-64. Sold 12 July, 1865.
Glide	232	6	Screw. Purchased 1864-65. Sold 15 Aug., 1865.
Glide	137	6	Paddle. Purchased 1862-63. Destroyed by fire at Cairo, Ill. February, 1863.
Gloucester	786	10	Screw. Converted Gunboat. Built 1891, Naval Academy, Md. Originally Corsair. Purchased 23 April, 1898.
Goldsborough	248	4	Two screws. Torpedo Boat. Built 1897-99. Mare Island.
Governor Buckingham	886	6	Screw. Purchased 1863-64. Sold 12 July, 1865.
Governor Russell	631	..	Paddle. Auxiliary Gunboat. Built 1898. Purchased 11 May, 1898. Sold 19 July, 1899.
Grampus	300	..	Paddle. Purchased 1863-64. Originally Ion. Sold.
Grampus	120	..	One tube. Screw. Submarine Torpedo Boat. Built 1900-01. Building Union Iron Works, California.
Grand Gulf	1200	11	Screw. Purchased 1863-64. Sold 30 Nov., 1865.
Granite City	315	7	Paddle. Purchased 1863-64. Captured 6 May, 1864.
Grape Shot	26	..	Screw. Captured 1861. Originally Tug New York.
Great Western	..	..	Purchased 1861-62. Western Flotilla. Sold 29 November, 1865.
Grossbeak	196	6	Paddle. Purchased 1864-65. Sold 17 Aug., 1865.

47

Name.	Tons.	Guns.	Remarks.
Guardoqui	42	3	Screw. Gunboat. Transferred from War Department, Asiatic Station.
Guerriere	2200	20	Screw. Built 1863-64. Sold 1872.
Gunboat No. 16	..	..	Contract not awarded.
Gwin	46	1	Screw. Built 1896-97. Torpedo Station, Newport, R. I.
Hannibal	4291	..	Screw. Collier. Built 1898. Purchased 16 Apr., 1898. Originally Joseph Holland. At Mare Island. California.
Harcourt	68	..	Screw. Purchased 1864-65. Sold 3 Oct., 1867.
Harriet Lane	619	4	Side-wheel. Purchased 1861-62. Captured at Galveston, Tex., 1 Jan., 1863.
Hartford	2790	18	Screw. Built 1858. Training ship for landsmen.
Harvard	13,000	16	Two screws. Auxiliary Cruiser. Originally New York. Chartered during 1898. Returned to International Navigation Co.
Harvest Moon	546	3	Paddle. Purchased 1863-64. Sunk by torpedo, 1 March, 1865.
Hassalo	2200	8	Screw. Purchased 1863-64. Never built.
Hastings	293	8	Paddle. Purchased 1864-65. Sold 17 Aug., 1865.
Hatteras	1100	3	Side-wheel. Purchased 1861-62. Sunk by Alabama, 11 January, 1863.
Hawk	375	6	Screw. Converted Gunboat. Built 1891. Purchased 2 Apr., 1898. Originally Hermoine. Navy Yard, Norfolk, Va.
Hector	2792	2	Screw. Collier. Built 1883. Originally Pedro (war prize). Sold 10 Oct., 1899.
Helena	1397	19	Two screws. Gunboat. Built 1894-96. Asiatic Station.
Heliotrope	238	1	Paddle. Purchased 1863-64. Sold 20 June, 1865.
Hendrick Hudson	400	..	Screw. Purchased 1862-63. Sold 12 Sept., 1865.
Henry Brinker	108	1	Screw. Purchased 1861-62. Sold 20 July, 1865.
Hercules	198	3	Screw. Tug. Built 1888. Purchased 26 Apr., 1898. Naval Station, Port Royal.
Hetzel	301	2	Paddle. Built 1861-62. Returned to Coast Survey, 1865.
Hibiscus	406	6	Screw. Purchased 1864-65. Sold.
Hist	472	3	Screw. Converted Gunboat. Built 1895. Originally Thespia. Purchased 22 Apr., 1898. Norfolk, Va.
Holland	74	1	Screw. Submarine Torpedo Boat. Built 1899. Purchased 11 Apr., 1900. Newport, R. I.
Hollyhock	300	3	Paddle. Purchased 1863-64. Sold 5 Oct., 1865.
Hollyhock	300	3	Paddle. Purchased 1864-65. Sold 5 Oct., 1865.
Home	713	3	Screw. Purchased 1863-64. Sold 5 Sept., 1865.
Honduras	376	3	Paddle. Purchased 1863-64. Sold 5 Sept., 1865.
Honeysuckle	234	2	Screw. Purchased 1863-64. Sold 15 Aug., 1865.
Hopkins	408	7	Two screws. Torpedo Boat Destroyer. Built 1898-1901. Building, Harlan & Hollingsworth, Wilmington, Del.
Hornet	425	9	Screw. Converted Gunboat. Built 1890. Originally Alicia. Purchased 6 Apr., 1898. Naval Militia, North Carolina.
Housatonic	1240	9	Screw. Built 1861-62. Sunk off Charleston by torpedo, 17 February, 1864.
Howquah	397	4	Screw. Purchased 1863-64. Sold 10 Aug., 1865.
Hoyt	19	..	Screw. Purchased 1864-65. Sold 10 Aug., 1865.
Hull	408	7	Two screws. Torpedo Boat Destroyer. Built 1898-1901. Building, Harlan & Hollingsworth, Wilmington, Del.
Hunchback	517	4	Screw. Purchased 1861-62. Sold 12 July, 1865.
Huntress	138	6	Paddle. Purchased 1864-65. Sold 17 Aug., 1865.
Huntress	82	2	Screw. Converted Gunboat. Built 1895. Purchased 7 June, 1898. Naval Militia, New Jersey.
Huntsville	817	4	Screw. Purchased 1861-62. Sold 30 Nov., 1865.
Huron	541	..	Screw. Built 1874. Wrecked 1877.
Huron	507	4	Screw. Built 1861-62. Sold 14 June, 1869.
Hyacinth	50	..	Screw. Purchased 1862-63. Sold 17 Aug., 1865.
Hydrangea	224	2	Screw. Purchased 1863-64. Sold 25 Oct., 1865.
Ibex	236	6	Paddle. Purchased 1864-65. Sold 17 Aug., 1865.
Ida	104	1	Screw. Purchased 1863-64. Sunk by torpedo, 23 Apr., 1865.
Idaho	2638	8	Screw. Built 1864-65. Converted into sailing vessel and sold in East Indies.
Illinois	2200	20	Screw. Built 1863-64.
Illinois	11,565	46	Two screws. Battleship. Built 1896-1900. Newport News Shipbuilding Co., Newport News, Va.
Inca	120	2	Screw. Converted Gunboat. Built 1898. Purchased 13 June, 1898. Naval Militia, Massachusetts.

GENERAL NAVY REGISTER.   739

Name.	Tons.	Guns.	Remarks.
Indiana	10,288	44	Two screws. Battleship. Built 1890-93. North Atlantic Station.
Indianola	442	2	Iron-clad. Built 1861-62. Captured 24 Feb., 1863.
I. N. Seymour	133	2	Paddle. Purchased 1861-62. Sold 20 June, 1865.
Infanta Maria Teresa	7000	32	Two screws. Armored Cruiser. Built 1890. Captured in Spanish-American War. Wrecked 1898.
Intrepid	330	..	Screw. Built 1874. Sold May 16, 1892.
Ion	230	..	Paddle. Purchased 1863-64. Re-named Grampus. Sold.
Iosco	974	8	Paddle. Built 1861-62. Sold.
Iowa	11,340	48	Two screws. Battleship. Built 1893-96. Pacific Station.
Iris	400	..	Paddle. Built 1847. Sold 1850.
Iris	483	2	Screw. Purchased 1863-64. Originally Shiloh. Sold 1874.
Iris	6100	..	Screw. Refrigerator Ship. Built 1885. Originally Menerosha. Purchased 25 May, 1898. Asiatic Station.
Iron Age	828	8	Paddle. Purchased 1861-62. Destroyed on Coast of North Carolina, 11 January, 1864.
Iroquois	1575	6	Screw. Built 1858. Transferred to Marine Hospital Service.
Iroquois	702	7	Screw. Tug. Built 1892. Originally Fearless. Purchased Apr., 1898. Naval Station, Honolulu, H. I.
Isaac Smith	453	9	Screw. Purchased 1861-62. Captured 20 Jan., 1863.
Isla de Cuba	1125	12	Two screws. Gunboat. Built 1886. Captured during war with Spain. Asiatic Station.
Isla de Luzon	1125	12	Two screws. Gunboat. Built 1887. Captured during war with Spain. Asiatic Station.
Isonomia	593	3	Paddle. Purchased 1864-65. Sold 12 July, 1865.
Itasca	507	4	Screw. Built 1861-62. Sold 30 November, 1865.
Iuka	940	4	Screw. Purchased 1863-64. Sold 1 Aug., 1865.
Ivy	50	..	Screw. Purchased 1862-63. Sold 17 Aug., 1865.
Iwana	192	..	Screw. Tug. Built 1891-92. Yard tug, Boston, Mass.
Jacob Bell	229	3	Paddle. Purchased 1861-62. Lost 6 Nov., 1865.
James Adger	1151	9	Paddle. Purchased 1861-62.
Jasamine	220	2	Screw. Purchased 1863-64. Sold 1866.
Java	2490	21	Screw. On the stocks, New York Navy Yard. Broken up in 1884.
Jean Sands	139	..	Screw. Built 1864-65. Sold May 16, 1892.
John Hancock	382	..	Screw. Built 1850. Sold.
John L. Lockwood	180	2	Paddle. Purchased 1861-62. Sold 15 Sept., 1865.
John P. Jackson	777	6	Paddle. Purchased 1861-62. Sold 5 Oct., 1865.
Jonquil	90	2	Screw. Purchased 1863-64. Sold 21 Oct., 1868.
Judge Torrence	600	..	Paddle. Purchased 1861-62. Western Flotilla. Sold 17 August, 1865.
Juliet	157	6	Screw. Purchased 1862-63. Sold 17 Aug., 1865.
Juniata	828	8	Screw. Built 1861-62. Sold 25 March, 1891.
Juniper	116	2	Screw. Purchased 1864-65. Sold 9 Nov., 1865.
Justin	3300	1	Screw. Built 1891. Purchased 23 Apr., 1898. Mare Island, California.
Kalamazoo	3200	4	Iron-clad. Built 1863-64. Re-named Colossus. On stocks 1874. Broken up in 1884.
Kanawha	507	4	Screw. Built 1861-62. Sold 1866.
Kanawha	175	6	Screw. Auxiliary Gunboat. Built 1896. Purchased 7 June, 1898. Transferred to War Department.
Kansas	410	3	Screw. Built 1863-64. Sold 27 Sept., 1883.
Katahdin	507	4	Screw. Built 1861-62. Sold 30 November, 1865.
Katahdin	2155	4	Two screws. Armored Ram. Built 1891-92. League Island, Pa.
Katarina	112	2	Screw. Purchased 1864-65. Sold 25 Oct., 1865. Not known at Navy Department.
Kate	242	6	Paddle. Purchased 1864-65. Sold.
Kearsarge	695	6	Screw. Built 1861-62. Wrecked Roncador Reef, 10 Feb., 1894.
Kearsarge	11,540	56	Two screws. Battleship. Built 1896-99. North Atlantic Station.
Kennebec	507	4	Screw. Built 1861-62. Sold 30 November, 1865.
Kensington	1052	3	Paddle. Purchased 1861-62. Sold 12 July, 1865.
Kentucky	800	11	Purchased 1862-63. Sold.
Kentucky	11,540	56	Two screws. Battleship. Built 1896-99. Asiatic Station.
Kenwood	232	6	Paddle. Purchased 1863-64. Sold 17 Aug., 1865.

GENERAL NAVY REGISTER.

Name.	Tons.	Guns.	Remarks.
Keokuk	677	..	Iron-clad. Built 1862-63. Sunk in battle off Charleston, S. C., 7 April, 1863.
Keosauqua	2200	8	Screw. Built 1863-64. Not built.
Kewaydin	2490	21	Screw. Re-named Pennsylvania. On stocks, Boston. Broken up.
Keystone State	1364	9	Paddle. Purchased 1861-62. Sold 15 Sept., 1868.
Key West	207	9	Paddle. Purchased 1863-64. Burnt to prevent capture, 4 November, 1864.
Kickapoo	540	4	Iron-clad. Built 1861-62. Re-named Kewaydin. Sold in 1874.
Kineo	507	4	Screw. Built 1861-62. Sold.
King Philip	..	..	Paddle. Purchased 1861-62. Sold 15 Sept., 1868.
Kinsman	..	..	Purchased 1862-63. Snagged and sunk, 23 February, 1863.
Klamath	483	2	Iron-clad. Built 1863-64. Sold 1874.
Koka	483	2	Iron-clad. Built 1863-64. Broken up 1874.
Kosciusco	..	..	Ram. Purchased 1861-62. Sold.
Laburnum	181	4	Screw. Built 1864-65. Sold.
Lackawanna	1026	10	Screw. Built 1861-62.
Lady Sterling	..	8	Paddle. Built 1864-65. Sold.
Lafayette	1000	8	Ram. Purchased 1861-62. Sold 1866.
Lancaster	3250	22	Screw. Built 1858. Training service.
Lancaster	..	..	Ram. Purchased 1861-62. Sunk by Vicksburg Batteries.
Larkspur	125	2	Screw. Purchased 1863-64. Sold 10 Aug., 1865.
Laurel	50	1	Screw. Purchased 1862-63. Sold 17 Aug., 1868.
Lavender	68	..	Screw. Purchased 1863-64. Wrecked 12 June, 1864.
Lawrence	400	7	Two screws. Torpedo Boat Destroyer. Built 1898-1901. Building Weymouth, Mass.
Lebanon	3375	4	Screw. Collier. Built 1894. Purchased 6 Apr., 1898. Norfolk, Va.
Lehigh	496	2	Iron-clad. Built 1861-62. League Island, Pa.
Lenapee	964	8	Paddle. Built 1861-62. Sold.
Leonidas	4242	1	Screw. Collier. Built 1898. Originally Elizabeth Holland. Purchased 16 Apr., 1898. League Island, Pa.
Leslie	100	2	Screw. Built 1861-62. Returned to War Department, June, 1865.
Lexington	500	7	Iron-clad. Purchased 1861-62. Sold 17 Aug., 1865.
Leyden	450	..	Screw. Built 1864-65. Naval Station, Newport.
Leyte	151	4	Two screws. Gunboat. Built 1890. Captured during Spanish-American War. Asiatic Station.
Lilac	129	2	Screw. Purchased 1863-64. Sold 12 July, 1865.
Lilian	630	2	Paddle. Built 1864-65. Sold 30 Nov., 1865.
Lily	50	1	Screw. Purchased 1862-63. Sunk by collision, 3 May, 1863.
Linden	177	6	Screw. Purchased 1862-63. Snagged and sunk, 22 February, 1864.
Lioness	..	..	Ram. Purchased 1861-62. Sold.
Little Ada	196	2	Screw. Purchased 1864-65. Sold 12 Aug., 1865.
Little Rebel	..	..	Ram. Captured 1861-62. Sold 29 Nov., 1865.
Lodona	860	7	Screw. Purchased 1862-63. Sold 20 June, 1865.
Louisiana	295	4	Screw. Purchased 1861-62. Used as powderboat off Fort Fisher, 23 December, 1864.
Louisville	468	13	Iron-clad. Purchased 1861-62. Sold.
Lupin	68	..	Screw. Purchased 1863-64. Sold 28 Oct., 1865.
Machias	1177	15	Two screws. Gunboat. Built 1890-92. North Atlantic Station.
Macdonough	400	7	Two screws. Torpedo Boat Destroyer. Built 1898-1901. Weymouth, Mass.
MacKenzie	65	1	Screw. Torpedo Boat Destroyer. Built 1896-97, League Island, Pa.
Mackinaw	974	8	Paddle. Built 1861-62. Sold 1867.
Madawasca	2840	23	Screw. Built 1865. Re-named Tennessee. Sold.
Madge	218	2	Screw. Purchased 1861-62. Sunk off Frying-Pan Shoals, 11 October, 1863.
Magnolia	843	3	Paddle. Purchased 1861-62. Sold 12 Jan., 1865.
Mahaska	832	6	Paddle. Purchased 1861-62. Sold.
Mahopac	2100	2	Iron-clad. Built 1861-62. League Island, Pa.
Malvern	627	3	Paddle. Purchased 1863-64. Sold 25 Oct., 1868.
Manayunk	2100	2	Iron-clad. Built 1861-62. Now Ajax, 1874. Sold 22 March, 1899.
Mangrove	..	..	Light-House Tender. Transferred in 1898. Returned.
Manhattan	2100	2	Iron-clad. Built 1861-62. League Island, Pa.

GENERAL NAVY REGISTER. 741

Name.	Tons.	Guns.	Remarks.
Maine	6682	29	Two screws. Battleship. Built 1888. Blown up 15 February, 1898, in Havana Harbor, Cuba.
Maine	12,300	44	Two screws. Battleship. Built 1899-1901. Building, Philadelphia, Pa.
Manila	1750	12	Screw. Transport. Built 1881. Captured during war with Spain, 1898. Asiatic Station.
Manileno	142	6	Screw. Gunboat. Transferred from War Department. Asiatic Station.
Manly	30	..	Screw. Torpedo Boat. Purchased during war with Spain. Naval Academy.
Manitou	2000	15	Screw. Built 1870. Name changed to Worcester. Sold 27 September, 1883.
Maple	700	2	Lighthouse Tender. Transferred during war in 1898. Returned.
Maratanza	786	6	Paddle. Built 1861-62. Sold.
Marblehead	507	4	Screw. Built 1861-62. Sold.
Marblehead	2089	20	Two screws. Cruiser. Built 1889-1892. Mare Island, Cal.
Marcellus	4400	1	Screw. Collier. Built 1879. Originally Titania. Purchased 13 June, 1898. Norfolk, Va.
Maria	170	2	Screw. Built 1863-64. Sunk by collision, 1870.
Marietta	479	2	Iron-clad. Built 1861-62. Sold 17 April, 1873.
Marietta	479	2	Iron-clad. Built 1863-64.
Marietta	1000	13	Two screws. Gunboat. Built 1895-97. Asiatic Station.
Marigold	115	2	Screw. Purchased 1863-64. Sold 1866.
Marion	910	8	Screw. Built 1874. Naval Militia, San Diego, Cal.
Mariveles	142	3	Screw. Transferred from War Department. Asiatic Station.
Marmora	207	8	Stern-wheel. Purchased 1862-63. Sold 17 August, 1868.
Martin	25	..	Screw. Purchased 1864-65. Sold 10 Aug., 1865.
Maryland	13,680	62	Two screws. Armored Cruiser. Built 1901-04. Building, Newport News, Va.
Mary Sanford	757	3	Screw. Purchased 1863-64. Sold 10 Aug., 1868.
Massachusetts	765	..	Screw. Built 1848. Transferred from War Department. Re-named Farralones and sold 1866.
Massachusetts	2107	40	Screw. Building 1866. Originally Passaconaway. On the stocks, Portsmouth, N. H. Broken up in 1884.
Massachusetts	10,288	46	Two screws. Battleship. Built 1890-93. North Atlantic Station.
Massasoit	974	8	Paddle. Built 1861-62. Sold 1867.
Massasoit	202	1	Screw. Tug. Built 1898. Originally A. W. Booth. Purchased 25 April, 1898. Keywest, Fla.
Mattabessett	974	8	Paddle. Built 1861-62. Sold 1867.
Maumee	593	4	Screw. Built 1861-62. Sold 8 June, 1869.
Mayflower	306	2	Screw. Built 1863-64. Sold 23 Sept., 1892.
Mayflower	2690	14	Two screws. Converted Gunboat. Built 1896 Purchased 19 March, 1898. Special service.
McKee	65	2	Screw. Torpedo Boat. Built 1896-97. Navy Yard, N. Y.
Memphis	791	4	Screw. Purchased 1861-62. Sold 8 June, 1869.
Mendota	974	8	Paddle. Built 1861-62. Sold 1867.
Mercedita	776	7	Screw. Purchased 1861-62. Sold 28 Oct., 1865.
Mercury	187	2	Paddle. Purchased 1861-62. Sold 1873.
Meredosia	1380	12	Screw. Not built.
Merrimac	3200	40	Screw. Built 1855. Captured at Norfolk by the Rebels.
Merrimac, 4th	684	6	Paddle. Purchased 1863-64. Foundered February, 1865.
Merrimac	7500	..	Screw. Collier. Purchased 12 April, 1898. Sunk in Santiago Harbor, Cuba, by Lieut. Hobson during war in 1898, to block Spanish fleet, 3 June, 1898.
Metacomet	974	8	Paddle. Built 1861-62.
Meteor	221	6	Paddle. Purchased 1863-64. Sold 5 Oct., 1865.
Miami	730	7	Paddle. Built 1861-62. Sold 10 Aug., 1865.
Miantonomah	3990	4	Iron-clad. Built 1861-62. Rebuilding. 1874. Chester, Pa. Laid up at League Island, Pa.
Michigan	685	8	Paddle. Built 1844. On Lake Erie.
Mignonnette	50	..	Screw. Purchased 1862-63. Sold 17 April, 1863.
Milwaukee	970	4	Iron-clad. Built 1861-62. Sunk by torpedo, 28 March, 1865.
Milwaukee	970	4	Iron-clad. Built 1864-65. Sunk by torpedo, 28 March, 1865.
Milwaukee	9700	68	Two screws. Protected Cruiser. Not yet contracted for.
Mindoro	142	3	Screw. Gunboat. Transferred from War Department. Asiatic Station.

GENERAL NAVY REGISTER.

Name.	Tons.	Guns.	Remarks.
Minneapolis	7375	28	Three Screws. Protected Cruiser. Built 1891-93. League Island, Pa.
Mindanao	83	..	Two screws. Gunboat. Captured during war in 1898. Lost in 1899.
Mingo	974	8	Paddle. Built 1861-62. Sold 1867.
Minnesota	3200	40	Screw. Built 1855. Naval Militia, Mass.
Minnetonka	2490	21	Screw. Built 1870. Re-named California. Sold May, 1875.
Mississippi	..	10	Paddle. Built 1841. Destroyed at Port Hudson 14 March, 1863.
Missouri	1700	10	Paddle. Built 1841. Burned at Gibraltar, 1843.
Missouri	12,230	44	Two screws. Battleship. Built 1898-1901. Building, Newport News, Va.
Mist	233	7	Paddle. Purchased 1864-65. Sold.
Mistletoe	50	..	Screw. Purchased 1862-63. Sold 29 Nov., 1865.
Moccasin	192	3	Screw. Purchased 1864-65. Sold 5 Oct., 1865.
Moccasin	120	1	Screw. Submarine Torpedo Boat. Built 1900-1901. Building, Elizabethport, N. J.
Modoc	483	1	Iron-clad. Built 1865. Broken up, 1875.
Modoc	241	..	Screw. Tug. Built 1890. Originally Enterprise. Purchased 29 April, 1898. League Island, Pa.
Mohawk	464	5	Screw. Purchased 1858. Sold 1864.
Mohawk	420	..	Screw. Tug. Built 1893. Originally T. P. Fowler. Purchased 23 April, 1898. Norfolk, Va.
Mohican	1900	8	Screw. Built 1858. At Mare Island.
Mohongo	1034	10	Paddle. Built 1863-64. Sold November, 1870.
Monadnock	1091	4	Iron-clad. Built 1861-62. Asiatic Station.
Monarch	..	..	Ram. Purchased 1861-62. Sold.
Mondamin	2348	13	Screw. Purchased 1864-65. Not built.
Monitor	776	2	Iron-clad. Built 1861-62. Original type of turreted vessels. Foundered off Cape Hatteras, 21 December, 1862.
Monocacy	1370	6	Paddle. Built 1864-65. Asiatic Station.
Monongahela	960	11	Screw. Built 1861-62. Training service.
Montauk	1875	2	Iron-clad. Built 1861-62. Navy Yard, League Island, Pa.
Montauk	844	4	Iron-clad. Built 1864-65.
Monterey	52	1	Screw. Purchased 1863-64. Name changed to Ivy. Stricken from Register, 7 October, 1892.
Monterey	4084	17	Two screws. Monitor. Built 1889-92. Asiatic Station.
Montgomery	787	5	Screw. Purchased 1861-62. Sold 10 Aug., 1865.
Montgomery	2089	20	Two screws. Cruiser. Built 1889-92. South Atlantic Station.
Monticello	655	7	Screw. Purchased 1861-62. Sold 1 Nov., 1865.
Moodna	677	2	Iron-clad. Built 1861-62. Sold.
Moose	189	6	Paddle. Purchased 1863-64. Sold 17 Aug., 1865.
Morris	105	4	Two screws. Torpedo Boat. Built 1896-98. Torpedo Station, Newport, R. I.
Morse	513	2	Paddle. Purchased 1861-62. Sold 20 July, 1865.
Moshulu	2000	15	Screw. Built 1867. Re-named Severn. Sold 1877.
Mound City	512	13	Iron-clad. Built 1861-62.
Mount Vernon	625	3	Screw. Purchased 1861-62. Sold 12 July, 1865.
Mount Washington	..	..	Paddle. Purchased 1861-62. Sold 21 June, 1868.
Muscoota	1030	10	Paddle. Built 1863-64. Sold 8 May, 1869.
Myrtle	50	..	Screw. Built 1862-63. Sold 17 August, 1865.
Mystic	464	5	Screw. Purchased 1858. Sold.
Mystic	541	7	Screw. Purchased 1863-64. Sold 20 June, 1868.
Nahant	1875	2	Iron-clad. Built 1861-62. At League Island.
Naiad	185	8	Paddle. Purchased 1864-65. Sold 17 Aug., 1868.
Nansemond	340	4	Paddle. Purchased 1863-64. Sold 12 Sept., 1865.
Nanshan	4950	..	Screw. Collier. Built 1896. Purchased 6 April, 1898. Asiatic Station.
Nantasket	523	7	Screw. Built 1867. Broken up.
Nantucket	496	2	Iron-clad. Built 1861-62. Sold 14 Nov., 1900.
Napa	614	2	Iron-clad. Built 1863-64. Broken up.
Narcissus	101	4	Screw. Purchased 1863-64. Sunk by torpedo, 8 December, 1864.
Narkeeta	192	..	Screw. Tug. Built 1890-92. Navy Yard, N. Y.
Narragansett	910	5	Screw. Built 1858. Sold 20 November, 1883.
Nashville	1371	17	Two screws. Gunboat. Built 1894-96. Asiatic Station.
Naubec	483	1	Iron-clad. Built 1863-64. Re-named Minnetonka. Broken up, 1874.
Naumkeag	250	6	Paddle. Purchased 1863-64. Sold 17 Aug., 1865.
Nausett	483	2	Iron-clad. Built 1863-64. Broken up, 1874.
Nebraska	14,020	62	Two screws. Armored Cruiser. Built 1901-04. Building, Moran Bros., Seattle, Wash.

GENERAL NAVY REGISTER.

Name.	Tons.	Guns.	Remarks.
Neosho	523	2	Iron-clad. Built 1861-62.
Neptune	1243	11	Screw. Purchased 1863-64. Sold 12 July, 1868.
Nereus	1244	11	Screw. Purchased 1863-64. Sold.
Nero	4925	1	Screw. Collier. Built 1895. Originally Whitgift. Purchased 30 June, 1898. Mare Island.
Neshaminy	3200	10	Screw. Built 1863-64. Not built.
Nettle	50	..	Screw. Purchased 1862-63. Sold.
Nevada	2019	23	Screw. Built 1870. Sold June, 1874.
Nevada	3235	16	Two screws. Monitor. Built 1898-1901. Building, Bath Maine.
Newark	4098	26	Two screws. Protected Cruiser. Built 1887-89. Asiatic Station.
Newbern	948	6	Screw. Purchased 1863-64. Sold.
New Era	157	6	Purchased 1862-63. Sold 17 Aug., 1865.
New Ironsides	3486	18	Iron-clad. Built 1861-62. Burned at League Island.
New Jersey	15,320	66	Two screws. Battleship. Built 1901-04. Building, Weymouth, Mass.
New London	221	5	Screw. Purchased 1861-62. Sold 8 Sept., 1865.
New National	379	1	Paddle. Purchased 1863-64. Returned to owners, 1865.
New Orleans	3769	30	Two screws. Protected Cruiser. Built 1896. Originally Amazonas. Purchased 16 March, 1898. Asiatic Station.
Newport	1000	13	Screw. Gunboat. Built 1895-97. Cadet practice ship.
New York		..	Sold and broken up on the stocks at Navy Yard, New York, May 12, 1888.
New York	8200	30	Two screws. Armored Cruiser. Built 1890-93. North Atlantic Station.
Nezinscot	156	2	Screw. Tug. Built 1897. Originally D. C. Ivans. Purchased 25 March, 1898. Norfolk, Va.
Niagara	5221	2	Screw. Distilling Ship. Purchased 11 April, 1898. Sold 19 July, 1899.
Niagara	4580	12	Screw. Built 1855. Sold 24 September, 1883.
Nicholson	174	3	Two screws. Torpedo Boat. Built 1898-1901. Building, Elizabethport, N. J.
Nina	357	2	Screw. Purchased 1863-64. Navy Yard, N. Y.
Niphon	475	9	Screw. Purchased 1863-64. Sold 17 April, 1865.
Nipsic	1375	6	Screw. Built 1863. Rebuilt. Naval Station, Puget Sound.
Nita	210	4	Paddle. Purchased 1863-64. Sold 25 May, 1868.
Norwich	431	5	Screw. Purchased 1861-62. Sold 10 Aug., 1865.
Nyack	410	3	Screw. Built 1862-63. Sold 20 Nov., 1883.
Nyanza	203	6	Paddle. Purchased 1863-64. Sold 15 Aug., 1865
Nymph	171	8	Paddle. Purchased 1864-65. Sold 17 Aug., 1865.
O'Brien	174	3	Two screws. Torpedo Boat. Built 1898-1901. Building Elizabethport, N. J
Octorara	829	6	Paddle. Built 1861-62. Sold 1866.
Oleander	263	2	Paddle. Purchased 1864-65. Sold 5 Sept., 1868.
Oleander	206	..	Screw. Purchased 1862-63. Sold 5 Sept., 1865.
Ohio	12,440	44	Two screws. Battleship. Built 1898-1901. Building San Francisco, Cal.
Olympia	5870	36	Two screws. Protected Cruiser. Built 1890-93. Navy Yard, Boston.
Omaha	1122	12	Screw. Purchased 1868. Transferred to Marine Hospital Service.
O. M. Pettit	165	2	Paddle. Purchased 1861-62. Sold 2 Sept., 1865.
Oneida	1023	9	Screw. Built 1861-62. Run down and sunk in Yeddo Bay, 24 January, 1870.
Oneida	150	6	Screw. Converted Gunboat. Built 1896. Originally Illawara. Purchased 31 May 1898. Naval Militia, Washington, D. C.
Oneota	1034	2	Iron-clad. Built 1862-63.
Onondaga	1250	4	Iron-clad. Built 1861-62. Sold.
Ontario	2490	21	Screw. Re-named New York. On the Stocks, New York. Sold May, 1888.
Oregon	10,288	46	Two screws. Battleship. Built 1890-93. Asiatic Station.
Oriole	137	6	Paddle. Purchased 1864-65. Sold 17 Aug., 1865.
Osceola	974	8	Paddle. Built 1862-63. Sold 1867.
Osceola	571	4	Screw. Tug. Built 1896. Originally Winthrop. Purchased 31 Mar., 1898. Tender to Amphitrite.
Osage	523	2	Iron-clad. Built 1861-62. Sunk by torpedo, 29 March, 1865. Subsequently raised and sold, 1867.
Osage	523	2	Iron-clad. Built 1863-64. Sunk by torpedo, 29 March, 1865.
Ossipee	828	8	Screw. Built 1861-62. Sold 25 March., 1891.
Otsego	974	8	Paddle. Built 1861-2. Sunk by torpedo, 9 December, 1864.

Name.	Tons.	Guns.	Remarks.
Ottawa	507	4	Screw. Built 1861-62. Sold 25 October, 1865.
Ouachita	720	14	Paddle. Built 1863-64. Sold 25 September, 1865.
Owasco	507	4	Screw. Built 1861-62. Sold 28 October, 1868.
Ozark	578	2	Iron-clad. Built 1861-62. Sold 29 Nov., 1865.
Ozark	578	7	Iron-clad. Built 1864-65.
Palos	306	..	Screw. Built 1866. Sold 12 October, 1892.
Pampanoosuc	2869	21	Screw. Built 1863-64. Re-named Connecticut. On the stocks. Broken up in 1884.
Pampanga	201	..	Screw. Gunboat. Transferred from War Department. Asiatic Station.
Panola	507	4	Screw. Built 1861-62. Sold 30 November, 1865.
Pansy	50	..	Screw. Purchased 1862-63. Sold.
Panay	142	5	Screw. Gunboat. Transferred from War Department. Asiatic Station.
Panther	4260	16	Screw. Auxiliary Cruiser. Built 1889. Originally Venezuela. Purchased 19 April, 1898. League Island, Pa.
Paragua	201	..	Screw. Gunboat. Transferred from War Department. Asiatic Station.
Passaconaway	3200	4	Iron-clad. Built 1863-64. Re-named Massachusetts. On the stocks, 1874. Broken up 1884.
Passaic	496	2	Iron-clad. Built 1861-62. Sold 10 Oct., 1899.
Patapsco	844	2	Iron-clad. Built 1861-62. Sunk by torpedo, 15 January, 1865.
Patroon	183	5	Screw. Purchased 1861-62. Sold.
Paul Jones	863	6	Paddle. Built 1861-62. Sold 1867.
Paul Jones, Jr	30	1	Steam Launch. Built 1863-64. Sold 17 August, 1865.
Paul Jones	420	7	Two screws. Torpedo Boat Destroyer. Built 1898-1901. Building San Francisco, Cal.
Pawnee	872	4	Screw. Built 1858. Converted into sailing vessel. Sold 3 May, 1884.
Pawnee	275	2	Screw. Tug. Built 1896. Originally John Dwight. Purchased 6 May, 1898. Navy Yard, New York.
Pawpaw	175	8	Paddle. Built 1863-64.
Pawtucket	225	..	Screw. Tug. Built 1898. Naval Station, Puget Sound.
Pawtuxet	974	8	Paddle. Built 1862-63. Sold 1867.
Peacock	1380	12	Screw. Built 1864-65. Not built.
Pembina	507	4	Screw. Built 1861-62. Sold 30 November, 1868.
Penacook	225	..	Screw. Tug. Built 1898. Port Royal, S. C.
Penguin	389	6	Screw. Purchased 1861-62. Sold 18 Sept., 1865.
Pennsylvania	15,320	66	Two screws. Battleship. Built 1901-1904. Building, Cramp & Sons, Philadelphia, Pa.
Penobscot	507	4	Screw. Built 1861-62. Sold 19 October, 1869.
Pensacola	2000	22	Screw. Built 1858. Training Ship Yerba. Buena Island. Cal.
Peony	180	2	Screw. Purchased 1864-65. Sold.
Peoria	974	8	Paddle. Built 1862-63. Sold.
Peoria	488	7	Screw. Gunboat. Built 1897. Originally Philadelphia. Purchased 23 May, 1898. Navy Yard, Boston, Mass.
Peosta	233	14	Paddle. Built 1863-64. Sold 17 August, 1865.
Pequot	593	4	Screw. Built 1861-62. Sold 1869.
Peri	159	8	Paddle. Purchased 1864-65. Sold 17 Aug., 1868.
Periwinkle	387	2	Screw. Purchased 1864-65. Sold.
Perry	420	7	Two screws. Torpedo Boat Destroyer. Built 1898-1901. Building, San Francisco, Cal.
Peterhoff	..	..	Screw. Purchased 1862-63. Sunk by collision off North Carolina, 6 March, 1864.
Petrel, 2d	226	6	Screw. Purchased 1862-63. Captured 22 April, 1864.
Petrel	892	10	Screw. Gunboat. Built 1886-87. Asiatic Station.
Petrita	200	1	Paddle. Captured 1847. Sunk off Alvarado, 1849.
Philadelphia	500	2	Paddle. Purchased 1861-62. Sunk by torpedo.
Philadelphia	4324	30	Two screws. Protected Cruiser. Built 1887-89. Pacific Station.
Philippi	311	2	Paddle. Purchased 1863-64. Destroyed in Mobile Bay, 5 August, 1864.
Phlox	317	2	Paddle. Purchased 1864-65.
Pike	120	1	Screw. Submarine Torpedo Boat. Built 1900-1901. Building, San Francisco, Cal.
Pilgrim	168	2	Screw. Built 1863-64. Sold 25 March, 1891.
Pink	184	1	Screw. Purchased 1863-64. Lost on Dauphin Island, September, 1865.
Pinta	550	2	Screw. Built 1863-64. Naval Militia, San Diego, Cal.
Piscataqua	2490	21	Screw. Built 1864-65. Re-named Delaware.
Piscataqua	854	4	Screw. Tug. Built 1897. Originally W. H. Brown. Purchased 11 May, 1898. Portsmouth, N. H.
Pittsburg	512	13	Iron-clad. Built 1861-62. Sold 29 Nov., 1865.

GENERAL NAVY REGISTER. 745

Name	Tons	Guns	Remarks
Planter	300	2	Paddle. Captured 1861-62. Sold.
Plunger	120	1	Screw. Submarine Torpedo Boat. Built 1901. Building, Elizabethport, N. J.
Plymouth	1122	12	Screw. Purchased 1858. Broken up in 1884.
Pocahontas	694	5	Screw. Purchased 1858. Sold.
Poinsett	250	2	Paddle. Built 1840. Transferred from War Department and sold 1845.
Pompey	3085	1	Screw. Collier. Built 1897. Originally Harlech. Purchased 19 Apr., 1898. League Island, Pa.
Pontiac	974	8	Paddle. Built 1861-62. Sold 1867.
Pontiac	401	3	Screw. Tug. Built 1891. Originally Right Arm. Purchased 23 April, 1898. Navy Yard, New York.
Pontoosuc	974	8	Paddle. Built 1861-62. Sold 1866.
Poppy	93	2	Screw. Purchased 1863-64. Sold.
Porpoise	120	1	Screw. Submarine Torpedo Boat. Built 1900-1901. Building, Elizabethport, N. J.
Porter	165	4	Two screws. Torpedo Boat. Built 1895-96. Special service.
Port Fire	85	1	Screw. Purchased 1863-64. Broken up at Portsmouth, N. H.
Port Royal	805	8	Paddle. Purchased 1861-62. Sold 1866.
Potomac	677	4	Screw. Built 1897. Originally Wilmot. Purchased 14 April, 1898. Special service.
Potomska	287	5	Screw. Purchased 1861-62. Sold 10 Aug., 1865.
Powhatan	2182	17	Paddle. Built 1850. Sold 30 July, 1887.
Powhatan	194	2	Screw. Built 1892. Originally Penwood. Purchased 8 April, 1898. Pensacola, Fla.
Prairie	6872	8	Screw. Auxiliary Cruiser. Built 1890. Originally El Sol. Purchased 6 Apr., 1898. Special service.
Prairie Bird	171	6	Screw. Purchased 1862-63. Sold 17 Aug., 1865.
Preble	420	7	Two screws. Torpedo Boat Destroyer. Built 1898-1901. Building, San Francisco, Cal.
Preston	128	..	Screw. Purchased 1864-65. Sold 30 Nov., 1865.
Primrose	94	2	Screw. Purchased 1862-63. Sold 17 March, 1871.
Princess Royal	828	7	Screw. Purchased 1863-64. Sold 12 Sept., 1865.
Princeton, 1st	672	..	Screw. Built 1843. First screw vessel of war ever built. Broken up.
Princeton, 2d	..	10	Screw. Built 1851. Sold 9 October, 1866.
Princeton	1100	13	Screw. Gunboat. Built 1895-97. Asiatic Station.
Proteus	1254	11	Screw. Purchased 1863-64. Sold 12 July, 1865.
Pulaski	395	1	Paddle. Purchased 1858. Sold at Montevideo, 1863.
Puritan	1870	2	Iron-clad. Built 1861-62. Broken up. Rebuilding at Chester. In commission. Naval Academy, Maryland.
Pushmataha	2000	16	Screw. Built 1867. Re-named Congress. Sold 24 Sept., 1883.
Quaker City	1600	9	Paddle. Purchased 1861-62. Sold 20 June, 1865.
Queen	630	7	Screw. Purchased 1863-64. Sold 13 Oct., 1868.
Queen City	212	9	Paddle. Purchased 1863-64. Captured 24 June, 1864.
Queen of the West	..	..	Ram. Purchased 1861-62. Grounded and captured, 14 February, 1863.
Quinnebaug	910	8	Screw. Built 1864-65. Sold 25 March, 1891.
Quinsigamond	2127	4	Iron-clad. Built 1863-64. Re-named Oregon. On the stocks, 1874. Broken up in 1884.
Quiros	350	4	Screw. Gunboat. Built 1896. Asiatic Station.
Rainbow	6206	..	Screw. Distilling Ship. Built 1890. Originally Norse King. Purchased 29 June, 1898. Navy Yard.
Raleigh	3213	25	Two screws. Protected Cruiser. Built 1889-93. Portsmouth, N. H.
Ranger	1110	12	Screw. Built 1874. Special service.
Rapido	..	..	On Asiatic Station.
Rattler	165	6	Paddle. Purchased 1862-63. Wrecked and abandoned, 30 December, 1864.
Red Rover	..	1	Paddle. Purchased 1862-63. Sold 29 Nov., 1865.
Reina Mercedes	3090	..	Screw. Cruiser. Built 1887. Captured during Spanish-American War. Norfolk, Va.
Reindeer	212	6	Paddle. Purchased 1863-64. Sold 17 Aug., 1875.
Reliance	90	1	Screw. Purchased 1861-62. Captured 23 Aug., 1863.
Republic	90	1	Screw. Purchased 1864-65. Sold 1 Aug., 1865.
Resaca	900	10	Screw. Built 1864-65. Sold 1874.
Rescue	111	1	Screw. Purchased 1861-62. Sold 25 March, 1891.
Resolute	90	1	Screw. Purchased 1861-62. Sold 23 June, 1868.

GENERAL NAVY REGISTER.

Name.	Tons.	Guns.	Remarks.
Resolute	4175	2	Screw. Built 1894. Originally Yorktown. Purchased 21 April, 1898. Transferred to War Department.
Restless	137	8	Screw. Converted Gunboat. Built 1887. Purchased 22 April, 1898. Navy Yard, N. Y.
Rhode Island	1517	7	Paddle. Purchased 1861-62. Sold 1867.
Rhode Island	14,948	66	Two screws. Battleship. Built 1901-04. Building, Weymouth, Mass.
Richmond	2000	14	Screw. Built 1858. Receiving Ship. League Island, Pa.
Rio Bravo	325	..	Paddle. Purchased 1875. Turned over to War Department, June, 1879.
Roanoke	3400	40	Screw. Built 1855. Converted into a three-turreted monitor. Sold 24 Sept., 1883.
Rocket	127	..	Screw. Purchased 1863-64. Sold 28 Dec., 1898.
Rodgers	142	3	Two screws. Torpedo Boat. Built 1895-96. Navy Yard, N. Y.
Rodolph	217	6	Paddle. Purchased 1863-64. Sunk by torpedo, 1 April, 1865.
Romeo	175	6	Paddle. Purchased 1862-63. Sold 17 August, 1865.
Rose	62	1	Screw. Purchased. Sold at Pensacola.
R. R. Cuyler	1202	8	Screw. Purchased 1861-62. Sold 15 Aug., 1865.
Rowan	182	4	Two screws. Torpedo Boat. Built 1895-97. Naval Station, Puget Sound.
Sachem	197	5	Screw. Purchased 1861-62. Sold.
Saco	410	3	Screw. Built 1865. Sold 20 Nov., 1883.
Sacramento	1367	9	Screw. Built 1861-62. Wrecked in East Indies, 19 June, 1867.
Sagamore	507	4	Screw. Built 1861-62. Sold 1866.
Saginaw	453	4	Paddle. Built 1858. Wrecked in Pacific, 29 October, 1870.
Samar	210	5	Two screws. Gunboat. Built 1889. Transferred from War Department. Asiatic Station.
Samoset	225	..	Screw. Tug. Built 1897. League Island, Pa.
Sampson	600	..	Paddle. Purchased 1861-62. Sold 17 Aug., 1865.
Sandoval	106	4	Screw. Gunboat. Captured during Spanish-American War. Portsmouth, N. H.
Sandusky	479	2	Iron-clad. Built 1861-62. Sold 17 April, 1873.
San Francisco	4098	30	Two screws. Protected Cruiser. Built 1887-89. Norfolk, Va.
Sangamon	496	2	Screw. Built 1861-62. Re-named Jason. At League Island, Philadelphia.
San Jacinto	..	6	Screw. Built 1848. Lost in West Indies, 1 January, 1865.
Santiago de Cuba	1567	10	Paddle. Purchased 1861-62. Sold 21 Sept., 1865.
Saranac	1238	11	Paddle. Built 1848. Sunk June, 1876.
Sassacus	974	8	Paddle. Built 1861-62. Sold.
Satelette	929	2	Paddle. Purchased 1861-62. Captured 23 August, 1863.
Saturn	6220	1	Screw. Collier. Built 1890. Purchased 2 Apr., 1898. Norfolk, Va.
Saugus	550	2	Iron-clad. Purchased 1862-63. Sold 25 March, 1891.
Scipio	6864	..	Screw. Collier. Built 1882. Purchased 5 May, 1898. Sold 28 December, 1898.
Scorpion, 2d	339	3	Paddle. Purchased 1846. Sold 1848.
Scorpion	850	12	Two screws. Converted Gunboat. Built 1896. Originally Sovereign. Purchased 7 Apr., 1898. North Atlantic Station.
Scotia	507	4	Screw. Built 1861-62. Sunk by torpedo, 14 April, 1865. Raised and sold 25 October, 1865.
Scourge, 3d	230	3	Screw. Purchased. Sold 1848.
Sea Gull	150	3	Paddle. Purchased 1822. Sold 1840.
Sebago	832	6	Paddle. Built 1861-62. Sold.
Sebago	130	1	Screw. Tug. Built 1893. Originally Hortense. Purchased 30 Apr., 1898. Navy Yard, Pensacola, Fla.
Selma	590	4	Paddle. Purchased 1864-65. Sold 18 Aug., 1865.
Seminole	801	3	Screw. Built 1858. Sold 20 July, 1870.
Seminole	123	3	Screw. Tug. Built 1879. Originally Kate Jones. Purchased 6 June, 1898. Transferred to War Department.
Seneca	507	4	Screw. Built 1861-62. Sold.
Serapis	1380	12	Screw. Not built.
Shakamaxon	3200	4	Screw. Built 1863-64. Re-named Nebraska, and broken up at Philadelphia Navy Yard. On the stocks, 1874. Dropped from Naval Register in 1875.
Shamokon	1030	10	Paddle. Built 1863-64. Sold 21 October, 1869.

GENERAL NAVY REGISTER. 747

Name.	Tons.	Guns.	Remarks.
Shamrock	974	8	Paddle. Built 1861-62. Sold.
Shark	120	1	Screw. Submarine Torpedo Boat. Built 1900-1901. Building, Elizabethport, N. J.
Shawmut	410	3	Screw. Built 1863.
Shawmut	593	3	Screw. Built 1864-65. Sold 27 Sept., 1883.
Shawnee	483	2	Iron-clad. Built 1863-64. Broken up, 1875.
Shawsheen	180	2	Paddle. Purchased 1861-62. Sold.
Shearwater	122	3	Converted Gunboat. Built 1887. Purchased 9 May, 1898. Naval Militia, Pennsylvania.
Shenandoah	929	11	Screw. Built 1861-62.
Shiloh	614	2	Iron-clad. Purchased 1863-64. Re-named Iris. Sold 1 Sept., 1866.
Shokokon	700	6	Paddle. Purchased 1863-64. Sold 25 Oct., 1865.
Shubrick	165	3	Two screws. Torpedo Boat. Built 1898-1901. Building, Richmond, Va.
Signal	190	6	Stern-wheel. Purchased 1862-63. Captured 5 May, 1864.
Silver Cloud	190	6	Paddle. Purchased 1863-64. Sold 17 Aug., 1865.
Silver Lake	212	6	Stern-wheel. Purchased 1862-63. Sold 17 Aug., 1865.
Sioux	155	2	Screw. Tug. Built 1892. Originally P. H. Wise. Purchased 26 March, 1898. Norfolk, Va.
Siren	232	8	Paddle. Purchased 1864-65. Sold 17 Aug., 1865.
Siren	315	4	Screw. Converted Gunboat. Built 1897. Originally Eugenia. Purchased 9 June, 1898. Naval Militia, Va.
Snowdrop	125	2	Screw. Purchased 1863-64.
Snowdrop	125	2	Screw. Purchased 1864-65.
Solace	4700	3	Screw. Hospital Ship. Built 1896. Originally Creole. Purchased 7 Apr., 1898. Special service.
Somers	145	..	Screw. Torpedo Boat. Purchased 26 March, 1898. Navy Yard, New York.
Somerset	521	6	Paddle. Purchased 1861-62. Sold.
Sonoma	955	6	Paddle. Purchased 1861-62. Sold 1867.
Sorrel	68	..	Built 1863-64. Sold 27 Sept., 1883.
Southery	3100	1	Screw. Collier. Built 1889. Purchased 16 Apr., 1898. Norfolk, Va.
Southfield	751	4	Paddle. Purchased 1861-62. Sunk by Rebel ram, 19 April, 1864.
South Carolina	165	6	Screw. Purchased 1861-62. Sold 1866.
South Dakota	13,680	02	Two screws. Armored Cruiser. Built 1901-1904. Building, Union Iron Works, San Francisco, Cal.
Sovereign	440	2	Paddle. Purchased 1862-63. Sold 29 Nov., 1865.
Speedwell	306	2	Screw. Built 1863-64. Sold March, 1891.
Spirea	406	6	Screw. Purchased 1864-65. Sold 5 Oct., 1866.
Spitfire, 4th	228	3	Paddle. Purchased 1846. Sold 1848.
Springfield	146	6	Paddle. Purchased 1862-63. Sold 17 Aug., 1865.
Spuyten Duyvil	116	..	Screw. Purchased 1864-65. Broken up, New York.
Squando	614	2	Iron-clad. Built 1863-64. Re-named Algoma, and broken up, 1874.
Standish	306	2	Screw. Built 1863-64. Naval Academy, Annapolis, Md.
Stars and Stripes	407	4	Screw. Purchased 1861-62. Sold 10 Aug., 1865.
State of Georgia	1204	9	Paddle. Purchased 1861-62. Sold 25 Oct., 1865.
St. Clair	203	4	Stern-wheel. Purchased 1862-63. Sold 17 Aug., 1865.
St. Clair	203	8	Paddle. Purchased 1864-65. Sold 17 Aug., 1865.
St. Louis	14,910	12	Two screws. Auxiliary Cruiser. Chartered during War in 1898. Returned to owners.
St. Louis	9700	68	Two screws. Protected Cruiser. Building, Neafie & Levy, Philadelphia, Pa.
St. Paul	14,910	18	Two screws. Auxiliary Cruiser. Chartered during War in 1898. Returned to owners.
Stepping Stones	226	1	Paddle. Purchased 1861-62. Sold 12 July, 1865.
Sterling	5663	1	Screw. Collier. Built 1881. Purchased 16 Apr., 1898. Navy Yard, Boston, Mass.
Stettin	..	..	Screw. Purchased 1861-62. Sold 22 June, 1865.
Stevens' War Steamer	4683	6	Screw. Built 1848. Commenced 1842. First placed on the Navy list, 1858. Relinquished to Mr. Stevens, 1864. By him presented to the State of New Jersey.
Stewart	420	7	Two screws. Torpedo Boat Destroyer. Built 1898-1901. Building Morris Heights, N. Y.
Stiletto	31	..	Screw. Torpedo Boat. Torpedo Station, Newport.
Stockdale	181	6	Paddle. Purchased 1863-64. Sold 24 Aug., 1865.
Stranger	546	5	Screw. Auxiliary Gunboat. Purchased 9 June, 1898. Naval Militia, Louisiana.
Stockton	165	3	Two screws. Torpedo Boat. Built 1898-1901. Building, Richmond, Va.
Stringham	340	7	Two screws. Torpedo Boat. Built 1898-1901. Building, Wilmington, Del.

GENERAL NAVY REGISTER.

Name.	Tons.	Guns.	Remarks.
Sumter	464	5	Screw. Purchased 1858. Sold.
Sumter			Paddle. Sunk by collision, 24 June, 1863.
Suncock	483	2	Iron-clad. Built 1863-64. Broken up, 1875.
Sunflower	294	2	Screw. Purchased 1863-64. Sold 10 Aug., 1865.
Supply	4460		Screw. Supply Ship. Built 1873. Originally Illinois. Purchased 30 Apr., 1898. Navy Yard, New York.
Susquehanna	2213	23	Paddle. Built 1848. Sold 24 Sept., 1883.
Suwanee	1030	10	Paddle. Built 1863-64. Wrecked.
Suwanee	2185	2	Light-House Tender. Transferred during War in 1898. Returned.
Swatara	910	8	Screw. Built 1864-65. Sold 3 Aug., 1896.
Sweetbrier	240	2	Screw. Purchased 1863-64. Sold 25 Oct., 1865.
Switzerland	500		Ram. Purchased 1861-62. Sunk by Pittsburg batteries, 25 March, 1863.
Sylvia	302	6	Screw. Auxiliary Gunboat. Purchased 13 June, 1898. Naval Militia, Maryland.
Sylph	152	1	Screw. Converted Gunboat. Built 1898. Originally No. 295. Purchased June, 1898. Special service.
Tacoma	3200	24	Two screws. Protected Cruiser. Built 1899-1902. Building, San Francisco, Cal.
Tacony	974	8	Screw. Built 1861-62. Sold.
Taghkanic	1380	12	Screw. Not built.
Tahgayuta	2200	8	Screw. Built 1863-64. Not built.
Tahoma	507	4	Screw. Built 1861-62. Sold 1867.
Talbot	47	1	Screw. Torpedo Boat. Built 1896-97. Navy Yard, New York.
Tallahatchie	171	6	Paddle. Not built.
Tallahoma	974	8	Paddle. Built 1862-63. Sold.
Tallapoosa	650		Paddle. Built 1863. Wrecked, 1892, and sold, 24 February, 1892.
Tawah	108	8	Paddle. Purchased 1863-64. Burned to prevent capture, 11 November, 1864.
Teazer	90	2	Screw. Captured 1861-62. Sold 23 June, 1868.
Tecumseh	1034	2	Iron-clad. Built 1861-62. Sunk by torpedo, 5 August, 1864.
Tecumseh	214	2	Screw. Tug. Built 1896. Originally Edward Luckenback. Purchased 2 Apr., 1898. Washington, D. C.
Tempest	161		Paddle. Built 1864-65. Sold 27 Nov., 1865.
Tennessee	1275	2	Paddle. Captured 1861-62. Sold 1867.
Tennessee	1273	6	Iron-clad. Built 1864-65. Sold 27 Nov., 1867.
Tensas	150	2	Paddle. Purchased 1863-64. Sold 17 Aug., 1865.
Terror	3990	10	Two screws. Monitor. Built 1874-1896. Norfolk, Va.
Texas	6315	33	Two screws. Battleship. Built 1889-95. Norfolk, Va.
Theta			Tender. Built 1864-65. Sold.
Thistle	50		Screw. Purchased 1862-63. Sold 17 Aug., 1865.
Thomas Freeborn	269	2	Paddle. Purchased 1861-62. Sold 20 July, 1865.
Thornton	165	3	Two screws. Torpedo Boat. Built 1898-1901. Building, Richmond, Va.
Thunder			Tender. Built 1864-65. Sold 8 August, 1865.
Ticonderoga	1019	11	Screw. Built 1861-62. Sold August, 1887.
Tingey	165	3	Two screws. Torpedo Boat. Built 1898-1901. Building, Baltimore, Md.
Tioga	819	6	Paddle. Built 1861-62. Sold 1867.
Tioga	819	8	Paddle. Built 1863-64. Sold.
Tippecanoe	1034	2	Iron-clad. Built 1861-62. Re-named Wyandotte. Sold 17 Jan., 1899.
Tonawanda	1564	4	Iron-clad. Built 1864-65. Re-named Amphitrite. Special service.
Traffic	280		Screw. Built 1891. Navy Yard, New York.
Topeka	1814	15	Two screws. Gunboat. Built 1881. Originally Diogenes. Purchased 2 Apr., 1898. Boston, Mass.
Trefoil	370	2	Screw. Built 1864-65. Sold.
Trenton	2300	11	Screw. Built 1876. Wrecked during hurricane at Samoa in 1889.
Thetis	1250	1	Screw. Purchased for Relief of Greely Expedition. Sold.
Triana	306	2	Screw. Built 1864-65. Sold 2 May, 1891.
Tristam Shandy	444	3	Paddle. Built 1864-65. Name changed to Boxer, 12 June, 1865.
Triton	212		Screw. Tug. Built 1888. Yard Tug, Washington, D. C.
Tritonia	202	1	Paddle. Purchased 1863-64. Sold 1866.
Tritonia	202	2	Paddle. Built 1864-65. Sold.
Truxtun	433	8	Two screws. Torpedo Boat Destroyer. Built 1898-1901. Building, Sparrows' Point, Md.

GENERAL NAVY REGISTER. 749

Name.	Tons.	Guns.	Remarks.
Tulip	183	5	Screw. Purchased 1863-64. Blew up and sunk, 11 November, 1864.
Tunxis	614	2	Iron-clad. Built 1863-64. Re-named Otsego. Broken up, 1874.
Tuscarora	726	6	Screw. Built 1861-62. Sold 20 November, 1883.
Tuscumbia	565	3	Iron-clad. Built 1861-62. Sold 29 Nov., 1868.
Tyler	600	9	Paddle. Purchased 1861-62. Sold 1 Sept., 1868.
Underwriter	341	4	Paddle. Purchased 1861-62. Captured 1 February, 1864.
Umpqua	483	2	Iron-clad. Built 1863-64. Sold at New Orleans, 1874.
Unadilla	507	4	Screw. Built 1861-62. Sold 9 November, 1869.
Unadilla	345	..	Screw. Tug. Built 1895. Yard Tug, Mare Island, Cal.
Uncas	192	3	Screw. Purchased 1861-62. Sold 1863.
Uncas	441	2	Screw. Tug. Built 1893. Originally Walter A. Luckenback. Purchased 2 Apr., 1898. San Juan, Porto Rico.
Union	956	..	Horizontal Submerged Paddle. Built 1841. Sold 1858.
Union, 2d	1114	4	Paddle. Purchased 1862-63. Sold 25 Oct., 1865.
Unit	56	..	Screw. Built 1864-65. Sold 12 July, 1865.
Urdaneta	42	3	Screw. Gunboat. Built 1882. Transferred from War Department. Asiatic Station.
Valley City	190	5	Screw. Purchased 1861-62. Sold 15 Aug., 1865.
Vandalia	981	8	Screw. Rebuilt 1874. Wrecked during hurricane at Samoa in 1889.
Vanderbilt	4000	15	Paddle. Built 1862-63. Presented to the United States by Mr. Vanderbilt. Sold 18 Feb., 1873.
Verbena	104	2	Screw. Purchased 1864-65. Sold 20 July, 1865.
Vesuvius	929	8	Two screws. Dynamite Cruiser. Built 1887-1890. Boston, Mass.
Vicksburg	886	6	Screw. Purchased 1863-64. Sold 12 July, 1865.
Vicksburg	1000	13	Screw. Gunboat. Built 1895-97. Training Station, Newport, R. I.
Victoria	254	3	Screw. Purchased 1861-62. Sold 30 Nov., 1865.
Victory	160	6	Paddle. Purchased 1863-64. Sold 17 Aug., 1865.
Viking	218	4	Screw. Converted Gunboat. Built 1883. Purchased 22 April, 1898. Transferred to War Department.
Villalobos	347	3	Screw. Gunboat. Transferred from War Department to Asiatic Station.
Vigilant	300	5	Screw. Tug. Built 1883. Purchased 19 Apr., 1898. Mare Island.
Vindicator	750	4	Ram. Built 1863-64. Sold 29 November, 1865.
Violet	146	2	Screw. Purchased 1863-64. Lost on Cape Fear Bar, 4 August, 1864.
Virginia, 2d	581	7	Screw. Purchased 1863-64. Sold 30 Nov., 1865.
Virginia	14,948	66	Two screws. Battleship. Built 1901-1904. Building, Newport News, Va.
Vixen	..	..	Paddle. Purchased 1846. Sold.
Vixen	806	8	Screw. Converted Gunboat. Built 1896. Originally Josephine. Purchased 9 Apr., 1898. North Atlantic Station.
Volunteer	..	5	Paddle. Purchased 1864-65. Sold 29 Nov., 1865.
Vulcan	3530	2	Screw. Repair ship. Built 1885. Originally Chatham. Purchased 2 May, 1898. Sold 19 July, 1899.
Waban	150	1	Screw. Tug. Built 1880. Originally Confidence. Purchased June, 1898. Naval Station, Port Royal.
Wabash	3200	40	Screw. Built 1855. Receiving Ship, Boston.
Wachusett	695	6	Screw. Built 1861-62. Sold in 1887.
Wahneta	192	..	Screw. Tug. Built 1891. Yard Tug, Norfolk, Va.
Wampanoag	2135	12	Screw. Built 1864. Re-named Florida.
Wamsutta	270	5	Screw. Purchased 1861-62. Sold 20 July, 1865.
Wando	645	3	Paddle. Purchased 1864-65. Sold 30 Nov., 1865.
Wanoloset	2200	8	Screw. Built 1863-64. Not built.
Wasp	521	3	Paddle. Purchased January, 1865. Originally Emma Henry. Sold January, 1876.
Wasp	630	6	Screw. Converted Gunboat. Built 1898. Originally Columbia. Purchased 26 March, 1898. Norfolk, Va.
Wassuc	483	2	Iron-clad. Built 1863-64. Broken up, 1875.
Watauga	2200	8	Screw. Built 1863-64. Not built.
Watch	65	2	Screw. Purchased 1864-65. Originally Alert. Sold 23 June, 1865.

GENERAL NAVY REGISTER.

Name.	Tons.	Guns.	Remarks.
Wateree	974	8	Paddle. Built 1861-62. Destroyed by an earthquake.
Water Witch	255	..	Paddle. Built 1845. Captured 3 June, 1864.
Water Witch, 2d	..	..	Paddle. Built 1845.
Water Witch, 3d	..	..	Paddle. Built 1846.
Water Witch, 4th	..	..	Paddle. Built 1852. Captured by Rebels.
Wave	229	6	Paddle. Built 1863-64. Captured 6 May, 1864.
Waxsaw	483	2	Iron-clad. Built 1863-64. Re-named Niobe. Broken up, 1874.
Weehawken	840	2	Iron-clad. Built 1861-62. Sunk off Morris Island, 6 December, 1863.
Western World	441	5	Screw. Purchased 1861-62. Sold 23 June. 1868.
Westfield	891	6	Paddle. Purchased 1861-62. Blown up in Galveston Bay, 1 January, 1863.
West Virginia	14,020	62	Two screws. Armored Cruiser. Built 1901-1904. Building, Newport News, Va.
W. G. Putnam	149	2	Paddle. Built 1861-62. Sold 20 June, 1868.
W. N. Brown	800	1	Paddle. Purchased 1862-63. Sold 17 Aug., 1865.
Wheeling	1000	13	Two screws. Gunboat. Built 1895-97. Pacific Station.
Whitehead	136	1	Screw. Purchased 1861-62. Sold 10 Aug., 1868.
Whipple	433	8	Two screws. Torpedo Boat Destroyer. Built 1898-1901. Building, Sparrows' Point, Md.
Wilderness	390	3	Paddle. Purchased 1864-65. Sold 7 Sept., 1865.
Wilkes	165	3	Two screws. Torpedo Boat. Built 1898-1901. Building, Morris Heights, N. Y.
Willamette	2200	8	Screw. Built 1863-64. Sold.
Wilmington	1397	20	Two screws. Gunboat. Built 1894-96. South Atlantic Station.
Winnebago	970	4	Iron-clad. Built 1861-62. Re-named Tornado. Sold.
Winnebago	540	4	Iron-clad. Built 1863. Sold 1874.
Winnipec	1030	10	Paddle. Built 1863-64. Sold 17 June, 1869.
Winona	507	4	Screw. Built 1861-62. Sold 30 November, 1868.
Winooski	974	8	Paddle. Built 1862-63. Sold.
Winooski	974	10	Paddle. Built 1864-65. Sold.
Winslow	142	3	Two screws. Torpedo Boat. Built 1895-96. Navy Yard, New York.
Wisconsin	11,565	46	Two screws. Battleship. Built 1896-1899. Union Iron Works, San Francisco, Cal.
Wissahickon	507	4	Screw. Built 1861-62. Sold 25 October, 1865.
Wompatuck	462	2	Two screws. Tug. Built 1896. Originally Atlas. Purchased 4 Apr., 1898. Navy Yard, N. Y.
Worden	433	8	Two screws. Torpedo Boat Destroyer. Built 1898-1901. Building, Sparrows' Point, Md.
Wyalusing	974	8	Paddle. Built 1861-62. Sold 1867.
Wyandank	399	2	Paddle. Purchased 1861-62. Store-hulk. Naval Academy. Broken up.
Wyandotte	550	2	Screw. Purchased 1858.
Wyoming	726	6	Screw. Built 1858. Sold 16 May, 1892.
Wyoming	3235	16	Two screws. Monitor. Built 1898-1901. Building, San Francisco, Cal.
Yale	13,000	16	Two screws. Auxiliary Cruiser. Originally Paris. Chartered during War in 1898. Returned to owners.
Yankee	328	3	Paddle. Purchased 1861-62. Sold 15 Sept., 1865.
Yankee	6000	18	Screw. Auxiliary Cruiser. Built 1892. Originally El Norte. Purchased 6 Apr., 1898. League Island, Pa.
Yankton	975	4	Screw. Converted Gunboat. Built 1893. Originally Penelope. Purchased 20 May, 1898. Special service.
Yantic	900	8	Screw. Built 1864. Naval Militia, Michigan.
Yazoo	483	2	Iron-clad. Built 1863-64. Sold and broken up, 1874.
Yorktown	1710	16	Two screws. Gunboat. Built 1887-89. Asiatic Station.
Yosemite	6179	18	Screw. Auxiliary Cruiser. Built 1892. Originally El Sud. Purchased 6 Apr., 1898. Lost during hurricane at Island of Guam, 13 Nov., 1900.
Young America	173	1	Paddle. Purchased 1861-62. Sold 12 July, 1865.
Young Rover	418	5	Screw. Purchased 1861-62. Sold 22 June, 1865.
Yucca	373	2	Screw. Purchased 1864-65. Sold.
Yuma	483	2	Iron-clad. Built 1863-64. Sold at New Orleans, 1874.
Zafiro	1200	2	Screw. Supply Ship. Built 1884. Purchased 9 Apr., 1898. Asiatic Station.
Zeta	..	..	Screw. Purchased 1864-65. Sold.
Zouave	127	1	Screw. Purchased 1861-62. Sold 12 July, 1865.

www.ingramcontent.com/pod-product-compliance
Lightning Source LLC
Chambersburg PA
CBHW052128010526
44113CB00034B/921